Concise Dictionary

of

American History

CONCISE DICTIONARY OF AMERICAN HISTORY

ADVISORY EDITOR
THOMAS C. COCHRAN
University of Pennsylvania

EDITOR
WAYNE ANDREWS

CHARLES SCRIBNER'S SONS, *New York*

Foreword

"During the last few decades, our history has been almost completely rewritten," the late James Truslow Adams noted in the preface to the *Dictionary of American History,* the last of his principal works. "New facts have been discovered; new interests have developed. A generation ago, historians had done the merest spade work in many departments of our national life. They were still chiefly concerned with political and military events. Today, our whole culture is their province and the public which reads history has widened with the widening of the historians' vision. . . . Until now the facts of the new history have not been readily available. They are scattered through thousands of volumes of general history or special studies. There has been an increasingly insistent demand for some one source to which an inquirer might go to find, and quickly, what he wishes to know as to specific facts, events, trends, or policies in our American past. It is this need which the *Dictionary of American History* is intended to fill."

The innovating five-volume *Dictionary of American History* to which these words served as an introduction was projected, organized and written by Dr. Adams with the collaboration of more than eleven hundred leading historical scholars. In a month or two after its first publication in 1940, it took its place among the few truly indispensable library reference works. Supplemented in 1961 by an additional volume which brought it fully up-to-date, the *Dictionary of American History* is still without a rival.

Twenty years and more have passed since the *Dictionary's* first publication, years full of event and shock, glory and anxiety, the widening of our horizons and the deepening of national responsibilities. Amid the complexities of our present course, a clear, accurate, unprejudiced knowledge of what we have been and what we stand for is demanded of every intelligent American. Realms of knowledge which were once comfortably regarded as of value only to the teacher and scholar are now of immediate importance to us all. Those for whom the *Dictionary of American History* was originally planned—thinking, concerned men and women who wanted to know the facts of our

national being so that they might make their present judgments with wisdom and without prejudice—are counted no longer by the thousands but by the tens of thousands. "The public which reads history," in Dr. Adams's phrase, is today a greatly expanded public.

Therefore, when Charles Scribner's Sons and the American Council of Learned Societies decided to publish a concise version of the *Dictionary of American Biography,* it was decided also to attempt a similar edition of the *Dictionary of American History.* In this endeavor to make a notable work of reference generally available in a format and at a price which would put it within the reach of the greatest number of readers, there was never any thought of reducing it to a mere handbook of dates, names and events, spiced with a sprinkling of over-condensed and foreshortened topic treatments. Unless the essential virtues of the six-volume *Dictionary*—its breadth and depth of treatment and its interpretative character— could be retained in a concise rendering, the work would be labor wasted.

Under direction of Dr. Thomas C. Cochran, and with the help of 109 contemporary scholars equal in reputation to the original staff, the *Concise Dictionary of American History* has been brought to completion. A carefully considered plan guided the choice, regrouping and concising of articles from the original work and its Supplement. The almost seven thousand topics and articles available for use were studied and evaluated in order to determine which were all-essential or "basic"; which were useful but did not require the extended treatment previously given them; and which might reasonably be omitted. The editors tried to make their decisions from the point of view of the ultimate users of the *Concise Dictionary*—an interested, general reader seeking elucidation of a reference in some book or magazine article, a perplexed parent attempting to find an answer to a child's question, a harried writer or newspaperman checking a fact, a college or graduate student hoping to deepen his understanding of a topic raised in his classes or assembling his notes for a term-paper. Any information which readers such as these might hope to find in a reference book was considered basic and was included.

In making choice of topics which the editors considered of secondary importance, the determining factor was whether the topic dealt with a fact or expressed an opinion. To a lesser degree, contemporary relevance played a part in the choice of secondary topics. In every case, the cutting down or trimming of the original articles was done with the utmost care to preserve their cores of fact. The method adopted for concising varied literally from article to article. The regrouping of several large categories of articles—the assembly of all data on Indian tribes in a single place, for example, and also the drawing together of all sketches of principal railroads—was done in the belief that the student and general reader would welcome an overall survey of these topics without the need to seek out each item in the Index under its specific initial letter. Lengthy articles of the

first importance, such as Labor, Education, Taxation, Reconstruction, The American Revolution, and the like, were incorporated into the *Concise Dictionary* without change.

There is no need to dwell here on the authority of the articles. They possess the same distinguished character as the pieces in the original work on which they are based. The interested reader is referred to the articles in the parent *Dictionary of American History* for the names of the writers and also for bibliographical aids to further study.

The thanks of the publisher and the editors are extended to all who by counsel or effort have helped to make this book possible. Many of the contributors to the original *Dictionary* were still happily available to review their work and direct such changes and additions as they considered necessary; where this was not the case, the help of outstanding contemporary authorities was sought and secured. We are particularly grateful to the following ladies and gentlemen:

Thurman Arnold
F. Clever Bald
Thomas S. Barclay
James A. Barnes
Clarence A. Berdahl
Hyman Berman
Donald C. Biggs
James K. Blake
Louise Ade Boger
Horace Mann Bond
Witt Bowden
Frederick A. Bradford
William W. Brickman
Dee Brown
Roger Burlingame
Alan Burnham
Charles S. Campbell, Jr.
Neil Carothers
Rudolf A. Clemen
Robert W. Coakley
Elbridge Colby
Kenneth Colegrove
Francis J. Colligan
Jacob Ernest Cooke
Edward Everett Dale
Robert W. Daly
Fred de Luca
Thomas E. Drake
Franklin Dunham
David M. Ellis
Joseph W. Ellison
Glen L. Evans
Carl N. Everstine
Arthur S. Flemming
Eleanor Flexner

Paul W. Gates
Roland Gelatt
George W. Goble
W. Brooke Graves
Theodore G. Gronert
Le Roy R. Hafen
Andrew G. Haley
John Henry Hammond, Jr.
Robert T. Handy
Thomas R. Hay
James P. Hendrick
Robert S. Henry
Harold L. Hitchens
Oliver W. Holmes
J. Edgar Hoover
Vincent C. Hopkins
Mildred McAfee Horton
John Tasker Howard
Richard H. Howland
Howard Mumford Jones
Donald L. Kemmerer
E. E. Keso
Harold Kirker
Charles B. Kuhlmann
Christopher Lasch
Richard M. Leighton
John McCoubrey
Marvin W. McFarland
Joseph McKenna
Neil MacNeil
W. C. Mallalieu
Jacob R. Marcus
Grace Mayer
E. K. Meade, Jr.
William L. Mitchell

Arthur E. Morgan
Richard K. Morris
Dana G. Munro
Jeannette P. Nichols
Waldemar Nielson
Peter H. Odegard
Forrest C. Pogue
Martin Quigley, Jr.
Sidney Ratner
Clinton Rossiter
Amy Lyon Schaeffer
T. R. Schellenberg
Arthur R. Schultz
Donald Shannon
Richard H. Shryock
Howard Sigmand
C. P. Stacey
Harold C. Syrett
Warren S. Thompson
Oliver Townsend
Robert Trisco
R. W. Tupper
Carl Ubbelohde
Wilcomb E. Washburn
Alan Waterman
E. Bradlee Watson
Sara Ruth Watson
Winston Weisman
F. W. Westervelt
Benjamin H. Williams
W. R. Willoughby
O. O. Winther
Catherine Bauer Wurster

Concise Dictionary
of
American History

CONCISE DICTIONARY

OF

AMERICAN HISTORY

A. B. C. CONFERENCE met at Niagara Falls May–July, 1914, after Argentina, Brazil and Chile tendered mediation to prevent a conflict between the United States and the Huerta regime in Mexico. The conference failed because Carranza, victorious in recent battles, rejected its proposal for a provisional government chosen by agreement between the contending factions. Huerta, however, resigned on July 15 and Carranza assumed the presidency on Aug. 22.

ABILENE, KANS., an early cow town, was established by Joseph G. McCoy in 1867 as a depot to which Texas cattle might be driven for shipment by rail to Kansas City. Attempts of trail drivers to reach market in 1866 had largely failed due to the hostility of the settlers of Missouri and eastern Kansas, who feared the introduction of Texas fever. Located on the Kansas Pacific Railway west of all settlement, Abilene was for two or three years a popular shipping point until the westward advance of settlers forced the drovers to new cow towns farther west.

AB-INITIO MOVEMENT was a controversy that originated during Reconstruction in Texas in 1866. In the constitutional convention of that year the question arose, "Was secession null and void from the beginning (*ab-initio*) or became null and void as a result of the war?" The staunch unionists or radicals took the position that it was null and void from the beginning and therefore all laws based upon secession were null and void and all public and private relations based upon such laws were null and void. This contention was rejected by the governor, military officers, both constitutional conventions and by the Republican State Convention, but it seriously divided the party of Reconstruction. Two brothers assumed leadership of the respective groups, Morgan Hamilton of the Ab-Initios and ex-Gov. A. J. Hamilton of the anti-ab-initios. This heated controversy continued over a period of three years. A. J. Hamil-

ton and the conservatives finally emerged victorious but not until compromises had been made.

ABLEMAN v. BOOTH, 1859 (21 How. 506), provided Chief Justice Taney with an opportunity for a masterly analysis of Federal and state powers. Sherman Booth, sentenced to jail by a Federal court for assisting in the rescue of a fugitive slave at Milwaukee, was released on a writ of habeas corpus issued by a judge of the Supreme Court of Wisconsin on the ground that the Fugitive Slave Act was unconstitutional. The case was carried to the U. S. Supreme Court which rendered a unanimous opinion pronouncing the Fugitive Slave Act valid and forbidding a state to interfere with Federal prisoners by habeas corpus writs.

ABOLITION MOVEMENT. The first recorded vote against slavery in the United States was that on Feb. 18, 1688, by the Monthly Meeting of the Germantown, Pa., Society of Friends. Long before that, even in 1624, protests were heard against slavery in the colonies, both in the South and in the North. When the Revolution came, it was plain to increasing numbers that slavery was inconsistent with the sentiments of the Declaration of Independence. In Jefferson's first draft of that document the slave trade was described as a "cruel war against human nature itself, violating its most sacred rights of life and liberty." Negroes were freed on enlisting in the Continental armies, in which many served.

The early formation of antislavery societies during and immediately after the Revolution showed the strength of the opposition to slavery which waxed until the invention of Eli Whitney's cotton gin in 1793 enthroned King Cotton, made slaves valuable and, together with the Missouri Compromise, caused the dying out of antislavery sentiment. With each year of cotton prosperity the bitterness against all who attacked the human property of the South rose. Still James G. Birney, William Swaim, Cassius M. Clay, John Rankin, John G. Fee, and other Southerners worked steadily in the South for Abolition.

For the corresponding appearance in the North by 1830 of a militant antislavery movement there were various reasons, among them the general awakening of a more humanitarian spirit as shown by the reforming of jails, hospitals and orphanages, the growth of the temperance movement, and the beginning of the agitation for women's rights and suffrage. At this time there appeared a number of leaders and agitators, among the first being Benjamin Lundy, who in turn inspired William Lloyd Garrison, the founding of whose *Liberator*, with his determined announcement: "I will be as harsh as truth and as uncompromising as justice . . . I will not retreat a single inch, and I will be heard," brought about instant repercussions in the South. Within a year the legislature of Georgia offered a reward of $5000 for Garrison's "arrest and conviction."

The Garrison wing was uncompromisingly for immediate emancipation, refused to act politically, violently denounced all who disagreed with its policies, had little to do with the Middle Western and political movements and was as offensive to the moderate wing as to the slaveholders. At first the Church in the North was hostile to the Abolitionists; every church in Boston was closed to them. But gradually there appeared a group of great preachers, such as Theodore Parker, William Ellery Channing, Samuel J. May, and, later, Henry Ward Beecher and others, to espouse the cause of the slave. Other outstanding leaders were Theodore D. Weld, Wendell Phillips, Albert Gallatin, and John Quincy Adams then in the House of Representatives, although he refused to ally himself directly with the Abolition movement. Soon Abolitionists entered Northern state legislatures and Congress, in which, prior to 1835, there was only one, William Slade of Vermont.

Thereafter, Abolition was in politics to dominate everything until Emancipation. To this end the annexation of Texas, the war with Mexico, the Fugitive Slave Law, the Kansas-Nebraska Act, "Bleeding Kansas," the determination of the slaveholders to extend their "peculiar system," all contributed and gave the Abolitionists their opportunity to appeal to the conscience of the nation and keep the country in a turmoil. To this, two books contributed enormously, Harriet Beecher Stowe's *Uncle Tom's Cabin* (1852) and Hinton Rowan Helper's *The Impending Crisis of the South* (1859). From 1850 on, the history of Abolition is the history of the nation, and John Brown's Harpers Ferry raid the curtain-raiser to the bloody years which ended in April, 1865.

ABOLITIONIST LITERATURE extended from 1820 to the Civil War and included many varieties, namely: newspapers, published letters, the *Annual Reports* and other publications of the antislavery societies, sermons and addresses condemning slavery, the narratives and lives of escaped slaves and kidnapped free Negroes, William Lloyd Garrison's *Thoughts on African Colonization* (1832), a denunciation of the principles and purposes of the American Colonization Society, some popular poems of John Greenleaf Whittier and James Russell Lowell and others, *The Liberty Minstrel* (a collection of songs by George W. Clark which passed through several editions), extended analyses and denunciations of the Fugitive Slave Act of 1850 (some of which were reprinted several times), *Uncle Tom's Cabin* and subsequent works by Harriet Beecher Stowe, and the Rev. W. M. Mitchell's *Underground Railroad* (1860), which gave a glimpse at the secret methods of helping the runaways.

The great number of antislavery newspapers began with Charles Osborne's *Philanthropist* (1820) and Benjamin Lundy's *Genius of Universal Emancipation* (1821), both originating at Mt. Pleasant, Ohio, and *The Castigator* (1824) at Ripley, Ohio. *Letters on American Slavery* (1826) by the Rev. John Rankin passed through five editions by 1838. Having read the little book, Garrison became Rankin's "disciple." The Rev. Samuel Crothers, Rankin's contemporary and not distant neighbor, also abhorred slavery, as shown in his *Life and Writings* (1857). Antislavery societies became numerous in the North after 1832 and often had hundreds of members, by whom their *Annual Reports* were read. These Abolitionists also read such publications as *The Anti-Slavery Almanac*, Theodore Dwight Weld's *Slavery as It Is*, *The Anti-Slavery Manual*, *The Cabinet of Freedom*, *The Liberty Bell*, Jay's *View of the Action of the Federal Government on Slavery*, Horace Mann's *Slavery: Letters and Speeches*, E. B. Chase's *Teachings of Patriots and Statesmen*, and the memoirs of escaped slaves, including Frederick Douglass' *My Bondage and My Freedom*, C. E. Stevens' *Anthony Burns*, the *Narrative of Henry Box Brown*, and J. R. Giddings' *The Exiles of Florida;* also the few but stirring memoirs of abductors of slaves. Occasionally a runaway's narrative sold up to 10,000 copies. *Uncle Tom's Cabin* (1852) quickly made a "mass appeal" and intensified Northern hatred of the Fugitive Slave Law of 1850. Mrs. Stowe's *Key to Uncle Tom's Cabin* (1853) fed fuel to the fire, and her *Dred* increased the excitement over the Kansas struggle and the assault on Charles Sumner.

ABRAHAM, PLAINS OF, on the west side of the city of Quebec, were named after Abraham Martin, a Quebec pilot, who once owned part of the land. They were the scene, in 1759, of the battle that brought an end to the dream of French empire in North America, and, incidentally, resulted in the death of two great generals, Wolfe and Montcalm. The site is now a Canadian national park.

ABRAHAM LINCOLN, FORT, was built by Gen. George A. Custer in 1873, on the Missouri River, just below Heart River. Fort McKean, on top a hill above this fort, was an infantry post, and though built first, was usually considered part of Fort Abraham Lincoln. In 1895, the fort was abandoned.

ACADIA AND THE ACADIANS. The name Acadia, whether of European origin or a derivative of the Indian word *Aquoddiake,* was first applied in letters-patent to the grant obtained by Pierre de Guast, Sieur de Monts, from the King of France, Nov. 18, 1603. The boundaries of Acadia, never clearly defined, roughly embraced the North American coast from Cape Breton to the shores below the Hudson (40° to 46° N. Lat.) and overlapped considerably the land claimed by England by virtue of Cabot's discovery and Sir Humphrey Gilbert's possessory claim in the 16th century. Such was the basis for the conflicting claims of England and France to North America which resulted in a hundred and fifty years of predatory warfare, during which time Acadia, unproductive and desolate, was traded back and forth between the two powers as English and French diplomats sought to adjust the balance of losses and acquisitions elsewhere.

Although by the Treaty of Utrecht, 1713, "all Nova Scotia with its ancient boundaries" was ceded to England, French empire builders saw the advantage of tacitly narrowing the indefinite limits of Nova Scotia to what is now the peninsula bearing that name, and England, faced with the necessity of holding the land from the Kennebec to the St. Croix, came to view the French inhabitants of the peninsula, the Acadians, with alarm. By 1755 new colonial wars had broken out. The Acadians, both the victims and oftentimes the participators in maundering warfare, charged by the English with disloyalty undoubtedly fostered by Jesuit priests, were believed to menace the English colonial possessions from within. By an act of extreme severity, immortalized by Longfellow in his *Evangeline,* over 4000 of these Acadians were uprooted from their homes and dispersed to other English colonies, principally Maryland and Virginia. Some made their way to the West Indies and Louisiana. Many found their way back, however, and today their descendants may be found in Nova Scotia as well as in Madawaska, Maine.

Acadians in Louisiana. It is not known that any of the Acadians came directly from their homeland to Louisiana. They came in irregular groups and at irregular intervals, having first attempted to settle at other places without success. Some came by ship to New Orleans from the New England and Atlantic seaboard colonies, but the majority came overland, from Maryland, Pennsylvania, and Virginia, by trail across the mountains and by flatboat down the Tennessee, the Ohio, and the Mississippi rivers. This accounts for the fact that some came after the first deportation, while others did not arrive until 1766. From New Orleans they were first sent some fifty miles up the river to what is now St. James Parish (county) and gave the name of Acadian Coast to that section of the river. Others pushed up the river as far as Pointe Coupée, in the parish of that name. Later arrivals were sent westward into southern Louisiana, from 70 to 100 miles from New Orleans, along Bayou Lafourche and Bayou Teche, into the region protected by the frontier *postes* of Attakapas and Opelousas.

ÁCOMA is the name of both an Indian tribe and its pueblo, perched on a bold rock extending 357 feet into the air in Valencia County, N. Mex. It was discovered by the Spanish in 1539 and at one time had a large population. The Indians gained subsistence by cultivating gardens near the base of the rock which they reached by a dizzy trail cut in the rock. In 1599 the rock was scaled by the Spaniards who, after a three days' battle, killed about 1500 Ácoma, or half the tribe.

ACT FOR THE IMPARTIAL ADMINISTRATION OF JUSTICE (one of the Coercion Acts), passed by Parliament in May, 1774, provided that whenever the governor of Massachusetts doubted whether a person accused of misconduct in suppressing a riot or executing the law could secure a fair trial in Massachusetts, he might, with consent of the Council, transfer the trial to another colony or to Great Britain. This act—known in America as the "Murder Act"—aroused the colonists' apprehensions that the British government intended to establish a military despotism by giving British soldiers the privilege of shooting down Whigs with impunity.

ADAIR v. U. S., 1908 (208 U. S. 161). In violation of a Federal law of 1898, William Adair, acting for the L. & N. Railroad, dismissed O. B. Coppage because he was a member of a labor union. The Supreme Court declared this law unconstitutional because it violated the right of personal liberty and of property guaranteed by the Fifth Amendment.

ADAMS EXPRESS COMPANY. In 1839 Alvin Adams, a produce merchant ruined by the panic of 1837, began carrying letters, small packages and valuables for patrons between Boston and Worcester. Adams rapidly extended his territory to New York, Philadelphia and other eastern cities. By 1847 he had penetrated deeply into the South, and by 1850 he was shipping by rail and stagecoach to St. Louis. In 1854 his company was reorganized as the Adams Express Co. Meanwhile, a subsidiary concern, Adams & Company of California, had been organized in 1850 and spread its service all over the Pacific Coast; but not being under Adams' personal management, it was

3

badly handled, and failed in 1854, causing a panic which shook California to its depths. The South was almost entirely covered by the Adams express service in 1861, when the Civil War necessitated the splitting off of another company, which, for political reasons, was given the name of Southern. There was a mysterious kinship between the two ever afterward, they having joint offices at common points. Southern stock was never quoted in the market, and it was even charged by some Adams stockholders that the Southern was secretly owned by the Adams. The parent company held a strong position from New England and the mid-Atlantic coast to the far Western plains. Its stock holdings were enormous. In 1910 it was the second largest stockholder in the Pennsylvania Railroad and the third largest in the New Haven, besides owning large blocks of American Express, Norfolk & Western and other shares. Its ante bellum employment of Allan Pinkerton to solve its robbery problems was a large factor in building the noted detective agency. Along with the other expresses, it merged its shipping interests into the American Railway Express Co., but continued its corporate existence as a wealthy investment trust.

ADAMS-ONÍS TREATY, signed at Washington, Feb. 22, 1819, by John Quincy Adams, Secretary of State, and Luis de Onís, Spanish Minister, closed the first era of United States expansion by providing for the cession of East Florida, the abandonment of the controversy over West Florida, which had previously been seized by the United States, and a boundary delineation along the Sabine River from the Gulf of Mexico to the 32nd paralled, N. Lat., thence north to the Red River, along it to the 100th parallel, W. Long., north to the Arkansas, along it to its source, thence directly north or south as the case might be to the 42nd parallel, N. Lat., and west on that line to the Pacific Ocean. The United States assumed claims of its own citizens against Spain, prorating them down to a maximum of $5,000,000. Nonconflicting articles of Pinckney's Treaty of 1795 were to remain in force. Spanish goods received certain tariff privileges in Florida ports.

Spain, weakened by European wars and colonial revolutions, was obliged to sacrifice her interests, especially after Andrew Jackson's seizure of Spanish property in the Floridas in 1818. Other nations declined to assist Spain in the negotiations. Ferdinand VII's ministers at first refused to ratify the treaty, using as a pretext the nullification of certain land grants made by Ferdinand in the Floridas. Evasion failed, and after a revolt made Ferdinand a constitutional monarch in 1820, his council was obliged to approve the treaty. Ratifications were exchanged at Washington on Feb. 22, 1821.

ADAMSON ACT, enacted under Administration pressure backed by a strike threat, was passed Sept. 2, 1916. It established, in place of a ten, an eight-hour day for railroad trainmen. The alternative of 100 miles of run remained unchanged. The railroads claimed the law raised wages rather than regulated hours, as normal operation required over eight hours work. The law was upheld, in Wilson v. New (243 U. S. 332), as hour legislation in the interests of interstate commerce.

ADDYSTON PIPE COMPANY CASE, 1899 (175 U. S. 211). The Supreme Court, by a unanimous decision based on the Sherman Antitrust Act, permanently enjoined six producers of cast-iron pipe from continuing an agreement eliminating competition among themselves. Justice Peckham, speaking for the Court, denied that the decision in the Knight case obtained saying that here was a definite conspiracy to interfere with the flow of interstate commerce and a positive scheme to limit competition and fix prices. This decision indicated that the Sherman Antitrust Act possessed "teeth" and tended to restrain similar activities.

ADENA PREHISTORIC CULTURE, a type of Mound Builder culture, takes its name from a mound at Adena, O. It apparently existed in southern Ohio and adjacent parts of Kentucky, West Virginia and Indiana. The culture is characterized by shapely conical mounds, burials in log cists (usually without cremation), skill in carving small objects in the round, the use of tubular pipes, and a limited use of copper for ornamental purposes. No dwelling sites have been found.

ADKINS v. CHILDREN'S HOSPITAL, 1923 (261 U. S. 525), was a Supreme Court decision holding invalid an act of Congress creating a Minimum Wage Board to "ascertain" and "fix" adequate wages for women employees in the District of Columbia.

The question before the Court was whether the act of Congress constituted a deprivation of "life, liberty or property without due process of law" under the Fifth Amendment. The Court held by a vote of five to three that the act was an unjustified interference by Congress with the freedom of employer and employee to contract as they pleased. Taft, Sanford and Holmes, dissenting, took the view that the Fifth Amendment did not stand in the way of reasonable legislation calculated to correct admitted evils. The case was expressly overruled by West Coast Hotel Co. v. Parrish (57 Sup. Ct. 578), 1937.

ADMIRALTY LAW AND COURTS. In the American colonies in the 17th century admiralty jurisdiction was generally exercised by the ordinary common law courts, although governors had the right to commission courts of vice admiralty; but by the end of the century royal patents were being issued for the establishment of vice admiralty courts, beginning in

New York in 1696. In addition to the jurisdiction of the English admiralty courts over such matters as prize, wreck, salvage, insurance, freight and passenger contracts, bottomry, charter parties and seamen's wages, the colonial vice admiralty courts enforced the Acts of Trade. Piracy, which originally was under the jurisdiction of the admiralty, was in the colonies normally dealt with by courts specially commissioned by the crown to deal with particular cases. Procedure in vice admiralty was *in rem* rather than *in personam*. As the vice admiralty courts exercised summary jurisdiction and did not have trial by jury, they attained a considerable degree of unpopularity among that element in the colonies opposed to the Acts of Trade, and in some colonies writs of prohibition were frequently issued by the common law courts against the vice admiralty on the ground that the latter court was incompetent to act in particular litigation. As a rule such writs were obeyed. Common law courts throughout the colonial period, as, for example, the Mayor's Court of New York City, continued to exercise a good deal of admiralty jurisdiction.

After the Revolution most of the states erected their own courts of admiralty, really continuing the provincial courts, but the Federal Convention gave to the Federal courts "all cases of admiralty and maritime jurisdiction." Among the anachronisms surviving down to the 20th century in American admiralty law has been the privilege of the shipowner to limit liability after a disaster to whatever the value of the vessel or wreckage may be after the occurrence of the act. The *Titanic* and *Morro Castle* are two notorious examples of the application of this rule. The evolution of the doctrine of continuous voyage by the Federal courts during the Civil War provided Great Britain during World War I with a convenient precedent to justify the seizure of our ships bound for neutral ports on the ground that their ultimate destination was Germany.

ADOBE HOUSES are structures made of earth and used principally in the Rocky Mountain plateau and in southwestern United States. The method came from North Africa via Spain and was introduced by the Spanish conquerors into the Southwest in the 16th century. Most of the Spanish mission buildings were made of this material. Wet clay and chopped hay or other fibrous material were mixed and the mass tramped with the bare feet. This was molded into brick and sun dried. The walls were laid up with mud mortar. In the Rocky Mountain plateau adobe houses were made by molding clay directly into the wall instead of making it into bricks.

ADOBE WALLS, BATTLE OF, was fought at the buffalo hunters' trading post by that name, on the north side of the Canadian River, in the Panhandle of Texas, June 27, 1874. The hide hunt was on, and the Adobe Walls post, established by hunters and traders from Dodge City, Kans., was the southern outpost.

The Comanche, Cheyenne and Kiowa were concentrated in Indian Territory, but during the spring of 1874 made several raids into Texas. Concentrating on the hunters who were killing their source of food, clothing and shelter, several hundred Indians attacked Adobe Walls. But they could not stand up against the fire of the Sharp's buffalo guns, and though three of the hunters were killed, the Indians, after losing heavily, abandoned the attack.

ADVENTISTS, OR MILLERITES, were followers of William Miller (1782–1849) who, during 1831–44, preached that, according to Daniel's and Ezra's prophecies, at Christ's second coming in 1844 fire would destroy the earth. The advent failing to materialize and opposition from existing sects becoming intolerant, a new church, Adventist, developed in 1845. The adherents believed in Christ's personal, visible return, the necessity for repentance and faith to obtain salvation, a physical resurrection, and a millennium spanning the period between the first and second resurrections. This organization finally disintegrated to form five extant groups, among them the Advent Christian Church and the Seventh-Day Adventist.

ADVENTURERS. Colonization demanded labor and capital. Settlers had to be transported across a hostile sea, properly equipped to build life anew in a virgin land, and supplied with food until self-sustaining. Many were able to help themselves, venturing both life and money. Many others in their poverty were dependent upon financial assistance. The demands upon capital were heavy.

The term "adventurer" runs far back into English history when there appeared a body of traders known as "merchant adventurers." The very name, adventurer, denoted a new age and spirit in mercantile life. With money to invest, these enterprising merchants sought opportunities beyond England's shores. They adventured or risked their capital in foreign trade. Groups of merchant adventurers existed in Bristol, London, York, Chester and other leading ports.

These adventurers supplied the capital and enterprise which built up England's profitable commercial dominion in the Old World in the 16th century. The New World offered new opportunities. The merchants of Bristol aided Gilbert's futile colonial venture in Newfoundland in 1583 and a few London merchants assisted Raleigh in his ill-fated attempt to settle Roanoke Island in 1585. A larger capital was necessary and the familar device of the joint-stock company was employed. Adventurers of Plymouth subscribed to the stock of the Plymouth Company whose colonial effort in Maine in 1607 promptly failed. London adventurers took stock in the com-

5

pany which by persistent effort succeeded in making Virginia a permanent colony. A group of London merchants risked their capital in aiding the Pilgrims to settle the colony of Plymouth in 1620. The colony of Massachusetts originated in an association of merchants living in and about Dorchester, England. Not all those who risked their capital were merchants. The charter of 1609 to the Virginia Company of London incorporated fifty-six companies of the city of London and 659 persons gathered from various walks of life.

ADVERTISING. Early American advertisements were usually of the legal-notice variety with a slight amount of display or illustration. The *Boston News Letter* in its third issue, May 1–8, 1704, carried a notice of real estate for sale, and two notices of lost articles. Soon there were also runaways to be advertised and slaves for sale. These were set solid as other matter, though with a larger initial letter. Franklin in 1735 used larger type at the head of a notice; and somewhat later began the use of small woodcuts—of ships, Negroes, horses, etc.—to give variety and interest to the page. Notices were usually column width, and the larger were elongated squares. Shortage of paper led printers to discourage large notices, and to set a limit to the size of cuts.

These advertisements furnish valuable information for social and economic history. Commodities listed by merchants and manufacturers show the variety of imports and extent of manufactures, as well as consumers' tastes. Details of transportation and communication are found in notices of the sailings of ships, of post-routes, and later of stage, canal, and steamboat schedules. Beginnings of the professions are indicated by such notices as Paul Revere's offer to make false teeth (1768), and those offering the services of barbers, schoolteachers and dancing masters. Morals of an earlier generation are revealed by advertisements for runaway apprentices and slaves, and by offers of slaves for sale, often with detailed descriptions; and when the head of a family inserted a notice for a wet nurse, or informed the public not to trust the wife who had left his "bed and board." Lotteries, theatrical entertainments, horse races, and exhibitions of animals were recorded in advertisements, while cultural advance was indicated by notices of schools, musical organizations, libraries and lists of books for sale.

Up to the time of the Civil War, advertising in America was mainly local, in such forms as signs, posted bills, cards, pamphlets, handbills and brief notices in the newspapers. Many merely identified a seller and listed his wares. Others aimed to bring together a specific need and a supply, and were often inserted by the prospective buyer, as in "Lost and Found" and "Wanted" advertisements. Even retailers' advertisements seldom contained much salesmanship before the adoption of the one-price policy.

Among manufacturers, almost the only ones who advertised were the proprietors of patent medicines. Most families resorted to self-medication, especially in districts where doctors were scarce and not readily accessible. There was a lively demand for sarsaparillas, bitters, liniments, pills and panaceas. Such items had a low transportation cost, a high profit margin to manufacturer and retailer, and enjoyed a good repeat sale. However, the task of inducing the first purchase required aggressive salesmanship. Medical advertising was usually full of sensational and exaggerated claims; much of it was fraudulent.

Medical advertisers used every available medium. A favorite form was the almanac, since it was likely to be kept for reference throughout the year. The newspapers were almost the only periodicals available. Their values varied greatly and their rates were elastic. The difficulty of bargaining for space in them was partly solved by the emergence of the advertising agency. The agent could secure the lowest possible rate and handle the details of billing and checking; later he undertook other services.

After the Civil War the agricultural papers and religious papers enjoyed a brief importance. The general magazines at this period were not highly regarded as advertising media, and most of the influential ones did not welcome advertising. Some inserted only advertisements of books issued by their own publishing house. But in the 1880's, the magazines began to be more receptive to advertisers whose products and claims they considered acceptable. Because they had a country-wide circulation of well-to-do people, and were comparatively free from objectionable medical advertising, they rose rapidly toward a position of leadership in national advertising.

By this time American inventive genius had brought forth many new types of articles, and the network of railroads had made it possible to ship them to all the states of the Union. Manufacturers of cameras, fountain pens, typewriters, bicycles and a host of other new articles found the magazine a convenient medium for educating the public regarding their products. Manufacturers of new types of old articles like shaving soap, or of articles that were not habitually used, like chocolate and canned soup, widened their markets by magazine advertising. Brands of staple articles competed for the consumers' choice. Service industries used institutional advertisements to build good will for their organizations.

The growth of national advertising was aided by the constantly increasing efficiency of transportation, by the cheapness of periodicals, by the gradual transition from homemade to factory-made products, and by the change from buying in bulk to buying in packages. Advertising, in turn, exerted a reciprocal action in hastening these changes. This action was most obvious in the field of periodical publishing, where early in the 20th century advertising had become the chief source of income. It made possible two-cent newspapers of 48 or more pages, and five-cent weeklies with as much editorial content as the old 35-cent monthlies.

Advertising in the small "standard-size" (6" x 9") magazine soon reached a point of saturation. Advertisements in a thick segregated advertising section had a poor chance of being seen. Advertisers turned to the larger-size flat publications, with reading matter distributed through the advertising section. Many of the older magazines changed their formats to meet the advertisers' wishes; others suspended. The losses were largely offset by the rise of new periodicals of various kinds, notably class publications with audiences selected on the basis of vocation or leisure interests.

In 1929 the highest peak of national advertising up to that time was reached in an issue of the *Saturday Evening Post* containing 272 pages, of which about 168 were advertising pages (many in four colors) with a total cost of $1,579,408. The actual advertising cost per inch of space, on the basis of audience reached, was lower than that of most magazines of the 19th century, for the publication reached nearly three million families.

Modern advertising would be unthinkable without the advertising agency which appears to have originated in the activities of independent space brokers early in the 19th century. Some of these were freelance advertising salesmen, or conveniently situated businessmen (such as postmasters), who as a sideline accepted advertisements for insertion in various newspapers. N. W. Ayer of Philadelphia, the oldest agency in existence in 1960, was formed in 1869. Probably the earliest to make space brokerage his sole business was Volney B. Palmer. Shortly after 1840 he had offices in Boston, New York and Philadelphia, and represented himself as a duly accredited agent to receive advertisements and subscriptions for "most of the best papers published in the United States and Canada." He assumed no responsibility for collecting money from the advertiser, but charged the publisher 25% for his service in selling the space.

Another agent, John L. Hooper, who began business in New York about the same time as Palmer, or a little later, inaugurated a policy that eventually became standard practice with agencies. He assumed the financial risk of paying the publisher himself and then collecting from the advertisers. By the time of the Civil War, at least twenty agencies were operating in the larger cities.

In 1865, George P. Rowell invented his "List System" which consisted in buying space at wholesale and selling at retail. His offer was "an-inch-of-space-a-month-in-one-hundred-papers-for-one-hundred-dollars." Similar methods were adopted by other agents and applied to other kinds of periodicals, such as religious papers, farm papers and general magazines. The system was an important factor in the early development of magazine advertising, but ultimately was

abandoned, and the commission basis of payment was re-established.

Throughout the early period, the chief service of the agent was that of buying space more efficiently than the advertiser could do it. Newspapers varied tremendously in advertising values and the publishers' claims of circulation were notoriously unreliable. Only an expert space-buyer could determine the value of advertising space in a given medium, and buy it at the lowest price. Secret knowledge of values and rates, together with bargaining ability, remained the chief assets of the advertising agent until 1869. In that year appeared the first volume of Rowell's American Newspaper Directory. This listed 5411 publications in the United States and 367 in Canada, with estimates of their circulation. Subsequent issues of this directory, and other media directories and services, gradually made information about circulations more accessible and reliable. Space buying had become a minor function of most agencies by 1914, when the Audit Bureau of Circulations was established to secure accurate and systematic information regarding the quantity and quality of circulation of periodicals.

In the meantime, the agencies were developing new and valuable services. Through their experience in placing advertising they accumulated funds of knowledge about planning and executing campaigns. They wrote copy, designed the pictorial and typographic display, supervised the art work, and handled the production of material used in the actual printing of the advertisements. Many agencies added research departments as well as departments for handling such media as industrial publications, direct mail and radio. Although most of these services could be performed by the advertiser himself, the bulk of national advertisers and many local advertisers found it expedient to employ the expert knowledge of an agency.

Thus, the advertising agents approached a professional status. However, they were in the anomalous position of regarding the advertisers as their clients, while receiving most of their compensation from the media in the form of a commission. The amount of this commission varied in the 1880's and 1890's, but ultimately became standardized at 15% for most newspapers and magazines. The amount of service rendered to the advertiser was not so easily fixed. Moreover, the competition for desirable clients resulted occasionally in "splitting commissions" or otherwise rebating a part of the compensation.

To correct such practices and other forms of unfair competition, local associations of agencies were formed, and in 1917 a national organization, known as the American Association of Advertising Agencies, was established. This included in its membership the majority of the "fully recognized" agencies in the country. An agency was "recognized" by a publisher when he granted it the commission on space purchased through it. To secure such recognition, an agency usually had to demonstrate its financial strength, its expert ability, its possession of several substantial clients, and its freedom from alliances with either publishers or advertisers.

The Association of Agencies adopted a code of Standards of Practice in 1924 by which the members agreed to refrain from unfair competition or rebates, from submitting speculative plans or copy, and from preparing or handling any advertising of an untruthful, indecent, or objectionable character.

ADVERTISING SINCE 1929. The key figure in advertising during the 1920's and 1930's was Albert Lasker of Lord & Thomas. The most famous advertiser of the period was George Washington Hill of American Tobacco Co., who tyrannized his agencies, partly by being difficult to satisfy, partly by being something of an advertising genius in his own right. He was satirized in *The Hucksters,* a novel by Frederic Wakeman, published in 1946. Meanwhile, from 1922 to 1941, radio advertising grew to billings of $247,000,000.

Even before Pearl Harbor, the advertising business was called on to enlist public interest in conserving vital materials, to spur enlistment in the armed forces, and to make appeals for funds. Since many corporations had no goods to sell in World War II, advertising was largely spent in promoting the war effort. This was organized by the Advertising Council, a group created for the purpose of promoting co-operation between the Government and business. Campaigns on worthy subjects were prepared by agencies and either run free by media or paid for by advertisers in the public interest.

Television, once the war was over, expanded to billings of $1,291,000,000 in 1957, without damage to newspaper billings which reached $3,283,300,000 in that year. Magazines accounted for $815,300,000, radio for $622,500,000, while direct mail rose from $277,000,000 in 1939 to $1,527,000,000 in 1958.

At the end of 1959, billings for the six largest agencies were as follows: J. Walter Thompson, $328,000,000; McCann-Erickson, $304,000,000; Young & Rubicam, $232,000,000; Batten, Barton, Durstine & Osborn, $216,000,000; Ted Bates, $120,000,000; and Leo Burnett, $114,000,000.

AFRICAN COMPANY, ROYAL (1672–1750), was one of a series of trading companies granted a monopoly of the African slave trade. In 1672 it took over the charter and African trading posts of the Company of Royal Adventurers to Africa established by the Duke of York and associates in 1662. In 1697 its monopoly was destroyed when independent merchants were permitted to engage in the trade upon payment for fourteen years of export duties which were turned over to the company to maintain its posts. From this time the trade was largely absorbed by the independents. During the 18th century most of the slaves were carried to the West Indies and North America in ships owned by Bristol, Liverpool and colonial merchants. The company endeavored to prevent independent traders from bargaining directly with native dealers. Most of the Negroes it secured were sold to the independents, to the English South Sea Company after it was granted the Asiento (1713), or even to foreign traders. The destruction of the monopoly, the competition of independent traders, the expense of maintaining its posts, and the imposition of poll duties on slave importations by Virginia, South Carolina, Jamaica and Barbados, all proved so disastrous to the company, that, in spite of annual grants by Parliament of £10,000 beginning in 1729, its affairs were wound up in 1750. By that year, of the 155 British ships in the trade, twenty were North American, nearly half from Rhode Island.

AFRICAN METHODIST EPISCOPAL CHURCH. The oldest and largest denomination of colored Methodists, organized in 1816 with Richard Allen as its first Bishop. The origin of this body was the result of friction in St. George's Methodist Episcopal Church in Philadelphia, due to a feeling of race discrimination and a consequent conviction on the part of the colored members that they would enjoy a larger measure of freedom in worship and service by themselves. The denomination grew in the first decade slowly, reaching a membership of nearly 10,000, but after the close of the Civil War increased rapidly.

AGAMENTICUS. Successively known as Bristol (1632), Agamenticus (1641), Gorgeana (1642), and York (1652), this early Maine settlement, equidistant from Mt. Agamenticus and the Piscataqua River, has the distinction of being the first municipal corporation in America (1642), created so by Sir Ferdinando Gorges whose special favor the settlement enjoyed.

AGRARIAN MOVEMENT. Efforts on the part of the rural classes to better their lot by concerted political action have been almost a constant quantity in American history. Even in colonial times the southern planters, forced to exchange their produce for British manufacturers on terms that left them permanently in debt to British merchants, protested to the point of revolt against the imperial regulations that they blamed for their distress. From their point of view the American Revolution was a movement to free American agriculture from the tyranny of British commercialism. Independence was no sooner won, however, than in some of the northern states the debt-ridden farmers of the back-country launched a similar protest against the political power of the well-to-do seaboard merchants. The latter, frightened by such episodes as Shays' Rebellion in Massachusetts and the paper money craze in Rhode Island, joined with the creditor classes generally in a movement to provide a national government strong enough to keep order and protect property. The Constitution of the United States was the result.

Differences between the devotees of commerce and of agriculture speedily produced a two-party political system for the new republic. The Federalists, under the effective leadership of Alexander Hamilton, made it their business to head off money inflation, establish the national credit, keep open the lanes of commerce, and minimize the rights of the states, in which occasionally the agrarians had the upper hand. When the need for more revenue required the levying of an excise tax, they singled out whisky, a by-product of the back-country farms, to bear the burden. These policies the Republicans, equally well led by the agriculturally minded Thomas Jefferson, criticized with increasing vehemence. When the "Revolution of 1800" made Jefferson President, the more offensive Federalist measures were repealed, and a new course, definitely favorable to agriculture, was charted. The purchase of Louisiana added new territory for the agricultural interest to exploit, while such measures as the Embargo and Nonintercourse gravely jeopardized the welfare of commerce. Under Jefferson's successor, Madison, the War of 1812 was fought, less to safeguard American commerce on the high seas than to end the British and Indian menace to the westward march of agriculture, and to pave the way for the conquest by farmers and planters of Canada and Florida.

Ironically, the commercial restrictions that preceded and accompanied the War of 1812 resulted in a new and formidable challenge to the supremacy of the agriculturalists. Domestic manufacturing, essential because commerce had languished, soon revealed possibilities of profit that could not be ignored. Factories, particularly in the Northeast, multiplied with amazing rapidity, and the agricultural interests, scarcely aware of what had been going on, awoke to find themselves almost displaced by factory owners and their satellites in the control of the Republican (Jeffersonian) party. Soon the very party that Jefferson had founded was chartering a new national bank, adopting a protective tariff and giving serious consideration to a nation-wide program of internal improvements. Jacksonian Democracy was in no small degree the inevitable response of the agriculturalists to this challenge of the industrialists, and with the elevation of "Old Hickory" to the presidency—"the Revolution of 1828"—much of the lost ground was recovered. The Bank was destroyed, the tariff was reduced, and the burdensome problem of internal improvements was relegated to the states and to individuals.

The solidarity of the agricultural front was not to be maintained for long. The planters of the South, now obedient to the dictates of "King Cotton" and devoted as never before to the system of slave labor, had little in common with the small free farmers who owned the West. Both wished for expansion, and they cheerfully joined hands against the Indians and against the Mexicans to take what they wanted. But each hoped to exclude the other from the spoils of war. The small free farmers wished a small-free-farmer West; the slave-owning planters wished a slave-owning-planter West. The southern planters, however, were far more gifted at the game of politics than their western rivals, and for a generation after Jackson left office they maintained an unbroken ascendancy in the national councils.

Distaste for the policies of the slave-holding South at length drove the free-farmer West into an open alliance with the industrial Northeast. The fruit of this union was a new Republican party, which promised to the West free lands, to the Northeast a protective tariff, and to both a Pacific railroad. Rather than submit to such a program the South fought, and lost, the Civil War. With southern protests stilled, the other sections voted themselves what they had promised, and, for good measure, a new national banking system as well. Slavery itself was abolished.

The leadership of the re-united nation fell naturally to the industrialists. This was not due solely to the War, for the rising tide of industrialism was world-wide, not merely national. In the United States, as elsewhere, population tended more and more to concentrate in cities; and whole new industries such as steel and oil, virtually unknown before the Civil War, extended the field of industrial operations far into the West and South. Against this growing strength of the industrialists the agriculturalists found it difficult to unite. Farmers in the industrialized sections ministered to the local city markets, and tended to accept without protest both the policies and the prices that were offered them, while the farmers of West and South, with their economic interests at best somewhat divergent, overcame with difficulty the rancors let loose by war.

The same forces that had been at work to transform industry, however, were bringing about a revolution in agriculture. The old system of production for use, to which the small free farmer had long been accustomed, gradually gave way to a system of production for sale. New machines transformed each farm into a kind of factory, designed often-times to turn out a highly specialized product. The farmers of the Northwest concentrated on wheat, or corn, or live stock, or dairy products. The farmers of the South still pinned their faith mainly to tobacco and cotton. Fruit-growers appeared in the Far West. All were dependent upon the railroads for transportation, upon the banks for credit, upon the merchants for all those necessities of life that farmers no longer produced for themselves, upon nation-wide or world-wide markets for the prices of the things they had to sell.

Land values, thanks in part to the greater economy of production with the new machines and in part to the disappearance of the frontier, rose persistently. But farm mortgages also mounted, tenantry increased, and each cycle of depression left the rural classes worse off, relatively, than they had been before.

Out in the upper Mississippi Valley, where the cost of transportation ate up all the grain growers' profits, and down in the reconstructed South, where the crop-lien system had forced the cotton growers into virtual peonage, the "embattled farmers" began fumblingly and reluctantly to unite in their own defense. Through their experiences with the Granger movement, the Greenback movement, and the Farmers' Alliances, they learned that, if only they could stand together as voters, they might force the governments of state and nation to restrain the railroads and the trusts, to scale down debts by some form of money inflation, and to protect in general the farmers' interests. They discovered, too, that by co-operation in marketing, in purchasing, and even in manufacturing they might hope, with adequate management, to help themselves. Efforts to unite the rural classes into a People's Party that would take over the government and administer it directly in the farmers' interest failed during the 1890's, but the drift toward closer organization and co-operation went on.

During the 20th century the rural classes brought persistent pressure upon state governments to attain desired ends. In Wisconsin, for example, the LaFollette progressives, composed mainly of rural voters, captured the Republican organization, instituted the primary system of making nominations for office, established close supervision of railroads and public utilities, and reformed the system of taxation. The Farmers' Nonpartisan League in North Dakota, Minnesota and other northwestern states attempted with less complete success to bring about state operation of elevators, flour mills, and other businesses deemed guilty of taking unfair advantages of the farmers. Alliances with labor became increasingly common, and paved the way for such organizations as the Farmer-Labor party of Minnesota, and the Farmer-Labor-Progressive federation of Wisconsin. In the South the rural whites, increasingly rebellious against the exactions of country storekeepers and landlords, put their trust in the promises of such demagogic leaders as James K. Vardaman and Theodore G. Bilbo of Mississippi, the "Hon. Jeff." Davis of Arkansas, and Huey P. Long of Louisiana. Numerous agricultural organizations, such as the American Society of Equity, the Farmers' Union, and the American Farm Bureau Federation, appeared both in the South and in the West. Most of these orders emphasized almost equally the need of political pressure and of farmer-owned business co-operatives.

On the national front the agriculturalists regained much of the unity they had known before the Civil War. Republican "insurgents" from the Northwest worked together with southern Democrats from agricultural regions against the high protective rates of the Payne-Aldrich tariff, and during Wilson's administration helped inaugurate a generous Federal farm loan system. When the overexpansion of agriculture during World War I led to a drastic deflation at its close, a congressional "Farm Bloc," aided by pressure from a multitude of agricultural organizations the country over, began an agitation for farm relief that led eventually to the establishment under Hoover of the short-lived Federal Farm Board, and under F. D. Roosevelt of the Agricultural Adjustment Administration. Both measures had as their main objective the stabilization of farm incomes at a high enough level to insure farmers a profitable return for their labor and investments. When in 1936 the U. S. Supreme Court held the "A.A.A." unconstitutional, the New Deal substituted for it a soils conservation policy designed to gain the same end in another way.

AGRICULTURAL ADJUSTMENT ADMINISTRATION (1933). The Agricultural Adjustment Act of 1933 was an emergency measure of the New Deal. In 1932 the platform of the Democratic party pledged the extension and "development of the farm co-operative movement and effective control of crop surpluses." Thus, it was at the instigation of Secretary of Agriculture Henry Wallace that President F. D. Roosevelt called representative farm leaders to Washington on March 10, 1933. Six days later the Chief Executive sent to Congress a bill drafted by the conference.

In his message of March 16, the President pointed out that while the measure followed "a new and untrod path," "an unprecedented condition" called for a "new means to rescue agriculture." By May 10 Congress had agreed to the provisions of the farm bill, and two days later the President signed the measure proposing to "relieve the existing national economic emergency by increasing agricultural purchasing power." The statute emphasized the emergency situation and attempted to increase farm income and to reduce farm surpluses. Using the years 1909–14 as a base period, the administrators hoped to establish and maintain a balance between production and consumption of agricultural products.

Included in the statute were provisions relative to credit extension and relief for farm mortgages; but more particularly the Secretary of Agriculture was given extensive authority to reduce productive acreage and to foster marketing quotas. To effect the program farm surpluses were removed from the market and prices were to be increased by placing restraints on production. Immediate payments were made to farmers participating in the program.

The much discussed tax levied upon processors was to "obtain revenue for extraordinary expenses incurred by reason of the national economic emergency." The tax was to help defray the administrative costs of carrying out the provisions of the enactment. And agreements drawn up by participating farmers were to prevent produce from burdening markets. To help administer the act, state and local committees, or associations of producers, were to assist the Federal officials. This was a concession to avoid the criticism of centralization. The entire plan was to be financed by an appropriation of $100,000,000.

After the Agricultural Adjustment Act was in operation three years the Supreme Court in 1936 declared, in U. S. v. Butler, that the statute was unconstitutional. It was held that the regulation of agriculture did not come within the jurisdiction of Congress, but was instead a function properly belonging to the states. Following this declaration, Congress enacted a Soil Conservation and Domestic Allotment program for farm relief.

AGRICULTURAL ADJUSTMENT ADMINISTRATION ACT OF 1938.

This act was the result of the unconstitutionality of previous New Deal farm legislation and the success of the Soil Conservation and Domestic Allotment Act passed in 1936. During the first session of the Seventy-fifth Congress an extension of the soil conservation plan was given consideration. Through the summer of 1937 hearings of farm leaders were conducted in various states; but the second session adjourned while the farm bill was still in the hands of a conference committee.

In his message of Jan. 3, 1938, President F. D. Roosevelt emphasized the work of the conference committee and hoped that a "sound, consistent measure" would be adopted. After some debate in Congress the President, on Feb. 16, signed the measure providing "for the conservation of national soil resources."

The Soil Conservation Act was to be continued as a permanent farm policy; and to promote the program, national acreage allotments were to be fixed at a point "to give production sufficient for domestic consumption, for exports, and for reserve supplies." To induce farmers to operate within the allotments, payments were to be made by the Government. In order that "an adequate and balanced flow of agricultural commodities" might be maintained, the statute incorporated a method for storing produce in years of shortage.

AGRICULTURAL EXPERIMENT STATIONS

were established to provide instructional materials for the colleges and to investigate occupational problems. Organization and method were modeled upon European stations and the work of state chemists. The first station was founded by Connecticut in 1875 and by 1887 fourteen states had definite organizations and in thirteen others the colleges conducted equivalent work. The Bussey Institution at Harvard (since 1871) and the Houghton Farm at Cornwall, N. Y. (1876–88), were privately endowed stations. Through the combined efforts of the colleges and the Department of Agriculture the Federal Hatch Act of 1887 provided an annual subvention for the stations. This aid has been increased by the Adams Act (1906) and the Purnell Act (1925).

AGRICULTURE.

When the first settlers landed in America, the Indians were engaged in agriculture which ranged from the most primitive to fairly advanced methods of cultivation. The natives' main crop was maize, but their crudely tilled fields also contained beans, squash, potatoes, peanuts, tobacco, and wild cotton plants.

At first the colonists existed on natural food plants, wild game and fish, and many would have starved but for supplies obtained from the Indians. Gradually they adopted the native maize culture pattern, their farms being almost counterparts of Indian cornfields. Beans and hilled corn were planted together, with pumpkins and squash between the hills. From the Indians the settlers also learned of pemmican, maple sugaring, and the use of native dye plants such as indigo. Faced with a shortage of metal tools, they adopted the natives' digging sticks, flint and bone hoes, winnowing baskets, cornhusking pegs, and they copied the design of the Indian corncrib set on posts to dry the grain. They also learned from more advanced tribes the practice of seed selection in corn growing, and achieved yields of thirty to forty bushels per acre as did some of their mentors.

The first farms were set in clearings along the coastal plain, land which probably had been used and abandoned by Indians for maize plantings. The soil was seldom good, and soon the colonists were moving into the interior, resorting to primitive slash-and-burn methods upon the forests to obtain suitable farm land.

From the very beginning, labor scarcities have influenced American agricultural practices, and except for periods of economic depression the shortage has existed to the present, acting as an incentive for the development of labor-saving tools, equipment and machinery. Labor was scarce at first because of cheapness of land, later because of the ready availability of manufacturing and other types of employment. This competition of low-priced land and high-priced labor forced most Northern farmers to rely on their own efforts, one man clearing from one to three acres of land yearly by the hardest and most primitive form of stoop labor.

During the 17th and 18th centuries apprenticeship systems—indentured servants and redemptioners—brought thousands of farm laborers into the middle colonies, but as most of these emigrants soon gained their independence and acquired farms of their own, the labor shortage still persisted. Slave labor, both Indian and Negro, was tried in all the colonies, but the male Indian considered physical labor a disgrace

11

and would not toil, and the Negro was found to be suited only to the plantation system of the Southern states. In the South, slave labor proved so effective it drove out most of the free labor—although only one fourth of the population owned slaves. Yet, even with slaves, labor supply was usually short in the rapidly expanding agricultural economy of the South.

Thus in the first decades of American colonization, agriculture established labor patterns which were to affect the stream of history. In the South it was slavery; in the middle colonies it was indentured servants, working toward freedom and new homes; in New England it was community farming evolving into independent family farms.

During the colonial period little was done to improve implements which might have helped overcome the shortage of manpower. Dependent upon the Old World for manufactured articles, American farmers worked with simple hoes, pitchforks, axes, harrows, shovels and scythes. Plows were always scarce, the first one on record in America arriving in Plymouth colony twelve years after its establishment. Owners of plows could earn a good living plowing for their neighbors—a forerunner of the modern practice of custom-hiring power machinery. In the South, tobacco required only a minimum of machinery, the capital investment of huge plantations consisting only of the land, slave labor, work animals, plows, carts, and a few simple tools which could be contrived by plantation blacksmiths. And so, by the end of the 18th century, there was but slight improvement in farm implements. The hand tools were heavy, clumsy, poorly designed for their purposes. Plows were still primitive, barely scratching the surface of the earth. Harvesting and threshing implements, the scythe and the flail, were little advanced over those of Biblical times.

The chief characteristic of agriculture during the colonial period was its reckless wastefulness of soil, forests, and water. To the immigrants, the New World appeared an inexhaustible continent. Land was so plentiful and so cheap that it was acquired with the expectation of wearing it out by continuous cropping. The pioneer farmer was a migrant, always moving westward, claiming new ground when his old fields lost their fertility. Before the end of the 18th century, however, the best of the farmlands east of the Alleghenies were under cultivation, and agricultural experimenters such as Thomas Jefferson were beginning to advocate rotation and fertilization practices.

After moving away from the open coastlands, settlers found it necessary to clear trees and brush from their claims before crops could be grown. Sometimes trees were cut and burned, sometimes only girdled. In the North, maize was almost invariably the first crop, then wheat and rye followed when the ground had been worked sufficiently. The South, which was to become the primary agricultural region of the new nation, was exporting great quantities of tobacco, sugar, rice and indigo before the Revolutionary War. Cotton, grown for home use from the time of the Jamestown settlements, did not become a commercial crop until after the war. And as in the North, maize was the principal grain crop, being more easily grown and harvested than the smaller grains.

As the American Indian had no domesticated animal except the dog, farm livestock had to be imported. Wild game provided a meat supply for the colonists, and the first importations were mainly oxen and a few draft horses. But by the 18th century, the typical Northern farm was equipped with a few cattle, swine and sheep to provide milk, meat and wool for the farm family.

The livestock industry was slower to develop in the South, and in fact was discouraged in several colonies because of the desire of land-grant owners to concentrate production of staple crops on the plantations. When cattle proved to be profitable in Virginia and the Carolinas, the open-range system was generally used, and thus it was in the South that the pattern of later far-western ranching was established—with brands and marks to denote ownership, annual roundups, and overland drives to markets.

As the young nation moved into the 19th century, agriculture expanded rapidly westward in ever sharper competition for labor with the industrial revolution. In northern areas the manpower shortage became so acute by 1840 that inventors of improved farm implements and machinery found ready markets for their contrivances. The period from 1840 to the Civil War saw a ferment of inventions for the farm, hundreds of new patents being registered for implements designed to save labor. Plows were improved, iron replacing wood in the moldboard, share and landside. Shovels, hoes, and forks were better designed and made of cast steel. The grain cradle replaced the sickle; the horse-drawn, four-wheeled wagon replaced the oxcart. Horse rakes, hay balers, seed drills, corn planters, and mowing machines enabled horsepower to replace manpower. In the 1850's steam plows were introduced, creating much excitement, but these early predecessors of modern power machinery were too cumbersome and heavy, inefficient as dinosaurs, unable to compete with the horse.

Competition arising from the West quickened interest in farm machinery in the eastern areas of the South. Inventors were particularly active in Virginia —where the McCormick reaper had its beginnings— and planters eagerly purchased new plows, straw cutters, hemp and flax breakers, and rice hullers. But all attempts to devise a mechanical cotton picker failed at this time.

One side result of these changes was the gradual disappearance of the ox, that now almost forgotten beast of burden which hauled families by the thousands to frontier claims, plowed the first fields, carried wood and water, and was eventually sacrificed for food and leather. In 1840 there were three oxen to every two horses on American farms; by 1860 these numbers were about equal. Soon after the Civil War the ox virtually vanished, and for the next sixty years the horse was to reign supreme as the power source on farms.

In the first half of the 19th century, livestock production gradually developed into importance in areas just west of the Alleghenies. Between 1840 and 1860, a large-scale beef cattle industry flourished in Ohio and the Kentucky Bluegrass regions, the finished animals being trailed overland to markets in the East. Sheep and swine production also shifted westward while dairying remained concentrated in the East, closer to markets. By mid-century, the South was taking the lead in animal husbandry, the great breeding centers being in the pasture regions of Kentucky and Tennessee. The highest types of animals were imported from abroad—Henry Clay was one of the active leaders in improving livestock breeds—and from these germinal areas livestock farming spread to other sections of the South. During the 1850's Texans were beginning to drive cattle into the midwest for fattening, foreshadowing the great western beef cattle industry which was to develop after the Civil War.

If there was ever a golden age of American agriculture it existed in the years immediately preceding the Civil War. This was the era of Currier and Ives prints, of John Greenleaf Whittier's "Barefoot Boy," of Stephen Foster's ballads—romanticizing and idealizing rural life. It was also the era of agricultural societies and fairs, of many new farm periodicals—all spreading the gospel of better tillage, improved livestock breeding, crop rotations, and conservation practices. The burgeoning cities and manufacturing centers provided ready markets for farm products. While not all American farmers were prosperous, by comparison with the times before the advent of new labor-saving inventions, life was easy-going, the future seemed bright, rural life was the national ideal.

As the era came to a close with the outbreak of the Civil War, the center of agriculture was shifting to the west, to the vast raw prairie lands. John Deere's invention of a steel plow which would scour in the clinging black humus of prairie soils opened the richest grain-growing region in the world, millions of acres which earlier settlers had avoided or passed over as unsuited to agriculture. Here the farms were more isolated, social events less frequent. Populations were of mixed nationalities. There was more machinery, but overproduction and uncertain markets created tensions and insecurities.

In the South, also, the plantation system was exploding westward on the basis of cotton production—made possible by Eli Whitney's cotton gin—moving out of the Carolinas and Georgia across the black prairies of Alabama to the rich deltas of the Mississippi and Red Rivers. With the westward movement marched the burning question of slavery. Would the farms of the Western territories, future American states, be worked by free men or slaves?

The old rivalry between western and eastern agriculture was diminished by this greater rivalry between North and South. From colonial days the latter sections had been moving in different directions, and the South's commercial cotton cultivation of the 19th century had accelerated the differences. In addition to its cotton the South produced more than half the nation's corn, almost all of its tobacco, all of its rice and sugar. As the Civil War approached, the self-sufficient Northern farmers were also struggling toward a commercial type of agriculture, but they were hindered by habits and traditions, most of all by lack of working capital.

The war's outbreak had little effect on agricultural labor supply in the South, few slaves being diverted to direct military efforts, and the major change was a switch from large cotton acreages to corn and other food crops. In the North, however, many rural young men went into the army, creating a great labor shortage on farms at a time when produce was bringing fancy prices because of increased demand. To solve the dilemma, output of farm machines was increased sharply; old men, boys, and women could operate horsepowered cultivators, mowers, and reapers. The pressure of wartime thus served as a further impetus to lighten human labor, and the latter years of the struggle and the decades following it saw a new wave of inventions. The sulky plow took the farmer out of the furrow and placed him on a seat. Multiple-row cultivators, gang plows, twelve-foot seeders, lister drills, corn harvesters and shellers made it possible for him to do the work of several men in one operation.

In the 1880's when huge bonanza grain farms were opened on the Great Plains, machines were developed to reduce the back-breaking work of harvesting. The steam engine replaced the treadmill and sweep horsepower in threshing. Steam-powered combines and traction engines appeared as the first threat to the supremacy of the draft horse and mule. Then shortly after the turn of the century, the gasoline engine reached the farm as a replacement for the vanishing "handy man," cutting silage, grinding feed, pumping water, sawing wood, shelling corn, digging postholes, churning milk. Hailed as a deliverer of the farmer from drudgery chores, the gasoline engine served only a generation—to be replaced after World War I by the electric motor.

During this period of rapid mechanization, the farm frontier moved across the western plains ten times as fast as it had moved across the wooded regions of the East. The Homestead Act of 1862 which provided free land for settlers who would live on it for five years (military service being deductible) was an accelerating force to settlement. A flood of European emigrants, mainly Germans and Scandinavians, joined this westward-moving army. Specialization of crops became relatively more important, with increasing need for additional capital to finance risks and necessary machinery.

Wheat was the principal crop in the West, and once again the old story of land abuse was repeated, with the added hazards of crop failures from drought or pests, and foreclosures from over-extended debts and mortgages. When prices of commodities began falling, the postwar boom failed, and farm life on the new frontier turned almost as hard and barren as on the old frontier of a century earlier.

This was the period also of a major shift of livestock production from East to West, the corn-hog pattern of farming developing in the Middle West, the cattle kingdom in the Southwest and on the Great Plains. The rise of the Western cattle industry was the most picturesque of all American agricultural endeavors—the long drives from Texas to Kansas railheads and Montana ranges, the romantic cowboys, the wars between cattlemen and sheepmen, cattlemen and homesteaders. Shorthorns and Herefords gradually replaced the scrawny Texas Longhorns, the open range was closed, and in the mountain states sheep outnumbered cattle. By the late 1880's, Western stockmen were in as dire straits as the homesteaders. Blizzards, droughts and overproduction brought threats of economic disaster to cattle barons and homesteaders alike.

From the end of the Civil War to the late 1880's, prices of commodities gradually fell, farmers receiving less and less for what they had to sell, paying more and more for what they had to buy.

In the year 1867, agricultural leaders organized the Patrons of Husbandry, or National Grange, to fight for lower railroad rates, more favorable banking practices, and the elimination of middlemen. In the 1880's an outbreak of farm unrest resulted in the organization of several militant Farmers' Alliances, their policies varying from region to region, but united in a determination to better the farmers' lot through political action. The power of these movements was concentrated in the central plains, where grain and livestock prices were most depressed, and under leadership of such colorful political figures as "Sockless Jerry" Simpson and Mary E. Lease in Kansas won a series of surprise political victories in 1890. By 1892 the Alliances had united into the People's Party or Populist Movement, and two years later—after the Panic of 1893—doubled their vote, and a national third party loomed on the political horizon. But in 1896 the weakened Democratic party moved to add Populists to its ranks by nominating William J. Bryan as candidate for president and almost won the election. By 1900, however, demand for commodities caught up with supply. Many farm workers had gone to the cities to become factory workers; immigration had increased, the newcomers

remaining in cities because there was no more frontier land. As a result, prices of farm products were rising, and pressures for a radical agrarian party were ended.

During the early years of the 20th century much of the old Populist program was put into law, just as after World War I much of the program of the unsuccessful Farmer-Labor party of the 1920's became law during the New Deal of the 1930's.

Vast as were the changes in American agriculture from colonial days to 1900, the first half of the 20th century brought an even more startling transformation—an agricultural revolution comparable in scope to the industrial revolution of the 19th century. As early as 1850 the nation's industrial structure was beginning to challenge the supremacy of agriculture. By the time of the Civil War, the percentage of population engaged in agriculture had dropped to 60; in 1900 it was only 37. By 1920 the percentage had dropped to 30, and in 1960 it was only 12. Not only did the percentage drop sharply, but the total numbers of farm population also declined by more than 10,000,000 during the first half of the 20th century. Although considerably more land was put into farms, the total number of farms declined by more than 1,500,000. The average size of farms grew steadily larger, small-scale operations becoming obsolete in the process of mechanization and technical development which made it impossible for unmechanized units to compete.

Production per acre and per man-hour increased phenomenally for many of the staple crops. Except for the harvesting of some perishable fruit and vegetable crops, mechanization and automation replaced hand labor. Tractors increased from less than 1000 in 1910 to more than 5,000,000 in 1960. In the same period, horses and mules declined from 25,000,000 to 3,000,000, the farm draft horse becoming almost as extinct as its predecessor, the ox. Rural electrification brought power to more than 95% of the nation's farms. Daily mail service, telephones, radio and television, paved highways and modern consolidated schools, all but obliterated differences between city and rural life. After World War II, widespread use of chemicals for plant nutrition, pesticides, and feed additives (vitamins, antibiotics, enzymes, etc.) further increased rates of farm production. Much of this progress was made possible through scientific research engendered by the U. S. Department of Agriculture and the land grant college experiment stations, with their extension services which transmitted discoveries through county agents and farm and home advisers directly to farm homes.

At the same time Federal controls growing out of the economic depression of the 1930's eliminated many of the risks of farming. The Agricultural Adjustment Acts of 1933 and 1938 were designed to restore purchasing power of basic agricultural products to levels of 1910–14, a period of relative stability. This

14

"parity" concept was modified by subsequent legislation, providing more flexible supports for individual commodities. Price and income support programs, along with soil conservation programs, stabilized to a degree one of man's most speculative occupations. In the half century preceding 1960, value of farm assets rose from 40 to 200 billion dollars. Much more capital was required to operate a farm, and various farmer organizations expressed fears for the future of the traditional family farm. Others objected to government control methods. Surpluses of some staples certainly continued to be a vexing problem. But for the most part, at mid-century, American agriculture was experiencing the most prosperous period of its history.

Department of Agriculture. As early as 1796, President George Washington recommended to Congress the establishment of a national board of agriculture. "In proportion as nations advance in population," observed Washington, "the cultivation of the soil becomes more and more an object of public patronage." Although a bill was brought up for consideration in that session, it never reached a vote, and another forty years passed before agriculture was represented by a Federal agency. From 1836 to 1862, national agricultural interests were promoted through the Patent Office, Commissioner Henry Leavitt Ellsworth helping to lay the foundations of the present Department of Agriculture through his activities in collecting and distributing seeds and in gathering and publishing statistical and other information on agricultural subjects, which led to the establishment of an agricultural division of his agency.

It was largely through efforts of the U. S. Agricultural Society during the 1850's that a law was passed in 1862 establishing the Department of Agriculture, with Isaac Newton as first commissioner. The duties of the new department as specified in the act of establishment were "to acquire and to diffuse among the people of the United States useful information on subjects connected with agriculture in the most general and comprehensive sense of that word, and to procure, propagate, and distribute among the people new and valuable seeds and plants."

To facilitate operations the Department organized into divisions of chemistry, entomology, statistics, botany, forestry, pomology, and vegetable physiology and pathology. In 1884 the Bureau of Animal Industry was created, and six years later the Weather Bureau was transferred from the War Department. After the Hatch Act of 1887 established agricultural experiment stations, an Office of Experiment Stations was formed in the Department.

Not until 1889 did the Department achieve cabinet status, after a long campaign by the National Grange. Norman J. Colman served a brief term as the first secretary, his successors being Jeremiah M. Rusk, 1889–93; J. Sterling Morton, 1893–97; James Wilson, 1897–1913; David M. Houston, 1913–20; Edward T. Meredith, 1920–21; Henry C. Wallace, 1921–24; Howard M. Gore, 1924–25; W. M. Jardine, 1925–29; Arthur M. Hyde, 1929–33; Henry A. Wallace, 1933–40; Claude R. Wickard, 1940–45; Clinton P. Anderson, 1945–48; Charles F. Brannan, 1948–53; Ezra Taft Benson, 1953–61; Orville L. Freeman, 1961–   .

Throughout the 20th century, the Department has reflected the dynamic character of American agriculture by entering into many new fields of activity. It conducts both basic and applied research, the results of which are made available to farmers through extension organizations in the states. It provides crop reports, commodity standards, meat inspection services; it administers the national forests, promotes soil and water conservation, directs price-support programs, sponsors the national school-lunch program. It provides special credit to farmers and farm cooperatives. The library of the Department, first organized in 1862, has become the national agricultural library with a collection of more than 1,000,000 volumes.

Influence of Transportation on Agriculture. For more than a century and a half after the first colonists settled in America, lack of transportation facilities kept commercial agriculture confined to a narrow strip of eastern seacoast. Navigable rivers were the natural travel routes westward, and as immigration and the demand for farm land increased, settlers moved inland by water. The pattern of agricultural production for markets was therefore restricted to lands bordering these river routes. For many years, Indian trails which led from one stream to another were used by travelers, but these land routes were unsuited for transporting agricultural commodities. Even after the narrow trails were widened to roads, the costs of moving grain were prohibitive for farmers who lived several miles from a river landing. In the colonial South the greatest obstacle to expanding tobacco production was lack of transportation facilities, a problem which was only partially solved by rolling the product overland in hogsheads attached to mules by an ingenious pole arrangement.

Not until the beginning of the 19th century were any considerable amounts of public monies spent for building and improving roads, the greatest single contribution to agriculture being the Cumberland, or National, Road, which was completed westward to Columbus, O., by 1833. As late as 1840, however, most of the so-called highways were still cluttered by stumps and brush, and were without weatherproof surfacing so that loaded wagons could not pass over them during many months of the year. It was but natural that, discouraged by such overland means of transporting their products, frontier farmers should turn to canals as the answer to the problem of reaching markets.

As early as 1784, George Washington was urging

construction of a canal to connect the tidewaters of the Potomac with the Ohio River, as an aid to development of the Northwest territories, but not until 1850 was the Chesapeake and Ohio Canal completed to Cumberland, Md. Meanwhile, in New York State, the Erie Canal had opened a new era for Western agriculture. During its first ten years of operation, 1825 to 1835, the Erie reduced its rates from $22 per ton to $4 per ton, so cheapening transportation costs that an immense wilderness was opened for agricultural exploitation. For almost half a century a flood of agricultural commodities moved through the Canal from Lake Erie to the Hudson River, contributing to the establishment of New York City as the great port and commercial center of the nation.

Although the success of the Erie encouraged canal construction in almost all the Northern states and some of the Southern, neither these man-made water routes nor rivers and turnpikes combined were ever adequate to meet the demands of expanding agricultural production. Not until railroads were extended to the interior during the period between 1840 and 1860 was commercial agriculture able to begin its great development west of the Alleghenies. By the time of the Civil War, more than two thirds of Middle-Western farm products marketed in the East was transported there by rail. After the war, railroads and agriculture moved westward simultaneously. Refinements in railroad transport services, such as faster schedules and the development of refrigerated cars, made it possible for meats and other perishables to be shipped to markets thousands of miles from points of production. Specialty crops could be grown in the most suitable climate and soil zones and shipped to centers of population, giving rise to vast fruit and vegetable farms in Florida, the Rio Grande valley, and along the Pacific coast.

The 20th century has seen another complete revolution in agricultural transport—the introduction of the motor truck. Trucks and modern highways have made location of farms relatively unimportant insofar as markets are concerned. Farm products which once had only short and limited markets can now be delivered to any part of the nation at almost any time of year. Already in wide use as a farm implement for applying pesticides, fertilizers and seeds, the airplane by 1960 was beginning to be used for marketing perishable and luxury products, but was not yet a competitive cargo carrier for regular farm commodities.

Agricultural Policies of the U. S. Some national agricultural policies are rooted deep in America's beginnings. Others are comparatively recent in origin. Almost all are compromises resulting from the constant shifting of attitudes and purposes of conflicting groups within the population. When the Constitution was adopted in 1788, the United States was almost exclusively rural, and for a century afterward most

aspects of national policy were influenced by agricultural interests.

Early land policies were hardly more than modified survivals of ownership and tenure patterns established by feudal systems of western Europe, with tendencies toward perpetuation of strongly entrenched privileged classes. Gradually, however, American land policy tended to favor the settlers of the land, founders of family-type farms. After the original states ceded their western territories to the Union, the Federal Government transferred these holdings as soon as possible to farmer-settlers, enacting liberal credit provisions, and acceding to pressures from squatter-settlers through preemption acts.

During the twenty years before the Civil War, Congress considered successive bills designed to grant free lands to settlers. Land-grant policy being closely linked with the slavery question, no effective act was passed until after the war had begun. The Homestead Act of 1862 provided free title grants for 160 acres of land to settlers maintaining residence for five years. After 1900, this act was modified by a series of laws which granted larger tracts in arid regions of the Western states. More recent changes reflect the virtual disappearance of the nation's once vast domain; during the 20th century land policies involve efforts to conserve and reconstruct soils, to exercise more public control over forest lands, waters, and mineral resources.

American farmers have always been concerned with federal tariff policies, quantitative trade restrictions, transportation subsidies, credit and monetary systems —any national policy which might affect either the prices of agricultural commodities or the costs of manufactured articles used in agricultural production. Not until after the Civil War, however, did farmers form organizations to represent them in creation of new national policies. The Granger movement developed out of farmer opposition to the railroad monopoly and high interest rates. The Greenback movement, the Farmers' Alliances, and the People's Party attempted to formulate new, or to change old, national policies affecting agriculture. After 1900, the Farmers' Union, the Nonpartisan League, and the Farm Bureau Federation arose as spokesmen for farmers' policy.

During World War I, the government encouraged expansion of farm output, but when foreign and military demands declined, a collapse of export markets followed and American agriculture fell into a severe economic depression which continued long after urban and industrial segments of the population were enjoying restored prosperity. To adjust the sharp differences, several proposals for "farm relief" legislation—notably the McNary-Haugen bills—were actively discussed and promoted during the 1920's. "Orderly marketing" of farm products was encouraged by passage of the Co-operative Marketing Act of 1922; other laws provided special credit facilities for farmers. The Agricultural Marketing Act of 1929 created a Federal Farm Board, designed to stabilize prices of commodities. Although the Farm Board failed in its objectives, its experiences paved the way for more successful legislation during the Great Depression of the 1930's when farm prices plummeted to their lowest levels.

In an attempt to raise prices by restricting supplies, the Agricultural Adjustment Act of 1933 established quotas limiting production of basic agricultural commodities. Declared unconstitutional by the U. S. Supreme Court in 1936, the original act was superseded by the Act of 1938, which was subsequently amended in 1948, 1949, 1954 and 1956, the basic aims being formation of a price-support program to bring farm income into balance with the national income. To establish a "parity" formula, prices were first based on the years 1910–14, a period in which farm and nonfarm prices were considered to be in reasonable balance. In 1950 the formula was changed to permit use of average prices paid and received during the immediately preceding ten-year period of any current year.

The Commodity Credit Corporation, formed in 1933 to replace the Federal Farm Board, was the principal agency through which price-supporting activities of the government were carried out. When it was not possible to support prices through loans or purchase agreements, the C. C. C. bought farm commodities outright. Commodities thus acquired were usually disposed of in ways which would not disrupt price levels. For instance, storable commodities were held for future resale into commercial channels whenever demand increased. Perishable commodities were disposed of outside normal commercial channels— by donation to relief agencies for direct distribution, by transfer to the national school-lunch program, or through special export sales or exchanges. In an effort to increase exports of surplus products, Congress passed Public Law 480 in 1954, authorizing the Secretary of Agriculture to accept up to $700,000,000 in foreign currencies as repayment for commodities shipped abroad to friendly nations.

By the end of the 1950's, the C. C. C. had more than $8,000,000,000 invested in inventories of commodities, loans, and purchase agreements. The twin problems of overproduction and depressed prices still had not been solved, although the Soil Bank Act of 1956, through its acreage reserve and conservation reserve programs, was expected to further the shifting of land from production of basic crops to pastures and other conservation uses.

Agricultural Societies and Farm Organizations. Although agriculture is generally considered to be an individual way of life, American farmers have been quick to organize for mutual advantage when circumstances warranted. During colonial days they joined forces to fight Indians, to improve schools, to secure roads and canals. Shays' Rebellion of 1786–87 was largely an organized farmers' revolt against disproportionate taxation in Massachusetts. The Whiskey Rebellion of 1794 was a Pennsylvania farmers' revolt against taxes on distilled spirits; Fries' Rebellion of 1799 in the same state was an uprising against a Federal land tax.

As the nation moved into the 19th century, such violent rural protest movements declined. In this comparatively calm and prosperous era a more genteel type of organization flourished—the agricultural society. The Philadelphia Society for Promoting Agriculture and the South Carolina Society for Promoting and Improving Agriculture were formed in 1785. During the following half century almost every state, region and county followed suit by organizing some sort of society or farmers' club to promote agriculture or its branches of horticulture, dairying, animal breeding, etc. For the most part agricultural society members were "gentlemen" farmers, distinguished intellectuals and political figures. Originally, very few rank-and-file farmers were active; in fact agricultural societies at first were ridiculed by frontier farmers who had little use for scientific theories of improving production in a time of cheap land and scarce markets.

Nevertheless the societies flourished, gradually winning the support of practicing farmers. They sponsored annual fairs and exhibits, and supported agricultural journals which spread information concerning new experiments and discoveries. In the 1840's efforts were made to establish a national society, and in 1852 representatives from local organizations met in Washington, D. C., to form the U. S. Agricultural Society, which in turn was largely responsible for passage of the law creating the U. S. Department of Agriculture a decade later.

In 1867, Oliver Hudson Kelley and six associates founded a national secret organization of farmers, the Patrons of Husbandry, or the Grange. Originally intended as a fraternal and educational organization, the Grange within ten years attracted a membership of nearly a million and gave its name to the "Granger Movement" of the 1870's. During this period of agrarian discontent, the Grange fought against low commodity prices, high freight charges, and political corruption. Considered too conservative in its political action by many farmers, the Grange lost membership heavily during the rise of the more radical Farmers' Alliances of the late 1880's. But after the Alliances were submerged into the Populist Movement, the Grange came back into influence and in the 1950's was the second largest farmers' organization in America, with almost 900,000 individual members.

The National Farmers Union, founded by Newt Gresham at Point, Texas, in 1902, was considered the natural successor to the 19th century Farmers' Alliances. Flourishing in the South during its first decade, the Farmers Union gradually moved into the wheat-growing states of the West where it was especially strong during the 1950's. Its national membership in this decade included more than 250,000 farm families. The organization's policies have advocated preservation of the family farm, more bargaining power with government for farm operations, close relationships between farmer and labor groups, special aids for low-income farmers.

In the years immediately preceding World War I, several county farm committees or bureaus were organized in various states to support the county agent and extension services of the Department of Agriculture. Before the end of the war a few states federated their county bureaus into state organizations, the basic objective being educational, to help farmers solve problems of production. When agricultural prices began falling after the war, several state representatives decided to create a farmers' organization which would be national in scope, and the American Farm Bureau Federation was formally organized in Chicago, March 1, 1920.

In 1921 the Farm Bureau organized the first farm bloc in Congress, and two years later was urging action to solve the mounting problem of farm surpluses. During the 1920's the Bureau supported the McNary-Haugen bills to control overproduction, and with the coming of the Great Depression of the 1930's proposed a price-parity, production-control bill which was similar in its essential features to the Agricultural Adjustment Act of 1933.

During World War II, the Farm Bureau was active in protecting farmers' interests under price controls and in directing programs necessary in the war effort. After 1947, the Bureau's attitude toward government controls shifted to a policy advocating reduction in the use of public funds to increase farm productive capacity, and a return to policies which would allow prices to respond to supply and demand. In the 1950's the Farm Bureau was the largest American farmers' organization, with a membership of more than 1,500,000 families.

Farm Credit Agencies, Federal. From the days of the first pioneers down to the 20th century, one of the major problems of American agriculture has been that of financing the farmer. As a political issue during the nation's first century, agricultural credit was overshadowed only by slavery and the tariff. After the Civil War, high interest rates and the unavailability of long-term mortgage loans brought farmer support to a succession of cheap money schemes, notably those of the National Greenback Party and the Free Silver Movement. When these movements faded with the political defeat of William J. Bryan, agricultural leaders turned to the Federal government for a solution of their perpetual credit difficulties.

In 1913 the Federal Reserve Act increased facilities of country banks for supplying seasonal credit needs of farmers, and in that same year, as a preliminary to establishing adequate farm mortgage credit facilities, Congress appointed a special commission to study European experiences in the field. Three years later, the Federal Farm Loan Act was passed, establishing a national system of twelve Federal Land Banks. The operational method of the land banks was to pool the mortgages of individual farmers and issue bonds with the mortgages as security. To keep mortgage interest rates low, the bonds were exempted from taxation.

As a result of the price depression which affected farmers immediately after World War I, a demand arose for short-term credit. This led to passage in 1923 of an amendment to the Federal Farm Loan Act, establishing twelve Federal intermediate credit banks. Largely because of a continued decline in prices of farm commodities, these credit agencies failed to solve the problem, and in an effort to provide farmers with both a greater share of the market price of their products and adequate credit facilities for production, Congress in June, 1929, established the Federal Farm Board. One of the Board's major functions was to advance loans to agricultural co-operatives from a revolving fund of $500,000,000.

With the coming of the severe depression after 1929, however, both the bank credit and Farm Board programs ran into serious difficulties. Sharp declines in farm income and real estate values brought on such an accelerated rate of foreclosures in farm property that emergency measures became necessary. In 1932 the Reconstruction Finance Corporation was authorized to establish twelve agricultural credit corporations to make loans directly to farmers and stockmen in their respective areas. At the same time the Federal land bank system relaxed requirements for obtaining loans.

In June, 1933, the Farm Credit Administration was created with the objective of bringing together under one agency all farm credit functions of the Federal government. The agency operated independently until 1939 when it became a part of the Department of Agriculture, and fourteen years later the Farm Credit Act of 1953 again made the F. C. A. an independent agency, with a thirteen-member board to determine policy. One member was appointed from each of the twelve farm credit districts by the President; the thirteenth was appointed by the Secretary of Agriculture as his representative. Since 1953 the F. C. A. has been responsible for operations of the Federal land banks and national farm loan associations, the intermediate credit banks, and the Central Bank for Co-operatives which provides credit to farmers' co-operatives.

All expenses of the agency are paid from assessments against the banks and associations it supervises. In its first quarter-century of operation, farmers and their co-operatives borrowed approximately $40,000,000,000 from F. C. A. for use in agricultural operations. During the postwar years of agricultural prosperity, farm co-operatives increased their investment in the Farm Credit System, and since 1947 the twelve Federal Land Banks have been completely owned by their farmer-borrowers through national farm loan associations.

Although the F. C. A. was meant to combine all credit operations, only four months after its establishment the Commodity Credit Corporation was created as an independent agency to make loans on commodities in connection with crop control and marketing problems. The C. C. C. operated in close affiliation with the R. F. C. until a general reorganization of governmental functions in 1939 transferred it to the Department of Agriculture. The corporation is managed by a board of six directors, subject to the supervision of the Secretary of Agriculture, and a five-member advisory board appointed by the President. Capitalized at $100,000,000, the C. C. C. has authority to borrow up to $14,500,000,000 in carrying out its program of price supports for specified farm commodities. Funds in loans and inventories fluctuated from total investments of less than two to more than eight billion dollars during the decade of the 1950's.

In 1935 the Resettlement Administration was created to provide funds for relief and rehabilitation of low-income farm families; the Rural Electrification Administration was also established in 1935 to make loans for financing construction and operation of plants and lines furnishing electric power to persons in rural areas. A later amendment in 1949 also authorized the R. E. A. to make loans for furnishing and improving rural telephone service. The Resettlement Administration was succeeded in 1937 by the Farm Security Administration, which became the Farmers Home Administration in 1946, with authority to provide credit to farmers who could not obtain financing elsewhere at reasonable rates and terms. The Farmers Home Administration specializes in loans for farm purchases, improvement of farm housing, and soil and water conservation.

AIR CONDITIONING. Mankind has tried to solve the problem of discomfort caused by hot, humid air for centuries. Caliph Mahdi of Baghdad in 775 A.D. built a summer palace with double walls which were packed with snow brought down from the mountains by slaves.

With the widespread acceptance of mechanical refrigeration in the United States, a variety of elementary comfort cooling systems was installed by 1900. A restaurant was cooled by embedding air pipes in ice and salt and then circulating the air. Broadway Theater in New York City was cooled by ice placed in a fan-ventilating system. And abroad, in a German home, refrigerated coils in the attic cooled air which was delivered by gravity through ducts to the rooms below.

But until 1902 the four basic functions of air conditioning had never been accomplished. These are: control of temperature; control of humidity; control of air circulation and ventilation; and air purification. In that year Dr. Willis H. Carrier designed the first system ever to include all of the basic functions of air conditioning. This first installation is known as a fan-coil system. Air is blown over coils containing cold water or a refrigerant supplied by refrigeration equipment. By balancing water temperature, number of coils, and air velocity, both air temperature and humidity can be regulated.

The term *air conditioning* was originated by an engineer and pioneer in textile air conditioning, S. W. Cramer of Charlotte, N. C., in May, 1906. During the first three decades of this century air conditioning was mainly used in the control of industrial processes. But by 1921 air conditioning also had been installed in a few theaters, hotels and office buildings.

The next major advance was the invention in 1921 by Dr. Carrier of the centrifugal refrigerating machine. Refrigerating equipment then in use was expensive to install, maintain and operate, and mechanically inefficient. Carbon dioxide, the safest refrigerant then available, was costly and could not be controlled automatically. The centrifugal refrigerating machine used nontoxic refrigerants, provided constant temperatures, was much more compact and completely automatic. It was the first major advance in mechanical refrigeration since David Boyle designed the ammonia compressor in 1872.

The centrifugal refrigerating machine also expanded the market to include for the first time large-scale comfort installations as opposed to industrial process applications. Department stores—the first was the J. L. Hudson Company in Detroit—motion picture theaters, and even the Senate and House chambers in Washington, D. C., were air conditioned during the 1920's.

Another type of refrigerating machine which was an important advance in technology is the absorption machine which, paradoxically, uses low pressure steam to produce chilled water for air conditioning. Invented in 1915, the first commercially acceptable unit was developed by Williams Air-O-Matic in 1937. Subsequent refinements have evolved a machine that is completely automatic, has a low noise level and little vibration.

The next great stride was the development by Midgley and Hene in 1931 of fluorinated refrigerants. This resulted in a completely safe family of refrigerants for use in large machines and also in a new range of reciprocating machines of small capacities where it permitted a production and installation cost half that of ammonia machines. It thereby paved the way for small, economical air conditioning equipment for the home.

By the late 1930's air conditioning equipment had been devised to serve economically all except one type of building—the skyscraper. Conventional methods involved the use of a central air conditioning apparatus which propelled large volumes of conditioned air into each room at low velocities through big supply ducts. More ducts, equally large, were required for air return. This was expensive because it consumed too much otherwise rentable space.

In 1937 Dr. Willis H. Carrier devised a unique solution. His conduit induction system only conditioned that 25% of the air needed for ventilation. This air was distributed into the room units in small conduits at high velocities. This primary air passed through nozzles inducing room air over the coil supplied with either heated or cooled water and then into the room. This system permitted considerable economy as well as individual room control of temperature.

The first centrally air conditioned residence was completed in 1914. However, it was not until the 1950's that a factory-assembled, year-round air conditioner began to reach homes in sizable numbers. The recent trend has been toward the use of air cooled condensers as opposed to water cooled. These are located outdoors with only the cooling coil (and fan if required) located near the furnace.

The heat pump first made its appearance in the United States during the 1930's. Although the basic principle was introduced by Lord Kelvin in 1852, early working models were primarily of laboratory interest. The first actual residential installation was probably made in Scotland in 1927. By 1960 the air source heat pump had become the most popular design. Its operation can be described in terms of a household refrigerator, which essentially moves heat from inside the box to the outside. If this action were reversed, room heat would be pumped into the box and cold air expelled. In summer, a heat pump actually pumps heat from indoors to outdoors. In winter, it reverses to pump heat from outdoors to indoors. Latent heat does exist in outdoor air even at zero temperatures.

AIR FORCE, UNITED STATES. Although observation balloons were used in the Civil War and the Spanish American War, the U. S. Air Force may be said to date from 1907, when the U. S. Army established an Aeronautical Division in the Signal Corps. It soon asked for bids on an airplane to carry two men, fly for an hour, and attain 40 mph. The Wright brothers met the specifications in 1909 and as part of their contract taught two Army officers how to fly. Others were trained later, and in 1911 and 1912 the Army opened its own pilot training schools.

In 1914 Army aviation received statutory recognition when Congress established an Aviation Section within the Signal Corps; it was authorized to consist of 60 officers and 260 enlisted men. The formation of the First Aero Squadron in the same year indicated appreciation of the tactical value of aviation, but most of the Army's minuscule aviation activity continued to be devoted to training and experimentation. During these early years Army pilots dropped the first bombs, fired a machine gun from the air, and tried out an airborne radio. However, other countries were making far greater progress. In the five years before World War I, Germany and France each spent fifty times as much on military aviation as the United States. When the United States entered the war in 1917 the Army had only 35 pilots.

The Allies felt that the United States could help most effectively by sending a powerful air force overseas. The idea caught the American imagination, and a tremendous aviation program was launched. Although production lagged badly, and most American combat units employed foreign-built aircraft, mammoth Congressional appropriations and a gigantic training program led to a great increase in the numerical strength of the nation's military aviation. By the Armistice 195,000 men were serving in the Air Service, which had been removed from Signal Corps control. At the front were 45 squadrons, with 740 airplanes and 77 balloons.

The U. S. Air Service saw combat in World War I for only seven months—May to November, 1918. Brig. Gen. William (Billy) Mitchell became the outstanding combat commander and drew much attention for the massed bombing raids he carried out on rear-area German supply and tactical centers. United States airplanes constituted only about 10% of Allied air strength at the end of the war, but American pilots had shot down some 700 enemy airplanes and about 70 balloons.

After World War I the size of the Air Service was cut sharply. By 1920 strength was down to 896 flying officers and less than 8000 enlisted men. Leaders such as Mitchell had hoped the prominent part played by aviation in the war would result in the creation of a separate air force. In this they were disappointed; the Army Reorganization Act of 1920 made the Air Service a combatant arm of the Army, with an authorized strength less than 10% of the Army as a whole. The tactical support emphasis of the small force was reflected in its composition; of the 27 squadrons, 19 were for observation or surveillance. There were only four bomber squadrons.

Mitchell used the latter units, particularly the one heavy bomber squadron, to demonstrate his belief in the dominance of air power, and especially its supremacy over warships. In 1921 and 1923 German vessels and obsolete United States battleships were sunk by test bombing attacks. Naval authorities opposed continuation of such tests and argued that the results did not really prove the vulnerability of ships to air attack. Mitchell continued to argue that command of the air should control American military strategy. His attacks on the generals and admirals holding traditional views of warfare led to his court-martial in 1925. He was suspended and soon resigned.

The Mitchell case coincided with renewed agitation for a separate air force. The Government rejected this, but in 1926 Congress changed the name of the Air Service to the Air Corps, approved a small increase in its strength, and gave it more prestige by providing for an Assistant Secretary of War for Air. By 1932 the Air Corps had 45 airplane squadrons, of which only 13 were for observation. Despite its small strength in the 1920's and early 1930's, the force achieved significant advances in such important areas as long-distance flights, high-altitude flying, inflight refueling, and fighter and bombardment techniques that were to prove significant in World War II.

Improvements in bomber construction and performance in the 1930's revived the hopes of the advocates of long-range strategic bombardment. In 1933 the Boeing Corporation was encouraged to develop its design for a four-engine bomber, and in 1935 the initial experimental model of the famous B-17 "Flying Fortress" made its first flight. In the same year another development marked a significant departure from the prevailing concept that the Air Corps had no function apart from direct support of Army units. The General Headquarters Air Force was organized and took control of most combat units away from the ground commanders of the Army's corps areas.

As war loomed in Europe, Air Corps strength was increased slowly until the fall of France. Then huge Air Corps training centers were established, airfields were built in large numbers, and plans were made to train 30,000 pilots annually. New airplanes were rushed feverishly into design and production. In June, 1941, all air units were combined into the Army Air Forces. The trend toward autonomy for military aviation continued, and early in 1942 the A. A. F. was designated as one of three semi-autonomous branches of the Army. The first head of the A. A. F. was Gen. H. H. Arnold. After the United States formally entered World War II, the A. A. F. expanded enormously. By 1944, when it reached a maximum strength of 2,386,000, it was the largest air force in the world.

The key A. A. F. operations in Europe were heavy bombing attacks on Axis-occupied territory, and then on Germany and Italy. Units participating were the Eighth Air Force, which began flying from England in 1942; the Twelfth, which operated in the Mediterranean area; and the Fifteenth, which was based in Italy. Ground support and fighter escort was furnished by the Ninth Air Force, based in North Africa and then in England.

Working in close cooperation with the Royal Air Force, the Ninth and Twelfth Air Forces defeated the Luftwaffe over North Africa and played an important role in the campaign that brought victory over all Axis forces there. They helped capture Sicily and aided in the invasion of Italy. From southern Italian bases the Fifteenth then began a long campaign against Italian, German, and Austrian factories and other strategic targets.

Eighth Air Force bombing raids from England increased in intensity in 1943, particularly after May, when the Joint Chiefs of Staff decided on a Combined Bomber Offensive against Germany. The daylight raids of the Eighth were complemented by the night bombing of the R. A. F. Bomber Command. Attacks by B-17's and B-24's on such vital Axis targets as Schweinfurt ball-bearing factories, aircraft plants at Regensburg, and oil refineries at Ploesti, did severe damage but resulted in heavy American losses. Development of long-range fighter escorts helped reduce losses, and by spring, 1944, the German Air Force had been defeated over Germany itself. Massive Allied air attacks weakened the Reich and facilitated the invasion of Europe by Allied ground forces. The A. A. F. thereafter gave close support to the ground forces, and its light and medium bombers disrupted the German transport system behind the lines and deep in Germany. Further strategic attacks reduced German oil production to 5% of capacity. In the final victory over the Axis, Allied air power, particularly the A. A. F., played a decisive role. It provided the air supremacy required for ground operations and, by destroying the fuel and transport systems, weakened German resistance.

In the Pacific the weak A. A. F. units were defeated and forced back in the first few months after Pearl Harbor. Later, the Fifth Air Force, operating at first from Australian bases, disrupted the Japanese advance and gained air control over New Guinea. Thereafter the Fifth, aided by the Seventh and Thirteenth, neutralized enemy air strength and paved the way for the advance across the Pacific toward the Japanese home islands. These came under attack by B-29's in 1944, and in less than a year their hammering blows had almost wiped out Japanese war-making capacity. Much of the nation was ready to make peace when the atomic bombs dropped from B-29's over Hiroshima and Nagasaki brought about the actual surrender.

The A. A. F. was reduced drastically after World War II, to a strength of less than 300,000 by 1947. The part played by American military aviation during the war accelerated the trend toward its autonomy, and on Sept. 18, 1947, the U. S. Air Force was established as a separate service, on an equal plane with the Army and the Navy. Emphasis was on developing the new Air Force as a peacetime force-in-being. Major combat commands were the Air Defense Command, the Tactical Air Command, and especially the Strategic Air Command. The last was developed into a mighty force of atomic- and later hydrogen-bomb carriers, maintained in instant readiness and intended to provide a deterrent against Soviet attack.

After World War II the capabilities of the

21

U. S. A. F. were increased by technical developments such as the application of jet propulsion to aircraft, major increases in aircraft size, speed, range, and load-carrying capacity, and the development of jet- and rocket-powered missiles.

In 1948–49 the U. S. Air Force played the major role in the Berlin Airlift. During the Korean War, 1950–53, Air Force units in Korea gained control of the air and helped the United Nations ground forces hold off the numerically superior Chinese Communists, whose strength was continuously built up north of the Yalu River, where American air power was not allowed to attack. In the last two years of the war most of the American air effort was devoted to an interdiction campaign, carried on by B-29's, B-26's, and fighter-bombers.

After the Korean War, Air Force strength, which had grown to about a million, was reduced somewhat and stabilized at about 850,000. In 1954 a defense policy change resulted in abandonment of the balanced force concept (of roughly equal land, sea, and air forces) and clear emphasis on air power, which was allotted the largest share of the defense budget. In the same year Congress authorized establishment of the Air Force's own service academy for the preparation of career officers. The Air Force Academy began its operations at Lowry A. F. B., Colorado, in 1955 admitted its first class of cadets, and in 1958 moved to its permanent site, near Colorado Springs. The Academy provides professional military training along with an academic curriculum balanced between the social sciences-humanities and scientific-engineering courses.

As missile development progressed in the 1950's the Air Force was made responsible for the development and employment of intermediate and long-range ballistic missiles to supplement the long-range bomber force. Fighter strength was reduced, as the major enemy threat appeared to shift to missiles. Air Force operations extended to increasingly high altitudes, and the Air Force played a major role in the American space exploration which became important in 1958. Missiles and satellites were developed, and the first steps were taken toward the achievement of manned space flight.

AISNE DEFENSIVE (May 27–June 5, 1918) was a sequel of the operations on the Somme in March, the Germans making a new attack southward between Soissons and Reims with the intention of drawing French reserves south so that they could renew their attacks in the north. The attack was successful even beyond their hopes, and reached the Marne near Château-Thierry, only forty miles from Paris. The Germans then attempted to establish a bridgehead on the Marne, and also to push westward toward Paris; both efforts were unsuccessful. Two American divisions took part in the defense—the Third opposing the crossing of the Marne, and the Second being

very heavily engaged at the Bois de Belleau and at Vaux, west of Château-Thierry.

AISNE-MARNE OPERATION (July 18–Aug. 6, 1918) was the Franco-American counter-offensive, following the German offensive of July 15 in the Marne salient. The French Tenth Army (Mangin) opened the attack, striking eastward into the salient just south of Soissons. The main attack was made by the XX Corps, with three divisions in front line, two American and one Moroccan. The Germans were taken by surprise, and their outpost line made little resistance, but the line soon stiffened and the fighting was severe. It was not until the 21st that control of the Soissons-Château-Thierry highway was gained. The total penetration was eight miles.

From July 21 on, the armies farther east joined in the advance—the Sixth (Degoutte) and the Fifth (Berthelot), along both faces of the salient. With the Sixth Army there were two American corps headquarters—the I (Liggett) and the III (Dickman)—and eight American divisions. The Germans conducted their retreat skillfully, making an especially strong stand on the Ourcq on July 28. But early in August they were back behind the Vesle.

The operations since July 15 had changed the whole aspect of the war. A German offensive had been suddenly stopped in mid-career, and the advance changed to a retreat. The Marne salient had ceased to exist, and the Germans were never again able to undertake a serious offensive.

AIX-LA-CHAPELLE, TREATY OF (Oct. 18, 1748), ended the War of the Austrian Succession. The chief term which concerned American history was the restoration of Louisburg to France, which irritated the New Englanders who had been active in the capture. The peace was merely an intermission in the protracted struggle for control of the St. Lawrence and Mississippi basins. Its final phase, the French and Indian War, began in 1754.

AKRON LAW (Feb. 8, 1847) resulted from a movement for a better public school system in Akron, O. The Ohio General Assembly passed a special law for the city, which provided for an elected board of education of six members, the organization of the city as a single school district, free admission of all children to the public schools, the adoption of a system for the classification of pupils and their promotion by examinations, and local taxation for financing the schools. The law was broadened in 1848 to apply to any incorporated town, if the voters by a two-thirds vote chose to adopt the plan. In 1849 a general law, modeled on the Akron Law, reduced this requirement to a majority vote, required that schools be kept in operation not less than thirty-six nor more than forty-four weeks per year, and limited to four mills the amount of taxes to be raised for school purposes in any one year. In 1850 townships and special districts were permitted to make use of this system. Thus the Akron Law, with some modifications, came to be applied generally throughout the state.

ALABAMA. The roots of Alabama's history reach back to the beginnings of contact between Europe and North America. Some of the earliest Spanish explorers visited the Alabama coast, and DeSoto in 1540 explored the interior of the state. Alabama was the patrimony of three of the celebrated royal houses of Europe. The Spanish founded at least two temporary settlements on its soil in 1559. The French occupied it from 1702 to 1763; the British from 1763 to 1783; and the Spanish again held the southern portion of it from 1783 to 1813. Spain held the strip below parallel 31° and the United States all above that line. The Spanish base at Mobile was crushed out in 1813. In 1817 the Alabama Territory was organized out of the Mississippi Territory, of which it had been a part since 1798, and was admitted to the Union as a state, Dec. 14, 1819.

Alabama was settled principally by farmers, planters and professional men. A unique incident in its settlement was the founding of a colony of prominent Napoleonic exiles at Demopolis in 1817. The social and economic life of the state prior to 1860 was like that of the cotton South generally. Agriculture was the dominant interest, and the plantation system flourished in all of its glory. Alabama ranked second as a cotton-producing state in 1860.

Prior to 1860 politics was colorful. Many professional politicians, who had held high official stations in other states, moved into Alabama and jousted with each other for position and leadership. The Democratic and Whig parties sprang up and under able leadership stimulated a vigorous political life. The Democratic party dominated, but the Whigs kept up a spirited contest and exerted a large influence. Though local questions, such as the State Bank and state aid to railroads, gave rise to sharp contests, politics usually revolved around national questions. The people generally supported Jefferson's agrarian policies and the South's cause in slavery. Andrew Jackson was the idol of the masses but Calhoun and Clay had many followers. The states' rights sentiment grew apace after the Creek Indian controversy of 1832–33, and became robust under the impact of sectionalism between 1845 and 1860. William L. Yancey and his colleagues put the state in the front ranks of defense of southern rights. The exponents of sectional reconciliation, headed by Henry W. Hilliard, however, stayed the progress toward secession for a decade.

Alabama seceded from the Union in 1861, and the Confederate Government was organized and set up at Montgomery, since known as the "Cradle of the Confederacy." During the war that followed, its soldiers distinguished themselves in battle and prominent men held high places in the civil and military counsels of the Confederacy. The cost of the war was terrific. Property losses, including slaves, have been estimated at $500,000,000. The white population was frightfully decimated, and more than 437,000 slaves were freed and for many years had small part in rebuilding the state. When the war was over Alabamans earnestly sought restoration to the Union. They set up a state government under President Johnson's plan of reconstruction, but this plan was repudiated by Congress and the people were subject again to enervating uncertainty and to military oppression. The state was restored to the Union under the Congressional plan in 1868.

ALABAMA, THE. In June, 1861, J. D. Bulloch reached England as Confederate agent to contract with private builders for warships. He first obtained the *Florida,* and on May 15, 1862, a second and more powerful ship, the *Alabama,* was launched at Liverpool. The United States Minister, C. F. Adams, who had previously demanded the detention of the *Florida,* now presented, on June 23, what he thought full evidence of the illegal character of the *Alabama;* but the British authorities were deplorably slow and the sudden insanity of a law-officer of the crown caused a five-day delay. Finally orders were telegraphed to hold the vessel, but she had already sailed under pretense of a trial trip. Earl Russell and other Cabinet members felt a sincere desire to keep her from leaving, and deeply regretted the evasion. Guns, munitions and coal were brought her at the Azores, and she became the terror of American vessels. Under Capt. Raphael Semmes, before her destruction in June, 1864, in the English channel, she sunk, burned, or captured more than sixty ships.

ALABAMA CLAIMS. American grievances against Great Britain during and just after the Civil War all clustered about this generic phrase; but they filled a broad category. The Queen's proclamation of neutrality, giving the South belligerent rights, was regarded by Secretary Seward and most Northerners as hasty and unfriendly. The Confederate cruisers, built or armed by Britons, not only destroyed American shipping, but did indirect damage by driving insurance rates high and forcing many American ships under foreign flags. The Confederates raised large sums of money in Great Britain and outfitted blockade runners there.

Early in the war Seward instructed Minister C. F. Adams to lay before the British Government, with a demand for redress, the losses caused by the *Alabama.* As a result the British authorities showed greater care. In April, 1863, they halted the *Alexandra* when Adams proved she was intended for the Confederacy; in September, Russell issued orders to detain the two armored rams which Laird was building. Only one other ship, the *Shenandoah,* clearly violated the British neutrality laws and she only after refitting at Melbourne. Ultimately, the United States entered claims against Great Britain for damage wrought by eleven vessels, totaling $19,021,000. Of these the damage done by the *Alabama* was estimated at $6,547,609; that by the *Shenandoah* at $6,488,320; and that by the *Florida* at $3,698,609. The American claims were repeated from time to time but met no response until 1868. The Johnson-Clarendon Convention, signed that year under Seward's close supervision, made no mention of the *Alabama* damages; but provided for a settlement of all Anglo-American claims since 1853. Partly because of the unpopularity of the Johnson Administration, the Convention was overwhelmingly defeated by the Senate (April 13, 1869). Sumner seized the opportunity to make a speech reviewing the whole American case against Great Britain. He declared that the *Alabama* and other cruisers had not only done heavy damage, direct and indirect, but with the Queen's proclamation and other moral and material support given by England to the South had doubled the duration of the war. His object in thus implying that the total American bill reached $2,125,000,000 was to lay a basis for demands, which could be met only by the cession of Canada. Fortunately Hamilton Fish, becoming Secretary of State in March, 1869, took a saner position. Playing for time, he soon adopted the view that the whole set of *Alabama* claims could be met by the payment of a moderate lump sum, an apology, and a definition of maritime international law meeting American wishes. When he mildly urged Canadian independence, the British Government refused to admit that the two questions could be connected. The impasse between the two nations was brief. Great Britain advanced to a more conciliatory position when Lord Granville succeeded Clarendon as Foreign Minister, and when the Franco-Prussian War and Russia's denunciation of her Black Sea pledges threatened European complications. Washington became more amenable when Canada showed distinct hostility to the United States, when the Santo Domingo controversy destroyed Sumner's influence over Grant, and when financial interests pressed for a settlement. With Sir John Rose, a Canadian prominent in London, acting as intermediary, Fish and Granville decided that a joint commission should settle the whole nexus of disputes—Canadian fisheries, northwestern boundary and Alabama claims. The Commission, meeting under Fish and Earl DeGrey, drew up the Treaty of Washington (signed May 8, 1871), which expressed British regret for the escape of the *Alabama* and other cruisers, laid down three rules of maritime neutrality, and provided for submission of the Alabama Claims to a board of five arbitrators, American, British, Italian, Swiss and Brazilian. This tribunal decided Sept. 14, 1872, that Great Britain had failed in her duties as a neutral, and awarded the United States $15,500,000 in gold to meet her direct damages, all indirect claims having been excluded. American opinion accepted the award as adequate.

ALAMANCE, BATTLE OF. To punish and suppress the Regulators of North Carolina, Governor Tryon ordered Gen. Hugh Waddell to Hillsborough with a force of about 1000 militia. The Regulators to the number of 2000 had assembled on the Alamance River, about one half without arms, and with no officer higher than captain. The provincial army had artillery and was adequately equipped. The battle, fought May 16, 1771, lasted two hours and ended in disaster to the Regulators. The provincials lost nine killed and sixty-one wounded while the Regulators had about twenty killed and a greater number wounded. As a result of their defeat, many of the Regulators migrated to the trans-Alleghany region to Tennessee in particular.

ALAMO, SIEGE AND FALL OF THE (Feb. 23 to March 6, 1836). When the revolting province of Texas swept its soil clear of weak Mexican garrisons in 1835 the commander-in-chief, Sam Houston, ordered a concentration on the theory that the Mexicans would return. He recommended the destruction and abandonment of the fortifications at San Antonio. For this cautious counsel Houston was deposed from command. A 27-year-old lawyer, Lt.-Col. William Barret Travis, found himself in joint command, with James Bowie, of about 145 men at San Antonio when on Feb. 23 Santa Anna appeared with between 6000 and 7000 men.

Travis and Bowie could have retreated safely. Instead they moved into the stout-walled Alamo Mission, answered a demand for surrender with a cannon shot and sent couriers for reinforcements. A message signed by Travis read: "I have sustained a continual Bombardment and cannonade for 24 hours and have not lost a man. . . . Our flag still proudly waves from the wall. I shall never surrender or retreat. . . . VICTORY OR DEATH." On the eighth day of battle thirty-two recruits crept through the Mexican lines, the last reinforcements the garrison was to receive. This brought their number to about 187. Though suffering from want of sleep, and with ammunition running low, the Texans had lost the services of only one man, Bowie, ill and disabled by a fall.

At four in the morning of March 6, the thirteenth day of battle, Santa Anna stormed the Alamo on all sides. The first and second assaults were broken up. Day was dawning when the Mexicans attacked again. The Texans' guns were hot, their ammunition nearly out and, though casualties had not been numerous, men were dropping from exhaustion. The walls were breached. From building to building and room to room in the mission compound the defenders fought, clubbing rifles and drawing knives. The last point taken was the church. There fell David Crockett and twelve volunteers who had followed him from Tennessee.

By eight o'clock the last of the 187 defenders was dead, though the Mexicans spared about thirty non-combatants. Mexican losses were about 1500 killed and died of wounds.

The first effect of the butchery was to sow panic through Texas, precipitating a flight of the civil population and of the government toward United States soil. Inwardly raging against Travis' disastrous stand, Houston gathered an army. Six weeks later, marching to meet Santa Anna, Houston paraded his men and in an impassioned address abjured them to "Remember the Alamo!" With that cry on their lips they vanquished the Mexicans at San Jacinto, establishing the independence of the Texas Republic.

ALASKA. The eastward movement from Tsarist Russia through Siberia to the Pacific paralleled and preceded by almost a century the westward movement in the United States and Canada. Reaching Okhotsk and Kamchatka on the Pacific, Russian exploration continued eastward, by sea, in the direction of the North American continent. In 1725, Tsar Peter the Great commissioned Vitus Bering, a Danish captain in the Russian service, to discover whether Asia and America were divided. Traveling across Siberia by land, Bering built a ship in the Kamchatka River. In 1728, he sailed eastward with his lieutenant, Chirikov, and sighted the Diomede Islands, one of which is off the Alaskan coast. Sailing through what is now called Bering Strait into the Arctic, Bering rightly concluded that the sea divided the two continents.

Although Bering was probably only a few miles from the American coast, heavy fogs prevented his sight of the mainland. On July 16, 1741, on a second expedition, Bering sighted the volcano of St. Elias, and thus discovered America from the east. Returning, he landed on the island of Kodiak. Hurrying back to Petropavlovsk before winter closed in, his vessel was wrecked in a heavy fog on Bering Island, off Kamchatka. Here, a rigorous winter brought death to the gallant Dane. The survivors built a new boat from the wreck of their ship, and reached Petropavlovsk in the following spring. They carried back a valuable cargo of furs, including pelts of the sea otter, hitherto unknown in Europe and Asia. The hunt for furs now led numerous Russians to venture eastward. By 1784, they made a permanent settlement on Kodiak. These adventurers proved a lawless crew. They abused the native Aleuts and slaughtered furbearing otters and foxes indiscriminately.

European and American adventurers found Alaska sparsely settled by Aleuts, Indians and Eskimos. The Aleuts were a branch of the Eskimo race, but brachycephalic rather than long-headed. They lived in small villages on the Aleutian Islands and along the coast of the mainland. The name Alaska came from their language, meaning "the great land." The Eskimos lived along the Bering and Arctic Seas. The principal Indian group was the Tlingits who inhabited the southern coast, and their food came from both the sea and the forest. The Aleuts numbered around 30,000 when the Russian explorers first appeared. In the following years, they were doomed to great suffering. The fur hunters killed many males, ravished the women, and enslaved both men and women. The Aleuts numbered less than 3000 at the end of the Russian period, many of them being half-breeds.

Following the Russians, other European explorers reached Alaska. In 1774, a Spanish expedition, under Juan Pérez, hugging the coast from Mexico, had touched southern Alaska, and found in the hands of natives a rusty bayonet and other iron pieces probably taken from earlier Russian explorers. In 1774 and 1778, expeditions under Bodega y Quadra made landings in Alaska. Such names on the map as Cordova and Valdez bear witness of Spanish attempts to gain a foothold. But the rigorous Arctic climate was not congenial to the southern nature of the Spaniards, who made no permanent settlements in Alaska.

In 1774, a British expedition under Capt. James Cook surprised the Russians at Unalaska. Cook was in quest of the Northwest Passage from the Pacific side. Entering Bering Strait, he found his passage eastward barred by the polar ice-pack. In 1792, George Vancouver, who had sailed with Cook to the Arctic, anchored in Nootka Sound in British Columbia, to receive the surrender of the post from the Spaniards. Vancouver made extensive surveys of the coast of Alaska as well as of British Columbia. In 1793, Sir Alexander Mackenzie led the first expedition overland, across the Rocky Mountains, to the Pacific coast, reaching Georgia Strait in British Columbia. This remarkable achievement preceded by eleven years the American expedition of Lewis and Clark across the Rockies to the mouth of the Columbia River. Both expeditions testify to the growing awareness of British and Americans as to the importance of the Far West.

The rich fur trade led to Russian colonization of Alaska. In 1786, Gerasim Pribilof discovered the islands which now bear his name. These islands were the breeding grounds of the great seal herds. Numerous small groups of hunters entered the fur trade. Eventually the Russian-American Company, chartered at St. Petersburg, acquired practically a monopoly of all trade. In 1790, the company employed a Finn by the name of Alexander Andrevich Baranov as its manager. For 28 years, under Baranov, the company made the most of its monopoly of trade and greatly expanded its trading posts. In 1799, the settlement of Old Sitka was established. In 1804, when its fort was destroyed by the Tlingit Indians, Baranov, with a Russian naval vessel, seized the present site of Sitka. A new town was founded, with a stockade and blockhouses, guarded by cannon. This became the commercial center of a vast region. Baranov planned to found a trading post in Hawaii. Reaching toward California, he established a post as far south as Fort Ross, north of San Francisco Bay. Under Baranov's rule, the Company flourished, and the settlements took on a permanent form. Sawmills, gristmills and tanneries appeared, and there was some shipbuilding. Eventually the Russian Orthodox Church was brought to the colonies and remains to this day; most of the remaining Aleuts now belong to this faith. Finnish emigrants brought the Lutheran Church.

In the meantime, British traders and Yankees from Boston, Salem and New York had appeared. Both British and Yankee ships engaged in carrying furs, purchased from the Russians, to Chinese ports which were closed to Russian vessels. By an imperial ukase, in 1821, Russia sought to exclude foreign ships from Alaska. Both Britain and the United States protested. Treaties with the United States in 1824, and with Britain in 1825, soon relaxed these restrictions. By this time, the British Hudson Bay Company had appeared on the Pacific coast as a formidable rival to the Russian-American Company. In 1834, the Russians built a fort at Wrangell to block British use of the Sitkine River. Shortly, the two companies reached an agreement for mutual trade, while the Hudson Bay Company leased a large section of southern Alaska from the Russian Company. This arrangement probably saved the properties of the Russian-American Company from seizure during the Crimean War when an Anglo-French squadron burned Petropavlovsk.

Baranov had founded Fort Ross with the intention of raising badly needed supplies for Alaska. In 1811, John Jacob Astor established Astoria at the mouth of the Columbia River, making an agreement with the Russian-American Company to supply Alaska with foodstuffs in exchange for furs which he sold in Canton at a handsome profit. Having no further need for Fort Ross, the Company sold it in 1841 to Capt. John A. Sutter.

In 1861 the charter of the Russian-American Company expired. The cost of maintaining naval protection for Alaska now far exceeded profits from the company. At the same time the Tsar's government suspected British designs to seize the territory. Thus the sale of Alaska to the United States seemed a logical solution of these problems, and all the more so inasmuch as the Monroe Doctrine had shown American opposition to further colonization by European states on the American continents. The Civil War checked negotiations on the subject. But in 1867, U. S. Secretary of State William H. Seward signed a treaty for the purchase of Alaska for $7,200,000. By the treaty of cession, all Russian citizens who wished to remain in Alaska became United States citizens.

The American people were slow to appreciate the value of the vast new acquisition, derisively called "Seward's folly" and "Seward's ice-box." For the first fifteen years the territory was governed first by the Army and then by the Navy. In 1884 Congress organized Alaska as a "district" under a governor, a district judge, a marshal and four commissioners; and $25,000 was appropriated for schools. In 1906, Congress allowed Alaska a delegate in Congress. Juneau became the capital in the same year. In 1912 Alaska was organized as a Territory under a governor and a popularly elected legislature.

The fishing industry prospered. Americans had engaged in salmon fishing even before the purchase of Alaska. New methods of preserving the product appeared. As early as 1865 the first American cannery was built on the Pacific coast. The whaling industry, operating from shore plants, began in 1890. Trade in the pelts of the fur seal proved highly profitable. But as the great seal herd of the Pribilof Islands was decimated, American attempts to regulate the trade led to international complications. In 1869 Congress provided for the leasing of the Pribilof Islands to a commercial company with strict regulations as to the number of male fur seals that could be killed each year. The Pribilof Islands were the breeding grounds of the largest herd of fur seals in the Pacific. By capturing the seals on land, indiscriminate slaughter could be avoided. Barred from the Pribilof Islands, numerous Canadians, Japanese and Russians engaged in pelagic sealing, or killing seals at sea. This practice led to indiscriminate slaughter of female seals which almost resulted in the extermination of the seal herd. An American effort to seize all vessels engaged in pelagic sealing brought vigorous Canadian protests and led to the Bering Sea Arbitration of 1893, in which the American claim to jurisdiction over the Bering Sea was lost. The arbitration finally resulted in the Convention of 1911 between the United States, Britain, Russia and Japan prohibiting pelagic sealing in the Pacific north of the 30th parallel.

In 1896, the discovery of gold on Klondike Creek in Canada led to a gold rush across Alaska. Many prospectors headed for the Klondike field by way of the overland route from Skagway in Alaska to Dawson in the Yukon. Others traveled up the Yukon River. New gold fields, particularly in Nome, brought another influx of prospectors. Later, gold lode mines were opened near Juneau, and copper mines north of the seaport of Cordova. In 1902, the U. S. Government began the construction of the railway from Seward to Fairbanks, and completed the project in 1923.

A favorable homestead act was passed by Congress in 1903. But soon, the industrial development of the Territory was hampered by a conservation policy which began in the administration of President Theodore Roosevelt. Prudence dictated that vast sections of the public domain should be placed in national reservations. But even so, large areas of mineral, forest and oil lands were withheld from suitable development by private enterprise. At this time, Alaskans were compelled to import fuel at great cost, while coal and petroleum fields in Alaska lay untapped. Ten years later, a new Federal policy of leasing lands for exploitation eased the situation.

Friction between Canada and the United States over the Alaskan boundary began during the gold rush of 1896 when the shortest route to the Klondike lay through Skagway in Alaska. The United States claimed the border defined by the Russians in the treaty of 1825. Canadians disputed the claim. By agreement, the controversy was arbitrated in 1903 by a mixed commission of three American and three British-Canadian jurists. The three Americans held for the Russian line. The two Canadian commissioners insisted on a boundary closer to the Pacific. The British jurist, Lord Alverstone (Lord Chief Justice of England) sustained the American claim. The decision was bitterly resented by Canadians, but it did not prove to be a permanent block to good relations.

The strategic importance of Alaska was little appreciated in World War I. It was more fully recognized in World War II, particularly after Japanese forces seized three of the Aleutian Islands, and bombed the naval base at Dutch Harbor. The Alaskan Highway, extending from Dawson Creek in British Columbia to Fairbanks in Alaska, was built by U. S. Army Engineers in order to furnish a protected inland route through Canada to the army posts in Alaska. New airports were also built, and Alaska became an important link in the air lines to Soviet Russia. After the war, with the rising tensions of the Cold War, Alaska as well as Canada became an important factor in preparation for detecting and resisting possible bombing attacks from the U. S. S. R. By 1956, the DEW (Distant Early Warning) Line was completed. It extended from Point Barrow in Alaska to Baffin Island in Canada. This radar defense of 3000 miles, costing half a billion dollars, was designed to detect the approach of hostile bombers.

In 1946 voters in Alaska declared in favor of statehood. Already bills for admission into the Union had been introduced in Congress. The movement was complicated by a similar demand by Hawaii for statehood. In 1956, a constitutional convention, meeting in Fairbanks, adopted a state constitution. In a referendum in April this Constitution was ratified by the Alaskan voters. Finally, in 1958, Congress approved the Constitution and admitted Alaska as the 49th state in the Union. The statehood act authorized the new state to select, from the national public domain, 103,550,000 acres of unappropriated and unreserved public lands to be opened to prospectors and farmers. On Jan. 3, 1959, President Eisenhower proclaimed the admission of the new state.

Alaska, Purchase of. Three alleged movements for the sale of Alaska before 1867 are disclosed by documents in the Soviet Foreign Office: in 1854, during the Crimean War, to prevent England from seizing the territory; in 1856, when Senator Gwin of California

and Secretary of State Marcy proposed its sale to this country; and in 1860, when President Buchanan contemplated its purchase. There is no record of these movements in the Department of State.

On Dec. 28, 1866, Russia decided to sell Alaska to the United States because of the financial decline of the Russian American Company and Russia's disinclination to administer Alaska and inability to defend it, and in order to avoid future difficulties with the United States. On March 9, 1867, the Russian Minister, Edouard de Stoeckl, broached the subject to Secretary of State Seward, who readily agreed. On March 30, 1867, a treaty was signed conveying Alaska to the United States for $7,200,000. The Senate on April 9 gave its advice and consent to ratification out of gratitude for Russia's having sent its fleet to American waters in 1863, supposedly as a demonstration against England and France, which were sympathetic to the Confederacy. Ratifications were exchanged June 20, 1867, and the treaty was proclaimed that day. The formal transfer took place at Sitka, Oct. 18, 1867.

The motives which induced Seward to purchase Alaska are not altogether clear, but we know that prior to the Civil War he had envisioned the United States as coextensive with the North American continent and that after the War he had embarked upon a program of expansion. While he was engaged in this program, Stoeckl appeared with the offer of Alaska. As Alaska fitted into his plan of expansion, Seward probably purchased it for that reason.

Alaska Boundary Question. Maps of Alaska, American, English, Russian, French or Spanish, dated after the treaty of 1825 between Russia and England, all represented southern Alaska as a thirty-mile-wide strip parallel to the coast. That is what the treaty stipulated in establishing a boundary between Russian territory and British. The line was to start from the southernmost point of Prince of Wales Island in N. Lat. 54° 40′, ascend along Portland Channel to latitude 56°, then follow a supposititious "range of mountains" running parallel to the coast to the intersection of the 141° of longitude; thence north on that parallel to the Arctic Ocean. If the supposed range of mountains at any point was found to lie more than ten marine leagues from the ocean, then the line was to follow "the sinuosities of the coast" and not more than ten marine leagues therefrom. Since such mountains were nonexistent, the thirty-mile strip was always reckoned as Russian, later American territory.

The Klondike placer mines, discovered in the upper Yukon country in 1896, were found to lie east of longitude 141°, therefore in British territory. The only practicable way to reach the Klondike was by ascending Lynn Canal to its head, thence following one of several passes to the Yukon. It would have been of vast importance to British interests to gain a duty-free entrance through Lynn Canal which they would have if the inlet could be shown to extend far into

British territory: impossible, however, on the theory that the line of demarcation ran, at the distance of thirty miles, parallel to the "sinuosities of the coast."

Now there began to appear Canadian maps representing an entirely different theory of the boundary line. This was based on a "coast" defined as international law defines the three-mile limit, namely, sinuosities except at inlets, then "headland to headland." This clash of theories made the Alaska boundary question. It was adjudicated under a treaty stipulating that the findings of a joint commission, three American lawyers and three British, should be accepted as final. The commission met in London during the summer of 1903 and found by majority vote in favor of the American claim.

ALBANY. In September, 1609, Henry Hudson moored his ship, the *Half Moon,* near the site of the present Albany, N. Y. No serious attempt at settlement was made, however, until the spring of 1624, when the Dutch West India Co. sent over a group of eighteen families, mostly Walloons, who built Fort Orange on the site of the present steamboat square. During the years 1630–36 the colony was augmented by the arrival of groups of colonists sent over by Kiliaen van Rensselaer, who had been granted a large tract of land near Fort Orange. In 1652 the village of about 100 houses, which had grown up in the protection of the fort, was declared independent of the Patroon's colony, and became known as Beverwyck. Shortly afterward, the fur trade, which had been under the control of the Dutch West India Co., having been thrown open to the citizens, rapidly increased.

On Sept. 24, 1664, Fort Orange surrendered to the English and Beverwyck became Albany, after the Scotch title of the Duke of York. On July 22, 1686, Governor Dongan granted the city a charter. For many years Albany was the key in the regulation of Indian affairs. Since the early days of the colony relations with the Iroquois had been friendly. During the period of the colonial wars many conferences including the famous Albany Congress of 1754 were held there.

By a law enacted on March 10, 1797, Albany became the capital of the State of New York.

ALBANY CONGRESS (1754), called by order of the British government for the purpose of conciliating the Iroquois and securing their support in the war against France, was more notable for the plans that it made than for its actual accomplishments. In June commissioners from New York, Massachusetts, Rhode Island, Connecticut, Pennsylvania, New Hampshire the Maryland met with the chiefs of the Six Nations. Encroachment on their lands, the trade of Albany with Canada, and the removal of Johnson (later Sir William Johnson) from the management of their affairs had aroused a dangerous spirit of disaffection among the Indians. Gifts and promises were bestowed

and the alliance renewed, but the Iroquois went away only half satisfied.

For the better defense of the colonies and control of Indian affairs it had long been felt that a closer union was needed than occasional meetings of governors or commissioners. Discussion of such a union now became one of the principal subjects of the congress. Massachusetts indeed had granted her delegates authority to "enter into articles of union . . . for the general defense of his majesty's subjects." The plan adopted was one proposed by Benjamin Franklin and frequently referred to at the time as the "Albany Plan." It provided for a voluntary union of the colonies with "one general government," each colony to retain its own separate existence and government. The new government was to be administered by a President General appointed by the crown and a Grand Council of Delegates from the several colonial assemblies, members of the Council to hold office for three years. This federal government was given exclusive control of Indian affairs including the power to make peace and declare war, regulate Indian trade, purchase Indian lands for the crown, raise and pay soldiers, build forts, equip vessels, levy taxes and appropriate funds. The home government disapproved this plan because it was felt that it encroached on the royal prerogative. The colonies disapproved of it because it did not allow them sufficient independence. Nevertheless this Albany plan was to have far-reaching results. It paved the way for the Stamp Act Congress of 1765 and for the Continental Congress of 1774. And when, during the troubled days which followed, the need of a closer union was felt, there was a definite plan to serve as a guide in the deliberations of the representatives of the colonies.

ALBANY REGENCY was the first American political machine. It was organized (1820) under Martin Van Buren, and acquired its name because his first aides, residing in Albany and nearby, managed the machine during his absence in the U. S. Senate. The Regency developed party discipline and originated the control of party conventions through officeholders and others subservient to it. The spoils system was the core of its philosophy. The Regency waned when Van Buren's star set in 1848.

ALBEMARLE, Confederate ram, built on the Roanoke River, under command of James W. Cooke on April 19, 1864, sank the gunboat *Southfield,* put the *Miami* to flight, and captured Plymouth, N. C. On May 5 she fought indecisively Capt. Melancton Smith's seven blockaders at the mouth of the Roanoke. But on the night of Oct. 27 Lt. William B. Cushing, with fifteen men in a small launch, bearing a torpedo ingeniously attached to a spar, sank her.

ALBEMARLE SETTLEMENTS. The first permanent settlement in what is now North Carolina was made in the Albemarle Sound region about the middle of the 17th century by Virginians, in quest of good lands. In 1653 the Virginia Assembly granted Roger Green a tract of land on Roanoke River south of Chowan, to be located "next to those persons who have had a former grant." In 1662 George Durant purchased lands from the Indians in this region, and there is evidence to indicate that others had done the same. When it was learned that the Albemarle settlements were not included in the Carolina proprietary grant of 1663, a new charter was granted in 1665, which included them. Government was instituted in Albemarle in 1664 and within a decade settlements extended from the Chowan River to Currituck Sound.

ALBUQUERQUE, N. MEX., originated, April, 1706, as the Spanish villa "San Felipe de Albuquerque," named for King Philip V and the Viceroy, Duke of Albuquerque. It was on the Chihuahua Trail and dominated the Rio Abajo (down river) part of the province. Exposed to Apache and Navajo inroads, the settlers were "reduced" (1779) to the plaza arrangement which survives in "Old Town."

New Albuquerque started a century later (1880) a mile to the east, as a railroad center. That year, the Santa Fe system built down the Rio Grande and the Atlantic and Pacific headed westward over the old United States survey (1853) along the 35th parallel. Connection southeast into Texas came only in 1907.

ALDER GULCH, MONT. Gold was discovered on Alder Gulch, and the first stampede reached there June 6, 1863. The people lived in brush wickyups, dug-outs and rocks, but later a town sprang up which was named Virginia City. The diggings were the richest gold placer deposits ever discovered and in three years $30,000,000 was taken from them.

ALDRICH-VREELAND EMERGENCY CURRENCY LAW, enacted May 30, 1908, as a result of the so-called "bankers' panic" of 1907, aimed to give elasticity to the currency through the next six years, by permitting national banks to issue circulating notes on securities additional to Federal bonds. It permitted issuance, under strict supervision, of additional currency, on bonds of states, cities, towns and counties, and on commercial paper. A tax graduated up to 10% discouraged abundant issues. The Act also created a National Monetary Commission to investigate systems of money and banking abroad and to advise Congress of desirable changes in the American banking system.

ALEUTIAN ISLANDS. The Aleutians were discovered in 1741 by Vitus Bering, a Dane in the service of Empress Anne of Russia. In returning to Kamchatka, Bering died, but his crew reached Petropavlovsk with a rich cargo of furs. Soon numerous Russian fur trad-

ers voyaged to the Aleutian Islands. Among these, Michael Novidiskov landed at Attu in 1745. By 1766, Unalaska became the chief trade center. The early adventurers enslaved the native Aleuts, and there was considerable lawlessness until Baranov, manager of the Russian-American Company (1790–1819), brought law and order. The Islands were included, in 1867, in the purchase of Alaska by the United States. In 1881, when the American Government sought to protect fur seals by prohibiting pelagic or open-sea killing, the United States revived the Russian claim that the Aleutian Islands enclosed the Bering Sea, making it a *mare clausum.* The claim was overruled in the Bering Sea Arbitration of 1893. In 1942, during World War II, the westernmost islands of Attu, Agattu and Kiska were occupied by Japanese forces. They were driven out by the Americans in the following year.

ALEXANDRIA, VA., on the Potomac River, below Washington, was an important trading center until early in the 19th century, particularly as a tobacco warehousing and deep-sea shipping port. Incorporated in 1748, on an original grant of 6000 acres, awarded in 1669, the site was owned for a century by the Alexander family. It was situated on the main stage route, the King's Highway, running southward into Virginia. Braddock departed from there on his fatal expedition. The Fairfax Resolves were signed in Alexandria, July 18, 1774. From 1791 to 1846 Alexandria was under exclusive Federal jurisdiction as part of the District of Columbia. Jefferson's Embargo Act destroyed its tobacco trade.

ALEXANDRIA CONFERENCE (March 28, 1785), between Maryland and Virginia, concerned navigation and commerce in Chesapeake Bay and the Potomac and Pocomoke rivers. Scheduled for Alexandria for March 21, it actually met at Washington's invitation at Mount Vernon. Daniel of St. Thomas Jenifer, Thomas Stone and Samuel Chase represented Maryland, George Mason and Alexander Henderson, Virginia. In ratifying the agreement, Maryland urged the inclusion of Pennsylvania and Delaware, while Virginia urged a meeting of all the states to adopt uniform commercial regulations. This produced the Annapolis Convention, the origin of the Convention of 1787.

ALGECIRAS, CONFERENCE AT. France made agreements with England and Spain in 1904 which allowed her to increase her influence in Morocco. Germany, angered because she was not consulted, demanded a conference of the signatories of the Morocco agreement negotiated at Madrid in 1880. Among the signatories was the United States to whom the German government now appealed for an extension of the open-door policy to Morocco. President Theodore Roosevelt, in an attempt to obtain a peaceful solution, helped Germany by persuading England

and France to attend a conference at Algeciras, Spain, in 1906. In the conference, however, the Germans appeared so uncompromising that Roosevelt supported France, which in the end won out by obtaining a privileged position in Morocco. The United States Senate ratified the resulting treaty but declared that this action was taken solely to protect American interests and should not be interpreted as an abandonment of a non-intervention policy toward Europe.

ALIEN AND SEDITION ACTS were enacted by Congress (1798) because of threatened war with France, and the desire of the Federalists to insure against Jeffersonian Republican success at the polls. The presence in the country of a considerable number of alien Frenchmen favorable to the Republicans, and intemperate newspaper opposition to the Federalists, were the principal factors in prompting these laws.

The act of June 18 decreed that instead of five years, aliens must reside in the country fourteen years before naturalization, and must declare such intention five years before applying for citizenship. This law was repealed by the Republicans (Jeffersonian) in 1802. The act of June 25, which expired in 1800 and was not renewed, empowered the President to deport any aliens he deemed dangerous to public peace. The third act, of July 6, was the most defensible. It empowered the President, in time of war, to arrest, imprison, or banish aliens with whose motherland this country might be at war. In the two years of its existence, it was never applied, but many French were frightened into leaving the country. The principal objection to these laws was the arbitrary power they granted the executive.

The Sedition Act of July 14 made it a high misdemeanor "unlawfully to combine and conspire" in order to oppose legal measures of the Government, to interfere with an officer in the discharge of his duty, to engage in or abet "insurrection, riot, or unlawful assembly or combination." The penalty was a fine of not more than $5000 and imprisonment up to five years. The publication of false or malicious writing against the nation, the President or Congress, was punishable by a fine of not more than $2000 and imprisonment not exceeding two years. The anti-Federalists held that this act was unconstitutional. Of all the Federalist leaders, only John Marshall opposed it openly. A decision of the Supreme Court in 1882 supports the view that the Sedition Act was unconstitutional. It is noteworthy that the act was used to punish Republican editors who had criticized President Adams, while the diatribes of Federalists against Vice-President Jefferson were ignored. Ten individuals, all Republicans, were fined and imprisoned under the Sedition Act. The most notable was Dr. Thomas Cooper, later president of South Carolina College. He paid $400 and spent six months in prison for saying that when Adams took office he "was hardly in the infancy of political mistake: even those who doubted

his capacity thought well of his intentions . . . nor had he yet interfered, as President of the United States, to influence the decision of a court of justice." Many others were tried but not convicted. In some cases the Federalist judges, especially Justice Samuel Chase, displayed violent partisan bias against the accused. As the public began to treat the victims of these prosecutions as martyrs and popular heroes, the Federalists realized their mistake and ceased to enforce the act. Four decades later, Congress refunded some of the fines.

The most conspicuous result of these four laws was the evocation of protests from many states. The extreme protest was voiced in the Virginia and Kentucky Resolutions written, respectively, by Madison and Jefferson.

ALIEN PROPERTY. During the Revolution several colonies sequestrated British debts and refused to restore right of suit. The United States in 1802 settled British claims, and subsequently by treaties with many countries affirmed the general doctrine of inviolability of enemy alien property during war. But in 1917 Congress authorized the conveyance of such property to a Custodian as trustee for management and "if necessary" for sale, to prevent its use by the enemy. Later the idea of trusteeship changed and the property was sold freely at very low prices, even after the Armistice. Several thousand coveted German chemical patents were bought (at $50 each!) by The Chemical Foundation, organized for this purpose by a former Alien Property Custodian and associates. By a series of acts since 1921, notably the Settlement of War Claims Act of 1928, Congress compensated Austrians and Hungarians in full. Of German property seized by the Custodian, 80% was returned. For ships and certain other property used by the Government, Germans were paid 50%. A similar office was created in World War II.

ALLEGHENIES, ROUTES ACROSS. The steep eastern escarpment of the Allegheny Mountains, about 3000 feet high, extending from the Mohawk valley to the Tennessee River was a serious impediment to the westward movement. Routes across the Alleghenies depended upon gaps and approaches to these along the tributaries of rivers. Probably buffalo first trod these routes. Later the Indians followed them as trails. In turn they were used by white explorers and fur traders.

The Susquehanna with its West Branch extending close to the Allegheny River furnished a route much used by the Indians, though whites other than fur traders made little use of it during the early period. The branches of the Juniata River led to two historic routes across the Alleghenies, one, the Frankstown Path, much used by Pennsylvania fur traders, and the other, the Traders Path, followed by Forbes' Expedition and the Pennsylvania Road. From the Potomac at Wills Creek ran the route over the Alleghenies, used by Gist, Washington, and Braddock. From the headwaters of the Potomac also ran a route over the mountains much used in later times as the Northwestern Pike. The headwaters of the James River determined a route overland to branches of the Great Kanawha, one branch of which, the New River, also provided a route from the headwaters of the Roanoke River. Farthest south Cumberland Gap offered easy passage from eastern Tennessee to central Kentucky making possible the much used Wilderness Road. In the light of the extensive use made of Forbes' Road, Braddock's Road and the Wilderness Road in the westward movement, probably no routes in the United States are more properly known as historic highways.

ALMANACS. In colonial days the almanac was a publication of prime importance second only to the Bible and widely used by farmers. Beginning as a publication of astronomical information and prophecy, it later grew into one of culture, occupying the position in the 18th century later taken by the magazine.

The first almanac printed in America was entitled *An Almanac Calculated for New England*, by Mr. Pierce, printed by Stephen Daye at Cambridge, in 1639; in 1676 an almanac was published in Boston; in 1686 in Philadelphia, Samuel Atkins, "A student in the mathematics and astrology," compiled *The American Messenger*. Almanacs were published in New York in 1697, in Rhode Island in 1728, and in Virginia in 1731. In content these almanacs were similar to earlier ones in Europe containing prophecies concerning human beings and the weather, based on astrology. The early almanacs were preserved from year to year and the blank spaces used for diaries, recording accounts, and attempts at poetry.

The most famous of the early almanacs are *The Astronomical Diary and Almanac* published by Ames in Boston (1725–64); and *Poor Richard's Almanac* by Franklin in Philadelphia (1732–57). The latter was unequalled in reputation for proverbs, wit, and wisdom, not all original. Nathaniel Ames, in his *Astronomical Diary and Almanac*, furnished perhaps a greater versatility than appeared in any other almanac of the century. Its tide charts, solar table calculations and eclipses, and changes of the moon were definite assets.

Foreign language almanacs were widely used. A prominent example was the *Hoch Deutsch Americanische* in 1739 and various almanacs published by the Pennsylvania Germans.

In the 19th century, almanacs were frequently issued for political and other propaganda and advertising purposes as indicated by the *Sun Anti-Masonic Almanac* (1831); *Harrison Almanacs* (1840–41); *Henry Clay Almanac* (1844); *General Taylor's Rough and Ready Almanac* (1848); *Cass and Butler Almanac* (1849); *Common School Almanac* (1842); *Temperance Almanac* (1834).

The Confederate Almanac and Register (1862) and *Uncle Sam's Union Almanac* (1863) gave military statistics somewhat as did *Hutchin's Almanac* of New York in the later 18th century.

Comic almanacs in the 1830's; *Josh Billings' Almanac* in 1870; *Fithian's Silk Growers Almanac* in 1840; *The Poultry Breeder's Almanac* of 1856 and the *Phrenological Almanac* of 1841 are typical of the times.

All the outstanding religious denominations published almanacs giving denominational statistics and other information. Medical almanacs of all types have been widely distributed. Encyclopedic information is well served by almanacs published by newspapers of which that of the *Tribune* (1846) and the later *World Almanac* are examples.

AMANA COMMUNITY. Consisting of approximately 1500 people, living in seven villages and owning 26,000 acres of land in Iowa, the Amana Community had for nearly a century conducted the most successful experiment in communism recorded in the annals of American history. Then in 1932 by unanimous vote this community reorganized as a joint stock company where stockholders are both owners and employees.

Born of religious enthusiasm, this unique community was founded in 1714 as the Community of True Inspiration in protest against the arbitrary rule of church and state. For mutual protection the Inspirationists congregated on several large estates in south Germany. But high rents and unfriendly governments forced them to seek a new home in America.

Under the leadership of Christian Metz the Inspirationists crossed the Atlantic in the early eighteen-forties and settled near Buffalo in Erie County, N. Y. Here they laid out six villages, called the place Ebenezer, built mills and factories, tilled the soil, and formally adopted communism as a way of life.

The rapid expansion of nearby Buffalo threatened that isolation which the Inspirationists had sought in the New World. After twelve years at Ebenezer they moved to the frontier state of Iowa where they located in Iowa County, incorporated as the "Amana Society," and once more built houses, churches, schools, stores and mills, and continued their community life of "brothers all" through communism.

AMBASSADORS. The grade of ambassador is the highest rank in the diplomatic service. An ambassador has direct access, when desired, to a sovereign. The United States did not appoint officers of this rank until the close of the 19th century, contenting itself with ministers. The first ambassador of the United States was Thomas F. Bayard of Delaware, commissioned to Great Britain on March 30, 1893. The first ambassador to the United States was Sir Julian Pauncefote of Great Britain, who was presented to President Cleveland on April 11, 1893. Following this exchange of ambassadors between the United States and Great Britain, similar officers were appointed and received for the principal European powers. The first ambassador to Japan was Luke E. Wright of Tennessee, appointed Jan. 25, 1906; to China, Nelson T. Johnson of Oklahoma, appointed Sept. 17, 1935. The first ambassador of the United States to a Latin-American republic was Powell Clayton of Arkansas, who received his commission to Mexico on Dec. 8, 1898. Although Matías Romero, who had long held the post of minister to the United States, had been appointed as first ambassador from Mexico with a commission dated Dec. 5, 1898, and arrangements had been made for the presentation of his credentials, his death prevented his reception; consequently the first ambassador received for a Latin-American republic was Manuel de Azpíroz of Mexico, who was presented to the President on March 30, 1899.

AMEN CORNER was a celebrated niche in the corridor of the old Fifth Avenue Hotel (1859–1908), New York City, where politicians and reporters gathered to discuss coming political events. It was here that Sen. Thomas C. Platt's "Sunday School Class" was held in the late 1890's, and when the Senator announced his decisions his associates would say "Amen."

AMENDMENT CLAUSE OF THE CONSTITUTION was adopted by the Convention of 1787 with little controversy. It is contained in Article V of the United States Constitution. It provides two methods for the proposal of Amendments: either by a two-thirds vote of both Houses of Congress or, on the application of the legislatures of two thirds of the states, Congress shall call a convention for proposing Amendments. In either case Amendments must be ratified in one of two ways: either by action of the legislatures of three fourths of the states or by conventions in three fourths of the same. Congress is empowered to provide either one of these methods of ratification.

AMERICA, DISCOVERY OF. "Traditionally, the history of America begins with the 'discovery' in 1492. Now, that date does mark an important episode—the first piloting of sailing vessels across the Atlantic Ocean, an episode comparable with the first piloting of airplanes across the same sea. But neither was a feat of discovery." (Edgar Lee Hewett.) In other words, America was populated before the continents were "discovered" by western Europeans. It is the consensus of opinion of anthropologists at the present time, that man did not develop, indigenously, in America, but that early man came from the Mongoloid groups of central Asia and probably "discovered" and entered North America by way of Alaska, either by crossing Bering Strait, or possibly by an isthmus or other land bridge which may have existed at the time.

About the year 1000 A.D. roving Norsemen, start-ing from the Scandinavian colonies in Greenland, may have reached the coast of North America anywhere between Labrador and the Chesapeake. If they did, they left no undisputed archaeologic evidences of their visit. The legends of the voyages of Leif Ericsson and Thorfinn Karlsefne depend upon three manuscripts of sagas written more than three hundred years after the possible "discovery" of that part of America which Leif called "Vinland the Good." Admitting Leif to have been the "discoverer" of America, Edward Channing aptly said, "The history of America would have been precisely what it has been if Leif Ericsson had never been born and if no Northman had ever steered his knorr west of Iceland."

On the other hand, it is an undisputed historic fact that on Aug. 3, 1492, the Genoese, Christopher Columbus, sailed from Palos, Spain, under the authority of the King and Queen of that country. On Oct. 11, 1492, he saw, and the next day Columbus and his party landed on, some island in the Bahamas which the Indians called Guanahani, and which Columbus rechristened San Salvador. Its exact identity today has never been conclusively established, but many good scholars have accepted Watling Island as his first landfall. Following this Columbus made three other voyages to the New World (1495, 1499 and 1502), during which he touched the coasts of South and Central America. But it must be remembered there is a documented story that one of the factors which induced Columbus to make his voyage was his actually meeting with, or knowledge of, a Spanish pilot who brought back news of having been wrecked on an island far west of the Madeiras as early as 1484.

Possibly independently, John Cabot sailed from Bristol, England, in May, 1497, and some time in June probably discovered the continent of North America. In 1499, Alonso de Ojeda and Juan de la Cosa visited South America, and with them went Americus Vespucius who wrote such popular accounts of his own deeds that the German geographer, Martin Waldseemüller, coined the word "America" in a book published in 1507. The inevitability of the so-called discovery of America by Europeans is illustrated by the fact that the Portuguese, Pedro Cabral, in 1500, tried to reach India by way of the African coast, and was accidentally blown to the west where unintentionally he reached the coast of Brazil.

The island of Española (Hispaniola-Santo Domingo) became the Spanish outpost from which further discoveries of the mainland were made. Thence Vasco Nuñez de Balboa went to Central America, crossed the Isthmus of Panama and discovered the Pacific Ocean, Sept. 25, 1513. The eastern coast of the mainland of North America had been seen and was cartographically traced by 1502. On Easter Sunday, 1513, Juan Ponce de León, from Española, found his way to the site of the present city of St. Augustine, Fla. Francisco Gordillo coasted as far north as Cape Fear (1521) and Lucas Vasquez de Ayllon followed and got as far as the James River in Virginia (1526). Meantime Hernando Cortés had landed in Mexico and conquered it in one of a series of the most amazing expeditions in all history (1519). Panfilo de Narvaez explored western Florida, and possibly Georgia (1528–36) while his treasurer Alvar Nuñez Cabeza de Vaca walked overland from Pensacola Bay, Fla., to the Gulf of California. In 1539 Hernando de Soto took an expedition from Tampa Bay, Fla., marched north to the Savannah River, turned west and proceeded overland until he reached the Mississippi in 1541.

By this time Antonio de Mendoza had become viceroy of New Spain (Mexico, as opposed to Peru) and from his bailiwick, Franciscan friars were pushing up into what is now "The Southwest" of the United States. Fray Marcos de Niza (1539) brought back such reports that Francisco Vasquez de Coronado started out in April of 1540 on an expedition which took him as far north as central Kansas (1541).

So much for the Spaniards. Meantime the French had entered the field of exploration. Giovanni da Verrazzano, acting under the favor of Francis I, came to North America in 1524 and possibly saw the Lower Bay of New York. Jacques Cartier coasted Labrador in 1534, and in the next year entered and explored the St. Lawrence to the La Chine Rapids above Quebec. The discovery of much of the present area of the United States from the north was the work of Samuel de Champlain, who found Maine in 1603–4, and Cape Cod in 1605, and got as far as central New York State in 1615.

Last, but most effective of the discovering nations was England. The Hawkins—William, John, and James—roamed the West Indies. Sir Francis Drake doubled Cape Horn and reached the coast of California, near, if not at, San Francisco Bay in June, 1579. In 1602 Bartholomew Gosnold reached the coast of Maine near Cape Porpoise, skirted Cape Cod (which he named) and found Narragansett Bay. George Weymouth in 1605 sighted Nantucket and then headed north to find the coast of Maine in the neighborhood of Monhegan and the Gorges Islands.

Mention should be made of an alleged discovery of America by Swedes and Norwegians from Greenland in the 13th century, through Hudson Bay and the Red River of the North into the present State of Minnesota. This theory rests on an inscribed stone and certain artifacts which need further study. There are also stories of pre-Columbian discoveries of America by the Chinese, Welsh, Irish, Phoenicians and others. These are all legendary.

AMERICA, THE. American yacht which in 1851 won the trophy cup presented by the Royal Yacht Squadron, the famous America's Cup. She served later as a Confederate despatch boat, was captured, served as practice ship at the Naval Academy, defended the Cup in 1870, was sold to Gen. B. F. Butler in 1873, and in 1917 to Charles H. W. Foster of the Eastern Yacht Club. She was permanently docked at the Naval Academy in 1921.

AMERICA FIRST COMMITTEE. Founded in 1940 to fight against our participation in World War II, it was endorsed at the outset by Henry Ford and the historian Charles A. Beard. Isolationists in all parts of the United States were involved, but the Committee was especially active in Chicago. By October, 1941, the organization began to disintegrate.

AMERICAN ANTISLAVERY SOCIETIES. The first two American antislavery societies were the New York "Society for the Promoting of the Manumission of Slaves" and the "Pennsylvania Society for Promoting the Abolition of Slavery, the Relief of Free Negroes unlawfully held in Bondage and Improving the Condition of the African Race." Under their auspices the first convention of abolition societies was held in Philadelphia in January, 1794. The Pennsylvania society was created in April, 1775, less than a week before the clash at Lexington and Concord; Benjamin Franklin and Dr. Benjamin Rush were among its presidents. John Jay, later Chief Justice, was the first president of the New York society on its organization in 1785. Other state societies were organized in Delaware, 1788, Maryland, 1789, Rhode Island and Connecticut, 1790, Virginia, 1791, and New Jersey, 1792. There were also abolition societies in Charlestown, Md., and Winchester, Va., and one for the State of Kentucky. The older societies withered and died after the Missouri Compromise of 1820.

The militant Garrisonian Abolition movement led to the formation of the New England Anti-Slavery Society later called the Massachusetts Anti-Slavery Society, on Jan. 6, 1832, and the National Anti-Slavery Society in Philadelphia, Dec. 6, 1833. The New York Anti-Slavery Society was mobbed on the day of its organization, Oct. 21, 1835. From then on such organizations multiplied rapidly throughout the North. In 1835 there were 200; by 1840, 2000 auxiliary societies with a membership between 150,000 and 200,-000. The American Anti-Slavery Society came to life in 1833.

AMERICAN AUTOMOBILE ASSOCIATION. Organized March 4, 1902, in Chicago, Ill., by representatives of nine automobile clubs, the AAA elected Winthrop E. Scarritt, of the Automobile Club of America (New York City), as its first president.

The purposes of the AAA, as outlined in the formal call for organization, included: enactment of liberal motor vehicle laws; protection of legal rights of motor vehicle users; improvement of public highways; "development and introduction of the automobile"; equitable regulation of racing and endurance tests; and the provision of a medium for "counsel and interchange of information, ideas, and suggestions tending to the development and advancement of the art."

One of the earliest activities of the AAA was the sponsoring, during the period 1905–13, of national reliability runs, popularly known as the "Glidden Tours." The AAA also sponsored the good roads movement which resulted in the establishment of the Federal aid system.

Gradually the motor clubs lost nearly all of their early social aspect and became primarily service and civic organizations. In 1958 there were approximately 750 motor clubs, state associations, and motor club branches, with about 6,000,000 members, federated under the AAA banner.

AMERICAN BIBLE SOCIETY. Organized in New York City in 1816 by delegates from 31 local societies to encourage the wider circulation of the Bible, the Society is governed by a Board of Managers, consisting of 48 laymen, one fourth of whom retire from office each year, but are re-eligible. There are four forms of annual membership and three forms of permanent membership in the Society. All members receive the Society's monthly magazine, the *Record*, and all those above associate membership ($1.00) have the right to vote at the Annual Meeting, held on the second Thursday of May.

Associated with the Society are auxiliary societies, which, with the Society's district and division offices, cover every part of the United States. The Society maintains depositories at New York, Atlanta, Chicago, Dallas and San Francisco.

The Society works outside the United States through its own agencies and in support of national Bible Societies in other countries.

The income of the Society is principally derived through gifts from individuals and from churches.

In 1957, the Society's 141st year of service, the American Bible Society distributed at home and abroad 1,051,061 Bibles, 1,681,424 New Testaments and 11,883,157 Gospels and other portions, a total of 14,614,642 Scriptures; this circulation employed more than 271 languages. In 1957 the Society began its second half-billion of Scripture distribution, presenting to the President volume 500,000,001.

AMERICAN COLONIZATION SOCIETY (1817–1912), labored to remove free Negroes from the United States to Liberia, and in addition, aided in manumitting slaves and in suppressing the slave trade. Local branches in every state, the churches and, in some cases, state legislatures supplied the money necessary to buy slaves, transport them, and establish them in Liberia. The Society transported 6000 Negroes between 1821 and 1867. Lack of funds, internal dissension and the opposition of extremists, North and South, hampered the efforts of the Society after 1840. After 1865, the Society functioned chiefly as trustee for the Liberian settlement.

AMERICAN EXPEDITIONARY FORCES. This term was used to designate the American troops serving in Europe during World War I. The declaration of war found us without plans for organizing a force that would be capable of offensive action in modern warfare. On May 26, 1917, Maj. Gen. John J. Pershing, who had been selected by President Wilson to command our land forces abroad, was directed to proceed with his staff to France. Shortly after his arrival, convinced that military assistance on a vast scale would be necessary to Allied success, Gen. Pershing cabled the War Department that its minimum undertaking should contemplate 1,000,000 men in France by the following May, and that plans should be based on an ultimate force of 3,000,000. When the Armistice came, approximately 2,000,000 men had been transported to Europe, where they were trained, subsisted and equipped through their own supply system, and took a decisive part in bringing the war to a successful conclusion.

In the spring and early summer of 1918 a series of powerful German offensives threatened defeat of the Allies. In the crisis Gen. Pershing placed the entire resources of the American Expeditionary Forces at the disposal of the Allied High Command, postponing until July 24, 1918, the formation of the American First Army.

The assistance we gave the Allies in combat began in May with the capture of Cantigny by an American division in the first independent American offensive operation of the war. This was followed early in June by the entrance into battle of two divisions that stopped the German advance on Paris near Château-Thierry. In July two American divisions, with one Moroccan division, formed the spearhead of the counter-attack against the Château-Thierry salient, which marked the turning point of the war. Approximately 300,000 American troops were engaged in this Second Battle of the Marne. In the middle of September the American First Army of 550,000 men reduced the St. Mihiel salient. The latter part of September our Meuse-Argonne offensive was begun. After 47 days of intense fighting, this great battle ended brilliantly for our First and Second Armies on Nov. 11. More than 1,200,000 American soldiers had participated.

With the cessation of hostilities, attention was immediately turned to repatriating the troops. By the end of August, 1919, the last American division had embarked, leaving only a small force in occupied Germany, and on Sept. 1, 1919, Gen. Pershing and his staff sailed for the United States.

AMERICAN EXPRESS COMPANY. In 1850 two express companies then operating in the Northeast, Wells, Butterfield & Co. and Livingston, Fargo & Co., were united to form a joint stock association with a capital of $150,000 known as the American Express Co. Henry Wells and William G. Fargo were the real governing geniuses of the company, and Wells became its first president. It operated on important lines in

New England, followed the Great Lakes into the Midwest and Northwest, and even thrust fingers into Canada. It played no small part in the commercial development of the State of Michigan. Its incorporators organized Wells, Fargo & Co. in 1852 as a sister organization for the western half of the country. The U. S. Express Co. was organized in 1854 as a subsidiary, but in the course of two decades the two companies drifted apart and became sharp competitors. In 1915 the American operated on 61,500 miles of steam and electric railroads, water and stage lines, this being the second largest territory among the express companies. In 1918 all the companies merged their shipping interests in the American Railway Express Co., the American Express Co. continuing as a banking and tourist bureau. In 1929 the Railway Express Agency, owned by the railroads, took over the American Railway Express Co.

AMERICAN FUR COMPANY was incorporated for a period of 25 years, under the laws of the State of New York by an act passed on April 6, 1808. Its capital stock was not to exceed $1,000,000 for two years; thereafter it might not exceed $2,000,000. John Jacob Astor was the sole stockholder. From being a poor immigrant German lad in 1784, Astor had risen by 1808 to a position where he felt he could challenge unaided and successfully the two great fur-trading companies of Canada that were securing a large part of their furs within the limits of the United States— the North West Company, with a capital of $1,200,000, and the Michilimackinac Company, capitalized at about $800,000. All that he needed was incorporation as a company. This might seem presumption on Astor's part, but events were to prove that his belief in himself was justified.

To get control of the fur trade of the Great Lakes, the American Fur Company first came to an agreement with the North West Company and the Michilimackinac Company, whereby the South West Fur Company, representing the three companies, was constituted Jan. 28, 1811, to last for five years. It was to confine its operations to the region south of the Canadian frontier. The War of 1812 stopped the normal course of the fur trade and by 1817 Astor was able to buy out his partners in the South West Company at a very low price. Thereupon the Northern Department of the American Fur Company was established, with headquarters at Mackinac.

The next aim of the Company was to secure the St. Louis and Missouri River trade. In 1817 it made a tentative arrangement with powerful St. Louis firms, but it was not until 1822 that the Company established its own branch in St. Louis. This became known as the Western Department of the American Fur Company.

Still another obstacle to be overcome in securing monopoly of the fur trade of the United States was the abolition of the system of United States trading factories, which had been in existence since 1796 and which were a step in the direction of a safe, enlightened and humane Indian policy. However, they could compete successfully with Astor for the trade and so he determined to get rid of them. With the aid of such interested men as Lewis Cass and Thomas Hart Benton, he campaigned successfully. In 1822 the system was abolished.

Private traders and other companies were treated in the same high-handed manner. Competition was stifled by fair means or foul. An act excluding foreigners from the trade was passed by Congress in 1816, probably at the instigation of the American Fur Company. In 1824 Congress passed another act, designating certain places at which trade might be carried on, which greatly hampered the Company's competitors while favoring the Company men.

In 1827 the greatest rival of the Company united with it—the Columbia Fur Company—which operated between the upper Mississippi and the upper Missouri, and known henceforth as the Upper Missouri Outfit of the American Fur Company.

By 1828 the Company had a virtual monopoly of the fur trade of the United States. In 1834, however, it became politic for the Company to withdraw from the Rocky Mountain area. In that year, too, Astor withdrew from the Company, whose charter had lapsed in April, 1833, though no notice had been taken of that fact. During the last decade of its existence, the Company made profits and declared dividends of over $1,000,000. After 1817 the Company had consisted (till 1823) of Astor, Ramsay Crooks, and Robert Stuart. After 1823 and until 1827 the only new partners were the St. Louis firms. In 1827 the Columbia Fur Company's men were added. In 1834 Astor sold out his interests: those in the Western Department to Pratte, Chouteau and Company; and those in the Northern Department to a group headed by Ramsay Crooks. This second group, of some ten stockholders, now became the American Fur Company. It lasted till 1842. During these eight years Ramsay Crooks was president of the Company. Its operations were confined roughly to the area between Detroit, the Ohio and the Red River of the North. It built vessels on the upper Great Lakes, established extensive fisheries on Lake Superior, marketed the furs of the St. Louis firm of Pratte, Chouteau and Co. (after 1838 Pierre Chouteau, Jr., and Co.), tried desperately to oust such important rivals as W. G. and G. W. Ewing of Fort Wayne and maintained something of a banking business throughout the area of its operations. After its failure in 1842 it seems to have been reconstituted once more in 1846 as a commission house.

AMERICAN LEGION. The American Legion is an organization of veterans of World War I, World War II, and the Korean Conflict. Any person who served honorably on active duty in the Army, Navy, Air

Force, Marine Corps or Coast Guard of the United States during any of the following periods is eligible for membership: April 6, 1917, to Nov. 11, 1918; Dec. 7, 1941, to Sept. 2, 1945; or June 25, 1950, to July 27, 1953. Mothers, wives, daughters and sisters of Legion members are eligible for membership in the American Legion Auxiliary.

Col. Theodore Roosevelt, Jr., is credited with the original idea for the formation of an organization of World War I servicemen. On Feb. 16, 1919, twenty members of the American Expeditionary Forces met in Paris to discuss the morale and welfare of servicemen during the period of demobilization. This small group made arrangements for a caucus of overseas servicemen, held at the Cirque de Paris on March 15–17, 1919, with some 1000 officers and enlisted men present. The organization dates its founding from this meeting.

A subsequent caucus of servicemen and veterans of World War I who had returned to the United States was held in St. Louis, Mo., on May 8–10 of the same year. Final organizational plans were made at this meeting, and the American Legion was chartered by an act of Congress on Sept. 16, 1919.

Early in its history, the American Legion announced its primary objectives. It declared itself a patriotic organization and dedicated its efforts to "service to the community, state and nation." During the years immediately following World War I, the Legion directed its major effort to creating in the Federal Government an adequate program of care for war-disabled veterans and for the surviving dependents of deceased veterans. In 1922 its efforts saw the creation of the U. S. Veterans Bureau (now the Veterans Administration). At the same time, the Legion organized its own veteran rehabilitation program with both volunteer and paid service officers to assist individual veterans with problems of hospitalization, medical care, claims, insurance, employment, etc.

Other major American Legion programs, most of which date back to the early years of the organization, include Americanism, child welfare, national security. Under the Americanism program a wide range of youth activities were developed, including junior baseball, a national high school oratorical contest, Boys States and the Boys Nation, and sponsorship of Boy Scout units. The child welfare program had as its original purpose adequate care for the children of deceased veterans but soon broadened its concern to include all children. By 1958 total expenditures of the entire organization in all forms of child welfare and youth work had passed $8,000,000 annually.

For many years the Legion has urged a system of universal military training to provide adequate manpower for national security without the burden of a large standing army. In 1958 it gave strong support to the movement for reorganization of the Department of Defense to give greater unity of command and planning in this agency.

In 1920, the first year following its founding, the Legion numbered 843,013 members. In the twenty years before the beginning of World War II, annual membership fluctuated between a low of 609,407 and a high of 1,078,119. With the close of World War II, Congress amended the organization's charter to make veterans of that conflict eligible for membership. Again in 1951 the charter was amended to extend eligibility to men and women who served honorably during the Korean police action. On Dec. 31, 1957, official membership stood at 2,749,778 in 16,931 posts.

With a membership of this size, the Legion from the very first has been a potent legislative force. Its constitution prohibits it from taking part in any partisan political activity, and elected officers of the Legion may neither be candidates for nor hold any elective political office. Legislative policies are determined each year through the votes of delegates at the annual national convention, and between conventions by the national executive committee.

The Legion counts as its most far-reaching legislative achievement the passage of the Servicemen's Readjustment Act of 1944, which received its popular title of GI Bill from a Legion publicist. Other areas in which the American Legion has been active legislatively include: payment of World War I bonus in 1936; establishment of a system of veterans' preference in Federal employment; centralization of services for veterans in a single agency—the Veterans Administration; outlawing of the Communist party in the United States and other internal security measures; opposition to the diplomatic recognition of Red China or its admission to the United Nations; increased emphasis on scientific research and development.

By mid-1950 many World War I veterans were demanding payment of a general pension to all living veterans of that war who had passed a prescribed age (usually mentioned as 60 or 65), such as had been paid to the veterans of earlier wars. Recommendations urging the Legion to support such a measure became a repeated subject for debate at annual conventions, but through 1958 were consistently voted down by large majorities. In lieu of a general pension, the legion supported the existing system of pensions for older veterans based upon need, but urged some liberalization of payments and eligibility requirements.

In addition to its activities specifically relating to veteran welfare, the Legion has sponsored a wide range of community service programs. Some of the activities carried on in this field have included teen-age driver training, scholarship information service, civil defense, disaster relief, training in flag courtesy, and support to local charitable campaigns.

The activities of its national rehabilitation and

child welfare divisions were supported in part from the earnings of a seven-million-dollar endowment fund, established in 1925. In 1954 an American Legion Child Welfare Foundation was incorporated with the broad purpose of financing "in whole or in part research demonstrations, or other special projects which will benefit children and youth." By 1958 this foundation had made grants totaling nearly $100,000 for research or special projects in such areas as mental retardation, juvenile delinquency prevention and treatment, mental health, social attitudes of teen-agers, etc.

Following the first national convention in November, 1919, the Legion's national headquarters was established in Indianapolis, Ind. The State of Indiana provided the headquarters building on a rent-free basis. In addition, a Washington office maintains liaison with the Federal Government, and a New York office houses editorial and advertising departments of the organization's national publication, *The American Legion Magazine,* published monthly.

AMERICAN LIBERTY LEAGUE was organized in August, 1934, with the express purpose of fighting radicalism and defending property rights and the U. S. Constitution. Among its organizers were many lifelong, though conservative Democrats, but it was clearly inimical to the "New Deal" and, because of this and its many wealthy members, was denounced by the F. D. Roosevelt administration as reactionary.

AMERICAN (OR KNOW-NOTHING) PARTY enjoyed a meteoric career during the 1850's. It was founded in New York in 1849 as a secret patriotic society known as the Order of the Star Spangled Banner, but experienced little success until after 1852. Expansion from that time on was so rapid that by 1854 a national organization could be perfected.

This phenomenal growth was due partly to the charm of secrecy with which the party clothed itself. Members were initiated and sworn not to reveal its mysteries; their universal answer to questions was "I know nothing about it," thus giving their organization its popular name: the Know-Nothing Party. All who joined were pledged to vote only for natives, to work for a twenty-one-year probationary period preceding naturalization, and to combat the Catholic Church.

More important in accounting for the party's success was the period in which it thrived. Older party lines had been disrupted by the Kansas-Nebraska Act and many voters, unwilling to cast their lot either with proslavery Democrats or antislavery Republicans, found refuge with the Know-Nothings. At this time, too, anti-Catholic sentiment, long fostered by churches, societies and the press, was reaching its height. The American Party attracted thousands of persons who sincerely believed that Catholicism and immigration menaced their land.

These factors account for the startling strength shown by the party. In the elections of 1854 and 1855 it was successful in a number of New England and border states and its supporters fully expected to carry the country in 1856.

By this time, however, the slavery issue had caused a split in Know-Nothing ranks. A pro-slavery resolution, pushed through the 1855 convention by Southern delegates, caused a lasting breach and the American Party entered the election of 1856 so hopelessly divided that its presidential candidate, Millard Fillmore, carried only the State of Maryland. This crushing defeat and the growing sectional antagonism over slavery brought about the party's rapid end.

AMERICAN PHILOSOPHICAL SOCIETY was founded by Benjamin Franklin in 1743 "for the promotion of useful knowledge among the British plantations in America." It is the oldest learned society in America and from its foundation to the present time has included in its membership the leading scientists, scholars, statesmen and public servants of this country and some of the most illustrious of foreign lands. Membership is limited to 500.

AMERICAN PROTECTIVE ASSOCIATION, a secret anti-Catholic society, was founded at Clinton, Iowa, in 1887 by Henry F. Bowers. It grew slowly in the Middle West until the Panic of 1893 brought home to natives the economic rivalry of second generation immigrants and this, combined with rural antagonism toward urban Catholics, the effective propaganda of nativistic newspapers and speakers, revived Catholic demands for a share in public school funds, and political instability following the Democratic victory in 1892 attracted a million members by 1896. This voting strength was utilized to gain control of local Republican organizations and carry elections throughout the Middle West but in 1896 the Association split over the question of supporting William McKinley, and its members deserted rapidly amidst the greater excitement of the free silver campaign. It lingered on despite steadily declining support until 1911.

AMERICAN RAILWAY UNION was started by Eugene V. Debs in June, 1893, in an attempt to unite all railroad workers. In June, 1894, it ordered its members not to handle Pullman cars in sympathy with the Pullman shop strikers. Violence resulting, President Cleveland sent troops to stop interference with the mails. The union officers were jailed for violating an injunction secured by the railroads under the Sherman Act. The strike was lost, and the union collapsed.

AMERICAN SYSTEM, a term applied by Henry Clay, in his tariff speech of March 30–31, 1824, by which he sought to justify the greater measure of protection that he was trying to secure in the tariff bill under discussion. His object was to create a home market and "to lay the foundations of a genuine American policy"; he wished to check the decline of American industry and offered a remedy which, he said, "consists in modifying our foreign policy, and in adopting a genuine American system." By this he proposed to eliminate the dependence upon the foreign market with the result that American industries would flourish and a home market for the surplus of agricultural products would develop. Such a program was presumed to offer attractions not only to the eastern manufacturer but also to the western farmer. Implicit in the arrangement was the availability of more revenue for internal improvements, upon which Clay had already taken a leading position.

AMERICAN TOBACCO CASE. In this decision, 1911 (221 U. S. 106), the Supreme Court, following the same line of reasoning as in the Standard Oil decision of the same year, found that the American Tobacco Co. had attempted to restrain commerce and monopolize the tobacco business in violation of the Sherman Antitrust Act. Restraint of trade, the Court declared, did not embrace "all those normal and usual contracts essential to individual freedom, and the right to make which was necessary in order that the course of trade might be free," but on the other hand, in view of "the general language of the statute, and the public policy which it manifested, there was no possibility of frustrating that policy by resorting to any disguise or subterfuge of form, since resort to reason rendered it impossible to escape by any indirection the prohibitions of the statute."

AMISH MENNONITES are followers of Jacob Amman. They separated from the Mennonites in Europe in the late 17th century because of a strict interpretation of the practice of "avoidance" and "shunning," i.e., ostracizing, socially and religiously, violators of church rule.

Ultraconservatism is the chief characteristic of their cult. They use hooks and eyes instead of buttons, wear beards but ban the mustache, the badge of the soldier.

They first appeared in Pennsylvania about 1714, and have settlements in Pennsylvania, Iowa, Maryland, Indiana, Illinois, Ohio, Delaware, Kansas, Michigan, Missouri, Montana, Nebraska, Oklahoma, Oregon and Virginia.

AMISTAD CASE (1839). The 54 slaves on this Spanish schooner mutinied near Cuba, murdered part of the crew, and caused the remainder to sail into Long Island Sound and the jurisdiction of American courts. Piracy charges were quashed but some salvage claims were awarded by legal proceedings in Connecticut. In 1841 the Supreme Court declared the Negroes free. Private charity provided their transportation back to Africa. This case offers an interesting comparison with the *Creole* affair.

ANACONDA COPPER, one of the largest copper mining companies of the world, and the principal producer of the Butte district of Montana, was organized in 1881 as The Anaconda Silver Mining Company, Marcus Daly having persuaded James B. Haggin, Lloyd Tevis and George Hearst to purchase for $30,000 the small Anaconda silver mine, then only sixty feet deep. The ore contained just enough copper to facilitate the recovery of the silver for which it was being worked, but at greater depth it became evident that its principal content was copper. A copper smelter was erected in 1884 and 3000 tons of ore was being treated daily by 1889. Continuing to expand through the purchase of other mines it was reorganized as the Anaconda Mining Company in 1891, with a capital of $25,000,000. The Hearst interests were sold to the Exploration Company, London, and the company was reorganized in 1895 as the Anaconda Copper Mining Company, three quarters of the stock having been bought by the Amalgamated Copper Company. In 1910 its capitalization was increased to $150,000,000 to take over all the properties of the Amalgamated in the Butte district and some of the William A. Clark interests, the purchase being completed by 1915 and the Amalgamated dissolved.

ANÆSTHESIA. Though it had been known from ancient times that certain narcotic preparations would deaden pain and though Sir Humphrey Davy had suggested in 1800 that nitrous oxide (popularly called "laughing gas") might be used in surgery, no anæsthesia was ever administered in an operation until 1842. On March 30, 1842, Dr. Crawford W. Long used sulphuric ether on a patient in Jefferson, Ga., and removed without pain a tumor from the back of his neck. Though local prejudice was strong against this practice, Long later used ether in performing a number of other operations, but he published no statement of the fact. In December, 1844, Dr. Horace Wells, a dentist of Hartford, Conn., having likewise discovered that "laughing gas" was an anæsthesia, had it administered to himself and had a tooth extracted without pain. In 1846 Dr. W. T. G. Morton, a Boston dentist and a former associate of Wells, using sulphuric ether, performed a like act. Soon thereafter he administered ether in an operation in the Massachusetts General Hospital. A long contest over the question of priority in the use of anæsthesia has followed, complicated further by the claims of Charles T. Jackson, a Boston chemist.

ANANIAS CLUB was an expression employed by the press in 1906–7 to avoid the "short and ugly word" (liar) in connection with the "mutual accusations of inveracity" which arose between President Theodore

Roosevelt and Sen. Tillman of South Carolina over the railway rate bill and later during the controversy between Roosevelt and the "nature fakers."

ANARCHISTS. The leading exponent of philosophical anarchism in the United States was Benjamin R. Tucker. In his magazine *Liberty,* published in Boston, he defined anarchism as the law of equal liberty, with self-interest the supreme law for man, abolition of the state to be achieved by education and passive resistance. His theories were set forth in *Instead of a Book* (1893). Another, an insurgent school, leaned to the Bakunin-Kropotkin theory that the state belongs to a low stage of evolution and must disappear since the trend of social progress is toward more and more liberty. It saw evolution and revolution as alternating processes, revolution and political assassination as an accelerated evolution and belonging to the unity of nature. While this school did not advocate deeds of violence it did not condemn, and sometimes condoned them. To it belonged John J. Most, who, after expulsion from Germany in 1878 and imprisonment in England for incendiary utterances in his periodical, *Freiheit,* made his home in New York. Until 1883, anarchists and socialists belonged to the same organizations, though theoretically they were diametrically opposed. In 1887, in Chicago, following the Haymarket riot, four men who confessed themselves anarchists but denied bomb throwing were hanged. It was a young Russian immigrant, Emma Goldman, a gifted orator, who in 1889 became an active leader of the insurgent school. She championed an anarchist of the deed, Alexander Berkman, when, having attempted the life of Henry C. Frick, he was sentenced to 22 years' imprisonment. When President McKinley was shot, Sept. 6, 1901, by another anarchist of the deed, Leon Czolgosz, Emma Goldman became the object of suspicion when she published an essay explaining the deed in its social and psychological aspect. In 1906 she published an anarchist magazine, *Mother Earth,* which Berkman edited on his release.

In July, 1917, Berkman and Emma Goldman were sentenced to two years in the penitentiary, with $10,000 fine and deportation to Russia for their activities in the anticonscription agitation.

ANDERSON v. DUNN (6 Wheaton 204, 1821). The right of the House of Representatives to charge, hear and punish contempt, and detain, arrest and imprison those so charged, was unanimously upheld on the analogy of the right of the judiciary to punish contempt—for the self-preservation of the institutions of the state.

ANDERSONVILLE PRISON (February, 1864–April, 1865) in Georgia was the largest and best-known of Confederate military prisons. Hastily established because the number of prisoners constituted a military danger and was a serious drain on the food supplies of Richmond, no adequate preparations were made for housing the captives. The poverty of the Confederacy, a defective transportation system and the concentration of all resources on the army, prevented the prison officials supplying barracks, cooked food, clothing or medical care to their charges. The prison consisted solely of a log stockade of 16½ acres (later enlarged to 26 acres) through which ran a stream of water. Rations to the prisoners generally consisted of corn meal and beans, and seldom included meat. Bad sanitary conditions, lack of cooking facilities, poor food, crowding and exposure soon produced respiratory diseases, diarrhoea and scurvy. The inadequate medical staff, without drugs, could not cope with the situation. During the summer the number of prisoners increased to 31,678. There are 12,912 graves in the National Cemetery at Andersonville. Estimates place the total number of deaths even higher. In September, the approach of Sherman's army caused the removal of all well prisoners to Charleston, S. C. Only enlisted men were confined in Andersonville; commissioned officers were held at Macon, Ga.

To the prisoners and to their friends in the North it appeared that the Confederates were deliberately murdering the captives. As a result of this belief, Capt. Henry Wirz, commander of the interior of the prison, was tried in August, 1865, on charges of murder and conspiring with Jefferson Davis to murder. Although found guilty by a military commission, and hanged, Nov. 10, 1865, subsequent investigation has revealed much in Wirz's favor. For many years Andersonville prison was a vital element in the "bloody shirt" issue in politics.

ANDRÉ, CAPTURE OF. Maj. John André, adjutant-general of the British Army in North America during the Revolution, was entrusted by Sir Henry Clinton with the correspondence between the British Headquarters and the American traitor, Brig.-Gen. Benedict Arnold, in the years 1779–80. On Sept. 21, 1780, he met Arnold at Joshua Hett Smith's house, just south of West Point on the Hudson, to complete the arrangements for the betrayal of West Point to the British. He had arrived on the British vessel *Vulture* which anchored opposite Haverstraw. While Arnold and André were in conference, American artillery fire compelled the *Vulture* to fall down-stream. Having lost his means of transport, André was persuaded to change his costume for a disguise and carry the treasonable papers back overland by horseback. He crossed the Hudson, started down the east bank, and was captured (Sept. 23) by three American irregulars, John Paulding, Isaac van Wart and David Williams who searched him, discovered the papers and turned him over to the American army. André explained himself to Washington, and Sir Henry Clinton demanded his release on the ground that he had gone to consult with Arnold under a flag of truce, which was true. But, in fact, his conduct had made him a spy, as he said in his own words: "The events of coming within an Enemy's posts and of changing my dress which led me to my present Situation were contrary to my own Inclination as they were to your [Clinton's] orders. . . ." He was tried before a court-martial (Sept. 29), of which Maj. Gen. Nathanael Greene was the president, convicted of being a spy and ordered to be hanged. Washington refused to intercede in his behalf, and he was executed on Oct. 2, 1780, at Tappan, N. Y.

ANIÁN, STRAIT OF. A mythical strait, supposed to connect the Atlantic and Pacific, sought by the Spaniards in the 16th and 17th centuries. In 1601 they tried to find a harbor on it beyond Quivira for direct intercourse with Spain. Until 1742 the Gulf of California was believed by many to join the west end of the strait.

ANNAPOLIS CONVENTION was the precursor of the Constitutional Convention of 1787. On Sept. 11, 1786, twelve commissioners from New York, New Jersey, Pennsylvania, Delaware and Virginia met in the State House at Annapolis, Md., to discuss reform of the vexatious restrictions placed upon interstate commerce by the various states. Among those present were Alexander Hamilton, John Dickinson and James Madison. The convention took no action except to recommend that a larger convention be held in Philadelphia the following May.

ANTIETAM, BATTLE OF (Sept. 17, 1862). Early in September, 1862, Gen. Lee's (C.) Army of Northern Virginia crossed the Potomac into Maryland. He concentrated at Frederick, then sent Jackson's corps south to take Harpers Ferry, and Longstreet's westward across the South Mountain. On the 14th McClellan's (U.) Army of the Potomac forced the mountain passes.

Lee began to concentrate toward the Potomac, and took position at Sharpsburg, on the Antietam Creek. While Longstreet was assembling here, Lee heard that Jackson had captured Harpers Ferry, and took the bold decision to stand and fight behind the creek, with the Potomac at his back. Longstreet took the right of the line; Jackson's troops, as they arrived, the left.

McClellan planned to strike Lee's left with three corps (Hooker's, Mansfield's and Sumner's); to follow this blow with an attack by Burnside's corps on the Confederate right; and to hold Porter's and Frankin's corps, with Pleasonton's cavalry, in reserve in the center.

But Hooker, Mansfield and Sumner attacked successively, not simultaneously, and each in turn was beaten. Burnside's attack on the other flank came still later. Longstreet's line had been weakened to reinforce Jackson, for Lee had no real reserve; hence

Burnside made some progress at first, but when fully engaged he was struck in flank by A. P. Hill's (C.) division, the last of Jackson's troops returning from Harpers Ferry. Burnside was driven back to the bridge by which he had crossed the creek, and darkness ended the fighting.

On the 18th Lee stood fast and McClellan did not renew his attack. On the 19th Lee effected his withdrawal across the Potomac. The numbers engaged are uncertain; perhaps a fair estimate is 50,000 Federal, 40,000 Confederate. But this was Lee's entire strength, and McClellan had 20,000 in reserve, never used. The losses may be estimated as 12,000 Federal, 9000 Confederate.

ANTI-MASONIC MOVEMENTS. Suspicion of secret societies was marked at an early date, but the fact that Washington and other patriots were Masons seemed proof that the Order was not dangerous. In 1826, however, when the Morgan Trials aroused western New York there was a widespread reaction, which assumed national importance with the organization of the Anti-Masonic party. Many Masons renounced their vows, membership in New York dwindling from 20,000 to 3000 between 1826 and 1836. The number of lodges was reduced from 507 before 1826, to 48 in 1832. In Vermont the Grand Lodge voted down a proposal for dissolution, but agreed to receive charters from chapters desiring to surrender them, and provided that funds of such lodges should go to the state public school fund. Many congregations were divided, especially Presbyterian, Baptist, Methodist and Congregational. Masons were excluded from membership, and pastors were barred from their pulpits. In Pennsylvania, anti-Masonry found favor among Quakers, Mennonites, Dunkards, Moravians and some Lutheran and German Reformed groups. A Vermont law of 1833 forbade extrajudicial oaths; and elsewhere Masons were deprived of local office and dropped from jury rolls.

Anti-Masonic newspapers were an index of the rapid growth of the Anti-Masonic party. Charging intimidation of printers and suppression of facts of the Morgan Trials, party leaders urged the establishment of "free presses." Thurlow Weed, who in 1828 had started the Rochester *Anti-Masonic Enquirer,* was given financial backing in 1830 for his *Albany Evening Journal,* the principal party organ. In 1832 there were 46 anti-Masonic papers in New York and 55 in Pennsylvania. In September, 1831, a national Anti-Masonic convention was held at Baltimore, naming William Wirt of Maryland for President. This, the first "third party," only drew support from Clay, and helped the sweep for Jackson in 1832. It received seven electoral votes from Vermont. The party also gained adherents in Pennsylvania, Ohio, New Jersey, Massachusetts, Connecticut and Rhode Island; but only Pennsylvania, through the leadership of

Thaddeus Stevens, and Vermont elected Anti-Masonic governors. In the late 1830's the excitement subsided, or was replaced by the antislavery agitation. By 1838 the party had merged with the Whigs.

After the Civil War there was another movement directed against secret societies. The National Christian Association was founded at Aurora, Ill., in 1868 to oppose secret orders, "Jesuitism, Mormonism, atheism, spiritualism and free love." It maintained a national organization and published a weekly, *The Christian Cynosure* (1867–71). This crusade was unsuccessful, and the 1880's and 1890's witnessed a great increase of fraternal orders.

ANTINOMIAN CONTROVERSY was a theological dispute begun in Boston by Mistress Anne Hutchinson in the fall of 1636. She had been a parishioner and devout admirer of John Cotton in Boston, England, and with her husband followed him to the new Boston, where they were admitted to the membership in the First Church. She was exceptionally intelligent, learned and eloquent, and began innocently to repeat on week days to small gatherings the substance of Cotton's sermons, but soon commenced delivering opinions of her own. At the height of her influence about eighty persons were attending lectures in her house.

She caused turmoil by putting a different conclusion from that maintained by the clergy upon the doctrine of the Covenant of Grace. The standard view held that the elect entered a Covenant with God on the condition of their believing in Christ, in return for which God contracted to give them salvation, but that thereafter the justified saints devoted themselves to good works, not in order to merit redemption, but as evidence of their having been called. Mrs. Hutchinson declared that stating the matter thus put too much emphasis upon "works" and denied the fundamental Protestant tenet of salvation by faith alone. Consequently she preached that the believer received into his soul the very substance of the Holy Ghost and that no value whatsoever adhered to conduct as a sign of justification.

This conclusion made for a disregard of morality such as Protestant theologians had everywhere endeavored to resist, and it could clearly lead to disastrous social consequences. The New England clergy, recognizing in her teachings a form of "Antinomianism," *i.e.*, a discarding of the moral law, could not possibly have tolerated her. She made matters worse by accusing all the clergy except Cotton of preaching a Covenant of Works, so that Winthrop says it began to be as common in Massachusetts to distinguish the party of works and the party of grace "as in other countries between Protestants and papists." Thus she threatened to split the colony into factions, particularly when she was supported by her brother-in-law, the Rev. John Wheelwright, and the young governor, Harry Vane. The other clergy and

magistrates believed that the existence of the whole enterprise was at stake; led by John Winthrop, and employing consummately clever tactics, they regained control of the government in May, 1637, then proceeded to disarm Anne's partisans and suppress the movement. Anne was examined by a synod of the ministers, which found her guilty of eighty erroneous opinions; John Cotton publicly repudiated her. Wheelwright was banished to New Hampshire; Anne was arraigned before the General Court, where she boasted of having received explicit revelations from the Holy Ghost, a possibility which no orthodox Protestant community could for a moment admit. She was excommunicated from the First Church in March, 1638, John Cotton pronouncing sentence upon her, and banished from the colony by the Court, whereupon she fled to Rhode Island.

ANTIRENT AGITATION, which swept New York, 1839–46, was a culmination of the resentment of farmers against the leasehold system, whereby the great landlords and land companies collected yearly tribute in produce, labor or money, and exacted a share ("quarter sales") of one quarter or one third of the amount realized from the sale of a leasehold. In 1839, when the heirs of Stephen Van Rensselaer tried to collect some $400,000 in back rent, the farmers rebelled. Gov. Seward called out the militia and issued a proclamation of warning. This sobered the rioters and ended the so-called "Helderberg War." Similar disturbances, however, soon broke out in the counties south of Albany.

In Columbia and Delaware Counties groups of men disguised as Indians tarred and feathered sheriffs and deputies who attempted to serve writs of ejectment. The murder of Deputy Sheriff Steele, August, 1845, led Gov. Wright to proclaim Delaware County in a state of insurrection. Antirent secret societies spread rapidly and became a political influence. The constitution of 1846 prohibited new feudal tenures and a court decision declared "quarter sales" illegal. There followed a general conversion of old leases into fee simple ownership.

ANTI-SALOON LEAGUE was founded at Oberlin, O., May 24, 1893. Creating this state-wide organization was the idea of the Rev. H. H. Russell. This "Ohio plan" was copied by many states and in 1895 a national organization, the Anti-Saloon League of America, was established at the Calvary Baptist Church, Washington, D. C. Soliciting and securing aid from the Protestant Evangelical churches, the league grew rapidly and came to regard itself as the "Church in Action Against the Saloon."

Prior to the Eighteenth Amendment the league centered its attention upon destroying the liquor traffic by legislation. To this end it sought and obtained local option, county option, state prohibition, regulation of interstate liquor shipments and finally national prohibition. Following national prohibition the league sought by propaganda and pressure to achieve enforcement and the maintenance of this policy.

ANZA EXPEDITION (Oct. 23, 1775–Jan. 4, 1776), was sent out by Antonio Bucareli, Viceroy of New Spain, to provide Alta California with the white population essential to its occupation in face of English and Russian threats. Led by Juan Bautista de Anza, who in 1774 had proved that a route existed from Sonora to California, 244 persons crossed the Colorado desert and reached San Gabriel. Local jealousies prevented Anza from founding the city he laid out but his capable lieutenant, José Joaquin Moraga, Sept. 17, 1776, dedicated a presidio on the site of modern San Francisco and there, Oct. 9, 1776, was started the mission San Francisco de Asís.

APACHE PASS EXPEDITION (Feb. 4–23, 1861). Cochise, a chief of the Chiricahua Apaches, was arrested Feb. 5, 1861, by Lt. George N. Bascom, 7th Infantry, on an unproved charge of having captured a boy. He escaped, led attacks on a nearby stage station and on a wagon train, captured three men and offered to exchange one of his prisoners for Indians held by Bascom. Bascom demanded all three. On his way to Bascom's relief, Asst. Surgeon B. J. D. Irwin captured three Indians. It was later learned that Cochise had killed his prisoners, and six Indians were hanged in retaliation. This incident was the reputed origin of the long warfare (1861–74) against Cochise.

APALACHE MASSACRE (1704), was an episode in Queen Anne's War. Having failed to take St. Augustine, Fla. (1702), ex-Gov. James Moore of Carolina with 50 Englishmen and 1000 Indians invaded the Apalache district in western Florida, defeating Capt. Mexia's force of 30 Spaniards and 400 Apalaches, destroying all (*i.e.*, 13) but one of the Franciscan mission settlements and carrying off considerable loot including about 1400 Christian Indians.

APARTMENT HOUSES. Horizontal dwelling was a new concept in this country when the Baroness Pontalba introduced it on her return from Paris in 1849 in the Pontalba Buildings, designed by James Gallier, Sr., on Jackson Square, New Orleans. Not until *ca.* 1858 did Arthur Gilman design the Hotel Pelham for Dr. John H. Dix in Boston. This was the prototype of apartment houses, borrowed from the French, complete with mansard roof. New York followed suit in 1869, when Richard Morris Hunt, recently returned from Paris, designed the Stuyvesant Apartments at 142 East 18th Street for Rutherford Stuyvesant. This was the first apartment house of note in New York City and was followed by ever increasing numbers each year thereafter. The apart-

ment hotel was the true forerunner of the apartment house; however, it rarely had cooking facilities in the apartments and residents ate in the main dining room. By the early '80's apartments had been built in Washington, Chicago, and other major cities.

The odium connected with the squalid tenement house, which had been introduced in New York City as early as 1833, delayed acceptance of the apartment house in this country. However, middle-income families were in dire need of the apartment with its simplified housekeeping all on one floor, as the cost of building, furnishing and staffing the average New York town house on its 25-foot lot became prohibitive. Attempts were made to reduce the width of lots, producing ridiculously narrow houses with their floors connected by ladder-like stairs.

At first it was thought immoral for several families to live under one roof in these French-type dwellings, but the post-Civil War housing shortage made such a solution necessary. It took the well-to-do to introduce them and to make them respectable. Here Stuyvesant had led the way with his upper-class apartments. They were followed by Haight House in 1871 (probably the first elevator apartment in the city), The Grosvenor, and Hunt's Stevens House, all on Fifth Avenue. Stevens House rose to a height of eight stories, made possible by the elevator, and was completely French in its concept, with stores on the first floor and a towering mansard roof. The Dakota, designed by Henry Janeway Hardenbergh, at 72d Street and Central Park West, begun in 1880, was the prototype of the superblock apartment house with central courtyard.

The co-operative apartment was introduced in 1879 with Rembrandt House at 152 West 57th Street as a "Home Club," designed by Hubert, Pirsson & Co. A New York State law (Jan. 23, 1881) made it possible for tenants to purchase their apartments, and The Knickerbocker, The Gramercy and finally, the great Navarro or Spanish Flats, designed for José de Navarro by Hubert, Pirsson & Co., followed in rapid succession. The Spanish Flats consisted of eight units, named after cities in Spain, surrounding a central courtyard and separated by open breezeways. Their spectacular failure in 1886 so discredited "Home Clubs" that the co-operative movement was in disfavor until the late '90's. In the early 1900's, "Studio Co-operatives" began to appear, foretelling the great co-operatives of the 1920's. The lesson of their troubles in the depression was not lost on the wise builders of co-operatives after World War II.

In 1800 one twenty-fifth of the population was urban; in 1880, one fourth. The growth of the apartment house in New York City was rapid; 200 were built in 1876 and 576 in 1880. At that time, of 243,-000 families in the city, only 13,000 owned their own homes. By 1957 there were 2,560,000 dwelling units or individual apartments in Greater New York, of which 640,000 were in Manhattan.

APIA, DISASTER OF. On March 16, 1889, one British, three American and three German warships were crowded into Apia Harbor, ready for hostilities due to the German attempt to set up a protectorate under a puppet native king. A hurricane swept in, destroying the German *Eber, Adler* and the *Olga,* with the loss of 134 men; the U. S. *Trenton* and the *Vandalia,* with a loss of 52 lives. The U. S. *Nipsic* was run ashore. The British *Calliope* escaped by steaming out to sea. The Berlin Conference followed, establishing for Samoa a tripartite government.

APPEALS FROM COLONIAL COURTS. In the latter part of the 17th century the new colonial charters, proprietary and royal, reserved for the King in Council the right to hear cases on appeal from provincial courts where the sum litigated exceeded £300 sterling. In the New England colonies particularly the appellate authority was at best grudgingly conceded, as the Connecticut and Rhode Island charters made no provision for judicial review. At times, as in the case of Frost v. Leighton (1739), an order of the Privy Council was deliberately ignored by the Massachusetts authorities. Pending appeals, executions of the colonial courts were suspended. Such appeals were both costly and protracted.

Through this appellate procedure the Privy Council sought to bring the legal systems of the colonies into conformity with that of England, particularly in such matters as the rules of evidence and the jury system. Major issues of colonial policy were reviewed in litigation brought on appeal, notably Indian relations, the colonial currency laws and intestate succession. Currency practices in the colonies were more generally dealt with by the Privy Council under its authority to disallow colonial legislation or by Parliament. In the suit of the Virginia clergy instituted to recover back salaries resulting from the disallowance of the "two penny act," the Council, in view of the constitutional storms raised by the Stamp Act, was prompted by political considerations to dismiss the appeal on a technicality. In the notable case of Winthrop v. Lechmere the Council held the Connecticut custom of divisible descent of intestate estates invalid as contrary to the common law, but reversed itself in Clark v. Tousey and in the Massachusetts case of Phillips v. Savage, a great victory for egalitarian property concepts in New England.

APPLESEED, JOHNNY. As the American frontier moved into Ohio, Indiana and Illinois, the settlers were deprived of fruit until orchards could be grown. Since the people lacked money, they could not have bought young trees were nurseries available; and horticulture languished. John Chapman therefore consecrated himself from 1801 to 1847 to the mission of bringing seed from Pennsylvania and planting flowers and fruits, especially apple seed, in the forests to be ready for the free use of the settlers when they ar-

rived. Meager documentary evidence and rich tradition have preserved Chapman's fame under the sobriquet of Johnny Appleseed.

APPOMATTOX, former courthouse (county seat) of the county of the same name in Virginia, and scene of the surrender of the Confederate Army of Northern Virginia to the Union Army of the Potomac, April 9, 1865, is twenty miles ESE. of Lynchburg. Gen. R. E. Lee, commanding the Confederate forces which evacuated Petersburg and Richmond on the night of April 2–3, had planned to withdraw into North Carolina, via Danville, and to join Gen. Joseph E. Johnston; but on the third day of retreat, Lee found the Federals across his front at Jetersville, on the Richmond and Danville Railroad. As he was dependent on the railways for supplies, he determined to move westward across country to the Southside Railroad at Farmville, where he hoped to procure rations for a march to Lynchburg. Thence he would turn south again toward Danville. En route to Farmville, Lee was attacked heavily on April 6, at Sayler's (Sailor's) Creek, where he lost about 6000 men. The next day at Farmville he was again assailed before he could victual all his troops. By that time, long marches without food had so depleted the Confederate ranks that Gen. Grant addressed Lee a proposal for the surrender of the army. Lee did not consider the situation altogether hopeless and pushed on toward Lynchburg by the Richmond Stage Road. When the army bivouacked around Appomattox Courthouse on the evening of April 8, the reflection of Federal campfires against the clouds showed that the surviving Confederates, now reduced to two small corps, were surrounded on three sides. Lee closed his column and prepared to cut his way out, but when he found the next morning that the corps of John B. Gordon faced impossible odds on the Stage Road, he sent a flag of truce to Gen. Grant. A suggestion that the army break into small bands and attempt to slip through the enveloping lines was rejected by Gen. Lee on the ground that it would carry a hopeless struggle into country that had escaped the ravages of war. After some delay in communicating with Gen. Grant, who had made his dispositions with the greatest skill, Lee rode, about 1 P. M., into the village and, at the house of Maj. Wilmer McLean, formally arranged the surrender of all forces then under arms in Virginia. Gen. Grant's generous terms, which allowed officers to retain their side arms and provided for the parole of all surrendered troops, were executed with the least humiliation to the defeated army. A full day's rations were issued the prisoners of war. When the troops marched into an open field to lay down their weapons and their flags, April 12, the Federal guard presented arms. The number of Confederate infantrymen surrendered at Appomattox with arms in their hands was 7892; the total number of troops paroled was 28,231. In an interview with Lee on April 10, Grant sought to prevail on the Confederate commander to advise that all the remaining Confederate troops cease resistance, but Lee insisted that this was a question to be decided by the civil authorities.

APPORTIONMENT, CONSTITUTIONAL, signifies the distribution of legislative membership among established units of government, usually allocated with more or less exactness upon an equality of population.

ARANJUEZ, CONVENTION OF (April 12, 1779), provided for the entrance of Spain, as an ally of France, into the war against Great Britain, in case Great Britain should reject (which she did) Spain's impossibly intrusive offer of mediation. Spain and France made a pact to fight the war jointly, and not to negotiate peace separately, and in any peace Gibraltar was to go to Spain. Other desirable acquisitions were stipulated for both allies out of anticipated conquests from Great Britain.

ARBELLA was the flagship of the "Winthrop Fleet" on which, between April 8 and June 12, 1630, Gov. Winthrop, other members of the Company and Puritan emigrants transported themselves and the Charter of the Massachusetts Bay Company from England to Salem, thereby giving legal birth to the commonwealth of Massachusetts.

ARBOR DAY, ORIGIN OF. On the motion of J. Sterling Morton the Nebraska State Board of Agriculture designated the tenth day of April, 1872, as a day to plant trees, naming it Arbor Day. Later the state legislature changed the day to April 22, the birthday of Morton, and made it a legal holiday. Other states followed this example.

ARBUTHNOT AND AMBRISTER, CASE OF. An incident of Gen. Andrew Jackson's raid into East Florida in 1818. Believing himself tacitly authorized to seize the Floridas in view of Spain's delay in diplomacy, Jackson attacked the Seminole Indians in Spanish territory. At St. Mark's, Fla., he captured Alexander Arbuthnot, a Scotch trader who had warned the Indians to escape. At the village of Chief Bowlegs on the Suwanee River he captured Robert Ambrister, an English trader, who had plotted an Indian uprising. After courts-martial, Ambrister was shot and Arbuthnot hanged, both at St. Mark's on April 29, 1818. The British government took no action, but Spain protested the invasion. Secretary of State John Quincy Adams vigorously defended Jackson in his published despatches to the United States minister at Madrid, and thus helped to force Spanish signature of the Adams-Onís Treaty of Feb. 22, 1819, which included the cession of East Florida.

ARCHANGEL, AMERICAN TROOPS AT. After the Russian revolution (1917) the Allies sent a joint expedition, under British command, to co-operate with the White Russians at Murmansk and Archangel against the Bolshevist forces. By President Wilson's order American troops, eventually numbering 5100, participated. On Sept. 4, 1918, the 339th Infantry and auxiliary units reached Archangel with other Allied forces. The mission of the Allies was limited to protecting the ports and surrounding territory. The Americans guarded a front of 450 miles south and east of Archangel, and between September, 1918, and May, 1919, suffered more than 500 casualties. The last American troops withdrew from north Russia in July, 1919.

ARCHITECTURE, AMERICAN. American architecture in the colonial period was commendable, but our achievements were minor compared with contemporary European developments. It was not until the formation of our government in 1789 that American architecture came into its own. Ever since, it has been the equal of that of any other nation, and from the late 19th century onward has set standards that have been the envy of designers the world over. Architecture as here defined does not refer to the average level of building—which is too vague to be defined—but to architecture as a fine art. If it is to be a fine art, the architect must be devoted to his task, and so must the client who pays the bills.

Colonial Period (1607–1789). The admirable buildings erected by the French and Spanish settlers have had slight influence on the course of American architecture. The artistic accomplishments of the immigrants from the British Isles loom larger. Incidentally, the very first colonists from Great Britain did not live in log cabins; the log cabin was introduced no earlier than 1638 by Scandinavians descending the Delaware. The half-timbered clapboard-sheathed houses of the 17th century were modelled after similar structures in rural Jacobean England. One of the finest examples is the Parson Capen house (*ca.* 1683) in Topsfield, Mass.

Architecture as a fine art may be said to date from the 18th century, when Northern merchants and Southern planters could at last spend money enough to indulge their tastes. The first American architect—that is, the first colonist to sketch buildings for others to erect—was Peter Harrison, the designer of the Redwood Library, Newport, R. I. (1750), Congregation Jeshuat Israel, Newport, R. I. (1761), and King's Chapel, Boston, Mass. (1761). These buildings reflected his study of books published by British architects. American architecture in the 18th century is best described as the re-creation on a more modest scale of that of Georgian England. Here as in England Sir Christopher Wren was an inspiration; he is even said to have prepared the plans for the brick building of the College of William and Mary at Williamsburg, Va. (1695–1702). Possibly he had a hand in the laying out of the Capitol and Governor's Palace at Williamsburg. These were restored (1928–34) by the generosity of John D. Rockefeller, Jr.

We do not know the names of the designers or builders of most of the distinguished buildings of the 18th century, but we may assume that many a town and country house was contrived by an enlightened owner in a leisurely moment with a book at his elbow. On the eve of the Revolution there was a respectable show of taste, stretching from Charleston, S. C., remarkable for the elegant brick house of the merchant Miles Brewton (1769), to Portsmouth, N. H., memorable for the simple but fastidious frame house of Mark Hunking Wentworth (1760). The plantation houses of South Carolina were delightful monuments to colonial extravagance. So were those of Virginia, and no account of American architecture could neglect mansions the like of William Byrd II's "Westover" (*ca.* 1730), Thomas Lee's "Stratford" (*ca.* 1730), Mann Page's "Rosewell" (*ca.* 1730), Carter Burwell's "Carter's Grove" (*ca.* 1753), and John Tayloe II's "Mount Airy" (*ca.* 1762). William Buckland was the indentured-servant-turned-architect who planned the interiors of George Mason's "Gunston Hall" (1758). Buckland also designed the refined town house of Matthias Hammond in Annapolis, Md. (1773–74).

Philadelphia, the second biggest city in the British Empire by the outbreak of the Revolution, offered some of the choicest examples of urban display. Here, not far from Independence Hall (1731–36), stood "Cliveden," the residence of Chief Justice Benjamin Chew (1761), "Mount Pleasant," the estate of the privateersman John MacPherson (1762), and "Lansdowne," the country seat of John, the grandson of William Penn (1773). "Lansdowne"—now destroyed —was purchased by the banker William Bingham who in 1789 erected one of the greatest Philadelphia town houses. This, too, has vanished.

Federal Period (1790–1820). Prominent in this era was Asher Benjamin, the first American to publish handbooks for the guidance of carpenters. Another outstanding figure was Samuel McIntire, the carver-turned-architect of Salem, Mass., who built his most splendid town house for the Salem merchant Elias Hasket Derby. This has been pulled down, but McIntire's name will be forever associated with the box-like frame and brick structures of this time along the New England coast. Their exteriors were austere; their interiors revealed that owners and architects alike were anxious to reproduce the elegance of the brothers Adam in 18th-century England. Far more talented than Benjamin or McIntire was Charles Bulfinch, the well-bred Bostonian credited with sketching the plans for all three of the Boston town houses of the Federalist politician Harrison Gray

Otis. He may also have had something to say about "Gore Place," the estate at Waltham, Mass., of Governor Christopher Gore (1806). Here the great elliptical drawing-room showed that Americans were already bored with the conventional 18th-century plan of rooms opening symmetrically off a central hall.

The foremost achievement of the Federal Period was of course the founding of Washington, D. C., whose city plan was laid out by the Frenchman Pierre-Charles L'Enfant. The first design for the Capitol was the work of the West Indian William Thornton, but the Capitol also owes much to the Englishman George Hadfield, the Frenchman Etienne-Sulpice Hallet, the Irishman James Hoban (who designed The White House in 1792), and most of all to Benjamin Henry Latrobe, the English immigrant who was the greatest of all our architects in the early 19th century. To him are attributed—correctly—the "corn-cob" capitals in the Capitol, but he deserves greater recognition than such a slight invention would confer.

Although three Frenchmen placed their brilliant talents at our service in this era—Maximilian Godefroy created the First Unitarian Church, Baltimore, Md. (1816), Joseph-Jacques Ramée laid out Union College, Schenectady, N. Y. (1813), and Joseph-François Mangin collaborated with the native American John McComb, Jr., on the New York City Hall (1811)— they could not offer quite the challenge of Thomas Jefferson, an architect in his own right. Spellbound by Roman architecture, aware of the latest developments in France, and a careful student of the achievement of the Earl of Burlington in 18th-century England, Jefferson was responsible for the Capitol of Virginia (1785–92), the first example in the modern world of a public building in the temple style. His own house "Monticello" (1769–1809) was a superb adaptation of a Palladian villa; his plans for the University of Virginia (1822–26) ensured a campus which went unrivaled until Frank Lloyd Wright laid out Florida Southern College in 1940.

The Romantic Period (1820–60). This is best understood as a revolt against the Renaissance, in other words against the inspiration of the Georgian architecture of the 18th century. Andrew Jackson Downing, the leading critic of the period, was one of those who urged our architects to exploit the poetry of far-off times. This may explain why this era was the heyday of the Greek, Gothic and many other revivals. Though we may smile at the notion of a businessman traveling into the Middle Ages once he retired to his Gothic villa, such was the way the prestige of the Renaissance was undermined. Once that was achieved, buildings could be planned, not to fit preconceived ideas of symmetry, but the desires of a growing family or business. The Gothic, by far the most important of these revivals, marked the end of the formal plan of the 18th century and the first step toward the planning-for-convenience of the 20th. Furthermore, once Gothic architecture was invested with mystery by the romantics, scholars could not help discovering the engineering achievements of the Middle Ages. And so the romantics reminded their descendants that architecture could be an adventure in engineering.

Both the Greek and Gothic Revivals are of English origin. The former was launched in 1762 with the publication of Stuart & Revett's *Antiquities of Athens;* the latter was encouraged by the building of Horace Walpole's Gothic castle "Strawberry Hill" in 1750. It was Latrobe who introduced the Greek Revival— with the Bank of Pennsylvania, Philadelphia (1799) —and the Gothic Revival—with William Crammond's house, Philadelphia (1799). These were too advanced for the Federal period, and have been long destroyed. But Latrobe's daring was an incentive to the romantics.

The greatest romantic architect was Alexander Jackson Davis of New York, whose practice extended from Rhode Island to Kentucky. In the Grecian style he collaborated on the Capitol of North Carolina. In the Gothic vein he designed "Lyndhurst," the house at Tarrytown, N. Y., of William Paulding (1838), "Walnut Wood," the house at Bridgeport, Conn., of H. K. Harral (1846)—since destroyed—and the original buildings of Virginia Military Institute (1851). He was also adept at the Italian villa style, another romantic effort to foster asymmetry. One of his best examples in this manner was the house of E. C. Litchfield, Brooklyn, N. Y. (1854).

Davis seldom attempted churches. The leading ecclesiastical architect was Richard Upjohn, a native of England, who completed Trinity Church, New York, in 1846. One of his competitors was James Renwick, Jr., who created Grace Church, New York City (1846), and St. Patrick's Cathedral, New York City (1858–79). These were three great monuments of the Gothic Revival; Renwick turned to the Romanesque when he designed the Smithsonian Institution, Washington, D. C. (1846).

Although Robert Mills, once a pupil of Latrobe, labored prudently but admirably in the Grecian style in Richmond and Charleston, besides conceiving the Washington Monuments in Baltimore and Washington, D. C., he got few commissions so splendid as Girard College, Philadelphia (1833), the Grecian masterpiece of Thomas U. Walter. Walter also designed "Andalusia," the Grecian villa of Nicholas Biddle at Andalusia, Pa. (1833), and went on to build the dome of the U. S. Capitol. Another great Philadelphia architect in the Grecian style was William Strickland, the creator of the second Bank of the United States, Philadelphia (1818–24), the Merchants' Exchange, Philadelphia (1832–34), and the Capitol of Tennessee (1854). Perhaps the greatest mansion erected in the Deep South in the Romantic Period was "Belle Grove," the Grecian villa of John

Andrews at White Castle, La. (1857). Since destroyed, this was the work of Henry Howard.

Practical considerations were not overlooked in this age of Grecian villas and Gothic castles. The balloon-frame method of speeding timber construction was introduced as early as 1833, cast-iron construction was patented by James Bogardus in 1850, and the first practical passenger elevator was put in service in the Haughwout Building, New York City, in 1857.

The Age of Indecision (1861–76). During and after the Civil War our architects were not certain which way to turn. The mansardic style, modeled after that of Paris in the Second Empire, was popular, and an attempt was made to propagate the Venetian Gothic advocated by John Ruskin in England, but most buildings in this era were brutal and confused.

The Age of Elegance (1877–1913). H. H. Richardson, a graduate of the Ecole des Beaux-Arts, brought order out of chaos with Trinity Church, Boston, Mass. (1872–77). Superficially Romanesque in inspiration, Trinity was one of the great monuments of the 19th century, so superb was its massing. Other great granite buildings by Richardson were the Marshall Field & Co. Wholesale Store, Chicago, Ill. (1885–87), and the Alleghany Co. Court House and Jail, Pittsburgh, Pa. (1884–87). He also revolutionized domestic architecture by designing the house of Watts Sherman at Newport, R. I. (1874–76) whose simplified half-timber façade inspired a generation to re-think the problem of the summer home.

One of Richardson's most successful competitors was Richard Morris Hunt, the first American to graduate from the Ecole des Beaux Arts. This was the era in which the great millionaires were establishing their position. Hunt solved, brilliantly, the problem of the millionaire's home by designing for Mr. and Mrs. W. K. Vanderbilt a French Gothic château in New York City (1879–81)—since destroyed. Hunt went on pleasing the Vanderbilts and other wealthy clients, but was soon eclipsed by the firm of McKim, Mead & White, who came to exercise the greatest influence of any architects in our history.

Since both Charles Follen McKim and Stanford White had been trained by Richardson, the partners naturally followed his example in their early years. But in their "shingle-style" houses in Newport and elsewhere along the seacoast, they equalled and even surpassed their master in stressing the nature of materials and informal planning. The Casino at Newport, R. I. (1881), for which White was responsible, was a model of ease and elegance; the house of W. G. Low at Bristol, R. I. (1887), for which McKim deserved the credit, was a masterpiece of simplification.

Challenged by Hunt's triumph for the Vanderbilts in 1881, McKim, Mead & White eventually abandoned the informality and originality for which they were famous, to urge a return to the Renaissance for inspiration. Their first, and perhaps their greatest, monument in the Renaissance manner was the complex of five houses for Henry Villard and his friends, New York City (1885). This was no stale copy, but a re-examination of the Renaissance for American needs. The firm went on from success to success as the partners continued their exploration of the Italian past, stressing the virtues of symmetry and formal planning. Among their finest achievements in this vein were The Boston Public Library (1887) and the University Club, New York City (1899). They also introduced the Colonial Revival with the H. A. C. Taylor house, Newport, R. I. (1886), since destroyed.

McKim was one of those who succeeded in imposing the Renaissance dream of a classic revival on the Chicago World's Fair of 1893. Out of the Fair grew such major developments in city planning as D. H. Burnham's plan for the Chicago lakefront, and the revival of L'Enfant's plan for Washington, D. C. But with the imposition of the income tax in 1913, the lavish spending of the very rich was threatened, albeit faintly at first, and the Renaissance ideal was gradually cheapened by the acceptance of the commonplace.

The Chicago School. The greatest feat of engineering in the 19th century was the completion of Brooklyn Bridge, New York City (1883), by John and Washington Roebling. But the marriage of engineering and architecture was consummated in Chicago, center of the great advances in building skyscrapers. In 1883 William LeBaron Jenney began The Home Insurance Co. Building in Chicago, since destroyed, which proved that a steel skeleton could perform the function of masonry; from that day forward walls could be as thin as silk. While the firm of Burnham & Root built many important business buildings in Chicago and elsewhere, the acknowledged master of the skyscraper was Louis Sullivan. Too easily dismissed as the coiner of the slogan "form follows function," Sullivan was no mechanical functionalist but an artist who understood that every successful building was the solution of a unique problem. With his partner Dankmar Adler, Sullivan designed the supremely successful Chicago Auditorium (1889), and the Guaranty Building, Buffalo, N. Y. (1895), which exhibited his command of the verticality of the skyscraper. Equally challenging was the horizontally-accented Schlesinger & Mayer Building (later Carson, Pirie Scott & Co.) Chicago (1904), for which he alone was responsible. He protested, violently, against the classic revival, both in the Transportation Building he conceived for the World's Fair, and in his reminiscences, *The Autobiography of An Idea.* Discouraged in his later years, he ended his career planning banks for country towns. To the last he kept his incredible skill at ornamentation.

Easily the most inventive and perhaps the greatest of all American architects was Sullivan's pupil Frank Lloyd Wright, who fought a lifelong battle for what he termed "organic" architecture. A building, he held, should grow easily from its site and be designed from within outward. Walls were to be screens instead of barriers, and he championed informal planning, besides emphasizing, as did few others, the texture of whatever materials he was using. To these principles he was as loyal in the early houses he designed in the Chicago suburbs as in his last great commission, the Guggenheim Museum, New York City (1943–59). As a domestic architect, Wright was most famous for the Avery Coonley house, Riverside, Ill. (1908), the E. J. Kaufmann house, Bear Run, Pa. (1936), and for his own homes "Taliesin East," Spring Green, Wis. (1925–59) and "Taliesin West," Phoenix, Ariz. (1938–59). As a contriver of business buildings he astonished his contemporaries with the Larkin Building, Buffalo, N. Y. (1904), since destroyed, the Johnson Wax Buildings, Racine, Wis. (1939, 1951), and the V. C. Morris Store, San Francisco, Calif. (1949). He also created an international sensation with his Imperial Hotel, Tokyo, Japan (1916–22) which easily withstood the earthquake of 1923.

The Architecture of the 1950's. Wright, who detested the Renaissance although he once tried his hand, successfully, at a classic revival house, was so violent an individualist that he was equally annoyed by the emphasis on the impersonal which characterized the so-called International Style of modern architecture. One of the leaders of the International Style was the German Ludwig Miës van der Rohe, the designer with Philip C. Johnson of the Seagram Building, New York City (1958). Another was Walter Gropius, who was made head of the Harvard University School of Architecture in 1937 after directing the Bauhaus in his native Germany. Of the two, Miës had the greater impact on advanced American architects. Almost as meticulous as Miës, but far more imaginative, were Eero Saarinen, who planned the magnificent General Motors Technical Center, Warren, Mich. (1952), and Minoru Yamasaki, the inventor of the fanciful McGregor Memorial at Wayne State University, Detroit, Mich. (1958). The firm of Skidmore, Owings & Merrill were more respectful followers of Miës in their Lever House (1952) and Manufacturers' Trust Building (1954), both in New York City. The United Nations Secretariat, New York City (1950), the work of Wallace K. Harrison and his associates, owed more to the example of the Swiss LeCorbusier than to Miës or Gropius. Unfortunately the wide-open spaces to welcome crowds, insisted upon by the planners of Rockefeller Center, New York City, in 1930's, were seldom imitated by skyscraper designers of the 1950's.

Although one of the leading California architects in the 1950's was the International Stylist Richard J.

Neutra, the West Coast was the center of a group of designers who appreciated Wright's principles without imitating his mannerisms. They also made much of the native California tradition, and looked back with admiration on the work of Sullivan's pupil, Irving Gill, in La Jolla and San Diego, and on that of the brothers Greene & Greene, whose bungalows in Pasadena and elsewhere showed an instinct for texture that recalled the shingle style of McKim, Mead & White. Still another idol of the Californians was the highly poetic and imaginative Bernard Maybeck, the creator of the First Church of Christ, Scientist, Berkeley (1912).

The dominant influence in the San Francisco of the 1950's was that of the firm of Wurster, Bernardi & Emmons, who designed the Institute for the Behavioral Sciences in Palo Alto (1954). Another very important Californian was Harwell Hamilton Harris, who moved to Texas in 1955. His most famous work was the Weston Havens house, Berkeley, Calif. (1940.)

ARCHIVES. The national archives of the United States consist of the records of all the agencies of the Federal Government. Although most nations long ago made special provisions for the preservation and administration of their noncurrent records, the United States until recently left them in the custody of the agencies that had accumulated them, with the result that some were inadvertently destroyed and many were stored in unsuitable places where they were subject to deterioration and were practically inaccessible to scholars or officials. In 1926 Congress made provision for the construction of an Archives Building in Washington, which, though not fully completed until 1937, was occupied in 1935. The National Archives, an independent agency of the executive branch, was created by law in 1934 to have the custody and administration of the records transferred to this building.

Under the direction of Dr. Robert D. W. Connor, the first Archivist of the United States, 1934–41, a comprehensive survey was made of Federal records both at the Capital in Washington and in field offices throughout the states. The information assembled as to the location, quantity, nature, custody, physical condition, and research values of these records was important in gauging the size and nature of the task ahead and in establishing priorities for accessioning. Space needs for burgeoning New Deal agencies and even more for World War II agencies caused the older records to be transferred to the Archives building at a much faster rate than anticipated. All but a few of the 19th century records, and, in bulk, even greater quantities of 20th century records, were in the building by the end of the war. A *Guide* (684 pp.) to the holdings, published in 1948, described the more than 800,000 cubic feet accessioned by June 30, 1947. For the first time scholars had a single agency in Washington to which they might go to consult the older records of the Federal Government or learn whether or not such records existed and where they might be if not in the Archives. Such a center of information was serving the Federal Government also in many ways—by cleaning up disorderly attics and basements, eliminating fire hazards, providing Congress with a systematic review of records proposed for disposal, and, in general, bringing order and economy into record practices and administration.

Greatly increased responsibilities were given the National Archives under Dr. Connor and his successors, Dr. Solon J. Buck, 1941–48, and Dr. Wayne C. Grover, 1948– . The Federal Register Act of 1935 provided that all regulations intended to have the force of law must first be filed at The National Archives and published in the daily *Federal Register*. Those of continuing effect are also printed in a cumulative *Code of Federal Regulations*. Responsibility for receiving the original laws and publishing the *Statutes at Large* was transferred from the State Department to The National Archives in 1950. Another area of responsibility has been that of presidential libraries, beginning with the Franklin D. Roosevelt Library in Hyde Park, N. Y. The Library was built with private funds but, together with its contents, including papers of Roosevelt and of many of his associates, was donated to the Federal Government and accepted by joint resolution of Congress in 1939. A resolution of 1955 provided for the acceptance, maintenance, and administration of such presidential libraries, and in accordance with its provisions, the privately constructed Harry S. Truman Library at Independence, Mo., was opened in 1957. Similarly, the Dwight D. Eisenhower Library at Abilene, Kans., was intended to receive President Eisenhower's papers upon his leaving office. All three libraries are administered by the Archivist, and their holdings serve to supplement the strictly archival material in his custody.

Still greater expansion of the Archivist's duties and responsibilities came with the Federal Records Act of 1950, the first comprehensive records act ever passed by the Federal Government. He was directed to assist agencies in the control and maintenance of their current records. An Office of Records Management was created to work in this area. Authority was also granted for the establishment of intermediate records centers to house records not needed immediately at hand by operating agencies but still having to be kept for an extended period or possibly permanently. Ten such regional records centers have been established in the United States, including one to serve the central offices in the Washington area. Other such centers that had been established by the Army, Navy, and other agencies during the War were taken over and fitted into the new system, so that by 1960 almost all World War II records were under the control of the Archivist, and these regional and special centers held over 5,000,000 cubic feet of records. The National Archives lost its independent status in 1949, becoming a bureau of the newly created General Services Administration, an agency established upon the recommendation of the first Hoover Commission on the Reorganization of the Executive Branch. It was renamed The National Archives and Records Service.

Well over 100 inventories of special record groups have been published along with many special lists, information circulars, and other finding aids. Selected series of records having high research value are made available to libraries and scholars through a program of microfilm publication whereby the Archives prepares a master negative and the purchaser pays a modest sum for a positive print. Over 10,000 rolls, totaling some 10,000,000 pages, are thus available. Consultation of the records by scholars and others has increased steadily over the years.

Many of the states preceded the Federal Government in making some provision for the centralized administration of non-current records, but these provisions were extremely diverse and frequently inadequate. Usually the archival functions have been assigned to a state historical society or commission, a state department of archives and history, a state library, or the Secretary of State, where they are but part of a larger program that absorbs most of the meager appropriations. There are only a few independent archival agencies, as in Delaware and Maryland. In recent years there has been some tendency, following the Federal example, to place the archives function in a department of administration or general services. Delaware, Hawaii, Illinois, Maryland and South Carolina have modern, especially constructed, separate buildings to house the State archives. In other states, like Virginia, Tennessee, and Nebraska, the archives share a modern state library or historical society building that has specially planned stacks and service areas. Often, however, the quarters for archives are woefully inadequate and most of the noncurrent records perforce remain in the custody of the offices that accumulated them. Most state archival agencies have a degree of authority over the records of counties, municipalities and other state-created local governing bodies, and in the East there has been some tendency to centralize the older local records, say of the colonial period at the state archives, or at least to assemble photographic copies of them there. Some states have full-time inspectors or examiners of local records. Municipal archival programs have been started in some of the larger cities, notably New York and Philadelphia.

After World War II a number of leading business corporations (Firestone Tire and Rubber Co., Ford Motor Co., Du Pont, etc.) established well-considered archives programs, including special buildings and equipment for their older records. Greatly increased interest in business, social, and cultural history in recent years has led to more widespread concern for the archives of all influential organizations of the past. No longer are archivists engaged solely in the preservation of the documents of political history.

The profession of archivist, although an ancient and honorable one in Europe, could hardly be said to exist in the United States in the first third of this century. With the establishment of The National Archives, the expansion of state archival activities, and growing interest in the subject in educational, business, and other organizations, a need for meetings and publication channels developed that led to the formation in 1936 of the Society of American Archivists, which in 1960 had some 800 active members. Its quarterly journal, *The American Archivist,* published without break since 1938, is the chief source for the history of archival development in America in these years.

ARIZONA was the 48th state admitted to the Union. The southwestern one third of the state is chiefly low desert, sloping toward the Gila and Colorado rivers and the Gulf of California; the northeastern two thirds being the high mountain deserts and forest lands of the Colorado plateau. Arizona contains some of the oldest human habitations in the United States, some Indian towns and cliff dwellings dating back 1000 years or more. A considerable population of sedentary Pima and Yuma Indians occupied towns and irrigated lands in the Gila valley, wherein they were often on the defensive against the attacks of Apache and other highland tribes.

Opinions differ as to who were the first white visitors to Arizona. Padres Juan de la Asunción and Pedro Nazal are said to have reached it in 1538, and Fray Marcos de Niza probably entered it is 1539. It is certain that Francisco Vásquez de Coronado's Spanish army crossed it en route to Cíbola (Zuñi, in New Mexico), in 1540; while detachments from his expedition reached the Colorado mouth and discovered the Hopi Indian towns and the Grand Canyon. In 1583, Antonio de Espejo seems to have worked gold deposits near Prescott, and in 1604–6 Juan de Oñate, conqueror of New Mexico, crossed northern Arizona and descended the Colorado to the Gulf. Franciscan missionaries were at work among the Hopis of northeastern Arizona between 1629 and 1680. Padre Eusebio Francisco Kino and other Jesuits penetrated southern Arizona from 1691 onward, founding Mission San Xavier del Bac in 1700 and other Pima missions soon afterward. A Pima revolt in 1750–53 led to the establishment of a Spanish presidio at Tubac in 1752, moved to the Spanish and Indian settlement of San Agustín de Tucson in 1776. The Jesuits, expelled in 1767, were replaced by Franciscans, who maintained a feeble hold upon the missions until about 1828. During Mexican rule, 1821–

56, the only important white settlements in southern Arizona were at Tubac and Tucson in the Santa Cruz valley, nearly all others having been abandoned because of frequent Apache raids.

Anglo-American fur trappers penetrated Arizona by way of the Gila valley as early as 1826, and were fairly common visitors thereafter. The Mexican War saw the passage of a number of American military expeditions through the Gila valley from New Mexico to California, one of which, the Mormon Battalion, captured Tucson Dec. 16, 1846. The Treaty of Guadalupe Hidalgo, Feb. 2, 1848, left nearly all of Arizona south of the Gila a part of the Mexican state of Sonora. The region north of the Gila became part of New Mexico Territory under the act of Congress of Sept. 9, 1850. Explorations for a proposed Pacific coast railway, 1848–53, seemed to indicate the acquisition of the southern Gila valley as necessary for such a line. Accordingly, the Gadsden Purchase was negotiated with Mexico, Dec. 30, 1853, by which Arizona between the Gila and the present Mexican boundary was added to New Mexico, official possession being taken at Tucson, March 10, 1856.

In 1856 a convention at Tucson petitioned Congress to grant separate territorial status to Arizona, but the movement was defeated. Texan Confederate troops occupied southern Arizona for a few months in 1862; but after their expulsion, Congress, on Feb. 24, 1863, established the Federal territory of Arizona (including at first the southern tip of Nevada). A movement for statehood took definite shape on Oct. 2, 1891, with the framing of a constitution by the legislature, at Phoenix, the new territorial capital. Nearly twenty years later, Aug. 21, 1911, President Taft gave a new state constitution his approval, conditioned upon the elimination of a clause providing for the recall of judges; and the acceptance of this condition led to Arizona's formal admission as a state, Feb. 14, 1912, although the troublesome provision was soon restored.

ARK AND DOVE were the two vessels which brought the first colonists, about 200 in number, to Maryland. These pioneers left England at the suggestion of and under instruction from Cecil Calvert, to whom, on June 20, 1632, Charles I had granted a charter which conferred proprietary powers and authorized the colonization of the territory in the vicinity of the Chesapeake Bay. Sailing from Cowes, on the Isle of Wight, on Nov. 22, 1633, the *Ark* and the *Dove* laid their course to the Chesapeake by way of the Canary Islands and the West Indies. Entering the Potomac during the first week in March, 1634, they explored the northern bank of this river until, on March 27, it was finally decided to make the first permanent settlement on a river which empties into the Potomac not very far from its mouth. This settlement was and still is known as St. Mary's.

ARKANSAS. The first white man to visit the region

known as Arkansas was DeSoto (1541). Next came Marquette and Jolliet (1673) and then LaSalle and Tonti (1682), who came to take possession of the Mississippi Valley for the French. In 1686 Tonti founded Arkansas Post, the first permanent settlement in the region. The name "Arkansas" is derived from that of a tribe of Indians living west of the Mississippi and north of the Arkansas rivers. It appears on a map of 1718 as "Akansas." Capt. Zebulon Pike spelled it "Arkansaw" (1811) and it so appears in some government documents, but "Arkansas" came into general use. The Arkansas legislature of 1881 adopted the pronunciation Ark' an saw.

This region became American territory with the purchase of Louisiana (1803). When the State of Louisiana was admitted to the Union in 1812 Arkansas District became a part of Missouri Territory and then a separate territory of the first type in 1819, when Missouri applied for statehood. Arkansas Post was the first capital, but Little Rock soon took its place. The growth of the population was slow at first, but some energetic leaders soon got the territory advanced to the third stage with a bicameral legislature elected by the people. The same class of ambitious leaders rushed it into statehood (1836), ahead of time, measured by the population.

In 1860, Henry M. Rector, a defender of slavery, was elected governor, and he moved for secession. The state convention submitted "secession" or "cooperation" to be voted on in August, but after the bombardment of Fort Sumter and Lincoln's call for troops, the convention reassembled and seceded with only one dissenting vote. Isaac Murphy cast that vote and he became the first loyal governor in 1864. Although the state government had been organized under Lincoln's plan of reconstruction, Arkansas subsequently had to endure four years of congressional Reconstruction which left the state and counties heavily in debt with no money in the state treasury. A new constitution was drawn up in 1874 and Augustus H. Garland was elected governor.

ARKANSAS, FRENCH POST AND MISSION AT. When LaSalle laid claim to the entire Mississippi Valley for France in 1682 he granted to Henry de Tonti a large concession at the Quapaw villages on the Arkansas River, and in 1686 Tonti established the Arkansas Post as the earliest French settlement in the lower Mississippi Valley. In 1689 Tonti established a Catholic mission at the post, and by 1700 Jean Couture, who was left in command of the post, had developed an extensive trade with the English of Carolina. The subsequent history of the coast is obscure until the Western Company took possession of Louisiana in 1718 and John Law sent 700 German colonists to develop his large concession on the Arkansas River. But Law's venture collapsed a few years later, and his colonists abandoned the settlement and located at the "German Coast" near New Orleans.

When French Louisiana was divided into nine districts in 1721, Arkansas Post became the administrative center for the Arkansas District, and in 1722 Bernard de la Harpe strengthened the stockade and placed a regular garrison there. Arkansas Post remained important until the end of the French regime in 1762 as the administrative and commercial center of the extensive Arkansas District and as the site of a Jesuit mission.

ARKANSAS, GREAT BEND OF THE, was an important landmark on the Santa Fe trail marking the first point at which the river was encountered, 278 miles from Independence, and roughly half way to Bent's Fort, which was 530 miles. At Walnut Creek, which joined the Arkansas at the apex of the bend, travelers commonly encountered the first fringe of the buffalo herds, and Pawnee Rock, fifteen miles beyond, was regarded as the beginning of the hostile Indian country. One hundred miles from Walnut Creek was the Cimarron Crossing where a short cut to Santa Fé could be obtained.

ARKANSAS RIVER, known to the early French as Rivière des Ark or d'Ozark, derived its name from the Arkansas Indians who lived on its banks. The river was first discovered and explored by DeSoto in 1541 on his journey into the Southwest. The French explorers, Jolliet and Marquette, reached its mouth in 1673, in their search for a river "coming in from California on the southern sea." The Arkansas Post, established in 1686 by Henry Tonti, was the first permanent settlement in Arkansas River region, and around the post centers the early history of the river.

Arkansas River to the French was the highway leading into the Spanish Southwest—Taos and Santa Fe. French traders preferred waterways as highways. The headwaters of the Arkansas were in Spanish territory. The Spanish explorer Uribarri in 1696 called the upper Arkansas by the name Rio Napestle, probably of native Indian origin. This name was applied to the river by the Spanish until the 19th century. The treaty with Spain in 1819 made the Arkansas River west of the 100th meridian a part of the western boundary of the United States. The name Arkansas, which had applied only to lower reaches of the stream, was carried westward by American traders and trappers and succeeded in replacing the name Rio Napestle, or Napeste.

Arkansas River was navigable with keelboats as far west as Grand River. In early days "Arkansas" and "Ozark" were used interchangeably and were applied to Arkansas River, the mountains north of it and the post near its mouth.

ARKANSAS RIVER ROUTE was the mountain or Pikes Peak division of the Santa Fe Trail, which avoided the dangerous Jornada desert of the Cimarron cut-off. Instead of turning south at Cimarron Crossing near the present site of Dodge City, this route followed up the Arkansas River to old Bent's Fort near present-day La Junta and there turned southwesterly to the mountains and crossed the difficult Raton Pass. Choice was now open to continue southward rejoining the other Trail and going through Las Vegas to Santa Fe, or to proceed westward, past the Maxwell Ranch, along the base of the mountains and over the range to Taos. The Trail then followed the Rio Grande down to Santa Fe. The Arkansas River Route, though longer, was extensively used because of the importance of Bent's Fort, the trading center of the trappers and Indians; the presence of water and the demand for freight at the settlements along the way. Also it was the route to the Colorado goldfields of 1858 and later and to Denver-Auraria.

"ARKANSAS TRAVELER" is not only the best-known piece of folklore that Arkansas can lay claim to but the favorite of all old-time breakdown fiddle tunes in America. The rollicky dialogue and the rollickier tune go back to the days of Davy Crockett, but the author of neither has been determined. Newspapers, books and articles of commerce have taken the title. As the tradition goes, a stranger traveling in Arkansas comes to a roofless tavern before which the proprietor sits fiddling. "Where does this road go?" asks the stranger. "It's never gone anywhar since I been here," the squatter answers, going on fiddling. Finally, after more such colloquy, the stranger asks, "Why don't you play the rest of that tune?" Immediately the squatter makes the stranger dismount and play. This "turn of the tune" brings forth civil, though still comical, answers, whiskey, food, shelter, horse provender, a hospitality having all the gusto of a country hoe-down.

ARKS were known also as flatboats, broadhorns, Kentucky or Orleans boats, etc. These craft until 1860 carried a large part of the downstream traffic on the rivers of the West. They were cheaply constructed of green wood, shaped like boxes with raked bows, roofed over in whole or in part, and were sold for lumber or firewood at their destinations. They were steered by a long oar, and two or more sweeps, or broadhorns, were used to move them into or out of the current. Three to five men constituted the crew. They averaged about fifteen by fifty feet and held forty to fifty tons of flour.

ARKWRIGHT MACHINERY. A spinning machine developed, rather than invented, by Richard Arkwright in England about 1770. It was a marked improvement over earlier forms of spinning machines. The English government prohibited the exportation of machines or drawings but a young immigrant, Samuel Slater, carried the idea to Providence, R. I., and under his direction Almy and Brown constructed a set of Arkwright machines carrying 72 spindles. These were installed in 1790 in a small building at the Falls of Pawtucket. This introduced the modern factory to this country.

ARLINGTON NATIONAL CEMETERY is on the Virginia bank of the Potomac, directly opposite Washington, D. C. Originally part of the estate of George Washington, it passed to his adopted son, G. W. Parke Custis. In 1831 Robert E. Lee married Mary Ann Custis. Mrs. Lee inherited a life interest in the estate, which after her death was to go to her eldest son, G. W. Custis Lee.

Upon the outbreak of the Civil War, the estate was seized by the United States, which acquired an alleged tax title, built a fort and hospital on the site and used the grounds as a cemetery. In 1882, after suit which reached the Supreme Court, G. W. Custis Lee was declared the legal owner of the property. The matter was settled by paying Custis Lee $150,000 indemnity.

The estate has become the site of one of the most important shrines maintained by the United States. In the cemetery are buried the dead of every war since the Revolution. In front of the Memorial Amphitheater built in 1920 is the Tomb of the Unknown Soldier, killed in France during World War I. On Memorial Day, 1958, two other unknown service men were entombed beside the Unknown Soldier of World War I. They represent the dead of World War II and the Korean War.

A bronze statue commemorating the raising of the United States flag on Iwo Jima by the Marines stands at the entrance to Arlington Cemetery.

ARMINIANISM, the Reformed theology which arose in opposition to the prevailing Calvinism, received its name from Jacobus Arminius (1560–1609), a mild and liberal-spirited Dutch theologian. It places chief emphasis upon man's freedom and holds that God's sovereignty is so exercised as to be co-operable with the freedom of man. Introduced into America in the early 18th century, its influence spread rapidly in spite of able opposition. Those who accepted it became the advocates of a larger tolerance. On the frontier it made even more rapid headway than elsewhere, since it emphasized the natural human duties rather than speculative theology and the equality of all men in the sight of God, rather than limited grace and the possibility of salvation only for the few, which was the Calvinistic position.

ARMISTICE OF NOV. 11, 1918. On Oct. 4, 1918, the German government appealed to President Wilson for an armistice with a view to peace on the basis of the Fourteen Points. As a prerequisite, Wilson insisted on the practical democratization of the German government and hinted openly at the abdication of

William II. Gen. Pershing, the American commander in France, wished to continue the war until Germany was thoroughly beaten, but the Allied commanders, including Marshall Foch, agreed to an armistice and Wilson accepted this view. On Nov. 5, the United States notified Germany that the Fourteen Points were accepted as the basis of peace, subject to two reservations: (1) the freedom of the seas was not to be discussed; (2) Germany must make reparation for the damage done to the property of Allied nationals during the war. The terms of armistice were communicated to Germany on Nov. 8 and signed on Nov. 11 at 5 A. M., to take effect at 11 A. M. Germany had to evacuate all territory west of the Rhine, which was to be occupied by Allied troops; a neutral zone was established ten kilometers east of the Rhine. Germany surrendered large quantities of artillery, machine guns, airplanes, motor trucks and railway rolling stock, as well as most of her navy: it was made impossible for her to resume fighting. She had also to renounce the treaties of Brest-Litovsk and Bucharest and to withdraw her troops from Russia, Rumania and Turkey. The blockade was to continue until peace was made, and a blanket financial reservation was added that "any future claims and demands of the Allies and the United States of America remain unaffected." The armistice was for one month, and was renewed from time to time until peace was signed.

ARMY, CONFEDERATE. Officially, the "Army of the Confederate States of America" was the small regular force established by an act of the Confederate Provisional Congress, March 6, 1861, to consist of one corps of engineers, one of artillery, six regiments of infantry, one of cavalry and four staff departments (adjutant and inspector general's, quartermaster general's, subsistence and medical). This force, incompletely organized when war began, was soon overshadowed by the volunteer forces known officially as "the provisional army." Other acts of Feb. 28 and March 6 authorized the President to assume control over military operations, to accept state forces and 100,000 volunteers for twelve months. By the end of April President Jefferson Davis had called for 82,000 men. On May 8 Congress authorized enlistments for the war and on Aug. 8, four more states having joined the Confederacy, 400,000 volunteers for one or three years' service. After the passage of the first conscription act in April, 1862, men were taken into the provisional army directly without the necessary aid of the state authorities.

The highest office in the Regular Army was that of brigadier general until Congress, on May 16, 1861, established the rank of general in order to give higher Confederate commanders control over major generals of state troops in the field. On Aug. 31 Davis nominated and the Congress confirmed Samuel Cooper, Albert Sidney Johnston, R. E. Lee, Joseph E. Johnston and G. T. Beauregard as generals of the Regular Army. On April 12, 1862, Braxton Bragg became a general in that army and in May, 1864, E. Kirby Smith a general in the provisional army. Major generals in the provisional army, under the act of Feb. 28, 1861, were first appointed in May of that year. In September, 1862, the rank of lieutenant general in the provisional army was created.

Serious difficulties were encountered in arming, clothing and feeding the troops. Most of the arms available in May, 1861, were obsolete or inferior and even these could not supply all the men. There was little powder. Only one foundry could cast cannon and only one small powder mill was in operation. The chief reliance for improved arms was in purchases abroad, but getting them through the blockade was a slow, risky and expensive process. The Government made contracts with private firms for arms, set up its own arsenals and powder mills. Shoes, clothing and blankets were hard to procure, for wool and leather were scarce and importations did not fill requirements. Food supplies, much more plentiful in the South, were often reduced by weak transportation facilities. By 1863 horses and mules had become scarce, thus reducing the mobility of the cavalry, artillery and baggage trains. Although the Confederate soldier was often poorly armed, clothed and fed, discipline in the larger armies was good and morale high until near the end.

The Confederacy was divided into military departments, fluctuating in number and extent, under commanders responsible only to the War Department and the President. Prompt co-ordination between these departments was often lacking. Other than President Davis himself, there was no commander-in-chief until R. E. Lee was appointed on Feb. 6, 1865, although Lee had been Davis' military adviser for a short time early in 1862 and Braxton Bragg from February to October, 1864.

Because of incomplete surviving records the number of enlistments in the Confederate armies has long been in dispute. Southern writers have estimated them at from 600,000 to 800,000 men, some Northern students at from 1,100,000 to 1,500,000. This last figure is obviously too high for a white population of about 5,000,000. The United States Census for 1860 indicates approximately 1,100,000 men of military age in the seceded states, but these figures are deceptive. Many sections where hostility to the Confederacy developed furnished few soldiers; other large areas were soon overrun by the Union armies. Apparently more men from the seceded states went into the Union Army than came to the Confederate colors from the nonseceding slave states. Exemptions, details for industrial work and other evasions of service cut down enlistments. Probably between 800,000 and 900,000 actually enrolled, but so many were never in service at any given date. Consolidated returns in the War Department showed:

	Total present and absent	Total present	Total effective present for duty
Dec. 31, 1862	449,439	304,015	253,208
Dec. 31, 1863	464,646	277,970	233,586
Dec. 31, 1864	400,787	196,016	154,910

Liberal allowances for scattered commands not reported and for irregular organizations would not bring the total enrolled to more than 600,000 at any of these dates. The state militia, serving short terms, uncertain in number and of dubious value, probably fell short of 100,000 at any given date. Losses from battle, disease, capture and desertion so reduced the numbers with the colors that only 174,223 surrendered in April and May, 1865.

ARMY, UNION (1861–65). When Fort Sumter was fired on, the United States had an army barely exceeding 16,000 enlisted men and officers, and the effectiveness of this organization was soon lessened by the resignations of Lee and other Southern officers. Northern states were feverishly passing laws for the raising, equipping and training of volunteers for three years of the war. And by April, 1861, the governors had offered some 300,000 such troops to the Federal Government. But President Lincoln, though determined to restore the Union by force, would not assemble Congress before July 4. Without new legislation there was no authority for an increase in the army, so all the recruiting fervor of the early spring was wasted.

The 75,000 militia, called for on April 15, could be used for only three months, and hence were rushed into battle at Bull Run in a futile effort to show the strength of the Union before their enlistment should expire. The lesson of Bull Run finally aroused Federal activity as it had not been stirred by the earlier agitation in the states. On July 22, 1861, and following, Congress authorized the creation of a volunteer army of 500,000 men and legalized the President's call of May 3 for 42,000 three-year volunteers and 22,700 regulars. The Regular Army at an authorized strength of 42,000, which was half-way approximated, was used throughout the war for border defense against the Indians. The volunteer army, with which the war was fought, was officered mainly by political generals chosen by the governors, and in the early months, at least, by regimental officers elected by the enlisted men. The result was a needlessly slow development of discipline and efficiency. Also, the competition of state governments with the War Department in bidding for uniforms, munitions, food and supplies led to a scandalous series of contract grafts, high prices and shoddy products.

The volunteering spirit so cooled off after Bull Run that the remainder of 1861 had passed before an acceptable army could be whipped into rudimentary shape. By the middle of 1862 the first army had been so badly depleted by disease and battle that on July 2 an additional 300,000 volunteers were called for, the governors again being left to care for recruiting and management of the new contingents till they were mustered into service. The troops were urgently needed and on Aug. 4, when volunteering proved sluggish, a draft of 300,000 nine months' militia was ordered under terms of an act of July 17, 1862. As a direct means of getting soldiers this draft proved a failure, only about 65,000 men being provided. But Federal, state and local bounties lured enough volunteers during the next few months to tide over the emergency.

Early in 1863 it was seen that continued heavy casualties, desertions, the expiration of short-term enlistments and scanty volunteering was likely to cause a collapse of the army before the close of the year. Consequently, the Enrollment Act of March 3, 1863, was passed to provide men by draft. The act was intended mainly to stimulate volunteering by threat of conscription, thus encouraging the states and localities to avoid this stigma by the offering of adequate bounties. Men of means were given an easy escape from the draft by the payment of a $300 commutation fee or the hiring of substitutes. By a later amendment the commutation fee was limited to conscientious objectors, but substitution was permitted till the end of the war. The direct product of two years of repeated drafting was about 50,000 conscripts and 120,000 substitutes. But in the same period over a million volunteers were procured by bounties. Thus for the last half of the war the army was relieved from the constant danger of extinction which had threatened the first half.

The total effective strength of the army on Jan. 1, 1863, before Federal conscription was begun, was just under 700,000. On May 1, 1865, at its highest point, the number was nearly 800,000. Including all men not fit for active service, each of these figures would be increased by about 200,000. The commissioning of 2537 generals alone (including brevet brigadiers) for an army of this size may be taken as an indication of the part spoilsman politics played in army organization. Nevertheless, after the first year the weeding out of incapable officers in high positions went on apace, proved capacity began to replace political favoritism and regimental elections for minor officers, and a tolerable degree of discipline was evolved. Contract grafts continued to lessen the efficiency of the army, but in a diminishing degree. An obtuse policy of the War Department prevented the supplying of the soldiers with modern weapons, which were available to the Union but not to the Confederacy, thus further restricting military efficiency.

Enlistment in the Union Army. Throughout the Civil War, enlistment was largely in the hands of state officials. Calls for troops were made by the President, quotas were assigned among the states and congressional districts by the War Department, and local

officials or, in the early months, independent organizations tried to arouse the volunteering fever. Bounties were offered from the start, and before each draft they often reached immense sums. On Dec. 3, 1861, Gen. McClellan decreed a complete reorganization of the recruiting service, which might have grown into an effective national system had not Secretary Stanton had a burst of overconfidence shortly afterward. On April 3, 1862, just as the machinery was getting in good working condition, he ordered the discontinuation of the recruiting service in every state from that date. The recruiting offices were closed, the furniture sold, and the officers called back to the army. Then came the military reverses which led to the army crisis preceding the militia draft and the Enrollment Act of March 3, 1863.

Enlistments during the war were for various periods: three, six, nine and twelve months; two, three and five years; thus complicating the problem of assignment of quotas. The system in the summer of 1862 was particularly complex. The President's delay in calling Congress in 1861 did much to cool off the fervor for enlistment at a time when there was a large labor surplus and a holiday attitude toward joining the army and crushing the "secesh." By the time the belated Congress could pass military legislation business prosperity was returning, farm activity was at its height, and Bull Run had stilled the notion that the war was to be a mere summer's picnic. Nevertheless, the seasonal agricultural labor surplus in the fall of 1861 made it possible to assemble a volunteer army of 640,000 by December.

The wasting of the army by death, desertion and sickness in 1862 finally convinced Stanton that a national recruiting service would have to be revived, and this was done on June 6. But it was too late to remedy the damage done in April. Enlistment had dropped almost to zero and the military situation was such that another call for volunteers might spread panic throughout the country. Hence, Seward engineered a scheme to get the governors to appeal to the President for a call for troops to clinch a final victory presumed to be in immediate prospect. The succeeding calls were for 300,000 each of nine-months militia and three-years volunteers. From that time on adequate enlistment was to be procured only by means of bounties stimulated by fear of the draft. By such means the total force was kept at from 900,-000 to 1,000,000 for the last two years of the war. The total number of enlistments for the four years was 2,865,028, but the number of short-term enlistments would reduce the aggregate, on a three-year basis, to 2,324,516. The elimination of duplications shows about 2,675,000 different men serving during the war.

ARMY, UNITED STATES. The U. S. Army of 1960 is directly descended from the Continental Army of the American Revolution and its accepted birthday is June 14, 1775, the day the Second Continental Congress voted to enlist the first troops directly in the Continental service. Its origins are to be found in colonial military institutions. Each of the thirteen colonies had militia laws requiring military service of every able-bodied man. Volunteer forces, drawn from the militia and enlisted in the service of an individual colony, were employed for protracted campaigns such as those of the French and Indian War. The Continental Army was recruited in similar fashion, except that the men were enlisted in the service of the Continent rather than that of the individual states. State authorities, nevertheless, continued responsible for initially raising, organizing and officering Continental regiments, and the whole body of the militia, members of which were used continually to supplement Continentals, remained under state control. The major elements of this system of state recruiting of volunteers for the Federal service in time of war, with the militia as the base from which recruiting was conducted, continued through the Spanish-American War, though militia as such ceased to play a role of any importance as an integral part of the Army after the War of 1812.

During the course of the Revolution, the Continental Army matured as a military organization, adopting an English system of staff and line organization and a system of drill introduced by the Prussian, General von Steuben. At the end of the war, it was almost entirely disbanded, reaching its nadir of 80 men in 1784. The need for protection of the frontiers soon led to a modest augmentation, and further augmentations followed to meet crises on these frontiers and in our relations with England and France. The Constitution gave Congress power to raise an army and the President power to command it. Washington's view that there should be a small regular army supplemented by "well regulated militia" available for Federal service in time of emergency prevailed, though the "well regulated militia" never became an actuality. The small regular establishment proved its utility in the Battle of Fallen Timbers in 1794 when it achieved a decisive victory over the Northwest Indians and thus began a task of policing the frontier that was to absorb most of its energies for a century afterward.

The Army was swollen in the War of 1812, the Mexican War, the Civil War and the Spanish-American War by state-recruited volunteers who were discharged when the war ended or before if their term of service expired. In each interwar period, the regular establishment underwent a progressive increase in size to meet added responsibilities. Between the War of 1812 and the Mexican War it averaged around 6000 men, between the Civil War and the Spanish-American War around 26,000, and after the Spanish-American War about 75,000. Graduates of the U. S. Military Academy at West Point furnished professional leadership of a high order after 1815 and largely accounted for the Army's efficient performance in the Mexican War as contrasted with the general ineptitude that characterized the conduct of the War of 1812. West Point graduates also furnished the higher leadership on both sides in the Civil War.

As the American nation began to look beyond its own frontiers after 1898, the composition, organization and role of the Army changed. The old task of policing the frontiers was largely superseded by new tasks overseas such as the pacification of the Philippines and occupation of Cuba and Puerto Rico. The militia gave way to the National Guard, originally composed of selected state volunteer units. In 1903 the Guard was given Federal aid and support, and in 1916 recognized as a component of the Army to be called to Federal service by the President in time of emergency. In 1903, also, a general staff was established in the War Department. Between 1903 and 1914 new Army schools were set up and older ones expanded, giving a new impetus to the development of professionalism.

The National Defense Act of 1916 also authorized the formation of both an Officers' and an Enlisted Reserve Corps. While only the first steps toward forming these corps had been taken when America entered World War I, graduates of Reserve Officer Training courses in civilian colleges did play a part in officering the new National Army, along with the Regulars. The National Guard was also ordered into Federal service, but the massive 4,000,000-man army of World War I was largely recruited through Selective Service and most of its junior officers were graduates of Officer Candidate Schools. Beyond initially furnishing the Guard units and administering machinery for conscription under Federal regulations, the states played little part in building the military machine of 1917–18.

At the end of the war, the usual rapid demobilization took place and until the beginning of the new emergency in 1939, the Regular Army stayed at an average strength of around 150,000. But the new military system had come to stay. The National Defense Act of 1920 established the Army of the United States as an organization of three components —the professional Regular Army, the National Guard, and the Organized Reserves—the latter two commonly identified as civilian components. Training of the Guard and Reserves now became a major peacetime task of the Regular Army, which was authorized at a considerable officer over-strength for this purpose. Congress prescribed that at least half of these officers should be non-Regulars who had served during the war. This over-strength and a Reserve Officers Corps of around 100,000 immensely facilitated the unprecedented expansion of the Army in World War II.

Between the two wars education of both regulars and reserves received a new emphasis. The Military Academy and the R. O. T. C.'s in civilian colleges furnished basic schooling for new officers, some 31 special service schools gave branch training, and the Command and General Staff School, the War College and the Army Industrial College educated officers for intermediate and top staff and command positions. These schools produced the Army's leaders of World War II.

In World War II, the U. S. Army truly came of age, waging battles in every corner of the globe under leaders drawn from its own ranks and trained in its own doctrines. Expansion to over 8,000,000 men was accomplished with considerably greater efficiency than expansion to 4,000,000 in World War I, the Selective Service system again serving as the main reliance for filling the ranks and the Officer Candidate Schools as the main source of junior officers. This global war required not only technical proficiency in the fighting of battles but also development of a corps of logistical experts to operate the longest supply lines in the history of warfare.

Rapid demobilization again followed World War II and by 1949 the active Army consisted of around 591,000 men in the United States and on occupation duty abroad. The Korean War reversed the trend. National Guard units and individuals from the Organized Reserve were called back to duty and Selective Service was reinstituted. By July, 1951, the Army had increased to 1,500,000 men. Reduction after the war was gradual, reflecting the continuing tensions of the cold war, and in 1960 the Army still had an active strength of around 870,000.

Meanwhile, rapidly changing technology and reorganization of the national military establishment were requiring adjustments. In 1947, the Department of Defense was created and the Air Force, which had grown to maturity within the structure of the Army, was established as a third separate service. Under this arrangement, the Army's mission was that of organizing, equipping and training forces for land operations and ground defense against air attack and the actual conduct of such operations under such systems of joint command as the Department of Defense established. In carrying out this mission the Army in the 1950's moved to revamp its organization, tactics and weapons with the goal of providing highly mobile forces capable of fighting either atomic or conventional war in any corner of the globe. The emphasis was placed on a highly trained and specialized active Army supported by civilian components who could be mobilized rapidly in time of war or emergency. Various pieces of legislation passed during and after the Korean War established a theoretical obligation for some form of military training or service for every able-bodied youth, thus providing a means of keeping the civilian components as well as the active Army up to authorized strength and of assuring that at least part of the reserves could be trained to the degree of readiness required.

Peacetime Work. In addition to its primary task of preparing for and fighting wars, the Army has throughout its history performed peacetime tasks that have contributed immensely to the development of the American nation. Among the most important of these have been the exploration of the West, protection of the settlements and lines of communication against the Indians, surveying of the transcontinental rail lines, improvement of rivers and harbors, and occupation work in the South during Reconstruction and in Cuba, Puerto Rico, the Philippines, Germany, Japan and other areas in later periods. Army engineers supervised the building of the Panama Canal and other important public works. Army doctors have made large contributions to the development of modern medicine, among them Dr. Walter Reed's discovery of the cause of yellow fever. The Army has also been called on at times to maintain order in civil disturbances, to assist in the enforcement of Federal laws and to aid in the relief of civil disasters.

Insignia of Rank. Insignia of rank date from the Revolution when Washington ordered that field grade officers wear colored cockades in their caps, general officers colored ribands across their coats, and noncommissioned officers stripes or epaulettes of colored cloth on arm or shoulder. In 1780, generals began to wear silver stars on their shoulders. The colonel's eagles date from 1832, and the various insignia for majors, captains and lieutenants from 1836, though not precisely in their present form. Originally infantry colonels wore gold eagles while other colonels wore silver ones. In 1851 the silver eagle was prescribed for all colonels, the silver leaf for lieutenant colonels, and the gold leaf for majors. Insignia for captains and lieutenants were standardized in 1917 when second lieutenants, who had previously worn no insignia of rank, were authorized to wear the single gold bar. Meanwhile, the various chevrons of the noncommissioned officers were evolving to their present form. Their location at the spot above the elbow dates from 1847.

Army Contracts. Army supplies have normally been procured through contracts with private persons and companies rather than by production in Government installations. Contracting has, at times, been extended beyond procurement to the actual delivery of supplies in the field though in this phase it has not been notably successful. In the early part of the Revolution, Congress maintained agents who purchased by contracts and otherwise and set up its own machinery for distribution of the supplies thus procured. When this machinery broke down in the latter stages of the war, the contractual system was used for both procurement and delivery of supplies to the Army. The same method was used to some degree in campaigns against the Indians and in the

War of 1812. Almost invariably it gave rise to numerous scandals. In the Civil War and other major wars since that time contracts have been used primarily for procurement and the Army has maintained its own distribution system. In both the Civil War and Spanish-American War, procurement contracts gave rise to considerable fraud and profiteering with a resulting growth of a large body of restrictive legislation to govern their placement and administration. With these restrictions, there were few scandals in World Wars I and II, though the device of cost-plus contracts gave rise to much criticism. On the average, however, the administration of Army contracts in World War II and after has been as efficient as circumstances would permit and has resulted in a most successful production effort for supply of the Army.

Contracts have also been used for procurement of services. For instance, in our early wars, wagoners and sometimes drivers for artillery were civilian contractor personnel. In modern times contracts have been used for construction, research and development, and varied types of housekeeping services.

Army General Staff. From the time of the Revolution, the Army has possessed a General Staff of some sort, but until 1903 it was hardly a real one in the modern sense of the word, being composed mainly of administrative heads of the various bureaus. An act of Congress in 1903, passed on the recommendation of Secretary of War Elihu Root, established a General Staff Corps and a Chief of Staff, the latter to replace the Commanding General of the Army and issue orders to the whole Army in the name of the Secretary of War. The initial General Staff organization consisted of three divisions—one concerned with organization, equipment and administration, the second with intelligence, and the third with war plans, military education and seacoast defense. Though the system was supposedly modeled on contemporary European practices, there was a significant difference in that the U. S. General Staff was charged with establishing policies for the administration of the Army while European general staffs concerned themselves solely with planning for, and the direction of, war.

The system did not work well in World War I and numerous special organizations had to be formed to carry out War Department work. The American Expeditionary Force in France developed its own General Staff, modeled on the French, and this in turn became the model for postwar reorganization. The General Staff of the 1920's and 1930's consisted of five divisions—G-1 for personnel, G-2 for intelligence, G-3 for training and organization, G-4 for transportation and supply and a War Plans Division. In World War II the three major commands—Army Air Forces, Army Ground Forces and Army Service Forces—took over most of the powers of the General Staff sections except for those of War Plans. This last section, renamed the Operations Division, became practically a general staff in itself serving as a command post for General Marshall, then Chief of Staff, in the conduct of the war overseas.

After World War II, Army Service Forces was discontinued and Army Air Forces was transformed into a separate service. The prerogatives of the General Staff were restored along with an organization closely paralleling that of the old G-system. It has since undergone considerable evolution. In 1960 the Department of the Army General Staff was composed of a Chief of Staff, Vice Chief of Staff, Deputy Chiefs for Plans and Operations, for Logistics and for Personnel, Assistant Chiefs for Intelligence and for Reserve Components, Chiefs of Research and Development and of Civil Affairs and Military Government, and a General Staff Committee on National Guard and Army Reserve Policies.

Army Hospitalization. The Army has, from its very beginnings, had to provide means for care of its sick and wounded. Medical care in the Army is under the general charge and direction of the Surgeon General of the Army, an office that dates from 1818. Hospitals of a primitive sort, often little better than pesthouses, were provided for soldiers during the Revolution, the War of 1812 and the Mexican War, usually in existing or improvised buildings. The Civil War saw a considerable advance with the adoption of the system of hospitalization and evacuation pioneered by Gen. Jonathan Letterman, Surgeon General of the Army of the Potomac. Letterman's system involved field hospitals set up in tents where the wounded and sick could get immediate attention and pavilion-type hospitals set up in permanent locations whence the more seriously wounded could be evacuated and given more careful treatment. After the war, at the various Army posts scattered throughout the country, Army surgeons established small hospitals to take care of their sick and wounded within the organization. The Spanish-American War saw the introduction of permanent general hospitals for soldier care and medical research.

Though further refined in the course of two world wars and by the general advance of medicine, the Army's hospital system still follows generally along the lines established during this period. Mobile field hospitals close behind the front lines receive wounded men from collecting stations and forward them to evacuation hospitals further to the rear. From evacuation hospitals, patients who require still greater care are sent to base hospitals in the theater of operations. Those whose treatment requires it are sent back to general hospitals in the United States. Station hospitals take care of the day-to-day needs of troops in training.

Army Supply. Army supply can be divided generally

into two phases—procurement and distribution. In the procurement phase, requirements must first be determined for a stipulated period in advance. Requirements are then translated into production programs and out of these programs goods flow into depots to be distributed to using troops and installations. Adequate distribution depends heavily on means of transportation.

The Army's supply system has evolved over the years in pace with the state of the military art and the political and economic development of the country. During the Revolution the Continental Army suffered continually from lack of supplies since the weak central government lacked money or power to procure them, native industries were few, transportation facilities poor and supply organization inadequate. Development of a system adequate to the needs of 19th-century warfare was largely a product of the emergence of a Federal Government with sufficient financial strength and power and of the industrial development of the country. The system was largely shaped around the War Department bureaus each of which had responsibility for certain types of supply and certain supply functions under the general supervision of the Secretary of War. The Civil War saw the emergence of such standard attributes of a military supply system as echeloned depots, classification of supplies, and methods of calculating requirements in terms of standard allowances for given bodies of men. The railroads served for the first time as the principal means of transportation.

The increasing complexity of supply for the mechanized army of the 20th century and its employment largely in overseas theaters led to increased reliance on ocean shipping and to development of far more complicated supply procedures and supply organization. The various bureaus, now become technical services, continued responsible for detailed functions of development, procurement, issue and maintenance of specified articles but were generally subject to over-all control and co-ordination of either a General Staff division or an over-all supply command. In World War II, Army Service Forces was primarily responsible for calculation of requirements, co-ordination of procurement, distribution in the Zone of the Interior and shipment of supplies overseas. Overseas commands had their own supply organizations for receiving supplies and distributing them to using troops. Specified reserve levels were maintained in depots and ports all along the line to insure a continuous flow. All available means of land, sea and air transport were used. This system, in all its fundamentals, was used again in Korea though air supply played a more important role than in World War II. Since the Korean War, the Army has been moving rapidly to develop new concepts of supply that will be better suited to atomic age warfare. Among these are greater mobility and dispersion in the logistical establishment, increased reliance on air supply, and use of speedy means of delivery from the source as a substitute for echeloned depot reserves.

Corps of Engineers. The Corps of Engineers is the only Army organization possessing civil as well as military functions. The history of the Corps goes back to the Revolution. On June 16, 1775, the Continental Congress created an office of Engineer for the Continental Army and on March 11, 1779, authorized the formation of a Corps of Engineers. Most of the engineers of the Revolution, however, were foreigners, among whom Thaddeus Kosciuszko and Louis DuPortail stand out. In 1783, the Corps was disbanded but was then re-established as part of the Corps of Artillery in 1794. The original title was restored permanently on March 16, 1802, when Congress authorized a Corps of Engineers with station at West Point to "constitute a Military Academy," and it has been in continuous existence ever since.

On the military side, the functions of the Corps have been primarily to carry out construction required for military operations and training, destruction to impede movements of the enemy, and development, procurement, issue and maintenance of engineer material for the entire army. These functions include an important role in combat operations. On the civil side, the Corps has carried out Army responsibilities for improving navigable waterways, flood control and other internal improvements.

U. S. Military Academy. The Military Academy at West Point has been the principal source of leadership for the U. S. Army. It was founded on March 16, 1802, as a school for military engineers, but existed largely on paper until 1817 when Sylvanus Thayer became superintendent. Thayer, often called the "Father of the Military Academy," instituted a broader curriculum, a system of instruction, organization and discipline for the cadets, and an honor system, the main principles of which still remain in force. In the period 1820–60, West Point was not only the source of a new professional class of officers, but also the principal American institution for training the engineers who played so prominent a role in the great internal improvements of that period.

In 1866 Congress revamped the Academy, recognizing it was no longer simply a training school for engineers but an institution for training officers for all branches of the service. Supervision of the Academy was transferred from the Corps of Engineers to the War Department. Since that time the physical facilities and staff of the Academy have been vastly expanded, the number of cadets progressively increased, and the curriculum kept abreast of the changing needs of the Army officer and the progress of the military art. The Military Academy has continued to furnish the majority of the higher leaders of the Army though its graduates no longer, since the passage of the National Defense Act of 1920, monopolize these positions as they once did.

National Guard. The National Guard had its origins in selected volunteer units of the state militias that maintained their organization and training when militia service in general fell into disuse. The name National Guard was first used by a New York unit in 1824 in honor of Lafayette who had commanded the French *Garde Nationale* in 1789, and it gradually came into general use. In 1903 the Dick Bill gave the National Guard formal status as the "organized militia," to be formed into standard Army units, trained in part by Regular officers, and supported jointly by state and Federal funds. The National Defense Act of 1916 made the Guard a component of the nation's military forces, to be made a part of the Army of the United States in time of war or emergency, empowered the President to prescribe the organization, strength and armament of units, and provided Federal pay for armory drill. Under the provisions of this and succeeding acts, the Guard contributed 17 divisions and supporting units to the Army in World War I and 18 divisions and supporting units in World War II.

The Guard has continued to occupy a dual status, since Guard troops are state troops subject to the command of the governors of the respective states until ordered or called into Federal service. Since World War II, the National Guard has been broken down into an Army National Guard and an Air National Guard. During the Korean War the Army National Guard furnished eight divisions and supporting troops for the Army and the Air National Guard, 45,000 officers and men for the Air Force. On Jan. 1, 1958, the Federally recognized strength of the Army National Guard was 404,095, that of the Air Guard 69,029. In 1958 the Army began reorganization and modernization of the Army National Guard along lines already adopted for the active Army and in keeping with the current program to insure immediate mobilization readiness of reserve forces.

Ordnance. Ordnance is a term used to describe the Army's weapons of war. The Ordnance Corps, not formally created until 1918 though it had various antecedents, is charged with their development, procurement, issue and maintenance. Army ordnance has undergone an amazingly rapid evolution during the period of our national existence. The smooth-bore muskets and cannon of the Revolution gave way during the 19th century to rifles and rifled artillery which by the end of the century were entirely breech-loading. Ammunition was vastly improved and the invention of the machine gun introduced the principle of automatic fire. Tanks were introduced during World War I and by World War II had been vastly improved in design and efficiency. Other combat vehicles also took their place in the ordnance family and ordinary motor vehicles were added to the ordnance classification. Artillery was increased in size, mobility, rapidity of fire and velocity. All these changes produced a veritable revolution on the battlefield but they proved to be only the beginning. Post-World War II developments have seen the addition of various rocket and missile weapons adapted to fire either conventional or nuclear warheads as well as a further variety of weapons and supporting hardware of almost unbelievable complexity. In keeping with the growth in numbers and variety of weapons, the Ordnance Corps has also undergone tremendous expansion and is today responsible for the major portion of the Army's equipment.

Uniforms of the American Army. The Continental Army had no standard uniform though there were attempts at times to prescribe one, particularly for the higher ranking officers. The most common dress was hunting shirt and overalls. As the Army took shape as a professional organization in the period between the Revolution and the Civil War, standard uniforms were adopted though there were differences between those worn by infantry, cavalry and artillery, and between officers and enlisted men. Various shades of blue and gray were worn at various times with colorful trappings of more brilliant hues. During the Civil War most Union soldiers wore blue coats with either dark or light blue trousers and a short visor forage cap.

The evolution since that time has been toward a uniform giving an increasing amount of protective coloration and increasing utility and convenience as battle dress. The more colorful designs of the earlier period were reserved for dress uniforms. Khaki was introduced during the Spanish-American War and in 1901 a uniform board adopted the olive-drab uniform for service wear, retaining the blue for dress occasions. During World War I the blue was discarded entirely and the olive-drab uniform with high-collared blouse prescribed for all occasions. Between World Wars I and II, the roll collar replaced the high collar and the Sam Browne belt was added. A more comfortable field service uniform of olive drab for winter and khaki for summer was adopted in World War II. Toward the end of the war the Eisenhower jacket was substituted for the roll-collar blouse. Since World War II a new green winter service uniform has been introduced along with a colorful blue one with gold trappings for dress occasions.

ARMY OF OCCUPATION (1918–23). As part of the Allied Army of Occupation, the American Third Army, commanded by Maj. Gen. Joseph T. Dickman, crossed into Germany in December, 1918, taking station in the North Sector of the Coblenz bridgehead. Units of the Third Army were stationed at various points within the American area and engaged in duties of occupation and training, including participation in civil administration of occupied territory, until July 2, 1919, when the Third Army was discontinued. It was succeeded by the "American Forces in Germany."

Maj. Gen. Edward F. McGlachlin, Jr., assumed command of this newly designated force until July 8, 1919, when its permanent commander, Maj. Gen. Henry T. Allen, reported. From January, 1920, Gen. Allen worked in conjunction with the Rhineland High Commission. At noon on Jan. 27, 1923, American troops having left the Coblenz area, Gen. Allen relinquished command of the American area.

ARMY ON THE FRONTIER. This term applies to the activities of the U. S. Army stationed near the frontier settlements from the beginning of national existence until about 1890, the end of the settlers' frontier. The principal functions performed by this army were: 1, guarding the frontier settlements from hostile Indians; 2, aiding the settlement of the West by developing and protecting the communication between the older settlements and the frontier, by exploring the West, constructing roads and defending the overland trails, water routes and later telegraph and railroad lines; and 3, policing the frontier until the civil governments could maintain order.

The western movement of settlers brought conflict with the Indians. Scores of Indian wars and campaigns were fought by the army. Some of the more notable Indian wars were: the Northwest Indians, 1790–95 and 1811–13; Seminole Wars in Florida, 1817–18, 1835–42 and 1856; Black Hawk War, 1832; Sioux War, 1862–67; War of the Plains Indians, 1863–69; Sioux and Cheyenne War of 1876–79; and Apache Wars, 1861–90. These wars were fought by the regular infantry and cavalry regiments occasionally aided by state militia and volunteers. The frontier soldiers were usually stationed in posts at strategic points defending the routes of communications, settlements and Indian reservations. The strength of this army, about one half of the Regular Army in time of peace, ranged from 1423 troops in 1790 in the Northwest Territory to over 26,000 in 1868, which was the height of the Indian wars on the Great Plains. The frontier posts had on the average a garrison of 200 troops. By 1867 over 100 posts were scattered throughout the West. As the Indian wars ended, after 1870, these posts were abandoned.

The army supplies were carried by boats, steamboats, ox and mule trains, pack mules and horses and later by railroads, which stimulated the development of trade, farming and ranching. The difficulty of supplying these remote army posts encouraged farming and urban enterprises around the posts, the beginning of permanent settlements.

The daily life of the frontier soldier was a hardy one. The soldiers built their shelter, escorted travelers, emigrants, and wagon trains on the trails, aided and protected surveying parties, constructed thousands of miles of trails and roads, supplied needy emigrants, patrolled trails and railroad lines, guarded river navigation, protected government and private property from hostile Indians and outlaws, assisted and fed friendly Indians, fought hostile Indians and gave police assistance to the weak civil authorities on the frontier. Their shelters were usually log, stone, adobe or sod huts constructed largely by their own labor. The hardships of the soldiers, the miserable quarters, inferior food and the lonely life encouraged many desertions.

The army on the frontier disagreed with the Indian Bureau and the frontier civil authorities over the Indian policy. The frontiersmen in general demanded the destruction or removal of the Indians. The Indian Bureau attempted to protect the Indians, and the army to coerce them. When the Indians revolted the army made war upon the entire Indian tribe, punishing the innocent with the guilty, even to the extent of killing women and children in raids on villages or camps. The Indian Bureau and the army officials accused each other of being responsible for the Indian wars.

ARNOLD'S MARCH TO QUEBEC. In the summer of 1775 Col. Benedict Arnold went to Cambridge, Mass., and laid before Commander in Chief George Washington a plan for attacking Canada. Washington was sympathetic. The old classic route by way of Lakes George and Champlain and the Richelieu River was assigned to Gen. Richard Montgomery. News of another passage by way of the Kennebec and Chaudière rivers had reached Washington. This route was assigned to a force under Arnold. On Sept. 19 Arnold's command left Newburyport, Mass., and went by sea to and up the Kennebec where 200 bateaux had been ordered to be ready. With these Arnold headed up the river. Made of green wood and ill-adapted to the upper rushing waters of the Kennebec, these bateaux were a tactical blunder which, however, did not daunt Arnold. Neither did he hesitate when Lt. Col. Roger Enos turned back with one fourth of the little army. On up the Dead River, full of ice and through snowstorms, with insufficient food and clothing, Arnold led his force. Oct. 28 found them going across the carrying place which was actually the divide between the St. Lawrence and Atlantic watersheds. Arnold plunged ahead with an advance guard while the remainder were reduced to eating dogs and shoeleather. At Sertigan, Arnold arranged for supplies which refreshed his exhausted detachment so that they were able to go down the Chaudière and reach the St. Lawrence on Nov. 9, 1775. In the meantime Montgomery had reached Montreal, but Arnold went on across the St. Lawrence and was actually in front of Quebec before Montgomery arrived. Guy Carleton, the British commander at Montreal, evacuated that place and got into Quebec before Montgomery could join Arnold on Dec. 2. Carleton had 1200 men while the combined American forces numbered scarcely 1000. Nevertheless, in a blinding snowstorm, Montgomery and Arnold assaulted Quebec on the night of Dec. 31, 1775. The effort failed, Montgomery was killed and Arnold wounded. Arnold's march through the wilderness of Maine has been regarded as a classic of perseverance and determination in the face of extreme hardship.

ARNOLD'S RAID IN VIRGINIA. In December of 1780 Commander in Chief Sir Henry Clinton of the British armies in North America determined to send an expedition into Virginia. Its purpose was to conduct desultory raids into the tidewater region of that state and to block the mouth of the Chesapeake. The command was given to the traitor, Benedict Arnold, because Clinton admired his intrepidity and believed he could induce some more Americans to desert. Leaving Sandy Hook on Dec. 20–21 and arriving at Hampton Roads Dec. 30, Arnold seized the small boats on the James River and pushed up that stream to Westover. Sending Simcoe's Rangers ahead, the force was moved on to Richmond, which Arnold occupied after a skirmish on Jan. 5, 1781. He destroyed the iron foundry at Westham and the American stores at Richmond. Arnold then re-embarked on the James and fell down to Portsmouth, which he fortified and whence he sent various marauding and pillaging expeditions into the neighborhood until March, when he was joined and outranked by Maj. Gen. William Phillips. In April Phillips and Arnold started another expedition up the James, reaching City Point on the 24th, whence they proceeded overland to Petersburg where 1000 hogsheads of tobacco were destroyed, as were the small boats on the Appomattox. Arnold then returned to Osborn's on the James where he destroyed a small American fleet, marched to Manchester where 1200 hogsheads of tobacco were destroyed, thence to Warwick where the flour magazines and mills were burned. In May the force fell down to Westover, thence to Brandon. Throughout these movements the British were harassed by the inferior forces of Lafayette and Wayne. Phillips died at Petersburg on May 13, 1781, and the chief command momentarily devolved on Arnold again. But at this time Lord Cornwallis came up with his superior forces and joined the detachments of Phillips and Arnold to his for the campaign of the summer of 1781.

ARNOLD'S TREASON. Brig. Gen. Benedict Arnold of the Continental Army had fought gallantly for the American cause from Ticonderoga (1775) to Saratoga (1777). But by the spring of 1779 several motives led him to open up a treasonable correspondence with the British headquarters in New York.

These were (1) irritation at repeated slights by Congress, (2) resentment at the authorities of Pennsylvania who had court-martialed him, (3) need for money and (4) opposition to the French alliance of 1778. Throughout the rest of 1779 and 1780 he transmitted military intelligence about the American Army to the British. July 12, 1780, he "accepted the command at West Point as a post in which I can render the most essential services" [to the British]. He demanded from the British £ 20,000 in case he could betray West Point and £ 10,000 in case he failed but himself went over to the British. Negotiations were carried out with Maj. John André, adjutant general of the British army. The latter visited Arnold at a point between the British and American lines Sept. 21, 1780. On Sept. 23, when returning from this meeting, André was captured by the Americans, and the incriminating documents found in his stocking were sent to Gen. Washington, who happened to be in the neighborhood. News of André's capture was also sent to Arnold, thus giving him time to escape down the Hudson River to the British before he could be arrested for treason. He became a brigadier general in the British army, went to England after the defeat of the British and died there June 14, 1801.

AROOSTOOK WAR was an undeclared and bloodless "war," from February to May, 1839, occasioned by the failure of the United States and Great Britain to determine the boundary between New Brunswick and what is now Maine. In 1820 Maine became a state. Almost immediately, ignoring the British contention that all land north of Mars Hill, in Aroostook, was British, the Maine legislature, jointly with Massachusetts, made grants to settlers along both branches of the Aroostook River. In 1831 Madawaska, in the disputed area, was incorporated by Maine. Finally, in January, 1839, Rufus McIntire was appointed land agent, with authority to take a posse into the disputed area and oust Canadians. Within two months 10,000 Maine troops were either encamped along the Aroostook River or were on their way there. At the insistence of Maine congressmen, the Federal Government voted a force of 50,000 men and $10,000,000 in the event of war. To prevent a clash Gen. Winfield Scott was despatched to negotiate a truce with the lieutenant governor of New Brunswick. This he did, and Great Britain, convinced of the seriousness of the situation, agreed to a boundary commission, whose findings were incorporated in the Webster-Ashburton Treaty.

ART, AMERICAN. Painting in the American colonies was almost exclusively portraiture. During the 17th century, artisans who depended upon other skills for their livelihood produced likenesses in the manner of those remembered in their homeland. Surviving work by New England limners, like the portraits of *John*

61

Freake and *Mrs. Freake and Baby Mary* (1674) reveal the flat, patterned style of Tudor England, while portraits from New Amsterdam remained closer to the baroque realism of The Netherlands. Although the names of a few New Amsterdam artists, Hendrick Couturier and the Duyckincks, for example, were recorded, no portraits can be attributed to them with any certainty.

A group of New England portraits can be ascribed to Captain Thomas Smith (active 1650–90) who attempted to follow the contemporary style of English court portraiture. Imitation of English models, known through mezzotints after Kneller and others, became prevalent during the 18th century, particularly among the patroon painters of New York. Most of these attempts to reproduce a courtly style are crude, and those that achieve some artistic merit, like the portraits of the De Peyster and Van Cortlandt children (*ca.* 1730) are remarkable for their naive charm rather than for their European sophistication.

While these native attempts to reproduce English court portraiture were being made, a number of immigrant painters began to arrive in the colonies. Most important among these new arrivals were Gustavus Hesselius (1682–1755) and John Smibert (1688–1751). Hesselius painted in the middle colonies before settling in Philadelphia where he did his portraits of the Indians *Tishcohan* and *Lapowinsa* (1735). He also did some religious painting, now lost, and some mythological subjects. John Smibert arrived in the company of Bishop Berkeley in 1729. His *Bishop Berkeley and Entourage* (1729), perhaps the most ambitious work in portraiture that had been undertaken on these shores, reveals his English training. Smibert set up practice in Boston where he remained until his death, and his collection of casts and copies made his painting rooms one of the few places in the colonies where artists could get some idea of European originals.

The most outstanding native-born artist during this period was Robert Feke (*ca.* 1705–50). The influence of Smibert is evident in his *Isaac Royall and Family* (1741), but the color and restrained linear patterns in his single portraits are distinctly his own and in marked contrast to Smibert's more painterly style. The precise finish and clarity of Feke's work are continued in the painting of John Singleton Copley (1738–1815), greatest of the colonial portraitists. Although he was exposed to the work of Smibert and that of his stepfather, Peter Pelham, Copley was essentially self-taught. He soon developed a personal style of penetrating realism, rarely flattering to his sitters, combined with a sumptuous and daring use of color in his treatment of accessories. Although he sometimes adopted elaborate portrait formulae, he was at his best directly observing his sitters in intimate portraits like those of *Peter Hurd* (1765) or *Isaac Smith* (1769). Copley soon became impatient with the provincial at-mosphere of Boston and, after his *Boy with a Squirrel* had been successfully exhibited in London in 1766, his thoughts turned increasingly to Europe. He left Boston in 1774 and never returned. In London Copley enjoyed some early success, but his slow working methods and his inability to master the delicate brushwork of his English competitors lost him sitters. His popularity declined, and in his last years he was virtually without work.

The appeal of London continued to be felt by nearly every American artist. Gilbert Stuart (1755–1828) spent seventeen years there achieving a mastery of the painterly portrait style which eluded Copley. Stuart returned to America in 1793 to paint Washington: the Vaughan portrait in 1795, the standing Lansdowne portrait and the more famous Athenaeum portrait of 1796. During a long and productive career in Philadelphia, New York and Boston, Stuart continued, despite an increasingly painterly technique and a fondness for the accidental effects of light and color, to record with great insight the personalities of the prominent men in the early Republic.

Quite opposed to Stuart's Europeanized style were the portraits of Charles Willson Peale (1741–1827) whose *Peale Family Group* (1773) and *Staircase Group* (1795) remain closer to Copley. Despite a brief London visit his art remained relatively free of European mannerisms. Ralph Earl (1751–1801), whose portrait of *Roger Sherman* (*ca.* 1777) continued in Connecticut the tradition of Feke and Copley, also discarded in his later works the effects of a stay in London.

With the early Republic came a rising hope for the future of history painting in America. The Philadelphian Benjamin West (1738–1820) had become by 1770 one of the leading history painters in London and was ever hospitable and encouraging to visiting American artists. Although West's fame came from his early adoption of the neo-classical style, which he brought to London from Rome with such pictures as *Agrippina with the Ashes of Germanicus* (1769), he also practiced a more dramatic baroque style seen in his *Death of General Wolfe* (1771). It was in the style of the latter picture that John Trumbull (1756–1843) executed his series on the American Revolution. Of this series, which occupied the painter for ten years, the *Death of Montgomery before Quebec* (1786) clearly shows his indebtedness to West. Trumbull's plan to have the series engraved and sold by subscription failed, as did nearly all attempts to bring history painting to America. Another history painter was John Vanderlyn (1775–1852), unique among Americans of his generation in that he was trained in Paris. His *Death of Jane McCrea* (1804) was an attempt to depict an incident from American history in the style of Parisian neo-classicism.

Washington Allston (1779–1843) and S. F. B. Morse (1791–1872) were, like Trumbull, idealistic, educated young men convinced of the necessity of bringing painting in the grand manner to America. Allston, after two extended stays in London where he benefited from the advice of West, returned home permanently in 1818 with his unfinished canvas, *Belshazzar's Feast*. This ambitious picture remained unfinished at the time of his death, a symbol of the failure of history painting in America. Allston's smaller pictures, such as *The Deluge* (1804) and *Moonlit Landscape* (1819), depicting nature in moods of terror and mystery, were more successful and typical of his romantic sensibility. Morse, after setting out to become a history painter in London under Allston and West, was forced upon his return to take up portraiture or to produce, with an eye toward profits, paintings like *House of Representatives* (1822) or *Gallery of the Louvre* (1832). By the 1840's, he was wholly occupied in his work with the telegraph.

American painters of landscape and genre subjects found a more receptive public than did the history painters. In Philadelphia, James and Raphaelle Peale turned out still-lifes with *trompe-l'oeil* fidelity during the first decades of the century, and in New York, John Quidor (1801–81) and William Sidney Mount (1807–68) were exhibiting genre paintings. Quidor's were drawn principally from the stories of Washington Irving, while Mount's were gentle, luminous scenes of his native Long Island, like *Eel Spearing on the Setauket* (1845). Exactly contemporary was George Caleb Bingham's (1811–79) *Fur Traders Descending the Missouri,* the first of his river paintings which remain classic expressions of that vanished segment of American experience.

A record of life beyond the frontier had already been made by George Catlin (1796–1872) who set out for the Indian country in 1832, by Alfred Jacob Miller (1810–74) who accompanied an expedition into the Rockies in 1837, and by John James Audubon (1785–1851) whose monumental *Birds of America* appeared between 1827 and 1838.

Our most original artists were landscape painters. The Hudson River School had no real existence as a school, but the term is customarily applied to a group of artists who painted the Catskills, the White Mountains, and the eastern coastline as well as the Hudson. Among these artists were Thomas Cole (1801–48), Asher B. Durand, Thomas Doughty, John F. Kensett, and John W. Casilear. Thomas Cole's early paintings like *Last of the Mohicans* (1827) give a rather dramatic account of nature, but such works as *The Catskills* (1833) represent nature sharply observed and also convey a sense of the vastness and silence of the wilderness. Doughty and Durand relied on traditional landscape composition in their treatment of space, but Kensett often gave a panoramic view implying in his pictures the continuation of great distance and great space beyond the limits of the frame. Kensett, too, like

Fitzhugh Lane (1804–65), was particularly sensitive to the quality of American light. Younger landscape artists, Cole's only pupil, F. E. Church (1826–1900) and Albert Bierstadt (1830–1902), continued in the basically realistic manner of the older men but traveled far in search of more sensational motifs for their paintings. By the end of the century, Bierstadt's views of the Rockies enjoyed wide popularity. Another artist who began in the tradition of the Hudson River School was George Inness (1825–94), but his late landscapes reveal a more personal and poetic view of nature.

The decades after the Civil War saw American artists turning more to Paris and to Munich. Of the Munich group, William M. Chase (1849–1916) and Frank Duveneck (1848–1919) returned to paint with the rich sensuous brushwork learned abroad. The French Barbizon School made its influence felt on William Morris Hunt (1824–79) and later on Alexander Wyant and Homer Martin. By 1890, John H. Twachtman, J. Alden Weir, Theodore Robinson and Childe Hassam were involved with French Impressionism. Other artists remained abroad to establish themselves in their adopted countries. James A. McNeill Whistler (1834–1903) evolved, under the influence of Dégas and Japanese prints, his own exquisite style in such compositions as *Portrait of Thomas Carlisle* (1872) or in ethereal pictures of the Thames by night like *Nocturne in Black and Gold—The Falling Rocket* (ca. 1874). Mary Cassatt (1845–1926) settled permanently in Paris in 1873 and worked closely with Dégas. Although she has a place in the history of French Impressionism, her work was little known at home. A third expatriate was John Singer Sargent (1856–1925) who studied in Paris and won an early success in London as a portraitist of fashionable society. His *Daughters of Edward Darly Boit* (1882) was never surpassed by later works which are noteworthy for the dazzling virtuosity of Sargent's brushwork.

Three masters of American painting remained untouched by this new wave of European influence. Winslow Homer (1836–1910) began his career as a free-lance illustrator. His paintings of the Civil War reveal a reportorial sharpness, but in pictures like *Long Branch, New Jersey* (1869) he was more concerned with problems of light and atmosphere than with the fashionably dressed ladies he depicted. Although Homer had spent a year in Paris, his concern with light and atmosphere owes nothing to the French and is more in the tradition of our native landscape art. After 1881 Homer withdrew to the Maine coast and concentrated on seascapes and on depicting the struggle of men against the sea. In Philadelphia, Thomas Eakins (1844–1916) surpassed Homer in his objective analysis of the visible world. Devoted to the science of perspective and anatomy, he occupied himself principally with the human figure. He was at his best portraying people in their professional surroundings as in the *Gross Clinic* (1875) where the details of surgery were treated with a frankness shocking to his contemporaries. His photographic study of human and animal motion resulted in the accurate rendering of the horses' gait in the *Fairman Rogers Four-in-Hand* (1883) and the diving nude in *The Swimming Hole* (1883). In 1886, Eakins was forced to give up his professorship at the Pennsylvania Academy of the Fine Arts where he had insisted upon the study of the living model. Deprived of his students and gradually of his sitters, Eakins lived in relative obscurity during the last years of his life. The third of these independents was Albert Pinkham Ryder (1847–1917), a self-taught, solitary artist who turned from the world of fact to paint scenes from Shakespeare and Wagner or to depict lonely boats moving across moonlit seas. Like Eakins and Homer, he achieved little recognition in his lifetime.

There are but few names of importance in the history of American sculpture in the 19th century. William Rush (1756–1853) turned from the carving of figureheads in Philadelphia to provide some public statuary for that city. In 1824, Horatio Greenough (1805–52) became the first of many American sculptors to take up residence in Italy, and in 1832 he received the first commission from the government of the United States. Also drawn to Italy by Italian marble and Italian stonecutters was Hiram Powers (1805–73) whose *Greek Slave* (1845) enjoyed a sensational success. Among the sculptors who remained at home were Erastus Dow Palmer, John Q. A. Ward and William Rimmer. After the Civil War, Paris replaced Rome as the center of study, and the belated classicism of the earlier men gave way to more pictorial conception of sculpture in the work of Augustus Saint-Gaudens, Frederick MacMonnies and Daniel Chester French.

The history of American art in the 20th century is one of great complexity as the revolutionary styles of European modernism made themselves felt here, and American artists either rejected modernism out of hand or sought to adopt its new formal vocabulary to American subjects. The first revolt against the reigning academicism came in 1908 when a group of artists, under the leadership of Robert Henri—"The Eight"—held an exhibition of paintings which depicted urban life with vigorous brushwork and earthy colors. Their revolutionary activity led them to the organization of the Armory Show of 1913, the first major appearance of European modernism in America. So great was the impact of the Post-Impressionists, Fauves and Cubists represented that the painting of the Eight, whose revolt had been largely one of subject matter, appeared outdated.

During the years between World War I and the depression, American painters, working in the styles of modern European art, slowly gained recognition. Abraham Walkowitz, Marsden Hartley, and John Marin revealed their indebtedness to Cézanne, the Fauves and the Cubists. Joseph Stella painted views of New York in a style based on Italian Futurism and Arthur Dove developed a highly personal abstract style. None of the Americans went as far as the Europeans in limiting art to purely formal considerations. In scenes of the New England coast by Marin and Hartley, in the urban subjects of Georgia O'Keefe, Charles Sheeler and Stuart Davis, the lessons of the French were adapted to American scenery and American places. In these years, too, American sculptors, William Zorach, John Flannagan and José de Creeft among them, turned to direct carving and to some degree of abstraction. More recently various techniques in metal sculpture have appeared, resulting in a new freedom of sculptural expression in the work of Seymour Lipton, Herbert Ferber, Theodore Roszak, David Smith and others.

A few artists stood against the modern movement. Most forceful in his opposition was Thomas Hart Benton who led, during the 1930's, a movement called Regionalism. This form of artistic isolationism, both anti-European and anti-New York, can be seen in the work of John Steuart Curry and Grant Wood who painted, like Benton, scenes of the South and Middle West in a more or less traditional style. Edward Hopper continued to paint his haunting views of silent streets and houses, and Reginal Marsh carried on the style of the Eight in his pictures of New York's slums.

In the 1950's, Abstract Expressionism became the dominant style in American painting. Its sources were found in the methods of Kandinsky, the Dada painters, and the Surrealists who minimized the role of conscious control in their paintings. The leaders in its formative stage in the late '40's were Willem de Kooning, Franz Kline and Jackson Pollock who owed something to the work of Arshile Gorky and the calligraphic paintings of Mark Tobey. With the advent of this controversial style, which seemed to deny all ideas of order and control and yet was capable of projecting on canvas abstract images of great emotional intensity, America assumed for the first time a position of importance in the development of western painting.

ARTICLE TEN of the League of Nations Covenant was of wholly American origin and was regarded by President Wilson as an extension of the Monroe Doctrine to the whole world. In Wilson's mind the undertaking "to preserve as against external aggression the territorial integrity and existing political independence of all Members of the League" was not a pledge to go to war in advance of congressional consideration and decision. He interpreted the obligations of the article as moral, not legal.

Opponents of the covenant in the Senate made Article X their principal target. They argued that it was not the proper business of the United States to guarantee either new boundaries or old empires or to intervene in cases of revolution against oppression. They contended that moral obligations would be found as binding as legal ones. Consequently the Senate adopted a ponderous reservation repudiating any obligation under the article except as the Congress should provide in any particular case. This was unacceptable to President Wilson not for its legal effect but for its embodiment of an attitude destructive to the principle of international responsibility. He contemplated territorial change accomplished through the peaceful operation of Article XIX rather than the traditional resort to violence.

ARTICLES OF CONFEDERATION. The Continental Congress decided even before independence that it was necessary to set up a confederacy based upon a written instrument. Several plans appeared in the press and the subject was embraced in R. H. Lee's motion of June 7, 1776, on independence. On June 11 Congress voted to appoint a committee. This body set to work at once and on July 12 reported through John Dickinson a set of Articles of Confederation, of which eighty copies were printed for the use of members. Congress was so engrossed in war problems, however, that debates on the scheme dragged through more than a year. The principal disputes raged over the questions whether taxes should be apportioned according to the gross number of inhabitants counting slaves or excluding them—the South of course wishing them excluded; whether large and small states should have equality in voting; whether Congress should be given the right to regulate Indian affairs; and whether Congress should be permitted to fix the western boundaries of those states which claimed to the Mississippi. On Nov. 15, 1777, Congress finally approved a draft and sent it to the states, on the understanding that all must ratify it before it went into effect. This draft, declared a circular letter of Congress, "is proposed as the best which could be adapted to the circumstances of all; and as that alone which affords any tolerable prospect of a general ratification."

The Articles did not become the law of the land until March 1, 1781. Nine states ratified as early as July, 1778, but several of the smaller ones held back because of the question of western lands. Maryland in particular had urged that these lands be regarded as a common possession of all the states, and felt aggrieved when the Articles contained a clause declaring that no state should be deprived of territory for the benefit of the United States. She first declared that she would not ratify until her powerful neighbor, Virginia, ceased to advance extravagant western claims. But when New York had yielded and Virginia seemed certain to do so, Maryland on March 1, 1781, signed the Articles through her delegates, and made them effective.

Although the Articles have been harshly criticized and the very shrewdest critics at the time saw their inadequacy, they were generally regarded in 1781 as offering a sound national constitution. They provided for a "perpetual union" or "firm league of friendship" between the states. Each remained sovereign and independent, and retained every right not expressly ceded by the Articles to the general government. A single agency of government was established—a Congress; the states were to appoint from two to seven delegates annually to it, and each state was to have one vote. Rhode Island thus obtained a parity with New York or Virginia. The costs of government and defense were to be defrayed from a common treasury, to which the states were to contribute in proportion to the value of their surveyed land and improvements. The states were likewise to supply quotas of troops, in proportion to the white inhabitants of each, upon congressional requisitions. To Congress was entrusted the management of foreign affairs, of war and of the postal service; it was empowered to borrow money, emit bills of credit, and determine the value of coin; it was to appoint naval officers and superior military officers, and control Indian affairs. But none of these powers was to be exercised save by vote of a majority of all states, and the more important could not be exercised save by the vote of nine. On paper, almost every important national authority was turned over to Congress save three: the authority to raise money directly, the authority to enlist troops directly and the authority to regulate commerce. But the paper powers proved to be very different from actual power.

It soon became evident that Congress was doomed to fail in its attempts to make the Articles workable. These attempts consisted chiefly in requests to the states for money that was never paid, pleas for troops which filled no army ranks, and petitions for special powers which the states never granted. At various points the powers of the states were supposedly limited. They were forbidden to enter into treaties, confederations, or alliances, to meddle with foreign affairs, or to wage war without congressional consent, unless invaded. Most important of all, they were to give to free inhabitants of other states all the privileges and immunities of their own citizens. A citizen of South Carolina, for example, who removed to Boston, at once became a citizen of Massachusetts. Interstate extradition of criminals was also provided. The states could impose duties, but not any which conflicted with the treaty stipulations of Congress. They were required to "abide by the determinations of Congress" on all subjects which the Articles left to that body. The states did respect each other's rights to a considerable extent (when two or more of them fell out, any one could submit the dispute to Congress). But they failed lamentably to respect the needs and requests of the National Government. They refused to do what they should have done, especially in supplying money and men; they frequently did what they should have refrained from doing. A circular prepared by Congress not long after Maryland's ratification in 1781 declared: "The inattention of the States has almost endangered our very existence as a people."

Demands for amendment and invigoration of the Articles were made even before they became effective. New Jersey served notice on Congress Feb. 3, 1780, for example, that it was absolutely necessary to give the nation power to regulate commerce and to fix duties on imports. A committee which reported May 3, 1781, pointed to the chief defect of the Articles— the fact that they gave Congress no power to enforce its measures, and suggested a new article authorizing the employment of armed forces to compel recalcitrant states "to fulfill their Federal engagements." This would have led straight to civil war, and the plan failed. The years 1782–86 witnessed earnest efforts by Congress to obtain state consent to a Federal impost, which would have furnished a stable revenue; earnest efforts also were made to obtain from the states a sufficient control over shipping to enable it to wage commercial warfare with nations discriminating against the United States. But some states, notably New York and Rhode Island, long proved stubborn; others were tardy; and when they did act, their laws were found to conflict. Again, while the states were bound to respect the treaties made by Congress, several of them indulged in gross violations of the Definitive Treaty of Peace. The close of the year 1786 found the Articles of Confederation in widespread discredit, and many national leaders eager to find a wholly new basis for union. Yet the Articles, soon to give way to the Constitution, should not be regarded with contempt. They had served as a stepping-stone to a new order; as John Marshall said later, they had preserved the idea of union until national wisdom could adopt a more efficient system. Had they not been agreed upon in time, the states might have fallen asunder after Yorktown.

"AS GOES MAINE, SO GOES THE UNION," a saying based upon the supposed accuracy of Maine's September election as a political barometer for the country, was originated by the Whigs after the presidential election of 1840.

ASH HOLLOW, BATTLE OF (Sept. 3, 1855). To punish the Sioux Indians for the Grattan massacre on the California Trail, Gen. Harney left Fort Leavenworth, Kans., Aug. 5, with 1200 troops. Proceeding west of Fort Kearny, Nebr., he encountered Little Thunder's band at Ash Hollow. The Indians fought desperately but were nearly exterminated, losing 136 killed.

ASIENTO (1713) was a license granted to the English South Sea Company by the Spanish government, as a result of the Treaty of Utrecht, whereby the company was given the exclusive right to sell a total of 144,000 Negro slaves in the Spanish colonies during thirty years or at the rate of 4800 a year. For this privilege the company paid the Spanish crown $200,-000.

ASSEMBLY, RIGHT OF, is guaranteed against interference by Congress in the Federal Constitution, and is supplemented by state constitutional provisions imposing similar restrictions upon state legislatures. In no place is the right absolute, but is subject to supervision in its exercise by local government officials. The right of assembly will not be sustained where its exercise threatens to disrupt the government or destroy the public peace. Here the assembly clearly becomes unlawful.

The Supreme Court in U. S. v. Cruikshank (1876) held that the right of the people peaceably to assemble for lawful purposes, with the obligation on the part of the states to afford them protection, existed long before the adoption of the Constitution. It had existed in English law from "time out of mind" as a distinct, separate and independent right. That the right was so recognized was made evident by the numerous statutes which restricted and regulated its use.

A statute passed by Parliament in the reign of George I fixed the limitations upon the right of assembly which are still observed in this country. According to this act, the right of assembly cannot be maintained if the meeting is for an unlawful purpose or is conducted in a tumultuous manner. Most of the cases in which the right has been challenged fall into the second category. Four notorious cases of the last century which come under the heading of unlawful assembly involved four different motives. These were a meeting in Philadelphia of the proposed "Native American Party," 1844; the "Astor Place Riot" in New York City, 1849, concerning a performance at the Astor Place Opera House; the disapproval of a stringent liquor law in the State of Maine, 1855, by a meeting in Portland; and the "Anarchists' Case" of 1886, arising from an attempt of the workingmen in Chicago to introduce the eight-hour day. Each of these cases contained the essential elements of an unlawful assembly, in fact they were almost riots. In more recent years, most of the cases of unlawful assembly have developed from meetings of communists and strikers.

The practical decision whether or not an assembly is unlawful rests with the local police authorities. The chief of police or other official is supposed to exercise his fair and honest discretion. His action is subject to review by the courts but relief from the courts, if relief is merited, is at best uncertain.

ASSOCIATORS were a military organization formed by Franklin, Nov. 21, 1747, to defend the Port of Philadelphia. Revolting against the pacific policy of the Quakers, they formed military companies and erected two batteries on the Delaware. The Associators disbanded after the peace of Aix-la-Chapelle in 1748.

ASSUMPTION OF, AND FUNDING OF, REVOLUTIONARY DEBT. At the time of the organization of the American National Government under the United States Constitution it was found that the national debt consisted of the following: foreign debt, $11,710,378; to domestic creditors, $42,414,085, including $2,000,000 of unliquidated debt. Alexander Hamilton as Secretary of the Treasury proposed to pay this at par in order that the credit of the National Government might be established, though the domestic debt had been selling as low as 25%. This was finally agreed to after much popular opposition, since it meant that speculators who had bought up the securities would make large profits. In addition Hamilton also desired that the National Government should assume the payment of the debts incurred by the individual states in carrying on the Revolutionary War. This assumption of the state debts would increase the national debt by $18,271,786. From this proposal arose the celebrated "assumption" issue.

Some of the states had paid part of their Revolutionary War debt while others had paid but little, also some states were in far better financial condition than others, since they had suffered but little from the direct effects of the war. The State of New York was in peculiarly advantageous position if an assumption measure was proposed. It was among the largest of the debtors, but aside from this obligation was in an unusually strong financial situation, due to the sale of public lands and the careful investment of state funds. The Southern states whose population was smaller than that of the Northern states were especially hostile to this assumption, which would place increased taxation for its payment upon the entire country, themselves included. Hamilton rightly claimed that assumption of the state debts would cause the creditors holding these securities to look to the National Government for their payment, and thus increase their support of the new government at the expense of the states. He favored this as a strong believer in nationalism.

At the same time quite a controversy arose concerning the location of the new national capital. The Southern states were especially anxious that it be placed on the banks of the Potomac River while other locations such as sites on the Susquehanna River in Pennsylvania and the Delaware River in New Jersey were advocated by the people of the Middle and Northern states. The issue of assumption was at first defeated in Congress but finally, with the assistance of Jefferson, Hamilton procured an agreement by which Southern votes in Congress were secured for the assumption of state debts in return for Northern votes to locate the national capital on the banks of the Potomac River at the present city of Washington, D. C. This agreement was accomplished by the adroit action of Thomas Jefferson, then Secretary of State, who invited the Secretary of the Treasury, Alexander Hamilton, to dine with him at his home. Also, a few other friends were present at this social meeting for an informal conference. Jefferson, himself, stated that reasonable men could form a compromise by mutual satisfaction, which compromise was to save the Union. Since it would take time to build the national capital it was further agreed that the Government, then located at New York, should be transferred to Philadelphia for ten to fifteen years, and after that to the present site of the national capital city at Washington.

As a result of this informal agreement both the measures with regard to the assumption of state debts and the location of the national capital were carried through Congress in the spring of 1790.

ASTOR PLACE RIOT in New York, May 10, 1849, grew out of long-standing jealousy between the American actor, Edwin Forrest, and the English tragedian, William Charles Macready, and was essentially an expression of anti-British feeling mingled with class hatred. When police failed to disperse a pro-Forrest mob outside the Astor Place Opera House where Macready was playing *Macbeth*, the militia was called out; twenty were killed.

ASTORIA. John Jacob Astor planned an organized fur trade on a continental scale some time before American occupation of the upper Missouri country. To his American Fur Company, chartered in 1808, he added the Pacific Fur Company, organized in 1810, and proceeded to extend his organization from St. Louis to the mouth of the Columbia. Two expeditions were sent to the latter point: one by sea, and the other along the route of Lewis and Clark. The sea-going party, under Capt. Jonathan Thorn, embarked Sept. 6, 1810, in the *Tonquin* and after a stormy voyage reached the Columbia, Mar. 23, 1811. Within three weeks Astoria was established under the direction of Duncan McDougal, acting resident agent. In June Capt. Thorn and a trading party were massacred by Indians in Nootka Sound, and the lone white survivor blew up the ship *Tonquin*, killing himself and many Indians.

July 15, 1811, a party of Canadians sent by the North West Company to forestall the Americans, arrived at Astoria. In January, 1812, a second party came from the rival North West Company post on the Spokane River. Then came the Astor Overlanders, thirty-four in number. They had left St. Louis March 12, 1811, under the leadership of Wilson Price Hunt, and had traveled up the Missouri and westward through the country of the Crows, over the Continental Divide to the Snake River, thence to the Columbia and the Pacific, where they arrived Feb.

15, 1812. In May, the Astor ship, *Beaver,* arrived. Activities were extended inland to the mouth of the Okanagan, to the Spokane, and to the Snake River. Robert Stuart and a small party of eastbound Astor Overlanders set out with dispatches for Mr. Astor in New York, June 29, 1812, ascended the Snake River to its head, became the first white men to cross the South Pass, wintered on the Platte, and arrived in St. Louis April 30, 1813. They did not return, for news of the War of 1812 sounded the doom of the Astor enterprise. While Hunt was absent, McDougal and his associates, whose sympathies were with the British, sold all the Astor interests on the Columbia to the North West Company. Hunt returned to find Astoria in rival hands, the post renamed Fort George, and the British flag flying where the Stars and Stripes had been. Astoria was restored to the United States in 1818 in accordance with the Treaty of Ghent.

ATLANTA CAMPAIGN (May to September, 1864). The Union advance southward to Atlanta began, May 5, 1864, simultaneously with Grant's advance to Richmond. Sherman's (U.) army numbered 110,000 men; Johnston's (C.) half that number. Sherman's superiority enabled him, with little risk, to maneuver Johnston from one position to another. If Johnston was to save his army and prevent Sherman from taking Atlanta, he could not afford to stand and fight unless conditions were favorable. He considered doing this at Cassville, half way to Atlanta, but his subordinate commanders believed the risk too great. Ten days later a fierce battle took place at New Hope Church.

As the Confederates retreated nearer to Atlanta, fighting became more frequent. At Kenesaw Mountain, Sherman made a frontal attack against prepared positions, but was everywhere repulsed. The flanking operations were resumed. By July 6 Sherman had moved so near Atlanta that Johnston transferred his army south of the Chattahoochee River, into prepared positions along Peachtree Creek. On July 17 Johnston was relieved by a subordinate, Hood (C.), because he had "failed to arrest the advance of the enemy." On July 20 Hood violently attacked, but was repulsed with heavy losses. The attack was resumed, but was again repulsed. Sherman's renewal of his flanking movements to cut Hood's line of supply and force him out of Atlanta brought on the battle of Ezra Church. During August, Sherman edged closer to Hood's supply line. By the 31st he was across it. On Sept. 1, Sherman (U.) telegraphed President Lincoln: "Atlanta is ours and fairly won." Sherman had finally forced Hood (C.) out of the city. The Confederate Army concentrated to the southward. All people remaining in Atlanta were deported. After a brief rest Hood started northward. Sherman followed, but soon returned to Atlanta. On Nov. 16, 1864, the famous march to the sea was begun.

Before setting out, Sherman ordered the complete destruction of the town. "Behind us," he wrote, "lay Atlanta smouldering and in ruins, the black smoke rising high in air and hanging like a pall over the ruined city." No city during the Civil War was so nearly completely annihilated.

ATLANTIC CABLE. The laying of the Atlantic Cable was mainly due to the perseverance of Cyrus W. Field. A company was organized in 1854. A survey of the cable route followed. The British and American Governments loaned ships for the expeditions. A broken cable frustrated the efforts of 1857 and likewise efforts made in June of 1858. A later attempt in July met with success and by Aug. 5, 1858, the cable was laid. England and America rejoiced. President Buchanan and Queen Victoria exchanged greetings. Records of these early cable messages, cut in paper, are preserved at the Smithsonian Institution in Washington. Enthusiasm in America reached a culmination in early September when a great ovation was given Field in New York. But on Sept. 1 the cable ceased to function properly. For a time the experiment was much discredited.

During the Civil War capital was raised with great difficulty. Nevertheless, in July, 1865, the steamer *Great Eastern* began laying a cable which broke after two thirds of it had been laid. Success crowned the efforts of 1866 and shortly after the cable of 1865 was recovered and operated.

ATLANTIC CHARTER. (Aug. 14, 1941). The Atlantic Charter was signed Aug. 14, 1941 by President F. D. Roosevelt and Prime Minister Churchill at a meeting in Argentia Bay off Newfoundland. The United States, still technically a neutral in World War II, already had taken a number of steps that brought it close to war. The Charter, though less explicit, may be compared roughly to President Wilson's Fourteen Points in that both declarations expressed idealistic objectives for a postwar world. Although only a press release as first issued, the Charter was nonetheless well understood to be a pronouncement of considerable significance; and it soon acquired further authority when 26 countries (including the United States and Great Britain) signed the United Nations Declaration, which included among its provisions formal endorsement of the Charter. The Charter's text reads:

Joint declaration of the President of the United States of America and the Prime Minister, Mr. Churchill, representing His Majesty's Government in the United Kingdom, being met together, deem it right to make known certain common principles in the national policies of their respective countries on which they base their hopes for a better future for the world.

First, their countries seek no aggrandizement, territorial or other;

Second, they desire to see no territorial changes

that do not accord with the freely expressed wishes of the peoples concerned;

Third, they respect the right of all peoples to choose the form of government under which they will live; and they wish to see sovereign rights and self-government restored to those who have been forcibly deprived of them;

Fourth, they will endeavor, with due respect for their existing obligations, to further the enjoyment by all States, great or small, victor or vanquished, of access, on equal terms, to the trade and to the raw materials of the world which are needed for their economic prosperity;

Fifth, they desire to bring about the fullest collaboration between all nations in the economic field with the object of securing, for all, improved labor standards, economic advancement, and social security;

Sixth, after the final destruction of the Nazi tyranny, they hope to see established a peace which will afford to all nations the means of dwelling in safety within their own boundaries, and which will afford assurance that all the men in all the lands may live out their lives in freedom from fear and want;

Seventh, such a peace should enable all men to traverse the high seas and oceans without hindrance;

Eighth, they believe that all of the nations of the world, for realistic as well as spiritual reasons, must come to the abandonment of the use of force. Since no future peace can be maintained if land, sea, or air armaments continue to be employed by nations which threaten, or may threaten, aggression outside of their frontiers, they believe, pending the establishment of a wider and permanent system of general security, that the disarmament of such nations is essential. They will likewise aid and encourage all other practicable measures which will lighten for peace-loving peoples the crushing burden of armaments.

ATOM BOMB. On Aug. 6 and on Aug. 9, 1945 respectively, atomic bombs were dropped from U. S. combat airplanes on Hiroshima and Nagasaki, Japan. These events signalized the controlled release of atomic energy, one of the most significant events in world history. A new kind of warfare was ushered in, a new tool of industry was born, new and vital problems in international relations were created.

In the years immediately preceding and during World War II, a practical method for separating element U235 from the heavier and more abundant U238 existing together in a uranium bloc and for combining the forces released in a nuclear chain reaction and fission that could be controlled by experiment had been developed. Several elements are employable for atomic reaction. Only one, the uranium isotope U235, occurs in nature, though it must be separated from U238. Another, plutonium (element 94), is a man-made by-product produced in the separation of U235. Events leading up to the atom bomb may be said to have started with the discovery of radioactivity in 1896, with the pioneer investigation of atom-smashing by Lord Rutherford, and with the discovery of the possibility of converting matter into energy as suggested by Einstein's equation of equivalence first made public in 1905. This conversion required atom-smashers of tremendous energy. Invention of the electrostatic generator and cyclotron in 1929 was followed in 1932 by the first success in atom-smashing by Cockeroft and Walton. The neutron was discovered in the same year as were other atomic facts determined by H. C. Urey, Irene Curie and F. Joliot, Enrico Fermi, Nils Bohr, E. O. Lawrence and their associates and co-workers. By 1940 the basic data concerning the release and control of atomic energy was known.

The production of the first atomic bomb was achieved through the collective efforts of United States, British and European war refugee scientists, working as a team. No particular individual can be assigned credit for the result. Dr. George B. Pegram of Columbia University, a physicist, who had himself done much work on the project, first brought the atomic bomb to the attention of Pres. Franklin D. Roosevelt and his civil and military advisers in March, 1939, after having on Jan. 25, 1939, helped to carry out the first successful demonstration in the United States of uranium fission. President Roosevelt and his advisers approved the proposal to study the feasibility of producing atomic bombs, but it was not until Dec. 6, 1941, that the project was begun under the direction of the uranium section of the Office of Scientific Research and Development. On June 18, 1942, the "Manhattan District" was organized for production of the bomb with Gen. L. R. Groves in charge. The pilot plant in the project was located in Clinton Laboratory at Oak Ridge, near Knoxville, Tenn. Later, a more isolated site on the Columbia River north of Pasco in northwestern Washington was chosen and named the Hanford Engineer Works. An atomic bomb laboratory was established on an isolated mesa at Los Alamos, N. Mex., about 20 miles from Santa Fe. On July 16, 1945, the first atomic bomb was exploded at Alamogordo air base in the desert 120 miles southeast of Albuquerque, N. Mex. Three weeks later an atomic bomb was dropped on Hiroshima, Japan.

In March, 1946, a "Report on the International Control of Atomic Energy," known as the Acheson-Lilienthal report, was made public. On August 1, 1946, the Atomic Energy Act was passed by Congress providing for assistance to private research in the field of atomic energy, the publicizing of test information consistent with public safety, the establishment of federally conducted research and development, ownership of fissionable material and the creation of an administration to achieve the purposes of the act. The Atomic Energy Commission was set up, Oct. 28, 1946, with David E. Lilienthal as its first chairman.

In the meantime, on Jan. 24, 1946, the United Nations had appointed its own Atomic Energy Commission. Bernard M. Baruch, the American member, proposed free access under United Nations supervision for international inspection of all atomic energy installations with specific punishments for illegal possession or use of atomic bombs or materials from which bombs would be made. Soviet Russia rejected the Baruch plan, proposing instead an international agreement to outlaw the production of atomic bombs and to provide for the destruction of existing stocks of bombs. Russia, however, resisted the plan of international inspection and any impairment of its U. N. veto power. This refusal caused the practical rejection of the plan for international control of atomic production and storage. A second report to the U. N. Atomic Energy Commission in 1947 elaborated details of the original Baruch plan. In 1948 a third report was given over to a further discussion of the Baruch plan and to a study of Soviet Russian counterproposals. Russia constantly charged that the United States sought a monopoly in the manufacture of atomic energy and refused to accept any plan of atomic control not subject to the veto power. In the absence of any international plan of control, experimental and research plants and laboratories under civilian control were set up, and the search for uranium deposits continued. Permanent proving grounds were established for developing and improving atomic weapons and for developing applications of atomic energy for commercial uses.

German scientists had also been at work developing an atomic bomb. Many believe that if Hitler had recognized its importance and destructive potential, the Germans would have dropped the atomic bomb more than a year before Hiroshima. Russian scientists with the aid of captured German experts and Western traitors hurried their own research. It was believed by many in the United States that it would be ten years before Soviet Russia could produce an atomic bomb, yet on Sept. 23, 1949, a new chapter in the history of atomic energy began when Pres. Harry S. Truman announced: "We have evidence that within recent weeks an atomic explosion occurred in the U. S. S. R." The monopoly of atomic weapons by the United States had ended. The loss of a monopoly and the attitude of the Soviet Russian bloc toward any system of international inspection and control of atomic weapons, as proposed by the U. N. General Assembly, November 4, 1948, created world-wide fear that through accident or design the United States and Soviet Russia might become involved in an atomic war. Both countries conducted extensive development and performance tests; both countries added to their stock piles of atomic weapons; both countries feverishly engaged in development and testing of ground-controlled intercontinental ballistic missles with atomic warheads; both countries appropriated huge sums for the development, production and testing of even more deadly atomic weapons. In the hope of controlling the production and possible use of all atomic weapons, the United States has continued to urge a treaty banning nuclear weapons tests, production and stock

piling as a step toward world disarmament, only to be met by obstacles set up by Soviet Russia as a condition of negotiation. The question of control of the atomic bomb remains unsettled.

ATOMIC ENERGY COMMISSION, UNITED STATES. This Commission was created by the Atomic Energy Act of 1946 (McMahon Act), signed by President Truman on Aug. 1, 1946. The adoption of this law followed a year-long public debate on the issue of whether the United States atomic energy program, started during World War II for military reasons and carried on by the Manhattan District of the Army Corps of Engineers, should function in peacetime under primarily military or civilian control.

The McMahon Act resolved this issue in favor of civilian control by placing the postwar program under the direction of a five-member Commission, appointed by the President, whose members were precluded from engaging in any other vocation, including active duty in the armed services.

The powers granted to the Commission by the McMahon Act were essentially complete. The Commission, for example, was made the exclusive owner of all nuclear explosives and fuels (primarily uranium-235 and plutonium) and all facilities in which such materials could be produced. The Commission was also empowered to control, through a licensing and regulatory system, all of the source materials (primarily natural uranium and thorium) from which nuclear explosives and fuels are derived, all of the radioactive by-products resulting from the use of such explosives and fuels, and all atomic energy information.

The McMahon Act provided that the atomic energy requirements of the military services be made known to the Commission through a Military Liaison Committee which, with the concurrence of the civilian head of the appropriate military department of government, was authorized to carry any dispute arising with the Commission to the President for resolution.

The McMahon Act also created a General Advisory Committee, appointed by the President, to advise the Commission on scientific and technical matters, and a Joint Committee on Atomic Energy of the U. S. Congress to consider all atomic energy legislation and to be kept fully and currently informed of the Commission's activities.

To guide the Commission in the discharge of its statutory responsibilities, the McMahon Act declared it to be the policy of the people of the United States that, "subject at all times to the paramount objective of assuring the common defense and security, the development and utilization of atomic energy shall, so far as practicable, be directed toward improving the public welfare, increasing the standard of living, strengthening free competition in private enterprise, and promoting world peace."

The first Commission was appointed by President Truman in the fall of 1946. David E. Lilienthal, former chairman of the Tennessee Valley Authority, was designated chairman. At midnight, Dec. 31, 1946, all of the scientific and technical personnel and all of the facilities and equipment (representing a public investment of approximately $2,000,000,000) of the Manhattan District were transferred to the Commission. Included were an atomic weapons laboratory at Los Alamos, N. Mex., where the first atomic bomb had been developed; a plutonium manufacturing plant at Hanford, Wash.; a research laboratory and uranium-235 production plant at Oak Ridge, Tenn.; a research laboratory at the University of Chicago, where the first self-sustaining nuclear chain reaction had taken place on Dec. 2, 1942, and a research laboratory at the University of California in Berkeley.

Following its establishment in 1946, the Commission concentrated its attention on rebuilding the physical and human resources of the organization it had taken over from the Manhattan District. This organization at the end of the war had been severely weakened by the departure of many key personnel and by the uncertainties stemming from the public controversy over civilian versus military control. The Commission during its early years also expanded the capacity of the plants at Hanford and Oak Ridge to produce nuclear explosives, established a new research laboratory at Brookhaven on Long Island, undertook a series of atomic weapons tests in the Pacific Ocean, launched a program of peaceful research and development to be carried out both within and outside of its own facilities, undertook the production of radioactive by-product materials (called radioisotopes) for sale to medical and industrial users, and began the development of nuclear reactors for the generation of electric power and the propulsion of submarines.

In 1949, following the explosion in that year of the Soviet Union's first atomic test bomb, a difference of opinion developed within the Commission on the question of whether or not the United States should undertake a program of developing and producing hydrogen bombs—weapons which potentially could be many hundreds of times more devastating than the atomic bombs used during World War II at Hiroshima and Nagasaki. This difference of opinion was resolved by President Truman in favor of proceeding with development, an action which supported the Commission's minority view, subscribed to by two of its five members: Gordon Dean and Lewis L. Strauss, both of whom subsequently became chairmen. Among those who had endorsed the Commission's majority view was Dr. J. Robert Oppenheimer, chairman of the Commission's General Advisory Committee and wartime director of the Manhattan District's atomic bomb program.

Also in 1949 the Commission became the subject of public controversy when the ranking Republican member of the Joint Committee on Atomic Energy, Sen. Bourke B. Hickenlooper, charged Chairman Lilienthal with "incredible mismanagement." The charge led to public hearings at which it was alleged that the Commission under Chairman Lilienthal had been imprudently lax regarding security matters and had generally failed to make as much progress as might reasonably be expected. At the conclusion of the hearings, the Joint Committee issued a divided report in which the Democratic majority, under the leadership of Sen. Brien McMahon (author of the McMahon Act and then chairman of the Joint Committee), generally endorsed the Commission's record and the Republican minority generally was critical of it.

In early 1950 Chairman Lilienthal resigned and Commissioner Dean was appointed by President Truman to succeed him. In the ensuing years, the Commission undertook an enormous expansion of its capacity to produce nuclear explosives. This effort, which ultimately cost $5,000,000,000, resulted primarily in a substantial enlargement of the production facilities at Hanford and Oak Ridge, plus construction of comparable new similar facilities at Aiken, S. C., Paducah, Ky. and Portsmouth, O. There was also established a 400,000-acre National Reactor Testing Station in Idaho and a new weapons test reservation in Nevada.

Concurrently with its expansion program, the Commission continued to carry forward the projects it had previously undertaken to develop the hydrogen bomb and to produce nuclear reactors to generate electricity and propel submarines. As a result, the first electricity to be generated from atomic energy was produced in a small experimental reactor at the Reactor Testing Station in Idaho in December, 1951; and in May, 1953, the first land-based prototype of a submarine propulsion reactor was successfully operated in Idaho, the first hydrogen bomb was tested in the South Pacific, and the keel of the first nuclear-powered submarine, the *Nautilus*, was laid at Groton, Conn.

The Commission during the same period also enlarged its reactor development program to include projects for the propulsion of surface ships and aircraft, let its first contracts for the harnessing of the hydrogen bomb reaction for peaceful purposes, carried on an intensive test program involving both large and small weapons, undertook development of the United States' first full-scale atomic power plant, and issued the Federal Government's first invitations to private industry to participate in atomic power experimentation. In furtherance of this last named endeavor, the Commission in the spring of 1953 proposed to the Congress that the Atomic Energy Act of 1946 be revised to permit persons and organizations other than the Commission to own atomic reactors and to possess atomic fuels under Commission license.

Upon expiration of Chairman Dean's term of office in June, 1953, President Eisenhower appointed former Commissioner (1946–51) Strauss, a New York financier and a retired rear admiral in the U. S. Naval Reserve, to succeed him. In the immediately ensuing months, the Commission undertook construction of the United States' first full-scale atomic power plant (60,000 kilowatts) at Shippingport, Pa., submitted specific legislative proposals amending the Atomic Energy Act of 1946, and, in a controversial divided opinion (with scientist Henry D. Smyth, author of the "Smyth Report" on the wartime atomic bomb program, dissenting), withdrew the security clearance of the former (1946 to early 1953) Chairman of its General Advisory Committee, Dr. J. Robert Oppenheimer, because of an alleged "willful disregard for the normal and proper obligations of security."

On Dec. 8, 1953, President Eisenhower, in a major policy address to the General Assembly of the United Nations in New York City, proposed the launching of an international "atoms for peace" program focusing on the establishment, as its principal implementing instrument, of an International Atomic Energy Agency. It was proposed that the Agency be empowered by treaty to carry on research and development, serve as a world clearing house for international traffic in peaceful atomic energy materials and equipment, and administer a system of safeguards to assure the safety and prevent the diversion to military use of projects voluntarily placed under its control by member nations. Such an agency came into being in 1957, with headquarters in Vienna, Austria.

In 1954 the Congress adopted and the President signed into law a major revision (Cole-Hickenlooper Act) of the Atomic Energy Act of 1946. The revised law, called the Atomic Energy Act of 1954, expressly authorized the United States to join the International Atomic Energy Agency and also to enter into agreements for atomic energy co-operation with individual nations and regional groupings of nations outside of Agency channels. As a result, the United States in succeeding years became a member of the International Agency, entered into an atomic power and research agreement with the European Atomic Energy Community (EURATOM), joined the Inter-American Nuclear Energy Commission of the Organization of American States, and entered into approximately fifty peaceful and eight military agreements for atomic energy co-operation with other individual countries.

Domestically, the 1954 law loosened Federal control over atomic energy to the extent of permitting persons and organizations other than the Atomic Energy Commission to own atomic facilities, including power plants, and possess atomic fuels under a Commission-administered licensing system. The law also for the first time permitted private ownership of patents, subject, however, to the compulsory cross-licensing of patents found by the Commission to be affected by the public interest. In another provision, the law authorized the Commission to generate electricity from atomic energy, but only as a by-product of its developmental or production activity and not as an end in itself. In a vigorously contested amendment, the law further specified that Commission-generated electric power must be sold preferentially to publicly-owned utility systems.

Following adoption of the 1954 act, the Commission inaugurated a Power Demonstration Reactor Program designed to assist utilities, both publicly and privately owned, to build a series of full-scale plants for the purpose of demonstrating the technical feasibility of atomic power and of introducing engineering refinements designed to make atomic power competitive with power generated from coal, oil and natural gas.

Soon after its inception the Power Demonstration Program became the subject of intensive controversy, both as to its scale and the relative extent of its involvement with publicly-owned and privately-owned utilities. In general, critics of the program, including particularly the Democratic majority of the Joint Committee on Atomic Energy, contended that the program was too small to maintain United States leadership vis-à-vis other nations, notably the United Kingdom and the Soviet Union, and that it should be augmented by a large Federal construction effort. The controversy was heightened by a concurrent effort by the Commission to contract for sufficient power from two privately-owned utilities to replace power drawn by the Commission from the publicly-owned Tennessee Valley Authority for use at the Commission's plants at Oak Ridge, Tenn., and Paducah, Ky. This contract, widely known as the Dixon-Yates contract (from the names of the presidents of the two utilities involved) was vigorously opposed by the Joint Committee majority and was eventually cancelled.

The atomic power controversy continued as an acute issue until June 30, 1958, when Chairman Strauss's term expired and he declined reappointment because "circumstances . . . make a change in the chairmanship of the Commission advisable." This was generally interpreted to mean that the differences with respect to atomic power between Strauss and the Democratic majority of the Joint Committee, led by Sen. Clinton P. Anderson, then chairman of the Committee, were of such magnitude that Senate confirmation of Strauss's reappointment would either not be forthcoming or would be forthcoming only after vitriolic debate. Subsequently, President Eisenhower's nomination of Strauss to be Secretary of Commerce failed to be confirmed by the Senate, with Sen. Anderson leading the opposition.

In the meantime, during Strauss's tenure, atomic power projects totaling approximately 800,000 kilowatts, and of relatively many different types, were undertaken in the United States, including approximately 370,000 kilowatts by private utilities without Federal assistance, 360,000 kilowatts by private utilities with Federal assistance, and 100,000 kilowatts by the Atomic Energy Commission in cooperation with public power organizations. In the same period there were undertaken similar projects totaling approximately 1,400,000 kilowatts, all of the same general type, in the United Kingdom, and several hundreds of thousands of kilowatts, of a few different types, in the Soviet Union.

In other fields, in the years 1953 to 1958, the Commission proposed, and there were held in Geneva, Switzerland, two United Nations conferences on the peaceful uses of atomic energy; construction was begun on the United States' first nuclear powered merchant ship, the *Savannah;* secrecy was removed from virtually all information of nonmilitary value; the nuclear propelled submarine *Nautilus* was commissioned; a program, called Project Plowshare, for the peaceful utilization of atomic explosives was commenced; the atomic power plant at Shippingport, Pa., was successfully operated, and work was started on the first atomic-powered aircraft carrier, cruiser and destroyer. In addition, in early 1958, the Commission adopted as an objective, concurred in by the Joint Committee, the achievement of economically competitive atomic power by 1968. Throughout the period work also continued on the development of a nuclear-propelled aircraft, a project which, like the atomic power program, became the subject of controversy between the Congress and the Administration as to its rate of progress and extent of financial support.

Following expiration of Chairman Strauss's term in 1958, President Eisenhower appointed John A. McCone, a businessman who had previously served as Undersecretary of the Air Force. During Chairman McCone's tenure, which extended through 1960, there was a marked abatement in the atomic power controversy, partly because of substantial reductions in the power objectives of other countries (a cutback of from 6,000,000 to 3,000,000 kilowatts by 1966 in Great Britain and from 2,000,000 to a few hundred thousand kilowatts by 1961 in the Soviet Union) and partly because of the commencement by the Commission of several new federally owned developmental projects.

Also in the period 1958 through 1960, the Commission suspended weapons testing activities while unsuccessful talks among the United States, the Soviet Union and Great Britain on a permanent test ban proceeded in Geneva, Switzerland.

In nonweapon fields, the merchant ship *Savannah* was launched, nuclear submarines (there were fourteen at sea by the end of 1960) made pioneering voyages under water around the world and under the Arctic ice cap to the North Pole, and the first

successful ground test of a nuclear powered rocket designed for the ultimate propulsion of space vehicles was conducted. In the legislative field, the Atomic Energy Act was amended in 1959 to create a Federal Radiation Council to recommend acceptable standards of radiation exposure of atomic energy workers. The same amendment also permitted the Atomic Energy Commission to enter into agreements with individual states providing that the states assume regulatory jurisdiction over all radioactive atomic energy materials not capable of being used as explosives or as nuclear reactor fuel.

In summary, the United States by the end of 1960 had spent over $23,000,000,000 on its atomic energy program, approximately $2,000,000,000 by the Manhattan District during World War II and the remainder by the Atomic Energy Commission. These funds had been expended approximately as follows: 15% for the purchase of uranium primarily in the United States, Canada, South Africa and the Congo; 50% for the production from uranium of nuclear explosives and fuels, primarily for military purposes; 17.5% for the development, fabrication and testing of atomic weapons; 7.5% for the development of nuclear reactors for military purposes, primarily for the propulsion of submarines and aircraft; 7.5% for research in biology, medicine and the physical sciences, and 2.5% for the development of nuclear reactors for civilian use, primarily for the generation of electricity.

At the end of 1960, the Atomic Energy Commission had approximately 6500 employees, over 1000 contractors employing over 100,000 additional people directly on Commission work, and approximately twenty major installations valued in excess of $7,000,000,000. In addition, the Commission had licensed approximately 6000 persons and organizations including doctors, hospitals, universities, industrial concerns and agricultural experiment stations to utilize atomic energy materials for research, therapeutic and production purposes.

The principal programs under way by the Commission at the end of 1960, in addition to the production of weapons, were to: achieve economically competitive atomic power by 1968, develop a nuclear-powered aircraft, utilize atomic explosives for peaceful purposes, harness the hydrogen bomb reaction for peaceful purposes, develop nuclear power sources to propel rockets and space vehicles, add to the United States' store of fundamental atomic knowledge, stimulate the utilization of radioactive materials in industry, medicine and agriculture, and improve nuclear ship propulsion techniques.

The principal policy issue involving the Commission at the end of 1960 was whether or not the Commission embodied a basic conflict of interest as between its developmental and regulatory responsibilities, and whether or not, as a consequence, it should either be reorganized into two agencies or be divested of some of its powers and duties so that these might be transferred to other Federal agencies.

AUDUBON SOCIETIES, NATIONAL ASSOCIATION OF. This organization, for many years the foremost in the wild-life-conservation field, was incorporated Jan. 5, 1905. Primarily concerned with conservation education, it came into being as a federation of a number of dissociated state and local Audubon clubs which, in turn, had stemmed from the original "Audubon Society," first formed in 1886 by Dr. George Bird Grinnell, editor of *Forest and Stream.*

AUGHWICK, Indian village on the Juniata River near the site of Shirleysburg, Pa., became in 1753 headquarters for George Croghan, trader and agent for Pennsylvania among western Indians. Friendly Indians, refugees from the vicinity of Fort Duquesne, were maintained at Aughwick and left there to join Braddock's expedition in 1755.

AUGUSTA, FORT, named for George III's mother. Constructed by Pennsylvania in 1756, at the site of present Sunbury, to defend the frontier after Braddock's defeat, and to forestall the French who supposedly intended to fortify the forks of the Susquehanna, it protected frontiersmen from Indians and and Tories until abandoned after 1780.

AUGUSTA, GA., was founded (1735) by Gen. James Edward Oglethorpe at the head of navigation on the Savannah River. Until 1773 it remained the northwestern outpost of Georgia, dominating Indian trade and relations. Largely loyalist, it fell twice into British hands (1779, 1780–81). For a short period ending in 1795, it was the state capital. There a convention ratified the United States Constitution. Upland cotton and steam transportation made it, temporarily, the greatest inland cotton market in the world. A government arsenal and a large powder mill made it a major source of supply for the Confederate armies during the Civil War.

AUGUSTA, TREATY OF (1773), was made by Gov. James Wright, of Georgia, and John Stuart, Superintendent of Indian Affairs in the Southern District, with chiefs of the Creek and Cherokee nations, at the suggestion of the Indians, who were hopelessly in debt to various groups of white traders. By this agreement Georgia was ceded two tracts of land, one between the Altamaha and Ogeechee rivers and the other lying between the upper stretches of the Ogeechee and Savannah rivers, comprising in all more than 2,100,000 acres, and from the sale of these lands the traders were to be paid. A great influx of settlers was attracted here just before the Revolution.

AUGUSTA COUNTY, VA., named in honor of Princess Augusta, wife of the Prince of Wales, was erected on Nov. 1, 1738, from that portion of Orange County lying beyond the Blue Ridge. The newly created county was to remain part of the parent county until the number of inhabitants warranted the establishment of a separate government, which was not until Oct. 30, 1745. Territorially it included the present states of Kentucky, Ohio, Indiana, Illinois, nearly all of West Virginia and a part of western Pennsylvania. Here the Virginians came into conflict with Pennsylvania's claims, for both colonies had settlers in those parts of Pennsylvania west of the Alleghenies. Becoming alarmed at the influx of Virginia settlers, Pennsylvania had erected, on Feb. 26, 1773, Westmoreland County, which included all of the present counties of Westmoreland, Fayette, Greene, Washington and parts of Allegheny, Beaver, Indiana and Armstrong. In 1774–75 Virginia created the District of West Augusta, which claimed the land of the newly created Westmoreland County. In 1776 Virginia attempted to strengthen title to these lands by dividing West Augusta into three new counties: Ohio, Yohogania and Monongalia. These conflicting jurisdictional claims produced the Pennsylvania-Virginia Boundary dispute which was not settled until 1780. The immense territory of Augusta County was thus cut down, first by the creation of Botetourt County in 1769, Fincastle in 1772, the three counties in West Augusta and later encroachments until it reached its present-day status.

AURARIA (COLO.), established in October, 1858, was one of the towns started at the juncture of Cherry Creek and the South Platte, following gold discoveries earlier that summer. In April, 1860, it was consolidated with Denver, its rival, on the opposite bank of Cherry Creek.

AURORA, a Philadelphia newspaper founded in 1790 by Benjamin Franklin Bache as the *General Advertiser.* When Freneau's *National Gazette* suspended, the *Aurora* took its place as the Jeffersonian Republican mouthpiece. It was notorious for its violent personal abuse and its attacks on Washington's administration.

AUTOMOBILE. The automobile was not invented by any one person but was evolved through the efforts of many experimenters in several nations. As early as 1787 Oliver Evans of Philadelphia petitioned the Maryland legislature for a patent on the manufacture and operation of steam-propelled vehicles, and in 1804 he ran through the streets of Philadelphia a strange vehicle consisting of a large wagon which carried, and was driven by, a steam-propelled flatboat. However, largely because of the atrocious roads of the period and because of concentration on railroad development, little progress was made in this country until almost the close of the 19th century and automotive development got its real start abroad.

In the 1830's steam-driven stage coaches—ponderous, clumsy and rough—were operating on regular schedules along several routes in England, but eventually they were driven from the road by excessive toll charges and restrictive legislation. Most of the real progress was made in Germany; in 1876 Dr. A. N. Otto built a four-cycle internal combustion hydrocarbon motor, the same in principle as those used in motor vehicles today; in 1885 Gottfried Daimler built the first motorcycle and Carl Benz the first automobile powered by a gasoline engine. The French quickly took up their ideas, and by 1895 the French firm of Panhard & Lavassor was producing horseless vehicles on a commercial scale.

Meanwhile, activity in America was practically dormant, with most of the experimentation during the period being concentrated on heavy steam-propelled traction engines. After 1890, however, American pioneers began working in homes and workshops, borrowing heavily on the ideas of their European colleagues, and by 1900 they had laid the basis for a new industry. Authorities differ over which of the United States experimenters deserves precedence, but the weight of evidence places Charles and Frank Duryea first with successful operation of a vehicle in September, 1893; Elwood Haynes in 1894; Charles Brady King and Henry Ford in 1896; with R. E. Olds and Alexander Winton following closely. At any rate, the Duryea cars were the first American vehicles to prove themselves in competition: A Duryea road wagon won the first road race held in this country—the *Times-Herald* contest, run over snow-covered streets of Chicago on Thanksgiving Day in 1895—and the following year three of the four Duryea entries took all the money in the New York-Irvington race.

The first automotive trade journal, *The Horseless Age*, was launched by E. P. Ingersoll in 1895, but the industry was to remain largely in the experimental stage until the close of the century. The next decade saw phenomenal advances in the art of road transportation. Twelve manufacturing firms in 1900 turned out 4192 vehicles; by 1910 there were 69 companies in the field and their annual production had leaped to 187,000. This whole decade was marked by tremendous enthusiasm and intense activity. Automobile clubs were formed; strenuous campaigns for construction of good roads were undertaken; a dozen or more reliability runs were staged each year; a craze for speed contests of all kinds sprang up on both sides of the Atlantic, climaxed by the fantastic race around the world from New York to Paris in 1908.

Most of the firms started during this period operated on little more than a shoestring, using credit advanced by the supply companies, demanding advance payments or cash on delivery from dealers, and financing expansion through reinvestment of profits. The Ford Motor Car Co. started business with a capital of $28,000, the Hudson Motor Car Co. with considerably less. Very little actual manufacturing was done by many of these early companies; their function was to buy the parts ready-made, assemble them, and sell the resultant vehicles as quickly as possible.

Mortality among the automobile firms was high. The tremendous profits realized by a few companies gave rise to many promotional ventures, based largely on hopes and extravagant claims, and a number of companies capitalized at many millions of dollars sprang into the picture, only to crash and disappear. As a result of the fierce competition in the industry, of the well over two thousand makes of vehicles that at one time or another were driven over America's roads, only a handful remained by the 1950's, with the market dominated by the Big Three—General Motors, Ford and Chrysler.

During the early years, the industry was wracked by a lengthy court battle over the Selden patent. In 1879, George B. Selden of Rochester, N. Y., filed application for a patent on a gasoline-propelled vehicle, but purposely kept the matter pending so that the patent was not granted until 1895. Rights under the patent were obtained by the Electric Vehicle Co., which had suffered serious financial reverses in attempting to operate a fleet of electric taxicabs in New York City. This company promptly filed infringement proceedings. Almost all the industry capitulated, forming themselves into the Association of Licensed Automobile Manufacturers. Henry Ford led the fight in opposition. After eight years of litigation, an appellate court ruled that while the patent was valid, it was not being infringed and therefore was not enforceable.

The principal effect of the protracted court battles over the Selden patent was to give the automobile companies a healthy fear of patent litigation, thus laying the groundwork for the cross-licensing agreement which has kept the automobile industry almost free of the patent difficulties that have plagued so many other lines of enterprise.

Despite the ups and downs occasioned by recessions, depressions and war, the long-range curve of American automobile production has been steadily upward. Total vehicle production, including cars, trucks and buses, reached and passed the million-per-year mark in 1916; surpassed two million in 1920; jumped to four million in 1923; dropped off to less than a million during World War II; and hit an all-time high of more than nine million vehicles (with a wholesale value of well over $14,000,000,000) in 1955.

Installment buying, liberal allowances on cars traded in, and the used-car market made individual transportation a possibility for families in even the lower-income brackets. Car ownership became a powerful prestige influence for some and a vital necessity for many, as population trends showed a shift to suburbia and exurbia from downtown and rural areas. Special taxation of the motor vehicle, especially the gasoline tax, provided a vast reservoir of funds for road building. At the turn of the century, America had the poorest roads of any civilized country; during the '20's, vast outlays on highway building brought it to the forefront. But good roads encouraged greater car ownership; traffic demands have almost invariably been far in advance of the facilities provided.

In the late 1950's, special taxation of the motor vehicle was approaching the ten-billion-dollar mark; but even the huge increase in road building, spark-plugged by the historic Federal Highway Act of 1956, offered only a catching up with, rather than a solution of, the monumental traffic problems resulting from the astronomic increases in car ownership and use.

By 1959, there were almost 70,000,000 vehicles registered, of which some 60,000,000 were passenger cars, the remainder trucks and buses. Forecasts for 1975 pointed to a hundred million vehicles or more, running up a total of a trillion vehicle-miles of travel annually.

During the 1950's, cars offered by the Big Three became lower, longer, more powerful and speedy and a great deal more expensive. This trend suddenly was reversed late in the decade. Having dominated world markets since 1920 or thereabouts, American makers saw first a trickle and then a flood of foreign imports. By 1950, imports accounted for 10% of all United States car sales. And a domestic economy-make—the Nash Rambler—rose to take fourth position among all types in that same year.

While continuing production of practically all their former models, United States manufacturers met this new challenge with introduction of "compact" economy cars of their own: Ford with its low-priced Falcon, Chevrolet with Corvair and Chrysler with Valiant were the earliest.

Throughout all these competitive efforts over the years, it is clear that the individual mobility brought about by the ownership of private passenger cars has wrought great changes in the American way of life. The full extent awaits evaluation by future social historians. A few may now be noted. First of all, it drove the horse from the highway, wrecking the fifty-million-dollar carriage-and-buggy industry in the process.

More than any other single factor, the automobile has broken down sectional differences. It has almost obliterated the former antagonism between the city-dweller and the farmer, while giving rise to a new suburban way of life. Shopping centers and drive-in facilities, ranging from movies to banks, tailor shops, flower stores and even churches, are outward manifestations of a profound change in American patterns of life that the automobile has brought about. Over a long period of years, the trend of population has been away from rural areas to metropolitan centers and most of the resettlement has been in suburban sections. The tremendous growth of suburbia in America would have been impossible without the freedom of movement provided by the motor car.

The explosive growth in population along with the growing desire to live in suburbia or exurbia has brought with it a whole host of new problems. In 1956, the nation embarked upon a new and greatly expanded program of building highways that would serve both rural and urban traffic. Questions as to mass transportation became ever more acute. Traffic fatalities hovered around 40,000 a year.

The beginning of the 1960's found the United States the most highly motorized nation in the world.

Automobile Racing. From the very earliest times, there was competition among the various makes of cars. Some sought for pre-eminence in speed, others in reliability over long distances and bad roads, some in hill-climbing ability. Much later, ability to accelerate to a high speed in a short period of time became a criterion.

America's first road race, held in the late fall of 1895, was won by a Duryea car at an average speed over the whole distance of something less than 6 mph. Alexander Winton brought out a car that won many records, but was soon defeated by Henry Ford's famous "999," named after a high-speed railroad locomotive, and piloted by cigar-chewing Barney Oldfield, a converted bicycle-racer.

The American Automobile Association from 1904 to 1913 conducted a number of reliability runs known as the Glidden Tours because of the handsome trophy awarded the winner by Charles J. Glidden, an early motoring enthusiast who had made a comfortable fortune in the telephone business. These reliability runs contributed greatly to the acceptance of the American automobile as a dependable vehicle capable of all-weather operation over the terrible roads of that time.

The most glamorous of the early competitions were the road races for the Vanderbilt Cup, started in 1904, usually won by Europeans over a special course in Long Island. The last race for the Vanderbilt Cup was run at Santa Monica, Calif., in 1916, and road racing virtually disappeared from the American scene although remaining popular abroad.

Many closed-circuit tracks sprang up around the country. Some were made of planks with high-banked curves to permit high speeds. Dirt-track racing became a feature at county fairs. Hill-climbing was popular for a while but disappeared except for the annual scramble up Pike's Peak. In later years, midgets, stock cars and sports cars competed in many places throughout the country. But the top feature of the auto-racing world has for many years been the Memorial Day 500-mile classic at the Indianapolis Speedway.

This 2½-mile track was built in 1908 by four Indianapolis business men; two years later, the track was surfaced with brick. The first 500-mile race, held in 1911, was won by Ray Harroun in a Marmon Wasp. It has been repeated each year since, except in wartime, attracting near-capacity crowds to the "Brickyard" and setting higher and higher speed averages which hovered around the 130 mph mark by the close of the 1950's.

Meanwhile on straightaway courses efforts were made to set high-speed records over various distances with the measured mile being the main objective. In 1904 Henry Ford hit over 90 mph on—of all places—a frozen lake. Two years later, a Stanley Steamer broke the 100 mph mark, being clocked at close to 128 mph. For years these races against time were staged on the sands of Daytona Beach, Fla. Later they were held on the Bonneville salt flats which at certain times of the year offer ideal high-speed conditions. The world's record of just under 400 mph—officially 394.196 mph—was established by John Cobb in a Railton Mobil Special on the salt in 1947.

Organized auto racing and time trials through the years were sanctioned and supervised by the American Automobile Association. In 1955, A. A. A. withdrew and these responsibilities were taken over by the newly-organized U. S. Automobile Club.

Following World War II a different type of competition sprang up—drag racing by hot-rodders. Here the big idea was maximum acceleration over a short distance in cars on which youthful enthusiasts had spent a great deal of time and a substantial amount of money. Early drags were held on public roads and streets which gave the hot-rodders a bad name; later their competitions were held on special off-highway drag strips, and the hottest of the jobs competed annually on the Bonneville salt flats.

Sports Cars. Interest in sports cars in the United States, beginning somewhat tentatively in the 1930's, flourished after World War II. A sports car is difficult to define; in general it is a car capable of more-than-ordinary highway performance but not specifically engineered for racing purposes. A number of organizations of sports-car owners have evolved, the principal one being the Sports Car Club of America, under whose aegis many competitions have been held. Speed contests have been held on roads especially closed for the purpose (as in the early days of motoring); subsequently they moved to closed circuits on little-used airports; and in the late 1950's were concentrated on specially-designed tracks suitable for car competitions of varying classes. Most of the sports cars were of foreign manufac-

ture. Domestic manufacturers attempted to meet this challenge with the Ford Thunderbird and the Chevrolet Corvette. At the close of the 1950's, the S. C. C. A. had branches in all parts of the United States and more than 10,000 members.

AVIATION, the art and science of operating heavier-than-air aircraft, began in the United States. Serious interest in the problem of mechanical flight was aroused in this country by the experiments of Octave Chanute with gliders and of Samuel P. Langley, third secretary of the Smithsonian Institution, with power models during the decade 1890–1900. Two attempts by Langley to fly a full-sized man-carrying machine in October and December, 1903, ended in failure and brought public derision to the luckless scientist. Nine days after Langley's second disaster, the first powered flights were achieved on Dec. 17, 1903, by Wilbur and Orville Wright, of Dayton, O., on the flat sand at Kill Devil Hill, near Kitty Hawk, N. C. The world paid far less attention to the success of the Wrights than to the failures of the many who had attempted flight.

Nothing daunted, the Wrights continued to perfect their airplane and gain skill as flyers. In 1904 they flew the first full circle and figure eights; in 1905, they flew continuously 24 miles in 38 min. 3 sec. Also in 1905, they offered their invention to the U. S. Government "for use in war." The War Department was not interested and they went abroad, hoping to interest foreign governments, but had little more success than at home. By 1908, the climate had changed in view of ominous political developments, and the Wrights obtained a contract for demonstration flights and the sale of an airplane with a French syndicate and with the U. S. Signal Corps. These public flights on two continents instantaneously changed the entire outlook for aviation. The Wrights were acclaimed as the conquerors of the air and made further demonstration flights in 1909 at Rome and Berlin.

The impetus to aviation was nearly as great in the United States as in Europe, although in America, after a brave start with the purchase of the world's first military airplane, military flying lagged behind flying by civilians. In 1908 Glenn H. Curtiss and Glenn L. Martin both came out with biplanes of their own design and before many months entered the airplane manufacturing business. The Wrights, who had obtained broad patents covering the basic principles of airplane control, in 1909 formed the Wright Co. to defend their patent claims as well as to manufacture airplanes and manage their exhibition business. Glenn Martin voluntarily sought and readily obtained a license from the Wright Co., but this Curtiss and others declined to do. As a result, American aviation found itself bogged down in a protracted patent war which divided manufacturers and flyers into the Wright camp and the

Curtiss camp. The record shows that the Wright claims were substantially upheld in all the actions in the American courts. This fact in no way detracts from the great contributions made to aviation by Glenn Curtiss who, on Aug. 29, 1909, won for America the Gordon Bennett speed race during the first International Air Meet at Rheims, France; then, in May, 1910, he captured the Pulitzer prize for his 142-mile flight between Albany and New York; and, in 1913, was awarded the Langley Medal for the "hydro-aeroplane" he had developed in 1911.

The early period of aviation was marked by exhibition flights by individual flyers or by teams who performed at county fairs and elsewhere across the country. Great verve and daring were evident as new speed, altitude, and endurance records followed one another in rapid succession. Acrobatic flying was the rage, and men like Beachey, Hoxsey, Johnstone, and Ely won immortality—and found death—practicing the new art. A few flyers, among them the handful of military and naval aviators—Lahm, Foulois, Milling, and Arnold of the Army, and Ellyson, Towers, and Bellinger of the Navy, for example—concentrated on developing the serious potentialities of the airplane (and of those named, all but Ellyson survived the pioneering days by many years). With little interest or support from their superiors in either service, flying officers pushed ahead with practice bomb-dropping, reconnaissance, night flying, ground-to-air and air-to-ground wireless telegraphy, and the firing of a machine gun from the air; soon there were maneuvers with ground troops in mock combat and with naval forces at sea.

For all the devotion, ingenuity, and sacrifice of its service flyers, the United States nevertheless found itself unprepared in the air when World War I came. Although designs were improving and the promise of future commercial operation was great, aircraft manufacturers were still catering largely to the demands of wealthy sportsmen seeking, for the most part, expensive, speedy, and dangerous playthings. In other countries, governments were realizing the importance of the airplane and, as the war approached, were spending larger amounts for aerodynamic research and for procurement. Though aviation had begun in America with the breakthrough of the Wrights, the United States by 1914 was well behind Britain, France, Germany, Russia, and Italy.

Although observation planes had been used by the Army on the Mexican border in 1916, it was almost literally true that, as one Army flyer put it, "not a single air officer in Washington had even seen a fighting plane" when the United States went to war in 1917. The Air Service was woefully short of trained pilots, had only one organized and equipped squadron, and under 250 airplanes, none of them combatworthy by European standards. From such an unimpressive beginning, the Army Air Service underwent a phenomenal change. By the end of the war, there were assigned at the fighting fronts 45 squadrons, 767 pilots, 481 observers, and 23 aerial gunners, to say nothing of ground crews. The whole Air Service numbered 20,000 officers and 170,000 men. American pilots shot down 781 enemy planes officially credited for a loss of 289 American craft. The performance of American naval aviation was equally creditable, with more than 500 planes operating in various areas of northwest Europe. Perhaps the greatest American technical accomplishment of the war was the development of the famed Liberty engine. A more lasting achievement was the creation of a generation of aviation leaders among whom Brig. Gen. William Mitchell and Admiral William S. Sims were perhaps the most outstandingly enthusiastic in voicing their belief of the future domination of the airplane in war.

With the Armistice and the return of the squadrons from France, a good measure of the old apathy returned as well. There was still nothing that could be called commercial air transport. The military services, reduced in manpower and budget, fell back on spectacular accomplishments to keep up their spirits and the mettle of their flyers. In 1919 the Navy achieved the first airplane crossing of the Atlantic with the flight of the NC-4's. In 1924, the Army staged the first round-the-world flight which took a total of 175 days, of which 15 days 11 hours were actually spent in the air. The culminating event of the 1920's and, after the first Wright flight, probably the most important single event of aviation history was the 33-hour non-stop solo flight of Charles A. Lindbergh from New York to Paris, on May 20-21, 1927. The Lindbergh flight must be credited with sparking the development of commercial flying, for the feat was a triumph not only of imagination and courage but of technology which proved the reliability of the monoplane configuration and of the radial air-cooled engine. After the flight, aviation could command capital as it never could before.

If the Lindbergh flight was the spark of commercial aviation, the bedrock underlying its development was the Kelly Act of 1925, the Air Mail Law, which offered the possibility that commercial flying could be done with profit. Many of the airlines and aircraft manufacturing companies of today trace their beginnings to the Kelly Act and to the Air Corps Act of 1926 which, under an enlightened purchase program, promised the aircraft industry a sound basis for expansion. Through the National Advisory Committee for Aeronautics, with its wind-tunnels and other test facilities and its cadre of scientific personnel, the partnership of airlines, the aircraft industry, and the military and naval air services were assured of strong technological support for the great expansion that lay ahead.

The advent of larger airplanes, capable of carrying greater payloads at lower rates, was in large measure the result of the emergence of the all-metal low-wing monoplane with internally braced thick wings and of such reliable engines as the Whirlwind, the Wasp, and the Cyclone. With this combination of airframe and powerplant, multi-engine aircraft which offered speed, safety, and economy became a reality. The Douglas DC-3 is the classical example of the kind of airplane that made modern commercial flying truly possible.

The vast developments of World War II and of the fantastic post-war period cannot be described in such brief compass as the present article. All this progress has been due largely to new technological advances in which the United States led the world before 1936. From that date until the war was well advanced, America was probably a good deal behind Britain and Germany, each of which seized upon the potentiality of reaction or jet engines before this country. As for rocket power, it was an American, Robert H. Goddard, who pioneered this development as the Wrights pioneered the airplane, but his work was little appreciated in the United States until after the Germans and then the Russians had gained a serious scientific advantage. For the future of aviation in the form of manned space flight, with its need for safe and economical means of exit from and re-entry of the atmosphere, the fruitful combination may yet well be the rocket or reaction engine with the aerodynamic or airplane-type vehicle, rather than the projectile or missile type.

AXES, FRONTIER. From the early contacts of Europeans with Indians in the 15th century, through all periods of fur trade and other commerce, the Indian demanded and received the iron axe and hatchet. The French in the 17th century distributed great numbers of axes with light polls and long blades, a type known as the French trade axe. Records show, however, that Holland and England both supplied this same "Biscay" hatchet. The tree-felling axe brought by Frenchmen for their own use was a large counterpart of the popular trade axe, with heavy blade and light poll. The axe taken to Jamestown and Plymouth differed little from that of the French, but before a century had passed, there had developed from this British tool a better-balanced Anglo-American implement with lengthened poll and somewhat shortened blade. Before 1776 American makers had developed the characteristic American axe with heavy squared poll that outweighed the bit, a tool unknown in other parts of the world. The Indian, however, refused to recognize the greater efficiency of this new axe and as long as frontier relationships endured the "French trade axe" persisted.

AYLLON, EXPEDITIONS OF. In 1521 Vasquez de Ayllon sent from the West Indies an exploring expedition which visited the present Carolina coast, returning therefrom with a number of captured natives. In 1526 de Ayllon sailed in three caravels with 600 prospective settlers, Negro slaves, scores of horses and orders to seek the ever-elusive Northwest Passage. The name of his settlement, San Miguel de Gualdape, is recorded, but its site has yet to be determined, some scholars having placed it south of Cape Hatteras, while others have placed it within the Chesapeake, either on the James or the Potomac. Since the most extended account refers to severe cold, acceptance thereof would point to the more northerly site. The Spaniards suffered all the ills subsequently endured by the English at Jamestown in the form of malarial fevers, dissensions and Indian assaults. The settlement was abandoned and the survivors returned to the West Indies.

BACON'S REBELLION was a revolt in Virginia in 1676 led by Nathaniel Bacon, Jr., a young planter, against the aged royal governor, Sir William Berkeley. The revolt has, since the time of the American Revolution, usually been interpreted as an attempt at political reform directed against the allegedly oppressive rule of the governor. Recent scholarship has questioned this thesis and emphasized the controversy over Indian policy, over which Berkeley and Bacon disagreed, as a fundamental cause of rather than a pretext for, the rebellion. When Indian depredations occurred on the northern and western frontiers in the fall of 1675 and spring of 1676, Bacon demanded the right to lead volunteers against all Indians, even those living peacefully within the colony, in retaliation. Governor Berkeley, fearing unjust dispossession and slaughter of the friendly Indians, refused. Bacon ignored the Governor's restriction and led volunteers to the southern frontier in May, 1676, where he slaughtered and plundered the friendly Occaneechee Indians. When the Governor attempted to call him to account, Bacon marched to Jamestown and, at gunpoint, forced the Assembly of June, 1676, to grant him formal authority to fight the Indian war, which he then prosecuted against another friendly tribe, the Pamunkeys. When Governor Berkeley attempted to raise forces to reestablish his own authority, Bacon turned on the Governor with his volunteers. Civil war ensued. Berkeley was driven to the eastern shore of Virginia. Jamestown, the capital, was burned. For a few months Bacon's word was law on the mainland. But suddenly, in October, 1676, he died. Berkeley, having recruited forces on the eastern shore, returned to the mainland, defeated the remaining rebels, and, by February, 1677, re-established his authority. Soon thereafter 1,000 troops, sent by Charles II to suppress the rebellion, arrived, accompanied by commissioners to investigate its causes. Berkeley's strict policy toward the defeated rebels was severely censured by the commissioners who attempted to remove him from the governorship. Berkeley returned to England in May, 1677, to justify himself but died July 9, 1677, before seeing the King.

79

BAD AXE, BATTLE OF (Aug. 2, 1832). The Sauk and Fox Indians, dissatisfied with lands to which the Federal Government had moved them, recrossed the Mississippi in April, 1832, and, under the leadership of Black Hawk, revolted against the whites. They were finally penned up against the Mississippi River at the mouth of the Bad Axe River, midway between Prairie du Chien and La Crosse, Wis., and there completely defeated by an American force of 400 regular infantry and 900 militia, commanded by Gen. Henry Atkinson.

BADLANDS OF SOUTH DAKOTA were created by precipitation of volcanic ash, sand and Fuller's earth, perhaps borne by wind, from eruptions in the Far Northwest which buried several hundred square miles more than 300 feet in depth. Water erosion carved this material into many fantastic forms. The precipitation engulfed vast herds of antediluvian monsters where they were feeding in the swamps, the remains of which were later exposed by erosion. The Federal Government has established the region as "The Badlands National Monument" and has built a system of highways into the more scenic regions of the park. The Badlands were discovered by fur traders early in the 19th century and for more than 100 years scientific societies, museums and educational institutions have been busily engaged in unearthing the paleontological treasures, so long entombed.

BAILEY v. DREXEL FURNITURE COMPANY (259 U. S. 20) was a case in which the U. S. Supreme Court (1922) invalidated an act of Congress (1919) levying a tax of 10% upon the net profits of business concerns employing children under the age of sixteen. The Supreme Court held that the measure was not a valid exercise of the taxing power, since it was an attempt to bring under congressional control matters whose regulation belongs solely to the states.

BALANCE OF TRADE. Following the mercantilistic tradition, an excess of merchandise exports over imports is usually called a "favorable" balance of trade, and the reverse an "unfavorable" balance, the original assumption being that the difference was paid in specie, the acquisition of which made a nation economically strong. This theory is fallacious but persistent. It confuses money with wealth and is incompatible with any demand-and-supply theory of the value of money. It leaves out of consideration all "invisible" items like capital loans, shipping charges, tourist expenditures, immigrant remittances and interest payments. Inclusion of these is necessary to calculate the more significant balance of international payments. In the long run the value of the wealth (including bullion) and services flowing out of a country tends to equal that of those flowing in except for excesses of bad debts or other losses in one direction or the other.

The American colonies had an "unfavorable" balance of trade because they were a new country and the settlers were constantly buying on credit or depending on England for capital for new undertakings. Mercantilistic England encouraged our extractive industries and discouraged manufacturing. In 1770 the colonies south of Pennsylvania had a nearly even trade balance with England; Pennsylvania and those north imported eight times as much from England as they exported to her, making up the difference largely by a very "favorable" trade balance with the West Indies and by their carrying business.

After the Revolution we still wanted English manufactures but found difficulty paying for them because England's markets were closed to many of our products and trade with the British West Indies was illegal. The new trade to China, treaties with Prussia and Sweden and finally Jay's Treaty improved matters a little, but the development of cotton growing and the outbreak in 1793 of what soon became the Napoleonic wars helped much more. Both France and England bought heavily of our agricultural products and made increasing use of our shipping services. Between 1790 and 1807 our merchant marine engaged in foreign trade tripled. After 1806 England took successful steps to stop our commercial growth and from this the War of 1812 developed. Following the war foreign manufactured goods flooded our markets and hurt our infant industries. Protection sentiment increased, producing progressively higher tariffs in 1816, 1824 and 1828. Thereafter rates fell (except in 1842). Higher tariffs here and abroad, a post-war depression and the greater interest in developing the West all cut down the rate of growth of our foreign commerce and its relative importance to domestic commerce. Foreign trade picked up after 1830. Europeans, particularly the English, invested approximately $250,-000,000, much of it in our internal improvements. This ended abruptly with the Panic of 1837 and defalcation by several states. Between 1838 and 1849 our trade balance was slightly "favorable." During the 1850's both imports and exports (notably cotton) expanded rapidly until the Civil War. Foreign trade declined during the war because of the Northern blockade and activity of the Southern cruisers.

During the prosperity following the war our foreign trade grew from $405,000,000 in 1865 to $1,164,000,-000 in 1873. The Homestead Act, wars in Europe, immigration, railroad building and increasing use of agricultural machinery caused a rise in food exports. A five-year depression began in 1873. In 1874 our trade balance again became "favorable," largely because interest payments on foreign capital here exceeded new foreign investments. The annual balance has been "favorable" with minor exceptions since 1876. A great expansion of foreign trade began after 1897. Then our capital loans abroad grew nearly as fast as foreign loans to us. Tourist expenditures and immigrant remittances became important.

During World War I we supplied the Allies with enormous quantities of food and war materials. Between July 1, 1914, and Dec. 31, 1919, our trade balance was "favorable" by $18,600,000,000, $4,000,-000,000 being paid in specie, $2,600,000,000 in returned securities, and the balance in capital loans, three-quarters governmental. In 1916 we ceased being a debtor nation and became a creditor.

The 1920's were a prosperous era. Since our high tariffs made imports difficult, the only way to continue to sell abroad was to make heavy loans. We loaned $12,000,000,000 during the decade, while foreigners invested $7,000,000,000 here. Of course a loss occurred from scaling down the war debts. Notable borrowers were Latin-American nations whose prospects were sometimes too optimistically regarded, and Germany, who was thereby helped to pay reparations to the Allies, who in turn were able to pay us on their war debts. Then came the crash of 1929. Numerous Latin-American nations, largely dependent on the marketing of one or two commodities, defaulted. Our loans to Germany declined, and after the Hoover moratorium in 1931 Germany ceased paying reparations and the Allies gradually stopped paying their debts. Losses on foreign investments, however, were no greater proportionately than on domestic ones.

Foreign trade improved after 1933. Devaluation of the dollar stimulated exports and greatly increased our large stock of gold. Since 1934 numerous reciprocal trade treaties have lowered our tariff walls substantially and encouraged the flow of trade. This is desirable for many reasons, one being to help our debtors pay us. After a nation has been a creditor for some time it should usually receive back annually more in interest and returned principal than it makes in new loans. Yet because of huge foreign-aid programs, the United States was long unable to achieve this preferable "unfavorable" trade balance. Between 1942 and 1945 merchandise imports were triple the merchandise exports. Nevertheless the exports represented Lend-Lease in large part or virtual "gifts" whereas a substantial part of the imports represented loans to us. Consequently for a brief time at the end of World War II the United States was again a "debtor" nation. When an excess of merchandise imports at last appeared in 1959, critics attributed it to high American labor costs, high foreign tariffs and unduly generous American aid programs. One thing is more than ever clear, in this age it is increasingly futile to analyze merchandise exports and imports without reference to the other items in the balance of international payments.

BALLINGER-PINCHOT CONTROVERSY (1909–11) was a bitter contention over the conservation of natural resources. Early in the Taft administration an order of former President Roosevelt withdrawing from sale certain public lands containing water power sites in Montana and Wyoming was cancelled. Chief Forester Gifford Pinchot protested and publicly charged Secretary of the Interior Richard A. Ballinger with favoritism toward corporations seeking water power sites. Pinchot defended L. R. Glavis, Land Office investigator, dismissed for accusing Ballinger of favoring the Cunningham syndicate's claims to valuable Alaskan mineral lands. Pinchot likewise was dismissed. A joint congressional investigating committee exonerated Ballinger. But failing to regain public confidence, Ballinger resigned.

BALL'S BLUFF, BATTLE OF (Oct. 21, 1861). Inconsequential as a military affair, this engagement along the Potomac near Washington, D. C. had important results. Col. E. D. Baker (U.), Senator from Oregon, a personal friend of President Lincoln, was killed; the Union troops, through mismanagement, were defeated. Discontented Radicals and a critical public blamed McClellan (U.). Congress inaugurated the Committee on the Conduct of the War to investigate Ball's Bluff and other Union failures. McClellan, on orders from the Secretary of War, arrested Gen. C. P. Stone (U.), charged with responsibility both for the defeat and for Baker's death. No formal charges were ever made. After six months' imprisonment Stone was released by a special provision in the Confiscation Act, July 17, 1862. The Army of the Potomac (U.) questioned their leader's ability. "A fatal hesitation took possession" of McClellan. A movement against Richmond was deferred pending further preparation.

BALTIMORE, MD. Baltimore was founded in 1729 at the fall line of the piedmont area of Maryland and on the Patapsco River, a deep-water estuary of the Chesapeake Bay. It was chartered as a tobacco port, but the first cargo exported some ten years later consisted of flour. The availability of water power and the proximity of grain lands led to the development of the port for grain exports. Later in the 18th century an iron works was added, and shipyards were built.

The city's history is epitomized in these early years. Grain, tobacco and other bulk exports (including coal) continue to this day. Light industry and commerce have thrived. Shipbuilding reached an historic zenith in the early 19th century, with the development of the Baltimore Clipper, a speedy and rakish sailing vessel; and the city's shipbuilding industry has had solid, if less romantic, achievements in constructing 20th-century merchant ships. In the early 19th century the city took the lead in constructing the Baltimore and Ohio Railroad, from Baltimore toward the Ohio River, as its answer to the competition from the Erie Canal. During the late 19th and 20th centuries the great factor in the port's success has been its relative proximity to the Middle West, as compared with other East Coast ports; the resulting "freight differential" has kept Baltimore's port a leader in the export of bulk cargoes. A thriving jobbing business with customers in the southern part of the country built up the commercial life of the city after the Civil War.

In the 1790 census the city had 13,501 inhabitants; by 1830, 80,620; by 1960, 939,024, which meant that Baltimore was the sixth biggest city in the United States.

The city took an active part in the War of 1812. Privateers from Baltimore plagued British shipping. In September, 1814, in retaliation, the British force which had burned Washington attempted to capture Baltimore. The invaders were repulsed in the land battle of North Point on Sept. 12, 1814, and on the following day a British approach by water inspired Francis Scott Key to write "The Star Spangled Banner."

Four of the great cultural institutions in Baltimore stemmed from gifts by four merchants. They are the Enoch Pratt Library, the (George) Peabody Institute, the (William T.) Walters Art Gallery, and The Johns Hopkins University and Hospital.

A devastating fire in 1904 destroyed about 140 acres of the downtown area. The business section was rapidly rebuilt and modernized, and about the same time other vital improvements were made in the water supply, sewer system, and streets.

BALTIMORE CLIPPER was a term applied to the fast topsail schooners developed in and around the Chesapeake Bay in the Revolutionary period and (later) to the square-rigged vessels having the same general lines which were built in the Chesapeake region. In post-Revolutionary days they came into general notice largely because their speed enabled them to be used effectively both in privateering and in the slave trade. *Ann McKim* (1833) was the ultimate expression of the type and by some is regarded as the link between the Baltimore clipper and the clipper ship. Her length (143 feet) was great by prevailing standards compared to her beam (31 feet). She had the characteristic Baltimore clipper drag in that she drew eleven feet forward and seventeen aft. Her stem was sharp but her greatest beam was so far forward that she was bluffer bowed than the later clipper ship. Her freeboard was low and her carrying capacity was small and hence she was primarily a speed model. The three masts were tall and light with a sharp rake, but she was ship-rigged with courses, topsails, topgallant sails and royals on each mast.

BANDITS, OLD-TIME. Highway robbery was comparatively rare before 1800, and usually consisted of the holdup of a traveler or a late walker by a solitary rough; the professional bandit was unknown. After 1800, holdups of mail coaches and post riders took place occasionally, sometimes with violence. A mail carrier was killed in Illinois in 1810 and a stagecoach driver near Baltimore in 1830. In the Middle West there were river pirates such as those of Cave-in Rock, and between 1795 and 1800 the Harpe brothers in Kentucky, and a little later the murderous

John A. Murrell in the same region—he was one of those who robbed travelers along the Natchez Trace—were much feared. The Gold Rush brought the scum of all the Western Hemisphere and Australia to California, and from 1850 on, robbery of stagecoaches, mounted express messengers and others was common. With the opening of the Idaho gold mines in 1860, robbery began there and developed into a virtual reign of terror. From there, some of the outlaws moved to the new Montana gold mines in 1863, where they robbed and murdered until virtually eliminated by Vigilantes two years later. In the 1860's and 1870's robbery was a commonplace in California, among the widely scattered Nevada mining camps, and in the Sierra Nevada passes. "Shotgun messengers," cool and deadly marksmen, rode on stagecoaches beside the drivers, to protect express and mail, and there were some hot battles between them and the brigands. The opening of the Black Hills gold mines in 1876 launched another era of robbery, in which Sam Bass earned a reputation which he later enhanced by train robbery in Texas.

East of the Mississippi banditry was a minor evil before the Civil War (1861–65), money being handled casually by express with little thought of danger; but a wave of lawlessness followed the war. A party of amateur robbers concealed themselves in a supposedly locked express car leaving New York on a January night in 1866, and decamped from it in Connecticut with $700,000 in cash, bonds and jewels. The first train holdup of record was perpetrated Oct. 6, 1866, in southern Indiana by the four Reno brothers, who had drifted into crime during the war. They and their gang continued these attacks, thus becoming the first organized band of train robbers in history. Train robbery next appeared in western Tennessee and Kentucky and in Nevada; and in 1873 the James-Younger gang took to it. The career of this band continued for ten years thereafter, or until Jesse James' death in 1883. They were succeeded in that region by the Daltons, whose career was finally ended in their attempted robbery of the banks at Coffeyville, Kans., Oct. 5, 1892, when two Dalton brothers and two others of the gang were killed and another Dalton captured. Bill Doolin carried on a remnant of the gang for three years thereafter. During the 1880's the Southwest swarmed with bandits and rough characters; stage and train robberies were numerous, even cowboys and townsmen of hitherto honest record sometimes taking to crime. Rube Burrow, a farm hand, was one who attained great notoriety as a train robber in Texas, Mississippi and Alabama, 1886–91, his career being ended by death. Around the end of the century the Hole-in-the-Wall gang, from an impregnable lair in the Wyoming mountains, harassed the Union Pacific Railroad. Dynamiting of express cars held by stubborn messengers began. During the decade 1890–99, the *Express Gazette* said that there had been 261 train robberies, in which 88 persons were killed and 86 wounded. Express cars now began to be built of heavier steel, carrying massive built-in safes, with time locks or combinations known only at terminals. "Arsenal cars," guarded by squads of heavily armed men, began running on important routes. Through these measures train robbery became more difficult and gradually less common.

BANK FAILURES. American financial history down to 1934 was characterized by an appalling number of bank failures, because the majority of banks were local enterprises, not regional or national institutions with numerous branches. Lax state government regulations and inadequate examinations permitted many banks to pursue unsound practices. With most financial eggs in local economic baskets it took only a serious crop failure or a business recession to precipitate dozens or even hundreds of bank failures. On the whole, state-chartered banks had a particularly poor record.

At the outset of the 19th century inability of a bank to redeem its notes in specie might cause it embarrassment, and later on states imposed penalties for this, but it did not automatically signify failure. The first bank to fail was the Farmers' Exchange Bank of Glocester, Rhode Island, in 1809. The statistics of bank failures between 1789 and 1863 are inadequate but the losses were unquestionably large. John Jay Knox estimated that the losses to note holders were 5% per annum. Bank notes were the chief money used by the general public. Not until after 1853 did banks' deposit liabilities exceed their note liabilities. During the 1830's to the 1850's weekly newssheets called *Bank Note Reporters* gave the latest discount quoted on the notes of weak and closed banks. Worthless bank notes were a risk that all businesses had to allow for. Although some states —such as New York in 1829 and 1838, Louisiana in 1842, or Indiana in 1834—established sound banking systems, banking as a whole was characterized by many failures.

The establishment of the National Banking System in 1863 introduced needed regulations for national (nationally chartered) banks. These were more numerous than state banks, down to 1891, and were larger on the average. But even their record left much to be desired. There were 515 national bank suspensions during the fifty years 1864–1913 and only two years passed without at least one suspension. State banks suffered 2491 failures in the same half century. The nation had 1532 banks in 1863 and 26,664 in 1913. The worst year was the panic year of 1893 with almost 500 bank failures. The establishment of the Federal Reserve System in 1913 did little to improve the record of national banks, all of whom had to join it. They suffered 825 failures between 1914 and 1929 and another 1947 failures by the end of 1933. In the same twenty years there were 12,714 state bank failures. By 1933 there were 14,771 banks in the United States, half as many as in 1920, and most of that half had disappeared by the failure route. During the 1920's Canada, employing a branch banking system, had only one failure. Half a dozen states had experimented with deposit insurance plans without success. Apparently the situation needed the attention of the Federal Government.

The bank holocaust of the early 1930's—9106 bank failures, 1947 of them national banks, in four years —culminating in a nationwide bank moratorium in March of 1933 at last produced the needed drastic reforms. In 1933 Congress forbade Federal Reserve member banks to pay interest on demand deposits and founded the Federal Deposit Insurance Corporation which it modified in 1935. Any commercial bank might join it by contributing annually $\frac{1}{12}$ of 1% of its average deposits. At the outset the F. D. I. C. insured each depositor in a bank up to $10,000, then in 1935 the figure was cut to $5000 and in 1950 it was raised again to $10,000. In recent years the F. D. I. C. has protected 97% of all banks and nearly half of all deposits. The number of bank failures fell to about fifty a year in the F. D. I. C.'s first ten years and to about five per year since. Between 1934 and 1957 depositors received partial if not complete protection in 436 of 550 bank failures. People of today are spared that traumatic experience of past generations, a "run on the bank" and the loss of a large part of their savings.

BANK NOTES have had wide use in the United States since the beginnings of the country. Prior to the introduction of national bank notes in 1863 the circulation consisted of state bank issues and notes of the United States banks (*see* Bank of the United States) during their chartered existences. Since 1866 state banks have been effectively prevented from issuing notes by a 10% Federal tax and, since 1913, Federal Reserve notes have assumed first place among bank-note issues of the country. Since 1935 the latter have been the only bank notes in general circulation.

BANK OF AUGUSTA v. EARLE, 1839 (13 Peters 519), involved the right of a Georgia bank to recover on a bill of exchange purchased in Alabama. The Supreme Court, speaking through Justice Taney, held that though a state might exclude the creature of another state, yet in the silence of any positive rule it would be presumed that foreign corporations were by comity permitted to make contracts. Taney's opinion became the leading authority on the law of foreign corporations.

BANK OF COMMERCE v. NEW YORK CITY, 1863 (2 Black 620). The Supreme Court held that the state could not tax capital invested in Federal securities— thereby strengthening the financial position of the Government in the midst of the Civil War.

BANK OF NORTH AMERICA, the country's first Government incorporated bank, was chartered by the Continental Congress in 1781 and commenced operations in Philadelphia on Jan. 7, 1782. Organized by Robert Morris, the bank supplied vital financial aid to the Government during the closing months of the American Revolution. Original depositors and stockholders included Thomas Jefferson, Alexander Hamilton, Benjamin Franklin, John Paul Jones, James Monroe, John Jay and Stephen Decatur.

BANK OF THE UNITED STATES, First and Second. An act incorporating the subscribers to the Bank of the United States was approved by Washington and became law on Feb. 25, 1791. Under the provisions of the law the bank, which was to be located in Philadelphia, was to have a capital of $10,000,000, composed of 25,000 shares of $400 par value. One fifth of the capital was subscribed by the Government, the rest by private investors. Private subscriptions were limited to 1000 shares, and no shareholder was to have more than 30 votes. Foreign shareholders were not permitted to vote by proxy.

The management of the bank was vested in a board of 25 directors, elected by the shareholders. The board of directors was authorized to elect a president who was to receive compensation, the directors serving without pay. Only American citizens might be directors of the bank.

The bank was empowered to carry on a commercial banking business, was not permitted to deal in commodities or real estate and was limited in the interest it might charge on loans to 6%. The bank was authorized to issue circulating notes up to $10,000,000, the amount of its capital.

The Bank of the United States opened its doors for business on Dec. 12, 1791. It was efficiently managed and furnished the country, through its main office and eight branches, with sound banking service throughout its chartered life of twenty years. The bank served satisfactorily as fiscal agent for the Government and exerted a salutary controlling influence on the note issues of the state banks by refusing to accept state bank notes that were not redeemable in specie. In spite of the manifest advantages of a national bank, the charter of the First Bank was not renewed in 1811, doubt as to its constitutionality being the controlling factor. The bank therefore wound up its affairs, eventually paying shareholders $434 on each share held.

After a brief and unsatisfactory period of state banking, the Second Bank of the United States was incorporated under a law of April 10, 1816. The charter provisions were similar to those of the First Bank except that the capital and note issue limits were increased to $35,000,000. The President of the United States was also authorized to appoint five of the 25 directors.

The Second Bank was badly managed under its first president, William Jones, who retired in 1819. Langdon Cheeves, who succeeded Jones, spent his administration in getting the bank back to a sound position. In 1823 Nicholas Biddle assumed the presidency, and from then until 1833 the bank was well and capably managed, extending sound banking service to the country through its main office and 25 branches.

A dispute between Biddle and President Jackson led to the withdrawal of Government deposits in 1833 and a severe contraction of the bank's business. Efforts to obtain a renewal of the Second Bank's charter proved futile and the institution ceased to function as a national bank upon the expiration of its charter in 1836.

BANK OF THE UNITED STATES v. PLANTERS' BANK OF GEORGIA (9 Wheaton 904). Chief Justice Marshall here (1824) enunciated the rule that a suit against a corporation chartered and partly owned by a state was not a suit against the state itself. "It is, we think, a sound principle that when a government becomes a partner in any trading company, it divests itself, so far as concerns the transactions of that company, of its sovereign character, and takes that of a private citizen." The rule was later applied to banks wholly owned by a state (Briscoe v. Bank of the Commonwealth of Kentucky, 11 Peters 257).

BANKING. The fundamental functions of a commercial bank in the last two centuries have been making loans, receiving deposits and lending its credit either in the form of bank notes or of "created" deposits. The banks in which people keep their checking accounts are commercial banks.

There were no commercial banks in colonial times, although there were loan offices or land banks, which made loans on real estate security with limited issues of legal tender notes.

Robert Morris founded the first commercial bank in the United States, the Bank of North America, chartered Dec. 31, 1781. It greatly assisted the financing of the closing stages of the Revolution. The second bank was the Bank of Massachusetts, chartered Feb. 7, 1784, the third was the Bank of New York which began without a charter June 9, 1784, and the fourth was the Bank of Maryland in 1790. By 1800 there were 28 state-chartered banks and by 1811 there were 88.

Alexander Hamilton's financial program included a central bank to serve as a financial agent of the Treasury, provide a depository for public money, and be a regulator of the currency. Accordingly the first Bank of the United States, the fifth chronologically, was founded Feb. 25, 1791, with a 20-year charter. It was also the nation's largest commercial bank. Its $10,000,000 capital (huge for that day) and favored relationship with the Government aroused much anxiety, especially among Jeffersonians. The Bank's sound but unpopular policy of promptly returning bank notes for redemption in specie and refusing those of non-specie-paying banks, together with a political feud, were largely responsible for the narrow defeat of its recharter bill in 1811. Stephen Girard bought the bank and building. Between 1811 and 1816 people and the Government were dependent on state banks whose numbers increased to 246 and whose note circulation quadrupled. Nearly all but the New England banks suspended specie payments in September, 1814, because of the war and their own unregulated credit expansion.

The country soon recognized the need for a new central bank and Congress established a second Bank of the United States, April 10, 1816, also with a 20-year charter. Its $35,000,000 capitalization and favored relationship with the Treasury likewise aroused anxiety. Instead of repairing the overexpanded credit situation that it inherited, it aggravated this by generous lending policies. These precipitated the Panic of 1819 in which it barely saved itself and incurred widespread ill will. Thereafter, under Nicholas Biddle, it was well run, but like its predecessor it aroused the enmity of state banks by constantly requiring them to redeem their notes in specie. This policy, President Jackson's prejudice against banks and monopolies, the memory of the 1819 panic, and Biddle's tactless decision to let rechartering be a main issue in the 1832 presidential election led to the Bank's demise. After Sept. 26, 1833, the Government placed all its deposits with the "pet banks" (politically selected state banks) until it set up the Independent Treasury System in the 1840's. Between 1830 and 1837 the number of banks, bank note circulation and bank loans all about tripled. Without the second Bank to regulate them, the banks overloaned to speculators in land. The Panic of 1837 resulted with specie payments suspended, many failures and a depression that lasted until 1844.

For thirty years (1833–63) the country was without an adequate regulator of bank currency. In some states the laws were very strict or banking was forbidden while in others the rules were lax. Banks made too many long term loans, especially on real estate, and they resorted to many subterfuges to avoid redeeming their notes in specie. Conditions were especially bad in parts of the Midwest and South where there was some "wildcat" banking. Such a bank would lend its notes at its town branches but would redeem in specie only at its main office hidden away in a remote spot where only wildcats abounded. This practice probably began in Michigan. Almost everywhere bank tellers and merchants had to consult weekly Banknote Reporters for the current discount on bank notes and turn to the latest Banknote Detectors to distinguish the hundreds of counterfeits and notes of failed banks. All this constituted an added business risk and necessitated somewhat higher mark-ups on merchandise. In this bleak era of banking, however, there were some bright spots. These were the Suffolk Banking System of Massachusetts (1819–56) which kept New England notes at par; the moderately successful Safety Fund (1829–66) and Free Banking (1838–66) systems of New York, the latter copied, but with less success in fourteen other states; the Indiana (1834–65), Ohio (1845–66), and Iowa (1858–65) systems; and the Louisiana Banking System (1842–62) which was the first to require a minimum per cent of specie reserve behind liabilities and insisted also that loans be short term. Inefficient and corrupt as some of the banking was before the Civil War, our expanding economy found it an improvement over the system of land banks, personal loans and long-time borrowing from merchants on which the 18th-century economy had depended.

Secretary of the Treasury Chase began agitating for an improved banking system in 1861, one important motive for which was his desire to widen the market for Government bonds. The National Currency Act creating the National Banking System was passed Feb. 25, 1863, and completely revised June 3, 1864. Its head officer was the Comptroller of Currency. It was based on several recent reforms, especially the Free Banking System's principle of bond-backed notes. But the reserve requirements for bank notes were high, the law forbade real estate loans and branch banking, it had stiff organization requirements and it imposed burdensome taxes. State banks at first saw little reason to join, but in 1865 Congress levied a prohibitive 10% tax on their bank notes, effective July 1, 1866, which drove most of these banks into the new system. There were 1644 national banks by Oct. 1, 1866, and they had to use the word "National" in their name. The use of checks had been increasing in popularity in the more settled regions long before the Civil War, and by 1853 the total of bank deposits exceeded that of bank notes. After 1865 the desire of all banks, both state and national, to avoid the various new restrictions on bank notes doubtless speeded up the shift to this more convenient form of bank credit. By the 1890's it was estimated that about 85% of all business transactions were settled by check payments. Since state banks were less restricted, their number increased again until it passed the national banks in 1894. Most large banks were national, however. Improvements in state banking laws began about 1887.

The National Banking System represented a substantial improvement over the pre-Civil War hodgepodge of banking systems. But it had three major faults and several minor ones. One major one was the perverse elasticity of the bond-secured bank notes whose supply did not vary in accordance with the needs of business. A second was the decentralization of bank deposit reserves. There were three classes of national banks, and the lesser ones kept part of their reserves in their own vaults and deposited the rest at interest with the larger national banks, especially with the New York City banks, and these in turn loaned a considerable part of the funds on the call money market to finance stock speculation. In times of uncertainty the lesser banks demanded their outside reserves, call money rates soared, security prices toboganned, and some good, as well as many weak banks were ruined by runs. The third major fault was that there was no central bank to take measures to forestall such crises or to lend to deserving banks in times of distress. Among the minor faults were a slow and cumbersome check collection system and inadequate use of commercial paper.

Four times, 1873, 1884, 1893 and 1907, panics highlighted the faults of the National Banking System. Improvised use of clearinghouse certificates in interbank settlements somewhat relieved money shortages in the first three cases; "voluntary" bank assessments collected and loaned by a committee headed by J. P. Morgan gave relief in 1907. After that, Congress passed the Aldrich-Vreeland Act to investigate foreign central banking systems and suggest reforms and to permit emergency bank note issues. The nation used these emergency issues on only one occasion when a panic occurred at the outbreak of World War I in August, 1914. The new law superimposed a central banking system on the existing national banking system. It required all national banks to "join" the new system which meant to buy stock in it immediately equal to 3% of their capital and surplus thus providing the funds with which to set up the Federal Reserve System. State banks might also join by meeting specified requirements but by the end of 1916 only 34 had done so. A majority of the nation's banks have always remained outside the Federal Reserve System although the larger banks have generally been members. The Federal Reserve System largely corrected the faults to which the National Banking System had been prey. Admittedly, the Federal Reserve had its faults and did not live up to expectations, especially in 1919–20, 1927–29, and after World War II. Nevertheless, the nation's commercial banks had a policy-directing head and a refuge in distress to a greater degree than they ever had before. The founding of the Federal Reserve System ended the need for the Independent Treasury System which finally wound up its affairs in 1921.

Between the establishment of the Federal Reserve System in 1914 and 1960, the commercial banking system has grown and changed as might be expected in a nation whose population has nearly doubled and whose real national income has quadrupled. The number of banks has declined from 27,864 to 13,998; the number of national banks, from 7518 to 4542. Bank failures, 1920–33, account for most of these declines, with mergers a minor reason. Demand de-posits have grown from $10,000,000,000 to $121,-000,000,000, and time deposits from $8,600,000,000 to $105,000,000,000. Loans grew from $15,500,000,-000 to $141,000,000,000, a ninefold increase, but investments rose from $5,700,000,000 to $88,600,-000,000, or nearly sixteenfold. In addition, every decade saw some other significant developments in commercial banking.

Few national banks gave up their charters for state ones in order to avoid having to join the Federal Reserve, but during World War I many state banks became members of the System: there were 1374 in it by 1920. All banks helped sell Liberty Bonds and bought Treasury bills between bond drives. As a result, their demand deposits doubled, which was the chief reason for a more than doubling of the price level by 1920.

By 1921 there were 31,076 banks, the all-time peak; many were small family-owned state banks. Every year local crop failures, or other disasters, or simply bad management wiped out several hundred of them. By 1929 there were 25,568 banks in all. Admittedly mergers eliminated a few names and the growth of branch, group or chain banking provided stability in some areas, the Bank of America in California being an outstanding example. But the 1920's are most remembered for stock market speculation. Numerous large banks, such as New York's National City and Chase National had a part in this chiefly through their investment affiliates which were essentially investment banks. The role of investment advisor gave banks great prestige until the Panic of 1929 when widespread disillusionment from losses and scandals brought them discredit.

The 1930's witnessed many reforms growing out of the 9000 bank failures between 1930 and 1933 and capped by the nationwide bank moratorium of March 6–9, 1933. To reform the commercial and central banking systems as well as to restore confidence in them, Congress passed two major banking laws, one on June 16, 1933, and the other on Aug. 23, 1935. These laws gave the Federal Reserve firmer control over the banking system, especially over the member banks. They set up the Federal Deposit Insurance Corporation to insure bank deposits and soon all but a few hundred small banks belonged to it. That greatly reduced the number of bank failures. Other changes included the banning of investment affiliates, prohibiting banks to pay interest on demand deposits, loosening restrictions against national banks having branches and making real estate loans, and giving the Federal Reserve Board the authority to raise, to as much as double, member bank legal reserve requirements against deposits. As a result of the depression the supply of commercial paper dwindled and interest rates fell sharply. Consequently banks invested more in Federal Government obligations, built up excess reserves and imposed service charges on checking accounts.

In World War II the banks once again helped sell war bonds. They also converted their excess reserves into Government obligations and increased their own holdings of these from $16,000,000,000 in 1940 to $84,000,000,000 in 1945. Demand deposits more than doubled. Owing to bank holdings of Government obligations virtually convertible into cash and to Federal Reserve commitments to the Treasury, the Federal Reserve had lost its power to curb bank-credit expansion. Price levels nearly doubled during the 1940's.

In 1951 the Federal Reserve regained its freedom to curb credit expansion and thereafter interest rates crept upwards. That improved bank profits and also led banks to reduce somewhat their holdings of Federal Government obligations. Term loans (5–10 years) to industry and real estate loans increased. Banks also encountered stiff competition from rapidly growing rivals such as savings and loan associations, personal finance companies and others. On July 28, 1959, Congress reduced the reserve requirements on deposits for national banks in larger cities and permitted banks to count cash in their vaults as part of their legal reserves.

In over 180 years commercial banks have come to serve the economy in several important ways. They provide a safe place in which to keep savings, they are an institution from which short term borrowers can usually borrow funds (thus savings do not lie idle and unproductive), and they supply the nation with most of its money. At first this was in the form of bank notes; in the past century it has been increasingly in the form of demand deposits subject to check. (*See also* Banks, Savings; Export-Import Bank; Federal Reserve System; Investment Banks; Savings and Loan Associations.)

BANKS, SAVINGS. The first savings bank in the United States was the Provident Institution for Savings in Boston which was chartered Dec. 13, 1816. The Philadelphia Savings Fund Society was chartered earlier, Dec. 2, 1816, but did not begin business until Feb. 25, 1819. Between 1816 and 1820 ten mutual savings banks were chartered, all in the Northeast, north of Virginia. By 1914 there were 634 mutual savings banks with nearly 8,000,000 depositors and $4,000,000,000 of savings. By the end of 1959 there were 518 of these banks in 17 states still chiefly in the Northeast, with $35,000,000,000 of deposits. Two thirds of these funds were invested in loans on real estate. Since 1935 mutual savings banks have been eligible for membership in the Federal Reserve System but very few have joined.

After the Civil War stock savings banks were organized in a number of states. Their number reached 1529 by mid-1915 and then declined to 341 in 1935 with $700,000,000 of deposits. Since then figures on them have not been published.

The Postal Savings System, founded in 1911 largely to serve immigrants, accepts savings at the post office but actually deposits them in nearby savings banks. It experienced a temporarily rapid growth during the early 1930's when so many banks were failing. Its peak year was 1947 with over 4,000,000 depositors and over $2,000,000,000 in deposits. By 1957 deposits were down to $354,000,000.

Both state-chartered and national banks offer customers savings account service and their time deposits totaled $70,000,000,000 in September, 1960. This was by far the most important form of savings institution.

In addition, savings and loan associations have given savings banks, and commercial banks, too, severe competition. Since 1945 their "deposits" have grown from $7,000,000,000 to nearly $60,000,000,000 in September, 1960. Actually these "deposits" are shares in the association but they are normally treated like savings deposits.

BANNOCK WAR (1878) was the last major uprising of Indians in the Pacific Northwest. It was waged by approximately 1500 malcontents, principally Bannocks and Paiutes. Gen. O. O. Howard's troops engaged most of the hostiles, who, dissatisfied with reservation policies in Idaho and Oregon, fought under Chiefs Buffalo Horn and Egan. In the skirmishes, about eighty Indians and approximately fifty whites were slain. The majority of Indian prisoners were transferred to Yakima Reservation, Washington Territory, in 1879.

BAPTISTS, the most numerous Protestant body in the United States, originated in England in the early 17th century and are not to be confused with the Anabaptists. They hold to five great principles: (1) separation of Church and State; (2) complete independence of the congregation; (3) the Scriptures as supplying the only standard of faith; (4) church membership based on a religious experience; and (5) immersion as the only Scriptural form of baptism. It has generally been held that Roger Williams was the father of the American Baptists and the church he founded at Providence (1638) was the mother church of the denomination in America. This is disputed, however, by recent Baptist historians, who have shown that Williams and his associates, though rebaptized, were not immersed. Rhode Island, however, became the center for the propagation of Baptist views and the first American college founded by Baptists was established at Warren, R. I., in 1764. Baptists were severely persecuted in the New England colonies, outside Rhode Island, though after 1691 a larger degree of toleration was secured. Up until the Great Awakening Baptists flourished most in the Middle Colonies, due largely to English and Welsh immigration. The first Baptist Association in America, made up of five churches, was formed in Philadelphia in 1707. In 1742 this body adopted a

Calvinistic Confession of Faith, and from that time forward the majority of American Baptists have been Calvinistic in their theology. By 1740 there were more than fifty Baptist churches in the colonies, the largest number being in New York, Pennsylvania, Maryland and Virginia.

As a result of the Great Awakening, the Separate, or revivalistic, Baptists, led by uneducated and unsalaried farmer-preachers, grew very rapidly in Virginia and North Carolina. This type of evangelism was particularly effective among the lower economic classes. By the end of the Revolution the southern Baptists were both numerous and influential. Separation of Church and State being one of the great Baptist principles, they naturally took a prominent part in the struggle to establish complete religious liberty in America. In both New England and Virginia, where that struggle was most severe, the Baptists were in the lead. Due largely to the farmer-preacher type of ministry, the Baptists proved one of the most effective of the churches in following moving population, and their churches were planted widely on every frontier.

In 1814 the General Convention of the Baptist Denomination in the United States for Foreign Missions was formed and in 1832 a similar organization for Home Missions was established. Opposition to missions developed on the frontier and after 1818 an antimission schism occurred, often called "Hard-Shells." Since Baptists were numerous in both North and South a slavery controversy arose, which in 1844–45 led to the formation of a Southern Baptist Convention. Since the Civil War the number of Negro Baptists has grown rapidly, largely due to the ease with which Baptist churches can be formed and the pageantry which they make of the rite of baptism by immersion.

BAPTISTS, SEVENTH DAY. These literal Bible-followers, accepting the seventh day for Sabbath, started in Newport, R. I. (1671). A German group at Ephrata, Pa., later joined them.

BARATARIA is the name of a bay, a lake and a bayou on the Gulf coast of Louisiana, sixty miles south of New Orleans and forty miles west of the mouth of the Mississippi. The Barataria region is inseparably connected in history and legend with the smuggling operations of Jean and Pierre Lafitte, who maintained headquarters there from 1810 to 1815. Though regarded as pirates by the United States, the Lafittes claimed to operate as privateers under letters of marque and reprisal issued by the Republic of Cartagena, on the northern coast of South America, which had declared its independence from Spain in 1810.

BARBARY WARS (1801–5; 1815). After the Revolution the United States, following the example of European nations, made annual payments to the piratical Barbary States of Morocco, Algiers, Tripoli and Tunis, for unmolested transit of merchantmen through the Mediterranean. Constant difficulties, however, ensued, such as the episode of the *George Washington,* and in 1801 Tripoli declared war and seized several Americans and their vessels. The war, entirely naval except for the Derna Expedition, was very feebly prosecuted by the commanders first dispatched, Commodores Dale and Morris, but in 1803 Edward Preble was sent out with the *Constitution, Philadelphia* and several brigs and schooners. His arrival galvanized the entire force into vigorous action. Making a naval demonstration before Tangiers which brought the Emperor of Morocco to make amends for treaty violations, Preble set up a strict blockade of Tripoli itself. Here on Oct. 31, 1803, the *Philadelphia* ran on a reef just outside the harbor and was captured by the Tripolitans, who a few days later floated her and anchored her under the guns of the citadel. But on Feb. 16, 1804, Stephen Decatur and eighty officers and men recaptured and burned her in a daring night attack.

During August and September, 1804, Preble, in addition to blockading, harassed the Tripolitan shipping and fortifications with frequent attacks, in which the small gunboats fearlessly entered the harbor to enable the crews to board and capture piratical craft while the larger ships kept up a protective fire on batteries. Such activity reached a climax on Sept. 4, when the *Intrepid* with its cargo of gunpowder and explosive shells was maneuvered into the harbor at night. Apparently the explosion occurred prematurely, for all the participants were killed and little damage was done to the Tripolitan shipping.

When, soon after, Preble was relieved by Commodore Samuel Barron, and he in turn the next spring by Commodore John Rodgers, the Bey was ready to conclude peace. He was partly induced to this by the success of the Derna Expedition, which had captured Derna and was threatening to march on Tripoli itself. The treaty, somewhat hastily concluded, June 4, 1805, abolished all annual payments, but provided for $60,000 ransom money for the officers and crew of the *Philadelphia.*

Although payments were continued to the other Barbary States, the absence of American naval vessels in the years preceding the War of 1812 encouraged Algiers to seize American merchantmen such as the *Mary Ann,* for which $18,000 was paid Algiers, and to threaten others such as the *Alleghany,* where an increased payment was demanded and secured. Immediately after the termination of the war, Decatur and Bainbridge were ordered to the Mediterranean with an overwhelming force. By June, 1815, within forty days from his departure from New York, Decatur, the first to arrive, had achieved his immediate mission. Capturing the Algerian flagship *Mashuda* in a running fight off Cape de Gat and appearing off

Algiers, he demanded and secured a treaty humiliating to the once proud piratical state—no future payments, restoration of all American property, the emancipation of all Christian slaves escaping to American men-of-war, civilized treatment of prisoners of war and $10,000 for a merchantman recently seized. As Tunis and Tripoli were forced to equally hard terms and an American squadron remained in the Mediterranean, the safety of American commerce was assured.

BARBED WIRE. "Free grass" and the open range were doomed by advancing values and population. Without absolute control of his land and stock, no ranchman could afford extensive improvement. If he provided ample water, the stock belonging to other men would tramp out his range in getting to it; if he bought high-grade bulls, his neighbors would get the use of them, while at the same time scrub bulls of other brands ran with his cows. Colorado alone of the range states enforced laws against scrub breeders.

Cattle, some rovers always excepted, would after being located normally remain on a given range; but droughts and blizzards made them drift, a hundred —sometimes two hundred—miles. Moreover, open range meant open road for thieves. "Slick" wire would not hold range stock; plank fences were too expensive; hedges of *bois d'arc,* wild roses and other growth proved impracticable. Only small bunches of cattle could thrive under herd, and herding was costly; the line-riders of the big outfits were helpless when northers and blizzards struck.

Following various patents on barbed wire, in 1873 J. F. Glidden, a prairie farmer of Illinois, gave it commercial practicability and the next year sold the first piece. Factories developed. Fencing proceeded outward from privately owned land near settlements. John W. Gates in the late 1870's put up a "bob" wire fence on Alamo Plaza in San Antonio to demonstrate its being "bull proof and horse high." Before the plains were fenced into pastures, cowmen cooperated to build drift fences across long distances. By 1890 most of the range land under private ownership had been fenced, but it was decades later before some of the Federal and state lands of Western states were fenced.

With fencing came wire-cutting "wars" in Texas and elsewhere, brought on by men accustomed to using land without owning it and resentful of being shut out. Many big outfits fenced in vast tracts to which they had no right. Bigfoot Wallace used to say, "Bob wire played hell with Texas." But barbed wire came to stay. It revolutionized the whole range industry, cutting off trail driving and free grazing, making the improvement of breeds and the watering of the range by wells and tanks inevitable. It developed stock-farming.

BARNBURNERS was the nickname of a faction of the Democratic party in New York State in the 1840's. They were first called Radicals and were the progressive element in the party. The name "Barnburner" was given them as early as 1843, and accepted by them at the State Democratic Convention of 1847. It was based on the story of the Dutch farmer who was willing to burn his barn to get rid of the rats. They opposed further expenditures for canals, wanted a limitation on the state debt, and a direct state tax. They advocated a Constitutional Convention, and when it was called in 1846, they controlled it. In national affairs, they favored the Wilmot Proviso and opposed the extension of slavery. They seceded from the State Convention of 1847 and from the 1848 Democratic National Convention. They nominated Martin Van Buren for President and then united with the Free Soilers. This movement defeated Cass, the Democratic candidate. After this election they gradually returned to the Democratic party, but when the Republican party was formed most of the younger Barnburners joined, bringing elements of leadership and voting strength.

BARRON v. BALTIMORE. The issue in this case was whether the first ten amendments to the Federal Constitution, and in particular the due process clause of the Fifth, were intended as restrictions on state as well as Federal authority. In 1833, in the last case participated in by John Marshall, the Supreme Court held that in view of the history of the adoption of the bill of rights, the prohibitions were directed against the Federal Government but not against the states.

BASEBALL. The game was born in obscurity, and in early history is a mishmash of mythology, unsubstantiated facts, and rampant sentimentality. Actually almost nothing is known of its origins. While some authorities have attempted to trace its ancestry back to various bat-and-ball games played by children even before George Washington became President, others insist with unconscious irony that the national pastime was derived from the English games of cricket and rounders. All experts agree, however, that a game in which a bat, ball, and bases were used was being played throughout the United States during the early years of the 19th century. In New England it was called town ball, which Oliver Wendell Holmes reported that he played as an undergraduate at Harvard College in the 1820's. In other parts of the country, it was apparently a team game that had evolved from one-old-cat. In both instances, the playing field was a square rather than a diamond, for the batter stood midway between what are now home plate and first base.

One of baseball's most enduring myths is that the game was "invented" by Abner Doubleday in Cooperstown, N. Y., in 1839, and the National Baseball Hall of Fame and Museum was built in Cooperstown in 1939 to commemorate this legend. But baseball scholars—and there are many of them—have conclusively demonstrated that Doubleday had nothing to do with either the game's beginnings or development, and that in all likelihood the first games bearing some resemblance to modern baseball were played in New York City rather than in Cooperstown. In any event, in 1845, a group of New York sportsmen—several years later A. G. Spaulding, one of the most famous of the early professional ball players, called them "gentlemen to the manner born" and "men of high taste"—organized the Knickerbocker Baseball Club and drew up a set of rules, among which were several provisions that would be readily recognized by present-day fans. For the next few years baseball was played almost exclusively in and around New York City by the Knickerbockers and other teams composed of gentlemen sportsmen. If democracy in sports is equated with mass participation, baseball in its formative years was undeniably an aristocratic game. In this respect, its history is similar to that of every other popular American sport except basketball.

In the decade preceding the Civil War several baseball clubs were organized in the larger cities of the Northeast. Many of these teams, moreover, were composed of players from all walks of life, for interclub competition put a premium on skills that had nothing to do with an individual's social background. By 1860 more than fifty clubs belonged to the National Association of Base Ball Players; several teams played regular schedules and charged admission; and one, the Excelsiors of Brooklyn, in 1860 toured from Buffalo to Baltimore taking on—and beating—all comers. The Civil War broke up the clubs and their schedules, but long before Appomattox baseball had become the most popular game among the troops (at least those in the Northern armies) behind the lines. The demobilized soldiers took the game back with them to their home towns. A short time after the war baseball was being played in most towns in the North and many in the South, and a year after the end of the war more than 200 clubs were members of the National Association. It is well to remember, however, that in 1865, the fielders still did not wear gloves, the catcher still caught the ball on the first bounce, and the pitcher still used an underhand delivery. It would be at least another 25 years before the game was standardized into the form in which it is played today.

Baseball, like most other American sports, soon became a business enterprise. Although amateur clubs had occasionally paid some of their stars, the first all-professional team was the Cincinnati Red Stockings, which in 1869 toured the nation without losing a game. In the next few years other professional teams were formed, but from the outset the success of professional baseball was jeopardized by repeated instances of bribery, the widespread gambling which attended almost every game, and the lack of any over-all organization. The club owners, however, were businessmen, and like other entrepreneurs of the period they quickly recognized the advantages of monopoly over unregulated competition and of organization over chaos. Accordingly, in 1876, teams from eight cities established the National League of Professional Baseball Clubs. This organization, which is still in existence, gradually eliminated competition, introduced regularly scheduled games, and formulated and codified most of the rules under which baseball is played today.

During the half century after the formation of the National League, professional baseball became a complex, ingeniously organized industry that was dominated by the major league club owners. The pattern was set as early as 1882 when the American Association was organized under rules set down by the National League. In subsequent years minor leagues were established with National League approval in every section of the country. The structure was completed with the formation of the American League in 1901 and the establishment of the World Series in 1903. The result was an economic pyramid that has fittingly come to be called organized baseball. At the top of the pyramid were the major league team owners, at the bottom the lowest minor league teams. All were held together by rules governing the exchange and contracts of players, who on at least one occasion banded together and complained that they were "bought, sold and exchanged like sheep." In that no team or league could be formed without the sanction of the organization, this was a monopoly. And like all monopolies it fought off interlopers, defeating the National Brotherhood of Baseball Players in the Brotherhood War in 1889–90 and a group of financiers who in 1914–15 attempted to operate the Federal League as a third major league.

Since World War I no two individuals have had a more profound effect on both the game and business of baseball than George Herman Ruth and Kennesaw Mountain Landis. Babe Ruth, an alumnus of a Baltimore orphanage who grew up to hit more home runs (60) in a season than any other player and to receive a higher salary than the President of the United States, was almost singlehandedly responsible for changing baseball from a defensive game characterized by the bunt, squeeze, steal, and hit-and-run, into an offensive contest in which strategy was subordinated to sheer power as represented by the home run. Landis, a U. S. district judge, was named commissioner of baseball by the club owners in 1921 as a result of the "Black Sox" scandal in which eight members of the Chicago White Sox accepted bribes to throw the 1919 World Series. Landis, who was to serve as "czar" of baseball until his death in 1944, barred from organized baseball the Chicago players who had accepted bribes and restored public confidence in the game by the strict discipline he imposed on the players and management. During his long reign the club owners introduced such innovations as night baseball, ladies' days, radio broadcasts of the games, and farm systems.

In recent years professional baseball has not been altogether immune to the forces that have reshaped so many other aspects of American life. Almost a decade before the Supreme Court decision on school integration, Jackie Robinson broke the color line in organized baseball, playing for the Montreal Royals in the International League in 1946 and the Brooklyn Dodgers in the following years. By 1960 Negroes were a commonplace in organized baseball. The major league clubs also were forced, although belatedly, to take cognizance of the westward movement of American population, and in the 1950's four big-league teams shifted their franchises from the East Coast to cities in the Far West and Middle West. Finally, baseball has been markedly affected by new patterns of recreation and leisure. Television, while making new fans, has not necessarily created new customers, and it has all but wrecked the minor leagues. The omnipresent automobile has made a stadium's parking lot as important as its hot dog (which was incidentally "invented" at a big-league ball park) concession, while it has taken many men, who formerly would have been in the bleachers, to the beach, to the mountains, or even to their mothers-in-law.

Baseball is a participant as well as a spectator sport, and for generations the game has been played by Americans from all classes on teams representing colleges, schools, towns, factories, and clubs. All American boys may not play—or even like—baseball, but it is virtually impossible for any American boy to grow up without knowing a great deal about the game. He learns it at the playground or in gym classes at school; he is urged—more often than not by his father—to play on a local Little League or American Legion team; and he is bombarded with news of professional baseball by his friends, by newspapers, and by radio and television announcers. It is true that fishing and bowling are more popular participant sports than baseball and that horse racing is a more popular spectator sport, but it is also true that baseball, if not the national pastime, is a national cult. The only other nations in which baseball enjoys a comparable status are Japan and some Latin American countries.

Baseball has always had certain features that set it off from other American sports. No other game combines team play and individual virtuosity with such felicity, and few other games provide both players and spectators with such sharp contrasts between the predictable and the unexpected. Baseball, moreover, is pre-eminently a game of statistics, for virtually every bit of action in a baseball game, season, and career can be reduced to figures, all of which eventually end up in the record books. These statistics are not only endlessly fascinating to many fans, but they also serve to give baseball a kind of continuity that is unique in the history of American team sports. Baseball, with its emphasis on statistics, may even have made a contribution to American education, for it is likely that many boys first learned about percentages, not from a grade school, but from their own efforts to figure out batting averages or the standing of a favorite big-league team.

BASKETBALL has the unique feature of being the one popular sport played in this country which is truly American in its origins. It was invented, in 1891, by James Naismith, an instructor at the Y. M. C. A. Training School in Springfield, Mass.

"BATTLE HYMN OF THE REPUBLIC," one of the most popular and inspiring of American patriotic hymns, was written (1861) by Mrs. Julia Ward Howe.

In the autumn of 1861 Mrs. Howe and her husband were in Washington, D. C., interested in hospital work under the Sanitary Commission. They had been outside the city on a mission in connection with their work and were returning in a carriage through an exceedingly dark night. They met a regiment of troops which was marching up the road and singing the familiar song known as "John Brown's Body," the music of which was written by William Steffe about 1852. Mrs. Howe remarked as the soldiers were passing that these were poor words to be set to such a glorious tune. Dr. Howe replied, "Julia, why do you not write better ones?" Mrs. Howe continued to turn the matter over in her mind and awakened from her sleep late that night when the words suddenly came to her, beginning "Mine eyes have seen the glory of the coming of the Lord." She arose and wrote down the entire hymn.

The poem was printed in the *Atlantic Monthly* for February, 1862. It at once became popular and spread over the entire country. Not only is it in all collections of patriotic American songs but is included in the hymnals of a number of churches as well.

BAY PATH was a trail from the Connecticut River to Massachusetts Bay at or near Boston. Conversely, the same trail from the Bay to the Connecticut River would be the Connecticut Path. Some writers reserve the name Bay Path for such a trail in Massachusetts and that of Connecticut Path for one in Connecticut. There seems no question that from 1648 there was the New Path westward through Weston, Sudbury, Marlboro, Worcester, Brookfield and Brimfield to Springfield. Similarly, there is no question that after 1683 a Path ran southwestward from the vicinity of Boston to Woodstock, Conn., and thence westward to Hartford.

BAY PSALM BOOK, so called from its origin in Massachusetts Bay Colony, was the earliest book known to have been printed within the present boundaries of the United States. Begun in 1639 and finished in 1640, it was printed in Cambridge, Mass., by Stephen Daye, the first printer of the English colonies. Eleven copies are known to exist of which six are imperfect.

BAYARD-CHAMBERLAIN TREATY, drafted by a joint commission at Washington, Feb. 15, 1888, was intended to clarify the respective powers and rights of Great Britain and the United States in the waters of Newfoundland and the adjacent provinces. The Treaty of Washington, extending valuable privileges to American fishermen in Canadian waters, had been abrogated as of July 1, 1885, and more stringent and somewhat obscure provisions of the Convention of 1818 were now effective. Rigorous enforcement by the Canadian authorities, seizure and forfeiture of American vessels, retaliatory legislation, jingoistic fulminations by press and politicians, had created a situation which threatened peaceful relations. The new treaty provided for a joint commission to define American rights in Canadian waters, recognized exclusive Canadian jurisdiction in bays whose outlets were less than six miles in width, remedied several minor American grievances and promised further concessions should the United States remove tariff duties on Canadian fish. The Senate rejected the treaty on Aug. 21, 1888, but more than twenty years later when the protracted fisheries dispute was arbitrated at The Hague, the substance of several of its more significant provisions appears in the award which that tribunal rendered against American claims.

BAYARD v. SINGLETON (N. C. Superior Court, 1787). This case is important because it is the first reported decision under a written constitution overruling a law as unconstitutional. (Four years earlier than cases cited in 1 Kent. Com., 450; State v. Glenn, 52 N. C. 324.) The defendant moved dismissal of the case according to an act of the legislature which required the courts to dismiss, upon affidavit, suits against persons holding forfeited Tory (enemy alien) estates. The court overruled the motion and declared that the constitution of the state gives every man a right to a decision concerning property by jury trial. If the legislature could thus alter or repeal the constitution it would thereby destroy its own existence, and might even take away, summarily, one's life.

BAYNTON, WHARTON AND MORGAN (1763–98) was a firm of Philadelphia merchants which virtually monopolized the rich western trade at the close of the French and Indian War and which by its contacts in Philadelphia, Lancaster, Pittsburgh, Kaskaskia and London exploited the West in one of the most significant commercial enterprises of the day. Before the legal opening of Indian trade, it sent the first cargo of goods westward (1765) under protection of passes by George Croghan, Deputy Superintendent for Indian affairs. This premature attempt to capture Indian trade infuriated the "Black Boys" who attacked the pack train and destroyed the shipment. Soon, however, the firm had 600 pack horses and wagons on the road between Philadelphia and Pittsburgh and some 300 boatmen on the Ohio.

BEAR FLAG REVOLT (1846) climaxed a decade of suspicion and jealousy between the Anglo-Californians of the Sacramento Valley and the Mexican authorities. Unlike the American residents of Monterey and Los Angeles, many of whom were closely connected with prominent California families through business relations, friendship or even marriage, the American residents of northern central California formed a community by themselves. Restive under Mexican rule and over-anxious to assert their racial superiority, they had a deep-seated fear of their fate if the California authorities should get them completely under control.

Some color was indeed given to this fear by the treatment accorded the fur traders Smith and Pattie in the previous decade and especially by the deportation in 1840 of Isaac Graham and some forty of his friends. Accordingly it is not surprising that, when the settlers learned of the Hawk's Peak episode and Frémont's expulsion from California in March, 1846, they should have believed the rumors that the government planned to seize and expel all foreigners in the province.

Uneasiness gave place to alarm when the news came (later proved false) that 250 Californians were advancing on Sacramento. The Americans immediately repaired to Frémont's quarters at the Marysville Buttes where, in the middle of May, he had encamped on his return from Oregon. This much criticized defiance of the local authorities by Frémont was declared by him to be "the first step in the conquest of California." The next step was the seizure, early in June, by Ezekial Merritt and a dozen other Americans of a large band of government horses which Gen. Castro had obtained from Gen. M. G. Vallejo at Sonoma and which were being driven to San José by way of Sutter's Fort. This was an act of war and it was decided that the third step must be the capture of Sonoma, the chief stronghold of the Californians north of the Bay Region. The actual capture of the quiet little pueblo at early dawn, June 14, 1846, was a rather ludicrous affair; "To whom shall we surrender?" demanded the kindly general's wife. After a scene of no little confusion and considerable imbibing of Vallejo's wine, simple articles of capitulation were arranged and signed.

Then followed the erection of the Republic of California under the leadership of William B. Ide. To signalize it, William Todd designed a flag from a piece of unbleached cloth five feet long and three feet wide. Facing a red star was a grizzly bear which gave both the flag and the republic its familiar name. A proclamation setting forth the justification and purposes of the revolution was prepared; but before the new government could get under way, July 10, 1846, the American flag was officially sent to Sonoma.

The actual accomplishments of the Bear Flag Revolt were thus of little importance, but had not the Mexican War intervened, either Ide or Frémont might have stood out as the creator of a new republic, the Sam Houston of the Pacific Coast.

BEAR PAW MOUNTAINS, INDIAN FIGHT AT (Oct. 3–5, 1877). At the end of their long campaign starting in Idaho, June, 1877, the Nez Percé Indians under Joseph (Hinmaton-yalatkit) were surrounded by Col. Miles' command in the Bear Paws of northern Montana. After a brave three days' resistance, Joseph surrendered, ending the Nez Percé War.

BEECHER ISLAND, BATTLE OF (1868). Col. George A. Forsyth, leading fifty experienced scouts, in search of Indians who had pillaged western Kansas, encamped, Sept. 16, 1868, on the Arickaree River, fifteen miles south of Wray, Colo. Attacked next morning by about 1000 Cheyennes and Sioux, led by Roman Nose, the scouts moved onto a sandy island and with butcher knives and tin plates scooped out rifle pits. In the first Indian charge, Roman Nose fell, Forsyth was wounded, and Lt. F. H. Beecher was killed. The Indians made several unsuccessful charges, then settled to a siege. Despite wounds, death and the stifling odor from their dead horses, the scouts held on. Emissaries eluded the Indians at night and sought help. On the ninth day troops arrived. Five scouts were dead, eighteen wounded and the remainder almost exhausted.

BEECHER'S BIBLES was the term applied during the Kansas troubles to Sharps Rifles. In March, 1856, at New Haven, Henry Ward Beecher addressed a meeting at which a subscription was taken to equip a company of free-state emigrants to Kansas. Beecher said that for slave holders in Kansas a Sharps Rifle was a greater moral argument than a Bible. The first rifle was subscribed by Prof. Benjamin Silliman, of the Yale College faculty, the second by the pastor of the church in which the meeting was held and Mr. Beecher pledged the last twenty-five for Plymouth Church, Brooklyn.

BEEF TRUST CASES. In 1902 three large packers —Swift, Armour and Morris—formed the National Packing Co. in an effort to secure control of packing houses in Kansas City, East St. Louis and Omaha. The Government promptly attacked these and three other concerns, charging monopolistic practices which had resulted in a large degree of control over the slaughtering and packing of meat. In 1905 the Supreme Court (196 U. S. 394) upheld the Government for the most part, but failed to order dissolution of the National Packing Co., and monopolistic practices continued. Thereupon the Government sought an injunction, but the individuals involved successfully pleaded immunity from criminal prosecution because they had previously been compelled to testify against themselves. In 1910 further attacks on the packers were again unsuccessful, but in 1920, after an extensive Federal Trade Commission investigation, the packers agreed to dispose of their varied stockyards interests, their retail meat markets and the wholesaling of lines not directly related to meat packing.

BELKNAP SCANDAL (1876) was one of the series of scandals which marked Grant's second administration. Secretary of War W. W. Belknap's first wife agreed to secure a lucrative post tradership at Fort Sill for C. P. March of New York on condition that she should receive one half the profits. The trader at the post paid March $12,000 a year not to take the place and March paid $6000 to Mrs. Belknap. After her death he paid the money to the Secretary. Just before a House investigation committee moved to impeach him, Belknap resigned. The impeachment trial in April and May resulted in acquittal, largely on the ground that the Senate had no jurisdiction over a resigned officer.

BELLEAU WOOD, BATTLE OF (June 2–July 7, 1918). The German 7th Army, under von Boehn, driving southward from the Chemin des Dames toward Paris, on May 31 approached the Marne at Château-Thierry. Just west of there the American 2nd Division (Bundy) hastened into support of the French 21st Corps (Degoutte), the left corps of Duchesne's French 6th Army. Forcing back minor French units, by June 3 the Germans uncovered the American front line, which stood fast and stopped them. On June 6 the Americans assumed the offensive. Against bitter resistance the 4th (Marine) Brigade (Harbord) recaptured Bouresches and the southern edge of the Bois de Belleau, while on its right the 3rd Infantry Brigade (Lewis) advanced nearly to Vaux.

Continuing their local offensive, the Americans took most of Belleau Wood on June 8–11, and despite desperate counterattacks completed its capture June 21. At noon, July 1, following an intense artillery preparation, the 3rd Infantry Brigade stormed Vaux and La Roche Wood. The division front, everywhere established on favorable ground, was turned over to the American 26th Division, July 9, the 2nd Division retiring to a support position.

BELMONT, MO., BATTLE OF (Nov. 7, 1861), was Grant's (U.) first Civil War battle and first defeat.

Frémont ordered the attack on Belmont to prevent Polk at Columbus, Ky., from aiding the Confederates in Missouri. Steaming from Cairo, Ill., Grant landed five miles above Belmont and drove Gen. G. J. Pillow's men to the river and set fire to their camp. Polk, crossing with reinforcements and aided by the Columbus batteries, drove Grant to his transports.

BELTRÁN-ESPEJO EXPEDITION. When the soldier-escort of the Rodríguez expedition returned from "New Mexico" (1582), the Franciscans on the frontier at Santa Bárbara (southern Chihuahua) were alarmed for the safety of two missionaries who had remained at Puaráy. With fifteen volunteer soldiers Fray Bernardino Beltrán started north (November, 1582) to rescue his colleagues. Upon reaching the Pueblo country, he learned that they had been killed; but the soldiers refused to return before exploring the country.

We have no account from Beltrán regarding what happened; our knowledge rests on later statements of soldiers, especially Luxán and Espejo. The latter, desiring to emulate Hernán Cortés by developing a "new" Mexico, largely financed the expedition and tried to dominate it. His report added much detailed information of the Pueblo country and people; his exaggerations regarding population, resources and mining prospects were somewhat discounted by Luxán.

The expedition failed in its immediate objective, but its favorable reports of the country strengthened the resolve of secular and religious authorities to colonize and evangelize New Mexico.

BENNINGTON, BATTLE OF (Aug. 16, 1777). Toward the middle of August Gen. Burgoyne planned a raid on the American stores at Bennington. His purpose was fourfold: to encourage the loyalists; frighten New England; replenish his stock of provisions; and mount a regiment of heavily equipped German dragoons. Accordingly, these dragoons, lumbering along on foot in their enormous jack boots and stiff leather breeches, were made the nucleus of the raiding force, which, under the command of the German Col. Baum, amounted, with Tories, Canadians, Indians and a handful of English, to about 800 men. On nearing Bennington, Baum, learning that Gen. Stark had assembled about 1600 troops at Bennington to oppose him, sent to Burgoyne for reinforcements. Col. Breyman, with 500 men, was accordingly sent to his assistance. In the meantime Gen. Stark, hearing of Baum's advance, marched to meet him. On Aug. 15 it rained, and both armies remained in their lines. The following afternoon Stark attacked. Baum's command was too widely dispersed. His auxiliaries were scattered and his regulars, hastily entrenched on a hill overlooking the Walloomsac, were surrounded and most of them captured. In the meantime Breyman, ignorant of what was going on,

approached. Stark, reinforced by Col. Warner with 350 men, re-formed and attacked. The Germans retreated and were pursued until dark. The Americans took about 700 prisoners. The fortunate outcome of the engagement did much to improve the morale of the American forces.

BENTON, FORT (1850–65). After 1830 the American Fur Company established several trading posts near the navigation-head of the Missouri River. One of these, Fort Lewis (established 1844), a large, bastioned, log structure, was moved in 1846 to the site of the present town of Fort Benton, Mont., where it retained its original name until 1850, when it was renamed for Thomas Hart Benton, who allegedly saved the company from prosecution for selling whiskey to the Indians. The post was subsequently rebuilt with adobe bricks. During the Montana gold rush, beginning in 1862, Fort Benton became a main port of entry to the mines. A town with the same name sprang up around it and the fur company sold out to a mercantile firm in 1865.

BENT'S FORT, first known as Fort William, was founded by William Bent and partners about 1832, on the north bank of the Arkansas, some seven miles east of present La Junta, Colo. The founders are said to have previously built a temporary stockade farther up the river. Located on the mountain branch of the Santa Fe Trail, Bent's Fort participated in both the mountain fur trade and the overland commerce to Santa Fe, becoming the outstanding trading post of the Southwest. It was rectangular in form, about 180 by 135 feet. The walls, of gray adobe, were two to four feet thick and fifteen high, with bastions at two diagonal corners. Within, low earth-roofed rooms faced an interior court. An adjoining adobe corral housed stock and equipment.

Cheyennes and Arapahoes brought buffalo robes and skins for barter at the fort and from it white traders carried wares to Indian villages. An annual wagon train freighted furs to Missouri and returned with Indian goods. The fort outfitted trappers and traders, sheltered early travelers, was a depot for military expeditions before and during the Mexican War. William Bent married a Cheyenne woman, reared his family at the fort and became Colorado's first citizen. According to unverified tradition, the Government desired the fort, but offered an inadequate price Bent thereupon deserted the fort and partially destroyed it in 1849. Moving forty miles down the river, he erected Bent's New Fort, 1853. This structure, built of stone, he leased to the Government in 1859. Next year additional barracks were built and the post was named Fort Wise, after the governor of Virginia. In 1861 the name was changed to Fort Lyon, honoring Gen. Nathaniel Lyon. Floods endangering the buildings in 1866, Fort Lyon was moved up the river to its present location.

BERLIN, TREATY OF (1921), is the separate peace treaty between the United States and Germany, entered into after the Senate rejected the Treaty of Versailles. This Treaty of Berlin is unique, first, because of its brevity, and secondly, because it is an "index-treaty," in that its provisions merely refer to provisions of the Treaty of Versailles which are either accepted or rejected by the United States. Provisions thus taken over were those with respect to colonies, disarmament, reparations and responsibility for the war. The most important features rejected were the League of Nations, the International Labor Organization and the boundaries provisions. Approximately two thirds of the Treaty of Versailles, including its harshest provisions, was thus accepted by the United States through the Treaty of Berlin.

BIBLES, PRINTING OF. The first book printed within the limits of the present United States of which any copy survives was a portion of the Bible (the so-called *Bay Psalm Book*, Cambridge, Mass., 1640). The first complete Bible produced was John Eliot's translation into an Algonquian language printed at Cambridge in 1663 (second edition, 1685). In 1688 William Bradford projected the printing of a Bible in Philadelphia, but nothing came of it or of John Fleming's proposal in Boston in 1770. Partly because the printing of the King James version was an Oxford monopoly, three editions of Martin Luther's Bible in German appeared in America (Germantown, Christopher Sower, 1743, 1763, 1776) before any were printed in English. Robert Aitken published the first American Bible in English in Philadelphia, 1781–82. Isaiah Thomas is responsible for the legend of an English Bible printed surreptitiously in Boston about 1752, but no such book was attested by contemporaries, nor is any copy known to exist. Thomas printed the first Greek New Testament, Worcester, 1800. The first printing of the Douay version (Roman Catholic) was in Philadelphia in 1790.

BICAMERAL LEGISLATURES. The bicameral system has long prevailed in the United States. Based on British precedent, it was firmly established in the Federal Government by one of the major compromises of the Convention of 1787. The large states won representation on the basis of population in the House, while the small states, fearful of the strength of the larger and more populous states, won equal representation in the Senate, as well as a constitutional guarantee that no state should ever be deprived of its equal representation without its consent.

In the states, with the specific exceptions noted here, bicameralism has been in universal use. After independence was achieved, three states set up or retained existing unicameral legislatures: Georgia, 1777–89; Pennsylvania, 1701–89; Vermont, 1776–1836. For a period of exactly a century, there were no further exceptions. Early in the 20th century, there was some agitation for unicameralism; several governors recommended it, and several states voted on it, rejecting it, in each case, by substantial majorities. However, under the leadership of Senator George W. Norris, Nebraska voters in 1934 adopted a constitutional amendment establishing unicameralism effective in 1937. This action served to revive interest in the matter in other jurisdictions; although many proposals for unicameralism were presented and considered, none were advanced even to the referendum stage. After nearly a quarter of a century of successful operation in Nebraska, unicameralism is still a subject of discussion, but there appears to be little serious interest in adopting it in other states.

In the cities, the bicameral system, with a large common council and a smaller select council, universally prevailed down to the period of widespread municipal reform early in the 20th century. At present, all American city councils are unicameral, nearly all with small membership, in both mayor-council and council-manager cities. The spread of unicameralism in the cities, its success in Nebraska, and its use in the provinces of Canada have been widely used as arguments for its extension among the states.

BIG BONE LICK is in Boone County, Ky., one and one-half miles east from the Ohio River. The earliest known white man to visit this place was Capt. Charles Lemoyne de Longueil, who came in 1729. Christopher Gist visited it in 1751; and in 1773 James Douglas, a Virginia surveyor, described the animal remains which he found on the surface. Here were found the bones of mastodon, Arctic elephant and other animals of the Glacial Age. In 1803 and 1806 Dr. William Goforth made a collection of fossils which he entrusted to the English traveler, Thomas Ashe. Ashe in turn sold these to the Royal College of Surgeons in London, and to private Irish and Scotch collectors. Thomas Jefferson made a collection of some of the bones, and natural history museums at Lexington, Cincinnati, Philadelphia and Boston collected the remaining skeletons. The large prehistoric animals were attracted to the Big Bone Lick by the seepage of brine from an underlying basal coal measure. Pioneers found that 500 gallons of this water made one bushel of salt.

BIG HORN MOUNTAINS are a range of the Rocky Mountains lying mainly in north central Wyoming, but extending into southern Montana. Discovered in 1743 by Chevalier Vérendrye, they were early frequented by American fur traders. In 1811 they were crossed by Wilson Price Hunt and the overland Astoria expedition. Here in 1866 occurred the so-called Fetterman massacre, and in 1876 Custer's force was annihilated in the Battle of the Little Big Horn.

BIG KNIVES or Long Knives was a term used by the western Indians to designate the English colonists. After 1750 it was restricted to the colonists of Virginia, in contradistinction to those of New York and Pennsylvania. George Rogers Clark spoke of himself and men as "Big Knives," or Virginians, in his speeches to the Indians in 1778 after the capture of Illinois. In the latter part of the Revolution, down to and during the War of 1812, the term was used to designate Americans. The origin is thought to have been the use of steel knives and swords by the colonists, perhaps contrasted with the stone knives of the primitive Indians.

BIG TREE TREATY (1797). Robert Morris' agreement with the Holland Land Company required the acquisition of the Indian title. At Big Tree (Geneseo, N. Y.) with the sanction of the United States Government, the Senecas, by a treaty concluded Sept. 15, ceded to Morris all of their land west of the Genesee River, except about 200,000 acres, for the sum of $100,000 to be invested in United States Bank stock.

BILL OF RIGHTS. The first ten amendments to the Constitution of the United States are generally referred to as the national Bill of Rights. At the time the Constitution was submitted to the people in 1787 there was much criticism of the document due to the fact that it did not contain a Bill of Rights. The explanation of this goes back to the original English common-law idea of government. According to this, individual rights exist of themselves as inborn and inalienable. The Constitution and government are merely an added protection to those rights which the people already possess. This idea underlies today the governments not only of Great Britain and the United States, but also those of the self-governing British Commonwealths.

In contrast to this should be mentioned the doctrine and belief that were and still are prevalent in other countries, such as the states of Continental Europe, which are under what might be termed a prerogative type of government. Even the most free of these countries in their written Constitutions make statements of individual rights that are based on the underlying thought that these rights are the gift of the state. Thus we find the Constitution of Switzerland (Article 55), "The freedom of the press is guaranteed. However, cantonal laws shall enact the necessary provisions to avoid abuse; these provisions shall be submitted to the approval of the Federal Council. The Confederation may also fix penalties in order to prevent abuses directed against itself or its authorities." This provision is characteristic of the most enlightened European democracies and is in direct contrast to the British and American common-law idea of protection for already existing, inalienable rights.

Naturally there was a general feeling among those who made the Constitution and who were advocating its adoption that a Bill of Rights was unnecessary, since it might grant rights that already existed or merely prohibit the Government from interfering with these rights, which it had no authority to do. Alexander Hamilton, in *The Federalist*, No. 84, wrote: " 'We, the people of the United States . . .' is a better recognition of popular rights than volumes of those aphorisms which make the principal figure in several of our State bills of rights, and which would sound much better in a treatise of ethics than in a constitution of government. . . . The truth is, after all the declamation we have heard, that the Constitution is itself, in every rational sense, and to every useful purpose, a bill of rights."

In contrast to this was a widespread popular feeling that it would be wise to make a definite statement of these fundamental rights since such a statement would have a beneficial and restraining influence on the minds of both rulers and the people and also might serve as a definite basis for future court decisions in protecting these rights. This feeling, amounting to a conviction, went back to the old British tradition inherited by the colonists from the Revolution of 1688. This great change in the government of England and her colonies had as one important result the Declaration of Rights of 1689 which formed the basis for the later American Bill of Rights.

Massachusetts, Virginia, New York and several other states ratified the new Constitution with the recommendation that a Bill of Rights be added which should specifically safeguard individual rights. This was done by the First Congress in the form of twelve proposed Amendments which, after some delay, were passed by that body on Sept. 25, 1789. Of the twelve Amendments submitted, ten were declared ratified by the necessary number of states on Dec. 15, 1791. They bind the National Government alone, but do not limit the power of the individual states. The material for these Amendments was drawn in large part from the Virginia Declaration of Rights which was adopted by a Virginia convention composed of members of the colonial House of Burgesses which met at Williamsburg in 1776. The preparation of this Declaration was in large part the work of George Mason. In a sense, it was intended to serve as an original compact for society by stating permanent and fundamental truths. Also, it was intended to be the basis for a new society and government to be independently organized in America. In plain language it stated specific and fundamental principles with regard to jury trial, cruel and unusual punishments, search warrants, freedom of the press, the subordination of military to civil power; the derivation of all authority from the people, who have an inalienable right to reform an evil government; the doctrine of the separation of executive, legislative and judicial powers; and it declared for a full grant of religious freedom. Likewise it stated that all men should have the franchise who had sufficient evidence of permanent common interests with the community.

Jefferson soon thereafter drew upon it when he wrote the Declaration of Independence, and it not only became the basis for these first Amendments to the Constitution but also furnished a model for the various Bills of Rights adopted soon after by other colonies and offered the basis for the later Bills of Rights in many of the present state constitutions.

The First Amendment provides that "Congress shall make no law respecting an establishment of religion, or prohibiting the free exercise thereof; or abridging the freedom of speech, or of the press; or the right of the people peaceably to assemble, and to petition the Government for a redress of grievances." These are among the most fundamental rights to be preserved in a free government. In contrast to the above quotation from the Swiss Constitution, they prohibit interference with individual rights that already exist.

More specifically they mean that the National Government has nothing to do with religion as such. The right of fair discussion of men and measures does not mean free license of utterance, but the right of a person to express his or her thoughts depends on the thoughts themselves and on time and place. The right on the part of citizens to meet peaceably for consultation in respect to public affairs and to petition for a redress of grievances is implied in the very idea of popular government. It is true that the right of petition has lost much both in use and influence during more recent years. This is due to the extension of the means for expression of the popular will or protest, by universal suffrage. On the other hand, it still holds great potential value as a ready means of popular influence upon the course of legislation or administration in time of crisis.

Amendment II provides: "A well regulated Militia, being necessary to the security of a free State, the right of the people to keep and bear arms, shall not be infringed." This may be summarized as the right to bear arms in common defense but not to carry such arms as the individual may desire in order to use them in private conflict.

The Third Amendment provides: "No Soldier shall, in time of peace be quartered in any house, without the consent of the Owner, nor in time of war, but in a manner to be prescribed by law," and the Fourth Amendment provides for the security of the people "in their persons, houses, papers, and effects, against unreasonable searches and seizures." These two Amendments are designed to protect the people against any acts of illegal force by the National Government that may infringe their personal rights.

The four Amendments numbered V, VI, VII and VIII control legal proceedings in the Federal courts and constitute a statement of the rights of accused persons by guaranteeing to them the rule of common law.

The provisions of Amendment V are: "No person shall be held to answer for a capital, or otherwise infamous crime, unless on a presentment or indictment of a Grand Jury, except in cases arising in the land or naval forces, or in the Militia, when in actual service in time of War or public danger; nor shall any person be subject for the same offence to be twice put in jeopardy of life or limb; nor shall be compelled in any criminal case to be a witness against himself, nor be deprived of life, liberty, or property, without due process of law; nor shall private property be taken for public use, without just compensation." The most important clause of this Amendment is that guaranteeing "due process of law" to every citizen under Federal law. This means "that the accused person be given the right to a fair hearing in a tribunal having jurisdiction of his case." (E. S. Corwin.)

Amendment VI lays down certain provisions that are designed to secure this due process of law. It provides that "in all criminal prosecutions, the accused shall enjoy the right to a speedy and public trial, by an impartial jury of the State and district wherein the crime shall have been committed, which district shall have been previously ascertained by law, and to be informed of the nature and cause of the accusation; to be confronted with the witnesses against him; to have compulsory process for obtaining witnesses in his favor, and to have the Assistance of Counsel for his defence."

Amendment VII provides that "in Suits at common law, where the value in controversy shall exceed twenty dollars, the right of trial by jury shall be preserved, and no fact tried by a jury, shall be otherwise re-examined in any Court of the United States, than according to the rules of the common law." This Amendment restricts the power of the Supreme Court of the United States in reviewing questions of fact upon appeal from lower Federal courts. Amendment VIII requires that "excessive bail shall not be required, nor excessive fines imposed, nor cruel and unusual punishment inflicted." The wording of this Amendment is taken almost verbatim from the English Bill of Rights of 1689.

The last two Amendments in the Bill of Rights numbered IX and X form a final restraint upon the National Government and require it to be one of enumerated powers only. Thus Amendment IX states that "the enumeration in the Constitution of certain rights, shall not be construed to deny or disparage others retained by the people," and Amendment X states that "the powers not delegated to the United States by the Constitution, nor prohibited by it to the States, are reserved to the States respectively, or to the people." It would seem that the sovereign people of the United States are ultimately the ones who enumerate the rights and reserve them to the states or to the people. In other words, as stated in the Preamble to the Constitution, "We, the people of the United States," did "ordain and establish" the Constitution, with the result that legally and politically it may be said that the United States *is* a Nation, rather than the more grammatical expression that the United States are a nation.

BILLS OF RIGHTS, STATE. In American history the Bill of Rights adopted by the State of Virginia in 1776 preceded those of the other states, and also was the model upon which the national Bill of Rights, the first ten amendments of the United States Constitution, was drawn up. The Virginia Declaration, in large part, was the work of George Mason and was adopted on June 12 by the colonial House of Burgesses which met as a convention. The Virginia document was in large part a restatement of English principles drawn from such sources as Magna Carta, the Petition of Rights and the Bill of Rights. It still stands in practically the original form at the beginning of the sixth or present Constitution of the State of Virginia, which was formed in 1902.

While other and later constitutions of the various states have copied the Virginia provisions in large part, they also have added other provisions according to local or contemporary needs. The second great Bill of Rights in point of time was "The Declaration of Rights of the Commonwealth of Massachusetts" which was adopted in 1780. It was stated in thirty provisions while that of Virginia was stated in sixteen. The Massachusetts Bill of Rights goes into greater detail than that of Virginia, stressing such things as the right of the people to bear arms, a condemnation of *ex post facto* laws, bills of attainder, and the quartering of soldiers in time of peace. The Puritan religious influence is shown in the statement that "it is the right as well as the duty of all men in society, publicly, and at stated seasons, to worship the Supreme Being, the great Creator and Preserver of the universe." The final article is a more lengthy and specific statement of the principle of Separation of Powers. This Bill of Rights also stands as a part of the original Constitution of Massachusetts and still remains in force today.

The Bills of Rights in other or later-formed states show the results of contemporary events and influence and are often much more lengthy. Thus, slavery is prohibited in the Bill of Rights of the State of Maryland; also in the State of Nevada, and in almost all the Southern states. This is a direct result of the Civil War and Reconstruction period. Also, the Constitution of the State of New Mexico contains such an odd and legally questionable statement as the following, that "the people of the State have the sole and exclusive right to govern themselves as a free, sovereign and independent State."

While many of the Bills of Rights of the various states set forth matters which are never questioned and establish prohibitions of powers already beyond the competence of the state governments, yet there is no doubt that their effect in general is healthy and constructive. They specifically state and emphasize the fundamental principles upon which American government and society are founded.

BINGHAM PURCHASE. In 1786, when Massachusetts, which then included Maine, disposed of large tracts of unsettled lands in Maine by lottery, William Bingham, a wealthy Philadelphia banker, drew several townships and purchased others, with a total area of 1,000,000 acres. Gen. Henry Knox had signed a contract to buy another tract of 1,000,000 acres, but his duties as Secretary of War prevented his developing it, and Bingham took that over also.

BIRCH, JOHN, SOCIETY, a radical, right-wing organization, was founded in 1958 by Robert H. W. Welch, Jr., a retired Massachusetts businessman. It was named after John Birch, a Fundamentalist Baptist missionary from Georgia. Welch never knew Birch who, while serving as a U. S. intelligence officer, was killed by Chinese communists ten days after V-J Day, 1945. The declared aim of the Society is to fight communism on a so-called "intellectual basis" apparently by adopting some of communism's own most vicious and ruthless tactics. Among other ancillary elements of its program are its advocacy of a return to minimum Federal Government and the abandonment of the Federal Reserve System, the Commodity Credit Corporation, the veteran's hospitals, etc. Violence is not advocated, but a number of public men and others have been charged with being "dedicated agents" of "the communist conspiracy." The organization is composed of a semi-secret network of cells of "Americanists" throughout the country. Membership was greatest in southern California.

BISHOP HILL COLONY, a theocratic communistic colony, was founded in Henry County, Ill., in 1846 by Eric Janson who brought there some 1500 emigrants from Sweden where they had been persecuted because of their conversion to perfectionism. The colony was incorporated in 1853 and was dissolved in 1860. In 1879 many members of the former colony lost their farms to liquidate its debts and the costs of years of litigation.

BIT. An archaic term for a currency value of one eighth of a dollar, used chiefly in the South and Southwest, when depreciation of colonial paper money, problems of exchange, coinage and lack of specie caused the circulation of the Spanish *real,* a silver coin of that value.

BLACK BALL LINE was the first and most celebrated of the lines of transatlantic sailing packets from New York. Its popular nickname came from the black disc carried on the fore-topsail and the house flag. On Oct. 27, 1817, came the announcement of regular monthly sailings. Service started at Liverpool on Jan. 4, 1818, and at New York the next day. In 1822 it was increased to semimonthly sailings with eight ships. It was started by five New York textile and cotton merchants, all but one of whom were Quakers. Jeremiah Thompson is credited with the original idea. After 1834 it was operated by Capt. Charles H. Marshall. The line continued for exactly sixty years, terminating in 1878. During that time 43 different ships were used.

BLACK BELT is a crescent-shaped area extending along the Alabama River in Alabama and up the Tombigbee in northeastern Mississippi. About three fourths of its 5000 square miles lies in Alabama, including seventeen counties which make up nearly one forth the entire area of the state. This region derives its name from the black soil which is prevalent here in contrast to the red clays to the north and south. The Black Belt is a prairie which lies much lower than the surrounding country due to the decomposition of the soft limestone rock which underlies the soil. This rock decomposition has given it a remarkably fertile soil which makes it one of the best agricultural regions of the entire South.

That portion of the Black Belt which lies in Alabama was first opened for settlement by the Creek cession of 1816. However, the pioneers were suspicious of the unusual black soil and it was not until the Jacksonian migration of the 1830's that the region began to be settled. The Mississippi portion was opened at this time, too, as the Choctaw and Chickasaw moved west of the Mississippi. On account of the high fertility of the soil and the accessibility to market at Mobile it was inevitable that the Black Belt should become a plantation region producing great crops of cotton by slave labor. The slave population, in fact, at one time reached 87% of the whole, and thus afforded an additional justification of the name. From 1830 to 1860 the Black Belt of Alabama was the most prosperous portion of the state, held the most slaves, produced the most cotton, and was the bulwark of the Whig party. All the rivers of Alabama, except the Tennessee, water the region, and three of the five state capitals—Cahaba, Tuscaloosa and Montgomery—were located there.

With the coming of the Civil War, the Black Belt turned from cotton production to the raising of foodstuffs and furnished throughout the war a great part of the food supplies for the Confederate armies. As it had almost no railroad connections with the West or North it remained practically untouched by the Northern armies. After the war it again became the leading cotton-producing region of the South until 1880. In recent times, unable to meet the competition of Texas cotton, it has turned more and more to diversified farming and the raising of food crops, although still the principal cotton region east of the Mississippi.

BLACK BOYS were Pennsylvania frontiersmen who, in 1763, 1765 and 1769, came together under the leadership of James Smith to defend the frontier against the Indians, and who, in 1765, burned a pack-horse train belonging to Baynton, Wharton and Morgan engaged in the Indian trade.

BLACK CODES were laws passed in the ex-Confederate states in 1865–66, which dealt with the status of the Negro as affected by the abolition of slavery. As a rule, the laws were not organized as a separate code, in the usual sense of the word, but were statutes in the different states which dealt with vagrancy, apprenticeship, penalty for crime, property rights, etc. For the most part they adapted old principles on these subjects to the new conditions. The Negro was defined usually as "a person of color," one who had a certain degree of African blood, usually fixed at one eighth. Intermarriage between the races was forbidden. Marital relations and family responsibilities were legalized. Vagrancy laws attempted to force Negroes to work when many wished to "enjoy their freedom." Apprentice laws aimed to provide for orphans and the destitute young by hiring them out, usually to their former owners. Labor contracts provided means by which the Negroes might be held to steady labor, such as was required for the production of staple crops. Laws gave to the Negroes the ordinary civil rights to sue and be sued, and to give testimony in court, but only in cases involving Negroes. The laws varied greatly among the states, being most restrictive to the Negro in Mississippi and South Carolina, where the colored population largely outnumbered the white.

From the point of view of the South the laws were constructive measures to prevent complete chaos when the whole social system embodied in slavery was suddenly destroyed. From the point of view of the North the legislation expressed an attempt to revive slavery under another guise. The black codes furnished evidence to the already dissatisfied Radical Republicans that the state governments set up by President Johnson gave inadequate security to the permanence of Union victory, and so encouraged their demand for more thorough reconstruction by Congress.

BLACK FRIDAY (Sept. 24, 1869) was the climactic day of an effort by Jay Gould, James Fisk, Jr., Abel Rathbone Corbin and one or two associates to corner the ready gold supply of the United States. The nation then being on a paper-money basis, gold was dealt in as a speculative commodity on the New York exchange. Gould and Fisk first enlisted Corbin, who had married President Grant's sister; they then drew the new head of the New York Sub-Treasury, Daniel Butterfield, into the scheme, and unsuccessfully tried to involve Grant's private secretary, Horace Porter. On June 15, 1869, they entertained Grant on Fisk's

Bristol Line steamboat, attempted to learn the Treasury's gold policy, and argued that it was important to keep gold high in order to facilitate sales of American grain in Europe. Grant was noncommittal. A gold corner did not seem difficult if government nonintervention could be assured, for New York banks in the summer of 1869 held only about $14,000,000 in gold, not more than a million was in local circulation and time would be required to bring more from Europe. On Sept. 2 Gould began buying gold on a large scale; on the 15th Fisk began buying heavily and soon forced the price from 135 to 140. The movement excited much suspicion and fear and on the 13th the *New York Tribune* declared it the "clear and imperative duty" of the Treasury to sell gold and break up the conspiracy. Secretary Boutwell visited New York but decided not to act; meanwhile Grant had gone to Washington, Pa., and was out of touch until he returned to Washington on Sept. 22. On the 23d, with gold at 144, the New York panic grew serious.

The climax of Black Friday found Fisk driving gold higher and higher, business profoundly disturbed throughout the nation, and the New York gold room a pandemonium as scores were ruined. As the price rose to 160 Boutwell in Washington urged the sale of three millions of the gold reserve, Grant suggested five, and the Secretary telegraphed an order to sell four. Gould, perhaps forewarned by Butterfield, had already begun selling and gold sank rapidly to 135; Fisk immediately found means to repudiate his contracts. The episode caused heavy indirect losses to business and placed an ugly smirch on the Grant administration.

BLACK HAWK WAR (1832), waged chiefly in Illinois and Wisconsin between the United States and a faction of the Sauk and Fox Indians, was led by Chief Black Hawk, whose home village was near Rock Island, Ill. In November, 1804, certain spokesmen of the two tribes had ceded to the Government their title to 50,000,000 acres of land, comprising the northwestern half of Illinois and much of southwestern Wisconsin and eastern Missouri. The validity of this cession was hotly denied by Black Hawk, who was supported by a formidable fraction of the two tribes. The issue became acute in 1831, when squatters pre-empted the site of Black Hawk's village, and the Chief threatened forcible resistance. An army of regulars and Illinois militia was embodied, however, and before this threat of force Black Hawk yielded and withdrew to the Iowa side of the Mississippi.

Early in 1832 he recrossed the river with several hundred followers, intent on joining the friendly Winnebago and raising a crop of corn. Gen. Atkinson ordered him to return to Iowa, and since he did not comply, the war was on. Black Hawk slowly retired up Rock River, the white forces pursued, and numerous killings and minor activities took place.

Before long Black Hawk perceived the futility of his foray into Illinois and made proffers of peace, which were ignored. The remnant of his despairing followers was pursued westward across southern Wisconsin to the mouth of Bad Axe River, where, on Aug. 3, they were practically annihilated. At Fort Armstrong, in September, Gen. Scott compelled the Winnebago to cede their possessions in Wisconsin and the Sauks and Foxes to cede all of eastern Iowa, by way of punishment for the war.

BLACK HILLS, lying chiefly in South Dakota and skirting over into southeastern Wyoming, are formed by an upthrust of the archean rock through the overlying strata to a maximum height of 7242 feet above sea level. Mount Harney is the granite (archean) core of the upthrust. Passing from the surrounding prairie through the foothills to Mount Harney, the explorer walks over the upcrop of each strata which rises in regular order: the shales, redbeds (gypsum), sandstone, schists, limestones, and granite as they are folded back, affording an unusual opportunity to study the geological formations underlying the region. The Black Hills were embraced within the Great Sioux Reservation as defined by the Laramie Treaty of 1868. Gold was found in the Hills by miners accompanying Gen. Custer's expedition of 1874 which set out from Fort Abraham Lincoln (Bismarck) to find a practicable highway to Fort Laramie. The "discovery" created much excitement, but the Federal Government sought to protect the rights of the Indians until they had been duly extinguished by treaty. When early efforts to accomplish this release failed by reason of the refusal of the Sioux to agree upon reasonable terms, the Government raised the embargo and gold hunters rushed into the diggings in vast numbers. This invasion led to the Black Hills War, the high feature of which was the destruction of Custer's command on the Little Big Horn in June, 1876. After this affair the Government forced a treaty of relinquishment and civil government was established.

The miners first assembled at Custer, where 15,000 passed the winter of 1875–76. Gold having been found in Deadwood Gulch, there was a stampede from Custer to the new diggings early in 1876 and Deadwood became in a day the most exciting and picturesque gold camp on the continent. The diggings at that time were entirely in placer gravel, but before autumn the Homestake lead had been located and passed into the hands of San Francisco capitalists. The Homestake Gold Mine was developed. Its engineers believe its stores of ore cannot be depleted for scores of years to come.

There are extensive gold deposits in and about Keystone and that region is very heavily mineralized. Mica, spodumine, ambligonite, feldspar, arsenic, gold, silver and galena are produced in commercial values. More than 100 valuable minerals are present. Custer

State Park is very extensive and scenically attractive. President Coolidge, with his staff, made it his summer home in 1927. The Needles Highway and Iron Mountain road within the park are nationally popular.

On Mount Rushmore, of the Harney Range, in the park, the Federal Government has authorized a colossal national memorial, consisting of massive sculptures of Washington, Lincoln, Jefferson and Theodore Roosevelt, by Gutzon Borglum. The memorial is located essentially in the center of the North American Continent, upon the highest range between Pikes Peak and the Matterhorn.

BLADENSBURG, BATTLE OF (Aug. 24, 1814). Maj. Gen. Robert Ross, with 4500 British troops, landed on the Patuxent River in Maryland, Aug. 19–20, thus compelling Commodore Joshua Barney to destroy his gunboat flotilla in that river. The British force then turned toward Washington. About 6000 District and Maryland militia, a few regulars and Barney's seamen constituted the defensive force under Maj. Gen. William Winder. Ross reached Bladensburg Aug. 24. Across the river, on rising ground, Winder hastily and unskilfully posted his army, already worn down by three days' futile maneuvering, sleepless nights and scanty food. The British advanced steadily under artillery fire, drove back the American light troops after crossing the bridge, and approached the second line. Showers of Congreve rockets so terrified the raw militia that two regiments disintegrated immediately. A Baltimore regiment offered some resistance but broke when ordered to fall back. Barney's naval contingent, firing eighteen-pounders, checked Ross for a time, retreating only when its flanks were uncovered by fleeing infantry supports, its ammunition expended and Barney wounded. A general retirement, ordered by Winder, was effected in fair order, the British being too exhausted to pursue vigorously. Halting briefly at Capitol Hill, the Americans marched on to Georgetown. Ross entered Washington and burned the Capitol, presidential mansion and public buildings. President Madison, Secretary of War Armstrong, Secretary of State Monroe and Attorney General Rush were on the field during part of the battle. American losses were insignificant, those of the British rather severe. A congressional investigation whitewashed all concerned, but the uselessness of undisciplined militia against British regulars was again demonstrated. Winder was exculpated by a court of inquiry, and Armstrong, made the scapegoat by the public, was compelled to resign. Failure of the Administration to adopt defensive measures in time may be considered the true explanation of the disaster.

BLAND-ALLISON ACT (Feb. 28, 1878), was the first of several U. S. Government subsidies to silver producers in depression periods. The five-year depression following the Panic of 1873 caused cheap-money advocates (led by Representative R. P. Bland of Missouri) to join with silver-producing interests in urging return to bimetallism. The silver dollar had been omitted from the list of coins by a mint reform act, which lent itself to the political soubriquet of "The Crime of '73," and silver had depreciated with other commodities. The allies demanded restoration of free coinage of silver at "16–1," approximately $1.29 an ounce.

Free coinage, as the symbol of justice for the poor, was seized upon by greenbackers and others determined to prevent resumption of specie payments and to make Government obligations payable in silver. When Bland's bill for free coinage, passed by the House, jeopardized Secretary of the Treasury Sherman's plans for resuming specie payments, Sherman substituted limited purchases for free coinage, through a Senate amendment sponsored by Sen. W. B. Allison of Iowa. The producers accepted the arrangement as likely to restore silver to $1.29.

The law required Government purchase, at market prices, of $2,000,000 to $4,000,000 worth of silver bullion monthly, and coinage into legal tender "16–1" dollars, exchangeable for $10 silver certificates receivable for public dues and reissuable. The President was directed to arrange an international bimetallic conference to meet within six months. These provisions signified:—victory for producers over inflationists, defeat of international bimetallists by national bimetallists, a drain on the Treasury through the customs in times of uncertainty and failure for the conference.

BLAST FURNACES, EARLY. From the earliest days of English colonization, Englishmen pointed out that the smelting of iron in the New World for England's manufacturers would be advantageous to the mother country in view of the diminishing English forests which furnished fuel for the production of iron. The first attempt to build blast furnaces in the colonies was made in Virginia by the London Company. The project was not successful. The Puritans in Massachusetts established the first successful ironworks as early as 1644. The colonial iron industry, however, made slow progress in the 17th century.

Not until the 18th century did the smelting of iron in America become important. The colonial iron industry then went through a process of remarkable development. By the outbreak of the American Revolution there were more blast furnaces in the American colonies than in England and Wales, and American furnaces produced more pig iron and castings than English furnaces.

Colonial blast furnaces were patterned after those of the mother country. Built of stone, they were usually about 25 feet square at the bottom and from 25 to 30 feet high. Although square, they were larger at the bottom than at the top; thus they resembled truncated pyramids. The blast, forced through a single tuyère into the furnace, was produced by large bellows driven by water power. Before 1800 blowing cylinders were substituted for bellows at a number of furnaces. American furnaces continued to use charcoal fuel and cold blast until just before 1840 when some ironmasters began using anthracite coal. Later, coke displaced anthracite and charcoal as a furnace fuel. The early iron industry was the foundation upon which the great iron and steel industry of the present was established.

BLEASE MOVEMENT IN SOUTH CAROLINA developed in the 1900's from the failure of the Tillman Movement to satisfy the ambitions of the white masses. By studiously imitating Ben Tillman's vehement attacks on Negroes, aristocrats and clerical politicians, Cole L. Blease became something of the popular idol Tillman had formerly been. Elected governor in 1910, his administration was bizarre, but not criminal. He pardoned extravagantly and answered the snubs of the opposition with abusive language. Although the combined opposition of Tillman and the upper classes could not prevent his re-election in 1912, his influence thereafter declined and his repeated attempts to win high office usually ended in failure. Blease lacked a constructive program and the prudence of a successful organizer. But his agitations had permanently quickened the political consciousness of the cotton-mill operatives and other poor whites.

BLENNERHASSETT ISLAND in the Ohio River below the mouth of the Little Kanawha River, an Indian rendezvous, was first known as Backus Island for Elijah Backus who purchased it in 1792. It is famous as the site of Blennerhassett House, where Aaron Burr and Harman Blennerhassett, who purchased the north end of the island in 1798, are alleged to have plotted treason against the United States.

BLIZZARDS. This word is applied to snowstorms or drifting snow accompanied by severe cold and strong winds. It probably first appeared in print in this sense about 1870, but was widely used by 1880.

The most famous blizzard in American history is that of March 11, 1888, in the northeastern states. The streets of New York City were piled with twelve feet of snow in many places; in Herald Square the drift was thirty feet deep. There were no means of transportation except sleighs. Fires started and burned themselves out because fire-fighting apparatus could not move through the streets. A food panic threatened, as thousands were marooned in their homes. The Stock Exchange suspended business, telegraph communication was cut, and railroads stopped running. For a while the East River was

frozen over. This blizzard took an unknown number of lives, including that of Sen. Roscoe Conkling, and caused a property loss of $25,000,000.

Another famous blizzard took place in Kansas in January, 1886. Almost 100 lives were lost, and stock by the thousands perished. Animals drifted with the storm until caught by fences or other obstructions, and froze to death in the drifts. After the storm, bodies of stock, rabbits, antelope and even wolves were found huddled together.

More than 200 people were said to have perished in the Dakotas and adjoining states during the blizzard of Jan. 12, 1888. In that storm the wind attained a velocity of sixty miles an hour, the temperature falling 60° in 24 hours.

The storm of May 3–4, 1905, in the Dakotas, caught stockmen and homesteaders unprepared. Stock had already been turned out on the ranges and had shed their winter coats, and fruit trees were in blossom. When the blizzard came, great drifts were piled in the streets of Rapid City. Stock were driven blindly before the wind, over canyon walls, and into the draws where they were buried deep in the drifts. This storm caused greater livestock loss than any other in the history of the region.

On Dec. 4–5, 1913, Denver, Colo., experienced its worst blizzard. Due to the comparatively high air temperatures, however, there was little suffering as a result of the unusually heavy snowfall.

On Jan. 27, 1922, a severe snowstorm occurred on the Middle Atlantic seaboard. In Washington, D. C., it was known as the Knickerbocker storm, because the collapse of the roof of the Knickerbocker Theater killed nearly 100 persons.

The blizzard of Feb. 13–14, 1923, was one of the worst on record in the Dakotas and Minnesota, marked by unusually low temperatures. Notwithstanding ample warnings from the Weather Bureau, good telephone connections and better housing than in the old days, more than twenty people froze to death.

One of the worst blizzards since 1886 swept the Plains states on March 26–27, 1931, and was especially severe in Colorado and Kansas.

The blizzard that struck the northwestern Great Plains Jan. 3–4, 1949, was also tragic in its consequences. At Rapid City, S. D., the winds averaged fifty miles an hour, hitting seventy miles an hour. A fourteen-inch snowfall created drifts fifteen feet high; the thermometer fell below zero, and visibility was less than five feet.

March 22–25, 1957, twenty inches of snow fell in the west central and southwestern Great Plains, drifting as high as thirty feet in the wake of winds ranging from 30 to 80 miles an hour.

BLOCS, as the term is used in the United States, are members of legislative bodies who, disregarding party lines, agree to act together for certain special purposes, and set up an organization to accomplish these purposes. The co-operation of legislators with similar interests, such as the tariff or silver, has occurred throughout our history, but deliberately organized blocs are relatively recent, beginning with the Farm Bloc, organized in May, 1921.

"BLOOD IS THICKER THAN WATER." Commodore Tattnall, in command of the American Squadron in Far Eastern waters, made this adage a part of American history when explaining why he had given aid to the British squadron in an attack on Taku forts at the mouth of the Pei-ho, June 25, 1859, thereby infringing strict American neutrality.

BLOODY ANGLE, at Spottsylvania (May 12, 1864), was the climax in the first phase of Grant's (U.) Wilderness Campaign. Union troop movements indicated Grant planned a heavy attack. Lee (C.) was uncertain where the blow would fall. Early in the morning Grant moved in force against "the salient," or "Bloody Angle" in Lee's line. Because of surprise, lack of artillery and the force of the onslaught "the salient" was overrun. To restore the broken line and save his army, Lee proposed to lead the counterattack. Officers and men remonstrated, crying "General Lee to the rear." Lee's example fired his troops with intense ardor. The opposing lines met; the Union advance was halted and forced back. Lee put in every available man. All day and far into the night the battle raged. Neither side could advance. Early next morning Lee retired to prepared positions. The fighting ceased.

BLOODY SHIRT, usually found in the expression, "waving the bloody shirt." It is used to describe the attempts made in political campaigns (especially in 1872 and 1876) by radical Republicans to defeat the Democrats by impassioned oratory designed to keep alive the hatreds and prejudices of the Civil War period.

Perhaps the most reasonable explanation of the origins of the phrase is the Scotch tradition that after the massacre of Glenfurin, 220 widows rode to Stirling Tower, each bearing aloft on a spear the bloody shirt of her murdered husband, thus arousing the people to take vengeance on their enemies.

BLOOMER DRESS, a loosely fitting costume of knee-length dress and "Turkish" trousers buttoned at the ankle, was introduced in Seneca Falls, N. Y., by Elizabeth Smith Miller in February, 1851, and popularized by Amelia Bloomer, editor of a feminist journal, *The Lily.* For its physical comfort and as a symbol of the suffrage movement, the dress survived six years of ridicule but was extinguished by the revival of the hoopskirt.

BLOUNT CONSPIRACY. Takes its name from William Blount, U. S. Senator from Tennessee in 1796–97. It was connected with the Yazoo land frauds of 1796 and its main purpose seems to have been to raise the value of Western lands by driving the Spaniards out of Louisiana and Florida. This was to be accomplished by a land force of Western frontiersmen and Indians with the aid of a British fleet. The British minister in the United States, Robert Liston, gave the conspirators some encouragement and sent one of them to London. The conspiracy was exposed when an incriminating letter written by Blount to one of his agents fell into the hands of the administration and was transmitted by President Adams to the Senate (July 3, 1797). Blount was promptly expelled from that body. Impeachment proceedings against him were considered but dropped because of his expulsion. The exposure of the conspiracy had repercussions in the domestic politics and foreign relations of the United States, and there is some reason to believe that Aaron Burr's later conspiracy was connected with this one.

"BLUE AND GRAY" are familiar names for the armies of the North and South during the Civil War, derived from the fact that the Union Army wore blue uniforms while the Confederates wore gray.

BLUE EAGLE EMBLEM was a blue-colored representation of the American "thunder bird," with outspread wings, which was proclaimed on July 20, 1933, as the symbol of industrial recovery by Hugh S. Johnson, the head of the National Recovery Administration. All who accepted the President's Reemployment Agreement or a special Code of Fair Competition were permitted to display a poster on which was reproduced the Blue Eagle together with the announcement, "Member N. R. A. We Do Our Part." On Sept. 5, 1935, following the invalidation of the compulsory code system, the emblem was abolished and its future use as a symbol was prohibited.

BLUE LAWS. Rev. Samuel A. Peters originated the account of the so-called Blue Laws of Connecticut in *A General History of Connecticut, by a Gentleman of the Province,* published in London in 1781. The term was taken up by various later editors of the laws to refer specifically to the legislation of the New Haven Colony. Such instances as punishments of a rebellious child by being forced to work for his father as a prisoner with a lock on his leg, and of a young unmarried couple by a fine of twenty shillings for kissing, were considered typical Blue Laws. Despite some distortions, it is perfectly true that rather rigid Sabbath, sex, and sumptuary regulations prevailed generally in Puritan New England. But Blue Laws were not original among the Puritans nor unique with them in this country. To some degree Blue Laws could be found in every one of the American colonies. Compulsory church attendance and laws forbidding sports, travel and work on the Sabbath were found in the South as well, perhaps the most sweeping Sunday law being the Georgia act of 1762. Blue Laws became in the main dead letters after the Revolution, but in more recent times there has been an attempt to revive them all along the line. National prohibition, anti-cigarette legislation, the activities of the Lord's Day Alliance and other groups attest to the survival of the Blue Law spirit to some degree.

BLUE LICKS, BATTLE OF (Aug. 19, 1782). An engagement between 182 Kentucky pioneers and 240 Indians and Canadians, in the British service, raiding into Kentucky from the Ohio country and the vicinity of Detroit. It occurred near the Lower Blue Lick Springs on the Middle Fork of Licking River. A precipitate attack was launched by Kentuckians, from several pioneer "Stations," against the foe lying in ambush. After a fierce conflict of a few minutes, the right wing of the Kentuckians gave way and the entire body retreated in confusion, with a loss of about seventy killed and captured. The loss of the Indians and Canadians was never definitely ascertained. Notwithstanding the adverse outcome of the battle, no invasion by Indians in force ever afterwards occurred within the borders of Kentucky.

BLUEGRASS COUNTRY comprises some 8000 square miles of east central Kentucky. It is bounded by the Ohio River on the north and the Knobs on the east, south and west. The terrain, with some exceptions, has a gracefully undulating surface over a limestone foundation. The land is specially adapted to the growth of bluegrass, for which the region has been named. The inner portion with Lexington at the center is a beautiful district of shaded, winding roads, fine farms and prosperous villages and towns.

To this region came the first settlers of Kentucky in one of the greatest migrations of American history. Over the Wilderness Road, by way of Cumberland Gap, trekked most of these multitudes. Here the pioneers, Daniel Boone and Simon Kenton became national heroes. At Harrodsburg the first permanent settlement in Kentucky was made; at Boonesborough the first Anglo-Saxon government west of the Alleghenies was organized; at Lexington the first college (Transylvania) in the West was established; at "Ashland" lived Henry Clay, the Great Pacificator; to Transylvania came Jefferson Davis to study; and to Lexington came Abraham Lincoln to court Mary Todd. These and many other places and incidents in the Bluegrass Country constitute a historic environment probably unequaled in the Mississippi valley.

BLUFFTON MOVEMENT (1844), in South Carolina, was an attempt to invoke "separate state action" against the tariff of 1842, after Calhoun's failure to secure the presidential nomination and the Northern

Democrats' abandonment of the South on the tariff had apparently destroyed hope for relief within the Democratic party. Though many of the "Blufftonites" undoubtedly contemplated disunion, the object of their leader, Robert Barnwell Rhett, seems rather to have been a "reform" of the Union giving further safeguards to Southern interests. The movement collapsed within a short time, largely through its repudiation by Calhoun.

BOARD OF TRADE AND PLANTATIONS was the main British colonial office from its creation, May 15, 1696, until the eve of the American Revolution. It replaced the older committee of the Privy Council, called Lords of Trade and Plantations. It was a paid board of five members, the chief officers of state being also ex officio members. It had charge of poor relief in England, regular commercial relations with other nations, the enforcement of the trade and navigation acts, the general supervision of colonial administration, the examination of colonial laws to see that they were not harmful to British interests nor contrary to the English common law. It heard and investigated complaints of merchants and recommended imperial legislation in its field. It supervised the negotiation of important commercial treaties and kept in touch with the regular consular service. Its voluminous records today are the chief source for American colonial history in its imperial aspects.

The Board was a part of the regular political party system and its members changed with the usual party shifts. Most of its business articulated with the office of the Secretary of State for the Southern Department, consequently the activities of the Board varied with the practices and desires of the Secretary of State. Under a dominant character like Newcastle it had little power—most of the business being transferred directly to Newcastle's office. In 1748 George Dunk, Earl of Halifax, was appointed president of the Board. He began at once to make his position important. Investigations were made and reports compiled of what had been going on in America for the past thirty years. Plans were developed for strengthening the position of the royal governors. Instructions were revised, judges were made dependent upon the crown for their salaries and their terms of office, and the struggle began between the agents of the crown and the leaders of the colonial legislatures. By his energy, Halifax made himself practically a secretary of state for the colonies, secured control of the colonial patronage and was admitted to the cabinet in 1756. His influence was powerful in colonial affairs many years after his retirement from the Board in 1761.

A group of rising young men received important political training as members of the Board under Halifax. Among these were James Grenville, Charles Townshend and Andrew Stone, the tutor of George III. Townshend was even president of the Board for a short time in 1763, to be followed by Lord Shelburne. He in turn was succeeded by Hillsborough, who became a full secretary of state for the colonies and was directly responsible for many of the unfortunate policies between 1764 and 1772 that ultimately led to the Revolution. His most offensive colonial activities were connected with his attempt to force Massachusetts to rescind its famous Circular Letter and his use of troops in Boston, culminating in the Boston Massacre.

The permanent secretaries of the Board were among the best-informed men on colonial affairs in England. At the head of these were the Popples—William, William, Jr. and Alured, all related—who occupied the office from 1696 to 1737, and John Pownall, 1758–61. Another important officer was a solicitor and clerk of reports whose duties were to prepare all formal reports, to assemble information for use of the Board and to represent it before other departments of the government. The most famous of these was John Pownall, who served from 1745 to 1758 and personally prepared the reports associated with the work of Halifax. Another important officer was an attorney to whom all colonial laws were sent for examination and report as soon as they arrived from America. These reports on colonial laws subjected every American statute to a constitutional test. Three men, Richard West, Francis Fane and Matthew Lamb, filled this important position from 1718 to the end of the active work of the Board.

BOISÉ, FORT, was a fur trading post of the Hudson's Bay Company in Idaho. First built in 1834 on the Boisé River about seven miles above its mouth, it was relocated in 1838 near the confluence of the Boisé and Snake Rivers. It was a small adobe-walled fort, famous as a stopping point on the Oregon Trail. Partially destroyed by flood waters in 1853, it was finally abandoned after the Indian War of 1855.

BOLLMAN CASE. In *ex parte* Bollman and Swartwout (1807) the Supreme Court upheld its power to issue a writ of habeas corpus to review a commitment by an inferior Federal court, and upon hearing ordered the release of two petitioners held on charges of treason as participants in the Burr conspiracy. Justus Erich Bollman and Samuel Swartwout, by separate routes, had carried copies of a letter in cipher from Burr to Gen. Wilkinson at New Orleans. Wilkinson arrested them and sent them to Washington, where they were committed for trial by the circuit court for the District of Columbia. While the case was pending in the circuit court President Jefferson attempted, unsuccessfully, to induce Congress to suspend the privilege of the writ of habeas corpus. In holding that the evidence had been insufficient to support a charge of treason, Chief Justice Marshall said for the Supreme Court that "there must be an actual assembling of men for the treasonable purpose,

to constitute a levying of war." But, he added, if that be proved, then a conspirator, however remote from the scene of action, would be guilty. This dictum proved embarrassing when, a few months later, Marshall presided at the trial of Aaron Burr.

BONANZA WHEAT FARMING in the Red River Valley of the North during the period 1875–90 was an important factor in the settlement and development of the spring wheat region. The Cass-Cheney farm, first and most widely known of the bonanzas, was established in 1875 when George W. Cass, president of the Northern Pacific Railroad and E. P. Cheney, a director of the road, exchanged almost worthless Northern Pacific bonds for land held by the railroad in the Red River Valley. Cass took ten sections, Cheney eight and an experienced wheat farmer contracted to handle operations. Yields for the next decade were uniformly high. Capital was attracted to the region, and many Northern Pacific bondholders followed the example set by Cass and Cheney. By 1890 over 300 farms in the valley exceeded 1000 acres; a half dozen or more exceeded 15,000 acres. Some of the farms were individually owned; others were corporations. Few bonanzas were established after 1890 and most of the older farms were broken up within the next quarter century.

BONHOMME RICHARD AND SERAPIS, ENGAGEMENT BETWEEN (Sept. 23, 1779), was one of the most notable of American naval victories. John Paul Jones's flagship the *Bonhomme Richard,* originally an Indian merchantman renamed in honor of Benjamin Franklin, was proceeding with Jones's tiny fleet up the east coast of England in quest of English cargoes. Although worn out and unseaworthy, she carried 42 guns. About noon, Jones sighted two enemy ships of war, the *Serapis* and the *Countess of Scarborough,* convoying ships loaded with naval stores. He maneuvered his ship close to the *Serapis* and both opened broadside fire. Jones had placed some of his guns below, and two of the larger ones on his lower deck burst, killing and wounding several men. This catastrophe necessitated using only the lighter guns and musketry. The slaughter on both sides was terrible and the American ship was leaking badly. After an hour's fighting, Jones answered the British challenge to surrender: "I have not yet begun to fight." The two vessels became locked together and the battle raged for more than two hours longer. Jones was hampered by treachery of a captain in his own fleet, but finally by using British prisoners to man the pumps, he stayed afloat and wore down the enemy to the point of exhaustion and surrender.

BONNEVILLE EXPEDITION. Capt. B. L. E. Bonneville, U. S. Army, headed a party of trappers and traders in the Far West which started from Fort Osage, May 1, 1832. The well-known Platte-South

Pass route was followed to Green River. Here, a few miles above the mouth of Horse Creek in a region favored by the mountain men as a place of annual rendezvous, Fort Bonneville was built. Abandoned shortly after completion, it was frequently called "Fort Nonsense." Bonneville moved to the headwaters of the Salmon, then continued to move during the most of the time that he was in the mountains. So thoroughly did he cover the Rocky Mountains and the Columbia drainage basin, and so good was his map making that he may be credited with having been the first to gain true geographic knowledge of the Far West. A branch expedition organized by Bonneville left Green River, July, 1833, under Joseph Reddeford Walker, crossed Salt Lake Desert, descended Humboldt River, crossed the Sierras north of Yosemite Valley and spent the winter at Monterey. In the spring, it returned through the Sierras via Walker's Pass, across the Great Basin, and up Bear River, joining Bonneville June 1, 1834.

Irving made of Bonneville's manuscript a compelling story, which ranks at the top of the literary contributions of the fur traders.

BONUS ARMY was a spontaneous gathering of unemployed World War veterans who, late in May, 1932, began marching and hitchhiking to Washington in small groups from all over the United States until about 15,000 were assembled there. The needy veterans, seeking some economic relief from Congress, eventually united in petitioning for immediate payment of the Adjusted Compensation, or "Bonus," Certificates.

The problems of food, shelter and sanitation for the impoverished veterans embarrassed Washington, and there was latent danger of disorder. But the leader, Walter W. Waters, maintained almost military discipline and expelled communistic agitators, while patriotism permeated the ranks. Though the chief of police, Gen. Glassford, tried to provide quarters, most of the men built wretched hovels in which they lived.

In mid-June Congress, by a narrow margin, defeated the bonus bill, but the disappointed "Bonus Expeditionary Force" stayed on, haunting the Capitol grounds. Late in July Glassford ordered the veterans to evacuate. They failed to do so and on July 28, by instructions from the President, United States troops drove them forcibly from their quarters in public buildings and from their camps.

BONUS BILL, CALHOUN'S. On Dec. 16, 1816, John C. Calhoun recommended that the House of Representatives appoint a committee to inquire into the expediency of creating a fund for internal improvements from the profits derived from the second National Bank. With the appointment of the committee, Calhoun, as chairman, introduced a bill on Dec. 23, 1816, to set apart as a permanent fund for internal improvements the $1,500,000 bonus exacted from the bank as a price of the charter and the profits from the $7,000,000 of the bank stock owned by the United States. Although the bill was passed, President Madison vetoed it, March 3, 1817, on the ground that it was unconstitutional, but suggested an amendment to the Constitution that would remove all doubts upon the subject.

BOOMER MOVEMENT is a term applied to attempts of settlers to occupy an area in Indian Territory during the period from 1879 to 1885. The Five Civilized Tribes of Indians formerly owned all of the present state of Oklahoma except the Panhandle. In 1866 as a punishment for having participated in the Civil War on the side of the South, they were compelled to cede to the United States as a home for other Indians the western half of their domain. During the next ten years several tribes of Indians were given reservations on these lands but a fertile region of some 2,000,000 acres near the center of Indian Territory was not assigned to any tribe and came to be known as the "Unassigned Lands" or "Old Oklahoma."

Early in 1879 E. C. Boudinot, a railway attorney of Cherokee blood, published a newspaper article stating that this was public land, and so open to homestead entry. Widely reprinted, this article created great excitement. Later in the same year a colony of homeseekers under the leadership of C. C. Carpenter sought to enter the Indian Territory and occupy this area but was prevented by troops under Gen. Pope.

In 1880 David L. Payne became the leader of these so-called "Boomers." Payne organized the movement, charging a small fee for membership in his "Oklahoma Colony." During the next four years he and his followers made eight attempts to settle the region but in every case were ejected by soldiers. Upon his death at Wellington, Kans., in 1884 his lieutenant, W. L. Couch, led an expedition to the forbidden area, but was promptly removed by the military. The struggle was then transferred to the national capital and on April 22, 1889, the Unassigned Lands were opened to settlement under the provisions of an act of Congress.

BOONDOGGLING. On April 3, 1935, Robert C. Marshall, a witness before the Aldermanic Committee to Investigate the Relief Administration in New York City, testified that he taught various crafts, including "boondoggling," to workers on relief, and described "boondoggles" as "gadgets" or useful articles made out of scrap material. The term boondoggling was thereafter rather loosely used by critics of the New Deal throughout the country to ridicule so-called useless made-work and unproductive educational, recreational and research projects of relief workers.

BOONESBOROUGH, on the south side of the Kentucky River, in the present county of Madison, was founded April 2, 1775, by Daniel Boone. Despatched from the Watauga treaty ground by members of the Transylvania Company to mark out a roadway to lands purchased from the Cherokees, Boone and his companions blazed a trail across Cumberland Gap and thence through the wilderness to the mouth of Otter Creek on the Kentucky. There they erected a stout stockaded fort which served as a rallying-point of defense for the harassed settlers throughout the Revolution. At Boonesborough, May 23–27, 1775, was held the convention called by the Transylvania proprietors to consider the needs of the colony. The novel proceedings and enactments were devoid of effective sanction, but they were timely and savored of the soil.

On July 14, 1776, three young girls, one a daughter of Boone, were captured near the fort by skulking savages, but within a day or two were rescued unharmed. On April 15, 1777, Boonesborough was subjected to a savage Indian attack, and on July 4 of the same year the assault was renewed on a larger scale. The fiercest siege and assault of all, however, occurred Sept. 7–20, 1778. The Shawnee chiefs, Black Fish and Moluntha, together with the French-Canadian, Lt. Antoine Dagneaux de Quindre, were in command of a formidable body of Indians supported by a few British militiamen from Detroit and this combined force assailed the little fortress with all the arts of bravado and cunning. But neither force nor guile could bring about its downfall, and, finding their efforts futile, the invaders finally desisted and withdrew.

BOOTLEGGING is a term, derived from the early Indian traders' custom of carrying a bottle of liquor in the boot, especially applied to illicit deliveries of alcoholic beverages. The bootlegger is a peddler whose name differentiates his activities from those of the merchant who unlawfully purveys from a shop known variously as a "blind tiger," "blind pig" or "speakeasy." The manufacture of illicit hard liquor is termed "moonshining."

Since the activity is illicit, no reliable estimates can be given as to the scope. The profits derived from bootlegging depend somewhat upon the source of the beverage and somewhat upon the methods of retailing. To supply thirsty citizens in the days of the Eighteenth Amendment liquor was smuggled across the borders, alcohol lawfully possessed for manufacturing purposes was sold for beverages and a relatively small amount was distilled without license, the annual consumption from all sources averaging perhaps 100,000,000 gallons of hard liquor (1920 to 1932). In the larger cities powerful organizations arose to cater to the bibulous. These gangs, headed by an unusually astute or intelligent man, corrupted the agencies of law enforcement, arranged for a steady supply and set up a complete system of retailing both through luxurious speakeasies, which furnished a variety of entertainment as well as food and illicit drink, and through the private calls of bootleggers upon regular customers. They tried to create a monopoly and were as ready to take a rival "for a ride" as they were thus to entertain a spy or a traitor. The unlucky recipient of this attention was likely to be found along an unfrequented road, filled with slugs from a machine gun; the methods of disposal were all quite final, however various. The St. Valentine's Day massacre of 1929 in Chicago was the slaughter of seven unarmed rivals by one of these bootlegging gangs.

To meet the rising tide of crime several steps were taken. An amendment to the National Prohibition Act was passed in February, 1929, raising the maximum penalty for bootlegging to a fine of $10,000 plus five years in prison, but this carried a rider stipulating that it was the intent of Congress to apply this drastic punishment to major offenders only. A year later, a Federal grand jury sitting at Chicago uncovered what was termed the largest liquor ring since the advent of prohibition.

BORDER SLAVE STATE CONVENTION (1861), also called the Peace Convention or Conference, met in Washington, D. C., Feb. 4–27, 1861, on call by the Virginia legislature, in an attempt to satisfy the states of the far South on the slavery issue. Twenty-one states were represented, with the border states most active. The seven states which had already seceded did not send delegates, nor did Arkansas, Wisconsin, Minnesota, California, Oregon. Ex-President Tyler of Virginia, chosen president of the Convention, stated its purpose—"to bring back the cotton states and thereby restore the Constitution and the Union of the States." The Crittenden Compromise plan, which formed the basis of discussion, was so modified by further compromise in the course of the deliberations that the final recommendations of the Convention satisfied no one. The recommendations, submitted to Congress on Feb. 27, 1861, constituted the last attempt at conciliation on the slavery question in the territories.

BORDER STATES was a designation applied to the tier of slave states bordering on the North, consisting of Delaware, Maryland, Virginia, Kentucky and Missouri. They were largely Southern in sentiment, though many of their economic ties were with the North. They owe their chief significance to their reaction toward secession and the Civil War. None seceded except Virginia, from which West Virginia separated. Kentucky set up and maintained for a few months in 1861 the unique policy of neutrality, and all except Delaware sent considerable numbers of soldiers to the Confederacy. Kentucky and Delaware were the only states to cling to slavery until the Thirteenth Amendment abolished it.

BORDER WAR (1854–59), on the Kansas frontier, resulted from the opening of the territory to slavery, promoted emigration from the Northeast, the arrival of squatters and speculators and the presence of an adventurous element recruited from both North and South. While claim jumping provoked dissension, the slavery issue was controlling. Recurring personal altercations led disputants to organize regulating associations and guerrilla bands. It is impossible to determine which side committed greater excesses in lynching, horse stealing, pillaging and pitched battles. The first eighteen months witnessed killings and robberies, but moderation and self-control prevented serious discord until the murder of a free-state settler, following a quarrel over a land claim, precipitated the bloodless Wakarusa War, December, 1855. "Bleeding Kansas" soon became a grim reality. The "sack" of Lawrence, May 21, 1856, by a posse of "border ruffians," and John Brown's massacre of five proslavery men at Potawatomie three days later started a four months' reign of terror. Free-state men won victories at Black Jack, Franklin, Forts Saunders and Titus, Slough Creek and Hickory Point; their opponents pillaged and later burned Osawatomie but were prevented from destroying Lawrence by official intervention. A semblance of order restored by Gov. J. W. Geary in the fall was of brief duration. The Marais des Cygnes massacre of nine free-state men, May 19, 1858, was the last wholesale slaughter. In the same year disturbances in Linn and Bourbon counties reached critical proportions. Cessation of these early in 1859 terminated major conflict, albeit sporadic disorders continued until the Civil War inaugurated a new chapter in Kansas-Missouri relations. Anticipating a congressional appropriation which did not materialize, territorial commissioners approved claims for losses resulting from border trouble totaling over $400,000, which, though greatly exaggerated, give some notion of the extent of property damage.

BORGNE, LAKE, BATTLE OF (Dec. 14, 1814), was the naval engagement preceding the Battle of New Orleans. The British, with a force of light barges commanded by Capt. Lockyer, captured the five American gunboats commanded by Lt. Thomas ap Catesby Jones guarding Malhereux Island Passage. This cleared the eastern approach to the city and avoided the fortifications along the river. The defeated Americans inflicted such heavy losses upon their captors as to contribute to the many delays which made it possible for the lately arrived Gen. Jackson to organize the defense of the city.

BOSTON. Capt. John Smith explored and mapped the vicinity of Boston in 1614. In 1621 a party from Plymouth visited the site of Boston, the peninsula called Shawmut by the Indians and other landmarks. Individual settlers in the next few years located there

and across the Charles River. Following the Great Migration of 1630 John Winthrop's group first settled at Charlestown, but soon moved over to the Shawmut peninsula. On Sept. 7 of that year it was ordained by the Court of Assistants, sitting at Charlestown, that the new town be named Boston. In 1632 it was made the capital of Massachusetts Bay Colony and that year the first meetinghouse was erected. The first post office was opened in 1639; in 1652 a mint began work and in 1686 the first bank in Boston as well as the first in the colonies was established. A printing press was set up in 1674 (though there had been one in Cambridge, across the Charles, since 1638) and in 1704 the *Boston News-Letter* appeared. By this time Boston was becoming the largest and most important town in America. Its population in the middle 18th century was about 15,000. It was one of the earliest and chief centers of rebellion against the government of England and the first armed conflicts of the Revolutionary War took place in its environs. But Washington forced the British to evacuate it in March, 1776, and thereafter its peace was undisturbed during the war.

In government it was merely a town administered by selectmen until 1822, when it received a city charter. During the 19th century it became the cultural center of the continent and took pride in its nicknames, "the Hub" and "the Athens of America." The names of Agassiz, Alcott, Aldrich, Dana, Eliot, Emerson, Hawthorne, Holmes, Howells, Longfellow, Lowell, Motley, Parkman, Prescott, Thoreau, Ticknor, Whittier and others which almost concurrently graced its golden age, its institutions of learning, its numerous literary, historical, scientific and musical societies, clubs and coteries, its Beacon Hill crowded with the homes of old, aristocratic families, its numerous colonial landmarks, all these gave it an unique distinction and atmosphere. It was the nation's leading port until the 19th century, when it lost the supremacy to New York because of its lack of water communication to the westward—though it still retained a considerable foreign commerce. The city suffered numerous disastrous fires in the 17th and 18th centuries but the worst in its history was that of 1872, when sixty acres in the business portion were swept, with a loss of $60,000,000. By the filling in of tidal marshes and inlets, the original area of 783 acres was greatly expanded. In 1960 Boston's population was 697,197.

BOSTON, SIEGE OF (1775–76). On the day after the battle of Lexington (April 19, 1775) the Massachusetts Committee of Safety called out the militia. On April 22 the Massachusetts Provincial Congress resolved that an army of 30,000 men should be raised, Massachusetts to furnish about half, the other New England colonies the rest. Progress was slow; the old militia regiments could not be held together and new ones had to be raised. On June 17 was fought the battle of Bunker Hill, which, while technically a British success, had the moral effect of an American victory.

On July 3 Washington, chosen as commander-in-chief by the Continental Congress, assumed command. He found the British holding Bunker Hill and Boston Neck; the Americans faced them, their left in Somerville, their right in Roxbury and their center in Cambridge. It was evident that the makeshift force could not be relied upon; so in the face of the enemy a beginning was made upon organizing a Continental Army in place of the colonial contingents.

During the winter no serious operations were undertaken. The Americans needed all their energies for organization; moreover, they were practically without artillery and ammunition. On the British side, the commanders could see no advantage in starting a campaign which they could not press to a finish.

In January, 1776, the guns captured at Ticonderoga (May 10, 1775) reached Cambridge. On March 4 Washington seized Dorchester Heights, from which his guns commanded the city and harbor. The British forces were now in an untenable position and on the 17th they embarked for Halifax. The Americans immediately occupied Boston.

BOSTON MASSACRE (March 5, 1770). Irritated by the presence of British troops in the city and emboldened by the weakness of the royal governor, an irresponsible mob of some sixty rioters set upon a squad of ten soldiers, under the command of Capt. Thomas Preston, which had gone to the rescue of a sentry attacked by the mob. While defending themselves, some of the soldiers, without orders, fired into the mob, killing three and wounding eight, two of whom later died. Public feeling ran high. To prevent further trouble, the two regiments of royal troops were withdrawn from the city. Capt. Preston and his squad were tried; the captain and six soldiers acquitted; two found guilty of manslaughter were branded in the hand and discharged. Public feeling, already aroused, was fanned to flame by such patriots as Samuel Adams and John Hancock. Biased propaganda, including the famous but historically inaccurate picture of the "massacre" issued by Paul Revere, was widely distributed. This minor outbreak, in which the rioters were largely at fault, was the first powerful influence in forming an outspoken anti-British public opinion and a demand for American independence.

BOSTON NEWS-LETTER was the first newspaper published without interruption during the colonial period. Number 1 included the week April 17 to 24, 1704. The original publisher was John Campbell, postmaster, and the first printer was Bartholomew Green. In 1727 Green became the owner and changed its name to *The Weekly News-Letter*. In 1763 the title

was changed to *The Boston Weekly News-Letter and New England Chronicle* and there were later changes of title. Publication ceased in 1776 with the evacuation of Boston by the British troops. No complete file is known but the New-York Historical and Massachusetts Historical Societies both have comparatively good files.

BOSTON POLICE STRIKE. About three quarters of the Boston police force went on strike, Sept. 9, 1919, when the police commissioner refused to recognize their right to affiliate with the American Federation of Labor. Mayor Andrew J. Peters and a citizens' committee headed by James J. Storrow made compromise proposals relating to pay and working conditions in order to prevent the strike, but the police commissioner rejected them. The strike thus precipitated left Boston almost unprotected and riots, disorders and robberies occurred.

The Boston police commissioner is appointed, not by the mayor of the city, but by the governor of the state. Before the strike occurred Calvin Coolidge, then governor, was urged by the mayor and the Storrow Committee to intervene, but refused to act. When the rioting occurred Mayor Peters called out the Boston companies of the militia, restored order and broke the strike. With the city already under control, Gov. Coolidge ordered the police commissioner again to take charge of the police and called out the entire Massachusetts militia, declaring: "There is no right to strike against the public safety by anybody, anywhere, any time." This action gave Mr. Coolidge a reputation as a courageous defender of law and order, which led to his nomination for Vice-President (1920) and his eventual succession to the Presidency.

BOSTON PORT ACT (one of the Coercion Acts) was passed by Parliament on March 31, 1774. To punish Boston for the Tea Party, the act ordered the port of Boston closed on June 1, 1774, until the townspeople paid for the tea destroyed on Dec. 16, 1773, and proved to the crown's satisfaction they were peaceable subjects. Because Boston alone was punished, Lord North believed the colonies would not "take fire." It was a costly mistake: the cry was raised in America that the Port Act was merely a prelude to a "Massacre of American Liberty"; the colonies rallied to Boston's aid; and the Continental Congress was called to concert opposition to the mother country.

BOSTON TEA PARTY took place on the night of Dec. 16, 1773, when 342 chests of tea belonging to the East India Company were thrown into Boston harbor by the patriots. This audacious destruction of British property was caused by the Boston Whigs' fear that if the tea were landed, its cheapness would prove an "invincible temptation" to the people. This, it was believed, would give the East India Company

109

a monopoly of the American tea trade and establish the right of Parliament to raise a colonial revenue by means of port duties. Therefore, when it was learned at the town meeting of Dec. 16 that Gov. Hutchinson was determined to refuse the patriots' demand that the tea ships be permitted to return to England without paying the duty required by law, Sam Adams exclaimed that the meeting could do nothing more to save the country. His words were the signal for a war whoop from the "Indians"—Sons of Liberty disguised with blankets and dusky complexions—waiting outside the meetinghouse. With the cry of "Boston harbor a tea-pot this night," the braves streamed down to the waterfront, where surrounded by an immense crowd of spectators, they made short work of the tea.

The Tea Party was "the boldest stroke which had yet been struck in America." It marked the beginning of violence in the dispute, hitherto waged chiefly with constitutional arguments, between mother country and colonies, and it put the most radical patriots in command throughout America. The efforts of the British government to single out Massachusetts for punishment, instead of isolating the Bay colony, served only to unite the colonies and hasten them into war with the mother country.

BOULDER (HOOVER) DAM, located in Black Canyon on the Colorado River between Arizona and Nevada, 422 miles above the mouth of the Colorado River, was authorized by the Boulder Canyon Project Act in 1928, for flood control, navigation improvement, irrigation, storage and power, subject to the Colorado River Compact; dedicated as Hoover Dam by Secretary of the Interior Ray Lyman Wilbur at the start of construction in 1930; and completed in 1936 by Six Companies, Inc., contractors for the United States Bureau of Reclamation. It rises 727 feet from bedrock, elevates the water surface 584 feet, creates a reservoir (Lake Mead) with a capacity of 30,500,000 acre feet and 1,835,000 horse power of electric energy. The cost was approximately $130,-000,000. In advance of construction, Secretary Wilbur secured power contracts disposing of 4,330,000,000 kilowatt hours annually, adequate to liquidate the Government's investment within fifty years, with large excess revenues. The City of Los Angeles and the Southern California Edison Co. were lessees of the power plant, which was placed in regular operation June 1, 1937.

BOUNTIES, MILITARY. When war forces were raised by volunteering instead of by conscription or militia obligations, bounties stimulated recruiting. For Indian and French campaigns, colonies offered cash inducements, sometimes solely to induce enlistments, sometimes for bringing clothing or weapons into service. The practice was adopted during the Revolution by both Congress and the states. In Janu-

ary, 1776, $6⅔ was offered to fill the Canada expedition; in June $10 for three-year enlistments or re-enlistments; in September $20 and 100 acres for enrollments "for the war." To fill militia quotas, states offered their own bounties, so that states and Congress bid against one another and sums mounted until Congress was offering $200 and New Jersey $1000. Bounty-jumping and re-enlisting were prevalent.

With the peace, bounties shrunk to $6 in 1791 for Indian campaigns, but climbed after the Whisky Rebellion to $16, three months' pay and 160 acres. During the War of 1812 cash offers increased to $124 and 320 acres. They were abolished in 1833 but were resumed in 1847 to raise and re-enlist men for the Mexican War. Civil War bounties repeated Revolutionary history. Disappearing after Appomattox, recruiting bounties were expressly forbidden by the Selective Service Act of 1917.

BOUNTIES, MILITARY, IN THE CIVIL WAR. The earlier system of land grants was not followed except for the favored position of service men under the Homestead Act, but from the start in 1861 states and localities stimulated recruiting by grants of money. This practice reached large proportions during the militia draft of 1862 when even the Federal Government offered $25 for nine-month and $50 for twelve-month volunteers. Since July, 1861, Congress had allowed $100 for three-year men and the latter bounty was offered during the draft, even to conscripts who would volunteer for the longer term.

The climax was reached after the Enrollment Act of March 3, 1863, which legalized the earlier practice of giving $100 to conscripts and substitutes. Also, since those able to do so could avoid the draft on payment of $300, for several months an equivalent sum was given to all three-year and $400 to all five-year volunteers. But, since these bounties were divided over the term of service and were included in the monthly pay, they merely served as an addition to the legal wages. A worse system prevailed for state bounties. It was considered a disgrace for any congressional district to have to submit to a draft, so funds were raised to the utmost limit to fill the quotas before the wheel was set in motion. In consequence, the richer districts by offering $1000 or more could entice volunteers from poorer localities and fill their quotas with ease, whereas the low-bounty regions were badly depleted of man power by the exodus and then had to give an additional quota by draft. Furthermore, a loathsome profession of bounty brokers arose, who not only recruited men and then robbed them of much of their bonus, but also resorted to bribery to secure the muster of broken-down derelicts who had to be discharged later. The problem of the bounty-jumper was greatly aggravated by these practices.

In four years' time the Federal Government paid over $300,000,000 in bounties, and in the last two years alone the states and localities paid about the same amount. The total mercenary fees for the war, including local bounties in the first two years and substitute fees, amounted to about three quarters of a billion dollars.

The bounty-jumper was a product of the system of military bounties. Aided and abetted by bounty brokers, men would enlist, collect bounties, desert and then re-enlist elsewhere, repeating the process until finally caught. One deserter was sentenced to four years' imprisonment after confessing to jumping bounties thirty-two times. The large initial bounty payments was one of the major causes of the more than 268,000 desertions from the ranks of the Union Army.

BOUQUET'S EXPEDITION (1763–65). At the outbreak of Pontiac's War Col. Henry Bouquet was sent with 500 regulars to relieve Fort Pitt. Leaving Carlisle, he marched westward, and after defeating the Indians at the battle of Bushy Run he relieved the beleaguered fort. Bouquet's force was too small to march against the Delaware and Shawnee in the Ohio country, but in 1765 the Pennsylvania Assembly voted an adequate force for the expedition. Desertions from the militia, however, forced Bouquet to call for Virginia volunteers to meet him at Fort Pitt. After many delays he collected some 1500 men and in October, 1765, marched unopposed to the Muskingum River, near the mouth of the Tuscarawas. There he was met by chiefs bringing in eighteen white prisoners and suing for peace. Bouquet demanded the return of all the captives; and, taking the principal chiefs as hostages, he moved south to the forks of the Muskingum in the heart of the Indian country. Here he waited until some 200 prisoners had been surrendered to him.

He then made peace with the Indians, directed them to go to Sir William Johnson to make treaties and took hostages for the performance of this obligation and for the delivery of about 100 prisoners still in the hands of the Shawnee. He returned to Fort Pitt, and the Indians subsequently kept their promises and delivered there the remaining captives. Bouquet's expedition overawed the Indians and ended the reign of terror on the border.

BOURGEOIS. The term was used in the fur trade, especially in the Northwest, and was applied to the leader of a unit. The bourgeois was governor of the pack train, master of the canoe brigade and despot of the trading post. His word was law and his orders were implicitly obeyed. His was the responsibility for the well-being of the men and the success of the trade venture. When the great companies were organized the bourgeois were the wintering partners. A collection of their diaries was published at Quebec in 1889 under the title *Les Bourgeois de la Campagnie du Nord-Ouest*, by L. E. Masson.

BOWIE KNIFE. Perhaps devised by Rezin P. Bowie, perhaps by his brother James, who died in the Alamo, the knife both in origin and use has been the subject of a cycle of heroic folk tales. It achieved fame in the Sandbar Duel in 1827. Although supplanted largely by the six-shooter, it was for four decades a part of the regular equipment of frontiersmen and backwoodsmen from Florida to California. The Mountain Men used a modified form of it. The Texas Rangers rode with it. The "pirates" of the Mississippi disemboweled their victims with it. Its steel of superb temper, the blade well guarded, handle and blade so balanced that it could be thrown as well as wielded, it was both economical and practical for skinning, cutting up meat, eating, fighting duels, stabbing enemies, hammering and performing other services.

BOXER REBELLION. In this antiforeign uprising in China beginning in May, 1900, a total of 231 foreigners and many Christian Chinese were murdered. On June 17 began the siege of the legations in Peking. The United States concerted with Great Britain, Russia, Germany, France and Japan to conduct a military expedition for the relief of the legations, sending 5000 troops for this purpose. The international relief expedition marched from Taku to Tientsin and thence to Peking, raising the siege of the legation on Aug. 4. The United States, however, did not join in the punitive expedition under the German Commander in Chief Count von Waldersee. In July Secretary of State John Hay issued a circular note to "preserve Chinese territorial and administrative entity," and during the Peking Congress (Feb. 5–Sept. 7, 1901) the United States opposed the demand for a punitive indemnity which might lead to the dismemberment of China. The Boxer Protocol finally fixed the indemnity at $332,000,000, provided for the punishment of guilty Chinese officials, and permitted the Powers to maintain legation guards at Peking and between the capital and the sea.

BOY SCOUTS OF AMERICA. This organization was incorporated Feb. 8, 1910, and granted a Federal charter from Congress in 1916. It was based on the English principles modified to meet the needs of American youth. The membership June 30, 1958, was as follows: total boys—3,281,119; total adult leaders—1,266,151.

The purpose is to develop character and to train for citizenship. The organization consists of a younger boys' program for boys from nine to eleven who are known as Cub Scouts; boys from eleven years upward are Boy Scouts, and boys who are fourteen and in ninth grade in school may become Explorers. Boys

111

fifteen years of age, regardless of grade, may join Boy Scouts or Explorers.

It supplements the work of the home, church and school, provides a constructive program of leisure-time activities, very appealing to boys. It aims, through outdoor projects, such as camping, hiking, signaling, cooking in the open and nature study, to teach boys to be self-reliant and resourceful and, through knowledge of first aid, life saving, swimming, etc., to enable them to be of service to others.

Volunteer leadership is a fundamental element in the Boy Scout scheme. Scouts are organized in Patrols, under a boy leader, and Troops, under a volunteer leader known as a Scoutmaster. The boy enters scouting as a Tenderfoot. As he advances in skill he advances in rank, receiving recognition. The official scout uniform is protected by Congress.

Since the beginning of the organization 28,000,000 boys and leaders have been connected with the movement in the United States. The world Scout membership in June, 1958, was 7,589,183, divided among some 64 different lands.

BOYCOTTING. A boycott is a collective refusal to purchase commodities or services from a manufacturer or merchant whose employment or trade practices are regarded as unfair. Occasionally the economic boycott has been used by consumers against aggressor nations. Its chief use is by organized workers to secure better conditions of employment. Means for effecting a boycott include the distribution of cards, handbills, fair lists, unfair lists and picketing.

In the United States the courts have made a distinction between "primary" and "secondary" boycotts. The former involves refusal of patronage by employees directly concerned in an industrial dispute; the latter involves attempts to persuade or coerce third parties to boycott an employer.

Considerable uncertainty and confusion characterize the law of boycotts in the United States, but a few general principles are fairly well established. In most jurisdictions it is not unlawful for an association of aggrieved workers to withold patronage. Moreover, it does not appear to be unlawful in the several states for such workers to ask or persuade others to assist in their cause. It is illegal, however, to use physical violence, coercion or intimidation. The behavior of pickets must be peaceful and customers must be accorded complete freedom in entering and leaving the boycotted establishment.

The pivotal point in the law of boycotts is the use of pressure against third parties. Because most manufacturers do not distribute their goods directly but through wholesalers and retailers, organized labor can make a boycott effective only by bringing pressure upon such dealers. This is in essence a secondary boycott, which is regarded as unlawful in most jurisdictions. In Arizona, California and Oklahoma, however, all peacefully conducted boycotts have been held legal, and some of the lower courts of New York have sustained them. In Missouri and Montana the printing and distributing of circulars for purposes of boycott may not be directly enjoined by the courts.

The boycott was held unlawful in the United States as early as 1886. In 1908 the U. S. Supreme Court in the Danbury hatters case decided that the secondary boycott constitutes a conspiracy in restraint of trade under the provisions of the Sherman Antitrust Law (1890). The Court held that treble damages might be recovered for losses sustained by the manufacturer through the interstate boycott. In the Buck Stove and Range Co. case (1911), the same tribunal decided that all means employed to make effective an unlawful boycott are illegal, even though in themselves such means are innocent. Disregard of an injunction in this case by certain officials of the American Federation of Labor resulted in citation for contempt and jail sentence for one year. Although the sentence was subsequently set aside, the decision greatly discouraged the use of the boycott in labor disputes.

An attempt to escape from the restrictions of the Sherman Act was made through Section 20 of the Clayton Antitrust Act (1914), which prohibits the use of the injunction to restrain employees from picketing, boycotting and advising others to withhold patronage from an employer when such activities are carried on by peaceful and lawful means. In the Duplex Printing Press Co. case (1921), however, the U. S. Supreme Court ruled that all methods employed to make effective interstate boycotts involving third parties are unlawful.

BOZEMAN TRAIL. Traced by John M. Bozeman, 1863–65, as the shortest and easiest route for emigrants to the Virginia City gold fields, the trail continued the route from the South Platte at Julesburg (Fort Sedgwick), past Fort Laramie, where it crossed the Oregon Trail, to the Powder River Crossing at Fort Connor. Thence is passed eastward of the Big Horn Mountains to the Yellowstone River and westward to Virginia City.

The first caravan used the trail in the summer following the Powder River Campaign. Notwithstanding the Treaty of Laramie in 1851 the Sioux Indians resented the invasion and when Forts Reno, Phil Kearny and C. F. Smith were established for emigrant protection they went on the warpath. Red Cloud's War followed. By 1868 all posts along the trail had been abandoned.

Following suppression of the Sioux in 1877 the Bozeman Trail became an important route for cattle moving north from Texas into Wyoming and Montana.

BRADDOCK'S EXPEDITION (1755). After the battle of Great Meadows, England and France prepared for war. Gen. Edward Braddock, appointed commander of all the British forces in America, was dispatched with two regiments for a campaign the first objective of which was Fort Duquesne. The regulars and the colonial forces rendezvoused at Fort Cumberland, to start for Fort Duquesne by the route later called Braddock's Road. Wagons and horses were secured from Pennsylvania with Franklin's aid; Indian allies came from Aughwick, but most of them deserted when Braddock ordered their families home.

The army, 2200 strong, started west June 7, but had advanced only to Little Meadows (near Grantsville, Md.) by June 16. Then, on the advice of Washington, his aide-de-camp, Braddock pushed on rapidly with some 1200 men and a minimum of artillery, leaving a command under Col. Dunbar to bring up the heavier goods. On July 9 the expedition crossed and recrossed the Monongahela near Turtle Creek. Up to this point every precaution had been taken against surprise, but apparently the officers now grew overconfident. A hill commanding the route was left unoccupied and the troops marched in an order too close for safety.

From Fort Duquesne Capt. Beaujeu led some 250 French and 600 Indians to oppose Braddock. He had not laid his ambush when the two parties unexpectedly met. The British opened fire, putting most of the French to flight and killing Beaujeu. His subordinate Dumas, however, rallied the Indians to seize the hill that Braddock had neglected and to surround the British line. The van of the English, falling back, became entangled with the main body so that order was lost and maneuvering was impossible. For three hours the British stood under a galling fire; then Braddock ordered a retreat. The general was mortally wounded; many of the officers were killed; the retreat became a rout. Washington, sent to Dunbar by Braddock, reported the defeat and dispatched wagons for the wounded.

Dunbar, now in command, ordered quantities of stores destroyed, and retreated rapidly to Fort Cumberland. Refusing the request of Virginia and Pennsylvania that he build a fort at Raystown (Bedford, Pa.) and defend the frontier, he marched to Philadelphia in August and left the border to suffer Indian raids. Though Braddock's expedition failed, it demonstrated that an army could be marched over the Alleghenies, it taught the troops something of Indian fighting and its very mistakes contributed to the success of the Forbes Expedition.

Braddock's road ran from the Potomac at Will's Creek (Cumberland, Md.) to the Monongahela at Turtle Creek. The section from Will's Creek to the upper Youghiogheny River was opened by the Ohio Company, probably in 1752. In 1754 Washington improved the road to Great Meadows and extended it to Gist's plantation (six miles northeast of the present Uniontown, Pa.). In 1755 Braddock's expedition used the road and extended it almost to Fort Duquesne. After Braddock's defeat the route he followed facilitated Indian raids; still later it became a highway for western emigration and part of it was incorporated in the National Road.

BRADSTREET'S EXPEDITIONS. After the disaster at Ticonderoga in July, 1758, Lt. Col. John Bradstreet led a successful raid which went far to restore American morale.

Taking command in early August of 2600 men secretly mobilized in the Mohawk Valley, Bradstreet moved swiftly forward along the waterways. He reached Oswego on the 24th and, crossing Lake Ontario, effected a surprise which enabled him to capture the fort at Cataraqui (present Kingston) on the 27th. Both the post and the French shipping were put to the torch. This bold campaign broke the French hold of the water routes by which the western posts were supplied, contributing to the evacuation of Fort Duquesne later in the same year and to the surrender of Fort Niagara in 1759.

Unfortunately, his record suffered from his next assignment, command of the expedition of 1764 to the Great Lakes area to place Indian relations on a peace footing following the uprising under Pontiac.

On the shores of Lake Erie, Bradstreet revealed ignorance of Indian affairs by concluding improper treaties with unimportant delegations of Delawares and Shawnees. In this he went beyond his instructions; worse yet, he did not recover possession of all prisoners held by the former foes. To Col. Bouquet, advancing from the Forks of the Ohio, fell the duty of pushing far into Ohio to restore white prestige.

Bradstreet proceeded to Detroit, where he was only partially successful. While returning, he failed to carry out instructions to move on mutinous Scioto villages, a dangerous situation in that quarter being saved by Bouquet's steadiness. Delaying too long on the Sandusky shore, Bradstreet's forces, near to mutiny, encountered severe hardships. His reputation as a popular hero did not survive.

"BRAIN TRUST." Prior to his nomination as the Democratic candidate for the Presidency in 1932, Franklin D. Roosevelt had brought together three close advisers, Raymond Moley, Rexford G. Tugwell and Adolph A. Berle, Jr., all professors in Columbia University. These three continued to aid Roosevelt during his campaign for election and, after his inauguration on March 4, 1933, they became prominent in the councils of the chief executive. To keep them in Washington they were given salaried offices, Moley in the Department of State, Tugwell in the Department of Agriculture and Berle in the Reconstruction Finance Corporation. They and all professors or "intellectuals" who subsequently joined the administration were indiscriminately dubbed the "Brain

Trust," whether or not they were close to the President. The impression was created that they were responsible for everything that was done, so the expression "Brain Trust" became a symbol for all New Deal experimentation.

BRANDY STATION, BATTLE OF (June 9, 1863). Ordered by Hooker (U.) to ascertain whether Lee's army was moving northward, Pleasonton threw the Federal cavalry, 7981 strong, with 3000 infantry, across the Rappahannock. At Beverly Ford, Buford's division drove part of Stuart's (C.) 10,292 cavalry toward Fleetwood Hill and Brandy Station. Gregg's and Duffie's divisions, crossing below, attacked Stuart's rear at Fleetwood. Stuart hurried troops thither, precipitating the greatest cavalry conflict of the war. The Confederates retained the field, but Pleasonton learned that Lee was marching toward Maryland.

BRANDYWINE, BATTLE OF THE (Sept. 11, 1777), was fought near Brandywine Creek, Chester County, Pa. The British and Hessian troops commanded by Howe, Cornwallis and Knyphausen composed a force of 18,000. The American Army under Washington numbered 11,000, of whom a large number were militia. Following a feint attack by the Hessians upon the Americans at Chad's Ford, the British crossed the East Brandywine at Jefferis' Ford, continued southward and suddenly attacked Sullivan's troops near Birmingham Meetinghouse. The Americans, though outnumbered, fought gallantly, but were compelled to retire. Washington had received faulty news concerning the approach of the British. At night Washington withdrew his army without demoralization to Chester, Pa.

BRANNAN PLAN, first proposed by Charles Brannan, Secretary of Agriculture, in April, 1959, is a farm price-support plan using direct payments to the farmer, under certain conditions, as a substitute for price supports. The proposal has aroused considerable opposition. Its opponents characterize it as unsound and fantastically expensive. Its supporters call it "a rational approach to income protection for agriculture" and consider it "a much more effective and cheaper way to subsidize the farmer when subsidy is needed." From time to time the plan has been urged in Congress, usually in amended form, but no Federal legislative approval has been given it.

BRETTON WOODS CONFERENCE (July 1–22, 1944). This was held in New Hampshire, July 1–22, 1944, to make plans for postwar international economic co-operation similar to the groundwork for political co-operation laid by the Atlantic Charter and the Four-Power Declaration at the Moscow Conference of Foreign Ministers. Agreement was reached for an International Monetary Fund of $8,800,000,-000, as assigned at the conference (American quota $2,750,000,000), to promote exchange stability and expansion of international trade, and an International Bank for Reconstruction and Development (the World Bank, as it came to be called) with authorized capital of $10,000,000,000 (American subscription $3,175,000,000). Signatories at the conference were: Australia, Belgium, Bolivia, Brazil, Canada, Chile, China, Colombia, Costa Rica, Cuba, Czechoslovakia, the Dominican Republic, Ecuador, Egypt, El Salvador, Ethiopia, France, Greece, Guatemala, Honduras, Iceland, India, Iran, Iraq, Luxembourg, Mexico, the Netherlands, Nicaragua, Norway, Panama, Paraguay, Peru, the Philippines, Poland, South Africa, the United Kingdom, the United States, Uruguay, Venezuela, and Yugoslavia. Haiti, Liberia, New Zealand, and Russia attended but did not sign.

BRIAND-KELLOGG PACT was signed in Paris by fifteen nations on Aug. 27, 1928. Eventually other governments adhered to the treaty. It grew out of negotiations which were begun between the United States and France. Article I provides that the parties renounce war as an instrument of national policy in their relations with one another. Article II provides that the settlement of disputes between the parties shall never be sought except by pacific means. Connected with the text of the pact are certain interpretations of Secretary of State Kellogg which were included as a part of the negotiations and which made clear that the treaty did not prevent wars of self-defense, that it was not inconsistent with the Covenant of the League of Nations and that it did not interfere with the rendering of aid under the Locarno treaties and the so-called treaties of neutrality.

BRICKS, EARLY MANUFACTURE OF. Brickmakers came with the earliest settlers, and bricks were made in Salem, Mass., as early as 1629, in Hartford, Conn., as early as 1638 and in New Haven as early as 1640. There was also no lack of brickmakers in New Netherland; kilns were in operation in New Amsterdam by 1628. To the south, there were brick buildings in Virginia in 1611, and a visitor to Charleston in 1682 reported there was excellent brick on hand. These facts should dispel the legend that building after building in colonial America was put together with imported bricks. "There is no doubt," concluded Hugh Morrison in his authoritative *Early American Architecture* (New York, 1952) "that after the first few years brick could be made locally far more cheaply than it could be imported."

BRIDGER, FORT, was a frontier trading post and later a fort of the U. S. Army, located on Black's Fork, Uinta County, Wyo. It was named after James

(Jim) Bridger, trapper and scout, who with his partner, Louis Vasquez, built it in 1843 and operated it for a number of years.

Although trading in pelts was carried on, Bridger's post is best known as a way station and supply point for emigrants bound for Oregon, Utah and California. Its establishment marks the beginning of caravan travel to the Pacific Coast. The post was taken over by Mormon colonists from Utah about 1855; was burned by the Mormons on the approach of United States troops in the Mormon War of 1857; was rebuilt as a military post by the U. S. Army in 1858; and was finally abandoned in 1890. For many years it was famous as a mail, express and telegraph station.

BRIDGES. In 1541 Coronado, on his way to the legendary city of Quivira, had his men build a bridge over the Pecos River. This structure, probably of wooden piles with a log deck, is believed to have been the first erected by white men in what is now the United States; probably it stood a little southeast of Santa Fe, N. Mex. The early permanent bridges were of similar design, because their builders were carpenters and wood was plentiful.

But no significant advance occurred until the early 19th century, with the work of three pioneer bridge-builders—Timothy Palmer, Louis Wernwag, and Theodore Burr. Their bridges were all combinations of the timber arch-and-truss and covered. Burr was the most prominent of the three; the majority of covered wooden bridges in the United States were of his design.

In 1820 Ithiel Town patented a lattice truss. It was a true truss, entirely free from arch action. Because it employed small pieces of lumber and was easy to erect, it became very popular.

During the 1840's four men contributed to the evolution of the truss. William Howe patented a truss destined to become the most popular one in America and the first one to be used extensively by the railroads. Representing the transition from wood to iron, the Howe truss used timber diagonals in tension and cast-iron verticals in compression. Then Caleb and Thomas Pratt invented their truss, the reverse of the Howe, with the diagonals, not the verticals, in tension and of iron. The fourth man was Squire Whipple of Utica, N. Y., who was the first to analyze correctly the stresses in trusses.

The introduction of cast iron led James Finley, of Fayette County, Pa., to patent his design for an eye-bar chain suspension bridge with the roadway suspended from the cables—the first instance of this feature since the 16th century. His bridges, however, were not large; his first one—a 70-foot span—was built in 1801. The first bridge to be built entirely of cast iron in the United States was an 80-foot arch, completed in 1836 over Dunlap's Creek at Brownsville, Pa., by Richard Delafield.

As the railroads spread, cast-iron bridges were found to be undependable. Consequently, after 1850, wrought-iron trusses were designed by engineers in the employ of railroads. Among these were Wendell Bollman, Albert Fink, John H. Linville, and George S. Morison.

During the 1870's and 1880's steel began to replace wrought iron, and bridge specialists appeared, for the new material and heavy loading required careful, detailed scientific designing. The truss began to be used in combination with the arch, the suspension, and the cantilever types, although the simple truss did not completely disappear.

The first all-steel bridge, a railroad truss bridge over the Missouri River at Glasgow, S. Dak., was designed by William Sooy Smith in 1878. Ten years before this James Buchanan Eads was designing his great three-span arch bridge across the Mississippi at St. Louis—the first structure to make extensive use of steel. Completed in 1874, it was far ahead of its time. Its three trussed-arch spans—502, 520, and 502 feet—utilized hollow tubular chord members of high-strength, chrome-nickel steel, and were built by the cantilever method of construction so that river traffic was not impeded. For the foundations, which had to go to bedrock, Eads employed pneumatic caissons—their first use in the founding of large piers.

Steel arch bridges followed. One of the heaviest was the Hell Gate Bridge over the East River at New York City. Completed in 1917 by Gustav Lindenthal, it had a main span of 977½ feet. In 1960 the longest steel arch in the world, with a span of 1652 feet, was the Bayonne Bridge over the Kill Van Kull, New York, opened in 1931.

The arch was also favored for concrete and reinforced concrete, when these materials were introduced in the late 19th century. The first reinforced-concrete bridge in the United States was a 20-foot arch, built in Golden Gate Park, San Francisco, in 1889. As of 1960, the longest reinforced concrete bridge in the United States was the George Westinghouse Bridge over Turtle Creek Valley, east of Pittsburgh. The total length of its five spans was 1510 feet—the longest single span being 460 feet. At mid-century, precast and prestressed concrete were relatively new forms of this material, being used for small spans on highways and turnpikes. Instead of the arch, girder and rigid-frame types were preferred, for they were better adapted to the nature of the material.

While Eads was at work in St. Louis, John A. Roebling was erecting suspension bridges, inventing the air-stringing method of building parallel wire cables and using the truss and auxiliary cables to stiffen the design. In 1867 he came to New York to build Brooklyn Bridge. At his death, his son Washington Roebling carried on the work, and in 1883 this great bridge with its main span of almost 1600 feet was open to traffic.

American engineers since Roebling have so far advanced the suspension-bridge type that its potentialities seem almost limitless. The George Washington Bridge over the Hudson River, the heaviest bridge of its type with a main span of 3500 feet, was designed by Othmar H. Ammann in 1931. Then six years later came the Golden Gate Bridge, designed by Joseph B. Strauss. Its span of 4200 feet made it the longest suspension bridge in the world. The Transbay Bridge system, with a total length of eight miles, contained two suspension bridges, each with a main span of 2310 feet. The Mackinac Straits Bridge system, with a total length of five miles, contained a suspension bridge with a main span of 3800 feet, the second largest in the world. Its designer was David B. Steinman.

During the era of railroad expansion, the truss-cantilever type became important because of its great rigidity. The longest cantilever in the world was the Quebec Bridge, with a span-length of 1800 feet. Cantilevers were constantly built as parts of bridge systems and great expressways. The cantilever of the Transbay Bridge, with its main span of 1400 feet, was the longest in the United States until superseded in 1958 by the span of the New Orleans Bridge, which was 1575 feet long—the third longest cantilever in the world. And cantilevers formed parts of the greater New Orleans Expressway, the longest highway bridge in the world, which extended for 24 miles across Lake Pontchartrain, and also of the "Sunshine Skyway" that crossed Tampa Bay for about 15 miles.

American engineers have made an important contribution to the evolution of bridge-building. They developed the truss, both in practice and theory. They originated the modern suspension bridge type and have carried it to incredible dimensions. They have pioneered in reinforced, precast, and prestressed concrete and in the use of steel alloys and aluminum. The first all-aluminum bridge in the world was erected at Massena, N. Y., by Alcoa in 1946—a plate-girder of 100-foot span.

BRISTOE CAMPAIGN (Oct. 9–22, 1863). Lee (C.) crossed the Rapidan, Oct. 9, turning Meade's (U.) right flank, and advanced toward Washington. Using parallel roads Meade marched rapidly to cover the capital. He reached Centreville first, his rear guard, under Warren (U.), severely repulsing A. P. Hill's (C.) corps at Bristoe Station, Oct. 14. A battle under favorable conditions proving impossible, Lee returned to the Rappahannock.

BRITISH DEBTS were the debts owed by the American colonial merchants and planters to British merchants before the Revolution and which, obviously remaining unpaid during the war, continued a subject of dispute between the United States and England till 1802. The debts were a natural conse-

quence of the economic system prevalent in the colonies. The merchants of the Northern colonies and the planters of the Southern colonies bought practically all of their manufactured articles from English merchants. The merchants of the northern colonies depended on their trade and the planters upon their prospective crops to pay the balances due in England. The result, from 1763 to 1775, was a rather constant indebtedness of some £3,000,000—most of which was owed by the Southern planters. Stoppage of payment on these debts was frequently resorted to by the colonies in their fight against the colonial legislation of Parliament in the period, 1763–75. And the possibility of wiping out the indebtedness by war was one of the contributing causes of the Revolution.

During the Revolution all of the states enacted laws affecting these debts. In the states north of Maryland most of the debts were due to Loyalists, while in the Southern states most of the debts belonged to the British merchants. Some of the laws confiscated Loyalist estates, including debts (England later claimed that debts due to Loyalists should be included with those due to British merchants); some laws sequestered the debts due to British merchants; others confiscated such debts; while still others banished or restricted the activities of the agents of the British merchants; other laws, such as paper money legislation, just as effectively abolished or barred the collection of the debts. In Maryland £144,536 of debts due to British merchants were paid into the state treasury; in Virginia about £287,000; and in North Carolina over £50,000.

These debts were an important problem in the negotiation of the Definitive Treaty of Peace in 1782–83. At one time the British ministers were ready to make peace without any guarantee for the Loyalists and merchants. However, John Adams, more interested in the fisheries than in the debts of the planters and having "no notion of cheating anybody," was responsible for the provision (Article IV) that the debts due before the war were to be paid in sterling. Article V required that Congress should recommend to the several states the restoration of the confiscated estates of the Loyalists. Article IV met with determined opposition in the Southern states and Article V in all of the states. Practically all of the states either delayed or refused compliance. British merchants and their agents were denied admission to some states; courts were frequently closed to the debt cases; installment laws were passed; wartime interest was disallowed; and in some cases the debts were declared to have been terminated by the war and the wartime legislation of the states. On the other hand, American Negro slaves were carried off by the British troops; American posts along the Canadian border were occupied by the British; and Indians were incited to attack the frontier.

With the adoption of the Constitution, opposed by many of the debtors, a new chapter in the debts controversy opened. The Federal courts facilitated the collection of many of the debts; and the new administration was able to negotiate more effectively with England relative to the infractions of the treaty of peace. After Gouverneur Morris' mission to London an English minister, George Hammond, was sent to the United States. However, the Jefferson-Hammond negotiations failed to settle the debt question. Nothing more was done till the strained relations of 1792–93 led to the mission of John Jay and the famous Jay's Treaty. By Article VI of this treaty the United States accepted liability for such of the debts as could not at that date be recovered due to legal impediments imposed by the states. A five-man commission, to adjudicate the claims, sat at Philadelphia from May 29, 1797, till July 31, 1799. Claims to the amount of £5,638,629 8s. 1d. were received. The commissioners, however, were unable to agree on such important matters as: the jurisdiction of the commission; the nature of legal impediments; the question of the solvency of debtors; wartime interest, etc. The entire matter, therefore, fell again into the regular diplomatic channels. A final settlement was negotiated by Rufus King and the Addington Ministry on Jan. 8, 1802. By the terms of this settlement the United States was to pay, in lieu of its liability under Article VI of Jay's Treaty, the lump sum of £600,000. An English commission sat till 1811 adjusting the claims. It found only about 20–25% of the claims good, but even so was able to pay, with the £600,000, only about 45% of the approved claims.

BRONCO, a Spanish word, was early used in America to characterize hostile savages as opposed to *Indios mansos*—gentle Indians. In time the Spaniards applied the adjective to wild horses, a usage peculiar to America. Frontiersmen borrowed the adjective and converted it into a noun, often misspelled *bronk* or *broncho*. The mustang is not synonymous with the bronco until caught and more or less broken. Loosely, a bronco is a range horse, a cow horse; more specifically and accurately, a range horse that pitches or bucks. Through Wild West shows, Rodeos, Cowboy Reunions, Frontier Days celebrations, the Calgary Stampede, etc., he is familiar to the American public; he is found in the *remuda* of every sizable ranch. The range horse is basically of Spanish (Andalusian and Arabian) stock, but in the Americas he developed a buck virtually unknown in Europe or Asia. There horses are traditionally "gentled"; but by Indians, cowboys, vaqueros and gauchos they are "broken," usually a rough process hardly conductive to gentleness.

BROOK FARM INSTITUTE OF AGRICULTURE AND EDUCATION grew out of the realistic social criticism of the day, touched by German Transcendentalism. George Ripley was the indefatigable and brave center of the group which moved to a farm of 200 acres in West Roxbury, Mass., in April, 1841. The members undertook to build a co-operative community in which manual and intellectual labor might be united and men and women live in a simple but cultivated society. They worked hard, erected new buildings and did their best with the poor soil.

Ripley came to believe more organization was necessary and an adaptation of the Fourier phalanx was adopted in 1845, with the primary departments of agricultural, domestic and mechanic arts. Since communal living and centralized efficiency were basic to their new doctrine, they built a large phalanstery. Fire destroyed it in 1846 while the members were celebrating its completion. Money was depleted, they could not pay the promised 5% on investments, and the experiment had to end, but not in great debt.

Though not a financial success, Brook Farm was a great social success. Gaiety, entertainment, music, spirited talk, a successful progressive educational program with outside pupils and a generous economic democracy were there. Although the great Transcendentalists had too little faith in external reform to join the group, Hawthorne, Charles A. Dana and John S. Dwight were members and the famous of Boston and Concord came often to talk or lecture. Their interest has kept the farm in memory.

BROOKLYN, N. Y. The first settlements within the present boundaries of Brooklyn were made at Gowanus and the Wallabout in 1636 and 1637. In 1642 a ferry was established connecting Long Island with New Amsterdam, and within four years a hamlet called Breuckelen, after a village in Holland, was laid out about a mile from the ferry slip. This community, with its neighboring settlements, was organized as the town of Breuckelen in 1646. The name finally became Brooklyn, although for a century there were variant spellings. The district near the slip, called "the Ferry," became a market for Long Island agricultural products. After the Revolution there was an influx of non-Dutch settlers. In 1801 Brooklyn Navy Yard was established at the Wallabout. A district covering a square mile, with the Ferry as its nucleus, having a population of about 4000, was chartered as Brooklyn village in 1816. Growth was now very rapid. In 1834 Brooklyn township, numbering 24,000, was chartered as a city. During the quarter century before the Civil War Brooklyn's population multiplied more than eleven times. In 1854 the city of Williamsburgh was annexed. A residential suburb of New York—the "city of homes and churches"—it was also a great manufacturing, shipping and commercial center.

Brooklyn Bridge was the first bridge built across the East River between New York and Brooklyn.

There had been talk of bridging the river as early as 1840. The corporation to build the structure was organized in 1867, the city of Brooklyn subscribing for $3,000,000 stock and New York for $1,500,000. John A. Roebling was chosen chief engineer, but he died in 1869, and his son Washington completed the task. The bridge was thirteen years in building, and cost $15,500,000. It was opened on May 24, 1883.

By 1896 Brooklyn had expanded to take in the entire county of Kings, and on Jan. 1, 1898, as the borough of Brooklyn, it became part of the city of New York. It is now the largest borough of the city, with an estimated population (1958) of 2,764,000. Subway tunnels and three great suspension bridges connect Brooklyn with Manhattan. The Brooklyn-Battery Tunnel (opened in 1950) connects the two boroughs under New York Harbor. It is the longest under-water tunnel in this country and the second longest vehicular tunnel in the world.

BROWNISTS, a term applied to groups in England (*ca.* 1580–1660) which openly separated from the established church, was derived from Robert Browne, author of *Reformation without tarrying for anie,* 1583. Browne advocated an essentially Congregational polity, a church made up only of the visible elect who were to choose and install their own officers. Later Separatists, including the Pilgrims at Plymouth, probably owed much to Browne, as also did the settlers of Massachusetts Bay, although the latter always insisted that they had never "separated" from the Church of England.

BROWNSVILLE AFFAIR. About midnight of Aug. 13, 1906, unidentified Negro soldiers of Companies B, C and D, 25th U. S. Infantry at Fort Brown, Brownsville, Texas, angered at slights from white civilians, marched into town and shot into houses and at citizens indiscriminately, killing one man and wounding a policeman. Their officers investigated next morning but learned nothing. President Roosevelt ordered a thorough investigation which resulted in proof that the guilty men were from these companies but failed to identify them because no soldier would give evidence against his comrades. On Nov. 5 the President ordered 159 privates and noncommissioned officers from these companies and eight others "discharged without honor from the Army" and "forever debarred from the Army or Navy" because of their "conspiracy of silence." Sen. J. B. Foraker championed the cause of the discharged men; but after the Senate Committee on Military Affairs had conducted a lengthy investigation the majority sustained the President.

BRYAN-CHAMORRO TREATY, between the United States and Nicaragua, was signed Aug. 5, 1914. It granted to the United States in perpetuity the ex-

clusive right to build an interoceanic canal in Nicaragua, subject to a subsequent agreement regarding details of construction and operation; and also a 99-year lease of Great and Little Corn Islands and a right to establish a naval base in the Gulf of Fonseca. Nicaragua received $3,000,000.

Costa Rica and El Salvador protested against the treaty. Costa Rica claimed that an arbitral award by President Cleveland in 1888 had bound Nicaragua not to make grants for canal purposes without consulting her, because of her interest in the San Juan River. El Salvador asserted that the waters of the Gulf of Fonseca belonged jointly to El Salvador, Nicaragua and Honduras. Both appealed to the Central American Court which decided that Nicaragua had violated her neighbors' rights and should take steps to restore the legal status existing before the treaty. It did not declare the treaty itself invalid, because it had no jurisdiction over the United States. Nicaragua refused to accept the decision and the treaty remained in force. The proposed naval base has not been established and the Corn Islands remain under Nicaraguan jurisdiction, except for a small area occupied by the United States for a lighthouse.

BUCKSHOT WAR (1838). As a result of the state election of 1838, both parties claimed control of the Pennsylvania House of Representatives. Two speakers were elected. A mob, largely from Philadelphia, assembled in Harrisburg, threatened violence and forced Thaddeus Stevens, Charles B. Penrose and Thomas H. Burrowes to escape from the Senate chamber through a window. Gov. Ritner called for United States troops which the President refused, whereupon the governor called out the Philadelphia militia, requisitioning among other equipment thirteen rounds of buckshot cartridges, whence the name "The Buckshot War." Three Whigs voted with the Democrats enabling them to organize the House, whereupon order was restored.

BUCKTAILS (1818–26) were a New York State party opposed to the canal policy of Gov. DeWitt Clinton; named from a Tammany insignia, a deer's tail worn in the hat.

BUENA VISTA, BATTLE OF (Feb. 22–23, 1847). During the Mexican War Gen. Zachary Taylor had advanced his army of 4700 men from Monterrey to a mountain pass south of Saltillo. Near the hacienda of Buena Vista he encountered a Mexican force under Santa Anna three times the size of his own. Though the Americans lost ground the first day, they won a brilliant victory on the second and the Mexicans withdrew. Taylor gained a reputation which made him President, but the further conquest of Mexico was entrusted to Gen. Scott.

BUFFALO, or more properly the American bison, at

118

the time of the discovery occupied about one third of the continent from 63° N. Lat. in Canada to about 25° N. Lat. in Mexico, and from the Blue Mountains of Oregon to the western portions of New York, Pennsylvania, Virginia and the Carolinas. The chief habitat was, however, the plains between the Missouri River and the Rocky Mountains. Fossil remains date to the mid-Pleistocene period.

Easily hunted and of large size—the males reaching 2000 pounds—the buffalo were everywhere a favorite source of food for the Indians and frontier whites. As civilization advanced westward the animals were exterminated and by 1850 few if any remained east of the Mississippi. The dry plains, however, still contained numbers so vast as to be almost impossible of computation. Gen. Phil H. Sheridan, in 1866, estimated 100,000,000 buffalo in the region between Camp Supply, I. T., and Fort Dodge, Kans., and this was only part of the western buffalo.

Plains Indians based their civilization and religion to a large extent on the buffalo, as those farther east based theirs on the maize. Methods of killing included stalking, stampeding herds over cliffs, and driving them into cul-de-sacs. When horses were introduced in the plains, the methods of pursuit and the surround were added. Every part of the buffalo was useful to the Indians, who depended on the bison for food, shelter, weapons and clothing. Natural increase, however, kept pace with the slaughter until the advent of the white man.

Building of the Union Pacific and Kansas Pacific railroads, the early trains of which were sometimes stopped by herds crossing the tracks, led to the disappearance of the animals in the central plains and by 1875 there were two distinct groups, the northern and southern. The railroads furnished transportation outlets and in the 1870's hide and meat hunters began a systematic and wholesale destruction, shipping robes and meat to the East. By 1878 the southern herd was practically extinct, although the four last survivors were not killed until 1889. Similarly the northern herd was exterminated by 1884, except for a few individuals. Buffalo bones, gathered by settlers, later were important in commerce.

Dr. William T. Hornaday, of the National Museum, first called the nation's attention to the virtual disappearance of the buffalo in 1886. He made a census in 1889 which showed a total of only 1091 American bison existing throughout the world. This was the low ebb. Many individuals became interested and in 1905 the American Bison Society was organized. Through its efforts public consciousness was aroused and today the danger of complete extinction seems ended.

In 1903 a census revealed in the United States 41 herds in 24 states, with 969 animals, and a total in the world of 1644. The 1933 census showed 121 herds in 41 states, with 4404 animals, while Canada contained 17,043 and the world total was 21,701.

BUFFALO CHIPS was the dried excrement of the American bison. It was widely used for fuel by the first white men on the Great Plains.

BULL BOATS. When Hudson's Bay Company traders first visited the Mandan Indians in 1790 they found that tribe possessed of tublike boats with framework of willow poles, covered with raw buffalo hides. Later, frontiersmen who ascended the Missouri noted this light, convenient craft. From 1810 to 1830, American fur traders on the tributaries of the Missouri regularly built boats eighteen to thirty feet long, using the methods of construction employed by the Indians in making their circular boats. These elongated bull boats were capable of transporting two tons of fur down the shallow waters of the Platte.

"BULL MOOSE" PARTY was a popular nickname given to the Progressive party of 1912–16 which nominated Theodore Roosevelt for the Presidency at a national convention in Chicago, Ill., in August, 1912. The Progressives seceded from the Republican party following the renomination of President William H. Taft. The name itself was a tribute to Roosevelt who often used the term "bull moose" to describe the strength and vigor of a person.

Thus he wrote, following his nomination for the Vice-Presidency on the Republican ticket in 1900, in a letter to Sen. M. A. Hanna, "I am as strong as a bull moose and you can use me to the limit." Also, when shot by a would-be assassin in Milwaukee, Wis., on the evening of Oct. 14, 1912, he insisted on immediately filling an engagement to speak, saying to the audience, "It takes more than that to kill a Bull Moose."

The party was in large part reunited with and reabsorbed into the Republican party during the campaign of 1916, after the nomination of Charles E. Hughes, who was acceptable to Roosevelt and the leading Progressives.

BULL RUN, FIRST BATTLE OF (July 21, 1861). This, the first major engagement, has been described as "the best planned and worst fought battle" of the Civil War. The principal Union army, under Gen. Irvin McDowell, was mobilized about Washington. Gen. Robert Patterson (U.), with a smaller army, was sent to "retain" Gen. Joseph E. Johnston (C.) in the Shenandoah Valley. Gen. P. G. T. Beauregard (C.) occupied the line of Bull Run Creek, which lies across the main highways from Washington southward. His advanced force under Gen. M. L. Bonham was based on Fairfax Courthouse to watch McDowell's army. McDowell had available about 30,000 men and 49 guns; Beauregard, about 24,000 and 35 guns; Johnston, about 9000 to Patterson's 12,000. None of these armies was thoroughly organized or disciplined.

Public opinion compelled President Lincoln to order McDowell to move forward. The Federal advance guard drove in Bonham's pickets on July 17. In accordance with previous orders, Bonham withdrew to Centreville, waited until dark, then retired behind Bull Run where the road from Washington to Richmond crossed at Mitchell's Ford and where Beauregard expected the main attack. The Confederates were disposed as follows: Ewell held the right at Union Mills Ford below the Orange and Alexandria Railroad; D. R. Jones protected McLean's Ford two miles upstream; Longstreet held Blackburn's Ford a mile above; Bonham was a mile and a half farther; Cocke guarded Ball's and Lewis' fords, one and one half and two and a half miles above Mitchell's; a mile farther Evans held the Stone Bridge where the Warrenton Turnpike crossed Bull Run. Thus the Confederate line extended about eight miles behind a shallow, meandering creek. Ewell was supported by Holmes' brigade, while Early was behind Jones and Longstreet. Tyler (U.), commanding McDowell's advanced force, on his own initiative, made a reconnaissance in force on July 18, but was sharply repulsed by Longstreet and Bonham aided by Early.

Eluding Patterson, Johnston and part of his army reached Bull Run on Saturday, July 20. Though the ranking officer, Johnston did not assume personal direction of the Confederate operations till the middle of the ensuing battle, meanwhile stationing his troops on the slope behind Beauregard's line. McDowell and Beauregard planned to turn each other's left flank. Ewell, on the Confederate right, was to cross Bull Run at daylight of July 21, the other brigades to follow. Beauregard's order did not reach Ewell. Longstreet, after crossing, waited in vain for word of his attack. By 7 A.M., when Jones received his orders, Sherman (U.) and Schenck (U.) were attacking the Confederate left at the Stone Bridge, Burnside (U.), at the same time, attempting to flank this end of the Confederate line. Evans, at the Stone Bridge, promptly deployed his scant half brigade to meet these movements. Johnston sent Jackson (C.) and Imboden (C.) to support Evans and soon Bee (C.) and Hampton (C.) followed. Fierce fighting raged from Bull Run to the Henry House plateau, to which the Confederates were driven. Here Bee lost his life and Jackson won his name of "Stonewall." The arrival of another portion of Johnston's army turned the tide in favor of the Confederates. The Federals were driven across Bull Run in disorder, pursued along the Warrenton Pike. No fighting of any consequence had taken place on the Confederate right.

When the break took place on the Federal right, Johnston ordered Bonham and Longstreet to move in pursuit. The Federal withdrawal turned into a rout as the troops streamed back in the direction of Washington. The Confederate pursuit started from Mitchell's Ford in the direction of Centreville at which point it was halted, the Confederates later returning to Bull Run. Bitter controversy afterwards ensued between Davis and Johnston and Beauregard as to the responsibility for not pursuing the defeated Federals into Washington. Military critics think this was not feasible. The staff work and courier service on both sides was miserable and a heavy rainstorm added to the confusion and uncertainty. From some 13,000 men actually engaged, the Federals lost about 500 killed, 1000 wounded and 1200 missing; the Confederates, with about 11,000 engaged, lost about 400 killed, 1600 wounded and 13 missing. They captured 25 guns and much other material. But it was a Pyrrhic victory. The South was made overconfident, while the North was spurred to earnest effort.

BULL RUN, THE SECOND BATTLE OF, was initiated by the decision of Gen. R. E. Lee, Aug. 24, 1862, at Jeffersonton, Va., to send the 23,000 troops of Maj. Gen. T. J. ("Stonewall") Jackson to break the communications of Maj. Gen. John Pope's Army of Virginia, which was unassailably placed on the upper stretches of the Rappahannock River, Virginia. Jackson started before daylight, Aug. 25, passed Thoroughfare Gap and, on the evening of the 26th, reached Bristoe Station. The next day Jackson plundered Pope's base at Manassas Junction and proceeded to Groveton Heights, five miles N. W. of Manassas. There, on the 28th, he attacked King's division. On Aug. 29 Pope in turn attacked Jackson, who with difficulty beat off repeated assaults. Lee, meantime, had brought up the remainder of his army, 32,000 men, and had formed them on Jackson's right. By nightfall of the 29th Lee's line formed an obtuse angle from N. to S. (Longstreet) and thence S. W. to N. E. (Jackson). Pope, re-enforced by a large part of the Army of the Potomac, renewed the attack on Jackson on the 30th, but failed to confront Longstreet with sufficient force. Lee accordingly ordered a general attack which swept Pope from his positions. Heavy rain on Aug. 31 delayed pursuit and made possible the retreat by Pope within the Washington defenses. Pope blamed his defeat on FitzJohn Porter, who was cashiered and was not vindicated until 1886, but Pope himself was not again trusted with field command. His losses, Aug. 16–Sept. 2, were 14,462; those of Lee were 9112.

BULLDOZE. During the Reconstruction period a Federal marshall was investigating an attempt to assassinate a registrar of voters in East Feliciana Parish, La. (1875). The natives refused him all information, and as the marshall stood pondering he was approached by a half-witted German who shouted, "Bull dooza mit der hooza!" The expletive had no meaning whatsoever, but to the frightened marshall it sounded like a threat from the Ku Klux Klan and he fled, which result was so satisfactory that the term "bulldoze" came into general use throughout the South, with the generic meaning to intimidate in a bullying manner.

BUMMERS. A nickname applied to foragers of Sherman's army during its March to the Sea and north through the Carolinas in the spring of 1865.

BUNCOMBE is a term which, by 1828, had come into general use in political Washington to mean speechmaking designed for show or public applause. It is reputed to have originated a few years earlier in connection with a speech which Felix Walker made in Congress to please Buncombe County, N. C., in his congressional district.

BUNDLING, a mode of courtship in colonial days where the parties instead of sitting up together went to bed together, with their clothes on. This custom, inherited from Europe, apparently originated as a matter of convenience and necessity where space and heat were lacking. It was confined largely to the poorer classes. Its prevalence seems to have ended in the late 18th century with the general improvement of living conditions.

BUNKER HILL (June 17, 1775). To force the British from Boston, on the night of the 16th of June the American militia besieging the town sent 1200 men to seize Bunker Hill, on the peninsula of Charlestown. Instead, the detachment built a small redoubt on Breed's Hill, nearer Boston but easily flanked. Working silently, they were not discovered until daybreak, when British warships, anchored below, opened an ineffective fire. Col. William Prescott, commanding in the redoubt, strengthened his left flank, toward the Mystic River, by a breastwork, a rail fence stuffed with hay, and a slight defense of stones on the beach. The defenders of these were joined by perhaps 2000 men, and were commanded by Maj. Gen. Israel Putnam, while in the redoubt Gen. Joseph Warren served as a volunteer. Meanwhile, under the command of Maj. Gen. Sir William Howe, 2000 British infantry, with a few field guns, landed below the redoubt.

Dividing his men into two wings, early in the afternoon Howe attacked both the redoubt and the rail fence, expecting first to turn the fence by a column along the beach, which would make it easily possible to storm in front. The attack was bloodily repulsed by the provincials, chiefly New Hampshire men under John Stark, and the remainder of the British withdrew after being but briefly in touch with the Americans. At the second attack the British advanced on both wings with great courage; but the provincials, as before holding their fire until the regulars were close, cut them to pieces and forced their withdrawal. Still trusting to the desperate frontal attack, in the final attempt Howe merely feinted against the fence, and for the first time attacked the redoubt with the bayonet. For the first time, also, his field-pieces got within effective range and drove the defenders from the breastwork. What would have

happened had the Americans had enough powder cannot be known; but Prescott's men were out of ammunition and, after a first severe fire, on his order, quitted the redoubt. In this assault fell Maj. Pitcairn, British commander at Lexington, and Joseph Warren. The defenders of the fence covered the American retreat. After an engagement lasting less than two hours, the British were masters of the peninsula, but with heavy casualties of 1054, while the Americans lost, in killed, wounded and prisoners, but 441. At first regarded by the Americans as a defeat, Bunker Hill, because of the way in which militia resisted regulars, came to be regarded as a moral victory, leading to a dangerous overconfidence in unpreparedness.

BURCHARD INCIDENT. This arose when Rev. S. D. Burchard, speaking from the same political platform as the Republican candidate, James G. Blaine, Oct. 30, 1884, described the Democracy as the party of "rum, Romanism and rebellion." Blaine's failure to offset the diatribe cost him Irish support and the election.

BURGHERS were those citizens of an incorporated city who, under the Dutch (1657), enjoyed great or small burgher rights, and under the English were entitled by birth or admission by the magistrates to the designation of freemen. In New York and Albany only freemen, who had paid the required fees, could do business or ply a trade.

BURGOYNE'S INVASION. In late spring, 1777, Gen. Burgoyne prepared to invade New York from Canada by the Lake Champlain-Hudson River route. Lt. Col. St. Leger was given command of a small expedition which was to ascend the St. Lawrence, cross Lake Ontario and advance on Albany by the Mohawk Valley. Both commanders were instructed that their principal objective was junction with Sir William Howe. An order was prepared, but, through a mischance, never sent from England, commanding Howe to proceed up the Hudson. In spite of this fateful blunder, Howe knew the British plans, for he had received a copy of Burgoyne's instructions.

Burgoyne's army was made up of 3700 British regulars, 3000 German troops, 250 Canadians and Tories and 400 Indians. With his well equipped force he proceeded up Lake Champlain in late June and on July 1 was within four miles of Ticonderoga, which, with Mt. Independence east of the lake, was garrisoned by about 2300 Continentals under Gen. St. Clair. In spite of militia reinforcements St. Clair wisely abandoned the fortress the night of July 5–6. Engagements with pursuing British at Hubbardton, Skenesborough (now Whitehall) and Fort Ann did not prevent St. Clair from saving his army to form the nucleus of later resistance. The taking of Ticonderoga increased the confidence of the British and was at first a severe shock to the patriots; later, it proved a stimulus to resistance.

Burgoyne's progress now became very deliberate. He was retarded by his extensive baggage and by the fact that the transportation of his artillery up Lake George required all available boats, while his army proceeded overland. To oppose him there were 2000 Americans under Gen. Schuyler at Fort Edward; but Schuyler was reinforced July 12 by about 1700 from St. Clair's command and 600 Continentals from Peekskill. Retreating before Burgoyne's slow advance, Schuyler felled trees across the roads and encouraged the country people to burn their standing crops and drive off their cattle. His steadiness was of the utmost value to the American cause.

Meanwhile Howe, evidently believing the rebellion nearly crushed and that Burgoyne did not require his active co-operation, left Clinton at New York to make a sortie up the Hudson with such troops as could be spared from the garrison and went to Philadelphia.

Fortune now began to turn against Burgoyne. A raiding force dispatched to secure patriot stores at Bennington was overwhelmed, Aug. 16, by Stark's New Hampshire militia and Warner's small force. St. Leger, besieging Fort Stanwix, managed, at Oriskany, to repulse a relieving body of militia under Herkimer, but his Indian allies fled in panic at news of the approach of a patriot force under Benedict Arnold and he abandoned his campaign.

Gen. Gates, now in command of the American army near the mouth of the Mohawk, had about 6000 effective troops. Reinforced by Morgan's Virginia riflemen, he moved northward and entrenched at Bemis Heights, about eight miles south of the hamlet of Saratoga, now Schuylerville. Burgoyne, whose Indian scouts had fled, was close upon the American army before he realized its presence. The first battle of Freeman's Farm was fought Sept. 19. Both armies remained in position and Burgoyne waited, hoping for news of Clinton's expected advance up the Hudson. Clinton got no farther than the Highlands, however. Meanwhile Gates' numbers were increasing, bodies of New England militia were gathering in Burgoyne's rear and the British supplies were running dangerously low. It was necessary to fight or to retreat. By Oct. 7 Burgoyne's effective troops numbered about 5000, while the Americans in front of him were nearly 8000. A reconnaissance in force to examine the American left was repulsed, the British were driven back into their lines and a determined attack led by Gen. Arnold threatened their whole position. Burgoyne now had no alternative and fell back toward Saratoga (Schuylerville). His movement was so deliberate that the Americans were able to surround him, and on Oct. 17, finding himself opposed by over 17,000 regulars and militia, with less than 3500 infantry ready for duty, he surrendered his army to Gates.

BURLINGAME TREATY (July 28, 1868) consisted of articles added to the Reed Treaty of 1858 between the United States and China. These acknowledged Chinese territorial jurisdiction in China, left trade privileges in China to the discretion of the Chinese government and established free immigration between the countries. It placed China on the "most favored nation" plane with regard to treatment of consuls, immunity and privileges in travel, residence and education of Chinese subjects in the United States. It guaranteed nonintervention by the United States in Chinese domestic administration. It was signed in Washington by William H. Seward, Secretary of State, Anson Burlingame, acting as "Envoy Extraordinary and Minister Plenipotentiary" of the Emperor of China, and two Chinese envoys.

BURNS FUGITIVE SLAVE CASE (1854) was one of three famous fugitive slave cases arising in Boston, Mass., after the enactment of the Fugitive Slave Law of 1850. Part of the Vigilance Committee (1850–61) planned to rescue Anthony Burns, an escaped slave, from an upper room of the courthouse. They battered in a door of the building at night, May 26, entered and one of them shot and killed Marshall Batchelder. Despite the committee's efforts, U. S. Commissioner Edward G. Loring remanded Burns to his owner, Suttle, of Alexandria, Va. On June 2 throngs witnessed the slave's departure. Several rich citizens paid $1300 and got him back early in 1855.

BURR CONSPIRACY is one of the most involved and mysterious episodes in early American history. Because it climaxed the dramatic struggle for power between Jefferson, the President, and Aaron Burr, a discredited political adventurer, it bulks large in the history of the period. Essentially it was a compound of personal and political rivalry, discredited ambition and land hunger.

Burr's exact intentions probably cannot ever be known. Following his duel with Hamilton he became a creature of circumstances, always hoping and scheming to regain at least something of his one-time popularity and power. To accomplish this he chose what he considered the most likely road to wealth and power—land conquest or seizure of Spanish territory west of the Mississippi.

Burr's first act was an attempt to attach England to his cause. Failing in this, he served out his term as Vice-President, meantime intriguing with those who might be of help, yet never disclosing his exact intentions. He went to the West, down the Mississippi to New Orleans and back overland, seeking friendly help and necessary funds. Returned to the East he sought successively to draw France and then Spain into his web of intrigue, but to no avail. Without the hope of foreign help, he was ready to accept funds from whatever source. Blennerhassett, a trusting, visionary Irishman, who lived on an island in the

Ohio River, was only one, though the most bizarre and reputedly the heaviest of the contributors to this weird venture.

Before leaving Philadelphia in the summer of 1806, Burr wrote his friend Gen. James Wilkinson, who commanded the American army on the Mississippi, that the expedition would start for New Orleans before the end of the year. But Wilkinson, thoughtful for his own safety and uncertain as to Burr, declined to be involved. Instead, when Burr's advance flotilla reached the lower Mississippi, Wilkinson ordered its members arrested. As Burr came down he, too, was seized and then paroled. He attempted to escape to Spanish territory, but was again captured and taken East for trial. Burr was acquitted, but the "conspiracy" had already collapsed.

BURR-HAMILTON DUEL was the culminating point in the early partisan struggles of New York. It grew out of aspersions by Hamilton upon his rival's character. Burr, some weeks after his defeat, in 1804, for the governorship of New York, asked for an explanation and when Hamilton sought to evade the issue, Burr peremptorily challenged. Hamilton, in principle opposed to dueling, averred that "peculiar necessity" forced him to accept the challenge. He wished to be useful, he explained, in those future crises which might affect the public weal. This enigmatical expression may be interpreted as a wish to break up plans to disrupt the Union. By facing Burr he may have thought to prevent his opponent from becoming a leader of disaffected New England Federalists. An alternative explanation was the prospect of war with Spain, which would carry with it leadership in the emancipation of Mexico. Both Hamilton and Burr wished to achieve this honor, and it seems to present a more compelling motive for the challenge and its acceptance.

The outcome of the duel at Weehawken, N. J., July 11, 1804, was fatal to both. Each fired once although Hamilton's friends claim that his shot was intentionally discharged in the air. Burr's reached its mark and his victim, mortally wounded, died the next day. Bankrupt in fortune and reputation and under indictment in New York and New Jersey, Burr thenceforth became a political outcast.

BURR TRIAL, CONSTITUTIONAL ASPECTS OF, have to do largely with the interpretation of the constitutional provision concerning treason. Aaron Burr was indicted for treason in 1807 and brought to trial in the U. S. Circuit Court at Richmond, Va., before Chief Justice John Marshall sitting as a circuit judge. The political passions of the times and the friction between President Jefferson and Chief Justice Marshall carried over into the trial and render appraisal difficult. An early incident of the trial was the Marshall opinion that a Federal court might issue a subpœna *duces tecum* to the President of the United States. In guiding the jury as to the law of treason the Chief Justice gave an interpretation so restricting the meaning of the words "levying war" that in the case at hand only the assemblage at Blennerhassett's Island could come within it. Burr, however much he may have counseled, advised or planned that assemblage, was not present. Under the Marshall interpretation his absentee connection was not sufficient to render him guilty of treason. Marshall held that the broader definition asked by counsel for the prosecution would include the English doctrine of constructive treason, which the phrasing of the constitutional provision was intended to exclude. This statement of the law resulted in a verdict of acquittal. The Chief Justice was sharply criticized for inconsistency and bias, in that in a dictum in an earlier case in the Supreme Court involving two of Burr's messengers (*see* Bollman case) he had stated the law in a way which seemingly should have linked Burr with the treasonable assemblage.

BUSINESS, PUBLIC CONTROL OF. When the Federal Constitution and the various state constitutions were adopted, it was in accordance with "due process of law" for legislatures to regulate those businesses which had been regulated at common law. But the types of business classed as common callings changed with economic conditions. The tailor, surgeon and smith, for example, soon ceased to be so classed, but the ferryman, wharfinger, innkeeper and common carrier continued in the category, with the addition in the 19th century of proprietors of turnpikes, bridges and canals. But the popularity of *laissez-faire* economics during the first half of the 19th century caused governmental regulation to reach its lowest ebb during that period.

About the middle of the 19th century the business corporation began to emerge, and for a time the view seemed likely to prevail that unless the state, in granting a charter of incorporation to a business, had imposed upon it a duty of public service, or granted it a special or monopolistic franchise, the corporation was free to conduct its business as it liked, though it partook of the nature of a public calling. But with the growth of business corporations controlling products or services upon which people greatly depended, the pendulum began to swing the other way, and, in a series of decisions beginning with the historic case of Munn v. Illinois in 1874, the U. S. Supreme Court developed the doctrine that all businesses, regardless of their franchise or charter powers, were liable to legislative regulation, if they were "affected with a public interest."

Statutes regulating the sale of foods and drugs, stockyard transactions, insurance rates, insurance agents' commissions and rents were passed and held valid. In 1890 the Sherman Antitrust Act, making monopolies illegal, was enacted by Congress and its validity upheld. The distinction between a public utility and a private business seemed to be breaking down in favor of a rule that any business is subject to regulation to the degree required by the public need. To the objection raised in each case that the "due process" clause of the Constitution was being infringed, the courts replied that the "due process" clause must yield to the police power, when regulatory legislation seemed reasonably calculated to correct recognized economic or social evils. There were occasional setbacks, but the march of state regulation was relentless. Other illustrations of the trend are statutes regulating the price of milk and of handling and selling leaf tobacco (Nebbia v. New York, 291 U. S. 502, 1934; Townsend v. Yeomans, 57 Sup. Ct. 842, 1937).

With the creation of the Interstate Commerce Commission in 1887, with power to regulate the rates and conditions of railroad service (later interstate motor carrier service and inland water traffic), there was inaugurated the policy of administrative regulation of public utilities. Since then, most states have created public utility commissions, charged with the duty of determining reasonable rates and conditions of service of light, heat, power, water and telephone companies, and have set up administrative officers to regulate insurance, banking, mining, etc. In 1920 Congress created the Federal Power Commission, at first composed of the Secretaries of War, Interior and Agriculture, but since 1930, of five commissioners appointed by the President. The commission has power to regulate the licensing of water-power rights on public lands, and since 1935, "the transmission of electric energy in interstate commerce." Congress has also created the Federal Communications Commission (act of 1934 and subsequent amendments) with wide regulatory powers over radio broadcasting and other agencies of communication. Usually such commissions have power to find the facts, but their acts are subject to judicial review on matters of law.

The Federal Trade Commission and the Clayton Acts, passed in 1914, and the Robinson-Patman Act, passed in 1936, extended the principle of administrative regulation to businesses usually classed as private, i.e., not public utilities. These acts, reinforcing and extending the Sherman Antitrust Act, made monopolies illegal, and prohibited interlocking directorates, price discrimination, "tying" contracts and other methods of "unfair" competition calculated to promote monopolistic control. Into this class of legislation also falls the National Labor Relations Act (1935) as amended by the Taft-Hartley Act (1947) which prohibits employers from resorting to unfair labor practices and sets up a board for administering the law; and also the Securities Exchange Act of 1934 which created the Securities and Exchange Commission with power to regulate security sales on stock exchanges and, since 1935, all securities issued or dealt in by public utility holding companies.

An act of Congress may be invalid not only because

it infringes the "due process" clause of the Constitution, but because it is not among the powers expressly delegated to Congress. Since power to regulate business has not been expressly granted to Congress, regulatory acts of this nature are valid only if they come within some other congressional power, such as that to regulate commerce among the states or to tax for the general welfare. This is illustrated by the abortive attempt of Congress in 1932 to set up the National Recovery Administration with power to impose upon business codes of fair competition, minimum wages and maximum hours for employees. The act was held invalid (Schechter Poultry Corp. v. United States) not because of violation of the "due process" clause, but because its subject matter did not come within the power of Congress over interstate commerce, or any other congressional power. Similarly the Agricultural Adjustment Act of 1933, designed to regulate agricultural production, fell because it involved an improper exercise of the taxing power (United States v. Butler). A second Agricultural Act, enacted in 1938, was held constitutional. Its purpose was "to establish and maintain . . . orderly marketing conditions for agricultural commodities." Among other things it gave the Secretary of Agriculture power to adjust acreage devoted to specified crops, to assign quotas of production to individual farmers and to provide for the storage of surplus products. The effect of the act (with subsequent amendments) was to subject agriculture to a degree of Federal control.

During the period from 1938 to 1958 most of the legislative acts that have been mentioned were amended and revised, usually in the direction of extending governmental control and regulation; and during this period acts were passed subjecting other businesses to regulation or placing government in competition with private enterprise. Among the more important of them are the Civil Aeronautics Act of 1938, the Atomic Energy Act of 1954, the Small Business Act of 1958 and several housing and home-financing acts. Whether or not governmental regulation has extended too far for the common weal, as believed by some people, it has been one of the most significant political and economic developments of the present century.

BUSINESS CLUBS, such as Kiwanis, Lions and Rotarians, were first organized on an international scale during the second decade of the 20th century. Rotary was the pioneer, dating its international beginning back to November, 1910. Kiwanis followed in 1916, and Lions in 1917.

These leaders among the business clubs have similar aims and purposes. Typical among them are civic improvement and beautification of various kinds, aid to underprivileged children, cultivation of high ideals of civic life, the promotion of a friendly spirit among business competitors and, in general, the making of one's home town a better place in which to live. Rotary advertises a motto, "Service above Self"; Kiwanis insist that "We Build"; and the Lions are named from the initial letters of "Liberty, Intelligence, Our Nation's Safety." These and similar organizations have international officers and conventions.

Rotary has the best claim to the adjective international and is the largest as well as the oldest of the groups. By 1959, there were approximately 10,000 Rotary clubs including 468,500 individual members in 111 countries. There were more than 14,118 Lions clubs numbering slightly less than 600,000 members in 91 countries. The 4600 Kiwanis clubs of 256,000 members were confined to the United States and Canada. The club magazine for each group is sent to every active member and keeps the individual alive to the activities, aims and achievements of his organization.

In addition to the three larger fraternities there are many others of the same nature. Among these should be mentioned: Altrurians; American Business Club; Association of 20–30 Clubs; Civitan; Cooperative Club; Gyro; National Exchange; National Monarch; Optimist; Round Table; and National Metro Clubs.

BUSINESS CYCLES. Recurring phases of depression, revival, prosperity and crisis or recession, have characterized American business since the founding of the nation. Although the different phases of the business cycle have usually followed each other in the order noted, their intensity and duration have varied in marked fashion from cycle to cycle. At times, moreover, the revival or prosperity phases have been interrupted by minor recessions or depressions in business, while crises, which usually mark the termination of a speculative boom, have occasionally occurred in a period of depression.

The first major depression occurred in the half-decade 1784–89 as a result of dislocations attributable to the Revolutionary War. A period of prosperity, interrupted by a minor depression in 1807–10, ensued and lasted until after the War of 1812 when a severe depression, lasting from 1815 to 1821, set in. This was followed, after a few years of moderate prosperity, by another depression of mild character which ran from 1825 to 1829. Prosperity followed, culminating in the Panic of 1837 and a long depression which continued to 1843. The next major depression took place in 1857–58, shortly before the Civil War.

Extended wars always breed depression, and the Civil War was no exception. A depression in industry occurred in 1865–66, according to some authorities, or in 1866–67, according to others. This was followed by recovery and prosperity which finally ended with panic in 1873. The long depression of the 1870's, lasting until 1879, ensued. The subsequent recovery was interrupted by the depression of 1883–85, which

began as a minor recession but was prolonged and intensified by the crisis of 1884. By 1887 prosperity had returned and continued until 1893 with the exception of a short depression in 1890–91. The Panic of 1893 ushered in a severe depression which lasted, with the exception of a few months of prosperous conditions in 1895, until 1897, when business again turned upward. The prosperity which followed was broken briefly by a very mild recession in 1900 and, later, by the "Rich Man's Panic" of 1903–4. The latter was a financial rather than an industrial depression. The Panic of 1907 was the forerunner of a comparatively short but severe depression which ran into the following year. Recovery from this depression carried business through until 1913, although there was an extremely mild recession in 1910–11.

The depression beginning in 1913 started out to be a comparatively mild one, but the outbreak of hostilities in Europe intensified it considerably. By 1915, however, war demands had induced renewed prosperity which continued, with the exception of a slight readjustment in 1919, until the late spring of 1920 when a crisis occurred followed by a rapid recession in business.

The depression of 1920–22 was severe, although not unduly extended. Recovery brought a long stretch of prosperity to the country, broken by minor depressions in 1924 and 1927, which ended with the stock-market crash in the fall of 1929. There followed a long and severe depression from which recovery did not set in until after the Banking Crisis of 1933. The ensuing recovery was not regular but was interrupted by recessions in 1933, 1934 and 1935, followed by a severe depression in 1937–38.

The recession of 1937–38 was the most severe the country has experienced since the Great Depression of the early 1930's. From the spring of 1937 to the spring of 1938, the adjusted index of industrial production fell 38% while unemployment increased from 7,900,000 to 11,100,000 in the same period.

Recovery from this depression, which had become substantial by 1939, was further stimulated by the defense program of 1940–41, followed by our participation in World War II. From the low point of 1937 to the high of 1943, industrial production increased 225% and unemployment fell to negligible proportions. Industrial production declined a bit less than 4% from late 1943 to early 1945. Then, after leveling off for a few months, fell sharply (by 26%) to a low point in May, 1946.

The 1945–46 decline in industrial production was not a result of business recession, but rather of the essential shift from a war to a peace economy. Unemployment remained low, prices were rising and, once the shift to a peacetime economy was accomplished, industrial production resumed an upward course, increasing roughly 15% by the late fall of 1948.

The first postwar recession began in the latter

months of 1948 and reached a low point approximately a year later. Industrial production fell 12%, nonagricultural employment about 5% and wholesale prices some 11%. The recession was short-lived and not severe compared with major recessions of earlier periods. Scarcities engendered by the war had not been eliminated and, after a period of rolling readjustment, business resumed its upward course.

Another relatively mild recession occurred in 1953–54. Industrial production declined 10% and nonagricultural employment 3% while the level of wholesale prices, which had been falling since early 1951 following a sharp upward thrust after the outbreak of hostilities in Korea, leveled off toward the end of 1952 and did not fall appreciably during the recession.

Business began to recover in September of 1954, the index of industrial production rising 16% by the end of 1955 and remaining in the neighborhood of that level until the fall of 1957. Meanwhile, unemployment decreased to a very low level, and the wholesale price level rose moderately, by about 7%.

The downturn in business from the 1957 peak ushered in the third postwar recession. Within six months, industrial production declined 14% and nonagricultural employment 5%. Contrary to past experience, on the other hand, both wholesale and consumer prices rose slightly during the recession period. Whereas, at the beginning of the recession in 1957, a number of business analysts anticipated a rather long depression, business actually began a sharp recovery before mid-1958. An increase of 23% in industrial production carried this index to a new high in June, 1959. A slight decline in the index in subsequent months was attributable to a steel strike of record length rather than to business factors making for recession.

The cyclical pattern of business since World War II had deviated considerably from that expected by numbers of experts. Earlier wars in which this country participated were followed by first a primary, then later a secondary, postwar depression. The primary depression was apt to be severe, but short-lived (as in 1920–21) while the secondary depression was also severe and long drawn out (as in 1930–33). Since 1945, however, the United States has experienced three recessions, none of them of extreme severity and all of them short. There are numerous reasons for this, but one of the most important is the lavish government spending which has frequently been in excess of revenues, at times by a wide margin. This has resulted in creeping inflation which, in the long run, would appear to be an excessive price to pay for shorter and less severe recessions.

BUTLER'S GENERAL ORDER NO. 28. Gen. B. F. Butler established himself as military commander in New Orleans, May 1, 1862. The marked hostility of the inhabitants of the city to the Federal Govern-

ment was exhibited in insults to which Federal officers and men were subjected by the women. Accordingly on May 15 Butler issued an order to the effect that any female insulting or showing contempt for any officer or soldier of the United States should be treated as a woman of the town plying her vocation. The order evoked a storm of protest at home and abroad, and was a cause of Butler's removal from command of New Orleans, Dec. 16, 1862.

BUTLER'S RANGERS (1777–84) was a regiment of Loyalists, recruited by Col. John Butler with the consent of Sir Guy Carleton to serve with the Indians against the colonists. Eight companies were recruited. Their uniforms consisted of a green coat and waistcoat faced with red, buff breeches, white leggings and a hat of the Foot Regiment pattern. From their headquarters at Fort Niagara, the Rangers embarked on forays which spread terror throughout New York and Pennsylvania. They perpetuated the Wyoming massacre in July, 1778, and took part in Johnson's raid on the Mohawk settlements in 1780. The regiment was disbanded in June, 1784.

BUTTERFIELD OVERLAND DISPATCH. Because of much travel to Colorado after the discovery of gold there, D. A. Butterfield, backed by New York capital, organized a joint-stock express and passenger carrying service between the Missouri River and Denver. In July, 1865, the route via the Smoky Hill River was surveyed and soon thereafter coaches were in operation. Ben Holladay, acting for a competing organization, bought the Butterfield Overland Dispatch in March, 1866, when Eastern express companies threatened to take it over and establish a service between the Missouri River and Sacramento, Calif.

BYRD'S POLAR FLIGHTS. On April 5, 1926, Commander Byrd sailed on the S. S. *Chantier* for Kings Bay, Spitzbergen, which he intended using as the base for a flight to the North Pole. The vessel arrived in the bay on April 29. The only pier in the harbor was occupied by a Norwegian gunboat; therefore, it was necessary to ferry the big trimotored Fokker airplane, *Josephine Ford,* ashore through the drifting ice, which choked the bay, on a raft constructed from four ship's boats. This operation was successfully accomplished, and preparations for the flight commenced. After being held up by defects in the skis for some days, Byrd and his pilot, Floyd Bennett, eventually took off for the Pole shortly after midnight on May 9. The flight proceeded uneventfully until the airplane was one hour's flight short of the Pole, at which time a leak was discovered in an oil tank. In spite of this they continued onward. At 9:02 A.M., Greenwich Civil Time, the Pole was reached. After circling around it, the course was set for Spitzbergen. The return flight was uneventful, and the motors continued to function in spite of the oil leak.

Early in the Antarctic spring of 1929 Byrd made a flight from his base at Little America to the foot of the Queen Maud Mountains and laid down a gasoline base. On Nov. 29, 1929, at 3:29 P. M., the polar flight party took off in the Ford airplane, *Floyd Bennett*, for the Pole. At 9:15 they started up the Liv Glacier Pass for the Polar Plateau. The plane was so heavily loaded that she could not gain enough altitude to clear the head of the glacier. It was necessary to dump several hundred pounds of emergency food to lighten the plane enough to clear the "Hump." Once over the plateau the plane made good time. At 1:14, Greenwich Civil Time, the Pole was reached. A few minutes later the course was changed to head back to the mountains. This part of the flight developed into a race against clouds moving in from the east. The party just managed to get down Axel Heiberg Glacier before it was enshrouded. After a short flight to the eastward the plane was landed at the fuel base. At six o'clock the return journey to Little America began. Shortly after ten the party landed at the camp.

CABEZA DE VACA, ALVAR NÚÑEZ, TRAVELS OF. In 1527, at about the age of 37, Cabeza de Vaca went to America as treasurer of the expedition led by Pánfilo de Narváez, which landed near the present city of Tampa, Fla., in April, 1528. After a brief and disastrous exploration of the country the colonists built five horsehide boats and sailed for Cuba. A hurricane sank all but the one commanded by Cabeza de Vaca, and soon it was wrecked on the Texas coast. From the fall of 1528 to the spring of 1536 Cabeza de Vaca and his companions endured untold hardships in a 6000-mile journey through the American Southwest and northern Mexico. Finally safe in New Spain, Cabeza de Vaca returned to Old Spain to request of Charles V the governorship of "La Florida." Instead he was given the governorship of Paraguay. His account of his travels was printed in 1555 at Valladolid, Spain, under the title *Relación y Comentarios*.

CABILDO was the Spanish governmental organization for the province of Louisiana. It was established by O'Reilly in 1769, superseding the French Superior Council, and was abolished by Laussat when France regained possession of the province in 1803. Besides the governor, who presided, it consisted of two ordinary *alcaldes* (judges in New Orleans), *alférez real* (royal standard-bearer), provincial *alcalde* (judge outside New Orleans), *alguacil mayor* (high sheriff), depository-general (treasurer and storekeeper), receiver of fines (collector), attorney-general-syndic (public prosecutor), *mayordomo-de-propios* (municipal treasurer of New Orleans) and *escribano* (clerk). It met in the Government House (*Casa Capitular* or *Principal*), commonly known today as the "Cabildo."

CABIN RIGHTS. At an early period in the settlement of the West, pioneers asserted their claims to parts of wild lands by blazing trees around the desired boundary, and later comers customarily recognized the claims: tomahawk rights, they were called. Building a cabin and raising a crop, however small, of grain of any kind, led to "cabin rights," which were recognized not only customarily but by law. The laws of the colonies and states varied in their requirements of the settler. In Virginia the occupant was entitled to 400 acres of land and to a pre-emption right to 1000 acres more adjoining, to be secured in either case by a land-office warrant, the basis of a later patent or grant from colonial or state authorities.

CABINET. The cabinet of the President is the result of custom and was created neither by the Constitution nor by statute law. The Constitution says (Article II, Section II) that the President "may require the Opinion, in writing, of the principal Officer in each of the executive Departments, upon any Subject relating to the Duties of their respective Offices." These offices were created by act of Congress at various times and their holders were considered to be the personal assistants of the President in the work of administration. Washington tried to carry out the intentions of the makers of the Constitution that the Senate should serve as a privy council on the British model, but he dropped the method of personal attendance and conference with the Senate when he found that this was creating friction with certain members of that body. Also in 1793 he tried to secure the advice of the U. S. Supreme Court at a time of crisis in our relations with France. He submitted to the Court a number of questions with regard to the interpretation of our treaties with France, but the justices refused to answer these questions on the ground that they lay outside their duties. Washington then turned to his three secretaries or department heads of State, War and Navy, and called them, along with the attorney general into a council of four. This conference in time was recognized by the public as the official council or cabinet of the President.

The name "cabinet" was first used about the year 1793. Congressional debates show that the term was used in Congress in 1798 and again in 1802, but it was only some twenty years after the establishment of the national government that the idea and name of a cabinet council was understood and accepted by the people. The name "cabinet" was not recognized in Federal statute law until the act of Feb. 26, 1907, which provided for an increase in the salary of those "heads of the Executive Departments who are members of the President's Cabinet." Thus it may be repeated that the name and establishment of the President's cabinet originated in custom as in England and in process of time became an accepted part of the National Government. Washington, at first, undertook to conduct his administration on a nonpartisan basis and his first cabinet was chosen equally between the two wings of his supporters—those who were of strong nationalist and those who were of states' rights tendencies. Finding that the emergence of vital issues of policy made necessary united support of his department heads or cabinet, he changed its membership so that it became united in support of his views.

At the time of the death of President William Henry Harrison his cabinet resigned and his successor, Vice-President Tyler, reconstructed his administration according to his own views. It has now become the understanding that the members of the cabinet are the personal appointees and advisers of the President, and Congress usually confirms a presidential nomination to one of these offices. Furthermore, while certain cabinet members, as the head of the Treasury Department or of the Department of Commerce, usually are business men especially fitted for the work of that department, yet in general cabinet positions are given upon a basis of geographical or political influence in order to consolidate party support behind the administration of a President. The actual influence of a cabinet depends in large part upon the desires and intentions of the President himself. In certain cases the cabinet may be a collection of political leaders, at another time of executive administrators. Also the personality of a specific cabinet member and his personal influence with the President may count for much. In recent years the creation of numerous departments or independent commissions has weakened cabinet influence. In addition, the private unofficial advisers of a President may have more influence than the cabinet as a united body. The so-called Brain Trust of Franklin D. Roosevelt is an illustration of this situation.

In 1960 there were ten members of the cabinet, each of whom presides over his respective department. These departments are: State (foreign affairs); Treasury; Defense; Justice; Post Office; Interior; Agriculture; Commerce; Labor; and Health, Education and Welfare. Each department has one or more "under secretaries" or "assistant secretaries" who act as assistants to or under the direction of the cabinet member. They may attend cabinet meetings in the absence of the head of the department or upon special occasions, but generally are not considered part of the "Ministry" as would be the case in Great Britain. The salary of each member of the cabinet is $25,000 a year. The term of office is four years or at the pleasure and discretion of the President. Cabinet meetings occur at least once a week when the President is at the seat of government. At times the Vice-President and other high officers attend the meetings.

CABOT VOYAGES (1497–99). Early in 1496 a petition was placed before Henry VII in the name of John Cabot and his three sons, Sebastian, Lewes and Sancto, for the privilege of making explorations in the New World. Letters patent dated March 5, 1496, were granted to the Cabots, and in the spring of 1497 they sailed west. Coasting southward they discovered Cape Breton Island and Nova Scotia. The following year (1498) letters patent were granted to John Cabot alone, authorizing him to make further explorations along the eastern coast of North America. The discoveries made on this voyage were supposedly recorded on a map and globe made by the explorer. Both are now lost. Because there is no firsthand data concerning the Cabot voyages, Sebastian Cabot has been called the "Sphinx of North American history." His identity is often confused with that of his father, John. Important contributions to geographical knowledge were made by the Cabots, though "the descriptions of the regions they explored apply to no portion of the United States."

CABRILLO EXPEDITION (June 27, 1542–April 14, 1543). In the hope of finding a direct route from Spain to the East Indies through Spanish waters, Juan Rodríguez Cabrillo and Bartolomé Ferrelo sailed from Navidad, Mexico, and, Sept. 28, 1542, reached a port, "closed and very good, which they named San Miguel." They were in fact at San Diego and thus were the discoverers of California. After getting as far north as Drake's Bay they were forced back to the Santa Barbara Islands where Rodríguez died. Ferrelo carried on and is believed to have reached the vicinity of the Rogue River in Oregon.

CAHOKIA, the first permanent white settlement of consequence in Illinois, was founded in March, 1699, when priests of the Seminary of Quebec established there the Mission of the Holy Family. Their chapel, which became the nucleus of the village, was located near the left bank of the Mississippi a short distance south of the present city of East St. Louis. Cahokia took its name from the adjacent Indian village, which in 1699 contained about 2000 Tamaroa and Cahokia.

The mission at Cahokia quickly attracted French settlers, principally from Canada, occasionally from Louisiana. Their number, however, was never large. A census in 1723 enumerated only twelve white residents, while at Kaskaskia and Fort de Chartres, the other principal settlements, 196 and 126 were counted. In 1767, after many French had removed to St. Louis because of the cession of the Illinois country to Great Britain, Cahokia contained 300 whites and 80 Negroes—about half the population of Kaskaskia. By 1800, however, its population had increased to 719, while that of Kaskaskia had dropped to 467.

CAHOKIA MOUNDS is a group of 85 prehistoric Indian mounds four miles northeast of East St. Louis, Ill. This group is the nucleus of a larger group, which is believed to have numbered originally between 200 and 300. Monks' Mound, 100 feet high with a rectangular base 1000 feet by 700 feet, is not only the largest mound in the group, but also the largest pre-historic monument in the United States. The Cahokia Mounds are believed to have been built between 1200 and 1500 A.D., perhaps much earlier.

CAIRO, ILL., the "Eden" of Dickens' *Martin Chuz-zlewit,* was founded in 1837 by the Cairo City and Canal Co., after an earlier effort (1818) had failed. For fifteen years the town grew slowly, but the sale of lots, which commenced in 1853, and the comple-tion of the Illinois Central Railroad attracted settlers, with the result that by 1860 the population exceeded 2000. During the Civil War Cairo was of great stra-tegic importance and for several months both Grant and Foote had headquarters there. Because of its low elevation, its existence depends upon extensive levees, but even these have failed to prevent several severe inundations.

CAIRO CONFERENCES. On their way to the Teheran Conference, Pres. F. D. Roosevelt and Prime Minister Churchill met with Generalissimo Chiang Kai-Shek at Cairo (Nov. 22–26, 1943) to discuss the war against Japan and other Far Eastern matters. (Stalin was not present because Russia was not then fighting Japan.) The three conferees issued a declara-tion of intent: to take from Japan all the Pacific islands occupied by her since 1914; to restore to China all territory "stolen" by Japan, such as Man-churia, Formosa, and the Pescadores Islands; and to give Korea her independence "in due course."

Returning from Teheran, Roosevelt and Churchill met with President Inönü of Turkey at the second Cairo Conference (Dec. 4–6, 1943). No significant agreements were reached, and Inönü declined to commit his country to entering the war.

CAJON PASS, the best route from the Mojave Desert to southern California, was probably first known to white men when, March, 1776, it was traversed by Father Francisco Garcés. The first American to dis-cover it was Jedediah Smith (November, 1826). Shortly afterwards it became a part of the route between California and Santa Fe.

CALDER v. BULL, 1798 (3 Dallas 386). The *locus classicus* wherein the Supreme Court defined an *ex post facto* law: one which makes criminal an act not punishable when committed; or retrospectively in-creases the punishment; or alters the rules of evidence in order to convict the offender. Thus it was not un-constitutional for the Connecticut legislature to grant a retrial in a civil case.

CALHOUN'S *DISQUISITION ON GOVERNMENT* represents John C. Calhoun's reasoned views on gov-ernment as seen from the point of view of the per-manent minority. Begun in 1843, finished to Calhoun's own satisfaction in five years' time, it elaborates the doctrine of his *Exposition.* Its keynote is the idea of a concurrent majority. Simple majority government always results in despotism over the minority unless some way is devised to secure the assent of all classes, sections and interests.

The argument is close-knit and convincing if one accepts the belief of Calhoun that the states retain absolute sovereignty over the Constitution and can do with it as they wish. This doctrine could be made effective by nullification. But Calhoun believed that the clear recognition of rights on the part of the states on the one hand and of the national majority on the other would prevent matters ever coming to a crisis. South Carolina and other Southern states, in the three decades preceding the Civil War, had provided legislatures in which the vested interests of land and slaves dominated in the upper houses, while the popular will of the numerical majority prevailed in the lower houses. This was done in conscious ac-ceptance of the doctrine of the *Disquisition.*

CALHOUN'S *EXPOSITION* (1828). After the pas-sage of the "Tariff of Abominations" the South Caro-lina legislature resolved that it was "expedient to protest against the unconstitutionality and oppressive operation of the system of protective duties" and appointed a committee to report thereon. At the re-quest of William C. Preston of the committee, John C. Calhoun prepared his *Exposition* in which he de-clared the tariff of 1828 "unconstitutional, unequal and oppressive; and calculated to corrupt public virtue and destroy the liberty of the country." Draw-ing on the "Resolutions of 1798" (*see* Virginia and Kentucky Resolutions), Calhoun proposed nullifica-tion as the constitutional remedy. South Carolina should call a convention which should interpose the state's veto, to be binding upon its citizens and the general government unless three fourths of the states should amend the Constitution. Amended and pub-lished, although not adopted, by the legislature, Cal-houn's *Exposition* was applied four years later in the nullification of the tariff acts of 1828 and 1832.

CALIFORNIA. *Spanish Exploration of.* The discovery and early exploration of California were the work of the Conqueror Cortés and his agents. Jiménez, one of his mariners, discovered the Peninsula in 1533. Two years later Cortés himself led a colony to the Bay of La Paz. In 1539 Juan de Ulloa, also sent by Cortés, rounded the Peninsula from the head of the Gulf to Cabo del Engaño, near N. Lat. 30°. Three years later Juan Rodríguez Cabrillo explored the entire outer coast of the Peninsula, discovered San Diego Bay (calling it San Miguel), the Channel Islands, Mon-terey Bay and perhaps Point Reyes, then returned to the Channel Islands, on one of which he died. The voyage was continued by Ferrelo (Ferrer), Cabrillo's second in command, who reached the vicinity of the Oregon border, returning thence to Mexico.

Because of English ravages on the Pacific (Drake and Cavendish) and the heavy toll of scurvy on the Manila galleons, Spain conceived the idea of founding a settlement on the Alta California coast to serve for defense and as a port of call. California would be a cabbage patch for the support of the Manila trade. On this errand Sebastián Vizcaíno sailed from Mexico in 1602. He retraced the route of Cabrillo, changed the name of San Miguel Bay to San Diego, explored and overpraised Monterey Bay and continued north to the vicinity of the Oregon border, about where the Cabrillo expedition had turned back. Plans to colonize Monterey Bay failed to mature and for nearly 170 years the California coast was seen by Spaniards only on the merchant galleons returning (southbound) from Manila. Under Spain (1769–1822) the interior of Alta California was extensively explored north from San Diego to Upper Sacramento valley and east to the Sierra Nevada.

Under Spain. In the 17th century Baja (Lower) California and Pimería Alta (now southern Arizona) were colonized by Spain, largely through the work of the Jesuit missionaries. After the expulsion of the Jesuits in 1767 their work was taken over by the Franciscans. There had been frequent talk of extending the settlements from these two bases northward into Alta (Upper) California, but the step was not taken until foreign danger threatened. As a result of Bering's explorations in the North Pacific (1728–41), Russian fur traders established posts on the Aleutian Islands and began their southward march down the Alaska coast. Fearing the loss of Alta California, Spain now decided to occupy the province. The plan was carried out under the vigorous direction of José de Gálvez, Inspector-General of New Spain. He made use of men and means at hand. Gaspar de Portolá, governor of (Lower) California, was put at the head of a colony and Father Junípero Serra, president of the (Lower) California missions, accompanied him with missionaries. Part of the colony went by sea, part overland up the peninsula. They met at San Diego Bay, and there founded the mission and presidio of San Diego. Continuing up the coast by land, over what is essentially the main railroad route, Portolá reconnoitered Monterey Bay and discovered San Francisco Bay, which all earlier explorers seem to have missed. Next year (June 3, 1770), Portolá and Serra founded the presidio and mission of San Carlos (Monterey), which became respectively the military and missionary capitals of the province. Within two years the missions of San Antonio, San Gabriel and San Luis Obispo were founded at intermediate points between San Diego and Monterey.

Two important problems were now solved by Juan Bautista de Anza, captain of the presidio of Tubac, in Pimería Alta (now southern Arizona). With twenty soldiers, Indian guides, cattle for food and

Fathers Garcés and Díaz as diarists, in 1774 Anza explored a land route from the Mexican mainland over the mountains to San Gabriel. Next year he raised in Mexico a colony of settlers for San Francisco Bay, and led them over the same trail to California. His leadership was superb. Starting with 240 persons, he arrived at Monterey with 242, one death on the way being more than offset by the birth of three children. With this colony San Francisco was begun in June, 1776. Next year Felipe de Neve became the first governor of Alta California, which hitherto had been nominally ruled from Loreto, in Baja California.

When fully developed California under Spain was divided into four military districts (San Diego, Santa Barbara, Monterey and San Francisco). There were twenty missions, extending from San Diego to San Rafael (on the north shore of San Francisco Bay). Another, San Francisco Solano, was added in the rule of Mexico. Most of these mission colonies have become towns or cities. Three municipalities were founded, San José 1777, Los Angeles 1781 and Branciforte, now Santa Cruz, 1798. The chief industries of the province were agriculture, stock raising, and trade in sea-otter skins, the greater part of which was carried on by the missions. Spain's rule in California came to an end in 1822, independence being officially celebrated at Monterey on April 11.

Under Mexico. For a quarter century, after 1822, California was a province of the Republic of Mexico. Outside of the missions this was a period of rapid and promising material development, whose direction was changed by the American conquest and the discovery of gold. Of nearly 1000 so-called "Spanish" land grants, all but about a score were made under Mexico. Mexican colonists entered the province in considerable numbers, obtained vast ranches, built substantial country homes, raised great herds of cattle, horses and other stock, sold hides and tallow, engaged in sea-otter hunting, enriched themselves by obtaining the property of the secularized missions and led a carefree pastoral life.

During this period California was invaded by foreign intruders on all sides. Sailors deserted their ships and remained in the province; Hudson's Bay trappers (Scots, French and half-breeds), came yearly from the north. Stockton, for example, was founded by them as French Camp. American hunters and rovers came overland, without asking leave; English and American hide and tallow traders visited the California ports and set up the large establishments described by Dana in *Two Years Before the Mast*. Many of these foreigners settled in the country, married señoritas, acquired ranches, engaged in business or mechanical pursuits. Some of them became citizens of substance and influence. In 1841, contemporaneously with the movement of the covered wagon into Oregon, American immigrants began to come to California in caravans, no less than fifteen of which arrived before the Gold Rush. Thus the forty-niners were by no means the pioneer Americans in California.

Politics were turbulent in these years. Mexico was disturbed and exercised little authority in the distant province. Governors sent from Mexico were generally unpopular and sometimes were ousted by local patriots. But native governors fared little better, because of the sectional rivalries between north and south California. Prominent in the politics of the period was the question of the secularization of the missions and the division of the plunder. The outstanding native Californian of this era was Gen. Mariano Vallejo, lord of the Sonoma March. Immigrants entered politics and became involved in the disturbances. After 1840 Sutter's vast estate, called New Helvetia, became the center of a quasi-independent community of Anglo-American immigrants, who had come with or without permission. Thus the way was being prepared for the Bear Flag Revolt and conquest by the United States.

Missions. California has no "old" missions and never had any. California was the very last province occupied, at the end of three centuries of mission founding, all the way from Buenos Aires to San Francisco and Jamestown. The missions founded by the Jesuits in Lower (Baja) California in the 17th and 18th centuries were taken over by the Franciscans in 1768. Next year the Franciscans advanced into Upper (Alta) California and three years later withdrew entirely from the southern district, yielding it to the Dominicans. The California Franciscans were members of the College of San Fernando in Mexico City, by which they were governed. The founder and moving spirit of the California missions was Father Junípero Serra. San Carlos Borromeo (Carmel) was his capital. Nine missions were founded in his presidency (1769–84) and nine under Lasuén (1785–1803), three more being added by 1823. They were established in the following order: San Diego, 1769; San Carlos 1770; San Antonio, 1771; San Gabriel, 1771; San Luís Obispo, 1772; San Francisco de Asís, 1776; San Juan Capistrano, 1776; Santa Clara, 1777; San Buenaventura, 1782; Santa Bárbara, 1786; La Purísima, Concepción, 1787; Santa Cruz, 1791; Soledad, 1791; San José, 1797; San Juan Bautista, 1797; San Miguel, 1797; San Fernando, 1797; San Luís Rey, 1798; Santa Inés, 1804; San Rafael, 1817; San Francisco Solano (Sonoma), 1823 (under Mexico).

The missions were both Christian seminaries and training schools in the rudiments of European civilization. The native Californians, except the Yumas, had no agriculture whatsoever and few of them had fixed abodes. Under the missionaries they became skilled in raising grain and fruits, tending cattle, horses and other stock; in building, spinning, weaving, tanning, leather work, blacksmithing, soap-

making and many other crafts. Under the direction of the missionaries they built a score of beautiful missions. A complete mission plant comprised church, living quarters for the friars, the Indian village, shops, irrigation works, tallow vats, orchards, fields and vast pastures for flocks and herds. At each mission there were usually two priests and a small soldier guard.

At their height in 1821 the missions had in residence over 21,000 neophytes. By 1846 the total number of baptisms had reached 98,000. Under Mexico the California missions fared badly. Laws providing for secularization brought on a struggle which ended in the dispersion of the neophytes and the passing of most of the mission property into the hands of secular owners. The buildings fell into decay. Most of the churches are still (or again) used for religious purposes, but the rest of the buildings have largely disappeared. At some sites extensive restorations have been made or are in progress.

Russians in California. It was fear of Russia which caused Spain to occupy California in 1769. Eventually the fear was justified. By the end of the 18th century Russian fur-trading posts were extended down the Alaska coast, a new Russian American Fur Company was established with Count Rezánof as its head and Baránof as chief factor at Sitka, the new capital. Shortage of supplies being a vital problem, Rezánof visited California (1806) with a view to opening trade in foodstuffs, but his success was only partial. His diplomacy included betrothal to Doña Concepción Arguello, daughter of the commander at San Francisco. This romance has been popularized by Bret Harte in a poem and by Gertrude Atherton in an historical novel. Rezánof died on his way back to St. Petersburg, but Russian interest in California continued. Without Spain's permission Kushkof in 1811 established north of San Francisco Bay the post called Fort Ross, which became the center of an agricultural colony and a base for an extensive sea-otter trade all down the California coast. A smaller settlement was founded on Bodega Bay. As a defensive move, first Spain, then Mexico, established settlements north of San Francisco Bay (San Rafael, 1817, and San Francisco Solano, or Sonoma, 1823). In 1824 Russia yielded all territorial claims south of 54° 40′. By this time profits in the sea-otter trade had dwindled and Mexico's liberal trade policy enabled Russia to purchase supplies in California, thus lessening the agricultural importance of Fort Ross. As a result, in 1841 the establishment was sold to Sutter of New Helvetia (Sacramento) and Russia withdrew. Considerable ruins of Fort Ross are still to be seen.

American Immigration to California (1826–48). The few Americans in California before 1826 were deserters from New England trading ships. Overland immigration began with the arrival of Jedediah Smith in 1826. During the next fifteen years, about thirty different groups came to California. The majority of these were trappers from the Hudson's Bay Company post in Oregon, or traders from New Mexico. Probably about 300 Americans had established themselves in California by 1841, the year that home seekers began their trek across the plains.

During the winter and spring of 1840–41 numerous small groups along the frontier, particularly in Missouri and Arkansas, discussed the advisability of a move to California. As a result, in May, 1841, small parties assembled at Sapling Grove, a few miles west of the present site of Kansas City, and organized under the leadership of John Bartleson and John Bidwell. These pioneers crossed the Sierras in the vicinity of the headwaters of the Stanislaus River and reached various destinations in California by Nov. 1. Meanwhile another company, the Workman-Rowland, traveling over the Gila-Colorado route, arrived in Los Angeles.

Apparently there was no organized overland expedition from the East to California in 1842, but the following year the movement was resumed. The Chiles-Walker party of 1843; the Stevens-Murphy Company of 1844 (the first immigrants to bring wagons into the settled part of California, and probably the first to enter California by way of the Truckee River route); the McMahon-Clyman, the Swasey-Todd, the Grigsby-Ide, the Hastings-Semple, the Sublette and probably other companies of 1845; various expeditions bringing approximately 500 people in 1846, including the ill-fated Donner party, can only be mentioned here. In the latter half of 1846, following the outbreak of the Mexican War, many immigrants to California were sailors or soldiers. The treaty of Guadalupe Hidalgo, ending the war, was concluded Feb. 2, 1848, and California became a part of the United States. After that the account of immigration to California merges into that of the gold rush period.

The Conquest of California (1846–47) is divided into two distinct phases. The first is characterized by considerable scurrying of men, by frequent raising of flags and by an absence of fighting. Frémont took over the command of the men at Sonoma on July 5, 1846, and ten days later led them through the streets of Monterey. Commodore Sloat raised the American flag at Monterey on July 7; it was unfurled at San Francisco and at Sonoma July 9 and two days later at Sacramento. On July 29 Frémont landed with his company at San Diego and Commodore Stockton succeeded Sloat as commander of the Pacific squadron and issued an offensive proclamation. On Aug. 4 and 6 Stockton raised flags over Santa Barbara and San Pedro respectively. On the 13th he met Frémont in Los Angeles, raised the flag and four days later issued another proclamation. The first phase of the conquest was over.

In the second phase there was fighting and blood-shed. It began in the early morning of Sept. 23, with an attack by Californians (Mexicans) on the American garrison stationed at Los Angeles under the command of Capt. Gillespie. Capt. Mervine, sent by Stockton from Monterey with 350 troops, joined Gillespie's defeated forces at San Pedro and attempted a march on Los Angeles, but was driven back following an engagement with Capt. Flores' Californians. Both Santa Barbara and San Diego were quickly retaken by the Californians. Annoying guerrilla warfare in the north culminated in the battle of Natividad, Nov. 16, between Californians and a band of American frontiersmen on their way to join Frémont. The Californians retreated and the Americans moved south with Frémont to aid in recapturing Los Angeles.

Out of the inhospitable desert on Dec. 2 came Gen. Stephen W. Kearny to Warner's ranch with about 100 exhausted United States soldiers. On Dec. 5 he was joined by thirty-five men sent from San Diego by Stockton. On the following day Kearny fought the battle of San Pascual—the most stubborn engagement of the period. The Americans were left in possession of the field, but their loss was about a score killed and an equal number wounded. Among the latter was Gen. Kearny. Additional troops sent by Stockton arrived Dec. 10 and relieved the Americans. Two days later Kearny joined Stockton in San Diego. The united forces moved north and after two minor engagements again raised the American flag over Los Angeles. Three days later, Jan. 13, 1847, papers were signed at Cahuenga Rancho by Gen. Andrés Pico and Col. Frémont. This concluded the second and final phase of the conquest just seven months, lacking one day, after the occupation of Sonoma.

Gold Rush. Gold was discovered by James W. Marshall at Coloma on the south fork of the American River on Jan. 24, 1848. Further discoveries were made in the surrounding country during the month of February. The earliest reports to reach the communities along the coast were received dubiously, but by the end of May all uncertainty was removed. By the middle of June people were deserting homes and towns for the gold fields. Already, on June 1, United States Consul Larkin had forwarded official news of the discovery and his information reached Washington by the middle of September. Further dispatches, carried by Lt. Beale and dated a month later, were also received in the national capital. On June 12 Gov. R. B. Mason left Monterey to inspect the mines. About the middle of August he sent his report to the adjutant general, accompanied by a sample of gold. From $30,000 to $50,000, "if not more," he estimated were taken daily from the mines, and "there is more gold in the country drained by the Sacramento and San Joaquin rivers than will pay the cost of the present war with Mexico a hundred times over." A pick, a shovel and a tin pan were all that was required to obtain it. Mason's report, with its sensational observations, was included with the President's message to Congress on Dec. 5, 1848, and was published in the principal newspapers throughout the country.

The effect was immediate. By Jan. 18, 1849, 61 vessels, each carrying an average of fifty passengers, left Boston, Salem, New York, Philadelphia, Baltimore and Norfolk for the Pacific coast. Other ships carrying an unknown number of gold seekers sailed from Charleston and New Orleans during the same period. In February sixty ships were booked to leave New York and seventy from Boston and Philadelphia. The demand for accommodations to California had become so great that vessels were diverted from various services to provide passage for eager emigrants.

Both in Europe and in Asia populations were aroused by sensational reports from the gold fields. Five California trading and mining companies were organized in London at a cost of more than £1,250,-000. Notices regarding the departure of vessels from the principal ports of Great Britain and from ports in France, Spain, Holland and Germany were published in foreign newspapers and magazines. Among the Asiatic peoples those most affected by the gold malady were the Chinese. The *Alta Californian* for May 10, 1852, estimates the number of Chinese in the territory Feb. 1, 1849, at 54. By Dec. 31 of the same year there were 791. A year later there were more than 4000. The Japanese apparently heard of the discovery with stolid indifference. But in Australia the excitement was given free play. Shipmasters circulated reports and streets of the principal cities were placarded with announcements of "Gold! Gold!" in California, and soon it became difficult to secure passage on departing vessels. Even the inhabitants of the Marquesas Islands were affected. Members of the French colony who were free departed immediately and were quickly followed by the soldiers, leaving the governor alone to represent the government.

The spring of 1849 brought overland migration from Mexico and from the United States. "The mania that pervades the whole country, our own camp included," wrote an army officer regarding Mexico, "is beyond all description or credulity. The whole state of Sonora is on the move. . . ." Four thousand left for the gold fields before the beginning of summer, while in various rendezvous along the Missouri River numerous parties had gathered by the first of April. Bancroft estimates the number at 20,000. Bayard Taylor thought 30,000 crossed the plains and reached the gold fields before the beginning of winter. Throughout the summer of 1849, he says, the rich meadows of the Platte "were settled for the time, and a single traveler could have journeyed for the space of a thousand miles, as certain of his lodging and regular meals as if he were riding through the old agricultural districts of the middle states." Peter H.

Burnett, later to be elected the first governor of the State of California, thought that at least "two thirds of the population of Oregon capable of bearing arms" migrated to the gold fields.

Probably more than 80,000 people came to California during 1848 and 1849. The Federal census for 1850 gives the total population, excluding Indians, as 92,597, but these figures do not include returns from San Francisco, Contra Costa and Santa Clara counties. The returns from the first were destroyed by fire and those of the last two were lost. Whatever the number, it was sufficient to create more intricate social, economic and political problems than had confronted any former frontier settlements in the history of the United States.

California after 1848. With the signing of the Treaty of Guadalupe Hidalgo, Feb. 2, 1848, California, along with other lands wrested from Mexico by war, was formally annexed to the United States. Thus was climaxed a half century of United States commercial and diplomatic interest in the region. The hide, tallow and fur trade had brought Americans to California during the Spanish and Mexican periods; organized American migrations had begun in the 1840's; Presidents Jackson, Tyler and Polk had futilely attempted the territory's purchase; annexation was the logical and inevitable outcome.

Two weeks before California formally became a part of the United States, gold was discovered in the Sierra Nevadas and soon pastoral California was invaded by a host of adventurers, among whom the vicious element was inevitably large. By 1852 the population had jumped from 10,000 in 1846 (including 4000 Americans) to 250,000, centered mostly in San Francisco and the gold fields. This turbulent influx and the resultant clash between native Californian and Anglo-American customs rendered inadequate the military government set up during the Mexican War. The establishment of effective civil authority was imperative. Yet Congress, harassed by the question of slavery in the Mexican Cession, for two years remained deaf to California's plea for territorial government. At length, exasperated Californians took the initiative, devising a state constitution, ratified Nov. 13, 1849. This emergency document outlawed slavery, wherefore Southern congressmen blocked Federal recognition of California's act for nearly a year. At last, on Sept. 9, 1850, President Fillmore signed the bill admitting California as a free state, as part of the Compromise of 1850.

CALUMET AND HECLA MINE is a copper mine in the Keweenaw Peninsula of Lake Superior in northwest Michigan. For some years previous to its discovery by Edwin J. Hulbert in 1859 copper exploration and mining had been taking place in the region. Hulbert uncovered the conglomerate lode in 1864. The geological deductions which led to this result were based upon the discovery of masses of breccia scattered upon the ground, which suggested to Hulbert a search for the mother lode. The Calumet and the Hecla mines opened as separate undertakings under Hulbert's management, but soon afterwards Alexander Agassiz was sent out from Boston to superintend the initial stages of development. The problem of separating the conglomerate copper from its rock matrix was solved with great difficulty. The country was then very remote and wild, having only water transportation in the summer and none in the winter. In spite of difficulties the two original mines paid dividends in 1869 and 1870, and were consolidated into the Calumet and Hecla Mining Co. in 1871. Other mining companies were opened in the vicinity, at first under distinct corporations, but by 1923 most of them had consolidated with the Calumet and Hecla Co. The venture proved especially profitable for large Boston investors, such as Quincy A. Shaw and Lee, Higginson & Co.

Several shafts reached a depth of over a mile on the vertical and considerably over that on the vein or incline. Early milling methods did not recover all the copper from the rock, and the old tailings have been reworked with modern methods with remarkable results. By 1933 the aggregate tonnage of ore mined and treated had been 165,000,000. The various mines of the Calumet and Hecla have produced 4,808,000,000 pounds of copper metal, which sold for $771,000,000.

CALVINISM in its broadest sense is the entire body of conceptions arising from the teachings of John Calvin. Its fundamental principle is the conception of God as absolutely sovereign. The statement of Calvinism most influential in America was the Westminster Confession (1647). Its doctrinal portion was accepted by the New England Congregationalists and embodied in their Cambridge Platform (1648). American Presbyterians coming from Scotland and North Ireland were sternly Calvinistic. The Synod of Philadelphia, the oldest general Presbyterian body in America, passed the Adopting Act in 1729, which required all ministers and licentiates to subscribe to the Westminster Confession. Other Calvinistic bodies in America are the two Reformed Churches, the Dutch and the German, and all other Presbyterian bodies.

CAMBRIDGE, MASS., was settled in 1631. Originally intended as the seat of government of the Massachusetts Bay Colony, the town was early abandoned by Gov. John Winthrop and others in favor of Boston, leaving Deputy Gov. Thomas Dudley and Simon Bradstreet as the principal founders of the "newe towne," as it was first called. For a time Rev. Thomas Hooker's company settled there (1632–36) before removing to Connecticut. Their places were taken by the company of Rev. Thomas Shepard, who

became the first permanent minister of the town. Harvard College was founded there in 1636. The following year the college set up the first printing press in North America with Stephen Day as printer. In 1638 the name of Newtown was changed to Cambridge.

CAMBRIDGE PLATFORM was drawn up by a synod of ministers from Massachusetts and Connecticut (August, 1648), which met pursuant to a request of the Massachusetts General Court. The New England authorities desired a formal statement of polity and a confession of faith because of the current Presbyterian ascendancy in England and the activities of local Presbyterians such as Dr. Robert Child. The declaration endorsed the Westminster Confession and for ecclesiastical organization upheld the existing Congregational practice. The Cambridge Platform remained the standard formulation in Massachusetts through the 18th century and in Connecticut until the Saybrook Platform of 1708.

CAMDEN, BATTLE OF (Aug. 16, 1780). Following Lincoln's disaster at Charleston, Gates was given command of the Southern army consisting of 1400 regulars under DeKalb and 2052 militia. Marching southward from Hillsborough, Gates occupied Rugeley's Mill, a strong position about thirteen miles northeast of Camden which had been occupied by the British under Lord Rawden. Gates unwisely sent 400 regulars to aid Sumter cut the British lines of communication far to the southeast. Then failing to attack promptly, he allowed Cornwallis time to arrive with reinforcements. The two generals decided to surprise each other. Cornwallis, with 2000 veterans, marched northward and met Gates marching southward early in the morning of Aug. 16. The Americans were exhausted from long marches, many helpless with dysentery, and more than half were militia who had never been under fire. At the first attack the militia fled. The regulars, standing their ground, were surrounded and almost annihilated. DeKalb was captured, mortally wounded. The Americans lost 2000 killed, wounded and captured, seven cannon, 2000 muskets and their transport. The British loss was 324. Gates fled to Hillsborough and vainly attempted to rally his demoralized army and call out more militia, but his day was over. Dec. 2 he was replaced by Gen. Nathanael Greene. Many Americans fled to the swamps and mountains and carried on guerrilla warfare.

CAMDEN-YORKE OPINION. A written opinion, professional and not judicial in character, was given in 1769 by Lord Camden, who was at the time Lord Chancellor of Great Britain, and Charles Yorke, who was later to be raised to the same eminent position. It related to the rights of private persons who had taken conveyances of lands from native tribes of

Indians, and supported such titles, grants from the king not being necessary. It was held that the king only had sovereignty over the inhabitants as English subjects. The opinion was seized on by certain western land companies in America as applicable to any purchases they might make from the aborigines as proprietors of the soil. Many public men and lawyers in America concurred in the soundness of the opinion, Patrick Henry among them. However, when the matter came to judicial test in this country after the Revolution, the contrary view prevailed: titles to lands acquired from the Indian tribes were void when the state had not given consent; the real title was held to be in the state as sovereign.

CAMELS IN THE WEST. At the close of the Mexican War the United States added 529,189 square miles to its area. This territory contained no railroads and the difficulties of transportation were so great that an effort was made to establish across this new country fast express routes by using camels. Congress (1855) appropriated $30,000 to purchase camels in Egypt and Asia. Seventy-six camels were brought to Texas. Twenty-eight of them were taken to California (1857) to be used on mail and express routes through the desert country, but after a few trips their use was discontinued. They were later (1864) sold at auction, most of them being taken to Nevada and used to carry freight to and from the mines. Those remaining in Texas were sold to circuses and zoölogical gardens. The only other importation of camels was in 1860–62. Forty-five animals were brought from Siberia to San Francisco by Otto Esche, a German merchant, who planned to use them on eastbound express routes. He never started this service, but sold most of the camels to a mining company in British Columbia. Years later wild camels were occasionally seen in the Northwest, in Nevada, and especially in Arizona. All are now extinct.

CAMP JACKSON AFFAIR (May 3–10, 1861). Capt. Nathaniel Lyon, in command of United States Arsenal in St. Louis, imbued with the idea that Missouri authorities were planning to capture the arsenal, collected and armed a number of politico-military organizations as Home Guards. With over 8000 of these, mostly Germans and other foreigners, Capt. Lyon seized, on his own initiative and without resistance, the 669 militiamen encamped at Camp Jackson, St. Louis. While being marched away several miles to prison, these men were fired upon, three of them killed, about 28 civilians killed and many men, women and children wounded. Many of the militiamen were opponents of secession and all were subsequently released on parole, subject to exchange as prisoners of war.

CAMP MEETINGS. Outdoor religious meetings were a feature of the evangelical revival in both England and America in the 18th century. Baptists held meetings similar to the later camp meetings during the American Revolution. The meeting conducted jointly by Presbyterian and Methodist ministers in Logan County, Ky., in July, 1800, is generally accepted as the first regular camp meeting. Held in a wood, near a supply of water, the encampments usually lasted four days or longer. There were several services each day and sometimes four or five ministers spoke at the same time from different parts of the camp ground. The animated evening services of the frontier assemblies, accentuated by pine knots flickering in the dense darkness, were usually tense with excitement and frequently marked by emotional irregularities such as jerking, falling, barking, rolling and dancing.

Camp meetings were not confined to the frontier, but extended throughout the United States during the early 19th century. Steamboats carried many hundreds of people at excursion rates from Eastern cities to near-by camp meetings. In many cases cottages replaced tents and permanent auditoriums were erected. During the late 19th century popular educational movements, such as Chautauqua, and summer resort communities, such as Ocean Grove, N. J., developed from camp-meeting beginnings. Many summer assemblies still function as outgrowths of the camp meeting.

CAMPAIGN OF 1788 AND OF 1792 had no formal nominations, only one presidential candidate, and little opposition to the second choice. The Constitution ratified, the Continental Congress delayed three months before fixing the first Wednesday in January, 1789, for choosing electors, the first Wednesday in February for their voting and the first Wednesday in March for starting the new government. Pennsylvania, Maryland and Virginia elected electors; Massachusetts' legislature chose hers from elected electors; New Hampshire's election failed and her legislature, as did those of the remaining states, appointed electors. Thirteen states could cast 91 votes; but two states had not ratified and one (New York) failed to elect or appoint; four electors failed to vote. Washington received the entire 69 votes cast. John Adams received 34 as second choice and the other 35 were scattered among ten different candidates. In 1792 fifteen states could cast 132 electoral votes, when Hamilton's financial measures and the consolidation of national power roused an opposition (Jeffersonian antifederalists) which centered its efforts on the defeat of Adams by the antifederalist George Clinton, as to defeat Washington was seen to be futile. The attempt failed. Washington's vote was again unanimous, and Adams defeated Clinton by 77 to 50.

CAMPAIGN OF 1796 was the first national election in American history to be contested by political parties. The French Revolution, Genêt and the Jay

Treaty resulted in bitter partisanship. Without the modern machinery of nomination the Federalists informally agreed upon John Adams as Washington's successor; with him they chose Thomas Pinckney. With more enthusiasm the Republicans chose their leaders, Thomas Jefferson and Aaron Burr. Electors were chosen in sixteen states—in six by popular vote, in ten by the legislature. Of the total electoral votes Adams secured 71, Jefferson 68, Pinckney 59, Burr 30 and the remaining 48 were divided among nine others, several of whom were distinctly not candidates.

CAMPAIGN OF 1800 AND OF 1804. The election of 1800 forms a turning point in American political history. Its preliminaries were expressed in the famous Virginia and Kentucky Resolutions, proffered by Jefferson and Madison as a party platform. Its party machinery, still more essential to success, was directed by Aaron Burr with supplemental support in Pennsylvania and South Carolina.

Burr had already established the nucleus of a political machine that was later to develop into Tammany Hall. With this organization he swept the City of New York with an outstanding legislative ticket, gained control of the state assembly and secured the electoral votes of New York for the Republicans. He had already secured a pledge from the Republican (Jeffersonian) members of Congress to support him equally with Jefferson. Hence the tie vote which gave him a dubious chance for the Presidency.

Publicly disclaiming any intent to secure that office, Burr was, nevertheless, put forward by the Federalists in order to defeat Jefferson and bring about another election. A slight majority in the House of Representatives enabled them to rally six states to Burr and divide the vote of two others, thus neutralizing the vote of the eight states that supported Jefferson. The contest was prolonged through 35 fruitless ballotings; on the 36th, by prearrangement, a sufficient number of Federalists cast blank ballots to give Jefferson ten states and the Presidency.

This narrow escape from frustrating the popular will led the incoming administration to pass the Twelfth Amendment to the Constitution. Jefferson covertly helped eliminate Burr in New York, and the party caucus brought George Clinton forward as candidate for the Vice-Presidency. Burr, already divining his political ostracism, attempted to recover ground as an independent candidate for governor of New York. Representative Federalists of New England sought his support in their plans for disunion, but he refused to commit himself to such a program. Jefferson, pre-eminently successful in the more important measures of his administration, was triumphantly re-elected in 1804 as President with George Clinton as Vice-President, the first to be elected as such under the new amendment.

CAMPAIGN OF 1808 AND OF 1812. Candidates for the Republican (Jeffersonian) nomination in 1808 were James Madison, the choice of Jefferson; James Monroe, somewhat tainted by affiliation with John Randolph and the "Quids," who were anathema to the outgoing administration; and George Clinton, a New Yorker not favored by the "Virginia Dynasty." Jefferson's own refusal to consider a third term confirmed the two-term tradition for a President. At the party caucus Madison received 83 votes; his rivals three each.

The Federalist opposition was led by Charles Cotesworth Pinckney and Rufus King, but the chief obstacle to the Madison slate came from his own party, notably in Virginia and Pennsylvania, where William Duane, a powerful journalist, was unreconcilable. The malcontents finally voted the party ticket, however, and in the electoral college Madison obtained 122 out of 176 votes. Clinton ran behind the ticket by 9 votes to be Vice-President. Defeated for the Presidency, the Federalists nevertheless made serious inroads upon the Republican majority in the House of Representatives.

In 1812 Madison secured his renomination by a tacit rather than a formal yielding to the demands of Henry Clay and the "War Hawks." The vice-presidential nomination, tendered first to John Langdon of New Hampshire, went to Elbridge Gerry of Massachusetts. Opposition to the party slate was led by DeWitt Clinton of New York, who finally accepted nomination from the Federalists, with Jared Ingersoll of Pennsylvania as his running mate. The electoral college gave Madison 128 votes, as against 89 for Clinton. Vermont and Pennsylvania stood by Madison, but New York was led by Martin Van Buren into the Clinton column. Gerry and the ticket could not carry the candidate's own state of Massachusetts, notwithstanding his recent election as governor. Thus, on the eve of the War of 1812, the Republican party was seriously divided.

CAMPAIGN OF 1816 AND OF 1820. There was no campaign by parties in 1816 worth the name, none at all in 1820. President Madison's choice was James Monroe, old Jeffersonian protégé, Secretary of State and of War. Some Republicans (Jeffersonian) favored Gov. Tompkins of New York. Younger Republicans, interested in nationalist measures following the War of 1812, including a bank, protective tariffs and internal improvements to speed the development of the West, preferred Crawford, Secretary of the Treasury, a citizen of Georgia. They gave him 54 votes in the congressional caucus to 65 for Monroe. Here was the election of 1816, for in the electoral college Monroe overwhelmed Rufus King, signer of the Constitution and statesman of note, but a Federalist whose party now was thoroughly discredited by the Hartford Convention. Monroe was given 183 votes to 34 for King. Newer sectional conflicts and rivalry among the younger leaders embittered the "Era of Good Feeling," but President Monroe was secure. He was re-elected in 1820, with only one dissenting electoral vote. Federalists saw a greater menace to their propertied interests rising with the democracy of the West; it was to dethrone "King Caucus" and the "Virginia Dynasty" in the free-for-all campaign of 1824.

CAMPAIGN OF 1824, preparations for which began with the second inauguration of Monroe, marked the beginning of the transition from federalism to democracy with resulting voter realignment under new party emblems. The five candidates were prominent in national affairs and represented sections or factions rather than parties. In general, the politicians supported Crawford; John Quincy Adams represented business; Calhoun, the South and the rising slavocracy; Clay, the expanding West; Jackson, the people everywhere. The first three were Cabinet members. Clay was Speaker of the House and Jackson was the country's most popular military figure.

Crawford was virtually eliminated by sickness; Jackson was brought in late by his friends; Clay's support was never impressive; Calhoun withdrew and became candidate for Vice-President on both the Adams and Jackson tickets. No candidate received a majority electoral vote. Jackson secured the greatest number, 99; Adams, 84; Crawford, 41; and Clay, 37. Selection was made by the House. Adams was chosen. Jackson's supporters could only charge a "corrupt bargain" and bide their time.

CAMPAIGN OF 1828 AND OF 1832. In 1828 President John Quincy Adams stood for re-election and Andrew Jackson of Tennessee made his second campaign for the Presidency. Designated the people's candidate by the action of friends in the legislature of his own State of Tennessee, Jackson won and held the necessary support of influential leaders in New York, Pennsylvania and South Carolina. The campaign was waged throughout the administration of Adams. It was not marked by any clear-cut declaration of political principle or program and Jackson came to think of it as a personal vindication. Of the 24 states, Delaware and South Carolina still expressed their choice by vote of the legislature. In 22 states the elections were held in the period from late October to early December. There was a great increase in the popular vote cast and both candidates shared in the increase; 643,000 being cast for Jackson and 507,000 for Adams. The electoral vote stood 178 for Jackson to 83 for Adams. John C. Calhoun of South Carolina was again elected Vice-President. In many parts of the nation there was evidence of a more effective organization of the vote than in any previous contest, yet, over and above all considerations in this election was the appeal that the frontier hero made to an increasing body of democratically minded voters. Jackson, himself, was the cause of an alignment of public opinion in the years that followed.

Jackson men controlled the Congress, and platforms and programs were supported by leaders and sections and groups, but not by clearly defined political parties. Naturally Jackson stood for re-election although he had spoken in favor of a single term, and the campaign to renominate him began at once. After December of 1831, when Henry Clay returned to the Senate, he, rather than Adams, received the support of most of those who were opposed to Jackson. This did not include Calhoun, who in 1830 had broken with Jackson. Clay was formally presented by a national convention that met in December of 1831. He was endorsed by a national convention of young men which prepared a platform in a meeting held in May of 1832. In that month a national convention of Jackson supporters nominated Martin Van Buren of New York for the Vice-Presidency. In this election the recently gathered Anti-Masonic party supported William Wirt of Maryland. The campaign not only witnessed the general use of the national party convention but platforms were presented and cartoons freely used, and there was concentration of popular attention upon the pageantry of parades. Aside from the personal contest between Jackson and Clay the issue between the two centered upon Jackson's attack upon the United States Bank and particularly upon his veto of the bill for the recharter of the bank, a bill which had the backing of the supporters of Clay in both Houses of Congress. Twenty-four states participated in this election and all except South Carolina provided a popular vote. The electorate endorsed the administration of Jackson, for the distribution of the vote in 23 states gave Jackson 707,000, Clay 329,000 and Wirt 255,000. In the electoral college the vote stood Jackson 219, Clay 49, Wirt 7, with 11 votes representing the vote of South Carolina cast for John Floyd of Virginia. Jackson had a greater proportion of the popular vote in 1832 than he had had in 1828.

CAMPAIGN OF 1836. Made up chiefly of Anti-Masons, National Republicans and anti-Jackson Democrats, the Whig party, formed in 1834, naturally lacked unity. Because of this, the Whig leaders decided to put forward several sectional candidates in the 1836 presidential campaign. Accordingly, Judge Hugh L. White was entered in the race through nomination by legislative caucuses in Tennessee and Alabama, held in January, 1835. At about the same time, Judge John McLean was nominated by a legislative caucus in Ohio, but he withdrew from the race in the following August. Sen. Daniel Webster was nominated by a Massachusetts legislative caucus, also in January, 1835. Still another candidate of the Whigs was Gen. William H. Harrison, who was formally nominated by both Anti-Masonic and Whig state conventions in Pennsylvania in December, 1835.

Meanwhile at a national convention held in Baltimore on May 21–22, 1835, Martin Van Buren, who was President Jackson's personal choice, had been unanimously nominated for the Presidency by the Democrats. No platform was adopted by the convention, but a committee was authorized to draw up an address. Published in the party organ, the Washington *Globe*, on Aug. 26, 1835, this address presented Van Buren as one who would, if elected, continue "that wise course of national policy pursued by Gen. Jackson." For all practical purposes, this address may be regarded as the first platform ever issued by the Democratic party.

When the election returns were finally in, it was found that Van Buren had won the Presidency with 170 electoral votes and a popular vote of 761,549 to 736,656 for his opponents. White received 26 electoral votes, Webster 14, and Harrison 73, while South Carolina bestowed its 11 votes on W. P. Mangum. No candidate for the Vice-Presidency received a majority of the electoral vote, so on Feb. 8, 1837, the Senate chose the Democratic candidate, Richard M. Johnson, over his leading rival, Francis Granger.

CAMPAIGN OF 1840. Distinctive in American history as the first national victory of the Whig party, the campaign of 1840 was unique for its popular and emotional appeal, organized on an unprecedented scale. To the Whigs belongs the credit of introducing into a presidential battle every political device calculated to sway the "common man."

The Whig convention, assembled at Harrisburg, Dec. 2, 1839, nominated Gen. William Henry Harrison of Indiana for President, and John Tyler of Virginia for Vice-President. No attempt was made to frame a platform; indeed, the only bond uniting the various groups under the Whig banner was a determination to defeat the Democrats. The Democratic convention held at Baltimore, May 5, 1840, was united on Martin Van Buren for President, but left to the state electors the choice of a Vice-President. A platform on strict construction lines was adopted.

The Whigs conducted their campaign at a rollicking pitch. Harrison was adroitly celebrated as the "Hard Cider and Log Cabin" candidate, a phrase which the Democrats had used in contempt. Popular meetings, "log cabin raisin's," oratory, invective against Van Buren the aristocrat, songs and slogans ("Tippecanoe and Tyler Too") swamped the country. In the election Harrison polled an electoral vote of 234, a popular vote of 1,275,016; Van Buren received 60 electoral votes and 1,129,102 popular votes. A minor feature in the campaign was the appearance of an abolition (the Liberty) party, whose candidate, James G. Birney, received 7059 votes. Although the causes for Van Buren's defeat should be traced back to opposition to Jackson, the Panic of 1837 and the unpopular Seminole War, the campaign methods employed by the Whigs contributed largely to Harrison's success.

CAMPAIGN OF 1844. No outstanding Democratic candidate could muster the necessary two-thirds vote in the convention, so James K. Polk of Tennessee, the first "dark horse," was nominated, with George M. Dallas of Pennsylvania as running mate, on a platform demanding "the re-annexation of Texas and the re-occupation of Oregon" and in favor of tariff reform. The Whigs nominated Henry Clay of Kentucky and Theodore Frelinghuysen of New Jersey, on a platform favoring protective tariff and a national bank but quibbling on the Texas annexation issue, which alienated some of the Whigs. Polk carried New York by a small popular majority and was elected, with 170 electoral votes to 105 for Clay. The popular vote was: Polk, 1,337,243; Clay, 1,299,062.

CAMPAIGN OF 1848 resulted in the election of the Whig nominee, Zachary Taylor, who side-stepped the burning issue of slavery extension and coasted to victory on his military reputation. His Democratic opponent, Lewis Cass, straddled the slavery extension question by advocating state sovereignty. The new Free Soil party, specifically opposed to extension and headed by Martin Van Buren, split the Democratic vote in New York and thus contributed materially to Taylor's triumph. Taylor carried half the states, eight in the South and seven in the North. The popular vote was: Taylor, 1,360,099; Cass, 1,220,544; Van Buren, 291,263. The electoral vote was: Taylor, 163; Cass, 127.

CAMPAIGN OF 1852. The Whig party was apathetic and demoralized, so Democratic victory seemed almost certain. The question of greatest interest was who would be the Democratic candidate. After many ballots, the leading Democrats, Cass, Buchanan and Douglas, were eliminated and a "dark horse," Franklin Pierce of New Hampshire, was nominated with William R. King of Alabama. The Whigs nominated Gen. Winfield Scott; and the Free-Soilers, John P. Hale. Both major parties endorsed the Compromise of 1850, so there were no issues and little contest. Pierce carried all states save Massachusetts, Vermont, Kentucky and Tennessee, though in the popular vote he received scarcely 30,000 majority. The popular vote was: Pierce, 1,601,274; Scott, 1,386,580; Hale, 155,825. The electoral vote was: Pierce, 254; Scott, 42.

CAMPAIGN OF 1856. The Republican party in this, its first presidential campaign, nominated John C. Frémont. Its platform opposed slavery expansion and condemned slavery and Mormonism as twin relics of barbarism. The American, or Know-Nothing, party nominated ex-President Millard Fillmore. The Democrats nominated James Buchanan. Their conservative platform stressed States' Rights, opposed sectionalism and favored a somewhat ambiguous plank, giving Popular Sovereignty to the territories. The electoral vote was Buchanan, 174; Frémont, 114; Fillmore, 8. The popular vote was Buchanan, 1,838,169; Frémont, 1,341,264; Fillmore, 874,534. The Republicans rejoiced in their showing, while the Democrats congratulated themselves upon having saved the Union.

CAMPAIGN OF 1860. The Democratic national convention met amid great excitement and bitterness at Charleston, S. C., April 23, 1860. The delegates from the eight states of the far South demanded the inclusion of a plank in the platform providing that Congress should guarantee slave property in the territories. This was refused, and after several days of useless wrangling and failure to unite the convention upon a candidate an adjournment was taken to Baltimore on June 18 following. At this meeting the convention nominated Stephen A. Douglas of Illinois for President, and later the national committee nominated Herschel V. Johnson of Georgia for Vice-President. The platform pledged the party to stand by the Dred Scott decision or any future Supreme Court decision that dealt with the rights of property in the various states and territories. Seceding Democratic delegates met at Baltimore on June 28 and nominated John C. Breckinridge of Kentucky for President and Joseph Lane of Oregon for Vice-President. The platform reaffirmed the extreme Southern view with regard to slavery. Meanwhile, the remains of the "old-line" Whigs and American ("Know-Nothing") parties had met in a convention at Baltimore on May 9 and adopted the name of the Constitutional Union party, also the platform of "the Constitution of the Country, the Union of the states and the enforcement of the laws." They nominated John Bell of Tennessee for President and Edward Everett of Massachusetts for Vice-President and attempted to ignore the slavery and other sectional issues, with a plea for the preservation of the Union.

Also, the Republican national convention had met in Chicago on May 16. By means of the platform issues of nonextension of slavery and of a Homestead law and by advocacy of a protective tariff, the agricultural elements of the northern and western parts of the country and the industrial elements of Pennsylvania, New England and other northern and eastern sections of the country were united. At first it seemed that the convention would nominate either William H. Seward of New York or Salmon P. Chase of Ohio, but a deadlock between their respective supporters being threatened the convention nominated Abraham Lincoln on the third ballot. Hannibal Hamlin of Maine was nominated for Vice-President on the second ballot.

The split in the Democratic party made possible the election of Lincoln. He received 180 electoral votes as against 72 for Breckinridge who carried the extreme southern states, and 39 for Bell who carried the border states. Douglas received but 12 (9 from Missouri and 3 of the 7 from New Jersey). The popular vote was far otherwise since it totaled 1,857,610 for Lincoln, 1,291,574 for Douglas, 850,082 for Breckinridge and 646,124 for Bell. The combined opponents thus received 930,170 over Lincoln who was a minority President during his first administration.

CAMPAIGN OF 1864. A national convention was called in the name of "the executive committee created by the national convention held in Chicago on the sixteenth day of May 1860." The use of the name Republican was carefully avoided. The convention met in Baltimore on June 7, 1864, and named itself the Union National Convention. The Republican leaders desired to appeal to Union sentiment and do away as far as possible with partisan influence. The platform, which was unanimously adopted, was a statement of "unconditional Union" principles and pledged the convention to put down rebellion by force of arms. Abraham Lincoln was nominated for a second term by the vote of every delegate except those from Missouri who had been instructed to vote for Gen. Grant. The nomination then was made unanimous. Andrew Johnson of Tennessee, a leading Southern Democrat who had been staunch in his loyalty to the Union, was nominated for Vice-President.

The Democratic party met in convention on Aug. 29, at Chicago. Its platform declared the war a failure and advocated the immediate cessation of hostilities and the restoration of the Union by peaceable means. The convention nominated Gen. George B. McClellan for President and George H. Pendleton for Vice-President. McClellan accepted the nomination but at the same time virtually repudiated the platform, for he was thoroughly loyal to the cause of the Union.

At first it appeared that the Democrats might defeat Lincoln, but the victories of the Union Army in the field proved that the war was not a failure and rallied the people to the support of Lincoln and Johnson and the Union cause. The election took place on Nov. 8. For the first time in our history certain states, those of the South, deliberately declined to choose electors for the choice of President. Lincoln carried every state that took part in the election but New Jersey, Delaware and Kentucky. He received 212 electoral votes. McClellan received 21. Lincoln was given a popular majority of only 494,567 in a total of 4,166,537. This election was one of the most vital in the history of the country since upon its result might depend the perpetuation of the national Union.

CAMPAIGN OF 1868 AND OF 1872. The issues in 1868 were Southern reconstruction and the "Ohio Idea." Horatio Seymour of New York and Frank Blair of Missouri, the Democratic nominees, ran on a platform calling for a restoration of the rights of the Southern states and payment of the war bonds in greenbacks. Alarmed by Democratic victories in 1867, the Republicans nominated the war hero, Grant, and Schuyler Colfax of Indiana. Their platform acclaimed the success of reconstruction and denounced as repudiation the payment of the bonds in greenbacks.

Personal attacks on the candidates and Republican "waving the bloody shirt" featured the campaign. An effort to replace the Democratic nominees in October failed but foreshadowed defeat. Grant received 214 electoral votes to Seymour's 80, and nearly 53% of the popular vote, receiving 3,012,833 votes to 2,709,-249 for Seymour. Seymour carried eight states. The result was a personal victory for Grant rather than for Republican policies.

Dissatisfaction with the reconstruction policy and a desire for reform led to a Liberal Republican organization, supported by tariff and civil-service reformers, independent editors and disgruntled politicians. The new party nominated Horace Greeley, with B. Gratz Brown of Missouri, to oppose Grant's re-election in 1872. Its platform demanded civil-service reform, universal amnesty and specie payment. The tariff issue was straddled to please Greeley, a protectionist. The Democrats accepted the Liberal Republican platform and nominees. The Greeley campaign lacked enthusiasm, and he was mercilessly lampooned. Grant received 286 electoral votes to Greeley's 66, and over 55% of the popular vote, receiving 3,597,132 votes to 2,834,125 for Greeley.

CAMPAIGN OF 1876 is memorable because it resulted in the famous disputed presidential election. The leading aspirant for the Republican nomination was James G. Blaine of Maine. His name was presented to the national convention at Cincinnati by Robert G. Ingersoll in a striking speech in which he dubbed Blaine "the Plumed Knight." Among the other candidates were Benjamin H. Bristow of Kentucky, Roscoe Conkling of New York, Oliver P. Morton of Indiana and Rutherford B. Hayes of Ohio. For six ballots Blaine led the field, but on the seventh a stampede to Rutherford B. Hayes resulted in his nomination. William A. Wheeler was named as his running mate. The platform endorsed the Resumption Act and eulogized the Republican party for its work during the Civil War and Reconstruction.

Thomas F. Bayard of Delaware, Allen G. Thurman of Ohio, Winfield Scott Hancock of Pennsylvania and Thomas A. Hendricks of Indiana sought the Democratic nomination, but the logical contender was Gov. Samuel J. Tilden of New York, who was named on the first ballot. Hendricks was then nominated for the Vice-Presidency. The scandals of the Grant administration were denounced in unsparing terms and "Reform" was declared to be the paramount issue. Repeal of the clause of the act of 1875 providing for the resumption of specie payments was advocated, but Tilden personally was known to be a sound-money man rather than a Greenbacker. The platform also declared in favor of civil-service reform.

In the campaign the Democratic speakers dwelt heavily upon the scandals under Republican rule and contended that only through a change of men and parties could there be any real reform. Republican orators resorted to "bloody shirt" tactics—that is, revived the Civil War issues—questioned Tilden's loyalty during that conflict and praised Hayes' military record: four honorable wounds and a brevet major generalcy. In the North the campaign was a quiet one, but in some of the Southern states attempts to intimidate Negro voters produced violent disorders and considerable bloodshed.

Early returns on election night indicated the election of Tilden, but presently it appeared that the result would be in doubt. When the electoral college met and voted, Tilden received 184 unquestioned votes, Hayes 165; with 4 votes of Florida, the 8 votes of Louisiana, the 7 votes of South Carolina and 1 vote of Oregon claimed by both parties. After a protracted, bitter dispute, Congress created an Electoral Commission of five Senators, five Representatives and five judges of the Supreme Court to help decide the result. Of the Senators, three were to be Republicans and two Democrats; of the Representatives three were to be Democrats and two Republicans; four of the judges, two Republicans and two Democrats, were designated by their districts and they were to choose the fifth judge. It was expected that the fifth judge would be David Davis, but his election to the Senate by the Democrats in the Illinois legislature gave him an excuse to decline the thankless task. The choice then fell upon Joseph P. Bradley, who had been appointed to the bench as a Republican, but some of whose decisions made him acceptable, temporarily, to the Democrats.

In case the two Houses of Congress voting separately refused to accept any return the dispute was to be referred to the Commission, whose decision was to be final unless it was rejected by both Houses. The two Houses, voting separately on strict party lines, did disagree. Decision, therefore, rested with the Commission, which, in all cases, by a vote of 8 to 7 (Bradley voting with the majority), refused to go behind the election results as certified by the state authorities (in the case of Oregon by the Secretary of State) and declared in favor of the Republican contenders. In each case the Senate accepted this decision, the House rejected it. All the disputed votes were therefore counted for Hayes and Wheeler and they were declared elected.

CAMPAIGN OF 1880 took place during a business revival and with no definite issue before the country. It was routine politics. The Republicans overcame a serious split between groups headed by James G. Blaine and Roscoe Conkling respectively, by nominating James A. Garfield, a member of neither faction, over President Grant, supported by the Conkling wing for a third term. Against Garfield the Democrats nominated Winfield Scott Hancock, a nonpolitical Civil War general; but their party had no positive program, was discredited by its factious opposition to the Hayes administration and was defeated by a close vote. The Republicans carried the "doubtful states" and regained control over Congress. The popular vote was: Garfield, 4,454,416; Hancock, 4,444,952. The electoral vote was: Garfield; 214; Hancock, 155.

CAMPAIGN OF 1884, fought primarily between James G. Blaine and Grover Cleveland as Republican and Democratic candidates respectively, was one of the most vituperative in American history. There were several reasons why it became relentlessly personal in character. From the moment of Blaine's nomination at Chicago on June 6 he came under heavy fire from the reform element of all parties. He was believed to be allied with the spoils element in Republican politics; he had an unhappy record for baiting the South; he favored certain big business interests; and his railroad transactions had raised a suspicion that he had used his official position for personal profit. To divert attention from these attacks certain Republicans published evidence that Cleveland, nominated on July 10 at Chicago, was the father of an illegitimate son born in Buffalo some ten years earlier. Of serious issues between the two parties there were virtually none; both had good reason not to meddle seriously with the currency question or tariff, and international affairs attracted little attention. One leading feature of the campaign was the secession of a large body of Republicans who could not stomach Blaine and who became Cleveland Democrats or Mugwumps. Another feature was the open enmity of Tammany Hall, under Boss John Kelly, for Cleveland, and the success of it and other malcontents in carrying many Irish voters over to Blaine or to the new Anti-Monopoly party headed by Benjamin F. Butler. After exchanges which one observer compared to the billingsgate of quarreling tenement dwellers, the two parties approached election day running neck and neck. Democratic victory was finally decided by the vote of New York state, in which the Rev. Dr. Burchard's "rum, Romanism and rebellion" speech at a reception to Blaine, the "Belshazzar's feast" of Republican millionaires and politicians at Delmonico's just before election and Roscoe Conkling's knifing of Blaine all played a part. Cleveland obtained a popular vote of 4,874,986 against Blaine's 4,851,981, and an electoral vote of 219 against Blaine's 182. Butler's popular vote was just over 175,000, and that of John P. St. John, Prohibition candidate, was just over 150,000.

CAMPAIGN OF 1888 turned chiefly on the tariff issue, and resulted in the election of Benjamin Harrison over Grover Cleveland by a majority of the electoral college but not of the popular vote. The Republicans had approached the election with scant hope of victory, for Cleveland had proved an admirable President, when his annual message of 1887, devoted entirely to arguments for tariff reform, gave them new heart. The issue was one on which they could rally nearly all manufacturers, most general business and perhaps a majority of workingmen. Benjamin Harrison, who represented extreme high-tariff demands, was nominated by the Republicans at Chicago on June 25, after Blaine had withdrawn for reasons of health, and John Sherman and Walter Q. Gresham, whose tariff views were moderate, had failed to gain strength. Levi P. Morton was named for Vice President. Harrison, supported by Blaine, by manufacturing interests who were induced by the Republican Chairman, Matthew S. Quay, to subscribe large campaign funds and by Civil War veterans hungry for pension legislation, waged an aggressive campaign. His speech-making abilities made a deep impression on the country. Cleveland, who was renominated by the Democrats at St. Louis early in June, felt that his presidential office made it improper for him to do active campaigning; his running-mate, Allen G. Thurman of Ohio, was too old and infirm to be anything but a liability to the party; and campaign funds were slender. Worst of all for the Democrats, their national chairman, Sen. Calvin S. Brice of Ohio, held high-tariff convictions, was allied with big business and refused to put his heart into the battle. Two weeks before election day the Republicans published an indiscreet letter by Lord Sackville, the British minister, hinting to a supposed British subject that Cleveland would probably be more friendly to England than Harrison; and though Cleveland at once had Sackville recalled, the incident cost him many Irish votes. Cleveland received 5,540,329 popular votes, Harrison but 5,439,853; but Cleveland had only 168 electors against Harrison's 233. Charles B. Fisk of New Jersey, Prohibition candidate, polled 249,506 votes; Alson J. Streeter of Illinois, Union Labor nominee, 146,935.

CAMPAIGN OF 1892 brought the re-election of Grover Cleveland over Benjamin Harrison by a majority the size of which surprised observers of both parties. Cleveland had been named on the first ballot at the Democratic convention in Chicago, although David B. Hill of New York had made a demagogic attempt to displace him. Harrison, who had estranged the professional politicians of his party, who had quarreled with its most popular figure, Blaine, and who had impressed the country as cold and unlikable, was reluctantly accepted by the Republicans at Minneapolis on June 10. It was impossible to repudiate his administration. However, the McKinley Tariff of 1890 had excited widespread discontent, the Sherman Silver-Purchase Act of the same year had angered the conservative East and heavy Federal expenditures had caused general uneasiness. Cleveland's firm stand on behalf of the gold standard and low tariffs and his known strength of character commended him to large numbers of independent voters. One factor adverse to the Republicans was the great strength manifested by the Populists, who polled 1,040,000 votes for James B. Weaver of Iowa and James G. Field of Virginia; most of this coming from old Republican strongholds in the Middle West. Another factor was the labor war at Homestead, Pa., which showed that the highly protected steel industry did not properly pass on its tariff benefits to the worker. Cleveland, with a popular vote of 5,556,543, had 277 electors; Harrison, with a popular vote of 5,175,582, had 145; while Weaver won 22 electoral votes.

CAMPAIGN OF 1896 ended a 22-year period in which neither major party had been able to control the National Government for more than the life of a single Congress; it ushered in a period of Republican domination which lasted until 1911. Favored by Mark Hanna's cannily managed campaign, William McKinley of Ohio was named on the first ballot by the Republican convention meeting at St. Louis. The traditional party platform was adopted with the exception of a declaration for the gold standard until bimetallism could be secured by international agreement. A bloc of Western delegates bolted and organized the Silver Republican party.

There was no dominant candidate for the Democratic nomination. The important contest was over the platform. As presented to the delegates, it was an anti-Administration document favoring free silver at the sixteen-to-one ratio, criticizing the use of injunctions in labor disputes and denouncing the overthrow of the Federal income tax. In its support William Jennings Bryan delivered his "Cross of Gold" oration and endeared himself to the silver delegates by his effective answers to the criticisms of the administration orators.

The enthusiasm growing out of that speech gave impetus to Bryan's candidacy for the presidential nomination. Back of this was also the long campaign he had waged by personal conferences, speeches and correspondence with the inflationist delegates from the South and West. Another factor was the bolting Republicans and the Populists, who saw themselves being forced to support the Democratic nominee and demanded some one not too closely identified with the regular Democracy. Bryan appealed to the delegates as the Democrat who could unite the silver and agrarian factions.

The Populists, Silver Republicans and National Silver party members joined the Democrats in support of Bryan. The Administration Democrats placed a National Democratic ticket in the field to hold conservative Democratic votes away from him.

The campaign was highly spectacular. The Democrats exploited Bryan's oratory by sending him on speaking tours back and forth across the country during which enormous crowds came out to hear him. In sharp contrast, the Republican management kept McKinley at his home in Canton, Ohio, where carefully selected delegations made formal calls and listened to "front porch" speeches by the candidate. More important were the flood of advertising, the funds for building local organizations and the large group of speakers on the hustings, which were maintained by Hanna's organization. The metropolitan press, like the other business groups—except the silver miners—was essentially a unit in opposing Bryan. The results showed a sharp city-versus-rural division, with Bryan carrying the Solid South and most of the trans-Missouri states. The remainder, including California, Oregon, North Dakota, Kentucky and Maryland, went to McKinley. With him were elected a Republican House and a Senate in which various minor party members held a nominal balance of power. The popular vote was unusually large, each candidate receiving larger totals than any previous candidate of his party, McKinley's vote being 7,098,474 and Bryan's 6,379,830. Their electoral vote was 271 and 176 respectively.

CAMPAIGN OF 1900 carried over the presidential candidates and most of the issues of 1896. With the trend of prices upward, the pressure for inflation had declined, and the expansion of American control over new territories had created the issue of imperialism.

At the Republican convention in Philadelphia a combination of circumstances forced Hanna and McKinley to accept Theodore Roosevelt as the vice-presidential candidate. The party's position on the new territories was defined as American retention with "the largest measure of self-government consistent with their welfare and our duties."

When the Democrats met at Kansas City, they were unwilling to accept the conservatives' proposal to forget the last platform and make anti-imperialism the only issue. The 1896 platform was reindorsed, an antitrust plank added and imperialism designated the "paramount issue."

The campaign lacked the fire of 1896. The Republicans emphasized the "full dinner pail" and the danger of threatening it from the Democratic platform; the Democrats stressed the growth of monopolies under the McKinley administration and the danger of imperialistic government. The result was a more emphatic Republican victory than in 1896, one generally interpreted as an endorsement of both McKinley's domestic and foreign policies. The popular vote was: McKinley, 7,218,491; Bryan, 6,356,734. McKinley obtained 292 electoral votes to 155 for Bryan. This election made Roosevelt's elevation to the Presidency automatic upon McKinley's death in 1901.

CAMPAIGN OF 1904. Theodore Roosevelt, who

succeeded to the Presidency on the death of Mc-Kinley in 1901, ardently hoped to be nominated and elected "in his own right." The death of Marcus A. Hanna of Ohio, whom the "big business" interests of the country would have preferred, made possible the President's nomination by acclamation when the Republican convention met in Chicago, June 21. Charles W. Fairbanks of Indiana was chosen for second place.

The Democrats, meeting at St. Louis, July 6, pointedly turned their backs upon "Bryanism" by omitting from their platform all reference to the money question and by nominating for President, Alton B. Parker, a conservative New York judge, who at once pledged himself to maintain the gold standard, and for Vice-President, Henry Gassaway Davis, a wealthy West Virginia octogenarian. Business leaders, however, more afraid of the Democratic party than of Roosevelt, contributed so heavily to the Republican campaign chest that Parker rashly charged "blackmail." Corporations, he said, were being forced to contribute in return for the suppression of evidence that the Government had against them. Roosevelt, indignantly denying the charge, won by a landslide that reclaimed Missouri from the Solid South, gave him 336 electoral votes to Parker's 140 and a popular plurality of 2,540,067. Prohibitionist, Populist, Socialist and Socialist-Labor candidates received only negligible support.

CAMPAIGN OF 1908. Theodore Roosevelt, though at the height of his popularity, refused to be a third-term candidate in 1908, but swung his support in the Republican convention to William Howard Taft, who was nominated.

The Democratic convention was as completely dominated by William Jennings Bryan, who became its nominee. Party differences were not significant. After an apathetic campaign Bryan carried only the Solid South, Kansas, Colorado and Nevada, though he received 43% of the popular vote, securing 6,409,-106 to Taft's 7,679,006. Taft's electoral vote was 321; Bryan's 162. The Republicans won the Presidency and both Houses of Congress.

CAMPAIGN OF 1912 marked the culmination of the progressive movement in national politics and resulted in the return of the Democrats after sixteen years of Republican Presidents.

The struggle for the Republican nomination became a sanguinary battle between the progressive and conservative wings, aided in each case by personal followings and some division of support from large interests. In the beginning it was the progressive, LaFollette, against the incumbent, Taft. But former President Theodore Roosevelt, who had been largely responsible for Taft's nomination in 1908, entered the race to rally behind him Republicans who believed Taft had been too friendly with the con-

servative Old Guard. The influence in Taft's hands was sufficient to return delegates pledged to him in most cases where they were named by conventions, but Roosevelt or LaFollette were successful in all states save one where presidential primaries were held. The conservative controlled National Committee placed Taft delegates on the temporary roll in all contests and the small majority resulting gave Taft the nomination. Roosevelt was later nominated by the newly organized Progressive party, consisting largely of Republican bolters.

The contest for the Democratic nomination was also hard fought with both of the leading candidates accepted as progressives. Champ Clark led from the beginning and had an actual majority in the convention for a time, but when Bryan transferred his support to the second progressive, Woodrow Wilson, a shift began which resulted in the latter's nomination. All three party platforms were unusually favorable to progressive policies. Wilson, backed by a united party, won easily and Roosevelt was second. There was an unusual amount of shifting of party loyalties, although most Democrats voted for Wilson and most Republicans for Roosevelt or Taft. Wilson's popular vote was 6,296,547, Roosevelt's was 4,126,020 and Taft's was 3,486,720. Their electoral vote was, respectively, 435, 88 and 8. The Democrats won majorities in both branches of Congress. In spite of the three-way contest, a fourth candidate, Eugene V. Debs, Socialist, secured approximately 900,000 votes, the highest percentage of the total vote his party ever received.

CAMPAIGN OF 1916 reunited the Republican party and determined that American foreign policy should be left in Wilson's hands. The Republicans reunited when, after the nomination of Charles Evans Hughes, Theodore Roosevelt, already nominated by the rapidly declining Progressive party, announced support of the ticket.

There was no opposition to Wilson's renomination. The Democrats defended the policies of the administration, especially the Underwood Tariff and the measures for the regulation of business. They also praised the foreign policy as one which had kept us out of war and preserved national honor.

The Republicans attacked the policies of the Administration, promised a "stronger" foreign policy and were supported by the more extreme partisans of both alliances in the European war.

The results were in doubt for several days because of the close vote in several states. Wilson won the Presidency, carrying Ohio, New Hampshire, the South and most of the border and trans-Missouri states, including California, with an electoral vote of 277, against 254 for Hughes. The popular vote was Wilson, 9,127,695; Hughes, 8,533,507. Congress remained Democratic only because independent members of the House were friendly.

CAMPAIGN OF 1920. The debate on the League of Nations determined the alignment of political forces in the spring of 1920. The Republicans were confident; the wounds of the intraparty strife of 1912 had been healed; the mistaken strategy of 1916 admitted; and the conservative mood of the country was easily interpreted. They met in convention in Chicago, could not agree upon any one of the leading pre-convention candidates, Frank O. Lowden, Hiram Johnson or Leonard Wood, and nominated Warren G. Harding, Senator from Ohio, on the tenth ballot. Calvin Coolidge, Governor of Massachusetts, was nominated for the Vice-Presidency.

The Democrats met in San Francisco. None of the discussed candidates, William G. McAdoo, Alfred E. Smith, John W. Davis, A. Mitchell Palmer or James M. Cox, commanded a great following. The last-named was nominated on the 44th ballot, with Franklin D. Roosevelt as vice-presidential nominee.

Neither platform was unexpected or significant on domestic issues. The Republicans attacked the President and opposed American entrance into the League.

The Socialist party, meeting in May, nominated Eugene Debs for the fifth time. A Farmer-Labor ticket appeared also. The Democratic national committee supported Wilson's appeal for a "solemn referendum" on the covenant of the League; Cox waged a persistent and vigorous campaign; Harding, remaining at his home for the most part, contented himself with vague generalizations. Neither candidate had been nationally known at the outset of the contest, and no clear-cut issue developed and no real contest transpired. The Nineteenth Amendment had been proclaimed in August and in every state women were entitled to vote. The popular vote was: Harding, 16,152,200; Cox, 9,147,353. Cox won the electoral vote in only eleven states, receiving 127 electoral votes to Harding's 404. The Socialist vote was 902,310, but the strength of all the third parties totaled only 5.52%.

CAMPAIGN OF 1924. As in 1920, so in 1924, the candidates were new in a presidential canvass. The Republican convention meeting in Cleveland, with a few scattering votes in dissent, nominated Calvin Coolidge, who as Vice-President had succeeded to the Presidency in the summer of 1923. The vice-presidential nomination, refused by several, was accepted by Charles G. Dawes. The platform was marked by extreme conservatism.

The Democrats met in New York and were in almost continuous session for two and a half weeks. Not only was there serious division upon the matter of American adherence to the League of Nations and upon the proposed denunciation of the Ku Klux Klan, but also upon the choice of the nominee. Each of the two leading candidates, Alfred E. Smith and William G. McAdoo, was sufficiently powerful to prevent the nomination of the other, and finally on

the 103rd ballot the nomination went to John W. Davis. Charles W. Bryan of Nebraska was nominated for Vice-President. The platform called for a popular referendum on the League of Nations.

A Conference for Progressive Political Action brought about a series of meetings and eventually a widespread support of Sen. Robert M. LaFollette in his independent candidacy, with Burton K. Wheeler as his running mate. LaFollette's platform, in which appeared most of the progressive proposals of the previous twenty years, was endorsed by the Socialist party and the officers of the American Federation of Labor. So real did the threat of the third party candidacy appear to be that much of the attack of the Republicans was upon LaFollette, who waged an aggressive campaign.

The total vote cast exceeded that of 1920 by two and a third million, but because of the vote cast for LaFollette (nearly 5,000,000) that cast for Republican and for Democratic tickets was less than four years earlier, Coolidge securing 15,718,211 votes, and Davis, 8,385,283. LaFollette carried Wisconsin. Coolidge topped the poll in 35 states, receiving 382 electoral votes, leaving the electoral vote for Davis in only 12 states, or 136 votes.

CAMPAIGN OF 1928. An Aug. 2, 1927, President Calvin Coolidge announced that he "did not choose to run" for President in 1928. The majority of the leaders of the Republican party were undecided with regard to the candidate they should support. A popular movement having its strength in the rank and file of the voters forced the nomination of Herbert Hoover on the first ballot at the Republican National Convention which met at Kansas City, Mo., on June 12, 1928. The platform contained strong support of the usual Republican policies such as a protective tariff and sound business administration. It advocated the observance and rigorous enforcement of the Eighteenth Amendment. Charles Curtis was nominated for Vice-President.

The Democrats met at Houston, Texas, and on June 28 nominated Alfred E. Smith for President. They then nominated Joseph T. Robinson for Vice-President. The platform did not differ strikingly from that of the Republicans. The contest became one between rival personalities. Gov. Smith, an avowed "wet," took a stand in favor of a change in the Prohibition Amendment, and advocated that the question of prohibition and its enforcement be left to the determination of the individual states.

At the election on Nov. 6 Mr. Hoover was overwhelmingly successful. He carried forty states, including five from the old South, with a total of 444 electoral votes. Gov. Smith carried eight states with an electoral vote of 87. The popular vote was: Hoover, 21,392,190; Smith, 15,016,443.

CAMPAIGN OF 1932 AND OF 1936. The presidential campaign of 1932 began in earnest with the holding of the Republican National Convention at Chicago on June 14–16. President Herbert Hoover and Vice-President Charles Curtis were renominated on the first ballot. The platform praised the Hoover record including his program for combating the depression. After a long debate a "wet-dry" plank on prohibition was adopted which favored giving the people an opportunity to pass on a repeal amendment.

The Democratic National Convention was also held at Chicago, June 27–July 2, 1932. On the fourth ballot, Gov. Franklin Delano Roosevelt of New York was nominated for the Presidency, defeating Alfred E. Smith and ten other candidates. The platform pledged economy, a sound currency, unemployment relief, old-age and unemployment insurance under state laws, the "restoration of agriculture" and repeal of the Eighteenth Amendment together with immediate legalization of beer.

After a campaign featured by Roosevelt's promise of "a new deal," the elections were held on Nov. 5. The popular vote for each party was as follows: Democratic, 22,821,857; Republican, 15,761,841; Socialist, 884,781; Socialist-Labor, 33,276; Communist, 102,991; Prohibition, 81,869; Liberty, 53,425; and Farm-Labor, 7309. The electoral vote was 472 for the Democrats and 59 for the Republicans.

In 1936 the Republican National Convention was held at Cleveland beginning on June 9. Gov. Alfred M. Landon of Kansas and Frank Knox, Chicago publisher, were nominated for the Presidency and Vice-Presidency, respectively. The platform strongly denounced the "New Deal administration," from both constitutional and economic viewpoints. It pledged the Republicans "to maintain the American system of constitutional and local self-government" and "to preserve the American system of free enterprise."

The Democratic National Convention assembled at Philadelphia on June 25 for what proved to be a ratification meeting for the New Deal. President Roosevelt and Vice-President Garner were renominated without opposition. The platform vigorously defended the New Deal and pledged its continuance.

When the election was held on Nov. 3, the Democrats again won an overwhelming victory, carrying every state except Maine and Vermont. The popular vote for each party was as follows: Democratic, 27,476,673; Republican, 16,679,583; Union, 882,479; Socialist, 187,720; Communist, 80,159; Prohibition, 37,847; and Socialist-Labor, 12,777. The Democrats received 523 electoral votes while the Republicans received only 8. The popular vote was the largest ever polled in an election in the United States.

CAMPAIGN OF 1940. Although either Robert A. Taft, Arthur H. Vandenberg or Thomas E. Dewey was expected to be the Republican candidate, the nomination was won by Wendell L. Willkie at Philadelphia, June 28, on the sixth ballot. As presi-

dent of a large utilities corporation Willkie had fought the New Deal, but in foreign affairs he was an internationalist, and with Europe at war, this fact commended him to the liberal element of the party, which carried his nomination against the "Old Guard." The nomination of a liberal by the Republicans, together with the international crisis, in turn made the nomination of Franklin D. Roosevelt by the Democrats (Chicago, July 16) a practical certainty, even though his running for a third term was unprecedented. Foreign affairs dominated the campaign. Both candidates promised aid to the Allies; both promised at the same time to keep the United States out of "foreign wars." Roosevelt and Henry A. Wallace received 27,243,000 popular and 449 electoral votes against 22,304,400 popular and 82 electoral votes for Willkie and Charles E. McNary of Oregon.

CAMPAIGN OF 1944. Thomas E. Dewey, Governor of New York, was nominated by the Republican convention in Chicago on June 26 with little opposition. John W. Bricker of Ohio was chosen as his running mate. President Roosevelt, running for a fourth term, encountered even less opposition at the Democratic convention in Chicago. The real struggle revolved around the choice of a Vice-Presidential candidate. With Roosevelt's support Vice-President Wallace could probably have been nominated for another term, but the opposition to Wallace from within the party convinced the President that a compromise candidate had to be found. James F. Byrnes of South Carolina was acceptable to the White House and to the party conservatives, but not to Labor, in particular not to Sidney Hillman of the C. I. O. Accordingly Sen. Harry S. Truman of Missouri was nominated on the second ballot, July 20. In the November election Roosevelt received 25,602,505 popular and 432 electoral votes to Dewey's 22,006,278 popular and 99 electoral votes. The Democrats preserved their control of both houses of Congress.

CAMPAIGN OF 1948. The Republicans, having gained control of Congress in 1946, confidently expected to turn the apparently unpopular Truman administration out of power in the autumn elections, and for the first time in the party's history renominated a defeated candidate, Thomas E. Dewey, at the convention meeting in Philadelphia on June 21. The Democrats, on the other hand, suffered from severe internal conflicts. Truman's nomination at Philadelphia on July 15 caused no enthusiasm. Radicals left the party and, meeting in the same city on July 22, nominated Henry A. Wallace and Sen. Glen Taylor of Idaho as the candidates of the Progressive party. Southerners, offended by the civil rights planks of the Democratic platform, also seceded and at Birmingham, Ala., July 17, formed the

States' Rights Democratic party, with Gov. J. Strom Thurmond of South Carolina and Gov. Fielding L. Wright of Mississippi as their candidates. Under these circumstances Truman's candidacy appeared to be hopeless. The President, however, proved to be a whistle-stop campaigner of unexpected ability. Moreover, he enjoyed the support not only of organized labor and of Negro voters but as it turned out, to the great surprise of prophets and pollsters, of Midwestern farmers as well. He and Alben W. Barkley polled 24,105,695 popular and 304 electoral votes against 21,969,170 popular and 189 electoral votes for Dewey and Earl Warren. Thurmond polled 1,169,021 popular votes and the 38 electoral votes of South Carolina, Alabama, Mississippi and Louisiana. Wallace won 1,156,103 popular votes. The Democrats regained control of Congress by small majorities.

CAMPAIGN OF 1952. After a long and bitter struggle, the internationalist wing of the Republican party succeeded on July 11 in bringing about the nomination of Gen. Dwight D. Eisenhower against the opposition of Sen. Robert A. Taft and his supporters. The Democrats, following the Republicans to Chicago ten days later, turned to Gov. Adlai E. Stevenson of Illinois, who consented to become a candidate only at the last moment. In the following campaign Stevenson suffered from revelations of corruption in the Truman administration, from the widespread dissatisfaction with the seemingly inconclusive results of the war in Korea, and from the vague feeling that it was "time for a change." Eisenhower's personal appeal, moreover, was immense. He and Richard M. Nixon polled 33,824,351 votes to 27,314,987 for Stevenson and Sen. John J. Sparkman of Alabama. The Republicans carried the electoral college, 442 to 89. They carried the House of Representatives by a narrow margin and tied the Democrats in the Senate.

CAMPAIGN OF 1956. Adlai E. Stevenson was renominated on the first ballot by the Democrats at Chicago, with Sen. Estes Kefauver as his running mate. President Eisenhower and Vice-President Nixon were renominated by the Republicans at San Francisco with equal ease. The campaign, however, was far from being a rehash of 1952. Stevenson, having been advised that his serious discussions of issues in 1952 had been over the voters' heads, agreed to pitch his campaign at a somewhat lower level. The results disappointed his more ardent supporters without winning him any votes. The Suez crisis, occurring on the eve of the election, further strengthened the administration's position by creating a national emergency. In the election the President polled 35,300,000 popular and 457 electoral votes to Stevenson's 25,800,000 popular and 73 electoral votes. As in 1952, Eisenhower broke into the solid

South, carrying not only Florida, Virginia and Tennessee, which he had carried in 1952, but Texas, Oklahoma and Louisiana as well. In spite of his personal triumph, however, the Democrats carried both houses of Congress.

CAMPAIGN OF 1960. The Democrats nominated Sen. John F. Kennedy of Massachusetts at Los Angeles in July, with Sen. Lyndon B. Johnson of Texas as his running-mate. The Republicans, meeting at Chicago two weeks later, nominated Vice-President Richard M. Nixon and Henry Cabot Lodge of Massachusetts. The most striking feature of the campaign was a series of televised "debates," in which the candidates submitted to questioning by panels of reporters. By sharing a national audience with his lesser-known opponent, Nixon in this manner may have injured his own cause. Indeed, the debates, in view of the closeness of the result, may have been the decisive influence in Kennedy's victory. The final vote was not known until weeks after the election. Kennedy received 34,221,531, Nixon 34,108,474, and minor candidates 502,773. Despite the fact that Kennedy won by only 113,057 votes and had only 49.7 percent of the total vote as compared with 49.6 percent for Mr. Nixon, the President-elect won 303 electoral votes to Nixon's 219. At 43, Kennedy was the youngest man ever elected to the Presidency (although not the youngest to occupy the office). He was also the first Roman Catholic ever to become President.

CAMPAIGNS, PRESIDENTIAL, have occurred in the United States every fourth year, beginning in 1788, and will so continue as long as the present constitutional provisions remain in force. Each campaign has been ushered in since the 1830's by the holding of national party conventions to select presidential and vice-presidential candidates and to draw up platforms. The method of selecting delegates to these conventions was for a long time wholly extralegal, and determined by local party traditions, but in many states presidential primaries are now held, by means of which the voters may register their preference for the supporters of a particular candidate. Each convention represents the various political units of the nation approximately according to population.

Sometimes, as in the case of a popular President desiring renomination, there is no contest in the convention, but often the nomination is awarded only after long balloting and much excitement. State delegations rally around their "favorite sons," and win or yield votes in accordance with backstage deals and promises. Doubtful states, that is, states that may vote either way in the election, have a decided advantage over the rest; New York and Ohio, for example, have furnished a disproportionate share of the presidential nominees. If the contest is not decided on an early ballot, a "dark-horse" candidate, one not previously regarded as a serious contender for the place, sometimes wins out. Until 1936 Democratic conventions required a two-thirds majority to nominate, but at that time the Democrats adopted the rule long current in Republican conventions that a simple majority would be sufficient. While military heroes, Congressmen, cabinet members and judges have all been accorded presidential nominations, in general the governor of an important close state has an advantage over all other contenders.

After the nominations are made the Chairman of the National Committee, an officer personally selected by the presidential candidate, takes command of the party forces. Under his direction the campaign treasurer raises and expends huge sums of money to send "stump speakers," campaign literature and funds for less circumspect purposes into the doubtful states. In earlier times presidential candidates either stood aloof from the campaign, or made only dignified and sedate appearances, such as were a part of McKinley's "front-porch" campaign of 1896. Of late, however, presidential candidates have become themselves the chief campaigners. Frequent "swings around the circle" take them to every part of the country; radio and television report their every utterance to millions of listeners. Indeed, there is some reason to think that the mass media will revolutionize the language of political discourse, until candidates will be sold to the public by the same methods as are used to sell soap and toothpaste.

Campaign speeches and documents are usually formulated with a view to pleasing the maximum number of voters and real issues are often sidetracked in favor of blind appeals to partisanship. Thus "waving the bloody shirt" was the chief reliance of Republican orators for a long time after the Civil War, while the desire to maintain white supremacy has at times outweighed all other considerations in the "Solid South." On the other hand, Bryan's battle for "free silver" and his attack on "imperialism," Wilson's advocacy of the "New Freedom," Franklin D. Roosevelt's defense of the New Deal, and Adlai Stevenson's speeches on foreign policy are instances in which important ideas were set before the electorate for rejection or approval.

CANADA, AMERICAN INVASION OF, 1775–76. In attempting the conquest of Canada, the Continental Congress wished not only to effect a diversion favorable to the colonial operations around Boston, but, still more, to deprive Britain of a base for attack upon the revolutionary colonies. The idea was encouraged by the capture of Ticonderoga and Crown Point, which secured the route northward. Hopes of success were increased by the knowledge that there were few regular troops in Canada, and the plausible expectation of a rising of the French Canadians. After some hesitation, Congress authorized Gen. Schuyler

(June 27, 1775) to undertake the invasion if he found it practicable. Active direction of the expedition fell to Brig. Gen. Richard Montgomery.

A first hasty enterprise against Montreal resulted only in the capture of Ethan Allen by the British (Sept. 25, 1775). The real gateway of Canada, St. Johns on the Richelieu, held by a large proportion of Canada's regular garrison, fell after a siege lasting from Sept. 17 to Nov. 2, during which the invaders were strengthened by ammunition and provisions obtained by the capture of Fort Chambly. Montreal was occupied Nov. 13, 1775.

Gen. Guy Carleton, governor of the province, fled to Quebec, which was already threatened by the force which Arnold had brought up by the tremendously difficult Kennebec route; but even after Arnold's junction (Dec. 2) with Montgomery's depleted army, the colonial troops available for the siege of Quebec numbered only about 1000. The one assault which was attempted (Dec. 31) failed completely, Montgomery being killed; and in spite of considerable reinforcements toward spring the siege ended abruptly with the opening of navigation, when the first of 10,000 regulars arrived from England (May 5, 1776). On May 16 a British force from the west captured 400 Americans at Cedars, above Montreal; on June 7 part of the American main force, strengthened by a brigade under Gen. John Sullivan, who assumed command, met disaster at Three Rivers. On June 15 Montreal was evacuated. Sullivan's force and the small body under Arnold from Montreal were reunited at St. Johns. On June 18 the last Americans left that fortress. Carleton's pursuit was delayed while he built a fleet, which destroyed Arnold's, but it was too late in the season for further operations, and invasion of the colonies was postponed until 1777.

The failure of the American invasion was due to inadequate military measures, to British sea power, and to the generally neutral attitude of the French-Canadians. It has been argued that the campaign was advantageous to the revolutionary cause in the end by forcing the British to divert the reinforcements of 1776 to the St. Lawrence, thus causing a dispersion of the royal forces which led to the decisive success at Saratoga in the following year.

CANADA, AMERICAN INVASION OF, 1812–14. Since the destruction of British power in Canada was a primary object of those responsible for bringing on the War of 1812 it was inevitable that the United States in the course of the struggle should attempt the conquest of the colony. In 1812 an attempted invasion on the Detroit frontier resulted in disaster and an enterprise on the Niagara met the same fate. The next year brought more success; Perry's victory permitted a successful invasion of western Upper Canada and the Detroit frontier region remained in American hands until the end of the war. Farther east, the Americans successfully raided York, but initial successes on the Niagara were followed by a check at Stoney Creek and no permanent foothold was gained; while the campaign against Montreal was a total failure. In 1814 invasion was again attempted on the Niagara, but though the American troops now gave a better account of themselves no conquest of territory resulted.

Among the causes of the American failures, the military unpreparedness of the United States and the large degree of skill with which the defense was conducted by the British regular troops in Canada were important. The determined resistance of the Canadian population was contrary to American expectations and was also a powerful factor. Finally, the American strategic plans were in general decidedly unsound, in that they wasted the country's military resources in ill-conceived enterprises against Canada's western settlements, instead of concentrating them in an effective offensive movement against the essential British line of communication in the St. Lawrence Valley.

CANADIAN-AMERICAN RELATIONS. The present relationship of mutual confidence between the United States and Canada is of comparatively recent growth. In their earlier history issues arising between the republic and the British Empire produced not only an era of armed conflict (ending in 1815) but a long period of mistrust and difficulty thereafter.

Canadian-American relations in their earliest phase took the form of the chronic hostility, fanned by four intercolonial wars, which existed between the French Catholic settlers of New France and the English Protestant inhabitants of the thirteen colonies. Though the last of these wars brought Canada under the British flag, the traditional animosities survived, and in the American Revolution which followed they undoubtedly tended to restrain the French-Canadians from active co-operation with the Americans. The Definitive Treaty of Peace, 1783, partitioned the continent between the new republic and a group of continuing British colonies in the north; and the arrival in those colonies of perhaps 40,000 Loyalists expelled from the States, who founded the provinces of New Brunswick and Upper Canada (now Ontario), went far to render the division permanent, for the views of these men, inevitably strongly anti-American, colored the political life of their communities for generations.

Relations between republic and colonies were stormy from the beginning. The allied questions of the western posts on American soil which the British persisted in retaining, despite the treaty, until 1796, and of the alliances which, as part of the Canadian defense system, they kept up with Indian tribes within the United States, rendered British rule in Canada obnoxious to the American frontiersman; and the latter factor was probably more instrumental than the problems of impressment and neutral rights

at sea in producing the American declaration of war in 1812. The repeated unsuccessful invasions of Canada that followed only strengthened anti-American prejudices in the provinces. Memories of this war contributed materially to the growth of Canadian nationalism; for just as American national feeling was largely founded on antipathy to England, that of Canada was nurtured on antipathy to the United States. Though the Treaty of Ghent in general merely restored the *status quo,* the provision of Jay's Treaty which had permitted British intercourse with American Indians was not renewed and one historic cause of Anglo-American friction was thus greatly weakened. The Rush-Bagot Agreement of 1817 prevented a perpetuation of the wartime naval rivalry on the Lakes, but no limitation was imposed on land armaments, nor has any such limitation ever been negotiated.

Increasingly pacific relations were abruptly interrupted in 1837 when rebellions in Canada inaugurated another period of strain. The activity of American "sympathizers" and filibusters produced serious border incidents, notably that of the *Caroline,* and these difficulties were soon reinforced by those over the Maine boundary, which led in 1839 to troop movements and apprehension of war. These matters were resolved by the Webster-Ashburton Treaty, but the Oregon question prolonged the troubles to 1846. The next fifteen years, on the whole peaceful, were marked by the large development of commercial intercourse fostered by the Elgin-Marcy Reciprocity Treaty of 1854. The Senate's acceptance of this treaty has been attributed to Southern politicians' desire to avert the increase of free-soil territory by the annexation of Canada, which was represented as inevitable unless commercial concessions were made. An annexation movement which temporary commercial distress had produced in Montreal in 1849 gave color to this argument.

With the Civil War there commenced a decade of extreme danger in Anglo-American relations. The *Trent* affair of 1861 caused the most serious threat of war since 1815 and the state of the border thereafter was one of armed and precarious peace. The *Alabama* affair and similar incidents inflamed Northern opinion, and there was talk of annexing Canada in revenge. In 1864 the Confederates made attempts at using Canada as a base of operations against the North and fortification projects undertaken on both sides of the border in this and the following year reflected the increasing tension. At the end of the war the recrudescence of filibustering in the form of the Fenian Raids maintained this dangerous atmosphere, and the abrogation of the Reciprocity Treaty by the United States in 1866 embittered it. Fear of American attack lent impetus to the movement for federation of the several British provinces, which bore fruit in the organization of the Dominion of Canada (July 1, 1867). The British Government was more than willing to transfer its own responsibilities in America to the new government at Ottawa, which henceforth played an increasingly important role in negotiations with Washington.

The year 1871 is an important turning point. In that year the Treaty of Washington, by providing for arbitration of the *Alabama* claims, ended ten years of tension, and simultaneously the withdrawal of British troops from central Canada encouraged the growth of a less military atmosphere along the border. The fundamental territorial controversies between the two communities had now been settled; furthermore the abolition of slavery in the United States and the attainment of responsible government in Canada had removed domestic problems which had invited foreign interference. As memories of old conflicts faded, the influence of common racial and political traditions was freer to assert itself and to open the way for more peaceful relations; and from 1871 it is possible to speak with some truth of the Canadian border as an "unguarded" frontier, for no fortifications have since been built. The worst difficulties of the next period were the chronic Atlantic Fisheries dispute and the Bering Sea fur-seal question, both ultimately decided by arbitration; but the repeated refusal of the United States (now committed to high protection) to consider a renewal of reciprocity caused constant irritation and influenced Canada's own decision to turn to protection (1878) and the subsequent maintenance of this policy. In 1895 the Venezuela Boundary crisis aroused fears of war, and President Theodore Roosevelt's handling of the Alaska Boundary question (1903) further revived old animosities. In 1911 these helped to defeat President Taft's project of a new reciprocity treaty; traditional Canadian patriotism, fearing American penetration, now combined with the influence of new business interests which had grown up behind the Canadian tariff to bring about the rejection of Sir Wilfrid Laurier's government in a general election on this issue. In these same years, however, there was created (1909) the International Joint Commission on boundary waters, which ever since has done unostentatious but valuable work in settling disputes arising along the border.

American neutrality in the early stages of World War I did not increase the popularity of the United States with Canadians; but the improvement in Anglo-American relations, produced by this conflict in the end, prepared the way for a new era in Canadian-American relations also. In the postwar years, the complete and obvious abandonment by the United States of any expansionist ideas combined with growing national self-confidence in Canada to create a more frank and generous atmosphere. The gradual growth of Canada's international status culminated in 1927 in the inauguration of direct diplomatic intercourse between Ottawa and Washington by an exchange of ministers; since that year all Canadian-American issues have been dealt with through these channels.

Since the outbreak of World War II, Canadian-American relations have grown both closer and more complex. No full account is possible here. A limited military *rapprochement* between the two countries beginning in 1937 was followed, after the collapse of France in 1940, by much more active collaboration. On Aug. 18, 1940, the Ogdensburg Declaration made by President Franklin D. Roosevelt and Prime Minister W. L. Mackenzie King announced the establishment of the Permanent Joint Board on Defense, which has existed since that time as an organ for international discussion of the mutual security problems of Canada and the United States. Only very limited direct menaces to North America arose during World War II, but the closeness of Canadian-American military co-operation was reflected in such enterprises as the construction of the Alaska Highway and the chains of airfields known as the North-East and North-West Staging Routes. Canadian forces played parts in the campaign against the Japanese in the Aleutian Islands.

Military co-operation continued after 1945, both directly and through the North Atlantic Treaty Organization, in which Canada and the United States joined at its inception in 1949. The cold war with Russia has encouraged it; the development of nuclear arms and missiles, and the steadily increasing complexity and expense of modern weapons generally, have complicated it. The two countries have collaborated in developing a radar defense system in the north, comprising the Pinetree, Mid-Canada and Distant Early Warning lines. In 1957 the North American Air Defense Command (N. O. R. A. D.) was set up under a United States commander with a Canadian deputy. Canada's cancellation of the production program for her CF-105 interceptor fighter and the substitution of the U. S. BOMARC guided missile and a fighter of United States type (1959) emphasized the difficulty of the problems involved. It is evident that North American defense must in future be increasingly a joint operation; the precise place of the Canadian forces, and of Canadian defense industry, in this operation remains to be defined.

Economic relations parallel the military ones in importance and complexity. The American Hawley-Smoot tariff and the Canadian emergency tariff of 1930 amounted to an exchange of economic blows. However, following the passage by Congress of the Trade Agreements Act of 1934 an agreement was negotiated with concessions on both sides (1935) and a further agreement was made in 1938. In recent years there nevertheless have been complaints in both countries of the effects of tariffs and other trade restrictions, and in view of the enormous volume of commerce that passes between the two countries, this is not surprising. The growing national consciousness evident in Canada since World War II has been sensitive to United States economic measures, and there has been some resentment of the apparently growing penetration of the Canadian economy by American industry working through Canadian subsidiary firms. It has appeared over such matters as the reported imposition on those firms of United States Government policy concerning trade with Communist China. International agreement on the construction of the St. Lawrence Seaway, long obstructed in the United States, was finally reached in 1952–54, and the Seaway was opened by Queen Elizabeth II and President Eisenhower on June 26, 1959. Concurrently, however, complicated and difficult negotiations were proceeding between the two countries on the development of the power potential of the Columbia River. Conditions both within North America and in the world at large continued to lend force to a remark of L. B. Pearson, then Canada's Secretary of State for External Affairs, in April, 1951: "the days of relatively easy and automatic political relations with our neighbor are, I think, over."

CANADIAN RIVER is a part of the Arkansas River system. Early French traders and explorers followed its course west into the Spanish territory. The name Canadian possibly was given to the river by early French hunters and traders who came from Canada. The upper part was called by the Spanish, Rio Colorado. By the Treaty of Doak's Stand in 1820, Canadian River was made the northern boundary of the Choctaw nation. Early emigrants to California followed the south bank of the Canadian on to Santa Fe.

CANAL BOATS. On the early American canals, the blunt, horse-drawn boats were of three general types—freight boats carrying from 25 to 100 tons each of various commodities; passenger "packets"; and so-called line boats, which carried both freight and passengers, the latter getting poorer accommodations than on the packets. On the passenger boats the traveler both dined and slept in a central "saloon," a species of narrow canvas hammocks being affixed to the walls in tiers at night for berths.

CANAL BUILDING was an early phase of the struggle to provide transportation facilities adequate to develop and to unite the country. The first problem was to get around the falls of the rivers flowing into the Atlantic. To accomplish this, some canals were completed by private companies between 1789 and 1802. The second problem was to connect the coast with the Ohio and Mississippi River valleys and the rivers with the Great Lakes. During this second phase, the mania for canal building by the states (with some Federal aid) can be understood only in the light of the success of the Erie Canal and the widespread speculation and wildcat banking which characterized frontier enthusiasm for the development of the resources of the West.

The Erie Canal, started in 1817 by New York State, and completed in 1825, gave the first low-cost transportation from the coast to the interior of the country. Following the lowest crossing of the Appalachians along the course of an old Indian trail, it was a great success. It carried a vast traffic, it was largely responsible for the development of New York City and the towns along its course and it paid for itself in a brief time.

Other states believed that the same success would crown their efforts. Canal building seemed essential both to those who wished to exploit the resources of the country and to those primarily interested in speculation. Wildcat bankers took long chances and viewed hopefully projects which now seem fantastic. Foreign investors carelessly assumed that state credit was as good as that of the Federal Government, which was practically out of debt in the 1830's. Thus the sound position of the Federal Government played a strange role, encouraging foreigners to buy state bond issues, the proceeds of which went into canal construction. In 1825 Ohio, with a population of about 700,000, undertook canal projects estimated to cost approximately $5,800,000, one tenth of its taxable wealth. In the end they cost more. By 1838 the debts of twelve states for canal construction amounted to over $60,000,000. The actual construction appears all the more remarkable when we remember that the builders had only human and horse power to remove soil, only black powder for blasting and that holes for blasting had to be drilled in the rock with hand drills.

The canals, together with the natural waterways, aided greatly in the development of the country. In fact, the superiority of the railroad over the canal was not clearly evident until the late 1860's. The peak load on the Erie Canal was in the late 1880's. The financial results, however, were not so favorable. Unlike the Erie, few of the canals were profitable, and there were defaults by states on canal debts as follows: Indiana, 1841–47; Maryland, 1841–48; Pennsylvania, 1842–45; and Illinois, 1842–47.

The Federal Government has played a large role in more recent canal building. The St. Mary's River Canal between Lake Superior and the other Great Lakes, built by Michigan in 1853–55, was improved by the United States in 1870–71. In 1880 the Federal Government took over the whole project. The Cape Cod Canal makes traffic to and from Boston possible without going around the Cape. The building of the Panama Canal, completed by the Federal Government in 1914, was marked by the utilization of modern machinery in moving vast quantities of earth and in the triumph of medical science over tropical diseases.

CANDLES lighted most American homes, public buildings and streets until kerosene lamps and gas replaced them. The housewives made many kinds, namely—bear grease, deer suet, bayberry, beeswax (expensive, for state occasions largely), tallow dip (commonest), from well-rendered mutton fat, and spermaceti (the waxy solid from the head of whales). Every autumn the housekeepers filled their leather or tin candle boxes to last through the winter. It was a long, hard task to dip or mold several hundred candles by hand. First, women prepared wicks from rough hemp, milkweed or cotton spun in large quantity. The homemaker was the only manufacturer until the 1700's when an itinerant candle-maker could be hired. Later, professional chandlers prospered in the cities. Although factories were numerous after 1750, the home-dipping was continued as late as 1880. There was a large market for sperm candles in the West Indies. In 1768 they bought over 500,000 lbs. of sperm and tallow candles from the colonies. The total production from both factories and homes reached an estimated $8,000,000 in 1810. The New England factories, which produced most, imported supplies of fat from Russia. There were large plants, also, in New Orleans, St. Louis, and Hudson, N. Y. South Carolina and Georgia produced quantities of seeds and capsules from tallow trees used extensively for candle-making in the South. Allied industries grew rapidly for making metal and pottery candleholders.

CANNING INDUSTRY has expanded in America due to simultaneous advances in the technique of manufacturing cans, agricultural research, the invention of automatic machinery and the art of canning. These have progressed rapidly during the past 140 years and the United States is in the forefront of canning nations, leading in volume and variety of canned products. Some 300 food products are canned and the enterprise has become one of the billion-dollar industries.

Pioneers of American canning were Thomas Kensett, Sr., and Ezra Daggett of New York, 1819, and William Underwood at Boston, 1821. They used the Appert process (sealing in air-tight containers and immersing in boiling water) on oysters, meats, fruits, berries and vegetables, packing in glass. The tin can, its name derived from the original English canister, was introduced here by Peter Durand in 1818. Underwood and Kensett changed from glass to tin in 1839. Canning sprang up rapidly thereafter in Maryland, Maine, New Brunswick, New York and Delaware, with new products added. Methods of obtaining higher temperatures were evolved, the cooking time thus shortened and pack volume rose.

The Civil War produced the first "boom" and canneries sprang up in the Midwest, to supply the armies. From about 5,000,000 annual cans, the national pack increased sixfold. Canning was introduced in California, now a leading producing state, in 1862. Two years later George W. Hume and A. S. Hapgood, Maine salmon canners, transferred their ac-

tivities to the Pacific Coast. David S. Page, Dixon, Ill., made the first condensed milk can in Switzerland in 1865, paving the way for a major expansion in that product, carried forward later by Gail Borden and others.

In the following decades machinery inventions and development led the way, while can-making refinements continued. Andrew K. Shriver, Baltimore, patented the first closed steam-pressure kettle in 1875. R. P. Scott of Ohio and Messrs. C. P. and J. A. Chisholm of Ontario evolved an automatic pea podder in 1885. William H. Sells, in 1892, built the first automatic corn husker, deriving his idea from the principle of the clothes wringer. Other revolutionary improvements in machinery were made.

Early in this century the can itself was radically improved. Solid food particles had been forced into the can through a hole in the top, over which a metal disc was soldered. Mutilation of food was common. An open-top can was developed by Charles M. Ams, W. Y. Bogle and George W. Cobb, Sr., which, known as the "sanitary can," has become the standard, modern tin container for food. Soon after this, scientific research laboratories sprang up throughout the industry, launching programs of investigation as to causes of spoilage and contamination. Nutritive values were analyzed and proved. Raw products research led to refinements in planting, growing and harvesting canning crops. Popular prejudices against canned foods waned and public acceptance grew, as the results of this work became trade practice.

CANOE. The canoe in American and Canadian history usually was made of the rind of the white birch tree. On occasions other materials were used for canoes, but never, apparently, if birch-bark could be secured.

The Algonquian Indians had learned both the secret of making and of guiding canoes expertly before white men reached North America. The latter adopted the canoe immediately. Until railroads became common—about 1850—the canoe was the chief vehicle for reaching much of northern North America. Thus it became the usual craft in the transportation of furs and is always associated with the great explorers and the fur traders. It was admirably adapted to the waterways of the continent, being light enough to be portaged easily, responsive enough to be guided with precision through rapids and over low waterfalls, and so built as to be capable of repair at almost any place on the route from materials to be found along that route. Besides bark these materials were cedar for the frame and paddles, wattape (tree-root fibers) for sewing pieces of bark together and for lashing the bark to the gunwales, and resin for gumming the seams. No metal was used in its construction.

There were several kinds of canoes: the Montreal canoe, or *canot du maître,* from thirty to forty feet

151

long, manned by ten to fourteen men; the *canot du nord,* or North canoe, from twenty to twenty-five feet in length, manned by four to eight men; a half canoe, somewhat smaller; and Indian canoes, still smaller. A light canoe was usually an express canoe without freight aboard. The Montreal canoes weighed about 300 lbs. and carried about five tons' weight of men and freight. They were used primarily on the St. Lawrence and the Great Lakes. The North canoes were used beyond the Great Lakes, in smaller rivers and on lesser lakes.

CANTIGNY, AMERICANS ATTACK AT. The American 1st Division (Bullard) on April 25, 1918, joined the French First Army. It occupied the sector facing Cantigny, held by the German XVIII Army. To test the Americans' offensive ability in their first active sector, the French command ordered the new division to capture Cantigny. After careful preparations the 28th Infantry attacked at 6.45 A. M., May 28. The assailants, assisted by French tanks, took all objectives, with 250 prisoners, in forty-five minutes. Thereafter the Americans repulsed several violent German counterattacks, losing 1067 killed and wounded, but maintaining their position.

CANTON, FUR TRADE WITH, developed from the search for some staple, other than specie, which American merchants could exchange for the teas and silks of China. Furs met with a ready sale; the cargo of the first American vessel to Canton, Feb. 22, 1784, included furs. But only such rare furs as otter, seal, beaver and fox were acceptable. Boston merchants decided to seek sea-otter skins on the Northwest coast. The *Columbia* (Sept. 30, 1787–Aug. 9, 1790) returned with a cargo of teas—product of sea-otter skins bartered from the natives. Others hastened to follow. By 1796 American vessels were engaged in contraband fur trade with the Californians and by 1804 were borrowing Aleutian sea-otter hunters, on shares, from the Russian governor at Novarkhangelsk. In 1783, in the Southern Pacific, had begun the mass slaughter of the fur seal. When, after the War of 1812, the fur trade with Canton was renewed, the growing scarcity of the sea-otter, increased competition and a consequent decline in profits reduced the American vessels engaged from thirteen in 1821 to two in 1830. Trading in furs with Canton became merely one aspect of a more general "Pacific trade." ". . . by 1837 the old Northwest fur trade . . . was a thing of the past."

CAPE COD was a landmark for early explorers, possibly the "Promontory of Vinland" of the Norse voyagers (985–1025). Verrazano in 1524 approached it from the south, and Gomez the next year called it Cape St. James. Gosnold in 1602 gave it the name that survives. Champlain charted its sand-silted harbors in 1606 and Henry Hudson landed there in

1609. Capt. John Smith noted it on his map of 1614 and at last the Pilgrims entered the "Cape Harbor" on Nov. 11, 1620. Aside from Barnstable and Sandwich (1638) and Yarmouth (1639) the cape's fifteen towns developed slowly. Provincetown was a group of huts until the 18th century. A channel from Massachusetts Bay to Buzzards Bay is shown on Southack's map of 1717, but the present canal was not completed until 1914. The Federal Government purchased it in 1928.

CAPE FEAR RIVER SETTLEMENTS (N. C.). In 1664 and 1665 several hundred Barbadians planted a colony on the lower Cape Fear, which was abandoned in 1667. Little interest was shown in this region until after the removal of the Indian and pirate menace during the second decade of the next century. About 1723 settlers from South Carolina and from Albemarle began to move in, and in 1725 the town of Brunswick was laid out on the west bank of the river, about fourteen miles from the sea. Eight years later Wilmington was begun and became the colony's chief port. From 1735 to 1775 thousands of Scotch Highlanders settled on the upper Cape Fear. Naval stores and rice became the most important products of the region.

CAPITALISM is an economic system in which the ownership and control of land, capital and natural resources, the production and marketing of goods, the employment of labor and the organization and operation of the system as a whole are entrusted to private enterprise working under competitive conditions. Private property, contract, freedom of enterprise and profit making are basic rules; acquisition of consumption goods (food, clothing, etc.) is the goal; and accumulation, control and use of capital, as the essential instrument, is the way the goal is most quickly reached.

Most economists think of capital as "produced goods intended for further production." Tools, machines, coal, oil, lumber, unfinished or unsold goods, supplies are all examples. Cash and bank deposits are sometimes called "liquid capital" because they may be directed to any use the possessor wishes, but they are really only titles to capital. Capital is manmade and can be created only through someone's saving. Interest is the rental price for the use of capital. Throughout history the capitalistic or indirect process of production—creating capital to make consumption goods, such as making a net to catch fish—has been found more efficient than the direct method, involving no capital, such as catching fish by hand. Generous use of capital is the secret of the economies of mass production, and the nations with the most capital per person have the highest standards of living.

Virginia and Plymouth were handicapped at the outset by lack of capital, lack of artisans and lack of the profit motive. The Pilgrims did not bring a horse, cow or plow, and their fishhooks and nets were too large for cod. When the meager supplies soon gave out there was a period of "starving" because there was little incentive in either colony for the individual to work hard to build up a surplus since the settlers were expected to put all their produce into a common fund from which all would be supported and out of which the companies financing the expeditions would receive repayment and profit, a system bordering on communism so far as the settlers were concerned. John Smith remarked "When our people were fed out of the common store and laboured jointly together . . . the most honest among them would hardly take so much true paines in a weeke, as now for themselves they will doe in a day: . . ."

When the settlers were permitted greater freedom of enterprise and allowed to accumulate private property, colonies grew and prospered. Although the English urged Virginia to produce wheat and naval stores, tobacco was far more profitable, so the Virginians grew it. All along the eastern seaboard capital was created when land was cleared, fenced and otherwise improved, sawmills, tobacco warehouses, corn cribs, indigo vats, blast furnaces, rope walks and ships were built; or when men fashioned countless household tools in the leisure moments of the evening. Usually the profits from their occupations were plowed back into the business, and since people were "skimming the cream" off the resources of a virgin continent, the profits were frequently sizable.

An outstanding factor in our economic development until the 20th century was the plentifulness of land and the scarcity of labor and capital, the reverse of conditions in Europe. Since most men preferred to work for themselves, even if only on a log-cabin farm, labor for hire was scarce and there were thousands of small capitalists. The problem of the dearth of labor was met by the indentured servant system and by Negro slavery. The lack of capital was not so well handled. Many confused capital with money and, presuming that the interest rates were high owing to a scarcity of money, urged the Government to provide more money somehow. Whether the consequent inflation in the colonies greatly retarded the inflow of capital, or whether it put to quicker use savings that would otherwise have been uselessly hoarded, is still disputed. The absence of banks of deposit and discount to pool and distribute the community's savings made the flow of "liquid" capital sluggish when its efficient use was highly desirable.

British interference with the operation of our capitalistic system was a major cause of the Revolution. Parliamentary taxation took private property without our leave; enforcement of trade and navigation acts, especially the Sugar Act of 1764 which threatened a profitable triangular trade, restricted our freedom of enterprise; and the laws forbidding

legal-tender paper money seemed to dry up the supply of capital.

When our weakly confederated Government broke down, propertied men were largely instrumental in drawing up and securing the adoption of the Constitution which restored some sanctity to contract, put an end to legal-tender paper money and gave increased protection to private property.

Numerous factors affected the growth of capital in the next few decades. European wars augmented the demand for our agricultural products and led to a tripling of our foreign merchant marine between 1790 and 1807. After the embargo and other decrees reduced the supply of foreign manufactures the North diverted its savings to manufacturing and after the war higher tariffs were imposed to protect this new capital. Meanwhile the invention of the cotton gin and the power loom at the close of the 18th century stimulated the demand for the South's cotton and revived slavery. Southerners grew cotton to buy more land and slaves to grow more cotton to buy more land and slaves, etc. By the middle of the century the supply of new cotton land had been greatly reduced, much land had been exhausted and little capital invested in its restoration, the output of the slave had not increased much, for that form of capital is not easily improved, and the South had little mechanical capital to show for its efforts, a fact that lost it the Civil War

This demand for food and cotton was a chief cause of the westward movement. Thomas Jefferson had estimated in 1800 that it would take 1000 years to fill up the region east of the Mississippi but thanks to improvements in transportation the period was much shortened. Turnpikes, canals and then railroads enabled people to market their goods more cheaply and brought about regional specialization. Growing knowledge of how to make iron and steel, the use of coke and the standardization of parts made possible larger-sized machines, which the small capitalist or artisan could not afford, and helped cause the shift from the domestic to the factory system. Yet without the corporation with its distinguishing features of limited liability and perpetual life, capital for railroads and factories could hardly have been obtained. Now that laborer and capitalist were no longer one, or working close together, their interests diverged. Skilled labor gradually organized to deal with organized capital.

The period following the Civil War was one of tremendous business expansion. A good index of capital increase is the amount of power used in industry which grew from 2,300,000 horse-power in 1870 to 22,300,000 in 1914. The number of iron and steel establishments increased about 63% between 1860 and 1910, their output 14,730% and the number of their wage earners 1296%, indicating the greater average size of the plants and the extent to which capital had enabled labor to accomplish more in a day. Profits were large: because regulations were few; many resources were being exploited for the first time; high tariffs kept foreign competition out of the great free-trade area within the nation; and our patent system and the relative scarceness of labor stimulated invention. Most of the capital for this expansion was drawn from within the nation. Jay Cooke set the precedent by selling government bonds to the general public during the Civil War and stocks later, and thus did much to arouse the interest of people of moderate means in securities. In 1886 New York stock exchange transactions first exceeded a million shares a day.

This get-rich-quick era produced giant railroad companies and industrial combinations known as "trusts," which frequently used unfair methods of competition against rivals, exploited the people and corrupted governments. Both the Interstate Commerce Act, appointing a commission to regulate the railroads, and the Sherman Antitrust Act, to break up the "trusts" and make the members compete, were at first rendered ineffective by court decisions. According to the census of 1900 there were 185 "trusts" comprising a half of 1% of all establishments in the country but owning 15% of the capital and turning out 14% of the products. Public reaction, under the leadership of Theodore Roosevelt, produced a "trust busting" and reform era. The trusts fought state laws to regulate them and to give labor and the public some measure of protection by citing the clause in the Fourteenth Amendment providing that a person may not be deprived of his property without due process of law. Attempts to establish by law the ten-hour day in bakeries (Lochner case) or set a minimum wage for women (Adkins case) were deemed by the courts to interfere with freedom of contract. Yet in the end human rights received greater recognition without capitalists suffering seriously. An increasing number and variety of businesses were declared "affected with a public interest" and put under commission supervision. The income-tax amendment and laws made inroads on former rights of private property. It is noteworthy that the Socialist presidential candidate in 1912 polled nearly a million votes, a sixteenth of the total cast in an election where there were two liberal candidates.

War is hard on capitalism, for it results in the destruction of capital and necessitates the curtailment of individual rights of private property, freedom of enterprise and contract if the economic forces of the nation are to be organized for victory. In World War I men were drafted into the army, a war industries board set prices and restricted non-war production and the railroads were run by the Government. With peace the nation attempted to return to "normalcy," however.

The decade following the war was one of great prosperity and at such times capital accumulates rapidly. The sale of Liberty bonds had made the public security-minded and now corporation stocks came to be more widely held. Between 1919–29 the number of common stockholders of the American Telephone and Telegraph Co. increased from 116,721 to 458,135 and private corporations issued $64,000,000,000 of new capital securities and reinvested about $20,000,000,000 of savings. The horsepower of the average manufacturing industry increased 49% and the number of wage earners declined about 7%. Many economists believe that overinvestment in plant and equipment was largely responsible for the depression beginning in 1929 but this theory also has many critics.

During the depression of the 1930's individuals and companies drew heavily on their savings. The 1934 income tax report showed that in the years 1931–34 industrial corporations operated at a loss of above $11,000,000,000. Between 1930 and 1939 private business acquired only $3,800,000,000 of new capital. To a growing degree Federal agencies, especially the Reconstruction Finance Corporation, became the country's chief financial institutions. By Dec. 31, 1939, 40% of commercial bank earning assets were in Federal Government securities.

The F. D. Roosevelt administration introduced radical innovations. For the first time in the nation's history the Federal Government made extensive efforts to relieve the unemployed, help the near-bankrupt and promote economic recovery. The severity of the depression and the disillusionment it had brought led to a revulsion against many of capitalism's major tenets such as competition, individual initiative, the profit motive and respect for thrift. The relief and reform measures endeavored to solve the problems of agriculture by setting up Government-sponsored monopolies (the Agricultural Adjustment Administration); of industry by suspending the antitrust laws (the National Recovery Administration, until 1935), and of labor by making it easier to organize unions (N. I. R. A.'s clause 7a, and the Wagner Act). In a sense the government was itself adopting a solution for which it had condemned the trusts of the 19th century. The Public Works Administration, the Works Progress Administration, the Civilian Conservation Corps were government efforts to stimulate employment. The Government adopted economic policies advocated by the English economist, J. M. Keynes; it assumed that we had inherited a mature and lethargic economy and sought to spend the country out of the depression. As a result, within six years the national debt doubled. For a time the Government discouraged corporate saving by a corporations undistributed-profits tax. Whereas the owners of capital had been influential in the 1920's, after 1933, and especially after 1935, they were on the defensive. Many of the new developments represented a departure from the conditions under which the country had developed up to that time. Emphasis was laid increasingly upon social security, on the human rights of labor in contrast to the property rights of capitalists, and on the curbing of "big business."

World War II, like World War I, saw many restraints imposed on business, especially price, rent and credit controls. The automobile companies ceased making cars in order to produce tanks and planes. But the war ended the long years of depression and unemployment. With war came also inflation, stimulated by the deficit spending of the 1930's, the wastes and shortages of war itself and the artificially low interest rates of the era.

Following the war, a drift away from government regulation set in and Congress removed price controls and consumer credit restrictions and the Federal Reserve System gradually ended interest rate controls. Congress also imposed restrictions on labor in 1947 by the Taft-Hartley law; also, in 1947 it enacted the Full Employment Act, making it national policy to promote a high level of employment.

By 1955 the real per capita gross national product was double the 1935 level, but organized labor's influence in economic and political affairs had grown to the point that some critics complained that the United States was no longer a capitalistic economy. Whereas before 1914 employees received about half the national income, by 1948 they were getting about 70% of it. Whereas in 1913 the highest 1% of income receivers took 15% of the national income, by 1948 their share had declined to 8%. And whereas in 1902 8% of the national income passed through government hands (Federal, state and local), by 1922 the figure had grown to 14% and by 1957 to 35%. Conservatives complained. Others regarded the trend as an inevitable result of a more specialized economy, of an increasingly employee attitude of the people, and of a more urbanized population. Several facts seemed certain in 1960: the American people were more concerned with having security than they used to be, yet they enjoyed the world's highest standard of living. The owners of capital had much less influence than they did sixty years ago, even thirty years ago, perhaps because capital itself had become more plentiful, and yet the United States remained one of the world's most capitalistic countries.

CAPITOL AT WASHINGTON. In a disappointing public competition in 1791 of amateur and professional plans, Stephen Hallet's, though not satisfactory, was judged the best. Dr. William Thornton, by permission, submitted a more artistic design and Hallet was employed to make working drawings of it, and to superintend the erection. Accused of substituting his own plan for Thornton's, he was dismissed in 1794 and George Hadfield, an English architect, succeeded him. The cornerstone was laid with Masonic ceremonies by President Washington, Sept. 18, 1793; but the center portion had not been erected when

the British burned the public buildings in 1814. Rebuilding commenced in 1815, under Benjamin H. Latrobe, and the center portion of Aquia freestone with a low dome, designed by Charles Bulfinch, was finished in 1827. The present north and south wings of Massachusetts marble (the fluted pillars are from Maryland) were begun in 1851, from designs of Thomas Ustick Walter, and finished in 1857–59. The present dome of cast iron, an adaptation of Michelangelo's St. Peter's (Rome) and Sir Christopher Wren's St. Paul's (London), was begun in 1856 and finished in 1865. It is surmounted by Crawford's heroic bronze of Freedom, 19½ feet high. The dome is, roughly, 300 feet in height.

CARAVAN TRAFFIC OF THE GREAT PLAINS existed from approximately 1825 to 1875 and reached its maximum development during the first few years after the Civil War. During this period both immigrant and trade caravans were employed, particularly after the beginning of the Oregon movement (1842), the Mormon migration (1847) and the discovery of gold in California (1848).

The first important caravan traffic across the Great Plains was via the Santa Fe Trail. William Becknell drove the first wagon from western Missouri to Santa Fe in 1822. This was eight years before Jedediah Smith, David E. Jackson and William Sublette took a party of eighty-one men and ten large wagons (drawn by five mules each) from St. Louis to the trappers' rendezvous on the Wind River; and it was ten years before Capt. L. E. Bonneville conducted still another wagon train across South Pass. Caravans of 25 wagons or more were used largely to transport trade goods over the Santa Fe Trail to the value of $35,000 in 1824, $90,000 in 1826 and $150,000 in 1828. The distance traveled from Franklin, Mo., to Santa Fe was 870 miles. After the first few years, Lexington, some 60 miles farther west, was the point of departure; and still later, Independence, 100 miles farther west, was the starting point.

Caravan movements over the Oregon Trail were equally significant, although perhaps not so important commercially. Elm Grove, about twelve miles southwest of Independence, was a favorite starting point; and later Westport. At the former place, beginning in 1842, immigrants came in covered wagons each spring, elected their captains, guides and other officers and began the long trek westward via the Oregon Trail. The caravan of 1842, organized by Dr. Elijah White, traveled as far as Fort Hall before the wagons were abandoned. From here the immigrants traveled on foot, horseback or by raft down the Snake and Columbia rivers. The following year upward of 1000 immigrants moved over the same route in many wagons, some of which reached the banks of the Columbia.

During the 1850's, caravans, large and small, were thronging all roads across the Great Plains. Randolph

155

B. Marcy conducted a caravan of 100 wagons from Fort Smith to New Mexico via the Canadian River in 1849, on the first leg of its journey to California; and agent William Bent (for the Comanches and Kiowas) estimated 60,000 immigrants to have crossed the plains along the Arkansas route in 1859. Heavy freight caravans plied the routes between San Antonio and Chihuahua, between Santa Fe and Chihuahua; and from points in Nebraska, Kansas and Colorado to the far West by 1860. From Council Bluffs to the Great Salt Lake via Fort Bridger was a well-known road over which thousands of Mormon pilgrims traveled from 1847 to 1860.

The Army Appropriation Bill of 1853 made available $150,000 to be spent by the Secretary of War, Jefferson Davis, to survey routes for western railways, and soon thereafter four surveys were made. This promised a new era that was formally initiated by the first Union Pacific Act of 1862. Seven years later the first transcontinental line was completed. But caravan trade and travel were to remain for a decade until railroads could offer adequate facilities.

CARAVANS, OUTFITTING OF. A visitor to the West in 1860 estimated that 20,000 wagons were in use transporting immigrants and supplies, requiring around 100,000 oxen and 40,000 mules to pull them. Western towns such as St. Louis, Fort Smith, Little Rock, San Antonio, Denver and Salt Lake City did a thriving business in consequence. At one of these (or others equally active), immigrants bound for the Far West had a last opportunity to purchase necessities. Food (such as meal, flour, sugar, coffee and bacon), clothing, blankets, guns and ammunition, farm implements (such as an ax, hoe, shovel or an occasional plow) were a few of the purchases. In addition, immigrant wagons were generally burdened with certain household goods (a bedstead, a framed picture of grandfather or grandmother, a favorite chair and perhaps one or more heirlooms), and other sundry things considered as necessities. Many an immigrant traveling the Oregon Trail to the Columbia or the Platte route to California discarded much of his impedimenta before he arrived at his destination. In consequence many intermediate towns and communities profited. Settlers at Salt Lake City and in the Great Basin did a thriving exchange trade with the Forty-niners, buying worn-out horses and cattle, or exchanging potatoes and flour for their excess burdens. Likewise Denver was to profit as a supply center during Colorado's gold-rush days, 1858–65.

The great rush for western lands following the enactment of the Federal homestead law of 1862 greatly increased caravan traffic; and in every town of considerable size along the frontier was one or more well-known supply firms. Guns and ammunition were generally bought. During the period of the destruction of the bison on the southern plains, a general supply store at Fort Griffin, Texas, during a one-day period (1877), sold goods to the value of better than $4000, of which $2500 represented guns and ammunition. Other supplies were plows, farm tools, staple groceries, wagons, kerosene, dry goods, seed and feed for livestock. Such quantities of supplies were required that numerous freighting firms were organized and long trains of wagons were on every well-traveled road.

CARLISLE (PA.) INDIAN SCHOOL was established in 1879 by Capt. R. H. Pratt, under whose twenty-five-year direction it grew from 136 to 1000 pupils (boys and girls), the equipment expanding accordingly. Instruction included practical training in farming, horticulture, dress-making, cooking, laundering, housekeeping and twenty trades. A distinctive feature was the "Outing System." Pupils were urged to spend a year working on farms, in homes or industries of the neighborhood. The school was closed in 1918.

CARLOTTA, CONFEDERATE COLONY OF. In 1865 many ex-confederates left their native land for Mexico. Emperor Maximilian encouraged this exodus by appointing Com. M. F. Maury Imperial Commissioner of Immigration. Military and civil colonies were to be established along the railway between Vera Cruz and Mexico City. The best-known colony, comprising 500,000 acres, was Carlotta, in the Cordova Valley, named in honor of the Empress. Among reasons for failure were a hostile American press; lack of funds; improper colonization methods; forcible land seizure and occupation; disturbed political condition in Mexico; local hostility and opposition of the United States Government.

CAROLINA, THE FUNDAMENTAL CONSTITUTIONS OF, the most pretentious of the attempts to establish a feudal aristocracy in English America, were drawn up in 1669 by John Locke under the direction of his employer and patron the Earl of Shaftesbury. Between that date and 1698 four revisions were issued by the Lords Proprietors. Outstanding features were the provisions for a provincial nobility of proprietors, landgraves and caziques having permanent ownership of two fifths of the land; for a Grand Council made up of proprietors and their councilors which should have the executive and judicial authority, and—through its control of the initiative— should likewise control legislation; for an established Anglican Church and religious toleration; and for serfdom and slavery.

Shelving the top-heavy system for a time at the beginning of settlement, the proprietors set up revised Grand Councils in North and in South Carolina, but in the former the Fundamental Constitutions had little weight. In South Carolina they greatly strengthened the tendency toward a dominant landed aristocracy, and to them may be traced the ballot and certain land ownership requirements for voting and officeholding. The attempts of the proprietors to force the complete system upon the assembly came to a climax and failure about 1690.

CAROLINA PROPRIETORS. The first Carolina patent was granted by Charles I to Sir Robert Heath in 1629. By its terms the province extended from ocean to ocean between the 31st and 36th parallels. This patent was declared forfeited on the ground of nonuse by Charles II, who in 1663 issued a charter with the same bounds to eight joint proprietors: Edward Hyde, Earl of Clarendon; George Monk, Duke of Albemarle; William, Lord Craven; John, Lord Berkeley; Anthony Ashley Cooper, Lord Ashley (later Earl of Shaftesbury); Sir George Carteret; Sir John Colleton; and Sir William Berkeley. In 1665 the boundaries were extended to include the territory from 29° to 36° 30′ N. Lat. "Declarations and Proposals," the first organic law, issued by the proprietors in 1663, promised land to settlers who should emigrate within five years, representation of freeholders in a provincial assembly and liberty of conscience. The Fundamental Constitutions of Carolina, formulated by John Locke in 1669, never went into effect in the colony.

The enterprise resulting in loss, proprietary neglect became chronic. Great discontent was caused by the indifference of the proprietors during the war with the Tuscaroras (1711–12), and the Yamasee War (1715–16) and by their lack of support when the province was threatened from the West Indies by the French and the Spanish (1706, 1719) and when it was attacked by pirates (1718). Proprietary orders destructive of provincial interests brought about a revolutionary movement in South Carolina (1719), which the crown thereupon took over as a royal colony, leaving North Carolina to the proprietors until purchase of the proprietorship of both provinces for the crown (1729). Lord Carteret retained his interest in the form of a strip of land lying south of Virginia and estimated at an eighth of the original grant.

CARONDELET INTRIGUE. Hector, Baron de Carondelet, was one of the governors of Spanish Louisiana who intrigued with western communities of the United States, notably Kentucky, for the purpose of detaching them from the Union. His purpose was to thwart the policy of the United States to secure unchallenged access to the Mississippi River, a tendency which made Spanish colonial officials fear for the safety of Louisiana and New Spain. The movement came to an end with the ratification (1795) of Pinckney's Treaty.

CARPENTERS' HALL, Philadelphia, on Chestnut Street between Third and Fourth Streets, was built by the Carpenters' Guild in 1770 as a meeting place for its members. It was here the first Continental Congress convened, on Sept. 5, 1774.

CARPETBAGGERS were persons from the North who went to the South after the Civil War and who, through affiliation with the Republican party, became exploiters of the South, sometimes as financial adventurers, but more often as officeholders. Carpetbagger was an epithet of approbrium applied by Southerners of the antebellum dominant class to these newcomers who were presumably settlers so transitory and propertyless that their entire goods could be carried in carpetbags, the characteristic hand luggage of the period. The term was used primarily of the Reconstruction period, 1865–77, but especially after the Reconstruction Acts of 1867 brought the states of the former Confederacy under radical control.

Many of the carpetbaggers were young men who had served in the Union Army during the war or in the Treasury Department and who, at the close of the war, became agents of the Freedmen's Bureau. Some were missionaries sent from the North to minister to the needs of the Negroes. Others went South not in any official capacity, but in search of their fortunes. All groups found their chance for political activity when the Reconstruction Acts of 1867 demanded a thoroughgoing reorganization of all the former Confederate states, except Tennessee. Because the old officeholding class was disqualified and because the new electorate was not experienced in holding office, there was opportunity for leadership which the newcomers avidly seized. Even before 1867 some of these newcomers in each state had become experienced in political activity as organizers of the Loyal Leagues, which attempted to bring the Negroes and the former white unionists together in loyalty to the Republican party.

In the constitutional conventions elected in 1867–68 in the South, carpetbaggers were strongly represented and took active part in shaping the new state constitutions. In the seven states which were restored to the Union in 1868, four of the governors were carpetbaggers. In Congress there were many carpetbaggers in the delegations from the newly reconstructed states, twenty out of thirty-five members in 1868 in the House of Representatives and ten of the fourteen members of the U. S. Senate. Among the newcomers from the North there were a few Negroes who rose to conspicuous position as leaders of their race. Such were Hiram R. Revels, a colored preacher who succeeded Jefferson Davis as Senator from Mississippi, and Robert Elliott, who rose to power in state politics in South Carolina. Within the states, as in Congress, carpetbaggers generally supported the various schemes of fraudulent bond issues and other extravagant and corrupt financial programs which helped to bring the radical reconstruction governments into ill repute. After the political machinery of radical reconstruction in the South collapsed in 1876 or earlier, many carpetbaggers returned to the North; others who remained in the South ceased to live by public office and were absorbed in the ordinary class of work-a-day citizens. With the restoration of home rule in the South carpetbaggers as a class disappeared.

CARVER'S TRAVELS (1766–68). The first Englishman to visit and publicly describe the region of the upper Great Lakes and the upper Mississippi was Capt. Jonathan Carver of Massachusetts. His tour, performed in 1766–68, was described in his *Travels*, first published in London in 1778. The book proved immensely popular, and many editions, in several different languages, were issued. In recent decades the reliability of the narrative has been keenly debated by scholars; examination of Carver's manuscript journal establishes that it differs in important respects from the published version. More recent research points to the conclusion that while Carver actually made the tour he describes, he suppressed the fact that he performed it as a hired agent of Maj. Robert Rogers, who was intent on finding the Northwest Passage to the Pacific Ocean, rather than on his own responsibility.

CASABLANCA CONFERENCE (Jan. 14–24, 1943). This meeting of President Roosevelt and Prime Minister Churchill was the first of several overseas conferences attended by the President during World War II. The two leaders discussed military problems of the new front in North Africa and decided on an invasion of Sicily and Italy. They made the important public announcement (Jan. 24) that the Allies would demand the "unconditional surrender" of their enemies, an announcement the wisdom of which has been much debated.

CASKET GIRLS were women imported into Louisiana by the *Compagnie des Indes* as wives for settlers. Their name derives from the small chests (*cassettes*) in which they carried their clothes. They were conspicuous by reason of their virtue. Normally women were supplied to the colonists by raking the streets of Paris for undesirables, or by emptying the houses of correction. The Casket Girls, however, were recruited from church charitable institutions and, although poor, were practically guaranteed to be virtuous. For this reason, says Gayarré, it later became a matter of pride in Louisiana to show descent from them rather than from the more numerous prostitutes. Aside from providing respectable ancestry for some Creoles, the Casket Girls are not important. The first consignment reached Biloxi in 1719; and New Orleans in 1727–28. They inspired Victor Herbert's *Naughty Marietta*.

CASTLE THUNDER was a tobacco warehouse in

Richmond, Va., used (1861–65) by the Confederates to confine political prisoners and occasional spies and criminals who were charged with treason. Similar in general purposes to the "Old Capitol" prison in Washington, it enjoyed an unsavory reputation and its officers were accused of unnecessary brutality toward their charges. Upon the fall of Richmond the prison was used by the Federal authorities to house Confederates charged with crimes under international law.

CASTORLAND COMPANY was organized in Paris in 1792 as the *Compagnie de New Yorck* to colonize French aristocrats and others dissatisfied with conditions following the French Revolution. Land in Lewis County, N. Y., part of the Macomb Purchase, was bought from William Constable. Settlers arrived in 1796; within four years the colony had failed. The transplanted French people, unfitted for the vigorous open life and hard work of the frontier, preferred more civilized communities.

CATHOLICISM IN THE UNITED STATES. Although Catholics lived in the English colonies from the foundation of Maryland (1634), they suffered persecution under the penal laws until the American Revolution. Even then they formed a barely tolerated minority and only gradually acquired full civil rights in the several states. Yet Charles Carroll of Carrollton signed the Declaration of Independence; Daniel Carroll of Maryland and Thomas FitzSimons of Pennsylvania served in the Constitutional Convention; and the majority of Catholics followed the example of John Barry and Stephen Moylan in fighting for American independence.

The spiritual care of the colonial Catholics had been provided mainly by Jesuits, who were subject to the jurisdiction of their provincial in England and also (after 1688) of the vicar-apostolic of the London district. After the suppression of the Society of Jesus and the severance of ecclesiastical ties with England, John Carroll, a native of Maryland and former Jesuit, was appointed superior of the mission in the United States in 1784, and five years later was elected first bishop of Baltimore. There were then about 35,000 Catholics living chiefly in the Middle Atlantic states and in the French villages of the western country. In 1808 Baltimore was raised to metropolitan rank, and four suffragan dioceses were created.

The infant Church owed its growth largely to European assistance. During and after the French Revolution many priests of that nationality came to the United States, and eventually they occupied many of the episcopal sees. Financial aid was furnished by the Society for the Propagation of the Faith (founded at Lyons in 1822), the Leopoldine Foundation (at Vienna in 1828), and the Ludwig-Missionsverein (at Munich in 1838). The principal obstacles to the Church's development before 1830 were the nationalistic opposition sometimes shown to the French clergy and hierarchy and the occasional insubordination of lay trustees to ecclesiastical authority.

Catholic educational and charitable institutions date from 1727, when the first French Ursulines arrived in New Orleans to conduct a school for girls, an orphanage and a hospital. In the East, Georgetown Academy was opened for students of every religion in 1791, and in the same year the first Catholic seminary, St. Mary's, was set up by French Sulpicians in Baltimore. Elizabeth Bayley Seton, after founding the first native religious community for women, the Sisters of Charity of St. Joseph, established a school for girls at Emmitsburg, Md., in 1809; members of this sisterhood also began the first Catholic orphanage and hospital in the East—both at Philadelphia in 1814 and 1828 respectively. By 1840 there were at least 200 Catholic schools in the country, half of which were located west of the Alleghenies. The first Catholic weekly newspaper was the *United States Catholic Miscellany*, founded at Charleston, S. C., by Bishop John England in 1822.

The same farsighted prelate promoted regular meetings of the American hierarchy in order to insure uniformity of discipline and cooperation in solving common problems. Accordingly, the bishops assembled seven times from 1829 to 1849 in the Provincial Councils of Baltimore. Then, after the erection of more metropolitan sees, three Plenary Councils were held at Baltimore in 1852, 1866 and 1884. After each council a pastoral letter was published. From 1890 until World War I the archbishops met annually in different cities.

Between 1830 and 1860 the Catholic population increased from 318,000 to 3,103,000; of the latter total nearly 2,000,000 were immigrants. This sudden influx of so many foreign Catholics gave rise to the American nativist movement, which vilified "Romish" beliefs and practices and impugned Catholic loyalty and patriotism by means of sensational newspapers, books and lectures exposing alleged plots against American democracy and fantastic cases of moral corruption. Anti-Catholic sentiment exploded violently in the wanton burning of the Ursuline convent at Charlestown, Mass., in 1834, and in the bloody riots in Philadelphia in 1844. Organized nativism attacked the Church through the American Protestant Association (founded in 1842) and, in the political field, through the Know-Nothing party in the 1850's. After the beginning of the Civil War anti-Catholic bias tended to subside and was generally dormant or active only locally except when it was aroused to concerted expression by the American Protective Association in the 1890's and the Ku Klux Klan in the 1920's.

On the questions of slavery and emancipation Catholics were divided along sectional lines, but the bishops maintained unity by refraining from official statements. Even in the North, Catholics—who mostly adhered to the Democratic party—were not opposed to slavery on principle, as if it were *per se* evil, nor did they in any way support abolitionism. During the Civil War, Catholics fought on both sides, the most renowned being William Rosecrans for the Union and Pierre Beauregard for the Confederacy. At the request of Lincoln's government John Hughes, Archbishop of New York, went to Paris to urge French neutrality; he also favored conscription and helped to quell the draft riots in his own city. On the battlefields and in the military hospitals Catholic sisters rendered generous service as nurses.

In 1863 there were in the country about 100,000 Catholic Negroes, slave and free, the majority of whom lived in Louisiana. In spite of the practical decisions of the Council of 1866, the Church has made little progress among this race because of a scarcity of men and means and a certain amount of timidity and aversion. Although the priests called Josephites (introduced from England in 1871), the Sisters of the Blessed Sacrament (founded by Katharine Drexel in 1891), and other religious communities are devoted to this apostolate, the number of Negro Catholics in 1960 was only 615,964. In recent years Catholic bishops have often anticipated public opinion and court decisions by ending segregation in churches and schools.

As far as relations with the Holy See are concerned, the Catholic Church in the United States was under the direct supervision of the Sacred Congregation de Propaganda Fide until 1908. It was not noticeably affected by the presence of an American minister at the papal court from 1848 to 1868. In 1869–70 it was represented at the Vatican Council by 45 bishops. The first American cardinal was John McCloskey, Archbishop of New York, who was elevated to this dignity in 1875. To keep a close contact with the American Church the pope has had a delegate residing in Washington since 1893. On the other hand, several American prelates served as apostolic nuncios and delegates in various countries after World War II. In 1960, there were six American cardinals, including one in the Roman Curia.

The greatest impetus to Catholic educational efforts was given by the Third Plenary Council of Baltimore in 1884. Not only were parents commanded to procure a religious education for their children by sending them, if possible, to Catholic schools, but priests also were ordered to erect an elementary school in each parish—a goal that is still far from realization. On the highest level the Catholic University of America in Washington was opened in 1889 as the first Catholic center for graduate study in both the sacred and profane sciences. To unify all these undertakings the National Catholic Educational Association was established in 1904. Archbishop Hughes tried to lighten the financial burden without success by requesting a share of the public school funds in New York in the 1840's, and Archbishop John Ireland of St. Paul also failed in his attempt to incorporate the parochial schools in the public school system of Minnesota in the 1890's. Bearing the expense alone, Catholics in 1960 counted 265 colleges and universities (excluding seminaries) with 302,908 students, 2,433 high schools with 844,299 students, and 10,372 elementary schools with 4,285,896 pupils. Religious instruction for Catholic children attending public elementary and high schools (3,301,401 in 1960) is provided by the Confraternity of Christian Doctrine.

Particularly through its school system the Catholic Church rendered a unique service to the country by adapting the immigrant children of widely varying backgrounds to American political and social ideals. Between 1881 and 1890 about 1,250,000 Catholics immigrated to the United States, and only slightly fewer came in the next decade, bringing the total Catholic population to 12,041,000 at the turn of the century. Within the following ten years 2,316,000 arrived. A certain natural antagonism was evidenced by the suggestion of Peter Paul Cahensly, the German founder of the St. Raphael Societies for the protection of Catholic European emigrants, and others that the newer nationalities be also represented in the hierarchy; the majority of the bishops, however, who were of Irish birth or descent, resisted this proposal as contrary to the rapid Americanization of the newcomers. The only large and lasting schism in the history of American Catholicism began in 1907 with the organization of the Polish National Catholic Church. It is probable, nevertheless, that relatively few of the immigrants have been lost beyond the normal leakage due to other causes. Most of the losses have occurred in cities, where approximately 80% of the Catholics now live. To promote the growth of the Church in isolated districts, especially in the Southwest, the Catholic Church Extension Society was founded in 1905, and to strengthen Catholicity in farming areas the National Catholic Rural Life Conference was founded in 1923.

American Catholics showed little interest in preaching the gospel in pagan lands before the First American Catholic Missionary Congress was held in 1908. Three years later the first native American religious community intended exclusively for the foreign missions was established with its headquarters at Maryknoll, N. Y. The Catholic Students' Mission Crusade was inaugurated in 1918. By 1960 American Catholics were contributing about two thirds of the general fund of the international Society for the Propagation of the Faith, and more than 6000 American Catholics of both sexes were working abroad; of these over 800 were members of the Society of Jesus.

Since most American Catholics have belonged to the working class, the Church has long been concerned with the social order. In 1887 James Cardinal Gibbons, Archbishop of Baltimore, and others defended the Knights of Labor against more conservative prelates who would have had the union condemned as a forbidden secret society. Certain recommendations of the bishops' statement of 1919 were so progressive that they were called socialistic by opponents. The most prominent thinker and writer in this field was the Rev. John A. Ryan. In 1937 the Association of Catholic Trade Unionists was founded, and in the same decade the first labor schools were opened in several cities. Catholics have also sought to forestall juvenile delinquency by various programs, the most successful being that of the Catholic Youth Organization, founded in Chicago in 1930.

In 1917 the National Catholic War Council was formed to co-ordinate the activities of the dioceses and societies with the national emergency. After World War I this council was transformed into the permanent National Catholic Welfare Conference, which acts in an advisory capacity under an administrative board of ten bishops and functions through various departments—for education, lay organizations, press, social action, legislation (proposed in Congress), youth, and (since World War II) the Catholic Relief Services. Reports are read and plans are laid at the annual meetings of the hierarchy held every November in Washington; joint pastoral letters are also issued on topics of current importance.

Vigorous as American Catholicism has been, it has produced few officially recognized examples of extraordinary personal sanctity. Its only canonized saint is Mother Frances Xavier Cabrini (died 1917), a naturalized citizen who founded the Missionary Sisters of the Sacred Heart for the care of the immigrants. Blessed Philippine Duchesne (died 1852), a French Religious of the Sacred Heart, labored for 34 years in Missouri. Also remarkable for heroic virtue were Mother Seton (mentioned above) and John Nepomucene Neumann, Bishop of Philadelphia (1852–60).

In recent decades Catholic laymen have come to play a more active role in the Church. Individuals, such as Orestes Brownson, were often editors of Catholic newspapers even before the middle of the 19th century, and local societies began to federate as early as 1855 in the German Catholic Central Verein. Lay organizations now for the most part are bound together in the National Council of Catholic Men and the National Council of Catholic Women, both of which sponsor various projects to diffuse information and to promote conversions. In union with the clergy, moreover, the laity have fostered the liturgical movement for a revival of congregational participation in the public worship of the Church, the Cana Movement and the Christian Family Movement for the application of Catholic principles to the married state, and the retreat movement for a deepening of the spiritual life amid secular occupations. Outside the Church, however, Catholic laymen since the turn of the century have not exercised a leadership or attained a prominence commensurate with their numbers.

In 1960, there were 40,871,302 Catholics in the United States. This total includes 227 archbishops and bishops, 53,796 priests, 10,473 brothers and 168,527 sisters. The country was divided territorially into 26 archdioceses and 114 dioceses with 16,896 parishes.

CATLIN'S INDIAN PAINTINGS. From 1830 to 1838 George Catlin, a young, self-taught artist, roamed the trans-Mississippi wilderness, sketching and painting some 600 Indian portraits, scenes of native life and landscapes. His expedition up the Missouri by the steamboat *Yellowstone* and downstream by canoe in the summer of 1832 with a long stay at Fort Clark produced a splendid Mandan ethnological series of portraits and ceremonies. In 1834 he accompanied the First Dragoons into Texas and the Comanche country, and spent the following two seasons on the upper Mississippi and Minnesota rivers among the Sioux and other northern tribes. Catlin exhibited his collection in Europe for years after 1838 and added the 603 items of the so-called Catlin Cartoon Collection. The original collection was presented to the Smithsonian in 1879 by Mrs. Joseph Harrison, Jr. While not a great artist, Catlin faithfully depicted the primitive Indians, their lives and surroundings.

CATTLE INDUSTRY. Introduced into what is now the United States about 1600 by Spanish colonists from Mexico, the industry expanded rapidly northward during the next two centuries due to Spain's liberal land grants to settlers, and by 1821, at the close of the Spanish regime in North America, large numbers of the lean, long-horned Spanish type of cattle were reared in California, Arizona, New Mexico and Texas.

In the meantime the early English colonists along the Atlantic seaboard brought over cattle of the breeds common to northern Europe. As English settlement advanced westward cattle growers tended to occupy lands along the frontier where pasturage was readily available. Once the Appalachians had been crossed the industry grew rapidly, since farm products could not be transported profitably across the mountains. Accordingly, the Westerners fed their surplus grain and hay to cattle which, when fully grown and fat, could be driven to market. By 1860 the cattle industry was very important in Kentucky and

the states of the Old Northwest and had extended across the Mississippi into Missouri, Iowa, Arkansas, Indian Territory and eastern Kansas.

In the Southwest the Republic of Mexico, as well as the Texas Republic, had continued the liberal land policy of Spain. Texas, when annexed to the United States in 1845, retained possession of its own unoccupied lands and often sold large tracts to cattle raisers. By 1860 Texas had more than 3,500,000 head of cattle.

During the Civil War the number of cattle in most states was reduced from 30% to 50%. Texas, little touched by the war, however, was at the close of that struggle overflowing with cattle. In 1866 Texas ranchmen began to drive large herds north to railway points in Kansas and Nebraska known as "cow towns." Here, the fat, mature animals were shipped to market for slaughter while young cattle were sold to stock new ranges on the Central and Northern plains. By 1885 some 5,500,000 cattle had been driven north from Texas and the so-called range area had come to cover a vast region reaching from Mexico to Canada and extending from eastern Kansas far beyond the Rocky Mountains.

Shipments of dressed beef to Europe, which began in 1875 and grew to over 17,000,000 lbs. in 1884, gave impetus to the industry and helped to bring much European capital into the business. By 1885 the cattle industry in the United States had grown to gigantic proportions. The range area supplied the corn-growing states with enormous numbers of cattle to be fattened for market and received from these states many registered or high-grade breeding animals to improve its own herds. Great packing plants and stockyards were built at the important market centers—Chicago, Kansas City and Fort Worth. Cattle brokerage companies and banks specializing in cattle loans were established to finance the industry and railways provided specially equipped cars for the shipment of cattle and meat products.

After 1885 the character of the industry began to change. Much of the range area was occupied by settlers, necessitating smaller scale operation. The Department of Agriculture through its Bureaus of Animal Industry and of Agricultural Economics, did much to promote better breeding, care and feeding of cattle, and the same is true of the various agricultural colleges. The cattle industry is still very important, but the great ranches have with few exceptions given place to smaller ones, or livestock farms, producing by scientific methods cattle of high quality that can be marketed for slaughter at a far earlier age than was formerly done.

Cattle Associations is a term applied principally to organizations of cattlemen after 1865 on the Western ranges. In scope these were local, district, sectional and national and, like miners' associations and squatter claim clubs, functioned on the frontiers. The

Colorado Cattle Growers' Association was formed as early as 1867. The Southwestern Cattle Growers' Association of Kansas and the Montana Stock Growers' Association began in 1884. The Wyoming Stock Growers' Association, organized in 1873, had memberships of 400 in 1886 from nineteen states. Its 2,000,000 cattle, real estate, plants and horses were valued in 1885 at $100,000,000. In 1884 the National Cattle and Horse Growers' Association was organized at St. Louis.

A president, secretary, treasurer and executive committee were the usual officials to administer an association's affairs and to make reports at the annual or semiannual meetings. In the Wyoming Stock Growers' Association brand inspectors supervised the sale and transportation of 1,000,000 cattle in 1885. Roundup districts were laid out, rules for strays or mavericks adopted and thousands of brands recorded. Associations co-operated with local and state officials and were alert to urge favorable legislation by Congress.

Cattle Brands, although traceable back to Egypt before Christ, are peculiarly associated with ranching. The institution of ranching as taken over from Mexico by Texas and California included brands. They are burned on range horses also. Attempted substitutions for fire-branding have proved impracticable. After all, suffering from the process is brief and not intense. The brand is a mark of ownership. If names and addresses were not so long, they would be branded on stock. Every legitimate brand is recorded by either state or county, thus preventing duplication within a given territory. Identification of range stock is necessary among honest people as well as against thieves, in fenced pastures as well as on open range.

In form, brands are made up of (1) letters, (2) figures and (3) geometric designs, symbols, or representations of objects. Combinations are endless. Because brands reduce the value of hides and also induce screw worms, they are now generally smaller and simpler than they were when cattle were less valuable. They may or may not signify something peculiar to the originator; usually they have a significance. A seaman turned rancher gave the Anchor brand; a cowman who won a big game of poker on a hand of four sixes adopted 6666 as his brand; a rancher honored his wife Ella with "E Bar." Brands are the heraldry of the range. Reading and calling them is an art known only to range men. A straight line burned on the side of a cow may be a "Dash," a "Bar," a "Rail." The letter H set upright cannot be misread; lying on its side, however, it is "Lazy H"; in an oblique position, "Tumbling H"; joined to a segment of circle under it, "Rocking H"; separated from the segment, "H Half-Circle," etc. Happily, the art of running out, or blotting, brands—burning one device into another—is obsolete.

Cattle Drives. Contrary to popular conception, long-distance cattle driving was traditional not only in Texas but elsewhere in America long before the Chisholm Trail was dreamed of. The Spaniards, always to be remembered as establishers of the ranching industry, drove herds northward from Mexico as far back as 1540. In the 18th century and on into the 19th the Spanish settlements in Texas derived most of their meager revenue from horses and cattle driven into Louisiana, though such trade was usually contraband. Meantime in the United States herds were sometimes driven long distances. In 1790 the boy David Crockett helped drive "a large stock of cattle" 400 miles from Tennessee into Virginia; twenty years later he took a drove of horses from the Tennessee River into southern North Carolina. In 1815 Timothy Flint "encountered a drove of more than 1000 cattle and swine" being driven from the interior of Ohio to Philadelphia. The stock in the states was gentle, often managed on foot. The history of trail driving involves horses as well as cattle.

Notwithstanding antecedent examples, Texans established trail driving as a regular occupation. Before they revolted from Mexico in 1836, they had a "Beef Trail" to New Orleans. In the 1840's they extended their markets northward into Missouri—Sedalia, Baxter Springs, Springfield and St. Louis becoming the principal markets. During the 1850's emigration and freighting from the Missouri River westward demanded great numbers of oxen, the firm of Russell, Majors and Waddell in 1858 utilizing 40,000 oxen. Texas longhorn steers by the thousands were broken for work oxen. Herds of longhorns were driven to Chicago; one herd at least to New York.

Under Spanish-Mexican ownership, California as well as Texas developed ranching and during the 1830's and 1840's a limited number of cattle were trailed thence to Oregon. But the discovery of gold in California arrested for awhile all development there of cattle industry and created a high demand for outside beef. During the 1850's cattle were occasionally driven to California from Missouri, Arkansas and perhaps other states; the big drives, however, were from Texas. Steers worth $15 in Texas were selling in San Francisco for as high as $150. One Texas rancher in 1854 hired for $1500 a famous Indian fighter to captain his herd of 1000 steers to California; 35 armed men accompanied it. These drives were fraught with great danger from both Indians and desert thirst.

During the Civil War Texas drove beeves here and there for the Confederate forces. At the close of the war she had probably 5,000,000 cattle—and no market. Late in 1865 a few cowmen tried to find a market. In 1866 there were many drives northward without a definite destination and without much financial success; also to the old but limited New Orleans market, following mostly well-established trails to the wharves of Shreveport and Jefferson (Texas). In 1867 Joseph G. McCoy opened a regular market at Abilene, Kans. The great cattle trails, moving successively westward, were established and trail driving boomed. In 1867 also the Goodnight-Loving Trail opened up New Mexico and Colorado to Texas cattle. By the tens of thousands they were soon driven into Arizona. In Texas itself cattle raising was expanding like wildfire. Caldwell, Dodge City, Ogallala, Cheyenne and other towns became famous on account of trail-driver patronage.

During the 1870's the buffaloes were virtually exterminated and the Indians of the Plains and Rockies were at the same time subjugated, penned up and put on beef rations. An empire was left vacant. It was first occupied by Texas longhorns, driven by Texas cowboys. The course of empire in America has been west, but over much of Oklahoma, Kansas, Nebraska, the Dakotas, Wyoming, Montana and parts of Nevada and Idaho the precursors of this movement were trail men from the South. The Long Trail extended into Canada. In the 1890's herds were still driven from the Panhandle of Texas to Montana, but trail driving virtually closed in 1895. Barbed wire, railroads and "nesters" closed it. During three swift decades it had moved over 10,000,000 cattle and 1,000,000 range horses, stamped the entire West with its character, given economic and personality prestige to Texas, made the longhorn the most historic brute in bovine history, glorified the cowboy over the globe and endowed America with its most romantic tradition relating to any occupation—a peer to England's tradition of the sea.

Cows were introduced into all the North American colonies to reproduce an essential phase of Old World husbandry. Losses in transportation were excessive, at times as high as a third of the shipment, but conditions in most sections favored rapid multiplication. In the North the lack of forage crops for the long winters was a hampering influence. In the New England open-field system pasturage was in common, with a cowherd in charge. Pasturage requirements contributed directly to the extension of westward settlement. In the "back country" region from Pennsylvania southward cattle roamed on the open range, were branded and rounded up by the owners, or hunted as game animals.

The "native" colonial cows were of four main strains, English, Dutch, Danish and Swedish, with some Spanish mixtures from Florida and French from Louisiana and Canada. By intercolonial trade there was an intermingling that in most cases obscured the original source. The classification of colonial stock was by color or size. Dairying and beef production were not generally specialized. Milk yield was small and butter and cheese generally inferior. The chief exception was in Rhode Island where special attention was given to the rearing and care of dairy herds and a cheese of superior quality was produced for export.

In the westward movement of production areas, whether plantation, range, or farm, the cow was an essential element of the enterprise—either for beef production, dairying, or a self-sufficing combination. With regional specialization attention was given to the selection and adaptation of breeds and types. By 1850 the East was giving increasing attention to milk and its products, and the Ohio and Upper Mississippi regions to the beef supply. Much time and effort were wasted in the vain effort to develop the "dual purpose cow." But the application of sounder principles of breeding and selection in response to increasing market demands led to the modern specialized types.

The Devon strain in New England, the Dutch cattle of New York, and a careful crossing in Pennsylvania were the bases of improvements. The new Shorthorns were imported at the close of the Revolution and by the 1830's were becoming the dominant type of the West. Herefords were introduced by Henry Clay's foundation herd in 1817, but the breed did not become prominent until the days of the cattle boom in the 1870's. The Holstein became localized in central New York in the first quarter of the century, and in the same period the other leading milk breeds, the Channel Island group and the Ayrshire, were imported in sufficient numbers to give permanent establishment of their breeds.

The existence of the open range or "cow country" for approximately two decades (1866-86) had a direct and determining effect upon the differentiation and improvement of beef breeds to meet the demands of a major industry. With the transition to the ranch and to the grazing-feeder relation of the Great Plains and Corn Belt, beef type selection has been still further perfected.

Paralleling the development of specialized breeding and adaptation of the beef cow to provide the supply for a main portion of the modernized meat industry have gone the demands upon the sister bovine with the extension of the area of supply and the perfecting of new processes for the utilization of milk. The newer dairy areas while profiting from the experience of the old in the selection and management of herds have made their own contributions to this branch of husbandry.

The problems of both the beef and dairy interests have been dealt with by a combination of public and private agencies. State and Federal departments of agriculture have enforced inspections, quarantines and various eradication measures to combat diseases. Experiment stations have conducted studies in breeding, nutrition and comparative production. Producers themselves have organized breeding co-operatives and cow-testing circuits. Associations of the leading breeders have been formed to regulate registry and to promote the interests of the group. The first herd-book to be issued was that of the Shorthorns in 1846, the Jersey followed in 1868 and the others date from the 1870's and 1880's.

Cow Country was the term frequently applied to that vast pastoral region in the West occupied by the range cattle industry. Its central portion was the Great Plains area. The cow towns came into existence in the decade following the close of the Civil War and grew rapidly until shortly after 1880, when it reached its greatest extent and the height of its importance.

At this time it included a region larger than the combined areas of all the countries of Western Europe, or more extensive than all that part of the United States east of the Mississippi devoted to agriculture. To assign to it definite boundaries even at any particular date is impossible since it was more than a geographic region. It was a state of society having for its economic basis cattle and the native pasturage on which they fed. At the time of its greatest extent, however, it included the greater part of the region extending from Mexico to Canada and from the central part of the second tier of states west of the Mississippi nearly to the Pacific Coast. To this region were brought herds of cattle from Texas as well as considerable numbers from the agricultural states farther east. These were spread over the ranges made available for grazing by the slaughter of the buffalo and the placing of the Indians upon reservations.

After about 1885 the cow country rapidly declined, due to the westward advance of settlers. Drilling deep wells and building dams to impound the rainfall made some additional lands available for grazing, but even so the range shrank rapidly. As railroads penetrated nearly every part of the West, more settlers came in, towns grew up, and society rapidly changed. By the close of the 19th century a definite cow country had virtually ceased to exist.

Cow Towns. With the beating out of the Chisholm Trail in 1867 and the great cattle drives accompanying the expansion of the cattle-range industry, which reached the crest of its boom just before the epic die-up and the concomitant depression of 1886, the cow towns of history arose in all their gaudy glory. The first was Abilene, Kans. Wichita, Hays, Ellsworth, Newton, Hunnewell, Caldwell and Dodge City succeeded it or shared its patronage by riders fresh off the long trail. Ogallala, Nebr., Cheyenne, Wyo., Miles City, Mont. and Medora, of the Dakotas, had their day as cow towns also. In the 1880's Dodge City boasted of being the "cowboy capital of the world." But Abilene, Tascosa, Amarillo, Fort Worth, Wichita Falls—all in Texas—Prescott, Ariz., Greeley, Colo., and Las Vegas, N. Mex., were among outstanding cow-country centers.

There were two kinds of cow towns: those that fed off the cow country—the towns marking termini of the trails; and those that fed the cow country—distributing points for vast range areas and, after railroads were built, shipping points.

Many of the cow towns were during their heyday enlivened by buffalo hunters, railroad construction gangs, freighting outfits, etc. Cattlemen, the owners, made these towns headquarters for buying and selling. Here cowboys, after months of monotonous work, monotonous fare and monotonous abstinence of all kinds, were paid off and turned loose. It was their night to howl, and their day to get shaved, re-clad in new clothes, and buy horseback equipment. Not only to release spirits but to maintain a reputation, many of them cut loose to shoot up the town. As a class they meant no more harm by this than schoolboys mean with firecrackers on the Fourth of July. They seldom looked on the wine when it was red, but probably a majority of them drank "white mule" straight. The painted women were there to lure them. Gambling devices of every kind, run by a class of bloodsuckers that their experience with nature gave them no knowledge of, were there to bleed them of their wages. Everything was wide open all night as well as by day.

Each cow town had its boot hill—its graveyard populated by men who had died with their boots on. Yet murders by the range men were almost unknown. "Killings" were something else. Violence and ebullient spirits called forth a kind of "peace officer" that cow towns made famous—the town marshall. Wild Bill Hickok and Wyatt Earp were perhaps the two best-known cow-town marshalls.

A few places like Fort Worth, Cheyenne, Magdalena, N. Mex., and Duncan, Ariz., still carry on the tradition, in modified form, of cow-town days.

Open Range Cattle Period. While cattle were pastured upon unoccupied public lands quite early and especially in Texas in the years before the Civil War, the period of open-range grazing, in a larger sense, began about 1866 and closed early in the last decade of the 19th century. During the years following the close of the Civil War a vast stream of cattle poured north out of Texas to cow towns in Kansas and Nebraska. From these the fat, mature animals were shipped to market while young steers and breeding animals were driven farther north or west to stock new ranges. It has been estimated that nearly 5,500,-000 cattle were driven north from Texas in the period from 1866 to 1885 and this does not include large numbers driven west or northwest into New Mexico and Colorado.

Most of these cattle driven north each year were spread out over ranges in the public domain throughout western Kansas, Nebraska, the Dakotas, Montana, Wyoming and other western states and territories. Here they were held for growth and fattening, the boundaries of each ranchman's pasture lands being determined by that unwritten law of the range known as "cow custom." A ranch headquarters was usually established near the center of the range and along its borders were placed "cow camps" at which riders were stationed to look after the cattle and keep them within the limits of their own range. In spite of their efforts, however, some would stray across the line onto the pasture lands of neighboring ranchmen which made it necessary to hold roundups each spring and autumn. At the spring roundup calves were branded and at the fall roundup the fat, mature animals of each ranchman were separated from the remainder and placed in the "beef herd" to be shipped to market for slaughter.

The roundups were participated in by all the ranchmen of a large area designated as the "roundup district." Each usually sent a wagon and several cowboys to share in the work. In some states or territories, notably Wyoming, the districts and the dates and manner of conducting roundups were designated by law. A "roundup foreman" was chosen to have charge of the work and the method of disposing of "mavericks," or unbranded animals, was often fixed by statute.

As cattle were driven northward from Texas and spread over the public domain of the central and northern Plains they also spread over the state lands of western Texas and the great Indian reservations of the Indian Territory as well as those farther north. All of this great region constituted the so-called "cow country." Settlers were steadily advancing westward along its eastern border and taking up homesteads, but the area lost to grazing was for a time compensated for by building dams across ravines and drilling deep wells from which water was pumped by windmills, thus opening up large tracts of hitherto unwatered lands to pasturage.

In 1875 began the first shipments of dressed beef to Europe which steadily increased until more than 50,000,000 pounds were exported in 1878, and over 100,000,000 pounds in 1881. Most of this was sent to Great Britain, and this enormous influx of American beef so alarmed the cattle growers of North Britain that a parliamentary commission was sent to this country to visit the range area and report upon conditions. Its report made in 1884 told of such great profits made in ranching as to cause much excitement among the English and Scottish investors and huge sums of British capital were sent to America for investment in ranching enterprises. Many individual Scots or English came to the cow country to give their personal attention to ranching, and the excitement extended even to the continent of Europe. By 1884 it was estimated that more than $30,000,000 of British capital had been invested in ranching on the Great Plains.

Among the large Scottish or English enterprises were the Prairie Land and Cattle Co., the Matador, the Espuela Land and Cattle Co. and scores of others. An enthusiasm for grazing cattle upon the open range amounting almost to a craze had also swept over the United States before 1885. Prominent lawyers, United States senators, bankers and other businessmen throughout the East formed cattle companies to take advantage of the opportunities offered for ranching upon the great open ranges of the West. The destruction of the buffalo herds made it necessary to feed the many large tribes of Western Indians and this resulted in the awarding of valuable beef contracts for that purpose with the privilege of pasturing herds upon the various reservations.

The invention of barbed wire and the rapid extension of its use after 1875 brought about the inclosure of considerable tracts of pasture land. Laws were enacted by Congress, however, forbidding the fencing of lands of the public domain and orders of the Indian Bureau prohibited the inclosure of lands on Indian reservations. While such laws and orders were not strictly enforced, yet they were not without effect.

Perhaps the year 1885 marks the peak of the open-range cattle industry. By that time most of the range was fully stocked and much of it overstocked. During the summer of 1886 large herds were driven north from Texas and spread over the ranges in the most reckless fashion possible. Then came the terrible winter of 1886–87 in which hundreds of thousands of cattle died of cold and starvation. Spring came to find nearly every ranchman on the Central and Northern Plains facing ruin. The open-range cattle industry never recovered from the results of this tragic winter. The range area was being rapidly settled by homesteaders. Large Indian reservations were thrown open to settlement. The use of barbed wire was becoming universal and the public domain was passing into the hands of private owners who inclosed their lands with wire fences. In many regions cattle were being replaced by sheep. No date can be given as the end of the open-range cattle period, but by 1890 it was close at hand and by the end of the century that period virtually belonged to the past.

CAUCUS is the term applied to a general meeting of party members in any community or legislative body for the purpose of discussing and promoting the affairs of their particular political party. There are, however, various applications of the term:

(1) In the first place, the *caucus* as such means a meeting of the respective party members in a local community, for the purpose of nominating candidates for office or for electing delegates to county or state party conventions. Such a local caucus is ordinarily open to all voters in the community who consider themselves members of the particular party involved, and it constitutes the first formal step in the nominating procedure. The caucus in this sense was used in the colonies at least as early as 1725 and particularly in Boston, where several clubs, attended largely by ship mechanics or caulkers, endorsed candidates for office before the regular election and which came to be known as "caucus clubs." The gentry also organized their "parlor caucuses" for the same purpose, and this

method of nomination soon became the regular practice among the political parties. It was for some time entirely extralegal, but abuses became so flagrant that legal regulation begun in two states (California and New York) in 1866, by the early 1900's had spread to virtually all the states, and was applied not only to the caucus but also to the party conventions. Now the caucus as a nominating device has quite generally been supplanted by the direct primary, although still retained in some areas for township and other purely local office.

(2) A second application of the term is to the *party caucus in Congress,* which is a meeting of the respective party members in either house for the purpose of determining their position on legislation and other matters. The Federalists certainly used this device as early as 1796, the Republicans followed suit, and the caucus was firmly established at least by 1825. In general this caucus has three purposes or functions: (1) to nominate party candidates for Speaker, President *pro tem,* and other House or Senate offices; (2) to elect or provide for the selection of the party officers and committees, such as the Floor Leader, Whip, Committee on Committees, Steering Committee, Policy Committee; (3) to decide what action is to be taken with respect to legislation, either in broad terms or in detail. The House Democrats and the Senate Republicans have formal caucus or conference rules, while the House Republicans and the Senate Democrats prefer to be governed by *ad hoc* resolutions; but in any case these specify the circumstances under which caucus decisions may be binding or merely advisory.

Whether formally binding or not, caucus decisions are generally followed by the respective party members, since bolting is likely to bring punishment in the form of poorer committee assignments, loss of patronage, and the like; and consequently the caucus has been an effective means for securing coherent party action and an important, although extraconstitutional, device in legislative organization and procedure. It was notably effective as used by the Democrats during the Wilson Administration and by the Republicans in the 1920's. In recent years there has been a tendency to consider these party meetings as mere conferences rather than as binding caucuses; and for many years since the New Deal period the Democrats, in particular, seldom held caucuses or conferences on legislation, probably because of fear that party disunity would be revealed. This neglect of the caucus inevitably enhanced the authority of the party leadership, and has been protested by party members who are anxious to participate more fully in party decisions. It has also been criticized by students of government, who have come to emphasize the concept of party responsibility and to consider the caucus as a device for promoting party unity and coherence in

respect to legislative policy. There is some indication that these pressures may bring about a revival of the party caucus in Congress.

(3) A very special application of the party caucus in Congress is the *Congressional Caucus* (1796–1824), which was the earliest method of nominating presidential candidates. No provision was made in the Constitution for presidential nomination, clearly on the assumption that the presidential electors should exercise their own individual choice; and no nominations were made for the first two presidential elections, since Washington was the choice of all. But Washington's retirement having been announced and political parties having been organized for the particular purpose of controlling the national administration, the Federalist members of Congress met in secret conference in 1796 and agreed to support John Adams and Thomas Pinckney for President and Vice-President, and shortly afterwards the Republican members met and agreed on Jefferson and Burr. In 1800 the respective party members met again for the same purpose, and after that date the Congressional Caucus, as it was called, met openly as a presidential nominating caucus. Since the Federalist party was almost wiped out by the election of 1800, the Republican caucus was the only one held thereafter, and its caucus nominations became practically nominations by Congress itself.

This system became increasingly unpopular. Many thought it contrary to the spirit of the Constitution, if not actually unconstitutional, for members of Congress thus virtually to select the President. The friends of Andrew Jackson were particularly bitter against the Congressional Caucus, since he was never its choice, and it was denounced by mass meetings throughout the country. In 1824 only about a fourth of the members of Congress attended, nominating William H. Crawford, who stood third in the electoral vote. The Congressional caucus never met again, being succeeded in the next decade by the national convention system.

CAVALIERS. The legend that a large number of the early settlers of Virginia were Cavaliers, *i.e.,* highborn followers of the Stuarts, was demolished in 1910 by Thomas Jefferson Wertenbaker, himself a native of Virginia. In *Patrician and Plebeian in Virginia,* Wertenbaker proved to the satisfaction of himself and other scholars "that but few men of high social rank in England established families in Virginia; that the larger part of the aristocracy of the colony came directly from merchant ancestors; that the leading planters of the 17th century were mercantile in instinct and unlike the English aristocrat of the same period."

CAVE-IN-ROCK is a cave in Hardin County, Ill., on the Ohio River, about thirty miles below the mouth of the Wabash. In pioneer times it was used as an inn patronized by flatboatmen. It often served as a rendezvous for outlaws who robbed flatboats going down the river. Among its early occupants were Sam Mason and his gang of river pirates and highwaymen and the bloodthirsty Harpe brothers.

CÉLORON'S LEAD PLATES (1749) mark one step in the French-English rivalry over the Ohio Valley. By 1749 the English were pressing across the Alleghenies into the rich valley beyond the mountains. Unable to make reply in kind, the governor of New France sent an army, led by Pierre Joseph Céloron, to enforce its authority on the Ohio. He descended the river as far as the Great Miami, where he turned northward toward Detroit. En route, in frequent councils, he urged the natives to cease all intercourse with the English and warned the latter to leave the country At strategic points along the Ohio, lead plates were planted, bearing an inscription reciting the French monarch's title to the country. One of them was found prior to 1821 at Marietta, O., and is now owned by the American Antiquarian Society (Worcester, Mass.). Another plate was found at Point Pleasant, W. Va., and since 1849 has belonged to the Virginia Historical Society at Richmond. Both the English and the Indians ignored the admonitions of Céloron; the ownership of the Ohio Valley remained to be determined by the French and Indian War.

CENSUS. Article I of the Federal Constitution, which provides that Representatives "be apportioned among the several States . . . according to their respective numbers," provides also for a decennial census to furnish the necessary basis for such apportionment. It was only as an incident to the establishment of its democratic political machinery that the United States in 1789 became the first nation in the world to provide by law for a periodic enumeration of its people.

The first two censuses, those of 1790 and 1800, gathered little more than the necessary population figures, distinguishing colored from white and slave from free because slaves were to count as three fifths the same number of free persons in apportioning representation. The census of 1810 was the first in which an effort was made to collect statistics on matters other than population, notably manufactures, but the results were uneven and incomplete. In 1840 an attempt, perhaps overambitious, was made to collect information on mines, agriculture, commerce, manufactures, occupations, schools, illiteracy, insane and idiots, pensioners and other subjects. The accuracy of the census figures for many of these subjects has been questioned, although the information gathered is of great value to the historian. In 1850 there was still further expansion of the categories to include, among others, newspapers and periodicals, libraries, religious bodies, criminals and mortality figures. The censuses of 1860 and 1870 were taken under the same law as that for 1850. Because of the difficulties of Reconstruction in the South, the results of the 1870 census for that region are somewhat under suspicion.

All censuses prior to that of 1880 were taken under the supervision of United States marshals who hired assistants of their own to do the actual work of enumeration. Very little control from Washington was possible over these temporary political appointees and the results became less reliable as the schedules grew more complicated. The act providing for the 1880 census substituted a field force of supervisors and enumerators directly under the control of the Superintendent of the Census. The census of 1880 was vastly larger in scope, its results being published in 24 volumes, whereas five volumes had sufficed for any previous census. The census of 1890 was still larger. It was the first in which use was made of punch cards and electric tabulating machines, inventions which made possible tabulations of many combinations which were previously impracticable.

After long agitation, a permanent Census Office was established by act of March 6, 1902. Previously, every ten years since 1830, when the returns were first checked in Washington, a temporary organization had been called into existence to compile, edit and publish the results. This temporary Office, after 1849, was always set up in the Interior Department, and the permanent Office was placed there too, only to be transferred in 1903 to the newly established Department of Commerce and Labor, where it gradually came to be known as the Bureau of the Census. From 1913 it has been in the Department of Commerce. Beginning in 1940 the Census Bureau has maintained a nucleus field organization.

Since the establishment in 1940 of the Census Bureau as a permanent statistical-gathering agency, the efficiency of census-taking and of the tabulation and publication of results has shown continued improvement. In the '50s under the supervision of the Bureau of Standards, an electronic device, the Universal Automatic Computer, called the UNIVAC, was constructed for the Census Bureau. The UNIVAC is expected eventually to replace much of the card tabulating equipment.

CENT, FIRST AMERICAN USE OF. Our cent came from the adoption of the dollar as the unit and its division decimally. Colonial accounts were kept in pounds, shillings and pence but the circulation was mostly Spanish dollars. A privately issued coin dated 1783 (called the Washington cent) had the word cent on it. Vermont and Connecticut in 1785 coined cents, but Massachusetts, in 1787, was the first state to have the word on its coin. The "Fugio" cent in 1787 was the first cent issued under the authority of the United States. Cents were minted regularly by the Federal Government starting with 1793.

CENTENNIAL EXPOSITION, Philadelphia (1876), celebrating the 100th anniversary of the Declaration of Independence, was the first great international exposition held in America. It was ten years in the planning and building; it covered more than 450 acres in Fairmount Park; its total cost was more than $11,000,000. Thirty-seven foreign nations constructed pavilions, many in their native architectural styles. The 167 buildings of the exposition housed more than 30,000 exhibitors from 50 nations. The gates were opened on May 10 and during the 159 days that followed there were 8,004,274 cash admissions. There were seven principal divisions in the exposition: mining and metallurgy, manufactured products, science and education, fine arts, machinery, agriculture and horticulture. The Woman's Building, an innovation in expositions, demonstrated the relative emancipation of women in America.

There was no midway or similar amusement, for nothing could have competed with the intense public interest in the working models of many new machines and processes. The architecture was confused, but impressive. The influence of various foreign exhibits evoked a new interest in interior decoration in America. In this exposition the world, for the first time, saw industrial America on display. Americans realized that the Machine Age had arrived and that their country was, in many ways, at last coming of age. The Centennial was honest, homely and revealing; it provided an immense stimulus to the growing aesthetic, social and industrial consciousness of America.

CENTRAL TREATY ORGANIZATION (C.E.N.T.O.), conceived by U. S. Secretary of State John Foster Dulles in 1953, is an outgrowth of the Baghdad Pact. It is a Middle East alliance formed in August, 1959, of Turkey, Iran and Pakistan, Great Britain later becoming a member. The United States, while participating in many of the alliance's activities largely concerned with security, economic developments and cultural activities, has declined to assume full membership because of a reluctance to stir up animosities and hostility in the Arab nations. The major accomplishment of the alliance has been the bringing together of the three "regional" countries into more intimate association.

C.E.N.T.O. has provided a means for the United States to explain its policies to key officials in the Middle East area. The sixth meeting of the ministerial council of the alliance held at Ankara, Turkey, the headquarters of C.E.N.T.O., in April, 1961, was attended by U. S. Secretary of State Dean Rusk.

CERRO GORDO, BATTLE OF (April 18, 1847). Advancing to the interior after taking Vera Cruz, Gen. Scott found a Mexican army under Santa Anna entrenched on the National Road, eighteen miles below Jalapa. Twiggs' division stormed two fortified hills after a turning movement suggested and guided by Capt. R. E. Lee. Shields' brigade gained the rear of the position and the Mexicans fled. Santa Anna escaped, leaving 3000 prisoners, guns, baggage and $11,000 in specie. The American loss was 431.

CHAMP D'ASILE. In 1817 a group of Napoleonic exiles under the leadership of Generals Lallemand and Rigaud made a fortified camp in Texas on the Trinity River, about thirty leagues from the coast, calling it Champ d'Asile. It was charged that they hoped to take Mexico and rescue Napoleon from St. Helena. Scarcely were the forts and dwellings completed when the Spanish, who claimed the territory, forced the colonists to withdraw to Galveston Island. There they remained for weeks, the victims of hunger, sickness and tropical storms. At last, aided by the pirate Lafitte, they made their way to the French settlements in Louisiana.

CHAMPAGNE-MARNE OPERATION (July 15–18, 1918). This German offensive had several objectives. One was to correct their faulty supply in the Marne salient; another was to draw reserves to assure success in the offensive planned against the British in Flanders. The attack was made by three armies of the German Crown Prince Group. The plan was for the 7th Army (Boehn) to cross the Marne east of Château-Thierry and advance up the valley to Epernay. The 1st Army (Mudra) and 3rd Army (Einem) were to attack east of Reims in the direction of Epernay, swing south of the forest of Reims and capture Epernay and Chalons. The attack was definitely halted east of Reims on the first day by the efficient defense plans of the 4th French Army (Gouraud). West of Reims some fourteen divisions crossed the Marne but, unaided by the attack east of Reims and without artillery support, this attack soon bogged down. Orders were given on the 17th for their withdrawal, preparatory to a general withdrawal, from the Marne salient. The 3rd, 42nd and part of the 28th American Divisions participated. The approximate number of Americans engaged was 85,000. The 38th Infantry Regiment (3rd Division) here won the sobriquet, "Rock of the Marne."

CHAMPLAIN'S VOYAGES. A sojourn of two years in Mexico and the West Indies (1599) prepared Samuel de Champlain for his first Canadian voyage (1603) when he served as geographer for the DeChastes expedition, authorized by Henry IV of France to make a general survey and fix settlements. Champlain justified his appointment by vigorously prosecuting a cartographic survey of the St. Lawrence region including the gulf, Gaspé and Isle Percé and the Saguenay River, resulting in a report prolific in valuable information. In 1604 under DeMonts, he explored Nova Scotia. A year later he explored the New England coast, mapping 1000 miles of coast line. Returning to France several times with his reports, he repeatedly voyaged to Canada, after 1607 being Lieutenant-Governor. Other voyages of 1610, 1611, 1613, made him the acknowledged master of all that related to New France. A final voyage in 1633 ended in his effort to win the friendship of the Iroquois, whom he had previously attacked.

CHANCELLORSVILLE, BATTLE OF (May 2–4, 1863). In April Hooker (U.), with almost 130,000 men, lay across the Rappahannock River from Fredericksburg, Va. Intrenched behind Fredericksburg Lee (C.) awaited another attack such as that of Burnside (U.) in the previous December. In the absence of Longstreet's (C.) divisions in southeastern Virginia, Lee had approximately 60,000 men.

Beginning April 27, Hooker in rapid movements got four army corps across the Rappahannock on Lee's left flank, while maintaining his old lines and sending an army corps of 20,000 men under Sedgwick across the river below Lee's right flank. On May 1, with the forces on Lee's left, Hooker advanced across the river beyond Chancellorsville, only to retire behind Chancellorsville on the approach of the enemy. Lee, threatened by Hooker's movements, ran the risk of having his communication with Richmond cut and of being caught in an encircling trap. The greatest danger being on his left, Lee, leaving a force of about 10,000 men at Fredericksburg under Early, marched with the remainder of his troops toward Chancellorsville. The opposing armies, late in the day of May 1, took position for battle on lines nearly perpendicular to the Rappahannock. At night Lee and Stonewall Jackson (C.), conferring upon their dangerous situation, decided on a daring measure, that of dividing their forces and having Jackson with about 30,000 men march the next day around Hooker's right flank, while Lee with less than 20,000 men held the line in front of Hooker. Accordingly on May 2, while Lee deployed his men in skirmishes against Hooker, Jackson moved rapidly around Hooker's right flank.

In spite of adequate information of Jackson's movement, the army corps on Hooker's extreme right were unprepared when Jackson, late on May 2, fell upon them with irresistible fury. Howard's (U.) corps was routed and another corps badly demoralized. In the confusion and darkness greater disaster might have happened had not Jackson been dangerously wounded by the fire of his own troops and carried from the battlefield. In the renewed conflict of May 3 a cannon ball struck a column against which Hooker was leaning. Dazed by the effect and in doubt about the security of his army, Hooker withdrew his troops to the banks of the river, where they remained throughout May 4 in disorder and uncertainty.

Lee, meanwhile, turned back to deal with Sedgwick's corps, which had routed the Confederate force under Early and was rapidly approaching Chancellorsville. Under the fierce attack of Lee's veterans,

Sedgwick likewise retired to the Rappahannock, which he crossed during the night of May 4. When, on May 5, Lee advanced again beyond Chancellorsville, Hooker withdrew the Union forces north of the river. In the battle Hooker lost 17,287 men and Lee 12,423. But Lee suffered the irreparable loss of Jackson, who after days of intense suffering died of his wounds.

CHAPARRAL, from Spanish *chaparro,* as used by Mexicans, who gave the word to the Southwest, generally means any kind of thick or thorny brush, but never timber. In California, chaparral is specifically the manzanita oak; in parts of Texas, the black chaparral. Chaparral peculiar to arid and semi-arid regions of the Southwest includes juajillo, granjeno, mesquite, all-thorn and huisache, the bushes often interspersed with various kinds of cacti, agaves and yuccas. Only dogs, horses and men used to the chaparral can run in it, and the "brush popper," armored in leather and ducking, is a distinctly different type from the plains cowpuncher. The leaves of chaparral growth are as slender as the thorns are sharp, preventing evaporation. Some varieties afford good browsing; others are as bitter as gall. Before the era of overgrazing, a solid turf and frequent grass fires kept the brush down. Now it usurps millions of acres once prairie. Cattle ranging in it tend to become wild. It hides rattlesnakes, coyotes and other "varments."

CHAPULTEPEC, BATTLE OF (Sept. 13, 1847). The western approaches to Mexico City were commanded by Chapultepec, a rocky eminence, 200 feet high, crowned with stone buildings. After vigorous bombardment, Gen. Winfield Scott launched Gideon J. Pillow's division against the southern slopes. The garrison resisted desperately, but the Americans mounted the walls on scaling ladders and carried the *Castillo.* John A. Quitman's and William J. Worth's divisions then attacked the Belén and San Cosme gates, and the city surrendered the next morning. The American loss (for the day) was 138 killed, 673 wounded. Mexican casualties are unknown, but 760 were captured.

CHARIVARI. A French word of unknown origin meaning rough music. Corrupted into *shivaree* in America it designates an old custom, particularly in the Middle West, of serenading newly wedded couples with every type of noise-making device, the object being to exact a "treat." Refusal to serve the serenaders with refreshments resulted in some form of hazing, the groom often being compelled to "ride a rail." The *shivaree* was a manifestation of mob instinct, and like the barn dance was a popular form of rural entertainment. In New England the custom took the name of *serenade* or *callathump.*

CHARLES RIVER BRIDGE CASE, 1837 (11 Peters 420). In 1785 the Massachusetts legislature incorporated the Proprietors of the Charles River Bridge, for the purpose of erecting a toll bridge between Boston and Charlestown. In 1828, long before the expiration of the charter, the legislature incorporated the Warren Bridge Company to build another bridge a few rods from the first. The new bridge was to become free to the public within six years. Was the second charter unconstitutional as impairing the obligation of the first?

The case was carried from the highest court in Massachusetts (6 Pick. 376, 7 Pick. 344) to the U. S. Supreme Court, where it was first argued in 1831. Chief Justice Marshall would have held the second grant invalid; but because of absences and disagreement it was impossible to reach a decision until 1837. By that time new appointments had worked a transformation in the Court, which now upheld the constitutionality of the second charter with only two dissenting votes. In an opinion which marked that leaning against monopolistic power which characterized Jacksonian political philosophy, Taney, the new Chief Justice, developed the rule that corporate charters are to be construed strictly in favor of the public.

CHARLESTON, CAPTURE OF (May 12, 1780). In March, 1780, the British, under Gen Clinton and Admiral Arbuthnot, besieged Charleston by land and sea. The Americans, commanded by Gen. Benjamin Lincoln, made little use of the bar at the entrance of the harbor and the adjacent sea islands, the natural defenses of the town. The fall of Charleston, after a brave but futile resistance, for a time paralyzed the American cause in the Carolinas.

CHARLESTON, S. C. In 1670 an English expedition under Gov. William Sayle founded a settlement—the first permanent one in the Carolinas—on the Ashley River, three miles from the present center of Charleston, and named it Charles Towne, in honor of King Charles II. Other immigrants settled on the present city site, and in 1680 the public offices were removed thither. This soon became the largest and wealthiest town south of Philadelphia. A definitely French tinge was imparted to its population by the coming of Huguenot refugees from France in 1685–86, of 1200 Acadian exiles in 1755 and 500 French Revolutionary refugees from Santo Domingo in 1793. In 1706 the city withstood an attack by a combined Spanish and French fleet. In February, 1776, the Provincial Congress met here and adopted the first state constitution. The city was unsuccessfully attacked by the British in 1776 and 1779, but fell into their hands in 1780 and so remained until 1782. Until it received a city charter in 1783 it was governed by ordinances of the legislature, which were administered in part by provincial officials, in part by the churchwardens. It continued as the state capital until 1790. It was the center of the nullification agitation of 1832–33, and of the secession spirit of 1860. The first fighting of the Civil War took place in its harbor. In the decades following the war, its beautiful old homes and churches, its aristocratic pride, its serenity and mellow atmosphere of the past gave it a charm all its own. It has suffered many calamities —not only sieges and bombardments, but hurricanes in 1699, 1752 and 1854, epidemics in 1699 and 1854, fire in 1740 and, on Aug. 31, 1886, the great earthquake which damaged nine tenths of its buildings.

CHARLESTON, SIEGE OF (1861–65). This popular term is a misnomer, for Charleston was never besieged, nor was any serious effort made either to fortify it or to invest it on the land side. The operations consisted in a blockade begun in May, 1861, with land and sea attacks upon the harbor fortifications. The harbor was well fortified and great ingenuity was displayed by the defenders in constructing an ironclad flotilla, a system of torpedo defense and even submarine boats. The wooden blockading fleet could not close in and even when Federal monitors arrived they could accomplish little against the land works. In 1863 Fort Sumter was bombarded and almost destroyed, but the ruins could not be taken. Battery Wagner was taken by formal siege operations, but no further progress could be made. It was in the course of these operations that the famous "Swamp Angel," an eight-inch 200-pounder Parrott rifle, was emplaced on a platform floated on deep mud, and fired five miles into the city, but burst on the thirty-sixth round. The city held out until February, 1865, and was finally evacuated on account of Gen. Sherman's advance northward from Savannah after his March to the Sea.

CHARLESTON, W. VA., took its name from Charles Clendenin, whose son George acquired lands at the junction of the Elk and Kanawha rivers in the year 1787. Here was located Fort Lee, a refuge for wilderness settlers for a generation following the French and Indian War. Here Gen. Andrew Lewis halted his army in his march from Lewisburg to Point Pleasant in Dunmore's War. In 1791 Daniel Boone lived in a cabin in the suburbs of the present city and represented the county in the Virginia Assembly.

Charleston was a pivotal point in the early part of the Civil War and changed hands between the Confederates and Union forces a half-dozen times.

CHARLESTON HARBOR, DEFENSE OF (1776). On June 1, 1776, a British squadron, led by Sir Henry Clinton and Peter Parker, anchored off Sullivan's Island, at the entrance to Charleston Harbor, S. C. The city was held by 6000 militia, while a much smaller force, led by Col. William Moultrie, was stationed on the island. On June 28 the British tried to batter down the island fort, only to find that their shots buried themselves in the green palmetto logs of the crude fortification. After the loss of one ship, the British retired and soon sailed for New York. Thus the Carolinas averted the threatened British invasion of the South.

CHARLEVOIX'S JOURNEY (1721) to America was an attempt on the part of the French authorities to discover a route to the Western Sea, through the continent of North America. The regent of France, not wishing to have his purpose known, disguised the journey as a tour of inspection of the posts and missions of interior America. Charlevoix left France in July, 1720, arrived at Quebec in September, too late to join the flotillas that ascended to the "Upper Country." In May, 1721, he went around the Great Lakes, arriving in Mackinac in time to accompany the new commandant at La Baye to his post. There he conversed with Sioux Indians on their knowledge of the Western Sea. Finding it too late for an excursion into Lake Superior, Charlevoix decided to visit Louisiana. He entered Illinois by the St. Joseph-Kankakee route, and at Kaskaskia spent the winter interviewing traders from the Missouri. Thence he went down the river to New Orleans where he spent fifteen days, and continued to Biloxi where in February, 1722, he fell ill. Not being able to remount the Mississippi as he had planned, he returned to France, where he arrived in December, 1722. His recommendations to the regent resulted in a post among the Sioux, established in 1727. His experiences in America he wrote in *Journal Historique* which was published in 1744, first translated into English in 1761.

CHARTER COLONIES were promoted through private enterprise under charters from the Crown. They were founded by trading companies, by lords proprietors and by squatters later incorporated. Colonies of the first type for the most part either disappeared or changed their status early. The Virginia Company lost its charter in 1624, the New England Council surrendered its patent in 1635, the Providence Island colony was conquered by Spain in 1641 and the Massachusetts Bay Company became a theocracy, leaving the Bermuda Company as the only one of its kind in control of a colony through the greater part of the 17th century. Connecticut and Rhode Island, founded as squatter colonies by dissenters from Puritan Massachusetts, received charters of incorporation early in the Restoration Period. The predominating type throughout the 17th century was the proprietary colony. Of this sort was Carlisle's Caribbean grant, Maryland and Maine, in the early part of the century, and after 1660 the Carolinas, New York, the Jerseys, the Bahamas and Pennsylvania.

Similar institutions of government developed in all of the charter colonies. All ultimately had gov-

ernor, council and house of representatives, the two former chosen by company or lord proprietors, and in the corporation colonies, indirectly by the people. The house of representatives, first the voluntary concession of the trading company, as in Virginia and Bermuda, later became a generally accepted institution in all chartered colonies except New York. Government in the corporation colonies was the freest from outside control. Perhaps because they were settled without the mediation of trading company or proprietor, the inhabitants of these colonies from the beginning cherished a conception of government based on sovereignty of the people.

When the restoration English government turned its attention to the building of a colonial policy, it found charters obstacles in the path. Several colonies were royalized, and, with the view of ultimate consolidation of all colonial possessions into a few large units, the Dominion of New England was established. Its failure brought temporary reaction in favor of charter colonies, but throughout the 18th century the process of royalization went on until by 1776 only two proprieties, Maryland and Pennsylvania, and two corporation colonies, Connecticut and Rhode Island, remained. Except in the corporation colonies the people seem to have preferred royal rule.

CHARTER OF LIBERTIES (1683), drafted by New York's first assembly, was approved by James Duke of York as an instrument of government for his province. Recalling the rights of Englishmen and the principles of the great liberty documents, this charter described the framework of government, the functions of governor, council and a legislative assembly representative of the qualified freeholders, and guaranteed the freedom of the assembly, which was to meet at least once in three years, trial by jury, due course of law in all proceedings, protection of the property of women, freedom from feudal exactions, exemption from quartering of soldiers and especially religious toleration for all Christians.

CHARTRES, FORT DE (1719–72), seat of civil and military government in the Illinois country for more than half a century, stood near the present village of Prairie du Rocher in Randolph County, Ill. Named in honor of the son of the Regent of France, it was commenced in 1719 and completed the following year. Built of wood, and exposed to the flood waters of the Mississippi, the fort quickly fell into disrepair. In 1727 it was rebuilt, but by 1732 it was so dilapidated that St. Ange, the commandant, built a new fort with the same name at some distance from the river. By 1747, when a general Indian uprising seemed imminent, this too had fallen into such bad condition that repair was considered impossible and the garrison was withdrawn to Kaskaskia. In 1751 the French government decided to build a new fort at Kaskaskia, but the engineer in charge,

Jean Baptiste Saucier, decided on a location near the old fort. Foundations were laid in 1753; three years later the structure was substantially finished. Costing 200,000 livres, the new Fort de Chartres was an irregular quadrangle with sides 490 ft. long and stone walls 2 ft. 2 in. thick. Ten years after its completion a competent English officer described it as "the most commodious and best built fort in North America." It was capable of housing 400 men, although its garrison rarely exceeded half that number.

Fort de Chartres, transferred to the British on Oct. 10, 1765, was the last French post in North America to be surrendered under the Treaty of Paris. Renamed Fort Cavendish, it was the seat of British rule in the Illinois country until 1772 when it was abandoned and destroyed.

CHASE IMPEACHMENT TRIAL (Jan. 2–March 1, 1805).

This was generally considered as part of a concerted Republican (Jeffersonian) effort to curb the power of the Federal bench. Justice Chase, an arbitrary personage with an abusive tongue and an unswerving confidence in the righteousness of the Federalist party which had elevated him to the bench was charged in the articles of impeachment with unbecoming conduct and disregard of law. The outcome of the trial before the Senate hinged largely on the question whether his conduct, admittedly objectionable, constituted "a high crime or misdemeanor." His acquittal, March 1, 1805, was probably a distinct gain for judicial independence.

CHÂTEAU-THIERRY BRIDGE, AMERICANS AT.

Having broken the French front on the Aisne, the Germans entered Château-Thierry on May 31, 1918. Gen. Foch, rushing troops to stop them, sent the American 3rd Division (Dickman) to the region of Château-Thierry, where, aided by French Colonials, the Americans prevented the enemy from crossing on May 31 and June 1. The German attacks then ceased.

CHATTANOOGA CAMPAIGN (Oct.–Nov., 1863).

Before the battle of Chickamauga the Union troops under Grant, released by the capture of Vicksburg, had begun to move eastward. Bragg (C.) had failed to follow through after Chickamauga. All he could do was to "besiege" Rosecrans' (U.) army in Chattanooga. Grant, placed in general command of all Union forces in the West, replaced Rosecrans by Thomas and instructed him to hold Chattanooga "at all hazards." Food was running short and supply lines were constantly interrupted. Grant's first act was to open a new and protected line of supply, via Brown's Ferry. Reinforcements arrived. Vigorous action turned the tables on Bragg, whose only act was to weaken himself unnecessarily by detaching Longstreet (C.) on a fruitless expedition to capture Knoxville. Bragg then awaited Grant's next move. President Davis (C.) visited the army and tried, unsuccessfully, to restore confidence.

On Nov. 24, 1863, Hooker (U.) captured Lookout Mountain on the left of Bragg's line. The next day Grant attacked all along the line. The Confederate center on Missionary Ridge gave way; the left had retreated; only the right held firm and covered the retreat southward into northern Georgia. A brilliant rear-guard stand at Ringgold Gap halted Grant's pursuit. The Union troops returned to Chattanooga; the Confederate Army went into winter quarters at Dalton, Ga.

CHAUTAUQUA MOVEMENT

had its beginning in an assembly held at Chautauqua, on the shore of Lake Chautauqua, N. Y., Aug. 4–18, 1874. Here John H. Vincent, a Methodist clergyman of New York, later Bishop, and Lewis Miller of Akron, O., who were interested in developing Sunday schools, planned a course of meetings to give instruction in Sunday-school organization, management and teaching, and study of the Bible. They also arranged to include some recreation and a few lectures not actually relating to Sunday schools. The visitors were at first housed in a sort of camp, which rapidly grew into a permanent summer colony. In 1876 the session was lengthened to three weeks and later, with the introduction of new subjects, it extended to two months. In 1878 the Literary and Scientific Circle (home-study courses) was launched, and 7000 persons took this work in the first year. At times in after years as many as 25,000 were enrolled at once. At the assembly grounds in 1879 a school for teachers in secular subjects was opened, also a school of languages, later known as the College of Liberal Arts. Other developments, year after year, were Schools of Mathematics and Sciences, of Library Training, Domestic Science, Music, Arts and Crafts, Expression, Physical Education, Practical Arts and–in co-operation with Cornell University in 1912–Agriculture. The growth of the institution was rapid. Although founded by Methodists, many churches were represented at the first gathering and there was never any disposition to make the teaching of religious subjects denominational. One after another there came to be built on the grounds lecture halls with seating capacities of from 200 to 5000, a theater, club-houses, gymnasiums, a memorial church, memorial library, a colonial market place, etc. Between 1924 and 1932 (when the attendance fell off considerably because of the industrial depression) about 45,000 persons attended the general assembly each season. A magazine, the Chautauquan, was published from 1880 to 1914.

Hundreds of local assemblies appeared within two or three decades in the United States and Canada, imitating in a limited degree the Chautauqua plan and often calling themselves "Chautauquas." At least two of these, the Catholic Summer School at Lake

Champlain and the Jewish Chautauqua Society at Atlantic City, N. J., have been permanent and extensive in their programs. Shortly after 1900 the traveling Chautauqua appeared—promoted by a lecture bureau, moving from town to town, giving a week or more of lectures, concerts and recitals, from two to three programs a day, usually in a large tent. This had a considerable popularity for more than a decade.

CHECKS AND BALANCES is the term used to denote the "separation of powers" of government that was the underlying principle upon which the Government of the United States was created by the Convention of 1787. This theory became popular in America in large part due to the writings of Montesquieu and William Blackstone. It consists in setting off legislative and executive departments from each other and the courts against both. Each department of government is supposed to operate as far as possible within a separate sphere of administration, but the co-operation of all three is necessary for the conduct of the government.

The makers of our Constitution were aware of the weakness of the Continental government under the Articles of Confederation. This consisted in the complete conduct of the government by the Continental Congress with practically no executive or judicial departments. For this reason the office of President of the United States was created and largely modeled upon the kingship of Great Britain. In order to prevent executive aggression, such as had caused the misgovernment of George III, the system of checks and balances was introduced and also provision was made for a Federal judiciary. Furthermore it was provided that the Senate and House of Representatives should act as checks upon each other in the national Congress.

CHEQUAMEGON BAY, on the southern coast of Lake Superior, is noted as the site of the first dwelling occupied by white men in what is now Wisconsin. The French traders, Groseilliers and Radisson, built a hut somewhere on the west shore of the bay, probably in 1658. Other traders dwelt on this bay 1660–63 and were visited in the spring of 1661 by Father Ménard, first missionary to the Northwest. In 1665 Father Claude Allouez built a mission house near the southwest end of the bay. There his successor, Father Jacques Marquette, came in 1669 and remained for two years.

CHEROKEE NATION v. GEORGIA (5 Peters 1). In 1791 the Cherokee made a treaty of cession with the United States wherein they were guaranteed the remainder of their territory. When Georgia, in 1802, ceded her western lands to the Federal Government she received the promise that all Indians should be removed from her limits as soon as it could be done peaceably and on reasonable terms. Embittered by the failure of the Government to effect removal and by the organization of an independent Cherokee government within her borders, Georgia in 1828 and 1829 extended her laws over the Indians and began to occupy their territory. The Cherokees could get no protection from President Jackson and therefore appealed to the Supreme Court, filing an original bill (Dec. 12, 1830) for an injunction restraining Georgia from interfering with the Cherokees or enforcing her laws within the Cherokee Nation. Georgia refused to defend the suit. The sympathies of the Court were with the Cherokees, but the majority opinion was that since the Cherokees were not citizens of the United States, nor, as contended by them, a foreign nation, they were not competent to appear as a party to a suit in the Supreme Court.

CHEROKEE STRIP is a term improperly applied to an area officially designated as "a perpetual outlet, West." Both the terms "Strip" and "Outlet" are used. Guaranteed to the Cherokee Indians by treaties of 1828 and 1833 as an outlet, it was not to be occupied for homes.

The area comprises about 12,000 square miles, and lies between 96° and 100° W. Long., and 36° and 37° N. Lat. The Treaty of 1866 compelled the Cherokee Nation to sell portions to friendly Indians.

The Strip was leased by the Cherokee Nation in 1883 to the Cherokee Strip Livestock Association for five years at $100,000 a year; the lease was renewed, but was terminated before expiration by the United States. In 1891 the United States purchased the Cherokee Strip for $8,595,736.12. Opened by a "run" on Sept. 16, 1893, it became part of the Territory of Oklahoma.

CHERRY VALLEY MASSACRE (Nov. 11, 1778), in which Butler's Rangers, with Indians under Brant, attacked this important outpost in the upper Susquehanna Valley, was marked by special Indian savagery in retaliation for their losses at Oriskany. Whole families were surprised in their homes. A few escaped, 30 were killed, while 71, taken prisoners, were mostly released next day. All the buildings were burned and cattle taken. Sixteen soldiers were killed but the remainder held the fort and cared for the returning refugees.

This massacre directly determined the Sullivan expedition against the Iroquois (1779).

CHESAPEAKE AND OHIO CANAL, popularly known as "the Old Ditch," was a joint project of the United States, Maryland and Virginia. It was the legal successor of the Potomac Company in the attempt to connect the Chesapeake Bay with the Ohio River by a system of water transportation. The plan was to construct a series of locks and canals around the rapids and falls of the Potomac from Georgetown to Cumberland. From there the Ohio was to be reached at one of its tributaries, the Youghiogheny. Ground was first broken on July 4, 1828, and the canal was completed to Cumberland by 1850. Funds were contributed principally by Maryland, the terminal cities and the United States. The fifty shares of stock in the Potomac Company which George Washington had donated to a proposed National University were also invested and lost, for the corporation was not successful in reaching the Ohio. It failed on account of the inherent difficulty of the task, and because of competition from the Baltimore and Ohio Railroad, which reached Wheeling about 1852. Continuing as a local enterprise on the Potomac River, it was placed (1889) in the hands of receivers, who, in 1938, sold the property to the United States.

CHESAPEAKE CAPES, BATTLE OF (1781). A naval engagement, Sept. 5–9, which led to the surrender of Cornwallis at Yorktown. When a British fleet of nineteen ships arrived at the entrance of the Chesapeake with reinforcements for Cornwallis, it found a French fleet of 24 ships, under DeGrasse, already there. The battle was fought on an easterly course in converging lines. The British lost one ship and had several badly damaged; as a result they could not attack again and Barras' French squadron of eight ships, transporting siege guns from Newport for the attack on Yorktown, was enabled to enter the Capes. The British fleet returned to New York and Cornwallis was trapped.

CHESAPEAKE CAPTURED BY SHANNON. On June 1, 1813, the United States frigate *Chesapeake*, 38 guns, Capt. James Lawrence, with an untrained crew sailed out of Boston on a cruise. At 5:45 P.M. she met H. B. M. frigate *Shannon*, 38 guns, 330 highly trained men, Capt. Philip Vere Broke commanding. In the opening maneuvers, Lawrence lost an opportunity to rake his enemy and exposed his own ship to a terrible bombardment at pistol range. By 5:55 all the American officers were killed or wounded and the crew was in a panic. Lawrence, dying, gave his last order "Don't give up the ship." Leading his crew personally Broke boarded, and at 6:05 had taken the *Chesapeake*.

CHESAPEAKE-LEOPARD INCIDENT (1807). On June 22, off Hampton Roads, the American frigate *Chesapeake* was stopped by the British ship *Leopard*, whose commander demanded the surrender of four seamen, claiming them to be deserters from the British ships *Melampus* and *Halifax*. Upon the refusal of the American commander, Capt. James Barron, to give up the men, the *Leopard* opened fire. The American vessel, having just begun a long voyage to the Mediterranean, was unprepared for battle, and to the repeated broadsides from the British replied with only one gun which was discharged with a live coal from the galley. After the *Chesapeake's* hull had been struck with fourteen round shot, her mainmast and mizzenmast had been "irreparably injured" (Decatur's letter to Secretary of Navy, July 4, 1807), her rigging had been greatly damaged and her crew had lost "three men killed and twenty wounded" (Log of *Chesapeake*), Barron surrendered his vessel.

The British boarding party recovered only one deserter, the others having left the *Chesapeake* before she sailed; but three American seamen were also removed by force. The British captain refused to accept the *Chesapeake* as a prize, but forced her to creep back into port in her crippled condition. Barron was court-martialed, found guilty of "neglecting, on the probability of an engagement, to clear his ship for action" (*Proceedings . . . Court-Martial . . . Barron*), and suspended from the navy for five years without pay. England's offer to make reparations enabled President Jefferson to avert war, in spite of the widespread anger throughout the United States. Negotiations were prolonged by Great Britain until 1811 when she formally disavowed the act and returned two of the men, one having meanwhile died and another having been hanged as a deserter.

CHEYENNE, WYO., was established in 1867 by the advancing Union Pacific Railroad. After a brief boom as "Hell on Wheels" it became the chief outfitting point for the hordes of gold seekers flocking into the mining booms in the Sweetwater region and the Black Hills, and, as home of the Wyoming Stock Growers' Association, "the administrative and social metropolis of the immensely larger cattlemen's range" of the Northern Plains. The collapse of the cattle boom of the 1880's ended its great days of glamour and romance.

CHICAGO, ILL. To the Indians the word Chicago is said to have signified "great," "powerful," "skunk," or "wild onion." To the discontented Chicago novelist Henry B. Fuller, this was "the only great city in the world to which all of its citizens have come for the avowed object of making money." It is true that Chicago is most famous for its businessmen. Its history may be said to begin neither in 1675, when Père Marquette visited the site where the Chicago River meets Lake Michigan, nor in 1812, when the Potawatomis massacred the retreating garrison of Fort Dearborn, nor in 1833, when the town was incorporated, but in 1852, when the Michigan Southern and Michigan Central railroads linked the future metropolis for the first time with the eastern seaboard.

Chicago's first mayor, the New Yorker William Butler Ogden, did not need to be told that here was the logical railroad center of the nation. With the Connecticut Yankee Walter Loomis Newberry (the future donor of the Newberry Library), he founded the Galena and Chicago Union (1836) out of which grew the Chicago and North Western. Encouraged by the enterprise of Ogden and other Chicagoans, the Virginian Cyrus Hall McCormick, the inventor of the reaper, settled here in 1847, convinced that his factory should be near the expanding wheat-fields of the Middle West. In 1855 came the New Yorker George Mortimer Pullman, who patented the folding upper berth in 1864 and the adjustable lower in 1865. In 1865 Marshall Field arrived. At first a clerk in the dry-goods house of Cooley, Wadsworth & Co., this diligent, cautious native of Conway, Mass., founded Field, Palmer & Leiter in 1865, Field, Leiter & Co. in 1867, and in 1881 Marshall Field & Co., which became America's biggest department store. The wisest of all Chicago investors, he died in 1906 leaving $120,000,000, the greatest of all Chicago fortunes.

As early as 1862 Chicago outdistanced Cincinnati to become the nation's pork-packing center. By 1875 Philip D. Armour from New York and Gustavus F. Swift from Massachusetts decided that here, on the edge of the stockyards, was the inevitable site for their packing plants. The Great Fire of 1871 was an incentive rather than a deterrent. By 1890 Chicago, with 1,100,000 inhabitants, was America's second city.

Chicagoans could not sing small with these statistics. Marshall Field's one-time partner Potter Palmer was world-famous for his great hotel, The Palmer House. When the hotel vanished in the fire, he built a more extravagant replica in 1873, and in 1882 erected a formidable Gothic castle (since destroyed) for his home on Lake Shore Drive.

At the same time Chicago was the scene of violent uprisings growing out of the unrest of the labor force. On May 4, 1886, occurred the Haymarket Riot, when someone, no one knows who, threw a bomb that killed one and injured seventy. Anarchists were involved. One agitator committed suicide; four were hanged; three were sentenced to prison, to be ultimately pardoned by Governor Altgeld who questioned the justice of their trial. Even more serious was the Pullman Strike of 1894, when U. S. Attorney General Olney, overriding Altgeld, enjoined the American Railway Union led by Eugene V. Debs from interfering with the mails and interstate commerce.

But Chicago in the late 19th century was equally remarkable for philanthropy, no matter if the University of Chicago owed its rebirth in 1891 to the New Yorker John D. Rockefeller. The Art Institute was founded in 1879, Jane Addams' Hull House for settlement work in 1889, the Chicago Symphony Orchestra in 1891, and the Field Museum of Natural History (later known as the Chicago Natural History Museum) in 1893. The most important civic enterprise of all was the World's Columbian Ex-position of 1893, or World's Fair, visited by 28,-000,000. Though the classic revival style in which most of the buildings were designed distressed such great Chicago architects as Louis Sullivan and Frank Lloyd Wright, no one could deny that the Fair had a beneficial influence on city planning. The lagoons and vistas conceived by architect Daniel H. Burnham led the public to appreciate the magnificent Chicago plan proposed by Burnham in 1897. To this plan the city is indebted for the dramatic development of the lake front.

The most flamboyant businessman to emerge since the Fair was the utilities expert Samuel Insull, whose holding companies collapsed in 1932. Insull owed his start in Chicago to Marshall Field, who lent him the wherewithal in 1892 to buy into the local Edison company. Another Chicagoan under an obligation to the merchant was Joseph Medill, who borrowed enough in 1874 to assume control of the Tribune. Medill's grandson, Robert R. McCormick, was publisher of the newspaper in 1941 when Field's grandson, Marshall Field III, challenged the Tribune by launching the Times (later known as the Sun-Times.)

The population in 1960 was 3,550,404, second only to New York.

CHICAGO FIRE (Oct. 8–9, 1871). Modern Chicago began its growth in 1833; by 1871 it had a population of 300,000. Across the broad plain which skirts the river's mouth buildings by the thousand extended, constructed with no thought of resistance to fire. Even the sidewalks were built of resinous pine and the single pumping station which supplied the mains with water was covered with a wooden roof! The season was one of excessive dryness. Up from the plains of the far Southwest blew week after week a scorching wind which withered the growing crops and made the structures of pine-built Chicago dry as tinder. A conflagration of appalling proportions awaited only the starting spark.

It began on Sunday evening, Oct. 8. Where it started is clear; how it started no man knows. Living in a hovel at the corner of Jefferson and DeKoven streets was a poor Irish family by the name of O'Leary. The traditional story is that Mrs. O'Leary went out to the barn with a lamp to milk her cow; the lamp was upset and cow, stable and Chicago were engulfed in one common ruin. But Mrs. O'Leary testified under oath that she was safe abed and knew nothing about the fire until she was called by a friend of the family.

Once started, the fire moved onward resistlessly to the north and east until there was nothing more to burn. Between nine o'clock on Sunday evening and ten-thirty the following night an area of three and one half square miles, including the business center of the city, was burned, over 17,000 buildings were destroyed, and 100,000 people were rendered homeless. From Taylor Street to Lincoln Park, from the river to the lake, the city lay in ruins. The direct property loss was about $200,000,000. The loss of human lives, while never known, is commonly estimated at about 300.

CHICKAMAUGA, BATTLE OF (Sept. 19–20, 1863). The Army of the Cumberland, under Gen. W. S. Rosecrans (U.), maneuvered an inferior Confederate force under Gen. Braxton Bragg out of Chattanooga, an important railway center, by threatening it from the west while sending two flanking columns far to the south. On finding that Bragg had evacuated the city and was retreating, Rosecrans pushed his forces eastward in a "general pursuit" until he found that the main Confederate Army had halted directly in his front. In order to unite his scattered corps he moved northward to concentrate in front of Chattanooga. Bragg attacked on the morning of Sept. 19 in the valley of Chickamauga Creek, about ten miles from Chattanooga. The effective strength was: Confederate, 66,000; Union, 58,000.

The fighting began with a series of poorly coordinated attacks in *échelon* by Confederate divisions which were met by Union counterattacks. From the start it was the concern of Rosecrans to keep open his communications with Chattanooga and this made him constantly anxious for the situation on his left wing. On the second day the battle was resumed by the Confederate right in such a way as to make Rosecrans fear a turning movement. A needless transfer of troops to the Union left, plus a blundering order which opened a gap in the center, so weakened the right that it was swept from the field by Longstreet's attack. Rosecrans and his staff were carried along by the routed soldiers. Thomas (U.), commanding the Federal left, with the aid of troops under Granger, held the army together and after nightfall withdrew into Chattanooga. Both commanding generals lost heavily in reputation, Rosecrans because of his ill-considered orders and his flight from the battlefield, Bragg because of his failure to follow up his subordinates' success and his subjecting his troops to needless slaughter. Rosecrans was presently superseded by Grant, but President Davis sustained Bragg, against his corps commanders' protests until after his defeat by Grant at Chattanooga.

CHILD LABOR has been virtually eliminated in the United States—except in agriculture—thanks to restrictive legislation passed by both the states and the Federal Government in the past two decades. Three Federal acts regulate the employment of children. The Fair Labor Standards Act (1938) sets the minimum age at 14 for employment outside of school hours in nonmanufacturing, at 16 for employment during school hours in interstate commerce, and at 18 for occupations called hazardous by the Secretary of Labor. The Public Contracts Act sets the minimum at 16 years for boys and at 18 for girls employed in firms that supply goods under Federal contract. The Sugar Act sets the minimum age at 14 for employment in cultivating and harvesting sugar beets and cane. State laws vary greatly both as to standards and coverage. They govern the ages, hours, and conditions of employment and prohibit certain occupations for minors.

Most of this important legislation, which succeeded in radically curbing the social evil of child labor, came about as the result of aggressive campaigns early in the 20th century. Before the early 1900's, child labor was rampant. Knowledge of its extent prior to 1870 is fragmentary due to the fact that child labor statistics were not available, but juvenile employment probably existed in the spinning schools established early in the colonies. Textile mills founded after the Revolutionary War are known to have employed children for excessively long hours, but there is no indication of an acute problem.

However, as the 19th century advanced, child labor became prevalent. Two fifths of the factory workers in New England were reported to be children in 1832. Agitation for compulsory school attendance legislation had appeared in the previous decade. In the 1840's Connecticut, Massachusetts, and Pennsylvania passed laws limiting the hours of employment of minors in textile factories.

The problem had grown to the point of national significance by the time of the census of 1870, which reported the employment of three quarters of a million children between ten and fifteen years of age. From 1870 to 1910, the number of children reported as gainfully employed increased steadily. Aroused to action, the Knights of Labor projected a campaign for child labor legislation in the 1870's and 1880's which resulted in the enactment of many state laws.

Conditions in canneries, the glass industry, anthracite mining, etc., began to attract considerable attention at the turn of the century. In the South, the threefold rise in numbers of child laborers in the decade ending in 1900 aroused public sentiment for child labor laws. In the North, insistence upon improved standards of legislation and their adequate enforcement led to the formation of the National Child Labor Committee in 1904. This committee, chartered by Congress in 1907 to promote the welfare of America's working children, investigated conditions in various states and industries and spearheaded the push for state legislation with conspicuous success. By 1920, census reports began to reflect the decline in child labor that continued in the 1930's.

However, the backwardness of certain states and the lack of uniformity of state laws after 1910 led to demands for Federal regulation. The U. S. Supreme Court set aside attempts at congressional regulations in 1918 and 1922 (Hammer v. Dagenhart; Bailey v.

Drexel Furniture Co.). Child labor reformers, nevertheless, began to push for a Child Labor Amendment. In 1924, the amendment was submitted to the states for ratification, which has not yet been achieved.

The enactment of the Fair Labor Standards Act in 1938 marked the beginning of the end of the widespread practice of child labor in the United States. In 1960, the major problem was in agriculture. Children who worked in the fields were exempt from the 14-year-minimum age outside school hours set by the Fair Labor Standards Act for most other children, and state laws usually ignored them. In addition, more violations of the 16-year-minimum set by the F. L. S. A. during school hours occurred in agriculture than in any other industry. Many of those illegally at work in commercial agriculture were the children of migratory workers. Numerous studies have shown that they were educationally retarded. According to the U. S. Office of Education, they constituted the nation's largest illiterate group.

CHIMNEY ROCK. A landmark visible at forty miles from any direction in western Nebraska east of the point where the River Platte cuts a way into the highlands and to the plains, listed by Johnson and Hunter in their *Guide Book to Emigrants,* 1847, as being 595 miles from Independence, Mo., and "where the trail leaves the river."

CHINA TRADE, 19TH CENTURY. Cut off from the West Indian Trade, important in the colonial period, American merchants in the years following the Revolution sought new opportunities. Such were discovered in the China trade, which grew rapidly after the *Empress of China* returned to New York in 1785 from a successful voyage. Although New York sent the first vessel, the merchants of Philadelphia, Boston, Baltimore, Providence, Salem and lesser ports were quick to grasp the new possibilities. In the early years the routes generally followed were from the Atlantic ports, around the Cape of Good Hope, across the Indian Ocean and by way of the Dutch East Indies to China. Until after the Treaty of Nanking (1842) the only Chinese port open to foreign trade was Canton.

The early cargoes carried to China comprised chiefly silver dollars and ginseng, a plant erroneously believed by the Chinese to have curative properties. When in 1787 Capts. John Kendrick in the *Columbia* and Robert Gray in the *Lady Washington* sailed from Boston for the northwest coast of America, and Gray with a load of sea-otter peltries continued to Canton where his furs found a ready sale, the problem of a salable commodity for the Chinese market was solved. For the next two decades Americans exchanged clothing, hardware and various knickknacks in the Northwest for sea otter and other furs, thus developing a three-cornered trade route. As sea otters gradually disappeared traders shifted to seals, found in large numbers on the southern coast of Chile and the islands of the South Pacific. Sandalwood, obtained in Hawaii and other Pacific Islands, also became early an important item of trade. In return American sea-captains brought back tea, china, enameled ware, nankeens and silks. The China trade was characterized by long voyages and frequently by great personal danger in trading with Indians and South Sea islanders. Success rested largely on the business capacity of the ship's captain. The profits, however, were usually large. At its height in 1818–19 the old China trade (combined imports and exports) reached about $19,000,000.

After the Opium War (1840–42) between Great Britain and China, the latter nation was forced to open four additional ports to British trade. Similar rights for Americans were demanded by Commodore Lawrence Kearny and, shortly after, by the Treaty of Wanghia (1844), such privileges were obtained.

CHINESE IMMIGRATION AND LABOR. Beset by wars and famine at home and attracted by the story of gold in California, Chinese began to come to America in large numbers in the middle of the 19th century. The first recorded Chinese immigrants reached San Francisco in 1848, though the first really significant immigration occurred in 1852, when some 18,000 Chinese arrived in San Francisco, which then had fewer than 37,000 inhabitants. The need for unskilled labor, created by the Civil War, and the construction of the Union Pacific Railroad, paved the way for the Burlingame Treaty of 1868 which, among other things, recognized the reciprocal rights of Chinese and Americans to immigrate at will. Until 1882, when coolie immigration was shut off, the yearly average of Chinese arrivals was around 16,000. Approximately 375,000 had entered the United States by that year.

Barred from staking claims or working virgin properties in California, the majority turned to other fields. At one time, of the 25,000 mechanics and laborers employed by the Central Pacific Railroad Co., 15,000 were Chinese. In the 1870's and 1880's many turned to the land for a living. In 1870, 90% of the agricultural labor in California was Chinese; in 1880, 75%; in 1930, less than 1%. The second generation moved from the land and by 1920 there were but 57 Chinese-owned farms in the United States. In lumbering camps and mills Chinese were cutters, scalers and road builders. Today they have almost disappeared from the industry. They were once important in Pacific Coast fisheries, as late as 1890 constituting one half of the 2000 permanent employees of canneries and 7000 to 9000 of the seasonal labor. Today less than 1000 Chinese work in fisheries and canneries. Chinese entered manufacturing and commerce: woolen mills, shoe and cigar factories, underwear factories, pork-packing and fish-drying industries, banking, wholesaling and retailing, exporting and importing. In coastal states approximately 100 important Chinese firms are now engaged in importation and sale of Oriental goods and wares.

With the completion of the Union Pacific Railroad thousands of Chinese were left without employment and so many white settlers had come to California that in 1871 there were said to be three men for every job. In the 1870's Chinese competition at low wages with white labor caused anti-Chinese feeling, expressed by boycotts, "queue" and laundry ordinances, antialien land laws, police taxes, etc. Typical of the times was the agitation led by Dennis Kearney in 1877.

In 1880 the Burlingame Treaty was modified and China recognized the right of the United States to "regulate, limit or suspend . . . but . . . not absolutely prohibit" immigration of Chinese laborers. The way was now paved for the Exclusion Law of 1882, marking the beginning of the policy of Chinese exclusion from the United States, which was extended to Hawaii and the Philippines in 1900 and 1902. Chinese are also subject to the general immigration laws of 1917 and 1924. Under the latter act all aliens not eligible to citizenship are excluded from the country. This applies to Chinese, as the courts have ruled that aliens of Asiatic race are ineligible for American citizenship. Allowances are made for students, business executives and visitors. American-born Orientals possess all the legal rights of citizenship.

CHINOOK JARGON is a medium of communication composed of a combination of about 300 Indian, French and English words. It was employed generally by Indian traders, missionaries and miners and known to Indian interpreters along the Pacific coast from northern California to Alaska. Several Chinook-English dictionaries and religious tracts have been published.

CHIPPEWA, BATTLE OF (July 5, 1814). On the north bank of Chippewa Creek, Gen. Riall had under his command a British force numbering about 2000. Gen. Jacob Brown with 4000 Americans was encamped near by. Riall began his attack at 4 P.M. Simultaneously, Brown ordered an advance of his left. The Americans were repulsed. Winfield Scott's brigade and the artillery were moved forward and engaged the British on the plain south of Chippewa Creek. Superior maneuvering and the effectiveness of the American artillery soon compelled the British to retire in confusion.

CHISHOLM TRAIL was a cattle trail leading north from Texas, across Oklahoma to Abilene, Kans. Much controversy has existed as to the origin of its name and even as to its exact location. It was apparently named for Jesse Chisholm, a mixed blood Cherokee.

who followed a part of this route in freighting supplies and may have guided a detachment of soldiers over it soon after the close of the Civil War. The southern extension of the Chisholm Trail originated near San Antonio, Texas, though there is considerable doubt as to whether or not the Texas portion of it was ever known by that name. From here it ran north and a little east to the Red River which it crossed a few miles from the site of the present town of Ringgold, Texas. It continued north across Oklahoma, passing near the sites of the present towns of Waurika, Duncan, Marlow, Chickasha, El Reno and Enid to Caldwell, Kans. It therefore ran not far from the line of the 98th meridian. From Caldwell it ran north and a little east past the site of Wichita to Abilene, Kans. At the close of the Civil War the low price of cattle in Texas and the much higher prices in the North and East caused many Texas ranchmen to drive large herds north to market. The establishment of a cattle depot and shipping point at Abilene, Kans., in 1867 brought many herds to that point to be shipped to market over the southern branch of the Union Pacific Railway. Many of these were driven over the Chisholm Trail which in a few years became the most popular route for driving cattle from Texas to the North.

The Chisholm Trail decreased in importance after 1871 when Abilene lost its pre-eminence as a shipping point for Texas cattle, due to the westward advance of settlement. Dodge City became the chief shipping point and another trail farther west, crossing the Red River near Doan's Store, Texas, became of paramount importance. The extension of the Atchison, Topeka and Santa Fé Railway to Caldwell, Kans., in 1880, however, again made the Chisholm Trail a most important route for driving Texas cattle to the North, and this position it retained until the building of additional trunk lines of railway south into Texas caused rail shipments to take the place of the former trail driving of Texas cattle north to market.

CHISHOLM v. GEORGIA, 1793 (2 Dallas, 419). The heirs of Alexander Chisholm, citizens of South Carolina, sued the State of Georgia to enforce payment of claims against that state. Georgia refused to defend the suit and the Supreme Court, upholding the right of citizens of one state to sue another state, under Art. III, Sec. 2 of the Federal Constitution, ordered judgment by default against Georgia. No writ of execution was attempted because of threats by the lower house of the Georgia legislature. The Eleventh Amendment ended such actions.

CHOUTEAU (P., JR.) AND COMPANY was the successor to Pratte, Chouteau and Co. The latter was the Western Department of the American Fur Company, which was sold out by John Jacob Astor to Bartholomew Berthold, Bernard Pratte, Pierre Chouteau, Jr., and Jean Pierre Cabanne in 1834. The company previously had been operated on a basis of an equal division of profits and losses with the parent company on returns from all posts on the Missouri River and its tributaries; those of the Mississippi below Prairie du Chien; posts in the Osage country in present Oklahoma; and in southwest Missouri. Some of the important forts controlled by this company were: Forts Pierre, Clark, Mackenzie, Union, Benton, Sarpy and John. Most of their business was on the Missouri River and its dependencies. The name of the company was changed in 1838 to Pierre Chouteau, Jr. and Company, with name Pierre being commonly abbreviated. The company carried on business until about 1866. P. Chouteau, Jr. and Co. made a practice of distributing shares of the company among its most capable agents.

CHOUTEAU'S TRADING POSTS. The Chouteau family had more extensive interests in the fur trade than the several posts established by them directly would indicate. Pierre Chouteau spent most of his time among the Indians. His brother Auguste attended to the purchasing of goods used by them in their trade and to the sale of the furs gathered therefrom. Trading largely among the Big and Little Osage, the Chouteaus, in 1794, erected a post called Fort Carondelet, of considerable size and well fortified, in what is now Bates County, Mo. The Chouteau brothers were given, by the Spanish government, the exclusive right to trade with these Indians for a period of six years. At the expiration of this time Pierre Chouteau persuaded the Osage to move to the Arkansas River, where a fur-trading rendezvous was established, about 1802, at the junction of the Verdigris and Grand rivers in the present State of Oklahoma. In 1809, Pierre and his son, A. P. Chouteau, became stockholders in the St. Louis Missouri Fur Company and were restrained by agreement from trading on their private account. Auguste Chouteau continued to send out trappers on his individual account. By 1820 the elder Chouteaus had retired from active participation in the trade.

In 1822 Col. A. P. Chouteau occupied the trading post called "La Saline," where Salina, Okla., now stands. The following years he enlarged his operations and established a trading house just below the falls of the Verdigris. In 1836 he built a stockade fort, near the present town of Purcell, Okla., where extensive trade was carried on with the Comanche, Kiowa, Wichita and allied tribes, until his death in 1838. These posts bore the name of Chouteau.

The only other trading post bearing the name was established by François G. Chouteau on an island three miles below the mouth of Kansas River. This was washed into the river in 1826 and another built about ten miles up the Kansas.

CHRISTIAN CHURCHES, formerly called Disciples of Christ, is an indigenous American denomination with an estimated membership of 1,943,599 (1958). Thomas Campbell, an Irish Seceder Presbyterian minister, came to America in 1807, preached in western Pennsylvania, and soon broke with his church because of his desire for a wider fellowship on a simple evangelical and nontheological basis. In 1809 he organized The Christian Association of Washington, Pa., and published *A Declaration and Address*, urging the unity of Christians by a restoration of primitive faith and practice in accordance with the dictum, "Where the Scriptures speak we speak, where the Scriptures are silent we are silent." The adoption of the immersionist position led to a union of the "reformers" with the Baptists in 1813, but this union, never without mutual reservations, lasted only until 1830.

Meanwhile Thomas Campbell's son, Alexander, a much more vigorous personality, had assumed leadership of the movement. He disseminated his ideas widely by publishing two magazines, *The Christian Baptist* (1823–30) and *The Millennial Harbinger* (1830–70), by extensive preaching and lecture tours, and by founding Bethany College, Bethany, W. Va., of which he was president for twenty years. The Disciples and a great part of the followers of Barton W. Stone, known as "Christians," united in 1832.

The movement expanded with the westward growth of the nation, never made great progress in the East, but became strong in the Middle West. Its first national organization for missionary work was formed in 1849. The Disciples escaped division on slavery and the Civil War, but a cleavage resulting from differences of policy regarding missionary societies led to the separation of a conservative element, known in statistics since 1906 as "Churches of Christ" The Disciples are congregational in polity. Their local churches are generally known as Christian churches, and the official name of the denomination is now Christian Churches (Disciples of Christ), International Convention.

CHRISTIAN SCIENCE is the religion founded by Mary Baker Eddy (1821–1910) and represented by the Church of Christ, Scientist. The Christian Science denomination was founded by Mrs. Eddy at Boston in 1879, following her discovery of this religion and science in 1866 and her issuing of its textbook, *Science and Health with Key to the Scriptures*, in 1875. It consists of the Mother Church, the First Church of Christ, Scientist, in Boston, Mass., and branch churches or societies composed of local congregations.

CHRISTINA, FORT, was established by Peter Minuit and the Swedes who landed with him at "The Rocks" on March 29, 1638. It was the capital of New Sweden until 1643 and was made the seat of authority again in 1654. The following year it was surrendered to the Dutch who in turn surrendered it to the English in 1664. The town that grew around the fort was not only the first permanent white settlement in Delaware and the whole Delaware River valley, but was also the antecedent of the present city of Wilmington.

CHURCH AND STATE, SEPARATION OF. Nine of the thirteen American colonies had established churches. In Massachusetts, Connecticut and New Hampshire the Congregational Church was established by law; in Maryland, Virginia, North Carolina, South Carolina and Georgia, and in New York City and three neighboring counties, the Anglican Church was established.

With the formation of new state governments following the Declaration of Independence, separation of church and state came about more or less as a matter of course where establishment had been more a matter of theory than of fact. Such was the case in all the Anglican states except Virginia. Here the church had been strongly intrenched and a bitter struggle ensued. Baptists, Presbyterians, Methodists and Lutherans, assisted by such liberal statesmen as Jefferson and Madison, combined to fight establishment. Petitions flooded the Virginia Assembly from 1776 to 1779 and in the latter year a bill was passed cutting off state support. In this year also Jefferson's "Bill for establishing religious freedom" was introduced and after six years of bitter debate finally passed (Dec. 17, 1785).

In the New England states disestablishment was much longer delayed. The unpopularity of the Anglican Church, due to its large Tory membership, aided in its disestablishment. In New England, on the other hand, the Congregational Church was the church of the patriots. The Revolution, nevertheless, brought with it a strong movement to separate church and state in New England, led by the Baptists. Though unsuccessful at the time, the agitation was continued, and with the growth of Methodism and Episcopalianism in New England after 1790, the nonconforming bodies united with a growing liberal element in Congregationalism to bring about separation. This was accomplished in 1818 in Connecticut, in 1819 in New Hampshire, but not until 1833 in Massachusetts.

CHURCH MEMBERSHIP. Although the religious motive was strongly present in the establishment of a majority of the thirteen colonies, yet the economic motive was far more powerful in bringing individual colonists. This fact, together with the barriers placed in the way of the average person becoming a church member in a new country, meant that only a relatively small proportion of the colonial population was actually churched. At the close of the colonial period there were, according to careful investigation, 3105 congregations of all kinds in the English colonies. Of these 658 were Congregational, 543 Presbyterian, 498 Baptist, 480 Anglican, 298 Quaker, 251

Dutch and German Reformed, 151 Lutheran and 50 Catholic. The German sectaries are not included, but their number was relatively small. New England was the best-churched section, though even here the proportion of church members to the total population was about one to eight. In the Middle colonies, where the German and Scotch-Irish element was large and widely scattered and had come largely without ministers, the proportion was much smaller, probably not more than one to fifteen. In the Southern colonies the proportion was still less.

With the opening of the national period the churches which formerly had Old World connections achieved national organizations and began to think in terms of national need. This was particularly true of the Presbyterian, Methodist and Baptist bodies, and these were the groups most successful in following population westward, resulting in rapid growth. Thus the Methodists, with but 15,000 members at the time of their organization into a separate church (1784), had grown to 740,459 by 1840. The Baptists numbered 740,026 in 1844. The Presbyterians at the time of their great division (1837) had more than 200,000. The Congregational and Episcopalian bodies, the two churches which had been established in nine of the colonies and for that reason had the largest colonial prestige, failed to develop any adequate method of following population westward and as a result lagged far behind. The great German and Irish immigration brought the Catholic membership to 600,000 by 1830; by 1860 it had increased to 4,500,000. The Protestant group to profit most from immigration was the Lutheran. In 1821 they numbered 41,201; by 1861 they had increased to 246,788, and by 1901 to 1,625,185, the latter figure showing the result of the large Scandinavian influx following the Civil War. In more recent years the Jews also have grown tremendously and now rank as one of the major religious bodies in America.

The last Federal census of religious bodies was taken in 1936. Estimates of church membership for the year 1958 were recorded in the *Yearbook of the American Churches,* edition for 1960. It was calculated that there were nearly 110,000,000 church members, or approximately 63% of the population, on the basis of estimates by 251 bodies. The larger bodies were the Roman Catholic Church (39,500,-000), the Baptist churches (27 denominations, 20,-500,000), the Methodist churches (21 denominations, 12,200,000), the Lutheran churches (18 denominations, 7,800,000), the Jewish congregations (5,500,-000), the Presbyterian churches (10 denominations, over 4,000,000), the Protestant Episcopal Church (3,000,000), the Eastern Orthodox Churches (21 communions, 2,500,000), the United Church of Christ (2,200,000), the Churches of Christ (2,000,-000), the Christian (Disciples) Churches (1,900,-000), and the Latter Day Saints (6 Mormon bodies, 1,500,000).

CHURCH MEMBERSHIP SUFFRAGE was the means used by New England Puritans to control their theocracies against dissent. When the Puritans in the trading company of Massachusetts Bay retreated to America with their charter they established a theocracy, but without disturbing the outer shell of the trading company structure. They could maintain this theocracy successfully only so long as they could control the General Court of freemen or stockholders, which necessitated limiting freemanship to those who approved of the theocracy. This they could do by refusing to admit new freemen, but when pressure from dissatisfied nonfreemen became too great, they decided to accept a limited number on condition of orthodox church membership. After the restoration the king demanded of Massachusetts that the church membership qualification be removed, but although the colony made a gesture of complying, the requirement was not essentially altered. Through the influence of Massachusetts the colony of New Haven also adopted the principle of church membership suffrage. Among the other New England colonies it did not exist by specific regulation, although voters had to be in good standing in Connecticut and Plymouth. By the fusion of Connecticut and New Haven in the charter of 1662 the narrow suffrage ended in the latter colony, as it did in Massachusetts when the charter was annulled in 1684.

CHURUBUSCO, BATTLE OF (Mexican War, Aug. 20, 1847). Victorious at Contreras, Scott the same day encountered Santa Anna's principal army at Churubusco, four miles below Mexico City. Mexican engineers had prepared scientifically constructed works of great strength covering the bridge over the Churubusco River and fortified a massive convent near by. These Scott assaulted simultaneously. The defenders resisted stubbornly, but after losing 6000 killed, wounded and prisoners, were routed and retreated to the capital. Scott reported 133 killed, 905 wounded and missing. Eighty American deserters, enlisted in a Mexican "Foreign Legion," were captured.

CÍBOLA, a native name for the Zuñi country, first heard by Fray Marcos de Niza in 1539. His report (garbled and exaggerated in Mexico City) of "seven very great cities" in the North resulted in the Coronado expedition. As exploration advanced, the name Cíbola came to mean the entire Pueblo Indian country, and was extended to the Great Plains which, until late Spanish times, were called *los llanos de Cíbola.* As an administrative term, Cíbola was soon changed to New Mexico, but in one way the older name survived. The strange "cows" found on the plains were first called *vacas de Cíbola;* later this was shortened to *cíbolos* (buffalo).

CIMARRON, PROPOSED TERRITORY OF, known as the Public Land Strip, or No Man's Land, extended in longitude from 100° to 103°, in latitude from 36° 30′ to 37°.

Settled by squatters and cattlemen, the territory had no law, so to protect the squatter claims a movement was started to organize the country into Cimarron Territory. In March, 1887, territorial representatives drew up resolutions assuming authority for the territory. The proposal was referred to the Committee on Territories in Congress. There it remained. The area now constitutes the panhandle of Oklahoma.

CINCINNATI was located opposite the mouth of the Licking River in the Symmes Purchase by three proprietors, Matthias Denman, Robert Patterson and John Filson. Israel Ludlow replaced Filson, who mysteriously disappeared in the fall of 1788. The first houses were built in the winter of 1788–89. The original name of Losantiville (*L* for Licking, *os* for mouth, *anti* for opposite, *ville* for city) was changed to Cincinnati (after the society of that name) by Gov. Arthur St. Clair, who made it the capital of the Northwest Territory, 1790–1800. Fort Washington added to the importance of the little town, which had 2540 people by 1800. It was incorporated as a town in 1802 and as a city in 1819.

The early inhabitants were chiefly of New Jersey and Pennsylvania origin, but the population became more cosmopolitan as the city grew. By 1860 Cincinnati had 161,044 inhabitants, 45% of whom were foreign-born. The large German element, arriving in the decades 1830–60, played a particularly important part in the city's history.

The importance of Southern trade, and prejudice against the many illiterate free Negroes, made Cincinnati hostile to abolitionists, a mob on one occasion destroying the press of Birney's *Philanthropist.* Know-Nothingism, directed against the Germans and Irish, flared up in the 1850's, but soon subsided. In the Civil War Cincinnati, though losing its Southern trade, was loyal to the Union. In 1862, when threatened by Confederate advances, its citizens quickly organized to defend it, but the danger soon passed. Morgan's raid of 1863 went around the city.

Well located on the Ohio River to command Western and Southern markets, for many years Cincinnati rightly claimed the titles of "Queen City of the West" and "Porkopolis." In manufacturing it ranked third among American cities by 1860. But iron ore and coal were too remote, meat packing moved westward to the newer farming states, trunk-line railroads reduced the importance of the Ohio River and Cincinnati's leadership passed away.

CINCINNATI, SOCIETY OF THE. In June, 1783, shortly before the disbanding of the Continental Army, an organization of its officers who had formed lasting friendships through service together was suggested by Gen. Henry Knox. At the headquarters of

Baron von Steuben near Fishkill, N. Y., the organization was consummated, with Washington as the first president, and was named in honor of Cincinnatus, the Roman dictator, in allusion to the approaching return of the officers to civil pursuits. Its first object was to raise a fund for the widows and children of those slain in the Revolutionary War and it also hoped to promote a closer union among the states. Its membership consisted of the army officers and their eldest male descendants, or if direct descent failed, collateral descendants were eligible. It was divided into state societies, and there was a branch in France, which was destroyed by the Revolution in 1792. The Society aroused antagonism at first among ultrarepublicans who believed that it was setting itself up as an aristocracy. Alexander Hamilton was the second president. Hamilton Fish (1808–93), son of Nicholas Fish, one of the founders, was president from 1854 until his death. Through failure of heirs, most of the state societies had disintegrated by 1900, but a revival of the general organization was effected in 1902.

CIRCUIT RIDERS (MINISTERIAL). Circuit riding was devised by John Wesley for carrying on his religious movement in England. A circuit consisted of numerous preaching places scattered over a relatively large district served by one or more lay preachers. The original American circuit riders introduced Methodism into the colonies. Robert Strawbridge, who came to America about 1764, was the first in the long line. John Wesley sent eight official lay missionaries to America (1769–76), and several came on their own responsibility. By the end of the American Revolution there were about 100 circuit riders in the United States, none of whom was ordained. With the formation of the Methodist Episcopal Church (1784), Francis Asbury was chosen bishop, several of the circuit riders were ordained and the system was widely extended wherever settlements were springing up. It was found peculiarly adaptable to frontier conditions, since one man, equipped with horse and saddlebags, served a great many communities, a circuit often having as many as twenty-five or thirty preaching places. In this way the riders kept pace with the frontier, bringing the influence of religion to new and raw communities. The salary of the preachers was at first uniform, $64 a year, which by 1800 had become $100. Marriage was discouraged, for it usually caused withdrawal from the work. Peter Cartwright is the best known of the frontier preachers. His active career covered the first half of the 19th century, the scene of his labors being Kentucky, Tennessee, Ohio, Indiana and Illinois. The circuit system largely accounts for the even distribution of Methodism throughout the United States. Other religious bodies partially adopted it, particularly the Cumberland Presbyterians.

CIRCUITS, JUDICIAL, AND CIRCUIT RIDING.

When the Federal judicial system, under the Constitution, was established, the country was divided into three circuits (Eastern, Middle and Southern) to each of which two of the justices of the Supreme Court were assigned. They were required to hold the courts twice a year, sitting with district judges. During the first three years of its existence, the Supreme Court had practically no business to transact and the Chief Justice and his associates found employment in riding the circuits and trying cases at *nisi prius*. The roads and accommodations were bad and the duty proved to be onerous. The opening of the first courts in the spring of 1790 found, for example, Justice Iredell, of North Carolina, presiding in Boston. The justices complained, and President Washington wrote in August, 1791, that he hoped Congress would give "relief from these disagreeable tours" to hold 27 courts from New Hampshire to Georgia. Some relief was granted in 1793 in a change by which only one justice was required to sit with a district judge; and thereafter the justices rode the circuits in turn, instead of being confined to fixed circuits. The development of the West added another and another circuit which meant yet more magnificent distances between court sites. The system was changed in 1869. Then circuit judges were appointed, most of whom traveled over several states. The bar, generally speaking, did not ride circuit with the Supreme Court justices or Federal circuit judges.

In the states, from the outset, circuit courts existed, and in the early days the judge, accompanied by many lawyers, rode large circuits. The system tended to develop lawyers of initiative, originality and resourcefulness. The "case lawyer" was a later product.

"CITIZENS' ALLIANCES" were formed first in Kansas, and then in the neighboring states of Iowa and Nebraska, by townsmen who sympathized with the Farmers' Alliances. When the Supreme Council of the "Southern" Alliance met at Ocala, Fla., in December, 1890, it recognized the value of such support and assisted in the organization of these groups into the National Citizens' Alliance as a kind of auxiliary. Even more eager than the farmers for third-party action, members of the Citizens' Alliance were prominent in the several conventions that led to the formation of the People's party, into which their order was speedily absorbed.

CITIZENSHIP may be defined as membership in a political community. During the colonial period, the American people were accustomed to calling themselves "subjects" of the English king, the term subject having a connotation appropriate to a monarchy. The English law, feudal in origin, made each person born within the colonies, save minor exceptions, a subject of the king. Through acts of Parliament and of the colonial assemblies, provisions were made whereby other persons, except certain classes disqualified on grounds of religious faith, could be naturalized as British subjects. With the signing of the Definitive Treaty of Peace of 1783, and especially with the adoption of the Constitution, the term "citizen" gained in favor as more descriptive of membership in a republican political community.

The Constitution recognizes a dual American citizenship, that of the United States and that of the state. It was not at first clear which carried the primary obligation. The earlier opinion, as expressed by Justice Story, was that "every citizen of a State is *ipso facto* a citizen of the United States." This view, that the state claim is antecedent, found acceptance in the Dred Scott Case of 1857. After the Civil War, however, the determination of the North to settle once and for all the status of the Negro led to the enactment of the Fourteenth Amendment, which provided that "All persons born or naturalized in the United States, and subject to the jurisdiction thereof, are citizens of the United States and of the State wherein they reside." Thus, United States citizenship is now primary, that of the state derivative.

The Fourteenth Amendment embodies the English principle of *jus soli*, which fixes citizenship according to the place of birth. As interpreted by the American courts, not only are Negroes, born in this country, citizens of the United States, but so also are Orientals (U. S. v. Wong Kim Ark, 1898). The Indians, living in tribal relations, were not at first deemed to be "under the jurisdiction" of the United States in the sense of the Fourteenth Amendment (Elk v. Williams, 1884), but in 1924 Congress conferred citizenship upon all non-citizen Indians born within the territorial limits of the United States. The principle of *jus sanguinis,* which bases citizenship upon parentage, and which is widely accepted on the continent of Europe, has had some influence upon American policy. By Federal statutes, children born of American parents resident in foreign countries are presumed to be American citizens, though, by the act of 1907, such presumption will lapse unless on attaining the age of eighteen they record at an American consulate their intention to become residents of the United States and to retain their citizenship.

The Constitution, moreover, authorizes Congress to establish "an uniform rule of naturalization." Our Government has from the beginning been friendly to the idea of "acquired" citizenship. An early Federal pronouncement dignifies expatriation as "a natural and inherent right of all people." Hence, laws have been passed making provisions for naturalization of individuals, and special acts have conferred collective American citizenship (with certain exceptions) upon the inhabitants of Hawaii (1900), Puerto Rico (1917) and the Virgin Islands (1927).

CITY MANAGER PLAN, a simplified form of municipal government, originated in Staunton, Va. (1908), but did not attract much attention until after its adoption in Dayton, O., six years later. Then it spread rapidly, particularly in states which have the home-rule charter system, until eventually it gained acceptance in several hundred cities, large and small. Its chief vogue, however, is in the smaller municipalities.

The essential features of the city manager plan are, first, a small council elected by the voters of the city on a nonpartisan ballot; and, second, the appointment by this council of a chief administrative officer known as the city manager who assumes full responsibility for the entire work of municipal administration. The manager is chosen for his administrative capacity; he holds office during the pleasure of the council, and is the most highly paid officer of the city government. In some cases a member of the council serves as titular mayor, but without any important administrative duties.

The city manager attends all meetings of the council, prepares the budget for the council's consideration and appoints all the administrative officials, with a few exceptions such as the city clerk and the members of the public library board. The city charter usually forbids all interference by members of the city council in the manager's routine work, but the council retains the power to enact the ordinances and to decide all questions of general policy. City managers may be chosen from outside the city and in many instances this policy has been pursued.

On the whole the city manager plan has operated successfully, but its success has been most uniform in the smaller municipalities. In the larger cities it has proved a more difficult problem to find competent managers and to keep the managerial office out of politics.

CITY PLANNING. America's strong tradition for good city planning—from the simple colonial settlements of the early 17th century to the complex metropolis of the atomic age—stems from the rich heritage of her cosmopolitan population.

One of the best early colonial city plans was the one prepared for New Haven, Conn., in 1638. Nine large square plots were arranged in rows of three with the central square serving as the town "common" or "green." This large tree-shaded community park, still preserved as part of the Yale University campus, became a distinctive feature of most colonial New England town plans and continued to appear as a prominent element in many towns settled after the Revolutionary War.

In contrast to the large open "green" of the New England town, the "architectural square" was characteristic of the courthouse towns of Virginia, consisting of a smaller green square closely surrounded by private residences, shops, a stately courthouse, and usually one or two churches. The courthouse town, like the New England town, influenced later city plans in the Midwest and South.

Of the important early commercial seaport cities, Boston contained an unplanned maze of narrow winding streets reminiscent of medieval London, while the plans for Charleston, Philadelphia, Annapolis, Williamsburg, and Savannah contained suggestions of Christopher Wren's plan for rebuilding London after the fire of 1666, incorporating axes, radials, diagonals, and squares patterned after the monumental renaissance plans of Paris, France, and Karlsruhe, Germany.

Penn's plan for Philadelphia, laid out in 1682, was an application of the "gridiron" pattern—with regular blocks and straight streets crossing at right angles—that appeared in the ancient Greek cities of Plato's time which were designed by Hippodamus, the first known city planner. Four public "greens" known as "residential squares," in addition to a central square which served as a civic center, expanded the idea of the New England town plan with its single "green."

Annapolis' plan, prepared in 1694, was the first to incorporate diagonal avenues and circles as a basic plan form, foreshadowing the more ambitious L'Enfant plan for Washington a century later.

Williamsburg's major axis, cross axis, and squares reflected accurately many renaissance European plans for cities and parks, designed for displaying palaces and public buildings.

Savannah's plan, prepared by Oglethorpe in 1733, was similar to Philadelphia's "gridiron" pattern but with a more liberal introduction of "residential squares," ovals, and circles.

The phenomenal growth of commerce following the American Revolution brought a new grandeur to city planning. Patterned after the "grand plans" of renaissance Europe were L'Enfant's plan for Washington, Verle's plan for West Philadelphia, Pease's plan for Cleveland, and Woodward's plan for Detroit —all incorporating sweeping radials and diagonals, squares, ovals, and circles, designed to provide better focus and nobler settings for the increasing profusion of imposing public buildings appearing throughout the new nation.

These artistic plans were ultimately overshadowed by the simplicity and popularity of the perennial "gridiron" pattern which virtually monopolized city planning expression until the "City Beautiful" movement of the late 19th century.

New canals, steamboats, and the steam engine appearing in the early 1800's provided better means of transportation into the interior of the country and encouraged the establishment of countless new cities away from the coastal areas. Concurrently, the demand for greater production of textiles for the rapidly expanding Republic created the first planned company mill towns in New England, while wooden boom-towns of "gridiron" pattern were being hastily developed by land speculators in the eastern coal fields and midwestern plains states assisted by cheap public lands, new railroads, and the invention of "balloon frame" construction of buildings.

Numerous linear "road ranches" and canal towns appeared at toll gates along the National Road system and at locks along the new canals during this period, as well as a number of planned religious communities—the most famous of which was Salt Lake City, Utah, the Mormon settlement conceived by Brigham Young in 1847.

After the railroad had extended the frontier to the west coast it continued to criss-cross the countryside, promoting new "railroad towns" everywhere, while the industrial revolution was creating "factory towns" along the railroads in the East, designed as complete communities for industrial workers close to the factories. In contrast to these notorious industrial slums, a few "model" company towns were designed, notable among which was Pullman, Ill., planned and constructed in its entirety for Pullman Company employees in the 1880's. The success of Pullman, noteworthy for its carefully-planned layout of public buildings, parks, and substantial homes, was shortened by a bitter strike, which discouraged further model company town planning.

The Civil War served to hasten industrial growth and urbanization. Cities rapidly being covered by building bulk in the unimaginative and cramped "gridiron" pattern were neglecting the environmental needs of residents in an effort to accommodate exploding urban populations resulting from uncontrolled foreign immigration and increased movement from rural areas to the cities.

Improvements in urban mass-transit were causing rapid fringe expansion along the main transportation routes, creating prototypes of today's suburban "dormitory" communities. Tall buildings and great bridges, products of steel construction and the elevator, appeared in the last half of the 19th century to relieve somewhat the monotonous horizontal pattern of urban development, while parks and landscaped residential avenues, such as New York City's Central Park and Cleveland's Euclid Avenue, sought to introduce much-needed open space into the crowded living environments of the large cities.

In 1893 the magnificent spectacle of Olmsted and Burnham's classic "Court of Honor" at the Columbian Exposition in Chicago launched the "City Beautiful" movement—an enthusiastic revival of civic design and grand planning. Cities throughout the nation inspired by this movement appointed special civic art commissions—forerunners of today's planning commissions—to carry out vast self-improvement projects which yielded scores of civic and cultural centers, tree-lined avenues, and waterfront improvements. L'Enfant's partially effectuated plan for Washington, dormant since the Civil War, was reactivated.

In the midst of this wave of civic improvement

generated by the Columbian Exposition, Hartford, Conn., established the first city planning commission in 1907, while Wisconsin in 1909, followed by New York and Massachusetts in 1913, passed city and village planning laws officially recognizing planning as a proper function of municipal government. Most of the other states enacted similar enabling legislation in the 1920's and 1930's.

The general scope of planning characterized by the "City Beautiful" movement was concerned with promoting civic beauty instead of improving neglected living environments. The almost universal disregard for environmental considerations in city plans up to that time aroused the disdain of literary writers and social reformers in the late 19th century. Among the reformers was the Scotsman Patrick Geddes, whose advocacy of social surveys ultimately led to their inclusion in the modern planning process, and Ebenezer Howard, whose ideas of a self-contained "garden city"—an ideal environment for living, working, and playing—took root in England with the construction of the garden cities, Letchworth in 1903 and Welwyn a few years later.

Among the earliest planned communities inspired by Howard's "garden city" idea in this country was Forest Hills Village, built in New York City in 1913 by the Russell Sage Foundation as a demonstration community, and several Federally sponsored communities for defense workers during World War I.

A number of imaginatively planned housing developments emerged following World War I, financed by large corporations and insurance companies. Among these was Sunnyside Gardens, Long Island, N. Y., designed by Henry Wright and Clarence Stein on standard city blocks to demonstrate the advantages which could be gained in appearance and open space over the traditional tight row tenement development by varying building design and overall layout.

In 1927 this same team planned America's first "garden city"—Radburn, N. J., "The Town for the Motor Age"—which introduced the concept of the "super-block"—a large residential planning unit free from vehicular encroachment providing uninterrupted pedestrian access from every building to a large recreation area within the center and pedestrian underpasses at major arteries.

During the depression of the 1930's the Resettlement Administration applied the planning principles of Radburn to the design of three new "greenbelt" towns—Greenhills near Cincinnati, Greendale near Milwaukee, and Greenbelt near Washington.

The legal framework for modern city planning practice began with the zoning ordinance, based on the police power, to control land use and thereby protect the interests of the individual and the community. New York City in 1916 adopted the first comprehensive zoning ordinance. The classic decision by the courts upholding the constitutionality of municipal zoning was handed down in Village of Euclid v. Ambler Realty Company (272 U. S. 365) in 1926. The growing number of abuses in zoning plus the lack of direction in its application caused the courts to insist on an accompanying comprehensive master plan for future land use to provide guidelines for zoning. This gradually resulted in the general acceptance during the 1920's and 1930's of the master plan as the official document showing the pattern of development for the community. Along with this came state legislation authorizing planning commissions to prepare and help administer master plans and to control land subdivision.

Contemporary city or urban planning, defined as "intelligent forethought applied to the development of the community as a whole," has evolved as a five-step planning process: (1) Formulation of developmental goals and long-range objectives; (2) Survey and analysis of existing physical, social, and economic conditions; (3) Diagnosis of problems, present trends, and future needs; (4) Preparation of the master plan in the form of proposals presented on maps and in reports and covering (a) land use, (b) circulation and parking, and (c) community facilities and other public improvements; and (5) Effectuation of the master plan through the preparation, adoption, and administration of a zoning ordinance, land subdivision regulations, an official map, a capital improvements program, other regulatory codes and ordinances, and through urban renewal.

Contemporary concepts applied in city planning include the "neighborhood unit" described by Clarence A. Perry as a residential segment of ¼ mile radius centered on an elementary school and having churches, shops, and a community center. Another concept expressed currently in the designs for new cities, downtown redevelopment, and modern shopping centers is the separation of pedestrian and vehicular traffic—with pedestrian malls and plazas, shopping arcades, and peripheral or underground parking areas and loading zones.

City planners in America are currently engaged in four major areas of activity: (1) Preparation or revision of comprehensive master plans, zoning ordinances, subdivision regulations, and capital improvements programs for cities, towns, and villages; (2) Preparation of regional master plans to guide the future development of large areas where contiguous communities, counties, or even states share common planning problems and objectives; (3) Design of new neighborhoods, shopping centers, industrial parks, and complete new cities; and (4) Urban renewal planning in older communities for slum clearance and redevelopment of areas too deteriorated to salvage, rehabilitation of salvageable sections, and conservation of quality neighborhoods.

The Federal government by the passage of the National Housing Acts of 1949 and 1954 with subsequent amendments has stimulated planning activity in the 1950's and 1960's particularly in the fields of (a) urban renewal for eliminating and preventing blight in older cities; (b) city planning for small communities; and (c) regional planning—through the authorization of planning grants to municipalities and regions which alone would be financially unable to undertake such projects.

American city planning today is a recognized profession, practiced mostly by a new generation of planners who are technically trained in universities offering undergraduate and graduate degrees in urban planning and who are subsequently certified as to experience and competence by their professional organization, the American Institute of Planners, founded in 1917. There were approximately 2,500 city planners in the United States in 1960. Their number grows rapidly as the demand for city planning services increases with the continual urbanization of the nation.

CIVIL RIGHTS. Individual rights and civil liberties are interchangeable terms in the field of social relations, economics, politics and the law. They are derived from the first ten amendments to the Constitution of the United States. The most important controversies in recent years in the matter of civil rights have concerned the rights extended to Negroes, as well as others, by the Constitution and the use of the First and Fifth Amendments to the Constitution concerning, respectively, freedom of speech, freedom of religion and assembly and freedom from testimony against oneself in any criminal trial.

Civil rights have of late been extended in use and application. "Jim Crow" laws applying to seating in buses, trains, railway and bus stations and other private places were declared unconstitutional by the U. S. Supreme Court. Poll-tax requirements were greatly weakened though registration for voting in some states presented difficulties. Restrictions in housing were eased in many states. An important step forward was authorization in 1947 of the President's Commission of 15 on Civil Rights which made recommendations with respect to the extension of civil rights to all without regard to race, color or creed.

Labor criticized and opposed the Labor-Management Relations (Taft-Hartley) Act of 1947 and the Landrum-Griffin Act of 1959 as being impairments of civil rights. A House committee on un-American activities generated much criticism as well as approval of its procedures particularly in relation to hearings in connection with the movie industry.

Communist activities in the United States in the years following World War II created a widespread demand for repressive measures which the American Civil Liberties Union charged were serious dangers to civil rights. The anti-communist fight was carried

on by the purging of disloyal employees from their government jobs, the passing of laws requiring loyalty oaths of public employees and teachers, and attempts to outlaw the Communist party and communist-front organizations by state and Federal hearings and criminal prosecution. Efforts to drive communists and communist sympathizers out of the radio, television and motion-picture industries were continued. Leaders of the Communist party in the United States were convicted and imprisoned, and the decisions were affirmed later by the U. S. Supreme Court, although Justice Hugo L. Black, one of the two dissenting justices, considered the convictions "a virulent form of prior censorship of speech and press, which I believe the First Amendment forbids."

The movement for enforcing the civil rights of Negroes reached a climax in the Supreme Court ruling handed down on May 17, 1954, which held unanimously that racial segregation in the public schools was unconstitutional under the 14th Amendment (Brown v. Board of Education, 347 U. S. 483). A companion case was decided on the same basis. To the arguments that the 14th Amendment applied only to the states, the court, though admitting the fact, held that segregation was also a denial of due process of law guaranteed by the Fifth Amendment which applies to the Federal Government (Bolling v. Sharpe, 347 U. S. 497). On May 31, 1955, the Supreme Court ruled that the process of desegregation should be carried out "with all deliberate speed" under the supervision when necessary of Federal district courts.

The pronouncement of May 17, 1954, did not rule on the constitutionality of segregation *per se*, but stated that segregation in the public schools of the nation on "a separate but equal" basis violated the 14th Amendment. In a series of decisions on May 24, 1954, the Supreme Court cleared up any misunderstanding as to the fundamental import of its ruling of May 17, by directing the lower courts to read into certain other cases the general rule laid down. In effect, segregation was outlawed in (1) tax-supported graduate schools; (2) in tax-supported colleges and universities; (3) in tax-supported junior colleges; (4) in public housing developments; and (5) in public park recreation and entertainment facilities.

In the Southern states where the Negro population is large, there was much criticism of the decision, largely on the basis of its infringement on state rights and as flying in the face of custom and long established social relations. It was contended that social prejudices and a long established way of life could not suddenly be overthrown by a court decision and enforcing legislation. The ruling has been met with varying degrees and types of opposition and enforcement, both by the courts, the Negroes themselves in the form of public demonstrations and sit-downs, by white boycott of schools accepting Negro students, and in other ways. Desegregation has taken place at varying rates in different localities, particularly in the South.

The year 1957 was marked by several important developments: (1) Congress passed the first Civil Rights Bill enacted since Reconstruction days following the Civil War; (2) President Eisenhower sent Federal troops to Little Rock, Ark., to compel compliance with a court order requiring the admittance of Negro pupils into an all-white high school; (3) the Supreme Court in a series of decisions balanced civil or individual rights guaranteed by the Constitution against state rights. The main provisions of the Civil Rights Bill, which became effective in September, 1957, were (1) the Attorney General of the United States was empowered to apply Federal court injunctions against any violation of individual voting rights or any threatened violation; (2) persons violating the laws may be tried without a jury, at the court's discretion, and, under certain conditions, a fine or jail sentence could be imposed on conviction; (3) establishment of a commission to make a two-year investigation of the civil rights problem in the United States was authorized; (4) creation of a civil rights division in the Justice Department was authorized; (5) requirements that Federal court jurors can serve only if qualified under the laws of the states in which they serve were eliminated; and (6) a Reconstruction law authorizing the President to use Federal troops to enforce local court decrees in civil rights cases.

Federal courts struck down racial discrimination laws in public places. Congress, in 1960, in spite of bitter opposition from Southern states in the form of filibusters and other delaying practices, plugged loopholes in the 1957 Civil Rights legislation, mainly in connection with voting rights. The Federal Government and private groups collaborated to enforce Negro registration and voting rights throughout the country. Desegregation was ordered in the nation's armed forces; the rights of representation and voting rights were also ordered to be observed and enforced in labor unions.

Meanwhile, in an increasing number of court cases involving a wide range of activities from membership in the Communist party and contempt of Congress to trials for gambling, murder, racketeering and smuggling, witnesses, under oath, repeatedly refused to answer questions by asserting their rights under the First and/or Fifth Amendments to the Federal Constitution. In these cases, the Supreme Court has not itself been consistent in its rulings.

Recent Supreme Court decisions upholding the right of government agencies to question persons about their communist activities together with a general public agitation for adequate protection against communist subversion is expected to work in favor of a House-approved bill designed to prevent suspected subversives from taking the Fifth Amendment to hide their activities.

CIVIL RIGHTS ACT (April 9, 1866) was the first Federal statute to define citizenship and to safeguard civil rights within states. "All persons born in the United States and not subject to any foreign power, excluding Indians not taxed," were declared to be citizens of the United States. Such persons, "of every race and color," should have rights equal with white citizens for the security of person and property, in any state or territory. Jurisdiction over enforcement was given to Federal courts. The purpose of the act was to nullify the Black Codes of various Southern states. Since there was some doubt in Congress as to the constitutionality of the act, the Civil Rights section was later incorporated in the resolution framing the Fourteenth Amendment. After President Johnson vetoed the act (March 27, 1866) the opponents of the President won a two-thirds majority in Congress to override the veto, and thereafter Congress was in full command of Reconstruction legislation.

CIVIL RIGHTS CASES, 1883 (109 U. S. 3). Individuals are protected from violations of their civil rights on the part of the Federal authorities by the Bill of Rights in the Federal Constitution. They are protected from such violations on the part of state authorities by the Fourteenth Amendment and by the bills of rights in their respective state constitutions. The Civil Rights Cases clearly establish the fact that individuals have no constitutional protection—Federal or state—from violations of their civil rights on the part of other individuals. They may secure redress, but by court action, and under statutory rather than constitutional authorization. Furthermore, the statute must be a state, and may not be a Federal, one.

During the period of Reconstruction, Congress adopted a series of acts known as the Force Acts, of which the Civil Rights Act was one. For years Sen. Charles Sumner of Massachusetts had urged the adoption of such a measure; upon his death his erstwhile colleagues waived their doubts as to the measure's constitutionality, in their anxiety to pay tribute to a departed friend. This act (March 1, 1875), which was the last to be adopted in the group of Force Acts, sought to guarantee to all citizens of the United States full and equal enjoyment of the privileges of inns, theaters, restaurants, public conveyances, etc., and stipulated that such enjoyment should not be subject to any conditions applicable only to citizens of a particular race or color, or who had been in a previous condition of servitude. Suit was brought against certain proprietors—Stanley, Ryan, Nichols, Singleton and the Memphis and Charleston Railroad Company—for violation of the law.

The Court sustained the arguments of the defendants, who alleged that the act was unconstitutional. It was held that the denial of such privileges is not an indication of slavery or involuntary servitude; that the Fourteenth Amendment applies to states, not to individuals; that no law had been made by a state abridging rights or denying equal privileges to citizens of the United States, and that the acts complained of were committed by individuals, hence the cases did not come within the meaning of the Fourteenth Amendment. ". . . [U]ntil some State law has been passed, or some State action . . . has been taken, adverse to the rights of citizens sought to be protected by the Fourteenth Amendment, no legislation of the United States . . . can be called into activity. . . ."

What constituted "state action" was not altogether clear. In particular it was not clear whether Congress could protect individuals against state officers who exceeded their authority and acted in violation of the laws of the state itself. Could Federal law, for instance, serve as the basis of the prosecution of a sheriff who had arrested a Negro and beaten him to death? In Screws v. U. S. (1945) the Supreme Court by a five-to-four majority held that such activities fell within the meaning of the term "state action" and could be prohibited by Congress. But conviction in this case was reversed because the prosecution had failed to prove that Screws had "specifically intended" to deprive his victim of his constitutional rights. In Koehler v. U. S. (1951) the Court reversed this last dictum on the grounds that "the intent is presumed and inferred from the result of the action."

Some rights, it should be noted, have been exempted from the doctrine of the Civil Rights Cases. Thus the Court ruled in U. S. v. Classic (1941) that Congress can secure citizens' right to vote in Federal elections—even in primaries—against violation by individuals as well as by states.

CIVIL SERVICE, as distinct from military, naval and foreign service, is the term applied to those public employees who provide an administrative liaison between the state and the individual. All governmental units are thus operated by a civil service, with classified and unclassified divisions, expansion of which keeps pace with an increase in governmental functions. The classified service is characterized by appointment through competitive examination, salary standardization, permanent tenure, merit promotion and pension compensation; the unclassified service, on the other hand, is characterized by political appointment and rapid turnover in positions.

Corruption of civil service in the United States dates from 1789, but it was not until the Jacksonian era that political rotation of governmental posts became a widespread abuse which ultimately reached unprecedented proportions immediately after the Civil War. Then it was that reform organizations launched a campaign to make "civil service" synonymous with the "merit system"—a campaign which has been continued for more than 80 years. Civil service reform has been undertaken during four major periods in United States history—namely, the post-Civil War era, the post-Spanish-American War era,

the post-World War I era and the post-Depression era. Three major pressure groups—the National Civil Service League, the Public Personnel Association (formerly the Civil Service Assembly of the United States and Canada), and the League of Women Voters—have concentrated their efforts on drafting better civil service laws, on improving relations between public employees and legislators, and latterly on improving relations between civil servants and citizens whom they serve.

A more recent trend has been the extension of civil service laws to include provisions for the training of public employees, improving efficiency by incentive awards, and introducing some flexibility into pay systems.

Significant landmarks in Federal civil service reform have been the laws of 1853, 1855, 1871, 1883, 1919, 1940. In 1853 and again in 1855 a simple system of "pass examinations" was inaugurated by Congress for Federal civil servants. In 1871 Congress gave the President power to determine a general system of personnel selection. However, it was not until 1883, by the Pendleton Act, which received the support of President Arthur, that a Civil Service Act of any moment was passed. This is still the basic statute. It has been supplemented by a major set of Civil Service Rules and Orders promulgated by President Theodore Roosevelt in 1903, which have been amended from time to time; and by the Classification Act of 1923 which was superseded by the Classification Act of 1949, as amended. In 1919 war veterans were granted special preference and given increased rights by the Veterans' Preference Act of 1944. An act extending the merit system to first, second, and third-class postmasters was passed in 1938, and in 1940 the President was empowered to bring into the competitive service a large number of positions previously in the excepted service.

In 1883 New York adopted the first state Civil Service Act, the principles of which were incorporated in the state constitution in 1894. Massachusetts adopted a civil service law in 1884; Wisconsin and Illinois in 1905 (the latter's act superseded by a new act in 1955); Colorado in 1907 (statute incorporated in the constitution, 1919); New Jersey in 1908 (incorporated in the state constitution in 1947); Ohio in 1912 (constitutional amendment, supplemented by a statute in 1913); California in 1913 (incorporated in the state constitution in 1934); Connecticut, 1913 (repealed 1921; new law enacted 1937); Hawaii in 1939; Kansas, 1915 (defunct in 1920 for lack of funds, and a new law enacted in 1941, amended in 1953); Maryland in 1920; Arkansas in 1937, repealed in 1939; Maine in 1937; Michigan in 1937 (amended in 1939 and incorporated in the constitution in 1940); Alabama in 1939 (and a constitutional provision adopted in 1951); Rhode Island in 1939, amended in 1951; Minnesota in 1939; Louisiana in 1940 (repealed in 1948, and a self-operating constitutional provision adopted in 1952); Oregon in 1945; Georgia in 1943 (constitutional provision in 1945, and substantial extensions of coverage in 1950–52); Vermont in 1950; New Hampshire in 1951; Montana in 1953 (the law becoming inoperative in 1955 through lack of funds); Nevada in 1953; Florida in 1955; Oklahoma in 1959; Kentucky, Washington and Alaska in 1960.

With the states named above, New Mexico, North Carolina, Virginia and Wyoming have personnel systems which perform many of the functions of a state merit system but do not include competitive examinations.

Since 1940 the Federal Social Security Act has required states to maintain state merit systems for employees of agencies which receive Federal grants under that act, such as unemployment security, public assistance and some highway departments.

Some other states have civil service laws for one or more departments in addition to those which operate under the Social Security Act. These are Arizona, Idaho, Indiana, Missouri, Pennsylvania, South Carolina, South Dakota, Tennessee, Utah, and West Virginia.

Puerto Rico adopted a civil service law in 1908, drastically amended in 1931 and 1947.

The first existing civil service systems for a municipality (those of New York City and Buffalo) were created in 1884. Many others date from the late 1800's. But the periods of most rapid growth in the number of cities with civil service laws were from 1908 to 1918 and from 1930 to 1960. At present, all cities of over 500,000 population, all but one of between 250,000 and 500,000, most cities of between 100,000 and 250,000, and many of smaller size, are under civil service laws. The total—counting small cities with only police and fire departments covered —is probably now close to 1000.

Most cities operate their own statutes, but there are exceptions. The New York and Ohio plans place counties and cities (and in New York, towns, villages and school districts, also) under the state civil service laws, with local administration which, in New York, is subject to general state supervision. (New York law permits, as an alternative, administration by the state personnel agency at the option of the governing body of a city.) Massachusetts law makes coverage by the state civil service law with administration by the state mandatory for cities and optional for counties and towns. In New Jersey, voters decide by referendum whether the state civil service law shall apply to local jurisdictions; there is no provision for local statutes or administration. Louisiana's civil service constitutional provision applies to cities of over 250,000. Many other states have laws covering cities of certain populations.

In thirteen states (Alabama, California, Connecticut, Florida, Georgia, Kentucky, Louisiana, Minnesota, New York, Oklahoma, Oregon, Rhode Island and Wisconsin) the state personnel agencies may perform technical and administrative services for localities on a cost basis. California cities have taken most advantage of this provision.

Somewhat over 200 of the 3056 counties have civil service laws or are covered by the state law. New York, New Jersey and California have the largest number of counties under civil service laws. There are half a dozen city-county systems, principally in Alabama, California and New York.

CIVIL WAR. In understanding the background of the struggle it is essential to distinguish such broad factors as Southernism in terms of culture types, economic and political motives of the planter aristocracy, Southern defense reaction to Northern criticism, the whipping up of excitement by agitators on both sides, economic sectionalism (agrarian v. industrial tendencies), Northern thought-patterns as to democracy and slavery, Republican party strategy and the highly overemphasized issue of slavery in the territories. Sectional tension grew ominously in the 1850's and a major Southern crisis, accompanied by intense popular excitement, followed the election of Lincoln in November, 1860. By early February, 1861, the seven states of the Lower South had withdrawn from the Union and had begun the erection of the Southern Confederacy. After a period of inaction, the sending of an expedition by President Lincoln to relieve the Federal garrison at Fort Sumter in Charleston Harbor precipitated a Southern attack upon that fort, which was surrendered on April 13. This specifically was the opening of the war. Each side claimed that the other began it. Southerners argued that Lincoln's expedition was an invasion of a sovereign state; the Washington Government maintained that it meant no aggression in "holding" its own fort and that the "first shot" had been fired by the South.

Lincoln's inaugural address of March 4, 1861, had been conciliatory in tone; nevertheless his decision to retain Sumter, which necessitated sending food to the garrison, placed the opening "incident" in precisely that area where peace was most unstable and where emotion had been roused to greatest sensitivity. Fort Pickens in Florida, though similar in status to Sumter, presented no such menace of emotional outbreak. Lincoln's Sumter policy involved two main points: the sending of the provisioning expedition, and, after the fort had been fired upon, the call for 75,000 militia to be furnished by the states. This policy, while it produced a united North, served equally to unite the South; it was not until after Lincoln's call for militia that the four important states of the Upper South (Virginia, Arkansas, Tennessee and North Carolina) withdrew from the Union and joined the Confederacy. In this sense Lincoln's April policy, interpreted in the South as coercion, played into the hands of the secessionists while Buchanan's avoidance of an outbreak had supplied the setting for compromise efforts.

On the side of the Union there were 23 states with 22,000,000 people as against 11 states and 9,000,000 (including 3,500,000 slaves) within the Confederacy. In wealth and population as well as in industrial, commercial and financial strength the Union was definitely superior to the Confederacy. On the other hand the South had the advantage of bold leadership, gallant tradition, martial spirit, unopposed seizure of many Federal forts and arsenals, interior military lines and unusual ability among its generals. Its military problem was that of defense, which required far less men than offensive campaigns and widely extended hostile occupation. Between the two sections was a populous middle region (the Union slave states of Delaware, Maryland, Kentucky and Missouri; the area that became West Virginia; and the southern portions of Ohio, Indiana and Illinois) within which the choice of the people was for the Union while on the other hand there was cultural sympathy for the South and spirited opposition to the Lincoln administration.

Legally the war began with Lincoln's proclamations: the proclamation of April 15, 1861, which summoned the militia to suppress "combinations" in the seven states of the Lower South, and the proclamations of April 19 and April 27, 1861, which launched a blockade of Southern ports. Internationally the Confederacy achieved recognition of belligerency, as in the British queen's proclamation of neutrality (May 13, 1861), but never achieved full standing in the sense of a recognition of independence by any foreign power. Nor did any foreign nation intervene in the struggle, though the British government seemed at times to be seriously contemplating it and the government of Napoleon III did offer mediation which was indignantly rejected by the United States (February–March, 1863).

Before Lincoln's first Congress met in July, 1861, the President had taken those measures which gave to Union war policy its controlling character. Besides proclaiming an insurrection, declaring a blockade and summoning the militia (definite war measures), he had suspended the habeas corpus privilege, expanded the regular army, directed emergency expenditures and in general had assumed executive functions beyond existing law. A tardy ratification of his acts was passed by Congress on Aug. 6, 1861 (U. S. *Statutes at Large*, XII, 326) and in 1863 these strongly contested executive measures were given sanction by the Supreme Court in a five-to-four decision sustained chiefly by Lincoln's own judicial appointees. In general, Lincoln's method of meeting the emergency and suppressing disloyal tendencies was not to proceed within the pattern of regular statutes, but to grasp arbitrary power by executive orders or proclamations, as in the Emancipation Proclamation (in which the President exercised a power which he insisted Con-

gress did not have even in time of war), and his extensive program of arbitrary arrests wherein thousands of citizens were thrust into prison on suspicion of disloyal or dangerous activity. These arrests were quite irregular. Prisoners were given no trial (usually not even military trial); they were deprived of civil guarantees and were subjected to no regular accusations under the law. Such measures led to severe and widespread opposition to the Lincoln administration. In their denial of the habeas corpus privilege they were denounced as unconstitutional in a hearing before Chief Justice Taney (*ex parte* Merryman, May, 1861), but in the Vallandigham case the Supreme Court, to which the Merryman case had not been brought, declined to interpose any obstacle to arbitrary arrest, thus in a negative way sustaining the President. (In 1866, however, the Court did overrule a wartime military commission in the Milligan case.) Yet it cannot be said that Lincoln became in the 20th-century sense a "dictator." He allowed freedom of speech and of the press, contrary examples being exceptional, not typical. He tolerated widespread newspaper criticism of himself and of the Government, interposed no party uniformity, permitted free assembly, avoided partisan violence, recognized opponents in appointments and above all submitted himself, even during war, to the test of popular election. This testing resulted in marked Republican loss in the congressional election of 1862, while in 1864, though the situation looked very dark for the Republicans in August, the election in November brought in a considerable electoral majority.

In the military sense both sides were unprepared; had any conceivable policy of prewar preparedness been promoted (under the Southern secretaries of war of the 1850's) it could hardly have given the Union side that advantage which military writers often assume. The battle of Bull Run (July 21) was the only large-scale engagement in 1861. Though a Union defeat, it was, like most of the battles, an indecisive struggle. Except during the generalship of McClellan (U.), Meade (U.), and Grant (U.) the Southerners had the undoubted advantage of military leadership on the main eastern front; Lee's (C.) notable, though indecisive, victories of Second Bull Run, Fredericksburg and Chancellorsville were won against Pope, Burnside and Hooker. At Antietam, however, McClellan stopped Lee's Northern invasion of September, 1862, while the ambitious Confederate offensive of 1863 was checked at Gettysburg. In the West most of the operations were favorable to the Union side. This was especially true of the "river war" (resulting in the capture of Columbus, Forts Henry and Donelson, Nashville, Corinth and Memphis), the Federal half-victory of Shiloh; and more especially the important Union victories of 1863 at Vicksburg and in the Chattanooga area. Later campaigns involved J. E. Johnston's (C.) unsuccessful operations against Sherman (U.) in upper Georgia,

Sherman's capture of Atlanta and his famous raid through Georgia and the Carolinas, Sheridan's (U.) devastating operations in the Valley of Virginia, the Grant-Meade operations against Lee in Virginia (involving the costly battles of the Wilderness, Spotsylvania and Cold Harbor), the Hood-Thomas campaign in Tennessee and final operations in the Petersburg and Appomattox areas, which culminated in the fall of Richmond and the close of the war. In the naval aspects Union superiority was impressively shown in the blockade of Southern ports which were eventually closed to the Confederacy's own warships, the capture and occupation of coastal positions, the co-operation of western flotillas with the armies, the seizure of New Orleans in April, 1862, the complete control of the Mississippi River after the fall of Vicksburg and Port Hudson in July, 1863, and the defeat and sinking of the Confederacy's proudest ship, the *Alabama,* by the *Kearsarge* (June 19, 1864). On the other hand Confederate cruisers and privateers did considerable damage to Union commerce, the Union Navy failed in the operations against Richmond, and several ports (Wilmington, Charleston, Mobile) remained in Southern hands till late in the war. Galveston did not yield till after the war was over, June, 1865. Privateering was authorized by both sides but practiced only by the Confederacy, and that chiefly in the first year of the war. The military decision in favor of the United States was registered in the surrender of Lee to Grant at Appomattox, April 9, 1865, and the surrender of J. E. Johnston to Sherman near Durham, N. C., on April 26.

Methods of military recruiting and administration were amateurish, haphazard and inefficient. Conscription was used on both sides but by neither side with real effectiveness. Such factors as commutation money, bounties, bargaining in substitutes, draft riots, irregular popular recruiting, undue multiplication of military units, lack of a general staff and inadequate use of the very small regular army, marred the Union system of army administration. Somewhat similar difficulties existed also in the South. Guerrilla warfare, though never a decisive factor nor a part of major strategy, was extensively practiced. The administration of the War Department under Secretary Cameron (to January, 1862) was marred by fraud and corruption; under Secretary Stanton the system was improved, but profiteering and military blundering existed to a marked degree throughout the war. In addition, the Union cause was weakened by state control of national military processes, congressional interference, anti-McClellanism (involving the unwise abandonment of McClellan's peninsular campaign in the summer of 1862), confusion and circumlocution among divers army boards, councils and advisers, undue control of army matters by such men as Halleck and Stanton, extensive desertion and atrocious inadequacy in the care of hundreds of thousands of prisoners, the last-named abuse being chiefly due to utter breakdown in the exchange or cartel system. Negro troops were extensively used in the Union armies. The Confederate Government, late in the war, authorized their enrollment, but this was never put into practice.

What happened behind the lines would constitute a very elaborate story. Civilian relief was supplied by the U. S. Sanitary Commission (similar to the later Red Cross); war propaganda was spread by the Union League and the Loyal Publication Society; antiadministration effort was promoted by the Sons of Liberty and Knights of the Golden Circle. Financial instability and monetary abnormality carried prices to fantastic heights in the South; in the North the disturbance was far less, but specie payments were suspended and treasury notes ("greenbacks") depreciated to such an extent that the paper price of gold reached $2.84 in July, 1864. Taxation was heavy, yet a Federal debt of approximately $3,000,-000,000 was accumulated. Federal bonds were marketed by the semiofficial efforts of Jay Cooke and Company. Currency and banking regulations were drastically modified by the establishment of the national banking system. Labor obtained from the war far less advantage than business entrepreneurs. Immigration was encouraged and the wartime increase of wages was not commensurate with the depreciation of the money system. Greed was widespread, stock speculation was rife, lobbying was rampant, contractors cheated the Government and large numbers of men became unjustifiably rich. High wartime tariff laws gave ample protection to manufacturers. Various reforms and progressive schemes were delayed or wrecked by the war, but laws were passed for assigning free homesteads to settlers, for encouraging Western railroad building and for Federal aid in the establishment of land-grant colleges. To a people once united but split asunder by the tragedy of war there came the inevitable horrors of war psychosis; this took manifold forms including unChristian sputterings of hatred in the churches. One of the most savage of the wartime fanatics was "Parson" (W. G.) Brownlow of Tennessee. Yet Quakers and other honest religious objectors to war were given, by administrative procedure and later by law, the alternative of noncombatant service when drafted. Efforts of peace groups to end the war in 1864 received notable support from Horace Greeley, but, being associated with partisan politics, they met failure in every case; even the official efforts of highplaced statesmen met a like failure in the Hampton Roads Conference of February, 1865. War aims changed as the conflict progressed; the declaration of Congress on July 22, 1861, that the war was waged merely for the restoration of the Union was belied by the Radical Republicans who by 1864 had determined in the event of victory to treat the South as a subordinate section upon which drastic modifications would be imposed. One of the striking examples of wartime Radical policy was seen in the second confiscation act (July 17, 1862) which, against Lincoln's better judgment, decreed the forfeiture to the United States of the property of all adherents to the "rebellion." The relation of the war to the slavery question appeared in various emancipating measures passed by Congress, in Lincoln's Emancipation Proclamation as well as his abortive compensated emancipation scheme, in state measures of abolition, and finally in the antislavery amendment to the Constitution. The distinction of Lincoln was discernible not in the enactment of laws through his advocacy, nor in the adoption of his ideals as a continuing postwar policy, nor even in the persuasion of his own party to follow his lead. Rather, the qualities which marked him as leader were personal tact (shown notably in a cabinet crisis of December, 1862), fairness toward opponents, popular appeal, dignity and effectiveness in state papers, absence of vindictiveness and withal a personality which was remembered for its own uniqueness while it was almost canonized as a symbol of the Union cause. Military success, though long delayed, and the dramatic martyrdom of his assassination must also be reckoned as factors in the emancipator's fame. On the other side Southern memory of a cherished lost cause has been equally identified with the lofty perfection of Lee's personality.

To measure the war in terms of man power and casualties is a highly controversial task made doubly difficult by sectional pride, popular tradition, amateur history writing and inadequate statistics. Gen. Marcus J. Wright, a Confederate officer, after the war attached to the War Department, estimated Confederate man power at 600,000 to 700,000 men. Others, including T. L. Livermore and J. F. Rhodes, have put it much higher. Col. W. F. Fox, a careful military statistician, considered that the Union forces did not exceed 2,000,000 separate individuals. Comprehensive records are especially lacking on the Confederate side, while the better statistics on the Union side are in terms of enlistments and have been only conjecturally corrected to allow for numerous cases of re-enlistment. Comparable units of military measurement have been hard to obtain in determining the totals involved in particular campaigns or battles, and inadequate attention has been given to the precise meaning of such terms as "effectives," men "present for duty," forces "actually engaged," etc. Grand totals include men in home guards, thousands who were missing and many other thousands who enlisted in the final weeks or were otherwise distant from fighting areas. On the Federal side in April, 1865, there were approximately 1,000,000 men in the field, with 2,000,000 of the "national forces" not yet called out. The number of those subject to military call at the North was actually greater at the end of the war than at the beginning. Confederate dead have been estimated at 258,000, Union dead at 360,000. The stupendous economic and material loss has never been more than roughly estimated.

Aside from the obvious consequences of slaughter and destruction, the results of the war (or concomitants of the war and postwar period) involved suppression of the "heresy" of secession, legal fixation of an "indestructible" Union, national abolition of slavery, overthrow of the Southern planter class, rise of middle-class power in the South, decline of the merchant marine, ascendancy of the Republican party, inauguration of a continuing high-tariff policy, far-reaching developments in terms of capitalistic growth associated with centralization of government functions and adoption of the Fourteenth Amendment (intended to consolidate party control by the protection of Negro civil rights but later applied as a shield to corporations). But with the mention of these factors the enumeration of long-time results is only begun. A full enumeration, impossible in these pages, would also include postwar intolerance, partisanship associated with the "bloody shirt" tradition, immense pension claims with their many abuses, a deplorable complex of "reconstruction" evils and excesses, carpetbag and scalawag corruption and, as the continuing result of all this, the "solid South."

(See also Army, Confederate; Army, Union; Confederate States of America; also, articles on specific battles by title.)

Civil War Diplomacy. The basic diplomatic policy of the United States during the Civil War was twofold: to prevent foreign intervention in behalf of the Southern Confederacy; and to gain the acquiescence of the great maritime powers, England and France, in the vast extension of maritime belligerent rights which was considered necessary in order to crush the South. The chief diplomatic figures in Northern diplomacy were Secretary of State William H. Seward, supported and advised by President Lincoln, Charles Francis Adams, minister to England, William Dayton, minister to France, John Bigelow, consul general in France and, after Dayton's death in 1864, minister in his stead, and Thomas Corwin, minister to the Juarez government of Mexico. The United States, of course, had its diplomatic representatives in all the other principal civilized nations. But since France and England were great maritime powers and none too friendly toward the United States at the time, they seemed to offer the only serious danger of foreign intervention, and at the same time they were the nations which had to be appeased because of aggression against their commerce in prosecution of the war against Confederate trade. So Federal diplomacy was largely concerned with these two nations as far as it related to the Civil War.

In the very beginning, Seward deliberately created the impression upon the British government that he was willing if not anxious for the United States to fight Great Britain should that country show undue sympathy for the Confederacy. The recognition of Confederate belligerency before war had really begun —except the firing on Fort Sumter—gave Seward and Charles Francis Adams a tangible and even bitter grievance against both England and France. It resulted in Seward's issuing an ultimatum to England, threatening to break off diplomatic relations should England receive, even unofficially, the Confederate diplomatic agents. This grievance was constantly held up by Adams and Seward; and the launching of the Confederate cruisers and the building of the Confederate rams in England—and France—gave other even stronger grounds upon which the American diplomats could complain. The sale of munitions and the colossal blockade-running business carried on with the Confederacy furnished further and constant complaints, particularly against England. French intervention in Mexico was an added score against France. The piling up of grievances by the United States against France and England, particularly the latter, cannot be overlooked as a powerful factor in making these two Western European powers extremely cautious with reference to even friendly intervention in the Civil War. It helped create the very definite belief that intervention meant a declaration of war by the United States. As for war, neither France nor England cared to pay such a price to see the United States permanently divided. These grievances of the United States were used to counteract the grievances of England and France in the blockade of their West Indian ports and the seizure of their merchant vessels, under the doctrine of "ultimate destination," hundreds of miles from the Confederate coast when apparently destined to neutral ports. England, of course, was glad to see the re-establishing of the paper blockade and the doctrine of ultimate destination; but the methods employed in the seizure and search of scores of vessels, including the *Trent*, created deep resentment in England, and Adams and Seward cleverly used the *Alabama* claims and other similar grievances as counterirritants.

The objective of Confederate diplomacy was to obtain foreign assistance in gaining independence. The Confederate government based its plans upon European dependence upon Southern cotton, at first; and finally upon the well-known desire of England to see a powerful commercial rival weakened, and of Napoleon III to see the champion of the Monroe Doctrine rendered impotent to frustrate his attempted annexation of Mexico. The Confederacy first sent William L. Yancey, Pierre A. Rost and A. Dudley Mann as joint commissioners to obtain European aid and recognition. Later Yancey resigned, the commission was dissolved, Mann was sent to Belgium as permanent commissioner and Rost to Spain. James M. Mason and John Slidell—taken prisoner by Wilkes and later released by the Federal Government on the demand of Great Britain—were sent to Great Britain

and France respectively as Confederate diplomatic agents. The Confederacy sent John T. Pickett to the Juarez government in Mexico and Juan Quintero to the government of Santiago Vadaurri, governor-dictator of Nuevo Léon and virtual ruler of several of the neighboring border states of Mexico. The Confederate diplomats were ably supported by propagandist agents in both England and France. Edwin DeLeon and Henry Hotze were the chief propagandist agents. The Confederate diplomatic agents were informally received in May, 1861, in England; but after that Lord Russell refused even that much recognition under the pressure of Seward's ultimatum. However, the British government did continue to deal with the Confederate agents by means of correspondence. In Belgium, Spain, France, Mexico and even at the Vatican, Confederate diplomatic agents were received informally but freely. In fact, Slidell in France was on such good terms with Napoleon that the latter made a practice of intercepting messages to U. S. Minister Dayton for him.

The causes for the failure of the Confederacy to obtain foreign intervention were that the things to be gained by war on the part of England and France would not offset war losses. Europe had a surplus of cotton during the first year of the war; and after this surplus gave out, war profits, particularly in England, from cotton speculation, linen and woolen industries, munitions, blockade running and the destruction or transfer of the American merchant marine to British registry, dwarfed the losses among the cotton-mill operatives and removed the chief economic motives for intervention. It is also contended that the wheat famine in England made that country dependent upon the United States for its bread supply, and that this operated as an important factor in preserving the neutrality of the British.

Munitions. The standard equipment of the Union Army was muzzle-loading Springfield or Enfield rifles and the type of cannon now so often found cluttering up courthouse lawns. Many early regiments, however, went to the front with nondescript arms of their own procuring. Other hundreds of thousands of rifles were furnished by contractors who took all the antiquated, castoff weapons which European governments could drag from the junk heaps of their armies. A large proportion of these, sold to the War Department at extravagant prices, had to be scrapped immediately. Others, which were issued to the soldiers, proved more dangerous to the man behind the breech than to the enemy before the muzzle. Before 1861 various American companies were making breech-loading repeating rifles which, by repeated testimony of experts, would fire fifteen times as rapidly as the best of muzzle-loaders, with equal accuracy and force, and with greater ease of manipulation. But the traditional backwardness of the War Department and its staff prevented the use of such improved weapons. All sorts of excuses, none of them valid, were conjured up against them. In the closing months of the war a new Chief of Ordnance, Alexander B. Dyer, equipped a few companies in the Southwest with repeating rifles, and with these weapons in their hands the men proved invincible. When the war was over the same arms were adopted for the regular army.

Throughout the war those persons responsible for its conduct preferred to set up huge armies with inferior guns to form a larger target for the enemy, rather than equip a smaller and more compact force with weapons of multiple effectiveness. Even Gatling guns, firing 250 shots a minute with frightful precision, were dismissed in cavalier fashion. A dozen of them were supplied to Gen. B. F. Butler, whose men proved their merits. But again, the weapon was not adopted for general use till after the war. Following a few initial blunders there was not much difficulty in procuring a plentiful supply of good muzzle-loading guns, or of powder and shot.

The munitions of the Confederacy were inferior to those of the North. Battlefield captures, raiding expeditions, imports from Europe and an increasing production from Southern munitions plants kept the troops armed. Largely cut off by the blockade from European supplies, and with little industrial development, manufacturing plants had to be built and manned, and materials had to be obtained and prepared. While saltpeter and sulphur in the raw state were plentiful in the Confederacy, machinery and labor for conversion were generally lacking. Yet, in 1864, lead-smelting works, bronze foundries, a cannon foundry, rifle, carbine and pistol factories were operating. The big problem of supply was the lack of adequate transportation.

The Navy in the Civil War. On account of divided personnel, scattered forces and inadequate appropriations, the U. S. Navy was near to demoralization at the outbreak of the war. But the new Secretary, Gideon Welles, and the Assistant Secretary, Gustavus V. Fox, approached their task with intelligence and force.

The year 1861 was marked by a great disaster and two victories. The disaster, eight days after Fort Sumter was fired on, was the abandoning of the Norfolk Navy Yard. The Federal Government not only lost eleven ships including the steam frigate *Merrimack,* but 3000 pieces of ordnance, 300 of them Dahlgren guns of the latest type. On the other hand, Admiral Stringham's squadron in August easily took the forts at the entrance to Hatteras Inlet, and Du-Pont's fleet in November captured two forts defending Port Royal, S. C.

The year 1862 began with successful military and naval operations on the Tennessee and Cumberland rivers as Grant and Foote took Fort Henry and Fort Donelson, breaking the Confederate line of defense in the West, and saving Kentucky for the Union. On the Mississippi Foote's squadron co-operated with the

Army under Pope in taking Island No. 10 and later advanced as far as Vicksburg. Farragut, at about the same time, coming from the Gulf with a strong seagoing fleet, succeeded in passing the strong forts of Jackson and St. Philip (April 24) and overpowering the Confederate Defense Squadron. New Orleans surrendered and the forts soon capitulated. This brilliant campaign prevented intervention on the part of France and possibly of England. On the Atlantic coast, the Confederate ironclad *Merrimack,* coming from Norfolk into Hampton Roads, destroyed the *Cumberland* and the *Congress* and threatened to break the Union blockade (March 8). But the *Monitor,* arriving most opportunely, engaged the champion on the following morning and effectually checked her career.

In 1863, the Union ironclads increasing in numbers, naval attacks on Charleston became more determined. But even the *New Ironsides,* probably the strongest ship afloat, was unequal to the task. However, the blockade of South Carolina and other parts of the Southern coast was now highly effective. Of the first importance was the service rendered by Porter commanding the Mississippi Squadron. By his aid Grant, campaigning against Vicksburg, was able to cross the Mississippi and attack the city from the south and east. When he captured it (July 4) the Union controlled the entire Mississippi basin and split the Confederacy in two.

In 1864 the *Alabama* was sunk by the *Kearsarge* off Cherbourg, France (June 11). The *Alabama, Florida* and *Shenandoah* were highly successful in their depredations on Northern commerce, and because all three had been built in British shipyards the United States claimed a heavy indemnity from England after the war. On Aug. 5, Farragut won his second decisive victory. With a fleet of wooden ships and ironclads he forced his way past Fort Morgan at the entrance to Mobile Bay. Later in the same morning he fought the Confederate ironclad *Tennessee* and compelled its surrender. Soon Mobile was barred from all approaches to the sea.

On Jan. 15, 1865, the South's one remaining access to the sea was closed when the fleet commanded by Porter and the military forces by Terry took Fort Fisher, the key to Wilmington, N. C. With the capture of Fort Fisher, a termination of the war favorable to the North was assured.

The service of the Navy consisted in establishing an effective blockade; in carrying on joint operations with the Army to capture strategic positions on the coast and to gain control of the Mississippi; and in pursuing and capturing the cruisers that preyed on Northern commerce. It was essential for the preservation of the Union.

CLAIM ASSOCIATIONS were frontier institutions designed to provide a quasi-legal land system in areas where no land law existed. Settlers who preceded the government surveyor into a new area and established their homes therein or who located on public land not yet offered at public auction sale made their improvements with no certainty of continued ownership. Before 1841 settlement in advance of survey and sale was contrary to law. Settlers had no protection against speculators buying their lands at the public auction; they had no protection against the "claim jumper" who sought to oust them and steal their improvements; nor had they means for registering, transferring or mortgaging their claims. Where squatters were fairly numerous it was natural that they should organize to protect their common interests. Claim associations or claim clubs appeared early in the 19th century and were found in practically every part of the public land area which received settlers before 1870. The squatters would come together, adopt a more or less stereotyped constitution or bylaws guaranteeing mutual protection to each claimant of 160 or 320 acres who met the simple requirements for improvements. Claim jumpers were dealt with in summary fashion by these associations. A "register" was selected who kept a record of all claims and their transfers, and a bidder was chosen to represent the group at the public auction sale.

The most important event in the life of the frontier was the government land auction and to it flocked the squatters, well armed and determined to defend their claims against any speculators who contemplated outbidding them. When the sale began, the bidder, flanked by the motley crowd of squatters, took a prominent position near the auctioneer, and as the squatters' sections were offered bid the Government minimum price and no more. If higher bids were made, drastic action was at once taken, the offending speculator being treated as roughly as the claim jumper.

The claim associations' registry made it possible to buy and sell claims without the Government patent and there frequently developed a large claim business, much of which was speculative. Early state and territorial law gave legal sanction to many of the practices of the associations, including the registering and transferring of claims. After the public auction and the establishment of state or territorial transfer laws the associations disappeared.

The Pre-emption Law of 1841 legalized squatting upon surveyed lands and gave the settler the right of pre-empting his claim before the public sale, thereby protecting him against competitive bidding, but only if he could raise the funds to pay for the land. Claim associations were still necessary to give community sanction and force to the quasi land regulations in areas where no legal system existed. The heyday of the associations was in the 1840's and 1850's in Iowa, Kansas and Nebraska, where practically every township had its protective organization.

CLAIM JUMPER was one who drove a squatter from his claim or, in his absence, seized it. Next to the horse thief he was the most detested person on the frontier. The squatter's only recourse was to appeal to the local claim association, which undertook to rid the community of such undesirable characters.

CLAIMS, THE FEDERAL COURT OF, was created by Congress (1855) under its power to appropriate money to pay the debts of the United States. The court investigates contractual claims against the United States brought before the court by private parties, or referred to it by an executive department or by Congress. In some cases the decisions of the court are final, subject to appeal to the Supreme Court; in others, the court merely reports its findings to Congress or to the department concerned.

CLARK'S NORTHWEST CAMPAIGN (1778–79). During the early years of the Revolution the British exercised undisputed control over the country northwest of the Ohio River. Their most important center of influence was Detroit, the headquarters of the posts and the key to the control of the fur trade and the Indian tribes. From Detroit emanated the influences which dominated the savages of the entire Northwest, and instigated the dispatching of uncounted war parties against the frontier settlements south of the Ohio. So terribly were the settlers of infant Kentucky harassed that they were considering abandoning the country altogether, when George Rogers Clark stepped forward as their leader and protector.

Clark perceived that Kentucky could best be defended by the conquest of Detroit, the center whence the raids were instigated. Too weak to make a frontal attack upon Detroit, or even upon Vincennes, he directed his first blow against the towns of the French in Illinois. Kaskaskia was occupied, July 4, 1778, and the remaining Illinois towns, and even Vincennes, were easily persuaded to join the rebel standard. Upon learning of these developments, Lt.-Gov. Hamilton of Detroit prepared to effect a counterstroke. Under great difficulties he marched upon Vincennes, which was retaken, Dec. 17; but instead of pushing on against Kaskaskia, Hamilton now dismissed his Indian allies and settled down for the winter.

The situation was thus placed in the balance and victory would favor the leader who struck first. Instantly perceiving this, Clark led his little army eastward across Illinois to tempt his fate at Vincennes. An untimely thaw flooded the prairies and drowned the river bottoms and the story of the difficulties encountered and vanquished surpasses many a flight of fiction. Even Clark himself said the recital of them would be too incredible for belief by anyone not well acquainted with him.

A bullet through the breast of a British soldier apprised Hamilton of Clark's arrival. After an investment of 36 hours, Hamilton yielded his fort and garrison to the rebel leader, Feb. 24, 1779. Although

Detroit, Clark's ultimate goal, was never attained, he retained his grip upon the southern end of the Northwest until the close of the war, and this possession proved an important factor in obtaining the Northwest for the United States in the Definitive Treaty of Peace of 1783.

CLAYTON ACT OF 1914 was the result of a growing conviction that the Sherman Antitrust Law of 1890 did not reach some important evils of big business. The Sherman law was leveled mainly at the evils of monopoly and restraint of trade, and at the time it was passed the dominant method of combination was the business trust, where properties were transferred to trustees, a legal form different from the corporation. In the years after the Sherman law, combinations began to organize as holding companies, interlocking directorates, under trade agreements of various kinds, and eventually as aggregations of non-related industries. A new situation had developed which the Clayton Act and the Federal Trade Commission Act, passed the same year, were designed to cover. The Clayton law provided mainly prohibitions against practices which "substantially tended to lessen competition," or "substantially" tended to create monopoly, such as discrimination in prices among different producers, acquisition of stock by one company in another, the use of interlocking directorates where restraint was involved, and under certain conditions, a similar provision relative to banks. Another clause placed restrictions on the relation of common carriers to construction and supply companies. In some respects the rigors of the Sherman law were relaxed with respect to labor and agricultural organizations. In regard to labor, in some jurisdictions certain customary activities of unions were interpreted as restraints of trade. It was provided in the Clayton Act that nothing in the Federal antitrust statutes was to be construed to prohibit the existence of "labor, agricultural, or horticultural organizations, instituted for the purposes of mutual help . . . or to forbid or restrain individual members . . . from lawfully carrying out the legitimate objects thereof." Section 20 of the law prohibited the use of restraining orders or injunctions "unless necessary to prevent irreparable injury to property, or to a property right, of the party making the application, for which injury there is no adequate remedy at law."

CLAYTON-BULWER TREATY (1850) was a compromise arrangement resulting from the conflicting interests of Great Britain and the United States in Central America. In the late 1840's Great Britain, on the basis of claims dating from the 18th century, was occupying the Bay Islands, which belonged to Honduras, and also the eastern coast of Central America, as "protector" of the pseudo-kingdom of the Mosquito Indians. After war broke out between the United States and Mexico the British government quickly saw that the assured American victory would stimulate American interest in a ship canal across the isthmus. Therefore, on Jan. 1, 1848, British authorities, acting for the Mosquito king, seized the mouth of the San Juan River, the logical eastern terminus of any future canal in the region.

Strained relations at once developed between the two governments, though each assured the other that it had no selfish designs on the transit route. Negotiations in England having failed to end the dispute, Sir Henry Bulwer was sent to Washington, where, with Secretary of State John M. Clayton, he negotiated the treaty which bears their names. This provided that the two countries should jointly control and protect the canal which it was expected would soon be built somewhere on the isthmus. The introductory article, drafted by Clayton with the aim of ousting the British from Central America, pledged the two countries not to "occupy, or fortify, or colonize, or assume or exercise any dominion over Nicaragua, Costa Rica, the Mosquito Coast, or any part of Central America." The agreement was ratified July 4, 1850.

Almost immediately, however, the interpretation of the self-denying clause just mentioned became the subject of a bitter dispute between the two governments. The United States held that the pledge not to "occupy" required that Great Britain withdraw. The British replied that if the agreement had been intended to be retroactive this fact would have been definitely stated; and they failed to get out of the Bay Islands and the Mosquito territory. War again threatened, but Great Britain, valuing her cotton trade with the United States more than she did her claims in Central America, finally acquiesced in the American interpretation and withdrew in 1858–60.

The Clayton-Bulwer Treaty had become very unpopular in the United States, however, and when, after several decades, the canal was still unbuilt, popular demand grew for abrogation of the agreement, to make possible construction of an American-controlled canal. Finally, in 1902, the Hay-Pauncefote Treaty superseded the Clayton-Bulwer arrangement.

Critics have charged that the latter treaty, by taking Great Britain into American partnership in controlling the proposed canal, violated the spirit of the Monroe Doctrine. But it should be noted that the United States, by insisting upon a retroactive interpretation of the treaty, forced the British to give up long-existing territorial claims, which was a unique triumph for the Doctrine.

CLEVELAND, OHIO. A trading post was located at the mouth of the Cuyahoga River as early as 1786; in the same year an Indian village named Pilgerruh was founded by three Moravian missionaries on a site ten or twelve miles upstream. In 1796 Moses Cleaveland, agent of the Connecticut Land Company, which had acquired from Connecticut a large part of the Western Reserve, laid out a town which was given his name. Granted a township government in 1800, made the seat of the new county of Cuyahoga in 1810, incorporated as a village in 1814, Cleveland in 1836 began its history of an incorporated city with a population of about 4000. Originally important commercially only as a post on the route from Pittsburgh to Detroit, with the opening of the Ohio Canal —to Akron in 1827 and to the Ohio River in 1832—it became an increasingly important outlet for products of the interior of the state, and for the Pennsylvania, West Virginia and Ohio coal that was soon brought in quantity to smelt the iron ore shipped from the Lake Superior mines. A railroad development, ambitiously planned in the 1830's but not realized until the 1850's, made additional contributions to the important iron industry of the Civil War period, since which time Cleveland has had the history of a rapidly expanding industrial city. Its population in 1960 was 876,050.

CLIFF DWELLERS were a prehistoric race of Indians who built their dwellings under overhanging cliffs in rocky canyon walls. Most of the cliff dwellings are found within a hundred miles radius of the point where the boundaries of Colorado, Utah, New Mexico and Arizona meet. However, some have been reported as far north as Lodore Canyon, Colorado, and as far south as Sierra Madre, Mexico. The most important groups of these ruins are being preserved as Mesa Verde National Park. Other groups have been declared national monuments, e.g., Canyon de Chelly, Hovenweep, Montezuma Castle, Walnut Canyon and Navajo.

The cliff dwellers were an agricultural people raising corn, beans, melons and turkeys. Cisterns, ollas or water jars and irrigation systems give evidence of their struggle against an arid climate. The attacks of roving Indian enemies, disease, superstition and an increased aridity in the region caused the complete abandonment of these dwellings before the white man discovered America. Some of the present-day Pueblo Indians may be their descendants.

The cliff dwellings vary from single isolated rooms to large communal villages built solid to the roof of the cave. Several are three and four stories containing over 100 rooms. They are built of stone, much of it quarried and hewn with stone hammers, and adobe mortar and plaster. Many of the lower chambers are circular ceremonial rooms called kivas. Ceilings are timbered and these timbers enabled Dr. Douglass with his tree ring calendar definitely to date these ruins between 919 and 1273 A.D.

The dwellings are hundreds of feet above the floor of the canyon. Their inaccessibility made them safer from attack by enemies. Further protection was furnished by tall watchtowers built on the top of the mesas overlooking the canyons.

CLIPPER SHIPS were long and narrow wooden sailing vessels, with lofty canvas. Their era lasted for a quarter of a century, from about 1843 to 1868, and gave to the world the greatest development of the sailing ship in speed and beauty. The word "clipper" had its origin, perhaps, in the verb "clip," meaning to run swiftly. The clipper ships were designed to do just that thing.

Tea from China quickly lost its flavor in the hold of a ship, and about 1843 the clippers began quicker delivery of that product. The discovery of gold in California induced many in the decade from 1849 to 1859 to take the voyage around Cape Horn in fast clipper ships. After carrying their cargoes of men and merchandise to California, the ships would either return to Atlantic ports for another such cargo, or would cross the Pacific to China in ballast, and load there with tea, silk and spices. The discovery of gold in Australia in 1851 also gave a great impetus to the building of clipper ships.

They were much more dependable than the old-type sailing vessel. In a heavy sea they strained less and were thus able to take better care of their cargoes; and they crossed belts of calm better than the low-rigged ships. The swift brigs and schooners built at Baltimore during the War of 1812 were known as Baltimore clippers; but the first real clipper was the *Ann McKim*, built there in 1832. Beginning about 1850 the California clippers increased rapidly in size, ranging from 1500 to 2000 tons register. Of this type the *Stag-Hound*, built in Boston in 1850, was the pioneer. Six of the clipper ships established speed records that have never been broken. Practically all of them were faster than the steamships of their day, and it was more than a quarter of a century before the steamship was able to break the record of the fastest clippers. Their great speed is attested by the fact that eighteen ships made passages from New York or Boston to San Francisco in less than 100 days. The four best passages were made by the *Flying Cloud*, built in Boston in 1851, in 89, 89, 105 and 108 days, an average of 97¾ days. Then came the *Andrew Jackson*, built at Mystic, Conn., in 1855, in 89, 100, 102 and 103 days, an average of 98½ days. Those records were followed by the *Flying Fish*, built in Boston in 1851, in 92, 98, 105 and 106 days, an average of 100¼ days.

By 1855 the "extreme" clippers were succeeded by the "medium" clippers, vessels that did not carry so much canvas, but that could be handled by a smaller crew. Shortly after the close of the Civil War, American shipbuilding for oversea carrying trade declined. Although some clipper ships were built, the steamships gradually displaced them.

CLOCKMAKING, EARLY. Clocks were brought to America by the early settlers, and contemporary colonial artisans repaired them and probably made new ones. By the 18th century, at least, both household timepieces and belfry clocks were made to order. Fine examples of these are still cherished by collectors. Connecticut, whose population was outgrowing its agricultural resources before the Revolution, early developed several mechanical industries, including clockmaking. Its craftsmen received their skill from Holland, through New York, as well as from Great Britain. Finer timepieces had metal works, but wooden clocks were made in America soon after 1700. Being cheaper, they were in more demand and until the middle 1830's dominated the market. Itinerant vendors, like "Sam Slick," peddled them, with tinware, through the country. Works were often sold separately from cases, and the more democratic shelf clocks supplanted the tall eight-day clocks of our grandfathers in the homes of the people. Even these, however, were long a luxury, the cheapest models costing fifteen dollars.

In the Connecticut Valley the use of interchangeable parts soon suggested itself to clockmakers, and early in the last century power machinery assembled in factories was used to shape wheels and other parts. Then quantity production began. The fact that Connecticut was already a brassworking center facilitated the transition to that metal. As a result American clocks, which could not be exported as long as they had wooden works affected by atmospheric changes, were soon sold throughout the world at prices incredibly low to foreigners. A long step toward this was the invention, about 1837, of one-day brass clocks, which could be manufactured for six dollars; in 1855 they were made to sell for seventy-five cents.

Notable pioneers who invented improvements which simplified and cheapened the American product were Ely Terry, who began making wooden clocks at Waterbury in 1793 and built up an extensive business at Thomaston, where the Seth Thomas clocks were subsequently manufactured; and Chauncey Jerome, once employed by Terry, who became the first large exporter and whose works developed into the New Haven Clock Company. Even earlier a family named Willard built up a business at Roxbury, Mass., which sold tall striking clocks and public timepieces in all parts of the country.

COAL. Bituminous coal and anthracite, sometimes called "soft coal" and "hard coal," are a major source of heat and power in the United States, accounting for 23.1% of the nation's total energy consumption in 1960, including noncompetitive products such as gasoline and jet fuel.

Bituminous (and the few million tons of other types which are normally included with it in statistics) is produced in over 333 counties in 26 states. However, over 90% of the total comes from the highly populated and industrial states east of the Mississippi. The leading state in 1957, with 28.9% of the total, was West Virginia, followed by Pennsylvania, 15.9%;

Kentucky, 15.5%; Illinois, 11.1%; Ohio, 8.2%; Virginia, 7%; Indiana, 3.8%; and Alabama, 3.1%.

Indians are credited with making use of coal before the first white exploration and settlement. A Jesuit missionary, for example, recorded as early as 1660 that he saw Algonquins "making fire with coal from the earth." Joliet and Marquette, however, were the first to make a definite reference to coal discovery, this in 1673 between the present cities of Joliet and Ottawa, in Illinois. Commercial mining started in the Richmond basin of Virginia prior to 1750, and possibly as early as 1700. The early 1700's also saw discoveries in Maryland and southern West Virginia, and exploration later in the century added Ohio, Kentucky and other states to the list.

Growing population and industry, bringing an increase in fuel needs, resulted in the development of a sizeable mining industry in certain areas by 1825, in which year the recorded bituminous production was 117,988 tons. By 1850, it had grown to 7,018,181 tons. Thereafter, production roughly doubled every decade until 1920, reaching 569,-000,000 tons, exceeded up to that time only by the 1918 total of 579,000,000.

World War I marked a pivotal point for coal. It was rationed, oil use was encouraged, and a drive for economy in use was initiated. The rising use of the automobile in the years that followed increased the volume of the residual products that had to find markets in competition with coal. Hydroelectric power, with government support, also grew more important, and the oil refining industry decided to try for the home market. Then, in the '30's, the first of the long-distance pipelines was built, ushering in an era of rapid expansion for oil and gas.

Both competition and efficiency in use have taken their toll—the latter a largely unknown but significant one. For example, the utility industry in 1960 used 0.88 lb. of coal to produce a kilowatt-hour of electricity and consumed 173,800,000 tons. If the World War I rate had still prevailed, the industry would have required not 173,800,000 but over 630,-000,000 tons. Less striking but nevertheless significant gains have been made in other fields of use. As a result of competition and efficiency, bituminous coal has exceeded its 1918 tonnage in only five years since, and since World War II has completely lost the once-big railroad market. By 1960, "normal" demand was approximately 450,000,000 tons a year. Depressed conditions made the actual demand in that year less, however.

Rising demands for energy and changes in the fuel picture, particularly the rapid rise in utility use, coupled with increases in use by steel and general industry, are expected to lift the level of output sharply in the future. In 1965, for example, consumption, including exports, is expected to reach 525,-000,000 to 535,000,000, with utilities accounting for around 240,000,000; steel and coke for 120,000,000 to 130,000,000; and general industrial for 80,000,000 to 90,000,000 tons.

One big reason for expecting a better position for bituminous is its ability to hold its prices while other fuels steadily increase. The average value of bituminous coal in 1960 was estimated at $4.75 per ton, compared to $4.86 in 1950. In that period, wages rose from $14.75 to $24.25 per day and payments into the United Mine Workers Welfare & Retirement Fund from 30¢ to 40¢ per ton.

The answer has been heavy investments in machines to raise output per man, which in the same 1950–60 period rose from 6.77 to over 13 tons per man per day. A level of 17 tons per man or more is expected by 1965 or earlier. Equipment being used in 1960 included such items as stripping shovels carrying 70-cu. yd. dippers and costing over $3,000,-000 each, operated by three men; and underground mining units, operated by four to six men, costing up to $250,000 each. In addition, a 115-cu. yd. shovel was under construction and an 85-cu. yd. dragline had been ordered.

Stripping—or the process of taking the overburden off by excavators and then loading the uncovered coal—and associated methods accounted for 31% of the total output in 1960 and mechanized methods underground for 60.5%, leaving only 8.5% produced by the old hand methods.

Anthracite is characterized by a high percentage of fixed carbon and a low percentage of volatile matter. The term "anthracite" usually is applied only to the output of a 480-sq. mi. area of eastern Pennsylvania.

Anthracite also was known and used by the Indians. Obadiah Gore employed it in a forge in Wilkes-Barre in 1769, and anthracite was shipped to the Carlisle arsenal in 1776. Jesse Fell, also of Wilkes-Barre, used it for nail manufacture in 1788, and in 1808 introduced it for heating homes by burning it in an open grate with natural draft.

With emphasis on heating, anthracite grew steadily until World War I, which was a pivotal time for it as well as bituminous. From its peak of 96,612,000 tons in 1917, it has steadily lost ground, reaching 18,080,000 tons in 1960. Competition from the convenience fuels—first oil and then natural gas—were the big reasons.

Like bituminous coal, anthracite has called on stripping equipment to cut cost, and this method in 1960 accounted for over one quarter of the output. Underground opportunities for use of machines are much less than in bituminous because of pitch and other conditions.

COAST AND GEODETIC SURVEY, UNITED STATES.

This agency of the U. S. Department of Commerce had its beginning on Feb. 10, 1807, when Congress authorized a "Survey of the Coast."

Acting on the advice of the American Philosophical Society, President Thomas Jefferson accepted the plan submitted by a renowned Swiss geodesist, Prof. Ferdinand Rudolph Hassler. The Survey was placed under the Treasury Department, with Hassler as its first superintendent. He spent several years in England and France supervising the design and construction of precise instruments required in the great undertaking. His purchases of scientific instruments were delayed by the War of 1812; field work did not get under way until 1816 when base lines were surveyed on Long Island and near English Creek in New Jersey. A small network of triangulation was developed around New York Bay.

Following this beginning the Bureau was transferred to the Navy between 1818 and 1832 with the work severely curtailed. In 1832, Congress broadened the scope of the initial act, reactivating the agency under the Treasury with the designation "Coast Survey." Operations were extended along the Florida coast, and the military value of the work in coastal defense was recognized. Congressional action in 1871 authorized the Coast Survey to establish geodetic connections between the Atlantic, Gulf and Pacific coasts. The significance of these continental surveys was recognized in 1878 by adoption of the present name of the Bureau.

Hassler was succeeded in 1843 by Prof. Alexander Dallas Bache, an eminent scientist and great-grandson of Benjamin Franklin. The first major activity by Bache was to begin surveying and charting the coastline on a regional basis, pursuant to the newly revised Hassler plan of April, 1843. Geodetic, topographic and hydrographic surveys, and chart production, were extended along the Gulf Coast and later along the Pacific Coast after the western territories were acquired. Upon acquisition of Alaska from Russia in 1867 the Coast Survey began the task of surveying the coastal regions of the new territory. Since 1843 the expansion of the United States across the continent and the acquisition of island dependencies have brought the total coastline under the Survey to approximately 90,000 miles.

Although the superintendents of the Bureau for the first 100 years were civilian, the officers manning the survey ships until the turn of the century and chiefs of field parties until 1860 were Navy and Army officers on special detail. The Commissioned Corps was created in 1917 as one of the uniformed services of the nation.

The Coast and Geodetic Survey was one of the original agencies comprising the Department of Commerce and Labor when it was created in 1903. When these functions were regrouped into separate departments in 1913, the Survey remained with the Department of Commerce.

Through the years additional functions have been delegated to the Bureau through congressional action. In 1925 the agency was charged with reporting on earthquakes, previously an activity of the Weather Bureau. Aeronautical charting was assigned to the Survey under the Air Commerce Act of 1926.

The work is carried on at the main office in Washington, D. C., at district offices and field stations, by about 40 survey parties throughout the country, and by a fleet of 15 survey ships. Field offices in nine coastal cities collect data for revision of nautical charts and co-operate with local engineers and organizations requiring specialized data; six offices are maintained for photogrammetric compilation, processing of hydrographic data, and computing geodetic data; and two offices are maintained for aeronautical chart liaison. In addition the Bureau operates two latitude observatories and six magnetic observatories.

Thus in 1960 the activities of the Coast and Geodetic Survey included: (1) surveying and charting the coasts of the United States, its territories and possessions and the printing of nautical charts to insure safe navigation; (2) the determination of geographic positions and elevations along the coasts and in the interior of the country, to co-ordinate coastal surveys and to provide a framework for mapping and other engineering work; (3) the study of tides and currents for making annual tide and current forecasts; (4) the compilation and printing of aeronautical charts for civil aviation; (5) observations of the earth's magnetism for information essential to the mariner, aviator, land surveyor, radio engineer, and others; (6) seismological observations and investigations to supply data for designing structures resistant to earthquakes; and (7) gravity and astronomic observations to provide basic data for geodetic surveys and studies of the size and shape of the earth.

The results of field investigations and surveys are analyzed in Washington and published as nautical and aeronautical charts, annual tables of predicted tides and currents, charts showing magnetic declination, annual lists of United States earthquakes, publications of geographical positions, coast pilots, and technical manuals on various Bureau operations.

COAST GUARD, UNITED STATES.

The Coast Guard covers a wide range; it is an armed force as well as the chief national agency for promoting maritime safety. Its work includes enforcement of the navigation and other maritime laws of the United States, the rendering of assistance to vessels in distress, the saving of life and property, the destruction of derelicts, the removal of obstructions and menaces to navigation, and the maintenance of an extensive merchant marine safety program. It also maintains the International Ice Patrol in the North Atlantic and the Bering Sea Patrol, and gives medical aid to deep-sea fishermen and the natives of Alaska.

Our country's oldest continuous seagoing service, the Coast Guard traces its history back to Aug. 4, 1790, when the First Congress, at the request of Alexander Hamilton, authorized the construction of ten vessels for the collection of revenue. Known in early times as the Revenue Marine and later as the Revenue Cutter Service, the Coast Guard received its present name on Jan. 28, 1915, under an act of Congress combining the Revenue Cutter Service with the Life-Saving Service. On July 1, 1939, the Lighthouse Service of the Department of Commerce was also consolidated with this unit. In 1942, the Bureau of Marine Inspection and Navigation was transferred temporarily to the Coast Guard, the transfer being made permanent in 1946. Through its antecedents, the Coast Guard is one of the oldest organizations in the Federal Government.

In peacetime, it operates under the Treasury Department. In wartime, or on direction of the President, it becomes part of the Navy, subject to the orders of the Secretary of the Navy. The Coast Guard has a present strength of about 30,600 officers and men, and its floating equipment includes about 178 vessels of the larger type. It also operates about 128 fixed and rotary wing aircraft.

COD FISHERIES

COD FISHERIES of North America lie off the coasts of New England, Newfoundland and Labrador. The earliest explorers to the northeastern coast of North America noted the presence of the codfish. Cabot spoke of it, and in 1602 Gosnold gave Cape Cod its name because of the abundance of the fish in its waters. The earliest fishermen came from Spain and France, attracted by the lure of the bank fisheries off Newfoundland. In the 16th century Englishmen made frequent fishing voyages to the "banks."

Capt. John Smith's successful fishing venture in 1614 off the New England coast helped to establish the popularity of that region. Within a few years fishing colonies were established in Massachusetts (Cape Ann) and Maine (Monhegan Island and Pemaquid). Massachusetts Bay early engaged in the codfishery. Within less than forty years after its settlement Boston was a busy trade center for fish.

England often exasperated the colonies by failing in treaties with France to accord a proper interest to the fisheries. In treaties from St. Germain (1632) to Ryswick (1697), the French fisheries benefited. British colonists were particularly bitter in 1697 when Acadia was returned to France. The Treaty of Utrecht (1713) awarded Newfoundland and Nova Scotia (Acadia) to England, but France retained the island of Cape Breton and some fishing privileges.

The final defeat of France in the great colonial struggle with England, concluded by the Treaty of Paris (1763), left France only the fishing islands of St. Pierre and Miquelon and restricted fishing privileges. The New England codfisheries expected to benefit by the triumph, but new discontent appeared when Parliament passed the Sugar Act of 1764. Its enforcement threatened to ruin the profitable trade with the French West Indies that was based on the exchange of the poorer grade of cod for sugar and molasses, which were manufactured into rum. Like the earlier Molasses Act of 1733 this, too, was ineffective, largely because of smuggling.

Codfishing suffered severely from the Revolutionary War, but expectations were held for its revival when the United States secured extensive fishing privileges from England in the Definitive Treaty of Peace (1783). This revival was delayed not only by the contraction of the market in Catholic Europe, but also by the immediate exclusion of Americans from trade with the British West Indies. Fishing bounties began to be paid in 1789, but did not become a real aid to the fisheries until considerably later.

The Peace of Ghent (1814) did not provide for the continuance of the fishing privileges which Americans had been enjoying in British colonial waters. The Convention of 1818 attempted to settle the fisheries question, but it continued to be a sore spot in British-American relations until the award of the Hague Tribunal of Arbitration in 1910.

After the War of 1812 the cod and mackerel fisheries entered on a long period of expansion. The European market for salt codfish declined, but the domestic market more than offset this loss. The Erie Canal provided access to the Mississippi Valley, and introduction of the use of ice for preservation opened a wide domestic market for fresh fish. Tariffs from 1816 to 1846 on imported fish greatly helped New England fishermen to control the home market.

After the Civil War the cod lost the distinction of being the principal food fish of the American seas. From about 1885 the codfisheries began not only to decline in relation to other American fisheries, but also in the amount of tonnage employed. Such cities as Boston and Gloucester in Massachusetts, and Portland in Maine, however, still serve as centers for an industry whose importance in American history is symbolized by Massachusetts' use of the "sacred codfish" as its emblem.

COERCION ACTS, also known as the Restraining Acts and, in part, as the Intolerable Acts, were a series of four measures passed by the English Parliament in the spring and summer of 1774, partly in retaliation for such incidents as the *Gaspee* affair and the Boston Tea Party, but also partly as the enunciation of a more vigorous colonial policy. The Boston Port Act, designed as a direct reply to the Tea Party, closed the harbor to all shipping until the town had indemnified the East India Company for the destruction of its tea and assured the king of its future loyalty, pending which Marblehead was made the port of entry. The Massachusetts Government Act deprived Massachusetts of its charter and the right to choose its own magistrates, reducing it to the

status of a crown colony. An Act for the Impartial Administration of Justice provided that judges, soldiers and revenue officers indicted for murder in Massachusetts should be taken to England for trial, and lastly, the Quartering Act removed all obstacles to the billeting of troops in any town in Massachusetts.

COEUR d'ALENE RIOTS, in the lead and silver mines of northern Idaho, resulted from a strike of union miners in 1892. The mine owners protected nonunion labor with armed guards, and obtained injunctions against the unions. On July 11, 1892, armed union miners expelled nonunion men from the district, a mill was dynamited, and a pitched battle was fought. State and Federal troops took charge and martial law was proclaimed. In 1893 the local miners' unions were affiliated with the Western Federation of Miners. There were strikes in 1894 and 1899, when Federal troops suppressed violence. The Cœur d'Alene labor trouble gained national attention when Idaho's former governor, Frank Steunenberg, was killed, Dec. 30, 1905. The murderer, Harry Orchard, a former miner, claimed that the crime was instigated by officers of the Federation. He was chief witness for the state in the trial of "Big Bill" Haywood, secretary of the Federation, held in Boise in May, 1907. In 1908 Orchard was sentenced to be hanged, a punishment later commuted to life imprisonment. Haywood was acquitted, as was George A. Pettibone, the Federation's president, and the prosecution against Charles H. Moyer, member of the Federation's official board, was dropped.

COHENS v. VIRGINIA, 1821 (6 Wheaton 264). The Supreme Court upheld its jurisdiction to review the judgment of a state court where, in a criminal case, it was alleged that the conviction violated some right under the Federal Constitution or laws. This was one of Marshall's greatest opinions establishing national authority over the states.

COINAGE. The history of United States coinage divides naturally into two eras, the period from 1607 to the outbreak of the Revolution and the period from 1776 to the present day. The immigrants, usually poor, brought little money. Those from England brought a few pounds, shillings, sixpences, threepenny pieces, and copper pence. The Dutch brought *guilders* and *stivers,* and the Swedes brought *dalers* and *skillings.* Pirates left in the ports silver coins from Spain and Germany, gold coins from Spain, Portugal, and Arabia.

The supply of these miscellaneous coins was never adequate for local trade, retail or wholesale. For a century the colonists resorted to barter. Beaver skins and Indian wampum became universal currencies in the northern colonies. Many other commodities served in retail trade, even packets of sugar. Massachusetts made "musket bullets" legal tender. Warehouse receipts for tobacco, rice and lumber were a currency in many areas.

Spain set up a mint in Mexico in the 16th century. For almost 300 years it sent out a stream of silver coins to all the world. A considerable portion reached the colonies, chiefly by way of the West Indies. The basis of this coinage was the *peso* or piece-of-eight, always called in the colonies the "Spanish dollar." The denominations were the dollar, the half-dollar, the quarter, the eighth, and the sixteenth. The eighth was a *real*, known in the colonies as a "real" or "Spanish bit." It corresponded in value to the English sixpence.

The individual colonies made their own legal-tender laws, and each colony, in an attempt to retain foreign coins, gave them arbitrary and fictitious values in terms of the shillings and pence in which all accounts were kept. In 1701 South Carolina made 14 foreign coins unlimited legal tender. From about 1660 to the Revolution, the Spanish silver coins were the one common currency. The supply was never sufficient. The coins, clipped and filed as they came into circulation, became mere thin disks. The colonists resorted to every device to carry on retail trade. Spanish dollars were chopped into eighths and sixteenths. Lord Baltimore personally imported a quantity of underweight English silver coins. During the entire colonial period the people endured inconvenience and heavy loss. A traveler from Boston to Virginia, for example, would pass through three colonies with varying local values for each of the miscellaneous coins he carried.

Copper was discovered at an early date. A number of colonies undertook to set up mints, notably New York, Maryland and Virginia. Only Massachusetts succeeded, in 1652. The Pine Tree shilling and its parts, debased to keep them at home, were useful and popular.

Finally, in 1690, the colonies resorted to issues of paper money, with the inevitable consequences of over-issue, inflation, depreciation, and repudiation. The British Government's neglect of the currency difficulties, repression of attempts to set up mints and suppression of paper money issues were a material factor in bringing on the Revolution.

In the period of the Confederation, 1775–89, the new states were on a paper-money basis, the Continental currency driving out all coins. The issues were in terms of Spanish dollars, constituting the first official recognition of the Spanish coin as the standard of America. The new states thought that each would provide its own coinage, and abortive efforts were made to establish mints. In 1786, Massachusetts provided by law for an elaborate coinage of gold, silver, and copper. The only result was an experimental coinage of a few copper pieces, 1/100 of the Spanish dollar. This was the first attempt at decimal coinage in history.

The Congress of the new Federal Government of 1789 put an end to coinage by the states and delegated to Alexander Hamilton, Secretary of the Treasury, the task of drafting a plan for a new coinage system. In all history no nation had ever undertaken to establish a completely new national coinage. The plan presented by Hamilton was new in the standard money adopted, new in the type of legal tender laws, and, above all, new in being the first decimal coinage system.

Historians have generally credited Hamilton with the creation of the new system. Actually the plan he presented embodied features long before considered and recommended by others. Thomas Jefferson, Robert Morris and Gouverneur Morris had been concerned with the matter for years. The law finally adopted by Congress in 1792 departed widely in some details from Hamilton's plan. Hamilton's great service was in combining many and diverse proposals into one concrete program. As early as 1785 Congress had endorsed the Spanish dollar as the standard unit.

The new system was to be bimetallic, with two standard coins. The silver unit was to be a new silver dollar of the value of the Spanish dollars in circulation. It was to contain 371¼ grains of fine silver. The amount of copper alloy of 1792 was later changed, but the silver content is today what it was originally. It is the only coin in our history which has not been changed in content.

Hamilton thought that the current ratio valuation of silver and gold was 15 to 1. The gold dollar, accordingly, would weigh 24¾ grains. The gold coins were to be in denominations of $10, $5, and $2.50. The silver coins were to be the dollar, the half-dollar, the quarter-dollar, the *disme*, and the half-*disme*. All these coins, even the five-cent half-*disme*, were to have unlimited legal tender. All foreign coins in circulation would be a legal tender for three years. After that time only Spanish silver would be legal tender. The copper cent and half-cent were to be of pure copper and of such great size that they would be impractical in trade.

The new system was a complete failure. The ratio of 15 to 1 was unfair to gold, and no one brought gold to the Mint. The weight of the silver dollar was based on a sample weighing of a number of current Spanish dollars. But all silver coins were regularly clipped and thereafter were worn by use until they were well below the new silver dollar weight. When the Bank of Baltimore, for example, took silver dollars to the Mint for recoinage into United States coins it suffered a loss. The first director of the Mint, David Rittenhouse, a man of culture and character but wholly unversed in business, objected to the excessive copper alloy because it made the coins "too dark." Entirely illegally, he added 3½ grains of silver to each dollar. This increased the loss to depositors of Spanish silver at the Mint. In 1806, Jefferson, without legal authority, ordered the suspension of coinage of silver dollars. The order remained in force long after Jefferson's death.

The failure of the new system forced the country to depend on a vanishing supply of worn Spanish coins. The coinage from the Mexican mint was irregular and never adequate. Instead of grappling with the problem, Congress merely redeemed the legal tender of Spanish coins decade after decade. It seriously considered abolishing the Mint and abandoning the national system.

After 1840 the situation became critical. Some trivial gold mines had been discovered in Georgia. To encourage this petty industry Congress in 1834 debased the gold standard. The fine weight of the gold dollar was reduced from 24¾ grains to 23.2 grains. In 1837, the weight was changed to 23.22, as the Mint officials were having difficulty with the arithmetic involved in the 23.2 weight.

The reduction of the weight of the gold dollar changed the ratio of silver to gold from 15 to 1 to almost precisely 16 to 1, a ratio that was to be the focus of bitter political controversy a half-century later. At this new ratio a silver dollar was actually worth about $1.03 in gold coin. No silver would be brought to the Mint. If in desperation merchants and bankers obtained silver and had it coined to enable them to stay in business, the coins immediately disappeared. The only coins which could circulate were Spanish coins so worn that they could not be sold for gold. The change of ratio was a national injury.

There was no excuse whatever for the failure of the national coinage system. At any time, from 1792 to 1850, it was possible to establish a perfect system, without cost, without risk, under a single standard or a double standard. The failure of the system was due to ignorance. The old records show that an occasional Congressman had a clear understanding of the problem and its solution. Presidents and Congresses ignored them. England in 1816 had literally blundered into the simple and obvious solution—a subsidiary coinage system. In a crisis the Royal Mint bought silver bullion, coined it into shillings containing less in silver than a shilling value in gold, and sold the silver shillings for a shilling in gold. Thus, England unconsciously established the first official subsidiary coinage in history and in so doing adopted the first official single gold standard.

In 1851 Congress adopted a three-cent postage rate. The people had long refused to use copper coins because of their size. And there were no three-cent pieces of silver. Congress provided for a new silver piece of three-cent denomination containing less than three cents' worth of silver. The wording of the law made it impossible in operation. The Mint officials ignored its terms. They bought silver bullion for gold, coined the new pieces, and sold them for gold, at a profit. As in England in 1816, the United States in 1851 blundered into a subsidiary coinage.

When the law was passed the retail trade of the country was in a state of paralysis. The three-cent piece poured into the void by millions. For three years there were practically no coins in circulation below the one-dollar gold piece, which had been authorized in 1837, except the new three-cent piece.

Finally, in 1853, a genuine subsidiary silver system was established. The denominations were fifty, twenty-five, and five cents. For weeks the Mint ran day and night. In 1857 the copper coinage was completely reformed, and the last surviving underweight and Spanish silver coins were withdrawn. After about 200 years as a colony and more than 60 years as a sovereign nation the country had an adequate currency.

With typical carelessness, Congress did not in the law of 1853 refer to the silver dollar. It was still the standard coin of 1792, of 371¼ grains. The law of 1837 had lowered the content of the gold dollar until the ratio was 16 to 1. Under this law the two dollars were equally a standard money. Legally, the standard was bimetallic. The silver dollar had been for sixty years a useless, forgotten coin. It had never circulated. After its suspension by Jefferson in 1806 there was no coinage until 1837. After that date coinage was impossible because of the unfavorable ratio. A handful were coined between 1837 and 1853, only for export to China. Actually the United States was on a Spanish silver-coin standard from 1792 to 1834 and a single gold standard after 1834. But in law the forgotten silver dollar was still a standard coin. The records show that some members of Congress thought the establishment of subsidiary coinage in 1853 actually established the single gold standard by law. The failure of Congress in 1853 to abolish the standard silver dollar, as it abolished the standard silver coins below the dollar, was one of the most costly blunders in our history.

In the Civil War period gold and silver coins disappeared, North and South, and the country was without a coin currency until 1876, except for an inadequate supply of bronze cent pieces authorized in 1864. For more than ten years retail trade was carried on with flimsy fractional notes issued by the Government.

In 1873 there was a major revision of the coinage laws. The new code dropped from the list of coins that might be produced the silver dollar, the standard coin which had never been in circulation and had never been coined except in fragmentary amounts. The law did not repeal the law of 1837 which made the dollar a standard in a bimetallic system. Without explanation of its intent Congress had adopted the single gold standard which had been actual since 1834. This came after three years of intensive study by Congress and by all available financial experts. The adoption of the single gold standard was excellent. The failure to amend the law of 1837 and to declare the intent to establish the gold standard was a monumental mistake.

This law of 1873 created an oversized silver dollar,

called the trade dollar. Ostensibly it was wholly for export to China. It was given free coinage. It was made a legal tender in payments to $5 in the United States. Enormous deposits of silver had been discovered in the Rockies. From 1860 down to the present day, the Western states have had Senators and Representatives determined to use the U. S. Government to enlarge the market for silver and to increase its price. These agents of petty mines have been tireless and conscientious. A legal tender quality for the trade dollar was indefensible. Conceivably it was a stupid accident in the law; more likely it was designed to give this strange coin wide circulation. It was a failure in trade with China. But unprincipled business men forced it on the poor and ignorant. Shortly after the law of 1873 there was a collapse of the price of silver, and a silver owner could take 97 cents' worth of silver to the Mint and get a one-dollar legal coin. Millions of the unsophisticated received these dollars, only to discover that they could not pass them on. For years the silver interests prevented repeal of the law. The coins were finally redeemed by the Government in 1887.

In 1933 the new President, Roosevelt, confiscated all gold in the country, repudiated the pledge of the Government to pay all United States bonds in gold, and installed a so-called "gold-purchase plan." Under it the Government was to buy all gold offered to it with paper money at steadily increasing prices. The theory of the plan was that the depressed price level of that time would rise in proportion to the increased price paid for gold. The law of 1837 gave a weight to the gold dollar of 23.22 grains, so that one ounce coined into $20.67. When in 1934 the price paid for gold reached $35, Roosevelt had Congress stop the program and establish a new gold-standard coin at that value for an ounce. The debasement of the standard dollar, from $20.67 to the ounce to $35 to the ounce, was approximately 41%.

The plan, promoted by Secretary of the Treasury Morgenthau, was an abject failure. It was condemned in advance by practically every financial authority in America, and European authorities regarded it as an incredible blunder.

After the adoption of the new gold standard the Administration embarked on a "managed currency program." All gold presented to the Government is paid for with paper money, and the gold bullion is buried in Fort Knox. It is illegal for private persons other than jewelers to own gold bullion or coins. The country has been since 1934 on an irredeemable paper money basis. No gold coins of the new weight have been produced.

The difficulties accruing from inadequate coinage before 1860 were aggravated in three ways: by a flood of privately made metal tokens, by vast issues of unauthorized paper notes by banks and business enterprises, and by widespread counterfeiting. The Government made practically no effort to cope with

counterfeiting until 1853. The discovery of gold in small quantities in Georgia and in much larger quantities in California led to private coinage on a large scale. The delays and costs involved in shipping gold to the Mints made private coinage profitable. The coins were neither counterfeits nor imitations of United States coins. The coins were not only easily identifiable but of high quality, most of them containing more gold than the Government coins. The coins of Georgia and California were widely circulated. In 1864 all private coinage was made illegal.

A new national system based on Spanish silver coins and grafted onto a British system of accounting gave rise to a novel nomenclature, with additional Latin forms to fit the first decimal system. The term "dollar" came from the very old "thaler," made of silver from the Joachimsthal mines in Germany. The English corrupted the word to "dollar." Shakespeare was making bad puns on the word as early as 1600. The *real* was equivalent to the six-penny "bit" of the colonies, and our new quarter-dollar of 1792 was equal to two of the Spanish bits. "Two bits," still used colloquially for a quarter-dollar, is the oldest native monetary term in our history.

The "cent," "disme," and "mille," wholly new decimal terms, are generally credited by historians to Gouverneur Morris, although the evidence is questionable. A colonial valuation in the East of true Spanish coins at eleven pence and five pence led to the use of "levy" for a dime and "fip" for the five-cent silver piece for many years. "Nickel," used colloquially to describe our five-cent piece, was first used to describe our first copper-nickel coin, a one-cent piece.

After nearly 200 years the origin of our dollar mark is still a subject of debate. There are various popular explanations. Almost certainly it derives from the very old Spanish symbol for the Spanish dollar or "peso." It has been found in United States documents before 1790.

This country has had the most confused, variegated, and heterogeneous coinage in all history. There have been four different weights of the standard gold coin. The standard silver dollar has had only one fine silver weight, but it has had two alloy weights. For a time it was coined at an illegal weight. Since 1878 it has been in fact an underweight, useless coin masquerading by a statutory falsehood as a standard coin. There have been standard silver coins of the value of fifty, twenty-five, ten, and five cents, and subsidiary silver coins of the value of fifty, twenty-five, twenty, ten, five, and three cents. The present subsidiary silver coins have absurd metric weights, so that it is impossible to state their weights in English terms. There have been eleven different types of cents or half-cents, of four different materials, of five different weights, and of three different legal tender qualities. Our present five-cent copper-nickel piece has a metric weight.

Every nation's coinage shows a few evolutionary changes dictated by economic or technical development. The endless changes in our nondescript coinages do not represent such evolutionary improvements. They represent nearly 200 years of legislative mistakes followed by mistaken efforts to correct mistakes. And from 1850 to the present day much of our coinage legislation has been tainted with demagoguery or corruption.

COIN'S FINANCIAL SCHOOL was written by W. H. ("Coin") Harvey to convert to bimetallism, at sixteen to one, people suffering from the hard times prevailing in 1894. It represented prominent bankers, editors and other gold monometallists as asking and taking instruction from "Coin, the smooth little financier." By graphic illustrations, homely allusions, glib arguments and the use of prominent names, the book obtained wide credence as a narrative of actual occurrences. Printed in cheap paper editions, it circulated very widely among farmers, debtors and other distressed classes, preparing many minds to receive Bryan's arguments.

COLD HARBOR (June 3, 1864). Following failures to smash and outflank Lee (C.) at Spotsylvania, Grant (U.) on May 20 directed the Army of the Potomac southeast on a turning movement. Lee retired behind the North Anna. Grant recognized this position's strength and continued "side-slipping toward Richmond" by successive marches and deployments until the Confederates stood on a six-mile front without reserves, their right on the Chickahominy, their center at Cold Harbor. Estimating Confederate morale low and Lee's center weak, Grant ordered a direct drive, 60,000 men on 4000 yards frontage. The assault at 4:30 P.M., June 3, against well-entrenched lines cost 5600 casualties and failed completely. Grant dug in, held Lee in position until June 12, then resumed "sideslipping" and, crossing the James, threatened Richmond through Petersburg.

COLD WAR refers to the state of continuing hostility, lacking a general peace settlement, between the Soviet with her close allies and the United States with her close allies, enduring from the end of World War II into the 1960's. Hostilities persisted because objectives proved irreconcilable: world communization after the "Peoples' Republic" pattern of the Soviet and China versus maintenance of private capitalism patterned after western representative democracy. The adjective "cold" was adopted because leading governments of the two blocs did not declare and wage traditional war with continuous military engagements fought over defined areas. Instead, they developed techniques of conquest and influence more flexible and pervasive.

Communist cold war tacticians avoided military bludgeoning where a neighboring state could be made into a satellite "Peoples' Republic" by an almost bloodless coup. Hard expert cadres of infiltrators gained control of key positions to win dominance over an ill-prepared, less-well-organized majority of the populace, as in Czechoslovakia. In less "ripe" regions they used guerilla warfare plus outside "volunteers" tirelessly, to wear down defense resources of a resistant government. Recourse to avowed warfare, against such persistent obstacles as those in Korea and French Indo-China spawned "splitting" techniques which created such unstable political and economic units as North and South Korea, North and South Vietnam; their southern sectors owed survival to United States military and economic aid. East-West splitting of Germany and Berlin became an impasse matched only by disarmament. Rarely did a popular uprising expose the nakedness of a "Peoples' Republic" by requiring imported Soviet forces to quell it, as in Hungary. Normally, the fiction of popular will and national independence was astutely fostered; it proved invaluable in communizing noncontiguous and emergent colonial areas, like Guinea and Ghana. Divisive factionalism was developed into a high art, on a global scale. Trained agents slipped into foreign countries, exploiting every real or fancied grievance —political, economic, social or racial—to convert unrest into violence, to unseat pro-Western governments, and to induce an economic misery and a political disorder which might seek refuge in communism, as in Cuba and Laos.

United States cold war tacticians spent billions on economic and military barriers against communism: the Marshall Plan prevented economic collapse of war-scarred western Europe; the Truman Doctrine prevented subjection of Greece and Turkey; a ring of aviation bases outside Soviet borders effectively threatened retaliation prior to development of intercontinental ballistic missiles. Strengthening of military potential in the North Atlantic and South East Pacific areas was undertaken in NATO and SEATO treaty organizations.

But after Stalin's death the cold war became a technological competition for military and prestige purposes——a race to perfect rockets, missiles and space shots and to provide political influence, grants, loans, personnel and tutelage to answer demands of "underdeveloped" areas for miraculous conversion into completely self-governing, industrialized entities. This phase maximized the disadvantages of the West, whose members held the colonies and the heavy foreign investments—possessions vulnerable to revolt, expropriation and nationalization. By 1960 the cold war was global and the "uncommitted" areas in Latin America, Asia and Africa held the balance of power.

COLLECTOR v. DAY. Probate Judge Day of Barnstable County, Mass., having paid the Civil War income tax upon his salary under protest, brought suit to recover it and obtained judgment. The tax collector then sued out a writ of error. The U. S. Supreme Court in 1870 decided that it was not competent for Congress to levy a tax upon the salary of a judicial officer; the judgment obtained by Day was affirmed.

COLLOT'S JOURNEY (1796). Gen. Victor Collot came to Philadelphia after the British took possession of Guadeloupe, West Indies, where he had been governor. When litigation prevented his departure for France, he undertook a boat journey into the western country. He left McKeesport, Pa., June 6, 1796, visited the Ohio River settlements, made an excursion into the Illinois country and then turned back down the Mississippi to New Orleans. His journal illustrates the enlightened appreciation of the potentialities of the American West displayed by many of his countrymen of the period.

COLONIAL AGENT was the representative sent to England by the colonies in America during the 17th and 18th centuries. Since the practice of maintaining an agent grew out of the exigencies of the times when communication was slow and uncertain, a representative formed an indispensable link between the mother country and her far-flung empire.

In the 17th century an agent went to England only on special missions. For instance, John Clarke was sent by Rhode Island to secure a charter for that community from the Restoration government. As soon as he had accomplished his arduous task, which took two years, he returned home. In the 18th century, however, when the business of colonial administration had greatly increased in volume and complexity, the agent, like the diplomat of today, remained at his post year after year. Benjamin Franklin was in England from 1757 to 1762 as agent of the Pennsylvania assembly.

The agent was not necessarily always a colonist; not infrequently an Englishman, especially interested in the American colonies, was appointed as, for example, the brilliant lawyer, Richard Jackson, who represented Connecticut during the Revolutionary period.

Though the agent was never an official member of the loose-jointed imperial machinery, yet his importance can hardly be overestimated. He served as a clearinghouse for information at a time when ignorance of colonial conditions was widespread; he attended hearings on various matters held by the Board of Trade and the Privy Council; he prepared petitions embodying specific claims or requests; he worked on the perennial Indian problems; and he wrestled with boundary disputes which, because of prodigal land grants, caused endless difficulties.

It can be seen that many of these tasks were of a routine nature requiring only industry and an understanding of colonial aspirations. At times, however, emergencies arose which made unlimited demands on the resourcefulness and indeed the strength of the representative. After 1660 the home government tried repeatedly to revise or revoke altogether the colonial charters in the interest of more centralized government. As this would mean a serious curtailment of precious liberties, the agent was always instructed to fight such action as forcibly as possible. In 1730 a bill establishing a monopoly in West Indian rum, sugar and molasses was introduced into Parliament. This obviously favored the West Indian sugar planters at the expense of the New England merchants. The struggle over this measure, the famous Molasses Act, lasted three years and absorbed the New England agents and their West Indian rivals almost to the exclusion of everything else.

Nothing throws more light on the management of the British colonies in its early years than a study of the colonial agent. In and out of the offices of the Board of Trade he passed, conferring with an army of clerks, committee members and minor officials, attending hearings, talking with influential members of Parliament, chatting with friends and colleagues. Faithful, alert, friendly, an ambassador of frontier philosophy to the Old World, he did much to facilitate the administration of the first British empire.

COLONIAL ASSEMBLIES had their beginnings in the Virginia House of Burgesses called by Gov. Yeardley in 1619. The first Virginia assembly was an outcome of a new policy inaugurated after the Sandys-Southampton group gained control of the Virginia Company. It was unicameral in organization and was composed of the governor, his council and two burgesses elected for each of the towns, plantations and hundreds. Subsequently the units of representation were certain privileged towns or cities and the counties. Not until the latter part of the 17th century did the elected element separate from the parent assembly, resulting in a bicameral legislative body. From the beginning the Virginia assembly claimed and exercised the right to initiate legislation, and under Gov. Harvey vindicated the right to control taxation. After the withdrawal of Gov. Berkeley from public life in 1652 the House of Burgesses exercised great authority scarcely checked by any outside interference except that embodied in the Navigation Act of 1651, which placed certain limitations upon commercial intercourse. When Berkeley returned to power he failed to call elections, and retained the old assembly for many years prior to Bacon's Rebellion in 1676. Popular resentment of this means of attempting to control the legislative branch by the executive had the effect of restoring the representative character of the assembly.

Plymouth colony set up a popular assembly consisting of all qualified freemen. With the growth of out-settlements this evolved into a representative bicameral body. In Massachusetts Bay an effort was made by Gov. Winthrop and his supporters to concentrate legislative authority in the Court of Assistants, with the Great and General Court limited to the activities of a court of election. This failed in face of the demand by deputies of the towns that the provisions of the royal charter should be fully observed. After experimenting with a primary assembly of all freemen of the company and with proxy voting, a representative bicameral system was evolved there as in Plymouth.

In Rhode Island, after the Federation of Providence, Portsmouth, Newport and Warwick, the towns were empowered to initiate legislation which was thereupon referred to the assembly; or, on the other hand, the assembly would refer measures to the towns for their approval or disapproval. The system was ineffective, and the charter of 1663 gave the assembly a dominating role in all matters of government.

Connecticut under its Fundamental Orders of 1639 had a General Court which was both a representative body and, upon sitting as a court of election, a primary assembly. The latter feature continued under the charter of 1662, although in the middle of the 18th century it disappeared in favor of local election of colonial officials. As in Rhode Island, the assembly was the real center of governmental authority and throughout the colonial period enjoyed great freedom from outside interference in the making of laws.

On coming into possession of his Maryland proprietary, Cecil Calvert, Lord Baltimore, called an assembly of freemen. However, he attempted to establish the principle that the proprietor alone might initiate legislation, and sent over drafts of a series of measures. The assembly rejected them, claiming sole powers of initiation, and passed a number of bills framed by its own members. Although these were rejected by Baltimore as in violation of his rights, he finally admitted the competence of the assembly to initiate laws, but insisted that all measures be submitted to him for acceptance or rejection.

During the 17th century law-making processes in Carolina were confused by the divergent aims of the eight proprietors and the settlers. The latter were determined to uphold the binding nature of the so-called Concessions and Agreement of 1665, which provided for a popularly elected assembly of freeholders. In opposition to this the proprietors attempted to enforce the feudal Fundamental Constitutions with its extraordinarily complicated lawmaking machinery, designed to guarantee proprietarial control of legislation.

Contemporaneously, New York under the Duke of York was ruled for many years without the aid of any popularly elected body, much to the dissatisfaction of the English-speaking population. However, with the retirement of Gov. Edmund Andros to England in 1680, the settlers refused to pay imposts, which made it necessary for the Duke either to send an army to subdue the people, or to grant an assembly. He chose the latter course in sending out Gov. Dongan; but the laws passed by the deputies were never ratified; and when James became king future assemblies were forbidden.

From the time of its founding Pennsylvania was provided with a popularly elected assembly. After the withdrawal of the charter of Massachusetts Bay in 1684, a process of consolidation took place in New England. With the establishment of the Dominion of New England, the assemblies were suppressed and law-making powers were centered in the appointed Dominion council. New York, East New Jersey and West New Jersey, the two last with popularly elected assemblies, were also embodied in the Dominion before it collapsed in 1689.

During the 18th century the assemblies frequently came into collision with the governors. In Massachusetts Bay such issues arose as those involving appropriations for a permanent establishment and for the building of forts and the control of the office of speaker of the house of representatives. In New York and New Jersey, as the result of the maladministration of Cornbury, joint-governor of those provinces, the assemblies gained new powers over financial disbursements and administration generally. In Pennsylvania, with the beginning of the French and Indian War a controversy developed over the force of proprietorial instructions to the governor, as well as over the issue of paper money, and the determination of the assembly, a unicameral body, to tax proprietorial lands. When Parliament threatened to compel all officeholders in Pennsylvania to take the required oaths rather than to affirm, in 1756 the Quaker majority in the assembly disappeared through resignations, with the result that for a short period harmony was restored between executive and legislature. Conflicts with the governors, as a rule, left the assemblies in a strongly entrenched position, in spite of the continued control of colonial legislation on the part of the Privy Council.

With the approach of the Revolution, breaches took place between the assemblies and their governors in all of the colonies except the two corporate colonies (Connecticut and Rhode Island), although the degree of friction varied from the violent manifestations in Massachusetts Bay to the not unsympathetic relations that subsisted between Gov. John Penn and the Pennsylvania assembly

COLONIAL CHARTERS. Royal charters represented the king's authorization of colonization under private enterprise and his definition of the relationship of the projected colony to the mother country. They were at the outset issued to two chief types of promoters, the trading company and the lords proprietors, the former interested chiefly in trade, the latter in land as a source of profit. In the Restoration period, charters of incorporation which very closely resembled those previously given to trading companies were granted also to two already well-established squatter colonies, Rhode Island and Connecticut.

Charters to trading companies vested powers of government in the company in England. That body could determine what officers, laws and ordinances were necessary for the colony, subject only to the condition that the laws must conform to those of England. In the proprietary charters the authority to govern was granted to the lord proprietor, who could determine the form of government, choose the officers and make the laws, subject to the advice and consent of the freemen. According to the corporation charters of Connecticut and Rhode Island, government was to be administered by governor, council and house of representatives; the latter chosen directly, the former indirectly by the people. In all types of charter the settlers who might go to the colonies were promised the rights and privileges of Englishmen, a phrase which, because of its vagueness, was to give considerable trouble later.

Toward the end of the 17th century the king began to find charters obstacles in the path of colonial control and tried to substitute the royal province for corporation and proprietary governments. In course of time he was almost completely successful, for by 1776 there remained only two proprietary provinces, Maryland and Pennsylvania, and two corporation colonies, Connecticut and Rhode Island. Massachusetts, though operating under a charter, was governed in the 18th century as a royal province.

COLONIAL COMMERCE took various forms. There was the two-way commerce: that between a colony and the mother country, as was the case with respect to the tobacco trade; or that between two colonies or between a colony and a British or a foreign West India port, such as characterized the provision trade of Pennsylvania and the limited commercial relations of Connecticut. However, a triangular trade was a common, if not the most common, form that colonial commerce took. This might involve a colony, the African coasts and the West Indies, typified by Rhode Island's trade in rum, slaves and molasses; or involve a colony, a European country, such as Spain or Portugal, and Great Britain, as in the case of the trade of Massachusetts Bay in prime fish, in wines and British commodities; or a colony, Newfoundland and the West Indies, as was characterized by the trade of the same colony in merchandise, including rum, prize fish and molasses; or a Northern colony, a Southern colony and Great Britain, involving provisions, tobacco or rice from the Carolinas and British and European merchandise.

This commerce was carried on, as a rule, in American-built ships. When ships themselves were articles of commerce they were generally built in New England, loaded in a Southern port and then sent to their destination in England. The two greatest colonial commercial centers before the American Revolution were Boston and Philadelphia, each exercising a dominating influence over an extended region. However, New York controlled the business of that province and of western Connecticut and east New Jersey; Newport that of Rhode Island and of southern Massachusetts Bay; and Charleston that of South Carolina, Georgia and southern North Carolina. This commerce involved not only barter, specie transactions in Spanish or Portuguese coins and bills of exchange, but credit extensions on a great scale. For example, as the result of credit extensions to Virginia planters by British merchants before the outbreak of the Revolutionary War, the former were in many instances hopelessly involved in debt.

The commercial relations of the colonies with the outside world were subject to some restrictions from the beginning as the result of the comprehension of the plantations within the English realm, such, for example, as the prohibition of the export of English specie. However, the development of restrictions with particular reference to the colonies, outside of early restrictions by the crown on the sale of tobacco, is associated with the body of legislation known as the trade and navigation acts, including the Woolen, the Molasses, the Hat, the Iron and the Sugar Acts. Under these, certain colonial products, such as American woolens or beaver hats, could not enter into commerce; other products, placed on the enumerated list, such as sugar, molasses, tobacco, dyewoods, indigo, cotton, rice, furs, ginger, copper, potash, hides, raw silk, ship-timber, naval stores and iron, could be carried directly only to the mother country or to another colony, with certain relaxations ultimately provided for the marketing in Europe of sugar and rice. Ships engaged in colonial commerce were confined, with certain exceptions in favor of prizes captured, to vessels of English, later British, or colonial construction and manned chiefly by those owing allegiance to the crown. All such vessels were required to have a British or colonial registry, to be commanded by British or colonial officers and to sail under British colors. Also it was incumbent upon colonial merchants who desired to import European commodities to do so through a British port, with the exception of a few specified articles such as salt for the New England and Newfoundland fisheries, Madeira and Azores wines, and servants, provisions and horses from Ireland and Scotland.

COLONIAL COUNCILS existed in all the colonies. In general they represented the same control as did the governor. In the royal provinces they were appointed directly by the Crown, usually on recommendation of the Board of Trade. In the proprietary colonies they were appointed by the proprietor, and in Massachusetts, Rhode Island and Connecticut the councils were elective. In the royal and proprietary provinces the members of the council served during good behavior. The governor could suspend members for cause, but they could be removed only by action of the Crown or the proprietors.

Councils varied in size, although the standard practice tended to a uniform council of twelve in the royal provinces. Rhode Island had ten, Pennsylvania a council of eighteen and Massachusetts one of twenty-eight. Colonial councils acted as the upper house of the legislature and when so acting the governor was directed (1736) not to be present. The council together with the governor formed a supreme court of appeals in civil cases. Finally the council was an executive and administrative body for the governor, and many of his acts could be carried out only with the approval of the council. The duties of the council were specified in charters or in instructions to the royal governor, although custom gradually changed practices.

COLONIAL DAMES OF AMERICA. Women are eligible for membership who are descended from some ancestor who came to reside in America prior to 1750, and who served his country in the founding of a town which has survived and developed, or who held an important position, or who contributed to the achievement of American independence. The society, organized in 1890, has as its objects the collection of relics and mementoes for preservation, the creation of interest in American history and the promotion of social fellowship.

COLONIAL GOVERNORS were the chief civil officers in the American colonies before the Revolution. Some were appointed by the king as, for instance, the governor of the royal colony of Virginia; others were nominated by a proprietor, such as William Penn, and were approved by the Crown; and a few, those of the chartered colonies, were elected by deputies of the freemen of the community.

Their duties were the usual ones of an administrative officer: defense, preservation of law and order, promotion of the general welfare. To these were added enforcement of the Navigation Acts and supervision of the collection of customs duties. And so necessary did those last-named functions seem to the home government, believing in the principles of mercantilism, that even the governors of the chartered colonies were required to give oath and bond that they would execute the commercial laws.

The tasks of the executive of the chartered colonies were relatively simple. Chosen by his own people and linked by only nebulous bonds to the mother country, he suffered under no conflict of loyalties, and consideration of local interests easily took precedence over imperial policies.

The position of the governor of the royal or proprietary colonies, however, was always uncertain and often unpleasant. Saddled with definite instructions, he faced provincially minded and stubborn assemblies. Therefore, he was forced to decide between either constant bickering and possible loss of salary —for the assembly controlled the purse strings—or jettisoning most of his instructions.

After the Restoration England attempted to reorganize her loose-jointed empire in order to establish uniform government in the colonies, but this was never accomplished Consequently the colonial assemblies, overshadowing the governors, became the real executives and soon learned the art of self-government.

COLONIAL JUDICIARY, THE, was created in each colony by act of the assembly and followed the general pattern of English procedure. Each colony had a system of local courts to try petty offenses. There was a county court in most of the colonies to try major civil and criminal cases, which was presided over by one of the superior judges who travelled on circuit. There was a superior court made up of the superior court judges sitting *en banc* and presided over by a chief justice. Each colony had an attorney general.

In the royal provinces the chief justice and the judges of the superior court were at first appointed directly by the Crown. Every effort was made to secure competent men. In some cases well-trained lawyers were induced to emigrate to America to fill such vacancies, as was the case when William Atwood was appointed chief justice of New York (1701). Apparently, the first commissions were at the will of the Crown, as were those of other important colonial officers. There were, however, no actual removals. The Act of Settlement had made English judges independent of the Crown, with commissions during good behavior. Governors were authorized by instructions to fill vacancies when they occurred. Their instructions were not very clear on this point, except they were not to impose "any limitation of time" in any commissions they might issue. By the middle of the 18th century many judges had received commissions during good behavior. Gov. Clinton's appointment of William DeLancey as chief justice of New York attracted the attention of the Board of Trade to the obscurity of the instruction and in 1754, it instructed every governor that in future all judicial officers should be appointed "during pleasure only." In Pennsylvania the assembly enacted a law providing that judges could only be removed on address of the assembly (1759). This act was promptly disallowed in England.

The death of George II in 1760 terminated all judicial commissions, many of which had been granted by the governors during good behavior. The Board of Trade insisted that all renewals should be "at the pleasure of the Crown." This precipitated a controversy with the assemblies, which refused to pay judges unless their commissions read as formerly "during good behavior." Gov. Hardy of New Jersey had already renewed commissions under the former terms (1761). These commissions were held void by the Privy Council in England and funds were found to pay the judges so as to make them entirely independent of the local assemblies. This enforced solution of the question rankled with the Americans, as it deprived Englishmen in America of rights guaranteed to Englishmen in England, and is one of the specific acts of tyranny charged against George III in the Declaration of Independence.

COLONIAL PLANS OF UNION (1643–1754). The separate founding of the colonies, coupled with difficulties of travel, prevented effective union until the Revolution. However, many proposals for union grew out of the common problems faced by the colonies. The most continuous problem was that of frontier defense against Indian attack. Rivalry with the Dutch and French aggravated this problem. Trade and boundary disputes emphasized the need of a common arbitrator. A common culture and allegiance suggested the reasonableness of unity. Moreover, the English home government, desiring to make the colonies an effective unit for imperial trade and defense, in some cases encouraged a union. The chief plans, which varied widely in origin and the number of colonies to be included, were: (1) The United Colonies of New England, 1643–1684. Massachusetts Bay, Plymouth, Connecticut and New Haven, united in a league largely for frontier defense. (2) Dominion of New England, 1688. The British Crown made Sir Edmund Andros governor-general of all the New England colonies, New York, East and West Jersey. (3) Intercolonial Congress, 1689–91. New York, Massachusetts, Plymouth and Connecticut entered a temporary military league for frontier defense. (4) William Penn's "Briefe and Plaine Scheam" for Union, 1697. Penn's proposal for a loose confederation grew out of the conditions prevailing during King William's War. (5) Union under the Earl of Bellomont, 1698–1701, who was commissioned governor of New York, Massachusetts and New Hampshire, and commander of the military forces of Connecticut, Rhode Island and the Jerseys. This step was taken by the Crown because of colonial failure to co-operate in defense. (6) Hamilton's Plan, 1699, for frontier defense and production of naval supplies for the Royal Navy proposed by the deputy-governor of Pennsylvania. An intercolonial assembly was to levy a poll tax to finance the work which was to be done by British regulars. (7) *A Virginian's Plan of Union*, 1701, was an anonymous publication issued in London which advocated abolishing all the proprietary governments and uniting the colonies under an intercolonial congress and governor-general. (8) Robert Livingston's Plan, 1701. In a letter to the Lords of Trade Livingston proposed that the colonies be grouped into three units, which would be co-ordinated by the Council of Trade for frontier de-

fense. (9) Earl of Stair's Plan, 1721, submitted by the Earl of Stair to the Board of Trade, was to include all the continental colonies and the British West Indies. There was to be a governor-in-chief appointed by the crown. An advisory council of two members from each colony was to assist this official. The governor and his council could levy assessments against the colonies for defense purposes. The scheme was to be established by action of Parliament. (10) The Lords of Trade Plan, 1721, was contained in a report given the king. It was essentially a brief outline of the Stair plan. (11) Daniel Coxe's Plan, 1722, appeared in a book of travel published in London. It proposed a union of all the continental colonies under one governor, represented by a lieutenant in each colony. A great council composed of two delegates from each colony was to advise the governor and make the allotments of money and men needed for colonial defense. (12) The Kennedy-Franklin Plan, 1751, was published by Archibald Kennedy, receiver-general of New York, in a pamphlet dealing with Indian trade and frontier defense. These were to be directed by a superintendent to be assigned to the colonies by commissioners representing the colonial assemblies. Benjamin Franklin added some details which closely resembled his later Albany Plan. (13) The Albany Plan, 1754. This best known of all the colonial plans was largely the work of Franklin. It called for an intercolonial council with membership apportioned according to wealth and population. The president-general was to be appointed by the Crown. Control of Indian affairs and frontier defense was to be under control of this royal officer and his council. The colonial legislatures rejected the plan and it was not pressed by the home government.

COLONIAL POLICY, BRITISH, is technically that policy that was laid down or was evolved after the union of England and Scotland in 1707. This policy was based largely upon the earlier English policy, which envisaged the promotion of domestic industry, foreign trade, the fisheries and shipping, and the planting of Crown lands in the New World with the establishment of colonial settlements, or the exploitation of the resources of America through such commercial companies as the Hudson's Bay Company and the South Sea Company. It also included the policy of encouraging the utilization of the vast labor resources of Africa in the establishment and maintenance of plantations for the production of so-called colonial staples.

The earliest manifestations of English colonial policy are embodied in the 16th-century patents to Gilbert and Raleigh; then in 1606 came those to the London and Plymouth companies of Virginia in connection with which a settlement policy was laid down which, among other features, embodied the idea of direct Crown control; but in 1609 this was modified in the charter of that year issued in favor of the

Virginia Company substituting indirect for direct control and providing for a definite and extensive grant of land; this new policy also found expression in the creation of the Council for New England in 1620. Direct control, however, made its reappearance in 1624 when with the withdrawal of the political powers of the Virginia Company, Virginia took its place as the first of the so-called royal colonies under a system of government that permitted the survival of the colonial assembly. Nevertheless, this new policy was not to become basic until the beginning of the new century, for the year 1629 saw the appearance of the corporate colony of Massachusetts Bay with a charter that was sufficiently broad to permit the transfer of the government of the company to the New World, and 1632 that of the proprietaryship of Maryland with the granting to the Baltimore family of very wide powers. Thus three types of colonial government appeared as the result of the formulation of colonial policy—or perhaps one might suggest more accurately as the result of the failure of the Government to formulate a policy—royal, proprietary and charter.

Up to the Interregnum, colonial policy emanated from the Crown and was directed by it. Then with the outbreak of the English Civil War the Long Parliament assumed control, acting mainly through a special commission or council provided for by the Ordinance of 1643, which gave to its president, the Earl of Warwick, the title of Governor-in-Chief and Lord High Admiral of all the English colonies in America. Moreover, between the years 1645 and 1651 Parliament laid down various regulations which looked to a strict control of colonial commerce in favor of English shipping and manufactures. Nor did this parliamentary interference with the colonies cease with the Restoration, which not only gave validity to these restrictions but added to them in a series of measures beginning with the so-called First Navigation Act of 1660 and culminating in the very comprehensive Act of 1696. During the Commonwealth period Cromwell introduced a striking but temporary departure in colonial policy in 1654 with his ambitious plan known as the Western Design which had a twofold purpose: the acquisition of the Spanish empire in the New World and in this connection the removal of Northern English colonists to the warmer climes.

The growth in importance of the colonies led, moreover, to various experiments in their supervision such as the Laud Commission appointed by Charles I, and the various councils of Charles II ending with the transference in 1675 of this function to the Lords of Trade, a committee of the Privy Council, which continued to function after a manner until in 1696 William III brought into existence the Lords Commissioners for Trade and Plantations, a body which survived until after the American Revolution and which in the main fully justified its existence.

Colonial policy in the 18th century was characterized not only by efforts to reduce the colonies to a uniform type—that of the royal colony—which met with considerable success, but also by increased restrictions upon colonial enterprise with such acts as the Woolen Act of 1699, the White Pine Acts, the Hat Act of 1731, the Sugar Acts of 1733 and 1764 and the Iron Act of 1750. With the middle of the 18th century an important modification of policy may be noted with the growing menace of French competition. Side by side with mercantilism (with the emphasis upon immediate economic gain), modern imperialism (with the emphasis upon power politics, territorial aggrandizement, centralization of authority and a unified Indian policy) made its appearance. With the collapse of French empire in North America Parliament also turned its attention to securing a direct revenue from the colonies, passing for this purpose the Stamp Act of 1765 and the Townshend Acts of 1767. Reliance upon these new policies helped to bring on a crisis in colonial affairs that led to the Revolution.

COLONIAL SETTLEMENTS. Various little colonies were planted along the coastal ribbon of the Atlantic for different reasons. Government encouraged them to serve the economic needs of the nation, capitalists hoped for profit and people sought better opportunities. Tragedy stalked the efforts to colonize. Ships, abundant capital, many people were demanded to found a prosperous colony. The loss of life and money was tragic. Some ventures were stillborn, others were nursed through a puling infancy to maturity, a few grew lustily from birth.

Humphrey Gilbert landed with his company on Newfoundland's shores in 1584. A few months saw them sail away. Walter Raleigh in 1585 settled a few colonists on Roanoke Island (Carolina coast), but sustained effort failed to keep the venture alive. The time was not ripe and the cost was too heavy for private purses. The close of the war with Spain in 1604 freed England to turn to America. Joint-stock companies, combining capital and credit, entered into colonization. In 1607 the Plymouth Company tried a settlement on the Kennebec River (Maine), the London Company on the James River (Virginia). A rigorous winter and the death of the chief promoter sent the Kennebec settlers soon away. The Council for New England (1620) proved to be only a land company whose subgrants resulted in a few fishing, trading, lumbering camps on New England's shores. Against heavy odds the London Company persisted. During its existence about 5500 emigrants left England for Virginia; in 1625 a few over a thousand were living in the colony. The distress on a long voyage, disease, starvation and Indians in the colony took a deadly toll. Virginia lived to be the first permanent English colony, with a population of 5000 in 1634, rising to 50,000 in 1690.

England was not the only mother of colonies. In 1624 the Dutch West India Company sent over thirty families which founded New Amsterdam and Fort Orange (Albany). Forty years of effort showed a population of only about 8000. The Dutch were not a migrating people, and a grasping company attracted few settlers. In 1638 the New Sweden Company began Fort Christina on the Delaware with a few people, but New Sweden never contained over a few hundred Swedes and Finns. Sweden's wars in Europe left her inadequate sources for colonial ventures. New Sweden ceased to be when captured by the Dutch in 1655.

The economic motive was not the only factor in colonial enterprise. Abundant land meant little without people. At first no urgent expulsive forces drove people away. Settlers were hard to secure until intolerable conditions sent them to the new land. This stream began in 1620 when the Pilgrims found their weary way to plant the colony of Plymouth. Villagers from northern England, denied freedom of worship, went to Holland for refuge, but finding Dutch life uncomfortable, they came to New England. The stream widened with the exodus of over 16,000 to New England during 1630–40. Various motives explain the migration, but primary was the purpose to establish in Massachusetts a city of God on Puritan lines. Unable to reform the Anglican Church, visited with harsh royal authority, the Puritan leaders found the answer in Massachusetts. Villagers from Massachusetts Bay, in 1635, founded the colony of Connecticut, where better land was available and a milder brand of Puritanism was practiced. A small band of devoted Puritans began the colony of New Haven in 1638. In 1662 New Haven was merged with Connecticut and thirty years later the greater colony numbered about 18,000 people. Intolerable conditions in Massachusetts peopled Rhode Island. The Bay colony dealt severely with dissent. The radical views of Roger Williams drove him to find refuge in the settlement of Providence in 1636. The strange ideas of Mrs. Hutchinson and her followers brought exile, some settling at Portsmouth, others at Newport. Rhode Island contained about 4000 souls by 1690. Massachusetts added Maine by purchase and secured Plymouth colony by merger and before 1700 the Bay province had over 50,000 people. New Hampshire was a slender little colony which harbored a few people under the proprietorship of Capt. John Mason. Maryland owed its genesis to Lord Baltimore, who under a royal charter in 1632 desired to find a refuge for Catholics and to build up a great landed estate. From small beginnings its population rose to 30,000 within sixty years.

After 1660 colonial expansion took on a renewed life. Again promoters sought profit and people better opportunities. The circle of English colonies was completed by the conquest of New Netherland in 1664, renamed New York and granted to the Duke of York. He subgranted New Jersey to Sir George Carteret and Lord John Berkeley. Carolina, granted to eight men by charter in 1663, divided into two colonies, North Carolina peopled from Virginia and South Carolina settled by discontented planters from Barbados and persecuted Protestants from France and England. After thirty years of effort neither colony had over 3000 people. Quakerism, with its democratic and mystical principles, came into tragic collision with orthodoxy in both Old and New England. The Quakers found a welcome in Rhode Island and established their own colonies on the Delaware. In 1674 Berkeley sold West Jersey, which finally came into the hands of the Quakers who settled along the Delaware at Burlington and other places. East Jersey, purchased from the Carteret estate in 1680, soon fell under the control of a large board in which the Quakers were prominent. Before the century closed East Jersey counted less than 10,000, West Jersey about 4000. In 1681 William Penn received a charter for Pennsylvania where he tried a "Holy Experiment" in Quaker principles. The province became a haven of refuge for the persecuted, welcoming English, Welsh and Irish Quakers, and Germans. It grew lustily, having a population, inclusive of Delaware, of over 12,000 within a decade. Delaware, granted to William Penn by the Duke of York, governed at first as part of Pennsylvania, in 1704 became a province with Penn as proprietor. Thus ends the founding of the original colonies except for Georgia, which came into existence in 1732, in response to humanitarian motives. Georgia harbored debtors from English jails, and Lutheran exiles from Germany.

COLONIAL WARS. Although English, French and Spanish colonies in North America were repeatedly plunged into war by the outbreak of hostilities in Europe involving their parent states, the colonial wars, from the outset, were much more than mere New World phases of Old World conflicts. America's natural resources and the supposed advantages of owning American markets led Europeans to seek vast holdings here, and economic rivalries among the colonials themselves were intensified by racial and religious antagonisms. Louis XIV, concentrating on aggressions in Europe, gave little practical support to offensives in America; thus Frontenac, in King William's War (1689–97), resorted to the employment of Indian allies in ruthless border raids. Similar raids were utilized, chiefly by the French, in the subsequent conflicts: Queen Anne's War (1702–13), King George's War (1744–48) and the French and Indian War (1754–63).

At the outset of hostilities, and in 1711, English colonials and English regulars tried, futilely, to capture Quebec, the ultimate conquest of which by Wolfe, in 1759, is the best known of many dramatic episodes of these wars. English forces, chiefly colonial, captured Port Royal in 1690 and again in 1710, although not until the Treaty of Utrecht (1713) was Acadia confirmed to the English, becoming then their outpost, Nova Scotia. At Utrecht the French also yielded Newfoundland and their claims to the Hudson Bay territory. During "the long peace" following 1713 (actually marred by hostilities in America and the West Indies) France established Louisbourg on Cape Breton Island, a base of operations against English participation in North Atlantic fisheries and trade routes. The restoration of Louisbourg to France (1748) after its capture by New Englanders (1745) embittered many colonials, already indignant at England's tragic mismanagement of colonial volunteers in an expedition against Cartagena (1740). Other friction between England and her colonies was caused by the former's attempts to dominate military operations and the latter's failure to meet, fully or promptly, English requisitions for men, money and supplies, as well as by the colonies' persistence in trading with the enemy. Spain entered the conflict in the second war, exchanging blows with the English in Florida and South Carolina. When King George's War began Spain and England already were engaged in the War of Jenkin's Ear. Spain, a late entrant in the last colonial war, lost Florida to England. This conflict, the French and Indian War, was precipitated by English expansion westward and French advances into the Ohio Valley, the link between New France (Canada) and French Illinois and Louisiana. Braddock's defeat (1755) near Fort Duquesne was followed by English disappointments and defeats at Crown Point, Niagara, Oswego, Ticonderoga and elsewhere, until the turning of the tide in 1758, usually accredited to England's new war minister, William Pitt. By the Treaty of Paris (1763) France retained most of her West Indian Islands and some fishing bases off Canada; her other North American possessions east of the Mississippi, except the neighborhood of New Orleans, she ceded to England.

COLORADO was first visited by white men under the banner of Spain. Coronado, seeking fabled wealth, penetrated the American Southwest. Returning, disillusioned, he probably touched the southeast corner of Colorado in 1541. New Mexico, settled about 1600, then included the Colorado region. Spanish slave-catching and prospecting expeditions reached this country during the 17th century. In 1706 Ulibarri crossed the upper Arkansas, took formal possession for Spain and called the region Santo Domingo.

Frenchmen, from the Great Lakes region, pushed toward the Rockies. The alarmed Spaniards countered. In 1719 and 1720 Valverde and Villasur led unsuccessful expeditions against the intruders. The Mallet brothers, in 1739, crossed Colorado territory and reached Santa Fe. With France eliminated in 1763, Spain was again in undisputed possession of the Colorado region.

Through the Louisiana Purchase, 1803, the eastern part of Colorado became American. Z. M. Pike, first official explorer, led a small party up the Arkansas in 1806. Failing to climb the peak that bears his name, he turned south and built a log fort on the Conejos River. From here he was taken, as a prisoner, to Santa Fe and was finally released on the Louisiana border. The western boundary of the Louisiana Purchase was fixed in 1819. Through Colorado, it followed the Arkansas to its source and thence north to the 42nd parallel. S. H. Long, 1820, Frémont on his five expeditions, 1842–53, Gunnison, 1853, were official explorers who gave enlightening reports on the Colorado country.

Unofficial explorers, trappers and fur traders thoroughly examined the region from 1800 to 1840. Barter with Indians created Bent's Fort and other trading posts in the region. This trade augmented the overland commerce to New Mexico that made the Santa Fe Trail, which cut the southeast section of Colorado. The Mexican War brought Kearny's army over this trail and added the rest of Colorado Territory to the United States in 1848.

Settlements in Colorado, established in the 1850's by New Mexicans, were typical Spanish towns, with dirt-roofed adobe houses enclosing a plaza. Irrigated agriculture and grazing were their economic bases. Need for Indian protection caused the establishment, in 1852, of Fort Massachusetts, first United States military fort in Colorado.

Anglo-American settlement resulted from gold discoveries. News of finds at Cherry Creek, in 1858, caused the Pikes Peak gold rush of 1859. As a result of the reports, and of the panic of 1857, some 100,000 persons set out for the new Eldorado. Fortunately, real discoveries saved the movement from collapse. J. H. Gregory found lode gold near present Central City, May 6, 1859. Other discoveries followed. Mining camps and towns sprang up in the mountains, and outfitting towns at their eastern base. The influx of population brought need for government. Jefferson Territory, locally organized in 1859, maintained some authority until replaced by Colorado Territory, created by Congress Feb. 28, 1861. Colorado troops sustained the Union in the Civil War, giving decisive aid in the battle of Glorieta. Colorado was admitted to the Union, Aug. 1, 1876.

COLT SIX SHOOTER, the invention of Samuel Colt, was the first practical arm of its kind. With the rifle, it had its place in revolutionizing methods of warfare, and was an important link in the development of arms from the muzzle-loading musket to the magazine rifles and machine-guns of today.

Its manufacture began at Paterson, N. J., in 1836. Colt's patent, secured Feb. 25, 1836, covered the revolution and locking of the cylinder firmly in place, so that the chambers of the cylinder came in line with the barrel by simply pulling the hammer back to full cock. From the first, all the barrels were expertly rifled to give the greatest possible accuracy to the bullet. Although various models were produced at Paterson, the arms did not at first receive the endorsement of Government officials, and the company failed in 1842.

A few Colt arms, used by army officers in the Seminole War and by Texas Rangers during the border troubles, proved the worth of the "revolving pistol," and a supply was ordered by the Government in 1847. As Colt had no factory at that time, the first 2000 or 3000 were made for him at the plant of Eli Whitney in New Haven, Conn. These were heavy revolvers of .44 caliber and soon became the standard of the U. S. Army and the Texas Rangers. Colt resumed the manufacture of revolvers at Hartford, Conn., in 1848. From 1856 to 1865 there were 554,283 of the powder and ball revolvers manufactured at the Hartford factory. Large quantities of these arms were used during the Civil War by both Union and Confederate troops. All Colt revolvers, up to the early 1870's, were made to shoot loose powder and lead bullets, the powder being ignited by a percussion cap. From that period, envelope cartridges, enclosing powder and bullet, were used until the advent of metallic ammunition.

Colt six-shooters played a prominent part in the development of the West. When first used in Indian fighting the six-shooter was a surprise weapon, as the savages did not look for more than one shot and when opposed by a single-shot arm it was their custom to draw fire and then rush the settler while he was reloading.

The six-shooter won its popularity in the West because it was easily carried, accurate and of high capacity. Sheriffs, cowboys and plainsmen quickly became expert marksmen. It was an ideal weapon for mounted rangers and cattlemen, and was used for hunting as well as for defense. The extinction of the buffalo can be laid, in part, to the efficiency of the six-shooter in the hands of hunting horsemen.

COLUMBIA, BURNING OF.

Sherman's army reached Columbia, S. C., Feb. 17, 1865, on its famous march through the Carolinas. The fact that Columbia was the capital city of the state which was held peculiarly responsible for the war, and the desire of the Union soldiers for vengeance, probably account for the burning of the city, which occurred that night. Sherman's assertion that the fire spread from bales of cotton ignited by evacuating Confederates under Gen. Wade Hampton is not acceptable, for the cotton appears to have been drenched by fire engines long before the fires of the night of Feb. 17 gained headway. The house fires, reported to have been started by Union soldiers, originated on the windward side of the long-extinguished cotton in the middle of a very wide street and swept over that street and eastward across the city. It is probable that only by

confining his men to camp could Gen. Sherman have prevented the conflagration. He later asserted that he would not have done that to save the city. In his memoirs Sherman wrote: "Having utterly ruined Columbia, the right wing began its march northward."

COLUMBIA RIVER, EXPLORATION AND SETTLEMENT.

The estuary of the Columbia was first seen, described and mapped in 1775 by Capt. Bruno Hezeta, who named it Bahía de la Asumpción, though Spanish maps showed it as Ensenada de Hezeta. In 1792 Capt. Robert Gray of Boston sailed ten miles up the river proper and six miles up Gray's Bay, naming it Columbia's River after his ship. The same year W. R. Broughton of Vancouver's party surveyed and charted to Cottonwood Point, 119 statute miles from the ocean.

In 1800 Lagasse and LeBlanc reached the upper river from the Rocky Mountains. Lewis and Clark, in 1805, explored from the mouth of the Yakima to Cottonwood Point, 214 miles. In 1807 David Thompson explored for 111 miles, from the mouth of Blaeberry Creek to the Columbia River's source in Columbia Lake; and in 1811 Finan McDonald navigated from Kettle Falls to Death Rapids, 255 miles. In the same year Thompson navigated the entire river.

Prior to the great wagon train of 1843, settlements had been started along the river in over forty localities. The posts of the fur traders included those of the North West Company, the Astorian posts and those of independent traders. Among the earliest were Fort Clatsop (1805) and Chouteau's post (1807). Other settlements were Fort Colville (1825); Willamette Valley, an agricultural settlement (1829); Bonneville's cantonment (1832); Whitman Mission (1836); and Cœur d'Alene (1842). After 1843 the wagon train rapidly opened the country, and subsequently the steamboat, railroads and highways have transformed the wilderness into a prosperous and populous region.

COLUMBIA RIVER TREATY.

A water-power and storage agreement between the United States and Canada, to run for sixty years, was signed in Washington, D. C., Jan. 17, 1961, and ratified by the U. S. Senate, March 16, 1961. The agreement, which must also be ratified by the Canadian Government, provides that the United States will build the Libby Dam in northern Montana, which was authorized by Congress in 1950, within five years after joint ratification of the pact. Joint protection against improper diversion of power by either party to the agreement is provided for. Canada will build dams in Canadian territory at Arrow Lake, Mica Creek and Duncan Lake, all in British Columbia. United States development costs are put at $756 million, including $322 million for the construction of the Libby Dam; Canadian development costs are put at something over $400 million. Water power and storage development will supply hydroelectric power to the states of Washington, Oregon, Idaho and Montana as required; Canadian distribution will be to British Columbia and Alberta provinces.

COLUMBIA UNIVERSITY, established by royal charter on Oct. 31, 1754, as the College of the Province of New-York, was known from the beginning as King's College. The first president, Rev. Samuel Johnson, D. D., began instruction with a class of eight students in the English charity schoolhouse, and degrees were first conferred in 1758. In 1760 the college moved into a new building on what is now Park Place, New York City. Rev. Myles Cooper of Oxford, who succeeded Johnson as president in 1763, developed the college and conformed it as much as possible to English patterns, adding a medical school in 1767. Upon the occupation of New York by the American army at the outbreak of the Revolution, the building was taken over for use as a military hospital, all teaching ceased, and the students were dispersed. The corporation maintained its existence during the subsequent British occupation, however, and was rechartered, in 1784, as Columbia College under the Regents of the University of the State of New York. This form of government proving unsatisfactory, in 1787 an act was passed confirming the royal charter of 1754, and vesting the property and franchises of King's College in the trustees of Columbia College in the City of New York, under which charter it has continued to operate. The medical faculty was revived in 1785, but discontinued in 1813, its work being carried on by the College of Physicians and Surgeons, which was again incorporated in the college in 1860. During the first half of the 19th century the enrollment remained at about 100 annually, with a small faculty and a traditional curriculum. The administration of Charles King (1849–64) saw the establishment of the Law School (1858), the Medical School (1860), the School of Mines (1864), the enlargement of the faculty and curriculum and the awakening of the university idea. During King's administration the college was moved (1857) from its original site to Madison Ave. and 49th St. Under President Frederick A. P. Barnard (1864–89), Columbia achieved university status, which was confirmed by the revised corporation statutes of 1891; the first graduate school, that of Political Science, was established in 1880; women were permitted to study for Columbia degrees (1883); and the library began to grow in size and usefulness. Under Seth Low, president from 1889 to 1901, Columbia was moved (1897) to its present site on Morningside Heights, and the graduate faculties of Philosophy (1890) and Pure Science (1892) were established. The trustees adopted the name Columbia University in 1896, and the corporate title was legally changed in 1912. During the presidency

of Nicholas Murray Butler (1901–45) Columbia's enrollment, faculty, and endowment increased roughly tenfold, and the university began to draw students from all parts of the world. Columbia University as of 1960 includes, in addition to the schools above mentioned, Barnard College (1889), Teachers College (1898), Schools of Architecture (1881), Pharmacy (1904), Journalism (1912), Business (1916), Dental and Oral Surgery (1916), Library Service (1926), Social Work (1940), International Affairs (1946), and General Studies (1947). Barnard College, Teachers College, and the College of Pharmacy are financially independent but affiliated corporations.

COMBINE, THE, is a farm machine that makes harvesting and threshing a single process. It was developed by 1828, but not perfected until the 1870's. Between 1870 and 1873 the U. S. Patent Office recorded the invention of six harvester-threshers; and by 1880 the combine was commercially established.

Until 1920 this machine was used primarily on the West coast, because fair weather and dry grain were considered essential to its operation. High grain prices and the popularity of labor-saving devices after World War I brought the combine to the states of the Middle West where large-scale farming was being practiced. About this same time a desire for efficiency in the harvesting of soybeans brought the harvester-thresher into extensive use.

COMMERCE, THE DEPARTMENT OF, was created, as the Department of Commerce and Labor, by an act of Congress, Feb. 14, 1903, "to foster, promote, and develop the foreign and domestic commerce, the mining, manufacturing, shipping, and fishery industries, the labor interests, and the transportation facilities of the United States." That law was modified by an act of March 4, 1913, establishing the Department of Labor. The Department of Commerce in the narrower sense came into being at the latter date. But many of the functions of the Department are almost as old as the Federal Government and many of its agencies, under various names, were organized early in our history.

After the formation of the Department of Labor in 1913, the Department of Commerce retained the Bureaus of the Census, Corporations, Fisheries, Foreign and Domestic Commerce, Lighthouses, Navigation, and Standards, and the Coast and Geodetic Survey and Steamboat Inspection Service. Lighthouse service and aids to navigation were authorized by law as early as 1789. The first census was taken in 1790. Coast and geodetic surveys, vital to shipping and defense, were authorized in 1807. The statistical work of the Bureau of Foreign and Domestic Commerce has been traced to an office established in the Treasury Department in 1820. Earlier agencies in the general field of the National Bureau of Standards included the Office of Standard Weights and Measures, attached to the Coast and Geodetic Survey before it became, in 1901, the nucleus of the Bureau of Standards. A Commissioner of Fish and Fisheries was appointed in 1871. The Bureau of Navigation was established in 1884.

Under Herbert Hoover as Secretary of Commerce and later as President, the Department acquired jurisdiction over the Patent Office and the Bureau of Mines and greatly expanded the work of many of its agencies (notably the Bureau of Foreign and Domestic Commerce and the Bureau of Standards), besides adding new services such as the Aeronautics Branch, the Radio Division, and the Federal Employment Stabilization Board.

The Department's fourteen agencies of 1931 had been reduced, by early 1940, to six: Foreign and Domestic Commerce, Census, Standards, Marine Inspection and Navigation, the Coast and Geodetic Survey, and the Patent Office. Among the agencies added thereafter, in reversal of the trend, were the Weather Bureau, the Bureau of Public Roads, the Maritime Administration and Maritime Board, the Defense Air Transportation Administration, the Office of International Trade Fairs, and the Business and Defense Services Administration.

The names, duties, and interrelations of the various agencies of the Department underwent many changes. Those changes betokened efforts throughout the Federal Government to meet emergency conditions and new ideas of governmental responsibilities. Many emergency needs were met, it is true, by temporary agencies but with the co-operation of Commerce and other old-line Departments. The residual duties of some of the emergency agencies were transferred to Commerce; the liquidation of those agencies led to the setting up in the department, in 1947, of the Division of Liquidation.

Adaptation to rapidly changing needs was aided by advisory groups in the 1920's, and the formation of trade association was encouraged. The advisory connections of business groups with the department were formally recognized in 1933 by the formation of the Business Advisory Council. Specialized groups associated with the Department included the National Inventors Council, the Advisory Committee on Export Policy, and various industry advisory committees. Nationwide contacts were maintained, notably by the Business and Defense Services Administration with its four Offices of Field Services, Area Development, Technical Services, and Distribution.

Notably illustrative of the enlarged role of fact-finding was the Department's use of data collected by it and other agencies in its reports on "the economy viewed through the national income accounts." The first comprehensive official study of national income was published in 1934. The transformation of statistical work was facilitated by the improvement of such techniques as sampling, modes of portraying trends and the electronic processing of data.

COMMERCE CLAUSE. Its judicial history properly begins with the famous case of Gibbons v. Ogden (1824) in which Chief Justice Marshall defined commerce as intercourse. On the basis of this definition, the Supreme Court has held that Congress' power to regulate commerce among the states is the power to govern commercial intercourse among them. This power of Congress Marshall considered to be plenary and unaffected by the states and their powers.

When Roger B. Taney became chief justice, the Court assumed a view more congenial to states' rights, and the rule was laid down that there is a field of jurisdiction which is exclusively reserved to the states. However, the supremacy of Federal power was asserted again four years later when the Court maintained that where the subject matter is local in character the states may act, but only until Congress chooses to legislate. Whatever subjects of commerce are in their nature national, or admit only of uniform regulation, must be left to the exclusive control of Congress (Cooley v. Bd. of Wardens, 1852).

Until the Civil War most interstate commerce was by water, and few questions of jurisdiction arose between the Federal and state governments. But the construction of railroads throughout the United States created new problems. Illinois undertook to regulate that part of an interstate journey which was entirely within the state. This exercise of state power the Supreme Court held unconstitutional (Wabash St. L. and P. Ry. Co. v. Illinois, 1886). In order that the railroads might not be wholly unregulated, Congress in 1887 established the Interstate Commerce Commission.

The growth of the regulatory power of Congress in the field of commerce after 1887 was rapid. The Sherman Antitrust Act in 1890 extended the power of Congress to prohibit combinations in restraint of trade among the states. This act was early given a judicial interpretation which greatly restricted its scope (U. S. v. E. C. Knight Co., 1895), but in subsequent decisions came to represent an important exercise of the Federal regulatory power. The act was applied to combinations of labor as well as capital (Loewe v. Lawlor, 1908), a step which aroused the opposition of the trade unions and led in 1914 to the passage of the Clayton Act. At the same time Congress established the Federal Trade Commission.

The field of transportation was gradually confided by Congress to the supervision of the Interstate Commerce Commission. Beginning with the Elkins Act in 1903, a series of measures strengthened the powers of the commission and enabled it to assume jurisdiction of steamship and railroad companies, express and sleeping-car companies, motor bus and motor truck concerns, power transmission lines, telephone and telegraph lines and oil pipe line companies when engaged in interstate commerce. The Supreme Court in the late 1890's ruled that the commission could forbid discriminatory and unreasonable rates but did not admit the right to impose any definite rate or schedules on a railroad. The rule was laid down that a common carrier was entitled to a fair return upon the value of the property dedicated to the public use (Smyth v. Ames, 1898). When Congress under the Hepburn Act of 1906 authorized the commission to fix rates for the future, the courts had to determine a basis upon which the value of the property of a common carrier was to be ascertained. In other words, the judges were obliged to delve into the realm of economic theory to discover a rate basis which could be applied.

Meanwhile, conflicts arose between the commerce power and the reserved powers of the states. Within the legitimate exercise of the police power, the states might forbid the running of freight trains on Sunday, prohibit the importation within their borders of diseased cattle, and enact many other laws designed to promote the health, safety, and moral welfare of citizens. But in 1918 a majority of the justices of the Supreme Court refused their assent to an act of Congress prohibiting the transportation in interstate commerce of goods the product of child labor. The field of production was therefore to be considered as falling within the reserved powers of the states (Hammer v. Dagenhart). However, the Supreme Court had already admitted a large sphere of police power to Congress. The Mann White Slave Act and the act forbidding the distribution of lottery tickets through interstate commerce were police regulations.

The Transportation Act of 1920 assumed the judicial rulings already laid down in behalf of the power of Congress. Among these was the rule that "wherever the interstate and intrastate transactions of the carriers are so related that the government of the one involves the control of the other," Congress is entitled to regulate both classes of transactions (Shreveport Case, 1914). The extension of Federal power to the regulation of the business of the commission men and of the livestock dealers in the great stockyards of the country was upheld by the Supreme Court (Stafford v. Wallace, 1922). In this case the Court held that stockyards are not a place of rest or final destination but a throat through which the current of commerce flows. While the Supreme Court clung to its decision in the child-labor case, it upheld an act of Congress forbidding the transportation in interstate commerce of goods made by convict labor into any state where the goods are to be sold or used in violation of its laws. This decision assumed that where state policy condemned a practice the power of Congress might be put forth to prevent interstate commerce from frustrating the policy (Kentucky Whip and Collar Co., v. Illinois Central R. R. Co., 1937).

While the Supreme Court was permitting these extensions of Federal power, it was confronted with a case involving the validity of the National Industrial Recovery Act, in which Congress sought to delegate to the President control over the entire field of production where it affected interstate commerce. The N. I. R. A. was overturned not only as an unconstitutional delegation of power to the President but also as an invasion of the reserved powers of the states (Schechter Poultry Corp v. U. S., 1935). Two years later the Court receded markedly from the position it had taken not only in the latter portion of this decision but also from its position in the child-labor case. In upholding the validity of the National Labor Relations Act, a majority of the justices agreed that manufacturing, although carried out wholly within a state, may affect interstate commerce in such a way that it comes within the scope of Federal power (N. L. R. B. v. Jones and Laughlin Steel Corp., 1937).

The judicial interpretation of the commerce clause has taken many bypaths since the decision of John Marshall more than a century ago. Most of these have been pointed out by states' rights, and it is only as the philosophy of particularism has succumbed to nationalizing tendencies that the Supreme Court has been able to return to the fundamental principles of the decision in Gibbons v. Ogden.

COMMITTEE ON PUBLIC INFORMATION was set up by executive order of President Wilson, April 14, 1917. Formally it was the Secretaries of State, War and Navy with Mr. George Creel as civilian chairman. Actually it was the latter and a far-flung organization abroad and at home presenting the war issues by pamphlets, films, cables, posters, speakers (Four-Minute Men). Its function was informational, not censorship. The first year's budget was supplied by the President ($1,600,000); the second year by an appropriation of $1,250,000.

COMMITTEES OF CORRESPONDENCE, organized as part of the transitional Revolutionary machinery to facilitate the spread of propaganda and coordinate the patriot party, were of three general types. Samuel Adams was the promoter of the first local committees on Nov. 2, 1772, and within three months Gov. Hutchinson reported that there were more than eighty such committees in Massachusetts. On March 12, 1773, Virginia organized the second type, the colony committees which were in reality standing committees of the legislature. The third type and the most important was the county committee which was chosen by the local units and acted as the agent of the central colonial committees. The importance of these committees as channels for the creation and direction of public opinion during the preliminaries of the Revolution can hardly be overemphasized. They exercised at times judicial, legislative and executive functions and, containing the germ of government, gave rise to the later committee system.

COMMITTEES OF SAFETY carried on and extended the work of the Revolutionary committees of correspondence, and with the breakdown of constitutional modes of government, anarchy might have prevailed had not these extralegal committees developed to guide and stabilize the Revolutionary movement. The Second Continental Congress on July 18, 1775, recommended the establishment of such committees in the various colonies to carry on the all-important functions of government. Many of these committees had been active since 1774 and with the sanction of Congress they rapidly developed into a unified system which supplied the armies with men and equipment, apprehended Tories and carried on other exacting and unceasing duties of government. With the adoption of state constitutions the committees were largely replaced by constitutional agencies, New Hampshire and Connecticut alone continuing their committees throughout the war. So useful, however, had the committees proved themselves to be that many of them continued unofficially throughout the greater part of the war.

COMMON LANDS in early New England towns were either lands held in common by the proprietors in which the individual owners had fractional rights and carried on farming in accordance with open field practices, or, more generally, undivided and unallotted land on the outskirts of the New England settlements, used for pasturage and woodland. In the latter part of the 17th century newcomers insisted on sharing these undivided lands with the proprietors, but the rights of the "noncommoners," as the newcomers were called, were seldom recognized. Statutes in the 18th century and court decisions upheld the town proprietors.

COMMON LAW, originally custom and usage, became the law "common" to all the people of England by judicial enforcement. Thus it originated in England, but has come to consist in great part in the principles which have been declared and developed in the decisions of the courts when adjudicating upon the private law in countries of Anglo-Saxon origins. It is usually not incorporated in the constitution or written statutes of a country but is the term generally used to describe that system of fundamental law which is in force among English-speaking peoples as contrasted with Roman Law and derivative systems based on an enacted code. The early settlers of the United States claimed, and were in fact supposed, to have brought with them to America their inherent common-law rights of person and property. It is the English common law which thus is recognized throughout the United States as the common law of the country and is the fundamental basis of our institutions of government.

The common law is enforced primarily by the governments of each of the states and territories. It has been influenced to some extent by the Code Napoleon in its development in the State of Louisiana due to the original French settlement there. It is, of course, subject to repeal or amendment by statute, but primarily the common law has been developed and extended by the state and Federal courts, past and present.

In those states where the common law has been codified, these codes consist in large part of a restatement of common-law doctrines and their later development up to the time of codification. In addition, the common-law rights of the individual, as generally accepted, have been stated to a greater or lesser extent at various times in American history. Among these statements is that in the Declaration of Independence which says that all men "are endowed by their Creator with certain unalienable rights, that among these are life, liberty, and the pursuit of happiness." Also the Bill of Rights or the first ten Amendments to the United States Constitution and the bills of rights in the various state constitutions are in whole or in large part made up of statements of common-law rights and of methods of protecting these rights which are inborn, inherent and inalienable, and not granted by any government, according to Anglo-Saxon and American theory. Thus, the American governments, national and state, are merely the added protection to the common-law rights which the citizens already possess.

COMMON SENSE, a tract by Thomas Paine, was published in Philadelphia, January, 1776. In contrast to writers who denounced British tyranny but insisted on colonial loyalty, Paine described reconciliation as only "an agreeable dream." He maintained that, being of age, the colonies were qualified for independence and that their future interest demanded it. While many men had similar beliefs, none had so graphically stated the case. With its circulation of 120,000 in the first three months, the tract greatly fertilized the independence spirit which flowered so brilliantly in July, 1776.

COMMONWEALTH v. HUNT. This case, decided by the supreme court of Massachusetts in 1842, held the Boston Journeymen Bootmakers Society, defendant, to be a lawful organization. Previously, associations of workers had been judged unlawful conspiracies. The doctrine of conspiracy rests upon the assumption that an act which is innocent and legal when performed by an individual becomes dangerous and illegal when performed by a group. The historical significance of the case lies in the fact that it marks the legal recognition of labor unions as lawful institutions, provided the methods of attaining their ends are "honorable and peaceful."

COMMUNISM in its widest sense is a social system in which wealth and the agencies for producing, distributing and exchanging wealth are owned in common. Movements seeking communal ownership have included the numerous utopian schemes beginning with Plato's *Republic* and reappearing periodically to the middle of the 19th century (*see* Communities, Communal.) But in recent years communism has been identified with the social philosophy of Karl Marx and Friedrich Engels, who launched their *Communist Manifesto* in 1848, as interpreted by the party leaders of the U. S. S. R. When the International Workingmen's Association was founded in London in 1864, Marx was in charge of expounding its doctrines. This first International was dissolved in Philadelphia in 1876. A second International was established in 1889, which up to 1914 served as the international organization of the socialist movement as a whole. In this organization the Bolshevik opposition was led by Lenin, who in 1919 inspired the founding of the Third International to guide the Communist parties throughout the world.

The American Communist party, dating from 1919, has never gained numerical strength, although it made great efforts to proselytize Negroes and the underprivileged. The Nazi-Soviet Pact of 1939 tended to restrict its influence in the United States. In 1940 the Smith Act made it unlawful for anyone to advocate or teach the overthrow and destruction of any government in the United States by force of violence, and in 1950 the McCarran Act (passed over Truman's veto) required the registration of communist and communist-front organizations, and also the internment of communists in national emergencies, in addition to prohibiting the employment of communists in national defense work. In 1954 a Communist Control Act was passed whose main intent was to strip the Communist party of all legal rights. Party members were put under severe penalties for failing to register under the McCarran Act, and communist-controlled unions were deprived of all bargaining privileges. President Eisenhower, in signing this Communist Control Act, declared it would "require careful study" to make sure it did not interfere with existing laws against communist activity. In the meantime eleven leaders of the Communist party were convicted in 1949 of advocating the violent overthrow of the U. S. Government. Federal Judge Harold R. Medina sentenced ten defendants to five years in prison each, and the eleventh, a war veteran, to three years in prison. The convictions were upheld in 1950.

COMMUNITIES, COMMUNAL. Among the earliest settlements that were deliberate communistic experiments were the short-lived community founded by Plockhoy, a Dutch Mennonite, on Delaware Bay in 1662; the Labadist Community of Protestant Mystics, founded in northern Maryland in 1680; the Mennonite Community at Germantown, Pa., founded in 1683; and the community of "The Women in the Wilderness" in Pennsylvania, in 1694. After the disappearance of the latter, Conrad Beissel, who had expected to join it, adopted the Dunker religion and founded, in 1732, the Ephrata Community.

The first of the Shaker communities, scattered over seven states, was the Jerusalem Community, founded in 1786 by Jemima Wilkinson in Gates County, N. Y. The main branch of Shakers were followers of Ann Lee; their first permanent community was established in 1787 at Mt. Lebanon, N. Y. Other important Shaker societies are at Watervliet, N. Y., Union Village, O., and East Canterbury, N. Y.

Two communities, the Harmony Community and the Zoar Community, were founded by groups of Separatists from Württemberg, Germany, led by George Rapp and Joseph Blaumiler, respectively. The Harmony Society was originally, in 1805, in Butler County, Pa.; in 1814 the Harmonists removed to Indiana; and in 1825 they located at Economy, Pa. Zoar was founded in Ohio in 1817 and maintained its community organization until 1898.

Other religious communities were those of Perfectionists, led by Noyes at Oneida, N. Y., Brooklyn, N. Y., and Wallingford, Conn.; the Hopedale Community, Massachusetts (1842–57); the Amana Community in New York, and later in Iowa (1842–); the Bishop Hill Colony in Illinois (1848–62); the Mormon Community at Orderville, Utah (1874–84), and the communities of the Huterian Brethren.

The nonreligious communities in America have been experiments in some economic or social philosophy. An example of the former was Robert Owen's unsuccessful communistic experiment at New Harmony, Ind., which he purchased from the Rappists in 1825.

In 1841 a group of Boston intellectuals established a literary community known as West Rexburg Community. In 1842, when the entire community was converted to Fourierism, they transformed their society into a Fourierist "phalanx," which was called the Brook Farm Association. Other Fourierist communities were the Wisconsin Phalanx (1844–50) and the North American Phalanx, New Jersey (1843–56).

Other settlements founded on social or economic communism were at Teutonia, Pa. (1843), Icania, Iowa (1848–98), Equity, Ohio (1830–32), Eutopia, Ohio (1847–51), Modern Times, Long Island, N. Y. (1851–60), Steelton, N. J. (1915–), the Ruskin Commonwealth, Tennessee, and later Georgia (1894–1901), New Llano, Calif., and later Louisiana (1914–), and Fairhope, Ala.

COMPACT THEORY involves the idea that the basis of government is in the agreement of the people. Its appearance in America coincides with the first settlements and it is implicit in the Mayflower Compact. Church covenants and trading company charters gave support to the compact philosophy. Thomas Hooker in his *Survey of the Summe of Church Dis-*

cipline (1648) declared that the foundation of authority in both church and state is in the consent of the people. The idea of compact is therefore equally valid as the basis of ecclesiastical and civil government. But the 17th-century theologians found no means of interpreting the compact, except by divine revelation. It was left for John Locke to find in natural law a means of interpretation. Following Pufendorf, the guide of Locke, an Ipswich clergyman named John Wise in 1717 developed the compact theory in the light of the newer currents of thought. It was not long before the New England clergy were appealing to natural law and the social compact to dismiss absolutism on both sides of the Atlantic. Their homilies undoubtedly paved the way for the adoption of the compact idea in the revolutionary philosophy. Jefferson as he compiled the Declaration of Independence could with truth declare that the ideas it contained were hackneyed. The theory as it existed in 1776 in America was distinctly more individualistic than the English prototype. Locke envisaged the reversion of power upon the dissolution of the compact to the whole community but many Americans were not satisfied unless the individual, from whom the rights were originally granted, regained possession upon the exercise of the right of revolution.

COMPROMISE OF 1850 is a designation commonly given to five statutes enacted in September, 1850, following a bitter controversy between the representatives of the North and of the South. The controversy reached a fever heat during the weeks following the assembling of Congress in December, 1849, while the election of a speaker under the customary majority rule was prevented by the unwillingness of the Free Soil members, who held the balance of power, to be drawn into an arrangement with either of the two major parties. In the course of the prolonged balloting criminations and recriminations passed between the hotheaded spokesmen of the two sections. Pointing to indications that the principle of the Wilmot Proviso might be enacted into law and receive the signature of President Taylor, Southeners insisted as a matter of right upon the recognition of the Calhoun doctrine that under the Constitution all the territories should be deemed open to slavery. There was talk of secession unless this principle was recognized in fact or as a basis for some adjustment. Plans were under way for the discussion of a satisfactory Southern program at a Southern convention called to meet at Nashville in June, 1850.

In the face of increasing sectional strife Henry Clay returned to the U. S. Senate and on Jan. 29, 1850, suggested a series of resolutions intended to provide the basis for the prompt adjustment of the main questions at issue between the two sections. His resolutions were shortly referred to a select committee of thirteen of which he was made chairman.

Its report (May 8), which covered the ground of Clay's resolutions, recommended an "omnibus bill" providing for the admission of California under its free state constitution, for territorial governments for Utah and New Mexico, silent on slavery, and for the settlement of the boundary dispute between Texas and the United States. It also recommended a bill for the abolition of the slave trade in the District of Columbia and an amendment to the fugitive slave law.

The hope of compromise was tied up with the fate of the omnibus bill. Clay rallied to his support the outstanding Union men, including Daniel Webster, Lewis Cass, Henry S. Foote and Stephen A. Douglas; the latter became the active force in the promotion of the necessary legislation. President Taylor wanted the admission of California but no action on New Mexico and Utah until they should be ready to become states; he was, therefore, a formidable obstacle to the plans of the compromisers until his death on July 9. Even the active support of his successor, however, did not offset the fact that the idea of compromise "united the opponents instead of securing the friends" of each proposition.

Compromise as such had clearly failed; the ground which it had contemplated was covered in five statutes each formerly included as sections of the proposed omnibus bill. The act establishing a territorial government for Utah (Sept. 9) contained the important "popular sovereignty" clause providing that any state or states formed out of this territory should be admitted with or without slavery as their constitutions should prescribe. An identical clause was appended to the New Mexico territorial act (Sept. 9), which also resolved the conflict between Texas and the Federal Government over the Santa Fe region by a cession, with compensation to Texas, to the newly created territory. On the same date the act admitting California under its constitution prohibiting slavery in the new state was approved. The Fugitive Slave Act of Sept. 18, 1850, which amended the original statute of Feb. 12, 1793, provided for the appointment of special commissioners to supplement the regular courts empowered after a summary hearing to issue a certificate of arrest of a fugitive "from labor," which authorized the claimant to seize and return the fugitive (with a fee of $10 when the certificate was issued and of only $5 when denied); in no trial or hearing was the testimony of the alleged fugitive to be admitted as evidence nor was a fugitive claiming to be a freeman to have the right of trial by jury; Federal marshals and deputy marshals were to execute the warrants under a heavy fine for refusing and were made liable for the full value of fugitives who escaped their custody; these officials were empowered to call to their aid when necessary any bystanders or *posse comitatus;* finally, any person wilfully hindering the arrest of a fugitive or aiding in his rescue or escape was subject to heavy fine and imprisonment, as well as to heavy civil damages.

These statutes were shortly presented to the country as a series of compromise measures. They did not, however, magically calm the sectional storm. In the North there was widespread denunciation of the "iniquitious" features of the Fugitive Slave Act and deliberate declaration that its enforcement would never be tolerated. At the same time the conservative forces organized a series of Union meetings and pleaded the obligations of the North to pacify the South. In the latter section the other four enactments precipitated the most serious disunion crisis that the country had ever faced. In the states of Georgia, Mississippi and South Carolina the "Southern Rights," or secession, forces were checkmated only by the most strenuous efforts of the Union or Constitutional Union elements. Both sides foreswore old party labels and fought under their new banners to win control over the official state conventions that were ordered. The Southern Rights forces lost in the first test fight in Georgia and had to carry this moral handicap in the remaining contests. It was not until 1852 that the country at large made clear its acquiescence in what at length became known by the oversimple label, "The Compromise of 1850."

COMSTOCK LODE, Virginia City, Nev., from its discovery in 1859 to its decline in 1879, held the spotlight of the world. During this period more than $500,000,000 in silver and gold were taken from these mines.

To mine this ore great hoisting machines, giant pumps, heavy stamps, drills, cables and hundreds of other things were manufactured. To drain hot water from underground reservoirs, Adolph Sutro completed a five-mile tunnel from the floor of the Carson River to the Comstock mines in 1878. To extract the silver from the rock, the old Mexican patio method was first used; later, the amalgamating process was employed for the reduction of the ore.

Water, for the 40,000 inhabitants of Virginia City and vicinity, was brought from Marlette, an artificial lake, thirty miles away in the Sierra Nevada Mountains, through pipes, tunnels, flumes and a large inverted siphon. The pipe and siphon were made, piece by piece, in San Francisco, to fit around mountains, to cross Washoe Valley and to extend up the Virginia Mountains.

The discovery of the Big Bonanza in the California Consolidated Mine, 1873, made multimillionaires of John W. Mackay, James G. Fair, James C. Flood, William S. O'Brien, William Sharon and William C. Ralston.

San Francisco was the residuary legatee of the Comstock wealth. With this money palatial homes were built; banks, the San Francisco Stock Exchange, and dozens of other businesses were established.

CONCORD COACH. Most famous type of American stage coach, so called because manufactured by Abbot, Downing & Co., of Concord, N. H., who began business about 1813 and before 1860 had the largest factory of its kind in America. The Concord, an unusually sturdy and handsome vehicle, was most famous in the West, and especially in California, which state began importing them around Cape Horn in 1850. Many Concord coaches were used in Mexico, South America, South Africa and Australia.

CONCORD GROUP. In 1834 Ralph Waldo Emerson moved to Concord. Henry David Thoreau lived there. Others were attracted by the quiet village and the residence of Emerson. Nathaniel Hawthorne came in 1842 to spend four years in the old Manse; A. Bronson Alcott, at Emerson's invitation, settled there in 1840 and brought up his "little women"; William Ellery Channing, drawn by Emerson, came in 1843 to remain for life. These men were less a group than a collection of lonely New England individualists separated by lack of warm affection and by an exaggerated idealization of lofty friendship.

CONESTOGA WAGON. This "vehicle of empire" had its origin among the Pennsylvania Dutch and has been described as "one of the most distinctively American devices of all our transportation history." Although it was in use by mid-18th century, it first became general on the overland routes across the Alleghenies just after the American Revolution, when new roads were being laid out to meet the needs of a great immigrant movement into the interior.

In size and appearance the Conestoga wagon was a huge structure, heavily built, with broad wheels suited to dirt roads and a bed higher at either end of the wagon than in the middle, so as to prevent its contents spilling out in going up and down hill. Its canvas-covered top presaged the Prairie Schooner of a later day. The under parts of these wagons were regularly painted blue and the upper parts red. They were drawn by four to six horses, with the drivers usually riding wheel-horses. Sometimes they moved in solitary grandeur but more frequently in long caravans. Urged onward to the accompaniment of rumbling wheels, creaking harnesses, the weeping and the singing of women and children, these empire builders heralded an advance that knew no retreat.

CONFEDERATE STATES OF AMERICA. On Feb. 4, 1861, delegates from six seceded states—South Carolina, Georgia, Florida, Alabama, Mississippi and Louisiana—met in the state capitol at Montgomery, Ala., to form a general government for themselves. They elected Howell Cobb of Georgia president of their body, which they designated a "Congress," and on Feb. 8 adopted for one year a "Constitution for the Provisional Government of the Confederate States of America" based upon that of the United States. They continued their own group as the Provisional

Congress in which each state should have one vote. On Feb. 9 they unanimously elected to the Presidency Jefferson Davis of Mississippi and to the Vice-Presidency Alexander H. Stephens of Georgia. Stephens, a delegate to the Congress, was sworn in on Feb. 11 and Davis, who arrived later, was inaugurated on the 18th. The new President quickly formed a cabinet of six members. Texas, whose secession ordinance had been ratified by popular vote on Feb. 23, was admitted to the new union on March 2. Meanwhile, the Congress had begun work on a permanent Constitution which was adopted on March 11 and was soon ratified by all the seceded states. This Constitution, with a few important modifications, was closely modeled upon that of the United States.

The Provisional Congress hastened to put the new government into active operation. It continued in force all laws of the United States as of Nov. 1, 1860, which were not inconsistent with the Constitution of the Confederate States; it declared the navigation of the Mississippi River free to the inhabitants of the upper valley; established the several executive departments; authorized a small loan of $15,000,000 in bonds and $1,000,000 in Treasury notes; made provision for a Confederate judiciary (though a Supreme Court was never established); extended the control of the Confederate government over all questions between individual states and foreign powers; and requested the President to appoint three commissioners to settle all issues with the United States. It also authorized the President to call out, for purposes of defense, state forces as a "provisional army," to accept the services of not more than 100,000 volunteers for twelve months and to procure arms and munitions by purchase or manufacture.

President Lincoln's inaugural on March 4 seemed to threaten war since he pronounced secession void and promised both to enforce the laws of the United States and "to hold, occupy and possess the places belonging to the Government" in the seceded states. The greatest immediate danger of conflict lay in the rival claims to Forts Sumter in Charleston harbor and Pickens at Pensacola, both within the Confederate States but still held by United States troops. The Confederates warned that reinforcement of the garrisons would be an act of hostility; but persistent rumors of impending evacuation dispelled much of the uneasiness and when the Congress adjourned on March 16 its members were evidently unaware that war was at hand. The commissioners sent to Washington were rebuffed by Lincoln and Seward, and Lincoln's sudden demonstration in April for the ostensible relief of Sumter caused the Confederates to attack that fort. Davis at once summoned Congress into session, while Lincoln called for 75,000 militia to suppress unlawful "combinations" and proclaimed a blockade of the Southern coasts. Davis called out volunteers to resist invasion. War had begun.

Four border slave states—Virginia, Arkansas, North Carolina and Tennessee—which had previously rejected secession, refused to fight against the South, then seceded and joined the Confederacy. In Unionist northwestern Virginia local leaders organized a "restored" state government which in 1863 obtained admission to the Union as West Virginia. A similar movement in eastern Tennessee failed. In Missouri and Maryland secessionist minorities were sternly repressed. Kentucky for a time maintained neutrality but soon gave majority support to the Union. The secessionists of Missouri and Kentucky, withdrawing southward, set up state governments which were recognized by the Confederate Congress and were admitted to membership in the Confederacy in November and December, 1861.

The Confederates hastened preparations to meet the expected invasion. On May 8 Congress authorized President Davis to accept volunteers for the period of the war. Davis endeavored to induce new regiments to enlist for the war and to persuade those already in service to re-enlist for that period. He succeeded only in part; but some confusion resulted and some dissatisfaction because the War Department, being short of arms, gave preference to those enlisted for the war. By September the Department was refusing to accept twelve-months regiments unless they were already armed. The Confederate government had only such arms as had been found in the local United States arsenals, mostly obsolete flintlock muskets. Some states had purchased similar ancient weapons, discarded by the U. S. Army a few years earlier, and some had purchased a few thousand improved arms immediately after the John Brown raid or during the excitement over secession. Such states armed many of their own volunteers for Confederate service (the Government paying them for these arms), but they reserved a portion for local defense. There were no manufacturing armories in the Confederacy when war began and only two very small privately owned powder mills. The War Department hurried agents off to Europe to buy arms and munitions, but it was late in the year before supplies from this source began to arrive. Because the blockade and uncertain credits made reliance upon foreign purchases too risky, the ordnance bureau made many contracts with private firms which, often with the aid of Government funds, undertook to manufacture arms and munitions; but the bureau itself, as quickly as it could, began to erect a powder mill, laboratories and armories. Of artillery, especially for field service, there was an alarming scarcity. Some guns were cast at the Tredegar Iron Works at Richmond and at other places; some were imported, some captured. The heavier cannon for coast defense were imported. The stock of arms of all sorts was gradually increased and improved in quality; but the Confederate armies were never, except in the matter of powder, as well provided for as those of the North.

The problem of feeding and clothing the soldiers

presented less initial difficulty. Many of the volunteers supplied their own clothing, blankets and haversacks; the cavalrymen furnished their own horses; and local relief organizations equipped their poorer soldiers until the quartermaster's bureau set up its own shops. As time went on a growing scarcity of raw materials severely hampered the production of shoes, woolen clothing, blankets, cooking utensils and medicines. The lack of adequate hospitals was sorely felt during the first year and even after better hospital facilities had been provided by local societies, state governments and the Confederate medical service, the scantiness of imported medicines (made contraband of war by the United States) resulted in much suffering and many deaths. Inefficient railroad transportation caused great difficulty in getting supplies to the troops at the front. Above all, the depreciation and final collapse of Confederate currency made the purchase of supplies in the open market virtually impossible.

Upon the invitation of Virginia the seat of government had been moved to Richmond in June, 1861. The victory at Bull Run in July and the minor one at Ball's Bluff caused so much popular overconfidence that it was hard to persuade the people and the state officials to prepare for a long war. Volunteering "for the war" declined during the winter. When, on Feb. 18, 1862, the permanent Constitution went into effect and Davis and Stephens, re-elected in the preceding fall, were inaugurated for six-year terms, military disasters in Tennessee and on the Carolina coasts had darkened the outlook. Davis and his generals knew that the expiration of the terms of the twelve-months men would leave their armies too small to cope with the much larger Union forces. The new Congress in response to Davis' urging passed, on April 16, the first conscription act which made liable to military service all able-bodied white men from 18 to 35 years of age. Certain necessary exemptions were allowed; but in September the age of service was raised to 45 and in February, 1864, it was moved down to 17 and up to 50 years. There was much trouble over some features of the law and especially over exemptions; but at first the act received general support and it kept armies in the field.

The greatest single handicap to the Southern cause was the state of Confederate finances. Beginning its existence without income, save for paltry customs dues, without a tax system and with but little coin available, the Congress resorted to bond issues and a paper currency in expectation of a short war. The blockade reduced tariff revenues to a minimum and the first war tax upon property, assumed by the states, was paid chiefly in state notes which merely increased the flood of paper money. Depreciation set in rapidly in 1862, thus raising prices, increasing the costs of the Government and forcing further issues of bonds and irredeemable treasury notes. The steady decline of currency values finally paralyzed the strength of the Government and inflicted extreme hardships upon the people. When finally, in April, 1863, Congress resorted to heavy taxation it was too late. An effort to reduce the redundant currency by a funding act, Feb. 17, 1864, failed to do more than check briefly the downward plunge.

The rise in the cost of living cannot be attributed wholly to the fall of the currency for it was largely the result of the scarcity of important commodities such as salt, leather, wool, coffee, medicines, metals and manufactured articles generally. By the fall of 1861 many such articles had reached unprecedented prices. Foodstuffs were rising also, but more slowly. Governors and legislatures attempted to stop "speculation in necessities" and to hold prices down, but their efforts failed. Agitation began for an increased planting of food crops and the reduction of cotton and tobacco; and by voluntary agreements the cotton crop was cut in 1862 to about 1,500,000 bales (about one third of that of 1861) and larger acreage was given to corn, wheat and other foods. In the following winter state legislatures enacted stringent laws to limit the planting of both cotton and tobacco. Cotton production fell to about 500,000 bales in 1863 and to around 300,000 in 1864. The tobacco crop also declined, though not to the same extent.

Despite the greater attention to food crops there was extreme privation in some sections. The withdrawal of men to the army depleted labor on the small farms; droughts or frosts caused crop failures in many places; the salt shortage reduced the yield of cured meats; the cost of clothing and shoes rose far beyond the meager resources of the poor whether on the farms or in the towns and the pay of the soldier was insufficient to provide his family with the coarsest food. To succor the needy families of soldiers and allay the discontent which was causing desertion, every state passed relief laws under which such families received allotments of money from county or state taxes or, after the currency had become worthless, donations of food and clothing. Administration of relief was difficult in regions overrun or threatened by Union armies or where deserters and outlaws congregated. The shortage of transportation facilities added to the burden. In the towns where business was depressed and work was scarce with wages small, the abnormally high cost of living brought suffering not only to the poor but to all who lived upon fixed incomes. Distress, evident in many localities in 1862, was practically universal before the end of 1863, and grew steadily worse as the war dragged on.

Trade everywhere declined except in army supplies and in goods run in through the blockade, and these exceptions benefited but few. Small manufacturers of cotton cloth, iron wares and the like enjoyed a brief prosperity, but the failure of the currency left them with mere paper profits, conscription took away many of their best workmen, the blockade hindered the replacement of worn-out machinery, and the rising cost of living forced them to set up expensive commissaries for their employees. The nearly universal resort to barter along with other difficulties reduced their volume of business and brought them to the verge of bankruptcy. In order to procure clothing for their soldiers or to relieve their poor, state governments engaged in foreign trade and manufacturing on their own account. In 1864 Congress, seeking to increase the importation of military supplies, prohibited the importation of certain luxuries and placed all foreign trade, except that of the states, under regulations to be prescribed by the President. When Davis promulgated rules which reserved for the Government one half the cargo space on every privately owned vessel, he aroused the determined opposition of those governors whose contracts with blockade runners were jeopardized.

Although conscription had saved the military situation in 1862 and had prolonged the life of the Confederacy, it had aroused the antagonism of states' rights doctrinaires such as Gov. Joseph E. Brown, Robert Toombs and Vice-President Stephens, as well as thousands of men who wished to escape military service. Grasping at technicalities, many sought the protection of the courts. In the absence of a supreme court of the Confederate States, the state supreme courts assumed jurisdiction of constitutional causes, and while they generally sustained the measures of Congress they did not always do so. Some individual judges gave great anxiety to the Richmond authorities. In one way or another thousands managed to avoid service, and the Government, despite its utmost efforts, was unable to fill up the thinning ranks. Every successive official report from the field after the summer of 1863 showed fewer men with the colors. The suspension of the privilege of the writ of habeas corpus, used by Davis with caution and only after explicit authorization by Congress (in marked contrast with its free use by Lincoln), was becoming unpopular even in Congress and was refused altogether after the third such act expired on Aug. 1, 1864. These constitutional issues caused acrid controversies, and Davis, strict constitutionalist that he was, did not escape charges of aspiring to a dictatorship. Numerous opponents of his administration were elected to Congress in 1863, but the President retained the support of the majority of the members until near the end, when stronger symptoms of revolt appeared.

In 1863 the entire line of the Mississippi River had been lost; by 1864 other large sections were occupied by the enemy or threatened. As the military situation became desperate, internal conditions grew worse and the problems of the Government multiplied. The finances were near collapse and without remedy; hard pressed for supplies for the fighting men, purchasing officers had resorted to rigorous impressment, which aroused widespread resentment; the railroads were

nearing collapse. Confederate diplomacy had failed either to obtain foreign recognition or to induce Great Britain or France to take action against the blockade. Unable to build a navy or to purchase one with which to break up the blockade, the Confederacy was slowly strangling. Administrative control had so weakened in regions remote from Richmond that local military officers did much as they pleased, and bands of lawless men plundered the helpless people who longed for peace. The mountain regions were full of disloyalists. Davis was implored to invite or consider overtures for peace; but negotiations achieved nothing because his oath of office and sense of official duty committed him to claims for Confederate independence which Lincoln would not consider. Only a military decision was possible.

Gen. Sherman's shattering drive from Atlanta to Savannah in the fall of 1864 and northward into the Carolinas early in 1865 showed clearly what that decision must be. When Gen. Lee, who had guarded the Confederate capital so long, was forced to abandon Petersburg and Richmond and to surrender to Grant the remnants of his gallant army at Appomattox on April 9, every soldier knew that further resistance was useless. The other Confederate commanders soon surrendered, the last, Gen. E. Kirby Smith of the Trans-Mississippi Department, on June 2. Three weeks earlier, Jefferson Davis, while trying to make his way westward to continue the struggle, was captured near Irwinsville, Ga., and taken to prison. The Confederate States of America had dissolved. (*See also* Army, Confederate, and Civil War.)

Blockade of Seceded States. On April 19, 1861, President Lincoln proclaimed a blockade of the seceded states in pursuance of "the law of nations." To conform with international law, which required enforcement of a blockade to the point of risk to blockade runners, the Federal Navy in 1861 purchased 136 merchant vessels and began the construction of 52 new craft to supplement the 44 vessels still in condition for service. The personnel of the Navy was likewise increased from 7600 to 22,000. During the first year, however, the blockade was not effective beyond creating the required risk. At first, the South contributed to the restriction of commerce by unofficially prohibiting the exportation of cotton, with the hope that England and France would then be forced to ally with the Confederacy to obtain cotton. In the autumn of 1861 the Federals sank stone-laden ships in the Charleston harbor to aid the blockading fleet. The next year the duel between the *Monitor* and the *Merrimack* preserved the blockade in Hampton Roads. After 1862 the blockade gradually became more effective as the number of ships increased and more Southern ports were captured. Roanoke Island, New Orleans, Pensacola and Norfolk were taken by 1862; Mobile and Savannah were closed in 1864; and Wilmington (N. C.) and Charleston were in Federal hands in early 1865. By this time every other block-ade runner was being captured, and by the end of the war 1500 vessels and $31,000,000 in property had been taken by the blockaders.

Europe was, of course, a third party involved in the blockade. The very proclamation of the blockade, by implying Confederate belligerent status, justified British and French recognition of Confederate belligerency. On the other hand, England and France recognized the legality of the blockade in spite of the objections and arguments of Confederate agents. The hopes entertained by the Southern commissioners in London and Paris that British and French cotton manufacturers would force their governments to break the blockade were shattered by 1864. These industrialists found themselves loaded up with high-priced cotton and did not relish a quick slump in price which the breaking of the blockade would probably bring. The seizure of the cargo of the British vessel *Springbok* set a new precedent, later costly to the United States, by asserting the doctrine of continuous voyage.

The blockade, resolutely maintained until August, 1865, was one of the major factors contributing to the downfall of the Confederacy.

Congress (1861–65). The convention at Montgomery, Ala., in February, 1861, which organized the Confederacy, became by its own resolution the Provisional Congress of the Provisional Government. On Feb. 18, 1862, after four sessions of the Provisional Congress, the final Constitution of the Confederate States went into operation with a legislature of two houses. The first regular Congress, in four sessions, covered two years. The second Congress, convening in 1864, continued in two sessions until the capture of Richmond.

E. A. Pollard characterized the Confederate Congress as utterly inane, without independence, and "a mere reflection of the will" of Jefferson Davis. But A. H. Stephens described it as the "ablest, soberest, most intelligent body," he ever knew. In personnel it may have been weakened by the tendency of the ablest men to seek military position and preferment. But any body including A. H. Stephens, W. L. Yancey, Robert Toombs, R. M. T. Hunter, L. T. Wigfall, H. V. Johnson and Benjamin Hill was hardly inane. In the light of the overthrow of the Confederacy, the legislation of the Confederate Congress may be criticized as inadequate to the exigencies, but the voluminous laws, suspending habeas corpus, establishing conscription, making financial provisions and attempting to regulate business, compare favorably with any legislation anywhere under similar circumstances.

Independence of judgment and spirit on the part of the Confederate Congresses was shown in refusal to confirm nominations, in resolutions inquiring into acts of executive authority, in active works in committees on military affairs and in timely resistance to encroachments on congressional rights. In the last year of the war, with waning hope of permanent Confederate independence, the Confederate Congress made important inroads on executive prerogative. The weakness of Congress was caused by the essential weakness of the Confederacy itself.

Constitution. The Congress of seceded states, which assembled at Montgomery, Ala., on Feb. 4, 1861, adopted the "Constitution for the Provisional Government of the Confederate States of America," four days later; and, on March 11, adopted the "Constitution of the Confederate States," which went into effect Feb. 18, 1862. The provisional constitution provided for continuity of Federal law and justice, and for assumption of a pro rata share of the assets and liabilities of the late Union. Both constitutions were modeled on the United States Constitution, but contained significant departures.

Under the permanent constitution, the President was elected for six years without re-eligibility. While he could remove cabinet and diplomatic officers at pleasure, subordinate officers were protected from the spoils system. He was given a budgetary control over appropriations breakable only by a two-thirds vote of Congress. The general welfare clauses were omitted, and expenditures were limited to the payment of debts, the common defense and carrying on the government. Internal improvements were restricted to those in aid of navigation, with their cost to be recovered by special duties laid on the commerce facilitated. Omnibus legislation, indefinite appropriations, bonuses above stipulated compensation, protective tariffs, industrial bounties and class benefits, were forbidden. The Post Office Department was required to be self-sustaining. Seats in Congress were allowed to cabinet members to discuss departmental matters. The African slave trade was prohibited but interstate rights of slaveholders were protected.

The Confederate keynote was elimination of political waste and keeping each echelon of the complex American plan of government within its appointed orbit.

Financial Policies. The Confederate States' undiversified economy made financing of the war one of its greatest problems.

During 1861–62, C. G. Memminger, the inexperienced Secretary of the Treasury, relied almost wholly on bonds and treasury notes for revenue. Confiscated United States funds, donations and taxes were relatively negligible.

On Feb. 18, 1861, the Provisional Congress authorized a bond issue of $15,000,000, bearing 8% interest, payable in ten years. Designed to acquire specie, the issue was quickly subscribed, largely because the revenue derived from the export tax of one-eighth of one cent a pound on cotton was used as a sinking fund.

With specie scarce the Government issued a nominal amount of interest-bearing, and $150,000,000 noninterest-bearing, Treasury notes during 1861 which were exchangeable for $150,000,000, 8%, twenty-year bonds, or, in some cases, ten-year, 8% bonds. The cotton acquired during the war by produce loans was used by the Government to support its foreign credit and as security for a foreign loan of $15,000,000, authorized by secret act, Jan. 29, 1863.

The large bond and note issues of 1862 were climaxed by the desperate legislation of Sept. 23, 1862, which provided for unlimited issuing of bonds and notes to meet congressional appropriations.

The first step in the direction of forced funding of notes into bonds as a means of reducing the volume of notes was taken through an act of March 23, 1863, providing for semicompulsory funding of various issues of notes. Funding diminished when banks and newspapers looked adversely on this breach of contract. Then was passed, Feb. 17, 1864, an act placing a 100% tax on notes outstanding Jan. 1, 1865, and making them fundable in twenty-year, 4% bonds. Notes not funded in 4% bonds by certain dates were exchangeable at the rate of $3 old for $2 new.

Public confidence in Confederate finances was undermined by this last act. Unpopular, Memminger resigned June 15, 1864, George A. Trenholm succeeding him.

On Oct. 1, 1864, the public domestic debt was $1,371,000,000, represented by $362,000,000 in bonds, $178,000,000 in interest-bearing notes, and $831,000,000 in noninterest-bearing notes, with $547,000,000 of these being old notes and $284,000,-000 being new.

During 1865, with bankruptcy imminent, reliance was placed in new issues of treasury notes, produce loans and produce taxes.

The Flag was three times described by the Confederate Congress (March 4, 1861; May 1, 1863; March 4, 1865), each time differently. The Stars and Bars was the first: length, one and one-half times width, three horizontal bars of equal width, the center bar white and the others red, and a blue union, two-thirds the width of the flag, bearing a white star for each state. This is the flag most commonly thought of as the Confederate flag. The battle flag was a square red field with a Greek cross of blue, bordered by white, bearing a white star for each state; different sizes designated different branches of the service. The second Confederate flag was a white field twice as long as wide, with the battle flag as a union two-thirds the width of the flag. The third design was similar except for proportions and the addition of a vertical red bar at the outer edge. There were still other designs for the navy.

Judicial System. Conformable to restrictions contained in the provisional constitution, the Judiciary Act of March 16, 1861, provided for one district court in each state and for a Supreme Court to sit at the seat of government on the first Monday in January to be composed of all the district judges. The district courts were vested with the powers of the late United States district and circuit courts, and were authorized to complete the business left unfinished by those courts. The restriction of one judicial district to each state was quickly found to be improvident, and was repealed by a constitutional amendment of May 21, 1861. Thereafter, Virginia, Arkansas and Texas were each divided into two districts and Tennessee into three. A court of admiralty and maritime jurisdiction was provided for Key West, two district courts for the Indian country (Oklahoma), and a system of territorial courts for Arizona. The United States judicial personnel resigned to follow their states, except two judges in Texas, two in Missouri and one in Florida; but only about half of the resigned judges were reappointed by President Davis. The first district court was opened at Mobile in the Southern Division of the District of Alabama on April 18, 1861. Under the permanent Constitution, which went into effect on Feb. 18, 1862, the Confederate courts lost jurisdiction in cases dependent solely upon diverse citizenship; nevertheless, they continued busy to the end of the war, handling numerous sequestration, prize and habeas corpus cases as well as a varied civil and criminal docket, and unhesitatingly imposed death sentences on counterfeiters. Though the Confederate courts were held by postwar decisions of the U. S. Supreme Court as invalid, their records are today regarded as part of the record of the homologous U. S. district courts.

Realizing the difficulties of time and space in the way of assembling the district judges in Richmond, and the consequent disruption in the district proceedings, the Provisional Congress on July 31, 1861, repealed the provision for the sitting of the Supreme Court until it should be reorganized under the permanent Constitution. At the first session of the First Congress a bill was introduced (April 10, 1862) to organize the Supreme Court with an independent bench; shortly followed by a bill to establish the Court of Claims to supersede the Board of Sequestration Commissioners, which was then functioning as a provisional court of claims. These or similar measures were fruitlessly before the Congress until the collapse of the government in 1865. The opposition to the Supreme Court centered on an effort to repeal the provisions of the Judiciary Act conferring appellate jurisdiction over the decisions of the state courts —a somewhat broader jurisdiction than that enjoyed by the U. S. Supreme Court. The series of legislative stalemates which prevented the organization of the Supreme Court was the result of dissensions perhaps as much personal as ideological in origin.

Navy, Confederate. Organized by act of Feb. 21, 1861. Stephen R. Mallory was appointed by President Davis to be Secretary of the Navy. Mallory served for the duration of the Confederacy. By act of April 21, 1862, the Navy was to consist of 4 admirals, 10 captains, 31 commanders and a specified number of subaltern officers. Some of these ranks were never filled on account of the lack of ships.

As the states composing the Confederacy seceded, they had attempted to create state navies. A few revenue cutters and merchant steamers were seized and converted into men-of-war. These were turned over to the Confederate Navy. Before the outbreak of hostilities, Raphael Semmes was sent North to purchase ships and materials. None of the former, but some of the latter were secured. Two shipyards fell to the Confederacy when the Gosport Navy Yard at Norfolk was abandoned, and the yard at Pensacola seized. All shipping in the Norfolk yard had been destroyed, but the Confederates raised the hull of the *Merrimack* and converted it into an ironclad ram. Much ordnance was secured from the Norfolk yard. The Pensacola yard was of little value. On May 9, 1861, Secretary Mallory commissioned James D. Bullock to go to England to secure ships for the Confederacy. Bullock had some success, contriving to secure several ships which did much damage, as Confederate cruisers, to United States commerce.

The Confederacy had ample naval personnel, as 321 officers resigned from the U. S. Navy by June 1, 1861, and tendered their services. Lack of all necessary facilities, however, and the increasing effectiveness of the Federal blockade, presented grave obstacles to the creation of a Confederate Navy. The Confederacy never possessed a mobile fleet. Her naval services may be roughly divided into three classes: (1) Ships serving in inland waters, both for offense and defense. Besides many miscellaneous craft, this group included 21 ironclads of varying armaments. (2) Commissioned cruisers, harrying the commerce of the United States abroad. This group numbered fifteen, including the *Alabama, Florida* and *Shenandoah,* whose operations gave rise to the *Alabama* claims against England. (3) Privateers.

The Confederacy is credited with introducing the ironclad vessel, thus revolutionizing naval warfare. Confederates also contributed to perfecting the torpedo.

Prisons. Approximately 200,000 prisoners were taken by the Confederates in the Civil War. Inadequate resources and no preparation for the task produced a severe drain upon both the material and human resources of the South. An exchange of prisoners, arranged in 1862, was ended in 1863, and captives were held in scattered prison camps until near the end of the war. Among the larger prisons were Libby (Richmond, Va.), Macon, Ga., and Columbia, S. C., for officers; and Andersonville, Cahaba, Millen,

Charleston and Florence for enlisted men. Deserters, spies and political prisoners were incarcerated at Castle Thunder in Richmond or in Salisbury, N. C. Throughout most of the war the provost marshal of Richmond exercised a general but ineffective supervision over the prisons. The majority of the prisons consisted of either tobacco warehouses or open stockades. Poor quarters, insufficient rations and clothing and lack of medicines produced excessive disease and a high death rate which was interpreted in the North as a deliberate effort to starve and murder the captives. In retaliation, Northern authorities reduced the allowances for rations and clothing to the prisoners they held. Some relief was obtained when Southerners permitted the Federal authorities to send food, clothing and drugs through the lines, but conditions remained bad and the Confederate prisons became the major "atrocity" in Northern propaganda.

Public Opinion in the South. While a great majority of the people were loyal to the Confederacy the South was never a unit in its support. Few denied the right of secession, but many doubted its expediency. There was a wide difference of opinion as to procedure and considerable opposition to secession arose in all the states except South Carolina. Unionists who furnished more than 50,000 troops to Northern armies were found in the mountain highlands, and a disloyal element among lower-class whites not only refused to fight for the Confederacy but defied and worked against it. President Davis never had the entire confidence of the loyal element and his policies aroused a spirit of disaffection among them. The suspension of the writ of habeas corpus and conscription and exemption were especially unpopular. The lower-class whites, without any direct interest in slavery, resented the exemptions extended the upper classes and condemned the "rich man's war and the poor man's fight." The inevitable result was wholesale desertion, totaling more than 100,000. State rights was a potent force for division among the political leaders. Governors Brown of Georgia and Vance of North Carolina bitterly opposed the tendency toward consolidation in the Confederate government. So strong was this spirit that the Richmond *Dispatch* (1863) asked "Can it be that after all we are not in earnest?" The press, too, was divided: Edward A. Pollard of the Richmond *Examiner* and Robert Barnwell Rhett of the Charleston *Mercury* were especially caustic in their criticism of the Administration. Another group had expected a short war and lost interest in the cause as the years dragged on. By 1865 many enthusiastic secessionists of 1860 had become despondent, and a powerful peace movement led by Vice-President Stephens swept the Confederacy.

CONGREGATIONALISTS, the direct offspring of the Puritan movement in England, were the most numerous and influential religious body to develop in colonial America. Their first church was that at Plymouth composed of Separatist Puritans who had come over in the *Mayflower* (1620). Because of the combined influence of the Plymouth congregation and the then prevailing ideas as to church polity among the migrating Massachusetts Bay Puritan leaders, other churches as they were formed adopted the Congregational polity. Thus, in about ten years, 33 Congregational churches had been organized. When the Connecticut and the New Haven colonies were formed, their congregations also adopted the Congregational polity. In all of these colonies, and later in New Hampshire, Congregationalism was established by law, and throughout the colonial period their ministers exercised a powerful political influence, though they held no political office.

Because of the necessity of defending the Congregational polity against its English critics, the Cambridge Synod was called. It adopted the Cambridge Platform (1648)—embodying the extremely Calvinistic Westminster Confession—which was little more than the putting together of the administrative experience of the early Congregational fathers.

With the coming of the large Puritan immigration (1640–60) Congregationalism greatly expanded. Harvard College was established (1636) to provide an educated ministry, and in 1701 Yale College was opened for the same purpose. Of great importance was the adoption (1662) of the Halfway Covenant providing for a kind of halfway church membership for those who could not profess a religious experience, which was true of a large majority of the third generation. As time went on their numbers tended to increase, which was one of the principal reasons for the growing religious inertia and for the liberal tendencies which began to manifest themselves toward the close of the 17th century. To check these tendencies the Massachusetts leaders attempted to force the adoption of certain Presbyterian features. These were rejected in Massachusetts, but adopted in Connecticut (Saybrook Platform, 1708) and from this time on Connecticut Congregationalism tended more and more toward Presbyterianism.

New England Congregationalism was revived as a result of the Great Awakening (1734–44) and added at least 25,000 new members. The revival, however, split numerous congregations, and produced doctrinal disputes which divided Congregationalism into contending groups. Out of these eventually arose Unitarianism (1820). Congregationalism gave almost unanimous support to the Revolution, the New England clergy having prepared the people to accept the Revolutionary philosophy through their preaching election sermons.

Though there was a large immigration of New England people to the West, Congregationalism failed to develop any adequate method of following them. In 1801 a Plan of Union with the Presbyterians was adopted by which they agreed to form joint congregations in frontier communities. Eventually a majority of these churches became Presbyterian, the net result being that Congregationalism has remained a relatively small body. Though recently united with the Christian Church, the combined membership is still less than one million.

In 1852 the Congregationalists rejected the Plan of Union and formed the American Congregational Union, their first national organization. The Congregationalists have been particularly notable for their missionary and educational activity. They formed the first national foreign missionary society in 1810, while the American Home Missionary Society (1826), predominantly Congregational since 1837, carried on an immense work in the newer sections of the nation. The colleges established by Congregationalists such as Williams, Amherst, Oberlin, Carleton and Grinnell are among the best of their kind in the nation. Their American Missionary Association has worked effectively among Negroes in the South since the Civil War, some of the outstanding Negro colleges being under its control.

CONGRESS, THE UNITED STATES, was indirectly modeled by the Convention of 1787 upon the British Parliament. It consists of two houses, of which the House of Representatives represents the people according to population and the Senate is composed of two members from each state. Both the form and the basis of representation were the subjects of compromise in the Convention of 1787, and the successful accomplishment of these made possible the formation and finally the adoption of the Constitution. Originally the two Senators from each state were elected by the state legislatures, but by the Seventeenth Amendment, which went into effect on May 31, 1913, the Senators are now elected by direct vote of the people.

The House of Representatives consists of "members chosen every second year by the people of the several States, and the electors [voters] in each State shall have the qualifications requisite for electors of the most numerous branch of the State legislature." (Constitution, Art. I, Secs. 1–2). The qualifications for a Representative are that he shall be at least 25 years of age, have been for seven years a citizen of the United States and when elected to be an inhabitant of that state in which he shall be chosen. Also, Representatives and direct taxes shall be apportioned among the several states which may be included within the Union according to their respective numbers.

The first census was taken in the year 1790 and has been repeated every ten years since that time. The number of Representatives shall not exceed one for every 30,000 inhabitants, but each state shall have at least one Representative. The Constitution provided for a definite apportionment of 65 members for the various states at first until a new apportionment could be made following the first census. The number of members was increased after each census but that of 1840, when there was a reduction from 242 to 232. This was in spite of an increase of population during the preceding ten years, but was accomplished by increasing the ratio of apportionment. The reapportionment act of 1929 definitely fixed the number of Representatives at 435 who are apportioned among the states according to the method known as major fractions by which each state receives one member for each ratio quotient and major fraction thereof. If, following any census, Congress fails to enact the necessary legislation for apportionment, the representation reported by the President to be based upon that census automatically goes into effect for the elections to the next Congress.

The state governments divide the territory or each state into districts, but the territory in each district must be "contiguous." It is possible to manipulate the shape of a district so as to include various counties and cities by means of a process known as "gerrymandering" with the result that large numbers of voters of one party can be included in one congressional district. The district thus may be lost to the opposing party by a large majority while a number of other districts can be won by the party in power by small majorities. When a state such as Delaware or Vermont has but one member, he is chosen "at large" by the voters of the entire state. There is nothing to prevent any or all members being chosen in this manner in any state, and frequently following a new apportionment the state government will prefer that any newly acquired member be elected at large rather than disturb the already existing districts. When vacancies occur the executive authority of the state issues writs of election to fill such vacancies. While the Constitution merely requires that a Representative shall be an inhabitant, that is resident, of a state, yet the custom has grown that a Representative also must be a resident of the district of the state from which he is elected. This custom is occasionally but not often broken.

The House of Representatives is presided over by a speaker and has such other officers as it may determine. The speaker is nominated by a caucus of the majority party. The candidate for the office honored by the vote of the minority usually assumes the position of floor leader of his party. The power and influence of the speaker increased rapidly from the beginning until it reached a position of real dictatorship. In the year 1910, a revolt against the power of Speaker Joseph G. Cannon deprived the office of most of its powers and placed them in the hands of the committees. Each party chooses a Whip to assist the floor leader in securing the organization and support of the party followers.

The House is organized in 19 standing committees. (Before the enactment of the Legislative Reorganization Act of 1946 there were about 50 standing committees.) The members are designated by a Committee on Committees chosen by the members. The party members of this committee meet separately and agree upon their respective members who then are submitted as a joint list of the Committee and voted upon by the House of Representatives. The membership of the committees is divided among the parties roughly in proportion to the total party membership of the House. In general, the oldest majority members in length of consecutive committee service serve as chairmen of the respective committees. The majority party controls the Committee on Rules which in turn determines the business to be brought before the House for consideration.

The term of Senators is six years, but the members are divided into three classes so that one third of the total membership changes or is re-elected every two years. By provision of the Constitution, the Vice-President of the United States presides over the Senate, but has no vote except in cases of a tie. The Senate chooses a president *pro tem*, who presides in the absence of the Vice-President. The Senate is organized into 15 standing committees (formerly 33) upon somewhat the same plan as is the House of Representatives. The Constitution (Art. I, Sec. 3, Paragraph 3) requires that a Senator shall be 30 years of age, shall have been nine years a citizen of the United States and an inhabitant of that state from which he has been chosen. Both Houses are given authority (Art. I, Sec. 5, Paragraph 1) to be judge of the elections, returns and qualifications of their own members.

While debate in the House of Representatives is strictly controlled and limited by the majority, debate in the Senate is almost uncontrolled. It can be shortened or closed only by a cumbrous procedure which can be put into effect upon a petition of 16 Senators followed two days later by a two-thirds vote. If the cloture is passed it then provides that a measure under discussion shall be the unfinished business to the exclusion of all other business until disposed of, but each Senator may speak for one hour and no longer on the measure under discussion. The rule seldom has been used. This makes possible a filibuster or delaying of business by opposing Senators who may hold the floor and discuss a measure for days or weeks in order to cause its final defeat by the pressure of other business.

According to the Constitution money bills must originate in the House of Representatives, but the Senate has complete freedom of amendment and this includes reduction or addition to the amounts at its discretion. The House may pass articles of impeachment against any executive and judicial official of the U. S. Government. The Senate then sits as a court following the presentation of charges or indictment by the House of Representatives. Condemnation can be accomplished only by a two-thirds vote of the members present. The Senate also confirms appointments by the President by simple majority vote and ratifies treaties by a two-thirds vote.

When the Convention of 1787 formed the Constitution it was anticipated that the House of Representatives would be the most powerful body since it was elected by the direct vote of the people. The Senate, however, soon began to gain at the expense of the House of Representatives until today it is the more powerful house. The longer term of office, smaller number of members, unlimited debate, influence over foreign affairs by ratification of treaties, and participation in the spoils of office through the confirmation of the President's appointments has much to do with this. Due to the fact that the Senators originally were elected by the state legislatures and hence did not exercise their great powers under popular control, the movement arose which resulted in the Seventeenth Amendment and the direct election of Senators by the people. This has not resulted in a lessening of senatorial powers; that house still has predominant influence in legislative matters. The Senate is one of the most powerful legislative bodies in the world.

The individual Senators and members of the House of Representatives are provided with clerks, secretaries and offices in the Senate and House office buildings, all at public expense. The salary is $22,500 a year and in addition the members of both houses have the franking privilege or free postal service and also a generous provision of "mileage" for traveling expenses from their homes to Washington and return for each session of the Congress of which they are members. While, of course, individual members of both houses must face the fortunes of party warfare, yet it has been the custom, especially in the South, for Senators to be re-elected for a number of terms, some of them serving from twenty to thirty years. The proportion of Representatives re-elected is much smaller. The power and influence of any specific Congress depend in large part upon the membership, party majorities and also the caliber or initiative of the man who may be President.

Congressional investigating committees, around which so much controversy has centered, originally sprang into being as a consequence of the separation of powers, owing to which the executive and legislative departments frequently found themselves in disagreement. Investigating committees have never confined themselves to investigating the executive. On the contrary they have conducted extensive and sometimes highly illuminating researches into all phases of national life. They have also tended to assume more and more of the powers of the judiciary with oftentime controversial effect. The main points in controversy are whether investigating committees can compel testimony and whether the executive is obliged to give them all the information they ask for. Rules governing investigations adopted by Congress in 1955 set up minimal standards of behavior to which committees were expected, perhaps unrealistically, to conform.

CONGRESSES, 1ST TO 87TH, TABLE OF. The second clause of Art. I, Sec. 4 of the Constitution, which has been superseded by Sec. 2 of the Twentieth Amendment, provided that Congress should assemble at least once yearly, on the first Monday of December, unless a different day should be appointed by law. However, the beginning and end of the terms of senators and representatives, and therefore the calendar limits of each Congress, were determined by the action of the Congress of the Confederation in designating March 4, 1789, as the day for the new government under the Federal Constitution to begin to function. The Twentieth Amendment, which declared that the terms of senators and representatives should end at noon on Jan. 3, and which thereby shortened the term of the 73rd Congress by two months, was adopted in 1933.

The accompanying table gives years within which each term of Congress from the 1st to the 87th began and ended, together with the names of speakers of the House of Representatives, and the presidential administrations.

CONGRESS	TERM	SPEAKER	ADMINISTRATION
1st	1789–91	F. A. Muhlenburg	George Washington
2nd	1791–93	Jonathan Trumbull	" "
3rd	1793–95	F. A. Muhlenburg	" "
4th	1795–97	Jonathan Dayton	" "
5th	1797–99	" "	John Adams
6th	1799–1801	Theodore Sedgwick	" "
7th	1801–3	Nathaniel Macon	Thomas Jefferson
8th	1803–5	" "	" "
9th	1805–7	" '	" "
10th	1807–9	Joseph B. Varnum	" "
11th	1809–11	" "	James Madison
12th	1811–13	Henry Clay	" "
13th	1813–15	{ Henry Clay { Langdon Cheves	" "
14th	1815–17	Henry Clay	" "

CONGRESS	TERM	SPEAKER	ADMINISTRATION
15th	1817–19	Henry Clay	James Monroe
16th	1819–21	{ " " { John W. Taylor	" "
17th	1821–23	Philip P. Barbour	" "
18th	1823–25	Henry Clay	" "
19th	1825–27	John W. Taylor	John Q. Adams
20th	1827–29	Andrew Stephenson	" "
21st	1829–31	" "	Andrew Jackson
22nd	1831–33	" "	" "
23rd	1833–35	{ Andrew Stephenson { John Bell	" "
24th	1835–37	James K. Polk	" "
25th	1837–39	" "	Martin Van Buren
26th	1839–41	R. M. T. Hunter	" "
27th	1841–43	John White	{ William H. Harrison { John Tyler
28th	1843–45	John W. Jones	John Tyler
29th	1845–47	John W. Davis	James K. Polk
30th	1847–49	Robert C. Winthrop	" "
31st	1849–51	Howell Cobb	{ Zachary Taylor { Millard Fillmore
32nd	1851–53	Lynn Boyd	Millard Fillmore
33rd	1853–55	" "	Franklin Pierce
34th	1855–57	Nathaniel P. Banks	" "
35th	1857–59	James L. Orr	James Buchanan
36th	1859–61	William Pennington	" "
37th	1861–63	Galusha A. Grow	Abraham Lincoln
38th	1863–65	Schuyler Colfax	" "
39th	1865–67	" "	{ Abraham Lincoln { Andrew Johnson
40th	1867–69	" "	Andrew Johnson
41st	1869–71	James G. Blaine	U. S. Grant
42nd	1871–73	" "	" "
43rd	1873–75	" "	" "
44th	1875–77	{ Michael C. Kerr { Samuel J. Randall	" "
45th	1877–79	Samuel J. Randall	Rutherford B. Hayes
46th	1879–81	" "	
47th	1881–83	Joseph W. Keifer	{ James A. Garfield { Chester A. Arthur
48th	1883–85	John G. Carlisle	Chester A. Arthur
49th	1885–87	" "	Grover Cleveland
50th	1887–89	" "	" "
51st	1889–91	Thomas B. Reed	Benjamin Harrison
52nd	1891–93	Charles F. Crisp	" "
53rd	1893–95	" "	Grover Cleveland
54th	1895–97	Thomas B. Reed	" "
55th	1897–99	" "	William McKinley
56th	1899–1901	David B. Henderson	" "
57th	1901–3	" "	{ William McKinley { Theodore Roosevelt
58th	1903–5	Joseph G. Cannon	Theodore Roosevelt
59th	1905–7	" "	" "
60th	1907–9	" "	" "
61st	1909–11	Joseph G. Cannon	William H. Taft
62nd	1911–13	Champ Clark	" "
63rd	1913–15	" "	Woodrow Wilson
64th	1915–17	" "	" "
65th	1917–19	" "	" "
66th	1919–21	Frederick H. Gillett	" "
67th	1921–23	" "	Warren G. Harding
68th	1923–25	" "	{ Warren G. Harding { Calvin Coolidge
69th	1925–27	Nicholas Longworth	Calvin Coolidge
70th	1927–29	" "	" "

CONGRESS	TERM	SPEAKER	ADMINISTRATION
71st	1929–31	Nicholas Longworth	Herbert Hoover
72nd	1931–33	John N. Garner	"
73rd	1933–35	Henry T. Rainey Joseph W. Burns	Franklin D. Roosevelt
74th	1935–37	Joseph W. Burns William B. Bankhead	" "
75th	1937–39	William B. Bankhead	" "
76th	1939–41	" "	" "
		Sam Rayburn	
77th	1941–43	" "	" "
78th	1943–45	" "	Franklin D. Roosevelt Harry S. Truman
79th	1945–47	" "	Harry S. Truman
80th	1947–49	Joseph W. Martin, Jr.	" "
81st	1949–51	Sam Rayburn	" "
82nd	1951–53	" "	" "
83rd	1953–55	Joseph W. Martin, Jr.	Dwight D. Eisenhower
84th	1955–57	Sam Rayburn	" "
85th	1957–59	" "	" "
86th	1959–61	" "	" "
87th	1961–	John W. McCormack	John F. Kennedy

CONNECTICUT. The Dutchman, Adrian Block, in 1614, was the first definitely known explorer of the Connecticut coast and river. The interior of the state was first explored by Edward Winslow of Plymouth in 1632. The Dutch from New Amsterdam established the first trading post, the House of Hope, within the present bounds of Hartford in 1633. A few weeks later, Lt. William Holmes, of Plymouth, pushed on up the river and established a post at the present Windsor. Both these undertakings were crowded out within a score of years by settlers from Massachusetts Bay Colony who, during 1635 and 1636, settled the three River Towns of Windsor, Hartford and Wethersfield. In 1635 John Winthrop, Jr. arrived in New England with appointment as governor to act for Lord Saye and Sele and others who claimed the Connecticut region under the so-called Warwick Patent. He established a fort at Saybrook and entered into an agreement, through the Bay Colony government, with the Massachusetts Bay settlers who were moving to the Connecticut Valley. Under this arrangement a commission chosen among the settlers was created to maintain civil government for the River Towns. When the commission expired by limitation at the end of a year, the towns carried on a provisional administration until January, 1639, when they adopted a frame of government called the Fundamental Orders, under which the affairs of the Connecticut Colony were conducted for over two decades. Because of this remarkable document, somewhat inaccurately described as a constitution and as the first written constitution, Connecticut has been called the Constitution State. The Connecticut Colony increased in population and expanded rapidly, acquiring Saybrook in 1644, and establishing the new towns of Farmington, Middletown, Stratford, Fairfield, Norwalk, New London and Norwich. In 1650 a code of laws, drafted by Roger Ludlow, was adopted.

Meanwhile other groups of settlers newly arrived from England established themselves independently on the shore of the Sound. In contrast with the people at the River Towns, for whom farming was the principal occupation and trade an incident, the followers of Theophilus Eaton and Rev. John Davenport located at New Haven in 1637–38 to establish a trading town with agriculture as a subordinate necessity. While Hooker and his companions sought an atmosphere in which religion and government would be less closely interwoven than in Massachusetts, Davenport's party desired an even more theocratic state as was shown in the Fundamental Articles of New Haven adopted on June 14, 1639. Other settlers located at Guilford, Milford, Stamford and Branford and joined with New Haven in 1643 to form the New Haven Colony. Gov. Eaton's code of laws adopted in 1656 by the New Haven Colony obtained later undeserved notoriety as the Blue Laws.

Territorial and governmental security were assured by the charter issued by Charles II in 1662 which combined New Haven with the Connecticut Colony. This charter permitted almost complete self-government and, with verbal changes in 1776 to assert independence, it remained in force till 1818. In the colonial wars with the French, Connecticut was an active participant and in the American Revolution bore its full share though very little fighting occurred within the state. Connecticut's delegates were active in framing the Federal Constitution of 1787 and the state was the fifth to ratify, Jan. 9, 1788.

The first three decades of the 19th century witnessed a slow democratic revolution whose principal product was the state constitution of 1818 which still remains in force.

CONNECTICUT: CHARTER OF 1662. Following the accession of Charles II to the British throne, the people of Connecticut believed that the time was favorable for petitioning the king to grant them a charter for the colony, as they considered that the Old or Warwick Patent, under which they then held their lands, gave them only a somewhat uncertain tenure. Whereupon they chose John Winthrop, their governor, to act in the matter. Carrying a draft of a charter (which evidently was not used) based upon the Warwick Patent and letters to several persons of note, he sailed for England on his mission in 1661. His efforts were rewarded by the granting of a charter bearing the great seal and dated April 23, 1662. So liberal were the terms of this document that it was almost a grant of freedom to the colony. This charter was written and sealed in duplicate. One of these originals Winthrop brought with him when he returned later in the year; the other he left in safe hands in England where it remained for many years, probably until 1697. All went well until King James II succeeded to the throne in 1685. James endeavored to annul many existing charters, including that of Connecticut. The colony in a petition to him asked that they might continue as they were; but if that could not be, that they might go under the government of Massachusetts rather than that of New York. This the English officials assumed to be a surrender of the colony's freedom, and Sir Edmond Andros was sent over late in 1686 to receive their charter on behalf of the king, "if tendered by you." Much unsatisfactory correspondence followed between Andros, in Boston, and the Connecticut authorities, resulting at last in Andros coming with an armed troop to take over the government. Arriving in Hartford late in the day on Oct. 31, 1687, he was received with due ceremony and held "some treaty" with the colony authorities that evening. The next day "they all together went . . . to the publique court house" where Andros read his orders and commission and formally annexed the colony to his Dominion of New England.

It was at this time, according to tradition, that Andros called for the charter and after it had been brought in, and while Gov. Treat was making a fervid speech against its surrender, the lights were suddenly extinguished and when they were relighted, the charter was gone—having been taken by Joseph Wadsworth and secreted in a hollow tree, known later as the Charter Oak. This tree fell in 1856, at the estimated age of one thousand years.

CONNECTICUT, FUNDAMENTAL ORDERS OF. As founded in 1635, Connecticut consisted of the three River Towns of Windsor, Hartford and Wethersfield, with Springfield temporarily included. The River Towns were established within territory to which the planters had neither patent nor title. And, apparently, without higher authorization than their own good right (unless a so-called commission, of no legal standing and doubtful acceptance, recorded by the Massachusetts Bay Colony may be considered authorization) they established a court, which, from April 26, 1636, until April 5, 1638, exercised jurisdiction over such matters as trade with the Indians, the appointment of constables, the organization of a militia, the punishment of offenders, the laying of taxes and the determination of boundaries; and which declared and conducted a war against the Pequot Indians. Then, during the spring of 1638, there was a general assembly of the planters, held apparently with a view to establishing a more satisfactory form of government than had hitherto existed. Out of this meeting came the Fundamental Orders: "voted" on Jan. 14, 1639. Exactly how these orders were arrived at, and whether an existing court or the whole body of planters voted them, can only be surmised. That they were put into their final form by Roger Ludlow is practically certain.

The document, consisting of a preamble and eleven orders, created a form of government for the three towns. It recognized no higher authority than the freemen of those towns. The preamble set forth that "where a people are gathered together the word of god requires that to mayntayne the peace and Vnion of such a people there should be an Orderly and decent Gouerment established." The ensuing orders provided for the calling of general assemblies; the election of a governor and magistrates; and the qualification of voters. They specified how the deputies to the Court were to be elected; how the elections were to be called; how the courts were to be organized and empowered; and how taxes were to be apportioned between the towns. It was pointedly stated that no Court was to be adjourned or dissolved without the consent of the majority of its members.

The sixth and tenth orders are particularly interesting in that they set forth in detail how, in case the governor or magistrates neglected or refused to call a General Court, the freemen had the power, of their own right, to give orders for the calling of a Court and to proceed to any act of power which a regularly ordered Court might do. In these provisions, promulgated on the banks of the Connecticut River in 1639, is to be found the first public expression of the revolutionary provisions embodied in the Triennial Act which was passed by the Parliament of England two years later.

Although superseded in 1662 by a charter from the royal hand which they had ignored, the essential features of the Orders were incorporated in the charter, which continued as the basis of government for Connecticut until the adoption of a new state constitution in 1818, which constitution in turn continued these fundamentals.

To what extent the Fundamental Orders influenced later constitutional development in America is still a subject for controversy; but that they establish a pattern which reappeared in the state constitutions of 1776ff cannot be questioned.

CONNECTICUT, THE OLD PATENT OF, is known only from conflicting claims made under its authority and from what purports to be a copy of a deed made by the Earl of Warwick, on March 19, 1632, of a strip of land including a part of the present State of Connecticut. Warwick had no right to make the grant; nor did the grantees—Lord Saye and Sele, Lord Brooke and others—make any move to take possession until, in 1635, actual settlement of the Connecticut country was under way by other groups at the River Towns. At that time the agents of the grantees announced their claim and began the erection of a fort at the mouth of the Connecticut. Their efforts did not prosper, however, and in 1644 the fort and, presumably, the rights under the patent were sold to the planters of the River Towns, who had from the beginning regarded themselves as the colony of Connecticut. At the Restoration, when this self-blessed colony sought a royal charter, the nebulous Warwick Patent was cited in support of the bounds desired, and undoubtedly played a large part in securing for Connecticut the limits set forth in the Charter of 1662.

CONNECTICUT COMPROMISE. In the Convention of 1787 the larger states supported the Virginia plan which would create a bicameral legislature in which "the rights of suffrage . . . ought to be proportioned to the Quotas of contributions, or to the number of free inhabitants." Anticipating the greater burdens, these states demanded a commensurate share of control. The small states, jealous of their welfare, refused to be moved from their demand for equality in a unicameral house. Here was the fundamental problem of balance in a federation of states differing so greatly in size. June 11, Roger Sherman, of Connecticut, proposed a compromise: two houses, the one with equal and the other proportional representation. Amendments linking direct taxes and representation in the House of Representatives and both of these with three-fifths or Federal ratio were added. In its amended form the proposal of Roger Sherman was finally adopted, and has since been known as the Connecticut Compromise.

CONNECTICUT'S WESTERN LANDS stemmed from her royal charter of 1662, granting the territory between Massachusetts on the north, the "Sea" on the south, Narragansett Bay on the east, and the South Sea on the west. In securing this charter, Connecticut's representatives cited the "Old Patent."

Little interest was taken in the vast strip to the westward until the middle of the 18th century, when many settlement petitions were made. One Connecticut enterprise, the Susquehannah Company which was granted lands in the Wyoming (Pa.) re-

gion, came into conflict with Pennsylvania in the Yankee-Pennamite Wars, and as a result Connecticut was forced to relinquish jurisdiction (1782).

In 1780, to overcome the menace of unsettled boundaries and provide a public domain, Congress asked the six states whose colonial charters granted western rights to cede their claims. New York responded first, others followed, but Connecticut withheld cession until she received the grant of an area extending 120 miles from Pennsylvania's western boundary along Lake Erie, considered equal to the Wyoming lands.

This Western Reserve, excepting the half million acres set off as the "Firelands," for compensating the losses of Connecticut families in British and Indian raids, Connecticut sold in 1795 to the Connecticut Land Company for $1,200,000, thereby establishing her educational fund. In 1800, to ensure clear land titles, she relinquished jurisdiction to the U. S. Government, the region being made Trumbull County, Northwest Territory.

CONQUISTADORES (conquerors) is the name properly given leaders of the Spanish conquest of the Americas, though their followers are also included by the term. Ponce de León, in search of the fabled Fountain of Youth, had landed on the shores of Florida (1513) before the great Cortés, in 1519, took Mexico. Immediately thereafter, other *conquistadores* began exploring and subduing lands northward. Notable among them were Narváez, whose shipwreck on the Texas coast (1528) resulted in the seven years' walk of Cabeza de Vaca, a survivor, across the continent to Sinaloa; DeSoto, who in 1539, with 550 men, 200 horses and a herd of hogs, marched north from Tampa Bay, reached Tennessee, wandered across Oklahoma and Arkansas, and was buried in the Mississippi River he had discovered before the wretched remnant of his men found succor in Mexico four years after their *entrada* began; Coronado, whose fantastic search (1540–42) for the mythical Seven Cities of Cibola took him into New Mexico, across the Staked Plains, and perhaps into Kansas; Espejo, who, looking for a lake of gold, discovered rich ores in Arizona (1583); Oñate, who in 1598 began the settlement of New Mexico; Alonso de León, who penetrated Texas (1688) to prevent French occupation of that territory and founded a colony. *Conquistadores* explored California thoroughly, seeking a passage to the Atlantic.

CONSERVATION means getting the maximum use of the greatest number of available natural resources that are valuable to the greatest number of people for the longest period of time. In other words it means wise use of our resources. The principal resources that need conserving are soil, water, minerals, forests, wildlife, recreational resources, and our people. Some resources are more or less unlimited, while others must be used wisely to make the supply last as long as possible. Conservation practices were common in Asia and Europe many centuries before the discovery of America, but in our country it appeared that our great abundance of resources would never be exhausted. The British government early discovered that the better forests in the American colonies were rapidly being destroyed and had certain trees marked that were to be reserved for the ships of her Navy and Merchant Marine. William Penn requested that one acre in five be left in forest on the lands that had been allotted to him and distributed to the settlers.

Very little was done by the U. S. Government until much later. Although George Washington and Thomas Jefferson had experimented with various methods of crop improvement and soil conservation on their own plantations, the first official step seems to have been taken in 1828 when President John Quincy Adams established a naval station in the timbered area at Pensacola, Fla., and withdrew 30,-000 acres of live-oak land on the nearby island of Santa Rosa for later use in building our Navy. Carl Schurz, Secretary of the Interior, 1877–81, recommended the scientific care of forests and the establishment of Federal forest reservations. The American Association for the Advancement of Science presented a memorial to Congress in 1873, requesting that suitable laws be passed to protect our supply of natural resources. The first forest reserve was acquired in 1891. President Benjamin Harrison set aside 13,000,000 acres as forest reservations while President Grover Cleveland withdrew 21,000,000 additional acres and placed them in reserve. Scientific, forestry, and wildlife societies kept up the interest in conservation while men like Maj. J. W. Powell, Director of the U. S. Geologic Survey, 1881–94, explored and wrote about the arid conditions of the West, and Gifford Pinchot, appointed Chief Forester in 1893, informed the people of the need for protection of our forest resources.

Very little was accomplished however, until the administration of President Theodore Roosevelt. He appointed the Inland Waterways Commission in 1907 to study flood conditions on the lower Mississippi River. This Commission found that the problem of floods was of interest to the entire country, as it included removal of forests from the watershed, soil erosion, soil depletion, range control and many other factors. At their suggestion the President called the White House Conference, May 13, 1908, and invited the governors of the states, justices of the Supreme Court, congressmen, scientists, and prominent politicians to find out the state of our natural resources. It was discovered that we had little knowledge of the extent or supply of our resources. The President then called the North American Conference on Feb. 18, 1909, and invited representatives from Canada, Mexico and Newfoundland only to find that they too had little knowledge of the resources of their countries. Theodore Roosevelt was successful in getting a partial inventory of our resources; but his efforts were handicapped by refusal of Congress to continue appropriations for the study or to pass laws to stop exploitation of our resources. However, he was able to set aside 234,000,000 acres of forest land for future use. During the next twenty years few public acts were passed, but the people became interested in the broader phase of conservation including wise use of our soils, minerals, range improvement, wildlife and water. Societies such as the Isaak Walton League, Audubon Society, 4-H Clubs, Future Farmers of America, and Bird Clubs were organized and kept up interest in the movement. The National Conservation Association was started in 1909. The Stockraising Grazing Act of 1916 permitted grazing land to be leased by ranchers. The National Park Service was established in 1917, the National Parks Association in 1919, and the Federal Water Power Act of 1920 created the Federal Power Commission which has become important in recent years.

Prosperity during World War I and succeeding years caused our people to overlook the exploitation of our resources until droughts, dust storms, water shortages and millions of acres of abandoned land caused them to take a second look at what had happened to the resource supply of our country. President Franklin D. Roosevelt immediately requested that all possible be done to remedy the situation and included people as one of our greatest resources. The Soil Erosion Service, 1933, was followed by the Soil Conservation Service, 1935, the Agricultural Adjustment Administration, then the Production and Marketing Administration, which included marketing as well as conservation practices. Earlier laws were revised, huge dams were built for flood control, irrigation, and for the generation of electricity. The Works Progress Administration and Public Works Administration were made-work acts for the unemployed, while the Civilian Conservation Corps and National Youth Administration were planned to help the youth of our country. The Tennessee Valley Authority in 1933 was planned to include the well-being of the people as well as flood control and generation of electricity. Since World War II most of the earlier acts have been extended to save our resources, more stress has been placed upon recreational resources and the Government has taken a greater interest in the welfare of our people.

CONSTELLATION-INSURGENTE ACTION (Feb. 9, 1799). Near Nevis Island, West Indies, during naval hostilities with France, Com. Thomas Truxtun in the frigate *Constellation* defeated the French frigate *Insurgente* in a sharp engagement. The *Insurgente* lost 29 killed and 41 wounded, compared with three men wounded in the *Constellation*. Despite a gale which separated the two ships, the prize with 173 prisoners aboard was brought safely into St. Kitt's three days later by Lt. John Rodgers, Midshipman David Porter, and a prize crew of only eleven men. In this and in the subsequent *Constellation-Vengeance* action, Truxtun not only gave vigorous backing to his government's policy of commerce protection, but set high standards for the new national navy.

CONSTITUTION. Authorized by Congress, March 27, 1794, she was designed by Joshua Humphreys, built in Edmund Hartt's shipyard, Boston, and was launched Oct. 21, 1797. In the Naval War with France, she served as Commodore Silas Talbot's flagship, and as the flagship of Com. Edward Preble in the War with Tripoli, participating in five different attacks on Tripoli, July 25 to Sept. 4, 1804. She was victorious in several notable single-ship engagements in the War of 1812. During the fight with the *Guerrière,* a seaman gave her the nickname "Old Ironsides," when, seeing a shot rebound from her hull, he shouted, "Huzza, her sides are made of iron." Ordered broken up in 1830 by the Navy Department, she was retained in deference to public opinion aroused by Oliver Wendell Holmes' poem "Old Ironsides." She was rebuilt in 1833, served as a Naval Academy schoolship, 1860 to 1865, was partially rebuilt in 1876, and, except for one cruise, has been docked at Boston since 1897.

CONSTITUTION AND GUERRIÈRE ENGAGEMENT (Aug. 19, 1812). The capture of the British frigate *Guerrière,* of 49 guns, by the *Constitution,* Capt. Isaac Hull, of 55 guns, mostly long 42-pounders, was the first important naval victory of the War of 1812, and did much to win enthusiasm for the war from New Englanders. It took place 750 miles east of Boston while Hull was watching for British merchantmen on their usual course between Halifax and Bermuda. Running before the wind, Hull finally came to within range on the *Guerrière's* port side, and gave her a staggering broadside which carried away her main yard. A 24-pound shot then struck her mizzenmast, broke it, and sent it crashing over the starboard side. The falling mast knocked a hole in the stern and threw the ship's head to leeward away from the *Constitution.*

Hull immediately took advantage of the situation by securing a raking position and pouring in two broadsides which swept the decks of the *Guerrière* and penetrated her sides. Capt. Dacres, of the *Guerrière,* tried to board, and ran his bowsprit into the shrouds of the *Constitution,* but the loss of his head-sails and mizzenmast made it impossible for him to maneuver his ship. During this period marksmen in the tops wounded or killed several officers on each ship.

As the two ships separated, the *Guerrière's* bowsprit, scraping along the taffrail of her opponent, weakened the forestay on the Britisher and caused the foremast to fall. This in turn fell upon the principal support of the mainmast and brought the latter down also. Thus in thirty minutes of close action the *Guerrière* had been totally dismasted. With a high sea running and the gunports rolling under water, Dacres could do nothing but surrender. The next day Hull was obliged to burn the *Guerrière* and return to Boston without his prize.

The British lost 23 killed and 56 wounded, including Capt. Dacres; the American loss was only seven killed and seven wounded. Although the *Constitution* was nearly 50% superior in all features such as size, sail area, weight of broadside, and accuracy of fire, it was Hull's superior seamanship which made these factors count. To the British the superiority of the new American type of frigate was the most important lesson.

CONSTITUTION, IMPLIED POWERS OF THE. The Constitution of the United States creates a national government of express or enumerated powers and state governments of reserved or residual powers. Thus the authority of Congress to enact laws is defined by the Constitution. This authority is found principally in seventeen express clauses in Article I, Section 8. These express powers are supplemented by a general grant of authority in the final clause of the section "to make all Laws which shall be necessary and proper for carrying into Execution the foregoing Powers, and all other Powers vested by this Constitution in the Government of the United States, or in any Department or Officer thereof." It is in this general clause that the doctrine of implied powers finds its basis.

No sooner had the Constitution gone into operation than a bitter controversy arose between those persons who favored a strong central government and those who favored a central government of limited powers with strong governments in the states. The first group was known as Federalist and the second as Anti-Federalist. The Anti-Federalists would have had the Constitution construed strictly, according to its letter; the Federalists favored a broad interpretation which would render the Constitution adequate to the expanding needs of the country. Thus the issue of strict versus broad construction of the Constitution, that is, whether or not Congress was to enjoy implied powers, became an important major issue between political parties.

Both Washington and Adams were Federalists as were Jay and Ellsworth, the first two Chief Justices of the U. S. Supreme Court. Jefferson, however, was the leader of the Anti-Federalists. After the success of the Anti-Federalists in the election of 1800, Adams appointed John Marshall, an eminent Federalist, as Chief Justice. He held office until his death in 1835. It is difficult to overestimate the influence of Marshall in shaping the direction in which the new nation was to move. The fundamental constitutional decisions made by the Court under his leadership have stood unchallenged as precedents for subsequent courts to follow.

Chief Justice Marshall first enunciated the doctrine of implied powers in the case of United States v. Fisher (2 Cranch 358, 1805), but it was not until fourteen years later that the principle won national attention. In his decision in McCulloch v. Maryland (4 Wheaton 316, 1819), Marshall took occasion to reassert the doctrine of implied powers. He upheld the validity of the act which created the Second Bank of the United States, notwithstanding the silence of the Constitution on the power of Congress to create corporations, or to establish banks. In this decision he said: "Let the end be legitimate, let it be within the scope of the Constitution, and all means which are appropriate, which are plainly adapted to that end, which are not prohibited, but consist with the letter and spirit of the Constitution, are constitutional."

He justified this doctrine on the necessities of constitutional interpretation. He said: "A constitution, to contain an accurate detail of all the subdivisions of which its great powers will admit and of all the means by which they may be carried into execution, would partake of the prolixity of a legal code, and could scarcely be embraced by the human mind. It would probably never be understood by the public. Its nature, therefore, requires that only its great outlines should be marked, its important objects designated, and the minor ingredients which compose those objects deduced from the nature of the objects themselves. . . . We must never forget that it is a constitution we are expounding."

Under this and subsequent decisions upholding the doctrine of implied powers the Constitution has been elaborated and expanded to meet the needs of a civilization which could never have been envisioned by its framers. Pure food and drug laws, lottery acts, a white slave law, a law against the transportation of stolen motor vehicles across state lines, a kidnapping law, a statute requiring the use of safety devices on interstate trains, and many others have been passed under the general authority given to Congress to regulate interstate and foreign commerce. The powers to tax and to establish post offices and post roads have similarly served as bases for Federal regulation. But when Congress sought to regulate child labor under the taxing and commerce clauses the Supreme Court denied that such a power could be implied. Thus the powers reserved to the states under the Tenth Amendment may not be usurped under the excuse that they may be reasonably implied from some express power conferred upon Congress. The decisions upholding the constitutionality of the Wagner Act, however, indicate a tendency to permit a very broad construction of the commerce power which may result in a considerable diminution in the powers reserved to the states.

CONSTITUTION, RATIFICATION OF THE. The Constitution was adopted by the Convention of 1787 on Sept. 17. On the same day the Convention adopted a resolution that the Constitution be laid before the Continental Congress of the United States with the suggestion that in the opinion of the Convention the document should be submitted to a convention of delegates in each state for their assent and ratification, said convention to be called by the recommendation of the state legislatures. Article VII of the new Constitution provided that "the ratification of the Conventions of nine States, shall be sufficient for the Establishment of this Constitution between the States so ratifying the Same." According to the Articles of Confederation, still in force, any amendments to them and changes in the existing form of national government could only become valid by the unanimous consent of all the states. This action of the Convention, in requiring ratification by only nine of the thirteen states, was therefore revolutionary from the standpoint of the constitutional provisions of the time. Also on the same day, Sept. 17, George Washington, as President of the Convention, wrote a letter to the President of Congress transmitting the document. The Continental Congress acted promptly and on Sept. 28 following unanimously passed a resolution that the Constitution and documents accompanying it be submitted to the legislatures of the several states in order that the Constitution be likewise submitted to a convention of delegates chosen in each state by the people thereof.

The first state to ratify was Delaware on Dec. 7, 1787, by the unanimous vote of the convention called for that purpose. This little state was anxious to preserve its independence from Pennsylvania, with which state it had been joined in administration before the Revolution. Delaware was followed by Pennsylvania by a two-to-one vote of its convention on Dec. 12, and New Jersey by unanimous vote on Dec. 18 of the same year. Georgia was the next in order with a unanimous vote of its convention on Jan. 2, 1788, and Connecticut followed on Jan. 9, by more than a three-to-one vote.

Following these five, the action was slower and in several states ratification was secured only after a protracted struggle. Massachusetts ratified on Feb. 6 by the close vote of 187 to 168, and was followed by Maryland by a good majority on April 28 and South Carolina by a like overwhelming vote on May 23. New Hampshire ratified June 21 by a vote of 57 to 46. This made up the number of nine states necessary to cause the Constitution to go into effect according to the action of the Federal Convention.

Virginia ratified on June 26 by the vote of 89 yeas to 79 nays, and New York on July 26 after a desperate struggle in her state convention at Poughkeepsie. Due to the remarkable eloquence and leadership of Alexander Hamilton, what was at first an adverse majority was turned into the favorable vote of 30 yeas to 27 nays.

Only these eleven states had ratified the Constitution when the new Government went into effect on March 4, 1789, and George Washington was inaugurated first President on April 30. North Carolina ratified on Nov. 21, and Rhode Island finally on May 29, 1790, by the very close vote of 34 to 32. Three other states, newly formed, in addition to the original thirteen, ratified the Constitution during the administration of Washington. They were: Vermont, on March 4, 1791; Kentucky, on June 1, 1792; Tennessee, on June 1, 1796. The other states followed in succession as they were settled and created by act of Congress during more than a century following.

CONSTITUTION OF THE UNITED STATES

WE THE PEOPLE OF THE UNITED STATES, in Order to form a more perfect Union, establish Justice, insure domestic Tranquility, provide for the common defence, promote the general Welfare, and secure the Blessings of Liberty to ourselves and our Posterity, do ordain and establish this Constitution for the United States of America.

ARTICLE I.

Section 1. All legislative Powers herein granted shall be vested in a Congress of the United States, which shall consist of a Senate and House of Representatives.

Section 2. The House of Representatives shall be composed of Members chosen every second Year by the People of the several States, and the Electors in each State shall have the Qualifications requisite for Electors of the most numerous Branch of the State Legislature.

No Person shall be a Representative who shall not have attained to the age of twenty five Years, and been seven Years a Citizen of the United States, and who shall not, when elected, be an Inhabitant of that State in which he shall be chosen.

Representatives and direct Taxes shall be apportioned among the several States which may be included within this Union, according to their respective Numbers, which shall be determined by adding to the whole Number of free Persons, including those bound to Service for a Term of Years, and excluding Indians not taxed, three fifths of all other Persons. The actual Enumeration shall be made within three Years after the first Meeting of the Congress of the United States, and within every subsequent Term of ten Years, in such Manner as they shall by Law direct. The Number of Representatives shall not exceed one for every thirty Thousand, but each State shall have at Least one Representative; and until such enumeration shall be made, the State of New Hampshire shall be entitled to chuse three, Massachusetts eight, Rhode-Island and Providence Plantations one, Connecticut five, New-York six, New Jersey four, Pennsylvania eight, Delaware one, Maryland six, Virginia ten, North Carolina five, South Carolina five, and Georgia three.

When vacancies happen in the Representation from any State, the Executive Authority thereof shall issue Writs of Election to fill such Vacancies.

The House of Representatives shall chuse their Speaker and other Officers; and shall have the sole Power of Impeachment.

Section 3. The Senate of the United States shall be composed of two Senators from each State, chosen by the Legislature thereof, for six Years; and each Senator shall have one Vote.

Immediately after they shall be assembled in Consequence of the first Election, they shall be divided as equally as may be into three Classes. The Seats of the Senators of the first Class shall be vacated at the Expiration of the second Year, of the second Class at the Expiration of the fourth Year, and of the third Class at the Expiration of the sixth Year, so that one third may be chosen every second Year; and if Vacancies happen by Resignation, or otherwise, during the Recess of the Legislature of any State, the Executive thereof may make temporary Appointments until the next Meeting of the Legislature, which shall then fill such Vacancies.

No Person shall be a Senator who shall not have attained to the Age of thirty Years, and been nine Years a Citizen of the United States, and who shall not, when elected, be an Inhabitant of that State for which he shall be chosen.

The Vice President of the United States shall be President of the Senate, but shall have no Vote, unless they be equally divided.

The Senate shall chuse their other Officers, and also a President pro tempore, in the Absence of the Vice President, or when he shall exercise the Office of President of the United States.

The Senate shall have the sole Power to try all Impeachments. When sitting for that Purpose, they shall be on Oath or Affirmation. When the President of the United States is tried, the Chief Justice shall preside: And no Person shall be convicted without the Concurrence of two thirds of the Members present.

Judgment in Cases of Impeachment shall not extend further than to removal from Office, and disqualification to hold and enjoy any Office of honor, Trust or Profit under the United States: but the Party convicted shall nevertheless be liable and subject to Indictment, Trial, Judgment and Punishment, according to Law.

Section 4. The Times, Places and Manner of holding Elections for Senators and Representatives, shall be prescribed in each State by the Legislature thereof; but the Congress may at any time by Law make or alter such Regulations, except as to the Places of chusing Senators.

The Congress shall assemble at least once in every Year, and such Meeting shall be on the first Monday in December, unless they shall by Law appoint a different Day.

Section 5. Each House shall be the Judge of the Elections, Returns and Qualifications of its own Members, and a Majority of each shall constitute a Quorum to do Business; but a smaller Number may adjourn from day to day and may be authorized to compel the Attendance of absent Members, in such Manner, and under such Penalties as each House may provide.

Each House may determine the Rules of its Proceedings, punish its Members for disorderly Behaviour, and, with the Concurrence of two thirds, expel a Member.

Each House shall keep a Journal of its Proceedings, and from time to time publish the same, excepting such Parts as may in their Judgment require Secrecy; and the Yeas and Nays of the Members of either House on any question shall, at the Desire of one fifth of those Present, be entered on the Journal.

Neither House, during the Session of Congress, shall, without the Consent of the other, adjourn for more than three days, nor to any other Place than that in which the two Houses shall be sitting.

Section 6. The Senators and Representatives shall receive a Compensation for their Services, to be ascertained by Law, and paid out of the Treasury of the United States. They shall in all Cases, except Treason, Felony and Breach of the Peace, be privileged from Arrest during their Attendance at the Session of their respective Houses, and in going to and returning from the same; and for any Speech or Debate in either House, they shall not be questioned in any other Place.

No Senator or Representative shall, during the Time for which he was elected, be appointed to any civil Office under the Authority of the United States, which shall have been created, or the Emoluments whereof shall have been encreased during such time; and no Person holding any Office under the United States, shall be a Member of either House during his Continuance in Office.

Section 7. All Bills for raising Revenue shall originate in the House of Representatives; but the Senate may propose or concur with Amendments as on other Bills.

Every Bill which shall have passed the House of Representatives and the Senate, shall, before it become a Law, be presented to the President of the United States; If he approve he shall sign it, but if not he shall return it, with his Objections to that House in which it shall have originated, who shall enter the Objections at large on their Journal, and proceed to reconsider it. If after such Reconsideration two thirds of that House shall agree to pass the Bill, it shall be sent, together with the Objections, to the other House, by which it shall likewise be reconsidered, and if approved by two thirds of that House, it shall become a Law. But in all such Cases the

Votes of both Houses shall be determined by yeas and Nays, and the Names of the Persons voting for and against the Bill shall be entered on the Journal of each House respectively. If any Bill shall not be returned by the President within ten Days (Sundays excepted) after it shall have been presented to him, the Same shall be a Law, in like Manner as if he had signed it, unless the Congress by their Adjournment prevent its Return, in which Case it shall not be a Law.

Every Order, Resolution, or Vote to which the Concurrence of the Senate and House of Representatives may be necessary (except on a question of Adjournment) shall be presented to the President of the United States; and before the Same shall take Effect, shall be approved by him, or being disapproved by him, shall be repassed by two thirds of the Senate and House of Representatives, according to the Rules and Limitations prescribed in the Case of a Bill.

Section 8. The Congress shall have Power To lay and collect Taxes, Duties, Imposts and Excises, to pay the Debts and provide for the common Defence and general Welfare of the United States; but all Duties, Imposts and Excises shall be uniform throughout the United States;

To borrow Money on the credit of the United States;

To regulate Commerce with foreign Nations, and among the several States, and with the Indian Tribes;

To establish an uniform Rule of Naturalization, and uniform Laws on the subject of Bankruptcies throughout the United States;

To coin Money, regulate the Value thereof, and of foreign Coin, and fix the Standard of Weights and Measures;

To provide for the Punishment of counterfeiting the Securities and current Coin of the United States;

To establish Post Offices and post Roads;

To promote the Progress of Science and useful Arts, by securing for limited Times to Authors and Inventors the exclusive Right to their respective Writings and Discoveries;

To constitute Tribunals inferior to the supreme Court;

To define and punish Piracies and Felonies committed on the high Seas, and Offences against the Law of Nations;

To declare War, grant Letters of Marque and Reprisal, and make Rules concerning Captures on Land and Water;

To raise and support Armies, but no Appropriation of Money to that Use shall be for a longer Term than two Years;

To provide and maintain a Navy;

To make Rules for the Government and Regulation of the land and naval Forces;

To provide for calling for the Militia to execute the

Laws of the Union, suppress Insurrections and repel Invasions;

To provide for organizing, arming, and disciplining, the Militia, and for governing such Part of them as may be employed in the Service of the United States, reserving to the States respectively, the Appointment of the Officers, and the Authority of training the Militia according to the discipline prescribed by Congress;

To exercise exclusive Legislation in all Cases whatsoever, over such District (not exceeding ten Miles square) as may, by Cession of particular States, and the Acceptance of Congress, become the Seat of the Government of the United States, and to exercise like Authority over all Places purchased by the Consent of the Legislature of the State in which the Same shall be, for the Erection of Forts, Magazines, Arsenals, dock-Yards, and other needful Buildings;—And

To make all Laws which shall be necessary and proper for carrying into Execution the foregoing Powers, and all other Powers vested by this Constitution in the Government of the United States, or in any Department or Officer thereof.

Section 9. The Migration or Importation of such Persons as any of the States now existing shall think proper to admit, shall not be prohibited by the Congress prior to the Year one thousand eight hundred and eight, but a Tax or duty may be imposed on such Importation, not exceeding ten dollars for each Person.

The Privilege of the Writ of Habeas Corpus shall not be suspended, unless when in Cases of Rebellion or Invasion the public Safety may require it.

No Bill of Attainder or ex post facto Law shall be passed.

No Capitation, or other direct, Tax shall be laid, unless in Proportion to the Census or Enumeration herein before directed to be taken.

No Tax or Duty shall be laid on Articles exported from any State.

No Preference shall be given by any Regulation of Commerce or Revenue to the Ports of one State over those of another: nor shall Vessels bound to, or from, one State, be obliged to enter, clear or pay Duties in another.

No Money shall be drawn from the Treasury, but in Consequence of Appropriations made by Law; and a regular Statement and Account of the Receipts and Expenditures of all public Money shall be published from time to time.

No Title of Nobility shall be granted by the United States: And no Person holding any Office of Profit or Trust under them, shall, without the Consent of the Congress, accept of any present, Emolument, Office, or Title, of any kind whatever, from any King, Prince, or foreign State.

Section 10. No State shall enter into any Treaty, Alliance, or Confederation; grant Letters of Marque and Reprisal; coin Money; emit Bills of Credit; make any Thing but gold and silver Coin a Tender in Payment of Debts; pass any Bill of Attainder, ex post facto Law, or Law impairing the Obligation of Contracts, or grant any Title of Nobility.

No State shall, without the Consent of the Congress, lay any Imposts or Duties on Imports or Exports, except what may be absolutely necessary for executing it's inspection Laws: and the net Produce of all Duties and Imposts, laid by any State on Imports or Exports, shall be for the Use of the Treasury of the United States; and all such Laws shall be subject to the Revision and Controul of the Congress.

No State shall, without the Consent of Congress, lay any Duty of Tonnage, keep Troops, or Ships of War in time of Peace, enter into any Agreement or Compact with another state, or with a foreign Power, or engage in War, unless actually invaded, or in such imminent Danger as will not admit of delay.

ARTICLE II.

Section 1. The executive Power shall be vested in a President of the United States of America. He shall hold his Office during the Term of four Years, and, together with the Vice President, chosen for the same Term, be elected, as follows

Each State shall appoint, in such Manner as the Legislature thereof may direct, a Number of Electors, equal to the whole Number of Senators and Representatives to which the State may be entitled in the Congress: but no Senator or Representative, or Person holding an Office of Trust or Profit under the United States, shall be appointed an Elector.

The Electors shall meet in their respective States, and vote by Ballot for two Persons, of whom one at least shall not be an Inhabitant of the same State with themselves. And they shall make a List of all the Persons voted for, and of the Number of Votes for each; which List they shall sign and certify, and transmit sealed to the Seat of the Government of the United States, directed to the President of the Senate. The President of the Senate shall, in the Presence of the Senate and House of Representatives, open all the Certificates, and the Votes shall then be counted. The Person having the greatest Number of Votes shall be the President, if such Number be a Majority of the whole Number of Electors appointed; and if there be more than one who have such Majority, and have an equal Number of Votes, then the House of Representatives shall immediately chuse by Ballot one of them for President; and if no Person have a Majority, then from the five highest on the List the said House shall in like Manner chuse the President. But in chusing the President, the Votes shall be taken by States, the Representation from each State having one Vote; A quorum for this Purpose shall consist of a Member or Members from two thirds of the States, and a Majority of all the States shall be necessary to a

Choice. In every Case, after the Choice of the President, the Person having the greatest Number of Votes of the Electors shall be the Vice President. But if there should remain two or more who have equal Votes, the Senate shall chuse from them by Ballot the Vice President.

The Congress may determine the Time of chusing the Electors, and the Day on which they shall give their Votes; which Day shall be the same throughout the United States.

No Person except a natural born Citizen, or a Citizen of the United States, at the time of the Adoption of this Constitution, shall be eligible to the Office of President; neither shall any Person be eligible to that Office who shall not have attained to the Age of thirty five Years, and been fourteen Years a Resident within the United States.

In Case of the Removal of the President from Office, or of his Death, Resignation, or Inability to discharge the Powers and Duties of the said Office, the Same shall devolve on the Vice President, and the Congress may by Law provide for the Case of Removal, Death, Resignation or Inability, both of the President and Vice President, declaring what Officer shall then act as President, and such Officer shall act accordingly, until the Disability be removed, or a President shall be elected.

The President shall, at stated Times, receive for his Services, a Compensation, which shall neither be encreased nor diminished during the Period for which he shall have been elected, and he shall not receive within that Period any other Emolument from the United States, or any of them.

Before he enter on the Execution of his Office, he shall take the following Oath or Affirmation:—"I do solemnly swear (or affirm) that I will faithfully execute the Office of President of the United States, and will to the best of my Ability, preserve, protect and defend the Constitution of the United States."

Section 2. The President shall be Commander in Chief of the Army and Navy of the United States, and of the Militia of the several States, when called into the actual Service of the United States; he may require the Opinion, in writing, of the principal Officer in each of the executive Departments, upon any Subject relating to the Duties of their respective Offices, and he shall have Power to grant Reprieves and Pardons for Offences against the United States, except in Cases of Impeachment.

He shall have Power, by and with the Advice and Consent of the Senate, to make Treaties, provided two thirds of the Senators present concur; and he shall nominate, and by and with the Advice and Consent of the Senate, shall appoint Ambassadors, other public Ministers and Consuls, Judges of the supreme Court, and all other Officers of the United States, whose Appointments are not herein otherwise provided for, and which shall be established by Law: but the Congress may by Law vest the Appointment of such inferior Officers, as they think proper, in the President alone, in the Courts of Law, or in the Heads of Departments.

The President shall have Power to fill up all Vacancies that may happen during the Recess of the Senate, by granting Commissions which shall expire at the End of their next Session.

Section 3. He shall from time to time give to the Congress Information of the State of the Union, and recommend to their Consideration such Measures as he shall judge necessary and expedient; he may, on extraordinary Occasions, convene both Houses, or either of them, and in Case of Disagreement between them, with Respect to the Time of Adjournment, he may adjourn them to such Time as he shall think proper; he shall receive Ambassadors and other public Ministers; he shall take Care that the Laws be faithfully executed, and shall Commission all the Officers of the United States.

Section 4. The President, Vice President and all civil Officers of the United States, shall be removed from Office on Impeachment for, and Conviction of, Treason, Bribery, or other high Crimes and Misdemeanors.

ARTICLE III.

Section 1. The judicial Power of the United States, shall be vested in one supreme Court, and in such inferior Courts as the Congress may from time to time ordain and establish. The Judges, both of the supreme and inferior Courts, shall hold their Offices during good Behaviour, and shall, at stated Times, receive for their Services, a Compensation, which shall not be diminished during their Continuance in Office.

Section 2. The judicial Power shall extend to all Cases, in Law and Equity, arising under this Constitution, the Laws of the United States, and Treaties made, or which shall be made, under their Authority;—to all Cases affecting Ambassadors, other public Ministers and Consuls;—to all Cases of admiralty and maritime Jurisdiction;—to Controversies to which the United States shall be a Party;—to Controversies between two or more States;—between a State and Citizens of another State;—between Citizens of different States;—between Citizens of the same State claiming Lands under Grants of different States, and between a State, or the Citizens thereof, and foreign States, Citizens or Subjects.

In all Cases affecting Ambassadors, other public Ministers and Consuls, and those in which a State shall be Party, the supreme Court shall have original Jurisdiction. In all the other Cases before mentioned, the supreme Court shall have appellate Jurisdiction, both as to Law and Fact, with such Exceptions, and under such Regulations as the Congress shall make.

The Trial of all Crimes, except in Cases of Impeachment, shall be by Jury; and such Trial shall be held in the State where the said Crimes shall have been committed; but when not committed within

241

CONSTITUTION OF THE UNITED STATES

any State, the Trial shall be at such Place or Places as the Congress may by Law have directed.

Section 3. Treason against the United States, shall consist only in levying War against them, or in adhering to their Enemies, giving them Aid and Comfort. No Person shall be convicted of Treason unless on the Testimony of two Witnesses to the same overt Act, or on Confession in open Court.

The Congress shall have Power to declare the Punishment of Treason, but no Attainder of Treason shall work Corruption of Blood, or Forfeiture except during the Life of the Person attainted.

ARTICLE IV.

Section 1. Full Faith and Credit shall be given in each State to the public Acts, Records, and judicial Proceedings of every other State. And the Congress may by general Laws prescribe the Manner in which such Acts, Records and Proceedings shall be proved, and the Effect thereof.

Section 2. The Citizens of each State shall be entitled to all Privileges and Immunities of Citizens in the several States.

A Person charged in any State with Treason, Felony, or other Crime, who shall flee from Justice, and be found in another State, shall on Demand of the executive Authority of the State from which he fled, be delivered up, to be removed to the State having Jurisdiction of the Crime.

No Person held to Service or Labour in one State, under the Laws thereof, escaping into another, shall, in Consequence of any Law or Regulation therein, be discharged from such Service or Labour, but shall be delivered up on Claim of the Party to whom such Service or Labour may be due.

Section 3. New States may be admitted by the Congress into this Union; but no new States shall be formed or erected within the Jurisdiction of any other State; nor any State be formed by the Junction of two or more States, or Parts of States, without the Consent of the Legislatures of the States concerned as well as of the Congress.

The Congress shall have Power to dispose of and make all needful Rules and Regulations respecting the Territory or other Property belonging to the United States; and nothing in this Constitution shall be so construed as to Prejudice any Claims of the United States, or of any particular State.

Section 4. The United States shall guarantee to every State in this Union a Republican Form of Government, and shall protect each of them against Invasion; and on Application of the Legislature, or of the Executive (when the Legislature cannot be convened) against domestic Violence.

ARTICLE V.

The Congress, whenever two thirds of both Houses shall deem it necessary, shall propose Amendments to this Constitution, or, on the Application of the Legislatures of two thirds of the several States, shall call a Convention for proposing Amendments, which, in either Case, shall be valid to all Intents and Purposes, as Part of this Constitution, when ratified by the Legislatures of three fourths of the several States, or by Conventions in three fourths thereof, as the one or the other Mode of Ratification may be proposed by the Congress; Provided that no Amendment which may be made prior to the Year One thousand eight hundred and eight shall in any Manner affect the first and fourth Clauses in the Ninth Section of the first Article; and that no State, without its Consent, shall be deprived of it's equal Suffrage in the Senate.

ARTICLE VI.

All Debts contracted and Engagements entered into, before the Adoption of this Constitution, shall be as valid against the United States under this Constitution, as under the Confederation.

This Constitution, and the Laws of the United States which shall be made in Pursuance thereof; and all Treaties made, or which shall be made, under the Authority of the United States, shall be the supreme Law of the Land; and the Judges in every State shall be bound thereby, any Thing in the Constitution or Laws of any State to the Contrary notwithstanding.

The Senators and Representatives before mentioned, and the Members of the several State Legislatures, and all executive and judicial Officers, both of the United States and of the several States, shall be bound by Oath or Affirmation, to support this Constitution; but no religious Test shall ever be required as a Qualification to any Office or public Trust under the United States.

ARTICLE VII.

The Ratification of the Conventions of nine States, shall be sufficient for the Establishment of this Constitution between the States so ratifying the Same.

done in Convention by the Unanimous Consent of the States present the Seventeenth Day of September in the Year of our Lord one thousand seven hundred and Eighty seven and of the Independence of the United States of America the Twelfth

In witness whereof We have hereunto subscribed our Names,

G⁰ Washington—Presidᵗ
and deputy from Virginia

New Hampshire	John Langdon Nicholas Gilman
Massachusetts	Nathaniel Gorham Rufus King
Connecticut	Wᵐ Samˡ Johnson Roger Sherman
New York	Alexander Hamilton

New Jersey	{	Wil: Livingston
		David Brearley.
		Wm Paterson.
		Jona: Dayton

Pennsylvania	{	B Franklin
		Thomas Mifflin
		Robt Morris
		Geo. Clymer
		Thos FitzSimons
		Jared Ingersoll
		James Wilson
		Gouv Morris

Delaware	{	Geo: Read
		Gunning Bedford jun
		John Dickinson
		Richard Bassett
		Jaco: Broom

Maryland	{	James McHenry
		Dan of St Thos Jenifer
		Danl Carroll

| Virginia | { | John Blair— |
| | | James Madison Jr. |

North Carolina	{	Wm Blount
		Richd Dobbs Spaight.
		Hu Williamson

South Carolina	{	J. Rutledge
		Charles Cotesworth Pinckney
		Charles Pinckney
		Pierce Butler.

| Georgia | { | William Few |
| | | Abr Baldwin |

Amendments to the Constitution of the United States.

Amendment I

Congress shall make no law respecting an establishment of religion, or prohibiting the free exercise thereof; or abridging the freedom of speech, or of the press; or the right of the people peaceably to assemble, and to petition the Government for a redress of grievances.

Amendment II

A well regulated Militia, being necessary to the security of a free State, the right of the people to keep and bear Arms, shall not be infringed.

Amendment III

No Soldier shall, in time of peace be quartered in any house, without the consent of the Owner, nor in time of war, but in a manner to be prescribed by law.

Amendment IV

The right of the people to be secure in their persons, houses, papers, and effects, against unreasonable searches and seizures, shall not be violated, and no Warrants shall issue, but upon probable cause, supported by Oath or affirmation, and particularly describing the place to be searched, and the persons or things to be seized.

Amendment V

No person shall be held to answer for a capital, or otherwise infamous crime, unless on a presentment or indictment of a Grand Jury, except in cases arising in the land or naval forces, or in the Militia, when in actual service in time of War or public danger; nor shall any person be subject for the same offence to be twice put in jeopardy of life or limb; nor shall be compelled in any criminal case to be a witness against himself, nor be deprived of life, liberty, or property, without due process of law; nor shall private property be taken for public use, without just compensation.

Amendment VI

In all criminal prosecutions, the accused shall enjoy the right to a speedy and public trial, by an impartial jury of the State and district wherein the crime shall have been committed, which district shall have been previously ascertained by law, and to be informed of the nature and cause of the accusation; to be confronted with the witnesses against him; to have compulsory process for obtaining witnesses in his favor, and to have the Assistance of Counsel for his defence.

Amendment VII

In Suits at common law, where the value in controversy shall exceed twenty dollars, the right of trial by jury shall be preserved, and no fact tried by a jury, shall be otherwise re-examined in any Court of the United States, than according to the rules of the common law.

Amendment VIII

Excessive bail shall not be required, nor excessive fines imposed, nor cruel and unusual punishments inflicted.

Amendment IX

The enumeration in the Constitution, of certain rights, shall not be construed to deny or disparage others retained by the people.

Amendment X

The powers not delegated to the United States by the Constitution, nor prohibited by it to the States, are reserved to the States respectively, or to the people.

Amendment XI

The Judicial power of the United States shall not be construed to extend to any suit in law or equity, commenced or prosecuted against one of the United States by Citizens of another State, or by Citizens or Subjects of any Foreign State.

Amendment XII

The Electors shall meet in their respective states and vote by ballot for President and Vice-President, one of whom, at least, shall not be an inhabitant of the same state with themselves; they shall name in their ballots the person voted for as President, and in distinct ballots the person voted for as Vice-President, and they shall make distinct lists of all persons voted for as President, and of all persons voted for as Vice-President, and of the number of votes for each, which lists they shall sign and certify, and transmit sealed to the seat of the government of the United States, directed to the President of the Senate;—The President of the Senate shall, in the presence of the Senate and House of Representatives, open all the certificates and the votes shall then be counted;—The person having the greatest number of votes for President, shall be the President, if such number be a majority of the whole number of Electors appointed; and if no person have such majority, then from the persons having the highest numbers not exceeding three on the list of those voted for as President, the House of Representatives shall choose immediately, by ballot, the President. But in choosing the President, the votes shall be taken by states, the representation from each state having one vote; a quorum for this purpose shall consist of a member or members from two-thirds of the states, and a majority of all the states shall be necessary to a choice. And if the House of Representatives shall not choose a President whenever the right of choice shall devolve upon them, before the fourth day of March next following, then the Vice-President shall act as President, as in the case of the death or other constitutional disability of the President.—The person having the greatest number of votes as Vice-President, shall be the Vice-President, if such number be a majority of the whole number of Electors appointed, and if no person have a majority, then from the two highest numbers on the list, the Senate shall choose the Vice-President; a quorum for the purpose shall consist of two-thirds of the whole number of Senators, and a majority of the whole number shall be necessary to a choice. But no person constitutionally ineligible to the office of President shall be eligible to that of Vice-President of the United States.

Amendment XIII

Section 1. Neither slavery nor involuntary servitude, except as a punishment for crime whereof the party shall have been duly convicted, shall exist within the the United States, or any place subject to their jurisdiction.

Section 2. Congress shall have power to enforce this article by appropriate legislation.

Amendment XIV

Section 1. All persons born or naturalized in the United States, and subject to the jurisdiction thereof, are citizens of the United States and of the State wherein they reside. No State shall make or enforce any law which shall abridge the privileges or immunities of citizens of the United States; nor shall any State deprive any person of life, liberty, or property, without due process of law; nor deny to any person within its jurisdiction the equal protection of the laws.

Section 2. Representatives shall be apportioned among the several States according to their respective numbers, counting the whole number of persons in each State, excluding Indians not taxed. But when the right to vote at any election for the choice of electors for President and Vice President of the United States, Representatives in Congress, the Executive and Judicial officers of a State, or the members of the Legislature thereof, is denied to any of the male inhabitants of such State, being twenty-one years of age, and citizens of the United States, or in any way abridged, except for participation in rebellion, or other crime, the basis of representation therein shall be reduced in the proportion which the number of such male citizens shall bear to the whole number of male citizens twenty-one years of age in such State.

Section 3. No person shall be a Senator or Representative in Congress, or elector of President and Vice President, or hold any office, civil or military, under the United States, or under any State, who, having previously taken an oath, as a member of Congress, or as an officer of the United States, or as a member of any State legislature, or as an executive or judicial officer of any State, to support the Constitution of the United States, shall have engaged in insurrection or rebellion against the same, or given aid or comfort to the enemies thereof. But Congress may by a vote of two-thirds of each House, remove such disability.

Section 4. The validity of the public debt of the United States, authorized by law, including debts incurred for payment of pensions and bounties for services in suppressing insurrection or rebellion, shall not be questioned. But neither the United States nor any State shall assume or pay any debt or obligation incurred in aid of insurrection or rebellion against the United States, or any claim for the loss or emancipation of any slave; but all such debts, obligations and claims shall be held illegal and void.

Section 5. The Congress shall have power to enforce, by appropriate legislation, the provisions of this article.

Amendment XV

Section 1. The right of citizens of the United States to vote shall not be denied or abridged by the United States or by any State on account of race, color, or previous condition of servitude.

Section 2. The Congress shall have power to enforce this article by appropriate legislation.

Amendment XVI

The Congress shall have power to lay and collect taxes on incomes, from whatever source derived, without apportionment among the several States, and without regard to any census or enumeration.

Amendment XVII

The Senate of the United States shall be composed of two Senators from each State, elected by the people thereof, for six years; and each Senator shall have one vote. The electors in each State shall have the qualifications requisite for electors of the most numerous branch of the State legislatures.

When vacancies happen in the representation of any State in the Senate, the executive authority of such State shall issue writs of election to fill such vacancies: *Provided,* That the legislature of any State may empower the executive thereof to make temporary appointments until the people fill the vacancies by election as the legislature may direct.

This amendment shall not be so construed as to affect the election or term of any Senator chosen before it becomes valid as part of the Constitution.

Amendment XVIII

Section 1. After one year from the ratification of this article the manufacture, sale, or transportation of intoxicating liquors within, the importation thereof into, or the exportation thereof from the United States and all territory subject to the jurisdiction thereof for beverage purposes is hereby prohibited.

Section 2. The Congress and the several States shall have concurrent power to enforce this article by appropriate legislation.

Section 3. This article shall be inoperative unless it shall have been ratified as an amendment to the Constitution by the legislatures of the several States, as provided in the Constitution, within seven years from the date of the submission hereof to the States by the Congress.

Amendment XIX

The right of citizens of the United States to vote shall not be denied or abridged by the United States or by any State on account of sex.

Congress shall have power to enforce this article by appropriate legislation.

Amendment XX

Section 1. The terms of the President and Vice President shall end at noon on the 20th day of January, and the terms of Senators and Representatives at noon on the 3d day of January, of the years in which such terms would have ended if this article had not been ratified; and the terms of their successors shall then begin.

Section 2. The Congress shall assemble at least once in every year, and such meeting shall begin at noon on the 3d day of January, unless they shall by law appoint a different day.

Section 3. If, at the time fixed for the beginning of the term of the President, the President elect shall have died, the Vice President elect shall become President. If a President shall not have been chosen before the time fixed for the beginning of his term, or if the President elect shall have failed to qualify, then the Vice President elect shall act as President until a President shall have qualified; and the Congress may by law provide for the case wherein neither

a President elect nor a Vice President elect shall have qualified, declaring who shall then act as President, or the manner in which one who is to act shall be selected, and such person shall act accordingly until a President or Vice President shall have qualified.

Section 4. The Congress may by law provide for the case of the death of any of the persons from whom the House of Representatives may choose a President whenever the right of choice shall have devolved upon them, and for the case of the death of any of the persons from whom the Senate may choose a Vice President whenever the right of choice shall have devolved upon them.

Section 5. Sections 1 and 2 shall take effect on the 15th day of October following the ratification of this article.

Section 6. This article shall be inoperative unless it shall have been ratified as an amendment to the Constitution by the legislatures of three-fourths of the several States within seven years from the date of its submission.

Amendment XXI

Section 1. The eighteenth article of amendment to the Constitution of the United States is hereby repealed.

Section 2. The transportation or importation into any State, Territory, or possession of the United States for delivery or use therein of intoxicating liquors, in violation of the laws thereof, is hereby prohibited.

Section 3. This article shall be inoperative unless it shall have been ratified as an amendment to the Constitution by conventions in the several States, as provided in the Constitution, within seven years from the date of the submission hereof to the States by the Congress.

Amendment XXII

No person shall be elected to the office of the President more than twice, and no person who has held the office of President, or acted as President, for more than two years of a term to which some other person was elected President shall be elected to the office of the President more than once. But this Article shall not apply to any person holding the office of President when this Article was proposed by the Congress, and shall not prevent any person who may be holding the office of President, or acting as President, during the term within which this Article becomes operative from holding the office of President or acting as President during the remainder of such term.

Amendment XXIII

Section 1. The District constituting the seat of government of the United States shall appoint in such manner as the Congress may direct:

A number of electors of President and Vice-President equal to the whole number of Senators and

Representatives in Congress to which the District would be entitled if it were a State, but in no event more than the least populous State; they shall be in addition to those appointed by the States, but they shall be considered, for the purposes of the election of President and Vice-President, to be electors appointed by a State; and they shall meet in the District and perform such duties as provided by the twelfth article of amendment.

Section 2. The Congress shall have power to enforce this article by appropriate legislation.

CONSTITUTIONAL CONVENTION OF 1787 was called by the Annapolis Convention of 1786 and by the Continental Congress to meet in Philadelphia, on Monday, May 14, 1787. On that day, only a small number of delegates had assembled. Finally, on Friday, May 25, delegates were present from seven states, so the Convention was organized and began its deliberations. Sixty-five delegates had been chosen by the legislatures of twelve of the original thirteen states. Rhode Island was at no time represented in the Convention. Of the delegates elected, but 55 members attended, of whom but 39 signed the completed document when the Convention adjourned on Monday, Sept. 17, of the same year.

The delegates included many of the leading men of the period. Among them were the experienced statesmen who had taken a foremost part in social, political and military contests. They were practical politicians who in many cases had held high office in the colonial and the state and national governments. Foremost among them were George Washington, who was elected president of the Convention, and Benjamin Franklin. These two men did not take a prominent part in the debates, but doubtless had great influence in smoothing away difficulties, in encouraging the other members and in securing the later approval of the Constitution when it was submitted to the states. Twenty-nine of these men were graduates of colleges or universities in America or Great Britain. More than half of them were lawyers and took a leading part in the debates. Eight of them had signed their names to the Declaration of Independence in 1776.

Among those of first-class ability may be mentioned, in addition to Washington and Franklin, Elbridge Gerry and Rufus King of Massachusetts; Roger Sherman and William Samuel Johnson of Connecticut; Alexander Hamilton of New York; William Paterson of New Jersey; Robert Morris, James Wilson and Gouverneur Morris of Pennsylvania; John Dickinson of Delaware; Luther Martin of Maryland; George Mason, James Madison, Edmund Randolph, and George Wythe of Virginia; William Richardson Davie of North Carolina; Charles Pinckney and Charles Cotesworth Pinckney of South Carolina.

Soon after the members began their deliberations they became convinced, first of all, that the main

purpose for which they had been called in convention, namely to amend the Articles of Confederation sufficiently to serve as a future frame of government, was impossible. They, therefore, cast aside their instructions and produced an entirely new document which was to supplant the Articles of Confederation as the supreme law of the land. As a matter of fact, the new Constitution, when finally made, provided that it was to go into effect when ratified by *nine* states. This was a direct breach of constitutional law since the Articles of Confederation had provided that any change or amendment in them must be ratified by unanimous vote by all the thirteen states. From a legal standpoint this amounted to a revolution as great as the rebellion against Great Britain, or the Declaration of Independence. Even when the new government became established and Washington became President in 1789, North Carolina and Rhode Island had refused their consent and did not ratify the Constitution until some months later.

In the second place the members of the Convention realized that unless they did their work in secrecy minor disagreements might stir up popular excitement or outside pressure even to the extent that the Convention might be broken up without coming to any conclusion. For this reason, they closed their doors and the proceedings of the Convention were held a secret for nearly sixty years. The Constitution was placed before the people as a completed document without any knowledge at the time of the proceedings by which the results had been reached. The official journal of the Convention was not printed until 1819. In 1821, Robert Yates, a delegate from New York who had withdrawn from the Convention, published what he entitled *The Secret Proceedings and Debates of the Federal Convention*. These were but partial disclosures, and the full account appeared only in the year 1840, when the U. S. Government published the records of the debates and proceedings of the Convention which James Madison had prepared at the time and revised during the later years of his life.

The main work of the Convention may be summarized as follows. On May 29, Edmund Randolph of Virginia submitted for the consideration of the Convention the Virginia plan of government. It had been privately prepared by the members of the Virginia delegation in which James Madison took a prominent part. It should be remembered that the great weakness of the Articles of Confederation lay in the fact that they provided for what might be called a league of thirteen nations rather than a national consolidation. This was a fundamental defect since it was impossible to coerce a state and require obedience to the mandates of the national government. The Virginia plan now provided for a national government that should operate directly upon individuals rather than upon states. Also, the plan provided for two houses of a national legislature modeled on the legislatures of the various states. The members of the lower house were to be chosen directly by the people. The members of the upper house were to be elected by the lower house from persons nominated for that purpose by the state legislatures. Each state was to have representatives in proportion to its wealth and the number of its inhabitants. This would give the more populous states such as Pennsylvania and Virginia an overwhelming proportion of representatives, whereas the smaller states such as New Jersey and Delaware would have but few. Moreover, since the members of the legislative body were to vote as individuals and not by state delegations as in the Continental Congress under the Articles of Confederation this increased the preponderance of the populous states. The taxing power and other such matters of legislation were given to the legislature; also there was to be a national executive and a Federal judicial system. This plan proposed fundamental changes and went to the very roots of national necessity.

On June 15 William Paterson laid before the Convention the so-called New Jersey plan. While this provided for an increase in the powers of Congress and the right to levy taxes in proportion to population, with control of foreign relations and various other powers suitable to a strengthened national government, yet in reality its object was merely to secure an adequate revision of the Articles of Confederation. The Federal legislature was to consist of one house and was to represent states instead of individuals, while the states were to vote equally, as heretofore under the already existing government. Of course, this meant only an alleviation and not a cure of the difficulties of the Government under the Articles of Confederation.

These two plans caused a long and at times an excited debate until, at the suggestion of Roger Sherman, William Samuel Johnson and Oliver Ellsworth, the so-called Connecticut Compromise finally settled the matter by the creation of a legislative body composed of a House of Representatives in which the states were to be represented according to population, and a Senate in which the states were to be equally represented. This body was called the Congress, instead of a Parliament. It perpetuated the name of the Continental Congress which first had met at Philadelphia in 1774.

Also there was a struggle over the question of representation of the slave population since it had been decided that representatives should be apportioned only according to population. The Northern states held that slaves were property and should not be counted on the basis of apportionment. The Southern states held that slaves were individuals and hence should be represented. This difference of opinion was finally compromised by the agreement that three-fifths of the slave population were to be counted in the apportionment.

A third so-called compromise concerned the slave trade to which the Northern states were opposed but which, of course, was supported by the Southern states led by South Carolina. It was finally provided that the foreign slave trade should not be prohibited for twenty years or until 1808, and in return the Southern states consented to the provisions desired by the Northern states which empowered Congress to pass navigation acts and otherwise regulate commerce.

The office of President was created, more or less consciously modeled upon the kingship of Great Britain, but of course with the provision that the executive should be elected instead of hereditary. The people had learned from the bitter experiences of the Revolution the need for an adequate executive authority. Also a Federal judiciary was provided upon the basis of appointment by the President for life tenure or during good behavior, and the power of judicial review was taken for granted in the debates of the Convention. To the Senate were given powers somewhat like those of a privy council. These consisted in the ratification of treaties by a two-thirds vote and the confirmation of executive appointments.

No regular provision was made for a cabinet, since the delegates were not aware of the fact that Great Britain already was under a cabinet from of government. But it may be said that the new government was modeled upon that of the contemporary British government or what the delegates at that time understood the British government to be. From Blackstone and Montesquieu came the idea of a government of "separation of powers" among the legislative, executive and judicial departments. These should be so adjusted by means of checks and balances of power and authority that no one part of the government could increase its authority at the expense of the others, with a resultant danger to the liberties or rights of the people.

Another fact of great importance is that the Constitution was in reality not so much a new invention as a codification of British law and government, and of the practical experience of the Americans during the preceding century and a half of colonial history. The practical statesmen and politicians among the members of the Convention formulated the provisions of the Constitution in the light of their actual knowledge and experience of the needs and desires of the people. The amount of new material is relatively small. A provision that perhaps came nearest to that of being a new invention was the method of choosing the President by means of an electoral college. But this provision was practically discarded within fifteen years after the new government went into effect, and the electors became merely what they are today, the instructed agents of the voters at the polls.

The Convention provided that the new Constitution should be submitted to the still existing Continental Congress and also expressed the "opinion" that the document should afterwards be submitted to a convention of delegates to be chosen in each state by the people thereof, under the recommendation of its legislature, for their assent and ratification.

The Constitution was written out under the supervision of a so-called committee on "stile" and arrangement, of which Gouverneur Morris and William Samuel Johnson were leading members. It was adopted and signed on Sept. 17, and the Convention adjourned. Among the sixteen who refused to sign, George Mason, Elbridge Gerry and Edmund Randolph were still present. Most of the others already had left the Convention and returned home.

The debates in the Convention were of a high order and ability. The results were of such a remarkable character that the Constitution has far exceeded the expectations of the members of the Convention in the success of its functioning. The growth of its influence has had a stabilizing effect upon the country. At the same time it has provided a basis for the extension of its authority through judicial interpretation and the growth of custom to meet the needs of a progressive government which also has been adapted to a changing and developing mode of life.

CONSTITUTIONAL UNION PARTY. Late in 1859 old line Whigs and members of the American (Know-Nothing) party, alarmed at excesses of partyism and sectionalism and fearing secession, began the formation of a new party under the leadership of Crittenden. Meeting in convention on May 9, 1860, in Baltimore they chose John Bell and Edward Everett as candidates. Affection for the Union was reflected in the meager platform which disregarded sectional issues and sought to rally moderate men to support "The Constitution, the Union and the Laws." Polling only 590,000 votes and carrying only Kentucky, Virginia and Tennessee, the party succeeded, nevertheless, in temporarily allaying disunion sentiment.

CONTEMPT, POWER OF CONGRESS TO PUNISH FOR. This power has been repeatedly questioned on the ground that it is essentially judicial in character and therefore not vested in a legislative body. In McGrain v. Daugherty (273 U. S. 135, 1927) the Supreme Court, after an exhaustive review of the history, precedents, statutes and judicial decisions involved, declared that "the power of inquiry—with process to enforce it—is an essential and appropriate auxiliary to the legislative function," and that when necessary information is not forthcoming "some means of compulsion are essential to obtain what is needed."

CONTINENTAL CONGRESS is the name customarily given to the body of delegates of the American colonies (afterward states) which was first assembled in September, 1774, and again in May, 1775, as an advisory council of the colonies, but eventually became the central government of the union, serving as such until it was superseded, March 4, 1789, by the new government under the Constitution.

The First Continental Congress, which sat at Philadelphia from Sept. 5 to Oct. 26, 1774 (the title officially adopted was simply "The Congress," although in popular usage the word "Continental" came to be prefixed to distinguish it from various provincial congresses), was called together to concert measures for the recovery of colonial rights and liberties held to have been violated by a succession of acts of the British government, culminating in a series of repressive measures primarily directed against Massachusetts, but believed to involve threats against all the colonies. The principal measures taken by this Congress were the adoption of a Declaration of Rights (Oct. 14), an Association (Oct. 20), whereby the colonies bound themselves in a nonimportation, a nonconsumption and a nonexportation agreement, and a resolution voicing the opinion that, unless the grievances had meanwhile been redressed, another congress should be assembled on the 10th of May following.

As the grievances had not been redressed, the Second Continental Congress met in Philadelphia at the appointed time. Meanwhile something like war had broken out between Massachusetts and the British military forces, whereupon Congress resolved to give aid to Massachusetts, took over the provincial army at Boston, and appointed George Washington Commander in Chief "of all the continental forces, raised, or to be raised, for the defence of American liberty" (June 15, 1775). With these steps Congress definitely advanced from being a mere clearinghouse for colonial opinion toward becoming the superintending power over the unified colonial cause. For nearly six years thereafter, with little authority other than a general acquiescence, Congress not only took general direction of the war with Great Britain, but became the collective voice of the colonies, soon to become states, for a multitude of their other common activities as well.

In the early months of the Congress of 1775 the objective was still the recovery of rights, though not less the restoration of union and harmony between Great Britain and the colonies; but before another year had passed, as the conviction gathered strength that only by the arbitrament of arms could the prized liberties be preserved, the idea of independence had laid its grip upon the public mind. The result was that, on July 2, 1776, Congress adopted a resolution "that these United Colonies are, and of right ought to be, free and independent States," and two days later adopted a formal Declaration of Independence.

Prior to the Declaration of Independence colonial jealousies had led Congress to draw back from every suggestion of a permanent union; but now the necessity for an effective organization of the states for the promotion of the common cause became evident; while some minds even glimpsed national unity as a consummation to be sought for its own sake. Accordingly, Congress at once set about endeavoring to frame an instrument of union. The task was an exceedingly difficult one, particularly that of reconciling the antagonistic views and interests of the small states and the large, so that it was not until after nearly a year and a half of effort, accompanied by numerous hot controversies, that Congress was able to come to an agreement upon that framework of government known as the Articles of Confederation (Nov. 15, 1777).

Ratification of the Articles by the several states was still necessary, and it was only on March 1, 1781, that the last of the thirteen ratifications, that of Maryland, was obtained. From that time forth Congress was on a constitutional basis, a distinction sometimes emphasized by employing for this period the title "The Congress of the Confederation." The passing from a régime of unwritten to that of a written constitution made, however, no great difference in the conduct of affairs by Congress. The principal change was that some things theretofore done in a manner more or less irregular were now regularized; such, for instance, as the election of delegates, which formerly had been entirely at the discretion of the states, whether it were the number chosen or the times and terms of their election.

That the Articles of Confederation were defective in several particulars, none knew better than the very men who had framed them. For one thing, the method of voting by states, each state having one vote, adopted in the beginning as a concession to the small states, was perpetuated, and it led to many unfortunate results. For another, no provision was made for the support of the central government other than through contributions by the states upon the requisition of Congress. This deficiency was not so clearly sensed in the outset, for the reason that Congress undertook to finance the war by means of its own bills of credit, and, so long as those bills were good as well as plentiful, Congress could speak and the states would hearken. When, however, Continental money depreciated, and Congress began to call upon the states for help, there was grumbling and worse. A third serious defect of the Articles was the requirement of unanimous consent of the states to any amendment; and it came about that every effort to obtain amendments was defeated by a single state. Still another defect was in the constitution of Congress itself. The sole embodiment of the government—legislative, executive, judicial—Congress was not a fit instrument for the conduct of a war or of the administrative business of a government. Long hesitant to part with even the semblance of power, largely restrained indeed by the fear of a strong executive that pervaded the states, Congress did little toward developing its administrative arm until the war was closing.

The war, with its impelling power for unity, at an end, the states lost in great measure their concern for the Congress of their union, and even drifted toward a dissolution of that union; while Congress, for its part, advanced, not from strength unto strength, but from weakness unto weakness. It was only the determination of a small group to save the union that led, through the Annapolis Convention, to the Convention of 1787, and finally to the new-framed Constitution. It is not to be understood that Congress was wholly hostile to a constitutional convention, for that plan had several times been broached in Congress, and more than once was all but espoused. Neither is it to be understood that the government inaugurated under the Constitution was the antithesis of that which existed under the old Congress. On the contrary, the new government found ready to its hand not only much of the essential governmental machinery, but also a considerable body of substantive law.

CONTRABAND, NEGROES AS, was a doctrine set up by Gen. Benjamin F. Butler, in May, 1861, as applicable to the problem of fugitive slaves of secessionist owners, who sought refuge in Union military camps. On May 23, 1861, three slaves of a Virginia secessionist took shelter at Fort Monroe, Va. When demand for their return was made under the Fugitive Slave Law, Gen. Butler refused on the ground that Virginians had no privilege under Federal laws since Virginia had declared herself out of the Union. In his official report to Washington, May 25, he did not mention the word contraband. Not until July 30, in reporting to the Secretary of War, did he use the term in explaining that he treated "the able-bodied negroes, fit to work in the trenches, as property, liable to be used in aid of rebellion, and so contraband of war." Contraband as doctrine disappeared after the passage of the Confiscation Act, Aug. 6, 1861, but "contraband" as a slang term for Negro or slave was widely used. Although some question later arose as to Butler's authorship of the term, it seems credible that he used the word in conference if not in official reports before Northern newspapers made the term popular.

CONTRERAS, BATTLE OF (Aug. 19–20, 1847), was an engagement in Gen. Winfield Scott's advance on Mexico City. As Gen. Santa Anna had fortified the causeway between Lakes Chalco and Texcoco on the National Highway to Mexico City, Scott decided to take the difficult road across the lava bed south of Lake Chalco. This route was commanded by the heights of Contreras, held by Gen. Valencia. After severe fighting, the Americans drove Valencia from Contreras and captured Churubusco the same day.

CONVENTION ARMY was the name used to designate Burgoyne's army after it had been surrendered by a "convention" rather than by the customary "capitulation." The troops were marched, under armed escort, to an encampment in Cambridge, Mass., it being intended to return them to England. The transports did not arrive. The troops remained a year at the expense of Massachusetts, when they were moved to Rutland, Mass., and then to Charlottesville, Va. After another year, the troops again moved, this time to Winchester, Va., and Frederick, Md. In the summer of 1781 some of the "Convention" troops moved to Easton, Pa., and some back to Rutland, Mass. The Definitive Treaty of Peace released all prisoners of war. By this time, the army had been reduced by paroles, exchanges, deaths and desertions to about half of its original 5000. Some of the men remained in the United States, but most of them returned to their native lands.

CONVENTION OF 1800. Talleyrand, French foreign minister, alarmed at the aggressive action of the United States in the undeclared naval warfare against France and fearful of a possible Anglo-American alliance right at the time when France was planning a revival of her colonial empire in the region of Louisiana, invited the United States to negotiate a convention. In the negotiations Murray, Ellsworth and Davie, the American commissioners, demanded compensations for French spoliations since 1793, and the annulment of the treaties of 1778. After an irritating interruption caused by Napoleon's Italian campaigns against Austria, the negotiations were finally completed. The terms of the Convention of Sept. 30, 1800, suspended the former treaties and the damages claimed under them, pending subsequent negotiations, and accepted the maritime principles of the Treaty of 1778, including "free ships, free goods" and a "most-favored-nation" clause. France also gave up the bothersome practice of demanding crew lists. After one rejection the U. S. Senate finally ratified the convention with the understanding that the treaties of 1778 were not merely suspended but completely abrogated. France then insisted that the respective claims of the two parties also be renounced. Both countries agreed to these reservations, and the convention went into force Dec. 21, 1801.

CONVENTIONS, PARTY NOMINATING. A national nominating convention is a complex organization composed, in the case of a major party, of over a thousand delegates. These delegates are chosen prior to the conventions in party primaries or in state conventions. Ever since the convention system was originated by the Anti-Masonic party in 1831, the size of each state's delegation has been determined, in general, by the electoral vote of the state. Representation is also granted to the District of Columbia and to the territories of the United States.

The convention city is selected by the party's national committee. As soon as the convention assembles, with each state delegation seated together, a temporary chairman, generally a person nominated by the national committee, is chosen. After he has delivered a "keynote" speech, praising the record of his own party and flaying the opposition, four committees are selected through roll calls of the states. Each state is entitled to one member on each of these committees which are: the committee on credentials, the committee on permanent organization, the committee on rules and order of business and the committee on platform and resolutions.

The committee on credentials has the duty of settling the rival claims of persons claiming membership in the convention. Usually there are only a few disputes but occasionally, as in the Republican convention of 1912, when there were 210 contested seats, the committee assumes great importance.

After the permanent roll of delegates has been determined, the committee on permanent organization brings in its report, nominating a permanent chairman and other convention officials. Ordinarily the nominations are accepted, and the newly elected chairman is escorted to the platform to deliver another partisan speech.

Next comes the report of the committee on rules and order of business. While it may deal with a wide variety of matters, this report customarily recommends the adoption of the rules of the previous convention, including the rules of the national House of Representatives. On rare occasions, the committee makes extraordinary recommendations. Thus, in 1912, the rules committee of the Democratic party secured a modification of the "unit rule" under which the vote of each state delegation was determined by the majority of its members. Again, in 1936, the committee secured the abrogation of the "two-thirds rule" making it possible for Democratic candidates for President and Vice-President to be nominated by a simple majority. Both rules had been in effect since the first Democratic convention in 1832.

Finally, the committee on platform and resolutions brings in a report which, when adopted, constitutes a statement of the party's views on the whole field of national politics.

CONWAY CABAL, so-called, marked the culminating effort (1777–78) of New England's coterie in the Continental Congress to regain control of the army and the Revolution, both of which passed from its hands when Congress took over the war and elected Washington Commander in Chief. Regaining that control seemed even more important to the clique than independence. Maj. Gen. Thomas Conway's indiscreet letter to Gen. Gates revealed the military side of the cabal, which aimed at the removal of Washington as the main obstacle to Massachusetts' regaining control of the army; later the

French alliance was also opposed as it would put an end, definitely, to all such maneuvers. Conway's letter and the subsequent public revelations rallied to Washington a support that overwhelmed the conspirators both in Congress and the army. Fastening Conway's name to the cabal has improperly stigmatized the least of its factors, and long diverted attention from the real purpose of the scheme.

COOKE, JAY, founder of a private investment bank, established in Philadelphia in 1861. Jay Cooke got his experience in E. W. Clark & Co., a domestic exchange and investment house. When the Treasury's sale of United States loans brought inadequate funds, early in the Civil War, Cooke was appointed special agent to sell the "five twenties." His firm sold the loan directly to the people by means of a comprehensive organization and effective publicity. Success led to close association with the Treasury until the war ended. By 1865 Jay Cooke & Co. was regarded as the leading American banking house, but peace brought serious difficulties. The Cookes, expecting much work from refunding, added a New York house to their wartime Philadelphia and Washington offices. The partners were close to Secretary of the Treasury McCulloch and worked for sound Federal finance, but political and rival-banker opposition, and the failure of early refunding bills in Congress, prevented the Treasury from giving them much work.

Failing to get sufficient government business, the Cookes, like other bankers, turned to railroad finance. First they sold minor issues, and in 1869 undertook to finance the Northern Pacific. Railways were built from Lake Superior to the Mississippi and Missouri. But Jay Cooke & Co. failed in 1873 because of heavy advances to the railroads.

CO-OPERATIVES, FARMERS', have been important in the marketing of farm products, buying supplies for farmers, issuing insurance, providing their members with credit and aiding in production. Organizations of a general nature were reported as early as 1785. Early in the 18th century local associations were established to process and sell farm products. Attempts to make and sell cheese and butter co-operatively were reported in Connecticut in 1808 and 1810. The first successful "cheese ring" was started in Rock Lake, Wis., in 1841, and the first successful co-operative cheese factory in Oneida County, N. Y., in 1851. Successful co-operative creameries were started in Orange County, N. Y., in 1857 and the following years.

The first farmers' co-operative organization to attain national prominence was the Patrons of Husbandry, popularly called the Grange, started in 1868 at Fredonia, N. Y. It had a very rapid growth, especially in the Upper Mississippi Valley and by 1875 it had over 500,000 members. The Grange was started as a social organization but soon became interested in economic problems and started co-operative purchasing agencies, stores, factories, grain elevators, livestock shipping associations, creameries and insurance companies. Most of these, with the exception of the insurance companies, either failed or passed into private hands. Following 1875 the Grange declined rapidly, although it later revived and is now very important. Other organizations such as the Farmers' Alliance, the American Society of Equity, the Farmers' Union, the American Farm Bureau Federation and the National Government have actively promoted co-operatives. Their growth has been especially rapid since 1920.

Memberships of farmers in their marketing, farm supply, and related service co-operatives have steadily increased from 2,700,000 in 1926 to 7,730,710 in 1956. Many farmers have memberships in two or more co-operatives. During this period the high point in the number of co-operatives was reached in 1930 when there were 12,000 associations. Since that time the number gradually decreased to 9876 in 1956. A major reason for much of this decrease is discontinuance of many associations through mergers or consolidations with, or outright purchase by, existing co-operatives. These reorganizations among farmer co-operatives are a part of the general economic trend toward larger and more efficient business entities.

Gross dollar volume of these co-operatives amounted to $12,700,000,000 in fiscal 1956. After eliminating duplication resulting from inter-association business, the total net volume was $9,800,000,000, 77% in products marketed, 21% in farm supplies purchased, and 2% in receipts for services performed for patrons.

COPPAGE v. KANSAS (236 U. S. 1). By 1915 thirteen states had enacted laws prohibiting the employer from requiring as a condition of employment the signing of individual contracts not to affiliate with unions. In Coppage v. Kansas (1915) the Supreme Court held that such statutes violated the Fourteenth Amendment, and that the ruling in the Adair case that employers could discharge workers because of their affiliation with unions implied the right to insist upon nonunion pledges as a condition of employment.

COPPER INDUSTRY. Prior to European occupation the natives of America were using virgin copper hammered into ornaments, knives and other artifacts without the intervention of smelting. The mining of cupric ores was begun by colonists in Connecticut and New Jersey, and slowly other copper deposits were discovered and exploited on the Atlantic slope. The deposits on the southern shore of Lake Superior were known to the Canadian Jesuits as early as 1667, but this information was not shared with strangers.

Dr. Douglas Houghton accompanied Gen. Lewis Cass to this region in 1830, rediscovered the copper and publicized his find; commercial operations, however, did not begin until 1846. These mines yielded pure copper, hence their product did not require expensive reduction. Vast new sources of copper were discovered in Arizona and Montana just at a time when they could satisfy the heavy demands which were to be created by the then infant electrical industry. Later the requirements of the automobile industry were satisfied by newly developed rich deposits in Alaska and the plentiful supply of ore in Utah.

Various processes are applied to different types of ore. In general, the operations following the first separation of grosser impurities are crushing, concentration, smelting—which ordinarily separates the dross from the matte (or blister)—and lastly, refining, where all remaining impurities as well as precious metals such as gold and silver are removed. After this stage comes the manufacture of sheets, shapes, rods and wire.

These operations involve the use of much capital and technical skill, hence the industry is largely concentrated into the management of a few corporations. Anaconda is the principal owner of the Montana mines; Kennecott, through a subsidiary, owns the Utah deposits; Phelps, Dodge Corp. controls much of the Arizona copper; Calumet & Hecla, the Michigan supply.

Copper, the first metal used by man, is essential in every phase of modern life, including industry, communication, transportation and building. In every period of man's development copper has played a vital role. It is just as important in the modern world of electronics, radar and missiles as it was in the days of the ancient Romans. The United States produces about one third of the world's copper, but consumes almost half of the world's supply and must rely on imports to complete its requirements.

COPPERHEADS, also Butternuts, were terms used to describe Democrats opposed to the war policy of Lincoln. The term Copperhead first appeared in the New York *Tribune* for July 20, 1861, and within a year was common. Strongest in Ohio, Indiana and Illinois, the Copperheads were encouraged by Democratic successes in the elections of 1862.

Generally described as treasonable, the Copperheads, or Peace Democrats, advocated a union restored by negotiation rather than war. They denounced military arrests, conscription, emancipation and other war measures. C. L. Vallandigham of Ohio was their chief spokesman. His arrest in May, 1863, for alleged disloyal statements embarrassed the Lincoln administration. Other leaders were Alexander Long of Cincinnati, Fernando Wood of New York, and B. G. Harris of Maryland. Prominent newspapers supporting the Copperheads were the Columbus *Crisis,* the Cincinnati *Enquirer* and the Chicago *Times.*

Their lack of sympathy for the Confederates was shown by the Copperheads in July, 1863, when they joined Unionists in defending Indiana and Ohio during the Morgan raid. Persecuted by the military and the Union League the Copperheads organized in 1862 the "Knights of the Golden Circle," borrowing the name and ritual of a "Southern rights" organization of the 1850's. The organization was known as the "Order of American Knights" in 1863, and the "Sons of Liberty" in 1864, when Vallandigham became supreme commander. He counseled them against treason and violence. In 1864 extremists of the order were charged with plotting the formation of a "Northwestern Confederacy" and planning the release of Confederate prisoners at Camp Douglas near Chicago, and elsewhere. The "plot" was uncovered before any overt acts took place. In the fall of 1864 six "Sons of Liberty" were tried for treason before a military court in Indiana, and three were condemned to death, including L. P. Milligan.

The Copperhead element in the Democratic party was able to control the party platform in 1864 which included a plank written by Vallandigham pronouncing the war a failure and demanding peace on the basis of a restored Federal union. The successful termination of the war discredited the Copperheads, but the Democratic party was handicapped for some years because of its wartime Copperhead affiliates.

CORINTH, MISS., BATTLE AT (1862). After the battle of Shiloh, the Union troops occupied Corinth. On Oct. 3, Van Dorn (C.) attacked with 20,000 men. The advanced lines of Rosecrans (U.), who had about equal numbers, were broken and next morning the Confederates assaulted his main position. A ferocious conflict ensued, the assailants actually entering the town. But, suffering heavy losses, the Confederates retreated to Holly Springs. Van Dorn lost 4838 in killed, wounded and missing; Rosecrans 2520.

CORN (Indian corn, maize), the king of American cereals, was found by European explorers in native cultivation from the Great Lakes southward. All available evidence points to its origin in the Western Hemisphere, though the area, as the ancestry of its genesis, is still largely conjectural. Historically the plant is known only in the cultivated stage, and by the time of colonization all of the fundamental varieties had been developed. The Indians of North America had worked out an elaborate culture system —selection of ground, fertilization where needed, field arrangement, planting with vegetable combinations, protection of seeds and young plants, cultivation, harvesting, storing, grinding and cooking—that was followed in essentials by American farmers down to the period of mechanization. The place that the great food plant had in the life and thought of the native peoples is indicated by the rites, ceremonies and legends which attended its growth and harvest.

Bayard Taylor's poem, "Mondamin," recounts the coming of the maize god to the Ojibways, and Longfellow describes Hiawatha's struggle with this deity. This popular attachment for a plant whose extent and value was to exceed that of all other cereals combined soon became and has continued a national tradition, reflected in its place in harvest festivals, native art—landscapes, decorative designs, corn palaces—in corn songs, and folk tales. The New World dominance of its native cereal is further evidenced in its usual designation by the generic term for grain, "corn," rather than by the European adaptation of the Indian name, "maize."

In the colonies corn was the basic food product that enabled the initial settlements to persist and contributed largely to the prosperity of all. European grains had to be acclimated, but the long-developed indigenous staple was ready at hand. The Jamestown settlement was preserved by timely purchases from Indian stores, and the Pilgrims soon learned how to grow their food in an inhospitable soil and rigorous climate. In the main production belts of the colonies—extracting, farming and planting—the adaptable plant found an essential place as food and feed. But the use of this home product, then as later, was largely at home.

In both colonial and national commerce but a trifling proportion of grain and meal was exported. Its liability to deteriorate in long shipment and the prejudice of Europeans against its use have limited its foreign market. As compared with wheat breadstuffs, the corn shipments in the colonial West Indian and southern European trade were insignificant. In the period 1840–60, before the rise of the large wheat trade, the value of corn and meal exports was less than a quarter of that of wheat and flour, and the percentage of the total crop was too small to have appreciable effect on the market. During the intensified European demand of World War I only about one and one half per cent was sent overseas. The main form of marketing, home and foreign, has always been through fattened livestock.

In the westward movement, North and South, corn proved the most available and dependable frontier crop. It flourished alike in forest clearings and on the freshly broken prairie where the first crop of sod corn brought quick returns. In the systems of commercialized production that emerged from the frontier its dominance persisted. Other monarchs of the field rose and declined but King Corn maintained his rule.

For the plantation economy corn and pork furnished the food standbys. In 1840 nearly one half the nation's crop was in the slave states and by the Civil War the per capita production was still far above the average. But by the time of that struggle of the sections the center of the basic cereal was moving steadily westward into a region where a diversified rotation, in which the main crop was used for fattening cattle and hogs, was establishing the Corn Belt economy. Here appropriate rotation has made for relatively progressive methods and physiography and large-scale production have facilitated the early introduction and wide use of machinery.

In the dairy regions, notably Wisconsin and Minnesota, corn has had its chief utilization in the ensiling process developed in the 1880's. The corn silo, making the fullest and most economical use of the most reliable crop, and one that permits a desirable rotation, has become an essential adjunct of the American milk industry.

While the great proportion of the crop has been fed to stock, the corn plant has provided the materials for manufacturing industries which consume normally about 15% of the total yield. Milling by various processes provides meal, grits, flakes and hominy. Corn refining dates from the 1880's, but the main advances have been made since World War II. Starches, sugar and syrup of various grades, and corn oil are among the leading products. From early times in home stills and distilleries corn has been made into alcohol, the output varying with fluctuating beverage and industrial demands. In addition to the processing of the grain, cobs, husks and stalks have been the basis of some of the new synthetic chemical industries.

With the general and basic importance of corn in American agriculture it has been natural that it should have been given a leading place in the investigations of the experiment stations. Adaptations have been made by cross-breeding to secure hardier, stronger resistant and larger producing strains, and constant efforts have been made to combat diseases and pests. Agricultural economists have given special attention to costs of production and marketing systems of corn and its products. The interrelation of all these problems of production, marketing and utilization was recognized by the establishment at the Iowa station in 1935 of a corn research institute.

CORONADO'S EXPEDITION (1540–42) resulted from imaginary tales told in Mexico by Friar Marcos de Niza of having seen boundless wealth in gold, silver and gems in the seven cities of Cibola. Niza's yarns met ready credence, for the golden harvests of Cortés in Mexico and Pizarro in Peru were of recent occurrence. Every footloose man in New Spain was eager to enlist for the conquest of Cibola under the banner of Don Francisco Vásquez de Coronado, governor of New Galicia, who was commissioned by the viceroy as commander.

With an army of 300 Spanish horsemen, several of them men of noble blood, and 800 Indian footmen, Coronado departed for the north Feb. 22, 1540. Since this was to be a colonizing as well as a gold-finding venture, herds of sheep and cattle were taken as food for the army and as stockers for the ranches.

The *conquistadores* traversed much of Arizona and New Mexico, discovered the Grand Canyon and captured the Cibola cities, which were nothing but pueblos, whose most precious gems were a few turquoises and abalone beads. The next summer the army was lured on a second rainbow chase by the lies of Turk, a Plains Indian living as a captive at Pecos pueblo, who, after being shown a piece of gold by a credulous *conquistador,* said that such stuff was so plentiful in Quivira that the people did not care for it. Early in July, 1541, Coronado and thirty other horsemen came to the grass wigwams of the Quivirans, where they feasted on luscious sand plums, but found no gold. George Parker Winship locates Quivira in central Kansas. It also has been located by others in six other Plains states. Coronado, disappointed, returned to Mexico, having added much to the world's knowledge of geography. Three of his Franciscan priests remained behind as missionaries and were slain by the Indians.

COTTON is a subtropical plant which, at maturity, produces bolls containing seeds covered with long white fibers. Cotton accounts for about 65% of all textiles made in the United States.

With the advent of the Industrial Revolution, raw cotton became important to England, and imports from the American colonies were encouraged. The invention of the flying shuttle by John Kay in 1738, the spinning jenny by Hargreaves of 1764 and the power spinning frame by Richard Arkwright in 1769 provided the textile machinery for mass production of fiber into cloth. In America, the invention of the cotton gin by Eli Whitney in 1793 mechanized the tedious job of separating the fibers from the seeds and made possible the mass production of fiber to supply England's textile mills.

Samuel Slater, "father of the American cotton textile industry," escaped from England with the secrets of Arkwright's spinning frame and built a cotton mill from memory. He opened the first American mill with 144 spindles at Pawtucket, R. I., in 1790. By 1815 there were 165 cotton mills in New England, which remained the nation's textile center until 1927, when the South for the first time assumed leadership in cotton spinning production. By the latter half of the 20th century, nearly 90% of all active cotton spindles were located in the South, with the Carolinas alone the site of 825 textile mills and about half the nation's spindles. As productive capacity has increased, the number of operating spindles in the United States has declined from a high of 36,000,000 in 1921 to less than 20,000,000 spindles in recent years.

Since colonial days, cotton has been a major farm crop and a potent political force: "Cotton is king," Sen. James H. Hammond of South Carolina told Congress in 1858. The cotton economy of the South, with its dependence on slave labor, was a major factor in secession and the outbreak of the Civil War. The Confederacy gambled—in vain—that England would come to its assistance in order to break a Union blockade and obtain cotton for the hungry mills of Lancashire.

With the end of slavery some plantations were broken into smaller farms. Others were operated on a sharecropping system with tenants performing the labor and sharing proceeds from the crop.

Since the 1930's, with more and more workers leaving the farm, cotton growers have been turning to mechanization. This has been true particularly in areas adapted to use of tractors and multiple-row equipment. They include those parts of Mississippi, Louisiana, Arkansas and southeast Missouri that lie in the Mississippi River delta; also the High Plains of Texas and Oklahoma, the Rio Grande Valley, and irrigated sections of New Mexico, Arizona and California.

There has been a westward shift in cotton production in recent years. Including the traditional cotton growing areas of Arkansas, Missouri, Louisiana, Oklahoma and Texas, more than two thirds of the United States cotton crop is produced west of the Mississippi River. The Far Western states of California, Arizona and New Mexico were becoming increasingly important as cotton producers in the 1950's.

Historically, the United States is the world's leading exporter, in some years accounting for nearly half the world's supply; however, in recent years, exports have fluctuated wildly under the influence of acreage controls, price supports and complex international factors; they dropped to a peacetime low of 2,215,000 bales in 1955–56, jumped to 7,800,000 bales in the following season, then fell to less than 6,000,000 bales in 1957–58 and 1958–59.

With the rapid development of new textile industries in nations which have gained independence since World War II, world trade in cotton cloth has been steadily shrinking. Briefly, in 1947, the United States became the leading exporter of cotton goods with a record 1,500,000,000 yards; but Japan, which in 1938 had surpassed England as the world's leading textile exporter, soon regained its leadership. In recent years, Japan, India, the United States and the United Kingdom have ranked in that order as cotton textile exporters.

Cultivation. Botanically, cotton is a member of the genus *Gossypium* of the mallow family. *Gossypium hirsutum,* or Upland cotton, represents the great bulk of the American crop. *Gossypium barbadense,* or extra-long staple cotton, averaging over 1⅜ inches in fiber length, includes Sea Island, Pima and Egyptian varieties. In the United States extra-long staple cotton is represented primarily by Pima S-1 grown on irrigated farms in the El Paso area of Texas, and in New Mexico and Arizona.

Upland cotton matures in about 21 weeks, producing bolls about an inch in diameter. The boll is shaped like a punching bag and made up of three to five segments. Each segment contains seven to ten seeds with hundreds of fibers growing out of each seed. As the boll expands, it splits open into segments, exposing puffs of fluffy fiber.

Cotton, which flourishes on loamy topsoil in a climate providing six months of frost-free weather and 20 to 30 inches of rainfall during the growing season, is an annual crop in the U. S. Cotton Belt. In the five-year period, 1953–57, the following states were leading producers, in the order named: Texas, Mississippi, California, Arkansas, Arizona, Alabama, Georgia, Louisiana, Tennessee, South Carolina, Missouri, North Carolina, Oklahoma, and New Mexico. Very small amounts also are grown in Florida, Virginia, Kansas, Kentucky, Nevada, and Illinois.

With the exception of weed control and harvesting, United States cotton production is about 90% mechanized. Multi-row, tractor-drawn equipment is used for land preparation, fertilization and planting. Hand hoeing for weed control is eliminated or greatly reduced by application of herbicides, by flame cultivators which sear and kill weeds and grass, and by rotary hoes and sweep cultivators which uproot young weeds and stir the soil. Insecticides or defoliants may be applied with ground rigs to cover eight rows at a time or with planes that can dust or spray as many as 1500 acres in a day. About one third of the United States cotton crop is harvested mechanically.

The picked cotton is loaded into trailers and hauled to a gin. Here it is cleaned and dried, if necessary. Then it is conveyed automatically to gin stands which separate the lint from the seeds. A modern gin can process five or six bales an hour. Bales may weigh from 450 to 600 pounds, but the standard is 500 pounds, including 478 pounds of lint and 22 pounds of burlap wrapping and steel ties.

Cotton linters, the fuzz left on the seed after ginning, are removed at the cotton mill for use as batting or cellulose pulp. The bare seeds then are crushed for their oil. Cake, meal and hulls remaining are used primarily for livestock feed. Cottonseed oil is processed into cooking oils and shortening, salad dressing, and margarine, and is an important ingredient of mellorine—a frozen dessert. It takes about 1400 pounds of hand-picked seed cotton to produce one 500-pound bale of cotton lint, 75 pounds of linters, and 130 pounds of cottonseed oil.

The bulk of the cotton crop is harvested in the fall, although some ginnings continue through the winter. The crop year runs from Aug. 1, when heavy ginning begins, to July 31. America's largest crop was 18,946,000 bales in the 1937–38 season, when 33,623,000 acres were harvested. The smallest in modern times was 8,640,000 bales in 1946. The 1958 crop totaled about 12,000,000 bales with a record yield of about 486 pounds per acre on 11,-960,000 harvested acres, the smallest acreage since 1876.

Manufacture. Nonperishable, cotton may be stored for many years in warehouses. On the basis of small samples cut from each bale, the fiber is classed for grade whiteness, freedom from trash, etc., and staple length and sold to textile mills. Spinning mills remove trash and impurities from the cotton in openers and pickers; separate and align the fibers on carding and combing machines; form them into ropelike "slivers"; draw the slivers out into slightly twisted "roving"; and draw out and twist the roving into yarn. Ring spindles on modern spinning frames may spin yarn at more than 12,000 revolutions per minute. Some machines, with drafts as high as 60, reduce the roving strand to $\frac{1}{60}$th of its original linear weight in one operation.

Yarn, wound on bobbins, cones, warks, and other packages, is next made into cloth by the weaving or knitting operations. Modern, automatic power looms may weave cotton at speeds up to 250 picks (or crosswise filling threads) per minute, making 300,000 interlacings of warp and filling threads per minute. They operate with self-threading shuttles, automatic thread cutters, feeler mechanisms which eject spent bobbins and replace them with full ones, automatic tying-in machines which find and tie together hundreds of warp threads with neat weaver's knots in less than a minute, and with many other automatic devices. The average annual output of broad woven cotton goods is about 10,000,000,000 yards a year, or 10 miles of cloth per minute from all the 300,000 power looms of America, working night and day all year long.

Unfinished goods produced by the looms are processed at finishing plants: they are bleached, dyed, mercerized, printed, embossed, impregnated with thermosetting resins for "wash and wear" characteristics, made mildew or flame resistant, shrink resistant, or treated in any of a number of different ways, depending on their end use.

While the great bulk of the cotton crop is consumed in woven goods, millions of pounds of cotton yarn also are used by the knitting industry, the lace-making industry, and by tufting machines in the fabrication of tufted products. Some fiber also is consumed in nonwoven cottons, similar to felt, in which fibers are bonded together with adhesives.

There are more than 1000 end uses for cotton, the heaviest consumers in 1960 being men's shirts, sheets, drapery and upholstery, trousers, towels, automobile uses, dresses, rugs and carpets, bags, and piece goods. In 1960 cotton accounted for about 50% of all household textiles, 61% of all apparel and 27% of all industrial textiles made in the United States. The lowest per capita use in modern times was 19.7 pounds in 1932, and the highest 41.8

pounds in 1942, with the figure averaging around 25 pounds in recent years. It is estimated that in 1960 some 12,000,000 Americans depended on cotton to some degree for a livelihood.

COTTON GIN is a machine designed to separate cotton fibers from the seed. Though cotton has been known for many centuries, the difficulty of separating the fibers by hand long prevented wide use in textiles, though a rude gin was in use in India perhaps 300 B.C. Such gins were, however, useless in dealing with the upland cotton grown in the Southern states.

In 1792 a young Yale graduate, Eli Whitney, was living in the home of Mrs. Nathanael Greene, widow of the Revolutionary general, near Savannah, Ga. Hearing of the need for a machine to separate lint and seed, he set himself to devise such a contrivance. Mrs. Greene's manager, Phineas Miller, financed the undertaking. On June 20, 1793, Whitney applied for a patent, which was granted March 4, 1794.

The model was absurdly simple, and it seems almost incredible that the idea had not occurred to someone centuries before. Rows of metal spikes were driven into a wooden cylinder. These spikes extended between closely set metal bars into a box filled with raw cotton. When a crank was turned the revolving spikes pulled the lint through the bars leaving the seed on the other side. A rotating brush cleaned the spikes. Whitney calculated that a hand machine would do the work of ten persons, and one run by water power the work of fifty. This simple machine, as improved, changed the history of the United States and the world. Hodgen Holmes, a mechanic of Augusta, Ga., received a patent, May 2, 1796, for a gin in which circular saws were substituted for the spikes. Though declared to be an infringement of Whitney's patent, all gins now use saws.

Whitney and Miller planned to monopolize the industry, owning all the gins and charging high toll for their operation. Owing to a fire they were unable to provide gins promptly. Later they offered to sell a gin for $500, and the right to make one for $400, subsequently reduced to $200. As the rude machine could be made at small expense by any blacksmith or wheelwright in a few days, many were made without authorization. Expensive litigation followed. Finally South Carolina agreed to pay $50,000 for the right to use the gin in the state. North Carolina levied a special tax for four years which produced about $30,000, and Tennessee paid $10,000. Little was received from Georgia. Though Whitney received only a small part of the wealth which his epoch-making idea created, the stories that he received nothing are manifestly untrue.

COTTON KINGDOM, THE, existed between 1830 and 1860 in the region reaching from South Carolina to Texas. Climatic conditions favored the production of cotton, and the entire life of the region was shaped by this interest. The most characteristic marks of the Cotton Kingdom were the plantation system and slavery. The plantation system developed because cotton was most cheaply produced on a large scale. Slavery supplied a cheap and abundant supply of unskilled labor.

COUNCIL FOR NEW ENGLAND was the name under which the survivors of the Plymouth branch of the Virginia Company, chartered in 1606, were reorganized and incorporated by a charter in 1620. The Council received the land on the Atlantic coast between 40° and 48° N. Lat., extending from sea to sea, within which huge area it was granted, along with the authority to colonize and to govern its colonies, monopolistic trade and fishing rights. Though in many respects the Council appeared to be a trading company, it more nearly resembled the royal council of the Virginia Company, for in the charter no mention was made of General Courts or freemen, and it was a closed corporation of forty members. From the outset its members, who were nobles and landed gentry rather than merchants, were more interested in developing the land than in trade. This they planned to do by granting the greater part of the region to its members as fiefs and manors organized as nearly as possible according to English land law. The rest of the land was to be given to others, singly or in groups, with rights of local self-government, but subject to the superior authority of the Council's governor general. Sir Ferdinando Gorges, president of the Council, was the dominating figure throughout its whole history. His son Robert was appointed the first governor general and went to New England in 1623 to take up his duties and to found a subordinate colony for himself and family. His project succeeded no better than those of most members of the Council, and he soon departed for England. From time to time the Council tried to reorganize so as to give more vitality to the enterprise, and considered exchanging the charter for one which better represented the landed interests of its members. Nothing, however, came of these attempts. The enterprise as a whole failed, but New England was colonized through the unexpected success of two small grants to nonmembers. These two were destined to alter the character of expansion in New England, and to substitute for the Council's conception of a single aristocratic landed Anglican province several small independent Puritan middle-class colonies. The first of these patents was that of the Pilgrims who settled on Cape Cod in 1620 and the other, the Massachusetts Bay patient of 1628, confirmed the following year by royal charter.

The significance of the Massachusetts grant was that the Council for New England was eliminated as intermediary and the grantees held land with powers of government directly from the king. This alien wedge spoiled the unity of the Council's plans for developing New England under its direction, and brought from that body the charge that the grant had been surreptitiously obtained. In order to bring about the annulment of the Massachusetts charter, the Council decided to surrender its "grand patent" and ask the king to regrant the whole region in eight parts to eight of its members previously chosen by itself. The process of negotiating the transfer would enable the eight new lords proprietors to require the confirmation of all previous grants by the Council, including the original one to the Massachusetts Bay group. In 1635 the Council therefore surrendered its charter and designated the eight members who would receive the land divisions by royal charters. *Quo warranto* proceedings were begun against the Massachusetts Bay Company, and Sir Ferdinando Gorges was appointed governor general of New England in order to preserve the administrative unity of the region as formerly planned. But this vigorous campaign was interrupted by the Puritan Revolution in England. Only one charter, that of Maine to Gorges, made its way through the seals, and the proceedings against Massachusetts Bay came to nought. On the other hand, twenty years of civil war in England gave the Puritans the necessary breathing spell in which to strengthen their foothold and develop the region into a number of little Puritan colonies more or less centering around Massachusetts, the only one of them to hold a royal charter until after the restoration.

COUNCIL GROVE, KANS., derived its name from a grove at the Neosho River crossing where early western travelers gathered to form wagon trains. There, Aug. 10, 1825, the Osages signed a treaty granting right of way to the Santa Fe trail. Seth Hays, in 1847, established at Council Grove the first settlement on the trail west of Westport, Mo. It became important as the "jumping-off" point for the seventy-day wagon trek to Santa Fe.

COUNTY FAIRS, a peculiarly American agricultural institution, arose in the second decade of the 19th century. Fairs for the purpose of buying and selling on the pattern of the mediaeval fairs had been held in colonial times, but the first county fair in its distinctly American interpretation was fostered by Elkanah Watson, a gentleman farmer who exhibited sheep in the square at Pittsfield, Mass. The first modern fair was held under his promotion in 1811 and was followed by the organization of the Berkshire County Agricultural Society, which held fairs regularly thereafter. Watson worked indefatigably to promote the Berkshire plan in every county in New York and New England. The movement had a mushroom growth, and Watson claimed that all the counties in New England with the exception of those of Rhode Island had county fairs. State aid was given in many places and during the 1820's the institution

reached a peak. A gradual decline then set in, and the fair almost entirely disappeared. With the renewed expansion of agriculture in the 1840's there was a revival of the institution with hundreds of societies springing up and holding fairs during the next three decades. This enthusiasm has continued to the present time with unabated interest.

COUNTY GOVERNMENT. The institutions of government in the approximately 3000 counties in the United States had their origins in the English counties; they have been maintained here through three centuries with surprisingly little modification. While the town or township forms of local government organization developed in the North Atlantic states, the county developed in the South and West, where a vast expanse of territory and predominantly agricultural pursuits were conducive to a larger local unit.

As of 1959, county government existed in all but three states, in numbers ranging from three in Delaware to 254 in Texas. In Connecticut, counties were abolished by legislative action early in 1959. A similar proposal had been made a number of times in New Hampshire, but had never been adopted. The constitution of Alaska, framed in 1956, sought deliberately to avoid the establishment of county government, authorizing the legislature to provide for division of the state into boroughs, both organized and unorganized, in a manner and according to standards provided by law. Counties are not organized as units of local government in Rhode Island, and in the New England states generally, they serve merely as units for judicial organization.

The size of the typical American county was determined, it has been said, by the family cow, and the distance that a man could travel between milking time in the morning and milking time at night. Consequently, these units are too numerous, and many of them are too small to serve adequately the needs of the people under modern conditions. Serious structural defects still further impair their usefulness and effectiveness. Each has a board of county commissioners of three or five members, or as in New York and Michigan, a larger board of supervisors. In each, there is the usual long list of elected "row officers,"—coroner, clerk, prothonotary, register of wills, register of deeds, sheriff, assessor, treasurer, auditor, engineer/surveyor, etc. There is a conspicuous lack of any central co-ordinating influence, or over-all executive power. Each county either constitutes a judicial district, with its own county court, or is a part of a judicial district composed of two or more counties.

Counties perform three different types of services: older services which have always been their responsibility, newer services, and in a limited number of urban counties, municipal-type services. The general nature of the original services is indicated by the names of the elected county officers. Included in this category are protection of life and property, clerical and recording services, fiscal functions, education (in some jurisdictions), construction and maintenance of highways and roads. For certain activities, some old (like military organization and administration of elections), some relatively new (like agriculture, public health, public welfare, or recreation), the counties serve as convenient units for the administration of programs that are primarily the responsibility of the state. Among the newer services assigned to the counties may be mentioned library services, planning and zoning, conservation of natural resources, rural housing, mental health clinics. The municipal-type services include urban housing; water, gas and electric services; fire protection; garbage and refuse collection and disposal; and sewage disposal.

Long the victims of neglect by public officials, students of government, and the public alike, the counties were aptly described early in the present century as the dark continent of American politics. Following many studies of county organization and administration, there has been in late years some improvement in organization, particularly in some states, and significant improvement in the quality of administration, especially in approximately 300 urban counties which are being called upon more and more to provide municipal-type services to a constantly growing population outside the borders of incorporated places. In many instances, in addition, they are providing municipal-type services, under contract, within the cities themselves. So much is this true that many observers have commented on the tremendous rejuvenation of the county form in the years since World War II.

COUREURS DE BOIS, or "bushrangers," is a term applied to the very considerable number of persons who left the early French settlements in Canada, in defiance of authority, and took to the wilderness, actuated by love of adventure and a desire to profit by the fur trade. During the latter half of the 17th century the migration assumed almost the proportions of a mass exodus, and seriously weakened the colony of New France. In spite of government edicts and the hostility of the Jesuits, the *coureurs de bois* flourished, some of the more prominent among them being Radisson, Groseilliers, Du Lhut and Perrot. While they were accused of debauching the Indians, they did render valuable service as explorers and pioneers in the fur trade. A picturesque, adventurous type, they are not to be confused with the *voyageurs,* or *engagés,* of the later fur trade.

COURT LEET, in English law, was a court exercising the jurisdiction of the sheriff's tourn over petty criminal matters. In colonial Maryland leet jurisdiction was exercised by the proprietors of manors of

2000 acres under authority issued by the proprietary in 1636. The only records extant are those of the Court Leet and Court Baron of St. Clement's Manor, held by Thomas Gerrard, and running from 1659 to 1672. Both freeholders and leaseholders sat in the court and a presenting jury was employed. Police-court matters were dealt with and tenants swore fealty to their lord and paid relief. This court was a curiosity which had no permanent influence on the American judicial system.

COURTHOUSE ROCK, a notable landmark on the Oregon Trail, is located about five miles south of the present town of Bridgeport, Nebr., and fifty miles from the Wyoming line. In 1846 the trail ran seven miles from this natural formation.

COVENANT, THE CHURCH, was the formal and public act of mutual engagement which, according to the theory of the New England clergy, should be entered into by the founders of a particular church and without which no church could come into being. It was called the "form" of a visible church; all New England churches were founded upon such an agreement and later recruits subscribed to the covenant; at times of revival the covenant was often unanimously "renewed." Insistence upon this theory was one of the peculiar characteristics of Congregational or Independent theologians as opposed to both Anglicans and Presbyterians, and the clergy of New England wrote more voluminously in defense of it than on any other single subject. Their argument contains the seeds of principles that were later to be transplanted to the realm of political theory, particularly the assertion that no society can have power over a man until he has voluntarily and explicitly contracted to accept its regulations.

COVERED WAGON, THE, has carried American history across the continent for two centuries. Born in Pennsylvania as the Conestoga wagon, constructed under various names but always of strength and capacity, it served nomadic America as no other vehicle could have done; the modern trailer continues the tradition.

It carried early migrants over the Cumberlands; it carried Forty-Niners to California, Mormons to Utah, Americans determined on "Oregon for America" to the Far Northwest. Survivors remain in museums, the Conestoga original at Pittsburgh, Ezra Meeker's prairie schooner at Tacoma. But thousands have gone the way of even the stoutest timbers, like the bones of thousands who started with them; time has disintegrated all.

It was fundamentally a wagon box with framework of hoop-shaped slats over which was stretched a canvas tent that made it into a "covered" wagon. Each was drawn by several teams of horses, mules or oxen. Many were boat-shaped with oarlocks, that the

258

wagon might be floated over streams, the animals swimming across.

The adventurers assembled at such points west of the Missouri River as Independence, or Council Grove, and organized into caravans for companionship and protection. On the way, at night, the wagons were formed into a hollow square as corral for the animals, sentinels were posted, and each man slept under his wagon, ready to defend his family and his goods against the perils of the unknown. It took four or five months to make the 2000-mile trek that lay between the Missouri and the Pacific.

COWBOYS. The legitimate American cowboy came into existence when, in 1821, settlers pushing westward into present-day Texas discovered the local Mexican ranches, the methods of the *vaqueros,* and commercial possibilities in the herds of ownerless horses and cattle that dotted the Texan and Western plains. These belligerent beasts were descended from the mettlesome steeds and long-horned Andalusian cattle—of the same breed as the bulls of the Spanish bull-ring—which Cortés and other *conquistadores* had imported into Mexico in and after 1519.

American ranching extended its area slowly until 1866 when, the Northern Indians being in process of confinement on reservations, it began quick expansion over all the Western plains. The resultant need for additional cowboys was met by adventurous youths from Texas, Eastern farms and cities, and the British Isles. Until well into the 1880's the "long-horns" and horses of Spanish descent were the dominant livestock on the range. The herding and handling of these brutes was highly technical and could be accomplished only by such men as, in addition to expertness in horsemanship and the use of a lariat, possessed courage, initiative, resourcefulness, stamina, so much instinctive acquaintance with animals' whims as to foretell and control stampedes, and ability to find the way unerringly by day or night in fair weather or in blizzard, past quicksands, across swollen rivers and through miles of uninhabited and rugged country. So dangerous was the life that seven years formed the limit of the average cowboy's riding activity.

The cowboy's costume he selected for utility and not for picturesqueness. *Chaparejos* (leathern armor for the legs) protected from thorns, goring cattle and falling horses; high heels prevented entanglement in the stirrup and furnished an anchorage when throwing the lariat afoot; a neckerchief drawn across mouth and nose made breathing possible amid stifling dust.

The cowboy was a keen and accurate observer of all that he saw and heard upon the range. Always abstemious while at his tasks, he nevertheless was apt, during infrequent visits to towns, to revel in drunkenness and gambling. Intensely proud of his vocation, he resented any belittling of it—his resentment tending to become fiery when, upon long trail

drives, enforced watchfulness against stampede made his nerves as taut as those of a race horse. He loathed the sheep men, whose flocks with their sharp hoofs obliterated the grass otherwise available to the cowboy's herds. His readiness to shoot has been grossly exaggerated.

Cowboys, because of their numbers, controlled the social and political life of the plains until approximately 1890, but thenceforth they gradually and grudgingly ceded their fenceless empire to the farmer and his barbed-wire enclosures.

As citizens of the cattle range rather than of any particular states or territories, the cowboys welded the entire West into a solidarity against the East and, due to the amicable relationship between Texan and Northern cowboys, prevented the sectional prejudices of Mason and Dixon line from extending onto the Western plains.

COWBOYS AND SKINNERS were bands of guerrillas and irregular cavalry who operated chiefly in the "Neutral Ground" of Westchester County, N. Y., during the American Revolution.

"Cowboys" was a name given to the Westchester Light Horse Battalion, a Loyalist provincial corps of the British Army, commanded by Col. James de Lancey, and should not be confused with Gen. Oliver de Lancey's Loyal Americans, or Royal Refugee Corps, which confined its operations principally to Long Island.

The Westchester Light Horse, sometimes called "De Lancey's Green Jackets," due to their uniform, was organized in 1777, and was an irregular unit of the British Army until the end of the war, taking part in some of the principal battles. They operated in Westchester County from 1778 to 1780, when not called into service elsewhere from time to time. They had their headquarters at Morrisania.

The "Skinners," ironically named after Gen. Cortland Skinner's Brigade of New Jersey Volunteers, had no regular organization. They were separate bands of mounted rascals, or banditti, who claimed attachment, sometimes to the British and sometimes to the Americans, but were owned by neither. They plundered, burned and ravished the "Neutral Ground" from 1778 to 1783, and sold their plunder, including horses and cattle, to both sides. Their services were occasionally employed by the British or Americans as scouts and spies, though the cavalry of both sides hung or shot them whenever they were caught.

COWPENS, BATTLE OF (Jan. 17, 1781), was one of the most brilliant American victories in the Revolution. In December, 1780, Nathanael Greene, who was in command of the American Army in the South, sent out Gen. Morgan with 600 men to threaten the British post at Ninety-Six. Cornwallis, who was encamped at Winnsboro, sent Tarleton against Morgan, while he himself marched northward, thereby hoping to get between the two wings of the American Army. Morgan, who had been recently joined by Pickens with several hundred men, marched northward rapidly, with Tarleton's army in pursuit. On Jan. 17, Morgan offered battle. He took position upon the slope of a hill at "the Cowpens" (S. C.) and drew up his forces in three lines, the first consisting of skirmishers who were to begin firing when the enemy was within fifty yards and then fall back to the second line, made up of Pickens' militia. This line was to wait the approach of the British, fire twice, and fall back to the third line, containing troops from Maryland, Virginia and Georgia. Morgan had 940 men, Tarleton 1150. As the British approached, the first two lines of Morgan's army fired and fell back. The British thought they had won an easy victory and advanced in disorder, only to be met by a deadly fire and bayonet attack. At the same time the cavalry struck them on the right flank and the re-formed militia on the left. Finding themselves surrounded they surrendered. The British losses were 600 prisoners and over 200 killed and wounded; the American losses were 72 killed and wounded.

COWPUNCHER as a word has been abbreviated to puncher, and, in places, transmuted to cow poke, just as *vaquero* (common in California and Texas) was corrupted into buckaroo. All mean the same thing as cowboy, cow hand, hand and waddie (obsolescent). Cowboy, as word and fact peculiar to American ranching, originated in Texas about 1836. The word cowpuncher came into use around fifty years later, when cowboys used prodpoles to force cattle through chutes into stock cars and, accompanying cattle on trains, carried prodpoles to punch up any animal that got down in a car. Thus cowboys became literally cowpunchers.

COXEY'S ARMY. Jacob Sechler Coxey, of Massillon, O., was a successful self-made business man and a reformer with a special interest in fiat money. During the depression following the Panic of 1893 he worked out a plan to save the country by the enactment of two bills providing for large issues of legal-tender currency to be spent for good roads and other public improvements, thus furnishing work to the workless. His device to arouse public and congressional interest in these bills—the march of a "living petition" of the unemployed to Washington—was attributed to his picturesque western associate, Carl Browne. As a result of Browne's curious religious notions the organization was called "The Commonweal of Christ." The Commonweal marched out of Massillon on Easter Sunday, 1894, with about a hundred men, followed by half as many reporters who gave the "army" plenty of free publicity. Instead of the 100,000 he had predicted, Coxey had about 500 men when he arrived in Washington in time for a great demonstration on May Day. His parade was cheered by an enormous crowd, but when he tried to speak from the Capitol steps he was arrested, fined, and sent to jail for carrying banners and walking on the grass in the Capitol grounds.

Meanwhile, "industrial armies" larger than Coxey's had been formed by the unemployed on the Pacific coast and elsewhere, the largest and best organized being Fry's from Los Angeles and Kelly's from San Francisco. They decided to join Coxey at Washington. When the railroads refused to give them free rides on freights they stole trains and ran them themselves. Sometimes, when local authorities were unable or unwilling to suppress them, Federal judges enjoined Coxeyites from stealing trains and the injunctions were enforced by United States marshals or the Army, setting precedents for the Government's action against the Pullman strikers in July. Armies that crossed the Mississippi found the population and the railroads more hostile, and disintegrated before reaching Washington, but remnants straggled in until about 1200 were encamped there. The District of Columbia finally paid their way home.

The "Coxeyites," "Commonwealers" or "Industrials," as they were called indiscriminately, demanded measures that were mainly Populistic, and were generally supported by Populists and organized labor. Although they failed in their objectives, they were significant as symptoms of the economic unrest of the period and as an unusual type of Populistic propaganda.

"CRACKERS," the "poor whites" of the pine barrens area of the South, are also referred to as "piney woods people," "sand hillers," and "clay-eaters." Chief Justice Anthony Stokes of colonial Georgia claimed that the Southern colonies were overrun with men from western North Carolina and Virginia known as "crackers." The term is said to have originated from the practice of teamsters "cracking" their huge whips as they drove their teams long distances to markets with farm produce.

CRÉDIT MOBILIER OF AMERICA was a company used by a group of leaders of the Union Pacific Railroad to enable them to pocket exorbitant profits in the construction of the line. Vice-President T. C. Durant in March, 1864, took possession of an old company called the Pennsylvania Fiscal Agency, changed its name to Crédit Mobilier, and with Oakes Ames and Oliver Ames brought the capital in 1865 up to $2,500,000. When the railroad had been finished to the 100th meridian, the managers split into two factions; Durant was thrust aside and Oakes Ames took charge of the Crédit Mobilier while Oliver Ames became president of the Union Pacific. In 1869 the Crédit Mobilier completed the building of the road. According to the subsequent Senate investigation, the sale of first-mortgage bonds, and of government bonds lent the road upon a second mortgage, provided it with $50,863,172, or slightly more than enough to pay the whole cost of construction; but the Crédit Mobilier also received some $23,000,000 in stocks, income bonds and land-grant bonds. In short, the managers stripped the Union Pacific of what Congress had intended should be a permanent endowment, and placed it in their own pockets. When Congress opened on Nov. 21, 1867, it was evident that the Union Pacific-Crédit Mobilier combination might come under fire. Oakes Ames therefore took 343 shares of Crédit Mobilier stock and distributed at least 160 shares among Senators and Representatives; he sold it at par, though he believed it worth at least double, and he allowed some to pay for it out of accumulated dividends. Late in the presidential campaign of 1872 the New York *Sun* made charges which resulted the ensuing winter in both House and Senate investigations, which ruined the reputation of Oakes Ames; of James Brooks, who also was formally censured by the House; of Sen. James W. Patterson, who was recommended for expulsion, though no action was taken; and of ex-Speaker Schuyler Colfax. Other men, including James A. Garfield, were badly damaged in public esteem.

CREEK WAR (1813–14) began with the massacre of Fort Mims, August, 1813, and closed with the Treaty of Fort Jackson, August, 1814. The Upper Creeks, called "Red Sticks," living on the Coosa River, precipitated hostilities and carried on the war, while the Lower Creeks, on the Chattahoochee River, remained friendly and aided the Americans. Incited by a visit of Tecumseh in 1811, emboldened by the British in Canada, and armed by the Spaniards at Pensacola, the "Red Sticks" sacked and burned Fort Mims, on the Alabama River, massacred most of its inhabitants, and ravaged the surrounding country. Armies for relief soon began organizing in Mississippi, Tennessee and Georgia; though the main campaign was conducted by Andrew Jackson and his Tennesseans. In October (1813) he sacked the Indian village of Talishatchee, and the next month crushed a Creek force at Talladega. About the same time, John Cocke led a force from East Tennessee into the Creek country and unwittingly killed or captured a band of friendly Creeks, much to Jackson's chagrin. A few days later John Floyd with a force of Georgians and friendly Creeks defeated the "Red Sticks" at Autossee, on the Tallapoosa River, and speedily returned to Georgia; and in December Ferdinand L. Claiborne, of Mississippi, with a mixed army of regulars, militia, volunteers and friendly Choctaws, destroyed Weatherford's Town and killed thirty Indians.

In the meantime Jackson was being harassed in a most exasperating fashion by mutinous troops and others whose enlistments had expired. Holding together with reckless determination a few of his soldiers, he called on Gov. Blount of Tennessee for new forces. Having finally collected an army of about 2000 men, Jackson invaded the heart of the Indian country in March, 1814, and on the 27th, aided by John Coffee, he fell upon the "Red Sticks" at the Horseshoe Bend of the Tallapoosa River and killed an estimated 850 or 900 warriors and made prisoners of about 500 squaws and children. The power of the Indians was broken, and in the Treaty of Fort Jackson, which followed, the Creeks were forced to give up the southern parts of Georgia and Alabama.

CREOLES are scientifically defined as people of pure European blood born in the western hemisphere. Derived from the Spanish "Criollo," the term "Creole" was originally employed to distinguish Europeans born in the American colonies from their fellow nationals born in the mother countries; but in later times its application has been restricted to individuals of pure French, Spanish or Portuguese blood born in the Americas.

CRESAP'S WAR was a desultory warfare with the Ohio River Indians in the spring of 1774. Capt. Michael Cresap was a leader in this warfare. Among other incidents, on April 26, 1774, he had a skirmish with Indians on the river. Four days later the family of Logan, a noted Indian chieftain, was lured across the Ohio from its camp on Yellow Creek, intoxicated and brutally murdered. Out of this affair came Logan's famous speech, included by Jefferson in his *Notes on Virginia*. Likewise, arose the revengeful ravages of Logan and his followers, which precipitated Lord Dunmore's War. Jefferson and others put the blame on Cresap. Later investigations have shown that Daniel Greathouse was the leader in the Yellow Creek massacre, Cresap being absent.

"CRIME OF 1873" is a phrase associated historically with the coinage law of Feb. 12, 1873. The 67 sections of the law constituted a virtual codification of the then extant laws relating to the mints and coinage, but only two sections are significant in this connection. Section fifteen reads in part: "That the silver coins of the United States shall be a trade dollar . . . a half dollar . . . and said coins shall be legal tender at their nominal value for an amount not exceeding five dollars in any one payment." Section seventeen reads, "That no coins, either gold, silver or minor coinage shall hereafter be issued from the mint other than of the denominations, standards, and weights herein set forth." The omission of the standard silver dollar from the list of silver coins became, for more than two decades after 1876, the "Crime of 1873."

The movement for the free coinage of silver began about 1876, when decreased use of silver as a monetary metal and increased production caused the price of silver to decline. The leaders of the movement defended the bimetallic standard and charged that the demonetization of silver was the result of a conspiracy entered into by British and American financial interests to secure in a surreptitious manner the adoption of the gold standard in the United States. The "silverites" clung tenaciously to the plot theory in spite of the fact that the act of 1873 was simply a legal recognition of an existing fact, *i.e.*, that the silver dollar had not been in circulation for decades; that the act was considered in five sessions of Congress, read repeatedly, debated exhaustively and discussed frequently by Treasury officials. This actual series of events is of interest only to historians. For two decades millions of people thought that a crime had been committed and voted their convictions at every opportunity.

CRIPPLE CREEK MINING BOOM began in the early 1890's. Previously the district, immediately southwest of Pikes Peak, was a cattle ranch. Robert Womack, cowboy, did occasional prospecting and finally discovered a promising vein, January, 1891. Spring brought many prospectors. On July 4 W. S. Stratton staked the Independence, that was to bring him wealth and pre-eminence as an operator. A mining district was organized. Bennett and Myers, owners of the cattle ranch, platted the city of Cripple Creek. This and other towns sprang into bustling life. Disastrous fires and serious labor strikes interrupted production. The district's gold output reached $10,-000,000 in 1897 and exceeded that annually for twenty years.

CRITTENDEN COMPROMISE was the most important proposal made in 1860–61 in the attempt to resolve the conflict between North and South by peaceful measures. The plan, presented to the U. S. Senate, Dec. 18, 1860, by Sen. J. J. Crittenden of Kentucky, included six articles proposed as amendments to the U. S. Constitution, and four resolutions. The heart of the compromise was in the first article, which provided that: north of 36° 30′, the line of the Missouri Compromise, in all territory then held or thereafter acquired, slavery was to be prohibited; south of the line slavery was to be protected as property. Crittenden's proposal referred only to territory then held, but an amendment was added, "or hereafter acquired." Other articles prohibited Congress from abolishing slavery in places under Federal jurisdiction in the slave states, or in the District of Columbia without compensation and consent of Virginia and Maryland. The last article provided that there should be no constitutional amendment to alter the other five articles of the compromise, and that Congress should have no power to interfere with slavery where it then existed.

This plan was the chief subject of consideration by the Senate Committee of Thirteen and the House Committee of Thirty-three, and by the Peace Convention in Washington. It was defeated by vote on Dec. 21, 1860, in the crucial Committee of Thirteen, chiefly because the Republicans, in consultation with Lincoln, then President-elect, refused to yield on prohibition of slavery in the territories. The resolution for an amendment to prohibit interference with slavery in the states passed Congress in February and March, 1861, but was never ratified by the states.

CROGHAN'S EXPEDITIONS TO ILLINOIS (1765–66). After Pontiac's uprising had been put down, England faced the old problem of how to occupy the French settlements clustering around Fort de Chartres on the Mississippi in the Illinois country. Thousands of savages were still sullen; Pontiac was still at large; to penetrate the "Black Forest" with troops and supply a garrison in far-off Illinois would be feasible only if the Indians were friendly.

To carry on the complicated Indian negotiations for peace, Gen. Gage and Sir William Johnson selected George Croghan, an Indian trader and agent of renown, who was well acquainted with the Ohio country and its savages. After surmounting great difficulties in organizing his expedition, Croghan left Fort Pitt on May 15, 1765, for Illinois, with two boatloads of presents. His party included a deputation of Delaware, Shawnee and Seneca chiefs. On June 8, near the mouth of the Wabash, he was attacked by hostile Indians, his stores plundered and several whites and Shawnee killed. Croghan himself was tomahawked, but, as he reported, "my skull being pretty thick, the hatchet would not enter." He was taken as a prisoner to Vincennes. Fear of reprisals caused his release and the Indian tribes, now alarmed, came to him with offers of peace. Even Pontiac came to meet him and promised not to hinder British occupation. Croghan sent word of this to Fort Pitt, and soon a company of English soldiers under Capt. Stirling floated down the Ohio and occupied Illinois. Croghan returned overland to Fort Pitt and there held another important Indian conference.

In 1766, Croghan, with 17 bateaux, once more started from Fort Pitt on a dangerous but successful voyage of over a thousand miles to make a final formal treaty with the Illinois Indians. More than a thousand came, representing 22 "tribes or bands," and on Aug. 25 and 26 presents were given and a "General Peace and Reconciliation" was declared. Croghan then returned by way of New Orleans to New York. For the first time in history, business connections between the Illinois country and the Atlantic seaboard had been established, and Indian traders, land speculators and settlers were greatly stimulated to exploit the West.

CROMPTON LOOM, the first successful power loom for making fancy cotton fabrics, was invented—and patented in 1837—by William Crompton, an English weaver who had settled in Massachusetts. Crompton subsequently adapted this loom to the manufacture of fancy cassimeres at Lowell and thus introduced a new era in the American wool manufacture.

CROSS KEYS, BATTLE OF, was an engagement (June 8, 1862) near Harrisonburg, Va., during "Stonewall" Jackson's (C.) retreat up the Shenandoah Valley. Gen. Ewell (C.), with 6000 infantry and 500 cavalry, repulsed an attack by Gen. Frémont's (U.) force of 10,000 infantry and 2000 cavalry. Frémont showed little skill or confidence in his direction of the battle. The Federal loss was 684 killed, wounded and missing; the Confederate, 288.

CROSS OF GOLD SPEECH (July 9, 1896). "You shall not press down upon the brow of labor this crown of thorns, you shall not crucify mankind upon a cross of gold." So William Jennings Bryan, a delegate from Nebraska, concluded his attack upon the single gold standard before the Democratic national nomination convention at Chicago. Bryan's speech was not so notable for the cogency of its reasoning as for the distinction of its rhetoric and the perfection of its delivery; all of which, in spite of the appearance of spontaneity, was carefully planned in advance. The free silver delegates, recognizing in Bryan the leader they had sought, made him the convention nominee.

CROSWELL LIBEL SUIT (1802–5). Harry Croswell, an editor of Hudson, N. Y., in 1802 published in *The Wasp* an attack on President Jefferson for which he was convicted of criminal libel. According to traditional legal procedure, as in the Zenger trial, no evidence except the fact of publication was admitted. In an appeal to the state supreme court Alexander Hamilton argued for the right to submit the truth of the case in evidence. His plea was instrumental in liberalizing the libel law of the state by an act of April 6, 1805, and so achieved an outstanding victory for the freedom of the press.

CROWN POINT, a promontory on the west shore of Lake Champlain in northern New York, was a bone of contention between New France and the English colonies. Champlain passed the spot in 1609 on his way to Ticonderoga. Either Crown Point or Chimney Point, situated directly across the lake in Vermont, was called by the French *La Pointe à la Chevelure*. This appellation may have referred to a growth of bushy trees resembling a head of hair or to some scalping incident.

In 1690 a scouting party from Albany erected a temporary "Little Stone Fort" near Crown Point. Gov. Beauharnois of New France in 1730 sent a small force to the point to intercept traders from Albany, and in the next year Louis XV ordered "a fort of stockadoes" built, which was soon strengthened by a "Machicoulis Redoubt," a citadel with projecting stories. The fort was named St. Frédéric.

Only three days' march (110 miles) from Albany, Fort St. Frédéric served as a base for French raiding parties against New York and New England. The English held that it was erected in violation of the Treaty of Utrecht (1713), in which France acknowledged the Iroquois to be English subjects. The fort was extremely vulnerable to an invading army, but England and her colonies usually did not work well together in military matters. Expeditions were planned by Governors Clinton of New York and Shirley of Massachusetts during King George's War; and others were commanded by William Johnson in 1755, and Abercromby in 1758, but they failed to reach St. Frédéric. Not until July 31, 1759, did Lord Amherst force Bourlamaque to blow up the fort and retreat. Amherst then built a huge new fortress, called by the British Crown Point or Amherst, but in 1773 it was almost completely destroyed by fire.

Col. Seth Warner and the Green Mountain Boys had no difficulty in taking Crown Point from its small garrison on May 12, 1775. It was of some importance during the Revolution, serving mainly as an advanced post of Fort Ticonderoga. In 1910 the property containing the ruins of the two forts was deeded to the State of New York for a state park.

CUBA. Strategically the key to much of the Western Hemisphere, Cuba has been important out of all proportion to her size and population. The island was settled by the Spanish in 1515, thereafter becoming a base for many expeditions to the mainland. In 1762 it was captured by the British, but returned to Spain by the Treaty of Paris, 1763. In 1777 Cuba was made a captaincy-general. Both before and after that date—except from 1763 to 1800—it included all Spanish Gulf territories from Florida to Louisiana.

At the turn of the 18th century occurred an influx of many French and Spanish from Hispaniola, primarily fugitives from the Negro rebellion. Hospitably received at first, the newcomers greatly stimulated Cuban economic and cultural life, but, with Napoleon's conquest of Spain, many of the French were persecuted and exiled.

Cuba was always strongly held by Spain, and remained loyal during the Hispanic-American wars of independence. Nevertheless, desire for separation was present and manifested itself sporadically throughout the century. At first, Cuban advocates of separation generally favored annexation to the United States, which country became the base for much of their propaganda. Climaxing this early phase of the movement were the abortive filibustering attempts of Narciso López, Venezuelan expatriate, who, during 1849–51, twice descended upon Cuba with expeditions recruited in the United States.

Meanwhile, in the 1840's and 1850's, the Cuban policy of the United States, which theretofore had generally favored Spain's retention of the island lest it fall to England or France, reacted sharply to the stirrings of "manifest destiny" and the imperialism of the slavery-extension group. Presidents Polk, Pierce and Buchanan endeavored to buy the island or gain its voluntary cession, while the Ostend Manifesto, drawn up in 1854 at a conference between the American ministers to London, Paris and Madrid, boldly claimed the right to annex Cuba should purchase offers be refused. These and other Cuban projects were defeated by Spain's unwillingness to sell and the opposition of the antislavery Northern states of the American Union. The Civil War ended United States efforts to acquire Cuba, although the question was temporarily revived during the Cleveland administration (1885–89).

In 1868 began the Cuban rebellion known as the Ten Years War. Though most Cubans now wanted independence, various annexation overtures were made to the United States. These were rejected, however, and the United States maintained neutrality, despite the pro-Cuban sympathies of President Grant. Following the cessation of hostilities, in 1878, the United States, whose Cuban commercial and financial interests were fast increasing, futilely endeavored to effect the relaxation of Spanish trade restrictions and the liberalization of Cuban government. With little prospect of Spain's granting such reforms, the Cubans again arose, on Feb. 24, 1895. After two years of brilliant insurrectionary victories, Spain gradually prevailed, as thousands died in the reconcentration camps established by the notorious Spanish general, Valeriano Weyler.

In the United States, anti-Spanish feeling rose to fever heat in response to pro-Cuban propaganda in sensational American newspapers, especially Hearst's *Journal* and Pulitzer's *World,* bitter New York rivals. Behind much of this propaganda was the Cuban junta in New York, which, indeed, was the real directing agency of the revolution.

Reacting to popular belligerent spirit, Congress authorized war April 20, 1898, and Spanish capitulation ended a brief struggle (*see* Spanish-American War). Formally placed under United States military government in January, 1899, Cuba became a republic in May, 1902, after guaranteeing certain United States interests by acceptance of the so-called Platt Amendment. Subsequent political turbulence brought formal United States intervention from 1906 to 1909, the landing of marines for a few weeks in 1917, and, in 1921, the mission of Gen. Enoch Crowder as advisor to the Cuban government. Though the Platt Amendment was abrogated in 1934, United States influence in Cuban affairs has continued to be strong.

In 1933, as the result of a revolution against the government of Pres. Gerardo Machado (who had been in office since 1924) and an army coup against Carlos Mendieta, Machado's successor, Fulgencio Batista assumed the presidency of Cuba and continued in that office for the next ten years. One of the last acts of the Mendieta government was to include in the treaty abrogating the Platt Amendment, a provision reaffirming the rights of the United States,

originally granted in 1903, to occupy and use Guantanamo Bay and a 28,000 acre plot surrounding it as a naval base in consideration of an annual payment of $2,000.00 in gold coin, later increased to $3,386.25. The United States was given indefinite use of the area under a treaty which can be terminated only by mutual consent.

Batista was followed as president by Grau San Martín (1944–1947) and by Carlos Prío Soccarrás (1947–1952). On March 10, 1952, Batista again became president as the result of a military uprising. Elections scheduled to be held in November, 1953, were put off until November, 1954, because of opposition to Batista. He was elected, however, without opposition, Nov. 1, 1954. Batista's second term was marked by much opposition, violence and internal discord, and the government was charged with use of widespread cruelty and oppression to maintain itself in power. The president and his supporters were also accused of all manner of irregular financial transactions. One of the groups opposing the Batista government was led by Fidel Castro. He led a descent on the shore of Cuba's easternmost province, Dec. 12, 1956, but his small force of 81 men was nearly wiped out. Castro escaped and established headquarters for guerrilla warfare in the mountains of eastern Cuba. An attempt to kill or kidnap Batista, March 13, 1957, was beaten off. On Dec. 9, 1958, Castro, well supplied with arms and men, launched a major offensive against the Batista forces at Santa Clara. On Jan. 1, 1959, Batista, unable to depend on his army, fled to the Dominican Republic. The Castro forces occupied Havana. Manuel Urrutia became Cuban Provisional President, but Castro, as head of the armed forces, was the real power. In February, Castro became Premier of Cuba; in March he made a brief tour of the United States and Canada. He resigned as Premier on July 17, but ten days later, on July 26, 1959, he returned to the office of Premier.

Because of his hostility to the U. S. government and his socialistic nationalization program he was severely criticized by U. S. officials and businessmen. He sought aid and assistance from Soviet Russia and as a result President Eisenhower on July 9, 1960, ordered an end to further purchases of Cuban sugar made under a preferential agreement that had been in effect for many years. Castro was accused of deliberate and premeditated hostility to the United States. As Cuba's economic life revolves about and depends primarily on sugar, it was necessary for Castro to seek a market for the product. Soviet Russia agreed to purchase large tonnages in return for which a one hundred million dollar credit, later increased, was set up for the purchase of machinery and consumer goods in Russia and for the construction of an iron and steel mill in Cuba.

In September, 1960, at Bogotá, Colombia, Castro denounced the United States and the Organization of American States (O.A.S.) and refused to sign the

Act of Bogotá; two weeks later he appeared before the United Nations General Assembly in New York and in a long, bitter harangue accused the United States of all manner of crime, including a planned military invasion of Cuba. The following month Castro ordered the seizure and nationalization of nearly 400 foreign firms, mostly United States-owned and some Cuban-owned, including sugar plantations, mining and petroleum enterprises, electric-power companies, telephone companies, many hotels and banks and privately owned business and urban properties. On Oct. 19, 1960, the United States banned all exports to Cuba except medical supplies and food. Relations between the United States and Castro-controlled Cuba were a succession of controversies, not the least of which was an increase of accusations against Castro of being a communist whose friendship with and support by Soviet Russia might lead to international conflict and the communist subversion of much of Latin America. By harassments, threats and attempted intimidation, Castro endeavored to force American evacuation of the naval base at Guantanamo.

As a consequence of Castro's liquidation of those who opposed him (over 500 Batista supporters were put to death by firing squads and many thousands were arrested and thrown into prison), because of constant police surveillance, restrictions on personal movements, the mounting propaganda of communism and the conversion of Cuba to what amounted to a police state with Castro himself as dictator, many Cubans fled to the United States. Nearly 50,000 congregated in and about Miami, Fla.

By the middle of April, 1961, the Cuban opposition felt strong enough to attempt to overthrow Castro and his government by landing troops on Cuban soil. The landings took place early on the morning of April 15, following air bombings on the previous day, but the force used was too small, too poorly armed and badly led. It was no match for Castro's troops using Soviet Russian airplanes, tanks and arms. The people did not rise against the Castro government as hoped and the invaders were driven off, killed or captured.

On May 1, 1961, at a May Day celebration, Castro in a long and bitter speech against his opponents and the United States, informed the Cuban people that Cuba was a socialist state and that there would be no elections as had been promised. He concluded by declaring war on the Catholic Church, the chief center of opposition to his regime. The immediate effect of these proclamations by Castro was to cause Latin American nations to become much less sympathetic to him and his government. Opposition, largely underground, continued, but Castro troops were merciless in their search for anti-Castro arms and opponents, both organized and unorganized. On Dec. 3, 1961, Castro publicly announced: "I am a Marxist-Leninist and will be one until the day I die."

CUBA, INTERVENTION IN, FIRST (1898–1902). The United States, though pledged by the Teller Resolution not "to exercise sovereignty, jurisdiction or control" over Cuba "except for the pacification thereof," found it necessary to occupy and administer the island for three and one half years after the termination of the Spanish-American War. Under the military governorship of Gen. John R. Brooke (Jan. 1, 1899–Dec. 13, 1899) and Gen. Leonard Wood (Dec. 13, 1899–May 20, 1902) notable reforms in the life and government of the island were instituted, including reorganization of the courts, increase in the power and responsibility of the municipalities, establishment of schools, sanitation of cities, the conquest of yellow fever, the legalization of civil marriage, the construction of hospitals, roads, bridges, telephone and telegraph lines and railways. The principal object of the military occupation, however, was to prepare the way for an independent and sovereign Cuban government.

After experiments with new electoral machinery in the municipal elections of June, 1900, Gen. Wood ordered an election of delegates to a constitutional convention, which was not only to frame a constitution for the Cuban Republic but was also to embody in that instrument an agreement with the Government of the United States "upon the relations to exist between that Government and the Government of Cuba." The Convention met in Havana in November, 1900. By February, 1901, it had completed work on the constitution, except that it had neglected to make any provision for relations with the Government of the United States. Elihu Root, Secretary of War, found it necessary, therefore, to formulate a statement of the relations between the two governments upon which the United States was prepared to insist, and this statement, known as the Platt Amendment, the Cuban Convention was required to attach as an appendix to the constitution before the United States would relinquish military control. In general, the Platt Amendment was designed to safeguard the independence of Cuba, to insure the permanence of the reforms instituted under the military government, and to permit the United States to establish naval bases in Cuban waters and to intervene to preserve the independence or the internal order of the island. After it had been, of necessity, accepted by the Cuban Convention, the Cubans were permitted to elect a President and Congress (Dec. 31, 1901), and with the inauguration of President Estrada Palma (May 20, 1902) the American intervention ended and Cuba assumed its place as an independent republic.

CUBA, INTERVENTION IN, SECOND (1906–9). The Cuban Liberal party, defeated in the election of 1905, revolted against President Estrada Palma's government in August, 1906. The president soon afterwards requested the United States to restore order, invoking the Platt Amendment. Though unwilling to intervene, President Theodore Roosevelt sent Secretary of War Taft and Assistant Secretary of State Bacon to render such aid as might be possible. When their attempts to bring about a compromise failed, Estrada Palma and his cabinet resigned, leaving the island without a government. Taft therefore assumed control as Provisional Governor on Sept. 29. He was succeeded in October by Charles E. Magoon. The Congress did not function, but other Cuban officials remained in office.

Order was re-established, and an advisory commission headed by Col. E. H. Crowder drafted important and much-needed laws, paving the way for new elections and reorganizing the administration. Cuban historians have charged that the Provisional Governor permitted undesirable and corrupt political practices and was unduly generous in granting pardons. North American investigators have considered these charges exaggerated. After an election in November, 1908, José Miguel Gómez, a Liberal, was inaugurated as President on Jan. 28, 1909, and the intervention ended.

CUBA, INTERVENTION IN, THIRD (1917–23).

Disputes over a presidential election led the Liberals of Cuba to revolt against President Menocal's administration in February, 1917. The movement collapsed after the United States announced that it would support the constitutional government, but American marines which had been landed to protect foreign interests remained in Cuba to prevent interference with sugar production during World War I.

Cuba declared war on Germany in 1917 and cooperated with the Allies by greatly expanding her production of sugar, which was delivered at a fixed price. With the removal of price restrictions after the armistice, there was a period of wild speculation followed by a disastrous collapse. Meanwhile disputes about the presidential election of 1920 threatened to produce a new civil war. Gen. Enoch H. Crowder was therefore sent to Havana as personal representative of President Wilson in January, 1921. He settled the electoral question, though over the protests of the opposition party, but emergency legislation adopted at his suggestion failed to prevent the collapse of nearly all of the country's banks. His insistence on reforms in the government's financial administration bore more fruit. The budget was reduced and $50,000,000 was borrowed in New York to refund the floating debt. To obtain the consent of the United States to this loan, President Zayas promised a number of much-needed reforms, and appointed the so-called "honest cabinet" to assure their realization. With the money in hand, however, he refused to submit longer to dictation from the United States. Gen. Crowder's status as personal representative of the President of the United States ceased when he was appointed American ambassador to Cuba in January, 1923.

CULPEPER'S REBELLION (North Carolina, 1677–79), one of the first popular uprisings in American history, was caused by the efforts of the Proprietary government to enforce British trade laws. When Gov. Miller arrested George Durant, the leader of the "popular party," John Culpeper and the "rebels" seized the governor and other officials, jailed them, convened a legislature of their own, chose Culpeper governor, and for two years efficiently administered public affairs. Culpeper was finally removed by the Proprietors, but was never punished.

CUMBERLAND, ARMY OF THE, evolved from the Army of the Ohio, originally commanded by Gen. D. C. Buell, was so designated when Gen. W. S. Rosecrans took command, Oct. 30, 1862. He was succeeded by Gen. George H. Thomas, Oct. 16, 1863. Operating mainly in the states of Kentucky, Tennessee and Georgia, it played an important part in the battles of Mill Springs, Shiloh, Perryville, Stone's River, Chickamauga, Chattanooga, Lookout Mountain, Missionary Ridge and in Sherman's Atlanta campaign —in the latter numbering 60,773 men. It comprised regiments chiefly from Ohio, Indiana, Illinois, Michigan, Minnesota and Wisconsin.

CUMBERLAND GAP, in the Appalachian Highlands, is comparable historically to South Pass in the Rockies. It has an altitude of some 1665 feet and is on the border of Kentucky, Tennessee and Virginia, about 60 miles northeast of Knoxville. For centuries before the white man came, the defile allowed the Warrior's Path of Kentucky to connect with the vast system of trails used by the Indians (and the buffalo too) in the southeastern part of North America. Dr. Thomas Walker named the Gap when he and his party came through it to the region westward in 1750, and by 1800 thousands of hunters and settlers had used this pass to enter Kentucky. Through it passed Daniel Boone's party and the Long Hunters in the late 1760's, and there the Indians relieved the Boone party of their pack horses and pelfries in 1771. This gateway again admitted Boone, with his axmen, in March, 1775, as they marked a trail to the Kentucky River for the Transylvania Company. The next month Judge Richard Henderson and others came over this Wilderness Road to make permanent the settlement at Boonesborough.

A mail route through the Gap to Danville was established in 1792, and the legislature of Kentucky appropriated a total of £2500 in 1795 and 1797 to build a road from Crab Orchard to the pass. Virginia improved the road on the other side of the opening in 1796. In 1797 the first tollgate in Kentucky was located on this road a short distance north of the defile, and for a time a body of armed men was necessary to compel the payment of tolls at the gate. For many years the people of the commonwealth drove their stock through the Gap to markets on the coast. The Southern and the Louisville and Nashville railroads reached the pass in 1889 and 1890, respectively, and today a great national highway also uses the gateway.

Cumberland Gap was a strategic point during the Civil War. The Confederates occupied it very early, but retired in June, 1862, to strengthen their hold on Chattanooga. Soon thereafter Gen. George W. Morgan, who had been trying to dislodge Gen. Kirby Smith, then in command there, fortified the place and from it distributed supplies to East Tennessee until after Smith's victory at Richmond, on Aug. 30, 1862, when the Confederates occupied the pass again. Gen. Bragg retreated through the defile after his defeat at Perryville in October, 1862, but the Federals did not retake it until September, 1863. They retained possession until the end of the war.

CUMBERLAND ROAD, sometimes called the United States or National Road (especially along its western portions), was the first national road in the United States. Its influence upon the development of the Ohio and upper Mississippi valleys was incalculable. Previous to the construction of this highway the only route through southwestern Pennsylvania to the West had been Braddock's Road. The latter, however, for many years had deteriorated, and travelers had come to prefer the more northerly Forbes Road. In April, 1802, Congress passed an enabling act for Ohio preparatory to its admission into the Union. One of the provisions of this law set aside 5% of the net proceeds of the public lands sold by Congress within Ohio for the building of a national road from the waters flowing into the Atlantic, to and through the state of Ohio. A second act passed in March, 1803, allocated 3 of the 5% for the construction of roads within Ohio and the remaining 2% for the road from the navigable waters draining into the Atlantic to the Ohio River. Congress in March, 1806, provided for the marking and construction of the road from Cumberland, Md., as the eastern terminus, to the Ohio.

The construction of the road began in 1811, and by 1818 the United States mail was running over it to Wheeling. In general the route followed older roads or trails, especially Braddock's Road. Immediately the popularity of the road was tremendous.

Although Maryland, Pennsylvania and Ohio each gave permission (in 1806, 1807 and 1824, respectively) for the building of the road within their boundaries, constitutional difficulties soon arose. In 1822 Congress passed a bill for the establishment of tollgates along the highway to permit the collection of revenues for the repair of the road. President Monroe, however, saw danger in the enforcement of such legislation, and vetoed the bill. Penalties to be inflicted upon those who violated the requirements of the law, in his opinion, would involve an unconstitutional assumption of the police power of the states by the Federal Government. Congress, nevertheless, soon voted

money for repairs and in March, 1825, appropriated funds for extending the road from Wheeling to Zanesville, Ohio. Over this route the highway followed the first road built in Ohio, Zane's Trace, which at Zanesville turned southwestward to Lancaster, Chillicothe and the Ohio River. Parts of the Cumberland Road were later turned over to Maryland, Pennsylvania, Ohio and Virginia (1831–34), tollgates in some cases being erected by the state authorities. From time to time Congress voted additional funds for the continuance of the road through Ohio, Indiana and Illinois. The highway, however, was only completed in Indiana and Illinois after the Federal Government had relinquished its control. The last important Federal appropriation for it was made in 1838, an additional small item on the account of the survey to Jefferson City, Mo., being voted in 1844.

CUMBERLAND SETTLEMENTS. The immense domain acquired by the associates known as the Transylvania Company from the Cherokees in March, 1775, by the Treaty of Sycamore Shoals, covered lands on the Cumberland River and below. Until the state line between Virginia and North Carolina was extended in 1779–80 it was not certainly known whether the country around the French Lick was in North Carolina. Richard Henderson, leader of the Transylvania Company, engaged James Robertson, for years a leader in the Watauga Settlement, to lead a party to French Lick, site of later Nashborough (Nashville), to found a settlement. Henderson accepted appointment as one of North Carolina's commissioners to survey and mark the Virginia-North Carolina line westward. Robertson and a small party set out from the Holston and Watauga on Feb. 6, 1779, for French Lick where cabins were built and corn was planted that bread might be made for the main body of immigrants who were to arrive in the fall. Robertson returned East to lead an overland party to the Cumberland, and Col. John Donelson led a flotilla of flatboats down the Tennessee and up the Cumberland, his daughter Rachel (later Mrs. Andrew Jackson) being one of the many passengers. Several rude forts were constructed, around which settlements formed. After the conclusion of the survey of the state line which demonstrated that the region was in North Carolina, Henderson went to French Lick in April, 1780, and proceeded to organize a government under articles drafted by him, known as the Cumberland Compact, bearing date, May 1, with supplementary articles of the 13th. This instrument embodied agreements between the Transylvania Company and the settlers respecting lands to be acquired from the company, and also some of the main features of the Watauga Association. The legislature of North Carolina, in 1783, declared the Transylvania purchase void, but provided for Henderson and his associates a consolation grant of 200,000 acres of land on Clinch and Powell Rivers.

CURRENCY. In the strictly technical sense a nation's currency is the physically circulating money which is approved by law. In a wider sense it is any form of money which serves as a medium of exchange. In our colonial history there were long periods in which the people used commercial commodities as currency, a great variety of coins of dubious legal standing, and many types of paper money with or without legal standing.

The standard money of a nation is that which is made by law the basic medium in which debts must be paid. Historically, it has been generally a single standard of gold, a single standard of silver, or a double standard of both metals at a fixed ratio. But all countries have undergone crises which drove out metallic money and made paper money the standard. Currency also includes the lesser subsidiary coins of silver and the minor coins of copper, nickel or other base metals. These coins are in various ways attached by law to the standard coin.

For almost two centuries the colonies had no unified currency standard. England's policy was marked by two features: one was complete neglect of the currency difficulties of the colonies; the other was repression of any action by any colony which appeared to contravene British authority or reduce British control of trade with the colonies. The English provided no coins, but frowned on any effort to set up mints in the colonies. They made no regulations to curb excesses in paper money issues until the overissues wrecked the local economy, and then suppressed all issues.

Afflicted by chronic shortage of currency, the colonies used the most inconvenient, confused, and heterogeneous currency in history. Each colony made its own currency laws, and the various colonies made commodities the standard currency along with coins from all parts of the world. Warehouse receipts may perhaps be considered substitutes for currency rather than money, but for decades large transactions were effected with receipts for tobacco and other commodities.

Gradually the Spanish silver coins came to predominate everywhere. They became the standard money. But all accounts were kept in terms of non-existent pounds, shillings, and pence. In the colonial period England had the double standard, but the colonies were not concerned with the English standard. The one local standard was the Spanish dollar, and it was valued in shillings at whatever rate the colony chose.

There were repeated issues of Chinese paper money in very early times, and in 1685 French officers in Canada paid the soldiers with promises to pay government money written on playing cards. But the first formal government paper money in history was issued by Massachusetts in 1690. At first the issues were in large denominations, and there was no intent to use the notes except in large transactions. In the end the notes were used for all government purposes. Inevitably the various colonies ran the gamut from parity with coin to depreciation and repudiation. "New tenor" notes were issued to redeem "old tenor" at a discount. Eventually the home government prohibited all issues.

In the Revolutionary period the Continental currency drove out all metallic money. The notes were issued by both the Continental Congress and the individual states. The issues were very large, and the conduct of the war was greatly hampered by inflation. The notes became practically worthless. After the war Spanish coin slowly returned, and the new government redeemed the notes at 40 to 1, but the mass of the notes had been destroyed or thrown away.

The legal establishment of a national coinage system in 1792 did not establish a national currency. It did commit the country to a bimetallic system, with a new coin standard of gold and a new coin standard of silver, the latter to be a silver-dollar equivalent to the current Spanish dollar. The new system was a humiliating failure. Congress did nothing to remedy the situation. On the contrary, Congress perpetuated the currency of Spanish coins for sixty years by making them legal tender.

By the laws of 1834 and 1837 Congress established a new bimetallic ratio of 16 to 1. These measures, which in the end brought financial and political upheavals, were passed for the benefit of trivial gold mines in Georgia and North Carolina. The immediate effect was to make impossible any coinage of silver. With the supply of Spanish silver inadequate, the country's retail trade was brought to a standstill by 1850. Finally, in 1853, Congress established a subsidiary silver coinage which by 1857 gave the country a satisfactory retail currency and drove out Spanish coins, Spanish denominations, and English accounting. The standard silver dollar, not affected by the laws of 1834 and 1837, was still the legal standard. It had never been in circulation. In 1860 it was an unknown legal fiction.

After 1800 a banking mania seized the country. The banks were under state control, and in most states there was no protection of depositors and no control of note issue. Thousands of banks were organized for the sole purpose of issuing notes to insiders for speculation. A few banks were excellently managed. The United States Bank, the Government's own institution, made strenuous efforts to bring efficiency into the banking business. Andrew Jackson, under pressure from the worst elements in banking, killed the United States Bank.

There were overissues, while redemption in gold was evaded or refused. The country was flooded with notes, the bulk of which were accepted at varying discounts. There were bankruptcies everywhere. This condition obtained until the end of the Civil War.

The Civil War resulted in the disappearance of gold coin, the only metallic money used in large payments. Subsidiary silver, having less value as metal than its currency value, did not disappear until the falling value of the paper money went below the metal value of the silver. This point was reached early in 1862. The United States Notes, known as greenbacks, became the basic currency of the North and, after the War, of the whole country except in California. The greenback era lasted from 1861 to January, 1879, when the notes became redeemable in gold at face value. Inflationist elements in Congress prevented their redemption and destruction.

The disappearance of subsidiary silver in 1862 created chaos. There was an immediate solution, without cost or risk. The quantity of silver in the coins should have been cut in half. The new coins would not have reached the melting point until about the end of the war. The Mint should have been turning out a stream of the coins as soon as Greenbacks went to a discount in gold in 1861.

Secretary Chase did nothing for days. Then, in panic, he asked Congress to make postage stamps a legal tender, and Congress passed the law. The Post Office had no available supply for currency purposes. There were runs on every office. In circulation stamps became a mass of unrecognizable sticky bits of dirty paper. Again in panic Chase, without authority, had the Treasury issue small-denomination paper notes, known as "postage currency." Later on Congress formally provided for fractional paper currency, popularly known as "shinplasters." At one time or another they were in denominations of 50, 25, 15, 10, 5, and 3 cents. They were the retail currency of the country until 1876, when a rising value of greenbacks made it possible for silver coins of the old weights to remain in circulation. In use the fractional notes became ragged and dirty. They streamed into the government by millions, and the cost of replacement was very high. The loss to the public from wear and tear and accidental destruction of the notes amounted to many millions of dollars.

When the silver coins disappeared early in the war, retail stores, ferries, hotels and railroads could not operate. An indescribable mass of substitutes for small change instantly appeared, in the form of physical tokens and fractional paper notes. The tokens were usually imitations of the one-cent piece. They were made in factories and sold to business enterprises. The paper notes had three sources. City governments, such as those of Newark and Wilmington, issued great quantities. Banks everywhere put out small notes. Private enterprises, especially stores and hotels, issued their own notes. All these private issues were illegal by local or Federal law. Most of them were irredeemable, and final holders lost the face value.

In 1873 the country suffered a severe depression.

In the same year the price of silver in terms of gold fell precipitately. These two events changed the history of the United States. For the first time 16 ounces of silver were worth less than one ounce of gold.

In the same year, 1873, while the country was still on a greenback basis, Congress made a general revision of the coinage laws. In this revision the silver dollar was dropped from the list of coins. From 1792 to 1873 the country was legally on a double standard, with free coinage of 371¼ grains of silver into a dollar. The 1873 statute merely put the country on the single gold standard in existence actually since 1834. The unknown silver dollar had never served as a standard or a currency.

In 1874 the silver weight of the old dollar was worth only 97 cents. The silver interests discovered that the law now prevented their making this unearned profit of three cents by coining the silver. They began a drive to restore bimetallism, at the old ratio. Bimetallism at that ratio would have destroyed the American economic system. That such an evil proposal should have been considered seriously seems incredible until it is realized that from the discovery of silver in the West to the present day the powerful corporations which own the mines have influenced elections in the mining states. The false charge was made that the dropping of the silver dollar was a trick perpetrated by Wall Street, the "Crime of '73." Popular support came from the millions of victims of the depression, who were told that bimetallism would bring recovery. The silver interests kept the country in political turmoil until 1900. In that year Bryan was defeated for the second time, and Congress passed a law declaring that the monetary standard of the country was to be the gold dollar. Silver Senators prevented its passage until they added a clause saying that the silver dollar was also a standard coin.

Unable to achieve bimetallism, the silver interests set out to obtain by political pressure measures which would give the silver mine owners a direct subsidy from public funds. This drive has been relentless from 1874 onward. Their first success was the Bland-Allison Act of 1878, passed over Hayes's veto. The law ordered the Treasury to buy not less than $2,000,000 worth of silver bullion per month and coin it into dollars. The public refused to accept the strange coins. The Secretary, without authorization, resorted to a device to force ownership of the coins on the public. He stored the coins and passed out to the public a new note, the silver certificate, redeemable only with the silver dollar.

In 1890 the Sherman Silver Purchase Act was passed. The Treasury was ordered to buy 4,500,000 ounces of silver per month. It was to be paid for by another new note, the Treasury notes of 1890. These notes were redeemable in gold. Adverse economic conditions in 1893 so reduced Government revenues that redemption of the Treasury notes exhausted the gold reserves and brought the Government to the brink of bankruptcy. The crisis brought on the severe depression of 1893. Cleveland, who fought the silver interests with courage and intelligence, called a special session and forced Congress to repeal the Silver Purchase Act.

In 1863 Congress established a new banking system. The new National Banks were to be under Federal control. State banks were permitted to continue, but note issue was to be the privilege of the National Banks only. Gold certificates, which were merely warehouse receipts for gold stored with the Government, had been authorized. They became the chief currency for large transactions, but the National Bank notes were soon the major paper money. By 1870 the commerce of the country was carried on with gold certificates, National Bank notes, greenbacks, fractional paper notes, and minor coins of small value.

The National Bank note system was basically unsound, inadequately serving business needs, causing annual currency stringencies, and giving little profit to the banks. Congress neglected the matter for fifty years. In 1913 the Federal Reserve System was established. Note issue was to be by the twelve Federal Reserve Banks only. The Federal Reserve Notes immediately became the chief currency of the country. For a time there was issued a special type of note, the Federal Reserve Bank note.

In 1933 a World Economic Conference was convened in London at the insistence of President Roosevelt and the English Prime Minister. Its purpose was to stabilize currencies in a world suffering grievously from depression and if possible to restore gold standards that had broken down. In the midst of the negotiations Roosevelt cabled the United States delegation to return home, as he was opposed to the gold standard. The Conference broke up in dismay and shock.

Roosevelt then announced a "gold purchase" program. He had already confiscated all gold in private hands and repudiated pledges to pay in gold on Government bonds; Federal Reserve notes were no longer redeemable in gold. The Government was to buy gold from any source, in arbitrary amounts, at arbitrarily increasing prices, so that the paper money used to buy the gold would represent, per dollar, a constantly declining weight for the gold dollar. At some later time the debased gold dollar was to be the new standard of value. This scheme was supposed to cause a rise in domestic prices proportionate to the debasement of the gold dollar.

Its first effect was to throw world trade into disorder. It did not increase domestic prices. By the end of 1933 the whole world was waiting for the financial structure of the United States to collapse. In January, 1934, Roosevelt halted the program, and Congress fixed a new standard. At the time Secretary of the Treasury Morgenthau was paying

$35 an ounce for gold. Since 1837 the coining value of an ounce of gold had been $20.67 an ounce. The old dollar contained 23.22 grains of gold. The new dollar would contain 13.71 grains. The debasement was 41%.

The gold standard was not restored. No coins of the new weight have ever been made. And no money of the United States is redeemable in gold. It is illegal for any private citizen, except jewelers and industrial users, to possess gold. Our billions in gold are owned by the Government. They lie in an inert mass, underground, at Fort Knox, Ky.

The silver interests were relatively quiet, after their failure to win the election of 1900, until 1933. Of their many devices for extorting a subsidy for silver owners only one seriously menaced the standard currency and needs to be described here. In 1934 on orders from Roosevelt Congress passed the Silver Purchase Act. This measure directed the Secretary to confiscate all silver bullion in private hands. It was to be paid for with paper money at a price about twice its value. The Secretary was then to buy foreign silver in arbitrary amounts at arbitrary prices. The silver was to lie in vaults, with silver certificates issued against it. The silver was to be valued on the books at $1.29 per ounce. When the dollar was created in 1792, with a weight of 371¼ grains, an ounce of silver coined into $1.29. The new law assured, falsely, that an ounce was still worth $1.29.

When the total of silver held, valued in this way, reached one third of the value of all the gold held, the purchases would stop. Stripped of its technicalities, the measure was intended to force the price of silver from around 40 cents an ounce to $1.29. At that point the President would establish a bimetallic system. It is not necessary to describe the extraordinary consequences of this measure. The one-third proportion of silver holdings to gold holdings was not even approached, although the Secretary continued to buy silver. The purchases of foreign silver were eventually stopped.

By 1960 the many varieties of paper currency legalized since 1860 had been almost completely withdrawn, leaving only two, Federal Reserve notes and silver certificates. The Reserve notes are not redeemable, although they are indirectly backed by our gold hoard. The silver certificates are redeemable only in silver dollars, which are in fact merely uncoined or noncirculating subsidiary coins. These two notes are our major currency in an irredeemable paper-money system. Our current coins are the 50-cent, 25-cent, and 10-cent subsidiary silver pieces and the 5-cent and 1-cent minor coins. For many years leading economists and a few members of Congress have urged the re-establishment of the gold standard with paper money redeemable in gold.

CURRENCY, COLONIAL, shows attempts to obviate

the expense of a metallic currency. Wampum beads for a time could be exchanged for beaver skins. But artificial dyeing and overproduction lowered their value. Another device was to make commodities legal tender at certain rates. Virginia in 1619 set a price on tobacco and it became the usual money for many years, but overproduction caused a fall in value and necessitated revaluation. Massachusetts in 1631 made beaver skins legal tender at 10s. a pound and corn at its market price, and in 1640 definite prices were set for grains. South Carolina in 1719 made rice receivable for taxes.

Massachusetts issued paper money in 1690 to pay its soldiers after an unsuccessful expedition against Canada. The example was widely followed and there were great abuses. The notes were rarely paid when promised. They depreciated greatly and creditors were forced to take them for debts. Besides issues for deficits there were issues to loan to farmers and businessmen. The Pennsylvania issue of this kind in 1723 was relatively well managed.

A bank meant an issue of paper money. The most persistent idea was that land might be used as security for notes. A famous case was the Land Bank of 1740 in Massachusetts. Its career was stopped when in 1741 the Bubble Act of 1720 was applied to the colonies.

Massachusetts attempted to remedy the shortage of coins; from 1652 to 1684 her mint coined pine-tree shillings, sixpences and threepences. In an attempt to keep them in circulation they were made about 25% lighter than the corresponding English coins.

The metallic money of the colonies was composed of various foreign coins, mostly Spanish. There was a competitive overvaluation of the coins by the colonies, who hoped in this way to attract the coins.

CURRENCY, CONTINENTAL,

CURRENCY, CONTINENTAL, consisted of bills of credit issued by the Continental Congress and the states to assist in financing the Revolution. The first issue, of $2,000,000, was voted on June 22, 1775, shortly after the battle of Bunker Hill. Between that date and Nov. 29, 1779, the Continental Congress authorized total issues of $241,552,780. In addition to this the states issued bills in the amount of $209,-524,776, and there were doubtless also some unauthorized issues.

This was a tremendous amount of currency, considering the population of the country, and it shortly began to depreciate—slowly at first, more rapidly later. In 1779 the depreciation, in relation to specie, rose from 8 to 1 on Jan. 14, to 38½ to 1 on Nov. 17. In spite of partial redemption and retirement after 1779, the old continental currency depreciated more rapidly than ever. By January, 1781, it was valued at 100 to 1 and by May had practically lost its value. The phrase "not worth a Continental" comes from this period. Finally, under the funding act of 1790, the old continental issues were accepted in subscription of United States stock (bonds) at the rate of 100 to 1.

CURRIER & IVES.

CURRIER & IVES. Nathaniel Currier, a lithographer, began issuing original colored prints in New York in 1835. James M. Ives became a partner in 1857. The firm's prints—sentimental, journalistic, sporting, humorous, etc.—became tremendously popular. When Ives, the survivor, died in 1895, the photograph was displacing the lithograph, and the partners' outmoded pictures, with their slight artistic value, seemed destined for oblivion. But within two decades the craze for antiques made them eagerly sought for, and their prices rose enormously, a single rare subject selling at auction for as much as $3000.

CUSHING'S TREATY

CUSHING'S TREATY (Treaty of Wanghia, July 3, 1844) marked the opening of political relations between the United States and China, and through establishment of the "most-favored-nation" doctrine in matters of commerce definitely secured for this country the trading privileges won by England as a result of the so-called Opium War. It introduced the principle of extraterritoriality in the relations between China and the West. Provision was made that citizens of the United States accused of committing any crime in China should be tried only by their own consul and according to the laws of the United States, and that disputes between American citizens in China should be regulated by their own government.

CUSTOMS, COLONIAL.

CUSTOMS, COLONIAL. Administration of customs in the colonies was the general responsibility of the royal governors or the resident officials. Until about 1675 there were usually no special customs officers. Work in this field was at the beginning chiefly concerned with export duties, often collected in kind. By the 18th century, however, emphasis had shifted to tariffs on imports, collected in cash. British control over the colonies limited imposition of these tariffs for the most part to raw materials, foods and luxuries, often with preferential rates for the British imports. The principal source of revenue for certain colonies was duties on slaves (10% and higher *ad valorem*) and wine (2s 4d per gallon). Discriminatory rates were imposed on intercolonial importations of slaves, food and liquor for protectionist reasons.

There was no uniformity in the colonial customs field. In many colonies duties were very small; but the range was wide—importation of Spanish slaves, for example, was taxed by South Carolina at £150 a head. Concepts of cost, price and value were developed, but without any very clear delineation by the colonial legislators. At the same time, enforcement was a major problem seldom successfully dealt with; distaste for British government taxes encouraged distaste also for colonial revenues, and smuggling was widespread.

Nevertheless, the general outline of what became

19th-century customs administration emerged in the laws of one or another of the colonies: appointment of various customs officers remunerated at least in part out of fees; the submission, under oath, of manifest and invoice declaring the quantity and value of dutiable goods; credit privileges in payment of duties; severe penalties for evasion of duties, the proceeds to be shared with informers or prosecutors; settlement of disputes over value of imports by an impartial board of appraisers.

The last colonial customs regulations were the short-lived laws passed during the Revolution. Most elaborate was New York's Act of 1784, model for the first customs law of the United States. It embodied all of the provisions listed above, plus the privilege of importation in bond, except that the salary of the collector of customs was independent of the fees of his office.

CUSTOMS ADMINISTRATION. The principal task of customs administration is to collect import duties and taxes on imported merchandise. In addition, special duties are collected to protect against injurious foreign dumping, foreign subsidies, improper marking, or false declarations as to antiques, and entry is denied to imports produced with convict or forced labor. Customs determines the payment to be made for drawback where duty-paid articles are processed and exported; it regulates the movement of merchandise in and out of foreign trade zones; it documents and admeasures vessels, collects tonnage taxes, and enforces laws in fields such as those relating to narcotics, purity of foods, export control (*e.g.*, arms and ammunition), and import control (*e.g.*, quotas).

Customs duties were originally either *ad valorem*, calculated as a percentage of value; or specific, assessed on the basis of physical units, *e.g.*, three cents per pound of sugar. Later, *ad valorem* and specific duties were sometimes combined, for example, 10% of value plus three cents a pound. As in colonial times, value was based on price for consumption in the foreign country. Starting in 1922, provision was made for use in certain cases of "United States value" (value of the import in the United States) or cost of production, or, for a limited number of products, notably coal tar, the competitive American product's selling price. The definition of value was further refined in 1922 to be the price in the country of export or the price to the United States importer, whichever was higher. A 1954 amendment to the law established the latter as the basis ordinarily to be used.

To settle inevitable disputes over import valuations Congress established six salaried boards of appraisement in 1818; provided in 1842 for an appeal procedure by "two discreet and experienced merchants" selected by the collector, and set up a Board of General Appraisers in 1890. The functions of this Board were taken over in 1926 by a newly created Customs Court. In the meantime questions of law, but not valuation decisions, were appealable to the Federal circuit courts and, after its creation in 1909, to the Court of Customs Appeals, later (1929) the Court of Customs and Patent Appeals.

Major responsibility for customs administration is vested in the Treasury Department and its Bureau of Customs, in association with the U. S. Tariff Commission, established in 1916, and the Department of Justice.

CUSTOMS REVENUES. Duties on imports were considered a natural source of revenue when the U. S. Constitution was adopted, preferable to the hated British stamp and excise taxes, relatively easy to collect, and "scarcely felt by taxpayers." In most pre-Civil War years they represented well over 95% of all revenues, except when proceeds from the sale of public lands ran unusually high.

As provided for in the first Tariff Act (1789) the customs duties were collected for two purposes: revenue and protection. In the early years collections averaged 8½% of the value of imports. Duties were doubled during the War of 1812, and further increased in 1816 to an average of 30% of the value of all imports. Twelve years later the average rate was up to 45% (the "Tariff of Abominations"), but improved fiscal conditions were thereafter responsible for a general reduction, to 15% in 1840, 23% in 1846, and 16% in 1857.

Fiscal problems generated by the Civil War were responsible for a rise in the over-all rate to 44% (1864). At the same time internal revenue taxes, until then of little or no importance, were imposed in amounts substantially equal to customs collections. In subsequent years the over-all rate of duty was lower, fluctuating between 21% (1894) and 30% (1876, 1897) of the value of all imports before the end of the century and going down to 14% by 1913. During none of these years was customs' share of the revenue much over 50%.

After enactment of a Federal income tax (1913), customs' share of the revenue became steadily less, dropping to under 5% at the conclusion of World War I. From then until World War II it varied between roughly 5% and 15% of total revenues; after World War II the amount of customs collections greatly increased, but its share of total revenues dwindled to around 1%. The ratio of duties to the total value of imports was 14.7% at the passage of the 1922 Tariff Act, and 14.8% at the passage of the 1930 Act. Starting in 1934, tariff reductions were made on a reciprocal basis with other nations, and over the next quarter century the ratio of duties to the total value of imports declined to between 5.5% and 6.5%.

DADE MASSACRE. On Dec. 23, 1835, at the outbreak of the Florida War, Maj. Francis L. Dade, with a force of 112, left Fort Brooke on Tampa Bay, to reinforce the garrison at Fort King, about 130 miles to the northeast. To prevent surprise Maj. Dade sent out flanking parties, but when open country was reached by Dec. 28 they were not considered necessary. It is believed that the Indians got information of the movement from the guide, Luis Pacheco, a slave, who from time to time left the troops. What they learned led them to choose the open country for an attack. The morning of the 28th was chilly, and the soldiers were unprepared, having buttoned their overcoats over their ammunition boxes. To conceal themselves the Indians hid in saw palmetto patches, and at eight o'clock they launched their attack. Ransome Clark, one of the four survivors, related that he heard the report of a rifle shot in the direction of the advance guard, and before he had time to think a volley was poured at the column, and half the command went down. The remaining men concealed themselves as best they could and opened a sharp fire of musketry. The force had a six-pounder, which frightened the Indians away until the unwounded soldiers could begin building a log breastwork, but it was only knee high when the Indians returned and finished their deadly work.

DAIRY INDUSTRY, the strongest and most stable single source of farm revenue in the United States, began its rise when, in 1611 at Jamestown, the colonists first imported cattle. The *Mayflower* carried no cows. During the first winter at Plymouth, malnutrition was a large factor in the nearly 50% mortality, which included every child under two years. In 1624 the *Charity* landed three Devon cows at the Massachusetts settlement and nutrition difficulties were markedly reduced. Into the extending colonies, importations were continued from England, Spain, Holland, Sweden, Denmark.

The early colonial town-dweller kept one or two cows, or bought milk from a neighbor. As the town grew, raw milk—of highly dubious quality and safety —was peddled in tin buckets. Later, milk was vended from a horse-drawn, victoria-like wagon. In the fall cows usually went dry, and there was a scarcity of milk in winter.

As pasturage within the city limits was crowded out, nearby farmers began the delivery of milk, but through the early 19th century, the lack of sanitation, refrigeration and rapid transportation severely limited the distance which milk could be transported without souring. Gradually, however, the use of ice became common, and in 1841 regular shipment of milk by rail began—from Orange County, N. Y., to New York City. Dairying could then be carried on at greater distances from markets. Still, as the economic value of dairying rose, the purity and quality of market milk long remained unsatisfactory. Herds were not tested for diseases, while conditions

of milking and handling were unsupervised. Milk quality and winter production were not significantly improved until after the mid-19th century, when more attention was given to feeding and breeding.

Toward the end of the century, advances in dairy technology revolutionized the industry. In 1878 DeLaval patented the centrifugal separator. More convenient and more sanitary distribution resulted from the invention of the glass milk bottle by Thatcher in 1884. Between 1880 and 1890 the spread of artificial refrigeration lowered prices and changed marketing methods. In 1890 Babcock devised a butterfat test which measured cream content and sped the development of commercial milk handling. In the same year, tuberculin testing of herds marked the start of dairying's unsurpassed achievements in disease control.

Meanwhile, milk-borne epidemics were common. Each summer, thousands of city children died from cholera infantum. Impressed by this dreadful mortality, Nathan Strauss of New York City financed the first distribution of pasteurized milk in 1893— then a new application of Pasteur's technique of killing germs by thermal treatment. When infant mortality significantly declined, commercial pasteurization won recognition. In 1908 Chicago, and in 1912 New York City, made pasteurization of milk compulsory. Today, almost all milk sold in cities and towns is thus made safe.

With the turn of the century, sanitary regulations and education were extended to the farm, and progress in milk sanitation has been still more rapid. Since the introduction of the U. S. Public Health Service Standard Ordinance in 1923 and strong local enforcement measures, milk sanitation has gone forward in even the most isolated areas of the nation. Safe milk is a commodity taken for granted.

In promoting the safety of milk, in inspiring confidence in its purity, and in stimulating demand, pasteurization had unique influence. Steady improvements in other dairy hygiene, in production per animal, in the efficiency of plant machinery, and in methods of refrigeration and distribution, have been basic in establishing the United States as the world's leading dairy nation. Bovine tuberculosis has been practically eliminated as a factor in national health; brucellosis and mastitis are being brought under control.

There has been a long-term downward trend in cow population which has declined every postwar year, except 1953, and which reached an all-time low of 19,300,000 head in 1959. Conversely, the trend in milk output per cow has been rising steadily. In 1850 the average annual yield per cow was 700 quarts; in 1959 it was more than 3300 quarts, and the trend may go higher.

Transportation of milk has been remarkably facilitated from farms to the great cities by insulated tank trucks (since 1914) and tank cars (since 1924) wherein milk may be shipped hundreds of miles without change. Further, nutritional science—ever considering milk the prime basis for research—has set forth the irreplaceable role of milk, particularly its balance of vitamins and minerals in the diet, especially for the young. National health has been immeasurably benefited, as milk and dairy foods have become an integral part in health education programs.

Since World War II the dairy industry has kept its products in line with latest scientific findings and applications. The process of homogenization has been applied to milk, giving it a more even texture and increasing its digestibility. New dry milk products have been developed and improved. Packaging techniques in glass and paper cartons have become more varied and in line with consumer demand.

The economics of the dairy farmer has been profoundly altered. Formerly he was able to sell his commodities direct to the consumer. Well over half of the money paid for milk and cream in cities represents the expenses of transporting from the farm, pasteurizing, bottling, delivering, cleaning and sterilizing equipment. More than half of this cost is labor. The remainder must support plants, plant equipment, facilities for distribution and other fixed overhead. The farmer's share of the money paid for milk and cream does, however, represent an assured and eminently constant income, as a result of the volume of city milk and cream consumption. In many areas, farmers and others in the dairy business have asked the Federal Government to set up milk marketing orders designed to regulate the handling of milk within a defined area. The milk marketing orders set minimum prices which handlers (bottlers) who distribute milk must pay to dairy farmers.

A cash income of more than $4,500,000,000 is annually derived by United States dairy farmers from milk and its products—the yield from over 19,000,000 cows distributed among 4,000,000 farm families. An estimated 250,000 workers are engaged in processing and delivering dairy products. The nation daily consumes over 80,000,000 quarts of fluid milk, which with the other products of milk constitute 25% by weight of the 1500 pounds of food consumed each year by the average individual. Approximately 50% of the total annual production is utilized as fluid milk and cream. The rest, except for that used on the farm, is chiefly made into butter, cheese, ice cream, evaporated and condensed milk, dry milk and casein. Farm usage of dairy products has become negligible.

In the 19th century butter was almost exclusively a product of the farmstead. Probably the first butter factory was built in 1856 at Campbell Hall, Orange County, N. Y. Although factories spread to the Middle West, greatest strides came with the advent of the cream separator permitting efficient separation of the butterfat, and of the Babcock test, permitting adequate rating of the richness of milk and cream. After 1890 butter became more and more a factory product. By 1960, almost all of this was creamery butter, made in about 4000 creameries with a total annual output of 1,350,000,000 pounds.

Though excellent cheese has been made in this country since colonial days, factory manufacture was not begun until 1851, in Oneida County, N. Y. By 1869, two thirds of the total production was from factories. By 1960 all commercial cheese was factory made. The industry is important in most states, though outstandingly so in Wisconsin and New York. Per capita consumption has increased for several years due in large part to aggressive merchandising. Annual per capita cheese consumption has risen from two and one half pounds forty years ago to eight pounds today.

Ice cream, advertised in the *New York Gazette*, May, 1777, and served at the White House by Dolly Madison, did not become a leading commodity until within recent decades. Annual production is now about 660,000,000 gallons with every indication that this popularity will increase. It is made in ice-cream plants throughout the nation, with Pennsylvania, New York, California, Ohio and Illinois ranking as the top producers in this field.

Sweetened condensed milk, first made in 1856, and unsweetened condensed milk—evaporated milk—together make up the major source of cash income for many dairy farmers. Because of convenience, sterility, high digestibility, and excellent nutritional value, these forms of milk are used in home cooking and infant feeding, as well as in making bread, candy and ice cream. There are condenseries in every area of the country. The annual per capita consumption of evaporated milk was six and one half pounds in 1920, in 1937 more than fifteen pounds, but has declined in recent years to about eleven pounds per capita.

The manufacture of skim-milk powder, attempted as early as 1883, attained importance only within the past generation. Baking and making of confections, ice cream and sausage offer most of the demand for well over 1,700,000,000 pounds produced each year. Dry whole milk is used in the baking and candy industries, and as an infant food. The annual production is over 95,000,000 pounds. Dry buttermilk, with an annual production of approximately 75,000,000 pounds, is a source of feed for poultry and livestock.

Casein, milk's chief protein, prepared commercially from skim milk by precipitation, has many uses: in making of plastics (buttons, buckles, combs, insulators, etc.), sizing for better grades of paper, cold-water paints, glues of high quality.

For milk and commodities derived from milk, United States consumers annually spent by 1960 a total of more than $10,000,000,000 of which farmers got over $4,600,000,000, while more than 25,000,-

000 persons were concerned in such production on the farm, manufacture and distribution. Further, the dairy industry contributed largely to other industries, such as those turning out equipment, vehicles and containers. Thus, millions of new milk bottles were required each year as well as many millions of cans, paper containers and barrels.

Milk and dairy foods are available from home delivery and stores; they are also available from vending machines and through special distribution plans in schools, camps and other institutions, with and without government support. The School Lunch Program and Special Milk Programs, supported in part by U. S. Government funds have helped stimulate milk drinking among youngsters and in their later life.

The U. S. Department of Agriculture points out that when total farm income falls, farm income from milk and milk products becomes proportionately greater because it is more stable through fluctuations of consumers' buying capacity. Moreover, agricultural areas are not benefited solely by the cash income from milk. Generations of agricultural experience demonstrate that soil fertility is uniquely maintained by dairying.

DAKOTA TERRITORY was created by act of Congress, April 2, 1861. It corresponded to the present states of North and South Dakota, and much of Wyoming and Montana. The greater part of this immense region was included in the Louisiana Purchase of 1803; an indefinite part, from the 49th parallel southward, was confirmed to the United States by the Convention of 1818 with England. All of it fell within the vast Territory of Missouri, created in 1812. That part of the Missouri Territory east of the Missouri and White Earth Rivers was added to Michigan Territory in 1834. In 1836 Dakota became part of Wisconsin Territory, in 1838 part of Iowa Territory, and in 1849 part of Minnesota Territory. From 1834 to 1854 the western part of the later Dakota Territory was known as Indian Country and in 1854 was included in Nebraska Territory. Dakota Territory, as created in 1861, included all of Minnesota Territory west of the present boundary of that state and all of Nebraska Territory north of the 43d parallel to the Missouri River with the exception of a small strip west of that river which was annexed to the State of Nebraska in 1882. Montana Territory with the present state limits was cut off from Dakota Territory in 1864. This reduced Dakota Territory to the area included within the present states of Wyoming, North and South Dakota. When Wyoming Territory was created, in 1868, Dakota Territory was reduced to the region comprising the two Dakotas of today.

So far as is known this region was first visited by white men in 1738. The first trading post was built by Jean Baptiste Truteau in Charles Mix County, S. Dak., in 1794. The Lewis and Clark Expedition wintered at the Five Villages in 1804–5. The most famous trading post on the Missouri River was Fort Union built at the mouth of the Yellowstone in 1829.

In 1851 and 1859, Indian reservations were created in this territory but were changed by act of Congress (1863) as a consequence of the Minnesota massacre. After the battle of the Little Big Horn these reservations were again reduced in size by act of Congress. Since that time their extent has been gradually reduced by allotments to individual Indians and the remainder of the land has been opened to white occupation.

The first legislative assembly of the territory convened at Yankton (now S. Dak.) on March 17, 1862. Yankton was the capital until 1883, when it was moved to Bismarck. Legislative sessions were held at Yankton in 1862–83 and at Bismarck 1885–89.

The discovery of gold in the Black Hills in 1874 resulted in the opening, two years later, of that section to white settlement. In 1889 the territory was divided into the existing states of North Dakota and South Dakota.

DAKOTAS, EXPEDITIONS OF GEN. SIBLEY AND GEN. SULLY IN (1863, 1864, 1865). In 1863 Gen. H. H. Sibley was ordered by Maj. Gen. John Pope to march from Camp Pope near Fort Ridgely, Minn., against the hostile Dakota Indians, who had taken part in the Minnesota massacre of 1862, and drive them west toward the Missouri River. At the same time Gen. Alfred Sully was ordered to proceed up the Missouri River and intercept the Indians before they could cross to the western side of the river.

Gen. Sibley set out on June 16, and established his field base at Camp Atcheson, in what is now Griggs County, N. Dak. He defeated the Indians in three battles at Big Mound, Kidder County, July 24, 1863, at Dead Buffalo Lake, July 26, and at Stony Lake, July 28, both of the latter in Burleigh County. The retreating Indians by these successive battles and by continual skirmishing held back Sibley's army until all their women and children had been transferred to the west side of the Missouri River.

Sibley established his camp at the mouth of Apple Creek, near the site of the present city of Bismarck, N. Dak., and waited several days for news of Gen. Sully's command. On Aug. 1 he began his return march by way of Camp Atcheson to Fort Abercrombie, which he reached Aug. 23, 1863.

Meanwhile, Gen. Sully had established his headquarters at Sioux City, Iowa, and organized his force for the march into the Indian Country. He was seriously delayed by lack of equipment and the low stage of the water in the Missouri River. The steamboat accompanying his army carried his supplies to the base camp at Fort Pierre, S. Dak. On Aug. 13 he left this fort with a well-organized force for a quick march northward. On the 30th he learned that Sibley's army had already gone and that a large number of

Indians had recrossed the Missouri River and were hunting buffalo in the vicinity. On Sept. 3 he fought a battle at the present site of the state park of Whitestone Hill, N. Dak. The Indian camp was broken up and their supplies destroyed. Sully returned to his camp at Fort Pierre with a large number of prisoners whom he left at Fort Randall, S. Dak., after which he took his army into winter quarters at Sioux City.

The second campaign was conducted by Sully in the summer of 1864. His army proceeded up the Missouri River from Sioux City, accompanied by two steamboats that carried his supplies to the point of rendezvous at the site of the new army post at Fort Rice, N. Dak. Here he met a force from Fort Snelling, Minn., with an emigrant train bound for the Montana and Idaho gold mines. Leaving a part of his force to construct the fort, he marched northwest to the Indian camp located on an elevated portion of the Bad Lands, still known as Killdeer Mountain. Here a battle was fought July 28, and the Indians were defeated and scattered. Sully then marched northward, forded the Yellowstone River and proceeded down this river to the Missouri which he crossed Aug. 20 by the aid of his steamboats that had been ordered to meet him at this point. He camped in the vicinity of Fort Union and here the emigrant train left for the gold mines. Sully made his return march along the east side of the Missouri River, reaching Fort Rice on Sept. 8, 1864.

The third expedition into Dakota Territory was made by Sully in 1865. His force moved up the Missouri River to Fort Rice and marched north of Devils Lake. On Aug. 2 he went to the Mouse River and then southwest to Fort Berthold. Here he met the famous Indian missionary, Father DeSmet. His force reached Fort Rice on Sept. 8, and went into winter quarters at Sioux Falls, S. Dak.

DALE'S LAWS OF VIRGINIA was a criminal code issued by Sir Thomas Dale for colonial Virginia (1611–16). When Dale arrived in Jamestown, he found the colonists rebellious and disinclined to work. He placed them under martial law and issued a code notable for its pitiless severity even in an age of barbarous punishments.

DALLES, THE, of the Columbia was known as one of the most dangerous points in the early fur trade of the Pacific Northwest both because of navigation difficulties and Indian hostilities. In 1837 it was made the site of a branch of the Oregon Mission (Methodist) to the Indians. During the Indian wars (1848–58) it was an important outpost and base of supplies.

The physical basis for its importance is found in the fact that the Columbia River falls some eighty feet in about twelve miles, its course being restricted to a narrow channel. The name was given by the French-Canadian *voyageurs* because the smooth water-worn rocks of the channel suggested flagstones (*les dalles*). The water backed up by the Bonneville dam now covers "the dalles."

"DAMN THE TORPEDOES." A reply by Admiral Farragut to a warning of the dangerous proximity of submerged torpedoes (now called mines) at the critical juncture of the battle of Mobile Bay (Aug. 5, 1864). As the Union fleet approached the harbor entrance, which was known to be nearly closed by mines, the monitor *Tecumseh* struck a mine and immediately sank. The *Brooklyn,* leading the main column, was consequently stopped unexpectedly, and the following ships closed into a disordered group threatened with early defeat by a heavy cross fire from Confederate forts and fleet. Farragut in the flagship *Hartford* took the lead, signalling the fleet to follow, and despite the warning cry from the *Brooklyn* steamed safely through the mine fields.

DANBURY HATTERS' CASE (Loewe v. Lawlor). In 1901–2 a union, the United Hatters of North America, attempted to force the unionization of the employees of Dietrich Loewe and partners, a hat-making concern in Danbury, Conn. The Loewe company resisted the move, and a strike and nationwide boycott were instituted by the union. Loewe thereupon brought action against the 191 members of the local union as violators of the Sherman Antitrust Law. A district court agreed with this contention and fixed $74,000 as the damages due the company. The circuit court of appeals overruled this verdict, but in 1908 the U. S. Supreme Court reversed the circuit court and sent the case back for retrial. In 1912 the court of appeals, thus instructed, decided upon $80,000 as Loewe's damage, which, under the law, was to be trebled, the total sum with costs being more than $250,000. The union not being incorporated, the defendants were individually liable for their share of the penalty. The union's central organization had agreed in 1903 to back the local members in their fight, and this agreement was later taken over by the American Federation of Labor; but in 1913 the Federation disclaimed further responsibility, though it took up a collection for the hat workmen. In 1917 the district court ordered the sale of the homes of 140 workmen in Danbury, Bethel and neighboring towns to satisfy the judgment. The men had already paid about $60,000, but the accumulated interest brought the total still remaining to about $250,000. The effect upon the city of Danbury was little short of a major calamity.

DANCING RABBIT CREEK, TREATY OF (Sept. 27, 1830), provided for the final extinction of Choctaw claims to land in Mississippi and the removal of the nation west of the Mississippi. Greenwood Le-Flore, a chief of the Choctaws, persuaded his nation to accede to the white demands and was rewarded. The cession totaled 7,796,000 acres; many speculative frauds followed.

DARK AND BLOODY GROUND was the name given Kentucky at the time of settlement. No Indian tribe possessed claim to Kentucky, and there was a tug of war for its possession between the northern and southern tribes. Because of this the land of Kentucky was truly "dark and bloody." When representatives of the Transylvania Land Company signed the Treaty of Sycamore Shoals in 1775, Chief Dragging Canoe of the Cherokees said that they had secured "a dark and bloody ground." The whites realized this in years of fighting the Indians. Later Kentucky has been called "a dark and bloody ground" because of its tragedies, feuds and civil outbreaks.

DARK DAY (May 19, 1780, in New England). The sun rose clear and bright. At about nine darkness gradually developed. That evening the moon appeared blood red and the earth was wrapped in impenetrable darkness. Religious people thought it a direct fulfilment of Bible prophecy. Scientists conjectured its cause to have been smoke from fires on the frontier.

D'ARTAGUETTE'S DEFEAT (1736). When Bienville, governor of Louisiana, decided in 1736 to exterminate the Chickasaws because of their long and successful opposition to the French, he ordered the Chevalier d'Artaguette, in command of Fort Chartres in the Illinois country, to lead a force from the north against the main Chickasaw villages in the northeastern part of the present State of Mississippi. Bienville, meanwhile, led a larger force up the Tombigbee from the south with the same objective. Obeying instructions, d'Artaguette collected 1200 Indians and arrived at the villages on May 9, the date specified. Here he waited in vain for Bienville, who was unavoidably detained, until the unrest of his Indians forced him into a fatal attack. In the course of the battle he was wounded, and together with a score of his countrymen, including Vincennes, captured by the Chickasaws. After the defeat of Bienville, who finally arrived towards the end of the month, the Indians burned their earlier captives at the stake.

DARTMOOR PRISON, located in Devonshire, England, was used for the confinement of American naval prisoners during the War of 1812. The first Americans were brought there April 3, 1813. Their number was increased until April, 1815, when 5542 Americans were confined in the prison. During this period there were 252 deaths. Discipline was strict and rations scanty, but hospital arrangements were excellent. On April 6, 1815, the captives, indignant because of their continued confinement after the conclusion of peace, and angry because of damaged hardtack issued them, staged a noisy demonstration. The commandant called for troops who fired on the Americans, killing seven and wounding sixty. A joint English-American commission, which subsequently investigated the incident, exonerated the commandant, but blamed the soldiers for firing after the prisoners had retreated. The British government provided for the families of the slain, and pensioned the disabled. The prisoners were released in April, 1815.

DARTMOUTH COLLEGE v. WOODWARD (1819) extended judicial interpretation by declaring private-corporation charters to be contracts and hence by the contract clause of the Constitution immune from impairment by state legislative action. Circumstances aligned Republicans against Federalists and equalitarianism against religious establishment to complicate an aggravated educational squabble. The president of the college, John Wheelock, was deposed (Aug. 26, 1815) by the self-perpetuating board of trustees established under the charter of 1769 whereby the British crown set up the college to minister to the Indians. Legislative enactments presently altered the charter and brought the institution under state control by enlarging the board, creating a board of overseers appointed by the legislature, with veto on trustee action, and changing its name to Dartmouth University. The College sued William H. Woodward, former secretary-treasurer, now an adherent of the University faction, for recovery of documents and seal. After a state court decision favorable to the University, Daniel Webster argued the case before the Supreme Court in a famous flight of oratory having little bearing upon the point at issue. John Marshall's opinion held that the College Acts were invalid since they impaired contractual (charter) obligations. This decision freed existing corporations from control by the states which created them, and became a bulwark of *laissez faire* and a boon to corporate development. Control was later largely restored by (a) state legislation reserving the right to alter or repeal subsequent charters; (b) judicial decisions forbidding legislatures (1) to grant, by charter, rights which menace the community, or (2) to surrender, by charter, its duty under the police power to protect the life, safety and morals of the community.

DAUGHTERS OF THE AMERICAN REVOLUTION. This is a patriotic society organized at Washington, D. C., Aug. 8, 1890. Its eligibility requirements are descent from one who in military or civil service rendered material aid in the cause of American independence, and acceptability to the local chapter. Its purposes are to perpetuate the memory and spirit of early patriots, to develop enlightened public opinion, and "to cherish, maintain, and extend the institutions of American freedom." In 1960 it had 186,288 members.

DAUGHTERS OF THE CONFEDERACY, THE UNITED (known in the South as U. D. C.), is a patriotic society organized in Nashville, Tenn., Sept.

10, 1894. It was first called National, then after 1896, United Daughters of the Confederacy. Eligibility consists in direct or collateral descent from a man or a woman "who gave personal service or loyal aid to the Southern cause during the war." Its purposes are benevolent, social and educational, "to collect and preserve the material for a truthful history of the War Between the States." Its membership in 1960 was 35,000 members.

DAVIS, JEFFERSON, IMPRISONMENT AND TRIAL OF. Jefferson Davis was imprisoned in Fortress Monroe in May, 1865, charged with treason and complicity in Lincoln's assassination. The Government decided to try him for treason in order to have it decided judicially that the rebellion was unlawful. As he must be tried in Virginia, where he had levied war against the United States, he could not be prosecuted until the Federal courts resumed their functions in that state. It was not until May, 1867, that the United States circuit judges were ready, but then it appeared that the prosecution was not prepared. In fact, the outcome was uncertain, for a Virginia jury might very well refuse to convict, which would be embarrassing. Davis, therefore, was released on bail after two years of confinement.

Public opinion was still bitter and the Johnson administration feared the effects of giving up the case officially. A new indictment was drawn and preparations made to try Davis in May, 1868. However, the Johnson impeachment trial interfered, and it was not until November, 1868, that proceedings actually commenced. Then Davis' counsel pleaded that the Fourteenth Amendment had already punished Davis, and a trial would put him in double jeopardy. Upon this point the judges disagreed, and it was referred to the Supreme Court for decision. In the meantime, on Christmas Day, 1868, Johnson issued a general amnesty proclamation and on Feb. 26, 1869, a *nolle pros.* was entered in the case. Davis was thereby legally freed from any further possible prosecution. He was not tried largely because the law officers of the Government and their advisers dreaded the possibility of an undignified trial or an acquittal.

DAVIS-JOHNSTON CONTROVERSY (1861–65). The Confederate history of the Civil War is shot through with the factional differences between Jefferson Davis and his friends on the one hand, and J. E. Johnston and his partisans on the other. First in the quarrel over relative ranking of general officers and in the aftermath of the First Bull Run; then on the Peninsula and Johnston's relief from command; later, because of Davis' refusal to restore Johnston to the Army of Northern Virginia, now commanded by R. E. Lee, but instead sending him to Tennessee where he served in the winter, 1862–63; then with J. C. Pemberton at Vicksburg in the summer of 1863; and finally, to a climax, in the Atlanta Campaign

with Johnston's relief by J. B. Hood and his restoration nearly a year later after Hood had wrecked his army and the Confederacy was near collapse—constantly this feud colored and determined action. For many years the arguments and accusations echoed savagely throughout the Southland. This feud was not the least of several important and many secondary events that acted to focus the violent anti-Davis, anti-administration sentiment of the winter, 1864–65.

DAWES COMMISSION, commonly called the Commission to the Five Civilized Tribes, was appointed by President Cleveland in 1893 to negotiate with the Cherokee, Creek, Choctaw, Chickasaw and Seminole Indian tribes. The object was to induce these Indians to whom the Dawes Act did not apply to take their lands in severalty, abolish their tribal governments, and come under state and Federal laws. The original commission consisted of Henry L. Dawes, Archibald S. McKinnon, and Meredith H. Kidd. Having secured the necessary agreements with these tribes, it made up tribal rolls, classified the tribal lands and allotted to each citizen his rightful share of the common property. It also had large governmental functions. Its work being finished, the commission was abolished by law on July 1, 1905.

DAWES GENERAL ALLOTMENT ACT OF 1887 provided for the breakup of the Indian tribal relationship and the abandonment of the *domestic nation* theory. Discretionary power was vested in the President to cause Indian reservations to be surveyed in whole or in part, lands so surveyed to be allotted to resident Indians. It did not apply to certain tribes, notably the Cherokee, Creek, Choctaw, Chickasaw and Seminole. If the total area permitted, and unless an existing treaty stipulated larger amounts, each head of a family could select for himself 160 acres and for each of his minor children forty acres. Every unmarried person in the tribe over eighteen years of age, and every orphan, was entitled to eighty acres. Should the land be suitable only for grazing, acreage allotted was to be doubled. After approval of the selections by the Secretary of the Interior, patents were to be issued, and the occupants of the lands became United States citizens, under local, civil and criminal jurisdiction. However, the Indian owners were denied the power of alienation for 25 years, when title in fee might be conferred unless further delay were deemed advisable.

DAWES PLAN, adopted Aug. 20, 1924, resulted from the German default on reparations in January, 1923. A group of experts headed by Charles G. Dawes was chosen in November, 1923, to devise a plan of payments that Germany could meet from year to year, though no total payment was set. The payments were to start with 1,000,000,000 gold marks in 1924–25 and rise to 2,500,000,000 in 1928–29, which thereafter was to be the standard year's payment. It would be increased if an elaborate index showed Germany able to pay more. After 1928 the amount paid was to be readjusted if the value of gold changed at least 10%. The source of payments was an external loan, revenue from bonds and preferred stock of a company organized to take over the German government railroads, debentures issued against German industry, a transport tax and the budget. Foreigners were given representation on the general board of the Reichsbank and the railroad company and certain control over customs and taxes. The obligation of Germany ended when the funds were turned over to the Agent General of Reparations. He had the problem of transferring them. The plan operated successfully until replaced by the Young Plan on May 17, 1930.

DAYLIGHT SAVING. The term commonly applied to a movement originated in England by William Willett in 1907 to utilize summer daylight by advancing the clock in spring and retarding it in fall. This would offset the tendency of inhabitants of cities to retire later than dark and arise after sunrise. The idea is not new. In 1784 Benjamin Franklin wrote about it from Paris. Willett's plan made a strong appeal to many nations after the outbreak of World War I. No interest for it was shown in the United States until 1916 when agitation for it began. A law on this matter was passed by the Congress of the United States and took effect March 30, 1918. (The law required the clock to be turned ahead one hour on the last Sunday in March of each year, and retarded the last Sunday in October.) There was much opposition to this movement, and especially to the way the law was applied, by farmers, as well as others, and a bill was passed repealing the daylight saving law, over the veto of President Wilson, on Aug. 20, 1919. Daylight saving has been adopted locally in the United States since.

DEARBORN, FORT (1803–36). The value of Chicago as a center of control for the region between Lake Michigan and the Mississippi had been recognized long before the American Government was established. At Greenville, in 1795, the cession of a tract six miles square at Chicago was exacted, to serve as the site for a future fort, and early in 1803 its establishment was decreed. In July, troops were sent from Detroit, and the construction of Fort Dearborn, at the mouth of the Chicago River, was begun. Capt. John Whistler was commandant until 1810, and Capt. Nathan Heald from 1810 to 1812. With the outbreak of the War of 1812 several hundred Indians assembled at Chicago. On July 29 Gen. Hull at Detroit ordered Heald to evacuate Fort Dearborn and retire to Fort Wayne. Complying, his command was destroyed by the Indians a short distance from the fort, on Aug. 15.

Four years later, July 4, 1816, Chicago was reoccupied and erection of the second Fort Dearborn

was begun. It was garrisoned until 1823, when the shifting of Indian trade and population induced the Government to withdraw the garrison. The measure proved premature, however, for increasing trouble with the Winnebago and other tribes compelled its restoration in 1828, and the establishment of new forts at Portage and Prairie du Chien, Wis. Three years later the Fort Dearborn garrison was again removed, but the outbreak of the Black Hawk War brought back the troops in 1832. The marvelous development of modern Chicago began in 1833. The red man vanished into the sunset and in 1836 Fort Dearborn was again, and finally, evacuated. For a third of a century it had guarded the midwestern frontier. Its military reservation was transformed into modern Grant Park, the magnificent front door to the thronging Chicago Loop.

DEARBORN WAGON was a light, four-wheeled vehicle, usually with a top, perhaps with adjustable side curtains, and ordinarily for one horse, said (Frances Wright Darusmont, 1821) to have been designed by Gen. Henry Dearborn. It generally had one seat (but sometimes two or three), which may have rested on wooden springs. In 1844 the spring dearborn, possibly a later improvement, is mentioned. The "station wagon" of its day, it was in almost universal use in the United States, from about 1819 to 1850 or later, by truck farmers, pedlars, emigrants, and people traveling for pleasure.

DEATH VALLEY, a desert valley nearly a hundred miles long, in California near the Nevada line, is principally known for its production of borax. It is the bottom of a volcanic fault or trough, partially filled by alluvial deposits and salts, the last of a series of dry lakes where the drainage from the Sierra Nevada Mountains finally settles at Bad Water, 276 feet below sea level.

Death Valley received its name from the Manly-Hunt party of emigrants, many of whom perished there in 1849. While coming south from Salt Lake City, twenty-seven wagons separated from the rest and tried to find a short cut to California. They were attacked by Paiute Indians and in the bottom of Death Valley killed their oxen, burned their wagons to cure the meat, and struck out on foot to the west. Thirteen died along the way. The rest succeeded in reaching California.

At Emigrant Spring a rich deposit of silver was found, the first of the many lost mines for which Death Valley is famous. In recent years that of Death Valley Scotty is best known.

DEBS, IN RE. Influenced by his attorney general, Richard Olney, and convinced that the Pullman strike of June–July, 1894, was interfering with interstate commerce and the delivery of mails, President Cleveland ordered troops into Chicago and moved against the strikers in the courts. Although the Sherman Antitrust Act had proved of little value in controlling monopoly and Olney himself considered it useless, he asked and secured from the United States court in Chicago an injunction based on this act and on the law prohibiting obstruction of the mails. Described as "one of the most sweeping injunctions on record," it forbade Eugene V. Debs, president of the American Railway Union, and other officers "from in any way or manner interfering with, hindering, obstructing or stopping" the business of the railroads entering Chicago. Arrested for alleged violation of the injunction on July 10, Debs and other leaders were found guilty, Dec. 14, of contempt and sentenced to jail, the sentences varying from three to six months (U. S. v. Debs, 64 Fed. 724). Carried to the Supreme Court on a writ of habeas corpus, the sentence was upheld, May 27, 1895, on the Government's constitutional authority over interstate commerce and the mails (In re Debs, 158 U. S. 564). Avoiding examination of the Sherman Act, the Court rested its decision upon "broader grounds."

DEBT, PUBLIC. With the establishment of the National Government, the problem of what to do with the debts that had been created by the Continental Congress and the states became of pressing importance. There was general agreement that the foreign debt, which, with arrears in interest, amounted to $11,710,000, should be assumed by the new Federal Government, but there was less unity of opinion about the assumption of the domestic debt, whether incurred by the states or the Continental Congress.

Alexander Hamilton, first Secretary of the Treasury, held that the Federal Government should assume the domestic, as well as the foreign, debt in order to assure a high rating to the public credit. Hamilton estimated that the domestic debt (exclusive of state debts) amounted to $27,383,000, plus accrued interest of $13,030,000, with an additional $2,000,000 for unliquidated debt. The question of the assumption of this domestic debt was debated at length in Congress. Hamilton's counsel finally prevailed and it was provided that all holders of outstanding certificates were to receive their face value with interest, except for outstanding Continental bills of credit which were to be redeemed at 100 for 1 in specie.

In spite of considerable opposition, Hamilton was also successful in carrying through his plan for the assumption of state debts, some $18,271,786 of these obligations being actually assumed by the Federal Government. The total of these items led to what was, at the time, a fairly large debt, amounting to $75,463,476 in 1791.

From 1791 on, the public debt varied between $75,000,000 and $87,000,000 until 1806, after which it was reduced to a low of just over $45,000,000 in 1812. The War of 1812 naturally brought about a sharp increase in the debt to $127,334,933 in 1816.

Thereafter it was again reduced steadily to only $37,513 in 1835. From 1835 on the debt varied considerably from year to year, but remained below $100,000,000 until 1862, the highest figure being $90,380,874 in 1861, with much smaller totals prior to that year.

As with all wars, the Civil War brought a heavy increase in the public debt to a peak of $2,332,-331,208 in 1866. Following this year, reduction of the debt again set in, although the interest-bearing debt did not fall below $1,000,000,000 until 1888, reaching a low of $585,029,330 in 1892. There was then a moderate expansion of the Federal debt to slightly over $1,000,000,000 in 1899, after which year it fell again slightly, remaining somewhat under $1,000,000,000 from 1901 through 1916.

Beginning in 1917, our participation in World War I, with its attendant issues of Liberty Bonds, brought an unprecedented increase in the public debt to the enormous total of $25,234,496,274 in 1919. As had been the policy following previous wars, the Government began to reduce the debt as soon as possible and had effected a reduction of $15,770,000,000 by the end of the year 1930.

As the recession in business became increasingly severe, government revenues fell off and expenditures increased. This combination brought with it the need for increased borrowing by the Federal Government. The debt increased steadily to $22,158,-000,000 at the end of June, 1933. Even with the recovery in business, which set in in the spring of 1933, the Government continued to spend huge amounts in excess of revenues and the debt rose to $37,000,000,000 in the spring of 1938. In addition, beginning in 1934, the Government guaranteed the obligations of certain Federal corporations, the amount of such guaranteed securities being $4,646,-000,000 in March, 1938. There was also, at that date, $556,000,000 of non-interest-bearing debt, so that the total gross debt, including guaranteed securities, amounted to $42,202,000,000.

Between March, 1938, and December, 1941 (when the United States entered World War II), the total gross debt had increased to $64,300,000,000, much of this increase being attributable to heavy expenditures in connection with the defense program of 1940–41. Our participation in World War II was accompanied by an enormous increase in the total gross debt to slightly over $280,000,000,000 in January, 1946. Between the latter date and mid-1948 the gross debt declined to approximately $252,300,-000,000, the low point of the postwar period.

The gross debt reached a new peak of $280,800,-000,000 at the end of 1955 as a result of expenditures attending the conflict in Korea. A reduction of some $10,000,000,000 was effected by mid-1957, since which time the total gross debt has risen to an all-time high of $291,400,000,000 (October 1959). This most recent increase in the public debt was a cause of grave concern since it resulted from a large increase in nondefense expenditures not covered by revenue in a peacetime period. Sound financing of the government calls for a sufficient decrease in such expenditures to permit a substantial reduction in the Federal debt, but the prospects for such action were bleak in 1960.

State and local government debt has been increasing rapidly since World War II, from about $12,000,-000,000 in 1946 to better than $55,000,000,000 in 1959. If the latter amount was added to the Federal debt, the total public debt of the United States totaled better than $345,000,000,000 as 1959 drew to a close. The fact that state and local government indebtedness was almost certain to show a continuous increase in the years ahead was another cogent reason for substantial reduction in the Federal debt.

DEBTS, COLONIAL AND CONTINENTAL. As custom, imperial restrictions and local circumstances led the colonies to raise extraordinary public funds by lotteries and emission of paper currency rather than by borrowing, colonial debts, in the present sense, were not heavy. However, just as extraordinary expenses of King William's War caused Massachusetts first to issue paper currency in 1690, the subsequent struggles with the French and Indians not only forced other colonies to follow suit but also to resort to other expedients which, by 1756, included borrowing funds for public purposes. In 1775 these debts, plus others incurred by British attempts at imperial reorganization, totaled over £2,500,000. Business depression, absence of capital, and lack of foreign credit notwithstanding, the states incurred heavy debts during the Revolution. As Jefferson wrote, "Nobody knew what those debts were, what their amount or what their proofs," but the states floated domestic and foreign loans, gave innumerable "certificates" for war supplies, and incurred debts totaling, according to Hamilton's estimate, $21,000,000. The Federal Government actually funded and assumed state debts (1790) in a total of $18,271,786, to which more than $3,000,000 was subsequently added.

Meanwhile, the Second Continental Congress and the Congress of the Confederation had incurred heavy Continental debts. Despite constitutional weaknesses, the Continental Congress (Oct. 3, 1776) authorized a domestic loan of $5,000,000. When interest was raised from 4% to 6% and the Congress began using foreign loans to pay interest on domestic debts, the domestic loans finally rose to $11,585,506 (specie value); certificates of indebtedness for war supplies added $16,708,000 (Hamilton's estimate), and the total domestic debt (1790) according to Hamilton's *Report* was $40,423,085. Moreover, the Congresses had gained credit abroad. Foreign loans negotiated between 1777 and 1783 totaled $7,830,517, of which $6,352,500 were French; $174,017, Spanish; and $1,304,000 Dutch. After the war, the Confederation

sank further into debt abroad. Dutch loans continued, totaling $2,296,000 (1784–89), and as Congress was unable to pay all interest and installments on foreign loans, the foreign debt rose to $11,763,110 by Jan. 1, 1790.

DECLARATION OF INDEPENDENCE. June 7, 1776, Richard Henry Lee, on behalf of the Virginia delegation, submitted to the Continental Congress a resolution stating that "these United Colonies are, and of right ought to be, free and independent States, . . . and that all political connection between them and the State of Great Britain is, and of right ought to be, totally dissolved" (*Journals of Congress*, Ford ed., V, 424). This resolution was voted by Congress on July 2, and is, strictly speaking, the official declaration of independence from Great Britain. Meantime, on June 10 Congress voted to appoint a committee to "prepare a declaration" in support of the above resolution. The committee consisted of Thomas Jefferson, John Adams, Benjamin Franklin, Roger Sherman and Robert R. Livingston (*Ibid.*, 428–31). June 28 this committee reported to Congress the draft of a declaration entitled, "A Declaration by the Representatives of the United States of America in Congress Assembled," which with some modifications was adopted on July 4 (*Ibid.*, 491, 510). This is the document popularly known as the Declaration of Independence.

The task of drafting the Declaration was intrusted to Jefferson (*Works of John Adams*, II, 514; *Writings of Jefferson*, ed. 1869, VII, 304). Before submitting his draft to the committee, Jefferson showed it to Adams and Franklin, who together made some 26 alterations, mostly verbal, but including three new paragraphs (C. L. Becker, *The Declaration of Independence*, 160). As thus corrected, the draft was submitted to the committee, and by it, unaltered, to Congress. During the debates in Congress further changes were made, the most important being the omission of the paragraph on the slave trade, and the rewording of the final paragraph (*Ibid.*, 174 ff.). In spite of these alterations, the famous document is essentially the work of Thomas Jefferson.

In its final form the Declaration is entitled, "The Unanimous Declaration of the Thirteen United States of America." Strictly speaking, therefore, the title "Declaration of Independence" is a misnomer. It is a misnomer, not only because the document does not bear that title, but because it was not the act by which independence was declared (that had been done on July 2) but a document proclaiming to the world the reasons for declaring independence. The purpose of the Declaration is stated in the first paragraph: "When in the course of human events it becomes necessary for one people to dissolve the political bands which have connected them with another, . . . a decent respect to the opinions of mankind requires that they should declare the causes which impel them to the separation." Having stated its purpose, the Declaration goes on to formulate a theory of government which made the separation legitimate, and then to state the specific events which made it necessary.

The theory of government is formulated in the second paragraph. It is a brief statement of the theory of "natural rights," commonly accepted in the 18th century: "We hold these truths to be self-evident, That all men are created equal, that they are endowed by their creator with certain unalienable rights; . . . that to secure these rights governments are instituted among men, deriving their just Powers from the consent of the governed; that whenever any form of government becomes destructive of these ends, it is the right of the people to alter or to abolish it, and to institute new government, laying its foundation on such principles and organizing its powers in such form, as to them shall seem most likely to effect their safety and happiness."

The implications of the theory are that the people of the colonies were a free people and not merely part of the British people, and that their governments were separate entities and not creations of the British Parliament. Both of these implications were contrary to the assumptions on which the colonists had conducted their quarrel with the British government since 1765. They had repeatedly and consistently claimed to be British subjects, and to desire no more than the rights of British subjects within the empire. That they were in some measure subject to the laws of Parliament was conceded; the controversy turned on what rights the British constitution accorded them, what limits it placed on the authority of Parliament to legislate for them. They did not claim that these rights could justify separation from Great Britain, or complete freedom from Parliamentary legislation. But as the quarrel developed, the rights claimed were extended to meet the practical exigencies of the conflict. In 1765 the claim was "no taxation without representation." In 1768, in connection with the Townshend Acts, the claim was that a customs duty intended to raise a revenue was a tax, or more broadly that colonial legislatures had an independent legislative jurisdiction in internal as distinct from imperial matters. But in 1768 Franklin went farther. "Something," he said, "might be made of either of the extremes: that Parliament has a power to make *all laws* for us, or that it has a power to make *no laws* for us; and I think the arguments for the latter more numerous and weighty than those for the former" (*Writings of Benjamin Franklin,* Smyth ed., V, 115). In the following year James Wilson developed this idea in a reasoned theory, designed to prove that since men are by nature free and equal no people, such as the British, have a right to govern any other people, such as the American, without that other's consent (*Works of James Wilson,* ed. 1804, III, 99). Although Wilson's pamphlet was not published at the time, his

theory is essentially the same as that used by Jefferson in the Declaration of Independence.

It was indeed the only theory upon which the claim for separation from Great Britain could be justified as a right. And by 1776 the colonists had been forced to adopt the policy of separation in place of the former policy of demanding the rights of British subjects within the empire. The reason for the change was that, since Great Britain was determined to fight rather than make further concessions, and since there was no prospect that the colonies could succeed in the war without French aid, it was necessary, in order to obtain French aid, to come out frankly for independence: France would fight to disrupt but not to consolidate the British empire. To justify the claim for independence, the Declaration therefore assumed that the colonies were and always had been "free peoples." Hitherto they had voluntarily associated themselves with the British people, by voluntarily professing allegiance to the same king, and voluntarily submitting to certain regulations of the British Parliament. The theory implied that the British empire was a confederation of free peoples, any one of which might, at any time it judged expedient, withdraw from the confederation. Now circumstances made it desirable that the American colonies should exercise this right. The circumstances were certain acts of the king which showed a design to subject the Americans to arbitrary control. The greater part of the Declaration consists of an enumeration of these arbitrary acts of the king: "He has refused his assent to laws, the most wholesome and necessary for the public good. He has forbidden his governors to pass laws of immediate and pressing importance," etc.

The Declaration thus consists, (1) of a theory of government which made it legitimate in natural law for the colonies to separate from Great Britain at any time they thought desirable; and, (2) of a list of specific acts on the part of the king which made it necessary in their own interest to do so at the present time. In Great Britain the Declaration was severely criticized for the speciousness of its political philosophy and for the disingenuousness of its charges against the king (John Lind, *An Answer to the Declaration,* 1776). In France Condorcet declared it to be a simple and sublime exposition of the rights so sacred and so long forgotten (*Oeuvres,* VIII, 11). Lafayette placed a copy of the Declaration in his house, leaving beside it a vacant space to be filled by a similar declaration of rights for France at some future time. (*Mémoires et correspondance,* III, 197). Throughout the 19th century it was regarded, by progressive and radical groups, as a great charter of freedom, a classic expression of the principles which they hoped to realize in their own countries.

DECLARATION OF INDEPENDENCE, SIGNING OF. Contrary to tradition early established and maintained, the Declaration of Independence was not signed on July 4, 1776. The *Journal* of the Continental Congress contains, for July 4, a copy of the Declaration in the form in which it was adopted, together with these words: "Signed by order and in behalf of the Congress, John Hancock, President." No other signatures are appended. The secret domestic *Journal* for July 19 contains the following entry: "Resolved that the Declaration passed on the 4th be fairly engrossed." In the margin there is added: "Engrossed on parchment with the title and stile of 'The Unanimous Declaration of the 13 United States of America,' and that the same when engrossed be signed by every member of Congress." On Aug. 2 occurs the following entry in the *Journal:* "The Declaration of Independence being engrossed and compared at the table was signed by the members." Certain members, being absent from Congress on Aug. 2, signed at a later date. (On this question, *see* Hazleton, *Declaration of Independence,* Ch. IX.) This parchment copy of the Declaration, signed by the members of Congress, is carefully kept in Washington. It is identical in wording with the copy in the *Journal* which was adopted by Congress on July 4, although the engraver used a system of punctuation and capitalization which appears to have no justification either in custom or common sense, and which at all events did not follow that of any of the previous copies.

DECLARATION OF INDEPENDENCE *(Text)*
In Congress, July 4, 1776.
The unanimous Declaration of the thirteen united States of America.

WHEN in the Course of human Events, it becomes necessary for one People to dissolve the Political Bands which have connected them with another, and to assume among the Powers of the Earth, the separate and equal Station to which the Laws of Nature and of Nature's God entitle them, a decent Respect to the Opinions of Mankind requires that they should declare the causes which impel them to the Separation.

WE hold these Truths to be self-evident, that all Men are created equal, that they are endowed by their Creator with certain unalienable Rights, that among these are Life, Liberty, and the Pursuit of Happiness—That to secure these Rights, Governments are instituted among Men, deriving their just Powers from the Consent of the Governed, that whenever any Form of Government becomes destructive of these Ends, it is the Right of the People to alter or to abolish it, and to institute new Government, laying its Foundation on such Principles, and organizing its Powers in such Form, as to them shall seem most likely to effect their Safety and Happiness. Prudence, indeed, will dictate that Governments long established should not be changed for light and transient Causes; and accordingly all Experience hath shewn, that Mankind are more disposed to suffer, while Evils are sufferable, than to right themselves by abolishing the Forms to which they are accustomed. But when a long Train of Abuses and Usurpations, pursuing invariably the same Object, evinces a Design to reduce them under absolute Despotism, it is their Right, it is their Duty, to throw off such Government, and to provide new Guards for their future Security. Such has been the patient Sufferance of these Colonies; and such is now the Necessity which constrains them to alter their former Systems of Government. The History of the present King of Great-Britain is a History of repeated Injuries and Usurpations, all having in direct Object the Establishment of an absolute Tyranny over these States. To prove this, let Facts be submitted to a candid World.

HE has refused his Assent to Laws, the most wholesome and necessary for the public Good.

HE has forbidden his Governors to pass Laws of immediate and pressing Importance, unless suspended in their Operation till his Assent should be obtained; and when so suspended, he has utterly neglected to attend to them.

HE has refused to pass other Laws for the Accommodation of large Districts of People, unless those People would relinquish the Right of Representation in the Legislature, a Right inestimable to them, and formidable to Tyrants only.

HE has called together Legislative Bodies at Places unusual, uncomfortable, and distant from the Depository of their public Records, for the sole Purpose of fatiguing them into Compliance with his Measures.

HE has dissolved Representative Houses repeatedly, for opposing with manly Firmness his Invasions on the Rights of the People.

HE has refused for a long Time, after such Dissolutions, to cause others to be elected; whereby the Legislative Powers, incapable of Annihilation, have returned to the People at large for their exercise; the State remaining in the mean time exposed to all the Dangers of Invasion from without, and Convulsions within.

HE has endeavoured to prevent the Population of these States; for that Purpose obstructing the Laws for Naturalization of Foreigners; refusing to pass others to encourage their Migrations hither, and raising the Conditions of new Appropriations of Lands.

HE has obstructed the Administration of Justice, by refusing his Assent to Laws for establishing Judiciary Powers.

HE has made Judges dependent on his Will alone, for the Tenure of their Offices, and the Amount and Payment of their Salaries.

HE has erected a Multitude of new Offices, and sent hither Swarms of Officers to harass our People, and eat out their Substance.

HE has kept among us, in Times of Peace, Standing Armies, without the consent of our Legislatures.

HE has affected to render the Military independent of and superior to the Civil Power.

HE has combined with others to subject us to a Jurisdiction foreign to our Constitution, and unacknowledged by our Laws; giving his Assent to their Acts of pretended Legislation:

FOR quartering large Bodies of Armed Troops among us:

FOR protecting them, by a mock Trial, from Punishment for any Murders which they should commit on the Inhabitants of these States:

FOR cutting off our Trade with all Parts of the World:

FOR imposing Taxes on us without our Consent:

FOR depriving us, in many Cases, of the Benefits of Trial by Jury:

FOR transporting us beyond Seas to be tried for pretended Offences:

FOR abolishing the free System of English Laws in a neighbouring Province, establishing therein an arbitrary Government, and enlarging its Boundaries, so as to render it at once an Example and fit Instrument for introducing the same absolute Rule into these Colonies:

FOR taking away our Charters, abolishing our most valuable Laws, and altering fundamentally the Forms of our Governments:

FOR suspending our own Legislatures, and declaring themselves invested with Power to legislate for us in all Cases whatsoever.

HE has abdicated Government here, by declaring us out of his Protection and waging War against us.

HE has plundered our Seas, ravaged our Coasts, burnt our Towns, and destroyed the Lives of our People.

HE is, at this Time, transporting large Armies of foreign Mercenaries to compleat the Works of Death, Desolation, and Tyranny, already begun with circumstances of Cruelty and Perfidy, scarcely paralleled in the most barbarous Ages, and totally unworthy the Head of a civilized Nation.

HE has constrained our fellow Citizens taken Captive on the high Seas to bear Arms against their Country, to become the Executioners of their Friends and Brethren, or to fall themselves by their Hands.

HE has excited domestic Insurrections amongst us, and has endeavoured to bring on the Inhabitants of our Frontiers, the merciless Indian Savages, whose known Rule of Warfare, is an undistinguished Destruction, of all Ages, Sexes and Conditions.

IN every stage of these Oppressions we have Petitioned for Redress in the most humble Terms: Our repeated Petitions have been answered only by repeated Injury. A Prince, whose Character is thus marked by every act which may define a Tyrant, is unfit to be the Ruler of a free People.

NOR have we been wanting in Attentions to our British Brethren. We have warned them from Time to Time of Attempts by their Legislature to extend an unwarrantable Jurisdiction over us. We have reminded them of the Circumstances of our Emigration and Settlement here. We have appealed to their native Justice and Magnanimity, and we have conjured them by the Ties of our common Kindred to disavow these Usurpations, which, would inevitably interrupt our Connections and Correspondence. They too have been deaf to the Voice of Justice and of Consanguinity. We must, therefore, acquiesce in the Necessity, which denounces our Separation, and hold them, as we hold the rest of Mankind, Enemies in War, in Peace, Friends.

WE, therefore, the Representatives of the UNITED STATES OF AMERICA, in GENERAL CONGRESS, Assembled, appealing to the Supreme Judge of the World for the Rectitude of our Intentions, do, in the Name, and by Authority of the good People of these Colonies, solemnly Publish and Declare, That these United Colonies are, and of Right ought to be, FREE AND INDEPENDENT STATES; that they are absolved from all Allegiance to the British Crown, and that all political Connection between them and the State of Great-Britain, is and ought to be totally dissolved; and that as FREE AND INDEPENDENT STATES, they have full Power to levy War, conclude Peace, contract Alliances, establish Commerce, and to do all other Acts and Things which INDEPENDENT STATES may of right do. And for the support of this Declaration, with a firm Reliance on the Protection of divine Providence, we mutually pledge to each other our Lives, our Fortunes, and our sacred Honor.

John Hancock

NEW-HAMPSHIRE.	*Josiah Bartlett,* *W^m· Whipple,* *Matthew Thornton.*
MASSACHUSETTS- BAY.	*Saml· Adams,* *John Adams,* *Robt· Treat Paine,* *Elbridge Gerry.*
RHODE-ISLAND AND PROVIDENCE, &C.	*Step. Hopkins,* *William Ellery.*
CONNECTICUT.	*Roger Sherman,* *Saml· Huntington,* *W^m· Williams,* *Oliver Wolcott.*
NEW-YORK,	*W^m· Floyd,* *Phil. Livingston,* *Fran^s· Lewis,* *Lewis Morris.*

NEW-JERSEY.	Richd. Stockton, Jno. Witherspoon, Fra^{s.} Hopkinson, John Hart, Abra. Clark.
NORTH-CAROLINA.	Wm. Hooper, Joseph Hewes, John Penn.
GEORGIA.	Button Gwinnett, Lyman Hall, Geo. Walton.
PENNSYLVANIA.	Robt. Morris, Benjamin Rush, Benja. Franklin, John Morton, Geo. Clymer, Ja^{s.} Smith, Geo. Taylor, James Wilson, Geo. Ross.
DELAWARE.	Cæsar Rodney, Geo. Read, (Tho M:Kean.)
MARYLAND.	Samuel Chase, Wm. Paca, Thos. Stone, Charles Carroll, of Car- rollton.
VIRGINIA.	George Wythe, Richard Henry Lee, Th^{s.} Jefferson, Benj^{a.} Harrison, Thos. Nelson, j^{r.} Francis Lightfoot Lee, Carter Braxton.
SOUTH-CAROLINA.	Edward Rutledge, Thos. Heyward, jun^{r.} Thomas Lynch, jun^{r.} Arthur Middleton.

DECLARATION OF RIGHTS. In response to an appeal from Massachusetts, representatives of all the colonies, except Georgia, met in September, 1774, in Philadelphia to deliberate upon redress of their common grievances. In this First Continental Congress a committee of two from each colony reported on the violation of the rights of the colonies. On Oct. 14 a resolution embodying the views of the Congress was passed, and became known as the Declaration of Rights. In the introduction it was asserted that the Parliament had assumed the authority of compelling the colonists to submit to a policy which deprived them of rights which, as Englishmen, they had every reason to expect would be recognized.

Then followed in these resolves eleven specific resolutions defining the rights and declaring that they had been violated. By the "principles of the English Constitution" the colonists were entitled to "life, liberty, and property." Removal to the colonies did not result in the loss of the rights of Englishmen, for they were entitled to "all the rights, liberties, and immunities of free natural-born subjects, within the realm of England." It was maintained that the colonists had no representatives in Parliament and "that the foundation of English liberty, and of all free government, is a right in the people to participate in their legislative council." The colonists were entitled to the benefits of the "common law of England" and the "privilege of being tried by their peers of the vicinage." The colonists were insistent that they were "entitled to all the immunities and privileges granted and confirmed to them by royal charters."

As loyal Englishmen they insisted "that they have a right peaceably to assemble, consider of their grievances, and petition the king." They regarded as a serious menace, "keeping a standing army in these colonies, in time of peace, without the consent of the legislature." It was maintained that it was "indispensably necessary to good government, and rendered essential by the English Constitution that the constituent branches of the legislature be independent of each other," and that the exercise of legislative power in several colonies by a council appointed by the king was "unconstitutional, dangerous, and destructive to the freedom of American legislation." It was insisted that the rights of the colonists were violated by the Stamp Act, the Townshend Revenue Act, the Coercive Acts of 1774 and the Quebec Act. It was hoped that this declaration would impress the British statesmen sufficiently to bring about the desired relief.

DECLARATORY ACT was intended to be an important constitutional compromise. The Stamp Act (1765) had aroused a constitutional controversy unequaled since the Revolution of 1688. The colonial empire had grown to large proportions but the relations of Parliament to that empire had never been defined. Parliament had developed as a supreme, unrestrained legislature in England, while each colony had been evolving a legislature of the same type for its own local affairs. The attempt to extend Parliament's general legislative powers, including the power to tax, to the colonies by means of the Sugar Act (1764) and the Stamp Act caused widespread denial in America of parliamentary authority, and individuals and legislative bodies challenged the exercise of such power as unconstitutional; at the same time the authority of Parliament was vehemently upheld by writers in England. Public opinion in England crystallized in favor of withdrawing from the attempt to tax the colonies, but in favor of maintaining the constitutional supremacy of Parliament. The result was a repeal of the Stamp Act, abandonment of any program of internal taxation of the colonies, and the passage of a Declaratory Act to clarify the constitutional question. Both passed the House of Commons on the same day (March 4, 1766) and the House of Lords a few days later. The Declaratory Act (1) recited the claims of the colonies to a legal exclusive right of taxation; (2) asserted that the colonies were subordinate to the Crown and Parliament; (3) declared the king and Parliament "had, hath, and of right ought to have the full power and authority to make laws and statutes of sufficient force and validity to bind the colonies and people of America, subjects of the Crown of Great Britain, in all cases whatsoever"; (4) declared all votes, resolutions and proceedings of the colonies calling in question the authority of Parliament as stated above "utterly null and void to all intents and purposes whatsoever."

A declaratory act clarifying the British constitution was favored by Pitt and other friends of America, but the act as passed went far beyond their wishes. The assumption by Parliament of authority to annul colonial legislation was an exercise of power entirely novel; and, when Parliament suspended the New York Assembly (1767), the powers claimed for Parliament began to assume a sinister aspect to the Americans. Every new regulatory act gave added meaning to the Declaratory Act and it thus became an active cause of grievance and a standing threat to colonial self-government, instead of the constitutional compromise as originally intended.

DECORATION DAY (May 30), or Memorial Day, has been formally observed since 1868, when Gen. John A. Logan, Commander in Chief of the Grand Army of the Republic, called on members of the order to decorate soldiers' graves with flowers on the 30th day of May.

DEERFIELD MASSACRE. From the time of its first settlement in 1669 the town of Deerfield was exposed to frequent attacks from the Indians and the French by reason of its situation in the open valley of the Connecticut River, a natural highway from Canada to the sea, and long the western frontier of the Massachusetts Colony. The Deerfield Massacre took place in the early morning of Feb. 29, 1704, when a force of 50 French soldiers and 200 Indian allies from Canada, under the command of Maj. Hertel de Rouville, easily entered the snow-drifted stockade and quickly overcame the sleeping inhabitants. No effective resistance was possible except at the Stebbins house where seven men and four or five women with their children successfully defended themselves. Of the 300 inhabitants about 50 were killed, 137 escaped and 111 were taken prisoners. During the harrowing journey to Canada seventeen of the captives died from exposure or at the hands of their Indian captors. Among the prisoners was Eunice Mather Williams, the wife of Pastor John Williams, who published a touching narrative entitled *The Redeemed Captive Returning to Zion*. After prolonged negotiations, lasting several years, sixty of the captives were allowed to return home. Some, however, preferred to remain in Canada, including Pastor Williams' daughter, who married an Indian.

DEFENSE, NATIONAL. Throughout most of its history, the defense policy of the United States has been shaped, in the main, by three factors: the relative immunity to foreign aggression conferred by distance and flanking oceans, a deep-rooted national aversion to standing armies as a potential instrument of executive tyranny, and the pressure of economy. Until recently, therefore, the United States has seldom maintained powerful armed forces in time of peace (except for naval forces in the present century), and in time of war has depended largely on what forces could be mobilized, organized, armed and trained after hostilities began.

In 1789 the new constitution created a strong federal government, with powers to provide for the common defense, balanced by state control of the militia and the right of the populace to bear arms. Within the Federal Government authority was divided. Congress received the power to levy taxes, declare war, raise armies, and provide for a navy. The President was named commander-in-chief of the Army and Navy and, under an act passed in 1795, received authority to call out the militia in order to execute the laws, suppress insurrection, and repel invasion. The chief curb upon his military powers was the constitutional limitation of army (but not navy) money appropriations to two years. The states retained the right to train the militia, according to discipline prescribed by Congress, and to appoint its officers. The Militia Act of 1792 established the principle of universal obligation to military service for all free, white male citizens between the ages of 18 and 45. Not until 1808 did the arming of the militia become a Federal responsibility.

Although Washington had extolled the value of a well-trained militia, the levies called up to flesh out the tiny force of Regulars during the chronic Indian troubles of the early years often proved unreliable. The Regular Army, as a result, was repeatedly augmented and, though as often cut back, grew from a strength of 750 men at the time of Washington's accession to about 9000 on the eve of the War of 1812. The Navy was reborn in 1794 during the tensions of the French Revolutionary Wars, when each of the major belligerents, France and Great Britain, was attempting to stifle neutral trade with the other. It gained valuable experience in an undeclared war with France (1798–1800) and in later operations against the Tripolitan corsairs. The Marine Corps was established in the same period.

Under Jefferson (1801–8), during a lull in the European conflict, both Army and Navy were sharply reduced, and for defense against invasion the country depended largely on harbor fortifications, supplemented by gunboats, and the militia. Jefferson also founded the U. S. Military Academy at West Point, which in later decades became the nursery of American military professionalism. By purchasing the vast Louisiana Territory in 1803, he added immeasurably to the nation's military potential. Both Jefferson and his successor, Madison, attempted through restrictions on American trade with Europe to halt the seizure of American merchantmen and impressment of American seamen by British warships, but without success. War broke out with Great Britain in 1812. The ensuing conflict (1812–15) demonstrated the inadequacy of a national defense system based on the militia and maritime commerce raiding. The British, though absorbed in the struggle with Napoleon until 1814, successfully defended Canada, swept the tiny American Navy from the sea, and penetrated the Atlantic and Gulf coast defenses at several points. Peace restored the *status quo ante*.

During the century following 1815 the United States poured its energies into economic growth, territorial expansion, and domestic politics. Successive boundary disputes with Spain, Great Britain and Russia as the frontier advanced were settled without bloodshed and generally to American advantage. Thanks largely to the silent support of British seapower, the hemispheric hegemony proclaimed by the Monroe Doctrine in 1823 met no serious challenge from Europe until the end of the century. Down to the Mexican War (1846–48) the Regular Army's normal strength hovered around 6000, mostly distributed along the great periphery of the advancing frontier, while the Navy's few frigates and sloops were scattered on lonely patrols "showing the flag" or watching for slavers in distant waters. Still committed to the militia tradition, Congress in 1821 rejected Secretary of War Calhoun's plan for a peacetime army that could be rapidly expanded in an emergency.

In both regular services during this period a new and efficient professionalism was emerging, nurtured at West Point and, after 1845, at the Navy's new academy at Annapolis. Both services managed, too, to keep abreast of the new military technology of the 1840's and 1850's—rifled shoulder arms and artillery, heavy naval and seacoast ordnance, steam-propelled (but not armored) warships. At the same time the development of railroads, steamboats, steamships, and mechanized industry was creating an immense military potential. In the war with Mexico (1846–48), a limited conflict growing out of the annexation of Texas, the militia system was largely abandoned in favor of volunteer forces raised by the states. These and the small professional army performed brilliantly, and victory resulted in annexation of most of the remaining areas west of the Mississippi.

The Civil War (1861–65) called forth a greater national effort than any other American war down to (and, for the South, including) World War II, while in loss of life (over half a million) it remains the most costly of American wars. For both sides it was a war of national defense: the North fought to preserve the Union, the South to survive as a nation. In many ways it revealed the inadequacy of the traditional system of national defense. The Southern states could hardly have contemplated resistance at all had the Constitution not preserved state control of the militia and raised effective barriers against a large Federally-controlled standing army, and it was President Lincoln's call for militia to coerce the seceding states that drove the border states into armed rebellion. Except for a handful of leaders who proved equal to the test of higher command, the tiny Regular Army made only a small contribution. Volunteers, short- and long-term, made up the bulk of the armies, but in order to induce men to volunteer in the masses needed, both sides had to resort, for the first time in American history, to nation-wide centrally directed conscription, along with the traditional incentives of bounties and purchase of substitutes. Militia, as such, served only as state local defense forces.

After the Civil War, national defense became again largely a matter of protecting frontier settlements and emigrant wagon trains against Indian raids, and, for the Navy, of patrolling distant stations. Down to the 1890's the Army's strength remained in the neighborhood of 25,000, including a strong cavalry component to combat the fast-riding plains Indians. The main defense against invasion continued to be the seacoast fortifications, which were modernized in the 1880's. In that decade, too, the Navy began belatedly to replace its wooden sail ships and smooth-bore guns with modern vessels and armament; by 1898 it had a powerful fleet built around five battleships.

The war with Spain (1898–99), fought ostensibly to protect Cuba from Spanish tyranny, was a response to expansionist pressures. Military operations were brief, and the war effort in general was badly mismanaged, especially in the administrative sphere. Perhaps half of the 225,000 volunteers drawn into Federal service came from the state-controlled National Guard units which, since the Civil War, had largely replaced the militia. There was no draft. Victory, won with relative ease, brought the United States a new overseas empire in the Caribbean and the Pacific.

To protect this new empire, United States military and naval power expanded considerably in the early 20th century. Though still small by European standards, the Regular Army was increased to four times its prewar strength and armed with modern rifles, machine guns, and artillery. Through the reforms of Elihu Root, the Army also developed a machinery of command and planning, a general staff organization, and a system of advanced professional education, all patterned after European models. These were to endure, in their fundamentals, through two world wars. In 1903 the Dick Act formally interred the corpse of the militia system, repealing the Militia Act of 1792 and recognizing the National Guard as the Army's first-line reserve—in Root's words, "the great school of the citizen soldier." Spurred by Alfred Thayer Mahan's doctrines of sea power and by its new imperial responsibilities, the United States had become by 1914 the third strongest naval power in the world.

The great European war which erupted in 1914 impinged directly on American interests in many ways—through the strangling of trade with European neutrals and with the Central Powers, through the growth of a munitions industry fattened by Allied arms contracts, and through loss of American lives and property on neutral merchantmen attacked by German submarines—and its very magnitude aroused fears of eventual American involvement. These fears prompted a growing clamor for large-scale military preparedness, including peacetime conscription, against threats seldom made explicit but increasingly identified in the public mind with German militarism.

Preparedness pressures were reflected in the Defense Act of 1916, which greatly expanded the Regular Army and, while rejecting the Army-proposed plan for a huge volunteer Federal reserve, expanded the National Guard, and removed most of the restrictions on its federalization and use in an emergency. In August, 1916, Congress also voted a huge naval building program. That summer the National Guard was mobilized to protect the southwestern border, where a crisis had arisen following President Wilson's dispatch of a punitive force into Mexico to track down Mexican raiders.

In April, 1917, following Germany's resumption of unrestricted submarine warfare, the United States intervened on the side of the Allied powers. Between then and November, 1918, when the Central Powers collapsed, some 4,000,000 men were mobilized, of whom about half were sent to France and played a decisive role in the final battles. These forces were raised mainly by an efficient, Federally-administered system of selective service, supplemented by volunteering. While largely dependent on its Allies for heavy armament, the United States manufactured large quantities of small arms and ammunition for its own and Allied forces, and contributed substantially in warships and merchant shipping to the defeat of the German submarines.

In the succeeding two decades the development of long-range aircraft and the naval aircraft carrier exposed the nation, for the first time since the disappearance of sailing navies, to the real possibility of attack and invasion from other continents. In the 1930's, moreover, the growth of Japanese power and ambitions threatened American possessions in the Pacific, while the rise of Nazi Germany in alliance with Italy and Japan again raised the specter of a hostile militarism wielding world-wide power.

The nation's "first line of defense" during these two decades was the Navy, which inherited strong surface forces from World War I and developed a striking force of carrier-borne aviation. But at the Washington Naval Conference of 1921–22, the leading nations agreed to a ten-year holiday in capital-ship construction and to a fixed ratio of capital-ship strength among the five principal naval powers. This had the practical effect of giving Japan naval supremacy in the western Pacific. Meanwhile, the Regular Army, National Guard, and newly created Federal Organized Reserve fell far below authorized strength as a result of meager appropriations and declining enlistments in a period of popular revulsion against war. The Army's air forces embraced the new gospel of strategic air power and gained partial autonomy, and the Marines experimented with amphibious landing techniques. But on the eve of World War II the Army had only a handful of modern aircraft and no mechanized or armored forces worthy of the name.

During the 1930's the Roosevelt administration sought to foster hemispheric solidarity against German propaganda and economic penetration in Latin America, and in 1938 broadened the national defense policy to include the Western Hemisphere. But in 1940, with the German conquest of most of western Europe and the isolation of Great Britain, the United States suddenly faced the prospect of German-Italian naval ascendancy in the Atlantic and possible invasion of South America from bases in West Africa, while her fleet was pinned down in the Pacific watching Japan. Reacting to this threat, the United States in 1940 and 1941 reinstituted selective service on the World War I model and began to rearm, while negotiating with other countries in the hemisphere for base rights and military collaboration against aggression.

Hemisphere defense was closely linked with an expanding program of material aid to nations opposing the Axis powers (Germany, Italy, Japan). Under the Lend Lease Act of March, 1941, the United States eventually transferred to anti-Axis nations $50,200,000,000 in war materials and services. During 1941, in collaboration with the British, United States troops also occupied Iceland, United States warships convoyed shipping in the Atlantic and fought German submarines, United States transports ferried British troops, and United States military staffs helped to plan the eventual defeat of Germany. By late 1941, with German armies bogged down in Russia and Great Britain apparently safe from invasion, these deterrent measures seemed to be succeeding, and American rearmament began to slow down. At this juncture, on Dec. 7, 1941, Japan struck without warning, crippling American power in the Pacific and plunging the United States into World War II.

In this conflict the United States mobilized some 15,000,000 men, mounted large-scale campaigns all over the world, and as an "arsenal of democracy" provided the sinews of a crushing material superiority for the whole anti-Axis coalition. While its most direct interest lay in the recovery of its Pacific possessions from Japan, the United States was already deeply committed to the defeat of Nazi Germany first, as the stronger, and in the long-run more dangerous, enemy. The Pacific was, therefore, merely one theater in a global war fought by the United States to prevent the establishment of a totalitarian world order incompatible with American security and the American way of life.

The atomic bombing of Hiroshima and Nagasaki in August, 1945, ushered in a period of rapid advance in nuclear weapons and long-range delivery systems, in which the United States and, after 1949, the Soviet Union held a virtual monopoly of nuclear weapons. United States defense policy after this date was dominated by two facts: the implacable hostility and aggressive expansionism of Soviet and Chinese communism, and the increasing vulnerability of both the United States and Soviet homelands to devastation by long-range nuclear attack. This mutual vulnerability produced a precarious "balance of terror" between the two nuclear powers.

To deter attack on its homeland the United States maintained long-range nuclear air striking forces ready for instant retaliation, and, with Canada, developed an air and antiaircraft defense and radar detection system for the whole North American continent. The United States also maintained strong ground and naval forces armed with conventional and nuclear weapons for action against limited aggression. The Army, Navy and Air Force were unified under a single Department of Defense (1949); in 1951, during the Korean crisis, peacetime selective service was instituted as a basic policy of national defense.

In the Korean conflict (1950–53) the United States, in association with other United Nations powers, successfully repelled Soviet-supported aggression by North Korean and communist Chinese forces in Korea. The United States also countered communist subversion and aggression in this period through economic and military assistance to non-communist nations, and through regional mutual defense alliances like the North Atlantic Treaty Organization (1949). Finally, through the "massive retaliation" policy announced in 1953, the United States sought to deter piecemeal local communist aggression by the implied threat of responding with strategic nuclear power "instantly and at places of our own choosing."

DEISM, the belief in the existence of a supreme being, but rejecting revelation and the supernatural doctrines of Christianity, was introduced into America in the latter 18th century. Its influence was particularly felt during and immediately following the Revolution. Thomas Jefferson and Thomas Paine were avowed deists and numerous other influential men of the time leaned strongly in that direction. It invaded all the colleges and the whole religious climate of America was greatly affected by it.

DELAWARE. With the adoption of the state constitution, Sept. 21, 1776, Delaware became a political unit. Known as the Three Lower Counties, it had been under the jurisdiction of Pennsylvania for 94 years. The struggle for a separate political power had dated from 1702. A convention which met on Oct. 21, 1775, to elect delegates to the Second Continental Congress ordered that the Lower Counties have an "equal voice in Congress with the other Colonies."

The first settlement within the limits of the Three Counties, made in Sussex County by the Dutch in 1631, was destroyed by the Indians the same year. Six years later, on the banks of Minquas Kill, now Christina River, the Swedes landed, naming the surrounding country New Sweden. Captured by the Dutch in 1655, it was under the rule of Peter Stuyvesant until 1664, when the English gained control of all Dutch territory and reduced New Castle, the only town in the Delaware River Valley.

With the coming of William Penn in 1682, the controversy with Lord Baltimore regarding the ownership of the land along the Delaware River was continued until 1750, when the boundary was decided by the Lord Chancellor of England. This boundary was surveyed in 1765–67. The conflicting claims of the two proprietors for Sussex County interfered greatly with its settlement.

Delaware ratified the Constitution of the United States on December 6, 1787.

DELAWARE, CROSSING OF THE. Generally recognized as the "turning-point of the Revolution," this exploit of Washington checked the British advance and restored the American morale, then in danger of collapse. Under his command, about three o'clock in the afternoon of Christmas Day, 1776, some 2400 men and 18 field pieces set out from a position west of the Delaware River above Trenton to surprise the British, chiefly Hessians, in their quarters between Trenton and New York. The weather was terrible, the river covered with floating ice, the supporting columns failed or refused to make the crossing. Between three and four o'clock the next morning Washington's command made its way across the river, marched to Trenton, surprised the Hessian garrison, killed some, including the Hessian commander, Rall, took 946 prisoners, 1200 muskets, 6 cannon and the regimental colors. Having accomplished this daring raid, the American troops recrossed the Delaware, with half of their number disabled by the cold. The Hessian commander, Donop, hearing of the defeat of his fellow officer, Rall, hastily retired to Princeton, leaving his stores, sick and wounded to be captured by Cadwallader, who, hearing of Washington's exploit on Dec. 27, crossed into New Jersey. On Dec. 29 Washington again crossed the Delaware, advanced to Trenton, and, attacked there by the British under Cornwallis, marched to Princeton, hoping to capture the British supplies at Brunswick. There ensued the battle of Princeton, in which the British lost some 200 men killed and more than that taken prisoner. Thence Washington retired to Somerset Courthouse, thence to Morristown, and meanwhile in various skirmishes at Springfield, Hackensack and Elizabethtown, the Americans were successful. Washington established his headquarters at Morristown, and for the moment the American cause was saved.

This was the most daring exploit of the Revolutionary War and not merely saved the American cause from collapse but raised the reputation and influence of Washington to a point where he could, at last, be free to carry out his plans with a minimum of hindrance from his rivals and the authorities. More than sixty years after this great campaign, a German-born American painter, Emanuel Leutze, in his studio at Düsseldorf, began a series of heroic historical paintings, chiefly dealing with American history. Among them his "Washington Crossing the Delaware" is the most famous and most popular. However stirring the conception, the execution has seemed to many critics absurd. The pose of Washington in the prow of a rowboat under such circumstances as those of the real crossing, is patently ridiculous. The flag is an obvious anachronism; the river covered with ice is the Rhine, not the Delaware. Nonetheless the picture has become a symbol of Washington's great exploit, and is perhaps the best known of Leutze's works and the most popular conception of the crossing.

DEMOCRATIC PARTY. The origin of the present Democratic party goes back to the early years under the Constitution, when Thomas Jefferson organized into a coherent party the various elements of opposition to the foreign and domestic policies of the dominant Federalist party. These Jeffersonian Republicans came in part from the small tradesmen and mechanics in towns along the coast, but mainly from the sparsely settled and frontier regions, especially in the South and West, where agriculture rather than trade was the dominant economic interest. Originally, the party advocated a strict, or narrow, interpretation of the powers of the National Government in the interest of states' rights and individual liberty. Since the Louisiana Purchase, however, these Republicans (or Democrats, as they were later called), whenever in power, have not hesitated to act upon more liberal constitutional doctrines.

Following the election of Jefferson in 1800, the Republicans remained almost continuously in power for the next sixty years. Between 1816 and 1832, indeed, all voters seemed to be merged in the party of Jefferson. In this transitional period, however, hostile factions developed around half a dozen outstanding personalities—John Quincy Adams, Henry Clay, Andrew Jackson, William H. Crawford, John C. Calhoun and DeWitt Clinton—all claiming to be followers of Jefferson and true exponents of Republican principles. By 1824 the followers of Adams and Clay, who favored enlarging the activities of the National Government, had coalesced under the name of *National* Republicans, a name they soon changed to Whigs. The success of this combination led the opposing groups to amalgamate under Andrew Jackson and take the distinctive name of *Democratic* Republicans. With the name soon abbreviated to Democratic, this party became the immediate ancestor of the present Democratic party. Successful in elevating its leader to the Presidency in 1828, the Democratic party, except for two short intervals, remained in control of the National Government until the end of Buchanan's administration in 1861. This long lease of power is to be explained largely by the party's homogeneity, superior organization and the skill of its leaders in harmonizing internal differences, especially those growing out of the slavery controversy. For the greater part, however, Democratic policies in this long period consisted chiefly of negations—opposition to a national bank, to a protective tariff, and to a general system of internal improvements by the National Government. Following the Mexican War, the party became increasingly divided over the proper course for the National Government to pursue in dealing with slavery in the territories. The repeal of the Missouri Compromise in 1854 and the Dred Scott decision in 1857 led to the nomination of two Democratic presidential tickets in 1860, thus enabling the new Republican party to win its first national victory. During the Civil War, most Northern Democrats loyally supported the Lincoln administration, and were known as "War Democrats." Others, some of whom publicly opposed the war, came to be called "Copperheads." The stigma of disloyalty, real or imagined, together with the enforced disfranchisement of Confederate leaders, for a time after the war severely hampered the Democratic party. Its return to its former strength was facilitated not only by the removal of these disabilities and the waning of the sectional issue but by the eventual triumph, in the 1890's, of "white supremacy" in the South, and with it, the triumph of a one-party system. Since then the South has remained the most dependable source of Democratic strength. The support of other sections has, however, been indispensable to national party success, notably, the agricultural areas of the West and the metropolitan districts of Boston, New York and Chicago. The absence of party unity during most of the time since the Civil War justified a Democratic Senator in saying that there is no national Democratic party: only a Southern, a Western and an Eastern Democratic party. The party has, nevertheless, been able to carry nine presidential elections and, more frequently, has been able to control one or both branches of Congress.

Down to the time of Woodrow Wilson the party retained its Southern and Western orientation, its strict interpretation of the Constitution, its low-tariff dogma, and its distrust of both big business and big Government. The competition of the Progressive Party, however, followed by the First World War, forced the Wilson administration to assume unprecedented powers over the national economy, something urban progressives had been demanding for years. Thereafter the Democrats found it difficult to return to their traditional policy of *laissez-faire*. During the 1920's, as an opposition party they were obliged to criticize the policies of the party in power, and those policies happened to be ultra-conservative. Finally the Great Depression, as a result of which the Democratic party returned to power, created another national emergency which could be met only by a continuing expansion of the national power to regulate and control. The Depression, moreover, together with the policies of the New Deal itself, enabled organized labor to rise to a position of commanding importance. Rather than risk alienating this new source of political power, the Roosevelt administration enthusiastically solicited its support. As a result of these various circumstances, the Democratic party has tended since the New Deal to find its mass support in the industrial centers of the North (and of the Pacific Coast), and its domestic policies—defense of labor unions against such measures as the Taft-Hartley Act and the "right-to-work" laws; welfare legislation; opposition to racial discrimination, at least in employment; liberal use of the Federal spending power—reflect this urban working-class support. At the same time the persistence of the one-party system in the South, which insures Southern Democratic control of important Congressional committees, makes it possible for those who oppose these policies to wield an influence out of proportion to the votes they represent. The result is that while the liberal element controls the national convention and therefore the choice of a presidential candidate, it rules in Congress, when it rules at all, only by sufferance of the South. Only the fear of defeat—and sometimes, as in 1948, not even that— holds such a coalition together.

DENONVILLE'S INVASION (1687). Determined to subdue the Iroquois, whose intrigues with the English menaced the French trade, the Marquis de Denonville summoned Tonti, Duluth and Durantaye to organize the French forces, including Indian allies in the Illinois country, and proceed to a rendezvous at Irondequoit Bay. The main army under Denonville embarked at Montreal, arriving at Irondequoit Bay where the western forces soon joined them.

Leaving a detachment to guard the fortified base, Denonville with 1600 French and Indians advanced against the Senecas, July 12. On the second day of the march, while approaching a village reported deserted, the army was ambushed and, before the Senecas withdrew, lost 100 soldiers and 10 Indians. The following day, Denonville ordered an advance against the village but the Senecas had burned it during their retreat. The French destroyed three other villages and surrounding fields before they returned to Irondequoit Bay. This part of the expedition was a failure, having little effect beyond the burning of the villages and fields, but on July 26, after destroying the base at Irondequoit Bay, the French army moved up Lake Ontario to the mouth of the Niagara River and there constructed Fort Denonville.

DENVER was founded by gold-seekers in the fall of 1858. Discoveries in Cherry Creek, at the mouth of which Denver was situated, were meager, but lodes and placers in the mountains made Denver a chief outfitting depot. The Civil War, an Indian uprising, and refractory ores retarded growth in the 1860's. Some saw doom for the city when the first transcontinental railroad passed to the north, but vigorous local leaders built a connecting branch line. Thereupon the city grew. It became the territorial capital in 1867. Its population of 5000 in 1870 increased to 35,629 in 1880, and to 106,713 in 1890. The great camps of Leadville and Aspen poured in their silver during the 1880's. Bonanza kings invested in Denver real estate. Railroads multiplied, nearby agriculture flourished, some manufacturing developed. With rapid and consistent growth in population Denver became, after 1900, the largest city between the Missouri River and the Pacific Coast. The acceleration in the 1950's was especially noteworthy, reaching a figure of 493,887 in 1960. It became the market, distribution, business, and cultural center of the Rocky Mountain Region.

DEPOSIT, RIGHT OF. By Article IV of Pinckney's Treaty (1795) Spain recognized the claim of the United States to the free navigation of the Mississippi River from its headwaters to its mouth. To facilitate the exercise of this right, Article XXII of this treaty gave the citizens of the United States the right or privilege of depositing and re-exporting their property duty free at New Orleans for a term of three years, with the stipulation that at the end of this period

Spain should either continue this permission or assign an equivalent establishment at another place on the banks of the Mississippi. First formally opened in April, 1798, the New Orleans deposit was extensively and uninterruptedly used until the intendant of Louisiana, acting under secret instructions from Spain, closed it by a decree of Oct. 16, 1802, without designating the equivalent establishment required by the treaty. Under threat of war, Spain reopened the deposit at New Orleans, May 17, 1803. It remained open until the United States took possession of New Orleans in December, 1803, by virtue of the Louisiana Purchase.

DESERET, STATE OF (taken from *Book of Mormon,* meaning "land of the honey-bee"), was a provisional or temporary government formed by the Mormons. It included the immense area of land in Upper California acquired in the Mexican War east of the Sierra Nevada Mountains and west of the Rocky Mountains. At a convention on March 4, 1849, a constitution was drafted and Salt Lake City made the capital. The government was divided as in other states, counties were created, and local government established. On March 12, Brigham Young was chosen governor and a full corps of state officers elected. Almon W. Babbitt was elected delegate to present a memorial to Congress to admit Deseret. Congress, after voting unfavorably on the bill, created the Territory of Utah in 1850. The Mormons, however, accepted the territory as a temporary measure. A shadow of the Deseret government was preserved and admission sought until 1883.

DESERT, GREAT AMERICAN. Many of the atlases and school geographies published between 1820 and 1850 contained maps on which, across the region eastward of the Rocky Mountains, were printed the words, "Great American Desert."

This myth of a Great American Desert originated in the reports of explorers and other early travelers. After his southwestern expedition of 1806–7 Zebulon M. Pike wrote of great desert-like prairies incapable of supporting any considerable white population and constituting a fortunate barrier to further expansion. Stephen H. Long, who explored the southern part of the region in 1820, described it as "uninhabitable by a people depending upon agriculture for their subsistence." He shared Pike's belief that the nation was benefited by having this providential limit to western settlement. Other later writers gave similar characterizations of the country.

Americans in general were therefore accustomed for years to think of the Missouri River and the western borders of what are now Arkansas and Louisiana as the western termination of settlements. Thus it was possible for the Government to formulate and carry out an Indian removal policy, and to remove Indian tribes from east of the Mississippi to the country between this line and the Rocky Mountains.

Even while the Indian removal policy was being inaugurated, however, the destruction of the myth of a Great American Desert was begun by the Santa Fe traders. Then, during the 1840's, came the migrations to Oregon, the hegira of the Mormons to Utah, the California gold rush, and vast new territorial acquisitions extending to the Pacific. Not only was the reality of a real desert disproved, but there could no longer be any thought of a barrier separating the settlements from the possessions along the Pacific.

DeSOTO EXPEDITION (1539–43). Hernando DeSoto, believing Florida another Peru, secured a royal grant for conquest. He was named governor of Cuba and *adelantado* of Florida, and many wealthy persons joined his expedition. Leaving the Spanish port of San Lucar (April 6, 1538), he inspected Cuba and, sailing from Havana, landed on Charlotte Bay, May 30, 1539. During the four-year search for a "golden city," many of his 550 followers were killed or died from exposure and disease while wandering over Florida, Georgia, the Carolinas, Tennessee, Alabama, Mississippi, Arkansas, Oklahoma and Texas. The first winter was spent at Appalachees (near Tallahassee), Fla. In 1540 the Cherokee and Creek country was visited, and, in October, the Spaniards came to Mauvila (Choctaw Bluff) on the Alabama River where the fiercest engagement with the Indians occurred. Marching northwestward, the expedition discovered the Mississippi (Chickasaw Bluff, May, 1541). Crossing the river, the Osage and Kansas tribes were encountered before turning back. While moving down the Arkansas River, DeSoto fell ill and died on May 21, 1542. Fearing the effect of the death on the natives, his followers sank his body in the Mississippi. The 320 survivors, under Luis de Moscoso, finally reached Panuco in Mexico on Sept. 20, 1543.

DETROIT, FORT (1701–1825). At different times, several forts bearing different names have existed at Detroit. The earliest, built in 1701, was Fort Pontchartrain du Détroit. It was a quadrangular stockade with four bastions, located on a bluff, with the Detroit River in front and the Savoyard in the rear. During the French period it was several times enlarged and once (during the Fox-French Wars) was greatly reduced.

In the long contest for dominance of the Ohio Valley, the French endeavored to strengthen Detroit, their center of western control, but the struggle ended in the conquest of New France. In November, 1760, Fort Pontchartrain du Détroit surrendered to the British. In 1763–64 the place underwent an Indian siege of unexampled duration.

Throughout the Revolution, Detroit was the chief center of British power in the West, and the goal, in consequence, of the American armies. All their efforts to reach Detroit were defeated, but the success of

Clark at Vincennes produced an important local effect. Across the Savoyard River rose a hill from which an attacking army could command the existing defenses. In anticipation of its arrival, the British hastily erected a new fort here, and named it Fort Lernoult (vicinity of modern Fort Street). Eventually, stockades were erected connecting it with the older fort, thereby greatly enlarging the enclosed area.

Throughout the post-Revolutionary Indian wars in the Northwest, Detroit continued to be the real center of opposition to the American armies. On July 11, 1796, in pursuance of the Jay Treaty, the British at length yielded Detroit to the Americans and retired to Amherstburg, where they established a new military and governmental center. In July, 1812, Gen. Hull invaded Canada from Detroit, but instead of conquering the country, he soon retreated and on Aug. 16 surrendered his army and all Michigan Territory to the British. For over a year the Americans made extensive but futile efforts to recover Detroit; Commodore Perry's victory on Lake Erie (Sept. 10, 1813) determined the issue. Conveyed across Lake Erie by Perry's fleet, Gen. Harrison quickly occupied Detroit and destroyed the retreating British army at the Thames (Oct. 5). To the fortifications of Detroit, as now restored, he gave the new name of Fort Shelby.

The Treaty of Ghent (Dec. 24, 1814) nominally restored the *status quo ante bellum;* but no treaty could bring back the vanished power of the northwestern Indians, or enable them again to withstand the American Government. With their might, passed also the importance of Fort Detroit. It continued for another decade as military headquarters of the Department of the Lakes, when the city it had guarded for over a century ceased to require its protection, and its site was devoted to peaceful pursuits.

DETROIT, FORT, SIEGE OF, BY PONTIAC (1763-64). Canada surrendered to the British in September, 1760; the ensuing year was consumed in taking over the far-flung western French posts. Before the task was completed, the dislike which the red men felt for the conquerors was stirring them to organized revolt.

The great leader of this movement was Pontiac, who himself undertook the conquest of Detroit. Having enlisted the co-operation of several tribes, he schemed to overcome the garrison by stratagem. Under pretense of holding a council, 300 warriors with sawed-off guns beneath their blankets gained entrance to the fort on May 7; but Maj. Gladwin had been informed of their plan, and his preparations for resistance were so effective that Pontiac was forced to retire without giving the signal for the intended slaughter.

The siege which followed is one of the most thrilling events in American history. Within the fort were about 100 defenders, scantily supplied, while in the river near by floated two tiny armed sailing vessels; without, were hundreds of warriors, led by a savage genius and enjoying the sympathy of the French settlers of Detroit. British pluck was pitted against savage wiles in a contest that continued into the second year. The besiegers were animated by transports of savage fury, while the defenders were keyed to an exalted pitch of resolution. Pontiac made earnest efforts to overpower the two sailing vessels, whose essential service in maintaining communications with Niagara and in bringing needed reinforcements of men and supplies probably turned the tide in favor of the defenders.

To end the war, Gen. Gage in 1764 launched two armies against the red men. Col. Bradstreet, leader of one of them, entered Detroit, Aug. 26, 1764, and the fifteen-month siege was over, although formal peace was delayed for another year.

DETROIT, MICH., was founded on July 24, 1701, by Antoine de Lamothe Cadillac. Named Fort Pontchartrain du Détroit, *i.e.,* on the Strait, it consisted of a few buildings within a high palisade. The records of Ste. Anne's R. C. Church, begun in February, 1703, are the second earliest in the United States. Although the post was built to exclude English traders from the upper lakes, Cadillac intended it to be a permanent settlement. With him were Antoine, Jr., age 9, and civilians as well as soldiers. Mme. Cadillac and Jacques, 6, arrived in the fall. Cadillac granted on feudal terms lots within the fort and ribbon farms fronting on the river. In 1710 his enemies in Quebec had him removed. He was appointed governor of Louisiana. After the French and Indian War, on Nov. 29, 1760, Maj. Robert Rogers took over the fort for the British. In 1763, because of British mismanagement of Indian affairs, Pontiac, chief of the local Ottawas, attacked the fort. Maj. Henry Gladwin held out during the siege of 153 days, aided by supplies and men from Fort Niagara. During the Revolutionary War, Detroit was the base for raids into Kentucky. After Lt.-Gov. Henry Hamilton was captured by George Rogers Clark at Vincennes in 1779, Capt. Richard Lernoult, fearing an attack by Clark, built a regular defensive work behind the town. The British held Detroit until 1796.

On July 11, an American force occupied Fort Lernoult. Detroit was the seat of government of Wayne County, Northwest Territory. It became the capital when Michigan Territory was established in 1805. A fire completely destroyed the town on June 11. When Gov. William Hull arrived, for lack of a building, a bower served as the capitol. Judge A. B. Woodward laid out a new town to consist of a series of adjoining regular hexagons with a park in the center of each. His plan was later repudiated. Of this unique design only Grand Circus Park and streets radiating from it to the south remain. When the War of 1812 began, Hull was both governor and commandant. Cut off from supplies by British control of Lake Erie and unable to subordinate his responsibility for the civilians to his military duty, without firing a shot he surrendered on Aug. 16, 1812, to Gen. Isaac Brock, who had warned that inhabitants of the farms would be massacred if any of his Indians were killed.

After Perry's victory on Lake Erie, American troops reoccupied Detroit on Sept. 29, 1813. Elements of culture gradually appeared. Father Gabriel Richard brought a printing press to Detroit in 1809. The Rev. John Monteith organized an interdenominational Protestant Church in 1816. In 1817 the Catholepistemiad or University of Michigania was established by the Governor and Judges. Monteith was president and Richard, vice-president. This was the progenitor of the University of Michigan. In 1824 city government was established. The motto on the seal, *Speramus Meliora; Resurget Cineribus* (We hope for better days; it will arise from the ashes), recalls the fire of 1805. When the Americans took over, the population was about 400.

Detroit was the state capital until 1848. As the center of rail and water transportation, it served the interior as a shipping point. Manufacturing was stimulated by the Civil War. Principal products were railroad cars, steam and gasoline engines, stoves, drugs, paint, varnish, and shoes. Making of automobiles began in the 1890's. Charles B. King and Henry Ford each built a gasoline buggy in 1896. The earliest manufacturers were The Olds Motor Works, 1899, the Cadillac Motor Co., 1901, and the Ford and Packard companies, 1903. A new city charter in 1918 provided for a strong mayor and a nine-man council elected at large on a nonpartisan ballot. Municipal ownership of the street railway system was achieved in 1922 under Mayor James Couzens.

During World War II Detroit was called the arsenal of democracy. Because of war tensions, lack of housing and recreational facilities, on June 21, 1943, serious race riots occurred. Since the war, Detroit has built an extensive system of expressways. Another important project has been the improvement of the waterfront by the erection of public buildings in a new civic center. An earlier center, uptown, contains the Institute of Arts, the Public Library, the Historical Museum, the Rackham Educational Memorial, and Wayne State University.

The population in 1960 was 1,670,144.

DEVALUATION. The gold dollar unit of the United States has been devalued or debased upon two occasions. Under the coinage law of June 28, 1834, the fine gold weight of the dollar was reduced from 24.75 grains to 23.2 grains, a reduction of just over 6%. Since gold was undervalued at the mint when this law was passed, however, the actual debasement was approximately 3%. Under the law of Jan. 18, 1837, the gold content of the dollar was raised to 23.22 grains for technical reasons.

The second case of devaluation of the dollar occurred on Jan. 31, 1934, when the President, under authority of the Gold Reserve Act of 1934, reduced the fine weight of the gold dollar from 23.22 grains to 13.71 grains, a debasement of nearly 41%.

The Gold Reserve Act of 1934 gave the President the power to vary the weight of the gold dollar between 40% and 50% of its former weight for a period of three years, and this power was extended three times by Congress to June 30, 1943. However, no further change in the weight of the gold dollar was made. Although the gold dollar has remained at 13.71 grains since Jan. 31, 1934, the tremendous rise in prices (approximately 300%) since that date has led to fairly widespread, but fortunately unsuccessful, demands for further devaluation.

DIME NOVELS. Mrs. Ann S. Stephens, a famous author and magazine editor, not dreaming of the odium that would later attach to such pamphlets, wrote the first novel of record published in paper covers for ten cents—*Malaeska; the Indian Wife of the White Hunter.* It was published in 1860 by Erastus F. and Irwin P. Beadle and Robert Adams, who had begun business in New York with the idea of publishing "dollar books for a dime." Their series, issued in rapid succession thereafter, quickly fell into the style which the dime novel was to maintain throughout its existence—continuous suspense, violent action and no little bloodshed, but a high standard of morals. Virtue always triumphed, evil was punished; there was vigorous language but no profanity, sex was practically invisible and drinking was minimized; in fact, the heroes never drank. Irwin P. Beadle left the firm in 1862, and in 1866 formed a partnership with George P. Munro, a former Beadle & Adams employee, to launch a series called New Dime Novels. Beadle & Adams about the same time tried a series of longer stories (50,000 words and upward) at twenty cents a copy, but they were not a great success. Munro in later years published two of the most famous series of all, those of "Old Cap Collier" and "Old Sleuth." This, by the way, was apparently the first usage of "sleuth," the old Scotch-English word for track or trace left by man or beast, to designate a detective.

Edward S. Ellis, "Ned Buntline" (Edward Z. C. Judson), Capt. Mayne Reid and Prentiss Ingraham were among the most famous and prolific early writers of the outdoor adventure stories. Authors were paid from $50 to $250 outright for the stories, though for the longer, the twenty-cent Beadle series, Reid is said to have received $700 for one manuscript in 1868. The writers worked at terrific speed; Ingraham once wrote a 35,000-word story in twenty-four hours. The *North American Review* published a grave discussion of the Beadle novels in 1864, but did not find them pernicious; but by 1880 and thereafter, they were being denounced as a menace to youth; alleged instances were adduced of boys led into crime by them —yet their circulation increased; one story is known to have sold nearly half a million copies. Some series of them now began to be sold for five cents, catering to the boys' trade. Edward L. Wheeler created another famous character, "Deadwood Dick," who first appeared in 1884. John R. Coryell is given credit for inventing the great detective, "Nick Carter," though two other men wrote most of the stories. A trend toward the urban is seen in the stories of "Jack Harkaway," a dashing city youth, in the 1880's and 1890's. By 1890 another publisher, Frank Tousey, was catering to boys with his *Wild West, Work and Win, Pluck and Luck* and other weekly series, including the stories of "Frank Reade" and his electric marvels. In 1896 William Gilbert Patten, under the pseudonym of Burt L. Standish, created for Street & Smith the youthful "Frank Merriwell," about whom he wrote more than 900 stories. By 1910 the newsprint or pulp paper magazines were replacing the paper-backed novels, though the character of the fiction remained much the same. Meanwhile, Erastus F. Beadle had died in 1894, worth between $2,000,000 and $3,-000,000, while Munro's estate was estimated at $10,000,000.

DINGLEY TARIFF (1897). The tariff was not an issue in the 1896 campaign, but increases were justified by depression and Treasury deficits. Wool and hide duties were reimposed and 1890 duties on flax restored. Complex compensatory duties were levied on woolens. Silk and linen rates were increased and made specific to prevent undervaluation. Rates on cottons were not greatly changed nor were those on most metals. Despite the Treasury's plight, protection rather than revenue was the motive, except in the case of sugar.

DISMAL SWAMP is an immense swampy section in southeastern Virginia, covering about 750 square miles. In the center is the beautiful circular Lake Drummond, three and one-half miles in diameter, immortalized in the poems of Thomas Moore and in Longfellow's "The Slave in the Dismal Swamp." The swamp was named by William Byrd in 1728. Four thousand acres of it were owned by George Washington, and he surveyed "The Washington Ditch," a canal through the swamp to the Nansemond River.

DISTRICT, CONGRESSIONAL, is the electoral unit from which individual members are elected to the national House of Representatives. This single-member district system was used in a few states from the beginning, and was established by Congress for the entire country in 1842, election at large being permitted only during the period of necessary readjustment of the districts from one apportionment to another. Congress prescribes the conditions for laying out these districts, but their actual mapping is under the control of the respective state legislatures, and the problem of gerrymandering is therefore exclusively a state problem.

The Constitution requires that a representative reside within the state from which he is elected, but there is no provision with respect to district residence. The custom of electing only residents of a district has, however, become so thoroughly established as to be virtually a rule, the only exceptions being in the large cities, where on rare occasion a person living in one section has been elected to Congress from a district in another section of the same city. Even such cases are likely to arouse controversy over the matter of residence. It is this custom of district residence that makes our representatives to a considerable extent local rather than national in their approach to the problems of legislation; and it is in this respect that American custom differs strikingly from that of Great Britain, in particular, where the leaders in Parliament are assured of seats through the opportunity to run from "safe" districts regardless of their residence.

DIXIE. Among the theories for the origin of the word Dixie, one is that of a large farm and slave owner in early New York, a kindly man named Dixie, who, when slavery in the North was abolished, took his Negroes with him to the South; but they always looked back upon their former home with longing and spoke of it as "Dixie's Land." A far more plausible theory is that in early Louisiana, because of its large French population, the word Dix (ten) was printed on ten-dollar bank bills. Louisiana thus came to be known as Dix's Land, and, expanded to Dixie, the name spread to the whole South. There is also a vague notion that the name had something to do with the Mason and Dixon Line. Daniel D. Emmett, a black-face singer, composed the song as it is known today and sang it for the first time as a "walk-around" with Bryant's Minstrels in New York in 1859. He said that he had gotten the idea from hearing touring actors who played in the South say in bleak winter weather, "I wish I was down in Dixie now," or "Dixie Land." The piece was a tremendous hit, and was promptly adopted by the South. It was first sung as a Confederate song at the inauguration of Jefferson Davis as President at Montgomery, Feb. 18, 1861. It was a favorite song and marching tune for the Confederate armies in the Civil War. Gen. Albert Pike wrote new words for the tune in May, 1861, and a third version with a Northern bias was written by T. M. Cooley, but Emmett's words are the ones that endure.

DODGE CITY, KANS., was noted in Santa Fe trail days as the site of several temporary army camps until Fort Dodge was built as a permanent post in 1864. Upon completion of the Santa Fe Railroad to this site in 1872, a town sprang up as an outfitting center for buffalo hunters, who shipped over 400,000 buffalo hides a year for three years. Cattle succeeded buffalo on the range and Dodge City became the rendezvous for cowboys and the shipping station of from 250,000 to 500,000 cattle a year until 1886 when the Government closed the free range. Reckless men infested the young town, committing 25 murders the first winter and giving rise to Boot Hill, cemetery for men dying with their boots on. To enforce order, the citizens employed dead-shot gunmen, whose half-legendary exploits afford wild-west plots for fiction and drama.

DOLLAR MARK. The origin of the dollar mark, the familiar $ symbol, has long been a subject of public interest. Popular belief ascribes it to a mark on government mail bags standing for U S or Uncle Sam, or to the pillars of Hercules on the Spanish dollar. It might easily be a conversion of the old Spanish symbol for the Spanish dollar. Most probably it is a conventionalized combination of the letters p s for pesos. Such a mark was used by a government clerk as early as 1788, and the present symbol came into general use shortly after this time.

DONELSON, FORT, CAPTURE OF (Feb. 15, 1862). In January, 1862, the Confederate line of defense in the West extended from Cumberland Gap westward across Kentucky to Columbus on the lower Ohio. The defeat at Mill Springs in eastern Kentucky and the projected Union movement against Forts Henry and Donelson forced a withdrawal into Tennessee to protect the threatened points. After the capture of Fort Henry, early in February, 1862, Fort Donelson, twenty miles westward on the Cumberland River, was the only remaining obstacle to a Union advance all along the line. Grant (U.) proposed to destroy the fort, but difficulties imposed by terrain, rain and cold weather delayed him more than the weak, muddled and disorganized Confederate opposition.

On Feb. 13 Grant's troops assaulted Fort Donelson unsuccessfully. The following day the river gunboats bombarded the fort, but were driven off. The next morning the Confederates counterattacked without great success. The failure to cut their way out induced the Confederate commanders to request the "best terms of capitulation," to which Grant replied: "No terms except unconditional and immediate surrender can be accepted." During the night of the 15th the fort and over 14,000 men were surrendered.

DONGAN CHARTERS. Gov. Thomas Dongan granted to New York and Albany charters for city governments which with some changes have continued to the present time. Gov. Richard Nicolls in 1665 chartered New Harlem and Manhattan as a city with a mayor, aldermen and minor officers. The

mayor and aldermen of New York City in 1683 petitioned Gov. Dongan for a new charter, which was granted Dec. 6, and set up a government consisting of a mayor, six aldermen, six common councillors, recorder, clerk, sheriff, treasurer, coroner, constables, overseers, assessors and courts. This charter was signed by Dongan on April 27, 1686, and recorded a month later. Meanwhile the village of Albany petitioned Dongan for a city charter, Peter Schuyler and Robert Livingston were sent to New York to obtain the charter, which Dongan signed July 22, 1686. It fixed the boundaries, set up a government like that in the city of New York, conveyed large franchises and went into effect at once. Dongan also granted charters to towns on Long Island, and Schenectady to the northward.

DONIPHAN'S EXPEDITION. After the capture of Santa Fe in 1846 Col. Alexander W. Doniphan, commander of the First Regiment of Missouri Mounted Volunteers, which was part of Gen. S. W. Kearny's command, was ordered to lead an expeditionary force southward. Doniphan first brought the New Mexican Indians to terms; then, on Dec. 12, with 856 men, he began his march from Valverde on the Rio Grande. On Christmas Day he defeated a force of 600 Mexicans at El Brazito. The village of El Paso was occupied two days later. On Feb. 8, 1847, now reinforced, Doniphan set out with 924 men for Chihuahua. Twenty miles north of Chihuahua City, Feb. 28, the Americans met over 3000 Mexicans under Gen. Pedro García Condé. Again Doniphan was victorious, in the battle of the Sacramento, and the city was occupied the next day. In the spring the bulk of the expedition marched eastward, and on May 22 joined Gen. John E. Wool's army near Saltillo. Together with the later Chihuahua expedition of Col. Sterling Price, 1847–48, Doniphan's campaign contributed to the demoralization of Mexican frontier defense.

DONNER PARTY (1846–47), of California emigrants, whose nucleus was the Donner and Read families from Sangamon County, Ill., was blocked by winter snows while following an unfamiliar route south of the Great Salt Lake. Camping at Truckee Lake in November, 1846, the party suffered indescribable hardships, the survivors escaping starvation only by eating the flesh of those who died. During the winter, successive rescue parties from California broke through, and led out, with heavy loss of life, those who were able to travel. In the end, forty-seven out of eighty-seven survived.

"DON'T FIRE TILL YOU SEE THE WHITE OF THEIR EYES." The origin of this alleged command to the patriots at Bunker Hill, June 17, 1775, may have been Col. Prescott's order (powder being scarce) to reserve fire and aim low. It is said to have been passed on by Israel Putnam in these words: "Men, you are all marksmen—don't one of you fire until you see the white of their eyes."

"DON'T GIVE UP THE SHIP" were the immortal words spoken by James Lawrence, commander of the American frigate *Chesapeake,* after falling fatally wounded in the engagement with the British frigate *Shannon,* thirty miles off Boston harbor, on June 1, 1813. The *Chesapeake* was captured, and Lawrence died four days later. When Commodore Oliver Hazard Perry won his famous victory over the British on Lake Erie, Sept. 10, 1813, he flew at the mainmast of his flagship a blue battleflag inscribed with Capt. Lawrence's dying words.

DORCHESTER COMPANY. Certain Western Merchants, having ships sailing from Weymouth to fish "off the Banks," in 1622 decided that a settlement on the coast of New England would be to their advantage because they had to "double-man" their ships to have, besides the crews, enough men for the fishing; the latter could be left on shore with sufficient provisions for the winter and employ their time, until the fishing-fleet returned, in building, curing fish, trapping fur-bearing animals and planting corn.

The Rev. John White, rector of Holy Trinity, Dorchester, England, was a prime mover in this enterprise; while at Oxford he imbibed the principles of the "Early Puritans," who believed the church could be purified from within, and therefore had little sympathy with the rigid Separatism of the Plymouth Colony, where all who joined their fellowship must denounce publicly the church, its ceremonies and its form of government. Not only could a clergyman of his persuasion reside on this new plantation to attend to the spiritual welfare of the settlers, but here would be a refuge for those likely to suffer from the strict enforcement of discipline in the church, already foreshadowed by Bishop Laud's actions.

The Western Merchants, represented by "Richard Bushrod and his Associates," obtained from the Council for New England on Feb. 20, 1622/3, a license, signed by Sir Ferdinando Gorges and others, to search for a site for their colony and a month later one associate, Sir Walter Erle, became a patentee. It was required of planters that they should reside for three years and build churches, schools and other public buildings before they could be incorporated by the Council.

A situation considered suitable being found, the promoters of the scheme met on May 26, 1624, at Dorchester, under the auspices of Sir Walter Erle and Rev. John White. Whiteway, a Dorchester merchant, in his diary described this meeting as the "New England Planters Parliament" and Sir Walter as the "Govenour of the New England Plantation." A joint-stock company was formed, £3000 subscribed and more promised. A ship, the *Fellowship,* was purchased, fitted out and despatched. In September, 1625, she made her home port with a cargo of "dry fish, corfish, train-oil, quarters of oak, and skins of fox, racons, martyns, otter, muskutache and beaver." Two ships were sent out next year; and three, one laden with kine, in 1625/6.

By that time about fifty men had been left at Cape Ann, and some men from Plymouth Colony who disliked the Separatist rule there joined them; among these were Rev. John Lyford and Roger Conant. Their experience as colonists was useful to the plantation; yet that undertaking did not flourish, chiefly because the place for fishing, and the "landsmen," were ill-chosen, for "fishermen would not work on land neither husbandmen make good fishermen."

The three years of residence had elapsed and the site proved unsuitable so, on Conant's advice, all who wished to remain in New England were transferred to Nahum Keike, afterwards named Salem. Great losses had about ruined the company, so it was decided to wind up its affairs and establish a new company. John White meanwhile undertook to provide the necessary supplies to the Nahum Keike colonists.

An appeal was made to certain London merchants holding similar views on religion and a new joint-stock company—the New England Company—was formed, and Capt. John Endicott was sent out to act as governor. It was upon the foundations laid by the Dorchester Company that the Massachusetts Bay Company was reared.

DORR'S REBELLION. As late as 1841 Rhode Island was still using as her constitution the charter granted by King Charles II in 1663. This out-of-date government was not in step with the trend toward democracy which was characteristic of the times. The limitation of the suffrage to the owners of freehold estates and their oldest sons disfranchised more than half of the adult male population. For some years the masses, under the leadership of Thomas W. Dorr, had been clamoring for a wider participation in the government. Finally a mass meeting of the malcontents took the initiative in calling a convention, which met (October, 1841) and drew up a constitution known as the "People's Constitution." The active discontent of the people convinced the conservatives that some concessions would have to be made. Accordingly, a convention chosen by the qualified electors met (November, 1841) and framed a constitution, called the "Landholders' Constitution." Both of these constitutions provided for an enlargement of the suffrage, but the voting franchise was to be somewhat more liberal under the "People's Constitution" than under the "Landholders' Constitution." The former constitution was submitted to the people for ratification (December, 1841), and all adult male citizens were asked to take part in the election. The constitution was ratified by a majority of those who had voted. The "Landholders' Constitution" was submitted

(March, 1842) to those who were qualified to vote under its provisions. It was rejected by a small margin and the regular government continued to function under the charter. In the spring of 1842 a new government was organized under the "People's Constitution" with Dorr as governor. As the insurgents were preparing to uphold their authority by force, Gov. King appealed to President Tyler to lend military assistance in his effort to put down revolt. Tyler recognized the legality of the old or charter government, and promised aid if violence should be committed by the insurgents. He urged both sides, however, to settle their differences without a resort to force. This advice was not heeded and Gov. King sent the state militia to attack the Dorrites, who were fortified in the northwestern part of the state. Many of Dorr's followers fled without a fight and he surrendered himself to the authorities. A sentence of life imprisonment was imposed upon Dorr, but this was afterwards rescinded. The conservatives had the good sense to yield to the demands of the people, and so a third constitution was adopted which provided for manhood suffrage with slight restrictions.

DOUBLOON was a Spanish gold piece, so called because double the value of a pistole. Its value varied from $8.25 in the period 1730–72, $8.00 during the American Revolution and later, to about $7.84 from 1786 to 1848. It was freely used in the West Indies and South American trade, and Southerners in the United States in the colonial period often had their cash assets in Spanish gold.

DOUGHFACES were Northern people who, before the Civil War, supported Southern policies relative to territorial expansion and slavery. The word was coined in 1819 by John Randolph of Virginia as a term of contempt for members of the House of Representatives from the North who voted against the proposed Tallmadge Amendment to prevent the further introduction of slavery into Missouri.

DRAFT. Conscription enrolls able-bodied men for military service. The choosing of those to service is the draft. During the Civil War selection was effected by dividing Northern loyal states into districts roughly corresponding to congressional districts. The act of March 3, 1863, exempted the palpably unfit, a few officials, and sole supporters of aged parents and orphaned children, and authorized release from service to any one furnishing a substitute or paying $300. The draft claimed both citizens and alien declarants from the ages 20–35, and unmarried ones to 45. Drawings were made with army officers as local functionaries. Prior militiamen and Federal volunteers were credited to states, and quotas established. Lists were posted and advertised, with corrections invited. Names transcribed on cards were then placed in revolving cylinders at district draft headquarters and

drawn out until the number of men demanded was secured. Drawings were not simultaneous, but were made as each state was ready, commencing with Rhode Island on July 7, 1863; and, except for a few objections and purely local draft riots, proceeded smoothly. Enrollments began on May 25; investigators and engrossers worked to complete and verify until midsummer when altogether 3,112,279 were listed. Later drafts were made in April, 1864, September, 1864, and February, 1865. Excepting California and Oregon, all loyal states participated in one or all of these, some being exempted from one or another because of calculated quotas already exceeded. For example, for the 1865 call Connecticut, Massachusetts, Rhode Island and Iowa completely escaped; New Hampshire and Vermont were called upon to furnish only eleven and twelve men respectively. An act of July 4, 1864, abolished the discriminating and irritating cash payments in lieu of service. From total quotas of 2,759,049 considered available, these four drafts produced directly about 170,000 men, including 120,000 substitutes. Simultaneously recruiting under the bounty system during the same period approximated 1,000,000 volunteers whose names and numbers were credited to state quotas. Indeed, although Gen. Grant considered conscripts far better than the mercenary, undependable "bounty" men, it was felt that "the spur of an impending draft" acted to "stimulate recruiting" and the draft announced Jan. 5, 1864, was frankly conditioned upon quotas not being previously filled by recruiting; 489,462 volunteered for a draft of 407,092. Quotas, however, were by states; half of these were unfilled; and twelve states held drafts. There was also great inequality between districts within states, but a majority of the governors decided against concentrating on backward districts. Their political minds eschewed potential sore spots and took advantage of less troublesome neighborhoods. However, the Union Army got its necessary replacements to pin Lee against Richmond while Sherman swept through Georgia and up through the Carolinas to break the backbone of the Confederacy, whose own conscription system, at first effective, had now completely broken down.

Draft under the Selective Service Act of 1917 was throughout carried along with more localized civilian control, and, because the administration which entered World War I had been the peace party at the preceding political election, it secured phenomenal popular support. Except for temporary recruiting for Navy and Marines, and to fill up the Regular Army and National Guard to about 900,000, volunteering was completely avoided. First age limits were 21–30; later 17–45. All males within the age limits were registered, citizens and declarants alike; exemptions were for alienage, physical unfitness and conscientious scruples in organized religion. Under three calls, June 5, 1917, June 5 and Aug. 24, 1918, and Sept. 12, 1918, men totaling 23,908,576 were registered, producing an access of 2,810,296 draftees. Local boards got nowhere near the bottom of the manpower pool. Prior volunteering was not recognized, as in the Civil War, as credit for quotas demanded, but was considered when apportioning quotas between districts. Through state governors, civilian boards were appointed for each country and one for each 30,000 inhabitants in large cities (totaling 4648 local boards) and similar district boards to handle appeals and coordinate policies in each Federal judicial district (totaling 155). This was "on the principle of their peerage with the men whose cases they were to decide." Locally appointed medical advisory boards were similarly selected and late in 1918 industrial advisory boards. So speedily was organization effected that within a week of the President's request legal advisory boards were in operation, involving selection and installation of 119,282 members. Approximately one fifth of the district board members served without remuneration. The willing co-operation of the American people in this draft was phenomenal.

Registrants were numbered in each district, though the order of call was not determined locally but by drawing in Washington simultaneously the "call-numbers" for the parallel series through the country. Local boards then notified their draftees, examined them, and shipped the proper number to camp. From the first it was realized that effort must be made to avoid interfering with essential industries. Most of the local and district board effort was therefore directed to retaining at home men indispensable in industries and workers in industries producing war materials, and sending for service those least necessary to home or work "to the end that the whole nation may be a team in which each man shall play the part for which he is best fitted." No rioting or disturbance marred this draft. A few professional radical agitators were silenced (Goldman v. U. S., 245 U. S. 474). Conscientious objectors were handled with kid gloves and almost all assumed non-combatant duties upon call, or soon after. Federal courts sustained the law (Arver v. U. S., 245 U. S. 366) and clarified points regarding aliens (Angelus v. Sullivan, 246 Fed. 54). Half the male population was registered; 60% of our armed forces were raised by draft compared to the 2% during the Civil War. A Regular Army and National Guard strength in 1917 of about 200,000 was, by volunteering and by "selection" for the National Army, increased to 3,757,624 in 18 months. This was accomplished by national solidarity, wise legislation, administrative genius, and intelligent and enthusiastic local co-operation.

At the armistice of 1918, the draft was discontinued and our armed forces returned to the traditional volunteer recruiting system. Only relatively small numbers being needed, this sufficed. In 1926, authorized by a provision of the National Defense Act of 1920, there was created a Joint Army and Navy Selective Service Committee which studied and planned for

manpower procurement in the event of a new emergency. In 1935, with the Nazi peril in Europe, there commenced a five-year series of annual two-week training conferences and correspondence courses for 100 selected reserve officers, to which were later added National Guardsmen from state staffs. At the invasion of Poland, the President declared a limited national emergency in 1939 and the next year asked for a billion-dollar appropriation to speed up defenses. In this atmosphere, by midsummer of 1940 a national selective service headquarters was established, so that when the Selective Training and Service Act of Sept. 16, 1940 (Burke-Wadsworth Bill) was passed, the machinery was laid out and ready, the experience of the former war was preserved, and many key individuals had been chosen and trained. The act required the registration of all citizens and declarants between 21 and 36 years of age, pronounced against bounties and substitutes, and—since prewar training seemed at that time the main desideratum—limited service to twelve months or less and the total drafted to be in service not to exceed 900,000. As in World War I, the initial priority of call was to be based upon the drawing of lots at a public ceremony in Washington. A Director of Selective Service was provided and appointed. Deferment was to be based on individual status, not by group, except that exemptions were authorized for family men, for conscientious objectors, and for persons on tasks of "national importance."

As in World War I, the detailed administration of the draft was placed on local boards of citizens, one for each county and additional boards for each 30,000 population. There were 6443 local boards created for 3071 separate counties and parishes, 650 medical advisory boards, and 279 appeal boards. Approximately 100,000 citizens performed duties in this work without pay, as a patriotic duty and as a result of the "faith in the people" held by the government. By December, 1941, these boards had registered 17,388,000 men and, from the beginning of inductions in November, 1940, had actually drafted 921,-722. Although there were a few minor, but peaceful, pacifist demonstrations against this draft, it was very generally completely accepted by the citizenry as a defense necessity. An opinion poll indicated that almost all the people thought that the administration of the act was entirely fair. It had been fully debated in the Congress, for over a week in the House and twenty days in the Senate, where it faced 27 amendments, of which 18 were accepted. For the first time in our national history, conscription was accepted in time of peace, although specifically as a training measure and obviously as a preparation for war.

The act was successful. Its gentle pressure induced many to volunteer so as to be able to choose the arms and services in which to be enrolled. It fleshed out the National Guard and Reserve units to suitable training strengths for maneuvers. By Aug. 16, 1941, men over 27 years were being released from service.

In the summer of 1941, there arose a clearer definition of purpose, as to whether this was merely a temporary and limited peacetime training measure or was actual preparation for entry into the war in Europe. As concerned the first, the act had had strong support. It met more opposition when it was necessary that summer to secure legislative extension of the draft beyond the twelve months originally provided. Many isolationists and "America First" agitators, and newspapers, too, of that slant, aggravated the situation. High officials knew the trend of world affairs, but could not use their knowledge too openly in debate lest there be international repercussions. As a result, a bill for extension to only 18 additional months had hard sledding and actually passed the House of Representatives by the margin of only a single vote. But it did pass. It was signed by the President Aug. 18, 1941, and the system was preserved for the coming crisis.

Immediately after the Pearl Harbor attack and the following declarations of war, the act was amended on Dec. 13, 1941, to extend for the duration of the war and six months thereafter. Registration was broadened to cover men from 18 to 64 years of age, and liability to call to those 20 to 44 years of age, those from 45 to 64 chiefly being registered only for occupational classification. In December, 1942, the drafting of men over 42 was discontinued. A total of 182,509 persons were busy in the Selective Service System, approximately 95% of them volunteers working without pay. From first to last, from November, 1940 to October, 1946, there were 10,110,104 inducted into the service, and approximately 5,000,000 were either called as reservists or were induced to enlist to avoid the draft.

It was a steady process, fitted to the industrial mobilization. In the first twelve months after Pearl Harbor, the number inducted totaled only about 2,-520,000. All the while, the local boards were deciding —aside from physical fitness—on dependency questions and needs in a civilian occupation. The task of Selective Service, it has been authoritatively said, "involved the duty of furnishing to the armed forces the numbers of men desired and the types they would accept; on the other hand, the responsibility of leaving on farms, in factories and mines, on railroads and ships, those men necessary to supply the implements of war to our armed forces and our allies, to feed and clothe them and to care for the welfare of the people at home." The seriousness of this second responsibility may be illustrated by the fact that our production rose from $13,800,000,000 in 1940–41 to $53,-500,000,000 the next year. Two exhaustive conflicts, World War I and World War II, showed the importance of economic and industrial factors in modern war. For such events, the broad principle of selective service in the 20th century superseded earlier dependence upon merely professional soldiers and upon volunteering.

Following the surrender of Japan on Aug. 14, 1945, the very next day the induction of all over 26 was discontinued and two weeks later voluntary recruiting was resumed. Inductions dropped to 53,239 in September, 1945, and declined steadily to August, 1946, when the number was only 922. The act expired March 31, 1947, by Congressional action on a presidential recommendation. Liquidation of the Selective Service System, which had commenced even before the defeat of Germany, was complete by Nov. 1, 1947. On March 31, 1947, the President signed a new act to create the Office of Selective Service Records, to liquidate the System itself, preserve the records in decentralized depots in the states, and to preserve also the knowledge and methods of administration. Training was carried on, manuals were prepared, correspondence courses and conferences were arranged. The aim was to avoid a serious lapse if selective service should again be needed.

It soon became apparent, with our postwar commitments and the delicate state of international affairs, that the draft, or the indirect pressure of the draft, would be necessary to maintain our armed forces. There was no decline as complete as after World War I. There was no withdrawal into isolationism and pacifism as in the 1920's. For the first time in our history, a peacetime draft was therefore reconstituted, not as in 1940 under the shadow of an imminent war, but plainly to fulfill our peacetime commitments.

In March, 1948, the President recommended that Congress re-create the draft for the armed forces and also establish universal military training. After long hearings and sharp debate, the Congress passed and the President approved on June 24, 1948, the Selective Service Act of 1948, without provisions for universal military training, but requiring registration of youths from 18 to 26 for possible call for 21 months of service with a subsequent 5-year reserve obligation. Under it, approximately 50,000 workers on 3700 local boards swung into action again, registering 8,584,476 men. The intent of this law was to make up the difference between volunteer enlistments and service personnel needs, within the strength limits prescribed by appropriations. Reservists and National Guardsmen were exempted. Students under 20 were also exempted. Youths of 18 were permitted to enlist for a single year of active duty and later reserve obligations. This law fulfilled its purpose, and kept the armed forces at authorized strength, both by direct inductions and because it acted as a spur to volunteering.

This law of 1948 would have expired in June, 1950, but on urgings from the Defense Department and under the stimulus of the Korea episode, was extended for one year, and then by the act of June 19, 1951, the draft was extended indefinitely. A few details were changed: ages were set from 18½ to 26, service was to be for 24 months, active and reserve obligations were to be for a total of 8 years, special provisions dealt with assurances of re-employment rights, and others were inserted for the benefit of competent high school and college students, so that youths could decide for themselves whether to perform their service immediately or postpone it until after graduation. Arrangements were provided for the call of doctors and dentists to serve as such and that conscientious objectors should no longer be deferred but would be required to perform civilian work pertaining to the "national health, safety, or interest." Also, in addition to citizens and declarants, this new law now made liable to the draft other aliens permanently resident here, and those temporarily resident for more than one year.

The need for manpower had been so slight that in the year 1949 only 10,000 were called, and there were no calls at all from February, 1949, through August, 1950. In September, 1950, there were 50,000 called and the numbers ran high through 1951 and partly into 1952, when in February 52,500 were called. Thereafter the drafts diminished to a lower level. Calls ran at first to an average of 7500 a month, although in a few years it was sometimes as little as 2000 a month. Selective volunteering cut the draftee total in service down to about only one fifth of service strength in 1959, as compared with the wartime two thirds. In March, 1959, with a current call for 6000 just being issued, there was practically no substantial opposition to the enactment of a four-year extension of the draft, the favorable vote in Congress being 381 to 20 in the House and 90 to 1 in the Senate. Although reenactment continued necessary in the climate of the time, the principle of selective service seemed to be generally accepted.

DRAFT RIOTS. Although there were minor disturbances connected with personal enrollments or "conscription" under the act of March 3, 1863, actual violence awaited the draft itself. Minor riots occurred in Rutland, Vt.; Wooster, O.; Boston, Mass.; and Portsmouth, N. H.; but none equaled in length or destructiveness those in New York City. Fanned by Democratic opposition to the war, indiscreet remarks by Gov. Horatio Seymour, and arguments alleging constitutional liberties, objection to the draft in New York rested chiefly on the provision for money payments in lieu of service, which distinguished between rich men's money and poor men's blood. Shortly after the drawing of lots commenced on July 13 at the Ninth Congressional District draft headquarters, a mob, mostly of foreign-born laborers, stormed the building, overpowered attendants, police, firemen and militia, attacked residences, other draft district headquarters, saloons, hotels and restaurants and even railway tracks, and for four days the city was a welter of conflagrations, assaults and defiances, costing a thousand casualties and $1,500,000 property loss. On

July 15 militia regiments sent toward Gettysburg began to return and order was restored. Picked troops from the Army of the Potomac were brought in and on Aug. 19 drawings proceeded peaceably.

DRAINAGE OF FARM LANDS. Using imported tiles, John Johnson, of Geneva, N. Y., laid the first tile ditch in 1835. On the prairies, ditches were made by "mole plows" from 1850 to 1870. In 1930, $211,-000,000 were invested in 23,000,000 acres of reclaimed swamp lands, notably in the South; $364,-000,000 in 53,000,000 acres of farm lands improved by systematic drainage, one half being in Indiana, Michigan and Ohio. The lowly ditch digger has probably doubled agricultural production in the United States.

DRAKE AT CALIFORNIA. Francis Drake, in 1577, left England with an expedition designed to open Oriental and Pacific trade and to deliver a blow at Spanish commercial and colonial monopoly. After harassing the Spaniards in the Atlantic, Drake passed through the straits of Magellan, and, in his one remaining ship, the *Golden Hind,* coursed the Pacific coast, plundering as he went. Prevented by unfavorable winds from sailing west to his goal, the Moluccas, Drake, in June, 1579, entered a "convenient and fit harborough," apparently Drake's Bay, Calif., to repair his ship. Claiming the land for England and naming it New Albion, Drake remained 36 days, meantime exploring and establishing friendly relations with the Indians. Before departing for the Moluccas, he left nailed to a "firm poste" a brass plate, as evidence of England's claim. In 1936 the very same plate, apparently, was discovered on the western shore of San Francisco Bay, where it had been discarded not long before, its value unrecognized, after having been brought from the vicinity of Drake's Bay.

DRAMA, AMERICAN. The first essentially American play on an American theme, and produced by an American professional company, was Royall Tyler's *Contrast,* staged in New York's John Street Theater April 16, 1787. To insure its publication, Gen. George Washington, a drama enthusiast, headed the subscription list.

Theaters were no novelty in America; the John Street was then twenty years old, and playhouses had long existed in Williamsburg, Charleston, Philadelphia, Baltimore, and elsewhere, presenting British repertory by their own or visiting players. There had also been scattered performances, less professionally staged, of original plays—now lost or forgotten—that had entertained explorers and colonists as early as 1598, when a play in Spanish by Capt. Farfan of invader Oñate's army was acted to celebrate their crossing of the Rio Grande. A play in English, *Ye Bear and Ye Cubb* (1665), had been staged by young Virginians, for which "offence" they were haled to court but pardoned.

The only literary play known to have preceded Tyler's *Contrast* was classic in style and on an ancient theme: *The Prince of Parthia* (1765) by Philadelphian Thomas Godfrey, staged at the famed Southwark Theater of his native city. Of plays on Indian life, Major Robert Roger's *Ponteach; or, the Savages of America,* was the first to win popularity in print. The political behavior of Yankees was satirized also in book form, by Mercy Otis Warren of Massachusetts in her *Adulateur* (1773) and *The Group* (1775).

The first author to make dramaturgy a career was William Dunlap (1766–1839), whose first play produced was *The Father; or, American Shandyism* (1789) followed by *André* and *Leicester* and sixty or more adaptations of French and German pieces, attesting his scholarly and stylistic aims. But in 1805 his brave endeavor ended in bankruptcy.

From that year to 1825 America's 19th-century drama gave promise in works by Philadelphia's James Nelson Barker, whose *Indian Princess* (Pocahontas); *or, La Belle Sauvage* (1808) and *Superstition,* with its complex plot of refugee regicides, Indians, and Puritans deluded by suspected witchcraft, were meaningfully American.

Far more widely admired have been the dramas of New York's John Howard Payne (1791–1852), whose *Brutus or the Fall of Tarquin* (1818) was hailed as America's outstanding contribution to classical drama. It was even acted by London's greatest tragedian, Edmund Kean. Payne, too, was the first American dramatist to exploit the new French *mélodrame* and its by-product, the "well-made play," that was to set the pattern before Ibsen's "naturalism of the 'behind-life'" disparaged all superficial dramatizing. Payne's *Charles the Second* (1824), adapted from Duval's *La Jeunesse de Henri V,* captivated London as well as New York—a triumph that was celebrated, upon Payne's return to New York in 1832, by benefit stagings of his *Brutus, Charles the Second,* and *Catharine and Petruchio.* In Boston as many as 25 of Payne's plays were staged annually, suggesting an immense advance in the popular support of American drama.

The actor's appeal, however, was still stronger than the dramatist's, in England as well as America, a tendency that more than doubled Payne's theater prestige, for his acting genius won wider acclaim than his playwriting. On his European tours Payne won the admiration of the French actor Talma, through whom he came to know the Parisian playwrights and their plays, one of which he was later to adapt, entitled *Thérèse* (1821).

Under the growing appeal of romance, over 150 mid-century American plays exploited colorful historic episodes, as did Robert Montgomery Bird's *Gladiator* (1831), which for more than forty years afforded America's leading tragedian, Edwin Forrest, his most popular role. Long-lived, too, were Bird's *Broker of Bogota,* Nathaniel Willis' *Tortesa,* and Robert Conrad's *Jack Cade.* Climaxing this repertory were George Boker's *Colaynos, Leonor de Guzman,* and *Francesca da Rimini.*

Favorites, too, were many dramatizations of Indian life, the War of the Revolution and the War of 1812. In these dramatizations realistic vividness increasingly became the writer's aim; this is especially noticeable in the treatment of the Mormon migration, or in social and domestic episodes, like those of Mrs. Mowatt's celebrated *Fashion; or Life in New York* (1845), the first modern social comedy. Such stage realism of speech and action acquired a lasting fascination in Joseph Jefferson's *Rip van Winkle* (1865). It was so popular that it crowded the theaters of America and England till his death in 1905, making it impossible for him, except on special occasions, to enact any of the 500 or more characters that had made him famous before his portrayal of *Rip.* He first acted that character as his father had done, in a crude adaptation of his own; in 1865, young Joseph, on a visit to London, paid the great melodramatist Dion Boucicault to perfect the part.

Such realistic evolution, to which were later added more masterly foreign and American examples of the well-made play, gradually prepared the public for the "naturalist" trend, under Ibsen's leadership, that reached America in the last decade of the century.

Adding to the refinement of the theater after 1860, several geniuses emerged. Among them Augustin Daly made his mark as dramatist (*Horizon, Pique,* and *Divorce*), and more notably as manager of acting companies in contemporary repertory as well as Shakespeare's comedies and tragedies. Daly sponsored a new generation of theater artists, raising to higher levels the standards of acting, scenic effects, and stage business. He was quick to discern talent in playwrights, as he did in Bronson Howard (1842–1908), staging superbly his *Saratoga* (1870), *Shenandoah,* and *The Henrietta,* the last netting both the dramatist and his producer half a million dollars.

New York's city life was vividly portrayed in plays be Edward Harrigan; domestic scenes were featured in James A. Herne's *Shore Acres* (1892), and in his tragedy, *Margaret Fleming* (1890). Best remembered and most frequently revived were William Gillette's stagings as dramatizer and actor of Arthur Conan Doyle's *Sherlock Holmes* (1899) and his own *Held by the Enemy, Secret Service,* and *Too Much Johnson.*

Recognized as the best dramatic literature of this period were the plays of Augustus Thomas: *Alabama* (1891), *Arizona, The Witching Hour, As a Man Thinks;* and the popular social comedies by Clyde Fitch: *Beau Brummell* (1890), *The Climbers, The Truth, The Girl With the Green Eyes.*

Still remembered at the turn of the century as an outstanding man of the theater was New York's David Belasco, who rose to popular heights of artistic refinement, realistic detail, and romantic charm that radiated from his *Madame Butterfly* and *The Darling of the Gods.* Like London's Granville Barker, he was admired for the artistically convincing realism of scenery and costumes, speech, and action, that gave distinction to all his Broadway productions.

Shortly after 1900 courses in playwriting, play production, and contemporary theater art were introduced at several colleges. Brander Matthews of Columbia, George Pierce Baker of Harvard, and Frederick Koch of the University of North Carolina were soon to inspire students like Edward Sheldon, whose *Salvation Nell,* after production in Baker's famous '47 Workshop, became the first student-written play (1908) to win wide acclaim in the public theaters. No less an actress than Minnie Maddern Fiske appeared in the title role.

Even more of a reputation was made by the folk drama of Paul Green, under Koch's tutelage: *When Witches Ride* (1918), *The Shuffletown Outlaws, The No 'Count Boy,* the Pulitzer Prize winner *In Abraham's Bosom* (1926), and *The House of Connelly,* suggestive of Chekhov.

The greatest of all American dramatists, Eugene O'Neill, son of the actor James O'Neill, enrolled at the age of 26 in Baker's course, after years of world-wandering as a common seaman, and brief periods as a minor actor in his father's company. By that time, as he told his biographer Barrett Clark, he had read "about everything I could lay my hands on: the Greeks, the Elizabethans—practically all the classics—and of course all the moderns, Ibsen and Strindberg, especially Strindberg." He also had written several short plays on his sea experiences that he hoped to improve, but his improvement was disappointing and very little that Baker taught the class was new to O'Neill. But he got from Baker what he needed most —encouragement, for Baker had detected his genius, a self-directing one. He spent only one year at Harvard, but later he could say: "Yes, I did get a great deal from Baker—personally. He encouraged me, made me feel it was worthwhile going ahead. My personal association with him meant a devil of a lot to me at that time." And ahead O'Neill did go, gaining further inspiration from his work with the Provincetown Players who staged his *Bound East for Cardiff,* the first of his plays to be publicly produced (1916).

In 1920 O'Neill's *Emperor Jones* created a Broadway sensation with its escaping Negro Emperor, played by John Gilpin; the use of the wildly accelerated drum-beats of the Emperor's enemies to foretell his doom and suggest his mounting terror was the first of many such devices that distinguish O'Neill's masterly inventiveness. The mask in *The Great God Brown,* the whispered thoughts that belie the words spoken by the characters in *Strange Interlude,* the symbolism of the Gorilla in *The Hairy Ape* —these told of the influence of Strindberg. O'Neill's

successful defiance of dramatic conventions prompted even George Bernard Shaw, in a lecture to the students of a London dramatic academy, to urge them to begin their study with the plays of O'Neill instead of his own.

Another outstanding student of Baker's was Philip Barry, whose Harvard Prize play, *You and I* (1922), was soon followed by such nationally familiar titles as *White Wings, Paris Bound, The Animal Kingdom, Hotel Universe,* and his most admired, *Here Come the Clowns* (1938). Gratefully appreciative of Baker, Barry, a Yale graduate, persuaded Baker to abandon Harvard University, (its president having refused to sanction Baker's fund-raising to build a theater for his '47 Workshop) and to assume the direction of Yale's new Theater and School of Drama, which, since the early '20's has taken the lead in supplying academically-trained men of the theater.

One of the outstanding figures of the 20th century was the poet-dramatist, Maxwell Anderson, who believed "the best prose in the world is inferior on the stage to the best poetry." Beginning in 1924 he endeavored with surprising success to convince the public that his belief was justified even in an era of theater prose. Many of his plays have been notably successful in London. Most popular have been his *Saturday's Children* (1927); *Elizabeth the Queen* (1930); *Knickerbocker Holiday* (1938), a musical comedy; *Mary of Scotland* (1933); *Both Your Houses,* awarded the Pulitzer Prize (1933); *Winterset* (1935) and *High Tor* (1937), both winning the Critics' Award; and *Journey to Jerusalem* (1940).

Later came the Armenian-American, William Saroyan, whose first Broadway successes were *My Heart's in the Highlands* (1939) and *Time of Your Life,* followed by *Hello Out There* (1942). Uninhibited emotionalism has characterized most of his sixty or more plays, short or long. And still later came Tennessee Williams, whose *Streetcar Named Desire* (1947) and *Cat on a Hot Tin Roof* (1955) have both won the Critics' Award and the Pulitzer Prize.

One of the most successful playwrights following World War II was Arthur Miller, author of *All My Sons* (1947). His *Death of a Salesman* (1949), a drama of sociological implications, won sobering popularity as well as the Pulitzer Prize. His vivid reproduction of Salem witchcraft trials in *The Crucible* (1953) was intended as a weapon against what he regarded as a perversion of democracy.

Supplementing collegiate stimulus has been the spread of innumerable "Little Theaters" organized by devoted groups to give expression to their own ideals, or, as is the case with most "summer theaters," to supply dramatic entertainment in localities not served by the professional theaters. Even in the "off-Broadway" districts of New York many such playhouses have risen to fame and success while the professional theaters have suffered a decline. They have also been productive of playwriting members, doing their utmost to encourage every type of theater talent, such as the Provincetown Players that fostered Eugene O'Neill, and the Group Theater that gave William Saroyan to Broadway. The Neighborhood Playhouse and the Washington Square Theater have had immense influence in the theater life of America. The leaders of the latter troop formed the Theater Guild in 1919, following the closing of their own auditorium on Washington Square. With managers like Lawrence Langner, scenic artists like Jo Mielziner and actors like Alfred Lunt and Lynn Fontanne, the Theater Guild established the highest standards of play production the nation had known. O'Neill's *Mourning Becomes Electra* (1931) and *Strange Interlude* (1928) were impressively staged in the Guild's new, perfectly equipped playhouse.

DRED SCOTT CASE was decided by the U. S. Supreme Court on March 6, 1857. The judgment in the case, as distinguished from the opinions delivered, was relatively narrow and of no great importance. The Court held that a Negro, a slave under the laws of Missouri, had no constitutional right to sue in a Federal court to obtain his freedom. The importance of the case is derived from the broader issues discussed in the opinions, involving current political controversies. The Kansas-Nebraska Act of 1854 repealed provisions of the Missouri Compromise excluding slavery from the northern part of the Louisiana Purchase. This repeal, and subsequent strife in Kansas, added to intense sectional bitterness over the issues of slavery. Southern leaders justified the new legislation in part by contending that Congress had never had the constitutional power to exclude slavery from the territories of the United States. Northern leaders hotly disagreed. The Supreme Court had not had an occasion to decide the constitutional question.

The Court at first arranged to decide the Dred Scott case without discussing the power of Congress over slavery in the territories. When it was learned, however, that two dissenting judges proposed to argue that Congress had the power in question, the majority decided to enlarge the scope of their discussion and deny the power. Some members hoped the pronouncement of the Court would settle the question, allay some of the strife, and perhaps save the Union. The seven majority judges wrote opinions. That of Chief Justice Taney is usually spoken of as the opinion of the Court, although on one of the contentions set forth in his opinion only two of his associates concurred. Dred Scott claimed his freedom on the ground that with the consent of his master he had resided in territory where slavery was forbidden. Taney held that, within the meaning of the Constitution, the Negro was not a "citizen" who had a right to sue in a Federal court by virtue of his citizenship. His argument may be summarized as follows:

First. When the Constitution was adopted Negroes were regarded as persons of an inferior order, and not as "citizens," and they were not intended to be included by the constitutional provision giving to citizens of different states the right to sue in Federal courts.

Second. Apart from the question as to whether *any* Negro could be a citizen in the constitutional sense, it was obvious that no slave could be such a citizen. Dred Scott had originally been a slave. He had not become free by residence in territory covered by the Missouri Compromise, since Congress had no constitutional power to enact the Missouri Compromise. Unless he had some other claim to freedom he was still a slave, and therefore not a citizen entitled to sue in a Federal court.

Third. Whatever the temporary effect of Dred Scott's brief residence in the free state of Illinois, his status after his return to Missouri was determined by Missouri law. The Missouri courts had held that he was a slave. Therefore he was not a citizen, and could not sue in a Federal court.

On the first point Chief Justice Taney expressed an opinion which he had long held, and which he had submitted officially 25 years earlier when Attorney General of the United States. It was a drastic commitment, however, and although others of his associates probably agreed privately in the opinion only two of them concurred in the statement as necessary to the decision of the Dred Scott case. The holding was never repudiated by the Court itself, but it was superseded by that part of the Fourteenth Amendment which declares that "All persons born or naturalized in the United States and subject to the jurisdiction thereof, are citizens of the United States and of the State wherein they reside."

The conclusions with respect to the second point went to the heart of the controversy raging over the extension of slavery. The decision that Congress had no power to exclude slavery from the territories struck a heavy blow at the contentions of antislavery forces. Although the discussion of the question was logically relevant as phrased by Chief Justice Taney, the case might have been decided on the third point alone, without commitment as to the other two. Justices McLean and Curtis, in dissent, denounced the unnecessary breadth of the decision. The abolitionist press and hostile politicians followed suit in attacks upon the Supreme Court the bitterness of which has never been surpassed in any other period. The inflamed discussions probably did much to precipitate the Civil War. The broad phrasing of the decision therefore had the opposite effect from that intended by those who planned it. Apart from the sectional issue, the case is important in that it was the first in more than half a century in which the Supreme Court held an act of Congress unconstitutional.

DREWRY'S BLUFF, BATTLE AT (May 12–16, 1864). As part of the overland movement against Richmond, Grant put Gen. Butler in charge of the

Union forces operating from the Yorktown Peninsula. Landing at Bermuda Hundred, Butler sought to attack Confederate forces in rear of Richmond. At Drewry's Bluff he was defeated by Beauregard (C.). Had President Davis adopted Beauregard's entire plan of operations, it is possible that Butler's army would either have been captured or destroyed; as it was, the Confederates succeeded in restoring their communications south and west of Richmond. In this battle, Union forces under Gen. William Farrar Smith made successful use of wire entanglements.

DROUGHTS. A large part of the earth's inhabited area is subject to periodic droughts which have plagued mankind throughout the course of history. For centuries China and India have suffered from occasional great droughts which induced famines and caused the death of millions of people. In America droughts have not reached such catastrophic proportions because its droughty area is more restricted and less populous, and because it has greater capacity for food production. But droughts have caused serious economic losses, and at one time or another have affected almost all parts of the country. They were an important deterrent factor in the settlement of the western states, and at different times have caused partial abandonment of established settlements in the Great Plains.

A drought is a period of below normal rainfall lasting long enough to cause severe damage to native and cultivated vegetation, and to other forms of life, including man, whose welfare is dependent on the vegetation. The vegetation of any area becomes adjusted to the average rainfall and will defoliate and die when the average supply is seriously reduced. Arid land vegetation grows prolifically on a supply of rainfall that is completely inadequate for the vegetation of humid climates.

Droughts occur in varying degrees of intensity in nearly all of the country's climatic environments. In the humid eastern states they are usually of short duration, but sometimes cause serious damage to crops, trees, and water resources. In the desert Southwest where dryness is perpetual a period of even drier weather has relatively little effect. In the intermediate climatic ranges of the Great Plains states, where grazing and dry farming are widely practiced, droughts have been most severe and have caused the greatest losses and the greatest amount of human suffering.

In the middle 1930's at the culmination of one of the worst droughts in the nation's history the "Dust Bowl"—as the core of the drought-stricken area was known—encompassed an area of 50,000,000 acres centering along the boundary between the panhandles of Texas and Oklahoma, and extending into adjacent parts of New Mexico, Colorado and Kansas. The Dust Bowl derived its name from the great dust storms which were spawned on its wind-scoured surface. Top soil from desiccated farms and ranges was swept into the atmosphere and accumulated into mountainous, black clouds of dust. Some of the worst of these "black dusters" drifted all the way from the Great Plains to the Gulf and Atlantic Coasts.

The Dust Bowl developed during successive years of scanty rainfall and excessive evaporation caused by continuous strong, dry winds. Cultivated crops yielded little or failed completely. Cattle grew emaciated on bone-dry ranges and had to be sold at sacrifice prices in glutted eastern markets, while others, too poor for marketing, died of suffocation and starvation. Residents of the area, long accustomed to a pattern of "dry years" which frequently intersperse the more bountiful "wet years," became alarmed at the increasing destructiveness of the Dust Bowl drought. There was a widespread belief that an unprecedented climatic change was converting the Great Plains into a permanent desert. Many impoverished residents abandoned their homes and moved to other parts of the country.

The United States weather records indicate numerous droughts in the plains states prior to the 1930's. One which culminated in 1894 and 1895 was comparable in severity to the Dust Bowl maker, but was less destructive because in that period fewer people lived on the plains, and more of the land was turfed and therefore less subject to wind erosion. Maps of the country made prior to 1850 had "Great American Desert" written across the plains region. The map makers' classification of the Great Plains as a desert was probably based on observations made during a severe drought that occurred before weather stations had been established.

A climatic pattern of alternating dry and wet intervals has prevailed in the West since long before the country was settled by Europeans. Tree ring studies show a centuries-long succession of prehistoric droughts. One of the most severe of these extended through the last quarter of the 13th century, and may have been the cause of the permanent abandonment of Pueblo Bonito and other highly developed Pueblo Indian villages of the Southwest. Geologic records show the occurrence of droughty intervals since early Pleistocene time. Large areas of the richest plains soils are underlain by layers of loess—a fine-grained, wind-deposited dust—which attest to dust storms of past ages that would have dwarfed those of the Dust Bowl period. Ancient dune fields developed at different times under essentially desert conditions underlie thousands of square miles of modern farm- and rangeland.

Because of the ever-increasing population and expanding use of America's droughty lands, future droughts are likely to be more destructive than any previously experienced. The Dust Bowl drought demonstrated the disastrous consequences of overgrazing and ploughing lands highly susceptible to erosion, and made people more aware of the practical limitations involved in exploiting the plains soil. Improved methods of dry farming have since been developed, irrigation has been greatly expanded and conservation of soil and water resources is now more generally practiced.

Droughts are periodic, but they do not occur in a predictable cyclic pattern. With increasing knowledge of the phenomena that control our climate, man may someday be able to predict the occurrence and severity of droughts, and the area that will be affected. In the meantime he has learned at least that they are inevitably recurrent, and he has begun to learn means of ameliorating their effects.

DRY FARMING is the conducting of agricultural operations, without irrigation, in a climate with a deficiency of moisture. In the United States, Anglo-American experiments occurred more or less independently at different points where settlement was established. In California, during the early part of the decade beginning with 1850, Americans began to raise crops, such as winter wheat, whose principal growing season coincided with the winter rainfall season. By 1868 dry farming was extensively and successfully practiced in certain areas. In some interior valleys of the Pacific Northwest beginnings were reported before 1880. In the Great Plains, with its summer rainfall season, adaptation to dry farming methods was associated particularly with the small-farmer invasion of the late 1880's and later. Experimental work for the Kansas Pacific railroad had been begun near the 98th meridian by R. S. Elliott between 1870 and 1873. H. W. Campbell carried on private experiments on the Northern Plains which resulted in the formulation of much of his "system" by 1895. His work attracted the attention and support of railroad interests. The state agricultural experiment stations of the Plains region inaugurated experimental activities under governmental auspices soon after their foundation, and the Federal Department of Agriculture created the office of dry land agriculture in 1905. Once definitely inaugurated, development of dry farming was continuous in the Great Plains proper, but the drought cycle of the 1930's intensified investigational work and the invention of machinery for special soil cultural processes both in the Plains and in the transitional subhumid country where it was neglected during wet periods.

DUCKING STOOL was a rude armchair in use from the 17th to the 19th century in England and the United States for the punishment of witches, scolds and prostitutes. The chair was strongly made and was usually fastened to a long wooden beam fixed as a seesaw on the edge of a pond or stream of water. The unfortunate woman was seated in the chair, an iron band being placed around her so that she should not fall out. Then she was immersed. The number of duckings she received depended upon the sentence of the court.

DUE PROCESS CLAUSES occur at two points in the Constitution of the United States. The first is a provision in the Fifth Amendment, adopted in 1791, providing that "No person shall . . . be deprived of life, liberty, or property, without due process of law." This provision applies only to the Federal Government. The second due process clause in the Constitution is a provision in the Fourteenth Amendment, adopted in 1868, saying, "Nor shall any state deprive any person of life, liberty, or property, without due process of law." Most states have similar restrictive clauses in their own constitutions. The concept of "due process of law," or "law of the land," with which judges have identified the term, can be traced backward through the channel of British institutions far into the Middle Ages, to Magna Carta and beyond. It came into American law and American thinking as a part of our British heritage.

Use of the term was relatively infrequent in the first three quarters of a century during which it occupied a place in the Federal Constitution as a restriction on the Federal Government. The principal reason was that during this period, as during its earlier development in the mother country, due process was usually regarded only as a restriction on procedure. It was thought of as a requirement that government procedure affecting the rights and liberties of the people should harmonize with the principles and machinery worked out over a long period of time for the protection of these rights and liberties.

On the other hand, the term was not generally regarded as a curb on the kinds of laws which legislatures might enact. There are two instances of fairly clear-cut exceptions to this interpretation in the American field prior to the Civil War. In Wynehamer v. New York (13 New York 378) the highest court of New York held a state law to be in violation of the due process clause of the state constitution because of the substantive content of the law. In the Dred Scott case (19 Howard 393,450) Chief Justice Taney spoke of an act of Congress denying rights of slave property in the territories of the United States as one which "could hardly be dignified with the name of due process of law."

It was only after the Civil War, however, and after the Fourteenth Amendment had made due process a Federal restriction on the states that judges began a definite retreat before the insistence of counsel, and admitted in increasing numbers that due process limited substantive legislative enactments as well as procedure. This change in interpretation accompanied a change in the content or emphasis of legislation in the same period. The development of railroads and industries, and the increase in the production of commodities of all kinds, and the increased complexity of commercial relationships, were accompanied by a rapid growth of legislation affecting property and property rights. Legislative interference with matters traditionally left free or largely free from Government regulation brought vigorous protests from affected parties. At the behest of counsel, courts steeped in doctrines of laissez faire used the due process concept as an instrument to curb legislation deemed unreasonable or arbitrary.

The growth of this use of the term was gradual, but it has spread so widely that few enactments of Congress or the state legislatures affecting the rights and liberties of the people avoid the gauntlet of the courts in appraisal of their reasonableness. That which is not reasonable is not due process, and therefore is not in accord with the Constitution. Reasonableness, like due process itself, has no legal definition save in so far as a definition is provided by assembling the instances in which it has been judicially applied in times past. The philosophy of the judge applying the term, his conception of what "ought to be," has much to do with the determination of constitutionality in due process cases.

The result has been a great complexity of interpretations, involved in a mass of litigation in a number of fields. In rate regulation, for instance, rates fixed must not be such as to deny a fair return on a fair value. Fair return and fair value are also terms left to judicial definition, however, and provide broad bases for controversy in endless litigation. Until recently due process has been held to prohibit government fixing of prices and rates in business not "affected with a public interest." Unfortunately, there was no adequate definition of businesses so affected, and much litigation turned on this point as well. This business classification apparently no longer stands in the way of regulation (see Nebbia v. New York, 291 U. S. 502), but due process still provides a basis for judicial scrutiny in each instance. Interpretations in another field illustrate variations in terms of changing conditions and changing personnel of the courts. Government violated due process by the act of prescribing minimum wages for women in private employment in 1923, but such a regulation was upheld by the U. S. Supreme Court in 1937.

The due process clauses, therefore, have been used by judges to harmonize or limit state and Federal legislation in terms of their conceptions of public welfare. The clauses have retained at the same time their quality as restrictions on procedure. In this field, as in the field of substantive legislation, there is development of due process with changing conditions. Contemporary illustrations are provided by cases growing out of the activities of regulatory commissions to which quasi-judicial powers have been allotted. The procedure of these agencies is developed under the careful scrutiny of the courts, and judicial reprimands in the form of adverse decisions on due process curtail developments deemed by the courts to be unjust.

DUELLING was a social practice common in various sections of the United States for a century prior to 1870, although individual combats were recorded back to the earliest colonial days, and as recently as 1901. Defined as "a private fight between two persons, prearranged and fought with deadly weapons, usually in the presence of two witnesses called seconds who regulate the mode of fighting and enforce the rules agreed upon, having for its object to decide a personal quarrel or to settle a point of honor," duelling was a legacy of the Middle Ages and was carried by the English settlers to America. The first such affair in the English colonies probably occurred at Plymouth in 1621, though available records show less than a score from 1624 to 1763. It lost favor in the North after the Revolution, but spread in the ante-bellum South, motivated by a growing planter class, French and Spanish influences, and an individualism which soon developed a high code of honor. The decline set in after the Civil War.

Duels were waged over differences of opinion, real or fancied wrongs, or insults. Arrangements usually were carried out with respect to the code, whether it was the English, the South Carolina or the New Orleans covenant. Communications, couched in formal, stilted terms, were exchanged between principals or seconds. Choice of weapons was left to the challenged, other details being arranged by seconds. Swords were generally used during the colonial period, but pistols came into favor after the Revolution. The American brand of duelling changed gradually from the European standard of the satisfaction of honor to the desire to kill one's opponent. The practice embraced all classes; and weapons, varying with individuals, included rifles, shotguns, sword canes, Bowie knives, lances and even harpoons. Among the famous duelling grounds were the field near Bladensburg, Md.; the "Duelling Oaks," New Orleans; and Bloody Island, St. Louis. In addition to the Burr-Hamilton duel in 1804, and that of Barron—Decatur in 1820, other notable American *affaires d'honneur* were Andrew Jackson—Charles Dickinson (1817); Thomas H. Benton—Charles Lucas (1820); John Randolph—Henry Clay (1826); Jonathan Cilley—William Graves (1838); John H. Pleasants—Thomas Ritchie (1846); and David Broderick—David S. Terry (1859).

Agitation against duelling began in the 17th century. Washington, Franklin and Jefferson were among the men in public life who opposed the practice, and most of the states of the young republic eventually decreed a challenge a breach of peace, the wounding of an opponent an attempt at murder, or the killing of a combatant a homicide, seconds being held equally guilty with principals. The army and navy condemned the practice late in the 18th century, and in the latter part of the last century public opinion and ridicule brought an end to a senseless custom.

DUGOUT. A temporary home of the plains country, built in the side of a ravine or hill. Three sides were made of earth. The front, made of logs or sod, had a door and a window. The roof, sloping back onto the hill, was made by forming a framework of poles, covered with a layer of brush, another of slough hay, and over all a layer of sod.

DUGOUT (BOAT). The craft universally used by the primitive American, and at once adopted by the invading white man, was the hollowed log or pirogue. The cottonwood tree, easily procured along the northern waterways, was a favorite in many parts of the continent, but the cypress, too, was worked into a durable boat in those sections where it abounds. Many journeys from the heart of the wilderness to St. Louis through 2000 miles of the Missouri River system were made in dugouts.

"DUKE OF YORK'S LAWS" was a code of laws drawn up in 1665 by Gov. Nicolls in anticipation of a meeting called by him in February to bring a more uniform system of government to the towns of the newly created shire of Yorkshire, and presented by him to the 34 delegates, mostly from Long Island, who met at Hempstead on March 1. This proceeding by no means corresponded with the representatives' idea of lawmaking and considerable dissatisfaction was expressed. Nicolls shrewdly accepted a few minor amendments, and the code was promulgated. As compiled by Nicolls the laws were drawn largely from the existing codes of Massachusetts and New Haven. A civil and criminal code was set up; elaborate provisions made for local governments; a general provincial organization of the courts and militia provided; Indian affairs, ecclesiastical establishments, social and domestic relations regulated; standards of weights and measures provided; and legal forms and methods of keeping records fixed. The code was gradually extended to include the whole province.

DULUTH'S EXPLORATIONS. Count Frontenac, governor of New France in the late 17th century, was eager to explore westward and to find, if possible, a route to the western sea. In 1678 he gave secret instructions to Daniel Graysolon, sieur Duluth (he himself spelled his name Dulhut) to explore westward from Lake Superior, from where one of Frontenac's agents, Hughes Randin, had just returned. Duluth made friends with the Chippewa near the Sault Ste. Marie and in the summer of 1679 moved across to the western end of the great lake, where he had a rendezvous with the Sioux, near the site of the city that now bears his name. Thence he accompanied the Sioux through the Savanna portage to Lake Mille Lac, and learned that he was near the source of the Mississippi.

Returning to Lake Superior he met the Assiniboine Indians on the Kaministiquia portage and explored part of the northern shore of the lake. In 1680 he de-

termined to open a new route to the Mississippi, via the Brulé-St. Croix portage, the most northern and western portage route from the Great Lakes to the great river. In the next years he attempted to push west by land from the Sioux country, and his men appear to have crossed Minnesota to the land of the Teton Sioux on Big Stone Lake. Thenceforward his efforts were utilized in the Iroquois wars, and in safeguarding the French in the West. In 1683 he built a post on the St. Croix portage route, the first interior fort in Wisconsin. Later he sent his brother Claude Graysolon, sieur de la Tourette, to build a post on Lake Nipigon and to intercept the furs going to the English posts on Hudson Bay.

In 1688 Duluth again visited the Sioux region, approaching via the Green Bay-Fox-Wisconsin route to the Mississippi. The next year he attempted to penetrate the interior via the Kaministiquia portage route, but was recalled to the colony and never came West again. His explorations opened up the shores of Lake Superior, the headwaters of the Mississippi, the land of the Sioux Indians, and the portage routes to the interior, which were utilized by his successors in the early 18th century.

DUNBAR'S EXPEDITION started after Lewis and Clark had left for the Northwest to explore a portion of the new Louisiana purchase in 1804. Jefferson asked William Dunbar, a scientist of Mississippi, to explore the Red River of the South. Dr. George Hunter, a chemist of Philadelphia, was appointed to aid him, and the two headed an expedition of 17 men leaving Natchez, Miss., in October, 1804. They entered the Red from the Mississippi, but higher up turned into its confluent, the Ouachita (on some maps termed the Washita), where they found a few French and Spanish families in scattered hamlets; also some German, Irish and American frontiersmen. One hundred ninety miles up the Ouachita at Fort Miró they discovered an American settlement of 150 families protected by a military force. After penetrating into Arkansas, as far as Hot Springs, they returned to Natchez in January, 1805.

DUNKARDS is the name popularly given to a group of five denominations officially designated German Baptist Brethren. Influenced by the Pietist movement in Germany, Alexander Mack and others organized a church in Schwarzenau with the distinctive feature of trine (three times) immersion, whence the name Taeufer, or Tunker, or Dunker ("Dipper"), or Dunkard. In 1719, due to persecution in Europe, a first group settled in Germantown, Pa., to be followed by others under Alexander Mack, until the church existed only in America. Still centered in Pennsylvania, they now have spread into some 35 states. The Dunkards have been characterized by plain dress, an unsalaried ministry, the prohibition to bear arms, take oaths and go to law, and by the practice of trine baptism, foot washing and the Love Feast.

DUNMORE'S WAR (1774). The Indians of trans-Ohio were much incensed at the encroachment of the frontiersmen, while the rivalry between the colonies of Pennsylvania and Virginia over the site of Pittsburgh increased the tension. Early in 1774 Col. John Connolly, agent of Lord Dunmore, royal governor of Virginia, took possession of Fort Pitt, renamed it Fort Dunmore, and attempted retaliation for Indian outrages. The Delawares, under the influence of Moravian missionaries, kept the peace; the Shawnees were eager for war. June 10, the governor called out the militia of southwest Virginia, which, embodying under Gen. Andrew Lewis, prepared for an expedition to the Shawnee towns beyond the Ohio. The inhabitants of the Virginia frontier meanwhile "forted," and defended their families against the raids of the incensed Indians.

Early in August the militia of Frederick County, Va., under Maj. Angus McDonald, raided the Wapatomica towns on the Muskingum River. Gov. Dunmore, in midsummer, advanced in person to Fort Dunmore, where he opened a land office, and in September called on the neighboring militia to join in an expedition against the hostiles. He intended to join Gen. Lewis, but before the junction of the two wings of the army the Shawnee warriors led by Cornstalk attacked Lewis' division, Oct. 10, at the mouth of the Great Kanawha. After an all-day battle at Point Pleasant, the whites won a decisive victory. The Indians fled back to their Ohio towns, and the chiefs sought Dunmore's camp and offered peace. Dunmore marched to the Pickaway Plains, where he established Camp Charlotte and made a treaty, which was sealed by the delivery of hostages. Dunmore returned to Virginia, while Lewis' forces made their way, after leaving a garrison at Point Pleasant, to their homes in southwest Virginia.

The effect of this victory over the Indians was decisive for the frontier during the early years of the American Revolution. While the Indians remained at peace, many officers and men joined the colonial forces where their experience in warfare was of value.

DUQUESNE, FORT. In 1753 the Marquis Duquesne, governor of New France, moved to occupy the Ohio Valley. On the route from Lake Erie to the Allegheny River, forts were erected at Presque Isle, Le Bœuf, and Venango. Washington's mission to the French merely stimulated an early campaign in 1754. In February, 1754, Contrecœur left Montreal with 800 men, and on April 17 took possession of the fort being built by the Ohio Company at the forks of the Ohio. The French destroyed this work and constructed Fort Duquesne on its site. The rivers protected two sides of the triangle; walls of squared logs and earth, twelve feet thick, protected its base. Out-

side the walls was a deep ditch and beyond that a log stockade.

Troops left Fort Duquesne to defeat Washington at Great Meadows in 1754, and to rout Braddock's expedition in 1755. After Braddock's defeat the French held undisputed possession of the Ohio Valley for three years, administering their military occupation from Fort Duquesne and stimulating Indian raids on the frontiers of Pennsylvania, Virginia and the Carolinas. Finally, on Nov. 24, 1758, when the Forbes expedition neared the forks of the Ohio, the French destroyed Fort Duquesne and retreated.

DUST BOWL is a term applied since 1933 to the High Plains eastward from the Rockies to about the 100th meridian; and especially to the Southwest High Plains. Lt. Zebulon M. Pike reported drought and the blowing of dust on these plains in 1806, as did succeeding travelers, who called the region the Great American Desert, although it nourished 5,000,-000 buffalo. Agriculture began about 1886 and, with development of the drought-resistant crops, expanded to include one third the area by 1930. The rest remained grazing land. As the sod was broken, dust storms became more intense during dry years. Unprecedented drought prolonged over several years in the 1930's brought Black Blizzards, sweeping powdery loam from tilled fields, filling the air five miles high with eddying swirls of choking dust, converting days into nights, halting traffic and burying lands with shifting dust drifts. Silt, carried to the Atlantic seaboard in 1934 and 1935, threw news and magazine writers into a panic of exaggeration. Agricultural science has accomplished much in drought control since the 1890's, but larger Federal and state appropriations since 1935 have resulted in greater control of wind erosion. Methods include contour tillage to prevent run-off of rain, use of drought-resistant cover crops, etc.

DUTCH WEST INDIA COMPANY was organized by a group of Dutch merchants in imitation of the Dutch East India Company, and was chartered by the States General on June 3, 1621. Under this charter the company was given enormous powers both political and commercial, which included the exclusive right to trade on the west coast of Africa, in the West Indies, on the east and west coasts of America, and in Australia. In addition the company was empowered to make alliances with the natives, to build forts and plant colonies. Nineteen directors administered the general affairs of the company. In 1624 the company planted a settlement at Fort Orange, and in 1625 one on Manhattan, forming the colony of New Netherland. Strict obedience to the orders of the company was imposed on all colonists. The director and council acted under instruction from the company. Although later important matters affecting New Netherland often came before the States

General, the continued despotic control of the company and its interest in trade rather than colonization, was detrimental to the welfare of the colony.

E PLURIBUS UNUM ("from the many, one"), motto on the seal of the United States, was selected by Franklin, Adams and Jefferson (1776); it appears in Virgil's *Moretum* and the *Gentleman's Magazine* (from 1732 to 1833). New Jersey copper coins bore it (1786), as have subsequent coins of the Union.

EAGLE, AMERICAN. The eagle, for ages a military emblem and symbol of strength, probably first appeared as an American symbol on a Massachusetts copper cent coined in 1776. In 1787 it appeared on a New York copper and two new coppers of Massachusetts. Meanwhile, it had been placed on the Great Seal of the United States, Charles Thomson, Secretary of Congress, specifying that it should be the distinctly American white-headed or bald eagle. It has appeared on the reverse of some of our coins since the beginning of coinage, notably the silver dollar, half dollar and quarter, and the gold coins, which were christened eagle, half eagle, quarter eagle and double eagle. It even appeared on a three-cent piece of 1851 and (in full flight) on the obverse of a cent of 1857. Many states are now protecting the bald eagle by law from killing.

EARTHQUAKES. The first earthquake recorded in the United States was in 1638 in Connecticut and Massachusetts; no great damage was done. The most famous earthquake of colonial times was that of 1663, which, while centered in Canada, was felt in New England. To the rank and file of people earthquakes are classed as great or small according to their destruction of human life and property, although scientifically a different standard determines an earthquake's importance. From the latter viewpoint among the most important earthquakes in the United States were those centering near New Madrid, Mo., in 1811 and 1812. That of Dec. 16, 1811, is listed among the greatest known earthquakes of history, and the later shocks of 1812 were nearly as intense. At this time the most extensive known change in topography took place in a region of moderate relief. An area of 30,000 square miles sank through varying amounts from five to fifteen feet. Other areas were raised by similar amounts. The total area over which the shock was felt was about 1,000,000 square miles. The Mississippi River changed its course in places. These earthquakes caused little damage to men simply because there were few in the region, and most houses were log cabins—a design peculiarly adapted to resist an earthquake. From the other point of view, and aside, of course, from the San Francisco earthquake, the most important earthquakes in the United States were those at Charleston, S. C., and at Helena, Mont. That at Charleston took place at 9:50 P.M., Aug. 31,

1886, just as the inhabitants were either asleep or retiring. Many persons were killed and more than three fourths of the buildings were rendered uninhabitable; the property damage was estimated at $8,000,000. The earthquake near Helena of Oct. 18, 1935, was accompanied by several hundred fore and after shocks beginning on Oct. 12. The property damage was estimated at $3,000,000.

EAST FLORIDA was established as a British province by the Proclamation of 1763. It consisted of the peninsula of Florida north to the St. Mary's River and a line from thence along the 31° to the juncture of the Flint and the Chattahoochee Rivers. The western boundary was the Appalachicola River. East Florida was returned to Spain by the English in 1783. In 1822, after the purchase of Florida by the United States, it was joined to that portion of West Florida lying between the Appalachicola and Perdido Rivers to form the Territory of Florida.

EAST INDIA COMPANY (1600–1858), one of the longest-lived and richest trading companies, exercised a pervasive influence on British colonial policy and thus indirectly on American affairs from an early date in its history. Its wealth and its commanding position both in England and in the world of commerce affected regions outside its major concern, the East. Nevertheless, not until the era of the American Revolution did the company figure specifically in American affairs, and then but briefly. At that time it was expanding its activities in the East, particularly in China, and in order to strengthen its rather precarious foothold at Canton, the company purchased increasingly larger amounts of tea. This development, coinciding with the outbreak of disputes between Great Britain and her American colonies, ultimately related to them. After the imposition of the tea tax in 1767, boycotts reduced American consumption from 900,000 pounds in 1769 to 237,000 pounds in 1772. With its warehouses overflowing and a financial crisis looming, the company surrendered part of its political power for the right to export tea directly to America. This right, acquired in 1773 under North's Regulating Act, had most unhappy results and precipitated a crisis. After the Revolution, the company had little or no contact with America.

EAST JERSEY as a separate province begins with the execution of the "quintipartite deed" in 1676. This deed divided New Jersey along a line running northwest from "the most southwardly point of the east side of Little Egg Harbor" to the Delaware River at the 41st parallel of latitude. (In 1719 41° 40′ was established as the "north partition point" giving West Jersey an excess of 1,000,000 acres.) The territory east of this line, henceforth East Jersey, went to Sir George Carteret. In 1682 the heirs of

Carteret sold their portion to William Penn and eleven associates, each of whom sold one half of his share to a new associate, thus making a board of 24 proprietors. Save for the two months of the Andros administration in 1688, and an interregnum from 1688–92, this board, though enlarged, governed the province until the close of the Proprietary period. The Concessions and Agreement formed the basic law. The population included Puritans from New England and Long Island, Scotch Presbyterians and some Quakers. To promote trade Perth Amboy was founded and became the capital in 1686. On April 15, 1702, the Proprietors surrendered their powers of Government to the Crown but retained all rights to the soil.

EASTLAND, THE, excursion steamer, overturned at its wharf in the Chicago River, July 24, 1915, at the moment of departure for a day's outing on Lake Michigan with some 2000 persons, of whom 812 lost their lives. Overloading of the top deck and insufficient water ballast were blamed for the disaster.

EASTON, TREATY OF (Oct. 8–26, 1758), was the fourth of a series of conferences held by the government of Pennsylvania from 1756 to 1758 in an effort to divert the Delaware Indians of the upper Delaware and Susquehanna River valleys from supporting their brothers of the Ohio Valley who were aiding the French by laying waste the white frontier settlements of Pennsylvania. Besides the Delawares, led by Teedyuscung, there were present at Easton representatives of the Iroquois, who were the acknowledged overlords of the Delawares. Peace was made possible when the Pennsylvanians, led by Gov. William Denny, and assisted by Conrad Weiser, George Croghan and others, persuaded the Iroquois to consent to the abrogation of the treaty made at the Albany Congress of 1754 by which they had ceded most of the lands of the western Susquehanna Valley to the English. The Iroquois also promised the Delawares the right to live and hunt in security in these western Susquehanna lands, to which most of the Delawares subsequently migrated. Negotiations looking toward a peaceful adjustment with the Ohio Valley Indians were furthered by representations brought from the West by the Pennsylvania agent Christian Frederick Post, and two western Delawares, but no agreement was made.

EATON, PEGGY, AFFAIR (1829–31). Margaret O'Neil, daughter of a Washington tavern keeper, at the age of sixteen, married John B. Timberlake, a purser in the U. S. Navy. In 1828, her husband died while serving on the frigate *Constitution*.

Meanwhile, for a decade, she and her husband had been on friendly terms with Sen. John H. Eaton of Tennessee, who stayed at the O'Neil establishment while in Washington. On Jan. 1, 1829, with the approval of President-elect Jackson, Eaton married her. Their relations had previously been a subject for the scandalmongers, whose tongues were not stilled by the marriage.

After Eaton was appointed Secretary of War, his wife became an issue. For over two years, Washington society was disturbed by an undercover social war revolving about Mrs. Eaton. The Calhouns and their friends led in the attempts to ostracize her.

Finally, in 1830, the President broke relations with Calhoun, the Eaton affair being, however, only one of several causes of the break. This was followed, in the next spring, by a cabinet reorganization, which brought the Eaton affair into the open. For months it was publicly discussed in the newspapers. The evidence indicates that political rather than moral considerations were chiefly responsible for the whole affair.

EDUCATION. The roots of the educational systems of the United States are to be found, ultimately, in the ideas and practices of the schools of ancient Judea, Greece, Rome, and early Christianity. The American college had its remote beginnings in the medieval university of Western Europe. The American secondary school is a direct descendant of the grammar school of the Renaissance.

The more immediate antecedents of education in the United States, however, are to be located in the Protestant Reformations and the Catholic Counter-Reformation, as well as in the scientific and commercial revolutions of the 17th and 18th centuries. The schools of colonial New England, New Netherland, and other colonies drew their religious ideas from the Calvinism of the Old World: English Puritanism, Scotch Presbyterianism, and Dutch Reformism. The educational work carried on in the peripheral regions—the West, Southeast and Southwest—were within the framework of Roman Catholicism. The growing impact of experimental science and of international trade brought about profound educational changes during the later colonial period in the 18th century with respect to aims, courses of study and school organization. In the same way, these forces operated to modify the structure, functions, content and organization of the American college.

England contributed many ideas and practices to colonial education, such as laws providing for vocational training for the poor, ecclesiastical control of education, textbooks, teachers, and patterns of content and organization for all schools from the elementary through the collegiate. Scotland—via Ireland —was a source of inspiration for the stress on the need for universal education, an objective also common to the other Calvinists and to the Lutherans. According to some historians, 17th-century Holland, small in size but vast in culture and learning, may have exerted a potent influence on early American education.

Colonial Period. The earliest educational efforts in the New World were in the home. Those children whose parents could not afford to pay or who had no parents were enabled, through apprenticeship laws passed by the various colonial legislatures, to obtain vocational training, the fundamentals of reading, and religion. An illustration of this practice was the law passed by the General Court, or legislative body, of Massachusetts in 1642. This law specifically called for the town authorities to see to it that children were trained "to read and understand the principles of religion and the capitall lawes of this country," with the power of imposing fines for neglect. Apparently, success was not achieved by this plan, and the General Court therefore passed in 1647 the "Old Deluder Satan Act" which required each township of fifty families to engage a teacher to instruct children in reading and writing, and each township of one hundred families to get up a "grammar schoole" capable of fitting youth for "ye university," again under the penalty of a fine. The aims of this law, which many historians regard as the foundation of the American public school system, were to frustrate the designs of "ye ould deluder, Satan, to keepe men from the knowledge of ye Scriptures" and to ensure "ye learning may not be buried in ye grave of or fathrs in ye church and commonwealth." In this law may be found three principles typical of the public school system at the present time: the obligations of the community to establish schools, local school administration, and the separation of the secondary from the elementary school.

Laws similar to the Massachusetts law of 1647 were enacted in all the New England colonies except Rhode Island, where education was considered a private matter. While there were private schools, such as the "dame schools" in the colonies, the most important educational work was accomplished in the town schools, where the teachers were paid by local taxes and supervised by the town authorities or by the education committee (later known as the school board). While these town schools were publicly supported and publicly controlled, they were sectarian in purpose and content, as well as in control, since for a goodly part of the colonial period there was cooperation between the Congregational Church and government. As the population grew, new schools were opened to meet the needs of education. Thus arose in the 18th century the "moving school," a term for the teacher who taught for a few months each in the villages surrounding the town. This gave way in time to the district school, which served sparsely settled areas with limited numbers of children. This system of district schools grew not only in New England, but also in rural settlements all over the country and served the needs of children, even if at times in a rudimentary and unsatisfactory way, all through the 19th century and even persisted in the present century.

Probably the most widely circulated elementary textbook in the colonial era was the *New England Primer,* first published in 1690 in Boston, which was reputed to have "taught millions to read and not one to sin." According to Paul Leicester Ford, a total of 3,000,000 copies came off the presses, many of these carrying differing titles but including much of the content of the original colonial edition. The primer, which came to the colonies from England where it had been used several centuries, taught reading, spelling and catechism, and other religious content. The alphabet was presented through the medium of rhymed couplets—for examples, "In Adam's Fall/ We sinned all" and "A Dog will bite/ A Thief at Night"—together with crude woodcut illustrations. The *New England Primer* was used in schools until the 1840's when it finally gave way to another very popular textbook, Noah Webster's *The American Spelling Book,* published in 1783 and known as "the blue-backed spelling book," and other textbooks.

Secondary education in New England began with the establishment of the Boston Latin School in 1635. Graduates of this and other Latin grammar schools were qualified for admission to Harvard College. These schools featured the teaching of the Latin language and literature and of Greek by men whose scholarship and ability, such as those of Ezekiel Cheever in Boston, were immeasurably above those of the teachers in the elementary schools. During the mid-18th century, a new type of school, the academy, which offered modern and practical subjects, became increasingly attended and it foreshadowed the decline of the Latin grammar school.

Higher education in New England was inaugurated when the General Court in 1636 decided to allot £400 "towards a schoole or colledge," later named Harvard College after a clergyman who donated £780 and his library of four hundred books to the new college. The aim of Harvard, as stated in the charter of 1650, was to educate colonial and Indian young people "in knowledge and godliness" and "in good literature Artes and Sciences." Three more colleges were opened in colonial New England: Yale in 1701, partially because it was believed that Harvard was too liberal in theology; Brown in 1764 —a Baptist institution whose charter rejected the religious tests of admission and provided that faculty and students "shall forever enjoy full free Absolute and uninterrupted Liberty of Conscience"; and Dartmouth in 1769—a Congregationalist college for the training of ministers and Indians.

Education in the Middle Colonies varied from area to area, because of the differences of origin of the settlers. The Dutch in New Netherland set up public elementary schools where reading, writing, religion, and sometimes arithmetic were taught, with many of these schools continuing to teach the Dutch language even after the English took over the colony in 1664. Under the English in the 18th century, the poor were taught in schools of the Society for the Propagation of the Gospel in Foreign Parts, an Anglican association primarily dedicated to missionary work among the Indians in the colonies. Grammar schools were available in New York, including one which prepared students for King's College. This college, now Columbia University, was chartered in 1754 under Anglican auspices and aimed in the words of President Samuel Johnson, "to set up a Course of Tuition in the learned Languages, and in the liberal Arts and Sciences," as well as in religious knowledge and piety·

The principle of religious toleration prevailed in New York, Pennsylvania, New Jersey and Delaware, with the result that the various religious sects— Quakers, Lutherans, Reformed, Anglicans, Presbyterians, Catholics, and Jews—with the exception at times of the Catholics in New Jersey, were enabled to establish elementary schools of their own. It is of special interest that the first work on teaching published in colonial America was a German book, *Schul-Ordnung*, by Christoph Dock, "the pious schoolmaster on the Skippack" (Pennsylvania), in 1770. With regard to secondary education, Pennsylvania led the other Middle Colonies with the founding in 1689 of the Friends' Public School of Philadelphia (now called the William Penn Charter School), with other secondary schools, organized by religious groups to train ministers, and especially with the Academy in Philadelphia which was proposed by Benjamin Franklin in 1743 and opened in 1751. Franklin's Academy was organized into Latin, English and Mathematical departments, with the Latin department developing into the University of Pennsylvania. The school, which offered such subjects as languages, science, history and geography, also intended "that a number of the poorer Sort will be hereby qualified to act as Schoolmasters in the Country."

In addition to King's College in New York City, higher education in the Middle Colonies comprised the College of New Jersey (Princeton University) founded in 1746 by Scotch-Irish Presbyterians to maintain orthodox religion in the spirit of the Great Awakening; the College of Philadelphia (University of Pennsylvania), founded in 1740 but not chartered until 1755, and devoted to the teaching of the sciences and other modern subjects in line with the principles underlying the Enlightenment; and Queen's College (Rutgers University), chartered in 1766, and designed by leaders of the Dutch Reformed Church to provide for "the education of youth in the learned languages, liberal and useful arts and sciences, and especially in divinity, preparing them for the ministry and other good offices."

If the New England school policy can be described as that of compulsory public maintenance and that of the Middle Colonies as parochial education, then the Southern colonial policy can be characterized, as many historians have done, as *laissez-faire* and pauper education. The geographical, social and economic conditions in the South resulted in a system of colonial laws for apprentice training of poor and orphaned children, charity schools for the poor, private schools and tutorial training for the children of wealthy parents, and Old Field Schools which were established on abandoned waste land. A particularly significant type of elementary school was the school with an endowment derived from a will or bequest. An example of this kind in Virginia was the Syms-Eaton School, which originated with the will of Benjamin Syms in 1634 and was enlarged with funds from Thomas Eaton's will of 1659. This school, probably the first endowed educational institution in the colonies, lasted into the 20th century and was the model for other such endowments. There were instances of educational provisions for Negro children, mainly because plantation owners were interested in teaching them Christianity. However, there was no serious, systematic, and successful attempt in the colonies in the South to legislate in behalf of public schools.

Perhaps the most famous of the colonial secondary schools in the South was King William's School, founded in 1696 at Annapolis by an act of the Maryland General Assembly. This free, public school became, nearly a century later, St. John's College. Apart from such secondary schools, there was little of great significance in the colonial South until the time of the Revolution.

The only college in the South during the colonial period was the College of William and Mary, which, although chartered in 1693, was only a grammar school in reality and did not confer degrees until 1700. The original objective of the college—training young men for the ministry—was modified in 1779 by Thomas Jefferson, who organized an institution with a modern curriculum of languages, law, social sciences and the physical and natural sciences. From William and Mary, "Alma Mater of statesmen," were graduated, Jefferson, James Monroe, John Tyler and John Marshall.

The Early American Republic. The Revolution, which disrupted education on all levels in many areas, led to a greater awareness on the part of Americans that new types and new policies were necessary for a new society. Proposals for a national school system based on democratic principles, many of them inspired by Thomas Jefferson, were made by Benjamin Rush, Noah Webster, and others. Rush and James Madison urged a national university, and George Washington bequeathed in 1799 his shares in the Potomac Company toward the establishment of such an institution of higher learning. Most of the early state constitutions included some provisions for education, mainly adding to the already existing facilities and providing for the children of the poor. Some states, such as Georgia in 1785, North Carolina in 1789, Vermont in 1791, and Tennessee in 1794, granted charters for state universities, but the only institution of this type to grant degrees in the 18th century was North Carolina. What gave some impetus to the growth and development of higher education in the United States was the decision of the U. S. Supreme Court in the Dartmouth College Case in 1819. This decision, which laid down the principle that a state cannot modify a college charter without the consent of the college, may have been, in part at least, responsible for the increase of both the private institutions and the state universities.

The United States Constitution makes no reference to education and, therefore, under the provisions of the Tenth Amendment to the Constitution, educational control is reserved to the several states. However, by virtue of the principle of "general welfare" in the Preamble and the doctrine of implied powers, the Federal Government has spent billions of dollars all through its history for the teaching of agriculture and vocational subjects, schools for Indians, the U. S. Office of Education, the United States Military Academy, the Library of Congress, and for a large variety of other educational projects.

Interestingly, in the Land Ordinance of May 20, 1785, Congress reserved a lot, known as Section Sixteen, in every township in the Western territory "for the maintenance of public schools." The Northwest Ordinance of July 13, 1787, expressed a remarkable policy in its third article: "Religion, morality, and knowledge, being necessary to good government and the happiness of mankind, schools and the means of education shall forever be encouraged." On July 23, 1787, a congressional ordinance concerning the contract for the sale of the Western territory confirmed the reservation of Section Sixteen for public education and stated that lot number 29 was "to be given perpetually for the purposes of religion," with "not more than two complete townships to be given perpetually for the purpose of a university. . . ." By means of the land grant policy, the Federal Government was able to furnish the basic aid necessary toward the promotion of a public school system, especially in the Middle West and the Far West. On the other hand, the efforts of George Washington and others in behalf of a national university, to a large extent as a substitute for the tendency of American young men to study in Europe, were to no avail. The Constitutional Convention defeated a proposal for a national university, and Congress likewise defeated in 1816 a bill to establish such an institution.

George Washington was but one of many American educators who showed a concern for educational matters in the early years of the New Republic. Thomas Jefferson submitted bills to the Virginia legislature for the organization of a public school system in which intellectual ability would be stressed, so as to enable the best minds to be selected as leaders of the state. Among the other educational activities of Jefferson were his curriculum reforms at the College of William and Mary, the founding of the University of Virginia, various writings on education, and a plan to transplant the University of Geneva to the United States. John Adams, James Madison, Benjamin Rush and others also devoted much attention to the need for educational reform. Rush and several other educators submitted plans for a national system of education on the occasion of a competition organized by the American Philosophical Society.

During the years following the Revolution, New England was the only region that could lay claim to anything resembling a public school system. Only eight of the first sixteen states inserted provisions regarding education into their constitutions. As a general rule, except for Connecticut and Massachusetts, school standards were rather low. The various political, industrial, and social changes brought about a decline in the system of apprenticeship education. The poor attended charity schools which were supported by religious groups.

The Massachusetts law of 1789, which made the district system legal, led to lower standards in primary and secondary schools. The district school was upheld by the law of 1827, which made the system compulsory. While democratic control was exercised by local government under these two laws, the fact remained that educational efficiency, as Horace Mann was to point out in later years, was sharply reduced. The frontier conditions which were in force had thus a dual type of influence on the development of education in early national history.

New York State was active in setting up a statewide school system during this period. In 1784 it organized and in 1787 it reorganized the University of the State of New York, a centralized school system according to the French pattern. The state also set up in 1812 a permanent system of administration with Gideon Hawley as the first state superintendent of schools. The leadership of Governors George and DeWitt Clinton and others made possible the early establishment of an educational system with provisions for teacher training and other reforms.

Considerable effort was expended all over the young nation to attain a system of education in the several states. Many conscientious persons saw the defects of the charity or pauper schools in many states and were determined to do what they could to remedy conditions. Voluntary groups, such as the Free (later the Public) School of New York City, offered educational opportunities from 1805 until a merger with the city's Board of Education in 1852. Typical of similar societies all over the country outside of New York was the Society for the Promotion of Public Schools of Philadelphia, which was founded in 1827.

Funds for education were raised by means of lotteries, which fell into disfavor with the rise of the level of public morality; permanent school funds derived from license fees, direct state appropriations, fines, sales of public lands, and other sources of revenue; rate bills, or tuition fees in accordance with the number of children of the family attending school; and local taxes, such as required by the Massachusetts law of 1827. The struggle for public schools in the first half of the 19th century involved the abolition of the rate bill and the enactment of state laws for free school systems. In this campaign for free and universal education a number of educational statesmen played a decisive role in addition to that of the political and social leaders. Among the influential educators were Horace Mann and James Gordon Carter of Massachusetts, Henry Barnard of Connecticut, John D. Pierce of Michigan, and Calvin H. Wiley of North Carolina. To their efforts must be added those of workers' organizations, the clergy, and the press. The combined campaign in behalf of a democratic school system was won over such objections as fear of governmental power, opposition of property owners to school taxes, indifference by many public figures, and competition with long-established private schools.

Teaching procedures in the early national era were largely memorization, repetition, and individual recitation, with the textbook as virtually the only source of knowledge. The new textbooks, many of them compiled with the purpose of fostering patriotism in the pupils, were written by Noah Webster, Jedediah Morse, Samuel G. Goodrich (Peter Parley), and others. Later, textbooks were prepared in accordance with the pedagogical principles of Johann Heinrich Pestalozzi, the Swiss educational reformer whose ideas were brought over to America by leading American educators in the 19th century. Among the writers of these textbooks were Warren Colburn (arithmetic), William C. Woodbridge (geography), and Lowell Mason (music). The new subjects introduced into the elementary curriculum were grammar, spelling, geography, drawing, physiology, and history. Moral training was promoted often in a religious context, so much so that Catholics, Jews, and various Protestant minorities found themselves forced to open their own schools to escape sectarian instruction in the public schools. From the over-all viewpoint the American elementary school in the early decades of the 19th century granted more freedom to the child than previously given, reduced or abolished corporal punishment, broadened the concept of education, and began to take into consideration the abilities and interests of the individual child. This generalization did not apply, of course, to the district school; the infant school, which was transplanted from England after 1810; or the Lancastrian (or Monitorial) schools, likewise of English origin, in which one teacher instructed hundreds of young children under the supervision of pupil teachers or monitors.

In secondary education, the Latin Grammar School of colonial times gave ground to the English Grammar School, the academy, and finally to the high school. Such schools as Exeter and Phillips Andover Academies, founded in 1771 and 1778 respectively, exist to this day, even with altered aims. The academy was characterized by a curriculum of many subjects, including astronomy, geology, and often theoretical and practical sciences; foreign languages; philosophy, art, and music; rhetoric and oratory; and English language and literature. The high school—a term borrowed from Edinburgh, Scotland—was first introduced into Boston as the English Classical School in 1821 and renamed the English High School in 1824. A high school for girls was opened in 1826, also in Boston. The Massachusetts legislature recognized the value of the new type of school by passing the law of 1827, under which each town or district with 500 families was required to maintain a tax-supported school offering American history, geometry, bookkeeping and other subjects, and every town with a population of 4000 was obliged to teach Latin, Greek, general history and the like. The high school in later decades in the century became established as an integral part of the public school system.

The American college, in recovering from the adverse effects of the Revolution, inaugurated a broader curriculum in response to social demands. The sciences, modern foreign languages, law and the social sciences made their appearance in the courses of study in Harvard, William and Mary, and other colleges. Studies for the profession of medicine were promoted as well. An effort was made for a while to discourage American youth from studying abroad, but this failed and Americans flocked all through the 19th century to foreign universities, especially in Germany.

A number of significant changes took place in the administration and control of higher education. Gradually the religious influence was replaced by the secular. Professional schools were opened for the training of engineers, physicians, clergymen and lawyers. The Dartmouth College decision handed down by the U. S. Supreme Court in 1819 prevented state control of a chartered private college. The ultimate impact of this important decision was such that, on the one hand, private and denominational schools were founded in large numbers and, on the other, state legislatures established their own colleges and universities. The state university had its beginnings in Georgia and North Carolina toward the end of the 18th century, but it did not develop to any great extent until the mid-19th century at the earliest.

One of the key problems in American higher

education was beginning to emerge prior to 1830. The influence of Jefferson at the University of Virginia and that of George Ticknor at Harvard led to experimentation with allowing students to choose to some extent among the courses. The elective system, which later entered higher education on a large scale, was favored in principle in the Amherst College faculty report of 1826 but it was repudiated by the Yale College faculty report of 1828 which upheld the traditional classical curriculum.

Teacher training received an impetus before 1830 through the publication of several treatises on pedagogy, such as Joseph Neef's *Sketch of a Plan and Method of Education* (1808) and Samuel Read Hall's *Lectures on School-Keeping* (1829); the opening of private teachers' seminaries by Hall in 1823 and by James Gordon Carter in 1826; and the publication of teachers' journals—*The Academician* (1818–20) and William Russell's *American Journal of Education* (1826–31). The press and the pulpit also joined in the clamor for better teachers, in line with the widely quoted maxim, "As is the teacher, so is the school."

Educational Development until 1900. The growth of the nation in population, territory and wealth was not accomplished without educational pains. Among the factors making for educational progress were the demands of labor groups for a public school system; the reports by American educators of school methods and progress in Europe; the pressures exerted by governmental, cultural and educational leaders; and the humanitarian influences to aid the poor, the immigrant, and the handicapped.

Through the efforts of Carter and Mann, Massachusetts set up in 1837 a state board of education, and, under the direction of Mann as secretary, it extended school facilities, increased teachers' salaries, instituted supervision and in-service training of teachers, and introduced other reforms. Later, in 1852, Massachusetts was the national pioneer in enacting legislation to make school attendance compulsory. Significantly, Mann's crusading zeal in promoting educational change and giving public expression to his satisfaction with the European practices he had observed resulted in a controversy with the educators of Boston. His insistence that no religion be taught in the public schools, but that the Bible should be read without comment in the class, also involved him in controversy. In spite of such criticism Mann became recognized as the most influential American educator of the century and as one whose ideas affected education in such far-off countries as Argentina and Uruguay.

Another highly effective educator was Henry Barnard who did for Connecticut and Rhode Island what Mann did in Massachusetts. Barnard edited the *American Journal of Education* (1855–82) and served as the first U. S. Commissioner of Education (1867–70). Virtually every state had an educational leader of comparable, if not identical, stature.

Elementary education underwent changes during the 19th century. The kindergarten, based on the ideas of the German educator, Friedrich Froebel, was first established on American soil in 1856 by Mrs. Carl Schurz as a German-speaking school in Watertown, Wis. This was followed by a private, English-language kindergarten opened in 1860 by Elizabeth Palmer Peabody in Boston and the first public school kindergarten, set up in 1873 by Susan Blow in St. Louis under the supervision of the prominent educator and philosopher, Superintendent of Schools William Torrey Harris.

The Pestalozzian ideas were revived, but in a more formal object teaching method, by Supt. Edward A. Sheldon of the Oswego, N. Y., schools after he had observed an exhibit in 1859 in a museum in Toronto. Toward the end of the century, the theory and the practice of Johann Friedrich Herbart were introduced especially in connection with the teaching of social studies and character. Also contributing to character training were the widely used readers of Prof. William Holmes McGuffey. New ideas which stressed a curriculum and a methodology based on child growth, development and interest were put into operation by Francis Wayland Parker in Quincy, Mass., and later in Chicago. The elementary school founded by John Dewey at the University of Chicago (1896–1904) experimented with these ideas and served as a model for the modern or Progressive type of education which is characteristic of much of the work of elementary schools in the present century. Also relevant was the beginning of the testing movement in the 1890's and its development as a significant educational force in the decades to come. The entire curriculum of the elementary school came under scrutiny in the *Report of the Committee of Fifteen on Elementary Education* prepared in 1895 under the chairmanship of William H. Maxwell for the National Education Association.

All through the 19th century, the high school grew in prestige and took the place of the academy as the favored form of secondary education in America. The high school received in 1874 its legal recognition, insofar as support by public taxes was concerned, by the Kalamazoo decision in the Michigan Supreme Court. The high school, accordingly, became the typically American school of the people—free, public, universal, comprehensive in curriculum, and both academic and vocational. Problems of secondary education were reviewed in two significant reports: one in 1893 by the Committee of Ten on Secondary School Studies, National Education Association, with President Charles William Eliot of Harvard as chairman; and the other in 1899 by the Committee on College Entrance Requirements. As the high school became increasingly popular among the American people, and also among the immigrants of the 20th century, it became evident that it had developed into what some educators called "the American road to culture."

Higher education in the 19th century showed several new tendencies: the emergence of new subjects, such as agriculture, sociology, anthropology, and education; the secularization of colleges and universities, in part under the influence of the Darwinian ideas; the steady increase in the number of private and public institutions of higher learning; and the greater stress given to creative scholarship, to a large extent following the example of the German universities. The subject of science received considerable emphasis during the century beginning with the theoretical courses in the established colleges and then with the applied science and engineering taught at the U. S. Military Academy at West Point (1802), the Rensselaer Polytechnic Institute at Troy, N. Y. (1824), the Sheffield Scientific School at Yale and the Lawrence Scientific School at Harvard (both in 1847) and the Chandler School at Dartmouth (1851).

The passing of the Morrill Act by Congress in 1862 made land grants available to the states for the establishment of colleges where the subject of "agriculture and the mechanic arts" would be taught. The law made a special point of including military science and "other scientific and classical studies" and of stating that the aim of these colleges was "to promote the liberal and practical education of the industrial classes in the several pursuits and professions in life." This law, as well as the Morrill Act of 1890, brought about an expansion of state universities in the Middle West and Far West, especially with reference to agriculture and engineering education.

Women's higher education was provided in parts of the country before the Civil War on a private, denominational basis. The earliest graduates were given the degree of *Domina Scientiarum*. High academic standards were characteristic of Elmira Female College (1855) and of Vassar Female College (1865), both in New York State. Coeducation began with Oberlin Collegiate Institute (1833) and Antioch College (1853), both in Ohio, and at the state universities of Utah (1850), Iowa (1856) and Washington (1862). Other important developments in the century were the granting of the Ph.D. degree in 1861 by Yale, the introduction of the elective system at Harvard by President Eliot, and the founding of the Johns Hopkins University in 1876 as the first graduate school in the United States.

Teacher education was characterized by the raising of standards of training in the normal schools and the admission of psychology, the history of education, and other courses in education into the university curriculum. With new textbooks, periodicals, and teachers' organizations, it was evident that education was on the way toward becoming a profession.

Professional education flourished with the opening of the Massachusetts Institute of Technology (1861), the establishment of the American Medical Association (1847) and the Association of American Medical Colleges (1890), and the founding of the Association of American Law Schools (1900). Adult education was promoted by the lyceum, a lecture movement organized in 1826 by Josiah Holbrook and the Chautauqua forum movement inaugurated in 1874 by Bishop John H. Vincent.

Religious education was given in parochial schools by the Episcopalians, Presbyterians, Lutherans, Catholics, and Jews. The Roman Catholic Bishops' Third Plenary Council in Baltimore (1884) decreed that all Catholic parents must send their children to the parochial schools to be erected in every parish. All through the century there was a debate concerning the role of religion in public education and the question of providing public funds for religious schools.

Some colleges were opened for Negroes before the Civil War, but, in general, the opportunities for their education were rather limited. After the Civil War, from the establishment of the Freedmen's Bureau in 1865 on, schools of all types, most of them on a segregated basis, were available to Negroes. The legal precedent for segregated schools—"separate but equal" education—was set by the decision of the U. S. Supreme Court in 1896 in the case of Plessy v. Ferguson. The pattern of Negro education, all over the South and in several states in the North, was now determined for the next six decades.

The Twentieth Century. The elementary school grew at a rapid pace after 1900, with the expansion of the population. One of the problems that had to be faced was the constant enrollment of new pupils of immigrant parents, at least until about 1920. The kindergarten became more accepted and was instituted in many public school systems all over the country. The nursery school was introduced around 1920 for children less than four years of age and this type of preschool education was supported by the Federal Government during the depression years and World War II, so that mothers who had to work would have no anxiety about their youngsters. In the late 1920's and early 1930's, the activity plan, which gave elementary children a more flexible learning program, came into vogue. In time, very few elementary schools made use of formal class teaching procedures in fixed seats. Curriculum changes in the 1950's involved an emphasis on science and the inclusion of foreign languages.

Tests of intelligence, achievement, diagnosis and prognosis were frequently used in elementary education. The doctrines and practices of John Dewey, Edward Lee Thorndike and William H. Kilpatrick exerted a deep influence on teachers, parents and school administrators. In fact, the parent-teacher association, which was promoted by the Progessive educators who followed the lead of Dewey and Kilpatrick, became an outstanding feature of the American elementary school in the 20th century. The Federal Government manifested interest in elementary education by way of the National School Lunch Act of 1946 and other temporary measures along these lines; the White House Conferences on Children and Youth in 1940, 1950 and 1960; and the White House Conference on Education in 1955. The U. S. Supreme Court handed down influential decisions in the Nebraska case in 1923 declaring invalid a state law against foreign languages in private elementary schools; the Oregon case in 1925 upholding the Constitutional status of the religious and other private schools; the Everson case in 1947, which allowed states to furnish bus transportation for pupils in parochial schools; the McCollum (1948) and Zorach (1952) cases, which permitted released time but only outside the public school; and the integration cases of 1954 and 1955, by which the public schools of the entire country were required to discontinue the practice of segregating the Negro pupils.

The high school, since 1890, became a very popular institution for the education of America's youth. About 1910, the junior high school appeared in Berkeley, Calif., and elsewhere. Many large cities reorganized their secondary education in terms of the new type of school.

The secondary curriculum was the subject of many investigations by the National Education Association (1918), American Mathematical Association (1923), the American Classical League (1924), the Modern Language Association (1929), the Progressive Education Association (1941), and other organizations. In addition, the Federal Government sponsored the National Survey of Secondary Education (1933) and the Commission on Life Adjustment Education for Youth (1949). The Regents Inquiry into the Character and Cost of Public Education in New York State (1938) received widespread attention.

A report by the National Education Association in 1918 set down the seven "Cardinal Principles of Secondary Education," which have exerted an influence on the curriculum of the American high school: health, vocation, command of fundamental processes, worthy home membership, worthy use of leisure, citizenship, and ethical character. Vocational education was promoted by the Smith-Hughes Act of Congress in 1917 and by subsequent laws. In the 1950's, secondary education applied the principle of tying two more courses together in the "core curriculum." The report by the former president of Harvard University, James Bryant Conant, on the American high school in 1959 made some specific recommendations toward improvement, but essentially upheld the system of secondary education in the United States. Dr. Conant's report in 1960 on the junior high school stressed the need for the learning of academic sub-

ject matter. Among the leading controversial issues in secondary education was the question of academic studies versus the vocational or life adjustment program.

The 20th-century history of higher education in America was inaugurated by the issue of the elective versus the prescribed curriculum, which was carried over from the previous century. In 1900, the Association of American Universities was formed to keep high standards among the institutions of higher education. The public junior college movement had its start in 1902 at Joliet, Ill. The junior college attained considerable popularity in such states as Texas and California, and in the period since World War II it began to multiply in the form of community colleges.

The college curriculum was very diversified and practical, so much so that professors, administrators, and other critics of the contemporary college began to express their opinions in literary and professional journals and in numerous books. Among these proponents of the liberal arts and the scholarly status of higher education were Albert Jay Nock, Irving Babbitt, Norman Foerster and Robert Maynard Hutchins. Perhaps the most widely read critique of undergraduate and graduate instruction, was Abraham Flexner's *Universities: American, English, German* (1930). One of the most devastating attacks on the college was the report on *American College Athletics,* issued in 1929 by the Carnegie Foundation for the Advancement of Teaching. The various criticisms and the rethinking of the curriculum by college officials led to the founding of experimental colleges and teaching programs, as well as the spread of the general education movement. Among the other significant developments in higher education were the Harvard faculty's report on *General Education in a Free Society* (1945), the *Report of the President's Commission on Higher Education* (1949), the founding of the Southern Regional Education Program (1949), and the establishment of the State University of New York (1949). Another development of outstanding importance was in the field of Federal activity in higher education. The U. S. Government aided higher education through the G. I. Bill of Rights for the veterans of World War II (Public Laws 16 and 346, 1943–44); the G. I. Bill of Rights for the veterans of the Korean War (Public Law 550, 1952); the Fulbright and the Smith-Mundt Acts of 1948 for the exchange of students, faculty, and research workers with foreign countries; and the National Defense Education Act of 1958, which promoted the teaching of sciences, modern foreign languages, and mathematics, and other aspects of education in the colleges and universities.

In the field of teacher education, the normal schools became teachers' colleges which granted degrees, and in the period after World War II many of them were transformed into state colleges with liberal arts programs in addition to professional teacher training. Teachers College at Columbia University, the University of Chicago, the George Peabody College for Teachers, and New York University were among the institutions which were influential in the training of teachers and administrators for the United States and for many foreign nations. From 1958 to 1960, professors of academic subjects and professors of education met every year at a national conference in an effort to arrive at a common policy with regard to the education and certification of teachers. For several decades members of both groups had criticized each other with some bitterness.

The standards of medical education were suddenly and sharply raised with the publication in 1910 of the report by Abraham Flexner for the Carnegie Foundation for the Advancement of Teaching. The other professions also concerned themselves with the modification of curriculum and the upgrading of standards. The fields of law, engineering, journalism, and business administration were particularly active in the matter of providing an adequate general education as a basis for professional study.

Adult education flourished through the programs of the Americanization of the immigrant, through the "Great Books" discussion programs, and through the various activities of organized bodies, such as the Adult Education Association of the U. S. A., the Fund for Adult Education, and the American Library Association. Moreover, universities, public schools, churches, labor unions, governmental agencies, various voluntary organizations, and the mass media of communications offered different programs of study, recreation and aesthetic enjoyment to adults.

Negro education, which had been encouraged by the philanthropy of George Peabody (1867) and John F. Slater (1882), was further benefited by the funds set up in the names of John D. Rockefeller in 1903, Anna T. Jeanes in 1905, Phelps-Stokes in 1909, and Julius Rosewald in 1911. Although opportunities increased for Negroes on all levels of public and private education, the South and part of the North practiced racial segregation in education. The main steps in the integration of higher education were the U. S. Supreme Court decisions in the Gaines (1938), Sipuel (1948), Sweatt (1950), and McLaurin (1950) cases. The case of Alston v. Norfolk School Board, decided by a Federal Circuit Court of Appeals in 1940, was the precedent for the practice of paying equal salaries to white and to Negro teachers in the public schools. But the most fundamental events were the U. S. Supreme Court decisions of 1954 and 1955 which declared segregation in public schools as contrary to the doctrine of equality as guaranteed by the Constitution, and which ordered desegregation to be carried out "with all deliberate speed." Although public schools were integrated in several Southern and Northern states as the result of these decisions, physical resistance in Alabama, Tennessee, Arkansas and Louisiana slowed down the process. In 1960,

only 6% of the total Negro pupils attended the same classes as white children. Full segregation on all levels of education was maintained in 1960 in Alabama, Georgia, Mississippi, and South Carolina. Negroes were admitted to the public colleges of Louisiana, but there was opposition to the integration of the public elementary and high schools.

Trends and Problems. According to an estimate by the U. S. Office of Education, the statistics of public and private school enrollment for 1960–61 were expected to be as follows: 34,380,000 in elementary education, from kindergarten through the eighth grade; and 3,980,000 in all types of higher educational institutions. The grand total of 48,650,000 in the fifty states and in the District of Columbia represented a record figure in the history of American education. Of special interest was the enrollment during 1959–60 of 48,486 students from 141 countries in 1712 colleges and universities all over the country.

The problems and controversies which face American education are manifold. Outstanding among these are the relative status of general and professional or vocational subjects in the curriculum; the emphasis on a particular subject, such as science; the procurement of an adequate number of scientists and engineers; the selection and education of the gifted child and adolescent; the admission of qualified students to higher education; the prescribed versus the elective or permissive attitude in studies in the various levels of education; the criticisms of the principles and methods of teaching in the elementary and high schools, especially of reading and mathematics; the Progressive versus the Essentialist or traditional approach to the curriculum and methodology; the emphasis on competitive athletics in the high school and college; the provision of Federal aid without Federal control of education; the equalization of educational opportunity to minorities, especially the Negroes; the relation of religion to public education, with respect to doctrinal teaching, religious ceremonies, Bible reading, bus transportation, released time, health and other fringe benefits, and other issues; the freedom of teaching in the face of pressures of war, international tension, economic situation, political ideology, religious views, and the like; the perennial shortage of qualified teachers and professors; the low salaries and unsatisfactory teaching conditions in schools and colleges; the continuing shortage of funds for school facilities and for the construction of new school buildings; the growth of juvenile delinquency and crime; and the opposition in some quarters to teaching about the work of such international bodies as the United Nations and the United Nations Educational, Scientific and Cultural Organization (abbr. UNESCO). All these controversies and problems were receiving much attention by the public, governmental agencies, voluntary groups of citizens, and the educational profession itself. If the problems were not easy to solve with speed, they were at least widely discussed at meetings, in the press, in periodicals, in books, and on radio and television.

EDUCATION, OFFICE OF, was established as a Department of Education by act of Congress approved March 2, 1867; but by an amending act, effective July 1, 1869, it was reduced to a Bureau under the Department of the Interior, where it remained until 1939 when it was transferred to the newly established Federal Security Administration. In 1953 the Office of Education was placed under the Department of Health, Education and Welfare. Primarily, it is intended to serve as a fact-finding and advisory agency, collecting and disseminating school statistics and information on the organization and methods of education. Dissemination of information may be through speeches, conferences and correspondence, but is chiefly through the many publications of the Office, notably its *Bulletins* and *Circulars,* its comprehensive *Biennial Survey of Education,* and its monthly magazine, *School Life* (est. 1918). An important phase of its advisory work, developed largely since 1910, is the making, upon invitation, of intensive and critical surveys of school systems of cities, counties or states. In recent years special study has been given to the possibilities of radio and television as educational channels. Also, there has been special promotion of adult education, including public forums, and of library facilities and service.

The duties of the Office of Education were greatly increased in 1933 when, under executive order, there were transferred to it the functions of the Board for Vocational Education, which board, originally established as an independent agency in 1917, was continued in existence in merely advisory capacity, its members to serve without compensation. Before Federal funds provided in the Smith-Hughes Act of 1917 and in subsequent vocational education legislation can be released to the states, the Office of Education must examine and approve vocational education plans and programs drawn up by the state boards. Upon the Office also devolves the responsibility for seeing that such programs are carried out and that, generally, the Federal aid is efficiently expended. Beginning in 1885, the Office of Education had charge of providing educational facilities for the children of Alaskan natives and also, after 1910, of providing for these natives medical and hospital service, but in 1931 these duties were transferred to the Indian Office. The Reindeer Service, also built up under the Office of Education, was, in 1930, put under the direction of the governor of Alaska.

ELECTION OF THE PRESIDENT. After prolonged discussions of various methods of electing the President the framers of the Constitution finally settled the matter with the provision: "Each State shall ap-

point, in such manner as the legislature thereof may direct, a number of electors equal to the whole number of Senators and Representatives to which the State may be entitled." This was a plan of election by assemblies of state notables expected to exercise independent personal judgment at meetings in their respective states. Since the presumption was that they would vote with no announced candidates, the ballots would normally be cast for so many different persons that a majority would be rare. They would, in Madison's opinion, fail to elect a President "nineteen out of twenty times." Hence the constitutional provision that in such cases the House of Representatives should elect the President from the three standing highest in electoral votes, with each state casting one vote. Thus the framers expected the Electoral College to serve as little more than a nominating agency.

Madison's prediction was upset by the unforeseen concentration of votes on two opposing sets of candidates by 1796, due to the unexpected emergence of political parties with candidates for President and Vice-President, selected in party caucuses of Congressmen. The third election produced a crisis due to the defect of the constitutional provision that electors shall "vote by ballot for two persons" without designating the office for which each vote was intended. This blind voting produced the tie vote on Jefferson and Burr, an inevitable result where each elector merely registered his party choices. This defect was corrected by the Twelfth Amendment's requirement that electors cast votes specifically for President and Vice-President.

Since the Constitution authorized state legislatures to determine the method of choosing a state's electors, they at first generally chose to perform that function themselves. By 1824, however, the present method of voting for electors in a general election was becoming prevalent enough to produce the conviction for the first time that the people were electing the President. Consequently when the House of Representatives in 1824 failed to elect Jackson, after he had received a plurality of the electoral votes among four candidates, it was widely regarded as a defiance of the popular will. Since the election of Jackson in 1828 the Electoral College has been regarded as merely formally registering the people's choice at the polls. This popular conviction has been strengthened by the fact that, since the 1830's, nominations of presidential candidates have been made by national conventions of delegates theoretically expressing the choice of the rank and file of the party.

ELECTIONS. An election is the choice of a person or persons for public office by legally qualified electors. It differs from appointment where designation is made by some official or body of officials. In the Federal Government of the United States there are only 537 places filled by popular vote, *viz.,* the

Presidency, the Vice-Presidency, 100 seats in the Senate and 435 in the House of Representatives; whereas in 1959 there were 2,000,000 appointive positions. In state and local governments the proportion of elective officials is somewhat larger, but here also as a rule the number of appointive officials is much greater.

In popular speech the term election is applied also to votes upon questions authoritatively submitted to the electorate, i.e., Initiative and Referendum proposals, the ratification of state constitutions and city charters or of amendments thereto. It seems preferable, however, to distinguish between votes which affect only constitutional and legislative policies, and elections proper which decide between candidates for office. Under the latter are included final elections, also Direct Primary elections where nominations are at stake, and Recall elections in which the tenure of an officeholder or group of officeholders is attacked before the expiry of the term fixed by law. It does not follow that an election in the more precise sense is concerned solely with candidates; they stand upon platforms or for certain principles and policies which the voter is presumed to take into account in deciding between them.

The prime although often lethargic factor in elections is the electorate. It is made up of all those persons who possess the qualifications as set down in constitutions and laws of state and nation for the exercise of the right of suffrage. In order to prevent frauds all states but one have passed Personal Registration laws which make it necessary for the otherwise qualified voter to appear before a Board of Registrars and give information necessary to identify him at ensuing primary or final elections. Owing to the diversity of state legislation on suffrage it is impossible to do more than estimate the number of qualified voters in the United States. Of the total population in 1960 about 60% were of voting age, but in any given election the disfranchisement of unnaturalized aliens and of persons not possessing residence requirements or temporarily disqualified for other reasons makes the proportion somewhat lower.

The active factors in elections are political parties, particularly the two major parties, each of which has an elaborate organization paralleling the official structure of Government from top to bottom. Its most important elements are National Committees, State Committees, District, County, City and Precinct Committees. After nominations have been made in Direct Primary elections or delegate conventions it is these elaborate party organizations which go into action. They raise large campaign funds, send out candidates and innumerable other orators, prepare and distribute enormous quantities of propagandist pamphlets and leaflets, make appeals by press, movies, radio and television, and resort at times to other less reputable or even criminal devices. All of these methods are employed with the purpose, first, of holding and strengthening the support of convinced partisans; and, second, of converting the lukewarm or even hostile elements of the electorate in sufficient numbers to achieve a victory on Election Day.

Elections may be either direct or indirect. In the former, decision rests upon the attainment of a majority or, more commonly, a plurality of the total number of popular votes cast. The principal form of indirect election still prevailing in the United States is in the choice of the President and Vice-President by an Electoral College, itself now chosen by the voters in the separate states. Ordinarily the result in the Electoral College exaggerates greatly the result of the popular vote in the country as a whole. However, there have been cases when the successful candidate for the highest office in the land has received less than a majority of the popular vote (Lincoln, 1860; Wilson, 1912, 1916). Cases have even occurred (Hayes, 1876; Benjamin Harrison, 1888) of successful candidates who did not even receive a popular plurality, actually standing lower in the scale than their principal rivals.

In addition to the simple and still predominant plan of election by direct majority or plurality vote, various preferential or proportional methods have found increasing acceptance of recent years. Their common purpose is to prevent the often greatly exaggerated success achieved by the largest party whenever candidates are chosen in single member districts. Among these new methods are the Limited Vote plan, according to which each elector votes for only two candidates where there are three places to be filled; the Cumulative Vote plan under which the voter is permitted to plump all his votes to the one or two candidates he favors particularly; and Preferential Voting, also known as the Grand Junction or Bucklin plan, which permits the voter's second or third choices to be considered in case no candidate receives an absolute majority of first choices. By far the most accurate and satisfactory plan of this character, however, is Proportional Representation, which in 1960 was in use in a few commission or commission-manager cities. Proportional representation was at one time in use, among other places in Cleveland, Toledo and even in New York, which adopted it in 1936; but all of these cities shortly abandoned it, and after a promising beginning proportional representation seems everywhere in retreat. The greatest weakness of the plan, and the one which has caused it recently to be opposed not only by machine politicians but by students of politics, is that it may fail to provide a working majority in the council or legislature. Insofar as the plan encourages factionalism it may lead, according to its critics, to scenes reminiscent of the French Chamber of Deputies.

Following old English tradition many of the earlier elections in the United States were viva voce affairs.

321

This method of voting died out during the earlier decades of our national history. Since the Civil War the use of election papers or ballots has been universal. Unfortunately, with the multiplication of elective offices, our "blanket-ballots" have become the largest and most complicated used anywhere in the world. To remedy the difficulties which they occasion, the Short Ballot idea has been advocated widely, its chief successes to date being in commission and commission-manager cities. Of recent years the rapidly increasing use of voting machines has contributed greatly to the speed and accuracy of election counts.

Participation in elections was large from the Jacksonian period onward. In presidential elections from 1856 to 1888 it amounted to 80% or better of the total number of qualified electors. Thereafter a slow decline set in, which continued more or less unabated until the age of Eisenhower. By 1920 the proportion of qualified voters actually voting had dropped to about 50%. In part this figure reflected the difficulties experienced by the newly-enfranchised women voters in making use of their hard-won rights; not only were many of them unfamiliar with election processes, but under the laws of some states they could not have registered before Election Day even if they had intended to do so. In any case, it is estimated that two fifths of the women voters failed to vote. But participation in American elections has continued to remain disappointingly small compared with that in European countries, and compared with what one might expect of a literate and seemingly enlightened electorate. In 1928, when interest was enlivened by the prohibition issue, only 57% of the qualified voters managed to vote. In 1936 and 1940, about 60% voted; in 1944, 56%; in 1948, 53%. In the election of 1952 the number of qualified voters voting reached 63%, and in 1956 it fell slightly to 61%.

From a constitutional point of view the most important presidential election was that of 1800, in which Jefferson and Burr received exactly the same number of votes in the Electoral College. To avoid such deadlocks in the future the Twelfth Amendment was added to the Constitution (Sept. 25, 1804), providing that thereafter separate ballots for the President and Vice-President should be taken. The contested election of 1876 created a most dangerous situation; even the possibility of civil war was widely feared. As a result a Federal statute was enacted in 1887 which endeavors to foresee and to provide for every possible case of disputed votes in the Electoral College. From a political point of view the election of 1800, which marked the accession to power of the Jeffersonians, and the election of Lincoln in 1860 are clearly of major importance. Among recent presidential contests those of 1896, 1912, 1928, 1936, and 1948 are of more than usual interest. It is perhaps not without significance that every presidential elec-

tion beginning with that of 1920, with the possible exception of the election of 1948, has been won by a landslide. Both parties have captured five of these contests. (*See also* Campaigns of 1940; 1944; 1948; 1952; 1956; 1960.)

ELECTORAL COLLEGE. The framers of the Constitution rejected popular election of the President because they feared that the scattered and relatively isolated communities of the Federal union could not become sufficiently informed about candidates. They provided instead for indirect election whereby a number of selected electors meeting in each state, and equal to its representation in the two houses of Congress, would each "vote by ballot for two persons" (Constitution of the United States, Article II). Since the voting was to be by separate state groups of electors, presumably without announced candidates, it was supposed that the electoral balloting would usually fail of the majority required for any election, in which case the House of Representatives, with each state casting a single vote, would choose the President, and the Senate the Vice-President.

As late as the third presidential election (1796) the electoral votes were scattered among thirteen candidates. Contrary to the expectations of the fathers, political parties were emerging and concentrating on distinct presidential candidates so that by 1800 every elector but one cast a party vote, which has since become the fixed custom.

Presidential electors in the earliest elections were chosen in a variety of ways, but since the Constitution permits state legislatures to determine the method, most legislatures were soon selecting them directly. In the late 1820's democratic tendencies compelled popular choice of electors, which is now universal.

After the voters in the November elections have chosen the presidential electors the latter meet in their respective state capitals on the first Monday after the second Wednesday in December to cast their ballots for President and Vice-President. These ballots are then transmitted to the President of the Senate where they are counted in the presence of the two houses of Congress in accordance with the provisions of the Electoral Count Act of 1887. The ones receiving majorities of the electoral votes are then declared elected, President and Vice-President respectively.

ELEVATED RAILWAYS. The first elevated line in America, a single-track structure running from Battery Place up Ninth Avenue to 30th Street in New York, was built in 1866–67, and operated by a continuous chain or cable for a short time, then with steam locomotives; but it was a failure, and the plant was sold for the benefit of creditors in 1871. A new company, organized in 1872, took over the line, and in the face of strong opposition to elevated railroads, extended it northward, besides building lines up Sixth and Third Avenues. The trains of from three to six cars were drawn by small steam locomotives until 1903, when the system was electrified. A company was organized in 1872 to build a line on which cars would be shot through pneumatic tubes suspended from lofty arches, but this project was abandoned before construction began. The "El" lines in Manhattan were later extended into the Borough of the Bronx, and a large system was built in Brooklyn. Chicago opened its first elevated line in 1893—later extended far out through the North and South Shore suburbs. Boston discussed elevated transit as early as 1875, finally chartered a company in 1894, and the system began operating in 1901.

ELEVATORS. An elevator must be equipped with an automatic safety device to keep the car from falling in case the hoisting ropes should break. Credit for this invention goes to Elisha Graves Otis of Yonkers, N. Y., who installed the first safety elevator in New York City on Sept. 20, 1853. A year later he demonstrated his device at the Crystal Palace in New York, eliciting such newspaper reports: "We may allude to an Elevator, or machine for hoisting goods (exhibited by Mr. E. G. Otis of Yonkers, N. Y.) which attracts attention both by its prominent position and by the apparent daring of the inventor, who, as he rides up and down on the platform occasionally cuts the rope by which it is supported." On March 23, 1857, Otis installed the first passenger elevator in the Haughwout on Broadway, New York; but the best known early passenger elevator was the "Vertical Screw Railway" patented by Otis Tufts and installed in 1859 in the Fifth Avenue Hotel. This elevator received a great deal of publicity because of the prominence of the building and the importance of the people, including the Prince of Wales, who rode upon it.

In 1860 the first direct-connected steam elevator was patented by Otis and the hydraulic elevator, having been tried in Paris as early as 1862 and in Boston in 1868, was first used in office buildings in 1878. Up to then these commercial buildings were seldom more than five stories high, but when it was found that the elevator caused a complete reversal in building operations, with the upper floors commanding higher rentals, building activity increased throughout the country. Elevator developments were consistently ahead of building construction, and after the first "skyscraper" with wrought iron and steel frame construction was completed in 1885, the *New York Times* said, "American architecture as an independent school began its existence with the invention and adaption of the elevator." In 1889 Otis developed the first direct-connected electric elevator, used for residences and smaller buildings, and in 1904 installed the first gearless traction machine, a high-speed electric elevator that could provide any desirable elevator speed and was capable of serving buildings as tall as anyone would wish to build. This type of machine soon replaced all other elevator equipment and is standard equipment for larger buildings today.

All recent elevator developments have been aimed at improving elevator service by eliminating the human element in elevator operation. In 1915 automatic self-leveling was developed for stopping the elevator platform level with a floor and holding it there. Although push-button elevators had been used in smaller buildings as early as 1894, it was in 1924 that the first automatic operation was installed in a tall office building. Known as Signal Control, this operation relieved the attendant in the car of all duties except pressing buttons and closing the doors. The speed of an elevator no longer was limited to the ability of a human operator.

It had long been a problem to keep a group of elevators operating on schedule to eliminate unnecessary delays, and starting in 1927 a series of automatic dispatching and control systems was developed for this purpose. In 1948 electronic computing systems were first used for elevator scheduling. Of even greater importance was the development of electronic detection devices for elevator doors. With this noninterference equipment no attendants were needed in the cars. Otis installed the first completely automatic elevator system for a busy building in Dallas in 1950. Operatorless elevators were by 1960 standard equipment for all new buildings, no matter how large, and this equipment rapidly was being applied to elevators in existing buildings.

ELEVATORS, GRAIN. The rise of specialized wheat growing in the Upper Mississippi Valley created a problem of grain storage. The farmer ordinarily could not provide storage on the farm. The railroads were unable to provide transportation facilities to carry the wheat to market immediately after harvest. Storage facilities had to be created both at country shipping points and terminal markets. In countries where labor was plentiful and cheap, grain was stored in sacks in sheds, under tarpaulins, or in ordinary "flat" warehouses. In the United States there developed a new type of grain storehouse.

American flour mills since the days of Oliver Evans (1755–1819) had used the "elevator" to raise the meal from the grinding to the bolting floor. This was an endless belt of leather to which were attached metallic cups, the whole in a tight casing either vertical or inclined. The use of this elevator to lift the grain from the farmers' wagons into the storage bins involved such a great saving of labor that the name was soon applied to the warehouse as well. This was a series of bins for storing the grain with a cupola on top. The elevator carried the grain up to the cupola, from which it was spouted to the storage bins. From there, in turn, it was discharged into cars or vessels.

The grain elevator rapidly displaced all other means of grain storage in the region of specialized wheat growing. The farmer could then store his grain until ready to sell. Or the elevator owner might buy the grain, shipping it to the terminal market. In order to do this the elevator developed facilities for weighing, grading and cleaning the grain.

As the country elevators grew in numbers and volume of business, terminal elevators were established at the milling centers and at the export market. These were usually built by the railroad companies at the start. By the 1920's about a third of the terminal elevator capacity was railroad-owned and much of it was railroad-operated. Since then operation has been largely taken over by milling or graindealing corporations. The concentration of terminal grain elevators is especially notable in Minneapolis-St. Paul, Kansas City, Duluth-Superior, Chicago and Buffalo.

In the early days many of the country elevators were built by milling companies or by the railroads. The ownership of the elevators gave them control over the marketing system, which in some cases was soon abused. In the 1870's wheat growers complained that they were compelled to accept unduly low grades, that deductions for dockage (weed seeds and other foreign materials in the grain) were unfairly large, and that elevator operators did not give them a fair price for their grain. The Patrons of Husbandry through local granges in Iowa and other states sought a solution for this problem through the establishment of co-operatively owned farmers' elevators.

Most of these early attempts at co-operation failed. The railroads often refused to lease trackage; there was bitter and unfair competition from the private companies, both independent and mill-owned. The farmers in many states were forced to go to the legislature for assistance. The first important law regulating the elevators was the Illinois Warehouse Act (1871). Operators of grain warehouses storing for the public were required to secure licenses, file bonds, and publish handling and storage rates. Legal maxima were prescribed. The constitutionality of this law was affirmed in Munn v. Illinois in 1876, and it became the forerunner of a detailed code of regulation based on the principle that the business is clothed with a public interest.

The failure of the farmers' elevator companies in the 1870's was not solely due to the opposition of railroad and elevator men. Many failed because inadequately capitalized or incapably managed. In the 1880's commission men and terminal elevator firms of the central markets began to build or acquire lines of elevators throughout the wheat region. At many points competition was suppressed completely. Renewed complaints from the farmers and a new wave of co-operative-elevator building under the leadership of the Farmers' Alliance followed. In Minnesota a law was passed in 1893 providing for a state-owned terminal elevator at Duluth. This law was held un-

constitutional by the state supreme court, but the idea was revived by the Nonpartisan League in North Dakota in the following decade.

Throughout the country, but especially in the Midwest, the grain-marketing co-operatives are very important. In recent years they have owned one fourth or more of the country elevators. The number of local co-operatives has decreased, but the membership and volume of business has steadily increased. From operation of country elevators they have expanded their activities to the supplying of both consumer and producer foods to their members. Through regional and national associations they have created selling agencies in terminal markets, have owned and operated terminal elevators and even attempted to stabilize the prices of grain by means of pools.

In the last two decades the storage of grain has become increasingly important, partly because of a tendency to speed up delivery from the farmer to the market, but mainly because of the Government's price-support policies and the increase in Government-owned surpluses.

ELKINS ACT, passed by Congress in 1903, primarily upon the initiative of the railroads themselves to prevent loss of revenue by rate cutting and rebates, supplemented the Interstate Commerce Act of 1887 by providing more specific methods of procedure and penalties for its nonobservance. The law provided prosecution and punishment of railroad corporations, as well as their agents and officers, for giving or receiving rebates, and made it a misdemeanor to deviate from published rates.

EMANCIPATION, COMPENSATED, was a device for eliminating slavery by having the Government buy the slaves. It was usually discussed in the United States in connection with schemes for colonizing freed Negroes. The constitutional convention of Virginia in 1829–30 proposed an amendment to the Federal Constitution giving Congress the power to appropriate money to purchase and colonize slaves. There were also proposals that the Government buy slaves and free them after they had earned their purchase price, and that profits from public lands be used to emancipate and transport slaves.

With the decline of the colonization movement, interest in compensated emancipation declined also. Strict constructionists believed it to be unconstitutional, and radical abolitionists believed that slave owners did not deserve compensation.

The Republican party revived interest in compensated emancipation. Their 1860 platform recognized it as desirable where slaves were legally held. President Lincoln believed it to be the best solution of the slavery problem. He insisted that it was just, that it distributed the financial burden of emancipation fairly, and that it was cheaper than war.

In a special message to Congress, March 6, 1862, he asked the adoption of a joint resolution pledging financial aid to any state adopting gradual emancipation. The resolution was passed and Lincoln tried to get the border states to accept the offer, but none of them did.

The only successful attempt at compensated emancipation was in the District of Columbia, where it was provided for by act of Congress, April 16, 1862. A bill was introduced into Congress to purchase the slaves in the border states also, but it never became a law.

The last effort in behalf of compensated emancipation was made in President Lincoln's message, Dec. 1, 1862. He proposed a constitutional amendment permitting an issue of Government bonds to any state adopting gradual emancipation. With the appearance of the Emancipation Proclamation, however, all interest in the scheme disappeared.

EMANCIPATION PROCLAMATION. Unhistorical tradition has surrounded the Emancipation Proclamation with an aura of misconception and exaggeration. That it was a central fact in Lincoln's administration and one of the great milestones of the 19th century may be admitted, but it is incorrect to think of it as a measure entirely new, or a striking of the shackles from millions of bondmen at a stroke of the pen, or as Lincoln's main solution of the slavery problem. By midsummer of 1862, despite its disclaimer of abolition as a war aim, Congress had imposed emancipation of slaves as a sweeping penalty upon "rebels" (by its ineffective confiscation acts), had prohibited slavery in the District of Columbia and the territories, and had decreed the liberation of slave-soldiers. Meanwhile Lincoln, whose caution and regard for border-state sentiment coexisted with an expansive concept of presidential authority, had withheld those bold strokes which Garrisonians had urged upon him, and had overruled Generals Frémont and Hunter when their premature measures of military emancipation seemed calculated to force his hand. In addition, with pathetic earnestness, the President had labored for the adoption of his main policy, *i.e.*, gradual emancipation by voluntary action of the states with Federal compensation to slaveholders. When compensated emancipation failed to advance beyond paper approval by Congress, and when the international situation called for some kind of stroke at slavery, Lincoln acted. That the main decision was his own and not that of his cabinet is clear from Lincoln's statement to the artist Carpenter (included in his *Works*, Feb. 6, 1864). He related how the proclamation came to be decided upon and prepared, showing the independence of his decision which was reached amid gloom and defeat, and stating that he put the proclamation "aside, . . . waiting for a victory" upon Seward's advice, lest it seem a "last shriek on the retreat." It was at the

Soldiers' Home that Lincoln finished the second draft of the preliminary proclamation. In his diary (June 24, 1864) John Hay quoted Carpenter as saying that Seward protested against the proclamation being taken as the "crowning act" of the Administration; the cabinet secretary is further quoted as considering the Administration's antislavery acts "merely incidental."

Having reached his decision, Lincoln announced his purpose in cabinet meeting on July 22, 1862; then, after waiting for victory, he issued his preliminary proclamation (Sept. 22, 1862) on the morrow of Antietam. Though repeating that union (not abolition) was the war aim of the Government and that his compensated emancipation policy was still active, he declared that "persons held as slaves" within areas "in rebellion against the United States" would be free on and after Jan. 1, 1863. When that day arrived the definitive proclamation specifically designated those districts "wherein the people . . . are this day in rebellion . . .," and ordered "that all persons held as slaves . . . [within said areas] are, and henceforward shall be, free. . . ." The final sentence invoking "the considerate judgment of mankind and the gracious favor of Almighty God" upon a measure of "military necessity" was mainly suggested by Salmon P. Chase. The edict was far from an abolition document, since it did not apply to Tennessee, nor to specifically excepted portions of Virginia and Louisiana, nor to the border slave states within the Union. Declaring liberation in areas not under Union military control, it had negligible effect as to the immediate freeing of any individuals held in thralldom, and in this sense it was sarcastically denounced by Lincoln's critics. Treating the unshackling of slaves as a device of war and as a penalty for rebellion, the document omitted any suggestion whatever of a blow directed by antislavery principle. Nonetheless Northern abolitionists and radicals in Congress hailed the proclamation with enthusiasm and it quickly became a kind of shibboleth for a new war aim. Thus, the actual provisions and legal consequences of the edict are in marked contrast to the garb and trappings which it wore as dramatized in the popular mind; nor are these trappings to be ignored in appraising its historic significance, since abolition did in fact become a war aim. Large numbers of conservatives in the North and on the border deeply deplored the measure, which they considered unwise, irrelevant to the main issue, and highly dictatorial. That Lincoln assumed war powers in a field where Congress might lack legislative authority is shown by a passage in his proclamation (July 8, 1864) concerning the Wade-Davis bill. In this proclamation Lincoln declared himself unprepared to admit the right of Congress to abolish slavery in the states.

In the South the proclamation was denounced as the act of a fiend who deliberately sought to stir up servile insurrection. Lincoln in his January proclamation took special pains to enjoin orderly behavior upon the Negroes, and no domestic uprisings of slaves occurred, but colored troops were extensively used by the Union Government, and the care of freedmen was progressively assumed by the military authorities as the armies advanced. Lincoln is quoted as having called the proclamation "the greatest question ever presented to practical statesmanship" (diary of John Hay, July 31, 1863); but there were times when he spoke almost apologetically of his most famous act, which he never regarded as a permanent solution. Ultimate emancipation as a national measure was effected by the antislavery amendment to the Constitution. To his last day Lincoln favored compensation for Southern slaveholders, declaring that the blame for slavery rested upon North as well as South, but the decisive refusal to extend such compensation was embodied in the Constitution itself in 1868.

EMBARGO, Thomas Jefferson's, represents a high point in the American quest for the formula of pacifism. Passed by Congress on Dec. 22, 1807, it was the practical application of a Jeffersonian principle long maturing, and the nation's reaction to the Napoleonic wars with their consequent injuries to neutrals, of which America was chief.

The underlying cause for an American embargo was a series of restrictions upon our commerce imposed by the European belligerents. In the early stages of the Napoleonic wars, the United States had grown wealthy as the chief of neutral carriers at a time when British shipping was dedicated to war purposes. Roughly speaking, this era of prosperity endured from 1793 to 1805, to the great enrichment of New Englanders, and to some extent of merchants in the Middle States, and to the corresponding enlargement of the American mercantile marine. Commercial restrictions then cut in upon these profits, although in 1806 there was some relaxation in the blockade which excluded Americans and other neutrals from the Seine to Ostend only. Subsequently, however, the Orders in Council of Jan. 7, and Nov. 11, 1807, and the Berlin and Milan Decrees of Nov. 21, 1806, and Dec. 17, 1807, respectively, threatened direst penalties to any neutral venturing into a port of the enemy of either.

Americans, as leading carriers, had ample cause for grievance, and, in the impossibility of armed vengeance upon both Napoleon and King George, some such expedient as the embargo might have resulted in any case. But for Americans there was the added goad of a distressing national humiliation—the *Chesapeake* incident, of June 22, 1807, in which years of the impressment of American sailors culminated in the overhauling of a national warship and the removal of four sailors on the plea that they were British. War would have been a logical reaction, but

this the policy of Jefferson forestalled. Instead, with a reliance upon the powers of commerce surprising in a Virginia country gentleman, it was determined to bring the proud belligerents to their knees by withholding from them the raw materials and finished products which they normally received from the United States. The embargo aimed to secure the benefits of war through the agencies of peace. A submission which armed forces could not dream of accomplishing was to be achieved by economic pressure.

To be effective—and it was effective to a degree, exports experiencing a decline, estimated at 75% against a 50% decline in imports—such pressure must presuppose considerable unity of national purpose, a high degree of administrative energy, duration of the experiment sufficient to exhaust existing stores of American goods in foreign hands, and pressure from the social classes adversely affected strong enough to influence the arbitrary government of Napoleon and the aristocratic government of Great Britain. The project represented a stronger policy than nonintercourse, which applied only to belligerents and did not prevent an indirect trade with them. It would bear hard upon America's commercial classes, as well as upon producers of raw materials dependent on foreign markets. Thus the embargo would test severely American cohesion and national unity. It constituted a major test of Jeffersonian and American idealism confronting concrete issues of economics and diplomacy.

Unity of national purpose proved greater than might have been supposed. True, geographical and social barriers already foreshadowed the sectional cleavage that colors so much of American history. But New England, which suffered most at the hands of the embargo, found some compensation, not complete, in the stimulus it gave to manufactures. In the Middle States, where commercial losses were less extreme, the offsetting stimulus was more adequate. Philadelphia, for example, underwent a positive boom, and progress was apparent in New York and Baltimore. The third great section, Jefferson's own Southland, suffered in its staples almost equally with New England in its commerce. But it was sustained by faith and hope; faith in Thomas Jefferson, and hope that it, too, would share in the profits to be anticipated from growing manufactures. Hope deferred eventually made the heart sick, but the South went along with the Middle States in a general support of the embargo, leaving New England as the most articulate spokesman for the opposition.

Administrative energy, our second requirement for a successful embargo, also exceeded expectation. Thomas Jefferson, whose fame is that of the philosopher, proved himself in the execution of this favorite project an administrator of uncommon energy. At the Treasury, moreover, where the brunt of administration naturally fell, he enjoyed the aid and counsel of Albert Gallatin, one of the three or four most brilliant men to hold that office. The embargo, like the Napoleonic decrees for that matter, provided certain loopholes which were taken advantage of, notoriously by Gov. Sullivan of Massachusetts. And there was much direct evasion, chiefly on the borders of Maine and Florida. But close study of the period reveals surprising efficiency in a government whose underlying theory of politics rejected any undue concentration of authority in the hands of the executive.

In the third requirement for success, namely, duration of the experiment, the embargo had scarcely a fair chance. The immediate effect in England, for example, of a cessation of supplies of cotton from the United States, would be not the ruin of the cotton manufacturer but rather his enrichment, temporarily at least, from a speculative increase in the value of his existing stocks. And even when supplies ran low and unemployment in the mills resulted, the classes most affected, the laboring proletariat, were not sufficiently articulate as yet to bring effective protest to their industrial overlords and to the government in power. Moreover, in the spring of 1808, just when economic pressure was becoming most unpleasant, the minds of Englishmen were turned from disagreeable facts in North America to roseate dreams in South America. British aid to Spain and Portugal in the Peninsular War against Napoleon was rewarded by the opening to British merchants of commercial opportunities in their respective South American dominions. Anticipation proved more dazzling than reality, but British hopes were buoyed as against the pinpricks of the embargo.

Great Britain was a more important objective for the embargo than was France, but several conditions applied to both. The French entrepreneur, like the English, might find immediate speculative profits in the cutting of staple imports. And the working classes which would feel the pinch of the embargo earliest were even less articulate than those in England. Napoleon's will was autocratic and only the most extreme and protracted pressure was likely to prevail against it. As the year wore on, moreover, it became increasingly apparent that America lacked the unity and energy to press the embargo to its ultimate conclusion.

Opposition to the embargo grew steadily. Letters to Jefferson from all parts of the country reveal an astonishing bitterness. Diatribes in Congress transcended the bounds of decency. Josiah Quincy, of Massachusetts, was continually insulting the Administration with an acrid wit which to contemporaries no doubt seemed funny; to posterity it seems a bit elephantine. Timothy Pickering, in the Senate, continued a feud with Thomas Jefferson which predated the embargo by many years. John Randolph of Roanoke, treacherous in all his affiliations, bored from within the Republican ranks to undermine the party unity. Debate in Congress led even to a duel, in

which George W. Campbell, of Tennessee, vindicated the Administration as against Barent Gardenier, of New York. John Adams, in retirement, lent moral support to the embargo. His son, John Quincy Adams, resigned his senatorial seat rather than misrepresent his constituents.

The closing months of Thomas Jefferson's second term were troubled scarcely less than the closing months of John Adams', eight years earlier. It became with Jefferson a point of honor that the embargo must survive his term of office. He drained to the full the cup of bitterness, therefore, when legislative action preceded his retirement. Jefferson and the embargo went out together, and to Madison was left only the emasculated version of nonintercourse.

EMBLEMS, PARTY, have long been used unofficially in the United States, *e.g.*, the black cockade of the Federalists. Officially they are placed at the top of party column ballots in fifteen states. A crowing rooster or a star usually serves for the Democrats, an elephant or a soaring eagle for the Republicans, hands clasped against the background of a hemisphere for the Socialists, the crossed sickle and hammer for the Communists, and so on. In New Mexico the Republicans adopted the national flag as their emblem whereupon the Democrats placed the national coat of arms at the top of their party column. A few states, among them Oklahoma and Delaware, prohibit by law the use as emblems on ballots of the national flag, the arms or seal of the state or of the United States. Party emblems enable the illiterate elector to vote a straight ticket without difficulty. He does not have to be able to read the names of the parties printed at the top of the ballot; all he needs to know is the difference between an eagle and a rooster. Hence practical politicians favor emblems; on the other hand reformers oppose them, hoping thus to discourage ignorant voters.

EMIGRANT AID MOVEMENT, designed to promote free-state migration to Kansas Territory, originated in the calculating mind of Eli Thayer in March, 1854. The movement was largely confined to the Northeast, where politicians, financiers, clerics and editors, typified by Gerrit Smith, Amos Lawrence, Edward Everett Hale and Horace Greeley, united in a "crusade" against the "slave power." In the Northwest, the deciding factor in making Kansas free, there was little organized effort. Settlers went at their own expense, but aid companies secured reduction in transportation costs and, with stock subscriptions and popular contributions, founded a few towns and forwarded supplies and mechanical equipment. Income was meager until the close of 1855, when renewed activity of promoters, passionate speeches on "border ruffian outrages" by Kansas radicals, and the inception of supplementary aid committees resulted in larger patronage. Northern sentiment was aroused, but tangible results were negligible, as only a few thousand went to Kansas under promoted auspices. The movement incited resentment in the South; Kansas expeditions, the largest recruited by Jefferson Buford of Alabama, hastened to the territory; but competition by assisted emigration proved impracticable. By 1857 the movement was rapidly waning.

EMINENT DOMAIN is the inherent right of a state as a sovereignty to take private property for public use with reasonable reimbursement. There is no constitutional limit to the state's power of eminent domain except that it shall be for a public purpose, by compensation, and in accordance with due process of law as provided in the Fifth and Fourteenth Amendments to the Constitution.

Contrary to the law regarding police power, taking property by the right of eminent domain requires compensation, the amount to be "just" and to be determined by a jury, commission, court or executive acting for the state. What constitutes a "public use" may have to be determined ultimately by a court. The usual procedure in the exercise of the right of eminent domain is for some official under legislative or congressional authority to requisition or condemn, that is, "take," the desired property and convert, or subject it to public use, as, for example, land for roads or streets, buildings, etc. The power of eminent domain is a sovereign, inherent power which cannot be contracted away or separated from the state.

EMORY'S MILITARY RECONNAISSANCE, in southwestern United States, was performed by Lt. W. H. Emory of the U. S. Topographical Engineers, together with Lieutenants Warner, Abert and Peck, as part of the military movement against Mexico in 1846. The party, with scientific instruments, was attached to Kearny's army of the West, which marched from Fort Leavenworth, Kans., to Santa Fe, N. Mex., and later to San Diego, Calif. After leaving Santa Fe, the reconnaissance included a portion of the Rio Grande River, the mountains, the Gila River to the Colorado, and thence to the California coast. This was the first American official survey of this region, and the report with accompanying illustrations is of great interest and value.

EMPRESARIO SYSTEM. In the Spanish language, an *empresario* is one who directs an *empresa,* an undertaking. It was the title of persons who obtained contracts to settle colonists in Mexican Texas. Contracts were granted by the governor, in accordance with Federal and state laws, authorizing the *empresario* to introduce a specified number of families into a designated area within six years. For his services, the *empresario* was entitled to receive from the state 23,025 acres of land for each hundred families that he introduced up to 800 families. The *empresario*

might also exact moderate fees from the colonists in return for very real local service. The *empresario* was obligated to introduce only families of Catholic religion and good moral character, to establish schools and erect churches, and to carry on official correspondence in the Spanish language. For the term of his contract, if not revoked, the *empresario* controlled the land within the generous limits of his grant, and no titles could issue therein without his consent; but he owned only those lands which he acquired by purchase or as "premium" for introducing colonists. Misunderstanding of the legal status of an *empresario* with relation to his grant was at the bottom of a considerable speculation in Texas lands in the United States.

ENABLING ACTS. Congress early established the policy of providing by law for the admission of each new state. The people of the territory desiring statehood petition Congress for such an act, which authorizes the holding of a constitutional convention, provides for the election of delegates, and which may seek to impose certain conditions upon the convention and the new state itself. Utah was required to prohibit forever the polygamous form of marriage while Oklahoma was forbidden to move its seat of government for a period of several years. Other examples might be cited. In Coyle v. Smith (221 U. S. 559, 1911) the Supreme Court held that such restrictions were not binding where they related to matters of domestic concern, to those matters concerning which the states have jurisdiction under the Federal Constitution. Otherwise, the states would have varying degrees of autonomy in the control of their affairs, and Congress would be able to extend its power over subjects and in ways never intended by those who framed the Constitution. When, however, the conditions imposed relate to the use of lands granted to a state by Congress, for a specific purpose, they are enforceable, in accordance with the conditions of the grant (Ervien v. United States, 251 U. S. 41, 1919).

ENGINEERING. The early settlers of the United States introduced engineering at the level of knowledge it had attained in the British Isles. Surveyors were in obvious demand in the colonial period. James Watt was probably the first to use stadia and a micrometer about 1770. Then Andrew Ellicott, in laying out the new city of Washington, about 1791, used a transit fashioned by his own hand. Finally, in 1831, William J. Young of Philadelphia invented a transit used in planning the routes of the first railroads in America.

Industries in the young nation counted on the inventions of tools and equipment to hasten the substitution of machines for hand labor—the spinning jenny in 1763, the circular saw in 1777, the cotton gin in 1794, the planer in 1802, Jethro Wood's cast-iron plow in 1819, the lathe for irregular shapes the same year, the electric dynamo in 1831, Cyrus Mc-Cormick's reaper in 1834, John Deere's steel plow in 1839, the magnetic telegraph in 1842, the sewing machine in 1846. Samuel Slater of Pawtucket, R. I., built in 1793 a spinning mill whose machines were powered by water; its operation marked the beginnings in America of mass production. In the year of the signing of the Declaration of Independence, the newly developed Watt engine was set to pumping water from coal mines in England, and it was largely restricted to that use until the end of the century. Oliver Evans of Philadelphia was one of the first to see the possibilities of utilizing the steam engine to operate machinery and vehicles. In 1803 he converted the low-pressure Watt engine into a more effective high-pressure engine; however, steam replaced water power only slowly in American factories. The same year marked the first steam-powered saw mill in New Orleans, and John Fitch used steam to propel a boat in 1788, but it remained for Robert Fulton to make steam navigation commercially successful in 1807. In 1799–1801 Benjamin H. Latrobe in Philadelphia used steam for pumping water through cast-iron water mains. And in 1814 Francis C. Lowell and Paul Moody perfected the power loom.

Gradually the steam engine and the railroad replaced the canals that had opened up the east-west transportation facilities. By 1850 more than 3200 miles of canals had been dug. The Erie Canal (1817–25)—the most famous one—had hardly been finished before it was already outmoded. In 1827 the Baltimore and Ohio Railroad was incorporated. So began a new era. The process of rolling iron shapes and rails and certain shop procedures in metal working had been born just in time to facilitate the growth of railroads.

The railroad ushered in the era of the truss bridge. In 1847 Squire Whipple developed the general solution for building framed structures, and in the wake of his analysis came the iron truss spans of Howe, Pratt, Bollman or Fink.

The old wrought-iron trusses began to be replaced by longer, stronger bridges of the arch, truss-cantilever, girder or suspension type about 1880, with the general adoption of steel. Although the Eads Bridge (1868–74)—the first across the Mississippi—used steel in its arches, the first all-steel bridge in America dates from 1878. Roebling's famous suspension bridges, notably Brooklyn Bridge (1883), followed immediately and established the use of steel wire for suspension bridge cables. Although the first modern suspension bridges were built in Europe, the United States has taken the lead in long-span suspension bridge design—the Golden Gate Bridge, the George Washington Bridge, the San Francisco-Oakland Bay Bridge being the longest ones in the world.

Like the suspension bridge, the skyscraper is a symbol of American urban culture. Although the first structures of metal frames and glass (curtain) walls were erected in Europe, the Chicago School of engineers and architects applied and developed this principle, thus creating the skyscraper. The invention of the elevator—the first practical passenger elevator was installed in a New York building in 1857—made the skyscraper possible. The first true skyscraper was the Home Insurance Building (1885) designed by the engineer William Le Baron Jenney. In the 20th century, New York took the lead with the Woolworth Building (1911–13) which is 769 feet high and then the Empire State Building (1930–31) which is 1250 feet, the tallest skyscraper in the world.

By the middle of the 19th century engineering began to branch out into many divisions—mechanical, mining and metallurgical, electrical, chemical, aeronautical. The invention of the rapid filter so reduced the cost of water purification that small cities were able to have good municipal supplies, and the separation of sanitary sewers from expensive huge storm-water conduits so reduced the cost of city sewerage that this great boon became available to small cities. From these two developments sanitary engineering became a subdivision of civil engineering.

Likewise, the invention of the arch dam in western United States gave a marked impetus to the hydraulics branch of civil engineering. In dam construction the United States is eminent. The Grand Coulee, the Hoover Dam, and Shasta Dam, one of the highest overflow dams in the world, should be mentioned.

In the 20th century, American engineering "know-how" built some large projects in the realm of roads and tunnels. First of all came the completion of the Panama Canal in 1914—a most significant major construction for international transportation. George Washington Goethals was the engineer in charge. In the realm of roads, the turnpikes and freeways have led to a revolution in road design and automotive transportation. These huge systems of roads, begun in this country by the Pennsylvania turnpike (1941), have spread like vast networks across the nation from coast to coast. In tunnel construction, the American engineer again has greatly extended the European concept, so that the subways and subaqueous tunnels of New York City, designed chiefly by Ole Singstad, have become models of tunnel design.

American engineers have pioneered in electrical engineering. The development of a practical electrical generator (1870) and motor, the incandescent light by Edison (1879) and the telephone by Bell (1875) caused electrical engineering to branch from mechanical engineering and to develop during the 20th century rapidly in respect to power, lighting, electric railways and appliances. Wireless telegraphy, electric signaling, the triode tube by DeForest (1909), the photo-electric cell, television, frequency modulation by E. H. Armstrong (1933), sonar and radar have brought about revolutionary changes in communications.

Electric power will probably never be replaced

altogether by atomic power. But electrical engineers at the present time are concerned with the potentialities of atomic power. Nuclear fission, first demonstrated by the American-Italian Fermi, has led to the building of large nuclear reactors—one of the earliest of which was the Hanford type—to furnish power for civilian and domestic uses.

Since 1900 chemical engineering has also greatly contributed to the ease of modern living. Dyes and other coal-tar derivatives, food preservation, packing, petroleum refinement, plastics, explosives, paints and sprays, ceramics, rayon and other cellulose products, rubber, nylon—all these are made by chemical processes.

The gasoline engine, imported from Germany about 1890, gave rise to the automotive industry and to aviation, which mark the notable changes of the 20th century in transportation. One of the most significant developments of engineering in America is the mechanization of industry (mass production) with the consequent use of labor-saving machinery. A minor branch of the profession—industrial engineering—has sprung from the need for effective distribution of products. Since World War II a major industrial revolution has been taking place in American industry: automation. Man-power and man-labor are rapidly being replaced by machines which are capable of performing difficult calculations and which seem almost to "think."

American ingenuity and resourcefulness have led to remarkable advances in applied engineering and technology, but, in almost every instance, American engineers have taken the invention, the idea, from Europe. Like the ancient Romans, the American engineers have built an extremely remarkable material environment upon the scientific theory and creativity of other nations. The problem of the future is for America to create an environment which will stimulate and foster scientific and engineering research.

ENTANGLING ALLIANCES (March 4, 1801). Contrary to common belief this phrase was turned by Thomas Jefferson and not George Washington. The latter advised against "permanent alliances," while the former in his inaugural address declared his devotion to "peace, commerce, and honest friendship with all nations, entangling alliances with none."

ENTERPRISE-BOXER ACTION (Sept. 5, 1813). Off Monhegan Island, Maine, the United States brig *Enterprise*, Lt. William Burrows, defeated the British brig *Boxer*, Capt. Samuel Blyth, in a hard-fought forty-minute action. Both commanders were killed almost at the first broadside, Burrows being ably succeeded by Lt. Edward McCall. The victory must be attributed chiefly to the larger complement of the *Enterprise*—102 men as compared with 66, and her slightly heavier armament—fourteen eighteen-pounder carronades and two long nine-pounders as compared with the *Boxer's* twelve eighteen-pounders and two long sixes, though, according to the findings of the British court-martial, the American fire was also directed "with the greater degree of skill." The American losses were thirteen killed and wounded; the British, twenty-one. The two commanders, as mentioned in Longfellow's poem "My Lost Youth," were buried in the Eastern Cemetery, Portland, Maine.

ENUMERATED COMMODITIES were articles originating in the British colonies and permitted to be exported only to limited destinations: generally to another British colony; or to England, Ireland, Wales, Berwick on Tweed and Scotland, after the union in 1707. The first article enumerated was tobacco in 1621, by Order in Council. Later enumerations were by specific acts of Parliament and included sugar, tobacco, indigo, ginger, speckle wood and various kinds of dyewoods in 1660; rice and molasses in 1704; naval stores, including tar, pitch, rosin, turpentine, hemp, masts, yards and bowsprits in 1705, although rosin was omitted in 1729; copper ore, beaver skins and furs, 1721; coffee, pimento, cacao, hides and skins, whale fins, raw silk, pot and pearl ashes, iron and lumber in 1764, and all other commodities in 1766–67. The object of much of this legislation was to prevent important colonial products from reaching European markets except by way of England. Enumeration did not apply to similar products from non-British possessions.

There was one important exception to the enumeration regulation. Direct trade from the colonies was permitted to points in Europe south of Cape Finisterre for rice, 1730; sugar, 1739; and all additional colonial products enumerated in 1766–67. Thus direct exportation from the colonies to the European areas north of Cape Finisterre was forbidden and permitted south of that point. Rice after 1765 could be exported to any place south of Finisterre and was not limited to Europe, thus American rice had an open market in the foreign West Indies and Spanish colonies.

ENUMERATED POWERS. Under the Constitution of the United States a National Government was created and to it were given definite powers in order that it might not encroach upon the limits of the states or the people thereof. Those powers given to Congress are contained in large part in Article I, and especially in Section 8 which also includes the right to lay and collect taxes "to pay the Debts and provide for the common Defence and general Welfare of the United States" and also "to make all Laws which shall be necessary and proper for carrying into Execution the foregoing Powers, and all other Powers vested by this Constitution in the Government of the United States, or in any Department or Officer thereof." These two clauses have furnished the basis for wide construction by the courts in order vastly to increase the enumerated powers of the National Government.

Article II creates the office of President of the United States and vests him with the Executive power in Section I and with other powers in detail, but of more restricted compass, in the rest of the sections. The judicial power of the United States was created in Article III and "vested in one supreme Court, and such inferior Courts as the Congress may from time to time ordain and establish." Other appropriate powers and regulations are included in the remainder of the Article.

In Article IV the Congress is given power to form and admit new states into the Union and also the power "to dispose of and make all needful Rules and Regulations respecting the Territory or other Property belonging to the United States." In Article V is a provision empowering the Congress to propose amendments to the Constitution.

In addition to these definite creations and locations of specific powers in the United States Government, other powers may be found throughout the Constitution, but the most important are as thus stated. These "enumerated powers" are, by the Ninth and Tenth Amendments in the so-called Bill of Rights, "not to be construed to deny or disparage others retained by the people," and also "The powers not delegated to the United States by the Constitution, nor prohibited by it to the States, are reserved to the States respectively, or to the people."

In contrast to this, in the Dominion of Canada enumerated powers are given to the Provinces and the unenumerated powers are left to the central government. This is exactly opposite to the arrangement and location of constitutional powers in the United States.

EPHRATA, near Lancaster, Pa., was a communal organization founded (1735) as a religious retreat by German Seventh Day Baptists led by Conrad Beissel. The institution comprised, besides householders, two monastic orders, Sisters and Brethren. Refusing a fixed creed, the society performed baptism by immersion, observed the seventh day and subscribed to pietist beliefs in simplicity. Their theosophy and rituals were drawn variously from Gottfried Arnold, Jacob Boehme, the Bible, primitive Christianity, Roman Catholicism, Rosicrucianism and Free Masonry. The community operated grist, saw, paper, oil (for ink), fulling and bark mills, a tannery, a bakehouse, a bookbindery and, most famous, a printing press. The Sisters did fine pen and needlework. Ephrata won renown for its vocal music, its Academy and its Sunday School. Although the congregation still exists, the monastic features at the Cloister had died out by 1800, and of the many fine buildings only two now remain.

EPIC. This alphabetical combination is the first letter of each of the following words: "End Poverty in California." The phrase was devised by Upton Sinclair, 1934 Democratic candidate for the governorship of California. The twelve principles of EPIC and its twelve political planks deeply appealed to fractions of an electorate distracted by the contemporary economic depression. Sinclair was defeated by a small margin. His scheme thereupon lapsed into the limbo of discarded American politico-economic panaceas.

EQUAL RIGHTS PARTY, a minor political party, 1884–88, had for its particular object the enfranchisement of women. It also advocated other measures, such as repression of the liquor traffic; uniform legislation with respect to marriage, divorce and property; civil service reform; and condemnation of war. The candidate for President in each year was Mrs. Belva A. Lockwood, a leader in the woman suffrage, peace and temperance movements. The party failed to receive any important support, even from the suffrage organizations, and polled at the most only about 2000 votes.

"ERA OF GOOD FEELINGS" (1817–24). A name originated by the *Columbian Centinel* (Boston, July 12, 1817) during President Monroe's Eastern tour, it was widely used to describe his two administrations. The demise of the Federalist party gave the appearance of a political union in strong nationalism, illustrated by the tariff act of 1816, the second National Bank and Western development. Monroe weathered the panic of 1819, and received all but one electoral vote in 1820. But shifting economic interests causing nascent sectional rivalries, and bitter personal conflicts leading up to the close election of 1824, made the accuracy of this name for the period questionable.

ERIE, LAKE, BATTLE OF (Sept. 10, 1813). The victory of the nondescript American fleet under Oliver Hazard Perry off Put-in-Bay, Lake Erie, was the major naval engagement on the Great Lakes in the War of 1812, and insured immediate American control of Lake Erie and thus the freedom to invade Canada. It also forestalled any cession of territory in the Northwest to Great Britain in the treaty of peace.

Perry's fleet of one captured brig and the ships he had built at Erie, two brigs and a half dozen schooners, blockaded Malden, the British base, thus obliging the British force of three brigs and three schooners to come out for supplies. The fleets met soon after noon in a light breeze, each side drawn up in a single line, but with Perry having the advantage of the windward position. On Perry's flagship, the *Lawrence*, which headed the line, flew a crudely made flag, now at Annapolis, inscribed with the words of the dying Lawrence, of the *Chesapeake-Shannon* action, "Don't Give Up the Ship."

As the lines slowly converged, Perry ordered the *Caledonia* and the *Niagara,* his better ships, but both armed only for short range fighting, to close up to support the *Lawrence* in concentrating on the head of the British line. Because of previous orders, Elliott, of the *Niagara,* seemed to have felt he must keep behind the *Caledonia* rather than use his superior sailing to pass ahead. As a result of the light air and the slow sailing of the *Caledonia,* the *Lawrence,* unsupported, sustained the fire of the larger British ships for two hours and a half until four fifths of her crew were killed or wounded and the ship itself badly damaged.

At 2:30 Perry assisted the purser and the chaplain to fire a final shot, and was then rowed through a dangerous fire to the *Niagara.* Once on board, he ordered her into close action, and she came up just as the two stronger British ships, the *Detroit* and the *Queen Charlotte,* had fouled each other in an attempt to wear and bring fresh broadsides into play. Securing a position ahead of them, Perry poured in raking broadsides, where at this close range the 32-pounder carronades of the *Niagara* could do great execution against an almost defenseless enemy. With forty dead in his squadron, and ninety-four, including himself, wounded, Barclay, the British commander, soon surrendered. So severe had been the early phase of the engagement that the American loss was little less, 27 killed and 96 wounded. From the *Lawrence,* to which he returned to receive the formal surrender, Perry sent his famous message to Gen. William Henry Harrison, the commander of the American Army in the Northwest, "We have met the enemy, and they are ours, two ships, two brigs, one schooner, and one sloop."

ERIE CANAL. After the Revolution the rapid settlement of upstate New York intensified the demand for an artificial waterway to the Great Lakes through the Mohawk Gateway. The legislature in 1808 authorized a survey and in 1810 set up a canal commission which selected Lake Erie for the western terminus. To DeWitt Clinton, canal commissioner and later governor (1817–22, 1824–28), must go the major credit for proposing and executing the undertaking. His speeches and memorial of 1815, giving details as to route, costs, and benefits, prodded the legislature in 1817 to authorize construction.

Untrained but able men such as Benjamin Wright overcame construction problems by developing new mortar, by inventing machines to cut roots and uproot stumps, and by building aqueducts such as the one across the Genesee River. The four-foot deep ditch was 363 miles long with 83 locks lifting boats a total of over 600 feet; it cost over $7,000,000. Farmers did most of the work but were reinforced by Irish laborers in difficult places. By 1823 boats from Albany reached Rochester and also Lake Champlain over the Champlain Canal. Two years later Clinton

led a procession of canal boats from Buffalo to New York.

The success of the Erie Canal in cutting transportation charges, raising land values, stimulating the growth of cities, capturing for New York City most of the western trade, led to a canal "mania." The legislature constructed branches: Oswego, Chenango, Genesee Valley, Black River, Cayuga and Seneca. During the 1850's, railroads began to capture freight; by the 1870's canal tonnage had fallen substantially. The abolition of tolls in 1882 did not check the Erie's decline.

ESCALANTE-DOMÍNGUEZ EXPEDITION. The year 1776 was momentous elsewhere besides in the Thirteen Colonies. New Mexico had then been occupied by Spaniards for nearly 200 years, whereas California had only recently been colonized and was difficult to reach. The viceroy in Mexico City wanted intercourse opened between Santa Fe and the new port of Monterey; while the Franciscan missionaries wanted to explore the intervening country for new Indian peoples to evangelize. Accordingly a party started from Santa Fe, July 29, 1776. It was headed by Fray Silvestre Vélez de Escalante from the Zuñi mission. With him went the Father Custodian, Fray Francisco Atanacio Domínguez; Don Bernardo Miera y Pacheco, retired captain and map maker; two other Spaniards; a "Yuta" interpreter, and four half-breeds and Indians as soldier-servants.

Following up the Chama River and across the San Juan (or Navajo), they had a glimpse of the Mesa Verde ruins and finally reached the Great Salt Lake Valley—far beyond any earlier exploration. With the season advanced, and unable to secure native guides, they abandoned the effort to reach Monterey. Turning south through Cedar Valley and "Dixie," they worked eastward through the "Arizona Strip," and finally succeeded in crossing the Colorado at the "Ford of the Fathers" (later, Lee's Ferry). After reaching Oraibi, they followed known trails to Zuñi, Ácoma, Laguna, Isleta, and arrived in Santa Fe, Jan. 3, 1777. In five months the little party had covered about 2000 miles, and strengthened Spanish exploratory claims northward nearly to the 42nd parallel and westward to the "Escalante Desert."

ESCALATORS. The word escalator was coined in the latter part of 1895 from the Latin *scala,* a ladder. Until April 3, 1950, it was an exclusive trademark of Otis Elevator Co. but on that date the U. S. Patent Office ruled that "escalator" had become a common descriptive term for moving stairways.

Although many schemes had been proposed through the ages for moving stairways, the first known patent for "revolving stairs" was granted to Nathan Ames of Saugus, Mass., in 1859. This patent suggested the use of equipment similar to that found in modern escalators, but forty years were to elapse before the first successful moving stairway was provided for public use.

In 1892 Jesse W. Reno patented an "inclined elevator," or endless moving ramp, and an experimental model was operated for a few weeks in 1896 at the Brooklyn Bridge. Also in 1892, a patent for a moving stairway with flat steps was granted to George A. Wheeler. This patent was acquired by Charles D. Seeberger, who coined the word "escalator." The first escalator of this type was manufactured by Otis Elevator Co. in 1898 and used at the World's Fair in Paris in 1900. This was the first escalator for commercial use, and after the fair it was sold to Gimbel Brothers, Philadelphia, where it continued in operation until replaced by modern equipment in 1939. On Sept. 5, 1900, Jesse Reno started to build an "inclined elevator" for the elevated railway station at Third Avenue and 59th Street, New York. This was the oldest moving incline in existence when the "el" was torn down in 1955.

Escalators soon were in wide use for stores, railway stations and factories. In 1911, Otis bought out the Reno Inclined Elevator Co. and shortly thereafter combined the better features of the Reno and Seeberger equipment to create the basic type in use, with many refinements, throughout the world in 1960. The highest escalator in this country was one of 53 feet in the New York subway system.

ESSEX, CRUISE OF THE (1812–14), inflicted a loss of $6,000,000 on British whaling in the South Pacific. The *Essex,* Capt. David Porter, 46 guns, after being the first American warship to round the Horn, refitted at Valparaiso, attacked and captured British whalers around the Galapagos, March to September, 1813. Overhauling his ship in the Marquesas, Porter returned to Valparaiso, outside which, in neutral waters, on March 28, 1814, he was attacked by the British frigate *Phoebe,* Capt. Hillyar, 44 guns, and the sloop *Cherub,* 26 guns. Hampered by the loss of his main-topmast in a squall, Porter was repeatedly raked by the enemy ships while his carronades could not reach them. He attempted to beach his ship and destroy her, but was prevented by the wind shifting, and, after resisting stubbornly for nearly two and one-half hours, was compelled to surrender. His losses were 58 killed, 65 wounded, and 31 missing; the British, 5 killed and 10 wounded.

ESSEX JUNTO was made up of "men of education and property," representatives of Essex County, Mass., who came together at Ipswich in April, 1778, to consider a new constitution for Massachusetts. Their adverse opinion, expressed in the "Essex Result," of the proposals of John Hancock caused him to characterize the group as the Essex Junto. They constituted the dominant group in the Federalist party, speaking of themselves as the "wise and good and rich," qualified by birth, education and property

to rule. They favored adoption of the Federal Constitution, supported Hamilton's financial program, and opposed Jefferson and all he stood for. They favored war with revolutionary France, opposed the embargo, and finally brought about its repeal. Because of bitter opposition to Jefferson and his policies and to the War of 1812, the Junto came to be called the "British faction." Nullification and secession were advocated. Though unsupported by general popular approval, continued opposition to the war and its conduct finally led to the calling of the Hartford Convention. The opposition within the convention, Jackson's victory at New Orleans, and the Treaty of Ghent ended the Junto's influence.

EUTAW SPRINGS, BATTLE OF (Sept. 8, 1781), was the last important engagement of the Revolution in South Carolina. The fight was forced by Gen. Nathanael Greene upon the British commander, Col. Alexander Stewart, to prevent aid to Cornwallis should the latter attempt a return to the state. The American force, about 2000 strong, was composed of Continentals and North and South Carolina militia; the British had a somewhat larger number, all regulars. Both commanders attacked successfully with their right wings, but the British, thanks to the gallantry of Maj. John Majoribanks and to the protection of a large brick house near their center, were able to force Greene from the field. Stewart, however, was unable to retain his position, and retreated next day toward Charleston. The Americans lost a quarter of their number, the British an even larger proportion. Although the battle had no effect upon the Yorktown campaign, the losses sustained by the British made it necessary for them to retire to Charleston for the remainder of the war.

EVANGELICAL UNITED BRETHREN CHURCH. Formed in 1946 by a merger of the Church of the United Brethren in Christ and the Evangelical Church, the United Brethren date from 1800. Philip William Otterbein and Martin Boehm were its joint founders. Otterbein came to America in 1752 as a German Reformed missionary, becoming pastor of a congregation at Lancaster, Pa. A deep personal religious experience caused him to become a zealous evangelist. He came into contact with Martin Boehm, a Mennonite minister of like views; they united their efforts and carried on extensive evangelistic work among the Germans of Pennsylvania, Maryland and Virginia. In 1774 Otterbein became the minister of an independent congregation in Baltimore where he continued his revivalistic work. Others joined in this work and in 1800 Otterbein and Boehm with eleven others formed the Church of the United Brethren in Christ. Otterbein was a close friend of Francis Asbury the Methodist bishop and the new church became Methodistic in both polity and doctrine, Otterbein and Boehm being chosen the first bishops.

The new church expanded into the Middle West following German settlement.

Jacob Albright, a Pennsylvania-born German of Lutheran background, gathered a group about him when he preached as a free-lance revivalist beginning in 1796. The first regular annual meeting of the group was in 1807; the name "Evangelical Association" was long used by the Albright followers. Methodistic in polity and doctrine like the United Brethren, the Evangelicals continued the use of the German language longer. The body suffered several schisms; the major one was healed in 1922, at which time the name, the Evangelical Church, was adopted. In 1946, the Evangelical United Brethren Church came into existence with 730,123 members; it has since increased to 749,188 (1958).

EVANGELISM is the effort by the Christian churches to bring the gospel of Christ to all men. Historically, evangelism in America has been carried out largely through revivalism, the emotional appeal to individuals collected in masses to accept Christian faith. Under the conditions of life during the colonial period and in the 19th century, with the large majority of the population not church members, revivalism proved to be an effective method of evangelism. The Great Awakening, in which such preachers as Congregationalist Jonathan Edwards, Dutch Reformed Theodore J. Frelinghuysen, Presbyterians Gilbert Tennent and Samuel Davies, and Anglican George Whitefield were conspicuous as revivalists, won many to the faith. In the early 19th century revivalism was influential both in the older communities of the East and in the frontier settlements of the West. Timothy Dwight, Lyman Beecher and Nathaniel W. Taylor were leaders of revivalism in New England Congregationalism. Not only was the number of church members significantly increased, but threats of "infidelity" were resisted. On the frontier, revivalism was more highly emotional, and was often associated with vast camp meetings. Barton Stone, James McGready, and Peter Cartwright were well-known frontier evangelists.

In the 1820's, Charles G. Finney synthesized some of the aspects of Eastern and Western revivalism in the "new measures," which included protracted meetings at unseasonable hours, the use of harsh and irreverent language in prayer and sermon, the specific naming of prospective converts in services, praying by women in mixed assemblies, and especially the "anxious bench" where the sinners were brought directly under the eye of the exhorting awakener. Methodists and Baptists in particular employed the techniques of revivalism in mushrooming into the largest Protestant denominations, but many other bodies also benefited, including Disciples and Presbyterians. In the later 19th century, Dwight L. Moody emerged as the most famous revivalist. In the 20th century, revivalism fell into decline, as can be traced in the career of Billy Sunday. At mid-century, there was a resurgence of mass revivalism, especially under the leadership of popular evangelist Billy Graham. Revivalism has tended to be quite conservative theologically.

In the 20th century there arose a new interest in other types of evangelism throughout the Protestant world. Attention was devoted to such approaches as personal evangelism, church evangelism, visitation evangelism, educational evangelism and evangelism through the mass communications media. Many denominations established departments of evangelism. The Federal Council of the Churches of Christ in America, later merged into the larger National Council of Churches, pioneered in new ways of evangelism, such as the National Preaching Mission. A special commission of evangelism of the National Council of Churches defined the task of evangelism as bringing "the whole mighty purpose of God . . . effectively into the conscious life of every people and every generation and to seek with all men, Christian and not-yet-Christian, its fulfillment in a growing community of faith and love." The renewed interest in evangelism has been an important aspect of the religious renewal that has characterized American religious life in the middle of the present century.

EXCHANGES developed during the 19th century. They have performed a highly useful function in the marketing of commodities and investment securities where the area of distribution is large, often nationwide, and sometimes world-wide. The transactions in marketing many products became so numerous and complicated for individuals, as the United States grew in population and expanded in size, that specialized groups of men were needed to carry on trading operations. For various commodities, groups were organized and rules made to facilitate the orderly conduct of their business. As an example, a grain exchange is a public market place where the nation's grain supply and demand meet. It is a place where the processor, storage elevator operator, and exporter go to buy the farmer's grain. A grain exchange governs trading activities by rules and regulations, but itself never buys or sells a bushel of grain, and in no way sets or fixes prices.

In the growth of commodity exchanges grading was very important, for commodities are not uniform. Private and governmental bodies certify that they are of a certain grade and, therefore, can be sold without inspection. But even if they are bought for cash, samples are presented. Ordinarily, the graded commodities are put in a public warehouse, and negotiable receipts are issued to the buyer as he takes delivery of the commodity. Banks make loans on such receipts. Usually one grade is commonly traded in, *e.g.*, "upland middling" cotton. Other grades can be substituted by paying differentials set by the exchange above or below the contract grade. On stock exchanges grading is unnecessary, for each share of a given class of stock or bond of a given issue is identical with every other. Elaborate provisions to prevent the fraudulent issues of listed securities make inspection unnecessary.

Exchanges may provide for future as well as cash (or spot) transactions. Either the futures or cash market provides opportunity for a form of speculation known as "hedging," which is really business insurance against loss, a useful function in rationing a seasonally-produced crop over its period of use. In futures markets, this speculation is regulated by the exchange and supervised by Federal authorities. For the use of traders the exchange usually makes available the figures as to visible supplies, arrivals, etc. It sets commissions and rules for trading.

The New York Produce Exchange was organized in 1850 and incorporated in 1862. It deals in grains, hay, lumber, naval stores, tallows, etc. The New York Cotton Exchange was started in 1870 and chartered in 1871. It deals only in cotton and is mostly a futures market. Coffee is dealt in on the New York Coffee and Sugar Exchange. The Commodities Exchange, Inc., has developed futures markets in a number of commodities. Separate exchanges were started for rubber, February, 1926; for silk, September, 1928; for tin, December, 1928; for copper, May, 1929; and for hides, June, 1929. These were combined in May, 1933; and in July, 1934, lead and zinc were added. Governmental regulation is provided by the Cotton Futures Act (1916), the Grain Standards Act (1916), the Security Exchange Act of 1934, and the Commodity Exchange Act of 1936.

The "Pit" is a specific location in a market where futures contracts for agricultural commodities are bought and sold. Most famous is the wheat pit of the Chicago Board of Trade, although this exchange also has "pits" for other commodities (corn, rye, oats, soybeans, soybean oil, soybean meal, milo, drummed and loose lard, and cotton) where world opinion on price is registered. By providing opportunities in these "pits" for the buying and selling of futures (the making of contracts for future delivery) and hedging (protection of owners against price changes), an exchange provides a continuous market for farm-grown commodities. The Chicago Board of Trade was organized on Monday, April 3, 1848, with a membership of 82. On Feb. 18, 1859, it was incorporated by a special act of the Illinois legislature. The Board is governed by a chairman, a vice chairman, second vice chairman, and fifteen directors elected by the membership. The original objectives were to promote uniformity in customs and usages; to inculcate principles of justice and equity in trade; to facilitate the speedy adjustment of business disputes; to acquire and disseminate commercial and economic information; and generally, to secure to its members the benefits of co-operation in the furtherance of their legitimate pursuits. The objectives are still the same in 1960. Chicago has always had the three characteristics needed for a grain market: closeness to areas of production; cheap transportation facilities; and a consumptive demand. The marketing facilities developed during the first decade after its charter was granted in 1859 were essentially the facilities offered today by the Board of Trade, viz., weighing, inspection and grading, warehousing, the market quotations service, arbitration of commercial disputes, the provision of floor facilities for cash and future trading. This statement is true for the many other commodity exchanges.

Members of the Chicago exchange, who buy and sell grain on the trading floor, represent commission houses, processors, exporters, cash commission men, and terminal elevator men. The procedure developed is a dual system of marketing. It permits the grain to take the shortest possible route from farmer-producer to consumer, with minimum speculative risks. It brings to grain the best terms of finance. It absorbs any amount of grain from a farmer's wagon load to a ship's cargo at the same price per bushel and without major price disturbances. It absorbs an entire crop and holds it against consumptive need with no sacrifice in price on the part of the farmer. It registers a constant price according to world supply and demand conditions. By accurate weights, grades and equitable rules of trade, it safeguards the interest of both producers and consumers. Through the Federal Trade Commission, the Future Trading Act of 1921, the Grain Futures Act of the same year, and the Commodity Exchange Act of 1936, the Federal Government has tried to prevent manipulation, excessive speculation, and fraud in the grain markets of the nation.

Trading in investment securities is carried on in stock markets, of which the most famous is the New York Stock Exchange. Considerable trading began with the formation of the Bank of the United States in 1791, the refunding of the Federal debt, and the assumption of the state debts, and with the new stocks of banks and insurance companies. In those early days the New York brokers met in the shade of an old buttonwood tree on Wall Street. On May 17, 1792, an agreement was signed regarding commissions by a group of 24 brokers. The War of 1812 caused such a growth of business that a formal organization was chartered on March 8, 1817. By that time trading was carried on in state and municipal securities. From 1830 on, another large group of securities was traded in with the development of canals and railroads. In the 1850's, petroleum and mining stocks came on the stock market. Naturally, the Civil War brought increased business with the large amounts of Government and other bond issues, and the securities of new industries of various kinds to provide the supplies for conducting the war. After the Civil War there arose another greater wave of new business. In addition to transcontinental railroad securities, the next group of securities to be traded in were those of industrial and utility origin, and the expansion of business in the form of trusts in the 1890's and early 1900's. A third time—World War I—a war brought rapid activity and speculative growth. Trading in the "war babies" and other stocks benefited the stock market. Both that war and the purchase of foreign bonds in the 1920's added greatly to the foreign list on the stock exchange. A crash took place in 1920, and then began the long upward movement in security prices which ended in the Panic of 1929.

On June 30, 1959, there were fourteen national securities exchanges registered with the Securities Exchange Commission: American Stock Exchange, Boston Stock Exchange, Chicago Board of Trade, Cincinnati Stock Exchange, Detroit Stock Exchange, Midwest Stock Exchange, New Orleans Stock Exchange, New York Stock Exchange, Pacific Coast Stock Exchange, Philadelphia-Baltimore Stock Exchange, Pittsburgh Stock Exchange, Salt Lake Stock Exchange, San Francisco Mining Exchange, and Spokane Stock Exchange. During the year from July 1, 1958, to July 1, 1959, the total market value of all securities sales on registered exchanges was $53,438,801,000, of which the New York Stock Exchange accounted for $45,209,865,000, and the American Stock Exchange (formerly the New York Curb Exchange) accounted for $4,214,669,000.

Membership in the New York Exchange is called a "seat" although there are no seats on the trading floor. By telephone, telegraph and cable, orders come from all over the United States and Europe to the brokers on the floor. When they have bought or sold, the transaction is carried by the ticker all over the country. The settling for the sales of securities is facilitated by the Stock Clearing Corporation started in 1920. Settlement is now made on the fourth business day after the transaction. The corporation enables the members to deliver or receive the net amount of shares he owes or is to receive. Also one check is received or drawn for the net amount of money owed or due the member.

Naturally, the stock market break in October, 1929, affected so many people adversely that unjust, as well as some just, criticism was uttered and written about the market and its procedures. Some of this criticism included alleged manipulation of prices of stocks, the lack of protection to unwise margin-buyers, and the use of inside knowledge by operators on the exchange. Following a congressional investigation of these complaints, Federal regulation of stock exchanges was provided by the Securities Exchange Act of 1934 which created the Securities Exchange Commission. The act provides for the registration and regulation of exchanges and of broker-dealers doing business off the exchanges, prohibits manipulation of stock prices by wash sales, matched orders, or certain other devices, and prohibits fraud in the sale of securities. The act also requires issuers of securities listed on exchanges to file certain documents and reports, regulates the solicitation of proxies with respect to listed securities, and contains restrictions upon the unfair use of "inside information" by the management of such corporations. The law also gives to the Federal Reserve Board power to regulate the use of credit in securities transactions and to fix margins for listed securities.

One of the excellent advantages of a stock market is the possibility it affords the owner of securities to sell them at once. This makes them good collateral for loans at banks. Again, the trading facilities at the various stock exchanges make easier and quicker the process of investment, since more people will invest if they know that they can get their money back when they need it.

The New York Curb Exchange (now the American Stock Exchange) formerly met in the open street. It has now moved indoors. It deals generally with newer securities and the securities of some companies which are less well-established and well-known than those listed on the New York Stock Exchange.

EXPLORERS, UNOFFICIAL. From the earliest period of American settlement private interest induced expansion beyond authorized exploration. The back country became the refuge of the independent and the lawless, and there were numerous unrecognized settlements, such as that of John and Samuel Pringle on the Buckhannon River after their desertion from Fort Pitt in 1761, and the Watauga settlement of James Robertson and John Sevier. Famous among early venturers across the Alleghenies was Daniel Boone, who made known Cumberland Gap and the Wilderness Road. Simon Kenton ranged over much of the Old Northwest, later rendering important military services. Not all early explorers were unlettered frontiersmen; William Bartram, botanist, wrote of his travels, 1773–78, through the Carolinas, Georgia and East and West Florida, and John James Audubon combed the wilderness for his *Birds of America,* as later George Catlin sought the Indian. Gurdon Hubbard marked the trail from the Wabash to Fort Dearborn.

The official expedition of Lewis and Clark made use of the findings of its unofficial predecessors; John Colter left it to trap, and was first to see Yellowstone Park, Green River and Jackson Lake. Meanwhile, the Columbia River had been discovered by Robert Gray, 1792, for a trading company. Manuel Lisa went as far as the Big Horn, and raced with Wilson Price Hunt's Astorians over a section of the Oregon Trail, 1811–12. John Day, of Hunt's party, has left his name prominently on the map, as have Jacques Laramie and Bill Williams.

William Henry Ashley's fur trading ventures, beginning in 1822, enlisted many of the "Mountain Men": Andrew Henry, first to trap west of the Rockies; James Bridger, discoverer of Great Salt Lake; Jedediah Strong Smith, first to cross the Utah-Nevada deserts to California and the Sierra Nevada on his return; Joseph Reddeford Walker, first to cross the Sierra Nevada from the east, who discovered Yosemite and left his name on Walker Lake and Walker's Pass; Thomas Fitzpatrick, guide of notable expeditions; William L. Sublette of Sublette's cutoff on the Oregon Trail; and Etienne Provost, who led independent trappers to the Uinta and Wasatch mountains.

The Santa Fe Trail was opened by William Becknell, Missouri trader. Antoine Robidou built Fort Robidou or Uinta in the Uinta Valley (Utah), 1832, a famous rendezvous. Ewing Young was an early Taos trapper and Oregon pioneer. Ceran St. Vrain and Charles and William Bent bartered with trappers and Indians. "Kit" Carson guided Frémont and other military explorers. John Bidwell went with the first emigrants to California and William L. Manly's train crossed Death Valley. The missionaries Jason Lee, Marcus Whitman and Pierre-Jean DeSmet made known much of the Northwest.

Prospectors also contributed largely to knowledge of America. Charles D. Poston and Herman Ehrenberg explored the Gadsden Purchase, 1854. Allen and Hosea Grosh discovered the Comstock Lode (Nev.), 1854; Green Russell, Auraria (Colo.), 1858; Bill Fairweather, Alder Gulch (Mont.), 1863; and Ed Schieffelen, Tombstone (Ariz.), 1877.

John M. Bozeman opened the Bozeman Trail from Fort Laramie to Virginia City, 1864. Jesse Chisum or Chisholm established the Chisholm Trail, 1866, one of several used in the heyday of the range cattle industry.

EXPORT-IMPORT BANKS. The First Export-Import Bank of Washington was created by executive order and chartered Feb. 12, 1934, to facilitate trade with Russia. By a law of Jan. 31, 1935, it continued as a Federal agency. The Second Export-Import Bank was organized in March, 1934, to finance the purchase and minting of silver for Cuba. In June, 1936, it was merged with the First Export-Import Bank. On July 31, 1945, the Bank became an independent Federal agency. The Reconstruction Finance Corporation provided most of its early funds; the Federal Government later subscribed to $1,000,-000,000 of its common stock. Trade with Russia did not materialize and the Bank has chiefly aided trade and internal development in Latin America, although China in the 1940's and a number of European countries and even Canada have felt its benefits. It has extended short-term credits for the export of agricultural products such as cotton and tobacco when financing was not available from private institutions. More important, it has granted one-to-five-year credits to firms seeking to export heavy industrial machinery, farm machinery and railroad equipment. Finally, it has extended credit to firms unable to withdraw their funds from countries with exchange restrictions. The Bank has co-operated with the State Department in encouraging projects that will promote the internal economic stability of friendly nations. In 1959 it had over $3,500,000,000 of loans outstanding.

EXTRADITION is the process through which one sovereign government secures from another the person of a fugitive from justice. In the United States the term has two different applications. First, it is used to denote the process by which the National Government of the United States requests the return of a person who is accused of violating a national or state law from some foreign country in which he has been found. Such requests are made only under definite treaty arrangements which usually establish reciprocity in such matters. Thus, the return of Samuel Insull from Greece in 1932 to stand trial in Illinois was retarded by the absence of an adequate extradition treaty between the United States and Greece.

The second meaning of extradition in this country refers to Article IV, Section 2 of the Constitution of the United States which provides that "A person charged in any State with Treason, Felony or other Crime, who shall flee from Justice, and be found in another State, shall on Demand of the executive Authority of the State from which he fled, be delivered up, to be removed to the State having jurisdiction of the Crime." This provision, although apparently mandatory, has been held by the U. S. Supreme Court to be discretionary (24 How. 66). The duty of the governor of the state of refuge is moral, not legal.

FAIR DEAL was the phrase adopted by President Harry S. Truman to characterize the program of domestic legislation he sought to have enacted into law during his years in the Presidency. The term did not become common till the President used it in his State of the Union message of Jan. 5, 1949. In a rudimentary way the Fair Deal existed from the time he took office on April 12, 1945. In September of that year he sent a lengthy message to Congress in which he proposed twenty-one points to be considered by that body as subject matter for legislation. In his opinion these proposals fulfilled the promises made in the Democratic platform of 1944 and he regarded them as continuing and extending the policies of his predecessor, Franklin D. Roosevelt.

Among these points was a request for a full-employment law. The National Government was to see to it that conditions were such that every man who was willing and able to work would have a worthwhile position. As he put it in 1953, "full employment means maximum opportunity under the American system of responsible freedom." He also requested that the wartime Fair Employment Practices Committee (F. E. P. C.) be put on a permanent basis. In other messages which followed he requested legislation on housing, health insurance, aid to education, atomic energy and the development of the St. Lawrence Seaway. In general it can be said that Congress did not respond to these requests. However, the Employment Act of 1946 carried out his wishes on that point. Under it the Council of Economic Advisers was set up which assists the President in the preparation of the annual Economic Report to Congress.

In the campaign of 1948 Truman succeeded in defeating the Republican candidate, Gov. Thomas Dewey of New York, despite the defection from Democratic ranks of numerous Southerners, the Dixiecrats who opposed his stand on civil liberties, and of numbers of Northerners who supported Henry Wallace and the Progressive Party of that year. After his surprising victory the President gathered together many of the proposals he had made in previous years in his annual message to Congress in January, 1949. He asked for laws on housing, full employment, higher minimum wages, better price supports for farmers, more organizations like the Tennessee Valley Authority, the extension of social security and fair employment practices. Filibusters prevented the passage of an anti-poll-tax law and a Fair Employment Practices Act. However, the Housing Act of 1949 facilitated slum clearance throughout the country, the minimum wage level was lifted from 40 to 75 cents an hour by an amendment to the Fair Labor Standards Act of 1938 and the Social Security Act of 1950 extended the benefits of that law to about 10,000,000 more people. The coming of the Korean War in July, 1950, the increasing complexity of foreign affairs and a general prosperity lessened interest in the Fair Deal program.

FAIR OAKS, OR SEVEN PINES, BATTLE OF (May 31-June 1, 1862). The action at Williamsburg on May 5, 1862, slowed McClellan's (U.) march up the Virginia peninsula on Richmond. Events in the Shenandoah Valley caused the wildest excitement in Washington; McClellan's repeated pleas for more troops were ignored. Union interests called loudly for successful action. McClellan was constantly urged forward. By May 27 his army was concentrating in the vicinity of Fair Oaks Station, about ten miles east of Richmond. J. E. Johnston (C.), knowing of McClellan's expectation of heavy reinforcements, resolved to strike before they could arrive.

The attack began piecemeal, in driving rain, on May 31. Confusion, misunderstanding of orders, and lack of effective staff work prevented proper advantage being taken of initial successes. The fight, first

on one wing and then on the other, continued with alternating advance and retreat throughout the day and into the night. About sunset Johnston was wounded and carried from the field. G. W. Smith succeeded him. The Confederate attack was renewed early the next day in the hope of cutting McClellan's line of communications up the peninsula, but with little chance of success. At the close of the day the Confederates retired to prepared positions to await McClellan's next move. Each side had used over 40,000 men. The Union loss totaled over 4400; the Confederate, about 6000.

In the midst of the fighting on June 1, President Davis (C.) placed R. E. Lee in command of the Confederate Army, which, henceforth, was to be known as the Army of Northern Virginia.

FAIR-TRADE LAWS. The moral and economic arguments used to support fair-trade laws run as follows. A manufacturer makes some highly specialized product like an electric toaster. He gives it a trade name like Sunbeam and spends large sums in advertising that name until it becomes in the minds of the public the symbol of excellence. As a result the public is willing to pay more for a toaster named Sunbeam than to take a chance on a less known product which may or may not be just as good. He fixes a retail price which gives the merchant a bigger margin of profit than he gets on most of the things he sells, thus giving the merchant an incentive to push the trade-marked article. The spread is so large that it gives price cutters the opportunity to offer bargains to the public by selling under the fixed and published retail price. If the manufacturer had not spent large sums in promoting the trade name this opportunity would not exist. Hence the price cutter, he claims, is in effect stealing the good will built up at great cost to the manufacturer. The price cutter is also engaged in unfair competition with those who respect the manufacturer's suggestion of prices. On the basis of this argument fair-trade laws were passed during the Great Depression in a majority of states permitting manufacturers, wholesalers and retailers to enter into agreements fixing resale prices.

Unfortunately state legislation by itself was entirely inadequate to protect the manufacturer. The Federal antitrust laws prohibited agreements to fix prices in interstate commerce. All products with widely advertised trade names have to move in interstate commerce. Therefore the Miller-Tydings Act was passed in 1937 under pressures from merchants and manufacturers. The drug industry, where trade names are of tremendous importance and the markup extremely large, was one of the most important pressure groups. The Miller-Tydings Act excepted from the antitrust laws agreements fixing the prices of advertised trade-mark goods. But this exemption proved not to be enough because in order to enforce fair trade prices against a retailer there had to be an agreement by that retailer. Manufacturers did not want to limit their market to persons who were willing to sign an agreement.

For this reason the fair-trade groups obtained additional state legislation which required all merchants to follow fair-trade prices whether or not they signed an agreement. In order to enforce this state legislation against persons shipping goods in from outside the state the fair-traders induced Congress to pass the McGuire Act in 1952. That act permitted State A to prevent the advertisement and the sale of articles at less than fair-trade prices of goods shipped in interstate commerce from State B *provided that State B was also a fair-trade state.* But if State B was not a fair-trade state, State A could not impose the condition of price maintenance on the advertisement or sale of goods shipped from State B.

The effect of this loophole permitted a price cutter to establish a mail-order business in a state where there was no fair-trade law in order to advertise and sell goods in fair-trade states in violation of the fair-trade laws of those states. In 1957 a decision of the U. S. Court of Appeals in New York interpreting the McGuire Act held that Masters, Inc., a New York discount house which had been enjoined from selling at less than fair-trade prices in New York, could nevertheless establish a subsidiary named Masters in Washington, D. C. (a non-fair-trade area) and hand out mail order blanks to its customers in its New York store enabling them to get fair-trade articles at bargain prices from Masters in Washington. This loophole has widened as more and more states have had their fair-trade acts declared unconstitutional and the whole fair-trade program is beginning to wither on the vine.

There is no economic justification for prohibiting consumers from getting bargains if they are willing to go to the trouble of seeking out high volume and low cost retailers. It is hard to see what legitimate interest a manufacturer has in preventing his retailer from selling at lower prices so long as the manufacturer gets his wholesale price. Much of the pressure for fair-trade laws comes from retailers which are hurt by the competition of the larger outlets able to give better bargains.

Yet the legal protection that retailers get from fair trade is illusory because manufacturers who impose fair-trade prices in fair-trade states are unwilling to abandon the market offered by discount houses in non-fair-trade states. Thus, a discount house in a fair-trade state can legally evade its fair-trade laws by handing out mail order blanks to its customers who order from its out-of-state subsidiary. Except in the case of liquor, where importation can be restricted and licenses taken away, fair trade enforcement has been a failure and large companies are gradually abandoning it as a sales policy.

FAIRFAX PROPRIETARY rested upon a patent issued by James II to Lord Culpeper in 1688, in pursuance of precedents and in fulfillment of obligations extending back to 1649, but counter to the strongly articulated wishes of the inhabitants of Virginia. The patentee was given rights to the soil in the region lying between the Rappahannock and Potomac Rivers and might make grants of land and collect quitrents just as the Crown did elsewhere. For purposes of government, however, the "Northern Neck" remained an integral part of Virginia. Following the death of Lord Culpeper in 1689, the proprietary passed through his daughter Catherine to her son Thomas, sixth Lord Fairfax of Cameron.

Westward expansion of settlement naturally precipitated an acute controversy as to the true purport of a grant which reflected the customary royal ignorance of American geography, but in 1745 a committee of the Privy Council reached a decision whereby proprietary rights over a vast area of more than 5,000,000 acres, including much of the best land in Virginia, were confirmed to Lord Fairfax. The latter, who had visited America in 1735 to safeguard his interests, returned in 1747 and took up his permanent residence at Greenway Court in the Shenandoah Valley. The American Revolution naturally reopened the question of his rights, but Fairfax, while declining to swear allegiance to the new state, held aloof from the conflict and was not molested. A year after his death in 1781, however, the Virginia Assembly sequestered the quitrents of the Northern Neck, and in 1785 abolished them, together with the other seignorial rights of the proprietors.

The Definitive Treaty of Peace (1783) having prohibited further confiscation of Loyalist property, and Virginia having pledged her adherence to this provision, the Fairfax heirs contended that the act of 1785 could not affect their title to lands held in fee, for against these no proceedings had been initiated in 1782. For a decade the matter hung fire. Eventually, in 1793, a syndicate represented by John Marshall undertook to acquire the interest held in fee under the Fairfax title. In 1796 a compromise was reached whereby the state was to relinquish claim to all lands specifically appropriated by Lord Fairfax to his own use either by deed or actual survey, and was in turn to be ceded all lands which were "waste and unappropriated" at the time of the death of Lord Fairfax. Subsequent litigation (*see* Martin v. Hunter's Lessee), while of considerable constitutional significance, did not materially modify this settlement.

FALL LINE is the line of junction of the tidewater region of eastern United States and the Piedmont or foothill region to the westward. Falls which mark the eastward passage of the streams across the line give it its name and much of its historical significance. The obstruction to navigation afforded by the falls rendered the Piedmont region less accessible to European commerce and influence than the tidewater region. When in the early part of the 18th century, due to the pressure of population below the falls, colonization of the upland region began, radical readjustments in modes of life were rendered necessary, justifying its being called the first American frontier. At the falls in the more important rivers crossing the line, cities grew up to which products of the Piedmont region were hauled or barged for shipment abroad. Examples of such cities are Richmond, Fredericksburg and Petersburg in Virginia, Raleigh in North Carolina and Camden and Columbia in South Carolina.

FALLEN TIMBERS, BATTLE OF (Aug. 20, 1794). When Wayne set out from Fort Greenville on July 28, 1794, on his march against the Indians, conditions in the Northwest Territory were in an uncertain state. Jay's Treaty was still unsigned and the border forts were still in British hands. The Indians, elated by their defeats of Harmar and St. Clair and encouraged by their British allies, were hopeful of defeating the Americans and driving them out of the country. Every obstacle was raised against Wayne's repeated proffer to negotiate questions in dispute, and the situation was only aggravated by an Indian attack on Fort Recovery.

Wayne, his army in a disciplined state and reinforced by Kentucky volunteers, decided to move. The British and Little Turtle, the Indian leader, warned of Wayne's advance, hastily gathered the scattered Indians. By mid-August about 1300 braves were assembled in northwest Ohio at the Rapids of the Maumee in a region called Fallen Timbers because of the large number of fallen trees in the vicinity. Less than 800 Indians were engaged in the two-hour battle of Aug. 20, in which Wayne decisively defeated and dispersed his opponent. This victory paved the way for the frontier enforcement of Jay's Treaty and the British evacuation of the border forts.

FALMOUTH, BURNING OF (Oct. 18, 1775), by the British, was one of the first acts of violence in the Revolution. Described by contemporary historians as "wanton" and "cowardly," this act was part of the British Admiralty plan to cripple seaport towns and punish rebels for openly giving aid to Continental troops in the besieged town of Boston. On Oct. 16 Capt. Henry Mowat, in command of the *Canceaux*, sailed into Falmouth harbor in Casco Bay, accompanied by three other armed ships, and demanded the surrender of the town. Unable to come to terms with the inhabitants, early in the morning of Oct. 18, the town was fired after the townspeople had withdrawn. By night Falmouth, largest of the eastern towns in wealth and population, was virtually reduced to ashes.

FANEUIL HALL, a market and public hall, the gift to the town of Boston of the merchant, Peter Faneuil, called the "Cradle of Liberty" because of the ringing speeches made there in Revolutionary times, has an unexcelled record as a meeting place for organized protest. It was built, 1740–42, with John Smibert as the architect, and much enlarged, 1805–6, by Charles Bulfinch.

FARIBAULT PLAN. In August, 1891, Archbishop Ireland made an arrangement with the Boards of Education in Faribault and Stillwater, in Minnesota, by which a parochial school in each of these two towns would be regarded during class hours as a state school, retaining, however, its own teachers, and preserving its character as a distinctly Catholic school during the remainder of each day. Although a similar system was quietly in vogue in scores of parishes, and in ten states of the Union, the Faribault-Stillwater plan evoked clamorous opposition not only from many Protestants, who saw in it a plot to squeeze from the state a subsidy for sectarian schools, but also from several Catholics, who feared that if it were widely adopted it would eventually obliterate the Catholic schools of America.

When the battle was raging at its height throughout the country, Archbishop Ireland in person presented the case to the Holy See for its decision. Five cardinals, commissioned to adjudicate, announced on April 2, 1892, their decision as follows: "The arrangement entered into by Archbishop Ireland concerning the schools of Faribault and Stillwater, taking into account all the circumstances, can be tolerated." The Pope approved the decision.

FARM MACHINERY. Although agriculture, well into the 19th century, continued to occupy most of the population, Americans from the beginning had been bad farmers from the European point of view. Throughout the colonial period, they were ignorant of the proper use of fertilizers, the rotation of crops, the effective care of livestock, farm management or efficient tools. Their implements remained primitive as late as 1820, when wooden plows and harrows, the sickle, the flail, the iron-shod wooden spade and hand sowing were still in general use—some of them much later. The only important agricultural implement invented in America in the colonial period was the scythe of Joseph Jenks (1646), which was the first step toward the modern, long, narrow, thick-backed bladed scythe.

The reasons for this backwardness were primarily the extent and cheapness of the land, and the delayed Industrial Revolution. With such abundance of virgin soil, the intensive farming long practised in Europe was unnecessary, but it was this very abundance which made labor-saving machinery a *sine qua non* of American agriculture, once the West was opened. Thomas Jefferson, whose thought, like Washington's, was much occupied with the improvement of agriculture, designed the first scientific mouldboard for the plow in 1798. Charles Newbold, the year before, had patented a cast-iron plow; but he had no success with the invention, partly because of a superstitious belief among the farmers that iron poisoned the ground. This prejudice was overcome after the cast-iron plow of Jethro Wood in 1819, which was so successful that Wood was obliged to fight patent infringements until his death in 1834. It was followed by the steel-faced plow of John Lane (1833), the saw-steel plow of John Deere (1838–47), and the chilled plow of James Oliver (1855), all of them more successful in the heavier soil of the West.

Americans made few original contributions to the harrow. Disk harrows, invented probably in Japan, did not come into general use in America until the latter half of the 19th century. Mechanical seeding was not greatly developed until the work of the Pennock brothers in 1842, although Jefferson had experimented with grain drills in the 1790's. Corn planters requiring a different technic were invented by D. S. Rockwell in 1839, M. Robbins in 1857, and John Thompson and John Ramsay in 1864, but they were not highly successful until 1875.

Harvesting machinery first became practical through the inventions of Cyrus Hall McCormick in Virginia and Obed Hussey in Cincinnati, though there had been 47 reaper patents, 23 of them American, before the celebrated McCormick reaper. McCormick's horse-operated machine utilized all seven of the principles which have since been found essential to successful mechanical harvesting. These are the side draft, the knife, the divider, the fingers, the reel, the platform and the wheel. Hussey's reaper, patented in 1833—a year before McCormick's patent, though probably McCormick's actual invention preceded Hussey's—had a wide sale especially in western New York, where McCormick's machine was unknown. It lacked, however, the vital principle of the reel.

The effect of the reaper was revolutionary. With two men, the McCormick machine could do ten or twelve times the work of two sickle harvesters. It is significant that less than fifteen years after his first reaper patent, McCormick was obliged to establish a factory in Chicago to meet the Western demand. By 1856, 4000 McCormick reapers were made and sold a year. The International Harvester Co., founded by the McCormick family, has continued to develop farm machinery up to the present day.

The use of McCormick machinery had, in the opinion of many historians, a profound effect on the outcome of the Civil War. It is an ironic commentary that the invention of a Connecticut Yankee, the cotton gin, was an important, indirect cause of secession, whereas the invention of a Virginian played a large part in winning the Civil War for the North.

Americans were backward in the invention of threshing and winnowing machines. Jefferson, in 1793, imported the model of a thresher from England and had a machine built from it which threshed "150 bushels of wheat in 8 hours with 6 horses and 5 men." It was not until 1828 that a practical thresher was patented in the United States. This was the invention of Samuel Lane, but it was superseded in 1834 by the machine for threshing and fanning into which John and Hiram Pitts put most of the principles now in use in threshers, including the apron conveyor. In 1844 Jerome I. Case designed a combined thresher and separator which eliminated the fanning mill. Three years later, Case established his plant in Racine, Wis., which by 1857 was producing 1600 machines a year.

The production of agricultural machinery owed its rapid rise to the use of the interchangeable parts system originally invented by Eli Whitney (1798). In the last half of the 19th century, the value of farm implements and machinery manufactured in the United States increased from less than $7,000,000 to more than $100,000,000. Between 1870 and 1900, the United States rose to the leadership of the world in the manufacture of agricultural machinery. During that time, machines had been developed which, in a single operation, plowed, harrowed and sowed, and which were drawn by traction engines. In the same period, hay stackers, potato planters, manure spreaders, reaper-and-binders, harvester-threshers and many other devices came into use. On the Western farms, gang plowing and harrowing became common. Since 1900 there have been great improvements. The tractor, which came into use in 1901, the caterpillar tread in 1904, the power-operated milking machine in 1905, have made revolutionary changes. The tractor and other automotive equipment caused the disappearance of some 9,000,000 horses and mules from American farms between 1918 and 1932. This released about 30,000,000 acres of crop land.

As a result of mechanization and other improvements, crop production, per male worker, has increased more than 100% between 1850 and 1930. Total power, per worker, has increased in this time from 1.5 to 7.4 horse power.

The latest inventions in machinery have solved difficult problems. These are the cane cutter, the corn harvester, and the cotton picker. The cotton picker represents the only important advance in mechanization of this field since the cotton gin of Eli Whitney (1793), which virtually established the American plantation. The delay in the use of the cotton picker is largely due to labor conditions in the South. Its effect is much dreaded because of the unemployment it may cause among Southern Negroes, but some of this will probably be absorbed as the new industrial uses for cotton, such as plastics, road building, explosives and film, are increased.

Indeed, the new industrial employment of agricultural products in a variety of commodities, lately evolved by organic chemistry, will undoubtedly increase farming in America, and, as the use of the soil increases, we may expect further improvements in the mechanization of agriculture.

From about World War I on, motorized farm equipment, knowledge of soil chemistry and biology, and the possible results of breeding for desired types of production had been available to farmers, but two decades of poor returns had checked investment of the capital needed to realize these advances. Excess demand for agricultural products in World War II and for nearly five years thereafter, brought all the stored-up learning and new mechanization into use with revolutionary suddenness. As a result the rate of growth in agricultural productivity was higher than in industry. Productivity per-man hour more than doubled from 1940 to 1960. Great advances were made in breeding cows for milk, chickens for eggs or animals for meat. Ceres wheat and hybrid corn increased grain yields, eventually flooding the market. In 1940 there were only a quarter as many trucks and about a third as many tractors as there were farms. By 1960 there was about one truck per farm and more than one tractor. The revolution in mechanization also included household electricity, radio and transportation of farm children to consolidated schools. In all, farm life probably changed more between 1940 and 1960 than in any equally brief period in history. By 1960 the most efficient quarter of the four million farms could probably supply the American people with food. Employing less than 10 per cent of the labor force, commercial agriculture had ceased being a general mode of American life, and had become a specialty like mining or transportation.

FARMER-LABOR PARTY OF MINNESOTA stems from the Nonpartisan League, which entered the state in 1916. League leaders with labor co-operation attempted to capture the Republican primaries in 1918 and 1920. Defeated in these attempts the coalition—again with little success—placed Farmer-Labor tickets in the general elections. Though in 1920 farmer-labor leaders in Minnesota, fearing loss of support locally, refused official support to the national Farmer-Labor party, the third-party idea was gaining strength. In 1922 Nonpartisan League tactics were in part abandoned. A Farmer-Labor ballot appeared in the primary, and the election that autumn of a U. S. Senator and a Representative indicated the desirability of giving the party a more permanent organization. In 1923 a joint convention of the Working People's Nonpartisan League (established in 1919) and the Farmers' Nonpartisan League organized the Farmer-Labor Federation. Sympathetic groups were invited to join the federation and local farmer-labor clubs were organized. Since 1923 the party has regularly been on the ballot in primary and general elections.

In 1930 Floyd B. Olson, outstanding leader of the party, was elected governor; re-elected in 1932 and 1934, he served until his death in 1936. Control of all branches of the state government, except the senate, was won in 1936, and in this year five Representatives and a second Senator were elected to Congress. While never abandoning entirely its original program of state ownership, in later years the party has stressed taxation reform, social-security legislation and protection for the farmers through moratorium and emergency credit legislation. In 1924 the party supported Robert M. LaFollette for the Presidency and in the campaigns of 1932 and 1936 played an important part in carrying the state for Franklin D. Roosevelt.

FARMER-LABOR PARTY OF 1920. Soon after World War I certain local trade-union officials began to organize labor parties, the first of which was formed by the munitions workers of Bridgeport, Conn., in 1918. These were followed by state organizations and in November, 1919, a convention forming the National Labor party was held in Chicago with delegates from forty states. The first platform, promulgated as "Labor's Fourteen Points," was based on the fundamental ideal that workers and farmers should exercise controlling power. It called for nationalization of all public utilities, basic industries and banks. At the presidential nominating convention of 1920 the name was changed to the Farmer-Labor party as an inducement to agricultural interests. After an unsuccessful attempt was made by remnants of the Progressive party of 1912 to stampede the convention into nominating LaFollette, Parley Parker Christensen of Utah was nominated with Max S. Hayes for his running mate. The party failed to secure the active support of the Nonpartisan League, the dominant farmers' political organization of the Northwest, and as a result polled but a quarter million votes. Its strength lay chiefly in Washington, South Dakota and Montana. At a convention held in Chicago in 1923, representatives of the Workers' Party of America (Communist) gained control, and the farmer-labor leaders withdrew from the movement.

FARMERS' ALLIANCE was the name commonly given to either or both of two powerful agricultural organizations of the 1880's and 1890's.

The National Farmers' Alliance, also known as the Northern, or the Northwestern, Alliance, was a nonsecret organization founded in 1880 by Milton George, editor of the *Western Rural,* a Chicago farm journal, as a means of combating the unfair discrimination of the railroads against the rural classes. Under George's leadership the order developed into a loose federation of powerful state alliances, with numerous locals in Kansas, Nebraska, the Dakotas, Minnesota and other Northwestern states. Its most active growth took place in the later 1880's, when the hard-pressed farmers of the "middle border" joined it by the hundreds of thousands with the hope that through it they could somehow curb the railroads and the trusts, lower interest rates and ease the mortgage burden. When pressure on the older parties failed to bring satisfactory results, the Alliance began to "go into politics," and by 1890 third-party tickets for state and local offices were general throughout the Northwest.

The National Farmers' Alliance and Industrial Union originated about 1874 in Lampasas County, Texas, when a group of frontier farmers united in a secret ritualistic "Alliance" against the local cattle kings and land sharks. The order soon spread into neighboring counties, but died out during the later 1870's owing to dissensions over the greenback issue. In 1879 it took new root in Parker County, Texas, and, as the Farmers' State Alliance, again began to grow. After 1886, with an aggressive new president, C. W. Macune, in control, it succeeded in absorbing the Louisiana Farmers' Union, the Arkansas Agricultural Wheel, and local farmers' clubs all over the South, into what remained, under varying names, a strongly centralized organization. Macune and his agents promised, among other things, to arrest through cooperative buying and selling the alarming decline in Southern prosperity that had followed the downward trend of cotton prices. A number of business "exchanges" were founded; but when most of them failed, the Southern Alliance, like its Northern prototype, went into politics. Third-party action, however, was carefully avoided, for most Southerners feared that such a split in white solidarity might pave the way for Negro participation in politics. Instead, the Alliance set out to capture the Democratic party of the South, and by 1890 it was well on the way to success. Meantime, a subordinate and well-disciplined Colored Farmers' Alliance and Co-operative Union had been founded to look after the welfare of the Negroes.

From time to time unavailing efforts were made to unite the two great sectional Alliances into one order. The divergent economic interests of Northwestern and Southern farmers account in part for this failure, but an even more effective obstacle was the formation, mainly under the auspices of the Northwestern Alliance, of the People's, or Populist, party. This development, indeed, proved to be disastrous to both Alliances. Northwestern Alliancemen forgot the old farm order in their enthusiasm for the new political party, while Southern Alliancemen deserted by the tens of thousands at the mere threat of party division. Thus, by the middle 1890's, the vitality had gone out of both Alliances.

FARMER'S ALMANAC(K). This is one of the oldest living periodicals in the United States, having been published continuously since its founding by Robert Bailey Thomas at Sterling, Mass., in 1792. Almanacs early gained prominence; the first was is-

sued at Cambridge, Mass., in 1639. With the popular reception of Franklin's *Poor Richard's Almanac,* this medium of information became an American institution. Thomas' *Farmer's Almanac* was timely in title and emphasis on agricultural affairs. Although this publication was most popular in New England, it spread throughout the United States, and its homely presentation of scientific subjects and its general moral and literary character were imitated by other writers and publishers. The later farmers' almanacs issued several editions aimed to appeal to sectional interests with similar basic information. Encyclopedic in its information, the almanac was often the only reading matter in the rural home; as patriotic and political views were intermingled with advice as to the proper time and method for planting, cultivating and harvesting, both might be accepted in like faith.

"FATHER OF HIS COUNTRY." This title seems to have been current in Pennsylvania in 1778 and the first known publication of it was by Francis Bailey, an Ephrata trained printer, a native American and a soldier at Valley Forge. The crudely engraved cover for his *Nord Americanische Kalender* for 1779 (Lancaster, Pa.) showed a flying Fame with a medallion of Washington, sounding from her trumpet the words "Des Landes Vater." The title appears in several of the many adulatory addresses inflicted on the General at the time he resigned his commission in 1783, and has persisted, in print, ever since.

FEDERAL AGENCIES. Under authority implied in the United States Constitution, numerous agencies to execute the law have been created by statute or executive order. The present article covers, with a few insignificant or local exceptions, the establishment and function of those organizational units which, in varying degrees of direct dependence on the President, execute or administer national legislation; these have no standard nomenclature and no uniform structure. Comment on several administrative entities which are agents of Congress or the courts will be found towards the end of this article.

The framework of the existing system as a whole has been considerably influenced by the recommendations of two major study groups which have examined the National Administration in recent decades: the President's Committee on Administrative Management (1936–37), and the (Hoover) Commission on Organization of the Executive Branch of the Government (1947–49). The Executive Reorganization Act of 1949, which is an outgrowth of the Hoover group's report, authorizes the President to create, abolish, transfer or modify any part of the executive branch virtually at his discretion; he must, however, lay the change before Congress, and either chamber may overrule it by passing a simple resolution within 60 days of the plan's submission.

The agency closest to the President himself is

the *Executive Office of the President.* This was set up by the Reorganization Act of 1939, principally as a staff aid, to assist him in effectively controlling and co-ordinating the rest of the executive branch. Within this agency, the White House Office helps the President maintain communication with Congress, the executive agencies, and the public; it handles his correspondence, appointments, engagements, and paperwork. The *Bureau of the Budget,* established in the Treasury Department in 1921 and transferred to the Executive Office in 1939, aids the President in collating, controlling, and presenting to Congress the agencies' budgetary requests; in co-ordinating legislative proposals which originate in the executive branch; and in improving governmental management methods and statistical activities. The *Council of Economic Advisers,* created by the Employment Act of 1946, informs the President of economic trends and suggests policies for adjusting to them. It also helps prepare the annual economic report to Congress. The *National Security Council* was instituted by the National Security Act of 1947. It advises the President on the integration of diplomatic measures, military programs, and domestic policies. Under its direction, the *Central Intelligence Agency,* established by the same act, co-ordinates the civil and military intelligence activities of other agencies. The *Office of Civil and Defense Mobilization,* formed under presidential Reorganization Plan 1 of 1958, brings together numerous planning and control functions on the civil side of war and disaster mobilization, such as the production and stockpiling of critical materials, the maintenance of communications, the relief of stricken areas, and the continuation of government itself.

There are ten agencies whose heads, by tradition, constitute the President's cabinet. These are the executive departments: State, Treasury, Defense (combining Departments of the Army, the Navy, and the Air Force), Justice, Post Office, Interior, Agriculture, Commerce, Labor, and the Department of Health, Education and Welfare. Except for the Post Office, accounts of all these and their constituent units will be found elsewhere.

The *Post Office Department* is an outgrowth of the Postal Service which was first established by an ordinance of 1782, passed under the Articles of Confederation. The Service in turn had antecedents in the postal system created under British colonial rule and continued—with Benjamin Franklin as the first Postmaster General—under the Continental Congress. The Service was made an executive department by statute in 1872. The original purpose of the postal system was to provide means "for conveying letters . . . through this continent." This purpose has gradually expanded to include such services as urban and rural delivery of mail (1863 and 1896), and the furnishing of facilities for money orders (1864), postal savings (1911), and parcel post (1913). Air mail service began in 1918.

Among agencies similar in structure to the executive departments but not bearing that name, the *General Services Administration* has perhaps the widest ramifications. This organization was established by the Federal Property and Administrative Services Act of 1949, to improve the efficiency of governmental "housekeeping." The act and several subsequent presidential reorganization plans have transferred to the organization such functions as the procurement, management, maintenance and disposal of real property, supplies, transportation facilities, and public utilities services for all agencies; the promotion of sound records management; and the preservation of valuable noncurrent records. The former functions of the State Department with respect to the publication of laws and the certification of constitutional amendments, presidential electors, and electoral votes have been transferred to the Administration. The agency's tasks on documentation are supervised by its National Archives and Records Service.

The *National Aeronautics and Space Administration* was created by Congress in 1958, partly out of concern for the lead in outer space technology which the Soviet Union's launching of the first artificial earth satellite seemed to demonstrate. It was felt that greater co-ordination of American study and operation in this field was needed. The agency is charged with conducting research and other activities on the problems of flight and on the exploration, scientific investigation and utilization of outer space. It has directed programs in aerodynamics, environmental physics and associated biological sciences, chemical and nuclear propulsion systems, space probes and manned flight in space.

The *Small Business Administration,* established by Congress in 1953, carried over and expanded in peacetime the essential functions of two wartime predecessors: the Smaller War Plants Corporation (1942–47) of World War II, and the Small Defense Plants Administration (1951–53) of the Korean conflict. The agency's task reflects a public concern to protect the competitive position of small businesses when massive demands for defense matériel tend to favor larger enterprises. The agency promotes research into the problems of small business, gives managerial counsel, makes loans to public and private small business investment institutions, lends money to disaster-stricken businesses, and seeks to distribute a fair proportion of government contracts—often through the subletting of prime contracts—to small establishments.

The *Veterans Administration* was created by executive order in 1930, under an enabling statute of the same year, in order to consolidate administration of the several programs which provided benefits to former members of the armed forces and their dependents. The agency manages pensions, insurance.

vocational rehabilitation, educational assistance, and certain loans to veterans; and provides medical care in veterans' hospitals, out-patient clinics, and domiciliaries.

The Federal Reserve System, which deals with banking and currency, is described elsewhere. The *Selective Service System* was set up by the Universal Military Training and Service Act of 1948. An earlier agency of the same name had been created by Congress in 1940 and had been liquidated in 1947. The System is responsible for the registration, examination, classification, selection, and delivery for induction into the armed forces of male persons liable to military service under the law. Much of the agency's operation is decentralized to the county level where it utilizes civilian boards serving without compensation. The records of its predecessor are managed by the new agency.

A 1958 statute created the *Federal Aviation Agency*, partly through the transfer of the Civil Aeronautics Administration and the safety regulatory activities of the Civil Aeronautics Board. These older organizations were based on legislation of 1938. The new agency is to promote civil aeronautics, with particular attention to safety and efficiency in the use of navigable air space. It promulgates safety regulations and air traffic rules; examines, inspects, and maintains surveillance over equipment and the regulated activities of airmen; plans, constructs, and operates aids to navigation and communication; administers grants-in-aid for airport development; and engages in research on traffic and safety measures and devices. For some purposes, its jurisdiction extends to military aviation.

The *U. S. Information Agency* was created by Reorganization Plan 8 of 1953, which consolidated several propaganda and informational activities directed to foreign countries. This move reflected concern for alleged lack of co-ordination and effectiveness in the psychological aspects of "cold war" diplomacy. The agency utilizes the media of open communication to demonstrate abroad that American policies promote the legitimate aspirations of other peoples for freedom, peace, and progress. For this purpose, it broadcasts radio programs to other nations; maintains or assists local information centers; produces or furnishes for foreign audiences motion pictures, television programs, press materials, pamphlets, and magazines, which delineate American life and interpret American policies. The agency's foreign field offices are subordinate to the respective chiefs of diplomatic missions.

The *Federal Mediation and Conciliation Service* was set up by the Labor Management Relations (Taft-Hartley) Act of 1947, to replace the U. S. Conciliation Service situated in the Department of Labor (1913). The agency seeks to minimize or prevent interruptions of commerce, caused by labor-management disputes. On its own motion or at the request of either party, it lends assistance in conciliating or mediating differences over new contract terms or over grievances arising under existing contracts. The Service has no law enforcement authority; refusal by either party to accept a recommendation of the agency violates no duty under the act. In its mediatory operations, the Service also tries to foster better day-to-day relations between labor and management.

The *Smithsonian Institution* was established to meet the terms of James Smithson's will. Smithson, an Englishman, in 1829 bequeathed his fortune to the United States to found at Washington an institution for the increase and diffusion of knowledge. Congress implemented his bequest by statute in 1846. The Institution fulfills its purpose through museum exhibits, scientific research and exploration, and publication. It maintains the U. S. National Museum which comprises collections on Natural History and on History and Technology, the National Air Museum, the Freer Gallery of Art, the National Gallery of Art, the National Collection of Fine Arts, the National Zoological Park, the Astrophysical Observatory at Cambridge, Massachusetts, the Canal Zone Biological Area in Panama, and the Bureau of American Ethnology which has promoted extensive research among indigenous peoples living within United States jurisdiction. A kindred agency, but more comprehensive in purpose than the Smithsonian Institution, is the National Science Foundation described elsewhere.

Several agencies, instead of having a single head, have plural leadership—often as a device to assure representation of diverse interests. The *Railroad Retirement Board*, created by Congress in 1935, follows this pattern. Two of the Board's three members are appointed by the President upon the respective recommendations of railroad carriers and railroad employees. The Board administers a system of retirement, disability, sickness, unemployment, and similar benefits for railroad employees and their dependents. The payments are made from a special fund in the national Treasury, to which the carriers and the employees contribute in stated ratios.

Congress established the *Renegotiation Board* in 1951, absorbing functions of the War Contracts Price Adjustment Board. The purpose of the agency is to eliminate excessive profits in national defense contracts. It does this by periodically reviewing and renegotiating contracts with their holders, and arranging for refunds when appropriate. Four of the Board's five members are appointed by the President upon recommendation of the agencies whose contracts are covered by the pertinent legislation.

The *Subversive Activities Control Board* was set up by statute in 1950. It is charged with determining, upon application, whether various organizations are

"Communist action," "Communist-front," or "Communist-infiltrated" organizations within the meaning of the Subversive Activities Control Act of 1950. No more than three of the Board's five members may belong to the same political party.

The *American Battle Monuments Commission*, created by law in 1923, administers American military cemeteries abroad; regulates the design of monuments erected in them; and plans, constructs, and maintains other memorials which commemorate the services of American armed forces in foreign countries.

The *Commission on Civil Rights* was established by statute in 1957, to investigate alleged interference with the suffrage on grounds of race, religion, or national origin; and to study and report developments concerning equal protection of the laws under the Constitution.

Congress created the *U. S. Civil Service Commission* in 1871. The Commission is bipartisan in membership. Its initial major task was to administer a merit system, under which appointments, tenure and promotions in government service would be assured on the basis of demonstrated capacity, regardless of partisan political considerations; the agency now concerns itself with more positive aspects of personnel administration as well. The Commission conducts competitive examinations of applicants for Federal employment and investigates their background, applies relevant provisions of veterans' preference laws, provides other agencies with lists of qualified job applicants, investigates complaints of discriminatory personnel practices, administers regulations restricting the political activities of governmental employees, and manages various insurance and retirement benefits for civil service personnel.

Congress instituted the *U. S. Tariff Commission* in 1916, and substantially augmented its functions in later legislation. Its central duty is to study questions associated with foreign trade and tariffs, chiefly for developments which threaten the well-being of American industries. Particularly with relation to the Reciprocal Trade Agreements program, it reports on these trends to the President, and to pertinent Congressional committees.

A special category of plural agency is the independent regulatory commission, which is characterized by unusual discretion in making rules for specified segments of the national economy, by some quasi-judicial power in applying the rules, by mandatory bipartisan membership (usually), and by special insulation of its members against arbitrary presidential interference—confirmed by the Supreme Court in the case of Rathbun (Humphrey's Executor) v. United States [295 U. S. 602 (1935)]. The exceptional powers of regulation and adjudication appear necessary for flexible control over technically complex activities, and the very scope of these powers occasions the requirement of insulation. The first agency of this kind and the prototype of the others was the Interstate Commerce Commission, discussed elsewhere; the latest such agency, also described in another place, is the Atomic Energy Commission.

The *Civil Aeronautics Board*, which is in this category, was established by Congress in 1938 as the Civil Aeronautics Authority, and renamed under a presidential Reorganization Plan of 1940. The Federal Aviation Act of 1958 transferred the Board's safety regulatory function to the Federal Aviation Agency, but continued its other tasks. The agency's central job is to regulate the economic aspects of commercial aviation. It authorizes carriers to engage in interstate and foreign commerce by air, permits foreign carriers to operate to and within the United States, regulates rates, supervises accounting, and maintains surveillance over mergers and other cooperative arrangements among carriers. It also investigates accidents for the Federal Aviation Agency and hears quasi-judicial appeals from some certification proceedings of that organization.

The *Federal Communications Commission*, set up by the Communications Act of 1934, brought together functions formerly scattered among agencies such as the Interstate Commerce Commission and the old Federal Radio Commission (1927). The new agency's purpose is to advance efficiency, economy and fair competition, and to promote national security and the safety of life, through telecommunications. Its jurisdiction includes telephone, telegraph, radio and television. The Commission authorizes extensions and reductions of communications services by wire or radio, licenses stations and operators, assigns frequencies, regulates rates, and monitors transmitting operations for adherence to its rules.

The *Federal Power Commission* was created by statute in 1930, replacing an earlier commission of the same name (1920). In the field of hydroelectric power and natural gas, the agency has purposes like those of the above institutions. It works with other agencies in planning multipurpose river-basin development; licenses construction of power projects on navigable waters or government lands; and regulates the rates, the securities, the accounting practices and the mergers of companies transmitting or wholesaling electrical energy. The Commission exercises similar controls over interstate commerce in natural gas.

Congress instituted the *Federal Trade Commission* in 1914, and substantially expanded its duties in later laws. The major objective of the agency is to curb monopolistic, unfair or deceptive trade practices including price-fixing, discriminatory pricing, deceptive advertising, and false labelling. The Commission normally seeks voluntary compliance with pertinent rulings through informal and confidential procedures, but is authorized to hold formal public hearings and to issue cease-and-desist orders.

The *National Labor Relations Board* was established by the Wagner Act in 1935 and modified by the Taft-Hartley Act in 1947. The Board is charged with preventing employers and labor unions from engaging in specified unfair labor practices—mostly subtle forms of coercion which interfere with the employee's right either to bargain collectively through representatives of his own choosing or to refrain from such activity. The agency may investigate complaints of prohibited conduct and issue cease-and-desist orders against it; pending final disposition of cases, it may also seek injunctive relief against certain types of action. The Board also conducts and certifies elections of bargaining representatives, and in some circumstances polls employees on their acceptance or rejection of the contract proffered by management.

Under the Railway Labor Act of 1935, the *National Mediation Board* was set up, to replace the U. S. Board of Mediation (1926). The new agency performs for railroads and airlines the general functions which the National Labor Relations Board performs for all other enterprises, and in addition seeks the prompt settlement of labor-management disputes on the carriers within its jurisdiction.

The *Securities and Exchange Commission* was created by statute in 1934, absorbing certain functions which the Securities Act of 1933 had assigned to the Federal Trade Commission; subsequent legislation has enlarged these. This agency is to protect the public and investors against malpractices—dramatized by the 1929 depression—in securities markets. Those who offer securities for sale must disclose pertinent information for investors before their offering can be registered with the Commission as required by law. The Commission also registers and supervises national exchanges, brokers, investment companies and investment counsellors; investigates malpractices; maintains surveillance over the transactions of public utility holding companies; and advises courts in bankruptcy proceedings. Its sanctions include the withholding and revocation of registration, and the initiation of prosecution.

The *Tax Court of the United States* does not readily fit any classification of executive agency. The Court was originally established by the Revenue Act of 1924 as the U. S. Board of Tax Appeals, and was renamed by the Revenue Act of 1942. The Court adjudicates controversies arising from administrative decisions on deficiencies, overpayment and refund of income, estate and similar Federal taxes. With few exceptions, the agency's decisions are reviewable by the U. S. Courts of Appeals.

Another type of Federal agency comprises those which furnish credit for certain types of private or public financial ventures. The *Development Loan Fund,* first established in the International Co-operation Administration by the Mutual Security Act of 1957, was given independent status by the corresponding act of 1958. The agency provides investment capital for projects which will contribute to the growth of economic resources in underdeveloped countries. The funds are made available as loans or credits to governments or to private enterprises, or as loan guarantees to private investors.

The *Export-Import Bank of Washington* is a banking corporation, first authorized by executive order in 1934 and subsequently continued by legislation. The Bank assists, either from its own capital or by borrowing from the U. S. Treasury, in financing exports and imports between the United States and foreign countries.

The Farm Credit Administration is described elsewhere. The *Federal Deposit Insurance Corporation* was organized under the Federal Reserve Act of 1933. Its chief purpose is to insure deposits in banks. Functions associated with this purpose include bank examinations; review of the establishment, consolidation, or merger of banks; loans to banks or purchase of assets in order to prevent closing; and payment of accounts to depositors in banks which have closed. The Corporation's activities have been financed completely by assessments on insured banks, although borrowing from the United States Treasury is authorized.

The *Federal Home Loan Bank Board* was first established by law in 1933, and has undergone several changes of name, status, and function through later legislation and Reorganization Plan 3 of 1947. The Board directs the Federal Home Loan Banks System and the Federal Savings and Loan Insurance Corporation. These two systems were created to provide credit reserves and insurance of savings for various home-financing institutions. Although they have authority to borrow from the U. S. Treasury, both systems have been fully supported by the participating institutions' assessments, premiums, and purchases of stock.

The *Housing and Home Finance Agency* was created by presidential Reorganization Plan 3 of 1947, which consolidated the administration of major governmental housing programs. Units of the agency include the Community Facilities Administration, managing programs concerned with public works and with student and faculty housing at institutions of higher learning; the Urban Renewal Administration, supervising assistance for slum clearance and urban planning; the Federal Housing Administration, insuring (not making) loans for property improvement, home mortgages, rental housing and urban renewal projects; the Voluntary Home Mortgage Credit Program, a committee of volunteers from interested enterprises which attempts to obtain, in difficult areas, private credit for housing under government-backed loans; the Public Housing Administration, which, as successor to two earlier agencies, extends assistance for low-rent public housing; and the Federal National Mortgage Association, aiding investment for several specialized programs.

The *Tennessee Valley Authority* is unique among executive agencies. The Authority is a corporation, established by Congress in 1933, but endowed with the right of eminent domain. Its central purpose, one which had concerned the Government for over a century, is the development of the Tennessee River Valley. Dams and other works constructed and maintained by the Authority have created a 9-foot channel extending 650 miles from Knoxville to Paducah, and have contributed to flood control and soil conservation in the area. Congress has also authorized the agency to develop new types of fertilizer for agricultural use, and to sell—in such a way as to promote wide use of electricity—surplus electric power generated at its installations; preference is to be given to municipalities and co-operative associations. The agency transacts its business as a commercial corporation, and is financed partly by congressional appropriation, partly by the revenues of its own operations.

A few agencies belong to the judicial or legislative rather than the executive establishment. Mention of them will nevertheless be useful. The *Administrative Office of the U. S. Courts,* created by statute in 1939, manages supplies, records, services, personnel, compensation, and statistical information for the federal court system. The *Government Printing Office,* established as a congressional agency by joint resolution in 1860, executes orders for printing and binding by any part of the Federal Government, and distributes or sells publications as may be appropriate. The *Library of Congress,* created by law in 1800 to serve Congress, continues its original function—chiefly through its Legislative Reference Service—but has also become, in effect, the national public library.

The *General Accounting Office,* headed by the Comptroller General of the United States, was established by the Budget and Accounting Act of 1921. It absorbed financial control functions enumerated in statutes as far back as the Treasury Act of 1789, and has acquired wider authority through later legislation. The principal purpose of the agency is to furnish Congress with an independent audit of governmental expenditure. To assure independence, the Comptroller General, although appointed by the President, has a term of 15 years and is removable only by joint congressional resolution. The Office sets accounting standards for all agencies, audits their books, examines their management of financial matters, reviews their expenditures for conformity with legislative intent, settles claims, and reports on all these to Congress and the President.

FEDERAL BUREAU OF INVESTIGATION. Established July 26, 1908, by Attorney General Charles J. Bonaparte, the investigative arm of the U. S. Department of Justice was known originally as the Bureau of Investigation. The internationally known name, Federal Bureau of Investigation, was adopted on July 1, 1935.

The investigative agency was reorganized in 1924 during the tenure of Attorney General Harlan F. Stone following the latter's appointment of John Edgar Hoover as Director. The policies which constitute the foundation of the present organization were inaugurated immediately. Political considerations were completely divorced from personnel appointments. Promotions were placed on a merit basis. A training program was developed.

Today, the Federal Bureau of Investigation is a fact-gathering and fact-reporting agency with headquarters in Washington, D. C. It has 53 field offices throughout the United States—including Anchorage, Alaska, and Honolulu, Hawaii—and in San Juan, P. R.

The jurisdiction of the F. B. I. covers more than 150 Federal investigative matters encompassing two major categories: domestic intelligence operations and general investigations. In the former field, the F. B. I. has responsibilities in matters of espionage, sabotage and subversive activities on a nationwide scale. In general, the F. B. I. is responsible for the enforcement of all Federal criminal statutes with the exception of those specifically delegated to other Federal agencies.

In addition to investigating violations of laws of the United States, the F. B. I. is charged with collecting evidence in cases in which the United States is or may be a party in interest, and with other duties imposed by law. It reports the results of its investigations to the Attorney General, chief legal officer of the United States, his assistants, and the various U. S. Attorneys in Federal districts throughout the United States for decisions as to prosecutive action. The F. B. I. is also a service agency which assists law enforcement agencies in identification, technical and training matters.

FEDERAL GOVERNMENT. The framers of the United States Constitution did not believe in extreme democracy or the direct rule of the people. Therefore, they created a government of limited powers. They believed that while the people might decide rightly in the long run, yet there should be limitation upon their actions so that they might have sufficient time to think and form their judgments. Otherwise there might be danger of mob rule instead of government by public opinion. Also, they adopted the system of "separation of powers" or "checks and balances" so that the executive, legislative and judicial departments might be independently administered. No one of these departments might gain such an amount of power as to endanger the liberties of the people.

Furthermore, in dealing with the governmental situation then existing they recognized the historic differences and independent feeling existing in the thirteen separate states so they formed a federation in which the rights of each state were carefully preserved insofar as they did not infringe upon the welfare of the United States or the new National Government which they created. Definite grants of power were made to this National Government with the intention that those powers not given to the National Government should be retained by the states or the people of the states.

It has been said in summing up the powers of the National Government (by Frederic J. Stimson) that the Constitution enumerates 65 powers which are given to the Federal Government which are contained in 57 clauses and the Amendments of that document. These powers are given to the three branches of the Government—legislative, executive and judicial—of which 19 are given to Congress, while 70 are expressly denied. Also, there are 66 things in 39 clauses which are forbidden to the United States Government and 13 more forbidden both to it and to the states. While these specific statements are at least approximately correct, of course there are many questions concerning the competence of the national or state governments which are bound to arise and these ultimately must be determined by the Federal or state courts with a final appeal to the U. S. Supreme Court.

The approximately nineteen powers given to Congress are classified under four heads (by Edward S. Corwin). They are: (1) enumerated powers that are contained and defined in the Constitution; (2) certain other powers which are specifically delegated by the Constitution; (3) the general grant of powers in the "necessary and proper clause" (Art. I, Sec. 8, Par. 18); (4) certain inherent powers which belong to Congress because it is the national legislative body.

The office of President of the United States was created upon the model of the kingship of Great Britain, but the Convention of 1787 placed such restraints and limitations upon the office that the evils which had been suffered or which were thought to have been suffered by the colonists at the hands of the British sovereign should not be repeated. In fact, the President has inherited, in large part, the powers of the British king and these have been combined with the political leadership that has grown up during the succeeding years. All these powers have resulted in the creation of the great and dominating presidential office of today. More specifically his authority extends to the administration of the executive departments of the National Government; the signing or vetoing of laws (which can be passed over his veto only by a two-thirds vote of both Houses of Congress); the calling of Congress into special session; the appointment to executive, diplomatic and judicial offices (with the confirmation of the Senate); the sending of messages to Congress upon the "State of the Union" and other matters at his own discretion; the pardoning power; the conduct of foreign affairs; and the command-in-chief of the Army and Navy. He must be a natural-born citizen, have attained the age of 35 years and have been fourteen years a resident within the United States. His term is four years, and he is eligible for re-election, although (since the Twenty-second Amendment) he may not serve more than two terms. In case of his removal, death, resignation or inability to discharge the powers and duties of his office, he shall be succeeded by the Vice-President for the remainder of the term for which he was elected. Although the electoral college is still retained, he practically is elected by the direct vote of the people. The President receives a stated salary of $100,000 a year, and in addition a yearly allowance of $90,000 for expenses of official duties, travel and entertainment.

Finally there must be some ultimate authority which possesses the power in case of dispute to say just what the Constitution means. This power has been placed in the hands of the Federal courts, which are intended, as Woodrow Wilson pointed out, to serve as a nonpolitical forum in which the questions "can be impartially debated and determined." It may be said that the Constitution has been formally amended 23 times on nine different occasions during the past 174 years of its existence. In addition to the actual provisions or text of the written document various customs or "conventions" have grown up which have the force of law through accretion of time and weight of popular opinion in their favor. These include such matters as the custom that requires presidential electors to vote for the nominee of their party. These conventions or customs, along with the statutes and precedents concerning the offices and duties connected with it, make a large addition to the actual Constitution and the consequent scope of the National Government of the country.

The American people, like most modern people, when they first came into independence or self-government, placed the larger part of governmental powers in the hands of the legislative body or Congress. They expected that the dominant power in the new Federal Government always should be in the hands of the House of Representatives, since it directly represents the people and has the power of originating money bills both of taxation and appropriation, while the Senate should play a secondary, balancing and restraining part. Owing to the longer term of six years of office, their election, originally, by the legislatures of the various states, which made them less responsible to the popular will, and the power to confirm appointments and ratify treaties, the Senate unexpectedly gained power steadily and soon came to the position of holding the dominant influence in the legislative department of the Government, and still holds it today. Nevertheless, during the first Congress and the few years thereafter, the House of

349

Representatives, which is composed of members elected by the direct vote of the people for a two-year term and apportioned to the states according to numbers of population, held a commanding position in the new Government until the gradual but steady growth of the Senate in power and influence practically displaced it from its commanding position.

On the other hand, the united power of the two Houses of Congress was the dominating influence in our Government during more than the first century after its creation. This was according to the usual method of development of popular government among various states in modern history. While several Presidents, due to vigorous personalities, foreign or domestic wars, or the critical state of national interests might temporarily contest this congressional supremacy, yet Congress always recovered its power until it reached its maximum during the thirty or forty years following the Civil War. The Reconstruction period (1865–77) was a time of almost complete congressional domination so that Woodrow Wilson designated the Federal Government in 1885 as a "Congressional Government" in his celebrated book by the same name.

It should be remembered that the "separation of powers," especially between the executive and legislative departments, required some outside authority or influence to make these two departments of government work together, and this outside influence was and is supplied by the American political party system. While the United States inherited the fundamental ideas of its party politics from England and developed under the British form of a two-party system, yet it was the added necessity and opportunity for a unifying force in our "government of checks and balances" that gave the commanding importance to the party system. But in some situations the party system, far from facilitating co-operation between Congress and the Executive, may make it almost impossible. If one party controls Congress and the other party the White House, co-operation may break down entirely, as during Reconstruction, or during the last two years of the administration of Woodrow Wilson. Either that, or, as was the case during the first Truman administration and the last six years of the Eisenhower administrations, opposition leaders in Congress must support the President against members of their own party, thus forfeiting their role as leaders of an opposition. Under these conditions, leadership of the opposition may fall to the more extreme members of the party in control of Congress. *Responsible* opposition, under conditions of "divided government," practically disappears.

Of course the parties grew in power only by gradual stages, and meanwhile there developed the custom of placing party leadership in the hands of individuals who held no office and often were known as "bosses." This led to an irresponsible form of government, for while the responsibility was in the hands of the various officeholders, nevertheless the actual power often lay in the hands of the irresponsible party leaders. It was only the growth of the power and influence of the national and state executives, who also have gradually assumed political leadership, that has made our party politics more responsible. Furthermore, this political leadership has increased proportionally with the same authority and power of the executives until the latter have come to the commanding governmental position of today.

It should be remembered that Washington, as our first President, was extremely careful with regard to the precedents he set, in order that the office might command the proper respect both at home and abroad and yet not lead to a dangerous centralization of power, which later might result in monarchy or some form of dictatorship. As above stated, the office of President varied in its influence directly with the personality of the man who occupied the office. Nevertheless, the growth in population and wealth on the part of the nation and its position of increasing importance in world affairs necessarily resulted in increased power for the President who administered its government. According to constitutional provision the conduct of foreign affairs lies in his hands, so that the importance of the foreign relations has had much to do with the power and influence of the President at any one time. About the year 1900 our Presidents began to take over more and more the leadership of the political party that had placed them in office. As a result of this assumption of political leadership the President gained directly in the extent of his power, until the last few years have seen the logical consummation in the supreme dominance of the office over our national affairs both at home and abroad at the hands of such men as Theodore Roosevelt, Woodrow Wilson and Franklin Delano Roosevelt.

By the mere necessities of government those people who make the laws must have a determining control over their administration, or those individuals who administer the laws must have a great influence in their formulation and passage. Such governments as Great Britain and France have developed the so-called parliamentary government. In this form a Committee of Parliament or a body of men completely responsible to the Parliament and known as a Cabinet has taken over the executive authority of the government and administers it in the name of the people and their representatives in the national legislative body. Since our constitutional system of separation of powers practically prevents this assumption on the part of our Congress we have developed the so-called presidential form of government. In this the President as political leader influences and leads Congress, when he acts as a national representative institution or what might be designated as a Prime Minister of the people. His position as national party leader enables him to do this. While the final dominance of the executive is not a determined matter nor its success a foregone conclusion, yet this status of executive aggression or executive leadership is the outstanding feature of the present American Federal Government.

The American cabinet, unlike that in parliamentary governments, is merely composed of the heads of the ten departments which have been created by acts of Congress. They occupy the position of assistants to the President in the administration of each respective department, and serve as a cabinet or advisory body entirely at the will or discretion of the person who occupies the office of President at any specific time.

In addition to the ten executive departments which have been created from time to time, there is a large and increasing number of independent administrative bureaus, boards and commissions. During recent years there has been a marked increase of such services in the National Government, especially since that Government has taken over a large and increasing amount of direction of the economic and social activities of our people. There are two main reasons for the creation of these departments and commissions. The nature of their duties is such that it would be difficult to include them in any one of the existing departments and, also, their creators desired to increase the importance of these agencies by giving them an independent status. Although they could not secure for them such rank as that of an executive department, they have been described as "floating islands of independent power in a sea of governmental administration." Also, they are an important attempt to increase the use of experts and the influence of the civil service or merit system without interference on the part of the President or any other department of government. This naturally has led to jealousy on the part of the President and other executive officials, and attempts have been made from time to time to include them in other departments of the Government or subordinate them to the direct control of the President. While these commissions add to the actual power of the President through his power of appointment, yet in the cases of several of them he cannot dismiss the members without the consent of Congress, and this is a check to his great powers already so largely increased through his political party leadership.

The same growth in administrative and political power on the part of the President naturally has led to a rivalry with the powers of the Federal judiciary, especially those of the U. S. Supreme Court, since that tribunal can at its own discretion check or nullify the authority or the policies of a national administration. Throughout our entire history there have been instances of congressional jealousy or opposition to the Supreme Court, but these have not resulted in any real curtailment of the powers of the tribunal. Parallel to the growth in authority of the Federal Government, especially during the period of change in our social system from that of an almost exclusively agricultural to that of an advanced industrial economy, the duties and powers of the Federal courts have increased in like proportion.

Up to the present time the growth of governmental powers has, to a large extent, been made possible by the growth in the customary or conventional part of the Constitution and also by the process of judicial interpretation. For the most part the people of the United States have been well satisfied with this process of orderly administrative and judicial progress, and the courts still hold a dominant position not only of influence but also of real reverence in the minds of the American people.

Contrary to the usual practice in other federal governments in the world, such as Canada or Switzerland, our state courts do not have the duty of adjudication upon Federal law within the respective states. Our system of so-called "dual sovereignty" extends from the administration of national and state affairs by different officials within the same districts, to that of a complete set of Federal courts and officials throughout the nation, and parallel with the judicial and administrative systems in each state, for the independent interpretation and enforcement of Federal law.

FEDERAL RESERVE SYSTEM, the central bank of the United States, was founded by the Owens-Glass Act of Dec. 23, 1913. It is unique in that it is not one bank but twelve regional banks co-ordinated by a central board in Washington. A central bank is a bank for banks: it does for them what they do for individuals and business firms. It holds their deposits (their legal reserves) for safekeeping; it makes them loans, and it creates its own credit in the form of created deposits (additional legal reserves) or bank notes (Federal Reserve notes). It lends to them only if they appear strong enough to repay the loan. It also has the responsibility of promoting economic stability insofar as that is possible by control of credit.

The nation's first bank, the Bank of North America, founded in 1781, was possibly its first central bank. Certainly the first Bank of the United States (1791–1811), serving as fiscal agent and regulator of the currency as well as doing a commercial banking business, was a central bank in its day. So likewise was the second Bank of the United States (1816–36) although it performed that function badly in 1817–20 but then well in 1825–26. The Independent Treasury System (1840–41, 1846–1921) was in no sense a central bank. A great fault of the National Banking System (1863–1913) was its lack of a central bank. The idea, and even the name, was politically almost taboo, which helps explain the form and name taken by the Federal Reserve System.

The faults of the National Banking System—perversely elastic bank notes, the paradox of dispersed legal reserves that were unhappily drawn as if by a magnet to finance stock speculation in New York, and the lack of a central bank to deal with the panics of 1873, 1884, 1893 and 1907—pointed to the need for reform. After the 1907 Panic a foreign central banker called the United States "a great financial nuisance." J. P. Morgan was the hero of the panic, saving the nation as if he were a one-man central bank, but in doing this he also showed that he had more financial power than it seemed safe for one man to possess in a democracy. The 1912 Pujo Money Trust Investigation further underlined his control over all kinds of banks. Meanwhile the Aldrich-Vreeland Act of May 30, 1908, provided machinery to handle any near-term crisis and created a National Monetary Commission to investigate foreign banking systems and suggest reforms. Sen. Nelson Aldrich proposed a National Reserve Association in 1911 consisting of a central bank, fifteen branches, and a top board controlled by the nation's leading bankers (critics said, in turn dominated by J. P. Morgan). It never passed, and the Democrats won the 1912 election. They accepted the groundwork done by Aldrich and others but President Wilson insisted that the nation's President choose the top board of this quasi-public institution. Congressman Carter Glass pushed the bill through Congress.

All national banks had to subscribe immediately 3% of their capital and surplus for stock in the Federal Reserve System to provide it capital to begin. State banks might also become "members," i.e., share in the ownership and privileges of the system. The Federal Reserve System was superimposed on the National Banking System and the new law corrected the major and minor shortcomings of the old one. In addition to providing a central bank, it supplied an elastic note issue of Federal Reserve notes based on commercial paper whose supply rose and fell with the needs of business; it required member banks to keep half their legal reserves (after mid-1917 all of them) in their district Federal Reserve Bank, and it improved the check clearing system. The seven-man Board took office Aug. 10, 1914, and the banks opened for business Nov. 16. World War I had begun and the new system was already much needed. But parts of the law which had been controversial were so vaguely written that only practice would interpret them. For that, the System needed wise and able leadership. This did not come from the Board in Washington, chaired by the Secretary of Treasury and often in disagreement on how much to co-operate with the Treasury, but from able Benjamin Strong, head of the System's largest Bank, that of New York. He was largely responsible for persuading bankers to accept the Federal Reserve System and for enlarging its influence.

At first the Federal Reserve's chief responsibilities were to create enough credit to carry on our part of World War I and to process Liberty Bond sales. A doubling of the price level by 1920 was one result.

In 1919 out of deference to the Treasury's needs the Federal Reserve delayed unduly long in raising discount rates, a step needed to discourage commodity speculation. That was a major mistake. In 1922 the System's leaders became aware of the value of open market buying operations to promote recovery and open market selling operations to choke off speculative booms. Governor Strong worked in the 1920's with Montagu Norman, head of the Bank of England, to help bring other nations back to the gold standard. To assist them he employed open market buying operations and lowered discount rates here so that America would not draw off their precious funds at the crucial moment of resumption. But plentiful funds in this country, for that and other reasons, promoted stock market speculation here. Strong's admirers feel he might have controlled the situation had he lived, but he fell sick in February, 1928, and died Oct. 16. As in 1919 the Federal Reserve did too little too late to stop the speculative boom which culminated in the Oct., 1929, crash. But the Federal Reserve helped many banks during the depression although it could do little for most of the 9000 that failed in the years 1930–33. This situation brought on congressional investigations and revelations in 1931–33, and demands for reforms and for measures to promote recovery. Congress overhauled the Federal Reserve System.

By the act of Feb. 27, 1932, Congress permitted the Federal Reserve to use Federal Government obligations as well as gold and commercial paper to back Federal Reserve notes and deposits. Shortage of commercial paper in the depression and bank failures that stimulated hoarding were creating a currency shortage and a new backing for the bank notes was essential. However much justified at the moment, the law made inflation in the future easier.

Four other measures about this time were very important. These were the Banking Act of June 16, 1933, parts of the Securities Act of May 27, 1933, and of the Securities Exchange Act of June 19, 1934, and the Banking Act of Aug. 23, 1935. Taken together, the four acts attempted to do four basic things, namely, (1) restore confidence in the banks, (2) strengthen the banks, (3) remove temptations to speculate, and (4) increase the powers of the Federal Reserve System, notably of the Board. To restore confidence, the 1933 and 1935 Banking Acts set up the Federal Deposit Insurance Corporation which first sharply reduced and after 1945 virtually eliminated bank failures. To strengthen the banks, the acts softened restrictions on branch banking and on real estate loans, and admitted mutual savings banks and some others. It was felt that the Federal Reserve could do more to control banks if they were brought into the System. To remove temptations to speculate, the banks were forbidden to pay interest on demand deposits, forbidden to use Federal Reserve credit for speculative purposes, and obliged to dispose of their investment affiliates. To increase the System's powers, the Board was reorganized, without the Secretary of Treasury, and given more control over member banks; the Federal Reserve Bank boards were given a more subordinate role; the Board was given more control over open market operations; and the Board got important new credit regulating powers. These last included the authority to raise or lower margin requirements, and also to raise member bank legal reserve requirements to as much as double the previous figures. The Board in 1936 had to raise reserve requirements, for reduced borrowings during the depression, huge gold inflows because of the dollar devaluation in January 1934, and the growing threat of war in Europe were causing the member banks to have large excess reserves. Banks with excess reserves are not dependent on the Federal Reserve and so can not be controlled by it.

During the Great Depression, World War II and even afterwards the Federal Reserve with Marriner Eccles as Board chairman (1934–48) kept interest rates low and encouraged member banks to buy Government obligations. The new economic (Keynesian) philosophy stressed the importance of low interest rates to promote investment, employment and recovery, with the result that for about a decade it became almost the duty of the Federal Reserve to keep the nation on what was sometimes called a "low interest rate standard." In World War II, as in World War I, the Federal Reserve assisted with bond drives and saw to it that the Federal Government and member banks had ample funds for the war effort. Demand deposits tripled between 1940 and 1945 and the price level doubled during the 1940's: there was somewhat less inflation with somewhat more provocation than during World War I. The Federal Reserve's regulation limiting consumer credit, price controls, and the depression before the war were mainly responsible. Regulation W was in effect Sept. 1, 1941, to Nov. 1, 1947, and twice briefly again before 1952. The Board also kept margin requirements high but it was unable to use its open market or discount tools to limit credit expansion. On the contrary, it had to maintain a "pattern of rates" on Federal Government obligations, ranging from ⅜ of 1% for Treasury bills to 2½% for long term bonds. That amounted often to open market buying operations which promoted inflation. Admittedly, it also encouraged war bond buying by keeping bond prices at par or better. Securities support purchases, 1941–45, executed for the System by the New York Federal Reserve Bank, raised the System's holdings of Treasury obligations from about $2,000,000,000 to about $24,000,000,000. The rationale for the Federal Reserve's continuing these purchases after the war was the Treasury's wish to hold down interest charges on the $250,000,000,000 public debt and the Truman administration's fear (based on Keynesian economics and memory of the 1921 depression) of a postwar depression. The Federal Reserve was not relieved of the duty to support Federal Government security prices until it concluded its "accord" with the Treasury, reported on March 4, 1951. Thereafter interest rates moved more freely, the Federal Reserve could again use open market selling operations and be freer to raise discount rates. At times bond prices fell sharply and there were complaints of "tight money." Board Chairman William M. Martin who succeeded Thomas McCabe (1948–51) on April 2, 1951, pursued a middle-of-the-road policy during the 1950's, letting interest rates find their natural level whenever possible, but using credit controls to curb speculative booms in 1953, 1956–57 and 1959–60, and to reduce recession and unemployment in 1954, 1958 and late 1960. Since the Full Employment Act of 1946 the Federal Reserve along with many other Federal agencies was expected to play its part in promoting full employment.

For many years the thirty member banks in New York and Chicago complained of the unfairness of legal reserve requirements which were higher for them, and bankers generally felt they should be permitted to count cash held in their bank as part of their legal reserves. By the law of July 28, 1959, member banks may count this cash as legal reserves and there are to be, after July 28, 1962, at the latest, only two classes (instead of three) of member banks, i.e., the 295 banks in 51 cities and about 6000 "country" banks elsewhere. Legal reserves against demand deposits will be 10–22% and 7–14% for the two, respectively.

As of Sept. 30, 1960, exactly 6200 banks of exactly 14,000 in the United States were members of the Federal Reserve System and they held 72% of all bank deposits in the nation.

FEDERALIST, THE, is a collection of essays written by James Madison, Alexander Hamilton and John Jay following the Convention of 1787 for the purpose of influencing the ratification in New York of the Constitution of the United States. All of them appeared over the signature Publius in reply to anonymous papers in the press condemning the new government. When 78 essays had appeared in the newspapers, these were collected and published in book form on May 28, 1788. Publication was resumed in *The Independent Journal* on June 14 until the remaining numbers had been completed on Aug. 16. The work is one of the few first-rate contributions made in the United States to the literature of political theory.

FEDERALIST PARTY secured much of its leadership from persons who supported the constitutional movement of 1787. It became identified during Washington's administrations with advocates of Hamilton's financial system, an attitude of neutrality in foreign affairs, and the firm enforcement of domestic laws. The Federalists associated the country's well-being with that of its prosperous citizens. Since their policies called for nationalistic legislation, they necessarily became advocates of loose construction of the Constitution.

Political demarcation was not clear until the struggle over the ratification of Jay's Treaty (1795), which gave Federalism a pro-British flavor that it never lost, and tended to lessen its Southern strength. The popularity of Pinckney's Treaty only partially offset criticism that the Administration favored commercial and aristocratic interests.

Warlike measures against France in 1798 stirred up popular enthusiasm for the Federalists; but party harmony was shattered by Adams' move toward peace in 1799. Adams was supported by such Federalists as John Marshall and Harrison Gray Otis; but his action was a factor in arousing Hamilton's opposition to him as Federalist nominee for the Presidency in 1800. In running for re-election, Adams proved stronger than his party, which bore a greater share of the odium attached to the Alien and Sedition acts of 1798.

Federalism was never restricted to Northern and commercial interests, although there was strong sectional feeling within the party. The national judiciary was a bulwark for Federalist principles; and even after 1800 there were Federalist strongholds in the South, despite the predominance of Jeffersonianism. Maryland maintained a staunch Federalist faction for many years, favored by the underrepresentation of Baltimore. In Virginia commercial centers, and in the Valley, the party remained important. A similar situation existed in North Carolina and in tidewater South Carolina. Even in the West, early settlements were seldom without those who scorned Republicans.

The opportunistic policy pursued by the Federalists after 1800 was suggested by their part in the disputed election of that year, when they tried far harder than did Aaron Burr to keep the Presidency from Jefferson. Subsequent mergers with moderate Republicans in Pennsylvania, and with the Livingstons or Clintonians in New York, demonstrated their steady influence in Northern state affairs. New England, moreover, still generally favored them. Many Federalists, especially a certain extreme New England element, never grasped the meaning of an opposition role in a democracy. They even viewed with suspicion younger members of their own faction. In 1804, a New England-New York secession scheme was contemplated. Federalist leaders elsewhere, such as Bayard of Delaware and the Pinckneys of South Carolina, were more temperate.

The embittered attitude of the New England Federalists during the War of 1812, resulting in the Hartford Convention, alienated some of their allies in other sections. Yet it was more the rise of new issues than criticism of the war which undermined the party's national importance. This, together with steady failure to attract new voters, and the growth of the West, explains the feeble showing made by its last presidential candidate in 1816.

FENCES AND FENCING LAWS. Fencing early became a problem in colonial America where unoccupied land was extensive and cultivated acreage was small. Virginia in 1632 required crops to be fenced and in 1646 defined a legal or "sufficient" fence. In Maryland the laws were similar and in North Carolina more rigid.

This type of law advanced with the movement of the frontier. Settlers with the concept of free range insisted upon using unsold public land. As settlement increased, the demand for fencing of pasture rather than crops arose and spread westward. Planters in Virginia secured some relief in 1835 and New Jersey made the change in 1842. The problem was general in the older states and became increasingly serious with the growing scarcity of timber. Yet in 1850 laws requiring the fencing of crops were the rule. In 1867 Illinois passed a permissive law allowing local units to require stock to be fenced in. Five years later a law for preventing stock from running at large was made general unless suspended by local option. In 1870 Iowa passed a local option law, the adoption of which within the state moved westward with the growth of settlement.

The type of fencing varied greatly with the region and the time. In sections of the East, stones from the fields were laid into fences. The zigzag or Virginia rail fence spread with the frontier wherever timber was available. As timber became more scarce post and pole, picket, and board fences became common, and wire fencing came into use. Prairie settlement was retarded by scarcity of fence material. Board and picket fences were common, and between 1850 and 1870 waves of enthusiasm for hedge fences swept from New England to Texas. When the frontier line reached the treeless plains only meager fence materials were available, and the need was acute.

Cattlemen had taken possession of large areas, particularly in the Southwest, and were driving cattle to the railroad. Settlers could not protect their crops until the advent of barbed wire, when the frontier again began to move. Advancing settlers fenced their farms and the free open range began to disappear, with bitter complaints, fence-cutter wars and frequent bloodshed. Stock farming succeeded open ranching with advantages in controlled grazing and opportunities for improvement in breeding. As cattle raising spread northward cattlemen fenced their own land, and until curbed by Federal legislation in 1885, they frequently inclosed the government land. In areas where mixed husbandry prevailed the woven wire fence came into use near the close of the century.

FENIAN MOVEMENT (1858–76) originated among Irish-Americans under the leadership of John O'Mahony. They planned to raise money, supply equipment and provide leaders to aid the Irish Revolutionary Brotherhood in an uprising against Great Britain. Membership in their organization rose to 250,000. In October, 1865, they established an "Irish Republic" in New York and ordered bond issues. O'Mahony's followers, failing in an earlier attempt against New Brunswick, participated in the republican revolutionary movement in Ireland, on March 5, 1867, and belatedly sent a vessel, *Erin's Hope*, loaded with arms and men. Those captured by the British attempted to use their American citizenship as a protective cloak and thus draw their adopted country into a naturalization controversy.

A dissatisfied group, called "the men of action," broke from the parent organization and conducted raids into Canada. On June 1, 1866, they crossed at Fort Erie, defeated Canadian troops, and returned to Buffalo, N. Y. The United States promptly halted reinforcements and arrested the raiders. Political pressure released them. Similar invasions from St. Albans, Vt., and Malone, N. Y., were checked by United States troops. Fenians captured by Canadians were treated as British subjects, intensifying unfriendly relations with Great Britain. May 25–27, 1870, Canadian and United States troops halted raids near Frankfort, Vt., and Malone, N. Y.

Unsuccessful in their objectives, and opposed by the Federal Government and the Catholic Church, members deserted to join the "Land League" and "Home Rule" movements. Their last congress was held Jan. 28, 1876. O'Mahony's death, Feb. 7, 1877, virtually ended Fenianism.

FETTERMAN MASSACRE (Dec. 21, 1866), the chief victory of the Sioux in their operations against Fort Phil Kearny, was the result of a clever ruse. Capt. William Fetterman, a brave but reckless officer, was sent with eighty men by Col. H. B. Carrington, commandant at the fort, to relieve a wood-transport train which had been attacked by the Indians. Although instructed by Carrington not to cross a line of hills called Lodge Trail Ridge, Fetterman was lured by a small party of mounted Sioux and Cheyenne warriors who acted as decoys, until his command was trapped on the other side of the hills.

Every man in Fetterman's command was killed in the fight which followed. High Backbone, a veteran chief, was the Sioux leader. The tragedy resulted in the removal of Col. Carrington from command at the post.

"FIFTY-FOUR FORTY OR FIGHT." The Oregon country lying between the Rocky Mountains and the Pacific Ocean and between California and Alaska, or between 42° and 54° 40′ N. Lat., was long claimed by both England and the United States, by virtue of discovery, exploration and settlement. Being unable to determine a definite division of the territory, they agreed to joint occupation. In July, 1843, an Oregon convention at Cincinnati adopted a resolution demanding 54° 40′ as the American boundary. In a speech in the Senate in 1844, William Allen, of Ohio, used the phrase "Fifty-four Forty or Fight." A plank of the Democratic platform of 1844 called for the reoccupation of Oregon, and the slogan, "Fifty-four Forty or Fight," became the battle cry of the expansionist Democrats. Stephen A. Douglas and Gen. Cass demanded all of the Oregon territory up to 54° 40′. At a public meeting in St. Clair County, Ill., it was maintained that Oregon extended to 54° 40′; and emigrants for Oregon in the spring of 1846 painted the legend "fifty-four forty" on their wagon covers. President Polk in his inaugural address and in his first annual message to Congress insisted on the whole of Oregon to which our title was "clear and unquestionable." All ardent expansionists expressed disappointment with Polk when he agreed in 1846 to compromise with England on the 49th parallel.

"FIGHT IT OUT ON THIS LINE IF IT TAKES ALL SUMMER," a phrase occurring in a letter of May 11, 1864, from Gen. Grant (U.) to Gen. Halleck (U.) written at Spotsylvania Courthouse after the battles of the Wilderness. The statement expressed Grant's determination to continue his plan of advance on Richmond in spite of heavy losses and only partial successes.

FILIBUSTER, CONGRESSIONAL, is the term used to describe obstructionist tactics employed by a minority in Congress, the purpose being to prevent a vote and thus to defeat legislation favored by a majority. For example, when President Wilson in 1917 proposed the arming of American merchant vessels, the House of Representatives passed the bill promptly by the overwhelming majority of 403 to 14, and 75 Senators signed a statement that they would vote for it if given an opportunity. Nevertheless, the bill failed because seven Senators, by filibustering until the term of Congress expired, prevented the measure from coming to a vote.

Filibustering has been occasionally indulged in from the beginning of our history, the most common methods being to deliver long speeches, to break a quorum, to offer numerous amendments and motions, and to force a roll call at every opportunity except on the measure itself. Since 1890 the rules of the House of Representatives have imposed such severe restrictions with respect to these practices as to make filibustering virtually impossible in that body. It still persists in the Senate, however, where the almost unlimited freedom of debate makes it possible for a determined minority to hold up legislation indefinitely by long speeches as well as by other devices.

For example, a filibuster against the United States Bank bill in 1842 lasted for 14 days, against Senate reorganization in 1881 for 47 days, against the silver purchase bill in 1883 for 64 days, against the armed ship bill in 1917 for 23 days, against the antilynching bill in 1938 for 29 days. On this last occasion Sen. Ellender (Louisiana) made a record by holding the floor for six successive days (about 28 hours), but the Senate recessed each night so that Ellender's speaking was not continuous. In 1957 Sen. Thurmond (South Carolina) made a new record by speaking continuously for 24 hours and 18 minutes in a lone effort to defeat the civil rights bill.

Speeches in the Senate need not even be confined to the subject under consideration, and during the filibuster in 1922–23 against the ship subsidy bill urged by President Harding, Sen. Sheppard (Texas) spoke at length on the League of Nations, Sen. Reed (Missouri) on a home for the Vice-President, Sen. Borah (Idaho) on the recognition of Russia, and Sen. McKellar (Tennessee) on the dismissal of certain employees in the Bureau of Engraving and Printing; and in 1949, when a new cloture rule was under consideration, fifteen Senators made extended speeches on entirely irrelevant subjects, such as foreign policy, military trials, N. A. T. O., the nomination of Louis Johnson as Secretary of Defense. In 1907 Sen. Stone (Missouri) filibustered against another ship subsidy bill by reading *Pilgrim's Progress* to the Senate, and in 1935 Sen. Huey Long (Louisiana) filibustered against renewal of N. R. A. by reciting the lives of Judah P. Benjamin and Frederick the Great and even reading to the Senate recipes for potlikker, fried oysters, coffee, and turnip greens.

By methods such as these important legislation clearly favored by the majority has on numerous occasions been defeated or seriously compromised, at least forty measures having been defeated by filibuster since the Civil War. These include such measures as the force bills of 1890 and 1891, the ship subsidy bills of 1907 and 1922, the antilynching bills of 1922, 1925, and 1937, the flood control bill of 1935, and anti-poll-tax bills of 1942, 1944, 1946, and 1948, the F. E. P. C. bill of 1946, and several civil rights bills.

The original Senate rules permitted debate to be closed by a motion for the previous question, and this was used on at least four occasions. However, that rule was dropped in 1806, and Senate debate has been virtually unlimited since. After the successful filibuster in 1917 against the proposal to arm merchant ships, and on the insistence of President Wilson, the Senate actually adopted a mild cloture rule which permitted debate to be closed after two more days, on petition of sixteen Senators and by vote of two thirds of those present and voting. In 1948 a new rule was adopted which plugged certain loopholes in the 1917 rule, but which otherwise made cloture more difficult by requiring two thirds of the entire Senate and by making cloture inapplicable to proposals to change the rules themselves. In 1959 the 1917 rule with respect to the two-thirds requirement was restored, but at the same time there was an express affirmation that the Senate is a "continuous body" and that therefore its rules carry over from session to session unless changed, whereas in the House of Representatives new rules have to be adopted, and by simple majority, for every new Congress.

The tradition of unlimited debate is so strong in the Senate, however, that even such modified cloture as is permitted under these rules has been seldom applied. Since the adoption of the first cloture rule in 1917, or in a period of more than forty years, there have been 23 attempts to close debate under the rule, but cloture has been applied only four times—on the Treaty of Versailles in 1919, on the World Court proposal in 1926, on the branch banking bill in 1927, and on the Bureau of Customs and Prohibition bill in 1927. Rather than apply cloture and thus formally assert the right to limit debate in the Senate, the Senate majority has been willing to engage in other tactics in the attempt to break a filibuster, principally to insist on continuous or "round-the-clock" sessions in an effort to wear out the filibustering minority through sheer physical endurance tests. In connection with the legislative battle over civil rights in 1960, all records for such round-the-clock sessions were broken with a session lasting 83 hours and 3 minutes without any recess or break, 125 hours and 31 minutes with a 15-minute recess, and 157 hours and 41 minutes before it finally ended.

The resulting spectacle of Senate sessions with only a half dozen Senators on the floor, of Senators sleeping on cots strewn around the Senate corridors, of frequent quorum calls in the middle of the night and Senators rushing in to answer roll calls while only partially dressed, to say nothing of the complete tie-up of normal Senate business, has aroused considerable public disapproval and disgust, so that minority groups have become increasingly reluctant to engage in open filibustering, and majority groups are increasingly disposed towards cloture. It is still true, however, that a determined minority which is skillfully organized and led can generally force at least important compromise in the Senate.

FILIBUSTERING. The word filibuster is an English corruption of the Dutch *Vrijbuiter* (freebooter) and was first applied to the English buccaneers of the 17th century, who gained a livelihood by plundering Spanish ships and settlements in the Caribbean. About the middle of the 19th century the term came to be applied to American adventurers engaged in armed expeditions against countries with which the United States was at peace. It is sometimes applied, incorrectly, to the clandestine enlistment of volunteers in neutral countries for service in a foreign war. It has also been wrongly applied to gun-running, as was the case during the Cuban insurrection preceding the Spanish-American War.

FIRELANDS was a tract of 500,000 acres, largely within the two westernmost counties (Huron and Erie) of the Western Reserve, granted by the State of Connecticut to citizens of nine "suffering towns" for losses totaling $538,495.26 suffered in British Revolutionary raids. The proprietors were incorporated by law of Connecticut (1796) and Ohio (1803). Indian rights were extinguished by the Treaty of Fort Industry (1805), the Firelands Company joining the Connecticut Land Company to pay $16,000 and an annuity of $175. Among the Indians dispossessed were Christian Delawares, refugees after the massacre at Gnadenhutten. Lands were partitioned among the proprietors in 1808, and settlement began at once. Eight of the Firelands townships took names of the "suffering towns" (New London, Groton, Danbury, New Haven, Fairfield, Norwalk, Greenwich, Ridgefield).

FIRES, GREAT. The first considerable fire in American history destroyed a large portion of the town of New York during the British army occupation in 1776, and was hotly ascribed by Americans to British vandalism. New York had another big fire Dec. 16–17, 1835, which burned 600 buildings in the business quarter, with a loss of $20,000,000. Fires were shockingly numerous in the 19th century, due to the preponderance of wooden buildings, to carelessness with inflammables and poor fire-fighting equipment. San Francisco, suddenly grown to an important city in 1849, was swept three times by flames in 1850, and finally built more carefully, using much brick and stone. A Gold Rush mining camp of several hundred population was apt to be wiped out completely in an hour or so on a windy day. The Chicago fire of 1871 was the greatest disaster of the sort in our history. Boston suffered a fire in 1872 which laid waste sixty acres of the city and did $60,000,000 worth of damage. In 1904 a great conflagration destroyed the business district of Baltimore with losses aggregating $125,000,000. In each case, much better construction followed. In that year of 1904 nearly 7000 persons lost their lives in fires in this country, or about nineteen per day. So great was the destruction in those early years of the century that there was much agitation for improved prevention and protection. It was pointed out in 1906 that the loss by fire during the past quarter century had been $3,500,000,000. Boston's fire loss at that time was said to be $1,500,000 yearly, or about ten times that of the average European city of similar size. But the disasters were bringing better practices —more fireproof buildings, stricter laws. The Iroquois fire, Chicago, 1903, caused more stringent regula-

tion of theater exits, asbestos curtains, etc., while the Triangle Waist factory fire in New York in 1911, in which 147 persons, mostly young women and girls, lost their lives, brought about reforms in factory inspection and safety measures. Our vast conifer forests, frequent droughts and native carelessness have brought greater losses from forest fires in this country than in any other. In pioneer days on the Great Plains, the giant grasses several feet in height, drying in late autumn, caused devastating prairie fires, often moving with incredible speed. For a week in November, 1869, one of these fires raged through central Kansas in a great arc more than 100 miles long, destroying farmsteads, railroad stations, cattle and whatever lay in its path.

"FIRST IN WAR, FIRST IN PEACE, AND FIRST IN THE HEARTS OF HIS COUNTRYMEN." These words were written by Gen. Henry Lee as a part of the resolutions offered by John Marshall in Congress on the occasion of the death of George Washington. They were repeated in Lee's memorial oration in Philadelphia, Dec. 26, 1799, and have become the best-known characterization of Washington.

FISHERIES DISPUTE, ARBITRATION OF. The Definitive Treaty of Peace of 1783 between Great Britain and the United States recognized the "liberty" of American citizens to fish within the territorial waters of British North America. This was a "liberty" and not a "right" which the American plenipotentiaries had at first contended for. The War of 1812 put an end to this treaty.

The Convention of 1818 respecting fisheries, boundary and the restoration of slaves again recognized the "liberty forever" but only in stipulated territorial waters: on the western and northern coast of Newfoundland, the shores of the Magdalen Islands, and the coast of Labrador, and expressly renounced "forever" liberties heretofore enjoyed elsewhere in British dominions, but allowed landing privileges for refreshment of fishermen in the renounced areas.

Various disputes over the exercise of these liberties and landing privileges were precipitated by the jealousies of Canadian and American fishermen between 1836 and 1854. In the latter year the fisheries question was again adjusted as a part of the Canadian-American Reciprocity Treaty. The Treaty of Washington of 1871, which was a comprehensive settlement of outstanding Anglo-American issues, restored again to American citizens the privileges renounced by the Convention of 1818 and temporarily recaptured by the reciprocity treaty.

The fishery article of the Treaty of Washington came to an end in 1885. From then on until 1909 the precise liberties of American fishermen in British territorial waters according to the Convention of 1818 were the matter of constant bitter and jealous dispute.

357

Controversies arose particularly concerning the territorial jurisdiction of Great Britain in nontreaty waters, over bays less than six miles across from headland to headland. Finally, the dispute was referred by an agreement of both governments, Jan. 27, 1909, to the Permanent Court of Arbitration at The Hague. That tribunal within its powers of reference laid down decisions, definitions and regulations which definitely settled the disputes and adjusted the whole affair. Since the award of the tribunal on Sept. 7, 1910, there has been no further trouble.

FITCH'S STEAMBOAT EXPERIMENTS.

John Fitch claimed to have projected the steam engine before he heard of similar plans by other inventors. In 1785 he made a model and sought funds from Congress and the Virginia Assembly. Though he found only polite interest and encouragement from these bodies he eventually received, from New Jersey in 1786 and from Virginia, Delaware, Pennsylvania and New York in 1787, the exclusive rights to steam navigation in their waters for fourteen years.

In April, 1786, he organized a joint-stock company in Philadelphia. An engine was built by Henry Voight, a watchmaker, and installed on a small boat to drive twelve paddles, six on a side. The vessel was successfully tried out, Aug. 22, 1787, on the Delaware River with members of the Constitutional Convention looking on. A more powerful boat went upstream to Burlington in July, 1788, but there the boiler broke down. William Thornton, the architect of the United States Capitol, now entered the company. After various heartbreaking experiments a third boat proved to be a mechanical success and in the summer of 1790 it made regular runs to Trenton, but failed to earn expenses. However, a United States patent was granted to the company in 1791. A fourth boat was begun, but was wrecked by a storm. Fitch and Voight quarreled, and their associates, discouraged of making profits, did not continue the enterprise.

FIVE-POWER NAVAL TREATY

(1922) was one of seven treaties negotiated at the Washington Conference on Limitation of Armaments and related to Far Eastern questions. Settlement of the latter, principally through the Four-Power and Nine-Power treaties, made possible the Naval Treaty of Washington, signed on Feb. 6, placing limitations upon capital ships, aircraft carriers and Far Eastern naval bases. Aggregate battleship tonnage was restricted to 525,000 for the United States and Great Britain, 315,000 for Japan and 175,000 for France and Italy. This quota required the United States to scrap 28 capital ships then building or completed. Competitive building of cruisers, destroyers and submarines continued until the 1930 London Treaty.

FIVE-TWENTIES

were a large issue of United States bonds sold during the Civil War. Redeemable after five, payable after twenty years, they bore 6% interest. Proposals to redeem them with greenbacks, since no specific provision for payment in gold had been made, resulted in much controversy.

FLAG DAY

(June 14). President Wilson in 1916, and President Coolidge in 1927, suggested and requested in proclamations addressed to "fellow-countrymen" that June 14 be observed as Flag Day. The date marks the anniversary of the adoption by Congress of the "Stars and Stripes" as emblem of the nation. Official recognition of the flag birthday is the result of efforts of various individuals and organizations since 1885.

FLAG OF THE UNITED STATES.

Among the oldest of the national standards of the world and in its development to a flag with fifty stars, the American flag embodies the military, naval and political history of the United States from the struggling colonies to the present day.

On June 14, 1777, the Continental Congress resolved: "That the flag of the thirteen United States be thirteen stripes, alternate red and white, that the union be thirteen stars, white in a blue field representing a new constellation." This flag, flown by Capt. John Paul Jones in the *Ranger*, received its first salute from a foreign state at Quiberon Bay, France, Feb. 14, 1778.

Vermont and Kentucky, after being admitted to the Union, made strong requests to be included in the symbolism of the flag. Congress provided from the first day of May, 1795, that the flag of the United States be fifteen stripes; that the union be fifteen stars in a blue field. For 22 years the flag of 1795 was hoisted ashore and afloat over civilian, military and naval activities. It was the conquering flag in 13 out of 18 naval battles of the War of 1812. It inspired in 1814, at Fort McHenry, Md., the words of the immortal "Star-Spangled Banner."

As time went on little uniformity was shown in the number of stripes in the flag. On April 4, 1818, President Monroe signed a bill providing from July 4, 1818: "The flag of the United States be thirteen horizontal stripes of alternate red and white; that the union have twenty white stars in a blue field; that one star be added on the admission of every new state in the Union. . . ." The exact proportions were finally established by executive order of Woodrow Wilson in 1916.

In 1958 and 1959 Alaska and Hawaii, respectively, were admitted as states, thereby giving the flag its present number of fifty stars.

Neither the Federal Government nor the states have enacted any laws as to the manner of displaying or saluting the flag. Navy, Army and Coast Guard have explicit regulations as to the display and honor to be rendered the flag. It has been left to the states of the Union to provide legislation to prevent misuse, abuse and desecration of the flag. All states and the District of Columbia have laws to this effect.

The best opinion and collected usage on flag etiquette is set forth in the Flag Code adopted 1923 and endorsed 1924 as a result of the National Flag Conference, convened by the American Legion at Washington in Continental Memorial Hall of the D. A. R., and directing that the flag should only be displayed from sunrise to sunset on buildings and at flagstaffs in the open. When the flag passes all persons should face the flag, stand at attention, holding headdress on the left side; women to place right hand over heart.

The flag and its stars symbolize an inspiring story of territorial expansion, for today the sun never sets on the American flag that flies over a domain of about 4,000,000 square miles.

FLATBOATMEN. Flatboating was an occasional rather than a full-time occupation. Flatboatmen were usually farmers or laborers out to see the country or to dispose of the products of their farms. All river cities were important terminals for flatboat commerce, but the most important was New Orleans. Flatboatmen often made annual voyages and there were probably few who did not make the journey more than once. They bore a reputation for thievery, debauchery and quarrelsomeness that probably should have been applied only to part of them, but their battles with keelboatmen are well known.

Wages varied greatly but were usually about fifty dollars for the voyage. In the early years flatboatmen returned north by sea or by the Natchez Trace, and in later years by steamboat. Many of them died by disease or violence or the perils of the voyage. Doubtless also many of those who made the voyage returned home to bring their families west or south.

Besides the regular flatboatmen there were the immigrant families on their way downstream who shared with the flatboatmen the distrust of the shore dwellers. Another class of flatboat people made annual voyages on boats fitted up as stores and outfitted with goods for sale to the farmers and to the people in the smaller settlements.

FLETCHER v. **PECK** (1810) was a Yazoo land fraud case in which the opinion was written by Chief Justice Marshall. Through various fraudulent activities the legislature of Georgia had been persuaded to authorize (1795) the issuance of grants of certain land belonging to the state. A later legislature passed an act (1796) annulling these grants on the ground of fraud. Meanwhile, a part of the land passed through several innocent holders to one Peck who conveyed to Fletcher with a covenant that the title had not been impaired by the subsequent act of the Georgia legislature. Fletcher sued Peck for a breach of this covenant. The question before the Court was whether or not the original grant by Georgia was a contract whose obligation was impaired by the later legislation of Georgia. Chief Justice Marshall held that the term contract included executed contracts as well as executory because an executed contract contains obligations binding on the parties; and that it applies to a grant from the state as well as to executed contracts between individuals; that as a contract it was not voidable in the hands of an innocent third party; and that therefore there was no breach of covenant by Peck.

FLOOD CONTROL. There is no uniform relationship between the capacity of a river channel and the maximum flow of the stream. The Hudson River channel between Albany and New York City, at the top of the depression through which it flows, would carry probably a hundred times the maximum flow. Through the Grand Canyon of the Colorado the capacity between the mile-high walls is more than a thousand times as large as necessary to carry the greatest flood.

At the other extreme, river channels through flat coastal plains may be totally inadequate for the flood flow. For instance, the natural channels of the St. Francis, Black and Little Rivers, as they leave the Missouri highlands to flow over the Mississippi River delta, have capacity for only about 1% of the extreme flood flow.

Where a river has cut a broad path or valley through higher land, because of the irregularities of its course, the channel commonly shifts gradually from side to side of its valley, cutting away the banks where the current is swift, and dropping the eroded material where the current is slack. During floods, a river which flows through a flat valley commonly overflows its banks, in moderate flood depositing fertile soil. In an unusually great flood, where the overflow current is rapid, it may tear away the surface, carrying off the fertile soil and leaving coarse gravel behind. Thus a river tends to build up the fertility of its overflow valley during periods of normal overflow, but in great floods may reduce fertile lands to worthless gravel beds.

Cities often are located in flat river valleys subject to overflow, at least during great floods, because the flat valley lands provide economical and convenient building locations, and because of the convenient water supply or for navigation facilities. For such cities, great floods may have disastrous consequences.

Flood-control engineering has evolved a wide variety of methods. Among the oldest are diking or leveeing the river channel to prevent its overflow, and the lining or "revetting" of the banks to prevent caving and shifting of the river channel. Building spur dikes into the channel where erosion is serious in order to divert the current is also an ancient device. Other methods include the straightening and deepening of a stream channel to give it greater carrying capacity and to prevent erosion of the banks. Especially in crooked channels which develop in flat valleys or in alluvial lands and deltas, it frequently is helpful to shorten the river channel by cutting across loops and bends, thus increasing the velocity of the flowing water. In tidal plains near the ocean it sometimes is feasible to construct "spillways" or bypasses which will let part of the water escape to the ocean by a short route. That method has been taken along the lower Mississippi above New Orleans, where it is desirable to avoid extreme high water in the city, but where, in the interest of navigation, it is desired to keep the main river channel through the city.

Until recent times the building of levees, and the protection of banks, were the chief methods of large-scale flood control, though the reforesting of uplands was practiced to some extent in the hope of reducing rapid runoff. In 1913 to 1921 a new method of controlling floods on a considerable scale was introduced with the building of flood control reservoirs or "retarding basins" to protect Dayton, O., and other cities along the Miami River (the Miami Conservancy District). After the great Mississippi flood of 1927, that method was added to those used for control of the Mississippi River, and flood control reservoirs are now an accepted part of the methods available. It is now recognized that in large-scale flood control, no one method can be wholly relied on. Modern flood control may use reservoirs, levees, bank protection, straightening and enlarging of channels, cut-off bypasses, and possibly the protection of the watershed by soil conservation and forestation.

In the earlier period of river control in America, the chief aim was the prevention of flood damage. To this was sometimes added the improvement of navigation and the supplying of irrigation water. Little by little, as other needs and possibilities developed, there has emerged the policy of unified control of rivers for all significant purposes. An example of this unified development is the river control policy of the Tennessee Valley Authority. Here the purpose of preventing flood damage is united with improvement of navigation; development of electric power; and storage for increasing low water flow to reduce pollution, to provide water supply for industrial, sanitary and domestic use, and to create recreation facilities. Thus river-control engineering, of which flood control is an important part, comes to be a process of using all engineering methods available and appropriate to meet all needs relating to water.

The behavior of water in contact with the earth is so varied and complex as often to defy mathematical or physical analysis. Until recent decades, engineers relied largely on general observation and judgment to forecast the effects of their works on river channels or related structures. There developed in Europe the use of hydraulic laboratories where the effects of water action could be tried out in advance on actual small scale models. The use of hydraulic laboratories was introduced to America in the 1920's through studies and reports of European practice by the great American engineer, John R. Freeman. Today hydraulic laboratories have become a normal part of large-scale water-control engineering.

Flood control, like irrigation, is a great socializing influence. In primitive life, each farmer in a river valley would build his own private dike or levee to protect his crops. The expensiveness and inadequacy of that process led to co-operation of groups of farmers. The process has eventuated in the great Mississippi River system control project costing billions of dollars.

There is no sharp line between the undertakings of single industries or cities or localities and far-reaching projects of state or national scope. The desire of members of Congress to bring benefits to their constituents, the craving of any public agency to increase its power and scope of operations, and the desire of industries, cities and local regions to shift their costs to the general government, all have combined to make even local flood control a Federal function, to be executed at national expense. The result is that we find conservative banking interests, industries and political officers, who would be shocked at the suggestion of socialism, nevertheless eagerly seeking Federal appropriations for private or local flood control works. Thus flood control has an effect on the structure of government. (*See also* Tennessee Valley Authority.)

FLORIDA became part of the United States, July, 1821, under the terms of the Adams-Onís Treaty, negotiated Feb. 22, 1819. Andrew Jackson, first American governor, was practically a military executive, being given, with certain limitations, all the powers formerly exercised by the captain general and intendant of Cuba and the Spanish governors of East and West Florida.

Congress authorized a territorial government in 1822 under which there was an appointive legislative council of thirteen members. This body was made elective in 1826 and its membership later increased. The abandoned Indian town of Tallahassee was made the capital in 1824. Florida was admitted as a state March 3, 1845.

Florida seceded from the Union, Jan. 10, 1861. During the four years of war its ports were taken by Federal forces and its coast line blockaded. The only major battle of the Civil War in Florida was Olustee, Feb. 20, 1864, in which the Federals were defeated.

The new constitution Florida formed in 1865 was unsatisfactory to Congress, because it did not give the Negroes suffrage, and the state was not readmitted into the Union until June 25, 1868, after a revised constitution had been adopted.

British Florida. England, to complete her possessions

east of the Mississippi and to end border troubles, forced Spain to cede Florida in the Treaty of Paris, 1763. The Proclamation of 1763 established colonial government and divided the region at the Apalachicola River into East and West Florida. The original northern boundary was 31° but, before government was finally organized, that of West Florida was advanced to 32° 20′ to encourage settlement along the Mississippi. East Florida developed slowly; much of the land was taken up by Englishmen as speculations. Among these were Andrew Turnbull, who planted the unsuccessful New Smyrna in 1767 with 1500 Greeks, Italians and Minorcans, and Dennis Rolles who founded Rollestown. After 1775 thousands of Loyalists poured into East Florida, founding numerous towns and plantations. East Florida was the objective of several attacks by the Americans from 1776 to 1778 and assisted the southern campaign of the British in 1778. West Florida was part of the Anglo-Spanish Mississippi rivalry. Efforts were made to lure settlers from Louisiana and plans laid to divert trade from New Orleans through the lakes to Mobile and Pensacola. The region became involved in the Revolution through the efforts of the Americans to get supplies at New Orleans (the Gibson-Linn Expedition in 1776 and the Willing Raid in 1778), and Spain's declaration of war against England (1779). Through Bernardo de Galvez's campaigns, 1779–81, West Florida surrendered to Spain. By the Definitive Treaty of Peace, 1783, both East and West Florida were returned to Spain.

French in Florida. Jean Ribaut, one of Coligny's ablest and most trusted naval captains, reached the upper east coast of Florida in 1562 with 150 colonists in three vessels and claimed this hitherto Spanish territory for France as an asylum for Huguenots. A settlement was also attempted in South Carolina. Two years later René de Laudonnière, who had accompanied Ribaut as lieutenant, was sent back to Florida by Coligny with another company of Huguenots. They settled near the mouth of St. Johns River where they built Fort Caroline. When in 1565 Ribaut returned with 300 additional colonists in a fleet of seven ships, he was attacked by the Spanish Admiral, Pedro Menéndez de Avilés. Subsequently Ribaut attempted to destroy the Spaniards, who were in the process of founding St. Augustine, but a storm wrecked his fleet. Starvation soon drove the stranded Frenchmen toward the Spanish settlement where most of them were massacred. Among the few who escaped a similar fate at Fort Caroline was an artist, Jacques LeMoyne, whose drawings of natives and animals are among the earliest made of the New World. Dominique de Gourgues avenged the French in 1568 by killing the Spanish garrison at San Mateo (Fort Caroline).

Spanish Florida, the southeastern portion of North America, was discovered in 1513 by Ponce de León, and explored by Ayllon, Narváez, De Soto and others Exploration extended as far north as the Carolinas and Virginia, and westward beyond the Mississippi. The first permanent settlement was made in 1565 by Pedro Menéndez de Avilés, whose purpose it was to drive the French from Fort Caroline and hold the region for Spain. Menéndez attempted to establish garrisons along the east and west coasts of the peninsula, and up the Atlantic coast as far as Santa Elena. In the 17th century Spanish settlement comprised a Franciscan missions system extending west, southwest, and north into the later Georgia, with St. Augustine as its garrison center. In 1698 Pensacola was founded to block French expansion in the Mississippi region.

French encroachments from the west and English pressure from the north limited the growth of Spanish Florida. The contest with the English led to the destruction of Spanish missions; frontier warfare in the debatable land between Florida and Georgia; and eventual cession to England. In 1783 Spain recovered Florida by treaty. Divided into the two provinces of East and West Florida, it extended to the Mississippi. The northern boundary was settled (1795) at 31° N. Lat. The United States (1803) claimed the territory west of the Perdido as part of the Louisiana Purchase, and by 1813 possessed it in fact if not legally. Florida was held by weak garrisons at St. Augustine, St. Marks and Pensacola. Border troubles with Seminoles and British adventurers led to Jackson's invasion in 1818, and purchase by the United census figures below:

Florida Land Boom. For years prior to 1925, there had been a great increase in activity in Florida real estate. The rapid growth of cities is indicated by the census figures below:

City	1910	1920	1925
Miami	5,471	29,571	69,754
Tampa	37,782	51,608	94,743
Orlando	3,894	9,282	22,225
Lakeland	3,719	7,062	17,051
St. Petersburg	4,127	14,237	26,847

Population of the entire state grew from 752,619 in 1910 to 1,263,549 in 1925, but neither growth of cities nor of the state by any means reflected the increase in property values. Real estate assessments between February, 1920, and February, 1925, went from $253,785,338 to $475,908,261. Hotel permits for construction valued at $8,724,350 were issued during the 1921–22 biennium; but during the next two years these increased to $35,948,043. Bank deposits more than doubled between Jan. 1, 1924, and Jan. 1, 1925.

The trend toward boom-time conditions in Florida was caused by no one thing, but the initial reason was the opening of far southern Florida to railway transportation prior to 1900. Drainage of the Everglades, begun in 1907, turned more people toward Florida. A constantly increasing tourist trade stimulated increased activities.

The ratification of a constitutional amendment prohibiting state collection of income and inheritance taxes, in November, 1924, turned men of wealth toward the state.

The rise in real-estate values until about the end of 1924 had been rapid, but orderly. Soon, however, the upward move in prices became so accelerated that before mid-1925 it had gotten completely out of hand. Orange groves were cut down to build subdivisions. Ordinarily practical persons took gamblers' risks in the hope of quick wealth. Bankers lost their usual business sanity. Visitors to Florida in July, 1925, exceeded any previous number coming in midwinter, and hotels constantly had to turn away guests.

By September it was evident that the beginning of the end had come; many who had made heavy down-payments on property could no longer "unload" it on others. Many who believed themselves rich in July, a few months later realized they were poorer than before the boom.

FLORIDA WAR (1836–43). The effort on the part of the United States to remove the Seminoles from Florida, in accordance with a devious interpretation of the Treaty of Payne's Landing (May 9, 1832), led to this, the second Seminole War. The presence of free Negroes and slaves, the unwillingness of the warriors to trust the whites, and the vitiating climate in the swamps to which the Indians fled, complicated the prolonged struggle. Many of the best officers in the army, including men of the caliber of Scott, Taylor, Macomb and Jesup, failed to bring it to a successful conclusion. Mediation by the Cherokees was of no avail. Gradually, however, by means of a few pitched battles, the destruction of villages and food supplies, the violation of sacred agreements (such as the capture of leading chiefs by means of a flag of truce), the continual scouring of the swamps and even the use of bloodhounds, the army was able to induce the Seminoles, in small groups, to emigrate. Peace, prematurely announced on several occasions, became a reality when Col. Hitchcock removed the last of the Mikasukis. By 1843 all except a few hundred of the estimated 5000 Indians had been moved west of the Mississippi, but at a cost of the lives of 1500 white soldiers, $20,000,000 and untold suffering on the part of the belligerents.

FLOUR MILLING. The first American manufacturing establishments were devoted to the grinding of grain. The earliest English settlers brought small hand mills with them. But growth of population and the spread of wheat growing soon made larger mills necessary. Gov. Winthrop mentions a windmill in his

Journal (1632). This was perhaps the first power mill in New England. In 1643 the exclusive right to grind corn for the public in Boston was offered to any one who would build a tide mill. Such mills were fairly common along the coast. Water power was also used in the interior. In 1786, according to Jefferson, there was "no neighborhood in any part of the United States without a water grist mill for grinding the corn."

New York, Pennsylvania and Maryland early produced a surplus of grain and began to export both wheat and flour. Shipments were made to Europe, the West Indies and the other colonies. Buhr millstones were imported from France and silk bolting cloth from Holland. Machinery was developed for cleaning the wheat as well as bolting the meal. Most of the mills ground the farmers' grain for a toll but merchant mills became common. New York City and Philadelphia developed a considerable flour trade.

At the end of the colonial period there was a concentration of mills at the Brandywine Creek near Wilmington, Del. Twelve merchant mills devoted themselves to the export business and ground annually over 50,000 barrels of "superfine" flour besides other products. European travelers commented on the high degree of mechanical excellence of these mills. The invention of the elevator and the conveyer by Oliver Evans (patented 1791) was largely responsible for the superiority of the best American mills.

After 1790 Baltimore and Richmond became important milling centers with a large export trade. A little later Rochester, with the fine white wheat of the Genesee Valley, came to the front. In 1835, the Rochester mills were producing 5000 barrels of flour a day. Just before the Civil War, St. Louis and Milwaukee became important milling centers. The soft red winter wheat from the regions tributary to those cities brought them to the front. After 1870 a concentration of wheat growing in Minnesota and the Dakotas, together with the water power of St. Anthony Falls, built up the mills at Minneapolis. The hard red spring wheat of that area was found unsatisfactory for bread flour until the invention of the middlings purifier by LaCroix in 1871. The Minneapolis millers were the first to adopt this machine. Soon after they began to substitute the roller process of grinding for the millstones used since ancient times. The first complete roller mill was built by Gov. C. C. Washburn in Minneapolis in 1878. These improvements made the flour from the spring wheat area supreme in the world market. Concentration of ownership and large-scale production made Minneapolis the largest milling center of the world after 1882.

After 1890 the introduction and rapid spread of hard red winter wheat in Kansas and the Southwest created a new milling area with Kansas City as the most notable center. But the greatest growth in recent years has been that at Buffalo. Cheap power, nearness to the great consumer markets, the opportunity to mill Canadian wheat in bond for the export market, and the relatively low rates on wheat on the Great Lakes have made Buffalo our largest milling center, with Kansas City the second. Of the states, Kansas produces more wheat flour than any other, with New York second and Minnesota third.

Flour milling shows increasing concentration of ownership. In 1954, of 694 companies, four shipped 40% of the total flour output, and eight companies shipped more than half the output. These larger companies, especially the two largest, have greatly diversified their products—not only in the grain products field but in others quite unrelated to grain. These diverse products are marketed with very heavy advertising and promotional expenditure and the producers also expend large sums for product research. Whereas formerly these large companies tended to concentrate their activities in a few milling centers, they now decentralize their activities so as to get closer to the markets for their products. The increased concentration of ownership and enlarged scale of production has caused the decline and disappearance of a multitude of small mills.

FLYING CLOUD, a famous clipper ship of 1780 tons, 229 feet long, was built at East Boston by Donald McKay, in 1850. Built in the heyday of the clipper-ship era, she was an extreme type of her class and long held top place for beauty and speed. She made the run from New York to San Francisco in the record time of 89 days, and to Hong Kong in 127 sailing days.

FOLSOM CULTURE COMPLEX is characterized by association of stone artifacts (chiefly projectile points, knives, scrapers, gravers and hammerstones) with extinct mammals (mainly bison, mammoth and camel). So far no skeletal remains have been found of this primitive nomadic hunting people, whose culture has been given a nominal age of 10,000 years. The typical implement is a laterally fluted projectile point named from finds (1926–28) near Folsom, N. Mex. This point and related forms have been found over much of North America, with a concentration along the high plains east of the Rocky Mountains.

FOOTBALL. This ancient game, to which references are found in the days of Edward II, was played occasionally in the colonies and during the first half of the 19th century. It was not until the 1870's, however, that the modern American game, the intercollegiate football which we know today, came into being. At that time a sport more closely resembling association football, or soccer, was being played in some of the colleges (Princeton and Rutgers holding the first recorded intercollegiate contest in 1869), but under the leadership of Harvard and Yale it was supplanted by a form of rugby which proved more popular than the older association game. In order to bring some order out of the chaos of differing styles of football, a set of rules to govern the American game, derived from those of the English Rugby Union, was adopted (1876) at a meeting of representatives of Harvard, Yale, Princeton and Columbia.

These rules were immediately subject to change and modification. The number of players on a side was reduced from fifteen to eleven; new provisions were adopted to govern running, kicking and passing which represented distinct innovations, and the modern scrimmage substituted for the rugby scrimmage. A start was made in that long process whereby American football has slowly evolved out of actual experience on the playing field with almost yearly changes in its governing rules. It has thus proved the most variable of games in methods of play, but when the principles noted above were accepted by the new Intercollegiate Football Association in 1880, the change-over from rugby was complete and what was virtually a new game had been established.

From its earliest days football awoke great spectator interest and even in the 1890's crowds of 50,000 were recorded at the games of the Big Three—Harvard, Yale and Princeton. For long, indeed, these Eastern colleges dominated the sport and public interest in it. Only gradually did football extend its sway to other parts of the country, but once it began to be played by other colleges, it rapidly forged ahead to become the foremost intercollegiate sport.

Throughout the 20th century football has occupied a unique position in the American educational system. In thousands of towns across the nation, high school football teams are enthusiastically—even fanatically—supported by students and townspeople alike, drum majorettes and cheer leaders are integral parts of the academic landscape, and football stars approach the status of folk heroes. In some institutions of higher learning, football has at times tended to overshadow all other forms of collegiate activity in the minds of undergraduates, alumni, and public. In many colleges receipts from football games finance the entire athletic program, and at some universities the football stadium is the most prominent and expensive structure on the campus. Because big-time football is often a profitable enterprise, it has produced many strange anomalies. At some colleges the football coach is the highest paid member of the faculty, the players receive larger scholarships than the members of Phi Beta Kappa, an alumnus' degree of devotion to alma mater depends on the team's record during the past season, virtually all the players major in physical education, and the members of the band practice almost as rigorously as the members of the squad. College football may be, as is often said, a distinctly American phenomenon; but it is just possible that some of the spectators at a college football game—as they view the prodigious efforts of the athletes, the lavish half-time displays, and the stretcher-bearers waiting on the sidelines—may occasionally be reminded of the Colosseum in ancient Rome.

Not all colleges have emphasized football to the same degree. In several small colleges, particularly in the Northeast, little effort is made to recruit star players, and the undergraduates consider the game no more important than several other forms of extracurricular activity. At least one college (Johns Hopkins) solved the problem of overemphasis by not charging for admission to its games, while several other colleges—particularly since World War II—have adopted the more drastic expedient of dropping football as an intercollegiate sport. In 1952, in an effort to save both the baby and the bath, the so-called "Ivy League," consisting of eight well-known colleges and universities in the Northeast, adopted a code of ethics which outlawed the most flagrant devices for recruiting athletes, participation in post-season bowl games, and the holding of spring practice. In recent years, moreover, there has been a marked trend toward the establishment of inter-collegiate associations or conferences made up of teams of roughly the same caliber. Although this device has not eliminated overemphasis, it has helped to produce a system under which those institutions that place a high premium on football victories play only among themselves.

In recent years professional football has rivaled—and in some areas surpassed—college football in popularity. Professional football originated in the industrial towns of Ohio and the mining regions of western Pennsylvania in the years immediately preceding the United States' entrance into World War I. Most of the teams were made up of ex-college stars who held other jobs or undergraduates who played professionally on Sundays under assumed names. In 1920 the American Professional Football Association was formed, and a year later the organization's name was changed to the National Football League. In its early years the league, which consisted for the most part of teams from the smaller cities in the Middle West, was in constant financial difficulties. By the 1930's, however, many of the nation's largest cities had obtained league franchises, and attendance figures for the league's regularly scheduled Sunday games approached or equalled those for important college games. In 1946 the All American Conference was established as a rival league, but after four years of intensive competition for players and spectators, it collapsed, and three of its teams joined the National Football League. Today professional football is a major spectator sport. Single-game crowds of 50,000 are commonplace, the season stretches from the first practice sessions in midsummer until the last bowl game in January, and the fans are fully as enthusiastic as those attending major college games.

Football has never been a static sport, for there have been frequent changes in the game's rules and strategic concepts. At various times rule changes have been made affecting—among other things—the position and width of the goal posts, the number of substitutions permitted in a game, and the ways in which a point or points after a touchdown could be scored. Originating as a game in which victories were achieved by sheer power or mass and in which the flying wedge was a characteristic formation, football has evolved into a game which combines power with deception, finesse, and precision of execution. More responsible than any other factor for making football something more than a pushing match between two opposing sets of behemoths was the forward pass, which, according to most football historians, was first used by a Wesleyan University team in a game with Yale in 1906. In subsequent years the forward pass became not only football's most spectacular offensive weapon, but it also gave the game a degree of variety that made it far more appealing to spectators than it had been in the past. At the same time football became an increasingly complex game, and in 1960 players have to learn to execute an appalling number of formations and plays, while coaches spend more time in their studies than on practice fields, and only a few of the nation's millions of football spectators know enough about the game either to understand or appreciate its intricacies.

FORBES EXPEDITION (1758), a major campaign of the French and Indian War, was directed against Fort Duquesne, focus of French territorial and trading control of the upper Ohio Valley. Commanded by Gen. John Forbes, the force of over 6500 men was composed of Pennsylvanians, under Colonels John Armstrong, James Burd and Hugh Mercer; Virginians, under Colonels George Washington and James Byrd; regulars, of the Highland and North American regiments; Marylanders, under Col. George Dagworthy. Arrangements for commissary, communications and finances were yet formative when in April Forbes was invalided by an ultimately fatal illness and reduced until mid-September to conducting his campaign by voluminous letter-writing. In the exigency Col. Henry Bouquet of the Royal Americans proved Forbes's brilliant mentor, directing the arduous training of the provincial volunteers and adapting the tactics of the regulars to conditions of wilderness fighting. Bouquet was most influential in the decision to cut a wagon-wide swath through Pennsylvania, the Forbes Road, against intense opposition from Washington and other Virginians who for military or land-speculative reasons favored adoption of the path of Braddock's disaster. From earlier rendezvous at Carlisle and Winchester, in July the main body and the Virginia troops advanced respectively to Fort Bedford and Fort Cumberland. Bouquet had occupied the advance post of Loyal-

FORBES ROAD · FORD FOUNDATION

hanna (Ligonier) when in mid-September, almost simultaneously with the costly defeat of a scouting expedition—the Battle of Grant's Hill—the Virginians moved to Fort Bedford and shortly, with Forbes's artillery, joined the main body for an anticipated final push. However, caution after the furious—although unsuccessful—attack of Indians and French upon Loyalhanna (Oct. 12), frequent rains which hampered communications and demanded heartbreaking additions to the prodigious labor of hewing the Forbes Road, vexations and uncertainties of the commissary, and an habitual tendency of the command to overestimate the strength of the enemy, induced a decision to entrench at Loyalhanna for the winter. But triumph for the English was smoothed by a successful council with the Six Nations at Easton (Oct. 8–26); the peace missions of Christian Frederick Post, a Moravian missionary, among the Ohio Indians; and the desperate situation of the French under François Marchand de Ligneris at Fort Duquesne —their Indian allies deserting, and their communication with Canada cut by the success of the Bradstreet expedition against Fort Frontenac. Apprised of conditions by three prisoners taken on Nov. 12, Forbes ordered a forward press. On Nov. 25, viewing the smoking remains of the just-abandoned fort, English-speaking people took permanent possession of the "Gateway to the West."

FORBES ROAD was built in 1758 across the rugged wilderness of western Pennsylvania for the use of the Forbes Expedition in the conquest of Fort Duquesne. Directed by Col. Henry Bouquet, working parties aggregating 1400 men linked a chain of advance fortifications, beginning just west of Bedford— in continuation of the established route from eastern Pennsylvania by way of Lancaster, Carlisle and Chambersburg—and passing through Ligonier to Pittsburgh. For thirty years the Forbes Road was the chief highway between the East and the Ohio Valley, its military values supplemented by civil, as streams of emigrants and freighting trains followed it. The original route is roughly paralleled by U. S. Route 30.

FORCE ACTS comprise the general name popularly applied to various Federal statutes passed to enforce certain national laws and constitutional amendments, particularly in the South. The act of March 2, 1833, authorizing President Jackson to use the Army and Navy, if necessary, to collect customs duties, was a reply to South Carolina's vigorous defiance of the tariffs of 1828 and 1832 in its ordinance of nullification, Nov. 24, 1832. With the Force Bill went moderation, however. Jackson had conferred with South Carolina Unionists like Joel Poinsett, and Henry Clay had composed a compromise tariff which substantially met Southern objections. The Force Act, signed on the same day as this new tariff, was therefore only a gesture of national authority to enforce a law already

in effect repealed. South Carolina meanwhile (March 18, 1833) maintained its theoretical sovereignty by nullifying the Force Act itself.

In order to maintain the political power of the Republican party and of the Northern industrial class against "white supremacy" aims in the South, as supported by the Ku Klux Klan and other similar organizations, Congress, between 1870 and 1875, passed four acts to enforce recognition of the freedmen's civil and political rights as guaranteed by the Fourteenth and Fifteenth Amendments. These statutes were: (1) The act of May 31, 1870, which re-enacted the Civil Rights Act of April 9, 1866; reaffirmed the Negro's political rights as guaranteed by constitutional amendment; authorized Federal courts, marshals and district attorneys to enforce penalties on states, groups and individuals who interfered with registrations or voting in congressional elections; and empowered the President to use the land and naval forces to enforce the act. (2) The "federal election law," Feb. 28, 1871, prompted by Republican reverses in the election of 1870, and passed after a Senate investigation, provided for Federal-appointed election supervisors. (3) The "act to enforce the 14th Amendment," April 20, 1871, was aimed particularly at the Ku Klux Klan and other "conspiracies" which were preventing Negro registration, voting, officeholding and jury service. It extended the earlier acts, provided additional Federal penalties for violations, and authorized the President to make summary arrests. Under this act nine counties in South Carolina were placed under martial law in October, 1871. Eventually over 5000 indictments and about 1250 convictions resulted throughout the South under this and the earlier statutes. (4) The Supplementary Civil Rights Act, March 1, 1875, passed as a memorial to Charles Sumner, just before the Republicans lost control of Congress, gave Negroes social equality of treatment in theaters, public conveyances, hotels and places of amusement. Meanwhile, the Supreme Court had maintained discreet silence on these acts, but between 1876 and 1883 in four decisions declared the severest of the measures unconstitutional. The Court maintained that the Fourteenth and Fifteenth Amendments permitted Federal protection against discrimination only by states and not by individuals or groups, that such protection was limited only to discrimination because of race and color, and limited only to civil rather than social discrimination; and finally, that the Fifteenth Amendment did not contain a positive grant of the franchise. Eventually (1894) Congress repealed most of the provisions of the force acts, after an unsuccessful attempt in 1890 to pass a new Force Bill.

FORD FOUNDATION. This is a private, nonprofit corporation, established in 1936 by Henry and Edsel Ford. It seeks to serve human welfare and strengthen American society by identifying problems of national and international importance and underwriting efforts toward their solution. By 1960 it distributed more than $1,000,000,000 in grants to some 6000 organizations and institutions in the United States and 54 foreign countries. About two thirds of the Foundation's grants have been for the support of education. The main fields of interest in the Foundation's program are: education, including teacher training and educational television; economics and business administration; the humanities and the arts; the engineering sciences; and the strengthening of democratic society, including the problems of public service and governmental affairs and urban and regional problems. Outside the United States, the Foundation has supported a number of significant research, training and development projects in Southeast Asia, the Middle East and Europe. The Foundation has also begun recently to extend its overseas work to Africa and Latin America.

The Foundation has helped finance and bring into being a number of independent, nonprofit corporations which carry on programs in specified fields. Among those currently in existence are: the Center for Advanced Study in the Behavioral Sciences, the Council on Library Resources, the Fund for Adult Education, the Fund for the Advancement of Education, the Fund for the Republic, the National Merit Scholarship Corporation and Resources for the Future.

FORDNEY-McCUMBER TARIFF (1922) was designed to protect "infant" war industries and farmers distressed by price declines. After prolonged debate, sharp tariff increases were granted grains, meats, sugar, wool and many minor farm products. The textile rates of 1897 and 1909 were generally restored, and duties were increased on dyes, ferro-alloys, chinaware, laces, etc. The President was empowered to change tariffs so as to equalize cost of production between American and foreign products—the "flexible" tariff. Some form of "American" rather than invoice value was authorized as a duty-base if "necessary." The improvement in structure of schedules and of administrative provisions was largely due to Tariff Commission drafting.

FOREIGN POLICY. The foreign policy of the United States, like that of other nations, has varied from time to time to meet changing circumstances. Generally speaking, its chief aims, again in common with those of other countries, have been the safeguarding of independence and of the set of values to which the United States has attached significance, and the promotion of the economic prosperity of its citizens. But, as has not been the case with other countries, the United States has frequently formulated doctrines or slogans of foreign policy, some of which have become virtual ends in themselves. Up to World War II the principal doctrines and slogans were: (1) Freedom of the Seas, or neutral rights (set forth in the Plan of 1776). (2) Abstention from European affairs (laid down in Washington's Farewell Address, 1796, and the Monroe Doctrine, 1823), sometimes called isolationism, and expressed most urgently in the injunction, No Entangling Alliances. (3) The Monroe Doctrine, 1823: no European interference with, or further colonization in, the New World republics; and in return no American interference in European affairs. (4) The Open Door Policy as stated in 1899 and 1900: equal commercial opportunity for all countries in China, and Chinese territorial and administrative entity.

The main questions with which American foreign policy has been concerned over the years fall under two headings: one, relations with Great Britain and Canada; the other, territorial expansion. During nearly half its history a part of the British empire, America naturally acquired a British population and many British traditions. Since independence, immigrants from Britain (including Ireland) have arrived in greater numbers than those from any other country; British books have constituted the largest part of those imported; and Britain and America have each provided a major (often, the leading) market for the other's exports. Moreover, Anglo-American relations have been profoundly influenced by Canada.

As for expansion, a vigorous people concentrated on the eastern seaboard of a rich, largely uninhabited continent were bound to move westward. And when the west coast became settled before the interior, attention was bound to turn to the narrow isthmus to the south, where a canal would provide easier and cheaper transportation from one coast to the other and from the centers of production on the east coast to the great markets of the Orient, and would enhance the effectiveness of the navy. The need to safeguard so strategic an area furnished the main motive for expansion outside continental North America up to World War II.

Victory in the Revolution did not bring freedom of action. British forts remained on American soil in the north; Spanish power threatened in the south; the French alliance, once so cherished, became an Entangling Alliance. Taking advantage of wartime difficulties in Europe, the United States negotiated a British withdrawal in 1794 (Jay's treaty), a boundary agreement with Spain in 1795 (Pinckney's treaty), the termination of the French alliance in 1800, and the procurement of the vast Louisiana territory in 1803. But the continuing and spreading European conflicts threatened to engulf the new, weak republic. It had a narrow escape from disaster in the War of 1812 (caused partly by American pressure for freedom of the seas), but emerged without loss of territory. Thereafter commenced a long period in which the United States, at length free of European entanglements and protected by a balance of power in Europe and an absence of power in Asia, could take the initiative. The age of defensive diplomacy had ended.

Spain came out of the wars in Europe much weaker; in the Adams-Onís treaty of 1819 she yielded East and West Florida and an enormous domain for American expansion right through to the Pacific Ocean. Territorial expansion was deeply affected by the growing sectional struggle between the free and the slave states. The South was unwilling to strengthen the North by permitting the incorporation of British North America (in accordance with the dictates of Manifest Destiny). Similarly the North was unenthusiastic about adventures in Texas, Mexico, Cuba, and Central America, though its attitude did not prevent the Mexican War, 1846–48.

The appearance of a substantial population on the west coast as a result of the Mexican War and the California gold rush laid the groundwork for new departures in foreign policy. A Central American canal, the acquisition of Cuba, influence in Hawaii—these became objectives of American foreign policy in the 1850's. The rise of industry also directed attention to a canal, as well as to potential markets across the Pacific. The United States followed hard upon Great Britain and France in demanding commercial privileges in China, and itself took the lead in opening Japan to foreign trade in 1854. But the fruition of these newer impulses was delayed half a century by the Civil War: first by the rising din of sectional controversy during the 1850's, then by the years of fighting, finally by the resulting dislocations during the 1870's and 1880's. Not until the end of the century could foreign policy turn with full vigor to the canal, Cuba, and Hawaii, the prime objectives of the "Large Policy" of the 1890's.

Thirty-three years elapsed between the end of the Civil War and the start of the Spanish-American War, years usually described as quiet in foreign affairs. Quiet some of them were, yet these years prepared the way for a diplomatic revolution that transformed Great Britain from the arch-foe into the principal associate. Despite bitterness felt by the victorious North toward Britain and Canada after the Civil War because of their allegedly unneutral conduct and sentiment, despite a still-strong tide of Manifest Destiny as evidenced by the desire of many governmental leaders to force Canada into the union, despite serious frictions over America's insistence on fishing rights in Canadian waters and assumption of the role of protector of fur seals in the open waters of the Bering Sea (this last a departure from the customary stand for freedom of the seas), the United States and Great Britain turned increasingly to a practice uncommon in international affairs: the arbitration of controversies that could not be settled by diplomacy. Thus the postwar bitterness was mitigated by British and Canadian concessions at the Treaty of Washington (1871) and by an award in favor of the United States at the Geneva arbitration of 1872; the Bering Sea dispute was eased by the Paris arbitration of 1893; and the fisheries controversy was settled by the Hague arbitration of 1910.

During the Spanish-American War Great Britain alone among the principal neutrals sympathized with the United States. Her sympathy, reflecting and enhancing the improvement in Anglo-American relations, facilitated a settlement after the war of the only dangerous controversies still outstanding: one concerning the construction of an isthmian canal, settled by the Hay-Pauncefote treaty of 1901; the other concerning the Alaska boundary, settled by an adjudication of 1903.

The war with Spain set loose the pent-up impulses of 1848; and all at once the old aspirations of a canal in Central America, bases in Cuba and the Caribbean, and supremacy in Hawaii were realized. Somewhat unexpectedly the United States also found itself in possession of the Philippine Islands. With the Stars and Stripes floating so close to the mainland of Asia, the country embarked upon a more active policy in China, now envisaged as a great potential market for a mounting "surplus" of American goods. The Open Door notes of 1899 and 1900, which had the modest aims of embarrassing Russian expansion and shoring up the potential market, became transmuted over the years into another dogma of American foreign policy, the Open Door Policy, conveniently applied in opposing Japanese expansion in China.

Between 1895 and World War I the United States pursued a more vigorous policy in Latin America, as well as in China. The Monroe Doctrine came into much greater prominence. The United States brandished it so belligerently in 1895 over a British-Venezuelan boundary dispute (settled by another Anglo-American arbitration, at Washington in 1899) that for a moment war with Great Britain seemed imminent. Theodore Roosevelt discovered a surprising "Corollary" to the Doctrine in 1905, according to which America's resolve to prevent others from intervening in the New World conferred an obligation to intervene itself. And the Doctrine was complemented by an emerging Pan American movement (which however made little headway before World War I) in the sense that Pan Americanism represented a policy of the United States to encourage the American republics to cherish New World economic and political associations rather than trans-Atlantic ones. During those years, too, the United States developed a Panama Canal policy. Its intervention insured the success of the Panama revolution in 1903. Rising German naval power and a German-British intervention in Venezuela in 1902 aroused American fears for the safety of the future canal, surrounded as it was by weak, debt-ridden little countries. Anxious to bring law and order to the strategic Caribbean area, the United States established protectorates (all terminated after World War I) over

Cuba, 1901; Panama, 1903; Santo Domingo, 1905; Nicaragua, 1912; and Haiti, 1915.

When World War I broke out in 1914 most Americans, nurtured on the Farewell Address, took for granted the desirability of keeping clear of this most unpleasant European affair. On the other hand Woodrow Wilson, with widespread backing, felt it a duty to uphold the freedom of the seas. The long-run incompatibility between these two dogmas of foreign policy resulted in American belligerency in April, 1917.

Having rejected membership in the League of Nations, the United States rationalized its decision by becoming confirmed in a renewed glorification of isolationism. In the 1920's its foreign policy attempted little more than to collect the war debts and to outlaw war by the Pact of Paris of 1928—and failed in both aims.

During the great depression which began in 1929 international order deteriorated alarmingly. Japan invaded Manchuria in 1931 and sponsored a new country there. Though resenting this affront to the Open Door Policy, the United States contented itself with a refusal to recognize the new situation (the Stimson Doctrine, 1932). Similarly, dangers in Europe prompted the country to renounce part of the traditional freedom of the seas, through the neutrality legislation of 1935–37. Another change from the past came with the Reciprocal Trade Agreements Act of 1934, which inaugurated a trend toward lower tariffs. When World War II broke out, neutral rights were largely forgotten; instead, America's unneutral support of Great Britain and stand against Japanese expansion resulted in a state of semiwarfare months before Japan attacked Pearl Harbor in December, 1941.

After World War II the United States found itself in an unprecedented situation that necessitated a revolution in its foreign policy. For the first time in its history it was not protected by a balance of power in the rest of the world. On the contrary, with Germany and Japan crushed, and Great Britain and France exhausted, the U. S. S. R. stood predominant in Europe and Asia. To the restoration of the balance of power destroyed by the war, the United States devoted itself. Its task was enormously complicated by the fact that the U. S. S. R. was controlled by men who, under the spell of a Marxist-Leninist "science" of society that taught the impossibility of protracted coexistence with non-communist countries, apparently dedicated themselves to pushing hard for world-wide communism. Thus the United States had to contain not only the Soviet Union but international communism as well. All this it had to do in the nuclear age when the feasibility of applying atomic and thermo-nuclear energy to warfare raised awesome possibilities of destruction. Never before had the stakes of foreign policy been so high.

At first the United States did not appreciate the ominous shape of affairs. Secure in sole (until 1949) possession of the atomic bomb, it solicited the friendship of the Soviet Union, and looked to the United Nations as a bulwark of peace. But when the hopes of the Yalta agreement of 1945 were shattered and when the U. S. S. R. rejected the offer of the United States (Baruch Plan) to destroy its atomic bombs in return for international control of fissionable materials, the country embarked upon a sweeping reorientation of its foreign policy. The turning-point came, characteristically, with the promulgation of another doctrine, the Truman Doctrine of 1947: the United States, the President announced, would "support free peoples who are resisting attempted subjugation by armed minorities or by outside pressures." Though with immediate reference to Greece (then resisting forceful communist infiltration) and Turkey, the Truman Doctrine had universal applicability. At the time of an earlier doctrine, that of Monroe in 1823, the American government had considered, but had decided against, an expression of sympathy for Greece, which then too was engaged in a struggle for freedom. Now in 1947 not only sympathy but economic and military assistance as well were extended to both Greece and Turkey.

Soon the United States was exerting itself to contain international communism in many other areas. It has done so partly by extending military aid to its friends and by participating in a far-flung network of defensive military alliances: the Pact of Rio of 1947, among the American republics; a Filipino-American treaty of 1951; the A. N. Z. U. S. treaty of 1951, between the United States on the one hand and Australia and New Zealand on the other; a Japanese-American treaty of 1951; a South Korean-American treaty of 1953; the South East Asia Treaty Organization (S. E. A. T. O.) of 1954, comprising the United States, Great Britain, France, New Zealand, Australia, the Philippines, Thailand, and Pakistan; a Chinese (Formosa)-American treaty of 1954. By far the most important alliance was the North Atlantic Treaty Organization (N. A. T. O.) of 1949, including eventually fifteen countries of North America and Europe. Although none of the alliances legally bound the signatories to extend armed assistance to an attacked ally, the moral obligation to do this was so strong, particularly in the case of NATO, as to be practically compulsive.

The United States has tried to contain communism not only through alliances but by helping non-communist countries economically. Under the European Recovery Program (Marshall Plan) of 1947, which together with N. A. T. O. constituted the essence of America's policy toward Europe, it gave many billions of dollars to European countries. (It offered to include the U. S. S. R. in the program but the latter refused.) And under the Technical Cooperation (Point Four) Program of 1949 it has extended economic and technical assistance to underdeveloped countries in Asia, Africa, and Latin America.

The destruction of Germany and Japan during the war created power vacuums which the United States has sought to fill. When it proved impossible to reach agreement with the U. S. S. R. on a common economic policy for the four zones of Germany, a policy prescribed by the Potsdam agreement of 1945, the United States, Great Britain, and France merged their zones into a West German Republic (1949). The United States (with Great Britain) "airlifted" supplies to Berlin over a Russian blockade in 1948 and 1949; it welcomed West Germany as a N. A. T. O. ally in 1955 and has extended considerable economic and military aid to her; it has tried without success to reunite all Germany with a government of the German people's choice. American policy toward Japan has been similar. After keeping Japan disarmed for several years, the United States in 1951 concluded a lenient peace treaty and a security treaty with her, and since then has helped her to rearm.

After World War II China was the scene of civil war between nationalists and communists. An American mission attempted throughout 1946, but failed, to reconcile the two factions. By the end of 1949 the communists controlled all mainland China, leaving the nationalists stranded on the island of Formosa and a few smaller islands. The United States has steadily refused to recognize the communist government in Peking. On the other hand it recognized Formosa as the Republic of China, and has given her considerable military and economic assistance. A major crisis broke out in 1950 when the communists of North Korea invaded South Korea. Acting through the United Nations and with help from fifteen other countries, the United States hastened to the aid of the South Koreans and, despite the intervention of communist China on the side of the North Koreans, succeeded in preserving South Korea's independence with essentially her pre-war boundaries. Since the outbreak of the Korean War it has been American policy to defend Formosa. Congress in 1955 authorized the defense also of the small nationalist islands of Matsu and Quemoy, provided their defense was necessary to the defense of Formosa itself. It appeared possible in 1958, when Quemoy was under heavy bombardment from the mainland, that the United States would fight should the communists attempt an invasion, which they did not.

Important elements of America's Latin American policy since World War II have been the Pact of Rio (1947) and the Charter for the Organization of American States (1948). The Charter, which provided a treaty basis for Pan Americanism, specifies the nature and structure of the international organization of the 21 American republics. The United States sponsored a resolution adopted by these republics in 1954 denouncing any attempt to extend international communism to the western hemisphere. The resolution had particular significance because there

was at the time a pro-communist government in Guatemala. The United States gave at least moral support to exiled Guatemalans who invaded their country and seized power later in 1954.

In the Middle East, where the bitter clash between Arab nationalism and Zionism produced turmoil favorable to communism, the United States has tried to create more stable and prosperous conditions. It promptly recognized Israel in 1948, thereby contributing to apprehension among the Arabs lest the new country expand at their expense. Partly in order to reassure the Arabs it joined Great Britain and France in a Tripartite Declaration of 1950 expressing their determination to prevent any violation of a Middle Eastern frontier by a Middle Eastern country. But in 1956, following Egypt's nationalization of the Suez Canal and Israel's attack on Egypt, Great Britain and France also attacked Egypt. The United States, with general support from the United Nations, took a strong stand against its principal allies, which withdrew their troops. With the policy of the Tripartite Declaration in ruins, the United States attempted to fill the void by putting forth yet another doctrine, the Eisenhower Doctrine of 1957, offering military assistance to any Middle Eastern country that might request help against communist attack. In 1958 the United States sent troops into Lebanon, rent by civil war, at the request of that country's government, and it supported a simultaneous British occupation of Jordan; all the troops left a few weeks later.

A survey of the history of American foreign relations since World War II shows the extent to which traditional foreign policy has been transformed. Freedom of the seas (which indeed was badly wounded by the prewar neutrality legislation) is dead: in a future war a neutral nation, if such should exist, would search in vain for freedom on the high seas. The injunction, "No Entangling Alliances," is dead: probably no nation has ever been so entangled as is the United States. The Open Door Policy for China is dead (except in a most limited sense for Formosa): the United States does not even recognize the mainland government. Of the principal policies of the past only the Monroe Doctrine remains, and even it has been shorn of much of its content by the Truman Doctrine and by the virtual disappearance of its basic assumption: that an essential difference exists between the political systems of western Europe and the New World.

But if there has been a revolution in particular foreign policies, there has been a general continuity in the principal matters with which American foreign policy has been concerned: territorial expansion and Anglo-American-Canadian relations. No longer is expansion territorial in the sense of acquiring title to land (although since 1947 America has administered the Marshall, Caroline, and Mariana Islands as a member of the United Nations Trusteeship Council), but rather in the sense of acquiring military bases overseas. Relations with Canada and Great Britain are marked by the usual close economic ties grown even closer especially with Canada, and also by a new intermingling of diplomatic (with signal exceptions) and military policies.

Such have been the transformations since World War II, and the continuities since the Revolution, of the foreign policy of the United States.

FOREIGN SERVICE OF THE UNITED STATES. The Continental Congress sent diplomatic representatives to several foreign countries during the Revolutionary War, and after the adoption of the Constitution an appropriation was made for the salaries of ministers and chargés d'affaires. A law of 1792 defined the powers and duties of American consuls. These were usually merchants established in foreign cities who were compensated by the fees collected for services to shipmasters and other merchants.

In the first decades of independence, several of the Republic's leading statesmen served abroad as diplomatic representatives. Benjamin Franklin, John Adams and John Jay negotiated the peace treaty at the end of the Revolutionary War. Later, John Jay, Rufus King and James Monroe were ministers to Great Britain, and Thomas Jefferson, Gouverneur Morris and James Monroe were ministers to France. After the War of 1812, there was less interest in foreign affairs, and it became customary to appoint both diplomatic officers and consuls solely as a reward for political services, with little regard for fitness or training. The consuls, especially, were notoriously incapable and sometimes dishonest.

By the act of Aug. 18, 1856, the diplomatic and consular services were given a more definite organization. Salaries for diplomatic representatives were fixed and the post of secretary of legation was established. Consuls at certain posts were placed on a salary and forbidden to engage in trade, and a fixed tariff of fees did away with the extortion which some officers had practiced. A provision for "consular pupils," selected on the basis of fitness, looked toward the creation of a trained service, but almost all important appointments continued to be made for political reasons.

Until 1893 the United States was represented abroad only by ministers or chargés d'affaires. At many of the European courts these representatives were at a disadvantage as compared with the ambassadors from other powers, who had higher rank and direct access to the head of the state, and in 1893 the American missions in Great Britain, France, Germany and Italy were raised to embassies. Ambassadors were appointed to Russia and Mexico in 1898, to Austria-Hungary in 1902, to Brazil in 1905, to Japan in 1906, and to Turkey in 1906. The number of embassies increased gradually before World War II and more rapidly afterward. In 1960 nearly all permanent diplomatic missions were embassies.

With the increasing responsibilities that the United States was assuming as a world power and the increasing interest in foreign trade, the inadequacy of the diplomatic and consular service became painfully apparent after 1900. Conditions in the consular service, which were conspicuously bad, were materially improved by the Act of April 5, 1906. This classified consular posts on the basis of relative importance, and fixed salaries accordingly. It further provided that each consulate general or consulate should be inspected at least once in two years by officers from within the ranks of the service. No consul general, consul or consular agent receiving a salary of more than $1000 was permitted to engage in commerce within his consular district. The reorganization thus effected made it possible to place the whole consular service under a merit system, and an executive order issued by President Theodore Roosevelt on June 27, 1906, provided that vacancies in the higher classes should thenceforth be filled by promotion on the basis of efficiency and those in the lowest classes by examination.

Diplomatic secretaries were given a civil-service status by President Taft's executive order of Nov. 26, 1909. New appointments were to be made only in the lower grades, and more important positions, under the rank of minister, were to be filled by promotion for efficiency. The order also directed the Secretary of State to report to the President from time to time the names of secretaries in the higher grades who had demonstrated special capacity for promotion to be chiefs of missions. This provision paved the way for the appointment of a few career men as ministers or ambassadors between 1909 and 1913.

In 1915 Congress authorized the appointment of consular officers to classes in the service rather than to posts, and authorized the President at his discretion to transfer men from one post to another. The same act authorized the assignment of diplomatic and consular officers for service in the Department of State for periods of not more than four years at one time.

The increasing importance of relations with foreign countries made further changes in both services imperative after World War I. The consular service, since the reorganization of 1906, had been built up into a fairly efficient and well-trained organization, but salaries were still inadequate to attract and hold a sufficient number of well-qualified men. In the diplomatic service salaries were ridiculously low, for secretaries of Class I, the highest grade below the rank of minister, received only $3000 per annum before 1920 and $4000 thereafter. The field of choice in making appointments was consequently practically confined to men who had considerable independent incomes. The opportunities for advancement were still small, for career men were only occasionally and exceptionally appointed as minister or ambassador, and several of those who had been promoted from the ranks had later been removed to make places for political appointees. The complete separation between the diplomatic and consular services was another factor which diminished the usefulness of both.

The Rogers Act of May 24, 1924, effected a complete reorganization. The Foreign Service of the United States, comprising both diplomatic secretaries and consular officers, was divided into ten grades, with salaries ranging from $1500 in the lowest or unclassified grade to $9000 in Class I. Any officer might be assigned to duty in either the diplomatic or consular branch. Initial appointments were to be made after examination and a period of probation, and promotions were to be made on merit. A Foreign Service School was established for the training of newly appointed officers, and a contributory retirement system was set up. The act also authorized a more generous system of allowances. After 1924, residences for diplomatic and consular representatives were built in many foreign cities, and there was a considerable increase in the number of career men appointed as ambassadors and ministers.

The organization set up by the Rogers Act was modified by the Foreign Service Act of 1946, which authorized a new class of Career Minister, enabling officers to serve in the higher posts without separating themselves from the career service. It also provided for a Foreign Service Reserve, consisting of technical specialists recruited for temporary duty, and a Staff Corps, in which clerks and administrative officers, and also scientific and technical specialists permanently connected with the Service, were organized as a career group.

After World War II it became obvious that the number of officers in the Foreign Service must be greatly increased. There were a number of newly independent countries where diplomatic missions must be established and the new military and economic commitments of the United States forced the missions, and also the consular posts, to deal with a far wider range of problems than ever before. Additional personnel was obtained during the war by the creation of a Foreign Service Auxiliary, consisting largely of technical specialists, and after 1946 through the Foreign Service Reserve. About 165 new officers were recruited under the Manpower Act of 1946, which authorized appointments from outside to higher grades in the career service, and many similar appointments were made under a provision of the Foreign Service Act of 1946, but the Service was still inadequate numerically for the tasks that faced it. Indeed, it lost many officers and found it increasingly difficult to recruit new ones in the early 1950's, when attacks in Congress and elsewhere impaired its morale and made it seem unattractive as a career. After several studies by various groups, the recommendations of a committee headed by President Henry M. Wriston of Brown University were substantially adopted after 1954. Most of the civil service personnel doing policy work in the State Department was integrated into the Foreign Service, greatly increasing the number of officers. Recruitment at the lower levels was made easier by modifying the entrance examination, and by abolishing the language requirement, which had eliminated many candidates. At the same time the program of training under the Foreign Service Institute was broadened, especially in connection with work in foreign languages.

In 1959, there were 3638 Foreign Service officers and 1040 officers in the Foreign Service Reserve. The staff corps had a total of 3457 officers and employees. About 71% of the ambassadors and ministers serving the United States abroad were career men.

FORESTS. Nearly one third of America is covered with forests. Of the 1,903,824,000 acres comprising the United States (excluding Alaska), 647,686,000 support tree growth. Of this area, 484,340,000 acres are classed as commercial forest land, *i. e.*, producing, or capable of producing, commercial crops of timber. Coastal Alaska contains 16,508,000 acres of forest land, of which 4,269,000 acres is commercial forest land, making a total of about 489,000,000 acres in the United States including coastal Alaska. There are also large areas of forest in interior Alaska, some of which may be of commercial value. Of the 489,000,-000 acres, three fourths are in the East with the greatest concentration in the Southeast, West Gulf, and Lake States regions. The Pacific Northwest has the greatest forest area in the West.

The noncommercial area, consisting of 163,346,000 acres in continental United States and 12,239,000 in coastal Alaska, is not suitable or not available for growing commercial timber crops. Much of it is valuable, however, for watersheds, livestock grazing, wildlife, and recreational use.

These forests include about 845 different species of trees, which vary from the immense redwoods and Douglas firs of the Pacific Coast to the small, scattered piñons and junipers of the southern Rocky Mountains and the stunted alpine fir, hemlock, spruce, and limber pine of mountaintops. More than 160 have commercial value. Species used in the production of lumber, plywood, and wood pulp include Douglas fir, ponderosa pine, southern pine, white pine, oak, hemlock, gum, maple, spruce, cypress, and redwood. Over forty of the states produce commercial tree crops, but all the states contain some forests.

Values of the forest may be divided into three major categories. They supply highly important raw materials which meet the many vital needs of American citizens. They help to protect the soil from erosion and to reduce the severity of floods by regulating the runoff of water. They also furnish appealing environment for recreation.

The following, in the order of timber volume which

goes into each annually, are the major products into which the wood cut from the forests is converted: lumber, pulpwood, fuelwood, veneer logs, posts, poles, mine timbers, cooperage, and ties. These products not only provide the people of America with essential materials but also give hundreds of thousands of people an opportunity to earn a livelihood in their harvesting and manufacture. About 60,000 companies —employing more than 1,750,000 workers, all told— produce lumber and related wood products, including the finished products like paper and furniture.

The value of the forests in reducing the severity of erosion and floods varies greatly from one region to another. The rougher the topography, the more important the conservation of the forest usually is. In all cases forest devastation has some bad effect.

About one fourth, or 27%, of the commercial forest land is publicly owned and managed. These lands are in Federal, state, county, or municipal ownership. The great majority of the Federal forest lands is in national forests. There are 151 national forests comprising 180,618,433 acres in 39 states and Puerto Rico. National forests are administered by the U. S. Forest Service, an agency of the Department of Agriculture, on the principle of multiple use and sustained yield management. Under this principle forest and related areas are managed in a manner that will conserve the basic land resource while at the same time producing high-level sustained yields of water, timber, recreation, forage, and wildlife harmoniously blended for the use and benefit of the greatest number of people. Through co-operative Federal-state programs authorized by Congress, state and private forest landowners are given assistance by the Forest Service in the management and protection of their properties.

Demands of the public for the products and services of the forests are increasing at a tremendous rate. In order to meet these increased demands on national forests, Secretary of Agriculture Ezra Taft Benson in March, 1959, presented to Congress a "Program for the National Forests," which is an intensified management and development plan. Under this program, the renewable resources will be more fully used and these public forests will be made to produce, and continue to produce for all time, their maximum benefits. It sets up long-range objectives looking to the year 2000 and a short-range action plan to cover what needs to be done in the next ten to fifteen years to meet current needs.

The other three fourths, or 73%, of commercial forest lands is in private ownership. Thirteen per cent is in industrial holdings, which for the most part represent fairly large areas of timberland. Some 60% is divided among 4,500,000 farmers and other private owners, mostly in small holdings averaging less than 100 acres. Generally these small ownerships, aggregating a large part of the country's total forest land, are in very poor condition, producing far below their capacity. Getting them under more intensive management has been termed the nation's chief forestry problem. Many large timberland owners, however, are managing their lands under good forestry practices which insure a continued yield of timber.

The rapidly growing population and expanding economy of America necessitate maximum use of her forests. Since most of the commercial forest lands are in private ownership, they will be called upon to supply ever-increasing amounts of raw materials for industry. Much more intensive forestry is needed to get these lands producing the timber they should. Forest industries and public ownerships are in better condition than privately-owned lands and more prepared to expand the productivity of their forests.

To keep the forests producing at full capacity, forest-fire damage must be kept to a minimum. Forest pests and diseases must be controlled. Good forestry practices must be applied. Denuded areas must be planted to trees. Additional recreational facilities must be developed.

If all of America's available commercial forest land is vigorously managed and protected so that it produces at or near capacity, the nation's steadily increasing population will continue to have the wood and other forest resources it will need in the future.

FORGES, EARLY IMPORTANCE OF. During the 17th century most of the meager amount of iron used in the American colonies was imported from England in the form of nails, locks, tools, implements and small quantities of bar iron. The few ironworks that were established near the bog ores of the coastal region of New England during this century added somewhat to the supply. It was not until the early part of the 18th century, when ironworks began to flourish in New England and were also erected in other colonies, that the iron industry became important in colonial economic life. Before the period ended, blast furnaces which produced pig iron and castings, as well as forges which furnished bar iron for manufactures, could be found in almost all the American colonies.

Two types of early forges existed: bloomery forges (bloomeries) and refinery forges. At the former, bars of wrought iron were obtained by the primitive process of heating iron ore to a semimolten mass and hammering it under heavy hammers driven by water power. At the refinery forges, pig iron from blast furnaces was heated and hammered, reheated and rehammered, under ponderous water-driven hammers until a refined form of wrought iron was produced. The bar iron was shaped into finished products by blacksmiths who occupied an important position in iron manufacture at this time. There were hundreds of blacksmith shops scattered over the colonies where bars of forged iron were wrought into axe-heads, hoes, shovels, chains, scythes, hinges and other forms of iron products.

By 1775 there were more forges in the American colonies than in England and Wales, and the output of bar iron was larger in America than in the mother country.

As the American iron industry grew in the 18th century, attempts were made by English forge masters to influence Parliament to pass laws prohibiting or restricting colonial forges. While several Parliamentary committees seriously considered such petitions and memorials, even suggesting bills in 1719 and 1738–39 to curtail the operations of colonial forges, all efforts resulted in failure. When the Iron Act of 1750 was passed, encouragement was given to the production of colonial pig iron and bar iron, but mills producing more advanced types of iron were restricted.

"FORGOTTEN MAN, THE," was the title of a public lecture delivered by William Graham Sumner, of Yale University, in 1883. By this term he identified the man who "pays" for political and social extravagance. The term was revived by Franklin D. Roosevelt in an address at Warm Springs, Ga., May 18, 1932.

FORT: All forts are indexed under the identifying name of the fort rather than under such headings as Fort ——, except where the designation has become attached to a continuing city.

"FORTY ACRES AND A MULE" was an expression common among the Negroes in the South after the Civil War. It described the homestead for each Negro family which they expected from the confiscation of plantations. This expectation, especially prevalent before Christmas, 1865, probably arose from the division among freedmen of lands on the Southeast coast by Gen. Sherman's order, January, 1865.

FORTY-EIGHTERS. The Revolution of 1848 in Germany led to the migration of many of the choicer spirits to the United States. German influence increased greatly in Cincinnati, Milwaukee, St. Louis, Chicago and elsewhere. It became of decisive aid to the Federal Union in the congressional election of 1862 and the national election of 1864. To Francis Lieber, political scientist and most eminent German of the earlier migration, were now added such leaders in war and politics as Franz Sigel and Carl Schurz; in medicine, as Dr. Abraham Jacobi; and in business, as Henry Engelhard Steinway and Henry Villard. Not brilliant as a general, Sigel's greatest service lay in marshalling pro-Union sentiment among the German-Americans of Missouri. Similarly, Carl Schurz, whose military accomplishments at Chancellorsville were overshadowed by his record as a "mugwump" politician and reformer, remained until his death in 1906 the most eminent of all German-Americans.

FORTY FORT, WYOMING VALLEY, PA. A frontier fort, erected 1772 in the original "Forty Township," now Forty Fort Borough, named for the "First Forty" settlers sent in 1769 by the Susquehannah Company of Connecticut to take up the Wyoming lands. Enlarged in 1777, it was the militia's mustering place before the battle (massacre) of Wyoming.

FORTY-NINERS. On Jan. 24, 1848, James Wilson Marshall discovered gold in the tailrace of a sawmill which he and John A. Sutter were erecting on the South Fork of the American River, about fifty miles northeast of the present city of Sacramento, Calif. The news, first published in the San Francisco *Californian*, March 15, eventually spread throughout the world. The earliest account reached "the States" about Aug. 1, when a courier brought it to St. Joseph, Mo.; but the first printed news in the East did not appear until Aug. 19 (*New York Herald*). A nationwide trek to California soon began.

Some argonauts traveled by sea but most proceeded overland. Leaving eastern and southern ports, thousands boarded sailing vessels or clipper ships; their routes, which were wholly or partly by water, were via Cape Horn, Panama, Nicaragua or Mexico; and their sufferings included seasickness, scurvy, yellow fever, poor food and short rations. Most emigrants went by land, traveling either northern or southern trails. Those who took the former started from Missouri or Iowa early in 1849 and journeyed west via the Platte River, South Pass and Humboldt River. Those who chose the latter started from Texas, Arkansas or Missouri, crossed the Great Plains to the eastern slope of the Rocky Mountains, and proceeded thence via northern Mexico, Cooke's wagon road, the Old Spanish Trail or Salt Lake City. The overlanders organized themselves into companies before venturing upon the plains, using prairie schooners or pack animals for transportation. Of the hardships endured, cholera, scurvy and dysentery were the most fatal. Other sufferings were heat, dust, mud, deep sand and a scarcity of water and provisions; some of the latecomers encountered snow, ice and severe cold in the mountains. One company suffered heavy losses crossing a desert in southern California, which was thereafter named Death Valley.

FOUNDATIONS, ENDOWED. The foundation in its broadest sense may be defined as an instrument for the contribution of private wealth to public purpose.

In America a foundation is a nongovernmental, nonprofit organization having a principal fund of its own, managed by its own trustees or directors, and established to maintain or aid social, educational, charitable, religious, or other activities serving the common welfare.

Only a few such organizations were established in the United States before the 20th century. The first notable funds approaching this conception were the two established in 1791 under the will of Benjamin Franklin in the cities of Boston and Philadelphia, to assist "young married artificers" of good character, each of whom might be lent $300 at 5%. Portions of these funds were to accumulate for 200 years, and are still accumulating. Over the years changes have been necessary, both in investment and proposed uses of these funds.

The Magdalen Society of Philadelphia was set up as a perpetual trust in 1800 "to ameliorate the distressed condition of those unhappy females who have been seduced from the paths of virtue, and are desirous of returning to a life of rectitude." Reorganized in 1918 as the White-Williams Foundation, it now aids girls and boys in the public and parochial schools of Philadelphia who are in need of financial assistance.

Smith Charities was established in 1845 to give aid in Northampton, Mass., and certain neighboring communities to indigent boys, indigent female children, indigent widows, and young women, the last through marriage portions. The Havens Relief Fund Society, established in 1870 by Charles G. Havens, is for "relief of poverty and distress, and especially the affording of temporary relief to unobtrusive suffering endured by industrious or worthy persons."

A number of similar special-purpose trusts were placed, or later fell under, the jurisdiction of local governments. For example, the Board of Directors of City Trusts, City of Philadelphia, organized in 1869 to supervise such funds, still administers 25 minor trusts which antedate its own organization. Oldest of these is the William Carter Fund, created in 1739 "for ye use and Service of ye alms houses belonging to ye sd City (Philadelphia), and for ye relief of ye poor people in the same forever." Like it, nearly all such funds are narrowly restricted trusts that scarcely meet the modern conception of a foundation.

Somewhat closer to this conception was the Smithsonian Institution, outgrowth of a bequest to the United States of America of $508,000, later increased, from James Smithson, an English scientist, "to found at Washington, under the name of the Smithsonian Institution, an establishment for the increase and diffusion of knowledge among men." However, as primarily an operating institution and a ward of government, it differs materially from the usual philanthropic foundation.

The first substantial foundation that meets the definition was the Peabody Education Fund, set up in 1867 by George Peabody with a principal sum of over $2,000,000 to aid the stricken South. It was followed by the John F. Slater Fund in 1882, the Baron de Hirsch Fund for the aid of Jewish immigrants in 1890, and a very few other examples in the 19th century.

But at the beginning of the 20th century the foundation idea began to take deep root in American soil, and with a significant difference. Substantial endowments were set up, often in perpetuity, as in England, but frequently with wide latitude in their use. "To promote the well-being of mankind throughout the world," the purpose-clause of The Rockefeller Foundation, was not unusual. Special-purpose funds were also set up, but characteristically the larger foundations had great freedom of action. Their trustees spent less time in conserving money than in exploring new and enterprising ways of spending it. The new doctrine asserted that the funds of foundations were largely the venture capital of philanthropy, best spent when invested in enterprises requiring risk and foresight, not likely to be supported either by government or the private individual. The usual purpose was not relief or even cure; it was research, prevention, and discovery. The very word "foundation" acquired in America connotations of freedom of action.

Andrew Carnegie was a chief proponent of these ideas, first in his essay *The Gospel of Wealth,* and then in the foundations he himself established. In 1902 he set up his first important foundation, the Carnegie Institution of Washington, "to encourage, in the broadest and most liberal manner, investigation, research, and discovery, and the application of knowledge to the improvement of mankind." In the same year came the General Education Board, a Rockefeller benefaction of which Mr. Carnegie was an active trustee.

Names which have become notable in foundation history followed rapidly. The Milbank Memorial Fund and Carnegie Foundation for the Advancement of Teaching were established in 1905; Russell Sage Foundation in 1907; the New York Foundation in 1909; Carnegie Endowment for International Peace in 1910; Carnegie Corporation of New York, largest of the Carnegie benefactions and the most general in scope, in 1911; The Rockefeller Foundation, giant of the early foundations, in 1913; the Cleveland Foundation, first of the community trusts, 1914.

A few other foundations were established during this period, but they were not large. Complete records of foundations and trusts do not exist, but a series of directories, based upon available knowledge, list 27 foundations in 1915, 54 in 1920, 179 in 1926, and 185 in 1930.

The following decade, the period of the great depression, was not conducive to accumulation of surplus wealth. Some previously existing foundations disappeared, or were seriously depleted. A 1938 directory records 188 foundations altogether. However, in 1936 The Ford Foundation was incorporated in Michigan with the modest endowment of $25,000; it was destined to become the giant among all the foundations, with assets exceeding $2,700,000,000 at market value in 1960.

By the mid-1940's a new wave of foundations was

beginning to sweep over the country, induced in part by high levels of taxation resulting from World War II. Many of these were family foundations, set up by a living individual, with both contributions and direction closely held within the family group. Another large segment were company-sponsored foundations, set up by business corporations to receive substantial contributions in years of high profits—or especially high taxes—and to disburse these funds, through good years and bad, in the customary patterns of corporation giving. Both family and company-sponsored foundations differed in one significant respect from the older, traditional type; they had usually no large initial corpus, but carried on their often substantial programs with moneys received currently. Although they may accumulate corpus, typically they are "in and out" foundations rather than the endowment type.

Further to complicate the picture, foundations constantly arose that did not fit any of these categories; for example, community foundations that were amalgamations of numerous small funds, and the wholly tax-supported National Science Foundation. Also, a number of organizations devoted primarily to fund-raising, propaganda, or subsidized research have assumed the prestigeful name "foundation," to which they can show no legitimate claim.

According to estimates made by the Foundation Library Center, there were by 1959 about 5200 foundations in the United States which fall within the aforesaid definitions, and have assets of a minimal $50,000 or made grants of at least $10,000 in the latest year of record. At least 7000 of smaller size are in existence. About 1200 additional organizations of the foundation type receive tax-exempt status each year, but most are small and some are not destined for survival. Also, a few existing foundations lose tax-exempt status, become inactive, or are dissolved each year.

Assets of all American foundations at market value in 1959 were in the neighborhood of $11,500,000,000; but since a substantial part of these assets were in common stocks, they were subject to wide fluctuation. More than half of the total assets were in the hands of the hundred largest foundations.

Figures on grants from the Foundation Library Center's current (1959) survey for a recent year approximated $625,000,000. The foundations distributed their grants in the following proportions: for support of education, 41%; health and health services, 16%; scientific research, with concentration on medical and biological science, 11%; the broad field of social welfare, 15%; international affairs, 5%; the humanities, 5%; religion, 5%; studies in government, 2%.

Foundations have undergone three major congressional investigations, and some of their operations have had airings at special hearings in the House or Senate. The first investigation was in 1915, by the U. S. Senate Industrial Relations Commission headed by Sen. Frank P. Walsh, which looked into the charge that foundations were dominated by big business and were exerting strong conservative and even reactionary influences. The next two investigations—by the Select (Cox) Committee of the House in 1952 and the Special (Reece) Committee in 1953–54—took the opposite position, questioning whether the grants and actions of foundations "tend to weaken or discredit the capitalistic system as it exists in the United States and to favor Marxist socialism."

Increasing use during the 1940's of the foundation as a tax shelter for business operations, led to certain provisions affecting foundations in the Revenue Act of 1950. Under this law, with subsequent refinements, foundation income derived from business operations not related to their exempt purposes was taxed; unreasonable accumulation of income was forbidden; and tax exemption was forfeited if the organization engaged in any of a variety of "prohibited transactions," resulting in special benefits to the donor or persons related to him. Annual information returns were required, and most of this information was opened to public inspection.

As of 1960, foundations were able to spend about eight cents of the total dollar of American private philanthropy. This did not support the popular assumption that they were a reservoir of almost unlimited wealth, able to undertake vast projects at will. But because they have had long experience in giving and most of them disburse their funds with care, they have built an enviable record of accomplishment from relatively meager resources. (*See also* Ford Foundation.)

FOUR FREEDOMS. After his triumphant third-term election (1940), President Franklin D. Roosevelt began to espouse the cause of Great Britain and her allies in World War II even more strongly than before. An indication of this came in a major speech before Congress (Jan. 6, 1941) in which he urged "a world founded upon four essential human freedoms": (1) "freedom of speech and expression everywhere in the world"; (2) "freedom of every person to worship God in his own way everywhere in the world"; (3) "freedom from want . . . everywhere in the world"; (4) "freedom from fear—which, translated into world terms, means a world-wide reduction of armaments to such a point and in such a thorough fashion that no nation will be in a position to commit an act of physical aggression against any neighbor—anywhere in the world." Two of these freedoms—"from fear and want"—are mentioned as desirable objectives in the Atlantic Charter.

FOUR-H (4-H) CLUBS. A rural youth movement which had its beginning in Macoupin County, Ill., in 1900, when selected seed corn was distributed to 500 boys with instructions to plant it and to exhibit at the next farmers' county institute. Similar clubs were organized in 1902 in Clark County, Ohio. Soon the scope of the work was broadened to include the growth of other products, soil conservation and the discussion of farm problems. The movement spread rapidly and in 1904 the Ohio organizations were united into a state federation. Meanwhile boys' and girls' clubs were being organized elsewhere; by 1909 they had extended to twenty states, and within recent years have become nationwide. With the passage of the Smith-Lever Act in 1914, the Federal Department of Agriculture took over the supervision of this work for the entire country. In 1960 the membership was about 2,254,000. The symbol, derived from the 4-H chart, which consists of a number of tests for the head, hand, heart and health, is a four-leaf clover with an "H" on each leaf.

"FOUR HUNDRED, THE." In 1892 Mrs. William Astor, finding that her list of guests exceeded her ballroom's capacity, asked Ward McAllister, social arbiter in the gilded age, to reduce it to 400. McAllister afterward boasted that "there were only about four hundred people in New York society."

FOUR-POWER TREATY, signed on Dec. 13, 1921, by the United States, the British Empire, France, and Japan, was one of seven treaties which emerged from the Conference on Limitation of Armament held in Washington from Nov. 12, 1921, to Feb. 6, 1922. It was a substitute for the Anglo-Japanese alliance which, under pressure from the Dominions and the United States, Great Britain had allowed to expire in 1921, and the necessary preliminary to the other treaties and resolutions of the conference. The signatories bound themselves to respect each other's "rights in relation to their insular possessions and insular dominions in the region of the Pacific Ocean"; to go into conference for the consideration and adjustment of any controversy "arising out of any Pacific question and involving their said rights which is not satisfactorily settled by diplomacy"; and to "communicate with one another fully and frankly in order to arrive at an understanding as to the most efficient measures to be taken, jointly or separately" in the event of "the aggressive action of any other Power." The treaty was to run for ten years, and thereafter until denounced by one of the signatories. A declaration of even date applied the treaty to the mandated islands of the Pacific, without, however, signifying the assent of the United States to the mandates or preventing it from negotiating about the mandates. By a supplementary treaty of Feb. 6, 1922, the signatories declared that "insular possessions and insular dominions," when applied to Japan, included only Korafuto (southern portion of Sakhalin), Formosa, and the Pescadores, and the islands under the mandate of Japan.

FOURIERISM takes its name from Charles Fourier

(1772–1837), a pioneer French Socialist. His harmonious society was based upon the assumption that human nature is unchangeable, and that therefore society must be adapted to the individual. His ideal community consisted of 1600 persons living on a self-supporting estate of several thousand acres. Out of the common gain subsistence would be provided and surpluses would be equitably distributed among the three groups: labor, capital and talent.

In 1834 Albert Brisbane (1809–90), a young humanitarian, returned to the United States from France, where he had studied under Fourier. He proceeded to introduce Fourierism to this country, by lecturing, writing books and contributing to newspapers. Some forty small and poorly financed experiments sprang up as a result of the excitement, although Brisbane had nothing directly to do with organizing them. Brook Farm was one of the more impressive experiments; its failure in 1846 marked the end of the "Association" movement in the United States.

FOURTEEN POINTS, PRESIDENT WILSON'S. In order to counteract the evil effects of the "secret treaties," published late in 1917 by the Soviet government, President Wilson addressed Congress on Jan. 8, 1918, and stated in Fourteen Points America's terms of peace. Briefly, they were: (1) "open covenants of peace openly arrived at"; (2) freedom of the seas; (3) removal of economic barriers and equality of trade conditions; (4) reduction of armaments to lowest point consistent with domestic safety; (5) impartial adjustment of colonial claims; (6) evacuation of Russian territory and unselfish treatment of Russian problems; (7) evacuation and restoration of Belgium; (8) evacuation of France and restoration of Alsace-Lorraine to France; (9) readjustment of Italian frontiers; (10) autonomous development for the peoples of Austria-Hungary; (11) readjustments in the Balkans; (12) autonomous development for the non-Turkish nationalities of the Ottoman Empire and opening of the Dardanelles; (13) restoration of Poland with access to the sea; (14) establishment of a general association of nations. No attempt was made to secure Allied acceptance of the Points until the German government in October, 1918, applied for an armistice and peace on the basis of the Fourteen Points. After an official interpretation had been communicated to the Supreme War Council, and Col. Edward M. House, the American representative, had threatened that the United States might make a separate peace with Germany, the Fourteen Points were accepted by the Allies on Nov. 4, 1918—with the reservation that they reserved to themselves "complete freedom" on the subject of freedom of the seas and with the further understanding that "compensation will be made by Germany for all damage done to the civilian population of the Allies and their property by the aggression of Germany by land, by sea and from the air." With these limitations, the Fourteen Points thus became the legal basis for the ensuing treaty of peace.

FOX-WISCONSIN WATERWAY, from the time of its discovery by French explorers, constituted one of the best-known portage routes from the upper Great Lakes to the Mississippi, and was the main artery of transportation through what is now Wisconsin. Wisconsin River flows southwest and south until just below the narrows, called the Dells, it makes a sharp elbowlike turn to the west and finally enters the Mississippi River at latitude 43°. Near the elbow bend the Fox River rises, which flows northeast and enters Green Bay in latitude 44°. Between the bend of the Wisconsin and the upper Fox River there is a carrying place called a portage about a mile and a half in length, over level ground. The Wisconsin River in high water occasionally overflowed the portage, and boats could pass without unloading. This waterway was known to the Indians from prehistoric times. An Indian legend relates that a great serpent came down the Wisconsin, leaped across the portage and wriggled its way to Green Bay, thus accounting for the sinuosities of the upper Fox. The first travelers by this route, of whom there are records, were the French explorers, Louis Jolliet and Jacques Marquette, sent in 1673 by the officials of New France to find the central river of the continent. They ascended Fox River from Green Bay to the Mascouten village, previously visited by French traders and missionaries. Thence they were escorted to the portage, of which Marquette wrote, "Thus we left, the waters flowing to Quebec four or five hundred leagues from here to float on those that would henceforth take us through strange lands." In this way was discovered the first portage route from the Great Lakes to the Mississippi, which continued in use until the era of railroads.

The first known eastward traverse was that of Duluth after he had rescued Hennepin from the Sioux Indians and brought him to Mackinac in 1680 over the Wisconsin-Fox route. Thereafter it was continually in use by French traders, travelers, soldiers and missionaries. Nicolas Perrot went this way in 1683 to build forts on the upper Mississippi. A French expedition of 1727 passed by this route to build Fort Beauharnois for the Sioux trade. The Fox-French wars deflected some traffic to the Chicago-Illinois route. The last French expedition was the retreat in 1760 of the soldiers of the garrisons of Forts Michilimackinac and LaBaye after the capture of Montreal by the British.

During the British regime, the Fox-Wisconsin waterway was in continuous use. Before the French left, a retired soldier had established a transit at the portage by means of an oxteam. Jonathan Carver found this veteran there when in 1766 he set out to find the Northwest Passage to the Pacific. Posts and towns were built at each end of the waterway, at Green Bay and Prairie du Chien. A British expedition passed over this route in 1814 in order to dislodge an American garrison that had been established at Prairie du Chien. The next year the last British troops in Wisconsin retired by this route to Mackinac.

The Americans in 1816 safeguarded the Fox-Wisconsin portage route by building Fort Howard at its eastern end, Fort Crawford at the western. In 1828, after a serious uprising of the Winnebago Indians, Fort Winnebago was built at the portage. Its garrison was maintained until the 1840's.

FRANCHISE. The term is used to denote the right of suffrage. Individuals upon whom this right is conferred are voters or electors; collectively, they make up the electorate which may be defined as that part of the people of a state who are legally qualified to declare their will authoritatively in the choice of public officials or as regards other political matters —in direct primaries, on initiative and referendum measures, in recall elections and the like.

Idealistic statements of qualifications for the right of suffrage usually include (1) loyalty to the Constitution; (2) a sufficient amount of political intelligence; and (3) willingness to use the vote according to one's conscience for the general good of the commonwealth. However desirable loyalty, intelligence and conscientiousness may be in the abstract, it is evident that tests to determine their existence would have to be numerous and complicated; moreover, opinions differ widely as to the nature of such tests. It is not strange, therefore, that actual qualifications laid down by Federal and state constitutions and laws should deal with more tangible matters, such as age, sex, nationality, literacy, payment of taxes and period of residence in various jurisdictions.

In the course of our suffrage history two broad developments have taken place: first, the lowering or abrogation of many of the legal qualifications noted above; and, second, the conferring upon the electorate of several heavy and important new duties. During colonial days property and tax-paying qualifications were high; as a result only about three fourths of the adult white males in the North, and somewhat less than one half in the South, were qualified to vote. Immediately prior to the Revolution religious tests were still in effect in Rhode Island, New York, Virginia and Maryland, but all of those which were of a sectarian character had disappeared by 1810. The enormous sweep of suffrage extensions throughout the nation subsequently is revealed by estimates indicating that the proportion of the total population which possessed the franchise increased from only 6% in 1789 to between 40% and 45% in 1931.

At the same time that this vast extension of suffrage took place, and particularly during its later phases, a large number of new duties were placed upon the electorate. Originally the prevailing idea was that voters should choose only representatives in the legislatures. With the rise of Jacksonian democracy they were given power to elect administrative and judicial officials as well. Also, the attempt of the Founding Fathers to keep the choice of the President away from too direct influence by the voters soon broke down. By 1800 the electoral college had been subjected to party control. Beginning with Wisconsin in 1903 a further striking addition to the powers of the electorate was made by the introduction of the direct primary. As a result of this device the voters who earlier had chosen only between candidates nominated by caucuses and conventions, now began to name the candidates themselves as directly as possible. In 1913 the Seventeenth Amendment to the Constitution took the choice of United States Senators away from state legislatures and placed it in the hands of the electors. Since 1898 the initiative and referendum laws of 22 states have given voters direct power over legislation. Finally by the recall they have been placed by 12 states in a position to determine at a special election whether certain officials shall be suspended before the legal expiration of their terms. Taking all these newer powers into consideration, it is evident that the electorate, which originally was considered a silent partner in government, speaking only at the intervals legally fixed and then only to pronounce judgment as between candidates, has now become a much more active and frequent participant in a wide variety of affairs of state. On this ground there is a certain justification for adding it as a fourth to the traditional three organs of government—legislative, executive and judicial.

Suffrage history in the United States falls into three periods: (1) extension of the franchise to the white manhood of the country beginning with 1789; (2) efforts to establish Negro suffrage from the Civil War to the present time; and (3) the movement for woman suffrage which triumphed in 1920.

Beginning with the adoption of the Constitution colonial limitations upon the right to vote were lifted in one state after another so far as white males were concerned, the process being substantially complete well before the onset of the Civil War. Jefferson's doctrines and Jackson's policies contributed to the success of this democratic movement. Fierce party competition characteristic of the period caused a continual reaching out for new blocks of voters. Strong economic forces were also at work. Newly formed states in the West offered to poorer settlers not only land and opportunity but the right to vote as well; indeed, several of the Western commonwealths permitted aliens to vote merely on declaration that they intended to seek naturalization. States on the eastern seaboard were compelled to reduce their suffrage qualifications in order to meet competition from beyond the Alleghenies.

Prior to the adoption of the Constitution the nearest approach to white manhood suffrage was in Vermont, which in its Constitution of 1777 provided that "every freeman . . . who has a sufficient interest in the community" might vote. A freeman's oath was also required, binding the elector to vote for the best good of the state as established by the constitution, "without fear or favor of any man." Kentucky and Tennessee came into the Union (1792, 1796) with white manhood suffrage practically established in their constitutions. Early in the 19th century the new states formed out of the territories of the old Northwest and Southwest followed suit. The repercussion of these developments upon the eastern seaboard states was shown by the fact that in 1820 Massachusetts admitted to the suffrage all citizens who paid a poll tax. New York granted the right to vote to all white male citizens in 1826. Thereafter the democratic solution of the problem was taken more or less for granted as state after state entered the Union.

In the whole period from 1789 to 1860, during which the right to vote was being conferred upon larger and larger masses of white males, the attitude in Northern states toward free Negroes remained hostile. Thus, in 1826 New York adopted a constitutional amendment which abolished property qualifications for whites but retained them for colored persons. In 1844 New Jersey disfranchised Negroes altogether. At the outbreak of the Civil War they were permitted to vote in four states only—Maine, Massachusetts, New Hampshire and Vermont. The colored population of these states in 1850 amounted to less than one half of 1% of the total.

By the Fifteenth Amendment to the Constitution (1870), it was provided that "the right of citizens of the United States to vote shall not be denied or abridged by the United States or by any State on account of race, color, or previous condition of servitude." Immediately a fight to nullify this provision in practice was begun in the Southern states, a fight which has continued with a large measure of success to the present day. At first violence and terror, culminating with the earlier Ku Klux Klan (1865–76), were employed to keep the Negro from the polls. Election crimes such as repeating, ballot-box stuffing, and ballot-box seizures were also resorted to freely in the effort to maintain white supremacy.

As a result of these violent and illegal measures colored voters in Southern states largely ceased to exercise the right conferred upon them by the Fifteenth Amendment. Following the bitter conflicts of the Reconstruction era resort was had to other deterrents, among them "moral suasion" and various legal restrictions. To cite one example of the latter, the Mississippi Constitution of 1890 bristled with clauses designed to exclude colored citizens from the polls—without referring to them specifically: increased residence requirements which disqualified nomadic

Negroes; deprivation of civic rights on the ground of conviction for petty crimes; heavy poll-tax requirements and literacy tests. Administered by white election officials the last-named tests seldom excluded voters belonging to that race; on the other hand Negro applicants, even if able to read and write, frequently found themselves called upon to deal with lengthy Latin quotations which had been inserted in the state constitutions with the express purpose of debarring them. However, the most notable legal device used to this end was the famous "grandfather clause," which was adopted by South Carolina (1895), Louisiana (1898), North Carolina (1902) and Oklahoma (1910). Essentially, it provided that while all the suffrage restrictions noted above should remain in force otherwise, they should be waived in the cases of applicants who had voted, or whose ancestors had voted, prior to 1866. In this way, while illiterate or otherwise disqualified whites secured enrollment, the illiterate or otherwise disqualified Negroes were excluded. Appearance of conflict with the Fifteenth Amendment was avoided, since colored persons were not specifically mentioned. Nevertheless, the Supreme Court pronounced the Oklahoma Grandfather Clause unconstitutional (Guinn v. U. S., 238 U. S. 347). Subsequently a number of Southern states have sought to exclude Negroes from the primaries in which, owing to the overwhelming predominance of the Democratic party, the real decisions are made rather than in the ensuing elections. Here again, however, the Supreme Court has handed down adverse decisions (Nixon v. Herndon, 273, U. S. 536). In general, the effect of the movement to enfranchise Negroes has been fully effective only north of the Mason and Dixon line.

Agitation for woman suffrage began between 1830 and 1840; organization to that end was first effected in 1851. Ten years later Kansas entered the Union with a constitution which conferred the franchise upon women in school affairs. Several other states followed with limited grants of the right to vote in local elections. The territory of Wyoming enfranchised its women in 1869. Its admission to the Union (1890) marks an epoch in suffrage history, for the men of the new state insisted upon retaining full suffrage rights for their women who thus, for the first time, became able to vote in all elections, national as well as state and local. Within six years three neighboring states—Colorado (1893), Idaho and Utah (1896)—enfranchised their women. Thereafter the cause hung fire until, caught up by the progressive movement from 1910 onward, it scored a succession of victories, among others in the great states of California (1911) and New York (1917). In 1912 the platform of the Progressive party declared in its favor. At the national election of 1916 women were voting in eleven states. As a result, the two major parties, hitherto discreetly silent on the subject, expressed themselves somewhat cautiously in favor of the further extension of woman suffrage by state action. Meanwhile, work for the passage of the Nineteenth Amendment was being pushed vigorously. It received ratification by the legislature of the 36th state in the course of the national campaign of 1920, and was duly proclaimed a part of the Constitution Aug. 26 of that year.

Review of the three periods of suffrage history in the United States brings out various similarities and contrasts. The movement for white manhood suffrage was carried through without Federal intervention by small additions to the electorate made first in one state, then in others. Negro suffrage originated with Federal action during the embittered conflicts of the Reconstruction era. In Southern states it has been fought illegally by a variety of means, legally by a long series of state enactments. Votes for women were sought and obtained by separate constitutional amendments and laws in a large number of Western and Northern states, the effort being crowned with success by the adoption of an amendment to the Federal Constitution. At present white manhood suffrage and woman suffrage are everywhere accepted; on the other hand resistance to Negro suffrage persists. In general the United States possesses a suffrage as inclusive as that of any other democratic country except England.

FRANCO-AMERICAN ALLIANCE OF 1778. The outbreak of the American Revolution found France waiting for an opportunity for revenge against Great Britain for the dismemberment enforced by the Treaty of Paris in 1763. That opportunity, which presented itself in the form of a chance to rend asunder the British colonial empire by intervention in the American Revolution, was quickly discerned by Beaumarchais, influential courtier and well-known French *littérateur*, who had conversations with Arthur Lee, agent of the Continental Congress in London, in 1775. Beaumarchais' perspicuous confidential memoirs on the subject of French intervention aided the French Minister of State, the Comte de Vergennes, to propose a policy of secret assistance to the revolted colonies. The King's Council decided in favor of this in May, 1776, before the Declaration of Independence, and before any agent of the Continental Congress had set foot on the soil of France, with the result that the French government immediately and covertly extended such assistance in the guise of sales of munitions, from French arsenals, through Beaumarchais' fictitious commercial company, Rodrigues Hortalez et Cie. The French government really had decided to donate these supplies, but when Vergennes and Beaumarchais saw the instructions of Silas Deane, first agent of Congress to appear in France, to buy these things on credit, Beaumarchais naturally sold, instead of gave, the munitions. Loans (a total of 1,000,000 livres) and subsidies (3,000,000 livres, plus 1,000,000 which the King of France induced the King of Spain to give) during the period of French neutrality, enabled the revolted colonies to carry on, and to win the important victory of Saratoga (October, 1777).

After the Declaration of Independence, Congress appointed a joint diplomatic commission to France consisting of Silas Deane, Benjamin Franklin and Arthur Lee. They sought, at first, French recognition of American independence and loans, later an actual alliance, when it became apparent that recognition was not possible without an alliance, since recognition would mean war for France with Great Britain. Until the end of 1777 Vergennes continued a policy of watchful waiting and refused formally to recognize the American mission; watchful waiting accompanied by secret assistance and deceitful neutrality; watchful waiting for some auspicious military event which would assure the ultimate triumph of the American cause should France intervene in its favor.

The surrender of Burgoyne at Saratoga proved the decisive event. After that stunning defeat the North government in England decided to send a peace commission to America to try to patch up a peace of home rule within the Empire. It became evident to Vergennes that he must act immediately. His decision was made all the more quickly when he found Franklin and Deane conspicuously flirting with secret emissaries of Lord North. Without consulting Spain Vergennes promised the commission (Dec. 17, 1777) that France would make a treaty with the United States, thus recognizing its independence. Several weeks of risky delay followed while Vergennes unsuccessfully endeavored to get Spain to come into a triple alliance. On Feb. 6, 1778, Vergennes signed two treaties with the independent United States, one a treaty of amity and commerce based on the freedom of the seas, the other a treaty of alliance in case recognition of the United States should bring war with Great Britain, as it did. The alliance provided that neither party would make peace without the consent of the other, and that there should be no peace until the independence of the United States, absolute and unlimited, should be secured by treaty or by truce. Thereafter, France would guarantee the independence of the United States, according to the boundaries established in the peace, and the United States would guarantee the possession by France of her West Indian Islands.

The alliance successfully weathered diplomatic vicissitudes during the war and during the ensuing peace negotiations, and brought the conflict to a victorious end, thanks to the joint efforts culminating at Yorktown, and to continued French loans (total 35,000,000 livres, or $6,352,000, paid back 1792–95) and subsidies (10,500,000 livres, or $1,996,500).

The conditional and preliminary articles of peace were not a violation of the alliance—indeed they were quite agreeable to the purposes of Vergennes' Spanish diplomacy. France did not invoke the alliance in 1793 during her next war with Great Britain, preferring the benefits of American neutral carriage. Jay's Treaty of 1794 with England did not violate the alliance either, but it provoked an imbroglio and undeclared hostilities with France, ended by the Convention of 1800 which re-established peace.

FRANKLIN, BATTLE OF (Nov. 30, 1864). The day following Gen. J. B. Hood's (C.) failure to cut off Schofield (U.) at Spring Hill, the Confederate Army under Hood's command pursued northward to Franklin. The Union troops were ready. Hood, chagrined by his previous failure and goaded by the necessity for a quick decision, rashly attacked. He suffered several bloody repulses with the loss of many men and thirteen general officers. After dark Schofield retired northward to Nashville, where he joined the force being gathered by Gen. George H. Thomas. Hood's defeat gave Thomas time to organize an effective defense.

FRANKLIN, STATE OF (1784–88). When North Carolina in 1784 ceded her western lands to the United States with a view to avoiding the expenses of protecting the western settlements, and in the interest of land speculators who had acquired large holdings under the state's land acts of 1782–83, the natural result was a movement, among the inhabitants of the eastern part of the region ceded, in favor of the formation of a new state. Encouraged by separatists in southwest Virginia and by the adoption in Congress of the Jefferson ordinance authorizing the establishment of new commonwealths in the West, the Wataugans assembled at Jonesboro in August and December, 1784, and organized the "State of Franklin," considering the action necessary for the maintenance of orderly government, defense from Indian attacks and protection of land titles. When North Carolina immediately repented her action, repealed the cession act, and attempted to remove some of the western grievances, John Sevier and other western leaders, fearing the effects of separation upon their land dealings in the Tennessee country and at the Muscle Shoals, advised reconciliation. Unable to check the Franklin movement, they seized the "reins of power," and adopted a constitution validating North Carolina land titles. With Sevier as governor, the state maintained a precarious existence for four years, characterized by Indian troubles, intrigues with the Spanish, and ineffectual efforts to obtain recognition from Congress and North Carolina. The chief cause of failure was the opposition of a rival faction led by John Tipton, which contributed materially to North Carolina's success in re-establishing jurisdiction by 1789.

FRANKLIN STOVE, invented 1742 by Benjamin Franklin, was a device for giving greater warmth, more comfort, and more healthful heating at a lower fuel cost. His idea, drafted in co-operation with his friend Robert Grace, master of Warwick Furnace, consisted of a low stove, equipped with loosely fitting iron plates through which air might circulate and be warmed before passage into the room. This "New Pennsylvania Fireplace" avoided drafts, gave more even temperatures throughout the room, and checked loss of heat through the chimney. The plan was probably a development of an earlier ten-plate stove, and was, in turn, supplanted by the newer cannon-stove invented at Lancaster a decade later.

FRAYSER'S FARM, BATTLE OF (June 30, 1862). After Savage Station McClellan (U.) got his force across White Oak Swamp while Lee hurried to hit the exposed Union column marching through thick country toward the James. Near Frayser's Farm and the settlement of Glendale, Longstreet and A. P. Hill (C.) struck east but were checked after slight successes, as Union troops there were numerically superior. Holmes and Jackson (C.) then failed to carry out Lee's converging plan and encircle McClellan, who withdrew to Malvern Hill.

FREDERICKSBURG, BATTLE OF (Dec. 13, 1862). Following Gen. McClellan's (U.) defeat at Sharpsburg, command of the Army of the Potomac was given to Gen. Burnside (U.) who made Richmond, instead of the Army of Northern Virginia, his objective. Gen. Lee (C.) outmarched him to Fredericksburg and placed his army of about 78,000 on the high ground from one to two miles south of the Rappahannock. His lines roughly paralleled the river for more than six miles. Burnside slowly concentrated his 122,000 on the northern bank, with difficulty drove the Confederate sharpshooters out of Fredericksburg and crossed to the southern bank, where he drew his lines for battle on Dec. 13. The Confederate right flank rested on no natural obstacle, but only one major assault was made on the right of Lee's line during the entire day, and this was repulsed. The main battle was fought at the base of Marye's hill, where a sunken road provided a natural breastwork for the Confederates. Wave after wave of Union infantry was broken and rolled back by the devastating fire from this road. Fourteen charges cost 6300 men before nightfall ended the battle along the entire line, after 10,208 Unionists and 5209 Confederates had been killed or wounded. Burnside planned to renew the attack on the 14th but was dissuaded by his commanders. His plans frustrated by his defeat, Burnside withdrew his demoralized army north of the Rappahannock during the night of the 15th and was subsequently relieved of his command, which was given to Gen. Joseph Hooker.

FREE SILVER. The movement for the free coinage of silver, superficially an agitation for the adoption of a specific monetary policy, was much more than that. Springing from the very roots of the American social order, it was the political manifestation of a theory of currency, of sectional antagonism, of class bitterness, and of conscienceless political intrigue. Condemned by competent authority as unsound and unworkable, "free silver" was nonetheless for millions a crusade for economic justice and social betterment.

In 1853 bimetallism was abolished for the five-, ten,- twenty-five- and fifty-cent silver pieces. Unhappily the law said nothing about the silver dollar, an unknown coin which had virtually never circulated. The oversight left the country, legally, on the double standard at the old 1837 ratio of sixteen to one. In 1873 a revision of the coinage laws, which had been before Congress three years and had been considered line by line by dozens of committees, dropped the silver dollar, thus establishing the single gold standard.

In 1873 a combination of events of world-wide scope resulted in a violent fall in the value of silver. The value of the silver in a dollar fell below that of a gold dollar and a little later below the value of the current greenback dollar. The owners of the silver bullion pouring out of the newly developed mines in the West, seeking desperately some artificial support, realized that if free coinage at sixteen to one were permitted they would have an unlimited market for silver, with a profit on every dollar of the difference between the metal value and the coinage value.

They started a drive for "free silver," their case resting on four unsound contentions: that the law of 1873 was secretly railroaded through Congress, that the silver dollar was the traditional currency of the common people, that the panic of 1873 was caused by the "demonetization" of silver, and that "restoration" of free silver would increase the monetary supply, raise prices and end depression.

The distressed farmers, the Populist and Granger elements, and the economically untrained in general accepted these propositions and demanded free silver. From the early 1870's to the middle 1900's the establishment of bimetallism was the leading issue in America. It was narrowly averted time after time, on two occasions only by the passage of laws giving silver producers a government subsidy.

These subsidy measures precipitated the panic of 1893. In the face of this fact the silver movement captured the Democratic party, up to this time less prone to yield subsidies than the Republicans. The bitter campaign of 1896, with its "Coin's Financial School" and "Cross of Gold" keynotes, resulted in the defeat of Bryan. In March, 1900, Congress passed the Gold Standard Act, but in the campaign of that year Bryan again made free silver an issue.

The economic aspects of the free-silver movement are inevitably a part of its history. With sixteen ounces of silver worth less than one ounce of gold, free coinage would destroy gold as a medium, put the country on a debased silver standard, cause chaos in foreign trade, and engender a crisis. During the entire period of the free-silver movement a silver dollar was worth less than a dollar in gold, and in the Bryan campaigns the value was around fifty cents. Adoption of free silver would have meant national financial suicide.

The world depression (1929 *et seq.*) drove silver to the lowest depths in history, a dollar being worth eighteen cents at the bottom point. But the movement was revived in Congress in 1933, and in that year 33 U. S. Senators voted for free silver at sixteen to one. Devaluation of the gold dollar in 1934 changed the actual ratio of the two dollars to twenty-seven to one, and "free silver at sixteen to one," never rational economically, ceased to have any significance traditionally.

FREE SOIL PARTY was the commonly accepted designation of the movement organized at Buffalo on Aug. 9, 1848. As antislavery-extension sentiment developed and found expression in the Wilmot Proviso formula, considerable Northern dissatisfaction with the evasive policy of the old parties appeared. The New York Democratic "Barnburners" not only broke away from the regular organization but, meeting on June 22 and 23, 1848, undertook the nomination of their leader, Martin Van Buren, for the Presidency. Simultaneously a convention at Columbus, O., dominated by "Conscience" Whigs proclaimed dissatisfaction with the regular parties and called a national convention to meet at Buffalo on Aug. 9. These elements, together with the Liberty party and a group of land reformers, now co-operated in the broader movement which nominated a ticket of Martin Van Buren and Charles Francis Adams. Their platform announced a policy of "no more slave states and no more slave territory" and of free homesteads to actual settlers. Van Buren polled 291,263 votes, largely in New York State and in the Northwest; by running second in New York he prevented the election of Lewis Cass. A dozen members of Congress, who later held the balance of power in the lower House, and a considerable number of state legislators, indicated a fair success for the movement. The campaign of 1852 in support of the candidacy of John P. Hale saw the Free Soil vote fall to 156,667. Two years later its disorganized remnants found a logical successor in the newly forming Republican party.

FREEDMEN'S BUREAU was a Federal agency created by an act of Congress passed March 3, 1865, and granted very wide powers by a second act passed in 1866 over the veto of President Johnson. The purpose of the bureau was to aid the former slaves in adjusting themselves to a life of freedom. It furnished food and clothing to needy Negroes and aided them to find employment. It provided homesteads on public lands and supervised labor contracts to insure justice to the ignorant slaves. It established hospitals and schools for the freedmen and protected their civil rights in unfriendly Southern communities.

The bureau operated under the War Department and maintained an elaborate organization in every Southern state. Gen. Oliver O. Howard served as commissioner, by presidential appointment, throughout the life of the bureau. He divided the South into ten districts with an assistant commissioner in charge of each. To carry out the manifold duties assigned to the bureau a large number of other officers were used in each division.

From the beginning the bureau was subjected to severe criticism. Democrats in Congress charged that it was unconstitutional and unnecessary. It was accused of engaging in politics in the interests of the Republican party. Its financial affairs were badly managed at times and some of its agents misappropriated funds. Much criticism came from the South where the bureau was accused of fomenting race hatred and advancing the Negro at the expense of the rights of the white population.

It was originally proposed to discontinue the bureau June 16, 1868, but by various acts of Congress it was continued until June 30, 1872, although many of its duties were abolished or transferred to other government agencies before that time.

FREEHOLDER. Tenure of land "in free and common socage" became the prevailing system in the colonies and with endless acreage available for settlement feudal survivals were greatly modified and eventually disappeared with the establishment of independence. The colonial laws, however, influenced by the county franchise system of England, attached great importance to the possession of a freehold both for suffrage and officeholding. Seven colonies restricted the suffrage to freeholders, the others permitting persons owning other forms of property of sufficient extent to vote. Statutes defined the minimum freehold for town or rural residents. The democratic forces released by the Revolution were soon directed against such restrictions on "the right to vote," and while the freeholder retained his privileged position in a few states until the Jacksonian era, universal suffrage became dominant in American politics.

FREEMAN'S FARM, FIRST BATTLE OF (Sept. 19, 1777); also known as First Battle of Bemis Heights, or Stillwater. On the morning of Sept. 19, Gen. John Burgoyne started his army south in three columns against Gen. Horatio Gates, intrenched on Bemis Heights, scarcely four miles distant. At Freeman's Farm, over a mile from Gates's headquarters the English right and center columns encountered troops under Colonels Daniel Morgan and Henry Dearborn. Here fighting centered. Throughout the day Americans dribbled into the firing line, failing to co-ordinate their efforts. Like true frontiersmen they took advantage of woods and gullies and employed their marksmanship to distinct advantage. The British used volleys and salvos with little effect; they succeeded better with spirited charges and the use of sword and bayonet. During the late afternoon reinforcements from the left enabled the Americans to hold firm. With darkness, firing ceased. The field of battle was left in the hands of the British, who had lost 600 "killed, wounded, or taken." American casualties were little over half the same number. Burgoyne had been thwarted in opening a way to Albany; the Americans began to feel that they could cope with the best British soldiers in close fighting on difficult terrain.

FREEMAN'S FARM, SECOND BATTLE OF (Oct. 7, 1777); also known as Second Battle of Bemis Heights, or Stillwater. With winter approaching and rations diminishing, Gen. Burgoyne was under the necessity of retreating or joining his forces with those of Sir Henry Clinton on the lower Hudson. During the morning of Oct. 7, Burgoyne sent out 1500 troops to reconnoiter Gates's position at Bemis Heights. By 2:30 P.M. they had reached the American left and were hotly engaged with troops that Gates had despatched to meet them. Suffering more than 400 casualties in less than an hour, the British began to fall back. Benedict Arnold, without orders, assumed a command, and pursued the enemy to their intrenched camp. Under his dynamic leadership the attack successfully continued to the late afternoon. Then he was wounded, and, almost simultaneously, recalled. Fighting ceased as darkness fell. Burgoyne had inflicted slight losses and had failed; his escape lay only in retreat.

FREEMEN. Throughout the colonial period this term was commonly used to mean freeholders, possessors of land in fee simple, and was so defined in the laws of Pennsylvania and other colonies. This class alone in the majority of the colonies had the right to participate in the government of the colony and to vote for members of the colonial assemblies. In some communities admission by the magistrates to the freedom was necessary in addition to ownership of land. In Massachusetts and some of the other New England colonies religious qualifications or guaranty of good conduct were required. Only in the chartered cities of New York and Albany in the colony of New York did the term freeman have economic significance. The charters of these two cities forbade any merchant to do business or any craftsman to ply his trade without admission to the freedom by the magistrates and payment of the required fees.

FREEPORT DOCTRINE was Douglas' doctrine that in spite of the Dred Scott decision slavery could be excluded from territories of the United States by unfriendly local legislation. Although propounded earlier and in other places, this solution of the apparent inconsistency between "popular sovereignty" and the Dred Scott decision came to be known as the Freeport doctrine because Douglas advanced it in answer to a question by Lincoln in the Freeport debate. By it Douglas was able to hold his Illinois followers and secure re-election to the Senate, but the extensive publicity it received killed his chance of Southern support for the Presidency in 1860.

FRÉMONT EXPLORATIONS. John Charles Frémont led five expeditions into the Far West. In the first, June to October, 1842, he crossed the plains and mountains to southern Wyoming and ascended Frémont's Peak. His most important expedition began in May, 1843, and ended in July, 1844. In this he explored the region immediately north of the Great Salt Lake, the Snake and Columbia River valleys, the Klamath Lake country, eastern Nevada, through Kit Carson Pass to Sutter's Fort, and returned east by way of the San Joaquin Valley and the Old Spanish trail. In July, 1845, crossing again to California, he ascended Sacramento Valley to Oregon and returned by way of that same valley to California where the last official expedition was terminated when Frémont became involved in the conquest, June, 1846. His fourth and fifth expeditions (October, 1848, to February, 1849; and September, 1853, to February, 1854) were organized to explore a route for a railroad across the Rockies in the vicinity of 37° and 38° N. Lat. They were privately financed, added nothing to Frémont's fame, and contributed no practical information for prospective railroads to the Pacific.

FRENCH AND INDIAN WAR, extending from 1754 to 1763, was the final struggle between the French government, and its colonies in America, and the English government and its colonies in America for imperialistic control of the North American continent. In its broader aspect, it was the result of the clash of French and English colonial frontiers. As such, it was a part of and was overshadowed by the Seven Years' War which embroiled Europe from 1756 to 1763. In its narrower aspect, however, it was the result of the rivalry of French and English colonists in North America.

The English settlements were confined to the region along the Atlantic seaboard from Maine to Florida, and to the west as far as the Appalachian Mountains, although some of the English colonies by their charters had claims to lands west of the mountains. The French settlements, developing from fur-trading posts, extended from the mouth of the St. Lawrence River up its course to the Great Lakes, with tentacles reaching southward to Lake Champlain; along the Great Lakes; and to the southward along the Mississippi River to St. Louis and New Orleans. Thus, the French by a so-called encirclement plan hoped and threatened to restrict English settlements to the relatively small area east of the mountains. From 1689 to 1784, throughout three previous wars, both the French and the English colonists struggled for control of the lucrative fur trade of the hinterland and for the land itself, primarily for speculative purposes because, as yet, there was an insufficient number of settlers to occupy the land. Furthermore, a rivalry between the French and English colonists along the Atlantic seaboard for fishing privileges off the Grand Banks of Newfoundland engendered animosities which contributed to the outbreak of the French and Indian War.

Both the French and English colonists attempted to project their control into the Ohio region in the period from 1748 to 1753 by means of peaceful penetration. A group of Virginia planters formed the Ohio Company for the purpose of fur trading and land settlement in the West, procured a grant of a half million acres south of and along the Ohio River, May 19, 1749, and sent Christopher Gist to explore the country in 1750. In 1749 Céloron de Bienville, for the French, made a journey by way of Lake Erie, the Allegheny River, the Ohio, the Miami and the Maumee, from whence he returned to Quebec by way of the Great Lakes. Céloron's task had been to plant leaden plates proclaiming French control of the region and to urge English fur traders to leave the region.

The French in 1753 began the construction of a chain of forts from Presque Isle, along the Allegheny River, to the Forks of the Ohio, thus invading territory claimed by the colony of Virginia under the charter of 1609. Gov. Dinwiddie of Virginia, alarmed by the actions of the French, sent George Washington in November of 1753 to warn the French that they were advancing on English soil, and to make observations upon a suitable site for a fort. The following year Washington was authorized to construct a fort at the Forks of the Ohio (Pittsburgh), but was unsuccessful because of the earlier and more aggressive efforts of the French who, in that year, completed the line of forts from Presque Isle to LeBœuf to Venango and Duquesne. The French even forced Washington to capitulate at Great Meadows and return with his forces to Virginia.

The following year, 1755, Gen. Edward Braddock cut his way from Virginia along the wilderness trails to the Monongahela River only to be surprised and badly defeated by the French whom he had expected to oust from Fort Duquesne. The French were thus left in control of forts extending from Lake Champlain to Lake Erie and to the Forks of the Ohio. The English activities were unsuccessful until after the reorganization of the English army by Lord Pitt.

In 1758 Lord Pitt projected a plan of war which included expeditions against the French at many points. Gen. John Forbes, marching across Pennsylvania, was ordered to reduce Fort Duquesne. Generals James Abercrombie and Lord Howe were to attack in the Lake Champlain region. Gen. Jeffry Amherst was expected to destroy the French fort at Louisburg, which fell July 26, 1758. The French fort, Frontenac, fell Aug. 27, 1758, thus breaking the French line of communication with the Ohio region. Fort Duquesne was abandoned and burned by the French prior to the arrival of Forbes' advance guard on Nov. 25, 1758. The following year an attack was made on Quebec, the capital of the fast crumbling French empire in North America. Gen. James Wolfe, scaling the Heights of Abraham, defeated the French under the Marquis de Montcalm, Sept. 13, 1759, and four days later Quebec was formally surrendered to the British. Montreal was surrendered Sept. 7, 1760. The French and Indian War was over and only the division of the French territory remained for treatment in the Treaty of Paris, 1763.

FRENCH EXPLORATION IN THE WEST (1609–1833) was actuated by a desire to extend the fur trade, to carry the gospel to the Indians, to find a route to China, and to satisfy a love for adventure. Although Spaniards were first in the South and Southwest, the French preceded the English beyond the Alleghenies, gave the French designation of *prairie* to the western grasslands and named the Rocky Mountains as well as numerous rivers, mountains and cities of the West.

No sooner had Champlain founded Quebec in 1608 than he and his men began exploring the St. Lawrence basin. He discovered Lake Champlain in 1609 and visited both Lakes Huron and Ontario in 1615, voyaging to Huron by way of the Ottawa so that he missed Erie. His subordinate, Jean Nicolet, discovered Lake Michigan while on his way to the Winnebagoes of the present Wisconsin in 1634. All five of the Great Lakes are located in their correct relative positions on a French map of 1650.

Systematic exploration of the Mississippi basin began with LaSalle, who may have descended the Ohio to the falls at the present Louisville as early as 1669. Jolliet and Marquette voyaged in 1673 from Green Bay up Fox River and down the Wisconsin to the Mississippi, descended the Mississippi to the Arkansas and came back to Lake Michigan by way of the Illinois. Exploration of the Mississippi to the Gulf was completed by LaSalle in 1682. In the north, Duluth pushed southwest from Lake Superior and there met Father Hennepin, who ascended the Mississippi from the Illinois in 1680.

Knowledge of the south was extended after LaSalle, attempting to bring a colony to the Mississippi by sea, landed through error at Matagorda Bay in 1684, and there built Fort St. Louis, the first Texas settlement. After his death, Henri Joutel, a lieutenant, led six of the colonists to Canada, exploring much of the present Texas and Arkansas en route. Henri Tonti, LaSalle's commander at Starved Rock on the Illinois, in a vain effort to find and rescue the surviving colonists, ascended the Red River from the Mississippi as far as Texas in 1690. Other exploration of the south was continued from Mobile and New Orleans after the founding of Louisiana in 1699.

The westward march across the Great Plains commenced in 1713 when St. Denis traveled from Natchitoches on Red River to San Juan on the Rio Grande in an unsuccessful effort to trade with Mexico. Four years later Gov. Bienville of Louisiana sent two expeditions to the Prairies. One under Bernard de la Harpe advanced from Natchitoches up the Red River almost to the Wichita Mountains, turned northeast to the Arkansas and followed it back to the Mississippi. The other, led by Claude Charles du Tisne, traveled from Kaskaskia up the Missouri and cross country from the Osage village to the Wichita village on the Arkansas. Bourgmont and other *coureurs de bois* became familiar with the Missouri River and the Missouri tribes as far north as the Platte during the dozen years he was a fugitive from punishment for desertion in 1706 from his military command at Detroit. His crime being condoned, he was reinstated in the army and he built Fort Orleans on the Missouri in 1723, whence he led an expedition to the Comanches in the Smoky Hill Valley of the present Kansas in 1724.

The first known Frenchmen to complete the crossing of the Great Plains to the Rockies were Pierre and Paul Mallet, who journeyed from the Missouri at the mouth of the Platte to Santa Fe in 1739 and returned down the Arkansas to the Mississippi the following year. They guided Fabry de Bruyere up the Canadian River in the present Oklahoma in an attempt to reach Santa Fe in 1742; but, owing to the incompetence of the commander, the expedition failed. First to arrive at the Rockies in the north were two sons of La Vérendrye. The father and two sons left their trading posts on the Manitoba Lakes in 1739 and blazed a trail to the Mandan village on the Missouri in the present North Dakota. Three years later the two sons passed the Big Horn Range to the Rockies.

Other traders and trappers, many of them unknown, threaded their way up every important stream of the Mississippi basin. They knew the West so well that they guided the Lewis and Clark expedition beyond the Yellowstone in 1805; and, even west of the Rockies, George Droulliard of St. Louis was invaluable to the expedition because of his skill in sign language and in hunting. Descendants of French pioneers continued to take an important part in the fur trade and exploration west of the Rockies until the beaver market collapsed in 1833.

FRENCH SPOLIATION CLAIMS. These claims may be divided into two general classes, those arising between 1793 and 1798 and those arising chiefly between 1800 and the end of the Napoleonic wars. The first were settled in part when, through ratification of the Convention of 1800, the United States relinquished claims, amounting to about $20,000,000, in return for a release from the 1778 treaty of alliance with France. The claims of American citizens against France for loss of ships and cargoes then became claims against the United States. After years of persistent effort by the original claimants and their descendants, Congress, between 1885 and 1925, made provision for paying the claims at the rate of about 25 cents for each dollar.

A further disposition of early claims was made in the Louisiana Purchase Treaty of 1803 which specified that the United States should pay "debts" due its citizens by France to an amount not to exceed 20,000,000 francs.

The second, and most controversial, class of spoliation claims grew chiefly out of French seizures and confiscations of American ships and cargoes under a series of decrees issued by Napoleon between 1806 and 1810. These were the Berlin decree of 1806, the Milan decree of 1807, the Bayonne decree of 1808, the Vienna decree of 1809, and the Rambouillet decree of 1810. Additional claims were based on actions prior to 1803. The total claims amounted to over $12,000,000, exclusive of interest.

During the administrations of Presidents Madison, Monroe, and J. Q. Adams, unsuccessful attempts were made to secure a settlement of these claims. When Andrew Jackson became President in 1829, he sent William C. Rives to Paris as minister with instructions to press the subject vigorously. Rives presented the claims, but they were rejected in June, 1830.

Following the July Revolution which brought Louis Philippe to the French throne in place of Charles X, Rives again took up the subject. A commission was appointed which, after considerable negotiation, decided that 25,000,000 francs should be paid in settlement of the claims. A treaty was accordingly concluded on July 4, 1831, and, after an exchange of ratifications, was proclaimed about a year later.

The amount promised was to be paid in six annual installments beginning one year from the date of ratification. When that time arrived, the American Government, through its financial agent, the Bank of the United States, presented a draft which was protested by France. No appropriation for the payment had been provided by the French Parliament.

There followed a heated controversy, which came to a climax early in 1836 when diplomatic relations were suspended. War clouds were dissipated, however, by a British offer of mediation. The French paid the four installments which were past due and paid the remainder when due. Thereafter, 1567 American claimants were awarded the money received pro rata. The final settlement was at the rate of about fifty-nine cents for a dollar, for the total awarded by a special commission was $9,352,193 while the six installments with interest paid by France yielded $5,558,108.

FRIES REBELLION (1799) is the term applied to the armed resistance of certain farmers in Bucks and Northampton counties in Pennsylvania to a Federal tax on land and houses. Their opposition grew out of a misunderstanding of the means of evaluating the houses, *i.e.*, by the number and size of their windows. The farmers understood this to mean that they were to pay a window tax. Women in protest poured scalding water on the assessors when they were measuring the windows, whence the term "The Hot Water Rebellion." John Fries, a traveling auctioneer or vendue crier, was their leader. The insurgents forcibly prevented the assessors from functioning in Bucks County, and compelled the release of men who had been imprisoned at Bethlehem in North-ampton County for similar resistance to the tax. Federal troops were sent, and the rebellion was put down. John Fries was captured, twice tried for treason, and along with two other men, sentenced to be hanged. The date of the execution had been set, when Fries obtained a pardon from President John Adams.

FRIGATES were large sailing cruisers of relatively high speed, carrying their main armament of 28 to 50 guns on one deck. Eighteen such vessels were built or purchased during the Revolution. In 1794 Congress ordered six vessels of this type, the *United States, Constitution, President, Constellation, Congress,* and *Chesapeake*. These, with other frigates built subsequently, were chiefly responsible for American success in the war with the Barbary States and the War of 1812.

FRITCHIE, BARBARA, AND THE FLAG. A famous Civil War legend, given long life by the poet Whittier, was that of the elderly Mrs. Fritchie, who lived in Frederick, Md., when the Confederate army passed through in September, 1862. Seeing a Union flag in her window, so the story ran, "Stonewall" Jackson ordered his men to fire at it. The old lady rushed to the window, seized the riddled flag and waved it defiantly. Jackson, touched by her bravery, thereupon decreed death to any soldier who molested her. The story was untrue. Mrs. Fritchie, who was aged 96 at the time, feebly waved a small Union flag from her porch when Federal troops marched through six days later, but the testimony both of Jackson's staff and of her own family is that she and Jackson never saw each other.

FRONTENAC, FORT, was erected at Cataraqui by Count Frontenac in 1673, within the present confines of Kingston, Ontario. On May 13, 1675, the seigniory was granted to LaSalle, who built Fort Frontenac on the earlier foundation, using it as a base for his explorations to the south. In 1683 the post was confiscated by LaBarre and became a storehouse for trade until abandoned in 1684.

In 1687, Denonville, en route with his expedition against the Iroquois, garrisoned the post. During the winter of 1688, the garrison suffered greatly from scurvy and starvation. The following year, the fortifications were blown up under orders of Denonville and further destroyed by the Indians in 1695. In 1696, Frontenac repaired the fortress and regarrisoned it, and from that period it was used as a base for trade. On Aug. 27, 1758, it was captured and destroyed by Col. John Bradstreet.

In 1789, when Kingston became a military depot, a wooden barracks for men and one-story houses for officers were constructed within the curtains of the old fort and enclosed with a stockade, the old French tower in the northeast angle being used as a magazine. In 1819 the fort was demolished.

FRONTIER, TURNER THEORY OF THE. In 1893 a young professor in the University of Wisconsin, Frederick Jackson Turner, produced a brief paper on "The Significance of the Frontier in American History." Born in a region just ceasing to be a frontier, schooled in a state possessing the greatest of manuscript collections relating to frontier experience, trained at a time when the results of economic forces were commanding study, Turner inquired why the United States was as it was. He noted that the solvent population of the United States, the whites, came only from the races that had built the civilizations of Western Europe. Yet in America the children of the immigrants had begun by the 18th century to play the part of changelings: they were not Europeans, but were Americans. He looked for causes of the transformation, finding no single variation of great consequence in the environment except in the fact that in the North American settlements of England the children of Europeans had come into contact with relatively unlimited quantities of cheap arable land.

Once glimpsing the notion that the open frontier with its cheap land might have been a causal force, Turner beheld the American picture in a new perspective. From the earliest settlements at Atlantic tidewater until the latest on the western edge of the high plains, Americans had lived within easy reach of cheap land. In their old homes they knew little but dependence for the dirt farmer, for whom nearly every language had a common name suggesting something less than freedom. In America there was independence for the taking; freedom at a low level to be sure; but freedom. Turner's inquiry as to the significance of this led him to the modest suggestion that in the process of occupying the continent forces were created or released that built the mental structure of the American, shaped his ideas of government and contributed to the development of his institutions.

The essay on "Significance" did little more than suggest the theme. For the rest of his life Turner, and his students, tested its applications in many places and many periods, while no important voices challenged the validity of his hypothesis until after his death. From his continuing studies came the third meaning of frontier: that of process. As a social process he conceived frontier as a state of society in which ancient life and old ideas were undergoing continuous adaptation to the requirements of new communities, usually freed from the dead hand of the past. For 300 years the process was under way without check, as young men created farms, as farmers created local governments, as states succeeded territories, and as National Government smoothed the processes of home rule. Throughout it all ran evidence suggesting that from the cheap land came influences to break down the definitions of conservative society, to encourage the initiative of the individual citizen, to build up a spirit for home rule, to encourage political democracy as teammate with economic equalitarianism, to advance at once the federal structure of the Government of the United States and the exercise of national authority by that Government.

FUGITIVE SLAVE ACT OF 1850, part of the Compromise of 1850, was the South's vain attempt to supplant the ineffectual Fugitive Slave Law of 1793 by one which would suppress the aiding of runaways or stop its heavy losses by the facility of their recovery. The new law added United States commissioners to the usual courts to issue warrants for the arrest of fugitives and certificates for their removal to the states or territories whence they had escaped. The claimant's affidavit established his ownership, and in an arrest without process he took his slave before the official, who determined the matter summarily. Citizens must aid in executing the law. Those harboring, concealing or rescuing a fugitive were liable to a fine of $1000, six months' imprisonment and civil damages of $1000 for each runaway so lost. The commissioner received $10 for issuing a warrant, but only $5 for discharging the Negro. A United States marshal or his deputies refusing to execute the warrant might be fined $1000, or, letting the fugitive escape, might be sued for his value. The new law produced an era of slave hunting and kidnapping in the North, drove hundreds of runaways from the free states to Canada, created some vigilance committees, increased underground railroad operations and stimulated Mrs. Stowe to write *Uncle Tom's Cabin.*

FUGITIVE SLAVE ACTS, in colonial days, applied to white indentured servants and Indian and Negro slaves. An early Massachusetts law required the

magistrates to recover runaways by armed force, and a later one imposed fines for harboring Negro servants without the owner's consent. In New Netherland indentured fugitives were required to serve double their absent time and pay damages to the master. The harborer was heavily fined. Other colonies had similar laws. The Virginia act of 1672 authorized killing a runaway who resisted arrest and public payment of his value. Maryland also had such a law. In North Carolina, by act of 1715, a person swearing he had killed a fugitive in self-defense while apprehending him was not held accountable, and a fugitive's harborer was required to pay the owner according to the time he had kept him. All persons were required to strive to arrest traveling slaves without passes and take them before magistrates for appropriate action. The law of 1741 rewarded the securer of a runaway, increased the harborer's fine and ordered him sold for not paying it. Persons convicted of abducting slaves from the province lost their lands and lives, or each was obliged to pay £25 to the owner if attempting it. In 1793 sea-captains were made liable as capital felons for abductions. Three laws of 1825–33, in force to 1860, imposed death for stealing slaves from the state, being aimed at underground railroad operators.

The South Carolina slave code of 1722 required patrols to punish slaves going without passes and treated abductors as in North Carolina. Runaways trying to leave the province suffered death. In Southern colonies generally slaves absent from their plantations were required to carry passes, and free Negroes to prove their status by producing certificates.

Emancipation in New England and Pennsylvania (1777–84) and the Northwest Ordinance (1787) rendered the status of fugitive slaves in free territory a problem, but the Ordinance recognized the owner's right of reclamation, and the Constitution declared that a person held to service in one state and escaping into a free one should be delivered to the rightful claimant.

The principles underlying the Federal Fugitive Slave Acts of 1793 and 1850 existed in the articles of confederation of the United Colonies of New England (1643). The act of 1793 authorized the claimant, or his agent, to arrest the runaway in any state or the territories northwest or south of the Ohio River, and prove orally or by affidavit before a circuit or district judge or a magistrate that the fugitive owed service as claimed. Thereupon the official issued a certificate to the applicant for removing the fugitive to the state or territory from which he had fled. Any person knowingly harboring a fugitive, or obstructing his arrest, was liable to pay $500 for each offense by action of debt and to a further suit for damages.

FULBRIGHT ACT AND GRANTS. The Fulbright Act (Public Law 584, 1946) was sponsored by Sen.

J. William Fulbright of Arkansas to initiate and finance certain international educational exchange programs with funds in foreign currencies accruing to the United States from the sale to other governments of property abroad considered surplus after World War II. Subsequent acts of Congress authorized the use of such currencies from other sources also as well as the appropriation of dollar funds as needed for the effective administration of the programs by the Department of State.

Proposed as an amendment to the Surplus Property Act of 1944, the Act was motivated, as Senator Fulbright stated, by the conviction "that the necessity for increasing our understanding of others and their understanding of us has an urgency that it has never had in the past." Programs were developed accordingly by executive agreements with interested, eligible nations. By 1960 these numbered more than forty, in every region of the world outside the Soviet Bloc. More than 16,000 Americans, awarded grants, had traveled abroad from every state and major dependency of the Union to study, teach, lecture, or conduct research, usually for one year. Nearly 22,000 foreigners with travel grants had visited the United States with similar projects, and almost 4000 more had been enabled to attend American-sponsored institutions in 17 countries—for example, a farm school in Greece and a training school for nurses in Burma. The total annual cost of the program in foreign currencies averaged the equivalent of about $6,300,000. The program had made possible many types of projects, among them the interchange of teachers and related professional activities; the training of personnel and other co-operative undertakings by American and foreign specialists in journalism, the physical sciences and social studies; and the promotion of American studies abroad and of foreign "area studies" in the United States.

Among the various acts supporting international educational exchange, the Fulbright Act with its amendments was notable. It encouraged the development of extensive co-operative relationships with binational foundations supervising the country programs abroad and the presidentially appointed Board of Foreign Scholarships selecting candidates for grants and supervising the program generally in Washington. While nongovernmental institutions and organizations provide numerous services, many contribute directly, as do participating governments to some extent, the dollars necessary to supplement the foreign currency grants.

The act was the first to allocate to such activities foreign currency funds accruing to the United States under agreements with other governments, thus establishing a precedent for the financing of other, related programs that were to follow. It anticipated, too, the need for systematic government financing of such programs to a substantial degree. It also committed the U. S. Government for the first time to long-term programs, potentially world-wide and on a scale more nearly commensurate with their current significance. It originated, in fact, the largest program in history consisting of international exchange grants made to individuals and thus helped demonstrate the value of such activities in increasing mutual understanding and broadening the community of interests among peoples.

"FULTON'S FOLLY." At least sixteen steamboats, including the successful experiments of Rumsey and Fitch, had been built before the *Clermont* was launched in 1807. Fitch had offered his invention to Congress for the free use of all, but had been refused. In 1787 he had secured from the legislature of New York the sole right to navigate steamboats on the Hudson. But public opinion was slow to realize that steam could be made of practical use in travel and transportation, and Fitch, failing to build a boat of the required speed in the time specified, lost his monopoly. In 1798 the exclusive privilege of navigating all boats propelled by steam on all water within the State of New York was given to Robert R. Livingston, who, also, failed to build a boat of the required speed and for a time abandoned the project. In Paris he became acquainted with Robert Fulton and in 1803 the monopoly was revived with Livingston and Fulton as joint beneficiaries. Livingston's financial backing and political influence gave Fulton his chance. In 1807 the *Clermont* was built. The snub-nosed little boat, with sparks roaring from her smokestack, made the 150-mile run from New York City to Albany in 32 hours. A regular passenger service was inaugurated and a new era in water transportation began. In 1809 Fulton applied for and obtained a Federal patent.

The Livingston-Fulton monopoly was the cause of much grumbling. It was asserted that Fulton had not invented the steamboat and had no right to a monopoly. In 1810 a rival company was started in Albany. The case was appealed and Fulton won, but was forced to compromise with the Albany company because of lack of means to enforce the verdict. During 1811 Fulton built two vessels for the Hudson, and a ferryboat, which he and Livingston operated successfully between New York City and New Jersey. The question of ferryboats from state to state and navigation on rivers which formed the boundaries between states became a source of endless litigation.

Spurred on by their success in New York, Livingston and Fulton became ambitious to gain monopolistic control of the steamboat traffic of the United States. They studied the Ohio and Mississippi. They advertised, offering to license steamboats on a percentage basis in territory over which they had no control. In 1811 Louisiana gave them a monopoly for a limited time on the Mississippi. Fulton accordingly built the *New Orleans,* the first steam craft to navigate a stream in the interior of the country. Litigation caused by the monopolies continued, until they were broken up by the decision of John Marshall in 1824 in the case of Gibbons v. Ogden.

FUR TRADE. Goods exchanged in the trade were weapons, utensils and tools, clothing and ornaments, tobacco and firewater—which were the things most desired by the aborigines. The primitive Indians having no knowledge of the working of metals, except small copper nuggets used chiefly for ornament, were greatly impressed with the value of metal objects, both as weapons and as implements. Knives, hatchets, axes of several shapes, tomahawks, awls and needles, scrapers for dressing skins, hoes, traps, wire for snares, fishhooks, spearheads, fire-steels and kettles were always in demand. They soon learned to covet the white man's guns, and in the 18th century a special weapon known as the "Northwest gun" was manufactured in England for the Indian trade. With these weapons went powder, lead, gunflints, worms for cleaning, and the several parts of the gun for repairs.

For clothing, the principal object was the blanket, made in various sizes called points—a three point blanket was the ordinary size, a two point was for a child. The women coveted combs and looking glasses. Ready-made clothing had good exchange value; shirts, cloth leggings, coats, hats with feathers for the chiefs, silk handkerchiefs, neck cloths and breechcloths were carried in the traders' packs, along with bolts of red and blue cloth (called stroud), ribbons, worsteds and braid for decoration. Other ornaments were known as *argenterie* or silverware, including armlets, rings, earrings, brooches of many shapes, and gorgets. These became standardized and were produced in France, in Canada and in England. Beads, used to replace the native wampum for ornaments and records, were made in Holland, France and Italy. Strings of beads were called *rassade* by the French traders. The bead belts were known as collars among the British. Bells were also used as ornaments. Even jew's-harps were occasionally included among the traders' wares.

The most universal and most devastating trade goods were different sorts of liquor. The French carried brandy (*eau de vie*) and high wines; the British and Americans carried whisky and rum. It was the universal custom to give the customer a small gift of an intoxicant, which the native could never resist. Then for more indulgence the Indian would barter everything he possessed. Although the tribesman had a native tobacco, called *Kinnikinnick,* he preferred "Brazil" tobacco, that he secured from his trader. Few traders went among the Indians without packages of vermilion which the natives used for personal adornment to paint their faces and parts of their person.

All these goods were traded on a system of credits, the Indian securing from his trader ammunition, blankets, kettles, etc., necessary for hunting. These credits were paid by the furs the native obtained; sometimes the traders took food—pemmican, wild rice, maple sugar—to repay credits.

Great Lakes Region. The area considered as this region may be regarded as an economic unit, with respect to the fur trade, and includes the St. Lawrence and Great Lakes system, and the upper Mississippi with its tributaries. At times the trade centering in this area was extended even beyond the limits indicated and included the region between the Ohio and Mississippi, as well as the valley of the Missouri. Until about the close of the War of 1812, the trade of this vast territory centered largely in Quebec or, later, Montreal. While traders operating from Canada were dominant, the region was at times invaded by outsiders—by French or Spanish from the lower Mississippi, or by New Yorkers approaching along the Hudson-Mohawk waterway. This regional unity affords a splendid illustration of the importance of the geographical factor in determining the general organization of the fur trade.

The region in question was one of the rich fur-bearing areas of North America, and the peltry trade flourished on a large scale for some 200 years. Beaver skins were the most important single item but the country also yielded the pelts of the raccoon, otter, mink, muskrat, fox and many other animals. The traders dealt with many different Indian tribes and a detailed study would have to take into account the characteristics of the natives, their intertribal relations and attitude toward the whites. The Iroquois, occupying the New York area, were an important factor in the Anglo-French rivalry prior to 1763 and determined to a certain extent the general channels of trade.

The Great Lakes fur trade may be divided into three fairly distinct periods, the first extending from the early French explorations of the 17th century to the completion of the military conquest of Canada in 1760; the second, or British period, from 1760 to the surrender of the Northwest posts to the Americans in 1796 and the third, or American period, from 1796 until the decline of the trade in the middle 19th century. The subject may be considered by treating these three periods in turn.

New France had its genesis largely in the fur trade, which began with the earliest contacts of French explorers with the natives in the 17th century. Quebec was founded by Champlain in 1608 and from this settlement as a base the trade was extended to the interior with amazing rapidity. The industry received the active support of the French authorities, who devoted much attention to matters of regulation and control, and at times the fur trade largely overshadowed all other interests. Every effort was made to establish the trade as a French monopoly and the privilege of exporting furs to France was vested in a succession of companies, including the Company of the Hundred Associates, founded in 1628, the Company of the West Indies, the Company of Canada, and the Company of the West. Commercial firms sprang up within the colony which carried on the trade with the "upper country" through agents or correspondents. At first the Indians were encouraged to bring their furs down to great annual fairs held at Three Rivers or Montreal, but gradually French traders penetrated the Great Lakes region, establishing themselves at various posts, among the more important of which were Niagara, Detroit, Michilimackinac, Sault Ste. Marie, La Baye, St. Joseph's and Vincennes. The French policy of control varied from time to time, but as a rule the trade of particular posts was farmed out to individuals with monopoly privileges. The *coureurs de bois* or unlicensed traders presented a considerable problem during the 17th and early 18th centuries. As time went on, forts were built at many of the trading posts of the interior. During the French period, methods were developed which were taken over in turn by the British and Americans. Routes were explored, methods of transport developed, and a trained personnel including merchants and *voyageurs* or *engagés* built up. Bitter rivalry grew up between the French and English traders from New York and Pennsylvania, and the struggle for the fur trade became one of the causes of the intercolonial wars, which finally resulted in the expulsion of French authority from the continent.

Following the capitulation of Montreal in 1760, and the fall of the interior posts, there was an influx of British merchants, including many Scotch, whose energy and ability led to rapid expansion of the trade during the next four or five decades. They took over the system built up by their predecessors, gradually supplanting the French merchants, and the furs exported from Canada were diverted to the great market of London. The British abandoned the system of government monopoly characteristic of the French regime, but there appeared a new trend toward economic monopoly, centered in the hands of a few great companies which arose during the last quarter of the 18th century. Of these concerns the North West Company became by far the most powerful. During this period the "merchants of Montreal" extended their operations to the upper Missouri and into the region northwest of Lake Superior. The British refusal to surrender the Northwest posts to the United States until 1796 strengthened their grip upon the trade of this vast country.

After 1796 American interests made a strong bid for commercial control and finally secured the trade south of the Canadian boundary, although British influence among the Indians remained strong until after the War of 1812. In 1795 the United States inaugurated a system of government **factories**, in order to undermine British influence. Trading houses were set up at Detroit, Chicago, Green Bay, Mackinac, Sandusky, Fort Wayne, Prairie du Chien, etc. The system was never a great success, however, and was discontinued in 1822. The figure of John Jacob Astor looms large during the American period and from the close of the War of 1812 until his retirement in 1834 he virtually controlled the trade of the Great Lakes region within the United States. His American Fur Company was chartered in New York State in 1808. There were successive reorganizations and by 1817 Astor's influence had become dominant on the American side of the boundary. In 1822 he set up the Northern and Western Departments, with headquarters respectively at Mackinac and St. Louis. In 1834 Ramsay Crooks took over the Northern Department, which continued under the name of the American Fur Company until it failed in 1842. While the Great Lakes fur trade continued sporadically thereafter, it was obvious by the middle of the 19th century that its great days were ended.

New England. Trade with the Indians in the New England area began with the visits of explorers and fishermen to these shores in the early 1600's and continued throughout the colonial period, although it declined in importance following the period of King Philip's War. In fact, the economic basis of the earliest settlements, especially Plymouth, consisted largely in the fur trade. Though the early New Englanders were in no sense lacking in energy, the geographical situation tended to circumscribe their trading activities, preventing any considerable expansion. There were no great waterways leading to the interior of the continent and the presence of New Netherland, later New York, on the west, and New France on the north, held New England trade in check, while the expansion of settlement exhausted the local supply of furs. There was at first keen rivalry with the Dutch in the Connecticut Valley and in the 1630's traders from Massachusetts succeeded in breaking their monopoly. William Pynchon founded a post on the site of Springfield, and he and his son John dominated the fur trade of this region for many years. Meanwhile, Massachusetts traders were pushing up the Concord and Merrimack Rivers and northeastward along the Maine coast, their trading posts often becoming centers for settlement. Simon Willard was one of the most prominent traders of the Merrimack region during the middle of the 17th century. The United Colonies of New England (1643) had as one object the protection of the trading interests of its members. Overseas commerce came to absorb a relatively larger share of the energies of New Englanders, though the fur trade continued in the Maine country. From 1694 until the Revolution Massachusetts Bay attempted to limit the trade to government truck houses, which showed no commercial profit but probably aided in keeping peace with the Indians.

Atlantic States. The trade in furs and coarser skins constituted an important element in the economic life of the seaboard colonies during the 17th and 18th centuries. As in New England, the first explorers and settlers took advantage of a traffic which afforded immediate returns. There was at first a tendency on the part of proprietary and governmental authorities to reserve the trade for themselves but it proved impossible to maintain an effective monopoly for any considerable period of time. Early settlers traded with the Indians as a side line to agriculture, but, owing to a need for capital and effective business methods, trade fell gradually under the control of the merchant class. Geographically, three fairly distinct regions are recognizable. There was New York, which dominated the Hudson-Mohawk route to the Great Lakes and the Northwest; secondly, the Pennsylvania-Virginia frontier and the Ohio Valley; and lastly, the area extending from the southern seaboard to the Mississippi, which was exploited by traders from the Carolinas and Georgia.

The trade of the New York area was established by the Dutch, monopoly rights being granted in turn to the New Netherland Company and the Dutch West India Company, the latter chartered in 1621. Important posts were established at Fort Orange, later Albany, and the "House of Hope," on the Connecticut. The Dutch at Fort Orange laid the foundations of the long-continued trade with the Iroquois, who acted as middlemen for tribes farther west. The English took New Netherland in 1664 and continued the trade along much the same lines followed by the Dutch. They soon came into conflict with the French and the fur trade became a vital factor in the Anglo-French rivalry which ended only in 1763. Vigorous efforts were made to undermine the French commercial system and as a part of this program the English in 1722 established Oswego to intercept the French trade with the interior. The English enjoyed a marked advantage in the form of cheap goods of superior quality, but the Albany merchants caused embarrassment by trading directly with the French at Montreal in spite of all regulations. After 1763 a considerable part of the New York trade was diverted to Canada, a trend which continued after the Revolution.

The Dutch and Swedes were pioneers in the fur trade of the middle region but were soon supplanted by the English. Traders from Virginia and Pennsylvania pushed forward during the 17th century, but Pennsylvania enjoyed the advantage of position in exploiting the Ohio region. By 1750 the traders' frontier had reached the Wabash and Maumee Rivers, where the English clashed with the French. Philadelphia and Lancaster became important centers of the Pennsylvania trade and prior to the Revolution

large companies grew up, among them Baynton, Wharton and Morgan, and David Franks and Company. Traffic with the upper Ohio was largely by pack train.

As early as the 1670's and 1680's, traders from Carolina were pressing toward the South and West. After the founding of Georgia in 1733 they met with competition from that quarter. As time went on there developed a three-cornered rivalry among English, Spanish and French for the trade of the region extending to the Mississippi, which had important diplomatic repercussions. Deerskins constituted the most important item in this southern trade, and, as in the middle colonies, transport was largely by pack train. The peltry traffic of this region was more valuable than has sometimes been assumed and in time a considerable part of the business was taken over by Scotch merchants. As in the region to the northward, the advance of settlement following the Revolution spelled the doom of the fur trade.

Rocky Mountains. The abundance and excellent quality of the furs to be obtained in the Rocky Mountains made this region, during the first half of the 19th century, the most attractive fur-trading area within the limits of the United States. Furthermore, the widespread activities of the fur traders were of great significance in exploring and making known an extensive region which might otherwise have long remained unknown and unoccupied. The trade was developed almost entirely by Americans. Frenchmen had pushed up the Missouri, and Spaniards had made a few attempts to trade for furs in the Southwest. But after the purchase of Louisiana and the return of Lewis and Clark, Americans entered vigorously into the trade of the newly acquired region. In 1807 Manuel Lisa, of St. Louis, led an expedition up the Missouri and Yellowstone Rivers and established a trading post at the mouth of the Big Horn River. The St. Louis Missouri Fur Company, founded in 1809, and the Missouri Fur Company, founded in 1814, extended their operations as far west as what is now southwestern Montana.

Before the Missouri Fur Company passed out of existence about 1830, a group of the most resourceful, energetic and picturesque men who ever pursued the fur trade under the American flag formed what was later known as the Rocky Mountain Fur Company. Beginning in 1822, these traders experienced two disastrous years along the Missouri River. Then, in 1824, they abandoned the river and the practice of establishing trading posts, struck out boldly into the mountains, and inaugurated the famous rendezvous at such places as Jackson Hole and Pierre's Hole. In this group were such well-known "mountainmen" as Jedediah S. Smith, Thomas Fitzpatrick, Kit Carson, David E. Jackson, Jim Bridger, and William L. and Milton G. Sublette.

For two years, from 1832 to 1834, the Rocky

Mountain Fur Company engaged in bitter rivalry with Astor's American Fur Company, which had actively entered the fur trade of the upper Missouri a few years earlier. During this contest the fur trade exhibited its worst features. The Indians were debauched with liquor and instigated to attack parties of the rival's traders. In the end, the American Fur Company won out, and thereafter dominated the trade of the northern mountain area. It was this company which introduced steamboats on the upper Missouri River.

All the American traders met effective competition on the part of the Hudson's Bay Company west of the continental divide in the old Oregon country.

In addition to the companies already mentioned, several smaller groups and numerous individual "free trappers" operated in the Rocky Mountain area. Some of these men, like Ceran St. Vrain and Charles and William Bent, erected forts or trading houses which were noted landmarks. Others, including Capt. Benjamin L. E. Bonneville, Nathaniel J. Wyeth, Jacob Fowler, Sylvester and James O. Pattie and Ewing Young, headed parties of traders who made extensive expeditions into the mountains.

The passing of the great days of the fur trade, around 1850, brought to a close one of the most colorful phases of the history of the Far West. The trappers and traders, with all their defects, were the pathfinders of civilization.

In the Southeast and Lower Mississippi. English traders from Carolina were already among the Indians on the Cumberland and Tennessee Rivers when LaSalle claimed the Mississippi Valley for France in 1682, and by 1700 they were passing down these rivers to the Ohio and Mississippi. Jean Couture, whom Tonti had left in command of Arkansas Post in 1686, deserted the French service and became a leader of the Carolina traders. Permanent French settlement in the lower Mississippi Valley after 1699 brought on a struggle for control of the trans-Allegheny fur trade, and by 1717 the French had won over all important tribes except the Cherokee and deprived the Carolina traders of half their Indian traffic. The new French policy of inducing traders to take up agriculture, their exorbitant prices for European goods and their war with the Natchez, enabled British traders to recover their former position by 1730.

The establishment of Georgia in 1733 diverted some British fur trade from Charleston, previously its center. After Louisiana reverted to royal control in 1732, French traders operating from Mobile offered English goods to the Indians, thus regaining part of the fur trade during the following decade. Wars between England and France, 1744–63, severely handicapped the French fur traders; and the expulsion of France from the Mississippi Valley in 1763 left British traders without serious competitors

in the entire region, though a small portion of the fur trade still centered in Spanish New Orleans. From their new posts at Mobile, Pensacola and Manchac, and their old ones in the Carolinas and Georgia, British traders controlled the southeastern fur trade until the close of the American Revolution. Though the Floridas became Spanish in 1783, British traders operating from Mobile and Pensacola maintained a thriving fur trade despite American efforts to stop it. The Louisiana Purchase of 1803 brought the fur trade centering in New Orleans under United States control, the War of 1812 loosened the hold of the British traders at Mobile and Pensacola, and the entire southeastern fur trade passed into American hands with the acquisition of the Floridas in 1821. The fur trade gradually decreased in importance with the expansion of agriculture in the trans-Allegheny region, and virtually ceased as an organized activity in that quarter with the removal of the Indians beyond the Mississippi in the 1830's, though it still provides a livelihood for a considerable number of individuals.

Fur Trade on the Upper Mississippi and Missouri Rivers was inaugurated in the latter part of the 17th century by alert French hunters. As early as 1694, Frenchmen from Illinois began dealing with the Osage Indians, which nation contributed more than any other to the profitable trade subsequently developed. French settlements were built up in Kaskaskia and Cahokia, about 1700, and in 1723 Bourgmont established Fort Orleans on the Missouri, in present Carroll County, Mo. The French were active upon the plains west of the Mississippi striving to control the trade of the Indians between the Platte and Missouri Rivers and the eastern limits of New Mexico. In 1763, when Great Britain acquired the territory east of the Mississippi, the French were carrying on trade by land and by water up the Mississippi, along the Wisconsin, Fox, Chicago and Illinois Rivers to the Great Lakes, and up the Ohio to the Wabash Indians. Under a license granted to Maxent, Laclede and Company, Pierre Laclede Ligueste moved up the Mississippi from New Orleans, reaching the present site of St. Louis late in 1763, where he established a trading post the following year. He became the principal Indian trader, so that it was said "the whole trade of the Missouri, that of the Mississippi northwards, and of the nations near La Baye, Lake Michigan and St. Josephs by the Illinois River, is entirely brought to him" (Hanna, *Wilderness Trail*, II, 48). However, after the English took possession of the territory east of the Mississippi, in 1765, there was a general exodus of the French to the western shore, and during the time that country remained in British control their competition restricted traders operating from St. Louis principally to the Mississippi below the Des Moines, and the Missouri with its tributaries. After the British lost this territory to the American colonies the St. Louis traders moved again into the upper Mississippi and Missouri to fight it out with the North West and the Hudson's Bay Companies. They had the advantage of a waterway to their hunting and trapping domain and also to New Orleans, to which their packs of furs were at that time taken for shipment to Europe.

In 1794 the Spanish Commercial Exploration Company was promoted by Lt. Gov. Zeñon Trudeau to exploit the fur trade of the upper Missouri, combining the capital and energies of the most prominent merchants of St. Louis, and subsidized by the Spanish government to the extent of $10,000. After the return of Lewis and Clark, the St. Louis Missouri Fur Company was organized and many expeditions went forth from St. Louis up the Missouri. Other companies and individuals followed and forts were erected along the Missouri and its tributaries. After the death of Manuel Lisa, who led most of the expeditions, and was the prime mover in the various reorganizations of the St. Louis Missouri Fur Company, John Jacob Astor entered the field successfully as the head of the American Fur Company. He had failed in his earlier enterprises in the West. In 1834 Astor withdrew from the company and left the field largely to P. Chouteau, Jr., and Company, which became the largest and most successful organization until its retirement in 1866. Conservatively speaking, the average annual value of furs received at St. Louis from 1808–47 was between $200,000 and $300,000, and from 1847–60 between $300,000 and $500,000.

FURNITURE. Early American furniture styles are frequently divided into two historical groups, Colonial and Federal. Under Colonial are grouped the styles that prevailed before and at the time of the American Revolution: Jacobean, before 1700; William and Mary, 1700–20; Queen Anne, 1710–55; and Chippendale, 1750–85. The Federal includes the styles in vogue after the Federal Government was established in 1789: the Hepplewhite, 1785–1800; Sheraton, 1795–1820; Directoire, 1805–15; and Empire, 1815–30. The dates are only approximate and of necessity overlap.

Philadelphia achieved its high rank in American furniture history during the Chippendale period, the golden age of Philadelphia cabinetwork. Philadelphia-style highboys and lowboys in the rococo taste are ranked among the finest specimens of American cabinetwork and are equaled only by the block-front furniture of Townsend and Goddard. Thomas Affleck, working in Philadelphia around 1763–95, was regarded in the 1950's as the outstanding figure among Philadelphia cabinetmakers. A few years earlier this leading position was held by William Savery (1721–87), and later by Benjamin Randolph, flourishing around 1762–92. Authenticated Savery pieces retain the high position that has always been accorded them. Among the celebrated chairs designed in the Chippendale style are the so-called sample chairs, comprising five side chairs and one wing chair, attributed to Randolph.

South of Philadelphia the most famous center among the colonies was Charleston. Of great value is the account book of Thomas Elfe, an eminent Charleston cabinetmaker, which covers the years from 1768 to 1775.

Practically all the block-front articles of furniture which were made from around 1750 to 1780 originated in New England, and the finest in quality of design and workmanship were made at Newport, R. I. It is generally accepted that block-front furniture was originally developed in the Newport workshops of John Townsend (1721–ca. 1809) and John Goddard (1723–85). The high position accorded to Newport in American furniture history is due to the Townsends and Goddards, twenty in all, of three generations, closely allied by intermarriage and their remarkable performance as cabinetmakers.

A well-known name is that of Samuel McIntire (1754–1811), the prominent architect and builder of Salem, Mass., who was also a most skillful carver. Presumably he executed the fine carvings on furniture made by various Salem cabinetmakers, such as the Sandersons. After his death the carving business was continued by his son, Samuel Field McIntire.

The names of the many American craftsmen who made the 18th and early 19th century a period of fine achievement in cabinetwork are almost endless. One of the most celebrated is Duncan Phyfe (1768–1854), listed in the New York City Directory of 1792. He worked in the styles that were fashionable during his career, that is, Sheraton, Directoire and Empire. Especially praiseworthy are his Directoire chairs inspired by the Grecian *klismos* and his sofas of lyre-form. Like that of Phyfe's, the work of Charles Honoré Lannuier, a New York City craftsman working about 1805–19, is representative of the American Directoire and Empire styles.

The furniture from around 1825 onwards showed a progressive coarsening of the declining American Empire style. The Victorian period in England and America is frequently divided into three phases: early, 1837–50; middle, 1850–75; late, 1875–1901. Victorian furniture displayed no fresh source of inspiration, nor a unified style, but only a pattern of imitation drawn from the exclusive cult of past traditional styles.

A notable amount of Victorian furniture, esteemed as examples of a local style, was produced from around 1840 to 1860 in the New York workshops of John H. Belter. Typical of his work are ornate chairs and settees in the revived rococo taste with pronounced curves and elaborate openwork frames. The furniture made in the 1860's in the Philadelphia workshop of Daniel Pabst is highly regarded for its workmanship; extant pieces, like sideboards, display a predilection for French Renaissance forms. Of interest in the history of American furniture literature is a book entitled, *The Cabinet Makers' Assistant,* by John Hall, published in Baltimore, 1840. Arranged on 44 plates containing 198 figures, it is believed to be the first completely illustrated furniture style-book published in America. The so-called Eastlake style prevailed for a few years from around 1868 when a book with furniture designs, entitled *Hints on Household Taste,* was published by Charles Locke Eastlake, an English architect. Oak Mission furniture, based on California mission designs, but in reality more American than Jesuit, was a turn-of-the-century development.

Contemporary furniture has not achieved that inner unity which could constitute a style. The use of new materials in furniture has not brought forth a clear objectivity. Radical designers work to become more radical; other designers, striving towards an almost classical concept, allow the past to enrich and stimulate their creative energy. This lack of unity may perhaps merely be indicative of the disunity of the times.

GADSDEN PURCHASE. The treaty of Guadalupe Hidalgo (1848) did not settle the "Mexican Question." The United States was soon charged with not enforcing Article XI which promised Mexico protection from inroads of American Indians. A boundary-line dispute also arose involving territory held necessary by some Americans for a southern railroad route to the Pacific Ocean. Diplomatic tension was increased by activities of American speculators in Mexico. In 1849 P. A. Hargous of New York City purchased the Garay grant made in 1842 by the Mexican government for opening a communication across the Isthmus of Tehuauntepec. This concession was nullified in 1851 by Mexico, but in 1853 A. G. Sloo was given an almost identical grant. Both Hargous and Sloo demanded American protection for their concessions.

In July, 1853, James Gadsden, minister to Mexico, was instructed by President Pierce to make a treaty not only settling the issues involved but also securing territory sufficient for the proposed southern railroad route. Financial needs of the Santa Anna administration aided negotiation of a treaty whereby territory in northern Mexico was sold to the United States. Article XI was abrogated, but the United States was to aid in suppressing Indian depredations. For these concessions the United States was to pay Mexico $15,000,000 and assume all claims of its citizens against Mexico, including the Hargous claim. The United States promised to co-operate in suppressing filibustering expeditions.

The treaty met strong opposition in the Senate. Antislavery Senators opposed further acquisition of slave territory. Lobbying by speculators gave the treaty a bad reputation. Some Senators objected to furnishing Santa Anna financial assistance. The Senate, by a narrow margin, ratified the treaty on April 25, 1854, but only after reducing the territory to be acquired to that considered essential for the railroad route. Article XI was abrogated without reservations. All mention of private claims and filibustering expeditions was deleted. The payment to Mexico was lowered to $10,000,000 and an article was inserted promising American protection to the Sloo grantees. A combination of the advocates of the southern railroad route and the friends of the Sloo grant made ratification possible.

By the Gadsden Treaty the United States secured 45,535 square miles of territory. This tract became known as the Gadsden Purchase and now comprises the southern part of Arizona and New Mexico.

GAG RULE, ANTISLAVERY. On May 26, 1836, the House of Representatives adopted a gag rule to hold back the flood of antislavery petitions which rushed in upon it following the growth of antislavery sentiment and the formation of the American Anti-Slavery Society in 1833. The gag rules, variously phrased, prevented discussion of antislavery proposals. Originally adopted by Southerners with the aid of Northern Democrats, the gag rule was repealed Dec. 3, 1844, after the Northern Democratic support had fallen away. The gag rule strengthened the antislavery movement by adding the issue of deprivation of the right of petition to the ordinary antislavery arguments.

GAINES CASE. Probably the longest lawsuit known to American jurisprudence, this case was instituted in 1834 by Myra Clark (then Mrs. Whitney, later Mrs. Gaines) to recover property in New Orleans allegedly alienated illegally from the estate of her father, Daniel Clark. The issues were Myra's legitimacy, and the validity of Clark's will made in 1813 and assertedly destroyed by his executor, Relf. Both points were eventually decided in Myra's favor, and in 1877 the nonexistent will was admitted to probate. During her lifetime Mrs. Gaines recovered property approximately worth $250,000. In 1890, five years after her death, the so-called Blanc Tract suit was decided against New Orleans, and four years later the city paid the Gaines heirs $1,925,667. This terminated the litigation, which throughout its progress had disturbed real-estate titles in New Orleans and retarded the development of the community.

GAINES' MILL, BATTLE OF (June 27, 1862). After the opening of the Seven Days' Battles at Mechanicsville and Beaver Dam Creek on June 26, the Federal right wing north of the Chickahominy under Gen. Fitz-John Porter was withdrawn by McClellan (U.) to high ground east of Gaines' Mill and south of Cold Harbor—this because of knowledge that Lee (C.) had sent Jackson's corps on a northward flanking detour. Lee attacked with the major portion of his army shortly after noon on June 27. When Jackson, who had moved with inexplicable slowness, arrived in midafternoon, Lee had approximately double Porter's numbers; but with the latter in a strong position, the battle was evenly and desperately waged for several hours. Just before dusk the Confederates pierced the Federal line at one point and captured 22 guns. That night Porter's force was withdrawn to the south side of the Chickahominy. The Union loss was 6800, the Confederate probably larger.

GALLEY BOATS ON THE OHIO. The use of the term "galley boat" was applied to small shiplike craft designed to use both sails and oars—the same craft known on the river in the two decades after 1800 as barges. The French and Spanish maintained galleys on the Mississippi for military purposes. James Willing's *Rattletrap* with which in 1778 he began his famous raid on the lower Mississippi was probably a galley boat. In the same year George Morgan built six gunboats at Pittsburgh which may have been galleys. George Rogers Clark used a small row-galley, the *Willing*, in his Vincennes expedition in 1779 and in 1782 he built a larger galley, the *Miami,* to aid in preventing British and Indian parties from crossing the Ohio. It was 73 feet in keel and had 40 oars. The galley *Mayflower* in which the settlers of Marietta descended the Ohio was probably a modified flatboat. During the troubles with France and Spain at the close of the 18th century the Federal Government built two galleys, the *President Adams* and the *Senator Ross,* which were launched at Pittsburgh, respectively in 1798 and 1799. Other gunboat-galleys were built at various points in the West during the next decade.

GALLIPOLIS, an early Ohio settlement, was founded in 1790 by French immigrants. Lured by glowing, but fictitious, accounts of the Ohio region, and holding fraudulent land titles innocently purchased from the Scioto Land Company, about 600 prospective settlers, called "The French Five Hundred," sailed from Havre. Upon disembarking at Alexandria, Va., they learned the true facts and the company disbanded. Some, however, determined to go on and were transported to a site on the right bank of the Ohio River about three miles below the mouth of the Great Kanawha. Here some cabins had been erected for them by Marietta settlers. The first two years were precarious ones, and the number was reduced by migration to other Western settlements and to Eastern cities. In 1795 Congress reimbursed about 100 of those who remained, with tracts of land located in the present Scioto County, Ohio.

GALLOWAY'S PLAN OF UNION, submitted to Continental Congress on Sept. 28, 1774, was an at-

tempt on the part of the moderate element in that body to settle the conflict between England and her colonies by the establishment of an American legislature which should have authority over all American imperial and intercolonial affairs, civil, criminal and commercial. Its organs of government were to be a President General appointed by the King, and a Grand Council chosen by the colonial assemblies. The distinctive feature of this plan was that the legislature was to be considered a branch of the British Parliament and the assent of both bodies necessary to make laws governing the colonies valid. Congress rejected it by the vote of one colony.

GALVESTON PIRATES were bands of lawless men, many of them former Baratarian pirates, and other restless adventurers who found Galveston Island an ideal place for their headquarters during the disturbed times when revolution was shaking Mexico and Spain's North American empire was crumbling. To give a semblance of legality to their practices, they swore allegiance to the revolutionary government of Mexico and pretended to be privateers engaged in capturing Spanish merchant vessels; but in reality they were slave traders and pirates. Their first leader was Luis Aury, who appeared in 1816 and was later joined by Capt. Perry, a survivor of the Gutierrez-Magee expedition. These men abandoned the island in November, 1816, but their place was taken by Jean Lafitte, the most notorious of the Gulf pirates, whose establishment soon harbored nearly 1000 desperadoes. A United States naval vessel put an end to their activities in 1821.

GARCIA, MESSAGE TO. This is a highly romanticized legend popularized by Elbert Hubbard's article in the *Philistine*, March, 1899. According to Hubbard's account President McKinley, shortly after the outbreak of war with Spain, wanted to send a message to Gen. Calixto Garcia, the Cuban revolutionary, whose whereabouts was unknown. Some one said: "There is a fellow by the name of Rowan who can find Garcia if anybody can." Then follows in the Hubbard account a series of trite observations on overcoming obstacles. In actual fact Lt. A. S. Rowan set out for Jamaica early in April, 1898, with Lt. Henry H. Whitney on a mission of inquiry about the size and location of Spanish and Cuban forces. When the war broke out Whitney went to Puerto Rico to secure information, and Rowan crossed to Portillo, Cuba, with the aid of Cuban sympathizers. He met Garcia on May 1, 1898, at Bayamo, conferred with him, left Cuba May 5 near Nuevitas and was picked up by sponge fishermen. He finally made his way to Washington with valuable messages *from* Garcia. The important part of his mission was the information he brought from Cuba.

GASPEE, BURNING OF THE (June 10, 1772). The many waterways and islands in Narragansett

Bay were very convenient for smugglers, and during the 18th century smuggling constantly increased. The British government sent revenue cutters to suppress these irregularities and much friction resulted. In March, 1772, H. M. S. *Gaspee* under Lt. Dudingston arrived in Narragansett Bay and proceeded to stop even small market boats and to send seized property to Boston. On June 9, 1772, the *Gaspee*, while chasing the *Hannah*, ran ashore on Namquit (now Gaspee) Point in Warwick. A group of angry men met at Sabin's Tavern in Providence and plotted to burn the ship. John Brown, a leading Providence merchant, supplied eight boats; the men armed themselves with guns, staves and paving stones, about 10 o'clock in the evening, and with muffled oars, proceeded down the river. When they neared the *Gaspee*, they were hailed by the lookout and also by Lt. Dudingston. Capt. Abraham Whipple (later Commodore, U. S. Navy) replied with some profanity that he had a warrant to arrest Dudingston. Joseph Bucklin then shot Dudingston, and the men from the boats boarded the *Gaspee* without resistance and drove the crew below decks. The captured sailors were bound and put on shore. The *Gaspee* was set on fire, and burned to the water's edge. A proclamation was issued to apprehend the participants in the raid, but although the personnel of the expedition was widely known in Providence, no one gave any evidence, except a Negro named Aaron whose story was disputed. No one was brought to trial, and a commission of inquiry could find no evidence sufficient to convict.

GATLING GUN, the most famous of multiple-barrel rapid-fire arms, was patented Nov. 4, 1862, by Richard Jordan Gatling, but there is no evidence of its having been in action during the Civil War. Adopted after successful trials in 1866, it appeared in the New Orleans riots of 1868 and on several expeditions against Indians, but took no conspicuous part until the siege of Santiago, 1898, by which time it was being superseded by the machine gun. The barrels, six to ten in number, were placed in a circular frame which was made to revolve by means of a crank, each barrel in turn being automatically loaded and fired. A rate of 400 shots a minute was attained.

GENERAL ARMSTRONG. Within the space of a few hours there arrived in Fayal, Azores Islands, Sept. 26, 1814, the American privateer *General Armstrong* and a British squadron. About sunset, longboats from the latter approached the former, were warned to stand away and then fired on. The American consul requested support of the port authorities. In the morning the *General Armstrong* was destroyed. The United States believed Portugal negligent of her duty as a neutral and pressed a claim for damages. The matter was finally submitted to arbitration. The award was in favor of Portugal, for, according to the arbiter, the Americans, opening fire before requesting assistance, put themselves beyond any claim upon the port authorities.

GENERAL COURT, COLONIAL. The Great and General Court was a New England institution. It originated with Massachusetts Bay colony whose charter gave full powers of governing, correcting, punishing and ruling to a body known as the General Court. This consisted of the governor, eighteen assistants and the freemen of the company. Only eleven of the assistants came to Massachusetts and very few of the freemen, consequently about a dozen men had a legal right to rule some 2000 settlers. The assistants voted themselves individually the power of British magistrates. The charter provided for four meetings of the General Court each year. At these meetings additional freemen were admitted, rules for the governing of the province were adopted, taxes levied, fines assessed, undesirable immigrants ordered returned to England and such other things done as the local situation seemed to demand. In the course of time the large meeting came to exercise mainly legislative powers, but at first and throughout the life of the first charter some judicial business was transacted. The name persisted and was used in the second charter.

The other colonies in New England followed the Massachusetts practice. New Haven was governed by a similar body, as were also Connecticut and Rhode Island. Plymouth called its smaller body assistants, the same as Massachusetts. Connecticut and New Haven used the term magistrates for this group. All used the term General Court for a meeting of the governor, the assistants or magistrates, and the freemen, or their representatives. Thus throughout New England there developed the idea that all reserve powers of government resided in a General Court or assembly of the people of each province.

GENÊT MISSION. Citizen Edmond Genêt, who had been designated by the Girondists, Nov. 19, 1792, as minister from France to the United States, landed at Charleston, S. C., April 8, 1793. He received a cordial civic welcome, which was amplified en route to the capital, then at Philadelphia, with an extravagance consciously designed by Anti-Federalists to exert pressure upon the Administration. Following a cool reception by President Washington, the minister became a factor in the conflict between Alexander Hamilton and Thomas Jefferson, the latter his natural friend. Even Jefferson was alienated, however, by Genêt's disingenuous handling of the *Little Sarah*, an interned privateer which in defiance of formal pledge was permitted to go to sea. In the matter of French privateers as well as the outfitting, with Andre Michaux and Stephen Drayton, of expeditions against Louisiana and also Florida, Genêt proceeded on the mistaken philosophy that he was the minister of a people to a people, not of a government to a government. The Administration demanded his recall but permitted him unofficial residence, because return in disgrace to a France now turned Jacobin would mean the guillotine. With Genêt's recall, that of Gouverneur Morris, American minister to France, could not be long deferred. Failure of both missions was convincing evidence that the Franco-American Alliance of 1778 had little further meaning.

GENEVA THREE-POWER NAVAL CONFERENCE. In 1927 President Coolidge invited Great Britain, Japan, France and Italy to a conference of five powers at Geneva in order to impose a limit on the tonnage of cruisers, destroyers and submarines. Great Britain and Japan accepted the invitation while France and Italy declined. The negotiations ended in ignominious failure, partly through the instructions of the American delegates for parity in tonnage with Great Britain and rejection of all political arrangements. The traditional American policy of "freedom of the seas" also clashed with the possible status of Great Britain as a belligerent in a war to fulfill obligations under the covenant of the League of Nations—a war in which Britain would interfere with neutral shipping as was done in World War I. The collapse of the Geneva Conference strengthened the agitation of the "Big Navy" adherents in the United States with the result that Congress entered the naval competition by passing an act authorizing the construction of fifteen cruisers and one aircraft carrier.

GEOGRAPHER'S LINE was surveyed by Thomas Hutchins, Geographer of the United States, according to the plan provided in the Ordinance of 1785. The line was to begin at the point where the Pennsylvania boundary intersected the Ohio River and was to run due west. The Seven Ranges, the first surveys under the Ordinance, were laid out south of this line, which extended westward 42 miles. The line is located at 40° 38′ 2″ N. Lat., but the inaccuracies of the survey, begun under many difficulties in 1785–86, caused it to deviate a mile to the north at its western end. Every six miles, at right angles to the line, were drawn the meridians marking the boundaries of the ranges, while parallel to it, at six-mile intervals, were east-and-west lines to complete the township boundaries.

GEOLOGICAL SURVEY, UNITED STATES, was constituted (March 3, 1879) a permanent bureau for closer co-ordination of government agencies assigned to the task of classifying the public lands and "the examination of the geological structure, mineral resources, and products of the national domain." At the same time the Geological and Geographical Survey of the Territories, the Geographical and Geological Survey of the Rocky Mountain Region (both under the Department of the Interior), and the Geographical Surveys West of the 100th Meridian (under the War Department) were discontinued.

The land west of the 100th Meridian was divided into four geological districts, headed by four geologists-in-charge. Later the field of geological survey was extended over the whole United States, and the territory east of the 102nd Meridian was divided into four divisions. The Mississippi Basin was made a geological unit by itself, consisting of two divisions.

Besides its extensive field work, the Geological Survey has issued many valuable publications through the Department of the Interior, including annual reports, monographs, professional papers, bulletins, water-supply papers and papers on the mineral resources of the United States. Map publications include the *Geologic Atlas of the United States,* the *World Atlas of Commercial Geology,* as well as topographic folios and maps, some with descriptive text. Additional base, contour and other maps of the United States and of the states have more recently been added to the list of publications of the Survey.

GEORGIA was the youngest of the original Thirteen Colonies. Motives for its founding, which varied with the groups interested, were: to erect a buffer against the Spaniards in Florida and the French in Louisiana; to produce silks and other special raw materials; to promote an experiment in rehabilitating the unfortunate debtors of London; and to offer a refuge for persecuted Protestants. James Edward Oglethorpe and Lord John Percival, first Earl of Egmont, were the leaders in securing the charter (1732), which provided for a Board of Trustees, made up of titled and other prominent Britons, to govern the colony for 21 years, after which control reverted to the Crown. The colony comprised that territory between the Savannah and Altamaha Rivers and lines drawn due west from their headwaters to the Pacific. The first colonists arrived in 1733 and settled Savannah. Opposed by Spain, Oglethorpe was forced into a war, which lasted from 1739 to 1744. Certain peculiarities of Trustee rule were: prohibition against slavery and rum, and a restricted land system.

The colony prospered little under the Trustees, and not until the Crown assumed control and appointed James Wright governor (1760–76, 1779–82) did life take hold. The chief population groups which came in during colonial times were: English, Germans, German Salzburgers, Moravians, Scotch Highlanders, Scotch-Irish, Irish, Puritans and some Jews. Friendly relations with the Indians were established in the beginning, and as a result no Indian wars occurred throughout the life of the colony. At the end of the French and Indian War the boundaries of the colony were fixed on the south by the St. Marys River and a line drawn from its headwaters to the Chattahoochee and thence along the 31st parallel to the Mississippi, which became the western limits.

Georgia was slow to join the agitation which led to the Revolution because of gratitude to England for the large grants of money made in maintaining the colony, and through fear of attack by the king's forces in Florida and by Creeks and Cherokees on the west and north. Though unrepresented in the Stamp Act Congress and the First Continental Congress, Georgia joined the Revolution in time to be represented in the Second Continental Congress. Not until 1778 was there any serious fighting in the state, when the British seized Savannah, and within the next few months almost subjugated the state. The next year royal government was restored and Sir James Wright returned to be governor. During 1779 the patriots won at Kettle Creek, lost at Briar Creek and aided by the French made a desperate assault on Savannah without success. Defeat elsewhere forced the British to evacuate Savannah in 1782.

Though characterized throughout her subsequent history by a passionate attachment to states' rights, Georgia was the first Southern state to ratify the Federal Constitution, which she did by a unanimous vote on Jan. 2, 1788. Her desire for protection against the Spaniards in Florida and from the hostile Creeks and Cherokees, and her feeling that with a territory larger than any other state in the Union, she would soon play a dominant part in the new government—these considerations led her in the beginning to adopt a strong national position, which she abandoned after the decisions of the U. S. Supreme Court in the Chisholm v. Georgia and the Brailsford v. Georgia cases.

Troubled by the Yazoo Land Frauds, the state, in an agreement known as the Georgia Compact, accepted the Chattahoochee River as her western boundary. As part of the same agreement the Federal Government promised to remove the Indians from the state. Their removal, completed by 1838, opened up rich cotton lands, which made Georgia for a time the greatest cotton producing region in the world.

Embittered by the sectional struggle, Georgia, urged forward by Gov. Joseph E. Brown, Robert Toombs and other leaders, seceded from the Union on Jan. 19, 1861. She was almost free from invasion until 1864, when Gen. Sherman made his famous march and left bitter feelings to rankle for a generation. Reconstructed with the other Confederate states, Georgia was first readmitted to the Union in 1868; but her expulsion of Negro members of the legislature led to her second reconstruction, which was completed by 1871.

GERMAN FLATS, N. Y., were the meadow lands south of the Mohawk River, opposite the present village of Herkimer, granted for settlement to the Palatines, who had been brought over to make naval stores and who at the failure of that enterprise were settled on the frontier as a protection against French attack. The exact date of settlement is not known, but it was probably in the year of 1723–24. In 1757 the settlement was attacked by the French and Indians and 200 persons killed or captured. During the Revolution the settlers suffered continual depredations. In September, 1778, German Flats was laid waste for ten miles along the river.

GERMANTOWN, BATTLE OF (Oct. 4, 1777). After his defeat on the Brandywine Sept. 11, Washington retired in good order, skirmishing with the British almost daily to prevent Lord Howe's sending assistance to Burgoyne. Confident, if this could be prevented, of Burgoyne's destruction, Washington conceived an idea for a decisive victory over Howe, who had disposed his main force around Germantown, just outside of Philadelphia, while Cornwallis' division occupied the city itself. This battle project was second in audacity only to that of Trenton, and came remarkably near to success. With his inferior and poorly trained force, Washington planned to converge by four roads upon Germantown at dawn, drive the British army back on the Schuylkill River and destroy it or force its surrender.

The night march of Oct. 3–4 was beset with the usual unexpected delays, and at dawn a dense fog prevailed, to which may largely be attributed the failure of the plan. The right wing under Sullivan struck an advance post of the enemy and drove it back to Judge Chew's large mansion, where the British took refuge, firing from the windows. A detachment was left to besiege them, and Sullivan pressed on. The left wing under Greene was a bit slower in reaching the scene; nevertheless, the British were being crumpled up and victory seemed assured, when an incident occurred which contributed to turn the tide of battle. Stephen, of the left wing, coming up behind Wayne of the right in the fog, mistook the latter for the enemy and fired upon his brigade. Wayne's men, thus beset on both sides, fell back in confusion upon Sullivan's other brigades. However, the Americans continued to press the attack after this incident, and then fell back in a panic, caused possibly by the firing of the Chew House in their rear, the fog and lack of ammunition. A general retreat began, and though the panic quickly subsided, the moment for success had been lost. Cornwallis, hearing the firing, rushed two battalions to the field, who aided in driving the Americans back. They retreated in good order, bringing off all their cannon as well as some captured British guns. One American regiment, however, was surrounded and made prisoners. The American loss was 1071, the British 535. Washington's daring and strategy created a deep impression in Europe, and Germantown is said to have done almost as much toward gaining the aid of France as Burgoyne's surrender.

GERONIMO'S CAMPAIGNS in New Mexico, Old Mexico and Arizona, coming after the general threat of Indian hostilities had been removed, caused more of a sensation than if they had been waged fifty years eariler. The Apaches, always independent, resented their removal from southern New Mexico to the San Carlos agency in Arizona, and Geronimo and his band decamped for Mexico in 1876. He later returned but after a time headed a revolt that ended as a raid into Sonora, and it was only after long trailing and hard fighting that the band was finally surrounded by the force of Gen. Crook in the Sierra Madre Mountains in 1882. After a third return to San Carlos reservation, Geronimo broke out again in 1884 and waged bloody guerrilla warfare in Arizona and New Mexico. Although his band had few fighting men, and had to live off the country while carrying their women and children with them, they led the American forces such a cleverly deceptive race that Geronimo won respect as a strategist. Not until Mexican troops and American forces under Gen. Miles had driven them to exhaustion did the little band surrender in 1886. They were sent first to Florida, then Alabama and later to Fort Sill, Okla.

GERRYMANDER. The word gerrymander was first used during Elbridge Gerry's second term as governor of Massachusetts, when a bill was passed (Feb. 11, 1812) redistricting the state in order to give the Jeffersonian Republicans an advantage in the election of state senators. It was derived from a caricature representing a strangely shaped three-member Republican district in Essex County as a salamander, which quickly became gerrymander.

Gerrymandering, or redistricting for partisan advantage, has been applied to congressional, state and city districts. Its purpose is to concentrate in a few legislative districts the minority voting strength. In order to protect rural areas, certain state constitutions and laws deliberately create an apportionment which is, in effect, an antiurban gerrymander. Because of the mobility and shifting of population, the gerrymander is a dangerous weapon in city districting.

To prevent its use, certain state constitutions and Federal laws have provided that legislatures must divide states into districts of compact territory and substantial equality in population. But none of these have destroyed gerrymandering. When provisions of this character have come before state courts, no uniform rule has resulted. Some courts permit wide legislative discretion; others, believing the injustice too obvious, have interfered.

GETTYSBURG, BATTLE OF (July 1–3, 1863), decided the outcome of the invasion of Pennsylvania and, with the simultaneous surrender of Vicksburg, forecast Confederate defeat in the Civil War. Pettigrew's (C.) North Carolina Brigade, attempting to raid Gettysburg, June 30, reported to Gen. R. E. Lee, then at Greenwood, that it had encountered Federal cavalry and had returned to Cashtown. Lee doubted that the enemy had reached Gettysburg so soon, but as he already had ordered a concentration in that direction of his 70,000 troops, he sent Hill's Third Corps toward the town. On July 1, near Willoughby Run, Hill was repulsed by Reynolds' (U.) I Corps; but the Second Confederate Corps (Ewell's), marching southward, arrived opportunely, turned the Federal right, cleared Gettysburg, and drove the Federals to Cemetery Hill, south of the town. Ewell, new to corps command and unused to discretionary orders, did not adopt Lee's suggestion that he storm Cemetery Hill that evening. Lee ordered up Longstreet's corps, then the rear guard, and advanced Hill to Seminary Ridge. Eastward and parallel to this ridge, at an average distance of 1300 yards, across the Emmitsburg Road, was another elevation, Cemetery Ridge, which ran northward almost to Gettysburg and, at Cemetery Hill, turned eastward to another summit, Culp's Hill. Lee reasoned that the Federals would occupy this entire ridge and, accordingly, he planned for Longstreet on the 2nd to attack diagonally across the Emmitsburg Road and to get astride Cemetery Ridge before the Union army could reach it. At daylight on the 2nd this seemed feasible, but before Longstreet could get in position, Meade (U.), hurrying up from the line March Creek-Manchester, had his II, III and V corps on Cemetery Ridge, the XII on Culp's Hill, and the XI in support of the battered I on Cemetery Hill. The VI Corps was in general reserve. When, therefore, Longstreet attacked in the late afternoon of July 2, he encountered heavy opposition. His only material gain was the capture of a good artillery position in Peach Orchard near the Emmitsburg Road. Ewell, who had orders to demonstrate when Longstreet attacked and to assault if Longstreet succeeded, easily captured Culp's Hill. One of his divisions, Early's, almost reached the Federal batteries on Cemetery Hill but had to fall back for lack of support. In these circumstances, Lee felt that his one hope of victory was to break the Federal center by a direct assault on Cemetery Ridge. For this purpose, on July 3, he intended to use the whole of the First Corps, but, when Longstreet objected that this would expose the right, Lee chose for the assault Pickett's fresh division of the First Corps, Heth's (temporarily under Pettigrew) of the Third Corps and two brigades of Pender's division, also of the Third. About 125 guns were placed to cover the advance. Ewell's orders were to co-operate substantially as on the previous day. It was two o'clock on the 3rd before Longstreet reluctantly ordered Pickett's Charge against the front of the II Corps. When this failed with bloody losses, Meade did not feel strong enough to deliver a counterstroke. The only attempt of this character, a cavalry attack on the Confederate right, was easily beaten off by Stuart's (C.) men, who had returned on the 2nd from their long raid. Back on Seminary Ridge with the survivors, in whose presence Lee took all blame for the failure, the commanding general learned that Ewell had been able to accomplish nothing that day. Retreat was the only course left to Lee. On the evening of July 4, in a torrential rain, he started for the Potomac. Behind him, or groaning in the ambulances, were 20,000 casualties. Meade, who had lost 23,000, was so slow and cautious in pursuit as to provoke criticism which temporarily silenced the praise he had received for his admirable defense. To the excellence of that defense, more than to anything else, victory was due. Overconfidence on Lee's part, poor co-ordination of attack, and the inferiority of the Southern artillery were the other major reasons for the Confederate defeat.

GETTYSBURG ADDRESS (Nov. 19, 1863) was delivered by Abraham Lincoln at the dedication of the national cemetery at Gettysburg, Pa. The address was not written on the train, as readers of *The Perfect Tribute* have been led to believe, but was completed in Washington, although Lincoln made minor changes at Gettysburg. At the dedication, the President read slowly from manuscript. Tired by the two-hour oration of Edward Everett, the crowd applauded without enthusiasm. Contrary to the general belief, some American critics recognized the literary merit of the address almost at once; others, for partisan reasons, belittled or denounced it.

GHENT, TREATY OF. The War of 1812 was scarcely begun when on June 26, 1812, the American Government made preliminary overtures for peace, on terms, however, unlikely of acceptance. Again, on Sept. 21, 1812, the Russian chancellor proffered a mediation, accepted at Washington, March 11, 1813, but rejected at London. Lord Castlereagh, however, on Nov. 4, 1813, offered a direct negotiation, which was accepted on Jan. 15, 1814, and Henry Clay and Jonathan Russell joined James Bayard, Albert Gallatin and John Quincy Adams, who were already named in response to the Tsar's preliminary mediation. The British representatives were Lord Gambier, Henry Goulburn and William Adams. Negotiations took place at Ghent.

America's chief demand, abandonment of impressment, was relinquished on June 27 as unattainable. In June, the British tone was high. Lord Castlereagh had returned from Paris with what Admiral Mahan calls a "consciousness of mastery." Far from concessions on impressment, England would protect her Indian allies with a buffer state, along with other territorial readjustments, and would demand military control over the Great Lakes. A position so advanced was unwarranted by the military situation, and proved untenable. When the United States re-

jected these proposals, Great Britain fell back upon a restoration of the Indians to their treaty rights as of 1811. The United States denied that the Indians were a subject for direct negotiation, but agreed that Indian rights should be respected.

On Sept. 27, news reached London of the capture and burning of Washington, but, out of deference for Tsar Alexander I, a conciliatory tone was not abandoned. Lord Bathurst did, however, on Oct. 18 and 20, contend for *uti possidetis*, or the principle that each party should retain existing holdings. On Oct. 21 news reached London of Commodore Macdonough's victory on Lake Champlain, thereby rather counteracting the capture of Washington, and on Oct. 24 the Americans rejected *uti possidetis*, insisting upon a basis of complete mutual restitution. A temporary deadlock ensued.

But larger forces wrought for peace. The Continental situation grew increasingly involved. British finances labored under an unprecedented strain. The Duke of Wellington refused an American command with a warning, Nov. 9, that a decisive victory in North America was hopeless without British supremacy on the Great Lakes. The opinion of Wellington fortified the ministry in receding from its extreme demands. *Uti possidetis* gave way on Nov. 13 to *status quo ante bellum,* which was mutually acceptable.

While Continental dangers hastened British acquiescence, America meanwhile abandoned not only impressment but also demands for commercial losses incurred in the war between France and England. American rights in the Newfoundland fisheries were acknowledged. Both parties agreed to employ their best efforts to abolish the slave trade. Boundary commissions were provided for subsequent negotiations.

A treaty was signed by the eight negotiators on Dec. 24, 1814. It reached the United States on Feb. 11, 1815, and was formally ratified on the 17th.

GHOST DANCE was a ceremonial dance in connection with the messiah religion, which originated among the Paiutes of Nevada in 1888, and spread through most of the plains Indian tribes. Originator of the doctrine was a Paiute named Wovoka (Cutter), known to the whites as Jack Wilson, who evolved it after a delirium during an illness.

Wovoka preached that belief in his doctrine would result in restoration to the Indians of their hunting grounds and reunion with departed friends. Certain symbolic dances and songs were prescribed and "ghost shirts" with specific markings were worn by the men. Hypnotic trances were features of the dances.

The Ghost Dance excitement led to the Sioux outbreak of 1890–91, during which Sitting Bull was killed, and the Wounded Knee fight occurred. The doctrine has disappeared except for reminiscent social dances.

G. I.; G. I. BILL OF RIGHTS. The initials "G. I." originally stood for anything of "government issue"; eventually they came in army slang to designate an enlisted man. Congress in June, 1944, passed the Servicemen's Readjustment Act, the so-called "G. I. Bill of Rights," which provided Government aid for veterans' hospitals and vocational rehabilitation; for the purchase by veterans of houses, farms and businesses; and for four years of college education—$500 a year for tuition and books and a monthly allowance of $50 (later raised to $65).

GIBBONS v. OGDEN (9 Wheaton 1) was decided by the U. S. Supreme Court on March 2, 1824. The case is important in American constitutional history chiefly because of the broad interpretation given by Chief Justice Marshall to the word "commerce" as used in the constitutional provision giving Congress the power to regulate commerce with foreign nations and among the several states. It had an immediate importance, furthermore, in checking the growth of strife among the states over the control of steam navigation.

Even before steam navigation was demonstrated as commercially feasible Robert R. Livingston and Robert Fulton had secured from the New York legislature a grant of monopoly rights for a period of years for the operation of steamboats on the waters of the state. In 1808, the year following the first successful demonstration on the Hudson River, the grant was renewed. The building and operation of steamboats developed rapidly in New York and other states. Many operators wishing to do business in part or wholly in New York waters secured licenses from the Livingston-Fulton monopoly, but the demands of the monopoly resulted in bitterness and retaliation in other states. The situation threatened the return of the strife among the states over interstate commerce which had necessitated the creation of a federal government stronger than that provided by the Articles of Confederation.

The case of Gibbons v. Ogden arose when Ogden, who held a license from the monopoly for operation between points in New York and New Jersey, sought an injunction in a New York court to eliminate competition from Gibbons, who had no such license, but did have a license from the Federal Government under an act of Congress regulating the coasting trade. The case was argued in the Supreme Court by William Wirt and Daniel Webster for Gibbons and Thomas Addis Emmet and Thomas J. Oakley for Ogden.

Chief Justice Marshall wrote an opinion in the case characterized by his biographer as one "which has done more to knit the American people into an indivisible nation than any other one force in our history, excepting only war." He interpreted the word "commerce" broadly, to include not merely buying and selling and barter, but other forms of intercourse as well, including navigation. He reasoned that commerce among the states must be commerce in the states, and could not stop at state lines. As against Federal regulations of interstate commerce in the waters of a state, conflicting state regulations must fall. The New York grant of monopoly rights was therefore unconstitutional insofar as it was in conflict with the act of Congress regulating the coasting trade.

The Court did not decide whether the state measure would have been unconstitutional as it affected interstate commerce because of the constitutional grant of power to Congress to regulate interstate commerce, in the event that Congress had passed no regulatory act. Justice Johnson wrote a concurring opinion, however, in which he took the position that the grant to Congress automatically excluded the states from the field. That subject remained one of bitter controversy for many years.

GILA TRAIL was an early trade and emigrant route following in general the course of the Gila River and its branches between Yuma, Ariz., and several points along the upper Rio Grande from Santa Fe to El Paso. It was occasionally followed by early Spanish travelers. American fur trappers used it as early as 1826. Gen. Kearny's march from Santa Fe to California, in 1846, descended the Gila from the copper mines to the Colorado River and thence reached the California coast towns; soon afterward Lt. Col. Cooke's Mormon Battalion marked a wagon road by way of Guadalupe Pass from the Rio Grande to Tucson, the Pima villages and the lower Gila. Subsequently the southern Gila routes were more frequently in use by California emigrants; and the Southern Pacific Railway still follows them in part through Arizona, as do a number of motor highways.

GILBERT'S PATENT. In 1578, Sir Humphrey Gilbert, leading promoter of the search for a Northwest Passage, was granted letters patent by Queen Elizabeth to discover lands and plant colonies in America within a six-year period. Lands which he discovered were to be held as a royal fief, reserving one fifth of all gold and silver to the Crown. Gilbert was authorized to transport English settlers, establish one or more colonies, set up a government, grant lands and make trade concessions "over a territory encompassing the settlement on all sides to a distance of two hundred leagues." All laws and religous policies were to conform to English practice. A carefully planned expedition in 1578 failed to materialize, but in June, 1583, Gilbert's fleet sailed and reached Newfoundland about the close of July. The colony failed and ended in the death of Gilbert, who was lost at sea. On March 25, 1584, Gilbert's patent was renewed in the name of his half-brother, Walter Raleigh, who had been associated with Gilbert in what may be considered the beginning of English colonization in America.

"**GILDED AGE**" was the period of currency inflation, widespread speculation, overexpansion of industry, loud booming of dubious enterprises, loose business and political morals, and flashy manners which extended from the end of the Civil War in April, 1865, to the Panic of September, 1873. It was the resultant of two main forces. One was the business boom produced by paper money, large government expenditures, high tariffs, such new invention as Bessemer steel, the rapid development of the Middle and Far West, and the exuberant confidence of the victorious North. The other was the moral laxity produced by wartime strain, easy money, the pressure of rich corporations on the Government and frontier influences. The title of "Gilded Age" was fixed upon the period by the novel of that name which Mark Twain and Charles Dudley Warner published in 1873.

GIRL SCOUTS OF THE U. S. A., a leisure-time organization for girls from seven through seventeen years old, was founded in Savannah, Ga., March 12, 1912, by Juliette Gordon Low after the pattern suggested by Lord Baden-Powell for the Boy Scouts and Girl Guides of England. It provides girls with opportunities for educational and recreational activities in four major areas: citizenship; outdoor activities; homemaking; and the arts. These activities are designed to build character and to develop personal resources and civic responsibility. The movement thus helps to fill the gap left in the education of youth by mechanical progress, urban living and other complications of modern civilization. Girl Scouting provides for democratic planning and execution of projects by girls under the supervision of trained adult leaders. Girl Scouts of the U. S. A. is a member of the World Association of Girl Guides and Girl Scouts, and fosters friendship with an appreciation of cultures in other countries through an annual interchange program as well as through printed material and international meetings. Girl Scout membership in 1958 was about 3,000,000 of which 2,300,000 were girls and 700,000 adults.

GIST, CHRISTOPHER, TRAVELS AND JOURNALS OF. In 1750 the Ohio Company sent Gist, a surveyor and frontiersman of North Carolina, to explore the Ohio Valley. He left Wills Creek on Oct. 31, crossed the Allegheny near the site of Pittsburgh and explored the country north of the Ohio as far as the Miami River. In March he crossed the Ohio at the Scioto and traveled in Kentucky nearly to the site of Louisville. Eighteen years before Daniel Boone, he made his way through Kentucky, reaching his home on the Yadkin May 18. From November to May, 1751–52, Gist explored lands between the Monongahela and the Little Kanawha. His journals of these expeditions discuss the suitability of the western lands for colonization and throw incidental light on Indians, fur traders and the conflict between France and England for the Ohio Valley. Gist also kept a journal of a third expedition in the West, when he went to Fort LeBoeuf with Washington.

"**GIVE ME LIBERTY OR GIVE ME DEATH!**" In the Virginia Provincial Convention, March 23, 1775, Patrick Henry offered resolutions to organize the militia and put the colony on a footing of defense. When this met with opposition, he delivered an oration in which he is quoted as saying, "Is life so dear or peace so sweet as to be purchased at the price of chains and slavery? Forbid it, Almighty God! I know not what course others may take, but as for me, give me liberty or give me death!"

GLASS was made by the Virginia colonists and at Salem immediately after settlement, but no permanent manufacture was established in America until the 18th century, when small bottle works were set up at several places. By 1740 flint hollow ware and window glass were produced in New Jersey. Shortly before the Revolution "Baron" Stiegel, a German industrialist, erected a glass house at Mannheim, Pa., comparable with those abroad. The best colonial glassware is still admired for quality and beauty.

During the next half-century about 100 glass works left records of their existence in the United States. The more important of these were in or near Boston and Sandwich, Mass., New York City, Philadelphia and Pittsburgh, which supplied an increasing share of the western market.

Abundant fuel, potash and glass sands favored the industry, but skilled labor was scarce. Workers from Poland, Germany and Italy made colored beads for the Indian trade at the first Virginia glass house. "Baron" Stiegel imported German workmen for his big enterprise. Early establishments at Boston, Pittsburgh and elsewhere owed their success to foreign workers.

After the Civil War the substitution of lime and soda for costlier fluxes accelerated migration westward, and the Pittsburgh-Wheeling area became the center of this industry. A few decades later the employment of natural gas for fuel intrenched the business more strongly in the Ohio Valley.

Soon after 1820 American makers perfected the manufacture of pressed glassware, thus lowering costs and extending popular demand. The same urge toward mass production 75 years later encouraged the invention of automatic glass-blowing machinery, which has made the manufacture of articles of huge quantity consumption, like electric light bulbs, possible. But America's cheap fuel and materials delayed the adoption of the Siemens furnace and the substitution of tanks for glass pots, and annealing improvements, which since 1890 have augmented productive capacity.

About 1850 household canning started a demand for fruit jars. Ten years later a great call for petroleum lamps and lamp chimneys further stimulated production. The next decade saw the plate-glass manufacture established in America to supply the needs of rapidly growing cities and display merchandizing. Before this impulse lost headway the advent of the automobile brought makers huge orders for plate and safety glass. Meanwhile the popularization of the camera widened the demand for optical glass, while in another field the rediscovery of Tiffany or iridescent glass recorded a step in the art use of this material.

GLEBE LANDS OF THE EPISCOPAL CHURCH.

A glebe is a farm owned by a parish, the use of which belongs to the incumbent minister and forms a part of his legal stipend. The first provision for such farms in America was made in Virginia in 1619. When the Church of England was established in the other Southern colonies, glebes were set apart in them likewise, in accordance with English custom. Some Northern parishes also acquired farms, either through purchase or by the gift of a wealthy individual or public official. The glebe was supposed to be furnished with the necessary farm buildings and to be stocked with cattle, and, sometimes, with slaves. After the Revolution the Episcopal Church was deprived of its glebe lands in Virginia, and they were sold (1802) for the benefit of the public treasury. In the other states, the title to the glebes was retained, but during the long vacancies which ensued in many parishes, much of the land fell into neglect and decay. In some parishes, however, particularly in Maryland and South Carolina, the use of the glebe continued, during the early 19th century, to form an important part of the minister's stipend. As the sense of professional differentiation increased, the actual cultivation of his glebe was thought beneath the dignity of a minister, and the farms were usually rented out instead. Outside of the South, due to the growing industrialization and urbanization of the country, the use of glebes died out almost entirely. Some parishes sold their farms outright. Others rented them and applied the rent to the general parish expenses.

GLORIETA, BATTLE OF.

On March 27, 1862, a Confederate force, following the Santa Fe Trail to capture Fort Union, N. Mex., encountered a Union force in Apache Cañon, and was defeated in a sharp engagement. The Federals fell back to camp near water at Pidgin's ranch, just east of Glorieta Pass. Next day, both sides reinforced to about 1700 men, they fought the battle which proved the turning point for the Confederate cause in the Far West. The Union force finally fell back to Kosloski's ranch, the Confederates holding the field but requesting a truce to care for their casualties.

In effect, the battle was a Union victory, since a detachment had gained the Confederate rear and destroyed their baggage and supply train in Cañoncito. Leaving many of their dead for the Federals to bury, the Confederate survivors retreated to Santa Fe and down the Rio Grande. Jefferson Davis' dream of revolutionizing New Mexico, Sonora and California was definitely ended.

GNADENHUTTEN, a Delaware village on the Tuscarawas River in Ohio, site of the present town so named, was founded in 1772 by Christianized Indians and Moravian missionaries, migrating from Pennsylvania. During the Revolution, the pacifism of the Moravian Indians made them suspect to both sides, and in 1781 hostile Indians forced their removal to the Sandusky Valley. Parties of them, however, returned for food during the ensuing winter; and in February, 1782, warriors who had accompanied them attacked settlers in Washington County, Pa. Some hundred militiamen under Col. David Williamson surrounded Gnadenhutten on March 7, intending to destroy the town and take the unresisting Indians to Fort Pitt. But when one of the Indian women was seen wearing the dress of a woman captured in Washington County, the enraged frontiersmen voted overwhelmingly to wipe out the entire band. The Indians made no resistance, and about a hundred men, women and children were brutally executed.

"GO WEST, YOUNG MAN, GO WEST," was first used by J. L. B. Soule in the Terre Haute, Ind., *Express,* in 1851. The expression attracted Horace Greeley, who wrote in an editorial in the New York *Tribune,* July 13, 1865: "Go West, young man, and grow up with the country." When the phrase gained popularity, Greeley printed Soule's article to show the source of his inspiration. The phrase greatly influenced clerks, mechanics and returned soldiers from the Civil War to move West to take up a homestead.

GODEY'S LADY'S BOOK was first published in Philadelphia in 1830 by Louis Godey as the *Lady's Book.* In 1837 Godey bought the *Ladies Magazine* of Boston and made its editor, Sarah Josepha Hale, the literary editor of his periodical. It was this combination of Godey and Mrs. Hale that gave the magazine its standing. In the forty years of their association Godey's became the most famous and influential periodical in America. In matters of fashions, etiquette, home economics and standards of propriety Godey's was the supreme arbiter, and was the model for the home magazine which still exerts such an enormous influence in American life. Shortly before the Civil War it had a monthly circulation of 150,000 copies. Following the sale of Godey's interests and the retirement of Mrs. Hale in 1877, the magazine was moved to New York where it finally expired in 1892.

GOEBEL AFFAIR. William Goebel was an active northern Kentucky politician who became known as a friend of the common people. In 1899 he obtained the Democratic nomination for the governorship from a riotous nominating convention. A warmly contested campaign followed, and his Republican opponent, William S. Taylor, was declared elected. Claims were made that voters had been intimidated, and that corporations were influential in bringing about Goebel's defeat. The election returns were contested, and mountaineers from the eastern counties came to Frankfort, the capital, in large numbers. On Jan. 30, 1900, Goebel was shot by an unidentified rifleman who was hidden in the state office building. However, the legislature declared him elected, and on Jan. 31, he was sworn in as governor of the state. He died Feb. 3. The tense situation in the state relaxed during the term of his successor, the Democratic lieutenant-governor, J. C. W. Beckham.

GOLD, DISCOVERY OF, IN CALIFORNIA (1848). Perhaps no other event in California's history has been of such far-reaching consequence as James W. Marshall's discovery of gold in the Sierra Nevadas, on Jan. 24, 1848, nine days before the formal transfer of the territory from Mexico to the United States. For three centuries a series of accidents had kept the Spaniards from settling California at all, or from doing so populously when at length they did establish themselves. Thus the gold remained hidden, away from the area of the Spanish occupation, and there was no rush of gold hunters who might have made this region Spanish instead of Anglo-American. Minor discoveries of precious metal near Los Angeles prior to 1848 were not great enough in amount to produce such a transformation.

Marshall, a Scotch-American carpenter, was building a sawmill in partnership with Capt. John A. Sutter, a Swiss soldier of fortune and prominent merchant-adventurer of early California. Sometime on Jan. 24—probably in the morning, although authorities differ—he was at Coloma, on the south fork of the American River and between forty and fifty miles from Sacramento, making his customary inspection of the tailrace. He noticed a number of yellow particles mingled with the earth, some of which he gathered. Finding them malleable, he announced, that evening, that he thought he had found gold. Four days after the discovery, with several ounces of the metal which he and his companions had meantime collected, Marshall rode off for Sutter's Fort, at present Sacramento. Convinced, after various tests, of the correctness of their conclusions, Sutter and Marshall agreed to keep the discovery secret until the completion of pending business operations, and pledged the others who knew of the find to silence. Nevertheless, the news was soon out, and both Sutter and Marshall were beggared by the gold rush, which so profoundly altered the California scene.

GOLD MINES AND MINING. Gold mining in the United States began in the foothills of the Appalachian Mountains of North Carolina following the chance discovery of a nugget of free gold in 1799. Limited but continuous activity there, and in Georgia after the opening of gold deposits in 1828–29, resulted in the production of an estimated $24,500,000 worth of gold in the years before 1848. This record was completely and dramatically eclipsed in the gold fields of California after the discovery at Coloma by James Wilson Marshall in January, 1848. The gold flakes that Marshall found in the run at Sutter's Mill were not the first gold found in California; Mexicans had worked placer deposits near Los Angeles since 1842. But the Coloma strike touched off a mass migration to the gold fields of the newly acquired province. The first decade of California mining, 1848–58, saw some $550,000,000 worth of gold extracted.

The early California mines were placer deposits of free, or pure, gold mixed with sand and gravel. The mining pan became the basic tool of the placer miner. He recovered the gold by agitating water and debris in the pan; the gold, being heavier than the sand or gravel, settled to the bottom of the pan. Refinements such as the rocker, sluice, tom, dredge, and hydraulic nozzle are all devices employing the same principle as the pan—a method of washing the gold-bearing debris with water. The only chemical process used was amalgamation of gold with mercury, and the heating of the amalgam to drive off the mercury as vapor, leaving the residue of free gold.

In time, as the easily worked California placer deposits began to be exhausted, interest turned to lode mining. Here the free gold occurred in streaks or veins embedded in quartz or rock. Lode mining required more expensive methods of crushing the ore. Early tools like the Spanish arrastre soon were replaced by steam-powered stamp mills. Washing and amalgamation followed the pulverizing of the ore to recover the gold. The Empire and the North Star mines at Grass Valley were California's most successful lode mines.

The California gold mining initiated a continuing series of gold strikes in the trans-Mississippi west, and the experiences of California miners proved valuable lessons in the new camps. Mining laws and mining methods, with many ingredients borrowed from Spanish mining via Mexico, were exported from California to the new fields. The California experience of early emphasis on placer deposits and a gradual turning to lode mining, was the general pattern throughout the West. Not all of the new fields provided the hoped-for lodes, but in most of them at least low-grade veins were found.

In 1859 the Comstock lode in Nevada, with its

rich gold and silver ores, gave rise to the boom-town of Virginia City. The year before small placer deposits had been found near Cherry Creek in what became Colorado, touching off the Pike's Peak rush in the spring of 1859. In the following decade camps were opened in Idaho and Montana, and the Black Hills region of South Dakota experienced the same pattern in the years after 1875. The Alaska fields were first mined in the 1880's, with later and richer discoveries in 1898 near Cape Nome and in 1902–3 in the Fairbanks region. Goldfield and Tonopah provided Nevada with a second rush in 1903–5.

Most of this gold was free gold, and mechanical methods of separation were sufficient for recovery. Gold also exists in chemical combination with other elements, and here the problems of extraction are more complex. Advances in metallurgical chemistry were necessary before such ores could be profitably worked. One of the first successful chemical processes for separation of refractory ores was the cyanide process, perfected in 1887. This process involved the placing of finely crushed gold ores in a solution of potassium cyanide, where the soluble gold cyanide that formed could be removed either with zinc or by electrolysis. This process, and others such as chlorination and, later, oil-flotation, were available when the Cripple Creek fields of Colorado were opened in 1891. The nation's richest mining district developed from the telluride ores of Cripple Creek, with the two biggest producers, the Portland and the Independence mines, accounting for more than $100,000,000 worth of gold in the years after 1891. The new chemical processes also made possible the reworking of older mines to recover gold from low-grade ores, and the development of areas like the San Juan region of Colorado, with its Camp Bird, Liberty-Bell, and Smuggler-Union mines.

After World War I gold mining decreased markedly in the United States. High-grade ores had been exhausted, and the costs of extraction and refining increased. The Homestake mine at Lead, S. Dak., after 1920, made South Dakota the leading gold producing state. Gold mining in Utah, Alaska, and California continued, but at a reduced pace.

The U. S. Bureau of Mines has estimated that from 1493 to 1957, throughout the world, 1,934,-528,100 ounces of gold were mined. The United States provided approximately 15% of the world's supply, worth an estimated $7,664,442,080.

GOLD STANDARD, THE, is a monetary system in which gold is the standard or, in other words, in which the unit of value, be it the dollar, the pound, franc or some other unit in which prices and wages are customarily expressed and debts are usually contracted, consists of the value of a fixed quantity of gold in a free gold market.

The United States' experience with the gold standard began in the 1870s. From 1792 down to the Civil War the country, with a few lapses during brief periods of suspended specie payments, was on a bimetallic standard. This broke down in the early days of the Civil War and from Dec. 30, 1861, to January 2, 1879, the country was on a depreciated paper money standard. In 1873 the currency laws of the National Government were revised and codified and in the process the standard silver dollar was dropped from the list of coins whose minting was authorized by law. The law of 1873 continued the free and unlimited coinage of gold and unlimited legal tender quality for all gold coins, and declared the gold dollar to be the unit of value. There was a free market in the United States for gold, and gold could be exported and imported without restriction. Nonetheless the country for six years longer continued on a *de facto* greenback standard with the greenback and national bank notes that comprised the principal money of the country circulating at a substantial discount from gold parity.

With the return of the nation to specie payments on Jan. 2, 1879 in accordance with the provisions of the Resumption Act of 1875, all the currency was brought to a parity with the gold dollar.

Under the gold standard as it then operated in the United States the unit of value was the gold dollar which contained 23.22 grains of pure gold. Inasmuch as a troy ounce contains 480 grains, an ounce of gold could be coined into $20.67 (480/23.22=$20.67). Under free coinage, therefore, any one could take pure gold bullion in any quantity to an American mint and have it minted into gold coins, receiving $20.67 (less certain petty charges for assaying and refining) for each ounce, while anyone melting down American gold coins of full weight would get an ounce of gold out of every $20.67. This was called the "mint price" of gold although to say that an ounce of gold was worth $20.67 was like saying that a yard was 3 feet long. Clearly mint price is not a market price that fluctuates with the changing demand and supply of gold.

The Gold Standard Act of 1900, following the monetary difficulties associated with the bimetallic controversy and the silver legislation of 1878, 1890 and 1893, made legally definitive a gold standard system that had existed *de facto* since 1879. This act declared that the gold dollar "shall be the standard unit of value, and all forms of money issued or coined by the United States shall be maintained at a parity of value with this standard and it shall be the duty of the Secretary of the Treasury to maintain such parity." That meant that the value of every dollar of our paper money and of our silver, nickel and copper coins, and the value of every dollar payable by bank check with which hundreds of billions of dollars of business annually were effected were equal to the value of a gold dollar, namely, to the value of 23.22 grains of pure gold coined into money. Anything that affected the value of gold in the world's markets affected the value of the gold dollar in terms of which this tremendous amount of business was being done and of which all of our debt obligations were expressed. If the supply of gold thrown on the world's markets relative to the demand increased, gold depreciated and commodity prices in the United States, as in all other gold standard countries, tended upward. If the world's demand for gold increased more rapidly than the supply of gold, gold appreciated and commodity prices in all gold standard countries tended downward.

It is highly desirable that the value of the monetary unit, namely, its purchasing power over goods and services, shall be stable; but owing to the widespread variations in the world's supply of gold and in the world's demand for gold, the value of gold, when viewed over any considerable periods of time, has usually shown substantial fluctuations. If we think of the gold dollar as a yardstick of value and represent the purchasing power of this dollar over commodities at wholesale in the year 1926 in the United States by a length of 36 inches, the length of this yardstick would have been as follows for the dates specified: 1913, 52 inches; 1920, 23 inches; 1921, 37 inches; 1929, 37 inches; 1932, 57 inches.

When the yardstick shrinks, we have inflation, a rising cost of living and excesses in speculation, and when the yardstick expands, we have deflation and depression. Inflation usually helps the debtor at the expense of the creditor, the exporter at the expense of the importer, the speculator at the expense of the man with a fixed income, the capitalist at the expense of the laborer. Deflation does substantially the opposite. Both inflation and deflation are undesirable.

There is little difference of opinion among economists on the desirability of obtaining a stable unit of value. The difficulty is in finding how to accomplish this purpose. This is the great monetary problem of the ages. While gold as a monetary standard during the half-century, 1879–1933, was far from stable in value, it was more stable than silver, its only competing monetary metal, and its historical record was much better than that of paper money standards. Furthermore, its principal instability was usually felt during great wars, or shortly thereafter, and at such times all other monetary standards were highly unstable.

During the 19th century, especially from 1870 on, the major nations of the world moved toward the gold coin standard. England, Germany, France and the United States all had dependable currencies because of it. It was considered the most dependable monetary standard yet devised and between 1873 and 1912 some 40 nations used it. World War I swept all of them off it whether they were in the war or not. At the Genoa Conference in 1922 the major nations resolved to return to gold as soon as possible (a few had already done so). Most major nations did so within a few years; over 40 had by 1931. But not many could now afford a gold coin standard and so they used the gold bullion standard (the smallest "coin" was a gold ingot worth say $8000) or the even more economical gold exchange standard. In the latter the so-called gold standard country would not redeem in its own gold coin or bullion but in drafts on the central bank of some gold coin or gold bullion standard country with whom its Treasury "banked." It was a parasitic gold standard. The central banks in England, France and the United States were preferred. It was a hazardous system for if the principal nation's central bank was in trouble, so were all the depositor nations. In the summer and fall of 1931 the gold standards of Austria, Germany and England successively collapsed, dragging other gold exchange standard nations with them. This was the beginning of the end of the gold standard in modern times. Many British blamed their financial difficulties in the latter 1920s on the alleged inflexibility of the gold standard. The trouble lay in the fact that England failed to face up to the fact that her pound had depreciated 60% during World War I and yet she refused to devalue the pound in 1925 before returning to the gold bullion standard. The failure to devalue, not the gold standard, forced Britain to lower prices and wages to try to hold her foreign trade: such moves were understandably unpopular with businessmen and wage earners. Politicians blamed depression and unemployment on the gold standard and England finally abandoned it in Sept., 1931.

Meanwhile in the United States the gold coin standard that had begun in 1879 continued in full operation until March of 1933 except to the small extent that the country departed from it during the World War I embargo on gold exports in effect from Sept. 10, 1917, to June 9, 1919. At first the Panic of 1929 which ushered in the long and severe depression of the 1930s seemed not to threaten the gold standard. True, England's departure from gold in 1931 was a shock. In the 1932 presidential campaign candidate Franklin Roosevelt was known to be influenced by those who wanted the United States to follow England's example. A growing number of bank failures in late 1932 severely shook public confidence in the economy, but it was not until February of 1933 that a frightened public began to hoard gold. Soon after President Roosevelt took office, on March 6, 1933, he declared a nationwide bank moratorium and forbade banks to pay out gold or to export it. On April 5 the President ordered all gold coins and gold certificates in hoards over $100 turned in for other money. The government took in $300 million of gold coin and $470 million of gold certificates by May 10. Suspension of specie payments was still regarded as temporary; dollar exchange was only a trifle below par. But the

President had been listening to the advice of infla-tionists, and it is possible that the anti-hoarding order was part of a carefully laid plan. Suddenly, on April 20, he imposed a permanent embargo on gold exports, justifying the step with the specious argu-ment that there was not enough gold to pay all the holders of currency and of public and private debts in the gold these obligations promised. Dollar ex-change rates fell sharply. By the Thomas Amend-ment to the AAA of May 12, 1933 Congress gave him power to reduce the gold content of the dollar as much as 50%. A joint resolution of Congress on June 5 abrogated the gold clauses to be found in many public and private obligations requiring the debtor to repay the creditor in gold dollars of the same weight and fineness as those borrowed. The Supreme Court in four cases later essentially upheld this abrogation.

During the autumn of 1933 the Treasury bid up the price of gold under the Gold Purchase Plan and finally set it at $35 an ounce under the Gold Re-serve Act of Jan. 30, 1934. This made the new gold dollar 13.71 grains of pure gold (480/35=13.71) although the act forbade the actual coinage of gold. The dollar value of our gold stock (formerly $4,033 millions was increased by 69% (23.22 is 169% of 13.71). Most of this profit was subsequently used as a stabilization fund and to retire our national bank notes. The reason for raising the price of gold by 69% was to push up the price level by 69%, for between 1926 and early 1933 wholesale prices had fallen by 41% and a 69% rise (the reciprocal of a 41% fall) was needed to restore them to the previous level. Some of the President's economic advisors naively believed that this rise in the price of gold would soon raise other prices and that this in turn would help restore prosperity.

The United States was now back on a gold stand-ard (the free gold market was now in London). It was a completely new kind and it came to be called a qualified gold bullion standard. It is at best a weak gold standard, having only external and not internal convertibility. In other words foreign central banks and Treasuries may demand and acquire gold coin or bullion when the exchange rate is at the gold export point, but no person may obtain gold for his money, coin or bank deposits. After France left gold in 1936 it was about the only gold standard left in a world of managed currencies. Although better than none at all, it was not a very satisfactory gold standard. In the first place the $35 an ounce price greatly overvalued gold, stimulating gold mining all over the world and causing gold to pour into this country. Our holdings grew from $6.8 billions in Jan. 1934 to $11.3 billions in Jan. 1937 to $17.9 in Jan. 1940 to $22.7 in Jan. 1943. This "golden avalanche" aroused considerable criticism and created many problems. It gave banks excess reserves and placed their lending policies beyond Federal Re-

serve control. For a while in 1936 the Federal Reserve solved this problem by "sterilizing" some of the gold. On the other hand citizens were not permitted to draw out gold to show their distrust of the new system or for any other reason. As for raising the price level the desired 69%, it did not do that either. Wholesale prices rose only 13% between 1933 and 1937 and except for a brief re-covery in 1937 the depression lasted throughout the decade of the 1930s. Finally a new economics was replacing the classical economics so characterized by the gold coin standard and its stable price level goal.

The appearance of J. M. Keynes, *The General Theory of Employment, Interest and Money* in 1936 and the influence of that British economist on the policies of the Roosevelt administration caused a revolution in economic thinking. The new economics deplored oversaving and the evils of *de*flation and made controlling the business cycle to achieve full employment the major goal of public policy. It advocated a more managed economy. In contrast, the classical economists had stressed capital accumu-lation as a key to prosperity, deplored the evils of *in*flation and relied on the forces of competition to provide a self-adjusting, less-managed economy. The need to do something about the Great Depression of the 1930s, then World War II, the Korean War and the "cold" war all served to strengthen the hands of those who wanted a strong central government and disliked the trammels of a domestically convertible gold coin standard. The rising generation of econo-mists and politicians held this view. After 1940 the Republican platform ceased to advocate clearly a return to domestic convertibility in gold. Labor leaders, formerly defenders of a stable dollar when wages clearly lagged behind prices, began to feel that a little inflation helped them. Some economists and politicians frankly urged an annual depreciation of the dollar by 2, 3 or 5 per cent, allegedly to prevent depressions and to promote economic growth. All of these attitudes are characteristic of a people whose economic value judgements have changed because capital seems more plentiful than formerly and thus requires less encouragement and protection.

There remained, however, a substantial segment of society that feared creeping inflation and that even advocated a return to the domestically convertible gold coin standard. Not a year has passed since 1934 but that one or more Congressmen or Senators have introduced such a gold standard bill. These rarely emerge from committee, however. In 1954 the Senate held extensive hearings on the Bridges-Reece bill but administration opposition killed it. In the academic profession the chief organization favoring such legislation is the Economists National Committee on Monetary Policy which has included many dis-tinguished monetary economists. These economists have deplored the inflation, much of it unnecessary, that has taken place since the 1930s (the dollar has lost 55% of its value since then), and the trend towards a more managed economy that it has brought in its wake. They feel that a gold coin standard is an ever-present voting device enabling the people to defend their savings and themselves against their economic managers just as the right to vote gives them protection against their political managers. Opponents of domestic convertibility and even of the weak gold standard in existence contend that it is an inflexible tool that deepens depressions and worsens unemployment or a dangerous device which a panicky public or a cold war enemy might use to wreck the nation's finances. They argue that government authorities can serve the public better by managing the currency than by relying on this "relic of barbarism" as Keynes called it. They ignore that even gold standards have been in part managed in the past and that the world has suffered far more from inflation which managed currencies sooner or later produce, than from deflation which has been a relatively rare historical phenomenon.

Somewhat apart from these two viewpoints, but important, is the less disinterested attitude of the gold mining interests in South Africa, Canada, the United States and elsewhere, who would welcome a return to the gold coin standard on a many nation basis just as the silver mining interests once wanted a return to bimetallism. In the 1930s the depression and devaluation greatly stimulated gold mining, the former because it lowered costs, the latter because it raised the price of gold by 69%. But a return to prosperity and a more than doubling of the price level with no change in the mint price steadily reduced gold mining profits. Gold mining companies have repeatedly urged a higher price for gold on the ground that all other prices have risen since 1934. They have ignored that a higher price for gold automatically means devaluation. For example, a $48 an ounce price for gold would mean a 10 grain gold dollar (480/48=10) and thus a 27% debasement or devaluation of the dollar. Regardless of their complaints, they have continued to produce in recent years between $700 million and $1200 million of gold a year and the managed currency nations have bought it just as gladly as we have. This has been about a 2% to 3% increase in gold per year, and that is roughly equivalent to world production increases in other commodities.

There are about $41 billions of monetary gold in the world today (1960) distributed as follows: the United States, $18 billions, and other nations, $23 billions, with $11 billions of it in their safe deposit vaults in New York. It is estimated that in addition Russia may have about $10 billion. The United States keeps its gold hoards chiefly in Fort Knox, Kentucky, New York, Denver and San Francisco. Since World War II American holdings of gold have varied between a high of over $24 billion in August 1949 and a low of $18 billions in October 1960. The outflow of several billions in 1942–45 and in 1949–51 caused some worry, but the larger outflow since early 1958 has caused greater concern. It was caused by large government expenditures abroad, increasing American investments abroad and prosperity in Europe permitting nations there to build up their gold holdings. It is what a gold standard nation should occasionally expect and be ready to face, just as banks must occasionally expect sizable withdrawals by their depositors. To the extent that it is a sign of loss of confidence, it is a healthy warning signal to repair the financial damage. The United States, despite some $11 billions required for money and banking reserves and additional fractional reserves needed against about $21 billions of short term liabilities to foreigners, could stand substantial further withdrawals before the gold standard would be seriously jeopardized. But the moment the nation puts a stop to external convertibility, it would remove its last claim to being on a gold standard.

GOLDEN HILL, BATTLE OF (Jan. 18, 1770). The Liberty Boys of New York City had for three years been at odds with the British soldiery, who felled their liberty poles now and then. On the day of the skirmish, three soldiers who were posting insulting placards were seized by Isaac Sears, a Liberty Boy leader, and some comrades. Other soldiers rushed to the rescue, followed by other citizens, and a street fight took place at a spot known as Golden Hill (in the vicinity of William Street above Wall). The sixty soldiers charged the citizenry with cutlass and bayonet; several of the latter were wounded, and it is said that one died of his injuries. There was another sharp clash on the following day.

GOLDEN HIND, originally named the *Pelican*, the first English vessel to circumnavigate the globe, sailed from Plymouth, Dec. 13, 1577. She was rechristened the *Golden Hind* by her commander, Sir Francis Drake, in Magellan Strait; sailed up the South American coast, plundering Spanish treasure ships; and reached the present vicinity of San Francisco, June 15, 1579. She sailed home round the Cape of Good Hope, reaching Plymouth, Sept. 26, 1580.

GOLIAD, MASSACRE AT (March 27, 1836). Col. James W. Fannin, Jr., of the Texan army, surrendered to the Mexicans his force of about 400 Anglo-Americans, near Goliad, Tex. They understood that they were surrendering as prisoners of war to be returned to the United States. Pursuant to a decree of the Mexican government that foreigners taken on Mexican soil be treated as pirates, they were shot down in merciless fashion one week after their surrender.

GONZALES, BATTLE OF (Oct. 2, 1835), the first battle of the Texas Revolution, was caused by the demand of the Mexican military commander at San Antonio that the people of Gonzales surrender a cannon which they had for protection against the Indians. The demand was refused, whereupon a force of 100 men was sent to seize the gun. A band of Texas volunteers engaged and routed them a few miles from Gonzales.

GOOD NEIGHBOR POLICY. In his first inaugural address, March 4, 1933, President F. D. Roosevelt said: "In the field of world policy I would dedicate this nation to the policy of the good neighbor—the neighbor who resolutely respects himself and, because he does so, respects the rights of others." Among subsequent acts of the Roosevelt administration in keeping with the policy may be mentioned the renunciation of armed intervention in Latin America in 1933; the abrogation of the Platt Amendment and the withdrawal of marines from Haiti in 1934; and participation in the Buenos Aires agreement of 1936 which presumably made the Monroe Doctrine a multilateral instrument for all the Pan-American republics.

GRAN QUIVIRA. Quivira was the name used by Coronado for the Indian villages he sought in the plains of Kansas in 1541, probably the native name for the Wichita and the Pawnee Indians. The name was later used as Gran Quivira, to designate the ruins of a Piro Indian village and its Spanish mission, built in 1629, abandoned in 1670, now a National Monument.

GRAND ARMY OF THE REPUBLIC was founded by Benjamin F. Stephenson, a physician of Springfield, Ill., who had served as surgeon of the 14th Illinois Infantry. Impressed with the desirability of a veterans' association which should exist for the mutual benefit of its members and for the aid of soldiers' widows and orphans, Stephenson and a small group of friends formed the nucleus of an organization at Springfield in the spring of 1866. On April 6, 1866, the first post was established at Decatur, Ill. By July 12, 1866, when a state convention was held to form the Department of Illinois, 39 posts had been chartered. At the first national encampment, held at Indianapolis on Nov. 20, 1866, ten states and the District of Columbia were represented.

The first commander in chief was Gen. S. A. Hurlbut of Illinois. Hurlbut was succeeded by Gen. John A. Logan, also of Illinois, who served three successive terms. Logan's successor was Gen. A. E. Burnside.

GRAND BANKS is a submerged tableland between Newfoundland and deep water, sea-covered by an average of approximately 240 feet, reaching south to the latitude of Boston, and east for 500 miles. Arctic current and Gulf Stream meeting produce almost constant fog. Basque fishermen knew this region as "Baccalaos," the land of codfish, probably before the time of Columbus. By 1578 Spanish, Portuguese, French, Breton, and English ships were fishing there for cod, whales, and walruses. Fishing boats still resort to the Grand Banks each year, catching cod in water from 50 to 750 feet deep.

GRAND CANYON OF THE COLORADO, in width from four to eighteen miles and in places more than a mile deep, winding some 280 miles from Marble Canyon, near the Arizona-Utah line, to Grand Wash Cliffs in northern Mohave County of Arizona, constituted a natural barrier to travel.

Pedro de Tovar, an officer of the Spanish expedition under Coronado, first heard of it during a visit to the Hopi Indians in 1540. To investigate Tovar's reports, García López de Cárdenas, with twelve companions left Coronado's camp at the Zuñi pueblo of Háwikuh, late in August of 1540, and after twenty days' journey, discovered the Canyon, the first description of which by white men is to be found in Pedro de Castañeda's narrative of the Coronado expedition. The Canyon was little known to the world until Lt. Joseph C. Ives and Dr. J. S. Newberry visited the lower end of it in April, 1858, and brought back the first geological description of the region. The first journey down the Colorado River through the Canyon was made by Maj. John Wesley Powell and nine men, from Green River in Wyoming to the Grand Wash Cliffs, May 24–Aug. 30, 1869. Powell made second and third voyages through the Canyon in 1871–72. Since that time many parties, for scientific or other reasons, have attempted the hazardous journey, sometimes with tragic results. The Grand Canyon National Park, an area of 1009 square miles, was created by Congress on Feb. 26, 1919, and two years later the completion of a railroad from Williams, Ariz., facilitated tourist travel to the Canyon.

GRAND PORTAGE received its name from *voyageurs*, who found the nine miles between Lake Superior and navigable waters on the Pigeon River the longest portage in their regular canoe route from Montreal to the Rocky Mountains. About 1780 the name came to be applied to the North West Company post at the lake end of the portage.

GRANDFATHER CLAUSE was a device in Southern state constitutions to circumvent the requirement of Negro suffrage in the Fifteenth Amendment. Exemption from property-owning, tax-paying, or educational requirements in state suffrage laws was granted to those who had had the right to vote on Jan. 1, 1867, and to their lineal descendants. Since Negroes in the South could not vote at that time, they were excluded from the privilege granted to impoverished or illiterate whites. The clause, applicable for a limited time, was adopted in South Carolina, 1895; Louisiana, 1898; North Carolina,

1902; Alabama, 1901; Virginia, 1902; Georgia, 1908; Oklahoma, 1910. In 1915 the Supreme Court declared the "grandfather clause" unconstitutional (*see* Guinn and Beal v. U. S.).

GRANGER CASES. During the years 1869 to 1874 the legislatures of Illinois, Iowa, Wisconsin and Minnesota passed a number of statutes, known generally as the "Granger Laws," for the regulation of railroads and warehouses within their respective borders. Most of these laws set maximum schedules of charges, and some of them established regulatory commissions with extensive authority. The railroad companies disliked the Granger laws intensely, and sought to discredit them with the public by blaming indifferent and expensive service upon them. The laws were, in fact, badly drawn, and were soon repealed, but better laws based upon the same principles were presently enacted, not only by the four states mentioned, but by most of the rest of the states of the Union as well.

Efforts to enforce the original Granger laws led to a large number of lawsuits, a series of which, the so-called "Granger Cases," were decided by the U. S. Supreme Court in March, 1877. The issue involved in each case was the same: Had a state the right to regulate, on the ground that the business concerned was public in nature, a corporation that was privately owned and managed? Attorneys for the railroads argued that any such assumption of power on the part of the state amounted to a deprivation of property without due process of law, and thus violated the Fourteenth Amendment of the Federal Constitution; also, that, within the meaning of Article I, Section 10, of the same document, the charters under which the railroads operated were contracts, the obligation of which was impaired by the Granger regulations. The Court held, however, that regulation, even to the setting of maximum rates, was within the constitutional right of the states. The cases most frequently cited in this connection are Munn v. Illinois and Peik v. the Chicago and North Western Railway. In 1886 the Court modified the doctrine of the Granger decisions to the extent of restricting state regulation to strictly intrastate business (Wabash, St. Louis and Pacific Railroad v. Illinois).

GRANGER MOVEMENT grew out of a farmers' lodge, the Patrons of Husbandry, founded in 1867 by Oliver Hudson Kelley, a clerk in the Post Office Department at Washington. The preceding year, Kelley, then in the employ of the Bureau of Agriculture, had made a tour of the South, and had been struck by the blind enslavement of Southern farmers to outworn and traditional methods of agriculture. This situation, he believed, could best be remedied by an organization that would bring farmers together in groups for the study and discussion of their problems. Accordingly, with the help of a few interested

friends, he devised a secret ritualistic order, equally open to women and to men, and became its first organizer. Each local unit, or Grange, was admonished to select among its officers a "Lecturer," whose duty should be to provide some educational diversion, such as a lecture or a paper, for every meeting.

Early in 1868 Kelley started west to his home in Minnesota, hoping to organize Granges as he went. He had little success, however, until he reached his destination, and began work among his former neighbors. There his organization won adherents, less for its social and educational advantages than for the opportunity it presented for farmers to unite against the monopolistic practices of railroads and elevators, and to institute for themselves co-operative methods of buying and selling. By the end of 1869 there were 37 active Granges in Minnesota, a year later the order had expanded into nine widely separated states, and when the panic of 1873 broke there were Granges in every state of the Union but four. Membership claims, always hard to substantiate, reached a maximum during the middle 1870's of about 800,000, with the total number of Granges set at about 20,000. The center of Granger activity remained during the entire period in the grain-growing region of the upper Mississippi Valley.

The grievances that drove the Northwestern farmers into organized revolt grew out of their almost complete dependence upon outside markets for the disposal of their produce, and upon corporation-owned elevators and railroads for its handling. The high prices that accompanied the Civil War in the United States and the Bismarckian wars in Europe enabled the farmers, while the wars were on, to pay the high charges that the corporations exacted, but afterward, when prices began to drop, the grain-growers found themselves in acute distress. In 1869 they paid at the rate of 52½ cents a bushel to send grain from the Mississippi River to the Atlantic seaboard, and nearly half as much to send it from an Iowa or Minnesota farm to Chicago. Elevators, often themselves owned in turn by the railroads, charged generously for their services, weighed and graded grain without supervision, and used their influence with the railroads to insure that cars were not available to farmers who sought to evade elevator service.

Rumblings of revolt were heard throughout the later 1860's, and in 1869 the legislature of Illinois actually passed an act that required the railroads to charge only "just, reasonable, and uniform rates"; but, because the act provided no adequate means of enforcement, nothing came of it. Next year, however, Illinois adopted a new constitution in which the legislature was definitely authorized to correct railway abuses and extortions by law. Acting on this authority, the legislature of 1871 set maximum freight and passenger rates, and established a board of railroad and warehouse commissioners to enforce them.

These laws the railroads flatly refused to obey, a position in which they were sustained by the state supreme court. But in 1873 a more carefully drawn law ran the gauntlet of a revised supreme court, for in the meantime at a judicial election the angered farmers had replaced one of the offending judges with a judge more Granger-minded.

By this time the Grange had become far more political than educational in nature, and, ably assisted by a host of unaffiliated farmers' clubs, was in the thick of the fight for state regulation of railroads and elevators. At Granger lodge meetings and picnics the farmers exhorted one another to nominate and elect to office only those who shared their views; and, in case corporation control over the Republican and Democratic organization could not be overthrown, to form "Independent," or "Reform," or "Anti-Monopoly" parties through which to carry on the fight. So many farmers made Independence Day, 1873, an occasion for airing these views that the celebration was long remembered as the "Farmers' Fourth of July." On this day many rural audiences listened with approval to the reading of a *Farmers' Declaration of Independence*, which recited their grievances and asserted their determination to use the power of the state to free themselves from the "tyranny of monopoly." Victories at the polls, as a result of this agitation, led, not only in Illinois but in several other Northwestern states also, to the passage of a series of so-called "Granger Laws" for the regulation of railroads and warehouses. These measures were not always well drawn, and for the most part they were soon repealed or drastically modified. Nevertheless, the U. S. Supreme Court in Munn v. Illinois, Peik v. the Chicago and North Western Railway, and a number of other cases, all decided in 1877, sustained the Granger contention that businesses of a public nature could, in accordance with the Federal Constitution, be subjected to state regulation—a precedent of far-reaching consequence.

Hardly less important than the political activities of the various Granges were their business ventures. Under Granger auspices numerous co-operative elevators, creameries and general stores were founded, although most of these establishments failed to survive the ruthless competition of private business. The Granges tried many other experiments also, such as buying through purchasing agents or through dealers who quoted special prices to Grangers, patronizing mail-order houses and manufacturing farm machinery. The last-mentioned undertaking, ill-conceived and overdone, resulted in serious financial reverses, and had much to do with the sudden decline in Granger popularity that, beginning about 1876, brought the movement to an untimely end.

In spite of its short span of life the Granger Movement had taught the farmers many things. They had learned that their political power, when they chose to use it, was very great; that business co-operatives,

although hazardous, might, if properly managed, limit the toll paid to middlemen; and that such social and educational activities as the Grange had fostered could greatly brighten rural life. The Patrons of Husbandry as a lodge survived the Granger Movement, won new Eastern adherents to replace the Western deserters, and in the 20th century even recovered some of its influence in politics.

GREAT AWAKENING. In the early decades of the 18th century religion was at a low ebb in both the New and the Old World. Liberalism in America and liberalism and skepticism in Europe were undermining theological orthodoxy on both sides of the Atlantic. Besides, religion had been conventionalized and wealth had brought materialism into the Church. The religious leaders throughout the British American colonies were conscious of this spiritual decline and felt the need of a revival that would renew a deeper interest in the cause of Christianity.

At this juncture there came the Great Awakening, a series of revivals that swept over the colonies. While there were local stirrings in New Jersey in the 1720's, the great revival began in New England (1734) under the leadership of Jonathan Edwards, a Congregational minister of deep piety, brilliant intellect, and great oratorical powers. After a brief lull the revival started up again under the preaching of George Whitefield, an eloquent minister from England. Whitefield traveled through the colonies preaching to immense audiences and arousing the greatest emotional excitement.

Whitefield and Edwards believed that conversion is the initial step in the religious life. Conversion involved first a realization of one's sinfulness (often accompanied by a torturing fear of eternal punishment) and then a consciousness of pardon that filled the soul with love and ecstatic joy. Thousands were brought under the spell of the earnest oratory of the evangelists and great numbers of them professed conversion. Many were doubtless victims of group excitement, but a large number exchanged a religion of cold, complacent formalism for one of joyous hope and active zeal.

The Great Awakening accentuated the differences between the conservatives and the liberals, and thus led to a schism in the two great Calvinistic denominations, the Congregationalists and the Presbyterians. Among the Presbyterians this disagreement widened into a temporary division of the denomination. On the other hand, the Baptist and Anglican churches were strengthened, for many of the converts became Baptists, as this denomination favored the revival; while quite a number of the opponents of the movement entered the Anglican Church, which disapproved of the methods of the revivalists.

The revival also gave a new impetus to higher education, which resulted in the establishment of four colleges (Princeton, Brown, Dartmouth and

Rutgers). It was favorable to the growth of religious toleration, as Whitefield advocated a broad tolerance in religion. A sense of responsibility for the unfortunate was aroused, and this found expression in humanitarianism. The movement tended to break down sectionalism, as the converts were bound together by a fraternal feeling that overleaped denominational lines and provincial boundaries. It was also in line with the trend toward democracy, since it broke the hold of the upper class on the Church and gave the common man a greater influence in religious affairs.

GREAT MEADOWS, ten miles east of the present Uniontown, Pa., on the Cumberland Road, was the site of an early battle in the French and Indian War. On May 24, 1754, a force of some 150 men under George Washington from a Virginia regiment commanded by Col. Joshua Fry, encamped at the open place known as the Great Meadows. Here on May 27 Washington learned that a small French force was hidden a few miles to the north. Leaving a guard at the Great Meadows camp, he made a night march and in a surprise attack soon after sunrise killed ten of the French, including the commander, Jumonville, and took 21 prisoners. This was Washington's first battle and the first engagement of the French and Indian War. Washington sent the prisoners to Williamsburg and, returning to Great Meadows, erected there a small fortification, which he called Fort Necessity.

In June the rest of the Virginia regiment and Capt. Mackay's independent company from South Carolina augmented the force to about 360. Col. Fry had died at Wills Creek, and Washington was now in command of the Virginians. Leaving Mackay's company to guard the supplies at Great Meadows, Washington pushed forward thirteen miles to Gist's plantation, cutting the road as he went. After further consideration, however, he decided to fall back to Great Meadows. Here Fort Necessity was enlarged and strengthened, and on July 3 it was attacked by about 500 French and 400 Indians. The distance from fort to forest made the encounter one of long-range firing in which both sides nearly exhausted their ammunition without sustaining great damage. At length, however, his provisions almost gone, Washington consented to capitulate. The English, allowed to leave the fort with arms and colors after giving hostages for the return of the French prisoners, marched on foot to Virginia, carrying their wounded.

GREAT MIGRATION. During the "Personal Government" of Charles I (1629–40) discontent in England and prospects for better things abroad grew to such proportions that approximately 60,000 persons emigrated. About one third of them went to New England, founding the colonies of Massachusetts Bay, Connecticut and Rhode Island. Others settled in Old Providence, other Caribbean isles, and elsewhere.

The great majority of these emigrants were religious or political Puritans, chiefly of the nonseparating Congregationalist persuasion, who found Laud's Anglicanism or Stuart government intolerable. Puritans were exasperated by the Stuarts' failure materially to assist the defeated Protestants on the Continent and dismayed when their efforts failed to "purify" the Anglican Church of vestigial "Popery" and to limit the Stuarts to constitutional procedures. Meanwhile, William Laud rose to power and applied the screws of conformity until Puritans had no choice but to conform or emigrate. Already, the Rev. John White of Dorchester, the Earl of Warwick and others pointed the way by organizing companies chartered for New World trade and colonization. Between 1627 and 1635 several such companies were organized under Puritan auspices. Of these, the Massachusetts Bay Company was most successful. With White's West Country enterprise, the New England Company, as nucleus, the Massachusetts Company was dominated by East Anglican Puritans. By the Cambridge Agreement, the latter bound themselves to go to Massachusetts provided the Company and the charter be legally transported thither by Sept. 1, 1630. Thus, the 140 West Country people who sailed from Plymouth (March, 1630) and founded Dorchester, Mass., were greatly outnumbered by East Anglicans who sent fourteen ships by June. The Great Migration had begun. During the next decade, about 20,000 people emigrated to the Bay Colony.

Of course, not all these emigrants were Puritans. Depression in agriculture and the cloth trade led many to emigrate for economic betterment—persons often discontented and troublesome in the Bible Commonwealth. Nor was there complete unity among Puritans themselves. Differences between the West Country group and the East Anglican majority which precipitated disputes in the General Court, perhaps were factors in the former's wholesale migration to Connecticut. But the basic cause for the Great Migration was Puritan discontent, as evidenced by its cessation when the English scene became more hopeful after the Long Parliament assembled. Meantime, Puritans had enlarged English Caribbean trade, garnered bullion from the Spanish Main, established fisheries in New England, laid the basis for shipbuilding and the West Indies trade, and founded permanent, populous colonies in New England.

GREAT REVIVAL (1801) was the apogee of a Western revival movement, chiefly in Kentucky, from about 1797 to 1805. The revival had its beginning under the vehement preaching of James McGready, a Presbyterian minister, in Logan County, Ky. Despite doctrinal differences the Methodists, Presbyterians and Baptists often united in conducting the larger meetings which generally were held in encampments. Strange bodily manifestations intensified the religious revival which quickly spread through most of the West. The climax was reached in a great sacramental meeting held at Cane Ridge, Bourbon County, Ky., in August, 1801. The number in attendance has been differently estimated between 10,000 and 25,000. Emphasis upon emotional appeal brought extravagances which checked many of the benefits desired by the leaders. Nevertheless, the revival altered the moral tone and contributed much of value toward developing the Western region. Church membership increased tremendously during the period. The Methodist and Baptist denominations were definitely strengthened, but the Presbyterians suffered from schisms which resulted from opposition to some of the methods used, as well as doctrinal differences. Out of the dissent developed the Cumberland Presbyterian Church which, with the Methodist Church, continued to use the camp meeting revival to stimulate religiously the frontier.

GREAT SALT LAKE, about 35 by 75 miles in size, averages only 25 or 30 feet deep. Its size varies somewhat from wet periods to dry, the constant salt content ranging from 15% to 28% by weight. The earliest reference to it may have been by Baron Lahontan, who claimed to have discovered the River "Long" and to have heard (January, 1689) Indians describe "a Salt Lake 300 leagues in circumference." Father Escalante described it from reports which he heard when crossing the adjoining valley, September, 1776. It was discovered December, 1824, by James Bridger, twenty-year-old Rocky Mountain fur trapper, who, because it was salty, mistook it for an arm of the Pacific Ocean. John C. Frémont made a preliminary instrument survey of the lake in 1843 and described it in his reports, while Howard Stansbury made a more thorough survey in 1849–50, published in two volumes. The most exhaustive lake studies were made in the 1880's by G. K. Gilbert for his celebrated monograph, *Lake Bonneville.*

GREAT SWAMP FIGHT (Sunday, Dec. 19, 1675) took place during King Philip's War, in the Narragansett Country, now South Kingstown, R. I. The combined forces of Massachusetts Bay, Plymouth and Connecticut, over 1000 soldiers, under the command of Gov. Josiah Winslow, with about a hundred and fifty Indian allies, marched on Saturday from Smith's Garrison House (now Wickford, R. I.) to Pettaquamscutt, where they spent the night. Sunday they pushed on through the snow to the island in the Great Swamp, which had been fortified by the Narragansett Indians. The first assault by the English, made about one o'clock in the afternoon, was turned back with terrible losses, but after three hours of desperate fighting the fort was forced at the rear and the Indians routed. The Indian wigwams were set on fire and many women and children lost their lives in the flames. The English lost six captains and 120 men and

the Narragansett's losses ran up into the hundreds This battle did not end the war, but it broke forever the power of the Narragansetts and thus contributed materially toward the final outcome of the struggle.

GREAT TRADING AND WAR PATH. The paths used by the Indians in going to war were for the most part those which had been beaten out by the buffalo, and followed lines of least resistance. Traders to the Indians used these paths, as did later hunters and emigrants. One of most utility and importance took the name of the Great Path. It ran down the Shenandoah Valley to the valleys of the New and Holston Rivers to the Overhill Cherokee towns in the Tennessee country, thence to the Coosa River where it connected with the war path of the Creek Indians. One of its prongs ran through Cumberland Gap from Long Island of Holston; another through Boone's Gap of the Alleghenies to the middle towns of the Cherokees. It was over this path that the Northern Indians, Iroquois and Shawnees especially, went to war with the Cherokees, and the last-named used it in retaliatory raids. A great stream of white migration flowed along it from Pennsylvania, Maryland and Virginia to the Southwest, 1770 onward. Merchandise southward, and horses, cattle and produce northward, were borne over the roads that succeeded the path, and followed it, generally speaking. Mail routes and railroads came later. It may be said that the buffalo was by instinct a civil engineer that located his trace, to be adopted by the Indians as a trail and later used for road and railway.

GREAT TRAIL was a famous Indian thoroughfare leading from the Forks of the Ohio to the present site of Detroit. It followed the north bank of the Ohio River to the mouth of Big Beaver Creek, traversed the watershed to the "Crossing-place on the Muskingum," where Bolivar (Fort Laurens) now is, and then bore northwest passing near the sites of the present towns of Wooster, Fremont and Toledo. During the last half of the 18th century it was the most important trail north of the Ohio. Important Indian villages were located along its route. Along this trail Indians passed long before the white man came. White traders' pack-horse trains used it to carry goods to the natives and to bring out furs. Col. Bouquet's expedition in 1764 followed it. It continued to be important until the 19th century when the building of the Cumberland Road, the Erie Canal and the railroad displaced it.

GREEN BAY (LaBaye, LaBaye des Puans) was the site of the earliest white settlement west of Lake Michigan. The region is known to have been discovered by the French explorer, Jean Nicolet, in 1634. It was not thereafter visited by other Frenchmen for more than twenty years. Traders like Nicolas Perrot and Jesuit missionaries like Claude Allouez visited this site, at the mouth of Fox River, in the late 17th century. A mission was founded at DePere, six miles above Green Bay, in 1671–72; the first French fort was built on the site of the present city in 1684 by LaDurantaye, called Fort St. François Xavier (the name of the mission at DePere). This post was evacuated in 1695 when the governor of New France called in all western garrisons.

A French post was rebuilt there in 1717 during the first Fox war, called Fort LaBaye. It was abandoned and re-established several times during the French regime, but was garrisoned until 1760, when the last officers and soldiers withdrew. British troops arrived next year, under Lt. James Gorrell, a Maryland officer, who repaired Fort LaBaye, renamed it Fort Edward Augustus, and maintained it until Pontiac's conspiracy, when he and his garrison were recalled to Mackinac.

Meanwhile a considerable settlement grew up composed of French traders and retired *voyageurs*. Although French in language and customs, the habitants took the oath of allegiance in 1761 to the British sovereign, and remained loyal throughout the British occupation. Fort Edward Augustus was never restored, but Green Bay became a fur-trade emporium. Commanding the eastern end of the Fox-Wisconsin portage route to the Mississippi, it increased in importance during the fur-trade era. Although the Americans in 1796 established a garrison at Mackinac, Green Bay traders were British in interests, and on the outbreak of the War of 1812 sided with Great Britain, and devoted their energies to supplying the hordes of Indians collected for attack on the American frontiers. Green Bay habitants were impoverished by their war contributions, and regarded with dislike the coming of the Americans and the building of Fort Howard in 1816. Soon afterward a few American settlers arrived at Green Bay, the old Franco-British inhabitants became naturalized and an American settlement grew up.

GREEN MOUNTAIN BOYS. In 1749 Gov. Benning Wentworth, of New Hampshire, began to grant lands in the region west of the Connecticut River which is today Vermont, even though New York put in a strong claim to the area. In 1764 the king decided that the jurisdiction belonged to New York, and the New York Supreme Court, in 1770, held that all Hampshire patents were invalid. This meant that settlers under New Hampshire must rebuy their lands.

The people of the New Hampshire grants west of the Green Mountains promptly resolved to keep their lands by force if necessary, formed military companies, and elected Ethan Allen colonel commandant of the Green Mountain Boys. Settlers under New York were terrorized. The "birch seal" cut into naked Yorker backs; fences were torn down; cattle disap-

peared; and cabins were burned or had their roofs taken off and replaced to symbolize "conversion" to the Yankee cause. The "Green Mountaineers" built rude fortresses on Otter Creek and Onion River. New York proclamations and laws of outlawry were disregarded, and New York sheriffs were driven off. The British government refused to use military force to put down the Green Mountain men and forbade New York to grant more land until the dispute could be settled.

With the coming of the Revolutionary War, the Green Mountain Boys espoused the Patriot cause, took Ticonderoga, raised a separate regiment under Col. Seth Warner, fought at Hubbardton, and were a potent factor in British defeat at the Battle of Bennington. Led by Ira Allen, Thomas Chittenden and Jonas Fay, they declared themselves an independent republic of Vermont, in 1777, and set about securing support from the New England delegates in the Continental Congress. At last New York ceased her opposition, and in 1791 the Green Mountain state was admitted into the Union.

GREEN RIVER. South and west from the Wind River Mountains, there flows the Green River, whose waters make the chief contribution to the Colorado. Hunt and his Astorians were probably the first Americans to visit the valley of the Green, but Spanish parties had noted its course and their name, *Rio Verde*, is probably the origin of the American appellation. Prior to the activities of Wm. Ashley and his Rocky Mountain Fur Company in 1824, but little attention had focused upon the Green, but with the advent of the rendezvous system, the fur trade levied heavy and remunerative toll upon the beaver of its rich valley. The upper reaches of the Green River became a favorite place of meeting for the powerful tribes: Snakes, Nez Percés, Flatheads, Blackfoot and Crows, who assembled for annual exchange of pelts for trade goods supplied by the Rocky Mountain Fur Company and the American Fur Company. Henry's Fork, Fort Bonneville, Ham's Fork and Horse Creek in the valley of the Green witnessed six of the annual fairs of the mountain men held between 1824 and 1840. From the Green River and its tributaries came the greater number of the beaver that yielded to William Ashley the $250,000 proceeds realized by him in five years of fur trading. In the valley of the Green were schooled many of those leading spirits of Far-Western adventure and commerce who later guided the government parties that explored the West.

GREENBACK MOVEMENT was a reaction against the tendency to re-establish specie payments in place of the greenback standard of exchange which had prevailed since 1862. It naturally made its strongest appeal to debtor farmers. It included the "Ohio Idea" of retiring at least the five-twenties among the

Federal Government bonds by issuing new greenbacks, and thus ending the Government's large interest payments as well as the tax-free character of a particular type of investment. Its most essential demand was that greenbacks be given complete legal-tender status, and be issued freely. Besides the debtor character of the movement, it united opposition to National Banks and their currency with resentment against the handsome profits which holders of the Civil War bonds were to take out of the funds raised by taxes.

Although these ideas had strong support in both major parties in rural areas and received partial endorsement in the national Democratic convention in 1868, thereafter the greenback movement became chiefly one for minor parties. The campaign of 1872 found the only organized support of greenback policies in the new Labor Reform party. The independent state Granger parties which sprang up following the panic of 1873 were inflationist in only a few instances, but two of them, Indiana and Illinois, furnished the leadership to create a new national party committed to greenback policies. The Indiana party issued a call for a conference at Indianapolis in November, 1874. It was attended by representatives from several states, including representatives from the Labor Reform party. A permanent organization was established, and a national nominating convention met at Indianapolis on May 17, 1876. This party, variously called "Independent National," "National" and "Greenback Labor," is commonly referred to as the Greenback party, and represents the most important political phase of the movement. Within the party the more extreme members organized the Greenback clubs, which agitated extensively, and in party conventions protested against local fusion with the major parties. For its first national campaign the party nominated Peter Cooper, the New York philanthropist, for President. Its platform demanded the repeal of the recently enacted Resumption Act and enactment of the greenback plans for a national currency. This first platform failed to go outside of the currency for an issue, and the party did not conduct an aggressive campaign. It was handicapped by the fact that in most districts where greenback ideas were popular they were supported by candidates of the two major parties. As a result, the vote received was only slightly more than 80,000, most of it coming from Midwestern farm states.

The most evident result of the campaign was the election of a number of members of the Illinois legislature who combined with the Democrats to elect Justice David Davis of the U. S. Supreme Court to the Senate, a move which in the judgment of some historians kept Tilden from becoming President.

The labor difficulties the next year made that part of the movement more active, and the Greenback party showed notable increases in state elections.

A broader orientation was evident in a party conference at Toledo in 1878, when to the older Greenback planks was added a denunciation of the demonetization of silver, as well as endorsements of legal restrictions upon the hours of labor, the abolition of Chinese immigration and the reservation of public lands for the use of actual settlers. In the congressional elections of that year, the Greenback party scored the most notable victory in its history by sending to the House of Representatives a large number of congressmen. Of these, fourteen or fifteen chose to act as party-conscious Greenbackers, the remainder staying with the major party which had also supported them. Historians credit the party with over 1,000,000 votes in this election, but this includes votes for some candidates who were also supported by one of the major parties. This striking success for the young party created a bloc in the House, which, under the leadership of James B. Weaver of Iowa, gave direction to the organization. The national character of its support is indicated by the fact that the bloc included representatives from every section except the Pacific coast.

This success raised high hopes among party leaders of a steady march toward major-party status. The successful resumption of specie payment in 1879 destroyed the most plausible argument the party had, and the convention of 1880 broadened its appeal by adding a graduated income tax, woman suffrage, government regulation of interstate commerce and social-welfare legislation to its program. Weaver was named the candidate for President, and high hopes were held for attracting a large vote. The disappointing result was a vote of 300,000, less than 4% of the total. The bloc in the House was reduced to ten members.

The decline of the party was steady. Although it nominated the peripatetic Benjamin F. Butler for President in 1884, it was impossible to revive the enthusiasms of 1878 and 1880. The earlier farmer support seemed to be passing away entirely, and Butler's vote was less than 200,000. A convention was hopefully called in 1888, but contented itself with a declaration of principles. Faithful Greenbackers supported the candidate of the Union Labor party, Alson J. Streeter, and its "greenback" platform. This furnished a bridge between the Greenback and the Populist parties.

In spite of its surprising success in 1878, the party had failed to maintain its strength. The achievement of the resumption of specie payments had undermined the appeal of its program. The growing disparity of values between silver and gold made free coinage of silver a far more feasible political goal than greenback inflation. It was, however, a predecessor of subsequent agrarian and labor political movements, and educated a group of voters toward political independence. It also trained leaders who were to play an active part in the Populist crusade.

415

GREENVILLE, TREATY OF, was the sequel to Anthony Wayne's defeat of the Indians at Fallen Timbers. Signed Aug. 3, 1795, this treaty was arranged between Wayne and the chiefs of the Delaware, Shawnee, Wyandot, Miami Confederacy and other tribes; and established a definite boundary between Indian lands and those open to settlement. Running up the Cuyahoga, the line followed the portage to the Tuscarawas, thence to Fort Laurens, to Loramie's Creek, to Fort Recovery and to the Ohio River opposite the mouth of the Kentucky. The land westward and northward of this line was conceded to the Indians, except Detroit and the other French settlements, and several trading-post sites with the highways between them. Also, the United States reserved 150,000 acres on the Ohio opposite Louisville, for bounties to the veterans of George Rogers Clark's campaign.

The Treaty of Greenville and the speedy surrender of the border forts ended British influence over the Indians east of the Wabash Valley, and raids virtually ceased beyond the new boundary line. Hitherto, fearing Indian attacks, settlers had not ventured far from the Ohio valley. Now they could live in safety throughout the greater part of Ohio, and in the "gore" in southeastern Indiana. The result was an era of greatly increased immigration into the Northwest Territory.

GRIERSON'S RAID (April 17–May 2, 1863). Col. B. H. Grierson (U.), commanding a small brigade, 1700 strong, successfully raided eastern Mississippi, starting from LaGrange, Tenn., and finally arriving at Baton Rouge, La. He covered over 600 miles in sixteen days, destroying bridges, railway and telegraph lines. He inflicted a hundred casualties, captured and paroled many prisoners, seized horses, mules and army supplies and suffered only a total of 24 casualties from all causes to his own forces.

GRINGO, a nickname, perverted from *griego* (Greek), applied in several Spanish-American countries to foreigners who "talk Greek," or unintelligibly. It did not originate during the Mexican War from the song, "Green Grow the Rushes, O," since it is defined in the Terreros y Pando *Diccionario Castellano* (Madrid, 1787).

GUADALUPE HIDALGO, THE TREATY OF, signed near Mexico City, Feb. 2, 1848, specified the terms of peace at the close of the Mexican War. It was negotiated by Nicholas P. Trist, the chief clerk of the Department of State under Secretary Buchanan.

In April, 1847, President Polk decided to send Trist secretly as a peace commissioner to Scott's army headquarters, with a definite project of a treaty prepared by Buchanan. Trist was given authority to receive expected Mexican peace proposals and to suspend hostilities. In late August Gen. Scott arranged an armistice to facilitate a conference for peace negotiations, which, however, proved entirely futile.

Polk then ordered (Oct. 1) Trist's recall, in order to discourage false Mexican views of American anxiety for peace. Trist delayed his departure, and finally (Dec. 3) decided to remain and to assume the responsibility of negotiating a treaty substantially on the basis of the territorial demands of his original instructions. On Jan. 24 he was able to secure a completed draft of the treaty, which was signed at Guadalupe Hidalgo, Feb. 2, 1848.

The treaty provided for the establishment of the American-Mexican boundary at the middle of the Rio Grande from the Gulf to a point where that river met the southern boundary of New Mexico (which southern boundary was then identical with the present southern boundary east of the Rio Grande); thence west on this southern boundary of New Mexico to the western line of New Mexico (identical at this point with the present western line); thence north along this western line until it intersected the first branch of the Gila River; thence down this branch and the middle of the Gila to the Colorado River; thence direct to the Pacific at a point one marine league south of the southernmost point of the port of San Diego; and for the cession to the United States by Mexico of the territory of New Mexico and Upper California for a payment of $15,000,000. It was promptly accepted by President Polk and ratified, with amendments, by the Senate, March 10, 1848.

Because of the inaccuracies of Disturnell's map, used by the negotiators of the treaty, and the difficulties which prevented the surveyors from agreement on the identity of the first branch of the Gila, the line between the Rio Grande and the Gila was never marked, and the dispute remained unsettled until its international importance was ended in the Pierce administration by the negotiation of the Gadsden Purchase.

GUILFORD COURT HOUSE, BATTLE OF (March 15, 1781). Following a masterly retreat northward through North Carolina, Greene crossed the River Dan into Virginia, closely followed by Cornwallis. Collecting recruits, Greene recrossed the Dan with 4404 men—3000 were militia—and marched rapidly to Guilford Court House. Placing the militia in two lines in the front, and the Continentals on a rise in the rear, Greene offered battle. On the afternoon of March 15, 1781, Cornwallis with 2213 veterans attacked. The battle that ensued was one of the most severe of the war. After five hours, Greene ordered a retreat, having lost 79 killed and 184 wounded, while nearly 1000 militia dispersed to their homes. Cornwallis lost 93 killed, 413 wounded and 26 missing, nearly one fourth of his force. The British held the field, but the battle was a strategic victory for the Americans. Cornwallis soon withdrew to Wilmington, abandoning all the Carolinas save two or three coast towns.

GUINN AND BEAL v. U. S., 1915 (238 U. S. 347), grew out of the attempt of Oklahoma to include in its constitution, on a permanent basis, the "grandfather clause" principle earlier applied on a statutory and temporary basis in other Southern states, and then discarded after it had served its purpose. The Supreme Court decided that this represented a clear violation of the purpose and intent, if not of the express provisions, of the Fifteenth Amendment.

HABEAS CORPUS, WRIT OF. Like jury trial, it has a history which runs well back into the Middle Ages. It is a device for freeing persons from illegal detention by governmental agencies. It is in the nature of an order of a court to the custodian of a person held, directing that the person be brought to a court hearing to determine whether he is lawfully detained. If the detention is deemed to be unlawful the prisoner is ordered released. The privilege of the writ was guaranteed in England by the Habeas Corpus Act of 1679, but it was suspended thereafter on occasion by special acts, so that its enjoyment was never fully assured. The American colonists valued it highly as a device for the preservation of civil liberties. In order to prevent suspensions of the privilege of the writ such as had taken place in England a provision was included in Section 9 of Article I of the Constitution of the United States to the effect that "The Privilege of the Writ of Habeas Corpus shall not be suspended, unless when in Cases of Rebellion or Invasion the public Safety may require it." Similar provisions are to be found in the constitutions of the several states.

The Judiciary Act of 1789 empowered the Supreme Court and the district courts of the United States to issue writs of habeas corpus in circumstances involving the exercise of jurisdiction by Federal authorities. In 1833, when the nullification controversy brought the threat of state interference with Federal officers in the performance of their duties, Congress authorized the Federal courts to issue writs of habeas corpus to state officials by whom Federal officers might be detained. In 1842, when the McLeod case in New York had indicated the power of a state to embarrass the United States by interference with the representatives of a foreign government, Congress authorized the Federal courts to issue writs to state officials when the persons detained were subjects of foreign governments and claimed to be acting under their sanction. The states, on the other hand, were held not to have a corresponding right to inquire by means of the writ of habeas corpus into the detention of persons held by the Federal Government (*see* Ableman v. Booth). Federal juris-

diction was expanded in 1867 to cover the broad field of cases in which detention was alleged to be in violation of the Constitution or of a law or treaty of the United States.

The Constitution does not say who may suspend the privilege of the writ of habeas corpus, within the exception clause which permits suspension. President Lincoln authorized its suspension at the beginning of the Civil War. In *ex parte Merryman*, a U. S. Circuit Court case decided early in 1861, Chief Justice Taney held that the power of suspension was in Congress and not in the President. President Lincoln ignored this opinion in preference for one of Attorney General Bates in which the power of the President to act in the absence of legislation was upheld. To meet the needs of this particular situation Congress later enacted a statute to cover suspension in circumstances arising out of the war. While the basic controversy has never been officially settled, the weight of opinion is now on the side of the interpretation given by Chief Justice Taney.

"HAIL COLUMBIA," our first national hymn, was the direct outgrowth of President Washington's neutrality policy in the war between France and England. Both countries had partisans in America, the Federalists generally favoring England, the Republicans (Jeffersonian), France. Those sympathetic to the French Revolution made the "Marseillaise" their song while those who wished to avoid war adopted "The President's March" which had been written in the early 1790's by Philip Roth, an American citizen and former bandmaster in the British army. In 1798 feeling ran high as a result of the publication of the "XYZ" letters, and George Fox, a popular Philadelphia actor, asked Joseph Hopkinson, a prominent young lawyer who had a reputation as a poet and patron of the arts, to compose a song to the music of the "March." Hopkinson, a strong Federalist and ardent admirer of Washington, avoided reference to either France or England, and gave voice to our national feeling of independence and our determination to protect our honor and rights. He succeeded so well that the song became popular with all classes and remained our national hymn until "America" was written.

"HAIR BUYER" was the epithet fixed upon Lt. Gov. Henry Hamilton of Detroit by his Kentucky opponent, George Rogers Clark. As governor, Hamilton promoted Indian raids upon the settlements of the Ohio frontier. All civilized governments have utilized the Indians as military allies; the gravamen of Clark's charge was that the governor encouraged the savages to commit inhuman acts, which Hamilton denied. The epithet was a partisan atrocity accusation provoked by wartime hatred and suffering, and unsupported by trustworthy evidence.

HAITI, INTERVENTION IN. Increasingly frequent revolutions, disputes between the Haitian government and American interests controlling the National Bank and the National Railroad, and a fear of European intervention were the principal reasons for the American military occupation of Haiti in July, 1915. The immediate occasion was the disappearance of organized government when a mob at Port au Prince, angered by the killing of 167 political prisoners, murdered President Guillaume Sam, after invading the French legation, in which he had taken refuge.

A new president, elected by the Congress under the protection of the American marines, signed the treaty of Sept. 16, 1915. Under this, Americans nominated by the President of the United States, but serving as officials of the Haitian government, assumed control of the country's finances, of its police force, of public works and of sanitation. The constitution of 1918, permitting foreign landownership, was adopted by a plebiscite, after the president and the American military authorities had arbitrarily dissolved the Haitian Congress.

The "caco" revolt of 1918, during which some 1500 Haitians were killed, led to an investigation by a committee of the U. S. Senate in 1921. The committee's report, criticizing the failure to co-ordinate the work of the American treaty officials and the general lack of a constructive policy, was followed by the appointment of Gen. John H. Russell as American High Commissioner, in 1922. Thereafter much constructive work was accomplished in road building, irrigation and sanitation. Order was maintained by a well-trained police force and the finances were placed on a sound basis. A $16,000,000 loan obtained in New York in 1922 provided funds for much of this development. In 1924 a fifth treaty service of "Agriculture and Professional Education" was established.

Under the transitory provisions of the constitution of 1918, an appointed council of state exercised the legislative power and elected the president. The indefinite continuance of this situation under President Borno (1922–30), as well as dislike of foreign control, caused much discontent. In 1930 President Hoover appointed a commission to study the problem of terminating the intervention. A popularly elected government under Stenio Vincent took office in 1930, and in 1931 American officials were withdrawn from the departments of public works, sanitation and agriculture. In 1934 the police was turned over to Haitian control and all American military forces were withdrawn.

HALDIMAND NEGOTIATIONS. When the Republic of Vermont, established during the Revolutionary War at New York's territorial expense, failed to gain admission to the United States which it had been loyally assisting, Lord George Germain authorized the British commanders in America to offer Vermont self-government under the Crown. In 1779 Sir Henry Clinton made overtures to Gen. Ethan Allen from New York, but these were not reciprocated. In 1780, however, the Vermont leaders sounded Gen. Frederick Haldimand, who commanded at Quebec, by proposing an exchange of prisoners. Haldimand sent Capt. Justus Sherwood to confer with Ethan Allen. In consequence, a cartel for exchange of prisoners was arranged and under this disguise Haldimand negotiated for the remainder of the war for the reunion of Vermont with Great Britain. These parleys were by conferences in isolated spots around Lake Champlain and by correspondence. On Germain's authority, Haldimand offered Vermont a liberal constitution, preferment for the leaders, confirmation of land titles and territorial expansion. The Vermonters, enjoying periodical truces because of the cartel, temporized and only promised to bring Vermont to neutrality. The defeat of Cornwallis in 1781 saved them from having to make a critical decision when Haldimand, impatient with delay, was threatening their frontiers. In 1782, considering that they had again been shabbily treated by Congress and that Vermont might even be suppressed after the war, they sent emissaries to Quebec with proposals for a reunion as soon as Great Britain could protect and subsidize them. But Haldimand, having received secret instructions to cease offensive warfare, temporized and avoided any commitment.

The Vermont negotiators were a small, influential group dominated by Ira and Ethan Allen, Gov. Chittenden and the Fays, whose guiding principles were to perpetuate Vermont and safeguard their landed interests irrespective of who won the war. Rumors were rife. Some Vermonters branded the negotiations as treason to America; others had confidence in the shrewd opportunism of their leaders; the loyalist minority, their numbers rapidly increasing by immigration, worked covertly for reunion. But the ruling clique was never forced by events to disclose precisely where it stood. Had the war ended in compromise—the Allens thought this likely—Vermont could have claimed favored treatment from Great Britain. The traditional view that the Vermonters negotiated only as a ruse and never seriously considered the British proposals is unwarrantable.

HALE, NATHAN, EXECUTION OF. In September, 1776, when Washington desired information as to the British strength and positions, Hale volunteered to act as a spy. Posing as a country teacher, he entered the British lines on Long Island and Manhattan, procured the information and was returning when he was arrested on Sept. 21 and executed the following morning. His last words are said to have been, "I only regret that I have but one life to lose for my country," a paraphrase of a line from Addison's *Cato*.

"HALF-BREEDS" represented the liberal wing of the Republican party during the Hayes and Garfield administrations. Favoring Hayes' liberal Southern policy and civil-service reform, the faction was nicknamed by the "Stalwarts" for its so-called "half-breed" Republicanism. Bitter factional rivalry continued for several years.

HALF MOON was the ship which the Dutch East India Company provided for the voyage of exploration made by Henry Hudson in 1609, in the course of which the Hudson River was discovered. A vessel of eighty tons, it was a flat-bottomed two-master, of a type designed to navigate the difficult approaches to the Zuyder Zee. Called by the Dutch a *vlieboot*, a term derived from the Island of Vlieland, it has been translated into English, without reference to its derivations as "flyboat." Later employed in the East India trade, the *Half Moon* was wrecked in 1615 on the shore of the Island of Mauritius, then owned by the Dutch.

HALFWAY COVENANT. If, as they reached adulthood, children of the founders of Massachusetts and Connecticut gave no acceptable proof of that spiritual experience called "regeneration," should they be granted full church membership? In June, 1657, an intercolonial ministerial conference at Boston attempted to answer through the "Halfway Covenant," whereby membership was granted but, pending regeneration, participation in the Lord's Supper and voting in the church were withheld. Liberals objected, and though a Massachusetts Synod proclaimed it for all Massachusetts churches (1662), controversy continued for more than a century.

HALL, FORT (Idaho), a fur-trading post located on the left bank of the Snake River near the junction of the Snake and Portneuf Rivers, was built in the summer of 1834 by Nathaniel J. Wyeth. It was named in honor of Henry Hall of Boston, one of Wyeth's financial backers. In 1837 the fort was sold to the Hudson's Bay Company, which operated the establishment until its abandonment in 1855. Fort Hall was a center for trade with Indians, and a stopping and trading point for Oregon Trail immigrants, 1841–55. Here Idaho's first Protestant religious service was held, July 27, 1834, by the Rev. Jason Lee, a Methodist missionary. Under the Oregon Treaty the United States Government reimbursed the Hudson's Bay Company for the value of the post.

HAMMER v. DAGENHART was decided by the U. S. Supreme Court in 1918 by a vote of five to four, in which the Court invalidated an act passed by Congress in 1916, designed to check the evil of child labor by excluding from shipment in interstate commerce the products of mines and manufacturing establishments in which children under certain ages had been employed. The Court held the act unconstitutional on the ground that it was not a regulation of commerce, but an attempt to regulate the conditions of manufacturing and production —a matter that has been reserved to the states.

HAMPTON ROADS CONFERENCE. In response to an unofficial attempt of Francis P. Blair, Sr., to bring about peace when the collapse of the Confederacy was evident, Jefferson Davis wrote that he was willing to enter into a conference "with a view to secure peace to the two countries." On seeing this letter Abraham Lincoln wrote Blair of his readiness to bring peace "to the people of our one common country." In spite of the opposing points of view a conference was held, Feb. 3, 1865, on the *River Queen* in Hampton Roads between Lincoln and Seward on the one hand and Alexander H. Stephens, R. M. T. Hunter and J. A. Campbell representing the Confederacy. A veiled suggestion made by Blair for an armistice during which Confederate troops could be sent secretly to Mexico to assist the nationalist movement was rejected by Lincoln, who offered peace on the basis of (1) reunion, (2) emancipation, (3) disbanding of Confederate troops, with a personal promise of sympathetic treatment. The Confederate representatives were not empowered to accept any terms except independence, and the conference adjourned without further agreement.

HANNASTOWN. When the Pennsylvania colonial government organized its westernmost lands into Westmoreland County in 1773, the county seat was established at Robert Hanna's tavern on the old Forbes Road, 35 miles east of Pittsburgh. Virginia claimed this area and sent Capt. John Connolly of Pittsburgh to arrest the Pennsylvania magistrates at Hannastown. The settlement continued to be the center of Pennsylvania county government during the Revolution, and was an important rendezvous for expeditions against the Indians who, on July 13, 1782, led by the Seneca, Guyasuta, attacked and burned it. In 1787 the county seat was moved three miles south to Greensburg on the newly created state turnpike.

HANNASTOWN RESOLUTION. Upon receipt of the news of the Revolutionary clash at Lexington, Mass., the frontier inhabitants of Westmoreland County, Pa., met at Hannastown on May 16, 1775, and declared it the duty of Americans to resist English oppression. Stimulated by the danger of a frontier Tory-Indian co-operation with the English, the Association of Westmoreland County was organized to be ready to resist force with force.

HARD LABOR, TREATY OF. At points along the frontiers the thrust of settlement in Virginia carried the whites across the Indian lines. One of these points was in southwest Virginia. To prevent war, Lord Shelburne sent from London instructions to the two superintendents of Indian affairs in this country that the Indian tribes who claimed the western lands be called into separate conferences in which dividing lines might be agreed upon. At the south, Supt. John Stuart convened the Cherokees at Hard Labor in South Carolina, where on Oct. 14, 1768, a treaty was signed which fixed the line: to run from Tryon Mountain of the Blue Ridge by a straight line to Chiswell's Mine on the New River; thence by a straight line to the confluence of the Kanawha with the Ohio River. Thus was recognized the claim of the Cherokees to lands west of that line. Virginians were not satisfied; the line as fixed left white settlers in the Indian country. Agitation led to a shift of the line farther west by the later treaty of Lochaber.

HARD MONEY is specie. But those who favor hard money have, at different times, fought different opponents. In the 1830's the fight was against banks, which were opposed because they drove out specie, mixed in politics, and defrauded the people. The specie circular of July 11, 1836, represents this point of view. In the 1870's and 1880's the fight was against the advocates of inconvertible Government paper money as represented first by the Greenback party and later by the Populist party. This later group of hard money advocates had no objection to bank notes if they were redeemable in specie.

HARLEM, BATTLE OF (Sept. 16, 1776). After the Battle of Long Island, Washington, finding himself unable to hold New York City, withdrew to Manhattan Island and established a line from the mouth of the Harlem River across the island to Harlem (Morningside) Heights. His army's morale was low, and groups of soldiers, sometimes whole companies, were leaving camp almost daily and going home. On the morning of Sept. 16 about 1000 British appeared on the Harlem Plains, and skirmishing began. Washington ordered Col. Knowlton's Connecticut Rangers and three Virginia companies under Maj. Leitch to strike at the enemy's rear. The movement was made too hastily, and both Knowlton and Leitch were killed; but with reinforcements sent down from the heights, the British were repulsed and driven back. This small victory greatly heartened the American troops, and Washington held his position for another month.

HARMAR, FORT, TREATIES OF. There were two Fort Harmar treaties, both negotiated the same day, Jan. 9, 1789, by Arthur St. Clair, governor of the Northwest Territory. The treaties were made separately so that the jealousy subsisting between the Six Nations and the more westerly tribes should not be lessened. The treaty with the Six Nations

(excepting the Mohawks, not represented) renewed and confirmed the Treaty of Fort Stanwix, negotiated in 1784. This treaty fixed the western limits of the possessions of the Six Nations. A separate article provided severe punishment for Indians or whites guilty of stealing horses. Goods to the value of $3000 were given the Indians for these considerations.

The other treaty, with the Wyandot, Delaware, Ottawa, Chippewa, Potawatomi and Sauk nations, renewed and confirmed the treaty of Fort McIntosh, of 1785. These nations were to serve as buffer nations against unfriendly Indians. For the consideration of $6000, the Indians relinquished all claim to lands beyond the limits set forth in the treaty.

HARMAR'S EXPEDITION (October–November, 1790). Before American settlers could occupy the Old Northwest, the Indian confederacy opposed to them must be conquered. The war began in 1790, and in October, Gen. Josiah Harmar marched from Fort Washington (Cincinnati) against the Indian towns at present-day Fort Wayne. Two hotly contested battles were fought (Oct. 18, 22) in or near Fort Wayne, in both of which important detachments of Harmar's troops were defeated, whereupon Harmar retreated to Fort Washington. The hostile confederacy had not been conquered, and the campaign is well characterized as a "mortifying failure."

HARMONY SOCIETY was established in Butler County, Pa., in 1804, by German Separatists under the leadership of George Rapp and his adopted son Frederick Reichert. The Harmonists emigrated from Württemberg to escape the persecutions to which their dissidence from the German Lutheran Church had subjected them. Economic necessity and the equalitarianism inherent in their pietistic beliefs led them to organize communistically Feb. 15, 1805. Their communism was based on contracts between the members and the trustees under which all property and authority was surrendered to the society in exchange for maintenance. In 1815 the society removed to Posey County, Ind., but returned in 1825 to a permanent home at Economy, Pa., twenty miles below Pittsburgh on the Ohio River. Here the Harmonists engaged in agriculture and industry with remarkable success, but toward the end of the century their wealth was dissipated by unwise investments and poor management. They had adopted celibacy in 1807 and despite the occasional accession of new members, their numbers gradually diminished. Most of the property was sold by 1903 and the society came to a practical end although it was continued as a legal entity for the support of the four surviving members.

HARPERS FERRY, CAPTURE OF. On Sept. 9, 1862, at Frederick, Md., Lee (C.) issued his famous

"Lost Order" outlining his plan of operations. To clear the enemy from his rear, Lee directed Jackson to make a wide march to the southwest, capture the garrison at Harpers Ferry as quickly as possible and then hurry northward to rejoin the main army, which was to advance westward through South Mountain, delaying McClellan (U.) as much as possible, and meet Jackson as he came northward from Harpers Ferry. The combined forces would then move through Hagerstown into Pennsylvania.

By Sept. 14, Jackson was beginning his investment of Harpers Ferry. The "Lost Order" had come into McClellan's possession and he knew Lee's plans. His movements became more energetic. On the 15th Harpers Ferry surrendered. Lee had advanced to Sharpsburg, expecting Jackson. Delayed by the unlooked-for opposition at Harpers Ferry, Jackson was 24 hours behind Lee's schedule, a delay that was nearly disastrous.

HARPERS FERRY RAID (Oct. 16–18, 1859) was the most positive blow struck by the antislavery forces in the half-century of agitation for the abolition of slavery in the United States. Yet it was not representative of the organized abolition societies; rather it was a one-man war upon the institution of slavery. The raid itself was abortive and ended disastrously, but it created such public discussion and political turmoil that, for the first time, national thought was thoroughly aroused on the issue with a resultant sharp cleavage between the proslavery and antislavery forces. In its influence on the stream of history, and as one of the chief contributing causes of the Civil War, the quixotical foray of Capt. John Brown and his small army of liberation looms up as a milestone.

John Brown, while yet following the peaceful pursuits of farmer and wool factor, nursed a plan to invade the South and forcibly liberate the slaves. As early as 1847 he talked of his scheme with Frederick Douglass, following in general outline the plan finally adopted for a series of raids along the line of the Allegheny mountains, liberating the slaves and organizing the country under a plan of government of his own devising. A convention was held at Chatham, Canada, on May 8, 1858, when a provisional constitution was adopted, a paper government set up, and a provisional army established of which Brown himself was selected as commander in chief. Brown's supporters in the Northern states were few in number and apparently none was in his full confidence; to them he imparted only the barest outlines of his scheme of liberation, not even disclosing the locale. Trusting him, and yet distrusting militant motives, these friends raised the necessary funds for the expedition.

Harpers Ferry, Va. (now West Virginia), was selected as the place of raising the standard of the new revolution because it offered an easy gateway to the South and the slaveholding sections and for the more practical reason that it was the site of the United States armory and arsenal where stores of arms and munitions were kept. Fresh from "bleeding Kansas" and slave raids into Missouri, John Brown made his appearance at Harpers Ferry on July 3, 1859, and established headquarters at the nearby Kennedy farm in Maryland. Men and material assembled, he moved to the assault on Sunday night, Oct. 16, heading his army of liberation of seventeen white and five colored men. Ironically enough, the first man to lose his life was a free Negro, who was shot down by one of the raiders when he attempted to escape. The venture failed for lack of support; not one slave willingly joined the army of liberation. Besieged by Virginia and Maryland state troops, the survivors of the raiding party were driven into a fire engine house on the government reservation. Early Tuesday morning, the 18th, a force of U. S. Marines, commanded by Col. Robert E. Lee and Lt. J. E. B. Stuart, battered down the doors and captured the insurgents. Seventeen in all, ten of whom were raiders, were killed in the fighting. Brown and six of his men were later hanged at Charles Town, the county seat; the leader on Dec. 2, 1859.

HARRISON LAND ACT (May 10, 1800), named after William Henry Harrison, first delegate from the Northwest Territory and chairman of the Committee on Public Lands responsible for its framing, is of the greatest significance in the history of the Federal Government's policy toward its public domain. It amended and democratized the terms of the act of 1796, reflecting the demands of the frontier.

The chief complaint against the system established by the act of 1796 was that it encouraged the purchase of land by speculators and inhibited the acquisition of farm tracts by settlers. Nor had its operation resulted in large returns to the Government, for less than 50,000 acres of land had been sold between 1796 and 1800. The act of 1800, therefore, while retaining the rectangular system of survey established in 1796, was designed to facilitate individual purchase of land on easier terms. Framed largely in accordance with the proposals of Harrison's report of Feb. 18, 1800, the act provided for the sale of land west of the Muskingum River in units as small as 320 acres. East of that river tracts of 640 acres were still to be offered. The credit system was made more flexible to meet the needs of the settlers, a four-year term being offered during which time payments might be completed, and the penalties for forfeiture abated. The minimum price of $2.00 an acre and the auction system were retained but the administrative machinery was revised in the interests of the small purchaser. Four land districts were established, each with its respective land office—Cincinnati, Chillicothe, Marietta and Steubenville. Annual auction sales at stipulated dates were to be held in each office but private sales might take place in the intervening periods. The office of register was instituted to administer the land sales and records in each district. The act thus laid the foundations for the Government's democratic policy, and remains a monument to Harrison and to the influence of the frontier.

HARRODSBURG. The earliest white settlement in Kentucky was begun at Harrod's Town (or -burg) in June, 1774, by James Harrod. Before the settlement was completed, however, Dunmore's War occurred, and Harrod and his men left to participate in this struggle, returning in 1775. Harrodsburg became the principal base of operation for the Virginia pioneers, and it was here that George Rogers Clark planned (1777) his campaign against the British in the Northwest.

HARTFORD, a wooden-screw steam sloop-of-war, of 2790 tons, 226 feet by 43 feet, was named for Hartford, Conn., and launched at the Charlestown Navy Yard, Boston, Nov. 22, 1858. She was armed with twenty-two 9-inch smooth-bore guns in broadside and two 20-pounder Parrott rifles. During the Civil War the ship became famous as the flagship of Admiral David Glasgow Farragut in the passage of Forts Jackson and St. Philip, in the bombardment and passage of the batteries at Vicksburg and later at Port Hudson, and in the Battle of Mobile Bay.

HARTFORD CONVENTION, called at the invitation of the Massachusetts legislature, was a meeting of 26 New England Federalists. Its inspiration was the opposition of New England mercantile interests, the Essex Junto and Federalists generally, to Jeffersonian Republican policies and to the War of 1812. Delegates, elected by the legislatures, were sent from Massachusetts, Connecticut and Rhode Island. Vermont and New Hampshire failed to co-operate, although two counties in the former and one in the latter sent delegates. The convention was held in secret sessions at Hartford, Conn. (Dec. 15, 1814–Jan. 5, 1815), for the declared purpose of considering the advisability of calling a general convention to revise the Constitution. It was a distinguished group, and, with one or two exceptions, was not drawn from the radical Federalist element, its most prominent figure being Harrison Gray Otis, who looked upon it as a safety valve for pent-up Federalist feeling.

Resentment in New England against commercial restrictions and westward expansion had been augmented by the unpopular war with England, which raised vexatious problems as to the control of state militia and the protection of the New England coast. The resolutions adopted for the consideration of New England legislatures recommended interstate co-operation in repelling British attacks, the use of Federal

revenues in state defense, and the protection of citizens against unconstitutional military acts. The New England states were also urged to support constitutional amendments which would limit Southern political power, commercial embargoes and trade restrictions, declarations of war, admission of new states into the Union and officeholding by naturalized citizens.

Having made tentative plans for calling another meeting in six months, the convention adjourned. Both because of its secrecy and the immediate end of the war it was laid open to ridicule and charges of treasonable intent, and the doctrines of state and sectional rights which it advocated were temporarily discredited throughout the nation.

HARTFORD WITS. In the last two decades of the 18th century a small group of youthful writers, chiefly Yale graduates, banded together as an informal literary club at Hartford, Conn., and achieved wide recognition through their timely satiric verse. The company was dubbed, first locally, later by a wider circle, "The Hartford (or Connecticut) Wits." The principal members were John Trumbull, Joel Barlow, David Humphreys, Timothy Dwight, Theodore Dwight, Richard Alsop and Lemuel Hopkins. Individually prolific writers, their chief productions in collaboration were *The Anarchiad, The Political Greenhouse* and *The Echo.* Contemporarily popular, but possessing scant literary merit, these effusions satirized educational curricula and the policies of Jeffersonian democracy.

HARVARD UNIVERSITY. Founded in 1636 with a grant of £400 from the Massachusetts General Court, Harvard is the oldest college in the United States. It has never moved from Cambridge, Mass., where the first classes were held in 1638. It owes its name to John Harvard, a graduate of Emmanuel College, Cambridge, who left the institution half his property and all his library. The first head, Nathaniel Eaton, was dismissed at the end of a year. He was succeeded by Henry Dunster, a graduate of Magdalene College, Cambridge, who in 1650 secured the charter (suspended from 1686 to 1707) under which Harvard has continued to operate. According to this charter, college affairs are administered by the Corporation (consisting of the president and five fellows, given perpetual succession) and by a second governing committee known as the Board of Overseers. The most distinguished president in the early days was Increase Mather (1685–1701), but he treated the office as a part-time job.

In 1780 Harvard became a university, in 1782 a medical school was established, and in 1815, a law school. Under John T. Kirkland, president from 1810 to 1828, the college acquired professors with European training. George Ticknor, who taught French and Spanish after studying at Göttingen and meeting

Goethe and Madame de Staël, was a Kirkland appointee. When he resigned after eighteen years as chairman of the modern language department, his place was taken by Longfellow and later by James Russell Lowell. Another Kirkland appointee was Edward Everett, who taught Greek after his immersion in Göttingen. When Everett himself became president (1846–49), he made Louis Agassiz professor of zoölogy and geology.

The greatest advances were made under Charles William Eliot, president from 1869 to 1909. Eliot laid the foundations of the graduate school in 1872, revived the law school by appointing Christopher Columbus Langdell dean, and reformed the medical school. He also secured the most brilliant faculty in the history of any American university. When Henry Adams declared that he knew nothing about mediaeval history, Eliot was adamant. "If you will point out anyone who knows more, Mr. Adams, I will appoint him," he said. Henry Adams and Edward Channing lent a sudden new distinction to the history department, Charles Eliot Norton headed the fine arts department inaugurated in 1874, and William James, Josiah Royce, Charles Sanders Peirce and George Santayana gave the philosophy department an unrivalled reputation. Painfully bored by teachers who expounded subjects to improve the minds of students, Eliot introduced the elective system, challenging Harvardmen to cultivate their particular interests.

Abbott Lawrence Lowell, president from 1909 to 1932, was also an exceptional administrator. "The teaching by the professor in his class-room on the subjects within the scope of his chair ought to be absolutely free," he maintained. When German-born Hugo Münsterberg of the psychology department was harried by patrioteers for expressing his sympathy with Germany in World War I, the Corporation refused to dismiss him, and he died a Harvard professor in 1916. When Harold Laski, an instructor in political science, was criticized for addressing the wives of the Boston policemen on strike in 1919, Lowell told the Corporation and the Board of Overseers that if Laski were sent packing, he would resign. Laski left shortly afterward for the University of London.

Tempering Eliot's emphasis on the elective system, Lowell asked undergraduates to concentrate in one discipline and introduced the tutorial system. One of his major achievements was the Society of Fellows. Under this plan 24 junior fellows, the graduates of any college, were freed from taking courses or studying for a degree, and given the opportunity to engage in any approved writing or research. But the greatest blessing of the Lowell years was the house plan, financed by $10,000,000 from Edward S. Harkness, Yale '97. The three upper classes were lodged with their tutors in residential units, virtually eliminating the social influence of the Harvard clubs.

Lowell was followed by James Bryant Conant, and by Nathan M. Pusey in 1953.

Among the architects who have contributed to the distinction of Harvard Yard and its environs, Charles Bulfinch of the class of 1781 must be mentioned. He designed University Hall. Henry Hobson Richardson of the class of 1859 planned Seaver Hall and Austin Hall for the law school. The firm of McKim, Mead & White was responsible for the gates of the Yard.

Five graduates of Harvard have become President of the United States—John Adams, John Quincy Adams, Theodore Roosevelt, Franklin D. Roosevelt and John F. Kennedy. A sixth President, Rutherford B. Hayes, attended Harvard law school for a year and a half.

HASTINGS' CUTOFF, named for Lansford W. Hastings who first advocated its use in 1846, followed a route to California which crossed the Salt Desert and the Sierra mountains instead of proceeding to Fort Hall, Idaho, and then branching southward. It shortened the route, but produced terrible suffering among emigrants driving slow-moving ox teams.

HATCHET, BURYING THE. This term appears in American literature as symbolizing a pledge of peace between Indian tribes or between Indians and whites. Often it is applied to an individual, Indian or white, who decides to withdraw from a controversy.

In the documents drawn up by historic Iroquois Indians (*Bulletin 184*, New York State Museum), explaining the principles of the League of the Five Nations, a symbolic tree is mentioned, which is dug up, and all weapons of war cast into the hole and the tree replanted. This concept is certainly prehistoric. One of the first acts of white traders was to introduce the metal tomahawk, in English, a hatchet, which soon became the symbol of Indian raids. Knox (1767), writing of Indians in New York and New England, tells that a hatchet painted red was thrown down in a friendly village as an invitation to join in a war. Acceptance was signified by picking it up or by "taking up the hatchet." In some instances war was declared by striking a hatchet into the ceremonial post in the center of the village. Priority in the literary use of "burying the hatchet" is usually credited to Washington Irving. Thus while the actual origin of the term is obscure, the concept is found in Iroquois tradition where the burying of all weapons symbolized the making of peace. It was probably the existence of this symbolism and the subsequent place of the tomahawk in colonial speech, that led to the phrase "burying the hatchet."

HATFIELD-McCOY FEUD was one of the most savage of mountain vendettas. Anderson (Anse) Hatfield, clan leader, and many of his kinsmen lived in or near Williamson, W. Va., the McCoys just across the border in Kentucky. Their animosity dated back to the Civil War, but the feud proper began in 1880, after a Hatfield had been accused of stealing a semi-wild hog belonging to Randolph McCoy. In 1882 three sons of Randolph were seized by a squad of Hatfields led by a constable and a justice of the peace, on pretense of arrest for the killing of Ellison Hatfield, but instead, were brutally murdered. The feud continued, with frightful atrocities, suffered mostly by the McCoys, until 1888, when Kentucky officers made several raids into West Virginia, killing at least two Hatfield clansmen and capturing nine more, two of whom were executed, the others sent to state prison. By 1890, except for occasional killings, the war was ended.

HAWAII (the Sandwich Islands) was visited by Robert Gray and the *Columbia* in 1789–90, eleven years after the discovery by Cook. Yankees trading in furs in the Pacific Northwest soon began visiting Honolulu. A thriving three-cornered trade developed; Hawaiian sandalwood was used in China in payment of goods for the American market. By 1820 American whalers began to make Honolulu a repair port, some 400 visiting Hawaii annually from 1840–60. In 1820 Boston missionaries began the successful promotion of American influence. By 1840 Honolulu with its Yankee whalemen, missionaries and merchandise appeared as an American outpost.

To supervise growing American interests in Hawaii, President Monroe appointed a resident agent in 1820. American, as well as English and French, warships began visiting Hawaii. In 1826 the United States and Hawaii signed a treaty of peace and friendship. Though it was not ratified by the United States, Hawaii continued to respect it. Fearing French and English designs, Secretary of State Webster announced in 1842 that the independence of Hawaii be respected; that no power seek undue control or exclusive privileges. In 1843 Washington was represented in Hawaii by a diplomat, the first of his kind sent by any foreign power.

The acquisition of Oregon and California in the 1840's enhanced American interest in the Pacific and Asia. Honolulu, queen of the north Pacific, 2100 miles from San Francisco, became valuable as a naval station, a half-way point between Asia and California. Americans, including President Pierce and Secretary Marcy, talked of the manifest destiny of their country to include Hawaii. Influential Americans in Hawaii favored annexation. Fearing revolution from within, attacks by California filibusters or by some foreign power, King Hamehameha III consented to annexation on his terms. His death put a stop to the project.

Urged by the American sugar interests, the insular government appealed in 1848, 1852 and 1855 to Washington for a reciprocity treaty. In 1855 Secretary Marcy agreed, but the Senate, responding to the sugar interests of Louisiana, rejected the treaty. Attempts to revive the idea were made in 1863. In 1867 President Johnson signed it, but the Senate defeated it June 1, 1870. At the persistent urgings of the American sugar interests in Hawaii, King Kalakaua visited Washington in 1875 to exert some influence. Fearing that the islands might turn to England, President Grant signed the reciprocity treaty Jan. 30, 1875, and the Senate approved it a month and a half later. The treaty provided for free access of sugar and other products into American ports. When the treaty was renewed the United States was given the "exclusive right to enter the harbor of Pearl River."

This treaty stimulated Hawaiian industries, and American capital poured into the islands. When the McKinley tariff of 1890 placed all sugar on the free list and Hawaii's basic industry lost its favored position, American growers demanded annexation as a means of restoring prosperity. When in 1893 Queen Liliuokalani attempted to eliminate American influence and restore autocratic rule, the influential Americans in Hawaii, with the connivance of United States Minister Stevens and the "moral" support of American marines, engineered a revolution, deposed the Queen, organized a provisional government, and opened negotiations with the United States for annexation. President Harrison signed the treaty, but before the Senate acted, Cleveland took office, withdrawing the document. When his special agent, Blount, reported the revolution a conspiracy between American planters and Minister Stevens, Cleveland ordered the restoration of the Queen. Refusing to obey, the provisional government converted itself into the Republic of Hawaii, soon recognized by foreign governments, including the United States.

The fear of Japanese designs upon the islands, and the value of the Hawaiian harbors, offered for the use of the United States during the Spanish-American War, strengthened sentiment for annexation in Washington. On July 7, 1898, Hawaii was annexed by a joint resolution and on Aug. 12, the islands formally transferred sovereignty to the United States. In reply to Japan's protests, Washington assured Tokyo that annexation would not affect the rights of Japanese in Hawaii.

By the Organic Act of April 30, 1900, Hawaii was made a full-fledged territory with American citizenship conferred on all citizens of the islands. The advantages of union have been mutual: practically the entire expanding Hawaiian trade is with the United States, while the islands furnish valuable naval bases for a strong American military and naval outpost. Hawaii favored even closer relations with the United States—statehood. Hawaii's "Bill of Rights," an act passed by Congress and signed by Coolidge April 10, 1924, meant greater benefits for the territory.

Hawaii was the first part of the United States to be attacked by Japan on the "Day of Infamy," Dec. 7, 1941, causing the destruction of many warships and total casualties of 4575 killed, wounded, and missing. "Remember Pearl Harbor" became America's war slogan. Martial law was declared in Hawaii and the writ of habeas corpus was suspended. It took a long legal campaign to restore it. Fears of sabotage and fifth-column activities, however, were unfounded. Hawaii was thoroughly loyal. The people subscribed to war loans of over $200,000,000. The Nisei outfit in the Italian campaign suffered heavy losses and won the name of the "Purple Heart Battalion."

The effects of the war on Hawaii were tremendous. At the peak of military strength in July, 1944, about 250,000 army troops were stationed in Oahu. The war brought much business to Hawaii and made the islands even more an integral part of the United States. While those of Japanese ancestry predominate, about one third of the marriages of descendants of Asian and European immigrants are across racial lines.

Economically Hawaii has progressed from a sort of feudalism to paternalism, to economic democracy. Much progressive legislation has been adopted and labor is strongly organized. A virile middle class is also appearing.

Statehood for Hawaii was first proposed in 1849, again in 1854, and during the negotiations following the Revolution of 1893. From 1903 to 1919 the territorial legislatures petitioned Congress for statehood, though some newspapers in the islands opposed it. Statehood bills were introduced in Congress but little attention was paid to them until 1935.

In 1940 the Hawaiians voted two to one for statehood and President Truman advocated statehood in 1946. A conference of western governors, chambers of commerce and church leaders likewise favored statehood for Hawaii. In 1959 Congress passed the statehood bill and on July 4 President Eisenhower signed the proclamation of statehood. During the election of 1959 the Republicans won the governorship and a U. S. Senator; the Democrats elected the second U. S. Senator and the only Representative. In August, 1959, President Eisenhower formally proclaimed Hawaii the 50th state of the Union. With her population of some 585,000 Hawaii is 47th in population, 44th in size.

HAWLEY-SMOOT TARIFF of 1930 was partly the outcome of unsatisfactory conditions in agriculture, and much of the discussion was concerned with farm products; but strenuous efforts were made to add further protection to certain manufactured products—a movement which the agricultural bloc was rather successful in stopping. On its way through Congress the bill was subjected to trading and log-rolling, and both in method of construction and in final form was the antithesis of scientific tariff making. In spite of opposition, the act continued in modified form the "flexible clause" of the previous tariff. One section of the law prohibited the importation after Jan. 1, 1932, of goods produced by convict, forced or indentured labor. Forced labor was defined as "all work or service which is exacted from any person under the menace of penalty for its nonperformance and for which the worker does not offer himself voluntarily." Under some interpretations this statement might have described certain types of labor under communistic, or dictatorial, forms of government. The tariff stirred an unusual amount of hostility abroad. European critics associated the act with the payment of foreign war debts to the United States, and urged that not only did the high duties impose additional burdens on debtors, but that these nations were further embarrassed because of the decline of prices which made larger payments necessary, measured in goods, than was contemplated at the time the debt agreements were signed.

HAY—BUNAU-VARILLA TREATY was signed on Nov. 18, 1903, by Secretary Hay and Philippe Bunau-Varilla, who, after the department of Panama revolted from Colombia, was made the envoy at Washington of the Panama Republic. This treaty provided that the United States should guarantee the independence of the republic of Panama, while that republic granted to the United States in perpetuity "the use, occupation, and control of a strip of land ten miles wide for the construction of a canal." Panama gave to the United States sovereign rights over this zone and the adjacent waters. In return, the United States agreed to pay the Panama Republic $10,000,000 when ratifications were exchanged and, beginning nine years thereafter, an annuity of $250,000. By this agreement the United States secured permission to construct the Panama Canal despite the fact that Colombia had refused to ratify the Hay-Herrán Treaty.

HAY-HERRÁN TREATY was signed by Secretary of State Hay and Minister Herrán of Colombia on Jan. 22, 1903. It provided that the New Panama Canal Co., which held an option on the canal route, might sell its properties to the United States. The treaty further provided that Colombia would lease to the United States a strip of land across the Isthmus of Panama for the construction of a canal. In return, the United States agreed to pay Colombia $10,000,000 cash and, after nine years, an annuity of $250,000. Although objections were made to this treaty because it did not give the United States complete governmental control over the proposed canal zone, yet it was ratified by the U. S. Senate. Evidently largely because of the expectation of securing greater financial returns, the Colombian Congress declined to ratify this convention.

HAY-PAUNCEFOTE TREATIES. The first Hay-Pauncefote Treaty, signed Feb. 5, 1900, modified the Clayton-Bulwer Treaty of 1850, which provided for a joint protectorate by England and the United States of any transisthmian canal, to permit the construction and maintenance of a canal under the sole auspices of the United States. It was amended by the Senate to provide that it should supersede the Clayton-Bulwer Treaty, and to give the United States the right to fortify the canal. Great Britain declined to accept the Senate amendments, and the second Hay-Pauncefote Treaty was negotiated, and signed Nov. 18, 1901. Article I declared that it should supersede the Clayton-Bulwer Treaty. Article II provided that a canal might be constructed under the auspices of the United States and that she was to have all the rights incident to such construction as well as the right to regulate and manage the canal. However, Article III stipulated that the canal should be free and open to the vessels of all nations "on terms of entire equality" and that the charges of traffic should be "just and equitable." The United States was virtually accorded the sole power to assure the neutrality of transisthmian transit. Fortification of the canal was not mentioned, but during the negotiation the British foreign secretary admitted that the United States would have the right to fortify. This treaty made feasible the construction of a canal through Central America by the United States and enabled her to consider the Nicaragua route as an alternative to the Panama route.

HAYBURN'S CASE (1792) was the first involving the constitutionality of an act of Congress to reach the Federal courts. It arose out of a pension law authorizing circuit judges to pass on claims subject to review by the Secretary of War and Congress. The decision of the Pennsylvania circuit on April 11, 1792, declining to hear the petition of William Hayburn on the grounds that it could not proceed because the law was inconsistent with the Constitution, led the Attorney General to appeal to the Supreme Court for a mandamus. The justices refused to act on the motion, but took under advisement one in behalf of Hayburn. Before a decision was announced other relief for pensioners was provided and, therefore, the Supreme Court never passed on the act. The decision in the Pennsylvania circuit is sometimes styled the "First Hayburn Case" to distinguish it from the motion before the Supreme Court.

HAYMARKET RIOT (May 4, 1886) arose as an incident of the militant eight-hour movement of that year in Chicago which was frequently accompanied by conflicts between strikers and police. In protest against the shooting of several workmen, August Spies, editor of the semianarchist *Arbeiter-Zeitung*, issued circulars demanding revenge and announcing a mass meeting at the Haymarket. Amidst general anticipation of violence, large police reserves were concentrated nearby and Mayor Harrison attended the meeting; soon the mayor left, judging the speeches to be innocuous. Despite Harrison's advice, Capt. Bonfield and 180 police advanced on the meeting and ordered the crowd to disperse. At this point, a bomb, thrown by an unknown hand, fell among the police, resulting in seven deaths and numerous injured. Popular fears of a general anarchist plot made impartial investigation impossible; eight alleged anarchists were convicted on a conspiracy charge and four were hanged. The eight-hour movement collapsed beneath the stigma of radicalism. Gov. Altgeld pardoned the three surviving prisoners in 1893, declaring that the trial had been a farce—an opinion severely condemned by the conservative press, but highly praised by organized labor.

HAYS, FORT (Kans.), built in 1867 by Gen. John Pope, was one of a system of military posts established to combat hostile Plains Indians. Gen. Phil Sheridan for a time made his headquarters at Fort Hays, as did Gen. George A. Custer in the campaigns of 1867–69.

Building of the Kansas Pacific Railroad to this point caused the rise of Hays City, which became the most turbulent town on the Plains while it was the rail head. Here James Butler Hickok, known as "Wild Bill," began his notable career as a frontier marshal in 1869. He maintained order with his revolvers until 1870, when, having killed three soldiers in an altercation, he fled to escape execution by Gen. Sheridan.

Moving of the rail head to Fort Sheridan, Colo., brought more peaceful conditions, although as late as 1874, citizens fought a street battle with Negro soldiers from the fort, in which six of the latter were killed.

HEAD RIGHT was the system used in most of the English colonies, especially in the 17th century, of granting a certain number of acres, usually fifty, for each settler, the grant being made either for himself or to the person who paid for his transportation. This principle was also found in the early land laws of Texas.

HEALTH, EDUCATION, AND WELFARE, U. S. DEPARTMENT OF, in 1953 replaced the Federal Security Agency. Its main components are the Public Health Service, Social Security Administration, Office of Education, Food and Drug Administration, Office of Vocational Rehabilitation and Saint Elizabeths Hospital (for the mentally ill). The Department also has legislative and budgetary responsibilities for three corporations—American Printing House for the Blind, Gallaudet College (for the deaf), and Howard University.

The Public Health Service, established in 1798, collaborates with the states in the control of epidemics, communicable and chronic diseases, and water and air pollution, and in the sanitation of milk and water supplies; conducts research in major diseases; and administers grants to research organizations.

The Social Security Administration, established in 1935, administers old-age, survivors', and disability insurance; the Federal aspects of the state-Federal public assistance programs; and grants to states to assist in developing services for mothers and children. It charters and supervises Federal credit unions.

The function of the Office of Education when it was established in 1867 was collecting statistics and facts regarding education. Added responsibilities include making grants to land-grant colleges, administering programs of Federal aid for vocational education and for schools in areas of large Federal employment, and administering the National Defense Education Act.

The Food and Drug Administration, established in 1906, enforces Federal laws to insure the purity, safety, and truthful labeling of foods, drugs, and cosmetics.

The Office of Vocational Rehabilitation, established in 1943, co-operates with the states in helping prepare unemployed handicapped people for useful work and in other activities to help the physically and emotionally handicapped.

HEALTH, PUBLIC. In modern society, public health is a broad concept which encompasses the varied preventive and protective health activities of public and voluntary agencies in the community, state and nation. These agencies—governmental and nongovernmental—join forces for the prevention of premature death, the reduction of disease, and the promotion of health and efficiency in the community and the individual.

In the United States, as elsewhere, quarantine and isolation were the first important measures adopted for the prevention and control of disease. When outbreaks of disease occurred during the 17th and 18th centuries, temporary committees or officers were appointed, or persons voluntarily grouped themselves together to meet the emergency. Public health activities were devoted chiefly to attempts to control smallpox, with spasmodic efforts to apply quarantine measures against yellow fever when it appeared in the cities of the Atlantic and Gulf coasts. To quarantine and isolation measures were added others, such as immunization and disinfection. Isolation measures were adopted early in New England, with local provisions concerning smallpox enacted in Boston and Salem as early as 1678. Inoculation against smallpox was championed by Cotton Mather in 1721; in time, the idea took hold, and 8000 persons were reportedly inoculated in Boston in 1792.

Inoculation was later abandoned in favor of the milder preventive measure of vaccination. Until fairly recently, disinfection was emphasized as all-important.

The discovery and adoption of vaccination against smallpox marked the beginning of a new phase of public health. Discoveries in bacteriology by Koch, Pasteur and others made new prophylactic measures possible. Improved water sanitation and methods of sewage disposal, protection of milk and food supplies, and better housing were among the important gains. Typhoid fever, tuberculosis, diphtheria, yellow fever, malaria and other communicable diseases began to give way before mass immunization and other large-scale control techniques. Decisive progress was made against hookworm. A growing knowledge of bodily chemistry provided keys for controlling vitamin- and food-deficiency diseases such as pellagra, endemic goiter, rickets and beriberi.

After 1900, medical methods and health education of the public began to receive increasing attention. New biological agents for the prevention and cure of communicable diseases, laboratory diagnostic techniques, pediatrics and pre-natal care, modern tuberculosis sanatoria, chemotherapy for venereal disease infections, all contributed to the increasingly important role of the physician in public health. New specialists—public health nurses, medical social workers, epidemiologists, engineers, and a host of others—were also added to the evolving public health team.

Recent decades have seen the development of new knowledge of the smaller micro-organisms. Previously unknown diseases such as rickettsial pox, and new reservoirs for previously known diseases such as Q-fever, have been identified. The Coxsackie group of viruses and other immunologically distinct disease agents have been discovered. The introduction of Salk vaccine and the development of oral live-virus vaccines give hope of eradication of poliomyelitis.

People today are safer from communicable diseases and live longer than earlier generations. This means that the chronic diseases—heart disease, cancer, mental illness and others—are correspondingly more important. Rapidly changing conditions have created new problems. Industrial expansion, the growth of cities, new housing conditions, the problems of water supply and pollution, population shifts, development of modern food processing, and changes in the general standard of living are among the 20th-century developments which have enlarged the responsibilities of workers in the field of public health. The constantly increasing use of the automobile makes for greater accident hazards and also contributes—together with industrial and urban growth, and other factors—to air pollution in cities. The use of ionizing radiation requires protection against undue public exposure to radiation.

To meet the many new problems, public health activities have expanded, at local, state, and Federal levels. Working within the framework provided by the American system of enumerated powers, the Federal Government develops health facilities and resources, conducts health research, provides medical and hospital services to designated beneficiaries, operates interstate and foreign quarantine, directs the collection and analysis of vital and public health statistics, works with state and local health agencies to improve public health services, and co-operates with other countries on international health problems. Federal agencies also make national surveys to identify health problems, to determine the needs for facilities and programs, and to develop plans of action for meeting the needs.

The U. S. Public Health Service, in the Department of Health, Education and Welfare, has the principal responsibility for carrying out these functions. The Public Health Service began as the Marine Hospital Service, created by Congress in 1798. By the middle of the 20th century, it was responsible for a wide range of health programs. Its major research arm, the National Institutes of Health at Bethesda, Md., constitutes one of the world's most comprehensive medical research operations. Its major focus is on such important contemporary problems as chronic diseases and disabilities—including cancer, heart disease, arthritis, and mental illness—and on infectious diseases which still resist modern science.

Public health activities are also administered by other agencies in the Department of Health, Education and Welfare, among them, the Food and Drug Administration, the Office of Vocational Rehabilitation, the Children's Bureau—and by the Departments of Agriculture, Commerce, and Labor.

Local health programs, undertaken in early days largely in response to epidemics and other emergencies or public nuisances, have developed to the point where today more than two thirds of the total population in the United States is covered by organized local health service under the direction of a full-time health officer. In some sections of the country, the city, town and municipality constitute the local health jurisdiction. In others, county health departments and multi-county health units known as local health districts have flourished. Supervision and sanitary control of water supplies, sewage disposal facilities, milk production and distribution, and food-handling establishments are among the important responsibilities of many local health departments, as are diagnostic laboratory services, school health services, nutrition services and general health education.

The first state department of public health was established in Massachusetts in 1869; by 1900, 38 other states had created similar departments, and today all states have boards or departments of health. Another major development has been the organization of full-time rural health organizations, a trend which began around 1908 and spread throughout the country in the following decades.

In the United States, an important public health role is played by voluntary and fraternal organizations, foundations, universities, and charitable and philanthropic groups. Such groups support research and professional training, promote health education of the public, provide medical and hospital care insurance, and help build hospitals and other health facilities. Voluntary health agencies—a unique American development—supplement the work of official health agencies in many ways. They work for new projects and programs, promote needed legislation and support exploratory work in a variety of new fields. Their activities have been vital in the history of American public health.

In the middle decades of the 20th Century, public health was branching out in important new directions. Popular interest in health and medicine reached new highs. The benefits of modern medical progress gave new meaning and promise to the goal of better health for all Americans.

HEATING. The early colonists knew of no means of heating buildings and of cooking other than by open fireplaces. For more than a century, wood was the only fuel used in America. The late arrival at an inn, during winter, found his bedroom miserably cold, though a fire was hastily lighted on the hearth and a warming pan used on the bed. This was a flattish metal box filled with live coals which was passed back and forth by its long handle between the sheets of a bed until the chill was taken off. Foot stoves, metal boxes filled with glowing charcoal, were used by well-to-do folk in church, in their traveling carriages and sometimes in stagecoaches, though often a hot brick or slab of soapstone wrapped in cloth had to serve. The first hint of new heating methods came between 1730 and 1740 when Christopher Sower of Germantown, Pa., invented a primitive stove which partly enclosed the fireplace. Benjamin Franklin in 1742 evolved what he called the Pennsylvanian Fireplace (Franklin stove), really a sort of stove, though with the front open, like a fireplace; the smoke passed over the top of a separate air-chamber and down behind it before going up the chimney; and through small apertures, this air-chamber emitted heat into the room. With the beginning of coal mining in Virginia in 1750, grates were introduced. The first enclosed stove, a box-shaped affair much like those used in the following centuries, was produced in 1752. Dozens of modifications were devised by succeeding generations. Mica windows and firebrick linings appeared in the early 19th century, and about 1830 the first base-burner, primarily for the use of anthracite, was introduced. The first hot-air furnace—then called a "basement stove"—is said to have been made and installed by William A. Wheeler of Worcester, Mass., about 1835. An early type of anthracite furnace was just a cast-iron stove surrounded by a brick air chamber; the smoke, hot gases and hot air passed through large sheet-metal drums on each succeeding floor above before escaping by the chimney. The hot-air furnace was the favorite type of central heating device for public buildings and large residences for half a century and more thereafter.

Hot water heating was brought to the United States from London in 1842 by Joseph Nason—who was also the first to warm a building in this country by steam, this in 1845–46. His first large steam-heating contract was that of the Eastern Hotel in Boston, his second, a woolen mill in Burlington, Vt. A few colleges and other institutions with groups of buildings were by 1880 warming them from a central steam-heating plant. Steam heat was one of several factors which contributed to the growing size and height of commercial buildings. After 1885 corporations in some of the larger cities distributed steam from central plants (frequently exhaust steam from electric lighting and power plants) through pipes under the street to customers. After 1895 many of these heating systems were made appendages of lighting and power organizations. In the latter 19th century gas, mostly natural, though some artificial, was much used for fuel, usually with fire-clay "gas logs" in grates and stoves. In the 20th century, as air conditioning was developed, heating, of course, became an element in the scheme. Gas and oil also began slowly but steadily to supplant coal as fuel in heating furnaces.

HELENA, BATTLE AT (July 4, 1863). A Confederate force of 7600 under Gen. T. H. Holmes attempted to take Helena, Ark., which was strongly fortified and held by Federal troops under Gen. B. M. Prentiss. The Confederate right wing stormed the Federal works, but the left was defeated, and the right was finally driven back, the whole attack failing. Confederate loss 1636, Federal 239.

HELENA MINING CAMP started in 1864 with the discovery of gold in Last Chance Gulch in Prickly Pear Valley, just east of the Continental Divide. John Cowan, Robert Stanley and others, after spending the summer in unsuccessful prospecting, in September tried their "last chance," thus opening the most productive mining camp in Montana. Gold seekers from Bannack and Alder Gulch and elsewhere hurried to the new "diggings," which soon adopted the name Helena, and the district took the name Rattlesnake. Red Mountain, Ten Mile and Unionville also produced large quantities of gold. On Silver Creek Thomas Cruse developed the Drum Lummon mine, which he sold in 1882 for $1,500,000. His North Star and Monarch mines showed almost equal wealth. As the placer mines were exhausted, quartz mining developed and silver and lead became important. In 1880, gold production was 8215 ounces, and silver 51,379 ounces; in

1904 it had increased to 29,437 ounces for gold and 331,091 ounces for silver. In 1937 gold production amounted to 35,805 ounces and silver to 138,512 ounces.

HELPER'S *IMPENDING CRISIS OF THE SOUTH*, published at New York in 1857, was an economic appeal to nonslaveholders of the South written by a North Carolinian of the small-farmer class. Using the census reports of 1790 and 1850 as sources, he contrasted Northern and Southern states to show that the South, with slave labor, was unable to keep pace with the "free" North in population, agriculture, industry and commerce. Applying opprobrious epithets to slaveowners, Helper claimed that they owed nonslaveholders of his section over $7,000,000,000 because slavery was responsible for the impoverished status of free labor. By selecting, twisting and misinterpreting his figures, he produced a volume which convinced many Northerners, who had been uninfluenced by the moral appeal, that slavery was an economic fallacy. By the end of 1857, 13,000 copies had been sold; by 1860, 142,000. A *Compendium*, published in 1859, was widely circulated as Republican campaign literature, and its endorsement by John Sherman was a factor in his defeat for the speakership. In the South newspapers and speakers refuted the work, copies were publicly burned, individuals were jailed for buying or possessing it, "Helperites" were dispossessed of positions and privileges, and a Virginian, Samuel M. Wolfe, wrote *Helper's Impending Crisis Dissected* (1860).

HENRY, FORT, CAPTURE OF (Feb. 6, 1862). Seventeen thousand Union troops under Gen. U. S. Grant, supported by gunboats under Commodore Foote, moved by water against Fort Henry on the Tennessee River, initiating the successful Mississippi campaign. Outgunned by the river boats, outnumbered by the troops put ashore downstream, Gen. Tilghman (C.) safely evacuated most of his small garrison and fought well with a few artillerymen before surrendering. Grant disregarded previous plans to delay and moved straightway on Fort Donelson.

HEPBURN ACT OF 1906 was regulatory legislation designed to clarify certain powers previously granted to the Interstate Commerce Commission and to further increase its authority over railroads and certain other types of carriers. It authorized the Commission to determine and prescribe just and reasonable maximum rates upon complaint and investigation; establish through routes and prescribe maximum joint rates and proper rate divisions between participating carriers; and determine, prescribe and enforce uniform systems of accounts. The Commission's orders upon carriers subject to its jurisdiction were made binding without court action, thus requiring the latter to assume the burden of initiating litigation that tested the validity of its orders. The law strengthened the Elkins Act of 1903 as regards personal discrimination; forbade railroads from transporting any commodity, other than timber and its manufactured products, in which they were financially interested, except that which was necessary for their own use; restricted the granting of free passes to certain groups of individuals; and increased the number of commissioners from five to seven.

HERD LAW v. FREE GRASS was a manifestation of the age-old question of inclosures. It was common in the newly settled Western states and territories during the last quarter of the 19th century. The point at issue was as to whether livestock or the growing or ungathered crops must be fenced. The livestock grower who planted little or no crops favored free grass, or the fencing of fields and allowing animals to run at large. This was especially true when a considerable part of the land was still a part of the public domain. The homesteader who owned merely a pair of horses and a milk cow or two believed in herd law, or that pasture lands should be inclosed and cultivated fields left unfenced. State laws usually provided that each township or county unit should decide the question for itself by local election. Since the proponents of herd law were usually poor homesteaders, and those favoring free grass were well-to-do cattle raisers, the controversy sometimes took the form of a class struggle resulting at times in violence, the destruction of property and even loss of life. As communities became more thickly settled and prosperous, adequate fences were constructed and the controversy died out.

HERRIN MASSACRE (June 22, 1922) was an outgrowth of an attempt to operate a strip mine in Williamson County, Ill., with nonunion labor during the coal strike of 1922. On June 22 forty-seven men working at the strip mine surrendered, under a promise of safe conduct, to an armed force of several hundred striking union miners. The captives were marched to a spot near Herrin and then ordered to run for their lives under fire. Twenty-one were killed, many more wounded. A special grand jury returned 214 indictments for murder and related crimes, but at the ensuing trial, which began on Nov. 13 and lasted nearly five months, local sentiment was such that convictions were impossible. On April 7, 1923, after several verdicts of acquittal had been returned, all the untried indictments were *nolle prossed.*

HESSIANS, a designation often indiscriminately used for all the German mercenaries fighting on the side of the British in the Revolution, were, strictly speaking, the 17,000 men hired out by the landgrave of Hesse-Cassel, whose first wife was a daughter of George II. The 12,000 sent in 1776 included some of his best regiments, all drilled on the Prussian system and officered by experienced men. They took part in every campaign except Burgoyne's, distinguishing themselves especially at Long Island, Fort Washington, Brandywine, Newport and Charleston. Their defeat at Trenton, Christmas, 1776, raised the morale of Washington's men, who learned that even the Hessians were not invincible. The Jäger Corps, light troops, who rivaled the American riflemen, were the best soldiers on the British side. As prisoners the Hessians generally fared better than the British. Many deserted, partly induced by Congress' proclamations; others were bought out of prison by farmers and artisans; and many remained in the country after the war had ended.

HIAWATHA was a Mohawk Indian chief known to the Iroquois Confederacy as Haionhwat'ha, who with Dekanawida and Jikonsasa founded the League of the Iroquois, a confederacy of the Mohawk, Oneida, Onondaga, Cayuga and Seneca tribes. The purpose of Hiawatha was to establish universal peace by uniting all known groups of the American continent. He began his mission among the Onondagas with whom he lived, probably attempting to build upon an older idea long prevalent among the Huron-Iroquois people. Since the Iroquois, later called the Six Nations, played an important part in colonial history, one must credit Hiawatha and his compeers with being the builders of one of the most formidable native empires on the continent, resulting in a military power entirely opposed to the peaceful plans of the founders. J. V. H. Clark is credited with relating the epic of Hiawatha to Henry R. Schoolcraft, whose writings attracted Henry W. Longfellow, who intermixed Algonkian and Iroquoian legends in the poem, "Hiawatha," but gave no facts relating to the hero's real character as a reformer and statesman.

HISS CASE. On Jan. 21, 1950, Alger Hiss was found guilty of perjury on two counts and was sentenced to five years in prison. An adviser to the State Department on economic and political affairs, he had served as secretary general of the San Francisco Conference for the Organization of the United Nations and had been appointed president of the Carnegie Endowment for International Peace. Hiss was tried and convicted of perjury for having denied under oath the charge of passing secret State Department documents to Whittaker Chambers, then acting as the agent for a communist spy ring. He also denied having seen Chambers later than Jan. 1, 1937.

HISTORICAL SOCIETIES. Organizations for the study of history existed in Europe long before they began in America: the Society of Antiquaries of

London was established as early as 1572. The first society of this sort in America was that of Massachusetts, founded in 1791 by Jeremy Belknap and a small group of Bostonians. John Pintard had attempted to attach a historical museum to the Society of St. Tammany in 1790 but this effort failed. The Massachusetts Historical Society grew out of the prevailing spirit of inquiry of the 18th century and also out of the Puritan atmosphere of New England which fostered a theistic interpretation of history—the latter a factor which helps to explain why such societies proliferated in New England, and in areas settled by New Englanders, more rapidly than in other sections of the country. Other historical societies followed that of Massachusetts in rapid succession: New York (1804), American Antiquarian Society, Worcester (1812), Rhode Island (1822), Maine (1823), New Hampshire (1823), Pennsylvania (1824), Connecticut (1825), Indiana (1830), Ohio (1831), Virginia (1831), Louisiana (1836), Vermont (1838), Georgia (1839), Maryland (1844), Tennessee (1849), Wisconsin (1849) and Minnesota (1849).

HOBKIRK'S HILL, BATTLE OF (April 25, 1781). After the Battle of Guilford Court House, Gen. Greene invaded South Carolina, detached a force to reduce Fort Watson, and himself, with 1200 men, marched toward the British post at Camden, where Lord Rawdon was in command. At Hobkirk's Hill, north of Camden, he was attacked by Rawdon with 900 men. Greene's plan of battle was good, but two regiments fell into confusion through the loss of a commander and a misunderstanding of orders, and the battle was lost, though the Americans retired in good order, losing 264 men. The British loss was 258. But the fall of Fort Watson in his rear had made Rawdon's position untenable, and on May 10 he retreated southward, abandoning Camden to Greene.

HOLLADAY OVERLAND STAGE COMPANY. From 1850 to 1870, before railways were generally available for express, mail and passenger service between the Mississippi Valley and the Pacific coast, overland stage companies were organized and extensive lines were maintained. Among these was a service provided by Ben Holladay on March 21, 1862, when he bought at public auction the interests of Russell, Majors and Waddell. By 1866 he operated over 2760 miles of western road, used 6000 horses and mules, 260 coaches, many wagons and employed hundreds of men. The Federal Government paid him annually $650,000 to carry the mail over these lines. In 1866 he sold his properties to Wells, Fargo and Co.

HOLLAND LAND COMPANY (1796–1846). Four Dutch banking houses, Stadnitski & Son, Van Stap-

horst, Van Eeghen and Ten Cate & Vollenhoven, decided to speculate in American funds, and in 1789, sent Theophile Cazenove to this country as agent.

In 1792 the other promoters, without Van Staphorst, authorized their agent to invest monies in lands in the United States. Regaining confidence, Van Staphorst soon joined, and the houses of Willink and Schimmelpenninck were added. Lands were purchased in the Genesees in November of that year. In December, Willink and others authorized Cazenove to purchase 500,000 acres in Pennsylvania.

Having decided to form a stock company, on May 20, 1795, the bankers made their declaration before a notary and on Feb. 13 of the following year the organization known as Hollandsche Land Compagnie was organized. The stock was divided into shares representing ownership of 1,300,000 acres in the Genesee, 900,000 east of the Allegheny and 499,660 west of that river. A director with six commissioners composed the management in Holland. In 1800 Cazenove was succeeded by Paul Busti as a general agent in America, and Joseph Ellicott became agent in the Genesees. The affairs of the Company in America were liquidated in 1846, or shortly thereafter.

HOLLAND SUBMARINE TORPEDO-BOAT, designed by John P. Holland, of Paterson, N. J., the most practical submarine built in the United States up to her time, was purchased, after exhaustive trials, by the Navy Department on April 11, 1900. Two months later Congress authorized the construction of five submarines of the Holland type. The Holland was a cigar-shaped craft, 53 feet long, propelled by a gasoline motor on the surface, and by an electric motor under water. The craft could dive, rise and be held at a desired level by the action of horizontal rudders placed at her stern. Air was furnished by compressors and reserve tanks. Her armament consisted of one bow torpedo tube, one bow pneumatic dynamite gun and three short Whitehead torpedoes. Holland had experimented with submarines for a quarter-century, and launched his first craft in 1877. He was the first to use an internal combustion engine in conjunction with an electric motor in a submarine.

HOLSTON TREATY. On June 26, 1791, Gov. William Blount of the Southwest Territory (now Tennessee) met the representatives of the Cherokee at White's Fort (Knoxville), some four miles below the junction of the French Broad and Holston Rivers. On July 2 a treaty was signed making the Cherokee-American boundary the watershed between the Little and the Little Tennessee rivers and guaranteeing to the Cherokee the possession of the lands still retained by them. This ended a period of warfare on the upper Tennessee frontier in which the Indians had endeavored to get the United States to enforce the more favorable Treaty of Hopewell of 1785 making the French Broad River the Cherokee-American boundary.

HOLSTON VALLEY SETTLEMENTS. James Patton of Augusta County, Va., claimed the honor of discovering in 1743 an unnamed river south of the New River. Stephen Holston about 1746 built his cabin at the headspring of the river. In 1748 Holston explored its lower reaches and in a canoe passed down the Tennessee, Ohio and Mississippi Rivers as far as Natchez. This adventure led to Holston's name being given to the river and valley. Progress of settlement down the Holston Valley was slow because of opposition of the Cherokees to encroachments south of New River. Not until 1768 were there settlers as far down as the North Carolina line; but the treaty of that year at Fort Stanwix caused an inrush and permanent settlements on the Holston and its tributaries below Virginia's southern boundary line. Donelson's line, run in 1771 under the Treaty of Lochaber, fixed the boundary between the Cherokees and Virginia at Holston River, severing this Holston Settlement from the one on the Watauga. The first named, even the large part in North Carolina until 1777, was governed by Virginia. West of Donelson's line was formed on the Holston a distinct settlement known as Pendleton District. Virginians largely predominated in both Holston settlements, and took active parts in Lord Dunmore's War and the Revolution.

HOLY EXPERIMENT was Penn's term for the ideal government he established in Pennsylvania (1681) which laid "the foundation of a free colony for all mankind" and guaranteed civil liberty, religious freedom and economic opportunity. The people shared fully in government with a constitution and code of laws chosen by them. No restrictions were placed on immigration; religious or political oppression was unknown; oaths were abolished and peace established, hence no provision for war by forts, munition or militia was necessary. This government succeeded for seventy years.

"HOME, SWEET HOME," was written by John Howard Payne while living in Paris, and was set to music by Henry Bishop from a Sicilian air which Payne had heard and with which Bishop was familiar. It was first sung by Maria Tree in Payne's operetta, *Clari,* produced at Covent Garden Theater, London, May 8, 1823, and at the Park Theater, New York, on Nov. 12. The version sung in *Clari* includes only the first two stanzas. The song became vastly popular and *Clari* was repeated on the American stage for over forty years.

HOMESTEAD MOVEMENT. It would be difficult, if not impossible, to fix a date for the beginning of the movement which culminated in 1862 in the passage of the Homestead Law. Free land was engrained in the thoughts and desires of westward-moving settlers from early colonial days, but until the West became politically powerful the demand passed unheeded. The revenue motive was basic in determining the public land policy of the new nation, and more than three quarters of a century were to elapse after the great land ordinance of 1785 before the advocates of free land to settlers were victorious.

Nevertheless, Congress began very early to receive petitions asking that land in certain regions be given without price to settlers. From the Ohio River came such a petition in 1797, and two years later one from Mississippi Territory. In 1812 Representative Morrow of Ohio presented a request from "The True American Society," whose members considered "every man entitled by nature to a portion of the soil of the country." Other instances could be cited to show that there was an insistence on the part of the pioneers that their services in making farms in the wilderness entitled them to land free of price. In 1825 Thomas Hart Benton moved that an inquiry be made into the expediency of donating lands to settlers. The House committee on public lands reported in favor of such a policy in 1828. In his message of Dec. 4, 1832, President Jackson expressed the opinion that "the public lands should cease as soon as practicable to be a source of revenue." Thus the basic doctrines of homestead legislation were steadily attracting adherents.

During the 1830's the Westerners gained an ally in organized labor. The National Trades Union Convention in 1834 and in 1836 adopted resolutions favoring the giving of land to settlers. Perhaps the most active leader in the movement was George Henry Evans, who became the editor of *The Working Men's Advocate,* established in 1844. About the same time there was organized the National Reform Association, which gave much of its attention to agitation for free land by means of public meetings, petitions and circulars. Horace Greeley also espoused the cause and brought it the powerful aid of his *New York Tribune.* In 1852, he presented a lengthy statement of the views of the "land reformers," the central idea being that the public land system should "be so modified that every person needing Land may take possession of any quarter-section not previously located, and that none other than a person needing land shall be allowed to acquire it at all."

The increasing public agitation was reflected in Congress by resolutions and petitions and finally, in 1846, by the introduction of homestead bills by Felix G. McConnell of Alabama and Andrew Johnson of Tennessee. The latter continued to be an ardent promoter of the homestead movement until success was achieved in 1862. It was not until 1852, however, that a general bill for free land actually came to a vote in Congress and then it was defeated in the Senate. Special laws donating land to settlers in Florida and Oregon, under certain conditions, were passed in 1842 and 1850, respectively.

The homestead movement first became a definite political issue in 1848, when the Free Soil party declared in favor of free land to actual settlers "in consideration of the expenses they incur in making settlements in the wilderness . . . and of the public benefits resulting therefrom." Four years later the same party gave its support even more vigorously, but on different grounds. Now they asserted that "all men have a natural right to a portion of the soil; and that, as the use of the soil is indispensable to life, the right of all men to the soil is as sacred as their right to life itself." Therefore, they contended, "the public lands of the United States belong to the people, and should not be sold to individuals nor granted to corporations, but should be held as a sacred trust for the benefit of the people, and should be granted in limited quantities, free of cost, to landless settlers." These two platforms contained the main arguments used from first to last by the advocates of free land, namely, reward for public service in developing the country, and natural right.

No major political party came to the support of a homestead policy until 1860, but the adherents of the idea were far more numerous than the small votes polled by the Free Soil candidates indicated. In Congress the defeat of the bill of 1852 did not discourage the introduction of similar measures in both houses in the succeeding sessions. Until 1860, however, the formidable opposition to free land made it impossible to get a law through both houses.

Most Southerners were opposed to homestead legislation, mainly because they believed it would result in the peopling of the territories by antislavery settlers. Many Easterners disapproved of the movement because of their fear of the effect of its success on the economic situation in Eastern states. It would, they contended, accelerate the westward movement, it would lower the value of land in the East, and it would deprive the Federal Government of an important source of revenue. Besides these sectional antagonisms to a measure so eagerly desired by Westerners, there was the opposition of the Know-Nothing party and other antialien groups to any proposal to give free land to foreign immigrants.

The forces of opposition were sufficiently strong until 1860 to prevent the passage of a homestead law. In that year, however, a bill, introduced by Galusha A. Grow of Pennsylvania, and amended in the process of debate and conference, passed both houses. Although this law as finally passed retained a price of 25 cents an acre, it was vetoed by President Buchanan, who used most of the arguments which had hitherto been advanced against free land, including unconstitutionality. The effort to override the veto failed by a small margin, and the defeat was a bitter disappointment to the homestead cohorts.

As a matter of fact, however, victory was approaching. The very sectional conflict which had raised the most formidable obstacle to homestead legislation soon led to a situation which left the road to success entirely open. The new Republican party in 1860 declared that "we demand the passage by Congress of the complete and satisfactory Homestead measure." The victory of the Republicans and the secession of the South left the triumphant party free to carry out its program. On May 20, 1862, Abraham Lincoln attached his signature to the Homestead Law, and free land—the goal sought by generations of Westerners since the inception of the public-land policy—was attained.

The Homestead Law gave to "any person who is the head of a family, or who has arrived at the age of twenty-one years, and is a citizen of the United States, or who shall have filed his declaration of intention to become such," the privilege of obtaining a quarter-section of land free of charge, except a small filing fee, by living on the land for five years and meeting certain conditions with respect to cultivation. With numerous modifications, the basic features of the law are in force today.

HOOKWORM DISEASE. The prevalence and importance of hookworm in the Southeastern states was first recognized by Dr. C. W. Stiles in 1901. In 1909 the Rockefeller Sanitary Commission was organized to study and control the disease in this country; it was out of this that the International Health Division of the Rockefeller Foundation eventually grew. The effect of this attack on hookworm disease was to awaken an intelligent public interest in rural hygiene and to establish permanent agencies for the promotion of health in rural areas, which in this country took the form of county health organizations.

HOOSAC TUNNEL, opened in 1876, extends 4.73 miles through the Hoosac Mountains of Massachusetts, a southern extension of the Green Mountains. It was started in 1855 by the Troy and Greenfield Railroad as part of a plan to divert western trade to Boston. The state aided, and was forced to take it over when the road failed in 1863. In 1887 it was turned over to the Fitchburg Railroad, now a part of the Boston and Maine. The first use of compressed air drills in the United States was in 1866 in the construction of this tunnel.

"HOOSIER" is a term applied to the inhabitants of Indiana since pioneer days. It had a meaning well understood in the state as early as 1830. "Hoosier" occurs in a poem of that year printed in the Indianapolis *Journal* and was often used in letters and addresses during the first half of the 19th century. Its origin is obscure—incapable of satisfactory explanation.

HOOVER COMMISSIONS. Two commissions on organization of the executive branch of government were set up by unanimous votes of the two chambers of the Congress of the United States. Both served under the chairmanship of Herbert Hoover, 30th President of the United States. The first functioned in 1947–49 to deal with growth of Government during World War II. The second dealt with growth during the Korean emergency. Both sought to reduce expenditures to the lowest amount consistent with essential services and to end duplication and overlapping of services or activities.

The commissions were nonpartisan. Of the personnel for each, four were named by the President, four by the Vice-President and four by the Speaker of the House. The first included: Herbert Hoover, Dean G. Acheson, Sen. George D. Aiken, Rep. Clarence J. Brown, Arthur S. Flemming, Joseph P. Kennedy, Sen. John L. McClellan, James V. Forrestal, Rep. Carter Manasco, James K. Pollock, George H. Mead, and James H. Rowe, Jr. The second included: Herbert Hoover, Rep. Clarence J. Brown, Herbert Brownell, Jr., Sen. Homer Ferguson (succeeded by Sen. Styles Bridges), James A. Farley, Arthur S. Flemming, Rep. Chet Holifield, Solomon C. Hollister, Joseph P. Kennedy, Sen. John L. McClellan, Sidney A. Mitchell, and Robert G. Storey.

The first commission created twenty-four task forces of experts to study as many phases of government; the second, nineteen. Task forces reported to the commission which, after studies by their staffs and members, reported their findings to Congress. The first commission made 273 recommendations, the second 314. Of these about half could be carried out by administrative action and the rest required legislation. More than 70% of the recommendations have been put into effect.

Mr. Hoover estimated that the first commission brought, in all, savings of $7,000,000,000 and the second, of better than $3,000,000,000 yearly.

Among reforms resulting from the commissions are: passage of the Military Unification Act of 1949; creation of the General Services Agency; formation of the Department of Health, Education and Welfare; cost accounting and modernized budgeting; reduction of Government competition with private business; development of a Federal career service; co-ordination of Federal research; and reduction of "red tape."

HOPEWELL, TREATY OF, was made at Hopewell, S. C., on Nov. 28, 1785, between the Cherokee Indians and commissioners of the United States; in the following January the same commissioners at the same place made almost identical treaties with the Choctaw and Chickasaw. These treaties fixed boundaries between the different tribes and between Indians and whites, gave the United States sovereignty over the three tribes, and control of their trade. The treaty of Hopewell is significant as the first general Indian treaty made by the United States; its most important provision was the establishment of a definite boundary of Indian lands.

HORNET-PEACOCK ENGAGEMENT (1813). On Feb. 24, off British Guiana, the United States sloop *Hornet,* Master-Commandant James Lawrence, captured the British brig *Peacock,* Capt. William Peake, after a spirited action of fifteen minutes. Soon afterward the *Peacock* sank. The British had five killed, including Capt. Peake, and thirty-three wounded; the Americans, one killed and four wounded.

HORSE. Developing in the Americas only to the prehistoric stage, horses were introduced into all the colonies from England and the continent. Before settled agricultural systems developed, oxen were preferred for draft purposes, but horses and ponies were essential for inland travel. For the colonies as a whole, horses were valued mainly for riding, hunting and racing. The latter was a leading form of recreation throughout the colonies; there were sectional and intersectional meets, and races were a usual attraction of the market fairs. The jockey club founded at Charleston in 1734 is claimed to have been the first in the world and a similar organization was formed at Annapolis in 1745. Long Island was another famous racing center. Relatively high stakes and the sporting spirit gave the incentive for improvements through importations and a degree of selective breeding. New England carried on the first extensive breeding on the basis of early English and Flemish importations. From 1650 the region was exporting increasingly to the other continental colonies and especially to the West Indies, where the sugar industry created a steady demand. Rhode Island developed one of the most distinctive and noted types of the period in the Narragansett pacer—a fast easy-gaited saddle horse but one not suited for driving or draft purposes. In direct contrast was the famous Conestoga of the Pennsylvania German farmers. The product of selection and careful handling, these animals were distinguished for size, strength and endurance. The development of such a suitable draft type was in harmony with the more settled and advanced cultivation and husbandry that prevailed in this region.

In all phases of the penetration, occupation and development of the continent the horse has played a major role. The stagecoach was the first interregional utility. The post-rider opened communication with outlying settlements. The peddler ministered to material needs, the doctor to physical and the circuit-rider to the spiritual. Horses and mules drew canal boat and rail car. The Western pony served the hunter, trapper and miner, and later provided the mounts for the long drive and herding activities of the cowboy. Pack horse, stager, freighter and express pony served the transportation needs of the Far West before the coming of the railroad. Extractive industries, manufactures and city distributive systems were all dependent on horse power. Cavalry mounts and supply teams were adjuncts of military organization and of campaigning on every front. Sport and recreation, organized and unorganized, made increasing demands upon equine standardization and specialization.

Speed desires motivated the first systematic efforts at high breeding. The English thoroughbred, "Messenger," imported in 1788, was to become the progenitor of a group of racing families of whom the most noted have been the Hambletonian and the Mambrino. "Justin Morgan," foaled in Massachusetts in 1793, founded a line notable not only for speed but for light draft and provided the nearest attainment to a distinct American breed. The modern runners have been highly developed from thoroughbred strains and such races are still associated with high society and equally high stakes. From the first quarter of the past century, increasing attention has been given to harness racing, and selective breeding, careful training and improvement of track and equipment have brought a steady increase in speed. Racers' pedigrees and records are officially recorded in the registers established by John H. Wallace in 1871. The saddle-horse has continued to be bred for ever-lessening demand in the Kentucky bluegrass region. The heavy harness type—cob, hackney, coach—were imported and bred for a special pleasure-driving demand in the pre-automobile days and still appear in horse shows. The polo game has utilized small thoroughbreds and Western ponies.

Less spectacular but far more significant have been the uses of the horse in carrying on the nation's production and transportation. By 1860 the age-old controversy of the ox versus the horse for farm traction had been decisively settled. The ox's availability at the self-sufficing stage was overcome by the needs of increased and bettered production and the requirements of the new machinery. The general use of the standard draft breeds, pure or grade, was a condition of the "new agriculture" before the tractor stage. The Percheron was widely imported in the 1850's to become the most popular type. The other leading heavy breeds—Belgian, Clydesdale and Shire—were bred for the market from the 1870's. The Corn Belt from Ohio to Iowa has been the center of the draft-horse supply.

The Cow Horse. The original cow horse was essentially of the mustang breed. Until the 20th century mares were seldom used for range work, and they are not much used yet, although a belled mare commonly led the *remuda*. The cow pony had to have bottom, surefootedness and "cow sense"—a quality lacking in many finely bred horses. The average did not weigh a thousand pounds and was around fourteen hands high—"enough horse" to hold 1500 pounds of beef at the end of a rope. The cow pony often maintained the pitching proclivities of a bronco. The elite of his kind were the cutting horses, agile, intelligent, superbly reined, trained to cut, or part, animals from a herd. The night horse was picked to stand guard, and to be relied upon when in pitchy darkness the herd stampeded across prairie-dog holes and gullies. In running after cattle, the cowboy's chief work often lay in staying with his horse, which would no more quit the running than a hound will quit a hot trail. "Cowboys are plentiful, good cow horses cost money," was a range saying.

The Spanish Horse. Brought to the West Indies at the close of the 15th century, the Spanish horse was rapidly acclimated, and within thirty years formed the chief supply for the mainland expeditions. By the middle of the 16th century there were outstanding horse breeders in Cuba, Jamaica, Nicaragua, Chiapas and Oaxaca, who sold their products in two continents.

From the islands and Mexico the horse advanced with the Spaniard into the northern mainland in four salient columns. While Jamestown was being settled by the English on the Atlantic coast, Oñate was establishing Spanish ranches in New Mexico. The tradition that the mustangs of the Southwest sprang from the early expeditions of Coronado and DeSoto is apparently incorrect. By 1630 horses were plentiful around Santa Fe, but the Plains Indians seemingly had none, and no records are found of mounted Indians for three more decades. By 1660 the Indians had learned the value of horses, and had begun to steal them. During the next forty years the horse spread into the plains and mountains with great rapidity. In 1719 Dutisne found the Pawnees near Kansas with 300 horses, some bearing Spanish brands. The Snakes had horses by 1730 and two decades later the Blackfeet in present-day Canada were mounted. By the end of the 17th century the French of St. Lawrence Valley were obtaining a regular supply of Spanish horses from the Indians west of the Mississippi.

Farther west Kino and his companions were pushing a second Spanish wedge into Arizona, where they established many stock ranches by 1700. Here also the horses multiplied and were acquired by the natives. Portolá from Lower California, and Anza from Arizona, took horses into Alta California, where they increased prodigiously. Exportation thence to Hawaii began in 1803 and reached extensive proportions by 1830. So numerous did horses become in California that thousands were slaughtered, or driven off cliffs or into the sea to drown. Simultaneously with the movement into Arizona, Spaniards from Coahuila introduced horses into Texas and Louisiana, where Patrick Henry, Daniel Boone, Philip Nolan and others from east of the Mississippi were buying stock before the end of the 18th century.

Just as the Western horse came from Mexico, so the foundation stock of the Atlantic coast came from the Spanish islands to Florida. By 1650 this district had many missions, several large towns, and two royal haciendas whence horses spread to the Indians —not from the remnants of DeSoto's mounts as has been commonly supposed. Indian revolts and English depredations at the close of the 1600's tended to spread the horse north into the English colonies. On the outskirts of Virginia they multiplied in a semiferal state—like the mustangs of the Southwest—until they were a menace to the crops and were hunted for sport. These horses were generally small, with bad points, but new blood was obtained from the Spanish stock west of the Mississippi.

HORTALEZ ET CIE owed its origin to Beaumarchais. The famous author of *Le Mariage de Figaro* in a pamphlet *La Paix ou la Guerre* influenced Louis XVI to secret assistance for the Americans. A corporation, nominally private, would safeguard the official neutrality of France while permitting substantial aid to the revolutionists. On May 2, 1776, the king authorized purchase of supplies to the value of 1,000,-000 livres. In July the Spanish king extended similar assistance. In August the company was officially organized, and within a year it had sent to the Americans eight shiploads of military stores worth over 6,000,000 livres.

Notwithstanding the formal alliance of 1778, the company continued in business until 1783. Its total disbursements exceeded 21,000,000 livres and were of immeasurable importance to the *matériel* of the American Revolution. Confusion in reimbursements was responsible for the "Lost Million" of Beaumarchais.

HOSPITALS. The medieval Church was the mother of hospitals, and its influence established hospitals in Catholic America before they were known in Protestant America. Still existent are the 16th-century Jesus Hospital of Mexico (1524) and the 17th-century Hôtels-Dieu of Quebec (1639) and Montreal (1644), but there was no general hospital on the soil of the United States until the 18th century. The orator's dramatic claim for the Philadelphia General Hospital, "This, Gentlemen, is the oldest hospital on this continent," is therefore incorrect. The Philadelphia General Hospital, known as Old Blockley, which opened as an almshouse (1732); Bellevue Hospital of New York, which opened as a workhouse (1736); and Pennsylvania Hospital, which opened as a hospital (1751), continue to contend for the title of "America's oldest hospital." William Shippen's private institution (1762) in Philadelphia, "a convenient lodging, under the care of a sober, honest matron, well acquainted with lying-in women," was our first maternity hospital. The Mad House (1768) at Williamsburg, Va., now the Eastern State Hospital, was the first insane asylum in the United States.

After the battle of Bunker Hill, in which the physician Joseph Warren died a hero's death, his youthful pupil and brother, John Warren, took charge of the wounded at Cambridge, "in several private but commodious houses," which may be regarded as our first military hospital (1775). James Tilton, who introduced the hut system in the "hard winter of 1779–80, when the army was hutted near Morristown," advocated the plan of the Indian hut as the best hospital in cold weather. The army hospital located on a pasture in Boston afforded John Warren the material for lecturing on the cadaver. His sessions were conducted behind locked doors, as hostility to dissection of the human body was intense (lack of caution in New York caused prejudice to flare up in the Doctor's Mob, quelled only with the aid of militia). Despite the attempt at secrecy, this early anatomical course could not be hidden, and when it was repeated for two years it originated Harvard's medical school (1782–83), in which John Warren served as first professor of anatomy and surgery. His son, John Collins Warren, who succeeded to the dual chair, founded the Massachusetts General Hospital (1811), where in his old age he consummated his labors by giving anesthesia its first public demonstration (1846)—"and a new era for surgery began."

In the log-cabin period, Daniel Drake (1785–1852) was the medical builder of Ohio. Drake, battle-scarred from the "Thirty Years' War" with colleagues, gave the impulse to the hospital movement in the Mississippi Valley with the words: "All the tendencies of the age are to the study of medicine and surgery in hospitals. The laboratory is not more necessary for the study of chemistry, or a garden of plants for the study of botany, than a hospital for the study of practical medicine and surgery." The classic appeals for hospital instruction in America were made by Oliver Wendell Holmes (*Scholastic and Bedside Teaching*, 1867), who was a truant of Aesculapius; and by Abraham Flexner (*Medical Education in the United States*, 1910), who was not a physician. The hospital, designed for the reception and treatment of the sick, has emerged as the training field and teaching center of medicine and nursing.

Not until the 20th century did American hospitals, in number and equipment and personnel, begin to keep pace with the needs of the nation. In 1957 there were 1,558,691 hospital beds in 6818 hospitals in the United States, of which 2218 were Government hospitals.

HOUSING. American housing has been shaped by two quite different historic influences. One stems from traditional values of American individualism: self-reliance, family independence, and private enterprise. The other, an older and more universal tradition, reflects civic values: community pride, and public responsibility for the collective welfare. This is perhaps oversimplified. But the history of housing progress in the United States is mainly the record of continuous efforts to resolve this dichotomy.

One obvious heritage from pioneering days is the bent for home-ownership. On each successive frontier the first dwellings were primitive self-built shelters, which were gradually replaced by better structures as family resources expanded. We are now a wealthy, highly urbanized nation, housing possibilities and requirements are entirely different, and most homes are produced by commercial builders, often with Federal aid. But the free-standing house, individually owned, is still the dominant and favored building type wherever land prices and convenience permit. Even the original form survives, in the shacktown type of slum. And there is also a prevalent feeling that individual initiative and private enterprise should be able to meet a larger share of our housing needs more satisfactorily.

But civic requirements have also influenced American homes from the start. The colonial towns of the eastern seaboard apparently exercised a relatively high degree of community responsibility for the period, in terms of elementary municipal services and regulations with respect to roads, fire safety, and minimal sanitation. In the higher density centers, wooden structures were outlawed in favor of a European dwelling form, the brick row house. Piped water systems were beginning to reach homes in several communities, before the Revolution. As the frontier moved westward in the 19th century, civic initiative may have been weaker on the whole, by comparison with rising standards elsewhere, while the homestead ideal had a stronger influence on urban patterns. Later, it was the midwestern bungalow and the western "ranch-house" that flooded eastern suburbs.

But economic progress, modern science and technology have steadily increased the burden of collective problems and responsibilities with respect to living conditions. In the early stages, industrialization and the immigrant flood led to factory enclaves with company-built housing, but the major result was big cities where poverty, crowding and land prices created slums which neither individual nor commercial enterprise have been able to remedy. Meanwhile, the great public health revolution created a new concept of "minimum standards," essential to the welfare of both rich and poor. And municipalities slowly began to develop the vast present-day network of sanitary services and housing regulations.

The modern bathroom and kitchen were great achievements in which America led the world. But they also raised both the direct and indirect costs of minimal housing, and helped to put lower-income families outside the market for acceptable accommodations. Rising central densities, with stricter regulation of new construction, likewise increased costs. The slums therefore remained, in many cases more crowded than ever.

Transportation technology started a new chapter in housing history. The automobile, following a start by the railroad and trolley-car, opened up vast areas of cheap suburban land for middle and upper class home-ownership, inaugurating the present era of chaotic metropolitan expansion. But the price of mobility was also high in terms of both consumer budgets and public expenditures, and is still rising more rapidly than incomes, in part due to the expensive remedies required for commuters' congestion in central districts. The old slums still accommodated the latest waves of low-income immigrants, who were increasingly of minority race, and in addition there were ever-widening rings of blight, decay and overcrowding in once adequate residential districts.

A demand for more positive measures to improve urban housing conditions began to take shape even before World War I, stimulated by European examples, but it was a series of national emergencies that sparked direct public action. In 1917 the Federal Government built English-type housing projects for war-workers. In the postwar shortage, several state and local governments took various tentative steps. And there were some civic-minded private experiments which had considerable influence on later housing and community design practice.

With the depression of 1929 came disaster in the housing market, critical unemployment in the building industry, and all kinds of Federal measures of which three have been operating ever since: over-all credit controls; mortgage insurance for private builders; and subsidies for low-rent public housing. World War II and its aftermath again brought emergency shortages, with a big Federal program for war-workers, then special aids for veterans.

To sum up American housing history since the war is a difficult task, because it has been lively but inconclusive. The decay in central districts has become a national issue, and Federal grants for redevelopment were inaugurated in 1949, with added incentives since 1954 for rehabilitation, conservation, broader physical planning, and private housing. The public housing program survives in 1960 despite continuous controversy. But it cannot be claimed that the slum problem is solved, or well on its way to solution. Federal mortgage insurance and other credit aids have stimulated millions of suburban tract houses, sporadic rental construction, a few co-operatives, and some housing initiative for the elderly, but the effective market is still quite limited, particularly for families of minority race. Several states provide additional housing aids, and most residential development is now subject to public guidance through local planning and zoning as well as building regulations, but as yet there is little effective planning or housing responsibility at the metropolitan level.

Suburbia is now seen as a "problem area" along with blighted central districts, and there is a rising but still uncertain push toward some form of metropolitan unification. Racial discrimination in housing is fast becoming a major issue at all levels of government. And there is a general feeling that large-scale private enterprise and governmental policies tend to produce overstandardized results, from the viewpoint of variegated human housing needs.

American housing, in short, is still a dynamic field where shifting individual, business and public interests must continually be resolved.

HUDSON RIVER. Verrazzano, an Italian explorer in French employ, was, so far as known, the first white man to have seen the Hudson River. In 1524, after entering New York Harbor, he wrote of "a very large river, deep at its mouth," which he had ascended for about half a league. The Spaniard Estevan Gomez noticed the Hudson in 1525. French traders traversed it, mostly from Canada, during that century, trading with the Mohawk Indians, and founded a small fort near the site of Albany in 1540, but this was later abandoned. Henry Hudson, exploring for the Dutch West India Company, ascended the river in 1609 as far as the neighborhood of Albany.

HUDSON'S BAY COMPANY came into being as a result of the western explorations of Radisson and Des Groseilliers in the middle of the 17th century. On trips into the Wisconsin and Minnesota country they learned from the Indians of a great fur country northwest of Lake Superior, which might be reached via Hudson Bay. This idea, linked with one of a probable Northwest Passage through Hudson Bay, led the Frenchmen to England in the middle 1660's. There a sort of syndicate of wealthy and influential men was formed to try out their ideas. Out of this grew the Hudson's Bay Company, which received its charter on May 2, 1670, as the Governor and Company of Adventurers of England Trading into Hudson's Bay. Under that charter and supplemental charters the company still operates, though it has now lost its monopoly of trade, its territory and its administrative rights in the West, which were granted by the first document. It is thus one of the oldest commercial corporations in existence. During the heyday of the fur trade, the company had posts in most parts of what is now Canada. It also had a few forts on United States soil, but fewer than is currently believed. These were mostly along the boundary line west from Grand Portage, in the area where the chief impact of the company on United States history was felt. Some of that impact came with the bitter struggle carried on between the Hudson's Bay Company and the North West Company, which resulted largely from the establishment of Lord Selkirk's colony on the Red River of the North in 1811. Selkirk, it needs to be said, was one of the largest owners of stock in the English company. Just before the differences were composed by a union of the two companies in 1821, Selkirk died, and for some years his colony was administered by the company. The colony's founding and struggles had a bearing on the founding of Fort St. Anthony (now Fort Snelling) in 1819; the misfortunes of the colonists led to the emigration of many of them to Fort Snelling to be Minnesota's earliest settlers; the need of a market for the colony led to the development of the Red River cart traffic with Minnesota settlements; and proximity to United States soil, and discontent of the colonists under company rule, led to annexation hopes and schemes both on the part of the colonists and the United States between 1849 and the surrender of the company's territories in 1869. Other effects of the company on Minnesota and North Dakota history are those resulting from the sending of missionaries to the Indians and half-breeds under the aegis of the company. Missionaries also played an important part in the company's relations to the history of the Oregon country, where company men appeared after the union of 1821 to carry on the fur trade begun years earlier by the North West Company, and where a joint occupation agreement between the United States and Great Britain was in force between 1818 and 1846. By welcoming American traders, explorers, missionaries and settlers, Dr. John McLoughlin, the company's chief factor, helped Oregon to become American, though the decline of the fur trade is probably the basic reason for Great Britain's consent in 1846 to abandon its claims south of the forty-ninth parallel and thus avert a war which threatened.

HUGUENOTS IN AMERICA. The term Huguenot, of unknown origin, probably a diminutive of Hugo, had been applied to the followers of Calvin during the religious struggles of the 16th and 17th centuries. Henry IV had granted religious toleration to his Protestant subjects by the Edict of Nantes (1598), but this was revoked by Louis XIV in 1685. Approximately 300,000 persecuted French Huguenots fled to Prussia, Switzerland, Holland, England and America. Attempted settlements in Florida and South Carolina (1562 and 1564) failed. In 1623 Huguenots, largely French-speaking Walloons, settled New Amsterdam. Peter Minuit was a Walloon, and Jean Vigne, first white child born on Manhattan Island, was French and probably Huguenot. Fort Orange (Albany), Kingston and New Paltz in New York were Huguenot settlements. Some 200 or 300 Huguenot families came to Boston after the Dragonades.

After 1685 increasing numbers came to America, settling in Rhode Island, in Hartford and Milford in Connecticut, and in New Rochelle, N. Y., mingling with other settlers in Delaware, Maryland and Pennsylvania, where they were called Dutchmen and confused with German settlers. In Virginia the first of the "French Protestant Refugees," as the name appears officially in the Virginia records, was Nicholas Martiau, coming before 1620 and being the earliest known Virginia ancestor of George Washington. The shipload coming to Manakintowne July 23, 1700, and two more shiploads in the same year, made up the largest single settlements of Huguenots in America.

This group with its local church and pastor was absorbed into the Church of England. King William Parish was set aside for them, but their blood soon mingled with the English people of the colony.

In South Carolina Huguenots began coming in 1670, played a large part in the settlement of Charleston in 1680 and by 1687 had established four settlements largely or wholly French: Jamestown on the Santee, "The Orange Quarter" on the Cooper, Saint John's Berkeley and Charleston. In 1732, 360 French-Swiss Protestants settled Purysburg on the Savannah, and in 1764 was founded the last French colony, New Bordeaux in Abbeville County. In South Carolina, Huguenots preserved their identity more completely than in other colonies. The only Huguenot church in America is in Charleston, preserving its service, doctrine and organization unchanged. The Huguenot religion was Calvinistic in theology, ritual in form, Presbyterian in government and tolerant in principle. Until well within the 20th century one service each year was conducted in French in the Charleston Huguenot church.

HUMPHREY'S EXECUTOR v. U. S. (1935) restricted the President's power to remove members of the so-called "independent" agencies. In the Federal Trade Commission Act, Congress provided that any commissioner might be removed by the President for inefficiency, neglect of duty, or malfeasance in office. In October, 1933, President Roosevelt removed Commissioner William E. Humphrey, not on any of the stipulated grounds, but because of differences of opinion as to policy. Humphrey denied the validity of this action, and after his death, his executor sued for recovery of the deceased's salary.

The Supreme Court held unanimously that Congress intended to create the Federal Trade Commission as an independent body of experts, and therefore meant to limit the President's removal power to the causes enumerated in the act. It denied the Government's contention, based on Myers v. U. S., that such limitation was unconstitutional. Whereas the Myers case involved a purely executive officer, the Federal Trade Commission's duties are predominantly quasi-legislative and quasi-judicial. Congress has authority, the Court declared, to require such a body to act independently of executive control, and may forbid removal except for cause.

HUNDRED. The hundred in England was of varying size but generally supposed to have been originally an area occupied by 100 families.

Very early in Virginia the hundred was adopted as a territorial division and included, in theory at least, 100 families, but was far more extensive than in England and soon became strictly territorial, without regard to the number of persons. In Virginia, as in England, it was the unit for judicial, military and political purposes. By 1619 the borough, which in-

cluded hundreds, was established and two burgesses from each borough were elected to the legislature. By 1634 Virginia was divided into eight large shires or counties. The hundreds thus gradually lost their influence but their names persisted because of their former importance.

In Maryland, as in Virginia, the hundreds were territorial units for elections, public levies and the preservation of the peace. The chief officer of the hundred, the constable or conservator of the peace, had the power of a justice of the peace in England. In the early period, the hundred was the unit of representation for the legislature (two burgesses from every hundred), also the unit for judicial, fiscal and military purposes. Even after counties were established, the importance of hundreds continued for a considerable period.

In Delaware under English control the hundred was adopted and was in operation by 1690. After counties were established the hundreds continued as the important subdivisions of them, persisting to the present. There are, for example, thirteen in Sussex County and the city of Wilmington has been made a separate hundred.

HURRICANES. The word hurricane has come, in the United States, to mean a marine storm or one of those destructive tropical gales which arise in the West Indies and sometimes cross to our continent. Of a list of 355 such storms, all that are on record between 1493 and 1855, it was found that 245, including all of the worst ones, occurred in August, September and October. They follow some curious courses. The great hurricane of 1848 crossed Florida and moved with somewhat diminished force northwest to Nebraska, then turned sharply eastward, past the southern Great Lakes. The great hurricanes of 1873, 1879, 1881, 1885, 1886, 1893 and 1911 all occurred in August. That of 1879 destroyed 300 vessels along the Atlantic coast. That of 1881 killed 335 persons in and near Savannah. Two days later, its center was near Memphis, the next morning in Iowa, then in Minnesota. That of 1893 ravaged the Georgia and Carolina coasts, killing 1000 and doing $10,000,000 damage, and finally passed across Lake Ontario into Canada. Very frequently these storms—those of 1875, 1878 and 1896 being notable examples—sweep from Florida up the Atlantic coast to New York or New England. That of 1878 did enormous damage in Philadelphia. The most destructive hurricane in our history was that which struck Galveston, Texas, on Sept. 8, 1900. It fairly lifted the waters of the Gulf and hurled them through the city, drowning 6000 persons, more than one seventh of the population, and doing $20,000,000 damage, leaving not a house in the city uninjured. The barometer there fell to 28.48, the lowest figure on record in America up to that time. The year 1915 saw two major disasters, in August and September. The August storm entered through Texas, passed up the Mississippi Valley, then swerved northeastward across the Great Lakes; the September gale ravaged the Louisiana and Alabama coasts. In each of these some 275 persons were killed, and the property damage ran into many millions. In 1920 it was calculated that in the twenty years from 1900 to 1919 inclusive, Gulf coast hurricanes caused $105,642,000 damage and took 7225 lives. The September, 1926, hurricane almost wrecked Miami, Fla., killed 400, and did $25,000,000 damage. Two years later, September, 1928, a more terrible storm passed diagonally across southern Florida, driving Lake Okeechobee out of its bed, doing less property damage, but killing, as nearly as could be ascertained, about 2300 people. On Sept. 21, 1938, a West Indian hurricane, which had missed the whole east coast until it touched the New Jersey shore, devastated large areas of Long Island and New England; Providence, New London and other cities suffered enormous damage. More than 600 lives were lost. The eastern coast of the United States suffered considerable damage and lost about 350 persons in a hurricane on Oct. 12–16, 1954, and another 400 persons on Aug. 18–19, 1955. Approximately 430 deaths were reported in a hurricane which hit Texas and Louisiana on June 27–30, 1957.

HYDROGEN BOMB. In this bomb the light elements of hydrogen and helium are fused to produce an explosive force greater by far in intensity than the atom bomb. On Sept. 13, 1949, Pres. Harry S. Truman revealed the fact that Soviet Russia had detonated an atom bomb. Some four months later, on Jan. 31, 1950, the President ordered the Atomic Energy Commission (A.E.C.) to proceed with the production of a hydrogen bomb, potentially one thousand times more powerful than the atom bombs that destroyed Hiroshima and Nagasaki, Japan, in August, 1945. In November, 1952, an A.E.C. and Defense Department task force detonated the first hydrogen bomb in an explosion sufficiently powerful to level a great city. These frightening developments, the atom and hydrogen bombs, were marks of the entry of the people of the United States and of the world into the thermo-nuclear age of potential mass destruction or of achievements for human progress heretofore unknown in the history of the world. Soviet Russia also soon announced the detonation of an hydrogen bomb.

HYDROGRAPHIC SURVEY. The U. S. Navy Hydrographic Office conducts surveys on the high seas and in foreign waters; the U. S. Coast and Geodetic Survey, Department of Commerce, conducts surveys of the coastal waters of the United States and its possessions, and the U. S. Army Engineer Corps conducts surveys on the Great Lakes and specific related waterways. The participation of the United States in the field of world-wide hydrographic survey

is characterized in the history of the Hydrographic Office, which commenced with the establishment of a Depot of Charts and Instruments in Washington in 1830.

The Depot of Charts and Instruments was established for the express purpose of supplying accurate nautical charts, books and navigational instruments to the Navy and American shipping interests which, prior to 1830, had been compelled to rely on foreign charts and various commercial sources. The Depot, in 1854, was separated into a Hydrographic Office and Naval Observatory which were given individual status in 1866 by an act of Congress.

The first survey made by the U. S. Navy was that of fishing banks off the coast of Massachusetts and resulted, in 1837, in the publication of four engraved charts. The Wilkes Exploring Expedition (1838–42), which ranged from the eastern Atlantic to the coasts of both the Americas and thence deep into the western and southwestern reaches of the Pacific, made surveys which formed the basis for charts issued prior to the Civil War. Extensive supplementary surveys were also conducted in 1848, 1850, and 1853. Matthew Perry's expedition to Japan in 1853 provided a wealth of data supplementing the earlier works of Wilkes.

In 1842, Matthew Fontaine Maury, in command of the Depot between 1842 and 1861 laid the foundation for systematic hydrographic survey by initiating an extensive uniform system for collecting meteorological and navigational data. The data, obtained from the logbooks of naval and merchant vessels, contributed to the issue in 1847, of a "track chart," the prototype of the modern pilot chart. The production of trade wind charts, thermal charts, whale charts, and storm and rain charts was commenced soon afterwards. Maury himself wrote the first authoritative sailing directions and, in 1855, published *The Physical Geography of the Sea*, a work which is the basis of modern oceanography.

The act of Congress creating the Hydrographic Office in 1866 also authorized the purchase of plates and copyrights of other existing charts and publications. Thus supplemented, the Hydrographic Office expanded its scope of operations. The expeditions of 1874–84 succeeded by use of the telegraph in accurately establishing the longitude of thirty positions girdling the globe and thus increasing accuracy of survey which was not improved until the advent of the radio time signal in 1911. The modern "pilot chart" appeared for the first time in 1883; gnomonic charts were begun in 1885. In 1921 the United States became a member of the International Hydrographic Bureau established in Monaco; this membership affording a facility for the exchange of information on an international basis, increasing tremendously the sources, amount of survey and research material available to the Hydrographic Office.

In 1922 the introduction of a practical sonic

depthfinder and the application of photogrammetry to aerial photography, both initiated by the U. S. Navy, marked the beginning of a new era in hydrographic survey. By means of the sonic depthfinder, bathymetric charts delineating the ocean floor were constructed; by means of aerial photography a true relationship of land and water areas was quickly shown. The years 1922–59 were marked by the development, especially during World War II and the conflict in Korea, of various electronic devices and similar developments in the scientific field. These brought into being new and more accurate methods of survey and greatly improved chart construction. The opening of a "Northwest Passage" by Canadian and American vessels in 1957 and the underwater passage of the U. S. S. *Nautilus* across the North Pole in 1958 marked the degree of development thus attained.

HYLTON v. U. S., 1796 (3 Dallas 171). The question of whether a tax on carriages imposed by an act of Congress (June 5, 1794) was a direct tax, and therefore subject to the rule of apportionment, was decided in the negative. Three Justices, Chase, Paterson and Iredell, sitting without their colleagues, decided unanimously that the tax was an excise or duty and not a direct tax. The case is chiefly interesting as the first in which the constitutionality of an act of Congress was directly reviewed by the Supreme Court.

"I HAD RATHER BE RIGHT THAN BE PRESIDENT." This expression was used by Henry Clay, early in 1839, in a conversation with William C. Preston of South Carolina. Clay, alarmed by the growth of Abolitionism in the North, had decided to attack the movement publicly. He consulted Preston, and the latter suggested that such a speech might be injurious to Clay's political fortunes. This advice, according to Preston, elicited the famous reply.

ICARIA was the perfect commonwealth described by the French communist, Etienne Cabet (1788–1856), in the *Voyage en Icarie*. In Icaria all property was to be held in common, and all the products of labor were to be divided according to need. The book became enormously popular and led to a succession of attempts to put the theory into practice in the United States.

The initial effort was made in Fannin County, Texas, in 1848, by an "advance guard" from France. The colony was a failure. In 1849, under Cabet's personal leadership, a new start was made at Nauvoo, Ill. Here, after a period of prosperity, dissension developed, and in 1856 Cabet himself was expelled. Shortly afterward he died at St. Louis, Mo. His personal followers soon set up a community at nearby Cheltenham, which lasted until 1864.

After Cabet's death, Iowa was the scene of the principal Icarian experiments. Near Corning, emigrants from Nauvoo established a settlement and incorporated in 1860. Factional differences led to its dissolution in 1878. The next year, one of the factions organized a new community on the old site, which disintegrated in a few years. The other faction formed the "New Icarian Community" nearby. Its members lived in harmony, but their number dwindled steadily, and in 1895 the property was turned over to a receiver for distribution.

In 1881 former members of the Cheltenham group founded a community at Cloverdale, Calif. (Icaria-Speranza). It was dissolved in 1887.

IDAHO was part of the Oregon Country and later (1859–63) was included in Washington Territory until the region achieved political organization as a territory in 1863. The first recorded events in the area were those associated with the journeys of Lewis and Clark (1805, 1806), and representatives of British and American fur companies. Between 1809 and 1834 the following posts were established: Kullyspell House, by the North West Company on Lake Pend Oreille (1809); Fort Henry, an American post near St. Anthony (1810); Fort Boise; and Fort Hall.

During the preterritorial era three missions were founded: Lapwai Mission; the Coeur d'Alene Mission of the Sacred Heart; and the Latter-day Saints or Mormon Lemhi Mission, in the modern Lemhi County (1855). Thousands of Oregon Trail emigrants crossed southern Idaho (1843–63) during the height of the emigration period, but made no settlements.

The discovery of placer gold by E. D. Pierce on Oro Fino Creek (August, 1860) was a forerunner of settlement. Other camps were soon located to the southward. The miners needed a seat of government in the Salmon River country, as the region of the gold fields was called. This resulted in the creation of Idaho Territory, March 3, 1863.

The Nez Percé Indian War (1877) is the best-known territorial event. During the decade 1880–90 the territory attained a population requisite to claim statehood. A state constitution was framed in August, 1889, and President Harrison signed an admission bill, July 3, 1890.

ILLINOIS. The Illinois Indians and their country were known to the French by report for years before Jolliet and Marquette in 1673 passed by the western edge of the present state in their exploration of the Mississippi River. Returning by the Illinois River and the Chicago portage, Jolliet sensed the possibilities of the fertile prairies and of a canal connection between the Mississippi and Great Lakes system. Between 1679 and 1687 Illinois was the center of the ambitious imperialistic schemes of LaSalle. In January, 1680, he established Fort Crèvecoeur at the present Peoria. Two years later, he built a fort on

441

Starved Rock, near the present town of LaSalle, on the Illinois River. This remained the base of operations for himself and, after him, of his lieutenants, Tonti and LaForest, until 1692, when their center of activity moved back to Lake Peoria. Near the beginning of the 18th century, the missions to the Kaskaskia and Cahokia tribes of the Illinois Indians, together with the chief French posts, were moved to the rich bottom lands on the east side of the Mississippi River from the mouth of the Missouri southward to the mouth of the Kaskaskia River. Here, stimulated by projects for mining and trade, grew up a permanent French settlement, with considerable numbers of Negro slaves, which, in the end, supplied foodstuffs both to New Orleans and to the French posts of the Great Lakes; here arose Fort de Chartres on the bank of the Mississippi.

The Treaty of Paris (1763) transferred the area of Illinois to the British. It was two years before they were able to send a garrison to Fort de Chartres. From it the territory was ruled during the British period by military authority. Although, intermittently, private persons and ministers considered establishing colonies within the area of the state with a measure of self-government, the Quebec Act of 1774 finally annexed the territory to the province of Quebec. July 4, 1778, George Rogers Clark took possession of Kaskaskia in the name of Virginia, and established Virginia's authority in the Mississippi River settlements and at Vincennes. Until 1782 the territory was included in the Virginia county of Illinois. Although Clark failed to occupy the whole territory of the present state, he kept the British out of it and maintained garrisons in the Illinois and Wabash villages. In 1783 the territory became part of the United States by the Definitive Treaty of Peace. It was part of the Northwest Territory, organized in 1788 under the Northwest Ordinance. It remained a part of Indiana Territory from 1800 to 1809, when Illinois Territory was established, including the present State of Wisconsin. At the outbreak of the War of 1812, the garrison of Fort Dearborn at Chicago was massacred by the Indians. Indian trouble continued in the state throughout the war, and one pitched battle was fought by the British and American forces near Rock Island.

At the end of the War of 1812 population flooded into the state. A series of Indian treaties between 1795 and 1833 cleared the state of Indian claims. On Dec. 3, 1818, it was admitted to the Union, with a population of about 40,000. In disregard of the Northwest Ordinance, the northeastern boundary of the state was set so as to include the site of Chicago within it.

ILLINOIS AND MICHIGAN CANAL (1836–1930),
connecting Lake Michigan and the Mississippi by a channel from Chicago to LaSalle on the Illinois River, was begun by the State of Illinois on July 4, 1836. In

less than a year came the panic of 1837, followed by a long period of stagnation. Financing become increasingly difficult with the result that in 1842, Illinois being virtually bankrupt, work was abandoned. However, under the leadership of Gov. Thomas Ford (1842–46), who saw in the revenues to be derived from the completed canal the only way to save the credit of the state, new methods of financing were devised and construction was resumed. On April 23, 1848, the first boat passed through the canal.

The Illinois and Michigan Canal became immediately profitable, and although the railroads which were constructed extensively in the next decade reduced its receipts, tolls exceeded expenses of operation until 1879. In the 20th century traffic dwindled almost to nothing, but sections of the canal were continued in use until 1930. So great was its influence on the development of its tributary region, that among North American artificial waterways only the Erie Canal outranked it in importance.

IMMIGRATION. The migration to the United States of over 41,500,000 persons (of whom 34,000,000 came from Europe) in the years between 1820 and 1959 is the greatest movement of population in Western history. In the strict sense immigrants are persons who voluntarily uprooted themselves from their native environment in order to seek sustenance and fortune in the United States.

For convenience the account of American immigration may be divided into three periods: (1) the colonial period, 1607 to 1776; (2) the "old" immigration, 1776 to 1890; and (3) the "new" immigration, 1890 to the present. Down to the close of the second period immigrants from northern and western Europe predominated, about 85% of immigrants arriving before 1883 having come from these areas. By contrast, the "new" immigrants originated primarily in the countries of eastern and southern Europe; in the year 1907, for instance, 80% of the arrivals were of southern and eastern European origin. Some idea of the magnitude of this migration is conveyed by the fact that included in the total population of 76,000,-000 in continental United States in 1900 were 10,500,000 born in Europe and 26,000,000 more of foreign or mixed parentage. According to the census of 1905, in a total white population of 135,000,000, the foreign-born and persons of foreign or mixed parentage amounted to 33,750,653, or exactly 25% of the total. The absolute figures have increased moderately since 1900, but in the last fifty years the percentage of "foreign stock" in our population has fallen from 38.7 to 25.0, thus reflecting the operation of our recent policy of quota restriction and limitation of immigration since 1924.

The Immigration Act of 1924, commonly known as the Johnson Bill, passed by Congress by overwhelming majorities and signed by the President on May 26, 1924, provided a more drastic limitation of immigrants than the Act of 1921 by reducing the quota from 3%, on the basis of the number of foreign-born of various peoples as recorded in the 1910 census, to 2%, on the basis of the 1890 census, thereby favoring prospective immigrants of the older racial stocks. Until 1920 there had been only a qualitative limitation on immigration, excluding certain individuals judged unfit in health, character, or by virtue of criminal record.

The act of 1924 provided for an annual quota of 164,667, until July 1, 1927, when the statute provided that the annual quota be 150,000 and that the admission of persons of any race eligible for naturalization should be the percentage of this basic figure which that national group bore to the total population of the country in 1920 with no nationality having less than 100. This act carefully defined immigrants and nonquota arrivals; it described the machinery of selection at American consulates in the country of departure; and it provided certain humane preferences as well as drastic provisions of enforcement against fraudulent admissions. Criticism has come on the score of the difficulties in determining scientifically national origins in this country: from employers who prior to the depression of 1929 feared a shortage of manual labor; from religious and racial representatives who feared a numerical limitation of their groups; and from internationally-minded persons who feel the free migrations of peoples should not be prevented.

The most recent step in legislation has been the Immigration and Nationality Act of 1952 (the "McCarran Act"), which simplified the national origins formula of the 1924 act by basing the annual quota on a flat one sixth of 1% of the population in the 1920 census. By presidential proclamation effective Jan. 1, 1953, new quotas were established for each quota area, totaling 154,657. Quotas were further revised during 1957, 1958, and 1959 by presidential proclamation, and the total now stands at 154,857. The Displaced Persons Act of 1948 authorized the entry of certain displaced persons and other refugees without regard to the current availability of quotas, but subject to charges made against future annual quotas. The Refugee Relief Act of 1953 authorized the issuance of 214,000 special nonquota visas until the end of 1956 to German, Italian, Greek, Far-Eastern and other refugees and expellees from the Soviet and other communist-dominated countries. An act passed Sept. 11, 1957, further provided for the reallocation of 18,000 of these visas which were unused. The act of July 25, 1958, authorized the adjustment of status to that of permanent residents for Hungarian parolees after they had acquired two years' residence in the United States, and the act of Sept. 2, 1958, authorized admission as nonquota immigrants from the Azores of victims of earthquakes and from Netherlands nationals displaced from Indonesia.

Total immigrants admitted in 1921–30, including the last years before the act of 1924 took effect, were 4,107,209. Of these, 2,477,853 came from Europe and 1,516,716 from Canada, Mexico and other countries of this hemisphere. In the decade 1931–40, the number arriving from Europe fell to 348,289, rising to 621,704 in 1941–50 and 954,726 in 1951–57. In 1959 the immigrants from Europe totaled 138,191; principal countries of origin were Germany with 32,039, Hungary with 24,103, Great Britain with 18,325, Italy with 16,804, Ireland with 6595, Austria with 5189, and Greece with 4612.

The colonial, the "old," and the "new," immigrations had their individual character, their unique forms and causes, and involved different levels and different groups of men within the respective countries of origin. In colonial times the Dutch colony of New Netherland for fifty years divided the British colonies of New England from those of the South. Throughout the English settlements the "American blood of 1776" was already decidedly mixed, though early American institutions remained basically Anglo-Saxon. There were large settlements of Scotch-Irish on the frontier, Huguenot French in the larger cities as far south as the Carolinas, small Jewish groups from Spain and Portugal in Rhode Island and elsewhere, Welsh in Pennsylvania, Germans in Pennsylvania and in scattered settlements throughout the South, Swedes in present-day Delaware, along with Danes, Scotch, Irish, and Finns in the highly cosmopolitan Philadelphia of the 18th century. In Pennsylvania, for example, the Germans were so numerous that it was feared that the colony was in danger of losing its "American" character. Proprietors, speculators, and others encouraged the flow of immigration as an adjunct to direct colonization. Thousands of true immigrants originating in countries other than England came in as indentured servants and redemptioners, apart from the thousands of Negro slaves. The influence of non-English immigrants on the social, economic and cultural developments of colonial America was significant. The diversity of religions in the colonies—to take one example—made religious toleration a necessity, and the final separation of Church and State, apart from its being a matter of democratic theory, became an inescapable necessity under colonial circumstances.

The Scotch-Irish and the Germans are numerically the most prominent of colonial immigrant groups. To assess the exact dimensions of Scotch-Irish immigration before 1820 is difficult. Statistics are lacking for the colonial era and even after 1820 the figures are unreliable, since large numbers of Irish persons sailed from Scottish and English ports or migrated from other British lands into America. In the 17th century there was a small number of arrivals as servants or migrants from the West Indies. In the 18th century there may have been 50,000 Irish Catholics among the half-million Presbyterians from

Ulster. In 1790, of the estimated Catholic adherents of 35,000, not over half were Irish, but on the basis of a name survey of the census of 1790, 3.7% of the national population was said to be of Celtic Irish stock. Immigrants from 1783 to 1820 are conventionally put at 250,000, of whom it is doubtful if more than a fifth were Irish Catholics. As late as 1820 there were less than 4000 Irish arrivals, and not for fifteen years was the United States more popular than British America with its official encouragement and cheaper fares, at least as a temporary resting place; nor did the Celtic surpass in numbers the Scotch-Irish division of the race. Though the Scotch-Irish entered through all the ports up and down the length of the colonies, and rapidly spread inland and westward to the frontier in all sections, the real mecca of the Scotch-Irish was Pennsylvania. By 1750, this element constituted approximately one fourth of the total population of the colony, and by 1776 Benjamin Franklin estimated it at 350,000, or one third of the total. Forced by their poverty to seek the area of free lands, and pushed along by the Quaker proprietary government, which wanted to get rid of a new, turbulent element by sending it to the frontier, the Scotch-Irish of Pennsylvania became the typical western "squatters," the frontier guard of the colony, the "cutting-edge" of the frontier. By 1776, 500 Scotch-Irish communities were scattered throughout the colonies, of which nearly 70 were in New England, from 40 to 50 in New York, from 50 to 60 in New Jersey, over 130 in Pennsylvania and Delaware, over 100 in Virginia, Maryland and Tennessee, 50 in North Carolina, and about 70 in South Carolina and Georgia.

German immigration came on the heels of the settlements of peoples from the British Isles, Sweden and The Netherlands. The German stream carried with it a great diversity of types. At the time of the Declaration of Independence, it is estimated that there were about 225,000 people of German blood in the United States, constituting a little more than one tenth of the total population. Of these, one third resided in Pennsylvania. This colonial migration was the product of religious, political, and economic persecution and distress. The great majority of immigrants came from the Rhine country, especially from the Palatinate and Württemberg, where humble people were under the yoke of political and religious persecution and the victims of economic disorders that accompanied and followed the Thirty Years' War and the wars of Louis XIV. In the first half of the 18th century, but especially from 1720 to 1750, Moravians, Mennonites, Dunkards, Lutherans and Reformed Germans settled in large numbers in the Middle and Southern Colonies. Books and pamphlets acquainted prospective immigrants with the opportunities awaiting them in the New World. Pennsylvania was the best advertised province; and the founder, William Penn, traveled among and preached to the people whose mode of life and religion resembled that of the Quakers. German-speaking Swiss established settlements in Pennsylvania and the Carolinas alongside their German brethren.

While the American stock in the Republic from 1790 to 1820 multiplied vigorously from roughly three to ten million, the influx of immigration was relatively slow in those years. With the close of the Napoleonic Wars and the War of 1812 the constant stream of immigration took its inception. It was at this point that the rapid modern growth of population in Europe suddenly made itself felt; it had roughly doubled between 1700 and 1800. This "old immigration" was stimulated by the rapid development of steamship and railroad transport and encouraged with vigor by the governments of the new states of the Midwest, whose primary need in these years was to build up a population. Thus, after the decade of the 1830's, wave after wave of immigration set down on American shores newcomers from practically every country of Europe. The movement of pre-Civil War immigration has been called the "Celtic" because of the prominence in it of Irish, Scotch-Irish, and Welshmen, and the years 1847–54 represent the crest of this wave. In the single decade preceding the election of Lincoln, and in spite of the temporary braking effect of the Panic of 1857, 2,598,214 persons, principally from Great Britain, Ireland, and Germany made their way across the Atlantic.

What were the forces that had set in motion and accelerated the flow of immigration? European peasants and artisans and intellectuals became expatriates out of dissatisfaction with conditions in Europe and a belief that they would be favorable in the United States. The ultimate forces that caused the individual to uproot himself and strike out on the great adventure of transplantation were most often, though not always, as we have seen, the expectation of economic betterment. Population pressure, land hunger, the Poor Law in England, and economic dislocation in Europe attendant on the rapid increase in agrarian population; the enclosure of the common lands; the rise of early industrial civilization in which many could not find their place—these forces made for hopelessness and frustration. Indeed, the emigration movement is part of the broad agrarian development which revolutionized the European countryside and made obsolete the traditional village economy. Whole sections of the rural and lower middle classes in one locality after another fell victim to a class movement —popularly known as "America fever"—which spread from parish to parish. This fever was transmitted most effectively by hundreds of thousands of letters written by immigrants to relatives and friends back home. "America letters" were read and pondered in cottages, at markets and fairs and church steps and broadcast by the newspapers. In naïve and simple language the writers discoursed—often inaccurately —on the vista of opportunities that opened for them in the "Land of Canaan": the absence of onerous class distinctions; democracy and equality in government, religion and social intercourse; opportunities for education; low taxes and high wages; food and clothing better and more abundant than anything dreamed of in Europe; freedom from compulsory military service; the feverish development of the country— industrial expansion, railway construction, the opening of new territories, cheap, free and fertile land and large farms whose owners counted their chickens by the hundreds and their livestock by the scores. In this land of great distances, with billowing prairies of endless grain fields, its rivers and lakes swarming with fish, its abundance of coal and metals, the Government was rich enough to give to every man a 160-acre farm (referring to the Homestead Act of 1862).

The immigrants' longings for all these good things awaiting them in the "Dollar Land" could not have been satisfied without cheap and rapid means of transportation. The steamship and the railroad, together with inventions that revolutionized agriculture and manufacturing, not only brought tremendous adjustments in the lives of individuals in Europe and America but also shortened the span of the Atlantic Ocean from eight weeks in the days of sailing vessels to eight days in the era of the steam engine and the screw propeller. Rate wars between steamship companies and between railroad companies made it possible for hundreds of thousands of immigrants to travel from Liverpool, Hamburg, Stockholm, Olso and Rotterdam to New York and Chicago for as little as $35.

During the last quarter of the 19th century and the opening years of the 20th, Europe was invaded by an army of emigration agents endowed with persuasive tongues and armed with broadsides and pamphlets published by steamship and railroad companies, land companies, and industrial establishments, as well as the immigration commissions established by many of the states. Spurred on by attractive commissions, these agents and the emigration societies which they organized portrayed Europe in dark colors and America as a land without shadows.

The "Celtic" Wave. Irish immigration increased rapidly in the decades after 1820, rising from 54,338 in 1821–30 to 207,381 in 1831–40. The industrial slack in England and Scotland, from whence unemployed Irishmen, some of long residence, were being deported back to Ireland, and the slow development of Canada popularized the United States for emigrants, with its wages of two dollars per day for artisans and a dollar for laborers in the busy season, its demand for labor attendant on the growth of factories and the coastal migration to the frontier, and its growing political and religious freedom. In general the Irish came as individuals and sent for their families and friends; they were of the artisan, small-farmer class, of sturdy physique and in the prime years of life; many were the victims of land clearances and consolidations; settling largely in coastal cities or in growing towns along the road, canal and railroad construction projects on which they worked, they accounted for the rapid growth of cities and provided the cheap labor necessary for the incipient industries.

In the two decades, 1841–60, official figures account for 1,694,838, exclusive of those entering via Newfoundland and Canada or of returning immigrants, and of those from the large Irish colonies in London and in the industrialized sections of north England and Scotland. The pressure upon peasants and laborers to emigrate was aggravated by a number of circumstances: Ireland had a population of 8,000,000; Great Britain was burdened with continuing economic difficulties and a wretched agrarian system. Potato famines occurred in the late 1840's. The small farms were consolidated in the interest of landlords' economy and there was a shift from tillage to grazing due in part to the competition of American agriculture. The cost of improved steerage passage was reduced from four to two pounds as the result of shipping competition and the rivalry between sailing and steam vessels. The attraction of America was in her free institutions, despite some misgivings aroused by organized nativism; in her demand for labor in the boom years between the two panics; in the inducements of Western states and labor agents to stimulate emigration; in the apparent success of their countrymen who were sending remittances as high as £2,000,000 in later years; and finally, in the growth of the Catholic Church in the United States which silenced Irish episcopal opposition to emigration. Despite the Civil War, during which Northern agents in Ireland sought labor, and, no doubt, potential volunteers, there was a fairly heavy emigration, so that the decade of 1861–70 saw 435,778 Irishmen enter. In the years from 1840 to 1870 the bulk of Irish immigration was of the so-called "Celtic" element and in some years amounted to as high as 80%.

Down to 1890 the influx continued to hold steadily at about a half million Irish per decade. In the century since 1820 over 4,250,000 entered the United States, a number roughly equal to the entire population of the home island at the end of that period. After 1890, Irish immigration declined as the Irish laborers in America came into competition with continental immigrants and as conditions in Ireland improved as a result of new land legislation, rising wages, and a stabilization of the population at lower levels. It was at this time, too, that the flow of immigration turned toward Australasia in preference to the United States. The subsequent rise of a new nationalism in Ireland in the early decades of the 20th century brought the number of immigrants down

445

to 146,181 for the decade 1911–20. In the years 1908–23, for which figures are available, the Irish returning home numbered 46,000 or about 11% of the immigration. Finally, under the Immigration Act of 1924 the Irish Free State quota was established at 28,567 as compared to 34,000 for the rest of the British Isles.

The "German" Wave. After the collapse of the Confederacy the stream of immigration assumed such great volume as to open a new phase, without bringing about, however, any significant change in patterns of origin. The seventh decade alone deposited on American shores more than 5,000,000 immigrants —a figure exceeded only in the two decades from 1900–19, when the respective arrivals were 8,795,386 and 5,735,811. In 1905, for the first time, the number arriving within a twelvemonth reached the million mark; and in 1907 the total was 1,285,349, the peak for all years before and since.

The wave of the period 1860–90 is strongly northern European in character, since the ranking countries were Germany (*i.e.*, the areas of Prussia, Saxony, and Bohemia), Ireland, England, Canada and Sweden. By contrast with this, the "new" immigration after 1890 was Mediterranean and Slavic, with Italy, Germany, Austria-Hungary, Russia and Ireland in the lead, but including also Slovakia, Poland, present-day Yugoslavia, Greece, and Armenia.

In three decades, from 1860 to 1890, Germany ranked highest in American immigration statistics; and in three decades—1840–60 and 1890–1900—it held second place. From 1820 to 1959 the total German immigration was 6,696,842 and if German-speaking immigrants were included, the number would be considerably augmented. Prior to 1850 emigration from Ireland had exceeded that from Germany; in the last decade of the century emigration from Italy forced Germany from first to second place.

Between the Declaration of Independence and 1820, when German immigration was temporarily ebbing low, the existing German-American population had made rapid progress in assimilation. Thereupon, at the close of the Napoleonic wars, the second wave began to gather momentum. It brought two distinct cultural groups. From eastern and northern Germany came peasants who were conservative in politics and religious belief. From southwestern Germany and the Rhineland came a rather liberal sprinkling of political exiles and agnostics, university-trained men and intellectuals who became prominent in various walks of life in the adopted country. They were called *Dreissiger* or "Grays" and "Forty-Eighters" or "Greens," the former having emigrated after the political disturbances of 1830 and the latter within a few years after the revolutions of 1848. The more impatient and radical "Greens" were the

more implacably revolutionary in theory and spirit, in their journalistic agitation and in their immodestly sweeping program for reforming America. The *Dreissiger* included such distinguished citizens as Gustav Körner, Judge J. Bernhard Stallo, Friedrich Münch, and Dr. Konstantin Hering. Even earlier, as the result of political persecution by Metternich in 1817, such distinguished men as Karl Follen, Francis Lieber, Robert Wilhelm Wesselhöft and Franz Joseph Grund were driven to these shores. There were many vocal and colorful figures among the "Greens," but among them all Carl Schurz stands out as the greatest. Many of these intellectuals tried a hand at farming in the rich lands of the new West. Being unaccustomed to manual labor and knowing more about Latin than about agriculture, they were called "Latin farmers." However, the great bulk of immigrants in this period before the Civil War were fairly well-to-do agriculturists, mechanics, laborers, and small tradesmen who were hungry for land rather than thirsty for release from persecution. It is significant, however, that a strong contingent of "Old Lutherans," whose attachment to confessional Lutheranism made the union of Lutheran and Calvinist churches odious, left Saxony and laid the foundations of the powerful Missouri Synod, in the decade of the 1840's. After the Civil War, political and religious considerations were overshadowed by the economic motive. It was still the impact of agricultural America on an agricultural civilization in the process of transition to industrial development. The Homestead Act remained the star of hope, although an increasing number of immigrants gravitated to cities. The eventual decline of immigration when it came in the 1890's may be attributed to the Bismarckian social legislation which gave greater security in days of unemployment and old age, to the relatively fewer opportunities in the United States, and to a governmental policy of discouraging emigration or of diverting it to the German colonies and to South America.

The German immigrants distributed themselves more uniformly throughout the United States than did any other immigrant stock, though certain sections and cities were more favored than others: the northern Mississippi Valley, Milwaukee, St. Louis, Chicago, Cincinnati, Cleveland, St. Paul, and Davenport, Iowa. According to the census of 1880, Wisconsin had a larger percentage of German-born residents than any other state. It stood fourth in the total German-born population. The hardwood-limestone soil areas along the western shore of Lake Michigan were very inviting, and Wisconsin offered further inducements: a suitable climate and products similar to those of the homeland; a liberal land policy; the right of suffrage extended to persons who had taken out their first papers; the prospect of attaining sufficient population density to establish and maintain German churches and parochial schools.

In spite of a vociferous Utopian element which had sought in the 1860's to realize separate German statehood and preserve a massive German-speaking enclave on this continent, the Germans tended to assimilate and Americanize as readily as did the members of other immigrant groups. Their farm communities radiated thrift and efficiency, and their vast numbers of German societies, like the *Männerchor* and the *Turnverein* fostered love for music and manly sports.

The Swiss immigration amounted to 278,187 between 1820 and 1924. Before 1881, the peak year was 1854, when nearly 8000 arrived, but the greatest influx was in 1881–83, with more than 10,000 arrivals. A number of group settlements were carried out by the Swiss, notably a colony in Switzerland County, Ind., shortly after 1800, and the farming community of New Glarus, in Green County, Wis., in 1845.

The "New" Immigration. The "new" immigration had its source in the crowded and relatively backward agricultural communities of eastern and southern Europe. Once upon our shores, however, these immigrants settled in the industrial centers and became factory wage-earners or laboring hands in the mining camps. In crowded city surroundings the "new" immigrants remained often quite segregated from the broad American life and institutions. Since the 1890's agitation for restriction on immigration was directed in large part against the alleged characteristics of this group. The objection was a protest of descendants of older settlers against the rapid increase of south European, Slavic and Oriental peoples; a religious protest against the large Catholic infusion which they represented; and finally, an economic protest from American labor against the competition of those who were willing to accept a lower standard of living than the accustomed American norm.

The Italians. New York City had more people of Italian stock than Rome—1,070,355 persons of Italian birth or parentage,—according to the census of 1930, out of a total of 4,651,195 of Italian stock living in the entire United States. In one year, 1907, more Italians were admitted than the presentday population of Venice. From 1820 to 1930, over 4,628,000 Italian immigrants arrived, and of this number over 3,500,000 came in the present century. Before 1860, at the time when emigration from northern and western Europe was getting under way in earnest, only about 14,000 Italians, mainly from the northern provinces, migrated to the United States—"fantastic vanguard of the brawny army to follow." Among these early arrivals there were a few political refugees, of whom Garibaldi was the most famous, and a few gold-seekers who founded the Italian colony in California. From the ranks of the California Italians a number have risen to political and cultural leadership, notably Anthony Caminetti, commissioner general of immigration during Wilson's administration. In fact, until the huge wave of Italian immigration washed up on American shores after 1900, there were more Italians on the Pacific coast than there were in New England. Since 1890 more than one half of the Italian population has resided in the Middle Atlantic states, about 15% in New England and slightly less than that percentage in the East North Central states.

Coming from a country with a rapidly increasing population, extensive tracts of unproductive soil, obsolete methods of agriculture, meager natural resources such as coal and iron, excessive subdivision of land, poor means of communication, heavy taxes, and especially in the South a high percentage of illiteracy, the Italian immigrants found inviting opportunities for employment on railroad construction gangs, on streets, in mines, in the clothing industry, as fruit venders, shoemakers, stonecutters, barbers, bootblacks and truck farmers. The great majority of these were single men who toiled long hours at hard work, lived frugally—even miserly—before returning to their native country in the expectation of living comfortably on their savings. Some of these immigrants were victims of the vicious *padrone* system.

Unlike most countries of Europe, the Italian government early embarked on a policy of protecting and encouraging emigration, instead of invoking restrictive measures. Knowing that large numbers of emigrants were "birds of passage" who would return after a few months or years, legislation was designed to protect them from exploitation en route and to furnish information about opportunities abroad.

French Canadians. Statistics pertaining to the immigration of French Canadians are incomplete and unreliable, chiefly because of lax immigration laws and loose inspection conducted along the international boundary. According to the Census Reports, French Canadians residing in the United States in 1890, 1910, and 1930 were 302,496, 385,083, 370,852 respectively, constituting roughly about one third of the total of 3,508,730 persons who emigrated from Canada and Newfoundland to the United States since 1820. The influx of French Canadians contributed to the transformation of New England into a highly industrialized section, with its large foreign-born population employed in textile mills and in shoe factories. However, a number settled on abandoned farms—a profitable undertaking in view of the cheap land and the growing industrial centers. The migratory interplay and cultural contact between New England and the French-Canadian provinces to the north are obviously products of proximity and opportunities for people who sought a higher standard of living. The history and laws of Canada explain the tenacity with which the French-Canadian immigrants and their children adhere to the Roman Catholic Church and the language and customs of their native provinces. They are relatively high in the percentages of illiteracy and relatively low in the percentages of naturalization.

During the years of World War I and after (1914–59), the extraordinary situation in Europe and in the United States, coupled with drastic restrictive legislation, reduced the stream of immigration to a trickle. When Congress enacted the Immigration Act of 1924 it closed a momentous chapter in American and European history. The generous, free-handed, laissez-faire policy was succeeded by laws designed to admit only a few who satisfied the strict requirements.

IMPEACHMENT and conviction as a method of removal from public office was introduced from England into the revolutionary state constitutions. It had been claimed in behalf of the colonial assemblies, but was denied except in the proprietary government of Pennsylvania. The Constitution of the United States provides that "The President, Vice President and all civil Officers of the United States, shall be removed from Office on Impeachment for, and Conviction of, Treason, Bribery, or other high Crimes and Misdemeanors." Most of the states have drafted their constitutional provisions on this subject in similar language. Some difficulty has arisen in defining offenses so that they fall within the last two categories. But impeachable offenses were not defined in England, and it was not the intention that the Constitution should attempt an enumeration of crimes or offenses for which an impeachment would lie.

Impeachments have been voted by the House of Representatives and tried by the Senate of the United States upon ten occasions; upon two other occasions the proceedings were abandoned. The two-thirds vote of the Senate necessary to conviction has been obtained in only three cases. The majority of impeachments have been directed against judges, who hold office during good behavior and whose removal can be effected in no other way. The first important use of impeachment was in the case of Samuel Chase, Associate Justice of the U. S. Supreme Court, in 1805. In obtaining an acquittal, counsel for Justice Chase insisted that indictable offenses alone were comprehended within the impeachment power. This restricted meaning of impeachable offenses was not transcended until the trial in 1913 of Robert W. Archbald, Associate Judge of the U. S. Commerce Court. The charges against Judge Archbald, set forth in thirteen articles of impeachment, presented no indictable offenses. In all cases they alleged instances of misconduct in office which, if true, constituted breaches of the good-behavior tenure granted judicial officers. The conviction of the judge was a triumph for the broad view of the impeachment power.

Within the states the impeachment power has not been used extensively, because the short terms attached to public offices make enforced removals unnecessary. Where impeachments have been undertaken they have usually been instruments of party warfare. The impeachment of judges from partisan motives was carried out in several instances in Pennsylvania and Ohio at the beginning of the 19th century. More than 100 years later, Gov. Sulzer of New York was impeached and removed, the charges resting upon broad grounds of unfitness and involving offenses committed by Sulzer prior to his election. Subsequently governors were removed upon impeachment and conviction in Texas and Oklahoma. Although partisanship was the motivating force in these impeachments, they have served to give broader scope to the power of impeachment.

IMPEACHMENT TRIAL OF ANDREW JOHNSON (1868). The greatest state trial in the United States was that of the impeachment of President Andrew Johnson in 1868. He was the first and so far has been the only American President to suffer this ordeal.

After an eventful career in both houses of Congress, he had been elected Vice-President in 1864 as Lincoln's running mate. On Lincoln's death he became President and promptly took his stand for Lincoln's plan of reconstruction. The Radical Republicans began at once maneuvering to thwart him. Above all else they wanted Stanton continued as the Secretary of War. This was the object of the Tenure-of-Office Bill passed on March 2, 1867, over Johnson's veto. It provided generally that all civil officers in whose appointment the Senate had participated could be removed only with the advice and consent of that body. A removal contrary to the act was made a "high misdemeanor." In August, 1867, Johnson found it impossible longer to tolerate Stanton, and when Stanton refused to resign, Johnson suspended him and appointed Gen. Grant as Secretary of War *ad interim*.

On Feb. 21, 1868, Johnson removed Stanton from office and on the following day the House of Representatives, by a vote of 126 to 47, decided to impeach the President for removing Stanton in defiance of the Tenure-of-Office Act.

The Constitution provides that the House of Representatives has the sole power to prefer charges against a President, *i.e.*, articles of impeachment, and that the Senate sits as a court for the trial of the charges and is presided over by the Chief Justice. A two-thirds vote of the Senators present is necessary for a conviction.

On March 13, 1868, the trial began. Benjamin F. Butler, a virulent partisan, opened for the prosecution with a vitriolic tirade, going far outside the charges. The evidence for the prosecution consisted largely in establishing that Johnson had in fact removed Stanton. The defense was that under the

Constitution the President had this right and that the Tenure-of-Office Act in seeking to deprive him of this right was unconstitutional. Johnson himself did not attend the trial.

The scene in the high court on May 16, 1868, when the vote was taken, was a dramatic one. For days the Radicals had been working feverishly in and out of Congress to bring pressure to bear upon the Senators to vote for a conviction. Finally the roll was called on the eleventh article (the first of the thirteen to be voted on). Sen. Grimes, suffering from a stroke of paralysis, was borne into the Senate chamber at the last moment to vote for an acquittal. In dead silence the galleries waited for the tally. At last it was announced that 35 senators had voted guilty and 19 not guilty. Two thirds not having pronounced guilty, the Chief Justice thereupon declared that the President was "acquitted on this article." He had been saved by one vote. But there were twelve articles which had not yet been voted on. The court thereupon adjourned to permit the Representatives and Senators to attend the National Republican Convention. It was hoped that on their return to Washington some of the wavering Senators might change their minds in favor of conviction. On May 28 the high court reconvened to vote upon the second and third articles. Again the roll was called, but again 35 senators voted for conviction and 19 for acquittal, and once more Johnson was saved by one vote. The remaining articles were never voted on. The court was then adjourned never to convene again, either for the trial of Andrew Johnson or thus far of any other President.

IMPRESSMENT OF SEAMEN was one of the harshest memories in the relations of Great Britain and the United States, which time and correct description have helped to soften. Recruits for the Royal Navy were forcibly mustered in the 18th century by the press gang. While neutral vessels appear to have been so victimized prior to 1790, the problem became acute between that date and 1815. Under cover of the belligerent right of search British boarding parties removed from the decks of foreign neutrals any seamen deemed British. The practice was steadfastly regarded in England as indispensable to sea power in the war with France. Improvement of the naval service and the application of psychological devices to induce enlistment, common to later days, were not then conceived of.

Although American seamen, in common with a few of other nationalities, were the occasional victims of the press gang in England, and although persons allegedly British subjects were removed from American ships in British ports, the real issue concerned the impressment of seamen *on the high seas*. The American merchant marine, prospering and expanding under wartime conditions, offered unexcelled opportunities to British seamen. It is estimated that between 1790 and 1815 twenty thousand of them—including deserters from the Royal Navy—signed up on American ships. The conflict between the traditional doctrine of inalienable allegiance, held to by England, and the new, revolutionary American doctrine of the right of the individual to change his allegiance made an insuperable difficulty. As Canning put it, "when [British] mariners . . . are employed in the private service of foreigners, they enter into engagements inconsistent with the duty of subjects. In such cases, the species of redress which the practice of all times has . . . sanctioned is that of taking those subjects at sea out of the service of such foreign individuals. . . ." In no circumstances was naturalization as an American citizen a protection to the seaman.

The British left the matter of determining nationality to the discretion of the press gangs and boarding officers. It is not recorded that these were careful in making distinctions. Use of the English tongue appears to have been the main test applied in the cases of likely-looking seamen. Of the 10,000 persons estimated to have been impressed from American ships, only one tenth proved to be British subjects.

The British returned native-born American seamen to the United States, without indemnity, *if* their citizenship could be established. But the British authorities themselves took little responsibility to determine citizenship, and each separate case had to be handled by the American Government. In the meantime the impressed person had to remain in the service and go wherever he was commanded. As early as 1796 the United States issued certificates of citizenship to its mariners in an effort to protect them. These "protections" were soon abused, however. They were easily lost or sold by sailorfolk to British subjects. An American sailor could buy a "protection" from a notary public for one dollar and sell it to a Britisher for ten. The British consequently refused to honor the certificates.

American protest against impressment dates from 1787. Jefferson in 1792 tried to proceed on the simple rule "that the vessel being American shall be evidence that the seamen on board of her are such." But legally this doctrine was defensible only for the high seas. It had no pertinency to American vessels in British ports. On the other hand, Great Britain refused any concessions whatever to the principle. Thrice the United States tried to negotiate a treaty in which each party would deny itself the right to impress persons from the other's ships, and offered various concessions thereto. Impressment was linked with other issues of neutral trade, but it came to assume first place in American diplomacy. The climax occurred in 1807 when four men were removed from the frigate *Chesapeake*. In 1812 Congress alleged impressment to be the principal cause of war, but in view of the ambitions of the Western "war hawks" this is subject to discount.

Impressment of seamen has been, since 1815, nothing but an historical curiosity. But there have been several modern derivatives: (1) On the basis of inalienable allegiance naturalized American citizens have been impressed into the armed services of the country of their birth upon their return to that country. (2) In the *Trent* affair the United States impressed citizens in rebellion from a British vessel. (3) In World War I the Allies removed enemy aliens, particularly military reservists, from American vessels.

"IN GOD WE TRUST" is the motto that has appeared on most issues of United States coins since 1864–66. There is no law that requires it to be used.

INDENTURED SERVANTS were usually adult white persons who were bound to labor for a period of years. There were three well-known classes: the free willers or redemptioners; those who were kidnapped or forced to leave their home country, because of poverty, political or religious reasons; and convicts. The first class represented those who chose to bind themselves to labor for a definite time, usually three or five years, to secure passage to America. The best known of these were the Germans, but a great many English and Scotch came in the same way. The scarcity of labor in the colonies led to various forms of "spiriting individuals away" to the ships bound for America. This varied all the way from enticing to open kidnapping. On arrival in America their services were sold to plantation owners or farmers for what they would bring and the victims indented for a period of years. The convicts and paupers were sentenced to deportation and on arrival in America were indented unless they had personal funds to maintain themselves. Seven years was a common term of such service. The West Indies and Maryland appear to have received the largest numbers of this third class.

Most of the colonies regulated the treatment of indentured servants. A common provision was that they must be provided with clothing, a gun and a small tract of land upon which to establish themselves after their term of service. These provisions applied especially to those who were unwilling servants. There was no permanent stigma attached to indentured service and the families of such persons merged readily with the total population. Children born to persons while serving their indenture were free. This class of labor outnumbered the slaves in the Southern colonies during the 17th century and always far outnumbered the slaves in the other colonies. In the 18th century they were most numerous in the Middle Colonies. Terms of an indenture were enforceable in the courts, and runaway servants could be compelled to return to their master and serve out their terms with additional periods added for the time they had been absent.

The treatment of indentured servants varied. Some

were mistreated, others lived as members of the family. The presence of so many redemptioners in the later years of the colonial period would indicate that the hardships were not considered excessive.

INDEPENDENCE, MO. In the 1820's when overland freighting from Missouri to upper Mexico began, the goods were shipped from St. Louis, Mo., to the town farthest west on the Missouri River. To meet the demand for a more western depot near the bend of the river, Independence was founded in 1827. For over twenty years this sprawling settlement, located ten miles from the Kansas border, served as a focal point for most of the Indian and Mexican trade and for many of the emigrants en route to the Far West. At the head of the famous Santa Fe and Oregon-California trails Independence became known as the "jumping-off place of the American frontier, the rendezvous of traders and trappers as well as of all the veriest rogues and scoundrels in America." At no time, however, did Independence outfit the whole emigration, that patronage being shared with St. Joseph, Mo., and the trading posts in eastern Nebraska and western Iowa known for years as Council Bluffs.

Independence supplied between six and eight thousand emigrants in 1849. This town, however, which claimed 1600 inhabitants, thirty stores, two "large and fine Hotels," numerous boarding houses, and twenty wagon and blacksmith shops was doomed by the geographic fact that it did not long remain the farthest west point on the Missouri from which emigrants and freighters could depart for the West. Towns more favorably located, a number of which rose after the Kansas-Nebraska Act of 1854, outfitted the emigration and served as headquarters for the freighters in the 1850's and 1860's.

INDEPENDENCE HALL, where the Declaration of Independence, Articles of Confederation and United States Constitution were signed, is a two-story, hip-roofed brick building, 100 feet long by 44 feet deep, on Chestnut Street, between Fifth and Sixth Streets, in Philadelphia. It was erected, 1732–41, after plans drawn by Gov. Andrew Hamilton. The white clock-steeple was added in 1781 to replace a wooden bell-tower.

Originally designed for provincial officers, it was used by the Second Continental Congress and later by the legislature and the state supreme court. Independence Hall contains a museum of furniture, uniforms, documents and relics of the Revolutionary period, together with an almost complete set of portraits, chiefly by Charles Willson Peale, of the Signers. In the central rotunda stands the Liberty Bell.

INDEPENDENCE ROCK, WYOMING. Its naming shrouded in legend, this granite boulder on the north bank of Sweetwater River is a famous Oregon Trail landmark. Pioneers to the Pacific stopped there for fresh water and trail information. The rock is approximately two fifths of the way from the beginning of the trail in Independence, Mo., to its terminus at Fort Vancouver, Wash.

INDIAN, THE. The aboriginal inhabitants of the United States were of one general anatomical type, regarded as Mongolian in origin. As to antiquity, there is now good evidence that the ancestors of the Indian of 1492 were in America before the mammoth, the wild horse and the ground sloth became extinct, perhaps ten to twenty thousand years ago. The Indian population of 1492 was not evenly distributed over the country, but was dense on the margins, as in the Atlantic Coastal Plain, the Gulf states and finally the Pacific Coast Belt. The sparse population areas were the Great Basin and the dry Plains. The total population in the United States at the time of white contact is variously estimated as from 800,000 to 1,000,000.

The political and social order of Indian life was tribal; each tribe was independent and a self-contained social unit. The number of such tribes is variously estimated at from 1000 to 2000. There were some confederacies of the tribes of which the most formally organized seems to have been the Iroquois League. There were several other less formal groups, as the Abenaki Confederacy in New England, the Creeks in the south, the Pawnee Republics in Nebraska and the Dakota tribes along the Missouri River. Even under the Iroquois League each separate tribe reserved the right of independent action at any time. Friction with European settlers formed a few temporary group alliances but with little solidarity. For the most part the tribes were hostile to each other and more or less engaged in predatory warfare, especially in scalp and head hunting. This condition made conquest easy for the white settlers, who, when sufficiently irritated, hired other Indians to assist in the extermination of the offending tribe.

The language status of the Indian was truly primitive, for, as might be anticipated, each independent tribe had language peculiarities. The classification of Indian languages is a credit to American scholarship. The task was first sponsored by a committee of the American Philosophical Society, appointed in 1816. The first linguistic tables and distribution map were compiled by Albert Gallatin about 1836; the final standard classification was made by Powell, about 1885. At that time 51 independent families of Indian languages were listed as spoken within the borders of the United States. Many of these families embraced a large number of mutually unintelligible languages, the total for the United States being in excess of 300. All the surviving Indians still speak their native tribal tongues, though more and more of them are learning English and thus becoming bilingual.

The geographical distribution of Indian languages is peculiar; of the 51 families, thirty are found west of the Cascade ranges, or on the Pacific coast; fifteen between these mountains and the Mississippi River and six east of the Mississippi; however, there is some overlapping. While some allowance must be made for the effect of population density upon language diversity, it nevertheless remains that most of the families are in the extreme West. The significance of this may be that the Pacific coast was the first area to be settled by Indian peoples, thus allowing a sufficient time for more languages to develop in the West. Yet this cannot be proved. The families occupying the largest territories are Algonkin, dominating in northeastern United States and eastern Canada; Siouan in the upper Mississippi and the Missouri country; the Uto-Aztecan in the western dry Plains and the Great Basin.

The economic types of Indian life were regional. Possibly excepting the village tribes of New Mexico and Arizona, the Indians of the United States were primarily hunters and gatherers of wild foods. Throughout the entire country east of longitude 100°, the secondary means of support was agriculture, with maize the chief crop. The only other area in which agriculture was practised intensively was in parts of New Mexico and Arizona, but even here hunting was of the first importance. Beans, squashes and sunflowers were the food plants of less economic importance. Tobacco was grown but for ceremonial uses and so a luxury. Cotton was grown in Arizona and New Mexico and the turkey was domesticated. Along the Great Lakes and the St. Lawrence, wild rice took the place of maize, in California the acorn was dominant and in the Great Basin area certain wild seeds were gathered.

Deer was the chief food animal except in the plains and prairies where the bison was the main staple. Fish and sea food became a staple only along the seashores and inland along streams in which the salmon and sturgeon "ran."

Skin dressing was an important craft everywhere as might be expected but most highly developed in the northern half of the United States. At the time of discovery the textile arts east of the Mississippi were primitive, but the Indians were skilled in the use of bark fibers from basswood, Indian hemp, nettle and milkweed, of which they made good cordage and some good cloth. The tribes on the lower Mississippi, when first observed, were said to weave fine cloth from vegetable fiber but trade soon destroyed this craft. Cotton was woven in Arizona and New Mexico. Along the Mississippi some coarse cloth was made from buffalo hair, and in the Columbia River country the hair of the mountain goat and the hair from a certain breed of dog were spun and woven. But in general the textile development among Indians in the United States was weak; they were predominantly a skin-and-fur-wearing people.

It is customary to divide the Indians of the United States geographically into culture areas, the tribes in each area having more or less similar modes of life. The areas are (1) the Northeastern Woodlands, all the country north of Mason-and-Dixon's Line and east of the Mississippi; (2) the Southeastern area, all the country south of said line and east of the Mississippi; (3) the Great Plains, the area between the Mississippi and the Rocky Mountains; (4) the Southwest, chiefly New Mexico and Arizona; (5) the California area, chiefly Nevada and California; (6) the Pacific area, the western parts of Oregon and Washington; (7) the Plateau area, Idaho and parts of Oregon, Washington and Montana. Among the more important tribes in history are—Area 1: Chippewa or Ojibwa; Delaware; Iroquois; Miami; Pequot; Sauk and Fox; Shawnee. Area 2: Cherokee; Creek; Seminole. Area 3: Blackfoot; Cheyenne; Comanche; Crow; Dakota Sioux; Pawnee. Area 4: Apache; Hopi; Zuñi. Area 5: Modoc; Paiute. Area 6: Chinook. Area 7: Nez Percé.

In the colonization of the United States the Indian was, first of all, an important economic factor. He offered a market for manufactured objects in exchange for which he was prepared to give furs, hides and food. He contributed maize, tobacco, maple sugar, beans, squashes and the knowledge of how to grow them. He instructed the colonist in woodcraft, the use of the birch canoe, snowshoes and the toboggan. He contributed many medicinal plants and superstitions to the folklore of the frontier. In all these respects he was an asset; but he was a hard fighter, resisted extermination and assimilation, thus becoming a liability. His conquest was expensive in blood and property, some 200 major battles were fought, and, when subdued, he was confined to reservations where he is still dependent upon government support.

Indian Art, within the United States, was limited to painting, modeling, drawing and carving. There were no large stone sculptures. The chief mediums were pottery, textiles, wood, bone and shell. Painting and drawing were weakly developed, except for conventional designs upon skins, rarely rising above the level of picture writing. On the other hand conventional geometric decorative art was highly developed in the 19th century, especially in bead and quill work among the Plains Indians, pottery and textiles in Arizona and New Mexico and basketry in California. In pre-Columbian times there was a high development in pottery along the Mississippi, especially between Cairo and Baton Rouge. It is agreed that the peak of pottery in New Mexico and Arizona was reached around 1100 A.D. (tree-ring dating). There were similar art peaks in Middle-America and in Peru. Mound builder art, expressed in carved-stone pipes and sheet-copper cutouts, reached its climax in pre-Columbian time also. It is believed that the art cultures of all Indian peoples were on the decline in 1492. Among the Plains Indians, the tribes of California, and the totem pole makers of Alaska, art reached a peak in the 19th century or in post-Columbian time. Eventually archeology may reveal the meaning of these changes.

Pottery, basketry and much painting on skins was the work of women. Totem poles were carved by men and so were the wooden "false faces" of the Iroquois. Pictographic drawing and painting was the work of men. The usual generalization is that Indian women specialized in geometric art, Indian men in realistic or pictographic art. In quality the art of the women is superior, possibly because beauty was the main objective, whereas the work of the men was crude, the objective being to convey information and to symbolize the mythical.

Since 1890 white people have shown an increasing appreciation for bead work, basketry, pottery and certain textiles, thus creating a market for the best Indian artists. Among the famous potters are Nampeo in the Hopi Pueblo of Hano, Arizona, and Maria Martinas in Pueblo San Ildefonso, New Mexico. Each of these women devised new techniques and achieved high levels of excellence. A number of Indian women are following the leadership of these two geniuses. Further, since 1900 an original, unique school in water colors has been developed by two Indian men, Creccencio and Awa Tsira, both in Pueblo San Ildefonso. There are now a number of Indian men proficient in this realistic art. In all this there is promise of a widespread revival of Indian art.

Indian Conception of Ownership of Land. To the Indian, land was not susceptible of individualistic sale and transfer. Tecumseh, the Shawnee, said, "Sell a country! Why not sell the air, the clouds, the great sea as well as the land?" Land was an integral, inseparable part of nature that sustained the beings that lived upon it. These beings lived by hunting and fishing in the unity of nature which must never be disturbed by vicious exploitation. An Ohio Valley Indian told the missionary, David McClure, in 1772, "When you white men buy a farm, you buy only the land. You don't buy the horses and cows & sheep. The Elks are our horses, the Buffaloes are our cows, the deer are our sheep."

The only conception that could correspond to ownership was that geographic sections of this unity of nature were capable of being used by different tribes. Friction and warfare could thus come about between groups. But as for individuals, the Indians believed, according to the 18th-century missionary, John Heckewelder, that the "Great Spirit made the earth and all that it contains for the common good of mankind. . . . Everything was given in common to the sons of men. Whatever liveth on the land, whatsoever groweth out of the earth, and all that is in the rivers and waters . . . was given jointly to all, and every one is entitled to his share."

Under such conditions it is easy to understand the reluctance with which Indians consented to the cession of their land at treaties.

Indian Council. This was, technically, a gathering of all the males of mature age, roughly over thirty years, belonging to a village or community. All matters of importance were passed upon by this body. The chief had no special authority, except as delegated by the council, or such as would be spontaneously accorded because of his forceful personality.

When there was some kind of confederation, as when a number of villages or camps were considered to form a tribe, each village council would send representatives to sit in a tribal council. The numbers were rarely fixed, it being understood that the few leading, or head men, in each village would attend. The active participants usually sat around a fire, hence the designation "council fire." For example, the Dakota recognized seven autonomous tribes, so spoke of themselves as the "seven council fires." The Six Nations used the symbol of Six Fires, referring to the council fires in the respective tribes.

The Council of the Delaware Indians as described by Zeisberger (1781) proceeded as follows: When the Chief had knowledge of matters to be referred to the council, a messenger was sent to notify the council members of the time for the meeting. When they were assembled, the Chief, or usually some one designated by him, presented in detail and with clarity the question at issue. All speakers stood, spoke forcefully and smoothly. No one interrupted a speaker, nor did they applaud, absolute silence being the rule. When all had spoken, one of the councillors summed up the discussion, formulating the prevailing opinion. This task was undertaken only by those who had special competence and experience. The discussions might be completed at one sitting, but often continued for a week or more. It was the duty of the women to bring in food at appropriate times. Each member brought his pipe, tobacco and pouch, for there was a great deal of smoking and pipe passing. These meetings were rarely secret, any one could listen, but there must be no noise. Women were rarely members or permitted to speak.

A house somewhat larger than a dwelling was used, frequently the residence of the Chief. In fine weather, the meeting might be around an outdoor fire.

Indian oratory was developed in the council, that being the only place where it functioned. The great Indian orators recorded in history, King Philip, Logan, Red Jacket, Keokuk, etc., came to notice in peace conferences with white government officials, but these conferences were not normal Indian councils.

Indian Land Cessions. The policies and procedures involved in the extinguishment of the Indians' rights to lands constitute an important chapter in the history of the United States, and present interesting comparisons with the practices of other nations in dealing with native peoples inhabiting countries over which these nations have claimed and maintained jurisdiction. At the outset it should be stated that, with a few possible exceptions, the Indians themselves had little or no conception of either individual or tribal ownership of land. To them land was like air or water —something that was necessary to life, but not capable of being bought or sold. Thus it was difficult for them to understand the full meaning of treaties in which they relinquished their rights. Furthermore, in some instances it was held by the Indians that no single tribe had the power to alienate land unless all the tribes living in a given territory were in agreement.

The English, like the other European nations colonizing North America, based their territorial claims upon discovery, exploration or settlement. Fundamentally, therefore, they ignored the rights of the Indians. That the newly discovered lands were inhabited by native peoples was no barrier to the making of grants to individuals and companies or the planting of colonies. In fact, it was not until near the close of the colonial period that the English home government formulated any definite policy in regard to the possessory rights of the Indians. The proprietors and other colonial authorities were left to deal with the Indians largely in their own way.

Policies and practices naturally differed among the various colonies. In general, it may be said that almost from the beginning it was conceded that the Indians possessed rights of occupancy of their lands which must be extinguished by purchase or treaty before such lands could be actually occupied by white men. While in many instances individuals purchased land directly from the Indians on their own responsibility, it early became the practice to prohibit such dealings without the permission of the colonial authorities. Indeed it soon became customary to require that treaties of any kind with the Indians be negotiated only by agents of the colonial government.

It would be difficult, if not impossible, to determine the date or terms of the first Indian land cession within the present boundaries of the United States. Furthermore, it would be an almost hopeless task to attempt to unravel the tangled and ambiguous accounts of Indian land cessions during the early colonial period. Boundaries were often exceedingly vague and indefinite. For instance, there were numerous "walking treaties" in which land areas were described in terms of distances which a man could walk in a day or a given number of days; and similarly, there were "riding treaties" in which the distances which a man could cover on horseback in given periods of time were used as measurements. Other treaties were even less specific in the matter of boundaries. There was also much overlapping, even in the land cessions of a single tribe to a single colony, to say nothing of the cessions by different tribes.

A few illustrations will serve to indicate something of the character of the Indian land cessions made during the colonial period. William Penn was notably successful in his dealings with the Indians, and one of his early acts was the holding of a council at Shackamaxon (1682) at which the Indians deeded to him a vaguely defined area in return for a considerable amount of merchandise which was itemized in the treaty. In the succeeding years several other treaties were made with the Indians of Pennsylvania, including the "Walking Treaty" of 1686. In 1744 representatives of Pennsylvania, Virginia and Maryland concluded a treaty with the Six Nations or Iroquois at Lancaster, Pa., in which these important tribes ceded their rights to land between the frontier of Virginia and the Ohio River. After the close of the French and Indian War a so-called "Indian Boundary Line" was established in a series of treaties, among which three are outstanding. First was the Treaty of Fort Stanwix in 1768 with the Iroquois in which they agreed to relinquish their claims to lands east and south of a line which ran roughly from the vicinity of Fort Stanwix in New York southward to the Delaware, then southwestwardly to the Allegheny, and down that river and the Ohio to the mouth of the Tennessee. By the Treaty of Hard Labor the same year and by the Treaty of Lochaber in 1770 the Cherokee Indians ceded their claims to lands in the present State of West Virginia. Finally, mention should be made of the remarkable but illegal privately negotiated Treaty of Sycamore Shoals in 1775, between the Transylvania Company and the Cherokee Indians, who ceded to the company approximately 20,000,000 acres of land lying between the Cumberland and Kentucky Rivers.

When the United States came into existence the Government from the beginning followed the policy adopted during the colonial period with respect to the rights of the Indians to their land. It has been held that the ultimate title to the soil resided in the Federal Government, but that the Indians had the right to the use and occupancy of the lands which they claimed, and that this right could be extinguished only by their consent. Negotiations for Indian land cessions could be conducted only by agents of the Federal Government except in certain cases in which the original states were permitted to act. Article IX of the Articles of Confederation gave Congress the power to regulate the trade and manage all affairs with the Indians. A proclamation of Sept. 22, 1783, prohibited any person from "purchasing or receiving any gift or cession of such lands or claim without the express authority and direction of the United States in Congress assembled." The Constitution made no specific reference to dealings with the natives except to give Congress power to regu-

late commerce with them. In practice, therefore, negotiations with the Indians were based upon the treaty-making power.

As a consequence, for nearly a century Indian land cessions were accomplished by means of treaties couched in all the formal verbiage of an international covenant. These treaties were negotiated with Indian chieftains and leaders by appointees of the executive branch of the Federal Government, signed by both parties, and ratified by the U. S. Senate. In 1871 the fiction of regarding the Indian tribes as independent nations was abandoned; and thereafter simple "agreements" were made with them. This change of practice seems to have been dictated mainly by the determination of the lower house of Congress to have a voice in the making of commitments entailing appropriations of money, for the "agreements" required the approval of both houses of Congress.

While the United States made a treaty with the Delaware Indians in 1778, the first Indian land cession to the new nation was that made by the Six Nations or Iroquois by the Treaty of Fort Stanwix in 1784, ceding land in northwestern Pennsylvania and in the extreme western part of New York. The following are brief summaries of selections from the long list of Indian land cessions made between 1784 and 1871. They furnish some indication of the rapidity with which the Indian title was extinguished as the tide of American settlers swept westward.

Treaty of Hopewell, 1785, with the Cherokee Indians, ceding land in North Carolina west of the Blue Ridge and in Tennessee and Kentucky south of the Cumberland River.

Treaty of New York City, 1790, with the Creek Indians, ceding a large tract of land in eastern Georgia.

Treaty of the Holston River, 1791, with the Cherokee Indians, ceding land in western North Carolina and northeastern Tennessee.

Treaty of Greenville, 1795, with the Wyandot, Delaware, Shawnee, Ottawa, Chippewa, Potawatomie, Miami, Eel River, Wea, Kickapoo, Piankashaw and Kaskaskia Indians, ceding large areas in southern and western Ohio comprising nearly two thirds of the present state, some land in southeastern Indiana, and small tracts around Michilimackinac in Michigan.

Treaty of Tellico, 1798, with the Cherokee Indians, ceding three tracts of land mostly in eastern Tennessee.

Treaty of Buffalo Creek, 1802, with the Seneca Indians, ceding lands in western New York involved in the purchase of the Holland Land Company. This was an unusual treaty in that the land was ceded directly to the company.

Treaty of Vincennes, 1803, with the Kaskaskia Indians, ceding a large area in central and southeastern

Illinois comprising about one half of the present state. Other tribes ceded their claims to this area in the Treaties of Edwardsville, 1818 and 1819.

Treaty of Fort Clark, 1808, with the Osage Indians, ceding land between the Arkansas and Missouri Rivers, comprising nearly half of Arkansas and two thirds of Missouri.

Treaty of Fort Jackson, 1814, with the Creek Indians, ceding large areas of land in southern Georgia and in central and southern Alabama.

Treaty of St. Louis, 1816, with the Ottawa, Chippewa and Potawatomie Indians, ceding land between the Illinois and Mississippi Rivers in Illinois, as well as some land in southwestern Wisconsin.

Treaty of Old Town, 1818, with the Chickasaw Indians, ceding land between the Tennessee and Mississippi Rivers in Tennessee and Kentucky.

Treaty of Saginaw, 1819, with the Chippewa Indians, ceding a large area surrounding Saginaw Bay and numerous other scattered tracts in the present State of Michigan.

Treaty of Doak's Stand, 1820, with the Choctaw Indians, ceding land in west-central Mississippi.

Treaty of Chicago, 1821, with the Ottawa, Chippewa and Potawatomie Indians, ceding land in southern Michigan and northern Indiana.

Treaties of St. Louis, 1823, with the Osage and Kansas Indians, ceding very extensive areas of land in the present states of Missouri, Kansas and Oklahoma.

Treaty of Prairie du Chien, 1830, with the Sauk and Fox, Sioux and other tribes, ceding land in western Iowa, southwestern Minnesota and northwestern Missouri.

Treaty of Fort Armstrong, 1832, with the Sauk and Fox Indians, ceding a fifty-mile strip of land along the west bank of the Mississippi in Iowa. This was the Black Hawk Purchase.

Treaty of Sauk and Fox Agency, 1842, with the Sauk and Fox Indians, ceding all of south-central Iowa.

Treaty of Traverse des Sioux, 1851, with the Sisseton and Wahpeton bands of Sioux Indians, ceding claims to lands in southern Minnesota, comprising more than one third of the present state, and in northern Iowa.

Treaty of Fort Laramie, 1851, with the Sioux, Cheyenne, Arapaho and other tribes of Indians, ceding land in North Dakota, Montana and Wyoming. The provisions of this treaty were altered by the Senate and were never ratified by the Indians.

Treaty of Table Rock, 1853, with the Rogue River Indians, ceding land in southern Oregon.

The treaties above listed have been selected to illustrate the rapidity with which the Indian tribes ceded their lands to the United States Government in the three quarters of a century following national independence. In 1854, in order to make way for the organization of Kansas and Nebraska territories,

there were signed a number of treaties in which land was ceded by Indian tribes most of whom had been located along the eastern border of the so-called Indian Country in accordance with the Indian removal policy. The center of interest now shifted to the Far West, and especially to the region of the Great Plains, where the powerful tribes were becoming increasingly restless. In 1861, for instance, the Arapaho and Cheyenne Indians ceded their claims to enormous tracts of land in the present states of Nebraska, Kansas, Colorado and Wyoming. Before the end of this decade the old Indian Country on the Great Plains was reduced to the area long known as the Indian Territory, which later became the State of Oklahoma. During the same period the extinguishment of Indian titles was proceeding rapidly from the Rocky Mountain region to the Pacific coast.

In fact, by 1871, when the making of formal treaties with the Indians was abandoned, there was comparatively little left to be done. By 1890 the process was practically complete, except for the Indian reservations on which the tribesmen resided either in accordance with treaty provisions or under authority conferred upon them by the Federal Government. Since that time many of these reservations have been abandoned, consolidated or reduced in area.

A total of 720 Indian land cessions is indicated by Charles C. Royce on the maps accompanying his digest of *Indian Land Cessions in the United States*, which covers the period from 1784 to 1894. It must be remembered, however, that it often required treaties or agreements with several tribes to clear the Indian title of a given area of land. Many treaties also dealt with the ceding of relatively small reservations set aside previously when a much larger area was relinquished.

Compensation to the Indians for the land ceded by them consisted of livestock, various kinds of merchandise (often including guns and ammunition) and annuities, or annual payments of money for a specified number of years. A government report (Donaldson's *Public Domain*, 1883) indicates that up to 1880 the Federal Government had expended more than $187,000,000 for the extinguishment of Indian land titles. How much of this sum actually reached the Indians, either in goods or in money, would be impossible to determine. In numerous instances traders gobbled up the annuities as fast as they were paid on the ground that the Indians were indebted to them. If these figures are accepted at their face value, however, it might be contended that the United States has dealt quite liberally with the native inhabitants, since the total sum paid to Spain, Mexico and Texas for the territory acquired from them was less than $75,000,000.

It has sometimes been asserted that the United States has never dispossessed the Indians of their right in the land without their consent. Literally speaking, with a few exceptions, this statement is true. If, however, the term "willing consent" were substituted, the case would be quite different. A survey of the history of Indian land cessions reveals the fact that they fall into three large general groups when considered in the light of the conditions or causes which produced them. In the first place, many of the cessions were made at the close of wars. In this group are the cessions made at the Treaty of Greenville, following Anthony Wayne's campaign; the Treaty of Fort Jackson, following Andrew Jackson's campaign in the South; and the Black Hawk Purchase of 1832. To be sure, the Indians signed these treaties, but scarcely voluntarily.

In the second place, there are the land cessions made after the Government had exercised pressure in order to accomplish purposes which it had in mind. Illustrations of this group will be found in the treaties with both eastern and western tribes when the Indian removal policy was being put into effect from 1830 to 1840, and the treaties insisted upon when the policy of an Indian Country was being abandoned after 1853. Finally, numerous treaties ceding land were clearly brought about by the demand for more land for settlement; as, for instance, the treaties negotiated by William Henry Harrison opening up land in Indiana. It would be difficult, indeed, to find a land cession made by the Indians entirely of their own volition.

Indian Legends. The term legend is often used to cover all fixed narratives heard among Indians. These include humorous tales, historical and migration narratives, and, finally, those accounting for the supernatural origins of life. The Indians usually distinguished between anecdotes of contemporary life and those legends assumed to have originated in the remote past, when animals could talk and perform miracles, as did the gods and supermen. While there were several hundred separate Indian tribes, each claiming a series of legends and tales as peculiarly its own, these tribal mythologies are found to have many tales in common, or at least with common plots. Fairly complete collections of tribal legends have been made for each of the more important tribes throughout the United States, the comparative study of which has produced a sizable body of literature. The American Folk Lore Society, organized in 1888, has been one of the chief agencies promoting the serious study of this subject.

Since none of the Indian tribes in the United States possessed systems of writing, these legends and myths constituted their literature. The aesthetic and literary qualities of Indian narratives seem about equal to those in the mythologies of the Old World. Some of the tales considered "classics" are "The Woman Who Married a Star," "The Twin Brothers," "The Lost Children," "Turtle's War Party," "The Bungling Host" and "Origin of the Pleiades." These are hero tales, versions of which are found in the collections from many different tribes.

One outstanding characteristic of Indian mythology is the belief in a culture-hero, a supernatural being who establishes the present order of the world by changing or transforming the then existing order. The philosophy of the Indians is to assume that the original world always existed, that there was no creator but a transformer who worked with the forms and materials at hand.

A puzzling characteristic of these transformers is that many obscene and immoral tales are associated with them. The favorite role is that of a rude, vulgar trickster, sometimes appearing to possess superhuman smartness, at other times the stupid dupe of ordinary mortals. However, when playing the hero in these antisocial antics, these transformers are masked as animals, such as rabbits, coyotes, etc. All such hero tales probably reflect the ideals, aspirations and emotions of the tribe concerned and, since human nature has much in common everywhere, Indian mythology has been enjoyed and appreciated by Americans generally.

Schoolcraft (1793–1864) was the first writer to make Indian mythology popular in the modern sense, though Longfellow's *Hiawatha* is the classic adaptation of such tales to modern literature, but good literal renderings of tribal collections are now available for the Iroquois, Ojibwa, Sauk and Fox, Dakota, Blackfoot, Crow, Pawnee, Micmac, Apache, Hopi and Zuñi.

Historians are interested in the class called migration legends. The best-known example is the Delaware or Lenape, *Walam Olum,* first published in 1836 by Rafinesque, and in revised form by Brinton in 1885. Though many tribes had such migration legends, few have been recorded fully by students of folklore, because they were regarded as sacred and in large part secret. For example the pueblo village tribes of New Mexico and Arizona are known to possess elaborate legends of this kind but none have been fully recorded. Judging from the known fragments, these migration narratives are in the form of a genesis, dwelling upon the miraculous but usually tracing the assumed migrations of the tribe from an unidentifiable country to the known historic habitat. A comparative study shows that these legends contain borrowed elements; thus, the same routes and events are claimed as peculiar to several tribes in turn. Since other evidence for a common history is lacking, the historical value of such Indian legends is highly questionable.

Indian Paths. Without doubt some of the principal paths or trails of the American Indians were made by the mound builders in traveling considerable distances between their towns. During the pre-Columbian period, as well as afterward, the buffalo was chief trail-maker. By instinct he was a civil engineer; he chose the line of least resistance through mountain gaps, across valleys and along watercourses. The Indians adopted his trails as their paths, and the hunters, traders and pioneers made the paths their trails, and, later, their roads. Today many of the main highways and railroads run, broadly speaking, where the buffalo had made location and broken the way. The forests, except where fires had produced "barrens," were unbroken; the trees grew thick and tall and beneath them was a mass of matted undergrowth and vines. On the mountain heights and sides, in certain latitudes, grew thick and tangled masses of laurel and rhododendron. Through such a terrain the buffalo, by reason of his form and thick skin, was best fitted to penetrate; his hoofs and compact weight beat out a trace where human beings must have measurably failed. When the pioneer came to use these forest highways he found them sunken one or two feet below the surrounding surface. This wearing was due to the hoof of the buffalo rather than to the soft moccasin of the red man. The paths were not wide, only two to four feet. At portages they were wider. The buffaloes and bears marched in single file, as did also the Indians when traveling beyond the domain of their nation. Many of the traces of the buffalo were intercolonial in extent; his lures were vast meadows of grass and cane and the far-separated salt licks.

The Indian, hunter, trader or home-seeker would sometimes blaze trees along a trail so that seasonal changes might not confuse him should he see fit to make a return journey and to guide others outbound.

The paths or trails of the American Indian were used for war and trade, and were usually along relatively high ground or ridges where the soil dried quickly after rains and where the fewest streams were to be crossed; stony ground was to be avoided where practicable, because of the soft footgear. In trade the paths were followed by Indian "burdeners" loaded with peltry; later, goods of traders were taken into the Indian country by pack horses, and peltry carried back to the seacoast or a trading point in the interior. The principal paths through the territory of one tribe connected with those which ran through the country of another; and there was an interlacing of minor with major trails. Long distances were traveled in the conduct of intertribal barter or in visits on occasions of ceremony.

Among the great trails of the Amerinds were: the Iroquois trail from Albany up the Mohawk River, through the site of Rochester on to the site of Buffalo on Lake Erie; the Occaneechi trail from the site of Petersburg, Va., southwest into the Carolinas; the Great Warrior Path leading from the mouth of the Scioto to Cumberland Gap into the Tennessee Country where at Long Island of Holston it joined the Great Trading Path which led to the Cherokee towns

on the Little Tennessee, and ran on into regions of Georgia and Alabama. Over the trail through Cumberland Gap flowed early migrations into Kentucky and Middle Tennessee. It became known as Boone's Trail or the Wilderness Road. The Chickasaw-Choctaw Trail became the noted Natchez Trace between Nashville and Natchez.

Indian Removal. This term is generally used to designate the removal by the Federal Government of Indian tribes from east of the Mississippi to the country west of that river, in pursuance of a national policy which received definite authorization by Congress in 1830 and was vigorously put into effect during the succeeding years. This policy was adopted in the hope and expectation that it would be a solution of the problems of conflict arising wherever whites and Indians came into contact during the rapid progress of the westward movement.

The idea of Indian removal seems to have originated with Thomas Jefferson at the time when he was troubled in his own mind regarding the constitutionality of the Louisiana Purchase. He drafted a constitutional amendment authorizing Congress to exchange lands west of the river for lands possessed by Indians east of the Mississippi. By this device apparently he sought to satisfy his own scruples concerning the great purchase, and at the same time to solve the Indian problems in Georgia and along the frontiers of settlement. This amendment was never submitted to Congress. The idea of Indian removal was not abandoned, however, for the act of 1804, establishing the Territory of Louisiana, contained a clause which authorized the President "to stipulate with any Indian tribes owning land on the east side of the Mississippi, and residing thereon, for an exchange of lands, the property of the United States, on the west side of the Mississippi, in case the said tribes shall remove and settle thereon."

Although the Indian removal policy received considerable support, especially in the South, for various reasons not much was achieved during the ensuing two decades. Certain tribes, such as the Delawares, the Kickapoos and a small portion of the Cherokee nation, were encouraged to migrate west of the Mississippi and there shift for themselves. Otherwise, during this period, there was a continuance of the old practice of extinguishing Indian titles by treaties which made no provision for new locations for the displaced Indians.

The year 1825, however, witnessed a definite revival of the idea of Indian removal. By that time it was evident that the entire region east of the Mississippi would soon be included within state boundaries, and that there would then be no further place to which Indians could move on that side of the river. But beyond the Mississippi lay the Great Plains, an area thought to be unsuited to white habitation, but abounding in wild game and therefore adapted to the use of the Indians. Few people at that time foresaw the day when white settlers would covet this region. John C. Calhoun, Secretary of War, was therefore doubtless quite sincere when in 1825 he recommended to President Monroe that he acquire a sufficient amount of land west of Missouri and Arkansas to provide a permanent home to which the Eastern Indians could be moved. The proposal received Monroe's endorsement as one of his last official acts. During the administration of his successor treaty-making was in progress, both among the Western Indians to make room for the migrating tribes and among the Eastern Indians to induce them to move.

The Indian removal policy was pursued with real vigor and relentlessness after Andrew Jackson's accession to the Presidency. In 1830 Congress definitely authorized the President to exchange land beyond the Mississippi for lands held by tribes within the states or territories. Within a few years there was created an Indian Country, to which the word "permanent" was confidently applied—a region inhabited by indigenous Western tribes and by Eastern Indians who had been moved to lands allotted to them. The Indian Intercourse Act of 1834 provided for agencies, schools and farmers and prohibited the intrusion of unauthorized white men. By about 1840 the Indian removals were nearly completed and the eastern boundary of the Indian Country extended along the western boundaries of Arkansas and Missouri, along the northern line of Missouri, through eastern Iowa, northward along the Mississippi and across northern Wisconsin.

The removal of the Northern Indians was accomplished with comparatively little difficulty. There were numerous tribes, most of which were small in numbers and weakened in strength by long years of conflict. Some of these tribes had been pushed about so frequently in preceding years that they cannot be said to have become deeply attached to a given area. Among the Northern tribes moved to new homes west of the Mississippi were the Chippewas who were pushed into northern Wisconsin and Minnesota; the Sauk and Foxes, Winnebagoes and Potawatomies who were located in what is now Iowa; and the Iowas, Kickapoos, Delawares, Shawnees, Ottawas, Kaskaskias, Peorias, Miamis, and the Iroquois and other New York Indians, all of whom were assigned tracts of land in the Indian Country along the western border of Missouri.

It was in the South that the Indian removal policy encountered the most stubborn resistance and led to the most tragic results. Here lived the Cherokees, Creeks, Chickasaws, Choctaws and Seminoles, known collectively as the Five Civilized Tribes because of the relative advancement of most of these tribes toward some of the features of civilization. Not only were these tribes large and powerful, but the Cherokees and the Creeks, especially, had permanent homes

and farms on which they maintained herds and raised varied crops, built grist mills, carried on trade, sent their children to missionary schools and had representative government. They loved their home lands, and they put up every resistance in their power to the arguments, threats, bribes and persuasions of the agents and commissioners sent to induce them to sign and obey treaties agreeing to remove to a new and more barren country. The Seminoles, particularly, were convinced of the inevitable only after a series of military campaigns. By 1840, however, all these tribes, numbering altogether about 60,000, were moved to the region immediately west of Arkansas.

The Government doubtless did not realize the difficulties and problems involved in removing large numbers of people such long distances. The officers and men of the regular Army units detailed to escort the migrating tribes usually performed their unpleasant duties efficiently and sympathetically. Locally recruited volunteers and civilian employees, however, were generally not much concerned for the welfare of the unhappy Indians, and contractors were not overscrupulous about the quality of the supplies furnished. As the result of all these factors the story of the removal of the Southern Indians, especially, is one of pathos and tragedy. Whether they traveled by steamboat or flatboat, in wagons or on foot, the migration of the Indians was characterized by suffering from hunger, exposure and disease and an abnormal number of deaths.

The later experiences of these Indians on the border of the Great Plains, and their conflicts with the native Western tribes, have no place in this account. It needs only to be added that the "permanent Indian Country" began to disintegrate almost before it had been completed. The Western tribes, such as the Sioux, Cheyennes, Arapahoes, Comanches, Apaches and many others were placed on scattered reservations. Beginning early in the 1850's the Eastern Indians affected by the Indian removal policy were required to move again. Ultimately they were crowded into the area long known as Indian Territory. In 1907 with the admission of Oklahoma into the Union even this last remnant of the old Indian Country disappeared.

Indian Revolutionary Service. In March, 1775, the Massachusetts Provincial Congress accepted the offer of the Stockbridge Indians to serve the Patriots as minutemen. This was followed by overtures to the Iroquois, Penobscot and St. Francis Indians seeking to attach them to the American cause. In turn, Lord Dartmouth, British Secretary of State for the colonies, instructed Sir Guy Johnson, British Superintendent of Indian Affairs in the North, to induce the Indians to take up the hatchet for England. The success of Sir Guy's plans, culminating in a council at Oswego in July, 1775, was prevented by the American invasion of Canada, which cut off supplies. This made possible a treaty of neutrality between Continental Commissioners and some of the Iroquois at Albany in September, and another at Fort Pitt in October, securing the neutrality of the Ohio and Lake tribes.

War first broke out on the Virginia-North Carolina frontier when the Cherokee, counting on English help in removing the white intruders from the Indian hunting grounds in the Watauga and Nollichucky valleys, plunged the frontier into a racial conflict that purged it of all Tories and resulted in an overwhelming defeat of the Indians, and the cession of the lands in question in the Treaty of Long Island on July 2, 1777.

In the North the failure of the Canadian invasion reopened the St. Lawrence and started the conversion of the northern tribes to the British. This process was stimulated by the financial inability of the Continental Congress to support the subsidy policy of Indian Agent George Morgan at Pittsburgh, as well as the inevitable border incidents accompanying frontier expansion. Supplied by the British, the tribes gradually went over to them, believing that British victory would save them their hunting ground and restore a satisfactory fur trade. First the Mingo, in 1776, sought to nip the Kentucky settlement in the bud. In 1777 the Mohawk, Brant, led the Iroquois (excepting the Oneidas and Tuscaroras) in co-operating in the Burgoyne-St. Leger campaign, and terrorized the frontier, after its failure, in such massacres as took place at Wyoming and Cherry Valley, until they were silenced by the Clinton-Sullivan-Brodhead campaign in 1779. In 1777 the Shawnee went over to the British after the murder, by Virginia militia, of Chief Cornstalk. In 1778 British supplies brought over the Wyandot, Ottawa, Miami and other Lake tribes who hesitated only momentarily in their British allegiance in 1779 until George Rogers Clark's campaign was shown not to be in the interest of the tribes. The Delawares went over in 1781 after years of vain waiting for the American reoccupation of Fort Laurens and a campaign against Detroit. The war ended in the Old Northwest with the Indians confident that they had successfully defended their hunting grounds as the result, in 1782, of the victory of Blue Licks and the defeat of the expedition of Col. William Crawford, and his torture in expiation for the Moravian Massacre.

In the South, with the revival of British fortunes, the Cherokee had resumed the hatchet in the fall of 1780 only to be crushed again by the Virginia and Carolina militia in the battle of Boyd's Creek with the inevitable result of the forced cession of more land. The Creek Indians in general refrained from warfare until 1781 when Gen. Anthony Wayne was completing the restoration of American control in Georgia. Then a band of Creeks, under Emistesigo, made a heroic but futile attempt to relieve the British forces besieged at Savannah.

Indian Trade and Traders. The expansion of Europe into the outside world was one of the most significant developments of the modern era, and as the movement proceeded Europeans invariably entered into trade relations with the native races. The Indian trade of North America, therefore, represents but one aspect of a larger world phenomenon. When explorers and settlers arrived in America they found vast potential wealth in furs and skins awaiting exploitation. The character and quality of the peltry available varied with topography and climate. The beaver was the most important fur-bearing animal and often the "beaver trade" was referred to as synonymous with the "Indian trade" in general. There were other important varieties, however, including otter, muskrat, raccoon, mink, sable, fox, etc. In southern latitudes there were few fine furs and the trade was mainly in coarser skins and hides, as those of the deer, bear and buffalo.

The goods offered in exchange for peltry were of almost infinite variety. There is often an impression that they consisted only of valueless trinkets, but they were, for the most part, articles of real utility to the Indians. Hardware was an important item of trade, including axes, knives, traps, kettles, awls, needles, etc. Then there were woolen blankets, including the "strouds" of English manufacture. A well-assorted lot would contain small ornaments and trinkets in the nature of luxuries. Firearms and ammunition needed by the Indians for the hunt came to form a large part of almost every cargo. Lastly, there was usually liquor—English rum or French brandy. The North American tribes thus became a valuable market for European, and, later, American manufactures.

As the Indian was drawn into the orbit of European commerce, his domestic economy underwent a profound change and he rapidly made a transition from the stone to the iron age. His manner of living and hunting was altered and he became increasingly dependent upon the white man's goods, to so great a degree in fact that an interruption of trade might threaten want or actual starvation. Whatever may have been the relations between settlers and natives, contacts between the traders and Indians were normally friendly, as each group depended upon the other. The liquor traffic, however, constituted one great obstacle to the maintenance of peace and order. It is also true that certain venal and irresponsible traders did, upon occasion, cheat and otherwise impose upon the Indians, thereby arousing their hostility. Various government agencies were tireless in their efforts to win and preserve the friendship of the various tribes, and it was generally the custom to give them periodical presents. Since these presents usually consisted of goods similar to those used in the trade, the merchants were constantly on the alert to see that they were not bartered for furs by Indian agents of doubtful probity.

The Indian trade, like other forms of business enterprise, became more complex and highly organized as it expanded. The average person is prone to think of the "Indian trader" as a wilderness hunter or trapper, wearing buckskin shirt and raccoon cap, but actually there arose a vast commercial hierarchy whose interests were tied up with the traffic in furs. The trade was at first carried on by settlers or small merchants, but conditions soon demanded new methods and forms of organization. Trade was based largely upon the credit system, which required a considerable capital outlay. In the case of the British trade, for example, two or three years might elapse between the time when goods were shipped from London and the sale of the furs received in exchange for them, the merchants in the meanwhile having large sums invested. Complex problems of marketing and transportation called for more efficient business methods, while the evils of unrestrained competition furnished an incentive to large-scale organization based upon the principle of monopoly. Small firms and partnerships were formed at important trade centers which often gave way to large companies with monopoly characteristics. Commission houses were established at such centers as Montreal, New York, Philadelphia, Charleston and St. Louis, which supplied goods to traders and attended to the marketing of furs for their correspondents. Sometimes, as has been suggested, these commission merchants established companies which directly managed the business in all its stages, from the wilderness hut to the European market. Among the better known of the larger concerns were the North West Company with headquarters at Montreal; Baynton, Wharton and Morgan of Philadelphia; Astor's American Fur Company and the Missouri and Pacific Fur companies. While the fur trade might be very profitable in some instances, its difficulties and hazards should not be minimized. A study of the correspondence reveals that all was not plain sailing by any means and one is impressed by the large number of business failures which occurred in almost every period.

Owing to the peculiar conditions under which it was carried on, the fur trade developed highly specialized methods. Transportation was a difficult and costly aspect of the business. Naturally traders followed the waterways wherever possible, tracing out a far-flung network of communication, utilizing rivers, lakes and portages. The most important single highway to the interior was the St. Lawrence-Great Lakes system. The traders made use of canoes, bateaux and even sailing vessels, and the northern trade employed large numbers of French-Canadian *voyageurs* or *engagés,* who performed the hard manual labor and added a colorful, romantic touch to the industry. Many of the *voyageurs* mingled their blood with that of the Indians, giving rise to a numerous half-breed population whose descendants are to be found scattered throughout the Northwest to this day. Where convenient waterways were not available, recourse was had to the more cumbersome and expensive method of transport by pack train. The life of the wilderness trader, who came into direct contact with the Indians, extending credit and watching over their annual hunts, was not without its picturesque side. The journals and diaries left by many of these persons afford a most interesting and valuable picture of a phase of frontier development. Here are to be found accounts of the long and lonely winters and of the thousand-and-one details which required the trader's attention. The appearance and habits of the Indians are described and there are vivid tales of the drunken "frolics" which almost invariably occurred when they visited the trader at his post.

As the Indian trade became more valuable, it frequently became involved in politics. Merchants and traders were decidedly conscious of their interests and often exerted an influence in local or international politics analogous to that of modern "pressure groups." British merchants, for example, protested vigorously against the boundary line which was agreed upon by the Definitive Treaty of Peace, 1783, and sought to delay the surrender of the posts upon the Great Lakes as long as possible. Again at the time of the War of 1812 they in vain sought the erection of an Indian barrier state between Canada and the United States. Commercial spheres of influence frequently became a basis for subsequent territorial claims.

A complete roster of the fur trade would include hundreds of persons, most of them obscure, but others well known to history. A few names, selected more or less at random, can do little more than suggest the great variety of types and the vast range of their operations. In the Great Lakes region we find Radisson and Groseilliers during the French period, and later, Alexander Henry, John Long, Peter Pond, Robert Dickson, John Askin, John Jacob Astor and Ramsay Crooks. The "merchants of Montreal" included such personages as Isaac Todd, James McGill, Simon McTavish and Benjamin and Joseph Frobisher. George Croghan and William Trent operated in the Ohio Valley, while the names of Pierre and Auguste Chouteau are associated with the trade based upon St. Louis. A great many of them attained prominence in fields other than the fur trade. A complete and connected story of the activities of these and hundreds of others remains to be written.

Indian Treaties. During the colonial period the Indian tribes were regarded practically as independent nations with the right of occupancy of the lands on which they lived. The relations of the mother country and of the colonies with the tribes were regulated by means of treaties, involving extinguishment of title to Indian lands and a variety of other matters, negotiated by colonial officials or direct representatives of the Crown, and signed by both parties. This same policy was adopted by the United States, which made its first Indian treaty with the Delawares in 1778. For nearly a century this practice was continued. During this period about 370 treaties, clothed in the same stately phraseology as characterized the most important international covenants, were negotiated by agents of the executive branch of the Federal Government and submitted to the Senate for ratification. Treaty-making with the Indians was abandoned in accordance with an act of Congress dated March 3, 1871. Thereafter the term "agreement" was substituted for treaty. As a matter of fact, the principal difference made by this change of policy lay in the fact that these agreements required the approval of both houses of Congress, instead of that of the Senate merely.

Many of these treaties came at the close of Indian wars. Illustrations are the Treaty of Fort Greenville in 1795 at the conclusion of Anthony Wayne's campaign in the Old Northwest; the Treaty of Fort Jackson in 1814 following Andrew Jackson's military activities in the Old Southwest; the Black Hawk Purchase Treaty of 1832; and the numerous treaties concluding the Indian wars on the Plains after the Civil War. A large number of other treaties were negotiated because of the pressure of the westward movement, or because the Government had plans which it wished to carry out. Examples in this group are the Treaty of Fort Wayne made in 1809 by William Henry Harrison; the scores of treaties with both eastern tribes and the Indians of the Plains when the Indian removal policy was being carried into effect; the treaties which marked the abandonment of this policy in the early 1850's; and the treaties of Fort Laramie and Fort Atkinson in 1851 and 1853, respectively, in which various plains tribes agreed to permit roads and military posts within their territories. (See also *Indian Land Cessions* under INDIAN, THE [*supra*].)

The pretense of regarding the Indian tribes as independent nations in any important sense had worn very thin before treaty-making was abandoned. The policy was unsatisfactory at best. The Indian chiefs met government commissioners in solemn councils where long speeches were made, and at the end the names or marks of the negotiators on both sides were affixed to the resulting document. But the Indians were slow to understand the meaning of the relinquishment of title to land; the members of a tribe were not bound by the promises made by their leaders; and the young and ambitious warriors were difficult to control. On the other side, the westward-moving settlers, avid for land, were supremely indifferent to the sanctity of agreements with the redskins. Altogether, the story of our treaties with the Indians is not a pleasant one.

Indian Village. In the period of exploration and colonization the term Indian village was used to designate a cluster of relatively permanent habitations in contrast to a temporary camp. Most Indians east of the Great Plains were hunters primarily, and agriculturists secondarily. Nevertheless, the latter practice required permanent residence near the cultivated plots for part of the season, at least, but permitted the use of temporary and movable shelters when engaged in hunting. The term village in historical writing of the 17th and 18th centuries, refers to the permanent places of habitation. A map of Connecticut, compiled from early historical records by Mathias Speiss, shows 106 Indian villages under seventeen sachemships, the number of villages under a sachem ranging from one to fifteen. This is typical of eastern United States. Regional variations in North American Indian house types were striking, as the Algonkins north of Virginia and Kentucky usually used dome-shaped houses covered with bark or mats; the Iroquois-speaking tribes, long, rectangular, one-story bark-covered, multifamily houses, known as "long houses;" in the South among the Muskogee-speaking tribes the houses were circular, with vertical walls and conical roofs.

In eastern United States many villages north and south were fortified by palisades and often by moats, and were occasionally called "forts" in colonial literature. The village ground plans varied greatly, but in general the houses clustered irregularly around a kind of plaza, in which the council fire was kindled, and around which the inhabitants gathered for business and pleasure.

The Indians of the Great Plains were mobile bison hunters, using dogs as pack animals, until the European horse was introduced. Their habitations were usually spoken of as camps, sometimes composed of 200 tents, or tipis, with an average of ten persons to a tent. Such a camp was always on a war footing, well organized and disciplined. In New Mexico and Arizona, the Indian villages go under the Spanish name, pueblo, the most characteristic being the terraced apartment houses. In many cases the entire pueblo was housed in a single building of three to four stories with 200 to 500 rooms.

The size of villages varied greatly but in eastern United States the lower limit approximated fifty persons, the upper limit was around 500. The increased efficiency of iron tools and firearms, secured in trade, made possible larger villages than before. Each village was a separate community and though there was a chief, or head sachem, for several such villages, each was usually autonomous, jealous of its independence and freedom of action. This was true of all United States Indians from the Atlantic to the Pacific. Even the so-called Iroquois Confederacy permitted a great deal of village autonomy.

Indian Wars and Campaigns. Classification of Indian hostilities into wars and campaigns must be largely arbitrary, and initial and terminal dates are not capable of exact definition. Prior to the Civil War, convenient grouping is not practicable but after that conflict Indian hostilities fall into three broad classifications, (1) Indian Wars of the Great Plains, including adjacent regions of the Rocky Mountains and Texas, (2) Indian Wars of the Southwest, in Arizona, New Mexico and adjacent regions, and (3) Indian Wars in the Northwest and adjacent regions.

In many instances given below, action was local but regular troops were involved and the engagements and campaigns were prosecuted under Federal authority. Reduced to chronology, the more important wars and campaigns are listed as follows:

1790–95, Northwestern Indian War (Ohio); 1811–13, Northwestern Indian War (Indiana); 1812, Florida or Seminole War; 1813, Peoria War (Illinois); 1813–14, Creek War (Georgia, Alabama, Mississippi, Tennessee); 1817–18, Florida or Seminole War (Florida and Georgia); 1823, Arickaree and Blackfeet War (Missouri River region and Dakota Territory); 1832, Black Hawk War; 1835–42, Florida or Seminole War (Georgia and Alabama); 1836–37, Creek War (Georgia and Alabama); 1836–37, Sabine or Southwestern Indian War (Louisiana); 1847–48, Cayuse War (Oregon); 1849–61, Campaigns against Navajos, Comanches, Cheyennes, Lipans and Kickapoos (Texas and New Mexico); 1850–53, Utah Indian War; 1851–52, California Indian War; 1851–56, Rogue River War against Yakimas, Klikitats, Klamaths and Salmon River tribes (Oregon and Washington); 1855–56, Campaign against the Sioux, Cheyennes and Arapahos; 1855–58, Florida or Seminole War; 1857, Campaign against Sioux (Minnesota and Iowa); 1858, Campaign against Northern Indians (Washington Territory); 1858, Campaign against Spokane, Coeur d'Alene and Paloos Indians (Washington Territory); 1858, Campaign against Navajos (New Mexico); 1858–59, Campaign against Wichitas (Indian Territory); 1861–90, Apache Wars, including campaigns against Victorio and Geronimo; 1862–67, Sioux War (Minnesota and Dakota); 1863–70, Campaigns against Cheyennes, Arapahos, Kiowas and Comanches (Kansas, Colorado and Indian Territory); 1865–68, Northwestern Indian War (Oregon, Idaho, California and Nevada); 1867–81, Campaigns against Lipans, Kiowas, Kickapoos and Comanches; 1872–73, Modoc War (Oregon); 1874–75, Campaigns against Cheyennes, Arapahos, Kiowas, Comanches and Sioux (Kansas, Colorado, Texas, New Mexico and Indian Territory); 1874–79, Campaigns against the Sioux and the Cheyennes (Wyoming, Nebraska, Dakotas, Nevada, Montana, Indian Territory and Kansas); 1877, Nez Percé War (Utah); 1878, Bannock War: Bannocks, Piutes, Shoshones or Snakes (Idaho, Washington and Wyoming Territories); 1878, Campaign against Utes (Colorado); 1879, Campaign against Sheepeater Indians (Idaho); 1879–80, Campaigns against Utes (Colorado and Utah); 1890–91, Sioux Campaign (South Dakota); 1895, Campaign against Bannocks; 1898, Campaign against Chippewas (Leech Lake, Minnesota).

INDIAN AFFAIRS, OFFICE OF. Congress entrusted the management of Indian affairs to the War Department between 1789 and 1849, but not until 1832 did it create the position of Commissioner of Indian Affairs within that department. The Commissioner had jurisdiction over trade with the Indians, negotiations for their concentration on reservations, the payment of annuities to them, their education, punishment for depredations against whites, and their protection from exploitation by white men.

Dissatisfaction early developed in the West over the control of Indian affairs by the War Department which, it was felt, was unresponsive to Western interests in that it did not press aggressively for Indian removal and granted appointments and lucrative contracts to Easterners. In 1849, the West triumphed; the Office of Indian Affairs was transferred to the newly organized Department of the Interior in which Westerners were dominant.

The new department was no more successful than its predecessor in preventing Indian wars, nor in eliminating the corrupt influence of the "Indian Ring," and demands were made for the return of the Office to the War Department but without effect. So shameful was the record of Indian exploitation and corruption that a Board of Indian Commissioners was created in 1869 to exercise joint control with Interior officials over the disbursement of appropriations.

The office of Indian Affairs developed into a land administering agency controlling the ceded trust lands which did not become a part of the public domain and the reservations with their valuable timber and minerals. It also had jurisdiction over the allotment of lands to individual Indians, a process which was speeded up after the adoption of the Dawes and Burke Acts of 1887 and 1906.

Growing dissatisfaction with government management of Indian affairs, the inadequacy of educational opportunities, the character of agents assigned the Indians, and the poverty of the Indians resulting in part from the allotment policy and the disposal of the surplus lands led to demands for change. The resulting Indian Reorganization Act of 1934 was planned to revive native crafts, restore the tribal councils to positions of importance and to rehabilitate the economy of the Indians by halting further sales of allotments and recover by purchase some that had long since passed into other hands. It did not bring all the expected benefits, and in the 1950's government policy took a new tack. A number of special acts provided for the dissolution of individual tribes and the division of their land and endowments among members. Reformers were sharply critical of the results of these measures.

Between 1789 and 1871 the Government through treaty negotiations had promised Indian tribes annuities, gifts, tools, the services of farm aids and advisors and educational opportunities. The payments on a per acre basis were slight, and the Indians long maintained that they were grossly underpaid for their land. They were unable to secure redress until 1946 when the nation, conscience-stricken because of its penuriousness, authorized identifiable Indian groups to sue for proper compensation for their earlier cessions. Over 800 claims were brought for a total in the billions, and substantial sums were won by some tribes. The Bureau of Indian Affairs had no direct part in adjudicating these claims, but its records were worked over by a host of historians, anthropologists, and appraisers to support or oppose the claims.

INDIAN AGENCIES, sometimes called superintendencies, are centers from which the U. S. Office of Indian Affairs administers one or more tribes. They were originated by the British Government which about 1763 appointed a crown agent to supervise the Indians of the Northern American colonies and another for those of the South. In 1786 the U. S. Congress followed this precedent by establishing two Indian districts in the West, one north of the Ohio River and one south of it, with a superintendent over each. The Constitution gives the control of Indian affairs to Congress, which in 1793 authorized the President to establish temporary agencies. A few were created before 1834 when Congress, by the Indian Intercourse Act, established the agency system still in force.

This act provided for twelve agencies and fixed their locations but authorized the President to transfer any of them to some other place. The removal of most large Eastern tribes to lands west of the Mississippi changed the Indian situation while the acquisition of Oregon and the Mexican Cession added enormously to the Indian population of the United States and forced the abolition of any limitation of the number of agencies.

After the Civil War many new agencies were created when the Army forced the roving Western tribes to occupy reservations. Eventually the number of agencies was over 100, but this had been reduced to about 80 by 1960. The agency head is the agent, a civil service appointee since about 1901. Under his direction are subordinates consisting of clerks, teachers, shop superintendents, and field officials. In densely populated areas the agency may be located in a single building in town, but on reservations the physical plant consists of a group of buildings. The agent is responsible for the health, education, and general welfare of all Indians under his jurisdiction.

Although the agent's powers are still great, they were reduced by the Indian Reorganization Act of 1934 giving the Indians more control of their own affairs. The experiences of the Indian agencies with people of a race, color, and culture wholly unlike our own have been of great value to United States officials dealing with similar peoples throughout the world.

INDIAN CITIZENSHIP. Congress in an act of June 2, 1924, granted citizenship to all Indians born within the United States who had not previously acquired that status. Previous to the enactment of this law the legal and political status of many American Indians was anomalous. In 1831 the Supreme Court defined their status as that of "domestic dependent nations," and other decisions contained similar statements. Indians were not citizens but neither were they aliens in the full sense of the term. Even the Fourteenth Amendment did not confer citizenship on Indians.

Prior to 1924 many Indians were granted citizenship by treaties and by acts of Congress. Certain culturally advanced Indians were made citizens at the time alienable allotments of tribal lands were conveyed to them, notably the Wyandots in 1855, some Potawatomies in 1861 and some Kickapoos in 1862. This practice was further liberalized in 1887 and made general when the Dawes Act provided that citizenship was to be conferred on all Indians receiving allotments or who had terminated the tribal relationship. Under the Burke Act of 1906 citizenship was postponed until individual Indians had received the patents for their allotments. In 1901 citizenship was extended to all Indians in Indian Territory and in 1919 it was granted to all Indians who had served in the Army or Navy in World War I. The Act of 1924 completed the piecemeal process by extending citizenship to all American-born Indians.

INDIAN RESERVATIONS are lands set aside for the use of Indian tribes. The first ones in what is now the United States were established by Great Britain and Spain in the 17th century and later approved by the U. S. Government. While the creation of Indian reservations was begun by the United States in 1786, few were set aside before 1830, but by 1860 there were many more. After the Civil War a reservation policy was inaugurated, and the wild roving tribes of the West were rounded up by the Army and placed upon reservations. As a result there were in 1960 reservations in all but three or four states west of the Mississippi and many in states east of it, including Wisconsin, Michigan, Maine, New York, North and South Carolina, Virginia, and Florida.

The exact number has varied from time to time because the allotment of lands in severalty begun in 1887 has abolished many former ones, but in 1960 it was about 250. They have been established by treaty, agreements, acts of Congress, and executive orders of the President. They are classified as "closed reservations," with all land held in common ownership and partially allotted, with some land allotted and some tribal, and they vary in size from only a few acres to the great Navajo reservation with an area of nearly 24,000 square miles.

INDIAN STREAM REPUBLIC. Since the international boundary around the sources of the Connecticut River, in the extreme northerly part of New Hampshire, was uncertain, the remote and somewhat lawless settlers based their land titles on an Indian purchase of 1796, and drew up their own government, admitting little control by New Hampshire. The denial by that state in 1824 of the validity of the Indian deed, and the attempted exertion of Canadian rule after 1827, increased a local desire to be free of both till the line was settled. An elaborate written constitution was adopted in 1832, and legislatures met in 1833, 1834 and 1835. The claim of independence, or, failing that, of belonging to the United States, but not to New Hampshire, was rejected by both state and Federal governments. This caused many to wish to join Canada; bad feeling and violence resulted, with both Canada and New Hampshire trying to enforce their laws. Finally, in November, 1835, New Hampshire sent up militia. In April, 1836, the people voted to join New Hampshire and were incorporated as the town of Pittsburg in 1840. The Webster-Ashburton Treaty of 1842 settled the boundary.

INDIAN TERRITORY, so-called, originally included all of present State of Oklahoma except the Panhandle. It was never an organized territory but was set aside as a home for the Five Civilized Tribes, who were removed to it in the period 1820–45. In 1866 they ceded the western half of this region to the United States as a home for other tribes. A part of this ceded area was opened to white settlement in 1899 and the following year was formed into the Territory of Oklahoma, which eventually came to include all the lands ceded in 1866. The reduced lands of the Five Civilized Tribes, then called Indian Territory, had an area about equal to that of Indiana and were occupied by more than 75,000 Indians. Lands were held in common and each tribe had its own government. In 1907 the two territories were again united and admitted to the Union as the State of Oklahoma.

INDIAN TRIBES. *Abenaki* were in colonial times a loose confederacy of Algonkian tribes occupying the present state of Maine and southern New Brunswick. In a restricted sense the term applied to the Indians of the Kennebec River (and sometimes in a wider sense it covered all the Algonkian tribes of the Atlantic coast). The New England settlers generally called them Tarrateens. Under missionary in-

fluence they were active allies of the French against the northern New England settlements, which they ravaged repeatedly, notably during King William's War. After the Peace of Utrecht the French maintained their influence, and in consequence of the resumption of irregular attacks on border settlements the New Englanders in 1724 destroyed Norridgewock on the Kennebec, the center of the French mission to the Abenaki. The Kennebec population was dispersed, mainly to Canada, where their principal settlement developed on the St. Francis River near its juncture with the St. Lawrence. The Penobscot and Passamaquoddy, and the Malecite to the east of them, did not move to Canada, and in 1749 the Penobscot made their peace with the English. Some Indians returned to Norridgewock, but it was attacked in 1749, and in 1754 its inhabitants migrated again to St. Francis, which, although ravaged in 1759 by Robert Rogers' Rangers, has remained the principal home of the remnants of the Abenaki tribe.

Algonkin (Algonquin) is a generic term for a linguistic stock or basic group of Indians having a wide distribution, their territory reaching from Newfoundland to the Rocky Mountains and from isolated areas in California to Pamlico Sound. This great family embraced numerous tribes and groups of tribes having a common linguistic affinity. The Algonkin were first met in Canada where the Weskarini provided the name now applied to the whole. The western group embraced the Blackfoot confederacy and the Arapaho and Cheyenne; the extensive northern division the Chippewa, the Missasaga, Nipissing, Abittibi, Algonkin and probably the Cree. The northeastern division embraced the Montagnais group, the Abenaki, including the Micmac, Malecite, Passamaquoddy, Arosaguntacook, Sokoki, and Norridgewock. The central division embraced the Sauk, Fox, Kickapoo, Mascoutin, Pottawatomi, the Illinois branch of the Miami group which included the Peoria, Kaskaskia, Cahokia, Tamaroa and Michigamea, the Miami group proper, including the Miami, Piankashaw and Wea. The eastern division embraced all the Atlantic coast Algonkian tribes, such as the Pennacook, Massachusetts, Wampanoag, Narragansett, Nipmuc, Montauk, Mohegan, Mahican, Wappinger, Delaware, Shawnee, Nanticoke, Conoy, Powhatan and Pamlico.

The Algonkian tribes were the first to sustain the shock of French and English penetration and suffered greatly from wars with the Iroquois. Most of the tribes except those of the north were sedentary and carried on agriculture with varying degrees of intensity. They possessed a degree of manual skill and their mental qualities are not to be despised. Among their great leaders were such men as Tecumseh, Pontiac, Samoset, Massasoit, King Philip, Powhatan and Nimham. Many eastern tribesmen embraced Christianity early in the colonial period.

Apache was a name applied to a number of banded warlike tribes in New Mexico, Arizona and west Texas, belonging to the Athapascan family. After the Spanish conquest the tribes increased and extended into northern Mexico. From their homes in the mountains they raided Mexicans and Americans alike, and became notoriously expert at hiding, trailing, ambushing and shooting. Apache campaigns were bloody and prolonged. Some bands were practically exterminated before they surrendered and the name has become synonymous with treachery and cruelty. F. W. Hodge believes some of their later hostilities were due to mismanagement. Their famous chiefs were Cochise, Victorio and Geronimo. The Chiricahua tribe held out longest; Geronimo was not captured until 1886, and a few bands were still at large in 1900.

Arapaho, a large and important plains tribe, and a branch of the Algonkian family, ranged from the head of the North Platte River to the Arkansas, when first encountered by the whites. Formerly they lived, according to tradition, east of the Missouri, probably in Minnesota. In warfare they associated themselves with the Cheyenne who were good fighters with a strong tribal organization and culture. Most white observers of the 1850's and 1860's found the Arapaho dirty, lazy and immoral to a degree. In war they were formidable enemies, especially under Cheyenne leadership, but they were more friendly and hospitable than their allies in times of peace. Some members of the tribe participated in the Fort Fetterman fight, raids in western Kansas, the Beecher Island fight, the Washita massacre, and a few were in the Custer fight on the Little Big Horn. They attended the Medicine Lodge Treaty of 1867 at which it was proposed to move them south of the Arkansas. In early days the Santa Fe trade was greatly harassed by raids from this tribe.

Arikara, Caddoan people, primitive inhabitants of central South Dakota, were strongly entrenched on Missouri River for centuries before white exploration. They lived in substantial houses in stockaded villages, and cultivated extensive gardens. They were expelled by the Sioux, August, 1794, and settled near present Mobridge, S. Dak. A remnant is now at Fort Berthold.

Arkansas, Akensas, Akansas, Acansa, a tribe of Indians belonging to the southwestern Siouan family, called themselves O guahpa or Akapa, signifying "those going down stream." They were mound builders. By DeSoto's time, 1541, they were in the lower Arkansas valley. DeSoto's chroniclers called them Pacaha and Capaha. The early French explorers called them Arkansea. LaSalle and Tonti found them living in three villages near the mouth of the Arkansas River, in 1683. The Arkansas were tall, well-shaped, nonwarlike, agricultural people. From the Arkansas

Post, France controlled their trade and made alliances with them. As a result of the Anglo-American westward movement, they were pushed west and south. The remnant of the tribe, now called Quapaw, is in northeastern Oklahoma.

Assiniboine or Stone Indians, of Siouan stock, left the parent nation in the 17th century, and shortly after 1800 settled on the upper Missouri. By the Treaty of Fort Laramie in 1851 they were assigned a reservation between the Missouri and Yellowstone Rivers. In the 1870's they were moved to the Fort Peck and Fort Belknap reservations.

Blackfeet, a confederacy of the Siksika proper, Bloods and Piegan sub-tribes, so called because of the color of their moccasins, are members of the Algonkian linguistic family and thus related to the eastern timber tribes. Acquiring the horse, they appear to have migrated to the Northwest, adopted the culture of the plains tribes and, existing chiefly on buffalo meat, came to occupy a territory some 300 miles in width along the eastern slope of the Rocky Mountains between the North Saskatchewan River, Canada, and the southern headwaters of the Missouri in Montana. They had great herds of horses and were in frequent conflict with neighboring tribes. While hostile to the white man in early days, they never waged actual war against the United States. In 1855 they were located in part on a reservation in northwest Montana where their descendants now reside.

Catawba, from the first contact with Europeans, have had their village or villages on the river of that name just below the North-South Carolina boundary. Wasted by rum, disease and their feud with the Iroquois, which latter was a plague to those colonies through which the war trail led, they had by 1760 declined to less than 100 fighting men. Save for their defection in the Yamasee War of 1715 they were the steadfast friends of South Carolina. Since 1840 they have resided on a square mile of their original lands and have subsisted largely on the bounty of the state.

Cayuse inhabited the Blue Mountain region in northeastern Oregon. They were a powerful, warlike tribe, allied to the Umatillas and Walla Wallas with whom they participated in the Whitman massacre and the early Indian wars of Oregon and Washington. They were noted for their wealth in horses. The tribal name has entered American dictionaries as denoting the sturdy type of Indian pony. The tribe now resides on the Umatilla reservation.

Cherokee, at the beginning of the 18th century, occupied or claimed all that region south of the Ohio and west of the Great Kanawha rivers, extending as far as the northern parts of South Carolina, Georgia and Alabama. DeSoto's march in 1540 gave them their first contact with white men. During the last quarter of the 17th century, first the Virginians and then the South Carolinians established commercial relations with them, and by 1700 French traders had come in. In 1730 Sir Alexander Cuming allied them to the British in a treaty and sealed it by taking a group of chiefs on a visit to England. In 1757 the British built for the Cherokee Fort Loudoun on the Tennessee River. During the French and Indian War the Cherokee remained true to their alliance, until near the end when trouble broke out which resulted in a fierce war lasting for two years (1760–61), in which the Cherokee captured Fort Loudoun and massacred many of the prisoners. During the Revolution they took up hostilities against the Americans, and for some years thereafter bloody encounters continued.

Beginning in 1721 the whites gradually whittled away by treaties the Cherokee country until, by 1819, the Indians were reduced to a small fragment of their former domain, most of which now lay in Georgia, but with small areas in North Carolina, Tennessee and Alabama. The Cherokee now determined to stand on their treaty rights and cede no more land. Under the tutelage of missionaries from New England and by the aid of the Federal Government they had already begun to take on much of the civilization of the white man, and in 1827 they organized a government with a written constitution. With an alphabet which Sequoyah devised, they published a newspaper, the *Cherokee Phoenix,* and issued from their printing press at New Echota many pamphlets. Unable to tolerate the organization of a nation within her borders, Georgia demanded the Cherokee country and the removal of the Indians to the reservations beyond the Mississippi. A bitter legal fight took place between Georgia and the Cherokee aided by the U. S. Supreme Court in two decisions, Cherokee Nation v. Georgia and Worcester v. Georgia, both of which the state ignored. With President Andrew Jackson sympathizing with Georgia, a treaty of cession was made in 1835 and within the next three years all the Cherokee with the exception of a few in North Carolina were removed to the Indian Territory.

Cherokee Wars (1776–81). In April, 1776, commissioners of the Continental Congress held a conference with the Cherokee at Fort Charlotte with the purpose of conciliating the tribe, restless because of continued enroachment on its lands. Notwithstanding this, the Cherokee, disregarding the advice of the British agents among them, and yielding to the incitement of Shawnee and other northern Indians, attacked the frontiers of Georgia and the Carolinas. Their most ambitious attacks—against Watauga and the upper Holston settlements—were beaten off, and in return, South Carolina, aided by Congress, ar-

ranged for retaliatory expeditions converging from Georgia, the Carolinas and Virginia. Against these the Cherokee, dispirited because of the refusal of the Creeks to aid them, offered little resistance; practically all their towns were destroyed, several hundred of them forced to find refuge in Florida, and the tribe purchased peace from the four states in treaties of June and July, 1777, only by extensive land cessions in the two Carolinas.

From 1776 to 1781 Cherokee affairs were under the supervision of North Carolina and Virginia, each of which appointed a Cherokee agent. James Robertson, the Carolina agent, resided at Echota, the Cherokee "capital," and exerted sufficient influence to keep the Cherokee at peace, except a disgruntled element which had built new towns down the Tennessee on Chickamauga Creek where the British agents established their headquarters. The Chickamauga, aided by some of the Creek towns, constantly raided the frontiers and in 1779 entered into an alliance with the northern Indians to aid Lt.-Gov. Henry Hamilton in his campaign against George Rogers Clark. At Clark's suggestion a company of Virginia militia moving down the Tennessee to Illinois stopped off at Chickamauga Creek and, with the aid of Watauga forces, destroyed the Indian towns and carried off great quantities of supplies gathered there by the British. The towns were rebuilt and the Indian attacks continued, with the result that in the fall of 1779 another joint expedition from Virginia and North Carolina repeated the destruction of the preceding spring.

In the fall of 1779 Robertson left Echota for the new settlement Henderson was establishing on the Cumberland and, with his influence withdrawn, the Overhill Cherokee relapsed into hostility, joining the Chickamauga and the Creeks in co-operating with Gen. Cornwallis and Maj. Patrick Ferguson by attacking the frontier. Joseph Martin, the Virginia agent, was unable to keep the Indians quiet, and again Virginia and North Carolina had recourse to a joint expedition, following the battle of King's Mountain. The devastation this time was as complete as in 1776. In the spring of 1781 Gen. Greene, now Federal Indian superintendent in the South, appointed commissioners to make peace with the Cherokee, which was done in April. This treaty, confirming the land cessions made at the treaties of DeWitt's Corner and Long Island in 1777, was thereafter steadily adhered to by all the Cherokee except the Chickamauga. Against the latter John Sevier led constant expeditions in 1781 and 1782 with the result that they moved farther down the Tennessee, where they built their Five Lower Towns and continued their hostility.

Cheyenne. An important tribe of Algonkian Indians, their name being a corruption of the Dakota *Shahiyena,* "people of alien speech." Originally living in

Minnesota, from where they visited LaSalle's Illinois River fort in 1680, they were pushed out on the plains by the Sioux, being reported by Lewis and Clark in 1804 as living west of the Black Hills.

They early confederated with the Arapahoes, but fought constantly with the Sioux, Crows and Hidatsas. In 1835 William Bent, who married a Cheyenne woman, induced about half the tribe, including part of the Arapahoes, to move south to the Arkansas River and hunt and trade near Bent's Fort. This artificial division between "Northern" and "Southern" Cheyennes still continues.

After Gen. W. S. Harney's Ash Hollow campaign of 1855, the Cheyennes joined the Sioux in hostility and from 1860 to 1878 were the most implacable foes of the whites, losing, according to James Mooney, more lives in fighting them than any other plains tribe, in proportion to their numbers.

They participated in the destruction of the commands of Capt. William J. Fetterman, Dec. 21, 1866, and Gen. George A. Custer, June 26, 1876. They were terrifically punished when their villages were destroyed by troops at Sand Creek, Nov. 29, 1864; Washita River, Nov. 27, 1868; Sappa Creek, April 23, 1875 and Crazy Woman Creek, Nov. 25, 1876. Other notable actions included Beecher Island, Sept. 17, 1868; Adobe Walls, June 27, 1874; Rosebud River, June 17, 1876, and the entire Dull Knife campaign of September, 1878, to January, 1879.

Throughout their wars the Cheyennes were characterized by desperate valor and they did perhaps more than any other tribes, save the Sioux and Apaches, to hold back settlement of the West.

Chickasaw. This important Muskhogean tribe was closely related to the Choctaw in language and custom, though formerly these tribes were mutually hostile. From their earliest history their habitat was northern Mississippi. They were noted from remote times for bravery, independence and warlike disposition toward surrounding tribes. Early in the 19th century they began sending their youth to Eastern schools, and mission schools in their nation, and in time became a literate people. As the result of white intrusion in their country, these Indians in 1832 entered into a treaty ceding their country to the United States. In 1837 they purchased from the Choctaw the western half of their domain in the Indian Territory and in that year the 6000 members of the tribe began emigration to the West. They first settled among the Choctaw and shared in a common government until 1855. The Chickasaw, considerably intermarried with the whites, possessed a constitutional government, a school system and became known as one of the Five Civilized Tribes. Early in the present century their communal land holdings were allotted in severalty to the individual members and tribal government was dissolved. Their citizens and land are now included in the State of Oklahoma.

Chippewa. This tribe, the name a corruption of Ojibwa, meaning "to pucker up," of Algonkian linguistic stock was living, about 1640, in the Sault Ste. Marie area of Michigan. During the first half of the 18th century, gradually moving westward along both shores of Lake Superior, they decisively defeated the Fox and the Sioux of northern Wisconsin and Minnesota and seized their lands. Meanwhile certain groups, such as the Ottawa and Potawatomi, split off to occupy the Lake Michigan area.

Typical forest culture Indians, using the dome-shaped bark and matting wigwam and the birch-bark canoe, the Chippewa eventually controlled splendid hunting, fishing and wild-rice areas. Although wars with the Sioux continued sporadically until 1858, no further territorial advances beyond the compromise Prairie du Chien Treaty line of 1825 were made. Successive treaties with the United States Government in 1837, 1854, 1855 and 1863 gradually transferred most of the Chippewa lands to the whites and restricted these Indians to relatively small reservations in Minnesota, Wisconsin and Michigan, where they still receive small government annuities from early timberland sales.

Choctaws were one of the Five Civilized Tribes of the southern United States, formerly in southeastern Mississippi and southwestern Alabama. They were encountered in 1540 by DeSoto. After 1699, when Louisiana was founded, they became allied with the French although an English faction existed which brought on civil war between 1748 and 1750. After the French surrendered their territories in 1763 Choctaws began to cross into Louisiana where a few of them still remain. Relations with the United States were uniformly friendly and, thanks to this fact and the personal eloquence of the great Choctaw chief Pushmataha, they refused in 1811 to join Tecumseh's coalition against the whites. In 1830, by the Treaty of Dancing Rabbit Creek, they ceded their lands to the United States and accepted in exchange a large area in the southeastern part of the present Oklahoma to which the greater part of them migrated between 1831 and 1833. Here they gradually evolved a government patterned somewhat after that of the United States which lasted until 1907 when their territory became an organic part of the new State of Oklahoma.

Comanche, a tribe or a group of tribes more or less closely related, belonged to the Shoshonean stock. There were once twelve divisions of the Comanches, the most important being the Yamparika, Kotsoteka, Nokini, Kwahadi and Penateka.

The Comanches appeared in New Mexico early in the 18th century. Soon they drove the Apaches out of the South Plains country. By the middle of the century they were causing the Spaniards at San Antonio considerable annoyance, and thereafter, for a century and a quarter they harried the frontier settlements of Texas. By 1840, when they had reached the limit of their southward migration, the Comanche country was the South Plains from the Arkansas River to the San Saba River in Texas. At peace with the Comanches lived the Kiowas in the northern part, and the Wichitas and other Caddoan peoples in the southeastern part, of the vast domain the Comanches claimed. War parties of Comanches frequently raided settlements as far north as the Platte River and as far south as Durango. They were not a numerous people; 20,000 souls, in 1800, and 10,000, in 1850, represent liberal estimates.

A reservation for Comanches, maintained in Texas from 1855 to 1859, did not lessen their marauding operations. A larger reservation assigned to them in southwestern Oklahoma, in 1867, was not occupied by the more warlike divisions until they were driven in by troops eight years later.

Superb horsemen, nomadic and warlike, the Comanches constituted the greatest human factor in retarding the settlement of the South Plains.

Creek Indians were living, when the Europeans came to the southeastern United States, in that region between the Atlantic Ocean and, roughly, the Tombigbee River. Those in Georgia came to be designated the Lower Creeks, while those in Alabama were called the Upper Creeks. Though the origin of their name has often been attributed to the large number of streams in their country, it seems more likely to have been a shortening of "Ocheese Creek Indians," as most of them lived on this stream, later called the Ocmulgee River.

The Creeks, unlike some of their kindred tribes, were tall and slender, and the women were not without positive elements of beauty. Bravery was the characteristic most sought after among the men, whose warriors defeated in battle all the surrounding tribes, including the Cherokee. In colonial America they were considered the most powerful Southern tribe. They could easily muster 3500 braves.

They were organized by clans, and descent of position came on the maternal side. They lived in villages, based on clans, composed of clusters of huts surrounding a public square. In the center of this square was the Great House, used for ceremonials, and the Council House, where secret deliberations took place. In the center of the square a perpetual fire was kept burning. In time of peace each village was ruled by a *mico* and a council of old men; when hostilities were on, a war chief led the braves into battle. All the Creek villages were held together in a loose confederation for purposes of defense only. There was no central authority; each village was autonomous and decided for itself whether it would go to war or not. The best known of their ceremonials was the green corn dance held at the time of the ripening corn. Though great hunters, they were primarily a sedentary people, engaged in agriculture.

Their geographical location gave the Creeks the most strategic position of any of the tribes of Southern Indians. With the French on the west, the Spaniards on the south, and the English on the north and east, they plotted with and among these rival nations, playing one off against another. When Oglethorpe founded Georgia he immediately made friends with them, and through three treaties of cession (1733, 1763, 1773), the English maintained this friendship down through the Revolution. After the Revolution, when only the United States and Spain sought their affections, the Creeks most of the time kept both guessing. Creek hostilities against the Georgia frontier were composed in the Treaty of New York in 1790.

But the onset against the Creeks, who occupied rich cotton lands, could not be stemmed. In the War of 1812 the Upper Creeks, casting their lot with the English, were finally crushed by Andrew Jackson at the battle of Horseshoe Bend. The Treaty of Fort Jackson in 1814 deprived the Creeks of much of their lands, and in the early 1820's George M. Troup, governor of Georgia, began a campaign to rid the state of the Creeks entirely, which nearly precipitated war with the United States. William McIntosh, a halfbreed chief friendly to Georgia, made a treaty of cession in 1825, which led the irreconcilable Upper Creeks to murder him. Finally in 1832 the Creeks were forced into a treaty which provided for the removal of the entire tribe to reservations west of the Mississippi. In 1918 there were about 12,000 Creeks living in Oklahoma. (*See also* Creek Wars.)

Crow Indians formerly were part of the Siouan tribe, Hidatsas (Gros Ventres) of the Missouri River, but separated from them late in the 18th century. Lewis and Clark found them in 1804 near their present site on the Big Horn River.

The Crows were warlike and of fine physique. Maximilian, in 1843, counted 400 lodges and herds totaling 10,000 horses, chiefly acquired in the Crows' constant wars with the Teton Sioux and Blackfeet. The Crows early adopted unwavering friendship for the whites and provided scouts for the Army in many Indian campaigns.

Dakota Indians. See Sioux.

Delaware. This tribe, known to themselves as Leni-Lenape, *i.e.*, real men, at the time of the first white settlement occupied the entire basin of the Delaware River in what is now the states of Pennsylvania, New Jersey and New York. After their famous treaty of peace and fair play with William Penn at Shackamaxon (Kensington, Pa.) in 1682, they were gradually forced to give up their original lands in a series of treaties and incidents, the best known of which was the Walking Purchase of 1737. As dependents of the Iroquois, they remained at peace with the whites until, in 1755, the section that had migrated to the upper Ohio Valley in the years following 1720, supported the French against the English. After their failure in this war, the tribe concentrated on the waters of the Muskingum Valley in what is now Ohio. They supported Pontiac's War in 1763, but remained neutral in Dunmore's War in 1774 and during the American Revolution until 1781. The British failure in this war led the Delawares to retire to the valley of the Maumee and upper Wabash where they were living when they joined the confederacy against the United States in the years from 1790 to 1795. After this final failure, sections of the tribe split off, going, some to Missouri and Arkansas, some to Texas and others to Canada. At present, the main body has incorporated with the Cherokee in Oklahoma.

Digger Indians originally meant one tribe of the Paiutes in southwestern Utah who subsisted on agricultural produce and roots. They were termed "digger" in distinction to hunting, flesh-eating tribes. They were poor and feeble fighters, and practically always were spoken of by early pioneers as degraded and thievish. Later the term was applied to other root-eating tribes in other Western states.

Flatheads were a sturdy tribe of Indians living in western Montana. Curiously enough, while other Indians of the Northwest flattened their heads, the tribe known in history by this designation did not practice this custom. They gained fame for their reputed delegation of 1832 (now much discredited) to St. Louis, which so stimulated zeal for missions to the Indians of the Northwest. They are best described in the writings of Father P. J. DeSmet, the "Apostle to the Flatheads" during the 1840's.

Fox were an Algonkian tribe, called "Reynards" by the French. Their native name was Outagami or Red Earth people. Their earliest habitat was near the western end of Lake Erie whence with other Algonkian kindred they fled westward in the middle of the 17th century, driven by the Huron-Iroquois wars. After wandering for some years in the forests of Wisconsin, they built, about 1665, a village called by the missionaries Ouestatinong on the Wolf River. There they were visited by Nicolas Perrot, who found them "destitute of everything." Want rendered them brutish and they were inimical to white culture. There Father Allouez established the mission of St. Marc.

By 1680 the Foxes were living on Fox River; there their enmity to the French led to the Fox-French wars. After their submission to the French officers (about 1740) they removed to the lower Wisconsin and to Prairie du Chien, where their chief, *le Chien*, gave name to the place.

After their union with the Sauk, which occurred during the French wars, the Foxes built villages on the Iowa side of the Mississippi River. During the American Revolution they sided with the Spanish and Americans; but in the War of 1812 their alliance was with the British. After the Peace of Ghent they made a treaty with the Americans in September, 1815. Thereafter the Foxes kept peace with the whites, until the Black Hawk War, in which many Foxes joined the Sauk. By the treaty of 1842 they agreed to remove from Iowa, but ten years later returned in such numbers that they were allowed a reservation in Tama County, where under the native name of Musquakie a remnant of the tribe still live.

Fox-French Wars (1712–18, 1727–38). In 1710 Cadillac, the French governor of Detroit, persuaded a part of the Fox Indians to leave their home in Wisconsin and live near Detroit. They had always been restive under French dictation, and in their new habitat became so insolent that, in 1712, the other tribesmen fell upon and defeated them during a native quarrel. The remnant of the tribe fled to Wisconsin, and joining those that had remained there spread war against the French and their allied Indians throughout the West. The Fox-Wisconsin waterway was closed to traders, and in 1716 a punitive expedition was undertaken by Sieur de Louvigny. He led an army of 800 whites and savages up Fox River to the Fox village on Little Lake Butte des Morts. The hostiles had there a palisaded town where they stood siege. Finally Louvigny obtained a truce from the Foxes sealed by hostages, and a promise to end the war. This expedition was really a huge trading enterprise and the indemnity paid by the Foxes was in the form of furs.

The Foxes kept the peace for about ten years, when continued attacks on the Illinois allies of the French led to retaliation, whereupon Kiala, a Fox chief, formed a vast confederacy embracing the Abenaki of New England, the Iroquois of New York, the Sioux of the upper Mississippi, and the tribes of Missouri. A second expedition in 1728 under Marchand de Lignery invaded Wisconsin, but the Foxes had fled. In 1730 in trying to escape and join the Iroquois, the Foxes were defeated in eastern Illinois and a large number killed. The Sauk about this time joined the Fox, their kinsfolk, and a French officer was killed in 1733 at the Sauk village where Green Bay now stands. A battle at the Butte des Morts followed, wherein several French officers were slain. The Sauk and Fox maintained for several years a guerrilla warfare which was finally ended by the conciliatory advances of Joseph Marin, who in 1740 took several chiefs to Montreal, where peace was made.

The Fox wars made a shift in the trade routes; the Fox-Wisconsin being insecure, the Chicago-Illinois and the Wabash routes came into use, shifting French trade into the region claimed by the English. They were thus an indirect cause of the loss of the French empire in North America.

Grosventres Indians (Big Bellies) were so named by the French who applied the term to the distinct tribes of Atsina or Hitunena, a band of the Arapaho; and secondly, to the Hidatsa, or Minitari. The more common distinction of later fur-trading days was Gros Ventres of the Missouri and Gros Ventres of the Prairie.

Hopi Indians, often called "Moqui," are a people of Uto-Aztecan stock, speaking a Shoshonean dialect but Pueblo in culture, occupying a large reservation in northeastern Arizona which centers around a cluster of pueblos atop, or close to, three mesas. They were evangelized during the 17th century, but from 1680 were persistently "apostates" and an asylum for numerous Pueblo fugitives from the Rio Grande towns.

Among the Hopi alone has survived the Snake ceremony; they are famous also for their footracers, and for their arts and crafts: pottery, textiles and basketry, sand painting and water-color work.

Hurons were a confederation of more advanced Iroquoian tribes, visited by the French under Champlain in 1615, and estimated at from 20,000 to 30,000 people. Occupying what is often referred to as Huronia, around Lake Simcoe and south and east of Georgian Bay, their towns were often palisaded, more or less permanent and the site of many early French missions. From prehistoric times the Hurons had been at war with the Iroquois tribes to the south. These latter, being the first to come into possession of firearms, fell upon the Hurons in 1648–50 with implacable fury. They ravaged their towns and country and killed or enslaved the greater part of the population. The history of the survivors is a tragic story. Some sought refuge with the French; others moved west to Michigan, Wisconsin and Illinois. Incurring the enmity of the Sioux, they were driven back to Wisconsin, moved to Michigan and finally to Ohio where, known as Wyandots, some were removed to Kansas in 1842 and, in the way of the white tide flowing westward, to what is now Oklahoma in 1867. Only a handful of this once great Indian people now remains.

Iroquois League consisted of a confederated group of five related tribes of the Huron-Iroquois linguistic stock, these being the Mohawk, Oneida, Onondaga, Cayuga and Seneca. Their territory in 1609 extended from a line near Schenectady to the Genesee River in New York.

Each group had a distinctive dialect but could understand each other. Archaeology traces the Iroquois from a point west and southwest of New York and also indicates that there were two divisions of these people, the Mohawk-Oneida-Onondaga division coming into New York from the northern bank of the St. Lawrence, and the Seneca-Cayuga by way of the hill country south of Lake Erie. Early in their history they seem to have been parts of a general group which included the Eries, Attawendaronks, Andastes and, remotely, the Tuscarora and Cherokee. Their traditions state that their league was organized sometime in the 16th century through the efforts of Hiawatha, Dekanawida, Totadaho and Jikonsasa, the five tribes agreeing to unite and the others rejecting the union. Calling their government "the great peace" they established a council of forty-nine sachemships, divided unequally among the tribes, but council action was by the unanimous voice of each tribe, the Onondagas, who acted as moderators, having the casting ballot in case of tie. The league had no authority to promote war, but two war captains were elected to resist invasion. Iroquois incursions and wars, in general, were the private affairs of war chiefs elected or recognized by the fighting men. A civil chief was compelled to abdicate his high position if he became a warrior. The league had no president, though the Totadaho of the Onondagas was nominally recognized as such. In practice a new chairman was chosen for each day's session of the council when convened.

Each tribe was divided into clans, the totem being hereditary through the mother. Certain hoyaneh (noble) families had the right to groom their sons for the office of civil chief, the nomination, in case of vacancy, being made by the women's council. The clans of the five tribes had three common totems, the bear, wolf and turtle, but such tribes as the Seneca had in addition the snipe, heron, hawk, beaver and deer, probably gens of the original stock.

The Iroquois were an agricultural, village-dwelling people living in stockaded towns of bark long houses. The dress of the people was as distinctive of the forest region as was their mythology. They called themselves Ongwehoweh, or the True People. Their metaphorical name was People of the Long House, because they lived in mutual peace in their chosen territory, as one family.

The cohesiveness of the league was never great but in general it stood united against invasion. Its war captains carried on a relentless war against the Erie, the Neutrals, the Hurons, the Andastes and other tribes, most of which were either exterminated or absorbed by 1675. The alliance of the French with the Hurons led the Iroquois to unite with the English during the mid-17th century in a war to destroy the power of New France. Before the American Revolution the Iroquois were generally friendly with the British colonial authorities under Sir William Johnson. This resulted in making the strongest tribes British allies in the American Revolution, though the Oneidas and the Tuscaroras (admitted as the sixth "nation" in 1722), fought for the colonists. After the Revolution the league was split, a portion going to the Grand River Valley in Canada. Those who remained accepted reservations in New York where many still dwell on six reservations. Most of the Oneidas later emigrated to Wisconsin. The present status of these Indians is that of semi-dependent people, being both wards under a treaty of 1794 and citizens under an act of 1924. They have produced a number of notable professional men, but those who remain on reservations are farmers and mechanics.

Kansas or Kaw Indians, who gave their name to the state of Kansas and to the Kansas River, are otherwise of little historical importance. They surrendered tribal lands by treaty in 1846, relocated on a small reservation in Morris County, and removed in 1873 to the Indian Territory, near the Osages. Of Siouan stock, they were closely related to the Osage Indians, and intermarriage produced much confusion in the making of tribal rolls.

Kickapoo Indians, an Algonkian tribe formerly living in Wisconsin. They later removed to Illinois and Indiana where they fought in the wars of Tecumseh. They then removed to Missouri and thence to northeastern Kansas where about 300 still live. In 1852 a large band migrated to Mexico. These so annoyed border settlers that in 1873 most of them were returned to the United States and settled on a reservation in what is now Oklahoma. Here they still live on individual allotments, their surplus lands having been opened to white settlement in 1895. A small band resides in Mexico.

Kiowa. A small but extremely warlike plains Indian tribe, formerly residing in Montana but driven south by the Sioux and Cheyennes, until they crossed the Arkansas River and confederated with the Comanches. With these allies they raided the frontier from northern Kansas to Durango, Mexico, during the 1860's and 1870's. They were finally subjugated after the outbreak of 1874–75 and now live near Fort Sill, Okla.

Mahican Indians, an Algonkian group of five divisions, occupied both banks of the upper Hudson River northward almost to Lake Champlain (*ca.* 1650). The Dutch called them the River Indians while the French classed them with the Munsees and Delawares under the name Loups. The Mahicans, who had about forty villages, joined the Wappingers on the south near the present Poughkeepsie and extended east into Massachusetts, holding the upper Housatonic Valley. Their capital was at Schodac Island near Albany. In 1730 they had lost most of their territory and had removed to Wyoming, Pa. A few survivors joined the Stockbridges and later the Oneidas.

Mandans belong to the Siouan family. Some evidence of their origin may be found in their most sacred relics, four huge turtle shells, claimed to have come from the Atlantic Ocean. They were sedentary in habit and lived in earth lodges of a fixed type in villages along the Missouri River from the Grand River, S. Dak., to Fort Berthold, N. Dak. They have been associated with the Hidatsa, also of Siouan stock, from about 1790, and were found by Lewis and Clark, 1804, at the Five Villages. After being almost entirely destroyed in 1837 by smallpox, they moved northward and were joined by the Arikara at Fort Berthold in 1861. A few survivors are located on separate holdings in the vicinity of Elbowoods.

Miami, of the Algonkian family, often referred to as Twightwees, were originally divided into six bands, of which the Weas and Piankashaws became practically separate tribes. Pushed from the Wisconsin region by other tribes, they settled in the St. Joseph, Wabash and Maumee (Miami of the Lakes) valleys and adjacent regions, finally spreading as far south as the Miami valleys of southwestern Ohio. After 1763 they retired to Indiana. By various treaties from 1795 to 1854, they ceded their Ohio-Indiana lands and moved west of the Mississippi, except for a band remaining permanently in Wabash County (Ind.). Though few in numbers and mild in disposition, they long resisted the white advance. Little Turtle, who signed the Treaty of Greenville, was their most famous leader.

Mingos, or Mingoes, were Indians of the great Mengwe family, better known as the Iroquois of the Five Nations, who once dominated the upper reaches of the St. Lawrence, Hudson, Susquehanna and Ohio Rivers. Their main habitat was in New York, but scattered groups dwelt elsewhere, sometimes as overlords of other Indians. These outlying Mengwes, as in the Ohio Valley were, by the whites, called Mingoes. They proved a great trouble to early frontiersmen.

Mohave Indians were a warlike Yuman tribe living on the Colorado River above Williams Fork. First visited by a Spaniard, Father Garcés, in 1776, they are frequently mentioned in the Spanish annals of California. The first Americans to contact them were fur men, Jedediah Smith, 1826, Kit Carson, 1829. Hostile to emigrants, the Mohaves were subdued in 1858, and in 1865 placed on a reservation in Arizona where the tribal remnant still lives.

Mohawk Indians were the most eastwardly division of the Iroquois Confederation, as late as 1755 occupying a large portion of the Mohawk Valley in New York. In 1650 they were estimated to number 5000 but ten years later these figures were reduced to 2500. Seven villages were reported in 1644, reduced to five in 1677. The Mohawks bore the brunt of the early conflict with the French and quickly allied themselves with the English, whose cause they espoused in the American Revolution. The surviving groups now live in Ontario, with a few hundred near Hogansburg, N. Y.

Mohegan Indians were an Algonkian tribe whose proper territory lay along the Thames River in Connecticut to a point eight or ten miles from the Massachusetts line, and whose claims of conquest extended north and east into Massachusetts and Rhode Island. After the destruction of the Pequots, the Mohegans claimed their lands (1637), for at the opening of white settlement the two tribes had formed one group under Chief Sassacus, a rebellion under Uncas having caused the separation. Uncas was favored by the English in his claims to supremacy and after the death of King Philip in 1676 the Mohegans were the only well-organized tribe south of the Abenaki. Selling most of their lands, the Mohegans retreated to a small reservation in New London County, where a small remnant of mixed bloods continue in occupation. They never had political relations with the Mahicans of the Hudson River.

Moqui Indians. See Hopi Indians.

Narragansett Indians were a tribe located in what is now Washington County, R. I., on the west side of Narragansett Bay. Shortly before the arrival of the English colonists in 1620, the Narragansett sachems had imposed their authority on the Niantics to the west, the Cowesets, Shawomets and Nipmucs to the north, the Wampanoags and Massachusetts on the east and northeast, and the tribes on Block Island and on the eastern end of Long Island. Their rule extended to Weymouth on the northeast and to Mount Wachuset on the north.

Roger Williams went among the Narragansetts, learned their language and was deeded by them the land where he built Providence. Subsequently they deeded land to the Rhode Island and Warwick settlers. The Narragansetts joined the English in the Pequot War in 1637. Their chief Miantonomi was killed in a war with the Mohegans in 1643, and in 1644 the Narragansetts for their own protection submitted themselves as subjects of the king of England.

They joined the Wampanoags in King Philip's War in 1675, and suffered a terrible defeat in the Great Swamp Fight. After the war the scattered Narragansetts merged with the Niantics, whose sachem Ninigret became sachem of the Narragansetts.

Natchez, a Muskhogean tribe, occupied nine villages on the east side of the Mississippi between the Yazoo and Pearl Rivers, including in 1700 about 1000 warriors. Of a high degree of civilization, evidenced by considerable skill in the arts, the Natchez for their livelihood depended primarily on agriculture. They practised an extreme form of sun worship and engaged in occasional human sacrifice. They exercised a powerful influence over neighboring tribes, and were at first friendly with the French who were allowed to build Fort Rosalie in 1716. Arbitrary and despotic action on the part of the latter led to serious outbreaks. In 1723 the Natchez were almost crushed by Bienville. An Indian conspiracy planned for 1728 proved abortive but on Nov. 28, 1729, over 200 Frenchmen were slain on the St. Catherine. This led to a war of extinction on the part of the French and their Choctaw allies. The Natchez, forced to abandon their villages in 1730, were dispersed but not exterminated. Nearly 450, captured in Louisiana, were sold into West Indian slavery, while some reached haven in northern Mississippi with the Chickasaws, others on a tributary of the Coosa River and still more in South Carolina.

Navaho. One of the most important tribes now resident in the United States, the Navaho so adapted themselves to the American occupation as to escape the usual prolonged hostilities and consequent loss of their land and property. At the outbreak of the Mexican War some 10,000 of them living in Arizona and New Mexico subsisted by primitive agriculture, sheep raising and pillaging the Mexicans.

Following the occupation of Santa Fe by American troops in 1846, Col. Alexander Doniphan concluded a treaty with nearby Navaho tribes, binding them to peaceful relations with Mexicans, Pueblos and Americans. This agreement was promptly ignored by the Navaho and a second military expedition under Col. John W. Washington penetrated to their famous stronghold, the Canyon de Chelly, in 1849 and another treaty was drawn by which the Navaho acknowledged the sovereignty of the United States. This treaty was also ignored by the Navaho, particularly after the outbreak of the Civil War, and in 1863 Col. Kit Carson was ordered to punish them until resistance was destroyed. This he did in a brief campaign during which he invaded the Canyon de Chelly, inflicting such severe loss on the Indians that they came, as ordered, to Fort Sumner at the Bosque Redondo. There they were retained as prisoners until 1867–68 when they were returned to their own country and given new flocks and herds. Since then they have been at peace. Their number has increased to over 80,000 and their blankets and silver ornaments are standard articles of commerce.

Nez Percé were one of the most powerful of the Indian tribes of the Pacific Northwest. The early contacts with the whites were friendly—they helped Lewis and Clark and later welcomed the missionaries, to whose instruction they were responsive. Under the leadership of Dr. Elijah White, the first Government Indian agent west of the Rockies, this tribe adopted a code of law in 1842. Despite these early friendly contacts, the last and most extensive Indian war of the Pacific Northwest was fought with this tribe. Hostilities broke out in 1876 as a result of efforts of the whites to settle in the Nez Percé country. The losing struggle was ably led by Chief Joseph. (*See also* Nez Percé War.)

Ojibwa. See Chippewa.

Oneida was one of the smaller confederated Iroquois tribes situated south of Oneida Lake where a few survivors still linger. They served the patriot cause in the American Revolution and were recognized in the Fort Stanwix Treaty of 1784.

Osage Indians, the most important southern Siouan tribe of the western division, were found in historical times in Missouri in two principal bands, the Great Osage and the Little Osage. In 1802 nearly half of the Great Osage under a chief named Big Track migrated to the Arkansas River, leaving the remainder of the tribe on the Osage River in Missouri.

By a treaty negotiated in 1808 the Osage ceded to the United States all their lands in Missouri and Arkansas, and subsequently they were found in the present Oklahoma. Entering into later treaties, they gave up more land and agreed to remove to what is now Kansas. By an act of Congress of 1870 their reservation was established comprising the present Osage County, Okla., where they now hold the lands on which they live. Their population was estimated at more than 5000 in 1845; but by 1855, after hundreds died from smallpox, they were reduced to 3500. In recent years they have enjoyed large incomes from the production of oil from their tribal holdings.

Ottawa Indians are members of the Algonkian family, probably related to the Chippewa and Potawatomie tribes. Great traders, they came early on the Ottawa River to the French settlements. Friendly with whites and Hurons, when the latter were defeated by the Iroquois, 1648–49, the Ottawa with the survivors joined the Potawatomi at Green Bay. Later, still traveling west, the Sioux drove them back into Michigan where, except for bands moved westward in 1832, most of them remained.

Paiutes, sometimes known as Pah-Utes, are difficult to identify because the name has been used by different writers to designate most of the Shoshonean tribes of western Utah, northern Arizona, southern Idaho, eastern Oregon, Nevada, and eastern and southern California. The great majority of the Paiutes are not on reservations but are attached as ranch hands to farms in their former country. Generally speaking, they have been friendly to the whites. They took part in the Bannock War of 1878 against what they considered aggression.

Pawnees, one of the great groups of plains Indians, were a confederacy of the Caddoan family, named probably for the stiffened scalp lock worn erect, curved like a horn. In the emigration of the Caddoan family, the Pawnees settled along the valley of the Platte River with the Cheyennes and Arapahoes to the west, the Omahas to the east and the Otoes and Kansas to the south. With establishment of the Oregon Trail across their country, the Pawnees succumbed early to the vices and diseases of the white man, and were left, finally, a handful of their once large population.

Pima Indians are a distinctive southwestern tribe which for unknown generations has inhabited the valleys of the Salt and Gila Rivers in Arizona. Frequently at war with the Apache, they aided the whites in their wars with this tribe. They are now associated on reservations with the Papago and Maricopa.

Potawatomi is an Indian tribe of the Algonkian family allied linguistically with the Ottawa and Chippewa, with whom they originally formed one people. The various bands were gathered in the 1840's on one reservation in Kansas, where they divided in the late 1860's into two groups, the larger one moving to the present Oklahoma, the other remaining in Kansas.

Pueblo Indians are a sedentary people, living from time immemorial in towns (*pueblos,* in Spanish) as hunters and farmers. Their habitat, today confined to New Mexico and Arizona, once embraced wide stretches of present Utah, Colorado and Nevada. Their lands were visited for the first time by Coronado and his army in 1540. Permanent settlement of Spaniards among them began in 1598. Practically all became Christians, the Franciscans achieving their conversion and thereafter serving their spiritual needs. Their rebellion against Spanish rule in August, 1680, cost the lives of some 300 Spanish settlers and 21 Franciscan missionaries.

Sauk Indians, a tribe of Algonkian stock, were first known to the French near Saginaw Bay, Mich. In the middle of the 17th century they retreated to Wisconsin and built villages on the shores of Green Bay and Lake Michigan. After uniting with the Fox Indians during their wars on the French, the Sauk retreated to the Wisconsin River, where they built a large village on Sauk Prairie, which Jonathan Carver described in 1766. After the American Revolution the Sauk retired to the mouth of Rock River and hunted on the western side of the Mississippi in Iowa. Tricked into a treaty in 1802, they sold all their land east of the Mississippi, but in 1832 one of their warriors, Black Hawk, began a border war. At its close the Sauk retired to Iowa, and thence to Kansas and Oklahoma. A small refugee band went to northern Minnesota and gave their name to place names in that region. United with the Fox they now reside in Iowa and Oklahoma.

Seminoles, now in Oklahoma and in Florida, were Lower Creeks who began their movement into Florida soon after the invasions of that area by Col. James Moore of South Carolina in 1702 and 1704, during which much of the native Indian population was wiped out.

The newcomers, who took the name of Simanoli (Semanole), meaning in the Creek language runaways or separatists (sometimes renegades), combined with or absorbed the remnants of the native red population. Their movement into Florida was slow and their beginning as a separate people did not occur until about 1750.

During and even before the American Revolution there were other Indian migrations to Florida, perhaps the chief of which was the Mickasuki from Georgia. Many Upper Creeks came after Jackson broke their power during the War of 1812. All of these became one resisting element, taking the general name of Seminole during the Seminole Wars. In the struggle of 1835–42 they were pushed into far Southern Florida and were there joined by the remnant of the ancient Caloosa tribe on the lower west coast.

Of the composite Seminole group 3824 were removed to the west of the Mississippi during the war of 1835–42, and more than 150 others were sent west between 1850 and 1859.

Seminole Wars (1816–18, 1835–42). The Seminole Indians, living in Spanish Florida adjacent to the United States, became a haven for runaway slaves and a victim of international rivalries. United States troops seeking escaped slaves blew up "Negro Fort" on the Apalachicola River in 1816, leading to retaliation by Negro and Seminole raiders. Andrew Jackson led an expedition against the latter in 1818, executed two British subjects, Arbuthnot and Ambrister, and routed the Seminoles. His arbitrary seizure of Spanish posts helped frighten Spain into signing the Adams-Onís Treaty of 1819 which included the cession of East Florida to the United States.

In 1832 and 1833 the treaties of Payne's Landing and Fort Gibson provided for the removal of the Seminoles westward. The Seminoles resisted, especially when their leader Osceola was arrested and imprisoned after a conference in 1835. Following his release they killed many troops and settlers, including Indian Agent Wiley Thompson and Maj. Francis L. Dade. Osceola was captured by deception in 1837, and later died in prison. The Second Seminole War then degenerated into a process of harassing, bargaining with and seizing Indian groups, who were deported to Oklahoma. The last hostile body was removed in 1842.

Senecas constituted the most populous division of the Iroquois Confederacy, when discovered, occupying the region about Seneca Lake westward to or nearly to the Genesee River. They were divided into eight clans and had eight civil chiefs, ranking with the Mohawks as "Elder Brothers." The group was warlike and engaged in many raids against surrounding tribes not affiliated with their league. Their warriors were largely responsible for the destruction of the Huron confederacy and Erie and Neutral tribes, the survivors of which they largely adopted (1648–54), giving the captives special consideration and ultimate political equality. The Senecas sided with the British in most of the colonial conflicts with the French and later suffered heavily for their espousal of the British cause in the American Revolution.

Shawnee (a term meaning Southerners) were the southernmost of the Algonkian Indian tribes, and are first recognized by anthropologists as inhabiting the Cumberland basin in what is now Tennessee with an outlying colony on the Savannah in South Carolina. The latter group was the first to abandon its southern hunting grounds in a migration lasting from about 1677 to 1707, caused by friction with the near-by Catawba who were favored by the whites. Their new homes were in the valleys of the Susquehanna and Delaware Rivers, but congestion soon caused them to remove to the waters of the upper Ohio Valley in a migration lasting from about 1725 to the years of the French and Indian War (1754–63). The Shawnee on the Cumberland began retreating north as the result of friction with the Cherokee and Chickasaw about 1710 and began to merge with their brethren from the east in a group of villages on the Ohio River from what is now Tarentum, Pa., to the mouth of the Scioto in Ohio—hunting in the forests on both sides of the river.

The Shawnee were the spearhead of resistance to advancing settlement in that period of frontier warfare lasting from 1755 to 1795, supporting and being supported, first by the French and then by the English. By 1795 their homes were in the valley of the upper Miami, and the Treaty of Greenville of that year forced them to retreat to the Au Glaize. A movement for confederated Indian regeneration and resistance to further white expansion developed under the leadership of the Shawnee brothers, Tecumseh and The Prophet, but met disaster in the battle of Tippecanoe in 1811. The loss to the Indians of British support, as the result of the War of 1812, hastened the rapid dispersion of the Shawnee. The main body is now incorporated with the Cherokee in Oklahoma.

Shawnee and Delaware Migration to the Ohio Valley (ca. 1720–53). This migration from the Susquehanna and Delaware river valleys was important in the prelude to the French and Indian War.

It not only brought Indian life and power to a French area that had been uninhabited, but it diminished English influence through the loss of those tribes. Moreover, in the Ohio region the eastern Shawnee merged with their western brethren who had migrated from the Cumberland Valley.

The migration was caused by the encroachment of whites, by such aggravations as the Walking Purchase of 1737, by the decline of hunting and knowledge of better hunting grounds in the West, by the probability that the Iroquois would not be able to keep them out of the new grounds and by encouragement from both French and English traders. In the competition for the furs of the new region the English got the lion's share. But the fact that the English trade was accompanied by uncontrolled rum selling and unpunished fraud caused many Shawnee and Delaware to prefer the French, with whom their leaders were in touch from the beginning of migration. They were well disposed toward French expansion, which culminated in the occupation of the Forks of the Ohio (1753) and the erection of Fort Duquesne. The English, first through the Pennsylvania colonial government and later through the Iroquois overlords of the Shawnee and Delaware, sought in vain to bring the migrants back to English protection. Although the Iroquois scolded their dependents, they went no farther; and the failure of the Pennsylvania government to establish an Indian department impressed the Indians with the inability of the English to make their traders behave.

During the French and Indian War when the western Shawnee and Delaware, supporting the French, sought to wipe out the interior Pennsylvania settlements, the status of those remaining in the East was imperiled. The reassertion of English supremacy caused most of these to join the western tribesmen. After 1763 all were again under English influence.

Sioux is the name commonly used to designate the Dakota confederacy of Siouan tribes which played an important role in western history. The word Sioux is abbreviated from Nadowessioux, a French spelling of a Chippewa word meaning "snake," hence enemy. Dakota, Nakota or Lakota, depending on whether the pronunciation is in Santee, Yankton or Teton dialect, means "allies."

The Sioux, numbering about 30,000, were the most numerous of the plains people, comprising many loosely confederated bands ranging from the Minnesota lake country to the Powder River Valley and from the Canadian border to south of the Platte. Three major divisions are listed: the Santees, including the Mdewakanton, Wahpekute, Wahpeton and Sisseton groups which occupied the most easterly hunting grounds along the upper Mississippi and Minnesota Rivers; the Yanktons and Yanktonais, the middle group, living in what is now eastern South Dakota; and the Tetons, subdivided into Oglalas,

Brules, Sans Arcs, Minneconjous, Hunkpapas and some lesser bands, who hunted in the high plains, the western end of the Sioux range.

The Sioux are mentioned as early as 1640 in the *Jesuit Relations*. They were continuously at war with the Chippewas, who, supplied by the French with firearms, drove the Sioux westward where they collided with other tribes already in the country and whom they successively defeated. During the Revolution and the War of 1812, the Dakotas aided the British. Lewis and Clark passed through their country in 1804–5, encountered most of their tribes, and described their habitat.

The Sioux were among the most determined of all Indians in resisting white encroachment in the West, the series of Sioux wars extending, with intervals of peace, over more than thirty years. They developed a number of celebrated chiefs whose names became well known, including Red Cloud, Little Crow, Spotted Tail, Crazy Horse, Gall and Sitting Bull. Chiefs ordinarily rose to power through demonstration of fitness for leadership, but their power consisted largely of the weight of their personal influence.

Early writers universally pay tribute to the Sioux for their great courage and skill with weapons and in horsemanship. Their women were chaste, their men exceptionally honorable considering their savage state. Mentally and physically they were among the finest of all the American Indians.

Sioux Council (July 26–Aug. 6, 1889). During the 1880's there was ever-increasing pressure for the reduction of the so-called Great Sioux Reservation, an area roughly extending from Nebraska's northern line to the 46th parallel and from the Missouri west to the 104th degree of the longitude. Several attempts to negotiate with the Sioux by commission failed. A law of March 2, 1889, provided for the setting aside of certain specified areas for seven reservation groups in Dakota Territory and the opening of the balance for sale to whites, the amounts received to be credited to Indian funds. But before the law became operative it required the consent of three fourths of the adult Indians. A three-man commission, after visiting several agencies concerned, began its most important council at Standing Rock (Dak. Terr.), July 26, 1889. Indian opposition, headed by John Grass, stressed failure to observe the Laramie Treaty of 1868, particularly payments, schools, etc. In successive sessions the commissioners patiently explained the provisions of the act and, by minor concessions, met the objections. Indian agent James McLaughlin in private conferences finally convinced Grass and Chief Gall of the wisdom of accepting the act, and the formal signing followed on Aug. 3, after Sitting Bull had failed to stampede the council. The compensation was estimated at upwards of $7,000,000.

Sioux Treaties. Negotiations and treaties with the Sioux Indians covered a period of some eighty-five years, from 1805 to 1889, and a geographical area extending from Fort Snelling (Minn.) and Portage des Sioux (Mo.) on the Mississippi to Fort Laramie in Wyoming. The terms of these treaties reflect in a general way the growth of American power as settlement crossed the upper Mississippi and advanced into the Great Plains country.

On Sept. 23, 1805, Lt. Zebulon M. Pike, at Pike's Island (Minn.), purchased from the Minnesota Sioux for $2000 in goods a tract roughly nine miles square at the mouth of the Minnesota River for a military post (the later Fort Snelling), to inaugurate the series of treaties. Termination of the War of 1812 necessitated peace treaties with England's Indian allies, and between 1815 and 1817 a series of peace agreements acknowledging the sovereignty of the United States were negotiated by Gen. William Clark and others at Portage des Sioux and St. Louis with various Siouan tribes.

The extension of fur trading operations up the Missouri River by Ashley, and the movement of troops up that stream under Gen. Atkinson produced friction with the Sioux and other tribes of the Missouri, some fighting, and then, in 1825, several treaties such as that of Fort Lookout (S. D.), providing for peaceful relations and the admission of traders to the country. The same year witnessed the great treaty council of Prairie du Chien (Wis.), where on Aug. 19, the Sioux and other warring tribes, by treaty under governmental supervision, agreed upon mutual boundary lines and the maintenance of intertribal peace. The treaty of July 15, 1830, negotiated likewise at Prairie du Chien, was concerned with peace measures between the Sauk and Fox Indians and the Minnesota Sioux and allied groups, but attempted to attain such results by setting up a block of neutral territory between tribal enemies.

By the Treaty of Washington of Sept. 29, 1837, the Sioux began the sale of their Minnesota lands, and the assignment of treaty funds to settle debts to traders. By the time the agreements of Traverse des Sioux and Mendota of 1851 and Washington in 1858 had been completed, they retained only a ten mile wide strip in that state. The Sioux uprising in Minnesota (1862) had its Dakota phases, and eventually the great treaties of Fort Laramie in 1868 attempted to end the Indian wars by setting up a vast Sioux reserve west of the Missouri River and promising certain annuities and payments. The Indians were to withdraw opposition to the building of railroads through their country.

The act of March 3, 1871 prohibited further treaty making with Indian tribes, but in order to secure Indian acceptance of laws applicable to them, periodic councils for ratification were held, of which those in the summer of 1889 with the Sioux are typical. Although similar to treaty councils, the Indians in these assemblies acted as individuals, not as agents for semi-independent tribal entities.

Sioux Uprising in Minnesota (1862). Concentration upon upper Minnesota River reservations, without hunting areas, following the cession of their lands, resulted in semistarvation for the Sioux. After wanton murders near Acton, Minn., on Aug. 17, the outbreak came at the Redwood Agency the following day, and for two weeks raiding bands swept through southwestern Minnesota, murdering and pillaging. Despite the loss of twenty-four soldiers from Fort Ridgely, ambushed at the Redwood Ferry late Aug. 18, the successful defense of New Ulm and Fort Ridgely (Aug. 19–24) against Little Crow's warriors, permitted the movement up from Fort Snelling of troops under Col. H. H. Sibley. The white victory at Wood Lake Sept. 23, following the Birch Coulee defeat Sept. 2, crushed the uprising, except for sporadic incidents like the Dustin murders. The Sibley and Sully expeditions in the Dakotas freed the frontier. Thirty-eight Sioux were executed at Mankato Dec. 26, 1862. The uprising cost about 450 lives.

Sioux Wars (1854–91). The Sioux were accounted warlike from earliest times but the first military clash with Americans occurred Aug. 19, 1854, when Lt. J. L. Grattan and eighteen men were killed near Fort Laramie, Wyo. The next year Gen. W. S. Harney, in retaliation, attacked a camp of Brulé Sioux, Sept. 3, near Ash Hollow, Nebr., killing about one hundred.

Treaty dissatisfaction led primarily to the Sioux uprising in Minnesota under Little Crow (Chetan Wakan Mani), beginning Aug. 18, 1862.

Troops pursuing fugitive Santees out on the plains spread excitement among the Teton Sioux. Not until 1865, however, were the Tetons generally hostile, when they aided the Cheyennes in raiding the stage lines and in the Platte Bridge fight, July 25–26. The Government's decision to erect forts along the Bozeman Trail aroused the Sioux in 1866. Under Red Cloud (Mahkpiya-luta) they harassed the trail and hampered construction at Fort Phil Kearny and Fort C. F. Smith. Capt. William Fetterman and eighty men were killed near Fort Phil Kearny, Dec. 21, 1866, Fort C. F. Smith was unsuccessfully attacked Aug. 1, 1867, and the following day Capt. James Powell defeated the Sioux in the Wagon Box fight. The so-called Red Cloud War was terminated by the Treaty of Fort Laramie in 1868, by which the Government abandoned the trail and forts.

Discovery of gold in the Black Hills, S. D., in 1874, caused a rush of prospectors, although the Laramie Treaty of 1868 guaranteed the hills to the Sioux. Fearing trouble, the Government ordered the wild Teton bands to come in to the agencies. The principal chiefs, Sitting Bull (Tatanka y Yotanka) and Crazy Horse (Tashunka Witko) refused and Gen. George Crook, in March, 1876, failed to drive them in.

Crook, Col. John Gibbon and Gen. Alfred Terry

each led columns into the Sioux country in June, 1876. Crook fought the hostiles on the Rosebud River, June 17, and was compelled to fall back. On June 25, Gen. George A. Custer, with a detachment from Terry's force, encountered the Sioux on the Little Big Horn River, suffering one of the greatest disasters in Indian warfare. Custer and 264 officers and men were killed.

The Sioux separated after the Custer fight. Crook defeated American Horse's band at Slim Buttes, Sept. 9; Dull Knife's Cheyenne village was destroyed in Crazy Woman Canyon by Col. Ranald S. Mackenzie, Nov. 25; and Sitting Bull was chased into Canada by Gen. Nelson A. Miles. Crazy Horse, defeated by Miles at Wolf Mountain, Jan. 7, 1877, surrendered with most of the hostiles the following spring, ending the Sitting Bull War.

The final Sioux uprising was due to religious excitement during the ghost dance craze of 1889–91. Sitting Bull was killed by Indian police, Dec. 15, 1890, and approximately 200 fanatical Sioux were slain by troops at the so-called Wounded Knee fight, Dec. 29.

Snake (or Shoshonean) Indians. The term Snake Indians was incorrectly applied by early explorers and fur traders, ignorant of native language, dialectic variations, cultures and political organizations, to groups of the Shoshonean family residing chiefly in the Snake River Valley of southern Idaho, and in contiguous areas of Montana, Wyoming, Utah, Nevada and Oregon. Among these Indians were the Wihinasts (along the Boise River), the Sheepeaters, the Lemhis, the Diggers, the "Dog-Ribs" (of Irving's *Astoria*) and the Bannocks. The confusing term was employed for over a century, but today the groups which formerly resided in southern Idaho are scientifically designated as Shoshoni and Northern Paiutes. The origin of the name "Snake" is obscure. Contrary to frequent assertions that Lewis and Clark conferred it upon a native group in 1805, modern research discloses that it was used by Upper Missouri River fur traders prior to 1770.

Twightwees. See Miami.

Utes are Indians belonging to the Shoshonean linguistic family. Their country once included eastern Utah, central and western Colorado, and part of northern New Mexico. Formerly there were thirteen or more Ute tribes or bands, seven in Utah being organized into a confederacy. By 1870 there were probably about 4000 Utes; their descendants continue to live on reservations in Utah and Colorado. They were nonagricultural and warlike. Before 1700 the Spaniards in New Mexico felt their strength and during the 19th century Anglo-Americans frequently clashed with them. Their first treaty with the United States was made in 1849.

Winnebago, an offshoot of the Siouan family, were closely akin to the Iowa, Oto, etc. They called themselves Otchungras, "people of the parent speech." When discovered by the French in 1634 they occupied all of southern Wisconsin. Their numbers declining, because of wars with the Illinois, they permitted the intrusion of the Algonkian tribes. They were most closely allied with the Sauk and Foxes and the Menominee. They were allies of Tecumseh, and their chief, Caramaunee, was with him when he died. The Winnebago opposed the advent of the Americans, but in 1828, 1832 and 1840 were forced to make treaties, ceding all their Wisconsin lands. Transferred to Minnesota, they were in 1862 carried away to the upper Missouri, where they had a reservation with the Omaha. About half the tribe now live in Wisconsin, on lands which they have purchased.

Wyandot Indians. See Hurons.

Zuñi, a tribe of village-dwelling Indians in New Mexico south of Gallup, were discovered in 1539 by Fray Marcos and the Negro Estevan, a survivor from the ill-fated expedition of Cabeza de Vaca. A story was current in Mexico that seven cities, rich in gold, lay in a country to the north, called Cíbola. Seven Zuñi towns were found by the Fray Marcos party, but Estevan, leading the advance, was killed, whereupon Fray Marcos turned back. The next year Coronado led an army into the country, which found no difficulty in capturing the Zuñi towns. The Spanish exercised intermittent control over them until their subjugation was complete. At the end of the Mexican War the Zuñi came under the control of the United States. In mode of life, economics, architecture, social organization, etc., they resemble the Hopi, Acoma and other pueblo Indians. Their speech is a distinct language, but bears a vague resemblance to Shoshoni and Aztec.

INDIANA. Until 1763, what is now Indiana formed a part of the colonial empire of France in North America. Certain of the scattered French communities were within the limits of the present state, the most important being Vincennes. Few changes occurred within the British period, which nominally ended in 1783. In 1778 George Rogers Clark took possession of Vincennes, which was retaken by the British late in the same year, and again captured by Clark in 1779. When the Definitive Treaty of Peace in 1783 made the Mississippi River the western boundary of the United States, the Old Northwest came under the jurisdiction of the Congress of the Confederation. In 1787, the Northwest Territory was organized.

In 1800 the original Northwest Territory was divided into the Northwest Territory and Indiana Territory. A Virginian, William Henry Harrison, was appointed to the governorship of the newly formed territory, which included about what is now Indiana,

477

plus much of Michigan, all of Wisconsin and Illinois and part of Minnesota. Settlers came slowly, and, for some years, most of the problems related to the restless Indians of the Northwest. The American claim to the region was partly established by the exploits of Clark and greatly strengthened by Anthony Wayne's victories of 1794 and his Treaty of Greenville in 1795. In spite of the Louisiana Purchase and the earlier accomplishments of Clark and Wayne, the final showdown came during the War of 1812, after which, for the first time, the United States was in real possession of the valley of the Mississippi. The organization of Michigan Territory in 1805 and of Illinois Territory in 1809 left Indiana Territory with practically the limits of the present state, though the exact boundaries were not fixed until statehood was conferred.

Colonization began in earnest after 1813. A territorial census of 1815 showed a population of something over 60,000. Indiana, having passed through the stages of government provided in the Ordinance of 1787, was admitted to the Union in 1816.

INDIANA STATE CANALS were one of the results of the mania for state-promoted internal improvements which swept the Middle West in the first third of the 19th century. The Wabash and Erie Canal, to connect Lake Erie and the Ohio River through Indiana, was that state's first project, begun in 1832. In 1836 a great internal improvement bill was made law, carrying total appropriations of $13,000,000—one sixth of the state's wealth at that time. It provided for the building of a canal along the Whitewater River northward from the Ohio, another, the Central Canal, from the Wabash west of Fort Wayne via Indianapolis and White River to Evansville; a railroad from Madison through Indianapolis to Lafayette; and some turnpikes. The panic of 1837 greatly disturbed the plans; also there were gross incompetence, mismanagement and fraud in the state commission's operations. By 1840 the state was well-nigh bankrupt. The short completed portions of the Central Canal were sold to private interests for $2425. Before the Wabash and Erie reached the Ohio River in 1853, railroads were destroying its reason for being. The Whitewater Canal, taken over by a private corporation in 1846, was dead before 1870. Financial failures though they were, the canals played a large part in the development of Indiana and the Middle West.

INDIGO CULTURE was introduced into South Carolina at the inception of that colony, but it was not until 1744 that Eliza Lucas, a youthful planter of St. Andrews Parish, demonstrated that its production was practical with slave labor. Neighboring planters promptly adopted her idea as a supplement to the cultivation of rice. Stability was given to the industry by the granting, in 1748, by the British government of a bounty of sixpence a pound on indigo shipped to

England, and by the coming to South Carolina in 1756 of Moses Lindo, an experienced indigo-sorter. For some thirty years indigo, after rice, was the colony's most important crop; on the eve of the American Revolution more than a million pounds were exported annually. But in the closing decades of the 18th century the production declined rapidly. The causes were the withdrawal of the bounty; the tedium and unhealthfulness of indigo-curing; and the development of cotton. The dyestuff, however, continued to be cultivated in South Carolina, mostly in Orangeburg District, for local consumption until the end of the Civil War.

INDUSTRIAL WORKERS OF THE WORLD was a revolutionary industrial union organized in 1905 as a protest against craft unionism and the conservative policies of the American Federation of Labor. The organization split in 1908 on the issue of political action. There emerged the Chicago I. W. W., the anarcho-syndicalist wing, which sponsored industrial unionism and opposed political activity; and the Detroit I. W. W., the socialist wing, which advocated political action in the class struggle. The latter group in 1915 became the Workers International Industrial Union, which was dissolved in 1925.

INFLATION. There is no generally accepted definition of inflation, but, from the standpoint of the public, inflation means rapidly rising prices of commodities and services. According to traditional analysis, such a price rise is caused by an increase in the quantity of money which is not paralleled by a corresponding increase in the quantity of goods and services coming on the market. The increased money demand for goods, without a corresponding increase in the amount of goods offered for sale, causes prices to rise and constitutes inflation.

In recent years (1949–59), a new analysis of inflation, which may be termed "the wage-cost push" theory, has received substantial support. Under this theory, it is maintained that higher money wages in excess of increased labor productivity engender higher operating costs and thus force producers to raise their selling prices to consumers, the result being an upward thrust in prices. The cause of inflation is thus transferred from the demand to the cost side of the picture.

Whether the initial force bringing about a rise in prices is excessive money demand or an increase in the money costs of producers resulting from higher wages, the fact remains that the inflation cannot be maintained without an increase in the quantity of money in excess of the increase in the flow of goods to market. And in the end money demand is the determining factor, since producers will not grant wage increases that necessitate higher prices for their products unless they feel sure that consumers will have the necessary money to buy these products at increased prices.

Another point worth noting is that inflation resulting from the wage-cost push is of the creeping variety, *i.e.*, relatively small but regular increases in the price level extending over a long period, as opposed to the more violent type of inflation that has occurred chiefly as a result of war and its aftermath.

The evils attending a violent inflation—the impairment or even destruction of savings and insurance policies, the near pauperization of those living on fixed or slowly changing incomes, hyperspeculative activity, etc.—are well known and universally deplored. Creeping inflation, on the other hand, prevents the attainment of equilibrium in the economy. It discourages saving and encourages investment, with resulting misallocation of capital and wrong investment and managerial decisions. It tends to foster uneconomic speculation, and it injures the country's position in international trade. Finally, it eventually engenders all the evils of violent inflation as well, but stretched over a longer period.

In some respects creeping inflation is more dangerous than inflation of the more violent sort, chiefly because its evils are not readily recognized by the public. This is bound to be the case when even some professional economists condone creeping inflation as essential to continued economic growth, although actually sound growth is impeded rather than furthered by inflation of this sort.

Prior to the Revolution, inflation occurred in many of the colonies where bills were issued by the government and made legal tender. The issue of such bills was prohibited by Parliament by acts passed in 1751 and 1764.

With the outbreak of the Revolutionary War, emission of bills of credit on a large scale by both the states and the Continental Congress occurred. From 1775 to 1779 inclusive, the latter body authorized the issuance of $241,552,780 in such bills, and the various states issued an additional $209,524,776 of bills during the same period. As there was no corresponding increase in goods and services, the purchasing power of these bills decreased rapidly. By January, 1781, this currency was valued at 100 to 1 in relation to specie and by May had lost its value almost completely. The Continental Congress and the various states attempted to fix prices by law, but without success.

Following the collapse of the Continental currency and the establishment of the Union, prices remained moderate until the War of 1812 when another inflation occurred. This, however, was the result of the overissuance of bank notes instead of the issuance of bills by the Government. The peak of prices was reached in 1814–15, and thereafter the price level receded sharply until 1821, after which a fairly long period of relatively stable prices ensued.

The next major inflation in the United States occurred at the time of the Civil War. In order to help finance the war, Congress authorized three issues of greenbacks of $150,000,000 each. The currency was thus inflated and prices rose rapidly, reaching a peak in 1864–65. At the same time, an even more intense inflation was occurring in the Confederacy. The price level dropped rapidly after 1865 until 1880.

Following the resumption of specie payments by the Government on Jan. 1, 1879, no major inflation occurred in the United States until the outbreak of World War I in 1914. Prices shortly began to rise rapidly and continued to mount after the United States entered the war in 1917. The peak was not reached until the spring of 1920 when the wholesale price index stood at 244% of the prewar level. People with fixed incomes and those receiving salaries and fees more or less fixed by custom suffered severely from the great increase in the cost of living.

The inflation during and following World War I differed from that of the Civil War period in that it was caused by an overexpansion of check currency and bank notes rather than by the issuance of fiat money by the Government. The Government sold bonds to the people, the people borrowed at the banks in order to buy the bonds and the banks created check currency in granting such loans. Thus monetary purchasing power was expanded much more rapidly than production, and prices rose accordingly.

The period from 1922 to 1929 was one of comparatively stable prices. It appeared to many economists, however, that prices should have fallen because of the vast increase in the production of goods, and that some inflation therefore existed. In any event, there was no doubt that a severe inflation of stock prices occurred between 1924 and 1929.

From the autumn of 1929 to the spring of 1933 a severe deflation occurred, and the Roosevelt administration shortly decided on what was popularly termed a policy of reflation; *i.e.*, the raising of prices of commodities to the predepression level. Actually, through the sale of government obligations to the banks, a large expansion of the check currency took place. Business, however, did not respond to the increase in monetary purchasing power for a number of reasons, and the commodity price level remained below that of the predepression period until the country's entry into World War II in December 1941.

Because of the introduction of price, wage, and other direct controls in 1942, official price indexes rose but moderately (10% to 15%) until the middle of 1946 when controls were removed, although the actual price rise was greater than indicated by the indexes which could take no account of prices obtained in black market transactions. With the removal of controls in mid-1946, however, the unleashing of monetary purchasing power built up during the war period drove prices up to a peak in the fall of 1948 which approximately equalled that of the inflation of World War I.

The price level fell moderately during the recession of 1949, but rose again sharply to a new peak with the outbreak of the Korean conflict in 1950. The price level declined somewhat from this peak through 1952, leveled off for a couple of years, and has since been inching upward to an all-time high in late 1959.

Of the periods of inflation in the United States only those of the Continental and Confederate currencies were comparable to the extreme inflations which took place in a number of European countries following World Wars I and II; however, our own war inflations, while severe, were controlled. The gradual increase in the price level of the last half-decade, on the other hand, represents inflation of the creeping variety which, as pointed out earlier, is especially insidious because its evils are not clearly recognized and are hence difficult to counter.

INITIATIVE. The process by which the people may propose legislation is known as the initiative. It may be either indirect or direct. The indirect type calls for the submission of the initiated law to a representative legislative body for enactment. If the body fails or refuses to act or makes changes in the proposal, the sponsors may secure its submission to a vote of the people. The direct type omits the consideration by the legislative body and proceeds at once to the popular vote. The initiative is one of two democratic devices for direct legislation; the other is known as the referendum.

INSCRIPTION ROCK (El Morro), a varicolored sandstone rising 200 feet out of a lava-strewn valley in Valencia County, west-central New Mexico, derives its name from a fancied resemblance to a castle and from inscriptions carved on its sides by early Spanish and subsequent explorers. That of Don Juan de Oñate, April 16, 1606 (an error for 1605), is the earliest. Lt. J. H. Simpson and R. H. Kern, an artist, visited it, September, 1849, and were the first to record the inscriptions and bring them to the attention of the public. It was created a National Monument June 8, 1906.

INSULAR POSSESSIONS OF THE UNITED STATES. The United States acquired its first important insular possessions in 1898, when it annexed Hawaii and obtained Puerto Rico, the Philippines and Guam as a result of the war with Spain. American Samoa was occupied in 1899, under a treaty with Great Britain and Germany and by agreement with the native chiefs. The Virgin Islands were purchased from Denmark in 1917, and responsibility for the Trust Territory of the Pacific Islands was assumed as a result of World War II. The United States also has a number of smaller islands, like the Midways, acquired in 1867, and Wake, occupied in 1898, which are important chiefly as stopping places on air routes or as sites for lighthouses or communications facilities. Canton and Enderbury Islands in the Central Pacific are jointly administered by the United States and Great Britain.

Some former insular possessions now have a different status. The Philippines became independent in 1946, Puerto Rico has been an autonomous commonwealth since 1952 and Hawaii became a state in 1959.

The Virgin Islands, Guam, Samoa, and the Trust Territory were formerly administered by the U. S. Navy, but the Interior Department assumed responsibility for the Virgin Islands in 1931 and for the other possessions after 1949. The Virgin Islands and Guam are organized but unincorporated territories of the United States and their inhabitants now enjoy American citizenship, since 1927 in the case of the Virgin Islands and since 1950 in Guam.

The Virgin Islands have an area of 128 square miles and a population of 30,000. Under the Organic Act of 1954, the governor is appointed by the President of the United States and there is a popularly elected unicameral legislature of eleven senators. The chief exports are rum and bay rum.

Guam, which was overrun by the Japanese in World War II, was retaken in 1944 and served as a major naval base in the months that followed. The people of the island, of mixed Spanish and Chamorro descent, had little self-government until the passage of the Organic Act of 1950, which provided for a governor appointed by the President of the United States and a unicameral elected legislature. The island has an area of 209 square miles and a population of 37,000. It produces chiefly foodstuffs for local consumption.

American Samoa includes Tutuila and Aunuu, occupied in 1899, the Manua Islands, occupied in 1904, and Swain's Island, annexed in 1925. Until its transfer to the Interior Department in 1951, the territory was administered by a naval governor. The governor was assisted by an advisory council of native chiefs until 1948, when a bicameral elected legislature was established. Since 1951 the governor has been a civilian, and a native of the islands was appointed to the position in 1956. Local administration is still controlled to a great extent by the native chiefs. The total area is 76 square miles and the population 20,000.

The Trust Territory of the Pacific Islands includes the Marshall, Caroline, and northern Mariana Islands, which are scattered over 3,000,000 square miles of ocean. The total land area is 687 square miles, with an estimated population of 67,000. These islands were German colonies before World War I when they were seized by Japan, which ruled them under a mandate from the League of Nations, and fortified them in violation of the mandate's terms. They were conquered by the United States in World War II. They are administered under an agreement made in 1947 with the United Nations. The Interior Department has had charge of the administration since 1951, except in the northern Marianas, where Saipan and Tinian were again placed under the control of the Navy in 1953. The American High Commissioner for the Trust Territory has his headquarters at Agaña in Guam. Some of the atolls have been used for nuclear experiments by the United States.

In the "Insular Cases," decided after the first overseas possessions were acquired, the U. S. Supreme Court held that certain fundamental rights guaranteed by the Constitution apply in all territory held by the United States, but that other provisions of the Constitution do not apply to territories which have not been incorporated as an integral part of the United States. The inhabitants of such possessions are not *ipso facto* American citizens.

INSURANCE, CASUALTY. The history of the casualty insurance industry begins in 1864 when one of the largest modern insurance companies (Travelers) was formed solely to issue travel accident policies. In 1868 a casualty insurance company was created to provide an inspection service for steam boilers (the forerunner of modern loss prevention) and to provide indemnification for accidents which occurred.

The first liability insurance company was formed in 1887 by the owners of some twenty Massachusetts textile and paper mills and machine works after the passage of a state Employer's Liability Act for workmen injured or disabled by accidents while on the job. This was the forerunner of workmen's compensation insurance.

By 1898 there were fourteen companies in the nation, sharing total casualty premiums of less than $11,000,000. In 1960 there were approximately 3500 property and casualty companies with casualty premiums alone in excess of $9,000,000,000 a year.

Casualty insurance is a broad field. It takes in all kinds of liability protection and includes such lines as automobile insurance, workmen's compensation, plate glass, boiler and machinery, burglary and theft, and liability for personal injury and property damage. While fidelity and surety bonds are not, strictly speaking, casualty insurance, they are closely allied and generally considered as belonging in the same branch of insurance.

Casualty insurance in 1960 was helping to usher in a new era, that of the Atomic Age, by providing liability protection for commercial nuclear reactor operations and a myriad of other radiation exposures such as the use of radioactive isotopes in research, commerce and medicine.

Perhaps nowhere is the growth of casualty coverages more strikingly illustrated than in the area of automobile liability insurance. The first liability policy to be written on an automobile was issued in 1896 to Gilbert J. Loomis of Westfield, N. J. In that year there were fewer than ninety automobiles in the country. From that total in 1896, automobile regis-

trations soared past the ten-million mark in 1921, past the twenty-million mark in 1926, to a high of 70,000,-000 in 1960. This vast increase in the number and expansion in the usage of motor vehicles was accompanied by widespread need for insurance protection. The volume in 1960 of automobile bodily injury and property damage liability premiums topped $3,700,-000,000.

Other casualty lines have similarly matched the pace of growth and expansion in the nation. Population growth, higher standards of living, new products and greater use of them—all have resulted in increased risks and the need for even greater financial protection.

To meet the risks of increased exposure to liability from such sources as new products and services as well as the increased use of boats, planes and sporting equipment, general liability coverage other than automobile has risen more than fifteen-fold, from approximately $58,000,000 in 1933 to about $950,000,000 in 1960.

Similarly, the phenomenal advances in manufacturing and the increased wages of the working man, together with the increase in total number of employed, have been reflected in the development of workmen's compensation insurance. Premiums for this coverage rose from $120,000,000 in 1933 to 1.2 billion dollars in 1958, a ten-fold increase in 25 years. In 1959, they rose to 1.3 billion dollars.

It was estimated that the assets of casualty insurance companies amounted to more than $28,000,-000,000 in 1960. They were invested in state, municipal, government transportation and utility bonds, high grade stocks, and to a modest extent, in real estate which the companies use for their own offices. A sizable portion of the securities was in U. S. Government bonds. In addition, the insurers were required by law to set aside vast sums as reserves against incurred but not reported claims.

The industry pays taxes, licenses and fees of about $500,000,000 a year. And, to perform its services to individuals and industries, the property-casualty industry employs hundreds of thousands of men and women with annual payrolls and commissions in the neighborhood of $3,500,000,000.

The industry plays a leading role in accident prevention and spends approximately $30,000,000 a year to promote traffic, industrial and home safety in the nation. In order to meet the problem of ever-increasing traffic accidents on the country's highways and streets, the casualty insurers organized the Insurance Institute for Highway Safety in 1959. This organization works with motor vehicle administrators, state safety co-ordinators, and police and traffic engineers in an effort to reduce the traffic accident toll.

INSURANCE, HEALTH. In the 1890's, accident coverage was expanded to include sickness benefits,

481

forming the basis of modern day health insurance. Early policies paid benefits for a limited number of serious illnesses, partially to replace wage or salary losses. With experience, insurers eventually included all common ailments, extended benefits to hospital and surgical expenses, and introduced noncancellable and guaranteed renewable disability income policies. Group health insurance plans became available in 1910.

In 1929, a group of Texas teachers arranged with a hospital to provide them with hospital care for which they paid on a prearranged pro-rata basis—the forerunner of Blue Cross. By 1939, a similar type program, sponsored by local and state medical associations, was established to help people pay surgical costs (Blue Shield).

Beginning in 1940, health insurance entered the most expansive period of growth in American history. Less than 10% of the population was covered in 1940; today over 70% have some form of health insurance. Contributing factors were: (1) More public awareness of rising hospital-medical costs and how to provide for them; (2) Employers utilizing hospital-medical insurance as a fringe benefit to reduce employee turnover; (3) Labor unions making health insurance a bargaining point in negotiations; (4) Insurance companies becoming more active in health insurance—especially in developing group coverages.

In 1960, health insurance was available to all age levels with protection against hospital, general medical, surgical, and loss of income expenses—as was major medical insurance, designed to help offset heavy medical expenses resulting from catastrophic or prolonged illness or injury.

INSURANCE, LIFE. Life insurance got off to an informal start in the coffeehouses of colonial America when individuals "wrote their names under" specific short-term life insurance agreements. Then in 1759 the Presbyterian Synods of New York and Philadelphia established the first formal American life insurance corporation, known today as the Presbyterian Ministers' Fund.

Fifty years later the Pennsylvania Company for Insurance on Lives and Granting Annuities was founded. This was the first commercial company organized for life insurance exclusively, and the first to collect and use American vital statistics.

During the 1830's several new stock life companies were formed, and also the first mutual, which was chartered in 1835. The 1840's saw the development of commercial life insurance as it operates today.

The protective power of life policies was strengthened immeasurably after the New York State legislature enacted a law in 1840 providing that the proceeds of a policy naming a widow as beneficiary would be paid to her and were exempt from creditors' claims. Similar laws were subsequently passed by

most states. The usefulness of life insurance to the living policyholder was also increased toward the end of the 1840's, when policy loans were first granted.

In 1859 New York established the first totally independent state insurance department. New Hampshire had been the first to establish a board of commissioners, in 1851. Today every state has a similar department to regulate the practices and policies of insurance companies. Massachusetts was the first state, in 1880, to require nonforfeiture or cash surrender values as part of life policies.

Policyholder rights and company operations were materially strengthened after the Armstrong investigation of life insurance by the New York State legislature in 1905, which resulted in many changes in insurance laws in New York that set the pattern for other states.

The last quarter of the 19th century saw the introduction of industrial life insurance, issued in relatively small amounts and on a weekly premium basis. Group life insurance, which today totals about one third of all life insurance in force, had its beginnings in 1911.

Life insurance has grown at its fastest rate since the end of World War II, with the full development of the income concept of life insurance benefits. From 1945 to the beginning of 1961 the amount of life insurance in force more than tripled, to well over $585,000,000,000. During the same period annual benefits paid by the companies increased from $2,600,000,000 to $8,120,000,000. Life company assets rose from $44,800,000,000 to over $119,700,000,-000 comprising an important reservoir of capital funds invested in a cross-section of the national economy. The amount of insurance per insured family placed with the legal reserve companies increased to over $12,500 and at the beginning of 1960 six out of seven families owned some life insurance.

INSURANCE, PROPERTY. The earliest record of the insurance business in America pertains to coverage on ships and cargoes. As the colonies developed and the need for financial protection from loss by fire became apparent, enterprising citizens ventured into the field of fire insurance.

The first such venture was in 1721 when John Copson of Philadelphia advertised that he was opening an "Office of Publick Insurance on Vessels, Goods and Merchandizes." Mr. Copson's venture then dimmed into obscurity. In 1735, the Friendly Society for Mutual Insuring of Houses against Fire was organized under royal charter in Charleston, S. C. The Friendly Society remained in business only six years.

The first successful property insurance organization was established in 1752 in Philadelphia with Benjamin Franklin as one of its founders. This was a mutual insurance organization known as the Philadelphia Contributionship for the Insurance of Houses from Loss by Fire. The Philadelphia Contributionship issued perpetual fire insurance policies to property owners who were eligible for membership and each contributed a single large premium which was then invested to produce income to pay losses suffered by the members. This organization continues in business on the same basis today, confining its operation to coverage on a few types of property in and near Philadelphia. The first capital stock insurance company was organized in 1792, also in Philadelphia. This was the Insurance Company of North America which developed over the years into one of the leaders in the business.

As the young nation developed, the property insurance business developed with it. During this period, the majority of insurers were mutual companies, but at the turn of the century more and more capital stock companies were created as business enterprises. Mutual insurers relied for strength upon the financial integrity of their members, whereas the capital stock insurance companies had their financial strength in the form of capital funds contributed by stockholders, plus growing reserves.

The growth of the property insurance business brought with it public scrutiny and the beginnings of state regulation. In 1837, the State of Massachusetts required that companies maintain a fund to insure their contracts to maturity and in 1849, a general insurance law was enacted in the State of New York.

State supervision of insurance companies began in 1851 when the New Hampshire legislature created a Board of Insurance Commissioners charged with the yearly duty of examining the affairs of all companies licensed in that state. In 1859, the State of New York established the first separate insurance department presided over by a full-time superintendent of insurance.

Standardization of fire insurance policies was first undertaken in Massachusetts in 1873 with the adoption of the Massachusetts Standard Policy. This was followed in 1888 by the adoption of a standard form of fire insurance policy in New York. The last revision of the so-called New York Standard Policy was in 1943 and at present the New York Standard Policy has been adopted in 35 states. Eleven other states have adopted the New York standard form with minor variations. The policies adopted in Maine, Massachusetts, Minnesota and Texas had more important variations from the New York standard form.

The need for property insurance protection grew as the population increased and cities spread out to accommodate more businesses and more dwellings. The American industrial development also increased the need for new types of insurance protection. Inland marine coverages, so called because the policies were based on the broad form of insurance written under ocean marine contracts, were issued to cover many forms of property not confined to a single location. These policies were referred to as "floaters" and covered property in transit or kinds of property not confined to a single location. The first property insurance coverage on an automobile was written in 1902 on an ocean marine form of policy. Later, specific automobile insurance policies were developed for this new form of vehicle. In the 1930's, new kinds of property insurance were made available through extended coverage endorsement, and in the 1940's, property insurance companies, as a result of changes in insurance laws permitting multiple line underwriting powers under their charters, undertook the development of so-called package policies which included in one policy of insurance many separate forms which previously had to be written as separate insurance contracts.

INSURANCE, UNEMPLOYMENT. Unemployment insurance was established under the Social Security Act of 1935 as a Federal-state system. States worked out and administered their programs, subject to a few very general requirements of the Federal act.

The act levied a tax on payrolls of employers in industry and commerce who had eight or more employees (four or more beginning in 1956) in twenty weeks of the year. An offset provision for employers taxed under state programs and Federal grants for administration encouraged passage of unemployment insurance laws in all the states by July, 1937. Wisconsin had passed the first such law in 1932.

About two thirds of all employed persons were covered by 1960, including Federal employees and ex-servicemen. Agricultural and domestic workers, the self-employed, and public employees in about half the states remained the principal exclusions.

Compensation varied in amount and duration in the different states. The amounts were commonly set at about one-half of the employee's wage, but subject to dollar maximums which brought benefits to about one third of prior earnings. Duration of the payments in 1959 ranged from 6 to 39 weeks.

The agency responsible for administering Federal aspects of the system is the Bureau of Employment Security in the Department of Labor. Before 1949 the Bureau was part of the Social Security Administration.

INTERCHANGEABLE PARTS manufacture grew out of Eli Whitney's plan for making muskets in 1798. Thomas Jefferson reports an earlier experiment with this method in France, but most authorities give Whitney credit for the first successful operation of the system. In the artisan era, gunsmiths made muskets by hand and eye, making one part at a time and fitting it to the next part until the musket was complete. Whitney's plan was to produce each part in quantity by machine and, when the full supply had been turned out, to assemble the required number of muskets, picking the parts at random. This could only be done if all of each kind of part were identical.

Identical parts were obtained by means of the jig—a device for guiding a tool. A simple form of jig is a metal plate, in which are several holes. When it is desired to repeat the pattern of these holes, the plate is placed over the material to be drilled and the drill guided through the holes. Each piece so drilled will have the holes at the precise distances apart, and in the same relationship to one another as in the jig. The jig was Whitney's independent invention, though forms of it existed before him in watchmaking.

Whitney's scheme for the production of firearms, by jig-guided, power-operated machine tools, was perfected by his own descendants, by Simeon North, by Samuel Colt and others. English attention was drawn to it in 1851. From that time on, it became known throughout the world as the "American system." Meanwhile, it had been widely adopted in the United States in sewing-machine and farm-machinery manufacture.

It was the basis for all mass production of machines. Its effect on industry was revolutionary. It brought the artisan era to a close. A primary reason for its development in America was undoubtedly labor shortage.

INTERIOR, DEPARTMENT OF THE, was established in 1849 as the sixth department of cabinet rank, upon the recommendation of Robert J. Walker, Secretary of the Treasury. At the time certain government bureaus had no departmental affiliation, and others were overburdening departments in which, functionally, they did not fit. Walker's recommendation that these various bureaus, including the General Land Office, then in the Treasury Department, the Indian Office in the War Department, the Pensions Office scattered in both the War and Navy Departments, the Census Bureau and other minor supervisory agencies, be united in one department, produced a new sectional controversy. Western interests had long complained that the General Land Office was too strongly influenced in its administration of the public domain by eastern control, and they now supported the measure to set up a new department which, they hoped, would be more friendly to the West. Conservatives from the East and South, however, opposed Walker's recommendation, fearing that it meant further bureaucratic growth and a more liberal land policy. Another criticism of Walker's recommendation was that it would bring together bureaus with no functional unity, that it would set up a "catch-all" department with no common objectives. Despite opposition the act to establish the "Home Department," as it was first called, was approved on March 3, 1849.

Throughout its history the Department of the Interior has been one of the most politically minded of government agencies and, consequently, has been subject to attack by special groups, or by other departments seeking to wrest from it some of its bureaus.

The War Department, smarting under the loss of the Office of Indian Affairs, made serious efforts to recover its lost child. During and after the Civil War, when the West was aflame with Indian troubles and the Army was barely able to suppress the warlike tribes, officials of the War Department argued that the troubles were caused by the bungling and corrupt administration of the Indian Office and that both war- and peacetime jurisdiction over the Indians should be restored to the War Department.

The Interior officials held their own in this controversy and gained a new but modest recruit in the Office of Education, a research and tabulation agency. Then followed the creation of the Geological Survey in 1879 as a combination of surveying, geological investigations and mapping work formerly conducted by a number of government agencies. In 1902 the Reclamation Service was organized to administer the reclamation and irrigation activity being undertaken by the Government. The Bureau of Mines was established in 1910 to conduct investigations into all phases of mining and to promote the health and safety of the workers. In 1916 Congress established the National Park Service to provide administrative control for the widely scattered parks and monuments of the Federal Government. Finally, in 1934 the Division of Grazing was created to administer the 142,000,000 acres of range lands withdrawn from homestead entry and placed under organized management.

Meantime, the Department had narrowed its scope and achieved more unity by dropping some of its ill-fitting bureaus. In 1903 the Census Bureau was transferred to the newly created Department of Commerce and Labor (later Commerce); the Patent Office was similarly transferred in 1925; and in 1930 the Pensions Office was made a part of the Veterans Administration. The Bureau of Mines was also lost temporarily to the rapidly growing Department of Commerce under its aggressive secretary, Herbert Hoover, but later was returned to Interior.

The New Deal placed additional burdens upon the Secretary of the Interior and made his department even more of a "catch-all" than when it first started. Either under his supervision or as bureaus in his department were established the Public Works Administration, with its program of public construction, the Subsistence Homestead Division and Soil Erosion Service which were later taken over by the Department of Agriculture, and the Division of Territories and Island Possessions.

In the Reclamation Service with its augmented construction program of high dams on Western rivers there was developing in the '30's a major public works agency, and thought was given to making the Department of the Interior the public works department to which might be transferred the Bureau of Public Roads from Agriculture and the Army Engineers from the War Department. Though Harold Ickes, Secretary of the Interior from 1933 to 1945, toyed with the notion for a time, he was pulled more strongly in another direction, that of centering the work of his department around conservation. To that end he fought long and bitterly to have the National Forest Service transferred from Agriculture but without avail, for conservation interests insisted that forest and range management was safer in the department where it had achieved such notable success in the past.

Interior officials continued to place emphasis upon conservation and sought to achieve greater efficiency in administering the natural resources by consolidating in the new Bureau of Land Management in 1946 the old General Land Office, the Division of Grazing and the revested Oregon and California Railroad Lands with their rich timber stands. Its forest and range management duplicated to some degree similar policies previously introduced within the National Forests and critics questioned the need for two bureaus performing the same services on adjacent tracts.

Since 1933 the Department of the Interior has developed into a major producer of hydroelectric power with its principal dams at Grand Coulee, Bonneville, Hungry Horse, McNary, Chief Joseph and Boulder Canyon.

INTERNAL IMPROVEMENTS. Early settlers in the American colonies were not seriously handicapped by the lack of roads because they had little surplus goods for exchange. Furthermore, water transportation was generally available to them because of their proximity to the coast and to navigable rivers. But as population pressed farther into the interior, the rivers were less accessible and frequently unsuited even to light rafts. Overland routes became necessary and the buffalo and Indian trails were commonly used. They could not stand heavy traffic, however, and when the commercial production of tobacco, salt, iron and lumber developed in interior communities, roads had to be constructed. Then was voiced the demand for internal improvements which, together with the demand for land and tariff reform, ranked as the three most vital issues of the day.

Many economic interests stood to benefit from internal improvements. Cotton and tobacco planters in the southern piedmont, the wheat producers of Maryland, Pennsylvania and New York, the grain and stock farmers of New England, the owners of western lands seeking settlers, western settlers who were beginning to produce surplus goods, iron and coal producers, traders, merchants, importers, even the artisans in eastern cities would profit from reduced transportation rates. These groups, though not always aroused to united action, provided the great bulk of sentiment for state and Federal aid to internal improvements.

The first internal improvements, such as turnpikes and some short canals around falls, were begun by private groups. Even the Middlesex Canal to connect Boston with the Merrimack River, the first important canal to be built, was completed without public aid in 1803. Though itself not financially successful, it brought the trade of an important industrial area to Boston and showed the commercial advantages of canal construction, something which the Erie Canal was soon to demonstrate on a larger scale. But few large improvements could be financed solely with private funds. State and local governments were first importuned for aid and they responded by adopting many enterprises, some of which were quite fantastic.

The proposal to connect the Hudson River with Lake Erie by a canal was suggested in the late 18th century and efforts were made to build small parts of the project but it was not until 1817 that New York State was induced to undertake it. By that time the merchants and commercial interests of New York City were competing with the merchants of Philadelphia, Baltimore and other eastern cities for the rich trade of the trans-Allegheny country and they threw their support behind the measure. The main canal was to connect the Hudson at Troy with Lake Erie at Buffalo by way of the Mohawk River and branch canals were to lead to Lake Champlain, Lake Ontario and the Finger Lakes. The Erie Canal was completed in 1825 and its success in rapidly developing upstate New York amazed the country. Towns sprang up along its route, the counties tributary to it were soon settled and the two termini, New York and Buffalo, enjoyed unprecedented growth. But more important, cheaper transportation was provided and an admirable route into the interior now made easier the great trek of settlers into the states of Old Northwest.

Other states, not to be outdone by New York and determined to prevent her from monopolizing the trade of the interior, attempted to duplicate her feat by building their own canals, but unfortunately they had to go through or across the Alleghenies and New York's canal did not. Pennsylvania spent millions of dollars in canalizing the Susquehanna, Juniata and Conemaugh, and Allegheny Rivers, Virginia subsidized the James River and Kanawha Canal and Maryland the Chesapeake and Ohio Canal, all of which were influential in developing the sections they were built through but none of which were financially sound. Most of the states which undertook canal construction severely strained their credit, some even defaulted on their obligations. Poorly developed frontier states naturally were not able to finance costly canal and road construction and they looked to the National Government for assistance.

The first national enterprise was the Cumberland Road to connect Cumberland, Md., at the head of navigation on the Potomac River, with Wheeling, on the Ohio River. The congressional act authorizing the road involved no constitutional hair-splitting because a portion of the receipts from public land sales was available for such purposes, and, furthermore, there could be no doubt that the road was interstate in character. Although the measure was adopted in 1806 the road did not reach the Ohio River, 130 miles distant from Cumberland, until 1818. Subsequently, it was extended through Ohio and Indiana and into Illinois but it never reached its objective, Jefferson, Mo. The road made possible overland transportation of heavy goods, and the flow of commerce over it was so heavy that parts were worn out before it was completed. The Cumberland, or National Road as it was later called, was the first great man-made thoroughfare into the interior of America and, like the Erie Canal, was important in opening up new areas to settlement and commercial farming.

Meantime, the insistent demand of other areas for aid to canal and road construction induced Albert Gallatin, Secretary of the Treasury, to prepare a report in 1808 on internal improvements in which he outlined a comprehensive system of canals and roads for Federal construction. No action was then taken but the agitation continued and came to a head in 1816 when Calhoun and others drove through Congress the Bonus Bill which provided that the $1,500,000 bonus to be paid by the Second United States Bank to the Government for banking privileges and also the Government's share of the interest on the bank's stock should be used for internal improvements. Calhoun argued that the post roads and general welfare clauses of the Constitution justified such an act. But President Madison, who was more familiar with the intentions of the Constitution's framers, was not convinced by Calhoun's eloquence and vetoed the measure. Madison and Monroe, his successor, insisted that there was nothing in the Constitution to authorize Congress to use public funds for internal improvements and urged that recourse must be had to an amendment to the Constitution. Madison was looking backward to a simpler age when the settled area was narrowly circumscribed, while Calhoun, then a farseeing nationalist, looked to the future and was keenly aware of the need for better transportation facilities throughout the country. Calhoun and his section were subsequently to revert to Madison's narrow constitutional views while the West as it grew in political power voiced an irresistible demand for Federal aid to internal improvements and found its champion in Henry Clay.

From his first appearance in the halls of Congress, Clay favored Federal aid to roads and canals. His so-called American system included protective tariffs to encourage the development of industries, and internal improvements to make possible the easy flow of domestic commerce. He championed the Cumberland Road, the Chesapeake and Ohio Canal and numerous other projects. Clay's brilliant maneuvering and the popularity of Federal aids put the opponents of internal improvements to rout and forced President Monroe to sign measures providing for a subsidy to the Chesapeake and Delaware Canal, a $150,000 appropriation for the extension of the Cumberland Road to Zanesville, O., and smaller amounts for surveys and roads elsewhere.

Clay's views on internal improvements had the sympathetic support of John Quincy Adams during whose administration financial subsidies were granted to the Louisville and Portland Canal, the Dismal Swamp Canal and the Chesapeake and Ohio Canal, and large land donations were made to aid the Miami, the Wabash and Lake Erie and the Illinois and Michigan canals to connect Lakes Erie and Michigan with the Ohio and Mississippi Rivers. At the same time the rivers and harbors appropriations, the "pork barrel" legislation of a later day, began to appear with ominous regularity. Few of these enterprises were of lasting significance, and most of them were scarcely completed before the railroads began to put them out of business. But they had their part in the settlement of the territories they served and in making possible the beginnings of commercial farming therein.

Andrew Jackson, though an ardent nationalist, like most of the early national leaders allowed his political and personal prejudices to affect his constitutional views and, finding that his chief enemy, Clay, supported internal improvements, he turned against them. He endeavored to stand on the same ground that Jefferson, Madison and Monroe had taken in their opposition to grants-in-aid, and in his ringing veto of Clay's Maysville Turnpike bill he rehashed all the old arguments and denounced the project as being of a local character. But Jackson could no more stay the tide of sentiment favorable to Federal aid than Monroe, and during his eight years as President annual expenditures for canals, roads, and rivers and harbors were at the same rate as they had been during the Adams administration. True, more liberal land donations were made under Adams but when Jackson retired from the White House he could well boast that, despite his veto of the Maysville Turnpike bill, Federal aids had been lavishly distributed for transportation improvements.

In the middle 1830's the craze for internal improvements seemed to seize most of the country to a degree hitherto unsurpassed. Schemes were adopted without consideration of their feasibility and ultimate cost, states piled up debts to fantastic heights to finance their elaborate programs, absurd prices were paid for necessary lands, and other costs, even wages, were driven to high levels as a result of the competition of contractors for employees. Pennsylvania with its far-flung canal system, Ohio with its three north-south canals and other feeders, Indiana with its Wabash Canal, Illinois with its Illinois and Michigan Canal and an intricate network of railroads, Michigan with its three cross-state railroads, and other states with equally extensive programs all vied with one another in their efforts to extend their transportation facilities. The panic of 1837 wrought havoc with these grand programs; many of the states were forced to suspend work, dismiss employees and subsequently default on their obligations. There was a revulsion against state ownership and construction and when business conditions revived in the late 1840's private capital generally was forced to take the initiative with little state assistance. Many of the state projects were sold to private groups, notably the Michigan Southern and Michigan Central railroads. Control over others, including the Wabash and the Illinois and Michigan canals, temporarily passed out of the hands of the states.

It was the misfortune of the canal promoters that so many of their projects were approaching completion about the same time that the railroads were being built to rival them. The Chesapeake and Ohio Canal suffered from the competition of the Baltimore and Ohio Railroad which was, in fact, begun in the same year, 1828. The Rock Island Railroad paralleled the entire line of the Illinois and Michigan Canal in less than a decade after the completion of the canal in 1848, and other canals enjoyed but a short period of predominance, except for such great thoroughfares as the Erie Canal and the local canals connecting the eastern hard coal section of Pennsylvania with the rivers.

In the Eastern states the early railroads were generally built to connect important cities such as Boston and Lowell, Worcester and Springfield, Syracuse and Rochester. The process of consolidation was slow, and frequent changes were necessary between such cities as Albany and Buffalo, New York and Boston, and Washington and New York. Nevertheless, by 1850, the railroad net was beginning to reveal its modern outline. Although constructed by private groups, many of the eastern railroads received aid from state and local governments. Massachusetts assisted the Great Western Railroad which connected Boston with Troy, South Carolina contributed to the Charleston and Hamburg, and Baltimore aided the Baltimore and Ohio. Eastern states and cities, despite their financial reverses in the 1830's, recovered quickly and were easily able to help finance railroads but the relatively undeveloped West was not as fortunate. Consequently, in that area the cry went up for Federal grants of land to aid railroads. Again the bogey of unconstitutionality was raised by that section which felt that it would profit the least from Federal aid to railroads, the states of the Old South, but it had lost its effectiveness.

In 1850 a new era in Federal aid to internal improvements began when Congress granted 3,750,000 acres of land to aid in constructing a line of railroad from Galena and Chicago in Illinois to the Gulf of Mexico at Mobile. In the next 21 years more than 131,000,000 acres of land were given as subsidies to railroads, and large loans were made to the Union and Central Pacific railroads. Even during such a Southern-controlled administration as that of Franklin Pierce Southern opposition failed to prevent liberal land grants. The generous land grants and the financial assistance rendered by the counties and cities, which subscribed liberally to the stock and bonds of those railroads which would build through or into them, were largely responsible for the great expansion of the railroad net in the Middle and Far West during the years 1850 to 1890. By the latter date all parts of the country were knit together by bands of steel, and it was thought the railroads would never be replaced by more modern transportation facilities.

INTERNATIONAL GEOPHYSICAL YEAR (I.G.Y.). This denominates a period from July 1, 1957, to Dec. 31, 1958, in which more than 60,000 scientists from all nations of the world, including Soviet Russia and its satellites, collaborated on an international scientific level in exchanging and correlating without restrictions interrelated geophysical data. Geophysics is the collective name for meteorology, oceanography, geology, volcanology, seismology, etc., all relating to the study of the earth from its hot metallic core to the radiation belts that are over the atmosphere. The results of this international study were published in 1961 in a book entitled *Assault on the Unknown*.

INTERNATIONAL MONETARY FUND. An international institution negotiated at Bretton Woods, N. H., in 1944, it is affiliated with but independent of the United Nations. Located in Washington, D. C., it began operations in 1946 and now has 68 member countries. Its purposes, set forth in the Articles of Agreement, are principally to assist members to establish convertible and stable currencies free from exchange restrictions, and to provide short-term financial assistance. A Board of Governors with each member represented meets annually. Operations are administered by a Board of Executive Directors and a technical staff. Each member has a quota ordinarily subscribed one fourth in gold and three fourths in its own currency. Total assets in 1959 were about $9,-200,000,000. Advances to members, ordinarily repayable in three years, are to assist them in meeting exchange difficulties and to provide financial support for stabilization programs. As of April, 1959, total advances by the Fund had amounted to $3,300,000,-000, of which about half had been repaid. Much of the Fund's energies have been directed toward the elimination of exchange restrictions, and the general move to currency convertibility in 1958–59 is an evidence of success in this direction.

INTERSTATE COMMERCE COMMISSION was set up by the Interstate Commerce Act of 1887, on the authority of the provision of the Constitution granting Congress power to regulate commerce among the states. The members of the Commission, originally five, later seven, and now eleven in number, are appointed by the President with the advice and consent of the Senate, for terms of seven years. Not more than six members may be of the same political faith. The original act, though it gave the Commission certain regulatory powers over railroads, did not give it the degree of control necessary to develop an adequate transportation system. As a result of incessant demand for increasing the power of the Commission, the Elkins Act of 1903, Hepburn Act of 1906, Mann-Elkins Act of 1910, Valuation Act of 1913, Transportation Act of 1920 and Motor Carrier Act of 1935 were enacted. This legislation granted to the Commission sweeping inquisitorial and regulatory powers over rates, the character and conditions of service of railroad, motor carrier, sleeping car, express and pipe line companies engaged in interstate commerce; as well as authority to inquire into their accounts, records, financial structures and management, and power to impose penalties for refusal to comply with the Commission's orders. By the Transportation Act of 1940, the authority of the Commission was extended over interstate transportation by water. This included coastwise, intercoastal, inland and Great Lakes traffic. In 1942 freight forwarders (i.e., agencies engaged in the business of assembling goods of different owners for shipment) were subjected to the regulation of the Commission. The decline in the passenger business of railroads and the strong competition of motor truck freight service during the 1950's seriously hampered the railroads in their maintenance and improvement programs. This prompted Congress to enact the Transportation Act of 1958, by the provisions of which the Commission was authorized to provide financial assistance to railroads, by guaranteeing needed loans made to them by lending agencies. Authority over telegraph, telephone and cable service, granted in 1888, was transferred to the Federal Communications Commission in 1934.

To expedite administration, the Commission has subdivided its membership into five divisions and has established several boards for the purpose of conducting hearings. The findings or orders of a member, division or board have the same effect as if made by the Commission itself. The Commission is required to publish its findings and decisions, and to make annual reports to Congress.

INTOLERABLE ACTS, in part also known as the Coercion Acts, were five acts of Parliament: the Boston Port Act (March, 1774); the Massachusetts Government Act; the Act for the Impartial Administration of Justice (May, 1774); the Quartering Act; and the Quebec Act (June, 1774). The first four acts were designed to punish Boston for the Tea Party and to reinforce royal authority at the expense of popular liberty by alterations in the Massa-

chusetts charter; the Quebec Act, although lumped by Americans with the Coercion Acts, was not a punitive measure, but in the hands of colonial propagandists it was made to appear a menace to the religious as well as the civil liberties of the colonists. To Lord North's consternation, these acts, intended to restore peace and order in America and to isolate Massachusetts, threw the colonies into ferment and became the justification for calling the first Continental Congress.

INVENTIONS, GREAT. The history of invention in the United States, up to about 1920, may be divided, roughly, into two phases. The Civil War marks the division. The inventions of the first phase worked, in the beginning, to bring about separation and expansion, but at the end of the period they worked toward union. The inventions of the second phase have tended to consolidate this union. Since 1920, revolutionary discoveries in physics have brought an entire new era of applied science.

The great needs of the first phase were presented by agriculture, distance and labor shortage. The flour mill of Oliver Evans (1780) which so combined machinery that the product passed from grain sack to flour barrel without human intervention responded to two of these needs. So did the cotton gin of Eli Whitney (1793). This device, however, designed as a labor saver, had the effect of multiplying slavery by increasing the planting of cotton. Thus it became a remote cause of the Civil War.

Far more important, technically, than the gin was Whitney's second labor-saving invention. In 1798 he designed for the manufacture of muskets what later became known throughout the world as the "American system." Working with jigs or patterns in automatic machines he produced identical, interchangeable parts in unlimited quantity. This was revolutionary in the period. It is, perhaps, the greatest invention in American history and forms the basis of all machine mass production.

Western emigration which made labor shortage acute in the East also revealed the problems of distance and soon made demands of its own. The steamboat, invented by John Fitch (1787) and made useful by John Stevens, Nicholas Roosevelt, Robert Livingston, Robert Fulton and others, overcame the difficulty of upstream river transport. Stevens, then, inspired the Americanization of the steam railroad. The peculiar American need of economy, because of the extent of track, was met by Stevens' son Robert with the T-rail (1830).

When agriculture increased in the fertile West the reaper of Cyrus H. McCormick (1831–34) turned subsistence-farming into mass production. This, with new methods of transport, began the centralization of food supply, making other parts of the country dependent on the West and thus establishing the necessity of union. The greatest psychological stimulus to unity came, however, with the electro-magnetic telegraph invented by Joseph Henry (1831) and brought into use by Alfred Vail and Samuel Morse (1844). Aided by the rotary presses of Richard Hoe (1847) and the resultant cheap newspapers, it unified public opinion and completed the process of democracy in the nation.

Industry, as well as agriculture, had now become centralized. Beginning with the reproduction of English machinery by Samuel Slater (1790), the textile industry had grown enormously in New England. The boot and shoe industry kept pace. Great impetus was given to both by the labor-saving sewing machines of Elias Howe (1844), Isaac Singer (1851), Benjamin Wilson (1850) and James Gibbs (1850–58). These machines created the ready-made garment industry.

It is commonly supposed that the post-Civil War period of American invention was the greater. In this second phase, however, comparatively little invention was basic. Most of it was improvement in the interests of unification, consolidation, speed and the cultural impulse.

The typewriter, probably invented by William Burt in 1829, played no part in business until the 1870's. Meanwhile, out of the efforts by Sholes, Glidden, Clephane and many others to perfect it, came one of the greatest inventions of the century, Ottmar Mergenthaler's linotype (1884). This revolutionized the one remaining slow process in printing and made modern American journalism possible.

The telephone (1876), of which Alexander Graham Bell is the accepted inventor, seems from the social point of view merely a new variety of rapid communication. Psychologically, however, its effect was far more unifying than that of the telegraph because of the illusion it gave of personal contact.

The phonograph, a great basic invention by Thomas A. Edison (1877), belongs to the cultural phase, along with inventions in photography, processes for the printing of pictures, and radio broadcasting. In this phase also the sound-record principle has combined with many inventions in celluloid film photography and projection to produce the modern motion picture whose social effect is highly unifying and standardizing. Bearing upon this and of immense effect also in the scientific world is the invention of the incandescent lamp usually attributed to Edison (1879).

The basic heavier-than-air flying machine by Orville and Wilbur Wright (1903–8) has depended for its present usefulness on the collateral science of metallurgy and the technology of the internal combustion engine. The cheap automobile, an American development, has resulted from improved industrial machinery and processes. It has tended to standardize, democratize and consolidate national unity.

In the new era since 1920, it has become increasingly difficult to give either individual or national credit for inventions. Most of the scientific theory on which nuclear technics, radio inventions and electronic devices are based was evolved in Europe. In the field of radiotelephony and broadcasting, two Americans have made significant contributions: Lee DeForest invented the audion tube, and Edwin Armstrong the regenerative circuit and frequency modulation (FM). Television became practical with the application of electronics; American industrial laboratories such as those of Bell and the Radio Corporation of America have done much for its progress. The same is true of the transistor and other inventions in the field of miniaturization. The relatively new technology of electronics is responsible for giant strides in the invention of computers, and these too are laboratory products.

The American chemical industry has made immense contributions in plastics, synthetic fibers and silicones. The United States has played a large part in the recent drug and pharmaceutical advance: cortisone has achieved production through the efforts of Edward C. Kendall and co-workers in the Mayo Clinic; Selman A. Waksman, American Nobel Prize winner, is credited with the invention of streptomycin; and ACTH has come out of the Armour Research laboratories.

Scientists from several nations were assembled in the United States to co-operate under J. R. Oppenheimer in the production, in 1945, of the atomic bomb. Other uses of atomic energy are being currently explored in American research centers.

In the latest phase, American invention has become mainly collective. Technology has grown so complex and it is now so dependent on discoveries in all branches of science that most inventions are made by laboratory groups or teams. The old-time "lone wolf" or "garret" inventor has largely disappeared.

INVESTIGATING COMMITTEES have frequently been used throughout our history to obtain evidence on which Congress, state legislatures and city councils have acted. Whether joint, standing, or special committees, they must be expressly authorized to subpoena witnesses and papers on a specific subject. The colonial assemblies, following English precedents, frequently authorized investigations of elections, finances, etc. Some state constitutions (e.g., Maryland, 1776) expressly authorized such committees, but for Congress and most legislatures it is an implied power.

Congressional investigations of elections and qualifications of members have occurred at almost every session. A bribery investigation in 1857 resulted in the expulsion of four Representatives, and an act making refusal to testify before congressional committees a misdemeanor. Later instances were the Crédit Mobilier scandal, the Silver Pool investigation (1891), sugar tariff bribery charges (1894), post-office graft (1884 and 1903), and the ship subsidy lobby (1910).

Presidents and members of the cabinet have been investigated at least 23 times, beginning with Alexander Hamilton (1793). Practically every administrative agency has been scrutinized, the War Department and the Indian Office perhaps most often. Nearly every war, including Indian wars, has been followed by one or more investigations. St. Clair's defeat caused the first (1792). The first senatorial investigation was of Jackson's Florida campaign. In 1861 was established the first joint investigating Committee on the Conduct of the War. Partisanship has often caused inquiry into alleged administrative abuses, as that into the Treasury Department (1793) in connection with the funding of Revolutionary debt, and those into the Jackson administration (1833, 1836, etc.) in connection with the removal of deposits, the spoils system, etc. Investigations of the political activities of officials frequently furnished campaign material for the opposition party. The height of inquisitorial activity was during the Grant administration, when 35 investigations occurred.

Investigations for legislative purposes have ranged widely in spite of the narrow definition of the investigatory power given by the Supreme Court in Kilbourn v. Thompson. If the resolution authorizing the committee states that the ultimate purpose is legislation, the courts can rarely interfere with its activities, as evidenced by the Townsend case (1938). Important legislation resulted from investigations of Southern Reconstruction (1866–67), Ku Klux Klan (1871), Nicaraguan Canal Project (1899), Philippine Islands (1901), money trust (1911–13), and many others. Lately, mere "fishing expeditions" have, in general, been replaced by preliminary expert investigations, as in the senatorial inquiries into banking (1933–34), stock exchanges (1934), munitions trade (1934–35), labor conditions (1936–38), holding companies (1936), and railways (1937).

A Senate rule adopted in 1928 allows the appointment of special commissions to take testimony in any part of the country. This and other Senate rules have made senatorial investigations overshadow in number and importance those of the House. Although temporary or permanent commissions have taken over some of this work, there remains a broad field for congressional investigations.

During World War II, Senate committees made important investigations of defense contracts (Truman Committee) and of price control. A House committee under Martin Dies investigated "un-American activities" (1938–44).

Under the Legislative Reorganization Act (1945) investigations are made by subcommittees; the House set up a standing committee on subversive activities. A Senate subcommittee under Joseph R. McCarthy investigated communists in government service (1950–54). The Senate censured Senator McCarthy for his unfair conduct in a dispute concerning the U. S. Army. A Senate subcommittee investigated labor union practices (1957–59). The courts have generally upheld investigations of subversive activities and beliefs, but witnesses have often hindered inquiries by claiming the right of non-self-incrimination under the Fifth Amendment.

INVESTMENT BANKS normally perform none of the three basic functions that commercial banks do; it would be more accurate to call them wholesale merchants of securities. The work of the modern investment bank is in three parts: (1) It investigates and judges the stocks and bonds that business concerns, seeking to raise capital, ask it to market for them. (2) It buys these securities for a negotiated price, frequently borrowing most of the funds needed from a commercial bank. To avoid a serious loss it invites each of several rival investment banks to "underwrite" a part of the issues. (3) In co-operation with other firms it markets the securities, either wholesale, retail, or both, at a profit. The presence of stock exchanges, on which buyers know they may resell securities, makes it easier for the investment banker to sell his wares in the first place. New York's stock exchange was informally founded in 1792, and formally established in 1817; Philadelphia's began in 1800.

Early in the 19th century well-known brokerage houses such as Prime, Ward and King of New York or Alexander Brown and Sons of Baltimore, or commercial bankers, such as Nicholas Biddle, sold securities, chiefly governments', to wealthy clients or to investment houses overseas. For a time so-called loan contractors also handled this business. It was not yet developed to the three-stage system described above. Nor were these people very conscientious about the quality of the securities they offered. But the English House of Baring, specializing in American securities, and the American, George Peabody of Baltimore, living in London in the 1840's and 1850's, realized the importance of selling only securities of institutions and companies from whom they could expect good performance. During the Civil War Jay Cooke developed a large organization of bond salesmen to sell Government bonds to the public. After the war he had less success with railroad bonds and failed in 1873. Thereafter the House of Junius Morgan and of his son, J. P. Morgan, assumed the leadership. Its efforts to improve the ethics of investment dealings in the corrupt era of Jay Gould did much to promote transportation and then industrial growth. But Morgan carried his dislike for wasteful competition and his dictation too far when he helped to found such monopolies as the Northern Securities Co., and the United States Steel Co. about 1901. In consequence, Theodore Roosevelt's trust-busting activities and later the Pujo Money Trust Investigation of 1912 followed. The latter found in essence that Morgan headed a huge security merchandising monopoly.

During the 1920's giant commercial banks such as New York's Chase National, headed by Albert Wiggin, and National City, headed by Charles Mitchell, developed large investment affiliates to market securities. Irresponsible management of these contributed to the 1929 Panic. Subsequent revelations before Congress in 1931–33 led to the prohibition of affiliates, and to the passage of the Securities Act of May 27, 1933, and the Securities Exchange Act of June 6, 1934. These laws regulated the exchanges and obliged the investment banker to "tell all" in his prospectus about the security he was offering under severe penalty if he failed to do so. It was said that the old adage of "Let the buyer beware" had changed to "Let the seller beware." Investment banking declined sharply in the depressed 1930's; indeed Government agencies such as the Reconstruction Finance Corporation headed by Jesse Jones were the big suppliers of capital of this era. Investment banking revived somewhat after World War II but now "private placements" plagued the profession. Huge insurance companies bypassed the investment bankers and bought up directly the offerings of well-known companies seeking capital.

IOWA. The recorded history of Iowa begins on June 17, 1673, with the advent of Jolliet and Marquette. The first explorers encountered such tribes as the Mascoutens, the Peoria and the Miami. Iowa belonged to France from 1673 to 1762, when Louisiana west of the Mississippi was ceded to Spain. The Spanish made three private land grants—to Dubuque in 1796, to Tesson in 1799, and to Giard in 1800. At Napoleon's command Spain reluctantly retroceded Louisiana in 1800, only to see the United States acquire it three years later.

Thereafter territorial jurisdiction over Iowa land was kaleidoscopic. Included in the District of Louisiana until 1805, in the Territory of Louisiana until 1812, in the Territory of Missouri until 1821, it was unorganized territory for thirteen years until attached to Michigan Territory in 1834. In 1836 Iowa formed a part of Wisconsin Territory.

The Sauk, Fox and Potawatomi, the Iowa, Winnebago and Sioux have been closely associated with the region. The only pitched battle between the Indian and the white man on Iowa soil occurred at present-day Des Moines in 1735. The Black Hawk War (1832), fought in Illinois and Wisconsin, resulted in the first Indian cession of Iowa land. Between 1832 and 1851 the United States quieted the Indian title to the land of Iowa for less than ten cents an acre. After 1851 only two significant Indian episodes occurred: the return of the Fox Indians in 1856 to purchase and establish the Tama Reservation, and the Spirit Lake Massacre in 1857.

The *Western Engineer* made the first steamboat voyage up the Missouri to present-day Council Bluffs in 1819, while the *Virginia* ascended the Mississippi to Fort Snelling in 1823. Ten years later, on June 1, 1833, permanent settlement began. After stubborn Southern opposition the Territory of Iowa, including the present state of Iowa, the present state of Minnesota and that part of the present states of North Dakota and South Dakota east of the Missouri River, was created on July 4, 1838. It was named by Albert M. Lea in 1836 from the Iowa River which derived its title from the Iowa Indians.

A clamor for statehood culminated in the constitution of 1844 featuring low salaries, limited debt and restrictions on banks and corporations. After a disagreement with Congress over boundaries, Iowa was admitted Dec. 28, 1846, with the present area (56,147 square miles), under a second constitution.

IRON AND STEEL INDUSTRY. The first attempt to build blast furnaces in the American colonies was made in Virginia while that colony was under the jurisdiction of the London Company. Before production was under way the works were demolished and the ironworkers slain during the Indian massacre of 1622. It was almost a hundred years later that Gov. Spotswood established his furnaces in Virginia. The first furnaces and forges to operate successfully were built by the Puritans under the leadership of John Winthrop, Jr., in 1646 at Lynn, and soon after at Braintree, Mass. While other ironworks followed in New England, especially at Concord, New Haven and Pawtucket, as well as at Shrewsbury, N. J., the American iron industry did not make much progress during the 17th century.

From the second decade of the 18th century, the development of the colonial iron industry was remarkably rapid. Before the Revolution, blast furnaces and forges had been built in every colony except Georgia. In 1775 there were more blast furnaces and forges in the American colonies than in England and Wales combined and the production of pig iron and bar iron was greater in the colonies than in the mother country. In 1700, the seaboard colonies produced about one seventieth of the world's supply of iron, while in 1775 they were producing almost one seventh. Although the industry was quite scattered, spreading from New Hampshire to South Carolina and westward to the frontier, there were forces that tended to concentrate it in certain regions. The most highly industrialized region was southeastern Pennsylvania.

The ironworks were usually organized on plantations or estates where large quantities of wood could be obtained for the charcoal fuel and where food for the workers could be raised. The ironmaster's mansion, the homes of the workers, the store, the woodlands, the farmlands, the mines, the ironworks, the gristmill, the sawmill and the blacksmith shop made up a largely self-sufficing community. This form of organization—a combination of agriculture and industry—continued until well into the 19th century.

From about 1800 to the Civil War, Northern river valleys, from the Hudson-Champlain region southward, became the important areas of iron production. The coastal iron industry of New England and the bog ore industry of southern New Jersey gradually disappeared as anthracite fuel was substituted for charcoal about 1850. The valleys of the Lehigh, Delaware, Schuylkill and Susquehanna became the chief centers of iron production. West of the mountains the industry developed rapidly in western Pennsylvania and eastern Ohio. Also, along the Cumberland River, in western Kentucky and Tennessee, much iron was produced.

The processes of early ironmaking did not change until after the opening of the 19th century. The first important change was the adaptation of the puddling furnace and rolling mill, the English invention of Henry Cort. In 1817 the first mill of this type was put into operation at the Plumsock ironworks in western Pennsylvania. Others followed in the Pittsburgh district and elsewhere. Most of the iron used in early railroad development was secured from England, but by 1860 one half the rails, axles and other forms of railroad iron were rolled in this country.

Significant changes were also made in blast-furnace production. In 1840, after a few years of experimentation, it was demonstrated that anthracite could be profitably used in smelting iron. By 1855 its use had surpassed that of charcoal in the country's output of pig iron. Attempts were also made to use raw bituminous coal as well as coke in blast furnaces. In 1850 several furnaces in western Pennsylvania and eastern Ohio used bituminous coal. For a few years there was an increase in the number of furnaces using this fuel; then came a decline and, like anthracite, it was displaced by coke, which was used successfully in blast furnaces in the United States as early as 1835. It did not surpass coal as furnace fuel until many years after the Civil War. The substitution of steam for water power in producing the blast and the utilization of the gases which escaped from the furnace for heating the blast were important blast-furnace improvements of this period.

From 1800 to 1860 many changes also took place in the production of secondary iron manufactures. An impetus was given to the metal industries through the contemporary revolutions in agriculture and manufactures. The increased use of machinery created unprecedented demands on the iron industry. Castings, especially, were required for steam engines, machinery, stoves and for other purposes. In 1860 almost every state produced machinery; Pennsylvania, New York, Massachusetts, Ohio and New Jersey led the others.

After the Civil War the age of iron gradually gave way to the age of steel. Until this time, relatively small amounts of blister and crucible steel were used, chiefly in making cutlery and the finer grades of tools. The bessemer and open-hearth processes revolutionized the industry. The bessemer method was invented in England in 1856 by Henry Bessemer, who in 1865 received a patent in the United States. Many years earlier, William Kelly of Kentucky had experimented independently and had discovered the principle of decarbonizing molten metal by forcing a stream of air through it—the essential principle of the bessemer process. The priority of Kelly's invention was recognized by the U. S. Patent Office in 1857 when a patent was granted to him. It was not until 1864 that a company in Wyandotte, Mich., operating under Kelly's patent, made steel by the new method. The next year, a company at Troy, N. Y., began operating under Bessemer's patent. In 1866 the Bessemer and Kelly interests compromised their conflicting claims and thus the way was clear for the production of steel in large quantities at comparatively low cost. The Thomas-Gilchrist invention, which substituted a basic limestone lining for the acid lining of the converter, made possible the application of the bessemer process to iron containing a high degree of phosphorus.

The open-hearth steelmaking process is based on the pioneering work of the Siemens brothers in France during the 1860's. First used successfully in this country in 1869, one of its principal advantages over the bessemer process is the use of much larger amounts of scrap iron and scrap steel as raw materials.

The United States has been the world's leading producer of steel since 1890 when production totaled more than 4,000,000 net tons. Annual production has increased to exceed 100,000,000 tons several times since the end of World War II. Approximately 90% of present production is made in open-hearth furnaces. While bessemer process production has declined, another pneumatic process, oxygen steelmaking, has increased rapidly in importance in recent years. Electric furnace production continues to grow, while crucible steelmaking is no longer a factor.

In 1960, the United States iron and steel industry was made up of approximately 260 companies, over 80 of which produce raw steel. The companies have more than 430 plants situated in some 33 states. There were 29 states in which raw steel is made and those with the largest capacities included Pennsylvania, Ohio, Indiana, Illinois and Maryland.

IRON CURTAIN. Winston Churchill at Fulton, Mo., March 5, 1946, spoke of eastern Europe as an area where an iron curtain had descended, behind which Soviet and Moscow control was increasing. The expression came particularly to connote controls over influences of any kind entering communist countries from the outside or circulating within them.

IRON MINING. Most of the early ironworks of America utilized iron ores outcropping on the surface of the earth, in veins, beds, irregular deposits and also taken from bogs and ponds. Especially in New England and southern New Jersey were bog ores important. All types of ores—magnetite, red hematite, brown hematite or limonite, and carbonate—were used during the colonial period. Since the ores were on the surface or just below, little or no technical knowledge of mining was necessary. The chief tools required were bars and pickaxes, for there was little boring, blasting or firing. Prior to 1800 few shaft mines existed, most mines being open trenches from which the ores were dug. In the 19th century, as the iron industry grew, the number of shaft mines increased, although old methods continued in many places.

A new era in mining began with the development of the ore deposits of the Lake Superior regions. While there were rumors of mineral wealth in this section as early as the 18th century, Michigan at the time of her admission as a state in 1836 bitterly opposed receiving the northern peninsula in lieu of a disputed strip in northern Ohio. Even after the discovery of iron ore deposits in 1844 by U. S. Government surveyors, near what is now Marquette, few realized the importance of the mineral wealth of this region. In 1852 a small amount of ore was shipped to New Castle, Pa., the first shipment of Lake Superior iron ore to the East. It was not until 1856 that the Marquette range began to ship ore regularly. These shipments, which marked the beginning of the development of this great ore region, were made possible by the construction of the canal around the rapids at Sault Sainte Marie in 1855 (St. Marys Falls Ship Canal). In the decades that followed many other ranges were opened up in Michigan and Minnesota, including the Menominee, Gogebic, Vermilion, Mesabi and Cuyuna. The Gogebic range straddles the Wisconsin-Michigan line.

An outstanding iron ore development in recent years is the beneficiation or improvement of low-grade ores. Now in operation at various ranges in the United States, beneficiation processes make available vast reserves of iron ores that were once considered uneconomic for use in blast furnaces.

The beneficiation of taconite, for example, requires special mining and preparation equipment and techniques. Taconite is a very hard rock containing about 32% iron that is found in the Lake Superior region. It must first be crushed to a fine powder and then reduced to a muddy sand. After unwanted elements are removed, the remainder is partially dried and formed into pellets containing about 62% iron. These are then baked hard to form an excellent blast furnace charge.

In addition, at steel plants, flue dust and fine ore particles that were once considered waste are now being processed into useful, solid forms such as sinter, pellets, briquettes or nodules.

Lake Superior ores are taken chiefly to Duluth, Minn., and Superior, Wis., and there loaded on large steel barges. Ingenious loading devices move the ores. The barges transport them to South Chicago, Ill., to Gary, Ind., and to Conneaut and Ashtabula, Ohio. At South Chicago and Gary are great iron and steel plants, but a part of the ores received at these two cities is transported by rail to Joliet, Ill., Milwaukee, Wis., and elsewhere. From the Lake Erie ports, the ores are shipped largely by rail to the furnaces of the great Pittsburgh district and others.

The ores of the Appalachian region, roughly from northeastern Pennsylvania to Alabama, are also utilized to some extent. The greatest mining development in this region is in the Birmingham district. These ores had been used to a small extent before the Civil War, but during the last two decades of the 19th century their development really began. Other ores used in the United States are obtained from mines in Utah, California, New York and a few other states.

IRONCLAD WARSHIPS. Thickening ships' sides against penetration by shot was common practice in the sailing-ship era. The early American frigates afford examples. The Crimean War demonstrated the great advantage of metal armor especially against shell-fire. The advent of rifled cannon hastened the development and nearly one hundred armored warships were built or building in Europe by 1861. The first ironclad undertaken in the United States was the *Stevens Battery*, of 4683 tons and 6¾-inch side armor, begun in 1842 but never completed. In the Civil War inadequate shipbuilding facilities forced the Confederates to fit armor on existing hulls, the former steam frigate *Merrimack* (renamed *Virginia*) being the first so converted, with a waterline belt and an armored central casemate having inclined sides. Similar conversions were made by both sides on the Mississippi River but the Federals generally relied upon newly constructed iron or wooden vessels designed to carry metal armor. The *Monitor* was the first completed and her success against the *Virginia* (*Merrimack*) on March 9, 1862, led to the construction of many others of the same type—characterized by a very low freeboard, vertically armored sides and armored revolving gun-turrets. Vessels of other types, designed for and fitted with armor, were also built simultaneously; the large, unturreted and very seaworthy *New Ironsides* being most successful. The demonstrated worth of armor in this war led to its universal adoption for large warships. Metallurgical developments have constantly enhanced the value of armor protection.

IROQUOIS THEATER FIRE (1903). This greatest of all American theater disasters occurred on the afternoon of Dec. 30, 1903, in the "loop" district of

Chicago, and resulted in burning or smothering 571 persons, mostly women and small children.

"IRREPRESSIBLE CONFLICT" was a term originating with William H. Seward in his Rochester speech on Oct. 25, 1858, in which he offered a forecast that the socio-economic institutions of the North and those of the South were headed for a collision the outcome of which would be the domination of the country at large by either a system of free labor, on the one hand, or, on the other, a system of slave labor. The same idea had been formulated by Lincoln in his famous "house divided" speech of June 16, 1858. It had taken form even earlier, however, among both the defenders and the opponents of slavery. It did not necessarily imply a program to secure one or the other objective. The use of this phrase did not include the assumption that the "irrepressible conflict" would necessarily find expression in violence or armed conflict.

IRRIGATION began in the arid area of the North American continent during the Spanish regime. By the time the United States came into possession of the Mexican cession, irrigation institutions seem to have been rather firmly established. Irrigation by Americans began with the activities of the Mormons in Utah. They established numerous farm villages of five or six thousand acres each and from this co-operative method grew the plan of reclaiming by the irrigation district. By 1860 the improved farm land of the Mormons was valued at more than one and a third million dollars.

After the gold rush, irrigation developed rapidly in California. By 1866 there were 617 ditches irrigating 37,813 acres and by 1879 there were 890 ditches irrigating 255,646 acres. In California litigation over water rights led to the establishment of what became known as the "California Doctrine" which recognized the common law of riparian rights on private land and the doctrine of prior appropriation on public lands.

During the decade of the 1860's irrigation developed along the trails to the Far West and in Colorado. Under the impetus of the *New York Tribune* several colonies were established, and from these colonies developed what became known as the "Colorado Doctrine" which held that an appropriator received his water right from the state and that the doctrine of prior appropriation should be recognized on both private and public lands.

In the following decade the people of the arid West began to urge that the Federal Government amend the land laws to aid the development of irrigation. This movement resulted in the passage of the Desert Land Act on March 3, 1877, which provided that the Government sell up to 640 acres, at $1.25 per acre on terms, to any one who would reclaim the land within a period of three years. In spite of this

encouragement, irrigation did not develop rapidly until after the break in the cattle industry in the middle of the 1880's. Land and irrigation companies then began to be formed and irrigation entered a boom period resulting in overexpansion and disillusionment in the 1890's. The census of 1890 reported 3,631,381 acres being irrigated by 54,136 irrigators.

The recession in the development of irrigation was attributed to the fact that under the Desert Land Act the land could not be made a security for the cost of reclamation since the Government did not give title until after the land was reclaimed. The West again urged a change in the land laws, and Congress, on Aug. 18, 1894, passed the Carey Act which provided for the transfer of land up to a million acres to each state that would provide for the reclamation of the land. Under this act the states contracted with construction companies which reimbursed themselves by the sale of "water rights" and there followed, in the first decade of the new century, another boom. However, by 1910 it was apparent that the irrigation industry was due for another collapse, and the Carey Act bubble burst. In 1913 the general land office reported that although more than 7,000,000 acres had been applied for under the Carey Act, less than 500,000 acres of public land had been reclaimed. Of this 62% was in Idaho and 22% in Wyoming.

The failure of private enterprise to enter the irrigation field in the 1890's led to a movement for the construction of irrigation projects by the National Government. On June 17, 1902, the Newlands Reclamation Act was passed which provided for government construction of irrigation works from the proceeds of the sale of public lands. Repayment of the cost of construction was to be by the users of water over a period of ten years, without interest on the deferred payments. Between 1902 and 1907 twenty-five projects were started. By 1910 395,646 acres had been brought under irrigation with 786,190 acres capable of being irrigated under the government system. But like private projects and the projects of irrigation districts, the projects of the Government were, in the main, financial failures; Congress was besieged to make advances to the reclamation fund and to extend the term of payment to the settlers, and, by an act of Aug. 13, 1914, the settlers were permitted to repay over a period of twenty years.

World War I was a boon to irrigation, but the close of the war, with the resulting changes in agriculture, spelled doom to success in the financing of irrigation, either private or government. Private irrigation projects were reorganized into irrigation districts and in a number of states irrigation districts had their bonds backed by the state governments. By 1930 better than 50% of the irrigation districts had failed and the states began to rescind the legislation guaranteeing the bonds. The Federal projects fared little better. A "fact-finders" committee reported in April, 1924, that the Government should write off as loss more than $27,500,000, which did not include the subsidy given to the projects by the no-interest provision.

In the United States the rate of recent increase is illustrated by California, which has led in irrigation, and which by 1960 contained a quarter of all the irrigated lands in the country. In 1870 there were 60,000 acres under irrigation, while by 1952 the area irrigated in that state amounted to more than 7,000,000 acres. This increase has been achieved by means of more and more imposing dams, reservoirs and other structures, such as the world never saw until the second quarter of the 20th century. The cost of arid land irrigation in the United States has been about $2,000,000,000, and the value of the annual crop production on the irrigated land is about a quarter of that total cost.

ISLAND NUMBER TEN, OPERATIONS AT (1862). From March 15 to April 7, six ironclads and ten mortar boats commanded by Flag-Officer Andrew H. Foote (U.) co-operated with Maj. Gen. John Pope's 25,000 men in capturing this island. Located in the upper part of a triple bend of the Mississippi, 55 miles below Cairo, it was protected by 49 guns on the island and the opposite Tennessee shore, a floating battery of 9 guns and 12,000 men. The decisive factor was the running of the batteries at night by the *Carondelet* and *Pittsburg*. This enabled Pope's forces to cross the river south of the island and capture about half the Confederate defenders. It was the first achievement in a campaign to divide the Confederacy by gaining control of the Mississippi.

ISOLATIONISM. In the first two terms of Pres. F. D. Roosevelt, the United States with decreasing tenacity held to a policy of isolation in world affairs. Before his first election President Roosevelt had stated: "We are opposed to any official participation in purely European affairs or to committing ourselves to act in unknown contingencies." However, he favored continued co-operation with the League of Nations in all matters "which bear on the general good of mankind." As President he did not favor "American participation" in world affairs, as he deemed it necessary to concentrate on domestic problems created by the depression of the 1930's. There was a certain willingness to co-operate in furthering the world disarmament program, but no effort was made by the Roosevelt administration to join the World Court. Isolation increased in the face of a growing threat of war in Europe. Congress insisted on a policy of strict neutrality, and the Roosevelt administration continued its deep involvement in domestic affairs. The bitter opposition of Sen. Borah, Hiram Johnson and Norris was vehemently supported by the Hearst press and the Detroit radio priest Father Coughlin.

Japanese efforts to establish dominance and control in the Far East, German occupation of Austria and the Sudetenland and the Munich conference were followed by the German compact with Soviet Russia and an attack on Poland in September, 1939. The United States could not stand by, indifferent. However, in spite of general public sympathy for England and France, isolationism persisted though with steadily diminishing power. The United States was gradually and inexorably drawn into the conflict. The lend-lease program of March, 1941, the revision of the neutrality law in November, 1941, and the Japanese "sneak" attack on Pearl Harbor, Dec. 7, 1941, in the words of Sen. Arthur H. Vandenberg, leader of the isolationists, "ended isolationism for any realist." The United States entered its second world war in 25 years as a belligerent.

The progress of World War II to a victorious conclusion on all fronts for the United States and its allies so broke down isolationist sentiment that the Senate, supported by public opinion in the move for collective international security, approved United States membership in the United Nations, July 28, 1945, by an all but unanimous vote. Four years later, on July 21, 1949, the Senate approved United States membership in the North Atlantic Treaty Organization (N.A.T.O.), characterized by President Truman as the result of "the collective judgment of the people."

JACKSON HOLE, a valley in western Wyoming, east of the Teton Range and south of Yellowstone Park, was for several years one of the best-known trappers' rendezvous. While no doubt seen earlier by trappers, it was apparently named for David E. Jackson who spent the winter of 1829 there.

JACKSON'S VALLEY CAMPAIGN (1862). In the early part of 1862, when McClellan (U.) removed his army to the Virginia Peninsula for a march on Richmond, all available Confederate troops were sent to that place except a small force left in the Shenandoah Valley under "Stonewall" Jackson. President Lincoln had directed that a large Union force under McDowell be detained at Fredericksburg and vicinity to be ready to protect Washington from attack and to watch Jackson. At the proper time it was planned to send McDowell to McClellan.

It became Jackson's mission to harass the Union troops in the valley, thus directing Lincoln's attention from Richmond to the defense of Washington. It was hoped to keep McDowell from joining McClellan. If his operations were successful, Jackson would join Lee. McClellan, as he advanced, constantly shifted his right to join with McDowell when he arrived.

In a masterly campaign of deception and unexpected maneuver, Jackson more than fulfilled his mission. Though greatly outnumbered, he usually managed to have a superior force at the point of contact. He struck first at Kernstown on March 23, 1862. Though repulsed, he created much alarm. Six weeks later, as McClellan approached Richmond, Jackson defeated Milroy (U.) at McDowell and drove him down the valley. Two weeks later, at Front Royal and at Strasburg, Jackson struck again. Lincoln cancelled McDowell's orders to join McClellan. Sharp fights at Cross Keys and at Port Republic followed. The Union forces were scattered; the Washington authorities were distracted. Jackson now controlled the situation in the valley. His objective had been accomplished. In 35 days he had marched 250 miles, fought four battles and won them all. On June 21 he began to transfer his command to Lee's army at Richmond.

JACOBIN CLUBS (Democratic Societies) were organized first in Philadelphia and later in other cities, after the arrival of Genêt in Philadelphia in 1793. Modeled after the Jacobin Clubs in Paris they sought to propagate democratic views on American politics and to arouse support for the principles of the French Revolution and for the French government in its struggle against the European powers allied against it. They opposed most of the measures of Washington's administration and bitterly assailed Washington himself.

JAMES RIVER AND KANAWHA CANAL began in 1785 as the James River Company. In 1832 the river improvement scheme was broadened to include a canal to connect Richmond with the Ohio by way of the James, Greenbrier, New and Kanawha Rivers. Virginia, Richmond and Lynchburg subscribed most of the funds, and the canal was finished to Buchanan in 1851, where construction was abandoned owing to growing financial difficulties. The canal contributed materially to the development of the James River Valley and to the growth of Richmond. After the Civil War it failed to regain its prosperity, due to railroad competition, and in 1880 was sold to the Chesapeake and Ohio Railroad which abandoned the canal and used its towpath for a railroad.

JAMESTOWN. The Virginia Company of London, or London Company, sent out three ships late in 1606 to found a colony in Virginia. They were the *Sarah Constant*, 100 tons, Capt. Christopher Newport, Admiral; *Goodspeed*, 40 tons, Capt. Bartholomew Gosnold, Vice Admiral and promoter of the Virginia enterprise; and *Discovery*, 20 tons, Capt. John Ratcliffe. They first sighted land at Cape Henry, April 26, 1607. The Company's sealed box of instructions was then opened, and Gosnold, Newport, Ratcliffe, Capt. John Smith, Edward Maria Wingfield, a London merchant, John Martin and George Kendall were found named as composing the governing council of the new colony. They paused at and christened Point Comfort, April 30, and on May 13 cast anchor at a marshy island 32 miles from the mouth of the James, one of the worst possible places to found a colony,

but quite near the spot where Ayllon's colony of 1526 had its brief existence. Wingfield was elected president of the Council, and the colonists were disembarked on the 14th. On an enclosure of slightly more than an acre, rude huts covered with sedge and earth were erected. A few even made dugouts in the ground. A small fort was built and on some higher ground farther back from the river wheat was sown. An Indian attack occurred almost immediately, but was beaten off with a loss of one killed and eleven wounded. Dissension and distrust appeared among the settlers at the very beginning. Newport departed for England with small cargoes on the *Sarah Constant* and *Goodspeed*, on June 22, leaving 104 to 108 persons in the settlement. An Indian siege followed, and the inhabitants were reduced almost to starvation. They had only the brackish river water to drink, for a well was not dug until the following year. Disease next appeared, probably for the most part malaria and dysentery, and more than sixty persons died, among them Gosnold on Sept. 1. Kendall, accused of treachery, was shot, and Wingfield was deposed as president of the Council. Wingfield had made charges against Smith and John Robinson, which brought about the first jury trial in Anglo-Saxon America, Sept. 17, 1607, Smith being awarded £200 damages for slander, and Robinson £100.

By September the Indians were friendly and were sending supplies of corn and wild meat. In December Smith went on an exploring trip up the Chickahominy, but was captured by Indians, who killed his two companions, though he—saved by Pocahontas, according to tradition—was spared and returned to Jamestown. On the same day Newport returned, finding only 38 or 40 colonists still surviving, but bringing 120 more. Five days after Newport's return, fire destroyed the village, even the palisades. Some persons died from exposure, and the buildings were only partially replaced during the winter. Newport departed again in April, 1608, and on the 20th another ship arrived with forty additional settlers. This vessel returned in June with a cargo of cedar timber. In October, seventy more recruits came, including two women, the first to arrive. In the winter of 1609–10 famine almost depopulated the colony, and the remnant, disheartened, were starting for England in June when they met Lord Delawarr, the new governor, at the mouth of the James with provision ships, and all turned back. The cultivation of tobacco, begun by John Rolfe in 1612, gave the colony new economic life, but in 1616 there were (according to Rolfe) only 351 inhabitants in Jamestown and thereabouts, and many were despondent. Thereafter growth was more rapid, however. In 1619 the first legislative assembly in America was held at Jamestown, and slavery was introduced when a few Negroes were brought from Africa. The fortified village was a place of refuge for those outside during the Great Massacre of 1622. In 1640 the first brick house on the continent was erected. In 1676 the town was burned during Bacon's Rebellion against Gov. Berkeley, so that it might no longer "harbor the rogues." It was during the rebuilding, between 1676 and 1684, that the brick church, whose ruined tower survives in the 20th century, was erected. But Jamestown was now doomed—in fact, it had been doomed from the very outset. Its population was dwindling, and for years there was talk of moving the capital elsewhere. When in October, 1698, another fire swept it and destroyed the little state house and the homes of the three or four families still remaining, it was decided to move the seat of government to the Middle Plantation (Williamsburg), which was accomplished in 1699. That was the end. Probably no other pioneer town had ever suffered such vicissitudes. Even the site of the place would have disappeared long ago from the river's erosion had not a sea wall been built through the efforts of the Society for the Preservation of Virginia Antiquities.

JAY-GARDOQUI NEGOTIATIONS. The beginning of Spanish-American diplomatic relations in 1783 found serious issues existing between the two nations: the question of the navigation of the Mississippi, which Spain claimed exclusively where it ran between Spanish banks; the southern boundary of the United States—Spain did not accept that established by the Definitive Treaty of Peace; sovereignty over the Indians within the disputed territory; and lack of any treaty of commerce. Diego de Gardoqui came to the United States in 1784 and endeavored to make a treaty with John Jay, Secretary of Foreign Affairs for the Continental Congress, to settle all these issues. The two diplomatists agreed on the main terms of a treaty (never signed, however) in 1786 by which the United States would have "forborne" to exercise the navigation of the Mississippi for thirty years in return for favorable commercial privileges in Spanish European ports, and the boundary presumably would have been settled by a compromise that would give the United States nearly all it claimed. Opposition of the Southern states, with their western (Mississippi) appanages, blocked any chance of ratification; indeed this opposition was one of the principal reasons which caused the inclusion in the national Constitution of 1787 of a provision requiring a two-thirds majority of Senators present for the ratification of any treaty.

JAYHAWKERS. A named applied to the Free State bands in the Kansas-Missouri border war (1857–59), particularly the band captained by Dr. (later Col.) Charles R. Jennison, and to the unionist guerrilla bands during the Civil War. It was applied also to the Seventh Kansas Cavalry, commanded by Col. Jennison. Because of real and alleged depredations committed by the Jayhawkers, the term became one of opprobrium. The origin of the word is uncertain, but it appears to have been coined by a party of gold seekers from Galesburg, Ill., in 1849, and to have

been used in early California. The traditional stories of its origin in Kansas are obviously apocryphal. Since the Civil War, Jayhawker has become the popular nickname for a Kansan.

JAY'S TREATY, signed Nov. 19, 1794, adjusted a group of serious Anglo-American diplomatic issues arising out of the Definitive Treaty of Peace of 1783, subsequent commercial difficulties, and distressing issues over neutral rights.

The principal issues arising out of the treaty of peace were: Great Britain's deliberate refusal to evacuate six controlling frontier forts in American territory along the northern river-and-lake boundary established by the treaty; obstacles of state courts to the collection of prewar debts by British creditors, despite the guarantees of the treaty of peace; alleged confiscation by states of property of returning Loyalists in violation of treaty protection against any such acts after the peace; and unsettled boundary gaps. To these grievances were added: the refusal of Great Britain to admit American ships into the ports of her remaining colonies in North America and the West Indies; to make a treaty of commerce, or even to exchange diplomatic representatives, during the period of the Confederation, 1783–89; and her active intrigue with the western Indian tribes, allies of Great Britain during the Revolution, now left within the boundaries of the United States. It was the hope of the British government to establish north of the Ohio River a "neutral Indian barrier state" as the price of any settlement with the United States, or even to put off any settlement at all in expectation of the ultimate breakup of the feeble American Confederation.

The new Constitution of the United States of 1787, and the National Government of President George Washington established in 1789 checked these expectations. New national navigation laws, championed by James Madison in Congress, and supported by Secretary of State Thomas Jefferson, leader of the crystallizing Republican party (Jeffersonian), revealed the possibility of serious discrimination against British trade by its best foreign customer and induced Pitt's (the younger) government to send a minister, George Hammond, to the United States in 1791, empowered to "discuss" issues. These discussions had produced nothing by the time war broke out between France and Great Britain on Feb. 1, 1793, largely because Alexander Hamilton, Secretary of the Treasury, assured Hammond that he would try to block any commercial discrimination against Great Britain. Hamilton had just restored American credit by a fiscal system that depended for its revenues on import duties, and nine tenths of that revenue came from taxes on imports from Great Britain. A commercial war might thus mean the collapse of American credit and with it of the newly established American nationality.

Arbitrary British naval orders in 1793 and consequent capture of hundreds of American neutral ships, combined with a bellicose speech of Lord Dorchester, Governor General of Canada, to the western Indians, precipitated the "war crisis" of 1794. Hamilton and the Federalist leaders pressed Washington to stop short of commercial reprisals (Congress did vote an embargo for two months) while Chief Justice John Jay was sent to London as Minister Plenipotentiary and Envoy Extraordinary on a special peace mission. In the negotiations with Lord Grenville, British Secretary for Foreign Affairs, Jay could have made more of the American cause. On Hamilton's secret advice (Jefferson had now been succeeded by Edmund Randolph as Secretary of State), Jay acquiesced in British maritime measures for the duration of the war, in return for the creation of a mixed commission to adjudicate American spoliation claims ($10,345,200 ultimately paid by 1802) for damages made "under color" of British Orders in Council (not in themselves repudiated); Great Britain agreed to evacuate the frontier posts by June 1, 1796 (executed on time); the United States guaranteed the payment of British private prewar debts, the total amount to be worked out by another mixed commission (£600,000 *en bloc* settlement made in 1802); and two mixed boundary commissions were set up to establish correctly the line in the northwest (this one never met) and in the northeast (agreed on identity of the St. Croix).

Washington got the treaty through the Senate and the House (where the Republicans tried to block the necessary appropriations) only with great difficulty. The temporary acquiescence in British maritime measures was the price which the Federalists paid for: (1) redemption of American territorial integrity in the Northwest, (2) peace with Great Britain when peace was necessary for the perpetuation of American nationality. On her part Great Britain was anxious for a treaty: (1) to keep her best foreign customer, (2) to keep the United States as a neutral during the European war then raging.

JAZZ is a distinctly American music developed primarily by the American Negro from harmonic, melodic and rhythmic sources of European and African origin during the latter half of the 19th century. The word "jazz" has been attributed to French, Arabian and Creole sources. Jazz differed from all other music because it was improvised and almost always played in strict tempo, four beats to the bar.

The earliest forms of jazz were: ragtime, a syncopated piano music developed largely in Missouri; vocal blues and work songs sung by the Negro throughout the South; spirituals evolved from English, French and Spanish religious music; and brass band music. Jazz was played for dancing by small combinations of three to eight pieces throughout the United States although largely concentrated in the major cities.

Few early jazz musicians had legitimate training

and they played in ensemble style, with only occasional improvised solos. Many musicians from New Orleans, perhaps the most important early source, toured on vaudeville routes to California, Chicago and New York and made lasting impressions on budding musicians everywhere. Trumpeter Freddie Keppard's Original Creole Band played the Pantages Circuit from 1912–17 and the white Original Dixieland Jazz Band played Chicago in 1915 and New York in 1917 and became the first jazz unit to record when Victor signed them that year.

Many of the best musicians left New Orleans after 1917, when the infamous Storyville section was closed by the Navy. Cornetist Joseph "King" Oliver soon established the leading jazz band in Chicago. Louis Armstrong joined him in 1922.

New York became the center of the commercial music industry. Pianist Fletcher Henderson, a graduate of Atlanta University working for composer W. C. Handy (creator of *St. Louis Blues* and other jazz standards), and conservatory-trained saxophonist and arranger Don Redman organized the first big band to play specially written arrangements.

Cornetists Red Nichols and Bix Beiderbecke, the New Orleans Rhythm Kings, the Original Memphis Five and other white combinations were playing and recording throughout the East and Middle West, establishing group and solo styles based to some degree on earlier pioneers' efforts. Combos throughout the country developed original styles and became the large orchestras of the late '20's and early '30's. Although clarinetist Ted Lewis represented jazz to the public, Fletcher Henderson and a handful of other leaders set the pattern for the Swing Era.

Vocal blues sung principally by Ma Rainey and Bessie Smith were extremely popular and were marketed on "race" records for sale only in Negro areas. Okeh, Paramount and the Negro firm Black Swan dominated the field until other major firms established their line.

Commercial music interests shifted to crooning vocals and heavily arranged, sweet music during the depression. Talking movies, radio, records and the jukebox closed many ballrooms and few jazz bands worked regularly. Others dropped their original scores and used publishers' stock arrangements. Louis Armstrong and Duke Ellington went overseas as had others since 1915, and American jazz bands played throughout the world until World War II.

In 1935 clarinetist Benny Goodman, who formerly worked in recording studios, ushered in the Swing Era with his touring orchestra. His success was largely due to specially written arrangements, made by Fletcher and Horace Henderson, Benny Carter and others, which took popular tunes of the day out of the music publishers' domain and swung them. For five years prior, Glen Gray's Casa Lomans and the Dorsey Brothers had tried and only partially succeeded. Small groups found work on New York's

52nd Street and vocalists Mildred Bailey, Billie Holiday and Ella Fitzgerald evolved new vocal styles. Goodman also helped break the color line by employing pianist Teddy Wilson and later, vibraphonist Lionel Hampton.

Swing soon became commercial and repetitious. Trumpeter Dizzy Gillespie, saxophonist Charlie Parker, guitarist Charlie Christian, pianist Thelonious Monk and drummer Kenny Clarke broke tradition in after-hours jam sessions in Harlem and Kansas City. Their music was called bebop by 1944. Their inspiration came from Art Tatum's and Count Basie's piano arrangements; Lester Young's and Buster Smith's saxophones; Jimmy Blanton's bass and Jo Jones' drums. Their improvisations and compositions were based on harmony and chord structure rather than on melody. Their music was difficult to play and required exceptional technique. It produced vocalist Sarah Vaughan, whose style was drawn from her church background.

By 1950 bebop retreated to an introspective "cool" jazz typified by Miles Davis' trumpet and the arrangements of Gil Evans and Gerry Mulligan. A movement to merge jazz with classical forms was unsuccessful.

The rhythms, harmony and fervor of the music of the gospel church have played a large part in the success of artists like Cannonball Adderley, Horace Silver, Ray Charles, Ray Bryant, Dakota Staton and Aretha Franklin.

JEFFERSON-BURR ELECTION DISPUTE. Jefferson and Burr were the Republican (Jeffersonian) candidates for the Presidency and Vice-Presidency, respectively, in the acrimonious campaign of 1800. Due to the growing effectiveness of the two-party system, the Republican candidates each received 73 votes in the electoral college, with the Federalist vote split 65 for John Adams, 64 for C. C. Pinckney and 1 for John Jay. Thus, the election went to the Republicans. But as the vote for Jefferson and Burr was exactly equal, the opportunity for a quibble was presented. According to the Constitution as it then stood, "The Person having the greatest Number of Votes shall be the President, if such Number be a Majority of the whole Number of Electors appointed; and if there be more than one who have such Majority, and have an equal Number of Votes, then the House of Representatives shall immediately chuse by Ballot one of them for President." Accordingly, the election was thrown into the House. But, again by the wording of the Constitution, "in chusing the President, the Votes shall be taken by States, the Representation from each State having one Vote; A quorum for this Purpose shall consist of a Member or Members from two thirds of the States, and a Majority of all the States shall be necessary to a Choice." The Federalists, still in control from the elections of 1798 and despite the opposition of Hamilton and other reputable leaders, and in cynical disregard of popular interest,

schemed to put Burr into the highest office of the land. Jefferson received the vote of eight states; Burr of six; while Maryland and Vermont were equally divided. Thus, there was no majority as among the sixteen states then belonging to the Union. For weeks a sordid intrigue went on amid rumors of forcible resistance should the scheme succeed. On Feb. 17, on the thirty-sixth ballot, the Federalist members of Maryland and Vermont declined to vote. Jefferson now had the votes of ten states and was declared elected. The Twelfth Amendment, correcting the procedure of the electoral college, became effective before the next election, but the "lame duck" Congress, an important factor in this sinister episode, remained unreformed until 1933.

JEFFERSON TERRITORY was a spontaneous provisional government which had a precarious existence in Colorado from 1859 to 1861.

JEFFERSON'S PROPOSED STATES. Virginia ceded her western land claims to the United States, March 1, 1784. The same day Thomas Jefferson as chairman submitted to Congress a committee report, drafted by himself, for the future disposition of the western lands. The report, variously amended, was enacted April 23, and is known as the Ordinance of 1784.

Although the ordinance never became operative, being superseded by the Ordinance of 1787, some of its provisions, as reported by Jefferson, contributed notably to the development of our nascent constitutional system. It provided for the division of the western country into convenient units, whose citizens might set up temporary governments, which on attaining 20,000 free inhabitants should be replaced by permanent state governments, republican in form and duly subordinate to the United States. Slavery (after 1800), nullification and secession were to be forever prohibited.

The solid merits of the document are sufficient to command for it the permanent interest of Americans. Unfortunately, however, the popular attention has too often been diverted from their appreciation by the impractical scheme of state boundaries and nomenclature which Jefferson embodied in the report. The area embraced by it was the entire West, from Florida northward to Canada and from Pennsylvania westward to the Mississippi. This was to be subdivided by parallels of latitude two degrees apart, beginning at the thirty-first, and by meridians of longitude running through the Falls of the Ohio and the mouth of the Great Kanawha, thereby making provision for sixteen future states. Since the states south of Virginia had not yet ceded their western claims, the report identified and named only the ten states included within the Virginia cession. Apart from that of Washington, which occupied the eastern part of modern Ohio, these states comprised two tiers, running from north to south. Beginning at the north, those comprising the eastern tier were named Cherronesus, Metropotamia, Saratoga and Pelisipia; the states of the western tier were named Sylvania, Michigania, Assenisipia, Illinoia and Polypotamia. Although Jefferson was a man of brilliant intellect, his theories frequently ignored the practical facts of life. Apart from the absurd nomenclature, the proposals for subdividing the western country into many small states, bounded by meridians and parallels, ignored the plainest facts of geography, with their consequent implications upon the economic and political interests of the people inhabiting the region. Thus the Lower Peninsula of Michigan, which constitutes a homogeneous geographical and political unit, would have been split between the four states of Cherronesus, Metropotamia, Michigania and Assenisipia; while, except for the State of Washington, the Ohio River, as a natural boundary, was completely ignored.

JEHOVAH'S WITNESSES are a religious group initiated by an American Congregationalist layman, Charles Taze Russell (1852–1916), in 1872. Witnesses believe that the rule of Satan over the world will soon be destroyed and that God's theocracy will be established.

JENKINS' EAR, WAR OF (1739–43), was a fouryear struggle between England and Spain, preliminary to and merging into the War of the Austrian Succession (King George's War), and ridiculously named for Robert Jenkins, a British smuggler who lost an ear in a brush with the Spaniards off the coast of Florida. Commercial rivalry on the seas and disputes over the ownership of Georgia were responsible for the conflict. War was declared in June, 1739, and was fought on land and water, with the Caribbean the center of naval operations and the Georgia-Florida borderlands the scene of military warfare.

Admiral Vernon captured Puerto Bello on the Isthmus of Panama in 1739, but the following year met with disastrous failure before Cartagena. James Edward Oglethorpe, after having clinched friendship with the Creeks at a great meeting on the Chattahoochee, invaded Florida in early 1740 and seized two forts on the St. Johns River. In the following summer he attacked St. Augustine, but failed to take it. In 1742 the Spaniards with a force of 5000 men sought to end the Georgia colony, but were turned back at the battle of Bloody Marsh, on St. Simon Island. The next year Oglethorpe again invaded Florida without success.

JERSEY PRISON-SHIP. This dismantled 64-gun British man-of-war, moored in Wallabout Bay, the present site of the Brooklyn Navy Yard, was used for the confinement of American naval prisoners during the Revolution. Though she was only one of several prison-ships moored in New York harbor, she became notorious for ill-usage of the prisoners. Rations were inadequate, often damaged and poorly cooked. Though as many as 1200 were confined aboard her at one time, all prisoners, able-bodied, sick and dying, were sent below at night, where the heat, vermin and stench were intolerable. Dysentery, smallpox and yellow fever were prevalent, and the death rate appalling.

JESUIT MISSIONS. The first Jesuits to labor in the territory which is now the United States were a Spanish group who conducted an abortive mission during the period 1566–71 in the vast region then known as Florida. In 1566 Father Pedro Martínez, founder of the mission, was slain by Indians and in 1571 Father John Baptist Segura and seven companions met the same fate, somewhere, it would appear, in the region of the Rappahannock. In the following century French Jesuits organized the Mission of Canada or New France, the initial post being set up in 1611 in Acadia, under Fathers Pierre Biard and Ennemond Massé.

In 1625 the Jesuits were at Quebec, which they made the headquarters of their missionary operations in New France. The first of their number to reach mid-America were Fathers Isaac Jogues, now a canonized saint, and Charles Raymbaut, who in 1641 journeyed west to attend an Indian powwow at the waters connecting Lakes Superior and Huron, the rapids of which were subsequently known as Sault Ste. Marie. They were followed in 1660 by Father René Ménard, Wisconsin's proto-missionary, who, until his death the following year, ministered to Indian groups of the Lake Superior region. He was in search of some scattered Hurons when he perished on the way, having been, in the course of this last journey, the first member of his order to penetrate the Mississippi Valley. Next to appear on the western missionary scene was Father Claude Allouez, who in 1665 founded at Chequamegon Bay near the western extremity of Lake Superior the Ottawa-Huron Mission of La Pointe du Saint Esprit. Other posts were established by him, among them, St. Francis Xavier's at Green Bay and St. Mark's among the Fox Indians. His career of 24 years, 1665–89, throbbed with activity, the range and success of his missionary labors earning for him the sobriquet of "the apostle of the West."

In 1668 Father Jacques Marquette began at Sault Ste. Marie an Algonkian mission, around which grew up the earliest white settlement in the State of Michigan. Two years later, in the winter of 1670–71, was established the Mission of St. Ignace on behalf of the Huron and other tribes driven from La Pointe by the Sioux. Located first on Mackinac Island, it was later moved across the straits to the northern mainland. From St. Ignace, where he was resident missionary, Marquette set out with his fellow explorer Jolliet on their famous Mississippi expedition of 1673. In 1675 the same Jesuit inaugurated among the Kaskaskia, an Illinois tribe, the Mission of the Immaculate Conception. This historic center of evangelical enterprise, the first in the Mississippi Valley, was moved in 1691 from its first location near Starved Rock on the Illinois River to Lake Peoria, thence, 1700, to the site of the future St. Louis and, finally, 1703, to the Kaskaskia River, where it was maintained until 1763.

Other centers of Jesuit missionary activity among the western tribes were the Sioux Mission of St. Michael the Archangel, 1727, on the west bank of Lake Pepin at the present Frontenac, Minn.; the station opened, *ca.* 1739, among the Wyandot Hurons settled at Sandusky Bay in Ohio; and the Huron Mission of the Assumption, located *ca.* 1742, on Bois Blanc Island in the Detroit River and later moved to the site of Sandwich, Ontario. Nor were the aborigines in other sections of the future United States left unattended. There were Jesuit missions among the Iroquois of the Mohawk Valley, the Abenaki of the Kennebec, Penobscot and St. John Rivers, and among the Yazoo, Alibamons, Choctaw and Arkansas of the South. In the Southwest the missionary career of Father Eusebio Francisco Kino, marked by the founding, 1700, of the famous Mission of San Xavier del Bac, near the site of Tucson, Ariz., was noteworthy. The California missions associated with the labors of the Jesuits Salvatierra and Kino were in Lower or Mexican California.

Owing to Indian wars, lack of personnel and other circumstances, the Jesuit missions of colonial America were gradually suspended. About the last to survive were those of the Illinois country and these were swept away by the expulsion of the missionaries from that region by the Louisiana authorities in 1763. The story of the missions has been put on record in the *Jesuit Relations*, a rich mine of religious, geographical and ethnological data indispensable to the historian of colonial America. Yet success in converting and civilizing the Indians was not on the whole conspicuous. Typical causes of the failure of the missionaries to achieve more substantial results are detailed by one of their number, Father François Philibert Watrin, in an informing memoir in the *Relations* (Thwaites, ed.), LXX, 211 ff.

Nineteenth-century Jesuit work among the American Indians is especially identified with the career of Father Peter J. DeSmet, 1801–73, founder of the Catholic Rocky Mountain Missions, the more notable of which were those for the Flatheads, Coeur d'Alènes and Kalispel. The Potawatomi and Osage of Kansas were also successfully evangelized by Jesuits from St. Louis.

In 1886 two Jesuits, Rev. Pashal Tosi, S. J.—later first Prefect Apostolic—and Aloysius Robaut, S. J., accompanied the future Archbishop Seghers from the states into Alaska to found the first permanent mission there.

At present, Alaska is divided into the diocese of Juneau—the southern coast of Alaska from Juneau to Anchorage—and the Vicariate of Alaska—the rest of the new state. The Vicariate under the direction of His Excellency, Most Rev. Francis Gleeson, S. J., Vicar Apostolic, is still missionary territory. From his headquarters in Fairbanks, Bishop Gleeson directs the work of 38 Jesuits who maintain sixteen parishes, many scattered mission stations, and three high schools.

JESUIT RELATIONS. Each Jesuit missionary was required to report every year to his superior the events of his mission, the prospects for exploration and all he had learned of the regions in which he dwelt. These reports were then made up into a yearly *Relation* and forwarded to the chief of the order in France or Rome. These *Relations* were published beginning with 1632 in order to stimulate the zeal and interest of the people at home. The Jesuit missionaries being educated men and careful observers wrote reports of the regions of Canada, the Great Lakes and the Mississippi Valley that could not be surpassed. They were published in annual volumes, which were known as the "Relation of 1632" or the corresponding year, sometimes including the name of the editor, as the "Relation of 1673 by Claude Dablon." In the latter year the publication was suspended; the missionaries, however, continued to send in reports, which remained in manuscript for almost two centuries.

There were in all 41 separate *Relations* published, and it has been the aim of collectors of Americana to complete their list of *Jesuit Relations*. Several American libraries have full sets of the originial *Relations*. In 1896 an edition was begun which included not only the published *Relations*, but other documents secured from many sources in America and Europe. This edition, edited by Reuben G. Thwaites, was known as the *Jesuit Relations and Allied Documents,* and extended in time from 1610 to 1791. It was published in 73 volumes, with the original French or Latin on the left-hand page, the translation into English opposite. It forms a source of unusual quality for the primitive conditions of the North American continent, the accounts of the fauna and flora, descriptions of the lakes, rivers and country, mention of indications of minerals and other resources. Especially is it valuable for the customs, habits, habitat and migrations of the tribesmen of this great continent, and of the impact of civilization on uncivilized barbarians. But for the *Jesuit Relations*, knowledge of the discoveries, explorations and conditions in North America in the 17th and early 18th century would be meager.

JESUITS is the conventional designation for members of the Society of Jesus, a religious order of men founded by St. Ignatius Loyola (1491–1556) and formally approved by the Holy See Sept. 27, 1540. The Jesuits were an influence in the development of colonial America, particularly through their explorations and missions. They were associated with the Calverts in the founding of Maryland, 1634; they inaugurated the Catholic ministry in the Middle Atlantic states, the upper Great Lakes region and the Mississippi Valley, making at the same time contributions of interest to the economic and cultural beginnings of the territory in which they worked.

Jesuit activities in post-colonial America date from the organization of the Maryland Mission of the order in 1805. From Maryland the order spread to the Middle West, opening in 1823 at Florissant, in Missouri, what proved to be a starting point of subsequent far-flung expansion. In 1841 it became established in the Pacific Northwest and in 1849 in California. Meantime, Jesuit houses had been opened in Kentucky, 1832, Louisiana, 1837, and New York, 1846. The activities of the Society of Jesus have been and continue to be highly diversified. They range from Indian missions and the parochial ministry to the preaching of popular missions, attendance in hospitals and prisons, and other sorts of ministerial or social service. But the major interest is education. The first American Jesuit college, Georgetown, dates from 1789. St. Louis University, oldest school of university grade west of the Mississippi, has been conducted by the Jesuits since 1829.

Educational institutions under their management in the United States, parochial schools apart, total 71, of which 28 are universities or colleges and 43 high schools. The American Jesuits, organized into ten provinces or administrative units, numbered 8052 in 1959, the total membership of the order being 34,016.

JEWS IN THE UNITED STATES. *The Sephardic Period (1649–1840).*

After the fall of Jerusalem, 70 A. D., Jewish life remained centered in the Orient for another thousand years. Then Jewry's spiritual focus shifted to Europe. Expelled from or driven underground in Spain and Portugal after 1492, many Spanish and Portuguese Jews (Sephardim) settled as crypto-Jews in the Iberian colonies of the Western Hemisphere. When the Dutch lost Brazil to the Portuguese in 1654, twenty-three Jewish émigrés took refuge in New Amsterdam in September of that year. This marked the beginning of Jewish community life in continental North America, although there had been a Jewish businessman in Boston in 1649.

Jews came to America from Europe during the 17th and 18th centuries to escape religious persecution and political disabilities as well as to advance themselves economically. By the 1720's, the majority here were of German or East European stock (Ashkenazim), although all congregations then followed the Sephardic synagogal ritual. Many lived in the six towns of Montreal, Newport, New York, Philadelphia, Charleston, and Savannah. By 1776 there were about 2500 Jews in England's North American colonies. They enjoyed civil rights, but could not hold honorific office. A large number were shopkeepers, merchants and merchant shippers. The Franks, of New York—who were also army purveyors—and Aaron Lopez, of Newport, were important merchant shippers. The religious community centered in the synagogue. Services were conducted by a cantor, and a measure of religious education was also available. At intervals, the New York synagogue provided secular education. Charities were also the concern of the synagogal community.

After the colonies seceded from the British Empire, New York was the first state to enfranchise the Jews completely (1777); New Hampshire, in 1877, was the last.

The Period of the Rise and Dominance of the German Jews (1841–1920). Central Europeans (Ashkenazim) started coming to the United States in large numbers after the Napoleonic wars, seeking economic advancement. Many of them remained in tidewater towns, but by 1840 they had reached the Mississippi. By 1849, those in California had begun moving east towards the Mississippi. For the most part, these German Jews pursued some form of commerce, starting as clerks and peddlers and ending up as shopkeepers, merchants, and wholesalers. By the Civil War some were garment manufacturers; a few were private bankers. With prosperity, in the post-bellum period, came an interest in general culture and in Jewish literature. Individuals entered the professions of law and medicine; there had been Jewish officeholders ever since the late 18th century. Jewish life moved towards some degree of secularization as lodges of a mutual-aid type were established and autonomous local charities provided for the Jewish poor, widows, orphans and aged. Hospitals were first founded in the 1850's.

Encouraged by American religious freedom, Reform Judaism, brought to this country from Germany, achieved organizational form under Rabbi Isaac Mayer Wise (1819–1900), of Cincinnati. Influenced probably by the traditionalist Isaac Leeser (1806–68), of Philadelphia, Wise organized a moderately liberal congregational union in 1873, established a religious seminary in 1875, and united many of the Reform rabbis into a rabbinical conference in 1889. This pattern of organization was later adopted by the Orthodox and the middle-of-the-road group, the Conservatives.

The Period of the Coming of the East Europeans and Their Bid for Hegemony (1852–1920). Although there were always East European Jews in America, they did not arrive in large numbers until the 1850's, when Russian Jews began to emigrate because of bad economic conditions. After the pogroms of 1881, they came by the thousands, and from that year to 1924, about 2,388,000 arrived. Feeling rejected by the older Jewish settlers, the East Europeans established communities of their own. Thus, after their arrival in the

1850's, there were two Jewish "communities" here until about 1920. Many of these newcomers remained in New York, settling on the East Side.

The East European Jews were characterized by their adherence to a traditional type of orthodoxy, by their knowledge of Hebrew and rabbinic lore, and by their devotion to Jewish ritual and the dietary laws. Their language was Yiddish, and here they developed an extensive and vital Yiddish literature, theatre and press. The rise of nationalism in the late 19th century, the hope for a Messianic utopian state, the oppression they had suffered in Russia and the appearance of anti-Semitism made them sympathetic to Zionism. Those who went into the back country frequently became peddlers and shopkeepers. Substantial numbers of those who remained in New York City became workers in the garment industry. Four unions were developed by them in the 20th century: the International Ladies Garment Workers Union; the Amalgamated Clothing Workers; the United Cloth Hat, Cap, and Millinery Workers; and the International Fur and Leather Workers' Union. After their initial struggles with the employers, the first three of these unions devoted themselves increasingly to bringing about industrial stabilization and union-management co-operation. They won many social-welfare and cultural benefits for their members. The East European immigrant Jew was rarely either the son or the father of a proletarian. Respectful of learning, the immigrants sacrificed to give their children excellent secular educations. These children are often among the cultural élite of mid-20th-century American Jewry.

The Period of the Emerging American Jewish Community, the Age of Fusion (1921 to date). The immigration quota laws of 1921 and 1924 effectually stopped Jewish immigration to America. The immigrants here speedily assimilated themselves to an American way of life, and both the Jewish natives and the Jewish newcomers began a process of fusion that is now well advanced. An "American"-type Jew, similar to the homogeneous English or French or German Jew, is now emerging. Though many Jews still remain in the garment factories, their general tendency, since 1921, has been to become self-employed white-collar workers. Many Jews have turned to the sciences, particularly the physical sciences, and to the graphic and tonal arts. In the political area, they have held almost every office except the presidency and the vice-presidency. The assimilatory influence of Americanism and the dominant Christian culture has brought about the decline of orthodoxy. Many of its adherents have moved into the Conservative synagogue which occupies a strategic position halfway between the Reformed and the Orthodox.

By the 1930's, American Jewry had begun, informally at least, to build socio-cultural-religious communities which include a variety of service agencies paralleling those available to every American citizen. The spur to this apparently duplicate community came from several sources: American sectarian traditions, the Jewish desire to "take care of their own," the impact of an intensive Jewish education, Zionism, the traumatic effect of American anti-Semitism, and the Nazi murder of some 6,500,000 Jews. The Jewish community today maintains health and welfare agencies, massive hospitals, "parochial" schools (about 3% of the school children attend such schools), religious schools of all types, bureaus of Jewish education, socio-cultural community centers, country clubs, vocational guidance bureaus, and community relations committees to promote civil and religious liberties. There is an extensive, though inadequate, Anglo-Jewish press, a growing Hebrew press, and a still vigorous, though rapidly declining, Yiddish press. Every community of any size has a number of synagogues following the Reform, Conservative, or Orthodox traditions, but an American type of Judaism is emerging, laying emphasis on decorum, art music, the organ, and the English sermon. Strong efforts are being made to develop a liturgy that is aesthetic and appealing. Both the Conservatives and the Reformers tend increasingly to balance the extent of the Hebrew and the English texts, stressing, in the English paraphrase, the universalistic rather than the particularistic elements in Judaism. Since the 1930's the attempt has been made to co-ordinate all Jewish community agencies through an over-all community council with authority to plan and guide community life. This attempt has not been successful, and most local agencies remain semi-autonomous.

The local institutions are paralleled on the national scene by a series of agencies, and in effect they constitute the organs of an American Jewish national community. There is, however, no liaison between these various national agencies. They work autonomously in the areas of religious co-ordination, social welfare, overseas relief, Zionism, aid to Israel, Jewish education, civic defense, leisure and group work, as well as providing for the needs of Jews in the armed forces. There are rabbinical seminaries, schools for religious teachers, publishing houses and presses, and Jewish-sponsored secular universities.

By 1958 there were about 5,260,000 Jews in the United States. About 60% live in the cities of New York, Los Angeles, Chicago, Philadelphia, and Boston. Many are moving into the suburbs of all large cities. Continuing a trend begun in the second quarter of the century, typical American Jews are self-employed white-collar workers engaged in some form of trade, as managers or sales workers. An unusually large percentage has college degrees and is heavily represented in the professions. The Jew of the approaching 21st century will be a member of the middle class, politically liberal, strongly opposed to the union of Church and State, friendly to Judaism and

Jewish culture, sympathetic to the state of Israel, ready to identify with his fellow-Jews, and eager to effect a synthesis of Americanism and Judaism.

JOHNSTOWN FLOOD. Occurring simultaneously with lesser floods in twenty Pennsylvania counties, it resulted from the collapse of the Conemaugh Reservoir during a period of exceptionally heavy rainfall. The dam, constructed in 1852 as part of the old Pennsylvania canal system, had been rebuilt during 1879–81 to a height of eighty feet by Pittsburgh sportsmen to quadruple the original size of Conemaugh Lake, situated 275 feet above the Johnstown low flats.

On Friday morning, May 31, 1889, startled engineers observed the rapid sinking of the lake as its waters poured into the reservoir. Emphatic warnings were disregarded by many inhabitants of Conemaugh Valley as exaggerated. At 3:30 P.M. the earthen walls of the dam yielded, quickly inundating the entire valley in a powerful downward thrust. Halted by the Pennsylvania railway viaduct, just above Johnstown proper, the flood receded, causing destructive vortices, inducing a huge conflagration in the Cambria Iron Works, and annihilating most of Johnstown and its suburbs. At least 2142 persons perished; careful estimates claimed fully 5000. Property losses totaled over $10,000,000. Generous assistance came immediately from almost every civilized country, furnishing $3,742,818.

Recriminations were severe. The London *Chronicle* declared that the disaster revealed the shoddiness of American engineering. In New York City a newspaper controversy raged over the construction of the Quaker Bridge dam. To these attacks American engineers replied that the Conemaugh Reservoir did not even represent the best professional practices of an earlier generation, being the only dam in the United States over fifty feet in height without a central wall of masonry or puddle. Despite popular demands for an official investigation, none was held, but the Pennsylvania legislature permitted the legal consolidation of the Johnstown area for more effective civic cooperation.

JOLLIET AND MARQUETTE DISCOVERY (1673). Louis Jolliet was a native of New France who, after being educated at the Jesuit schools of Quebec, embarked on a career of exploration in the then far western country. On one of his voyages to Lake Superior in 1669 he met the Jesuit missionary, Jacques Marquette, then at the mission of Sault Ste. Marie. Three years later the authorities of New France commissioned Jolliet to undertake the discovery of the great central river of the continent, which the Indians had described and spoken of as the Mississippi. Jolliet requested that Marquette be appointed chaplain of the expedition, and late in the autumn of 1672 set out for the Northwest to prepare for the voyage.

Jolliet found Marquette at the mission of St. Ignace on the north shore of Mackinac Strait. Together they prepared maps and planned for the discovery during the ensuing winter; the map Marquette then drew still exists; later he traced the route of his discovery thereupon.

May 17, 1673, the two explorers left St. Ignace in two canoes with five *voyageurs*, "fully resolved to do and to suffer everything for so glorious an undertaking." They went by way of Lake Michigan, Green Bay and Fox River. As far as the upper villages on Fox River the way was well known; at the Mascouten village guides were obtained to lead them to the portage. Friendly Indians tried to dissuade the explorers, enlarging on the difficulties of the voyage; but the travelers pressed on, and a month from the time of departure their canoes shot out from the Wisconsin into a great river, which they instantly recognized as the stream they sought. Marquette wished to name the river the Conception for the immaculate conception of the Virgin Mary; Jolliet called it first the Buade, the family name of the Count de Frontenac, governor of New France. Ultimately he christened it the Colbert for the prime minister of France; but the Indian name has persisted.

The two explorers in their canoes drifted down the river as far as the Arkansas; they met few Indians and these for the most part friendly. They saw no monsters except painted ones on the cliffs high above the stream. They encountered no falls or whirlpools, and the voyage, while memorable, was not dangerous. From the Arkansas they turned back upstream, fearing to encounter Spaniards on the lower river. Acting on Indian advice they did not return to the Wisconsin-Fox waterway, but ascended the Illinois and the Des Plaines, portaging at Chicago to Lake Michigan. They were thus the first white men to stand on the site of that great city.

Returning by Lake Michigan and Green Bay to the mission at DePere, Marquette remained there to recruit his health. Jolliet, after a winter of exploring around the lake, went in 1674 to Canada to report his discovery. Just before reaching Montreal his canoe overturned in the rapids, and he lost all his journals, notes and maps, his own life being saved with difficulty. Thus Marquette's journal has become the official account of the voyage, and Jolliet's share has been somewhat minimized. Jolliet was an expert map maker, later the official hydrographer of New France; his maps of the expedition, however, were drawn from memory, and the Jesuit maps superseded his. The discovery was widely heralded in France, and formed the basis for the exploration and exploitation of the Mississippi Valley by LaSalle and other French voyagers in the late 17th century.

JUDICIAL REVIEW is the power of courts to declare legislative acts unconstitutional and thus invalid. It is the most important power possessed by the American Judiciary and, along with federalism, has been considered America's unique contribution to political science. Judicial review in the United States consists specifically of: (1) the power of Federal courts to decide whether or not an act of Congress is consonant with the provisions of the U. S. Constitution and hence to declare such acts valid or invalid; and (2) the power of courts to invalidate acts of state legislatures and overrule state court decisions in violation of the Constitution. Judicial review also includes the power of state courts to invalidate state legislation which conflicts with the state constitution. Although "state judicial review" has been important in U. S. constitutional history, it is no longer of great significance, a fact chiefly attributable to the great ease with which state constitutions are amended.

Many scholars have attempted to trace the origins of judicial review to the institutions of colonial America. Such attempts have been largely unsuccessful, although the review of the acts of the colonial assemblies by the judicial committee of the Privy Council in England is similar to the later review of state legislation by Federal courts. The first state constitutions, adopted soon after the outbreak of the Revolution, did not contemplate judicial review, although in three states (Pennsylvania, New York and Vermont) the constitution was protected by a council of censors or of revision. These early constitutions emphasized legislative supremacy as well in the interpretation as in the enactment of law. The abuses to which this supremacy led were responsible for several cases during the 1780's which most scholars consider precedents for the later exercise of judicial review by Federal and state courts. Chief among these was Rutgers v. Waddington, a New York case, Trevett v. Weeden, a Rhode Island case, and Bayard v. Singleton, a North Carolina case.

Judicial review is not explicitly provided for in the Constitution but is deducible from its general provisions. Such a power logically can be inferred from the "supremacy clause" and from the section of Article III defining the judicial power of the United States. The supremacy clause enjoined the state judiciaries to uphold the laws and treaties of the United States against any conflicting state law or state constitutional provision. Article III established the right of appeal in all cases "arising under this Constitution" to the Federal courts, including the Supreme Court. Members of the Constitutional Convention, furthermore, probably believed that the Federal courts would exercise judicial review. It was one method (separation of powers and federalism were other methods) by which the framers hoped to impose restraints on the power vested in the central government. It was also a device which they fashioned to curb the impulsive desires of the majority. In the later numbers of *The Federalist,* for example, Alexander Hamilton demonstrated a keen apprecia-

tion of judicial review as a means of protecting individual liberty.

The Judiciary Act of 1789, the foundation stone of the Federal judicial system in the United States, was silent on the question of the Court's power to review acts of Congress but explicitly gave it the power to pass upon the validity of state legislation and to review decisions of state courts in which claims founded upon the Constitution, acts of Congress or treaties of the United States had been disallowed. This power was not immediately exercised, but was firmly established during the chief-justiceship of John Marshall: In Fletcher v. Peck (1810) the Court invalidated a state act in violation of the provisions of the Federal Constitution and in Cohens v. Virginia (1821) Marshall asserted the power of the Court to revise state court decisions in order to make them square with the "supreme law."

The first case in which the Court declared an act of Congress unconstitutional was Marbury v. Madison (1803), the most important decision in Supreme Court history. In that case Chief Justice John Marshall compared the disputed section of the Judiciary Act of 1789 with the applicable section of the Constitution and ruled that "the authority given to the Supreme Court by the act establishing the judicial courts of the United States, to issue writs of mandamus to public officers, appears not to be warranted by the Constitution." The importance of Marbury v. Madison consists not only in the fact that it established the doctrine of judicial review of acts of Congress but in Marshall's assertion that the ultimate power to interpret the Constitution resides neither with the President nor Congress. "It is emphatically the province and duty of the judicial department to say what the law is," the Chief Justice asserted.

It was not until the ill-fated Dred Scott decision, 54 years later, that the Supreme Court again declared an act of Congress invalid. In the meantime, however, the Court continued to review the acts of state legislatures and, in a few instances, sustained acts of Congress.

For a brief time after the Civil War it seemed that this self-imposed restraint might continue, for the Court appeared belatedly to have accepted the Jacksonian doctrine that the will of the people might best be discovered at the ballot box and in the legislative halls. In 1877, for example, Chief Justice Waite told aggrieved litigants to resort to the polls, not the courts, for protection against alleged wrongs inflicted by a state legislature (Munn v. Illinois). These same sentiments were expressed by Justice Joseph Bradley in 1890. By that time, however, the trend toward judicial aggrandizement had reached the point that he was forced to speak in dissent, a dissent which in succeeding years was echoed in the dissenting opinions of Justices Oliver Wendell Holmes, Louis Brandeis, and Harlan Fiske Stone.

The high tide of judicial review in the United

States was from 1890 to 1937. In contrast to the two acts of Congress invalidated by the Court before the Civil War, 69 such acts suffered judicial censorship between 1889 and 1937. Of even greater significance was the control exercised over acts of state legislatures. Although the Court set aside fewer than 20 state enactments before 1860, it disallowed 228 state statutes between 1890 and 1937. During these years the justices succeeded in making the Constitution a bulwark of *laissez faire*. They denied at once the right of the Federal Government to enact legislation dealing with the problems presented by an expanding national economy, and the right of the states to manage those economic interests which the National Government could or would not regulate. Both the commerce clause and the Tenth Amendment were used to inhibit the exercise of national powers. The due process clause of the Fourteenth Amendment was the formula used to defeat state action under the police power. From a merely technical procedural requirement affecting the exercise of legislative power, due process was transformed into a substantive limitation on all government power. The term "liberty" in the Fourteenth Amendment, furthermore, was extended by the Supreme Court to cover "liberty of contract" and "freedom of competition." The discretionary veto over state legislation which the Court thus assumed was exercised vigorously from 1890 to 1910, sparingly from 1910 to 1920, and with renewed vigor from 1920 to 1930. The way in which it was applied depended more on the social and economic predilections of the justices than on the preciseness of Constitutional law.

The fact that the Court had set itself up as a "super-legislature" led to an insistent demand that bold measures be taken to curb its power. Among the reforms proposed during the first two decades of this century were the recall of judges and of judicial decisions, and the amendment of the Constitution.

The Court, however, was more than a match for its opponents. Wrapping itself in the mantle of judicial independence and dignity, the Court continued to wield due process as a club with which to strike down state legislation that offended its economic predilections and the commerce clause to strike down national legislation with which it disagreed. The apogee of its power came under Chief Justice Taft. Of the 53 Congressional acts set aside up to 1925, nearly one fourth were handed down in the 1920's. Senator Frank Norris of Nebraska put the matter bluntly: "We have a legislative body, called the House of Representatives, of over 400 men. We have another legislative body, called the Senate, of less than 100 men. We have, in reality, another legislative body, called the Supreme Court, of 9 men; and they are more powerful than all the others put together."

If the period from 1890 to 1937 constituted the high mark of judicial supremacy, the most significant

brief period in the history of judicial review was from 1935 through 1937. In the three years beginning with the October, 1933, term, the Court held acts of Congress unconstitutional in twelve decisions, thus nullifying much of the New Deal program. One decision negated the National Industrial Recovery Act, a main prop of the New Deal. Another judgment invalidated the Agricultural Adjustment Act, the New Deal's answer to the desperate plight of American farmers. In other decisions, congressional acts providing for farm debtor's relief, railroad pensions, municipal bankruptcy relief, and regulation of the bituminous coal industry were struck down. The climax of judicial supremacy was reached just before the 1936 election, when the Court ruled that neither the states nor the National Government had the power to enact a minimum wage law.

Believing his program for the nation's recovery from the worst depression in its history "fairly completely undermined," Franklin D. Roosevelt determined to secure judicial approval of the New Deal through the President's appointing power and through congressional control over the Court's size. On Feb. 5, 1937, he submitted to Congress his program for reorganization of the judiciary, a program which immediately was dubbed "Court-packing." Although the Congress rejected his proposals, Roosevelt's purpose was achieved. On March 29, 1937— even as the Court Reorganization Plan was under consideration—the Court sustained a minimum wage law of the State of Washington similar to the New York statute invalidated only nine months before. On the same day, the Court also upheld laws providing for farm debtor's relief, collective bargaining in the nation's railroads, and a tax similar to one struck down only a few years before in the case invalidating the Agricultural Adjustment Administration. More important in demonstrating the drastic change in constitutional jurisprudence was the important case of National Labor Relations Board v. Jones and Laughlin Steel Corporation, handed down on April 12, 1937. In this case the constitutionality of the National Labor Relations Act of 1935 was upheld. Ignoring its own decision in the National Industrial Recovery Act case in which Congress had been denied the right to regulate local business activities even when those activities affected interstate commerce, the Court gave the Federal power over interstate commerce its maximum sweep. Six weeks later, judicial sanction was given the Social Security Act of 1935. In approving this measure, a major New Deal innovation, the Court gave an exceedingly broad interpretation to the power of Congress to tax and spend for the general welfare.

Students agree that the somersault of 1937 represented a near revolution in the jurisprudence of the Supreme Court—a revolution which aptly has been described as "Constitutional Revolution, Ltd." It was a transformation which, in terms of scope and speed of execution, is unprecedented in the annals of the Supreme Court.

Since 1937 judicial review of acts of Congress has been an inconspicuous feature of the judicial process. In the field of economic activity by the Federal Government the Court presumes constitutionality and thus has allowed Congress virtual freedom. In general it may be said that since that date the Court has returned to the idea expressed by James Madison that dependence on the people is America's primary safeguard against abuses of government power. So too has the Court's substantive review of state legislation passed into desuetude. By 1949, Justice Hugo Black, speaking for the Court, declared that "due process" as a substantive limitation on the states was rejected "at least as early as 1934." Since then, the Justice declared, the Court has "consciously returned closer and closer to the earlier constitutional principles" that the states may regulate injurious practices, so long as specific constitutional provisions or Federal laws are not thereby violated. This has not meant, however, an abnegation of power by the Court, for the commerce clause remains as a potent weapon for striking down state legislation. It rather has signified a return to the judicial humility of Supreme Court statesmen like John Marshall, Oliver Wendell Holmes, and Harlan Fiske Stone.

Having abandoned judicial guardianship of property as a preferred freedom, the Court soon was emphasizing another category of preferred freedoms. The debate on the exercise of judicial review in the past two decades has often centered on the duty of the Court to use its veto to invalidate legislation infringing freedom of speech, thought, and religion. During the years of the Roosevelt Court (1937 to about 1949), the Court frequently gave to First Amendment rights a "preferred" position—a phrase which means that in this sensitive area the Court presumes invalidity. In recent years, however, the doctrine of preferred freedoms, although not explicitly disavowed, has not been accepted by any majority opinion.

Since 1954 the Supreme Court has nevertheless given preference to at least one type of freedom—the freedom against discrimination because of race or color. In its historic decision of May 17, 1954 (Brown v. Topeka) the Court unanimously upset sixty years of precedent to rule segregation in public schools unconstitutional. In an opinion notable both for its brevity and for its emphasis on sociological and psychological factors, Chief Justice Earl Warren declared that "separate educational facilities are inherently unequal." Despite vociferous opposition from parts of the South, the Federal courts resolutely have implemented the Supreme Court order.

Its unanimity on the unconstitutionality of state legislation that discriminates on the basis of color excepted, the Supreme Court under the chief-justiceship of Earl Warren (1954–   ) has been deeply divided on the exercise of judicial review. The majority (of which Justice Felix Frankfurter is the spokesman) advocates judicial restraint, the obligation of the Court to use sparingly its power to infringe congressional or executive authority. The other group (currently labelled "judicial activists" and led by Justice Hugo Black) argues that the Court boldly should resist government encroachments on the rights and liberties of the people.

Such a division is not new. Both exponents and practitioners of judicial review have faced throughout our history a serious dilemma. At issue is not only the preservation of our Federal system (for whose smooth operation some arbiter of the conflicting claims of nation and state must exist), but the age-old question of minority rights. There may be, as the late Robert H. Jackson said, "a basic inconsistency between popular government and judicial supremacy." The Americans, however, have not been willing to risk democracy without judicial restraint.

JUDICIARY, THE, of the United States has its historical background in the legal and political institutions of England. The tribunals set up in the colonies were similar to those of the mother country, and acts of Parliament and the principles of the common law and equity were enforced in the new country as in the old, with the added responsibility on colonial courts of enforcing the enactments of colonial assemblies. The office of justice of the peace, for dealing with minor civil matters and minor offenses, was well established. Above this office was the court usually known as the county court, having original jurisdiction in more important matters. A right of appeal to the colonial assembly existed in some colonies, analogous to appeal to the House of Lords in England. There was in some cases a right of appeal from colonial courts to the judicial committee of the Privy Council in England.

After the colonies became independent states the courts remained fundamentally the same, except for the development of courts of appeals with full-time professional judges. Constitutions prescribed the governments of the states, pursuant to which state laws were made and enforced. The application of common law and equity principles was continued.

No provision for an adequate Federal judiciary was included in the Articles of Confederation. Congress was given the power, however, to set up commissions to settle disputes among the states. This power was infrequently exercised, but the Confederation Congress did set up a court of appeals to decide cases appealed from state courts involving prizes of war and piracies and felonies on the high seas. The lack of an adequate judiciary was one of the major defects of the Confederation. All the proposed plans of government submitted to the Constitutional Convention of 1787 provided for a national judiciary distinct from the judicial systems of the states.

The first three articles of the Constitution provided respectively for the establishment of the legislative, executive and judicial branches of the Government. The judiciary article provided that the judicial power of the United States should be vested in a Supreme Court and in such inferior courts as Congress might ordain and establish. All Federal judges were to hold office during good behavior, and their salaries were not to be diminished during their continuance in office. By Article II, dealing with the executive, the President was authorized to nominate, and, by and with the advice and consent of the Senate, to appoint Supreme Court judges and certain specified officers. It also defined the original jurisdiction of the Supreme Court and prescribed the content of Federal judicial power. The jurisdiction of particular Federal courts, however, was left to congressional determination. The sixth article established a basis for review by the Federal judiciary of state court decisions involving the Federal Constitution, laws or treaties by providing that state judges should be bound by them notwithstanding any contrary provisions in the constitutions and laws of the states. The first ten amendments, added in 1791 to meet criticism voiced in the ratifying conventions, included additional prescriptions with respect to the courts. Among them, suits at common law involving more than twenty dollars were to be tried by jury; criminal trials, with certain exceptions, were to be preceded by indictment by grand jury; and the resort to excessive bail, excessive fines, and cruel and unusual punishments was prohibited.

The judiciary provisions of the Constitution were given effect in the Judiciary Act of 1789, enacted after eleven states had ratified the Constitution. The judicial system was headed by a Supreme Court consisting of a Chief Justice and five associate justices. Below the Supreme Court were three circuit courts, which had no judges of their own but were conducted by two Supreme Court judges and a district judge. Below the circuit courts were thirteen district courts, for each of which a district judge was to be appointed by the President in the same manner as Supreme Court judges.

The district courts were given original jurisdiction in minor offenses against Federal laws, and in a wide range of admiralty cases, the latter making up the burden of their work in early years. In some cases a right of appeal lay to the circuit courts. The circuit courts had original jurisdiction in cases involving larger amounts and more serious offenses. The major portion of their work in the early years was with cases involving state laws, in which Federal jurisdiction depended on the fact that the parties were citizens of different states. The Supreme Court was given the jurisdiction allotted to it by the Constitution, and appellate jurisdiction in certain cases from decisions of the circuit courts and the highest state courts.

The history of the Federal judiciary has been the history of the steady expansion of business and the consequences of this expansion. The expansion has been one of territory, an increase in the settled area requiring judicial service. It has been one of population, in that growth of population within given areas has added to the work of the courts. It has been one of legislation, in that the bulk of Federal legislation to be applied by the courts has grown with the growth of the country and the increasing complexity of the conditions of living.

Although the district courts survived and increased in number, they underwent drastic jurisdictional changes by which they were crowded into the field originally occupied by the circuit courts. The circuit courts had a more difficult task of survival. Modified early in 1801 by an act of Congress creating a number of circuit judgeships and abolishing the requirement that Supreme Court judges ride circuit, the old circuit court system was largely restored within a few months. In 1869 Congress provided for the appointment of nine circuit judges for the circuits, thereby relieving the judges of the Supreme Court of part of their circuit responsibilities. The increase in the appellate work of the Supreme Court led to demand for further relief. Congress responded with a new measure in 1891. This measure added a new circuit judge to each circuit, withdrew all appellate jurisdiction from the circuit courts, and by implication relieved Supreme Court judges of the obligation to ride circuit. The same act provided for the creation of a circuit court of appeals in each circuit. Upon these courts was conferred the appellate jurisdiction hitherto exercised by the circuit courts, and a portion of the appellate jurisdiction hitherto exercised by the Supreme Court. The circuit courts were finally abolished in 1911 because of the extent to which their work overlapped with that of the district courts.

The Federal judicial system, therefore, now consists of the district courts, the circuit courts of appeals, and the Supreme Court. The Federal district courts are at the bottom of the regular judicial hierarchy. Between the Supreme Court and the district courts is a Court of Appeals in each of the eleven circuits into which the United States is divided (by an act of Congress of 1948, the former circuit courts of appeals were renamed United States Courts of Appeals, and the District of Columbia was recognized as constituting one of the eleven circuits).

Provisions with respect to appellate jurisdiction of the Federal courts are exceedingly complex. For example, some cases are taken directly from the district courts to the Supreme Court. Some go from the district courts to the courts of appeals, and thence to the Supreme Court. Some cannot go beyond the courts of appeals. The purpose of Congress in prescribing the appellate jurisdiction of the several courts is to provide for the expeditious appeal to the highest court of cases of greatest public importance, while limiting or cutting off altogether the right of appeal in those of lesser importance. The appellate jurisdiction of the Supreme Court is almost entirely discretionary. By the Judiciary Act of 1925, the Court itself was constituted the judge, with only a few exceptions, of what cases it will hear on appeal.

The Federal judiciary, in a narrow sense, consists only of these several courts which are created pursuant to the provisions of the third article of the Constitution. In the exercise of other powers conferred upon it, however, such as the powers to govern territories, to grant patents, and to appropriate money to pay claims against the United States, Congress may create other tribunals to exercise judicial functions. These are known as legislative courts, in contrast with the so-called constitutional courts organized under Article III. Among them are the courts established in the territories of the United States, the Court of Claims, and the Court of Customs and Patent Appeals. Bearing some resemblance to legislative courts are independent agencies such as the Interstate Commerce Commission, the Federal Trade Commission, the National Labor Relations Board and other agencies within some of the departments of the Government, which exercise judicial functions but which are not usually classified as judicial tribunals.

Since the business of the Federal courts is clearly defined and limited by the Constitution and acts of Congress, most law cases in the United States are handled by state and local courts. In every state the courts are organized in a progressive series. At the bottom of the scale is the justice of the peace, an office of ancient origin which was early established in the United States and which has persisted to the present day. The jurisdiction of the court of justice of the peace is confined to petty civil disputes and breaches of the peace. In cities this jurisdiction is exercised by police courts and municipal civil courts rather than justices of the peace. Above the petty courts are the trial courts which hear most of the civil and criminal cases arising in the states. These intermediate courts are variously called "county courts" (usually of limited jurisdiction), "superior courts," and "circuit courts." At the head of the judicial system of every state is a court of last resort (known as "the Supreme Court," or by other names such as "the Court of Appeals") for all cases arising under the state constitutions and laws. The states, finally, usually have special tribunals for particular purposes. There are, for example, probate courts, small claims courts, children's courts, chancery courts, and administrative courts, such as industrial commissions.

The state judicial systems differ greatly among themselves and from the Federal system in matters of appointment and tenure. In the early years the selection of judges was made largely by the legislature or indirectly under its control. The Jacksonian period saw a movement toward popular election, particularly in the newer states. In some of the states, including

a number of the original thirteen and other older states, judges of appellate courts and courts of general jurisdiction are selected by legislatures or governors or by co-operation between governors and legislatures or senates. The other states resort to election by the people—in more than one half the states on a partisan ballot. The latter method is generally regarded as defective as it involves the judiciary in politics and often fails to result in the selection of the best personnel. Tenure varies greatly from state to state and from court to court. The term is usually shortest in the lower courts, and longest in those of the highest rank. In a few states (Maryland, Pennsylvania, Massachusetts, and New Hampshire) judges of the higher courts have long terms that often are tantamount to life tenure. Removal of a judge before the expiration of his term is difficult. The machinery of impeachment is available but is cumbersome and hard to use. A few states authorize removal by the governor on address of both houses of the legislature without resorting to impeachment procedure.

Complexities of procedure have embarrassed the states as well as the Federal Government. In the middle of the 19th century a movement was started for the codification of procedure with the elimination of unnecessary technicalities. It was carried forward under the leadership of David Dudley Field, of New York, and spread to many other states. A similar movement was started for the codification of substantive law. Codes were adopted in a number of states, and have been satisfactory in part, but they have never entirely fulfilled their intended purpose. More recently, the American Law Institute has attempted to achieve simplification by a restatement of law in the several fields.

Although there is no complete separation of powers in any state or in the Federal Government, the several judiciaries have maintained their strength against legislative and executive departments. There has been little interference with the personnel of the bench, once the personnel has been chosen. There has been little interference with the work of the courts through the alteration of their jurisdiction. On the other hand the courts have strengthened their position down through the years by resort to judicial review, making themselves final authorities as to the meanings of state and Federal constitutions. By keeping their interpretations in harmony with conservative sentiments of the times they have maintained a prestige which has given added authority to their interpretations. There have been popular outbursts against particular courts at particular times, but seldom against the courts as institutions.

JUILLIARD v. GREENMAN, 1884 (110 U. S. 421), upheld the implied power of Congress to make the United States' own notes legal tender (and therefore money) in peacetime as well as in wartime. In the case of Hepburn v. Griswold, the Supreme Court first held the legal-tender acts unconstitutional. Immediately thereafter in the legal-tender cases the Supreme Court (it is claimed after it had been packed by President Grant) reversed this decision and upheld the legal-tender acts as a war measure. Juilliard v. Greenman upheld them without reference to the war power, and in this decision all the members concurred except Justice Field. In this case the Supreme Court implied the power from the express power to borrow money, and the implied power to issue bills of credit.

JUSTICE, DEPARTMENT OF, had its official beginning July 1, 1870. The office of Attorney General, however, which became the nucleus of the Department, had been established in 1789, along with the departments first created. Until 1870 the principal duties of the Attorney General were the argument of government cases in the Supreme Court of the United States, and the giving of legal advice to the President and the heads of the departments in connection with official business. He had no control over United States attorneys and marshals until 1861, and he was given nominally full control only after he had been designated the head of the new department.

The duties of the Attorney General for many years after the adoption of the Constitution were very light, and he devoted much of his time to private practice. Official responsibilities expanded gradually, and by the 1850's they took most or all of his time. The multiplicity of California land cases arising just before and during the Civil War added burdensome duties for the Attorney General, and made it necessary to provide assistance. Problems arising from the war, and the necessity of co-ordinating legal advice and litigation, lent weight to arguments made intermittently for a number of years for the creation of a law department of the Federal Government. The organic act was passed June 22, 1870.

The growth of litigation and of advisory legal responsibilities, and the bringing together of a variety of functions in the Department of Justice, required the Attorney General to give much of his time to problems of administration. The Solicitor General, whose office was created when the Department was organized, assumed principal responsibility for the argument of cases in the Supreme Court. That work came to be handled by or under the direction of the Solicitor General and the Assistant Attorneys General who head the five functional divisions of the Department. Likewise, official opinions, while appearing in the name of the Attorney General, have long been prepared by subordinates, and are now the responsibility of the Assistant Solicitor General.

The work of the Department, and the establishment and expansion of divisions and bureaus for handling it have grown with the growth of the country and the extension of Federal control over varied public and private activities. The Antitrust Division, for instance, which had its formal beginning in 1903, was the product of need for organization to enforce antitrust legislation. The enactment of other laws based on the commerce clause of the Constitution has brought to the same Division work rivaling antitrust enforcement in importance. The growth of Federal criminal legislation has greatly expanded the work of the Criminal Division, and has also stimulated the growth of the Federal Bureau of Investigation. Likewise the cold war and the fear of subversion has given rise to an elaborate security system, administered by the Department of Justice; in recent years this has been the most publicized and the most controversial of the Department's activities. The growth of a Federal prison system has been responsible for the development of the Bureau of Prisons. Other agencies, such as those having to do with claims against the United States, tax problems and the acquisition of title to land, have expanded in similar fashion.

KALAMAZOO CASE was decided by the Michigan supreme court in 1874. Charles E. Stuart and others, citizens of the village of Kalamazoo, sought to restrain the school authorities from collecting taxes for the support of a public high school and a nonteaching superintendent. The opinion of the court, written by Chief Justice Thomas M. Cooley, held that the levying of taxes for these purposes was consistent with the educational policy of Michigan since 1817 and was legal under the provisions of the constitution of 1850. Education beyond the rudiments, it was affirmed, had never been regarded by the state as having a merely cultural value, but rather as being "an important practical advantage" to be supplied to rich and poor alike at the option of the school district. The decision confirmed the right of the state to establish, at public expense, a complete system of education from the elementary school through the university, and, as such, constituted an important precedent in many other states.

KANSAS was admitted into the Union Jan. 29, 1861. It occupies the geographic center of the United States. Dominated by political considerations, the boundaries were drawn without reference to geographical unities. The northern part lies in the Smoky-Kansas River watershed, the southwestern part in the Arkansas River basin, and the southeastern part is drained by large tributaries of the Missouri and Arkansas.

Early European contacts were quite casual and some of the generally accepted accounts are subject to controversy, notably of the Coronado expedition. The earliest economic penetration of the area was in exploitation of furs under the French regime, otherwise no important natural resources were subject to development until the period of Anglo-American settlement after 1854: agricultural, coal, oil, gas, salt, gypsum, lead and zinc. After 1830, in view of apparent barrenness, the southwestern trans-Missouri

River region of the United States was designated as permanent Indian country, and in the portion which became Kansas, tribes from northeastern United States were relocated. For frontier defense three early forts were established: Leavenworth in 1827, Scott in 1842 and Riley in 1853, and later others farther westward.

Much of the region fell within the so-called Great American Desert and as such constituted a barrier to be crossed in pursuit of trade, lands, or gold beyond, by the Santa Fe Trail to the Spanish Southwest, by the Oregon Trail to the Pacific Northwest, and later to the gold region of California. When Kansas was organized as a territory in 1854, the primary incentive was not settlement and development for its own sake; but partly, rivalry between the North and the South over a railroad to the Pacific, partly, rivalry between North and South over the issue of slavery extension which became involved with the first.

KANSAS CITY, MO., an outgrowth of two frontier settlements, Westport and the Town of Kansas, is named from its location at the confluence of the Kansas (Kaw) and Missouri Rivers.

About 1800 Louis Bartholet (or Bertholett) established a trading camp there, but the first permanent settlement was a trading post at Randolph Bluffs, built by François Chouteau in 1821. Floods submerged this post in 1826, causing its removal two miles upstream to a point near the mouth of the Kansas. The place became important because, at the apex of the big bend of the Missouri, it was the nearest water approach to the Santa Fe and California trails.

On the Santa Fe Trail, a few miles west of Independence, its terminus, John McCoy laid out Westport in 1833. It was four miles south of the Kaw's mouth. A company headed by William Sublette, noted fur trader, platted the Town of Kansas on the river above Chouteau's warehouse in 1838, but a clouded title prevented its development until 1846, and it was called derisively "Westport Landing." Bent and St. Vrain, the Indian traders, hauled merchandise direct from the Town of Kansas to Fort Bent in 1845 and by the next year the settlement was competing for its share of the Santa Fe trade with Independence, Westport and Leavenworth, its strategic location being a deciding factor.

In 1853 the name was changed to the City of Kansas and in 1889 to Kansas City. During the border difficulties preceding the admission of Kansas to statehood, it was a focus of proslavery activity, and near Westport the Civil War battle of that name was fought, Oct. 23, 1864. Kansas City became a railroad and packing center after the Civil War and absorbed Westport. Kansas City, Kans., a separate municipality, lies west of the Kaw's mouth. In 1960 its population was 478,539.

KANSAS-NEBRASKA ACT (1854), which repealed the Missouri Compromise and led to a general re-

alignment in American politics, was initiated to aid Midwestern efforts to build a transcontinental railroad line. For a decade, the South and Central West sought to best one another in this race for the Pacific. A chief Southern advantage was that the whole region through which its road would pass was already organized, while the region immediately west of Missouri and Iowa was in the hands of Indian tribes and had no political organization. From 1850 on, Midwestern Senators and Representatives introduced bill after bill to organize a Territory of Nebraska. Stephen A. Douglas, Chairman of the Senate's Committee on Territories, was particularly active for such legislation. These efforts were thwarted by stubborn Southern opposition, arising from the fact that the new territory, being north of the Missouri Compromise line, would therefore be free rather than slave territory. In December, 1853, a new Nebraska bill, introduced by Sen. Augustus C. Dodge, Iowa, caused Douglas to renew his quest of a formula by which it could be passed. There is some ground for believing that he thought the Missouri Compromise unconstitutional, and that climate and natural resources in the Nebraska area would ban slavery there in fact, whatever its status in law. On Jan. 4, 1854, he reported a Nebraska bill based on the principles of Popular Sovereignty, as employed in the Compromise of 1850.

But leading Southern ultras termed the bill "delusive" and insisted on the Missouri Compromise's explicit repeal. Douglas soon found this was the only way a territorial bill could be passed. Jefferson Davis and others secured President Pierce's active support, and the whole Administration force was put behind explicit repeal of the Missouri Compromise, so that the citizens of the new area would themselves determine whether it would be free or slave territory. Likewise, because of differences in political and railroad interests between Missouri and Iowa, the Nebraska area was cut into two new territories, one west of Missouri, to be known as Kansas, the other, west of Iowa, retaining the name Nebraska.

Even before the new bill was reported to the Senate, such congressional abolitionists and antislavery leaders as Sen. Salmon P. Chase, of Ohio; Charles Sumner, of Massachusetts; and William H. Seward, of New York, saw the chance to raise a storm of passion against Douglas and the Administration. Late in January they issued the "Appeal of the Independent Democrats," denouncing Douglas' original bill "as a gross violation of a sacred pledge; as a criminal betrayal of precious rights," a "monstrous" plot, a sacrifice of the people's dearest interest to "the mere hazards of a presidential game." Their appeal flamed through the antislavery states, Douglas was burnt in effigy from Iowa to Maine, and the abolitionist storm became a hurricane.

All through February Douglas defended himself stoutly in the Senate, showing by detailed historical recital that the very men who now assailed him for seeking to repeal the Missouri Compromise had, until 1848, opposed it might and main; likewise that acts of Congress had never really excluded slavery from an inch of United States soil—the free states had actually become such by self-determination rather than because of Federal law.

Closing the Senate debate, March 3, Douglas extracted Seward's admission that his chief attack on the bill had been based on a "misapprehension." Chase offered a personal apology; Sumner's egotism was pierced and he sat speechless in his seat. A few hours later the Senate passed the Kansas-Nebraska Bill, 37 to 14.

Douglas then took charge of the effort for it in the House, where the abolitionist crusade had had chief effect. Partisans went wild, fighting talk was heard, weapons were drawn. But through March and April the Administration applied pressure; the wavering were made firm, many backsliders were brought in line. Finally, May 22, 1854, the bill passed, 113 to 100. President Pierce signed it, and it became the law of the land.

KANSAS STRUGGLE, THE, began in May, 1854, with the passage of the Kansas-Nebraska bill, which repealed the slavery-extension restriction of the Missouri Compromise and applied the doctrine of popular sovereignty to the two territories. Competition for the rich lands of Kansas began immediately. Emigrant aid societies were formed in the East to promote settlement, but the lure of opportunity, a more potent factor than promotion, brought settlers from every section, especially from Missouri and the Old Northwest. Important proslavery settlements were made along the Missouri River; Free-State migrants sought homes in the Kansas Valley. In elections for a delegate to Congress in November, 1854, and for a territorial legislature in March, 1855, there was illegal voting on both sides, but the proximity of Missouri gave the proslavery party an advantage and it won both contests. A slave code was enacted, friction developed between the legislature and Gov. Andrew Reeder, and he was replaced by Wilson Shannon.

Antislavery men, now a majority of the population, assembled at Big Springs in September to form a Free-State party, and a few weeks later inaugurated the "Topeka Movement" for statehood, with James H. Lane chairman of an executive committee. A *de facto* government, set up early in 1856 with Charles Robinson as "governor," unsuccessfully sought recognition from Congress. At Washington acrimonious debates over Douglas' proposal to authorize a constitutional convention culminated in Sumner's "Crime against Kansas" speech, May 19–20, and in Brooks' assault upon the Massachusetts senator. Open warfare in the territory had been narrowly averted the previous December by Shannon's intervention to

prevent "border ruffians" from attacking Lawrence. As Sumner was making his speech, proslavery men again appeared at Lawrence and destroyed considerable property. This act was avenged by John Brown, who, with sons and neighbors, murdered five proslavery advocates. Such proceedings greatly aroused public sentiment North and South and led to renewed activity of aid companies and committees. Sporadic outbreaks continued and "Bleeding Kansas" caused Shannon's removal in favor of John W. Geary, who established peace and thereby contributed to Buchanan's election.

Robert J. Walker, appointed governor in March, 1857, realized that slavery was doomed and labored to save Kansas for the Democratic party. Free-State men declined to participate in the framing and ratification of the Lecompton Constitution which guaranteed protection of slave property already in Kansas regardless of the decision on the slavery clause, the only one submitted to the voters. Walker's rejection of fraudulent votes in the October election gave the Free-State party control of the legislature but cost the governor his position. A special session early in 1858 provided a referendum on the whole Lecompton Constitution. As proslavery men declined to vote, it was rejected almost unanimously. Despite the hostility of the great majority of actual settlers, Buchanan recommended that Kansas be admitted under it. The Senate approved notwithstanding Douglas' opposition; however, his following in the House helped to defeat it there. Congress then passed the compromise English bill offering Kansas a gift of land upon becoming a state, but the bribe was rejected. The state was finally admitted Jan. 29, 1861.

KASKASKIA (1703–*ca.* 1910), metropolis of the Illinois Country in the 18th century, was founded in April, 1703, when the Jesuit Gabriel Marest removed the Mission of the Immaculate Conception from the site of the present city of St. Louis to the right bank of the Kaskaskia River seven miles above its then junction with the Mississippi. With him went the Kaskaskia tribe of the Illinois Indians, former inhabitants of the Great Village of the Illinois.

For fifteen years Kaskaskia was primarily an Indian village in which a few French lived permanently, while more drifted in and out. Growth commenced in 1717, when it became a part of the district of Louisiana. In 1723 its white inhabitants numbered 196; in 1752, 350 whites and 246 Negroes were enumerated. By 1770, after the high point of its 18th-century growth had been passed, it was said to contain 500 whites and nearly that many Negroes.

Meanwhile, the French and Indian villages had been separated (by Boisbriant in 1719). The population of the latter fluctuated greatly, but the trend was steadily downward. By the end of the century only a handful of indolent, degenerate Indians remained.

Under Boisbriant, commandant from 1718 to 1724, the characteristic land system of the French village was established—large commons, and common fields in narrow strips. Throughout the French period agriculture flourished, and grain was shipped as far as Detroit and New Orleans. Especially notable was the plantation of the Jesuits, which had become an "extensive estate" by 1763, when the order was dissolved.

During the last third of the 18th century many changes took place in Kaskaskia. In 1765, after the cession of the Illinois Country to Great Britain, a British garrison was established there, and traders and their employees replaced in part the former inhabitants, who moved across the Mississippi. On July 4, 1778, British rule ended with George Rogers Clark's capture of the town. For a decade after the Revolution, American rule was ineffective, and Kaskaskia was sunk in anarchy. During these years its population declined to such an extent that only 349 white inhabitants were counted in a census taken in 1787.

By 1800 Kaskaskia had recovered somewhat, and had become perhaps half American. The creation of Illinois Territory in 1809, and its designation as the territorial capital, resulted in further revival. In the following decade growth continued, and by 1818, when it became the first state capital, Kaskaskia had regained its former position as the metropolis of Illinois. But its primacy was short-lived. When the state offices were removed to Vandalia in 1820 rapid decline set in, and the town soon sank into somnolence. A disastrous flood in 1844 almost destroyed it, and led to the removal of the county seat three years later. In 1881 the Mississippi broke through the tongue of land on which Kaskaskia stood and began to flow through the channel of the Kaskaskia River. Gradually it encroached upon the town site. By 1910 it had obliterated the ancient settlement.

KEARNY, FORT. It was with a view to protecting the frontier that Congress passed a law on July 2, 1836, providing for the opening of a military road from some point on the Mississippi near its junction with the Des Moines River, to the Red River. In accordance with this act, in the spring of 1838, Col. Stephen W. Kearny and Nathan Boone selected a site (present Nebraska City) for a fort on the Missouri River. A military post named Fort Kearny was established there in the spring of 1846, but was abandoned two years later in favor of one on the Platte. From this time on little is heard about the old fort. Lt. W. P. Woodbury was the founder of Fort Kearny on the Platte. This location on the Oregon Trail, near Grand Island, was selected to furnish protection for emigrants who might be en route and to hold the Indians at peace. In 1851 the War Department, because of lack of appropriations, seriously considered abandoning this post. However, the Indian troubles which followed made the idea impracticable, and the fort remained in use until 1871, by which time travel on the Oregon Trail had ceased and the Indian fighting frontier had been pushed farther west. For several years, the Fort Kearny reservation remained under the control of the U. S. Government. Finally, by act of Congress, July 21, 1876, the land was surveyed and offered for sale to "actual settlers at a minimum price in accordance with the provisions of the homestead laws."

KEARNY, FORT PHIL, named after the general who fell at Chantilly, principal military post on the Bozeman Trail, was built by Col. H. B. Carrington in the Big Horn foothills on Piney Fork, in northern Wyoming. Construction, starting in July, 1866, was opposed by the Sioux, whose warriors harassed it constantly. In the first six months of its existence, Indians made 51 hostile demonstrations before the fort, killed 154 persons, and drove off 700 head of stock.

The Fetterman disaster, Dec. 21, reduced the garrison to perilous weakness, but Portugee Phillips, a frontiersman, rode 236 miles to Fort Laramie and secured help. The Wagon Box Fight, Aug. 2, 1867, was a sharp defeat for the Sioux, but at no time were there enough troops at Fort Phil Kearny for anything but defense. The fort was burned by Indians after its abandonment under the terms of the Treaty of Fort Laramie, 1868.

KEARNY'S MISSION TO CHINA (1842). Despatched to the Far East to protect American trading interests in China, Commodore Lawrence Kearny arrived in Canton at the close of the Anglo-Chinese War, generally known as the Opium War. After issuing through the American consul a statement that the United States would not under any circumstances sanction trade in opium, he sent a note to the Chinese High Commissioner, on Oct. 8, 1842, expressing the hope that in any new arrangements governing foreign trade which might be made as a result of the war, the trade and citizens of the United States would be "placed upon the same footing as the merchants of the nation most favored." The reply of the Chinese High Commissioner gave assurance that this would be done. By establishing the "most favored nation" doctrine as the standard for American trade relations with China, subsequently incorporated in our first treaty (Cushing's) with China, this exchange of notes constituted the genesis of the Open Door doctrine proclaimed by Secretary Hay some 57 years later.

KEARSARGE AND ALABAMA (June 19, 1864). The C. S. S. *Alabama*, 1050 tons, 8 guns, 149 men, Capt. Raphael Semmes, arrived at Cherbourg, France, on June 11, for repairs and to land prisoners of war. Three days later while the Confederates were awaiting Napoleon III's permission to use the imperial drydock, the U. S. S. *Kearsarge*, 1031 tons, 8 guns, 162 men, Capt. John A. Winslow, entered port for the purpose of securing the released captives. Winslow's intention being denied by the French authorities, he withdrew beyond the neutrality limits. Meanwhile, Semmes sent him word that he intended to come out and offer combat as soon as he could take on coal.

The engagement, fought five days later, on Sunday morning, within sight of crowds gathered on the Norman cliffs, was one of the most deliberately staged naval conflicts in world history. The opening gun was fired by the *Alabama* at 10:57 A.M., and the battle ended at 12:24 noon with the *Alabama* plunging stern first into the sea. Semmes sought to lie alongside his adversary to allow his well-disciplined crew to fight it out with pistol and cutlass; but the battle was decided by superior speed and ammunition. The *Kearsarge,* fresh from overhauling in a Dutch dockyard, enjoyed every advantage of condition over the *Alabama,* whose bottom was foul and powder dull from 22 months continuously at sea.

The *Kearsarge's* loss was one killed and two wounded; the *Alabama's,* nine killed, twenty-one wounded, and ten drowned. Little effort was made by Winslow to rescue the Confederates, most of whom were taken from the water by the boats of French and British spectators.

KEELBOATS. A type of craft that was used on American rivers, chiefly in the West. The first keelboats seem to have been skiffs with a plank nailed the length of the bottom to make the boat easier to steer, but by about 1790 it had become a long narrow craft built on a keel and ribs and with a long cargo box amidships. It was steered by a special oar and propelled by oars or poles, pulled by a cordelle, or occasionally fitted with sails. Keelboats were forty to eighty feet long, seven to ten feet in beam, two feet or more in draught, and with sharp ends. A cleated footway on each side was used by the pole men. The success of Shreve's shallow draft steamboats drove the keelboats from the main rivers by about 1820, except in low water, but they were used quite generally on the tributaries until after the Civil War. The chief utility of the keelboat was for upstream transportation and for swift downstream travel. It was used extensively for passenger travel.

KELLY'S INDUSTRIAL ARMY was born of the panic of 1893. It numbered about 1500 when it left California in box cars at the insistence of the police. Charles T. Kelly, 32, was the "general." At Council Bluffs, Iowa, the railroad ejected the army, and after camping in the mud for a week, and being fed by sympathizers, its members started on foot for Washington. The remnant which reached the Capitol failed to impress Congress and eventually disbanded.

KENDALL v. U. S. (12 Pet. 524, 1838) held that administrative officers must conform to the law when entrusted by Congress with purely ministerial duties having no executive or discretionary character. Postmaster General Kendall had maintained that he was responsible only to the President in performing such duties with respect to certain postal claims, but the Court unanimously overruled his argument because its acceptance would clothe the President with dispensing powers not contemplated by the Constitution. There was a difference of opinion whether the circuit court of the District of Columbia could command his obedience by a writ of mandamus, the majority holding that it could by virtue of its general common-law powers. Jackson's opponents made political capital of the decision, and President Van Buren criticized it in his annual message to Congress, but the law remained unchanged.

KENESAW MOUNTAIN, BATTLE OF (June 27, 1864). As Sherman (U.) advanced southward from Chattanooga in his campaign to Atlanta, he usually was able by flanking movements to force J. E. Johnston (C.), his opponent, to retire without serious fighting. As he neared Atlanta, Sherman came upon the Confederate Army, drawn up with its center occupying the crest of Kenesaw Mountain. He decided on a frontal attack. After a furious cannonade, the Federal troops moved forward, but were everywhere repulsed with heavy losses. Several days later Sherman resumed his flanking movements, forcing Johnston southward to the line of the Chattahoochee River. This unnecessary assault was one of Sherman's few serious errors in the campaign.

KENNEBEC RIVER, SETTLEMENTS ABOUT THE. The English idea of colonizing what was later called the Province of Maine dates from the return of David Ingram, survivor of a crew marooned on the Gulf of Mexico in 1558, who started homeward on foot, walked the length of the Atlantic seaboard, and was picked up at Norumbega on the Penobscot. His tales of jewels and furs fired English imaginations. Queen Elizabeth sent her great captains Raleigh, Davis and Gilbert westward. The Virginia Company was formed. Bartholomew Gosnold, 1602, Martin Pring, 1603, and George Weymouth, 1605, visited the Maine coast and reported rich resources there.

In 1607 the Popham plantation was established at the Kennebec's mouth. But in 1608, because of the severity of the winter, the death of its leader and the character of the colonists, it was abandoned.

The next settlements are shadowy. The settlers were unchurchly men, without patents; no records were kept. Since the 16th century English fishermen had been busy along the coast; by 1615 they were using Monhegan Island and Pemaquid Point as bases for curing fish. A mutinous crew built a village on Monhegan. The Pilgrims of Plymouth got supplies from English fishermen there in the lean year of 1622. Fishing folk doubtlessly were the first permanent settlers on the Kennebec. In 1625 the first deed drawn up in Maine was given John Brown of New Harbor by Abenaki sagamores. He had probably been there some time. Abraham Shurt settled on Monhegan in 1626. By this time, there were some families on the Kennebec. Before 1630 Thomas Purchase had selected Pejepscot Falls (Brunswick) for a settlement. The Pilgrims established a trading post at Cushenoc, far up the Kennebec, and encountered bitter competition with settlers near by. According to Sullivan, early Maine historian, there were 84 families near the Kennebec's mouth in 1630. There was a stout fort at Pemaquid. The Lygonia and Plough patents to Kennebec lands date 1630 and 1631. A settlement sprang up on Sheepscot Bay. John Parker acquired the lower west bank of the Kennebec in 1648; he bought Georgetown Island from Robinhood, a Kennebec chief. Robert Gutch bought and settled in 1661 on the site of what is now Bath. These settlements on or near the Kennebec flourished until the Indian wars, when, at one time or another, most of them except Monhegan were destroyed and had to be rebuilt by former inhabitants or newcomers.

KENTUCKY. The territory which is now Kentucky first attracted the attention of English settlers in Virginia during the latter half of the 17th century. In this century one or two expeditions were successful in crossing the Appalachian ranges into the Ohio Valley, but the first practical exploration of the territory did not come until 1750 when Dr. Thomas Walker, scouting for the Loyal Land Company, crossed through Cumberland Gap into eastern Kentucky. In 1751 Christopher Gist entered Kentucky through the Ohio Valley. Following these early expeditions many whites came to the territory, among whom were Mrs. Ingles, John Swift and John Findley. It was Findley who brought Daniel Boone to Kentucky in 1769. Between 1769 and 1775, Kentucky was visited by numerous hunters and surveyors. The Virginia Assembly created Fincastle County in 1772, and in 1774 James Harrod located and began building Harrodstown, but because of Dunmore's War was forced to withdraw until the cessation of hostilities. The year 1775 saw the beginning of the first permanent settlements at Harrodstown, Boonesborough, McGary's Fort and St. Asaph.

Richard Henderson, leader of the Transylvania Company, called a meeting of delegates from these four Kentucky forts to meet at Boonesborough on May 23, 1775, to discuss western problems. Jealousy between the Virginia settlers and those representing the Transylvania Company resulted in the settlers at Harrodstown calling a meeting and selecting George Rogers Clark and John Gabriel Jones to represent them before the Virginia assembly. The Virginia government, in answer to the Kentuckians' petition, agreed to protect their western county, and on Dec. 6, 1776, Kentucky County was created out of the western part of Fincastle. Between the years 1775 and 1785 Kentucky immigrants were forced to protect their homes against the frequent Indian attacks. During this period there occurred the siege of Boonesborough and the battle of the Blue Licks.

By 1780 the Kentucky population had increased, and in that year Kentucky County was divided into three parts, which became Fayette, Jefferson and Lincoln counties. Ten conventions were held between 1784 and 1792—preparatory to the creation of the independent state of Kentucky—and on June 1, 1792, Kentucky became a member of the Union.

When the Civil War began in 1861, Kentucky was carrying on a prosperous trade between both the North and the South. Because of its geographical location the state was a keystone between the two sections, but in reality belonged to neither. Many families were divided in sentiment and brothers went off to fight in opposing armies. Despite its neutrality, the war was brought to Kentucky when the Confederates invaded the state on Sept. 3, 1861.

KENTUCKY, INVASION OF (1862). In July, 1862, following the lull after the battle of Shiloh, Gen. Braxton Bragg (C.) moved his army from northern Mississippi to the vicinity of Chattanooga, preparatory to beginning a movement through middle Tennessee into Kentucky. Much of both states was strongly pro-Southern. A successful movement to the Ohio River, it was hoped, would bring many recruits into the Confederate ranks, open rich resources to the Southern cause and relieve the pressure on Lee (C.) in Virginia. Interior lines would give a controlled, well-led army an opportunity to reach the Ohio in advance of any large Union force.

Bragg's army left Chattanooga late in August and marched rapidly northward, arriving at Bowling Green, Ky., in mid-September. Buell, commanding the Union defense, hastily gathered troops to oppose Bragg. On Sept. 14, the Confederate leader, unnecessarily, digressed to attack Munfordville. He wasted five valuable days of which Buell made good use.

When Bragg finally resumed his march, instead of hurrying to Louisville, his proper objective which was only weakly garrisoned, he went to Bardstown. Buell rapidly concentrated his forces at Louisville. The first phase of the campaign was over. Up to this point the advantage had been with Bragg. While Buell prepared to march southward, Bragg waited for an independent army under Kirby Smith (C.) coming from eastern Kentucky, in the meantime himself going to Frankfort to help inaugurate a secession governor of Kentucky. This ceremony completed, Bragg returned to his army.

Confused by Buell's energy, Bragg was uncertain what to do. Finally, he decided to move eastward toward Kirby Smith. Buell had gained the initiative. On Oct. 8, 1862, Bragg gathering his now scattered troops unexpectedly encountered Buell's army near Perryville. A bloody battle followed, considering the numbers involved. Only portions of the two armies were engaged. Bragg achieved a tactical success, but after dark withdrew to join Kirby Smith. Two days later it was decided to withdraw from Kentucky rather than chance defeat in enemy territory.

Divided command, unnecessary diversions and Buell's aggressive leadership all contributed to failure. Nothing of importance had been accomplished. Buell's army had not been defeated nor had the Kentuckians been persuaded to rise in revolt.

KILLDEER MOUNTAIN, BATTLE OF (July 28, 1864). July 23, 1864, information reached Gen. Alfred Sully's Northwestern Indian Expedition on the upper Heart River (N. Dak.), of a heavy concentration of Indians on Knife River. Coralling his heavy wagons and accompanying emigrant train, with 2200 mounted men and light wagons carrying provisions and supplies, Sully marched northward, and on July 28 found the united Sioux forces, estimated at some 5000, strongly posted on Tahkahokuty or Killdeer Mountain (N. Dak.), in rugged, timbered country.

With dismounted men as skirmishers, supported by light artillery, flanking cavalry and reserves, Sully pushed forward, while the rear guard protected the wagons. Through skillful use of cavalry charges, while artillery shelled the ravines, the mountain was reached and fully occupied by dark, together with the abandoned Indian camp. Vast quantities of Indian provisions and equipment were destroyed. Sully's casualties were fifteen killed and wounded, while the Indian losses were estimated at upwards of one hundred.

"KING COTTON" was an expression much used by Southern authors and orators before the Civil War. The idea appeared first as the title of a book by David Christy, *Cotton Is King*, in 1855. In a speech in the U. S. Senate, March 4, 1858, James H. Hammond declared, "You dare not make war upon cotton! No power on earth dares make war upon it. Cotton is king."

KING GEORGE'S WAR (1744–48). Nominally at peace from 1713 to 1744, France and England developed irreconcilable colonial conflicts over boundaries of Acadia and northern New England and possession of the Ohio Valley. When England's commercial war with Spain (1739) merged into the continental War of Austrian Succession (1740–48), England and France, first fighting as "auxiliaries" on opposite sides, threw off the mask and declared war (March 15, 1744). The Louisburg French first learned of the war (May 5, 1744), surprised and captured Canso (May 13) but failed to take Annapolis (Port Royal). In retaliation New Englanders captured Louisburg (June 15, 1745), the most daring

and decisive victory in the colonial war, and planned, with English aid, simultaneously to attack Quebec and Montreal. Seven colonies co-operated to raise forces, ready in 1746, but promised English help did not arrive and the colonials finally disbanded (1747). Meanwhile, France sent a great fleet under Duc D'Anville (June, 1746) to recapture Louisburg and devastate English colonial seaports, but storms, disease, death of D'Anville and suicide of his vice admiral frustrated the attempt. A second fleet sent (May, 1747) was defeated on the open sea by combined British squadrons. Gruesome raids along the New England-New York borders by both conflicting parties and their Indian allies characterized the remainder of the war, with no result except temporary check upon frontier settlement. Weary of futile, costly conflict, the warring parties signed the Peace of Aix-la-Chapelle (October, 1748), granting mutual restoration of conquests (Louisburg for Madras), but leaving colonial questions unsolved.

KING PHILIP'S WAR (1675–76). No longer of value to New Englanders, who, by 1660, produced their own food and valued fishing and commerce above fur trade, Indians played little part in New England economy. Their lands were coveted, their presence denounced, as New Englanders pushed forward the frontier. Conversely, Indians suspected English motives, chafed under English laws, resented missionary efforts. When Massasoit died (1662), new Indian leaders rejected friendship with the English, ignored the Pequots' fate, and were suspected of conspiring against New Englanders.

Chief conspirator was Massasoit's second son, Metacom, or Philip, sachem of the Wampanoags after his elder brother died (1662). Philip renewed the peace covenant with Plymouth Colony, but repeated reports of plots with Narragansetts, the French, and others led Plymouth (1671) to demand an account. Philip haughtily protested peaceful intentions, and agreed to surrender firearms. Sullen peace followed, but the Wampanoags surrendered suspiciously few arms and when three Wampanoags were executed for the murder of John Sassamon, a Christian Indian informer, the warriors got out of hand, plundering and firing farms. Philip's alliances were not concluded, but the English were unprepared, widely scattered, tempting. On June 18, 1675, Wampanoag marauders provoked Swansea settlers to begin hostilities. Swift, devastating raids upon Swansea and neighboring towns threw the colonists into panic, intensified when the militia found no Indians to fight —for the Indians were will-o'-the-wisps and never made a stand. The war was a series of Indian raids with retaliatory expeditions by the English.

The English counter-attack was ill-planned, indecisive and antagonized other tribes. Jealous colonial commanders and troops co-operated badly, the soldiers were poorly equipped and ignorant of

Indian warfare, the troops lacked scouts to track the enemy and, at first, refused to employ friendly Indians. When (June 30) combined Plymouth and Massachusetts forces drove Philip from Mount Hope into Pocasset swamps, he easily slipped into central Massachusetts. Then, suspicious of the Narragansetts, colonial forces raided their country, compelled a few lingerers to sign a treaty of neutrality (July 15), but the warriors, led by Canonchet, had joined in Philip's War. English sale of captives into West Indian slavery and slaughter of innocent Christian Indians drove Nipmucks, Abenaki and even some converted Indians into opposition—though they never united under one leader.

Before the end of 1675, disaster overtook New England on all sides. Middleboro, Brookfield, Deerfield, Northfield and other towns were devastated, abandoned, or both; two colonial forces (Beer's and Lathrop's) were ambushed and destroyed (Sawmill Brook, Sept. 3; Muddy Brook, Sept. 18). Similar raids devastated New Hampshire and Maine settlements. The English in turn destroyed the Narragansetts in the Great Swamp Fight. As winter came on, the Indians encamped at Quabaug and Wachusett. Philip and a small band wintered at Scaticook, near Albany, in hopes of gaining aid from Mohawks and the French.

In 1676 the war began adversely for the English. Planning to attack the eastern settlements in order to concentrate English forces there while they planted crops in the Connecticut Valley, the Indians (Feb. 9) fell upon Lancaster—where the famous Mrs. Rowlandson was captured—and threatened Plymouth, Providence and towns near Boston. Meanwhile, the colonies reorganized their forces, destroyed Narragansett food supplies (December–January, 1675–76), and, though they temporarily fell into the Indian strategical trap, Maj. Palmes (April 3) captured and executed Canonchet; the Mohawks threatened to attack the valley Indians from the west, thereby helping the English; and (May 18–19) Capt. Turner with 180 men surprised and massacred the Indians at Deerfield and broke their resistance in the valley. By the end of May the tide had turned in the west. Capt. Benjamin Church, assisted by able scouts, harried Philip and his followers in swamps near Taunton and Bridgewater, captured his wife and son (Aug. 1), surrounded his camp, and shot Philip as he tried to escape (Aug. 11).

Philip's death marked the end of the war, though hostilities continued in New Hampshire and Maine, where the Abenakis and others, supplied with French arms and encouragement, wreaked havoc upon settlement after settlement. Finally, April 12, 1678, Articles of Peace were signed at Casco, with mutual restoration of captives and property. Since June, 1675, sixteen towns in Massachusetts and four in Rhode Island had been destroyed, no English colonist was left in Kennebec County (Maine), all along New

England frontiers expansion was retarded. But the Indian problem in southern New England was solved; thereafter it was confined to the northeast and northwest where it merged with the struggle with France for control of the continent.

After the Great Swamp Fight (Dec. 19, 1675), the Narragansetts were dispersed and, as the war went against Philip in 1676, scattered bands of Indian refugees, harassed by the English and their Indian allies, fled, some westward to the Mahicans and others northeastward to the Abenaki. Some Nipmucks and Narragansetts joined the Abenaki, later fled to Canada; others, with Pocumtucks, Wampanoags, Mohegans and some Pennacooks and Abenaki, fled to Scaticook on the east bank of the Hudson, where, subsequently, they were adopted by Mohawks. In the 18th century, decimated by disease and the Iroquois, they were induced to join French Indians at St. Francis, Quebec, or driven westward to the Illinois Country.

KING WILLIAM'S WAR (1689–97). This first of the French and Indian wars was already smouldering on the New England frontier at the time of the English declaration of war with France in May, 1689. Angry at the plundering of St. Castine's Trading House, the French had incited the Abenaki tribes of Maine to destroy the rival English post of Pemaquid, and to attack the frontier settlements. The Revolution in England, which forced James II from his throne, was followed by revolt against his representatives in the northern English colonies. The Dominion of New England split into ten or a dozen independent parts, each jealous of its own frontiers. In New York, the civil and military officers of Albany, the key point for Indian relations, were at odds with Jacob Leisler, who had usurped control of the southern part of the province.

In Canada conditions were little better. When Count Frontenac arrived in 1689 to begin his second term as governor, he found the colony terror-stricken by Iroquoian raids. To revive the courage of the French and to regain the allegiance of his Indian allies, he sent out during the winter of 1690 three war parties, of which the first destroyed Schenectady, the second attacked and burned the little settlement of Salmon Falls on the New Hampshire border and the third forced the surrender of Fort Loyal, an outpost at the site of the present city of Portland.

Terror spread throughout the English colonies, and Massachusetts raised a fleet of seven ships, under the command of Sir William Phips, who captured and plundered Port Royal. In May, 1690, at the invitation of Leisler, representatives of Massachusetts, Plymouth, Connecticut and New York met in New York City. A united attack by land on Montreal was planned with the promised co-operation of the Iroquois; Massachusetts and the other New England colonies undertook to attack Quebec at the same time by sea.

Both expeditions were failures. Although a small number of New York and Connecticut troops under the command of Fitz-John Winthrop set out from Albany, they were unable to advance farther than the foot of Lake Champlain. Sir William Phips, who commanded the New England fleet, fared no better. Realizing that neither their financial resources nor their military organization were equal to the task, the leaders of the northern English colonies made repeated appeals to the English government for help. In response, in 1693, a fleet was despatched under the command of Sir Francis Wheeler. This fleet, after operating in the West Indies, reached Boston with fever-stricken crews, and as no preparations had been made to co-operate with it, nothing was accomplished. Frontenac, also, made urgent appeals for help, with no better luck, for the French squadron sent to capture Boston, was delayed by head winds, ran short of provisions and could do nothing.

With both the French and English colonies thus thrown back on their own resources, the results were altogether favorable to the French. Their numerous Indian allies were always available for raids on the English frontier. Pemaquid, which had been rebuilt, was again captured by the French, and the New England frontier suffered cruelly. New York suffered less, but the Iroquois, frightened by French attacks, were with difficulty held to their alliance. The peace of Ryswick (1697) ended the fighting, but did little to settle the questions under dispute.

KING'S MOUNTAIN, BATTLE OF. In the autumn of 1780 Maj. Patrick Ferguson, in command of a detachment of about 1000 soldiers from the army of Lord Cornwallis, made a foray into the western part of North Carolina. The "mountain men," as the dwellers in the back country were called, had been stirred up by the ill conduct of the British troops in the South; and from the western Carolinas and Virginia, as well as from the present states of Kentucky and Tennessee, there gathered about 2000 American frontiersmen under the leadership of Col. Isaac Shelby, Col. William Campbell, Col. John Sevier, Maj. Joseph MacDowell and Maj. Joseph Winston. Hearing of this possible resistance, Ferguson beat a hasty retreat, but the American forces caught up to him at an eminence called King's Mountain, which is in what is now York County, South Carolina, about a mile and a half south of the North Carolina boundary. Here Ferguson took his position atop the mountain on Oct. 6. The next day he was entirely surrounded by the Americans. On the afternoon of the 7th the Americans attacked up the mountain from all sides. The part of the ridge which the British occupied was extremely narrow. The Americans, equipped with long rifles, but without bayonets, assaulted the hill, and the British tactics consisted of charging down the side of the hill with bayonets. However, the cover of trees and shrubs was such that

the Americans were able to retreat only a little way and conceal themselves while the British had to retreat to the summit and charge down the other side of the mountain. As Light Horse Harry Lee pointed out, the hill was "more assailable by the rifle than defensible by the bayonet," and the British lost heavily from rifle fire as they tried successively to regain the height. After about an hour's fighting, Maj. Ferguson was struck by several bullets, one of which killed him. Capt. Abraham DePeyster succeeded to the command, and observing that he was being overwhelmed, raised the white flag. The British force was composed principally, not of regulars, but of Loyalists, and the bitterness felt by the mountain men against their erstwhile Tory neighbors was exceedingly deep. There were charges of atrocities on both sides, possibly with some justification. Practically all the British were either killed, wounded or captured, and they lost over a thousand stand of arms to the Americans. The significance of the battle was best pointed out by Sir Henry Clinton, the British commander in chief, who wrote that this battle "proved the first Link of a Chain of Evils that followed each other in regular Succession until they at last ended in the total Loss of America."

"KITCHEN CABINET" was a title derisively applied by President Jackson's political enemies to an informal group of advisers who were credited with exercising more influence on the President than his regular cabinet. From 1829 until 1831 when the cabinet was reorganized, the "kitchen cabinet" or "lower cabinet," as it was often called, was especially influential. Thereafter, President Jackson relied less on his informal advisers and more on regular members of the cabinet. The most important members of the "kitchen cabinet" were Amos Kendall, Francis Preston Blair, Sr., William B. Lewis, A. J. Donelson, Martin Van Buren and John H. Eaton.

KLONDIKE RUSH. On Aug. 16, 1896, gold was discovered on Bonanza Creek of Klondike (Ton-Dac) River, a tributary of the Yukon River in the Canadian Northwest Territory, by George Carmack and his two Indian brothers-in-law, allegedly on a tip from Robert Henderson. Carmack made known his discovery at the town of Forty Mile, and the miners from that place and other settlements came up and staked claims. At the confluence of the two streams Joseph Ladue laid out Dawson City.

News of the discovery reached the United States in January, 1897, and in the spring of that year a number of persons made preparations to depart by boat via St. Michael up the Yukon or up the Inside Passage to Lynn Canal and over the Chilcoot and White passes and thence down the upper tributaries of the Yukon. On July 14, 1897, the steamer *Excelsior* arrived at San Francisco with $750,000 in gold; on July 17, the *Portland* arrived at Seattle with $800,000.

As no compelling news event was before the country when the ships arrived, the press played up the strike. Thousands of inquiries were received by chambers of commerce, railroads, steamship lines and outfitting houses, and these agencies, seeing the commercial possibilities, commenced a highly financed propaganda which precipitated the rush.

The peak of the rush occurred during 1897–99, when some 100,000 persons departed for Alaska. The passage to the Klondike was facilitated by the progressive construction of the White Pass and Yukon Railroad from Skagway to White Horse. The miners worked their claims for the coarse gold and then sold them—principally to the Guggenheim Exploration Co., which sent up dredges and introduced scientific methods of gold recovery.

The Klondike Rush had far-reaching economic results, particularly for Alaska. Those who were unable to secure claims on the Klondike spread over Alaska, finding gold at Nome, Fairbanks and at numerous lesser places. Many turned to other pursuits. Taken together, the participants in the rush were the principal factor in the diffuse settlement of Alaska and the economic development of the territory.

KNIGHTS OF LABOR was founded by Uriah Stevens and other garment workers in Philadelphia in 1869. For a time the order grew slowly, but during the early 1880's its membership increased in spectacular fashion and in 1886 it included between 600,000 and 700,000 persons. Organized into mixed local and district assemblies, the whole labor movement was to be welded into a single disciplined army. All gainfully employed persons except lawyers, bankers, professional gamblers or stockbrokers, saloon keepers and (prior to 1881) physicians were eligible.

The natural consequence of this all-inclusive membership and of the structural arrangements of the order was a bent in the direction of political action and broad social reform. The underlying premise was that of an abundance of opportunity to be shared among all workers of hand and brain, and the mission of the producing classes was conceived to be to regain for themselves and to protect this opportunity.

Several factors contributed to the rapid decline after 1886. Of immediate and circumstantial character were the unsuccessful outcome of the strike policy, internal friction, and depletion of union finances consequent upon failure of the producers' co-operatives which were supported. Of more basic importance were the structural characteristics of the order and the fallacies in assumption. The centralized control and the mixed character of local and district assemblies inevitably invited difficulties with the "job-conscious" trade unions which, affiliated in the Federation of Organized Trades and Labor Unions called American Federation of Labor after 1886, had evolved a program of worker control of jobs that attracted and held the mass of skilled craftsmen; and by 1890 their federated organization overshadowed the Knights of Labor.

KNIGHTS OF THE GOLDEN CIRCLE, a secret order first recruited in the South, was formed about 1855 by a Cincinnati physician to support proslavery policies and promote conquest of Mexico. During the Civil War the organization was introduced into Indiana as an order of Peace Democrats or Copperheads to oppose Lincoln's war policy. Connected with many acts of minor violence, under this name the order did not promote any serious plots against the Federal Government. It was reorganized in 1863 as the Order of American Knights and in 1864 as the Sons of Liberty, the last being involved in the Northwest Conspiracy.

KNIGHTS OF THE GOLDEN HORSESHOE. So named were the gentlemen who accompanied Gov. Alexander Spotswood of Virginia on his journey to the Blue Ridge in the summer of 1716. Spotswood's companions were presented with miniature golden horseshoes.

KNIGHTS OF THE WHITE CAMELIA arose in New Orleans in 1867 and spread rapidly over the South as an organization to maintain the supremacy of the white race, which was threatened by Radical Reconstruction. Secret, it was organized similarly to the Ku-Klux Klan in councils along state, county and community lines.

KOREA, WAR WITH, 1871. Undeclared hostilities in Korea in 1871 resulted from the murder of Americans, who had illegally entered closed ports, and from the subsequent refusal of Korean isolationists to open the Hermit Kingdom to foreign trade.

By ancient custom, violation of Korean seclusion was a capital offense. In August, 1866, W. B. Preston, an American merchant of Chefoo, despatched the armed schooner *General Sherman* to Ping-yang (now Heijo) in the extreme northwest of Korea to open trade. The schooner grounded on a sandbar in the Ping-yang River. The Koreans, acting by royal command, burned the ship and murdered the entire crew.

The U. S. S. *Shenandoah,* despatched from Chefoo to investigate, was denied all communication with the capital on the ground that it had not come "in obedience to direct instructions from the sovereign of the United States." On the advice of George F. Seward, Consul General at Shanghai, a punitive expedition was authorized. Rear Admiral John Rodgers was instructed to convey Frederick F. Low, American minister to China, to the Korean capital to demand an audience with the king and to secure satisfaction for the *General Sherman* affair. The *Monocacy, Palos* and four steam launches arrived at the mouth of the Han River (then called Salée, or Seoul,

River) on May 26, 1871. Local officials were advised that the squadron was friendly and sought merely to survey the coast and to confer with the king. When no favorable reply was received, the ships started up river. On June 1, masked batteries situated on either side of the stream suddenly opened fire. Two Americans were wounded. The Americans returned the fire, silenced the batteries, and shelled the ravines in which the Koreans sought cover. The Korean loss is unknown. The *Monocacy* then struck a rock and was compelled to withdraw.

Guardian-General Li, of Fu-ping prefecture, formally complained of the American penetration of Korean waters, but declared himself too humble a person to dare communicate the American message to his king. The Americans answered by sending a second expedition, June 10, to reduce the Korean forts. Five batteries were taken and burned. In the battles, which occurred June 11, 250 enemy dead were left on the field. The American loss was three killed and nine wounded. But no satisfactory reply was given the American requests for an audience, and on July 2 Edward B. Drew, acting secretary of legation at Peking, announced that the squadron would withdraw to consult with Washington concerning further steps. No treaty was secured until 1882.

KOREAN WAR (1950–53). The Russians' opportunistic land-grab of Japanese Manchuria during the last week of World War II was halted in Korea by the American occupation northward to the 38th parallel of the Korean peninsula. The parallel became the divider between zones of trusteeship scheduled to end within five years by the establishment of an independent, united Korea. Elsewhere, however, the "cold war" commenced. By late 1947, the United States despaired of forming a provisional government and invoked the jurisdiction of the United Nations, which in November sought to arrange Korean-wide free elections. The North Koreans, refusing to participate, established in February, 1948, a Soviet satellite form of government called the "Democratic People's Republic of Korea." The following July, U. N.-sponsored measures resulted in the creation of the "Republic of Korea," (abbreviated R.O.K.) with Syngman Rhee as President.

Shortly afterward, U. S. military government formally ended, but left forces at Rhee's U. N.-endorsed request to maintain order pending the development of an R. O. K. Army. To the majority of the U. N. General Assembly, Rhee's government had the legal status for ruling all Korea: the Soviet bloc claimed the same for the D. P. R. The views were unreconcilable. Revolts, sabotage and the inexperience of Rhee's administration found his political power waning in the May, 1950, elections. The North Koreans, ostensibly seizing an opportunity to win by legitimate methods, in early June masked

plans for military action by asking the U. N. to supervise elections for an all-Korea government. Then, on June 25, 1950, the North Korean Army, trained and armed by the Russians, suddenly attacked across the parallel with 100,000 troops plentifully supplied with tanks, artillery and modern equipment.

By then, U. S. military commitments had been reduced to 500 advisers training the 95,000 recruits of the new R. O. K. army, whose tactics and equipment were incomplete. The North Koreans advanced irresistibly, ignoring a U. N. cease-fire. President Truman accepted a mandate to intervene and then authorized Gen. Douglas MacArthur to commit U. S. occupation forces in Japan. Other disputes had caused the Soviet delegate to boycott the U. N. Security Council, which on June 27 appealed for military units from the 53 member nations who condemned the North Koreans as aggressors. Ultimately, the R. O. K. and U. S. forces were joined by substantial or token contingents from Australia, Belgium, Canada, Colombia, Ethiopia, France, Great Britain, Greece, Luxembourg, Netherlands, New Zealand, Philippines, South Africa, Thailand and Turkey.

At the outset, except for U. S. Air Force sorties from Japan and U. S. Navy carrier strikes, the R. O. K. Army fought desperately alone. Seoul, the capital, fell on June 28. On July 7, 700 men, constituting the first U. N. aid in ground action, spearheaded the understrength U. S. 24th Infantry Division being airlifted from Japan to Pusan. The U. S. 1st Cavalry Division landed on July 18, a U. S. Marine brigade on Aug. 2, and the U. S. 2nd Infantry Division and 5th Regimental Combat Team on Aug. 3. These sufficed to stiffen the battered R. O. K. formations and to check North Korean momentum. A perimeter was established enclosing a meager 500 square miles hinged upon Pusan.

MacArthur, commanding the U. N. forces after July 7, now exploited U. N. sea and air supremacy to plan a bold "end-run" around the victorious North Koreans which would cut their communications by striking amphibiously at Inchon, the port of Seoul, and the invaders' logistic base. On Sept. 15, 1950, U. S. Marines took Inchon and a firm beachhead. On the 17th, American forces captured Seoul. Almost simultaneously, the U. N. forces at Pusan commanded by U. S. Gen. W. H. Walker broke out of the perimeter and advanced northwards towards Seoul, meeting a southward drive of the Marines on Sept. 26. The North Koreans, fatally overextended, hit in rear and front, became disorganized and fragmented. As they retreated, MacArthur was authorized by a large majority of the U. N. membership to pursue across the border and to demilitarize the aggressors. Pyongyang, the D. P. R. capital, fell on Oct. 19. Terrain features and overconfidence began to divide the advancing, road-bound U. N. troops into eastern and western segments. Between these, a gap of eighty miles opened as they neared the Yalu River which was the border with Red China.

The Korean War was dominated by the possibility of World War III. Consequently, Red China observed the letter of neutrality but freed large numbers of "volunteers" in organic formations which suddenly and skillfully struck between the U. N. columns. In turn caught overextended, the U. N. forces were compelled to retreat. Pyongyang was given up on Dec. 5 and Seoul on Jan. 4, 1951, before the Red Chinese attack was checked. The retreat was brightened by the famous march to sea evacuation at Hungnam by the U. S. Marines. Against great odds, the Marines brought out their casualties and equipment and remained battle-ready.

MacArthur was forbidden to strike across the Yalu, and nuclear armament, still a U. S. monopoly, was withheld. Under these conditions, the war could not be concluded on satisfactory military terms, especially after increasing numbers of Russian-built jet fighters based on trans-Yalu fields began to contest command of the air. Of necessity, MacArthur's objective became the destruction of communist forces actually in Korea. That was to be achieved by "Operation Killer," wherein control of territory was subordinated to the purpose of creating tactical situations in which maximum losses could be inflicted. In two months, "Killer" restored a defensible battle line slightly north of the parallel. But "Killer" could not win while the trans-Yalu area remained a secure staging and regroupment area for the communists. MacArthur's publicized conviction that the war could not be won without decisive measures against Red China itself, led President Truman to replace him with Gen. M. B. Ridgway on April 11, 1951.

A few trials of strength failed to restore decisive movement to the war of attrition. In October, 1951, peace negotiations commenced at Panmunjom and dragged out to an armistice signed on July 27, 1953.

In general, except for a slightly rectified frontier, the *status quo ante bellum* was restored and the basic problem of Korean unity left unsolved. Both sides claimed victory. On balance, if strategic and tactical victory remained out of the grasp of the military on either side, the war was a political success for the U. N. which had undeniably (1) fielded an international fighting force to oppose aggression, (2) held the aggressors back from their objective, and (3) confined the conflict to limited and non-nuclear bounds. Some students of the Soviet scene contend that there was an even greater long-range victory, insofar as the solidarity of the communist bloc might be undermined by communist yielding on the fundamental issue of prisoner-of-war exchange, which was the main cause for delay in reaching an armistice. In the course of World War II, Western powers had conceded the Soviet demand of forced repatriation of Soviet nationals wherever and however found. At Panmunjom, the U. N. representatives finally established the principle of voluntary repatriation of prisoners-of-war. It was underscored by the decision of 114,500 Chinese and 34,000 North Korean prisoners to stay in the free world, while only 22 Americans elected to stay with their captors.

The United States put 1,600,000 servicemen into the war zones. Losses were about 24,000 killed, 9000 missing, 2675 captured, and some 100,000 wounded. The war cost about $20,000,000,000. After the first few months, the American public became almost apathetic towards the war in strong contrast to the national patriotism that burned through World War II. President Truman set the tone with his description of it as a "police action." (*See also* Air Force, U.S.; Army, U.S.; Defense, National; Draft.)

KU-KLUX KLAN. As a movement, the Ku-Klux Klan was relied upon by Southern whites to recoup their prestige destroyed by Radical Reconstruction. Spontaneously organized, May, 1866, in Pulaski, Tenn., by a group of young veterans to provide activity for their unoccupied energies, its potentiality as an agency for disciplining forward freedmen was soon discovered. Its quick flowering over the South was encouraged by unprecedented economic, political and social conditions.

At least one design of Radical Reconstruction was to abolish the once dominant political power of the agrarian South by attaching the recently enfranchised freedmen to the Republican party. With leading southern whites disfranchised and with elections conducted by Federal troops, state and local governments were soon in the inexperienced and unscrupulous hands of ex-slaves, carpetbaggers and scalawags.

At Nashville, in 1867, the Ku-Klux Klan was organized into the "Invisible Empire of the South" ruled by a "Grand Wizard"; the "Realms" (states), were ruled by "Grand Dragons"; the "Provinces" (counties) were headed by "Grand Titans"; the individual "Dens" were under the authority of a "Grand Cyclops." The "Dens" had couriers known as "Night Hawks." The organization's objective was to open the way for the reassertion of the supremacy of the whites politically and socially.

To intimidate Negroes and to escape being identified by Federal troops, the Klansmen covered their bodies in white robes, masked their faces, wore high, cardboard hats, and rode robed horses with muffled feet. One of their favorite practices was to ride out of woods, surprising Negroes walking home in the darkness from meetings of the Union League, an organization which sought to direct the Negroes' votes into the proper Republican channels. The Klan invariably rode at night.

The Klan also intimidated carpetbaggers and scalawags and played unseen influential roles in many trials in the South. It was responsible for floggings and lynchings in extreme circumstances. The trying times led it into inexcusable acts on occasions. The Klan was formally disbanded in the spring of 1869, but it did not die.

In April, 1871, a "joint Select Committee" of seven Senators and fourteen Representatives was selected "to inquire into the Conditions of Affairs in the late Insurrectionary States. . . ." In 1871 the Ku-Klux Act was passed, empowering the President to use Federal troops and to suspend the writ of habeas corpus in an effort to abolish the "conspiracy" against the Federal Government in the South. The gradual reassumption of political power by the whites saw the activities of the Klan gradually decline.

KU KLUX KLAN (20TH CENTURY) traced its inspiration to the intolerance of Know-Nothingism rather than to the Ku-Klux Klan of the Reconstruction era. It was founded in Georgia in 1915 by Col. William J. Simmons but remained small and local until 1920 when two professional publicity agents, Edward Y. Clarke and Mrs. Elizabeth Tyler, began a nationwide membership campaign. Their slogan of "native, white, Protestant" supremacy found favor in the United States of the 1920's, and by 1925 between four and five million Americans had enrolled. Fiery crosses, the symbol of the new order, were burned in every part of the country, and the hooded members denounced Negroes, bootleggers, Jews, pacifists, Bolshevists, internationalists, Catholics and evolutionists with equal impartiality. This rapid growth led eventually to the Klan's downfall, for popular interest precipitated a congressional investigation and newspaper exposures of its terroristic methods and of the floggings and killings for which it was responsible. Its decline was inadvertently hastened by politicians who used the Klan's ready-made political machine to elevate themselves to positions of power in Texas, Louisiana, Oklahoma, Maine, Kansas, Indiana and other states. Their corrupt administrations, particularly in Indiana, did much to discredit the order. By 1928, when the Klan abandoned its secrecy, most of its strength was gone.

LABOR DAY. On May 8, 1882, Peter J. McGuire, carpenters' union founder, proposed to the New York City Central Labor Union the designation of an annual "labor day," recommending the first Monday in September as midway between July 4 and Thanksgiving Day. This resulted in a parade and festival of the New York group the following Sept. 5. Oregon (Feb. 21, 1887) declared the first holiday, 31 states having followed this example when Cleveland signed the national bill (June 28, 1894).

LABOR IN AMERICA. Unsuccessful in attempts to utilize native (Indian) resources as a labor force, the sponsors of colonies in the 17th century looked to Western Europe for their source of supply. Impoverished or propertyless laborers were induced to migrate to the far from Utopian Middle Atlantic and Southern colonies through the promise of a better life. The labor force of the New World was recruited either as workers for chartered companies (in Virginia to 1624), as indentured servants, as redemptioners later in the 18th century, or as apprentices. An agreement stipulating that after the period of servitude the laborer would receive his freedom, and possibly land besides, proved attractive to the unemployed and hopeless in Western Europe who came from England, from among the Scots settlers in northern Ireland and from the western states of Germany.

Involuntary laborers, convicts, debtors, stranded seamen, and Negro slaves were also brought to the colonies to meet the insatiable demand for hands. At first almost all the work was performed on the soil; but with growing population and consequent specialization of function, urban centers such as Boston, Philadelphia, New York, Baltimore and Charleston arose with their demands for mechanics, artisans, apprentices and wage laborers.

Throughout the colonial period, and in fact, throughout the history of the United States—with the possible exception of 1920–60—labor has been in short supply. During the 17th and 18th centuries impressment and co-operation were often resorted to in order to meet labor needs. Roof-raising and barn building were usually co-operative community activities, and crops were saved from ruin in some of the New England colonies by authorizing constables to impress mechanics and artisans to harvest the neighborhood fields.

Labor shortages required in some instances colonial controls over wages. Jonathan Winthrop remarks in his *Journals* that the cupidity of the artisans in Massachusetts knew no bounds. In 1633, as a consequence of high wage demands, the Massachusetts General Court set a maximum wage for most skilled mechanics. Employers and employees violating this law were to be penalized as were workers who refused to toil. Three years later, after the general penalties were removed and this law proved inoperative, the towns were given jurisdiction over wage determinations. Hours of toil were the traditional agricultural norm of "sun-up to sun-down."

Common interests of artisans resulted in some degree of organization in the 17th century, but it was not until the end of the 18th century that labor unionism, as now understood, came into being. During the agitation regarding taxation and home rule which rocked the colonies after the French and Indian War (Seven Years' War), urban laborers were to be found in the forefront of the anti-Parliament cause. The Sons of Liberty in New York recruited many of its members from among the workers and the famous Boston Massacre was in large part the outgrowth of a labor conflict.

The appearance of merchant-capitalists, organized

into associations of master employers seeking to reduce costs and increase profits by undercutting wages and extending hours of labor of their workmen, caused the laborer, usually of the skilled variety, to turn to organization for protection. As early as the 1780's short-lived local craft groups were founded, but not until the 1790's did more permanent unions appear. In 1792 the Philadelphia shoemakers formed a protective organization and in 1794 the Typographical Society of New York was founded. In addition to the usual union aims found in later organizations, such as higher wages, shorter hours and better working conditions, these bodies of workmen also sponsored fraternal benefits for sickness and burials.

These early unions, concentrating in the few large urban centers, invented some of the techniques later used extensively by labor organizations. Strikes, boycotts, business agents, collective bargaining and the closed shop appeared early in the history of trade unionism. More usual, however, was the attempt made by the New York typographers to control the number and duration of apprenticeships in order to protect wage standards and work quality.

Employers' associations, organized both to protect the interests of employers and to combat the unionized artisans, early questioned the legal right of workers to combine into labor organizations. They argued that the English common law, which held that any combination of workers whose aim was to improve their financial lot constituted a conspiracy against the public weal, was applicable in the United States in the absence of any statute law on this point. From the turn of the 19th century until 1815 in almost all of a number of separate conspiracy trials the English common law contention was upheld. As a result of these decisions the embryonic labor unions formed at the end of the 18th century soon foundered and disappeared.

The destructive nature of these conspiracy decisions, particularly those in the Philadelphia cordwainers' (1806) and New York cordwainers' (1809–10) cases, was not overcome until a new political climate prevailed. Although democracy under Jackson did not completely free unions from legal disabilities, it gave an impetus to more liberal interpretations of labor's rights. The decision of Chief Justice Lemuel Shaw in the 1842 Massachusetts case of Commonwealth v. Hunt, recognizing the legality of unions and their right to strike for a closed shop, was the most important case in eliminating the effects of the conspiracy decisions upon trade unions.

During the first half of the 19th century wage scales for both skilled and unskilled labor were generally from one-third to one-half higher than those for similar workers in Western Europe. The unskilled factory worker received from 90 cents to $1.00 a day which was approximately half the amount received by a skilled worker. Farm workers received

up to $15.00 a month with board and from 50 cents to $1.50 a day without board. Even though these wages were often inadequate to support a family unless more than one member of the family was working, the evils associated with the introduction of the factory system in England were largely avoided.

Hours of labor continued to be extremely long during this period, generally varying between twelve to fifteen actual work hours. The early factory mills were frequently unhealthy and unsanitary work places.

Initially the newly formed textile factories recruited their labor force from among single women, daughters of New England farmers, who worked for marriage dues or for a trousseau. Humanitarian factory owners, such as Francis Cabot Lowell, attempted to introduce sorority-like living in the factory dormitories and many foreign visitors (Harriet Martineau, 1835) commented favorably on factory life in Waltham, Mass. Overlooked by these visitors was the excessive paternalism, minute supervision of the workers' lives by the employer, the requirement of purchasing goods in the company stores and worshipping in the company churches.

Increased immigration from Western Europe during the 1840's and renewed agreements among employers as to wages, hours, conditions and blacklists ended the Waltham system. The growing competition for jobs and the extended use of child labor in the factories, coupled with the depressing effects of the panic of 1837, resulted in wage reductions for factory workers and increased paternalistic supervision over their lives by the employers.

The extension of democratic ideals in the 1820's created a more favorable climate for trade union organizational success. Renewed trade union activity found expression in the first recorded strike of women workers when in 1824 the Pawtucket, R. I., women weavers left work for higher wages. In Philadelphia, Boston, New York, New Orleans and Paterson, N. J., carpenters, weavers, tailors, cordwainers, cabinet makers, masons, stevedores, hatters and riggers formed fairly stable trade unions. The recognition by many of the workmen that, regardless of craft, they had many problems in common, prompted fifteen Philadelphia unions in 1827 to form the first city central trade council, the Mechanics Union of Trade Associations. By 1836 thirteen other cities followed the Philadelphia mechanics' lead.

Under the leadership of Thomas Skidmore and William Leggett in New York and John Ferrol and William English in Philadelphia, labor sought to achieve certain of its objectives through political action. In 1828, first in Philadelphia and then in New York and Boston, Workingmen's Parties were formed. Among their goals were the reduction of the workday to ten hours, abolition of imprisonment for debt, abolition of prison contract labor, enactment of mechanics' lien laws, curbs on banks and other monopolies, universal education and free public land to settlers. In a few years these parties disappeared, either having been absorbed by the Jacksonian Democracy or the Whigs or forming radical factions (Loco Focos) of the New York and Pennsylvania Democratic party.

Despite organized labor's support of Andrew Jackson, the first use of Federal troops in a labor dispute was ordered under his administration, in January, 1834. When Irish workers on the Chesapeake and Ohio Canal in Maryland struck for a closed shop and violence ensued, Jackson directed the War Department to halt the "riotous assembly" and restore peaceful conditions at the canal works. In that same year the New York General Trades Union, a city central, called a convention of delegates from other city centrals to discuss nonpolitical trade union objectives. From this meeting emerged the first national federation of labor organizations, the National Trades Union, under the leadership of Ely Moore, a New York printer and union leader who was elected to Congress from New York and served as labor's first Congressman from 1834 to 1839. The depression which followed the panic of 1837 saw the disappearance not only of the National Trades Union, but also of the various city centrals and almost all of the local trade unions.

Social panaceas, utopianism and the ten-hour day movement dominated the thinking of labor during the next decade and a half. Associationism of either the Fourierist or Owenite variety captured the imagination of the leaders of labor and co-operation of the Rochdale variety was attempted unsuccessfully in both production and consumption by elements of organized labor. Labor was also attracted to the agrarian reform movement espoused by George Henry Evans, editor of the *New York Working Man's Advocate.* Evans called for free homesteads and many workers believed this to be the answer to their propertyless state. Lack of success of these reform attempts slowly alienated the workers and they turned increasingly to the more immediate economic gains which they hoped to achieve through trade unionism.

The ten-hour day movement was, on paper, more successful. In 1836, as a result of the initiative of Ely Moore and the National Trades Union, Jackson's Secretary of the Navy ordered a ten-hour day in the Philadelphia Navy Yard. President Martin Van Buren in 1840 extended the ten-hour day to laborers working on Federal public works. Ten-hour legislation was passed in seven states during the 1840's and '50's, but in all cases loopholes in the laws allowed workers to toil longer if they contracted a longer work day. By 1860, although the ten-hour day was widely accepted for skilled craftsmen, it still was not the universal norm for unskilled workers.

The improved economic conditions spurred on by increased industrialization and fortuitous gold finds in California caused a resurgence of labor union activi-

ties. Many locals were formed and some ten national unions were organized in the 1850's. In 1852, the National Typographical Union, which has had a continuous existence to this day, was founded; the Iron Molders formed a national union under the leadership of William Sylvis in 1859. The Hat Finishers (1854), Journeymen Stone Cutters Association (1855), United Cigarmakers (1856), Machinists and Blacksmiths (1859) were organized. Rejecting utopias and stressing immediate economic gains, these unions were so solidly formed that even the panic of 1857 did not destroy all of them.

The outbreak of the Civil War occasioned a severe labor shortage, what with the needed wartime industrial expansion in the face of large scale military recruitment from among labor's ranks. Congress, in 1864 authorized the importation of contract labor to fill this need. Inflation, a usual partner of war, caused real wages to decline by one third from 1860 levels by 1865. Although few strikes were called by unions during the war, labor considered the Draft Law of 1863 as unfair and consequently displayed some sympathy for the Irish laborers who rioted against the draft in New York.

Favorable wartime conditions acted as a further spur to trade union organization. National organizations and city centrals expanded their hold; an attempt was even made in Louisville, Ky., in 1865 by delegates from eight city centrals to form a national federation of unions but the "International Industrial Assembly of North America" never really came into being. During and immediately after the war the Railway Brotherhoods were founded; the Locomotive Engineers in 1863, the Railway Conductors in 1868 and the Firemen in 1873. The shoemakers organization, the Order of the Knights of St. Crispin, started in 1867, had attained a membership of over 50,000 by 1870. The introduction of machinery into the shoe trade transformed the industry by allowing unskilled hands to replace skilled shoemakers. The Crispins sought to overcome this by creating producers' co-operatives. Failure of these ventures to succeed spelled the doom of the Knights of St. Crispin early in the 1870's.

The iron molders under Sylvis and the anthracite coal miners, organized into a Workingmen's Benevolent Association by John Siney in 1868, were the two most powerful unions during the immediate post Civil War period. Both organizations were weakened in the early 1870's however; the molders by concerted employer opposition and the miners by increasing competition from immigrant labor. At their height, however, both unions could claim a membership of over 300,000 each.

Encouraged by the national unions and by local associations of workers and reformers seeking to establish the eight-hour day—a movement pioneered by Ira Stewart of Boston—a national organization of labor, the National Labor Union, was established in

Baltimore in 1866. Under the leadership of William Sylvis of the Molders and Richard F. Trevellick of the Ship Carpenters and Caulkers International, the National Labor Union concentrated upon producers' co-operatives and national political action to achieve its aims. The failure of the co-operatives and the minimizing of trade union methods and objectives caused many of the national unions to withdraw from the federation after Sylvis' death in 1869. In 1872 the organization converted itself into the National Labor Reform party which nominated David Davis of Illinois for President. Davis' withdrawal, after failing to capture the nomination of the Democratic party, resulted in the collapse of both the party and the National Labor Union. This short-lived federation was not a complete failure for through its efforts Congress passed a law in 1868 limiting the hours of Federal employees (laborers and mechanics) to eight a day. Furthermore, the National Labor Union was the first body of organized American workers to make contact with its European counterparts when it sent a delegate to the First International in Basel in 1869 to discuss means of limiting migration of European workmen to the United States.

The depression following the panic of 1873 saw the trade unions lose a substantial number of members so that of the thirty national unions in existence only some eight were able to survive. More significantly, the growth of the corporate form of industrial organization forced a wider separation of workers from employers. Consequently impersonal corporations did not consider the human price of layoffs, wage cuts and other forms of extracting more labor from workmen at lower costs. Defensive actions by workers, organized or unorganized, often resulted in violence and other manifestations of labor turbulence. Before the depression had run its course armed clashes between workers, private police and Federal and state militia had become a commonplace.

One casualty of the depression was the miners' union. In its absence anarchy ruled the anthracite fields. In eastern Pennsylvania a secret organization of Irish miners, called by the newspapers of the time "Molly Maguires" but actually an outgrowth of a fraternal order, the "Ancient Order of Hibernians," was accused of murdering opponents, not only miners competing for the jobs of their members but also foremen and mine bosses carrying out the policies of the Philadelphia and Reading Railroad, the operators of the local mine fields. As a result of the testimony of a Pinkerton detective, James McParlan, 24 Molly Maguires were convicted of murder in 1875 and ten were hanged in 1876, even though the evidence seems spurious in 1960.

A series of wage reductions sparked a most militant labor demonstration in 1877 when a veritable general strike tied up the railroads of the country. Strikes and spontaneous work stoppages began on July 17 on the Baltimore and Ohio Railroad system

and before the month was over had spread to the Pennsylvania, the New York Central and to many western lines. At Martinsburg, W. Va., the strikers clashed with the state militia and after nine persons were killed, President Rutherford B. Hayes dispatched Federal troops to restore order. General rioting followed at Baltimore, Pittsburgh, Chicago and St. Louis. The violent climax of the strike was reached in Pittsburgh, where on July 21 the strikers, joined by sympathetic bystanders, fought a pitched battle with a company of Philadelphia militiamen. The Pittsburgh militia was considered unreliable for it sided with the strikers; thus Philadelphia troops were called in. After surrounding the defeated state troops in a railroad roundhouse, the enraged mob burned down machine shops, destroyed the Union depot and damaged property valued at $5,000,000. Twenty-six people were killed in Pittsburgh before the Federal troops put down the disturbances and broke the strike. Many state legislatures reacted to the violence of the great strikes of 1877 by re-enacting conspiracy laws; labor reacted by turning to politics and, temporarily at least, to radical movements.

The Greenback party was the immediate recipient of labor's support when locally organized Workingmen's parties combined with the Greenbackers to form the National Greenback-Labor party at Toledo in 1878. The success of this party in the election of 1878—it elected fifteen members to Congress and gained over a million votes—was misleading. The resumption of specie payment on Jan. 1, 1879, and the cleavage between the aims of the currency reformers and the labor people in the party caused its rapid decline.

Marxian and Lassallean socialism had some influence on the labor movement after 1876. The headquarters of the First International was moved to New York City during its declining years. The Marxists organized a Workingmen's party in 1876 and a year later its name was changed to Socialist Labor party. This party attempted to work within the trade union movement, but succeeded only among those unions like the Cigarmakers and the Furniture Workers, which had a high proportion of German immigrants among its members. In 1878–79 the Marxists, through their short-lived International Labor Union, attempted unsuccessfully to organize unskilled textile workers in Fall River, Mass., and Paterson, N. J. Only in Chicago did the socialists have any success in the city trades council, but this was dissipated in 1880 as a result of the friction between the Marxists and the newly formed anarchist faction within the labor movement.

In San Francisco, the Workingmen's party of California, under the domination of Dennis Kearney, gained some degree of political success with its program of Chinese immigration restriction. Anti-Chinese riots in 1877 were stimulated by this party and it elected a mayor of San Francisco in 1879. Although the party disintegrated by 1881, its anti-Chinese agitation bore fruit when in 1882 Congress enacted a law prohibiting Chinese immigration to the United States for twenty years.

Antagonism to labor organizations which dominated the public mind throughout the depression years led to the prevalence of secret societies and orders among the workers. The one labor group which had a rapid rise in membership and influence and equally rapid decline in the 1880's, the Noble Order of the Knights of Labor, began as a secret society. Founded in 1869 by a group of Philadelphia garment cutters led by Uriah S. Stephens, it did not gain strength until after the violence of 1876–77. By 1881 the Knights had a membership of 19,000 which increased to 111,000 in 1885 and swelled to some 700,000 a year later.

In form the Knights resembled a national union of all workers. Organized into local and district assemblies, some of which contained workers of a single craft but most of which were mixed as to crafts and skills, the Knights were constitutionally a highly centralized group, with the assemblies being directly responsible to the general executive board and the Grand Master Workman. All gainfully employed persons except lawyers, bankers, gamblers, stockbrokers, saloon keepers and physicians were eligible for membership.

Under the leadership of Terence V. Powderly, Grand Master Workman from 1879 to 1893, the secret nature of the Order was abolished in 1881 and the Knights for a short time became the most powerful single labor organization in the United States. They favored the eight-hour day, advocated such reforms as the graduated income tax and prohibition of imported contract labor, sponsored consumers' and producers' co-operatives and condemned the growing monopoly power of banks and railroads. Despite Powderly's emphasis on the boycott and arbitration as the means for achieving labor's economic advances, a spontaneous strike movement among the Knights' railroad members in the Gould system resulted in large additions to the Order's ranks.

After a number of successful strikes conducted by the Knights against Western railroads in 1884 and 1885, Jay Gould agreed to discontinue discriminatory practices against members of the Order. A year later, when the Texas and Pacific Railroad did not live up to the agreement, the District Assembly immediately involved, led by Martin Irons, called another strike against the Gould system over the objections of Powderly. Marked by violence, arrests and pitched battles, the strike was doomed to failure by the adamant refusal of Jay Gould to arbitrate the dispute as requested by Powderly. The failure of the Knights in this strike and in other actions in 1886, coupled with the growing antilabor sentiment which stemmed from the public reaction to the Haymarket massacre of May 4, 1886, resulted in the serious decline of the Order as a labor organization.

Even before the catastrophic demise of the Knights the revived craft unions, seeking a federated home, had deserted the Order, feeling that the latter was organizationally impractical for autonomous, job-conscious trade unions. The Knights of Labor thus remained a shadow of its former self, mainly dominated by its agrarian western members. In 1893 when James R. Sovereign of Iowa replaced Powderly as Grand Master Workman the order virtually ceased to exist as a labor organization.

The brief but spectacular career of the Knights of Labor was not devoid of results. Many weak unions were strengthened and some new unions were established through affiliation with the Order. Its lobbying activities were instrumental in the passage of the Foran Act in 1885 which aimed at cutting off the migration to the United States of contract labor. The House of Representatives established a standing Committee of Labor in 1883, and in 1884 a Federal Bureau of Labor to gather data was created. The railway strikes conducted by the Knights prompted Congress to pass a law in 1888 calling for the settlement of railway labor disputes by arbitration if both parties agreed. Most important, the Knights emphasized once again that only through organization could labor achieve even minimum economic benefits.

The eight-hour movement, strongly endorsed by all segments of organized labor, reached its climax in May, 1886. The national unions set the first of that month as the deadline for achieving an eight-hour day. Labor demonstrations were called for as the day approached and clashes with the police were commonplace. Aroused by the shooting of several workmen in Chicago, the anarchist newspaper, *Die Arbeiter Zeitung*, called for a mass meeting of protest at the Haymarket. Although the circulars issued were inflammatory, the speeches were innocuous. Despite the Mayor's advice, Capt. Bonfield, leading 180 police, advanced on the meeting and ordered the crowd to disperse. A bomb was thrown causing the death of seven policemen and injuring many. Fears of an anarchist plot made impartial investigation impossible. Eight anarchists were convicted on a conspiracy charge, four were hanged and one committed suicide. In 1893, Gov. Altgeld pardoned the three surviving prisoners on the ground that they did not receive a fair trial. The Haymarket affair served to hasten the demise of the Knights of Labor even though the Order had nothing to do with the events in Chicago. The eight-hour movement, branded as radical, also suffered in consequence of the tragic event of May 4.

In the wake of the disastrous effects that the depression years of 1873–79 had upon the national trade unions, many leaders of labor began considering means to make their organizations more effective. Realizing that lack of central control, absence of strike funds, striving after monetary reforms and advocating social panaceas had not achieved results, men like Samuel Gompers and Adolph Strasser of the New York Cigarmakers Union looked to the British trade unions and their Trade Union Congress as models. After a catastrophic strike of long duration had virtually destroyed the Cigarmakers Union in 1877, Gompers and Strasser reorganized the union along the lines of the British unions. Centralized control of the locals, effective collection of strike funds and concern only over immediate economic objectives of the cigar workers were the prinicipal guides of this "new unionism."

To the promoters of the "new unionism" the reorganization of the Cigarmakers Union was only a first step. In emulating the British Trade Unions Congress they felt that a national federation of trade unions embodying business union principles was essential in order to mold labor unity for national acts of defense against aggressive employer groups, to lobby for favorable legislation and to prevent the energies of organized labor from being dissipated in political and social utopian schemes. Consequently Gompers and Strasser seized upon a call for a national convention of laboring groups issued by two secret societies in 1881 to accomplish this aim. On Nov. 15, 1881, the Federation of Organized Trades and Labor Unions was formed in Pittsburgh. For a short time this federation and the Knights of Labor tried to co-operate, but when the essentially anti-trade-union approach of the Knights was reflected in its sanctioning of trade assemblies or dual unions competing with Federation affiliates, the trade unions called another convention at Columbus, O. There on Dec. 8, 1886, the American Federation of Labor was organized with the Federation of Organized Trades and Labor Unions disbanding in favor of the newer federation.

From its beginnings to 1924, with the exception of one year, Samuel Gompers was elected president of the A. F. of L. Organized on the principle that each constituent national union was autonomous, the federation had only those powers that were delegated to it by the constitution or by the convention. City central unions and state federations co-ordinated economic and political actions of the A. F. of L. affiliates on the local or state level and also joined with the executive council in helping to organize new craft unions. Co-ordinating councils or departments within a single industry, such as the building trades department, consisted of delegates from the various unions in that industry. They sought to promote their common interests and to settle any jurisdictional disputes between member unions. The executive council, consisting of a president, several vice-presidents, a treasurer and a secretary, administered the affairs of the federation between annual conventions. A per capita tax on all members provided funds for the work of the federation.

Through collective bargaining and through the use of such weapons as the strike, boycott and picketing, the A. F. of L. sought to improve the economic status of the members of its affiliates. It sought public support through a campaign to popularize the union label among consumers. Being an organization of craft unions whose members were mainly skilled workers, the A. F. of L. stressed job security, favored the curbing of immigration, espoused the enactment of national and state laws favorable to labor, demanded relief from technological unemployment and endeavored to achieve these objectives through collaboration with employer and consumer groups. It rejected independent political action, seeking only to lobby on behalf of its members. Only rarely did the federation deviate from its political principle of rewarding its friends and punishing its enemies.

The A. F. of L. made slow progress in its attempted organization of the workmen during the early years. The membership of its affiliated unions rose from somewhat less than 200,000 in 1886 to slightly more than 1,750,000 in 1904. Gompers, as president, vigorously acted as organizer, conciliator and peace maker within labor's ranks. Jurisdictional conflicts between member unions were resolved and in the 1890's the electrical workers, teamsters, musicians and building laborers were formed into national unions. Despite this activity the proportion of workers organized in unions lagged behind the growth of the labor force. With rapid industrialization utilizing unskilled immigrant labor, the A. F. of L. persisted in concentrating its attention on the skilled crafts. Only the United Mine Workers, founded in 1890 as a result of an amalgamation of the A. F. of L. miners with those affiliated with the Knights, was initially organized along industrial lines and succeeded in winning over Slavic and Italian miners in the bituminous fields after a successful strike in 1897.

More typical was the experience of the Amalgamated Association of Iron, Steel and Tin Workers. In 1890 this union, which restricted its membership to skilled workers, claimed a total of 24,000 members in the steel industry. In 1892, the union had a contract with the Carnegie Co. at Homestead, Pa., which was to be renegotiated. Henry Clay Frick, manager of the steel works, realizing that the union did not represent the majority of the Homestead workers, who by this time were mainly Slavic unskilled laborers, refused to accord recognition to the union and ordered a reduction in wages. The strike which followed had the support of the entire labor force of the steel works. When on July 6 Frick hired some 300 Pinkerton guards to keep the mills open for strikebreakers and had them brought to Homestead on river barges by night, the strikers prevented the guards from landing and a battle broke out causing a number of deaths. Although the Pinkertons surrendered, the state militia was summoned and under its protection the strike was broken even though it dragged on for four more months. Thus, organized labor's first struggle with large-scale capital ended in failure; the Amalgamated Association of Iron, Steel and Tin Workers lost support in other steel mills and the steel industry was destined to be free of union controls for many more years.

The Coeur d'Alene district of northern Idaho was rocked by violence at the same time as Homestead, Pa. A strike of lead and silver miners who became part of the Western Federation of Miners, a sometime A. F. of L. affiliate, was marked by pitched battles, dynamiting of a mill and the proclamation of martial law when the owners sought to run their mines with strikebreakers and sweeping injunctions. Federal and state troops restored order and the strike was broken, but in 1894 and again in 1899 the events of 1892 were repeated.

Concern over the failure of the A. F. of L. unions and the Railroad Brotherhoods to attempt to recruit large numbers of unskilled workers into their ranks caused some to question the basic premises of craft union philosophy. The socialists in particular were critical of the job-conscious skilled labor monopoly approach to unionism of Gompers and the A. F. of L. Largely as a result of their efforts, Gompers was defeated for the presidency of the federation in 1894 but returned to office in 1895 when his successor proved unequal to the task of supervising the loose federation. Failing in their attempt to capture the A. F. of L., the socialists, led by Daniel DeLeon, sought to win control of the almost defunct Knights of Labor. In 1895, when this also failed, the Socialist Labor party established an independent federation, the Socialist Trade and Labor Alliance. This deliberate creation of a "dual federation" alienated many socialists who believed it to be a cardinal sin in the labor movement. Many defected from the Socialist Labor party and in 1897 formed a rival organization, the Social Democracy. In 1900, this organization united with still another moderate faction of the Socialist Labor party to create a new group, the Socialist Party of America which became the largest socialist group in the United States and continued to challenge Gompers' policies, but from within the ranks of the constituent unions of the A. F. of L.

The failure of the Railroad Brotherhoods to create a federation of railroad unions after the unsuccessful strike on the Burlington Railroad in 1888 caused Eugene Victor Debs, a former secretary of the Locomotive Firemen, to attempt a new type of organization. In 1893 the American Railway Union was founded as an industrial union open to all railroad workers including the unskilled switchmen and maintenance workers who had been ignored by the Brotherhoods. Despite the depression which followed the panic of 1893 and resulted in widespread unemployment, the new American Railway Union was able to attract a membership of 150,000 after it had conducted a successful strike against the Great

Northern Railroad in April, 1894. Instead of consolidating its gains, the Debs'-led union was forced almost immediately into a strike by members working for the Pullman Co. This quickly assumed nationwide proportions.

Wage reductions averaging 25% ordered by the Pullman Co. to offset the heavy losses caused by the depression were not matched by any reductions of rents or fees charged the workers living in the model town run by the company, Pullman, Ill. Disgruntled, about 4000 employees joined the American Railway Union and on May 11, 1894, they quit work. The Pullman Co., receiving revenues from the rental of its equipment to the railroads, was not willing to arbitrate or negotiate a settlement with the union. The union, therefore, called upon its members on the railroads not to handle Pullman cars. As a result of this boycott call, 24 railroads centering in Chicago were tied up and by June 28 the whole West was affected. By June 30, the railroads in the entire country were affected.

The strike seriously curtailed the movement of mail; consequently, at the request of the railroad's General Managers' Association, Richard Olney, President Cleveland's Attorney General, secured injunctions against the union's interference with interstate commerce. Defiance of the injunction of July 2 led to the arrest of Debs and the ordering of Federal troops into Chicago by Cleveland. Gov. Altgeld of Illinois protested against this violation of state rights and the presence of the Federal troops triggered mob violence and destruction of railroad property. Riots were reported as far west as Oakland, Calif., and Federal troops were ordered to strike duty there. By July 13 some trains were running under military guard and a week later the strike was broken. Thus the first and only attempt to create a single railroad union ended in failure. More significant was the dramatic and successful use of an injunction to curb the strike. The U. S. Supreme Court upheld the right of Federal judges to issue such injunctions in the case In re Debs (158 U. S. 564) and for many years organized labor campaigned to abolish the use of injunctions by Federal and state courts in labor disputes.

Labor leaders, disappointed by the results of the Pullman strike and by the march on Washington of a jobless army led by Jacob S. Coxey for unemployment relief and Federal work projects in 1894, turned once more to political action. Debs, who spent six months in prison, read Marxist literature and became a socialist. Other labor leaders attempted a coalition with the Populists. The A. F. of L. remained true to its nonpolitical position and consequently when the depression subsided after 1897 and the Populist party virtually disappeared after the election of 1896 it was prepared to take advantage of better times to continue its organization of skilled workmen into labor unions.

From 1898 to 1904, a time called "the honeymoon period of capital and labor," the A. F. of L. unions received wide recognition from employers and with the assistance of such middle-class organizations as the National Consumers' League, National Civic Federation, National Child Labor Committee and the American Association for Labor Legislation, was able to increase its membership substantially. The organizational success of the A. F. of L. unions as well as the new progressive mood of the nation were reflected in the action of President Theodore Roosevelt when John Mitchell, the president of the United Mine Workers, in attempting to organize the anthracite miners, called a strike in 1902. Roosevelt compelled the mine owners to accept arbitration by a commission appointed by the President. The commission's award of a 10% wage increase for the anthracite miners was the first known example of the Federal Government's intervention in a labor dispute on the workers' behalf. A number of new national unions chartered by the A. F. or L. were founded during this period; notable among them was the International Ladies' Garment Workers' Union (1900).

Trade union success caused a noticeable stiffening of attitudes among some employers. The National Association of Manufacturers, organized in 1895, spearheaded a campaign against trade unionism by sponsoring an open-shop drive which appreciably slowed down union organizational achievements after 1904. The unions were dealt a heavy blow by the courts during this open-shop campaign when boycotts were ruled to be violations of the Sherman Antitrust Act. The D. E. Loewe Co. of Danbury, Conn., was awarded triple damages under the Sherman Act when the Supreme Court in 1908 upheld its contention that the 1902 boycott of its wares initiated by the hatters' union was illegal. Gompers was cited for contempt of court in 1909 in another boycott case, that against the Bucks' Stove and Range Co.

At the same time, the A. F. of L. trade union concepts of craft exclusiveness and autonomy were challenged from the left. In Chicago in June, 1905, delegates from the Western Federation of Miners, from DeLeon's Socialist Trade and Labor Alliance and some individual socialists like Eugene V. Debs founded the Industrial Workers of the World (I. W. W.) whose object it was to unite all workers, regardless of skill, race or ethnic origin, into one centralized industrial organization. Emphasizing the class struggle, the I. W. W. called for the abolition of the wage system and stressed direct action, the general strike, boycott and sabotage, as the means of accomplishing this end. Factionalism and defections weakened the organization from the beginning, but after the elimination of the DeLeon faction in 1908, William D. Haywood and Vincent St. John were able to achieve a certain degree of success for the industrial union. In the West, the unskilled and migratory lumber, shipping and farm laborers were organized. In the East, the "Wobblies" provided English-speaking leadership for immigrant workers, especially those in textile factories. Under Haywood's leadership these textile workers won wage increases after strikes at Lawrence, Mass., in 1912 and Paterson, N. J., in 1913. The I. W. W.'s syndicalist philosophy, its rejection of collective bargaining and its extreme tactics, prevented any but the most desperate workers from joining, so that at its height in 1913 the organization did not have more than 70,000 members. Federal prosecutions of its leaders during World War I coupled with effective vigilante action, notably at Centralia, Wash., eliminated the I. W. W. as an effective labor federation, but not before it had called attention to the need for organizing the millions of unskilled workers who were flocking to the labor force to man new mass industries. Furthermore, the attention it paid to the migratory farm and lumber workers in the West underscored the problems of this underprivileged group.

Meeting the challenge of both the open-shop, antiunion employer groups and the militant industrial union advocates, Gompers sought to emulate the British Labor Representation Committee by appealing to Congress and to the two major parties for a redress of labor's grievances. Rebuffed by Congress and the Republican party, the A. F. of L. unofficially supported the Democratic party in the presidential campaigns of 1908 and 1912. That not all the workers followed Gompers' lead can be seen in the large vote polled for Debs, the Socialist candidate for President, who received close to 900,000 votes in 1912. Nevertheless, Wilson's election in 1912 and his subsequent use of Gompers as his unofficial and official labor advisor meant that organized labor for the first time had access to an administration which paid serious attention to its needs.

The early years of the 20th century saw a marked change in the public attitude toward the problems of the worker and during this "progressive era" protective legislation for labor's benefit was enacted in most states as well as on the national level. State laws were passed limiting child labor, setting hours and wage standards for women workers, providing controls over sanitary and safety conditions of factories and attempting to establish systems of accident insurance. Uncertain as to the reception these laws would receive from a usually hostile Supreme Court, many states held off until their constitutionality was determined. Arguing that the state's police powers gave it jurisdiction to protect its children, the state child labor laws were invariably upheld. A New York law limiting the labor of bakers to ten hours a day was upset on the grounds that this restricted the worker's freedom of contract (Lochner v. New York, 1905). When an Oregon statute limiting the maximum working hours for women was challenged, the

Supreme Court, following the sociological arguments submitted in favor of the law by Louis D. Brandeis, upheld it (Muller v. Oregon, 1908). By 1917, 39 states had such laws on their statute books. In 1911 Wisconsin set up an industrial commission to establish safety and health standards in the factories. New York revamped its factory laws after the tragic Triangle fire in March, 1911, took a toll of 146 women shirtwaist workers. In 1912 Massachusetts established a minimum wage board with authority to establish minimum wages for women and minors. Although the first workmen's compensation laws of Maryland (1902), Montana (1909) and New York (1910) were upset by the courts, those framed after 1910 met the tests of constitutionality and when enacted gave an economic incentive to employers to improve industrial safety in their factories.

Under friendly pressure from the Wilson administration, Congress passed several laws favorable to labor. In 1913 the Newlands Act created a four-member Board of Mediation and Conciliation for the settlement of railroad labor disputes. In 1915 the LaFollette Seamen's Act regulated conditions for maritime workers. A year later the Adamson Act established an eight-hour day with time and a half for overtime for workers on interstate railroads. During the same year the Keating-Owen Act sought to bar the products of child labor from interstate commerce but the Supreme Court in 1918 ruled against this law. A subsequent act passed in 1919 sought to tax the products of child labor out of existence but this too was declared unconstitutional in 1922. When, early in the Wilson administration, the Department of Labor was created separate from the Department of Commerce and Labor which was established in 1903, William B. Wilson, a former official of the United Mine Workers, was appointed as its first Secretary.

Of greatest concern to organized labor, however, was the use by the courts of the Sherman Antitrust Act to frustrate its organizational drives. Injunctions and prohibitions against secondary boycotts by the courts were often justified through the use of the antitrust law. Consequently, when the Wilson administration in 1914 sponsored a revision of the antitrust laws, the resulting Clayton Act contained provisions which prompted Gompers to call it "the Magna Carta of labor." Under its provisions labor was not to be considered a commodity; labor organizations were not to be held as illegal combinations in restraint of trade and the injunction was not to be used in labor disputes except when necessary to prevent irreparable property damage. Strikes, boycotts and peaceful picketing were recognized as legal rights of labor under Federal jurisdiction and jury trials were mandated in contempt cases except where the offense was committed in the court's presence. Judicial interpretation soon substantially weakened most of the labor provisions of the Clayton Act (Duplex

Printing Press Co. v. Deering, 1921) making possible a renewal of the campaign against trade unions after the end of World War I.

During World War I the number of organized workers increased from 2,750,000 in 1916 to 4,250,-000 in 1919. This gain resulted partially from favorable action of Government agencies responsible for maintaining war production, and partially from the workers' better bargaining position as labor scarcity grew during the war. To offset this shortage of available workmen approximately a million women were recruited into the labor force; countless thousands of Negroes migrated North from the rural South and the U. S. Department of Labor expanded the activities of its Employment Service. Since the A. F. of L. enthusiastically supported the war effort, officers of the federation were appointed to most of the war boards organized by the Government. Gompers was appointed to the Council of National Defense and the Advisory Committee of National Defense. A Mediation Commission (1917) and a War Labor Board (1918) were created to settle disputes and maintain continuous production. A Railroad Wage Commission and adjustment boards were established to assure unhampered movement of the railroads even after the Federal Government took over their operation. Through these means strikes were kept to a minimum and the trade unions grew in importance and size. In recognition of labor's role in winning the war, an international conference was sponsored by the victorious powers in Washington in 1919 out of which came the recommendation that an organization to promote the international improvement of labor conditions be created under the auspices of the League of Nations. Thus was established the International Labor Organization.

Although the standard work day, in the main, declined to the desired eight-hour norm during the war and money wages rose appreciably, real wages actually declined from 1913 levels by 1919. By 1920, however, real wages had risen some 12% above the 1913 levels. The failure of wages to keep significantly ahead of rising prices, coupled with the public's growing hostility to organized labor resulting from the opposition of labor's left wing to the war, meant a resurgence of labor unrest after the armistice.

In 1919 over 4,000,000 wage earners were involved in strikes as compared to 1,250,000 the year before. The bituminous coal strike called by the new president of the United Mine Workers, John L. Lewis, was broken by an injunction secured by Attorney-General Palmer under a wartime measure. A railroad shopmen's strike collapsed under Government opposition. A general strike tying up Seattle, Wash., and a policemen's strike in Boston, Mass., spread a fear of radicalism. The most significant strike in 1919 was one called under A. F. of L. auspices against the U. S. Steel Corp. The strikers sought to end the notorious twelve-hour day in steel, and to gain union recognition, collective bargaining rights and wage increases. The adamant refusal of Judge Elbert H. Gary, U. S. Steel's chairman, to bargain, the successful use of Negro strikebreakers and the division of the strike committee into 24 craft committees spelled the doom of the walkout. The steel corporation effectively called the public's attention to the alleged radicalism of the leader of the strike, William Z. Foster.

The 1920's, a decade of massive economic growth resulting from the expansion of new industries and the increase of productivity, was also a decade of rapid decline of organized labor. Paradoxically, the prosperity decade which saw real wages and per capita income rise, except for the textile workers and the coal miners, saw the membership of labor unions decline from 5,000,000 in 1921 to 3,400,000 in 1929. Unions lost another 500,000 members during the depression years from 1929 to 1933. This decline can be attributed to the failure of defensive strikes during the sharp recession of 1921; to the resurgence of strong, organized opposition to unions by employer associations and to the unfavorable decisions rendered by the Federal courts. Furthermore, the continued failure of the craft-oriented leadership of the A. F. of L. to organize the growing army of unskilled labor allowed this task to be defaulted to a new militant revolutionary movement working within the ranks of labor, the communists.

Under the guise of the "American Plan," manufacturers' associations and chambers of commerce conducted a successful open-shop drive. Company unions, organizations founded and controlled by management, grew in number and influence; by 1926 some 400 such unions had a membership of 1,400,000 and by 1935 they had 2,500,000 members. Labor spies and *agents provocateurs* were used in increasing number to destroy legitimate unions. Expansion of freely given fringe benefits, such as medical services, vacations with pay, profit-sharing devices, insurance and pension schemes, and promotion of stock ownership by employers, helped to discourage workers from remaining in unions. Finally, effective publicity campaigns blamed organized labor for the high cost of living and for increased radical and communist activities.

The actions of the Supreme Court in rejecting labor's contention that the Clayton Act protected it from injunction proceedings (Duplex v. Deering, 1921) and the dismissal of a Washington, D. C., minimum wage law for women (Adkins v. Children's Hospital, 1923), convinced the A. F. of L. leadership that it must reverse its traditional attitude to political action. Consequently, the A. F. of L. joined with the Railroad Brotherhoods, disgruntled liberals, reformers, farm groups and socialists in endorsing the candidacy of Robert M. LaFollette for President of the United States on the Progressive party ticket in the 1924 election. LaFollette polled only 4,800,000 votes and labor's power to affect the votes of its members was shown to be faint indeed.

William Green of the United Mine Workers succeeded Samuel Gompers as president of the A. F. of L. after the latter's death in 1924 but the policies of the federation remained unchanged. Jurisdictional claims among rival affiliates of the federation frustrated Green's hope to organize the automobile industry and the hoped for extension of unionism into the newly born Southern industries was thwarted in part by the failure of the A. F. of L. unions to contribute funds for this purpose.

Agitation for industrial unionism and for militancy came from the communists who, under William Z. Foster, set up a Trade Union Education League. Seeking to take over existing unions, the communists succeeded with the furriers and came close to success in the needle-trades unions. Failing to control these unions, they sought to create dual unions but, when the line changed, the communists reverted to their "boring from within" tactics. Under communist leadership, several violent strikes were conducted in the textile mills in Gastonia and Marion, N. C., in 1929, but they were just as unsuccessful as the strikes conducted at the same time by the A. F. L. United Textile Workers Union.

Civil war in the West Virginia coal fields early in the decade, the Herrin massacre in which strikebreakers were killed in retaliation for the murder of two strikers by mine guards in Williamson County, Ill., in 1922, and the internal conflict between the communists and John L. Lewis decimated the ranks of the United Mine Workers. The membership in that union dwindled from 500,000 in 1921 to not quite 150,000 in 1933.

The economic collapse of the nation which began in 1929 found the labor movement completely unprepared to cope with the disastrous consequences. Unemployment surpassed 13,000,000 by 1933 and countless millions of workers were employed only part time. Although employment declined 35.4% from 1926 levels by 1933, the total national payroll declined 56%. Local relief and private charity sought to ameliorate some of the more extreme effects of the depression but soon these funds were exhausted. Families doubled up in apartments and some were forced to improvise dwellings using packing cases and boxes. The Communist party organized hunger marches, but the largest demonstration by veterans in Washington in 1932 demanding the payment of bonuses was not run by them. Until 1932 President Hoover sought to extend aid indirectly by assisting needy businesses and expecting that this would affect the workers. When the extent of the need became clear, the President authorized direct Federal assistance by means of loans to the states for emergency relief.

Union membership declined during the early years of the depression; the A. F. of L. by nearly 1,000,000 from 1929 to 1933. William Green, in the face of the depression, had the federation reconsider its opposition to legislation establishing compulsory welfare schemes. In 1932, the A. F. of L. began advocating a compulsory system of unemployment insurance as well as large-scale public works projects while attempting to hold the line on wages. In that same year, Wisconsin enacted the first unemployment insurance law in the United States. A Congress more friendly to organized labor than previous postwar Congresses passed the Norris-LaGuardia Act in 1932, which curtailed the Federal courts' power to issue injunctions against unions conducting peaceful strikes and made antiunion ("yellow dog") employment contracts unenforceable in the courts.

In the depths of the depression the New Deal of Franklin D. Roosevelt came to power with the announced objectives of "relief, recovery and reform." Seeking to minimize the effects of unemployment, the new administration set up a Federal Emergency Relief Administration under Harry L. Hopkins with an initial appropriation of $500,000,000 for direct grants to the states. A Civilian Conservation Corps was authorized by Congress for the purpose of providing work for jobless young people. Under the National Industrial Recovery Act (N. I. R. A.), a Public Works Administration headed by Harold L. Ickes was established with an authorized fund of $3,300,000,000. The cautious approach of the administrator prevented the rapid expansion of public works, consequently a Civil Works Administration was created to employ 4,000,000 jobless on public works in order to cushion the economic distress of the winter of 1933–34. With the passage of the National Employment Service Act, the U. S. Employment Service was expanded and the state bodies were co-ordinated with the Federal agency. These measures sought to minimize the effects on the worker of joblessness while at the same time they sought to expand employment, even if it were under public auspices. In 1935 the Federal Government withdrew from the area of direct relief when Congress created the Works Progress (after 1939, Projects) Administration (W. P. A.) with Hopkins as administrator, for the purpose of establishing a massive national public works program for the jobless. During its lifetime till 1943 the W. P. A. spent $11,000,000,000 and employed 8,500,000 different people on some 1,400,000 projects. These measures of relief were necessary, for despite efforts at recovery, it was not until the defense and war production demands of the 1940's caused industry to boom that the rolls of the unemployed declined appreciably.

To improve the security of the American worker, the New Deal enacted a series of measures which resulted in the establishment of a system of social reforms closely paralleling the systems in operation in Western Europe for a number of decades. The codes of industrial self-regulation drawn up under the National Recovery Administration (N. R. A.) prescribed minimum wages, maximum hours and elimination of child labor. The Walsh-Healey Government Contracts Act of 1936 sought to establish fair labor standards among contractors accepting Government work. Finally in 1938 the Fair Labor Standards Act established minimum wages, maximum hours and abolition of child labor for all businesses engaged in interstate commerce. To provide for the further security of the wage earner, a joint Federal-state system of unemployment insurance financed by a tax on employers' payrolls, coupled with a system of old-age and survivors' insurance financed by a payroll tax on both employers and employees, was adopted as the Social Security Act of 1935.

Strengthening the power of organized labor was a further objective of the New Deal. Section 7(a) of the N. I. R. A. proclaimed the workers' "right to organize and bargain collectively through representatives of their own choosing," and prohibited the employers from any "interference, restraint or coercion" on this process. A National Labor Board, chaired by Sen. Robert F. Wagner, was created to settle differences arising from this act, and in 1934 this board was authorized to hold elections of employees to determine their bargaining representatives. After the N. I. R. A. was invalidated by the Supreme Court, Congress reenacted the labor provisions of Section 7(a) when it passed, in 1935, the Wagner-Connery National Labor Relations Act. A new three-man National Labor Relations Board was created by this act with the function of supervising elections of workers, designating the appropriate bargaining agents, and holding hearings to determine unfair employer practices. The Board was authorized to issue cease and desist orders which were made enforceable through the Federal circuit courts of appeals.

Reacting to the stimulus of New Deal legislation and favorable governmental actions, the labor movement reawakened from its decade-long lethargy to begin a massive organizational drive. Supported by a shift of public opinion which began looking with favor upon unions, noncompany union membership increased from 3,000,000 in 1933 to 4,700,000 in 1936, then to 8,200,000 in 1939, reaching a total of 15,400,000 in 1947 and 17,000,000 in 1953.

The almost defunct national unions affiliated with the A. F. of L. made rapid organizational progress on the heels of the N. I. R. A. The three industrial unions within the A. F. of L.—the United Mine Workers, the International Ladies' Garment Workers' Union and the Amalgamated Clothing Workers' Union—re-established themselves as effective bodies of organized workers through the membership drives they conducted as early as 1933. The executive council of the A. F. of L. and its national convention authorized an organizing campaign in the mass production industries, but when it became clear that the newly recruited members were to be distributed among existing craft unions no appreciable headway was made. At the 1935 A. F. of L. convention the delegates split on the question of craft vs. industrial unions for the mass production industries and after the traditional craft-oriented position of the federation won out, the minority leaders established a Committee (after 1938, Congress) for Industrial Organization (C. I. O.) with John L. Lewis as chairman. Although the A. F. of L., after warning the dissidents, first suspended and then expelled the unions which went along with the minority, the existence of a militant rival federation in the C. I. O. caused the leaders of the older federation to intensify and make more forceful their own organizing drives. Consequently, as the C. I. O. successfully carried out its efforts in the mass production industries, the A. F. of L. unions also continued to expand. The Teamsters Union, for example, grew from 95,000 to 350,000 in the 1930's and became the largest union in the A. F. of L.

Financed from the coffers of the United Mine Workers, the C. I. O. set up organizing committees to establish unions for rubber, automobile, steel, electrical and textile workers. Using a dramatic technique, the sit-down strike, a device whereby the workers remained in the plants rather than vacating them and giving the companies an opportunity to utilize strikebreakers, the C. I. O. United Automobile Workers Union was able to receive recognition from General Motors and Chrysler Corp. early in 1937. By September, the automobile union had bargaining agreements with every automobile producer except Ford and boasted of a membership of over 300,000. Even Ford finally capitulated and recognized the union in 1941. Earlier sit-down strikes were successful in establishing union control in the rubber industry and the C. I. O. organizers had some measure of success in establishing unions and attaining bargaining agreements in the electrical industry, among the West Coast longshoremen and in the maritime trades.

After careful spadework, the Steel Workers Organizing Committee which was led by Philip Murray was ready to tackle the U. S. Steel Corp. in 1937. Rather than risk a strike, what with the Government friendly to labor and with public opinion aroused against management by the disclosures of the La Follette Committee's inquiry into industrial espionage and violence, the U. S. Steel Corp. capitulated to the union and in March, 1937, its subsidiaries signed agreements granting union recognition, wage increases and the 40-hour week. It was expected that the rest of the steel companies, known collectively as "Little Steel," would follow the lead of U. S. Steel but, except for Inland Steel which agreed to recognize the union in July, 1937, the others offered stiff resistance. The strike which followed was marked by violence; special deputies of Republic Steel killed two strikers in Massillon, O., and the South Chicago police killed ten strikers and wounded many at the Republic Steel plant on Memorial Day, 1937. The LaFollette Committee's investigation of the strike which revealed that the companies violated the Wagner Act, maintained an army of spies and had collected weapons for use against the strikers, combined with an N. L. R. B. demand that the companies bargain in good faith with the union, resulted in Little Steel's capitulation in 1941. Thus, when the United States entered World War II, the entire steel industry was organized and the steel workers' union reported over 600,000 members.

Not so successful was the attempt made by the Textile Workers Organizing Committee headed by Sidney Hillman and financed by his Amalgamated Clothing Workers' Union to penetrate the Southern cotton mills. Local opposition, which often resulted in violent attacks against the union organizers and which was reinforced by vigilante groups, frustrated this first all-out attempt to bring the benefits of unionism to the South.

Organized labor recognized its debt to the Roosevelt administration. In 1936 John L. Lewis contributed heavily to Roosevelt's re-election campaign, the New York labor leaders organized the American Labor party as a vehicle for garnering votes for the President, and the A. F. of L. cautiously and quietly worked for the President's re-election through the Labor's Nonpartisan League. The situation was quite different in 1940 when Roosevelt ran for a third term. Lewis, piqued that he did not become the President's labor adviser and critical of Roosevelt's international policies, backed Wendell Willkie for the Presidency. Although Lewis was supported within the C. I. O. by the communists who, in obedience to the Stalin-Hitler Pact phase of the party line, also opposed Roosevelt's policy of aiding the allies, the majority of the members, led by Hillman, supported the President. When Roosevelt won, Lewis, as threatened, resigned as president of the C. I. O. and was replaced by Philip Murray, a former colleague in the United Mine Workers whom he had chosen to head the steel workers' union.

Production and employment boomed with the increase of United States defense spending and shipments of war materials to the Allies in 1940. The necessity for continuous production at the same time that the labor unions were militantly expanding their influence, dictated vigorous executive actions. Hillman was made co-director of the Office of Production Management in October, 1940, and in March, 1941, a National Defense Mediation Board was established. With no effective powers to enforce decisions and with labor split on foreign policy questions, this body soon proved ineffective. Strikes of coal miners in April and September, 1941, raised Roosevelt's ire and caused public opinion to turn against "selfish" unions which put their own interests ahead of the national interests.

When the United States entered the war, a no-strike pledge was given at a conference of labor leaders called by President Roosevelt. A National War Labor Board with powers to enforce decisions was created in January, 1942. To the demand of the unions for the spread of the closed shop in war industries, the W. L. B. devised a compromise of "maintenance of membership" by which unionized workers were obliged to remain in their unions in order to continue employment. By war's end some 4,000,000 workers were employed under such conditions.

The necessity to hold the wage and price levels stable caused further difficulty for the W. L. B. In July, 1942, the Board devised the "Little Steel" formula by which it tied wage increases to rises in the cost of living since January, 1941. President Roosevelt ordered the freezing of wages and prices in April, 1943, causing discontent within the ranks of labor. John L. Lewis dramatized this discontent by refusing to appear before the W. L. B. and calling a strike of soft-coal and anthracite miners in May, 1943. The seizure of the mines by the Federal Government under the President's war powers quickly halted the strike, but not before Congress acted in haste in passing the Smith-Connally War Labor Dispute Act over the President's veto. In December, 1943, the railroads were temporarily taken over by the Army in the face of a strike threat and in December, 1944, Montgomery Ward was seized after the firm refused to follow a W. L. B. directive.

Despite these strikes and seizures the actual time lost in wartime walkouts was exceptionally small. The dramatic challenge of Government authority by Lewis, however, caused some public revulsion and opened the way for more restrictive legislation after the war. In fact, many Southern and Western states outlawed the closed shop during the war period.

The need to expand the labor force during wartime was met by the increased utilization of women workers and the opening of opportunities for Negro workers. To curb discriminatory employment, the Fair Employment Practice Committee was established by executive order in June, 1941, and in May, 1943, the Government required nondiscrimination clauses in all war contracts. Attempts to make the national F. E. P. C. permanent failed to pass the Senate after the war, but by 1946 five states had created such commissions.

Political activities undertaken by the C. I. O. were more vigorous than those attempted by the A. F. of L. Avoiding the prohibition against union funds being used for political purposes, which was part of the Smith-Connally Act, the C. I. O. organized a Political Action Committee to work for Roosevelt's re-election in 1944 and to support congressional candidates favorable to labor's cause. Sidney Hillman was asked to give labor's approval before Harry S.

Truman could be nominated for the Vice-Presidency by the Democratic party in 1944. The A. F. of L., although supporting Roosevelt in 1944, continued to refuse to give him its open endorsement.

The end of the war saw the beginning of a wage and price rise cycle which frightened the public into an antiunion attitude, even though the responsibility of labor for this inflationary spiral was not exclusive. Strikes to keep up with the rising cost of living were widespread in 1945 and 1946 with the most dramatic being the two strikes of the miners in 1946, the second of which resulted in the union being held in contempt of court and fined $3,500,000 (sustained by Supreme Court in 1947, but fine reduced to $700,000). When the railroads under Government control were struck by the Brotherhoods in 1946, President Truman threatened to draft the strikers. Walter Reuther, president of the United Automobile Workers' Union, demanded the right to inspect the company's books during the 1945 strike against General Motors to determine whether the firm could raise wages without raising prices. In all cases the wage demands of the workers were met when Government boards, intervening in the strikes, recommended both wage raises and price increases. A new means of increasing compensation, which had its origin during the war, was expanded in the postwar period when fringe benefits in the form of pension plans, insurance and vacation grants became part of the collective bargaining agreement.

The inflationary spiral, the feeling that unions had grown too powerful with the help of favorable legislation, the existence of a few corrupt labor officials, and the control of some unions by communists, resulted in public hostility to unions which was translated into congressional action. In June, 1947, the Taft-Hartley Act was passed over the veto of President Truman. Designed as a measure to redress the balance between union and management rights, the act modified the Wagner Act by changing the structure of the N. L. R. B., by limiting some of the unions' freedoms and by spelling out the rights of employers in industrial disputes. The act prohibited the closed shop, forced the unions to wait 60 days before striking, ended the system whereby employers collected union dues ("check-off"), made the unions liable for broken contracts and damages during strikes, and required union leaders to take a non-Communist oath. The U. S. Conciliation Service was removed from the Department of Labor and made an independent body, the Federal Mediation and Conciliation Service.

Organized labor called the new law a "slave labor act" and campaigned for its repeal. Although the need for amending the act was proclaimed by Sen. Taft before his death and by President Eisenhower throughout his terms in office, only minor changes were made in its provisions. In response to the same antiunion climate, many states adopted "right to work" laws which outlawed union shops as well as closed shops. Effective political activity of labor, however, limited these laws almost exclusively to non-industrial states.

The purge of the communists from the C. I. O. in 1949 and 1950, the appearance of new leaders of the rival federations when George Meany and Walter Reuther succeeded Green and Murray as presidents of the A. F. of L. and C. I. O. upon the latters' death in 1952, the beginning of vigorous anticorruption activity by the A. F. of L. as reflected in the expulsion of the International Longshoremen's Association in 1953, paved the way for the long-desired merger of the two federations in 1955. During the Korean war the two federations formed the United Labor Policy Committee and in 1953 they approved a "no-raiding" agreement. Negotiations removed jurisdictional obstacles, sought to remove the racial discriminatory policies of some A. F. of L. unions and guaranteed the principle of industrial organization. The merged federation, calling itself the A. F. L.-C. I. O., elected Meany president with Reuther heading the industrial union department. Autonomy of affiliates was recognized, with equality of status between industrial and craft unions specifically stated in the constitution. The executive council was given authority to investigate and suspend affiliates accused of corruption and totalitarian control. At the time of the merger in 1955, the A. F. L.-C. I. O. consisted of 6 trade and industrial departments, 139 national unions, 50 state or territorial federations, 60,000 local unions, 1000 city central bodies and approximately 16,000,000 members.

The most urgent task facing the merged federation was the elimination of corrupt elements from the labor movement. Despite the creation of an ethical practices committee which investigated and recommended the expulsion of a number of national unions, notably the Teamsters Union in 1957, the evidences of sharp practices uncovered in the labor and management field by a Senate committee headed by John L. McClellan, resulted in legislation which further restricted the freedom of action of organized labor. The Landrum-Griffin Labor-Management Reporting and Disclosure Act of 1959 restricted secondary boycotts, called for precise controls over union elections, demanded strict reporting of a union's financial transactions, outlawed extortion picketing, authorized state jurisdiction over labor disputes not handled by the N. L. R. B. and modified union security provisions for the construction and garment industries. Labor reluctantly accepted this law, pledging to continue its efforts to clean its own house.

On the eve of a new era of labor history, the organized workers, numbering some 18,000,000, faced the reality that they were plagued with many unresolved problems. With the growth of the number of service and clerical employees, the proportion of manual workers in the labor force was steadily declining. With the advent of automation, this proportion will decline even more precipitously. How to meet this challenge looms as labor's major problem. Decline of certain industries, notably coal mining and railroading, and the regional shifts of certain industries; textiles from the Northeast to the South, automobiles from the Midwest to the West, poses another major problem. The existence of a body of unorganized, underprivileged workers, agricultural migrants, poses still another problem. The manner in which the labor movement solves these and other problems will determine whether organized labor has reached the limit of its development or is able to surmount the challenge of a new industrial frontier.

"LAFAYETTE, WE ARE HERE." On July 4, 1917, Paris enthusiastically celebrated the American Independence Day. A battalion of the 16th U. S. Infantry was reviewed by President Poincaré and then marched to the Picpus Cemetery, where several speeches were made at the tomb of Lafayette, the principal one by Brand Whitlock. Gen. Pershing was present but spoke very briefly, having designated Col Charles E. Stanton, of his staff, to speak for him. The historic words uttered on that occasion, "Lafayette, nous voilà," translated as, "Lafayette, we are here," have been popularly, but erroneously, attributed to Gen. Pershing. He himself has stated positively that they "were spoken by Col. Stanton, and to him must go the credit for coining so happy and felicitous a phrase."

LAFAYETTE ESCADRILLE, an organization of American volunteers in French Aviation Service, was formed in April, 1916, as Escadrille Americaine No. 124. On Nov. 16, 1916, at the protest of the German ambassador, the name was changed to "Volunteer Escadrille No. 124" and on Dec. 6, 1916, it became known as "Lafayette Escadrille," continuing as such until Jan. 1, 1918, when it entered our Army as the 103rd Pursuit Squadron.

LAFAYETTE'S VISIT TO AMERICA. In February, 1824, President Monroe invited the Marquis de Lafayette to visit the United States. Lafayette accepted, but would not permit a government vessel to be sent for him, as Congress wished to do. He sailed, however, in an American ship, and reached New York Aug. 16, 1824. He was so reduced in fortune that he feared he could not meet the expense of a long stay, but to his surprise, he was not permitted to pay for anything while here. After a tumultuous reception in New York and a four days' stay, he toured New England, including Albany, N. Y., visited the Harvard Commencement, returned to New York twice, then moved slowly southward through Philadelphia and Baltimore, making leisurely stays everywhere. After a long stop at Washington, where all government officials joined in doing him honor, he visited Jefferson at Monticello and went down through the Coast states, then westward to New Orleans. Coming northward into the Middle West, he suffered shipwreck when a steamboat sank with him on the Ohio below Louisville but, despite his age, he came through the disaster without severe shock. His progress everywhere was one continuous ovation; bands and military escorts went miles along the roads to meet him, banquets and fetes greeted him at every stop. He visited Braddock's Field, Lake Erie, Niagara and other American war scenes, returned to Boston for the celebration of the fiftieth anniversary of the Battle of Bunker Hill, visited New York for the fourth time, and finally returned to Washington, from which he sailed for home on Dec. 7, 1825, having spent nearly sixteen months in this country. A steamboat carried him from Washington to the frigate *Brandywine*, which awaited him at the mouth of the Potomac, and on that vessel he returned to France. Congress made him a gift of $200,000 in cash and a township of land.

LaFOLLETTE (PROGRESSIVE) PARTY.

As a part of the general progressive movement in the United States, led by Sen. Robert M. LaFollette of Wisconsin, there was formed in 1922 the Conference for Progressive Political Action, a loose federation of various progressive groups in the country, such as the farmers' Nonpartisan League, the Farmer-Labor party, the Single Tax League and several labor organizations, including particularly the sixteen railroad brotherhoods. The purpose at first was not to organize another political party, but to secure the election of progressives to Congress, regardless of party, and to promote the enactment of progressive legislation.

A national convention was held in Cleveland, July 4–6, 1924, at which, in view of the dissatisfaction with the presidential nominations made by both major parties, Sen. LaFollette was nominated or "endorsed" for President and Burton K. Wheeler, Democrat, of Montana, for Vice-President. The new party, officially named the Progressive party, although generally known as the LaFollette party, was also endorsed by the Socialist party and by the American Federation of Labor. The platform was largely a reproduction of LaFollette's personal views on public questions, with particular emphasis on the needs of agriculture and labor. It polled nearly 5,000,000 votes (about 17%), chiefly in the Middle and Far West, displaced the Democratic party as the second party in eleven states and carried Wisconsin. The results were, however, disappointing to LaFollette and the other leaders of the movement, plans for a permanent party organization were abandoned, and Sen. LaFollette himself died soon thereafter.

LAKE CHAMPLAIN IN THE WAR OF 1812.

Lake Champlain was teeming with martial activity during the War of 1812 as in previous wars, with England threatening by both land and water from the north and considerable bodies of United States regulars and militia, supported by a naval force, being stationed at Burlington, Vt., Plattsburg, N. Y., and vicinity.

In command of the American fleet was Lt. Thomas Macdonough. On June 3, 1813, the Americans lost two vessels to the English. The next month Col. John Murray, with over 1400 British troops and marines, destroyed several military buildings near Plattsburg. A few days later, Aug. 2, three British ships appeared off Burlington, but were driven off by Macdonough's ships and the shore battery. At about the same time the English burned the abandoned barracks and other government property at Swanton. Macdonough sought out the English fleet, but it declined battle. In a thrust by Col. Isaac Clark several of the enemy were killed and 101 taken prisoners. Gen. Hampton, with several thousand men, crossed the border and was defeated by a smaller body of English. On the morning of March 30, 1814, the American army, 4000 strong, advanced for an unsuccessful attack upon LaColle Mill.

Meanwhile Macdonough had gone into winter quarters at Vergennes in Otter Creek and was strengthening his fleet. On April 14 the British fleet attacked the battery at the mouth of the creek and was repulsed. Land skirmishes during the summer were frequent. In the fall came the general advance of the English, the decisive engagement taking place Sept. 11, 1814, when Sir George Prevost led upwards of 14,000 British troops against an American force of some 4700 regulars and militia under Gen. Macomb, who had taken up their position on the south bank of the Saranac River near Plattsburg. At the same time the British fleet attacked Macdonough off near-by Cumberland Head. The American land and naval force were both victorious, and the outcome had an important bearing on the peace which was signed at Ghent on Dec. 24.

LAKE GEORGE, BATTLE OF (1755).

With 3500 provincials, William Johnson (then Major General of New York militia) moved north against Crown Point in midsummer, 1755. At the southern end of Lake George, his encamped force was threatened by Baron Dieskau commanding 1700 French and Indians. Sept. 8, Johnson sent 1200 men south to locate the French. Division proved costly; the French drove the surprised Americans back with severe losses, killing Col. Ephraim Williams and Hendrik, Mohawk chieftain.

At the camp barricades the reunited provincials beat off repeated charges; the day ended with the French retreating. Both commanders were wounded, Dieskau captured. Provincial forces lost 260 killed, 91 wounded; the French about as many, including most of the regulars. The battle is regarded as a draw. Johnson could not proceed, and capture of their commander stopped the French offensive.

LAKE OF THE WOODS BOUNDARY PROBLEM was projected by the Definitive Treaty of Peace, 1783, which provided that the northern boundary should extend westward from the "most northwestern point" of the Lake of the Woods to the Mississippi. Since such a line was geographically impossible, it was agreed in 1818 that the boundary should be drawn south from the northwest point of the lake to the 49th parallel—an arrangement that resulted in the creation of the Northwest Angle.

LANCASTER PIKE, the first turnpike built in the United States, was begun in 1791, opened to travel in 1797 and freed from tolls, by state purchase, in 1917. Need for a public highway to connect Philadelphia with Lancaster had been felt since the founding of the latter town by Scotch-Irish and German immigrants in 1728. In 1770 commissioners were appointed to lay out a sixty-foot road, but the plan failed, probably because of war conditions. William Bingham then secured a charter for the Philadelphia and Lancaster Turnpike Co., offering for public sale 1000 shares of stock, $300 par, to be one tenth paid up at once. The offering was heavily oversubscribed, and the surplus was reduced by a lottery. In 1807 the charter was made perpetual.

The Lancaster Pike opened the interior to settlement. Conestoga wagons rumbled westward in great numbers. A twelve-hour night stage service connected Philadelphia with Lancaster beginning with the spring of 1798. The Pike, however, lost heavily when the main line of the Pennsylvania Railroad, begun in 1846, paralleled its course. Free roads built by the state close by the Lancaster Pike also cut away its trade. The perpetual charter was, accordingly, surrendered.

LAND ACT OF 1796. This was the first great land act adopted by the Federal Government. It established the office of Surveyor General and re-enacted the rectangular system of survey with townships of six miles square and sections of 640 acres which the Confederation had embodied in the Land Ordinance of 1785. One half of the townships were to be offered in 5120-acre blocks and the smallest unit which could be bought was 640 acres. The lands were to be sold at public auction to the highest bidder at or above the minimum price of $2 per acre. Full payment was required within a year after purchase and 10% reduction was offered for advance payment. Although it was the basic law of the American land system, the act of 1796 was a failure from the start because the high minimum price and the large unit of entry deterred purchasing.

LAND ACT OF 1820. The credit system in the disposition of the public lands, inaugurated by the Land Act of 1796 and extended by the Harrison Land Law of 1800, had become an evident failure by 1820.

Large numbers of settlers found it impossible to make the deferred payments on their lands. Other hard-working farmers, seeing that nothing happened to those who failed to meet their obligations, decided to let their own installments lapse. Arrearages piled up rapidly and Congress was forced to pass law after law for the relief of the settlers. After considerable agitation Congress finally enacted the law of April 24, 1820, abolishing the credit system. The minimum price at the public auctions and at private sale thereafter was reduced from $2 to $1.25 per acre, the entire amount to be paid at the time of purchase. The smallest purchasable unit of land was fixed at eighty acres.

LAND DISTRIBUTION BILL, CLAY'S. Land policies, tariff rates and public revenue questions were inseparable during the years 1834 to 1842. The old policy of using the public lands as a major source of income for the Government remained in effect, and throughout the boom years 1834 to 1837 Federal revenues were enormously swollen by the receipts from land sales. Faced with a surplus, the politicians sought means to rid the treasury of its unwanted millions. The West wished the Federal Government to dispose of its public domain either by ceding it to the states, by granting free homesteads or by selling the land at low rates; the Old South opposed liberalization of the land policy and favored a lower tariff as a means of reducing the Federal revenue; the Northeast opposed tariff reduction and a liberal land policy and favored Clay's proposal for the distribution of the net proceeds from the public land sales among the states. Clay's distribution bill, first introduced in 1832, provided that 10% of the net proceeds of the land sales be distributed to the states in which they were located and that the remaining 90% be distributed among all the states and territories in proportion to their population. To gain support for this measure the advocates of distribution made a concession to the West by adding to Clay's bill a provision for pre-emption. Before the bill was adopted it was further provided that if tariff rates were raised above the 20% level which they reached in 1841, distribution would automatically be suspended. In 1842 the tariff was raised and Clay's great political measure was suspended.

LAND GRANTS, COLONIAL. Claims to land as between European governments rested upon discovery, exploration and occupation which, when completed, vested the title in the sovereign of a particular state, who alone could terminate the claims of the natives. Consequently the title to all English America was in the king and from him all later titles stemmed. Royal land grants took the form of charters and the whole Atlantic seaboard, except Florida, was, between 1606 and 1732, parceled out to the London and Plymouth Companies, the Council for New England, James,

Duke of York, William Penn and associates, Lord Baltimore, Clarendon and associates and James Oglethorpe and associates. From some of these in turn came grants to individuals and groups which were gradually incorporated into regular colonial governments with boundaries based upon the earlier charters. Many of the original grants ran westward to the sea, and became the foundation for the western claims of the original states, which were finally surrendered to the National Government between 1778 and 1781.

Local land titles came from the colonial government or the proprietor, depending upon who held the direct title from the king. The practice of New England was for the General Court in each colony to grant a considerable tract, called a township, to a body of settlers who in turn issued deeds to individual settlers. This practice tended to prevent speculation in vacant lands and engrossment.

In Maryland there were some manorial grants of 1000 acres or more, although most of the grants were small and made to actual settlers. The practice in Pennsylvania was to grant land to actual settlers in small parcels, but to retain title to vast acreage in the settled areas. Thus the proprietor not only held title to the ungranted regions but was also the largest landowner in the developed eastern counties and collected rents as from any other private estate.

In Virginia there was at first a system of grants based upon head rights—fifty acres for each person arriving in Virginia—and belonging to the individual who paid the transportation. This led to abuses and gradually degenerated into a simple fee system at the land office. Any one who could pay the fees could acquire original title to as many acres as he could pay for. Under this system large plantations grew up in excess of any possible cultivation, such as those of Byrd, Fairfax, Randolph and Spotswood.

Grants were not infrequently used to promote settlements in the back country. These were usually conditioned upon the transportation and settlement of a minimum number of families within a limited time. The best known is the Ohio Company grant of 500,000 acres near the forks of the Ohio in 1749. The practice was common on a smaller scale in all of the colonies south of Maryland.

In New York and South Carolina there were vast individual grants and extensive engrossment. In New York the practice had begun under the Dutch by the creation of the patroon estates which were recognized as valid by the English. Cornbury and other royal governors issued enormous grants to their favorites. In this way the Van Rensselaer, Philipse, Van Cortlandt and Livingston estates were built up and perpetuated, paving the way for the serious antirent difficulties in New York, 1840–45.

A grant to be valid had to come from the colonial government in which the land was situated. Undefined boundaries led to conflicts over titles, such as the troubles in Vermont where settlers claimed land under grants from both New York and New Hampshire, and the bitter dispute in the Wyoming Valley where settlers from Connecticut were expelled as trespassers by those with titles from Pennsylvania.

Land grants as bounties for military service became especially important after 1750. The Virginia grants were made in what is now West Virginia. Individual soldiers or officers could either use their warrants or sell them, the purchaser in turn could use them singly or in groups. Thus George Washington came into possession of his vast western properties by purchasing Virginia military warrants. The British government made extensive military grants in the Floridas after their acquisition from Spain.

Indian titles were presumed to be extinguished by the local colonial government as the representative of the king before land was granted to individual settlers. This was not always done and after 1750 there was a growing custom of frontiersmen purchasing lands directly from the Indians and securing confirmation later. In other cases, settlers secured grants before the Indian titles were extinguished; this was one of the causes of Pontiac's conspiracy. The Proclamation of 1763 was issued to stop encroachments of this kind. On the other hand, the expansion into Kentucky and Tennessee by Boone, Henderson, Robertson and their followers was based upon the assumption that Indian titles alone were valid.

The vast interior of the continent tempted Americans and Englishmen to seek grants to the rich lands west of the mountains. On the eve of the Revolution patents were pending in England for property grants to form four new colonies in the region west of the Alleghenies and south and east of the Ohio-Mississippi Rivers. These were called Vandalia, Transylvania, Georgiani and Mississippi. Large additional purchases from the Indians north of the Ohio River also awaited confirmation.

Colonial land grants were not limited to the eastern part of the United States. Spain and France made grants similar to those made by England. When new areas came under the control of England or later the United States, the earlier foreign colonial land grants were accepted as valid. As many of these had very obscure descriptions, the boundaries became elastic and were used as the foundation for claims to large tracts of government lands. One of the most famous of these is the Maxwell land grant in Colorado and New Mexico which involved litigation as late as 1887. Many of the large landed estates of the southwestern part of the United States go back to old Spanish colonial land grants confirmed after annexation to the United States.

LAND GRANTS, SPANISH AND MEXICAN. By treaty at the close of the War with Mexico, the United States agreed to recognize all the land grants made by Spain and Mexico in the ceded territory. Besides the usual purposes of granting large estates for agricultural and pastoral pursuits, after the revolt of Texas a definite effort was made to colonize the frontier with Mexicans, and protect the Santa Fe trade from the Indians and, especially, the aggressive *Americanos* (*e.g.*, the Tierra Amarilla, the Maxwell, the St. Vrain, the Mora and the Las Animas grants). When these lands were ceded to the United States, many Americans rushed in and squatted on the new public lands. Innumerable conflicts arose. Three steps in the settlement of these claims followed. (1) March 3, 1851, Congress established a commission of three which confirmed 538 claims involving over 8,000,000 acres of land in California. (2) July 22, 1854, Congress provided a surveyor-general for New Mexico to investigate thoroughly all private land claims. Upon his reports, Congress confirmed 71 additional grants. (3) In a final effort to quiet title on these grants, Congress established "A Court of Private Land Claims" of five judges from different states. From 1891–1904, this court heard all remaining claims (301 in all) and confirmed 87 grants for 3,000,000 acres.

LAND GRANTS FOR EDUCATION. The practice of making land grants to aid in supporting schools was generally followed by the American colonies. The Confederation, borrowing from the New England land system, provided in the Land Ordinance of 1785 that the sixteenth section of each township, or one thirty-sixth of the acreage in the public-land states, should be granted to the states for the benefit of common schools. New states after 1848 were granted two sections in each township and Utah, Arizona, New Mexico and Oklahoma (in part) were given four sections in each township when they entered the Union. Each public-land state on entering the Union was also given a minimum of two townships of 46,080 acres to aid in founding "seminaries of learning," or state universities. Such great institutions as the Universities of Michigan, Wisconsin and Indiana benefited from these grants.

The next important step in Federal aid to education came in 1862 as a result of an energetic campaign undertaken by Jonathan Baldwin Turner of Illinois, the farm and labor journals, and Horace Greeley and the New York *Tribune*. This was the Agricultural College Land Grant Act which was fathered in the Senate by Justin S. Morrill of Vermont and is generally called the Morrill Act. This measure gave to the states 30,000 acres of public lands for each Representative and Senator they had in Congress to aid in establishing Agricultural and Mechanical Arts Colleges. States which contained no public lands received scrip which could be located elsewhere on public land "subject to entry." As a result of this act agricultural colleges have been established in every state in the Union. Special land grants have, in addition, been given by the Federal Government to endow normal schools, schools of mines,

military institutes, reform schools, a girls' college and a colored university.

These numerous grants reflect the ever growing interest of the United States in free public education. They encouraged the states early to create liberal educational systems and aided in financing them at a time when local resources were unequal to the task. The total acreage granted by the Federal Government for educational purposes is 118,000,000, or an area practically four times the size of the State of New York. Some of the states recklessly disposed of their lands for small sums; others, like Minnesota, have received large amounts from the sale of their land grants.

LAND OFFICE, U. S. GENERAL, is a bureau of the Federal Government, established in 1812, which has as its chief functions the survey, management and disposition of the public lands, and the maintenance of records thereon. The Ordinance of 1785, the cornerstone of Federal land policy, provided for a Geographer to direct surveys of the public lands. In 1796 the Geographer was succeeded by a Surveyor General who, with his deputies, continued to survey and map the public domain until 1836, independently of any other official or agency. Land sales, according to the Ordinance of 1785, were to be managed by a board of treasury consisting of three commissioners. Under the Federal Constitution this function was inherited by the Secretary of the Treasury.

The first district land offices were set up in 1800 at Chillicothe, Cincinnati, Marietta and Steubenville, all in Ohio. By act of Congress, approved April 25, 1812, the General Land Office was established as a bureau in the Treasury Department, with a Commissioner as its chief officer. Friction between the Commissioner and the Surveyor General resulted in the latter officer being placed under the Commissioner in 1836. For the next five years the Commissioner was made responsible to the President direct, but in 1841 the Secretary of the Treasury was given the power to hear and decide appeal cases. However, the Commissioner continued to enjoy considerable independence and influence for some years after the transfer of the Office in 1849 to the newly organized Department of the Interior, where it has since remained.

Up to 1910 surveying was done in large part by a system of contracts with private surveyors; it has since been executed by a force employed directly by the Land Office. There has been an increasing amount of resurvey work in recent years, some of it necessitated by reason of fraudulent original surveys when the work was handled through contracts. Map compiling and drafting have always been an important part of the work of the General Land Office, including the preparation of original plat maps, state maps, a biennial edition of the large United States map and many special maps. Through the years the Land Office has administered the long series of acts providing for the disposal of the public domain, including the pre-emption and homestead laws. When the acreage of public land in any district is reduced to less than 100,000 acres, the Secretary of the Interior is required by law to close the district office and transfer its business to a neighboring district office. The records of the General Land Office in Washington, which are complete from the beginning, are the basis for all land titles in the 29 public-land states.

LAND SPECULATION. The favorite object of speculation in America before the era of "big business" was the public lands. They could be bought cheaply in large quantities and withheld from market, if one had sufficient capital to carry them, until rising prices brought profits to the investors. Memories of high land values in the old world and of the social prestige which the possessor of broad acres enjoyed, combined with the natural land hunger of all races, produced in the American people an insatiable lust for land.

Land speculation began with the first settlements in America. The proprietors of Virginia, disappointed at the meager returns from their investment, granted to themselves great tracts of land from which they hoped to draw substantial incomes. Similarly, the Penns and Calverts in Pennsylvania and Maryland and the early proprietors of New York, New Jersey and the Carolinas speculated in an imperial way in lands. Later in the colonial period a new crop of land companies composed of English and colonial speculators sought both title to and political control over great tracts in the Mississippi Valley. The Vandalia, the Mississippi, the Georgiana, the Wabash, the Indiana, the Loyal and the Ohio land companies attracted some of the ablest colonial leaders into their ranks, among them being George Washington, Richard Henry Lee, Benjamin Franklin, the Whartons and George Croghan. The struggles of these rival companies for charters and grants played an important role in British colonial policy during the pre-Revolutionary years. Company rivalries were matched by the rival land claims of the colonies, one of the most notable being the conflict between Connecticut and Pennsylvania for the Wyoming Valley which the former had granted to the Susquehanna Land Company. In western Virginia, Richard Henderson and his Transylvania Company, which claimed title to a great tract received from the Indians, came into conflict with Virginia and was successful in having only a small part of the area confirmed to him.

Most influential colonials tried their luck at speculating, either through the land companies or by operating on their own account. George Washington was a large land owner in Virginia, Pennsylvania and the Ohio country; Robert and Gouverneur Morris, William Duer, Phelps and Gorham and William Johnson acquired princely domains in Pennsylvania, New York and Maine. The Morrises negotiated a number of large purchases and resold tracts to others, per-

haps the largest of which went to the Holland Land Company. This company was composed of Dutch capitalists who bought the Holland Reserve in western New York and who were busily engaged in settling it during the first third of the 19th century. Meantime, most of upstate New York was parcelled out among speculators, some of the most prominent of whom were the Wadsworths of the Genesee country, John Jacob Astor and Peter Smith, father of Gerrit Smith. These men, unlike Robert Morris, were able to retain their lands long enough either to resell at high prices or to settle tenants upon them.

The largest purchase and the most stupendous fraud was the sale in 1795 of 30,000,000 acres of western lands by the legislature of Georgia to four Yazoo companies for one and a half cents an acre. The next legislature cancelled the sale, but the purchasers, frequently innocent third parties, waged a long fight to secure justice, claiming that the obligation of the contract clause in the Federal Constitution prevented the Georgia legislature from reversing the original sale (*see* Fletcher v. Peck). The Yazoo frauds became a *cause célèbre* in which John Randolph, Thomas Jefferson, John Marshall and other notables took prominent parts.

When the public domain of the United States was created by the donations of the states with western land claims, speculative interest converged upon Congress with requests to purchase tracts of land north of the Ohio. In fact, the craze for land speculation was partly responsible for the adoption of the Ordinance of 1787 which provided for the government of the ceded territory north of the Ohio. A group of New England capitalists known as the Ohio Company of Associates wished to buy a tract of land in southeastern Ohio for a New England settlement. To get the measure through Congress it seemed necessary to enlarge the original project and to create a second organization, the Scioto Company, which was composed of members of Congress and other influential people who planned to buy some 5,000,000 acres of land. The formation of the Scioto Company made possible the enactment of the Northwest Ordinance, but the company itself was a failure because it could not fulfill its contract with the Government. The Ohio Company of Associates did, however, succeed in planting a little New England outpost at Marietta. John Cleves Symmes of New Jersey likewise bought a large tract from the Congress in 1788. These purchases virtually defeated the purpose of the Land Ordinance of 1785 and the Land Act of 1796 because the speculators whom Congress had allowed to acquire large tracts of land at lower prices than were offered to individual settlers were thus enabled to undersell the Government.

There were three great periods of land speculation after the creation of the public domain, 1816–19, 1835–37 and 1854–57. Outstanding Easterners like Daniel Webster, Caleb Cushing, Edward Everett,

Amos Lawrence, Moses and John Carter Brown and James S. Wadsworth, and Southerners like John C. Breckinridge, John Slidell, Eli Shorter and William S. Grayson bought western lands in large quantities. Land companies again were organized and they entered great tracts embracing entire townships. The New York and Boston Illinois Land Company acquired 900,000 acres in the Military Tract of Illinois, the American Land Company had great estates in Indiana, Illinois, Michigan, Wisconsin, Mississippi and Arkansas and the Boston and Western Land Company owned 60,000 acres in Illinois and Wisconsin.

The adoption of the Homestead Law in 1862 did not end land speculation and some of the largest purchases were made thereafter. William S. Chapman alone bought over 1,000,000 acres of land in California and Nevada, Henry W. Sage, John McGraw and Jeremiah Dwight, benefactors of Cornell University, entered 352,000 acres of timberland in the Northwest and the South and Francis Palms and Frederick E. Driggs bought 486,000 acres of timberland in Wisconsin and Michigan. Not until 1889 were effective steps taken to end large speculative purchases and by that date the Government had parted with its best lands.

Meantime, the canal and railroad land grants and the lands given to the states for drainage and educational purposes were also attracting speculative purchasing.

The accumulation of vast quantities of land in advance of settlement created many problems for the West, some of which have never been satisfactorily settled. The Indians were pushed back more rapidly than the actual needs of the population dictated and the frequent clashes between settlers and Indians might have been avoided had there been more social control of westward expansion and land purchases. In some places "speculator's deserts" were created where large amounts of land were owned by absentee proprietors who withheld them from development while waiting for higher prices. Settlers were widely dispersed because they could not find land at reasonable prices close to existing settlements. The problem of providing transportation facilities was consequently aggravated and as a result of the importunities of settlers, thousands of miles of railroads were built through sparsely settled country which could provide but little traffic for the roads. Nevertheless, the speculators and land companies were an important factor in the development of the West. Their efforts to attract settlers to their lands through the distribution of pamphlets and other advertising literature which described the western country lured thousands from their homes in the eastern states and countries of northern Europe to the newly developing sections of the West. They also aided in building improvements such as roads, canals and railroads to make easier the life of the immigrant.

LAND SYSTEM, NATIONAL. Our land system was, almost as a matter of course, an adaptation of European land systems brought over by the colonists, or in some instances imposed by England, or Holland, on their respective colonies. The land in the English colonies, according to English law, in the first instance, belonged strictly to the Crown.

Land was granted liberally to single individuals, groups of individuals, or joint-stock companies, proprietors who undertook settlements. These proprietors in turn granted land to settlers, generally pretty freely, but often under the stipulation that rents should be paid. Down through these patentees, sometimes three or four in succession, title to the land passed into the hands of occupier and tiller. The latter usually paid little if anything for it, in the way of a purchase price. He was in many colonies granted a fee simple title. Such was the case in the New England colonies. In most of the others there was an attempt to collect quitrents in the form of very small payments, such as a halfpenny per acre, or a shilling per hundred acres. Money being scarce, provision was made for payment in kind, usually in wheat or tobacco.

There was much difficulty attendant upon the collection of the rental payments, and eventually it gradually fell into disuse, although under its provisions title to much land was lost. This was no great calamity, since land was so plentiful, and the colonies so anxious to have it settled that almost any one who wanted land could get it. Land, thus, came to be widely distributed in ownership, held in fee simple, and serving at once as a homestead and a farm.

Two general land systems, so far as the character of the holding was concerned, prevailed. In New England the holding was patterned after the farms of England and consisted of several separate pieces of land, although making a small unit. There was the "home lot," usually in a village; a modest sized tract of arable land; a smaller piece of meadow, in typical localities where such were available; a wood lot; and last, but not least, a share in a commons. This latter right might also include woods in lieu of a separate wood lot. The commons was used largely for pasturage, available for feeding all kinds of farm animals. These farm lands were parcelled out under direction, located within a prescribed "town." The surveying was done in advance of distribution of the parcels, and the distribution carried out by lot. Thus the whole procedure was democratic in the extreme.

In the South the farm was essentially different in character. To begin with it was large. The grants of land were generally, to a family, a matter of a few hundred acres, and not infrequently, to the influential, a few thousand acres, some reaching the equivalent of a modern township. These tracts were surveyed privately, and the sites chosen by the grantee virtually at will. Through these liberal grants, coupled with the adaptation of the country to large field undertakings in the growing of staple products, the foundation was laid for the plantation system which long characterized the South.

The system of the North was found suitable for the settlers as they moved farther west. The complications characterizing the New England farm were broken down, even before the Green Mountains were reached. Farms came to be of one piece. The village idea was abandoned as fear of the Indians disappeared. For a long time the farms of the North were small, due to the fact that each family did most of its own work, and, until about the middle of the 19th century, with comparatively little machinery.

All told, the land system as found in the United States is adapted to a regime of extreme, individualistic, private ownership, modified mainly by the power of taxation. More recently a system of zoning has been applied, first to city property, now to much land adapted to agriculture, forestry and recreation. The proportion of public land to private is still, however, small. Zoning implies, and embodies, the right of the public to decide, in general terms, the use to which land shall be put: whether or not, for example, a given tract, large or small, shall be provided with schools or roads, or shall be designated as forest, or recreational land.

The general plan respecting land, for a century and a half, has been to put the public domain into the hands of the user as fast as possible. Recent movements have been in a contrary direction.

LANDGRAVE was the title proposed for the second order of provincial nobility provided for in the Fundamental Constitutions of Carolina by the Lords Proprietors. Their inability to enforce the Constitutions made the title of little meaning save as an occasion for gifts of land to favorites, and as a title for the governors.

LANDRUM-GRIFFIN ACT. This labor act, passed on Sept. 14, 1959, which has as important objectives (a) to protect the rights of individual union members from "dictatorial, iron-fisted" actions by labor-union officials and (b) to insure free and democratic elections by secret ballot, was characterized by labor-union officials as a "killer" law just as the Taft-Hartley Act of 1947, amended in 1951, was called a "slave labor act." The experience record has not justified the charges. The act also restricts union strike and picketing activities for organizing purposes, and imposes a tighter ban on so-called "hot cargo" clauses in building trades and garment union contracts. In the first 18 months of its operation, more than 1200 cases involving violations of the act were resolved out of court, 80 of them being disputed elections. Only 25 complaints filed by workers required court action, a slow process because of crowded court dockets. The first court action against an employer, under the act, was filed by the Federal Government in May, 1961.

LANSING-ISHII AGREEMENT was concluded by an exchange of notes between Secretary Robert Lansing and Viscount Ishii on Nov. 2, 1917. Its ostensible purpose was to reconcile conflicting viewpoints in American and Japanese policy in the Far East as a measure of wartime co-operation, but Japan also undertook to win from the United States recognition of what Viscount Ishii termed Japan's "paramount interest" in China. Secretary Lansing opposed this move but finally accepted a compromise whereby the two governments' reaffirmation of the Open Door policy and of the territorial integrity of China was supplemented by American recognition of Japan's "special interest in China, particularly in the part to which her possessions are contiguous." Despite Secretary Lansing's disclaimers, Viscount Ishii subsequently insisted that this clause in the agreement implied definite acknowledgment of Japan's special position in Manchuria. His interpretation was generally accepted in the Far East and the agreement was widely condemned in China as a betrayal of the principles of the Open Door. Its ambiguity was recognized at the time of the Washington Conference and soon thereafter, on March 30, 1923, a further exchange of notes between the American and Japanese governments declared that "in the light of the understanding arrived at by the Washington Conference," the correspondence between Secretary Lansing and Viscount Ishii would be considered canceled and "of no further force or effect."

LAPWAI MISSION (1836–47) was established in November, 1836, by the Rev. and Mrs. Henry Harmon Spalding, co-workers of Dr. Marcus Whitman, at a site eleven miles above Lewiston, Idaho, where the Lapwai Creek empties into the Clearwater River. Here Spalding had the first white home, church, school, flour mill, sawmill, blacksmith shop and loom in what is now Idaho. In 1839 the mission secured a printing press from Hawaii and sent it to Lapwai. This was the first press in the Pacific Northwest. The mission was closed by the Whitman massacre. In 1871 the Presbyterian Church resumed the work.

LARAMIE, FORT, was established in June, 1834, by William Sublette and Robert Campbell, fur traders from St. Louis, Mo. The first structure, built of logs, was named Fort William for the senior founder. Located near the junction of the Laramie and North Platte Rivers, in the land of the Sioux and Cheyennes, it became the trade center for a large area, serving white trappers and Indians alike. The American Fur Company purchased the fort in 1836. They replaced the log stockade with adobe walls in 1841 and christened the structure "Fort John." But the name did not "take"; "Fort Laramie" supplanted it.

First missionaries to Oregon and earliest overland emigrants used this fort, on the Oregon Trail, as a supply and refitting depot. The growing emigrant tide, greatly augmented by the goldseekers of 1849, demanded protection from Indians. The Government purchased the post from the trading company on June 26, 1849, for $4000 and converted it into a military fort. New wooden and adobe buildings were erected. It became the great way station on the principal road to the Far West. The Grattan (1854) and the Harney (1855) massacres near the fort foreshadowed the general Indian war that followed. Fort Laramie became headquarters for the military campaigns. When the Indians were finally subdued and placed on reservations, need for the fort ended. It was abandoned April 20, 1890.

LARAMIE, FORT, TREATY OF (1851). Thomas Fitzpatrick, first Indian agent to the tribes of the upper Platte and Arkansas, asked, in 1849, authorization and funds for a general treaty with his wards. In February, 1851, Congress responded with a $100,000 appropriation. Couriers were sent to the Indians appointing a council for Sept. 1 at Fort Laramie. Sioux, Cheyennes, Arapahoes and Shoshones were the principal tribes that gathered, forming perhaps the largest and most colorful Indian council ever assembled in the West. For twenty days negotiations continued, being prolonged to await arrival of the wagon train of presents. Indian feasts and demonstrations occurred daily. Companies of soldiers placed between tribes hereditarily hostile avoided conflict. The treaty as signed provided peace, territorial boundaries for individual tribes, a $50,000 annuity to the Indans and permitted establishment of forts and roads in the Indian country.

LARAMIE, FORT, TREATY OF (1868). In 1866 the Sioux had agreed to permit the opening of the Bozeman Trail to Montana. Before negotiations were completed, Col. Carrington arrived with troops and began erection of forts on the new road. The Indians objected, attacks began and war ensued. Peace advocates in the East now won ascendancy with the slogan "cheaper to feed than to fight the Indians." The Government changed policy and in 1867 sent Peace Commissioners, but the hostiles refused to negotiate while the new forts remained. The Commissioners came again in April, 1868, acceded to Indian demands and drafted a treaty. They agreed to withdraw the Bozeman Trail forts and to recognize the country north of the North Platte and east of the Big Horn Mountains as unceded Indian territory. No whites might settle in this region. All that part of present South Dakota, west of the Missouri River, was formed into a Sioux Reservation. To induce Indians to settle upon it the Government agreed to construct an agency building, a schoolhouse, sawmill, gristmill, etc., on the Missouri River and to furnish

food supplies for four years and clothing for thirty years. The Indians promised to refrain from capturing and killing whites, attacking coaches and wagon trains, and to withdraw all opposition to the construction of railroads being built across the plains. Some of the Indians signed the treaty in April, but Red Cloud and the distrusting bands refused to sign until November, after the hated forts in the Powder River country had actually been abandoned. With these concessions made and with annuities provided, generally peaceful relations were to prevail until gold discoveries in the Black Hills brought a new white tide into Dakota and precipitated the wars of the middle-1870's.

LaSALLE, EXPLORATIONS OF. Until New France became a royal colony in 1663, its development was painfully slow. Following this change, a period of marked progress set in. The Iroquois were subdued, industry and commerce were fostered and geographical expansion was vigorously prosecuted.

Foremost in promoting this renaissance of New France were Intendant Jean Talon and Gov. Frontenac. Among the galaxy of explorers whose names adorn the period, the most notable was René Robert Cavelier, Sieur de LaSalle (1643–87), who came to Canada in early manhood in 1667 and began near Montreal the development of a seigniory. Soon, however, his active mind became absorbed in the possibilities inherent in the Indian trade, and the coming of Count Frontenac as Governor in 1672 offered him an opportunity to exploit them.

Frontenac was an imperialist and the fur trade offered the prospect of recouping his ruined fortune. In 1673 he founded Fort Frontenac (modern Kingston) in the Iroquois country, and next year sent LaSalle to France to enlighten the king concerning his expansionist designs. The royal approval was obtained, and LaSalle returned with a patent of nobility for himself and the grant of Fort Frontenac as a seigniory.

In 1677 LaSalle again went to France to seek royal approval of a far greater design. He now desired to establish a colony in the country south of the Great Lakes, and to this end desired a trade monopoly of the region to be developed, and authority to build forts and govern it. The king was willing to approve all but the idea of colonizing, and in 1678 LaSalle was back in New France making preparations for the actual invasion of the West, to be launched the following season. A small vessel, the *Griffon,* was built above Niagara and in August, 1679, LaSalle set sail for Green Bay. Here the *Griffon* was sent back to Niagara, laden with furs, while LaSalle himself journeyed southward by canoe around Lake Michigan to the mouth of the St. Joseph.

Here he tarried until December, building Fort Miami and awaiting the return of the *Griffon,* which had vanished forever on its maiden voyage. At length he ascended the St. Joseph to South Bend, where he crossed to the Kankakee and descended that stream and the Illinois to Lake Peoria where he built Fort Crèvecoeur and a vessel in which to descend the Mississippi. He also dispatched Father Hennepin and two companions to explore the Upper Mississippi, while he himself set out in midwinter for distant Fort Frontenac to procure badly needed supplies.

Iroquois raids and other obstacles were now encountered, but LaSalle doggedly fought on and the close of 1681 found him again at Fort Miami, ready to renew his push for the sea. Descending the Illinois, he reached the Mississippi on Feb. 2, 1682, and on April 9 was at the Gulf of Mexico, where with fitting ceremony he formally claimed the entire Mississippi Valley for his king and named it Louisiana.

The way to Mexico was open, and the realization of his plans seemed assured, when Count Frontenac was replaced by a new Governor who proved a bitter enemy of LaSalle. Facing utter ruin, he again went to France to appeal to his monarch in person. His requests were approved, and in 1684 he sailed for the Gulf of Mexico, equipped with men and means to establish a post on the Lower Mississippi to serve as the southern outlet of his colony. Unable to find the river-mouth, however, the colonists were landed on the coast of Texas, where most of them eventually perished. LaSalle himself was murdered in 1687 while still seeking to find the Mississippi and establish contact with his post in Illinois. Although his life closed in seeming failure, his dream survived and in the following century Louisiana became the fairest portion of New France. In the eyes of history, LaSalle will forever be deemed its father.

LATIN AMERICAN RELATIONS WITH THE UNITED STATES. The United States entered into diplomatic relations with Colombia in 1822 and with other Latin American governments soon afterward. Though the Monroe Doctrine, enunciated in 1823, became a basic principle of its foreign policy, such relations as the American Government had with the Latin American states during the 19th century were principally with Mexico and the republics in the Caribbean region. The United States was at war with Mexico in 1846–48, and about the same time was involved in a diplomatic conflict with Great Britain over the control of the Nicaraguan canal route. Before the American Civil War it frequently manifested a lively concern over the fate of Cuba, which was coveted by several European powers as well as by some North American statesmen. In 1869–70 President Grant made an unsuccessful effort to annex the Dominican Republic. North American investments and trade became important in Mexico in the latter part of the 19th century. There was less contact with South America, where European capital and trade were predominant, and whence persons who traveled for trade or for study usually went to Europe rather than to the United States.

The first important step toward closer relations with the Latin American republics as a group was taken when the United States convened a Pan American conference at Washington in 1889. This was the first of a series which were held at irregular intervals thereafter. The earlier meetings dealt chiefly with commercial matters, and they accomplished little because most of the participants failed to ratify the agreements that were adopted. The South American countries continued to trade principally with Europe and to look to Europe for intellectual leadership.

This situation changed with World War I. During and after the conflict Latin American trade with the United States increased rapidly and much North American capital was invested in mines, public utilities, and railroads. The war also brought closer political relations. A majority of the Latin American republics manifested their support of the United States by breaking diplomatic relations with Germany or by actually declaring war. The Pan American conferences that met after the war began to discuss political as well as economic matters. During the 1920's, however, Latin American dislike of the policy that the United States had been following in the Caribbean region was an obstacle to thoroughly friendly relations.

The United States had begun to show an increased interest in the internal affairs of the West Indian and Central American republics soon after the Spanish-American War. When the American Government decided to build the Panama Canal it became even more important than before, from the standpoint of national security, that the small states in the vicinity of the waterway should not fall under the control of a potentially hostile power. In accord with Theodore Roosevelt's corollary to the Monroe Doctrine, the United States endeavored to help some of these states to eliminate the political disorder and financial mismanagement which had frequently exposed them to European intervention. These efforts led to an increasingly active interference in their internal affairs, culminating in military interventions in Haiti in 1915, in the Dominican Republic in 1916, and in Nicaragua in 1912 and again in 1926–27. These events aroused alarm and distrust in other Latin American countries.

The United States' policy changed after 1929. President Hoover withdrew the remaining Marines from Nicaragua and initiated measures to end the control that the United States had been exercising in Haiti under the Treaty of 1915. President Franklin D. Roosevelt specifically repudiated intervention as a policy, and Secretary of State Hull, at the Seventh Pan American Conference in 1933, agreed to a convention which provided that no state had a right to intervene in the external or internal affairs of another. The "Good Neighbor Policy," combined with a growing realization that the American republics had a common interest in the defense of democracy against totalitarianism, paved the way for much closer economic and political co-operation after World War II began.

When the war broke out in Europe, the Foreign Ministers of the American republics met at Panama to discuss measures for maintaining the neutrality of the Western Hemisphere and for alleviating the economic effects of the conflict. Another meeting after the fall of France agreed to act if necessary to prevent any European colony in America from falling into the hands of the Axis powers. After Pearl Harbor, all of the American states except Argentina, which was ruled by the pro-Axis Perón dictatorship, co-operated in the war effort. Brazil and Mexico sent troops to the fighting fronts and several countries permitted the United States to use air or naval bases that were of great military value. Latin American governments endeavored to increase the production of strategic raw materials and to control espionage and sabotage. On the other hand, economic and technical aid from the United States helped to offset the effects of the cessation of trade with Europe.

Plans for strengthening the Inter-American System were formulated at a conference at Mexico City in 1945, and were put into effect in the Inter-American Treaty of Reciprocal Assistance signed at Rio de Janeiro in 1947 and in the Charter of the Organization of American States, adopted by the Ninth Pan American Conference at Bogotá in 1948. In the 1947 treaty, the signatories pledged themselves to aid any American state that was the victim of an attack if the attack occurred in the Western Hemisphere. Aid might take various forms, ranging from the recall of diplomatic representatives to the use of armed force. The Charter of the Organization of American States set up a regional arrangement within the framework of the United Nations to promote political, economic, and cultural co-operation among the member states.

The "supreme organ" of the O. A. S. is the Inter-American Conference, which normally meets every five years. Between conferences, major problems are dealt with by meetings of Ministers of Foreign Affairs or by the Council of the Organization, sitting in Washington with a representative from each state. The Council directs the activities of a number of specialized agencies, including the Inter-American Economic and Social Council, the Inter-American Commission of Jurists, the Inter-American Cultural Council, and many others. The Pan American Union, set up by the first Pan American Conference in 1889, is the secretariat of the O. A. S. After 1949 the Council successfully used its good offices on several occasions to settle disputes which threatened to cause or had already caused armed strife between member states.

After World War II, the United States increased its financial aid to Latin America. In addition to the Technical Assistance and other direct-aid programs, it made loans through the Export-Import Bank and the Development Loan Fund, chiefly for industrial development. It contributed a large part of the capital for the Inter-American Development Bank, which began operations in 1960. Much North American private capital also went into Latin America, in spite of obstacles created in many countries by a spirit of economic nationalism. Economic and social discontent continued, however, to be a major problem in inter-American relations, partly because discontent was utilized by the communists in their efforts to destroy the O. A. S. In 1960, the President of the United States proposed a broad attack on the problem of poverty and discontent through land reform, housing, and education. The Congress authorized an appropriation of $500,000,000 as an initial contribution by the United States, and the other American states approved the program at a conference which met in the same year at Bogotá.

Most of the American states have had to deal with subversive communist activities. The Inter-American conferences at Bogotá in 1948 and at Caracas in 1954 adopted resolutions condemning the intervention of international communism in the affairs of the American republics. A communist-controlled government in Guatemala was overthrown by revolution in 1954, but in 1959–60 the growing influence of communists in Cuba seriously threatened the peace of the Hemisphere. The O. A. S. endeavored to discourage the revolutionary activities which were apparently directed from Cuba against other Caribbean states, but the principle of nonintervention was an obstacle to any very effective measures.

While political and economic relations between the American nations were growing closer, there was also a great increase in other contacts. With the establishment of direct passenger service between the United States and South American ports after World War I and the establishment of airlines after 1929, there was an increasing flow of students and other visitors both north and south. Inter-American conventions provided scholarships for students, and the U. S. Government invited large numbers of distinguished Latin Americans to visit the United States as its guests. Binational centers in most Latin American countries promoted cultural interchange in other ways, especially by teaching English to many thousands of people. Another helpful factor in inter-American relations was the work of private foundations, which began with the Rockefeller Foundation's great health program in the period of World War I.

LAWRENCE, THE SACK OF (May 21, 1856), was the beginning of actual civil war in the Kansas conflict. A proslavery grand jury had indicted several of the Free-State leaders for treason, and had "presented" the Emigrant Aid Company's Free-State

Hotel, believed to have been built as a fort, and the newspapers, the *Herald of Freedom* and the *Free State,* as nuisances. A United States marshal appeared before the village with a posse of seven or eight hundred men to serve the warrants. Having made his arrests unopposed, he relinquished his posse to the proslavery sheriff S. J. Jones who, since the Wakarusa War, had sought the destruction of this "hotbed of abolitionism." Led by Jones, ex-Senator Atchison of Missouri, Maj. Buford of Alabama and others, the mob entered the town and, making a pretext of the grand jury "presentment," burned the hotel and wrecked the newspaper offices. Accounts disagree as to how much more property was destroyed or stolen. A few days later John Brown retaliated in the Pottawatomie Massacre, while, at the request of Gov. Shannon, troops were sent to Topeka to effect the dispersal of a Free-State legislature. News of the sack aroused the entire North, led to the formation of the National Kansas Committee and provided the Republican party with the issue of "Bleeding Kansas."

LEADVILLE MINING DISTRICT, named for a lead carbonate ore which abounded in the region and contained large amounts of silver, is located near the headwaters of the Arkansas River. The first settlement resulted from the discovery in 1860 of rich placer deposits in California Gulch, which yielded over $3,000,000 in gold before they were exhausted in 1867. For nearly ten years sporadic prospecting was carried on, which finally culminated, in 1875, in the discovery of the true nature of the carbonate ore by W. H. Stevens and A. B. Wood. Then occurred a mining rush on a grand scale. The Little Pittsburgh, Matchless, Robert E. Lee and other famous mines were developed. On Jan. 26, 1878, the city of Leadville was organized with H. A. W. Tabor, who was to become the district's best-known Bonanza King, as the first mayor. During the period 1858–1925 the district produced nearly $200,000,000 of silver and over $50,000,000 of gold.

LEAGUE OF NATIONS, THE, in the words of President Wilson, "is a great idea which has been growing in the minds of all generous men for several generations . . ., the dream of the friends of humanity through all the ages." William Penn's *Essay Toward the Present and Future Peace of Europe* (1693) and William Ladd's *Essay on a Congress of Nations* (1840) were notable American contributions to this remarkable literature on world organization. On the practical side, the framers of the Covenant relied upon the experience of the numerous public administrative unions—such as the Universal Postal Union—the Permanent Court of Arbitration and the international conferences like those of 1899 and 1907 at The Hague of which the purpose and result were the provision of principles and rules of international law. In all of these steps toward an integrated in-

ternational system the United States had participated, American official and private effort having been particularly directed toward the establishment of international judicial machinery.

During World War I various societies were formed in the United States, as in European countries, to consider and plan for an international political structure that would, *inter alia,* provide legal methods of settling controversies and thus reduce the likelihood of war. The most effective of these societies was the League to Enforce Peace, organized at Philadelphia in June, 1915. William Howard Taft was its president, and its 22 vice-presidents were highly distinguished leaders in public life, business and the professions. Political party lines were disregarded in its membership. Henry Cabot Lodge and A. Lawrence Lowell as well as Mr. Taft were ardent advocates of its four-point program: (1) a world court, (2) a council of inquiry and recommendation to deal with political issues, (3) economic and military sanctions and (4) periodical law-codification conferences. Ninety-six per cent of American Chambers of Commerce voted "that this country take the lead in forming a league of nations," 77% for economic sanctions and 64% for military sanctions.

President Wilson made the conception of a league the fourteenth point of his peace program laid before Congress on Jan. 8, 1918: "A general association of nations must be formed under specific covenants for the purpose of affording mutual guarantees of political independence and territorial integrity to great and small states alike." Col. House further revised the document. The plan submitted to the commission appointed by the Versailles Conference to "work out the details of the constitution and functions of the League" was a combination of British and American ideas.

President Wilson insisted that the Covenant should be part of the Treaty of Versailles. He was chairman of the Peace Conference commission to draft the Covenant, of which Col. House also was a member.

The Treaty of Versailles was submitted to the Senate on July 10, 1919. Sen. Lodge, who had previously withdrawn from his advocacy of a league, was, as chairman of the Foreign Relations Committee, the principal opponent of the Covenant. Outside the Senate, George Harvey, editor of *Harvey's Weekly* and the *North American Review,* was vigorously antagonistic. Because of the strong popular feeling favoring entrance into the League, the senatorial opposition feared a direct vote and resorted to reservations and delay. This opposition was motivated by party politics, by traditional repugnance to "entanglement" in foreign affairs and by resentment against certain sections of the treaty. On the final vote upon the treaty with fifteen reservations, taken on March 19, 1920, the ayes mustered but 49 votes (seven less than the required two-thirds majority of those present); the nays mustered 35 votes. Although by that date public sentiment had cooled, it was still so favorable to League membership that Warren G. Harding, the Republican candidate in the 1920 election, felt obliged to propose an "association of nations," thereby confusing the electorate as to his real attitude.

For six months after President Harding took office the Department of State ignored all communications from the agencies of the League. Undoubtedly Secretary Hughes was controlled in this procedure by the feeling among the "irreconcilable" Republican Senators. However, American interest in many of the subjects of League conferences soon forced a cooperative attitude. At first "unofficial observers" were sent to such meetings, but as these men and women were usually experts and sincerely concerned, their participation was of great value to the League's activities. Beginning in 1924 the American Government was officially represented in various League conferences, among them the Second Opium Conference of 1924–25 and the Opium Conference of 1931, the Conference on the Traffic in Arms of 1925, the Conference for the Limitation and Reduction of Armaments, 1932–34, and the Economic Conferences of 1927 and subsequent years. It also appointed official representatives to such League committees and commissions as the Preparatory Commission for a Disarmament Conference, the Economic Committee and the Opium Advisory Committee. In 1931 an official of the American Government represented the United States as a full voting member of the Council Committee on assistance to Liberia. In 1934 the United States agreed to register all treaties and other international agreements with the Secretariat. A special group of Foreign Service Officers was maintained at Geneva to observe and have contact with the work of the League.

Co-operation in political questions began with the Sino-Japanese controversy in Manchuria, 1931–33. Secretary Stimson not only sent notes of protest paralleling those of the Council but appointed a representative to sit with Council for consultation upon the applicability of the Pact of Paris and approved the acceptance by Maj. Gen. McCoy of membership in the Lytton Commission of Inquiry. Approval of the League's nonrecognition resolutions, which were similar to the statement of Secretary Stimson on Jan. 7, 1931, and of the Assembly resolution of Oct. 6, 1937, in which Japanese action in China was declared to be contrary to Japan's treaty obligations, was expressed by the incumbent secretaries of state. However, the American Government gave no direct intimation of readiness to co-operate with the League in economic or military sanctions.

The relation of this country to the Italo-Ethiopian case was indirect, but the application of the Neutrality Act of 1935, like the public endorsement by President F. D. Roosevelt and Secretary Hull of League measures in the premises, was assurance to the League that the United States at least would not support Italy morally or by the sale of arms and munitions of war.

On April 15, 1946, the League of Nations was disbanded, and the assets surrendered to United Nations.

LEAVENWORTH, FORT. In 1824 some citizens of Missouri, at the suggestion of Sen. Benton, petitioned Congress for a military post at the Arkansas Crossing of the Santa Fe Trail to protect traders journeying to New Mexico. Although no action was then taken, the Secretary of War in 1827 decided to erect a fort near the western boundary of Missouri, which would, at least in part, meet the wishes of the petitioners. On March 7 the adjutant-general ordered Col. Henry Leavenworth to select a site for the cantonment, an assignment which he completed on May 8. It was named Cantonment Leavenworth. Due to an epidemic of malaria between 1827 and 1829, it was practically evacuated in May, 1829; but late that summer it was reoccupied. During 1832 it was renamed Fort Leavenworth.

The post became important as a starting point for a number of military expeditions to the Far West, as a meeting place for Indian councils and as a supply depot for forts and camps on the frontier. Before 1846 its garrison usually included portions of the Sixth Infantry or First Dragoons. It rose to national prominence during the Mexican War, when the Army of the West was organized there and began a long march to occupy the Far Southwest. Throughout the 1850's it continued to be a point of departure for many military expeditions. Occupying a strategic position in the West during the Civil War, it was at various times headquarters of the Department of the West, the Department of Kansas and the Department of Missouri. Although the Fort Leavenworth military reservation was for a time the seat of an arsenal (1859–74) and of the U. S. Disciplinary Barracks (1874–95, 1906–29), today it includes, in addition to a military post, the U. S. Penitentiary (since 1895) and the Command and General Staff School (since 1881), the latter an important training school for officers.

LeBOEUF, FORT, WASHINGTON'S MISSION TO. In 1753 the French erected forts at Presque Isle and at LeBoeuf (Waterford, Pa.) and, seizing an English trader's house at Venango, converted it into a French fort. Gov. Dinwiddie of Virginia selected the youthful George Washington to deliver a letter to the French demanding their withdrawal. With Christopher Gist and five others, Washington traveled from Wills Creek over the trail later known as Braddock's Road to the forks of the Ohio and thence to Logstown. Guided by friendly Indians, the party then proceeded to Venango and LeBoeuf. St. Pierre, the commandant at LeBoeuf, received Dinwiddie's letter and answered that he would forward it to Duquesne.

547

At LeBoeuf Washington and his companions noted the strength of fort and garrison and the large number of canoes there, indicating a contemplated expedition down the Ohio.

After two narrow escapes from death on the return journey, Washington arrived at Williamsburg Jan. 16, 1754, and delivered to Dinwiddie his journal and St. Pierre's letter. The journal, published and widely reprinted in the colonies and in England, not only helped arouse the English against the French advance, but also brought Washington for the first time to the attention of the world.

LECOMPTON CONSTITUTION was framed by a convention of proslavery Kansans, Sept. 7–Nov. 7, 1857, Free State men having abstained from voting at an election of delegates on the preceding June 15. The convention adjourned on Sept. 11 to await the outcome of the territorial legislative election; a Free State victory discouraged moderates and the convention, which reassembled on Oct. 19, could not obtain a quorum until the 22nd. A constitution was framed which provided the usual forms and functions of a state government. A clause in the bill of rights excluded free Negroes. The slavery article declared slave property inviolable, denied the power of the legislature to prohibit immigrants from bringing in slaves or to emancipate them without compensation and the owners' consent, and empowered that body to protect slaves against inhuman treatment. The schedule provided a referendum on the alternatives, the "Constitution with Slavery" and the "Constitution with no Slavery." If the latter prevailed, the slavery article should be deleted, but there should be no interference with slave property already in Kansas. Other provisions prevented amendment before 1865 and placed responsibility for canvassing returns upon the presiding officer.

On Dec. 21 the slavery clause was approved, 6226 to 569, Free State men declining to vote. The legislature called an election for Jan. 4, 1858, at which the whole constitution was submitted. Proslavery men did not participate and the document was rejected, 10,226 to 162. Against the advice of some of his friends, Buchanan recommended on Feb. 2 that Kansas be admitted under it. The constitution was approved by the Senate, but Republicans, Douglas Democrats and other opponents in the House united to defeat it. Congress then passed the English bill which provided a referendum on the whole constitution and promised the future state over 5,000,000 acres of land if the instrument were ratified. An election on Aug. 2 rejected it, 11,300 to 1788.

LEDERER'S EXPLORING EXPEDITIONS. John Lederer, a German traveler, in 1670–72 made tours of western exploration for Sir Wm. Berkeley, governor of Virginia and one of the proprietors of Carolina. Lederer, starting from the site of Richmond, claimed to have reached the summit of the Appalachian Mountains, but in fact he only reached the eastern foothills of the Blue Ridge. In a town of the Occaneechi Indians he met "stranger Indians" who lived two months' distance to the westward and who well described their country as marked by waves (mountain ranges). From this Lederer drew the wild conjecture that "the Indian Ocean does stretch an arm or bay from California into the continent as far as the Apalataean Mountains." The explorer did reach as far south as upper South Carolina, visiting as he went a number of Indian tribes, some of whose customs he recorded in a book published by Sir Wm. Talbot in London, 1672.

LEGAL TENDER is anything which, by law, a debtor may require his creditor to receive in payment of a debt, in the absence of any agreement for payment in some other manner, appearing in the contract itself. The tender is an admission of the debt and in some jurisdictions, if refused, discharges the debt.

There were two periods of American history when the question of legal tender was an important political issue. The first was in the period between 1776 and 1789; the second was in the years just after the Civil War. In the first case the question was whether the states should be permitted to print currency and require its acceptance by creditors regardless of its severe depreciation in value. In the second case it was whether Congress had power, under the Constitution, to cause the issuance of paper money (greenbacks) which would be legal tender in payment of private debts.

The amount of circulating medium in the newborn states was insufficient to finance a costly war. Nearly every state early had recourse to the printing presses in order to meet its own expenses and the quota levies made by the Continental Congress. At first, these issues were small and notes passed at their face value. Soon, however, they began to depreciate and the state legislatures resorted to laws requiring the acceptance of state bank notes at par. In Connecticut, in 1776 for example, the legislature made both continental and state notes legal tender and ordered that any one who tried to depreciate them should forfeit not only the full value of the money he received but also the property which he offered for sale. Attempts were also made at price regulation. The South particularly went to excess in the abuse of public credit. Virginia, for example, practically repudiated her paper issues at the close of the Revolution.

The leaders in business and finance in the states were not slow to see the undesirability of a repetition of this financial orgy. So when the Constitutional Convention met in 1787 there was general agreement upon the desirability of providing for a single national system of currency and of prohibiting note issues by the states. Accordingly Article 1, Section 10 of the Constitution contains the following prohibitions upon the states, "No State shall . . . coin Money; emit Bills of Credit; make any thing but gold and silver Coin a Tender in Payment of Debts; pass any . . . ex post facto Law, or Law impairing the Obligation of Contracts. . . ."

The question raised after the Civil War related to the constitutionality of the Legal Tender Act passed by Congress in 1862. It was alleged that Congress, in requiring the acceptance of greenbacks at face value was violating the Fifth Amendment, which forbade the deprivation of property without due process of law. It is now a clearly recognized power of Congress to make paper money legal tender. The Constitution itself clearly denies such powers to the states.

LEGAL TENDER ACT (1862). To provide funds to carry on the Civil War, Congress issued fiat money. By the act of Feb. 25, 1862, and by successive acts, the Government put into circulation about $450,000,000 of paper money dubbed "greenbacks." No specific gold reserve was set aside nor any date announced for their redemption. To insure their negotiability, Congress declared these notes legal tender in "payment of all taxes, internal duties, excises, debts and demands of every kind due to the United States, except duties on imports, and of all claims and demands against the United States . . . and shall also be lawful money and legal tender in payment of all debts, public and private, within the United States." Wall Street and the metropolitan press opposed this measure. On the Pacific coast the law was frequently evaded through the passage of a "specific Contract Act." In 1870 the Supreme Court declared the Legal Tender Act unconstitutional and void in respect to debts contracted prior to its passage. Upon filling two vacancies, however, the Court reversed its decision.

LEGAL TENDER CASES involved the question of the constitutionality of the measures enacted during the Civil War for the issue of Treasury notes to circulate as money without provision for redemption. The constitutional question hinged not on the power of the Government to issue the notes, but on its power to make them legal tender for the payment of debts, particularly those contracted before the legislation was enacted. The U. S. Supreme Court decided the question on Feb. 7, 1870, in the case of Hepburn v. Griswold (8 Wallace 603). The majority of the Court held that Congress had no power to enact the legal-tender provisions. The vote of the Court members, when taken in conference, had been five to three, with the obvious senility of Justice Grier, one of the majority, casting doubt on the weight of his opinion. He retired before the decision was announced, leaving the alignment at that time four to three. The opinion against the constitutionality of the legislation was written by Chief Justice Salmon P. Chase, who

as the Secretary of the Treasury had shared responsibility for the original enactments.

Nominations of two new members of the Supreme Court were sent to the Senate on the day on which the decision was announced. At the ensuing term, over the protest of the four members who had hitherto constituted the majority, the Court heard the reargument of the constitutional question in another case. On May 1, 1871, the Court reversed the Hepburn decision in Knox v. Lee and Parker v. Davis (12 Wallace 457), which are listed in the United States Reports under the title of The Legal Tender Cases. The question as to whether President Grant deliberately packed the Court to bring about a reversal of the original decision is still a matter of debate. Some of the notes issued were withdrawn by the Treasury but some were reissued under a later statute enacted without reference to wartime conditions. This statute was upheld on March 3, 1884, in Juilliard v. Greenman.

LEGISLATURE, THE, in the United States is one of the three major organs of national and state governments, the others being the executive and the judiciary. Its function is to enact law—to declare the public will in objective form.

Colonial legislatures usually consisted of an assembly, elected by vote of the freemen of the colony, and a council, appointed by the Crown or proprietor. There were no councils in Georgia or Pennsylvania, resulting in legislatures of but one house. The first state legislatures followed colonial models, except that senates were substituted for councils as the upper house. Suffrage was restricted by property or tax-paying qualifications, often larger for the upper than for the lower house. The legislature appointed the governor and judges. Its powers were not subject to check by gubernatorial veto or judicial review. This was the period of legislative supremacy.

The first half of the 19th century witnessed the rise of gubernatorial and judicial power in the states and the corresponding decline of legislative authority. The state legislature has never regained its early position of supremacy over the other two branches of state government. In addition state constitutions have become longer and contain more and more limitations upon the power of the legislature. Initiative and referendum have increased popular control over legislative questions. The impossibility of dealing with administrative details in a general law has led to the delegation of rule-making power to administrative officers, boards and commissions further restricting the sphere of legislative action.

The form of the legislatures in the states has generally followed the national model. Georgia and Pennsylvania entered the Union with single houses but abandoned them in 1789 and 1790 respectively. Vermont used but one house from 1777 to 1836. In 1934 Nebraska amended its constitution to substitute one house for two. Unicameralism is a live issue in most of the states. One important reason lies in the fact that rural areas retain representation in one of the houses out of all proportion to their population. A single house consisting of members chosen on the basis of population is widely advocated as a remedy.

LEISLER REBELLION (1689). The revolution in England, which forced James II to abdicate, was followed by revolution in America. May 31, 1689, Fort James on Manhattan Island was "seized by the Rable" and shortly afterward Capt. Jacob Leisler usurped complete control of southern New York. The following spring at his suggestion representatives of Massachusetts, Plymouth, Connecticut and New York met in New York City to concert measures for a united offensive against Canada. Leisler assumed energetic charge of operations, but lack of co-operation from the other colonies, and his own tactlessness, spoiled his efforts. In March, 1691, Col. Henry Sloughter was commissioned governor of New York by William and Mary. Leisler was tried for treason and executed, but the flame which he had kindled burned long and the agitation caused a further examination of the case in England, resulting in a reversal of the attainder and restoration of his estates.

LEVEE SYSTEM. The fertility of flat river-valley land is usually due to the deposit of silt during the overflows of the stream. Yet when such land is planted to crops, that same flooding may destroy them. To prevent this it is customary to build dikes or levees along the stream to prevent its overflow. This practice goes back to the distant past.

The world's greatest levee system is that along the Mississippi River, beginning in Louisiana in 1717 with small private levees about three feet high, built by individual planters. As these proved inadequate the works were enlarged and administered by parishes (counties), and then by levee districts organized under state law. With settlements further upstream, levees were built over most of the length of the river. Little by little the Federal Government began to assist in the process, in the guise of improving navigation, since the Federal Constitution made no provision for such works as river control for agricultural benefits. The role of the Federal Government grew more and more important. The fiction of benefiting navigation gradually lost emphasis, and by the process of usage and interpretation the Federal Constitution was modified to include flood control as a proper Federal function, though by custom the habit of referring to navigation benefits persists.

For about a century the control of the Mississippi River has been administered by the U. S. Army Engineers, and for a long period was one of their major peacetime activities. Through the years the Mississippi levees were increased in length until they now total more than 2000 miles. They were built higher and higher until the average height reached nearly 25 feet, with some short reaches 40 feet high.

For many years the doctrine of "levees only" dominated the work of the U. S. Engineer Corps. The levee system was finally held to be adequate, and for a number of years the Annual Report of the Chief of Engineers stated that the Mississippi River area was safe from disastrous effects of floods. Then came the 1927 flood which broke through the levees in about fifty places, covered nearly 2,000,000 acres of land, and submerged the homes of 750,000 people.

Thereupon the doctrine of "levees only" was abandoned, and Mississippi River flood control now includes levees, cutoffs of bends, spillways and by-passes for relieving the channel, and the construction of reservoirs. The cost since 1927 of completing the supposedly adequate system is approaching $1,000,000,000. Yet for the Mississippi River the levee system, containing about 1,000,000,000 cubic yards of earth, is the largest single factor in this, the greatest of all flood control projects.

LEWIS AND CLARK EXPEDITION (1804–6). The problem which Lewis and Clark undertook to solve originated with the dawn of American history. Columbus was intent upon finding a new way to the Orient, and the accidental discovery of America was for him a great tragedy. As soon as contemporaries perceived that America barred the way to the Indies, they took up the task of finding a way around or through the troublesome continent, and for centuries this goal afforded one of the chief incitements to further American exploration. President Jefferson was deeply interested in scientific discoveries, and the acquisition of Louisiana in 1803 afforded him a pretext for sending an expedition to explore the western country.

Meriwether Lewis, Jefferson's private secretary, was appointed to command the expedition, and he associated his friend, William Clark, younger brother of Gen. George Rogers Clark, in the leadership. The party was assembled near St. Louis late in 1803 in readiness to start up the Missouri the following spring. This season it ascended the river by flatboat and keelboat to the group of Mandan and Arikara towns in west central North Dakota.

Here the winter was passed, and from here on April 7, 1805, while the flatboat returned to St. Louis, the explorers, in six canoes and two keelboats, set their faces toward the unknown West. Besides the two leaders, the party included 26 soldiers, George Drouillard and Toussaint Charbonneau, interpreters, Clark's Negro servant, York, and last but not least, Charbonneau's squaw-wife, Sacajawea (the Bird Woman), and her infant son.

On Nov. 7, 1805, the explorers gazed upon the Pacific Ocean. They had ascended the Missouri and its Jefferson fork to the mountains, which by a rare combination of skill, perseverance and luck they had crossed to the Snake; thence down the Snake and the Columbia to the sea. The winter was passed in a shelter (named Fort Clatsop) near present-day Astoria, and in March, 1806, the return journey was begun. After crossing the Rockies the explorers separated into three groups to make a more extensive examination of the country than a single party could accomplish. Thus both the Missouri and the Yellowstone were descended, near whose junction the groups reunited. From here the party passed rapidly down river to St. Louis on Sept. 23, 1806, where the expedition ended.

A great epic in human achievement had been written. Thousands of miles of wilderness inhabited by savage beasts and savage men had been traversed; an important impulse to the further extension of American trade and settlement had been supplied; important additions to the existing body of geographical and scientific knowledge had been made; in the person of humble, patient, loyal Sacajawea a precious addition to the world's roster of heroines had been disclosed.

LEXINGTON AND CONCORD. On the evening of the 18th of April, 1775, the British military governor of Massachusetts sent out from Boston a detachment of about 700 regular troops, to destroy military stores collected by the provincials at Concord. Detecting the plan, the Whigs in Boston sent out Paul Revere and William Dawes with warnings. The detachment consequently found at Lexington, at sunrise on the 19th, a part of the minute-man company already assembled on the green. While it was unwillingly breaking ranks at the command of the British Maj. Pitcairn, the regulars fired and cleared the ground. Eight of the Americans were killed, ten wounded. The regulars marched for Concord after but a short delay.

Here the provincials, outnumbered, retired over the North Bridge and waited reinforcements. The British occupied the town, held the North Bridge with about a hundred regulars, and searched for stores. Of these they found few; but the smoke of those which they burned in the town alarmed the watching provincials who (reinforced to the number of about 450) marched down to the bridge, led by Maj. John Buttrick. The regulars, seeing them, hastily formed on the farther side to receive them, and began to take up the planks of the bridge. Buttrick shouted to them to desist. The front ranks of the regulars fired, killing two provincials and wounding more. Buttrick gave the famous order, "Fire, fellow soldiers, for God's sake, fire!" The response of his men, and their continued advance, were too much for the British, who (with two killed and several wounded) broke and fled. The Americans did not follow up their success, and after a dangerous delay the British marched for Boston about noon.

At Meriam's Corner their rear guard was fired upon by the men of Reading, and from there to Lexington a skirmish fire was poured upon the British from all available cover. By the time they reached that town the regulars were almost out of ammunition and completely demoralized, and were saved from slaughter or surrender only by the arrival of a column from Boston, under Lord Percy, with two fieldpieces which overawed the militia and gave the troops time to rest. When they marched on again, however, the militia closed in once more and dogged the regulars all the way to Charlestown, where before sundown the troops reached safety under the guns of the fleet.

The casualties of the day bear no relation to its importance. Forty-nine Americans were killed, 73 British, with a total of the killed and wounded of both sides of 366. But the fighting proved to the Americans that by their own methods they could defeat the British. In that belief they stopped, before night, the land approaches to Boston, thus beginning the siege of Boston.

LIBBY PRISON was, after Andersonville, the most notorious of Confederate prisons. When the captives from the battle of First Bull Run arrived in Richmond, Gen. John H. Winder, provost marshal of the city, commandeered a number of vacant tobacco warehouses, among them one belonging to the firm of Libby and Son. Commissioned officers were confined here until after the fall of Richmond. The prison contained eight rooms, 103 by 42 feet, each equipped with a stove upon which the prisoners cooked their rations. After the failure of the cartel for the exchange of prisoners, Libby became crowded and a shortage of food supplies during December, 1863, and January, 1864, caused extensive suffering among the inmates. In February, 1864, 109 officers escaped through a tunnel, and 61 made their way to the Union lines. Feb. 28 and March 4, 1864, saw two Federal cavalry raids on Richmond for the purpose of releasing the prisoners. As a result of these events, the Confederates established a new officers' prison at Macon, Ga., in May, 1864. Thereafter Libby Prison was used only as a temporary station for captives en route to Macon.

LIBERAL REPUBLICAN PARTY represented a revolt of the reform element in the Republican party during Grant's first administration. They advocated a conciliatory Southern policy and civil service reform, and condemned political corruption. Some favored tariff revision. The movement was led by B. Gratz Brown, Carl Schurz, Charles Sumner, Charles Francis Adams, Horace Greeley and others. Greeley was named for President and Brown for Vice-President in 1872. Both candidates were later endorsed by the Democrats. In the ensuing campaign Greeley was overwhelmingly defeated by Grant.

LIBERATOR, THE, was a weekly antislavery newspaper edited by William Lloyd Garrison and published in Boston, Jan. 1, 1831, to Dec. 29, 1865. Its circulation never exceeded 3000. The subscription price was $2. Though never a success financially, this paper was largely influential in changing the anti-slavery movement from the advocacy of gradual emancipation to a demand for immediate, uncompensated emancipation. It greatly aided Garrison's work in organizing the New England Anti-Slavery Society in 1832 and the American Anti-Slavery Society in 1833. In its first issue he sounded its keynote in these words: "I am in earnest—I will not equivocate—I will not excuse—I will not retreat a single inch—AND I WILL BE HEARD."

LIBERTY BELL first proclaimed American independence from the State House, Philadelphia, following the reading there on July 8, 1776, of the Declaration of Independence. Originally ordered by the Provincial Council in 1751 for the Golden Jubilee of Penn's 1701 Charter of Privileges, it was cracked in testing upon arrival and recast by Pass and Stow, Philadelphia. During the Revolution it was hidden in Allentown (1777–78). Rung frequently for celebrations, it was first strained tolling the obsequies of Chief Justice Marshall (1835), but was fatally cracked and silenced on Washington's birthday, 1846. The antislavery movement in 1839 first called it Liberty Bell. It weighs over 2080 pounds, cost £60, and is inscribed: "Proclaim Liberty throughout all the land unto all the inhabitants thereof."

LIBERTY POLES, or Liberty Trees, were symbols before which Sons of Liberty assembled and "pledged their fortunes and their sacred honors in the cause of liberty." Numerology played a part in the erection of poles, particularly the numbers 92 and 45. *Forty-five* symbolized the issue of John Wilkes' newspaper which had criticized the king. *Ninety-two* typified the votes in the Massachusetts legislature against rescission of the Circular Letter. Ninety-two Sons of Liberty raised a Liberty Pole 45 feet high, or dedicated a tree with 92 branches after 17 had been lopped off in detestation of the 17 Tories who had voted to rescind the Circular Letter.

The best-known Liberty Pole was erected in New York City (1766), with approval of the royal governor, in celebration of repeal of the Stamp Act. Raised in harmony, it soon became the focus of brawls between British soldiers and Liberty Boys, attended by lively street fights and bloodshed.

The original Liberty Tree was an elm at the intersection of Washington and Essex Streets, Boston; a rallying place for Sons of Liberty who met under its boughs, denounced British oppression, drank toasts, sang songs and hanged unpopular officials in effigy. It was cut down by British soldiers in 1775, and converted into fourteen cords of firewood.

LIBRARY OF CONGRESS was established by the act of Congress, approved April 24, 1800, that made

provision for the removal of the Government of the United States to the new Federal City, Washington, D. C. It provided for "the purchase of such books as may be necessary for the use of Congress" and for "fitting up a suitable apartment" in the Capitol to house them.

The original collections of the Library, obtained from London, consisted of 152 works, in 740 volumes, and a few maps. To administer them, Congress, in an act of Jan. 26, 1802, provided that a Librarian be appointed, and three days later President Jefferson named John James Beckley, Clerk of the House of Representatives, who held both posts until his death.

When British troops burned the Capitol in 1814, the Library of some 3000 volumes was lost. To replace it, Congress purchased for $23,950 the personal library of Thomas Jefferson, consisting of an estimated 6487 books. This fine collection, far-ranging in subject matter, was "admirably calculated for the substratum of a great national library," proponents of its purchase contended. In 1851 a Christmas Eve fire destroyed some 35,000 volumes, including two thirds of the Jefferson library. By the end of 1864, the collections had grown to some 82,000 volumes, but they were far from distinguished and national only in the sense that the Government owned them. Then Congress, in less than three years, passed four laws that cast the Library in the mold of greatness: an act of March 3, 1865, requiring the deposit in the Library of a copy of all books and other materials on which copyright was claimed, with loss of copyright for failure to deposit; an act of April 5, 1866, depositing in the Library of Congress the Smithsonian Institution's unique collection (40,000 volumes plus future increments) of scientific materials and transactions of learned societies, gathered from all over the world; an act of March 2, 1867, strengthening international exchange of official publications and making the Library the beneficiary; and an appropriations act of March 2, 1867, providing $100,000 for the purchase of the Peter Force Collection of Americana—the first major purchase since the Jefferson library and the Library's first distinguished research collection. The 19th century also saw the creation (1832) of the Law Library in the Library of Congress, the assignment (1870) to the Library of responsibility for the administration of the copyright law, and the first substantial gift to the Library of a private citizen —Dr. Joseph Meredith Toner's collection of medical literature and of materials for the study of American history and biography, which was accepted by Congress in 1882.

In 1897 the Library, which had grown to nearly a million volumes, moved from the Capitol to its own building. In preparation, Congress, in an appropriations act of Feb. 19, 1897—the nearest to an organic act the Library has—provided for the appointment of the Librarian by the President, by and with the advice and consent of the Senate, and vested in the

Librarian the authority to make regulations for the government of the Library and to appoint members of the staff "solely with reference to their fitness for their particular duties."

During the 20th century, the Library of Congress emerged as a library "universal in scope, national in service," as Librarian Herbert Putnam termed it. By June 30, 1960, the collections, acquired by gift, exchange, purchase, official transfer, and the operation of the copyright law, totaled nearly 39,000,000 items and constituted unparalleled resources for research. They included more than 12,000,000 books and pamphlets on every subject and in a multitude of languages. Among them are the most comprehensive collections of Chinese, Japanese, and Russian materials outside the Orient and the Soviet Union; 1,500,-000 volumes relating to science and technology and nearly as many legal materials, outstanding for foreign as well as American law; the world's largest collection of aeronautical literature; and the most extensive collection of incunabula in the Western Hemisphere, including a perfect copy of the Gutenberg Bible printed on vellum. The manuscript collections totaled more than 16,500,000 items relating to American history and civilization and including the personal papers of 23 of the Presidents. The music collections, from classic to modern, contained more than 2,049,000 volumes and pieces, manuscript and published. Other materials included more than 2,500,-000 maps and views; 3,000,000 photographic items, from those of Mathew Brady to date; 107,000 recordings, including folksongs and other music, speeches, and poetry readings; 583,000 fine prints and reproductions; and newspapers and periodicals from all over the world, motion pictures, microfilms, and many other kinds of materials.

These collections are housed in the "old" or Main Building and in the Annex, which was occupied in 1939. In 1960, Congress appropriated $75,000 for the making of plans and specifications for a third Library building.

The functions of the Library have been extended by Congress until it is now, in effect, the national library, serving the Congress, Federal agencies, other libraries, scholars, and the public. It provides research and reference services to members and committees of Congress. Its comprehensive collections are open to adults for reference use, and some reference service is also provided by mail. It participates in a nationwide interlibrary loan service, which enables it to share collecting responsibilities and to supplement local research resources. For a fee, it furnishes photoduplicates of unrestricted materials in the Library. It publishes bibliographies and other guides to its collections. It administers the national library service for the blind. It contains the national office for the registration of claims to copyright, and its collections are enriched from the copyright deposits. It is the United States partner in the official, intergovernmental exchange of publications and has thousands of exchange agreements with private research institutions throughout the world. It receives gifts to the nation in the form of personal papers, rare books and other valuable materials. It develops a subject-classification system and cataloguing codes, which are nationally accepted standards. It serves as the national center for co-operative cataloguing and provides a national catalog card distribution service, to which some 10,000 libraries subscribe. It maintains national union catalogs on cards, which show the location of important research materials in American libraries, and it publishes a national bibliography in book form— the *National Union Catalog*. It presents exhibits of its materials, which are open to the public and some of which are circulated in the United States and abroad. The Library of Congress Trust Fund Board, created by an act of March 3, 1925, accepts, with the approval of the Joint Committee on the Library, and administers gifts and bequests that enable the Library to develop tools for research, to enrich the collections, and to present cultural programs in the fields of music, art and literature.

There have been 11 Librarians of Congress: John J. Beckley, 1802–07; Patrick Magruder, 1807–15, who also served as Clerk of the House of Representatives; George Watterston, 1815–29, the first to hold the separate post of Librarian; John Sylva Meehan, 1829–61; John G. Stephenson, 1861–64; Ainsworth Rand Spofford, 1864–97; John Russell Young, 1897–99; Herbert Putnam, 1899–1939; Archibald MacLeish, 1939–44; Luther Harris Evans, 1945–53; and L. Quincy Mumford, 1954–.

LICKS were saline springs or oozes to which herbivorous animals resorted for the quota of salt needed in their diet, which they obtained by licking the mud banks or rocks near the water. In some cases the lick was not near a flowing spring, but was a spot, usually muddy and, in at least one case, nearly an acre in extent, where the earth was so impregnated with salt that the animals licked it until they excavated considerable depressions. Important deposits of salt were frequently found thus. That prehistoric animals used the licks is indicated by the mastodon fossils found near Big Bone Lick in Kentucky. Well-beaten trails made by the animals led to the licks, which therefore became favorite places for the stalking of deer and buffalo, both Indian and white hunters constructing blinds nearby for the purpose. Licks were numerous in New York, Pennsylvania, the Middle States, Louisiana, Texas, etc. Their frequency in Kentucky accounted for the swarms of game found there when the white men came, and there they left behind them more place-names, such as Bank Lick, Berry's Lick, Paint Lick, Lick Creek—not to mention the Licking River—than in any other state. It has been said that it was the discovery of the licks and saline springs along the Holston, the Kanawha and Kentucky Rivers which enabled colonization to cross the mountains. Daniel Boone located his first settlement, Boonesborough, at a salt lick on the Kentucky River. It was while making salt at the Blue Licks some thirty miles distant, that he and several other colonists were captured by Indians in 1778. The Blue Licks later became a fashionable health resort. When Boone in after years moved to Missouri, he settled near another lick, which thereafter bore his name.

LIGHTING. The first American settlers employed candlewood or pine knots, which were dipped in pitch and burned with a bright but smoky flame. When they could afford it they used candles, which were generally manufactured at home, but the mass of the people used grease lamps with wicks of reed or twisted rag. The so-called Betty lamps, small oval or triangular basins of metal with a short spout and a handle and chain for carrying or hanging, were popular. In the more elaborate colonial homes candle fixtures of crystal and brass imported from France and England were installed.

At the beginning of the 18th century whale oil, abundant and cheap, was used extensively, although tallow candles were much preferred. Wealthy colonists used astral oil burned in glass shades to protect the flame from drafts. With the discovery of oil in Pennsylvania about 1860 kerosene was the accepted illuminant and is still in common use in communities with no electric or gas service.

Illuminating gas produced by distilling coal was a real advance in artificial lighting. Tried experimentally in England in 1798, it did not reach America until 1816. By 1875 it was the accepted method of lighting in all the cities. The "fish tail" burner was used exclusively until Welsbach's invention of the mantle, which gave a whiter and more brilliant light than any previous source. Gas lighting was widely used until about 50 years ago for stores, factories, theaters, churches and the better-class homes within reach of the mains.

The electric arc lamp was a practical thing before the incandescent lamp and in the late 1870's began to be introduced for street lighting using the series system. Electric lighting indoors, however, had to await the development of Edison's multiple system, the incandescent lamp and the establishment of central stations to supply current. The first permanent central station in the world was that of the Edison Electric Illuminating Co. in Pearl Street, New York City, which started operation on Sept. 4, 1882, with 59 customers who had a total of 1284 sockets.

For nearly thirty years all that was available for electric lighting were high-powered arc lamps and rather weak (2, 4, 8, 16 and 32 candlepower) carbon lamps. General illumination in stores, theaters and other public buildings was accomplished by arc lamps or clusters of incandescent lamps in a single reflector. In most offices and factories lighting was provided by individual lamps in tin or glass shades, known as drop lights. There was little general illumination and extreme contrasts between the brightly lighted work area and the rest of the room. In the homes most of the fixtures were converted gas chandeliers and table lamps.

With the introduction of the efficient and more powerful tungsten filament lamps, general lighting for all types of interiors became common.

LINCOLN COUNTY WAR was a struggle between two rival groups of ranchers and businessmen in southeastern New Mexico. One faction was headed by Maj. L. G. Murphy and the other by John Chisum and Alexander A. McSween. Murders and depredations extending over a long period culminated in July, 1878, in a three days' battle at the town of Lincoln, in which McSween and several others were killed. William H. Bonney, better known as Billy the Kid, was a prominent figure in this struggle.

LINCOLN-DOUGLAS DEBATES, the most noted events in Abraham Lincoln's senatorial campaign in Illinois against Stephen A. Douglas, took place at Ottawa, Freeport, Jonesboro, Charleston, Galesburg, Quincy and Alton, Aug. 21–Oct. 15, 1858. The Little Giant's opening speeches in his re-election drive, with their effective frontal attack on Lincoln's "House Divided" doctrine, alarmed Lincoln's managers and led him to challenge Douglas, "for you and myself to divide time and address the same audiences the present canvass." Douglas' speaking dates were already set through October, but he agreed to one debate in each of the above seven congressional districts.

About 12,000 gathered at Ottawa, Aug. 21, for the first debate, which was preceded and followed by parades, and punctuated by shouts and cheers. Douglas was well-dressed, with a ruffled shirt, a dark blue coat with shiny buttons and a wide-brimmed soft hat. Lincoln wore a rusty, high-topped hat, an ill-fitting coat with sleeves too short and baggy trousers so short as to show his rusty boots. Their speaking manners likewise contrasted. Douglas talked fast and steadily, in a heavy voice. He would shake his long, black hair and walk back and forth across the platform with great effectiveness. Lincoln's voice was light, almost nasal, and at the start had an unpleasant timbre, but carried well. Both gave a sense of profound earnestness.

Douglas' theme at Ottawa was the sectional bias, the strife-fomenting nature, of Republican doctrine. He read a series of resolutions he mistakenly believed had been adopted when the party was formed in Illinois in 1854, and pressed Lincoln to deny his own indorsement of them. Douglas likewise assailed the "House Divided" doctrine. Lincoln seemed troubled by the questions.

He went to Freeport determined to impale Douglas on the horns of a dilemma. There he asked the famous Freeport questions, as to the Dred Scott decision. Either Douglas must accept the Supreme Court's decision, which would mean that slavery could go anywhere; or he must cease urging the sanctity of Supreme Court decisions.

It was not a new question for Douglas, who was more realist than dialectician. "Slavery cannot exist a day," he answered, "or an hour, anywhere, unless it is supported by local police regulations." This was an effective counter in debate, and would seem one in fact. Without the support of local laws and administration, no national law can be effectively enforced, as was shown in the national prohibition experiment.

The other debates were hard fought and colorful, but Ottawa and Freeport had set the main tone for the rest of them. The third took place Sept. 15 at Jonesboro. At Charleston, three days later, the crowd was fairly evenly divided. Lincoln, smarting under Douglas' Negro equality charges, toned down his earlier statements.

Three weeks later the fifth debate occurred at Galesburg, an Abolition stronghold. On Oct. 13 the two men grappled at Quincy, and the last debate was two days later at Alton. Here the two men epitomized again their points of view. Lincoln repeated the charge that the trouble with Douglas was "that he looks to no end of the institution of slavery." But Douglas said: "I care more for the great principle of self-government, the right of the people to rule, than I do for all the Negroes in Christendom. I would not endanger the perpetuity of this Union."

The Lincoln of the debates was a strong antagonist at grips with one quite as strong. At times both men seemed political wrestlers crafty in verbal clutches, who spent much time in fumbling about for or escaping from effective holds. Judged as debates, they do not measure up to their reputation. On neither side did the dialect compare with that in the debates between Webster, Hayne and Calhoun.

LINCOLN HIGHWAY. The idea of a coast-to-coast highway originated with Carl G. Fisher of Indianapolis in 1912, when the automobile was in comparative infancy and when there was no system of good roads covering even one state. In September, 1912, Fisher laid the proposition before the leaders of the automobile industry, and, giving $1000 himself, obtained pledges of more than $4,000,000 for the building. To add a patriotic touch, he gave the name "Lincoln" to the road in 1913, and the Lincoln Highway Association was formed to further the project. States and individuals the country over made contributions, cement manufacturers donated material for "demonstration miles." By an act of 1921 the United States increased its aid to states in road building, which greatly helped this project. From Jersey City the route chosen passed through Philadelphia, Gettysburg, Pittsburgh, Fort Wayne, near Chicago, through Omaha, Cheyenne, Salt Lake and Sacramento to San Francisco. The original course was 3389 miles, later cut by more than fifty miles. Work began in October, 1914, but proceeded slowly. When the Association closed its offices on Dec. 31, 1927, and $90,000,000 had been spent, the road was usable throughout its length, though there were still sections of gravel, some even of dirt road, which were slowly improved thereafter. In 1925 the road became U. S. Highway No. 30.

LINCOLN'S ASSASSINATION. On April 14, 1865, at 10:15 P.M., while attending a performance of "Our American Cousin" at Ford's Theatre, Abraham Lincoln was shot in the back of the head by John Wilkes Booth. As soon as the fatal nature of the wound was apparent, Lincoln was carried to a lodging house opposite the theater. There, without regaining consciousness, he died at 7:22 on the following morning.

In spite of the fact that Booth broke his leg in jumping from the presidential box to the stage, he made his way from the theater, and, with David E. Herold, escaped from Washington in the direction of Virginia before midnight. All the forces of the Government were directed toward his capture, but hysteria, greed for the reward and incompetence hindered the pursuit to such an extent that it was not until April 26 that Booth and Herold were surrounded in a tobacco shed on the Garrett farm near Port Royal, Va. There Herold surrendered, but Booth defied his captors and was shot—possibly by Boston Corbett, possibly by his own hand.

Before the death of Booth, the Government had implicated nine persons in the assassination—George A. Atzerodt, Lewis Payne, David E. Herold, Mary E. Surratt and her son John H. Surratt, Edward Spangler, Samuel Arnold and Michael O'Laughlin. All except John H. Surratt were tried before a military commission, May 9–June 30, 1865. All were found guilty, although the verdict in the case of Mrs. Surratt was certainly a miscarriage of justice. Atzerodt, Payne, Herold and Mrs. Surratt were hanged on July 7; the others were imprisoned in Fort Jefferson, Dry Tortugas. John H. Surratt was brought to trial in 1867, but the jury failed to agree, and his case was later dismissed.

The assassination of Lincoln was a national tragedy in the broadest sense. It removed a President who was averse to vindictive measures, and by transforming widespread Northern inclination to leniency into a passion for retribution, gave Reconstruction its popular sanction.

LIND, JENNY, TOURS AMERICA. Opening at Castle Garden, New York City, Sept. 11, 1850, Jenny Lind toured the eastern United States under the astute management of P. T. Barnum, giving 95 concerts, the last one on June 9, 1851. Tickets were auctioned before the concerts and often sold at fantastic prices (one at $650!). Miss Lind received $176,675 for her services and Barnum cleared over $500,000. Thereafter the singer gave a number of concerts under her own management before returning to Europe in 1852.

LINDBERGH FLIES THE ATLANTIC. The first nonstop flight between New York and Paris, and the first one-man crossing of the Atlantic by air, was made by Charles A. Lindbergh on May 20–21, 1927. Previously, several attempts had been made to win the Orteig prize of $25,000, offered in 1919, for the first continuous flight between New York and Paris over the Atlantic. In 1926 Fonck had crashed when taking off from Roosevelt Field, two American naval officers had been killed on a trial flight and the French aviators, Nungesser and Coli, had been lost over the Atlantic while attempting the difficult east-to-west crossing.

Backed by a group of St. Louis businessmen, Lindbergh supervised the construction of a Ryan monoplane, christened the "Spirit of St. Louis." It had a wing spread of 46 feet and a chord of seven feet, weighed 5135 pounds, and was propelled by a 225-horsepower Wright Whirlwind motor. On the morning of May 20, 1927, taking advantage of an area of high pressure reported over the Atlantic, Lindbergh took off from Curtiss Field on Long Island with a load of 425 gallons of gasoline. Encountering fog and sleet, the aviator was compelled to fly blind part of the way at an altitude of 1500 feet. Later he dropped closer to the water, flying at times ten feet above the waves. Sighting the coast of Ireland he turned his course toward France. Flying over England, he crossed the Channel and at ten o'clock in the evening saw the lights of Paris. After circling the Eiffel Tower he made for the field Le Bourget where he landed after having flown 3605 miles in 33 hours and 39 minutes.

The reception of the young aviator in the capital of France was cordial and demonstrative. Under the guidance of Myron T. Herrick, the American ambassador at Paris, Lindbergh made a most favorable impression on the French public. A round of fetes in his honor failed to mar his attractive modesty, and he became a symbol of daring, courage and international fraternity. In Brussels, Berlin and London he was received with equal enthusiasm. He returned to America from Cherbourg on the U. S. S. *Memphis* sent by command of President Coolidge.

LINDBERGH KIDNAPPING CASE. On the night of March 1, 1932, the eighteen-months-old son of Col. Charles A. Lindbergh was abducted from his parents' country home near Hopewell, N. J. The kidnapper climbed to the window of the second-story nursery by

a ladder brought with him. He left a note demanding $50,000 ransom. After some futile attempts at closer contact with him, Dr. John F. Condon, a retired New York teacher, acting as intermediary, succeeded in having two night interviews with the man in a cemetery. On the second occasion, April 8, the money was paid to the latter upon his promise to deliver the child—a false promise, as it had been slain immediately after the abduction. Its body was found on May 12 near its home. The serial number of every note of the ransom money was made public. On Sept. 15, 1934, a carpenter named Bruno Hauptmann passed one of the bills at a New York filling station and was arrested. More than $14,000 of the ransom money was found concealed about his home. At his trial at Flemington, N. J., in January—February, 1935, the ladder was identified as having been made with plank taken from his attic. He was convicted, and executed on April 3, 1936.

LINOTYPE (1886), the most important printing invention since movable type, transformed typesetting into a mechanical process. Many had sought faster composition when J. O. Clephane, Washington stenographer, promoted an experiment in multiplying typewriting in 1876. This failed but it inspired Ottmar Mergenthaler, Baltimore machinist, who for a decade worked on a series of machines, each nearer the goal. Finally, Mergenthaler devised a machine for casting molten metal in lines, automatically spaced, from individual matrices, assembled by keyboard and returned to a magazine after use. The first patent was issued in 1884. On July 3, 1886, a "Linotype" was successfully operated by the New York *Tribune*. Within eighteen months there were sixty machines in newspaper composing rooms; by 1895 more than 3100 were in use. An immediate effect was impetus to afternoon newspapers through faster news presentation. The tramp printer was dispossessed, but the way opened for undreamed-of publishing expansion.

LINSEY-WOOLSEY was a stout homespun cloth having a wool weft and commonly a flax warp, though hemp or cotton was sometimes used, extensively manufactured in the American colonies and on the frontier. Its name, which is of British origin, first appears in colonial records soon after settlement. It was a homely fabric suitable for backwoods use, conveniently made in country households from materials raised on the farm. Not only was it widely used for men's and women's garments by servants, laborers and rural workers and therefore consumed for the most part in the households where it was made, but it also appeared in local store accounts and was occasionally receivable for taxes. No trustworthy statistics of the quantity produced in America exist but linsey-woolsey probably formed a substantial fraction of the eighteen or twenty million yards of mixed fabrics reported by the census of 1810.

LISA (MANUEL) & CO. consisted of Manuel Lisa, Gregoire Sarpy, François M. Benoist and Charles Sanguinet. After Auguste and Pierre Chouteau failed in their endeavor to renew their monopoly, and moved their activities to the Arkansas River, Manuel Lisa & Co., in the year 1802, sought and obtained the exclusive trade with the Osage Indians on the waters of the Missouri and Osage Rivers. The territory involved was about 120 miles from the mouth of the Missouri. This monopoly ended with the transfer of Upper Louisiana to the United States in 1804. In 1807 another firm called Manuel Lisa and Company was organized by Lisa, William Morrison and Pierre Menard, with a capital of $16,000. An expedition consisting of about 25 men left St. Louis for the Upper Missouri River country on April 19, 1807. The party reached their wintering ground Nov. 21, 1807, and immediately built a trading house. In the following spring Fort Raymond was built on the Yellowstone at the mouth of the Big Horn River.

LITERATURE, AMERICAN. If American literature be confined to belles-lettres, the story of literary art in the United States begins with the random appearance of occasional poetry in the 17th century, broadens into a general acceptance of the patterns of British imaginative writing in the 18th century, and comes to something like fullness only after the republic is well established. But if American literature include the literature of knowledge as well as the literature of power, it begins in the bosom of the Renaissance, speaks maturely from its beginnings, and continues to be full and rich until the present time, when American literature is commonly regarded as one of the most important expressions of thought and imagination in the modern world.

On the first line of development one would have to go back to two minor figures—Anne Bradstreet (*The Tenth Muse Lately Sprung Up in America,* 1650) and Edward Taylor (his *Poetical Works,* however, were not printed until 1939) for formal utterances by the muse. The literary magazine is not effectively established in this country until 1741 when Andrew Bradford printed *The American Magazine,* and Benjamin Franklin established his *General Magazine and Historical Chronicle,* both in Philadelphia. American fiction begins even later with *The Power of Sympathy* by William Hill Brown and *Charlotte Temple* by Susanna Haswell Rowson in 1789. The great body of imaginative writing in the United States comes after the Revolution.

But the American mind has its truer beginnings in the great literature of discovery, exploration and settlement from Hakluyt's *Principal Navigations, Voyages, Traffiques & Discoveries* (1589) onward. A vast library of narratives by Capt. John Smith, Gov. William Bradford, Gov. John Winthrop, Edward Johnson, Thomas Morton, George Alsop, Mary Rowlandson, and others vigorously describes and thought-fully interprets the first ventures of the English people into the New World. These books have the vitality of English prose of the 17th century. This writing shares the intellectual excitement of the eras of Bacon and Milton; it develops theories of history, of salvation, and of the relation of church and state that are to have their profound influence on American thought. The highest expression of the New England mind comes in the next century in the work of Jonathan Edwards: *A Faithful Narrative of the Surprising Work of God* (1737) and *Enquiry into the Modern Prevailing Notions of Freedom of the Will* (1754). Virginia, which has never lacked a literary culture, neatly counterpointed the metaphysics of Edwards with the secularity of William Byrd, whose *History of the Dividing Line* (written 1738, first printed 1841) remains a humorous minor masterpiece, whose secret journals, recently published, reveal an American Pepys, and whose career is a curious blend of the Renaissance and the Enlightenment. Byrd carried his considerable learning lightly like a flower; Cotton Mather—whose *Magnalia Christi Americana* (1702) ends, as it were, the New England 17th century and brings the New England mind face to face with the Enlightenment—boasts of erudition. More widely read than any of these, the first American to have a world-wide influence, was Benjamin Franklin, whose masterly *Autobiography* is a classic of Western literature, and whose letters, satires, bagatelles, almanacs, and scientific writings are the expression of a citizen of the world.

The intellectual brilliance of American thought between the ending of the Seven Years' War (1763) and the creation of the Federal Government (1789) is among the wonders of the history of ideas. The constitutional issues of the 18th century could not be more ably debated, as Burke, Pitt, and other British statesmen testified. Franklin, too, participates, but so do Samuel Adams, John Adams, Thomas Paine, Thomas Jefferson, and a company of others. Of this group Tom Paine the propagandist, whose *Common Sense* (1776) and *The Crisis* (1776–83) awakened American enthusiasm, and Thomas Jefferson, the principal author of the Declaration of Independence and of an unrivalled collection of letters and papers that reveal an encyclopedic mind, are best remembered today. The obsession of modern literary theory with problems of symbolism, depth psychology, and the like has turned attention away from this body of great argumentative prose, albeit many are willing to grant with Carl Becker that Jefferson's prose has a haunting felicity.

The Revolution, the Peace of Paris and the adoption of the Federal Constitution created a drive towards cultural independence. The satires of Philip Freneau, Francis Hopkinson, and John Trumbull are mainly of interest to scholars, but Freneau in lyric poetry and in an exercise in Gothic romanticism, *The House of Night* (1779), marks the transition from the

Enlightenment to romanticism. Trumbull is one of the Connecticut Wits, a group conscientiously endeavoring to create a national literature. The romances of Charles Brockden Brown have more vitality; *Wieland* (1798), *Arthur Mervyn* (1799) and *Edgar Huntley* (1799), compounded of Gothicism, romantic "science," propaganda, realism, and rhodomontade, attracted Shelley by their power.

Maturer years begin with the appearance in literature of three writers associated with New York. William Cullen Bryant, whose "Thanatopsis" (1817) was the product of a Wunderkind, and whose philosophical poems, such as "The Prairies," have intellectual dignity, edited the New York *Evening Post* from 1829 to 1878, giving space in its columns to liberal and radical movements. More popular was Washington Irving, whose *History of New York by Diedrich Knickerbocker* (1809) equipped that city with a symbolic figure, whose *Sketch-Book* (1819–20), gave us Rip Van Winkle and Ichabod Crane, and whose *Alhambra* (1832), an exercise in the sentimental exotic, scarcely prophesied his *Tour of the Prairies* (1835) or his substantial biographies, that of Columbus (1828) being the best. The third was James Fenimore Cooper, of world-wide fame, whose Leatherstocking series (*The Pioneers*, 1823; *The Last of the Mohicans*, 1826; *The Prairie*, 1827; *The Pathfinder*, 1840; *The Deerslayer*, 1841) has been called an American prose epic. Natty Bumppo is immortal. Cooper's sea novels, of which *The Pilot* (1823) is most often read, were the best in the language before Conrad. Widely misjudged as a critic of American society, Cooper in later novels and expository prose endeavored to stem the tide of Jacksonian democracy by plumping for a doctrine of *noblesse oblige* among a governing elite.

Of those who sought the cosmopolitan solution to the question of what literary culture should be, the Cambridge poets—Lowell, Holmes, and Longfellow—are characteristic. The most influential was Longfellow, who appealed to religious, patriotic and cultural desires, in translations (his version of Dante, 1865–69, is notable), short lyrics, remarkable sonnets, and narrative poems of special appeal to the American 19th century—*Evangeline* (1847), *The Song of Hiawatha* (1855), *The Courtship of Miles Standish* (1858), and *Tales of a Wayside Inn* (1863, 1872, 1873). Holmes, in verse and prose, sought to liberate Americans from the tyranny of theology, and Lowell from that of cultural provincialism. Associated with this group is the Quaker abolitionist, John Greenleaf Whittier, whose *Snow-Bound* (1866) in an unforgettable vignette of rural America.

Moderns find the Concord group—Emerson, Thoreau, Hawthorne, and at some distance, Herman Melville—more exciting. Emerson was, par excellence, the mover and shaker in 19th-century American idealism, with "The American Scholar" (1837), *Nature* (1836), "The Divinity School Address"

(1838) and the *Essays* (1841; 1844). His crisp Yankee accent penetrated where metaphysics could not reach. Industrial society pays more attention to Henry David Thoreau, whose *Walden* (1854) is today more widely read than anything by Emerson, and whose vigorous essays on what we today would call civil rights are applicable to present problems. Twentieth-century interest in neo-Calvinist theories of human nature has considerably heightened the appeal of Nathaniel Hawthorne in such books as *The Scarlet Letter* (1850), *The House of the Seven Gables* (1851), and *The Marble Faun* (1860), not to speak of his short stories. A more drastic revolution in values has placed Herman Melville among the literary giants for much the same reason; and *Mardi* (1849), *Moby Dick* (1851), *Pierre* (1852), and *Billy Budd* (not available until 1924) are studied as problems of symbolism for evil and for good.

The South and the West, meanwhile, had been developing writers of their own, but no ante-bellum author save one quite rose to the importance of the names just surveyed. The exception of course is Edgar Allan Poe, if he can be called a Southern writer; and though the present tendency is to derogate his genius, his influence has gone round the world as critic, as short-story writer (*Tales of the Grotesque and Arabesque*, 1840), and as poet. The reputations of fictionists like John Pendleton Kennedy and William Gilmore Simms are local in comparison, nor does the West speak with unmistakable authority until Mark Twain's *Roughing It* (1873).

The age of radio and television cannot believe that oratory was ever a branch of literature, but in the second quarter of the century the speeches of Daniel Webster and of his great rivals, Calhoun and Clay, approached Roman dignity in discussing the constitutional issues that led to the Civil War. Abolitionism, however, lacked this large discourse; yet the *Uncle Tom's Cabin* (1852) of Harriet Beecher Stowe, partisan, sentimental, and melodramatic, went round the world. After a great deal of unsuccessful hack-writing, Walt Whitman produced the first version of *Leaves of Grass* (1855), a work he continued to rewrite and expand until 1882. Famous as metrical experimentation, this gospel is part of the Religion of Humanity in the Western 19th century. In *Drum Taps, Specimen Days and Collect, Calamus, Democratic Vistas* and other later works Whitman caught the epic quality of civil war, as Lincoln caught its mystic quality in *The Gettysburg Address* (1863); or denounced political corruption as did Mark Twain and Charles Dudley Warner in an uneven novel, *The Gilded Age* (1873), that gave its name to the postwar period.

The Civil War is an historical watershed dividing the culture of agrarian America from that of industrial America. But one of the results of that vast conflict was curiosity about the far-flung nation; and the increasing effectiveness of literary periodicals, symbolized by the creation of *The Atlantic Monthly* in 1857, gave rise to a vast literature of local color. The South found comfort in glamorous or sentimental pictures of a slavery culture, as in George Washington Cable's *Old Creole Days*, 1879 (Cable was later to become a vigorous proponent of Negro rights), Joel Chandler Harris' *Uncle Remus: His Songs and Sayings* (1880), now dismissed as "Uncle Tom-ism" but a treasury of folklore, F. Hopkinson Smith's *Colonel Carter of Cartersville* (1891), a sentimental picture of the Confederate colonel, and Thomas Nelson Page's *Red Rock* (1898), an equally sentimental version of life in Old Virginia, which the novels of Ellen Glasgow in the 20th century were to correct. New England salved its hurts during its "decline," in the charming, and occasionally powerful, genre stories of writers like Sarah Orne Jewett, Mary W. Wilkins Freeman, and Alice Brown. New York State produced *David Harum* (1898) by Edward N. Westcott, Tennessee was pictured by Mary Noailles Murfree ("Charles Egbert Craddock") whose *In the Tennessee Mountains* (1884), preludes the literary (and popular) exploitation of the mountaineer, and California occasioned Bret Harte's *The Luck of Roaring Camp* (1870). This survey runs from East to West; chronologically Harte comes first, and through him the influence of Charles Dickens was filtered into the whole school. Local color verse by John Hay, Joaquin Miller, Will Carleton, James Whitcomb Riley, sometimes in dialect, sometimes "straight," accompanied the vogue.

After the Civil War the vigorous philosophic idealism of Concord deliquesced into the cultural propriety of the genteel tradition. The moderns find it difficult to be fair to the work of this tradition, exemplified by the poetical theories of Edmund Clarence Stedman (*The Nature and Elements of Poetry*, 1892), the aesthetic teachings of Charles Eliot Norton, and the neo-Platonic poetry and criticism of George Edward Woodberry. But the disciplinary quality of genteel criticism (for example, that of Brander Matthews) in curbing the excesses of romantic self-expression was an important contribution; and the postwar years also saw the rise of a mature literature of biography, history, and expository prose. Biography was of moment to the Puritans, but American biography struck its stride with James Parton's *Life and Times of Benjamin Franklin* (1864) and has continued to produce masterly works ever since. American achievement in historical writing begins early and matures in such books as William Hickling Prescott's *History of the Conquest of Mexico* (1843) and Francis Parkman's distinguished series, *France and England in North America* (1851–92). These two are commonly classed as "romantic" historians; the influence of European scholarship is more directly evident after the Civil War in the work of Henry Harrisse, Justin Winsor, James Schouler, John

Bach McMaster, James Ford Rhodes, and others. Stylistic craftsmanship is most evident in the work of Henry Adams, whose *History of the United States of America during the Administrations of Jefferson and Madison* (1884–89) challenges the literary supremacy of Parkman. All the world knows his *Mont-Saint-Michel and Chartres* (1904) and *The Education of Henry Adams* (1907; 1918).

Historians had no monopoly of expository scholarship or of propaganda. The *Personal Memoirs* of U. S. Grant (1885) have the clarity and simplicity of Caesar; Henry George's *Progress and Poverty* (1877–79) and Edward Bellamy's *Looking Backward* (1888) were as influential in their way as Paine had been in his; and a vast literature of science, philosophy, and theology develops as the country discovers Darwin. Andrew Dickson White's powerful, if uneven, *History of the Warfare of Science with Theology in Christendom* (1896) is perhaps the single best monument of this debate, though writers as excellent as Asa Gray, John Fiske, Josiah Royce, and their like participated. All this is the background for William James's classic *Principles of Psychology* (1890), the prelude to pragmatism. *The Will to Believe and Other Essays* appeared in 1897.

As a literary genre American fiction came of age in the latter 19th century, however great the contributions of Hawthorne's generation. In *The Adventures of Huckleberry Finn* Mark Twain created a classical work, and if his collected writings are uneven, he moved steadily from the "oral" manner of *The Innocents Abroad* (1869) to the Voltairean irony of *The Mysterious Stranger* (1916) as hilarity gave way to pessimism. But the gathering forces of realism—evident, for example, in the work of John William De Forest, Albion W. Tourgée, and others—found their typical spokesman in William Dean Howells. His *Criticism and Fiction* (1891) summed up realistic, though not naturalistic, theory, and in novels like *A Modern Instance* (1881), *The Rise of Silas Lapham* (1884) and *A Hazard of New Fortunes* (1890), he showed that the business of literature was with the here and now, not with the trumpet-and-drum romances and the sentimental tales beloved of the populace. Beneath the serene surface of his prose there is a sardonic feeling, an ironic vision. About him there were grouped realists and naturalists (none of them consistent) like Hamlin Garland, Stephen Crane, Frank Norris, and others; and presently out of the excitement there emerged the slow, awkward genius of Theodore Dreiser, whose *Sister Carrie* (1900) marks the transition in fiction between the realism of the 19th century and that of the 20th.

While realists and sentimentalists, naturalists and idealists argued the case, Henry James, self-exiled, opened the modern manner in fiction by concentrating upon the subjective world within. His progress from *The American* (1877) through *The Portrait of* a Lady (1881) to The Wings of the Dove (1902), The Golden Bowl (1904), and The Sense of the Past (1917) is for admirers a march towards subtlety of insight and of craftsmanship. For others he becomes so difficult, the game is not worth the candle. He was a theorist of literary art (for example, Notes on Novelists, 1914); and his example has profoundly influenced contemporaries and successors of the rank of Edith Wharton (The House of Mirth, 1905), Ellen Glasgow (The Sheltered Life, 1932), and Willa Cather (A Lost Lady, 1923), not to speak of living novelists. Indeed, the way leads from Henry James through William James to the stylistic experimentation of Gertrude Stein.

The end of the 19th century and the opening of the 20th saw a pause in the rhythm of American literature, as if the country awaited the coming of World War I and, so far as writing is concerned, the scarcely less powerful impact upon the literary imagination of Sigmund Freud. For a moment poetry seemed to recapture the great audiences it had lost since Longfellow, when writers like Vachel Lindsay, Edgar Lee Masters, E. A. Robinson, Carl Sandburg, and Robert Frost achieved vast reading publics. But foreign influences (from France and Italy) and the impact of the war, summed up in T. S. Eliot's The Waste-Land (1922) and in the energetic propaganda of Ezra Pound, diverted poetry into the more difficult manner of Conrad Aiken, Wallace Stevens, Hart Crane and Marianne Moore. More recently the pendulum has swung back to a more public manner in verse, a greater responsibility for communication to audiences wider than an elite.

Reacting with extreme violence against the canons of the 19th century, critical theory, whether it concerned literature or culture, took on new importance about 1910. Preluded by Joel Spingarn, Randolph Bourne (cut untimely off), John Macy, and their elder fellow, George Santayana, critics turned to a total re-examination of the American present and a total revaluation of the American past. Van Wyck Brooks, in America's Coming-of-Age (1915), campaigned for a "usable past," which he furnished in later volumes; Henry Louis Mencken demanded "sophistication" in various books of Prefaces (1919–27); and Walter Lippmann in Preface to Morals (1929) and Joseph Wood Krutch in The Modern Temper (1929) declined to accept traditional canons about the dignity of man. It was vain for the neo-humanists —Irving Babbitt, Paul Elmer More, Stuart P. Sherman and others—to assert that long-run sagacity lay with tradition. Meanwhile the distinguished prose of Lewis Mumford, in such books as Sticks and Stones (1924) and The Brown Decades (1931), demonstrated that the modern spirit was not identical with iconoclasm.

In retrospect the 1920's resemble the 1850's—a great creative decade. The 1920's open with the smashing success of Sinclair Lewis's Main Street

(1920) and close with the troubled rhetoric of Wolfe's Look Homeward Angel (1929), a singular specimen of the confession literature one associates with the European romantics. It was, in truth, a brilliant ten years, including Fitzgerald's The Great Gatsby (1925), James Boyd's Drums (1925), which first maturely demonstrated modernity in the historical novel, and a spate of "sophisticated" writers like James Branch Cabell, Joseph Hergesheimer, and Carl Van Vechten, Cabell's Beyond Life (1919) setting forth a theory of "sophistication" that governed the whole movement of literary smartness. Possibly the soundest product of the self-conscious school was Thornton Wilder's philosophical and lengthy conte, The Bridge of San Luis Rey (1927).

The cry was for "freedom," though no one quite knew what kind of freedom was meant; and the angry '30's, as they have been called, took revenge by nourishing proletarian fiction that included the Studs Lonigan trilogy (1935) of James T. Farrell, the huge national canvas of John Dos Passos' U. S. A. (1937), and the emergent genius of William Faulkner, whose The Sound and the Fury (1929) announced both a new method in fiction and a somber view of human failure. It more and more appeared that America was not promises; and foreign reporting of unexampled brilliance and penetration by John Gunther, Vincent Sheean and others not only pictured the death of Europe but prepared the Americans for World War II. The spate of novels concerning World War I—Dos Passos' Three Soldiers (1921), Cummings' The Enormous Room (1922), and Hemingway's The Sun Also Rises (1926) and A Farewell to Arms (1929) are characteristic; these were at once the result of shock and a return upon European literary techniques. The novels of World War II lacked the shock technique, but were frequently powerful, their somber episodes being sometimes lighted by humor. Typical are James Gould Cozzens' Guard of Honor (1948) and Norman Mailer's massive The Naked and the Dead (1948). Thomas Heggen's Mr. Roberts (1946) illustrates the humor, but frivolity faded before the apocalyptic vision of total destruction in John Hersey's Hiroshima (1946).

The last two decades have seen powerful streams of criticism at work in both literature and literary scholarship, writers like Lionel Trilling (The Liberal Imagination, 1950) and Edmund Wilson (The Wound and the Bow, 1941, is a typical volume) striving to reunite social interpretation and aesthetics. Historical prose has improved (except in the textbook field), as is evidenced by the work of Carl Becker (The Declaration of Independence, 1922) and of C. Vann Woodward. Science fiction, commonly ignored by the academic world, has risen to the imaginative brilliance of Ray Bradbury's The Martian Chronicles (1950) and unites with disturbing social comment in his Fahrenheit 451 (1953).

Social and political comment is still on a high plane when written by experienced commentators. On the other hand, the short story has declined in scope, and fiction seems to many persons to be fighting a desperate battle against mass amusement and a queer economic life, a battle it must win if it is to survive as an important expression of literature. Poetry, though frequently interesting, has on the whole lost the place it had in Longfellow's day—save always for the phenomenal success of a writer like Robert Frost. The old-fashioned informal essay has virtually disappeared, its place taken, if at all, by columnists, the *New Yorker* type of special article, and, oddly enough, highly personalized books, such as those by E. B. White. This brief survey does nothing with the American theater and touches only in passing on American humor. But perhaps enough has been said to indicate the wide range and variety of recent and contemporary American writers.

LITTLE BIG HORN BATTLE (June 25, 1876). The Indians in Dakota territory bitterly resented the opening of the Black Hills to settlers in violation of an earlier treaty. Owing also to official graft and negligence they were facing actual starvation for the coming winter. In the fall of 1875, therefore, they began to leave their reservations contrary to orders, to engage in their annual buffalo hunt. Here they were joined by lawless tribesmen from other reservations until the movement took on the proportions of a serious revolt. The situation was one that called for the utmost tact and discretion, for the Indians were ably led and the treatment they had received had stirred the bitterest resentment among them.

Unfortunately, by some inexplicable blunder, an order, originating with the Indian Bureau, was sent to all reservation officials early in December, directing them to notify the Indians to return by Jan. 31, under penalty of being attacked by the U. S. Army. This belated order could not be carried out in the dead of winter even if the Indians had been inclined to obey it.

Early in 1876 Gen. Sheridan, from his headquarters at Chicago, ordered a concentration of troops on the upper Yellowstone River, to capture or disperse the numerous bands of Dakotas who were hunting there. In June Gen. Terry, department commander, and Lt. Col. George A. Custer with his regiment from Fort Abraham Lincoln, marched overland to the Yellowstone, where they were met by the steamboat *Far West* with ammunition and supplies. At the mouth of Rosebud Creek (a tributary of the Yellowstone) Custer received his final orders from Terry: to locate and disperse the Indians. According to official records there is now no longer any doubt that Gen. Terry gave Custer absolutely free hand in dealing with the situation, relying upon his well-known experience in this kind of warfare.

With twelve companies of the 7th Cavalry, Custer set out on his march and soon discovered the Indians camped on the south bank of the Little Big Horn River. He sent Maj. Reno with three companies of cavalry and all the Arikara scouts across the upper ford of this river to attack the southern end of the Indian camp. Capt. Benteen, with three companies, was sent to the left of Reno's line of march. Custer, himself, led five companies of the 7th Cavalry down the river to the lower ford for an attack on the upper part of the camp. One company was detailed to bring up the pack train.

This plan of battle, thoroughly typical of Custer, was in the beginning completely successful. Suddenly faced by a vigorous double offensive, the Indians at first thought only of retreat. At this critical juncture, Reno became utterly confused and ordered his men to fall back across the river. Thereupon the whole force of the Indian attack was concentrated upon Custer's command, compelling him to retreat back from the river to a position where his force was later annihilated. The soldiers under Reno rallied at the top of a high hill overlooking the river and here they were joined by Benteen's troops and two hours later by the company guarding the pack train.

LOCAL GOVERNMENT. *Units of Government.* Prior to 1932, when the first census of governments was taken, nobody knew how many units of government there were in the United States. The results of this census, with the three official counts which have been taken since, are shown in the accompanying table(*). Most significant facts revealed by these figures covering a quarter of a century are: (1) addition of two new states—Alaska in 1958, Hawaii in 1959; (2) no significant change in the number of counties, municipalities, and townships; (3) drastic decrease in the number of school districts; (4) some decline, followed by an increase, in the number of special districts; (5) a notable decline in the total number of units, chiefly attributable to the decrease in the number of school districts.

The town and the county were the two original forms of local government. The climatic and physiographic conditions in New England, together with dangers from the Indians and from wild animals, were all such as to encourage the establishment of small, compact settlements. The presence of water power, and the eventual development of industrial communities tended to preserve the established governmental traditions. In similar manner, the climatic and physiographic conditions in the South, and the virtual absence of danger from the Indians, made possible the more extended settlements out of which developed the Southern counties. The soil was fertile, and the types of crops for which it was adapted encouraged the maintenance of the plantation system, as did the absence of water power and other influences toward industrialization. Thus the town form was indigenous to New England, the

* GOVERNMENTAL UNITS IN THE UNITED STATES, 1932–1957
Source: U. S. Bureau of the Census, *Governmental Units in the United States*, 1932, 1942, 1952, 1957.

TYPE OF UNIT	1932	1942	1952	1957
U. S. Government	1	1	1	1
States	48	48	48	48[1]
Counties	3,062	3,050	3,049	3,047
Municipalities	16,442	16,220	16,778	17,183
Townships	19,978	18,919	17,202	17,198
School Districts	128,548	108,579	55,346	50,446
Special Districts[2]	14,572	8,299	12,319	14,405
Totals	182,651	155,116	104,743	102,328

[1] Now fifty, with the admission of Alaska and Hawaii.

[2] Includes drainage, road, park, sanitary, irrigation, reclamation, fire, lighting, cemetery, navigation, port, waterworks, etc.

county to the South, the strength of each form varying directly in proportion to the distance from the locale of its origin. (The states in the South and Far West, which followed the lead of the South in this matter, were: Alabama, Arizona, *California,* Colorado, Delaware, Florida, Georgia, Idaho, Kentucky, Louisiana, Maryland, Mississippi, *Montana, Nevada,* New Mexico, *North Carolina,* Oregon, *South Carolina,* Tennessee, Texas, Utah, Virginia, Washington, West Virginia and Wyoming. Townships exist in those states whose names appear in italics, but they are merely justice of the peace districts and do not possess the characteristic township organization.)

In the Middle Atlantic States, where the two types came in contact with each other, hybrid forms developed. The North Central type, characterized by New York, had both the town and the county, with the town stronger and more important. The South Central type, characterized by Pennsylvania, had both the township and the county, with the county the stronger and the more important. As the settlers moved west, they took with them the forms cf local government to which they had become accustomed in the East, making only such changes in these forms as were required to adapt them to the conditions of the frontier. (The North Central group includes Illinois, Michigan, Nebraska, New Jersey, New York and Wisconsin, while the South Central group includes Arkansas, Indiana, Iowa, Kansas, Minnesota, Missouri, North Dakota, Ohio, Oklahoma, Pennsylvania and South Dakota.)

Regardless of the form of local government established, there were certain important functions which it was expected to perform; among these were the maintenance of peace and order, the administration of justice, the settlement of estates, the conduct of poor relief, the maintenance of the schools, the protection of the public health, the construction and maintenance of roads, the administration of elections and the record-

ing of land titles. The local units also served as units for military purposes. Vitally important to all of these was the assessment and collection of taxes.

The Town. The New England town was an excellent illustration of the functioning of pure democracy, perhaps the best available. The freemen of the community came together in the town meeting to select town officers and to determine questions of public policy. As the settlements spread out and increased in size, as the danger from the Indians and wild animals decreased, it became necessary to develop the representative principle, in partial substitution for that of pure democracy. The character of the General Court was changed by the dispersion of the towns, a portion of the membership consisting of deputies of those who, on account of numbers and dispersion, could not themselves attend the court. In time, the district system developed, with small districts and a consequently large total membership. The tradition of local self-government, however, was firmly established; included in the setup were such institutions of English origin as jury trial, the grand jury, the justice of the peace, etc. The town form of organization, characteristic of New England, appeared also in New York, became the township in Pennsylvania, and ceased to exist in Maryland and other states to the south.

The County. The county seat constituted the political and economic center of a number of adjacent plantations. Its location and the size of the county itself were largely determined by the distance that a man could travel between morning and nightfall, allowing some time at the county seat in which to transact his business. The prevailing form of organization called for a board of county commissioners, consisting usually of three or five members, who had the power to levy taxes and to provide for the usual governmental functions. There was no executive officer, but the county court was a very important institution. This form appeared in Pennsylvania, but in New York the board of commissioners became a board of supervisors, in which each town or city was represented by at least one member, often resulting in a body of considerable size. While counties were laid out in New England, they had no important functions of government to perform; in Rhode Island, for instance, they served only to establish the limits of the judicial districts. In Connecticut, they were abolished by legislation enacted in 1959.

The other county officers included that group of elected officers often referred to as the row officers: the sheriff; the prosecuting attorney, district attorney or state's attorney; the coroner; the county clerk; the court clerks; the treasurer, auditor or comptroller; the register of wills; the register of probate, the probate judge or the surrogate; the recorder of deeds; and such others as the jury commissioners, jail commissioners, prison wardens, prison inspectors, mercantile appraisers, election boards, superintendent of schools; director, overseer or superintendent of the poor; superintendent of the workhouse; surveyor or engineer; road or highway commissioner; board of assessors; and board of review. The more important of these offices were closely patterned after the English models, particularly the sheriff and the coroner.

City Government. City government in the United States has passed through several different forms or stages of development—the weak mayor and council plan, the strong mayor and council plan, the commission type, and the manager type. The first of these, once universally used, was a reproduction in miniature of the machinery of the Federal Government. There was a mayor, who had little real power. The council consisted of two chambers, a large common council and a smaller select council. While the judges in the courts were selected locally, the courts themselves were a part of the state judicial system. The Federal form of governmental organization is best adapted to meeting the needs of a large number of people in a broad expanse of territory; the effort to adapt it to the needs of even a fairly large number of people in a small and compact area was a dismal failure. It was of cities so governed that Bryce was able to say, in all truthfulness, that municipal government was the one conspicuous failure in American politics. It was in cities so governed that the Tweed Ring developed in New York, the Gas Ring in Philadelphia, and similar rings of one sort or another in cities throughout the land.

Out of these experiences grew a general dissatisfaction with the existing situation. This first found expression in the strong mayor and council plan, in which the powers of the mayor were considerably increased, he being authorized to appoint the heads of the various administrative departments in the city

government. These department heads formed an advisory body frequently called the cabinet, the members of which were directly responsible to the mayor. It thus became possible for the mayor to be in fact as well as in theory the head of the administration. The old, cumbersome, bicameral council was abolished and a small, compact, unicameral council substituted for it. The judicial branch of the government was not affected by this reorganization. Where the mayor and council form of municipal organization is still in use, it is of this type, since the old weak mayor and council form has practically passed out of existence.

While some cities were trying to remodel and improve the existing machinery for municipal government, others were experimenting with new devices. First of these was the commission form, originated in Galveston following a great natural disaster in 1900, and later adopted in Des Moines, Newark, and many other cities. Although it represented some measure of improvement over the old weak mayor and council form, it had serious built-in weaknesses which detracted greatly from its successful operation, and which prevented its acquiring any permanent standing as a form of municipal government. As of 1959, it had all but disappeared from the scene.

Next to develop was the city manager form, now commonly referred to as council-manager government. More or less by accident, in 1908 the city of Staunton, Va., evolved the precedents upon which the city manager form is based. A railroad maintenance engineer was employed by the city to make some repairs in the water supply system, at a considerable saving to the city as compared with contractor's estimates. The idea was extended to other similar operations, with the result that the engineer, Charles E. Ashburner, was retained by the city as a sort of business manager. After a rather unhappy two years, this creator of a new profession resigned in disgust, and vowed never again to undertake such an assignment. He showed up again, however, as manager of the city of Norfolk, and later in California, where he served for many years. In the meantime, the city of Dayton adopted the plan, attracting nation-wide attention to it. In the years since, it has been adopted in an ever increasing number of cities and other local units in all sections of the country, until today it is functioning in some 1,641 communities.

Under the council-manager plan, there is a small council with the members elected from councilmanic districts. For a time (as in New York from 1937 to 1947, Cleveland from 1923 to 1933, in Cincinnati from 1924 to 1957, and in a few other cities) council members were selected by proportional representation, but for various reasons this practice has been largely abandoned. The mayor, who has little power, is usually selected by the council from their own number, while the manager, selected by and responsible to the council, is a professional man with training and experience in municipal administration, chosen without regard to his political beliefs, and preferably without regard to his place of legal residence.

He serves as the administrative head of the city government, appointing and removing heads of departments and other subordinates, subject, of course, to civil service limitations prescribed by the charter or by state law. It is his duty to carry out the policies adopted by the council, the details of administration being left to him. His responsibility to the council is for the results achieved. A number of the larger mayor-council cities have accomplished a comparable result in improved administration through the use of the administrator or administrative manager, appointed by the mayor. By thus being freed from much of the normal administrative routine, the mayor is able the better to perform his other duties of civic and political leadership in policy determination.

Home Rule. The question of home rule has long been a troublesome one in the field of local government. All of the units—counties, cities, boroughs, towns, townships, villages and special districts— were created by, and the nature and extent of their powers were defined by, the legislature. The legislature can today abolish most of the units, and modify or withdraw their powers as it sees fit, except insofar as the units themselves are protected by the provisions of home rule amendments, such as exist in about one third of the states. For many years, nearly every small detail in the government of any city had to be submitted to its state legislature; this was bad for the cities and bad for the legislature, until the powers of the latter to adopt special legislation were restricted by constitutional prohibitions, or by provision for the classification of cities according to population.

Home rule, or the power of local self-government, gives to the local units to which it is extended the right to select their own form of governmental organization and either draft their own charter or select one to their liking, under an optional charter plan. Home rule may be granted by constitutional provision, by legislative act, or by a constitutional provision which becomes effective only upon legislative implementation. As of 1959, constitutional provision for home rule had been adopted in more than half of the states (consult the accompanying table [**])— in four states before 1900, in eight since 1950. The home rule concept was first limited to cities, but in late years has been made applicable in many states to counties as well. Implicit in the home rule idea is the conflict between the right of local self government, on the one hand, and the right and the duty of the state to exercise reasonable regulatory and supervisory powers over its political subdivisions, on the other.

Metropolitan Areas. Metropolitan areas, long in process of development, today constitute the most pressing domestic problem confronting the nation. As a result of unprecedented, unregulated and largely unanticipated urban growth, the 186 Standard Metropolitan Areas (SMA) now contain 14% of all local governments, nearly 60% of our population, but only 7% of our continental area. 100,000,000 of our people make their homes in these areas, and the end is not in sight. Population experts predict that by 1975, there may be 60,000,000 more metropolitan area residents; that by the year 2000, the nation may have some 300,000,000 people with 220,000,000 of them concentrated in these areas; that the entire eastern seaboard from Portland, Me., to Norfolk, Va., will be one vast and continuous metropolitan development.

What this means governmentally may be illustrated by reference to the nation's four largest metropolitan areas, the 1957 figures for which are presented in the accompanying table (***). All units of government are involved in the metropolitan area problem, from the largest to the smallest. Of the multitude of major problems confronting these areas, four may be mentioned here: (1) policy determination on matters of area-wide concern, and overall enforcement of such policies on a uniform basis, once they have been decided upon; (2) planning and economic development of the area; (3) the problem of mass transit; (4) public work affecting the entire area, notably water supply, sewage disposal, and highways.

As of 1959, no generally acceptable solution had been found for the first of these problems: the dilemma posed by the need for uniformity throughout the area, on the one hand, and on the other, the desire of each local unit within a given metropolitan area to preserve intact and without any impairment whatsoever its geographical integrity and legal powers. Several different attempted solutions are now being tried on an experimental basis. One of these involves creation of a new, federated overall government to handle area-wide problems, as was adopted first in Toronto in 1953, in Montreal in 1959, and in this country in Miami-Dade County, and Seattle-King County. Under this plan, control over matters of purely local concern remains with the previously existing political subdivisions.

Another proposed solution places strong reliance on special-purpose authorities created by act of the legislature, or—in interstate areas—through interstate compact. The oldest and best known of these is the Port of New York Authority which owns and operates a vast network of airports, terminals, tunnels and other transit facilities in the New York metropolitan area. Other and more recent examples are to be found in the Philadelphia, St. Louis, and Washington, D. C., metropolitan areas.

A third solution places reliance upon the county

** CONSTITUTIONAL HOME RULE STATES—1959

Table originally appeared in the author's *American State Government*, Fourth Edition (Heath, Boston, 1958), p. 801, and revised here in cooperation with Professor Arthur W. Bromage, University of Michigan, and Miss Patricia Shumate of the National Municipal League Staff.

STATES	CITIES	COUNTIES	STATES	CITIES	COUNTIES
Alaska	1958	1958[1]	Nevada	1924[3]	
Arizona	1912		New Jersey	1947[8]	
California	1879	1911	New York	1923	1958[9]
Colorado	1902		Ohio	1912	1933
Connecticut	1951		Oklahoma	1907	
Florida		1956[2]	Oregon	1906	1958
Georgia	1954[3]		Pennsylvania	1923[10]	
Hawaii	1959	1959	Rhode Island	1951	
Louisiana	1952[4]	1946–	Tennessee	1953	
		1956[5]	Texas	1912[11]	1933[12]
Maryland	1954[6]	1915	Utah	1932	
Michigan	1908		Virginia	1920[3, 13]	
Minnesota	1896	1958	Washington	1889	1948
Missouri	1875[7]	1945	West Virginia	1936	
Nebraska	1912		Wisconsin	1924	

[1] No counties; for units to be known as boroughs.

[2] Applies to Dade County only.

[3] Authorization to the legislature to grant home rule, rather than a direct grant of power to the cities.

[4] Amendments in 1946, 1948 and 1950 had previously authorized home rule for individual cities (Baton Rouge, Shreveport, and New Orleans, respectively); in 1952, home rule was granted to any municipality.

[5] Authorized adoption of a charter in Jefferson Parish; an earlier amendment, in 1946, had given similar authorization to East Baton Rouge Parish.

[6] Baltimore had been granted home rule in 1915.

[7] Only to cities of more than 100,000 population; extended in 1945 to all cities of over 10,000, and to counties of over 85,000 population.

[8] Constitution of 1947 authorized a type of "permissive" home rule; a 1950 law, with subsequent amendments, makes available sixteen optional charter plans, with variations.

[9] This state has been moving toward home rule for counties, as evidenced by amendments adopted in 1935 and 1958, and a number of optional laws enacted between 1935 and 1952.

[10] Legislation necessary to carry out the grant was not enacted until 1949, and then only for cities of the first class (Philadelphia).

[11] Amendment has proved unworkable; consideration is being given to simplifying proposals.

[12] Limited to counties of more than 62,000 population; implementing legislation enacted in 1946.

[13] Implementing legislation enacted in 1946.

*** GOVERNMENTAL UNITS IN THE FOUR LARGEST METROPOLITAN AREAS

Figures from U. S. Bureau of the Census, *Local Government in Standard Metropolitan Areas* (Washington, December 1957) except for New York for which the following source was used: Davies, Audrey M., *Political Units in the New York Metropolitan Area* (Institute of Public Administration, New York, March 1959).

	NEW YORK– NEW JERSEY– CONNECTICUT	CHICAGO	LOS ANGELES– LONG BEACH	PHILADELPHIA
Counties	17	6	6	7
Municipalities	367	198	68	140
Towns & Townships	182	108	...	199
School Districts	560	355	157	332
Special Districts	330	287	92	27

to render municipal-type services to the inhabitants of the unincorporated and fringe areas lying outside the borders of the core cities, or by contract within the core cities themselves. Out of 125 urban counties replying to a questionnaire sent out by the National Association of County Officials in 1958, over half were providing health, prison, election and planning services for their cities on a co-operative basis. Many were co-operating with cities in assessing property and collecting taxes; in operating airports, libraries, and recreation facilities; in supplying water, maintaining streets, inspecting buildings; providing services for government personnel; and in law enforcement, fire fighting, and sewage disposal services. Dozens of other government services were being provided jointly by cities and counties. Los Angeles County, for example, was providing forty-two different municipal services for at least one city, and some cities in that county were contracting for nearly all of their municipal services. "Intergovernmental cooperation . . . was the most notable characteristic of urban county government in 1958," the survey concluded.

LOCHABER, TREATY OF (Oct. 18, 1770), with the Cherokees, was negotiated by Col. John Donelson for Virginia. Its purpose was to exclude from the Indian lands many whites who had settled west of the line fixed by the Treaty of Hard Labor. The treaty effected these changes: the dividing line was moved westwardly to begin six miles east of Long Island of the Holston, running thence to the mouth of the Kanawha River. However, in the running of Donelson Line a wide departure from the treaty was made in fixing the northern terminus.

LOCHNER v. NEW YORK (198 U. S. 45, 1905). At about the same time that Utah attempted to regulate hours of labor for men in dangerous industries, New York sought to extend this type of regulation to workers in baking and confectionery establishments. While the Supreme Court upheld the Utah statute in Holden v. Hardy (169 U. S. 366, 1898), it declared the New York statute invalid seven years later. The law provided for a maximum sixty-hour week, with an average ten-hour day. Lochner, proprietor of a Utica bakery, was arrested, tried and convicted for violation of the law. On appeal to the Supreme Court, attorneys for the defendant argued that while such protections might be justified in dangerous industries, they were quite unnecessary in industries which, by their very nature, required extreme care in matters of cleanliness and sanitation. The court accepted this reasoning, holding the act void as a violation of freedom of contract. It held that this right is a part of the liberty of the individual, protected by the Fourteenth Amendment, along with the right to purchase or sell labor. The statute did not come under the legitimate police power of the state as a proper regulation of the health, safety or morals of the people.

LOCO FOCO PARTY was a radical faction of the Democratic party in New York allied with Jacksonian Democracy. At a meeting in Tammany Hall, Oct. 29, 1835, it wrested control of the city caucus from the conservatives by producing candles, lighting them with loco foco matches and continuing the meeting, when their opponents turned off the gas. Newspapers derisively called this faction the "Loco Foco Party." Its program embraced suppression of paper money, curtailment of banking privileges and protection of labor unions. From 1837 to 1860, the term was applied to the National Democratic party by its opponents.

LOCOMOTIVES. In 1825 Col. John Stevens of Hoboken, N. J., constructed an experimental locomotive, operating it on a circular track. The "Tom Thumb," built in 1829 by Peter Cooper, made its first run, Aug. 25, 1830, on the Baltimore and Ohio Railroad between Baltimore and Ellicott's Mills, Md. "The Best Friend of Charleston," the first locomotive built in the United States for actual service on a railroad, was constructed in 1830 for the South Carolina Canal and Railroad Co., at the West Point Foundry in New York City, which also built the "De Witt Clinton" for the Mohawk and Hudson (1831).

Matthias Baldwin's "Old Ironsides," the beginning of construction by the Baldwin Locomotive Works, went into service in 1832. The American Steam Carriage Co. of Philadelphia announced in 1833 its readiness to build locomotive engines and tenders. In 1838 a report on "Steam Engines" submitted by Secretary of the Treasury Levi Woodbury contained the names of 27 American builders of locomotives. In following years, other locomotive works were organized and some of the railroads began construction, the Altoona Works of the Pennsylvania Railroad building its first locomotive for passenger service in 1866. With its tender, this locomotive weighed 137,700 pounds—about equal to the weight of two pairs of drive wheels of today's standard passenger locomotives. How far the making of locomotives in America has extended may be judged by a comparison of the engines of the early period with the steam, electric and Diesel locomotives of the present day.

LODE MINING. Gold, silver and other metals are generally found in narrow streaks from a few inches to many feet in width and frequently traceable for a mile or more in length. This is a lode or vein or ledge. A lode has been legally defined as mineral-bearing rock in place. Extracting this mineral-bearing rock from the earth is lode mining. It is hard rock mining and almost entirely underground, as distinguished from placer mining in which the metals are found in alluvial deposits near the surface. The ore is mined either by shafts sunk vertically downward or by tunnels driven horizontally into the mountainside.

The discoverer of a new lode, according to the

laws of the early mining districts, could stake out two claims, but no more, along the lode. Others could stake one claim. Local laws and regulations determined the size of the claim—usually 100 or 200 feet—which was recognized by the first United States mineral patent law (1866). May 10, 1872, Congress fixed the size of lode claims at 600 feet wide and 1500 feet along the lode. Consequently, there can be many rich mines on the same lode. Famous lodes are the Mother Lode in California and the Comstock Lode in Nevada.

LODGE RESERVATIONS. In the duel between Woodrow Wilson and his opponents over incorporation of the League of Nations Covenant within the Treaty of Versailles, the Lodge Reservations played an important part. Designed to safeguard national sovereignty, they were unacceptable to Wilson. Nevertheless, had Sen. Henry Cabot Lodge secured his Reservations, Wilson might have had his League.

Including the preamble, there were fifteen resolutions, notably the following: (2) In the event of her withdrawal from the League, the United States must be sole judge of whether its obligations had been met; (3) No obligation existed to uphold the celebrated Article X, insuring permanence to existing territorial boundaries; (5) The United States reserved the sole determination of what questions fell within domestic jurisdiction; (6) The Monroe Doctrine was specifically exempted from foreign interference; (7) Full liberty of action was reserved concerning certain contingencies that might arise between China and Japan; (8) No American might represent his country in organizations created by the League, save in accordance with an Act of Congress; (10) All contributions toward League expenditures must first be authorized by Congress; (11) Any agreements covering a limitation of armaments must be subject to reversal by the United States if "threatened with invasion or engaged in war"; (12) Nationals of a Covenant-breaking nation residing in the United States might continue their usual relations with our citizens; (14) The United States must assume no responsibility toward "the government or disposition of the overseas possessions of Germany." Finally (15) The United States must be the exclusive judge of what questions affected "its honor or its vital interests."

These Reservations, first ordered printed on Nov. 6, 1919, were modified somewhat as the controversy gained momentum. In the calm of retrospection they seem mild enough and probably quite unavoidable. To Wilson at the time they seemed a base betrayal of idealism. He fought them to his own paralysis and death. The Reservations ultimately gave way to entire negation of the League and to a policy of isolation.

LOEWE v. LAWLOR (1908). In this case, commonly known as the Danbury Hatters' Case, the Sherman Antitrust Act was held to have been violated by a combination of members of a labor organization in the nature of a boycott to prevent the manufacture and sale of hats intended for interstate commerce. The Court emphasized that where the general purpose and effect of the organization was to restrain trade the separate acts, though in themselves acts within a state, were illegal as tested by Federal law.

LOG CABIN. Twentieth-century scholarship has shattered the myth that the early settlers of Virginia and Massachusetts erected log cabins. In *The Log Cabin Myth* (Cambridge, 1939), Harold R. Shurtleff proved that this type of building was imported no earlier than 1638 by the Scandinavians who descended the banks of the Delaware.

LOG COLLEGE (1726–42), at Neshaminy, Pa., was a log schoolhouse, about twenty feet square, erected and conducted by William Tennent, an Irish Presbyterian minister. It served to emphasize the need for an institution for the instruction of Presbyterian ministerial candidates. The Presbyterian Synod recognized this need and in 1746 the charter for the organization of Princeton University was issued.

LOGAN'S SPEECH, popularly regarded as the most famous example of Indian oratory, was made by the Mingo warrior, Capt. James Logan, sometimes called John Logan (Indian "Tahgahjute"), to John Gibson who had been sent from Camp Charlotte (in present Pickaway County, Ohio) by Gov. Dunmore of Virginia to persuade Logan, then at his cabin a few miles distant, to attend the peace negotiations at the close of Dunmore's War (1774). The Indian refused to come and recited his grievances in a speech so strangely moving that Gibson translated and recorded it from memory after returning to Dunmore's camp. Thomas Jefferson later inserted it in his *Notes on The State of Virginia,* but the family and friends of Capt. Michael Cresap, whom Logan mistakenly charged with the murder of his relatives, took offense at the speech and denied its authenticity. A long controversy ensued. Most historians since have reached the cautious conclusion that Gibson probably caught at least the spirit of Logan's impassioned remarks, if not the exact words.

LOGSTOWN, an Indian village eighteen miles below the forks of the Ohio near the present Ambridge, Pa., was probably established by the Shawnee some time after 1728, but it later became a mixed village of Shawnee, Delaware and Iroquois. In the critical period from 1747 to 1753 it was the most important Indian village on the upper Ohio, the center of trade and the scene of Indian councils. It was visited by Conrad Weiser in 1748; by Céloron's expedition in 1749; by Christopher Gist in 1750; by Washington on his journey to Fort LeBoeuf in 1753; and by Christian F. Post in 1758. When the French and Indian War began, most of the Logstown Indians removed to Aughwick, and parties of them fought for the English in the battle of Fort Necessity and joined Braddock's expedition.

LOGSTOWN, TREATY OF (June 13, 1752), opening to settlement lands west of the Allegheny Mountains, was negotiated with Iroquois, Delaware, Shawnee, Wyandot and Miami Indians resident in what are now western Pennsylvania, Ohio and Indiana. In 1751 negotiations with the same Indians had been conducted at Logstown by George Croghan of Pennsylvania and presents had been distributed, but the Pennsylvania Assembly had refused funds for erecting forts to hold the region against the French. In 1752 commissioners from Virginia distributed a royal present to the Indians and, with the help of Croghan and of Christopher Gist representing the Ohio Company, secured permission for the Virginians to make settlements south of the Ohio and to build two fortified trading houses on the river. One of these was erected on the Monongahela at Redstone Old Fort, and the other, in process of erection at the site of Pittsburgh, was surrendered to the French at the outbreak of hostilities in 1753.

LONDON NAVAL TREATY OF 1930. Through the efforts of Ramsay MacDonald, British prime minister, a naval conference met at London in 1930 attended by representatives of the United States, Great Britain, Japan, France and Italy. The object was an agreement to limit the size and number of warships left unlimited by the Washington Treaty of 1922. The clash between the United States and Great Britain over parity and large cruisers which had disrupted the Geneva Conference was settled by a compromise arranged by Premier MacDonald with President Hoover prior to the conference. The success of the conference was endangered, however, by the French demand for a tonnage beyond Italian needs and for a security pact with Great Britain, and by the Japanese claim for a 10:10:7 ratio in place of the 5:5:3 ratio of the Washington Conference. The British were unwilling to give a guarantee to the French without American support, and the United States utterly rejected the idea. The final treaty thus was confined to a three-power pact with provisions to include France and Italy if agreeable in the future. The 5:5:3 ratio was applied to large cruisers, but Japan won a 10:10:7 ratio in small cruisers and destroyers, and equality in submarines, each nation being permitted to maintain a tonnage of 52,700 in the latter category. Not including capital ships and aircraft carriers the total tonnage limitation under the treaty was 541,700 tons for Great Britain, 526,200 tons for the United States and 367,050 for Japan. In order to meet the situation caused by the fact that neither France nor Italy signed the treaty, the so-called "escalator clause" provided that if the national security of any signatory power was endangered by the new construction of ships by a nonsignatory power, the signatory power might increase its tonnage. Ratification of the treaty in Japan was obtained only after a struggle with the militarists. In 1931, after the invasion of Manchuria, the Japanese government took an expanded view of the naval requirements of Nippon. Japanese demands for parity were rejected by the United States and Great Britain in parleys in London in 1934. Accordingly, under the provisions of the treaty, on Dec. 29, 1934, the Japanese government gave notice of its denunciation of the Washington Naval Treaty of 1922, to take effect on Dec. 31, 1936.

LONDON NAVAL TREATY OF 1936. The Japanese government having, on Dec. 29, 1934, denounced the Washington Naval Treaty of 1922, a conference of the principal naval powers was held in London from Dec. 9, 1935, to March 25, 1936. Great Britain and the United States refused to recognize the Japanese claim to parity or to accept a "common upper limit" for naval construction. Japan thereupon withdrew from the conference. By the treaty of March 25, 1936, Great Britain, France and the United States agreed to maximum limits of the various types of warships which they would not exceed (35,000 tons and 14-inch guns for battleships) and to exchange information concerning their building programs. But it was provided that the limits agreed upon might be set aside in the event of war or if these limits were exceeded by a power not a party to the treaty. Italy, indignant at the application of sanctions in the Ethiopian war, refused to sign the treaty, which was, however, left open for her adherence and that of Japan. The treaty, unlike those of 1922 and 1930, contained no provisions for quantitative limitation. In 1938 the contracting parties, unable to obtain information from the Japanese government about its building program, agreed to set aside the limit of 35,000 tons for capital ships.

LONG, HUEY, ASSASSINATION OF. On Sept. 8, 1935, U. S. Sen. Huey Pierce Long of Louisiana was shot at the state capitol at Baton Rouge by Dr. Carl A. Weiss. He died two days later. Nicknamed "Kingfish," Long had been governor of Louisiana and had organized a Share-the-Wealth Society, which promised a homestead allowance of $6000 and a minimum annual income of $2500 for every American family.

LONG HOUSES OF THE IROQUOIS were structures of heavy poles covered with large sheets of bark, and varied from 50 to 160 feet or more in length. The roof was either angular or arched but usually the latter. Long houses sheltered several families and had individual compartments for each,

LONG ISLAND, a part of New York State, 118 miles long, and 1682 square miles in area, lies parallel to the southern shore of Connecticut. As early as 1620 it was included in the grant given by James I to the Virginia Company of Plymouth. In 1635 the territory held by the Plymouth Company's successor, the Council for New England, was divided into eight parts, and Long Island was assigned to William Alexander, Earl of Stirling.

In 1636, when Wouter Van Twiller was director general of New Netherland, Jacobus Van Curler (or Corlaer) was given the first Dutch patent for land on Long Island. During the Dutch period farms spread along the Long Island shore opposite Manhattan, and several settlements, both Dutch and English, sprang up in the interior, Hempstead, Flushing, Gravesend, Newtown and Jamaica being English; and Breuckelen (Brooklyn), Midwout (Flatbush), Amersfoort (Flatlands), New Utrecht and Boswyck (Bushwick) being Dutch.

While the western end of the island was thus being settled as a part of New Netherland, Puritan towns which reproduced the characteristic features and religious polity of New England were planted along the northern and southern shores of its eastern end. In 1640 English settlers from New Haven laid out Southold, and others from Lynn in Massachusetts Bay settled Southampton. Similar New England communities were established elsewhere, such as that at Oyster Bay in 1653 and those at Huntington and Setauket in 1660. An attempt was made to settle conflicting Dutch and English claims by means of a treaty signed at Hartford in 1650, which fixed a boundary by drawing a line southward across the island from the point where Oyster Bay was afterward located. The eastern towns in time fell under Connecticut jurisdiction, and thus eastern Long Island was politically a part of New England when the English conquered New Netherland (1664). Charles II at that time granted all of Long Island to his brother, James, Duke of York, who cleared his title by promises of payments to Stirling and to Lord Berkeley who had bought a half interest. Reconquest brought the Dutch back to the western district in 1673, but the Treaty of Westminster (1674) finally established Long Island's status as part of the English colony of New York.

Long Island has become one of the most prosperous and populous areas of its size in the United States. Its primary industries were agriculture, fishing and shipbuilding, but during the past century there has been a varied and constantly increasing industrial development. Its two western counties comprise two of the five boroughs of the city of New York, the boroughs of Brooklyn and Queens.

LONG ISLAND, BATTLE OF (Aug. 27, 1776). Howe brought all but one of his brigades across from Staten Island, landing them on Gravesend Bay beach.

Washington's outpost line was along Brooklyn Heights, a series of low hills crossed by four roads, through Jamaica, Bedford and Flatbush passes, and along the shore from the Narrows. He strengthened his force by placing nearly a third of the entire American army on Long Island—under command of Putnam.

The night of Aug. 26–27, Howe attacked, captured Miles' rifle regiment and most of Stirling's command. Following this victorious outpost action, the British struck Washington's main position. Had this attack been pushed, all American forces on Long Island could have been captured. Instead, Howe switched to siege tactics. Realizing his danger, Washington determined to withdraw his forces to Manhattan, while giving the impression he was reinforcing. Withdrawal, begun the night of Aug. 29–30, was successfully completed, without interference from the British, by 7:00 A.M., on the 30th.

LONG ISLAND OF HOLSTON, TREATY OF. The militia of southwest Virginia and North Carolina under Col. William Christian and Col. Joseph Williams made a successful punitive expedition in the fall of 1776 against the Cherokees, following the Indians' raid and the battle of Long Island Flats. A pledge was extorted from the Cherokees that they would come into a treaty the following year. In June and July, 1777, the Indians met and negotiated with commissioners of the two states at Long Island, and ceded lands. North Carolina received a cession, the south line of which ran from Chimney Top Mountain past the mouth of McNamee's Creek of the Nolachucky to the Allegheny range.

LONGHORNS, TEXAS. Although predominantly of the blood that Spaniards began bringing to Mexico in 1521, the longhorn achieved character and fame (roughly 1845–95) as a Texas product. A strain out of cattle imported from southern states and the climate and ranges of Texas combined to develop an animal heavier and more "rangy" than straight Mexican cattle but at the same time severely differentiated from the "American" cattle of Colorado, Kansas and elsewhere. In color the breed was earthlike, brindles, duns, smokies, blues, browns, dull reds, blacks, paints of many variations, all mingling. Long of legs, body and tail, a "Texas steer" carried a pair of horns that spread from three to five feet from tip to tip, occasionally over eight feet.

LONG'S EXPLORATIONS (1819–20, 1823). In the summer of 1819, Maj. Stephen H. Long, in the steamboat *Western Engineer*, left St. Louis in command of the scientific part of the Yellowstone Expedition. Because of the delay and expense of the latter expedition, Congress refused further funds. As a compromise Long was authorized to make a scientific exploration to the Rocky Mountains.

On June 6, 1820, Long and twenty men set out to explore the Platte, the Arkansas and the Red. Marching up the Platte to the mountains, he discovered Long's Peak. Dr. Edwin James of his staff climbed Pikes Peak. Capt. J. R. Bell marched down the Arkansas with part of the force; but Long, misled by Spanish information, explored the Canadian River and found it was not the Red when he came to its confluence with the Arkansas. The expedition added little to the world's knowledge of geography; but the four scientists of the party, including Dr. Thomas Say, added much to knowledge of the botany, zoology, geology and Indian lore of the Plains.

On April 20, 1823, Long set out on another exploration, from Fort Snelling and thence up the St. Peter's (Minnesota) River. His mission was to explore the country, locate the 49th degree of latitude and take possession of all the territory below this newly authorized boundary line. Lord Selkirk's Colony at Pembina and North West Company posts in the Red River country were visited. The return trip was begun in August, the party going down Red River to Lake Winnipeg and thence eastward to Lake Superior, through the Great Lakes to Niagara Falls, and on southward to Philadelphia where they arrived Oct. 26, 1823.

LOOKOUT MOUNTAIN, BATTLE ON (Nov. 24, 1863), was an action in which Hooker (U.), commanding the right wing of Grant's army of about 56,000 men, cleared Lookout Mountain of the enfeebled and disheartened Confederate troops who had held it since the battle of Chickamauga. This initial stroke in Grant's effort to raise the siege of Chattanooga was dramatic, even if easily accomplished. It is popularly known in history as the "battle of the clouds" owing to the fact that low-hanging clouds hid the contending forces from observers below in the valley of the Tennessee. The withdrawal of Longstreet's (C.) corps from Lookout Mountain had left the Confederate left wing dangerously weak. Hooker's troops scrambling up the mountain drove off the remaining Confederates, swept on across Chattanooga Creek and the next day participated in the fighting on Missionary Ridge, lying farther to the east. The battle, though not a hard fight, marked the beginning of final Union triumph in the Chattanooga campaign.

LOOM. Primitive English looms, brought to America by the first settlers, were soon displaced by improved Dutch looms to which the fly shuttle, which speeded their operation, was added before 1800. Power looms were invented in England, but original American types were perfected by the Boston Manufacturing Co., and adapted from the Scotch loom. Between 1825 and 1850 Samuel Bachelor, William Mason and William Crompton of Massachusetts improved these looms to weave wool as well as cotton and to make pattern as well as plain fabrics, and Erastus Bigelow of the same state invented machinery to weave ingrain and eventually Brussels and Wilton carpets. Another era of rapid improvement occurred after the Civil War when James Northrop and George Draper perfected improvements which automatically changed shuttles and stopped a loom when a single warp thread broke. Early in the present century further refinements were embodied in the Crompton and Knolls looms and their successors.

LORDS OF TRADE AND PLANTATIONS. Constitutional practice provided that English provinces outside the realm were charges of the Privy Council. Beginning in 1624, British colonial administration was directed by special committees advising the Privy Council. As these committees were short-lived and often unskilled, confusion and inefficiency in imperial control resulted. To create an informed personnel with vigor and continuity in colonial policy, Charles II organized, by Order in Council (March 12, 1675), the Lords of Trade and Plantations of 21 Privy Councillors, nine of whom held "the immediate Care and Intendency" of colonies, any five constituting a quorum. Though the Lords represented nothing new in method and held powers only advisory to the Privy Council, because they were men of informed ability and great administrative capacity and had continuous existence for twenty years with relatively few changes in personnel, they achieved more systematic administration than any previous agencies for colonial affairs, serving as a transition to and a model for the Board of Trade and Plantations which succeeded them (May 15, 1696). Holding 857 meetings (1675–96) and maintaining permanent offices in Scotland Yard, they established a permanent, salaried secretary (Sir Robert Southwell), assistant secretary (William Blathwayt) and clerical staff to handle colonial correspondence; became a bureau of colonial information by sending inquiries to colonial governors, and agents (notably Edward Randolph) to colonies; recommended appointees as royal governors to Crown colonies and prepared their commissions and instructions; developed the technique of judicial review of colonial cases appealed to the Privy Council; assaulted, in the interests of unity and efficiency, the charters of colonies—forcing surrender of two and instituting *quo warranto* proceedings against five others by 1686—and instituted the policy of consolidating colonies (the Dominion of New England). Though vigorous in its early years, the Popish Plot (1678) lessened activity, and as death took older members and political disorders (1685–89) interfered, the Lords of Trade became weak and ineffective. Their last meeting was on April 18, 1696, a month before the Board of Trade superseded them.

"LOST BATTALION" (Oct. 2–8, 1918) is a misnomer applied to part of the American 77th Division which, during the Meuse-Argonne offensive, was surrounded in Charlevaux Ravine by German troops. The force was composed of Companies A, B, C, E, G and H, 308th Infantry; Company K, 307th Infantry; and two platoons from Companies C and D, 306th Machine Gun Battalion, all under command of Maj. Charles W. Whittlesey. Adjoining French and American attacks launched Oct. 2 failed, whereas Whittlesey penetrated to his objective where he was promptly encircled. For five days (morning of Oct. 3–evening Oct. 7) he maintained a heroic defense against great odds until American relief troops broke through. Strictly speaking, Whittlesey's force was not a battalion nor was it at any time lost.

LOST ORDER, LEE'S (September, 1862). As the Confederate Army advanced into Maryland, Lee planned to capture Harpers Ferry and concentrate his army for an advance into Pennsylvania. Accordingly, on Sept. 9, 1862, he issued Special Order No. 191, outlining routes and objectives. Copies were sent to division commanders concerned. D. H. Hill's division, heretofore under Jackson's orders, had been transferred. Jackson, receiving the order before learning of Hill's transfer, sent him a copy in his own hand. Hill preserved this copy. Another copy from Lee's headquarters, also sent Hill, in some manner was lost and later found by a Federal soldier. It was sent to McClellan (U.) who was thus informed of Lee's plans. It is not certain that Lee knew until several days later that McClellan was informed as to his plans. The loss nearly brought about Lee's complete defeat and created one of the most unusual situations in American military history.

LOTTERIES, until a comparatively recent time, were considered in this country a legitimate method of raising money for a wide variety of purposes. Their history dates from 1612, when James I authorized the Virginia Company to make "a good supply to ye colonie" by this means. Although this venture was apparently restricted to England, the idea was speedily transmitted across the Atlantic, and by 1699 lotteries were sufficiently numerous here for a New England ecclesiastical assembly to denounce them as "a cheat" and their agents as "pillagers of the people." Nevertheless, the earliest printed reference to a lottery occurs in Bradford's *American Weekly Mercury*, for Feb. 23, 1720. Thereafter, throughout the remainder of that century, lotteries were increasingly employed on behalf of schools, roads, bridges, canals, etc. In 1748 part of Philadelphia's fortifications were built with funds thus obtained. Lotteries for churches were especially popular. Franklin's *Pennsylvania Gazette* announced one in 1759 "Solely for the promotion of honor and religion . . . in imitation of . . . neighbors in this and adjacent provinces." The idea of lotteries for private gain was largely a growth of later days.

The fact that the early lotteries were generally projected for public causes long blinded to their evils many who would otherwise probably have opposed them. Franklin, Washington, Jefferson and other distinguished citizens favored them. As late as 1826 a lottery was considered a dignified method of relieving Jefferson's financial embarrassments.

Philadelphia was the principal center of lottery activities in this country in the 18th and early 19th centuries. There were, however, lotteries in many other places, some sporadic, some permanent. Boston, for instance, built the existing Faneuil Hall with the proceeds of a lottery in 1761. Harvard, Dartmouth, Yale, Williams and other colleges replenished their building funds by the same device. In 1793 the District of Columbia commissioners paid for improvements in Washington through a lottery. In New York City, in 1790–91, lotteries were numerous and permanent enough for the lists of drawings to fill half a column in a local newspaper.

Between 1820 and 1833 the traffic in lottery tickets rose to extraordinary proportions. Philadelphia's lottery offices, of which there were three in 1809, increased by 1833 to more than 200. In 1830 New York had 52 drawings, involving prizes aggregating $9,270,000. It is estimated that 420 lotteries were then functioning in the country, offering annual prizes of about $53,000,000. Most were indigenous enterprises, but many were foreign-owned.

The earliest legislation restricting lotteries was enacted by Pennsylvania in 1729, but affected only those not operating under special legislative grants. No consistent attempt was made to suppress lotteries, as such, until about 1831. Pennsylvania and Massachusetts passed laws to that purpose in 1833; New York followed in 1834. The earliest antilottery society appeared in Philadelphia in 1833. Its educational work did much to direct attention to the essential immorality of lotteries. During the ensuing two decades one state after another took steps to end them. Louisiana, after chartering in 1868 the greatest lottery in American history, abolished it in 1892. In 1890 Congress made illegal the distribution of lottery tickets or advertising through the mails. In 1895 they were excluded from interstate commerce. These acts proved a deathblow to the business.

LOTTERY CASE. The issue was whether the Lottery Act of Congress, passed in 1895, prohibiting the sending of lottery tickets through interstate commerce, was a valid exercise of power under the commerce clause. In 1903 the Supreme Court held, in Champion v. Ames, that Congress could do so, in order to guard the people of the United States from the "pestilence of lotteries." This has given rise to what some authorities term a "Federal police power" and in line with this principle Congress has passed and the Supreme Court has upheld laws excluding from interstate commerce such articles as obscene literature, impure food, prize-fight films and other articles deemed injurious to the health, welfare or morals of the people.

LOUDON, FORT (southeast of the present Loudon, Pa.), was built by Col. John Armstrong of the Pennsylvania militia in 1756 as a protection against Indian forays into the Conococheague Valley. During the Forbes expedition it was used as a military storehouse and convalescents' camp. Lt. Charles Grant with a detachment of Highlanders occupied the post when, in November, 1765, the "Black Boys" demanded the return of several guns which Grant had impounded following an assault upon a pack train of trading goods. Refused, they fired upon the fort, forcing its surrender and evacuation.

LOUDOUN, FORT. In 1756, to meet the French menace in the Old Southwest, two forts were erected on Little Tennessee River west of the Alleghenies, one by Virginia and the other by South Carolina. The latter, named in honor of the Earl of Loudoun, commander of the British forces in America, was garrisoned by troops from South Carolina, and stood until 1760, when, under French incitement, it was besieged by the Cherokees, and surrendered on Aug. 7. The troops marched out only to be attacked by the Indians early in the morning of the 10th, when 4 officers, 23 privates and some women and children were massacred. The fort was burned.

LOUISBURG EXPEDITION (1745). After the loss of Acadia (1713), France settled Louisburg (Cape Breton Island), constructing a mighty fortress and naval station to dominate the North Atlantic. A seat of Popery, privateers and pirates, Louisburg threatened Nova Scotia and preyed upon New England commerce, fishing and peace of mind, though after long peace (1713–44) France neglected it. When King George's War began (1744), New Englanders, led by Gov. William Shirley of Massachusetts, determined to attack Louisburg. Well advised about French conditions, Shirley prevailed upon the General Court (Jan. 25, 1745) to raise 3000 men and necessary supplies, and enlisted support from neighboring colonies. Without assurance of English assistance, Shirley hoped to capture Louisburg before the French spring fleet arrived. On March 24 about 4300 men, commanded by William Pepperell, sailed from Boston. Landing at Canso, they were cheered by the arrival (April 23) of Commodore Peter Warren with three English warships (eight others arrived later). On April 30, while Warren blockaded Louisburg harbor, Pepperell landed his men at Gabarus Bay and laid siege to the town. Fortunate in capturing (May 3) the French Royal Battery of thirty heavy cannon, which they turned upon the town, the colonials forced Louisburg to capitulate (June 15), and captured the vessels of the French fleet as they arrived. Primarily achieved by colonial

troops, this first important English victory in America was the result of careful planning, reckless fortitude and good luck. The colonists held Louisburg despite ill-fated attempts at recapture, and were embittered when, in the Treaty of Aix-la-Chapelle (1748), England sacrificed Louisburg for Madras, though England's reimbursements to the colonies for their expenses in the capture rescued Massachusetts, at least, from financial doldrums.

LOUISIANA. *As a French and Spanish Colony.* Spanish explorers touched the Louisiana coast before 1520, and DeSoto died in the interior in 1542 while searching vainly for mines of precious metals. Spain then abandoned the region, which remained a sort of no man's land for nearly a century and a half, until LaSalle, coming from Canada, followed the Mississippi to its mouth in 1682 and claimed the entire valley for Louis XIV of France, in whose honor it was named "Louisiana." LaSalle's expedition to plant a colony at the mouth of the Mississippi in 1684 missed its intended destination and landed on the Texan coast, and in 1687 he was assassinated while trying to make his way back to Canada by land. The War of the English Succession delayed the completion of LaSalle's project, but when peace returned Iberville and Bienville planted the first permanent French colony on the Gulf coast in 1699 (Biloxi). The War of the Spanish Succession forced France to neglect the colony. In 1712 Louis XIV, still anxious to develop Louisiana but with an empty treasury, granted to Antoine Crozat the exclusive privilege of exploiting Louisiana. Crozat exhausted his resources in futile searches for sources of quick wealth, and in 1717 surrendered his charter without having effected much development in the colony.

John Law, a Scotchman recognized in France as a successful banker and financier, organized the Western Company, which assumed control of Louisiana on Jan. 1, 1718. The scope of the company's operations was soon enlarged and its name changed to the "Company of the Indies." The anticipated immense and immediate profits were not realized, and in 1720 the company failed, the "bubble" burst and Law passed off the scene. However, the company retained control of Louisiana until a series of bad harvests and the disastrous war with the Natchez Indians caused the surrender of the charter in 1731. Profiting by Crozat's mistakes, the company brought some substantial development to the colony, but failed to make it a financial success.

Louisiana then passed under French royal control, thus to remain for three decades. The colony developed slowly, handicapped by strife between France and England. France undertook to unite Louisiana with Canada by erecting fortified posts to exclude the English from the Mississippi Valley. The British quickly accepted the challenge, and the ensuing War of the Austrian Succession and the Seven Years' War, culminating in the expulsion of the French from the mainland of North America, seriously retarded the progress of Louisiana. In 1762 Louisiana west of the Mississippi and the Isle of Orleans were ceded to Spain, and the remainder of Louisiana was surrendered to England in 1763.

Resentment of the French inhabitants at the transfer, Spain's tardiness in taking possession of the colony, general economic distress and the unpopular measures of Antonio de Ulloa, the first Spanish governor, led to his expulsion in the so-called Revolution of 1768. But Alexandro O'Reilly crushed the "Revolution" and firmly established Spanish authority in 1769. Louisiana experienced a steady development under Spanish rule, in spite of many difficulties. The international confusion accompanying the American and French revolutions kept alive the hope of the Louisianians for eventual reunion with France. Spanish Louisiana played an important part in the American Revolution. Needed supplies were forwarded from New Orleans to the patriot forces in the West, and when Spain entered the war as an ally of France in 1779, Bernardo Galvez, operating from Louisiana, captured the British posts in West Florida. Spanish discontent with the Definitive Treaty of Peace, 1783, led to intrigues with the Indians and with some of the western leaders for protecting Louisiana by holding back the influx of American settlers, or detaching the trans-Allegheny region from the United States. The Nootka Sound controversy between England and Spain in 1790 and the Genêt episode of 1793, involving threats of western attack upon Louisiana, alarmed the Spanish authorities. Disputes between the United States and Spain over navigation of the Mississippi and the northern boundary of West Florida were adjusted by the Pinckney Treaty of 1795, but Spain still feared the outcome of American expansion in the Southwest.

When Napoleon became head of the French government in 1799, he planned a new colonial empire, and by the Treaty of San Ildefonso (Oct. 1, 1800) Spain retroceded Louisiana to France. But Napoleon's inability to subjugate the blacks in Haiti, threat of renewal of the European war, discontent of the United States over commercial restrictions at New Orleans, and his pressing need for money induced him to sell Louisiana to the United States by the Louisiana Purchase Treaty of April 30, 1803, before he had taken possession of the colony. In spite of Spanish resentment and threats, Louisiana was formally transferred by Spain to France on Nov. 30, 1803, and by France to the United States on Dec. 20, 1803.

State of Louisiana, the first carved from the Louisiana Purchase, was admitted to the Union in 1812.

The sectional crisis of 1861 found Louisiana definitely aligned with her sister slave states. The sixth state to secede, she early suffered from Federal mili-

tary and naval superiority, New Orleans being captured on May 1, 1862, and vital sections of the state remaining in Federal hands throughout the war. Reconstruction began earlier and lasted longer in Louisiana than in any other Confederate state, and during the war Lincoln used this state as an experimental laboratory for testing his reconstruction theories. Louisiana was readmitted to the Union in 1868.

LOUISIANA LOTTERY was chartered by the Louisiana legislature August, 1868, for a period of 25 years. The capital stock was fixed at $1,000,000, but operations were to begin when $100,000 was paid in. In return for its monopoly of the lottery business in Louisiana, the company paid $40,000 annually to the state, but was exempt from other taxation. The business soon became immensely profitable. In March, 1879, the legislature repealed the charter, but the U. S. District Court for Louisiana held that this was a violation of contract. In 1890, when the charter was about to expire, the company, through John A. Morris, one of its founders, offered the state $500,000 annually for an extension of 25 years. This offer was subsequently raised to $1,000,000 and then to $1,-250,000. Opposition immediately developed. Gov. Nicholls sent to the legislature a message denouncing the proposal. Nevertheless, an act calling for a constitutional amendment embodying the lottery company's franchise was passed. This was vetoed by Nicholls. The House passed the bill over his veto, but the Senate failed to do so. The latter body, however, approved a resolution denying the governor's right to veto a bill proposing a constitutional amendment, whereupon the House sent the bill to the Secretary of State to be promulgated. This the official refused to do. Morris took the matter into the courts, which decided against the Secretary of State. On Sept. 19, 1890, the U. S. Post Office Department denied the lottery company the use of the mails. Morris thereupon withdrew his proposition. In the meantime a political organization unfavorable to the lottery had been formed, and held a convention in Baton Rouge, Aug. 7, 1890. The agitation thus initiated resulted in the election of Murphy J. Foster to the governorship. After his election, Foster approved acts (June 28 and July 12, 1892) making the sale of lottery tickets unlawful in Louisiana. The lottery company continued in business in New Orleans till 1895, when it transferred its domicile to Honduras. Thence it continued to sell tickets in the United States till April, 1906, when the U. S. Department of Justice succeeded in breaking up the business.

LOUISIANA PURCHASE. The province of Louisiana embraced the Isle of Orleans on the east bank of the Mississippi and the vast area between that river, the Rockies and the Spanish possessions in the Southwest. The purchase of the colony from Napoleon by the United States in 1803 ended forever

France's dream of controlling the Mississippi Valley, and began a program of expansion destined to carry the American flag to the Pacific.

For a generation Louisiana had been a pawn in European diplomacy. France ceded it to Spain in 1762. Genêt planned to attack it from the United States in 1793, but France turned to diplomacy as a means of recovering it between 1795 and 1799. By the Treaty of San Ildefonso, Oct. 1, 1800, and the Convention of Aranjuez, March 21, 1801, Napoleon acquired Louisiana in return for placing the Prince of Parma, son-in-law of the Spanish king, on the newly erected throne of Etruria.

The acquisition of Louisiana was part of an ambitious plan by which Napoleon and Talleyrand hoped to build a colonial empire in the West Indies and the heart of North America. The mainland colony would be a source of supplies for the sugar islands, a market for France and a vast territory for settlement. Two million francs were spent upon an expedition for Louisiana assembled in Holland, at Helvoët Sluys, in the winter of 1802–3. Fortunately for the United States the ships were icebound in February, just as they were ready to sail.

By the Treaty of San Lorenzo, Spain, in 1795, had granted American citizens the privilege of depositing their goods at New Orleans for reshipment on ocean-going vessels. The United States was deeply aroused when Juan Ventura Morales, the acting intendant of Louisiana, revoked this right of deposit on Oct. 16, 1802, and failed to provide another site, as the treaty required. It was assumed at the time that France was responsible for the revocation but all available documentary evidence indicates that the action was taken by Spain alone, and for commercial reasons.

President Jefferson handled the crisis in masterly fashion by appointing James Monroe as a special envoy to assist Robert R. Livingston, the minister at Paris, in securing American rights. Monroe's instructions authorized an offer of $10,000,000 for the Isle of Orleans, on which New Orleans stood, and the Floridas, erroneously thought to be French. If France refused this proposition the ministers were to seek a commercial site on the Mississippi, or at least permanent establishment of the right of deposit at New Orleans.

In the meantime, Livingston had pursued his country's interests with a zeal deserving better results. He proposed the cession of New Orleans and the Floridas, belittled the economic value of Louisiana for France and, after the closing of New Orleans, urged the cession to the United States of the Isle of Orleans and all the trans-Mississippi country above the Arkansas River. This was the first hint by any one that France surrender any part of the right bank of the Mississippi.

By the spring of 1803, Napoleon's plans for his American empire had all gone astray. Spain refused to round out his possessions by ceding the Floridas.

Negro resistance and yellow fever thwarted the attempt to subjugate Santo Domingo. War with Great Britain was imminent. In the United States there was growing hostility to France and talk of an Anglo-American alliance. Particularly disturbed at such a prospect, Napoleon decided to reap a nice profit and placate the Americans by selling them all of Louisiana.

When Monroe arrived in Paris on April 12, the first consul had already appointed François Barbé-Marbois, Minister of the Public Treasury, to conduct the negotiations. On April 11 Talleyrand had amazed Livingston by asking what the United States would give for the entire colony. Barbé-Marbois conferred with Livingston on the evening of April 13, thereby initiating the negotiations before the formal presentation of Monroe. Some jealousy arose between the American ministers but it did not handicap their work. Monroe was at first less inclined than Livingston to exceed their instructions and purchase all of Louisiana. By a treaty and two conventions, all dated April 30, the United States paid $11,250,000 for Louisiana, set aside $3,750,000 to pay the claims of its own citizens against France and placed France and Spain on an equal commercial basis with the United States in the colony for a period of twelve years.

Serious barriers to American ownership of Louisiana yet remained. Napoleon's action required the confirmation of the French legislature, and the sale was a violation of his solemn pledge to Spain never to alienate the colony to a third power. There was also grave doubt regarding the constitutionality of such a purchase by the United States. None of these dangers materialized. Napoleon ignored the legislature, Spain did nothing more than protest and Jefferson put his constitutional scruples conveniently aside. On Nov. 30, 1803, Spain formally delivered the colony to Pierre-Clément Laussat, the French colonial prefect, who on Dec. 20 transferred the territory to William C. C. Claiborne and Gen. James Wilkinson, the American commissioners. The Anglo-Saxon had vanquished the Latin in the long struggle for the Mississippi Valley.

Boundaries of the Louisiana Purchase. The United States purchased Louisiana "with the same extent that it now has in the hands of Spain, and that it had when France possessed it; and Such as it Should be after the Treaties subsequently entered into between Spain and other States." The treaty of cession, incorporating these words, quoted verbatim from the treaty by which Spain retroceded Louisiana to France in 1800. When the United States commissioners requested a definition Napoleon is reported to have said that "if an obscurity did not already exist, it would perhaps be good policy to put one there." The resultant series of diplomatic and territorial controversies is still not settled.

France, original settler of Louisiana, had not re-occupied it at the time of our purchase, but the extent of the region as then "in the hands of Spain" was ill defined. Before 1763 France claimed the entire Mississippi watershed eastward to the Alleghenies and westward to undetermined limits, as well as the Gulf Coast eastward to the Perdido River. French explorers had traversed Texas, and French traders controlled the Texas Indian trade, but the Arroyo Hondo, between Nacogdoches (Tex.) and Natchitoches (La.), was tacitly accepted as the frontier in the 18th century. Between French Louisiana and French Canada no clear line had been drawn.

France ceded western Louisiana to Spain in 1762, but there is no evidence that they made a boundary delineation. Great Britain, by the Treaty of Paris, in 1763 completed her possession of all North America east of the Mississippi except New Orleans, making that river the eastern boundary of Louisiana. The province of West Florida was joined with the province of Louisiana, in administration only, from 1783, when Spain recovered both Floridas, until 1803 when Louisiana was surrendered to France and in turn to the United States. But Spain governed West Florida separately after 1803 and asserted its independence of Louisiana. The United States claimed it and took over part of it in 1810, further complicating the West Florida controversy.

Meanwhile Spain's acquisition of Louisiana in 1762 had postponed the need for a Texas-Louisiana delineation. Frontier disturbances began after 1803, and in 1806 rival commanders effected the "Neutral Ground Agreement," mutually limiting their activities by a strip between the Arroyo Hondo and the Sabine River. The United States took French colonial exploration and the instructions to the intended French captain general of Louisiana in 1802 as bases for its claim that the purchase extended to the Rio Grande.

The State of Louisiana as admitted in 1812 included part of West Florida and employed the Sabine River as its western limit, though without treaty sanction. In the Adams-Onís Treaty of 1819 Spain relinquished West Florida, though the negotiators consciously avoided saying whether or not it belonged to Louisiana before 1819, and in exchange for other concessions the United States yielded Texas beyond the Sabine.

The natural limit between New Mexico and Louisiana was at the headwaters of the Río Grande and the Arkansas River. But to keep the line far from Santa Fe, the Adams-Onís delineation left the Red River at 100° W. Long., and proceeded west along the Arkansas to its source. Since colonial occupation gave no ground for boundary claims farther north, it was logical to assume that the purchase included the natural watershed of the Mississippi. Jefferson's claim that Oregon was included had no foundation and no international recognition. The drawing of the line to

the Pacific on the 42nd parallel, N. Lat., in the Adams-Onís Treaty was the result of bargaining on a larger scale.

An assertion that the northern boundary was defined in the Treaty of Utrecht of 1713 was ignored. In the Convention of 1818 a practical agreement between this country and England placed the boundary at 49° N. Lat., from the Lake of the Woods to the Rocky Mountains. The United States had thus effected its ownership of practically the whole western Mississippi watershed through rights acquired in the Louisiana Purchase.

LOVEJOY RIOTS. The Rev. Elijah P. Lovejoy established a weekly newspaper, *The Observer*, at St. Louis (1833). Threatened with violence by pro-slavery men for editorials against slavery (1834), he made a point of his rights to free speech and free press. Moving his press to free soil (Alton, Ill.) in 1836, it was smashed on the Alton dock by local citizens. Sympathizers helped to purchase a new press, but when Lovejoy came out for immediate abolition and a state antislavery society (July, 1837), a mob destroyed the press (August), smashed a third (Sept. 21) and, in an effort to destroy the fourth (Nov. 7), shot its defenders and killed Lovejoy who immediately became a martyr to the cause of Abolition.

LOVEWELL'S FIGHT occurred at Pigwacket (Fryeburg), Maine, Sunday, May 9 (o.s.), 1725. Capt. John Lovewell, with 33 volunteers, was out for scalp bounty, and Chaplain Frye had just scalped an Indian, when the troop was ambushed by about eighty Indians. Twelve white men, including Lovewell, fell at the onset; one deserted under fire; twenty-one were left. Ensign Seth Wyman, the only officer, placed his men for a finish fight, a pond at their backs and two large, fallen pines for breastworks. Toward nightfall, seeing the Indians powwowing for a fresh attack, Wyman still-hunted and shot the medicine man at his incantations. This ended the fight. Eighteen of the men eventually reached home. Rev. Thomas Symmes in his account changed the date from May 9 to May 8, supposedly to divert from Chaplain Frye, who died, the odium of scalp hunting on Sunday.

LOWER COUNTIES-ON-DELAWARE, which comprised the counties of New Castle, Kent and Sussex, or the present state of Delaware, evolved from the earlier Swedish and Dutch settlements. They were conveyed by the Duke of York in 1682 to William Penn, and shortly afterward annexed to the Province of Pennsylvania by the Act of Union. Because of disagreement in the Provincial Assembly the Lower Counties, in 1704, seceded from that body and formed, at New Castle, their own assembly, by which, and the provincial governor of Pennsylvania, they continued to be governed until the adoption of the constitution of the State of Delaware in 1776.

LOYAL LAND COMPANY (1748). The spirit of speculation in western lands was rife in Virginia in the later years of the first half of the 1700's. The first grant to a company organized to deal in such lands was to the Loyal Land Company. A grant of 800,000 acres was made to it by the Council of State of Virginia, on July 12, 1748, John Lewis, founder of Staunton, Va., being the leading spirit for four years. In launching the company's activities Dr. Thomas Walker was chosen on Dec. 12, 1749, as field agent, and soon became the directive force of the enterprise. In 1750 he led a group on a tour of exploration into the Tennessee and Kentucky country in the interest of the company and kept a journal which is one of the most valuable sources on the early history of that region. On that tour Walker named the Cumberland Mountains, Gap and River in honor of the Duke of Cumberland.

However, the lands actually taken up by the company were located east of the Cumberland Mountains. By the autumn of 1754 lands were sold to about 200 settlers. The French and Indian War brought a cessation of activities for some years; and the Proclamation of 1763 gave Walker and his associates concern and trouble. In order to render lands west of the proclamation line available, Walker took an active part in removing the claims of the Indian tribes to the region. He participated in negotiating the treaties of Fort Stanwix and Lochaber. Until his death in 1794, Walker was persistent in salvaging all he could for the company. Southwest Virginia owes much to his enterprise and assiduity in bringing in settlers.

LOYALISTS, OR TORIES, those who were loyal to Great Britain during the Revolution, comprised about one third of the population of the thirteen revolting colonies. In Georgia and South Carolina they were a majority; in New England and Virginia a minority; elsewhere they were more or less evenly matched by the patriots. Included in their ranks were all classes: great landowners such as the DeLanceys, Jessups and Philipses of New York; rich merchants like the Whartons and Pembertons of Philadelphia, and the Higgins and Chandlers of Boston; large numbers of professional men—lawyers, physicians and teachers; prosperous farmers; Crown officials and Anglican clergy and laity; and dependents of Loyalist merchants and landlords. While a few of the more conservative stood for the rigid execution of imperial law, the majority opposed the objectionable acts of the British Parliament, served on the early extralegal committees and were not hostile to the calling of the first Continental Congress in 1774, in fact working hard to elect delegates of their own convictions to it. Although anxious to maintain their rights by means of petition and legal protest, and in some cases not even averse to a show of force, they were strongly opposed to separation from the British Empire. The Declaration of Independence gave finality to their position.

Before April, 1775, few efforts were made to arrest or suppress the Loyalists, but after the battle of Lexington the war fervor rapidly grew more intense. Great numbers of Loyalists flocked to the royal colors or, in a few instances, organized militia companies of their own under commissions from the Crown. Although they probably contributed 60,000 soldiers, yet much to the disappointment of the British authorities their military service was not commensurate with their numerical strength, their only outstanding exploits being an expedition against the coast towns of Connecticut; frontier raids in conjunction with the Indians; and a savage guerrilla warfare between patriot and Loyalist in the South.

As the struggle progressed the patriots resorted to more and more drastic measures against the Loyalists. All who refused to take an oath of allegiance to the new governments were denied the rights of citizenship, and could not vote, hold office or enjoy court protection. In many cases they were forbidden to pursue professions, or to acquire or dispose of property. Free speech was denied them, and they were not allowed to communicate with the British. When these laws failed to accomplish their purpose, the more ardent Loyalists were jailed, put on parole, sent to detention camps, and tarred and feathered. Nearly all of the new state governments eventually enacted legislation banishing those who refused to swear allegiance. Before the war was over probably 200,000 Loyalists died, were exiled, or became voluntary refugees to other parts of the Empire—a large number of citizens for struggling frontier communities to lose.

To banishment was added confiscation of property. In the early days of the Revolution Thomas Paine advised confiscation of Loyalist property to defray the expenses of the war, and several states followed this suggestion. The definition of treason by Congress on June 24, 1770, supplied a legal basis for action. Late in 1777 Congress advised the states to confiscate and sell the real and personal property of those who had forfeited "the right of protection" and to invest the proceeds in Continental certificates. Although some of the more conservative patriots protested that confiscation was "contrary to the principles of civil liberty," statutes of condemnation and forfeiture were enacted in all the states before the end of the war.

Many persons were inevitably the victims of private grudges and persecution. Evidence abounds that the execution of the sequestration laws was frequently attended with scandal and corruption. The amount of property seized is uncertain. Claims totaling £10,000,000, however, were filed with the commission established by the British Parliament, and less than £1,000,000 were disallowed.

On the whole, throughout the conflict the Loyalists

lacked organization and good leadership. They were conservatives who were suspicious of the innovations demanded by a crisis. The triumph of the patriots accentuated their hesitancy. They had placed implicit trust in the invincibility of the British army, and the unexpected development of the conflict dazed them.

All things taken into consideration, the treatment of the Loyalists was moderate and fair. The period was one in which the most bitter and most harsh human emotions were aroused—a civil war within a state. Although the laws of banishment and sequestration were severe, there was no such slaughter and terrorism as prevailed in the French Revolution, and surprising care was taken to make sure that punishment of Loyalists was carried out only in accord with law.

LUNDY'S LANE, BATTLE AT (July 25, 1814). Three weeks after his victory at Chippewa, Maj. Gen. Jacob Brown's invading army encountered the British under Riall at Lundy's Lane, in Canada near Bridgewater and Niagara Falls. Winfield Scott's First Brigade failed to carry the position in a frontal attack and was reinforced by Ripley's and Porter's brigades. Jesup, with the 25th Infantry, executed a turning movement, driving in the British left and capturing Riall himself. Lt. Gen. Drummond, arriving with reinforcements, took command. Protracted and savage fighting ensued. Miller's 21st U. S. Infantry stormed the hill and took the British artillery, the Americans repulsing determined counterattacks until midnight. Brown and Scott, both severely wounded, withdrew. Ripley, left in command, brought off the army when ammunition failed, but lacking horses, abandoned the captured cannon. Both sides claimed victory, but Drummond remained in possession of the field. Losses were heavy, the British 30%, American slightly less.

LUSITANIA, SINKING OF THE. The Cunard liner *Lusitania* was sunk without warning by the German submarine U-20 off Old Head of Kinsale, Ireland, on May 7, 1915. Of the 1959 passengers and crew, 1198 perished, including 128 (out of 197) Americans. Since on May 1, the day of sailing, the German embassy in Washington had published an advertisement in American papers warning Atlantic travelers that they sailed in British or allied ships at their own risk, it was widely believed that the sinking was premeditated. The log of the U-20, published years later (*Journal of Modern History,* VIII), shows, however, that the submarine had sunk other ships, met the *Lusitania* by chance, and sank her from fear of being rammed. The ship carried 4200 cases of small-arms ammunition and 1250 shrapnel cases, this being allowed by American law; this cargo, stored well forward, about 150 feet from the spot where the torpedo struck, may have exploded and contributed to the

rapid (18 minutes) sinking of the ship. A thorough examination prior to sailing revealed no evidence that the liner was armed. Why the captain of the ship had reduced speed, failed to follow a zig-zag course and kept close to shore, in violation of orders from the British admiralty, was not satisfactorily explained.

The catastrophe created intense indignation in the United States. On Feb. 10, 1915, the American Government had denied the legality of submarine warfare (as practised by Germany) and had warned that it would hold the German government to "a strict accountability" for the observance of American rights on the high seas. In May, President Wilson resisted considerable popular clamor for war (chiefly in the East), and in three successive notes (May 13, June 9, July 21, 1915) demanded that Germany make reparation for and disavow the sinking; the last note concluded with the statement that a repetition of the act "must be regarded by the Government of the United States, when they affect American citizens, as deliberately unfriendly." Secretary of State Bryan thought the American demands too severe and likely to lead to war, and resigned on June 8. The German government agreed to make reparation and eventually gave a promise (after the sinking of the *Arabic*) that liners would not be sunk without warning and without safety for the lives of noncombatants; but it steadfastly refused to disavow the sinking of the *Lusitania.* No settlement of this question was reached before the United States entered World War I.

LUTHERANS. One of the largest denominational families in the United States, the Lutherans had an estimated membership in 1958 of 7,800,000 in eighteen separate bodies. The Dutch in New York and the Swedes on the Delaware formed the first Lutheran congregations in America. Of much greater importance, however, was the large 18th-century German immigration. Congregations began to be formed among these German settlers as early as 1703, Daniel Falckner being one of the first Lutheran ministers among them. Salzburg Lutherans settled in Georgia in 1734. The outstanding personality among colonial Lutherans was Henry Melchior Mühlenberg who came to America in 1742. Through his influence the first Lutheran Synod, the Ministerium of Pennsylvania, was formed in 1748.

The first national Lutheran organization, the General Synod, dates from 1820, the earlier synods being state organizations. The Civil War caused the formation of the United Synod of the South, and in 1867 the more conservative element withdrew to form the General Council. In 1918 these divisions were healed when the United Lutheran Church was organized.

The large influx of Germans after 1830 and the great immigration from Scandinavian countries after 1860 resulted in the formation of numerous independent Lutheran bodies, their maintenance as separate bodies being largely due to language differences. The principal German bodies are the Missouri Synod, the Wisconsin Synod, and the American Lutheran Church formed in 1930 through the merger of three independent synods. The largest Scandinavian churches are the Norwegian Synod, the Augustana (Swedish) Synod and the United Danish Synod.

Although there are eighteen Lutheran denominations in the United States, there are strong unifying trends within the tradition. Eight of the churches have co-operative relationships with each other through the National Lutheran Council, and five others through the Evangelical Lutheran Synodical Conference of North America. Furthermore, the merger of the Evangelical Lutheran Church, the American Lutheran Church, and the United Evangelical Church has been effected; a union of the United and Augustana churches together with several smaller churches is also planned.

All the Lutheran bodies maintain colleges and theological seminaries and several of the more conservative synods have important parochial school systems. Altogether, American Lutherans support more than 100 periodicals and maintain numerous boards of missions, education and other charities.

LYNCHING, or the extralegal execution of an offender by a mob, has long been practised in the United States. The word is thought to have been derived from a Virginian named Lynch, who in Revolutionary times led a small organization which meted out punishment to desperadoes and Tories. Under frontier conditions, when regular law enforcement agencies were weak or lacking, lynching served as a substitute method of social control. In the South, however, lynching has crystallized into a traditional method of summary execution, particularly of Negro offenders against white people.

Fairly reliable statistical data on lynching have been available only since 1882. A compilation made at Tuskegee Institute and published in *The Negro Year Book* shows that from 1882 to 1936 there were 4672 persons lynched in the United States, of whom 3383 were Negroes and 1289 were whites. All states except the six New England states had one or more lynchings during this period and all except eleven lynched one or more Negroes. Although the annual number of lynchings fluctuates considerably, the trend has been consistently downward for the past sixty years. The annual average number of lynchings was 154 for the decade 1890–99; 31 for the decade 1920–29; and 15 for the period 1930–37. Lynching tends more and more to be confined to the South and to Negro victims. Whereas from 1890 to 1899, 13% of the lynchings were outside the South, since 1930 fewer than 5% have been outside. In the decade of 1890–99, 72% of mob victims were Negroes but in the period 1930–37, 91% were Negroes.

MACKINAW BOAT, a light, strongly built, flat-bottomed boat, pointed at both ends, was utilized for travel more especially for transportation of goods, on the rivers of the interior of the continent. Mackinaw boats varied greatly in size; they were commonly propelled by oars, and when conditions permitted, by a sail. Apparently the Mackinaw boat was adapted from the Indian Northwest canoe, long the favorite vehicle of the fur trader and explorer.

MACOMB PURCHASE. In accordance with an act of the legislature for the sale and disposition of lands of the State of New York, Alexander Macomb contracted with the commissioners in 1791, for the purchase of 3,635,200 acres of land in the present counties of St. Lawrence, Franklin, Jefferson, Lewis and Oswego at eight pence per acre. The application was accepted and a patent issued to Macomb who, soon becoming financially embarrassed, deeded the tract to William Constable and others.

MACON'S BILL NO. 2 was enacted May 1, 1810, for the purpose of compelling Great Britain and France, the major belligerents, to desist from their illegal seizures of American commercial vessels. Designed as a substitute for the unsuccessful Nonintercourse Act, it forbade British and French armed vessels to use American waters, unless forced in by distress, except for the carrying of dispatches. The measure opened American trade to the entire world. If France removed its restrictions on neutral commerce by March 3, 1811, and Great Britain failed to do likewise within three months, the President should continue to trade with the former and prohibit it with the latter and vice versa.

MAFIA INCIDENT (March 14, 1891) caused an interruption of diplomatic relations between the United States and Italy (1891–92). David C. Hennessey, chief of police, was assassinated at the gate of his home in New Orleans (Oct. 15, 1890) by a lurking group of men with sawed-off shotguns. Hennessey had been relentless and courageous in efforts to curb local groups which, using the name made infamous by a Sicilian secret society, Mafia, had a record of a dozen murders. His murder was certainly the work of such a group. Nineteen Italians were indicted, and nine of these were the first put on trial. The case made by the state was overwhelming. Yet the jury brought in a verdict of acquittal for four; there was a mistrial for three; two were cleared by direction of the judge, and by public feeling. There was strong conviction that improper influences had defeated elementary justice. A mass meeting of the most prominent citizens the next morning (Saturday, March 14) denounced this, and marched from Canal and St. Charles Streets to the old Parish Prison, on what was then Congo (now Beauregard) Square. Eleven accused Italians were put to death by the leaders of this committee, most of them being shot; the two known to be innocent were not harmed; there was no rioting. President Harrison and Secretary Blaine expressed regrets to Italy, and paid a small indemnity.

MAINE, a part of Massachusetts until its separation in 1820, has had a long and involved history. Situated in the extreme northeastern part of the United States, covering approximately 31,500 square miles, the state is strategically located with reference to the Atlantic seaboard and the St. Lawrence River. Historians differ as to possible visits by Europeans before the 17th century, but that Gosnold (1602), Pring (1603), Champlain (1604), Weymouth (1605), Popham (1607) and Capt. John Smith (1614) visited Maine before the first permanent settlement in New England in 1620, there can be no doubt.

First falling within the colonial schemes of France, Maine was included in the patent obtained by Sieur de Monts from the king of France, November, 1603, and was subsequently explored by Champlain in 1604–5. However, Maine also fell within the limits of the grant made to the Plymouth Company by the king of England in 1606, confirmed in 1620 by the king in his grant to the Council for New England, and included in the charter given to Capt. John Mason and Sir Ferdinando Gorges in 1622. By this latter grant the proprietors had possession of all the lands between the Merrimac and Kennebec Rivers, reaching sixty miles inland, with all the islands within five leagues of the shore. The name "Maine" was first used in this charter, and therefore antedates the names of all other states with the exception of Virginia and Massachusetts. In 1629 Mason and Gorges divided their claim, Sir Ferdinando taking for his share the land between the Piscataqua and Kennebec Rivers. Ten years later, 1639, Georges' charter was renewed by Charles I, and in it was inserted a clause to the effect that the land "shall forever, hereafter be called and named the Province or County of Maine & not by any other name or names whatsoever."

MAINE, DESTRUCTION OF THE (Feb. 15, 1898). In January, 1898, the second-class battleship *Maine,* Capt. Charles D. Sigsbee, was ordered from Key West to Havana on a friendly visit but before the objections of the Spanish authorities were ascertained. For three weeks the ship lay moored to a buoy 500 yards off the arsenal. There was considerable ill feeling against the United States among the Spaniards, but no untoward incident took place until 9:40 P. M., Feb. 15, when two explosions threw parts of the *Maine* 200 feet in the air and illuminated the whole harbor. A first dull explosion had been followed by one much more powerful, probably that of the forward magazines. The forward half of the ship was reduced to a mass of twisted steel; the after part slowly sank. Two officers and 258 of the crew were killed or died soon

afterward. Most of these were buried in Colon Cemetery, Havana.

Investigations were soon made by the American and Spanish authorities separately. Their decisions differed: the Spaniards reported that an internal explosion, perhaps spontaneous combustion in the coal bunkers, had been the cause; the Americans that the original cause had been an external explosion which in turn had set off the forward magazines.

News of the disaster produced great excitement in the United States, and accusations against the Spaniards were freely expressed by certain newspapers. Without doubt the catastrophe stirred up national feeling over the difficulties in Cuba, crystallized in the slogan "Remember the *Maine.*" The wreck remained in Havana harbor until 1911, when U. S. Army engineers built a coffer dam about the wreck, sealed the after hull of the ship, the only part still intact, and floated it out to sea. There, on March 16, 1912, appropriate minute guns boomed as it sank with its flag flying. The remains of 66 of the crew which were found during the raising were buried in the National Cemetery, Arlington.

During the removal of the wreck a board of officers of the Navy made a further investigation. Their report, published in 1912, stated that a low form of explosive exterior to the ship caused the first explosion. "This resulted in igniting and exploding the contents of the 6-inch reserve magazine, A–14–M, said contents including a large quantity of black powder. The more or less complete explosion of the contents of the remaining forward magazine followed." The chief evidence for this was that the bottom of the ship had been bent upward and folded over toward the stern. European experts, perhaps influenced by several internal explosions in warships in the intervening years, still, however, maintained the theory of an internal explosion. No further evidence has ever been found to solve the mystery.

MAIZE, or Indian corn, was extensively cultivated in aboriginal America. It was the chief cereal for the civilizations in Mexico, Central America and the highlands of South America. Archaeology has demonstrated that the earliest agriculture in prehistoric United States was based upon such native plants as the sunflower and the giant ragweed. Later maize and beans were introduced from Mexico. Tree-ring dating for Arizona and New Mexico suggests that maize appeared there about the fifth century B.C. and beans about 200 A.D.

Presumably these plants reached the mound builders a few centuries later and were handed on to the proto-historic Indians east of the Mississippi. The only Indians depending primarily upon maize and beans were the pueblo dwellers of Arizona and New Mexico. Hunting was with them secondary. In addition, maize was grown by most of the tribes east of the 100th meridian and south of 48° N. Lat. The modern cultivation of maize is limited to the same areas.

The colonists planted maize in the Indian way, in hills, tended it with hoes and used fish for fertilizer. In the making of meal, corn bread and hominy, the Indian methods were followed. The Indians planted beans and squashes among the maize, which is still the white custom. Both popcorn and sweet corn were developed by Indians. Throughout the Mississippi Valley and eastward, the historic Indians were primarily hunters, using maize as a reserve food. Traders encouraged the forest Indians to abandon agriculture and to become more nomadic in order that all their time be given to hunting and fur production.

MALVERN HILL, BATTLE OF (July 1, 1862), last of the Seven Days battles, ended Gen. McClellan's (U.) Peninsular Campaign. After the battle of Frayser's Farm, McClellan fell back to a prepared position on Malvern Hill, a plateau protected by streams on its flanks, with an open field of fire at the immediate front. When Gen. Lee's (C.) artillery attack failed, through poor organization and staff inefficiency, several divisional attacks were launched against Malvern Hill. These assaults were not successful in driving the Union Army from its position that day, but on July 2 McClellan felt forced to withdraw to his base at Harrison's Landing.

"MANIFEST DESTINY" was a phrase in common use in the 1840's and 1850's, suggesting the supposed inevitability of the continued territorial expansion of the United States. The phrase first appeared in the *Democratic Review* for July-August, 1845, in an article in which the editor, John L. O'Sullivan, spoke of "our manifest destiny to overspread the continent allotted by Providence for the free development of our yearly multiplying millions." While this article referred specifically to the annexation of Texas, the phrase was quickly caught up by the expansionists of the period and utilized in the controversy with Great Britain over Oregon and in the demand for annexations of territory as a result of the war with Mexico in 1846–48. It was also used, in the next decade, in connection with the desire to annex Cuba.

Believers in "manifest destiny" derived their faith in part from the phenomenal rate of population growth in the United States, in part from a conviction of the superiority of American talents and American political institutions over those of neighboring countries. Though at first a tenet chiefly of the Democratic party, "manifest destiny" also had its devotees among Whigs or Republicans—notably William H. Seward, who as Secretary of State purchased Alaska and sought vainly to annex sundry Caribbean and Pacific islands. "Manifest destiny" was revived as a Republican doctrine in the 1890's and was in evidence in connection with the annexation of Hawaii and the islands taken from Spain in 1898.

MANILA BAY, BATTLE OF (May 1, 1898). Selected for the Asiatic command through the influence of Assistant Secretary of the Navy Theodore Roosevelt, Commodore George Dewey thoroughly fitted out at Hong Kong his four cruisers, *Olympia* (flagship), *Baltimore, Boston* and *Raleigh* (6000–3000 tons), and the gunboats *Concord* and *Petrel*. Upon the declaration of war with Spain he received orders to attack Admiral Montojo's fleet at Manila—"You must capture vessels or destroy." On April 30 Dewey was outside Manila Bay and entered safely at midnight, disregarding serious risks from shore batteries and mines. Off Manila at dawn, he sighted Montojo's force ten miles westward under the guns of Cavite dockyard. It consisted of some ten small, wretchedly equipped cruisers and gunboats, mounting not one third the American broadside. At 5:41 A.M. Dewey opened fire, swinging his column in long ovals past the enemy ships at 5000–2000 yards' range. On a mistaken report of ammunition shortage he withdrew at 7:35, but renewed action at 11:16 and ended it an hour later, when the shore batteries were silenced and every Spanish ship, to quote Dewey's report, "was sunk, burned, or deserted." The Spanish suffered 381 casualties, the Americans but nine slightly wounded. Manila was blockaded, and surrendered Aug. 13 after merely formal bombardment. For his easily won victory Dewey's promotion to full admiral (1899) was high reward, yet justified by his prompt, resolute movements, and correct discounting of the dangers in entering enemy waters defended by mines and heavy guns on shore.

MANITOU is an Algonkin Indian word of uncertain meaning, but used with reference to supernatural beings or gods, or to a quality or power of an animistic kind which may reside within any specified object, temporarily or permanently. Manabus, Nanabozho, etc., is a supernatural hero in Algonkin mythology, or the chief manitou. The term Kitchi Manito is often used for Great Spirit.

MANORS were self-sufficient agricultural communities, embracing one or more villages or towns over which seignorial rights and privileges generally obtained and within which both independent farmers and servile tenants lived. At the time of colonial settlement the manor was the prevailing mode of agricultural life in the mother country, but the manorial lord was becoming more and more a country proprietor and less and less an administrative figure. It was owing to the desire of the country gentlemen to secure landholdings in the New World that the manorial system was established in the proprietary colonies, principally in New York, Maryland and South Carolina.

Under the Dutch regime in New Netherland numerous patroonships, virtually manors, were authorized, but only one, that of Rensselaerswyck, was successfully established. The early English governors of New York created numerous manors in Westchester, on Long Island and elsewhere, whose legal and political characteristics were feudal, and confirmed the manorial jurisdiction of Rensselaerswyck. The manorial jurisdiction, however, could not withstand the encroachments of town and county authority, although the manorial landlords, through their control of the sheriffs and the manorial or local courts, and through their influence in the provincial legislature, dominated for long the local government of the province. From the point of view of the tenants the chief grievances in the manor system were insecurity of tenure and perpetual rents. The tenants on the Van Rensselaerswyck manor agitated against their leasehold estates and perpetual rents, and the controversy was a burning one down into the 19th century.

In Maryland the proprietors set up the manorial system extensively, erecting some sixty manors in the 17th century, not including those which the proprietary and his relations laid out in 6000-acre tracts, each for his own use. The manors were divided more or less unevenly into demesne land reserved for the lord and freehold lands, both called plantations, where tobacco was cultivated.

Under the Fundamental Constitutions of Carolina of 1669 an aristocratic system of landholding was set up, two fifths of the land being granted to the hereditary nobility and three fifths to the manorial lords and the common freeholders. Seignories, baronies and manors were provided for, although no seignory or barony ever contained more than 12,000 acres, and there is no evidence available of any manor in the strict sense actually having been set up. In these large estates manorial jurisdiction such as found in Maryland and New York in the 17th century does not appear to have existed. Over a hundred proprietary manors were set up by Penn for his colony, but in no case does it appear that manorial jurisdiction was ever exercised.

MANUEL'S FORT (1807–11), first American outpost in the present Montana, was built by Manuel Lisa, St. Louis fur trader, at the junction of the Yellowstone and Big Horn Rivers in 1807, to serve as a trading post for Crow Indians and as headquarters of trapping brigades. Various trapping expeditions started from this post and explored the region. Most noted were two ventures of John Colter, who, traveling alone, explored what is now Yellowstone Park and first reported the geysers. He later explored a route to the three forks of the Missouri, where he narrowly escaped the Blackfeet Indians.

Hostility of the Blackfeet caused the abandonment of the fort, first in 1810, and finally in 1811. Trappers returning to the site after the War of 1812 found no remains of the fort. Later trading posts built at this location were headquarters for trappers who explored most of the present Wyoming.

MANUFACTURES, RESTRICTION OF, IN COLONIES. During the 17th century the colonies were regarded by Englishmen as sources of supplies, chiefly raw materials, which England did not produce herself. By the 18th century the plantations came to be prized as markets for English manufactured goods in addition to being reservoirs of raw materials. English manufacturers now felt that it was imperative to keep the colonies from manufacturing goods which they themselves could produce. For this reason, attempts were made in various ways to restrict the development of colonial manufactures. It was partly for this reason, also, as well as to free Great Britain from dependence on Baltic countries for naval stores and other supplies that a policy of granting bounties on such commodities was inaugurated in 1705.

Restrictions of colonial manufactures were attempted not only through the passage of laws, but also by administrative action. For instance, the Board of Trade in its inquiries and reports was constantly concerned with the problem. In its instructions to royal governors the Board frequently emphasized that the restriction of colonial manufacturing was one of the duties of governors, but in few cases were such instructions taken seriously. Another example can be seen in the action of the Privy Council, when in 1724 it ordered the colonists to refrain from imposing tariffs on English goods, thus discouraging colonial legislation which favored manufacturing.

The first important step in the direction of Parliamentary restriction of colonial manufactures was made in connection with the production of woolens. In 1699, at the demand of English woolen manufacturers, a law was passed which forbade the export of wool, raw or manufactured, from one colony to another "or to any other place whatsoever." The law was not prohibitory, for any colony could still manufacture woolen goods for consumption within its own borders.

Another colonial enterprise which became the subject of restrictive legislation was the beaver hat industry. An inquiry in 1731 disclosed that thousands of hats were being manufactured annually in the colonies, especially in New England and New York. The Hat Act of 1732 provided that no American-made hats could be exported from any colony, that no one could engage in hat making who had not served an apprenticeship of seven years, that no hat maker could have more than two apprentices, and that no Negroes should be employed in the industry. The Iron Act of 1750 prohibited in the colonies the further erection of slitting mills, steel furnaces and plating mills. However, it also encouraged the production of colonial pig iron and bar iron by relaxing the duties when imported into England.

The colonists, whenever they wished, disregarded all administrative measures and laws which restricted manufactures. The reason why manufacturing did not develop more rapidly in the colonies was due to other causes, such as the difficulty of securing skilled labor, poor transportation, the lack of capital, and competition from agriculture.

MANUFACTURING, EARLY. Most manufacturing in the United States was still in the handicraft stage when Washington became President. The only power-using plants were mills for making flour, lumber, paper and gunpowder and for grinding plaster. Establishments in the fuel-using industries were limited to charcoal furnaces and forges for working iron, kilns for making lime, tar and potash, distilleries, brickyards, and a few small glass works and potteries.

During the next quarter of a century, ending with the War of 1812, such enterprises increased in size and number. More significant, however, was the introduction of machine spinning and weaving, the erection of nearly 200 cotton mills in New England and the middle states and the use of steam to move machinery. Meanwhile a manufacturing interest, which had been vocal in a small way when the first Federal revenue laws were drafted in 1789, had acquired sufficient influence by 1816 to give a protectionist color to subsequent customs legislation.

Between the War of 1812 and the Civil War American manufacturing acquired its characteristic pattern. Faced by a scarcity of accumulated funds and entrepreneurial experience, its leaders adopted corporate organization as a device for assembling capital and economizing management. This was particularly true in New England. Funds came at first from the accumulations of merchants engaged in the European and Far Eastern trade. Later the investment reserves of insurance companies and other financial institutions were a source of capital. The mercantile origin of many factories accounted for the early appearance of the agency or factor system and through it of larger corporation groups.

During this period the growth of manufacturing was encouraged by a rapidly expanding market protected to some degree by tariffs, and held together by canals and steam transportation on land and water. Factories specialized in the quantity production of standardized goods to supply the multiplying demands of middle-class consumers. Native ingenuity and scarcity of labor stimulated the use of power devices. Yankee inventors designed textile machinery that enabled relatively inexperienced operatives to make cheaply and efficiently plain fabrics for common use. Americans developed interchangeable mechanism and its correlative, automatic machinery, for working wood and metals, in order to produce on a large scale and at low cost the tools, agricultural implements, household utensils, firearms, shelf clocks and vehicles demanded in ever larger quantities by the expanding population of the older settlements and the rapidly growing West. Simultaneously imperative traffic demands called into being shops and

foundries to build steamboat machinery and locomotives, and improved transportation hastened the urbanization of industry.

During these fifty years the advent of factory goods in place of household and homespun manufactures revolutionized consumption. Although in 1860 plain fabrics, hats, footwear, axes and nails, plowshares and hoes still dominated manufacturing output, refinements and modifications of these staples as well as new inventions and novelties already held a conspicuous position in the market. The production of machine-knit goods, collars and cuffs, garment accessories and silks had become important industries. Manufactures of rubber were familiar. Pressed glass and porcelain, plated metal wares, lamps and numerous minor conveniences turned out in quantities by machinery had ceased to be luxuries. Changing fashions increasingly determined consumer demand and the industries that served it.

Quantitative evidence of progress was even more imposing. Between 1810 and 1860, or within the memory of people still alive at the latter date, the number of factory cotton spindles in the country increased from a few hundred thousand to over 5,000,000, each doing far more work than its predecessors. Output of pig iron rose from less than 60,000 tons to nearly 1,000,000 tons. The factory system extended from textiles to the production of clocks and watches, firearms, sewing machines and other metal manufactures. In 1853 American methods of making interchangeable mechanism with automatic machinery had aroused European attention and were studied by special commissioners from Great Britain.

Meanwhile a division of labor developed along sectional lines so that by 1860 the northeastern states were engaged chiefly in mechanical production, the South in growing staple crops like cotton, and the West in producing and processing other raw materials and provisions.

MANUFACTURING SINCE THE CIVIL WAR. The outcome of the Civil War gave the industrial states control over Federal policies and inaugurated a period of high protection during which new branches of manufacture were brought to America from Europe. The discovery of petroleum, the introduction of Bessemer steel, the opening of new mines on Lake Superior and in the South, the growth of inland cities, and a great influx of immigrants from Europe combined to turn the nation's energy increasingly toward manufacturing and to move industries from older sites to centers near new sources of raw material and recently created markets. This phase of American manufacturing development was passing at the close of the century and ended by World War I.

Inventions and scientific discoveries multiplied at an accelerated rate as the industrial organism grew more complex. Some of these, suggested at first by an immediate need, later created new industries. In the 1840's, ten years after the advent of railways, the electric telegraph arrived to facilitate their operation. But a major electrical industry did not arise until forty years afterwards, when the incandescent lamp and alternating current changed illumination and power distribution and substituted electric power for shaft and belt transmission in large plants. In 1851 William Kelly, a Kentucky ironmaster, invented a rudimentary Bessemer-type process for steel which enabled him to make better boiler plates for steamboats. The perfected process came to America, however, nearly twenty years later, after heavier traffic made steel rails and bridges a necessity. Petroleum appeared at the opportune moment to provide lubricants for millions of machine-age bearings and subsequently suggested the development of internal combustion engines which made oil an indispensable source of power.

Public enthusiasm for industrial development was increased by a series of international expositions. Two years after the Crystal Palace Exhibition at London in 1851, where American manufacturers first exhibited their skill to Europe, a similar though smaller exhibition in New York testified to a national awakening on the subject. America was officially represented at the Paris Exposition of 1867 and at subsequent international fairs in Europe and learned much from this participation. At home the Centennial Exhibition at Philadelphia in 1876 for the first time enabled the public to compare in a systematic way foreign and domestic manufacturing attainments.

The economy continued the rapid rate of expansion of the pre-Civil War decades. By 1890 the United States had surpassed its nearest rivals, England and Germany, in the production of iron and steel, and was by almost any method of reckoning the leading industrial nation. Between 1869 and 1914 the number of wage earners engaged in manufacturing more than trebled. Meanwhile, however, the horsepower employed in factories increased nearly tenfold and the gross value of manufactured products rose from $3,400,000,000 to $24,200,000,000.

Before the turn of the century important manufacturing enterprises had begun to assemble under unified control all operations from extracting raw materials to marketing finished products. Along with this vertical integration occurred a horizontal grouping of plants engaged in similar processes of production but situated in different parts of the country under the ownership and direction of giant companies such as the United States Steel Corp. formed in 1901. This movement necessitated large-scale financing from a center like New York City and caused control over many big companies to pass from the large stockholders to investment bankers. Simultaneously management was entrusted increasingly to professional salaried administrators rather than to the chief owners. Although proprietary establishments and moderate-size corporations continued to grow in numbers, big companies dominated the highly capitalized industries and made big business a characteristic of American manufacturing.

During the 19th century most manufacturing consisted of processing or shaping materials with hand tools or power machinery. The development of new substances was a relatively minor part of industrial activity. The factory overshadowed the laboratory. Only in the 20th century was organized research, made possible in part by the concentration of industrial capital in great corporations, directed consciously and continuously to the discovery of processes and products hitherto unknown. As early as the Civil War, to be sure, when Abram Hewitt watched his furnace assays and introduced gun metal from Great Britain, research into the structure and qualities of metals and alloys began slowly to emancipate American metallurgy from rule of thumb limitations. A line of advance indicated by the requirements of the Bessemer process in the 1870's and of high-test armor plate in the 1880's, and the development of electrolytic processes and the commercial production of aluminum in the same decade eventually gave industry the metals that make airplanes and automobiles possible. Meanwhile, plastics such as celluloid film led to motion pictures, and development of synthetic fibers such as rayon greatly changed the textile industry. While the domestic dye industry was largely the result of interrupted trade with Germany in World War I, in general chemical processes were gaining greatly in importance. Up to 1940 continuously pursued research was largely confined to the electrical, chemical, rubber and power machinery industries; in other lines innovation came from outside, or by chance more than by design. World War II added aircraft and scientific instruments, over 60% supported by Government orders or grants, to the research oriented industries.

Research directed to the perfection of existing processes inevitably spawned ideas for new ones, and firms engaged in research tended to diversify their products. Large corporations also saw added security in product diversification, while high corporate taxes added an incentive to absorb companies with "carryover" tax losses regardless of the type of product. Thus rubber companies came to produce moving pictures, and chemical companies made scores of unrelated items. By the second quarter of the 20th century the control of production was so well understood that companies did not fear the problems of managing plants making strange products; the difficulties came in marketing. Here there were a number of failures by very big concerns that found that their dealer organizations educated for a particular purpose could not efficiently take on radically different tasks.

The unusual needs and taxes of World War II

increased the pace of diversification. Whereas in World War I the United States had been chiefly a supplier of raw materials and semi-finished goods, in World War II it became the chief source of finished military supplies. And these supplies took on a complexity never dreamed of before. The automobile industry converted to military products was the great mass supplier of motors and various assemblies. Wartime needs expanded small electronics operations into the manufacture of radar, computers and other devices that had continuing postwar importance. Meanwhile, Government-financed research penetrated some of the secrets of atomic fission and fusion and laid the base for atomic power in future decades. The development of rockets, confined in the United States to hand and traditional artillery weapons, was also to lead quickly to navigation in outer space. The war also raised real wages and thereby created a permanently larger consumer demand.

Outwardly, the most striking change in United States industry between 1940 and 1960 was its relocation. The break-up of large urban industrial complexes with their high land values and congestion of population had always been inherent in the use of electricity and motor transportation, but it only occurred rapidly after 1940 when massive Government and private investment led to the construction of new plants, and the underwriting of new housing. Electric power that could make the small plant as efficient as the large, and automobiles and trucks that could carry small shipments more cheaply than the railroads, opened the whole countryside to factory location. Typically, the movement of factories was from central cities to urban fringe areas, and plants that used highly skilled or middle income employees moved before those requiring large numbers of unskilled workers.

In spite of all of these changes in processes, products and location, the major types of United States industry remained about the same. In 1920, textiles and their products, primary metals industries, machinery and foods held the first four places in value added by manufacture; at mid-century, machinery was first, and textiles had dropped to third, behind primary metals, while food products remained fourth.

MAPS, COASTAL (1492–1900). Every phase of exploration and discovery in America is represented by one or more contemporary maps. Columbus plotted his course to the westward in 1492 either from Toscanelli's world map (1474) or from Martin Behaim's globe (1492). On his return to Spain with news of islands in the "Great Western Sea" between Europe and the Orient, Columbus drew a map of his discoveries. Only a copy, after the original, survives in the "Admiral's Map" (*ca.* 1507), first published in the 1513 edition of Ptolemy's *Geographia*. By the end of the 15th century several voyages had been completed, a series of explorations which probed the coastlines of both North and South America in an attempt to find a passage through the land barrier to the Orient. The mapping of America was a slow process, made slower by the unwillingness of navigators to exchange information and maps. In 1500 Juan de la Cosa, experienced navigator and pilot, compiled a large map of the world based on his own voyages across the Atlantic with Columbus and also Ojeda. On it he incorporated all he knew of the Spanish, Portuguese and English discoveries in America, including those of Vespucius and the Cabots. Two years later (1502), the discoveries of Corte-Real were outlined on a map drawn by Alberto Cantino. But only four maps are known which were actually printed between 1492 and 1510, so closely were new discoveries guarded in Spain and Portugal. And those four were printed in other countries. The earliest, by Giovanni Contarini (1506), was closely followed in 1507 by a globe and large wall map by Martin Waldseemüller. The globe gores of Waldseemüller were published with a text (*Cosmographiae Introductio*) which suggested for the first time that the New World be called America. The fourth printed map, by Johann Ruysch, appeared in 1508.

Two general theories became current regarding the size and shape of America. The first, propagated in a series of maps by Oronce Finé, whose heart-shaped world was published in 1531, assumed that America was joined to Asia, that by sailing far enough north or south along the Atlantic coast a passage would be discovered which would lead to Asia, lying not far beyond. Others believed that America was a continent beyond which, at some distance, lay the Orient. But just how far beyond, nobody knew. This second theory was championed by Waldseemüller, whose ideas were developed and extended in a long series of maps by Johannes de Stobnicza. After Magellan had circumnavigated South America in 1520, and Cortés had launched several expeditions in the Pacific Ocean, the western coast of America began to take shape. It was first drawn on a map in 1529, but there was no other good map of the coast until 1544, when one attributed to Sebastian Cabot was published, probably based on the *Padron Real* in Seville. This master chart, maintained under the supervision of the Casa de Contraction, was supposed to have added to it all new discoveries, as soon as they were made. Many inaccuracies crept into this chart, and many discoverers failed to report their findings. The first authentic map of the coast of California, undated, but based on the discoveries of Cortés in 1535, was followed by a map of the same region by Alonso de Santa Cruz (1542–45).

The latter half of the 16th century saw many map-publishing firms spring up in Europe. From them issued hundreds of maps of America and parts thereof, strange combinations of factual and legendary information. Two cartographic productions by Gerard Mercator (Krëmer) led to a revolution in the mapping of America. On his world map of 1538 and his globe of 1541, Mercator, though unfamiliar with the discoveries of Cortés, separated America from Asia and rejected the Asiatic names commonly found in the heart of the New World. Meanwhile, three manuscript maps were produced in the Dieppe school of cartography (1541–53), to which we owe our cartographic knowledge of the three voyages of Jacques Cartier along the northeast coast. These maps incorporated much that was new, including the discoveries of Giovanni Verrazzano (1524–28). With the publication of Gerard Mercator's large-scale chart of the world (1569), revised and improved by Edward Wright in 1655, the science of cartography came into its own, and mariners were able to navigate with a degree of certainty. Mercator's projection, in a modified form, is still in use today.

In the 17th century, three maps made by Capt. John Smith added to the knowledge of the Atlantic coast; these were a map of Virginia, 1608, a map of New England, 1614, and a general map of the Atlantic coast, 1624. Samuel Champlain's map of the northeast coast, published in his *Voyages*, 1613, represents the first attempt to lay down the latitudes and longitudes of the region, at the same time adding a great deal of information on the interior of the country. On the west coast, beginning with a map in the 1622 edition of Herrera, and later on the Briggs map of 1625, California was shown as an island. This erroneous idea persisted for many years, although not all cartographers subscribed to it. Chief among the notable maps of the west coast printed in the 17th century were those of Robert Dudley, an expatriated Englishman who explored the entire west coast. His large-scale map of the region was included in his atlas, the *Arcano Del Mare*, Florence, 1646–47. On this map he supplied the world with a precise and elaborate nomenclature for the west coast.

In the 18th century an elaborate survey of the Atlantic coast was projected by the British government. The work was begun in 1765 under the direction of Capt. Samuel Holland, who worked with a detail of men until 1772. At that time it was estimated that it would take five more years to complete the job. In 1774 Capt. J. F. W. Des Barres replaced Capt. Holland, and from that date until 1781 his charts were printed and published as they were completed. Later they were bound in various atlas formats and issued under the title *The Atlantic Neptune* (1774–81). On the west coast Capt. George Vancouver completed two years of surveying in 1792 and published his findings in three volumes (1798) including a valuable atlas, giving the world the first accurate maps of the region. Surveys of the Pacific coast were climaxed by Alexander von Humboldt and Aimé Bonpland, whose monumental works including many maps, published over a period of nearly fifty years, added greatly to our knowledge of the Northwest. The mapping of the United States by the Coast

Survey, a branch of the Federal Government, began in 1807; the field work of this agency has been practically uninterrupted since its inception. After the Civil War geodetic operations were added to the function of the Coast Survey, and in 1878 the name of the agency was changed to Coast and Geodetic Survey.

MAPS, INTERIOR (1600–1900). Early explorations along the coasts of North America established the New World as a potential source of wealth to European nations. France had visions of a large-scale trade with the Indians. England was interested in establishing colonies and growing silk. Rumors of mines of precious metals were inviting, but the great incentive for exploring and mapping the interior of North America was the probability of finding a northwest passage to the Orient. The early penetration of the interior by Europeans, led by the French, yielded information which stimulated further exploration. Foremost among 17th-century explorers and observers in America was Samuel (Sieur) de Champlain, whose voyages into the interior by way of the St. Lawrence Valley and the Great Lakes from 1603 to 1632 resulted in several important maps and valuable journals. Further intelligence on the St. Lawrence and Acadia was compiled on maps drawn by Marc Lescarbot (1609). Reports were brought in by adventurous *voyageurs* such as Etienne Brulé, who penetrated the interior beyond Lake Huron (1618?). Jean Nicolet explored and mapped the interior (1634–35) in the interests of the fur trade, as far west as Sault Ste. Marie, Green Bay and the Wisconsin River. As early as 1650 the five Great Lakes had been at least partially surveyed, and appeared for the first time on Sanson's map of that year. In 1673 Louis Jolliet and Father Marquette reached the Mississippi River. Jolliet's map of the river is probably the earliest survey based on actual knowledge. Daniel Greysolon DuLhut, a trader, explored the Sioux country beyond Lake Superior (1678–79) in the region of Mille Lacs, Minn. Jesuit and Recollect missionaries, devoted to the conversion of the Indians, introduced the compass and astrolabe into the interior; they drew maps and made detailed scientific reports on the physical features of the country and the inhabitants. The reports or *Relations* of the Jesuits (1632–73) are authentic, scholarly records of great value. In 1679 Jean Baptiste Louis Franquelin began to make maps of the French explorations in New France. These appeared between 1679 and 1684, when he climaxed his efforts on a great map which has been termed "the most remarkable of all the early maps of the interior of North America." Other cartographic records were made by the Baron Lahontan (1683) and by the Recollect missionary, Louis Hennepin, the same year. Westward exploration by the English, Dutch and Swedish settlers along the Atlantic seaboard was limited by the natural barrier of the Appalachian Mountains, and by the

French domination of the land beyond this barrier, as far west as the Mississippi River. However, many regional surveys and maps were made by colonial surveyors along the Atlantic seaboard during the 16th and 17th centuries. Two important surveys were made by Capt. John Smith: one of New England (1614) and one of Virginia (1608). The latter was improved and enlarged in 1673 by Augustin Herrman. Detailed maps of the various colonies were made to facilitate the settlement of disputes relative to overlapping boundary claims. Many of these maps were incorporated in the numerous geographical atlases then popular in Europe.

During the 18th century the mapping of the interior was advanced by several able cartographers of the French school. Foremost among these were Guillaume Delisle and Guillaume D'Anville. The former published numerous maps, but his great *Carte de la Louisiane*, 1718, was for many years the basis of all maps of the Mississippi River and the Far West. During the first half of the century maps of the coastal region, "The British Dominions in North America," were enlarged and improved by cartographers of the French, Dutch and English schools. Herman Moll (1729) produced the first postroad map of North America and in 1732 the first large-scale map of North America was published by Henry Popple, English cartographer. Three important maps published in 1755 had a pronounced effect on all later maps of the interior east of the Mississippi. The first was John Mitchell's map of the British and French dominions in North America. The second, by the colonial surveyor Lewis Evans, treated the "Middle British Colonies." The third, by Joshua Fry and Peter Jefferson, mapped in detail the extensive lands claimed by Virginia, as well as part of Maryland and Pennsylvania. The Treaty of Paris (1763) activated the further mapping of the French and British claims in the interior. The British territory established by the treaty was surveyed in great detail by army engineers and officers attached to regiments stationed in North America. Prominent among these men were Thomas Hutchins, Phillip Pittman, Bernard Romans, John Stuart and Joseph Purcell. Their maps received widespread attention in Europe, and remained standard throughout the 18th century. The American Revolution emphasized the need of detailed topographic maps of all parts of the "Theatre of War in North America," from Newfoundland to Florida. The colonies were resurveyed, and improved road maps were made. The search for the northwest passage went on sporadically; a few hardy explorers investigated the territory west of the Mississippi. Franciscan monks from Lower California, led by Silvestre Velez de Escalante and Francisco Domínguez (1776–77), journeyed through New Mexico, Colorado, Utah and Arizona, recording their observations of the country. After the Definitive Treaty of Peace (1783) between the United States and Great Britain resulting in the birth of the United States, American maps began to appear. In 1784 Abel Buell, Connecticut printer and type-founder, produced the first map of the United States printed in this country, based on all available surveys. Other important American maps of this period were McMurray's map of the United States, 1784, which outlined the ten Jeffersonian states proposed to be laid out northwest of the Ohio River, and John Fitch's map of the Northwest, 1785. The first series of maps of the individual states appeared in Carey's Atlas of 1795. Discoveries made by the members of the Hudson's Bay Company in the north were recorded on Aaron Arrowsmith's important map of the "Interior Parts of North America," 1795 *et seq.*

The purchase of Louisiana (1803) stimulated the surveying and mapping of the vast region beyond the Mississippi River. The expeditions made by Lewis and Clark (1804–6) resulted in the discovery of the first overland route to the Pacific. The military reconnaissances of Zebulon Pike (1805–7) resulted in valuable maps of Louisiana and New Spain. A group of enterprising fur-traders, headed by William Henry Ashley and Andrew Henry, launched several exploring expeditions which resulted in valuable contributions to the knowledge of the Far West. Under their direction Jedediah Smith made explorations between 1827 and 1829, and discovered a second overland route to the Pacific Ocean. Joseph C. Brown, leading a United States surveying expedition (1825–27), opened and mapped the Santa Fe Trail. The first good map of the river system between the Rockies and the Pacific was made by Capt. B. L. E. Bonneville on expeditions made between 1832 and 1836. The extensive surveys made by John Charles Frémont (1842–46) beyond the Rockies were incorporated on a map made by his cartographer, Charles Preuss, published in 1848. Capt. Bonneville was one of the first of a long list of military engineers, surveyors and geologists working in the field during the first half of the 19th century. Throughout this period, map publishers exerted themselves to keep up with the new discoveries made by explorers and surveyors. Among the more prominent publishers were Samuel Augustus Mitchell, John Melish, Henry Schenk Tanner and John Disturnell. In 1853 an act was passed by Congress which aimed to co-ordinate the various government mapping agencies in an effort to survey all possible railroad routes from the Mississippi River to the Pacific Ocean. Five routes were surveyed over a period of seven years. Four expeditions were in the field between 1867 and 1879, two directed by the Department of the Interior and two under the War Department, making familiar the names of Hayden, Powell, King and Wheeler, their leaders. Voluminous reports, accompanied by maps, gave a scientific analysis of the country, but the expense of the field work and publications made imperative further economy and co-ordination. It was to this end that the United States Geological Survey was inaugurated by an act of Congress on March 3, 1879. The agency has functioned continuously since that date.

MARBURY v. MADISON (1 Cranch 137) was decided by the Supreme Court on Feb. 24, 1803. The importance of the decision in American constitutional history lies chiefly in the position taken that the Court would declare unconstitutional and void acts of Congress in conflict with the Constitution. By this decision the doctrine of judicial review was firmly entrenched in the governmental system, and the position of the judiciary was strengthened in the balance of powers among the legislative, executive and judicial branches of the Government.

The case grew out of the attempt of William Marbury to compel James Madison, Secretary of State, to turn over to Marbury a commission as justice of the peace which had been made out to Marbury by Madison's predecessor in office. The Supreme Court had to decide whether it could and should issue a mandamus to compel the Secretary of State to act. Intimately involved were issues of contemporary politics. The appointments of Marbury and other Federalists to newly created offices had been made as the Federalist administration under John Adams retired to be succeeded by Republicans under the leadership of Thomas Jefferson. At the head of the Supreme Court was Chief Justice John Marshall, a staunch Federalist. Granting the writ of mandamus would therefore be regarded not merely as an exertion of judicial power upon the Executive, but of Federalist power upon Republican (Jeffersonian) party leadership as well. The customs of the Constitution were not yet well established, and it was not known whether the writ would be obeyed even if issued.

The opinion of the Supreme Court, written by the Chief Justice, began not with the constitutional question, the existence of which was not generally recognized, but with the question as to Marbury's right to the commission. He found that Marbury had such a right. Reasoning from accepted principles of government he concluded that the laws of the country must provide a remedy for the violation of a vested legal right, and that the writ of mandamus was the proper form of remedy. The remaining question was whether the Supreme Court could issue the writ. The power was not included among the grants of original jurisdiction made to the Supreme Court in the Constitution, but it was given by a section in the Judiciary Act of 1789, which had the effect of expanding the original jurisdiction of the Court beyond the group of powers enumerated in the Constitution. The Chief Justice argued that Congress could not expand the original jurisdiction of the Court. The act was therefore in conflict with the Constitution, and it became necessary to decide whether an act repugnant to the Constitution could become the law of the land. The Court answered in the negative. It held the statutory provision unconstitutional, and decided that the writ of mandamus could not issue from the Supreme Court.

Contemporary interest lay less in the doctrine of judicial review than in the political aspects of the case. The Chief Justice succeeded in condemning the acts of the Jefferson administration, and then, by a step which appeared superficially an act of judicial self-restraint, avoided a resulting decision which might have terminated in mutiny when it came to enforcement. It was only gradually that emphasis in appraisal of the case shifted to the topic of the power of the courts to invalidate Federal legislation deemed by them to be in conflict with the Constitution.

MARCY'S EXPLORING EXPEDITION of 1852 was ordered by the War Department for the purpose of exploring the Red River to its source. Capt. R. B. Marcy by reason of his previous exploration of the territory between Fort Smith (Ark.) and Santa Fe to determine the best route to California from the Mississippi, and his experience in exploring the Canadian and locating sites for forts in that region, was selected to command the expedition. His report, printed by Congress in 1853, disclosed that there were two main branches of Red River, whereas earlier treaties, including the one between Mexico and Texas, admitted but one. Between the two stretched valuable lands which were made the object of litigation between the United States and Texas in 1896. No survey of the Red to its source had been made before Marcy's expedition. In addition to mapping the country, Marcy brought back much valuable scientific information and wrote one of the most interesting reports of the Southwest which we possess.

MARIETTA, the first settlement made under the provision of the Ordinance of 1787, was settled on April 7, 1788, when 48 men under the leadership of Gen. Rufus Putnam of the Ohio Company of Associates concluded their journey from Massachusetts to the mouth of the Muskingum River in the present State of Ohio. It was at first named Adelphia, but on July 2, 1788, in honor of Queen Marie Antoinette of France, the name was changed to Marietta. The machinery of government in the Northwest Territory first functioned here, on the arrival of Gen. Arthur St. Clair, governor of the Territory, July 9, 1788.

MARINE CORPS, UNITED STATES. The U. S. Marine Corps dates from the resolution of the Continental Congress on Nov. 10, 1775, authorizing two battalions of Marines. Never larger than one battalion in actual strength, the Continental Marines served gallantly throughout the Revolution. They carried out the first American overseas expeditions in the raids on New Providence, Bahama Islands (1776, 1778). With Washington they fought in the Trenton-Princeton campaign (1776–77). They served on the Mississippi and with Clark in the West (1778–79) and were part of John Paul Jones's descent on Whitehaven, England (1779). They participated in the ill-fated Penobscot expedition (1779) and in the defense of Charleston (1780). And they fought in most of the important sea battles of the war from the Alfred v. Glasgow (1776) to the Alliance v. Sybil (1783). Not to be mistaken for Continental Marines were the many Marines in the various state navies of the revolutionary era.

After independence was won, the Marines, like the rest of the Continental forces except for one minuscule Army unit, went out of existence. During the trouble with Algerian pirates in 1794, Marines were authorized by Congress to complement the small naval force contemplated at the time. When the crisis passed without war, however, naval construction was cut back to such an extent that Marines were not required. Marines were not actually recruited until the revival of the Navy in 1797 during the controversy with France over American neutrality at sea. After the separation of the Navy from the War Department in April, 1798, the Marines already in service, as well as those to be raised thereafter, were brought into one corps by the act of July 11, 1798.

During the "quasi-war" resulting from the diplomatic impasse with France, the Marines fought in all the major sea actions, as well as the innumerable encounters with privateers and pirates in the West Indies. They also carried out landings on Curaçao (1800) and at Puerto Plata, Santo Domingo (1800), and guarded French prisoners of war in the United States.

In the War with Tripoli commencing in 1801 Marines took part in the naval engagements in the Mediterranean and in the blockade of Tripoli City. The only land campaign of the war, the capture of Derna (1805), was carried out by Marines after an overland march from Egypt. Decatur's brief expedition against Algiers in 1815 again took Marines to the Barbary Coast.

In the War of 1812, the Marines fought in every major naval engagement, including the Battle of Lake Erie. On land they are best remembered for the attack on Fort George, the defense of Sackets Harbor, N. Y., and Norfolk, Va., (1813), and the Battles of Bladensburg (1814) and New Orleans (1815).

General lawlessness in the Caribbean and the Gulf of Mexico growing out of the collapse of the Spanish Empire led to many naval encounters with pirates and revolutionaries in the second and third decades of the 19th century. Marine landings against pirate strongholds were made at Grand Barataria (1814), Amelia Island (1817), Port-au-Prince, Haiti (1817, 1821), and Fajardo, Puerto Rico (1824). On the other side of the world, plundering of American merchantmen in the East Indies led to Marine landings in Sumatra in 1832, 1838, and 1839. Under the provisions of the act of June 30, 1834, which enlarged the land warfare responsibilities of the Marine Corps, Marines commenced in 1836 a seven-year land campaign against the Creek and Seminole Indians in Georgia and Florida in conjunction with the Army. Marines were also active with the "Mosquito Fleet" which the Navy sent into the Everglades during the war.

Marines with the Wilkes Exploring Expedition (1838–42) made several landings in the Fiji, Samoan, and Gilbert island groups to pacify hostile inhabitants or redress injuries to American merchant seamen. Attacks on merchant vessels by coastal tribes took Marines ashore in West Africa several times in 1843. The Marines got their first acquaintance with China in 1844 when they landed at Canton during an anti-American riot.

Marines served in both theatres of operations in the Mexican War. In eastern Mexico they supported Taylor's advance to the Rio Grande by the landing at Point Isabel and the Burrita expedition (May, 1846). A provisional regiment of Marines formed part of Scott's army moving on Mexico City and provided shock troops in the assault on Chapultepec (September, 1847). From their duty as guards for the National Palace in Mexico City the Marines added the sobriquet of "the Halls of Montezuma" to "the shores of Tripoli" earned some forty years before. In the West, Marines made the landings which initially secured the coast of California (July–August, 1846), fought ashore in the reconquest of the interior (December, 1846–January, 1847), and occupied several towns in Lower California (March, 1847–May, 1848).

A number of landings in support of American commerce were carried out by Marines in the 1850's, the most important being the reduction of the Barrier Forts at Canton, China (November, 1856). A formidable Marine guard accompanied Perry's mission to Japan in 1853–54. In the United States, Marines were the only regular troops involved in the capture of John Brown at Harpers Ferry, Va. (October, 1859).

Although their part in the Civil War was comparatively minor, Marines were among the first United States troops to feel the impact of the coming conflict, when the barracks at Pensacola, Fla., and Norfolk, Va., were compelled to surrender to local forces (January, April, 1861). A Marine battalion fought in the first battle of Bull Run (July, 1861). Marines were aboard all major vessels of the blockading fleets, and a Marine battalion serving in Admiral DuPont's Squadron (October, 1861–March, 1862) carried out a number of armed reconnaissances along the South Atlantic coast. Other operations of the war in which Marines took part were the landing at Hatteras Inlet, N. C., (August, 1861); the attacks by the *Virginia* on the *Cumberland* and *Congress* (March, 1862); the Battle of Drewry's Bluff, Va., (May, 1862); the siege of Charleston, S. C., (1863–1864); suppression of the New York Draft Riots (July, 1863); the defense of Gunpowder Bridge, Md., (July, 1864); the Battle of Mobile Bay (August, 1864); the expedition up Broad River, S. C., (November–December, 1864); and the capture of Ft. Fisher, N. C., (January, 1865).

In the 33 years of peace following the Civil War, the Marines saw action on foreign soil some 32 times, most memorably in the assault on the Yom River Forts in Korea (June, 1871) and on the Isthmus of Panama (March–May, 1885). Establishment of formal Marine guards for American diplomatic posts also dates from this era.

At Guantanamo Bay, Cuba, (June, 1898) Marines, for the first time in the Age of Steam, seized an advance base for naval operations. With the fleet, Marines manned secondary batteries in the Battles of Manila Bay and Santiago (May, July, 1898) and provided the landing parties which took possession of Guam (June, 1898) and various ports in Puerto Rico (July–August, 1898). Marines on occupation duty in the Philippines after the Spanish surrender were drawn immediately into the suppression of the insurrection attendant upon the American occupation (June, 1898–July, 1902). During the Boxer Rebellion, Marines defended the American Legation in Peking and formed part of the allied relief column which captured the Chinese capital (June–August, 1900).

Unrest in various parts of the world claimed the attention of Marines in the early years of the 20th century, particularly China (1900, 1905, 1911–13), the Isthmus of Panama (1901–4), Cuba (1906, 1912), Nicaragua (1912), and Mexico (1914). In 1915 and 1916, Marines began occupations of Santo Domingo and Haiti which were to last until 1924 and 1934, respectively.

A Marine regiment was in the first contingent of the A. E. F. to go overseas in World War I (June, 1917). On the western front, a Marine brigade stopped the last German drive on Paris at Belleau Wood (June, 1918) and fought in the battles of Soissons (July, 1918), St. Mihiel (September, 1918), Blanc Mont and St. Etienne (October, 1918), and the final Meuse-Argonne offensive (November, 1918). In the air, Marine aviators flew with the northern bombing group in Flanders and maintained an anti-submarine patrol out of the Azores. Marines served with the Army of Occupation in Germany until June, 1919.

Commencing in 1922 and extending to 1941, Marine units of varying sizes were maintained in China to protect American lives and property. Nicaragua, torn by internal strife, was the scene of a Marine occupation from 1927 through 1932. In the face of widespread banditry Marines guarded mail trains in the United States in 1921 and 1926.

Concentration on development of large-scale amphibious warfare during the 1930's amply fitted the Marine Corps for the task ahead in the Pacific in World War II. Before commitment to that area, however, there remained the occupation of Iceland by Marines from July, 1941 to March, 1942.

Rebounding from initial defeats in which their comrades on Wake and Guam, in China and the Philippines were overwhelmed (December, 1941–May, 1942), Marines opened the American offensive against Japan at Guadalcanal in August, 1942. Thence a succession of amphibious assaults carried the Marines forward to the threshold of the Japanese homeland: New Georgia (June, 1943), Vella Lavella (August, 1943), Treasury Island (October, 1943), Bougainville (November, 1943), Tarawa (November, 1943), New Britain (December, 1943), Kwajalein (January, 1944), Eniwetok (February, 1944), Saipan (June, 1944), Guam and Tinian (July, 1944), Peleliu (September, 1944), Iwo Jima (February, 1945), and Okinawa (April, 1945). Close air support for ground troops had been a Marine combat principle since the jungle fighting in Nicaragua. This concept was given full play by Marine aviation throughout World War II in support of both Marine and Army operations, the latter notably in the Philippines (October, 1944–July, 1945). After the war, Marines participated briefly in the occupation of Japan, but a sizable force was maintained in North China until July, 1947.

At the outbreak of the Korean War a Marine brigade, including an air group, was rushed from the United States (July, 1950) to aid in the defense of the Pusan perimeter. In September, 1950, a Marine amphibious assault took Inchon and captured Seoul, thus breaking the back of the enemy thrust into South Korea. Thereafter, one Marine division and one aircraft wing served continuously in Korea until the armistice (July, 1953). Because of the necessity of guarding the United Nations truce line, the last Marine ground troops were not withdrawn until March, 1955. Marine air units remained in Korea until July, 1956.

In October, 1956, Marines assisted in the evacuation of American and foreign nationals from Alexandria, Egypt, during the Suez War. Marines were the first troops into Lebanon during the United States intervention of July, 1958. On both occasions these Marines were drawn from units serving with the Sixth Fleet in the Mediterranean, an assignment dating from 1948.

"MARK TWAIN." On the old Mississippi River steamboats, the leadmen created a series of characteristic terms for the various markings on the leadline which were chanted as they called the soundings, thus: "quarter twain" indicating two and one-quarter fathoms; "mark twain," two fathoms or twelve feet. "Mark Twain" was first used as a *nom de plume* for newspaper articles by the old Mississippi River pilot, Isaiah Sellers. It was later adopted and made famous by Samuel L. Clemens.

MARQUE AND REPRISAL, LETTERS OF, are papers from a belligerent government authorizing privately owned vessels, commonly known as privateers, to engage in warfare against enemy commerce. The Constitution gives Congress power to

589

"grant letters of marque and reprisal, and make rules concerning captures on land and water." According to former practice, the legality of captures was decided in prize courts, and the profits went chiefly to the privateer owners, officers and crews. During our earlier wars, privateering was widely practiced and highly profitable. In the Revolution, letters of marque were issued by both Congress and state governments to 1150 vessels, and in the War of 1812 privateers numbering 515 captured about 1450 prizes. Among European nations privateering was abolished by the Declaration of Paris (1856). It was practiced only briefly by the South in the Civil War, and in subsequent wars commerce destroying has been limited to government-owned vessels.

MARQUETTE IRON RANGE is in upper Michigan near the midpoint on the south shore of Lake Superior. The oldest and largest mines are at Negaunee and Ishpeming, where iron was first discovered in the Lake Superior district, September, 1844, by United States land surveyors. The Jackson Mining Co. was incorporated in 1848, and others were soon established. There was in the district abundant wood for charcoal to weld the iron into blooms and smelt it in blast furnaces, and Lake Superior charcoal iron became a standard product in the American market until superseded by coke furnace iron produced in the lower lake region. In order to connect the ore with the Great Lakes transportation routes it was necessary to build first a road and then a railroad from mines to ports. The "Iron Mountain" railroad, built in 1857 to serve this range, was the first railroad in the Upper Peninsula. The known ore resources will last for many years.

MARSHALL PLAN is the popular name of the European Recovery Program (1948–52) which grew out of a proposal of Secretary of State George C. Marshall in a speech at Harvard University, June 5, 1947. Designed to revive European economy in order to provide political and social conditions in which free institutions could survive, the plan proposed that European countries take the initiative in assessing their resources and requirements in order to show what they could do to give effect to American economic aid.

Sixteen countries, led by Britain and France, established the Committee of European Economic Cooperation to outline a four-year recovery program. This was later replaced by a permanent Organization of European Economic Cooperation (O. E. E. C.) to which Western Germany was also ultimately admitted. The U. S. Congress in April, 1948, enacted legislation for a recovery program which was placed under the control of the Economic Cooperation Administration (E. C. A.), headed by Paul J. Hoffman. In an effort to restore agricultural and industrial production to prewar levels, create financial stability, promote economic co-operation, and expand exports, the United States in a four-year period appropriated some $12,000,000,000 (plus $1,150,000 for assistance on credit terms). This period saw great efforts made towards European reconstruction; the gross national product of western Europe rose 25% or 15% over prewar levels. The Soviet Union and its satellites refused to participate in the program.

MARTIAL LAW, in American procedure, is the exercise of control by a state or by the National Government over the civil population, through its military forces, after civil authority has shown itself ineffective in meeting the emergency. The term does not apply, though often employed, to the exercise of authority by a belligerent in enemy territory under the laws of war, as in Puerto Rico following American occupation of the island in 1898. A more common error in terminology appears in the frequent confusion of "military aid to the civil power" with martial law. The President may legally furnish aid, short of a declaration of martial law, to a state government whose authority has been impaired by domestic disturbances, and may move separately to protect United States property, with or without the consent of the states in which such property may be located. Correspondingly, the state executive may act on his own initiative in parallel situations.

An historical summary of the instances of actual martial law in the United States may be divided into three classes: first, where the President of the United States promulgated the declaration *eo nomine*; second, where such proclamations issued from state executives; lastly, where military commanders on their own initiative invoked the law of necessity during an emergency, either in peace or war. There are but two instances of the first type: the presidential proclamations of Sept. 24, 1862, and July 5, 1864. The authority invoked under the latter led to the decision by the U. S. Supreme Court in the case of *Ex Parte Milligan* (1866). The court was unanimous in holding that the President and his military subordinates had violated the constitutional rights of the defendant, a citizen of Indiana, in denying trial by jury. The results of the case were summarized later by Charles Evans Hughes: "Outside the actual theater of war, and if, in a true sense, the administration of justice remains unobstructed, the right of the citizen to normal judicial procedure is secure." The Whisky Insurrection, in 1794, and President Cleveland's use of regular army troops in Chicago to prevent interference with the mails during the Pullman strike were not instances of actual martial law.

More frequent have been the declarations of martial law by state executives. Among the more notable instances was the Dorr Rebellion, which occurred in Rhode Island in 1842. It gave rise to a declaration of martial law by the state legislature, probably the one instance in our history of such an occurrence. In 1877 widespread strikes in fourteen states, from New York to Texas, caused conditions which state executives attempted to meet by the use of state military forces. Where such forces were inadequate, President Hayes dispatched Federal troops; but in all instances where it did not appear that state authorities had used all means at their disposal for the restoration of order, Federal troops were under orders only to protect United States property as in the Railroad Strike of 1877. Idaho in 1892 and again in 1899 was the scene of martial rule, declared by the governor during Coeur d'Alene Riots. Federal troops were used in each instance to support the civil authorities. Colorado went through three serious periods of domestic disturbance: 1903–4, 1913–15, 1927–28, and in each instance martial rule was established in the disaffected areas. In West Virginia, 1912–13, Gov. Glasscock declared the existence of a "state of war," and exercised war powers through military commissions and the state militia. Demobilization after World War I virtually stripped several states of armed forces, and in consequence regular army units were used to restore order in Gary, Ind. (1919), and in the West Virginia coal fields (1920–21).

An instance of the third class of martial law—when a military commander acts on his own initiative—occurred in December, 1814, when Andrew Jackson, facing the threat of a British attack against New Orleans, established martial law in that city and its vicinity. There were many cases of martial law in the zone of operations during the Civil War. A notable peacetime instance occurred when Gen. Funston, immediately following the San Francisco earthquake of April, 1906, declared himself martial-law ruler of the stricken community. Floods and other disasters have similarly impelled the nearest military commander to assume full control.

MARTIN v. HUNTER'S LESSEE (1 Wheaton 304, 1816) upheld the right of the U. S. Supreme Court to review the decisions of state courts, which right had been challenged by the Virginia court of appeals. The opinion of Justice Story (Chief Justice Marshall not participating because of personal connection with the litigation) held that the Supreme Court's jurisdiction depended upon the nature of the case rather than upon the court from which it was appealed, and that Congress could confer appellate jurisdiction upon the Supreme Court in all cases involving the laws, treaties and Constitution of the United States.

MARYLAND. The Province or Palatinate of Maryland was carved out of Virginia by virtue of the patent granted in 1632 by Charles I to George Calvert, Lord Baltimore. George died before the patent had passed the royal seal, so that the province was colonized under the direction of his eldest son, Cecil. On Nov. 22, 1633, the *Ark* and the *Dove* sailed from Cowes via the West Indies, the settlers landing on Maryland soil early in March, 1634. On March 25, a cross was erected at St. Clement's Island in the Potomac; and, two days later, permanent settlement was begun some twenty-odd miles down the river. Here the provincial government was proclaimed, an event of peculiar interest in that it marked the separation of church and state, whereby religious freedom was first established on the American continent. The first capital was named St. Mary's City. The province was granted by an Anglican monarch to a Roman Catholic subject; and while Lord Baltimore provided a refuge for coreligionists, he welcomed without distinction all who cared to unite in the enterprise.

From 1634 to 1649 governmental attention to religious differences was confined to penalties imposed upon those who sought to interfere with the practice of "security of conscience." In 1649, after the advent of a number of Virginia-exiled Puritans, the General Assembly passed an Act Concerning Religion. The first part of this act affirmed the principles of toleration previously practised but imposed penalties upon non-Trinitarians. This restriction was invoked in the trial of Jacob Lumbrozo, a Jew. Prosecution, however, was delayed and finally abandoned on the restoration of the Calvert regime subsequently to the Cromwell interregnum. The Act Concerning Religion has been described as the "Toleration Act," whereas it delimited the practice of religious freedom that had preceded its enactment.

Following his brother's instructions, Gov. Leonard Calvert was careful to initiate and maintain friendly relations with the nearby natives. Although Sir John Harvey paid Calvert a friendly visit in the first conference of American colonial governors, the people of Virginia resented the intrusion of a separate colony under Roman Catholic leaders, whom they associated with the church and government of Spain. Furthermore, William Claiborne, secretary of state for Virginia, had established a settlement at Kent Island. This planting, Claiborne declared, invalidated Calvert's charter covering land "hitherto uncultivated." Lord Baltimore had, however, the ear of the king, and Claiborne was dispossessed in 1638. In all controversies affecting the principles underlying the management of his province, Cecil Calvert showed a high degree of courage. In 1666–67 he defied the will of the autocratic Sir William Berkeley, governor of Virginia, who attempted to force Maryland into an agreement to limit tobacco production and fix prices. Again, in the matter of acquiring and holding land within the bounds of his grant, he long contended with members of the Society of Jesus until his position was vindicated by the General of the Order and at the Vatican.

Cecil Calvert died in 1675, so that he did not live to see the encroachments upon his domain by William Penn, whose claims for a proprietary province below the 40th parallel were unsuccessfully disputed by

Charles Calvert. Following the accession of William and Mary, Calvert was deprived of his political prerogatives. In 1694 the seat of government was removed from St. Mary's to Anne Arundel Towne (Annapolis), where King Williams School, now St. Johns College, was founded in 1701. Albeit William III had issued instructions "to permit freedom of conscience to all," the Anglican Church was established. Benedict Calvert renounced the Roman Catholic faith, and proprietary rights were restored to his son Charles in 1715.

While Maryland declared her independence and formulated a constitution in 1776, she did not become a member of the Confederation until 1781, when Virginia yielded her claims to the Northwest. Maryland adopted the Constitution on April 28, 1788.

"MARYLAND! MY MARYLAND!" was written by James Ryder Randall in April, 1861. Randall, a college professor in Louisiana but a native of Maryland and a strong Southern adherent, was inspired to write this famous poem when he heard that Massachusetts troops had been attacked as they passed through Baltimore. In the hope that this episode would swing Maryland to the Southern cause, Randall made his appeal to the people of his state in verses that, set to the music of the old German song, "O Tannenbaum," soon became one of the marching songs of the Confederate Army.

MASON AND DIXON LINE (1763–69) is the southern boundary line of Pennsylvania, and thereby the northern boundary line of Delaware, Maryland and a part of Virginia which is now West Virginia. It is best known historically as the dividing line between slavery and free soil in the period of history before the Civil War, but to some extent has remained the symbolic border line between North and South, both politically and socially.

The present Mason and Dixon Line was the final result of several highly involved colonial and state boundary disputes, at the bottom of which was the Maryland Charter of 1632, granting to the Calverts lands lying "under the fortieth degree of Northerly Latitude." Acute trouble arose with the grant and charter to William Penn in 1681, containing indefinite and even impossible clauses in regard to boundaries. The terms of the two charters were inconsistent and contradictory. A full century of dispute in regard to the southern boundary of Pennsylvania was the result. At first the trouble was between Pennsylvania and Maryland. Had all Pennsylvania claims been substantiated, Baltimore would have been included in Pennsylvania, and Maryland reduced to a narrow strip. Had all Maryland claims been established Philadelphia would have been within Maryland. There were conferences, appeals to the Privy Council, much correspondence, attempted occupation, temporary agree-

ments, all without permanent solution. The Maryland and Pennsylvania proprietors continued the quarrel until 1760, when an agreement was finally made, and under its terms, in 1763, two English surveyors, Charles Mason and Jeremiah Dixon, began the survey of the boundary line. Completed after four years' work, it was ratified by the Crown in 1769. In the meantime, Virginia contested the boundary west of Maryland in a dispute which lasted for many years and ended finally with the extension of the Mason and Dixon Line westward, a settlement not completed until 1784. Historically the line embodies a Pennsylvania boundary triumph.

MASONRY. Jonathan Belcher, governor of Massachusetts 1730–41, became a Freemason when in England in 1704, and on his return to Boston, was said to have been the only member of the order in the city. A lodge of Masons, supposed to have been British soldiers, met for a time in King's Chapel, Boston, in 1720. A Masonic lodge is believed to have assembled in Philadelphia as early as 1730. Benjamin Franklin, in his weekly newspaper published there, printed an alleged exposure of Masonry, written in England; but a year later he was initiated into a Masonic lodge. A Philadelphia member installed a lodge in Boston in 1733. Masonry died out in Philadelphia in 1738, but was revived by Franklin in 1749. Lodges appeared in other cities. George Washington was initiated at Fredericksburg, Va., in 1752; he took the oath of office as President upon his Masonic Bible, and in laying the cornerstone of the Capitol at Washington, he used a Masonic trowel. The participation thereafter of Masons in cornerstone layings was often strongly opposed by anti-Masonic factions. The first Scottish Rite lodge in America was installed at Albany in 1768. The first Grand Encampment of the Knights Templar of which there is record was in South Carolina in 1780. The first shaft on the site of the present Bunker Hill Monument was a memorial to Dr. Joseph Warren, a Grand Master of the order, who was killed in the Battle of Bunker Hill. The Masons donated this with its plot of ground to the Bunker Hill Monument Association, on condition that a model of the original structure be kept in the base of the newer one. Lafayette, a French Mason, laid the cornerstone of the great monument in 1824. At its dedication in 1842, Daniel Webster, the chief orator, made no reference to Masonry, to the indignation of members of the order. Anti-Masonic feeling was at its height then. John Quincy Adams was a bitter opponent. Henry Clay had joined the order in youth, but in later life practically disowned it. Strong feeling had been aroused in 1826 by the kidnapping and alleged slaying of one William Morgan of Batavia, N. Y., who had revealed Masonic secrets, and an anti-Masonic political party existed for some years thereafter. The feeling against secret orders died away in the later 19th century.

MASS PRODUCTION, in general practice, may be described as the application of machinery in simultaneous or successive operations to the manufacture of identical articles. Standardization of process and continuity of operation are two essentials and the corollaries are large, continuous and standardized markets. In this sense it is probably American in origin though its background is large-scale production (from which economists differentiate it sharply) which began in the English industrial revolution. As attention came to be concentrated on operation rather than organization—on efficient mechanization and close co-ordination of all contributory processes rather than mere departmentalism, specialization and division of labor—the influences are primarily American.

For the origin of the pattern of all mass production of machines, we must go far back to Eli Whitney who, in 1798, with jigs and machine processes of his own invention, introduced the interchangeable parts system in the manufacture of firearms. In mass production of goods other than machines, a great pioneer was Oliver Evans in the same period; his contribution was the combination of several different operations in the same machine and in the co-ordination of different machines in a continuous process.

Following Whitney's pattern, manufacture moved toward mass production through other firearms, notably the Colt revolver, through the sewing machine and farm machinery to the automobile in which true mass production may be seen at its highest degree of perfection. From Evans' card-making machine and flour mill, we may trace the steps toward mass production of hardware, shoes, ready-made clothing, food products and many other manufactures. In the late 19th century, new methods introduced by William Richard Jones in the steel industry and by the first efficiency engineer, Frederick Winslow Taylor, were further American steps, though mass production did not reach anything approaching its present stage of efficiency until the 20th century.

Probably Henry Ford contributed most to true mass production. In his design of multiple assembly lines leading into a final assembly line and in the co-ordination of men and machines, the simplification of processes and the reduction of work to a point where each man or machine unit in a long series performs a single specialized operation, he evolved what seems to the observer a miracle of timing and continuity. His cardinal principles are that the work must be brought to the man (in practice by conveyor belts); that no portion of the entire process must at any time be idle; and that all material shall be in constant transit. This last principle is carried to the point where there are no warehouses or static inventories in a Ford plant.

MASSACHUSETTS. *The Bay Company* (1629–84). The royal charter of 1629 confirmed to a group of mer-

chants and others land already granted to them, presumably, by the Council for New England in 1628, with power to trade and colonize in New England between the Merrimac and the Charles Rivers. Under the Council's patent the Massachusetts group had local powers of self-government, subject to the general government to be established by the Council over all New England. The royal charter removed Massachusetts from its position of dependence on the Council's general government and allowed the company to establish whatever government it chose for its colony, subject to no superior authority except that of the king. The company in its beginnings closely resembled other trading companies operating in the New World, but almost immediately after receiving its charter, it changed the emphasis of its interest from trade to religion. Puritan stockholders who considered prospects for religious and political reforms in England increasingly hopeless under Charles I, decided to migrate to New England with their families, possessions and the company charter. Some compromises concerning the business administration were made with the merchants remaining behind, but control of the enterprise for the future lay with those who left England in the Great Migration of 1630, and the government designed for the trading company in England became that of the colony of New England.

The charter of 1629 provided for the usual organs of government; governor, assistants, and General Court of the stockholders, but omitted the clause requiring the company to hold its business sessions in England. This omission made it possible for Puritan leaders among the stockholders to transfer the company with its charter to the colony in New England and to superimpose upon the colony the government designed for the company. By so doing they could use the power of the General Court to admit new members as a means of limiting the suffrage in the colony to those of their own religious faith and in a few years to transform the enterprise from a trading company existing for profit into a theocracy practically free from outside control. As a further safeguard, the assistants tried to govern the colony without the share of the General Court except in annual elections, but when this breach of charter terms was objected to, the General Court received back its legitimate authority. With the expansion of settlement, representative government evolved and the General Court came to be comprised of deputies from the towns, who sat with the governor and assistants until a bicameral court was established in 1644. Dissent within the theocracy resulted in the voluntary exile of the group which founded Connecticut, and the forced exile of Roger Williams and Anne Hutchinson, founders of Rhode Island towns.

The Council for New England under the leadership of its president, Sir Ferdinando Gorges, almost immediately charged that the charter had been surreptitiously obtained, and, aided by leading officials of government, including Archbishop Laud, began a campaign to have it annulled. In 1635 the Council surrendered its own charter and asked the king to regrant the land in eight charters to eight members of the Council, a process which would give to the new patentees an opportunity to inspect all previous grants for purposes of confirmation. It was expected that the Massachusetts charter would be caught in this net. The plan failed of its purpose because only one of the eight patents, that for Maine, passed the seals before the outbreak of the Puritan Revolution.

Massachusetts Bay Company remained neutral during the Puritan Revolution in England, but joined with Plymouth, Connecticut and New Haven in a defensive confederation in 1643, perhaps partly as a protection against being drawn into the struggle. Although the Massachusetts government considered itself an independent commonwealth after 1649, nevertheless when the monarchy was restored in 1660 the company recognized the relationship to the mother country which the charter defined. After the passing of the Navigation Acts, however, the leaders in the theocracy found it extremely difficult to be reconciled to the dependent position of the colony. Because they refused to accept many features of England's new colonial policy, they gradually incurred the displeasure of the Crown. The commission sent over in 1664 to conquer New Netherland was instructed also to visit the New England colonies and investigate conditions. The commission and others reported Massachusetts at error in many respects: coining money without authority, extending government over the region of Maine and New Hampshire at the north, restricting the suffrage to church members, denying freedom of worship to dissenters, and, most important of all, refusing to obey the Navigation Acts or to recognize Parliament's authority over them. The company avoided trouble for a while by a policy of procrastination and evasion, but in 1676 Edward Randolph was dispatched on another mission of investigation. His report was even more damning than that of the 1664 commission. At the king's demand the company sent over agents to negotiate some sort of compromise, but thereafter failed to fulfill the promises made by the agents. The Lords of Trade, exasperated by the long delays and the failure to accomplish results, finally recommended annulling the charter on the ground that the company had not lived up to its terms. Formal charges were made against the company and the charter withdrawn by *scire facias* proceedings in 1684, after which the company as a corporation ceased to exist. Its government, however, continued to function without legal status until the establishment of the Dominion of New England in 1686.

Although the company very early lost its character as a trading company, and became a theocracy, the charter itself was necessary to the maintenance of that theocracy because of the almost complete governmental control it gave to the company's General Court. Under that outer shell the colony developed a very close union of church and state, a theocracy more or less on the Calvin pattern. To maintain the purity of the religious ideals of the leaders, the very limited suffrage was necessary, as was the weeding out of dissenters, the control of the school system and the refusal to recognize the power of Parliament over them. Yet the colony was too weak to resist the authority of the mother country by force and therefore had to resort to strategy. The faith of the leaders in God's protection of them led them to believe that in a crisis He would come to their aid. It was this faith which made them dare to procrastinate and at times even to defy the mother country. If they had been more conciliatory they might have preserved the charter. As it was, their actions and attitude made England believe that no policy of colonial administration could ever be successful as long as the Massachusetts Bay theocracy existed. The only way to destroy it was to destroy the company through its charter.

Massachusetts as a Royal Colony (1684–1774). This new phase in the history of the colony may be considered as lasting from the annulment of its charter in 1684 to the revolutionary establishing of the Massachusetts Provincial Congress to administer government in 1774. The insistence of the Massachusetts leaders on a larger measure of independence than could be allowed at the time by the British authorities if they were to exert any imperial control had, in 1684, laid the colony prostrate. It now had no charter, and in 1686 a royal government was inaugurated provisionally with a native son, Joseph Dudley, as "president." He was soon replaced by Sir Edmund Andros who as royal governor of the Dominion of New England (including New York) greatly irritated the colonists by lack of tact and unwise laws, though not essentially tyrannical. When word came of the overthrow of the Stuarts in Britain Andros was imprisoned, and in 1691 the colony received a new charter, adding Maine and Plymouth to the former Massachusetts. Although it much diminished the power of the old theocratic party it was a reasonable instrument, and the colony was not harshly treated, though henceforth it would have a royal governor. The first under the new charter was Sir William Phips, a New England man who had unsuccessfully attacked Quebec in 1690, almost bankrupting the colony by a debt of £200,000.

It was the lowest period in the colony's history and the most sterile intellectually. In 1691–92 came the witchcraft delusion, but after the turn of the century Massachusetts began to take a larger share in the life of empire, and her troops played honorable parts in imperial expeditions against Jamaica, 1702, Canada, 1709–11, and Cartagena, 1740. The colony was also chiefly responsible for the capture of Louisburg in 1745, and the loss of the old charter was proving a benefit rather than a detriment to its life. It had got into serious financial difficulties with over-issues of paper money but the payment to it of £183,000, sterling, by England for its services in the Louisburg expedition enabled it to redeem about £2,000,000 of its depreciated currency, which greatly assisted its now rapid economic development. Thought had also become much more liberalized, including Harvard.

Commerce had expanded and during the French and Indian War there had been much smuggling and trading with the enemy. In 1756 England introduced a system of general search warrants (already authorized locally by the Massachusetts courts), against which James Otis made his famous speech opposing Writs of Assistance in 1761. The colonists were conscious of their growing wealth and power, and protested vigorously against the measures passed by Parliament after the peace of 1763, notably the Stamp Act. In especial, Samuel Adams, an extremely able agitator, organized resistance and manipulated public opinion. Building up his system of Committees of Correspondence, he probably did more than any other man in America to prevent any settlement with the mother country.

In 1768 British troops were stationed in Boston and on March 5, 1770, a clash occurred between them and citizens, of which latter five were killed. The mob, led by a halfbreed Negro, had been the aggressor, but the affair was skilfully employed to stir public emotion and was dubbed the "Boston Massacre." New laws as to trade had led to acts of violence and in 1773 the famous "Boston Tea Party" was staged. A band of Bostonians, slightly disguised as Indians, boarded a British ship and threw overboard the cargo of tea, estimated to be worth £15,-000. The repercussion of anger in England was immediate and Parliament closed the port of Boston to all trade. This Boston Port Bill went into effect June 1, 1774, and on that day the royal governor, Hutchinson, sailed for England, turning over the administration of the colony to the British commander in chief in America, Gen. Gage.

Meanwhile, there was mob violence in many parts of Massachusetts and government was rapidly breaking down. Members of the colonial council who lived in the country were hunted from their homes and forced to resign or take refuge with Gage in Boston. Gage canceled the writs for the autumn elections to the General Court, and the towns, claiming this to be illegal, elected representatives to a "Provincial Congress," which became the revolutionary government of the colony. The royal government had ended, and this may be taken as the close of the period, though Gage was still in Boston with his troops. Meanwhile, in wealth, population and influence, Massachusetts and Virginia had become the most important colonies in America, and were to take the lead in the struggle now to follow.

State of Massachusetts. The events which marked the end of Massachusetts as a royal colony presaged war, and in April, 1775, an effort of Gen. Gage to secure military stores of the colonists brought on the first battles at Lexington and Concord. On June 17 occurred that of Bunker Hill and the following month Washington arrived to take charge of the colonial forces with the resultant evacuation of Boston by the British and large numbers of Loyalist Bostonians. During the remainder of the war the tide of military operations flowed to other colonies though Massachusetts contributed liberally in men and money. On February 6, 1788, Massachusetts ratified the Constitution.

MATAMORAS EXPEDITION was an incident in the Texas Revolution. After the capture of San Antonio in December, 1835, many Texans wished to carry the war to Mexico by launching an expedition to seize Matamoras. The provisional government of Texas was divided over the plan; a violent quarrel between Gov. Smith and the council disorganized the military forces of Texas and wrecked the proposed expedition. Meanwhile, the rival commanders, Fannin and Johnson, who had been commissioned by the council to lead it, were left on the frontier where their forces were annihilated by the Mexicans early in 1836.

MAVERICK. In 1845 Samuel A. Maverick, lawyer in San Antonio, Texas, reluctantly took over 400 head of stock cattle on a $1200 debt. He kept them for eleven years under charge of a thriftless Negro and had fewer cattle than he started with. Neighbors had done most of the branding of the increase. They came to refer to any unbranded animal too old to suck and running at large as "one of Maverick's." The usage spread, the noun becoming common. After the Civil War there were hundreds of thousands of maverick cattle in Texas. Mavericking became an occupation that sometimes bordered on and often led to thieving, though any range man had—and yet has—a right to brand any maverick found on his range.

MAXIM GUN. Hiram S. Maxim (1840–1916), a native of Maine, invented the first automatic, quick-firing gun. He conceived the idea and made the first drawings while on a visit to Paris, and going thence to London, perfected the gun in 1884. It used a belt of cartridges, the first model firing more than ten times per second. Maxim manufactured automatic guns of various calibers (up to 12-pounders) for many governments, modifying them to suit the ideas of each. His guns' aid to Great Britain in winning the Egyptian campaigns of 1897–99 brought about his knighting in 1901. He had become a British subject several years before.

MAYFLOWER, a three-masted, double-decked, bark-rigged merchant ship of 180 tons, with a normal speed of 2½ miles per hour, Christopher Jones her master since 1608 and in 1620 quarter owner, was chartered in London to take the Pilgrims to America. They left Leyden, Holland, on July 31, 1620 (all dates are New Style), for Delfthaven, from where, the next day, they sailed for Southampton, England, aboard the *Speedwell,* a smaller but older craft which they had outfitted for the voyage to America. There they met the *Mayflower,* took on supplies for the voyage and the two ships sailed on Aug. 15, but put back into Dartmouth harbor about Aug. 23 because of the leaky condition of the *Speedwell.* They sailed again about Sept. 2, but the *Speedwell* continued unseaworthy and they were again forced to return, this time to Plymouth harbor, where the smaller ship was abandoned, some of the passengers returned to shore and 102 passengers and crew finally sailed on the *Mayflower* on Sept. 16, sighted Cape Cod on Nov. 19 and arrived in what is now the harbor of Provincetown, Cape Cod, on Nov. 21. Some time was spent in taking on wood and water, in mending their shallop and in exploring the bay and land, so that they did not reach the site of Plymouth until Dec. 21, 1620. The *Mayflower* followed the land-exploring party and sailed into Plymouth harbor on Dec. 26, where she remained until houses could be built for the new settlement. She finally sailed for England on April 5, 1621, reaching London safely. She was in the port of London again in 1624, after which her history is uncertain because of confusion with several other contemporary ships of the same name.

"MAYFLOWER COMPACT" was the agreement signed on Nov. 11, 1620, by the male passengers on the *Mayflower,* before coming ashore, that they would form a body politic and submit to the will of the majority in whatever regulations of government were agreed upon. Its purpose, according to Bradford, was to hold in check the restless spirits on board who had threatened to strike out for themselves when the Pilgrim leaders decided to land in New England instead of Virginia. The Pilgrims held a patent from the Virginia Company granting rights to the soil and to local self-government, but this patent was of no use after they began settlement in New England. The compact appears therefore to have been a voluntary agreement to establish a local government which, though having no legal status until a patent could be obtained from the Council for New England, would at least have the strength of common consent. Its significance lies rather in its similarity to later ideas of democratic government than in any new philosophy of popular government in the minds of its authors. Plymouth Colony, though never so completely theocratic as Massachusetts, nevertheless leaned more toward theocracy than toward democracy.

MAZZEI LETTER. A letter by Thomas Jefferson to Philip Mazzei, April 24, 1796, was published in translation at Florence, Jan. 1, 1797. Retranslated for the French *Moniteur,* it was republished in English for the *Minerva,* May 14, 1797. An attack upon Washington and the Federalists, it precipitated a permanent rupture between Washington and Jefferson.

McCARRAN ACT (June 27, 1952). This is America's basic immigration law. It revised all previous laws and regulations regarding immigration, naturalization and nationality, and brought them together into one comprehensive statute. The law retains the national-origin system of the Immigration Act of 1924 under which the United Kingdom, Germany and Ireland are allotted more than two thirds of the annual maximum quota of 154,657 persons (380 more than the previous maximum). The most significant changes effected by the law are: (1) It removes race as a bar to immigration and naturalization; thus, countries whose citizens were previously ineligible for naturalization are assigned annual quotas of not less than 100 persons. (This change was expected to have a favorable effect particularly on American relations with Far Eastern countries, which had bitterly resented the exclusion policy.) (2) It removes discriminations between sexes. (3) It gives preference to aliens with special skills needed in the United States. (4) It provides for more rigorous screening of aliens in order to eliminate security risks and subversives, and for broader grounds for the deportation of criminal aliens.

The law has aroused much opposition, mainly on the grounds that it discriminates in favor of northern and western European nations, and that its provisions for eliminating undesirable aliens are unduly harsh. It was passed over President Truman's veto.

McCARTHY-ARMY DISPUTE. On March 11, 1954, the Army charged Sen. Joseph McCarthy and members of his staff with improperly attempting to obtain preferential treatment for G. David Schine, an assistant of McCarthy's who had been drafted into the Army. McCarthy replied that the Army was seeking to interrupt his investigations of subversion at Fort Monmouth. Both charges and counter-charges were substantiated by the subsequent investigation by the Subcommittee on Investigations of the Senate Committee on Government Operations. But they were incidental to what proved to be the real though unintended object of the inquiry: the role McCarthy was to play in American politics. The hearings made it clear, if further proof was needed, that McCarthy had exerted an influence on almost every branch of government. That he was not to continue to do so was the eventual unspoken verdict arrived at not by the subcommittee but by the millions of Americans who from April to June watched the televised hearings. Chiefly as the result of the prodding of the Army counsel Joseph B. Welch, McCarthy's methods were revealed in rather an unfavorable light, and the Senator emerged from the investigation with his prestige and popularity considerably impaired. The Senate on Dec. 2, 1954, censured his conduct as "unbecoming a member of the United States Senate."

McCREA, JANE, MURDER OF (1777). Jane Mc-Crea of Fort Edward was seized by some Indians and accidentally shot when her captors were pursued by the colonials. She was scalped by an Indian in revenge for losing the reward given for white prisoners. This act contributed to Burgoyne's defeat, for the frontiersmen were greatly aroused and rallied to Gates' support. Many Indians deserted Burgoyne, angered by his orders to end murder and pillage, leaving the English without sufficient scouts or guides.

McCULLOCH v. MARYLAND (4 Wheaton 316) was decided by the U. S. Supreme Court on March 6, 1819. The immediate question involved was whether the State of Maryland could tax notes issued by the Baltimore branch of the Second Bank of the United States, which had been created pursuant to an act of Congress of April 10, 1816. The present-day importance of the case lies in Chief Justice Marshall's discussion and broad interpretation of the implied powers of Congress, and in the denial of the power of a state to tax an instrumentality of the Federal Government. The Bank of the United States was created as the successor to an institution of the same name which had gone out of existence in 1811. It was intended to aid in restoring stability to currency and credit after the chaos created by the War of 1812. The power which it exerted over state banks and a measure of looseness in its own operations resulted in jealousy and distrust which expressed themselves in hostile legislation in a number of states. The Maryland tax measure was one such piece of legislation. Similar measures were enacted in other states. The case was undoubtedly argued and decided with the situation as a whole in mind. William Pinkney, Daniel Webster and William Wirt argued for the bank, and Luther Martin, Joseph Hopkinson and Walter Jones for Maryland.

Chief Justice Marshall wrote the opinion for a unanimous court upholding the power of Congress to charter a bank as a government agency, and denying the power of a state to interfere with the agency by taxation. The establishment of a bank or the creation of a corporation was not listed in the Constitution as among the powers granted, but such an instrumentality might facilitate the exercise of powers which

were specifically granted. The Chief Justice measured the discretion of Congress in such matters as follows: "Let the end be legitimate, let it be within the scope of the constitution, and all means which are appropriate, which are plainly adapted to that end, which are not prohibited, but consist with the letter and spirit of the constitution, are constitutional."

The denial of state power to tax the notes of the bank was based on the argument that "the power to tax involves the power to destroy." This part of the decision became the parent of a long line of subsequent decisions dealing with the power of state and Federal governments to tax the instrumentalities of each other. Important issues remain unsettled, however, and still provide grounds for serious controversy.

McHENRY, FORT, built in 1799 on a small island in Baltimore harbor at the time of Franco-American difficulties, was named for James McHenry. After the burning of Washington a British fleet in Chesapeake Bay bombarded the fort (Sept. 13, 1814). A spectator, Francis Scott Key, who watched through the night, was moved to write a poem, "The Star-Spangled Banner." Subsequently the fort was used as a storage depot and an army headquarters post.

McINTOSH, FORT, TREATIES OF (January, 1785). After the second treaty of Fort Stanwix in 1784 it was thought desirable to extinguish the claims of western Indian tribes to some of the lands covered by the Iroquois cession. United States and Pennsylvania commissioners therefore met at Fort McIntosh with representatives of the Wyandot, Delaware, Chippewa and Ottawa Indians. By the treaty, signed Jan. 21, these tribes ceded much of what is now the State of Ohio and agreed to give hostages for the return of prisoners taken during the Revolution. By the Pennsylvania treaty, signed Jan. 25, the Wyandot and Delaware, for a consideration of goods worth $2000, deeded to Pennsylvania the lands previously claimed by them within the limits of that state. Many of the western Indians later repudiated these treaties, and stable peace in the region involved was not secured until the Treaty of Greenville.

McLOUGHLIN LAND CLAIM (1829–62). Dr. John McLoughlin, a chief factor of the Hudson's Bay Company, laid claim in 1829 to the land at the falls of the Willamette River where he later platted Oregon City. Because of disputed national possession until 1846 all land claims rested upon squatters' rights. As a nonresident, Dr. McLoughlin found his claim contested by a group of early settlers, which contest was settled by a compromise. Even after becoming a resident at Oregon City in 1846 his claim was disputed, and by the terms of the Federal law known as the Donation Land Law of 1850 a portion of McLoughlin's claim was given to a rival claimant, and the remainder, with its valuable water power rights, was given to the territory of Oregon for the benefit of a university. While this injustice was not corrected within McLoughlin's lifetime, the land claim was restored to his heirs by act of the state legislature in 1862.

McNAMARA CASE. Efforts of union labor to organize Los Angeles culminated Oct. 1, 1910, in the bombing of the plant of the *Times*, which had campaigned for an open shop. Twenty persons were killed, and the building demolished. Labor leaders claimed the explosion was due to escaping gas, but James B. McNamara, his brother, John J. McNamara, and Ortie McManigal, an accomplice, were arrested and charged with the crime. McManigal confessed, but the brothers pleaded "not guilty."

Following their arrest, the prisoners became symbols of labor's struggle against capital, and their trial a national issue. Employers' organizations supported the prosecution, while the American Federation of Labor issued an official appeal to the working class to stand by the McNamaras. Samuel Gompers visited the brothers and declared the trial a "frame-up." McNamara Defense Leagues raised a large fund, with which Clarence Darrow was hired as defense attorney.

The trial began on Oct. 11, 1911, coinciding with a heated political campaign in Los Angeles. It proceeded slowly, and was marked by the arrest of two of Darrow's agents on charges of jury-bribing. After asserted negotiations with the prosecution, the defense on Dec. 1 withdrew its pleas of "not guilty." James B. McNamara pleaded guilty to bombing the *Times*, and John J. McNamara to bombing the Llewellyn Iron Works, a Los Angeles concern. They were sentenced to life imprisonment and fifteen years respectively. Their confessions were a decided blow to the organized labor movement throughout the country.

McNARY-HAUGEN BILL had for its purpose the rehabilitation of American agriculture by raising the domestic prices of farm products. At the end of 1920, overexpansion of agricultural lands, the decline of foreign markets, the effects of the protective tariff, the burdens of debt and of taxation had created a serious agricultural depression. It grew steadily worse in the middle 1920's. The basic idea of the McNary-Haugen, or equalization-fee, plan was to segregate the amounts required for domestic consumption from the exportable surplus. The former were to be sold at the higher domestic price (world price plus the tariff), using the full advantage of the tariff rates on exportable farm products, and the latter at the world price. The difference between the higher domestic price and the world price, received for the surplus, was met by the farmers of each commodity, in the form of a tax or equalization fee. The legislation was before Congress from 1924 to 1928. It received power-

ful and united support from the agricultural interests in 1927 and in 1928, respectively, when it passed both houses, only to meet two vigorous vetoes by President Coolidge.

MEAT INSPECTION LAWS in the United States originated with the campaign for pure food legislation. After 1887 the publications of the Department of Agriculture, under the supervision of H. W. Wiley, did much to stimulate national and state interest. Spurred to action by the "embalmed beef" scandal at the time of the Spanish-American War, Congress passed in 1906 a comprehensive meat inspection statute. This act gave the Secretary of Agriculture, under the interstate commerce clause, power to inspect all meat and condemn such products as are "unsound, unhealthful, unwholesome, or otherwise unfit for human food." Although modified and amended, this enactment has remained the basis of activity by the Federal Government.

MECHANICSVILLE, BATTLE OF, sometimes called Beaver Dam Creek (June 26, 1862). Aware that McClellan (U.), endeavoring to contact McDowell's (U.) advance from Fredericksburg, had dangerously extended his right, consisting of Porter's 5th Corps, north of the Chickahominy, Lee (C.) determined to crush the exposed wing. Leaving 21,000 troops east of Richmond to contain the 75,000 of McClellan's center and left, he threw 36,000 across the Chickahominy toward Porter's front, east of Mechanicsville. Jackson (C.), marching from the Shenandoah Valley via Ashland with 18,500 troops, was to envelop the Federal flank. Five brigades of A. P. Hill's and Longstreet's divisions of Lee's army assaulted McCall's (U.) division, entrenched behind Beaver Dam Creek, and were severely repulsed. Jackson arrived too late to participate. During the night McCall withdrew and Porter concentrated behind Boatswain's Creek.

MECKLENBURG DECLARATION OF INDEPENDENCE (May 20, 1775). On April 30, 1819, the *Raleigh Register* printed what was purported to have been a document adopted by the citizens of Mecklenburg County, meeting at Charlotte, N. C., May 20, 1775, in which they declared themselves "a free and independent people, are and of right ought to be a sovereign and self-governing association under the control of no other power than that of our God and the General Government of Congress." This account was based on the recollections of old men, who insisted that there had been such a meeting and that the original records had been destroyed by fire in 1800. Jefferson denounced the document as "spurious," but its authenticity was not seriously questioned until 1847, when a copy of a Charleston newspaper of June 16, 1775, was found containing a full set of the Resolves adopted at Charlotte, May 31, 1775.

The available evidence leads one to believe that there was only one meeting. Confusion as to dates probably arose because of the old style and new style calendars. The Resolves of May 31 did not declare independence and they were drafted by the same men who claimed the authorship of the May 20 document, and who, after 1819, insisted that there was one meeting and one set of resolutions. Although the date May 20, 1775, is on the state seal and the state flag, most historians agree that the Mecklenburg Declaration of Independence is a "spurious document."

MECKLENBURG RESOLVES. On May 31, 1775, a committee of Mecklenburg County (North Carolina) citizens, meeting at Charlotte, drew up a set of twenty resolves, declaring "that all laws and commissions confirmed or derived from the authority of the King and Parliament are annulled and vacated and the former civil constitution of these colonies for the present wholly suspended." One resolve stated that the Provincial Congress of each colony under the direction of the Continental Congress was "invested with all legislative and executive powers within their respective Provinces and that no other legislative or executive power does or can exist at this time in any of these colonies." The committee proceeded to reorganize local government, elected county officials, provided for nine militia companies, and ordered these companies to provide themselves with proper arms and hold themselves in readiness to execute the commands of the Provincial Congress. Any person refusing to obey the Resolves was to be deemed "an enemy to his country." The Resolves were to be "in full force and virtue until instructions from the Provincial Congress shall provide otherwise or the legislative body of Great Britain resign its unjust and arbitrary pretensions with respect to America." This revolutionary document must not be confused with the so-called Mecklenburg Declaration of Independence of May 20, 1775, the authenticity of which has never been established.

MEDICINE AND SURGERY. For more than a century after the founding of the first settlements, no medical institutions appeared in the American colonies. Rural isolation and poverty delayed the transit of medical culture from Europe, and the English government (unlike the Spanish) made no effort to project a medical code overseas. Hence the colonies long possessed no medical schools, societies or hospitals. Most routine care was based on folk medicine, including that borrowed at times from the Indians, but families sought professional attention during serious illness.

Both men and women engaged in medical practice at will, often combining it with other pursuits. A few had had some European education, others were learned provincials (magistrates, clergymen), but most were trained at best by apprenticeship. London guild distinctions were not recognized, but in effect American "doctors" resembled the surgeon-apothecaries of provincial Britain—engaging in surgery and drug-selling as well as general practice. Only after about 1730 did increasing wealth enable a few Americans to secure M.D. degrees abroad and to return to the colonies as "physicians" in the London sense. Such men took the lead after 1750 in founding the earliest professional institutions.

Thus, Dr. Thomas Bond led in founding the Pennsylvania Hospital in Philadelphia in 1751 on English "voluntary" models; and Dr. John Morgan, with the Edinburgh faculty in mind, set up the first medical school in association with the College of Philadelphia (University of Pennsylvania) in 1765. Meantime, local professional groups were organized, and the first state medical society appeared in New Jersey in 1761. State legislatures provided after 1790 for licensing practitioners by societies or by state boards—either on the basis of examinations or by virtue of the possession of a medical degree. The first real journal, the *Medical Repository*, appeared in New York in 1797. Thus, by 1800, a beginning had been made in creating both institutions and a learned profession.

The scientific information available to practitioners before 1800 was very limited. Surgery, although improved by greater knowledge of anatomy, dealt chiefly with structural emergencies (fractures, amputations, superficial growths). Only two or three drugs were known to be "specifics" against particular diseases. Pathologic theory, indeed, gave little heed to particular diseases, emphasizing rather the state of the patient's "system" (feverish, bilious, etc.) which was treated by bleeding, sweating, purging, and by various drugs. Under the influence of teachings at Leyden and Edinburgh, such treatments were moderate until about 1790, but thereafter "heroic" practice was popularized by Dr. Benjamin Rush of Philadelphia on the basis of later Edinburgh doctrines. Rush and others were inspired by the Revolution to seek medical as well as political independence from Britain, and became convinced that American practice was the most effective in the world.

Health conditions, nevertheless, were very bad by modern standards. Average life expectancy at birth has been estimated for 1800 at only 35 years. Chronic infections (tuberculosis, malaria), as well as acute ("children's diseases," enteritis), were widespread and fatal. Most feared though not most destructive were sudden epidemics of smallpox and of yellow fever, which elicited legislation on quarantines and rudimentary sanitation. The chief American contribution made to medical knowledge before 1800 was the demonstration, by the Rev. Cotton Mather and Zabdiel Boylston at Boston in 1721, that inoculation with smallpox "virus" usually prevented serious attacks by that disease. Here was the beginning of modern preventive medicine.

After 1800, marked scientific advances were made in Europe. The so-called "Paris school" rejected all pathologic theories, viewed diseases as specific and as localized in the body parts, and sought to identify them by correlating clinical observations with autopsy findings. This program involved hospital research, in the course of which most old methods of treatment were found useless. American physicians, attracted to Paris between 1820 and 1850, brought these views back to medical schools and hospitals in the larger cities. But there was neither public nor private support for research which could not yet promise cures.

The view that diseases were localized did open up new vistas in surgery, since surgeons could repair or remove diseased parts. American surgeons revealed much ingenuity after about 1840, as in the gynecologic operations of Marion Sims of Mobile. A great obstacle to surgical advances was removed, moreover, when the dentist W. T. G. Morton demonstrated the possibilities of inhalation (ether) anesthesia at Boston in 1846. American dentists became outstanding by this time, and the transit of culture was reversed in this field when Europeans began to look to the United States for leadership.

While science advanced, however, professional conditions seemed to deteriorate. All practitioners now wanted the medical degrees which conferred the right to practice. State legislatures permitted practitioners to open easy, proprietary schools, and gave the same opportunity to medical sectarians (homeopaths, Thomsonians). By 1850, almost any man could become a "doctor" after a year's training. The "regular" physicians founded the American Medical Association (1847) in an effort to reform the schools, but that body accomplished little because of the mediocrity of its own membership. When the Civil War began in 1861, the military medical services were quite inadequate, and—as in previous wars—deaths from wounds were far exceeded by those caused by illness in the camps.

Reform of the medical schools, and thus of the profession, awaited further scientific advances. These came, at first largely in France and Germany (1850–1900), in terms of the cell theory in pathologic anatomy, the development of physiology (biochemistry, endocrinology), and the emergence of bacteriology. The latter revolutionized surgery by the introduction of antiseptic techniques and also made possible new preventive measures in public hygiene. American physicians flocked to German universities, 1870–1914, and brought this "modern medicine" back to their schools and hospitals. This medicine demanded research and better educational standards. Such leaders as William Osler and W. H. Welch of the new Johns Hopkins School (1893) promoted reform in medical colleges and in the profession at large. They were aided by two circumstances; (1) the fact that medicine could now promise prevention and cures, so that even the most "practical" of

peoples could appreciate its values; and, (2) that enough wealth was accumulating after 1875 to maintain the more expensive programs involved. The states soon co-operated by requiring all "M.D.'s" to pass board examinations in order to practice. Finally, supported by one of the Carnegie foundations, Abraham Flexner made in 1911 a national survey of medical schools which revealed conditions which could no longer be tolerated. Under public and legislative pressures, nearly all the weaker schools were closed by about 1920.

World War I brought an end to dependence on German medicine, but better schools and hospital facilities had assured independent achievements by that time. American surgery was already outstanding, as in the work of the Mayo brothers at Rochester, Minn. Other Americans had made major contributions to public hygiene, as in Walter Reed's demonstration of the insect vector of yellow fever (1900). Further contributions were made after 1930 toward the prevention or cure of malnutrition disease (pellagra), of pernicious anemia, and of endocrine disorders. World War II saw a rapid development of the new "wonder drugs" (the "sulphas" and antibiotics) and of new psychiatric methods introduced originally from Europe. By this time, more effective medical science —combined with rising standards of living—had brought about unprecedented improvements in the health of the people. As late as 1900, average life expectancy at birth had only been about 50 years, but by 1950 it was close to 65.

To some degree after 1930 and particularly after 1945, American medicine attained world leadership— as was evident by the number of Nobel prizes awarded in this country. Some critics hold that, despite this scientific pre-eminence, the United States has been socially backward in not providing medical care to the masses through such national health insurance as is provided in most European countries. The Federal Government has, nevertheless, taken an increasing interest in health conditions and is now the chief source of support in medical research.

MEEKER MASSACRE (1879). Because of his arbitrary ways, Agent N. S. Meeker of the Ute agency on White River, Colo., created so much ill will among the Indians that on Sept. 10, 1879, one of them assaulted him. He asked military aid and Maj. T. T. Thornburgh marched with 200 men, Sept. 24, from Fort Fred Steele, Wyo., bearing also orders to arrest Indians suspected of setting forest fires in the district. The Utes ambushed this detachment near Milk River, Sept. 29, killing Thornburgh and nine men and wounding 43 others. The survivors were besieged six days in hastily prepared barricades. Meanwhile, on Sept. 29, other Utes attacked the agency, thirty miles south of Milk River, killing Meeker and seven employees, and carrying away three women. Gen. Wesley Merritt relieved Thornburgh's men Oct. 5, the Utes disappearing. Through efforts of Ouray, Ute chief, who was absent deer hunting during the fights, further hostilities were averted and the three captured women released.

MEIGS, FORT, was built in 1813, on order of Gen. William Henry Harrison, on the south bank of the Maumee River opposite the present town of Maumee, Ohio, primarily as a general depot for supplies and a base of operations against Detroit and Canada. It was in the form of an irregular ellipse, with block-houses equipped with cannon. April 28 to May 9, 1813, it was besieged, unsuccessfully, by Gen. Proctor with a force of British, Canadians and Indians, aided by Tecumseh. During this siege Col. Dudley exceeded orders given him by Harrison, and, as a result, he and his men were ambushed and killed by the Indians.

MENNONITES. This religious body was founded in 1525 in Switzerland by Conrad Grebel, and in 1533–36 in Holland by Obbe Philips and Menno Simons, orthodox in theology, but advocating separation of church and state, nonresistance and renunciation of war, and mutual aid. It spread to South Germany (1650 f.). From Switzerland and South Germany about 5000 Mennonites went to eastern Pennsylvania 1683–1756, founding settlements in Bucks, Montgomery, Chester, Berks and Lancaster counties. A second emigration from the same regions (1815–60) brought about 3000 to Ohio, Indiana, Illinois, Iowa and Ontario. Their descendants constitute today the main body of the Mennonite Church, with about 71,000 baptized members in 1958, located chiefly in compact rural settlements in eastern Pennsylvania, the Shenandoah Valley of Virginia, east central and western Ohio, northern Indiana, central Illinois, eastern Iowa, eastern Nebraska and southern Ontario. There are a dozen other Mennonite bodies with an estimated total membership of about 100,000. The Amish Mennonites are represented chiefly by the so-called "Old Order Amish" with about 17,000 baptized members. From 1873 to 1880 about 10,000 South Russian-German Mennonites settled in the prairie states and Manitoba, and in 1923–25 about 20,000 more went to western Canada. American Mennonites have created outstanding rural communities by their industry, intelligence, solidarity, piety and simple living. In recent years there has been a tendency toward assimilation in their respective communities.

MENOMINEE IRON RANGE. About 85% of the iron produced in the United States comes from six iron ranges adjacent to Lake Superior. Three of these are in Michigan and three in Minnesota. Of these six ranges, the Menominee is the second to have been developed, the Marquette Range being the oldest. The Menominee Range is situated mainly in the valley of the Menominee River which lies on the boundary between the Upper Peninsula of Michigan and northern Wisconsin. That iron was located here seems to have been known before the Civil War, but mining dates from the 1870's. The Breen Mine was opened in 1872 and other locations were made soon thereafter, but active shipments had to await the construction of a branch of the Chicago and North Western Railroad from Powers on the main line of the Peninsular Division, which reached the district in 1877. The best outlet for the Range was at Escanaba on Bay De Noc of Lake Michigan, to which the North Western constructed a direct line. The Chicago, Milwaukee and St. Paul Railroad also penetrated the region and shipped ore over the Escanaba and Lake Superior line until it reached a pooling agreement for shipment over the North Western. Mines were opened at Vulcan, Norway, Iron Mountain and Iron River, and at Florence, Wis., from which eventually more than 180,000,000 tons of iron were shipped to the end of 1936. The most remarkable producer was the Chapin Mine at Iron Mountain which produced nearly 26,000,000 tons of iron ore from its opening in 1879 to its closing in 1934. Most of this ore reached Lake Michigan at Escanaba where ore docks were erected whence bulk freighters carried the ore to lower lake ports. A few well-integrated corporations operate the mines.

MERCANTILISM, as applied to the British colonies, did not follow the general theories of that doctrine very closely. It was always tempered by the fact that the colonies were self-governing subdivisions of the British Empire, inhabited by Englishmen. The mercantilist trading company was used to initiate the first colonies, but was soon abandoned for direct imperial control. This control took the form of many measures intended to regulate the trade, production and manufacture of both England and the colonies with the object of promoting the prosperity of all. These included the Navigation Acts by which the trade within the Empire was confined to English seamen and English ships. The word English in these and subsequent acts referred to nationality and not to residence, thus a merchant from Boston was just as English as was a resident of London.

Other phases of the Navigation Acts enumerated certain colonial products and required that they be shipped from their place of production to England, or to another British or colonial port, and not directly to a foreign country. Asiatic goods and European manufactured goods were in turn required to reach the colonies only by way of England. This program permitted the profits from colonial trade and commerce to center in England, promoted English shipping, and enabled the British government to support itself by taxing this trade as it flowed through England.

The colonies were chiefly producers of raw materials, homes for surplus British population, and markets for goods produced in the home country. Colonial manufacture for an export trade that competed with that of the home country was discouraged by prohibitive legislation: wool in 1699, hats in 1732, and wrought iron and steel in 1750. On the other hand, colonial production of articles needed within the Empire was encouraged. The sugar islands were given a practical monopoly of the colonial market for molasses (1733). Virginia and her neighbors were given a monopoly of the tobacco market in England by acts forbidding the growing of tobacco in England and by prohibitive tariffs on competing Spanish tobacco. Direct bounties, paid from the British treasury, were used to promote the colonial production of hemp, tar, pitch and other naval stores, and very large sums were paid out for this purpose between 1705 and 1774. Other colonial products that benefited from bounties were raw silk, masts, lumber and indigo. Payments from the British treasury on this account averaged more than £15,000 a year in the decade preceding the Revolution. Preferential tariffs gave colonial products favored treatment in the British markets. Colonial products like sugar and tobacco that were not needed for the British market were, on exportation, assisted by drawbacks of the import duties so that they reached their European markets burdened by a minimum of British taxes. Drawbacks were used to promote American colonial use of goods from the British colonies in Asia, as tea after 1767. The total export drawbacks paid out by Great Britain in an average year, as 1772, amounted to £2,214,508 in a total export trade valued at £16,159,412, nearly one third of which was exports to America. Exports from Scotland show a similar relationship. Thus colonial and foreign goods flowed through Great Britain to the colonies without too much burden.

The colonial markets were developed by favors instead of compulsion. The usual inducement was export bounties, especially in the case of British manufactures that had foreign competition. The chief articles so aided were cordage, gunpowder, linen, sail cloth, silk manufactures and refined sugar. The total payments by England alone averaged about £40,000 a year at the close of the colonial period, but amounted to more than £61,000 in 1771, according to treasury reports. In this way the British market was made attractive to colonial purchasers. Both England and the colonies profited from this 18th-century policy of enlightened mercantilism.

The opposition to mercantilism in its later stages came from free traders like Adam Smith, who admitted that the system worked, but insisted it was wrong in theory. It is difficult to find opposition to the system among Revolutionary Americans, so long as measures were purely regulatory and did not levy a tax upon the colonists. The system was specifically approved by the First Continental Congress in the Declaration of Rights of Oct. 14, 1774.

MERCHANT MARINE. The history of American shipping in the foreign trade has been spectacular, but not invariably profitable. There was marked activity, especially in New England, in the colonial period. The Revolution brought short-lived dislocations of trade; then, in the neutral trading during the long Anglo-French conflict, the merchant fleet quickly expanded and prospered until enmeshed in the War of 1812. Shortly after that, the New York sailing packets began to give American seamanship high prestige. The old merchant marine reached its peak between 1845 and 1855. This was followed by a long depressed period in which the American flag was virtually withdrawn from the distant sea lanes. After World War I, the United States returned to foreign trade with the largest merchant marine in the world.

Less familiar has been the less spectacular but steadier story of the long major role in the nation's transportation of the domestic "enrolled" shipping. The lack of adequate statistics comparable to the wealth of "commerce and navigation" figures for foreign trade, doubtless accounts for part of the failure to appreciate the full significance of the domestic merchant marine which, since 1817, has been protected by law from foreign competition. Many American coastal runs have been longer than many foreign ones in Europe. A voyage equivalent to the Boston-New Orleans passage, for instance, would carry a vessel from London on a "foreign" run to numerous nations in Western Europe. Until the early 20th century, a large share of the cargo movements in the Atlantic, Gulf, and Pacific coastal regions were seaborne; so, too, was a considerable part of the passenger traffic. The protection against foreign competition from foreign shipping was extended to the lengthy "intercoastal" routes between Atlantic and Pacific ports, whether by clippers around Cape Horn or, later, by steamships through the Panama Canal. Likewise protected in later days was commerce with the "noncontiguous" possessions: Alaska, Hawaii and Puerto Rico. In the meantime, steamboats on the Mississippi and other western waters, and barges on the Erie and other canals, handled a large amount of internal transportation from about 1820 to 1860, when the railroads began to take over. Then, in the second quarter of the 20th century, barge traffic on the inland waterways revived in vigorous fashion. The most consistently flourishing segment of domestic shipping has been the Great Lakes movement of ore, grain, and other heavy cargo in great ships specially designed for the purpose.

The New England colonists took to the sea almost at once. Their rocky acres were poor for farming, but they had a rich supply of oak and pine to build vessels that they could load with lumber and fish which could be swapped and reswapped until they got what they wanted. Much of that cargo went to the West Indies to be exchanged for sugar, molasses or rum; some went along the coast to get grain or flour; and some crossed the Atlantic. England's Navigation Laws, aimed at developing a self-sufficient empire, benefited them, for a vessel built and manned on Massachusetts Bay or Casco Bay counted as an English ship with an English crew; many of the cheaply built New England vessels, moreover, were sold to English owners. By 1700, Boston ranked third, after London and Bristol, among all English ports in the tonnage of its shipping. By 1730, Philadelphia passed it in commerce, but the New England coast remained the center of shipping activity.

After the Revolution, American vessels no longer enjoyed British registry, could not be sold in England, and were barred from the profitable and mutually-advantageous triangular trade with the British Caribbean sugar islands. On the other hand, American ships no longer had to buy all their return cargoes in Britain, and were free to trade with the Mediterranean, the Baltic, India and China. Salem, in particular, was quick to take advantage of this. The long Anglo-French wars, starting in 1793, put a premium on the neutral status of American-flag shipping, which could visit ports where the British or French belligerent flags would be vulnerable. At the risk of occasional capture and confiscation in this "heroic age" as they ran afoul of belligerent regulations, the Americans reaped a rich profit. Their registered tonnage rose from 346,000 tons in 1790 to 981,000 in 1810, while the combined exports and imports in those same years jumped from $43,000,000 to $152,000,000, about 90% of which was carried in American bottoms. Eventually, the American Embargo and Nonintercourse Acts hurt the trade, while the British blockade during the War of 1812 eventually almost cut off the United States from the sea. The difficulty in bringing Southern cotton and other products overland to New York and New England during the blockade was to illustrate the importance of the normal coastwise trade.

In the fairly quiet period between 1815 and 1845, the two principal developments were the rapid expansion of steam navigation and the performance of the transatlantic sailing packets. Though there were numerous early American, British, and French experiments in steam, successful steam navigation is normally dated from the voyage of Robert Fulton's *Clermont* up the Hudson River from New York to Albany and back in 1807. New York quickly utilized the sheltered waters of Long Island Sound as a steam approach to New England, while other local uses of steam for ferries and tugs developed. The ability of steamboats to ascend the Mississippi and its tributaries quickly revolutionized and promoted traffic on the western waters. On the longer ocean runs, however, the early engines required so much coal, in contrast to wind which was free, that steam did not pay. The pioneer ocean crossing of the auxiliary steamer *Savannah* (1819) was not a success.

Permanent transatlantic steam navigation dates from 1838 when two British steamships, the *Sirius* and *Great Western,* arrived at New York the same day. In the meantime, the American sailing packets from New York to Liverpool, London, and Havre had dominated the North Atlantic run since 1818. These "square riggers on schedule," sailing on specified dates with passengers, mail and fine freight, had demonstrated the value of regular line service, previously unknown.

By the 1840's, the Irish potato famine, Britain's repeal of her Corn Laws and Navigation Laws, and the discovery of gold in California were combining to bring the American merchant marine to its "golden age" in the early 1850's, almost equalling Britain's shipping in tonnage and surpassing it in quality. The starving Irish swarmed across the Atlantic in huge numbers, followed shortly by a large migration of Germans. The Yankee ships which brought them over could now, with the repeal of the Corn Laws, carry back American grain. The California gold rush led to the construction of large numbers of beautiful, fast clippers in which cargo capacity was sacrificed for speed, and also to the establishment of subsidized steamship lines converging from New York and San Francisco upon the Isthmus of Panama. The British example of subsidizing the mail steamers of Samuel Cunard led Congress to support steamship lines to Bremen and Havre. Finally, it gave even more generous support to Edward K. Collins for a line to Liverpool to "beat the Cunarders." For a while, he achieved that; his *Baltic's* speed won the "blue riband." But after that, speed led to the loss of two ships; Congress withdrew its support, and the line failed.

By the late 1850's a decline, which would lead to the long "Dark Ages" of the merchant marine, had already set in, accentuated by the Panic of 1857. The clipper craze had been overdone; it no longer paid to sacrifice one third of a vessel's cargo capacity for a few extra knots of speed. The building of square-rigged ships, which reached its peak in 1855, fell off sharply but the total tonnage registered for foreign trade was a trifle higher in 1860 than it had been in 1855—at 2,379,000 tons, a level which would not be equalled again until World War I. With the tonnage enrolled or licensed for domestic trade, however, it was a different matter. In 1860, at 2,974,000 tons, it was well ahead of the registered tonnage and would gradually increase. But the ocean-going shipping would suffer during the Civil War from the depredations of the *Alabama* and other British-built Confederate naval raiders. Actually, they caught barely one Northern ship in a hundred, but the panic they generated so raised war-risk insurance rates that shippers sought foreign flags which called for no such extra expense. Scores of the finest American square-riggers were consequently transferred to foreign registry and were not permitted to return afterwards. After the war, the shift of the nation's interest, and also its capital investment, from the sea to the opening of the West contributed to this decline.

Probably the basic cause of the decline in American oceangoing shipping stemmed from the upward surge in the use of steam. The development of the compound, reciprocating marine engine at last made it practicable to transport bulk cargoes such as coal, wheat and sugar by steamship rather than by sailing vessel; the opening of the Suez Canal in 1869 further accentuated the trend, for sailing ships had great difficulty in traversing it and the adjacent Red Sea. Steam gradually pushed sail off all except a few of the longest runs to Europe, such as grain from California, nitrates from Chile, jute from India, and wool and grain from Australia. The big American "Down Easter" square-riggers found employment on some of these runs for a while, but gradually were crowded out. The most important cause of the new difficulties, however, probably lay in the effect of the cost of steam and also iron or steel on shipbuilding. In the past, wooden vessels had been built more cheaply on this side of the Atlantic because of the ample supplies of ship timber close to the seaboard. Now Europe had that advantage of lower costs because of its iron deposits and technological advantages for manufacture.

Congress tried to stimulate American shipping with subsidies for lines to Brazil and the Far East and with the 1891 program for mail subsidies in general, but they accomplished little. The tonnage registered for foreign trade fell off from 2,379,000 in 1860 to 782,000 in 1910. Although the value of foreign commerce in that half century grew from $762,000,000 to $2,983,000,000, the share carried in American bottoms shrank from 66% to 8%.

With the protected domestic trade, it was a different story. From the 2,974,000 tons of enrolled and licensed shipping in 1860, it fell off slightly during the '60's and '70's but by 1890 it had climbed to 3,496,000 tons, continuing on to 6,726,000 by 1910, almost nine times the foreign trade total. Certain river, Great Lakes, and Long Island Sound steamers were of too specialized construction for oceangoing use, but between the major coastal ports some quite substantial and effective vessels performed regular cargo and passenger service, which long held its own against railroads parallel to the coast. Much of the coastal bulk cargo was still carried by sail, especially in the Northeast, in little two-masted schooners for lumber, granite, anthracite coal, and lime. Gradually, larger schooners came into use, with three- and four-masters carrying ice and Southern lumber. Eventually, big five- and six-masters competed with barges and later with steam colliers in carrying bituminous coal northward from Hampton Roads. Tankers began to carry Gulf petroleum up around Florida to ports "north of

Hatteras." On the West Coast, small "steam schooners" carried lumber southward to California, while big second-hand square-riggers brought the salmon catch down from Alaska. The sizable fishing fleet, operating chiefly out of Gloucester and other Northeast ports, consisted chiefly of two-masted schooners for fishing from rowed dories on the Grand Banks.

The experiences of World War I produced a drastic transformation in the American merchant marine, leading it once more back to the distant sea routes. On the eve of the war, some 92% of the nation's foreign commerce was carried by British, German and other ships which offered generally satisfactory service. When that was suddenly disrupted by the war in 1914, the United States suddenly realized how serious it was to lack shipping flying its own flag. This was especially brought home to the nation when South America, Africa, Asia and Australia suddenly offered rich opportunities for American exporters. American-owned vessels, which had been under foreign flags for reasons of economy, were now glad to be admitted to neutral registry under the American flag, while sailing vessels were to have their last chance for large-scale useful service in supplying those distant markets. In 1916, Congress established the U. S. Shipping Board, the first body specifically charged with supervision of the merchant marine.

The amazing expansion of American shipping resulted from the emergency building program undertaken in 1917 to offset the heavy Allied losses from Germany's unrestricted submarine warfare. The Shipping Board's ambitious program set up numerous new yards, the largest being at Hog Island just below Philadelphia. Much of this activity was continued after the war suddenly ended late in 1918. By 1921, the United States had overtaken Great Britain for first place among the world's merchant fleets; she had some 700 new large steel freighters and 575 smaller ones.

About a third of those new large ships found employment in a new "intercoastal" trade between the East and West coasts through the Panama Canal, opened in 1914, which cut the New York-San Francisco run from 13,122 to 5263 miles. It was now possible to carry steel, machinery and similar heavy cargo westward and to bring back lumber and canned goods at rates about one-third cheaper than by rail.

More permanent in national merchant marine policy, however, was the use of many of the other new freighters on Government-supported "essential trade routes" to all parts of the world. The wartime experience had shown how important it was to have regular service on certain runs to provide outlets for American exports and dependable sources of essential imports. At first, the new lines were operated directly for the Shipping Board, which absorbed the initial deficits, but as soon as they were on a paying basis, the ships were auctioned off at bargain rates to private operators who would agree to maintain regular service on their lines for a period of years. In 1929, the Jones-White Act provided generous grants, in the name of mail payments, to those approved lines which agreed to build new ships. The falling-off of trade during the depression which started that year left the shipping industry in difficulties, particularly because of competition against cheaper foreign costs of operation and construction.

To meet that situation, Congress in 1936 passed a Merchant Marine Act which would still be the basis of American shipping policy a quarter-century later. The former supervisory functions of the Shipping Board now passed to a Maritime Commission which in 1950 would give way to a Federal Maritime Board for policy and a Maritime Administration for operation. To enable American-flag vessels to compete with the foreigners, Congress established "operating-differential" and "construction-differential" subsidies which would meet the difference between American and foreign costs both in the operation and building of vessels.

The operating subsidies went only to lines approved for specific "essential trade routes"; there would usually be a dozen to fifteen such lines on thirty-odd routes from Atlantic, Gulf or Pacific ports. To avoid excessive profits in boom periods, the Government would "recapture" half of all profits in excess of 10%. About three quarters of the operating subsidies went to meet the difference in pay between American and foreign officers and crews. Aggressive action on the part of new maritime unions at just about that same 1936 date began to push American wages far ahead of foreign levels; the daily wage cost on a medium-sized American-flag freighter would rise from $141 in 1938 to $552 in 1948, and $1234 in 1960. (That final figure would be about four times as much as in the principal foreign merchant marines.) Consequently, unsubsidized vessels found it increasingly difficult to operate under the American flag, and large numbers of them shifted to the "flags of convenience" of Panama or Liberia. In 1960, the subsidized fleets, in order of size were: United States Lines, Lykes Brothers, Moore-McCormack, Grace Line, American President Lines, American Export Lines, Pacific Far East Lines, Farrell Lines, Mississippi Shipping Co. (Delta Lines), Oceanic Steamship Co., American Mail Lines, Gulf & South America Line, Prudential Steamship Co. and Bloomfield Steamship Co.

The construction-differential subsidies, designed to keep American shipyards going, absorbed up to half the cost of construction in foreign yards. Lines receiving operating-differential subsidies had to build in American yards, and certain other shipowners were also eligible. For replacement, as vessels approached the conventional 20-year age limit, the Maritime Commission developed several standard types of freighters designated as "C" for "cargo"—especially the "C-2" and "C-3."

During World War II, the subsidized merchant marine fully demonstrated its high value, through its adequate ships, trained mariners, overseas contacts, and operational skill, which did much to provide logistical support for the far-flung military operations across the Atlantic and Pacific. Once again the Government undertook a tremendous emergency building program which produced 5777 vessels, about half of them slow, capacious "Liberty ships."

The foreign services on the essential trade routes continued on a fairly successful basis after the war, and some of the other shipping also benefited by the congressional "50-50" stipulation that at least half of the cargo sent abroad in the various foreign-aid programs must be carried in American-flag vessels. Domestic shipping, however, fell off sharply in the coastal and intercoastal trades. Part of this was blamed by the shipping industry on the "railroad-minded" Interstate Commerce Commission which in 1940 was given control of all transportation rates. Part of the trouble also arose from the still mounting wages of mariners and longshoremen, and also from the competition of trucks. Efforts were made to combat the stevedoring costs by "containerization," with truck bodies, railroad freight cars or other preloaded containers carried aboard ship. Barge traffic on inland waterways, on the other hand, gained heavily during the middle years of the century, while the Great Lakes traffic, stimulated by the St. Lawrence Seaway, likewise flourished. In 1959, the shipping in domestic trade, at 13,284,000 gross tons, was almost equal to the 15,000,000 tons in foreign trade.

MERIT SYSTEM is the method of recruiting personnel on an open, competitive basis. Though frequently so used, it is not synonymous with the term Civil Service, since the latter applies to the entire civil personnel no matter how recruited. Thus the Federal Government has had a Civil Service from its origin in 1789, but did not have a merit system until 1883 when the Pendleton Act was passed.

MERRY MOUNT, or Mount Wollaston, in Quincy, Mass., was the site of an early conflict between the public interest and commercial greed. About 1625 one Thomas Morton, Gent., established an Indian trading post there, and later added a Maypole, around which he and his men sported with the "lasses in beaver coats." Of the dozen settlements then scattered along the New England coast only that at Plymouth would have objected to the customary May Day promiscuity which Morton, according to his own story, gleefully introduced, and Plymouth was too busy trying to get out of debt; but the combination of neglected Indian husbands, liquor and gunpowder was recognized as a public menace. Every settlement from Maine to Nantasket (none of them Puritan) complained. Plymouth, being near by, was asked by the others to suppress Morton. Twice the Pilgrims protested to him that he was endangering the common safety, but each time he insisted that he would "trade peeces [guns] with the Indeans in despite of all." As a result, Miles Standish was sent in June, 1628, to arrest him in the king's name. Fortunately Morton's crew was so drunk that the only bloodshed came from one of his men who ran his nose onto a sword. Morton was sent off to England, whence he returned shortly to set up the Maypole again and resume his practices. The Massachusetts Bay Colony having been founded in the interval, it was Gov. Endecott who cut down the pole this time. The Puritans offered to take Morton into the fur-trading monopoly, but he refused because its methods were less profitable than his practice of getting the Indians drunk before trading. So he was again shipped off to England, where he got revenge by writing his amusing *New England Canaan,* the first of the attacks on the New Englanders.

MERRYMAN CASE (1861) involved President Lincoln's exercise of extraordinary war powers, specifically his right to suspend habeas corpus. John Merryman, a Baltimore County secessionist, was imprisoned in Fort McHenry by military order, May 25, 1861. The commanding officer refused to comply with a writ of habeas corpus issued by Chief Justice Roger B. Taney, on the grounds that he had been authorized by the President to suspend the writ. Taney wrote an opinion, widely denounced in the North, that it could be suspended constitutionally only by Congress, not by the President. Lincoln, however, did not alter his policy.

MESA VERDE, PREHISTORIC RUINS OF. In the southwest corner of Colorado stands Mesa Verde National Park, created in 1906 to preserve the ruins known as the "cliff dwellings." Not all the remains of cliff dwellings are found in Colorado; many have been located in the adjacent parts of New Mexico, Arizona and Utah. But the most extensive and best preserved, particularly the communal houses, lie in the canyon walls of this sloping plateau. There are hundreds of ruins scattered through these canyons, among the most important being Spruce Tree House, Cliff Palace, Balcony House and Sun Temple. The builders were a race of Indians, supposedly the predecessors of the present Pueblos. For purposes of defense, they constructed their communal houses in recesses high up on the sides of precipices, the dwellings and temples being composed of stone, clay and supporting poles. The cliff dwellers flourished in the 11th and 12th centuries, and it is supposed that they were forced to abandon the mesa canyons by a severe drought which came upon the land in the year 1276.

MESABI IRON RANGE of Minnesota became of economic importance with the discovery of workable iron ore in November, 1890, though references to the region occur as early as 1810. Over 4000 tons of ore were shipped from the district in 1892; railroads reached the deposits the following year; and ten years later the output had increased to over 13,000,000 tons annually. Steam shovels were used for mining the ore almost from the beginning, and in 1916 the output from the district was over 40,000,000 tons. The Merritt brothers, who discovered the first ore, early secured the financial participation of John D. Rockefeller in a program of opening mines and building railroads and ore docks. Following the panic of 1893 the properties fell into Rockefeller's hands, and were later sold to Andrew Carnegie and his associates, who subsequently merged them, as the Oliver Iron Mining Co., into the U. S. Steel Corp. Various other mining companies have since operated in the region, which is the most important iron-ore producing district of the world. The Hull-Rust-Mahoning-Susquehanna pit is the largest surface excavation made by man.

MESAS (Spanish for table) are flat-topped areas of land with bluffy walls, sometimes hundreds of feet high, standing above eroded terrain. A mesa may comprise an acre or a thousand acres. This geological formation is characteristic of the Southwest. Ácoma, the "city in the sky," is a noted example.

MESQUITE. This shrub characterizes the Southwest. Its astounding root system enables it to withstand the severest droughts and produce beans, which horses thrive on, cattle can exist on, and of which Indians and Mexicans make brew and bread. Its leaves afford browse, its trunks fence posts, its limbs and roots aromatic fuel. The more arid the land, the slimmer are its leaves—to avoid evaporation. It is always spinous. For many a man it connotes "home on the range."

MESSIAH WAR (1890–91) was an outgrowth of the Ghost Dance excitement, which so affected the Sioux Indians that R. F. Royer, the agent at Pine Ridge, S. Dak., wired for troops. On the arrival of the soldiers, Oct. 19, 1890, thousands of Indians fled to the Badlands, and many settlers left their homes in fear of a major Indian war.

Gen. Nelson A. Miles, commanding the troops in the area, ordered the apprehension of the chief, Sitting Bull, then living on Grand River, but on Dec. 15 the chief was killed, together with six Indian police and eight of his own followers, while resisting arrest.

Skirmishing in the badlands followed, but on Dec. 28 Maj. S. M. Whitside, 7th Cavalry, discovered the principal band of hostile Indians, under Big Foot, camped on Wounded Knee Creek. Big Foot surrendered but the following morning while his warriors were being disarmed by the troops, fighting broke out, and the so-called Battle of Wounded Knee, really a massacre of the Indians, followed. An estimated 200 to 300 Indians were killed and 29 whites lost their lives.

This was the only important action. After a few more skirmishes, the overwhelming force under Miles overawed the Sioux and compelled their surrender at Pine Ridge Agency early in January, 1891.

METHODISTS. Although their origin in England dates from 1739, the Methodists did not begin in any organizational sense in America until 1766. By that time two Methodist classes had been formed in the colonies, one under the leadership of Robert Straw-bridge, one of Wesley's Irish preachers, on Sam's Creek in Maryland, and the other in New York by Philip Embury, also an immigrant from Ireland. News of these beginnings in America caused John Wesley to send out two missionaries in 1769. Two years later (1771) two others were sent, one of whom, Francis Asbury, was to become the principal leader of the Methodist movement until his death in 1816. Later four others came, making eight in all. Meanwhile a native ministry was arising, largely in Maryland and Virginia, while Devereux Jarratt, an evangelical Anglican minister in Dinwiddie County, Va., gave full co-operation, administering the sacraments to the newly gathered Methodist classes wherever possible.

With the approach of the Revolution all of Wesley's missionaries, with the exception of Asbury, returned to England. Wesley's political pamphlets and his activity in support of the policies of King George III complicated the situation for the American Methodists and led to the persecution of some of the preachers in Maryland and Virginia. Once independence was won the American Methodists were not content to remain under Wesley's control, and he was wise enough to see the necessity of setting them apart as an independent body. Up to this time none of the American Methodist preachers had been ordained and the people were demanding the sacraments. Accordingly, Wesley ordained two of his English preachers and sent them to America with Dr. Thomas Coke, an Anglican clergyman, whom Wesley appointed superintendent of the American Methodists. He also appointed Asbury as joint superintendent with Coke. Asbury, unwilling to accept his appointment without the consent of the preachers, called a conference to meet at Baltimore in Christmas week, 1784. Here within eleven days the Methodist Episcopal Church was formed, preachers were ordained, and a book of discipline and a service and hymn book adopted.

The circuit system which had been brought from England by Asbury and his co-laborers proved to be ideally suited to the task of following a moving population, while the Methodist gospel of free grace and individual responsibility won a ready response on the democratic frontier. As a result Methodism grew rapidly, and by 1820 there was a Methodist membership

in America of 259,890. Twenty years later (1840) it had increased to 740,000.

American Methodism has had two great controversies, each of which resulted in a serious division. The first culminated in 1830 with the formation of the Methodist Protestant Church; the second in 1845 with the organization of the Methodist Episcopal Church, South. The first was over the question of the power of the bishops; the second grew out of the slavery controversy. Three large Negro Methodist churches have also arisen.

Until 1831 the American Methodists had established no permanent colleges, but after that date a national educational policy was adopted and by 1860 thirty-four colleges had been formed. In the development of Methodism the press has had an influential place. The Methodist Book Concern was formed in 1789 and in its present form as the Methodist Publishing House is one of the largest publishing houses in the country, issuing a large number of official papers as well as books.

Since 1872 a movement had been under way to unite the three main Methodist bodies. After years of negotiation a plan of unification was finally worked out and in 1938 was adopted by the Methodist Episcopal Church, the Methodist Episcopal Church, South, and the Methodist Protestant Church to form a united body of nearly 8,000,000. The union was consummated in 1939. The Methodist Church had an estimated membership of 9,670,690 in 1958. There are twenty other Methodist bodies, of which the African Methodist Episcopal Church (1,166,301), the African Methodist Episcopal Zion Church (780,-000) and the Christian Methodist Episcopal Church (392,167) are by far the largest.

MEUSE-ARGONNE OFFENSIVE (Sept. 26–Nov. 11, 1918). Marshal Foch entrusted to the American army the task of beginning the Allied general offensive which he designed to disrupt the German Western front. Gen. Pershing planned to attack in the sector Argonne plateau (inclusive)—Meuse River, and advance northwest on the axis Montfaucon-Romagne-Buzancy toward Sedan, 35 miles distant. At Sedan breaking of the enemy's main railways would compel evacuation of his four entrenched zones from that place to the English Channel.

Nine American divisions supported by 2700 guns attacked the eleven small German divisions of Gen. Gallwitz' Army Group holding the 20-mile Argonne-Meuse front. This was the pivot of the enemy's salient in France, protected by three of his entrenched zones, ten miles in total depth. Co-operating constantly with Gen. Gouraud's 4th French army, west of Argonne, the Americans captured Montfaucon, Sept. 27, and by the 29th had progressed six miles in places, piercing the second entrenched zone. Gallwitz now introduced six more divisions and progress became slower. However, on Oct. 7 and 8 attacks on the Argonne heights and those east of the Meuse deprived the Germans of formidable flanking positions and relieved the American center of artillery cross fire.

In mid-October Gen. Liggett took the 1st American army and Gen. Bullard the new 2nd army, Gen. Pershing assuming command of the Group of American Armies. The 1st army's renewed general attack, Oct. 14, encountered bitter resistance, but Romagne was taken and the line straightened by Oct. 31 confronting the third German retirement position, held by 31 divisions.

Attacking Nov. 1 with seven divisions west of the Meuse and six east of it, the 1st army immediately broke the German center, advancing five and one-half miles the first day. Nov. 2 Buzancy was captured and the Gallwitz Army Group began withdrawing east of the Meuse. When hostilities ceased, Nov. 11, the Americans had crossed in pursuit at many points and their left had reached Sedan, interdicting the German rail communications.

This was America's greatest battle in World War I. Aiding and aided by French and British advances averaging fifty miles between the Argonne and the sea, the 1st American army employed over 1,000,000 troops during seven weeks, broke the hinge of Germany's defenses, defeated 47 divisions, more than one fourth of her total, and captured in action 26,000 prisoners and 4000 cannon and machine guns. American losses totalled 117,000 killed and wounded.

MEXICAN BOUNDARY. The history of the boundary between the United States and Mexico may be said to begin in 1803 with the Louisiana Purchase; thereby the frontier of the United States marched with the possessions of Spain along the western limits of the Louisiana Territory; but the western boundary of the Louisiana Territory was not, either then or thereafter, internationally or juridically delimited.

After prolonged negotiations, a conventional line was established between American and Spanish sovereignties by the Adams-Onís Treaty of Feb. 22, 1819. The boundary fixed by that treaty, with a reference to Melish's Map of 1818, began in the Gulf of Mexico at the mouth of the Sabine River, ran up that river to latitude 32°, thence north to and up the Red River to longitude 100°, and thence north to and up the Arkansas River; from the source of the Arkansas the line extended north to the 42nd parallel and followed that parallel from near longitude 109° (in Wyoming) west to the Pacific. Adams had given up the American claim to Texas and in return had acquired for the United States the Spanish rights to the Oregon country, north of California, as well as a definitive cession of all Spanish territory east of the Mississippi, *i.e.*, the Floridas.

The treaty of 1819 did not go into effect until Feb. 22, 1821; in the same year came Mexican independence; so the line of the treaty of 1819 became the first boundary between the United States and Mex-

ico. This was declared by the two countries in the treaty of Jan. 12, 1828, which did not enter into force until April 5, 1832; before survey of the line, events intervened; the independence of Texas (March 2, 1836) was recognized by the United States on March 7, 1837. Accordingly, the boundary of the treaty of 1819 was not demarcated either with Spain or with Mexico.

The boundary between the United States and Mexico during the period of Texan independence (1836–45) is not internationally definable; not only was there great divergence of view as to the western and northern limits of Texas, but the independence of Texas was at no time recognized by Mexico; and there was but a brief interval between the admission of Texas into the Union (Dec. 29, 1845) and the outbreak of the Mexican War on May 13, 1846.

The boundary of the treaty of peace, signed at Guadalupe Hidalgo on Feb. 2, 1848, ran from the Gulf of Mexico up the Rio Grande to the southern boundary of New Mexico (*i.e.*, Nuevo-México) "which runs north of the town called Paso" (Ciudad Juarez), thence along the southern and western boundaries of New Mexico (as those boundaries were laid down in Disturnell's Map of 1847) to the intersection of the western boundary of New Mexico with the river Gila, thence down the Gila to its junction with the Colorado, and thence by a straight line to a point on the Pacific one marine league due south of the southernmost point of the Port of San Diego (as shown on a plan of that port drawn in 1782).

Owing to inaccuracies of Disturnell's Map, controversy arose during the demarcation of the boundary between the Rio Grande and the Colorado. The Mexican Boundary Commissioner proposed a line beginning on the Rio Grande at latitude 32° 22' north (this being the latitude at the Rio Grande of the southern boundary of New Mexico according to Disturnell's Map), running thence about one degree west to the Mimbres, up that stream to its source, and therefrom by direct line to the Gila. The line agreed upon by the two Boundary Commissioners (April 24, 1851) ran from the Rio Grande at 32° 22' three degrees west, and thence due north to the Gila; but the Surveyor of the United States, whose assent was necessary under the treaty, did not accept the line of the Commissioners, and contended (correctly) that the beginning point at the Rio Grande should be at 31° 52' N. Lat., according to the position of the Chihuahua-New Mexico boundary on Disturnell's Map relative to the true latitude of Paso; this starting point is some thirty miles south and a few miles east of the point on the Rio Grande at latitude 32° 22'; the line of the Surveyor ran from the Rio Grande at 31° 52' three degrees west and thence due north to the Gila. The territorial difference between the line of the Surveyor and the line of the Commissioners was about 6000 square miles. Congress approved the line of the Surveyor; the work of demarcation ceased;

the boundary of the United States with Mexico between the Rio Grande and the Colorado under the Treaty of Guadalupe Hidalgo was never internationally agreed upon.

Dispute as to the boundary from the Rio Grande to the Colorado under the Treaty of Guadalupe Hidalgo was ended by the Gadsden Purchase; by the Gadsden Treaty of Dec. 30, 1853, as it went into force on June 30, 1854, after extensive Senate amendments, the line westward from the Rio Grande ran, as it does now, from 31° 47′ N. Lat. due west one hundred miles, thence south to 31° 20′ N. Lat., thence along that parallel to 111° W. Long., thence in a straight line to a point on the Colorado River twenty English miles below the junction of the Gila and Colorado, and, finally, up the middle of the Colorado some twenty miles to a point nearly seven miles to the west of the junction of the Gila and Colorado and about ten miles by water below that junction, meeting at that point the boundary from the Colorado to the Pacific. That line of the Gadsden Treaty is now the boundary with Mexico of the states of New Mexico and Arizona, and throughout its entire course from the Rio Grande to the Colorado is well to the south of any possible line under the Treaty of Guadalupe Hidalgo. No change from the treaty of 1848 was made by the Gadsden Treaty in the line from the Pacific to the Colorado River (the southern boundary of California) or in the boundary of the Rio Grande between Texas and Mexico, from 31° 47′ to the Gulf of Mexico.

The boundary resulting from the treaties of 1848 and 1853 remains the boundary between the two countries, except for the reciprocal elimination, pursuant to various agreements, of *bancos,* which have been defined as "small tracts of land in the valleys of the Rio Grande and the Colorado which are isolated by the river when it cuts through a sharp bend and forms a new channel"; and from the shifting course of the Rio Grande arose one question of the boundary which technically has not been settled; this involves the Chamizal Tract of some 630 acres in El Paso, Tex.

MEXICAN WAR. Its remote or indirect cause was the increasing distrust arising from diplomatic indiscretions, quibblings and misunderstandings of the first decade of American-Mexican diplomatic relations. Its more immediate cause was the annexation of Texas, which the Mexican government regarded as equivalent to a declaration of war and which was followed by withdrawal of the Mexican minister from Washington in March, 1845, and the severance of diplomatic relations. Another cause was the American claims against Mexico arising from injuries to and property losses of American citizens in the Mexican revolutions.

The American Government strove to preserve peace. It adopted a conciliatory policy and made the first advances toward renewal of diplomatic relations. Recognizing that the chief American foreign policy was the annexation of California, Polk planned to connect with that policy the adjustment of all difficulties with Mexico, including the dispute concerning jurisdiction in the territory between the Nueces and the Rio Grande.

In September, 1845, assured through a confidential agent that the new Mexican government of Herrera would welcome an American minister, and acting upon the suggestion of James Buchanan, Secretary of State, Polk appointed John Slidell as envoy-minister on a secret peaceful mission to secure California and New Mexico for fifteen to twenty million dollars if possible, or for $40,000,000 if necessary—terms later changed by secret instructions to $5,000,000 for New Mexico, and $25,000,000 for California. In October, before Slidell's departure, Secretary Buchanan sent to the American consul Larkin at Monterey, in California, a confidential statement of the American "good will" policy to acquire California without war and with the spontaneous co-operation of the Californians.

However, Mexico refused to reopen diplomatic relations. In January, 1846, following the first news that the Mexican government under various pretexts had refused to receive Slidell, partly on the ground that questions of boundary and claims should be separated, Polk ordered Gen. Taylor to advance from Corpus Christi to the Rio Grande, resulting shortly in conflicts with Mexican troops.

On May 11, after arrival of news of the Mexican advance across the Rio Grande and the skirmish with Taylor's troops, Polk submitted to Congress a skillful war message, stating that war existed, and that it was begun by Mexico on American soil. He obtained prompt action authorizing a declaration of war, apparently on the ground that such action was justified by the delinquencies, obstinacy and hostilities of the Mexican government; and proceeded to formulate plans for military and naval operations to advance his purpose to obtain Mexican acceptance of his overtures for peace negotiations.

The military plans included an expedition under Col. Stephen W. Kearny to New Mexico and thence to California, supplemented by an expedition to Chihuahua; an advance across the Rio Grande into Mexico by troops under Gen. Taylor to occupy the neighboring provinces; and a possible later campaign of invasion of the Mexican interior from Vera Cruz.

In these plans Polk was largely influenced by assurances received in February from Col. Atocha, a friend of Santa Anna, then in exile from Mexico, to the effect that the latter, if aided in plans to return from Havana to Mexico, would recover his Mexican leadership and co-operate in a peaceful arrangement to cede Mexican territory to the United States. In June, Polk entered into negotiations with Santa Anna through a brother of Slidell, receiving verification of Atocha's assurances. Polk had already sent a confidential order to Commodore Conner who later, Aug. 16, permitted Santa Anna to pass through the coast blockade to Vera Cruz. Having arrived in Mexico,

Santa Anna promptly began his program which resulted in his own quick restoration to power, but he gave no evidences whatever of his professed pacific intentions.

On July 3, 1846, the small expedition under Col. Kearny received orders to go via the Santa Fe Trail from Fort Leavenworth to occupy New Mexico. It reached Santa Fe on Aug. 18, and a part of the force (300 men) led by Kearny marched to the Pacific at San Diego. From there it arrived (Jan. 10, 1847) at Los Angeles to complete the work begun at Sonoma by insurgents under Frémont, and at Monterey and San Francisco Bay by Commodore Sloat, shortly succeeded by Stockton.

The expedition of Gen. Taylor into northern Mexico, which was organized to carry out the plan for an advance southward into the interior of Mexico, began to cross the Rio Grande to Matamoras on May 18, 1846, and advanced to the strongly fortified city of Monterrey, which after an attack was evacuated by Mexican forces on Sept. 28. Later, in February, 1847, at Buena Vista, Taylor stubbornly resisted and defeated the attack of Santa Anna's Mexican relief expedition.

Soon thereafter the theater of war shifted to Vera Cruz, from which the direct route to the Mexican capital seemed to present less difficulty than the northern route. In deciding upon the campaign from Vera Cruz to Mexico City, Polk probably was influenced by the news of Sloat's occupation of California, which reached Washington on Sept. 1, 1846. In November, 1846, Polk offered the command of the Mexico City expedition to Gen. Winfield Scott, who promptly accepted. After the capture of the fortress of Vera Cruz, March 29, 1847, Scott led the army of invasion westward via Jalapa to Pueblo, which he entered May 15, and from which he began (Aug. 7) his advance to the mountain pass of Cerro Gordo.

Coincident with Scott's operations against Vera Cruz, Polk began new peace negotiations with Mexico through a "profoundly secret mission." On April 15 Secretary Buchanan had sent Nicholas P. Trist as a confidential peace agent to accompany Scott's army. In August, after the battles of Contreras and Churubusco, Trist arranged through Scott an armistice as a preliminary step for a diplomatic conference for discussion of peace terms—a conference which began on Aug. 27 and closed on Sept. 7 by Mexican rejection of the terms offered.

Scott promptly resumed his advance. After hard fighting (Sept. 7–11) at the battles of Molino del Rey and Chapultepec, he captured the city of Mexico, Sept. 14, and with his staff entered the palace over which he hoisted the American flag.

Practically, the war was ended. Santa Anna, after resigning his presidential office, made an unsuccessful attempt to strike at the American garrison which Scott had left at Pueblo, but was driven off and obliged to flee from Mexico.

The chief remaining American question was to find a government with sufficient power to negotiate a treaty of peace to prevent the danger of American annexation of all Mexico. Fortunately, Trist was still with the army and in close touch with the situation at the captured capital. Although recalled, he determined (Dec. 3–4) to assume the responsibility of remaining to renew efforts to conclude a treaty of peace even at the risk of disavowal by his government. After some delay, he was able to conclude with the Mexican commissioners a treaty in accord with the instructions which had been annulled by his recall. The chief negotiations were conducted at Mexico City, but the treaty was completed and signed, Feb. 2, 1848, at the neighboring town of Guadalupe Hidalgo. By its terms, which provided for cessation of hostilities, the United States agreed to pay $15,000,000 for New Mexico and California. Polk received the treaty on Feb. 19, and promptly decided to submit it to the Senate, which approved it on March 10 by a vote of thirty-eight to fourteen. Ratifications were exchanged on May 30, 1848.

Among the chief results of the war were the following: expansion of American territory; increased American interest in problems of the Caribbean and the Pacific and in the opening and control of isthmian interoceanic transit routes at Panama, Nicaragua and Tehuantepec; and ebullitions of "manifest destiny" in the period of "Young America" from 1848 to 1860. In domestic affairs the result of the large acquisition of territory was reflected in political controversies relating to the slavery problem.

MEXICO, FRENCH IN. In October, 1861, England, France and Spain signed a treaty by which they undertook coercive action to secure reparation for their subjects and the execution of certain obligations contracted by Mexico. They agreed to refrain from intervention in Mexico's internal affairs and neither to make any territorial aggrandizements nor to influence her form of government. Armed forces of Spain promptly seized Vera Cruz. After French and English soldiers arrived on the Mexican coast, a conference of commanders of the allied forces held at Orizaba could not agree. The English and the Spaniards decided to withdraw from Mexico. The French army, which was strongly reinforced, captured the city of Mexico in June, 1862. An Assembly of Notables, convoked there by the invaders, decided in favor of the establishment in Mexico of a monarchy headed by Ferdinand Maximilian, Archduke of Austria, who had been selected by Napoleon III.

Attracted by the glittering dream of a throne in a fair land over which his ancestors had ruled, Maximilian accepted the invitation. He expected that Napoleon III would support the exotic empire for a term of years. After Maximilian's arrival in Mexico, he sought to secure recognition by the United States, but that government continued to support the republican leader, President Juárez, who took refuge on the northern frontiers of his country.

The fortunes of the Empire of Maximilian largely depended upon the outcome of the Civil War. During that struggle the United States made mild protests against French intervention in Mexico, but after Lee's surrender, the French secretary of foreign affairs was informed by Secretary Seward that the "presence and operations of a French army in Mexico and the maintenance of an authority there resting upon force and not the free will of the people of Mexico is a cause of serious concern to the United States." In vain did France attempt to secure the recognition of Maximilian's government by the United States or to postpone the withdrawal of her troops. Finally, in the spring of 1867, the last detachment of French soldiers left Mexican soil. The soldiers of Juárez soon captured Maximilian, who was deserted by his Mexican followers. The unfortunate prince was court-martialed, and, despite the pleas of the United States for mercy, was shot on June 19, 1867. Thus a clear violation of the Monroe Doctrine was repelled and republican government restored in Mexico.

MEXICO, PUNITIVE EXPEDITION INTO (1916). As a result of Villa's attack on Columbus, N. Mex., on the night of March 8–9, 1916, Gen. John J. Pershing was directed to pursue Villa into Mexico for the purpose of capturing him and preventing any further raids by his band. On March 15 Gen. Pershing crossed the border with a force consisting of a provisional division, mostly cavalry. The advance was conducted in two columns, each column engaging in minor skirmishes with small groups of Villa's troops. Progress was exceedingly difficult, both because the Carranza government refused Pershing's troops the use of railroads and because the United States had given instructions that villages could not be occupied. The Mexican government troops were also hostile to what they considered an invasion, and on two occasions, one at Parral and one at Carrizal, clashed with Pershing's forces. These clashes occurred in spite of the fact that the U. S. Government had agreed to withdraw its troops as soon as the Mexican government could give assurance that the border situation could be handled by the Mexicans themselves. Pershing's force advanced 400 miles into Mexico and, although it was unable to capture Villa, his followers were scattered into small, unorganized bands. On Feb. 5, 1917, Pershing's punitive force was ordered to return to the United States. In the meantime sufficient troops of the National Guard and Regular Army were stationed along the border to prevent further incidents such as occurred at Columbus.

MIAMI PURCHASE, the next important colonization project in the Old Northwest after the grant to the Ohio Company of Associates, was first settled about eight months after Marietta. The Miami Purchase represented an important step in the American advance on the north bank of the Ohio. Extending northward from the Ohio, between the Miami and the Little Miami Rivers, in addition to the increasingly important Ohio River route it commanded the Miami-Maumee roadway to Lake Erie, while southward the Licking River gave ready access to the Kentucky bluegrass region. Benjamin Stites, an Indian trader, represented the possibilities of the Miami country to Judge John Cleves Symmes, of Morristown, N. J., an influential member of the Continental Congress. After a personal inspection Judge Symmes enlisted the support of Jonathan Dayton, Elias Boudinot and other important men, to found a colony between the two Miamis. A contract with the Treasury Board, Oct. 15, 1788, granted Judge Symmes and his associates 1,000,000 acres, for which, under the Land Ordinance of 1785, they agreed to pay $1 per acre, with certain deductions, in Continental certificates, and one seventh in military warrants. As in the Ohio Company Purchase, section 16 in each township was reserved for the support of education, and section 29 for that of religion. Also, one entire township was set aside for a college. Eventually, Judge Symmes could not meet the payments in full, and in 1794 he received a patent for the Miami Purchase that covered only 311,682 acres.

Judge Symmes started for his new colony in July, 1788, and made a temporary stop at Limestone, Ky. The first permanent settlement in the Miami Purchase was made Nov. 18, 1788, by Benjamin Stites, at Columbia, at the mouth of the Little Miami. The next settlement, Dec. 28, 1788, opposite the mouth of the Licking, was led by Israel Ludlow and Robert Patterson, and was given the fanciful name, Losantiville, which Gov. St. Clair changed to Cincinnati, in honor of the Society of the Cincinnati. The third settlement Judge Symmes himself founded, Feb. 2, 1789, at North Bend. At first the constant danger of Indian attacks confined the settlers, the majority of whom were from New Jersey, to the vicinity of Fort Washington, but gradually they went up the watercourses into the interior. Fort Hamilton, founded in 1791, became the nucleus of an advanced settlement, and after the Treaty of Greenville, population quickly spread through the Miami Purchase.

MICHIGAN. The Northwest Territory, to which Michigan nominally belonged, was created by the Ordinance of 1787. By the Jay Treaty the British agreed to evacuate the northwestern posts, and on July 11, 1796, the American flag was raised at Detroit. Shortly thereafter Wayne County, with boundaries embracing almost all of Michigan and much of Ohio, Indiana and Wisconsin, was organized, with Detroit as the county seat.

Until 1800 Michigan remained a part of the Northwest Territory. On the organization of Indiana Territory, it was divided between the two, and when

Ohio became a state in 1803 all of Michigan was attached to Indiana. The resounding complaints of Michigan's residents over this status were soon heeded by Congress, which created Michigan Territory, July 1, 1805. Until 1818 the territory embraced only the southern peninsula plus the eastern end of the upper one. When Illinois was admitted in 1818 the remaining portion of the Old Northwest, north of Illinois and west of Lake Michigan, was attached to Michigan. Finally, in 1834, the boundary was extended to embrace Iowa and Minnesota and the eastern half of the Dakotas.

Michigan's territorial era was prolonged and stormy. Separated from the settled portion of the United States by a wide wilderness, there was almost no immigration, and as late as 1820 the white population was less than 9000. The extinction of the Indian title to the land, and the completion of the Erie Canal in 1825 finally brought Michigan within the sweep of the westward movement of American settlement. From 1830 on, the tide of immigration rose steadily higher and the territory quickly became eligible for statehood.

The story of Michigan's transition from territory to state is unique in American history. The Ordinance of 1787 provided that Congress should organize three states in the Northwest Territory, and at its discretion might create two more north of a line due east and west through the southern extreme of Lake Michigan. Five states were eventually created, but the boundary provision proved a fruitful source of discord among them. Indiana in 1816 and Illinois in 1818 were admitted with material extensions northward of the Ordinance line. When Michigan applied for admission with this Ordinance line as its southern boundary, Congress, catering to Ohio's demands, required the people, as the *sine qua non* of admission, to assent to the present Ohio-Michigan boundary, which is the eastward projection of a straight line drawn northeastwardly from the southern extreme of Lake Michigan to the northeast corner of Maumee Bay. The tract in dispute was a triangular strip about 470 square miles in area and seven miles wide at its eastern end, running from Lake Erie to the western boundary of Ohio, and embracing the mouth and lower portion of Maumee River. But few issues have so united the people of Michigan as this one. Under its influence a political revolution was consummated; the territorial government was banished and a state government established, which functioned for a year and a half unrecognized by the United States. This impasse was finally resolved by a characteristic political subterfuge, and Michigan, "compensated" for the loss of the southern boundary by the unasked donation of the Upper Peninsula, was admitted to the Union, Jan. 26, 1837.

MICHILIMACKINAC (MACKINAC) STRAIT AND ISLAND. The waters of Lakes Michigan and Su-

perior unite with Lake Huron by the Strait of Michilimackinac and the St. Marys River. Lying at the crossroads of the Upper Lakes, in the middle of the Strait and within striking distance of the outlet of the St. Marys, is Michilimackinac Island.

The name Michilimackinac applies not only to the Strait and to the adjacent mainland, but also specifically to three distinct place-sites, the Island, Point St. Ignace on the northern mainland and Mackinaw City on the southern mainland. Although today the final syllables of both Island and mainland names— *nac* and *naw*—are pronounced alike (rhyming with "paw"), originally the French pronounced *nac* as they spelled it (rhyming with "pack").

For almost a century prior to 1761 Michilimackinac was under French rule. From 1761 to 1796 and from 1812 to 1815 the rule of Britain prevailed; from 1796 to 1812 and since 1815 Michilimackinac has belonged to the United States. The advent of the railroad wrought the doom of Michilimackinac as a military and commercial center, but its scenic beauty and its rich and colorful history remain as permanent possessions. A Jesuit missionary labored for some months on the Island (1670–71); thereafter until 1706 white activity centered at St. Ignace; from about 1712 to 1781 it was at Mackinaw City; for two generations following 1781 both military and commercial activities again centered on the Island; since the advent of American settlement communities have existed at all three places.

MIDDLE PASSAGE was the term applied to the trip from Africa to America, the second leg of the triangular voyage of a slave ship. During the passage the slaves, packed in holds eighteen inches to five feet deep, and allowed above only for air, food and exercise, died in large numbers.

MIDNIGHT JUDGES refers to the judicial appointments made by John Adams just before he was succeeded in the Presidency by Thomas Jefferson. The action of Adams was assailed as an attempt "to make permanent provision for such of the Federalists and Tories as cannot hope to continue in office under the new administration." Congress, dominated in the next session by the partisans of Jefferson, reconstructed the inferior courts and legislated out of their commissions most of the midnight judges. In the case of a justice of the peace for the District of Columbia the delivery of his commission was refused. This led to the famous case of Marbury v. Madison.

MIER EXPEDITION. Mexico refused to recognize the independence of Texas in 1836 and as late as 1842 made an invasion and took possession of San Antonio for a short time. A counter expedition into Mexico was ordered by President Houston. This expedition left San Antonio for the border in November, 1842, under Gen. Somervell, with 750 troops. Because of lack of enthusiasm of the leaders and dissension among the troops, only 250 crossed into Mexico and these surrendered to an overwhelming Mexican force at Mier on the lower Rio Grande. After an attempt to escape, one tenth were shot and the others marched to a prison near Mexico City. Here some died, some escaped and the others were released two years later.

MILITARY TRACTS. Military land bounties were offered in the early national period by the states and the Federal Government to attract people into the armies or to reward soldiers and officers for their services. In the Revolutionary War such bounties varied in size according to military rank, the upper limit being 5000 to 10,000 acres in some cases. To satisfy the warrants issued for these bounties military tracts were set aside in which the warrantee must locate his land. New York set up two such reserves, one in the Finger Lakes district and the other in the extreme northern part of the state. North Carolina created a military tract in the Cumberland basin of Tennessee, and Virginia established a similar tract in western Kentucky. When it was seen that the Kentucky tract would not satisfy outstanding warrants of Virginia a second military tract, consisting of 3,850,000 acres, was created in south central Ohio which Virginia reserved to itself from the cession it made of its western lands to the Federal Government. In this latter tract the United States had no control over the lands and it is the only part of Ohio which was not surveyed in rectangles in advance of lawful settlement.

The United States created four military tracts to satisfy its warrants given in the Revolutionary War and the War of 1812. The first of these was located in central Ohio, adjacent to the Virginia Military Tract, and consisted of 2,539,000 acres. Warrantees of the Revolutionary War located their lands here. The other three tracts of 2,000,000 acres each were originally located in Michigan, Illinois and Arkansas; but when it was reported that the Michigan tract was poorly drained and unsuited to farming, it was abandoned and the Illinois tract was increased to 3,500,000 acres and a tract of 500,000 acres was established in Missouri. In these three tracts soldiers of the War of 1812, who received 160 acres each, were required to locate their warrants by lottery.

Most of the soldiers or their heirs refused to move to these tracts to take up their claims, as the law contemplated, because they were too far distant from zones of settlement. Instead, they sold their warrants or locations to speculators for prices as low as ten cents an acre. The result was a high percentage of absentee or speculative ownership in each of the military tracts. For example, 24 persons, including such well-known individuals as Nathaniel Massie, Duncan McArthur and Thomas Worthington, owned 1,035,000 acres in the Virginia Military Tract of Ohio. In the Military Tract of Illinois, located in the triangle between the Illinois and Mississippi Rivers, the New York and Boston Illinois Land Company acquired 900,000 acres, Romulus Riggs of Philadelphia owned 40,000 acres and other easterners had large possessions.

Such large-scale land monopolization in the military tracts aroused all the latent frontier hostility against absentee speculators. Squatters settled upon the absentee-owned lands, plundered them of their timber, defied ouster proceedings and flouted all efforts to make them pay rent for their use of the land. Local governments frequently levied discriminatory taxes on absentee-owned lands, raised their valuations and built public improvements in their vicinity to force higher taxes. The speculators with little capital might lose their lands at tax sales; others, better financed, sooner or later would sell or lease to tenants. Residents of the military tracts long cherished their dislike of nonresident proprietors.

MILLIGAN CASE (1866). This decision by the Supreme Court invalidated the trial and conviction of Lambdin P. Milligan by a military commission in 1864. Milligan had been arrested at his Indiana home by order of the general in command of the military district of Indiana charged with conspiring against the United States, with giving aid and comfort to the enemy, and with inciting insurrection and disloyal practices. The charges grew out of Milligan's activities as an officer of a secret order whose general purpose was to co-operate with the Confederate government. Milligan was tried before a court-martial established under the authority of the President, found guilty, and sentenced to be hanged. Before execution of sentence, proceedings were instituted in the Federal circuit court denying the legality of the military trial, and asserting that Milligan had been deprived of his constitutional right to trial by jury.

The Supreme Court held that neither the President nor Congress has the power to set up military tribunals except in the actual theater of war, where the civil courts are no longer functioning; and that elsewhere courts-martial have jurisdiction only over persons in the military or naval service of the United States. Milligan was not in the military or naval service; war did not exist in Indiana; nor was the state invaded or threatened with invasion; and the civil courts were open and in the proper and unobstructed exercise of their jurisdiction. The substitution of trial before a court-martial for the regular civil procedure was therefore unwarranted, and Milligan had been deprived of his constitutional right. He was released, after having been held in confinement for eighteen months. Later, because the decision seemed to cast grave doubt upon the legality of the military government established by Congress in former rebellious states, the Court was widely denounced, especially by Radical Republicans.

"MILLIONS FOR DEFENSE, BUT NOT A CENT FOR TRIBUTE" was a toast offered by Robert Goodloe Harper, Congressman from South Carolina, at the dinner given by Congress in Philadelphia on June 18, 1798, in honor of John Marshall on his return from the diplomatic mission to France, which eventuated in the XYZ affair. The naval war with France followed soon afterwards.

MIMS, FORT, MASSACRE AT, occurred Aug. 30, 1813, when the fort was attacked by a force of about 1000 Creeks. The fort was a mere stockade built the preceding July around the house of Samuel Mims on the eastern bank of Lake Tensaw, near Mobile. In it the white and half-breed families of the vicinity had taken refuge, fearing a Creek uprising in revenge for the Burnt Corn attack in July. At the time of the massacre there were 553 people within the fort, about 100 of whom were enlisted soldiers. Deceived as to the intentions of the Creeks and not expecting an attack, the commanding officer, Maj. Daniel Beasley, neglected to keep out patrols, to maintain a watch, or even to keep the gates closed. The Creeks surprised the fort, entered through the open east gate, and after desperate fighting burned the fort and massacred all the people except thirty-six who managed to escape. The Creeks themselves lost heavily.

MINERAL PATENT LAW OF THE UNITED STATES. When gold was discovered in California and Colorado the United States had no mining code. Mining law consisted of the rules and regulations drawn up and enforced by the miners themselves. Based on these laws, Congress passed the first national mining act July 26, 1866. This law, amplified by the act of May 10, 1872, established the rules for obtaining patent to the mineral lands of the United States. The principle adopted was the sale of the lands, even those containing gold and silver mines, to the first occupant for a nominal sum. Upon discovering a mineral lode any citizen could stake off a claim 1500 feet long by 600 feet wide and obtain title to it after making $500 worth of improvements and paying $5 per acre. Placer claims were limited to twenty acres at a price of $2.50 per acre. No great nation has been as liberal as the United States in disposing of its mineral deposits. Special acts govern mining in the Philippines and Alaska. The mineral patent laws apply only to the public domain of the United States, hence do not apply to the original thirteen states or Texas. Some lead mining states like Michigan, Wisconsin and Minnesota are governed by the agricultural land laws instead of the mineral patent law.

MINIÉ BALL was invented in 1849 by Capt. Minié of the French army. This bullet had a deep tapered cavity in the base with a hemispherical iron cup fitted into it. The bullet was easily fitted into a muzzle-loading rifle, and the force of the explosion expanded the base of the bullet against the rifling of the barrel with resultant greater accuracy and range. The Minié ball was used extensively in the Civil War in the Model 1842 U. S. Rifle, caliber .69. In the American service a wooden plug was substituted for Capt. Minié's iron ring, the force of the explosion driving the plug into the cavity and expanding the bullet.

MINNESOTA bears a Sioux name, meaning sky-tinted or turbid water, which originally was applied to the river that joins the Mississippi near the Twin Cities. Among geographic factors that have influenced the state's history are its more than ten thousand lakes and its central position. Within its borders are three river systems, the Mississippi, St. Louis and Red, flowing, respectively, southward to the gulf, eastward to the St. Lawrence and northward toward Hudson Bay.

French explorers, taking advantage of this water highway system, were early on the scene. Radisson and Groseilliers, traders and adventurers, probably visited Minnesota on their "voyages" to the Northwest between 1654 and 1660, and they were followed by a long line of explorers, including Duluth from 1679 to 1689, Father Hennepin in 1680, LeSueur in 1700, LaPerrière in 1727, and the Vérendryes in the 1730's and 1740's. Among French outposts in the Minnesota wilderness were Forts L'Huillier, Beauharnois and St. Charles.

Eastern Minnesota remained under French control until 1763, when it became British. Among the explorers and traders of the British period were Jonathan Carver, 1766–67; Peter Pond, 1773–75; and David Thompson, noted cartographer, 1797–98. The British developed an extensive Indian trade, with Grand Portage on the north Superior shore serving as the western headquarters of the North West Company until about 1803. Minnesota east of the Mississippi came under American sovereignty by the Definitive Treaty of Peace of 1783, and four years later it became part of the Northwest Territory. British traders continued to operate in Minnesota, however, until after the War of 1812. The American Fur Company then took over the field.

White men in Minnesota came into contact with two Indian nations, the Sioux and the Chippewa. About the middle of the 18th century, the Chippewa, an Algonkian people migrating westward and armed with guns, forced the Sioux from their ancient wooded lands into the prairie country farther south and west. Conflict between these tribes continued until well after Minnesota was settled by white men. Zealous missionaries worked among both the Sioux and the Chippewa.

Minnesota west of the Mississippi was nominally part of the Spanish empire for forty-one years preceding its transfer to the United States as part of the Louisiana Purchase. To explore the new region, conciliate the Indians and obtain fort sites, Zebulon M. Pike was sent into the Minnesota country in 1805. At the mouth of the Minnesota River he secured from the Sioux the site of the post later known as Fort Snelling, established in 1819.

Explorers of the Northwest henceforth made this fort the objective or point of departure for their expeditions. Among them were Lewis Cass, 1820; Giacomo C. Beltrami and Maj. Stephen H. Long, 1823; Henry R. Schoolcraft, who discovered Lake Itasca, the source of the Mississippi, in 1832; and Joseph N. Nicollet, who mapped the Northwest in the late 1830's.

By treaties in 1837 the United States purchased from the Indians the triangle of land between the lower St. Croix and the Mississippi. Settlements, such as Stillwater, Marine and St. Paul, began to appear as lumbermen, farmers and town builders arrived. In 1849 Minnesota Territory was established, its boundaries extending northward from Iowa to the Canadian line and westward from Wisconsin to the Missouri. Alexander Ramsey of Pennsylvania was appointed its first governor.

Much of the southeastern and central part of Minnesota was opened to settlement by treaties with the Sioux in 1851; and large areas farther north were made available by Chippewa treaties in 1854 and 1855. After 1851 southeastern Minnesota was rapidly settled, large numbers of Germans, Scandinavians, Irish and English joining the native American pioneers. A great boom came on and Minnesotans, increasing from 6077 in 1850 to 157,037 in 1857, asked for statehood. The Kansas question delayed admission, but finally, on May 11, 1858, Minnesota took its place among the states.

MINSTREL SHOWS. The first appearance of a comic Negro character on the stage is said to have taken place in Boston in 1799. There were few such appearances until 1830, when Thomas D. Rice introduced his enormously popular song, "Jim Crow," in blackface make-up. The first known minstrel troupe was a quartette—including Dan Emmett, who later wrote "Dixie"—which appeared on the Bowery in 1843. Thereafter, many new troupes sprang up and grew in size. By 1857, when the famous Christy Minstrels appeared, the performance had settled into the standard pattern which endured ever afterward; a "first part," with the company seated in a semicircle, a white interlocutor and two "end men" who bandied jokes with him between vocal solos by others in the circle. Following this came the "olio," a variety entertainment, with dances, comic sketches and acrobatic turns. In the latter 19th century, when such entertainment was highly popular and there were scores of companies on the road, Haverly's was perhaps most famous, though Lew Dockstader, Primrose & West, Al G. Fields and others shared popularity

with him toward the end and carried on after him. Beginning in 1853, Philadelphia had a permanent minstrel organization for three quarters of a century. Minstrelsy gradually died in the 20th century and was practically extinct by 1930, though the "first part" was heard in its original form on the radio as late as 1935.

MINT, FEDERAL. Robert Morris, Secretary of Finance, urged the Continental Congress, in 1782, to establish a mint. In 1786 Congress ordered the Board of the Treasury to study the subject, but not until April 2, 1792, three years after the birth of the new government, was the creation of a mint authorized. It was set up in Philadelphia, then the national capital, in 1793, and remained there permanently after other government agencies had been removed to Washington. Silver coinage began in 1794 and that of gold in 1795. The staff at first consisted of eleven officers and clerks, nineteen workmen in the coining department and seven at the furnaces. The total coinage produced in 1794–95 was less than $500,000. Not until 1807 did the output exceed $1,000,000; but in 1851 nearly $63,500,000 was struck, all of it gold save about $800,000. In the earlier years the mint often lacked gold and silver with which to work. In 1820 it operated only part of the time because of this scarcity and the small demand for copper coins. In 1835 Congress established three branch mints—one at New Orleans and two in the new gold fields, at Charlotte, N. C., and Dahlonega, Ga. The one at New Orleans was taken over by the Confederates at the beginning of the Civil War and operated thus from Jan. 26 to May 31, 1861, then suspended. It did not resume work until 1879, ceased to coin in 1909, and became an assay office. The mint at Dahlonega closed in 1861; that at Charlotte was used as barracks by Confederate soldiers and never operated thereafter. A branch mint was installed at San Francisco in 1854. Another was legally established at Denver in 1862, but no coins had yet been made there when in 1870 it was turned into an assay office. In 1895 it was again authorized to coin, but no money was made there until 1906. A sixth branch mint began work at Carson City, Nev., in 1870; but its production was not great, and it closed in 1893. Another, authorized in 1864 at The Dalles, Oregon, was in process of construction in 1871 when destroyed by fire, and the project was abandoned. A mint authorized in 1902 at Manila, P. I., has had comparatively small output. By acts of 1846 and later, the various mints were made public depositories. The Bureau of the Mint was created by Congress, Feb. 12, 1873.

MINUTEMEN. While the phrase "minute-man" goes back at least to 1756, the famous body developed under that name first appeared in the reorganization of the Massachusetts militia by the Worcester con-

615

vention and the Provincial Congress in 1774. To get rid of Tories in the older militia, in September resignations of officers were called for in the three Worcester regiments, which were broken into seven and new officers elected. These officers were to enlist a third of the men in new regiments, which were specifically called (Sept. 21) regiments of minutemen, who were to elect their officers. The Provincial Congress, meeting in October, found the same process voluntarily going on in the militia of other counties, and directed its completion (Oct. 26). Thus a double system of regiments was established in the province, the minutemen to be ready for any emergency "at a minute's warning."

The formation of the minuteman regiments proceeded slowly. On Feb. 14, 1775, as returns which had been called for were not forthcoming, the Provincial Congress set May 10 for a complete return. None was ever made, and only scattered records show that while Marblehead organized its company on Nov. 7, 1774, Woburn, though close to Boston, did not vote to establish its minutemen until April 17, 1775, two days before the outbreak of war. No complete list of minutemen companies and regiments was possible, and only from town records, a few lists and the "Lexington alarm lists" of minutemen and militia alike can a fragmentary roster be patched together of an organization that never was finished.

On April 19 militia and minutemen turned out together to resist the British expedition to Concord. The men whom the British killed on Lexington green were minutemen, and minutemen led the march down to Concord bridge. But militia were also in the column, and men of both kinds harried the British back to Boston. The minuteman organization was then abandoned by the Provincial Congress in organizing the Eight Months Army. As this was formed, it drew men from both minutemen and militia; those who could not join went back into the militia, and the minutemen thenceforth disappeared in Massachusetts.

Other colonies organized their minutemen on the recommendation of the Continental Congress (July 18, 1775) to enlist them for rounds of service on special brief enlistments. Maryland (August), New Hampshire (September) and Connecticut (December) are on record as accepting this plan, and Connecticut minutemen are credited with resisting Tryon's expedition against Danbury. There are statues to minutemen in Concord and Lexington, Mass., and Westport, Conn.

MISCHIANZA was the most elaborate, extravagant and romantically feudal *fête champêtre* given in 18th-century America. It was held at the Wharton estate, "Walnut Grove," on May 18, 1778, in honor of Sir William Howe, then occupying Philadelphia as commander of the British forces. The directing geniuses were Maj. John André and Capt. Oliver DeLancey. The entertainment lasted from four o'clock on the afternoon of May 18 until four o'clock in the morning of the following day. Seven hundred and fifty invitations were issued, 330 covers were laid. The staff officers paid 3312 guineas and a London firm sold, it is said, £12,000 worth of silks, laces and other fine materials.

MISSIONARY RIDGE, BATTLE OF (Nov. 25, 1863). To prevent reinforcement of Longstreet (C.), besieging Knoxville, Tenn., on Nov. 24, 1863, Grant (U.) ordered Hooker to attack Bragg's (C.) left on Lookout Mountain. The movement was successful. The next morning Thomas (U.) was directed to assault the Confederate center on Missionary Ridge; Sherman (U.) was ordered to turn Bragg's right and sever his communications southward; Hooker was to advance from Lookout Mountain and get across Bragg's line of retreat. Sherman made repeated unsuccessful attacks against the Confederate right commanded by Hardee and Cleburne; Hooker's attack was held up. To prevent Bragg from reinforcing either wing of his army, Thomas, about noon, was ordered forward.

Bragg's defense was faulty. He had disposed one half his center at the foot of Missionary Ridge, with orders to retire and join the other half, stationed on the crest of the Ridge, if Thomas' advance should get within 200 yards. Bragg's artillery was nearly useless as it could not be sufficiently depressed to sweep the slope of the Ridge effectively. The Union troops had orders to halt at the foot of the Ridge, but as the Confederates promptly retreated, the Union soldiers took matters into their own hands. They must either go forward or retreat. Stopping only momentarily, the men rushed on, driving the disorganized Confederates from their positions on the top. Bragg's routed center and left moved eastward to the protection of Cleburne's command, which had successfully resisted Sherman. Before dark the battle was practically over. It only remained for Bragg to withdraw his defeated troops as best he could southward to Chickamauga Station and Dalton. Cleburne covered the retreat, halting Hooker's vigorous pursuit at Ringgold Gap. A week later Bragg relinquished his command of the Army of Tennessee. Hardee, temporarily in command, was soon succeeded by Gen. J. E. Johnston.

MISSIONS OF THE SOUTHWEST. As a Spanish frontier institution the mission was meant to be a temporary, not a permanent, device. It envisaged the training of the aborigines for citizenship and economic self-dependence, a process which the first lawmakers expected would last some ten years only, after which period the mission regime was to give way to civil and parochial organization. Along with the mission went the presidio or military guard. The two mutually supporting institutions formed in combination the essential spearhead of the Spanish advance into the wilderness.

In 1539 Fray Marcos de Niza made his famous journey along the road to Cíbola, and the year following Coronado led his expedition in the same direction. With the latter were four Franciscans, whose missionary activities in present New Mexico and beyond are the earliest recorded for the Southwest. One of their number, Fray Juan de Padilla, settled among the Indians of Quivira, but while on his way to evangelize a tribe farther afield was slain by the natives, *ca.* 1544, being the first missionary so to die on American soil. In the religious sphere the Southwest was pre-eminently Franciscan land, the bulk of missionary enterprise in that region being due to members of the Order of St. Francis.

Numerous missions were established within the limits of present-day New Mexico, Arizona and Texas. In New Mexico Fray Francesco de López and the lay brother Agustín Rodríguez were at work as early as 1581 among the Tigua Indians at Puaray, now Sandía, where they were martyred. Mission centers multiplied with the years. In 1630 they were 25 in number, staffed by 50 friars and serving 90 pueblos with a Christian population of some 60,000. In 1680 the New Mexico missions, then numbering 33, were destroyed in the great Pueblo revolt of that year, which cost the lives of 21 missionaries. With the reconquest of New Mexico under Gov. de Vargas, in the last decade of the 17th century the missions were restored. In Arizona the three missions set up among the Hopi or Moqui Indians, the first of which dated from 1628 or 1629, were swept away in the Pueblo revolt. Near the site of Tucson the Jesuit, Eusebio Kino, "superb missionary, church-builder, explorer and ranchman," founded in 1700 the Mission of San Xavier del Bac. Within the two years following he founded also San Gabriel de Guevavi and San Cayetán del Tumacácori, all three missions being within the limits of Arizona. On the expulsion of the Jesuits in 1767 the three missions were taken over by the Franciscans, one of whom, Fray Francisco Garcés, labored at San Xavier del Bac with distinguished zeal. The first of the Texan missions was planted among the Jumano of La Junta near the present Presidio, 1683; the last foundation, Refugio, on Mission River, was in 1791. Outstanding among the Texan missionaries was the saintly Fray Antonio Margil de Jesús.

The missions of the Southwest declined during the 18th century and by the time of the Mexican War were practically nonexistent. Chief among the causes of decay was the process of secularization, which withdrew the Indians from the tutelage of the friars and transferred administration of the mission temporalities from the latter to civil functionaries.

MISSISSIPPI, TERRITORY AND STATE OF, was first explored by DeSoto who entered the present limits of the state in 1539. In 1682 LaSalle descended the Mississippi River to its mouth and claimed possession of the entire basin for France, giving it the name Louisiana. Biloxi, near the present town of that name, was founded by Iberville in 1699, and Natchez was founded by Bienville in 1716. France ceded Louisiana to Spain in 1762, but Great Britain gained the portion east of the Mississippi as a result of the Treaty of Paris, 1763. The lower third of the present states of Mississippi and Alabama was made part of the new British province of West Florida. Spain occupied West Florida during the American Revolution, but the United States claimed that part north of the 31st parallel under the treaties with Great Britain of 1782 and 1783. Spain accepted this parallel as the northern boundary of West Florida in 1795.

Mississippi Territory was organized under the act approved April 7, 1798. It included the area between the 31st parallel and the parallel of the mouth of the Yazoo River, and between the Mississippi and Chattahoochee. The addition, in 1804, of the country south of Tennessee, and, in 1812, of the region between the Pearl and Perdido Rivers, enlarged the Territory to what is now included in Alabama and Mississippi.

The territorial government was similar to that provided for Ohio under the Ordinance of 1787 except that slavery was permitted.

Mississippi was admitted as a state Dec. 10, 1817, and at the same time the eastern half was organized as Alabama Territory. Mississippi seceded Jan. 9, 1861, and one of her citizens, Jefferson Davis, was elected President of the Confederacy.

The struggle for control of the Mississippi River inevitably made the state a main theater of the war. Corinth, Iuka, Holly Springs and Oxford were occupied in 1862. The capital, Jackson, was captured in May, 1863, and the state government was moved first to Columbus, and then to Macon. The surrender of Vicksburg, July 4, 1863, was followed by Sherman's march from Meridian across the state in January, 1864. By the end of the war most places had at some time been occupied by Federal troops.

Mississippi was readmitted Feb. 23, 1870, but continued under a reconstruction government until 1875.

"MISSISSIPPI BUBBLE" is the term commonly applied to the disastrous failure of John Law's scheme for exploiting the resources of French Louisiana. After Antoine Crozat surrendered his charter in 1717, John Law, a Scotchman who had previously gained an enviable reputation in France as a successful banker and financier, organized the Compagnie de l'Occident (Western Company), also known as the Mississippi Company, to assume control of Louisiana on Jan. 1, 1718. Law's reputation caused the stock to sell readily, and the organization soon enlarged the scope of its activities by absorbing several other commercial companies, its name then being changed to the "Company of the Indies." Enormous profits were anticipated from the operations of the company, and the increasing demand for its stock led to wild speculation which drove the price of shares to high figures, without any sound basis in tangible assets. Many Frenchmen invested their all in the company's stock. A few, who sold at the right moment, reaped fortunes from their speculation; but the majority held their stock in expectation of greater profits. The anticipated immense and immediate profits were not realized, and soon the scheme revealed itself as a purely speculative venture. In 1720 the company failed, the "bubble" burst, and the stockholders lost their entire investments, many being completely ruined. Law's connection with the venture ceased, but the company retained control of Louisiana until 1731.

MISSISSIPPI COMPANY OF VIRGINIA (1763) was organized by a group of men, most of whom were members of the original Ohio Company of Virginia, including Thomas and Arthur Lee, George Washington and others, for the purpose of procuring a huge tract of land at the junction of the Ohio and Mississippi Rivers. Their hopes were soon dampened, however, by the Proclamation of 1763 which prohibited land grants and settlements west of the Appalachian Mountains. The company continued its existence, however, and Arthur Lee was its representative in London in 1768 when the Treaty of Fort Stanwix again opened opportunities for western settlements. He pressed the claims of the Mississippi Company which was now asking for 2,500,000 acres to lie between the Alleghenies and the Ohio and the 38th and 42nd parallels. From that time to 1775 the British secretary of colonial affairs was besieged by the Ohio Company, the Indiana Company and the Vandalia Company for grants of land which overlapped the grant sought by the Mississippi Company. The approach of the American Revolution terminated the hopes of the Mississippi Company, as well as the hopes of the other companies.

MISSISSIPPI PLAN (1890 f.), disfranchising the Negro, adopted by the Mississippi constitutional convention of 1890, required every citizen, aged 21 to 60, to be able to display his poll tax receipt; one had to be able to read the Constitution, or understand it when read to him, or give a reasonable interpretation thereof. This permitted registration officials to discriminate between white and black illiterates. Furthermore, citizens were disfranchised for crimes Negroes were prone to commit, as theft, arson and wife beating. Six other Southern states made similar constitutional changes, 1895 to 1910. In Williams v. Mississippi (1898) the Supreme Court upheld these suffrage provisions.

MISSISSIPPI RIVER. Although other Spaniards had doubtless seen the mouth of this great river, its discovery is rightly accredited to Hernando DeSoto, who reached it near the site of Memphis, Tenn., early in May, 1541. There is no indisputable evidence that another European saw the Mississippi River until 1673, and then the new discoverers were Frenchmen. On June 17 of that year Louis Jolliet and Father Jacques Marquette paddled their canoes out of the Wisconsin River into the larger stream. They proceeded down the river to a point near the mouth of the Arkansas River, where they turned back. In 1682 LaSalle explored the river from the Illinois to its mouth, where on April 9 he took possession of the country for France and named it Louisiana.

LaSalle realized the full significance of the Mississippi River, and planned to establish a colony at its mouth. Unfortunately, when in 1684 he sailed from France to carry out the purpose, he missed the mouth of the Mississippi and landed on the coast of Texas. Three years later he was murdered by one of his followers and his plan for a French colony seemed to have perished with him.

Scarcely more than a decade elapsed, however, before two Frenchmen, Iberville and Bienville, sailed from Brest in two vessels carrying 200 soldiers and colonists. In March, 1699, they entered the Mississippi, explored it for some distance and warned away an English vessel which had arrived on a mission similar to their own. The French established themselves first at Biloxi, then on Mobile Bay, and in 1718 they founded New Orleans. Thereafter for nearly a half-century the Mississippi was used and controlled by the French.

At the close of the French and Indian War France lost her possessions in the New World, and the Mississippi River became an international boundary. From 1763 to 1783 Spain and Great Britain confronted each other across the "Great River." During the American Revolution the river witnessed hostilities between the British and the Spanish, and was the avenue for the supplies by means of which George Rogers Clark was able to maintain his hold on the Illinois country. According to the Definitive Treaty of Peace, 1783, the United States was to extend to the Mississippi between Spanish Florida and the Canadian boundary, and Americans were to have the free navigation of the river.

The Spanish were not party to this treaty and they had their own ideas about the navigation of the Mississippi—ideas which they were able to enforce because they controlled the mouth of the river. They imposed duties which were regarded as exorbitant and prohibitive by the settlers in the Ohio Valley for whom the river was the only feasible outlet to market. The West seethed with unrest, intrigues and threats of disunion, and the "Mississippi Question" became one of the most troublesome problems facing Federal officials and diplomats. Finally, in 1795, in accordance with Pinckney's Treaty with Spain the river was opened to Americans. In 1800, however, Spain ceded Louisiana back to France. Shortly afterward the river was closed once more and again there was consternation and turmoil in the West until the Louisiana Purchase settled the question and made the Mississippi an American river.

Thereafter the Mississippi River served without restriction as the great artery of trade and commerce for the whole upper valley. The first successors of the canoes or pirogues of the Indians and traders were the flatboats on which the farmers floated their produce to market. Then came the keelboats which could be propelled upstream by prodigious effort. But river transportation received its greatest impetus in 1811 when the steamboat *New Orleans* made its historic trip from Pittsburgh to New Orleans. The number of steamboats on the Mississippi and Ohio increased slowly at first, but by 1825 there were 125, and by 1860 more than 1000 were in service. It was not without reason, therefore, that the Southerners counted on the Mississippi to bind the Middle West to them in economic interest. That it failed to do so at the critical time was due to the counteracting influence of the railroads and other factors.

Opening of the Mississippi River (1861–63). The strategic importance of controlling the Mississippi was recognized by both Federals and Confederates early in the Civil War. In the hands of the former it would afford an easy avenue for penetrating into enemy territory and separating the important states of Arkansas, Louisiana and Texas from the rest of the Confederacy; to the latter it served as a valuable artery for transporting troops and supplies and a connecting link between two important sections of their territory.

Thwarted in 1861 in their plan to hold the line of the Ohio River, the Confederates fortified Columbus, Ky., on the Mississippi; but the Federal capture of Forts Henry (Feb. 6, 1862) and Donelson (Feb. 16, 1862) led to the evacuation of Columbus. Island No. 10, in the Mississippi River near the Kentucky-Tennessee boundary, was then fortified by the Confederates, but Federal gunboats captured the island on April 7, 1862, leaving Fort Pillow, about midway between Island No. 10 and Memphis, as the northernmost river defense. However, Federal occupation of Corinth, Miss., soon rendered Fort Pillow useless to the Confederates and it was abandoned; and on June 6, 1862, Memphis fell into Federal hands, thus opening the Mississippi as far south as Vicksburg.

Meanwhile, a Federal squadron under Farragut, operating from the Gulf of Mexico, had forced its way past the Confederate defenses at Forts Jackson and St. Philip, some sixty miles below New Orleans, and appeared before that city on April 25, 1862. New Orleans surrendered on May 1, 1862, and other river points as far up as Baton Rouge soon fell into Federal hands. The Confederates now strongly fortified the high bluffs at Port Hudson, twenty-five miles above Baton Rouge, and at Vicksburg, 200 miles to the northward, in an effort to preserve the valuable communi-cation between the fertile Red River Valley and Confederate territory east of the Mississippi.

After several months of preliminary operations, Grant closed in on Vicksburg in the early summer of 1863, and Banks soon attacked Port Hudson from the rear, after Farragut had made an unsuccessful attempt to pass the fortifications with his gunboats on March 14, 1863, to go to the aid of Grant before Vicksburg. After a siege of nearly two months Vicksburg surrendered on July 4, 1863; and when the news reached Port Hudson that post also surrendered on July 9, 1863, being no longer of value to the Confederates. This completed the opening of the Mississippi, and Lincoln could write: "The Father of Waters again goes unvexed to the sea."

MISSOURI history virtually begins in the last half of the 17th century. The French were the first real explorers, traders and white settlers, the Canadian-French being in the majority among the settlers and the Louisiana-French in the minority. Chief among the explorers between 1673–1723 were Jolliet, Marquette, LaSalle, LaHontan, DuTisne and Bourgmont. Others followed and a large part of Missouri was explored by 1804. Lead mines and salt springs were discovered and made productive, and profitable fur trading was established. Trade with Santa Fe and the upper Missouri was attempted, and war and peace were made with the Indians. A temporary settlement was made as early as 1700 when French Jesuits from Canada established a mission where St. Louis now stands. The first permanent settlement was Ste. Geneviève, possibly about 1735. St. Louis, the second permanent settlement, was founded by Laclede in 1764. In 1762 France secretly ceded her territory west of the Mississippi to Spain. It was 1767, however, before the first Spanish officer came to St. Louis, and 1770 when the French lieutenant-governor in St. Louis, St. Ange de Bellerive, officially surrendered upper Louisiana to Don Pedro Piernas, Spanish lieutenant-governor and military commandant. French population increased after England won the eastern side of the Mississippi, and American immigration began during the Revolutionary War, increasing after 1795 because Spain encouraged American settlement. The simple Spanish government did not affect the character of the easygoing French and more energetic Americans, and French influence remained dominant in colonial Missouri.

The Louisiana Purchase was consummated by the United States in 1803 but upper Louisiana was not formally transferred to the United States until March 10, 1804, when Capt. Amos Stoddard took command in St. Louis. Following a period of military government (March 10–Oct. 1, 1804), the area which became Missouri passed through three stages of territorial government as a part of the District of Louisiana (Oct. 1, 1804–July 4, 1805), the Territory of Louisiana (July 4, 1805–Oct. 1, 1812), and finally the Territory of Missouri (Oct. 1, 1812–1820). In 1818 and 1819, when popular and legislative petitions from Missouri Territory were presented asking for statehood, Congress engaged in a bitter sectional controversy of nationwide significance. The Missouri Compromise, effected in 1820, gave Missouri the right to form a state constitution and government without restriction on slavery, and also provided that slavery should not exist elsewhere in the Louisiana Purchase north of 36° 30′, N. Lat. Missouri drafted and adopted a constitution on July 19, 1820, held a state election and on Aug. 10, 1821, Missouri became a state.

MISSOURI COMPROMISE. The Missouri Territory comprised that part of the Louisiana Purchase not organized as the State of Louisiana in 1812. Ever since it had been a French province slavery had existed in the Territory. From 1817 to 1819 the Missouri Territorial Assembly petitioned Congress for statehood, with boundaries limited to approximately those of the present state. In 1819 there was an equal number of slave and free states. When the House of Representatives reported a bill authorizing Missouri to frame a constitution, James Tallmadge of New York proposed an amendment prohibiting the further introduction of slaves into Missouri and providing that all children born of slaves should be free at the age of twenty-five. The amendment was passed, Feb. 16–17, 1819, but rejected by the Senate. Congress adjourned without further action but the South was stricken with fear.

When Congress reconvened in December, 1819, Maine had formed a constitution and was requesting admission as a free state. The House passed an act admitting Maine. The Senate joined this measure to the one admitting Missouri without mention of slavery. Sen. J. B. Thomas of Illinois offered an amendment to the Senate bill for the admission of Missouri as a slave state, but with the provision that, in the remainder of the Louisiana Purchase, slavery should be prohibited north of 36° 30′ N. Lat. A debate followed that startled the nation. It came, said Thomas Jefferson, "like a fire bell in the night." A sectional alignment threatened the Union.

The House passed a bill, March 1, 1820, admitting Missouri as a free state. The Senate took up the measure, struck out the antislavery provision, and added the Thomas amendment. A compromise was effected by admitting Maine as a free state, March 3, 1820 (effective, March 15), and by authorizing Missouri to form a constitution, with no restriction on slavery, March 6, 1820. The region of the Louisiana Purchase north of 36° 30′, except the State of Missouri, was thus dedicated to freedom.

Missouri called a constitutional convention to meet at St. Louis, June 12, 1820. The constitution empowered the legislature to exclude free Negroes and mulattoes from the state. This restriction caused another bitter debate in Congress. A second compromise was, therefore, effected, March 2, 1821. This stipulated that Missouri would not be admitted until she agreed that nothing in her constitution should be interpreted to abridge the privileges and immunities of citizens of the United States. The pledge was secured. On Aug. 10, 1821, Missouri became a state.

The Compromise was respected and regarded as almost sacred until the Mexican War, when the power of Congress to exclude slavery from the territories was again questioned. In 1848 Congress passed the Oregon Territory bill prohibiting slavery. President Polk signed it on the ground that the Territory was north of the Missouri Compromise line. Soon afterward proposals were made to extend the Compromise line of 1820 through the Mexican Cession to the Pacific. These efforts failed to secure the extension of the 36° 30′ line across the continent. Instead, the principle of popular sovereignty prevailed in the Compromise of 1850. The admission of California in 1850 gave the free states a majority of one. In 1854 the Missouri Compromise was repealed by the Kansas-Nebraska Act.

MISSOURI RIVER, known to Marquette in 1673 as the Peki-tan-oui, so named on some of the early maps, and later as Oumessourit, drains a watershed of nearly 600,000 square miles. Stretching from its source northwest of the Yellowstone Park, where the Jefferson, Gallatin and Madison Rivers join together in southern Montana, it winds around hills and bluffs, through the most fertile valley in the world, a distance of 2546 miles to its junction with the Mississippi. The Missouri River was first explored from its mouth to its source by Lewis and Clark. The lower part of the Missouri was known to the French trappers, traders and *voyageurs*, who ascended it as far as the Kansas River in 1705. In 1720 a Spanish caravan was sent from Santa Fe to the Missouri to drive back the French. The early French called the river "St. Philip." They probably did not go higher than the Platte, which was considered the dividing line between the upper and lower river. In 1719 Claude Charles du Tisne and party went up the Missouri in canoes as far as the Grand River. Credited with being the first white man to visit the upper Missouri country, Sieur de la Vérendrye led a party from one of the posts of the Hudson's Bay Company in 1738 to the Mandan villages. Other explorations followed, searching for the "Western Sea" by way of the Missouri River. Although it was thought for years that no keelboat could ascend the Missouri, it later became the great highway into the West. While Gregoire Sarpy is said to have first introduced the keelboat, the real father of navigation on the Missouri was Manuel Lisa. The first steamboat ever to ascend the river was the *Independence* which pushed off from St. Louis in 1819, reached Old Franklin in thirteen days and turned back at Old Chariton, in Missouri. In 1831 Pierre Chouteau ascended the Missouri in his *Yellowstone.*

MOBILE BAY, BATTLE OF (1864). On Aug. 5, a Union fleet of four monitors and fourteen wooden vessels of war, commanded by Admiral David G. Farragut, forced an entrance into Mobile Bay through a narrow passage protected by mines, by Fort Morgan and by the ironclad *Tennessee* and three small wooden gunboats, commanded by Admiral Franklin Buchanan. The Federal monitor *Tecumseh* was sunk by a mine; "Damn the torpedoes!" cried Farragut, as his *Hartford* took the lead. All his vessels eventually reached the Bay, though some were injured by Fort Morgan and the *Tennessee*. Then followed a terrific battle between the *Tennessee* and the whole Union fleet. Three of the larger wooden vessels were injured, but the powerful guns of the three monitors finally forced the ironclad to surrender. Farragut lost 52 killed, 93 drowned and 170 wounded. Buchanan lost 12 killed and 20 wounded. Fort Morgan surrendered on Aug. 23, and the city of Mobile was completely blockaded.

MOCCASIN, from an Algonkian word for shoe, is specifically a foot covering of soft skin, with soft or hard soles. All the Indian tribes of the United States wore moccasins except a few of those in our western deserts and in parts of California. The eastern Indian moccasin had a soft sole and was often made by folding a piece of soft tanned skin up over the foot, the seams at the top. The uppers and the toes offered fields for decoration with quills and beads. The Plains Indians preferred a moccasin with a hard sole, but decorated the uppers with attractive designs in porcupine quills and beads. There were tribal styles in shape and other unessentials which made possible the identification of tracks in soft earth. Women made the moccasins and both sexes of all ages wore them. Moccasins were adopted by the whites, universally worn by early traders and trappers and are still in use in parts of Canada and the United States. To some extent Indian models have influenced certain modern styles of shoes.

MODOC WAR (1872–73), the last Indian war to affect southern Oregon and northern California, was started in 1872 when a Modoc chief known as Capt. Jack went on the warpath to resist efforts to force him and his followers to live on the reservation assigned to them. Capt. Jack commanded scarcely fifty warriors, but the lava beds centering in the Tule Lake region offered a country which was almost impenetrable to the United States troops.

Gen. Edw. R. S. Canby, commander of the troops sent to capture the Indians, and one other unarmed member of a peace commission which met the band were treacherously murdered (April 11, 1873) and other members wounded. The War Department and the Department of the Interior dealing with Indian affairs took opposing views of the struggle and worked at cross purposes. The Indians finally gave up the struggle, and Capt. Jack and three other Modoc leaders were tried by a military court and hanged on Oct. 3, 1873. The surviving tribesmen were removed to a distant reservation.

MOLASSES ACT (1733) laid a prohibitive duty of ninepence on every gallon of rum, sixpence a gallon on molasses and five shillings a hundredweight on sugar imported from foreign colonies into his majesty's American colonies, to be paid before landing.

The act originated in the conflicting economic interests of continental and island colonies. Barbados, which was suffering from the effects of a recent hurricane, the exhaustion of her soil, the restraints of the Navigation Acts and a burdensome export tax, led the other British sugar colonies in petitioning Parliament that the "bread colonies" be prohibited from selling provisions to, or buying sugar products from, the more fertile foreign West Indies. The continental colonies had a sound economic answer, that the British West Indies could not consume all their provisions nor satisfy their demand for molasses; but the sugar colonies had the better political connections in Parliament.

Colonial smuggling minimized the act's effects. Although one cannot measure the exact extent of the illicit trade, it is clear that New England distilled considerably more rum than could have been produced from legally imported molasses. Yet it was expensive to evade officials or to procure their connivance, and the act probably served as a mildly protective tariff in favor of the British West Indies until its repeal in 1764 by the Sugar Act.

MOLINO DEL REY, BATTLE OF (Sept. 8, 1847). Believing it to contain an operating gun foundry, Gen. Winfield Scott ordered William J. Worth to storm the "King's Mill," a stone building near the base of Chapultepec hill. Worth's tactics proved uninspired, the Mexican defense unexpectedly resolute, and it was only after a bloody initial repulse that the "Mill" was captured. The victory proved disappointingly barren, the foundry nonexistent. The heavy casualties, including valuable senior officers, temporarily depressed the army's spirits. Later the "Mill" provided cover from which Pillow assaulted Chapultepec.

"MOLLY MAGUIRES," a secret and eventually criminal society also known as the "Buckshots," "White Boys" and "Sleepers," terrorized the anthracite region of Pennsylvania from about 1865 until finally broken up in a series of sensational murder trials from 1875 to 1877.

The Molly Maguires used their power in labor disputes for the benefit of their members, and intimidated or murdered recalcitrant mine bosses and colliery superintendents.

In 1874, at the height of their power, Franklin B.

Gowen, president of the Philadelphia Coal and Iron Co., determined upon their suppression. A Pinkerton detective, James McParlan, posing as a counterfeiter, holder of fraudulent pension and ex-killer, established himself in the coal regions, joined the organization and rose to be secretary of his division.

After a particularly outrageous murder in 1875, one assassin was condemned to death, the first capital conviction of a Molly. In view of evidence brought out at the trial, suspicion arose that a detective was at work and quickly centered on McParlan. Evading one plot to murder him, he continued his pose for some time and then quietly withdrew. The murder prosecutions which followed were based largely on his evidence and shattered the organization forever.

MONEY, PURCHASING POWER OF,

is the reciprocal of the general level of prices, and changes in purchasing power can be measured by changes in an index of the price level. We have no index of the general level of all prices in the United States prior to 1875, but the Bureau of Labor Statistics, in conjunction with Warren, Pearson and Stoker, has constructed a wholesale commodity price index which runs back to pre-Revolutionary times and gives at least an approximation of changes in the value of the dollar.

The first drastic change in the dollar's purchasing power occurred in the Revolutionary War, the dollar falling from $1.96 (1926 = $1.00) in 1775 to a low of $0.67 in most of 1779 and 1780. Thereafter it rose to around $1.67 and maintained a fair degree of stability until the War of 1812, when it again fell to $0.76 in December, 1814. From 1820 on, the purchasing power of the dollar fluctuated above and below $1.43 until the time of the Civil War when it fell to $0.65 in August and September of 1864. From then on the trend of the purchasing power of the dollar was irregularly upward to a high of $2.13 in 1896-97, after which a declining trend set in which carried the dollar down to about $1.43 in 1915.

With the progress of World War I the purchasing power of the dollar again declined rapidly, reaching $0.60 in May, 1920, from which low point it rose drastically to $1.10 in early 1922. Thereafter it fell to $0.99 at the end of the year and fluctuated moderately above and below $1.00 until 1929. With the onset of the great depression the purchasing power of the dollar rose rather steadily to $1.67 in the spring of 1933, then, following the settlement of the banking crisis, fell irregularly to $1.14 in the summer of 1937, after which it rose to $1.21 in 1939.

During the defense program of the two years (1940–41) preceding our entry into World War II, the purchasing power of the dollar declined to $1.15 in 1941. A further decline during the war, to $0.95 in 1945, was moderated by the existence of price and wage controls. With the removal of controls in 1946, however, purchasing power dropped sharply to $0.61

in 1948. Since then it has fallen further, with two minor interruptions to $0.54 in January, 1959, a new low point in this country's history.

Consideration of the figures presented indicates that, up to our entry into World War II, the really violent changes in monetary purchasing power in the United States have resulted from war inflations and their subsequent reactions. Severe inflation during World War II was held in check through the institution of direct controls, but the years since have witnessed almost continuous depreciation in dollar purchasing power. The outlook in late 1959 did not indicate any change in this unfortunate trend.

MONITOR AND MERRIMACK, BATTLE OF (MARCH 9, 1862).

The ironclad principle was introduced by the French during the Crimean War. There were about 100 ironclads built or projected, none in the United States, before the American Civil War. Since 1851, Stephen Mallory had been chairman of the Senate Committee on Naval Affairs, so that he was exceptionally well informed when he became Confederate Secretary of the Navy. He saw the Confederacy's only chance at sea in beating the North to ironclad production. Unfortunately for Mallory, his program was subordinated to the greater needs of equipping the Confederate Army from meager industry. He managed to commission thirty-two, of which less than a dozen were ever fully ready.

The U. S. S. *Merrimack* was scuttled in the Union evacuation of Norfolk. Upon her sound hull the Confederates built a sloping casemate of twenty-inch-square heart-pine, sheathed by four-inch-square live-oak, and a double layer of two-inch-thick iron, the outermost vertical. The conversion dragged for months that allowed the Union to recognize the danger and commence a program. The *Merrimack* was rechristened the C. S. S. *Virginia,* a name that did not gain contemporary usage. She was unique in not having a captain, inasmuch as Flag-Officer Franklin Buchanan preferred to have her commanded by her Executive Officer, normally second. This officer was able young Lt. Catesby Jones.

On March 8, 1862, the *Merrimack* sortied from Norfolk to demonstrate Buchanan's conviction that she could vitally assist Maj.-Gen. John Magruder if he wished to expel Union forces from the lower "Yorktown" peninsula. Control of Hampton Roads and the James River was the issue. The wooden warships *Cumberland* and *Congress* were protecting the water flanks of the Union position at Newport News, and Buchanan sank them easily, being himself painfully wounded by imprudent exposure during the fight with the *Congress*. The Union squadron on duty at the blockading station outside the Roads hastened in and were driven back by the ironclad. The *Minnesota* was stranded beyond the *Merrimack's* reach and Jones brought her to anchor for the night off Sewell's Point.

During the night, the U. S. S. *Monitor* arrived after a dramatic dash from New York on March 6, into blue water that nearly foundered her (and would do so on New Year's eve).

When Jones got up steam on March 9 to destroy the *Minnesota,* she was no longer helplessly alone. The *Monitor* under Lt. John Worden successfully engaged the *Merrimack* until tide and cumulative damage required Jones to head for Norfolk. Worden was blinded and shocked by a shell explosion.

Union claims of victory were founded upon the misconception that the *Merrimack* was trying to break the blockade. For multiple reasons, the lumbering *Merrimack* was incapable of making headway three miles into the open Atlantic. She was aimed by Buchanan at clearing Hampton Roads and did so. By naval semantics, both antagonists won: the *Monitor tactically* because Worden kept the *Merrimack* from destroying the *Minnesota,* the *Merrimack strategically* because the Union Navy thenceforward stayed out of the Roads until she was destroyed by her own crew upon the Confederate evacuation of Norfolk on May 11, 1862. By then, Gen. McClellan, who had initially planned upon using the Roads and the James for a swift stab at Richmond, was fully committed to the limited wharfage of Fort Monroe, safely outside the Roads, to mount tediously and slowly his famous peninsular campaign which ended in defeat.

The strategic victory of the *Merrimack* in buying time for the Confederacy to shift forces from the Potomac to defend Richmond is an American classic illustration of the influence of sea power upon history.

MONROE DOCTRINE (Dec. 2, 1823). From the very beginning of our Federal history there has been a strong tendency to differentiate America from Europe, and to assume that as little political connection should exist between the two as is possible. Expressions of this viewpoint can be found in Washington's Farewell Address and in Jefferson's First Inaugural. Monroe's message of Dec. 2, 1823, supplemented this previous formula by seeking to exclude European intervention from the New World. The message was due to two different sets of circumstances. The pretensions of the Russian government to exclude all but Russian vessels from the Northwest coast of America north of 51° precipitated a diplomatic controversy in the course of which Monroe's Secretary of State, John Quincy Adams, laid down the principle that European governments could establish no new colonies in the New World, every portion thereof having been already occupied. Monroe, in the message of 1823, repeated Adams' formula virtually in Adams' own words, declaring that "the American continents, by the free and independent condition which they have assumed and maintained, are henceforth not to be considered as subjects for future colonization by any European powers." A second reason for the message lay in the fear that the continental European powers were planning the reconquest of the Spanish American republics which had declared their independence of Spain. Suggestions of such a purpose came to Monroe and his cabinet from Richard Rush, the United States minister in London, who got them from George Canning, the British Foreign Secretary, and more directly from the language of the Tsar Alexander in a memorandum addressed to the American Government in October, 1823. After long cabinet discussions, the President fixed upon a pronouncement which warned against intervention, and, with regard to the Spanish colonies, declared that "we could not view any interposition with the view of oppressing them or controlling in any other manner their destiny by any European power, in any other light than as the manifestation of an unfriendly disposition toward the United States."

While the message was enthusiastically received in the United States, it had little practical influence at the time. The European powers never intended intervention on any considerable scale and viewed the message with irritation and contempt.

The United States itself, on four separate occasions in the years immediately following 1823, refused to make any commitments looking to the carrying out of the policy outlined by Monroe, and the debates on the Panama Congress in 1826 showed that, beyond the shadow of a doubt, American opinion was hostile to any alliance with the new states. They themselves, as a matter of fact, became economically and financially, if not politically, more dependent on Great Britain than on the Republic to the north.

For some time after 1826 Monroe's message remained virtually unnoticed, and minor violations of it occurred in the encroachments of Britain in Central America and in the acquisition by Great Britain of the Falkland Islands.

The first great revival of interest in it came in 1845 and was produced by the intrigues of Great Britain and France to prevent the annexation of Texas to the United States, by the difference of opinion over Oregon, and fear of British purposes in California. On Dec. 2, 1845, President Polk reiterated the principles of President Monroe, condemning not only intervention, but the application of the principle of the balance of power to the New World. He emphasized particularly the significance of this principle with regard to North America. Again, as in 1823, the immediate results were not important, but the principle had begun to sink into the American mind, and Polk gave it new expression.

On April 29, 1848, in a message in which he declared that an English or Spanish protectorate over Yucatan would be a violation of the principles of 1823, Polk declared that the threat of such action might compel the United States itself to assume control over the region in question. In this message, for the first time, the Monroe principle was made the basis for measures of expansion. No action was taken, however.

In the 1850's, the message figured again and again in connection with the dispute over the Central American question and attained increasing popularity (*see* Clayton-Bulwer Treaty). From a partisan or Democratic dogma, it began to rise to the rank of a national principle. It was cited in international correspondence and its significance was recognized (though its validity was denied) by more than one European statesman.

The Civil War offered to the powers of Europe an excellent opportunity to challenge Monroe's principles. Taking advantage of the situation, Spain intervened in Santo Domingo and France sought to establish in Mexico an Empire under the rule of the Austrian Archduke, Maximilian. When, at the outbreak of the war, Secretary of State Seward attempted to invoke the Monroe Doctrine against the first of these powers, he received a sharp rebuff, but learning from experience, he waited before challenging the French in Mexico until the success of American arms made it possible for him to assert the Doctrine with increasing vigor. While other circumstances contributed to the collapse of Maximilian's Empire, there can be no question that the diplomatic pressure exerted by the American Government in 1865 was keenly felt in Paris, and that fear of the United States was a factor in the French decision to withdraw its troops from Mexico. The Doctrine, in the meantime, had attained an immense popularity at home.

The events of the 1870's and the 1880's are less dramatic, but a steady tendency developed to expand the scope of the Doctrine. The principle that no territory might be transferred in the New World from one European power to another, not altogether unknown in the previous epoch, became more and more closely linked with Monroe's principles, especially through the efforts of President Grant and his Secretary of State, Hamilton Fish. The Doctrine was cited even less in consonance with its original terms, or with Polk's interpretation of it, as forbidding the construction by Europeans of a trans-isthmian canal (*see* Panama Canal), and still more as implying that such a canal must be under the exclusive guarantee of the United States. This point of view, the cause of acute diplomatic controversy in the 1880's, was accepted by Great Britain toward the end of the century in the famous Hay-Pauncefote Treaty.

One of the most dramatic extensions of the Doctrine was Grover Cleveland's assertion that its principles compelled Great Britain to arbitrate a boundary dispute with the Republic of Venezuela over the limitations of British Guiana. President Cleveland's position produced a serious diplomatic crisis, but the moderation displayed by the British government permitted a peaceful solution of the difficulty.

The growing nationalism of the United States toward the end of the 19th and the beginning of the 20th century was not without its effect upon the Doctrine. The joint intervention of Great Britain, Germany and Italy against Venezuela, looking to the satisfaction of pecuniary claims, we now know quite definitely, concealed no ulterior purpose, but it produced widespread irritation in the United States. The story of German designs of conquest is pure legend, but that the Theodore Roosevelt administration, which began with an attitude of great moderation, was gradually rendered more and more nervous by the intervention, and was considering diplomatic measures to bring it to an end, is certainly true. On President Roosevelt himself the effect of the intervention was important. He moved toward the position that the United States must assume a measure of control of the more unruly of the Latin-American states in order to prevent European action against them, and in 1905 a treaty for American control of customs in Santo Domingo was negotiated. While it met with opposition in the Senate, it was ratified in 1907. In the meantime the President, in his message of 1904, had definitely laid down the doctrine that chronic wrongdoing by a Latin-American state might compel American action. The precedent which he established has more than once been applied, or attempted to be applied, especially in the Caribbean area, and, in general, in the not infrequent interventions in the affairs of Caribbean states the Doctrine has figured as justification.

Of recent years, however, there has been a change. Increasing resentment against American interference in the affairs of the Republics of Latin America has been reflected in actual policy. The interventions of the United States in Haiti and Santo Domingo in 1915 and 1916, during the administration of President Wilson, were liquidated, respectively, in 1934 and 1924. The intervention in Nicaragua in the Coolidge administration was short-lived. Under President Franklin D. Roosevelt, pledges against armed intervention were given, and at the Seventh Pan-American Conference at Montevideo a definite treaty was signed, pledging the signatories not to intervene in the internal and external affairs of one another. At Buenos Aires in 1936 the practice of collecting pecuniary obligations by armed force was declared illegal.

The Monroe Doctrine has never obtained a true international status. At the World War Peace Conference in 1919, in order to placate domestic opposition to the covenant of the League, President Wilson was obliged to incorporate in that document an article declaring that nothing therein contained should affect the legal validity of a regional understanding such as the Monroe Doctrine. The exact interpretation of such a phrase, however, must remain doubtful, and it is difficult to maintain that it implies complete European recognition of the American dogma. It was certainly far from acceptable to the more nationalistic supporters of Monroe's principles in the United States.

In America, as the evolution of the American attitude toward intervention shows, there has been somewhat of a reaction against extreme interpretations of the principles of 1823. Secretary Hughes attempted to dissociate our various interventions in the Caribbean area from the Monroe Doctrine. In 1929 the Committee on Foreign Relations of the Senate of the United States, in transmitting the Briand-Kellogg Pact, added a gloss or separate report in which the Monroe Doctrine was conservatively interpreted and based upon the principle of self-defense. The Roosevelt Corollary of 1904 was definitely excluded.

On the other hand, there is no question that the words "Monroe Doctrine" are still words to conjure with in the United States, and that there is a very great sensitiveness with regard to all European activities in this hemisphere. Emotionally the phrase has an immense appeal which operates to fortify a purely isolationist policy on the part of our own Government. Abroad, the intensity of this feeling is well understood. It is extremely doubtful whether any nation would challenge it directly, nor indeed has it been so challenged for more than ninety years.

The Monroe Doctrine is not international law. Its principles may be deduced from other principles truly legal, such as the right of self-defense and self-preservation, but fundamentally the Doctrine is an article of faith, all the more powerful because it has its roots in emotion rather than in reason.

MONROE MISSION TO FRANCE (1794–96). The rapid development of the French Revolution made Gouverneur Morris unpopular as the American minister to France. His sympathies were strongly monarchial. The French government suggested his recall when Citizen Genêt was recalled from the United States. James Monroe was selected to replace Morris because of his known friendship for the French Republic. He arrived in Paris in August, 1794, and found the French Revolution rapidly changing. He took a fraternal tone toward the revolutionary government and immediately became popular. Monroe, however, faced a double difficulty which eventually deprived him of the confidence both of the French government and of President Washington. Jay's Treaty was negotiated with England in 1794. Monroe, having been kept in ignorance of the real character of Jay's mission, was instructed to allay French suspicions. He informed the French government that Jay had been positively forbidden to weaken the engagements between the United States and France. Monroe was in no position to defend the Jay Treaty when its text was revealed, containing provisions harmful to our ally France. Monroe tried to palliate what seemed to him to be the ill faith of Washington's cabinet. The Federalist leaders were able to convince Washington that Monroe's conduct was disloyal to the administration and the President recalled him. Washington's decision was approved by many Americans whose sympathies had been alienated by the bloody excesses of the French Revolution. The French government refused to receive Charles Cotesworth Pinckney, appointed as Monroe's successor, and this led to the XYZ affair.

MONTANA. The eastern part of Montana became an American possession in 1803 by the Louisiana Purchase; the western portion was a part of the Oregon Country, conceded by Great Britain to be American territory by the Oregon Treaty of 1846. The primary exploration of both sections was by Lewis and Clark in 1805–6; a trip up the Missouri by Prince Maximilian of Wied in 1833 added to the ethnology and geography of the region; and the survey by Maj. I. I. Stevens (1853) of a railroad route from St. Paul to Puget Sound brought additional information. At this time the Blackfoot confederacy occupied the area north of the Missouri, the Crows held the region south of the Yellowstone, Siouan tribes contested the terrain near the confluence of these rivers, and the central rolling plains were neutral hunting grounds shared with the Shoshone by all of these peoples. The Flatheads occupied the Bitter Root Valley, and among them Father Jean Pierre de Smet (1842) founded his mission.

Manuel Lisa opened the fur trade on the upper Missouri in 1809. After migration to Oregon began, the number of traders was augmented by some who had aimed for the Willamette but had compromised with the hardships of the trek by going no farther than the Bitter Root, the Yellowstone or the Missouri headwaters. Thus was created that small settlement in Bitter Root Valley which requested Washington Territory to erect for them a county government. In response, the region east of the 117th meridian and west of the Rockies was designated in 1860–61 as Missoula and Shoshone counties.

Gold had already been discovered in the region. Capt. John Mullan's report on a feasible wagon route from Fort Benton, head of navigation on the Missouri, to Fort Walla Walla in the Columbia Valley, described a route to gold deposits at a time (1863) when many men were anxious to get away from war. This information swelled the number of gold seekers. Gold was found at Bannack in 1862, at Virginia City in 1863, and at Helena in 1864. Each locality had its own provisional government, and the law of the mining camps prevailed. Increase of population, however, had made necessary a civil government, and in 1864 the Territory of Montana was created.

Placer mining gave way to quartz mining. At Butte, the Asteroid produced Montana's first silver in June, 1866, but it was not until January, 1895, that the mine was really worked. Silver, then copper, replaced gold as the most valuable mineral product. Statehood was gained in 1889.

MONTERREY, BATTLES OF (Sept. 21–23, 1846). In the Mexican War, Gen. Zachary Taylor's invading army of 6000 attacked Monterrey in northeastern Mexico, defended by Gen. Ampudia with 9000 men. The first day's fight outside the city paved the way for the assault upon three fortified hills which guarded the approach, and which were carried before daybreak on the 22nd. On that day and the next the Americans completed the conquest of the city. An eight-weeks' armistice was agreed upon, but repudiated by Congress, and the fighting was renewed within six weeks.

MONTGOMERY CONVENTION, THE, assembled at Montgomery, Ala., Feb. 4, 1861, to organize the Confederate States of America. Representatives were present from six states of the lower South (South Carolina, Georgia, Alabama, Mississippi, Florida and Louisiana).

The convention drafted a provisional constitution for the Confederate states. It then declared itself a provisional legislature and set up a government without waiting for the ratification of the constitution.

The next important step in setting up this government was the selection of the President and Vice-President. For President, the convention selected Jefferson Davis of Mississippi, a conservative who had not actively supported secession. For Vice-President, Alexander H. Stephens of Georgia, who had actively opposed secession, was chosen.

The convention continued to sit in Montgomery until May 20, 1861, when it adjourned to meet in Richmond on July 20. It added new members as other states seceded and acted interchangeably as a constitutional convention and a provisional legislature. It completed a permanent constitution (adopted March 11, 1861), and supervised its ratification. It directed the election in November, 1861, at which a Congress and a President and Vice-President were elected; it also passed all laws which were necessary to adapt the existing laws and machinery of the Government of the United States to the needs of the new government. With the inauguration of the permanent government (Feb. 22, 1862) it adjourned.

MONTICELLO was the home of Thomas Jefferson near Charlottesville, Va. Begun in 1770 and completed in 1809, it was designed by Jefferson himself. Like the Earl of Burlington in 18th-century England, Jefferson was inspired by the villas of the Italian architect Andrea Palladio. But in his awareness of the changes compelled by climate and site he was closer to the work of Inigo Jones, the first Englishman to follow Palladio's example. The estate has been opened to the public by the Thomas Jefferson Memorial Foundation.

MONTREAL, CAPTURE OF (1760). Wolfe's victory at Quebec in 1759 was followed on Sept. 8 of the following year by the surrender of Montreal. The spirits of the French had been raised by the success of the Chevalier de Lévis at Ste. Foy on April 28, but not for long. Everything depended upon whether the French or the English fleet would first come to the rescue. On May 15 the vanguard of the English ships appeared below Quebec. Lévis, abandoning hope of help from France, raised the siege and retreated up the river. The English, knowing that Montreal was doomed, prepared at their leisure for the final stroke. The plan of campaign had been carefully prepared. While Gen. Geoffrey Amherst moved north from New York to Lake Ontario and descended the St. Lawrence, Gen. James Murray with another army and the fleet moved up the river, and Col. Haviland approached by way of Lake Champlain. On Sept. 8, 1760, the governor, the Marquis de Vaudreuil, at Amherst's demand, surrendered Montreal, and with it Canada.

MONTREAL, CAPTURE OF (1775). After the fall of St. Johns, Nov. 2, 1775, the main body of the American force under Gen. Montgomery pushed on toward Montreal, which Ethan Allen had failed to take by a *coup de main* in September. Gov. Carleton was in the city, but, as the fortifications were weak and ruinous, he made no attempt to defend it, and on Nov. 11 slipped away with the garrison down the river toward Quebec. American batteries at Sorel barred the way, and the flotilla and the troops were captured; but Carleton himself reached Quebec in safety. On Nov. 13 the American troops marched into Montreal without encountering resistance. The city remained in American hands until June 15, 1776.

MOORE'S CREEK BRIDGE, BATTLE AT (Feb. 27, 1776), was a decisive victory of North Carolina Whigs over North Carolina Loyalists. Aptly called "the Lexington and Concord" of the South, this battle, fought 18 miles above Wilmington, crushed the Loyalists, aroused the Whigs, stimulated the independence movement and prevented British invasion of the state in 1776. In the battle, which lasted only three minutes, 1600 Loyalists were overwhelmed by 1100 Whigs. The latter had one killed and one wounded; the former fifty killed or wounded and 850 prisoners. The Whigs also captured 350 guns, 150 swords, 1500 rifles, 13 wagons, medical supplies and £15,000 sterling.

MORAVIANS. The name is generally applied in America and England to a German-speaking sect of Protestants, known originally as The *Unitas Fratrum* or The Unity of the Brethren. This evangelical church arose in eastern Bohemia before the Reformation; spread to Moravia, Poland and Austria; was almost crushed out of existence during the Thirty Years' War; and was revived on the Saxon estate of Count Zinzendorf in the first half of the 18th century. Their desire to escape persecution and their missionary zeal led Zinzendorf, their leader, to make an agreement with the Georgia Trustees, whereby a colony of Moravians was to be planted in Georgia, with the assurance that they would not be required to bear arms. Bishop Augustus Gottlieb Spangenberg and nine of his followers landed in Savannah in 1735, followed by twenty-seven other Moravians during the next five years. The outbreak of war in Georgia in 1739 made the Moravians very unhappy and they removed to Pennsylvania in 1740. The next year they purchased land in "the Forks of the Delaware" and founded the town of Nazareth. Meantime, other Moravians from Europe, including Count Zinzendorf, were arriving in the province, and a large tract of land was purchased at the junction of the Lehigh River and Monocacy Creek, where the town of Bethlehem was begun about 1741. This settlement grew rapidly, having 800 settlers by 1756, and from the first it has been the Moravian center in America. By 1775 there were about 2500 Moravians in Pennsylvania. At first the Bethlehem and Nazareth Moravians adopted a communism of labor, called the General Economy, with the lands being owned by the Church, its members working them and receiving in return the necessities of life. This plan was abandoned in 1762.

In 1752 the Bethlehem Moravians sent out a party headed by Spangenberg to select a place for settlement in North Carolina. After a careful survey the party selected a tract of about 100,000 acres, which Spangenberg named Wachovia. This land was purchased from Lord Granville in August, 1753, and a few months later the town of Betharaba was founded by twelve Moravians from Bethlehem. Bethania and Salem were founded a few years later, and the latter town, now a part of Winston-Salem, became the Moravian center of the South.

The Moravians stressed missionary work among the Indians more than any other religious body in the English colonies. Quite early they established churches and mission schools among the Pennsylvania Indians, and also among the Mahicans, Iroquois and other New York tribes. During the French and Indian War the Pennsylvania government gave special protection to the "Moravian Indians." Although conscientiously opposed to war, the Moravians have rendered valuable assistance in wartime.

The Moravians have always emphasized education. Linden Hall at Lititz, a boarding school for girls, was started in 1749; the same year a Seminary for Young Ladies was founded at Bethlehem; Nazareth Hall, a boys' boarding school, began in 1759. Salem Female Academy was founded in 1802. At present the Church maintains one theological seminary, one college for men, two colleges for women and a number of smaller schools. The Moravians probably had the most highly developed church music in colonial America.

The Moravian Church in America (*Unitas*

Fratrum) claimed a membership of 60,415 in 1958. A smaller Moravian body, the Evangelical Unity of the Czech-Moravian Brethren in North America, had 6028 members.

MORGAN'S RAIDS (1862–64). After taking part in some minor engagements as a Confederate cavalry leader, Col. John Hunt Morgan began his real career as a raider by a spectacular dash into Kentucky from Knoxville, Tenn., July, 1862, going as far as Georgetown and Cynthiana and causing alarm in Cincinnati and Lexington before retiring with 1200 men across the Cumberland after having destroyed quantities of Federal arms and supplies with little actual fighting. He assisted Kirby Smith's northward advance in September, 1862, captured a Federal force at Hartsville, Tenn., in December and continued his activities the next spring, but his most spectacular achievement came in July, 1863, when he led 2460 men across Kentucky, reaching the Ohio River in five days. Without authority from his superiors and pursued by Federal cavalry, he crossed the Ohio River at Brandenburg, Ky., drove off some Indiana militia, dashed northeastward into Ohio at Harrison, and passing through the suburbs of Cincinnati at night, bewildered Federal and state forces by the speed of his march and the boldness of his plan. His dash across southern Ohio ended disastrously in a battle at the ford at Buffington Island but Morgan and 1200 men escaped, only to be captured finally at Salineville, Ohio, on July 26. After several months' confinement in the Ohio penitentiary Morgan escaped, with six others, to resume his military career as commander of the Department of Southwestern Virginia. His raiding activities ended suddenly when he was surprised and killed in eastern Tennessee, September, 1864. His raid of 1863 had given Indiana and Ohio a bad fright, had inflicted property damages of over $500,000 in Ohio, and had helped relieve the pressure on the Confederate forces in Tennessee.

MORMON BATTALION. A company of United States soldiers who served in the War with Mexico (1846–48). They were enlisted from the Mormon camps in Iowa Territory, and were furnished by Brigham Young. In all, there were 549 persons, including several families, who marched to Fort Leavenworth, where the battalion was properly equipped with clothing and firearms. Under the command of Col. Philip St. George Cooke, the Mormon volunteers marched to California by way of Santa Fe and the Gila River. Due to short rations, lack of water and excessive toil in road making and well digging, there was much sickness, and some deaths. San Diego, Calif., was reached in January, 1847, where the battalion was disbanded, and most of the members joined the Mormon company under Brigham Young, which had arrived in the valley of the Great Salt Lake, July, 1847.

MORMON EXPEDITION (1857–58) was caused by refusal of the Mormons, led by Brigham Young, to obey Federal laws. President Buchanan ordered the 5th and 10th Infantry and two batteries of Artillery from Fort Leavenworth, Kans., to subdue them; the force totaled about 1500 officers and men. The 2nd Dragoons were to follow with Col. Albert Sidney Johnston, designated as commander of the expedition. The lateness of the season—it was September before the troops crossed Green River—and the guerrilla tactics of the Mormons compelled the troops to go into winter camp near Fort Bridger. Col. Johnston arrived at the fort on Nov. 11; despite continuous Mormon depredations on Federal supplies, he found that by strict rationing his force could remain there until the following summer. However, the shortage of animals caused by hardships of the journey and Mormon raids was serious and on Nov. 27, 1857, Capt. Marcy and 35 volunteers started an almost incredible journey to Fort Massachusetts, N. Mex., from which they returned on June 8, 1858, with 1500 horses and mules and an escort of five companies of infantry and mounted riflemen. Meanwhile, promises of amnesty by President Buchanan, coupled with the threat of Federal military intervention, induced Young and his followers to submit, and on June 26, 1858, Col. Johnston's expedition marched into Salt Lake City without bloodshed.

MORMON TRAIL. The Mormons, after expulsion from Nauvoo, Ill., in February, 1846, took a westerly route along a well-beaten trail, through what is now Iowa, to the Missouri River. By permission of the Omaha Indians, they crossed the Missouri River into Nebraska Territory, and established winter quarters, where they remained during the winter of 1846–47. In April, 1847, the first company, consisting of 143 men, 3 women and 2 children, started west, under the leadership of Brigham Young. They followed the north bank of the Platte River to Fort Laramie. At this point they continued their journey over the old Oregon Trail, until they reached Fort Bridger in Wyoming. Traveling to the southwest through Echo Canyon to the Weber River, they ascended East Canyon, crossed Big and Little Mountains of the Wasatch Range, and entered the valley of the Great Salt Lake through Emigration Canyon, on July 24, 1847.

MORMON WAR (1844–46). A series of disorders between the Mormon residents of Nauvoo in Hancock County, Ill., and the non-Mormon population of the neighboring territory. Upon their settlement at Nauvoo in 1839 the Mormons had been warmly welcomed, but resentment at the excessively liberal terms of their city charter, fear of their political power, which they demonstrated by mass voting, and envy of their apparent prosperity soon generated suspicion and then hate on the part of the non-Mormon population.

By June, 1844, mutual antagonism had reached such a pitch that the Mormon militia was under arms in Nauvoo, while at least 1500 armed men, bent on the expulsion of the Mormons, had assembled in the county. The situation was so critical that Gov. Thomas Ford took personal charge. When Joseph Smith, leader of the sect, surrendered on a charge of riot, a peaceful solution appeared possible, but on June 27 Smith and his brother Hyrum were murdered by a mob in the county jail at Carthage. The state militia, however, kept peace throughout the winter of 1844–45. The summer of 1845 was relatively quiet, but violence flared in the fall, and the militia was called out again. On Oct. 1 the Mormons promised to leave Illinois in the following spring. Their migration commenced in February and continued steadily, but the anti-Mormons, professing to believe that many intended to remain, moved in force against the city in the fall of 1846. A general engagement, with several casualties, resulted. Peace was patched up and the Mormons hastened their exodus. By mid-December, when nearly all had gone, the trouble came to an end.

MORMONS is a common pseudonym for the Church of Jesus Christ of Latter-day Saints, which was organized by Joseph Smith and five others at Fayette, N. Y., April 6, 1830. Being troubled in spirit over the question of salvation, one day in the spring of 1820 Joseph Smith retired to the woods and earnestly prayed. Soon, he said, he was surrounded by a brilliant light and two glorious personages stood above him in the air. One of them spoke to him calling him by name and, pointing to the other, said: "This is my beloved Son, hear him." He then asked the personage which of all the churches he should join in order to obtain salvation, and was told to join none of them. He declared that he was also told to wait and eventually the fullness of the gospel which had been withdrawn from men would be restored. Returning to his home he made these things known to his parents who believed him, but when he presented them to the leaders of religion he met with harsh treatment and was told that there was no need for the appearing of heavenly beings in those days, therefore he was deceived. From that time opposition against him commenced and his life was sought by enemies.

Three years later he again proclaimed that the heavens had been opened to him and that on Sept. 21, 1823, a heavenly messenger, who said his name was Moroni, appeared and quoted freely from the Bible and said that many of the sayings of the ancient prophets were about to be fulfilled. This messenger, Joseph said, informed him of a record, engraved on plates of gold, buried in a hill, not far from his home, which was the sacred history of the ancient inhabitants of the Western World. After several visits from this angel, covering a period of four years, the record was placed in his hands by the messenger who also gave him the Urim and Thummim, prepared for the purpose of translating the record. By the aid of these instruments and with the help of Oliver Cowdery, a young man near Joseph's own age, he said he translated the record which was published in 1830 as the *Book of Mormon.*

The Latter-day Saints claim that this book contains the gospel taught among the people on the American continent before and immediately subsequent to the days of Christ, who visited these people after His resurrection, and established His Church among them.

Joseph Smith now had a witness in Oliver Cowdery, and these two men claimed that while engaged in the work of translating they received a visitation from John the Baptist, in May, 1829, who conferred upon them the "Aaronic Priesthood," which is the authority given to Aaron and his sons. Later that same year, the "Melchizedek Priesthood" was conferred upon them by heavenly messengers. By this authority and the command of the Lord, they said, they organized the Church April 6, 1830. From that day forth it grew rapidly. When the membership numbered several hundred souls, headquarters were transferred to Kirtland, O. Settlements were also attempted in Jackson County, Mo., where, the Mormons teach, the city of Zion, or New Jerusalem, is eventually to be built.

From the first, persecution followed this band of Mormons. The bitterness of the Missourians against them became intense, partly due to their religion and partly because they were abolitionists. By the summer of 1833 a large settlement of Mormons had been made in Jackson County. In July of that year they were ruthlessly driven from their homes. For a short time they found refuge in Ray County, but persecution followed them and they were forced to move to a sparsely settled portion of Missouri in Daviess and Caldwell counties. In 1838, spurred on by the bitterness of their enemies, Gov. Lilburn W. Boggs issued an exterminating order against the Latter-day Saints and demanded that they leave the state forthwith. Joseph Smith and his brother Hyrum, with other leaders, were taken prisoners, court-martialed by the mob-militia and ordered shot, although they were not men of arms and were not engaged in rebellion. This order was given to Col. Alexander W. Doniphan to execute; disobeying his superior officer, he said: "It is cold-blooded murder. I will not obey your order. My brigade shall march for Liberty tomorrow morning, at 8 o'clock; and if you execute these men, I will hold you responsible before an earthly tribunal, so help me God." His action calmed the feelings against the Mormons and saved the lives of the Smiths. They were, however, thrown into prison and kept there six months, enduring many hardships before they were released, no real charge having been sustained against them.

At the time of the exodus from Missouri the Church numbered about 12,000 souls. Their property was confiscated and, poverty-stricken, they sought refuge in Illinois. On the banks of the Mississippi they built the city of Nauvoo and began to prosper. A liberal charter was received from the state. They founded a university and commenced to build a temple which, when completed, cost $1,000,000. The bitterness which followed them while in Missouri still pursued them, and their enemies stirred up many of the citizens of Illinois who joined in the opposition against the Church, which finally resulted in the murder of the Smiths, at Carthage, Ill., June 27, 1844, while awaiting trial on charges made by their enemies.

Brigham Young became the presiding officer after the death of the Smiths. He took command, and order was restored. In 1845 hostilities again broke out and the Mormons were forced again from their homes. In the month of February, 1846, the first bands of refugees crossed the Mississippi River, with cannon pointing at them to hasten their flight. In poverty and inclement weather they commenced their journey westward, seeking a more friendly locality. Temporary settlements were formed in the territory of Iowa, and in the spring of 1847 the first company of 143 men pushed on westward in search of a new home. This company arrived in the Salt Lake Valley, July 24, 1847. Later that same year other companies arrived and, because of the proximity of the inland sea, the settlement was called Salt Lake City. From this point the people radiated in all directions making settlements in many parts of the Rocky Mountains. Contrary to the impression of some writers, the Mormons in migrating were not attempting to get out of United States territory, but only to be removed from persecution.

It was claimed that during the Nauvoo period Joseph Smith received a revelation on "celestial marriage," including plural marriage, or that it is in accord with the will of heaven, under proper conditions, for a man to have more than one wife. Celestial marriage is marriage for eternity. This practice resulted in great opposition and Congress passed laws prohibiting it. After these laws were declared constitutional, the Mormon people, by proclamation of President Wilford Woodruff in 1890, abandoned the practice of plural marriage.

MORRILL ACT. Long agitation by agricultura societies, farm journals and other advocates of vocational training for farmers and mechanics—Jonathan Baldwin Turner of Illinois being the most important—influenced Justin S. Morrill of Vermont to introduce into Congress a bill to aid in the establishment of agricultural and mechanical arts colleges in every state in the Union. The measure passed Congress in 1858, but constitutional objections induced President Buchanan to veto it. A similar measure, since called the Morrill Act, was signed by President Lincoln in 1862. States were offered 30,000 acres of land for each

Representative and Senator they were entitled to in the national legislature, as an endowment for the proposed schools. In some states the lands were given to existing institutions, as in Wisconsin where the state university was the beneficiary; elsewhere they were conveyed to newly established agricultural and technical colleges such as Purdue University or the Illinois Industrial University, now the University of Illinois. Sen. Morrill was henceforth called the "Father of the Agricultural Colleges."

MOSBY'S RANGERS, an irregular body of Confederate troops commanded by Col. John S. Mosby, operated, 1863–65, south of the Potomac behind the Union lines. This organization began with a scouting assignment from J. E. B. Stuart (C.) in January, 1863. From a few troopers the Rangers gradually grew to eight companies in 1865. Apart from participation with Stuart in the Gettysburg campaign, their main activities consisted of sudden attacks on Union outposts, followed, when pursued, by quick dispersion. To Sheridan, Custer and others, Mosby's men were a veritable thorn in the flesh. Efforts to destroy the Rangers were provokingly unavailing.

MOSCOW CONFERENCE OF FOREIGN MINISTERS (Oct. 19–30, 1943) was held by U. S. Secretary of State Hull, British Foreign Secretary Eden, and Soviet Foreign Commissar Molotov. Hull and Eden had some success in allaying Russian suspicions over the failure to open a second front in Europe, and in promoting closer co-operation with Russia. In addition, a European Advisory Commission was established to make studies of European questions, with a view to a peace settlement; and a Four-Power Declaration (signed also by China) was made pledging the four countries to set up at the earliest practicable date an international organization for peace.

To implement the declaration, steps were taken after the conference which led eventually to the Dumbarton Oaks Conference and the United Nations Conference, San Francisco.

MOTION PICTURES. Scientists of many lands acquired over a period of centuries the knowledge needed for motion pictures. Motion pictures involve three elements: (1) a working knowledge of light and vision; (2) camera and projector apparatus; and, (3) photography, including a flexible base for the emulsion. Only the third is of modern origin. The key to motion pictures was the discovery of a suitable plastic, a flexible film base. Motion pictures were the first great modern industry founded on plastics.

As a commercial activity motion pictures are a modern development paced by Americans. Thomas A. Edison deserves more than anyone the title of "father of motion pictures." He made the first thoroughly workable camera and viewer for motion pictures.

The first practical projectors in the United States and elsewhere were based on his apparatus. In 1887 Edison began his quest for apparatus to do for sight what his phonograph had done for sound, ultimately wishing to reproduce both pictures and sounds. The same year Hannibal Williston Goodwin obtained a United States patent on a photographic pellicle described as "transparent, sensitive and like celluloid." In 1889 Edison and an assistant, Kennedy Laurie Dickson, obtained from George Eastman film stock that proved workable. On Dec. 10, 1889, Eastman applied for a patent on "the manufacture of flexible photographic films." This patent was issued in 1898, after a legal battle with the Goodwin estate had been compromised.

In 1891 Edison's Kinetograph camera and Kinetoscope viewing apparatus were completed, and application was made for a patent which was issued in 1893. The peep-show Kinetoscopes went on public display on April 14, 1894, at 1155 Broadway, New York City. Later that year they were shown in Paris and London. These demonstrations influenced many here and abroad who finally solved the problems of projecting on a screen continuous motion pictures.

Screen projection was achieved in 1895 in France by Louis and Auguste Lumière with the Cinematographe; by Robert W. Paul in London with films made by Birt Acres shown in the Bioscope; and by Thomas Armat, C. Francis Jenkins, Grey, Otway and Woodville Latham and others in the United States. In 1896 motion pictures were commercial successes on screens in many parts of the world. In New York the significant premiere was held at Koster & Bial's Music Hall, Herald Square on the evening of April 23, 1896.

The first "movies" were only brief sequences, inserted in a vaudeville show. Before long personalities of the stage agreed to appear in films. Productions became more elaborate as pictures began to tell a story. Public interest grew rapidly, especially among immigrants in the large industrial cities of the United States. In the movies these people found a universal language as well as inexpensive recreation. In April, 1902, the first modest theater was established to show movies exclusively. It was the Electric Theater, Los Angeles, owned by Thomas L. Tally. Early in 1903 Harry Warner and brothers opened the Cascade Theater in New Castle, Pa. These and other early theaters soon became known as "nickelodeons" because the admission price was five cents.

Initial production centers in the United States were in and adjacent to New York City and in Chicago and Philadelphia. In larger cities throughout the country "exchanges" were established which serviced the nickelodeons with complete programs at a fixed weekly rental. Such a system did not encourage quality or experimentation.

The Motion Picture Patents Company which controlled the industry through patented devices in the early years of the 20th century did not believe that the public would accept "features." The Patents Company came under attack by independent producers led by Carl Laemmle, William Fox and others. In 1912 Adolph Zukor imported a four-reel film made in France, "Queen Elizabeth," with Sarah Bernhardt. The success of this long film was a spur to American producers to attempt more ambitious subjects. In 1913 Jesse Lasky formed an association with Cecil B. De Mille and Samuel Goldwyn. The resulting picture was "The Squaw Man" with Dustin Farnum. It was the first feature made in Hollywood. The lure of good weather and remoteness called producers west and Hollywood became the American production headquarters while corporate management, financial and sales departments became centered in New York.

During the period of World War I American films first achieved important stature. In 1915 the film classic, D. W. Griffith's "The Birth of a Nation," was released. That film was popular with the public and also made intellectuals realize the dramatic power of the screen. At this time Mary Pickford and Charles Chaplin were so popular that stars became more important than stories. From then on American films were usually made with players selected for "star value."

Hollywood, in the period of the golden age of the silent film, from the days of World War I to the mid-1920's, sought out story material and creative workers from the whole world. This gave the American film a flavor that was an important factor in developing international appeal. While Hollywood films had a substantial export market from the early 1920's, by the 1950's almost half the gross revenue of American pictures was being earned abroad.

At a time when many observers felt the silent films were becoming routine, sound became a reality. At first the industry leaders did not view "talkies" with favor, but the public wanted them and in 1927 and 1928 the entire industry shifted to talking pictures. Although Edison and others had experimented with sound, the first acclaimed talking picture was Al Jolson in "The Jazz Singer" made by Warner Bros. and shown in 1927. On Aug. 6, 1926, the first sound film (synchronized with music on discs but with no dialogue), "Don Juan," Warner Bros., was presented at the Warner Theater, New York. Also in 1927 the first pictures with sound-on-film, Movietone, were shown. In 1928 came the first all-talking picture, "The Lights of New York" (Warner Bros.).

As pictures and sound were improved there was increasing interest in color. Experiments of Dr. Herbert T. Kalmus of Technicolor and others resulted in successful three-color features, the first being "Becky Sharp" in 1935. Although there had been experiments with color from the beginning of motion pictures, Technicolor was the first commercially

successful process and long remained the standard of comparison of other screen color systems. From the time of the release of the record-breaking "Gone With the Wind" in 1939 an increasing proportion of important motion pictures were in color.

Following record attendance enjoyed during World War II, the American motion picture industry entered upon a long-deterred period of technical improvement. This took two forms—one, the "large screen" and the other, improved sound. The traditional screen proportions of four (width) to three (height) had been set by Edison. In order to compete with television's "small screen" and to give a "new look," motion picture theaters, first in the United States and then throughout the world, installed large screens permitting pictures to be two to three times as wide as high. Cinerama, a three-film strip process developed from an aerial gunnery trainer of World War II, which opened in New York on Sept. 30, 1952, stimulated interest in "wide screens." Cinerama also introduced a highly developed multi-track stereophonic sound system. CinemaScope, introduced in 1953 by Twentieth Century-Fox with "The Robe," became an important wide-screen and stereophonic sound system.

The American motion picture industry had difficulty adjusting to increased competition for the public's leisure time in the booming 1950's. Television was the principal competition. Several thousand theaters, including many obsolete ones, closed but over 4000 drive-in theaters were opened. Readjustment was complicated by the results of a government antitrust suit filed in 1938 and concluded in 1950 which resulted in the divorcement of the five largest circuits from the major producing-distributing companies.

Over the years American films have had a stormy battle over censorship. A series of U. S. Supreme Court decisions in the period 1952–58 struck down much local and state censorship. In 1930 the industry had established a Production Code and self-regulatory machinery. By the late 1950's there were renewed pressures for censorship or some form of official regulation resulting from the nature of some popular imported films and a general relaxing of moral standards in the United States.

Emphasis of Hollywood in the later years of the 1950's was on the unusual screen subject, on the big picture, the spectacular, and anything thought to have appeal to youth because the majority of theater patrons were in their teens or early twenties. When a picture hit the public's fancy, grosses were higher than ever both in the United States and throughout the world.

MOULTRIE, FORT, BATTLE OF (June 28, 1776). Throughout a ten-hour bombardment, this palmetto fort on Sullivan's Island in Charleston (S. C.) harbor, commanded by Col. William Moultrie, successfully beat off a British attack under Clinton and Parker. American loss was slight, while that of the British, both in lives and damage to ships, was large. The victory kept the British out of the South for the next two years.

MOUNDS AND MOUND BUILDERS. The terms are used to designate respectively the numerous ancient artificial structures of earth and stone, widely scattered over the eastern United States, and the primitive peoples responsible for their construction.

What may be termed the General Mound Area corresponds approximately to the basins of the Mississippi and its tributaries, particularly those to the eastward, and the Gulf and Southeastern seaboard regions. There are few major remains east of the Appalachians, from the Carolinas northward through New England.

In its broader interpretation, the word Mounds comprises all major remains of prehistoric man within the area: conical mounds, truncated mounds, effigy and linear mounds, defensive earthworks, geometric enclosures, and shell heaps. Conical mounds are artificial hillocks of earth, earth and stone, and occasionally entirely of stone, more or less conical in form, and ranging in size from almost imperceptible elevations to structures of seventy feet in height. They occur generally throughout the Mound Area, and were intended mainly as places of interment and as monuments to the dead. Two striking examples of conical mounds are the Grave Creek Mound in Marshall County, W. Va., and the Miamisburg Mound in Montgomery County, Ohio, each of which is a trifle short of seventy feet in height.

Truncated mounds occur mostly in the lower Mississippi Valley. They are mainly quadrangular flat-topped pyramids, and served as bases or platforms for sacred and domiciliary structures. Surprisingly enough, the greatest of the truncated mounds lies near the northern limit of their occurrence—the great Monks Mound, near East St. Louis, Ill. This tumulus, but one of more than eighty comprising the Cahokia Group, is 100 feet high and covers sixteen acres of ground.

The Effigy Mounds, so called because they are built in the images of animals, birds and men, and the associated linear mounds, center in southern Wisconsin and adjacent parts of Iowa, Minnesota and Illinois. Within this area are numerous examples, occurring both singly and in groups, particularly in and adjacent to the city of Madison. The greatest of the Effigy Mounds, however, is the Serpent Mound, in Adams County, Ohio. This effigy, following the sinuous coils of the serpent, measures 1330 feet in length. The Effigy Mounds supposedly were adjuncts of the religious observances of their builders.

The defensive earthworks, or fortifications, usually occupy the more or less level tops of isolated hills, and consist of walls of earth and stone following the outer circumferences of such areas, supplementing the natural barriers against intrusion. The walls usually were further fortified by means of pointed upright stakes or pickets. They are of general occurrence, with their greatest development in southern Ohio, where the noted Fort Ancient, in Warren County, is the most striking example.

Geometric enclosures, as contrasted with the defensive works, invariably occur in level valley situations, without consideration of defensive factors, and are strictly adjuncts of the so-called Hopewell culture of southern Ohio and adjacent regions. They usually are low walls of earth, in the form of circles, squares, octagons and parallel walls, occurring singly or in combination. Their function apparently was social and ceremonial, rather than defensive. Examples are the Hopewell, Mound City and Seip groups, in Ross County, Ohio; and the Newark works, at Newark, Ohio.

Shell mounds are accumulations of shells of both marine and fresh-water mollusks, and are incidental to the use of these as food. They occur to some extent adjacent to inland streams, but mainly along the Atlantic tidewater, particularly in Florida, and often are of great extent. Other major fixed remains of aboriginal occupancy are village-sites, cemeteries and flint quarries, occurring generally throughout the area.

Builders of the ancient Mounds originally were thought to have been a separate and distinct race of people. Archaeological investigations, however, have demonstrated that they were members of the single great race to which the historic Indian, the highly evolved Aztecs, Mayans and Incas of Mexico, Central and South America, and others of the native stocks pertained. While some of the cultures of mound-building peoples cannot be directly identified with historic tribes and nations, it is probable that for the most part they were the ancestors of Indian nations living in the same general area at the time of discovery. It is further probable that the Creeks, Choctaws and Natchez to the southward, the Cherokee and Shawnee in the Ohio Valley, and the Winnebago and some others of the Siouan family, at some time and to some extent, were builders of mounds. DeSoto and other explorers of the 16th century found certain tribes in the South using, if not actually building, mounds. The occasional occurrence of objects of European manufacture as original inclusions in mounds toward the southeast and to the west of the Great Lakes indicates a limited survival of the trait in early Columbian times. However, for unknown reasons, the American tribesmen mostly had lost or abandoned the trait prior to the discovery, and it appears to this writer that some at least of the more important carriers thereof had become extinct as the result of conquest, subjugation, pestilence or some other of the many causes contributing to the decadence of peoples and their cultures.

Since the Mounds and their builders antedate the

historic period of America, their age can only be approximated. Peopling of the Americas by Mongoloid immigrants from Asia, subsequent to the most recent glacial invasion (estimated variously at 10,000 to 20,000 years since) presumably led to earlier settlement to the west and south than in the eastern portions of the continent. The main stream of migration appears to have passed southward into Mexico, with an infiltration through the mountain passes across Canada and the Great Plains. To the latter may be attributed many of the nonmound-building Indians, while the settlement of the Mound area seems to have derived from the South and Southwest, at a comparatively late date. The most that can be said of the mound-building stocks is that they were pre-Columbian, but probably not extending backward beyond the beginning of the Christian era.

While the mound-building peoples were still in the Stone Age era, certain of them had achieved a considerable degree of advancement. Copper was hammered into implements and ornaments; very creditable potteryware was made; and woven fabric of several types was produced. In the lower Mississippi Valley and to an even greater extent in the Ohio Valley, a surprising artistic development, in the form of conventional design and small sculptures in the round, probably was not surpassed by any people in a similar stage of development.

MOUNT VERNON, the home of George Washington, is situated on the south bank of the Potomac River, sixteen miles below the city of Washington.

The Washington family acquired title to Mount Vernon by division of a 5000-acre grant in 1690. The central part of the existing house was built about 1743 for Lawrence, elder half-brother of George Washington. Lawrence died in 1752 and the property passed to George Washington a short time later.

In 1759 Washington married Martha Custis, widow of Daniel Parke Custis, and established his household at Mount Vernon. Here he lived until the outbreak of the Revolution. At the close of the war he returned to his home and completed improvements that had been started under his own supervision in 1774 and carried forward by his manager during his absence. Buildings, gardens and grounds were developed substantially to their present form and extent during this period. The mansion and thirteen subsidiary structures have survived. Several others have been reconstructed.

Mount Vernon has been restored and maintained by the Mount Vernon Ladies' Association, founded by Miss Ann Pamela Cunningham of South Carolina.

MOUNTAIN MEADOWS MASSACRE occurred in southern Utah, in September, 1857. In the summer of that year, two companies of emigrants, one from Arkansas, and the other from Missouri, passed through Salt Lake City on their way to California. In south-

ern Utah, as they reached the country beyond the fringe of settlement, the Missouri company was attacked by the Indians, and was saved by the help of the "Mormon" militia. This company reached the Pacific coast in safety. The Arkansas company met with a terrible fate. It numbered thirty families, aggregating some 137 persons, including a lawless band known as the "Missouri Wild-cats." At a point forty miles from Cedar City, a party of Indians, and a few white men, led by one John D. Lee, a farmer, attacked the company, and all were massacred, except seventeen children, who were spared. It was primarily an Indian outbreak, and was due to the insolent and lawless conduct of certain members of the emigrant party. Gov. Brigham Young had admonished his people to allow all emigrants to pass through the territory unmolested, to furnish them food when necessary, and to protect them from the Indians. John D. Lee was later executed for the crime on the spot where it was committed.

"MOUNTAIN MEN," the pioneers of the Rocky Mountain West, came first as fur trappers, lured to the West by beaver as these animals were lured to traps by castor bait. With virgin streams producing the prize catches, there was reward for trail blazing and the trappers thus became the explorers of the Far West. Frenchmen, most experienced of fur gatherers, mingled with Americans and Spaniards at St. Louis in the first decade of the 19th century, and made this the great Western emporium of the fur trade. From here went trapping parties and trading company caravans laden with supplies and Indian goods for the mountain trade. A season or two of trapping and the adventurer boasted the sobriquet of "Mountain Man."

Mingling with the Indian, he adopted the aborigine's manner of life, his food, shelter, morals and frequently his superstitions. He took on the Indian love of adornment, bedecking himself in moccasins and fringed buckskin suit, adorned with dyed porcupine quills or colored glass beads. An Indian buffalo skin lodge provided winter shelter. His rifle, steel traps, skinning knife and horse made him independent and free. Jim Bridger, Kit Carson, Thomas Fitzpatrick and Bill Williams were examples of the fraternity. There were three classes: the hired trapper, paid annual wages by a fur company; the skin trapper, who dealt with one company only; and the free trapper, who trapped and disposed of his furs when and where he pleased.

The summer rendezvous at Green River, Wyo., or other appointed mountain valley, became the most interesting and typical institution of fur trade days. To it white trappers and Indians gathered. Fur companies from Missouri brought out their supplies and trade goods, and barter flourished. With drinking, gambling, racing and contests of skill the "Mountain Man" made holiday. His regular meat diet was now varied by limited supplies of flour, coffee and similar luxuries from "the States." In a few days of prodigal living he frequently spent his year's earnings.

With the introduction of the silk hat and the consequent decline in beaverskin prices, from $6 or $8 apiece to $2 or less, the "Mountain Man" forsook his traps and became a trader with the Indian. Buffalo robes replaced beaver pelts, the trading post supplanted the rendezvous. With the coming of emigrant homeseekers and government exploring and military expeditions, the trapper-trader became scout and guide to lead newcomers over the paths he broke. Advancing civilization "rubbed out" the "Mountain Man."

MUCKRAKERS. A group of young reformers who, through novels and popular magazines, laid bare the abuses which had crept into American political, social and economic life. The era began in 1903 with the publication of Lincoln Steffens' "The Shame of the Cities" and Ida M. Tarbell's "History of the Standard Oil Company" in *McClure's Magazine.* These were followed by numerous others, delving into every phase of American life—the most important of which were Ray Stannard Baker's "The Railroads on Trial" (*McClure's,* 1905–6), Thomas W. Lawson's "Frenzied Finance" (*Everybody's,* 1905–6), and David Graham Phillips' "The Treason of the Senate" (*Cosmopolitan,* 1906–7). *Collier's* exposed food adulteration, traffic in women and children, and fraudulent advertising of patent medicines. Of the novelists, the most important was Upton Sinclair who, in *The Jungle* (1906), revealed the unsavory conditions in the packing plants of Chicago. Although the authors were specific in their charges, no major suit was ever entered.

President Theodore Roosevelt in two addresses (March 17 and April 14, 1906) likened the authors of the exposure literature to the man with the rake in Bunyan's *Pilgrim's Progress,* who was more interested in the filth on the floor than in a celestial crown, and referred to them as "muckrakers." He declared that the time had come to cease exposure for its own sake and to turn to constructive reform. From then on "muckraking" declined, only to be revived in 1909, when it attached itself to the Progressive movement. The "muckrakers," primarily responsible for most of the progressive legislation of the period, passed into oblivion after 1912.

MUGWUMPS was one of many derisive terms applied to those liberal, or independent, Republicans who bolted the party ticket in the presidential campaign of 1884 to support actively the candidacy of Grover Cleveland and thus were credited with being a strong factor in the defeat of James G. Blaine. They held one national and many regional meetings.

MULES, while introduced into the colonies from Spain, became of significance in America in 1785

with the receipt by Washington of an Andalusian jack and jennets from the King of Spain, and shortly after of a similar Maltese group from Lafayette. By crossing the two breeds Washington secured a mule stock that found ready favor with fellow planters. Another center of origin was in Kentucky where Henry Clay and other leading stockmen imported asses from the two main sources that included the famous jack, "Warrior." The mule proved particularly adapted to plantation needs and by 1860 nine tenths were in that region, with the source of supply in the Ohio Valley. Mules were extensively used in the Civil War in the supply trains, and from that time the "army mule" has become proverbial. Mules have been classified according to the main uses to which they have been put, as plantation, heavy draft, mine and farm. Extensive breeding has developed only since the 1880's and has centered in the Southwest. In contrast to the horse the mule demand has remained steady.

MULLAN TRAIL (1859–62), one of the most important wagon trails of the Pacific Northwest, was 624 miles long, from the head of navigation of the Missouri River (Fort Benton) to Walla Walla. It was built largely for military purposes, but played an important part in opening the Montana mines. Lt. John Mullan directed the building of the trail. Work started at Walla Walla, July 1, 1859, and the trail reached Fort Benton in 1860. Work during the summers of 1861 and 1862 made it a passable pioneer road.

MULLIGAN LETTERS were letters written by James G. Blaine during the years 1864–76 to Warren Fisher, Jr., a businessman of Boston. On May 31, 1876, James Mulligan, an employee of Fisher, testified before a committee of Congress that he had such letters in his possession. On motion of a member of the committee, who pleaded illness, the committee immediately adjourned. That afternoon Blaine obtained possession of the letters, promising to return them. On June 5 he read the letters on the floor of the House and defended himself of the charge that he had used his official power as speaker of the House to promote the fortunes of the Little Rock and Fort Smith Railroad which it was alleged the letters indicated. Friends of Blaine claimed a complete vindication. Eight years later, however, when he was the Republican candidate for the Presidency, the letters were published and were probably an important factor in his defeat.

MUNN v. ILLINOIS (1877), one of the Granger cases, involved the validity of an Illinois law of 1871 that fixed maximum rates for the storage of grain. A Chicago warehouse firm, Munn and Scott, found guilty in 1872 of violating the law, appealed first to the state supreme court, where the decision of the lower court was affirmed, and then to the U. S. Supreme Court, which upheld the Illinois statute. To the argument that the fixing of maximum rates constituted a taking of property without due process of law, the Court replied that the warehouse business was sufficiently clothed with a public interest to justify public control; and to the argument that Congress alone had the right to regulate interstate commerce, of which the storage of grain was a part, the Court replied that until Congress made use of its power a state might act, "even though in so doing it may indirectly operate upon commerce outside its jurisdiction."

MURFREESBORO, BATTLE OF (Dec. 31, 1862–Jan. 2, 1863). After Perryville, Gen. Braxton Bragg withdrew his Confederates through eastern Tennessee. The Union Army of the Cumberland under Rosecrans concentrated at Nashville. Both forces were reorganized and refitted during November and December, Bragg facing and annoying Rosecrans from Murfreesboro thirty miles away. After a five-day deployed advance Rosecrans confronted Bragg drawn up astride Stone River protecting Murfreesboro. Each general aimed against his enemy's right on Dec. 31. Bragg, striking first against the flank and rear of McCook's (U.) unready corps, would have won save for inspired resistance by Sheridan's division and stern pertinacity by Thomas' (central) corps. Rosecrans' attack lagged. He recalled Crittenden's advancing (left) corps and hurried reinforcements to the Union right, bent back, repeatedly charged, dented, but not broken. By nightfall the two nearly equal armies had fought themselves into fatigue, with ground, spoils and many prisoners in Confederate hands, and Rosecrans' Unionists clinging desperately to the Nashville pike and pinned against the river. For a full day the forces took breath as sporadic Confederate advances were checked. Instead of withdrawing his shaken army, Rosecrans was awaiting ammunition and moving one of Crittenden's divisions back across the river. Jan. 2, Bragg sent nearly 10,000 men against Crittenden's division and broke it, but an insane counterattack made without orders by 1500 Indianians across the stream cracked the assault; sudden artillery concentration shattered it; and the battle stopped. Next day Bragg's nerve broke and that night he retreated toward Chattanooga.

MUSIC. The first music heard on the North American continent was that of the Indians, but its primitive nature was so far removed from the formalized structure of European music that it had little effect on the music of the white settlers. The Spanish who captured Mexico City in 1521 founded a music school three years later, and their missionaries carried their liturgical music into what are now the states of Texas, New Mexico, Arizona, and California. The French Huguenots who settled along the eastern seaboard as far south as Florida in the 1560's undoubtedly used music in their worship, and the settlers of Jamestown in 1607 probably sang the English ballads and madrigals they had known at home. Unfortunately there are no references to music in the contemporary records of these southeastern settlements.

It is definitely known that the Pilgrims who came to Plymouth (1620) and the Puritans who settled Massachusetts Bay (1630) brought Psalters they had used in England. Psalm-singing was an integral part of their religious worship. In 1640 the Massachusetts Bay settlers published a psalm collection of their own, popularly known as the Bay Psalm Book. Records of musical instruments in 17th-century New England colonies are very few, for the rigorous tasks of opening up and settling a new territory, as well as Puritan distrust of secular amusements, allowed little opportunity for indulgence in nonreligious music. By 1700 psalm-singing in the Puritan churches of New England had become a haphazard practice, and the younger members of the clergy urged reform. Singing-books that contained the rudiments of singing by note were issued. Itinerant singing-teachers traveled from town to town instructing classes that later developed into church choirs. One of these teachers, William Billings (1746–1800), became widely known as a composer of "fuguing-pieces," anthems with crude attempts at imitative counterpoint. Billings published six collections of vocal music (the first in 1770), each containing a number of his anthems and "fuguing tunes." While Billings was largely untutored musically his work had a rugged vitality that reflected his pioneer surroundings.

At the beginning of the 18th century importation of both musical instruments and printed music made the enjoyment of secular music possible. The first public concert to be recorded in newspapers was given in Boston in 1731. Charleston, S. C., followed in 1732, New York in 1736, and Philadelphia in 1757. In 1762 a St. Cecilia Society was formed in Charleston which had its own concert hall and imported foreign musicians who were paid a yearly salary to give periodic concerts. In Philadelphia a group of amateurs gathered regularly in each other's homes to play ensemble music. One of its leading members was Francis Hopkinson (1737–91), a signer of the Declaration of Independence, who is credited with being the first native-born American composer. His songs, the first dated 1759, have been revived in modern times. One group of them was dedicated to George Washington.

Various of the minority groups that settled in Pennsylvania are known to have had an active musical life. The Swedish Gloria Dei Church in Philadelphia had an organ as early as 1703, and at the Ephrata Cloister near Lancaster the worshipers sang chorales in as many as seven parts. The founder of this Dunker sect, Conrad Beissel (1690–1768), is believed to have composed more than 1000 of these chorales. At the Moravian colony established in Bethlehem in 1741 the settlers formed an orchestra and chamber-music group to play works of Haydn and later of Mozart. A number of their members were composers.

The War of the Revolution interrupted the musical life of the colonies, but when the new nation was founded, hundreds of well-trained musicians emigrated from England and France. Settling here permanently, they became for a time our leading performers and teachers. Native performers and composers found it difficult to compete with the newcomers, and the growth of such native expression as had been achieved by men like Billings was temporarily arrested.

Numerous musical societies were founded during the first half of the 19th century. Several have continued in existence, notably the Boston Handel and Haydn Society (1815), the Musical Fund Society of Philadelphia (1820), and the Philharmonic Society of New York (1842), which has lived to be the oldest permanent orchestra in the United States.

In 1836 Lowell Mason (1792–1872) persuaded the Boston school board to make music a regular part of the curriculum and, by establishing "musical conventions" in various parts of the country where teachers could be trained in class methods, he became the founder of our present public school music, a movement that has reached its ultimate fulfillment in the 20th century. Mason was himself a composer of hymn tunes.

New Orleans was probably the first American city to hear grand opera. A foreign company gave a performance there as early as 1791 and by 1810 the city had three theaters. In 1825 Manuel Garcia brought an opera troupe to the Park Theater in New York, and from that time various opera companies gave performances in the city each season. None had continued success until the Academy of Music was built in 1854. This was the home of opera in New York until the Metropolitan Opera House was opened in 1883.

From the early years of the century virtuosi from Europe toured the country, dazzling audiences not only in cities but also in smaller communities in the Middle and even the Far West. Ole Bull, the Norwegian violinist, made his first visit in 1843; Jenny Lind made her New York debut under the management of P. T. Barnum in 1850; and from 1853 the New Orleans-born Louis Moreau Gottschalk (1829–69), trained abroad, enraptured all who heard him with the elegance of his piano playing and of his own compositions. Gottschalk's piano pieces were marked not only by Parisian polish and refinement but also by the use of Creole melodies the composer had heard in his youth.

At mid-century the nation experienced another wholesale immigration of foreign musicians, this time caused by the Central European revolutions of 1848. Thousands of Germans sought new homes in the United States. The musicians among them were better trained than native Americans and when they settled in both the seaboard cities and in such inland centers as Milwaukee, Cincinnati, and St. Louis they became the principal musicians and teachers of those communities. Germanic ideals and standards became the norm of our musical life for a full half-century. In contrast to the programs in concert halls and opera houses, the minstrel shows that became popular in the 1840's and 1850's were typically American. Originating with black-faced performers, they presented a caricature of the American Negro. While the dialect songs written for the shows were by no means Negro folk songs, they were nevertheless indigenously American. It was for these minstrel shows that Stephen Foster (1826–64) composed most of his songs. At that time they were considered nothing more than popular songs of the day, but they have proved to be far more enduring than the more ambitious works of mid-century concert composers who wrote in accordance with contemporary European styles.

By the closing years of the 19th century a number of American cities had permanent symphony orchestras: New York (1842); St. Louis (1880); Boston (1881); Chicago (1891); Cincinnati (1895); Pittsburgh (1895); and Philadelphia (1900). The establishment of these orchestras was largely the result of the annual visits of a touring orchestra organized and conducted by the German-born Theodore Thomas (1835–1905), who came to America at the age of ten and spent his entire adult life acquainting the American public with the world's finest symphonic music.

While American composers were still under the influence of foreign masters, and such men as John K. Paine (1839–1906), George W. Chadwick (1854–1931), and Horatio Parker (1863–1919) were writing according to academic formulae, the Bohemian composer Antonin Dvořák spent four years (1892–95) teaching composition at the National Conservatory of Music in New York. An intense nationalist himself, Dvořák felt that American composers should express their own nation by turning to the folk songs of the American continent—particularly the Negro spirituals and Indian music. As an example of what might be done with Negro-like material he composed his *New World Symphony*. Immediately a group of American composers grasped at this method of breaking with European models and of writing a truly nationalist music. Others were not impressed by such an objective method for realizing an American idiom, particularly Edward MacDowell (1861–1908), a composer who had developed a style that was definitely recognizable as his own. MacDowell felt that Americanism must be portrayed subjectively in order to be valid.

With the new century the number of resident orchestras continued to increase and during the first three decades symphony societies were founded in Minneapolis (1903); San Francisco (1908); Baltimore (1916); Cleveland (1918); Los Angeles (1919); Rochester (1922); Indianapolis (1930); and Washington, D. C. (1931). By 1960 there were thirty major orchestras in large cities and the number of secondary organizations in smaller cities had grown from 100 in 1920 to over a thousand. Many of the secondary orchestras are composed of both amateur and professional players. The conservatories and music schools that had been founded in the 19th century (notably the Oberlin Conservatory in Ohio, 1865; New England Conservatory in Boston, 1867; Cincinnati Conservatory, 1867; and the Peabody Conservatory in Baltimore, 1868) were joined by the Institute of Musical Art in New York (1904), and three institutions heavily endowed by philanthropists—Eastman School of Music in Rochester (1919); Juilliard School of Music in New York (1920); and the Curtis Institute in Philadelphia (1924). The existence of such institutions, together with that of excellent music departments in leading universities, has enabled American musicians to procure their training in their own country.

World Wars I and II had a profound effect on American music. The wars themselves and the persecution of minority groups in Europe brought hundreds of refugee musicians to this country. Among them were many of Europe's leading composers—such men as Stravinsky, Schoenberg, Hindemith, Milhaud, some of whom became teachers in our universities. The effect of these 20th-century immigrations was very great, but it was altogether different from the results of the late 18th- and mid-19th-century immigrations. By the 20th century music in the United States had become integrated and developed. American musicians were rooted firmly in their own country and the best of them were as well trained as their foreign colleagues. Americanisms were apparent in the music our composers were writing, and some of them, particularly ragtime and jazz, were being imitated abroad.

The appearance and development of jazz in the years around 1915 had a more far-reaching effect on American music than did the Negro spirituals or the Indian music that had impressed Dvořák. Although jazz had its origin among Negroes, particularly in New Orleans, it has been practiced and developed also by white musicians, and even though some of it became highly commercialized among the songsmiths of "Tin-Pan-Alley," it has nevertheless remained a typically American expression, recognized as such throughout the world. The incorporation of its idioms in the music of symphonic composers has led to a merging of the so-called "popular" music of the nation with the formal music of the concert hall. This has resulted in ridding our formal music of some of its self-consciousness and pompousness, and in raising the quality of our "popular" music itself.

George Gershwin (1898–1937) facilitated this merger of concert and popular music by writing his *Rhapsody in Blue* (1924), a piece for piano and orchestra that developed symphonically the racy elements of jazz music. Gershwin was himself a highly successful composer of popular songs, and he brought to his serious works a thoroughly subjective incorporation of the idioms of jazz and the Broadway theater.

The hundreds of American composers who have come into prominence in the first half of the 20th century are in a far happier position than were their immediate predecessors. The existence of major and secondary orchestras, as well as of capable symphonic groups in universities and even in high schools, has provided a medium through which American works may gain performance and become part of the standard repertoire. Opera workshops in colleges and schools afford opportunity for the production of stage works by Americans, so that composers are no longer limited to the few opportunities for performance offered by the mere handful of major opera companies in the nation.

Many of our outstanding composers are as well known abroad as they are in this country, and the work of many of them is marked by individual characteristics and by a viewpoint and a flavor that are unmistakably American. A few of those who have gained international reputation are: Aaron Copland (1900–   ); Samuel Barber (1910–   ); Henry Cowell (1897–   ); Norman Dello Joio (1913–   ); Charles T. Griffes (1884–1920); Howard Hanson (1896–   ); Roy Harris (1898–   ); Charles Ives (1874–1954); Douglas Moore (1893–   ); Walter Piston (1894–   ); Wallingford Riegger (1885–1961); William Schuman (1910–   ); Deems Taylor (1885–   ); and Virgil Thomson (1896–   ).

MUSTANGS. "After God, we owed the victory to the horses," wrote Bernal Diaz, the great chronicler of the Conquest of Mexico. When Cortés landed, 1519, he had sixteen horses and a colt born on the ship that brought them—all mares and stallions, no geldings. In time the Spaniards brought other horses. They explored the New World on horseback. They raised horses on unfenced ranges. For 24 years after the landing of Cortés a royal edict prohibited an Indian's riding a horse. But horse stock strayed from the *haciendas;* on explorations that took their riders thousands of miles into the unknown, horses were lost. The wild increase of these lost and estrayed animals were called *mesteños*—mustangs. Indians learned to master what, "next to God," had mastered them.

With the development of ranching, mustangs were recognized as a nuisance and were killed off. The

637

wild horses ranging today in certain places of Arizona, Wyoming and other Western states are not of the unmixed Spanish mustang breed. This wonderfully hardy breed is not being preserved in North America as its counterpart, the *criollo*, is being preserved in South America. The wild horses along the Carolina seaboard were another breed. The mustang—even though Mark Twain satirized "A Genuine Mexican Plug"—influenced tremendously the history of the West.

"MY COUNTRY, 'TIS OF THEE." In 1832 Lowell Mason, musical educator and hymn writer of Boston, handed Samuel F. Smith—then a theological student at Andover and becoming known as an amateur poet—a book of German songs, asking him to look over it and if he found any good tunes, to make an English translation of the words thereto, or write original songs to the meter, for use in schools. One air, simple yet strong and pleasing, gave Smith a patriotic inspiration, and within half an hour he had written five stanzas of the now familiar hymn to his native land, "My Country, 'Tis of Thee." The third stanza he later discarded, and the remaining four stand almost as originally written. Not until some time afterward did Smith learn that the tune he had used was that of the British national anthem, "God Save the King," which had been taken over into the musical literature of several other lands. Even the melody is of gradual growth, though in its present form it is generally attributed to the early 18th-century English composer, Henry Carey. Smith's hymn was first sung in the Park Street Church, in Boston, July 4, 1832. Anti-British feeling was still strong in the United States then, but strangely enough, the knowledge that the air was that of the British national anthem did not deter the growth of the song's popularity. It was first published in Mason's collection, *The Choir*, in 1832. With the tune rechristened "America," and without any official action, the song—simple, melodious, easily sung and remembered—became within two or three decades as nearly a national anthem as anything we have—perhaps even nearer than "The Star-Spangled Banner," which is essentially a paean to the national flag, and is frequently under attack because of its alleged unsuitability.

"MY OLD KENTUCKY HOME" (1853) is the work of our greatest composer of folksongs, Stephen Foster. Though its origin is shrouded in legend, it seems probable that the original inspiration came from a visit that Foster made to Federal Hill at Bardstown, Ky., sometime in the 1840's. This old Southern mansion was the home of Judge John Rowan, a relative of Foster's.

MYERS v. **U. S.** The Constitution definitely confers upon the President a broad power to appoint Federal officers "by and with the advice and consent of the Senate," but is silent upon the President's right to remove officers so appointed. Since 1789, however, Presidents have assumed that their power to appoint and their duty to see that the laws are faithfully executed implied the power to remove without senatorial consent, even though Senate approval may have been necessary for the original appointment. In 1876 Congress restricted the power of removal by requiring senatorial approval for removals of postmasters. In 1920 President Wilson, without consulting the Senate, removed Frank S. Myers, postmaster at Portland, Oregon, who brought action to test the legality of the President's action. The Supreme Court, by a vote of six to three (1926), upheld the removal, declaring that the act of 1876 was an unconstitutional invasion of executive authority, and giving the Court's sanction to the executive assumption stated above. Incidentally, the Tenure-of-Office Act of 1867—partly repealed in 1869 and wholly in 1887—was pronounced to have been unconstitutional, thus supporting the contention of President Johnson at the time the act was passed over his veto. The broad doctrine that Congress may not limit the President's power of removal has, however, been somewhat narrowed by the Court's decision (1935) in the case of W. E. Humphrey's removal from the Federal Trade Commission.

NAPOLEON'S DECREES. Throughout his long struggle with Great Britain, Napoleon was torn between the desirability of excluding British commerce and the undesirability of economic suffocation for Continental Europe. His policy alternated between impositions such as the Berlin, Milan and supplementary decrees, and a system of licenses accorded from time to time as exceptions to the major decrees.

To particularize, the Berlin Decree of Nov. 21, 1806, in belated response to the Orders in Council of May 16, 1806, imposed a paper blockade of the British Isles, outstripping in its defiance of neutral rights Britain's own blockade. The Milan Decree, of Dec. 17, 1807, eclipsed even this, by declaring lawful prey ships submitting to the British Orders in Council. The Bayonne Decree, of April 17, 1808, further mocked the neutrals by representing the seizure of American shipping as co-operation with Jefferson in enforcing the Embargo. Similarly, the Rambouillet Decree, drafted March 23, published May 14, 1810, legalized seizure of American shipping as retaliation for a proviso in the Nonimportation law. Climaxing Napoleonic hypocrisy was the Cadore Letter, of Aug. 5, 1810, deceptively revoking the Continental Decrees contingent upon British abandonment of the Orders in Council.

NARVÁEZ EXPEDITION. Pánfilo de Narváez received from Charles V on Nov. 17, 1526, a patent to explore and reduce to Spanish rule all the lands from Soto la Marina northeastward around the Gulf of Mexico to the "Isle of Florida." With 400 men and 80 horses, he landed from his five ships at Tampa Bay, April 14, 1528. Marching north along the coast in search of the Indian country of Apalache, he lost contact with his ships, and, after battles with the Indians at Apalache, he and his men were reduced by famine to the desperate plan of building crude flatboats in which to follow the coast from Apalache Bay westward to the Spanish settlements on the Rio Pánuco. Despite bad weather and starvation the surviving 247 men managed to follow the Gulf coast as far as Texas, where the flotilla broke up among the coastal islands near Galveston Bay, Narváez perishing there in a storm in November, 1528. The treasurer of the expedition, Alvar Nuñez Cabeza de Vaca, with a few survivors lived among the coastal Texan Indians for about six years. Then, utilizing their reputations as healers and traders, Cabeza de Vaca and three companions, including a Moorish slave, Estebanico, sought to reach the Pánuco on foot. Turned back in northeastern Mexico, they performed the justly famous feat of traversing the continent by ascending, in general, the Rio Grande Valley, crossing the Sierra Madre ranges and wandering down through Sonora to be rescued by Spaniards near Culiacán, in modern Sinaloa, in March of 1536. The account of their journey and of the Indian lands they had visited or heard about seems to have been a stimulus to the viceroy of New Spain, Antonio de Mendoza, in despatching the Coronado expedition in 1540. Narváez's patent was taken over by Hernando DeSoto in 1537.

NASHVILLE, BATTLE OF (Dec. 15–16, 1864), was the dramatic winter conflict in which George H. Thomas, with a hastily organized army of heterogeneous troops, moved out of Nashville and fell upon the Confederate forces of John B. Hood. On the first day the Confederates were pushed back. On the following day, while feinting and holding on his left wing, Thomas pressed forward on his right and drove the Confederates in disorderly retreat from the battlefield. Sometimes described as perfect tactics, this victory of Thomas' freed Tennessee of organized Confederate forces and marked the end of Hood's Tennessee campaign.

NASHVILLE CONVENTION (June 3–12, Nov. 11–18, 1850). Many Southern statesmen believed that a united Southern party was necessary if slavery and Southern rights were to be maintained within the Union. A caucus of Southern delegates in Congress adopted and published an "Address . . . to their Constituents" in 1850, but the leaders felt that a Southern convention would be more effective. John C. Calhoun wrote a letter to Collin S. Tarpley of Mississippi suggesting that his state issue the call for the convention. The Mississippi state convention (Jack-

son, Oct. 1, 1849) resolved "that a convention of the slave-holding States should be held in Nashville, Tenn., . . . to devise and adopt some mode of resistance" to Northern aggressions. In response to this call delegates from nine states, chosen by popular vote, by conventions, by state legislatures or appointed by governors, assembled at Nashville. Both Whig and Democratic delegates were chosen but the latter predominated. Many of the outstanding political leaders of the South were among those elected. The Convention unanimously adopted 28 resolutions which maintained that slavery existed independent of but was recognized by the Constitution. They asserted that the territories belonged to the people of the states, that the citizens of the several states had equal rights to migrate to the territories, that Congress had no power to exclude them but was obligated to protect them. The resolutions then expressed a willingness to settle the matter by extending the Missouri Compromise line to the Pacific. The Convention also adopted an address to the people of the Southern states which condemned the Clay resolutions then before Congress. Reassembling six weeks after Congress had adopted the Compromise of 1850, with a changed and more radical membership, the Convention rejected the Compromise and called upon the Southern states to secede from the Union. The second session of the Convention was a fiasco, however, for Southern sentiment rapidly crystallized in support of the Compromise.

NATCHEZ TRACE was a road running more than 500 miles from Nashville, Tenn., to Natchez on the Mississippi River, following roughly an old Indian trail. When in 1795 the United States acquired a clear title from Spain (*see* Pinckney's Treaty) to the Old Southwest, and when eight years later it purchased Louisiana from Napoleon, the economic and military necessity of adequate roads through the southwestern wilderness to the Gulf spurred the Government into action. By far the most famous and important of the roads which resulted was the Natchez Trace. In 1801 Gen. James Wilkinson obtained the right of way by treaties with the Chickasaws and Choctaws, and in 1806 Congress authorized President Jefferson to begin construction. In a few years wagons were using the road, but for several decades most of its traffic was northward, since settlers would float their produce down the Mississippi to market on flatboats and return over the robber-infested Trace by foot or on horseback.

NATIONAL COUNCIL OF THE CHURCHES OF CHRIST IN AMERICA is a national co-operative organization officially supported by 33 Protestant and Orthodox communions. It was formed in 1950 by the merger of a number of general interdenominational agencies, including the Federal Council of the Churches of Christ in America, the Foreign Missions

Conference of North America, the Home Missions Council of North America, the International Council of Religious Education, and the United Council of Church Women. The leading objects of the Council are: to manifest the common spirit and purpose of the co-operating churches in carrying out their mission to the world; to do for the churches such co-operative work as they shall authorize; to encourage fellowship and mutual counsel concerning the spiritual life and religious activities of the churches; to promote co-operation among local churches and to further the growth of local and state councils of churches; and to maintain fellowship and co-operation with the World Council of Churches and other international Christian organizations.

NATIONAL ROAD, a name often given to the Cumberland Road, the latter being the legal name. West of Wheeling this famous artery of communication (macadamized) was commonly called the "United States" or "National" Road for it was the first, and for a long period the greatest, of such enterprises undertaken by the Federal Government. This western portion was probably not so significant as was the earlier built section, for much of the traffic in the West was diverted to steamboats on the Ohio River. As the interior of Ohio developed, however, the National Road through that state became a crowded highway and as many as a hundred teams often would be encountered in a journey of twenty miles. For some years construction west of Wheeling was uncertain because of constitutional scruples, held especially by Old School Republicans. The work was begun from Wheeling toward Zanesville, however, in 1825–26, following to that place the celebrated Zane's Trace. By 1833 the road was opened to Columbus. The last appropriation for the road—in Ohio, Indiana and Illinois—was made by Congress in 1838. Following President Monroe's veto of a bill for the collection of tolls by the Federal Government (1822), parts of the road had been surrendered to the states, which undertook repairs and erected toll gates to insure the financing of such operations. The road through Indiana was completed only in 1850 by a state corporation. When Illinois received the custody of her portion, it was unfinished, although graded and bridged as far west as Vandalia, then the state capital.

The road meant less to Indiana and Illinois than to Ohio; and after 1850 the canal, the railroad and the telegraph contributed generally to the decline of its importance. But today, as U. S. Route 40, it is a primary route for motor travel in the United States.

NATIONAL SCIENCE FOUNDATION. This organization was created by Congress in 1950 (Public Law 507, 81st Congress, as amended) "to promote the progress of science; to advance the national health, prosperity, and welfare; to secure the national defense; and for other purposes." The Foundation resulted from the recommendations of Dr. Vannevar Bush who, in *Science, the Endless Frontier,* a report to the President in July, 1945, stressed the growing need for Federal support of basic research and education in the sciences and for the development of national science policy. The Foundation supports basic research, principally in the universities, in all the natural sciences and in selected areas of the social sciences.

The Foundation also contributes support for capital research facilities that cannot be provided by other means and for the development of graduate research laboratories. Two major astronomy facilities supported by the Foundation are the National Radio Astronomy Observatory at Green Bank, W. Va., and the Kitt Peak National Observatory (optical) near Tucson, Arizona.

Efforts to improve education and training in the sciences are directed towards students, teachers, and course-content. The programs include several types of fellowship awards at predoctoral and postdoctoral levels; summer institutes, academic-year and in-service institutes for college and secondary-school teachers of science and mathematics; university-centered projects for the revision of the basic secondary-school curricula in physics, chemistry, mathematics, and biology; and a variety of special projects including conferences, visiting lecturers, and traveling lecture demonstrations.

The Foundation has been assigned a leading role in strengthening and co-ordinating governmental and private efforts for more effective handling of the results of scientific research in the form of scientific information.

As a basis for its own operations and for policy studies, the Foundation surveys and analyzes research and development expenditures by industry, educational and other nonprofit institutions and the Federal Government. A scientific manpower program provides information on the characteristics and numbers of scientists, engineers, and science teachers, and projected national requirements.

The Foundation operates as an independent Federal agency under its director, appointed by the President, and under the policy guidance of the National Science Board, also appointed by the President.

NATIONAL TRUST FOR HISTORIC PRESERVATION IN THE UNITED STATES. The National Trust of Washington, D. C., is a nonprofit, nongovernmental organization founded in 1949 to promote the preservation of sites, buildings and objects significant in American history and culture. It maintains and exhibits five historic properties: Casa Amesti, Monterey, Calif.; The Wayside Inn, South Sudbury, Mass.; Decatur House, Washington, D. C.;

Woodlawn Plantation, Mount Vernon, Va.; The Shadows, New Iberia, La. The Trust's especial interests lie in encouraging public participation in historic preservation. To this end it has developed not only a wide individual membership, open to all, but has established an organization of 310 affiliated groups, both national and regional in character, for which the Trust serves as a central clearinghouse for information and advice. The Trust does not offer direct financial aid. The principal educational media are a quarterly publication, *Historic Preservation,* participation in a six-week summer course in preservation and administrative techniques, and regional seminars or short courses offered in co-operation with local affiliates.

NATIONAL UNION ("ARM-IN-ARM") CONVENTION (Philadelphia, Aug. 14–16, 1866) was an effort by President Johnson's supporters to unite opposition to the Radical Republicans. The convention platform stressed conciliation, state equality and acceptance of the results of the war, and called for election of conservatives to Congress. Copperhead delegates withdrew to preserve harmony. Widely acclaimed at first, Radical successes in the congressional elections of 1866 demonstrated its failure.

NATIVISM, the policy of favoring native inhabitants of a country as against immigrants, has through the course of American history fostered antagonism toward the Roman Catholic Church rather than toward any particular alien group. Until recent times many natives have consistently held to the belief that this Church endangered both the traditional Protestantism and the democratic institutions of the United States, and have viewed foreigners with alarm because they were Catholics rather than because of their alien birth.

This antipapal sentiment, brought to America by the first English colonists, was fostered in the new country by the 18th-century wars with Catholic France and Spain. Colonial laws and colonial writing both reflected this intolerance. The Revolution abruptly changed the American attitude toward Catholics; the liberal spirit of the Declaration of Independence and the French Alliance of 1778 both contributed toward a more tolerant spirit which endured until the 1820's, despite the efforts of New England Federalists who were largely responsible for the antialien sections of the Alien and Sedition acts and the proposals of the Hartford Convention.

Anti-Catholic sentiment reappeared in the late 1820's, inspired by a mounting Catholic immigration and by the English propaganda which accompanied the passage of the Catholic Emancipation Act. Protestants, under the influence of the Finney revivalism, quickly rushed to the defense of their religion. A No-Popery newspaper, *The Protestant,* was founded in 1830 and a year later the New York

Protestant Association began holding public discussions to "illustrate the history and character of Popery." By 1834 intolerance had grown to a point where the mob destruction of an Ursuline convent at Charlestown, Mass., was condoned rather than condemned by the mass of the people. This sign of popular favor resulted in the launching of two new anti-Catholic papers, the *Downfall of Babylon* and the *American Protestant Vindicator,* the releasing of a flood of anti-Catholic books and pamphlets, and the formation of a national organization, the Protestant Reformation Society (1836).

The sensational propaganda spread by this society probably convinced many Protestants of the evils of Catholicism but it remained for the New York school controversy of the early 1840's to win over the churchgoing, middle class. In this controversy Catholic protests against the reading of the King James version of the Scriptures in the public schools were immediately misrepresented by propagandists who convinced Protestants that the papists were opposed to all Bible reading. Alarmed by this, the churches took up the cry against Rome, giving nativists sufficient strength to organize the American Republican party with an anti-Catholic, antiforeign platform. Before more than local political success could be gained, a series of riots between natives and foreigners in Philadelphia in 1844 turned popular sentiment against the whole No-Popery crusade. For the remainder of the decade the Mexican War and the slavery controversy absorbed national attention.

Nativistic leaders, recognizing that the stigma of past sensationalism could be wiped out only by a new organization, in 1844 formed the American Protestant Society to take the place of the Protestant Reformation Society. This new body, by promising a labor of "light and love . . . for the salvation of Romanists," won the endorsement of nearly all Protestant sects and influenced hundreds of clergymen to deliver antipapal sermons. Its methods proved so successful that in 1849 a merger was effected with two lesser anti-Catholic organizations, the Foreign Evangelical Society and the Christian Alliance, to form the most important of the pre-Civil War societies, the American and Foreign Christian Union, pledged to win both the United States and Europe to Protestantism.

The propaganda machinery created by these organized efforts, combined with the heavy immigration from famine-stricken Ireland and Germany, so alarmed Americans that political nativism seemed again feasible. The Compromise of 1850, apparently settling the slavery question for all time, opened the way for the Know-Nothing, or American, party, which enjoyed remarkable success in 1854 and 1855, carrying a number of states and threatening to sweep the nation in the presidential election of 1856. Its brief career was abruptly halted by the passage of the Kansas-Nebraska Act, for as Americans became absorbed in the slavery conflict they forgot their nebulous fears of Rome, and the Civil War doomed both the Know-Nothing party and the American and Foreign Christian Union to speedy extinction.

After the war the nation's attention was so centered on the problems of reconstruction and economic rehabilitation that nativistic sentiments remained dormant until the 1880's. By this time mounting foreign immigration and unsettled industrial conditions had created a state of mind receptive to antialien propaganda. Instead of being directed against the foreigner, however, this propaganda was again aimed almost exclusively at the Catholic Church. A "Committee of One Hundred" from Boston flooded the country with anti-Catholic documents, newspapers bent on exposing the errors of Rome were founded, and an alleged "Papal Bull" calling for the massacre of all Protestants "on or about the feast of St. Ignatius in the Year of our Lord, 1893" was widely circulated and believed. The American Protective Association, formed in 1887 to crystallize these prejudices, although pledging its members neither to vote for nor employ Catholics, scarcely mentioned Protestant aliens, indicating that religion and not birthplace was the point of objection.

The political failure of the American Protective Association combined with the interest aroused by the Free Silver campaign of 1896 to check nativistic agitation. In the years after 1898 there was another brief flurry occasioned by the continuing immigration and two events that centered attention on the Church: the celebration of the centenary of the erection of the diocese of Baltimore into a metropolitan see and the meeting in Chicago of the first American Catholic Missionary Conference. This resulted in the inevitable formation of anti-Catholic organizations. Most prominent were the Guardians of Liberty, the Knights of Luther, the Covenanters and the American Pathfinders. No-Popery newspapers, led by the *Menace*, began to appear, but before this phase of the movement could be translated into politics World War I intervened.

The next burst of nativistic excitement occurred during the 1920's. The United States, in the restless period which followed the war, developed an intense nationalism which bred antagonism toward immigrants and Catholics—toward all groups that were not conservative, Protestant Americans. During the early part of the decade the Ku Klux Klan shaped and fostered this prejudice. The Klan's excesses and political corruption brought about its decline, but intolerance did not abate—a fact clearly shown by the presidential campaign of 1928. The presence of Alfred E. Smith, a Catholic, as the Democratic candidate aroused a bitter nativistic propaganda which was an important factor in causing his defeat. No such trend was evident in 1960, when the Catholic John F. Kennedy defeated Richard M. Nixon.

NATURAL RIGHTS are deemed to be those which inhere in the individual anterior to the creation of government and which are not relinquished upon entrance into civil society. The concept was brought to the American colonies through the writings of John Locke and was stated in the New York assembly as early as 1714 by John Mulford. It was developed by the dissenting clergy in New England and became a part of the revolutionary philosophy. Samuel Adams conceived natural rights to be guaranteed by the British constitution, but the radical Thomas Paine thought they existed independently of charters and constitutions. His conception of popular sovereignty involved the basic notion that rights inhere in the individual, and governments exist only for the further protection of individual rights. This idea was in the mind of Jefferson when he wrote into the Declaration of Independence that all men "are endowed by their Creator with certain inalienable rights," to secure which governments were instituted. Among these rights are "life, liberty and the pursuit of happiness." From the revolutionary philosophy the idea was embodied in the state constitutions with some changes in phraseology.

Both Hamilton and Jefferson subscribed to the doctrine of natural rights, but neither permitted speculative theories to interfere with practical statesmanship. The first attack upon natural rights came in the slavery controversy when Dr. Cooper of South Carolina repudiated the doctrine as a fabrication "by theoretical writers on a contemplation of what might usefully be acknowledged among men as binding on each other." There are no rights, he maintained, except those which society considers it expedient to grant. He was followed by Calhoun, who rejected the individualistic political theory of the earlier centuries. In his opinion, government was not a matter of choice but was a fundamental necessity to the existence of man. It was therefore fallacious to assume a state of society anterior to the creation of government and from this attempt to rationalize the formation of political institutions. Thus the whole theory of natural rights appeared to him to be worthless when its foundations were proved to be unsound. Not all of the defenders of slavery, however, were willing to relinquish the doctrine of natural rights. But those who relied upon the doctrine gave it an interpretation which obviated any objection to slaveholding.

Since the Civil War, political theory in the United States, as elsewhere, has not adhered to individuality before organization. Recent tendencies, reflected in the writings of Burgess and Willoughby, hold that natural rights have, at most, ethical significance and have no place in political science. However, the doctrine is asserted occasionally in judicial decisions as a basis for the protection of the individual against what is deemed to be the arbitrary action of government.

NATURALIZATION. Citizenship in the United States is acquired either by birth or by naturalization. Naturalization is the formal, legal adoption of an alien into membership in a political community. In the 17th and early 18th centuries, its principal function was to remove the alien's disabilities for holding and bequeathing property; subsequently, it was viewed as admitting him to full civil rights and to political participation through the suffrage and the holding of public office.

The American development of naturalization represented a departure from European practice. In Great Britain naturalization had been granted, sparingly, only by special acts of Parliament or (in the attenuated form of "denization") by royal decrees. Wishing to attract immigrants for land settlement, the separate colonies in the New World, with no sound legal warrant but with little interference from home before the mid-18th century, bestowed naturalization liberally by various methods. An enabling act of Parliament, passed in 1740, was little used because its residency requirement was long. England's increasingly stringent control of naturalization, particularly in measures of 1760 and 1773, became one of the grievances memorialized in the Declaration of Independence.

During the Revolutionary and Confederation periods, the desirability of a uniform system of naturalization in the several states was discussed, but fructified only in the new Constitution (Art. 1, Sec. 8, Cl. 4) which authorized Congress "to establish an uniform rule of naturalization." James Madison, in *Federalist* No. 42, cited this provision as an argument for ratifying the new charter. The Supreme Court ruled, in Chirac v. Chirac (1817), that Congress possessed this power exclusively rather than concurrently with the state governments.

Naturalization may be conferred collectively. Thus, through the respective treaties of acquisition, all or many inhabitants of the Louisiana Purchase, Florida, the Mexican cessions and Alaska were admitted to the American body politic. Texans were given citizenship by a joint resolution of Congress (1845). Statutes granted citizenship to natives of Hawaii (1900), Puerto Rico (1917), Guam (1950), and to inhabitants of the Virgin Islands who did not opt for Danish citizenship (1927). The congressional bestowal of citizenship on American-born Negroes (1866) and American Indians (1924) was not properly naturalization, but recognition of their status as native-born citizens.

The first general legislation governing individual naturalization was an act of 1790. In this, Congress empowered courts of record to confer citizenship on free white aliens who had resided two years in the country, had satisfied the court of their good character, and had taken an oath to support the Constitution. Later legislation (including the basic Naturalization Act of 1906 and the major codification in the

Immigration and Nationality [McCarran-Walter] Act of 1952) has added significant details, but has followed the fundamental pattern of this law.

In 1870, naturalization was opened to persons of African descent; in 1940, to "descendants of races indigenous to the Western Hemisphere"; in 1943, to Chinese; and in 1946, to natives of India and the Philippines. The McCarran-Walter Act ended all racial restrictions. The two-year residence requirement was extended to fourteen in 1798, but reduced to five from 1802 onwards. Between 1795 and 1952, the process of naturalization consisted of three stages: a preliminary declaration of intention to become a citizen ("first papers"); after a stated period of residence which was regarded as probationary, the petition for citizenship; and the oath itself. Since 1952 the declaration of intention has been unnecessary. Under prevailing judicial interpretation from the 1920's to the 1940's, pacifists were ineligible for naturalization because their oath could not signify their will to bear arms in support of the Constitution (Schwimmer v. U. S., and Mackintosh v. U. S.; reversed in Girouard v. U. S.). The 1952 legislation accepts a will "to perform work of national importance under civilian direction" as sufficing for the required allegiance.

The collective methods of naturalization are all legislative in character. They admit to the political community through general acts without the issuance of citizenship papers. But the naturalization of individuals, though controlled by legislation, is judicial and administrative. The alien petitions a court, and his case becomes the subject of investigation and hearing in which the judge is assisted by executive agents.

Under the Immigration and Nationality Act of 1952, citizenship papers may be granted by national district courts, or by state and territorial courts which have a seal, a clerk, and jurisdiction in actions at law and equity. The applicant must first file with the court his petition together with sworn evidence in support of his qualifications for citizenship. The applicant must be at least 18 years old; must have been lawfully admitted to the country and resided here for five years continuously since his admission; must be reasonably able to understand, speak, read and write simple English words and phrases; and must understand the fundamentals of American history and government. He must demonstrate that he is of good moral character (a qualification which courts interpret in accordance with contemporary, flexible, community standards). The applicant must also show that he is "attached to the principles of the Constitution of the United States and well disposed to the good order and happiness of the United States." The 1906 statute excluded from citizenship aliens who espoused anarchist principles. Acts of 1940 and 1950, along with that of 1952, exclude those also who within ten years prior to the prospective naturalization have espoused, advocated, or belonged to organizations espousing or advocating other doctrines of political subversion. Moreover, membership in such an organization within five years after naturalization is to be regarded as *prima facie* evidence of fraud in obtaining naturalization; a person thus involved is therefore liable to cancellation of his citizenship certificate (denaturalization) and deportation.

The Immigration and Naturalization Service, which was established in 1906 within the Department of Labor and transferred in 1940 to the Department of Justice, examines and investigates the petitioner and his affidavits; it then reports to the courts. Not less than thirty days after the petition has been filed, the judge conducts a final hearing in open court, administers the oath of citizenship—which includes a renunciation of all foreign allegiance—and authorizes the issuance of letters of citizenship (final papers).

Children, 16 years old and under, are derivatively naturalized with their parents. Since the Cable Act of 1922, a woman's citizenship status in American law has not been altered by marriage. An American woman marrying an alien does not lose her citizenship, and an alien woman marrying an American does not automatically acquire citizenship. The alien wife or husband of an American, however, may now be naturalized after only three years of residence.

Despite judicial assertions that naturalized citizens have equal rights with native citizens, some differences remain. The Constitution itself requires the President to be a natural-born citizen (Art. 2, Sec. 1, Cl. 5). Its requirements that Senators be citizens of nine years standing (Art. 2, Sec. 3, Cl. 3), and Representatives be citizens of seven years standing (Art. 2, Sec. 2, Cl. 2), are of practical importance only for the naturalized. The Immigration and Nationality Act of 1952, moreover, lays down several grounds for loss of naturalized citizenship, which are not applicable to native-born citizenship. These include fraud in the acquisition of citizenship, subversive associations within five years of naturalization, and residence for specified lengthy periods in foreign countries.

NAUVOO, MORMONS AT (1839–46). In 1839, upon their expulsion from Missouri, the Mormons, or Latter-day Saints, purchased the embryonic town of Commerce in Hancock County, Ill., changed its name to Nauvoo, and prepared to make it the capital of their faith. The city grew rapidly, attracting Mormons from the East and converts from Europe, especially England. Figures are unreliable, but its population was at least 12,000 in 1845, which was larger than any other city in Illinois at the time.

Nauvoo seemed also to be prosperous. Evidences of wealth were the temple, begun in 1841 and completed five years later at a cost of $1,000,000, the Nauvoo House and other pretentious structures. But the prosperity was hollow, being dependent principally upon the money brought to the community by the ever-growing stream of newcomers. By 1845

poverty was widespread, and if the exodus forced by the Mormon War had not taken place, economic collapse probably would have occurred.

NAVAL OIL RESERVES were suggested to President Taft by Secretary of the Interior R. A. Ballinger in September, 1909, and after the necessary legislation had been passed the President permanently withdrew from entry Naval Petroleum Reserve No. 1 (Elk Hills) on Sept. 2, 1912; No. 2 (Buena Vista, Calif.) on Dec. 13, 1912; and No. 3 (Teapot Dome) April 30, 1915, altogether involving about 50,000 acres of public land. Less than a tenth of the total area withdrawn from entry was free pending prior claims, and though Secretary of the Navy Josephus Daniels, in his report to President Wilson on Dec. 1, 1913, urged the passage of legislation permitting the Navy Department to take possession of the reserves, drill wells, erect refineries and produce its own supply of fuel oil, such permission was not given. The reserves lay dormant until 1920 when an act of Congress authorized the Navy Department to take possession of that part of the reserves against which no claims were pending, to develop them, and to use, store and exchange the products therefrom. It had become evident, meanwhile, that petroleum beneath the withdrawn area was probably being drained away through wells on adjoining land, and some leases for protective drilling were given during the few months Secretary Daniels remained in office. Edwin Denby, who became Secretary of the Navy under President Harding, requested early in 1921 that the custody of the Naval Petroleum Reserves be transferred to the Interior Department, which had not only been engaged in producing helium for the Navy Department, but was the official agency for settling claims to public land. The power to determine general policy in regard to the reserves remained with the Navy Department, and it was at the suggestion of the latter that it was eventually determined to lease the Elk Hills and Teapot Dome reserves as a unit, exchanging the royalty oil not only for fuel oil, but for storage facilities at Pearl Harbor, Hawaii, and other strategic points. This was done in comparative secrecy, imposed by the Navy Department on the grounds that the action taken was part of its war plans, but early in 1922 it came to the attention of the Senate, which began an investigation. It was disclosed that Secretary of the Interior Fall had received $100,000 from the president of the company that had leased Elk Hills and had engaged in involved financial dealings with the president of the company that leased Teapot Dome. Through the ensuing litigation the leases were cancelled and Secretary Fall was convicted on a charge of bribery, but the others were acquitted.

NAVAL WAR WITH FRANCE. In consequence of the Franco-American misunderstanding of 1798–

1800 the French, with no declaration of war, began to seize or plunder American merchant vessels. Despite our attempts to settle the matter diplomatically no solution could be reached. In March–July, 1798, Congress passed acts empowering our merchant marine to "repel by force any assault"; commissioning privateers; and ordering our navy to seize all armed French craft on our coast, or molesting our trade. Washington was recalled from retirement and appointed commander in chief of the army. Our three-ship navy was rapidly enlarged by construction, purchase and gifts to 55 vessels. The first got to sea May 24, 1798. France, occupied with European wars and knowing the weakness of our untrained navy, sent no heavy vessels to the western Atlantic, but placed her reliance on privateers supported by a few frigates and sloops of war.

As our vessels were commissioned, they were organized into small squadrons to guard the chief trade areas in the East and West Indies with single vessels detailed to convoy duty. Aside from numerous actions with privateers, the only engagements, each an American victory, were between the *Insurgente,* 40 guns, and the *Constellation,* 36; the *Vengeance,* 50, and the *Constellation,* 36; and the *Berceau,* 24, and the *Boston,* 32. Capt. Thomas Truxtun, commander of the *Constellation* in both engagements, was presented with two gold medals by Congress. Two vessels, the schooners *Enterprise* and *Experiment,* had especially notable careers, the former taking thirteen prizes on one cruise. No attempts to seize the French islands were made, but Capt. Henry Geddes with the ship *Patapsco* on Sept. 23, 1800, successfully dislodged the French forces which had taken possession of the Dutch island of Curaçao. About 85 French vessels were captured, not including recaptures of American craft and small boats; the French took one American naval vessel, the schooner *Retaliation* (ex-*LaCroyable*), the first American capture in the war. However, several hundred American merchant vessels were seized by France both abroad and in home waters. These were condemned at farcical admiralty trials, the crews in most instances being imprisoned and brutally treated.

On Sept. 30, 1800, a "Convention of Peace, Commerce and Navigation" was concluded, and shortly thereafter hostilities ceased. Claims arising from France's failure to meet her obligations under this treaty helped bring about the purchase of Louisiana.

NAVIGATION ACTS had their origin in the British regulations of the coastwise trade. When colonies developed overseas an extension of the coastwise regulations followed. The first formal legislation affecting the colonies was enacted by Parliament in 1649 and 1651. These laws were modified, consolidated and re-enacted in 1660 and became the basic Navigation Act. This law and others were revised in the final act of 1696. The object was to protect British shipping against competition from Dutch and other foreign seamen. Under these acts no goods could be imported into or exported from any British colony in Asia, Africa or America except in English vessels, English-owned, and with crews three-fourths English. Other clauses limited the importation of any products of Asia, Africa or America into England to English vessels and provided that goods from foreign countries could be imported into England only in vessels from such foreign countries or in English ships.

Wherever the word English was used in these and subsequent acts it referred to the nationality of individuals and not to their place of residence. Thus American colonists were just as much English as their compatriots who resided in London. The net effect of these basic laws was to give Englishmen and English ships a legal monopoly of all trade between various colonial ports and between colonial ports and England. Even the trade between colonial ports and foreign countries was limited to English vessels. Thus foreign vessels were excluded entirely from colonial ports and could trade only at ports in the British Isles.

Another field of legislation had to do with commodities. Certain important colonial products were enumerated and could be exported from the place of production only to another British colony or to England. At first this list included tobacco, sugar, indigo, cotton wool, ginger, fustic and other dyewoods. Later, enumeration was extended to naval stores, hemp, rice, molasses, beaver skins, furs, copper ore, iron and lumber.

Asiatic goods and European manufactures could be imported into the colonies only from England. An exception was made in the case of salt or wine from the Azores or the Madeira Islands, and food products from Ireland or Scotland.

The enumerated clauses of the Navigation Acts were enforced by a system of bonds which required the master of the vessel to comply with the provisions of the acts. These operated in such a way as to give American shipowners a practical monopoly of the trade between the continental and West Indian colonies. Residents of great Britain in turn had a general monopoly of the carrying of the heavy enumerated goods from the colonies to the British Isles.

Closely related to the Navigation Acts was another series of measures called "Trade Acts," and usually confused with the Navigation Acts proper. These were enacted mostly after 1700 and gradually developed into a most complicated system of trade control and encouragement. The general plan was to make the entire British Empire prosperous and the trade of one section complementary to that of other sections.

Colonists were largely limited to buying British manufactures. This was not necessarily a disadvantage, because an elaborate system of export bounties was provided so that British goods were actually cheaper in the colonies than similar foreign goods. These bounties averaged more than £38,000 per year for the ten years preceding the Revolution. From 1757 to 1770 the bounties on British linens, exported to the colonies, totaled £346,232 according to the British treasury reports. Added to this was a series of rebates or drawbacks of duties on European goods exported to the colonies. These, too, ran into formidable sums. Those to the West Indies alone amounted to £34,000 in 1774. The average payments from the British treasury in bounties and drawbacks on exports to the colonies in 1764 amounted to about £250,000 sterling per year.

Colonial production of articles desired in the British markets was encouraged by a variety of measures. Colonial tobacco was given a complete monopoly of the home market by prohibiting its growth in England and placing very heavy import duties on the competing Spanish tobacco. Other colonial products were encouraged by tariff duties, so levied as to discriminate sharply in favor of the colonial product and against the competing foreign product. Some colonial products, not fully needed in England, were given rebates on re-exportation so as to facilitate their flow through the British markets to their foreign destinations. In other cases surplus colonial products, like rice, were permitted to be exported directly to foreign colonies and to southern Europe without passing through England. In still other cases colonial products such as hemp, indigo, lumber and silk were paid direct cash bounties on arrival in England. These alone totaled more than £82,000 from 1771 to 1775. Naval stores also received liberal bounties, totaling £1,438,762 from 1706 to 1774, and at the time of the Revolution were averaging £25,000 annually.

In the main the navigation system was mutually profitable to colonies and mother country. An occasional colonial industry was discouraged by parliamentary prohibition, if it threatened to develop into serious competition with an important home industry. The outstanding illustrations are laws forbidding the intercolonial export of colonial-made hats, colonial grown or manufactured wool, and the act forbidding the setting up of new mills for the production of wrought iron and steel. These laws produced some local complaint, although they evidently affected very few people.

So long as the Trade and Navigation laws were limited to the regulation of trade and the promotion of the total commerce of the empire they were generally popular in America; at least that was true after 1700. The attempt to use them as taxation measures was resisted. The enumerated products came largely from the colonies that remained loyal. The bounties went largely to the colonies that revolted. The New England shipping industry rested directly upon the protection of the Navigation Acts. These are among the reasons why the First Continental Congress in its resolutions approved the navigation system and why Franklin offered to have the acts re-enacted by every colonial legislature in America and to guarantee them for a hundred years, if taxation of America was abandoned.

NAVY, UNITED STATES. As colonials, Americans had served in the British Navy and merchantmen. Against Britain's foes, they had been expert privateers. In seeking independence, it was natural for them to carry the struggle to sea. Such effort was spontaneous and opportunistic, the most consequential resulting from the issuance of some 2000 letters-of-marque.

1775–1860

For essential duties that privateersmen shunned, the Continental Navy was founded by Congress on Oct. 13, 1775. Of 27 small men-of-war at sea, only three survived hard fighting and cruising. Continental captains such as Jones, Barry, Wickes and Biddle were distinguished from privateersmen by eagerness to engage warships: the last captain mentioned blew up with the 32-gun frigate *Randolph* against the 64-gun ship-of-the-line *Yarmouth* on March 7, 1778, while the first gave the Navy its battle cry of "I have not yet begun to fight!" in conquering the fine 44-gun frigate *Serapis* with the 32-gun merchantman *Bon Homme Richard* on Sept. 23, 1779. Eleven colonies also had navies which, when totaled, exceeded Continental numbers; Pennsylvania's was particularly aggressive under leaders like Joshua Barney.

All maritime branches brought in about 800 prizes, whose cargoes were indispensable to the cause, especially before 1779 when the French alliance and seapower became effective. The British were further humiliated by the capture of 102 minor men-of-war mounting 2622 guns, besides 16 privateers with 226 guns.

American navies vanished in peacetime. Independence, however, brought problems. Barbary pirates and then warring British and French preyed on United States commerce. Consequently, the Navy Department was founded on April 30, 1798. Benjamin Stoddert as first Secretary directed 12 frigates and sloops commissioned to protect trade in the West Indies against French freebooters. Appropriately, the first man-of-war afloat was the 44-gun frigate *United States*.

In the quasi-war with France (1798–1801), the Navy expanded to 41 vessels through converting merchantmen. Three French warships and 81 privateers were captured. Thomas Truxtun was the outstanding captain. In the 36-gun *Constellation,* he took the 40-gun *Insurgent* and shattered in night battle the 40-gun *Vengeance.* More enduringly, Truxtun as a squadron commander infused professional order and attitude. Similarly, the inconclusive Tripolitan War (1801–5) was most important for the example and training provided by Edward Preble.

By 1805, the officer cadre was firmly established. Jefferson, alarmed by the implications of having fought offensively overseas, turned to gunboat construction to manifest intent to fight only defensively. His 176 gunboats proved useless in the War of 1812, while 22 seagoing vessels won glory. The *United States* and her sister *Constitution* under Decatur, Hull or Bainbridge won dazzling victories before preponderant British power closed American ports. Losing twelve, the Navy captured 15 minor warships and 165 merchantmen. The ubiquitous privateers took an additional 991 merchantmen and five small men-of-war. Significant as such successes were in injuring British trade and shortening the war, more significant were the victories of "pigmy fleets" on inland waters. Perry's victory on Erie (Sept. 10, 1813), buttressed by Macdonough's on Champlain (Sept. 11, 1814), settled much of the Canadian boundary. Defending New Orleans, Patterson's handful was essential. The war stabilized the Navy, which was rewarded by a few 74-gun ships-of-the-line, *Independence* the first.

The Algerian War (1815), suppression of West Indian pirates (1816–29), anti-slaver patrols (1820–50), provided training for the Mexican War. Then unchallenged afloat, the Navy of 63 vessels conducted blockade and amphibious operations, the latter destined to become a United States specialty. Sloat and Stockton helped secure California. Conner and Matthew Perry had the bulk of the fleet in the Gulf of Mexico, making possible the transportation to and landing at Vera Cruz (March 13, 1847) and maintenance of the lifeline for Scott's triumphal march to Mexico City.

1861–1940

When the Civil War commenced, the Union Secretary Welles had only 8800 personnel and 42 of 76 vessels ready to close 185 registered harbors in 12,000 miles of indented coastline, exclusive of rivers. Confederate Secretary Mallory began with 3000 personnel and 12 sequestered vessels. By war's end, the Union Navy had mushroomed to 58,000 sailors in 671 vessels. Following Confederate confiscation of Federal ships, the Union lost 109. In action, 34 warships were sunk conventionally and 14 by mines, while 16 were captured. The rigors of blockade were witnessed by 38 men-of-war lost to the sea, including the famous *Monitor*. Seven more burned accidentally. Confederate figures can only be approximated. Extant official records indicate that Mallory about doubled manpower and commissioned 209 vessels, always too little and too late.

The Union Navy had three main missions: blockade, Army co-operation and commerce protection. Blockade was mounted through capturing a coaling base at Port Royal (Nov. 7, 1861) between Charleston and Savannah and was finalized by the amphibious capture of Wilmington seaport (Jan. 15, 1865).

Altogether, 1504 blockade-runners were captured or destroyed. Co-operating with the Army, the Navy helped take the Mississippi, notably by seizing New Orleans (April 24, 1862) and at Vicksburg (March 13–July 4, 1863). Even more decisive was naval support along the rivers feeding Chesapeake Bay. Only on the high seas did the Confederate Navy conspicuously succeed, as the *Alabama* and eleven sisters took or sank 250 merchantmen. Prudently, a third to a half of Northern shipowners sought foreign registry. Such shipping did not return to the United States flag. Since then, government subsidy of the merchant marine has been increasingly necessary.

The Navy withered in peace until given rationale by Mahan, whose writings (1890–1914) are the classics of sea power. A small "new Navy" of only 21 modern warcraft was far readier than the Spaniards for the War of 1898, which was signalized by easy victories won by Dewey at Manila (May 1) and Sampson at Santiago (July 3). The Navy won national support and began expansion to supremacy. Unpleasant duty in helping suppress insurrection in the newly acquired Philippines was followed by the world cruise of the "Great White Fleet" of 16 new battleships (1907–9), which demonstrated the superb maturity of American engineering as well as the substance for the "Big Stick" then popular.

Through World War I, the Navy had 497,030 personnel to man 37 battleships and 1926 lesser vessels. Contracts for 949 others, including 32 battleships and battle cruisers, would have made the Navy almost equal to all others combined, if completed. Operations were unglamorous. Since the British after Jutland (1916) contained the German Navy, the prime mission of the United States became "the Bridge to France" for 2,079,880 troops and their supplies. The submarine was the foe, combatted defensively by convoy and escort, and offensively by mine fields and the airplane. The Navy was brilliantly successful. Although primitive submarines sank nearly 13,000,000 tons of shipping, including 124 American merchantmen, no American soldier was lost in France-bound convoy. Only one of 178 submarines sunk fell to an American destroyer, but the stupendous North Sea Mine Barrage, 80% laid by the United States, sank or damaged about 17 more and reputedly broke the morale of German submariners. The war was close to bloodless for the Navy, which lost 1142 lives in 45 miscellaneous men-of-war: 13 were sunk by U-boats, 3 by mines, and 29 by collision or mischance. The heaviest combat loss was the Coast Guard Cutter *Tampa*, which went down with 111 men. (The Treasury Department's "Navy" has been under naval control in all wars except those with the Barbary States.)

Besides the portents of the submarine and airplane, the war had unveiled the amphibious potential which the Navy had in the combat readiness and excellence of the Marines. Quintupled from prewar strength to

67,000, the Corps won immortality in France and a firm place in naval plans. In 1933, the Fleet Marine Force was created, a heavy infantry organization dedicated to amphibious assault at a time when the perfecting of the airplane-carrier and naval gunfire promised to revolutionize sea-war.

1941–1960

When the storm of World War II broke, the Navy had concepts if not the numbers for bold, flexible operations. Rebounding from the surprise of Pearl Harbor, the Navy expanded to 3,400,000 men and women serving new construction of 8 battleships, 48 cruisers, 104 aircraft carriers, 349 destroyers, 203 submarines, 2236 convoy-escort craft, 886 mine craft, 4149 large and 79,418 small amphibious craft, 1531 auxiliaries, and 22,045 others. American combat losses to Oct. 1, 1945, were 2 battleships, 5 heavy and 7 escort aircraft carriers, 10 cruisers, 79 destroyers, 52 submarines, 36 mine craft, 69 PT-boats, 172 large amphibious craft, and 254 other types. Casualties of the Navy, Marines and Coast Guard totaled 56,206 dead, 8967 missing and 80,259 wounded. The Navy destroyed 132 German and eight Italian submarines in supplementing air and British naval operations, but as the major combatant in the Pacific annihilated the initially triumphant Japanese, sinking 11 battleships, 15 fleet and 5 escort aircraft carriers, 33 cruisers, 119 destroyers, and uncounted lesser craft.

Fleet Adm. Ernest J. King, who commanded through 1941–45, in his *U. S. Navy At War* divided the Pacific War into four stages. Phase One was defensive from Dec. 7, 1941, to June, 1942. The period had ten naval engagements capped by the Coral Sea, May 7–8, 1942, when Rear Adm. Fletcher with the *Yorktown* and *Lexington* carrier task-forces stopped a superior Japanese thrust at southeast New Guinea. Superb intelligence procedures detected Japanese intensions to take Midway. The ensuing battle (June 3–6, 1942) was the turning point of the war. Outnumbered American carriers decisively decimated their opposites in the first sea fight by fleets whose ships never sighted each other.

The defensive-offensive period of Midway was a brief Phase Two, merging with Phase Three, the offensive-defensive which committed the Marines to the long fight for Guadalcanal (Aug. 7, 1942–Feb. 8, 1943) and produced a dozen night battles amid shallows and islands as well as supporting open-sea carrier engagements, together exacting battle losses exceeding Jutland's. The Japanese, rebuilding carrier strength after Midway, improvidently fed idle naval aviation into the fray, thus undermining their carrier potential in trying to stop the Marine drive up the Solomons to join pressure with General MacArthur's combined forces outflanking the Japanese naval and air bastion of Rabaul on New Britain. About this time, American submarines hit stride with a deadliness

that sank two thirds of Japanese shipping, an attrition in itself sufficient to have produced eventual victory through starvation of Japan.

The pure offensive, Phase Four, opened with the Navy thrusting westward into the Marshalls. The battle nicknamed "Marianas Turkey Shoot" (Philippine Sea, June 19–20, 1944) disclosed the fatal deterioration of Japanese carrier aviation when 402 Japanese planes were downed with an American loss of only seventeen. Saipan, Guam, Tinian, Peleliu and Ulithi milestoned the drive, forging a logistic line for naval juncture with the successful MacArthur and his Southwest Pacific command in a two-fisted campaign for recapture of the Philippines. On Oct. 20, 1944, MacArthur landed at Leyte. Japanese naval counterattack produced a complex of farflung actions (Oct. 23–26) which crushed Japan as a naval power and left the home islands completely vulnerable. Japan itself became the objective. To add fullest weight of air power to the assault on Japanese home industry and to supplement the mounting submarine blockade, Marines took Iwo Jima at heavy cost (Feb. 19–Mar. 1, 1945), which thereafter provided essential fighter-cover for long range bombers. On April 1, Marines and Army landed on Okinawa, within easy reach of southern Kyushu. Desperate *kamikaze* (suicide-plane) attacks failed to dislodge the supporting fleet, which sustained 5000 fatalities, 368 damaged ships, and 36 minor vessels lost. When atomic attacks on Hiroshima and Nagasaki ended the war, the Navy was preparing for the invasion of Kyushu and a drive on Tokyo itself. Strangulation by sea and air had produced the first unconditional surrender of a major nation without such invasion.

In the war with Germany, the Navy was preoccupied anew with defense of sea communications and began as a junior partner to the British, who were mastering effective antisubmarine warfare in the period before United States belligerency. Concurrently, the Germans were perfecting submarine tactics, making "the Battle of the Atlantic" bitter and too often close. In the summer of 1943, the advent of American escort-carrier groups ("hunter-killers") gave defense the decisive edge. Allied forces destroyed 753 of a phenomenal 1170 U-boats (figures by Doenitz), which sank 197 warships and 2828 merchantmen totalling 14,687,231 tons (Morison).

The liberation of Europe was predicated upon re-entry onto the Continent, which American amphibious techniques made possible. Commencing with a meager 102 vessels for landings against French Morocco (Nov. 8, 1942), the Navy multiplied amazingly to 2489 amphibious craft for the Normandy invasion (June 6, 1944) and loaned an equal number to the British. The liberality of such "lend-lease" is the most convincing evidence that America had noncompetitively supplanted England as "Mistress of the Seas." The erstwhile Mistress was the recipient, besides amphibious craft, of an impressive navy in the

Insignia of Rank

RANK	DATE ESTAB.	NO. GOLD STRIPES ON SLEEVE 2″ ½″ ¼″			COLLAR DEVICE	SHOULDER MARKS	MILITARY EQUAL
Fleet Admiral	1944	1	4	x	5 silver stars	Anchor over 5 stars on gold epaulette	General of the Army[1]
Admiral[8]	1865	1	3	x	4 ditto	4 ditto	General
Vice Admiral	1864	1	2	x	3 ditto	3 ditto	Lieut. General
Rear Admiral	1862	1	1	x	2 ditto	2 ditto	Major General
Commodore[2]	1862 1943	1	x	x	1 ditto	1 ditto	Brigadier General
Captain	1775[3] 1797	x	4	x	Silver eagle	Corps device[4] over same no. and widths of sleeve stripes	Colonel
Commander	1838	x	3	x	Silver oak leaf	ditto	Lieut. Colonel
Lieut. Commander	1862	x	2	1	Gold oak leaf	ditto	Major
Lieutenant	1775[3] 1797	x	2	x	2 silver bars	ditto	Captain
Lieutenant (Junior Grade)	1883	x	1	1	1 silver bar	ditto	First Lieutenant[5]
Ensign	1862	x	1	x	1 gold bar	ditto	Second Lieutenant
Midshipman[6]	1775[3] 1797	various ⅛″			small gold anchor	Same as sleeve stripes	Cadet
Chief Warrant Officer	various	x	1[7]	x	Gold bar & corps device	Same as sleeve	Same
Warrant Officer	ditto	x	x	1	ditto	ditto	Same

[1] The Marine Corps has all ranks below this.

[2] From 1775 to 1862, "Commodore" was not an actual rank but a courtesy title accorded a senior captain cruising with juniors, and later politely used by them ashore. In the years indicated, the rank was commissioned for special command purposes during war.

[3] In the Continental Navy, "Captain," "Lieutenant" and "Midshipman" were the only ranks and were reaffirmed during the organization of the Navy Department, 1797–98.

[4] In qualification and duties, officers are divided into "line" and "staff." The line officer, distinguished by a gold star above his sleeve rank, commands *tactical* units. Each of the eight staff Corps has its own device. The Corps are: Medical (established in 1775), Dental (1912), Medical Service (1916), Hospital (1916), Nurse (1861), Chaplain (1799), Supply (1775) and Civil Engineer Corps (1867).

[5] In the Navy, "First Lieutenant" is a shipboard duty assignment, principally dealing with deck seamanship. Any officer from Ensign to Commander may be a "First Lieutenant."

[6] The position of Midshipman has been complex. Today he is a nascent officer-in-training and an officer in a qualified sense ranking above the warrant officer and below the chief warrant officer.

[7] The gold stripe on sleeves is broken by blue every two inches and collar devices and shoulder marks are similarly broken at midpoint. The Chief Warrant Officer ranks with but after an Ensign. He is a specialist par excellence in one of the basic naval ratings, such as Boatswain, Gunner, etc.

[8] The Coast Guard has all ranks below this and identical uniforms, distinguished by a different cap device and a gold shield instead of a star where used on sleeve and shoulder in the Navy.

form of 38 escort-carriers, 189 blue-water convoy-escorts, 9 submarines, 187 minesweepers, and 415 specialized craft. The U. S. S. R. was second, receiving some 615 naval and military vessels and 90 merchantmen. France was third, with 145 minor men-of-war.

In the postwar uncertainties of the nuclear age, the Navy continued to perfect the potentials of carriers, submarines and amphibians. Gradually budgeted down to 238 major combat craft, 393,893 personnel and 74,396 Marines, the Navy was professionally keen in 1950 upon the outbreak of the Korean War, which proved to be an extension of conventional arms. Besides vital close air support from carriers, and amphibious outflanking such as at Inchon, naval gunfire proved invaluable in interdicting free communist use of their coasts. The 16-inch guns of battleships, editorially consigned to join mastodons in museums, were unexpectedly useful in firing across communist territory from the seaward rear to knock out positions on reverse slopes of mountains, where communist forces were otherwise safe from front-line fire. By the armistice of July 27, 1953, the Navy operated 408 major and 720 minor vessels, with Reserves swelling manpower to 800,000 personnel and 248,612 Marines. The Navy lost 5 ships and had 87 damaged, while 564 downed aircraft added heavily to the 458 killed or missing and 1576 wounded.

In the tensions since Korea, the Navy has been a powerful support of United States policy, while ceaselessly striving to exploit and adapt advancing technology. Whatever shape tactical instruments may take, the indefinite future will require the Navy in some form for as long as the United States must use and hold the sea.

Fleets. The "squadron" concept which began in the quasi-war with France was the basic tactical organization until 1907, when the Atlantic, Pacific, and Asiatic Fleets were formed. Within this structure, the "force" concept grew into the now-familiar "task-force." In World War II, there were eleven Fleets with specific geographic areas of operations, except for the Tenth which was charged with antisubmarine warfare. Odd-numbered Fleets were Pacific, and even numbers, Atlantic, persisting to today. The most famous in wartime were the Third, Fifth and Seventh Fleets, the latter with MacArthur. The Third and Fifth were in the Central Pacific and consisted largely of the same ships, designated Third Fleet when under Halsey and Fifth Fleet when under Spruance.

Students reading World War II naval history may encounter numeral designations such as "Task Element 38.4.6.2." In this, subdivision is indicated by italics:

3–.–.–.– = *Third Fleet*
38.–.–.– = *Task Force 8* of Third Fleet
38.4.–.– = *Task Group 4* of Third Fleet 38
38.4.6.– = *Task Unit 6* of Task Group 38.4
38.4.6.2 = *Task Element 2* of Task Unit 38.4.6

For administration, etc., ships are also organized into "type commands," such as "submarines, Atlantic" (SUBLANT); "submarines, Pacific" (SUBPAC); "destroyers, Atlantic" (DESLANT), etc. Basic tactical organizations are: division—two or more vessels of the same type; squadron—generally two or more divisions; flotilla—generally two or more similar squadrons.

United States Naval Academy. Founded at Annapolis, Md., in 1845 to graduate career officers equipped to meet the demands of the dawning age of steam, the Naval Academy throughout its growth into the dawning nuclear age has conservatively reflected the soundest trends in engineering institutions, keeping uppermost the fundamental mission of educating professional officers rather than technicians. Bancroft Hall, named in honor of the Secretary who started the Academy, is by far the largest dormitory in the world, and is the heart of the program, providing the naval milieu and discipline 24 hours a day which infuses professional attitude. The basic curriculum is 156 college-level hours, approximating five years' work in four. The curriculum is rigidly constructed for the purpose of best preparing a young officer for efficient service. Since 1959, a midshipman satisfying certain scholastic requirements may voluntarily superimpose a collegiate major and/or minor in many fields of science and humanities through an "elective" program.

The Brigade of Midshipmen is kept at a strength of approximately 3700 by a dozen methods of entry, in which Congressional appointment supplies the greatest number. As the curriculum changes, so, too, do the requirements for entry.

Naval War College. Established in 1884 at Newport, R. I., with Com. Stephen B. Luce, its principal proponent, as first President, the College had its purpose and value crystallized in the publications of its most famous faculty member, Capt. (later Rear Adm.) Alfred Thayer Mahan.

Today, about 360 students below captain, primarily from the Navy but including members of other armed services, civilian specialists in government departments, and foreign officers, systematically explore and reflect upon the philosophy of war, strategy, tactics and logistics. They also study staff requirements and techniques in courses of senior and junior levels. Since 1954, the course has been two years. In addition to instructing, the 125 members of the faculty conduct a strong correspondence course program for officers in the field.

One of the oldest of postgraduate officer institutions, the College has had considerable influence upon the other services, notably in the adoption by all of the "estimate of the situation" and "completed staff study" concepts.

Naval Reserve. During the years the American merchant marine was expanding, its seamen made a virtual reserve, epitomized by the "volunteers" who filled the ships of the Civil War. The ensuing decline of American shipping, however, created a need for formal organization and recruiting. Massachusetts led the way on March 18, 1890, by founding a naval militia, soon adopted by other seaboard states. Development was paralleling the National Guard until militias were brought under Federal control on Feb. 16, 1914. The National Naval Volunteers Act of Aug. 29, 1916, created the "Naval Reserve" as such, which absorbed the militias on July 1, 1916. Thereafter the Naval Reserve proliferated in conformance with technological advances to a complexity which in World War II provided about 90% of naval personnel.

The act of July 9, 1952, made the present Ready, Standby and Retired categories, primarily differentiated by liability to recall to active duty. Normally, a reservist passes from the Ready Reserve through Standby to Retired status. He maintains qualifications through drills in a broad program of some forty different types of pay and non-pay units, through two-week active-duty-for-training periods, officer schools, correspondence courses, and in other manners approved by the Chief of Naval Personnel. The success of the 1946 "Week-end Warrior" program for aviation units has recently resulted in a "Selected Reserve" program for small ships, principally antisubmarine warfare types, which are kept ready by a small, permanent crew to be manned in a matter of hours by Reserves who year-round train afloat one week end a month.

To supplement the traditional appointment of qualified officers from the merchant marine or with applicable civilian specialties, "the Student Navy Training Corps" was established in 1917 at 90 colleges and universities. This became the basis for normal peacetime procurement and evolved into the present N. R. O. T. C. at 53 colleges. Selected appointees receive pay throughout the four years of college work in fields of individual choice and concurrently take six hours a week of naval training plus appropriate summer cruises. After graduation and commissioning, they serve a stipulated time on active duty and have then the option, if recommended, of transferring into the regular Navy for a career. The same N. R. O. T. C. units also have "Contract" candidates who, after satisfactory grades and aptitude for the first two years are paid during the last two. For non-N. R. O. T. C. collegiate institutions, there is the "Reserve Officer Candidate" or "R. O. C." program wherein a college student may earn a commission by satisfactory completion of two six-week training courses in summertime. The Naval Aviation Cadet program is a fourth major means of entry. The Navy and Naval Reserve through such programs have the largest percentage (1960) of college graduates in the armed services.

NEAGLE, IN RE (135 U. S. 1, 1890), was a case in which the U. S. Supreme Court asserted the supremacy of Federal over state law. Under his authority to see that the laws are faithfully executed, President Benjamin Harrison, by executive order, directed David Neagle, a deputy United States marshal, to protect Justice Stephen J. Field of the Supreme Court against a threatened personal attack. At Stockton, Calif., as the Justice was traveling in the performance of his official duties Neagle shot and killed David S. Terry as the latter made a murderous assault upon Justice Field. Arrested by California state authorities and charged with murder, Neagle was brought before the Federal circuit court upon a writ of habeas corpus, and released upon the ground that he was being held in custody for "an act done in pursuance of a law of the United States"; and his release was upheld by the Supreme Court.

NEBBIA v. N. Y. (291 U. S. 502, 1934) sets forth a broad view of business "affected with a public interest." New York State in 1933 established a Milk Control Board empowered to fix maximum and minimum retail prices. A dealer, convicted of underselling, claimed that price fixing violated the Fourteenth Amendment's due process clause, save as applied to business affected with a public interest, that is, to public utilities or monopolies. The Supreme Court, upholding the law five to four, declared "there is no closed class" of businesses "affected with a public interest"; it includes any industry which, "for adequate reason, is subject to control for the public good."

NEBRASKA, the Otoe name for the Platte, was used by the French explorer Bourgmont in 1714. The purchase of Louisiana and the exploration of Lewis and Clark in 1804–6 awakened American interest in the region. Manuel Lisa established Fort Lisa (1807–19) as a fur-trading post on the approximate site of Fort Calhoun. Fort Atkinson in the same region served as a military encampment and fort (1819–27). The expeditions and reports of Maj. Long (1819–22) suggested the Great American Desert. Bellevue, above the mouth of the Platte, became a permanent trading post in 1819 and remained the nucleus of white settlement. There Peter Sarpy became a renowned figure among both whites and Indians.

Nebraska, as a designation of the area of the Platte watershed, was used by Frémont in 1843. Proposed as a political territory by Secretary of War

Wilkins, in 1844, the name appeared as the title of the bill presented to Congress. Douglas' first Nebraska bill defined a territory extending from the Missouri River on the east to the Continental Divide on the west; from the Niobrara River on the north to the Kansas and Arkansas Rivers on the south. The Nebraska Act ten years later changed the north and south boundaries to the Canadian border and the 40th parallel, respectively. Within those ten years the Overland Trail had become the great continental highway. It was necessary to organize Nebraska Territory in order to compete with the Southern routes for the transcontinental railroad. Nebraska's area was restricted to approximately its present size by the creation of Colorado and Dakota territories in 1861. The northern boundary was changed from the Niobrara River to the 43rd parallel between the Keyapaha and the Missouri Rivers in 1882.

Francis Burt of South Carolina became territorial governor Oct. 16, 1854, at Bellevue. Two days later he died, and Secretary Thomas B. Cuming of Michigan became acting governor. The first territorial legislature was assembled at Omaha Jan. 16, 1855.

In 1866 Congress passed an enabling act for the admission of Nebraska to statehood, but the constitutional convention regarded statehood as too expensive and adjourned *sine die*. Two years later the territorial legislature submitted to the voters a constitution produced by its own committee, and it was declared adopted by a vote of 3938 to 3838.

NEGRO IN AMERICA. The 19 "Negars" brought to Jamestown, Va., in 1619, in a Dutch man-of-war, had grown to some 18,000,000 by 1960, constituting 10% of the population of the United States. The first importations by the Dutch and Swedes doubtless came from the slave forts established by these nationals on the Gold Coast (now Ghana), and were mainly directed to their American settlements in the Delaware Valley and around New Amsterdam, during the first half of the 17th century. As the English took over the Danish, Swedish and Dutch slave depots on the Guinea coast, and extended their domination of the slave trade along the neighboring Slave Coast (Nigeria), it may be presumed that the 5,000,000 to 10,000,000 Africans exported to the present-day United States from 1619 to 1864 came principally from that area of West Africa. There was some trans-shipment by way of the West Indies, where the famous triangular trade in rum, slaves and molasses found a way-stop to the terminus in the prosperous slave-trading, capital-building enterprises of New England.

The Spaniards had discovered that the African could flourish in the arduous Seven Labors of the New World, where the Indian perished. The plantation system was practicable only in the South. In North America the slave was indispensable in six of the seven great tasks. There were no gold or silver mines; but he cleared the forest; tilled the soil for necessary foodstuffs; provided the labor for cash plantation crops, first tobacco, then indigo, then sugar, and finally cotton—after the clever Yankee, Eli Whitney, made its plantation culture profitable.

More than fifty years were required, in Virginia, to establish a legal basis for holding black slaves for life, as contrasted to holding indentured white and black slaves for the Biblical period of seven years. Once established, the distinction became one of the most profound forces in American history, moulding thereafter every aspect of the life and fortunes of the American colonies, and of the peoples of the United States.

The Negro provided cheap labor. The free whites without property, in the South, could not compete with the slave black, and were driven from the fertile lowlands to the barren hill and mountain country. It was profitable to train Negroes to carry on all of the skills necessary to the maintenance of the self-sustaining plantation, and required only a second step to put these skilled craftsmen into the urban labor market. Negro slave labor thus came to be the greatest single factor in moulding the economic, social, and political structure of the region; through the region, the nation was influenced. In the North, the Negro artisan was barred from competition with the white mechanics, largely derived from foreign immigration. These antebellum attitudes were to persist to contemporary times.

The Emancipation Proclamation, and the end of the Civil War, conferred only partial freedom on the Negro laborer, whether in the field, or in the city. The slave plantation system was reconstructed on the basis of the sharecropping system, a form of tenantry made necessary by the total lack of fluid capital in the Southern region after the War, but ready-made for landlord abuses. The rapid industrialization of the North after the Civil War yielded few benefits to the Negro laborer, as the predominant crafts structure of the burgeoning labor movement retained old attitudes that viewed the Negro with suspicion, and excluded him from membership.

In the South, the introduction of textile manufacturing as the first step toward industrialization, at the end of the 19th century, clothed itself in the vestment of a humanitarian movement frankly aimed at alleviating the plight of the marginal "poor white" worker. Negroes came, therefore, to be excluded from the new Southern industry.

Negro labor began a new phase in history when European migration was interrupted by World War I, and the booming war industries of the North demanded mass supplies of labor from a new source. More than 500,000 Negroes moved to the North between 1916 and 1920, and an even larger number from 1921 to 1925, when wartime barriers to foreign immigration were reinforced by the National Quotas Immigration Acts. Since that time, the trend has continued, slowed up by industrial depression, but accelerated by industrial boom and the increasing needs of World War II. The pull of industrialization has been aided by the push of the mechanization of Southern agriculture; indeed, analyses of migration trends during the last decades show that the movement of rural whites to the cities, and to the North, has been as pronounced as that of the Negroes. In similar fashion, the recent heavy migration of Negroes from the West South Central states, to the Pacific Coast states, followed a pattern first set by the "Okies" and their drought-distressed brethren during the Great Depression of the 1930's.

Only during World War II did the old pattern of Negro employment begin to change, and with it, the relationship of the Negro to the labor union movement. In the South, Negroes frequently retained their strong position in the construction crafts, established in ante-bellum days, and in the trades unions that had developed in these crafts. Elsewhere, they were principally relegated to the heavy, dirty industries, as unskilled labor, whether in the South, or in the North, or to domestic and personal service. The development of industrial unionism in the North combined with wartime expediency to give Negroes a foothold in the new C. I. O. industrial unions, in the steel industry, in new metals fabricating, and in the automobile industry. This foothold was strengthened by Federal Fair Employment Practices regulations, stemming from President Roosevelt's Executive Order 8802, issued in 1941. The status and bargaining position of the Negro worker has been additionally improved by Fair Employment legislation on the state and municipal level, by continued presidential executive action, and by action from within a newly federated national union movement (A. F. L.- C. I. O.).

The status of the Negro as a person before the law, and as a citizen, has ebbed and flowed with the changing tides of national experience. The colonial slave system rested on variations of the "black codes" first elaborated in French and Spanish dependencies in the Caribbean. The marginal economic utility of slavery, combined with revolutionary enthusiasm for the natural rights of man, first promised a speedy and voluntary abolition of the institution. The entrenchment of the three-fifths compromise in our Constitution governing congressional representation suggested that a slave was not quite a whole man, but more than half of one. As early as 1752, Benjamin Franklin was in correspondence on the subject with Adam Smith and the *Philosophes* (among them Du Pont de Nemours); they agreed that chattel slavery was uneconomic in both French and English colonies, and advocated the formation of free black republics in West Africa to supply Europe and the New World with sugar and other tropical produce. As late as 1818, the Virginia legislature came within one vote of passing a resolution to abolish slavery in the state.

Eli Whitney's invention of the cotton gin brought such liberalism to a stop. As the slave traffic became more profitable, all talk of emancipation ended; the Southern states, faced with a series of slave revolts and the horrible memory of successful slave insurrections in the West Indies, re-enacted the harsh slave codes of the colonial period that in many instances had been allowed to lapse. The slave-owning interest in the national Congress, and in the higher courts, reached the peak of denigrating the right of the Negro, as a person and as a citizen in the Dred Scott decision of 1857.

Meanwhile, the voice of the absolute equalitarian began to be heard in the land. Theodore Weld and his followers sounded the trumpet through the length and breadth of the Western Reserve; Garrison and other abolitionists agitated effectively in the Northeast. The stage was set for the great conflict.

The outcome of the Civil War—the Thirteenth Amendment in 1865, the Fourteenth Amendment in 1868, and the Fifteenth Amendment in 1870—was the apparent victory of the forces set in motion thirty years before by Garrison and Weld and their followers, and seemed to affirm, forever, the attainment by the Negro of full stature in the dignity of his person, and full enjoyment of citizenship rights by every man. But brief Reconstruction in the South, marked by full exercise of citizenship rights by the newly enfranchised Negroes, quickly yielded to co-operating Northern and Southern conservatives; the great Compromise of 1876 was a bargain that put Hayes in the White House, assured the stability of Northern capital investments in the South, and promised an era of good feeling between the sections on the platform of economic development, Southern states' rights, and gradual elevation for the Negro.

The bargain did not reckon with the fundamentally depressed nature of the agrarian economy everywhere in America, and particularly in the South. The "rule of the Generals" was overturned in the 1890's, and the rule of the Southern demagogue began. New constitutions and new statutes were everywhere enacted, repealing the previous sanctions guaranteeing the Negro franchise, and instituting new sets of segregatory laws even more rigid than the customary separation of the races in ante-bellum times. "Jim Crow" was a child of thirty years of freedom, not of slavery. The ripples of the new wave extended across borders into the North, and resulted in the segregation of the races in school systems, in public places, and in discrimination in employment.

Changes in race relations may be as good a subject for the study of the cyclical theory of history as our society can afford. Whether because of the influences of the processes of an urbanized and industrial economy on an incompatible and irrational system of racial discrimination and segregation; or because of the growing educational attainments of the Negro; or because of the rapid growth of political power in the masses clustered in the great industrial centers of the North; or because of an expansion of the democratic sentiment sharpened by heroic testing of the idea of democracy elsewhere in the world—for whatever reason, it is clear that since the mid-'30's the public image of the Negro as a person and as a citizen has been greatly altered in American life. Beginning with the interposition of executive authority to remedy economic discrimination against Negroes during the Great Depression; passing through the wartime period when the Executive, again, required adherence to policies of nondiscriminatory employment policies; attaining in the postwar period the elimination of segregation in the American armed forces, for the first time since the War of the Revolution—the cycle (if it is one), may have reached its zenith in the decision of the U. S. Supreme Court in 1954 that declared the segregation of the races in public schools to be "inherently" unequal and unconstitutional. The decision has implications, already apparent in subsequent decisions of the courts, that extend far beyond the sphere of education, to which it had immediate application. As the nation entered the seventh decade of the 20th century, it appeared that a new chapter of American history was opening that would include the Negro as a person and a citizen, enjoying at long last the full rights and privileges of his fellow-Americans.

Culture and Religion

There is controversy over the question of the existence of a distinct Negro "culture" in the United States. Some social historians insist that the enslaved Africans were recruited so haphazardly, dispersed by preventive design to avoid insurrections by conspiratorial former fellow-tribesmen, and subjected, as slaves, to so overwhelming and novel a culture, that no traces of the African culture were preserved. Other scholars claim to have identified numerous African survivals in secular and religious customs, practices, and in the language. Lorenzo D. Turner has identified 4000 African personal and place names, and other African words, drawn from numerous tribes, and used contemporaneously among the Negroes of the Southeastern coastal areas. Survivals in the dance and in music have yet to be carefully studied, in spite of the immense speculative literature developed around these subjects.

To whatever degree the African culture has persisted, there can be no doubt that the American Negro has developed, in this country, unique adaptations of social and artistic institutions. The Negro family has tended to be strongly matriarchal, whether as a result of the survival of that tradition from African backgrounds, or in response to the conditions of slavery and the social disorganization characteristic of an economically depressed class of the population. The Negro church, as a separate entity, has existed since the beginning of the National Period, when

in cities such as Savannah, Philadelphia, Richmond, Baltimore and New York, separatist Negro churches were constituted among the Baptists, Presbyterian, Methodist and Episcopalian denominations. A sign of the spirit of the times was that they universally adopted the descriptive adjective "African," e.g., the First African Baptist church of Savannah, Ga. (1785), and Richmond, Va. (1795); the First African Meeting House of Philadelphia (1788); and the First African Presbyterian Church of Philadelphia (1804). Benjamin Rush sponsored a subscription list for the First African Meeting House in Philadelphia founded by his friend Richard Allen; in those enlightened times, an African was a child of nature and thereby one of God's noblemen, and proud to call himself so. Allen later organized the African Methodist Episcopal Church (1816).

These separatist churches yet persist; the two largest separate Methodist denominations still preserving the word, "African," in their official designations are the African Methodist Episcopal church (reporting 1,116,000 communicants) and the African Methodist Episcopal Zion Church (with 758,000 communicants). The Baptists enroll the largest number of Negroes; in 1950, one convention (Boyd Group) reported 2,645,000 members, while the National Baptist Convention reported 4,445,000. Smaller numbers belong to nominally interracial church denominations, though worshipping, for the most part, in separate churches: 368,000 Methodists, 64,000 Episcopalians, and 21,000 Congregational-Christians. It is estimated that there are 400,000 Negro Catholics in the United States, two thirds of them communicants in predominantly Negro parishes. One spectacular characteristic of the religious life of the Negro has been the appearance of "cults" that have flourished among the newly urbanized inhabitants, principally in Northern Negro ghettoes. Most famous has been that of Father Divine, whose followers include numerous white persons; his sect and others have given rise to an extensive literature. The "Black Muslims" are a new phase.

Education

The education of Negroes began with religious instruction, as part of the "divine plan" that justified African slavery as a means by which the heathen savage could be brought to Christ. In Northern cities, such as Philadelphia, the Quakers initiated elementary schools for Negroes as early as 1745. The churches established special missions to bring the gospel to plantation slaves and masters were under church injunction to provide for the religious instruction of their slaves when no regular white pastor or missionary was available. Clandestine schools were maintained in various Southern cities, although in violation of the "black codes."

A violent reaction against any form of instruction for slaves set in over the South, following the Southampton, Va., slave insurrection of 1831. The revolt had been led by Nat Turner, a literate Negro slave preacher, who drew his inspiration from reading the Bible. Stern penalties were established for teaching Negroes to read and write, and convictions and punishments were not infrequent. Nevertheless a number of slaves were taught by kindly owners or members of owner families. A survey of the biographies of Negroes who reached adulthood as slaves and attained prominence as freemen shows how frequently such clandestine teaching and learning took place.

Immediately on the conclusion of the Civil War, agencies of Northern Church Missionary Societies set up numerous schools for the freedmen in the South. These early foundations were materially aided by the Freedmen's Bureau. Titled "colleges" and "universities" by optimistic founders, these institutions perforce had to begin on the lowest level. They rejoiced in the finest type of the "New England schoolmarm," and dealing with a clientele dazzled by the promise of learning, their work was strikingly effective.

Public education in the South had its origin, legally, in systems patterned after Midwestern prototypes and enacted by combinations of "carpetbaggers," Negroes and "poor white" (Scalawag) members of Reconstruction constitutional conventions and legislatures. The destitution of the South prevented any considerable development of the ambitious schemes devised. The wave of anti-Negro discriminatory laws enacted in the 1890's eliminated constitutional guarantees of "separate but equal" provision for education. Local systems diverted state educational funds to the support of schools for white children. In some black-belt counties, per capita distributions reached the proportion of $40 to $1 spent, respectively, on the white and Negro child.

With growing prosperity in the South, and a lessened proportion of Negro children in the population, these vast differences began to decrease in the 1920's. Disparities were further reduced in the period 1935–54, as the result of greater tax resources, successful litigation to equalize teachers' salaries, and a genuine desire on the part of Southern states to make the schools "equal" as well as "separate." The unanimous Supreme Court decision of 1954, urging "all deliberate speed" in desegregating the schools, by 1960 had resulted in almost total compliance in the border states, isolated compliance in the middle tier of Southern states, and "hard core" resistance in South Carolina, Georgia, Alabama, and Mississippi. The measure of the effectiveness of the schools for Negroes is a reduction in illiteracy from an estimated 95% in 1865 to less than 7% in 1960.

The higher education of Negroes in the United States began in 1774, when two African seamen from the Gold Coast were enrolled from Providence, R. I., in the College of New Jersey, to be educated for missionary service in their native land. Several abortive efforts to found colleges for Negroes in the North led, in 1854, to the founding of Ashmun Institute (later Lincoln University), by persons devoted to the cause of African colonization. The end of the Civil War encouraged the founding, in the South, of numerous colleges for freedmen. There are in 1960 more than fifty fully accredited colleges for Negroes in the South, some of them enrolling white students. Meanwhile, litigation, first successful in 1937 and greatly accelerated by the 1954 Supreme Court decision, has opened higher institutions, formerly for white students only, to Negroes in all but three "hard-core" resisting states, South Carolina, Alabama and Mississippi. Technically, the University of Alabama has been "opened" by litigation, but the attendance of the one student so enrolled was never consummated, because of mob violence. It is now (1960) estimated that there are more than 125,000 Negroes enrolled in colleges and universities in the nation, a proportion of the age-group less than one third that characteristic of the national average.

NESTERS AND THE CATTLE INDUSTRY. Following the slaughter of the buffalo, cattle grazing on the open range of the Western plains from Texas to Montana became the major industry. The cattlemen divided the public domain into large grazing tracts, some of which they fenced. When the farmers, contemptuously called nesters, attempted to settle on the range, the cattlemen kept them out by intimidation and in some rare instances by murder. The contest of the ranger and the granger continued from 1867 to 1886. Congress passed a law, Feb. 25, 1885, prohibiting interference with settlers, and President Cleveland followed this with an enforcement proclamation, Aug. 7, 1885. Of greater potency was the great blizzard of January, 1886. Freezing rain encased the buffalo grass, on which the cattle depended for winter feed, in a glare of ice. There followed driving snow with zero temperatures. Range cattle died of freezing and starvation, and most of the cattle barons were ruined.

"NEUTRAL GROUND." During the American Revolution, Westchester County, N. Y., especially The Bronx, then within that county, was known by this term because it was not consistently occupied by either side, and the sympathies of its inhabitants were divided. Gen. Howe in 1776 began there his advance to White Plains.

After 1806 the region between the Arroyo Hondo, near Natchitoches, La., and the Sabine River, near Nacogdoches, Texas, received this name as a result of the "Neutral Ground" agreement between Gen. James Wilkinson and the Spanish Lt. Commander Simon de Herrera.

Another area received the name in 1830, when the Sioux on the north and the Sauk and Fox on the south each ceded twenty miles of land along a line from the Mississippi to the Des Moines River, leaving a forty-mile "Neutral Ground" in which they could hunt, but must remain peaceful.

NEUTRALITY, PROCLAMATION OF (1793).When news arrived in the United States in April, 1793, of the declaration of war by France against Great Britain, and the extension of the wars of the French Revolution into a great maritime war, it was the general disposition of the Government and the people, despite a strong predilection for the old ally, France, to remain neutral—in fact, France preferred her ally to be neutral, as a storehouse of foodstuffs and naval stores to be moved in American neutral ships to France despite the preponderant British Navy, under the protection of the freedom of the seas if possible. President Washington hurried to Philadelphia from Mount Vernon, and after earnest discussion with his cabinet decided on a policy of strict neutrality. A proclamation to that effect was drawn up by Attorney General Edmund Randolph and signed by the President and Secretary of State Thomas Jefferson. At the latter's suggestion, it studiously avoided the word "neutrality," hoping that the absence of this would be noted by Great Britain and persuade that power to make concessions of maritime practice to the United States in order to keep it neutral. The proclamation of April 22, 1793—a landmark in the history of international law and neutral rights and obligations—enjoined upon citizens of the United States a friendly and impartial conduct and warned them against committing or abetting hostilities against any of the belligerent powers under penalty of "punishment or forfeiture under the law of nations," particularly if they should carry "articles which are deemed contraband by the modern usage of nations." Jefferson thought the use of the word "modern" very significant in that it might dispute the British traditional practice of including foodstuffs and naval stores in the category of contraband, which was contrary to American practice.

Despite the absence of the word "neutrality" in the proclamation, the belligerent powers, and the neutral world, regarded it as a genuine proclamation of neutrality—as indeed it was—and even the U. S. Government soon lapsed into the usage of referring to the document as the proclamation of neutrality. The policy fixed by this proclamation was carefully carried out, in adherence to the strict letter of treaty obligations, and the executive rules proclaimed to enforce it were soon legislated into the Neutrality Act of June 5, 1794. It set American precedent and law for neutrality, which institution, and the problems connected with it, have since constituted a major part of the diplomatic history of the United States.

NEUTRALITY ACTS OF 1935, 1936 AND 1937 represented an effort to reorient American neutrality in anticipation of another conflict in the Old World. Taken together, the principal provisions of this legislation were: (1) prohibition, in time of war between foreign states, or of foreign "civil strife," of the export from the United States of "arms, ammunition or implements of war," as the same shall be defined by presidential proclamation, "to any port of such belligerent state, or to any neutral port for transshipment to, or the use of, a belligerent country," with the exception of an American republic at war with a non-American state and not co-operating with a non-American state in such a war; (2) prohibition of loans or credits to a belligerent state (with the same exception) by an American national; (3) discretionary power to the President to forbid exportation on American ships to belligerent countries of articles or materials other than arms, ammunition or implements of warfare, and to forbid the exportation of any American property in such articles or materials in foreign ships (the so-called "cash-and-carry" feature limited to two years, which expired May 1, 1939); (4) government licensing and control of the munitions industry in time of peace and war; (5) power to the President to forbid to belligerent submarines or armed merchant ships the use of American neutral ports; (6) prohibition of the arming of American ships trading to belligerent countries.

Except for the first and second provisions, which were mandatory, the President retained a large measure of discretionary power in the execution of this act, and even these provisions were brought measurably under his discretion (a) by the power he had to decide what was or was not a war (he did not recognize the second Sino-Japanese War as a war within the meaning of the act, although he did so judge the Italo-Ethiopian War), (b) by phraseology which might exclude contiguous states like Mexico and Canada from the operation of the "cash-and-carry section."

After the outbreak of war in Europe on Sept. 1, 1939, this legislation was superseded by the Neutrality Act of 1939.

NEUTRALITY ACT OF 1939. Impending war in Europe made the administration of Franklin D. Roosevelt and, in general, the public of the United States, in the spring and summer of 1938, apprehensive lest the Neutrality Acts of 1935, 1936 and 1937 would prevent Great Britain and France from purchasing arms, ammunition and implements of warfare in the United States during the next war. Under international law, as unamended by domestic legislation, belligerents would have a perfect right to purchase contraband of all kinds in a neutral state, and the power which controlled the seas would be able to secure their safe delivery. But the existing neutrality acts had superimposed restrictions and self-denials on American neutrality beyond that called for by international law. These self-denials, particularly the embargo on the export of arms, ammunition and implements of warfare to belligerents in time of war, had been accepted under the theory that, profiting by our experience during World War I, they would serve to keep us out of the next war. If this legislation were to be repealed without any deviation from strict neutrality, it was necessary to do so before the next war should break out, but isolationist sentiment in Congress prevented any amendment of the existing domestic neutrality legislation before Congress rose in the summer of 1939.

The Neutrality Law of 1939 was approved on Nov. 4, after the war between Germany, on the one hand, and Poland, France and the British Empire, on the other hand, had commenced in September. It was therefore a relaxation, after the war began, of previously self-imposed obligations of neutrality. To this extent the act was a deviation from strict juridical neutrality. It was in fact a diplomatic instrument, the purpose of which was to help the Allies win the war without the United States joining the war. Briefly summarized, the act provided:

(1) "Whenever the President, or the Congress by concurrent resolution, shall find that there exists a state of war between two states, and that it is necessary to promote the security, preserve the peace of the United States or to protect the lives of citizens of the United States, the President shall issue a proclamation," putting into effect the statute. By the provisions of this section it is clear that the act did not apply to all wars: it did not apply to civil wars (as did the previous Neutrality Act of 1937); and it did not apply to those wars which both the President and Congress believed not to affect the peace or security of the United States or the lives of its citizens; for example, the law was immediately applied to the war between Germany and its enemies, but not to the subsequent war between Russia and Finland.

(2) The act omitted any embargo on arms, ammunition or implements of war, or on anything else (in contrast to the neutrality legislation of 1935–37) but forbade American ships to carry arms, ammunition or implements of war.

(3) It forbade American ships to go to belligerent ports in Europe or North Africa, i.e., as far south as the Canary Islands.

(4) It prohibited arming of American merchant ships.

(5) It gave discretionary power to the President to forbid American ships to enter such "combat zones" as he should proclaim. He immediately proclaimed a zone which included the waters around the British Isles and European Atlantic waters from the Spanish boundary to Bergen, Norway, including all the Baltic coasts.

(6) It prohibited American citizens traveling on belligerent vessels.

(7) It allowed American ships to carry all goods except arms, ammunition and implements of war, but not excluding other contraband, to belligerent and neutral ports other than in Europe or North Africa or east of 66° W. Long. and north of 35° N.

Lat. (this excluded them from the St. Lawrence estuary and the port of Halifax, but allowed them to go to St. John, Yarmouth, Jamaica and the Caribbean, Vancouver and all belligerent ports in the Pacific and Indian oceans). They could carry any goods—except arms, ammunition and implements of war—to such ports without previous divesting of American title on leaving the United States.

(8) All goods shipped to European belligerent ports on foreign ships must first have their title transferred from American ownership, so that they might never be the source of spoliation claims of any citizen of the United States (this was in effect a pass-title-and-carry provision, not a "cash-and-carry" clause as popularly called).

(9) Like the Neutrality Act of 1937, the act of 1939 forbade "any person within the United States to purchase, sell, or exchange bonds, securities, or other obligations" of a belligerent state, "or any person acting for or on behalf of any such state," but allowed dealing in old securities, issued previous to the act and did not prohibit "renewal or adjustment of existing indebtedness."

(10) Like the previous neutrality legislation, the Neutrality Act of 1939 provided for the licensing of all munitions exports in time of peace or war.

NEVADA, "snow-covered," was the 36th state admitted to the Union. Although this area was claimed by the Spaniards, in 1776, it was not explored by them. After Mexico came into possession of it, in 1820, trails were made across it by explorers, trappers, traders and emigrants. By the Treaty of Guadalupe Hidalgo, 1848, it became a part of the United States. By the Compromise of 1850, the territories of Utah and New Mexico were organized on the principle of squatter sovereignty. Nevada was a part of both of these territories.

The first permanent settlement, Mormon Station, was made in 1851 by John Reese and a party of Mormons on the west side of Carson Valley. In 1854 the station was renamed Genoa, and made the county seat of Carson County, Utah Territory. A number of Mormons settled in the neighboring valleys. In 1857 most of these settlers returned to Salt Lake City to fight in the Mormon War.

With the discovery of the Comstock Lode at Virginia City in 1859 large numbers of Californians settled in Carson County. Not wishing to be under Mormon rule, they petitioned Congress to create Nevada Territory out of western Utah, March 2, 1861. In 1862 and again in 1866 land was added to Nevada from Utah; in 1866 the western part of Arizona Territory was added to Nevada. The history of Nevada Territory was similar to other mining states. Problems peculiar to the territory were secession sentiment, corrupt officials, boundary disputes, lawlessness and mining litigation.

President Lincoln, wishing to insure the enactment

of the Thirteenth Amendment, urged the admission of Nevada to secure three needed votes. Due to an unwise tax measure, the first constitution submitted, 1863, was rejected; a second one was approved and telegraphed to Lincoln, who proclaimed Nevada a state, Oct. 31, 1864.

NEW DEAL is a term used to describe the various measures proposed or approved by President Franklin D. Roosevelt from his inauguration in 1933 to 1939 when, as he put it in 1943, "Dr. New Deal" had to make way for "Dr. Win-the-War." He first used the expression on July 2, 1932 when he addressed the Democratic Convention in Chicago which had nominated him.

These measures fall into three general categories—relief, recovery and reform—although there were some overlappings. Some were aimed at relieving the hardships caused by the economic depression which had started in October, 1929. Others had as their chief purpose the recovery of the national economy. Others were intended to reform certain practices which the President and his advisers regarded as harmful to the common good or were measures which they thought would further the general welfare. In many ways these laws curtailed traditional American individualism and through them the Government regulated aspects of its citizens' lives hitherto regarded as beyond its competence. The New Deal has been distinguished into two phases, the First New Deal which lasted from 1933 to the beginning of 1935 and had as its primary aim, recovery, and the Second New Deal, running from 1935 to 1939, during which the chief objective was reform.

In implementing his program Roosevelt had the assistance of the members of his cabinet and numerous other advisers who were called the "New Dealers." Not all of those so termed, however, agreed on principles or practices. There was much variety of opinion among them. As Secretary of State, the President chose Cordell Hull of Tennessee, a Wilsonian Democrat with long congressional experience who was interested in free trade. William Woodin, a Pennsylvania industrialist, was made Secretary of the Treasury but, due to ill health, he was succeeded after a few months by Henry Morgenthau, Jr., of New York, a Dutchess County neighbor of the President. Henry A. Wallace, a progressive Republican from Iowa, an agricultural expert and the son of the Secretary of Agriculture under Harding, was named to the same post as his father. As Secretary of the Interior, Roosevelt appointed another progressive Republican, Harold Ickes of Illinois. Frances Perkins, a New York social worker, became Secretary of Labor and the first woman to hold a cabinet post. James A. Farley of New York, who had done so much as Chairman of the Democratic National Committee to bring about Roosevelt's victory, became Postmaster General. As Secretary of Commerce, the President chose Dan-

iel Roper of South Carolina, a former commissioner of Internal Revenue who practiced law in Washington, and he appointed George Dern, a former governor of Utah, and Claude Swanson, a Senator from Virginia, chiefs of the War and Navy Departments respectively. Homer Cummings of Connecticut was named Attorney General. Those on whom Roosevelt leaned for advice who were not members of his official family became known as the "Brain Trust." Membership in this group shifted rather frequently. It included professors, social workers, lawyers, labor leaders and financiers. Leading members of the group at one time or another were Raymond Moley, a Columbia professor who had worked under Roosevelt when he was governor of New York on ways to improve the administration of justice in the state, Rexford Tugwell—at one time a member of the faculties of the Universities of Pennsylvania and Washington and Columbia University—who was concerned about the plight of the small farmers, and Adolph A. Berle, Jr., a lawyer and an authority on corporations who was also on the Columbia faculty. Iowa-born Harry Hopkins, a social worker who headed the New York State Temporary Relief Administration under Roosevelt, remained close to the President as director of relief agencies, Secretary of Commerce and roving diplomat.

On March 6, 1933, in order to keep the banking system of the country from collapsing, the President, availing himself of the powers given by the Trading with the Enemy Act of 1917, suspended all transactions in the Federal Reserve and other banks and financial associations. He also embargoed the export of gold, silver and currency till March 9 when Congress would meet in special session. On that day the Emergency Banking Act was passed and signed. This gave the President the power to reorganize all insolvent banks and provided the means by which sound banks could reopen their doors without long delay. On March 12 Roosevelt delivered the first of many "fireside chats" to reassure the country and win support for his policies. The Civilian Conservation Corps (C. C. C.) was established on March 31 to provide work for young men in reclamation projects and in the national parks and forests. About 250,000 youths were so employed at a wage of $30 a week, $25 of which was sent to their families. The Federal Emergency Relief Administration (F. E. R. A.) was set up on May 12 and placed under the direction of Harry Hopkins. This agency had an appropriation of $500,000,000 and it was authorized to match the sums allotted for the relief of the unemployed by state and local governments with Federal funds. In 1933 there were nearly 13,000,000 out of work. By the Home Owners Loan Act of June 13 the Home Owners Loan Corporation (H. O. L. C.) was authorized to issue bonds to the amount of $3,000,000,000 to refinance the mortgages of home owners who were about to lose them through foreclosure.

The first major recovery measure of the Administration was the Agricultural Adjustment Act which created the Agricultural Adjustment Administration (A. A. A.). Passed on May 12, the act empowered the A. A. A. to control the production of wheat, cotton, corn, rice, tobacco, hogs and certain other commodities by paying cash subsidies to farmers who voluntarily restricted the acreage planted with such crops or who reduced the number of livestock. These cash subsidies were to be paid out of the proceeds of a tax levied on the processors of farm products. The act also authorized the Federal Government to make loans on crops to farmers so that they could hold them for better prices and to buy surpluses outright. By these means it was hoped that demand would catch up with supply and that farm prices would rise. Those who favored inflation as the remedy for the country's ills succeeded in adding an omnibus amendment to the Agricultural Adjustment Act, proposed by Sen. Elmer Thomas of Oklahoma, which gave the power to the President to inflate the currency by the coinage of silver at a ratio of his own choice, by printing paper money or by devaluating the gold content of the dollar. Secretary Wallace and George N. Peek, a former associate of Bernard Baruch on the War Industries Board during World War I and of Gen. Hugh Johnson in the Moline Plow Co., the first Administrator of the A. A. A., undertook the job of persuading the farmers to curtail production.

Having tried to assist the farmer to recover, the Administration turned its attention to industry and labor. The National Industrial Recovery Act (N. I. R. A.), passed on June 16, set up the National Recovery Administration (N. R. A.). Under governmental direction employers, employees and consumers were to draft codes by which the various industries would be controlled. The employers were assured that these regulatory codes, which were similar to those drawn up by a number of trade associations in the '20's, would be exempt from prosecution under the antitrust laws and that production would be limited to raise prices. Under section 7a the employee was promised collective bargaining and that minimum wages and maximum hours would be established. The N. R. A. was placed under the direction of Gen. Hugh Johnson, a West Point graduate who had drafted and applied the Draft Act of 1917. Johnson threw himself into the work of code-making with great energy and considerable showmanship. A great many codes were drawn up and the subscribing companies were allowed to stamp their product with the "Blue Eagle," the symbol that they had conformed to the code of their industry and were helping the country to recover. The second section of this act set up the Public Works Administration (P. W. A.). Charge of this was given to Secretary Ickes to the disappointment of Johnson who did not think the N. R. A. would be effective unless one office controlled both the regulation of industry and the disbursement of funds. The P. W. A. was an extension of the Hoover policy of providing employment by the construction of public works. Under Ickes it was administered honestly but too slowly to be of assistance in recovery.

Three measures which were passed during the "Hundred Days" of this special session of the 73rd Congress belong more to the reform category than to relief or recovery. One was the Tennessee Valley Authority Act of May 18 which set up the Tennessee Valley Authority (T. V. A.). In general this agency was to develop the economic and social well-being of an area that embraced parts of seven states. A corporation was organized and it was given the right of eminent domain in the valley. It was authorized, among other things, to erect dams and power plants, to improve navigation and methods of flood control, to undertake soil conservation and reforestation projects and to sell electric power and fertilizers. Arthur E. Morgan, President of Antioch College, was named Chairman of the T. V. A. and David Lilienthal was made counsel. He soon became the driving force in the Authority.

Another reform was the Securities Act of May 27. New issues of securities were to be registered with the Federal Trade Commission along with a statement of the financial condition of the company of issue. This statement was also to be made available to all prospective purchasers of the securities. The bill contained no provision for the regulation of stock exchanges. It was revised in 1934 and such regulatory power was entrusted to the Securities and Exchange Commission (S. E. C.). The Glass-Steagall Banking Act, passed on June 16, separated investment from commercial banking so that there could no longer be speculation with the depositors' money. Another provision gave the Federal Reserve Board power over interest rates to prevent speculation with borrowed money. It also set up the Federal Deposit Insurance Corporation by which the government guaranteed bank deposits below $5000, later increased to $10,000.

By Dec. 5, 1933, three fourths of the state legislatures had ratified the Twenty-first Amendment to the Federal Constitution which repealed the Eighteenth. The states were to decide whether they would allow the sale of alcoholic beverages or not. As a national experiment, the "dry era" ended. Revenue from liquor taxes helped finance state and Federal expenditures.

Despite all this legislation and activity, farm prices, industrial employment and payrolls declined and there was dissatisfaction with the recovery program. In an effort to raise prices the President experimented with an inflationary devaluation of the dollar by reducing its gold content, the third of the methods allowed him by the Thomas Amendment to the Agricultural Adjustment Act. This move in the direction of economic nationalism, based on the "commodity dollar" theory of Prof. George Warren of Cornell, nullified the work of the International Monetary and Economic Conference then meeting in London. The resulting cheapening of American goods in foreign markets convinced European manufacturers that the United States was seeking an unfair advantage in world trade. It also was a blow to the more conservative advisers of the President such as Lewis Douglas, the Director of the Budget, and the banker James Warburg who wished to maintain the gold standard. The dollar was eventually stabilized by an executive order of Jan. 31, 1934, which fixed the gold content of the dollar at 59.06% of its former value. Title to all gold in the Federal Reserve banks was transferred to the Government which was also buying gold in the world market above the current price. By the Gold Clause Act of 1935 no one has the right to sue the Government because of gold-clause contracts or claims arising out of changes in the gold value of the dollar. The President also set up the Civil Works Administration (C. W. A.) to "prime the pump" of recovery by increasing the purchasing power of the people at large. This was not intended to be a permanent solution to the problem of unemployment and was ended on April 1, 1934.

While the President's policy of a managed currency was nationalistic in the sense that it was aimed at raising prices at home, it did not mean American isolation from world commerce. Partly to increase American foreign trade Roosevelt, after securing certain guarantees for American citizens from Maxim Litvinoff, Commissar for Foreign Affairs of the U. S. S. R., recognized the Soviet Union in November, 1933, and diplomatic representatives were exchanged. The Reciprocal Trade Agreement Act, which was passed on June 12, 1934, was also aimed at stimulating foreign commerce. After a long struggle between Secretary Hull and George Peek, whom Roosevelt had made Foreign Trade Adviser after he left the A. A. A., over the interpretation of the act, Hull's more international policy won out over Peek's idea that the act did not intend a general tariff reduction but merely provided a means for drawing up bilateral agreements with various countries. By the end of 1935 reciprocal trade agreements had been negotiated with fourteen countries and the process continued. Such treaties fitted in with the "Good Neighbor" policy of the Administration which brought an end to United States' intervention in the internal affairs of Latin America and created a mutual security system for both continents.

During 1934 attempts were made to control the monopolistic tendencies of the larger companies under the N. R. A. codes. During June the Railway Retirement Act was passed and the President appointed a committee to prepare plans for a general program of social security. In the same month the Frazier-Lemke Farm Bankruptcy Act became law. This made it possible for farmers to reacquire lost farms on reasonable terms and to stay bankruptcy proceedings for five years if creditors were unreasonable.

In his message to Congress of Jan. 4, 1935, Roosevelt emphasized the idea that reform was essential to recovery. He called for legislation which would provide assistance for the unemployed, the aged, destitute children and the physically handicapped. He asked for laws concerning housing, strengthening the N. R. A., reforming public utilities holding companies and improving the methods of taxation. Recovery was to be achieved by placing purchasing power in the hands of the many rather than by encouraging price rises in the hope that the benefits would seep down to the employees in the form of higher wages. This marks the opening of the Second New Deal.

The Social Security Bill was introduced on Jan. 17, 1935. A Federal tax on employers' payrolls was to be used to build up funds for unemployment insurance. States which had approved insurance systems could administer up to 90% of the payments made within its borders. A tax of 1%, which would reach 3% by 1949, was levied on the wages of employees and the payrolls of employers to provide funds for old-age pension insurance. The bill was opposed by various groups. Among them were Dr. Francis E. Townsend's Old Age Revolving Pension Movement, the American Federation of Labor (which was against the tax on wages), the National Association of Manufacturers and the Communist party. It became law in August. On May 6, 1935, the Works Progress Administration (W. P. A.) was established with Hopkins as director. Many projects were organized to spread employment and increase purchasing power. Critics of the Administration considered many of them to be trivial and called them "boondoggling" as they had termed the jobs provided by the C. W. A. Among the agencies it established was the Resettlement Administration (R. A.), under Tugwell in the Department of Agriculture, the purpose of which was to remove farmers from submarginal to better land and to provide poorly paid workers with "Greenbelt Towns" outside cities where they could supplement their salaries by part-time farming. An enthusiastic supporter of these ideas was Mrs. Eleanor Roosevelt, the President's wife, whose political and social interests ranged widely. Another was the Rural Electrification Administration (R. E. A.) which offered low interest loans to farmers' co-operatives to build power lines with W. P. A. labor in localities where private companies thought investment unjustified. A third was the National Youth Administration (N. Y. A.) which aimed at keeping young people at school and out of the labor market. Money was turned over to school administrators who paid it out to students for various types of work about the school. The Federal Theatre Project provided work for many actors, directors and stage crews; the Writers' Project turned out a series of state guides; the Historical Records Survey brought to light many documents in local archives. The wages paid W. P. A. workers were higher than relief payments but lower than those paid by private enterprise. In 1936, after considerable pressure from the workers, the Government raised wages on W. P. A. projects to the prevailing level but reduced the number of hours worked a month so that wage totals remained at security level. The Government wished the workers to return to private enterprise as soon as possible.

In June, 1935, the President sent a special message to Congress on tax revision. Tax burdens, he said, should be redistributed according to ability to pay. Higher taxes on large individual incomes, inheritances and gifts would lead to a wider distribution of wealth. The principle of ability to pay should also be extended to corporations. The Wealth Tax Act, which embodied these proposals, was opposed by Sen. Huey Long of Louisiana and his "Share Our Wealth" movement as too moderate but it was passed on Aug. 30. Taxes on large individual incomes were steeply scaled to 75% on those over $5,000,000. Taxes on estates were increased. Excess profits taxes on corporations ranged from 6% on profits above 10% to 12% on profits above 15%. Income taxes on corporations were graduated from 12.50% to 15%. The act was regarded by many as a "soak the rich scheme" and as a punitive measure on the part of the Administration which had parted company with "big business" by this time.

The President submitted a Public Utility Holding Company Bill to Congress which was designed to prevent abuses in that field, especially those made possible by the pyramiding of such companies. The bill did not require the abolition of such companies but imposed a "death sentence" on those which could not prove their usefulness in five years. The act as finally passed on Aug. 28, 1935, permitted two levels of holding companies but otherwise retained the "death sentence" clause.

Roosevelt requested the extension of the much criticized N. R. A. for two more years. The Senate voted to extend it for ten months. At the same time it was considering the Wagner-Connery National Labor Relations Act which was designed to strengthen section 7a of the N. I. R. A. The bill proposed to outlaw employer-dominated unions and assure labor of its right to collective bargaining through representatives chosen by itself. While a number of the Senators thought this bill and section 7a overlapped, it passed on May 16. The bill, which did not become an Administration measure till the N. I. R. A. was declared unconstitutional, became law on July 5, 1935. By it the National Labor Relations Board (N. L. R. B.) was set up to determine suitable units for collective bargaining, to conduct elections for the choice of labor's representatives and to prevent interference with such elections.

The constitutionality of this controversial legislation became a central issue in 1935. Of the nine justices who then sat on the bench of the Supreme Court four were considered to be conservatives: Justices Van Devanter, Sutherland, McReynolds and Butler; three to be liberal: Justices Brandeis, Cardozo and Stone; while Chief Justice Hughes and Justice Roberts were thought to occupy an intermediate position. On Jan. 7 the court decided that section 9c of the N. I. R. A. was an unconstitutional delegation of legislative authority by Congress to the executive. This led to doubts about the constitutionality of the whole act. On May 6 the court invalidated the Railroad Retirement Act which raised the question of the constitutionality of the Social Security Act which was before Congress. On May 27 the Frazier-Lemke Farm Bankruptcy Act was declared unconstitutional because under it private property was taken without compensation. On the same day a unanimous court declared, in Schechter Corp. v. the United States, that the legislature's delegation of the code-making power to the President in the N. I. R. A. was an unconstitutional surrender of its own proper function. The court also found that the Schechter Corporation's activities, the sale of chickens in Brooklyn, N. Y., had only an indirect effect on interstate commerce. Roosevelt termed this a "horse and buggy" interpretation of the commerce clause.

A way out of this impasse was found in part by rewriting some of this legislation so as to meet the objections of the court. The Frazier-Lemke Farm Mortgage Act and the Wagner-Crosser Railroad Retirement Act replaced those found unconstitutional. The Guffey-Snyder Bituminous Coal Stabilization Act, passed on Aug. 30, practically re-enacted the whole bituminous coal code of the N. R. A. The Wagner National Labor Relations Act replaced section 7a of the N. I. R. A. When the court found the A. A. A. unconstitutional in Jan., 1936, because the tax on food processors was an unjust expropriation of money and because the powers of the states were invaded, it was replaced by the Soil Conservation and Domestic Allotment Act of March 1, 1936, and later by the second Agricultural Adjustment Act of 1938. Rewriting, however, did not save all this legislation. On May 18, 1936, the Guffey-Snyder Act was invalidated. When, on June 1, a New York minimum wage law was declared unconstitutional because it violated freedom of contract, the President said that the court had created a "no man's land" where neither a state nor the Federal Government could act.

At the Democratic Convention held in Philadelphia in June, 1936, Roosevelt and Vice-President Garner were nominated practically without opposition. Al Smith and a number of conservative Democrats, who had joined with others to form the Liberty League, attempted to lead "Jeffersonian Democrats" out of the party but without much success. The Convention also repealed the two-thirds rule with which Democratic conventions had been so long saddled. In his acceptance speech Roosevelt defended the measures of his administration and attacked his opponents whom he termed "economic royalists." The Republicans nominated Gov. Alfred Landon of Kansas, who was strongly supported by William R. Hearst, the publisher, for President and Frank Knox of Illinois for Vice-President. A third party was formed out of the followers of the Rev. Gerald L. K. Smith who had taken over Long's "Share Our Wealth" movement after the Senator was assassinated, of Dr. Francis Townsend and of the Rev. Charles Coughlin of the Social Justice movement who had become strongly anti-Roosevelt. It was called the Union Party and it nominated Congressman William Lemke of North Dakota for President. The Socialists nominated Norman Thomas and the Communists, Earl Browder. Labor took a very active part in the campaign and the new industrial labor organization, the Committee on Industrial Organization (C. I. O.), under the leadership of John L. Lewis and Sidney Hillman, set up Labor's Nonpartisan League and raised a million dollars for the support of Roosevelt and other pro-labor candidates of either party. After a stormy campaign the popular vote was 27,500,000 for Roosevelt and 16,700,000 for Landon. The electoral vote was 523 to 8. Only Maine and Vermont cast their votes for the Republican candidate.

After this resounding victory at the polls the President sent a proposal to Congress to reorganize the Federal judiciary on Feb. 5, 1937. In his message he pointed out Congress's power over the Federal judiciary and the difficulties arising from insufficient personnel, crowded dockets and aged judges. He suggested that the number of Federal judges be increased when the incumbent judges did not retire at seventy. He asked that cases involving the constitutionality of legislation be removed from the lowest court to the Supreme Court immediately and that such cases should have precedence there. This proposal shocked a great many people and Roosevelt was accused of trying to "pack" the court with judges who favored his legislation. During the debate over this bill the Democrats in Congress and throughout the country split. The situation was helped at this point by certain decisions of the Supreme Court. On March 27 it upheld, by a vote of five to four, both the Washington State Minimum Wage Act, which was similar to the invalidated New York law, and the Frazier-Lemke Farm Mortgage Act. Justice Roberts joined Chief Justice Hughes and Justices Brandeis, Cardozo and Stone in these decisions. On April 12 it found the Wagner Act, which had been declared unconstitutional by the Circuit Court of Appeals in San Francisco, valid. On May 24 it declared the Social Security Act constitutional. Despite this change on the part of the court and the fact that his party was divided on the matter, Roosevelt continued to press his Judiciary Reorganization Bill. A substitute was proposed and the Judicial Procedure Reform Act

was passed on Aug. 24. No mention of the appointment of new judges was made in the bill. This was the President's first important defeat at the hands of Congress.

During the summer of 1937 an economic "recession" started which lasted through 1938. Many attributed it to the Administration's hostility to business and capital. High taxes, it was said, discouraged business expansion and personal initiative. Roosevelt again resorted to "pump priming" and expanded bank credits.

On Feb. 16, 1938, Congress passed a second Agricultural Adjustment Act. Like the first, it aimed at controlling surpluses but used different means. Whenever a surplus in an export crop which would cause a fall in prices appeared likely the A. A. A. would fix a marketable quota and the farmers who agreed not to market more than the product of the acreage allotted to them could store their surpluses under government seal till a shortage developed. In the interim they could receive loans on them. The A. A. A. would also fix a parity price which represented the purchasing power of a unit of the crop concerned during the years 1900 to 1914. The farmer was to sell his surplus when the price was at parity or above. So the "ever normal granary," a favorite project of Wallace, would be established. The act also had provisions taking care of the special problems raised by conditions in the Dust Bowl, the area of the semi-arid high plains, and for soil conservation.

On June 25 the Fair Labor Standards Act was passed. The law sought an eventual minimum wage of 40 cents an hour and a maximum work week of 40 hours. Time-and-one-half was to be paid for overtime and labor by children under sixteen was forbidden. Exceptions were made for various localities. The Housing Act of 1937 made low-rent housing available in many cities. The Second New Deal was written into law.

These measures had not gone unopposed. In addition an Executive Reorganization Bill which had been proposed by Roosevelt, like many of his predecessors, was defeated largely because it was regarded as connected with his Judiciary Reorganization Bill. The legislature also repealed the graduated tax on the undistributed profits of corporations of 1936. The President personally entered the congressional campaigns of 1938 and urged the voters not to re-elect certain Democratic members of Congress who had not supported his program in recent sessions. Leading targets were Sen. Walter George of Georgia, Sen. "Cotton Ed" Smith of South Carolina, Sen. Millard Tydings of Maryland and Congressman John O'Connor of New York. Except for O'Connor the President was unsuccessful in his attempt to "purge" the party and for the first time since 1928 the number of Republicans in Congress increased.

By 1938 the world situation had become very tense.

Japan, Italy and Germany were threatening international peace. The Democratic party was divided on foreign policy. The South, while not enthusiastic about all of Roosevelt's domestic policies, supported his program of resistance to aggression. The Middle West and West were in favor of his domestic reforms but tended to isolationism. The Northeast alone supported him in both. In the face of world conditions, especially after the Munich Crisis of September, 1938, the President felt compelled to subordinate his domestic reforms to keep southern support for his foreign policy. His failure actively to support an anti-lynching bill indicated a new outlook. Henceforth he would strive chiefly for party and domestic unity as the nations prepared for war.

NEW ENGLAND, DOMINION OF (June, 1686–April, 1689), represented the application of a principle which the English government had long had in mind, the consolidation of the American colonies into a few large provinces for the sake of better administration of defense, commerce and justice. The experiment in dominion government was first tried out in New England because of the necessity of replacing the old charter government of Massachusetts Bay Colony, after the annulment of the charter in 1684, with some form of royal control. The dominion was established in June, 1686, in temporary form, under the presidency of a native New Englander, Joseph Dudley, but was formally inaugurated in December, 1686, upon the arrival of Gov. Edmund Andros, under whose rule the former colonies or regions of Massachusetts, Plymouth, Rhode Island, Connecticut, New Hampshire, Maine, the County of Cornwall (northern Maine) and King's Province, a disputed region in southern New England, were consolidated into one province.

Governmental power was vested in the governor and a council, appointed by the king, but there was no representative assembly. Andros' strict administration of the Navigation Acts, his attempts to establish English land law, and above all the menace of taxation without representation (though taxation under him was not excessive in amount) drew all groups into opposition. To strengthen the line of defense against the French, New York and New Jersey were added to the dominion in 1688, making a unit too large for one man to administer well. Upon arrival of news that James II had abdicated, the Puritan leaders rose in revolt against Andros and overthrew him (April, 1689).

NEW ENGLAND COMPANY (1628–29) was the successor to the Dorchester Company which began settlement of the Massachusetts Bay region, and precursor to the Massachusetts Bay Company. The New England Company came into existence as an attempt to revive the dying Dorchester plantation, which had originated chiefly as a fishing venture, but which had failed to establish a strong settlement. A new group of men, interested primarily in making a plantation for religious purposes, took over the Dorchester enterprise, then applied to the Council for New England for a patent, which they are reputed to have received under date of March 19, 1628. The New England Company thus formed was an unincorporated, joint-stock affair, like so many which had attempted plantations under patents from trading companies but, under the leadership of John White, there was from the first a strong Puritan influence in the enterprise. With funds subscribed the company despatched a fleet with prospective settlers and supplies, and appointed John Endecott as governor of the tiny settlement already existing at Naumkeag (later Salem). Within the company doubts arose concerning the efficacy of their patent, which made the members decide to seek royal confirmation. Supported by important men at court, they succeeded in their endeavor and were able thenceforth to proceed in their project under the royal charter of March 4, 1629, which released them from further dependence upon the Council for New England.

NEW ENGLAND EMIGRANT AID COMPANY (1854–66), an important factor in the Kansas conflict and in the rise of the Republican Party, was first incorporated by Eli Thayer, April 26, 1854. Its plan of operations was to advertise Kansas, send emigrants in conducted parties at reduced transportation rates, and invest its capital in improvements in Kansas, from which it hoped to earn a profit. It sent to Kansas about 2000 settlers who founded all the important Free State towns. It established ten mills and two hotels, and assisted schools and churches. It aided the Free State party in various ways, and its officers sent the first Sharps rifles. It raised and spent, including rents and sales, about $190,000. Its activities furnished the pretext for the fraudulent voting by Missourians. It was blamed by President Pierce, Stephen A. Douglas, and the proslavery leaders for all the troubles in Kansas. Although the company failed financially, its friends believed it had saved Kansas from slavery. After the Civil War it undertook unsuccessful colonization projects in Oregon and Florida.

NEW-ENGLAND PRIMER, THE, first published about 1690, combined lessons in spelling with the Shorter Catechism and with versified injunctions to piety and to faith in Calvinistic fundamentals. Crude couplets and woodcut pictures illustrated the alphabet. Here first was published the child's prayer, "Now I lay me down to sleep." This eighty-page booklet, four and a half by three inches in size, was for a half century the only elementary textbook, and for a century more it held a central place in infant education. It is one of the most important colonial American cultural documents.

NEW FRANCE. For a century after the discovery of America the kings of France, preoccupied with dynastic and civil wars, devoted little attention to New World enterprises. In 1524 Francis I sent out Verrazzano, whose expedition provided a paper claim to much of North America, while the three expeditions of Cartier (1534–42) served to fix French attention upon the region adjoining the Gulf of St. Lawrence. The short peace which Henry IV afforded the distracted country (1598–1610) made possible the first permanent French establishment in America (Quebec, 1608). For over half a century the government followed the policy of granting the colony to various companies to exploit, and despite the splendid devotion of Champlain, the "Father of New France," its growth was painfully slow.

In 1663 Louis XIV assumed direct control of the colony and a notable renaissance ensued. Soldiers were sent out to defend it and maidens to supply it with homes. Numerous measures looking to its economic betterment were instituted, and the Iroquois, whose warfare had been a nightmare hitherto, were thoroughly humbled. These things prepared the way for a remarkable geographical expansion whereby the boundaries were extended over the Great Lakes and the entire Mississippi Valley—the work of St. Lusson, Jolliet, LaSalle, Hennepin, Duluth and others.

The revolution of 1688 which placed William III on the English throne initiated the second Hundred Years' War between France and England. To Old-World rivalries the colonies added their own, and the period 1689–1763 witnessed four world wars, in each of which the American colonies participated. The long conflict ended with the surrender of Canada to England (Montreal, Sept. 8, 1760), while the remainder of New France was divided between England and Spain.

New France as a political entity thus ceased to exist. Upon both Canada and the United States, however, the colony has left an indelible influence, while the French race and culture remain permanently seated in the valley of the St. Lawrence.

NEW FREEDOM is a term generally accepted as descriptive of the political and economic philosophy underlying the domestic policies of President Wilson at the opening of his first administration. The more significant utterances of Wilson in the campaign of 1912 were published under the above title early in 1913. They constituted an earnest plea for a more humanitarian spirit in government and business, political reforms which would restore government to the people and break the power of selfish and privileged minorities. The growth of corporate power had, he argued, rendered obsolete many traditional concepts of American democracy. Government must have not merely a negative, but a positive, program and use its power "to cheer and inspirit our people with the sure prospects of social justice and due

reward, with the vision of the open gates of opportunity for all."

NEW HAMPSHIRE. Its brief coast and Isles of Shoals were visited by many fishermen in the 16th century. In 1603 Martin Pring sailed up the Piscataqua; Champlain landed there in 1605, as did John Smith in 1614, whose *Description of New England* gave wide publicity to the region. The Council for New England granted much of what is Maine and New Hampshire, in 1622, to Sir Ferdinando Gorges and Capt. John Mason, and in 1629 regranted to Mason alone an area which he called New Hampshire. Later grants added to the Mason title. Under smaller grants from the Council, David Thomson settled at Odiorne's Point near Portsmouth in 1623, the first settlement in New Hampshire, and soon after Edward Hilton founded Dover. The Laconia Company settled Strawberry Bank as a trading post in 1630. Rev. John Wheelwright with other religious dissenters from Massachusetts founded Exeter, and Massachusetts encouraged the settlement of Hampton in 1639. These four towns were practically independent, but weak. Massachusetts, disliking their Anglican or Antinomian tendencies, laid claim to the region, holding "3 miles north of the Merrimac" to mean its source, and assumed control in 1641, making some religious concessions, especially in voting requirements. There was little religious persecution in New Hampshire, and no witchcraft trial, but several Quakers were hanged in 1659–60. Farming, lumbering, shipbuilding, fishing and the fur trade were the chief occupations. No Indian troubles developed till King Philip's War, but only one more town was settled by 1675.

Mason's heirs succeeded in 1679 in having New Hampshire created a separate royal province, with governor and council chosen by the Crown, and an elected assembly. It was again ruled by Massachusetts for a time after the fall of Andros, becoming separate permanently in 1692, although having the same governor, 1699–1741. The boundary with Massachusetts was settled by the king in 1741. Soon after conflict developed with New York over the western line, and New Hampshire granted out 138 towns, the New Hampshire Grants, in what is now Vermont. The king settled this line in 1764.

Severe Indian attacks, as at Salmon Falls, Exeter and Durham between 1689 and 1725, slowed up settlement. Immigration was chiefly from Massachusetts and Connecticut, with an important group after 1719 in the Scotch-Irish. After the wars the province grew rapidly. By 1776 about 80,000 persons were living along the coast, inland to the Merrimac and in the west along the Connecticut. The northern half of New Hampshire was still unsettled, and much of the rest so recently occupied as to be under frontier conditions. Portsmouth, the capital, was the only town of size and wealth. Economic differences were not great, and the colony was distinctly rural, provincial and democratic. The first newspaper, the *New Hampshire Gazette,* was founded in 1756, and Dartmouth College in 1769.

The Revolution found few of the people Tories. The majority, after an attack on Fort William and Mary in 1774, drove out Gov. Wentworth, and created a new government in January, 1776, the first of the colonies to do so. New Hampshire regiments contributed their share; scores of privateers sailed from Portsmouth; three ships of the new navy were launched on the Piscataqua; Gen. Stark won the battle of Bennington (1777) with local troops. The economic distress after the war produced at Exeter a mild copy of the efforts of Daniel Shays, and a close contest in the ratification of the Constitution, which was finally secured June 21, 1788. New Hampshire was the ninth and decisive state.

NEW HAMPSHIRE GRANTS. This term was applied in the early settlement to that section of territory now known as the State of Vermont. Benning Wentworth, first governor of New Hampshire, which colony claimed jurisdiction over the territory, began granting land to the settlers in 1749 in the name of the king of England. The first of the grants bore the name of Bennington. By 1761 the grants began to be issued rapidly, and a total of 131 townships had been chartered by 1764. At this point New York, which had set up counterclaims to the territory, with the attendant right to make grants, gained the support of the Crown, and in 1765 began to charter townships within the grants, some of which conflicted with grants already made by New Hampshire. New York contended that the prior titles were invalidated, and the historic controversy between the settlers and the government of New York was born.

NEW HARMONY SETTLEMENT, of Posey County, Ind., was founded in 1825 by Robert Owen, the English philanthropist and industrialist, on the site previously occupied by the Harmony Society of Pennsylvania. Here Owen attempted to put into practice the theories of socialism and human betterment he had evolved. By December, 1825, New Harmony had attracted a heterogeneous population of about 1000 men, women and children of all sorts and conditions. Following a preliminary organization, the constitution of "The New Harmony Community of Equality" was adopted Feb. 5, 1826. This provided for absolute equality of property, labor and opportunity together with freedom of speech and action. The absence of any real authority in the community government resulted in virtual anarchy, and after several abortive attempts to better conditions, Owen admitted the failure of the experiment on May 26, 1827. A number of communities modeled on New Harmony which sprang up in other states at this time were equally short-lived.

NEW HAVEN COLONY. Dissatisfied with government by king and council and with growing high-church Anglicanism in England, in the spring of 1637 John Davenport, Puritan divine, and Theophilus Eaton, merchant, led a group of Londoners to Massachusetts Bay. Both Davenport and Eaton were members of the Massachusetts Bay Company and probably intended to found a plantation within the limits of the Bay Colony, where the group already had many friends. They were sympathetic to the principles of Congregationalism, to the attempt to limit political privileges to members of Congregational churches, and to "Moses his judicials," a code of laws recently prepared by John Cotton for Massachusetts and at the moment under consideration in that colony. They intended to found a commercial settlement, however, and by 1637 the best harbors of Massachusetts had been occupied. Moreover, at the time of their arrival the Antinomian controversy was at its height in Massachusetts, and must have discouraged a group of Puritans seeking a new Jerusalem. Finally, the Pequot War had cleared the territory on the northern shore of Long Island Sound of Indians, and glowing reports of this region had reached Massachusetts. In the fall of 1637 Theophilus Eaton and others set out to investigate this "promised land," and as a result of their explorations, the group decided to settle at Quinnipiac, later known as the town of New Haven.

With recruits gained in Massachusetts, the Davenport-Eaton company set out for Quinnipiac in the spring of 1638. They soon attracted kindred souls from Massachusetts, from Wethersfield on the Connecticut River, and from England. In addition to the town of New Haven, settlements appeared at Guilford, Milford, Stamford, Southold on Long Island, and, somewhat later, Branford. Without royal charter authorizing them to take possession of the soil and to organize a government, the settlers purchased land from the natives. In each town a church was gathered according to Congregational principles, and, following the gathering of a church, a plantation government based upon the Cotton Code (*see above*), adapted to meet the needs of a new and smaller community, was established. At first Guilford and Milford were independent plantations but Stamford, Southold and Branford acquired their land from New Haven and always recognized the jurisdiction of the mother town. As a result of the formation of the United Colonies of New England in 1643, a colonial government, also based upon the Cotton Code, was established, and the New Haven Colony took its place as the smallest of the Puritan colonies of New England. Of this colony, Theophilus Eaton was governor until his death in 1658. Throughout the existence of the colony, political privileges were restricted to members of Congregational churches. To train leaders for church and state, John Davenport endeavored to found a colony grammar school and college at New Haven. A grammar school opened its doors in 1660 but closed two years later. The college of which Davenport dreamed did not materialize until long after his death (*see* Yale University).

During the early years of the colony the leaders had high hopes of establishing a commercial commonwealth which would extend from the western boundary of Saybrook to the Delaware River. As early as 1641 they acquired title to land on the Delaware from the Indians. These plans brought the New Haven Colony into conflict with New Sweden and New Netherland. Probably more than the other colonies of New England, the Puritans on Long Island Sound desired the English conquest of New Netherland. The first Anglo-Dutch War seemed to further their designs but Massachusetts, not yet awakened to the possibility of extending her territory across the continent, balked the plans of the merchants of the New Haven Colony and Connecticut in 1653, and the end of the war in Europe halted an expedition which Oliver Cromwell had sent across the Atlantic to seize New Netherland in 1654. Hemmed in by Connecticut and the Dutch, the New Haven Colony failed to develop into the great commercial commonwealth its founders had envisaged, and turned to agriculture.

The Restoration in England found the New Haven Colony without a leader capable of representing it at the court of Charles II. William Leete, governor, suggested that John Winthrop the Younger, about to visit England to secure a royal charter for Connecticut, procure one charter under which two colonial governments might function. Winthrop succeeded in securing a charter which unquestionably included the New Haven Colony, and, disregarding Leete's suggestion of two colonies, the magistrates of Connecticut hastened to extend their authority over their southern neighbor. The New Haven Colony fought absorption, but a royal grant of the territory between the Connecticut and Delaware Rivers to James, Duke of York, and the surrender of New Netherland to royal commissioners convinced the leaders that they would be better off under Connecticut than as part of the province of the Duke of York, and, reluctantly, in December, 1664, the New Haven Colony ceased to exist.

NEW JERSEY. With the grant of New Netherland by Charles II to the Duke of York, that portion located between the Hudson and Delaware Rivers was conveyed by the latter, through a deed of lease and release, to John Lord Berkeley and Sir George Carteret as joint proprietors (June 23, 24, 1664). By the terms of this conveyance the province was "hereafter to be called . . . New Caesarea or New Jersey" and boundaries were fixed as at present. Assuming powers of government the proprietors drew up the Con-

cessions and Agreement and appointed Philip Carteret governor. Carteret chose for his capital Elizabethtown and called his first assembly in May, 1668. Berkeley's western portion now passed, first to John Fenwick and Edward Byllynge (1674), and later to Quaker interests headed by William Penn, who secured a division of the province into East Jersey and West Jersey (1676). The latter division became a refuge for persecuted Quakers, who founded the towns of Salem and Burlington, while the former, offered at auction by Carteret's heirs, was purchased by Penn and 23 associates for £3400 (1682). In East Jersey, settled mainly by Puritans from Long Island and New England, proprietary government was resisted, especially in Elizabethtown and the towns of the Monmouth Purchase, which held their patents from Gov. Nicolls of New York. After the fall of the Dominion of New England, during which the Jerseys were joined to New England (August, 1688–April, 1689), proprietary authority disintegrated and, with the surrender of their government to the Crown (1702), the two divisions were reunited.

Until 1738 New Jersey was joined with New York under one governor, but retained its own assembly. This body, though chosen by restricted suffrage, was usually aligned against the governor and council, which represented the important landed and mercantile interests. Agriculture was the chief occupation and, especially in West Jersey where the farms were large, slavery existed despite the exhortations of John Woolman. As the conflict with England approached, the refusal of Gov. William Franklin to have delegates sent to the Continental Congress (1774) led to the meeting of a committee at New Brunswick for that purpose. From this committee grew the Provincial Congress of New Jersey, which assumed authority in all branches of government (May, 1775). Meeting at Burlington it elected the delegates to the Continental Congress (June 22, 1776) who signed the Declaration of Independence, adopted a state constitution (July 2) and, after taking the name "The Convention of the State of New Jersey," declared the state independent (July 18). To New Jersey the Revolution was a terrible ordeal: the people were divided in their sympathies; the state lay in the path of armies contesting for control of the Hudson and Delaware Rivers. The victories at Trenton (Dec. 26, 1776) and Princeton (Jan. 3, 1777), imparting new vigor to the American cause, and the battle of Monmouth (June 28, 1778) are numbered among the important battles of the war, while the hardships of the Continental Army at Morristown are only matched by Valley Forge. In the Convention of 1787 William Paterson introduced the New Jersey Plan and, later, at Trenton, the state convention unanimously ratified the new Federal Constitution (Dec. 18, 1787). That city was made the permanent state capital in 1790.

NEW LIGHTS. George Whitefield, appearing in New England in 1740, gave impetus to a religious reaction led by Jonathan Edwards toward the old doctrine of sanctification by faith alone. This became a cult known as the New Lights, which split the Congregational establishment in New England and drew from other faiths also. It brought on a religious revival known as the "Great Awakening," with extravagant demonstrations—shoutings, contortions of face and body—the first of the sort in our history. Connecticut, where the controversy was violent, passed a law in 1742 to restrain the revivalists. Many New Light leaders, including Edwards, eventually had to leave their parishes.

NEW MARKET, BATTLE OF (May 15, 1864). Moving down the Shenandoah Valley from Winchester, Sigel (U.) engaged the combined Confederate forces of Imboden and Breckinridge at New Market, Va. The engagement, fought in a driving rain, resulted in a Confederate victory, important in that it afforded Lee (C.) the opportunity of concentrating all his resources to the defense of Richmond.

NEW MEXICO. Alvar Nuñez Cabeza de Vaca, one of the castaways on the Texas coast of the Pánfilo de Narváez expedition, 1528–36, was probably the first white man to see New Mexico. Equally important was the reconnaissance of Fray Marcos de Niza in 1539, which led to Coronado's expedition, 1540–42. Coronado conquered the pueblos at Zuñi, July 7, 1540, and his captains proceeded to explore the surrounding country, finding the province of the Hopi Indians, the Grand Canyon of the Colorado River and the fertile province of Tiguex, near where Albuquerque now stands. After exploring the entire pueblo country, they sought the rich kingdom of Quivira, penetrating in vain the vast plains area of northwestern Texas, Oklahoma and Kansas.

In 1581 a group of nine soldier-colonists and three missionaries, led by Capt. Francisco Sánchez Chamuscado and Fray Augustín Rodríguez, entered the pueblo country from the Rio Grande Valley, and explored most of the area in which Pueblo Indians lived. They were received in peace, and the next spring the soldiers returned to Mexico to tell of their adventures, but the friars did not return and soon suffered martyrdom. A small rescue party led by Antonio de Espejo set out in November, 1582, pushed up the Rio Grande Valley in New Mexico, and re-explored the pueblo land. The news brought back by these two expeditions revived old tales of wealth, and the King of Spain ordered that the northern land be added to the empire. Many sought the honor of conquering the region, Juan de Oñate being the winner. In 1598 he proceeded up the Rio Grande Valley to the Chama River. Here he established his capital, San Juan de los Caballeros. A year later it

was moved to the near-by San Gabriel. Oñate failed to find the expected wealth, and maintained his authority with difficulty. He resigned in 1607, and in 1609 Pedro de Peralta became governor. Peralta founded a new capital at the Villa de Santa Fe, probably in 1610.

New Mexico now became a great mission field. Celebrated among the missionaries was Fray Alonso de Benavides, whose *Memorials* on New Mexico in 1630 and 1634 gave a history of the province. Till 1680 Spanish rule was not seriously challenged, but in that year an Indian rebellion practically cleared the province of Spaniards. Diego de Vargas, Marquis of Brazinas, became governor, and (1692–1704) succeeded in re-establishing control. Santa Fe again became the capital, the missionaries came back, Albuquerque was laid out (1706) and other settlements were founded.

Throughout the colonial period the province was exposed to the attack of the Navajo, Ute, Apache and Comanche; and after 1700 there were increasing rumors of French invaders. Occasionally French traders came to Santa Fe. In 1776 New Mexico was made part of the Provincias Internas, a commandancy general set up to provide more effective government on the frontier, its capital at Chihuahua.

Spanish rule ended in 1821, as Mexico became independent, and henceforth the province was governed from Mexico City. However, Mexican authority was weak on the frontier, and for the most part New Mexico went its own way until the Americans came. First among them was Zebulon M. Pike, in 1806–7. William Becknell, founder of the Santa Fe Trail, came in 1821. Year after year, trade with the United States increased. New Mexico easily fell before the invasion of Gen. Kearny, who occupied Santa Fe, Aug. 19, 1846. It became legally part of the United States by the Treaty of Guadalupe Hidalgo. Military rule continued until it became a territory by the Compromise of 1850.

After repeated attempts, New Mexico succeeded in obtaining statehood in 1912.

NEW NATIONALISM is the term used to describe the political philosophy of Theodore Roosevelt that the nation is the best instrument for advancing progressive democracy. In more detail, it meant emphasis upon the need for political, social and industrial reforms, such as government regulation and control of corporations, better working conditions for labor, conservation of natural resources and more power directly in the people; the ineffectiveness of the states in dealing with these problems; and the consequent necessity of using the powers of the National Government and of increasing those powers to the extent necessary.

NEW NETHERLAND. No serious attempt was made to plant a colony in New Netherland before the organization of the Dutch West India Company in 1620. In the spring of 1624, however, a group of thirty families, most of whom were Walloons, were sent over in the ship *New Netherland*. A few of the emigrants remained at the mouth of the Hudson, but the greater part were settled up the Hudson River at Fort Orange, where the city of Albany now stands. A fort was also built on Nut (Governors) Island and shortly afterward Willem Verhulst received the appointment of *commies* and sailed for New Netherland. Three months after Verhulst's arrival the thinly settled colony was reinforced by the coming of 42 new emigrants. In addition one of the directors of the company sent 103 head of livestock, including horses, cows, hogs and sheep. In July, 1625, the settlement was moved from Nut Island to Manhattan and called New Amsterdam. A new fort was built.

Verhulst did not remain long in New Amsterdam. His own council found him guilty of mismanagement. He was dismissed and Peter Minuit appointed in his place as the first director-general. Minuit negotiated the purchase of Manhattan from the Indians, paying the value of sixty guilders in trinkets, thus legalizing the occupation already in effect. In 1626 because of trouble with the Indians, Minuit moved the families at Fort Orange to Manhattan, leaving only a small garrison behind under Sebastian Crol.

Members of the settlement had no voice in its administration. Power was centered in the hands of the director and his council, who were appointed by and represented the company. The colonists for the most part were not free agents, but were bound by contracts to the company. Although farmers were allotted free land, they were obliged to stay in the colony for six years. The company had right of first purchase of the produce from their fields, and they could sell their farms only to one of the other colonists. Indentured husbandmen, under still more rigid restrictions, worked the company farms. Instructions in considerable detail were sent to the director by the company, and only in cases of urgent necessity was he allowed to modify his orders. New legislation was submitted to the executive committee of the company, as were, also, appeals in judicial cases. Later, important matters often came before the States-General. The Reform Church was supported though freedom of conscience was granted.

The first few years showed a moderate profit to the company from trade, but the efforts at colonization proved a loss. Among the directors of the company two parties appeared, one favoring active colonization of the province, the other desirous of restricting the company to its trading function. The former group was successful in 1629 in the passage of the Charter of Freedoms and Exemptions, which provided for the grant of great estates, called patroonships, to such members of the company as should found settlements of fifty persons within four years. The effect of patroonship under the charter

has been overemphasized. With the single exception of Rensselaerswyck, they were unsuccessful. Another type of landholding provided for in the charter was destined to be of far greater importance. "Private persons" were allowed to take possession of as much land as they could properly cultivate. In 1638, further to encourage colonization, trade restrictions in the colony were reduced, better provision was offered for transportation of settlers and their goods and the fur-trade monopoly was discontinued. The revised charter of 1640 reduced the size of future patroonships and held out promises of local self-government.

In 1632 Minuit was recalled, and Wouter Van Twiller named as his successor. The administration of Van Twiller was marked by violent quarrels with his council and prominent colonists. In 1637 his failure to send reports to the company resulted in his recall, and the appointment of Willem Kieft as director-general. An adventurer with a bad record, Kieft did nothing to improve it during his administration. By the summer of 1641 his brutal and unwise Indian policy had created so dangerous a situation that he was constrained to ask the colonists to elect a board to advise with him. The Twelve Men were chosen, and although they had been called only to give advice on Indian affairs, to Kieft's annoyance, they drew up a petition asking for much-needed reforms. The Indian difficulties died down temporarily, but in September, 1643, an unprovoked night attack, instigated by Kieft, on an Indian encampment, caused the tribes to rise in fury. Safety was to be found only in the immediate vicinity of the fort. Distant Fort Orange alone was not molested. Kieft once more called for an election of representatives, and the Eight Men were chosen. In October and again in the following year they petitioned the company for aid, bitterly criticizing Kieft's management of Indian relations. Conditions in the province were desperate. The frightened settlers huddling in or near the fort faced starvation. Hostile bands of Indians, estimated as totaling 15,000, threatened attack. Fortunately, however, the Indians had no common and concerted plan of attack. June brought reinforcements, but hostilities dragged on and it was not until August, 1645, that a general peace was signed. The Indian war had not extended to Fort Orange and the patroon's colony of Rensselaerswyck, although trade suffered. Despite the restrictions imposed by the company, this little settlement had grown by 1645 to a sizable colony.

The complaints of the Eight Men and similar protests from private persons resulted in the recall of Kieft, and on May 11, 1647, Peter Stuyvesant, his successor, arrived in New Amsterdam. The new director was honorable, active and conscientious, but his autocratic disposition and his hostility to popular demands led to continual friction. Conditions in the province were bad, trade was in a state of confusion, morals low and money urgently needed. In September, 1647, as a means of raising revenue, Stuyvesant called for an election of representatives. The Nine Men were chosen. They met the requests of the director-general fairly, and expressed themselves as willing to tax themselves to help finish the church and to reorganize the school. And then, despite protests from Stuyvesant, they drew up and sent to Holland two documents known as the Petition and Remonstrance of New Netherland. The Petition was a concise statement of the unsatisfactory condition of the province, with suggested remedies, and the Remonstrance a longer document, furnishing in detail the facts on which they based their appeal. In April, 1652, the company, inclined to grant some of the concessions asked, instructed Stuyvesant to give New Amsterdam a "burgher government."

Although Stuyvesant made a sincere attempt to maintain friendly relations with the Indians, yet he had to fight three Indian wars. The first broke out in 1655 in New Amsterdam and extended to the Esopus and Long Island settlements. Five years later there was a serious outbreak at Esopus, which was aggravated when Stuyvesant sent some of the Indian captives to Curaçao as slaves. This incident rankled, and the Indians rose again, so it was May, 1664, before a general peace was signed.

The gradual encroachment of settlers from New England on territory claimed by the Dutch had been a source of trouble since the beginning of the colony. Rivalry over the fur trade and complaint from the English traders against the tariffs levied at New Amsterdam increased the ill feeling. Stuyvesant took up the quarrel vigorously. No decision was reached over the tariff and Indian trade disputes, but the question of boundaries was finally settled by the Treaty of Hartford in 1650. The last year of the Dutch regime in New Netherland was fraught with grave anxiety of Indian wars, rebellion and British invasion. Stuyvesant tried vainly to put the province in a state of defense, but on Aug. 29, 1664, was forced to surrender to an English fleet, which came to claim the province in the name of the Duke of York.

NEW ORLEANS, located 100 miles above the mouth of the Mississippi, where the river approaches nearest to Lake Pontchartrain, was founded by Bienville in 1718 as a strategic trading post, and became the capital of French Louisiana in 1722. The original town, now called the "vieux carré," developed slowly during the French and Spanish periods, being nearly destroyed by fires in 1788 and 1794. Following the fires, substantial buildings replaced the former flimsy structures, and by 1803 it was a small European type of city with 8000 population.

The rise of steamboats on the Western waters and the rapid developments of the interior made New Orleans the commercial and financial emporium of the entire Mississippi Valley and the second port of the United States in ante-bellum days, with a population of 160,000 in 1860. The rapid influx of American settlers and traders, Latin-American political refugees, and German, Irish and other European immigrants made ante-bellum New Orleans the most cosmopolitan and most foreign city in the country. There, Latin and American culture and vice flourished side by side, the city becoming noted for its French Opera, American Theater, quadroon balls, cafés, gambling houses, exchanges and its "wide open" character in general.

Located behind the Mississippi levees, it has been periodically threatened by the river and menaced by heavy rainfall; but the Bonnet Carré spillway adequately protects it from river inundation, and the world's greatest drainage system quickly disposes of surplus rainfall. In 1960 the population was 627,535.

NEW ORLEANS, BATTLE OF. The United States declared war upon Great Britain in June, 1812, but the contest did not threaten Louisiana until near its close. After Napoleon's abdication early in 1814, England was free to concentrate her energies upon the American war. A veteran army was despatched to attack the South and West, the home of the "War Hawks," leading proponents of the war. In the autumn of 1814 a British fleet of over fifty vessels, carrying 7500 soldiers under Sir Edward Packenham, appeared in the Gulf of Mexico preparatory to attacking New Orleans, the key to the entire Mississippi Valley. The defenses of the city had been neglected, since the war up to that time had been waged mainly on the Canadian border. Under threat of British attack, Gov. Claiborne undertook such defensive measures as he could with the limited means at his command. Gen. Andrew Jackson, who commanded the American army in the Southwest, reached New Orleans on Dec. 1, 1814, and immediately began preparations for defense.

Instead of coming up the Mississippi River as was expected, the superior British navy defeated the small American fleet on Lake Borgne, landing their troops on its border and marching them across the swamps to the banks of the Mississippi, a few miles below New Orleans. Jackson had succeeded in assembling a force of between 6000 and 7000 troops, mainly Kentucky, Tennessee and Louisiana militia, with a few regulars. After a few preliminary skirmishes late in December, 1814, the British withheld their attack until their full strength could be brought to bear. The decisive battle, lasting less than a half-hour, was fought on the morning of Jan. 8, 1815, when the British undertook to carry the American position by storm. So effective was the American defense that the British were completely repulsed, losing over 2000 men, of whom 289 were killed, including Gen. Packenham and most of the other higher officers. Due to the protection of their breastworks, the Americans lost only 71, of whom 13 were killed.

The British soon retired to their ships and departed.

New Orleans and the Mississippi Valley were saved from invasion. Coming two weeks after the treaty of peace, the battle had no effect upon the peace terms; but it did have a tremendous effect upon the political fortunes of Andrew Jackson, the "hero of New Orleans."

NEW ORLEANS, CAPTURE OF (1862). At the outbreak of the Civil War the Federal authorities recognized the strategic importance of seizing New Orleans, the commercial emporium of the entire Mississippi Valley and the second port of the United States. Because of pressing needs elsewhere and over-estimation of the strength of their defenses, the Confederates had failed to render the approaches to New Orleans impregnable. In the spring of 1862 a naval squadron under Admiral David G. Farragut, carrying an army commanded by Gen. Benjamin F. Butler, entered the lower Mississippi. The chief defenses against approach by river to New Orleans were Forts Jackson and St. Philip, about sixty miles below the city, between which had been stretched a heavy chain cable, supported upon rafts, with a secondary defense beyond it, consisting of a group of fire-rafts loaded with pine knots and some armored rams. After firing upon the forts for some days, Farragut succeeded in cutting the chain and passing the forts in the night, without any very serious damage to his fleet, and shortly thereafter he appeared before New Orleans. Gen. Mansfield Lovell had only 3000 Confederate troops to protect the city, and, realizing that resistance was useless, he withdrew to the northward, leaving the city to fall into the hands of the Federal forces on May 1, 1862.

NEW PLYMOUTH, COLONY OF, was founded by a group of about 100 English emigrants who came over on the *Mayflower* in 1620. The dominant element in this group consisted of religious dissenters who had separated from the Anglican Church because of their dissatisfaction with its doctrines and practices. Some of these Separatists had come from Leyden in the Netherlands, where they had been living for more than a decade since leaving their original homes in northern England to escape persecution and the religious contamination incident to association with their Anglican neighbors. After a brief sojourn in Amsterdam, they settled in Leyden, where they organized a flourishing church. Although they enjoyed religious freedom, they became dissatisfied in their new home. They were unwilling to give up the language and customs of England for those of Holland, had difficulty in making a comfortable living in a foreign land, and were disturbed over the enticements to worldliness and immorality to which their children were subjected. Accordingly, some of them (thirty-five in number) decided to join others of their coreligionists in England and go to the New World. Both groups sailed on the *Mayflower* from

Plymouth, England, Sept. 16, 1620. On Dec. 26, after five weeks spent in exploring Cape Cod, the *Mayflower* anchored in the harbor of what came to be Plymouth, Mass. The task of erecting suitable houses was rendered difficult by the lateness of the season, although the winter was a comparatively mild one. Nearly all of the Indians in the vicinity had been destroyed by pestilence and the few survivors gave no trouble. On the contrary, their deserted cornfields afforded the settlers quite an advantage. Partly owing to poor housing facilities, and largely because of the rundown condition of the emigrants as a result of lack of proper food on the voyage, there was great suffering the first winter and nearly half of their number died. By spring there had come a turn for the better, and in a few years the menace of a food shortage was permanently removed.

The capital for the undertaking was furnished by a group of London merchants. An agreement was entered into between these "adventurers" and the settlers whereby a sort of joint-stock company was formed. The arrangement proved unsatisfactory to both the adventurers and the planters, and in 1627 the former sold their interests to the latter and thus withdrew from the venture. From this time on the planters were the sole stockholders of the corporation which had become a colony.

During the first decade Plymouth was the only settlement, but gradually other villages were established and so the town of Plymouth widened into the colony of New Plymouth.

Before embarking for America the Pilgrims had received assurances from James I that they would not be molested in the practice of their religion. A patent was also received from the Virginia Company authorizing them to settle on its grant and enjoy the right of self-government. But as they had landed outside the limits of the Virginia Company this patent was of no avail. The settlers, therefore, had no title to their lands and no legal authority to establish a government. It was not long, however, before a valid title to the land was obtained in the form of patents issued (in 1621 and 1630) by the Council for New England. But the power to form a government was not conferred by these patents. The Pilgrims had, however, before landing organized themselves into a body politic by entering into a solemn covenant that they would make just and equal laws and would yield obedience to the same. This agreement, known as the Mayflower Compact, was signed by all the adult male settlers except eight, who were probably ill at the time. On the basis of this covenant a liberal government was founded for the colony. Laws were made by the General Court, which was at first a primary and later a representative assembly of one house, the members of which were chosen annually by popular election. Administrative and certain important judicial functions were performed by the governor and the assistants, who were elected each year by the "freemen," or qualified voters. On the death of the first governor, John Carver (April, 1621), William Bradford was chosen as his successor. He was continued in office by re-election for more than thirty years.

New Plymouth was not well adapted to agriculture, as there was a scarcity of cultivable land in the colony. Nor was the location of the settlement as favorable for a profitable business in fishing and fur trading as were those of the other Puritan colonies. Consequently, the Pilgrims did not play a leading role in the history of colonial New England although it was largely due to their initiative that the Congregational form of church government was adopted in that section. New Plymouth was quite overshadowed by its neighbors, Connecticut and Massachusetts Bay, and was finally (1691) absorbed by the latter.

NEW SOUTH is a general and somewhat indefinite phrase signifying the social and economic changes and developments since Reconstruction. While the phrase had been used before, universal acceptance followed the famous oration of Henry W. Grady, editor of the *Atlanta Constitution,* delivered before the New England Society of New York, in December, 1886.

NEW SWEDEN, COLONY OF. In March, 1638, two ships, *Kalmar Nyckel* and *Fogel Grip,* brought to the Delaware River 23 Swedish soldiers and two officers to establish the first and only Swedish colony in the New World. They built a fort on the shore of a small river emptying into the Delaware, which stream they named Christina (after their queen) Kill. The site of this first permanent settlement in the entire Delaware River Valley, including Delaware, New Jersey and Pennsylvania, is now within the boundaries of the city of Wilmington, Del. Having bought from the Indians a tract of land on the western side of the Delaware extending from Sankikan (Trenton, N. J.) to Cape Henlopen at the mouth of Delaware Bay, they claimed this territory for their country, calling it New Sweden.

In 1640 a second expedition arrived with supplies and new colonists, their first governor, Peter Hollandaer, and the first clergyman, Rev. Reorus Torkillus. Another expedition arrived in 1641 and a fourth in 1643, bringing a new governor, Johan Printz.

Printz started at once to extend his domain, building small forts on the eastern or New Jersey side of the Delaware, at Tinicum, near the present site of Philadelphia, at Upland (Chester, Pa.) and at the mouth of the Schuylkill River. More ships came and more colonists, the forests were cleared, farms cultivated, a village, Christinahamn, was laid out behind Fort Christina, their first establishment.

Johan Printz ruled New Sweden with despotic power. Military leader, as well as civil governor, law-giver, chief judge and head of all the colony's activities, he was supreme over the whole Delaware Valley south of Sankikan. He was "a man of brave size, weighing over 400 pounds," headstrong, tyrannical, rough, violent, overbearing, arrogant and arbitrary, but an intelligent man, a brave soldier, a strict disciplinarian, an able administrator. In all, he was a colonial governor whose character and achievements have been unjustly slighted. He monopolized the fur trade, driving out English who came from New Haven and Dutch who came from New Amsterdam seeking to establish trading posts and settlements. By successive expeditions the colony increased to nearly 400 people.

Peter Stuyvesant, Dutch governor of New Amsterdam, built a fort at Sandhook (New Castle, Del.) called Casimir. Printz's successor, Johan Rising, in 1653, captured it and again gave Sweden the control of the whole valley. This so angered the Dutch in Holland that in 1655 they sent a warship to New Amsterdam, where it was joined by six others. With 300 fighting men Stuyvesant came down from Manhattan, took his fort back again and, after a ten days' bloodless siege, captured also Fort Christina. Thus New Sweden disappeared from the map and a Dutch province took its place.

NEW YORK CITY. Was founded as New Amsterdam, July, 1625, when the little settlement planted by the Dutch West India Company on Nut (Governors) Island was transferred to the lower end of Manhattan. In accordance with the instructions of the company directors, a fort, pentagonal in shape, was built, and a street connecting the two gates was laid out, with a market place in the center, houses around it to be used as offices for the company and homes for the director and members of his council. In 1626, because of Indian troubles, the families settled at Fort Orange were moved to New Amsterdam. Two roads, now known as Whitehall and Pearl Streets, and two canals, now covered by the pavements of Broad and Beaver Streets, formed the limits of the settlement. A wagon road led from the fort along the present Broadway, Park Row and Fourth Avenue up to about East 14th Street, east of which lay the five company farms and that of the director of the province.

The inhabitants of New Amsterdam had no voice in the government of the settlement, which was administered by the director of the province and his council, who were appointed by the directors of the company. Implicit obedience to the orders and laws of the company was expected. Life in New Amsterdam in the early years of the settlement was far from pleasant. The directors were autocratic, members of the council quarreled with the director and with each other. Jonas Michaelius, the first ordained minister to New Netherland, who arrived in 1628, was sharply critical of conditions. He declared the people oppressed, the food supply scarce, and many of the inhabitants loafers who needed to be replaced by competent farmers and industrious laborers. Housing conditions were little better than at the beginning of the settlement. Although the population then numbered 270 men, women and children, the majority of the people were still lodged in primitive huts of bark, huddled near the protecting ramparts of the fort.

In spite of difficulties the town grew and made progress. A new fort, girded with stone, was built. A barracks for the soldiers, a bakery and more houses for company servants were constructed; and a wooden church to replace the loft of the horse mill, in which Michaelius had held services, was begun. Shortly afterward a house for Domine Bogardus, who had succeeded Michaelius, was built.

In 1637 the brutal and unwise Indian policy of Director Willem Kieft resulted in an Indian war, which threatened to wipe out the settlement. Peace was made in 1645, but when Peter Stuyvesant arrived in 1647 to succeed Kieft, he found New Amsterdam in a state of complete demoralization. New ordinances were passed to curb drunkenness in the town (Domine Backerus reported seventeen taphouses). Three street surveyors were appointed to remedy the deplorable conditions of the houses, streets and fences; and steps taken to raise money to repair the fort, finish the church and build a school.

In 1652, as a result of much popular agitation, Stuyvesant was instructed to give New Amsterdam a "burgher government." Accordingly, in February of the following year, a schout, two burgomasters and five schepens were appointed. These officials together constituted a court, which met once a week, had both civil and criminal jurisdiction, and continued to function until merged in the supreme court of the State of New York in 1895. The magistrates met in the Stadt Huis, which had originally been built by Kieft as a tavern. At first Stuyvesant claimed the right to preside. In 1654 the magistrates received the power, if permitted by the council, to levy taxes and to convey lands. A painted coat of arms, a seal and a silver signet were delivered to them with impressive ceremonies. In 1658 they were allowed to nominate their successors, and two years later the company granted the separation of the office of city schout, an office which had previously combined the duties of sheriff, prosecutor and president of the magistrates. In 1657 burgher rights were granted, and from that time on no merchant could do business, or craftsman ply his trade, without admission to the freedom of the city by the magistrates.

In 1655 an Indian war again threatened the city, but after some show of force a truce was patched up. A census taken in 1656 showed 120 houses and 1000 inhabitants in the city. From the earliest days New Amsterdam had a cosmopolitan character, Father Jogues reporting in 1644 that eighteen different languages were spoken in or about the town. New Amsterdam became New York City, 1664, taken by a squadron of English vessels under Capt. Richard Nicolls, who became the colonial governor, and served for four years. He changed the name to New York, honoring the Duke of York (later James II), brother of the reigning British monarch, Charles II. The city continued until the Revolution as the seat of government of New York colony. Francis Lovelace, the second governor, called the merchants of the town to meet once a week under the bridge across the Heere Graft, which was essentially the beginning of a merchants' exchange. That spot, at the crossing of Broad Street and Exchange Place, continued to be a meeting place for 250 years thereafter, the Curb Market finally developing in the street, where it functioned until it decided to erect its building and went under a roof in 1921. In 1670 Gov. Lovelace bought from the Indians Staten Island, destined, two centuries later, to become a borough of the city. In 1673 he inaugurated the first mail service (monthly) to Boston. On Aug. 9, 1673, during Lovelace's absence, a Dutch squadron entered the harbor, and the county sheriff surrendered the city to its commander. Anthony Colve was the Dutch governor until Feb. 19, 1674, when news came of the ending of the war between Holland and Great Britain, and the colony was returned to British rule.

In 1689 occurred the Leisler rebellion. During Leisler's rule, Peter Delanoy, the first mayor elected by popular vote of the freemen, served from Oct. 14, 1689, until March 20, 1691. The next popular election of a mayor did not take place until 1834. The streets were first lighted and a night watch established in 1697. The first great epidemic of yellow fever occurred in 1702. William Bradford, who had set up a printing press in 1693, published the first newspaper, the *New-York Gazette*, on Nov. 8, 1725. The first stage line to Philadelphia was established in 1730, and the first coach to Boston left the present Chatham Square, June 24, 1772. A fire department was organized in 1731, and in that same year Harlem, though at several miles' distance, was declared annexed to the city. New York became revolutionary in spirit as early as any part of America. With the passage of the Stamp Act in 1765, the Sons of Liberty were organized, and there was rioting in that year and the next. New York had its "tea party" in 1773, as did Boston, though a less spectacular one than the latter. At the beginning of the Revolution, the city, including the Bowery suburb, scarcely extended as much as a mile and a half up Manhattan Island from the Battery, or about one tenth of the full length of the island. Washington occupied it with a portion of his army in April, 1776, but his defeat in the battle of Long Island on Aug. 27 forced him to evacuate it, and it remained in the hands of the British until the close of the war. Some patriotic citizens fled from the city, many were imprisoned. On Nov.

23, 1776, a great fire swept through the heart of the city, destroying 500 buildings, or about one third of it. The British asserted that the fire was accidental, but America imputed it to their vandalism, and was greatly incensed by it. On Nov. 25, 1783, the city was formally evacuated by the British, and Washington led the American army down the Bowery Lane and Pearl Street to the waterfront amid scenes of tumultuous rejoicing. He said farewell to his officers at a dinner at Fraunces Tavern (still standing), originally built as the town residence of Etienne De-Lancey, a prominent Huguenot immigrant. Until well into the 19th century, Evacuation Day was as important a holiday in New York City as the Fourth of July.

The city was the capital of New York State from 1784 until 1797, when the seat of government was removed to Albany. In 1785 it became the capital of the confederated nation, and in 1789 of the new republic. Washington was sworn in as first President on the balcony of Federal Hall, and took up his residence at No. 1 Cherry Street, whose site is now occupied by one of the great towers of the Brooklyn Bridge. The first national Congress met in the city that year, but in the following year, the capital was removed to Philadelphia.

The first national census, taken in 1790, showed New York's population to be 33,131. Its growth in the next few decades was amazing. In 1810, with 96,373, it was already the nation's biggest city. In 1860 its population reached 813,669. In seventy years it had multiplied 24½ times. It became the nation's most important seaport. Immigration, mostly from the British Isles and Germany, played no small part in this rapid growth. The immigrants were coming far too rapidly to be assimilated, and before 1800 a slum district began to appear in what is now known as the lower East Side, where it still existed in the second half of the 20th century.

Serious fires occurred in 1778, 1796 and 1804, and on Dec. 16–17, 1835, the greatest conflagration in the city's history raged on the east side of the main business district, destroying 600 buildings, with a loss of $20,000,000. In 1845 another fire in somewhat the same locality swept away 300 buildings and 30 human lives, and caused a loss of $10,000,000.

The mayors were chosen by the board of aldermen or the common council until 1834, when they began to be elected by popular vote. In 1808 engineers plotted the city streets as far north as 155th Street, and made the mistake of establishing the streets running east and west only 200 feet apart, while the avenues running north and south are often from 800 to 875 feet apart, a process exactly the reverse of what it should be, and the principal cause of the great traffic problems of the 20th century. The city was blockaded by a British fleet in 1813. Two small stone blockhouses, erected during this war, still survive in Central and in Morningside Parks.

The city's first public water supply, pumped from wells and delivered to users through wooden pipes, was undertaken in 1799 by the Manhattan Company, organized by Aaron Burr. The city's great project by which water was brought from the Croton River, about thirty miles distant, through a large aqueduct, was opened in 1842. The Crystal Palace Exhibition of 1853, Tammany Hall's rise to power in the city government, the Draft Riots and the Tweed Ring scandals are treated in separate articles. The population passed the million mark before 1880 and by 1890 it was 1,441,216. In 1874 more than twenty square miles of territory north of the Harlem River, comprising the most of what is now the borough of the Bronx, was annexed. By the Legislative Act of 1896, what was known as "Greater New York" came into existence on Jan. 1, 1898. This included the existing City of New York (which was coextensive with New York County), Kings County (Brooklyn), Richmond County (all of Staten Island), practically all of Queens County and parts of Hempstead, East Chester and Pelham. Under the new charter, adopted in 1899, this territory of 359 square miles was divided into the boroughs of Manhattan, the Bronx, Brooklyn, Queens and Richmond. The borough of the Bronx was given a county government of its own in 1914. The greater city had in 1900 a population of 3,437,202. Robert A. Van Wyck was the first mayor of the new corporation.

Until the opening of the Brooklyn Bridge in 1883, the original New York (Manhattan) could be reached from New Jersey, Brooklyn and other parts of Long Island and Staten Island only by ferries. The creation of the greater city began to bring new connections rapidly. Two new bridges, the Williamsburg (1903) and Queensborough (1909), were opened across the East River and other bridges and tunnels followed shortly. In 1921 the Port of New York authority was created, which within a few years built the George Washington Bridge, the first to span the Hudson at or near New York (completed 1931), the Holland Tunnel and the Triboro Bridge.

New York has from very early days been the seat of a number of institutions of higher learning. Some of the largest are Columbia University, founded in 1754; New York University (1831); Fordham University (1841); College of the City of New York (1848); Manhattan College (1853); Hunter College (1870); and Barnard College (1889).

The population of New York City in 1960 was 7,781,957. Bigger still were the suburbs, with a population of 7,794,441.

NEW YORK COLONY AND STATE. *Duke of York's Proprietary* (1664–85) had its origin in the new nationalism of the Restoration Period. The passing of the Navigation Acts and the program to draw the colonies into a closer relationship with the mother country in the interests of mercantilism demanded the elimination of the Dutch as competitors on the American continent, where they had established themselves on lands which had been granted by the English Crown to the Council for New England. The king decided to conquer New Netherland and to bestow it upon his brother the Duke of York. After purchasing the claims of the Stirling heirs which included also northern Maine, the king conveyed to the Duke, in March, 1664, several months before the conquest, New Netherland and other scattered territories, a proprietary stretching from the Connecticut to the Delaware River and Bay, including the near-by islands of Martha's Vineyard, Nantucket and Long Island, and the region north of Gorges' Maine, between the St. Croix and the Pemaquid.

The Duke's charter created him lord proprietor with complete authority to rule his province unchecked by a representative assembly. In him was vested all legislative, executive and judicial power, subject only to appeal to the king. He delegated his authority to governors whom he carefully instructed as to policy. Though he had no faith in democratic government, he expected his governors to consider the well-being of the people. Regions preponderantly English like Long Island were governed by laws of neighboring colonies, drawn up in a code called the Duke's Laws. Liberty of conscience prevailed throughout the province. Two features of his government the people found hard to bear, his inordinate interest in revenue from the province and the absence of a representative assembly. Though he at first denied petitions for representation, he finally instructed his governor, Andros, to call an assembly, which met for a few sessions in 1683–85 and adopted a Charter of Liberties. The new institution came to an abrupt end with the ripening of plans for the Dominion of New England.

Rival claims and failure of the Duke to appreciate the potentialities of his new proprietary as a unit resulted in periodic dismemberment of the once princely domain. Even before the conquest of New Netherland, the Duke leased to his friends, Berkeley and Carteret, the rich farm lands of the Jerseys. Another piece was soon to go to Connecticut whose charter of 1662 overlapped the Duke's grant, since it gave jurisdiction over the west bank settlements, including those of the former New Haven colony. Long Island was likewise included in both grants. The Nicolls commission settled the dispute in 1667 by assigning Long Island to New York, but surrendering to Connecticut the lands west of the river to within twenty miles of the Hudson. The Duke, however, did not accept this decision as final. When his province was restored to him in 1674, after the Dutch conquest, he reopened the issue by instructing Gov. Andros to assume jurisdiction over western Connecticut. Andros marched to Saybrook with an armed force and asserted the Duke's authority there. Connecticut refused to recognize these claims and the

matter hung fire until 1687 when Connecticut with its boundaries of 1667 was incorporated into the Dominion of New England.

The Duke's possessions on the west bank of Delaware Bay were given to William Penn in 1682, probably in deference to the Duke's regard for Penn's father, Admiral Penn. To these lands the Duke had no strict legal title. They were not included in his charter, but from the time of the conquest of New Netherland, the Duke considered himself possessor by right of conquest of all lands taken from the Dutch, including those which they in turn had taken from the Swedes. Gov. Andros introduced the Duke's Laws there in 1676 and a little later created three counties, New Castle, Kent and Sussex. Penn, after receiving Pennsylvania, realized that he might be shut out from the ocean by the possessor of the territory to the south, along the west shore of the river and bay, and he therefore applied to the Duke for a grant. After some hesitation the Duke finally agreed. In 1682 he executed two leases, one for New Castle and the land within a radius of twelve miles, and the other for the land to the south as far as Cape Henlopen. The Duke then made an effort, perhaps at Penn's instigation, to obtain a royal grant, and received one on March 22, 1683. Though this charter appears on the patent rolls, it apparently was incomplete. Doubt as to its validity prompted James, after his accession to the throne, to grant Penn a royal charter, but he was prevented by his abdication.

The last sizable outlying section of the Duke's proprietary to go was Pemaquid, which, as the County of Cornwall, was added to the Dominion of New England in June, 1686. James, now king, apparently had no further interest in preserving the scattered pieces of his proprietary intact, but turned his attention to experimenting with dominion rule throughout the English provinces. In the belief that a more satisfactory colonial policy could be maintained by organizing the colonies into a few large units, the New England colonies were combined into a dominion, but, before a middle group of colonies could be formed into another unit, danger from French attack suddenly decided the king and the Lords of Trade in 1688 to add New York and New Jersey to the Dominion of New England. After the overthrow of the dominion in 1689 by revolutions in Boston and New York City, New York became a royal province of the regular type with the representative government which its people had so long desired.

Capture of New York (1673). During the summer of 1673 rumors of the approach of a Dutch squadron with a design of recapturing the city reached New York. Gov. Lovelace failed to take them seriously, however, and in July made a long-deferred visit to Gov. Winthrop of Connecticut, leaving Capt. Manning in charge at Fort James. On July 28 a fleet of

23 ships, under the joint command of Cornelius Evertsen, Jr., and Jacob Binckes, appeared off Sandy Hook. Manning, putting up as brave a front as possible, demanded of the Dutch why they came "in such a hostile manner," and hurriedly dispatched an express to Lovelace, in New Haven, begging him to return at once. The Dutch commanders replied they had come to take that which "was theyr own." Manning tried frantically to raise volunteers. On July 30 the fleet came within musket shot of the fort. Manning parleyed for delay until morning. He was given a respite of half an hour. When the time expired the Dutch fleet opened fire. The fort held out for four hours and then surrendered.

Colony of New York (1689–1776). The year 1689 was a time of anxiety, violence and unrest in the colony of New York. A declaration of war against France had followed the accession of William and Mary to the throne of England. A revolt in New England caused the arrest of Gov. Andros. His representative in New York, Capt. Francis Nicholson, fled and Capt. Jacob Leisler seized control of the government. Albany attempted to resist Leisler's authority, but the burning of Schenectady by the French and Indians in 1690 forced the magistrates to yield. The government of William III, too weak to attempt anything in America, had left the colonies to their own resources. In the spring of 1690, with the co-operation of Massachusetts, Leisler called a meeting of the northern colonies in New York City. An attack on Montreal was planned. The expedition was a failure, and Leisler with a tactlessness which spoiled all of his efforts attempted to throw the blame on Fitz-John Winthrop of Connecticut, who had been in command. The following spring, upon the arrival of Col. Sloughter, who had been commissioned governor of the province by William and Mary, Leisler and his chief associates were tried for treason and Leisler and Milbourne executed. Leisler and anti-Leisler factions continued, however, to disturb the colony for many years.

Fletcher, who succeeded Sloughter in 1692, interested himself energetically in the problems of defense and Indian relations. Acting on the advice of Peter Schuyler of Albany, he conciliated the Five Nations, and bound them to a renewed alliance with England. This alliance, which had become a cardinal point of British policy in New York, was further strengthened during the administration of Bellomont by the action of the Iroquois in conveying to the care of the king of England the western lands which they claimed by conquest. Bellomont was shocked by his predecessor's generosity in granting enormous tracts of land to favored individuals, and managed to have some of these grants set aside. An able man, and a friend of the small landowner, his administration was cut short by his death in 1701.

Lord Cornbury, who arrived in 1701, renewed the policy of making extravagant grants. His arrogance and corruption greatly antagonized the assembly, which had been slowly growing in power and importance, and hastened the contest over the power of the purse, which was to agitate the province throughout the remainder of the colonial period. A short respite was granted the colony between the peace of Ryswick in 1697 and the second (Queen Anne's) war with the French. Although New York furnished her quota of men and money requested by the home government, the influence of the Albany traders tended to keep the colony neutral, when not specifically asked to take action. This tendency to neutrality and the trade between Albany and Montreal was the occasion of bitter complaint from the New England colonies.

Gov. Robert Hunter, whose administration (1710–19) witnessed the close of the war, was one of the ablest of the royal governors. By skillful management he compromised with the assembly and was able to bring a reasonable amount of stability and peace to the colony. One of the major problems of his administration was that of the Palatine refugees, who had been brought over to make naval stores. This unfortunate enterprise strained Hunter's personal credit in caring for the refugees. Gov. Burnet inherited the Palatine problem, which was finally solved by the settlement of most of them on the Mohawk frontier to form a barrier against French attack.

The arrival of William Cosby as governor in 1732 witnessed the beginning of a period of violent popular agitation. Smarting under the accusations of maladministration printed in Peter Zenger's small newspaper, the *New York Weekly Journal,* Cosby ordered Zenger's arrest. In the trial that followed the principle that truth is the justification for making a public statement was established.

The French continued their encroachments on territory claimed by New York. In 1727 a fort was built by the British at Oswego to offset the rival French post at Niagara. In 1731 the French occupied Crown Point. Hostilities broke out again in 1744. George Clinton, then governor of New York, was a man of courage and ability, but possessed little tact. His furious feud with James DeLancey, chief justice of the province, caused a bitter fight over the conduct of the war and the appropriation of funds by the assembly. As a result, the only effective action taken by the colony was through the exertions on the western frontier of Sir William Johnson, who was able to exercise sufficient influence over the Six Nations to keep their friendship.

In 1754 DeLancey was acting head of the provincial government. He presided over the famous Albany Congress, and in the fourth and final war with the French which followed, he gave firm support to the king's commanders. In 1759 Amherst compelled the French to abandon Ticonderoga and Crown Point, and Johnson, assisted by 900 Indians, captured Niagara. Throughout the war until the reduction of Montreal by Amherst in 1760 the western frontier of New York suffered cruelly.

The conviction had been growing in America that taxation should originate only in the colonial assemblies. The passage of the Stamp Act in 1765 aroused a storm of opposition. In October delegates from nine colonies met in New York to protest, and the following spring the act was repealed. In 1767, however, the Townshend Acts, putting a duty on paint, paper and tea, were passed. In protest the merchants of New York signed a nonimportation agreement, boycotting British goods. To add to the discontent in New York the currency bill of 1769 was disallowed. The Sons of Liberty again became active, and in 1770 the disturbances came to a climax in the battle of Golden Hill. The duties on glass, paint and paper were repealed and the agitation died down until the fall of 1773. In January, 1774, a committee of correspondence was appointed to write to "our sister colonies." In April of that year a group of "Mohawks" threw eighteen cases of tea into the harbor. Local and state revolutionary committees took over the government of the colony. On July 9, 1776, the Provincial Congress of New York approved the Declaration of Independence, and on the following day declared that New York had begun its existence as a free state.

New York State. Following the recommendation of the Continental Congress on May 10, 1776, the Provincial Congress on May 27 declared New York's right to self-government and henceforth assumed that the royal provincial rule had come to an end. Finality to this new status was expressed in New York's adoption of the Declaration of Independence on July 9. A convention proceeded to frame a new state constitution which was accepted by the legislature on April 20, 1777. The election of George Clinton as the first state governor was announced on July 9 and the new legislative bodies met two months later. Meanwhile, the continuation of the colonial courts and local government was authorized. On Feb. 6, 1778, New York joined the Confederation of the United States and, to perfect the new "league of friendship," ceded its western lands to Congress. A decade later the state ratified the national Constitution by a narrow margin after a bitter struggle.

Among the serious problems confronting New York were boundaries. By the Treaty of Hartford in 1786 New York's sovereignty over 19,000 square miles in the western part of the state was acknowledged by Massachusetts which retained a pre-emptive right to the land. The old dispute over Vermont was settled in 1790 when New York recognized Vermont's independence in return for a payment of $30,000. The remaining boundaries were also amicably adjusted. The feudal land system in the older counties, which gave rise to antirent riots, was not

adjusted until the adoption of the Constitution of 1846.

New York adopted the Federal Constitution July 26, 1788, becoming the eleventh state.

NEWBURGH ADDRESSES (March, 1783). Revolutionary officers, long unpaid, suspected, after Yorktown, the inability or disinclination of Congress to settle their claims before demobilization. Respectful memorials begging relief availed nothing. At Newburgh (N. Y.) winter quarters, exasperated officers were anonymously summoned to meet on March 11, to consider measures redressing grievances. An eloquent, unsigned address was circulated, urging direct action—an appeal from "the justice to the fears of government." Coercion of Congress was pointedly suggested. Washington, who was present in camp, with characteristic firmness intervened, denounced the "irregular invitation" and called a representative meeting for the 15th. A second anonymous address from the same pen then appeared, less vehement in tone. The Commander in Chief met a delegation and advised patience and confidence in the good faith of Congress. His enormous influence calmed the agitation, resolutions approving his counsel and reprobating the addresses being adopted. Maj. John Armstrong, Jr., a brilliant young soldier on Gen. Gates' staff, afterward general, minister to France and Secretary of War, was the writer of the two papers. Washington later expressed belief that his motives were patriotic, if misguided. Armstrong, writing in the *United States Magazine* (1823), admitted his authorship.

NEWPORT, R. I. Founded in 1639 by William Coddington, an Antinomian seeker after the truth preached by Anne Hutchinson, Newport was an ideal haven for the persecuted, welcoming Quakers as early as 1657 and Jews as early as 1658. An important seaport in the 18th century, Newport was ruined by the Revolutionary War but revived in the 19th century to become a summer resort for Southern planters and a quiet paradise for intellectuals like the novelist Henry James and the painter John LaFarge. After the Civil War it became *the* summer resort for millionaires.

Its architectural heritage is unique. In no other community in the United States are so many choice buildings to be seen in so small an area; from the 18th century to the 20th our greatest architects have collaborated to make Newport an unparalleled architectural museum. In 1945, with the founding of the Preservation Society of Newport County under the presidency of Maude A. K. Wetmore, an intelligent campaign was launched to preserve this heritage. Certain colonial structures were restored and the Breakers, the gigantic palace of Cornelius Vanderbilt II designed by Richard Morris Hunt (1892–95), has been opened to the public in the summer. By the fall of 1960, half a million visitors had explored the interior of the Breakers.

The earliest designer to contribute to the distinction of Newport was the local builder Richard Munday, who created Trinity Church (1725) and the Old Colony House (1739). Later came Peter Harrison, America's first architect, who was responsible for the Redwood Library (1748) and Congregation Jeshuat Israel (1759–63). In the romantic period A. J. Davis designed Malbone, a Gothic castle for Prescott Hall, and Richard Upjohn, later famous for Trinity Church, New York, fashioned the Gothic cottage of George Noble Jones.

After the Civil War came H. H. Richardson, who planned the greatest of all his houses for W. Watts Sherman (1874–76). In 1960 this was serving as an old people's home for the Baptist Church. Still later came McKim, Mead & White who endowed Newport with many of the most distinguished examples of their early shingle style. The Casino (1881) must be mentioned, as must the residences of Isaac Bell, Jr. (1883) and Robert Goelet (1883). Among the palaces of McKim, Mead & White at the resort, Rosecliff for Herman Oelrichs (1902) and the residence of E. D. Morgan (1891) cannot be overlooked. Besides the Breakers, Hunt designed Belcourt for O. H. P. Belmont (*ca.* 1890), Marble House for the W. K. Vanderbilts (1893–95) and Ochre Court (1889–91) for Ogden Goelet. This last palace was serving as the headquarters of Salve Regina College in 1960.

NEWSPAPERS. *Colonial Period.*

The first newspaper in the American colonies, entitled *Publick Occurrences,* was published in Boston, Sept. 25, 1690, but, after a single issue, was suppressed by the authorities. The first regularly published newspaper was *The Boston News-Letter,* established in Boston, April 24, 1704. This was followed by other papers in Boston, then in Philadelphia, New York, Annapolis, Charleston, Newport and Williamsburg, all before 1750. By April, 1775, there were 37 newspapers in eleven of the colonies on the Atlantic seaboard. The colonial newspaper was a small folio weekly, almost invariably of four pages, including foreign news on the first page, domestic news on the second, local news on the third and advertisements on the fourth. Political news and the proceedings of legislative bodies aroused a lively interest, and important documents and letters were often quoted at length, providing a means of disseminating information throughout the colonies, which more than any one cause welded the people together in their resistance to the mother country. Local news was negligible, and in fact the greatest amount of local information comes from the advertisements. Yet the history of no town could be written without access to its file of newspapers. Essays and poetry filled a considerable portion of the papers, especially the *Pennsylvania Gazette,* published by Benjamin Franklin in Philadelphia. Because of the scarcity of all but theological books, secular literature was almost unread in the colonies except through the newspapers. Outside of the Bible and the almanac, the newspaper was the only printed matter found in most colonial families.

National Period. In the period immediately following the close of the Revolutionary War, the newspaper press of the United States found innumerable opportunities for expansion. The extent of this expansion is indicated by the fact that where about 100 newspaper enterprises had been undertaken in seventy years under the colonial governments before the Revolution and about fifty more had made a beginning during the course of the war, some 500 new newspapers were started within the original thirteen states in the seventeen years between the treaty of peace and the end of the century. And in the first two decades of the new century about 700 more newspapers were started within the same area. Altogether, in less than forty years of independence, we find some 1200 such enterprises, to contrast with the 150 newspapers established during eighty years before independence.

But the expansion of the American newspaper press was by no means confined to the area of the thirteen original states. The Definitive Treaty of Peace in 1783 made available for settlement the vast "Western Country" between the Appalachian Mountains and the Mississippi River, and the resultant waves of westward migration opened up wholly new fields for newspaper enterprise. The new settlements in the West had their distinctive problems and aspirations, and it became the function of their newspapers to give expression to the life of the frontier and to assist in molding the institutions of pioneer communities.

The first newspaper west of the mountains was the *Pittsburgh Gazette,* established July 29, 1786, by John Scull and Joseph Hall, two young printers from Philadelphia. The moving spirit of this enterprise was Hugh Henry Brackenridge, a lawyer and former Revolutionary officer, who had visited the site of Pittsburgh and visualized its possibilities. A newspaper, he believed, was essential to the development of the recently plotted town, and it was at his instigation that Scull and Hall moved westward with their printing equipment.

A patriotic resident of Kentucky, John Bradford, a surveyor by profession with no previous knowledge of the printing craft, brought the press into his community as a measure of public service. Representatives of the "District of Kentucky" were in convention for the purpose of effecting separation from Virginia and attaining independent statehood. There was need of a newspaper to publish the deliberations of the convention to the widely scattered citizens of Kentucky. No Eastern printer would accept the invitation to venture so far into the wilderness, so Bradford undertook the task. He sent to Pittsburgh for press and type and founded the *Kentucke Gazette* at Lexington, on Aug. 11, 1787.

As new areas were settled and territorial governments were set up, the means of printing the laws and other official documents, with newspapers for the information of the public, were primary essentials. It was to meet such demands that George Roulstone and Robert Ferguson left North Carolina to establish the *Knoxville Gazette* at Hawkins Courthouse, now Rogersville, Tenn., on Nov. 5, 1791, nearly a year before Knoxville, the intended site of their operations as public printers for Tennessee, had even been laid out. Similarly, William Maxwell, after a brief career as a printer in Kentucky, moved across the Ohio to establish the *Centinel of the North-Western Territory* at Cincinnati on Nov. 9, 1793. In 1804 Elihu Stout, who had been trained as a printer in Kentucky, moved to Vincennes and there became public printer for Indiana Territory, and established the *Indiana Gazette* on July 31. On July 12, 1808, Joseph Charless, who had been a printer in Philadelphia and later for some years in Kentucky, founded the *Missouri Gazette* at St. Louis, while that region was still a part of Louisiana Territory. And Matthew Duncan, another printer from Kentucky, answered the call of the governor of Illinois Territory and set up his press at Kaskaskia, where he began the *Illinois Herald* in May, 1814.

Meanwhile, an attempt had been made to publish a newspaper at Detroit in 1809—the *Michigan Essay,* of which only one issue is known to have been printed. The newspaper press of Michigan did not make a successful beginning until July 25, 1817, when John P. Sheldon and Ebenezer Reed, both printers from the State of New York, founded the *Detroit Gazette.*

In a widely different part of the "Western Country," the pioneer newspaper in the Mississippi Territory was the *Mississippi Gazette,* established, according to all available evidence, by Benjamin M. Stokes at Natchez late in 1799 or early in 1800. The history of the newspaper press in Alabama dates from May 23, 1811, when Samuel Miller and John B. Hood began the *Mobile Centinel* at Fort Stoddert, being unable at the time to enter Mobile itself.

All in all, the "Western Country," including Missouri, gave birth to about 250 newspapers before 1821. The mortality rate of these enterprises, however, was exceedingly high. Few survived more than a few years, and many perished within a few months or even weeks. But each represented a great amount of pioneering effort in the face of innumerable difficulties, and each testifies to the laudable intentions, at least, of its founder to serve the needs of a frontier community while struggling to make an often inadequate living for himself and his family.

Until after the Civil War the typical American newspaper, especially outside of the larger cities, was printed on one sheet folded to make four pages. As long as they had to be printed on flat-bed platen presses, their dimensions were limited to the size of the sheet that such presses could accommodate, and pages of about 12 by 18 inches were the rule. The contents of those little papers were meager. There was little if any strictly local news. Letters from correspondents in other places and from local subscribers, extracts from other newspapers received in exchange and especially their foreign news, occasionally some legislative acts or local ordinances, legal notices, a bit of commercial news, with short poems, anecdotes or literary extracts as "fillers"—this was the typical reading matter. A presidential or a gubernatorial message might give occasion for the printing of an additional half-sheet or an "extra." There was but little editorial comment at first, but by 1820 the press was becoming markedly partisan and free expression of editorial opinion was the rule. By 1830 the introduction of the cylinder press with steam power made larger sheets possible, and there was an increase in the amount and variety of reading matter. Also there was more opportunity for editorial expression, and the newspapers gave themselves wholeheartedly to political, religious and even personal controversy, often of the bitterest and most vindictive nature.

Advertising in the early newspapers was inconspicuous. There was no attempt at display, and advertisements as a rule would run for months with no change in copy. If other matter pressed for space, advertisements were simply dropped to make way for it. Although advertising was a source of revenue, it seems to have been rather incidental in the earlier years of our newspapers.

The limitations of the hand-operated flat-bed presses, together with relatively high costs of paper, kept circulations within a few hundred copies except in the large centers, where a thousand or so was a notably large circulation until the means of production had improved. Income from subscriptions and advertising was often insufficient to maintain the printer, who also did job printing, printed and sold books, kept a book store or sold general merchandise. Distribution of newspapers was a problem, and innumerable early publishers were also postmasters. There was keen rivalry for the public printing as an important and dependable source of revenue.

The cities demanded more frequent news service, and even in colonial days there were semiweeklies. Some of these became triweeklies, and just at the close of the Revolution a need was felt for a daily in Philadelphia. Benjamin Towne, in May, 1783, began publishing there the *Pennsylvania Evening Post and Daily Advertiser.* This was followed in September, 1784, by the *Pennsylvania Packet and Daily Advertiser* of John Dunlap and David C. Claypoole. Also in 1784 a daily was begun in Charleston, S. C., and in February and March, 1785, two dailies were started in New York City within a few days of each other, including the *Daily Advertiser* by Francis Childs, the first daily newspaper to start as such without a previous history as a weekly, semiweekly, or tri-weekly. In 1790 there were eight daily newspapers in the country; in 1820 there were forty-two.

The first Sunday newspaper was the Baltimore *Weekly Museum* in 1797. It ran for only a few weeks. Somewhat more successful was the New York *Observer*, which started in 1809 and continued for about two years. These papers were both weeklies, of eight pages in magazine format. Sunday papers were severely condemned and did not become at all common until after the Civil War.

Also bitterly denounced by the more conservative press were the first "penny" papers. The New York *Sun* was the first to succeed with a one-cent newspaper in 1833. It competed with old-established papers which sold for six cents and it featured news that appealed to the common people but which the older papers ignored as beneath their notice. With the cheap newspaper also appeared the newsboy, to hawk the papers on the streets.

Improved means of production rapidly changed newspaper history. The first steam-power press in the United States appeared in 1822, but power-driven presses were not in common use until the 1830's. The first cylinder press was imported into the country in 1824; it made possible the use of a much larger sheet of paper than had previously been possible, as well as a much greater speed of production. A rotary press, with the type ingeniously fitted to its cylinder, made its appearance in 1846. Stereotyping had come into use in the 1830's, but it was not until 1861 that curved stereotypes could successfully be fitted to the cylinders of the rotary presses. Paper was always cut into sheets for feeding into the press sheet by sheet until 1863, when paper began to be delivered to the pressroom in rolls. Roll-fed rotary presses were in use by 1871, folders were added to the presses in 1876. Rotary presses were next assembled in gangs, each press producing its own part of a many-paged newspaper, all the parts being assembled and folded at the delivery point.

Another revolutionary development was the appearance of wood-pulp paper about 1870, to take the place of the expensive rag papers. The general use of newsprint made from wood pulp effected a startling reduction in the cost of production of a newspaper.

Telegraphic news first found its way into the news columns about 1844. Syndicated matter sold to newspapers all over the country in stereotyped form known as "boilerplate" appeared in the 1870's. The new process of photoengraving made its debut in newspapers in March, 1873, when the New York *Daily Graphic* printed the first line engraving produced by that process. In 1880 the same newspaper printed the first halftone made direct from a photograph.

In spite of numerous attempts to perfect a mechanism for setting type, all type was set by hand until July, 1886, when the New York *Tribune* made the first practical use of Ottmar Mergenthaler's linotype. With later improvements, the linotype entirely superseded the hand composition of single types for body matter of newspapers, and invention of the monotype and Ludlow greatly facilitated the setting of display heads and advertising.

Among the latest developments in the newspaper field are the use of the rotogravure process for pictorial supplements, the wide adoption of comic sections printed in color and the printing of color for advertising or editorial features on the regular news pages of weekday issues.

But with the rapid development in recent years of mechanical facilities for newspaper production, the capital investment in a modern newspaper plant has enormously increased.

There follows a list of the first newspapers established in each state and the District of Columbia, with the dates of their establishment, and the names of their printers or publishers:

ALABAMA
1811: May 23. Fort Stoddert: *Mobile Centinel.* Samuel Miller and John B. Hood

ARIZONA
1859: March 3. Tubac: *Weekly Arizonian.* William Wrightson, publisher; Edward E. Cross, editor; Jack Sims and George Smithson, printers

ARKANSAS
1819: Nov. 20. Arkansas Post: *Arkansas Gazette.* William Edward Woodruff

CALIFORNIA
1846: Aug. 15. Monterey: *Californian.* Walter Colton and Robert Semple

COLORADO
1859: April 23. Denver ("Cherry Creek"): *Rocky Mountain News.* William Newton Byers

CONNECTICUT
1755: April 12. New Haven: *Connecticut Gazette.* James Parker

DELAWARE
1762: Wilmington: *Wilmington Courant.* James Adams. (This newspaper is known from tradition only and was perhaps never published.)
1785: June. Wilmington: *Delaware Gazette.* Jacob A. Killen

DISTRICT OF COLUMBIA
1789: Feb. 12. Georgetown: *Times, and Patowmack Packet.* Charles Fierer

FLORIDA
1783: April ? Saint Augustine: *East Florida Gazette.* John and William Charles Wells

GEORGIA
1763: April 7. Savannah: *Georgia Gazette.* James Johnston

NEWSPAPERS

IDAHO

1862: Aug. ? Lewiston: *Golden Age*. Alexander S. Gould

ILLINOIS

1814: May. Kaskaskia: *Illinois Herald*. Matthew Duncan

INDIANA

1804: July 31. Vincennes: *Indiana Gazette*. Elihu Stout

IOWA

1836: May 11. Dubuque: *Du Buque Visitor*. John King, editor; William Cary Jones, printer

KANSAS

1835: March 1. Shawnee Baptist Mission: *Siwinowe Kesibwi* (The Shawnee Sun). Johnston Lykins, editor; Jotham Meeker, printer (a semimonthly newspaper in the Shawnee Indian language)

1854: Sept. 15. Leavenworth: *Kansas Weekly Herald*. William H. Adams

KENTUCKY

1787: Aug. 11. Lexington: *Kentucke Gazette*. John and Fielding Bradford

LOUISIANA

1794: March ? New Orleans: *Moniteur de la Louisiane*. Louis Duclot

MAINE

1785: Jan. 1. Falmouth (Portland): *Falmouth Gazette*. Benjamin Titcomb and Thomas Baker Wait

MARYLAND

1727: Sept. Annapolis: *Maryland Gazette*. William Parks

MASSACHUSETTS

1690: Sept. 25. Boston: *Publick Occurrences* (one issue only). Benjamin Harris, publisher; Richard Pierce, printer

1704: April 24. Boston: *Boston News-Letter*. John Campbell, publisher; Bartholomew Green, printer

MICHIGAN

1809: Aug. 31. Detroit: *Michigan Essay* (one issue only). James M. Miller

1817: July 25. Detroit: *Detroit Gazette*. John P. Sheldon and Ebenezer Reed

MINNESOTA

1849: April 28. Saint Paul: *Minnesota Pioneer*. James M. Goodhue

MISSISSIPPI

1799: Natchez: *Mississippi Gazette*. Benjamin M. Stokes.

MISSOURI

1808: July 12. Saint Louis: *Missouri Gazette*. Joseph Charless

MONTANA

1864: Aug. 27. Virginia City: *Montana Post*. John Buchanan, editor and proprietor; Marion M. Manner, printer. (Preceded, probably as early as 1863, by several issues of newsletters printed at Bannack and Virginia City.)

NEBRASKA

1854: Nov. 15. Belleview: *Nebraska Palladium*. Thomas Morton, publisher; D. E. Reed & Co., editors and proprietors

NEVADA

1858: Dec. 18. Genoa: *Territorial Enterprise*. William L. Jernegan and Alfred James

NEW HAMPSHIRE

1756: Oct. 7. Portsmouth: *New-Hampshire Gazette*. Daniel Fowle

NEW JERSEY

1765: Sept. 21. Woodbridge: *Constitutional Courant* (one issue only). "Andrew Marvel," pseudonym for William Goddard

1776: Sept. 21. Newark: *New-York Gazette* (previously published in New York City). Hugh Gaine

1777: Dec. 5. Burlington: *New-Jersey Gazette*. Isaac Collins

NEW MEXICO

1834: Santa Fe: *El Crepúsculo de la Libertad* (The Dawn of Liberty). Antonio Barreiro, editor and publisher; press of Ramon Abreú; Jesús María Baca, printer

1847: Sept. 10. Santa Fe: *Santa Fe Republican*. Oliver P. Hovey and E. T. Davies

NEW YORK

1725: Nov. 8. New York: *New-York Gazette*. William Bradford

NORTH CAROLINA

1751: July ? New Bern: *North-Carolina Gazette*. James Davis

NORTH DAKOTA

1864: July 7. Fort Union: *Frontier Scout*. Company I, 30th Wisconsin Volunteers, proprietors; S. C. Winegar and ? Goodwin, publishers

OHIO

1793: Nov. 9. Cincinnati: *Centinel of the North-Western Territory*. William Maxwell

OKLAHOMA

1844: Sept. 26. Talequah: *Cherokee Advocate* (in Cherokee and English). William Potter Ross, editor

OREGON

1846: Feb. 5. Oregon City: *Spectator*. Oregon Printing Association; William G. T'Vault, editor; John Fleming, printer

PENNSYLVANIA

1719: Dec. 22. Philadelphia: *American Weekly Mercury*. Andrew Bradford and John Copson

RHODE ISLAND

1732: Sept. 27. Newport: *Rhode-Island Gazette*. James Franklin

SOUTH CAROLINA

1732: Jan. 8. Charleston: *South-Carolina Gazette*. Thomas Whitmarsh

SOUTH DAKOTA

1858: June ? Sioux Falls. *Dakotah Democrat*. Samuel J. Albright

TENNESSEE

1791: Nov. 5. Rogersville: *Knoxville Gazette*. George Roulstone and Robert Ferguson

TEXAS
  1819: Aug. 14. Nacogdoches: *Texas Republican.* Horatio Bigelow, editor; Eli Harris, printer

UTAH
  1850: June 15. Salt Lake City: *Deseret News.* Willard Richards, editor and publisher; Horace K. Whitney and Brigham H. Young, printers

VERMONT
  1780: Dec. 14. Westminster: *Vermont Gazette and Green Mountain Post-Boy.* Judah Padock Spooner and Timothy Green IV

VIRGINIA
  1736: Aug. 6. Williamsburg: *Virginia Gazette.* William Parks

WASHINGTON
  1852: Sept. 11. Olympia: *Columbian.* James W. Wiley and Thornton F. McElroy

WEST VIRGINIA
  1790: Nov. 15? Shepherdstown: *Potowmac Guardian.* Nathaniel Willis

WISCONSIN
  1833: Dec. 11. Navarino (Green Bay): *Green-Bay Intelligencer.* Albert G. Ellis and John V. Suydam

WYOMING
  1863: June 24. Fort Bridger: *Daily Telegraph.* Hiram Brundage

NEZ PERCÉ WAR (1877). In June, 1877, southern Nez Percés defied efforts of the Government to deprive them of their reservation in the Wallowa Valley of Oregon. Gen. O. O. Howard marched against them but found in Joseph, their chief, an amazingly able opponent. The Nez Percés defeated the troops at White Bird Canyon, Idaho, June 17, and held their own at the Clearwater River, July 11.

Seeing he could not continue to hold off the troops, Joseph, late in July, led his people across the Bitter Root Mountains. Evading a small fort he turned south. Gen. John Gibbon surprised him on the Big Hole River, Mont., Aug. 9, but was sharply defeated. Joseph continued south, almost trapping Howard at Camas Meadows, then turned north through Yellowstone Park. He beat off Col. Samuel D. Sturgis at Canyon Creek, Mont., Sept. 13, and marching northward, reached the Bear Paw Mountains, where, June 30, Gen. Nelson A. Miles surrounded him and forced his surrender.

In this remarkable campaign Joseph, with only 300 warriors, opposed 5000 soldiers, and actually met in battle 2000, of whom he killed or wounded 266. His own loss, including many women and children, was 239. He marched 2000 miles through enemy country, carrying his noncombatants, and came within thirty miles of his goal, the Canadian border.

NIAGARA, CARRYING PLACE OF. Passage by water between lakes Ontario and Erie being obstructed by the great falls, a portage road of fourteen miles in length on the east side of the Niagara River was maintained by the French. In 1720 Louis Thomas de Joncaire, who was appointed master of the portage, having obtained permission from the Senecas, constructed the Magazin Royal, a trading house of bark surrounded by a palisade, at the lower landing of the portage, now Lewiston, N. Y. This storehouse of the French trade was occupied by the elder Joncaire until his death in 1739. Realizing the importance of this road, which was the means of communication between the posts below the falls and the upper lakes as well as the coveted Ohio region, Daniel de Joncaire, who had succeeded his father, erected Fort Little Niagara in 1751 at the upper landing. This was a palisaded post on the east shore of the river at the head of the portage road. The thoroughfare facilitated transportation of supplies destined for the new posts and those already established to the south and west. Although the English had established a post at Oswego they were prevented from entering the upper lakes.

Fort Little Niagara was destroyed by its commandant July 7, 1759, when the British attacked Fort Niagara. After becoming masters of the portage, the British fully realized its importance, and in 1764 received from the Senecas by treaty the full right to its possession. Its importance was demonstrated in the relief of Detroit, during Pontiac's War, and in control of the upper lakes until relinquished, under the Jay Treaty, in 1796.

NIAGARA, FORT. Permission having been obtained from the Senecas by the French, a stone castle was built on the eastern shore of Niagara River at Lake Ontario in 1726, six and one-half miles north of the Niagara Carrying Place. Palisades, ramparts and other buildings soon followed and this post became the principal guard of the coveted gateway to the rich fur lands in the West. A projected attack by the English under Gen. Shirley in 1757 failed. Two years later, a force of British and Indians under Generals Prideaux and Johnson besieged the fortress. Prideaux was killed and Sir William Johnson, succeeding to the command, captured the post on July 25. As a British fortress, it was the scene of several Indian treaties, and during the Revolution the irregulars under Butler and Johnson issued from its gates bound on their devastating forays. After the war, the surrounding territory was governed from Niagara until the fortress was relinquished to the American troops in August, 1796, in accordance with the Jay Treaty. Captured by the British on Dec. 19, 1813, it was returned to the United States under the Treaty of Ghent.

NIAGARA, GREAT INDIAN COUNCIL AT (1764). Sir William Johnson notified all of the rebellious Indian nations of the intended expeditions of the English under Bradstreet and Bouquet, requesting those desirous of making peace to meet him at Niagara, in July. In response, deputations including

Ottawas, Hurons, Menominee, Chippewa, Iroquois and others began to arrive at Fort Niagara. By the time the council convened on July 9, 2060 Indians were assembled—the largest number ever gathered together for a peace conference. On the 18th of July a treaty was concluded with the Hurons which ceded lands in their country lying on both sides of the strait to Lake St. Clair. The Senecas who arrived later signed a treaty on Aug. 6, which ceded to the Crown the four-mile strip on each side of the Niagara River, and gave the islands above the falls to Sir William Johnson. The other nations made no formal treaties, declaring they had come only to renew their friendship.

NIAGARA CAMPAIGNS (1812–14). On Oct. 13, 1812, Gen. Van Rensselaer crossed the Niagara River and attacked the British at Queenston, but lack of reinforcements finally caused the Americans to retire. On May 27, 1813, Col. Scott, assisted by Chauncey's fleet, captured Fort George, and the British abandoned the entire Niagara frontier to the American troops. Gen. McClure, destroying Fort George and Newark on Dec. 10, retreated to Fort Niagara. The British captured Fort Niagara on the 19th, and burned the villages of Youngstown, Lewiston and Manchester. Again crossing the river on Dec. 30, they defeated the Americans at Black Rock, burning that settlement and the village of Buffalo. The Americans, under Generals Brown and Scott, captured Fort Erie, July 3, 1814, and marching north, defeated the enemy at Chippewa on the 5th. After the battle of Lundy's Lane on the 25th, with both sides claiming victory, the Americans withdrew to Fort Erie. The British army under Lt. Col. Drummond arrived before the fortress, Aug. 1, and began a siege which was raised, Sept. 17, by the sortie of Gen. Porter's volunteers. This was the last important engagement in the campaigns on the Niagara.

NICARAGUAN CANAL PROJECT, for an interoceanic waterway along the San Juan River and Lake Nicaragua, has long been considered. A Spanish engineer first surveyed the route in the 18th century. Independent Central America was interested and Napoleon III considered the project. The route was the object of six treaties between the United States and Nicaragua during the 19th century, as well as of a treaty and an arbitration between Nicaragua and Costa Rica. England had claims which were considered in the negotiation of the Clayton-Bulwer (1850) and the Hay-Pauncefote (1901) treaties. The Nicaraguan Canal Association, an American corporation, made a contract with Nicaragua in 1887 to build a canal, and the Maritime Canal Co. was formed to carry it out. After a survey, construction was undertaken but suspended when funds could not be secured. The U. S. Government in 1895 began investigations and received a favorable report on the

project from the Ludlow Commission. In 1897–99 the Isthmian Canal Commission made a complete survey and report. By the Hay-Corea (1900) and the Sanchez-Merry (1901) protocols with Nicaragua and the Hay-Calvo with Costa Rica (1900) steps were taken by the United States looking toward a Nicaraguan canal. Political and other factors resulted in the adoption of the Panama route, and the Nicaraguan project was postponed. It, however, played an important part in the relations between the United States and Nicaragua after 1910. The Bryan-Chamorro Treaty (1914) gave the United States an option on the route. Interest in this project was given by President Coolidge in 1927 as the reason for the return of the marines to Nicaragua. A new survey of the Nicaraguan route by army engineers was authorized by Congress (March 2, 1929). The report (1931) was favorable to a Nicaraguan canal whenever the Panama Canal should become inadequate; hence, interest in a second interoceanic canal continues.

NICOLET, EXPLORATIONS OF. The personal explorations of Champlain terminated with his voyage to Georgian Bay and Huronia in 1615–16. Soon thereafter he adopted the policy of selecting promising youths to send among the Indians, to master, by such residence, the lore of the American wilderness.

Jean Nicolet was a native of Cherbourg who came to Canada in 1618 and was immediately sent by Champlain to Allumettes Island in the Ottawa River. After a two-year apprenticeship here, he was assigned to the distant Nipissing, living northward of the lake which bears their name. Here he remained several years, sharing the life of the natives and keeping, for Champlain's benefit, a careful memoir of his observations.

In 1633 he was called back to civilization and appointed interpreter at Three Rivers. From here, the following year, he was despatched in search of the "People of the Sea" who were at war with the Huron tribe, and who were surmised to have some connection with the realm of Tartary, which Marco Polo had described.

No direct record of Nicolet's voyage remains. Chiefly from contemporary Jesuit reports we learn that he journeyed by the Ottawa River north to Georgian Bay, passed through the Straits of Mackinac, and skirted the coast of Lake Michigan as far as Green Bay. Thereby he became the first known white visitor to Michigan and Wisconsin and the discoverer of Lake Michigan.

Upon this achievement his fame chiefly rests. From the scanty contemporary sources, several modern historians have spun tales of the voyage which are largely fanciful; the solid achievement of Nicolet stands in need of no embellishment.

NINE-POWER PACT, between the United States, Belgium, the British Empire, China, France, Italy,

Japan, the Netherlands and Portugal, was concluded at the Washington Naval Conference on Feb. 6, 1922. Japan's "Twenty-one Demands" on China in 1915 and the Japanese "Monroe Doctrine" had created a delicate international situation impairing the territorial integrity of China and endangering the Open Door principle.

In order to stabilize conditions in the Far East and to safeguard the rights and interests of China, the powers agreed to respect her sovereignty, independence, and territorial and administrative integrity, maintain the principle of the Open Door, and refrain from seeking special rights or privileges for their own citizens. The pact was an international guarantee of the Open Door and China's integrity, and effected (1923) the cancellation of the Lansing-Ishii Agreement of 1917.

Completely disregarding the treaty, Japan in 1931 seized Manchuria. Protesting, the United States proclaimed the Stimson nonrecognition doctrine (1932). Following Japan's invasion of China in 1937, the Brussels Conference (November, 1937) censured Japan and reaffirmed the principles of the pact. Refusing to recognize Japan's "special position" in China, the United States in July, 1939, notified Japan of her intention to terminate, at the end of six months, the Treaty of Commerce and Navigation of 1911.

NINETY-SIX, a village in western South Carolina, and a British fortified post during the Revolutionary War, was besieged by the Americans under Gen. Greene for 28 days in May and June, 1781. A desperate assault on June 17 failed, and the approach of Lord Rawdon with 2000 British forced Greene, who had only 1000 men, to raise the siege on the 19th. But the post was too far inland for Rawdon to hold, and he abandoned it June 29 and retired toward the coast.

NOMINATING SYSTEM. In the operation of the American representative system of government some method of nominating candidates for the various offices is essential. To meet this need three chief methods have been devised. These are the caucus system, which prevailed prior to 1824; the convention system, which became the chief method about 1830; and the direct primary system, which was introduced in 1903.

Originated early in the 18th century, in connection with local elections, the caucus system was later adapted to the nomination of governors and other state officers. Members of the legislature belonging to the same party would meet to recommend candidates. The next development was the congressional caucus wherein members of Congress having the same party affiliation would assemble for the purpose of recommending presidential and vice-presidential candidates.

Used first in 1800, the congressional caucus functioned for the last time in the campaign of 1824. In a country which was becoming increasingly democratic, it was denounced as being out of tune with the times.

Meanwhile there was developing in the states the delegate convention system. Delaware took the lead in setting up a convention during the administration of Jefferson. By 1830 state conventions prevailed everywhere except in the South.

Before the system was adapted to the national scene, there was a period of transition from the congressional caucus. In the campaign of 1824, Crawford received the caucus nomination, but three of the presidential candidates, Adams, Clay and Jackson, were nominated more informally by mass meetings, by newspapers, or by state legislative caucuses. In the next campaign, both Adams and Jackson were nominated by similar methods.

In 1831, however, the Anti-Masonic party, after a preliminary convention held in the previous year, inaugurated the national nominating convention. The National Republicans and the Democrats followed the example, with the result that the national nominating convention became the accepted method of nominating party candidates for the Presidency and Vice-Presidency while state conventions controlled the selection of candidates for state offices.

From the beginning the convention system was subjected to much severe criticism. As the years passed, the conviction grew that party conventions were so easily controlled by political bosses that their selections were not representative of the will of the party members. As an outgrowth of the dissatisfaction, the direct-primary system was developed. Originated in Wisconsin in 1903, the primary election system provides for the direct selection of party candidates by popular vote under state supervision. Generally, but not always, the primary election is "closed" to all but party members.

Advocated as a device to "return the government to the people," the primary system was adopted in some form in all but five states, by 1915. By the next year, it had been adopted in 22 states for the selection of delegates to national nominating conventions. Though subjected to severe criticism, some of which has certainly been merited, the direct-primary system has been firmly established as the most important nominating method in the 20th-century United States.

NONIMPORTATION AGREEMENTS were the colonies' chief weapon against Great Britain in the struggle for American liberty waged from 1765 to 1775. For a decade before the outbreak of war, Americans attempted to force the mother country to recognize their political rights by means of economic coercion; the failure to achieve their purpose by this means led many colonial Whigs reluctantly to regard war as the only safeguard of their liberties.

Nonimportation was first used against Great Britain by the New York merchants when, in 1765, they countermanded their orders for British merchandise and declared that they would order no more goods until the Stamp Act was repealed—an example that was quickly followed by the Boston and Philadelphia merchants. Thoroughly alarmed at the prospect of losing their lucrative colonial trade, the British merchants and manufacturers lobbied so vigorously in Parliament that the Stamp Act was repealed largely through their efforts.

Many colonial Whigs concluded from this victory that they had found a certain defense against the centralizing schemes of British imperialists. Although Englishmen might be deaf to appeals to natural law and charter rights, they seemed to lose no time in coming to terms with the colonies when pinched in their pocketbooks. Therefore, when the Townshend duties threatened colonial liberty, Americans again resorted to a boycott of British goods. Beginning in Boston in 1768, the nonimportation agreement was rapidly extended over the colonies with varying degrees of thoroughness and effectiveness. Tory merchants who refused to join the agreement were terrorized by mobs and compelled to cease importing British goods. Leadership of the movement soon passed from the Whig merchants to the radical Sons of Liberty who insisted that it be protracted until all colonial grievances, not merely the Townshend duties, had been redressed.

In 1769 the British government repealed all the Townshend duties except the tax on tea. This concession proved fatal to the nonimportation agreement. The New York merchants, outraged by Newport's open flouting of the agreement and suspicious of Boston's good faith, determined in 1770 to open their port to all British merchandise except tea. Although Boston and Philadelphia attempted to continue the struggle, New York's defection soon brought about the collapse of the boycott.

Economic coercion of the mother country was again attempted by the formation of the Continental Association in 1774. This differed from previous colonial boycotts inasmuch as it was imposed by the Continental Congress, contained provisions for non-exportation as well as nonimportation, and was controlled by the people, working through committees, rather than by the merchants. Nevertheless, the Continental Association failed to fulfill the hopes of conservative patriots who regarded it as a certain means of averting war. The British merchants and manufacturers, upon whom Americans relied to exert pressure upon the British government for a redress of colonial grievances, discovered new sources of trade to replace the lost American market; and, instead of rallying to the defense of the colonies, they permitted the Ministry a free hand in dealing with the American controversy. The supineness of the British merchants and manufacturers destroyed the plans of conservative American Whigs for a peaceful settlement; and the Continental Association had not been in effect six months before it was clear that the dispute between mother country and colonies was not to be decided by a bloodless economic war.

NONINTERCOURSE ACT. Commercial restrictions were an early and prominent ingredient in American foreign policy. Washington and the Federalists experimented with them, but it remained for Jefferson and his Republicans to realize their fullest possibilities. In the first decade of the 19th century there were four major acts restricting commerce: the partial Nonintercourse Act, of April 18, 1806, suspended on Dec. 19 of that year; the Embargo Act, of Dec. 22, 1807, which expired in March, 1809; the total Nonintercourse Act, of March 1, 1809; and the so-called Macon's Bill Number Two, of May 1, 1810. Of these four acts, the Embargo was the most significant, its two successors marking a progressive weakening of confidence in the efficacy of commerce as a coercive instrument.

The act of March 1, 1809, was, indeed, the rather impotent successor to Jefferson's pet measure, the Embargo. A face-saving device, it was far from comforting to the retiring President; at the same time it testified to the American commercial desperation. Designating Great Britain and France as countries with which the United States would hold no commercial relations, it offered to restore relations with whichever of those nations first withdrew its obnoxious orders and decrees. Here was, indeed, a marked recession from the late Embargo, which retained our shipping in home ports, for there was nothing in nonintercourse to prevent a general European trade in which the offender nations might indirectly benefit.

The attempt to pit the French and English against each other in a rivalry for America's commercial favors was rather an entreaty than a threat. And even this was further weakened by a time limit on the act, limiting enforcement at the outset to the close of the next session of the Congress.

While the Nonintercourse Act prohibited direct commerce, it permitted indirect. Its successor, Macon's Bill Number Two, was even milder. Direct commerce with Great Britain and France was reopened, saving only that restrictions should be renewed against one nation in the event that the other repealed its offending legislation. The restrictive system had been tried and found wanting, the Embargo alone being a true pathmarker on man's despairing road to peace.

How the European powers responded to these successive acts is another story. In the diplomatic duel of which they were a part, Napoleon played probably the shrewder role. At any rate when war supplanted these commercial gestures, the United States was at his side.

NONPARTISAN LEAGUE, NATIONAL (1915–24), an agrarian uprising in the Northwest, aroused one of the most bitter political controversies in recent American history. In immediate origin it was a revolt of the spring wheat farmers against the evils of the grain trade, but in part it was a culmination of the progressive movement in the Northwest. Marketing unrest, centering in North Dakota, was directed chiefly against the Minneapolis Chamber of Commerce, which, it was charged, exercised a monopolistic control over the wheat trade. Led by the Equity Cooperative Exchange after 1908, the farmers of North Dakota attempted to break the hold of the combine by establishing their own terminal facilities. When in 1915 the conservative administration of Gov. L. B. Hanna refused to carry out plans—twice approved by the voters—for a state-owned terminal elevator, the state was ready for revolt.

The man of the hour was A. C. Townley, "busted" flax farmer of western North Dakota and Socialist party organizer. In the spring of 1915 Townley, with the assistance of Equity and Socialist party leaders, launched the Nonpartisan League, demanding state-owned elevators, mills, packing plants, etc., state hail insurance, state rural credits and taxation reform. Capitalizing the bitterness aroused by the Equity conflict and directed by men skilled in the art of organizing farmers, the League swept the state. In 1916 a ticket headed by a dirt farmer, Lynn J. Frazier, captured the primaries of the Republican party, and was easily elected. In 1918 and 1920 the League was again successful. In 1919 the entire League program was enacted into law. The North Dakota Mill and Elevator and the Bank of North Dakota are still in operation.

After 1916 the League spread into neighboring states, its growth facilitated by a series of poor crops in the spring wheat region. Many progressive leaders, such as Charles A. Lindbergh, Minnesota League candidate for the Republican gubernatorial nomination in 1918, joined the movement, and the organizing genius of Townley, coupled with an effective publicity service, built up a formidable organization. Strong financial resources, which came from high membership fees, enabled the League to carry the fight to its enemies. North Dakota, Minnesota, South Dakota and Montana were most strongly organized, but many members were reported in Wisconsin, Iowa, Nebraska, Kansas, Colorado, Oklahoma, Idaho, Washington and Oregon. In each state the program of the League was modified to take advantage of local conditions, but state ownership of marketing facilities was the principal point in each platform. In states having large industrial populations, League leaders broadened their program to include the demands of the workingman and were generally able to effect a coalition of farmer-labor forces. In no state was the League so successful as in North Dakota. The strategy of the League was to capture the primaries of the dominant party; this was accomplished in several states, but outside North Dakota conservative elements were powerful enough to prevent victory at the general elections. No attempt was made by the League to influence the presidential election of 1920.

The strength of the League began to wane after 1920. The post-World War I depression, severe in the agricultural states by 1921, made difficult the payment of dues, and without money the organization weakened. The nationalistic reaction which followed the war also weakened the movement. During the war the League's advocacy of conscription of wealth had resulted in accusations of disloyalty, and these, combined with the cry of socialism, brought the League into disrepute in many quarters. In North Dakota, influenced by charges of mismanagement of the industrial program and by several banking scandals involving League leaders, the voters recalled Gov. Frazier in 1921. By 1924 the organization had practically disappeared; but the left-wing political revolt which it had created lived on—in Minnesota as the Farmer-Labor party, in North Dakota and other states as a faction within existing parties.

NOOTKA SOUND CONTROVERSY arose from conflicting British and Spanish claims to the northwest coast of North America. In 1789 expeditions from both countries arrived to occupy Nootka Sound, on Vancouver Island. The Spaniard seized the Englishman, his associates and vessels, and sent them to Mexico. The viceroy referred the matter to Madrid. The Spanish court demanded that the British court disavow the acts of its commander. The British refused, making counter demands. Each prepared for war and applied to its allies for assurances of support. Britain's responded affirmatively; Spain sought support under the Family Compact. Being in the throes of the French Revolution, France responded tardily and unsatisfactorily; and revolutionary contagion was feared by Spain. By a convention signed Oct. 28, 1790, Spain conceded most British demands. In the Oregon controversy Britain claimed all she thought she had gained in 1790; and the United States claimed what Spain retained, having acquired Spain's claims in the Florida Purchase Treaty, 1819.

"NORMALCY." In an address before the Home Market Club at Boston, May 14, 1920, Sen. Warren G. Harding said, in part, "America's present need is not heroics but healing, not nostrums but normalcy. . . ." The word normalcy came quickly to symbolize to many powerful American economic interests the immediate abandonment of the chief foreign and domestic policies of the Wilson administrations. Specifically, it signified a return to high protection, a drastic reduction in income and inheritance taxes, "putting labor in its place," a restoration of subsidies and bounties to favored corporate groups, no government interference in private enterprise, and a vigorous, nationalistic foreign policy. The "back to normal" slogan was used with great effectiveness by the Republicans in the campaign of 1920.

NORSEMEN IN AMERICA. In the 9th century the Norsemen discovered the Faroes and Iceland, and sighted the east coast of Greenland (Gunnbjarnarsker). In 982 Erik the Red, exiled from Iceland, discovered Greenland, explored its west coast and founded a colony of Icelanders there in 986 which existed for five centuries, but its ultimate fate is still unknown. The *Tale of the Greenlanders* tells of Bjarni Herjólfsson seeing in 986 three lands which by some are supposed to have been the American continent. The story, however, is doubtful, as is the account in the same source of five successive expeditions to Vinland. The *Saga of Erik the Red* appears to be more reliable. According to it Leif Eriksson, on his voyage from Norway to Greenland, accidentally discovered, in the year 1000, Vinland, a country where wild grapes and "self-sown" wheat grew. An expedition of exploration and attempted colonization of the newly discovered land followed in 1005, led by Thorfinn Karlsefni, an Icelander, with three ships and 160 men. They first came upon a land they called Helluland, then another they called Markland; thereupon they sailed by long, sandy and desolate beaches they called Furdustrands, and settled for the winter in Straumfjord, an attractive place in summer, but with a severe winter climate. Next summer one of the ships returned home while the others proceeded southward and came to a place they called Hóp, where wild grapes and "self-sown" wheat were to be found. One winter was spent there, but the settlement had to be abandoned because of the hostility of the aborigines, the Skraelings. Karlsefni returned to Straumfjord and spent there the third winter, returning in the summer of 1007 to Greenland. There were no more expeditions, but the Greenlanders apparently kept up the connection with Markland long afterward, probably for securing timber.

No Norse remains have so far been found on the American continent, hence any identification of the places mentioned in the sources is difficult, if not impossible. Helluland is generally supposed to be northern Labrador, Markland farther south on the Labrador coast, Furdustrands, the south coast of Labrador, and Straumfjord possibly Chaleur Bay. If the story about the wild grapes is authentic, Vinland and Hóp must be sought somewhere on the coast of New England south of Passamaquoddy Bay, the northern limits of wild grapes.

It has not been proved that these voyages influenced in any way the discoverers of America in the 15th century.

NORTH ATLANTIC TREATY ORGANIZATION (N.A.T.O.) was constituted under a treaty signed April 4, 1949 in Washington, D. C., by a group including the United States, Britain, Canada, France, Denmark, Iceland, Luxembourg, the Netherlands, Norway, Portugal and Turkey. Greenland also signed, but in 1951, a definitive agreement for the joint defense of Greenland by the United States and Denmark was signed. Sweden, adhering to its traditional policy of neutrality, did not sign, though it sympathized with the aims of the organization. Belgium and Italy joined in 1949, Greece in 1951 and West Germany in 1954.

N.A.T.O. is a mutual assistance pact under which the members agree to regard an attack on one member as an attack on all. It is a protective military shield over free Europe and aims at containing communism within its present (1961) limits. To achieve its military objectives the member nations announced plans for re-armament. At a meeting in Brussels, Dec. 18–19, 1950, approval was given to plans for unifying all N.A.T.O. forces under a single commander. General Dwight D. Eisenhower was named to the position; General Alfred M. Gruenther succeeded to the command, July 17, 1953, after General Eisenhower had resigned to become President of the United States. Gruenther served until Nov. 20, 1956, when he resigned and was succeeded by General Lauris Norstad.

N.A.T.O. was constituted when the nuclear weapon could be regarded as a United States monopoly. But that day passed when Soviet Russia exploded its first atomic bombs in the fall of 1949. Since that time N.A.T.O. has become essentially a deterrent force and it has become increasingly less likely to become effective in case of an all-out Soviet Russian attack in western Europe. Although N.A.T.O. is the most formidable barrier to Russian aggression, it has been weakened by Europe's uncertainty as to American plans for participation in it, to the resentment, in some countries, to the pre-eminence of the United States in the alliance, and to the cost of nuclear weapons. The alliance cannot be saved by any one nation, but only by the positive collective efforts of all its members. It has been said that an effective N.A.T.O. depends on knowledge by its members of what the United States wants to and will do and that its decisions are for the best course. This course may be the strengthening of conventional military ground, naval and air force by the European membership and occupation forces and the building of nuclear weapons by the United States with such assistance as may be possible from the European membership. In any case, N.A.T.O. is caught between a nuclear weapon it is increasingly reluctant to use, and an insufficiency of what it could more safely use if it had it. The obvious solution to the problem would be total disarmament or at least a total ban on nuclear weapons of any character, all under the observance and control of international inspection. However, Soviet Russia's unwillingness to such an agreement has prevented any acceptable solution.

In spite of these limitations and uncertainties, on May 10, 1961, N.A.T.O. met in Oslo, Norway, and resolved to meet the Soviet Russian-Chinese Communist bloc anywhere in an "ever-increasing area" of threat and its members reiterated their determination "to maintain the freedom of West Berlin and its people" and to do all possible to achieve "an equitable and just settlement of outstanding political questions."

In addition to the military aspects of the N.A.T.O. compact, it should be noted that Article II states: "The parties will contribute toward the further development of peaceful and friendly international relations by strengthening their free institutions, by bringing about a better understanding of the principles upon which these institutions are founded and promoting conditions of stability and well-being. . . ."

N.A.T.O., however, has done little to develop these expressed aims, though the protective shield of N.A.T.O. has permitted other organizations to till and fertilize the ground of political and economic unity. This is evident in such movements as the pre-N.A.T.O. Marshall Plan organization, the "Schuman Plan" coal and iron pool, the European Common Market, Benelux, Council of Europe, European Payments Union and other similar unifying bodies and projects. In spite of government hesitation to make use of Article II, people and their legislators have succeeded in giving to N.A.T.O. important social and political aspects.

NORTH CAROLINA. In 1585 the first English colony in America was planted on Roanoke Island, with Ralph Lane as governor and Walter Raleigh as promoter. This colony failed, as did another colony sent out in 1587, with John White as governor. In 1629 Charles I granted "Carolina" to Sir Robert Heath, who failed to plant a colony. About 1650 settlers from Virginia began to locate along the Albemarle Sound, and in 1663 Charles II granted Carolina to eight lords proprietors. A second charter, in 1665, fixed the boundaries of Carolina at 36 degrees and 30 minutes on the north, 29 degrees on the south, and westward to the Pacific Ocean. In 1664 the proprietors created two "counties" in what is now North Carolina—Albemarle and Clarendon (Cape Fear region), and offered land grants, tax exemption and other inducements to settlers. Clarendon was soon abandoned, and it was half a century before the Cape Fear country was settled. Until 1691 Albemarle had a proprietary governor and an elective legislature. From that date to 1711, North Carolina, as the northern portion of Carolina came to be called, was ruled by a deputy governor from Charles Town, although it had its own legislature. In 1712 an independent governor was appointed for North Carolina. In 1729 it became a royal colony.

North Carolina grew slowly during the proprietary period because of its dangerous coast and other geographical handicaps; neglect of the proprietors; weakness and inefficiency of its governors; Indian wars; piracy; friction over the Established Church; uncertainty of land titles and unpopularity of quit-rents and the greater attractiveness of other colonies. Only five towns were founded during this period—Bath (1705), New Bern (1710), and Edenton, Beaufort and Brunswick.

From 1729 to 1775, government improved, population increased and spread, agriculture and industry developed, many churches and a few academies were established, and three newspapers began publication. The lower Cape Fear was settled about 1725, and the upper Cape Fear after 1740. During the next thirty years thousands of Scotch-Irish and Germans moved from Pennsylvania into the Piedmont, and by 1775 settlements had reached the mountains.

North Carolina patriots openly resisted the Stamp Act; organized nonimportation associations to boycott British goods; called a meeting in defiance of the governor and chose delegates to the Continental Congress; set up a temporary government in 1775; crushed the Tories at Moore's Creek Bridge, Feb. 27, 1776; and, at Halifax, April 12, 1776, authorized their delegates in the Continental Congress to vote for independence—the first state to take such action. Guilford Courthouse was about the only important Revolutionary battle in the state, but North Carolina troops fought valiantly in other states, and also conquered the Cherokees in the West. The state's first constitution was drafted in 1776, and set up a government characterized by a weak executive, property and religious qualification for voting and officeholding, and a bicameral legislature elected annually.

The chief problems confronting the new state were: lack of specie and depreciation of paper currency; backwardness of agriculture, industry, commerce and education; Tories and their property; transmontane lands, and relations with the central government. The state ceded its western lands in 1790, and Tennessee was created therefrom. North Carolina rejected the Federal Constitution in 1788, but ratified in 1789, thus being next to the last state to accept that document.

NORTH CHURCH, Boston, whose real name is Christ Church, was erected in 1723, the second Episcopal Church to be established in Boston, and is the oldest church edifice in the city. Probably the first peal of bells used in this country—cast in England in 1744—is in its tower. It was in the steeple of this church that the signal lights were hung for Paul Revere's guidance on the night of April 18, 1775.

NORTH DAKOTA was formed by a division of the territory of Dakota in 1889. The enabling act was passed by Congress on Feb. 22, 1889; the state constitution was adopted by popular vote the same year and President Harrison issued the proclamation of statehood on Nov. 2, 1889.

NORTH WEST COMPANY was never an incorporated company like its chief rivals, the Hudson's Bay Company and the American Fur Company. It might be said rather to resemble more closely a modern holding company, the constituent parts of which were chiefly Montreal firms and partnerships engaged in the fur trade. It came into existence during the period of the American Revolution and ended by coalescing with the Hudson's Bay Company in 1821. In the interim it had reorganized in 1783, added the firm of Gregory, McLeod & Company, its chief rival in 1787, split into two factions in the later 1790's, reunited in 1804, joined forces with the American Fur Company, temporarily in 1811, been ejected from effective work on the soil of the United States (1816), and established its posts over much of Canada and northern United States. Its main line of communication was the difficult canoe route from Montreal, up the Ottawa River, through Lakes Huron and Superior, to its chief inland depot (Grand Portage before 1804, Fort William thereafter). Beyond Lake Superior the route to the Pacific was the international boundary waters to Lake of the Woods, the Winnipeg River, the Saskatchewan River, the Peace River and the Fraser River. Many lines branched from this main one, south into the Wisconsin, Dakota, Minnesota and Oregon countries, north to Lake Athabasca and the Mackenzie River area. Attempts were made by the company, but unavailingly, to get access to the interior through Hudson Bay, whose basin was the exclusive trading area of the Hudson's Bay Company. It was only when excessive competition between the two companies, raised to fever pitch after the Earl of Selkirk established his colony in the Red River Valley in 1811, had led to actual warfare that the North West Company got its cheaper transportation route, and then only at the cost of sinking its individuality under the charter rights and acquiring the name of the Hudson's Bay Company. When this union came in 1821 the Scotch, Yankee, English and French-Canadian employees of the North West Company had had nearly fifty years of valorous exploration and trail blazing; they had forced the Hudson's Bay Company to build forts in the interior; they had developed the *voyageur* to the acme of his unique serviceability; they had discovered the way to maintain a canoe route to the Pacific, through the use of pemmican, a concentrate of buffalo meat and grease; and they had contributed an éclat to the fur trade that gives it a charm forever in American and Canadian annals.

NORTHEAST BOUNDARY (1783–1842). The Definitive Treaty of Peace of 1783 designated the north-

eastern boundary as the St. Croix to its source, thence a line due north to the highlands dividing the rivers tributary to the St. Lawrence from those tributary to the Atlantic, thence along the highlands to the most northwestern head of the Connecticut, down the latter to the parallel of 45° and thence on 45° to the St. Lawrence. The controversy concerning the identity of the true St. Croix was settled in 1798 by a mixed commission selected under a provision of the Jay Treaty. Unsuccessful attempts to decide upon the line of the highlands were made in 1803 and 1807 by the negotiation of draft treaties which were never ratified. Another attempt was made by a provision of the Treaty of Ghent (1814), resulting in the appointment of a joint mixed commission of two representatives which, after working on the problem for six years (1816–22), by examination of costly joint frontier surveys and acrimonious arguments, reached no agreement except an agreement to disagree and adjourned without resorting to the provision for selection of a friendly umpire.

Under a treaty of 1827, the question of the location of highlands and the ratification of the old survey of 1774 west of the Connecticut was submitted for arbitration by the King of the Netherlands who, in 1831, proposed a compromise line along the upper St. John and the St. Francis tributary and westward to the line claimed by the United States. This proposal, not contemplated in the terms of the arbitration, the American Government after some delay declined to accept.

Confronted by new border controversies and irritations, resulting from the advance of settlements in part of the disputed territory, President Jackson suggested a renewal of diplomatic efforts, which were delayed for various reasons. The negotiations were continued with a tone which became more and more acrid until it impressed upon both contesting parties the necessity of a peaceful compromise to prevent border conflict in territory where each party had agreed to refrain from any extension of jurisdiction during the period of the negotiations for peaceful adjustment. From the devious negotiations and increasing danger finally emerged a friendlier attitude which in 1842 found practical expression in the Webster-Ashburton Treaty.

Early in 1838 Secretary of State Forsyth contemplated the expediency of an attempt at direct negotiations for the establishment of a conventional line, but he obtained no encouragement from Massachusetts, while Maine, early in 1839, precipitated the border clash known as the Aroostook war. Meanwhile the situation was complicated by unsettled questions concerning the British destruction of the *Caroline* on the Niagara River.

In 1841 Webster, who succeeded Forsyth, determined to end the long dispute by conciliatory compromise. After declining Palmerston's proposal for arbitration by a commission of three European kings he stated his decision to attempt a settlement on the basis of a conventional line, resulting in the British decision to appoint Lord Ashburton as a special minister to conduct the negotiations at Washington. Webster tactfully prepared the way for the co-operation of Maine and Massachusetts.

The negotiators finally were successful in reaching an agreement to accept as the boundary the upper St. John to the St. Francis, the latter to Lake Pohenagamoot, thence a direct southwest line to a point near the southwest branch of the St. John, thence a line via the crest of the hills to the northwest branch (Hall's Stream) of the Connecticut River and west of the Connecticut on the old survey line of the parallel of 45° to the St. Lawrence. These agreements, and provisions for certain equivalents for loss of American territory in Maine, and other coincidental agreements, were included in the famous Webster-Ashburton Treaty which was signed at Washington on Aug. 9, 1842.

NORTHERN SECURITIES CASE (193 U. S. 197, 1904) started out as a rather ordinary contest between competitive railroad trunk lines over control of an intermediate "feeder" line and ended up as a struggle for supremacy between the Morgan and James J. Hill group on one side and Edward H. Harriman and affiliated financial interests on the other. The former controlled the Northern Pacific and Great Northern railways. The latter controlled the Union Pacific system. The immediate occasion of the rivalry was an effort by Harriman to wrest from Morgan and Hill a special interest in the Chicago, Burlington and Quincy, thereby effecting an entrance into Chicago.

When Harriman had contrived to acquire, at first by stealthy moves and then by frenzied bidding culminating in the "Northern Pacific panic" of 1901, a sufficient interest to give him a majority of the voting rights outstanding in Northern Pacific stock, he was checkmated by Morgan's threat to call for redemption the preferred stock, which represented a large part of Harriman's holdings. Negotiations ensued for a friendly settlement out of which emerged the Northern Securities Company. This was a holding company which took over all of the contestants' stock interests in the Great Northern, Northern Pacific and Burlington lines, and in this company the Morgan and Hill group held a controlling interest.

Challenged as a violation of the Sherman Antitrust Act the defendants contended that that act did not embrace, and that if it were held to embrace it was beyond the constitutional power of Congress to regulate, *a fortiori* to prohibit, the mere transfer of proprietary interests in any enterprise from one person to another. It was especially urged that if, as in this case, the purchasing party was a corporation duly organized by a sovereign state and expressly authorized to make the acquisitions here attacked, the application of the Sherman Act's prohibitions would invade powers constitutionally reserved to the states.

The decision of the Supreme Court upheld the Government's contention that the holding company had been used as an illegal device for restraining trade, since its necessary effect was to eliminate competition in transportation service over a large section of the country.

NORTHWEST BOUNDARY CONTROVERSY. The Definitive Treaty of Peace of 1783 with Great Britain provided (Article 2) that the boundary between the United States and British North America should proceed by various streams from the western head of Lake Superior to "the most Northwestern point" of the Lake of the Woods, "and from thence on a due west course to the Mississippi River." The negotiators had before them Mitchell's Map of North America of 1755, which shows the Mississippi flowing out from under an insert map of Hudson Bay which had been set into the northwest corner of the Mitchell. They assumed that the river rose north of a line due west from the northwesternmost point of the Lake of the Woods. Actually, the source of the river is 152 miles south of that latitude. Thus a serious boundary gap was left by the peace settlement. It first became a matter of dispute in 1792 when Great Britain unsuccessfully proposed to close it by a boundary rectification which would have extended British territory south to the navigable waters of the Mississippi, thus giving Canada an access to that river, the free navigation of which had been guaranteed by the treaty of peace to the citizens and subjects of both parties. Jay's Treaty of 1794 established a mixed commission to determine the northwestern boundary, but it never met. In 1803 Rufus King signed a convention to close the gap by drawing a line from the Lake of the Woods to the source of the Mississippi River, but the Senate did not ratify it for fear of prejudicing the northern boundary of Louisiana just acquired from France. In 1807 the United States proposed drawing a line north or south from the northwestern corner of the Lake of the Woods to 49° N. Lat. and thence west along that parallel. The British negotiators accepted this, provided the words were added "as far [along the line of 49°] as the territories of the United States extend in that quarter." James Monroe and William Pinkney, the American negotiators, rejected this phraseology because it implied a limitation of American territory anywhere along that line. During the negotiations for peace at Ghent in 1814 the British negotiators reverted to the project of setting up between the Ohio, Mississippi and Great Lakes a "neutral Indian barrier state"—a proposal first introduced in 1792— and when this fell to the ground they eluded discussion of the boundary west of the Lake of the Woods lest they might recognize the American title to Louisiana which they desired to annul. The peace treaty provided for mutual restoration of occupied territory without stipulating boundaries.

After the Napoleonic wars Great Britain's need for repose caused her to cease contesting the American title to Louisiana, and the northwestern boundary gap disappeared in the Convention of 1818, which provided that the boundary should proceed from the northwesternmost corner of the Lake of the Woods to 49° N. Lat. and along that degree of latitude to the Rocky Mountains. Beyond the mountains the western territory and rivers claimed by either party were to be free and open for a term of ten years (extended indefinitely in 1826) to the vessels, citizens and subjects of both parties to the treaty without prejudice to the claims of either. The Northwest boundary controversy thus graduated from the closed Northwest boundary gap to the Oregon Question terminated in the Oregon Treaty of 1846 by extending the line of 49° N. Lat. through to the Pacific Ocean.

NORTHWEST PASSAGE. The search for an all-water route around the northern coast of North America began at the end of the 15th century and lasted 400 years. It may be divided roughly into two periods: (1497–1800) expeditions sent out to find a route to Asia for purposes of trade; (1800–1906) expeditions sent out for the purpose of acquiring geographical knowledge. It is impossible to mention all the numerous voyages, but the following are the most important.

1497–1800. John Cabot (1497–98) explored the American coast from Labrador to Florida. Jacques Cartier (1534–35) discovered the St. Lawrence River and explored it as far as the site of modern Montreal. Martin Frobisher (1576) discovered Frobisher Sound in Baffin Land and entered Hudson Strait. John Davis (1585–87) made three voyages to Davis Strait. Henry Hudson (1610) discovered Hudson Bay. William Baffin (1616) thoroughly examined the coast of Baffin Bay and pronounced the bay to be landlocked, a decision that discouraged further exploration in this direction for 200 years. Luke Foxe (1631) explored Fox Channel north of Hudson Bay. In the first half of the 18th century the Hudson's Bay Company sent out several expeditions to search for a passage along the western coast of the bay.

1800–1906. After the Napoleonic wars there began a series of voyages by British naval officers under the supervision of John Barrow, second secretary of the Admiralty. W. E. Parry (first voyage, 1819–20) penetrated from Baffin Bay through Lancaster Sound to McClure Strait; (second voyage, 1821–23) went through Hudson Strait to Fury and Hecla Strait. John Franklin and John Richardson (1819–27) made two overland expeditions to the Arctic Ocean and ranged its coastline from Point Turnagain westward to

longitude 148° 42'. John Ross (1829–33) sailed well into Prince Regent Inlet and crossed Boothia Isthmus to discover Victoria Strait. John Franklin (1845–47) sailed through Lancaster Sound, down Peel Sound, to Victoria Strait, where he perished. R. J. L. M. McClure (1850–54) was sent out to find Franklin. He sailed around South America to Bering Strait and thence to McClure Strait where he abandoned his ship. Marching eastward over the ice he joined Belcher's expedition coming from Baffin Bay. He was the first to find an all-water route from ocean to ocean, though heavy ice rendered it unnavigable. Roald Amundsen (1903–6) was the first to sail from the Atlantic to the Pacific. He sailed through Lancaster Sound, down Peel Sound, through James Ross Strait to the American coast, then westward to Alaska.

NORTHWEST TERRITORY, officially "the Territory Northwest of the River Ohio," included the Old Northwest when it was established by Congress July 13, 1787. Already the Ordinance of 1785 had provided for the survey of the public land in townships, each six miles square and divided into 36 sections of 640 acres. Payment for the land was permitted in specie, or in Continental certificates, and, for one seventh, the land warrants issued to Revolutionary soldiers were accepted. Section sixteen in each township the Ordinance set aside for the support of education.

The Ordinance of 1787 outlined the governmental framework. At first there would be an arbitrary administration, with a governor, three judges and a secretary elected by and responsible to Congress. When the population included 5000 free white males of voting age, the Territory would have practically local autonomy, with a legislative assembly, although Congress would still choose the governor. Finally, when any one of the stipulated divisions contained 60,000 free inhabitants it would be admitted into the Union as a state. An important clause in the Ordinance forbade slavery in the Old Northwest.

The two ordinances, modified to meet changing conditions, remained the basic principles for the organization of the Old Northwest, and set precedents for later territorial development.

In 1787 the Northwest Territory had a widely scattered population of some 45,000 Indians and 2000 French. The first legal American settlement was at Marietta, April 7, 1788. Gov. St. Clair inaugurated the territorial government, July 15, 1788, forming Washington County between the eastern boundary and the Scioto. January, 1790, he established Hamilton County between the Scioto and the Miami, and in March he set up St. Clair County along the Mississippi north of the Ohio. Winthrop Sargent, Secretary of the Territory, then organized Knox County between the Miami and St. Clair County, and in 1796 he formed Wayne County with Detroit as the county seat. From these basic counties others were set off as population increased.

The Indian menace confined the earliest settlers to the Ohio Valley, but after Wayne's decisive victory at Fallen Timbers, Aug. 20, 1794, and the subsequent Treaty of Greenville the greater part of Ohio was opened up. Population now increased so rapidly that the autonomous stage of government was inaugurated Sept. 4, 1799, with the first meeting of the territorial assembly. Owing to the distance between many of the settlements a division of the Territory became necessary, and in 1800 the area west of a line north from the mouth of the Kentucky was set off as Indiana Territory. The diminished Northwest Territory was further decreased in 1802 when Michigan was annexed to Indiana.

A movement for statehood now began, which was aided by the Republican (Jeffersonian) national victory in 1800. Although the Territory had approximately only 42,000 inhabitants, April 30, 1802, Jefferson approved the Enabling Act. With the first meeting of the state legislature, March 1, 1803, the Northwest Territory gave place to the State of Ohio, the "first fruits" of the Ordinance of 1787.

NUECES RIVER, which empties into Corpus Christi Bay, was the subject of a boundary dispute, first, between the Texas Republic and Mexico (1836–46), and next, between the United States and Mexico (1846–48). Though as a Spanish or a Mexican province Texas had never extended westward of the Nueces, the Texas Republic claimed the Rio Grande as its boundary. After annexation to the United States, Texas saw its claims supported when President Polk sent troops beyond the Nueces, and then asked Congress to declare war against Mexico for attacking them because they were on American soil. Mexico claimed they were invaders. By the Treaty of Guadalupe Hidalgo, the Rio Grande became the boundary of Texas.

NULLIFICATION is the act by which a state suspends, within its territorial jurisdiction, a Federal law. The right of nullification was first asserted by Virginia and Kentucky in their Resolutions of 1798. The Kentucky Resolutions of 1799 boldly asserted that "nullification" was "the rightful remedy" for infractions of the Constitution. The doctrine of nullification was based upon the theory that the Union was the result of a compact between sovereign states, that the Constitution was a body of instructions drawn up by the states for the guidance of the general government, that the states were the rightful judges of infractions of the Constitution, and that the states were not bound by the acts of their agent when it exceeded its delegated powers. The fundamental principles of nullification underlay the action of the Hartford Convention (1814); Georgia not only nullified the decisions of the Supreme Court in the Cherokee Indian controversy but prevented their enforcement (Cherokee Nation v. Georgia); and

several Northern states nullified the Fugitive Slave Law (1850) by the passage of Personal Liberty Laws.

The most noted example of nullification, however, occurred in South Carolina. Opposition to the protective tariff began to develop in the South in the 1820's. This hostility mounted to such proportions that the legislature of South Carolina printed and circulated Calhoun's *Exposition* (1828). This paper reaffirmed the doctrines of 1798 and formulated a program of action: the interposition of the state's veto through the people in sovereign convention assembled. The South Carolinians then rested upon their oars, expecting the Jackson administration to reduce the tariff. Later, when Congress enacted a tariff act (1832) that proclaimed protection a permanent policy, the nullifiers carried the issue to the people. They won control of the legislature and called a state convention (Nov. 19, 1832). This body adopted an Ordinance of Nullification declaring the tariff acts of 1828 and 1832 oppressive, unconstitutional, null and void and not binding on the people of South Carolina. Appeals to the Federal courts were forbidden and state officials were required to take an oath to support the Ordinance. The legislature later passed acts necessary to put the Ordinance into effect. South Carolina expected other Southern states to follow her lead, but none supported nullification, although several protested against protective tariffs.

President Jackson issued a proclamation (Dec. 10, 1832) in which he denounced nullification as rebellion and treason and warned the people of South Carolina that he would use every power at his command to enforce the laws. In a message to Congress he urged modification of the tariff and, later, asked the passage of a "Force Bill" to enable him to use the army and navy in enforcing the law. Before the date set for the Ordinance to take effect (Feb. 1, 1833) measures for reducing the tariff were introduced into Congress. Consequently, a committee, empowered by the convention to act, suspended the Ordinance until Congress should take final action. Both the Force Bill and the Compromise Tariff were passed by Congress and approved by the President. The convention reassembled (March 11, 1833) and rescinded the Ordinance of Nullification, but nullified the Force Bill. The nullifiers, who had claimed their action peaceable, now argued that the reduction of the tariff duties amply justified their position and action.

OCALA PLATFORM, adopted at a meeting of the National Farmers Alliance and Industrial Union at Ocala, Fla., December, 1890, demanded, among other things, the abolition of national banks, increase of money to $50 per capita, graduated income tax, free and unlimited coinage of silver, establishment of subtreasuries where farmers could obtain money at not exceeding 2% on nonperishable products, and election of U. S. Senators by a direct vote of the people.

"OH! SUSANNA," a song of the old Negro minstrel or nonsense type, was written and composed by Stephen Collins Foster and published in the spring of 1848. It was one of Foster's earliest successful songs, though he is said to have received only $100 for it. It became very popular that summer, when there was much immigration to Oregon. Parodies began to be written in which "Oregon" was substituted for "Alabama" in the original version. In the spring of 1849, when the Gold Rush started, "California" was the next substitution, and the whimsical ballad became in effect the theme song of America's most remarkable mass movement. It was sung on vessels rounding Cape Horn and by the campfires of the overland voyagers. In the East, it was played at balls as a polka or quadrille and by military bands as a quickstep, and was arranged with variations for band and solo piano. It became popular even in foreign countries.

OHIO. The legislature of the Northwest Territory, under the influence of Gov. Arthur St. Clair, Federalist, and his following, chiefly from Marietta and Cincinnati, favored dividing the territory along the Scioto River, but a Chillicothe Republican group, led by Thomas Worthington, won the support of the Republican Congress. The Enabling Act of April 30, 1802, defined the western boundary as the meridian from the mouth of the Great Miami northward to a line drawn eastward from the southern bend of Lake Michigan and authorized a constitutional convention to meet in November.

The 35 delegates drew up, in 25 days, a simple, democratic constitution which was sent to Congress without being referred to the voters. Its chief characteristics were a weak governor, with no veto and very limited appointing powers, and a powerful general assembly, which appointed state officials and both supreme court and common pleas judges. White adult male taxpayers could vote.

Congress extended Federal laws over the state, Feb. 19, 1803, and the first legislature convened on March 1.

OHIO COMPANY OF ASSOCIATES (1787) developed from the interest in western settlement of a group of Revolutionary War officers. Two New Englanders, Generals Rufus Putnam and Benjamin Tupper, were its leading spirits. Due to their activity, "A Piece called Information" appeared in several Massachusetts newspapers in January, 1786, inviting officers and soldiers to form "an association by the name of the Ohio Company." All persons interested were to elect delegates to meet at the Bunch of Grapes Tavern in Boston on March 1. Eleven men met on that date and organized the company. They planned to raise $1,000,000, to be subscribed for in shares of $1000 each, payable in Continental certificates, plus ten dollars in gold or silver, the fund to be used to purchase land "north westerly of the River Ohio."

A year elapsed before 250 shares had been subscribed and the company was ready to ask Congress for land. Gen. Samuel Parsons proving unsatisfactory as an agent, Rev. Manasseh Cutler was selected to represent the company before Congress. By skillful lobbying and by effecting an alliance with a group of New York speculators headed by William Duer, Cutler arranged a joint purchase: nearly 5,000,000 acres for the Scioto Company and 1,500,000 acres for the Ohio Company. Reservations of one section in each township for schools, another for religion, three for later disposal by Congress and two whole townships for a university increased the Ohio Company's total to 1,781,760 acres. It was to pay $500,000 down and the same amount when the survey was completed, but payment could be made in government securities, worth perhaps twelve cents on the dollar. The tract lay north of the Ohio River between the Seventh Range and the western limit of the Seventeenth. Cutler also helped in the formation and adoption of the Ordinance of 1787.

The Ohio Company later encountered financial difficulties and could not complete its payments. However, Congress granted title to 750,000 acres, and added 214,285 acres to be paid for with army warrants and 100,000 acres to be granted free to actual settlers. More than two thirds of the shareholders remained in the East, thus adding absentee ownership to the complications of inaugurating settlement on the exposed frontier. It required many years to arrange for the division of the lands and other assets among the 817 shareholders. Meetings were still being held as late as 1831 although nearly all the assets had long since been allocated. The great achievement of the company was the successful beginning of organized settlement north of the Ohio River at Marietta in 1788.

OHIO COMPANY OF VIRGINIA was a partnership of Virginia gentlemen, a Maryland frontiersman and a London merchant organized in 1747 to engage in land speculation and trade with the Indians in the territory claimed by Virginia west of the mountains. The company petitioned the Crown for a grant of 500,000 acres of land in the upper Ohio Valley or elsewhere in the West, 200,000 acres to be granted at once on condition that 200 families be settled on the land within seven years. Early in 1749 the governor of Virginia was directed to make the grant. The company built a storehouse for trade goods on the Potomac opposite the mouth of Wills Creek and sent Christopher Gist on exploring expeditions in 1750 and 1751. The Indians having been induced at the Treaty of Logstown to permit settlement south of the Ohio, a road was opened across the mountains, probably in 1752, and in 1753 Gist and a number of others sent out by the company settled in what is now Fayette County, Pa. In the same year the company built another storehouse on the Monongahela at the site of Brownsville, and early in 1754 it began, with the co-operation of the governor of Virginia, the erection of Fort Prince George at the Forks of the Ohio. The capture of this uncompleted fort by the French, and the war that ensued, resulted in the withdrawal of the settlers, and plans of the company to renew its activities in the region after the fall of Fort Duquesne were frustrated by the prohibition of settlement west of the mountains. An agent dispatched by the company to England to seek a renewal of its grant was unsuccessful in his quest, and in 1770 he exchanged its claims for two shares in the Vandalia Company. The Ohio Company was significant as a manifestation of the intention of England, and also of Virginia, to expand across the mountains into the Ohio Valley; and its activities played a part in bringing on the final contest between the French and the English for control of the interior.

OHIO RIVER, EARLY DISCOVERY OF THE, cannot be fixed with certainty. In the first half of the 17th century, rumors came to the French in Canada and the English in Virginia of the great river beyond the mountains, and occasional explorers may even have reached the Ohio Valley. From the scanty records the one justifiable conclusion is that a party of Frenchmen led by LaSalle first discovered the Ohio River.

From the Indians LaSalle had heard of the "Great River," in the Iroquois tongue, Ohio, that, flowing westward, plunged over a waterfall, and he became convinced he could descend it to the Gulf of California and perhaps even to China. Leaving Montreal, July 6, 1669, LaSalle with twenty men went up the St. Lawrence, along the southern shore of Lake Ontario, and across country to the Grand River Valley in northeastern Ohio. From there they pushed on to the Allegheny, and down the Ohio to the marshy country below the Falls at Louisville. Here, deserted by his men, LaSalle abandoned his original plan of going down to the mouth of the Ohio, and returned to Canada.

News of LaSalle's voyage quickly spread. Jolliet's map in 1674 gave the general course of the Ohio as far as the Falls, and Franquelin's map in 1682 showed that it flowed into the Mississippi. Later French explorers located the chief tributaries from the north, notably the Wabash, the Ouabache of this early period. Frequently these early maps showed the Wabash as the main river into which the Ohio flowed, and to the latter many of them gave the alternative name, *La Belle Rivière.*

The Virginians, too, sought the great river west of the mountains that reputedly flowed into the South Sea. About 1648 Gov. Berkeley proposed an expedition across the mountains, and other adventurous souls followed his example, although none of these plans materialized. It was left to Abraham Wood, a fur trader at Fort Henry, now Petersburg, on the Appomattox, actually to mark the path from Virginia across the mountains. According to unverified reports Wood himself, between 1654 and 1664, discovered several branches of the Ohio and the Mississippi. If so, he even preceded LaSalle in the Ohio Valley. Certainly in 1671 he despatched a trading party that crossed to the New River on the western slope. In the 18th century Gov. Spotswood urged an English advance from Virginia, and in 1716 at the head of the romantic Knights of the Golden Horseshoe he reached the south branch of the Shenandoah.

OIL INDUSTRY. The existence of petroleum deposits in the United States has been known for over 300 years, but the oil industry itself is comparatively young. The earliest mention of petroleum in the United States occurred in a letter dated July 18, 1627, from Joseph de la Roche D'Allion, a Franciscan missionary, which described a visit to the oil springs near what is now the town of Cuba, N. Y. The letter was published in G. Sagard's *Histoire du Canada et Voyage des Missionaires Récollets* in 1636.

Many brine wells, which were drilled for salt, as early as 1806 produced some oil; however, it was considered a nuisance, and little effort was made to collect it. A few of the more enterprising operators burned the oil to evaporate the water and obtain the salt.

The Indians, and later the white settlers, used the petroleum as a medicine and for lighting although it burned with a smoky flame and an offensive odor. It was skimmed from the creeks and oil seeps, bottled and sold as a medicine, purporting to be a sure cure for, among other things, blindness, rheumatism, burns, coughs, colds, sprains and baldness. In 1833 S. P. Hildreth, writing about the early uses of petroleum, mentioned that it was well adapted to prevent friction in machinery and that when filtered through charcoal made a fairly satisfactory lamp fuel.

In 1840 Samuel M. Kier, a Pittsburgh druggist, began bottling and selling crude oil as a medicine for fifty cents per half pint. The expense of obtaining, bottling and peddling it absorbed most of the profits, so he attempted to improve it for lighting purposes. He went to a chemist, who suggested distillation. In 1849 he constructed a crude still consisting of a kettle with a cover and worm-cooling coil; by double distilling the oil he made a fairly satisfactory lamp fuel. The heavier product of distillation he sold to a factory in Cooperstown, Pa., for cleansing wools. This apparently was the first commercial petroleum refinery, and initiated the replacement of coal oil by kerosene as a lamp fuel.

The first scientific investigation of petroleum was made by Benjamin Silliman, Jr., at the request of

George H. Bissell. His report, dated April 14, 1855, gave important information on the chemical and physical properties of Pennsylvania "rock oil," and pointed out its economic value. In December, 1854, Silliman wrote to Bissell and painted a bright picture of the commercial possibilities of the "rock oil," based on his findings to that date. On the basis of this letter George H. Bissell and Jonathan G. Eveleth organized the Pennsylvania Rock Oil Co. (Dec. 30, 1854) for the expressed purpose of drilling or mining for oil. This company was dissolved before a well was drilled, and Bissell and associates organized the Seneca Oil Co. which leased a plot of land on Oil Creek near Titusville, Pa. "Col." E. L. Drake, engaged to supervise the operations, hired two former brine-well drillers to drill the well, which was completed Aug. 27, 1859, at a depth of 69½ feet. The initial production was about 25 barrels per day, and during the remainder of the year the well produced approximately 2000 barrels of oil.

The Drake well marked the real beginning of the petroleum industry. News of its success soon spread, and Oil Creek Valley and the Allegheny River banks, above and below Oil City, were rapidly developed. For these early leases no rent was charged, a royalty of one eighth to one fourth of the oil produced being paid to the landowner. Many of these wells were drilled by the spring pole method, although even at that early date some were drilled with steam power, the rigs having all of the essentials of the American cable tool-drilling rig. (The rotary drilling rig was the most widely used in 1959.)

The first of many oil boom towns was Pithole. From January to September, 1865, Pithole mushroomed from a population of less than 100 to an estimated 14,000. In September, 1865, its post office ranked next in importance to those of Philadelphia and Pittsburgh. However, the production rapidly declined, the population shifted to other more active areas, and within two years the town was practically deserted.

During the period of early development the principal methods of transporting crude oil were by teams and barges. In 1865, much to the chagrin and anger of the teamsters, who attempted to destroy it several times, the first successful screw joint pipeline was built from Pithole to a railroad, a distance of five miles. It had a capacity of eighty barrels per day. This line was later purchased by the Allegheny Transportation Co., the first pipeline company in the United States. In 1879 the first long-distance pipeline was completed by the Tidewater Pipeline Co. It extended from Coryville, Pa., to Williamsport, a distance of 102 miles. The National Transit Co. constructed the first pipeline from the oil region in western Pennsylvania to the Atlantic seaboard. It was completed in 1881.

Since this early boom development in northwestern Pennsylvania the history of the American petroleum industry has been one of constant expansion in geographical distribution and quantity of production, in transportation systems, in refining technology and marketing facilities. While Pennsylvania remained the principal source of supply for several years, small quantities of oil were produced in New York, Ohio, West Virginia, Kentucky, Tennessee and California. After 1884 production in Ohio and West Virginia increased rapidly. In 1894 Wyoming came into the picture as a producing state. Near the turn of the century development was under way in Texas, Indian Territory (Oklahoma), Kansas, Louisiana and Illinois. In 1904 California production was 30,000,000 barrels. About this time appreciable quantities began to come into the markets from Colorado and Indiana, and Kansas and Texas were being developed rapidly. Active development of New Mexico and Michigan began in 1924 and 1925 respectively.

In 1959 oil was found and produced in 31 states at an average rate of 6,750,000 barrels per day. This production came from some 569,000 producing oil wells, averaging 12.8 barrels per well daily. The largest producing well ever drilled in the United States was in the Spindletop field near Beaumont, Texas, which at its peak produced 148,000 barrels a day. The deepest well in the world, which has been drilled to a depth of more than 25,000 feet, is in Pocos County, Texas.

The United States alone produced 2,461,000 barrels of crude oil in 1958, or about 38% of world production. Although oil men in this country have continued to find and produce more oil year after year, production in the rest of the world has been increasing at an even faster rate. Production outside the United States has increased from 881,000,000 barrels in 1945 (34% of world production in that year) to 4,100,000,000 barrels in 1958. In 1958 principal producing nations (other than the United States) were: Venezuela, the Soviet Union, Kuwait, Saudi Arabia, Iran, Iraq and Canada. The total oil produced in the United States from 1859 to Jan. 1, 1959, was 60,310,000,000 barrels, or over 55% of the total production of the entire world.

About 202,000 miles of pipeline, 96,100 railroad tank cars, 470 oil tankers and 42,000 tank trucks were used in 1958 for transporting American crude oil and refined products.

From Kier's first simple still to a modern refinery was a far cry. Some of the giant refineries currently in operation in 1958 turned as many as 355,000 barrels of crude oil into products daily. There were then 318 refineries in the United States, with a daily capacity of 9,744,000 barrels.

Prior to 1900, the most important products of petroleum were kerosine (i.e., the illuminant made from petroleum, as distinguished from that made from coal) and lubricating oils. With the advent of the automobile age, gasoline became the oil industry's principal product. During the past 25 years, ending in 1958, it has accounted for approximately 43% of domestic demand for all petroleum products. Along with gasoline, heating oils, diesel fuels, and in recent years, petrochemicals, have assumed great economic importance. In 1957, for example, 38,000,000,000 pounds of all chemicals produced were petroleum-derived.

Probably no other mineral resource has done more to change the lives of the American people than has oil. Over two thirds of our energy in 1958 came from oil and natural gas, and more than 2500 products were derived from petroleum. The American petroleum industry employed gross assets of $58,500,-000,000 in 1957, making it the third largest industry in the country, exceeded only by agriculture and the combined public utilities.

OISE-AISNE OPERATION, AMERICAN TROOPS IN (Aug. 18–Nov. 11, 1918).

Exploiting the success of the Aisne-Marne operation in reducing the Marne salient, Gen. Pétain ordered Degoutte's 6th French army and Mangin's 10th French army to continue their offensive between the Aisne and the Oise. The American 3rd Corps (Bullard) was in Degoutte's army east of Soissons when the attack was resumed, with the 77th Division (Duncan, Johnson, Alexander) and the 28th Division (Muir) in line, left to right, behind the Vesle. After indecisive fighting along this stream the two divisions crossed, Sept. 4, with the general French advance, and, against strong opposition by Von Boehn's 7th German army, pushed across the watershed toward the Aisne. The 28th Division was relieved Sept. 8; the 77th on Sept. 16, after progressing ten kilometers and crossing the Aisne Canal.

Placed in line in Mangin's army north of Soissons, the 32nd Division attacked toward Juvigny on Aug. 28. This place was taken Aug. 30, and on Sept. 2, after repeated attacks, the division reached the National Road at Terny.

OKLAHOMA.

The first Europeans to visit the region included in the present State of Oklahoma were a few Spanish soldiers under the leadership of Coronado who crossed it in 1541 seeking for the fabled land of Quivira. The expedition gave Spain a claim to this region, but no permanent settlements were made and the claim was lost to France by the explorations of Jolliet and LaSalle in the next century. By the Treaty of Fontainebleau France ceded her claims to the western half of the Mississippi Valley to Spain, but the latter retroceded it to France in 1800 by the Treaty of San Ildefonso. In 1803 France sold Louisiana, including all of Oklahoma except the Panhandle, to the United States. American explorers visited it during the years following the Louisiana Purchase, and in 1824 Col. Matthew Arbuckle founded Forts Gibson and Towson as the first military posts.

Few Indians were found by the early explorers except some Osage and small bands of Kiowa, Comanche and Wichita. During the period from 1820 to 1840, however, the Cherokee, Creek, Choctaw, Chickasaw and Seminole were removed to Oklahoma from their former homes in the Gulf Plains region and given all the land included in the present state except the Panhandle and a small area in the northeast assigned to the Quapaw tribe. Here these five great Indian nations, known as the Five Civilized Tribes, established little Indian republics, all except the Seminole having written constitutions and written laws. The Five Civilized Tribes held slaves and joined the Confederacy during the Civil War. At the close of that struggle they were forced to give up the western part of their lands, constituting roughly the western half of the present state, as a home for other Indians. During the next few years some twenty tribes were located here upon thirteen reservations.

One area of about 2,000,000 acres near the center of the state was not included in any reservation. This came to be known as the "Unassigned Lands" or "Old Oklahoma." Efforts were made to settle this area by the so-called "boomers," but they were removed by soldiers. On April 22, 1889, it was opened to white settlement in accordance with the terms of an act of Congress and a proclamation of the President of the United States. This opening was the first of the so-called "Oklahoma runs." In May, 1890, from these "Unassigned Lands" and the Panhandle, a region at this time outside the limits of any state or territory, the Territory of Oklahoma was created.

During the next sixteen years the remaining Indian lands west of the Indian Territory, as the country of the Five Civilized Tribes was called, were opened to white settlement and attached to Oklahoma Territory. Some were opened by "runs," the Kiowa-Comanche-Wichita reservation by lottery, and Greer County, claimed by Texas, was added by a decision of the Supreme Court. In the meantime the Five Civilized Tribes had continued to live under their own governments. Many white people came in to live among them, and a demand that these governments and the system of holding lands in common be abolished grew steadily stronger. In 1893 the Dawes Commission was created by the United States Government to achieve these objectives. After many years it was successful, and in 1906 Congress passed an Enabling Act permitting Oklahoma and Indian Territory to make a constitution for a new state which should include both regions. The convention, consisting of 112 delegates, met at Guthrie and formed a constitution, and Oklahoma became the 46th state of the Union on Nov. 16, 1907.

"OLD DOMINION."

When Charles II was restored to the throne in 1660 his authority was promptly and enthusiastically recognized by the Virginia burgesses. Thereupon Charles elevated Virginia to the position of a "dominion" by quartering the arms of the old seal of the London Company on his royal shield along with the arms of England, Scotland and Ireland; and the burgesses, recalling that they were the oldest as well as the most loyal of the Stuart settlements in the New World, adopted the name, "The Old Dominion."

"OLD FUSS AND FEATHERS" was a nickname applied to Gen. Winfield Scott. The connotation was affectionate or derisive, depending on the user's opinion of Scott. The sobriquet referred to the general's love of military pageantry, show uniforms and meticulousness in military procedure and etiquette. Soldiers, who appreciated his talents, seldom used it maliciously.

"OLD HICKORY." Because of his endurance and strength, this nickname was given to Andrew Jackson in 1813 by his soldiers during a march from Natchez, Miss., to Nashville, Tenn. By this name he was affectionately known among his friends and followers for the rest of his life.

OLD SOUTH CHURCH, Boston, was built in 1729 to replace the original structure of 1670. Here was held the Boston Massacre town meeting which forced the royal governor to withdraw the British troops from Boston in 1770; here were delivered Massacre anniversary orations by Warren, Hancock and others; and here was held the Tea Party meeting from which the "Indians" went to dump the hated tea into Boston Harbor.

"OLIVE BRANCH PETITION." After the first armed clashes at Lexington and Bunker Hill in 1775, the newly organized Continental Congress decided to send a petition to George III, setting forth the grievances of the colonies. Knowing the king's violent opposition to the idea of dealing with the colonies as an united group, the congressional delegates each signed the paper as an individual. Further to show their amicable intent, Richard Penn, descendant of William Penn and a staunch Loyalist, was made their messenger. But when Penn reached London on Aug. 14, 1775, the king refused to see him or to receive his petition through any channel.

OLNEY COROLLARY OF MONROE DOCTRINE. In his dispatch of July 20, 1895, to Thomas F. Bayard, Ambassador to Great Britain, Secretary of State Richard Olney applied the Monroe Doctrine to the Venezuelan situation by a much broader interpretation than that previously current. He declared that the Doctrine as a part of "public law" had made it the traditional policy of the United States to oppose a forcible increase by any European power of its territorial possessions in the Americas; that by withholding from arbitration part of the territory in dispute with Venezuela, Great Britain was constructively extending its colonization; and that since the United States was "entitled to resent and resist any sequestration of Venezuelan soil by Great Britain, it is necessarily entitled to know whether such sequestration has occurred or is now going on." On the basis of this extension of the Doctrine, Cleveland in December asked Congress to appoint a commission to fix the true boundary, beyond which Britain should not be allowed to push. Olney's loose construction of the Doctrine went much beyond the language used by Monroe and Adams, and was at once challenged by various American authorities on the subject.

OLNEY-PAUNCEFOTE TREATY was a general treaty of Anglo-American arbitration drafted primarily by Secretary of State Richard Olney and Sir Julian Pauncefote, British minister to the United States. Such a treaty had been considered for some years, and was suggested anew by Lord Salisbury in January, 1896. Salisbury proposed one of limited terms; Olney believed in giving arbitration the greatest possible scope, and in making the awards securely binding. The treaty he and Pauncefote drew up during 1896 made pecuniary and most other nonterritorial disputes completely arbitrable; territorial disputes, and any "disputed questions of principle of grave importance," were arbitrable subject to an appeal to a court of six, and if more than one of the six dissented, the award was not to be binding. Parliament promptly ratified the treaty. Cleveland sent it to the Senate on Jan. 11, 1897, with his strong approval, but it lay over until the Republican administration came into office. Then, although McKinley and Secretary John Hay earnestly supported it, ratification failed.

OÑATE'S EXPLORATIONS (1598–1608) were in reality rediscoveries of regions previously seen by Coronado, Espejo and Humaña, but they brought to light better trails and established Spain on the Rio Grande. Juan de Oñate, who previously had colonized San Luis Potosi, was appointed in 1595 to colonize and govern a new Mexico to be founded on the Rio Grande. He advanced from the Mexican frontier with 400 men, of whom 130 had families, and took formal possession near El Paso on April 30, 1598. Later in the summer he founded San Juan, north of the present Santa Fe. In the next three years he and his subordinates explored and subjugated the present New Mexico and northeastern Arizona. Oñate's first extensive journey from the Rio Grande was eastward in 1601, down the Canadian River and northeastward to the grass-house Indian village of Quivira, which was located on the Arkansas in the present Kansas. Returning to New Mexico, Oñate suppressed a brewing revolt. Late in 1604 he marched westward across the present northern Arizona to Bill Williams Fork, followed it to the Colorado River, and marched down that stream to the Gulf of California, returning in 1605. He was recalled from the governorship in 1608.

ONEIDA COLONY, N. Y., was America's most radical experiment in social and religious thinking. From literal concepts of Perfectionism and Bible Communism the colony advanced into new forms of social relationship: economic communism, the rejection of monogamy for "complex marriage," the practice of an elementary form of birth control (*coitus reservatus*), and the eugenic breeding of "stirpicultural" children. John Humphrey Noyes, leader of the group, was a capable and shrewd Yankee whose sincere primitive Christianity expressed itself in radically modern terms. His fellow workers had experienced complete religious conversion and boldly followed him into a communal life which rejected the evils of competitive economics while it kept realistically to the methods of modern industry, believing that socialism is ahead of and not behind society.

From the inception of the colony in 1848 the property grew to about 600 acres of well-cultivated land, shoe, tailoring and machine shops, canning and silk factories, great central buildings, houses for employees and a branch colony in Wallingford, Conn. Assets were $550,000 when communism was dropped. Health was above the average, women held a high place, children were excellently trained, work was fair and changeable, and entertainment was constant. They made communism work by adapting social theory to native facts and background.

In 1879, forced by social pressure from without and the dissatisfaction of the young within, monogamy was adopted, and within a year communism was replaced by joint stock ownership. In the new form, Oneida has continued its commercial success, but as a conventional group.

ONONDAGA, GREAT COUNCIL HOUSE AT. The capital of the Five (Six) Nations Confederacy was in the domain of the Onondaga nation situated (*ca.* 1600) south of Onondaga Lake. The group may or may not have had an official council house at the capital town, Onondaga, but it was presumably not possible for the meetings of the Iroquois Confederacy to be held within a single building unless strictly limited to the civil chiefs and their attendants. The term "great council house" is used in a symbolic sense, as is also the expression "the unquenched brands of the Great Council Fire of the League." In 1743 John Bartram described the Onondaga Long House giving a ground plan showing the building to have been eighty feet long and seventeen feet wide.

OPEN-DOOR POLICY. The expression "open-door policy" made its appearance toward the end of the 19th century in connection with official efforts to ensure equality of opportunity and treatment—that is, to prevent discrimination—in the field of trade in certain parts of the world where there were keen political and commercial rivalries.

In the General Act of the Conference of Berlin, in 1885, there was made provision that the commerce of all nations should enjoy in the basin of the Congo and its tributaries equality of access, and that there should be in those regions no discrimination in official treatment either of ships or of goods. Thereafter the expression "open door" came into popular usage in connection with discussion of competition and policies in the Far East, and especially of desiderata in regard to China. Ultimately that expression became particularized, especially in the United States, in reference to principles and procedure proposed by the American Secretary of State, John Hay, in the years 1899 and 1900, to the governments of the great powers most concerned, with the objective of preventing discrimination in the treatment of trade with and in China. Toward his objective, Hay, taking full cognizance of the *status quo*, first (in 1899) gave and asked for a pledge of equality of treatment for commerce in the various "spheres of interest or influence" in China, and then (in 1900, while the Boxers were besieging the legations) declared to the governments of the great powers represented in China that "the policy of the Government of the United States is to seek a solution which may bring about permanent safety and peace to China, preserve China's territorial and administrative entity, protect all rights granted to friendly powers by treaty and international law, and safeguard for the world the principle of equal and impartial trade with all parts of the Chinese Empire." (Circular Note, July 3, 1900, to "powers co-operating in China.")

In its broad application, "open-door policy" is an abbreviated and popular rendering of "policy of equality of commercial opportunity"—opportunity being envisaged in that connection from point of view of treatment officially accorded. It has frequently been affirmed that this expression is accurately descriptive of the practice of "most-favored-nation" treatment. In relations with China, the British government in 1842 and 1843 and the American Government in 1844 (Cushing's Treaty) induced the Chinese government to enter into treaties, and China then and therein undertook to accord that treatment. The United States had before and has since, in its relations with all countries, asked always for equality of commercial opportunity (treatment). The principle underlying the "open-door policy" has been regarded in American opinion as the most equitable and the most practicable that can be applied toward guidance of international conduct in the commercial field. The American people have come to believe that practical application of that principle makes for stability and peace, and the American Government has consistently urged universal adoption of and adherence to it.

ORDERS IN COUNCIL are executive edicts in Great Britain, issued in the name of the king, "by and with the advice of his privy council." They have the force of law until superseded by acts of Parliament. Among the many orders in council promulgated in British history, two are of primary interest for their influence upon the United States. They are the Orders in Council of Jan. 7 and Nov. 11, 1807, Britain's reply to the Berlin Decree of Napoleon.

Aimed at neutral commerce in general, in an endeavor to overthrow the economic foundations of Napoleon's power, they affected principally the United States as the chief of neutral carriers. The Orders of Jan. 7 placed French commerce under a blockade and forbade neutrals to trade from one port to another under Napoleon's jurisdiction. Commercial strangulation advanced a further step when, by the Orders of Nov. 11, it was stipulated that neutral ships, meaning American, might not enter any ports "from which . . . the British flag is excluded, and all ports or places in the colonies belonging to his majesty's enemies, shall, from henceforth, be subject to the same restrictions . . . as if the same were actually blockaded by his majesty's naval forces, in the most strict and rigorous manner."

These Orders were superseded on April 26, 1809, by a blockade of the Netherlands, France and Italy; and in June, 1812, too late to avert the War of 1812, the Orders were actually repealed, subject to certain modifications, in what constituted a major victory for American diplomacy.

ORDINANCES OF 1784, 1785 AND 1787 were enacted in connection with the development of a policy for the settlement of the country northwest of the Ohio River (*see* Northwest Territory). The establishment of the government of the Confederation was delayed several years over the issue of the disposition of the western lands. Seven states had western land claims, six had none; and the latter refused to join the Confederation until the former should cede their lands to the new government, to be utilized for the common benefit of all the states.

In 1780 New York led the way, whereupon Congress passed a resolution pledging that the lands the states might cede to the general government would be erected into new states which should be admitted to the Union on a basis of equality with the existing states. This vital decision made possible the future extension of the nation across the continent, for it is unthinkable that without it the people west of the Alleghenies would ever have submitted to a state of permanent dependence upon the original states.

Connecticut and Virginia followed New York, and the Confederation was established, March 1, 1781. With the close of the war the problems of reorganization which success entailed became more insistent, and among them the disposition of the western country loomed foremost. Among various projects propounded, one by Thomas Jefferson, which Congress enacted (April 23), became known as the Ordinance of 1784. It provided for an artificial division of the entire West into sixteen districts, eligible to statehood upon attaining a population of 20,000. Although subsequently repealed, the Ordinance of 1784 contributed to America's developing colonial policy its second basic idea—the establishment of temporary governments, under the fostering oversight of Congress, until a population sufficient for statehood should be attained.

Next year (May 20, 1785) the Ordinance "for ascertaining the mode of disposing of lands in the Western territory" was enacted. Since the dawn of civilization individual landholdings had been bounded and identified by such marks as trees, stakes and stones, and in the absence of any scientific system of surveying and recording titles of ownership to them, intolerable confusion, with resultant disputes and individual hardships, existed. In its stead, the Ordinance of 1785 provided a scientific system of surveying and subdividing land with clear-cut establishment of both boundaries and titles. The unit of survey is the township, six miles square, with boundaries based on meridians of longitude and parallels of latitude. The townships are laid out both east and west and north and south of base lines crossing at right angles; within, the township is subdivided into 36 square-mile sections, and these, in turn, into minor rectangles of any desired size.

In March, 1786, a group of New Englanders organized at Boston the Ohio Company of Associates. The leaders were able men of affairs who had very definite ideas concerning the colony they proposed to found. They opened negotiations with Congress, which made the desired grant of land and on July 13, 1787, enacted the notable Ordinance (which the petitioners had drafted) for the government of the territory northwest of the Ohio. It provided for a temporary government by agents appointed by Congress; but when the colony numbered 5000 adult free males, a representative legislature was to be established, and upon the attainment of 60,000 population the territory would be admitted to statehood.

The Ordinance also provided for the future division of the territory into not less than three nor more than five states; and it contained a series of compacts, forever unalterable save by common consent, safeguarding the rights of the future inhabitants of the territory. These established religious freedom, prohibited slavery, guaranteed the fundamental rights of English liberty and just treatment of the Indians; and a notable summary of the fundamental spirit of New England was supplied in the declaration that "religion, morality, and knowledge being necessary to good government and the happiness of mankind, schools and the means of education shall forever be encouraged."

The Ordinance of 1784 contributed a fundamental

idea to America's colonial system. Those of 1785 and 1787 still remain as landmarks in the orderly development of the American scheme of life. Under the operation of the policies they first established, millions of Americans today enjoy a security of life and property and a degree of liberty to which most of the people of the earth are still strangers.

OREGON. Long before the name Oregon became restricted to the present state it designated the Pacific coast region west of the Rocky Mountains, north of California and south of Alaska. Three nations were chiefly responsible for the exploration of its coastline, Spain, England and the United States. The first European known to have sighted the Oregon coast was Sir Francis Drake (who, escaping from the Spaniards after one of his raids in 1577, sailed along a portion of the southern Oregon coast). Aroused by this incident, the Spanish sought to secure the control of the coast by exploration. Juan Perez in 1774 reached the southern part of Alaska, and one of Bruno Heceta's ships reached the latitude of 58° in 1775. The English government sent one exploring expedition to the Northwest coast under Capt. Cook (1776), and one under Capt. George Vancouver (1792). Early American exploration was of a private character and incidental to the coastal fur trade; but one of the most important discoveries, that of the Columbia River, was made in this trade by Robert Gray (1792).

The first governmental exploring expedition to reach Oregon overland was sent by President Jefferson under the leadership of Meriwether Lewis and William Clark (1804–6).

American fur traders entered the region with the Pacific Fur Company's establishment of their post at the mouth of the Columbia River (1811). During the War of 1812 British fur interests supplanted the American interests. Before 1830 British fur-trading posts were scattered from the upper waters of the Columbia to California. The British retained the dominant place in the trade until after the boundary settlement (1846), successfully excluding American interests such as those of Jedediah Smith and Nathaniel Wyeth.

Missions for the Indians opened in 1834 when Jason Lee established the Oregon Mission of the Methodist Church in the Willamette Valley. The American Board Mission under Marcus Whitman and Henry Spalding was established in the interior in 1836. The missions became a major factor in arousing the interest in the Oregon Country, which resulted in the coming of the independent settler.

Each year after 1842 saw large numbers of settlers coming over the Oregon Trail to make their homes in Oregon, most of the first settlers taking up land claims in the Willamette Valley. No legal title to land was possible for the country was held jointly by Great Britain and the United States under the Convention of 1818 and no provision had been made for

such title. Essentially, all land was held by "squatters' rights." The settlers established a government by compact (Provisional Government—1843) which met the civil and military needs of the community until the territorial government was established (1849).

Oregon was the subject of frequent negotiations between the United States and Great Britain for almost thirty years before they adjusted their rival claims by the Oregon Treaty of 1846. This treaty extended the boundary along the 49th parallel from the Rocky Mountains to the Pacific Ocean, deflecting southward around the end of Vancouver Island to leave the island a unit under the British control.

The territory of Oregon as first established included not only the present State of Oregon but also Washington, Idaho and a portion of Montana. Washington was first separated from the parent territory (1853); Idaho was next carved out (1863); and Montana was the last to become a separate territory (1864).

The original movement of settlers to Oregon had been to the Willamette Valley, hence south of the Columbia River. This center of settlement determined that Oregon should first receive the full status of statehood. In 1857 the people voted to seek statehood and elected delegates for a constitutional convention. On Feb. 12, 1859, Congress passed a law admitting Oregon as a state.

OREGON MISSIONS. Attention was called to the need for Christian work among the Indians of the Pacific Northwest by an appeal made to Gen. William Clark of St. Louis in 1831 by four Flathead Indians who had journeyed from the Oregon Country asking that they be given religious instructors. A description of this visit was first published in the *Christian Advocate and Journal* of New York in 1833, and was widely copied in other religious journals. The Methodists immediately recommended the establishment of an Oregon mission, and Jason Lee, a young New Englander, was appointed to head it. By September, 1834, he and his party had reached Vancouver. A mission among the Flatheads being found to be impracticable, Lee established a mission in the Willamette Valley. A year later (1835) the American Board of Commissioners for Foreign Missions resolved to found a mission in the Pacific Northwest and commissioned Marcus Whitman and Henry H. Spalding to carry out the enterprise. Work was begun near what is now Walla Walla and soon a prosperous mission was in operation. Both Lee and Whitman became interested in bringing colonists to Oregon, a policy which their mission boards did not approve. Largely because of this fact Lee was removed. Whitman and his wife with twelve others were brutally murdered by the Indians in 1847.

The Catholics were also active in the same region, where their work was favored by the Hudson's Bay Company as being less likely to interfere with the fur trade. Under the intrepid Jesuit, Father P. J.

DeSmet (1840–50), Catholic missions were established in the region and within a few years 6000 converts were claimed.

OREGON PAROCHIAL SCHOOL CASE. In 1925 the Supreme Court by unanimous opinion (Pierce v. Society of the Sisters of the Holy Names of Jesus and Mary, 268 U. S. 510) invalidated an Oregon statute adopted in 1922 by initiative and referendum under which all children would have been required to attend the public schools. Ostensibly an education law and as such within the reserved powers of the state, it was well known from discussion in the course of the referendum that it was aimed at the parochial schools. It was not a compulsory education law or a reasonable regulation of school standards. The Supreme Court ruled, in effect, that children are not public wards, that parents have a right to control the selection of schools for their children, and that the owners and teachers of those private schools have a right to conduct their activities. The statute was an obvious abridgment of liberty under the due process clause of the Fourteenth Amendment. This decision, generally regarded as a wise and wholesome exposition of American ideals, was frequently cited in refutation of the common misconception that the Fourteenth Amendment is useful only as a protection of "property rights."

OREGON QUESTION. By successive treaties the territory of the Pacific Northwest was defined until it meant the territory west of the Rocky Mountains, north of 42° and south of 54° 40′. All or major portions of this vast territory were the subject of the conflicting claims of ownership of Spain, Great Britain, the United States and Russia.

Spain's exclusive claims, based upon discoveries of her seamen along the coast and her special claims of dominance in the Pacific, were successfully challenged by Great Britain in the Nootka Convention (1790); and in the Adams-Onís Treaty (1819) Spain surrendered to the United States all claims north of 42°. Russia, whose claims were the weakest of any of the four powers, withdrew all claims south of 54° 40′ by separate treaties with the United States (1824) and Great Britain (1825). With the boundary between the United States and British America having been drawn as far west as the Rockies by the Convention of 1818, the boundaries of Oregon were determined, and the territory was left by the same treaty in joint occupation of the two claimants, the United States and Great Britain.

Until the final division of the territory between the two powers in June, 1846, by the extension of the 49th parallel to the sea, deflecting southward to leave Vancouver Island to the British, the Oregon question was the subject of intermittent correspondence between the two governments. British claims were repeatedly summarized as depending upon the discoveries of Sir Francis Drake, Capt. James Cook and Capt. George Vancouver, the Nootka Convention with Spain, the exploration and occupation of the British fur companies. The American claims were based upon the discovery of the Columbia River by Capt. Robert Gray (1792), explorations of the Lewis and Clark expedition (1802–6), the establishment of Astoria (1811) by the Pacific Fur Company and its restoration under the Convention of 1818, the Spanish claims, and American settlements which started with the Oregon missions (1834) and had constantly increased after 1842.

American public interest became centered upon Oregon by successive unsuccessful efforts to make land claims available for American settlers. Under the leadership of John Floyd of Virginia such an effort was first made in 1821. Later congressional leadership concerning Oregon passed to Sen. Lewis F. Linn of Missouri. The first missionary settlements aroused widespread interest, and each successive group of settlers which poured into Oregon after 1842 built up the interest. By 1844 the popular feeling over Oregon found expression in the political slogan of "Fifty-four Forty or Fight," which was widely used in the campaign in which James K. Polk was elected President. Action followed quickly upon Polk's taking office. On April 27, 1846, Congress authorized the President to give Great Britain notice of the termination of the Joint Occupation Treaty. The British government was distinctly a peace government, and the American Government clearly overstated its claims, so by June 18, 1846, a compromise treaty settled the Oregon question by continuing the boundary east of the Rockies (49°) to the sea.

"OREGON SYSTEM." In 1902 Oregon adopted a constitutional amendment establishing a system of direct voter participation in lawmaking. The initiative permits a specified percentage of voters to place a law, or constitutional amendment, before the voters for their final action without reference to the legislature. By the referendum a law, passed by the legislature, can be referred to the people for final acceptance or rejection. Closely associated with these two features were other features commonly known as parts of the "Oregon system," including the recall, direct primary, presidential preference primary, and state printed campaign textbooks.

OREGON TRAIL, first dimly traced across the country from the Missouri River to the Columbia River by explorers and fur traders, after 1842 was worn into a deeply rutted highway by the pioneers in their covered wagons. In 1805 the course of Lewis and Clark in the Snake and Columbia Rivers region covered a portion of what was later to be the famous pioneer highway. A few years later (1810) a party of the Missouri Fur Company traveled through the South Pass and thus discovered an important part of the Trail. A party of Astorians, under Robert Stuart, returning to the East in 1812 largely followed the route which later became the Oregon Trail. Two independent American fur traders, Capt. Benjamin Bonneville and Capt. Nathaniel J. Wyeth, between the years 1832 and 1836, led their companies over this route. Knowledge of the Trail as a passable route was current among the traders on the frontier and became common property. This knowledge became available for the use of companies of settlers in two forms: traders who had been over the route and were willing to hire out as guides; and in the form of printed guide books compiled by enterprising travelers. These guide books appeared surprisingly early and the copies which reached the end of the Trail were thumbed and worn.

The distances on the Trail were calculated with a high degree of accuracy. One of the old guide books gives a tabulation of the distances which shows the established Trail. The points used to mark the way were selected for a variety of reasons, such as conspicuous landmarks, difficult streams to ford, the infrequent posts at which a few supplies might be obtained. This old guide book (J. M. Shively, *Route and Distances to Oregon and California*, 1846) marks the way from Missouri River to the mouth of the Columbia River as follows:

	MILES
From Independence to the Crossings of Kansas	102
Crossings of Blue	83
Platte River	119
Crossings of South Platte	163
To North Fork	20
To Fort Larima [Laramie]	153
From Larima to Crossing of North Fork of the Platte	140
To Independence Rock on Sweet Water	50
Fort Bridger	229
Bear River	68
Soda Springs	94
To Fort Hall	57
Salmon Falls	160
Crossings of Snake River	22
To Crossings of Boise River	69
Fort Boise	45
Dr. Whitman's Mission	190
Fort Walawala [Walla Walla]	25
Dallis Mission [The Dalles]	120
Cascade Falls, on the Columbia	50
Fort Vancouver	41
Astoria	90

The author could well have left off the last ninety miles and given the distance into the Willamette Valley, which was the destination of most of the travelers.

The interest in Oregon became so widespread along the frontier about 1842 that emigrating societies were formed to encourage people to move to Oregon. By lectures, letters and personal visits, members of these societies secured recruits for the long journey. Independence, Mo., was the most frequent place of departure, and shortly after leaving there the companies commonly organized a government by electing officers and adopting rules of conduct. The emigrants gathered in time to leave in the early spring to take advantage of the fresh pasturage for their animals and to allow all possible time for the long journey.

From Independence the companies followed the old Santa Fe Trail a two days' journey of some forty miles to where a crude signpost pointed to the "Road to Oregon." At Fort Laramie, where the Trail left the rolling plains for the mountainous country, there was an opportunity to overhaul and repair wagons. The next point where repairs could be made with outside help was Fort Bridger, some 394 miles beyond Laramie and about 1070 miles from Independence. The Trail used South Pass through the Rockies. It is a low pass less than 7500 feet above sea level and was easily passable for the heavy covered wagons. The difficulties of travel greatly increased on the Pacific side. Much barren country had to be crossed under conditions which wore out and killed the already exhausted horses and oxen. At Fort Hall, in the Snake River country, the first immigrants gave up their wagons and repacked on horses; but shortly, determined individuals refused to do so and worked a way through for their wagons. The Grande Ronde Valley offered grass to recruit the worn beasts of burden before the immigrant attempted the almost impassable way through the Blue Mountains. Emerging from these mountains the immigrant followed the Umatilla River to the Columbia, which he followed to Fort Vancouver, the last portion often being made on rafts. The journey of some 2000 miles over the Oregon Trail was the greatest trek of recorded history.

The wagon travel during the 1840's and 1850's became so heavy that the road was a clearly defined and deeply rutted way across the country. When the ruts became too deep for travel, parallel roads were broken. So deeply was the Oregon Trail worn that generations after the last covered wagon had passed over it hundreds of miles of it could still be traced. To the awed Indians it seemed the symbol of a nation of countless numbers.

The over 2000 miles of the Oregon Trail tested human strength and endurance as it has rarely been tested. The Trail was littered with castoff possessions, often of considerable monetary as well as great sentimental value. Worn draft animals could no longer drag the heavy wagons and even the most prized possessions had to be left standing beside the Trail. The carcasses of the innumerable dead cattle and horses were left along the Trail while the bodies of the human dead were buried in shallow graves. The diaries of the overland journey note with fearful monotony the number of new graves passed each day on the Trail. Cholera was the terrible scourge which struck the bravest heart with terror.

From 1842 through the 1850's the companies came over the Trail in large numbers, to dwindle away in the 1860's. The bitter experiences of the first companies, who knew so little about equipment, were passed on to the later companies, and as the years went by better adapted equipment was used. Especially constructed wagons were used, oxen largely replaced horses, and supplies were selected more wisely. The way became better established, even including crude ferries at some of the most difficult river crossings; but to the day that the last covered wagon was dragged over the rutted Oregon Trail it was the way of hardship and danger which tested the pioneer stock of the West.

ORGANIZATION FOR ECONOMIC COOPERATION AND DEVELOPMENT (O.E.C.D.). Adherence of the United States to this organization was insured by Senate ratification of the treaty of membership, March 16, 1961, and represents the first step the United States has taken in economic internationalism. In fact, it represents an attitude at the opposite pole of economic isolation epitomized by the Smoot-Hawley Tariff Act of 1930.

O.E.C.D., a 20-nation association (18 European nations and the United States and Canada) which became effective Sept. 19, 1960, has three major kinds of activity: (1) to develop a common approach to internal economic policies calculated to foster economic growth; (2) to coordinate, improve and increase aid to underdeveloped countries; and (3) to coordinate trade policies and to increase international trade. The two major operating elements are the Common Market and the European Free Trade Association (E.F.T.A.), the successful functioning of which depends on western European unity.

ORISKANY, BATTLE OF (Aug. 6, 1777). The British threefold plan of campaign for 1777 included in its strategy the advance of Lt. Col. Barry St. Leger across New York from Oswego to meet Burgoyne and Howe in Albany. On Aug. 3, St. Leger with an army of approximately 1200, mostly Tories under Col. John Butler and Sir John Johnson and Indians led by Joseph Brant, appeared before Fort Stanwix and demanded its surrender. In the meantime Gen. Nicholas Herkimer had called out the Tryon County militia, and on Aug. 4 with an army of about 800 men he left Fort Dayton. The following evening he sent three messengers to advise Col. Peter Gansevoort, the commanding officer at Fort Stanwix, that he planned to fall upon St. Leger's rear when Gansevoort attacked in front. Three guns were to be fired as a signal. The next morning the Americans advanced to a point about eight miles from the fort. Here, Herkimer wished to stop until he received the signal. His caution seemed excessive to his officers. A violent quarrel followed, and against his better judgment Herkimer gave the order to advance.

Brant's Indians had reported Herkimer's approach to St. Leger and a detachment of Tories and Indians under Sir John Johnson had been sent to ambush the advancing Americans. About two miles west of Oriskany Creek the main body of the Americans entered a ravine, followed by the heavy baggage wagons. A deadly volley from both sides met them. The rearguard, still on the hill above, retreated. The main body was thrown into confusion, but rallied and one of the bloodiest battles of the Revolution took place. A sudden thunder shower added to the tumult. Early in the conflict a ball killed Herkimer's horse and shattered his own leg. He had his saddle placed at the foot of a beech tree and lighting his pipe calmly continued to give orders. Suddenly the signal guns were heard. The expected sortie was taking place. The Indians fled and the Tories retreated from the Oriskany battlefield, but the weakened American forces were unable to proceed to the relief of the fort. Much-needed supplies and ammunition were, however, captured during the sortie from Fort Stanwix, and St. Leger, unable to force the surrender of the fort, on Aug. 22 retreated to Oswego.

OSAGE HEDGE, or *Maclura,* universally used on the prairies for fences, is a thorn-bearing plant producing a pale-green fruit larger than an orange from which the plant gets its name—Osage orange. The French discovered the Osage Indians using the tough, springy yellow wood for bows, and named the plant *bois d'arc* or bow wood. The first nurseries on the treeless prairies raised millions of these Osage orange, or, as they were commonly called, "hedge" plants, and sold them to the settlers for fences. The wood, although knotty and crooked, was used for tool handles, tongues for implements, and for fence posts which lasted for years. When allowed to grow, hedge furnished excellent wood for fuel. The thorn on the Osage orange gave an inventor the idea for perfecting barbed wire, which largely replaced hedge as a fencing agent. In the 20th century hedge has fallen into disfavor because it saps crops and obscures the roadway. Miles of this once-prized fence have been grubbed out at great expense.

OSAWATOMIE, BATTLE OF (Aug. 30, 1856). The town was attacked by about 250 proslavery men (supposedly Missourians) and was defended by John Brown with 40 men. The Free State men were soon dislodged from their position along the creek bank and fled, after which the village was sacked. Each side lost about six killed and several wounded.

OSTEND MANIFESTO. Expansionist ardor, unsatisfied even by the Mexican cession, was largely responsible for this blunder in our Cuban diplomacy. American slaveholders had dreaded the possibility of emancipation or revolution and the creation of a new Santo Domingo almost within sight of our shores.

Cuba, furthermore, offered tempting possibilities for annexation and the establishment of another slave state. On April 7, 1853, President Pierce appointed Pierre Soulé minister to Spain with instructions to negotiate for the purchase of Cuba. Soulé failed completely; but in 1854 Spain was embarrassed by revolutionary outbreaks, and it was hoped that holders of Spanish bonds, tempted by the prospect of American cash reinforcing a dubious security, might exert pressure on the Madrid government. Soulé, James Buchanan, minister to Great Britain, and John Y. Mason, minister to France, were instructed by Secretary of State Marcy to confer on the Cuban situation. They met at Ostend in October, 1854, signing the notorious "manifesto" on the 15th. In effect, the conferees declared that should Spain refuse to sell, and should the United States consider Spain's further possession of Cuba inimical to our domestic interests, forcible seizure would be fully justified. The document caused a profound sensation, and amid a storm of denunciation, foreign and domestic, Secretary Marcy disavowed the declaration.

OSWEGO. In 1722, in spite of French claims to the region, English and Dutch traders began to assemble at Choueguen (Oswego) where they carried on a thriving trade with the Indians. In 1726–27 Gov. Burnet dispatched a number of soldiers and workmen to construct a fort on the west bank of the Oswego River near its mouth. Intruding into the line of French fortifications which controlled the Great Lakes and the waterways to the south, this post was the most important English fortification west of the Hudson, for it created a barrier to further French encroachments into northern New York.

From this point, on June 28, 1755, was launched the first English vessel to sail on the Great Lakes, and on Aug. 18, Gen. William Shirley arrived with an expedition destined for an attack on Fort Niagara. This move was deferred, but on the east side of the Oswego River, a quarter of a mile from Fort Oswego, the British erected a post which they named Fort Ontario. In 1756 these establishments were under attack by the French under DeVilliers, and on Aug. 13–14 they were captured and destroyed by the Marquis de Montcalm. Abandoned by the French, the ruins were later converted into a fortified camp for the British troops under Prideaux.

In 1759–60 the British rebuilt Fort Ontario, and it again became a base for military operations. In July and August, 1760, it was the rendezvous of Amherst's army, augmented by 1300 French Iroquois who came to make peace with the British. It was there, in July, 1766, that Sir William Johnson met in council the great Ottawa chieftain, Pontiac, who signed a treaty of everlasting peace with Great Britain.

Fort Ontario continued as a peaceful trading post, and in 1774 was dismantled, with only a few men left to keep it from falling into decay. In 1777, however, it was St. Leger's base in his operations in the Mohawk Valley in connection with Burgoyne's invasion.

In the War of 1812, Oswego was a naval base, and the headquarters of Commodore Chauncey. On May 6, 1814, it was attacked and captured by the British. The settlement was incorporated as a village in 1828 and chartered as a city in 1848.

"OUR COUNTRY, RIGHT OR WRONG." At a dinner in his honor at Norfolk, Va., April 4, 1816, Stephen Decatur offered the following toast: "Our Country! In her intercourse with foreign nations may she always be in the right and always successful, right or wrong." This toast, popularly incorrectly quoted, was a reflection of the development of nationalism incident to the War of 1812.

"OUR FEDERAL UNION! IT MUST AND SHALL BE PRESERVED!" President Jackson's volunteer toast at the Jefferson anniversary dinner, April 13, 1830, was a rejoinder to previous speakers who had eulogized states' rights and hinted at disunion. Delivered in a most dramatic setting, with John C. Calhoun the exponent of nullification at the table, and described by onlookers as ringing through the banquet hall like one of the old warrior's strident commands on the field of battle, it not only clarified the position of the Chief Executive on the nullification question but served to strengthen the hearts of Unionists throughout the nation. It unquestionably contributed to the successful meeting of the ominous crisis of 1833.

OVERLAND COMPANIES, or Overland Emigrant Companies, were composed of groups of families who traveled from points east of the Mississippi River to the Pacific coast, usually Oregon or California, by wagon train, across country, as opposed to those who went by ship around Cape Horn or by the Isthmus of Darien.

The first of the large overland movements was the "Great Migration of 1843" to Oregon which established the Oregon Trail. The second large movement was the California gold rush of 1849. A company was usually organized among a group of friendly families although sometimes others unattached were accepted into membership. Rules to regulate the movement of the train and the action of individuals were drawn up and accepted before the start. One of the members, usually the most influential man, was elected captain; he had as much authority as a sea or army captain in making and enforcing the orders of the day. A council of ten or twelve older men was sometimes chosen for policy making; other active younger men were appointed hunters to supply the party with meat. All able-bodied men were regarded as a standing army if defense against an Indian attack was necessary.

OVERLAND FREIGHTING (1850–70). Before the railroads were built, a large portion of the freight was carried by wagons. More specifically the term "Overland Freighting" has been applied to the carrying industry on the Overland Trail from points on the Missouri River to the Rocky Mountains or California.

As soon as Salt Lake City was founded and gold discovered in California, a certain amount of hauling began. This was greatly increased during the campaign of Gen. Johnston against the Mormons and the discovery of gold in Colorado in the late 1850's. Large outfitting towns along the Missouri River were the eastern termini of the freighting routes which for the most part ran up the Platte Valley or the Kansas Valley to the Rocky Mountains.

Large freighting companies were established to take care of this business. The best known of these was the firm of Russell, Majors and Waddell, which started from Atchison and Leavenworth, Kans., St. Joseph, Mo., and Nebraska City, Nebr. At the outfitting town there were acres of wagons, huge herds of oxen, great pyramids of extra axletrees and battalions of drivers and other employees. In 1859 this firm alone used 45,000 oxen and from April 25 to Oct. 13, 1860, shipped from Nebraska City 2,782,258 pounds of freight. There were many other, both large and small, concerns in the business. Even pioneer farmers with one or two wagons sought a share of the lucrative business. In 1864 an army officer estimated that for several months during the summer no less than 1000 tons of merchandise a day poured into Denver, Colo.

Russell, Majors and Waddell ran 26 wagons in a train with an average load of 6000 pounds each. Each wagon was drawn by six yoke of oxen. The train was presided over by the wagon boss. An assistant boss, a night herder, a man to drive the extra animals and a spare driver or two brought the number of men in a train up to at least thirty-one. Their covered wagons strung out in line of travel like a fleet of ships with their white sails unfurled. The wagon master was admiral of this little fleet, and his word was law. He rode ahead, directed the course, selected a camp site and started and stopped the train. He and his assistant were on hand at once when one of the wagons had trouble.

It was customary to rise at three in the morning, get onto the road early, and drive until ten, when breakfast was eaten. The oxen were then allowed to rest until afternoon when a second drive was made. The train averaged from twelve to fifteen miles a day. When it reached the bedground, the boss directed the "bullwhackers," as the drivers were called, in forming an elliptical corral with their wagons.

The time required for a trip from Kansas City to Salt Lake City was about fifty days; the return trip was made in about forty. The freight rate differed with the season and danger from Indians.

Some freighting concerns used mule teams. In 1860 a "steam wagon," made on the order of a modern steam tractor, was tried out at Nebraska City, Nebr., with the idea of hauling freight overland, but its great weight, its imperfect mechanism, and the difficulty with which fuel could be secured for it, caused its promoters to abandon the plan. As the railroads were built across the plains the freighting outfits continued to operate over the gradually narrowing gap until finally the railroad usurped their prerogative.

OVERLAND MAIL AND STAGECOACHES followed the covered wagon into the trans-Missouri West. Monthly government mail services were established from Independence, Mo., to Santa Fe and to Salt Lake City in 1850. Thirty days were allowed for the one-way trip on each line. A similar service was begun between Salt Lake City and Sacramento, Calif., in 1851. With small remuneration, but one team was usually used for the trip and no way stations were maintained. With such facilities, practically all mail for California went by steamer, via Panama, with a thirty-day schedule from New York to San Francisco.

Proponents of overland service advocated an adequate subsidy for the maintenance of stations and changes of teams. They finally pushed their bill through Congress. Under it, the semiweekly Southern, or Butterfield, Overland Mail on a 25-day schedule was inaugurated in 1858. The choice of a southern route, via El Paso and Tucson, angered proponents of the central route (via Salt Lake City). The Postmaster General defended the southern route as the only one feasible for year-round travel. To disprove this, the Pony Express was established on the central route (1860) by the contractors carrying the semimonthly stagecoach mail on this road.

With the outbreak of the Civil War the Southern Overland Mail was removed to the central route, in Union-controlled territory, and was made a daily service. Coaches were to carry the letter mail from the Missouri River to California in twenty days, other mail in 35 days. The contract provided annual compensation of $1,000,000. Ben Holladay purchased the line and contract in 1862. A vigorous organizer, he quickly improved the line, extended branches to Oregon and Montana, and earned the appellation, "The Napoleon of the Plains." Indians interrupted the coaches and destroyed many stations in 1864, but the distribution of additional soldiers cleared the road. Wells Fargo purchased Holladay's lines in 1866 and continued operations until completion of the first transcontinental railroad (Union Pacific Railroad). Coaches continued for many years to serve localities not reached by rail.

The Concord stagecoach, manufactured by Abbot-Downing of Concord, N. H., was the great overland carrier of passengers, mail and express before 1869. It was swung on leather thorobraces in lieu of springs, and accommodated nine inside passengers and others on the top. Leather boots at front and rear carried the mail and express. The coach was drawn by four or six horses or mules, and usually made 100 miles in 24 hours. The driver was the lion of the road, the only one, as Mark Twain on his stage trips says, "they bowed down to and worshipped." His fancy whip was his pride. The stagecoach was a symbol and an institution of the prerailroad West.

OVERLAND TRAIL OR ROUTE was a variation of the Oregon Trail, being a short route from near the forks of the Platte to Fort Bridger, Wyo. It was popularized and named in 1862 when Ben Holladay's Overland Stage Line was moved to it from the old emigrant road along the North Platte. Shorter distance and less Indian danger induced the change of stage route. The Overland Trail followed the south bank of the South Platte to Latham, near present Greeley, Colo., up the Cache la Poudre, across the Laramie Plains, over Bridger Pass and thence west to Fort Bridger. Its route west of Latham was previously called the "Cherokee Trail," having been traversed by Cherokee goldseekers in 1849. The Lincoln Highway and the Union Pacific Railroad approximately follow the Overland Trail through western Wyoming. Some emigrants used this trail in the middle 1860's, but it was never so popular as the older route, the Oregon Trail.

OXEN were used from the time of the early settlements in America as draft animals and for plowing. Their slowness of pace was counterbalanced on rough, muddy pioneer roads by their great superiority to the horse in strength and endurance. They were used in logging and in early canal and railroad building. On the Middlesex Canal in Massachusetts, about 1805, one yoke (two) of them, in a test, drew a raft containing 800 tons of timber, but at the rate of only one mile per hour, which was considered too slow to be permitted on the towpath. During the 19th century, the small farmers, white and colored, in the South, were happy to have a yoke of "steers," or even one steer for general use, and an occasional one might be found working there as late as the third decade of the 20th century. Oxen drew many of the household wagons of the pioneers in all the great westward migrations—to the Ohio country, to Tennessee, Kentucky, to the prairie states, and finally, in 1848–49, on the long treks over plains and mountains to Oregon and California. Next they were employed in enormous numbers for freighting in the West. Two large loaded wagons were often hooked together and drawn over rough trails by six, eight or ten yoke of oxen. Several rigs of this sort, traveling together for safety, were called, in western parlance, a "bull train." Russell, Majors and Waddell, while they were hauling supplies for the army from the Missouri River to Utah in 1857–58, are said to have worked 40,000 oxen and only 1000 mules. When the gold rush to the Black Hills began in 1875, one company, freighting from Sioux City, Iowa, to Deadwood, S. Dak., used from 2000 to 3000 oxen and

1000 to 1500 mules. Another concern, operating between Yankton and Deadwood, was working 4000 oxen at the height of the rush.

PACK TRAINS. For the conversion of Western products into the indispensable articles which the trans-Allegheny pioneers could not wrest from their environment, caravans of pack horses were the means of transport. After crops were secured in autumn, the neighbors of a frontier community organized a pack train. Each horse was girthed with a wooden packsaddle and laden with goods for barter—mainly peltry, some ginseng, potash, flax, whiskey. Feed also was carried, part to be cached in the mountains for the return journey. The string of customarily ten to twenty horses, under command of a master driver and two or three "understrappers," followed usually an old Indian trail; the belled horses plodded in single file some 15 to 25 miles before they were hobbled for the night's bivouac. The main Pennsylvania trails were the Kittanning from the Allegheny River down the Juniata Valley, and the Raystown Path from the Ohio to the Eastern cities; on the main southerly route Baltimore, the earliest depot, was replaced as trading spread farther west by Frederick, Hagerstown and Cumberland. The pack trains returned with salt, iron, sugar, lead, perhaps some urban "luxuries" such as crockery.

From its communal beginnings, packing became a professional vocation. Widening of the trails to permit wagon passage, James O'Hara's enterprise in bringing salt down the Allegheny River to Pittsburgh, and the safety of keelboat transportation on the Ohio after 1795, pushed the primitive pack trains into farther frontiers. They shared the Santa Fe Trail with freighters' wagons, served remote fur-trading and mining posts, and were much used by troops operating against hostile Indians.

PACKERS AND STOCKYARDS ACT, passed in August, 1921, after several years of controversy, made it unlawful for packers to manipulate prices, to create monopoly, and to award favors to any person or locality. The regulation of stockyards provided for nondiscriminatory services, reasonable rates, open schedules and fair charges. The administration of the law was under the direction of the Secretary of Agriculture who entertained complaints, held hearings and issued "cease and desist" orders. The bill was a significant part of the agrarian legislation of the early 1920's.

PACKETS, SAILING. The packet proper, or sailing liner, as distinguished from the "regular trader" and the transient or tramp, was one of a line of privately owned vessels, sailing in regular succession on fixed dates between specified ports; it rendered a service later continued by the steamship lines. The New York packets in their day served as the chief link between the Old World and the New; played an essential part in attracting the movements of commerce toward New York; demonstrated the value of line arrangement; and incidentally made more money than most clippers or whalers. Nor was adventure lacking in their grim assignment, driven to the limit through ocean gales at all seasons.

The British government mail brigs, which carried no freight, and local New York steamers were partial precedents for the Black Ball Line which began monthly service between New York and Liverpool in 1818. By 1822 the Red Star Line, the Blue Swallow-tail Line, and doubled Black Ball service gave weekly sailings between the two ports, augmented later by the Dramatic Line and "New Line." Meanwhile New York inaugurated similar service with London and Havre between 1822 and 1824. Rival efforts of Philadelphia, Boston and Baltimore met with slight success.

The history of these New York ocean packets falls into three periods of some twenty years each. Until 1838 their functional importance was at its height, for they conveyed most of the news, cabin passengers, and "fine freight" between Europe and America. During the next twenty years, with steamships cutting into those lucrative fields, they changed to the immigrant business; but the ships themselves increased in size and in speed until the mid-1850's. In their later years, losing even the steerage trade, they became mere freighters on schedule. The last ocean packet sailing was made in 1881.

The packet principle was successfully extended to coastal runs. By 1826 lines of full-rigged ships were connecting New York with the cotton ports, while lesser lines of brigs or schooners plied other coastal runs. The former group brought cotton to New York for shipment to Europe and helped to distribute New York's imports.

"PAIRING," a practice whereby two members of opposing parties who plan to be absent agree that, during a specified period, they will refrain from voting in person, but will permit their names to be recorded on opposite sides of each question, appeared in the national House of Representatives as early as 1824, was first openly avowed in 1840, but not officially recognized in the Rules until 1880. Pairing is also permitted in the Senate, and is customary, though not universal, in state legislatures.

PALO ALTO, BATTLE OF (May 8, 1846), was the first battle of the Mexican War. Gen. Zachary Taylor's army of 2228 men met a Mexican force more than twice its number under Gen. Mariano Arista twelve miles northeast of the modern city of Brownsville, Texas. Almost entirely an artillery duel, it demonstrated the superiority of Taylor's cannon, strengthened American morale, and resulted in an American victory the full effect of which was not felt until the following day at Resaca de la Palma.

PAN AMERICAN CONFERENCES. James G. Blaine conceived the idea of a Pan American conference while he was Secretary of State under Garfield, but the invitations that he issued were withdrawn by his successor after Garfield's death. Blaine returned to the State Department in time to preside over the First International Conference of American States when it convened at Washington, at the invitation of the United States, in 1889. The chief purpose of the meeting was to promote trade, and the conference discussed several commercial and financial questions. It adopted a convention for the compulsory arbitration of pecuniary claims and created the International Bureau of American Republics, which later became the Pan American Union.

The Second and Third Inter-American Conferences, at Mexico City in 1901–2 and at Rio de Janeiro in 1906, also dealt with commercial and financial matters. Like the first, they accomplished little of lasting value. The Fourth, at Buenos Aires in 1910, adopted important conventions for the protection of copyrights and patents.

The first Inter-American conference to discuss political questions was the Fifth, which met at Santiago, Chile, in 1923. The conference adopted the Gondra Peace Treaty, which pledged the signatories to submit disputes to a commission of inquiry before going to war, but it was unable to agree on proposals for disarmament or for closer political cooperation. Both at the Fifth Conference and at the Sixth, at Havana in 1928, there was evidence of a growing opposition to the Caribbean policy of the United States, and at the Sixth Conference a resolution condemning intervention by one state in the affairs of another was blocked only after a disagreeable debate.

At the Seventh Conference, which met at Montevideo in 1933, Secretary of State Hull signed with minor reservations a convention on the Rights and Duties of States which specifically forbade intervention. This made possible a new era of inter-American co-operation. In 1936 a special Inter-American Conference for the Maintenance of Peace agreed that the American Republics would consult with one another if the peace of the continent were menaced. The Declaration of American Principles and the Declaration of Lima, both adopted by the Ninth Inter-American Conference at Lima in 1938, further stressed the American states' determination to act together in upholding civilized procedures in dealing with international problems.

During World War II questions affecting the defense of the continent were dealt with by meetings of the Foreign Ministers of the American Republics. At Panama, in 1939, standards for maintaining neutrality and measures to counteract the economic effects of the war were adopted. The Havana meeting in July, 1940, agreed that any European possession in the Americas which was in danger of a change of sovereignty, should be placed under a provisional administration representing the American Republics. The third meeting, held at Rio de Janeiro in January, 1942, adopted measures for continental defense and recommended that all of the American Republics break off diplomatic relations with the Axis powers.

In February, 1945, an Inter-American Conference on Problems of War and Peace adopted further measures for wartime co-operation and worked out plans for a more effective organization of the Inter-American System. These were given definite form at a conference at Rio de Janeiro in 1947, at which the Inter-American Treaty of Reciprocal Assistance was signed, and at the Ninth Inter-American Conference at Bogotá in 1948. Though the proceedings of the Bogotá meeting were interrupted by the riots which occurred while it was in session, the conference drew up the Charter of the Organization of American States, which created an effective international organization within the framework of the United Nations. Under the Charter, the general Inter-American Conferences, which are the "supreme organ" of the Organization, will meet every five years.

The Tenth Inter-American Conference, which met at Caracas in 1954, adopted conventions on territorial and diplomatic asylum and a convention for the promotion of cultural relations, and proclaimed a "Declaration of Solidarity for the Preservation of the Political Integrity of the American States Against the Intervention of International Communism." The Eleventh Conference was to have met at Quito in 1960, but was postponed.

The Ministers of Foreign Affairs met four times between 1951 and 1960 to discuss the growing danger from communist activities in America and other problems that endangered the peace of the Hemisphere. There have also been many special inter-American conferences to deal with a great variety of matters of common interest. An example was the economic conference that met at Bogotá in 1960 to consider plans for industrial development and social reform.

PANAMA CANAL. Proposals for a transisthmian canal were made soon after Spanish America became independent. In 1846, the United States made a treaty with New Granada, now Colombia, guaranteeing the neutrality of the Isthmus of Panama and the sovereignty of New Granada there in return for a promise of free transit across the Isthmus by any mode of communication that might be constructed. Under this treaty the United States frequently intervened to maintain freedom of transit in times of political disturbance. The Panama Railroad, built by American enterprise, was completed in 1855, and was for some years extensively used by travelers from the east coast to California.

In 1881 a French company, sponsored by Ferdinand de Lesseps, began the construction of a canal at Panama, under a concession granted by Colombia in 1878. After doing a substantial amount of excavation this company failed, partly because of financial mismanagement and partly because of the ravages of yellow fever among its employees. A new company took over the concession, but without the necessary capital to continue the work. Meanwhile an American company had also failed in an attempt to build a canal across Nicaragua.

After the voyage of the *Oregon* around South America at the beginning of the Spanish-American War emphasized the need for a canal, the U. S Government undertook the task of construction. The Clayton-Bulwer Treaty of 1850, by which the United States and Great Britain had agreed that neither would attempt to control any transisthmian canal, was replaced by the Hay-Pauncefote Treaty of 1901, which gave the United States a free hand but provided that the Canal should be open to ships of all nations on equal terms. A commission established in 1899 studied the Panama and Nicaragua routes and recommended that Panama be chosen if the French company would sell its rights for $40,000,000 and if adequate arrangements could be made with Colombia.

The French company agreed to sell, but the ratification of the Hay-Herrán Treaty of January, 1903, by which Colombia would have authorized the building of the Canal, was prevented by opposition in the Colombian Congress. This caused disappointment in Panama, and on Nov. 3, 1903, local leaders aided by the commander of the garrison seized control at Panama City and declared independence. The conspiracy had been encouraged by officials of the Panama Railroad Co., which was now a subsidiary of the French canal company, and it was financed by Philippe Bunau-Varilla, who had been connected with the French company. Officers of the railroad company refused to provide transportation for Colombian troops at Colón to cross the Isthmus to suppress the revolt, and were supported in this action by the commander of the U. S. S. *Nashville*, which had just arrived. On Nov. 6, the United States recognized the independence of Panama; and on Nov. 18 Bunau-Varilla, as representative of the new government, signed a treaty by which the United States was given the right to build a canal, and in return guaranteed Panama's independence. Thereafter the United States refused to permit Colombia to make any attempt to restore her authority on the Isthmus.

The Colombian government asserted that the revolt had been instigated and aided by the United States, and that the action of the American forces in preventing Colombian troops from crossing the Isthmus was improper. President Theodore Roosevelt and Secretary Hay denied that any responsible American official had been in communication with the revolutionists before the revolt. They defended their actions as justifiable under the treaty of 1846, and insisted that the people of Panama had a right to revolt when confronted by action that affected their vital interests. Nevertheless, the United States paid Colombia $25,000,000 as compensation for what had occurred, under a treaty signed in 1914 and ratified in 1922.

The treaty of Nov. 18, 1903, granted to the United States in perpetuity the "use, occupation and control" of a zone ten miles wide for the "construction, maintenance, operation, sanitation, and protection" of the canal, with the right to add to this zone such other lands as might be needed for the purposes indicated. Panama was paid $10,000,000, and in addition an annuity of $250,000 beginning nine years after the exchange of ratifications.

Construction began in 1904, and the Canal was opened to commerce in 1914. Its original cost was approximately $400,000,000, but subsequent improvements and additions greatly increased this amount. The man chiefly responsible for the work of construction was Col., later Maj. Gen., George W. Goethals. Dr. William C. Gorgas also contributed greatly to the success of the enterprise by his work as Health Officer, which brought about the elimination of yellow fever and the control of other tropical diseases which had long made Panama notoriously unhealthy.

The Panama Canal Act of 1912, passed in anticipation of the Canal's opening, exempted American coastwise vessels from canal tolls. Great Britain protested that this was a violation of the Hay-Pauncefote Treaty. The United States did not officially admit this contention, but President Wilson procured the repeal of the exemption in 1914.

The occupation of the Canal Zone, and measures deemed necessary in connection with the construction and operation of the Canal raised many delicate problems. Panama's two principal cities formed continuous urban areas with American settlements in the Zone, so that conditions within them directly affected the welfare of the Canal working force. The Canal Treaty had consequently authorized the United States to intervene if necessary to maintain public order in Panama and Colón. This right was exercised only on a few occasions, but threats of disorder frequently led the United States to use its good offices in internal political disputes in the early years of the republic. The treaty also gave the United States control of sanitation in Panama City and Colón.

From the beginning, there were disputes about the interpretation of Article III of the treaty, which granted to the United States "all the rights, power, and authority within the Zone" which it would possess "if it were the sovereign of the territory." Panama maintained that these rights were granted only for the construction, maintenance, operation, sanitation and protection of the Canal, and consequently objected to any acts of the United States in the Zone which were not strictly necessary for these purposes. The first controversy began in 1904, when the United States opened the Zone to com-

merce and established post offices there, but a compromise was reached in December, 1904, when Secretary of War Taft visited the Isthmus and ordered that imports at Zone ports be limited to supplies for the Canal and persons connected with it, to supplies for ships passing through, and to goods in transit. These principles continued to govern the policy of the United States after the "Taft Agreement" was abrogated in 1924.

The underlying legal question, however, was not settled, and frequent disputes occurred, especially in connection with the operation of the commissaries in the Zone. An effort to settle outstanding questions failed when a treaty signed in 1926 was rejected by the Panamanian Congress for internal political reasons, but important concessions to Panama's wishes were made in a treaty signed in 1936 and ratified in 1939. The United States' guarantee of Panama's independence and its right to intervene in Panamanian territory were abrogated, and the United States gave up its right to use Panamanian territory as it deemed necessary for the defense of the Canal. It also accepted further limitations on its freedom of action in the Zone. The Canal annuity was increased to 430,000 *balboas,* equivalent to $430,000, to make up for the devaluation of United States currency. Concern in the U. S. Senate about the effect on the defense of the Canal delayed the ratification of the treaty until 1939.

The Panamanian government co-operated in the defense of the Canal during World War II by permitting the United States to occupy air bases. The United States wished to continue the use of a few of these after the war, but the Panamanian Congress, influenced by an outburst of popular nationalistic sentiment, refused to agree. The defense sites were consequently abandoned.

By a treaty signed Jan. 23, 1955, the United States increased the Canal annuity to $1,930,000 and agreed to curtail certain business operations in the Canal Zone that competed with merchants in Panama. At the same time, it promised to seek legislation for the establishment of a single basic wage scale for North American and Panamanian employees of the Canal, in order to eliminate a discrimination against locally employed labor. This discrimination, with its concomitant of racial segregation, had existed since the beginning of the construction period, but had for a long time aroused little concern in Panama because most of the common labor in the Zone was imported from the West Indian islands. It became an issue when the descendants of the immigrants, who were Panamanian citizens, began to enter the Canal's employ.

Though this treaty met Panama's principal demands, nationalistic groups agitated for further changes in the status of the Canal, and grew more active after Egypt's seizure of the Suez Canal in 1956. There was dissatisfaction with the way in which some provisions of the 1955 treaty were carried out, and there were demands for a larger share in the Canal's income and for a more explicit recognition of Panama's sovereignty in the Zone. There were riots in November, 1959, when mobs attempted to raise the Panamanian flag in the Zone.

The administration of the Canal was reorganized in 1951 when the Panama Canal Co., with the Secretary of the Army as its "stockholder," was set up to operate the Canal and to carry on all business operations connected with the enterprise. The governor of the Canal Zone, who has charge of the civil administration in the Zone, under the supervision of the Department of the Army, is president of the Company.

PANAY INCIDENT. On Dec. 12, 1937, Japanese bombers, engaged in an attack upon China, sank the United States gunboat *Panay* and three Standard Oil supply ships 27 miles above Nanking on the Yangtze. Three were killed and more wounded. Secretary of State Hull demanded full redress. Japan accepted responsibility, made formal apologies, promised indemnities and appropriate punishment and gave future assurances. Hull accepted these assurances and the incident was closed. Indemnities were later set at $2,214,007.

PANIC OF 1791. The economic prosperity which accompanied the launching of the Federal Government developed into a speculative boom by 1791. Schemes for internal improvements, the chartering by state legislatures of inadequately financed banks, speculation in bank scrip, government securities and western lands brought a collapse. Much of the bank scrip proved to be of no value, and there were many failures for large amounts.

PANIC OF 1819 resulted from a sharp contraction of credit initiated by the second Bank of the United States. Overexpansion by the banks during the preceding years had encouraged speculation in commodities and land. A period of severe depression followed the contraction. Many banks suspended specie payments; the Bank of the United States went through a trying period of incrimination, congressional investigation and financial rehabilitation. Prices declined; cotton, for example, fell 50% within a year. Niles, a contemporary editor, was "sickened to the heart" at the large numbers of sheriff's sales and imprisonments for debt. Although the situation alarmed the administration, John Quincy Adams, who was then Secretary of State, believed that the Government could do nothing "but transfer discontents, and propitiate one class . . . by disgusting another." Nevertheless, manufacturers clamored for more protection, and debtors demanded relief legislation. The Order of Tammany called for "a fundamental change in morals and habits."

PANIC OF 1837 was due to a number of factors. Between 1830 and 1836 huge state debts were piled up in the construction of canals and railroads and in the chartering of new banks. At the same time the banks expanded their credit; land speculation prevailed in all sections of the country; and imports exceeded exports. In 1836 three events occurred which precipitated a crisis. To check the land speculation President Jackson on July 11, 1836, issued the Specie Circular which required all payments for public lands to be made in specie. This cramped the operations of the banks which had been financing the western land speculation. On June 23, 1836, Congress passed an act to distribute the surplus revenue in the Treasury among the states, thereby causing the depository banks to contract their credit. To make matters worse, there was a financial crisis in England and British creditors began to call in their loans, while the failure of the American crops lessened the purchasing power of the farmers. On May 10, 1837, the New York banks suspended specie payment; and they were followed by most of the banks in the country. The depression lasted until 1843, and was most severely felt in the West and the South. There was a general suspension of public works; a demand for more stringent banking laws; great unemployment; state defalcations and repudiations. The Independent Treasury system was established and the universal distress contributed to the return of the Whigs to power in 1840.

PANIC OF 1857 was a typical "bust" following a typical American "boom." The decade following the Mexican War saw speculation run riot in railroad construction, growth of manufacturing, expansion of the wheat belt, land speculation, and expansion of poorly regulated state banking. The opening of the California gold fields contributed to the general spirit of speculation.

The failure of the Ohio Life Insurance Co. of Cincinnati in August of 1857 pricked the bubble. The panic spread from the Ohio Valley into the urban centers of the East and with the approach of winter unemployment grew, breadlines formed and ominous signs of social unrest appeared.

The depression was more serious in the rising industrial areas of the East and wheat belt of the West than in the cotton South. Faced by British competition and balked by Southern low tariff policies, the industrial East turned to the Republican party. The Middle West, hit by bank failures and faced with Southern hostility to free land, likewise turned into the new party. The Cotton Belt was less affected by the panic. Cotton crops were good, prices were high and banks were sound. These factors brought overconfidence in the South, an impulse to protection in the East and a drive for free land in the West. The election of 1860, therefore, must be viewed against this economic background which was no less potent than the "moral" issue of slavery.

PANIC OF 1873 was precipitated by the failure of a number of important Eastern firms: the New York Warehouse and Securities Co. on Sept. 8; Kenyon, Cox and Co. on Sept. 13; and worst of all, Jay Cooke and Co. on Sept. 18. Days of pandemonium followed, President Grant hurrying to New York, the Stock Exchange closing for ten days and bankruptcy overtaking a host of companies and individuals. Some of the causes of the panic and ensuing depression were world wide: a series of wars, including the Austro-Prussian, Franco-Prussian, and American civil conflicts; excessive railroad construction in middle Europe, Russia, South America and the United States; commercial dislocations caused by the opening of the Suez Canal; and world-wide speculation, overexpansion and extravagance. Other causes were more peculiar to the United States: currency inflation and credit inflation; governmental waste; the losses from the Boston and Chicago fires; overinvestment in railroads, factories and buildings; and an adverse trade balance. Even in 1872 the United States had suffered more than 4000 failures for a total of some $121,000,000. The depression following the panic proved one of the worst in American history. For the two years 1876–77 business failures numbered more than 18,000. A majority of American railroads went into bankruptcy; more than two thirds of the iron mills and furnaces lay idle; by the beginning of 1875 fully 500,000 men were out of work; and in the absence of organized public relief, destitution and hunger far outstripped the efforts of charity to keep up. Wage reductions caused strikes among the coal miners of Pennsylvania and textile operatives of New England in 1875–78, and a railroad walkout in 1877 accompanied by appalling violence. Beggary, prostitution and crime increased, while political and economic radicalism gained ground. But in 1878 the clouds began to lift and the following year the depression gave way to good times.

PANIC OF 1893. The background of this spectacular financial crisis is found in the usual factors of the business cycle, together with an inflexible banking system. Capital investments in the 1880's had exceeded the possibilities of immediately profitable use, and the trend of prices continued generally downward.

The uneasy state of British security markets in 1890, culminating in the Baring panic, stopped the flow of foreign capital into American enterprise, and the resale of European-held securities caused a market collapse in New York and substantial exports of gold. Panic seemed pending that autumn but instead turned to uneasy stagnation. The huge exports of agricultural staples the next two years re-established gold imports and postponed the crisis. A high degree of uncertainty returned in the winter of 1892–93, aided by the well-publicized danger that the country would be forced off the gold standard by the decline in the Treasury's gold reserve, which bore the brunt of the renewed exports of gold and also suffered from decreased Federal revenues and heavy expenditures, including the purchases of silver under the Sherman Silver Purchase Act of 1890.

The Philadelphia and Reading Railroad failed in February and the gold reserve fell below the accepted minimum of $100,000,000 in April. The National Cordage Co. failed in May and touched off a stock-market panic. Banks in the South and West were especially hard pressed, and nearly 600 in the entire country suspended, at least temporarily. Commercial failures followed in great numbers. This condition continued throughout the summer and all currency was at a premium in New York in August.

Many of President Cleveland's advisers had been urging him to force repeal of the silver purchase act, since his election the previous November. The panic atmosphere furnished the opportunity, and repeal was advanced as the one absolute cure for the depression. By Oct. 30 it had passed both houses of Congress. In the meantime, imports of gold had stabilized the monetary situation in New York somewhat, but the depression continued. The winter of 1893–94, and the summer following, witnessed widespread unemployment, strikes met by violence, and a march upon Washington of "Coxey's Army"—all part of the human reaction to the tragedy. The depression did not lift substantially until the poor European crops of 1897 stimulated American exports and the importation of gold. The rising prices which followed helped to restore prosperous conditions.

PANIC OF 1907. Business prosperity characterized the opening months of the year 1907 and continued until autumn, although prices of corporate securities and commodities declined sharply in the spring. The failures of the Knickerbocker Trust Co. of New York City on Oct. 22, and the Westinghouse Electric and Manufacturing Co. on Oct. 23 were followed by a stock-exchange panic. Bank suspensions and failures dotted the country. The U. S. Treasury Department and J. P. Morgan & Co. each loaned $25,000,000 to the New York banks to alleviate the situation, and the acute stage of the panic passed in December.

PANIC OF 1929 began as a stock-market panic. The trend of stock prices had been upward since 1924. In 1927 the Federal Reserve authorities inaugurated an easy money policy, partly to assist business which was experiencing a slight recession and partly to assist foreign nations which had been losing gold to the United States. Unfortunately, the low money rates resulting from this policy fanned the flames of speculation in the stock market and prices of stocks began to rise with alarming rapidity.

Early in 1928 the Federal Reserve Board began to feel somewhat uneasy over the stock-market situation. In January and February discount rates at the Federal Reserve banks were raised from 3½% to 4%. From

April through June a further advance to 4½% occurred at all the Reserve banks, and by the end of the year rates had been raised to 5% at all but the four western Reserve banks. Reserve bank holdings of government securities were also sharply reduced during the year and open market rates hardened decidedly, the call loan rate reaching 8.6% by December.

In spite of the rate increases noted, speculation in stocks continued unabated. Accordingly, in February, 1929, the Federal Reserve Board changed its policy to one of direct pressure on member banks not to increase their loans to brokers. This policy was continued until Aug. 9, when the Federal Reserve Bank of New York was allowed to raise its discount rate to 6%. The policy of direct pressure, although effective as far as member-bank loans to brokers were concerned, was not effective in breaking the speculative mania, because of a huge increase in nonbanking loans to brokers, placed through the agency of the New York banks.

Although there was a recession in stock prices in March and declines in certain stocks at various times throughout the spring and summer, the final crash did not come until Oct. 24, 1929. On that day the market broke badly and prices hurtled downward with unprecedented rapidity. The bankers formed a pool to support the market with temporary success, but the bull market was definitely broken and the trend of stock prices moved inexorably downward until they reached appalling lows in the summer of 1932.

Despite the enormous crash in stock prices, no money panic ensued. The New York banks, in conjunction with the Federal Reserve Bank, met all legitimate demands for credit and the liquidation was carried out on as orderly a basis as the terrific collapse in stock prices would permit. No losses on call loans to brokers were reported.

PAPAL STATES, DIPLOMATIC SERVICE TO.

During the period 1797–1867 eleven American consuls resident in Rome were accredited to the papal government. There were also consulates in Città Vecchia and Ancona. Formal diplomatic relations were inaugurated in 1848 with the appointment of Jacob L. Martin as chargé d'affaires for the United States, a post which later carried with it the title of minister. The last American minister to the papal states was Rufus King, the legation being suppressed in 1867 through failure of Congress to continue the appropriation for its support. This action was protested by King as being based on misunderstanding of a papal regulation regarding Protestant services in Rome. While the legation lasted relations between the two governments were friendly. During the Civil War the papal authorities withheld recognition from the Confederacy on the ground that the North represented legitimate government in the United States and, after the conflict, delivered over to Washington the American, John H. Surratt, who had enlisted in the papal army while under indictment for complicity in Lincoln's assassination.

PAPER MONEY in the United States has consisted of three types, bills of credit or government notes, paper certificates representing deposited coin or bullion, and bank notes. Beginning with Massachusetts in 1690, the various colonies issued bills, usually in excessive amounts, until stopped by English legislation in 1751 and 1764. The issue of paper bills was revived during the Revolutionary War, the Continental Congress authorizing forty issues totaling over $241,000,000 in 1775–79, while the states put out an additional $210,000,000 in the same period.

Following the Revolution, the new government refrained from issuing paper money, with the exception of a $3,000,000 issue of Treasury notes in 1815, until the Civil War when large amounts of greenbacks were issued, as well as substantial amounts of fractional paper currency. The Confederacy also issued huge volumes of paper notes during the Civil War with disastrous results.

The next issue of Treasury notes occurred in 1890 when such notes were authorized to purchase silver under the terms of the Sherman Silver Purchase Act of that year. Between then and 1893, when the purchase clause was repealed, nearly $156,000,000 of these notes were issued. They have since been retired.

Gold certificates were first authorized in 1863 and silver certificates in 1878. The Gold Reserve Act of 1934 provided for a new type of gold certificate, which is not allowed to circulate, but silver certificates are still in circulation and provide the bulk of small-denomination paper currency.

Bank notes have been permitted since the beginning of the country and have constituted a large, but variable, proportion of total paper money. Prior to the Civil War, state bank notes and notes of the Banks of the United States amounted to half or more of the circulating medium. Between 1866 and 1935, national bank notes were an important element in the currency which is now in process of retirement. Since 1914 Federal Reserve notes and, on three occasions, Federal Reserve bank notes have occupied a significant place.

In 1959 Federal Reserve bank notes were also in process of retirement, and gold certificates were used only as reserves of Federal Reserve banks and could not be paid out into circulation. Hence, aside from small amounts of Federal Reserve bank notes and national bank notes which have not yet been retired, our paper money in circulation consisted of Federal Reserve notes, United States notes and silver certificates. Federal Reserve notes comprised 90% of paper money in circulation and 84% of total money in circulation.

PARIS, TREATY OF (1763), between Great Britain, France and Spain brought to an end the French and Indian War. In 1755 Great Britain had been willing to limit her jurisdiction in the interior of the continent by a line running due south from Cuyahoga Bay on Lake Erie to the 40th parallel and thence southwest to the 37th parallel, with the proviso that the territory beyond that line to the Maumee and Wabash Rivers be a neutral zone. She claimed, however, an Acadia that would have included all the land between the Penobscot and St. Lawrence Rivers and the Gulf of St. Lawrence and the Bay of Fundy, as well as the peninsula of Nova Scotia. The result of the British victory was an extension of British demands upon France to include the cession of all of Canada to Great Britain and the advancement of the boundary of the continental colonies westward to the Mississippi River. Both these demands, together with the right to navigate the Mississippi, were granted to Great Britain in the treaty. Similarly, Britain's claim to the "greater Acadia" was recognized, and Spain ceded Florida to Britain to offset the return of Cuba, which the British had conquered. As compensation for its losses, Spain received from France by the Treaty of Fontainebleau all of Louisiana west of the Mississippi River, and the island and city of New Orleans. France retained only the islands of St. Pierre and Miquelon in the Gulf of St. Lawrence, together with the privilege of fishing and drying fish along the northern and western coasts of Newfoundland as provided in the Treaty of Utrecht. In the West Indies, Great Britain retained the islands of St. Vincent, Tobago and Dominica; St. Lucia was given to France. The Treaty of Paris left only two great colonial empires in the Western Hemisphere, the British and the Spanish.

PARIS, TREATY OF (Sept. 3, 1783), between Great Britain and the United States, marked the final consummation of American independence. Coincidentally were signed peace treaties between Great Britain and each of two other belligerents, France, the ally of the United States, and Spain, the ally of France. A preliminary peace between Great Britain and the Netherlands (nobody's ally) had been signed on Sept. 2, 1783.

The definitive treaties marked the end of a complicated negotiation in Paris between Great Britain and her several enemies, begun in March, 1782, by the Rockingham Ministry, and continued by the government of Lord Shelburne through its agent, Richard Oswald, who had conducted the American negotiation from the first, and other British diplomatic officers. It was featured by the separately negotiated preliminary and conditional articles of peace between the United States and Great Britain, signed Nov. 30, 1782, which were not to go into effect until peace should be signed between the American ally, France, and the common enemy, Great Britain. France, in

turn, deferred her peace until her ally, Spain, should have also reached a settlement with Great Britain. The French and Spanish preliminaries were signed on Jan. 2, 1783, on which date the American preliminaries went into effect, and a general armistice took place pending signature of a final and definitive treaty of peace. The three sets (Anglo-American, Anglo-French and Anglo-Spanish) of preliminary articles of peace were thus in the nature of armistice agreements which accompanied a cessation of hostilities but did not end the legal state of war.

The definitive treaties, which ended the war, were deferred for several months in the hope of securing more concessions from the British, and to give the Dutch time to make a satisfactory peace with Great Britain. The Anglo-Dutch preliminary articles of peace were signed on Sept. 2, 1783, and the next day the definitive treaties (American, French and Spanish) were signed in essentially the same form as the respective preliminary articles. The Anglo-Dutch definitive treaty was not concluded until May 20, 1784.

Conflicting interests of the United States, France and Spain, but particularly of the United States and Spain, made each distrustful of the other and imperiled the success of the allies and associates in the war against Great Britain, and in the peace negotiations. The United States strove to get recognition of its independence within boundaries as wide as could be obtained, including Canada. Spain wanted Gibraltar from England and hoped to see the boundaries of the United States kept well to the east of the Mississippi. France desired primarily to cripple her traditional enemy, Great Britain, by detaching the United States from the Empire, thus fulfilling the obligations of the Franco-American alliance of 1778 by securing the independence of the United States, absolute and unlimited, either by treaty or by truce; and it was the hope of France to induce Spain to make peace with Great Britain, if necessary, without securing Gibraltar, which France had pledged to Spain by the Convention of Aranjuez.

In these negotiations it was the strategy of the French Minister of State, the Comte de Vergennes, to defer the definitive peace until all could sign their respective treaties simultaneously, and meanwhile to steer the negotiations so as to preserve France's essential objective, the independence of the United States, without leaving that republic powerful enough to get along without French patronage. To do this he endeavored to reconcile Spanish and American differences by suggesting limitations of American boundaries east of the Mississippi, which would have left both banks of the river, and its lower valley south of the Ohio, to Spain; and which would have left the Great Lakes and territory north of the Ohio and east of the Mississippi to Great Britain.

Vergennes' compromise suggestions helped to precipitate the signature, separately and secretly from

France, of preliminary and conditional articles of peace with Great Britain by the plenipotentiaries of the United States, Benjamin Franklin, John Adams, John Jay and Henry Laurens. Despite perfunctory protests at this conditional signature without the privity of France, Vergennes did not seem much displeased with the separate American conditional articles, because it enabled him to suggest to his Spanish ally the hopelessness of continuing the common war in order to secure Gibraltar, particularly after the British had broken up a Franco-Spanish siege of that fortress. Aranda, Spanish Ambassador at Paris, signed on his own responsibility a peace with Great Britain which gave Florida but not Gibraltar to Spain.

The principal terms of the Anglo-American definitive treaty were: independence of the United States; evacuation "with all convenient speed" of British troops; guaranty against legal obstacles for the collection, in sterling money, of private prewar debts to British creditors; boundary on the north corresponding to the present one as far west as the Lake of the Woods, on the west the Mississippi, on the south Florida; and "liberty" to fish in Atlantic inshore fisheries of remaining British North America. A secret article in the preliminary articles had stipulated that if Florida should remain to Great Britain in the final peace, then the northern boundary of Florida should be made more favorable to Great Britain (the latitude of the mouth of the Yazoo River—present Vicksburg—instead of 31° N. Lat.). Since Spain took Florida in the final peace this article was omitted from the definitive Anglo-American Treaty.

PARIS, TREATY OF (1898), terminated the Spanish-American War. Under its terms Spain relinquished all authority over Cuba and ceded to the United States Puerto Rico, the Philippine Islands and Guam, receiving from the United States $20,000,000 as the estimated value of public works and improvements of nonmilitary character in the Philippines. Hostilities had been suspended Aug. 12, and on Oct. 1 the five United States commissioners, headed by former Secretary of State William R. Day, opened negotiations with the Spanish commissioners in Paris. The most difficult questions encountered were the disposition of the Philippines, which Spain was reluctant to relinquish, and of the Spanish debt charged against Cuba, which the Spanish wished assumed by either Cuba or the United States. Eventually, Spain yielded on both points. An attempt by the United States commissioners to secure the island of Kusaie in the Carolines was blocked by Germany, which had opened negotiations for the purchase of these islands. The treaty was signed Dec. 10. The Senate, after a memorable debate over the adoption of a policy of "imperialism," exemplified in the annexation of the Philippines, consented to ratification by a close vote on Feb. 6, 1899. The treaty was proclaimed April 11, 1899.

PARKS, NATIONAL. The national park idea was born when a group of Montana citizens seated around a wilderness campfire in 1870 visualized reservation of an area on the upper Yellowstone River for perpetual public use. In 1872 Congress, acting on the recommendations of leaders in this party, established the Yellowstone National Park "as a pleasuring ground for the benefit and enjoyment of the people." The ideals of these first national park enthusiasts have persisted; today national park development is recognized as a major land use. The national parks of the United States, 29 in number, run the gamut in scientific interest, scenic beauty and historic importance. Yellowstone, in Wyoming, Montana and Idaho, is characterized by its geysers, varicolored canyon, and its herds of buffalo, elk and other animals that once abounded throughout the West. Yosemite, in California, is renowned for its spectacular valley, plunging waterfalls and beautiful granite high country. Sequoia and Kings Canyon, also in California, are distinguished by many groves of California Big Trees —the largest of living things—and by mountain grandeur of the High Sierra. Mount Rainier National Park, in Washington, presents a glacier system exceeding in size and beauty any other in the United States. The mountain itself, an extinct volcano helmeted in snow, is visible at a distance of more than 150 miles. Crater Lake, in Oregon, offers a lake of unbelievable blue, held within the abrupt walls of a tremendous crater in a mountaintop. Mesa Verde, in Colorado, is America's treasure house of prehistoric cliff dwellings. Glacier National Park, in Montana, boasts more than fifty glaciers and two hundred beautiful lakes. Rocky Mountain National Park, in Colorado, is distinguished by spectacular peaks in the heart of the Rockies. The Trail Ridge Road climbs to the crest of the range and follows the ridge, offering spectacular views of mountain peaks and lovely valleys. Lassen Volcanic National Park, in California, holds the only recently active volcano in the United States proper. Hawaii National Park boasts the world's largest active volcano, Mauna Loa, and Kilauea's lake of fire. Mount McKinley National Park, in Alaska, features the highest mountain in North America, more than 20,000 feet high. Its wild animal paradise protects great herds of caribou, white mountain sheep, Alaska moose and the tundra brown bear. Grand Canyon, in Arizona, offers an unparalleled spectacle of multihued canyon walls, cut by the Colorado River to a depth of a mile and fretted by wind and rain to produce a scene that defies description—a magnificence beyond comprehension. Acadia, in Maine, is a varied exhibit of seacoast, mountain and eastern forest; this was the first land within the United States reached by Champlain in 1604. Zion and Bryce Canyons, in Utah, are characterized by vividly colored and fantastically carved canyon walls of sandstone. The Grand Teton National Park, in Wyoming, features the towering and most historic summit of the West. The Grand Teton was well known throughout the fur trade period (beginning 1807) to both American and British fur companies. Carlsbad Caverns, in New Mexico, are characterized by many miles of impressive chambers 750 to 1000 feet beneath the surface of the earth containing magnificent limestone formations of infinite variety of sizes and shapes. The bat spectacle is one of its great attractions. Great Smoky Mountains, North Carolina-Tennessee, includes the most massive mountain uplift in the eastern United States covered with characteristic Appalachian flora—which includes 132 native tree species. Shenandoah, in Virginia, preserves a section of the heart of the Blue Ridge Mountains. Newest of the national parks is the Virgin Islands, occupying three fourths of colorful, tropical St. John Island in the Caribbean, with its lush green hills, white sandy beaches, prehistoric Carib Indian relics, and remains of colonial sugar plantations. Other national parks not mentioned above, historical, military, and memorial parks, battlefield parks and sites, monuments, cemeteries, memorials, historic sites, parkways, seashore and other recreational areas, and the parks in and adjacent to the Nation's Capital make up the system of Federal areas administered by the National Park Service. Nearly 60,000,000 visits were made to these areas (exclusive of the National Capital Parks) in 1958.

The ten-year Mission 66 park conservation and improvement program initiated by the National Park Service in mid-1956 is designed to equip and staff these areas for an anticipated 80,000,000 visits by 1966. In that year the Service will observe the 50th anniversary of its establishment.

PARSON'S CAUSE was a Virginia issue. Tobacco was a medium of exchange and ministers' salaries had been fixed (1748) at 17,200 pounds a year. To remedy the distress from fluctuating crops and prices, laws were passed in 1755 and again in 1758 permitting tobacco payments to be commuted in paper money at two pence per pound. As tobacco sold for six pence a pound the ministers considered themselves losers, assailed the law both in Virginia and England, and obtained a royal veto in 1759 which was not published in Virginia till 1760. In the meantime, ministers' salaries for 1758 had been settled in paper money at the prescribed rate. With the announcement of the veto, ministers started suits for the difference between what they were paid and the value of their tobacco quota at current prices. In Hanover County the court ruled the act of 1758 was invalid from its passage, and the Rev. James Maury brought suit to recover on his salary (1763). Patrick Henry defended the parish, presenting no witnesses but assailing the ministers and the practice of vetoing laws necessary for the public good. The jury awarded Maury one penny damages. In 1764 the General Court of the province held the law good until it was vetoed and left the

ministers without any remedy. This was appealed to the Privy Council where the appeal was dismissed (1767). A general twopenny act was passed in 1769, and the ministers gave up the agitation. Henry's speech was publicized about fifty years later when he had become a national hero, and the reference in the Declaration of Independence to vetoing "laws the most wholesome and necessary for the public good" probably referred to this issue.

PARTY GOVERNMENT. In the United States, party government dates from the latter part of Washington's first administration, when two rival political parties, the Federalists and (Jeffersonian) Republicans, began to take shape. Since then, down to the present day, two rival major parties, under varying names—Whig, Democratic, Republican—have sought to control government through the winning of elections and the holding of public offices. American parties, however, have formed no part of the Government, as do British political parties; they have existed, rather, as extraconstitutional and largely extralegal institutions. Nevertheless, all through our national history, parties have tended to reduce the friction and deadlocks that result from the constitutional separation of executive and legislative departments. Party government has functioned at its best, in the national sphere, during periods when the President and a majority of both branches of Congress have belonged to the same party; and likewise in state affairs, when a corresponding situation has existed. On numerous occasions, party attitudes upon governmental policies, expressed in party platforms, have determined the fate of momentous national issues; although since the Civil War, platform utterances have generally been of less significance than in the thirty years preceding. In fact, all through our national history, the chief function of political parties has not been so much to declare what laws shall be made, nor to control those who administer them, as to choose the persons who are to make the laws and to name those who are to administer them. Party responsibility, as the term is used in British politics, however, can hardly be said to have existed at any time in the United States. In the latter, party government has appeared far less in the formulation of legislative and administrative policies than in electoral activity. Indeed, American parties have always been primarily agencies for the nomination and election of candidates for national, state and local government offices, for placing party adherents in appointive positions and for serving in a way as sureties for the faithful performance of official duties.

For more than 100 years, electoral activities have been carried on through a national nominating convention and a series of national party committees, supplemented by an elaborate scheme of state, county and local committees. In the executive and administrative branch of government, parties have been chiefly concerned with the nomination and election of President, Vice-President, state governors and the other chief state officers; also with the appointment of fellow partisans to the thousands of subordinate administrative posts. In Congress and the state legislatures, party government has meant not only the nomination and election of members through party agencies (except in recent years in Minnesota, Nebraska and California), but also that in each legislature the dominant party has chosen the presiding officers, named the various legislative committees, and filled the numerous staff positions with members of the party. Frequently such arrangements have been effected, and party attitudes upon outstanding measures have been determined, through the agency of an irresponsible majority-party caucus. The vast majority of legislative measures, both in Congress and state legislatures, have always been of a nonpartisan nature. Party government, in the sense in which the term is here used, has also long existed in counties and municipalities, although, in recent decades, it has been superseded to some extent by a system of nonpartisan nomination and election of county and local officials.

In performing these electoral functions, American parties have furnished the motive power that runs the inert governmental machine outlined in the national and state constitutions, and has provided a lubricant that has kept its various parts operating with some degree of smoothness. From their first appearance, moreover, parties have been the most important channel through which the ordinary citizen has been able to exert a direct influence upon the policies and conduct of public officials.

PASSES, MOUNTAIN. America is traversed from north to south by two mountain chains, the Appalachians and Rockies, which formed barriers to the westward movement. Early hunters in search of pelts, and pioneers who coveted western lands, met the difficulty by finding natural outlets through the mountains. In the Appalachians these were generally called "gaps" and in the Rockies "passes." Early trails were, when possible, water trails so that the Mohawk and the Ohio Rivers were the key routes to the Great Lakes and the Mississippi Valley. The Iroquois and French barred the Mohawk route on the north, as did the Cherokees and other confederated tribes the lowlands south of the Appalachians. Accordingly, the confluence of the Allegheny and Monongahela Rivers to form the Ohio at Pittsburgh, and the breaks in the mountain ridges in the corner between Virginia and North Carolina leading into Kentucky, were the points of easiest passage. Such gaps in the Appalachians were frequently the result of troughs cut through the mountain slopes by rivers seeking an outlet to the Ohio or the Atlantic Ocean. The Virginia coast range was low but early maps show three passes into the Shenandoah Valley—Williams, Ashby and Vestal gaps, all in Fairfax County.

The most important pass in the Kentucky approach is the Cumberland Gap which led by way of the Holston and Clinch Rivers over and through the mountains and thence along Kentucky rivers to the Falls of the Ohio. This was known as Boone's Wilderness Road and gaps noted by early travelers include Flower Gap, from tidewater to the sources of Little River; Blue Ridge Gap, another passage from tidewater to the Shenandoah Valley; Moccasin Gap between the north fork of the Holston and Clinch Rivers.

On the Virginia road by Braddock's route to Pittsburgh were encountered Chester's Gap in the Blue Ridge Mountains. On the Forbes road, running west from Philadelphia to Pittsburgh, Miller's Run Gap was crossed northwest of the present site of Ligonier.

The Rockies, because of their uninterrupted length and great height, offered a more serious problem. Their secrets were unlocked for the most part by early Spanish missionaries at the south, by fur traders, emigrants and army explorers at the north and center. The earliest approaches were made in the south by the Spaniards pushing into California from New Mexico. After Mexico revolted and American trade with Santa Fe began, fur trappers thrust westward from Taos and Santa Fe to San Diego and Los Angeles. The river valleys unlocking the southern route to the West were the Gila and the Colorado. The Colorado trail, known as the Spanish trail, went north from Taos, crossed the Wasatch Mountains and Mohave desert and entered California by the Cajon pass. The Gila route which was the shorter from Santa Fe went west across the mountains and, by way of Warner's pass, reached San Diego.

By following the Arkansas River west to Pueblo, Colo., and crossing the mountains by a choice of three or four different passes—the Williams or Sandy Hill, the Roubideau or Mosca, the Sangre de Cristo or Music passes—Taos could be reached by turning south, or California by turning northwest on a route traced by Frémont. This route crossed the Great Basin of Utah and Nevada and surmounted the high Sierra Nevada passes. The most important of these passes were the Walker, the Carson, the Virginia, the Frémont, the Sonora, the Donner and the Truckee. After the eastern escarpment had been scaled, there still remained mountain folds in the Sierras which impeded progress to the coast. The Tehachapi pass into San Joaquin Valley crossed one such fold.

The central approach to the Rockies is by way of the Platte River which sends fingers high up into the mountains. The most important pass in the entire Rocky Mountain chain, South Pass, is on this route. It has easy grades and was used by many bound for California who turned south at Fort Hall, Idaho.

Of all river approaches the Missouri is the most effective and was the route used by Lewis and Clark who crossed the Rockies by Lemhi, Clark and Gibbon passes. Other useful passes of the northwest are the Nez Percés and Lo Lo through the Bitter Root

Mountains. The Bozeman pass offers access from the valley of the Gallatin to that of the Yellowstone. For traveling south from Oregon to California the Siskyou pass proved useful.

Important passes in the mid-continental region are the Union, crossing the Wind River Mountains from Wind River to the Grand; Cochetope pass over the San Juan Mountains, used by Frémont and others in passing from Colorado to Utah; and Muddy pass, two degrees south of South Pass, useful in crossing the Atlantic and Pacific divides from Platte headwaters. Bridger's pass, discovered in the early days of the fur trade, crossed the divide south of South Pass and saved distance on the California route and, in consequence, was used by the Pony Express.

PATENT OFFICE. The U. S. Patent Office was established to administer the patent laws enacted by Congress in accordance with Article I, section 8, of the Constitution. The first of these laws was enacted April 10, 1790 (1 Stat. 109), but the Patent Office as a distinct bureau in the Department of State dates from the year 1802, when an official who became known as the Superintendent of Patents was placed in charge. The general revision of the patent laws enacted July 4, 1836 (5 Stat. 117), reorganized the Patent Office and designated the official in charge as Commissioner of Patents. Another general revision of the patent laws was made in 1870, and since that date numerous acts of Congress relating to patents have been passed; these were revised and codified, effective Jan. 1, 1953, by an act approved July 19, 1952 (66 Stat. 792; 35 U. S. C. 1–293). The Patent Office was transferred from the Department of the Interior, in which Department it had been since 1849, to the Department of Commerce by Executive Order on April 1, 1925, in accordance with the authority contained in the act of Feb. 14, 1903 (32 Stat. 830). In addition to the patent laws, the Patent Office administers the Federal trade-mark laws, the present statute being the act approved July 5, 1946 (60 Stat. 427; 15 U. S. C. 1051).

The chief functions of the Patent Office are to administer the patent laws as they relate to the granting of letters patent for inventions, and to perform other duties relating to patents. It examines applications for patents to ascertain if the applicants are entitled to patents under the law, and grants the patents when they are so entitled; it publishes issued patents and various publications concerning patents and patent laws, records assignments of patents, maintains a search room for the use of the public to examine issued patents and records, supplies copies of records and other papers, and the like. Analogous and similar functions are performed with respect to the registration of trade-marks.

PATRONS OF HUSBANDRY, beginning as a farmers' lodge, was founded Dec. 4, 1867, in Washington,

D. C., and served as the vehicle through which the Granger Movement operated. It had a secret ritual like the Masons, and admitted both men and women to membership. Each local unit was known as a "Grange." In 1876 the order reached its peak membership of 858,050, but by 1880 the collapse of the Granger Movement had reduced this figure to 124,420. Thereafter, by abandoning business and politics for its original program of social and educational reforms, the order began a slow and steady growth which, by 1934, enabled it to claim again over 800,000 members, mainly in New England, the North Central states, and the Pacific Northwest. Of late years it has not hesitated to support legislation, both state and national, deemed of benefit to the farmers.

PATROONS. On June 7, 1629, the directorate of the West India Company granted, and the States General of the Netherlands approved, a Charter of Freedoms and Exemptions, which provided for the grant of great estates, called patroonships, to such members of the company as should found settlements of fifty persons within four years after giving notice of their intentions. The patroon, after he had extinguished the Indian title by purchase, was to hold the land as a "perpetual fief of inheritance" with the fruits, plants, minerals, rivers and springs, thereof. He swore fealty to the company and had the right of the high, middle and low jurisdiction. Before the end of January, 1630, patroonships had been registered by Pauw, for Sickenames and Pavonia; by Godyn, for the west side of the Delaware River; by Albert Coenraets Burgh, on the east side of the Delaware River; by Blommaert, for the Connecticut River; and by Van Rensselaer for Rensselaerswyck, about Fort Orange. With the single exception of Rensselaerswyck, these grants were unsuccessful. The difficulties of transportation across the Atlantic Ocean, lack of co-operation from the company, quarrels with the authorities at New Amsterdam, Indian troubles, and the difficulties of management from 3000 miles away, were all factors in their failure. In 1640 the revised charter reduced the size of future patroonships, but the same factors contributed to prevent the success of these smaller grants. At the close of Dutch rule all but two of the patroonships had been repurchased by the company.

PAWNEE ROCK was a famous pioneer landmark of uplifted sandstone, since largely quarried away, on the old Santa Fe Trail near what is now Pawnee Rock, Kans. It was not only the scene of bloody tribal warfare, especially between the Pawnees and Cheyennes, but was notorious in frontier days as furnishing cover from which marauding bands of plains Indians frequently launched savage attacks upon passing wagon trains.

PAXTON BOYS. During the so-called Pontiac Conspiracy (1763) the frontier of Pennsylvania felt for the second time in its history the horrors of Indian warfare. Henry Bouquet, a seasoned soldier, defeated the Indians at Bushy Run on Aug. 5, the most important engagement with the Indians in the history of Pennsylvania. While the Indian raids lasted, Shippensburg was crowded with 1300 fugitives, Carlisle was filled. These depredations filled the frontiersmen, chiefly Scots-Irish, with an intense hatred of Indians: they demanded a scalp bounty and utter extermination of the natives. Out of this grew the Conestoga Massacre—the killing of twenty defenseless and peaceable Conestoga Indians, who lived by their handicrafts near Lancaster. Some 57 rangers from Paxton committed this atrocity in 1763. Gov. Penn issued two proclamations commanding magistrates to bring the culprits to trial, but the juries and justices of the frontier towns were sympathetic, and nothing was done. Aside from the brutality of this event, it possesses importance as an evidence of the hatred of the frontiersmen for the eastern domination of the province, a hatred that grew out of unequal representation in the assembly and the assembly's failure to provide defense for the frontiers. The Conestoga Massacre projected the Paxton Boys into one of the bitterest political campaigns in the history of Pennsylvania (1764). Numerous pamphlets were written (one by Franklin) and in January, 1764, 600 armed "back inhabitants" marched on Philadelphia, intent on destroying their political opponents. Franklin was chiefly responsible for quelling this rebellion.

Lazarus Stewart, as head of the Paxton Boys, disgusted with the proprietary government and with writs hanging over him, moved with his followers to the Wyoming Valley in 1769, was granted a township by the Susquehanna Company of Connecticut, engaged in the Pennamite Wars that followed, and was killed in the Wyoming Massacre of 1778.

PAYNE-ALDRICH TARIFF (1909). Bowing to public conviction that protection was fostering monopolies, the Republican platform in 1908 promised tariff revision, offering the equalization of cost formula as the solution of the tariff problem. But no painstaking study of costs was made and Congress generally accepted the testimony of petitioning firms. Although the House increased some rates, it attempted downward revision and put coal, iron ore and hides on the free list. But in the Senate, under the leadership of Nelson W. Aldrich, an extreme protectionist, duties were voted on iron ore, hides and coal, while scores of increases were made. In conference Taft brought pressure for lower rates and forced hides on the free list. The tariff, however, remained distinctly protective and led to the decisive defeat of the Republicans in the congressional elections of 1910.

PAYNE'S LANDING, TREATY OF, was made on the Ocklawaha River, Florida, May 9, 1832, by James Gadsden for the United States, with fifteen Seminole chiefs, providing for a delegation of Indians to proceed to the West and decide whether land set apart for them there was acceptable. If so, the Seminoles were to remove within the next three years, giving up all their Florida lands and receiving an equal amount in the West in addition to certain money compensations. Disputes over this treaty and other problems led to the second Seminole War.

PEA RIDGE (ELKHORN), BATTLE OF (March 7-8, 1862). In the struggle for control of the trans-Mississippi, a Confederate Army under Van Dorn maneuvered against a Union Army under Curtis, of about equal strength. They met in northwestern Arkansas. A fierce two-day fight ensued with alternating success for each side. In the first day's fighting, at a critical moment, two of the Confederate leaders were killed. Superior leadership and equipment finally brought victory to the Union Army. This battle ended organized fighting in the trans-Mississippi. All troops were soon transferred to the line of the Mississippi.

PEABODY FUND. This, the pioneer educational foundation in the United States, was established in 1867 by George Peabody, a native of Massachusetts who subsequently became a banker in London. His first gift was $1,000,000 to which two years later he added a like sum to encourage and assist educational effort in "those portions of our beloved and common country which have suffered from the destructive ravages, and not less disastrous consequences, of civil war." When he made his second gift, Mr. Peabody said to the trustees of the fund: "This I give to the suffering South for the good of the whole country." To administer the fund he named sixteen Northern and Southern men of prominence and distinction, who selected Dr. Barnas Sears, president of Brown University, as the first general agent of the fund. Upon his death in 1880 he was succeeded by Dr. J. L. M. Curry, president of Howard College in Alabama, who was succeeded by Dr. Wyckliffe Rose, of Tennessee, as general agent. Through the tactful and energetic work of these agents the fund greatly assisted general education and teacher training for both whites and Negroes in the states that had formed the Southern Confederacy, and in West Virginia, and proved to be a most wholesome influence during the dark days that followed the war. When the fund was dissolved in 1914 the bulk of the capital went to the endowment of The George Peabody College for Teachers, Nashville, Tenn.; some went to Southern universities for schools of education; and some to the John F. Slater Fund. During its life the Peabody Fund distributed from income about $3,650,000.

PEARL HARBOR NAVAL BASE, on the south coast of Oahu, Hawaiian Islands, six miles west of Honolulu, is large enough to accommodate nearly the entire United States Fleet. In 1845 Lt. I. W. Curtis, an

American marine officer, called attention to the harbor's vast importance for the Islands' defense, and in 1873 an American military commission reported favorably on Pearl Harbor as a port of refuge in wartime and pointed out its ease of defense. The Hawaiian government in 1887 granted the United States exclusive use of Pearl Harbor, and the right to maintain coaling and repair stations there. In 1908 the Navy Department dredged an entrance channel 600 feet wide and in 1926 deepened and widened this channel. A huge dry dock was completed in July, 1919. In April, 1922, our Government awarded a contract to the Pan American Petroleum and Transport Co., headed by E. L. Doheny, for the construction and filling with fuel oil at Pearl Harbor of storage for 1,500,000 barrels, to be paid for with oil from the Navy's petroleum reserves in California. Though the Government subsequently declared this contract illegal, the oil tanks were completed in 1925. In addition, a marine railway, fueling stations, ammunition depots, machine shops, radio towers, a hospital, and a flying base on Ford Island were built.

On Dec. 7, 1941, the U. S. Pacific Fleet, consisting of 86 ships at anchor at Pearl Harbor, was attacked by 100 Japanese planes and a number of submarines. The battleship *Arizona* was lost. Four other battleships, three destroyers, one target ship and one mine layer were greatly damaged. Also damaged but ultimately repaired were three battleships, three cruisers, one seaplane tender, one repair vessel and one dry dock. Eighty Navy and 97 Army planes were lost. The Navy casualties amounted to 2117 officers and men killed, 960 missing and 876 wounded. The Army casualties amounted to 226 officers and men killed and 396 wounded.

Within 24 hours the United States was a belligerent in World War II.

PEARY'S POLAR EXPEDITIONS (1891–1909). Robert Edwin Peary, U. S. N., was sent in 1891 by the Philadelphia Academy of Natural Sciences to explore northern Greenland. Wintering at McCormick Bay near latitude 78° he started April 30, 1892, with Eivind Astrüp, and crossed the ice cap to Independence Bay on the northeastern coast of the island. The following year he returned to Greenland in the *Falcon,* and after spending two winters at Bowdoin Bay repeated the feat in 1895, with H. J. Lee and Matthew Henson.

In 1898 The Peary Arctic Club was organized in New York to finance an expedition under Peary to discover the North Pole. He sailed that year in the *Windward,* wintered at Cape d'Urville and spent the following year exploring Ellesmere Land and Grinnell Land. Proceeding along the Greenland coast in 1900 he reached Cape Morris K. Jesup in Hazen Land where he struck northward over the ice to latitude 83° 52'. Here he was forced back, but continued eastward along the coast to Wyckoff Island. Two years

later he made another attempt, starting this time from Cape Hecla in Grant Land, only to be stopped by snow in latitude 84° 17'.

The Peary Arctic Club was still willing to back him, and in 1905 sent him out in the specially constructed *Roosevelt* to make another attempt. He wintered at Cape Sheridan, and the following year started northward from Point Moss with Capt. Robert A. Bartlett, equipped with dogs and sledges. In six weeks he reached latitude 87° 6' when open water forced him to turn back. Later in the season he led an expedition westward along the coast to Cape Thomas Hubbard, the northern extremity of Axel Heiberg Land.

Elated at his success the Club again sent him out in the *Roosevelt* in 1908. Wintering once more at Cape Sheridan he gathered a large party at Cape Columbia the following February, which he divided into detachments that were to precede him, establish caches and return. At latitude 87° 47' he parted from Capt. Bartlett and proceeded with only Henson and four Eskimos. On April 6, 1909, he reached the North Pole. Widely acclaimed as the discoverer of the Pole, Peary in 1911 was given the rank of Rear Admiral by Congress.

PEDDLERS. As soon as the settlements in America were sufficiently advanced to produce surpluses, and to demand the surplus commodities of each other, these commodities were transported by pack on back, by horse, by boat or by carriage. Clocks and tinware are outstanding examples of commodities distributed by the colonial peddler. At times the peddler provided the back settlements with their only contacts with the rest of the world, and at times he was guilty of gross deception in selling his wares. With improvements in transportation and communication, peddling as formerly understood declined in importance, although there were 16,594 people in the United States who followed the occupation in 1860. In more recent times the peddler has been referred to as a door-to-door salesman.

PEMAQUID, the peninsula on the Maine coast between the Kennebec region and Penobscot Bay, plays an important, if shadowy, role in the early history of American colonization. Pavements there, never satisfactorily explained, give weight to legends of very early occupation by Europeans. Mystery shrouds its beginnings, but it, with nearby Monhegan Island, was a center of European fisheries probably from the late 16th century on.

There was an Abenaki settlement there when Weymouth landed, June 3, 1605, at New Harbor. Rosier describes the peninsula. The English seized five Indians and took them home for exhibit. Men of the Popham plantation visited the place in 1607. In 1616 Capt. John Smith found a dozen European fishing vessels there. Pemaquid was linked for many years with the colonial interests of Bristol, England; Robert Aldworth and Giles Elbridge, Bristol merchants, farmed its fisheries and furs. John Witheridge, a Devonian, was trading with the natives there in 1624. Englishmen were settled permanently at Pemaquid by 1625; and that year John Brown bought land from the great chief Samoset, whose "Welcome, Englishmen!" is like an invocation to American history. Abraham Shurt obtained a grant at Pemaquid in 1631–32 and built a palisaded post. The ship *Angel Gabriel* was wrecked at Pemaquid in 1631. Dixie Bull, the pirate, captured the place and got £500 worth of furs. It was the most vital eastern outpost against the French colonization of Maine. Together with New York, New Jersey and Delaware, it was granted to the Duke of York in 1664, and was administered as a part of the "County of Cornwall" and the colony of New York under Andros. It was reclaimed by Massachusetts after the Duke of York became King James II.

Pemaquid was a key position, heavily fortified, in the Indian wars. The early fort was taken by the Indians in 1676; the second, Fort Charles, in 1689; and Fort William Henry, built by Sir William Phips at a cost of £20,000, with walls six feet thick and twenty-two high, was captured by the French and Indians in 1696.

PEMMICAN was the product of the Indian method of curing and preserving buffalo meat, which later authorities maintain was equal to modern preserving methods. The meat was cut in thin strips and dried in the sun or the smoke of a wood fire until it was hard. It was then reduced to powder on a stone, and seasoned with wild cherry. Finally, an equal amount of buffalo marrow fat or tallow was added, and, while still soft, the mixture was shaken down in skin bags and sealed with tallow. Pemmican would keep indefinitely and could be eaten without cooking. The trappers borrowed the idea from the Indians and later passed it on to emigrants.

PENDLETON ACT (Jan. 16, 1883), written by Dorman B. Eaton, was sponsored by Sen. George H. Pendleton of Ohio, and forced through Congress by public opinion. It exempted public officials from political assessments. A Civil Service Commission was established to prepare rules for a limited classified civil service which classified service the President could expand at discretion. Competitive examinations were to determine the qualifications of applicants while appointments were to be apportioned among the states according to population.

PENINSULAR CAMPAIGN. This advance against Richmond began on April 4, 1862, when Maj. Gen. George B. McClellan got his Union Army of 100,000 under way from Fortress Monroe, its base, to attack the Confederate capital by way of the peninsula

formed by the York and James Rivers. McClellan had counted on a larger force and on aid from the Navy on the James. Because his arrangements for the defense of Washington were unsatisfactory to the Administration, 45,000 troops were withheld from his command. The Navy was unable to help because of the menace of the *Merrimack* and Confederate shore batteries.

The campaign had three phases. The early Union advance was marked by Confederate resistance behind entrenchments across the peninsula from Yorktown. McClellan besieged Yorktown, which was evacuated on May 3. He then pushed slowly forward, fighting at Williamsburg on May 5, reaching and straddling the Chickahominy on May 20 and facing a strengthened Confederate force under Gen. Joseph E. Johnston.

Help expected from McDowell's 40,000 men was lost to McClellan in May when Jackson's Shenandoah Valley campaign scattered or immobilized the Union armies before Washington. The first phase of the campaign ended with the indecisive two-day battle of Fair Oaks or Seven Pines, May 31 and June 1. Johnston was wounded on June 1 and Robert E. Lee succeeded to his command.

After Fair Oaks came the second phase, three weeks without fighting, marked by Stuart's spectacular cavalry raid around the Union Army on June 11, 12 and 13.

McClellan, reinforced, intended to take the offensive again, but Lee forestalled him and opened the third phase of the campaign by attacking the Union right at Mechanicsville on June 26. This began the Seven Days' Battles, during which McClellan changed his base to the James and retreated, fighting at Gaines' Mill on the 27th, at Allen's Farm and Savage's Station on the 29th, at Glendale on the 30th and at Malvern Hill on July 1. On the night of July 1 the Union Army withdrew to its base at Harrison's Landing and the unsuccessful Union campaign ended. With the appointment on July 11 of Gen. Henry W. Halleck to command all land forces of the United States, withdrawal of the Army of the Potomac from the peninsula began.

Union casualties in the campaign were 15,000, with 1700 killed; Confederate losses were 20,000, with 3200 killed. The Union forces greatly outnumbered the Confederate at the start of the campaign; toward its close the opposing forces were nearly equal.

PENNSYLVANIA. Early in the 17th century the territory which is now Pennsylvania was disputed among the English, the Dutch and the Swedes. Henry Hudson's voyage in the *Half Moon* established the Dutch claim; that of John Cabot and his "sea to sea" charter, the English claim; and both founded trading posts along the Delaware River (1623). The Swedes, under Peter Minuit (1638), built Fort Christina and effected the beginnings of the first permanent settlement within the present boundaries of the state, with their capital at Upland (now Chester). The Dutch captured Fort Christina (1655) only to bow to the English with the fall of New Amsterdam in 1664. Until 1681 the prevailing government was known as the "Duke's Law" under the grant of Charles II to his brother, the Duke of York.

However, on March 4, 1681, William Penn, in return for a debt of £16,000 owed to his father by the Crown, secured a grant to this territory for settlement by the persecuted English Quakers. As proprietor, he drew up his charter (1681) and his Frame of Government. Penn thus initiated his Holy Experiment, and his Charter of Privileges (1701) was the established government until 1776. Disputes were so frequent between the proprietor's deputy governor and the assembly in the years following Penn's return to England (1702) that he threatened to return the grant to the Crown (1712). His broken health prevented this action and, upon his death in 1718, the proprietorship descended to his sons, John, Richard and Thomas.

The peaceful, industrious Quakers, settling mainly in and about Philadelphia, prospered, and by 1730 there was an influx of oppressed German and Scotch-Irish immigrants to Pennsylvania. Many Germans, under Pastorius, settled in Germantown, but the majority sought the farmlands near Reading and Lancaster, while the hardy Scotch-Irish moved on to the frontiers near Pittsburgh and southwestern Pennsylvania. Redemptioners contributed great numbers to this later immigration.

Pennsylvania's boundaries were early the basis for controversy: the Pennsylvania-Maryland dispute was settled by the survey of Mason and Dixon (1769); the Pennsylvania-Connecticut claim was amicably settled in 1782 only after bloodshed in the Yankee-Pennamite Wars; and the Pennsylvania-Virginia altercation was solved by court action in 1779.

By 1755 the settlement program laid out by Penn after the Treaty of Shackamaxon with the Indians (1682) was completely disrupted. The Scotch-Irish frontiersmen complained of unequal representation in the assembly, and consequent neglect of their needs by the wealthy, lawmaking, metropolitan Quakers. Ever pushing forward, the Scotch-Irish pioneer often invaded Indian territory, inciting the Indians; and finally, the rivalry of the French and the English for supremacy in the Ohio Valley projected the French and Indian War.

Near Fort Duquesne, established on the present site of Pittsburgh, was the scene (July 9, 1755) of Braddock's overwhelming defeat by the French. After suffering many Indian attacks, the frontier settlers sought protection in the forts established in part by the aid of Franklin. In this period, the pacific policy of the Quaker had been tested, found inadequate, and Quaker political domination waned as revolutionary forces sought to overthrow the proprietary govern-

ment. Gen. Forbes recaptured Fort Duquesne (1758) for the English and named it Fort Pitt. With the conquest of Montreal (1760) all Pennsylvania became English territory. Pontiac's War (1763) visited another Indian war upon Pennsylvania settlers. Col. Bouquet, after his victory at Bushy Run, reached Pittsburgh in time to save Fort Pitt, and inflicted heavy losses upon the Indians

Fettered by a large Quaker and Loyalist population, Pennsylvania could not early join the Revolutionary cause. However, the pressure of forces generated by a strong East-West sectional antipathy and by unequal representation in the legislature, as well as the aid of such leaders as Dickinson, Mifflin and Reed, finally hammered away the last shackle, and the state joined in the Declaration of Independence, which was signed at the State House or Independence Hall in Philadelphia. The two Continental Congresses (1774 and 1775–81) were also held here. During Howe's occupation of Philadelphia (1777–78) Congress moved to Lancaster, York and Princeton; the Liberty Bell was hastily removed to Allentown; the British held the brilliant Mischianza here; Washington and his army encamped at Valley Forge; while Lafayette and Von Steuben joined the American forces. Franklin's diplomacy in completing, at this time, the French alliance is comparable to Washington's military prowess.

The Pennsylvania line under Wayne in the Continental army, the navy and the militia comprised Pennsylvania defense in the Revolution, and battles were fought at Brandywine (1777), Paoli (1777), Fort Mifflin (1777) and Germantown (1777).

A direct result of the coming of the Revolutionary War was the overthrow of proprietary government in Pennsylvania, and the adoption of a new state constitution (September, 1776), providing for a unicameral legislature. At Philadelphia, Dec. 12, 1787, Pennsylvania ratified the Federal Constitution, and in 1790 revised its own liberal constitution of 1776 in conformity with the general reaction to the excessive liberalism of the Revolution; the council of censors was abolished, the office of governor restored and the bicameral legislative system adopted.

PENNSYLVANIA, INVASION OF (1863). Chancellorsville presented Lee (C.) with two problems —army reorganization and what to do next. As to the first, Lee decided to divide his army into three corps —Longstreet remained in command of the first; Ewell and A. P. Hill commanded the other two. The cavalry was increased and the artillery reorganized. All this involved the mixing of old and new units, the breaking up of associations of long standing and the introduction of many new leaders. "To explain this reorganization is to explain Gettysburg."

While these changes were being made, Lee was developing a plan for future operations. He thought a victory on Northern soil an essential to Confederate success. He would free Virginia and meet and destroy his opponent. Davis, not appreciating the tremendous moral effect of the Emancipation Proclamation, still looked to foreign recognition as a means of saving the Confederacy, meantime adhering to his original military policy of holding territory regardless of its importance or strategic value. Others urged troop transfers on interior lines within the Confederacy. Key areas were menaced—Grant (U.) was threatening Vicksburg and Bragg (C.) in Tennessee felt too weak to take the offensive. Lee's plan of invasion was adopted. He believed that success would relieve pressure on other areas and that Northern public opinion would force a peaceable settlement.

The delicate operation of maneuvering Hooker (U.) out of his positions behind the Rappahannock was begun on June 3, 1863. Lee planned to use the Shenandoah and Cumberland valleys as covered avenues of approach into Pennsylvania. By June 12 Hooker had begun to move northward so as to keep between Lee and the capital at Washington. On June 23 the Confederate Army was crossing the Potomac; Stuart (C.) and his cavalry rode off to harass Hooker's army and then to pass between it and Washington, cross into Maryland and rejoin Lee in Pennsylvania. In retrospect it was a fatal detachment. On June 27 Hooker, feeling he had lost the support of his government, resigned. Meade succeeded him. The Confederate Army, living off the country, was moving into Pennsylvania, when Lee, learning that Meade was in pursuit, on June 29, ordered a concentration of his scattered army. Stuart's unfortunate absence had deprived Lee of exact knowledge of enemy movements and position. As a result, A. P. Hill's troops, investigating the character and strength of a Union cavalry force in Gettysburg, inadvertently and accidentally brought on the three-day battle that ended in Confederate defeat.

All during July 4 Lee waited in position for Meade's counterattack, but none was made. After dark the Confederate Army began to withdraw. The retreat, skilfully conducted, was made in driving rain that turned the roads into quagmires. By the 6th the army was at Hagerstown drawn up to repel Meade's expected attack. But Meade did not begin pursuit until July 5, moving cautiously as he went. Lee moved back slowly to the Potomac at Williamsport, where flood waters compelled another halt. Meade, following, hesitated to attack and by the time he reached a decision the river had fallen sufficiently to permit Lee's army, during July 13 and 14, to cross over into Virginia. Early in August the Confederate Army had taken position south of the Rapidan River to protect Richmond from any move by Meade's army. On Aug. 8 Lee, assuming complete responsibility for the failure of the campaign, asked President Davis to select someone else to command the army. Davis refused, asking, "Where am I to find the new commander?" In disaster Lee blamed no one but himself and in disaster his faith was unshaken.

PENNSYLVANIA, THE UNIVERSITY OF, located in Philadelphia, was founded by Benjamin Franklin (*Proposals Relating to the Education of Youth in Pensilvania,* 1749) and traces its beginnings to a Charity School established in 1740. Associated with it were ten signers of the Declaration of Independence, nine signers of the Constitution and 24 members of the Continental Congress. Although not the oldest institution for higher learning in this country, it was the first to become a university (1779). Its college curriculum instituted in colonial days was the first in this country to provide instruction in modern languages, physics, mathematics and economics, in addition to the classics. Among the university's 21 schools and colleges and its many other divisions in 1959 were North America's first school of medicine (1765), this country's first university school of business (1881) and the world's first psychological clinic (1896). In 1959 the university had 17,000 students; its endowment funds totaled $60,000,000, and its property was valued at $70,000,000.

PENNSYLVANIA CANAL SYSTEM. Not only was Pennsylvania jealous of New York's fame through the building of the Erie Canal, but Philadelphia's western trade was menaced by it. In 1826 the Pennsylvania legislature passed an act for state construction of a waterway from Philadelphia to Pittsburgh, and ground was broken at once. From Philadelphia to Columbia on the Susquehanna, 81.6 miles, a railroad instead of a canal was built, and opened in 1834. From Columbia the canal followed the Susquehanna and Juniata Rivers to Hollidaysburg whence the Portage Railroad carried the line over the mountains to Johnstown; from there the canal continued to Pittsburgh. Several auxiliary canals were authorized, and work on them began in 1828. Leaving the Main Line at the mouth of the Juniata, one of them ran up the Susquehanna to Northumberland, where it forked, one line following the West Branch of the Susquehanna past Lewisburg and Williamsport, the other the North Branch past Wilkes-Barre toward the New York state line. The Delaware Division, following the Delaware River from the mouth of the Lehigh down to tidewater at Bristol, was in effect a continuation of the Lehigh Canal, privately built from mines at Mauch Chunk and above, down to the Delaware. Some short branch canals were built, the Monongahela River was improved with locks and dams, and a canal was projected from the Ohio River near Pittsburgh to Lake Erie, of which only 31 miles were ever built. By 1840 there were 606 miles of canal and 118 miles of railroad in the system, and the expense incurred and authorized then stood at $32,000,000, though the original estimate had been $5,000,000. On Feb. 1, 1840, for the first time in her history, Pennsylvania defaulted in the payment of interest on her bonds. Thoroughly alarmed, the legislature halted construction throughout the whole system, and in some places it was never again begun. Although the tolls could not pay expenses and interest, the system was enormously useful in getting the state's coal and other products to market, in capturing a considerable portion of the trade of the Ohio and Mississippi valleys, and, in general, in developing Pennsylvania into one of the nation's greatest commercial and industrial states.

In 1846 the Pennsylvania Railroad was chartered to build a line paralleling the main canal from Philadelphia to Pittsburgh; but prosperity was returning, and though the canal debt had by 1848 risen to $40,000,000, the state was still hopeful. But the yearly balance sheets proved that these internal improvements were being operated at a loss, and the governor was authorized to offer the Main Line for sale. In 1857 the Pennsylvania Railroad bought it for $7,500,000, and promptly shut down the Portage Railroad. In 1863–64 it abandoned the west end, from Johnstown to Pittsburgh. The eastern section in 1866 was turned over to a subsidiary corporation, the Pennsylvania Canal Co. In 1858 the state sold the Delaware, Susquehanna, North and West Branch divisions to the Sunbury & Erie Railroad for $3,500,-000. The railroad resold all these to companies organized to operate them. The North Branch was extended to Athens, where it connected with the New York state canal system, but the portion of it above Wilkes-Barre was wrecked by a flood in 1865, and the Lehigh Valley Railroad was built on its right of way. In 1871 the Pennsylvania Canal Co. was operating 358 miles of the old system—the east end of the Main Line and portions of the Susquehanna, North and West Branch divisions—and carried over 1,000,000 tons of freight that year, but thereafter its business declined. In 1889 the eastern fragment of the Main Line was wrecked by a flood and never fully rebuilt. In 1904 the last mile of canal along the Susquehanna was abandoned. The Delaware Division, leased in 1866 by the Lehigh Coal and Navigation Co. continued to operate as long as its sister canal, the Lehigh, functioned. Both ceased operation in 1931.

PENNSYLVANIA GERMANS, commonly but erroneously called "Pennsylvania Dutch," are a distinctive people with a history all their own and are not to be confused with the general mass of German-Americans. Entering Pennsylvania among the first settlers under Penn's charter, they increased somewhat slowly at first but after 1727, when the heavy Palatine immigration set in, their increase was rapid. At the time of the Revolution they composed about a third of the population of the province.

Settling in the southeastern part of the colony, between the English on the east and the Scotch-Irish on the west, they occupied a well-defined geographical area, frequently referred to as Pennsylvania-German Land, where they predominate overwhelmingly. This region embraces the present counties of Northampton, Lehigh, Berks, Lancaster, Lebanon and York, and adjacent districts, though many Pennsylvania Germans are found elsewhere in the state.

PENNSYLVANIA HOSPITAL, of Philadelphia, is the oldest hospital in the United States. Chartered in 1751, it was founded by Benjamin Franklin and Thomas Bond. The buildings originally erected for it, 1755–94, at 8th and Spruce Streets, are still in use. John Morgan, William Shippen, Jr., Benjamin Rush and Philip Syng Physick were early members of its staff, and the board of managers has always consisted of representative citizens of Philadelphia. Its records show the admission of many victims of the French and Indian wars, including soldiers from Braddock's army. During the Revolution its facilities were made use of by both the British and Continental armies during their occupation of Philadelphia. The earliest clinical lectures in America were given in its wards by Thomas Bond, and the oldest clinical amphitheater (1804) is still shown.

PENNSYLVANIA-VIRGINIA BOUNDARY DISPUTE. This dispute had its origin in the ambiguous terms of the grant of 1681 to William Penn and the claim of Virginia to extend "from sea to sea, west and northwest" over any territory not covered by royal grants. The questions at issue were whether the 39th or the 40th parallel was the southern boundary of Pennsylvania and how the western boundary, which was to be five degrees west of the Delaware River, should be drawn. In 1779 joint commissioners of the two states agreed to settle the dispute by extending Mason and Dixon's line, which is about a quarter of a degree south of the 40th parallel, to a point five degrees west of the Delaware River and by running the western boundary of Pennsylvania due north from that point. The Pennsylvania assembly promptly ratified the commissioners' decision, but the Virginia assembly waited until commissioners had confirmed the land claims of Virginians in the region and then ratified with the proviso that such claims should be valid.

PENOBSCOT (later Castine), the peninsula at the mouth of Maine's largest river of the same name, near the almost mythical Indian Norumbega, city of jewels and furs, held by five different nations in turn, was the strategic center of the battleground of the French and the English for the possession of Maine. Explored by both, the site of a trading post of the Plymouth plantation, sacked by the French in 1631 and captured in 1633, it was held, in spite of Myles Standish's attack, by the Frenchman Aulney, until its recapture by the Puritans in 1654. Returned to the French by the Treaty of Breda in 1670, it became the seat of the picturesque Baron Castine, who left the French army to become an Indian nabob and philosopher, husband of a Penobscot princess and a lord of furs. But this noble experiment in "going Indian" was interrupted by King

Philip's War, and Baron Castine and his half-breed son became the leaders of the Indians in the fighting for many years. This important stronghold of Castine never became completely English until Quebec fell in 1759.

PENOLE, originating in the Spanish Southwest, was of great value to early travelers whose rations were reduced to essentials. It was compounded of crushed parched corn, sugar or molasses, and cinnamon, although the last could be dispensed with. The traveler, without necessarily cooking it, mixed penole with water and found it nutritious if not delicious. A man could live for a month on a half bushel. Lt. Brewerton called penole invaluable to travelers in the Far West.

PENSACOLA, FLA. The first settlement at Pensacola, soon abandoned, was that of Tristan de Luna in 1539. Over 100 years later, in November, 1698, Arriola reached Pensacola Bay and established San Carlos de Austria, near the present site of Fort Barrancas, as a protection against French encroachments. Within a few months the French settled the lower Mississippi region. In 1719 when war was declared, Bienville seized the town, only to have his prize at once recaptured. The French attacked a second time and burned the settlement; but after peace was made Pensacola was restored to Spain (1723). The Spaniards now made their settlement on Santa Rosa Island, whence a hurricane in 1754 drove them back to the mainland.

In 1763 the British obtained Florida and divided it at the Apalachicola into two provinces, Pensacola becoming the government seat of West Florida. The trading house of Panton, Leslie & Co. was organized with headquarters at Pensacola, and the city, until then a wretched place of "forty huts and a barracks," rose to its most prosperous period prior to the Civil War. During the American Revolution, Pensacola was involved in intrigues, and after Spain entered the war against England it was captured by Bernardo de Galvez in May, 1781.

Florida was restored to Spain in 1783 and Pensacola lost its importance, although it remained the headquarters of Panton, Leslie & Co. During the War of 1812 the British attempted to use it as a base of operations, whereupon the city was seized by Andrew Jackson (1814) and the British were expelled. Jackson again occupied Pensacola in 1818 on the grounds that Spain was harboring hostile Seminoles. After fourteen months it was restored.

When the United States obtained Florida, the formal cession took place in Pensacola July 17, 1821. In 1822 the first legislative council met there, and the town was soon full of land speculators, who were attracted by the road then being started from Pensacola to St. Augustine. A second real-estate boom took place because of a projected railroad, but the scheme collapsed and by 1839 Pensacola's population was less than 2000.

On Jan. 12, 1861, Fort Barrancas and the navy yard were surrendered to the Confederates. Fort Pickens on Santa Rosa Island remained in Union hands, and from this base Federal troops retook the city (1862).

PENSIONS, MILITARY AND NAVAL. The United States has granted pensions to participants in all its wars, including Indian wars, and to the regular Army and Navy in peacetime. They may be classified as (1) pensions for injuries incurred in the service or to dependents of those whose death was caused by the service; (2) qualified service pensions for service of specified length combined with some other qualification, such as age, disability, or indigence; and (3) for service alone, usually granted to aged survivors long after the war. These pensions developed independently of the retirement system for regular and lengthy service which was generally accorded half-pay after a stipulated minimum service. Since World War II, even the reserve components of the services have a retirement schedule. It is based upon $2\frac{1}{2}\%$ of highest base pay per full year of active duty or cumulative years of training through a minimum of twenty years of satisfactory Federal service, such a year being one in which a reservist earns the equivalent of at least fifty days' duty. Payment for the regular commences upon retirement; for the reservist, it is deferred to age 62. Even retirements for physical disability are not true pensions, since all recipients are liable to recall to active duty in wartime or national emergency.

The systems grew haphazardly. Before 1817 our wars were fought mainly by volunteer armies. Pensions were offered as inducements to enlistment in colonial wars and in the Revolution. Early Federal enactments granting Revolutionary pensions provided only for disabilities incurred in the service. The first service pension law was in 1818, and the first pensions for widows of Revolutionary soldiers in 1836.

A separate system for the regular Army and Navy was established in 1790. The acts raising troops for the War of 1812 and the Mexican War promised the volunteers the same pensions as the regulars, and acts increasing these pensions before 1862 applied alike to the Army and Navy, the War of 1812 and the Mexican War. The first service pension was granted for the War of 1812 in 1871, and for the Mexican War in 1887.

Two innovations appeared during the Civil War. First, the "general laws" of 1862, providing uniform pensions on account of death or disability of service origin for both regulars and volunteers of the armed forces, applied to future wars. Second, certain "specific disabilities" were pensioned in 1864 at higher rates than under the general laws. Thereafter both the number of these disabilities and the rates rose rapidly.

A combination of political factors, including

patriotism, the soldier vote, veterans' lobbies and pension attorneys, helped to give the United States the most generous pension system in the world. Cleveland's vetoes of private pension bills and of the Dependent Pension Bill of 1887 made the subject an issue in the election of 1888. The act of 1890 gave a qualified service pension to Civil War veterans who, from any cause, were incapacitated for performing manual labor. In 1904 an administrative order made age above 62 years a pensionable disability under this act. Congress recognized this principle in acts of 1907 and 1912, which graduated payment according to age and length of service. The first Civil War pension for service alone was enacted in 1920. At the beginning of the Spanish-American War volunteers and state militia were specifically granted the same pensions as regulars. In 1920 a qualified service pension was given to all above 62 years old.

The philosophy of veteran treatment was transformed by World War I and its aftermath. Since then, the able-bodied veteran has shared immediate and substantial benefits with his less fortunate comrades-in-arms. It began during the war with enactments of a liberal life insurance program and a $60 discharge allowance. Thereafter, benefits progressively grew, largely through the persistent, indefatigable efforts of the American Legion, organized in 1919 almost simultaneously with a Federal Veterans Bureau created to oversee the traditional caretaking of casualties. Able-bodied veterans were soon lobbying for what was called the "Bonus Bill," predicated upon $1 per day of domestic service and $1.25 per day of overseas service. In 1924, Congress passed the bill over Coolidge's veto. Sums exceeding claims of $50 were paid in life insurance certificates maturing in 1945, when the principal was to be paid. Compound interest and an adjustment scale made an average claim of $400 worth $1,000 at maturity. The depression came and veterans' organizations militated for preferential treatment. In 1931, Congress overrode Hoover's veto to authorize veteran borrowing from the Treasury of amounts up to 50% of a certificate. The next year, the Bonus Expeditionary Force (B. E. F.) marched on Washington in a futile effort to force premature, lump-sum payment. In 1935, Roosevelt's veto of a bill for such payment was sustained. In 1936, his veto was overridden and the then enormous sum of $2,491,000,000 was disbursed. It was an omen. From the Revolution to 1930, all Federal disbursements to veterans totaled about $15,000,000,000; by 1960, that sum would meet Veterans Administration disbursements for only two and one half years.

Established in 1930, the Veterans Administration expanded rapidly in complexity and scope, especially after the passage of the "G. I. Bill of Rights" in 1944 (see Title 38 of the U. S. Code, 1958). By 1959, the V. A. had the fourth largest budget in the Government, annually expending about $6,210,-812,000. This was justified by the following veteran population: From the regular establishment, 95,000; Spanish-American War, 43,000; World War I, 2,778,-000; World War II, 15,243,000; Korean War, 4,507,-000; totaling 22,666,000 veterans. Survivors of deceased veterans and present or potential beneficiaries of living veterans number about 58,000,000. Hence, veterans and their beneficiaries constitute a substantial 40% of the national population.

The V. A. provides medical care, insurance, education and training, loans, and guardianship of minor and incompetent beneficiaries. About half of the budget is expended in compensation and pensions, the former designed to compensate veterans for the loss of earning power arising from injury or disease incident upon military service. Pensions constitute recognition of obligations arising from war service when a non-service-connected disability cripples or a non-service-connected death imposes hardship upon a veteran or his family.

The V. A. operates 171 hospitals with 120,411 beds. These in fiscal 1959 provided 42,000,000 days of inpatient care. Where hospitalization may be expected to increase with the aging of the veteran population, the insurance program, which now makes the V. A. the second largest ordinary life insurance operation, should gradually contract, since the insurance privilege is no longer automatically extended to servicemen. Since World War II, the G. I. Bill gave education or training to some 10,800,000 veterans or beneficiaries. For World War II veterans, the education benefit expired on July 25, 1956; for Korean War veterans it will end on January 31, 1965. Monthly subsistence of $65–$160 up to 48 months is provided in addition to tuition, fees and study materials. Since 1944, the V. A. has guaranteed or insured some $46,800,000,000 in nearly 6,000,000 home, farm or business loans. The guardianship program is slowly increasing; on June 30, 1959, the V. A. administered estates for 118,386 incompetents and 262,457 minors.

On the same date, the V. A. had a staff of 171,416 people. This is almost exactly ten times the size of the U. S. Army at the outbreak of the Civil War, and underscores the enormous gains in veteran benefits over a century.

PEQUOT WAR. Prior to any white settlement in Connecticut trouble had developed between Dutch traders and the Pequots, located in the southeastern part of the region, who claimed control over the tribes farther west. Capt. Stone, an English trader, and several companions were killed by Pequots in 1633, as was Capt. John Oldham in 1636, which led to a fruitless attack by a Massachusetts Bay expedition.

Both sides began preparations for further hostilities. Capt. John Underhill with a score of men arrived early in 1637 to strengthen Saybrook Fort, while in

April some Pequots made an attack on Wethersfield, killing nine persons. It was this latter event that led the general court of the recently settled river towns on May 1, 1637, to declare war on the Pequots. Ninety men were levied, supplied and placed under command of Capt. John Mason. Accompanied by eighty Mohegans under Uncas, they soon made their way down the river to Saybrook. Joined by Capt. Underhill and twenty Massachusetts men, Mason took his party in boats to the country of the Narragansetts, where he conferred with their chief, Miantonomo, and received further aid. A two days' march overland brought the party to the Pequot fort at Mystic, which was surprised and burned. Only seven Indians escaped the slaughter. Some 300 braves, from other Pequot towns, decided that their only safety was in flight, and started with their women and children for the Hudson. Meanwhile, the Mason party reinforced by Capt. Patrick with forty Massachusetts men, returned to Saybrook, while Capt. Israel Stoughton and 120 additional Massachusetts men arrived at New London harbor. After a conference, it was decided to pursue the fleeing Pequots, who were soon caught in Sasqua swamp, near present Southport, Conn. Through the intervention of Thomas Stanton the women and children were led out of the swamp before the attack was made. The fight (July 13) resulted in the escape of about 60, and the capture of 180 Pequots who were allotted to the Mohegans, Narragansetts and Niantics and absorbed into their tribes. Many of those who escaped were hunted down, while the chief, Sassacus, was slain by the Mohawks and his scalp sent to Hartford. The Pequots, as a separate tribe, ceased to exist.

PERDICARIS AFFAIR (1904) was a spectacular prelude to United States secret participation in the Algeciras Conference. On May 18, 1904, John Perdicaris, an American citizen, and his stepson, Cromwell Varley, a British subject, were abducted from their villa near Tangier by the Riffian bandit, Raisuli. The United States, with British support and using French good offices, demanded that the Moroccan sultan secure Perdicaris' release, and despatched the warship, *Brooklyn,* to Tangier. Meanwhile, the State Department came to suspect that Perdicaris had divested himself of American citizenship, but ultimately determined the question in his favor. On June 22 Secretary Hay sent the famous despatch demanding "Perdicaris alive or Raisuli dead," just as Perdicaris was in fact being released. Hay's despatch, hailed as robust-Rooseveltian, took the country by storm, but the dubious character of Perdicaris' citizenship was concealed until after the election.

PERRY'S EXPEDITION TO JAPAN. As a consequence of a growing desire in the United States to enter into commercial relations with Japan, for almost two and a half centuries hermetically sealed against all foreign intercourse except for a carefully restricted trade with the Dutch, an expedition was despatched to that country in 1852 under the command of Commodore Matthew Calbraith Perry. Its objective was threefold: to effect some arrangement for the protection of American seamen and property wrecked in Japan; to obtain permission for American vessels in the Asiatic trade to secure provisions, water and fuel; and to induce the Japanese government to open up one or more of their ports for trade. A further goal in the mind of Commodore Perry was the possible acquisition of one of the outlying islands of the Japanese archipelago as an American naval base or coaling station, but this proposed move was rejected by President Pierce.

While the mission was pacific in character, it was decided to impress upon the Japanese the determination of the United States to enter into treaty relations by a show of force, and a considerable squadron, first of four war vessels and later of seven, was provided Commodore Perry. A first visit was made to the Bay of Yedo (Tokyo) in July, 1853, and formal delivery made of the President's letter to the emperor of Japan. Perry informed the Japanese authorities that he would return early the next year for a definite answer to the proposals embodied in the letter, and then withdrew his ships to the China coast.

A second visit took place in February, 1854, and conversations were commenced, near the modern site of Yokohama, looking toward conclusion of a treaty of peace and amity. Commodore Perry's firm insistence upon American rights, backed up by the strength of his naval force, and internal conditions of the empire had combined to convince the Japanese authorities of the necessity for abandonment of their traditional policy of seclusion. On March 31, 1854, the treaty of Kanagawa, opening Japan to trade and also providing for the care of shipwrecked Americans and for facilities for provisioning American ships, was duly signed. The success of the expedition, so fruitful in its consequences for Japan and for the entire Western World, was in no small part due to the skill with which Commodore Perry combined diplomacy and naval power in overcoming Japanese reluctance to the breakdown of their isolation.

PETERSBURG, SIEGE OF (1864–65). Severely repulsed by Lee (C.) at Cold Harbor, Grant (U.) decided to approach Richmond from the south, through Petersburg. On June 12, 1864, he started his army to the James River, which it crossed by ferry and pontoons at Wyanoke Neck, June 14–17. His leading corps attacked Petersburg, June 15. After three days of fighting, the Federals captured the eastern defenses. Lee's army then arrived, occupied a shorter line nearer the city and repulsed the last assaults.

Grant then began siege operations on the eastern front, meantime persistently pushing his left flank southwestward to envelop Petersburg and cut the railways leading south. His first advance, June 21–22, was driven back. The battle of the Crater, July 30, resulted in another Federal repulse. Again striking westward, after severe fighting, Aug. 18–21, around Globe Tavern, the Federals succeeded in cutting the Weldon Railroad. In September Grant's extension of his right across the James and capture, Sept. 29, of Fort Harrison, eight miles south of Richmond, compelled Lee, also, to move much of his army north of the James and to keep it there. Thus weakened southwest of Petersburg, the Confederates lost further territory, Sept. 29–30, when Grant's left pushed forward to Peebles Farm, within two miles of the Boydton Plank Road. But an attempt to cut this highway by advancing across Hatcher's Run, Oct. 27, was decisively repulsed by Lee and field operations virtually ceased during the winter.

Foreseeing that when spring came his attenuated line, now 35 miles long, would be broken by superior numbers, Lee on March 25, 1865, assaulted Fort Stedman, desperately attempting to penetrate Grant's right and cut his supply railroad to City Point. The attack failed and Grant countered by sending Sheridan with heavy cavalry and infantry forces to Dinwiddie Courthouse, March 29, to destroy the Southside Railroad. Sheridan, worsted, March 31, by Pickett's and other divisions, received reinforcements and on April 1 routed Pickett at Five Forks, rendering the railroad indefensible. Lee evacuated Petersburg and Richmond April 2 and retreated westward.

PETITION, THE RIGHT OF, was claimed in England from an early date when the king was asked by individuals as well as groups to redress grievances. The right was exercised in Virginia as early as 1619, when the first House of Burgesses assumed that its function was to hear the governor's instructions and petition for a redress of grievances. But the later assemblies, especially in New England, came to regard themselves as the custodians of popular rights under the charters. The Massachusetts General Court in 1646 was petitioned by Dr. Child, who hoped that in this way his appeal might reach Parliament. Thus the idea was established that the legislature was the authority from which a redress of grievances must be sought. When the state legislatures were set up under the revolutionary constitutions, the idea prevailed that they assumed all the powers of a British Parliament. Among these was the power to receive petitions.

The Federal Convention in 1787 did not embody in the Constitution guarantees of individual rights, but these were required by the states as they ratified the document, and became the first ten amendments. It is not surprising that the First Amendment asserts the right of petition. Affirmed in the colonial Declaration of Rights in 1765 and mentioned in the Declaration of Independence, the right of petition was recognized as one of the rights reserved to the people. That is not to say that a petition must be read or acted upon. In the course of the slavery controversy Henry Clay insisted that the right of petition required that Congress give consideration to all petitions, stating reasons for their final disposition. This view found few supporters in Congress, and in 1836 the House of Representatives voted that all abolition petitions be tabled without reading. This "gag rule" was bitterly contested by John Quincy Adams and was finally rescinded in 1844. Occasionally attempts to exercise the right of petition have been accompanied by demonstrations. Coxey's Army, an organized group of the unemployed, marched upon Washington in 1894 and trampled the grass in the Capitol park, for which the leaders were arrested by the local police. Petitions have been presented by individuals, organized groups and state legislatures. In recent years the use of formal petitions has been supplanted largely by letters and telegrams to members of Congress. Propaganda has proved more effective than petitions. But petitions in the form of resolutions by meetings of organized groups continue to make their appearance. The constitutional right of petition today seems to be satisfied when a petition is officially received.

PHILADELPHIA. Boston and New York were half a century old when Philadelphia was founded. Cornelis Jacobsen Mey brought a party of Dutch settlers to the Delaware in 1623, but they located above and below the site of Philadelphia. The New Sweden Company, which sent out colonizers in 1638, placed short-lived trading posts at the mouth of the Schuylkill River and had many clashes with the Dutch; but the English took over the whole territory in 1664. More Swedes had come and settled between the Schuylkill and the Delaware, on the site of central Philadelphia. They built a blockhouse there in 1669 and called their settlement Wicaco. William Penn having obtained his charter in 1681, visited his land in 1682, chose the site of his capital city between the Schuylkill and Delaware, had it surveyed and christened it. By August, 1683, Philadelphia had 75 or 80 families, mostly Quaker in religion. The first colony of Germans came that year and founded Germantown. There were other notable migrations of them in 1694 and 1709. In 1701 Philadelphia became a chartered city. In 1741 the *American Magazine,* the first magazine on the continent, was produced here by Andrew Bradford; and the *Pennsylvania Evening Post and Daily Advertiser,* founded in 1775, became in 1783 the first daily newspaper in America. In 1752 one of the first American fire insurance companies was organized. The University of Pennsylvania was founded here in 1740. The American Philosophical Society, founded in 1743, had among its early members Franklin, Rittenhouse, the astronomer, and Godfrey, inventor of the mariner's quadrant.

Philadelphia, the second biggest city in the British Empire on the eve of the American Revolution, was the chief center of events during the Revolutionary War. The first Continental Congress met in the city in 1774, and it continued meeting there through most of the war period. There the Declaration of Independence and the Constitution were written. The British under Howe occupied the city from Sept. 26, 1777, to June 18, 1778. Philadelphia was the capital of the nation from 1790 until 1800, and the state capital until 1799.

At the beginning of the 19th century it was considered the cultural center of the country, though its eminence in science and philosophy, as attested by numerous societies and institutions for their study, was greater than that in literature. It had developed its old aristocracy, too, centering about Rittenhouse Square in the city proper and in Germantown and Chestnut Hill in the suburbs.

Philadelphia became a great manufacturing city in the 19th century; but despite its industrialism, its strong infusions of Quaker and German cultures imparted to it a placidity, a conservatism and leisureliness of pace which persist even in the 20th century and have given it a distinctive character among American cities.

Fourth in size in 1960, outdistanced by New York, Chicago and Los Angeles, Philadelphia had a population of 2,002,512.

PHILADELPHIA, CAPTURE AND BURNING OF USS. On Oct. 31, 1803, during the Barbary Wars, this frigate, commanded by Capt. William Bainbridge, and temporarily unattended by other American warships blockading Tripoli, sailed too near the shore while pursuing an enemy craft and struck a hidden reef. Heroic efforts to release her proved unavailing, and in the end she and her crew of 307 men were captured. This incident prolonged and made more difficult American negotiations with and operations against Tripoli—although the ill effects were subsequently somewhat minimized in consequence of Stephen Decatur's daring exploit in destroying the captured frigate after the Tripolitans had refloated her. With some eighty men, in the ketch *Intrepid,* Decatur, during the night of Feb. 16, 1804, boarded the *Philadelphia,* cleared her of the enemy, set her afire and escaped from the harbor.

PHILADELPHIA CORDWAINERS' CASE (1805). When in the fall of 1805 the journeymen cordwainers of Philadelphia went on strike to enforce their demand for the wage scale prevailing at New York and Baltimore and a discontinuance of the rebate of wages for export work, eight union leaders were arrested on a charge of criminal conspiracy and tried in the Mayor's Court of Philadelphia. The court accepted the arguments of Jared Ingersoll for the prosecution and relied upon British authorities, since refuted, to establish the doctrine that "a conspiracy of workmen to raise their wages" was criminal at common law. Despite efforts of defense counsel, Caesar A. Rodney, the defendants were found guilty, but, as the court was chiefly concerned in establishing the principle, they were each fined $8.00. The strike was broken and an important precedent was set for the criminal prosecution of labor union activities which had multiplied with the rise of wholesale manufacturers. This was the first of six criminal conspiracy cases brought against union shoemakers in this period, four of which were decided against the journeymen.

PHILIPPINE INSURRECTION (1899–1902). Cession of the Philippine Islands to the United States by Spain in 1898 disappointed native expectations of immediate independence. Filipino insurgents already in arms against Spain proclaimed a republic, and friction between them and American authorities culminated on Feb. 4, 1899, in open hostilities. Regular and volunteer troops under Generals Anderson, Merritt, McArthur, Otis, Wheaton and Lawton defeated the *insurrectos,* driving them into northern Luzon. The Filipino "capital," Malolos, fell on March 31, the native government under Emilio Aguinaldo withdrawing to Tarlac. Sharp fighting with organized troops occurred along the Manila Railway and at successive entrenched river positions. Tarlac was taken in November, the insurgent armies then disintegrating. Aguinaldo fled to inaccessible northeastern Luzon.

Guerrilla warfare ensued throughout the archipelago until suppressed in April, 1902, when the last important chieftain surrendered. Aguinaldo was captured by stratagem in March, 1901.

More than 120,000 American soldiers were engaged in the war, a maximum of 69,000 at any one period. Barbarities practised by the Filipino guerrillas, especially against their own people, necessitated stern retaliatory measures. In Samar, an entire company of American regulars was surprised and massacred. The principal insurgent leaders were Aguinaldo and Gregorio del Pilar (Tagalogs), Antonio Luna (Ilocano), and Vicente Lucban (Visayan). Their troops, undisciplined, ill-armed and without artillery, were easily defeated, but with great difficulty dispersed. Generally speaking, the Filipino people supported the insurrection, although little effective co-operation was evident between tribes or islands. The Mindanao and Jolo Moros held aloof, to be subjugated later.

PHILIPPINE ISLANDS. This archipelago consists of over 7000 islands, of which more than 1000 are habitable. Europeans first became aware of it when Magellan landed there in 1521. Spanish occupation, under Miguel López de Legazpi, was begun in 1566. With the exception of a partial occupation by the British, 1762–64, the islands remained in Spanish possession until the Spanish-American War of 1898. The greatest single result of the Spanish occupation was the establishment of Christianity among the eight principal peoples (who became the Filipinos proper) and the consequent inculcation to some degree of Western ideas. The rising tide of Islam was restricted to Mindanao and adjacent regions where that religion still has many adherents.

The islands were ceded to the United States by the Treaty of Paris of 1898. An insurrection against American forces by Filipinos under Emilio Aguinaldo, which began in 1899, was finally suppressed in 1902. The outstanding result of the occupation by the United States was the development of the people along Western lines in the fields of education, agriculture, industry, law, government, and public health. The government evolved over a period of 48 years (1898–1946) from military occupation to independence, and the Philippines have been regarded as something of a showcase, exhibiting the successful conversion of an Asiatic colonial people into an independent democracy. Civil government was set up in 1901 under the Philippine Commission, and William Howard Taft, president of the commission, became the first civil governor. In 1907 a native Philippine Assembly was created, which, with the American-controlled Philippine Commission, operated as a legislature under the American governor general, a title adopted for the chief executive two years before. In 1913 the Commission was reconstituted with a Filipino majority of four out of seven members. In 1916, in the Jones Act, Congress provided for an elective House of Representatives and Senate, known as the Philippine legislature, but legislative enactments were still subject to the veto of the governor general and the President of the United States. In 1934 Congress passed the Philippine Independence (Tydings-McDuffie) Act which set up the conditions for complete independence, to take place on the first Fourth of July after an interval of ten years following compliance with the conditions of the act. In the interim the islands were governed as the Commonwealth of the Philippine Islands with a Filipino president. A high commissioner represented the United States at Manila.

In the controversy over the passage of the Philippine Independence Act, some definite factional divisions were revealed. The Democratic party, since the presidential campaign of 1900, had favored greater speed in bringing about independence than had the Republicans. By 1930 the friends of independence had been joined by representatives of certain economic interests that desired protection for their products against the competition of imports from the Philippines, and organized labor supported independence to avoid further infiltration of Philippine labor into this country. Opposition to independence came from American investors in the Philippines.

In 1935 the Philippines adopted a constitution modeled on that of the United States. It was accepted by President F. D. Roosevelt, Philippine elections were held, and the ten-year Commonwealth period was under way. World War II came during the Commonwealth period. After the attack upon Pearl Harbor, December, 1941, the Japanese occupied the principal points in the islands. Groups of Filipinos, with American support, conducted much resistance activity. When the returning American forces under Gen. Douglas MacArthur defeated the Japanese, the Government of the Commonwealth was restored. Manuel Quezón, who had been elected president under the Commonwealth, died in the United States in 1944, and his place was taken by Vice-President Osmeña. Early in 1946, in anticipation of independence, Manuel Roxas was elected president of the Philippine Republic. On July 4, 1946, independence became an established fact.

The Japanese occupation had seriously damaged the Philippine economy. Production was reduced, exports were low, and the great demand for consumer and producer goods had to be met mainly from imports. Such a situation tended toward inflation and created fiscal troubles. The United States contributed much to stabilizing the economy, and, during the first eight years of independence, it was estimated that the American contributions totaled about $2,000,-000,000. In more recent years the United States has offered development loans to enable the Filipinos to purchase materials and machinery for restoring and improving transportation and industry. There has been criticism in some Philippine circles to the effect that the amounts thus made available are not sufficient to bring about the desirable rate of industrial progress. The United States has undertaken to pay Filipino claims for war damage, and large sums have been spent in making partial payments. There is strong sentiment in Manila that these claims should be more promptly liquidated. Finally there has been criticism of the United States on account of American military bases in the islands, the continuation of which was authorized in the bases agreement of 1947. Extreme nationalists demand the abolition of the bases. Others desire some readjustment of the terms by which the United States exercises jurisdiction over military personnel accused of offenses against Philippine law. The rise of Philippine nationalism has increased the strength of these criticisms.

The threat of communist influence in the Philippines has risen and fallen since World War II, but it cannot be disregarded. The Hukbalahap movement from 1946 to 1950 was a serious menace to the government. The Huks, as the members were called, had constituted a resistance group during Japanese occupation. After the war they turned against the Philippine government and sought to establish a communist regime. Impoverished farmers and other discontented Filipinos were recruited. Villages were terrorized, and the overthrow of the government itself seemed a possibility. At that time one of the outstanding figures in Philippine history came into prominence. In 1950 Ramon Magsaysay was made Secretary of Defense and vigorously reorganized the armed forces. Within a year the backbone of the Huk movement had been broken, and the Huks were pushed into the hills where they were subjected to a mopping-up process. In 1953 Magsaysay was elected President by a large majority. He instituted economic and social reforms and did much to restore confidence in the government. Unfortunately his brilliant career was cut short by a fatal airplane accident in 1957. No one of equal stature has succeeded him, and the confidence in government which he inspired has been somewhat diminished. Meanwhile the communists have thrown their support to such Philippine nationalists as desire to eliminate American influence in the islands.

The Philippine government has co-operated with the United Nations and the free world. In 1951 it signed a mutual defense treaty with the United States. In 1954 it joined in the formation of the Southeast Asia Treaty Organization (SEATO). The policy of the United States toward the Philippines is that of encouraging the development of a strong, stable, and democratic government which will serve as an example to Asiatics and act as a deterrent against the further spread of communism in the Far East. There are influential elements in the Philippines that are cordial to the United States and friendly toward these aims. There are also counter forces of some strength, and, considering the volatile nature of Asiatic politics, the success of the American policy cannot be complacently taken for granted.

PHONOGRAPH. Thomas Edison's invention of the phonograph in 1877 is comparable in importance to Gutenberg's invention of the printing press in the 15th century. It has accomplished the dissemination of music on a scale undreamt of in the time of Bach, Mozart, and Beethoven, and it has conferred immortality on the previously evanescent art of the performing musician. Not only the invention of the phonograph but also its major improvements have all been of American origin.

The original apparatus, for which Edison applied for a patent on Dec. 24, 1877, consisted of a metal cylinder and two diaphragm-and-needle units—one to be used for recording, the other for reproduction. A piece of tin foil was wrapped around the cylinder, and on it the recording needle indented a pattern of the sound vibrations directed onto the diaphragm via a mouthpiece. On replaying, the reproducing needle converted these indentations on the tin foil back into sound. Wax and plastic cylinders were later used instead of tin foil, but eventually the cylinder phonograph gave way to the more advantageous disc phonograph, or Gramophone.

The device for recording and reproducing sound on flat discs was invented by Emile Berliner, an American of German birth, in 1887. Modified and refined by Eldridge Johnson, founder of the Victor Talking Machine Co., the disc phonograph quickly established itself throughout the world. The most celebrated vocalists of the day were persuaded to make records for it.

For almost half a century, discs continued to be recorded by the "acoustic" process invented by Edison—the recording needle being driven directly by the actual sound vibrations emitted by singer or instrument. In the early 1920's, a team of American engineers working for the Bell Telephone Laboratories perfected an "electrical" process of recording —the recording needle being driven by electrically amplified sound vibrations transmitted via a microphone. This process, which came into general use in 1925, greatly extended the frequency and dynamic range of records and for the first time made possible the effective registration of large orchestral and choral ensembles.

In 1948 another team of American engineers, working for C. B. S. Laboratories, developed the first successful long-playing record. By slowing down the speed from 78 to 33⅓ revolutions per minute, greatly decreasing the width of the grooves, and introducing an electronic equalization system, the C. B. S. engineers were able to increase playing time from four to 23 minutes without an accompanying decrease in fidelity. The LP microgroove disc, soon adopted by all companies throughout the world, together with high-fidelity techniques of recording and reproducing sound, have tremendously heightened interest in recorded music and vastly expanded the repertoire available on records.

PHOTOGRAPHY. America's introduction to photography dates back to April 20, 1839, when the New York *Observer* published a letter from Samuel F. B. Morse, describing his March 7th visit to Daguerre. The daguerreotype process (photographs on silver-plated copper) flourished here and was used almost exclusively until the middle 1850's, with Southworth and Hawes, John A. Whipple, the Langenheim and Meade Brothers, M. M. Lawrence and Mathew B. Brady as its most successful practitioners. The collodion or wet-plate process announced in 1851 by the Englishman, Frederick Scott Archer, was slow in taking over. Ambrotypes (photographs on glass) patented by James A. Cutting of Boston, achieved great popularity in 1856 and 1857. Carte-de-visite photographs in their decorative family albums began to grace parlor tables in 1859, and the tintype started a flourishing industry. In 1866 the larger cabinet-size photograph became the portrait favorite. Meanwhile, the stereoscopic views introduced by the Langenheims in 1850 brought America's natural wonders into the homes of America, and by the summer of 1863 one firm alone—E. & H. T. Anthony & Co., precursors of Agfa-Ansco—had published over 1100 subjects.

Notable achievements of wet-plate days include

the Civil War coverage of Mathew B. Brady, Alexander Gardner and their associates; the recording of the westward expansion and the construction of the transcontinental railroads; attempts to capture the illusion of motion by Coleman Sellers in 1861, continued by Henry R. Heyl, Eadweard Muybridge and Thomas Eakins, ultimately resulting in the motion picture; and efforts to reproduce illustrations in facsimile for books, magazines and newspapers, culminating in 1880 in the halftone process connected with the names of F. W. von Eggloffstein, Stephen H. Horgan, Frederick E. Ives and Louis E. and Max Levy.

Modern gelatin dry plates had first been manufactured in this country in 1878, but were slow in winning professional approval. The Rev. Hannibal Goodwin's celluloid flexible film (patent applied for in 1887) and George Eastman's Kodak of 1888 brought about the popularization of amateur photography.

At this time, too, the sociologist Jacob A. Riis became America's first crusading journalist-photographer, using documentation by flashlight as a weapon in his "Battle with the Slum." In 1905, Lewis W. Hine began to make his sociological records of immigrants, later delving into child labor and "Men at Work."

Meanwhile, in 1902 Alfred Stieglitz, Edward Steichen, Frank Eugene, Gertrude Käsebier, Joseph T. Keiley, Clarence H. White and others launched a movement "to advance photography as applied to pictorial expression." Known as the Photo-Secession, its inspiriting quarterly (*Camera Work*, 1903–17) and the widespread participation of its members in national and international exhibitions furthered the recognition of photography as a fine art. As early as 1912, the sense of abstraction began to make itself felt in photography.

During World War I, Edward Steichen as chief of the photographic division of the Army Air Service changed from the "soft focus" to the "straight" photographic approach that was to influence photographers in the United States from that time on.

Fertile years in the history of American photography lay ahead, with the impress of Paul Strand's direct approach; the emergence of the "West Coast school" in the pure photography of Edward Weston and Ansel Adams, exponents of the large-format camera; and the conception of the "Equivalents" which represented the sum-total of Alfred Stieglitz's life and experience. In this era both *Vanity Fair* and *Vogue* attracted the genius of Edward Steichen and the talents of others to bring forth many innovative and pioneering aspects of photography in interpretive portraiture, theatre, fashion and advertising.

In 1924 the German-invented 35mm camera began to exert a powerful effect, furthered by the introduction of the electric photoflash bulb, while constantly increasing speed in film advanced the development of photography.

During the depression of the 1930's, Roy E. Stryker's Farm Security Administration group (Ben Shahn, Walker Evans, Dorothea Lange, Arthur Rothstein, Russell Lee, Marion Post Wolcott and others) documented the saga of the underprivileged third of the nation. The 1930's also saw the beginning of the "picture book," a happy union of photography and text, and with the advent of *Life* (Nov. 23, 1936) modern photo-journalism was born.

While color photography in America has had a long history, dating back to 1851, it did not come into extensive popular use until 1935, when the Eastman Kodak Co. announced Kodachrome film. Recent advances, notably the experiments in color perception made by Edwin Land of the Polaroid Co., have opened revolutionary vistas.

In 1932, The Museum of Modern Art became the first art museum in the world to make the art of photography an integral part of its program, and, in the latitude and extent of this recognition, the Museum still stands without a peer. In 1955, Edward Steichen (Director of its Department of Photography since 1947) created "The Family of Man"—an exhibition seen by over 9,000,000 people in 37 countries. In 1959, The George Eastman House—the greatest museum entirely devoted to the history of photography—under the directorship of the outstanding photographic scholar and historian, Beaumont Newhall (formerly Curator of Photography at the Museum of Modern Art) celebrated its tenth anniversary with a major international exhibition, "Photography at Mid-Century."

The standard of American photography has been raised in recent years by the work of Alfred Stieglitz, Edward Steichen, Paul Strand, Edward Weston (in 1937 the first photographer to receive a Guggenheim Fellowship), Man Ray, Ansel Adams, Dorothea Lange and Margaret Bourke-White, to cite a few. Outstanding among the younger men are Aaron Siskind, Minor White, Frederick Sommer, W. Eugene Smith, Harry Callahan, Paul Caponigro, Steven Trefonides, and the Swiss national, Robert Frank.

In 1960, 52,000,000 Americans were taking still and motion pictures.

PICKAWILLANY, an Indian village near the site of the present Piqua, Ohio, was the western outpost of English traders before the French and Indian War. It was founded about 1748 by Miami who left their village at the site of Fort Wayne, Ind., desiring British rather than French trade. In 1749, when Céloron's expedition reached Pickawillany, Céloron ejected two employees of English traders and urged the Miami to return to their old village. He was, however, answered evasively by the chief LaDemoiselle, or "Old Britain," as the English called him. By 1750 English traders had built storehouses at Pickawillany and several were in residence there. Early in 1751 Christopher Gist reported that the village consisted of about 400 families and was "daily encreasing." George Croghan, Gist's companion, was so successful in cementing the friendship of the Miami that they refused to return to their old home at the request of a party of "French Indians."

Later in 1751 Gov. Jonquière sent to Pickawillany a party of eastern Indians under Bellestre and Longueuil to eject the English traders by force if necessary. Though the Ottawa forbade its passage through their territory, a small group reached Pickawillany, took some scalps, and increased the Miami's hostility to the French. Longueuil, Jonquière's successor, feared a general revolt of the Indians with LaDemoiselle as a leading spirit. Finally, on June 21, 1752, Charles de Langlade and over 200 Ottawa attacked Pickawillany, destroyed the traders' storehouses and confiscated goods worth £3000. Five English traders were captured and sent to France; several Miami, including LaDemoiselle, were killed; and the chief was cooked and eaten. After the treaty of Logstown Capt. Trent met some of the fleeing Miami and gave them their share of the royal present; but the English influence among them waned, and they returned to their old village, leaving Pickawillany deserted.

PICKETT'S CHARGE (July 3, 1863), more properly the Pickett-Pettigrew charge, was the culminating event of the battle of Gettysburg. Having failed on July 1 and 2 to drive the Federals, Gen. Lee decided to assault their center. For this purpose he designated Pickett's division, the division of Harry Heth, temporarily commanded by J. J. Pettigrew, and two brigades of Pender's division. After a preliminary bombardment by 125 guns, these troops, 47 regiments, 15,000 men, were ordered to advance an average of 1300 yards eastward from Seminary Ridge to a "little clump of trees" on the front of the II Corps along Cemetery Ridge. The assault, delivered with the utmost gallantry after 2 P.M., carried the column of attack to the Federal position, but failed for lack of support when the Federals closed in from three sides. The Confederates, who were compelled to retreat under heavy fire, lost about 6000 men. Three of Pickett's brigade commanders and most of his field officers were killed.

PICTURE WRITING, INDIAN, is a term loosely applied to all Indian pictures. In the United States many prehistoric pictographs, found upon rocks, may be symbolic but not necessarily intended for writing. Yet the historic Indians made some use of picture writing to convey information. In 1823 the traveler West, in the Red River country, noted his guide making pictures upon a piece of wood to be left on the trail as a message, indicating the number of persons in West's party, the direction taken and instructions to follow. The Plains Indians recorded their deeds upon buffalo robes and upon the covers of tipis in a similar manner, but a full understanding of such pictures was scarcely possible without help from their authors. The Kiowa and Dakota tribes kept crude calendars, each year indicated by some unique event: as in our year 1828 a man by the name of Chadron built a house at Cheyenne River; it was represented by the outline of a white man's house, encasing the head and shoulders of a man wearing a hat. In such cases it is obvious that the form of picture writing is little more than a mnemonic system. After contact with white people, Indians often signed their names by a graph, for example, as in a petition of Pennsylvania Indians to the English king, 1701. However, in this case the names of Indians are written in English but accompanied by Indian symbols called "totems," representing their respective hereditary families or clans.

The nearest approach to true writing among United States Indians appears in the song records of the Ojibwa, made by pressing the point of a stylus upon strips of birch bark.

PIECES OF EIGHT were Spanish silver coins of eight *reales* ("eight bits"), first authorized by a law of 1497. Also known as *pesos* and Spanish dollars, they were minted in enormous quantities and soon became recognized and accepted throughout the commercial world as a reliable medium of exchange. In 1728 the Spaniards began coinage of the milled dollar to replace the old piece of eight, the new coins being more difficult to "clip" or "shave" than the old ones. Subsidiary coins of four *reales* ("half dollar"; "four bits"), two *reales* ("quarter dollar"; "two bits"), etc., were also minted. The Spanish piece of eight or milled dollar had become familiar as the metallic basis of the monetary system in the British colonies in America, and consequently Congress adopted the Spanish milled dollar in 1786 as the basis of the coinage system of the United States, the first American dollars containing approximately the same amount of silver as their contemporary Spanish counterparts.

PIEDMONT REGION is geographically the area of the eastern United States lying at the foot of the easternmost ranges of the mountains of the Appalachian system, but, historically considered, is all the territory included between these ranges and the fall line on the rivers. Below these falls many of the rivers are tidal estuaries and the region is known as Tidewater. Upcountry or back country is other terminology sometimes given to the Piedmont region. The division of the Atlantic coastal plain into these two regions has been profoundly important in American history. First settled, the Tidewater region became the locale of conservative planters, merchants and politicians. To the Piedmont region went later, and often less wealthy and cultured, settlers. There they became small farmers rather than great planters or merchants. Socially and economically democratic, Piedmonters were generally at odds with the Tidewater population. Early sectionalism in America was based mainly on this differentiation. The gradual elimination of political discrimination and improved transportation have decreased but not eliminated the sectional significance of the Piedmont region.

PIERRE, FORT, developed from a small trading post established by Joseph LaFramboise, at the mouth of the Bad River on the west bank of the Missouri in October, 1817. The Columbia Fur Company took the business over in 1822 and named the post Fort Tecumseh. In 1828 the Astor interests bought the plant and in 1832 built a new post and named it Fort Pierre Chouteau. The Chouteau appellation did not become popular and was dropped. In 1855 the Government bought the plant, but dismantled it a year later. The village of Fort Pierre now occupies the area. For several decades Fort Pierre was the only place indicated on the maps of the Dakota country. There in 1743 the Verendrye brothers made claim to the Northwest for France and planted an inscribed plate in testimony to the taking. This plate was recovered in 1913.

PIERRE'S HOLE, BATTLE OF, was fought at the scene of this noted trappers' rendezvous in the Teton Mountains (in present eastern Idaho) between Gros Ventres Indians and American fur traders July 18, 1832. It was the most renowned struggle of the trapping era, and witnessed the exploits of such prominent trappers and pathfinders as William L. Sublette, Nathaniel J. Wyeth and Antoine Godin. The whites surrounded their outnumbered enemy in a fort protected by brush, but after an all-day fight were unable to dislodge them. During a parley the interpreter for the whites wrongly announced that more Blackfeet were at their camp and the attack was abandoned.

PIETISM is the name given to the movement in German Protestantism which arose in the 17th and 18th centuries to combat the growing formalism in the Lutheran and Reformed churches. The father of the movement was Philip Jacob Spener (1635–1705), a Lutheran minister in Frankfort-on-Main, who began the formation of *Collegia Pietatis* or societies of piety for the promotion of Bible study and prayer. He stressed Christianity as a life rather than as a creed; lay people were urged to take a larger part in the work of the church. In 1694 the University of Halle was established through Spener's influence, and became the principal pietistic center. Spener's work was continued by August Herman Francke (1663–1727) at Halle and pietism spread throughout Germany, influenced John Wesley and the Methodist movement in England and swept into the Scandinavian countries. In the American colonies its influence was chiefly exerted through the German Lutherans, the German Reformed and the Moravians. Henry M. Mühlenberg was sent to America largely through the exertions of the Halle pietists and his leadership among the colonial Lutherans in the

formative period served to emphasize that phase of Lutheranism. Count Zinzendorf was a pietist, having spent six years at Halle, and the American Moravians were the most pietistic of all the colonial religious bodies. Pietism was from the beginning strongly missionary in emphasis, and for that reason had large significance in colonial America particularly.

PIKE'S EXPEDITION TO THE UPPER MISSISSIPPI (1805–6). The acquisition of Louisiana initiated a notable period of western exploration in which Lt. Zebulon M. Pike played a leading role. On Aug. 9, 1805, he left St. Louis with twenty soldiers on a 70-foot keelboat to explore the Mississippi to its source, conciliate the natives, assert the authority of the United States, and procure sites for military posts. Near Little Falls, Minn., Pike built a substantial log fort, after which he traveled for weeks in midwinter by sled and toboggan, ascending to the upper reaches of the Mississippi, replacing the British flag with the American, hobnobbing with the natives and making geographical observations. He reached St. Louis, April 30, 1806, with a record of achievement which won the appointment to lead an expedition to the far Southwest (*see* Pike's Southwestern Expedition). Although he had accomplished all that had been expected of him, the Government neglected to follow up his achievement, whose chief practical result was its addition to existing geographical knowledge.

PIKE'S SOUTHWESTERN EXPEDITION (1806–7). This expedition, performed by Lt. Zebulon M. Pike and a small band of U. S. soldiers, was one of exploration, and of conciliation of the Indian tribes in the newly acquired territory of the United States extending southwestward toward Sante Fe and the Spanish border. Leaving Fort Bellefontaine (near St. Louis) July 15, 1806, the party traveled to the Pawnee towns in Kansas (precise location undetermined), and thence by way of the Arkansas River into Colorado. From here it crossed, in midwinter, the Sangre de Cristo Range to a tributary of the Rio Grande, where it was made captive by a detachment of Spanish soldiers from Santa Fe. The Spanish authorities conducted Pike to Chihuahua, and thence by a circuitous route to the American border at Natchitoches, on July 1, 1807.

Pike's narrative, published in 1810, afforded his countrymen their first description of the great Southwest which he had traversed. Few in number, and with the scantiest of material equipment, his men had braved the treachery of the savages, the perils of starvation, the awful exposure of the Colorado Rockies in midwinter, and the prospect of perpetual confinement in a foreign land. They wrote a new chapter in the annals of human daring and devotion, and added a volume of abiding worth to the literature of New World exploration.

PIKES PEAK (altitude 14,110 feet), the most famous of the Colorado mountains, was first described by Zebulon M. Pike in his *Journal,* Nov. 25–27, 1806; first ascended by Dr. Edwin James, July 14, 1820; named James Peak by Maj. Long, but became officially Pikes Peak through popular usage by trappers and others. It is the center for the region of Garden of the Gods, Manitou Hot Springs, the Ute Pass Highway and Cripple Creek mines.

Pikes Peak is of historical significance as a landmark of early traders and trappers and as the name of the region now known as Colorado. Discovery of gold in Colorado brought large numbers to the region in 1858. Many returned in disappointment, but further discoveries in 1859 attracted thousands who crossed the plains with the slogan "Pikes Peak or Bust," and gradually opened up the various mining camps or settled in the valleys of the state.

PIKES PEAK GOLD RUSH. Gold was discovered at Ralston Creek, near present Denver, in 1850 by Cherokee gold seekers bound for California. Reports of this find, augmented by rumors of other discoveries, led in 1858 to the organization of parties to prospect the region. The Russell-Cherokee expedition, comprising miners experienced in the gold fields of Georgia and California, was most important. Parties went also from Missouri and Kansas. Most of these prospectors, discouraged after a few days of unsuccessful search, returned to their homes. The remnant of the Russell party discovered some placer gold in Cherry Creek and other affluents of the South Platte in July, 1858. Word of these finds brought new hopefuls to the region in the fall. Exaggerated stories of the reputed gold fields circulated through the press of the country during the winter of 1858–59. Inasmuch as Pikes Peak was the best-known landmark, though 75 miles from the site of the discoveries, the region was called the "Pikes Peak Gold Country," or "Cherry Creek Diggings." The meager amount of dust found in 1858 hardly warranted so much excitement. But the country, suffering from the recent panic of 1857, grasped avidly at any hope of rehabilitation. Merchants and newspapers in the Missouri River towns, with an eye to spring outfitting, spread golden stories, which the Atlantic coast papers generally ridiculed and denied. Sixteen guidebooks (some by interested outfitting towns) were issued to instruct amateur prairie travelers and win them to particular routes. This directed publicity through the winter built a great flood of gold seekers that burst across the plains with spring. The principal routes were up the Platte, the Arkansas and the Smoky Hill, converging at the mouth of Cherry Creek. With wagons, on horseback and afoot the argonauts rushed mountainward. The Leavenworth and Pikes Peak Express established the first stage line to Denver. Many early arrivals, finding the creek sands were not yellow with gold, and unenriched by a few days' futile search, turned back, crying a "Pikes Peak Humbug." Fortunately, rich gold veins were found in the mountains (Gregory lode, near present Central

City, the first, May 6, 1859) in time to save the movement from complete collapse. It is estimated that 100,000 persons set out for the gold region, that half of them reached the mountains, and that only half of these remained, to found Colorado.

PILGRIMS, THE, consisted of 35 members of an English Separatist church in Leyden, Holland, who, with 66 English sectarians and servants, sailed from Plymouth (Sept. 6/16, 1620) on the *Mayflower* and founded Plymouth Colony in New England. Though outnumbered by the English contingent, the Leyden group were the prime movers and the backbone of the migration, and the Pilgrims are generally associated with the Leyden congregation of which they were a part. This congregation, one of many Puritan sects which opposed the Elizabethan church settlement, originated at Scrooby, Nottinghamshire, England, an obscure village on a manor of the Archbishop of York. Led by William Brewster, the Archbishop's bailiff (1590–1608) who had become a Puritan while at Cambridge (1580–*ca.* 1582), the sect formed as a Separating Congregationalist church between 1590 and 1607. By 1607 the congregation embraced 100 or more rural folk, including, besides "Elder Brewster," William Bradford, son of a prosperous Austerfield farmer, and John Robinson, nonconformist Cambridge graduate who became their minister in 1607.

A minority of Scrooby village, the congregation was persecuted by conforming neighbors and (November, 1607) mildly "investigated" by the Ecclesiastical Commission of York. However, to avoid contamination in England they determined to insure religious and ecclesiastical purity by emigrating to Holland where other English sectaries found liberty to worship, and lucrative employment. After embarrassing difficulties with English officials, about 100 escaped to Amsterdam by August, 1608. Amsterdam heterodoxy troubled them, however; in May, 1609, with Dutch permission, they settled at Leyden where the local cloth industry largely employed their labors and the university stimulated their leaders. At Leyden the congregation approximately tripled in numbers (1609–18), and its polity and creed crystallized under the able leadership of John Robinson and Elder Brewster.

But after seven years they grew troubled and discontented. Their work was hard, their incomes small, their economic outlook unfavorable, their children became Dutchified, and they lacked that ecclesiastical and civil autonomy deemed necessary for their purity and proper growth. Thus, they decided (winter, 1616–17) to move to America, to the northern part of the Virginia Company's grant, under English protection, where they hoped to establish a profitable fishing and trading post. Deacon John Carver and Robert Cushman negotiated (summer, 1617) with the Virginia Company, hoping for official guarantees against English ecclesiastical interference. The Virginia Company encouraged them, and gave them a charter (June 9, 1619). But they needed capital. When (February-March, 1620) Thomas Weston, London Puritan merchant, proposed they employ a charter which his associates held from the Virginia Company (dated Feb. 2, 1620, in the name of John Peirce and associates) and form a joint-stock company for seven years to found a trading post in America, the Leyden people accepted. Specific terms were drawn up.

A bare majority, however, voted to remain in Leyden. The minority, taking Brewster as their "teacher," prepared to depart (April-May, 1620). A sixty-ton vessel, the *Speedwell,* was outfitted. All was in readiness to sail when difficulties with the London financiers paralyzed the enterprise until June 10, when Cushman persuaded Weston to continue co-operation. The London associates hired the *Mayflower*; by mid-July it was provisioned and ready to sail from London. Aboard were some eighty men, women and children, most of them engaged by Weston as laborers or servants, and probably not of the Separatist persuasion. On June 22/July 1, the Leyden people left Delftshaven in the *Speedwell* and joined the *Mayflower* at Southampton. There they quarreled over business terms with Weston, who finally left them "to stand on their own legs" and, with no settlement, they sailed (Aug. 5/15). But the *Speedwell* proved unseaworthy and, after repairs at Dartmouth and Plymouth, the decision was made to sail on the *Mayflower* alone, with as many as it would carry and who still wished to go. On Sept. 6/16, 1620, with some 87 passengers, 14 servants and workmen, and a crew of 48, the *Mayflower* sailed from Plymouth. Only two of those aboard—Brewster and Bradford—came from the original Scrooby congregation.

After an uneventful voyage land was sighted (Nov. 9/19) and proved to be Cape Cod, north of the limit of their patent. There, deliberately abandoning their patent—which had given them legal departure from England—they determined to settle without legal rights on Massachusetts Bay. To quiet murmurs of the London men and maintain order, 41 adult males drew up and signed the famous Mayflower Compact (Nov. 11/21, 1620). The same day they landed in Provincetown harbor. After considerable searching they discovered Plymouth harbor (Dec. 8/18), landed the *Mayflower* there (Dec. 16/26), and spent the remainder of the winter building the town, combating illness (which reduced their number by 44 by April). In March, 1621, they chose a governor and other officers, but not until November (1621), when Weston arrived in the *Fortune,* did they come temporarily to terms with the London financiers and receive from the Council for New England a charter (dated June 1/11, 1621) which gave legal birth to Plymouth Plantation.

PINCKNEY'S TREATY (1795), or the Treaty of San Lorenzo, was the climax of twelve years of dispute with Spain over the western and southern boundaries of the United States and the navigation of the Mississippi River. Spain was nervous lest territorial acquisitions along that river should lead to contraband traffic in the colonies of Louisiana and Florida, and was alarmed lest commercial navigation of the river should lead to economic and political penetration dangerous to Spanish sovereignty in New Spain itself. The United States contended that its treaty of peace with Great Britain had made the Mississippi River and 31° N. Lat. its recognized boundaries, and that riparian territorial sovereignty rights upstream gave a "natural right" to free navigation in and out from the ocean, even though the lower reaches of the river were in undisputed Spanish possession.

The United States and Spain attempted, 1784–86, to reconcile their differences, but the effort failed; and despite the new vigor of President Washington's administration, the United States was unable to make headway until Spain became involved in the wars of the French Revolution. Then Europe's distress became America's advantage. By the Treaty of Basle (July, 1795) Spain made a separate peace with France. Fearing English vengeance, and perhaps Anglo-American alliance to guarantee the free navigation of the Mississippi, Spain suddenly gave in and met the American demands in a treaty signed by Thomas Pinckney at San Lorenzo, Oct. 27, 1795. This accepted the boundary claims of the United States, established commercial relations with Spain, and provided for the free navigation of the Mississippi by American citizens and Spanish subjects, with the right of deposit—for the first three years at New Orleans, later at some other convenient place in Spanish territory. The treaty also provided for the adjudication by a mixed claims commission of spoliation claims arising over Spanish arbitrary captures of American neutral vessels.

PINE TREE FLAG was a colonial flag of Massachusetts used as early as 1700. The pine tree of Massachusetts was the emblem of New England in general, and seems to have been one of the earliest symbols of the union of the thirteen colonies, as an evergreen tree was incorporated into the flags of the American forces from 1775 to 1777 in various ways, often with the motto, "An Appeal to Heaven." The pine tree and this motto were sometimes combined with the rattlesnake flag of the southern colonies with its motto, "Don't tread on me." In September, 1775, two American floating batteries attacked Boston under a pine-tree flag. The six armed vessels commissioned by Washington, Feb. 1, 1776, also flew a pine-tree flag. In April, 1776, the Massachusetts council resolved that for its sea service "the colors be a white flag, with a green pine tree, and the inscription, 'An Appeal to Heaven.'" An American flag of 1775 with a blue (sometimes red) field had a white canton bearing a red St. George's cross; in the upper corner of the canton next to the staff was a pine tree.

PINE TREE SHILLING. To secure relief to a certain extent from a great need of currency, Massachusetts established a mint in 1651. In the following year there was issued a crude silver coin about the size of our modern half dollar but weighing only one third as much. On the obverse was MASATHVSETS IN., between two beaded circles: within the inner circle was a pine tree from which the coin gets its name. On the reverse was NEWENGLAND. AN. DOM., between two beaded circles, and 1652, XII, within the inner one. The Roman numerals indicated the number of pence in a shilling. The mint was closed in 1683.

PINKSTER was the Dutch Whitsuntide, or week of Pentecost, celebrated in colonial New York, and to some extent in Pennsylvania and Maryland, with picnicking, picking "pinkster" flowers, and neighborly visiting. Gaily decorated booths were erected, as on Pinkster Hill (Capitol Hill), Albany, for the sale of gingerbread, cider and applejack. The Negroes later usurped the festival, electing a Negro governor or "King Charley," dressed in colorful regalia, and paying him mock respect amid hilarious drinking, singing and dancing to African tom-toms. In *Satanstoe*, Cooper described an 18th-century celebration in Long Island, where whites continued to participate. Forbidden in Albany (1811), Pinkster disappeared during the 19th century.

PIPE, INDIAN. The smoking of tobacco in the United States was pre-Columbian. Archaeologically, the pipe appears on the pottery level and is about contemporaneous with maize.

Every important ceremony involved the use of a pipe and its presentation to the heavens, to the four directions and to the earth. It was also passed back and forth among the chief participants.

The calumet, or peace pipe, is the best known form of pipe, characterized by a specially decorated stem, and presented as a guarantee of peace and protection. A stranger carrying a calumet was safe from all enemies. Such a pipe came to be used at every official conference with white men and in the making of peace treaties, the passing of which between representatives of a government and an Indian tribe was a guarantee of friendship. Frequently two pipes were used, each party presenting a pipe to the other, to be kept as a pledge of good faith.

PIPELINES, EARLY. In order to eliminate the risk, expense and uncertainty of transporting oil by boat or wagon, Heman Jones proposed in November, 1861, at a meeting at Tarr farm on Oil Creek, Pennsylvania, the laying of a four-inch wooden pipe to Oil City. The idea met with favor but on account of the teamsters' opposition, the state legislature refused to charter the company. In 1862 Barrows and Co. of Tarr farm began operating the first successful pipeline, conveying oil from the Burning well to their refinery,

about 1000 feet away. Other early experiments with pipelines met with only partial success owing to poor quality pipes, leaky lead joints and faulty pumps. They demonstrated, however, the feasibility of the pipeline.

In the fall of 1865 Samuel Van Syckle began trenching and laying a two-inch wrought-iron pipe from Pithole to Miller farm on the Oil Creek Railroad, about five and a quarter miles distant. From the time Van Syckle started work until he completed the project and demonstrated its usefulness, he was the subject of ridicule. Just prior to its completion, disgruntled teamsters, who saw their occupation threatened, maliciously cut the line in several places. Nevertheless, on Oct. 9, Van Syckle finished his line and made the first test, in which 81 barrels of oil were forced through the pipe in one hour, doing the work of 300 teams working ten hours per day. The experiment worked perfectly and Van Syckle had the pleasure of seeing his persecutors silenced. Two weeks later another pipeline was completed from Pithole to Henry's Bend on the Allegheny River. The Van Syckle line proved so successful that a second pipe was laid to Miller farm and commenced delivering oil on Dec. 8, 1865. Four days later the Pennsylvania Tubing and Transportation Co. completed a gravity line from Pithole to Oleopolis on the Allegheny River; it had a capacity of 7000 barrels every 24 hours. Aroused over the prospect of the oil trade being diverted to other points, some of the Titusville businessmen organized the Titusville Pipe Co., laid a pipe to Pithole, about nine miles away, and began pumping oil in March, 1866, at the rate of 3000 barrels per day. During the same month, Henry Harley and Co. laid two pipelines from Bennehoff Run to Shaffer farm on the Oil Creek Railroad, a distance of two miles.

While the pipelines reduced the cost of shipping oil to the uniform rate of $1.00 per barrel, they proved to be monopolies of the worst sort, keeping their prices just below the teamsters' in order to eliminate teaming, yet high enough so that producers derived little benefit. Even before the first pipeline to Miller farm had been completed, teamsters began leaving the oil fields and when the Harley lines were completed, more than 400 teams left at one time. Those teamsters who remained made threats against the pipelines and even set fire to the Harley storage tanks at Shaffer, causing a loss of about $10,000. Rather than continue the violence, teamsters reduced the price of teaming, but their ruin was inevitable.

Not long after the completion of the Van Syckle line, his partners failed financially. Van Syckle assumed payment of the debt and agreed that the First National Bank of Titusville should operate the line until the debt had been liquidated. Owing to unforeseen difficulties, however, Van Syckle never regained control. W. H. Abbott and Henry Harley bought Van Syckle's line and combined it with Harley's in 1867, to form the Allegheny Transportation Co., the first great pipeline company.

735

During the next few years short pipelines multiplied, crossing and paralleling one another in every direction. Competition was keen and ruinous rate wars ensued. These, and other, factors soon brought about the consolidation of the lines.

PIPE STAVES, barrel staves and hogshead staves were important articles of commerce and of domestic use in early America. All were rived from straight-grained logs of varying lengths, shaved smooth with a drawknife or plane and given shape with a slight bulge of width in the middle, so that when hooped together from each end the resulting barrel, hogshead, or cask would be a double conoid. A pipe was a large cask, holding usually half a tun, that is, two hogsheads or 126 wine gallons. Inasmuch as a large cask when filled was very heavy, pipe staves had to be thicker and stronger than barrel staves. Pipe staves were sent in large quantities to the wine-producing countries of Europe and the West Indies. The standard length of pipe staves was 4½ feet; the width only a few inches; and they were usually made of oak, white or red. Prices ran from £6 to £18 a 1000, depending on the quality, stage of manufacture (whether rough as rived, or shaved and shaped); also depending on the commodity or currency given in exchange, the time and place of the transaction, etc. Staves packed close in shipping, hence were preferred in outgoing cargoes to finished empty casks, which required much room. The trade in pipe staves began early and continued long.

PIRATES AND PIRACY ON AMERICAN COASTS.

From 1632 to 1827 our Atlantic and Gulf coasts were infested by numerous pirates who preyed upon our shipping and cost us great losses in ships and lives.

From New England's earliest settlement, its shipping suffered from pirates on its coast. In 1653 Massachusetts made piracy punishable with death; and its governors sometimes sent out armed ships to attack offshore pirates. Our colonial governors after 1650 granted many "privateering" commissions to sea desperadoes and winked at their piracies—a popular procedure then. The Navigation Acts led to colonial smuggling—and eventually to piracy. Colonial merchants and people bought pirates' stolen goods and thus obtained necessary commodities—cheaply, too. New York, Newport and Philadelphia were rivals in this scandalous trade, with Boston, Virginia and the Carolinas also engaging in it.

The Earl of Bellomont was made governor of New York and New England with orders to "suppress the prevailing piracy that was causing so much distress along the [American] coast"—and in 1697 reported general colonial connivance with pirates, especially in New York, Rhode Island and in Philadelphia, "where they not onlie wink at, but Imbrace Pirats, men and shippes." One New York merchant secured $500,000 in seven years through pirate promoting.

Legal privateering ended in 1697—but many privateers then became avowed pirates and preyed on shipping along the coast. The period 1705–25 was memorable for the maximum of piracies; and 1721–24 saw a reign of terror on the New England coast. English men-of-war ended this pirate peril, but, after the Revolution, piratical attacks on our ships by French "privateers" brought on the Franco-American misunderstanding (1798–1801) and forced the United States to create a navy. Piratical operations of English men-of-war and "privateers" on our coasts and the high seas—including impressment of our seamen—led to the War of 1812.

The period 1805–25 witnessed a vast resurgence of piracy. This led to the maintenance and increase of our navy, then very busy at suppressing piracy and convoying our ships. Over 3000 piracies were recorded between 1814 and 1824 alone—half of them on our shipping.

The Gulf coast long was haunted by pirates; and after 1805 our navy was engaged in warring on pirates on the Louisiana and Gulf coast. The Barataria pirates were driven out in 1814; the Aury-Lafitte pirates from Galveston in 1817. In 1816–24 we faced a perplexing problem in handling the piratical "privateers" of the new Latin-American republics. Congress finally was so angered by these freebooters' depredations that in 1819 it passed an act, prescribing the death penalty for piracy.

The Spaniards of Cuba and Puerto Rico sent out many pirates who captured our ships, murdered their crews, and nearly brought on a war with these two colonies of Spain. Congress denounced "this truly alarming piracy" in 1822. In 1823–24 we despatched a strong naval squadron to suppress these pirates; and 1827 saw the end of piracy on all our coatsts.

PIROGUE, the dugout canoe common on the western waters, was hollowed by fire or adz, usually from the sycamore, cypress or cottonwood tree, and had one or both ends square. Its capacity could be increased by splitting it lengthwise and inserting planks between the two halves, spiking them in place or binding them with thongs and filling the interstices with clay, rosin or oakum. The word had many variations; it probably originated from a Carib and Arawakan word which became the Spanish *piragua*.

PITT, FORT. A temporary structure, commonly known as Fort Pitt, was begun soon after the British forces of Gen. John Forbes arrived at the forks of the Ohio, on the present site of Pittsburgh, Pa., Sept. 25, 1758. It was completed about Jan. 1, 1759, and stood on the banks of the Monongahela River, approximately 200 yards above the site of Fort Duquesne. On Sept. 3, 1759, Gen. John Stanwix personally directed the beginning of the work on a permanent fortification, correctly known as Fort Pitt and sufficiently formidable to assure British supremacy in the region.

Although this fort was occupied in 1760, it was not completed until the summer of 1761 and the Redoubt, the only standing remains and now known as the Blockhouse, was added in 1764 by Col. Henry Bouquet. Fort Pitt was a five-sided structure, surrounded by a ditch, occupying the point between the two rivers, although situated nearer the Monongahela than the Allegheny. A brick revetment supported the ramparts on the two sides facing the land. The three sides facing the rivers were supported by pickets. The British maintained a garrison at Fort Pitt to aid in preserving order among the settlers and Indians until late in 1772, when the troops were withdrawn. In the interim between 1772 and January, 1774, only caretakers occupied the fort until Dr. John Connolly of Virginia took possession of it. Capt. John Neville, with a company of Virginia patriots, held control from September, 1775, to June, 1777, relinquishing his command to Gen. Edward Hand of the Continental forces. Except for one short interval, the fort was a base of operations for western Revolutionary campaigns. Gen. William Irvine repaired the fort in 1782 but thereafter it was permitted to deteriorate, although parts of it were occupied by army officials after 1792 and the ramparts were still standing in 1800.

PITTSBURGH. Situated at the point where the Allegheny and Monongahela Rivers form the Ohio, Pittsburgh was laid out in 1764 by John Campbell, and the small trading post which had survived Pontiac's Conspiracy became successively county seat in 1788, borough in 1794 and city in 1816. That same strategic situation that had made it the logical point for the fort controlling the upper Mississippi Valley also made it the entrepôt for the waves of migration to the westward. With the opening of the Mississippi, Pittsburgh began her period as a commercial city. Her manufactures found their way to New Orleans and ultimately to Baltimore and Philadelphia, first on flatboats, then by keelboat and river steamboat. The impetus given to nascent industry by the demands of westward migration was renewed by the War of 1812. Western armies found one of their chief sources of supplies in that city, and Perry at Lake Erie drew heavily upon the community. At the same time western and southern areas that had been drawing upon the city now began sending her raw materials by steamboat. This demand for manufactured products, combined with the relative abundance of certain necessary raw materials, soon made the iron and glass industries of Pittsburgh of national importance. During the Civil War, Pittsburgh iron foundries and mills played an important role in supplying Union armies with cannon and armor plate. The transition from iron to steel was neither long nor difficult, and the city, under the guidance of her Carnegies, Fricks and Olivers, soon served a world market. In less than a century and a half this village of 1200 inhabitants had evolved into the leading industrial area in the heart of the richest market in the world. In 1960 its population was 1,628,587.

PLACER MINING. A placer deposit is one in which the gold or other minerals are found loosely mixed with the sand at the bottom of a stream bed or similar alluvial deposit. It differs from lode mining where the minerals are always found in place. It was placer gold which started the gold rushes to California, Pikes Peak and the Klondike. The pure gold is washed from the sand or debris by means of a gold pan. Because of its weight gold, if present, will gravitate to the bottom of the pan. Here the "colors" (tiny specks) or nuggets of gold are picked out with a tweezer or amalgamated with mercury. Improvements in placer mining, such as the rocker, sluicebox, long tom, hydraulic nozzle, boom dam, or dredge, are all designed to wash more gravel with a given amount of time and labor. The richest placer deposits have been in California and Alaska.

PLAINS, THE GREAT. For purposes of historical discussion, the Great Plains may be roughly defined as the region lying between the 98th meridian and the Rocky Mountains. With some exceptions, the area has a relatively level surface sloping gradually upward to the foothills of the mountains; it is almost treeless; and it is subhumid or semi-arid, with respect to rainfall. In the two latter respects it presented an environment strikingly different from that to which American settlers had previously been accustomed in their westward march. Before the period of white occupation the Great Plains were the grazing area of huge herds of buffalo, and the home of virile, warlike Indian tribes such at the Sioux, the Cheyennes, the Arapahoes, the Pawnees, the Comanches and the Apaches.

The Great Plains first appeared in recorded history in the reports of early Spanish explorations, especially that of Coronado, 1540–42. During the next two centuries the Spanish established themselves in what are now New Mexico and Texas, and extended their knowledge of the country to the northward at least as far as Nebraska or Wyoming. During the first half of the 18th century, French explorers and traders saw many portions of the Great Plains area, as did other traders working out of St. Louis after 1763, while the whole region was in Spanish possession. However, Americans in general knew very little of the region when the northern portion was transferred to the United States by the Louisiana Purchase Treaty.

Discouraging reports concerning the habitability of the Great Plains were given by the explorers, Lewis and Clark (1804–6), Zebulon M. Pike (1806–7), and Stephen H. Long (1820). As a result, the region came to be known as the Great American Desert—a barrier to the further westward expansion of American settlements. It was this belief, in part at least, that led to the Indian removal policy, formulated by Calhoun and Monroe in 1825 and carried into effect during the administration of Andrew Jackson. By 1840 the Great Plains were included in what was confidently designated as the permanent Indian Country.

Even before 1840 the observations of traders going to and from Santa Fe began to modify the general belief in the desertlike character of the Great Plains. Then, during the 1840's, the region was crossed by emigrants to Oregon, by military and exploring expeditions, by the Mormons on their way to Utah, and by thousands of gold seekers rushing to California. During this decade, also, the territorial jurisdiction of the United States was greatly expanded by the annexation of Texas, the acquisition of Oregon and the Mexican cession. Not only did the entire Great Plains region now belong to the United States, but it was no longer thinkable that an inviolable Indian country should bar the way to the free movement of Americans to the new and desirable possessions.

During the 1850's the Great Plains region was alive with activity. Commissioners and Indian agents were busy making treaties with the Indians, in which the tribesmen ceded territory, agreed to move, or gave permission for the laying out of roads and the establishment of military posts. Emigrants continued to pour over the trails to California and Oregon, and in 1859 there was a stampede to the Colorado gold fields. Following the congressional act of 1853 the region was crossed by parties surveying routes for a railroad to the Pacific. Stagecoaches carrying mail and passengers to California began running early in the decade, and by 1858 John Butterfield's famous Overland Mail was operating over a southern route.

The discoveries of gold in the entire Rocky Mountain area during the early 1860's greatly stimulated the service of transportation and communication across the plains. Not only were stagecoach lines expanded, but a vast wagon-freighting business was developed, and the famous pony express greatly expedited mail service. By the close of the Civil War the Great Plains area was aflame with Indian wars, which continued until the close of the decade, with frequent outbreaks still later. During this same period the Union Pacific Railroad was built westward, to be followed soon by other transcontinental railroads.

Thus far the Great Plains had been regarded mainly as an unattractive country to be crossed in order to reach more desirable localities. Beginning late in the 1860's, however, and during the ensuing two decades the region was the scene of the rise and decline of the great range cattle industry, with its succession of "cow towns," its long drives from Texas to the northern ranges or to shipping points on the railroads, its roundups, and its huge areas of illegally fenced public land. The decline of this colorful activity was due to various factors, but chiefly to the relentless pressure of the settlers who, after the Civil War, launched themselves onto the Great Plains and year by year steadily narrowed the open range until it

finally disappeared before the end of the century. The later history of the last American frontier is largely concerned with problems of agricultural adjustment to an unfavorable environment, particularly during the 1930's when terrific dust storms devastated many sections of the Great Plains.

PLANK ROADS, introduced into the United States from Canada about 1837, were first constructed in New York, later being widely adopted in South Carolina, Illinois, Ohio, Michigan and other states. Thousands of miles were built at a mileage cost of from $1000 to $2400. Roadways were first well drained, with ditches on either side. Then planks, three or four inches thick and eight feet long, were laid at right angles to stringers which were placed lengthwise of the road. Planks were prepared by portable sawmills which were set up in neighboring forests. For a time, plank roads successfully competed with railroads.

PLATFORMS, PARTY. Some historians have argued that the Virginia and Kentucky Resolutions constituted the first party platform, but while there were numerous party manifestoes and declarations of principle in the ensuing thirty years, the platform in its modern sense appears in the fourth decade of the 19th century. Since 1840 it has been a regular feature of political campaigns.

PLATT AMENDMENT was the basis for Cuban-American relations from 1901 to 1934. Following the Spanish-American War the problem of the future relations between the United States and Cuba became a matter of earnest consideration in both countries. For the purpose of finding a solution, Gen. Leonard Wood, upon convening the Cuban constituent assembly on Nov. 5, 1900, instructed it to render an opinion on what the future relations "ought to be." Two unsatisfactory proposals were later submitted, whereupon the United States drew up its own plan. Although the product of many minds, it became known as the Platt Amendment after Sen. Orville H. Platt of Connecticut, chairman of the Senate Committee on Cuban relations. To insure its passage it was attached as a rider to the army appropriations bill for the fiscal year ending June 13, 1902. It contained eight articles, the substance of which were: (I) Cuba was to make no treaty which would impair its independence, nor was it to alienate Cuban territory to a foreign power; (II) Cuba was not to assume or contract any public debt beyond its ability to meet out of "ordinary revenues"; (III) Cuba was to permit the United States "to intervene for the preservation of Cuban independence, the maintenance of a government adequate for the protection of life, property and individual liberty, and for discharging the obligations with respect to Cuba imposed by the Treaty of Paris on the United States now to be assumed and undertaken by the government of Cuba";

(IV) all acts of the United States during the occupation were to be validated; (V) Cuba was to continue the sanitation program started by the United States and, if necessary, extend it; (VI) title to the Isle of Pines was to be decided later; (VII) coaling and naval stations chosen by the United States were to be sold or leased; (VIII) the articles were to be embodied in a permanent treaty with the United States.

When the articles were submitted to the Cuban convention with the demand that they be incorporated into the Cuban constitution, a storm of indignation arose. The convention at first refused to agree and sent a delegation to Washington to protest. Particularly objectionable was Article III, which was viewed as depriving Cuba of its sovereign rights. In spite of assurances given by Elihu Root that the United States interpreted its right to intervene as applying only when Cuban independence was threatened by internal anarchy or foreign attack, the convention continued to balk. Not until the United States threatened to remain in the island did the convention, on June 13, 1901, agree to accept it. On May 22, 1903, the articles were written into a formal treaty. The arrangement, never popular in Cuba, aroused increasing bitterness as time went on, especially when later administrations at Washington showed a tendency to ignore the Root interpretation. While armed intervention was seldom resorted to, there have been numerous occasions when the United States has exerted pressure of some sort. This so-called "intermeddling and interference" strengthened the demand for the repeal of the Platt Amendment, to which the United States acceded on May 29, 1934. Since then the right of the United States to intervene has rested on the general rules of international law.

PLATTE RIVER TRAIL (1825–69) owed its importance to South Pass, gateway of the Rockies. The Platte heads at the pass, and the most direct route from the pass across 780 miles of plains to the Missouri is down the Platte, which provides water for men and horses. Robert Stuart's Astor Overlanders traversed the route upon their return from Oregon in 1812–13, and Long's Expedition followed it part way to the Rockies in 1819. A brigade of Ashley's Fur Company definitely established the trail in 1825 while carrying supplies from the Missouri to trappers in the Rockies. From then on the route was traveled every year by trappers, missionaries and homeseekers. Branches of the trail, with eastern termini on the Missouri at Westport, Fort Leavenworth, Atchison and St. Joseph, all converged on the Platte near Grand Island. In 1843, when a thousand Oregon homeseekers traversed the Platte Trail, they regarded it as merely a part of the Oregon Trail. It also was known as the California Trail, Mormon Trail and Overland Route. The building of the Union Pacific, 1863–69, ended its importance.

PLATTSBURG, BATTLE OF (Sept. 11, 1814). Sir George Prevost, governor general of Canada, invaded New York with 14,000 veterans, recently arrived from the Duke of Wellington's victorious army in Spain. He was opposed by Gen. Alexander Macomb's 1500 American regulars and 2500 militia, who were strongly entrenched south of the Saranac River in the village of Plattsburg. Macomb's army was supported by a naval squadron of four little ships and ten gunboats under Commander Thomas Macdonough. The British invaders were assisted by another flotilla of about the same size commanded by Capt. George Downie.

Prevost planned a joint attack by land and by sea. He goaded Downie, whose fleet was not fully fitted, into attacking Macdonough, who lay at anchor in a well-chosen position in Cumberland Bay. Downie lost his ships and his life in a bloody battle. Macdonough's victory was chiefly due to his success in swinging about his flagship, the *Saratoga*, so as to make use of her uninjured broadside. Meanwhile, Prevost failed to fight his way across the Saranac and support Downie. Deprived of naval support, the British army was forced to retreat. Its defeat made peace more certain and cut short British designs of obtaining sole control of the Great Lakes by the peace treaty.

PLOW. The plows brought from England were crude wooden affairs with share and coulter of wrought iron and a wooden mould board covered with iron plates. When these plows wore out, those made locally were more adapted to the environment. Because of the early shortage of draft animals, plows were of lighter construction, but, because much of the plowing was heavy breaking, attention was paid to improving the shape so that greater efficiency might be obtained without increasing the weight. Through mathematical calculations, such as Jefferson's, the design was bettered and, through the development of the cast iron plow, such improvements were standardized. This step was taken when, in 1817, Jethro Wood's cast iron plow went on sale.

In the heavy, sticky soils of the West, this plow worked badly. The share broke easily and soil clung to the rough, pitted surface. Indeed, the heavy wooden plow was preferable. Sometimes, the Westerner plated his plow with the steel of old saw blades to obviate constant scouring.

In 1837 John Deere began his experiments on a steel plow. Ten years later, he had started a factory in Moline, Ill. At first, sheet steel was attached to cast iron, then later a cast steel plow was made. By 1857 prairie farmers were buying 10,000 of these yearly. They were, however, expensive and brittle. The Bessemer process reduced the cost, and the development of the chilled steel plow by James Oliver in 1868 increased durability and produced a smooth, hard surface.

Improved harvesting machinery meant a demand for faster plowing. About 1864 the riding, or sulky, plow appeared. Then came the gang plow used on the extensive wheat farms of the West, drawn first by many horses and then by steam tractors. With the coming of the gasoline tractor, plowing caught up with the harvesting methods.

PLOWDEN'S NEW ALBION was the first English colonizing grant of the present New Jersey area, the second in the United States giving religious liberty. Two years after petitions to King Charles I, the New Albion charter was issued June 21, 1634, to nine persons, including Sir Edmund Plowden (1592–1659), soon its sole owner. At their request it claimed title under the Irish Crown. It was issued by Strafford, Lord Deputy of Ireland, upon authority from King Charles I, and enrolled in Dublin, where Plowden was stationed when the grant was made. The charter's religious provisions copied those of Lord Baltimore's Maryland: Plowden, of a Shropshire Catholic family, apparently planned New Albion as another Catholic haven.

Plowden tried four times to settle his province. Financial troubles with his wife Mabel, daughter and sole heiress of Peter Marriner, delayed his start several years. On Aug. 30, 1639, Plowden wrote to Lord Baltimore that he would settle in New Albion next spring. Again domestic troubles intervened. In 1641 Plowden's colonizing prospectus appeared, *A Direction for Adventurers to New Albion*. Also, at this time, King Charles I and Parliament requested Gov. Berkeley in Virginia to help Plowden settle his province on the Delaware, the Swedes having now been established there four years. In August, 1642, just as the Civil War began in England, Plowden sailed with his colonists to Virginia where they spent the winter. The articles of his indentured settlers specified service in New Albion. Their predominant religion is not yet known.

Early in May, 1643, a party of Plowden's people, while sailing with him outside Chesapeake Bay, apparently en route to settle his province, successfully mutinied against him, as recorded by the Swedish governor, Printz. Legal records thereafter indicate Plowden resided continuously in Virginia, reportedly hopeful of more settlers in spite of the English Civil War. In the spring of 1648, he sailed to England, reporting at New Amsterdam and to Gov. Winthrop in Boston his intention to return to America and "dispossess the Swedes."

In December, 1648, there was published in England, *A Description of the Province of New Albion*, with a long foreword signed "Beauchamp Plantagenet." This prospectus fancifully described New Albion; detailed with considerable accuracy the New Albion charter, Virginia, and Plowden's life; and reprinted the 1641 *Direction*. Plowden's third colonizing attempt, a large project, now developed. Last

minute lawsuits blocked it in April, 1649. In 1650 "Plantagenet's" *Description* was reprinted, slightly revised, and on June 11, 1650, Cromwell's Council of State issued a pass to New Albion for "seven score persons." This last venture collapsed, doubtless from political pressure, for it had been planned, after Cromwell's triumphs, as a Royalist asylum.

Numerous land suits kept Plowden in England until his death in 1659. He was buried July 20, that year, at St. Clement Danes, London. He had made his second son his heir, and additional confusion arose when the New Albion charter document became lost. Consequently, no Plowden contested King Charles II's grant of these lands to the Duke of York in 1664. In 1772 chance disclosed the enrollment of Plowden's charter in Dublin. Francis Plowden, Sir Edmund's great-great-grandson, immediately but vainly petitioned King George III for restoration of the province. In 1784 he sent to America an agent, Charles Varlo, whose recovery efforts also failed.

PLUMMER GANG. Henry Plummer, elected sheriff of Bannack District (now Montana) May 24, 1863, organized a band of fifty outlaws, called "The Innocents," against whom 102 murders are charged. A Vigilance Committee, with which Wilbur Fisk Sanders, later Senator, was associated, was formed in December, 1863, and within six weeks hanged most of the band. Among 33 executions was that of the notorious Joseph A. Slade.

PLYMOUTH, VIRGINIA COMPANY OF (1606–20), was one of the two companies incorporated in the first Virginia charter of 1606. In 1605 a group of men representing the City of London and the outports of Bristol, Plymouth and Exeter petitioned for a charter which would accord them the privilege of planting colonies in America. Though the petitioners were men bound by the ties of relationship, friendship or common interest, the rivalry between London and the outports was such that the leaders wished to proceed with the project under separate companies. The charter of 1606 therefore created two companies, the Virginia Company of London, with permission to plant a colony in southern Virginia between the 34th and the 41st degrees of northern latitude, to be called the First Colony of Virginia, and the Virginia Company of Plymouth, whose plantation, to be called the Second Colony of Virginia, was to be located to the north between the 38th and 45th degrees of latitude, the overlapping area to be considered a neutral zone in which the colonies could not come within one hundred miles of each other.

The Plymouth Company, like the London Company, was to be under the jurisdiction of the royal council for Virginia, but had its own resident council of thirteen as government for its projected plantation. The enterprise was commercial in character, but to what extent the company could control the trade of its colony is not clear in the charter. The leaders in the Plymouth Company were Sir John Popham, an old man of seventy-five, and Sir Ferdinando Gorges, who became the mainstay of the enterprise after the death of Popham in February, 1608.

The Plymouth Company sent out its first expedition in the summer of 1606 to seek a place for a plantation. Unfortunately the vessel was captured by the Spanish near Puerto Rico where it was driven by adverse winds, and the men carried off as prisoners to Spain from where a few of them made their way back to Plymouth with difficulty. A second vessel dispatched in the autumn of 1606 reached the coast of Maine in safety, and returned with such glowing accounts that the company sent out two ships in May, 1607, the *Gift of God* and the *Mary and John,* carrying settlers. A plantation was begun near the mouth of the Sagadahoc, but from the outset it did not prosper. Gorges ascribed its failure to an insufficiency of food supplies and "childish factions." The men were apparently not of the right type, lacking the self-discipline and the will to work, necessary to all pioneer ventures. The winter cold, the burning of the storehouse and many dwellings, and consequent shortage of supplies weakened the interest of the planters, while the death of some of the leaders, including Popham, discouraged the company in England from pushing the enterprise further. Some of its members, however, continued their interest in the fisheries and sent out several expeditions to fish and trade with the Indians. Profits from these activities were sufficient to convince men like Gorges of the potentialities of the region, and thus to pave the way for the reorganization of the project in 1620 under the new company, the Council for New England.

PLYMOUTH ROCK. There is no contemporary record that the Pilgrims landed on Plymouth Rock when they disembarked on Dec. 11 (Dec. 21, New Style), 1620, and it is not known who first set foot on the rock. Thacher states, on the authority of "the late venerable Deacon [Ephraim] Spooner," that when the latter was a boy, about the year 1741, he saw "Elder [Thomas] Faunce," then ninety-five years old, identify the present Plymouth Rock as that on which, according to his father (John Faunce, who came in the *Ann* in 1623), the Pilgrims landed. This tradition is accepted by Winsor and later historians. Ann Taylor wrote in 1773 that her grandmother, Mary Chilton, was the first to step on the rock and a similar tradition persists regarding John Alden, but Winsor states that they both landed at a later date. The rock has been moved back from its original location in order to better protect and display it.

POINT FOUR of President Truman's 1949 inaugural urged international co-operation to teach self-help to poverty-stricken peoples, through provision of tech-

nological knowledge and skills and through capital investment, whereby living standards might be raised and democracy strengthened. A 1950 appropriation of $35,000,000 introduced United States outlays reaching $400,000,000 by 1954 and this country supplied most of the aid from "free world" sources during the decade. Being vastly inclusive, espousing economic and social development throughout the free countries of Asia, Africa and Latin America, Point Four necessarily confronted age-old institutions, customs and vested interests. Its technicians encountered obstacles difficult to understand, capitalize, alter or eradicate. Moreover, few areas possessed many facilities essential to that rapid industrialization recipient governments urgently sought. Yet, progress appeared in agriculture, conservation, water power, technical skills and installations. Although the Eisenhower administration tended to avoid use of the term, the validity of the Point Four principle continually widened its application. Offers of technical facilities and capital loans and grants to underdeveloped, uncommitted countries became a weapon sharpened by universal use in the cold war.

POINT PLEASANT, BATTLE OF (Oct. 10, 1774), was one of the most notable conflicts between Indians and frontiersmen in the annals of the West. Col. Andrew Lewis with about 1100 men from the frontier of southwest Virginia marching 160 miles from Camp Union, on the levels of Greenbrier, to join Gov. Dunmore on the Ohio, arrived at the mouth of the Great Kanawha, Oct. 6, where they made camp in the point of the two rivers called Point Pleasant.

While resting and recruiting the men, and awaiting the arrival of Col. William Christian with 250 of the rear guard, Lewis' army was attacked early in the morning by a large force of Shawnee, led by Chief Cornstalk, which had crossed the Ohio in the night. Lewis sent out two divisions under his brother, Col. Charles Lewis, and Col. William Fleming; both officers were soon wounded, the former fatally. The Indians fought desperately, hoping to drive the whites into the rivers. The fighting was in frontier fashion, individual combats, sheltering behind trees and logs.

About one o'clock the Indians grew discouraged, but continued desultory fighting until sunset, when they withdrew across the Ohio. The losses on both sides were heavy, the Virginians having nearly fifty killed and twice that number wounded. The losses of the Indians were never known.

The effect of the battle was to break the power of the Shawnee, who soon met Gov. Dunmore and made a treaty with him. This treaty saved the West from the horrors of Indian warfare during the first years of the American Revolution. The battle was a victory of colonial troops without support of regulars. Most of the officers and men soon enrolled in the Revolutionary forces that opposed Great Britain.

POLITICAL PARTIES. Modern democratic states have developed innumerable voluntary organizations which endeavor to influence government. Among these various "pressure groups" the political party is distinguished by the fact that it makes nominations to public office. In addition to this basically characteristic function the political party also as a rule formulates principles and policies in platforms which are put forth as superior to all others for the conduct of government; it wages campaigns for the election of its candidates; finally, if successful at the polls, it brings influence to bear upon officeholders to secure the realization of its principles and policies. For the defeated party, of course, the latter function is transformed into that of opposition to the activities of the party in power.

In spite of the progress made by democratic ideas toward the end of the 18th century, the views then prevailing of political parties, for which indeed abundant historical evidence could be quoted, was that they were incorrigibly violent, destructive, oppressive and corrupt. Much chicanery and dishonesty have marred their record since; nevertheless parties have shown themselves to be peaceful, constructive, and absolutely essential to the successful conduct of a democratic state.

Regardless of the prejudice against them, loosely organized parties existed in the American colonies from the latter part of the 17th century onward. Chief among them were the Tories and the Whigs, who with the advent of the Revolution came to be known respectively as Loyalists and Patriots. Later the controversy over the Federal Constitution produced two parties or factions, one in favor of, the other opposed to, adoption of the Constitution; but these were hardly organized parties in the modern sense. During this period and much of the early national period, real political organizations existed only in the states, and even these tended to be little more than factions springing up around some forceful and colorful personality. National parties may be said to have come into being when Jefferson, finding himself in disagreement with the policies of the Washington administration, resigned from the cabinet in order to build up an organization which would support his own ambitions for the Presidency. Thus perished the hope of the Founding Fathers that all shades of opinion would be represented within the administration itself. Henceforth competition for the Presidency, as well as for other elective offices, tended increasingly to center, not around a number of eminent individuals, but around candidates supported by rival organizations, representing the consensus of their membership. After 1832 candidates were selected by nominating conventions of the parties. The multiplication of Federal offices and the practice of distributing them as rewards among the party faithful —a practice which grew up during the democratic revolt of the Jacksonian period and which was justified under the honored principle of "rotation in office"—immeasurably increased the importance of parties. The "spoils system," indeed, gave the party system its enduring vitality.

The organization of the two major parties (Republican and Democratic) is similar, each party having a national committee, state committees, county committees and city committees in the larger cities. Below the city committees are ward committees, and at the bottom of the organization are the precinct leaders. Also, each of the major parties has a senatorial committee primarily concerned with the election of party members to the U. S. Senate, and a congressional committee which functions to promote the election of party members to the lower house.

State, county and city organizations were in existence long before the parties were organized on a national scale, although the national committees of the two major parties have had a long existence. The Democratic National Committee was established in 1848 by the Democratic Convention in Baltimore which appointed one member from each state to take charge of the campaign. The Republican National Committee was formally established by a resolution of the party at its convention in 1856 providing for the selection of one member from each state and territory to serve on the national committee during the ensuing four years. The Republican Congressional Committee was organized and has had continuous existence since it was established in 1866, being an outgrowth of the conflict between President Johnson and the Republican members of Congress. The Democratic Congressional Committee was established a few years thereafter. The senatorial campaign committees of both major parties were established in 1916 following the adoption of the amendment to the Constitution providing for the direct election of United States Senators.

Party organization in the United States has developed into a hierarchy of committees. But due to the manner in which the committees are selected in the major parties, there is no direct line of authority extending from the top of the organization to the bottom. The members of the national committees of the two major parties, 106 members on the Republican and 108 on the Democratic, are chosen by various methods: by delegates from the states to the national conventions, by state conventions, by direct primary election, or chosen by state committees. The senatorial committees, composed in the Republican party of seven members, of six members in the Democratic party, are appointed in each party by the chairman of the party caucus. The congressional committee of each party is made up of one member from each state party delegation in the House of Representatives and is elected by the delegation. State committees vary in size from eleven members in Iowa to several hundred in California, and are chosen primarily by two methods, by direct election and by conventions. County committees are usually composed of representatives from each precinct within the county and are required in most states to be elected by the voters, in some states by conventions while in others the choice is left to the party rules.

Since there is no direct line of authority running from top to bottom in the party organization, the whole machine is made to function by securing co-operation among the various units. The chief methods used for securing co-operation are through over-lapping membership on committees, by various forms of patronage—public positions, granting public business, privileges and immunities—by securing legislative enactments and by funds supplied by one committee to another.

Since 1789 the party history of the United States may be divided into three periods during the greater part of which two major parties were pitted against each other.

(1) From 1789 to 1824 the Federalists, who in many cases were the original champions of the Constitution, opposed the Republicans (Jeffersonian), who were the ideological heirs of those who had opposed it or supported it only with reservations. In general the former accepted the doctrines of Hamilton, the latter those of Jefferson. The Federalist party was supported principally by commercial and industrial elements, the Republican party by the agrarian element. Following Jefferson's election in 1800 the Federalists went downhill steadily; in 1820 they made no nomination for the Presidency. Shunning at first the title "democratic" as smacking of the French Revolution, the party of Jefferson came to be known later as the Democratic-Republican party. Toward the end of this period during the so-called "era of good feeling," which was really an era of intense personal politics, voters generally accepted the Republican label but followed various leaders—Adams, Clay and Calhoun; Crawford, Clinton and Jackson.

(2) From 1824 to 1860 the two principal parties were the Whigs, earlier known as National Republicans, who accepted the Federalist tradition largely and were supported by the same classes plus the rising manufacturing element then chiefly centered in New England, and the Democratic elements, no longer fearful of being called by that name. Fused by Jackson, these were powerfully reinforced by Western settlers and newly enfranchised laborers in the older parts of the country. Minor political groups, some of them mere factions confined to one or a few states, made their presence felt during this period, among them the Anti-Masons, Nullifiers, Barnburners, Hunkers, Loco-focos, Cotton Whigs, Conscience Whigs and the Know-Nothing (or American) party. By far the most successful of these, however, were the Liberty party and its successor, the Free Soil party, out of which grew the Republican party—the only case in our history of a third party which became one of the two major contenders for power.

With the rise of the slavery issue party lines were badly broken. The Whigs were moribund in 1852 and virtually dead in 1856. Four years later the Democratic party split hopelessly over the same issue.

(3) From 1860 to the present time the two great political rivals have been the Republican and Democratic parties. To secure support of the War Democrats the former rebaptized itself as the National Union party during the campaign of 1864. Issues were chiefly those of war and reconstruction from 1860 to 1876; subsequently they have been predominantly economic in character except during and immediately after World Wars I and II. Since 1860 third parties have been numerous. Prohibitionists made their first presidential nomination in 1872. Greenbackers, dating from the late 1860's, gave expression to agrarian discontent and were succeeded by the People's (or Populist) party, which flourished from 1890 to 1896. The Farmer-Labor party in the Northwest continued the tradition of agrarian protest into the period of the 1920's (in Minnesota, up to the present time), and was perhaps its last authentic embodiment. Similarly labor unrest has found expression through the Union Labor, Socialist Labor, Social Democratic, Socialist and Communist parties. Twice during this period the Republicans suffered heavy defections: in 1912 when Theodore Roosevelt bolted and formed the Progressive party, and again in 1924 when Robert M. LaFollette led an agrarian revolt of Independent Progressives. In 1948, neither Strom Thurmond, campaigning as the States' Rights candidate for President, nor Henry A. Wallace, campaigning under a Progressive label, diverted many votes from Truman and Dewey.

All things considered, the two-party tradition has shown remarkable vitality in the United States. If one considers the Republicans as descendants of the Federalists and Whigs and the Democrats as a continuous organization, the major contending organizations have enjoyed an almost equal measure of success.

POLLOCK v. FARMERS LOAN AND TRUST CO. (1895). The Supreme Court ruled in this case that the income tax provision of the Gorman-Wilson tariff was unconstitutional on the ground that it was a direct tax and hence subject to the requirement of apportionment among the states according to population. In a prior hearing, only the tax on real-estate income had been declared unconstitutional and the Court had divided evenly, four to four, regarding other forms of income. On a rehearing, the Court decided five to four against the income tax on personal property, due to the fact that one Justice, evidently Brewer, now reversed himself to oppose the income tax and another, Jackson, who had not participated in the earlier hearing, voted with the minority. This decision inspired a popular attack on "judicial usurpation" resulting in the Democratic income tax plank of 1896, and leading ultimately to the passage of the Sixteenth Amendment.

PONCE DE LEÓN'S DISCOVERY (1513) added the mainland of North America to the Spanish dominions. In 1512 Juan Ponce de León secured a royal grant, with the title of *adelantado*, to conquer the island of Bimini to the northward of Cuba where the Fountain of Youth presumably was located. Sailing from Puerto Rico, March 3, 1513, he sighted the mainland on the 27th and on April 2 landed near the mouth of St. Johns River. In honor of the Easter season the region was named Florida. Re-embarking, Ponce de León explored the eastern shore of Florida, doubled the cape, and passed along the Florida Keys which he called The Martyrs. He continued along the western coast, probably reaching Pensacola Bay, and returned to Puerto Rico on Sept. 21. Besides taking possession of Florida, he discovered the Bahama Channel. Returning to Spain in 1514, he received a grant to colonize the islands of Florida and Bimini, but it was not until 1521 that he undertook the second expedition from Puerto Rico to Florida. Reaching the peninsula, he began a settlement, probably on Charlotte Bay. The Indians were hostile, and in a battle the *adelantado* was severely wounded. Thereupon, the effort at colonization was abandoned, and the expedition returned to Havana where Ponce de León died.

PONTIAC WAR (1763–64). Montreal and Canada surrendered to the English Sept. 8, 1760, and immediately Maj. Robert Rogers was sent to take over the western posts. Detroit was reached Nov. 29, but the advent of winter prevented the occupation of Mackinac and the posts around Lake Michigan until the following summer.

Although New France had been conquered, it remained to reckon with the western Indians, who had not been consulted in the surrender. Their dissatisfaction found expression almost at once in a plot to expel the English from the country. It was discovered, and at a great council at Detroit (September, 1761), Sir William Johnson strove to allay the native discontent. Although he succeeded temporarily, the underlying causes of dissatisfaction—resentment of the arrogance of officials and the dishonesty of the traders, fear of the advancing tide of frontier settlement, regret over the passing of their French "father"—remained.

In the spring of 1763 the gathering tempest broke, and almost simultaneously the posts from Niagara and Fort Pitt to Mackinac and St. Joseph were attacked. Sandusky fell on May 16; St. Joseph, May 25; Miami, May 27; Ouiatanon, June 1; Mackinac, June 4; Presque Isle, June 16; Venango about the same date; and LeBoeuf on June 18. Of all the forts scattered over a thousand miles of wilderness, only Niagara, Fort Pitt and Detroit stood fast. In most cases the attack was begun by stealth, and savage success was immediate. Following the initial attacks the frontier settlements were ravaged with fire and axe, and more persons (chiefly settlers) are said to have perished in 1763 than in 1759, when the French and Indian War was at its height.

Because of the central location and the military importance of Detroit, where Pontiac directed the attack, the struggle has become known as the Pontiac War. Here the vigilance of Maj. Gladwin defeated the attempted surprise, and his vigorous leadership maintained the defense against heavy odds during many desperate weeks. At the close of July, Capt. Dalzel arrived with 250 Redcoats and a small number of Rangers led by the redoubtable Rogers. A night attack upon Pontiac's camp followed, resulting in the death of Dalzel and the disastrous defeat known ever since as the battle of Bloody Run. The siege was discontinued with the approach of winter, but the garrison was not finally relieved until the arrival of Col. Bradstreet's army in the summer of 1764.

In a great council held at Detroit in August, Bradstreet dictated terms of peace which the forest diplomats, who completely outgeneraled the white leader, accepted with no intention of observing. Meanwhile Col. Bouquet, a keener soldier than Bradstreet, was fighting his way across Pennsylvania to Fort Pitt. From here, in October, he advanced into Ohio, where his stern measures reduced the savages to submission. Finally, in a council at Oswego in July, 1766, Sir William Johnson confirmed and completed the treaty begun at Detroit two years earlier. The Indians acknowledged the sovereignty of King George, surrendered their white captives, and agreed to deliver to the nearest commandant individuals guilty of committing violence upon Englishmen. Pontiac was pardoned by the English, but his meteoric career practically ended with the defeat of his race in the war. In 1769 he was slain at Cahokia by an Indian who was supposed to have been bribed by a trader to commit the deed. His siege of Detroit in 1763–64 has become classic in the annals of Indian warfare; his failure illustrates the common inability of a savage people to wage successful warfare against a civilized nation.

PONY EXPRESS. During the late 1850's the question of the best route for the overland mail to California was a topic of great interest in the Far West. In September, 1857, a contract was granted to John Butterfield and his famous Overland Mail, which began operation one year later over a circuitous southern route. The shortest time made on this route was twenty-two days. Many Californians, including Sen. William M. Gwin, believed that a central route was entirely feasible and would expedite the carrying of mail to the coast. It was Sen. Gwin who, early in 1860, induced William H. Russell, of the great freighting firm of Russell, Majors and Waddell, to demonstrate the practicability of a central route in a dramatic manner by establishing a pony express.

The project was pushed vigorously. Starting at St. Joseph, Mo., the route in general followed the well-known Oregon-California trail, by way of Fort Kearny, old Julesburg, Scotts Bluff, Fort Laramie, South Pass, Fort Bridger and Salt Lake City. From the latter point, however, the trail went around the southern end of the Great Salt Lake, by way of Fort Churchill, Carson City and Placerville to Sacramento. Stations were built at intervals of about fifteen miles, where stage stations did not already exist. Fleet, wiry, Indian ponies were purchased; and young, courageous, lightweight riders were hired. On April 3, 1860, the service was inaugurated. It was like a giant relay, in which about 75 ponies participated in each direction. At each station the riders were given two minutes in which to transfer the saddlebags to fresh ponies and be on their way again. After riding a certain distance, one rider would hand the mail over to another, and so on, until the destination was reached. Day and night, summer and winter, over dusty plains and dangerous mountain trails, and frequently in the midst of hostile Indians, the ponies and their riders galloped at their best speed over the sections of the route allotted to them.

During the eighteen months of the operation of the pony express only one trip was missed. The service was weekly at first and later semiweekly. The best time ever made was in November, 1860, when news of Lincoln's election was carried in six days from Fort Kearny, Nebr., to Fort Churchill, Nev., then the termini of the telegraph lines which were being built from the Missouri River and California. When the two telegraph lines were joined in October, 1861, all need for the pony express was eliminated.

The pony express was disastrous to the fortunes of Russell, Majors and Waddell. The cost of operation was greatly in excess of the revenue. In fact the company was virtually ruined by the experiment, and was disappointed in its hope of gaining a valuable mail contract, which went to another firm. Furthermore, the enterprise was not even necessary, as things turned out, as a demonstration of the feasibility of a central route. The outbreak of the Civil War made the selection of such a route inevitable. Nevertheless, the pony express is one of the episodes in the history of the Far West which still fires the imagination and is depicted in frontier pageantry.

POOR RICHARD'S ALMANAC (1732–96), within a year of its first appearance, became the most popular book, excepting the Bible, in the American colonies. Any almanac was an important publication in 18th-century America, for it contained information necessary to every American farmer. In view of the fact that seven were published in Philadelphia in 1732, it would have seemed unlikely that another would be successful. However, Benjamin Franklin had new ideas which he felt would insure the success of his venture. Along with the usual information on the weather, tides, eclipses and medicinal remedies, Franklin printed the maxims, saws and pithy sayings which were even then making him famous. Each edition saw an increase in sales until 10,000 copies were printed annually, approximately one for every hundred people in the colonies.

It is probable that Franklin ceased to write for the almanac after 1748, when he began to devote most of his time and energy to public affairs. In 1757 he disposed of the almanac which, however, continued to appear until 1796. In 1758 Franklin collected the best of his writings from *Poor Richard's Almanac* in *Father Abraham's Speech* more commonly known as *The Way to Wealth*. In this form, the sayings of Poor Richard have become a permanent part of our literature.

POPHAM COLONY. Though English and European fishermen had long been taking cod along the coast, the first attempt by England to colonize the New England region was the ill-starred Popham plantation on the Kennebec, 1607–8.

On May, 31, 1607, the Plymouth Company of Virginia, proprietors of northern Virginia, spurred on by hopes of profitable farming of the rich resources of fish, lumber, furs, minerals and medicinal herbs reported by the navigators, Gosnold (1602), Pring (1603) and Weymouth (1605), sent out about 120 colonists in two ships, the *Mary and John* and the *Gift of God*. George Popham, brother of Sir John Popham, Chief Justice of England and sponsor of the venture, was President, and Raleigh Gilbert was Admiral.

These men, having reached Seguin Island, landed at the mouth of the Kennebec (Sagadahoc) River, on the western bank, in the middle of August, 1607. They built a fort and named it St. George, after England's patron saint, a storehouse, fifty dwellings and a church. The first Protestant church service was conducted here by the colony's Anglican clergyman, Richard Seymour. The settlers began the construction of a ship, a pinnace of thirty tons, *Virginia of Sagadahoc*, first ship built by Englishmen in North America; they explored the river up to Merrymeeting Bay, the Androscoggin branch to Pejepscot, Casco Bay on the coast to the west, and eastward to Pemaquid. They made friends with the Indians and traded with them. But things went wrong with the colony from the first. The reason for failure may lie in John Aubrey's statement that the colony was stocked "out of all the gaols of England." Quarrels arose, all but 45 men had to be shipped home when the second ship left, in December. On top of that disaster, there came a savage Maine winter. President Popham died. Though ships brought supplies in the summer of 1608, news of the death of Sir John Popham, sponsor, and of Gilbert's brother came also. So, in September, the settlers pulled up stakes and went home. A story, never verified by documentation, persisted for years that some colonists remained and joined the semi-permanent fishing settlements to the east.

POPULAR SOVEREIGNTY. In a general sense, this term means the right of the people to rule. "Squatter sovereignty" literally means the right of people living anywhere without a government to form a body politic and practise self-government. When the theory that the people of a Federal territory had the right to determine the slavery question for themselves was first enunciated, it was dubbed "squatter sovereignty" by its opponents. The term has persisted and is often used as the equivalent of popular sovereignty.

When Lewis Cass, writing to A. O. P. Nicholson on Dec. 24, 1847, declared that he was "in favor of leaving the people of any territory which may hereafter be acquired, the right to regulate it [slavery] themselves, under the great general principles of the Constitution," he made the first clear statement of the principle of popular sovereignty. Acts organizing the territories of Utah and New Mexico were passed in 1850. In neither territory was slavery prohibited or protected. It was simply provided that each of the territories should be admitted with or without slavery as its constitution might specify.

Sen. Stephen A. Douglas made the Kansas-Nebraska Bill a popular sovereignty measure which repealed the antislavery provision of the Missouri Compromise of 1820. That popular sovereignty would produce a bitter struggle for Kansas was as difficult to foresee as was the Civil War. The conflict which followed the passage of the Kansas-Nebraska Act was really decided by the forces controlling the westward movement of the 1850's. So superior were the drawing qualities of northern and southern frontier areas in competition with Kansas that only a small proportion of the migrating colonists reached that territory before 1860. The conditions prevailing between 1854 and 1860 were such that those interested in making Kansas a slaveholding state had no chance of success. Even the modest contingent from the North, largely from Ohio, Indiana and Illinois, greatly outnumbered the contribution from the entire South to Kansas. The Southerners who settled in the territory were mainly nonslaveholders from the upper South, and many of them voted with the free-state element, when, on Aug. 2, 1858, it was finally determined by a large majority that Kansas would not become a slaveholding state. The Lincoln-Douglas debates came after the people of Kansas had made this decision and there was no remaining Federal territory where the conditions were so favorable to slavery.

Douglas opposed the admission of Kansas under the Lecompton Constitution on the ground that popular sovereignty had not been fairly applied when that constitution was first submitted to the people. Through the aid of Republicans, he won the Lecompton fight, which preceded the debates with Abraham Lincoln. The Dred Scott decision had come a year before the Lecompton contest. The opinion of Chief Justice Roger B. Taney troubled the leaders of the new Republican party, because it ran directly counter to the Wilmot Proviso principle. Lincoln believed that Taney had played havoc with popular sovereignty also, though Douglas declared that he had accepted the Court's decision. Before the beginning of the debates, the logic of the situation caused Douglas to discuss the effects of the decision on his principle of nonintervention. His Freeport Doctrine in response to Lincoln's famous second question was new to neither of the senatorial candidates. The assertion of Douglas that slavery could not exist in any territory where the territorial legislature refused to provide the necessary police regulations squared with the facts, and the people of a territory really could decide for themselves regardless of how the Supreme Court might in the future decide the abstract question of the right of a territorial legislature to prohibit slavery. When Sen. Albert G. Brown of Mississippi complained on the floor of the Senate on Feb. 23, 1859, that "Non-action goes a great way to exclude slave property from a Territory, further perhaps than to exclude any other property," he was virtually repeating what Douglas had asserted at Freeport. On the basis of his belief that territorial legislatures would exclude slavery by non-action, Sen. Brown voiced the demand that Congress provide the necessary legislation. It was then that Douglas added the second and final corollary to the doctrine of popular sovereignty, when he proclaimed that he would "never vote for a slave code in the Territories by Congress."

POPULATION, GROWTH AND MOVEMENTS OF. There are only two factors influencing the size of the population in any given area: (1) the natural increase, that is, the difference between births and deaths within a specified time period, which at times may be a negative quantity, and (2) immigration, the net physical movement of people into or out of the area during the same period. In the United States, as a whole, since the earliest colonial days the annual difference between the births and the deaths has been a positive quantity. On the other hand, there have been several periods when net annual immigration has been insignificant and there have been a few years of net emigration. Here we are almost exclusively concerned with these two movements as they have affected the growth of population in the United States as a whole. Their effects on population growth in particular areas and in different types of communities will be given only brief notice.

Table 1 shows the estimated growth of the population from early colonial times to 1790 and the results of the censuses since 1790—the date of our first actual count.

For the first few decades of settlement the rate

of growth was very largely determined by net immigration and was highly variable. However, after 1660 a very high rate of natural increase, *i.e.,* a large annual excess of births over deaths per 1000 of the population, seems to have been achieved, although there can be no reasonable doubt that for the century 1660–1760 net immigration was a significant factor in total growth. The abundance of new land made the necessities of life relatively easy to come by and encouraged early marriages in a population which was overwhelmingly agricultural. The dispersed character of settlement also probably modified significantly the ravages of those contagious and infectious diseases which were responsible for such a large proportion of all deaths in those days. Hence, it is not surprising that natural increase remained at a very

high level during most of the two centuries in which agriculture remained so greatly predominant in the life of the nation. However, a study of the age data in our censuses after 1800 leaves no doubt that by 1820 the birth rate had begun to decline (Table 2). From 1800 it also became possible to calculate with reasonable assurance the contribution of net immigration to total growth (Table 3). These data justify the belief that in the first three decades of the 19th century, 1800–30, the natural increase was about 30–32 per 1000 per year, since immigrants constituted only about 5% of the total increase, which averaged over 34% during this period. It is also reasonably certain that much the same natural increase prevailed during the period 1760–1800, for there can be no doubt there was very little net immi-

TABLE 1

POPULATION, AND AMOUNT AND RATE OF INCREASE, 1610–1960[1]

YEAR	POPULATION (THOUSANDS)	INCREASE DURING DECADE ENDING IN YEAR INDICATED		YEAR	POPULATION (THOUSANDS)	INCREASE DURING DECADE ENDING IN YEAR INDICATED	
		NUMBER (THOUSANDS)	PER CENT			NUMBER (THOUSANDS)	PER CENT
1610	..[2]	..	...	1800	5,308	1,379	35.1
1620	2	2	1090.0	1810	7,240	1,931	36.4
1630	6	3	128.1	1820	9,638	2,399	33.1
1640	28	22	390.3	1830	12,866	3,228	33.5
1650	52	24	85.0	1840	17,069	4,203	32.7
1660	85	33	64.0	1850	23,192	6,122	35.9
1670	114	30	35.0	1860	31,443	8,251	35.6
1680	156	41	35.9	1870[3]	39,818	8,375	26.6
1690	214	58	37.2	1880[3]	50,156	10,337	26.0
1700	275	62	28.8	1890	62,948	12,792	25.5
1710	358	82	30.0	1900	75,995	13,047	20.7
1720	474	117	32.7	1910	91,972	15,978	21.0
1730	655	181	38.1	1920	105,711	13,738	14.9
1740	889	234	35.7	1930	122,775	17,064	16.1
1750	1,207	318	35.8	1940	131,669	8,894	7.2
1760	1,610	403	33.4	1950	150,697	19,028	14.5
1770	2,205	595	37.0		(151,132)[4]	(19,463)	(14.7)
1780	2,781	576	26.1	1960	(179,200)[5]	(28,100)	(18.6)
1790	3,929	1,148	41.3				

[1] For 1610–1780, estimated population as given in Table I, p. 9, from *A Century of Population Growth;* 1790–1930 from *Fifteenth Census of the United States, 1930,* Vol. I, p. 6 except 1870 and 1880 (see Note 3).

No Indians prior to 1860; civilized Indians in 1860, 1870 and 1880; all Indians from 1890 to date.

[2] Less than 500 population (210 in Virginia).

[3] Data as revised by the Bureau of the Census (see *Fourteenth Census of the United States, 1920,* Vol. II, pp. 15, 29).

[4] It is assumed that the census figures for 1930 and 1940 are comparable. Since forces overseas were small at both dates these figures closely approximate the *total* population. However, in 1950 the census did not include the armed forces overseas. The figure including the armed forces is given in parentheses and is believed to represent total increase during this decade (1940–50) more accurately than the census figure. This is the figure used in arriving at the increases and per cents of increase (in parentheses) for 1940–50 and 1950–60.

[5] The figure for 1960 is the writer's rough estimate of the total population as of April 1, 1960. In making this estimate it was assumed that the total growth of population for the eight months, Aug. 1, 1959 to April 1, 1960 would be the same as that estimated by the Bureau of the Census for the eight months, Dec. 1, 1958 to July 31, 1959, the last census estimate available. A deduction of 200,000 has been made for Aug. 1, 1959 in order to exclude Alaska from all the figures in this table. (See Bureau of the Census, Population Estimates, Series P-25, No. 205, Sept. 11, 1959.)

TABLE 2

RATIO OF CHILDREN TO WOMEN BY RACE, AND ESTIMATED WHITE BIRTH RATE, 1800–1930[1]

| | CHILDREN 0–4 PER 1000 WOMEN 15–44 | | ESTIMATED WHITE BIRTH RATE[2] | |
YEAR	WHITE	NEGRO	PER 1000 POPULATION	PER 1000 WOMEN 15–44
1800	952	...	55.0	278
1810	953	...	54.3	274
1820	905	810[3]	52.8	260
1830	835	830[3]	51.4	240
1840	797	785[3]	48.3	222
1850	659	741[3]	43.3	194
1860	675	724	41.4	184
1870	610	692	38.3	167
1880	586	759[3]	35.2	155
1890	517	621	31.5	137
1900	508	582	30.1	130
1910	484	519	27.4	117
1920	471	429	26.1	113
1930	386	393	20.1	87

[1] Mexicans are included with whites from 1800 to 1920, inclusive.

[2] Estimated white births divided by the white census population.

[3] Include an unknown but probably small and unimportant proportion of other colored; for example in 1860 there were 725,051 colored children 0–4 and the colored ratio of children to women was 721, only slightly different from the figures for Negroes in that year.

gration at that time, although no satisfactory figures are available.

By 1830, after a lapse of 60–70 years, net immigration began to rise rapidly and for the next century contributed a substantial proportion of the total increase in every decade. The proportion varied considerably from time to time but fell below 20% in only two decades, 1830–40 and 1910–20, (Table 3). Clearly by 1820 the number of children 0–4 years of age to 1000 white women aged 15–44, which is a rough measure of the birth rate, had begun to decline. However, in spite of the fairly rapid decline in the birth rate there was no decline in total rate of growth until after 1860.

During the decade of the Civil War (1860–70) there was a very marked decline in the rate of population growth, from over 35% in 1850–60 to 26.6%. There was only a slight decline in total rate of growth during the next two decades although the birth rate was declining fairly rapidly. In the decade 1880–90 it is estimated that net immigration contributed almost 43% of the total increase.

In the two decades following 1890 the rate of growth again declined significantly, to about 21%, in spite of a large net immigration, especially during 1900–10, for the birth rate continued to fall. In the next two decades (1910–30) there was a further decline of about five points in the rate of growth, to about 15.5%. The birth rate continued to decline (see adjusted rates in Table 5) and net immigration contributed a substantially smaller proportion to the

TABLE 3

ESTIMATED GROWTH OF THE WHITE POPULATION FROM NATURAL INCREASE AND NET IMMIGRATION, BY DECADES, 1800–1930[1]

| DECADE | WHITE POPULATION GROWTH (THOUSANDS) | NATURAL INCREASE | | IMMIGRATION | | ADJUSTMENT PER CENT |
		THOUSANDS	PER CENT OF POPULATION GROWTH	THOUSANDS	PER CENT OF POPULATION GROWTH	
1800–10	1,556	1,494	96.0	62	4.0	4.4
1810–20	2,005	1,934	96.5	71	3.5	5.2
1820–30	2,671	2,548	95.4	123	4.6	4.7
1830–40	3,658	3,165	86.5	493	13.5	5.3
1840–50	5,357	3,937	73.5	1,420	26.5	3.4
1850–60	7,369	4,811	65.3	2,558	34.7	3.6
1860–70	7,415	5,341	72.0	2,074	28.0	5.3
1870–80	9,066	6,486	71.5	2,580	28.5	2.7
1880–90	11,581	6,617	57.1	4,964	42.9	4.0
1890–1900	11,708	8,019	68.5	3,689	31.5	2.4
1900–10	14,923	8,680	58.2	6,243	41.8	2.8
1910–20	13,089	10,864	83.0	2,225	17.0	1.6
1920–30	15,466	12,131	78.4	3,335	21.6	0.7

[1] For method of calculation see Warren S. Thompson and P. K. Whelpton, *Population Trends in the United States*, page 303.

total growth (about one fifth) than it had at any time since 1840. The rate of population growth in the United States had now fallen to a moderate level in spite of a fairly large immigration.

Little has been said up to this point about changes in the death rate in the United States as a variable in determining natural increase. This is because there are no reliable figures for the death rate for the entire country before 1900. It may be of interest to note, however, that studies based on fragmentary data for Massachusetts indicate a probable death rate around the end of the 18th century in the neighborhood of 28; also that at that time the death rate for Boston was perhaps four to six points higher. By 1850 it would appear probable that the Massachusetts rate had fallen to about 21–22 per 1000 and to around 19 by the end of the 19th century. During the second half of the century registration data from a few other states became available, and a death rate of around 17 per 1000 in 1900 is now believed to be reasonably accurate. These rather scanty data on the death rate appear to justify conclusion that the death rate probably fell by about 10–12 points during the century 1800–1900. Since it appears rather probable that the birth rate fell by about twice as much (22–25 points) the rate of natural increase may have fallen by as much as 12–14 points or even a little more.

Since 1900 more adequate death rates are available and since 1910 birth rates adjusted for the non-registration of births are available (Table 5). These data show a natural increase of about 15 in the decade 1910–19, and of about 13 in 1920–29.

During the depression of 1930–40 the birth rate averaged only a little over 19 per 1000 as compared with about 25 per 1000 during the 1920's, which in turn had been about four points below that of 1910–19 (Table 5). The death rate, on the other hand, declined only from an average of about 12.0 during the 1920's to 11.0 during the 1930's. Hence,

the average rate of natural increase fell by about five points—to approximately eight per 1000—during this decade. It is not clear why this natural increase should be about one-tenth higher than the census increase, since there was also a very small net immigration during the decade (Table 4) in spite of a small net emigration in several years.

During the 1940's the birth rate began to rise slowly, and even during the war (1940–44) it averaged two points above that of the 1930's. It rose a further 2.9 points during 1945–49, so that the average for this decade was approximately 3.4 points above that of the 1930's. The death rate continued to decline but the decline was small, from an average of 11.0 for 1930–39 to 10.4 for 1940–49. Hence the decline in the death rate contributed but little to the rise in the rate of natural increase during the 1940's. However, net civilian immigration (Table 4) began to increase significantly even during the war and for the years 1940–49 amounted to 1,898,000, or to 10.1% of the total increase.

The rise in the birth rate in the immediate postwar years was to be expected as a consequence of the rapid demobilization of the armed forces. Under similar conditions after World War I the birth rate had risen significantly in 1920 and 1921 but then had begun to decline, and by 1929 had fallen by about seven points, or about one fourth from the high postwar level. It seemed reasonable to assume that a somewhat similar decline would take place after 1948 or 1949. But though there was a substantial decline from 1947 to 1948 there has not been any further significant decline as of 1959 (Table 5). Since the birth rate during the 1950's has averaged about the same as during the 1920's while the death rate has averaged about 2.5 points lower, the rate of natural increase has averaged about one-fifth higher than it was thirty years earlier. Moreover, during the 1950's net immigration has furnished a slightly

TABLE 4

TOTAL NET CIVILIAN IMMIGRATION, 1939–1960[1]

DECADE	NUMBERS (THOUSANDS)	PER CENT OF TOTAL INCREASE
1930–40[2]	68	0.7
1940–49	1,898	10.1
1950–59[3]	2,917	10.4

[1] This table cannot be compared directly with Table 2 since that table relates only to the white population. However, the differences, if they could be calculated, would be insignificant.

[2] This figure is taken from Taeuber and Taeuber, *The Changing Population of the United States* (Census Monograph; New York: Wiley,1958), p. 54 It probably is not exactly comparable with net civilian migration as calculated by the Bureau of the Census for following decades, but even a relatively large difference would have almost no effect on the contribution of immigration to our population growth 1930–40.

[3] The latest of the Population Estimates, Series P-25, showing the components of growth after 1940, *viz.* No. 195, Feb. 18, 1959 shows a net civilian immigration for the nine years Jan. 1, 1950, to Jan. 1, 1959, of 2,625,000. The figure given here is for ten years to Jan. 1, 1960, and is arrived at by adding one ninth, or 292,000, to this nine-year figure. It is believed that any error due to using calendar years rather than the year beginning April 1 is negligible.

749

larger proportion of the total increase than it did during the 1940's (Table 4). Hence, the total increase during the 1950's has been much larger (about 8,600,000) than during the 1940's. The increase during the 1950's will equal our total population of about a century ago (1857).

The future growth of population cannot be told with any certainty. However, it is of some interest to note that if natural increase for the next two decades remains at about the rate of 1959 (17% in a decade), and if net immigration adds about 10% to this (17% plus 1.7%), the population in 1970 will be a little over 212,000,000 and a little over 252,000,000 by 1980. It should be said regarding this calculation that although the death rates at certain ages will probably decline significantly during the next twenty years, any further decline in the crude death rate for the population as a whole will almost certainly be slow, so that the maintenance of a natural increase in the vicinity of 1.6 per year, or about 17% in a decade, will depend almost entirely on the maintenance of present birth rates.

Thus far there has been no discussion of the effects of differential birth rates and death rates, nor of the variations in the volume of net in-migration or out-migration, on the growth of population in different regions and different types of communities within the nation. In the broadest terms the birth rates in rural communities have been substantially higher than in urban communities, and the death rates have been lower. Thus the rural communities have had substantially higher rates of natural increase. In both types of communities, but especially in cities, the upper economic groups have had lower birth rates and death rates than the lower economic groups. However, these differentials have been declining for the past few decades and may be in process of disappearing.

Migration within the country as well as immigration has always played an important role in determining the rate of growth in different regions and in different types of communities. The westward movement on to the land always consisted chiefly of natives, but there were times when immigrants also played an important role in the agricultural settlement of certain areas. The volume of this westward migration has varied from time to time but the movement still continues, as is witnessed by the rapid growth of certain of the mountain and Pacific states in recent decades, the best example being California.

Since the revival of immigration on a relatively large scale in the 1830's the cities have regularly attracted a large majority of these newcomers; but they were not sufficient to supply city needs, and great numbers of natives from the rural areas also moved to cities. There can be little doubt that in the aggregate this movement from rural to urban areas has been larger than the movement of immigrants to cities. Since about 1890, by which time the better agricultural areas of the west were largely in the hands of *bona fide* farmers, even the westward movement of population has been also chiefly a cityward movement.

Throughout our national history, with the exception of 1810–20 and 1930–40, the rate of growth of the cities has been far higher than that of rural communities, often several times as high. Much of this city growth must be attributed to the cityward migration of rural youth.

In 1950 the census, under a new definition of "urban", classed 64% of the population as urban, but because of the changing pattern of distribution of people working at nonfarm jobs this figure still understates significantly the "urbanized" population.

In 1790 approximately one fifth of the population of the United States consisted of Negroes. This proportion fell almost steadily until in 1930 less than one tenth (9.7%) consisted of Negroes. The large immigration of whites during much of that period will account for some of this proportional decline of Negroes. However, there can be no reasonable doubt, although reliable figures are lacking, that the chief factor in this relatively slow growth of Negroes was their high death rate, for it also appears probable that their birth rates have been consistently higher than those of the white population as a whole. Since 1930 the Negroes have grown faster than the whites chiefly because their birth rates have declined more slowly and their death rates have declined more

TABLE 5

BIRTH RATES[1] AND DEATH RATES[2]—1910–1959 (TOTAL POPULATION)

YEARS	BIRTH RATES[3] (AVERAGE)	DEATH RATES (AVERAGE)
1955–59	24.9[4]	9.5
1950–54	24.9	9.5
1945–49	24.1	10.1
1940–44	21.2	10.6
1935–39	18.8	11.0
1930–34	19.7	11.0
1925–29	23.2	11.8
1920–24	26.8	12.0
1915–19	28.3	14.4
1910–14	29.8	13.9
1905–09	[5]	15.3
1900–04	[5]	16.2

[1] Source: Grabill, Kiser and Whelpton, *The Fertility of American Women* (Census Monograph; New York: Wiley, 1958), p. 26.

[2] Source: National Office of Vital Statistics, *Vital Statistics of the United States*, Vol. I, 1950, Table 8.02 and later Monthly Reports.

[3] Adjusted for underregistration and estimated for nonregistration states to 1932.

[4] 1959 estimated on the basis of data for the first six months.

[5] Not available.

rapidly than those of the whites. In 1950 Negroes constituted just 10% of the total population. With the increasing urbanization of the Negroes their birth rate can be expected to decline more rapidly, and since their death rate already approaches that of the whites it seems probable that their rate of natural increase will decline, although it may remain higher than that of the whites for another decade or two. Since early in the 19th century immigration has had no significant effect on the growth of the Negro population.

POPULIST PARTY grew out of the deflation of the late 1880's and early 1890's as an agrarian protest against falling prices, poor credit and marketing facilities, and crop failures. The members of Farmers' Alliance and other organizations were driven into politics by these conditions. The campaign of 1890 found them active in the Democratic party in the South, while those in the West sponsored independent parties. As a result, nine Congressmen and two Senators went to Washington as party-conscious agrarians.

These same elements united to form the People's party, as it was officially called, at a convention in Omaha in July, 1892. Its platform embodied the demands of the alliances, and its resolutions included labor legislation and proposals for a more direct political democracy. In the subsequent campaign, its most effective issue was the free coinage of silver, on which the major parties had each adopted a straddle plank. After failing to secure Judge Walter Q. Gresham as a presidential candidate, James B. Weaver was named and a vigorous campaign instituted. Over 1,000,000 votes were cast for Weaver, and he received 22 electoral votes, including all votes from Kansas, Colorado, Idaho and Nevada, and one vote each from North Dakota and Oregon. Small delegations went to the House and Senate, and a generous sprinkling of state officials was elected.

As economic conditions grew worse, the support for the party program seemed to grow. An energetic campaign in 1894 was indecisive, for the party found itself handicapped by the widespread support of the Populist program by Democratic and Republican candidates in those states where these ideas were popular. The prospects for 1896 seemed much brighter, especially if neither major party endorsed free silver as seemed probable. The complete victory of the silver Democrats over the Cleveland administration at Chicago in 1896 destroyed these prospects. The Democrats declared for free coinage and nominated Bryan.

With the Republican party committed to the gold standard, the Populists had a choice of either placing a third candidate in the field and thereby helping to defeat free coinage, or endorsing Bryan and thereby killing their own organization by merging it with the larger Democratic party. The long struggle at their convention was over this issue, with the Southern delegates against the fusion and the Westerners for it. The resulting compromise favored fusion as it provided for the nomination of Bryan, and a separate Populist candidate for Vice-President.

The defeat of Bryan marked the end of the effectiveness of the Populists, although representatives of the party stayed in Congress for several years. The majority faction of the party nominated Bryan again in 1900, but its support was no longer important. Still less so were the remnants which placed candidates in the field in 1904.

The significance of the Populists lies in their agitation of most of the causes which later became part of the progressive movement. Then, too, the third party tended to break up major party regularity, and many who left the locally dominant party to vote Populist remained independents, or they affiliated later with the alternative major party, Republican in the South, and Democratic in the West.

PORT AUTHORITY. This is a quasi-public, tax-free organization, generally regarded as the fastest growing unit of local government in the United States. The Port of New York Authority is the oldest in the United States and was modeled after the Port of London (England) Authority. It has made precedents and fashioned most of the law for many similar organizations and regional authorities throughout the country which have come into being since World War II.

The Port of New York Authority was created in 1921 by the joint efforts of Gov. Alfred E. Smith of New York and Gov. Walter Edge of New Jersey with a view to solve the problems caused by the artificial New York-New Jersey boundary line down the middle of the Hudson River which split the natural unity of the port. Because it was an interstate pact, approval of Congress was required. By the compact of organization, the Port of New York Authority is permitted "to purchase, construct, lease and/or operate any terminal or transportation facility" and "to make charges for the use thereof." Its sphere of jurisdiction extends over a 25-mile radius from the Battery, the southern extremity of Manhattan. Jurisdiction may be extended beyond this limit if approved by both New York and New Jersey governors and legislatures. The scope of the port authority may extend to road transport terminals, shipping facilities such as marine docks and terminals, also to airports, heliports, bridges and tunnels.

Many of the larger port cities in the United States, in addition to New York, have established port authorities with varying degrees of power and coverage as in Boston, Baltimore, Savannah, Mobile, Toledo, San Francisco, Los Angeles, Pensacola, Norfolk, etc. In some cases, the port authority is a state controlled unit, as in Maine, North Carolina, New Hampshire, Virginia, South Carolina, Georgia, Alabama and Puerto Rico, but the jurisdiction of these port authorities is usually restricted. Many of the larger port authorities or port commissions have as extensive and varied jurisdiction as the Port of New York Authority.

Port authorities as a rule cannot levy taxes, but derive income from tolls, largely from bridges and tunnels, and rentals from airports, heliports and marine and bus terminals. They can also borrow money, secured by tax-free bonds. The port authority is relatively free from political interference. Its operating head is usually an executive director, who is controlled by a board of commissioners of which he may be a member.

PORT ROYAL, on the Annapolis Basin, Nova Scotia, was the most important outpost of the French in Acadia against colonial New England. The earliest settlement of the name was begun across the Basin in 1605 by Sieur DeMonts, deserted in 1608, reoccupied in 1610, and destroyed by Capt. Argall from Virginia in 1613. French settlers were, however, left in the vicinity. The Huguenot Claude de la Tour brought some Scotch settlers in 1630 in behalf of Sir William Alexander to whom Charles I of England had granted the region, calling it Nova Scotia. Charles D'Aulnay obtained control in 1636, moved the fort to the site of the present town in 1643, and began a long rivalry with La Tour's son Charles, who, as governor of the French fort St. Louis at St. John, controlled much of the trade. On D'Aulnay's death in 1650 La Tour had possession until the place was captured by a New England expedition under Maj. Robert Sedgwick in 1654. Returned to the French in 1670, Port Royal in 1684 became the seat of their government in Acadia. It was the center from which they attacked New England shipping and the scene of much illicit trade with New Englanders. Captured by Sir William Phips in 1690 it was restored to the French by the Treaty of Ryswick, 1697. Several times threatened with attack from Boston, which in turn lived in daily fear of attack by a French fleet using Port Royal as a base, the town was finally taken by a great expedition in 1710 under Col. Nicholson and Col. Vetch. Acadia was ceded to England by the Treaty of Utrecht. In the face of the Acadian citizenry, England's hold was precarious after the French built Louisburg on Cape Breton Island. Twice attacked and several times threatened in King George's War, Annapolis Royal (as it was called by the English) lost its strategic importance and also its position as seat of the government with the building of Halifax by the English at the close of the war.

PORT ROYAL (South Carolina). The French diplomat, soldier and Huguenot leader Jean Ribaut in May, 1562, settled 28 or 30 Frenchmen, almost all Huguenots, on Parris Island in present South Carolina, and named the harbor containing the island Port Royal from its size. It lies twenty miles north of the mouth of Savannah River. Spanish navigators from Mexico and West Indies had already named the harbor Santa Elena and continued so to call it. Ribaut having gone to France for reinforcements, the settlers, soon discouraged, abandoned their frail fortification Charlesfort (confused by some writers with Fort Caroline on the St. Johns, Fla.), and after fearful sufferings, including slaying and eating one of their number, reached France after being rescued from a vessel of their own construction. Spain to prevent further trespass in the region built St. Augustine, 1565, destroyed the French Fort Caroline, built in 1564 on the St. Johns, and built Fort San Felipe on Parris Island, Port Royal, 1566, introduced farmers and missionaries, and explored the interior as far as the North Carolina mountains and eastern Alabama. Indians expelled the Spaniards and burned their fort in 1576, but in 1577 Spain rebuilt near the same spot on Parris Island under the name Fort San Marcos. Drake's burning St. Augustine in 1586 forced Spain's abandonment that year of Port Royal. The English who under the authority of the Lords Proprietors of Carolina settled South Carolina in 1670 landed at Port Royal, but in a few days removed to the site of Charleston as in less danger from the Spaniards. In 1684 51 Scotch Covenanters settled at Port Royal, but were driven off by Spaniards from St. Augustine in 1686.

The modern town of Port Royal, immediately above Parris Island, was captured Nov. 7, 1861, by a Federal fleet. The region became the scene for raising Negro Federal troops and for Northern missionary enterprises. The Federal Navy Yard was removed to Charleston in 1901–2.

PORTSMOUTH, TREATY OF (Sept. 5, 1905), brought to a close the Russo-Japanese War and gave formal sanction to Japan's supplanting of Russian interests and political influence in Korea and southern Manchuria. It represented Japan's first forward step in territorial expansion on the Asiatic mainland. From the opening of the peace negotiations Russia had agreed to cede the special rights the Czarist government held in southern Manchuria (notably the Liaotung Peninsula lease and what was to be called the South Manchuria Railway), but the conference almost broke up over Japan's demand for the further cession of the island of Sakhalin and payment of an indemnity. At this point President Theodore Roosevelt, whose earlier intercession had been instrumental in bringing about the conference and for its being held in Portsmouth, N. H., again intervened, and both directly and through the German Kaiser he brought such pressure as he could on the Russian and Japanese governments in favor of peace. As a result, Russia, while refusing to pay any indemnity, agreed to cede the southern half of Sakhalin, and Japan accepted these terms. Roosevelt was widely hailed for his contribution to peace, but bitter resentment was created in Japan through loss of the expected indemnity.

POST ROADS. The earliest colonial mail carrying, between New York and Boston, and later, between New York and Albany, in the latter 17th century, traced routes which became great highways and are still known as the Post Roads. The names "Boston Post Road" and "Old (Albany) Post Road" on two meandering streets in New York City mark their lower courses. The Continental Congress began creating post roads during the Revolutionary War. To designate a highway as a post road gave the Government the monopoly of carrying mail over it; on other roads, anybody might carry it. At first the mail was conveyed on horseback; later in stagecoaches. But as late as 1825 the Postmaster General reported that "The intelligence of more than half the Nation is conveyed on horseback." That a highway was a post road did not prevent its being impassable from mud at times, for little road improving was done in the early decades of our history. Hugh Finley, postal inspector, declared in 1773, for example, that the road between New London and Providence was "bad past all conception." In early days, horseback travelers often sought the company of the post rider for guidance and protection; later, the mail coach was an important passenger carrier as well. The inns where the post rider stopped overnight or the mail coach paused for meals became noted and prosperous hostelries, and the post roads were the first to be improved. In 1787 connecting stretches of road reaching as far north as Portsmouth and Concord, N. H., as far south as Augusta, Ga., and as far west as Pittsburgh were declared post roads, not to mention others in the more settled area between; but many of the new routes were not expected to be self-supporting, and so were let out to contractors. Between 1790 and 1829 successive acts of Congress increased the post road mileage from 1875 to 114,780. Steamboat captains carried many letters in early days and collected the fees therefor, until in 1823 all navigable waters were declared to be post roads, which checked the practice. Private letter-carrying companies after 1842 did much house-to-house mail business in the larger cities; but the Postmaster General circumvented them in 1860 by declaring all the streets of New York, Boston and Philadelphia to be post roads.

POSTAGE STAMPS. Although adhesive stamps were invented in Great Britain in 1840, their use in the United States was not authorized until 1845, and even then, Congress made no provision for printing them. During the two following years, a number of postmasters produced their own stamps, each in individual design, which are now among the greatest of philatelic rarities. On July 1, 1847, the Post Office Department issued its first stamps—a five-cent bearing the head of Franklin and a ten-cent (Washington)—and ordered all the postmaster stamps destroyed. Letter postage was then five cents per ounce. Meanwhile, there had been a great number of local delivery companies which—as the Government had no house-to-house delivery—carried mail in the larger cities and had their own stamps. One of these, the United States Despatch Post, issued in 1842 the first adhesive stamp used in America. Express companies even carried mail between cities in the East, and during the California gold rush and for two decades thereafter in the Far West, though only three or four of them used adhesive stamps. The pony express of 1860–61 had its own stamps. With the second issue (1851) of United States stamps, rates were reduced, and 1-, 3-, 5-, 10- and 12-cent values were issued; in 1856, 24-, 30- and 90-cent denominations appeared. Thereafter, other denominations were added from time to time. During perhaps two decades in these early years, stamps were often used as currency, for making purchases, paying street-car fares, etc. When the Confederate government was set up in 1861, there was a brief period when local post offices printed their own stamps before the government issue appeared.

Up to 1873 government mail was franked without stamps. For a decade thereafter the various government departments used stamps, each in its own design, at the regular postal rates; then these were dropped and the plain franked envelope returned. In 1869 the first stamps printed in two colors appeared—a novelty not repeated until 1901. In 1893 the first commemorative series appeared—large stamps in sixteen denominations, all picturing Columbus and the discovery of America, in celebration of the World's Columbian Exposition. The Trans-Mississippi Exposition of 1898 brought another series of nine; the Pan-American Exposition of 1901 a bicolored series of six values. Thereafter, commemoratives increased in popularity, and by 1930 and after, floods of them in rich designs were pouring from the presses at brief intervals. In 1913 a special series of stamps for parcel-post service was issued, but after 1917 these were discarded and the ordinary stamps used on packages. The inauguration of air mail in 1918 caused the designing of a 24-cent air stamp for letters; and as rates were thereafter reduced, air stamps in various denominations were issued. By 1938 there was a stamp for every value from ½ cent (and including 1½ cents) up to and including 22 cents, and others thereafter up to $5; and in that year a complete series bearing the portraits of the deceased Presidents from Washington to Coolidge (there is a rule against using the portraits of living persons on stamps) was begun—Franklin's portrait being placed on the ½-cent, Martha Washington's on the 1½-cent and the White House on the 4½-cent to complete the series. When we took over the Panama Canal Zone and the Philippine Islands, our low-value stamps were surcharged or overprinted with their names for use in those possessions. The increasing volume of stamp sales to collectors, and the philatelists' special requisites, caused the opening for their benefit at Washington in 1921 of a Government Philatelic Agency.

POSTAL SERVICE. When the Federal Constitution became operative, there were in the United States scarcely 2400 miles of post roads, of which the greater part was represented by a "main post road" paralleling the Atlantic coast from Maine to Georgia. Less than a dozen "cross posts" branched from this trunk route. There were but 76 post offices, of which 51 were along the main post road. The annual gross revenues of the entire "Post Office Establishment" were under $25,000, which meant that 3,000,000 people were sending less than 250,000 letters per year. Great portions of the country, including all rural areas, were without official postal service and had to send and receive mail by private means.

Some Federalists, particularly Hamilton, expected the Post Office to be a revenue-producing agency which would each year turn into the Treasury a profit on its operations. This view was challenged by those who argued that any surplus should be used to extend and render more efficient so useful a service, with the profitable eastern routes helping to support those on the frontiers. The latter principle was put into full effect by the Jeffersonians. The mileage of official post roads reached 20,000 by 1801; in 1812 it was over 50,000. Expansion at a still greater rate followed the close of the War of 1812 as the Post Office made an effort to serve adequately vast areas of new settlement in the Ohio Valley and the Old Southwest.

Stagecoaches, first employed in 1785 as carriers of the mail on the main post roads, reached their heyday in the Jacksonian era. The first contracts for railroad service were let in 1835, and railroads thereafter were used as carriers as rapidly as they were constructed. The costs of railroad transportation were much higher, however, while at the same time, the railroads brought into existence a host of express companies, which, challenging the supposed constitutional monopoly of the Post Office, carried letters between the large eastern cities at bargain rates, skimming the cream of the business. The expresses flourished because of the high official postage rates. The charge for a "single letter," *i.e.*, a single sheet, ranged from six cents for a hundred miles to twenty-five cents for over four hundred miles. Another sheet or an enclosure doubled the postage and additional sheets and enclosures increased the amount proportionately. The competition from expresses came when under Jacksonian auspices frontier routes had been vastly extended and also when, following the Panic of 1837, there was stagnation in business. A series of annual deficits resulted. As postal facilities were curtailed, revenues declined further. The people sided with the expresses, and in 1843 a powerful press and congressional faction demanded the abolition of the Post Office as an "odious monopoly." The service was saved in this crisis only by "cheap postage," a reform forced through Congress in 1845 by popular pressure over strong protests from postal officials who argued that the reform would not succeed in a country of great distances and sparse population. Cheap postage, however, at once eliminated the competition of the express companies. In two years the department was again on a paying basis, and in 1851 postage rates were further reduced. Payment was simplified by the introduction of postage stamps in 1847, and the general use of envelopes followed.

Railroads increased the speed of the mail only to have it delayed at overtaxed central distributing offices. Successful experiments in distributing on board trains in 1864 led to the establishment of the Railway Mail Service in 1865. The first ocean-mail contracts were authorized in 1845. Previously, foreign mails had been dispatched as opportunity offered, postmasters at the ports making the arrangements. Between 1847 and 1874 postal treaties regulating the exchange of mails were negotiated with many nations; these were replaced for the most part by the International Postal Convention of Berne, 1874. The registry service, designed to provide special security for letters containing money or other valuable matter, was established in 1855. The Money Order system, which went into operation in 1864, largely eliminated "money letters" from the mails and provided a convenient and safe method of transferring funds.

Gradually the Post Office has expanded its services to an extent undreamed of in the days of the "cheap postage" controversy. Free city delivery service was inaugurated in 1863. The Special Delivery service dates from 1885. In 1896, over much opposition and at great cost, the Rural Free Delivery service was established, lessening the isolation of farm dwellers. Also, of special benefit to the farmer was the Parcel Post service, which came into existence in 1913 despite the opposition of express companies and of retail establishments in country villages. The Parcel Post law represented a major enlargement of Post Office functions. The Postal Savings system, established in 1911, had less relation to the mail function, but represented a further development of the banking facilities provided by the Money Order system.

Air mail was inaugurated in 1918 with an experimental line between Washington and New York. By 1920 a transcontinental service was in operation. The Post Office Department financed and operated its own planes and ground facilities until the service had developed to a point where private capital was encouraged to enter the field. Most of the routes were placed under contract to private companies in 1927 and 1928. In 1934 a brief experiment was made with Army pilots. Foreign air mail routes were added to the domestic system until the service reached into Canada, Mexico, Central and South America, the West Indies and Bermuda. In 1935 the transpacific air mail was inaugurated via Hawaii and the Philippines to China. Transatlantic service was begun in 1939. As rates were reduced, the volume of air mail grew tremendously until in 1938 the air mail branch of the service first operated at a profit.

POTAWATOMIE MASSACRE was the calling out and murdering by free-state men of five proslavery settlers near Dutch Henry's Crossing of Potawatomie Creek, Franklin County, Kans., on the night of May 24–25, 1856. The principal facts became known almost immediately. Many free-state men denounced the act, named six members of the John Brown family and two others, made affidavits on which warrants were issued, and one arrest was made (Townsley), but the case never went to trial. Some proslavery newspapers gave fairly accurate statements of facts, but were confused in attributing motives. The free-state press misrepresented both. Brown's first biographer, James Redpath, endorsed by the Brown family, denied (1860) that Brown was present or even had prior knowledge of it. Not until the statement of a participator, James Townsley, was published in December, 1879, did the Brown family and friends (with a few exceptions) admit the truth. From that date the Brown controversy centered upon motives and justification rather than denial, but with little success in establishing either.

The primary issue in the spring of 1856 was enforcement of the so-called "bogus laws." In various parts of the territory, threats were made against the courts and enforcement officers. The significant fact about the Potawatomie victims is that, except for the younger son of Doyle, they were members of the Franklin County grand jury or were associated otherwise with the session of court of April 21–22. These facts place the massacre in the category of political assassination with a view to preventing enforcement of law by resort to a reign of terror.

POTOMAC, ARMY OF THE (1861–65). The demoralization of the Union forces after the first Bull Run left Washington in an undefended state which might have proved disastrous had the Confederacy been able to take advantage of its opportunity. Immediately after congressional authorization for the acceptance of volunteers the Division of the Potomac was created (July 25, 1861), and two days later Gen. George B. McClellan was placed in command. The immediate purpose was to guard the approaches to the Potomac River, and thus to protect Washington. McClellan fell heir to "a collection of undisciplined, ill officered, and uninstructed men," already demoralized by defeat. On Aug. 1 there were only about 37,000 infantry in the ranks, and the terms of many regiments were expiring. Four months later there were some 77,000 effectives available for active operations, aside from regiments on garrison and other duty, but the army was still growing.

McClellan's first job was to whip this heterogeneous mass of raw recruits into an effective fighting unit. The men were from all walks of life and every part of the country. Some were volunteers from foreign nations and many could not speak English. McClellan was not allowed to expand the regulars or break them up to head volunteers, and many of the political generals at his disposal were worse than useless. Also, he was hampered by the officious meddling and machinations of political leaders, while his own temperament was not such as to smooth out such difficulties. Nevertheless, in a very few months he evolved the best army the United States had had to that time, and so inspired it with a spirit of loyalty and feeling of destiny that all the interference from Washington during the remainder of the war could not permanently harm its morale.

Such an army was not allowed to exhibit its true worth until the war was half over. If McClellan overestimated the enemy in the Peninsular Campaign, it must be remembered that he was not allowed control of the intelligence service. Also, Washington officialdom far outdid him in that respect by withholding McDowell's 40,000 to guard against a possible attack on Washington by a third as many men under Stonewall Jackson. When the Seven Days' Battles resulted in the army reaching the James, and in a better position to advance on Richmond than was to be achieved for two more years, McClellan was demoted beneath the incompetent Pope and the pick of the army was removed to join the latter at Acquia Creek. In caution McClellan was exceeded by Thomas, in blunders by Grant, in egotism and insubordination by Stanton. His tardiness in pursuit after Antietam was at least as excusable as that of Meade after Gettysburg. But by July, 1863, Washington officialdom had learned to give a general a chance while he was winning. In 1864 and 1865, with Meade still in command but a Grant rather than a Halleck giving the superior orders, the Army of the Potomac was allowed to complete the work which McClellan had outlined and begun in 1862.

POTOMAC COMPANY (original spelling Patowmack) was organized in 1785 with the idea that it would eventually achieve a waterway connection between the Potomac and Ohio Rivers. George Washington was one of the incorporators and was elected president. Work was begun that summer on a short canal with locks around the Great Falls of the Potomac, near the present site of Washington—the first corporate improvement of navigation for public use in America. This canal was not completed until 1802. By 1808 there were four more short canals between Washington and a point above Harpers Ferry, the longest one 3814 yards in length. These were of great assistance to boatmen and raftsmen in bringing their products down to tidewater; but the project was not a paying one, and, when the Chesapeake and Ohio Canal Company was organized, the Potomac Company willingly surrendered its charter and rights to the new corporation in 1828.

POTOMAC RIVER drains the western slopes of the central Allegheny Mountains into the Chesapeake

Bay. Two main streams, the North Branch and the South Branch and several minor streams unite to form the upper Potomac. A fresh-water river for about 300 miles, the Potomac below Washington, D. C., is a tidal estuary 125 miles in length and from two to eight miles wide.

Spaniards probably reached the Potomac estuary before 1570. Capt. John Smith visited, described and mapped it in 1608. Capt. Samuel Argall and others sailed its waters in the next decade. In the following decade Virginia traders frequented its waters and shores. Probably agents of George Calvert before 1632 explored the upper Potomac. After the founding of Maryland in 1634, the Potomac was the early passageway of the colony. In following decades its southern shores were gradually settled by Virginians. But owing to the falls above Washington, D. C., and at Harpers Ferry the upper Potomac was long unimportant. In the second quarter of the 18th century, however, Germans and Scotch-Irish crossed it into the Shenandoah Valley, and about 1740 Thomas Cresap, militant Marylander, settled at Old Town, fourteen miles below the mouth of Wills Creek. Slowly the Potomac Valley became a pathway to the Ohio Valley, utilized by the Ohio Company of Virginia, by Washington and by Braddock. Over this route traveled the first settlers to the Monongahela country. Its utilization was the basis of later enterprises, such as the Potomac Company of 1785, the Cumberland Road of 1807, the Chesapeake and Ohio Canal Company of 1828, and the Baltimore and Ohio Railroad of 1827.

POTSDAM CONFERENCE (July 17–Aug. 2, 1945). This was the last meeting during World War II of the three allied chiefs of state. Already Germany, but not Japan, had surrendered. President Truman, Prime Minister Churchill (who was replaced during the conference by the new Prime Minister Attlee after the British elections), and Marshal Stalin fixed terms of German occupation and reparations, and replaced the European Advisory Commission (set up at the Moscow Conference of Foreign Ministers) with a Council of Foreign Ministers of the United States, Great Britain, France and Russia, charged with preparing peace terms for Italy, Rumania, Bulgaria, Austria, Hungary and Finland. Since Russia had not yet declared war on Japan, the Potsdam Declaration (July 26, 1945) was signed by the United States and Great Britain only, though with China's concurrence; it called for Japan to surrender but gave assurances that she would be treated humanely. Although the discussions were fairly cordial, the American delegation, disturbed by indications of Russian non-cooperation, left Potsdam in a far less optimistic mood than Roosevelt's delegation had left Yalta.

POTTERY, INDIAN, takes a prominent place in the history of aboriginal culture, partly because of its indestructibility, but chiefly because it serves as an index to time sequence in pre-Columbian history. Pre-Columbian pottery is found practically everywhere in the United States east of the Rocky Mountains. Washington, Oregon, northern California and parts of Idaho return no pottery. The outstanding prehistoric developments in pottery were in New Mexico and Arizona, the flood plain of the Mississippi River between St. Louis and New Orleans, and in Alabama and Georgia. In New England, New York, Kentucky and generally west of the Mississippi, archaeologists find the remains of cultures using pottery overlaying no-pottery cultures. This has been interpreted as giving a prehistoric horizon, as between the early hunting cultures and the later more sedentary modes of life. Pottery forms and styles vary from century to century, which in turn mark time sequence horizons; thus in New Mexico and Arizona at least six successive prehistoric culture periods are indicated by changes in pottery styles. In parts of the Mississippi Valley four such horizons are known.

Indian pottery was made by hand, the wheel being unknown. Decorations were by incised and stamped designs, in the East, while in the West, painted designs prevailed. Practically all pre-Columbian pottery was unglazed.

POWELL'S (JOHN W.) EXPLORATIONS of the Colorado River of the west were two in number. The first and more important, in 1869, was the pioneer passage by a white man of the entire length of this river with its precipitous canyons and long series of treacherous rapids and waterfalls. Entering the river where the Union Pacific Railroad crosses Green River in May, 1869, the company of eight, in four boats, did not emerge until August 29, after a journey of 900 miles. So dangerous were the rapids that three of the party deserted before the end of the journey. Powell reported the expedition to Congress and that body appropriated additional funds for the exploration of adjacent streams and territories, which Powell undertook and again descended the river in 1871, 1874 and 1875. As a result of his success Powell was named director of the Survey of the Rocky Mountain region in 1877, but in 1879 all local surveys were merged in the U. S. Geological Survey of which Powell became chief in 1881. The geological value of Powell's descent of the Colorado was slight but the hazard of the adventure and his picturesque reports concerning it did much to establish the popularity of scientific expeditions and to secure government support for them. His first report was revised and enlarged in 1895 under the title *Canyons of the Colorado.*

PRAIRIE DOGS are burrowing rodents which formerly infested the plains in immense numbers from Texas to Canada and the western slope of the Rocky Mountains. Since they lived underground in large colonies, threw up craters of earth at the surface of their burrows (excluding rain) and lived on grass, they destroyed vast areas of good grazing land. The cattlemen considered them pests for this reason and also because horses broke their legs by stepping in their holes. Prairie dogs do not require any drinking water and do not, as commonly believed, associate on friendly terms with rattlesnakes and owls. Both of the latter are found in prairie dog colonies but live in abandoned burrows. They are natural enemies. One prairie dog colony in Trego County, Kans., extended one hundred miles with a breadth of a half to five miles. Many prairie dogs are still to be found but for economic reasons ways have been found to keep them in check.

PRAIRIE DU CHIEN was a French settlement commanding the western end of the Fox-Wisconsin waterway from the Great Lakes to the Mississippi. The site was first visited in 1673 by Jolliet and Marquette. About 1683 a French officer built at this site Fort St. Nicolas, which was maintained until 1689 or later. It was not until the 18th century that the place acquired its present name from a Fox Indian chief named Le-Chien, who had a large village on this prairie. The settlement of French traders and *voyageurs* began about the middle of this century. Jean Marie Cardinal from the Illinois is known to have been there by 1754. After the cession in 1763 of all this region to the British, their traders mingled with the former French, and during the expansion of the fur trade Prairie du Chien became an important mart. Jonathan Carver, who visited here in 1766 and 1767, mentions the great concourse of traders, which met at this place each spring, and the rivalry with the British of the Spanish traders from St. Louis and New Orleans.

PRAIRIE DU CHIEN, INDIAN TREATY AT (1825). The two great tribes of Chippewa and Sioux had been enemies for over a century, and had drawn neighboring tribes into the feud. In 1824 a deputation to Washington requested the Federal Government to set up boundaries between the tribal lands. The treaty of 1825 was called for that purpose. Gen. William Clark of St. Louis and Gov. Lewis Cass of Detroit were the American commissioners. The tribal chiefs assembled to the number of over 1000—a magnificent spectacle of the Indian in his native finery and physical strength, before he had been debauched by white contact. The Philadelphia artist, J. O. Lewis, was present, and painted many chiefs from life. A bower was built outside Fort Crawford, the garrison of which preserved order.

This treaty, unlike others made with the Indian, contained no cession of land. Boundaries were established, which the several tribes agreed to respect. The parties to the treaty were Sioux, Chippewa, Sauk and Foxes, Potawatomi, Winnebago and Iowa.

PRAIRIE SCHOONER was a large wagon originally made with the sides of the box sloping outward. Six or seven arching wooden bows supported a canvas cover which, seen in the distance, so resembled a ship at sea as to suggest the name. The descendant of the old Conestoga wagon in which Pittsburgh "stogies" were early transported to Philadelphia, the prairie schooner was also the ancestor of the modern truck and trailer. First brought into common use in the Santa Fe trade soon after 1821, it was later used by the Mormons, California gold seekers, emigrants to Oregon, freighters operating on the Great Plains, and, in a modified form, by settlers seeking homesteads on the western prairies. Among the first used in the West were the "Murphy wagons" with iron axles made in St. Louis. Other types were made in Indianapolis, Chicago and Kenosha. The prairie schooner was usually drawn by three to six yoke of oxen or four to six mules. Its importance in the settlement and development of the Great West was enormous. It was not only the chief means for the transportation of goods, but it also provided a home for the family of the pioneer emigrant as he journeyed west in search of land.

PRAIRIES are a geographical region whose eastern border is an irregular line crossing Minnesota and Wisconsin in a southeasterly direction and extending into western Indiana, thence southwest through Illinois, Missouri, Oklahoma and Texas, and whose western boundary merges into the Great Plains. It is a vast area of grasslands as differentiated from the forest lands on the east. When the Americans first discovered this region it caused some alarm since it was thought the land was too infertile to produce trees. One result of the feeling that the valuable farming land was about all occupied was that the frontiersmen, with an eye on the Canadian forests, clamored loudly for war against Great Britain in 1812. So strongly did the idea persist that prairie land was poor soil that the timberland was almost always settled first. For this reason the rough, rocky portions of Missouri were settled before the rich prairies of the northeast. The prairie land had the advantage of being much easier to bring under cultivation. In a very few years a whole quarter section was bearing crops whereas in forested areas a decade often found the settler with only a patch of ground, comparatively, cleared. The objection to the prairie as a place for pioneering was the lack of timber for fuel and fencing.

PRE-EMPTION. Compact orderly settlement in groups or colonies and a continuous source of income for the Federal Treasury were the principal motives for the land policies adopted in the early years of our national history. To this end settlement was restricted to surveyed areas and the surveys were not made far in advance of demand. Inevitably, however, the lack of restraint and social control on the frontier broke down these policies. Settlers pushed farther into the unsurveyed territory, even into the Indian country, and, if forcibly removed, would promptly return and reconstruct their homes when the troops had withdrawn. As all lands when first brought on the market were put up at auction and sold to the highest bidder, the threat of the forthcoming government sale hung over the squatters like the sword of Damocles. Their improvements might give value to their land but they did not provide the necessary cash, always scarce on the frontier, to buy the land at the auction sale and there was always the danger that speculators might purchase their claims. Furthermore, in the absence of land laws, squatters had difficulty in protecting their improvements against claim jumpers before the day of sale arrived.

The squatters early besought Congress to grant them the right of pre-empting their claims in advance of the land sale so they would not be obliged to bid for them against speculators. Congress, increasingly responsive to demands of the West, granted pre-emption rights to sixteen special groups before 1830, and between 1830 and 1840 gave pre-emption rights on five occasions to all squatters then residing upon the surveyed lands. In 1841 the general pre-emption law was passed which gave the pre-emption right to all squatters then located or who in the future should take up locations upon the surveyed public lands. This act, although a victory for the West, by no means satisfied the settlers on the frontier. It neither applied to Indian reservations nor to unsurveyed lands; it did not provide for free grants to actual settlers, and it retained the minimum price of $1.25 per acre.

Squatters on surveyed lands before and on unsurveyed lands after 1841 were not sure of obtaining pre-emption rights. To provide mutual protection in the absence of such rights they organized claim associations. But such associations were powerless to aid, nor did the pre-emption law protect the penniless settler who was threatened with the loss of his claim if he could not raise the $200 necessary to buy it before the government auction.

The pre-emption law remained in effect until 1891, but in the later years it was subject to serious abuses. In areas where only limited entries of public lands could be made, predatory interests found it possible to acquire large tracts by employing "floaters" to pre-empt land for them. False swearing, bribery of the land officers, laxity of supervision and general Western approval of such practices made evasion of the law easy. Finally, in 1891, when sentiment against the monopolization of the public lands by corrupt groups had become sufficiently aroused, the land system was given a thorough overhauling and the pre-emption law was repealed. For thirty years it had outlived its usefulness.

PRESBYTERIANS. The Presbyterians in the United States arose out of the commingling of large numbers of Scotch-Irish Presbyterian immigrants with Puritan Presbyterians who came chiefly from New England. The father of American Presbyterianism was Francis Makemie (1658–1708), a Scotch-Irish licentiate who came to the eastern shore of Maryland in 1683 where he began preaching in several Scotch-Irish communities, and in 1684 formed the Snow Hill church. His appeal for assistance to the Presbyterian Union of London brought additional helpers, and in 1706 he took the leadership in forming the Philadelphia Presbytery. As Scotch-Irish immigration increased the number of congregations grew, particularly following the great middle colony revival. In 1716 the Synod of Philadelphia was formed, of four presbyteries and thirty ministers. The early colonial ministerial supply came partly from New England—Jonathan Dickinson and Aaron Burr, Sr., both graduates of Yale College, are notable examples. After the founding of the College of New Jersey (Princeton University) a majority of the ministerial supply came from that source. With the adoption by Connecticut of the Saybrook Platform (1708) Connecticut Congregationalism tended more and more toward Presbyterianism, a fact of large importance to both denominations. The passage by the Synod in 1729 of the Adopting Act, requiring all ministers to subscribe to the Westminster Confession, was an influential factor in keeping American Presbyterianism conservative.

Though the colonial revival caused a temporary division (1745–58) into Old Side and New Side bodies, Presbyterianism grew rapidly and by the beginning of the Revolution ranked only second to Congregationalism as the most numerous religious body in the colonies. Their almost unanimous support of the patriot cause added to their prestige, while the formation of a national organization in 1788 with a general assembly as the lawmaking body placed them in a particularly favorable position for national expansion.

The Presbyterians proved to be one of the most influential of the frontier churches, though their rigidity of doctrine and polity together with their relatively high educational standards for their ministry proved a handicap in competition with the Baptists and Methodists. They were, however, the great college founders, and up to the Civil War exercised the largest cultural influence in the West.

The Plan of Union of 1801, providing for co-operation between Presbyterians and Congregationalists on the frontier, at first seemed to work in favor of Presbyterians, and a large number of Congregational churches became Presbyterian. This very fact, however, was to be the main cause of controversy and eventual schism, and in 1837–38 the main body of American Presbyterians was divided into Old School and New School bodies. The Civil War further divided these bodies into northern and southern divisions. The southern bodies united in 1864 to form the Presbyterian Church in the United States; the northern wings merged in 1869–70 as the Presbyterian Church in the U. S. A. The United Presbyterian church was formed in 1858 by the union of two covenanter groups, the Associate Reformed and the Associate. In 1958 the Presbyterian Church in the U. S. A. merged with the United Presbyterian Church as the United Presbyterian Church in the U. S. A. with a total membership of 3,110,572. The southern Presbyterian church has an inclusive membership of 869,452 (1958).

PRESIDENT. The President of the United States enjoys a measure of authority, prestige, and independence that is unique among all chief executives in countries governed on constitutional principles. His authority derives from the vague and frugal words of Article II of the Constitution and from literally thousands of statutes passed by Congress, some of them granting almost dictatorial powers for use in national emergencies. His prestige derives from his position as the directly elected representative of the people, from the fact that he fills the office held by Washington and Lincoln, and from his dual capacity as head of government and chief of state. His independence derives from the division of power in the Constitution, and is matched by the unique independence of Congress.

The Presidency of today is the joint creation of the framers of the Constitution, of the circumstances of America's rise to world power, and of the outstanding men to hold the office.

The men most influential in shaping the Presidency on the floor of the Convention of 1787 were James Wilson, James Madison, Gouverneur Morris, and, by simply acting the part of the man universally expected to be the first President, George Washington. In the course of the Convention these men were able to persuade most of their colleagues that, contrary to the Whiggish sentiments of the Revolution, a strong and independent executive was an essential element of constitutional government. The framers rejected outright the example of the Articles of Confederation, under which there was no distinct executive. They also shunned, although somewhat less peremptorily, the solutions to the problem of executive power worked out in such early state constitutions as those of Pennsylvania and North Carolina, under which the governors were "mere cyphers." In the New York Constitution of 1777 and the Massachusetts Constitution of 1780, each of which had provided successfully for a strong, independent, and yet "safe" executive, they found the working models for the Presidency. It was not easy for them to reach the many decisions that together produced Article II, but in the end they made at least eight that pointed to strength rather than weakness and to independence rather than dependence. Some of the key decisions

	DATE OF IN- AUGU- RATION	AGE AT INAU- GURA- TION	STATE OF RESI- DENCE	POLITICS	DATE OF DEATH
George Washington	1789	57	Va.	Fed.	1799
John Adams	1797	61	Mass.	Fed.	1826
Thomas Jefferson	1801	57	Va.	Dem.-Rep.	1826
James Madison	1809	57	Va.	Dem.-Rep.	1836
James Monroe	1817	58	Va.	Dem.-Rep.	1831
John Q. Adams	1825	57	Mass.	Dem.-Rep.	1848
Andrew Jackson	1829	61	Tenn.	Dem.	1845
Martin Van Buren	1837	54	N.Y.	Dem.	1862
William H. Harrison	1841	68	Ohio	Whig	1841
John Tyler*	1841	51	Va.	Whig	1862
James K. Polk	1845	49	Tenn.	Dem.	1849
Zachary Taylor	1849	64	La.	Whig	1850
Millard Fillmore*	1850	50	N.Y.	Whig	1874
Franklin Pierce	1853	48	N.H.	Dem.	1869
James Buchanan	1857	65	Pa.	Dem.	1868
Abraham Lincoln	1861	52	Ill.	Rep.	1865
Andrew Johnson*	1865	56	Tenn.	Dem. (Union)	1875
Ulysses S. Grant	1869	46	Ill.	Rep.	1885
Rutherford B. Hayes	1877	54	Ohio	Rep.	1893
James A. Garfield	1881	49	Ohio	Rep.	1881
Chester A. Arthur*	1881	50	N.Y.	Rep.	1886
Grover Cleveland	1885	47	N.Y.	Dem.	1908
Benjamin Harrison	1889	55	Ohio	Rep.	1901
Grover Cleveland	1893	55	N.Y.	Dem.	1908
William McKinley	1897	54	Ohio	Rep.	1901
Theodore Roosevelt*	1901	42	N.Y.	Rep.	1919
William H. Taft	1909	51	Ohio	Rep.	1930
Woodrow Wilson	1913	56	N.J.	Dem.	1924
Warren G. Harding	1921	55	Ohio	Rep.	1923
Calvin Coolidge*	1923	51	Mass.	Rep.	1933
Herbert Hoover	1929	54	Cal.	Rep.	...
Franklin D. Roosevelt	1933	51	N.Y.	Dem.	1945
Harry S. Truman*	1945	60	Mo.	Dem.	...
Dwight D. Eisenhower	1953	62	N.Y. (Pa.)	Rep.	...
John F. Kennedy	1961	43	Mass.	Dem.	...

(Those men whose names are marked by an asterisk were Vice-Presidents who succeeded to the office upon the death of an incumbent President.)

were those to make the Presidency a one-man office, to give it powers of its own (including the veto), and to place the machinery of election outside of Congress. The title of President was affixed to the office of chief executive almost without discussion. The presiding officer of the Continental Congress was thus styled, and his title was a natural one for the framers to select.

One of the outstanding features of American constitutional development has been the sporadic but irreversible growth of presidential power and prestige, particularly at the expense of Congress. Among the circumstances that are usually credited with contributing to this development are the growth of the Federal administration in response to the challenges of a mighty industrial civilization, the deep involvement of the United States in foreign affairs, the three great wars since 1861, and emergencies like the Pullman Strike of 1894 and the Depression of 1933. The difficulties experienced by Congress in the 20th century and the refusal of the major parties to divide sharply on principle have also forced more authority on the President. Perhaps the most important circumstance of all has been the conversion of the Presidency to an office greatly admired and trusted by the people.

None of these circumstances would have had such influence on the Presidency if strong, alert, capable men had not occupied the office. The list of Presidents is a spotty one, yet in it can be found a substantial number of notable men.

The first President, George Washington, was also the first notable President. With the aid of Thomas Jefferson and especially of Alexander Hamilton, whose role as Secretary of Treasury went beyond administration to the forming of high policy in every field, he brought the words of Article II to life and rendered the Presidency acceptable to men of all factions. By lending his fame and dignity to the untried office of President he gave it prestige, by acting forcefully on such occasions as the proclamation of neutrality in 1793 and the Whisky Rebellion of 1794 he demonstrated its power, and by observing carefully the limits of his own authority he proved the point that Hamilton had argued in *The Federalist:* that strong executive power was "consistent with the genius of republican government." Of all Washington's contributions to the Presidency, his observance of the forms and spirit of the Constitution, symbolized by his refusal to serve beyond two terms, was perhaps most important.

The Presidency went into a long decline in the next three decades. John Adams was a doughty figure with lofty notions of executive independence, but he lacked Washington's self-confidence, tact, and aura of legitimacy. Thomas Jefferson, a notable President because of his skillful leadership of Congress, weakened the office for those who followed him by the very success of his highly personal, behind-the-scenes methods. The purchase of Louisi-ana, however, was a major precedent for future assertions of presidential authority. Neither Madison, Monroe, nor J. Q. Adams enjoyed the political ascendancy of Jefferson, and under them the Presidency became much too closely identified with the cabinet and dependent upon Congress, a condition made visible in the establishment of the congressional caucus as the chief source of candidates for the office.

Andrew Jackson's tenure was a virtual remaking of the Presidency. He re-established its independence of Congress, especially through his bold use of the veto power, and gained absolute command over the cabinet. Most important, he converted the Presidency into a popular office, relying heavily upon the fact that he was the first President who could claim to have been elected by the people. So dramatic was his assertion of the presidential prerogatives that the party of the opposition styled itself the "Whigs," a title that harked back to the suspicions of executive power entertained by the men of the Revolution. Jackson, however, was in touch with the new realities of American democracy, and although the Presidency suffered another decline under the debilitating influence of the slavery issue, it never again fell to the low point it had reached under Monroe. James K. Polk is generally recognized as the most effective President between Jackson and Lincoln.

The highwater mark of the Presidency in the 19th century was set in the administration of Abraham Lincoln. In sharp contrast to the vacillating Buchanan, who had denied his own authority to coerce a state to remain in the Union, Lincoln drew upon his authority as commander-in-chief to set in motion a broad program aimed at crushing the rebellion. In the process of enlarging the army and navy beyond their statutory limits, closing the mails to "treasonable correspondence," authorizing the arrest of potential traitors, and suspending the writ of habeas corpus, he brought the power of the Presidency to a new plateau, and there, despite the protests of Congress, he kept it throughout the war. Few assertions of presidential authority have ever been so bold as Lincoln's issuance of the Emancipation Proclamation.

Lincoln, like Jefferson, left the Presidency temporarily enfeebled, and the pendulum of power and prestige swung sharply back toward Congress in the next three decades. Andrew Johnson was impeached and almost removed from office, General Grant failed badly to measure up to the high expectations of the country, and both Chester Alan Arthur and Benjamin Harrison found Congress in an unco-operative mood. Only R. B. Hayes and Grover Cleveland made better-than-average records, chiefly by demonstrating their independence of Congress in controversial matters. The last President of the 19th century, William McKinley, was a man of solid virtues who had much success in dealing with a Congress whose temper he shared and whose leaders he knew well.

The first President of the 20th century, Theodore Roosevelt, was quite another kind of leader. A historian of considerable merit, he liked to separate the Presidents of the past into the "Jackson-Lincolns" and the "Buchanans." Throughout his years he did his best to join the first of these groups, and his maneuverings in diplomacy, his leadership of Congress, and his constant preaching to the people from the "bully pulpit" of the White House did much to shift the center of gravity in the government back to the Presidency. The ground broken by Roosevelt in his astute dealings with Congress was plowed deeper by Woodrow Wilson, a former professor who liked to think of himself as a kind of prime minister under obligation to mobilize the legislators in his party in support of a comprehensive program of progressive statutes. The undoubted successes of Wilson's first term have been overshadowed by the sad failures of the second, yet he carried the Presidency to new moral and political heights. His journey to Europe in December, 1918, was a herald of the world leadership destined to fall upon the Presidency during and after World War II. The strength of Wilson's days can be measured in the weakness of those that followed; few Presidents left so faint a mark on history as did Warren G. Harding and Calvin Coolidge.

No President, not even Washington or Lincoln, left so vivid a mark as did Franklin Roosevelt, the first (and presumably the last) to be elected not merely two or even three but four times to the office. Roosevelt achieved his universal reputation as a "strong President" by rising enthusiastically to two demanding occasions: the Great Depression, against which he directed a congressional assault that spread dozens of notable new laws on the statute-books, and World War II, in which he acted like a combination of Lincoln and Wilson in his breath-taking assertions of constitutional power and forceful leadership of Congress. Like these two men, he was an acknowledged master of politics who used his mastery for great ends, and thereby proved that political skill is an important ingredient of presidential effectiveness. Unlike them, he died as he lived: a figure around whom controversy swirled intensely.

Roosevelt was the first strong-minded and effective President whose successor did not suffer, sadly or gladly, a sharp decline in status and authority. By the time that Harry S. Truman succeeded to the Presidency in 1945, the office had become so clearly the center of gravity of the American government that it resisted all efforts to reduce it to an abode for "Buchanans." Truman overcame a woeful lack of preparedness for the position, a lack that must be largely blamed upon Roosevelt's failure to instruct him, and went on to become one of the most forceful Presidents in American history. His successor, General Eisenhower, was less "strong" a President, but no one could deny that he occupied a strong

Presidency. Perhaps the most noteworthy aspect of his tenure was the fact that, despite his immense popularity, he was faced by a Democratic Congress in 6 of his 8 years. This Congress proved itself unusually co-operative, and many Americans have expressed the pragmatic opinion that the purposes of 20th century America may be served by a division of the White House and the Capitol between the two major parties.

The Presidency, it may be seen, is eminently a product of history, and no quality of the successful President is more evident or essential than a "sense of history." As he bends to his demanding tasks of diplomacy, command, administration, legislation, politics, public opinion, and ceremony, he cannot help being conscious of the mighty examples of Washington, Jefferson, Jackson, Lincoln, Wilson, and the two Roosevelts. If he is now, in addition, a figure of importance for the whole world, it is because the United States has risen to a position of unimagined power. The strength of the Presidency is a reflection of the strength of the United States.

PRESIDIO was a Spanish institution established primarily to hold the frontiers in America against foreign aggressors and to protect the missions. *Presidios* were forts or posts where soldiers lived with their families and cultivated the land around them. The number of soldiers varied; along the northern frontier there were seldom more than fifty residing at a *presidio*. The *presidios* were not entirely self-supporting because they received subsidies from the viceroy of Mexico. They were located in California, Arizona, New Mexico, Texas, the West Indies, and Spanish Florida which at the time included Georgia and the Carolinas.

PRESQUE ISLE, FORT, was constructed on the shore of Lake Erie at the present site of Erie, Pa., under the direction of the engineer, Le Mercier, attached to the French command of Capt. Pierre Paul Marin. Work was begun in the late spring of 1753 and was completed in June or July of that year. Thenceforth to 1759, this fort of chestnut logs fifteen feet high, "about 120 feet square, a log house in each square [each corner], a gate to the southward and another to the N.ward," served as a base of operations for the further projection of the Pennsylvania line of French forts, LeBoeuf, Machault and Duquesne, and for the transportation of troops and supplies from Montreal to Duquesne. After the French abandoned it on Aug. 13, 1759, the British utilized it as a frontier outpost in dealing with hostile Indians of the region. During the general Indian uprising of 1763, however, the Indians captured the fort on June 22 and burned it. A subsequent fortification, designated as Presque Isle, was erected on a near-by site in the summer of 1795 to protect the commissioners who were laying out the town of Erie, but nothing was done to restore the original French fort.

PRESSURE GROUPS. Those organized minorities which seek to influence decisions concerning issues of public policy and administration are properly called pressure groups. Although most pressure groups represent special interests of one kind or another—organized labor or agriculture, business or industry, law or medicine—some are more ostensibly committed to broader interests of a civic or social nature. The League of Women Voters, for example, may be contrasted in this respect with the Middle Tennessee Burley Tobacco Growers, and the Americans for Democratic Action with the Association of Umbrella Manufacturers and Suppliers of America. Nearly all groups, however, strive to identify, or to reconcile, their own "special" interests with the "public" interest.

Most pressure groups are nonpartisan in their approach to decision makers. The partisan affiliation of a candidate or an incumbent in public office is less important than his attitude toward particular issues in which a pressure group is interested. Nevertheless it should be said that some pressure groups find their own interests more compatible with those of one party than another. Thus organized labor for many years has been generally pro-Democratic, whereas organized business and industry have been generally pro-Republican. Evidence of these partisan sympathies is discernible in the distribution of campaign contributions from members or officers of interest groups to the major parties.

Contributing to political campaigns, however, is but one of the methods used by pressure groups and their members to influence decision makers. Dissemination of propaganda in favor of certain candidates, factions, or officials and against their opponents is a common practice both during and between campaigns. Negotiation with and pressure upon party leaders are other methods employed.

Upwards of 1000 organizations maintain special representatives—so-called lobbyists—in Washington. At some state capitals the number of such representatives will run to several hundred. Among their more common duties are appearances before legislative committees, administrative bureaus, boards and commissions. Through almost daily contact with officials they consult with and advise decision makers concerning issues of policy and administration of special interest to their clients. Often they supply technical and specialized information to legislators and administrative officers. Occasionally they assist in drafting legislation, in formulating administrative rules and regulations, and in preparing draft decisions for the consideration of official decision makers.

Representatives of pressure groups also do a good deal of entertaining of key persons in political party organizations or in the public service. But the influence of the so-called "social lobby," although still important, is easily exaggerated, as are the frequent rumors one hears of open or covert bribery of public servants by agents of these "special interests."

Campaigns of "education" and propaganda on a state-wide, regional, or national scale are often carried on to create a friendly public opinion among rank and file citizens in whose hands, in final analysis, rests the fate of responsible public officials. It is not unusual for such campaigns to operate on "million-dollar budgets" and to make use of every known device of modern mass indoctrination and persuasion. Indeed, no small part of the daily content of mass communications media has its origin with specialized "public relations" personnel of pressure groups.

To reinforce their influence on decision makers, pressure groups often mobilize public opinion on a pending issue by inducing their own members and others, the so-called "folks back home," to send petitions, memorials, letters and telegrams of protest or commendation to public officials. On some critical issues, where extensive and powerful pressure groups are involved, such communications often run into hundreds of thousands within the space of a few days. In some cases delegations of influential persons are brought to the capital to present their pleas in person. Thus is implemented the constitutional "right of the people peaceably to assemble, and to petition the Government for a redress of grievances."

Although the literature on pressure groups is extensive, little scientific research has been done on the nature, processes and significance of political influence. It is often said that ease of access to decision makers is a crude measure of the influence of pressure groups and their representatives. But this is by no means always the case. Access to decision makers may be direct or indirect. Representatives of pressure groups may establish formal or informal face-to-face relations with public officials. They may also work through agents of other sympathetic groups, having easier access. Not infrequently professional "independent" counsel, schooled in the complex organization and procedures of the governmental process may be employed, sometimes on continuous retainer, sometimes on *ad hoc* assignments. When, as is often the case, such counsel are themselves former officials, then ease of access to decision makers may reflect a personal influence only coincidentally associated with the pressure group or groups they represent.

Although no accurate measure of the differential influence of pressure groups is available, some are patently more influential than others depending on (1) the size of the group, (2) its financial resources, (3) its internal cohesion, (4) its ability to mobilize public opinion in strategic political areas, (5) the quality of its leadership.

Pressure groups have played, and no doubt will continue to play, an important role in American political history. Countless illustrations could be cited of legislative and administrative decisions in the making of which the influence of organized pressure groups has been important if not decisive. So important, in fact, has "pressure politics" become in the process of government that the representatives of pressure groups have been collectively described as an "invisible government," and as a "Third House of the Legislature."

To those who view democracy as a direct relation between independent and rational individuals and their government, the influence and even the existence of organized pressure groups represents something sinister. Special interest groups clamoring for attention, seeking and often succeeding in exerting major influence in the decision-making process, seem inconsistent with the rule of the majority and the public interest which classical democratic theory assumes to be the goal of all legitimate government. Other students of democratic theory, however, see the governmental process as involving not only a dynamic interaction of individuals with one another and the political state, but also as a continuous effort by competing groups or "factions" to influence public decision makers along lines compatible with the special interests which group members share with one another. The public interest or the general welfare, they argue, is discoverable only when these "interest groups" are free to compete for access to decision makers either directly or indirectly through appeals to the general public or the electorate. In a pluralistic democratic society, pressure groups thus become major factors in a system of "countervailing powers" maintaining a kind of dynamic equilibrium which at any particular time corresponds to the public interest or public welfare.

To make sure that this group process of government operates in the open and with substantial equality of access for all groups, is a major problem for any democratic society. Constitutional guarantees of freedom of speech, press, and assembly are calculated to insure a "free competitive market for ideas." Legislation protecting the right to organize and bargain collectively, other laws against monopoly and unfair competition and against "corrupt practices" in election campaigns help to legalize and institutionalize the group process of government. More specifically are the laws which prohibit certain improper practices by "lobbyists" and require representatives of pressure groups to register and make public reports of their receipts and expenditures. Over thirty states and the Federal Government have such laws. Under Title III of the Legislative Reorganization Act of 1946, "lobbyists" seeking to influence Congress are required to register and report. Lack of any effective sanctions or methods of enforcement in these laws, their ambiguous terminology, and the narrow scope given to them by the Supreme Court have significantly reduced their effectiveness. Nevertheless they reflect a continuing concern in Congress and state legislatures to insure some measure of control over pressure groups in the process of government.

Pressure groups are no longer regarded as a unique feature of American politics. In recent years students of government have disclosed that no country is wholly free of this phenomenon.

PRIGG v. THE COMMONWEALTH OF PENNSYLVANIA (1842). In 1832 a slave fled from Maryland to Pennsylvania. Five years later Edward Prigg, an agent, seized her and, upon a magistrate's refusal to take cognizance of the case, returned her to the owner. Prigg was then indicted for kidnapping, in the York county court, under a Pennsylvania statute of 1826 relating to fugitive slave labor. Judgment for the Commonwealth was affirmed by the supreme court of Pennsylvania in 1840. The State of Maryland then prosecuted a writ of error to the Supreme Court. The unanimous opinion of the Court, written by Justice Story, declared the Pennsylvania statute unconstitutional because the Federal Fugitive Slave Act of 1793 superseded all state legislation on the subject. But the Court sharply divided over Story's statement that the power of Congress was so exclusive as to render invalid every state statute on the subject, a statement denounced by both proslavery and antislavery men. Many Northern states expressed dissatisfaction by passing so-called Personal Liberty Laws.

PRIMARY, DIRECT. Historically, the direct primary is the third major device employed by American democracy in making nominations to public office. It was preceded (1) by the congressional caucus which dated from the colonial period and was continued to about 1830; and (2) by the delegate convention which prevailed generally from 1830 to the beginning of the present century. Credit for the invention of the direct primary is ascribed to Crawford County, Pa., in which as early as 1842 power to make nominations was taken by the Democratic party from the county convention and placed in the hands of the voters. Hailed as a revival of true democracy, the "Crawford County Plan" was adopted subsequently by many counties in Middle, Western and Southern states. In all cases, however, it rested solely on the basis of local party rules. Not until 1903 was the principle of nomination by direct vote of party members enacted into law by the legislature of Wisconsin acting under the influence of LaFollette progressives. At present the direct primary has been established by law in all but three of the states.

Like the initiative, referendum and recall the operation of the direct primary begins with the circulation of petitions which must be signed by a certain number or percentage of the voters of a party in the local government district or state concerned. Requirements range from five signatures in the case of minor local offices to a thousand or more for higher state offices. In a number of states percentages of the party vote ranging from ½% to 4% are required.

Candidates who receive the required number of signatures thereby gain the right to have their names printed upon the official ballot, decision among them following by vote of party members at the ensuing primary election. Direct primaries are of two kinds, "open" or "closed." The former, used in Wisconsin and Montana, impose no test of party allegiance. In closed primaries, which are becoming the general rule, some evidence of party affiliation is required of the voter.

PRIMOGENITURE. In general, primogeniture implies seniority by birth though legally it connotes the right of the eldest son to inherit the estate of a parent to the exclusion of all other heirs. Its wide use in mediaeval England followed the introduction of Continental feudalism by the Normans who stressed the wishes of a lord to keep his holdings intact so as to insure the rents, fees and military services arising from these tenures. Otherwise, a vassal might distribute his tenure among his sons in a way that would defeat the economic basis of the feudal structure. By the 14th century practically all free tenures were subject to primogeniture, though by a statute of 1540 land held in fee simple, as well as many feudal tenures, could be willed. Feudal tenures were abolished in 1662, since which all freehold land could be willed. By this time feudalism, except for the manorial system, had seen its best days. And while feudalism influenced institutional development in America, it was chiefly in its manorial aspects that primogeniture affected the New World.

Primogeniture existed in all of the original thirteen colonies. In New England, except for Rhode Island, stout opposition gradually reduced this form of inheritance so that by the Revolution it had practically disappeared. In Massachusetts, however, the parent had to will a double share to the eldest son. This was also true of Pennsylvania. In New York and the Southern colonies, where economic and social forces favored large estates, primogeniture generally prevailed, much to the dissatisfaction of those who viewed the institution as an alien and undesirable practice. The movement for free and equitable inheritance was fostered by those sponsoring the American Revolution. Stimulated by the democratic philosophy of Thomas Jefferson, the Virginia assembly attacked the system and finally in 1785 abolished it. Georgia and North Carolina had done the same in 1777 and 1784 respectively. The other states followed this lead, though it was not until 1798 that Rhode Island abolished primogeniture. Since that date primogeniture has not operated in America, though in some states entailed estates descend to the eldest son.

PRINCETON, BATTLE OF (Jan. 3, 1777). Leaving three regiments at Princeton, Cornwallis arrived at the Delaware toward sunset, Jan. 2, to avenge Trenton. Here he found Washington's army of 5000 men occupying a precarious position along Assunpink Creek. Convinced the latter had no means of escape and ignoring Sir William Erskine's counsel to attack immediately, he decided to "bag him" in the morning. Washington, advised by St. Clair, executed a brilliant military maneuver. At midnight, leaving his camp fires burning, he quietly withdrew his main body along an unpicketed road, and gained the British rear. Approaching Princeton, about daybreak, the Americans encountered a force under Col. Mawhood, just leaving that village to join Cornwallis. Gen. Mercer's brigade engaged Mawhood's troops at close range but was driven back with the bayonet. Rallied by Washington and joined by new arrivals, the patriots, with deadly rifle fire, drove the enemy from the field and village with losses estimated between 400 and 600 in killed, wounded and prisoners. Cornwallis, outgeneraled, withdrew his entire army in feverish haste to New Brunswick to save a £70,000 war chest, while Washington, his army wearied, took up a strong position at Morristown, having freed New Jersey and infused new life and hope into a cause that appeared all but lost.

PRINCETON UNIVERSITY. Founded in 1746 as the College of New Jersey, Princeton was the fourth college established in the British colonies. It was inspired by the Great Awakening, and six of the seven original trustees were leaders in the New Light faction of the Presbyterian Church. The first president was the Rev. Jonathan Dickinson; the first classes were held at his home in New Brunswick. On his death the institution was transferred to Newark, and the Rev. Aaron Burr (the father of Jefferson's Vice-President) became the second president. In 1756 the college was moved to the town of Princeton, and Nassau Hall, the first building, was erected to the plans of Robert Smith of Philadelphia. This progress might not have been possible if still another Presbyterian minister, the Rev. Gilbert Tennent, had not succeeded in raising funds in England and Scotland.

Princeton played a distinguished role in the American Revolution. The Scottish divine John Witherspoon, president from 1768 to 1794, was one of the signers of the Declaration of Independence, and one out of every six members of the Constitutional Convention was a Princeton graduate. James Madison of the class of 1771 was the first Princetonian to become President of the United States.

The highly respected physicist Joseph Henry was made professor of natural philosophy as early as 1832. A graduate college was launched in 1877 under the presidency of James McCosh. But Princeton's faculty was strengthened and her academic prestige enhanced in the fullest manner by Woodrow Wilson, who became president in 1902, six years after the college was renamed Princeton University.

Wilson introduced the "preceptorial" system of instruction, under which small groups of students meet to discuss together their assigned reading under the guidance of a member of the faculty. He urged dividing the college into smaller segments, "quadrangles" (a system later adopted by Harvard and Yale thanks to the generosity of Edward Stephen Harkness), but he was unsuccessful in this effort.

The University grew, both in physical facilities, faculty and curriculum under the presidencies of John Grier Hibben (1912–33) and Harold Willis Dodds (1933–57), but the enrollment has remained relatively small (3000 undergraduates and 850 graduate students). Robert Francis Goheen became the 16th president of Princeton in 1957.

PRINCIPIO COMPANY. A bloomery forge, built in Maryland in 1715 at the head of the Chesapeake Bay, was the origin of the Principio Iron Works. In 1718 the first quantity of bar iron exported from the colonies to England was made at this forge. In 1722 the members of the Principio Company included Joseph Farmer, Stephen Onion, William Chetwynd, Joshua Gee, William Russell, John England and John Ruston, English capitalists, ironmasters and merchants. They built the Principio Furnace, which went into operation in 1724. The next year the company made an agreement with Augustine Washington, father of George Washington, by which the former became a member of the company. Mines were opened on Washington's lands and the Accokeek Furnace, Virginia, was built. On the death of Augustine Washington, Lawrence Washington fell heir to his father's iron interests. Not long after the death of Lawrence in 1752, the company abandoned the Accokeek Furnace. By this time the company owned the Principio Furnace and Forge, North East Forge, Kingsbury Furnace and Lancashire Furnace, all in Maryland. Though changes occurred from time to time in the partnership through death and the sale of interests, the company remained intact until the Revolution. In 1780 when Maryland confiscated British property within the state, the existence of the company came to an end. The Washington interests as well as those of Thomas Russell were not affected, since they were loyal to the American cause.

PRINTING IN AMERICA. Printing was first introduced into the Americas in Mexico City, certainly in 1539 by Juan Pablos and perhaps still earlier by Esteban Martín. These early dates are accounted for by the interest of the church authorities in providing books of devotion for the religious instruction of the Indians. For details of the history of the press in Latin America see *La Imprenta en México*, and other works by José Toribio Medina.

The first press in English-speaking North America was landed late in 1638 and set up early in 1639 in Cambridge, Mass. The press, types, paper and workmen to operate the equipment were brought to this country by Jose Glover, a nonconformist English clergyman who visited the Massachusetts Bay Colony and, deciding to make it his home, returned to England to get his family. Because he believed a printing press would be helpful to the colony and to the newly established Harvard College, he acquired the printing equipment in England and brought it with him on the return trip.

Glover died on this return trip, but his widow had the press set up by Stephen Day and his two sons, who had been employed in England for this purpose. The first job known to have been printed was the single-sheet Freeman's Oath; the second an almanac for 1639. No copies of either are known to have survived. The third product of the press was a consequential volume of local authorship as well as printing, *The Whole Booke of Psalmes*, which was newly translated from the Hebrew by the local Cambridge divines. This ambitious volume appeared in 1640 and constitutes the earliest extant product of the press in what is now the United States.

The books and pamphlets produced by the earliest Massachusetts printers were religious in character. The crowning achievement of the early Cambridge press was the printing of the entire text of the Bible translated into the Massachusetts Indian language by Rev. John Eliot. This book was completed in 1663, being printed by Samuel Green and Marmaduke Johnson.

In 1682 William Nuthead set up a press in Virginia and began to print, but the colonial governor, Sir William Berkeley, promptly suppressed the enterprise before Nuthead's first publication was completed. The printer then moved to Maryland, where he is known to have printed at least as early as 1685, and probably earlier.

Pennsylvania was the third colony to have a press, William Bradford setting up a printing office in Philadelphia in 1685. Wearied by interference by the religious and civil authorities, he moved in 1693 to New York, becoming the first printer in that city and colony.

From this point onward the most important products of the early presses became colonial laws, gubernatorial proclamations and other public documents. Connecticut's first laws were sent to Massachusetts to be printed, but in 1709 the colony secured its first press, set up at New London by Thomas Short.

Demand for the printing of laws and documents was responsible for the establishment of presses in South Carolina in 1731, in North Carolina in 1749 and in Georgia in 1763. The French king granted exclusive license to print in his American colony of Louisiana to Denis Braud, whose first duty was the melancholy one of printing in 1764 the notice of the transfer of that colony to Spanish sovereignty.

In the latter half of the 18th century the initial function of a printer was usually the production of a newspaper. Thus it was in New Hampshire in 1756, in Georgia in 1763, in Florida in 1783, in what is now the District of Columbia in 1789.

The westward migration of the printing press is told in the article on Newspapers. Where the dates of the first presses were far in advance of normal settlement, or of settlement accelerated by the discovery of gold or other metals, we find that evangelistic zeal was responsible for their establishment. Thus the young Baptist missionary Jotham Meeker took a press to Kansas in 1834 to educate and convert the Indians. Printing began at Union, now in Oklahoma, in 1835, to provide for the spiritual and educational needs of the transplanted Cherokee Indians, and devoted missionaries set up a press in 1839 in what is now Idaho to evangelize the Nez Percés.

The establishment of governmental functions in newly formed territories was the other important influence responsible for the spread of the press throughout the Middle West.

The following schedule gives the dates of the first printing in each state, and the name of the first printer, in accordance with the present state of knowledge on this subject:

ALABAMA
1807: [Wakefield] "On the Mobile." Printer unidentified
ARIZONA
1859: Tubac: Jack Sims and George Smithson (?)
ARKANSAS
1819: Arkansas Post: William Edward Woodruff
CALIFORNIA
1834: Monterey: Agustín V. Zamorano (minor printing at earlier dates)
COLORADO
1859: Denver ("Cherry Creek"): William Newton Byers
CONNECTICUT
1709: New London: Thomas Short
DELAWARE
1761: Wilmington: James Adams
DISTRICT OF COLUMBIA
1789: Georgetown: Charles Fierer
FLORIDA
1783: Saint Augustine: John and William Charles Wells
GEORGIA
1763: Savannah: James Johnston
IDAHO
1839: Lapwai: Edwin O. Hall
ILLINOIS
1814: Kaskaskia: Matthew Duncan
INDIANA
1804: Vincennes: Elihu Stout
IOWA
1836: Dubuque: John King and William Carey Jones
KANSAS
1834: Shawanoe Mission: Jotham Meeker
KENTUCKY
1787: Lexington: John and Fielding Bradford

LOUISIANA
1764: New Orleans: Denis Braud
MAINE
1785: Falmouth: Benjamin Titcomb and Thomas Baker Wait
MARYLAND
1685: Saint Marys: William Nuthead
MASSACHUSETTS
1639: Cambridge: Stephen Day
MICHIGAN
1796: Detroit: John McCall
MINNESOTA
1849: Saint Paul: James M. Goodhue
MISSISSIPPI
1798?: Walnut Hills: Andrew Marschalk
MISSOURI
1808: Saint Louis: Joseph Charless
MONTANA
1863: Virginia City: Daniel W. Tilton
NEBRASKA
1847: [Omaha]: Unidentified Mormon printer
NEVADA
1858: Genoa: William L. Jernegan and Alfred James
NEW HAMPSHIRE
1756: Portsmouth: Daniel Fowle
NEW JERSEY
1723?: Perth Amboy?: William Bradford
NEW MEXICO
1834: Santa Fe: Jesús María Baca
NEW YORK
1693: New York City: William Bradford
NORTH CAROLINA
1749: New Bern: James Davis
NORTH DAKOTA
1864: Fort Union: S. C. Winegar and ——— Goodwin
OHIO
1793: Cincinnati: William Maxwell
OKLAHOMA
1835: Union: John F. Wheeler
OREGON
1846: Oregon City: Oregon Printing Association (John Fleming, printer)
PENNSYLVANIA
1685: Philadelphia: William Bradford
RHODE ISLAND
1727: Newport: James Franklin
SOUTH CAROLINA
1731: Charleston: George Webb
SOUTH DAKOTA
1858: Sioux Falls: Samuel J. Albright
TENNESSEE
1791: Rogersville: George Roulstone and Robert Ferguson
TEXAS
1817: Galveston: Samuel Bangs
UTAH
1849: Salt Lake City: Brigham H. Young

VERMONT
    1781: Westminster: Judah Padock Spooner and Timothy Green
VIRGINIA
    1682: Jamestown: William Nuthead
WASHINGTON
    1852: Olympia: James W. Wiley and Thornton F. McElroy
WEST VIRGINIA
    1790: Shepherdstown: Nathaniel Willis
WISCONSIN
    1833: Green Bay: Albert G. Ellis and John V. Suydam
WYOMING
    1863: Fort Bridger: Hiram Brundage

PRINTING PRESS, EARLY AMERICAN. For over 100 years printing in America was on presses imported from Europe. Then in 1750 Christopher Sower of Germantown, Pa., contrived a press for himself; but American manufacture did not begin until 1769 when Isaac Doolittle, a clock-maker of New Haven, Conn., built a press for William Goddard of Philadelphia. About 1800, however, Adam Ramage, a Scotsman, began to manufacture in Philadelphia the presses which bore his name. All of these presses were of the primitive plan, operated by a hand lever which applied pressure to the platen by a central screw, held in a framework of wood. Ramage improved the press, enlarged the screw and used more metal parts. He adapted or copied European innovations, and carried on an extensive manufacture. In 1813 George Clymer made his Columbian press which substituted direct leverage for the screw; and Otis Tuft used a toggle joint in place of the screw. Other press makers were John I. Wells of Hartford, and Samuel Rust and Peter Smith of New York. The latter brought out the Washington hand press, but sold the patent in 1825 to R. Hoe and Company. The power press was then coming into use, but these hand presses were used in smaller offices for many years.

The first regular manufacture of type in America was by Abel Buell of Killingworth, Conn., whose foundry was aided by the Connecticut assembly, although various printers had made sorts before this time. German type was cast in 1770 by Christopher Sower, Jr., of Germantown. That of Binny and Ronaldson of Philadelphia in 1796 was the first extensive type foundry in America.

PRISON CAMPS, NORTHERN, IN CIVIL WAR. During the first months of the Civil War, most prisoners were released on parole, but officers captured were confined in Forts Warren, Lafayette, McHenry, on Governors Island, at Camp Chase, Ohio, at McDowell's College in St. Louis and the penitentiary at Alton, Ill. This proving unsatisfactory, in October, 1861, Lt. Col. W. H. Hoffman was appointed Commissary General of Prisoners, and began preparations of a prison camp at Johnson's Island in Lake Erie. The fall of Fort Donelson gave the North more prisoners than could be cared for on the island, and only officers were sent there. Enlisted men were confined at Camps Douglas in Chicago, Butler in Springfield, Morton at Indianapolis, Randall at Madison, and Chase at Columbus. Except Camp Randall, these former training camps became more or less permanent prisons. In addition, before the war closed, camps were established at Elmira, N.Y., Point Lookout, Md., Fort Delaware, and Rock Island, Ill. Prisoners were confined in barracks, closely guarded, and given regulation army rations. Savings from rations went into a camp fund to supply books, entertainment and hospital facilities. Although Southerners attempted to circulate atrocity stories about conditions in the prisons there were no unusual hardships imposed until 1863 when Secretary Stanton ordered reduction in rations until Northern prisoners were receiving "Precisely similar treatment . . . in respect to food, clothing, medical treatment, and other necessities" to that accorded Union prisoners held by the South. Under the regime of retaliation, disease and death increased in Northern prison camps until the total casualties approximated those in Southern prisons. In the last months of the war an agreement was made for each side to supply its soldiers in the enemy prison camps. Shipments of cotton to the North enabled the Confederates to furnish rations and clothing to Northern prisoners.

PRISON-SHIPS were used by both Americans and British during the Revolution for confining naval prisoners. The former maintained such ships at Boston and New London, and the latter at Halifax, Antigua, and at Wallabout Bay, Brooklyn. Conditions varied greatly according to the character of the officers and subordinates in charge, but the ships moored in Wallabout Bay, particularly the *Jersey*, became notorious for the harsh treatment accorded the captives. Provisions were scanty, of bad quality and poorly cooked. Fever and dysentery prevailed, the guards were brutal, and at night the prisoners, both able-bodied and sick, were herded below decks in intolerable heat and stench. Both Washington and the Continental Congress protested against this treatment, and Vice Admiral John Byron, Royal Navy, labored hard to better conditions. At least thirteen different prison-ships were moored in Wallabout Bay or in the East or North Rivers from 1776 to 1783. It has been estimated that some 11,500 men died on these ships.

PRIVATEERS AND PRIVATEERING. While the operations of Hawkins, Drake and other Elizabethan freebooters are often taken as the starting point in the history of privateering in America, the private-armed participation of American colonists in the wars of England practically began with King William's War (1689–97). During Queen Anne's War (1702–13) a considerable number of privateers were commissioned by the colonial governors, but relatively few took to the sea during the short war with Spain in 1718. Under royal warrants the American governors in 1739 again issued letters of marque and reprisal against Spain. In King George's War (1744–48) privateering began to assume the proportions of a major maritime business; and it is said that during the French and Indian War (1754–63) 11,000 Americans were engaged in private-armed operations.

Upon the commencement of hostilities with the mother country in 1775, most of the colonies, notably Massachusetts and Rhode Island, issued letters of marque and reprisal; and the Continental Congress three months before the Declaration of Independence sanctioned privateering "against the enemies of the United Colonies." The 1151 privateers of the Revolution captured about 600 British vessels, of which 16 were men-of-war. During the last three years of the war, the privateers carried the brunt of sea operations. By 1781 there were in commission only three public cruisers, but 449 private-armed cruisers mounting 6735 guns were in service. Although the operations of the privateers had been not only financially profitable but also an invaluable aid to the navy, the Government soon joined the sentimental movement in Europe for the abolition of privateering, but abandoned it in 1798 in the face of the arrogant depredations of armed vessels sailing under the authority of republican France. The Congress met the issue first (act of June 25) by allowing American merchantmen to arm themselves for defensive purposes, and then (act of July 9) by authorizing them to apply for special commissions to make offensive war on all armed French vessels. By the close of 1798, at least 428 merchantmen had been armed, probably three fourths of which had received official commissions; and before the close of hostilities in 1801, upward of 1000 vessels had been armed. As the armed merchantmen were not allowed to prey on unarmed commerce, fighting was generally secondary to trading; nevertheless, there were some notable encounters and valuable captures. In the War of 1812, 515 letters of marque and reprisal were issued, under which 1345 British vessels are known to have been taken. While all the seaboard states from Maine to Louisiana sent privateers to sea against England in one or both of these wars, Massachusetts led with a total of at least 457, Maryland followed with 281, and New Jersey and North Carolina closed the column with probably not more than four each.

With the return of world peace in 1815, many American and European privateers were unwilling to return to peaceful pursuits; some took service in Latin-American revolutions, and others became pirates. For the next 25 years the U. S. Navy was much engaged in the suppression of piracy. The Republic of Texas resorted to privateering in the early stage (1835–37) of its protracted war with Mexico. The United States with its naval superiority did not find it expedient to issue letters of marque and reprisal during the Mexican War. The United States declined to accede to the Declaration of Paris (1856), outlawing privateering among the principal world powers; but when the Confederate States issued letters of marque, Lincoln endeavored to treat the Confederate privateersmen as pirates until he was checked by retaliatory measures. The privateersmen sailing from Louisiana and the two Carolinas in 1861 enjoyed as profitable cruises as their brothers of 1812; but Confederate privateering declined after the first year, and a volunteer naval system was instituted. The United States' attempt at privateering in 1863 proved abortive, likewise Chile's attempt against Spain in 1865; and privateering ended throughout the world with the downfall of the Confederacy.

PRIVY COUNCIL. In the performance of its duties the English Crown acted on the advice of the Privy Council, which, at the time English colonization began in America in the 17th century, filled a place roughly corresponding to that filled now by the cabinet. This body of royal councillors contained all of the ministers of state, who held leading positions in administration. Its sphere of activity was approximately co-extensive with all the Empire, and, as colonies grew up, they fell, naturally, under the special care of the council. The duty of hearing appeals from colonial courts, together with receiving colonial laws referred to it for approval or veto, became the duty of the council. And, successive bodies formed for the oversight of the colonies, culminating in the Board of Trade and Plantations of 1696, were either committees of the Privy Council, or boards acting under its control and reporting to it.

PRIZE MONEY was derived from the sale of a captured ship or cargo. Generally privateers received the entire net proceeds, the officers and crew of a warship one half, shared according to pay. Captures in the Revolution and the War of 1812 sometimes were worth $500,000 and gave the captain $15,000 and the Negro waiters $1121. Privateering was abolished by the Declaration of Paris in 1856, but Union blockaders earned large amounts during the Civil War. The largest, according to Gideon Welles, was Rear Admiral S. P. Lee's $150,000. Prize money was finally abolished by Congress on March 3, 1899.

PROCLAMATION OF 1763 was prepared in part by Lord Shelburne, president of the Board of Trade, but was completed after his resignation by his successor, Lord Hillsborough, and was proclaimed by the Crown on Oct. 2. By it parts of the territory in America acquired at the Treaty of Paris were organized as the provinces of Quebec, East Florida, West Florida and Grenada, the laws of England were extended to the provinces, and provision was made for the establishment of general assemblies in them. Settlement within the new provinces was encouraged by grants of land to British veterans of the French and Indian War.

The part of the proclamation most significant for American history, however, was that aimed at conciliating the Indians. The governors of the provinces and colonies were forbidden to grant lands "for the present, and until our further Pleasure be known . . . beyond the Heads or Sources of any of the Rivers which fall into the Atlantic Ocean from the West and North West." An Indian reservation was thus established south of the lands of the Hudson's Bay Company, west of the province of Quebec and the Appalachian Mountains, and north of the line of the Floridas, the 31st parallel. Settlement upon the Indian lands was prohibited, and settlers already upon such lands were commanded "forthwith to remove themselves." Furthermore, private purchases of land from the Indians were forbidden, those that had been made in the Indian reservation were voided, and future purchases were to be made officially, by the governor of the colony involved, for the Crown alone. Indian traders were to be licensed and to give security to observe such regulations as might be promulgated.

Though the proclamation was issued hurriedly at the time of Pontiac's War the sections relating to the Indian lands and Indian trade had been maturely considered. For more than a decade successive ministries had been dissatisfied with the management of Indian relations by the different colonies. The rivalry of the colonies for Indian trade, and in some cases for western lands, had led to abuses by the governors of their power over trade and land grants. Attempting to advance their own interests or those of their respective colonies, they ignored the interests of the Indians and aroused a justified resentment. The success of the French in conciliating the Indians was an argument in favor of a unified system of imperial control of Indian affairs and the restriction of settlement.

The appointment in 1756 of two superintendents of Indian affairs, for the northern and southern districts, was the first step toward the home government's control of Indian relations. Thereafter the letters of Sir William Johnson, superintendent of the northern Indians, informed the Board of Trade of Indian grievances and urged the fixing of a line west of which settlement should be prohibited. The danger from the Indians during the French and Indian War automatically fixed such a line at the Appalachian Mountains, and after the war proclamations by the military authorities continued this line. Settlers, however, disregarding the proclamations, swarmed over the mountains, and their encroachments were one of the causes of Pontiac's War. The Proclamation of 1763 was an attempt to check the advance of settlement until some agreement securing the Indians' consent to such settlement could be made. It fixed the line temporarily at the watershed—

a conspicuous landmark—but did not and was not intended to change the boundaries of the old colonies; nevertheless, it was resented in the colonies as an interference in their affairs. After Pontiac's War, negotiations with the Indians resulted in the treaties of Hard Labor, Fort Stanwix and Lochaber, by which a new line, more acceptable to the colonists, was drawn; and in 1774 the Quebec Act added the remainder of the reservation north of the Ohio to the province of Quebec.

PROGRESSIVE MOVEMENT (1908–24) had its roots in the political and social philosophy prevalent about 1908, when Theodore Roosevelt dominated the Republican party and the Bryan element had recovered the leadership in the Democratic party. The failure of Taft, elected in 1908, to carry out the Roosevelt policies, brought severe criticism from a group of western Republicans and induced an "insurgent" movement in Congress which manifested itself particularly in a revolt against the Payne-Aldrich Tariff Bill, and against dictatorial powers of the Speaker, these revolts being led in the House by George W. Norris of Nebraska and Victor Murdock of Kansas, and in the Senate by Beveridge of Indiana, Dolliver and Cummins of Iowa and LaFollette of Wisconsin. A National Republican Progressive League was formed on Jan. 21, 1911, at the Washington residence of Sen. LaFollette, a program of progressive measures was agreed upon, and LaFollette was brought out as the progressive candidate against Taft for the Republican presidential nomination. Later LaFollette was shelved for Roosevelt, Taft won renomination after a bitter campaign and a violently contested convention, and Roosevelt organized the Progressive party. The resulting split in the Republican party gave an easy victory to the Democrats, now definitely under progressive control, and there followed, under President Wilson, a period of thoroughly progressive legislation until interrupted by World War I. The progressive movement was revived after the war, being manifested in renewed insurgency in Congress, the organization of the Agricultural and Progressive Blocs, and finally the launching by LaFollette of his Progressive party in 1924. LaFollette's defeat and later death, together with the conservative control of both parties after 1924, practically ended the progressive movement as originally conceived, although it may be said to have been revived around new issues and in a more far-reaching manner in the New Deal led by Franklin D. Roosevelt.

PROHIBITION. The ratification of the Eighteenth Amendment, Jan. 29, 1919, and the subsequent enactment by Congress of the Volstead Act, marked the culmination of a long campaign in the United States against the liquor traffic. Although the origin of the movement is to be found in colonial protests against the excessive use of intoxicants, the temperance crusaders did not turn from moral suasion to legal coercion until the middle of the 19th century. Three periods of legislative activity thereafter are apparent. Between 1846 and 1855, following the lead of Maine, thirteen states passed prohibitory laws. Within a decade, however, nine of these measures either had been repealed or had been declared unconstitutional. After Kansas in 1880 had written prohibition into its constitution, there was a revival, stimulated by the persistent efforts of the Prohibition party (1869), the Woman's Christian Temperance Union (1874) and, most powerful of all, the Anti-Saloon League (1893). Again results were impermanent, for by 1905 only Kansas, Maine, Nebraska and North Dakota were prohibition states.

The failure of the brewers and distillers to set their houses in order, and the judicious political tactics of the Anti-Saloon League, prepared the way for the final drive to outlaw the saloon. A wide range of motivation influenced the voters, as they went to the polls under local option laws in the various states. The ardent reformers relentlessly pressed their arguments that the liquor interests represented a demoralizing force in American politics, that the mechanization of industry placed a premium upon the sober employee and that the taxpayer really paid the bills for a business which was filling the poorhouses and prisons with its victims. On the eve of the entrance of the United States into World War I, twenty-six states had prohibitory laws, of which thirteen could be described as "bone-dry." Wayne B. Wheeler, Ernest H. Cherrington and other leaders of the Anti-Saloon League, who had already mobilized the forces of evangelical Protestantism, were quick to associate prohibition with the winning of the war. Congressional action reinforced their arguments.

By December, 1917, both Senate and House had approved a resolution, originally proposed by Sen. Morris Sheppard of Texas, to add an amendment to the Constitution prohibiting the "manufacture, sale or transportation" of intoxicating liquors for beverage purposes. Within thirteen months ratification by the legislatures of three quarters of the states had been secured, and a year later the Eighteenth Amendment went into effect. Meanwhile, Congress had placed restrictions upon the manufacture of intoxicants, as a war measure to conserve grain, and had provided that from July 1, 1919, until the end of the war no distilled spirits, beer or wine should be sold for beverage purposes.

The opponents of prohibition soon directed their attack against the efforts of governmental agents to enforce the law. They approved the banishment of the saloon, but they insisted that it had been replaced by illegal "speakeasies" and night clubs. The illicit traffic in intoxicants was breeding "rum runners," racketeers and gangsters; corruption was rampant in Federal and state enforcement units; and disrespect

for all law was becoming a characteristic of those who flouted the liquor laws with impunity. The supporters of the Eighteenth Amendment, on the other hand, admitted that enforcement was far from perfect, but proclaimed prohibition's benefits—reduced poverty, increased bank deposits and expanding industry. For them it was a basic factor in the nation's prosperity from 1923 to 1929.

But popular disgust over the failure of enforcement grew so steadily, partly as a by-product of the depression, that the Democratic National Convention in 1932 demanded repeal of the Eighteenth Amendment. The Democratic landslide in the November elections persuaded Congress that the time for action had come. In the short session (Feb. 20, 1933) a resolution was approved providing for an amendment to accomplish repeal. Submitted to conventions in the several states, the Twenty-first Amendment was ratified within less than a year.

Before ratification Congress, on March 22, 1933, had legalized sale of beverages containing no more than 3.2% of alcohol, wherever state law did not contravene. Repeal ended the first experiment on the part of the American people in writing sumptuary legislation into the fundamental law of the land. The liquor problem was turned back to the states.

PROHIBITION PARTY, oldest of the third parties, was organized in 1869 after nearly three quarters of a century of temperance agitation had failed to impress the major parties. The campaign of 1872 marked its initial appearance in national politics. Nine states were represented at its first national convention in Columbus, Ohio, Feb. 22, 1872. James Black of Pennsylvania was nominated for President. Prior to 1872 candidates for state offices had been nominated in some states. In its early years the party was strongest in Ohio and New York, holding the balance of power in the latter in the presidential election of 1884. Candidates have appeared in every presidential campaign, although never winning an elector. The peak of its popular support was reached in 1892 with 271,000 votes, and the low ebb in 1928 with a total of 20,000. In 1896 the money question temporarily split the party.

Through its educational activities and its strong appeal to the moral sentiment of the people, the party exerted an influence for a more effective governmental policy toward the liquor problem. While its primary object has been the prohibition of the manufacture and sale of intoxicating liquors, it has advocated other political, economic and social reforms, many of which have been endorsed by the major parties.

PROMONTORY POINT, Utah, marked the dramatic completion of the first transcontinental railroad (May 10, 1869). A motley crowd gathered to witness final ceremonies. Following prayers and brief but grandiloquent speeches, President Leland Stanford of the Central Pacific nervously drove the last golden spike into a polished California laurel tie with a silver sledge hammer. Western Union telegraph apparatus was connected with the spike, and these final strokes were instantly heralded in all cities of the land. Two locomotives, *Juniper* and *119*, hastened to move forward until their noses touched; and a cheering crowd confirmed a single word telegram: "Done."

PROPERTY. The most important classification of property is that which divides it into real and personal. In general, real property has reference to land and things permanently attached to land, which are immovable or which ordinarily go with the land when it is conveyed, such as trees, buildings and fences. Personal property, on the other hand, has reference to all other property which is capable of ownership.

Another classification, cutting across both of the above classes, divides property into corporeal and incorporeal, the former referring to tangibles, such as land, livestock, implements, furniture, automobiles and the like, and the latter referring to intangibles, such as contract rights, franchises, claims against others because of personal injuries, notes, stocks, bonds, insurance policies and rights of action of various kinds. Corporeal personal property is also known as chattels or goods.

In a popular sense, property usually consists of concrete things or substances; but more frequently, in the eyes of the law, it consists of legal relations between a person called the owner and other people. The owner's legal rights constitute his property. Hence, when one owns property he has a "bundle of legal rights," the essential one of which is the power of more or less exclusive control. Such things as air, light, water in streams, birds, fish and wild animals, not being capable of exclusive control, are not capable of ownership, until reduced to possession.

The feudal system of land tenures introduced in England by William the Conqueror was based upon the theory that all land was owned by the king, who allotted it among his lords, who in turn parcelled out its use among the villeins, who tilled it. The interests thus created, however, were not absolute, but conditional upon military and other services being rendered to the lord and king. Through the years the rights of the lords to such services were gradually reduced by statutes, until a more or less absolute ownership (called free and common socage) was created in the villeins.

This was the type of land ownership in England when the American colonies were settled, and it was this system that was transplanted to America. Hence the American law of real property is based on that of England after the feudal system had disappeared. Though all land titles in the United States originate with the state, the state, having no right to services,

is not an overlord in the feudal sense. There are, however, important limitations on ownership of land. No type of ownership can be said to be absolute. An owner may not use his land in such a way as to create a nuisance or injure his neighbor. Property may be taken for taxes, and is subject to execution for the payment of debts. It is also liable to escheat in the event of the death of the owner without a will or heirs, and is subject to the power of eminent domain and to curtailment under the police power.

The subjection of both real and personal property to the police power is of growing importance. Public utilities, such as transportation, communication, electric light and power companies, are said to be businesses "affected with a public interest." In contradistinction to a strictly private business they must serve all who apply and are subject to close legislative regulation as to rates charged and quality of service rendered. Since a business is property, this constitutes an encroachment upon ownership. But the line between such a business and one that is said to be private has grown less distinct with the years. Many businesses formerly classed as private are now subject to such governmental supervision as the public interest seems to demand. A law prohibiting the manufacture and sale of intoxicants is valid, though it curtails the use of property devoted to distilling and brewing. Similarly, the laws prohibiting the slaughtering of cattle within certain areas, regulating the hours and wages of labor for women, prohibiting construction of business houses in specified zones have been held valid, though they restrict the use of property and sometimes materially reduce its value. These are but illustrations of the many ways in which individual private property rights may be invaded in the interest of the public welfare. Though state and Federal legislative power to curtail the use of private property is limited by the "due process" clauses of the Constitution, recent decisions indicate that this protection is less obstinate than formerly. Property interests once regarded as immune from interference have now been brought within the scope of legislative treatment, with the approval of the courts.

Though title to land or an interest therein may be acquired by adverse possession, statutes in all American states provide for the conveyance or transfer of land by deed, a document required to be signed by the grantor and delivered to the grantee.

Interests in land that are inheritable under the law, upon the death of the owner pass to the owner's heirs, in most states, or if there be a will, to the devisees named in it. Statutes in all American states provide for the recording in a public office, of deeds, mortgages and other instruments affecting title to land, so that notice may be given to the world of the facts relative to the title. Instruments not so recorded, though valid as between the parties to them, do not affect others who have no notice of them. A document in which are copied the various links in the chain of title so that the history of ownership may be examined is known as an Abstract of Title.

Title to personal property may be transferred by delivery merely or by agreement. No formal document of transfer comparable to a deed is usually required. An exception to this rule is found in the sale of automobiles. Statutes of most states now provide that such transfers require the delivery and registration of certificates of title. Upon the death of the owner of personal property, the title passes to the executor or administrator. The next of kin of the owner have no rights with respect to the property until the debts of the owner have been paid and the estate finally settled.

Statutes regarding property interests have been passed in all states. Many of them are simply a codification of certain common law rules. Others have materially changed the law. Examples of the latter are: the broadening of the scope of the term "heirs" by the abolition of the doctrine of primogeniture; the abolition or modification of the fee tail estate; the granting to married women of the power to own and control both real and personal property; the providing for a system of recording deeds, mortgages and other instruments affecting property titles; and the simplification of the form of such instruments.

As affecting the ownership and transfer of various types of personal property in the United States, a noteworthy movement is that in the direction of uniformity in the law of the various states. This is being brought about through enactment by the several states of identical statutes covering such subjects as negotiable instruments, bills of lading, warehouse receipts and the sales of goods.

PROPRIETARY AGENT. The Duke of York in New York, the Carolina board, Lord Baltimore in Maryland, and Penn in Pennsylvania found it necessary to employ agents to attend to colonial business both in London and in the province. Sir John Werden served as the Duke of York's agent in England and John Lewin went to the colony as special agent to report on financial conditions. Before 1700 Henry Darnall served Lord Baltimore as a private agent in Maryland and this office was continued through the colonial era. Proprietors frequently acted as their own agents in London. Until his health failed William Penn transacted in London all important business relating to his province. F. J. Paris frequently acted during the 18th century as London agent for the Penn family and other private interests. For long years James Logan was the efficient agent of William Penn and his sons in the Quaker colony, looking after the survey and sale of lands, the collection of proprietary revenue, and the management of estates.

PROPRIETARY PROVINCES. The proprietorship succeeded the trading company as a device employed

to build England's colonial empire. The proprietary provinces had a familiar precedent in English history, being patterned, in general, upon the ancient Palatinate of Durham in which the feudal lord enjoyed large powers which enabled him to guard the English border against Scotch forays. Originating in a royal grant bestowing broad territorial and political powers upon a single person or a small group (the lord proprietor or the lords proprietors), the proprietary province was virtually a feudal jurisdiction in which, with specified exemptions, the lord proprietor exercised sovereign powers. He could appoint all officials; create courts, hear appeals, pardon offenders; make laws, issue decrees; raise and command a militia; establish churches, ports and towns. The charters of Maryland and Pennsylvania contained the important limitation requiring the proprietor to make laws by and with the consent of the freemen. These provinces were, thus, feudal only in name. The proprietors were forced to hearken to the insistent demands of the people and to yield to them political privileges and powers. The land of the proprietary province, however, constituted a great private domain. The proprietor granted it to settlers on his own terms. He could mortgage it for debt, as William Penn did. New provinces could come into existence by subgrants. Estates could be transferred into new hands by purchase.

By 1630 the trading company venture of the Virginia Company had proved a failure, the Council for New England was moribund, and when the next important royal grant was made, that of Maryland to Lord Baltimore in 1632, it was of the feudal or proprietary type described above. And when, seven years later, Sir Ferdinando Gorges received a royal charter for Maine, as compensation for his part in the Council for New England, the grant was also of the feudal or proprietary type, and as such was sold by Gorges' heir, in 1678, to Massachusetts.

When, in 1664, an English fleet drove Dutch power from New Netherland the king granted the region, including what came to be known as New York, New Jersey and Delaware, to the Duke of York as a proprietary, but when, in 1688, the Duke became James II, New York, being the part still remaining in his hands, became a royal colony.

The area of New Jersey had, in 1664, been subgranted by the Duke of York to John, Lord Berkeley and Sir George Carteret, and in 1682 the Duke had subgranted Delaware to William Penn. In 1674 Berkeley sold his share of New Jersey for £1000 and West Jersey, as the region was known, soon came into the hands of a board of Quakers. In 1680 another group purchased East Jersey from the Carteret estate. The proprietary right, so far as the land is concerned, to both of these areas still exists in the Councils of the Proprietors of New Jersey.

By the charters of 1663 and 1665 a group of eight men, royal courtiers and colonial planters, received the broad area of Carolina in which two colonies came into existence under one board which continued until 1729 when the proprietors, wearying of the unprofitable colonial business, sold their proprietary rights to the king, with the exception of one parcel which came to be known as the Granville Grant.

Pennsylvania, founded under a charter issued to William Penn in 1681, was the last of the proprietary colonies. Thereafter the policy was definitely in the direction of the royal colony. At the outbreak of the Revolution there remained of the proprietary colonies only Pennsylvania and Delaware, in the hands of the Penn family, and Maryland, in the hands of the Calvert family.

The American Revolution cut the political ties between England and the colonies and thereby placed the ultimate power in the people of the several states. Popular and independent state governments were promptly created. It was certain that the great proprietary estates would be swept away in the flood of democracy. The great estates of the Penn and Calvert heirs were confiscated by the popular assemblies and disposed of in harmony with popular desires. The state governments were not generous in the process of confiscation. The largest estate was that of the Penn family valued at about one million pounds sterling. The legislature paid the Penns £130,000. The Maryland government gave Lord Baltimore £10,000 for the confiscated land, a sum deemed so inadequate that the British government paid him an additional £90,000. The Granville estate also passed into the control of the state.

A feudal and proprietary land system thus ceased to be. These great areas became public property. The legislatures abolished quitrents paid into the pockets of the proprietors. The land was sold in smaller portions, thus making for economic democracy. And the sale of confiscated lands helped to pay for the war.

PROSLAVERY LITERATURE. The weight of Southern public opinion was always in support of slavery. Even during the Revolutionary period, when natural rights philosophy was generally accepted, Southerners used "hackneyed arguments" in defense of slavery. Proslavery sentiment, quiescent for some years, became vocal after the heated sectional dispute over Missouri, and Whitemarsh R. Seabrook and Thomas Cooper, pioneers in the philosophical defense of slavery, touched upon almost every defense later used by the slavery apologists. They wrote that slavery was practically universal, was nowhere forbidden in the Bible, was profitable to the whites, and beneficial to the Negroes. Thomas R. Dew, however, penned the classic statement of the positive good theory in his *Review of the Debate in the Virginia Legislature of 1831 and 1832* (1832). William Harper, James Henry Hammond and William Gilmore Simms elaborated Dew's views but added little thereto in *The Pro-Slavery Argument* (1852). They attacked the theory

that all men are equal and possessed of natural rights, and argued that slavery was the ladder from barbarism to civilization. John C. Calhoun did much to secure the acceptance of this philosophy through his writings and speeches in Congress. Edmund Ruffin popularized similar views in his essays, and James D. B. DeBow circulated the philosophy in his *Review*. George Fitzhugh in *Sociology for the South* (1854) and *Cannibals All* (1857) argued that slavery was the best defense against socialism and communism. J. C. Nott and J. H. Van Evrie, noted physicians, added the weight of ethnology and medical science to the historical, social and Biblical defense of slavery, all of which ministers expounded from their pulpits.

PROTESTANT EPISCOPAL CHURCH is the name adopted after the Revolution by the body formerly known as the Church of England in the Colonies. Its first task when the war closed was to develop a national organization and obtain the episcopal succession. The latter objective was secured by the consecration of Samuel Seabury, of Connecticut, by Scottish bishops in 1784 and the consecration by English bishops of William White of Pennsylvania and Samuel Provoost of New York in 1787 and of James Madison of Virginia in 1790. A general convention, organized under the leadership of William White and William Smith, succeeded in uniting the whole church under one government in 1789.

During the years following, the Episcopal Church recovered slowly from the wounds of war until 1811, when a period of active revival began which brought it, by 1850, to sixth place among American denominations, the position it still holds. This was also a period of important institutional growth. The first seminary of the church was established in 1817, and a general missionary society was formed in 1820. Between 1810 and 1830, Sunday schools were started in most parishes. The winning of the Low Church party by the Evangelicals made that section of the church sympathetic to revivalism, though the High Churchmen opposed it.

The Oxford (Tractarian) Movement, an effort to restore Catholic ideals in the church, began in England in 1833 and came to America during the 1840's, gradually superseding the old High Church party and intensifying party conflict. After the Civil War, at the close of which the northern and southern parts of the church, necessarily divided by secession, were quickly reunited, the ecclesiastical controversy became yet more bitter when the younger Tractarians sought to introduce ritualistic practices in harmony with their doctrinal position.

The dispute culminated in the withdrawal of some Evangelicals to organize the Reformed Episcopal Church in 1873 and the passage of an antiritual canon by the general convention of 1874. The canon was never enforced and the controversy died down in the decades following, partly because the formation of a strong liberal group was directing the attention of the church to other issues, notably, social reform, church unity and the critical study of the Bible. After 1890 these objectives began to engage the interest of the Anglo-Catholics also, so that during the present century the church has shown a tendency toward unity upon a program of conservative liberalism in respect both to theological and social questions. The estimated inclusive membership of the Episcopal Church for 1957 was 3,042,286. The Reformed Episcopal Church had a membership of 8928.

PROVIDENCE PLANTATIONS is the original name for the first colonial settlement in Rhode Island, made by Roger Williams in June, 1636, and so called for "God's providence to him in his distress," after he fled from Massachusetts to escape persecution. Williams bought a large tract of land from the Indians, and in 1638 associated with himself twelve other settlers as a land company. A covenant was drawn up in 1637 providing for majority rule "only in civill things," that is, for religious liberty. The first home lots were laid out along the present North Main Street of Providence. Under the parliamentary charter of 1644, Providence was joined with Newport and Portsmouth as "The Incorporation of Providence Plantations in the Narragansett Bay in New England." A communal gristmill was established by John Smith in 1646. Thirty years later, during King Philip's War, the growing town of 1000 people suffered severely from Indian attack. Although not as important a center of colonial commerce as Newport, Providence began to develop wharves and warehouses in 1680. The city's first newspaper, the *Providence Gazette*, was established in 1762 by William Goddard, and in 1770 Rhode Island College (Brown University) moved there from Warren. The term "Providence Plantations" still remains as part of the official title of the State of Rhode Island.

PROVINCIAL CONGRESSES. The extralegal, or revolutionary, assemblies that sprang up in most of the colonies in the earlier stages of the American Revolution and became the agencies whereby the transition was effected from dependent colony to independent state are generally known as "provincial congresses," although in some instances the term "convention" was used. Some colonies preferred one, some the other. Distinct connotations seemed not yet to have crystallized, although there was some donning and doffing of the one title or the other, as if making a distinction. The word "convention" had had its part in the long struggle against autocratic power, but "congress," long used in the colonies to designate occasional or irregular assemblages of delegates or agents for purposes of a conference, was the more familiar term, if not also the more adaptable to these new purposes. New Hampshire, Massachusetts and North Carolina inclined to the title "provincial con-

gress"; Virginia uniformly called its extraordinary assemblies "conventions"; New York used both titles at different times. In any case, however, for the last of the revolutionary assemblies, that upon which devolved, by virtue of its call or of its own decision, the task of formulating a system of government, the name convention was generally employed, the name which has become the accepted designation of a constitution forming body.

These congresses or conventions had various though similar origins. For the most part they were generated by or through the local committees, which flourished in the towns and counties of every colony (committees of correspondence; committees of safety). In some instances the colonial assembly was the promoting agency. In Massachusetts, for instance, the assembly merely transformed itself into a provincial congress. Virginia pursued a similar course. In several other cases the assembly, shorn of participation by governor and council, became virtually a provincial congress without change of name. Rhode Island and Connecticut, for instance, effected their transformation under their old charters.

The earliest of these colonial gatherings (they were recorded under a variety of titles, including such as "general meeting," "meeting of the principal gentlemen," etc.) were called together primarily for the purpose of choosing delegates to the proposed Continental Congress (September, 1774); the next for the similar purpose of choosing delegates to the second Continental Congress (May, 1775), to take action on the proposed "Association," in general, and to take into consideration the parlous state of affairs. The Continental Congress, in its turn, further promoted the provincial congresses by tentatively advising certain of them (New Hampshire, South Carolina and Virginia, on Nov. 3, 4 and Dec. 4, 1775, respectively) to set up their own governments; then on May 10, 1776, urging that counsel upon all of them.

To a greater or less degree that very process had meanwhile been going on. First called as advisory rather than as lawmaking bodies, these provincial congresses had already severed virtually every strand of British authority, and, presumably as representatives of the sovereign people, had little by little taken over the functions of government, either directly or through committees of safety of their own creation. It remained but for them definitely to set up their own systems of government; and upon this task, from the adoption of the Declaration of Independence, every colony, now an independent state, became busily engaged.

"PUBLIC BE DAMNED." On Sunday afternoon, Oct. 8, 1882, as a N. Y. Central R. R. train bearing W. H. Vanderbilt, president of the road, was approaching Chicago, two newspaper reporters boarded the train and interviewed Mr. Vanderbilt on various phases of the railroad situation. In the course of the interview

Vanderbilt was asked concerning his plan to meet the "express passenger" service just inaugurated by the Pennsylvania Railroad. Vanderbilt remarked that such service did not pay expenses, and to a question about "the public benefit," is reported to have replied, "The public be damned," adding that the public's only interest in the railroads was to get as much out of them as possible for the least consideration. Vanderbilt did not know how the interview had been reported until it was printed in the New York *Times* and other papers, whereupon he wired the *Times* denying that he had used the "language reported," stating that "both my words and ideas are misreported and misrepresented." The reporters, however, alleged that Vanderbilt's language had been reported correctly and stood willing to "make affidavits as to the correctness of their reports." Publication of the interview caused widespread critical comment.

PUBLIC DOMAIN is to be distinguished from national domain. The former pertains to land owned by the Government, the latter to political jurisdiction. By public domain we mean in this country land owned by the Federal Government, although all states have owned much land and some still do.

The public domain was created by (1) cession of land by old states, (2) purchase from other countries and from Texas, (3) division of the disputed Oregon country and (4) annexation. A number of the original thirteen states with Western land claims ceded a portion of these claims to the Federal Government, but they retained the public lands within their present boundaries as did the other original states and Maine, Vermont, West Virginia, Kentucky, Tennessee and Texas as now bounded. These cessions of Massachusetts, Connecticut, Virginia, the Carolinas and Georgia of 1781–1802 provided the beginnings of the public domain in the Old Northwest and in Mississippi and Alabama. In the next 65 years huge additions of territory were made both to the national domain and to the public lands of the Federal Government through the Louisiana Purchase, the Florida purchase, the annexation of Texas and the Texas cession, the division of Oregon territory, the huge purchase from Mexico, the Gadsden Purchase and finally the purchase of Alaska and the annexation of the Hawaiian Islands.

From the outset there were two different views concerning the policy that should govern the disposition of the public domain. The first, associated with Alexander Hamilton's name, was that the Government, being in need of money to retire the Revolutionary War debt and to meet its expenses, should pledge the public domain for the payment of that debt. The other view, held by Thomas Jefferson and his followers, was that unimproved wild land remote from settlement had no value until farm makers moved on it and by their improvements made it valuable; hence, it should be transferred to them at little or no cost.

Hamilton's view held sway for a time almost of a necessity and, indeed, was reluctantly accepted by many Jeffersonians. The basic price varied from one to two dollars an acre until 1820 when credit was abolished and the minimum price was made $1.25 an acre. This was not high to a speculator seeking to engross tens of thousands of acres of potential cotton land in Alabama, but to a frontiersman lacking resources or credit it was more than he could raise. His solution was to squat upon public land, clear the trees, fence, build his cabin, and raise cotton, corn or wheat in the first year or two in such quantities as to be able to buy the land before his trespass was discovered and he was ejected.

The squatter, as the first pioneer settler was called, wanted protection on his claim against speculators who might try to buy it from under him. Specifically, squatters wanted pre-emption, that is, the right to hold and improve public land for a limited period before the public sale and then to purchase it for the minimum price without interference from speculators. Pre-emption was increasingly assured settlers, whether by claim associations which provided mutual protection to all squatters or by special pre-emption laws before 1841. In that year the prospective pre-emption law permitted persons to settle anywhere on the surveyed lands in advance of sale, improve them and when the auction sale was announced purchase them at the $1.25 an acre price.

Squatterism, first tolerated and then sanctioned in 1841, had thus prevailed and a major breach was made in the revenue policy of Hamilton. In 1854 the Graduation Act provided a further breach by reducing the price of land that had been on the market for ten or more years in inverse ratio to the length of time it had been subject to sale, the lowest price being 12½ cents an acre. Finally, in 1862, the West gained its greatest triumph in the Homestead Act which made public lands free to settlers who would live upon and improve tracts for five years. By 1862, however, numerous acts had been adopted which greatly minimized the effects of this liberalization.

To aid the newly developing public land states the Federal Government granted them land, the proceeds of which were to help them meet the costs of constructing public buildings, draining swamps, building internal improvements and endowing education. Altogether 236,000,000 acres were given the states for these purposes. In addition over 100,000,000 acres were promised railroad companies to help finance the construction of their lines. All this land, and much of it was among the best land, whether for farming, grazing, lumbering or mining, was to be sold, not given to settlers, and generally it was sold at high prices. The free homestead policy, as won in 1862, was not, then, the complete victory which land reformers had sought.

Individual speculators and land companies, attracted by the ease with which government land

	NATIONAL DOMAIN ACRES	PUBLIC DOMAIN ACRES
13 original States Treaty of 1783	200,414,180	....
5 States cut out of original States, but not included in above	92,741,760	....
Western land cessions of original States	213,985,880	205,981,080
Louisiana Purchase	552,513,280	552,513,280†
East and West Florida	43,342,720	43,342,720†
Annexation of Texas	246,777,600	....
Oregon Compromise	180,644,480	180,644,480†
Mexican Cession	334,479,360	334,479,360†
Purchase from Texas		78,842,880
Gadsden Purchase	18,961,920	18,961,920
Alaska Purchase	378,165,760	378,165,760
Hawaiian Acquisition	3,110,720	....
TOTALS	2,265,137,660	1,792,931,480

* The island possessions outside of Hawaii are omitted.

† The English, French, Spanish and Mexican governments had made many grants in areas later transferred to the United States which, when title was satisfactorily proved to United States officials, were patented to the claimants. Technically, these 28,000 claims and the 33,000,000 acres patented were not a part of the public domain.

could be purchased in unlimited amounts and held at slight cost in taxes until it could be sold at large profits, bought heavily in the three great boom periods of 1816–19, 1833–38 and 1853–57. Holdings of 10,000 to 50,000 acres were thus established, and land and partnership holdings ran up from 100,000 to close to a million acres. By anticipating settlers, speculators raised the costs of farm making, dispersed population widely, delayed the introduction of roads, schools, churches and transportation facilities, contributed to the introduction of tenancy, aggravated problems with Indians, and in some regions were responsible for the development of rural slums. On the other hand, they provided credit to hard-pressed pioneers, their advertising and promotional work aided in bringing many settlers to the West, and some of the more advanced estate builders introduced high farming techniques on their property that by example contributed to better agricultural practices elsewhere. However, at the time public attention centered on the damaging effects of speculator intrusion in the West and led to demands for limitation in the sale of public lands. Consequently, after the adoption of the Homestead Law little newly surveyed land was opened to unlimited purchase, though lands already

offered at public sale and unsold continued to be subject to unrestricted entry.

Unfortunately, the movement of settlers into the high plains where rainfall was less than 20 inches was proceeding at the time when restrictions on land acquisition were being introduced. The 320 acres an individual could acquire beyond the 100th meridian was insufficient for some types of farming. Congress met this difficulty by again broadening basic land acquisition through the Timber Culture Act (1873), the Desert Land Act (1877), and the Timber and Stone Act (1878) which increased the amount of land individuals could acquire from the Government to a possible 1120 acres. There was reason for these measures but they quickly became subject to abuse by grasping individuals anxious to engross as much land as possible through the use of dummy entrymen.

Notwithstanding the speculators' abuse of the land system and the incongruous features that somewhat minimized the effectiveness of the measures designed to aid homesteaders in becoming farm owners, the public land states enjoyed a remarkable increase in settlement. In the 1850's, the first decade for which there are statistics, 401,000 new farms were created in the public land states. The number grew even more rapidly thereafter. By 1890, 2,000,000 additional farms had been established in the public land states. Never before had so many new farmers subjected such a large area to cultivation as occurred in the 19th century in the United States.

The censuses of 1880 and 1890, with their alarming figures of mortgage debt outstanding on farms and the high proportion of farms that were tenant-operated, combined with the growing feeling that soils, minerals and forests were being destructively used, turned people's thoughts toward reform in land management and conservation, the cautious and wise use of natural resources. Instead of a policy of transferring all the public lands to individuals, railroads and states as rapidly as possible it was decided to retain a portion of the lands in public ownership. The National Forest Reservation Act of 1891 marked the big change in philosophy, though it authorized, not required, the President to withdraw from public entry forest lands on which organized management policies could be introduced. Under Theodore Roosevelt's vigorous leadership withdrawals were pushed to nearly 160,000,000 acres.

Next came the Reclamation Act of 1902 which authorized the use of income from the public lands for constructing dams on Western rivers to store water for irrigating the dry lands. Extensive areas of public lands were withdrawn from entry to prevent speculators from anticipating actual settlers on lands to be irrigated.

In 1916 the National Park Service was created to administer the areas of superlative natural beauty which were being set aside as reserves, such as Yosemite, Yellowstone, Hot Springs, Glacier, Sequoia,

Mt. Rainier and Crater Lake. These and other natural beauty spots were thus prevented from falling into the hands of commercial interests that might despoil them of their unusual attractiveness.

Meantime, the minerals underlying the public lands, such as coal, oil, potash, uranium and iron, had been withdrawn from sale and the subsurface rights were reserved on large acreages the surface of which was transferred under various entry laws to private ownership. The Government thus became charged with responsibility for controlling the utilization of these minerals, and from them it has received a swelling income that goes into construction of reclamation projects. Also, valuable water power sites on public land were reserved which made possible the great hydroelectric power development of the Federal Government in the 1930's and 1940's.

Finally, when the harmful effects of overgrazing on the ranges of the West became evident, the livestock industry agreed to the closing of the public domain, the end of alienation of public lands save for scattered tracts, and the establishment of a Division of Grazing to administer the range lands. The new agency, later the Bureau of Land Management, sought to prevent overgrazing by limiting the number of livestock on the ranges and to improve the carrying capacity by reseeding and by weed and shrub elimination.

Nearly a century and a half of unparalleled prodigality in dealing with the public domain had made possible the alienation of most of the best agricultural, forest and mineral lands, but there still remained a noble fragment in Federal ownership, mostly under organized management. In the National Forests were 160,000,000 acres, only a small portion of which had come from other sources than the public domain. Included were rich stands of sugar pine and Douglas fir, as well as some mountain country that had little or no timber but was included for watershed protection. The grazing districts and other range lands leased for grazing and the revested Oregon and California lands with their heavy timber stands together amounted to 179,000,000 acres. Other miscellaneous reservations brought the total of Federal lands within the 48 states to 455,000,000 acres.

In Alaska the Federal Government owned practically all the land, but with admission in 1959 the new state became entitled to select 102,550,000 acres of the total of 378,000,000 acres for schools, colleges and other purposes. Since selection of these lands could not be made until surveys had been made, it would take many years before they could all be transferred to state ownership. There were 20,848,000 acres in national forests in Alaska, and an estimated 88,000,000 acres were withdrawn for their minerals, power sites or for defense purposes. The balance of Alaska's public lands were thought to be of little value. The admission of the 50th state—Hawaii—in 1959–60, added little or no public lands to

Federal responsibility. In a nation where the wide open spaces were rapidly being closed in and people sought them the more, the public lands were being increasingly cherished by wildlife enthusiasts, hunters, tourists and persons seeking to get away from the crush of the city.

PUBLIC LANDS, SURVEY OF. The first settlers in America measured out their lands for individual or public holdings on the basis of "metes and bounds," the shape of the tracts being determined by any convenient circumstance pertaining to the particular tract, such as the shore lines of ocean, lakes or rivers; the ridges of hills and mountains; or even the desirability of certain land as compared with other adjoining land. The lack of system permitted the first settlers to pick and choose to an almost unlimited degree. There had been in Europe some attempt at regular surveys, but they did not predominate, and were not introduced at all promptly in America.

The colonies had begun a system of surveys for outlining towns, Massachusetts attempting to lay them out in six-mile square tracts. Connecticut had likewise attempted a five-mile square town. The square town, or township, was, in a small way, attempted in South Carolina. To indicate further that the idea of a rectangular system of surveys was not altogether new in 1785, it may be noted that several land schemes provided for the "township" system of subdivision soon after the middle of the 18th century.

The difficulties connected with the indiscriminate surveys of most colonies, especially the Southern, including both Kentucky and Tennessee, had impressed a large number of men interested in a feasible system of measurements and designations, with the desirability of a rectangular survey. In the debate on this subject many objections were brought forth. The genuine objections were such as those pertaining to cutting across streams, valleys and ridges in undesirable and awkward ways, shutting one division off from a suitable building site, another from a watercourse; giving all of one kind of land to one tract, and all of another kind to another tract.

Our present rectangular survey was adopted as a feature of the Ordinance of 1785. It provides for the survey of all public land into townships six miles square. The townships are numbered both ways, to the north and the south, from certain east and west "base lines." Certain meridians are designated as "primary" meridians. Lying parallel to these meridians a north-and-south row of townships is called a "range." Such rows are numbered both to the east and to the west of the "primary" meridians. A township is divided into 36 sections, each a mile square, and numbered from the northeastern corner toward the west, forth and back, bringing no. 36 to the southeastern corner. This system applies, with a few local exceptions, to all states of the Union except the thirteen original states and Vermont, Maine, Kentucky, Tennessee, West Virginia and Texas, the last-named state having a similar system of her own.

Under this system it is possible to designate a certain forty-acre tract of land with a few words and numbers. The designation is absolutely definite and could not apply to any other land whatever. For instance, a tract of land numbered: Sec. 10; T. 94 N.; R. 40 west of the Fifth Principal Meridian could be found nowhere else than in northwestern Iowa. The Fifth Principal Meridian runs north from the mouth of the Arkansas River in Arkansas. The "base line" governing this part of the country runs west from the mouth of the St. Francis River in the same state. Thus the particular Section 10 designated will be found in the 94th township to the north of this base line, and in the 40th one to the west of the line designated as the Fifth Principal Meridian.

The rectangular survey system, with all its inaccuracies, is a system of great convenience, and, even though we did not literally devise the system, our use of it established its acceptance over a large portion of the newer parts of the world.

PUEBLO. The village Indians of New Mexico and Arizona developed a unique type of architecture culminating about 1000 A.D. in large apartmenthouse-like structures of several hundred rooms.

In the modern pueblos, as Hopi, Zuñi, Ácoma, Laguna, Taos, etc., are the surviving forms of this architecture. The type ground plan is 200 to 300 rectangular rooms, averaging about ten by twelve feet, grouped around two courts in the form of the letter "E." The second, and each succeeding story, was of less width than the preceding, thus forming successive terraces, facing the courts. All rooms in the lower story were entered through the roof. The walls were of stone and adobe, the whole easy to defend. In pre-Columbian time such a building stood alone and housed about 1000 people. The agricultural lands were on favored spots within a radius of two to five miles.

PUEBLO REVOLT (1680–96) was led by Popé, a Tewa medicine man who had suffered cruelties under the Spaniards. There were over 3000 Spanish settlers in New Mexico by 1680 and he desired to drive them out. Several hundred settlers were massacred, and the rest escaped to the El Paso region. The Indians ravaged the country and held sway under Popé, whom they soon disliked as their economic conditions grew worse. In 1692 Gov. Pedro de Vargas led an expedition to recover New Mexico. After some stiff resistance, the Pueblos were reconquered, and Taos, the center of the conspiracy, burned.

PUERTO RICO was one of the less important Spanish colonies. The aboriginal Indians soon died out and there was little white immigration until the latter part of the 18th century. Thereafter the island gradually became more prosperous, with coffee, sugar, and tobacco the chief crops. Despite the autocratic character of the Spanish government, there were no serious political disturbances.

The island was ceded to the United States as a result of the Spanish American War. The Foraker Act of 1900 authorized the President to appoint a governor and an executive council, consisting of the six heads of administrative departments plus five Puerto Ricans. This council was the upper house of the legislature, the lower being elected by the people. The inhabitants were not given American citizenship. In the "insular cases" the U. S. Supreme Court upheld the right of Congress to treat newly acquired territories as not fully incorporated into the United States and hence not subject to all of the provisions of the Constitution.

The native inhabitants of the island were given full American citizenship and a larger measure of self-government by the Jones Act of 1917. The President of the United States continued to appoint the governor, the attorney general, the commissioner of education, and the auditor, but the heads of the other executive departments were appointed by the governor with the advice and consent of the Puerto Rican senate, which was elected by popular vote.

A desire for more complete self-government persisted. A few leaders advocated full independence and a larger group desired statehood in the Union, but many felt that either status would be ruinous economically. The Puerto Ricans were given an opportunity to decide the question after World War II. In 1947, the U. S. Congress authorized the choice of the governor by popular election, and in 1950 it authorized the election of a constitutional convention. Under the constitution adopted in 1952 the island continued to be a part of the United States but as a self-governing commonwealth which retained a peculiarly favorable situation with regard to Federal taxes.

Under the leadership of Luis Muñóz Marín, who was elected governor in 1948 and re-elected 1952, 1956 and 1960, the Commonwealth government made a largely successful effort to improve standards of living in the island. Though Puerto Rico had been more prosperous than most Caribbean countries, there was much poverty, and an excessive dependence on sugar production, which provided only part-time employment, made the economic situation precarious. The government took advantage of the fact that the United States collects no income or excise taxes from Puerto Rico to persuade many new enterprises to establish themselves in the island, with a resulting great increase in industrial production. It also endeavored to diversify agriculture and to encourage small farming under an agrarian reform program. The emigration of several hundred thousand Puerto Ricans to the mainland helped to relieve the pressure of population, which had been one of the island's chief problems.

PUJO COMMITTEE. In February, 1912, the House of Representatives by resolution directed its Committee on Banking and Currency to ascertain whether there existed in the United States a concentration of financial and banking power, "a money trust." A subcommittee, headed by Rep. Arsène Pujo of Louisiana, with Samuel Untermyer of New York as counsel, conducted hearings, at which J. P. Morgan, George F. Baker and other financiers testified. After examining a great mass of evidence, the majority report declared that existing banking and credit practices resulted in a "vast and growing concentration of control of money and credit in the hands of a comparatively few men."

PULLMAN STRIKE. As a result of the panic of 1893, various railroad companies suffered heavy losses which led them to curtail their operations and to reduce the wages of their employees. Because of depression conditions, the Pullman Palace Car Co. likewise reduced the wages of its employees an average of 25%. This company, organized in 1867, carried on its chief operations at Pullman, a town which it owned just south of Chicago. When wages were reduced no reduction was made in the rentals and fees charged employees in this town. About 4000 disgruntled employees joined Eugene V. Debs' American Railway Union in the spring of 1894. On May 11, 1894, about 2500 employees quit work and forced the closing of the shops. Thereafter attempts were made to arbitrate the differences between the company and its employees but the former took the view that there was nothing to arbitrate. Nor would the company consent to bargain with the union, though its officials expressed readiness to deal with employees individually.

The local strike soon developed into a general railroad strike when members of the American Railway Union refused to handle Pullman cars. First, 24 railroads centering in Chicago, whose affairs were handled by the General Managers' Association, were tied up. This led to a general railroad tie-up throughout the whole West by June 28. Two days later the strike had spread to practically all parts of the country. Serious delay in the transportation of mail resulted. At this juncture Federal Judges C. D. Woods and P. S. Grosscup issued a "blanket injunction" prohibiting all interference with trains. The injunction was defied and the strikers resorted to violence. Thereupon President Cleveland ordered Federal troops into Chicago on July 4. Following their arrival there was much mob violence and destruction of railroad property. Rioting occurred in other cities as far west as Oakland, Calif., so that, on July 5, Federal troops were ordered to strike duty in that state. By July 13, some trains were running under military guard and a few days later the strike was broken. By July 20 all Federal troops were out of Chicago. A feature of the strike was the arrest of Debs, and his subsequent conviction for violation of the injunction. This led to a long-drawn-out campaign to curb the use of "blanket injunctions" in labor disputes.

PULLMANS. In 1836–37 the Cumberland Valley Railroad of Pennsylvania installed sleeping-car service between Harrisburg and Chambersburg by adapting the ordinary day coach to sleeping requirements. Each car was divided into four compartments of three bunks each, built on one side of the car with one rear section for washing facilities. Passengers were given no bed-clothes, could read only by candlelight, and were warmed by box stoves. The seats on most cars were foul with boot scrapings, the floors receptacles of filth, and personal arrangements were usually crowded. Travel under such circumstances could be justified only as a painful duty. A New York cabinetmaker, George M. Pullman, arrived in Chicago during 1855 to apply his inventive ability to altering these conditions. At Bloomington, Ill., in 1858, Pullman remodeled two Chicago and Alton coaches into sleeping-cars each of which contained ten sleeping sections, two washrooms and a linen locker. Although this venture proved unprofitable, Pullman decided in 1864 to create a more elaborate car, which was equipped at a cost of $20,178.14, a huge amount for car construction in that day. The *Pioneer* contained a folding upper berth, sliding seats, artistically decorated furnishings, special car springs, better lighting, heating and ventilation, and was enlarged in height and width. In 1867 came the incorporation of the Pullman's Palace Car Co. with a capitalization of $1,000,000. That year the new luxurious model, the *President,* included a kitchen, the predecessor of the dining car. In 1870 the Pullman car completed its first transcontinental journey. The Pullman Company introduced to America the brilliant Pintsch gas light as an illuminant in 1883 and was a pioneer in the introduction of electric lighting. Other improvements followed, and competitors were outdistanced. Pullman service, by introducing comfort to transportation, revolutionized travel both in the United States and abroad.

PULTENEY PURCHASE (1791), the residue of the Phelps-Gorham Purchase, comprised over 1,000,000 acres in Steuben, Ontario and Yates counties and parts of Monroe, Wayne, Allegany, Livingston and Genesee counties, all in western New York. These "Genesee lands" were purchased for £75,000 from William Franklin, Robert Morris' London agent, by an association styled "The Pulteney Associates." Charles Williamson, the first American agent, laid out Bath, N. Y., in 1792. The last transaction of the "Associates" was recorded in December, 1926.

PUNISHMENTS, COLONIAL. The New England and Quaker colonies of Pennsylvania and West Jersey had in general a more humane set of criminal punishments than prevailed in New York and the South. In the former, larceny was punished by multiple restitution and whipping. In the South the death penalty was at times enforced in accord with English law whereby larceny from the person in an amount above twelve pence was a nonclergyable felony. In the majority of instances, however, multiple restitution was also exacted in the South for this offense, as in Maryland under the act of 1715.

In Massachusetts barbarous or inhumane tortures were forbidden almost from the beginning. However, the Puritan code leaned in the direction of exemplary and humiliating punishments, such as the ducking-stool for the scold, the stocks for the vagrant, the letter sewn on the garment for the adulterer, branding for the burglar, or riding a wooden horse with an empty pitcher in one hand to indicate a propensity to strong drink. Hanging was the normal method of capital punishment, and it was by this method, not by burning, that the New England witches were executed. In West Jersey only treason and murder were capital offenses and in Pennsylvania murder alone was punishable by death. Imprisonment at hard labor was prescribed in most cases for noncapital crimes, but by 1700 the Quakers had abandoned their early humane theories with regard to punishment.

In New York and the South two tendencies stand out conspicuously—the extreme severity in penalties prescribed and the almost exclusive employment of fines or some form of corporal punishment as the prevailing modes of executing the penalty imposed. Whipping, branding, mutilating, confinement in the stocks or pillory, and ducking were among the most popular of these forms of punishments, and in Delaware the whipping post is still in use. At times whippings were carried to excess. The New Englanders observed the Mosaic law setting 39 stripes as the maximum penalty. In addition to hanging, burning and quartering were also employed in New York and the South. The large number of Negroes convicted in the Negro Plot of 1741 were burnt at the stake. Others were transported, a method used in New England also for dealing with captive Indians in wartime. Treason was punished by disposing of the body of the executed person variously, the head to be set up one place, and the quarters set up in other communities. For the murder of an overseer, a Maryland Negro in 1745 was sentenced to have his right hand cut off, to be hanged and then quartered. Except in New England, for treason and felony all the offender's goods and chattels were forfeited to the king and the attainder also brought with it an incapacity to inherit or transmit property to one's heirs.

Both in New England and in the South mutilation was not uncommon. In the South for contempt of court, an ear might be cut off or a tongue pierced with a hot iron. In Virginia an ear might be nailed to the pillory and then cut off as a punishment for runaway slaves. For slander in Virginia the tongue might be bored through with an awl and the convicted party forced to pass through a guard of forty men and be "butted" by each, and then be kicked down or "footed" out of the fort, or trailed behind a boat. For criticizing the authorities in Virginia one might be pilloried with a placard, lose both ears, serve the colony a year, or be unable to become a freeman, or worse, have his ears nailed to the pillory or be laid "neck and heels" in irons and fined. Castration might be ordered by the court of any slave convicted of attempting to rape a white woman.

PURE FOOD AND DRUG ACTS. The demand for a national Pure Food and Drug Act became insistent after the "embalmed beef" scandal of the Spanish-American War. Some states had already passed laws to protect against adulteration, but measures were limited in scope and application. Upton Sinclair's *Jungle* and the articles of Harvey W. Wiley attracted the attention of President Theodore Roosevelt, who began the reform by securing the passage of the Meat Inspection Act of 1906. He also sponsored the Pure Food and Drug Act passed in 1906, to become effective Jan. 1, 1907. The act, applying to goods shipped in foreign or interstate commerce, was designed to prevent the adulteration or misbranding of foods or drugs. Confectionery was declared to be adulterated if it contained poisonous color, flavor or other ingredients detrimental to health. Food was held to be adulterated if it was composed of filthy or decomposed animal matter, if it contained poisonous or deleterious ingredients, or if anything had been added to conceal inferior goods. Proprietary medicines must be labeled so as to indicate the percentage of narcotics, stimulants or other ingredients that might be harmful. Misleading statements as to the composition or purity of package foods or drugs rendered the offending distributor or manufacturer subject to Federal prosecution, provided that a distributor was not liable where he could show an adequate guarantee from the vendor.

The original act proved inadequate in several particulars and amendments were added in 1912, 1913 and 1923. The first amendment provided a penalty against false statements as to the curative quality of drugs, and the supplementary law of 1913 provided for the stamping or marking of the weight of packaged goods. The 1923 law defined "filled" milk and prohibited its shipment interstate.

In 1933 a demand arose for more stringent control of the advertised commodities subject to regulation under the Pure Food and Drug Act. Congress, in response to this demand, passed the Wheeler-Lea Act which became effective May 21, 1938. This act extended the scope of the original act by providing for the prosecution of individuals or agencies who engage in the presentation of false or misleading statements concerning "foods, drugs, diagnostic and therapeutic devices, and cosmetics," provided that such advertising is disseminated outside the boundary of any individual state. Radio stations, newspapers and magazines are not held liable if they disclose the name of the distributor or manufacturer responsible for the false advertising. The sections of the act dealing with advertising are enforceable by the Federal Trade Commission, and the question of misbranding is left to the Food and Drug Administration.

In 1940 the administration of the act of 1938 was transferred from the Department of Agriculture to the Federal Security Agency. After World War II the advances in use of chemicals in plant infestation and the development of antibiotics brought new problems of control.

In 1954 a Pesticide Amendment was passed providing for stricter control of dusts and sprays. The Agency also initiated an extensive campaign against contaminated foods and drugs.

Antibiotic drugs were carefully inspected before certification and court injunctions were secured to stop the sale of nostrums offered as a cure for cancer and other diseases.

In 1957–58 appropriations for research and for educational programs for the consumer were increased. The great increase in processed foods and the marketing of new drugs have caused emphasis to be placed on a constructive program supported by the states as well as the nation.

PURITANS AND PURITANISM. These terms originated in England in the 1560's, when they were used to describe the men who wished to reform the Church of England beyond the limits established by Elizabeth and who strove to "purify" it of what they considered the remnants of Popery. Puritanism was first formulated as an ecclesiastical protest and was at the beginning devoted to attacking clerical vestments, the use of medieval ceremonial, and the structure of the official hierarchy; it wished to substitute a church government modeled upon the example of the Apostles in the New Testament. However, this preoccupation with polity and ritual is to be interpreted as an expression rather than the substance of Puritanism. Puritans were men of intense piety, who took literally and seriously the doctrines of original sin and salvation by faith; they believed that true Christians should obey the will of God as expressed in divine revelation, and they condemned the Church of England because they found its order impious and anti-Christian. After 1603 their opposition to the Church became allied with the parliamentary opposition to the royal prerogative, and in the 1640's Puritans and Parliamentarians united in open warfare against Charles I.

Puritanism was thus a movement of religious protest, inspired by a driving zeal and an exalted religious devotion, which its enemies called fanaticism, but which to Puritans was an issue of life or death.

At the same time, it is to be connected with the social revolution of the 17th century and the struggle of a rising capitalist middle class against the absolutist state. It was a religious and social radicalism that in England proved incapable of maintaining unity within its own ranks and during the 1650's split into myriad sects and opinions. The process of division began in the 16th century when "Separatists" broke off from the main body of Puritans; a small congregation of these extremists fled to Plymouth in 1620, though the major contribution of Puritanism to American life was the settlement of the Massachusetts Bay Company at Salem and Boston in 1629–30. This band of Puritans was inspired to migrate by a conviction that the cause had become hopeless in England after the dissolution of the Parliament of 1629. Within the next decade some 20,000 persons came to Massachusetts and Connecticut and there erected a society and a church in strict accordance with Puritan ideals. Ruled by vigorous leaders, these colonies were able to check centrifugal tendencies, to perpetuate and to institutionalize Puritanism in America long after the English movement had sunk into confusion and a multiplicity of sects. Yet in so far as Puritanism was but the English variant of Calvinism, and was theologically at one with all Reformed churches, New England Puritanism must be viewed as merely one of the forms in which the Calvinist version of Protestantism has been carried to America, and its influence must be considered along with that of Scotch-Irish, Dutch, or French Protestantism. In the American setting the word Puritanism has become practically synonymous with New England simply because New England (except for Rhode Island) achieved a social organization and an intellectual articulation that trenchantly crystallized the Puritan spirit. Puritanism can be said to have affected American life wherever Calvinism has affected it, but most markedly at those points where America has been at all determined by persons of New England origin.

QUAKERS, or The Society of Friends. Quakerism reached America from England through the followers of George Fox, founder of the Society of Friends, who began to preach in 1647. Ann Austin and Mary Fisher went to Barbados in 1655, and reached Boston in 1656, whence the Puritans deported them and prohibited further Quaker immigration. Other zealous Quaker preachers continued to invade the Bay Colony, in spite of fines, floggings and banishment. Three men and one woman who returned after being banished suffered hanging on Boston Common (1659–61). Quakerism took root, however, in Sandwich on Cape Cod, in 1657, and in tolerant Newport the Friends organized the first "Yearly Meeting" in the world in 1661. In the New Netherlands toleration succeeded persecution, and the Friends settled first on Long Island (1657), whence they spread to Manhattan and the mainland. They appeared in Mary-

781

land (1656) and in Virginia (1657). When Fox himself visited America in 1676 he found Quakers scattered from the West Indies to Carolina, and from Carolina far up the New England coast.

Meanwhile Fox and others laid plans for a major emigration of British Quakers to the New World to escape persecution at home. Settlements at Salem, in West Jersey (1675), and in Burlington (1677), preceded the "Holy Experiment" which William Penn, a distinguished young convert to Quakerism, undertook in Pennsylvania in 1681. Penn's colony became a haven for thousands of Quakers from the British Isles, as well as for many Rhineland German sectarians. Uniting with their brethren in New Jersey and Delaware, the Pennsylvania Quakers organized a Yearly Meeting in 1682, which became the most influential in America. Other Yearly Meetings, independent but in close touch with one another and with London Yearly Meeting, appeared in New York, Maryland, Virginia and North Carolina. Each contained subordinate Quarterly Meetings, which in turn were made up of local Monthly Meetings, the basic congregational units in the Society of Friends. Democracy in church government and equality of opportunity for religious expression evolved from the Quaker doctrine of the Inner Light, which the Friends believe illumines the heart of every man. The Quakers met in their religious meetings silently to wait upon the Lord, while occasional sermons or prayers were offered by those who felt moved to speak. They renounced ritual and the sacraments, and banned music and art; but the very simplicity of their meeting-houses made for dignity and charm, and the uprightness of Quaker lives lent grace to their puritanical plainness of speech and apparel.

Active proselytism in the 17th century gave way to quietism in the 18th. Persecution thereupon ceased, except when Quakers refused to give military service or pay church tithes. They perfected a rigid discipline, and punished breaches of it, such as marrying out of the group, by expulsion or "disownment." Thus the Friends became a "peculiar people." The westward movement after the Revolution drew them over the mountains, some to Kentucky and Tennessee, but mostly to the slave-free soil of the Northwest Territory. Gradually they spread to the Pacific Coast, establishing Yearly Meetings in Ohio (1813), Indiana (1821), Iowa (1863), Kansas (1872), Illinois (1887), Oregon (1893), California (1895), and Nebraska (1908). Another stream of migration led into western New York and across Lake Ontario into Canada, where a Yearly Meeting was organized in 1834 (Hicksite; Orthodox in 1867).

The evangelical movement in American Protestantism in the first half of the 19th century brought schism to the Society of Friends. A "Great Separation" in 1827–28 produced the Orthodox and Hicksite groups, one evangelical, the other unitarian in tendency. The Hicksites avoided further schism, and

their Yearly Meetings united in a biennial "General Conference" in 1902. Opposition to the evangelical trends in the Orthodox body resulted in a small separation of Wilburite or Conservative Friends in New England in 1845, and later in New York, North Carolina, and some of the western Yearly Meetings. Philadelphia Yearly Meeting forestalled such a separation by ceasing to correspond with the other Orthodox bodies in 1857, and refusing to join in their united Five Years Meeting, which began to function in 1887. Evangelical tendencies increased in the Five Years Meeting bodies, with revivals, hymn-singing and salaried pastors being as common to Friends' "churches" as to Baptists, Methodists, and Presbyterians. Quakers abandoned their peculiarities of speech and dress in all but the Conservative groups, and by the early years of the 20th century they had ceased to be outwardly different from other Americans.

The Quakers' religious doctrine of the Inner Light found frequent expression in humanitarian activity. As they had attacked war and the slave trade and slavery in the 18th and early 19th centuries, and made notable contributions in the fields of Indian relations, prison reform, education, temperance, and the care of the insane, so their descendants sought to apply Quaker principles to the 20th century problems of war and social maladjustment. The American Friends Service Committee, organized in 1917 to enable Quakers to engage in noncombatant relief work as an alternative to military activity, united all the Quaker groups in effecting their peace testimony. After World War I the Committee continued as a relief and service agency abroad and at home. In 1920 American Friends attended an All-Friends Conference in London. In 1937 they joined Quakers everywhere in a World Conference at the Quaker Colleges of Swarthmore and Haverford, near Philadelphia. Out of this grew a Friends World Committee for Consultation.

In World War II the American Friends Service Committee, acting under the authority of the Director of Selective Service, operated Civilian Public Service camps for Friends and others who had religious scruples against service in the armed forces. In 1947 the Committee shared with its British counterpart, the Friends Service Council, in receiving the Nobel Prize.

Theological differences among Canadian and Eastern American Quakers diminished in the 20th century, until complete union occurred in Canada in 1944, among the Orthodox and Wilburite bodies in New England in 1945, and between the Orthodox and Hicksite Yearly Meetings in Philadelphia and in New York in 1955.

On the other hand, evangelism took fresh life in the West from the fundamentalist-modernist controversy of the first quarter of the present century, until several Yearly Meetings, notably Oregon (1926) and

Kansas (1937), withdrew from the Five Years Meeting as insufficiently evangelical and missions-minded.

It was estimated in 1960 that there were approximately 125,000 Quakers in the United States and Canada. Rural meetings and membership seemed to be declining, but the appearance in urban and university centers of new Quaker meetings indicated a growing interest there in basic Quaker principles and their application to religious worship and the problems of modern life.

QUANTRILL'S RAID (Aug. 21, 1863). William Clarke Quantrill, at the head of a band of 448 Missouri guerrillas or "bushwackers," fell upon Lawrence, Kans., in the early dawn. The town was taken completely by surprise and was undefended; the local militia company was unable to assemble, and the few Federal soldiers were stationed across the river. The raiders first stormed the Eldridge Hotel. After it had been surrendered, and set on fire, the raiders scattered over the town, killing, burning and plundering indiscriminately, though they did respect women and small children. Generally, the more prominent men, knowing what to expect, managed to escape. All the business buildings and more than half of the dwellings were totally or partially destroyed. The known dead numbered 142. Withdrawing at the approach of Federal troops, the guerrillas, although pursued, were able to reach Missouri with few losses. Unlike other border raids of the Civil War, this was not a mere harrying foray, but was a general massacre. It was no doubt prompted by the old bitterness against Lawrence for its part in the Kansas conflict, but the excuse given was reprisal for Lane's raid on Osceola, Mo. Quantrill, who had lived in Lawrence under the name of Charlie Hart and had been driven out as an undesirable, was probably motivated by a personal grudge.

QUARTERING ACT (one of the Coercion Acts) was passed by Parliament in June, 1774, to permit effective action by the British troops sent to Boston after the Tea Party. In 1768 the Boston Whigs, taking advantage of the absence of barracks in Boston, attempted to quarter the troops in Castle William rather than in the town itself where they were urgently needed. To forestall a like effort, the Quartering Act of 1774 provided that when there were no barracks where troops were required, the authorities must provide quarters for them on the spot; if they failed to do so, the governor might compel the use of inns or uninhabited buildings. The Boston patriots, however, forced the British troops to remain camped on the Boston Common until November, 1774, by refusing to allow workmen to repair the distilleries and empty buildings Gen. Gage had procured for quarters.

QUEBEC, CAPTURE OF (1759). The year following Louisburg's fall James Wolfe was given command of 9280 men, mostly regulars, with which, supplemented by naval aid, he was ordered to capture Quebec. Assembled at Louisburg in May, 1759, steadily drilled and trained, Wolfe's force sailed June 4, 1759, for the St. Lawrence. June 27 he landed on the Ile d'Orleans below Quebec and for two months, while the fleet dominated the river, made many abortive attempts against the city.

The French under Montcalm defended the north bank from the city to the Montmorency, a distance of seven miles; Wolfe went ashore east of this stream, and thus partially encircling Quebec with soldiers on the east, batteries on the south bank, and the fleet upstream, conducted a long-range bombardment and siege. July 31 he aimed a powerful but unsuccessful stroke by land and water at the Montmorency end of the French shore entrenchments. August was a month of discouragements.

September 1–3, the British skilfully abandoned the Montmorency camp. Wolfe secretly moved 3000 soldiers to the ships upstream. His fleet threatened several well-entrenched landing places. On the calm and cloudy night of Sept. 12, he slipped a strong force downstream in small boats, effected a surprise landing at a small cove near the city, overpowered a small guard, captured an adjacent battery, and made it possible for other troops, rowed over from the south shore and brought downstream by the ships themselves, to land safely and climb to the heights 5000 strong by six in the morning.

In this position, Wolfe threatened Quebec's communications with Montreal and inner Canada and the bridge across the St. Charles. Montcalm had to assemble and fight for the possession of Quebec from the outside. In the formal 18th-century manner, Wolfe had his force arrayed by eight o'clock. Although skirmishing intervened, it was ten o'clock before Montcalm formed for a conventional assault. This was met by formal volleys from the British battalions. Shots were exchanged for a few moments only, then the French wavered, the British charged, and the French fled. Wolfe was killed on the field. Montcalm was carried off mortally wounded. Wolfe's successor entrenched and closed in, and the surrender of Quebec on Sept. 17 made inevitable the conquest of Canada and the close of the French and Indian War with the capture of Montreal the following year.

QUEBEC ACT (one of the Intolerable Acts), passed by Parliament in June, 1774, was intended to pacify the French-Canadians by granting the free exercise of the Roman Catholic religion and re-establishing French civil law in Quebec. The boundaries of Quebec were extended to the Ohio on the south and to the Mississippi on the west, to be governed by an appointive governor and council without benefit of a representative legislative body. The interior was thereby closed to the expansion of the free institutions of the seaboard and the hopes of colonial land speculators were blasted. Colonial propagandists effectively used the Quebec Act to widen the breach between mother country and colonies by declaring that the British government intended to employ the "Popish slaves" of Quebec to establish the doctrines of royal absolutism and Roman Catholicism throughout the American colonies.

QUEEN ANNE'S WAR was the American counterpart of the War of the Spanish Succession which was fought in Europe from 1701 to 1714. Fundamental issues, including the rivalry of France and England in America, had been left unsolved by the Treaty of Ryswick (1697). They were revived upon the acceptance of the Spanish throne by a grandson of Louis XIV of France in November, 1700. The threat of Bourbon domination in Europe and in French and Spanish America caused William III of England and the Dutch Netherlands to ally (September, 1701) with the Holy Roman Emperor, a member of whose Hapsburg family claimed the Spanish throne. Two months after Anne had succeeded William as sovereign of England, the three allied powers jointly declared formal war on France (May, 1702).

In America the war was fought in the West Indies and on the Carolina and New England frontiers. In the summer of 1702 the English captured the island of St. Christopher, but Admiral Benbow's action against a French squadron along the Spanish Main was indecisive. After the English failure to take Guadeloupe in 1703, military activity in the West Indies was restricted to privateering, from which English colonial trade suffered. In the autumn of 1702 South Carolinians destroyed the town, not the fort, of Spanish St. Augustine; and in 1706 a Franco-Spanish fleet was repulsed from the harbor of Charleston.

In the North, New England bore the brunt of the war against the French in Canada. Until 1709 neither New York nor England rendered material assistance. English settlements, including those at Wells, Saco, Deerfield, Reading, Sudbury and Haverhill, became the victims of barbarous French and Indian raids. After retaliatory attacks on Port Royal, led in 1704 by Benjamin Church and in 1707 by John March, had failed, the English colonists secured in 1709 Great Britain's promise of aid for expeditions against Quebec and Montreal. These projected campaigns under Samuel Vetch and Francis Nicholson were abandoned (October, 1709) after the promised British force had been diverted to Portugal. In the following year a British contingent, secured by Nicholson and Peter Schuyler in London, arrived. With that support colonial troops, led by Nicholson and Vetch, took Port Royal in October, 1710. The capture of Port Royal, renamed Annapolis Royal, signified the fall of Acadia to Great Britain.

The new Tory government in England, dominated by Harley and St. John and interested in obtaining the Asiento for the projected South Sea Company, disavowed Marlborough's contention that the European fronts were alone decisive. That government sent Admiral Walker and Gen. Hill with military aid to support colonial troops in attacks on Quebec and Montreal. However, on Aug. 23, 1711, ten of the expedition's ships were wrecked with the loss of nearly 1000 men on the rocks above Anticosti. Thereupon Walker and Hill returned to England.

Meanwhile in 1711 peace negotiations had begun in Europe. In October, 1712, American colonial governors received a royal proclamation of an armistice; and in 1713 Queen Anne's War was concluded by the Treaty of Utrecht.

QUEENSTON (QUEENSTOWN) HEIGHTS, BATTLE OF (Oct. 13, 1812), the second serious reverse sustained by American arms in the disastrous campaign of 1812, arose out of the attempt of Maj. Gen. Stephen Van Rensselaer to invade Canada across the Niagara River. The advanced units of the American force (which amounted in all to about 3100 men) successfully established themselves upon the steep escarpment overlooking the village of Queenston, and defeated the first attempts of the British forces to dislodge them. In one of these attempts the British commander, Maj. Gen. Isaac Brock, was killed. American hopes of victory, however, were dispelled by the refusal of the main body of American militia to cross the river to support the troops already engaged; and later in the day Maj. Gen. Sheaffe, upon whom the British command had devolved, collected a force of about 1000 men, gained the summit of the heights by a flanking movement and enveloped and captured the whole force which had crossed. The British reported the capture of 925 prisoners, of whom 417 were regulars; among them was Lt. Col. Winfield Scott. The Americans had about 90 men killed; the British had 14 killed, 77 wounded and 21 missing.

QUITRENT originated in England from the commutation into a fixed money equivalent, of the annual food and labor payments due the lord of the manor. By the period of colonization the quitrents had become firmly established and were being enforced by distraint upon personal property, and in extreme cases by forfeiture of the land. As it was transplanted to the American colonies, the quitrent was a feudal due payable by freeholders to the proprietaries to whom the land had been granted. Later, after the proprietary rights were taken over, as in Virginia and the Carolinas, it became a Crown revenue in the royal colonies.

Customarily, the right to charge quitrents was included in all the early charters. But in Plymouth and Massachusetts Bay the title to the land was soon vested in the freeholders, and this system of free tenure soon spread to the other New England colonies. So firmly did it become one of the "Liberties of New England," that an attempt to exact quitrents was one of the chief grievances in the overthrow of Gov. Andros. Quitrents were nominally due in all the American colonies outside of New England, but they were more effectively enforced in Pennsylvania and the colonies to the southward. Also, they were proposed, but not always collected, in the West Indies, in the Floridas, in Nova Scotia and in other outlying colonies, and were included in the several schemes to set up British colonies west of the Appalachians.

The annual amount of the quitrent was nominal, varying in individual colonies from 2s to 4s per 100 acres, with occasionally 1d per acre, yet payments became a frequent source of irritation. Distraint was the usual means of enforcement, and efforts to secure forfeiture of the land, where necessary, met with determined opposition. The medium of payment, likewise, stirred up much controversy. With specie scarce, it was necessary to use commodities, such as wheat, tobacco and other native products. Consequently, many disputes arose between the assemblies and the representatives of the proprietaries or the Crown over the rate of exchange, grading, the cost of transportation and the place of payment. Actually, the quitrents produced a sizable revenue in the colonies in which they were enforced. In Pennsylvania, by 1776, nominally £10,204 7¾d was annually due, of which about a third was collected. In Maryland, in 1774, practically the entire rent roll, £8518 6s 2d, was being collected, but in Virginia, excluding the Northern Neck, which had been granted to Lord Culpeper, the net return from the quitrent in 1771 was only £3885 16s, not quite half the total rent roll. In South Carolina, toward the close of the colonial period, the annual return averaged between £2000 and £3000.

In both the proprietary and royal colonies the quitrents constituted an independent revenue for which there was no public accounting. But, especially as the Revolutionary period approached, they were collected with much less friction in the royal than in the proprietary colonies. As early as the Andros Rebellion in New England, colonial leaders appreciated the dangers inherent in a revenue that was altogether independent of popular control. After the outbreak of the Revolution the assemblies summarily ended these feudal dues upon the land, notably in Maryland where the Act of Abolition showed how galling this sign of perpetual dependence upon an absentee landlord had become. The quitrent, in short, was a feudal charge that was transferred to the American colonies, and the attempts to enforce it caused a constant irritation which had an important part in stirring up the Revolutionary spirit.

RADICAL REPUBLICANS were extremists who strongly influenced Union policy in Civil War days and became dominant during Reconstruction. Their main characteristics were antislavery zeal as a political instrument, moralizing unction, rebel-baiting intolerance and hunger for power. From the beginning these men made trouble for Lincoln by demanding a radical cabinet, rallying round Frémont in his most embarrassing maneuvers, intriguing against McClellan, denouncing West Point officers and pressing for a war of legislation against Southerners as persons. Their distrust of military expertness was combined with eagerness to seize the reins of army management. In their Committee on the Conduct of the War they used the weapon of congressional investigation, with deadly effect, to ruin the usefulness of valuable generals (*e.g.*, McClellan, Fitz-John Porter, Charles P. Stone), while their own military pets were urged for high command. Typical of their spirit and method was the second Confiscation (or treason) Act of 1862 by which the private property of Southerners as "rebels" was made subject to sweeping forfeiture. Lincoln disapproved of this bill and planned to veto it, but by a last-minute arrangement his unwilling signature was obtained. After the law was passed the Lincoln administration did little to enforce it. It was thus, in general, with Lincoln. He disapproved of the Radicals (or "Jacobins," as John Hay called them) but was in part swept along with them. The reconstruction issue found Lincoln in utter disagreement and hopeless deadlock with these "ultras" of his party, who showed clearly in 1864 that they did not wish his renomination.

Among the leaders of the Radicals may be mentioned Sumner, Wade, Stevens, Zachariah Chandler, Henry Winter Davis, J. A. Logan, James M. Ashley, Boutwell and Julian. By 1866 these vindictives had made themselves masters of Congress through the Republican party (now no longer a Lincoln party) and the drastic Reconstruction regime was peculiarly their work. In this they encountered the determined resistance of President Johnson, and the height of Radical vengefulness was reached in the almost successful effort to remove him on impeachment. As used in this article, the term "Radical" does not mean "liberal." The Radicals had small regard for civil rights, and some of their fiercest denunciations were hurled at the Supreme Court for upholding civil rights (in the North) in the Milligan case of 1866. Historians now recognize that there was an economic motive in Radical policy, for their control of the National Government favored Northeastern manufacturing and financial interests against those of the West and South.

RADICAL RULE IN THE SOUTH began in 1868 and 1870 when the government of ten Southern states was assumed by officials believing in equal rights for the Negroes. The main support of the new regimes was 931,000 newly enfranchised freedmen who, under prevailing conditions, formed majorities in five states and who had effective and unscrupulous leadership in the carpetbaggers. These Northern adventurers frightened the blacks with stories of white conspiracies against freedom, and stimulated hopes of overcoming the social and economic inequalities normally imposed upon Negroes in this country. The freedmen wanted to use their political rights as a means of securing land, education and even social equality.

The Radical governments accomplished certain constructive reforms. They established modern state constitutions and the principles of universal education and of equality before the law. There were visions of a truly Radical program designed to give the blacks opportunity to participate fully in the social and economic as well as the political rights of American citizenship. But such plans were overshadowed by the unparalleled incompetence and venality of the leaders. Illiterate field hands became legislators and minor officials, vying with each other in accepting bribes. Many of the carpetbag governors were corrupt and those who were personally honest were vindictive and unscrupulous in politics. Extravagant expenditures, heavy taxes and extensive increases in bonded debts were universal. Part of the public revenues was used for legitimate purposes, but the rest filled the pockets of embezzlers and thieves who garishly spent their gains. A continuation of a previously inaugurated policy of endorsing railroad bonds by the state was a fruitful source of easy money for the dishonest official and crooked speculator. Bonds were sometimes endorsed for roads which were never constructed. In extenuation of Radical rule it should be said that it was only one example of the several national political scandals of the post-bellum era and that its baneful effects were narrowly political. No successful attempt was made to subvert Southern society, and disorders in statehouses did not prevent notable progress in economic and social spheres.

Between 1869 and 1877 the Radical state governments collapsed. This process was hastened by divisions in Radical ranks and by the gradual withdrawal of Northern support because of the conviction that Negro rule was both scandalous and impractical. But the principal cause was the unrelenting opposition of the normally dominant white caste to an experiment which challenged Southern conceptions of the proper relations between races. As soon as the whites had recovered from the demoralization caused by war and the initial phases of Radical Reconstruction, they exercised their superior powers of organization to put an end to Negro rule. The scandals of carpetbaggery and Negroism were used to justify this action, but it would have come had the Radical governments been models of rectitude.

RADIO. In the years following World War I, radio grew from a medium used for experimental and specialized purposes into the largest mass medium in the United States, and the most nearly universal means of mass communication throughout the world. There were 156,400,000 radio sets and 4086 AM and FM stations on the air in the United States by Jan. 1,

1960. According to United Nations estimates, by 1958 there were 350,000,000 radio sets in the world, or more than the total circulation of all daily newspapers.

The invention of the three-electrode vacuum tube in 1906, by Dr. Lee DeForest, ushered in the electronic age. There followed a period of experimentation, largely by amateurs, or "hams." They included many leading engineers and inventors, and were of distinct importance in the development of radio. In 1909, an experimental forerunner of Station KCBS, San Francisco, became what is believed to be the nation's first radio station.

During World War I, the U. S. Navy controlled all private wireless facilities. Radio was then considered primarily a marine service. In 1919, radio returned to private enterprise; the Radio Corporation of America was incorporated in October, 1919. The station credited with presenting the first previously announced radio broadcast is Station KDKA, Pittsburgh. It is perhaps significant that this historic broadcast, on Nov. 2, 1920, consisted of the reading of the Harding-Cox election returns. In later years, radio was to make its most enduring contribution in the area of news and public affairs presentations.

In 1922, there were 30 radio stations and 60,000 sets in the United States; by 1927, 733 stations and 7,300,000 sets. Two radio networks were then in operation. The National Broadcasting Company began in 1926 and the Columbia Broadcasting System in 1927. The Mutual Broadcasting System was formed in 1934, and a fourth network, the American Broadcasting Company (first called the Blue Network), was established in 1942.

With the advent of networks, it became possible to present an advertising message simultaneously to large numbers of people throughout the country. Advertising interest in the medium grew accordingly. In 1930, advertisers spent $60,000,000 in network and local radio. The total increased to $215,600,000 by 1940, and to $643,000,000 by 1959.

In the 1930's and 1940's, radio reached its peak as an entertainment medium. Upwards of 15,000,000 people listened regularly to such favorites as Jack Benny, Fred Allen, Bob Hope and others. By 1948, there were 2079 radio stations and 76,991,000 sets in the United States. Major developments of the two decades also included: unprecedented use of radio by President Franklin D. Roosevelt; the introduction, during World War II, of the "roundup" technique in radio news reporting, with correspondents abroad reporting from the scene; the growth of frequency modulation (FM) broadcasting; and, late in the 1940's, the emergence of commercial television.

Government regulation of radio began with the Radio Act of 1912, in which licenses were granted to all citizens "upon application therefor." By the time of the Radio Act of 1927, the congestion of licensees made it impossible, in many places, to receive an adequate broadcast signal. The 1927 act, as incorporated into the broader Communications Act of 1934, is essentially the legislation under which all United States radio services have operated ever since. This act made provision for an administering body, the Federal Communications Commission.

Section 315 of the Communications Act, the so-called "equal time" provision, has been the subject of continuing disagreement. It requires equal broadcast treatment for all candidates for public office. In practice, this has meant equal time for all those representing special-interest and "fringe" groups, along with major party candidates. In 1960, for the first time, the Congress suspended Section 315 as it relates to the presidential and vice-presidential nominees, for the duration of the election campaign. This made possible historic, face-to-face discussions by the two major presidential candidates on radio and television.

During World War II, the importance of wire and radio communication, both for military and civilian uses, was amply demonstrated. As a result, in the postwar years, these facilities have formed an integral part of the national defense program. The CONELRAD System (Control of Electromagnetic Radiation) was established by the F. C. C. in 1950 at the request of the Department of Defense. The CONELRAD System minimizes the navigational aid which an attacking force might obtain from radio emissions, by confining all broadcast activity in an emergency to two radio frequencies, 640 and 1240 kilocycles.

In the 1950–60 decade, radio continued to move in new directions. Growing listener interest in FM is reflected in the increase of FM-equipped sets from 7,000,000 in 1950 to 15,000,000 in 1960. Large-scale international short-wave activity by the United States was another development. By 1960, the Voice of America, operated by the Broadcasting Service of the U. S. Information Agency, was broadcasting in 37 languages over a network of 87 transmitters. The Armed Forces Radio and Television Service brought United States servicemen and women stationed abroad full information on current affairs, as well as entertainment, using 12 powerful transmitters and 80 outlets around the world. An innovation, at the end of the decade, was the presentation of broadcast editorials. In 1959, the National Association of Broadcasters adopted a resolution favoring and encouraging editorials by broadcast licensees. The broadcast editorial was defined by N. A. B. as "an on-the-air expression of opinion (clearly identified as such) on a subject of public interest, by a station licensee or his designated representative."

During the 1950's, the character of radio programming and listening gradually changed to meet the new conditions created by television. Entertainment became more informal; it was no longer directed to a family audience in the living room but to individual listeners apt to be engaged in various other activities while listening. Music of all kinds became an important part of local station programming, and the role of radio "personalities" also emerged strongly.

In this period, too, radio listening in automobiles reached major proportions. The number of car radios increased from 14,800,000 in 1950 to a 1960 total of 40,400,000 sets. The mobility of listening was furthered by improvements in portable sets, notably the transistor in 1954. In the home itself, radios are found in many rooms. The 1960 national average set ownership was three radios per home, and 96% of all homes were radio-equipped. Usage averaged an estimated 16 hours a week per listener.

RADISSON'S RELATION. Pierre Esprit Radisson was long thought to have been one of the two traders sent by Gov. Jean de Lauson of New France in 1654 to seek out and get the trade of the Huron, Ottawa and other Western tribes that had been scattered by the Iroquois in the later 1640's and early 1650's. It is now regarded as certain that he was in Quebec in 1655, since a document of that date, signed by him there, has been found. He could not have been on the expedition, therefore, for it consumed two years. His brother-in-law, Médard Chouart, Sieur des Groseilliers, does appear to have been one of the governor's two men. It is probably Chouart's story that Radisson has given in his *Voyages*, derived in all likelihood from Chouart's oral accounts of his trip into and about Lake Huron and Lake Michigan. The book was printed from a manuscript, written about the year 1669, which is a defective, contemporary translation of an original French document now lost. The translation is among the papers of Samuel Pepys in the Bodleian Library at Oxford.

Radisson's account of the trip is inaccurate, confused and ambiguous, but it does give an inkling of the culture of the Indians and of trade methods in the West at a very early date. Other parts of the same manuscript are the narratives of two of Radisson's sojourns among the Iroquois in the 1650's and a trip made by Radisson and Des Groseilliers in 1659 and 1660 from their homes in Trois Rivières on the lower St. Lawrence to the end of Lake Superior and even a little south and west of that lake. This account is fairly detailed, exact and explicit. Its chief value lies in its descriptions of Indians before they were influenced by white men. On this trip the two men learned from the Indians of an easy route for fur-trading from Hudson Bay to the great beaver country northwest of Lake Superior, and of a supposed Northwest Passage in that area. It was these ideas that led the two men successively to France, New England and Old England in an endeavor to get aid to explore the possibilities of Hudson Bay, both for trade and for finding a route to Asia. In England they succeeded. Here, after many disappointments, the Hudson's Bay Company was founded on May 2, 1670, after Des Groseilliers' return from a successful trip to Hudson Bay in 1668 and 1669. The two explorers' lives between 1670 and Radisson's death in 1710 do not touch the history of the United States closely, though they are full of significance for English and French empires in North America, for Canada, and for the Hudson's Bay Company.

RAIL FENCES. For many years following first settlement in America, rail fences were common. Tree trunks easy to split were abundant, and an axe was the only tool necessary to make rails and fence. Rails could be split with an axe and wooden wedges made with an axe. Pine, oak and chestnut were favorite woods for rails, the tree trunks being cut into 11-foot lengths. A 10- or 12-inch log would make five or six rails, all three-cornered; a 20- or 24-inch log would turn out twelve to eighteen rails, those next the heart of the log three-cornered, those outside four-cornered, all four or five inches through. The ground rails, laid zigzag, were the "worm"; the top rails, the "riders." The worm zigzagged across the line two feet or more on each side, the fence thus covering a strip of land five feet wide. If stakes were dug in at the corners to support the riders, they toed out still farther. In a cap-fence, upright stakes (posts) clamped each corner and the worm was more nearly straight. The caps were short clapboards, with an auger hole in each end, fitted down over the tops of the posts, holding them together. The best rail fences came last—straight on the line, with the ends of the rails mortised into heavy posts. Soldiers in the Revolution, the War of 1812 and the Civil War found old dry fence rails handy for campfires, and burned millions of them.

"RAIL SPLITTER." The term originated in the Illinois State Republican Convention at Decatur, May 9, 1860, when Richard J. Oglesby and John Hanks marched into the convention hall with two fence rails placarded, "Abraham Lincoln, The Rail Candidate for President in 1860." The sobriquet caught on at the national convention at Chicago, spread quickly over the North, and became a valuable campaign asset.

RAILROAD SURVEYS, EARLY GOVERNMENT. Interest in a railroad to the Pacific, already aroused by the writings and activities of John Plumbe, Asa Whitney and others, became keen and widespread after the territorial expansion resulting from the Mexican Cession of 1848. The question of the best route now became the subject of a great deal of discussion, especially since each state along the Mississippi and each Midwestern city of any size from the Canadian border to the Gulf evinced a direct and active interest in the selection.

In 1853, therefore, Congress added the sum of $150,000 to the army appropriation bill to defray the expenses of surveying feasible routes to the Pacific.

Under the direction of Jefferson Davis, Secretary of War, parties were sent into the field and five routes were surveyed. The northernmost survey, between the 47th and 49th parallels from St. Paul to the mouth of the Columbia, received widespread publicity because of the enthusiasm of the leader, Gov. Isaac I. Stevens of the New Territory of Washington. Data regarding a route in general along the emigrant trail to California was secured by a party under Lt. E. G. Beckwith. A difficult route between the 38th and 39th parallels was surveyed by Capt. J. W. Gunnison, who was killed during an Indian ambush. A survey following the 35th parallel as closely as possible from Fort Smith to Los Angeles was conducted by Lt. A. W. Whipple. Finally parties under Capt. John Pope, Lt. J. G. Parke and others explored a far southern route along the 32nd parallel.

The reports of these surveys, later published in copiously illustrated volumes, contributed greatly to geographical and scientific knowledge concerning the Far West. The surveys, however, did not bring agreement as to a route. Jefferson Davis championed the southernmost survey, but sectional rivalry was too great to permit the choice of a route until after the Southern states had seceded from the Union, when the Pacific Railroad Bill was adopted in 1862.

RAILROADS. The earliest railroads in the United States were short wooden tramways connecting mines or quarries with nearby streams, upon which horses could draw heavier loads than on the common roads. The idea of the railroad as it came to be, tracks on which trains of cars are pulled by mechanical power in common carrier service, was first expounded by Col. John Stevens of Hoboken, N. J., who in 1812, published his *Documents Tending to Prove the Superior Advantages of Rail-Ways and Steam Carriages Over Canal Navigation.* On Feb. 6, 1815, the Colonel secured a charter from the New Jersey legislature authorizing the building of a railroad across the state but he was unable to enlist the capital necessary for construction.

The first charter under which a railroad was actually built in the United States was that of the Granite Railway of Massachusetts, a three-mile long line built in 1826, which used horses to haul stone for the building of the Bunker Hill monument from quarries at Quincy.

The first railroad incorporated as a common carrier of passengers and freight, the Baltimore & Ohio, was chartered by the State of Maryland on Feb. 28, 1827. Construction was started with due ceremony on July 4, 1828, and the first passengers were carried in January, 1830, in single cars drawn by horses.

Already, however, experiments with steam locomotion were under way. Col. Stevens had built a tiny locomotive which ran on a circular track on his estate in 1825. More significant was the "Stourbridge Lion," imported from England by the Delaware &

Hudson Canal & Railroad for use on the line of rails connecting its mines with its canal. On its one trial trip on Aug. 8, 1829, the "Lion" proved to be too heavy for the track and was not used again as a locomotive. In August, 1830, the Baltimore & Ohio experimented with the "Tom Thumb," an engine whose diminutive size was indicated by its name. It was built and operated by Peter Cooper.

The essential elements of a railroad in the modern sense—track, trains of cars, mechanical locomotive power and public service as a common carrier—were first combined on the South Carolina Canal & Rail Road Co. (now included in the Southern Railway System) when, on Dec. 25, 1830, it inaugurated scheduled service on the first six miles of its line out of Charleston with the steam locomotive "Best Friend," the first to pull a train of cars on the American continent. Three years later the line was opened to Hamburg, a terminus across the river from Augusta, Ga., 136 miles away, making it at the time the longest railway in the world.

Railroads opened for operation by steam power in the early 1830's included the Mohawk & Hudson, earliest link in the future New York Central System, over which the locomotive "DeWitt Clinton" pulled a train of cars between Albany and Schenectady on Aug. 9, 1831; the Camden & Amboy, now part of the Pennsylvania system, on which the British-built "John Bull" was placed in service at Bordentown, N. J., also in 1831; the Philadelphia, Germantown & Norristown, now part of the Reading, on which the Baldwin-built "Old Ironsides" first ran in 1832; and the railroad connecting New Orleans with Lake Pontchartrain, afterward part of the Louisville & Nashville, on which the first locomotive in the Mississippi Valley made its initial scheduled run on Sept. 17, 1832.

By 1835 railroads ran from Boston to Lowell, the beginnings of the future Boston & Maine; to Worcester, first link in the Boston & Albany; and to Providence, the genesis of the New York, New Haven & Hartford. The Petersburg Railroad, now part of the Atlantic Coast Line, ran from the Virginia city whose name it bore south into North Carolina. The Baltimore & Ohio had built a branch to Washington, D. C., and had pushed its main line westward to the Blue Ridge.

Countering this effort by Baltimore to reach out for the trade of the West, New York had started the New York & Erie, headed westward for Lake Erie through the southern tier of counties of the state, and the State of Pennsylvania, not to be outdone, had opened a hybrid route between Philadelphia and Pittsburgh, using two stretches of canals, a railroad operated with both locomotives and horses, and a series of inclined planes by which cars were raised and lowered over the Alleghenies.

Pennsylvania was not the only state to undertake the building of a railroad. North Carolina, acting through corporations in which the state was a majority stockholder, built and owns lines that today constitute a substantial segment of the Southern Railway, which operates them under lease. Georgia, acting directly, built, still owns and leases to the Louisville & Nashville an important link in Georgia and Tennessee. Virginia is a large stockholder in the Richmond, Fredericksburg & Potomac. Less fortunate were the railroad ventures of the states of Michigan and Illinois, which embarked prematurely on ambitious state transportation schemes which failed and were sold to private companies. One of the most successful ventures in public ownership is the Cincinnati Southern, a line built and owned by the city and operated under lease by the Southern Railway system.

1840–1860

By the end of the first decade of the railroad era, in 1840, 2800 miles of railroad were in operation in the United States, with mileage in every seacoast state and in Kentucky, Ohio, Indiana, Michigan and Illinois. In the second decade of railroad development, mileage more than trebled, with a total of 9000 miles. Lines had been opened in Vermont and Wisconsin and missing links had been supplied so that by 1850 it was possible to travel by rail between Boston and Buffalo, with numerous changes of cars, and between Boston and Wilmington, N. C., with occasional gaps covered by steamboat.

By 1850, also, there had been developed a standard American-type locomotive, with a four-wheel swivel leading truck and four driving wheels, coupled. The design was simple, powerful, and easy on the track. It became the "ancestor" of a variety of heavier and more powerful types for freight and passenger service, but itself remained as the backbone of the locomotive fleet until near the end of the century.

In the decade of the 1850's railway mileage again more than trebled, as the ambitious efforts of the Atlantic seaports to reach the "Western waters" were fulfilled. New York was connected with the Great Lakes both by the Erie Railroad and also by way of Albany and the New York Central, formed in 1853 by the consolidation of a dozen small railroads between the Hudson River and Buffalo. Philadelphia likewise established an all-rail connection with Pittsburgh, and Baltimore reached the Ohio at Wheeling early in the 1850's.

Before these lines reached their trans-Allegheny goals other lines were being built across the more open and level country of the Middle West. Chicago was entered from the East in 1852 almost simultaneously by two lines, the Michigan Central and the Michigan Southern, both of which are now included in the New York Central system. Already, lines were building west from Chicago—the Galena & Chicago Union (now the Chicago & North Western), which brought the first locomotive to the future rail center on a Great Lakes sailing vessel, and the Chicago &

Rock Island, which reached the Mississippi River in February, 1854. Only a year later, a route between Chicago and East St. Louis afforded another rail connection between the East and the Mississippi, while in 1857 two such connections were added— the direct route from Baltimore via Cincinnati and, to the south, a route between Charleston and Savannah, on the Atlantic, and Memphis, on the Mississippi.

But before the rails reached the great river from the east, railroads had started from the west bank. The first locomotive to turn a wheel beyond the Mississippi ran on Dec. 9, 1852, on the Pacific Railroad of Missouri (now the Missouri Pacific) from St. Louis five miles west. In 1856, the Iron Horse crossed the Mississippi on the first railroad bridge, that of the Rock Island line, which added "& Pacific" to its name. Before the end of the decade, the steed reached the Missouri on the tracks of the Hannibal & St. Joseph, now part of the Burlington Lines.

For the most part these routes had been built as separate local lines, in many instances lacking the physical connections without which through movement of freight and passengers was impossible. One road built as a unit was the Illinois Central, a north-south line connecting East Dubuque and Cairo, with a "branch" from Centralia to Chicago. Chartered in 1851, the line of more than 700 miles was completed in 1857.

One factor in the successful building at one time and as one project of what was then the world's longest railroad was the grant by the Federal Government to the State of Illinois, and through that state to the railroad corporation, of vacant lands from the public domain in Illinois as an aid to financing the construction of the line. This grant, and a like grant of lands in Alabama and Mississippi to the Mobile & Ohio Railroad which was to be built northward, was the beginning of a policy of making such grants in aid of railroad building, following an earlier precedent of such grants in aid of canals and wagon roads. Lands were granted to railroads in alternate sections of one mile square, for distances of from six to twenty miles on either side of the line. The Government retained title to alternate sections, making a "checkerboard" pattern of private and government ownership.

The purposes of the grants were to use vacant and unsaleable lands lacking transportation, to encourage the building of railroads into undeveloped regions, thereby attracting settlers, adding value to the lands retained by the Government, increasing production and taxable wealth, and unifying the nation.

During the 21 years in which the policy was in effect, from 1850 to 1871, Federal land grants were made to aid in the building of less than 10% of the railroad mileage of the United States, by which there were transferred to private ownership some 131,000,000 acres of the approximately 1,400,000,000 of the public lands owned in 1850. The value of

the lands granted as of the time of the grants was approximately $125,000,000. In return for the grants the railroads carried government freight, mail and troops at reduced rates until 1946, when the arrangement was ended by act of Congress. By that time land grant rate deductions for the Government amounted to a total of more than $1,000,000,000.

In the same decade of the 1850's, railroad building was started in newly annexed Texas, where the Buffalo Bayou, Brazos & Colorado was opened from the present-day Houston westward toward Richmond in 1853, and in the new state of California, where the Sacramento Valley was opened in 1856 from navigable waters at Sacramento to Folsom. Both lines are now part of the Southern Pacific system.

1861–1865

With the coming of the Civil War, the building of new railroads was slowed down somewhat but the existing railroads were called upon to play essential roles in the great struggle. Even before war started, the east-west railroads, tying the Northwest to the Northeast rather than to the lower Mississippi Valley, had been largely decisive in determining the attitude of the interior states of the North. More than two thirds of the 1861 mileage and an even greater proportion of railroad transportation capacity lay in the states which adhered to the Union. Invasion soon reduced further even the small percentage of the railroad mileage in Confederate hands. It is not too much to say that relative railroad strength was a decisive factor in the "first railroad war."

On the railroads of both sides, however, there were remarkable transportation achievements. The outcome of the first Battle of Bull Run was determined by troops shifted by rail from the Shenandoah Valley to the vicinity of Manassas. A major rail movement was the transfer of the Confederate Army of Tennessee from Tupelo, Miss., to Chattanooga, Tenn., via Mobile and Atlanta, preparatory to the launching of Gen. Bragg's Kentucky campaign. A more remarkable accomplishment was the movement of Gen. Longstreet's army corps from Virginia through the Carolinas and Georgia, just in time to win the Confederate victory of Chickamauga. Most remarkable of all was the movement of Gen. Hooker's two corps of 22,000 men over a distance of 1200 miles from Virginia to the vicinity of Chattanooga, via Columbus, Indianapolis, Louisville and Nashville.

More important even than these spectacular shifts of large army units from one strategic field to another was the part played by the railroads in the day by day movement of men, food, ammunition, materiel and supplies from distant sources to the combat forces. Movements of this sort reached a climax in Gen. Sherman's campaign for the capture of Atlanta in the summer of 1864, when his army of 100,000 men and 35,000 animals was kept supplied and in fighting trim by a single-track railroad extending nearly 500 miles from its base on the Ohio River at Louisville.

1865–1916

There had been agitation for a transcontinental railroad since 1848, at least, and during the 1850's the Topographical Engineers of the Army had explored five routes. Ultimately railroads were built on all of these routes but sectional jealousies and the immensity of the task prevented such an undertaking until the Civil War removed the southern routes from consideration and, at the same time, made imperative the need for better communication with the Pacific Coast. Congress accordingly passed and President Lincoln signed on July 1, 1862, a bill authorizing a railroad between the Missouri River and California, to be built on the central or, as it came to be called, the Overland route.

The President designated Council Bluffs, Iowa, as the starting point. Construction was undertaken by the Union Pacific, building westward from Omaha and by the Central Pacific (now part of the Southern Pacific), building eastward from Sacramento. On May 10, 1869, the construction crews met and joined tracks at Promontory, Utah, in the mountains north of the Great Salt Lake. The junction was celebrated by the ceremony of driving the Golden Spike, as the telegraph instruments clicked out to the waiting and rejoicing United States the message: "The last rail is laid . . . the last spike driven. . . . The Pacific Railroad is completed."

The first transcontinental route was built as a "great military highway," in the words of Gen. Sherman, and was not expected to be self-supporting. Construction was aided by land grants and by government loans, frequently and erroneously described as gifts, despite the fact that the loans were repaid in full with interest. Later transcontinental routes were not aided by loans but in most instances received grants of land in return for which they carried government traffic at reduced rates.

The second transcontinental connection was supplied in 1881 when the Atchison, Topeka & Santa Fe, building westward, met the Southern Pacific, building eastward, at Deming, N. Mex. The Southern Pacific continuing to build eastward, met the Texas and Pacific at Sierra Blanca in 1882, and by further construction and acquisition of lines established a through route to New Orleans in 1883. In the same year California was reached by a line built by the Santa Fe westward from Albuquerque, forming still another transcontinental route.

In the same year the first route to reach the Pacific Northwest was opened by the Northern Pacific, built through the northernmost tier of states. A second route to the Northwest was opened a year later when the Oregon Short Line, built from a junction with the Union Pacific, joined tracks with the Oregon

Railway & Navigation Co. Both are now part of the Union Pacific system.

In 1893 a third route to the Pacific Northwest, and the first to be built without the aid of land grants, was completed by the Great Northern. The extension to the coast of the Chicago, Milwaukee & St. Paul, which added "Pacific" to its name, was completed in 1909, also without the aid of land grants.

The present Union Pacific route to Southern California was completed in 1905 by the San Pedro, Los Angeles & Salt Lake, while another route to northern California was opened in 1910 when the Western Pacific effected a junction at Salt Lake City with the Denver & Rio Grande Western.

Meanwhile, railroad construction continued in the older settled portions of the United States, as the gaps in the rail net were closed and additional routes were added. Between 1860 and 1870, despite the interruption of the Civil War, total mileage increased from 31,000 to 53,000 miles. This rate of growth was exceeded in the 1870's when 40,000 miles of new line were built.

The decade of the 1880's recorded the greatest growth in railway mileage, with an average of more than 7000 miles of new line built each year. By the end of the decade the conversion from iron rail to the stronger, more durable and safer steel rail was largely completed. The same decade saw also the standardization of track gauge, of car couplers, of train brakes, and of time, all essential steps toward a continent-wide commerce by rail.

The earlier railroads were built to serve the interest of particular points and, for the most part, without thought of future inter-connection with other lines. Under such circumstances the question of gauge, or the width of track between rails, was of small importance. There have been altogether 24 different gauges used in the United States, ranging from two feet to six feet. By the 1880's gradual adjustment had brought about general agreement on two gauges. One of five feet predominated in the South. The other, predominant in the rest of the country, was 4 feet 8½ inches, a width originally used in England by George Stephenson which had spread to the United States through the importation by early railroads of English-built locomotives. In 1886, the railroads of the South changed their gauge to conform and the odd figure of 4–8½ became "standard gauge" for all but a limited mileage of "narrow gauge" railroads.

Along with standardization of track gauge there had to be, of course, standardization of cars and locomotives to make it possible for the cars of any railroad to run on the tracks and in the trains of every other railroad. Car couplers, for example, had to work not only with other couplers of like design but as cars went from road to road they had to work with those on other lines. Also, as new models of couplers were introduced, they had to work with those already in use. As early as 1869, the Master Car Builders' Association, one of the ancestors of the present Association of American Railroads, had begun tests of various types of couplers designed to replace the simple but unsafe and unsatisfactory "link-and-pin" device. Altogether more than 3000 patents were issued for various forms of safety couplers. Forty-two were considered sufficiently practical to warrant consideration in a series of tests at Buffalo beginning in 1885, which resulted in the adoption, in 1887, of the design of Eli H. Janney as standard. Vastly modified and improved, the basic principle remains standard today.

As in the case of couplers, interchange of freight cars among railroads required standardization of brakes. Early trains were stopped by hand brakes, set on each car by brakemen. Efforts to control the setting of brakes from the locomotive were unsuccessful until, in 1869, George Westinghouse devised his first air brake for passenger trains. Three years later he developed an improved system in which the brakes would be applied automatically if the train was accidentally separated. These brakes were installed on most passenger cars within the next decade but the problem of a satisfactory brake for freight trains remained. In 1886 and 1887 exhaustive tests were conducted on the Chicago, Burlington & Quincy at Burlington, Iowa, which resulted in the adoption of a quick-acting brake for freight trains. With further improvements, especially those adopted in 1933 after exhaustive laboratory and road tests, the air brake remains fundamental in train operation.

Another feature of railroad operation standardized in the 1880's was time. Previously, each locality used its own sun time, while each railroad had its own standard, usually the local time of its headquarters or of some important city on the line. There were altogether nearly 100 different railroad times, with unimaginable confusion. On Nov. 18, 1883, under an arrangement put into effect by the General Time Convention (another predecessor organization of the Association of American Railroads) all railroad clocks and watches were set on a new standard time with four zones one hour apart. Within a short time most localities abandoned their particular times and conformed to the system of Eastern, Central, Mountain and Pacific time zones set up by the railroads. The system of standard time continued under railroad auspices until 1918, when by act of Congress it was placed under control of the Interstate Commerce Commission.

The Interstate Commerce Commission itself dates from the 1880's. Early attempts to regulate railroad rates and practices by action of the states had been only partially successful, although in 1876 the so-called "Granger Laws" had been upheld by the U. S. Supreme Court for intrastate application. In 1886, however, the Court held in the Wabash case that Congress had exclusive jurisdiction over inter-state commerce and that a state could not regulate even the intrastate portion of an interstate movement. Efforts had been made for a dozen years before to have Congress enact regulatory legislation. The decision in the Wabash case brought these efforts to a head and resulted in passage on Feb. 4, 1887, of the Act to Regulate Commerce which created the Interstate Commerce Commission. Subsequent enactments, notably those of 1903, 1906, 1910, 1920, 1933 and 1940, have broadened the Commission's jurisdiction and responsibilities, increased its powers and strengthened its organization.

In 1888 the first Federal legislation dealing with relations between railroads and their employees was passed. This enactment applied only to employees in train and engine service, who were the first railway employees to form successful unions—the Brotherhood of Locomotive Engineers in 1863, the Order of Railway Conductors in 1868, the Brotherhood of Locomotive Firemen in 1873, and the Brotherhood of Railroad Trainmen in 1883. These, with the Switchmen's Union (organized in 1894) constitute the "operating" group of unions. Other "nonoperating" crafts formed organizations at various dates—the telegraphers (1886), the six "shop craft" unions in the period 1888–93, the maintenance-of-way employees (1891), the clerks and station employees (1898), the signalmen (1901). Nevertheless, the Erdman Act (1898) and the Newlands Act (1913), providing various measures of mediation, conciliation, arbitration and fact-finding in connection with railway labor disputes, dealt with train service cases only.

Between 1890 and 1900 another 40,000 miles were added to the railroad net, which by the turn of the century had assumed substantially its present main outline. After 1900, however, there were built still another 60,000 miles of line, to bring the total of first main track to its peak of 254,000 miles in 1916. Mileage of all track, including additional main tracks, passing tracks, sidings and yards reached its maximum of 430,000 miles in 1930. Between the above dates and 1960 mileage of line declined to approximately 220,000, with 390,000 miles of tracks of all sorts.

This reduction in mileage is due to many factors, including the exhaustion of the mines, forests or other natural resources which were the reason for being of many branch lines, the effects of intensified water competition and the new element of highway competition, and the co-ordinations and consolidations which have made many lines unnecessary. In 1916 more than 1400 companies operated 254,000 miles of line; in 1960, fewer than 600 companies operated 220,000 miles of line—but the reduced mileage had more than double the effective carrying capacity of the more extensive network.

1917–1941

Railroad mileage was at its peak when, in April, 1917, the United States entered World War I. Immediately the railroads established the body known as the Railroads' War Board to co-ordinate their work in meeting increased transportation demands. Increases were achieved but, by December, it was apparent that a voluntary organization of this kind could not cope with difficulties such as congestion due to abuse by government organizations of the privilege of demanding priority and preference for loading cars regardless of whether they could be unloaded promptly at destination; also those resulting from refusal to suspend for the emergency the application of the antitrust laws and the antipooling provisions of the Interstate Commerce Act. On Dec. 26, 1917, President Wilson issued his proclamation taking over the railroads for operation by the government, to start Jan. 1.

Operation of the railroads by the United States Railroad Administration lasted for 26 months, until March 1, 1920. From the standpoint of meeting the transportation demands of the war the operation was creditable. From a financial point of view, it resulted in losses, largely due to increased wages and prices not compensated for by increases in rates and fares, which amounted to an average of nearly $2,000,000 a day for the period of government operation.

The Congress voted to return the railroads to private operation and set up the terms of such operation in the Transportation Act of 1920. Among the changes in government policy was recognition of a degree of responsibility for financial results, found in the direction to the Interstate Commerce Commission to fix rates at such a level as would enable the railroads as a whole, or in groups, to earn a fair return on the value of the properties devoted to public service. This provision was frequently described as a government guarantee of railroad profits although there was no guarantee of earnings. Commercial conditions and competitive forces have kept railway earnings well below the contemplated level and the Government was not called on to make up the deficiency.

Another shift in government policy was the reversal of its attitude toward consolidation of railroads, previously frowned upon but encouraged by the Act of 1920. Consolidation in one form or another has been from early times the way of growth of the major systems, some of which include properties originally built by a hundred or more companies. The 1920 law directed the I. C. C. to work out a scheme of consolidation for the railroads, a requirement of which the Commission was relieved at its own request in 1933.

The 1920 act also, for the first time, set up a U. S. Labor Board with jurisdiction extending to all crafts of employees and with power to determine wage rates and working conditions, although without power to enforce its decisions otherwise than by the force of public opinion. The first nation-wide strike on the railroads took place in 1922, when the shop-

men struck against a Labor Board decision reducing wages. The strike failed but its aftereffects were such that in the Railway Labor Act of 1926, agreed to by both the unions and the railroads, the Labor Board was abolished and the principles of the earlier labor legislation with their reliance on mediation and conciliation were restored with improved machinery for making them more effective. The 1926 law was amended in important particulars in 1934, at the instance of the Railway Labor Executives Association, an organization of the "standard" railway unions formed in 1929.

In 1934, also, a Railroad Retirement Act was passed as the first of the social security measures of the New Deal period. This legislation was declared unconstitutional but in 1937 a retirement and unemployment insurance system was set up under legislation agreed upon by the Railway Labor Executives Association and the Association of American Railroads, an organization of the industry formed in 1934.

While railway mileage was shrinking in the two decades between World Wars I and II, the same years saw the introduction of numerous innovations in railroad plant, equipment and methods which greatly increased capacity and efficiency. The wooden car virtually disappeared. The steam locomotive became more powerful and more efficient. The diesel locomotive was introduced in passenger service in 1934 and in freight service in 1941. Passenger car air-conditioning was introduced in 1929 and the first all air-conditioned train was operated in 1931. Streamlining was added to passenger train service, beginning in 1934. Passenger train speeds were increased and overnight merchandise freight service for distances of more than 400 miles was inaugurated. Centralized traffic control and train operation by signal indication multiplied the capacity of single track lines and even made it possible to take up trackage that was no longer required. Car retarders increased the speed and capacity, as well as the economy, of handling trains in terminal yards. Methods of operation, including car supply and distribution, particularly through the operations of the Car Service Division of the Association of American Railroads, were so improved that periodic general car shortages were no longer experienced.

1942–1960

The combined effect of these and other improvements in plant, methods and organization was such that the railroads, continuing under private operation, were able to meet all transportation demands during World War II. With one-fourth fewer cars, one-third fewer locomotives and nearly one-third fewer men than they had in World War I, the railroads handled double the traffic of the first war and did it without congestion or delay.

In spite of wartime increases in wages and the

prices of materials and supplies, railway rates and fares were no higher at the end of the war than they were when war began. As a result of postwar increases in wages, average hourly earnings of employees have gone up from approximately $1.00 an hour to more than $2.50 an hour, and the level of prices paid for materials and supplies has more than doubled in fifteen postwar years. In the same period, the average revenue received for hauling a ton of freight one mile has gone up from the neighborhood of one cent to 1½ cents, and the average charge for carrying a passenger one mile has gone up from about two cents to a little less than three cents. At the same time, competitive forces have reduced the railroads' share of the total transportation movement.

In May, 1946, President Truman, acting under his war powers, seized the railroads as a means of dealing with a nation-wide strike by the engineers and trainmen which paralyzed the railroads for two days. Similar strike threats by other groups of unions brought similar seizures by the Government in 1948 and again in 1950, the latter lasting nearly two years. In 1951 Congress amended the 1934 Railway Labor Act by removing the prohibition against compulsory union membership as a condition of holding a job on the railroads, thereby permitting the establishment of the union shop by negotiation. Such agreements have been negotiated on most railroads.

Throughout the postwar years the railroads have carried forward a program of capital improvements, with expenditures for such purposes averaging more than one billion dollars yearly. The most striking and significant change has been the virtual displacement of the steam locomotive by the diesel-electric. Other major developments include the wider use of continuous welded rail in lengths of a quarter-mile, a half-mile, and even longer; the wide use of off-track equipment in maintenance of way work; the development of new designs of freight cars which ride more smoothly; the introduction of container or trailer-on-flat-car service, commonly called "piggy backing"; and the development of the automatic terminal with electronic controls, known as the "push-button yard."

In passing the Transportation Act of 1958 Congress somewhat relaxed regulatory requirements on the railroads providing, in effect, that competitive cost factors be given greater consideration in determining the lawfulness of rates, so long as the rate proposed is compensatory to the carrier and not discriminatory as among shippers.

In 1959, Congress amended the Railroad Retirement and Unemployment Insurance acts, increasing the benefits and the taxes levied to pay them. Retirement is financed by taxes on both companies and employees, half and half; unemployment insurance is financed by taxes on the companies alone, without contribution from the employees.

As 1959 ended, railroads and employees were engaged in negotiations over wages and working conditions. The companies were seeking changes in rules which, it was charged, compelled payment for work not done and not needed. The operating unions denied the charge, maintaining that the rules under criticism are necessary for safety and the protection of the rights of employees. Besides the dispute over so-called "featherbedding," which is with the operating unions only, negotiations over wages were also in progress with all the employee organizations.

RAILROADS: SKETCHES OF PRINCIPAL LINES

Atchison, Topeka & Santa Fe. Chartered in 1859 to connect Atchison and Topeka, Kan., the Santa Fe has expanded eastward to Chicago, westward to the Pacific Coast, and southward to the Gulf of Mexico. The system of 13,150 miles includes the Gulf, Colorado & Santa Fe and the Panhandle & Santa Fe, and the former Kansas City, Mexico & Orient, operating lines in Texas.

Atlantic Coast Line. Chartered in 1836 to connect Richmond and Petersburg, Va., the A. C. L. has stretched southward through acquisition of lines serving the Carolinas, Georgia, Alabama and Florida. The present name was adopted in 1900, when the parent company absorbed its southern connections. A. C. L. operates 5600 miles of line and has substantial interests in the Louisville & Nashville, the Clinchfield and other roads.

Baltimore & Ohio. Chartered in 1827 (the oldest charter under which a railroad is now operated), the B. & O. has expanded eastward to Philadelphia and New York and westward to Chicago and St. Louis, through construction and acquisition of lines. Present mileage is 6000.

Boston & Maine. The first of the 111 companies which have been absorbed into the B. & M. was the Boston & Lowell, chartered in 1830. The name "Boston & Maine" dates from 1835. The railroad operates 1700 miles of line in Massachusetts, New Hampshire, Maine, Vermont and New York.

Central of Georgia. Chartered in 1833 as the Central Railroad & Banking Co. of Georgia to build from Savannah to Macon, the C. of Ga. now operates 1700 miles of line in Georgia, Alabama and Tennessee. Not to be confused with the Georgia Railroad between Augusta and Atlanta, built and owned by the Georgia Railroad & Banking Co., also incorporated in 1833, and operated under lease since 1882. Neither is it to be confused with the Western & Atlantic Railroad, under which name the State of Georgia built a line between Atlanta and Chattanooga, which is still owned by the state and is operated under lease by the Louisville & Nashville.

Chesapeake & Ohio. The 22-mile Louisa Railroad, chartered in Virginia in 1837, has grown into the 5300-mile C. & O. system, extending from Hampton Roads and Washington, to Louisville, Chicago, the Straits of Mackinac and the western shore of Lake Michigan (by car ferry). The latest railroad to be absorbed into the system was the Pere Marquette, in 1947.

Chicago, Burlington & Quincy. The original unit of the Burlington system was the Aurora Branch Railroad, a 12-mile line chartered in Illinois in 1849. This has expanded through the amalgamation of some 200 railroads into the present system of 11,000 miles, extending from Chicago and St. Louis to the Twin Cities, Montana, Wyoming, Colorado, and, through control of the Colorado & Southern and the Fort Worth & Denver, to the Gulf Coast of Texas.

Chicago Great Western. The present name of the company dates from 1892, when the system was formed as a result of the combination of pre-existing lines, the earliest of which was the Iowa Pacific, chartered in 1870. The C. G. W. operates 1,450 miles of line between Chicago, the Twin Cities, Des Moines, Omaha, St. Joseph and Kansas City.

Chicago, Milwaukee, St. Paul & Pacific. The earliest "ancestor" of the Milwaukee Road was chartered in 1847 to build a line across Wisconsin to the Mississippi River. By 1900 the C., M. & St. P. operated between the Great Lakes and the Missouri River. Between 1905 and 1910 the line was extended to the Pacific Coast. In 1921, it was extended into Indiana, with a total of more than 10,000 miles of line built by some 150 companies consolidated in the present system.

Chicago & North Western. Chartered in 1848 as the Galena & Chicago Union, the C. & N. W. was the first railroad in Chicago and the first to connect that city with the Missouri River at Omaha. The North Western name dates from 1859. It presently operates 9,400 miles in the region between the Great Lakes and the Rockies. The organized "Safety First" movement started in the railroad industry on the North Western in 1910.

Chicago, Rock Island & Pacific. Incorporated in 1847 to build from Rock Island to LaSalle, Illinois, but, under an amended charter, built from Chicago, the Rock Island was the first railroad to bridge the Mississippi, in 1856. It presently operates 8,000 miles of line, extending from Chicago, St. Louis and Memphis, on the east, to the Twin Cities on the north, Colorado and New Mexico on the west, and the Texas and Louisiana Gulf Coast, on the south.

Delaware & Hudson. The original company, chartered in 1823, built a canal and a railroad to bring out its coal from Carbondale, Pa., to Rondout, N. Y., on the Hudson. It was on this line that the first steam locomotive to turn a wheel on an American railroad made its first, and only, run in 1829. The present system, extending through upstate New York to Montreal, has been built up by acquisition and construction. The original canal was abandoned in 1898.

Delaware, Lackawanna & Western. This company originated as the Liggitt's Gap Railroad, chartered in 1851 to build an outlet for the coal of the Lackawanna Valley in Pennsylvania. Subsequently, it was extended west to Buffalo, north to Lake Ontario and east to New York (Hoboken). In 1960 it merged with the Erie Railroad.

Denver & Rio Grande Western. Chartered in 1870 by Denver interests, the D. & R. G. built a narrow gauge line which reached a large part of southern and western Colorado and extended to Salt Lake City, Utah. By 1890 main lines had been converted to standard gauge. Consolidation with the Denver & Salt Lake, with its Moffatt Tunnel through the crest of the Rockies, and construction of a new cutoff connection with the original main line, shortened the distance between terminals by 175 miles. The road presently operates 2150 miles, of which 250 miles remain narrow gauge.

Erie. Chartered as the New York & Erie, in 1832, to build from Piermont, N. Y., on the Hudson to Dunkirk, on Lake Erie, a six-foot gauge track was completed in 1851. The financial and corporate history of the road was checkered in the extreme but after its last reorganization, completed in 1941, it has had a career of solid success. Before merging with the Lackawanna in 1960, the Erie operated 2300 miles, extending from New York to Buffalo, Cleveland and Chicago.

Florida East Coast. This line, extending from Jacksonville to Miami, is the result of the vision and determination of one man, Henry M. Flagler. Retiring from the Standard Oil Co. at the age of 53, he came to St. Augustine, then reached only by a narrow gauge railroad from the St. John's River. Acquiring the railroad in 1885, he steadily pushed it southward, reaching Miami in 1896. The overseas extension, built across the Florida keys and stretches of open sea, reached Key West in 1912, the year before Flagler's death. In 1935 the extension suffered severe hurricane damage and was abandoned as a railroad, to become the overseas highway to Key West.

Grand Trunk Western. The G. T. W. is a subsidiary of the Canadian National Railways, operating nearly

1000 miles across Michigan and Indiana to Chicago, which was reached in 1881, and to Milwaukee, reached by cross-lake car ferry. The tunnel under the St. Clair River, connecting the western extension with the parent Grand Trunk, was completed in 1891. Other Canadian National subsidiaries in the United States include the Grand Trunk to Portland, Maine, opened in 1853, and the Central Vermont, acquired in 1899.

Great Northern. The original line included in the present Great Northern was the St. Paul & Pacific, which started in 1862 to build northward and westward from St. Paul. After James J. Hill secured control the emphasis was on building to the west, although the line was completed north to Winnipeg. The transcontinental line was opened in 1893. The company presently operates 8300 miles of line, extending from the Twin Cities and the head of the Great Lakes to Vancouver, Seattle and Portland, and owns a one-half interest in the Spokane, Portland & Seattle and the Burlington Lines.

Gulf, Mobile & Ohio. The G., M. & O. dates from 1940 when the present corporation was formed by the consolidation of the Gulf, Mobile & Northern (itself a 1917 consolidation of earlier small railroads) with the Mobile & Ohio, which in the decade before the Civil War, built a through line from Mobile to Columbus, Ky., and afterward extended it to St. Louis. In 1947 the G., M. & O. absorbed the Alton Railroad, originally the Chicago & Alton, dating from 1847. The company presently operates 2800 miles, extending from Chicago and Kansas City to Mobile and New Orleans.

Illinois Central. Incorporated in 1851, the I. C. still operates under its original charter. The 700-mile charter lines, located in the state of Illinois, were built as one project. By construction and acquisition, the road has expanded to 6500 miles extending from Chicago west to the Missouri River and south to New Orleans and Birmingham, Ala. Oldest segment of the line, and the first interstate railroad in the United States, is the West Feliciana Railroad, connecting Bayou Sara, La., and Woodville, Miss., chartered in 1831, opened for traffic in 1835, and acquired by the I. C. in 1892.

Lehigh Valley. Originally chartered as the Delaware, Lehigh, Schuylkill & Susquehanna for the purpose of hauling coal from the vicinity of Mauch Chunk, Pa., the present name was adopted in 1853. The line has expanded to 1200 miles, reaching the Niagara Frontier on the west and New York on the east. In the process it has acquired numerous other lines, some dating back to 1836.

Louisville & Nashville. The L. & N. was chartered in 1850, completed its line between the cities whose

names it bears in 1859, and is today operated under its original charter. Construction and acquisition of some 75 other lines has created a system of 5,700 miles, extending from Cincinnati and St. Louis to Memphis, Atlanta and New Orleans. Oldest existing part of the system is the line between Lexington and Frankfort, Ky., chartered in 1830, opened for traffic in 1834, and acquired by the L. & N. in 1881.

Missouri-Kansas-Texas. The present-day "Katy" started with the incorporation of the Union Pacific Railway, Southern Branch, in 1865. The new company was in nowise connected with the U. P. but was formed to build a line southward from Junction City, Kan., with the ultimate destination of New Orleans. The name Missouri, Kansas & Texas was adopted in 1870 and the line was opened across the Indian Territory into Texas in 1872. Subsequent expansion has created a system of some 3000 miles extending from St. Louis and Kansas City to San Antonio and Houston.

Missouri Pacific. The Pacific Railroad of Missouri, earliest part of the present system, was chartered on July 4, 1851, to build a line of 5 foot 6 inch gauge from St. Louis to the west coast. On the first five miles of this road the first locomotive west of the Mississippi ran in December, 1852. By construction and consolidation, the road has extended from St. Louis, Memphis and New Orleans, to Omaha, Pueblo, Colorado, Laredo, Tex., and the Gulf Coast, operating some 11,000 miles.

New York Central. The earliest of the many companies which have gone to make up the present system, the Mohawk & Hudson, was incorporated in 1826 and ran its first train in 1831. To the New York Central, organized in 1853, was added the Hudson River Railroad, in 1869, to be followed in the course of time by the Lake Shore & Michigan Southern, the Michigan Central, the Big Four, the Boston & Albany, the West Shore, the Toledo & Ohio Central and other railroads, including the separately operated Pittsburgh & Lake Erie. The system consists of more than 10,000 miles, extending from Montreal, Boston and New York to the Straits of Mackinac, Chicago, and St. Louis. On Jan. 12, 1962, the directors voted to merge with the Pennsylvania.

New York, Chicago & St. Louis. The Nickel Plate Road, as it is usually called, was opened for operation between Buffalo and Chicago in 1882, with the last spike, driven at Bellevue, O., nickel-plated. Control soon passed to the New York Central, which acquired the road rather than have it fall into unfriendly hands. In 1916, control was sold to the Van Seringen brothers of Cleveland, O., who added the Lake Erie & Western and the Toledo, Peoria & Western, to the Nickel Plate. Subsequently the Wheeling & Lake Erie was added to the system which now operates 2200 miles, extending from Buffalo and Wheeling, W. Va., to Chicago, Peoria and St. Louis.

New York, New Haven & Hartford. Earliest of the approximately 125 companies which have gone into the New Haven was the Boston & Providence, chartered in 1831 and in operation by 1834. The Hartford & New Haven, incorporated in 1833, connected New Haven with Springfield, Mass., by 1844, the year in which a railroad was chartered to connect New Haven with New York. This line, providing the first all-rail service between Boston and New York via Springfield, was opened in 1848. The Shore Line, operating between New Haven and Providence, was leased in 1870. The New Haven Railroad operates 1800 miles, serving southern New England and New York. Between 1907 and 1914 the New Haven installed the first railroad electrification using high voltage alternating current transmission from New York to New Haven.

Norfolk & Western. The City Point Railway, a nine-mile line between Petersburg, Va., and the James River, chartered in 1836, is the oldest part of the N. & W. It grew into the Southside Railroad, which with its connections stretched across southern Virginia from tidewater to Tennessee, and which, with extensions westward into the coal fields, became the basis of the N. & W. The latest addition to the system is the Virginian, consolidated in 1959, and bringing the system mileage to 2700, extending from Hagerstown, Md., and Norfolk to Durham and Winston-Salem, N. C., Bristol, Tenn., and Cincinnati and Columbus, O.

Northern Pacific. The first of the Northern transcontinental lines, the N. P., was chartered by an act of Congress signed by President Lincoln on July 2, 1864. Construction of a line to connect the head of the Great Lakes with Portland, Ore., was started in 1870 and completed in 1883. The company presently operates 6700 miles of line, extending from St. Paul-Minneapolis and Duluth-Superior to Seattle, Tacoma and Portland, and owns a one-half interest in the Burlington Lines and the Spokane, Portland & Seattle.

Pennsylvania. The Pennsylvania Railroad operates under its original charter, issued in 1846, authorizing the building of a line between Harrisburg and Pittsburgh, paralleling the state of Pennsylvania's canal and inclined plane system. By purchase, construction and lease, the line has expanded to a system of 10,000 miles, extending eastward to Philadelphia, New York, Washington and Norfolk and westward to the Straits of Mackinac, Chicago, and St. Louis. Oldest segment of the system is the pioneer Camden & Amboy, chartered by New Jersey in 1830 and completed in

1834. The first "T" rail was rolled in a design whittled out by Robert Stevens, son of Col. John, while on a voyage to England to purchase rail for the Camden & Amboy. The design became the basis of rail now in use all over the world. On Jan. 12, 1962, the directors voted to merge with the New York Central.

Pullman Company. George M. Pullman built his first sleeping cars (rebuilt coaches of the Chicago & Alton Railroad) in 1858. His first completely Pullman-built car was finished in 1864. By the end of the century the name "Pullman" was substantially synonymous with the sleeping car business. The company also manufactured passenger and freight cars. As a result of an antitrust suit, the enterprise was required to divest itself of either the car manufacturing or the car operating business. In 1947, the latter was taken over by 57 railroads, which have continued it under the Pullman name.

Railway Express Agency. The express business as a special service started in 1839 when William F. Harnden, a conductor running between Boston and Worcester, offered such services, at first on a personal basis. Organized express companies operating under contracts with the railroads soon followed. When the Federal Government took over the operation of the railroads in World War I, the business was carried on by the Adams, American, Southern, United States, Wells-Fargo and other companies, all of which were consolidated in 1918 into the American Railway Express Co., which in 1929 was succeeded by the present organization of an agency owned by participating railroads.

Reading. The Reading Company, which now operates 1300 miles of line in Pennsylvania, New York and Delaware, is a successor company to the Philadelphia & Reading Railroad, incorporated in 1833, although parts of the line had been built by still earlier companies. It was on one of these predecessor lines, the Philadelphia, Germantown & Norristown, that "Old Ironsides," the first locomotive built by Matthias Baldwin, ran in 1832. The Reading owns a majority of the stock of the Jersey Central Lines.

St. Louis-San Francisco. The "Frisco" started in 1866 to build from Springfield (afterward from St. Louis), Mo., to the Pacific Coast but never reached the goal of the city whose name it bears. Instead, it developed as a system of some 5000 miles, stretching from St. Louis and Kansas City to Oklahoma and north Texas, on the southwest, and to Alabama and Florida, on the southeast. The Frisco is one of the few systems to operate in both the West and the Southeast.

St. Louis-Southwestern. The "Cotton Belt," as the line is commonly called, started as the Tyler Tap

Railroad, chartered in 1871, to build a connection from Tyler, Texas, to a main line railroad. From this beginning, the enterprise expanded to a system of 1500 miles, connecting St. Louis and Memphis with Ft. Worth, Dallas and Waco, Texas. The present name of the company dates from 1891.

Seaboard Air Line Railroad. The name "Seaboard Air Line" was first applied in 1889 to a loose operating association of a half a dozen separate connecting railroads in Virginia and the Carolinas. Oldest of these lines was the Portsmouth & Roanoke, chartered in 1832, which built the line from Portsmouth, Va., to Weldon, N. C. In 1900 the several railroads were consolidated and, by acquisition and construction, have grown into a system of 4000 miles extending from Norfolk and Richmond through the Carolinas, and Georgia to Birmingham and Montgomery, Ala., and both coasts of Florida.

Soo Line (Minneapolis, St. Paul & Sault Ste. Marie). Chartered in 1873 by business men of Minneapolis to build a line eastward to the Canadian border at Sault Ste. Marie, the line reached the Sault in 1887. By the same time it had extended westward into the Dakotas, finally building to a western connection with the Canadian Pacific at Portal. Since 1909 the Soo Line has operated the Wisconsin Central, effecting an entrance into Chicago. The 4200-mile system is a separately operated subsidiary of the Canadian Pacific.

Southern Pacific. The beginnings of the Southern Pacific were found in Louisiana, Texas and California. In Louisiana the New Orleans, Opelousas and Great Western Railroad was chartered in 1850 to build from New Orleans westward. In the same year, in Texas, the Buffalo Bayou, Brazos and Colorado was chartered and was in operation by 1852. In California, in the same year, the Sacramento Valley Railroad was started. Central Pacific, incorporated in California in 1861, undertook the task of building a railroad eastward over the Sierra Nevada and, in 1862, was selected to build the western leg of the first transcontinental route. The Southern Pacific, incorporated in California in 1865, built south and east, to become part of the second transcontinental route. The interests of the C. P. and the S. P. were closely linked as early as 1870. In 1934 the twelve companies making up the S. P. interests in Texas and Louisiana were consolidated into the Texas and New Orleans Railroad. The S. P. system operates more than 13,000 miles of line.

Southern Railway. The present corporation was formed in 1894, authorizing the purchasers of the Richmond & Danville to acquire the East Tennessee, Virginia & Georgia and other railroads, among them the pioneer South Carolina Railroad. The system includes the separately operated Cincinnati, New Orleans & Texas Pacific, Alabama Great Southern, New Orleans & Northeastern, Georgia, Southern & Florida, and Carolina & Northwestern railroads. Total mileage of 8000 extends from Washington, Cincinnati and St. Louis to New Orleans, Mobile and Florida.

Texas & Pacific. Chartered by act of Congress in 1871, the T. & P. took over the barely started projects of the Southern Pacific (a company in no way related to the present company of that name), formed in 1856, the Memphis, El Paso & Pacific, also formed in 1856, and the Southern Transcontinental, organized in 1870. From Marshall and Texarkana lines were built westward toward El Paso and eastward to New Orleans. In 1881, at Sierra Blanca, Texas, 90 miles east of El Paso, the T. & P. met the crews of the Galveston, Harrisburg & San Antonio, building the Southern Pacific line eastward. Joint trackage was arranged, effecting an entrance into El Paso for the T. & P. The line to New Orleans was completed a year later. The company presently operates 1800 miles of line.

Union Pacific. The U. P. was incorporated by act of Congress in 1862 to build westward from the Missouri River to meet the Central Pacific of California, building eastward. To the approximately 1000 miles of the original main line, the company has added the Kansas Pacific, Denver Pacific, Oregon Short Line, Oregon-Washington Railway & Navigation Co., San Pedro, Los Angeles & Salt Lake and other railroads. The property was extensively improved after it came under the control of E. H. Harriman in 1897. It now operates nearly 10,000 miles of line, extending from Council Bluffs, Omaha, St. Joseph and Kansas City to Portland, Seattle, Spokane and Los Angeles.

Wabash. The "Northern Cross" railroad, 12 miles long, built in 1838, was the first railroad in Illinois and the earliest part of the present Wabash. The system of nearly 3000 miles, one of the few operating in both the East and the West, stretches from Buffalo and Toledo to St. Louis, Kansas City, Omaha and Des Moines. Separately operated is the subsidiary Ann Arbor Railroad and its car ferries across Lake Michigan.

Western Pacific. Newest of the transcontinental connections in the United States is the Western Pacific, organized in 1903 and opened for service between Salt Lake City and Oakland-San Francisco in 1909. A branch line connecting with the Great Northern, opened in 1931, added a north-south route to the original east-west line of the railroad. Total mileage, including the subsidiary Sacramento Northern, is approximately 1500.

RAISIN RIVER MASSACRE (Jan. 22, 1813). Following Gen. Hull's surrender of Detroit and Michigan in August, 1812, the Americans raised two new armies to recover these places. Late December found Gen. Winchester encamped at Maumee Rapids (above Toledo), facing the British Gen. Procter at Amherstburg. On Jan. 14, 1813, Winchester sent 650 Kentuckians to recover Frenchtown (modern Monroe) from a British-Indian force, and shortly afterward himself led 300 more to the support of his force. Procter advanced from Amherstburg and at dawn, Jan. 22, assailed the American army. Winchester was captured and one wing of the army cut to pieces, whereupon the other surrendered under promise of protection from Procter's Indian allies. This pledge was disregarded and a frightful massacre followed. The affair stirred American opinion deeply and "Remember the River Raisin" became a rallying-cry throughout the war. A capable British official, castigating Procter's conduct, wrote: "within my hearing protection was promised for those poor people, be assured we have not heard the last of this shameful transaction. I wish to God it could be contradicted."

RALEIGH'S LOST COLONY.

The group usually designated as the Lost Colony sailed from Plymouth in three small ships May 8, 1587, and reached Roanoke Island in the Albemarle region of the present North Carolina July 22, 1587. The region was then vaguely known as Virginia. The colony as listed in White's account consisted of 91 men, 17 women and 9 children, or 117 persons. Raleigh named Capt. John White governor of the colony, which was incorporated as "the Governour and Assistants of the Citie of Raleigh in Virginia."

The colonists had not meant to stop permanently on Roanoke Island, which was not believed adapted to colonization, but were instructed by Raleigh to pick up fifteen men left by Sir Richard Grenville, and to proceed on to the Chesapeake region. They were balked in this plan by the pilot of the expedition, who set them ashore on the island, where they occupied the houses and fort abandoned the previous year by Lane's unsuccessful colony.

From the first the Roanoke colonists, inheriting the enmity Lane had provoked, encountered the hostility of the Indians on the mainland opposite the island, although they enjoyed the friendship of Manteo and his kinsmen from the island of Croatoan to the southward. On Aug. 18 Eleanor White Dare, daughter of Gov. White and wife of Ananias Dare, gave birth to a daughter, the first English child born in America. The child was christened Virginia. Soon thereafter controversy arose as to who should go back to England for supplies. It was decided that Gov. White should return, and on Aug. 25 he sailed.

When White reached England the danger of the threatened Spanish Armada overshadowed all else. White was not able to come back to Roanoke Island until August, 1591. He discovered no trace of the colony except the letters C R O carved upon a tree, and the word CROATOAN graven on a doorpost of the palisade.

The fate of Raleigh's colony remains a mystery. It has usually been assumed that they went to the friendly Croatoans. Some have thought that they were victims of the Spanish. A stone recently discovered in Chowan County, N. C., which purports to bear a message from Eleanor White Dare to her father, would indicate that they followed Albemarle Sound up the Chowan River, suffered sickness and war, and of the twenty-four survivors in 1591, all but seven were massacred by the Indians. It is presumed these seven were absorbed by the Indians.

RALEIGH'S PATENT AND FIRST COLONY.

On March 25, 1584, Queen Elizabeth renewed Humphrey Gilbert's patent of 1578 in the name of Gilbert's half-brother, Walter Raleigh, giving him and his heirs and assigns the right to explore, colonize and govern "such remote, heathen, and barbarous lands not actually possessed of any Christian prince, nor inhabited by Christian people." The settlers planted within this grant were to have "all the privileges of free Denizens, and persons native of England," and all laws passed must be in harmony with the laws of England.

On April 27, 1584, Raleigh sent out an expedition led by Philip Amadas and Arthur Barlowe, who were instructed to explore the country and decide upon the site for a future colony. Coming via the West Indies, they reached the North Carolina coast early in July. They entered Albemarle Sound, took possession of the country in the name of the queen, and a few days later landed at Roanoke Island. After two months spent in exploring and trading with the Indians, they returned to England with reports of the beautiful country, the friendly Indians, the abundance of game and fish and the soil which was "the most plentiful, sweete, fruitfull and wholsome of all the worlde." Queen Elizabeth was pleased; she named the new land "Virginia" and knighted Raleigh.

In April, 1585, Raleigh sent out a colony, consisting of 108 men, with Ralph Lane as governor and Sir Richard Grenville in command of the fleet. This colony landed at Roanoke Island on July 27. About a month later, Grenville returned to England, leaving behind the first English colony in America. Lane built a fort and "sundry necessary and decent dwelling houses," and from this "new Fort in Virginia," Sept. 3, 1585, he wrote Richard Hakluyt in London the "first letter in the English language written from the New World." The Lane colony spent most of its time in a vain quest for gold. Soon supplies began to run low and had to be obtained from the Indians, who were becoming more and more unfriendly. War finally broke out in the spring of 1586. Lane won an easy victory, but unrest and distress continued to increase. When Sir Francis Drake's fleet appeared along the coast and offered to take the colony back to England, Lane consented and they departed after having been on Roanoke Island for about ten months.

About two weeks later, Grenville arrived with supplies. He soon returned to England, but being "unwilling to loose possession of the countrey which Englishmen had so long held," he left fifteen men on Roanoke Island, "furnished plentifully with all manner of provisions for two years." When the next Raleigh colony headed by John White, arrived at Roanoke in 1587, they found only the bones of one of the men Grenville had left and the fort and houses in ruins.

RALSTON'S RING, so-called, was a group of financiers in San Francisco, headed by William C. Ralston, who, in the early 1860's, sought to capitalize for their benefit the profits of the Big Bonanza of the Comstock Lode in Nevada. Stocks were driven up to soaring heights and the opposition of Adolph Sutro was fought by the election of one of the ring, William Sharon, to the U. S. Senate. The panic of 1873 almost overthrew the ring but it survived until a second crash in 1875. Ralston, with a deficit of $1,500,000, was ousted from the bank and was found dead on the beach on the following day.

RAMS, CONFEDERATE. The distinguishing feature of these vessels was a massively constructed bow carrying an iron beak or ram, which enabled them to revive the smashing tactics of the ancient galleys. The novelty of their design was the armor-plated casemate constructed amidship to house the artillery. The sides of this citadel were sloped to cause the enemy's cannon balls and projectiles to ricochet. The *Virginia,* first and most famous of this type, was designed by a board consisting of Chief Engineer William P. Williamson, Lt. John M. Brooke and Naval Constructor John L. Porter, appointed by the Confederate Navy Department, June 23, 1861. It was constructed on the salvaged hull of the United States frigate *Merrimack,* which had been sunk at the evacuation of the Norfolk Navy Yard. The rams were used with much success by the Confederates, who put in service or had under construction 44 ironclad (armor 4 to 8 inches), 14 partially protected, and 6 cottonclad vessels of this general type.

RANDOLPH'S COMMISSION (1676) made him the special agent of the king to carry to Massachusetts Bay Colony the king's orders that agents be sent to England authorized to act for the colony concerning the boundary disputes with Mason and Gorges. As with the royal commission of 1664 he was also commanded to investigate conditions there, by which it was apparent that the real matter at issue was the king's decision to face the problem of the uncertainty and confusion as to the relationship between Massachusetts and the mother country. During Randolph's month in New England he was to make a complete investigation concerning the governments of the colonies; their methods of defense, finance, religion, trade; character of their laws; and attitude in general, toward each other and toward England. Needless to say, Randolph did not meet with a cordial reception. The government of Massachusetts personally affronted Randolph, and ignored the king's demands, although agents were actually dispatched after Randolph's departure. Upon his return to England he made a comprehensive report, adverse as far as Massachusetts was concerned. Many people had complained to him of religious and political discriminations, and neighboring colonies resented the arrogant attitude of Massachusetts toward them. Most serious of all offenses listed were the flagrant breaches of the Navigation Acts and the denial of parliamentary legislative authority over the colony. Randolph's report caused grave concern at court and was chiefly responsible for the reopening of the fifty-year-old question as to the legal position of the Massachusetts Bay Company which ended in the annulment of the charter in 1684.

RANGERS, COLONIAL (1742–83), were irregular provincial forces used in frontier defense, in scouting and in service against Indians. "It is impossible for an Army to act in this Country without Rangers," wrote Loudoun in 1756. Braddock in 1755 asked for one troop of Horse Rangers and four companies of Foot Rangers, "or six, if I can get them." Abercromby appointed Robert Rogers major of a battalion of rangers. Four companies raised by him were taken to Louisburg by Amherst in 1758. Wolfe "devised an extended order formation for his light infantry, to work either with line troops, or with rangers." Virginia had five companies, Maryland, one, and North Carolina, one, at Will's Creek, June 8, 1755. These consisted of captain, two subalterns, three sergeants, drummer and fifty-three rank and file. New Hampshire, New Jersey, New York and South Carolina companies served under Rogers. The loyalist Queen's Rangers served under Simcoe in the Revolution. The colonies, notably Pennsylvania, used rangers for frontier defense in the Revolution.

RAYSTOWN PATH derives its name from John Wray, an Indian trader who settled sometime before 1750 at what is now Bedford, Pa. It led from a point near Carlisle, Pa., in the Susquehanna Valley to Shannopin's Town (now within Pittsburgh) and Logstown, eighteen miles below Pittsburgh. The trail, in terms of present-day towns, went from Carlisle through Shippensburg, Chambersburg, Fort Loudon, Fort Lyttleton, Bedford and Ligonier; then north toward Latrobe, Harrison City, Trafford and Shannopin's Town. This route in the main was the same as that followed by Gen. Forbes in 1758 and by Col. Henry Bouquet in 1763. Much of it today parallels closely the Lincoln Highway west from Chambersburg to Pittsburgh.

REAPER, INVENTION AND DEVELOPMENT OF.

The modern tractor-combine is distinguished from the cradle-scythe of a century ago by five chief steps in mechanical development, *viz.*, reaper (1840–60), self-rake reaper (1860–70), harvester (1870–75), wire binder (1875–80), and twine binder (1880–1915). These dates indicate approximately when each implement exemplified the latest method of reaping, and not that it was then cutting most of the world's grain. This machine sequence does not include the header, header-thresher, header-binder, and tractor-header-combine which evolved during the same century for use in dry-farming areas where grain, without damage from sweating, can be reaped and threshed simultaneously.

The notable contribution of invention to the Industrial Revolution probably stimulated the three-score Englishmen and Americans between 1785 and 1830 who tried in vain to construct a practical horse-power grain-cutter. The machines of Henry Ogle of England and Patrick Bell of Scotland, however, included elements prophetic of the earliest successful reaper, the 1831 invention of Cyrus Hall McCormick of Midway, Va. His machine first combined harmoniously the seven principles or parts essential to efficient reaping, *viz.*, side draft, reciprocating horizontal knife, main ground wheel, divider, fingers, reel and platform.

Obed Hussey's rival invention of 1833 foreshadowed the modern mower as developed after 1850 by Lewis F. Miller and Ephraim Ball of Ohio, and Cyrenus Wheeler, Jr., and Moses G. Hubbard of New York. Hussey, at Baltimore, and Hiram Moore of Michigan greatly improved the knife and fingers.

Competition between manufacturers in the late 1850's, and the spur given to invention by labor scarcity during the Civil War, brought the self-rake reaper to perfection and encouraged experimentation with harvesters and automatic binders. William H. Seymour and Samuel Johnston of New York, and Owen Dorsey, Benjamin Fitzhugh and McClintock Young of Maryland merit remembrance for their self-rake attachments. In 1858 Charles W. and William W. Marsh of Illinois discovered how to elevate grain over the main wheel to a table where it could be bound by riding bandsters. This harvester had no wide sale for about a decade. Shortly thereafter Sylvanus D. Locke, Charles B. Withington and S. D. Carpenter, all of Wisconsin, and James F. and John H. Gordon of New York substituted their wire-binding attachment for the human binders on the harvester. Protests of millers and cattle raisers against "wire in wheat" assured an early and ready acceptance of the twine binding device of John F. Appleby of Wisconsin. He co-ordinated into an efficient whole the separate inventions of Marquis L. Gorham, Jacob Behel and George H. Spaulding, all of Illinois. Compared with the early McCormick reaper, the self-rake reaper and harvester-binder

greatly reduced the labor (rather than the time) cost of harvesting. Inventors after 1860 were usually in the employ of the big manufacturers.

Twentieth-century "power-farming" demands that a tractor shall draw the harvester-binder, windrow harvester, or harvester-thresher (combine) and operate its moving parts. C. W. Hart and C. H. Parr of Iowa in 1901 adapted the Otto internal combustion engine to movable use on the farm. Thereafter, they and the larger harvesting manufacturing concerns, as well as Henry Ford between 1918 and 1928, lightened and perfected the "all-use" tractor; made it less expensive, and convinced many farmers that kerosene or gasoline could well supplant animals, or even steam, as the motive power in harvesting.

REBATES.

A rebate has been defined by the Interstate Commerce Commission as "transportation at a less rate in dollars and cents than the published rate which the shipping public are charged." The intent of a carrier in granting a rebate is usually to discriminate in favor of a particular shipper by giving him a secret rate which is less than that charged his competitors. This practice developed out of the spectacular railroad rate wars that took place during the latter half of the 19th century and which often proved disastrous to carriers and public alike. These costly rate wars led carriers to avoid general rate cuts and to develop the practice of making secret agreements with certain shippers whereby the shipper would get some form of rate reduction in exchange for his promise to ship his goods over the line offering the concession. Such concessions enabled the favored shippers to undersell their competitors, and thus increase their business and the business of the railroad offering the rebates.

The public objected bitterly to the practice of rebating because of its obvious unfairness and because the process of building up one shipper at the expense of others promoted the development of monopolies with all of their attendant evils. Rebating also proved objectionable to those carriers who practiced it because it did not take long for competing carriers to size up the situation and attempt to make secret arrangements of their own with other shippers, and if they were successful, none of the carriers enjoyed an increase in traffic. And if a carrier did succeed in building up a shipper to a monopolistic position, that carrier was at the mercy of the shipper, and such shippers sometimes secured enormous concessions by playing one carrier off against another.

The outstanding recipient of railroad rebates was the Standard Oil Co., and much of its early success may be traced to the advantages it enjoyed in the way of rate concessions. In one case the published rate on oil between two points was 35¢ a barrel, but on each barrel shipped the Standard received a 25¢ rebate, making its rate 10¢ while its competitors paid 35¢. Not only did the Standard receive the 25¢ refund on all the oil it shipped, but it also received 25¢ for every barrel shipped by its competitors. This type of rebate in which a particular shipper is given a part of the rate paid by his competitors is known as a drawback. The packers were also notorious recipients of rate concessions.

The Interstate Commerce Act (1887) prohibited rate discrimination and established a fine of $5000 for each violation, and two years later violation of the law was made a penitentiary offense. However, it was necessary to prove that a rebate actually resulted in discrimination, and this was difficult to do. Furthermore, juries were reluctant to send men to prison for civil offenses even if proven guilty. Hence the act did not stop the practice of discrimination and further legislation was necessary. Under the Elkins Act (1903) any departure from a printed rate was considered an offense, thus eliminating the necessity of proving that discrimination existed. At the same time the penalty of imprisonment was dropped, the maximum fine raised to $20,000, and the law applied to shippers who received rebates as well as to carriers who granted them. The Hepburn Act (1906) restored the penalty of imprisonment and subjected the receiver of a rebate to a fine equal to three times the value of the rebates received during the preceding six years. Subsequent acts brought a further tightening of the law, and today rebating is practically unknown.

RECALL is a special election to determine whether a public officeholder shall be superseded before the expiration of his term. First introduced in the Los Angeles charter of 1903 this device found wide acceptance subsequently in municipal charters, chiefly of the home rule, commission and city-manager types. Oregon was the first state to make the recall applicable by constitutional amendment to its elective officials (1908); eleven other states have since followed the example thus set, *viz.*, California, Arizona, Nevada, Colorado, Idaho, Washington, Michigan, Kansas, Louisiana, North Dakota and Wisconsin. Particularly bitter controversy broke out early over the application of the recall to the judiciary. President Taft vetoed the enabling act admitting Arizona to the Union because its proposed constitution included a provision making judges subject to recall. The offending clause was accordingly stricken out, but a year after the admission of Arizona (1912) it was restored to the constitution. Of the twelve recall states four expressly exempt judicial officials, *viz.*, Idaho, Washington, Michigan and Louisiana.

Besides opposition to the recall on the above ground, it was attacked as unconstitutional, even revolutionary, in that it substituted a dangerous form of direct democratic rule for representative republican institutions. Experience has dissipated exaggerated views of this character; as a rule the states and cities in which the recall exists regard it as useful in a

cautionary way against officials tempted to neglect or malfeasance.

All recall laws guarantee a certain period of grace, usually six months, before it can be invoked. After the expiration of this period petitions may be circulated against the erring official or officials. To be effective petitions require the signatures of a certain percentage of the voters of the district concerned, ranging from 10% to 35%, 25% being the most common. After the required number of signatures is secured a special recall election is ordered to take place within from twenty to ninety days. At this election the fate of the official under fire is determined in competition with a candidate or candidates nominated against him.

RECIPROCAL TRADE AGREEMENTS. The Democrats, in their successful campaign of 1932, advocated "a competitive tariff for revenue . . . [and] reciprocal trade agreements with other nations. . . ." On June 12, 1934, Congress approved an amendment to the Tariff Act of 1930. This so-called Trade Agreements Act authorized the President, whenever he finds that import restrictions of the United States or foreign countries are unduly burdening American foreign trade, to enter into foreign trade agreements and to proclaim the changes in duties necessary to carry out such agreements, provided that existing rates are not changed by more than 50% and that no change is made in the free list. By providing for executive agreements rather than treaties, Congress made Senate ratification unnecessary.

The act further provided that the proclaimed duties should apply to imports from all foreign countries unless the President discovers evidence of discriminatory treatment of American commerce by any country. In other words, the unconditional "most-favored-nation" policy, followed since 1922 in American commercial treaties, was to be continued in these executive agreements.

RECONSTRUCTION. Following the close of the Civil War in 1865 the people of the United States passed through a troubled decade which showed how unfortunately a military victory may be used when matters fall into the hands of partisan extremists. Had kindlier counsels prevailed the seceded states might quickly have been restored, for popular detestation of the Union had never been as violent as the language of Southern leaders and to many of the war-weary the failure of Southern independence, besides being a patent fact, seemed almost a minor thing when compared to the relief of having the war over. Southern pride was not so much broken as it was now dissociated from the motive of preserving a separate Confederacy, just as "Southern rights" before the war had been far from synonymous with secession. Every one of the seceded commonwealths, in fact, stood ready to renounce secession, repudiate the anti-United

States debt and abolish slavery. Many a Southern leader in this postwar phase reviewed his former attitude with emphasis upon his original opposition to secession. Military leaders labored to promote a rapid and easy restoration, the main terms of such a policy being actually embodied in the Johnston-Sherman articles of surrender which were rudely overruled by Secretary of War Stanton. Surrender terms as applied, however, did involve the important provision that men and officers of the Confederate Army, going home on parole, would be unmolested and held to no prosecution by the Federal Government. Military imprisonment without trial was imposed upon some of the Southern civil leaders, the terms being short except in the case of the two-year imprisonment of Jefferson Davis.

The war ended with no restoration policy in operation. Lincoln's generous plan of reconstruction, announced in December, 1863, had been attempted in several states without being made legally effective; nor had the anti-Lincoln faction of Republicans (the Radicals) succeeded in enacting their own severe measure (the Wade-Davis Bill) which fell before a presidential veto. Lincoln's last speech (April 11, 1865) was an ardent and reasoned appeal for statesmanlike reconstruction, and President Johnson, keeping Lincoln's cabinet, strove earnestly to promote the essentials of his predecessor's program. Constitutional devices for state remaking were readily available, and in the interval between his accession and the assembling of Congress (April–December, 1865) Johnson made such use of these democratic methods that by July, 1865, "all Secessia" was well advanced on the road to reorganization. Except for congressional approval the process was practically completed by early December.

The 1865 phase, however, was but prelude or interlude. The men who controlled Congress, seeing the Republican party doomed if Southern state governments were restored with Federal representation, seized the reins of government and held them in opposition to the President and the moderates who agreed with him. Soon they became masters of party machinery and of Congress, denounced as traitors all except their own brand of Republicans, and succeeded by the end of the "critical year" (1866) in making their will dominant at Washington and in the occupied South. For this purpose they used the caucus and the party lash; ostracized those who would not travel with them; set up a dictatorial Joint Committee on Reconstruction; denied congressional seats to opponents; and enacted measures to bring the states, the army, the electoral college, the cabinet, and even the Supreme Court, within the orbit of their control. In the impeachment and trial of President Johnson they failed by only one vote to seize the Presidency, but such seizure was hardly necessary since the overriding of vetoes had eliminated Johnson as a force that could obstruct radical legislation. The failure to

fasten any proved accusation upon the President did not prevent his opponents from besmirching his name by innuendo, whispering campaigns, perjured slander and unfair propaganda. The attack upon the Supreme Court included a whole vocabulary of denunciation and an arsenal of weapons held in reserve, a potent weapon being actually used when the Court's jurisdiction was curtailed by Congress to prevent a review of the McCardle case involving military power associated with reconstruction. That the Radicals did not go much farther in this field was probably due to judicial acquiescence. Annihilating the Court, remodeling or packing it, modifying its procedure, and denying it jurisdiction over reconstruction cases were among the Radical proposals of this period, and in 1869 by a vote of 99 to 50 (*Congressional Globe,* 41 Cong., 1 Sess., p. 345) the Republican House of Representatives passed a judiciary-bill amendment which provided that any Federal judge on reaching the age of seventy after ten years of service might retire on full pay, or, for every case of a failure of a judge to retire at this age, the President might appoint an additional judge with the same powers and duties. The whole bill was passed by the House with this amendment by a vote of 90 to 53 (*ibid.*), but in the enacted law this clause was dropped.

How far the American people willed what was happening will always be a question. Both Lincoln and Johnson, elected by popular vote in 1864, had favored nonradical reconstruction as had also the Democratic candidate, McClellan. In 1868 the Republicans avoided Negro suffrage as a campaign issue. Much of the support that was obtained resulted from propaganda which represented the South as defiantly determined, as in its "black codes," to re-establish slavery, despite Southern ratification of the Thirteenth Amendment which became a part of the Constitution in December, 1865. That there was sizable opposition to the Radicals even in Congress is shown by the fact that the veto of the Freedmen's Bureau Bill was overridden in the House by a vote of 104 to 33, with 45 not voting (July 16, 1866). There were various absentees, and the South, as in this whole period, was unrepresented.

While the South was held under by Federal troops the Radicals slowly developed their legislative program. The multifarious activities of the Freedmen's Bureau of the War Department were pushed deep into Southern local affairs, while the agents of the Bureau, as well as those of the Union League in the South, functioned as party emissaries. By the Civil Rights Act of 1866 citizenship was given a new definition and civil rights a Federal guarantee against state interference. Though speaking unctuously in constitutional terms the Radicals showed in reality as little regard for the Constitution as they did for judicial standards in the impeachment proceeding. Finding their Fourteenth Amendment defeated when submitted for ratification because of Southern unwillingness to disfranchise their leaders, the Radicals revived it, made adoption the price of state readmission, promoted ratification by fabricated governments in the South, and by an unprecedented action (an undebated concurrent resolution, July 21, 1868) took over the promulgation of the amendment after the proclamation of Secretary of State Seward had left the question of its proper adoption dangling in ambiguity. In the sequel this amendment, by court interpretation, proved a mighty protection to corporations against regulation by state governments while the courts did but little to apply it as a guarantee of equal rights for the Negro. The Fifteenth Amendment (1870) has been likewise ineffective as a means of practically guarding the Negro from discrimination in the matter of suffrage.

By a remarkable series of "reconstruction acts," 1867–68, some of which had to be altered directly after passage, the Congress launched its artificial system for the South. Major generals in command of military districts were put over the Southern people, newcomers from the North were enfranchised after the briefest residence and native Southeners were disfranchised for supporting the lost cause. Negro voting and officeholding became an important feature of the system years in advance of the Negro-suffrage amendment. Election procedures, including registration of voters, were put into the hands of "boards" operated as party machines. What followed was the regime of the carpetbagger and the scalawag with its bogus political devices, fraudulent balloting, bribery, extravagance, Negro-militia excesses and numerous episodes of exploitation and plunder.

Some of the Southerners preserved a quiescent attitude during this period, some adopted the "Mississippi plan" of worrying Republican meetings, some labored through party conventions for an increasing application of conservative influence; others, especially the rougher element, struck back by the violent methods of the Ku-Klux Klan. Counter retaliation by the Federal Government led to various "force acts" and the vigorous suppression of the Klan which became virtually extinct by 1871. Through all this, the Negro, whose record under slavery had been in the main that of faithful servant, was more the tool of scheming white politicians than the perpetrator of abuse. Similarly Negro officeholding (e.g., in state legislatures and Congress) was less a formative factor than a sensational spectacle. It is a significant fact that the worst abominations of reconstruction came after the readmission of the states to representation in the Federal Congress, a process mainly achieved in 1868 and completed in 1871. In the old historiography, as in the Congress of postwar days, this readmission was played up as the main factor in reconstruction, though it is now recognized that intrastate conditions, especially in the social and economic sense, were far more vital. It is even true that those states whose "reconstruction" in the congres-

sional sense was delayed, were the more fortunate ones. Reconstruction history as now rewritten also recognizes the tariff and the influence of eastern bankers in the whole story. Indeed the "gilded age" is hardly intelligible (e.g., as to the sectional character of the national banking system) if the postwar capitalistic upswing is left out of account.

Gradually self-rule came to the states of the South, though not without a vicious period of civil strife between rival governments, especially in Louisiana. In 1876 only three states (Louisiana, Florida, South Carolina) remained under Radical Republican rule, but the use of party machines in these states proved an essential factor in the seating of President Hayes. The prompt withdrawal of Federal troops in 1877 signified Republican recognition of the failure of the postwar regime to whose processes Hayes (a minority candidate) owed his office. From that period Southern commonwealths have been torn by feuds between Bourbon and populist and have witnessed demagogic appeals which hark back to the 1860's and 1870's, but at least these commonwealths have been their own masters in state affairs. The transition in 1877 was not altogether abrupt. In a real sense the new South dates from Appomattox which was in truth the "end of an era." Economic and social rehabilitation proceeded through the darkest of carpetbag days, so that a down-trodden or self-pitying South was never the whole picture. Time, intertravel, investment, Northern philanthropy, the rise of Southern literature and the friendly approach of the Cleveland administration are among the factors that have stimulated progress on the "road to reunion." Confederate disabilities were ended by the amnesty act of 1898, executive clemency having been fully applied by 1868. By 1900 the old wounds had been measurably healed. Yet it would be an exaggerated optimism to overemphasize the success of reconciliation. Southern effects of the sequel of Appomattox have not been easy to live down. Memories of vindictive rule have outlasted the scars of war, and such a persisting pattern as the "solid South" takes its character largely from deep-seated feelings in the carpetbag years.

Lincoln's Plan of Reconstruction. In his proclamation of Dec. 8, 1863, President Lincoln offered pardon, with certain exceptions, to those who would take oath to support the Constitution of the United States and abide by Federal laws and proclamations touching slaves. When oath-takers equal in number to one tenth of the state's voters in 1860 should "re-establish" a government in a seceded commonwealth, Lincoln promised executive recognition to such government without commitment as to congressional recognition. Both the "plan" and the whole Southern policy of Lincoln were denounced as far too lenient, and there followed a storm of controversy with the Radical Republicans who by their control of Congress prevented any settlement of this vital problem during

Lincoln's life. The hopeless deadlock between President and Congress was seen in the Radical Wade-Davis Bill which Lincoln killed by a pocket veto. After this Lincoln issued a proclamation (July 8, 1864) explaining that he could not accept the Radical plan as the only method of reconstruction and was promptly answered by Wade and Davis in a truculent manifesto. No state was actually restored in accordance with Lincoln's plan, though he considered his terms fulfilled in Tennessee, Arkansas and Louisiana. In Virginia he considered that a loyal government already existed. Lincoln's secretary, John Hay, was sent to assist in the reorganization of Florida, and the President's policy became entangled with intraparty rows concerning delegates' votes for 1864. In his last public speech Lincoln urged generosity in restoring the states and in his last cabinet meeting (April 14) he advised leniency toward the defeated South.

Reconstruction Acts. Success in the election of 1866 gave the Radical Republicans both the authority and the opportunity to put an end to President Johnson's plan of reconstruction and to substitute one of their own, that would give them complete control of the "conquered provinces." The so-called reconstruction acts, enacted over presidential vetoes, put the South under military control. The basic act of March 2, 1867, divided the seceded states, excepting Tennessee, into five military districts, each in command of a major general authorized to perform civil functions necessary to insure complete control of the district. It further provided for the establishment of permanent state governments, based on Negro suffrage, but because the existing governments preferred to remain under military rule rather than to have their affairs controlled and directed by legislative bodies based on Negro suffrage, no move was made to provide for the authorized changes. Consequently, March 23, 1867, Congress passed the first supplementary reconstruction act authorizing the military commanders to provide the machinery for constituting the new governments. They took over the control of registration and voting. The electorate was enlarged and changed in character by the disfranchisement of the former governing class, most of which had served the Southern Confederacy, and substitution of the Negro, the carpetbagger and the scalawag. A second supplementary act was passed July 19, 1867, which interpreted and further extended the powers and duties of the military commanders, particularly in respect to the unlimited right of removal and appointment of state officers. This gave complete control of the personnel of the civil administration to the military commanders. On March 11, 1868, a final supplementary act was enacted providing that the approval of a majority of those voting, regardless of registration, should be regarded as sufficient for ratification of the proposed state constitutions.

The chief aim of these reconstruction acts was politi-cal and the result was the creation of class government subject to and supported by the military. In addition the acts were designed to cripple and so handicap Southern business and industry as to eliminate them as effective competitors of Northern business.

Reconstruction and the Churches. Religious bodies in the United States were particularly concerned with public affairs during and following the Civil War. Most of the major Northern churches had entered the South during the war, having won the consent of the War Department to take over church buildings abandoned by Southern ministers. Their refusal to return them to their owners at the close of the war led in some instances to court action and recriminations on the part of the Southern church leaders. The Northern churches generally looked upon the South, at the close of the war, as a new mission field and new organizations were formed to carry on work in the South, especially among the freedmen. Numerous Northern ministers found employment in the Freedmen's Bureau, some of whom became involved in carpetbag and Negro politics. The great exodus of Southern Negroes from the churches of their former masters and the large influx of Northern Negroes into the South, together with the activity of the Northern white and Negro churches, soon created an entirely new religious situation in the former slave states. The former slaves were gathered into independent congregations all over the South, a great majority being Methodists and Baptists. The Negro's religion at this time, quite naturally, was tinged with politics, and Negro churches were used by unscrupulous carpetbag and Negro politicians to gain control of the Negro ballot. Generally speaking, the Negro ministers were the first recognized leaders of the freedmen and under their direction freed Negroes took their first steps as American citizens.

RED CROSS, THE AMERICAN, was organized in 1881 through the efforts of Clara Barton, who was also largely instrumental in persuading Congress to ratify, in 1882, the Treaty of Geneva. Four months after its founding, the Red Cross gave its first disaster relief. Services for members of the armed forces began during the Spanish-American War. Congress granted a charter in 1900.

In World War I, the Red Cross organized base hospitals, recruited nurses, and staffed and supplied ambulances for the army. Through Home Service in chapters and field staff at military posts here and overseas, the Red Cross was the link between the people and their armed forces. Volunteers made millions of dressings and other supplies, worked in canteens, and gave motor service. Widespread civilian relief activities were carried on overseas. The Junior Red Cross was organized. Assistance was extended to veterans and their families. By the end of the war, Red Cross had spread into every community.

In the 1920's, the public health program developed into a major activity. Pioneer work was done in nutrition education for children and adults. Safety, home nursing, and accident prevention courses became increasingly popular. A series of major disasters called for extensive relief operations.

With the outbreak of World War II, the Red Cross again began a civilian relief program overseas, assisting in six years over 75,000,000 needy persons in about sixty countries. After Pearl Harbor, world-wide welfare and recreational programs were carried on for the U. S. armed forces. The Red Cross recruited 90% of the nurses who served in the armed forces and trained more than 200,000 volunteer nurse's aides to help care for civilian patients. It organized and carried on the first national blood program in American history. Through volunteer donors, more than 13,000,000 pints of blood were obtained for the armed forces by late 1945. Millions of volunteers responded for work. Many packed food and medical parcels for prisoners of war. During the war, some 12,500,000 certificates were issued to persons trained in first aid, water safety, and home nursing.

With the war's end, service to veterans and their families became increasingly heavy. In 1947 the Red Cross launched a blood program to provide whole blood and derivatives for civilians without charge for the products themselves. During the Korean War this program and others expanded rapidly to meet the needs of the armed forces.

The Red Cross is a membership organization deriving its support from the people. Currently there are 3700 chapters and more than 45,000,000 senior and junior members. Stated briefly, the organization serves members of the armed forces, veterans, and their families; provides emergency relief for disaster victims and needed assistance in restoring them to normal living; provides blood and derivatives; gives training in first aid, water safety, and home nursing; enrolls nurses for community services; trains volunteers for chapter and community activities; gives Junior Red Cross members an opportunity to serve others, locally, nationally, and internationally; and assists foreign societies in time of disaster or other emergency. Program emphasis is peacetime service that can be expanded as needed in national emergencies.

RED LINE MAP. Soon after the signature of the preliminary articles of peace and independence with Great Britain in 1782, Benjamin Franklin, as one of the American plenipotentiaries, marked the boundary of the United States, for the reference of Vergennes, French foreign minister, in a "strong red line" on a copy of Mitchell's Map of North America, which map has never since been located in the French archives, despite its vital relationship to American boundary disputes, notably the northeast boundary. In 1932 a transcript of the map, red line and all, was discovered in the Spanish archives.

RED RIVER CAMPAIGN (1864). Early in 1864 Gen. H. W. Halleck (U.) ordered an invasion of the great cotton-growing sections of Louisiana, Arkansas and Texas. The thrust, to be under the command of Gen. N. P. Banks, was to move up the Red River. The advance of the expedition was begun in March to take advantage of the spring rise in the river, which that year did not come.

Banks' command and a force from Mississippi under Gen. A. J. Smith, together with a river fleet, were to converge on Alexandria, La., after which the combined force would move on to a junction with troops under Gen. Frederick Steele coming southward from Arkansas. The two armies would then sweep up the Red River Valley to Shreveport, the Confederate headquarters, and on into eastern Texas. Scattered Confederate troops, of half the Federal strength, under Gen. E. Kirby-Smith, were available to oppose the invasion.

By the middle of March the fleet and Banks' army had taken Fort DeRussy and occupied Alexandria, there to await the arrival of reinforcements marching overland from the Mississippi. The retreating Confederate troops under Gen. Richard Taylor, receiving reinforcements as they retired, halted at Mansfield, La. Posted in good defensive positions, Taylor, on April 8, with less than half his opponents' numbers, sustained Banks' attack. The Federals were defeated and driven back in confusion.

The next day Taylor's troops advanced against Banks' army posted in a strong position at Pleasant Hill and in their turn were repulsed. Banks failed to follow up his success. In the night the Federals retreated to Grand Ecore and thence to Alexandria. The withdrawal of the army placed the Federal fleet in jeopardy. On account of continued low water it was uncertain if the ships could pass the rapids at Grand Ecore. However, engineering skill and resourcefulness got them safely through in time to escape capture or destruction.

When the threat of Banks' advance was removed, Kirby-Smith, at Shreveport, undertook both to pursue Banks and to crush Steele. He attacked at Jenkins Ferry on April 30. Steele retreated to Little Rock. Kirby-Smith then turned southward to join Taylor for a final blow against Banks. He was too late. Banks had re-embarked and started on his way back to the Mississippi, where the troops were dispersed.

The defeat of Banks' expedition ended important operations in the trans-Mississippi. The Confederate forces held out until May 26, 1865, when Kirby-Smith surrendered, thus ending the war in that area.

RED RIVER INDIAN WAR (1874–75). As a result of the Treaty of Medicine Lodge (Barber County, Kans.), in October, 1867, the Comanche, Kiowa and Kataka were put on a reservation about the Wichita Mountains, and the Arapaho and Cheyenne on another farther north (both within western Oklahoma).

But the Indians, not content to accept a sedentary life, again and again slipped away to raid the borders of Kansas, Colorado, New Mexico and Texas. During the summer of 1874 Gen. P. H. Sheridan was ordered to conduct a punitive campaign against the refractory Indians. Soon thereafter both cavalry and infantry under the command of Cols. Nelson A. Miles, George Buell, J. W. Davidson, Ranald S. Mackenzie and Maj. William Price advanced from their posts in Texas, New Mexico and Indian Territory against the hostile Indians who were encamped along the Red River, its tributaries and the canyons of the Staked Plains. More than fourteen pitched battles were fought before the Indians submitted and returned to their reservations. Seventy-five of their leaders were sent to Florida for confinement. This brought to an end Indian depredations along this part of the frontier.

RED RIVER RAFT. An obstruction of logs and other debris, accumulating for many years, had become lodged and fastened together so as to form an almost solid mass which blocked the channel of Red River (of the South) for a distance of 180 miles above Coushatta Bayou, stopping steamboat navigation at Natchitoches, La. About 1830 the War Department complained of the heavy expense of transporting supplies from Natchitoches to Fort Towson in the Indian country, and Congress made an appropriation for removing the raft and improving the navigation of Red River. Capt. Henry Miller Shreve, who had already won a reputation by his success in removing obstructions to navigation on the Ohio and Mississippi, was placed in charge of the work, and between 1833 and 1839 he entirely removed the raft, leaving the river navigable for over 1000 miles. Shreveport, named in honor of the raft-remover, arose as the commercial center of the region thus opened to settlement. After the removal of the original raft, new obstructions formed from time to time at different points in the channel, and Congress made additional appropriations for their removal in almost every decade from 1840 to 1890, when railroads superseded steamboats as the chief transportation agencies in the Red River Valley. The removal of the Red River raft was one of the most important internal improvement projects undertaken by the Federal Government in the ante-bellum Southwest. Total congressional appropriations for that project approximated $1,000,-000, but the value of the lands thus opened to settlement amounted to many times that sum.

REDEMPTIONERS were white immigrants who, in return for their passage to America from Europe, sold their services for a period varying from two to seven years. Upon arrival in port, captains of vessels having redemptioners aboard advertised in newspapers the sale of their services to persons who should advance the cost of their passage. From 1681 until after the Revolution, these indentured servants migrated here primarily to settle after working off their debt. Scarcity of slaves in Pennsylvania created a brisk demand for this type of labor, and farm laborers, skilled craftsmen and domestic servants were included in their lists. Until 1730 this traffic emanated chiefly from England; after that date, the majority were Germans and Scotch-Irish.

REDSTONE OLD FORT was the pioneers' name for a mound builders' entrenchment at the confluence of Dunlap's Creek with the Monongahela, in southwestern Pennsylvania. A focus of conflict in the preliminary expeditions of the French and Indian War, here in 1759 Col. James Burd of the Pennsylvania militia erected Fort Burd. It served as a refuge from Indian alarms, rallying point for scouts and rangers, and depot for military stores, to the close of the Revolutionary War. "Redstone Old Fort" persisted as the common appellation for the fort and for the village of boat builders and traders which grew about it. In 1785 the site passed into private ownership and was rechristened Brownsville.

REFERENDUM. Although usually mentioned in connection with the initiative, the referendum is distinguishable from it logically and legally. The initiative is a means whereby legislation may be passed by popular vote as against a hostile or indifferent legislature; the referendum is a means whereby measures which have passed the legislature may be defeated by popular vote. Maryland and New Mexico have the referendum but not the initiative. With few exceptions state constitutions and amendments thereto are now submitted automatically to the electorate for approval or rejection. America may claim the credit for the invention of this form of constitutional referendum, the first case of its use being the adoption of the constitution of Massachusetts in 1780. More commonly, however, the term referendum is applied to popular votes upon ordinary legislative enactments. This form of the device was imitated in the United States from Swiss models. It was first adopted by South Dakota in 1898; twenty-one other states have since installed the legislative referendum. Most of these are west of the Mississippi but Maine, Michigan, Ohio, Maryland and Massachusetts are included in the list. In addition, the referendum applying to municipal ordinances has been incorporated in the charters of many cities, particularly those with commission or city manager types of government.

Referendum procedure is inaugurated by the circulation of a petition against some measure which has passed the legislature. To be effective, signatures of a certain percentage of the voters must be secured, the requirements ranging from 5% to 10%. Decision by the electorate follows, usually at the first ensuing general election.

Both referendum and initiative are vigorously used. In the elections of presidential years the people of the various states possessing these devices of direct popular rule are accustomed to pass upon a total of from 150 to 200 constitutional amendments and legislative acts. Measures dealing with prohibition, public utilities, the direct primary, finances and relief are frequently subjected to popular vote in this way.

REFORMED CHURCH IN AMERICA. Known informally as the Dutch Reformed Church, its first congregation was organized in New Amsterdam, in 1628. Colonists from the Netherlands and France, occupying the river valleys of New York and New Jersey, established congregations which for many years were the prevailing religious organizations in those areas. Until late in the 18th century they were subordinate to the classis or synod of the Reformed Church of Holland, their American independence being about coincident with the independence of the colonies. The growth of the church has been in New York, New Jersey, Michigan and adjacent states; in 1958 there were also strong congregations in the Middle and Far West. The name of the church was changed from Reformed Protestant Dutch Church to Reformed Church in America, 1867–69. Estimated membership for 1958 was 216,096.

A group of Dutch Calvinists dissented from the Reformed Church in 1857 and formed the Christian Reformed Church. Strengthened by later immigration, it eventually surpassed the parent body in size, claiming a membership of 228,905 (1958).

REFRIGERATION. Man has known for centuries that cooling foodstuffs will preserve them. When the colonists arrived from Europe the Indians were already making primitive use of ice. Later, on the frontier, food was placed in cool caves, springs, deep wells and storage cellars. In the hot Southwest cooling was often achieved by evaporating water on the sides of earthenware jars.

Ice quickly became a marketable commodity. By 1800 New England was shipping large quantities of natural ice to insulated warehouses in the Southern states, the East and West Indies, South America and India. But transporting ice over long distances was expensive and, beginning in 1836, experiments were begun which led to the building of the first mechanical ice-making plant in America at Shreveport, La., in 1846.

All modern mechanical refrigeration is based upon the principle that a gas which passes from a liquid back to a gaseous state will absorb heat in the process. As early as 1775 it was proven that water evaporated in a vacuum would produce cold.

In 1849, Dr. John Gorrie invented an ice machine which was the forerunner of today's compressed air refrigerating machines. Two years later, Ferdinand Carré of France designed the first ammonia absorption refrigerating machine. Prof. C. P. G. Linde of Germany introduced an ammonia compression refrig-

erating machine in 1873. The electrically driven compression and absorption systems have remained the two basic principles in household refrigeration.

The mechanical production of ice for preservation of food in insulated cold-storage houses located in large cities was first used by the Pictet Artificial Ice Co. in New York City in 1881.

The railroad refrigerator car was developed during this same period. The first insulated car for the shipment of meat and dairy products was produced by W. W. Chandler in 1857. D. W. Davis in 1868 patented a car which could be filled with ice in transit. Nine years later through service was begun, making it possible for the first time for refrigerator cars to be re-iced en route.

Although by 1960 ice-packed refrigerator cars were still in the majority, food shippers were beginning to install direct-drive refrigeration units which would run on either diesel fuel or standby electric power. Thermostatically controlled, these units maintain proper humidity and either heat or cool the car automatically depending on the climate. Perishables can now be shipped unattended from coast to coast.

The refrigeration principle found its newest application in the quick-freezing process. Quick freezing is accomplished at temperatures of $-45°$ Fahrenheit and lower. At such temperatures meat and other foods freeze before ice crystals can form in the tissues and tear them, releasing the juices.

REGICIDES IN NEW ENGLAND. When the members of the High Court of Justice which condemned Charles I were exempted from amnesty at the Restoration, three, variously called the Colonels, the Judges, or the Regicides, escaped to New England. Edward Whalley, an own cousin of Oliver Cromwell, and William Goffe, Whalley's son-in-law, arrived in Boston on July 26, 1660. After a sojourn with Maj. Daniel Gookin in Cambridge, safety required them to move to New Haven in March, 1661, where they were sheltered by the Rev. John Davenport and his neighbor, William Jones. In May, agents in pursuit of them were cleverly delayed and thrown off the scent by Gov. Leete and the other magistrates. Meanwhile Whalley and Goffe made their escape and seem to have lived for some time in what is still known as "the Judges' cave" on West Rock, near New Haven, receiving succor from a near-by farmer, Richard Sperry.

From June, 1661, they lived at Milford with Micah, or Michael, Tomkins. As circumstances rendered their further stay dangerous, they took refuge with the Rev. John Russell at Hadley, Mass., in October, 1664. Whalley appears to have died there late in 1674 or early in 1675. During King Philip's War Hadley was one of the centers of military operations and, when attacked one day, a strange and venerable person, presumably Goffe, suddenly appeared and assumed leadership of the defenders and as promptly disappeared. Since further residence there seemed too perilous, Goffe moved to Hartford not later than September, 1676, where he lived with Capt. Thomas Bull or his son, Jonathan, perhaps until his death in the latter part of 1679, though he may have spent his last days at either New Haven or Hadley.

The third regicide to seek refuge in New England was John Dixwell who had had a distinguished but less prominent career in England and whose life in New England was less romantic. He had escaped to Germany in 1660 and appeared at Hadley in February, 1665. The next record of him is at New Haven in 1673 under the name of James Davids. There he was twice married and lived quietly until his death on March 18, 1689. His grave is still pointed out in the rear of Center Church.

During their residence in New England all three of the judges maintained correspondence with their relatives in England through the Rev. Increase Mather of Boston.

REGISTRATION OF VOTERS prior to elections has been adopted in most states as the result of grave election frauds, such as voting by "repeaters" under fictitious names or the names of persons who have died or moved from the precinct. Prior to the requirement of registration, election frauds and violence at the polls were very common in American cities.

The first registration law was enacted by Massachusetts in 1800. It provided that the assessors should compile a list of qualified electors, which was posted and revised before election day. Other New England states soon followed the lead of Massachusetts, but elsewhere legislation was delayed. New York did not enact such a law until 1840. It was repealed two years later and was not re-enacted until 1859. Most states with large cities adopted registration laws between 1850 and 1900, but many of them were essentially defective and failed to curb election frauds. However, there has been a general trend toward tightening and extending these laws. Only Texas and Arkansas do not require registration, and in these states the lists of poll-tax payers are used at the polls as a registration list. In many states, however, registration is required only in cities.

Many of the older laws did not require the voter to register personally, permitting registration officials to list the names of all persons whom they believed to be qualified. Such lists commonly contained names of persons who had died or moved away, and thus afforded little protection. Personal application is now generally required. Many states formerly permitted unregistered electors to "swear in" their votes at the polls, a provision now discontinued except in a few states where court decisions have required it. Formerly registration laws provided for a new general registration of all voters annually, or every two or four years. Periodic registration laws have given way in many states to permanent registration, under which the voter does not renew his registration while continuing to reside at the same address. Under most such systems the voter is required to sign his registration record, and his signature is required at the polls for identification; in large cities there is a house-to-house check by police or election officials; and if the voter fails to vote for a specified period (usually two years), his name is dropped from the list.

REGULATORS OF NORTH CAROLINA (1764–71). A long struggle of the settlers in the then back counties of North Carolina against the oppressive administration of the laws by corrupt officials, and excessive fees charged by them and by attorneys, began (1764) in Anson, Orange and Granville counties. Serious disturbances led to the issuance by Gov. Arthur Dobbs of a proclamation forbidding the taking of illegal fees. This for a time measurably allayed the discontent. Not until the spring of 1768 was there any further organized resistance to the official class. The protestants then organized what they termed "The Regulation," the center being Orange County. The new governor, William Tryon, was in the western counties in July and August, 1768, and assembled at Hillsborough a body of militia to suppress a threatened uprising and protect the courts. Before this show of force the Regulators wilted and agitation subsided.

The second phase of the regulation covered the years 1769–71. Suits brought against extortioning officials failing to afford adequate relief, the movement took the form of driving local justices from the bench and threatening the officials of the courts with violence. At the September, 1770, session of the superior court at Hillsborough the Regulators presented a petition to the presiding judge, Richard Henderson, demanding unprejudiced juries and a public accounting of taxes by sheriffs, which concluded, "Though there are a few men who have the gift and art of reasoning, yet every man has a feeling and knows when he has justice done him, as well as the most learned." The court had hardly convened when 150 Regulators, equipped with sticks, switches and cudgels, crowded into the courtroom and insisted that one of their number be permitted to speak. Jeremiah Fields, in their behalf, demanded that their cases, based on extortion, be tried at that term and by jurors newly chosen. A leading lawyer, John Williams, starting into the courthouse, was given a severe thrashing. Peaceful methods cast aside, the crowd rushed upon Edmund Fanning who was, in their eyes, their chief oppressor, and he, with three others, was whipped. Fanning's house was looted and demolished. Judge Henderson had promised to comply with the demands the following day, but at night he mounted his horse and rode away to his home in Granville County. The November following, Henderson's home, barn and stables went up in flames.

Gov. Tryon ordered the arrest of the leaders concerned in these outbreaks. Energetic preparations were made for a military expedition to Orange County, and there resulted the battle of Alamance. A large majority of North Carolina historians vindicate the Regulators.

RELIGION IN AMERICA. European settlers brought with them the religious traditions and forms with which they were familiar, so that there was a diversity of religious bodies on the American scene from the early 17th century. Two groups, however, were especially important throughout the colonial period. English settlers in Virginia established their Church of England under the law, and attempted to curb dissenting groups. The church was administered under the general supervision of the Bishop of London, who appointed commissaries to provide for some oversight and discipline. England's internal struggles of the 17th century led to a neglect of colonial religious affairs, and this, coupled with the fact that colonial parishes were often far too large and were left unstaffed for long periods, meant that the Anglican establishment was not too effective. After the Glorious Revolution and the Toleration Act of 1689, one fruit of a more direct interest of the mother country in colonial affairs was the establishment of the Church of England in other Southern colonies: Maryland (1702), South Carolina (1706), North Carolina (1715), and Georgia (1758). A ministry act in New York (1693) was sometimes interpreted as establishing Anglicanism in certain counties of that colony.

English Puritans were dominant in the settlement of the areas that became the colonies of Massachusetts, Connecticut and New Hampshire. In belief, they were adherents of Calvinist covenant theology; in polity, they were predominantly Independents or nonseparatist Congregationalists. One of their major reasons for migrating to North America was that they might follow what they believed to be the plain teaching of Scripture in matters of religion. They also established their churches by law, and dealt severely with dissenters. By the close of the colonial period, the Congregationalists were the largest American religious body, though they were largely localized in New England.

These were the only religious groups to maintain established status for any length of time. The Dutch had established their Reformed Church in New Netherland, but lost this privileged position when the English took the area as New York in 1664. The Dutch Reformed, protected by a liberal charter, retained their ties with the Classis of Amsterdam until the Revolutionary epoch. When the German Reformed churches began to multiply in the 18th century, they looked to their Dutch Reformed brethren for support and guidance.

Among the early settlers, however, were minority groups which were opposed in principle to state churches. Roger Williams (1603?–1683) was a Puritan separatist who could not accept the establishment of religion as provided by his nonseparatist brethren. Driven out of Massachusetts, he founded Rhode Island on the principles of religious liberty and the separation of church and state. English Baptists, also devoted to religious liberty, began to appear in New England in the late 1630's; some migrated to Rhode Island, and Williams for a short time joined with them, though he later became a Seeker. The Quakers appeared first (1656) in the colonies as missionaries, anxious to witness to their faith in the "Inner Light" and to protest against all establishments of religion. They were dealt with harshly, especially in Massachusetts, where four of them were hanged (1659–61). Many took refuge in Rhode Island. Quakers played an important part in the settlement of New Jersey, Delaware and especially Pennsylvania, where Quaker leader William Penn (1644–1718) made full provision for religious liberty. This helped to attract from Europe many persecuted religious minorities which were seeking a place of refuge. Prominent among them were the Mennonites, Anabaptists who followed the pacifistic teachings of the Dutch reformer Menno Simons (1492–1559). Especially in the four colonies in which no establishments of religion were ever effected did a richly diversified religious situation develop from the beginning. The arrival of a Jewish group on Manhattan in 1654 made the situation there still more religiously complex. Small Jewish communities arose also in Newport, in Philadelphia, and in a number of the Southern cities.

Some groups which had adhered to established church patterns in Europe came to accept or to prefer the free situation they found in parts of North America. The Lutheran churches of various European states were there established, but in America the Lutheran minorities were never strong enough to attempt establishment (except briefly in the Swedish colony on the Delaware). When German Lutherans arrived in sizable numbers in the 18th century, many settled in freedom-loving Pennsylvania. Their great leader, Henry Melchior Muhlenberg (1711–87), recognized on his arrival in Pennsylvania in 1742 that the churches would have to depend on their own resources alone for survival and growth.

The Presbyterian church in Scotland was established, but in America Presbyterianism was to move in a different direction. This church was formed by the confluence of two streams, New England Puritans who moved southward out of New England, and immigrants from Scotland and Ireland. The Scotch-Irish group was chiefly made up of Scots from northern Ireland, where they had to live under a minority Anglican establishment and had come to see the value of religious toleration. The first conspicuous Presbyterian leader, Francis Makemie (1658–1708), under whose leadership the first presbytery was formed in

Philadelphia in 1706, is also remembered for his contribution to the cause of religious toleration in a famous court case (1707). As Presbyterian growth centered in the middle colonies with their religious multiplicity and lack of establishment, the preference for freedom increased.

In Maryland, settlement had begun in 1634 as a refuge for Roman Catholics. Religious toleration was extended to all Christians. Protestants outnumbered Catholics from the start; by the early 18th century the Anglicans were strong enough to establish their church there. The number of Roman Catholics in the colonies remained very small throughout the colonial period. They were subjected to legal disabilities and harassments almost everywhere, finding their fullest freedom in Pennsylvania.

By the early 18th century, there had therefore developed a religious situation of increasing multiplicity, necessitating some toleration even where there were established churches. But by this time there occurred a serious decline in religious interest. The high hopes of the founders, especially of the Puritan Bible commonwealth, had largely been frustrated. The familiar patterns for maintaining church life in Europe were not very effective in the new situation. Many of the settlers had not renewed church ties in the New World.

New patterns for maintaining religious vitality were developed in a series of revival movements familiarly known as the Great Awakening. Paralleling the Pietist thrust in Germany and the Evangelical Awakening in Britain, the Awakening focused attention on the winning of new converts to the faith. The revival waves first became conspicuous in the 1720's in New Jersey Dutch Reformed churches under the leadership of Theodore J. Frelinghuysen (1691–1748). The revival spread to Presbyterian churches, where it was championed especially by Gilbert Tennent (1703–64). In New England, awakening broke out in 1734 under the preaching of Calvinist Jonathan Edwards (1703–58); in the early 1740's the Great Awakening, aided by the fervid oratory of Anglican itinerant George Whitefield (1714–70), brought hundreds into the Congregational churches, and stimulated also the growth of dissenting groups, especially the Separate Congregationalists and Baptists. Then the Awakening swept south, where there were successively Presbyterian, Baptist, and finally, on the eve of the Revolution, Methodist phases. The Awakening did much to strengthen the churches in the Enlightenment period. It also emphasized the emotional and pietistic aspects of the faith at the expense of its classical and organic patterns. It stressed persuasion in religion, the personal appropriation of faith, and toleration.

Jonathan Edwards was not only an Awakening leader, but also a most able theoretical defender of revivals. His description of the outbreak of revival in Northampton, Mass., *Narrative of the Surprising*

Work of God in the Conversion of Many Hundred Souls (1737), is a classic. Of greater theological significance was his effort to distinguish between true and false revivalism, *A Treatise Concerning Religious Affections* (1746). Edwards' theological talents were also devoted to the defense of Calvinism against Arminianism, especially in the famous *Treatise on the Will* (1754), and in *The Great Christian Doctrine of Original Sin Defended* (1758). He did not live to complete the vast systematic theology which he had planned, but the fragments of it that we have, in his *Miscellanies* and in such essays as *The Nature of True Virtue* (posthumously published, 1765), show him to have been a thinker of extraordinary profundity, dealing boldly with the problems posed by the ablest scientific and philosophic minds of his age. Long after his passing, the theological debates turned largely on the questions which he had raised. An Edwardsean school, in which Joseph Bellamy (1719–90), Samuel Hopkins (1721–1803), Jonathan Edwards, Jr. (1745–1801) and Nathanael Emmons (1745–1840) were leaders, followed the theological tradition set forth by Edwards, not slavishly, but with less imaginative power.

The last quarter of the 18th century saw the success of the drive to keep church separate from state in the life of the newly independent nation. In this effort, religious rationalists worked with orthodox groups which had come to believe in religious liberty to sweep away many of the state establishments of religion and to provide that there should be no religious tests for office and no establishment of religion under the Constitution. (The last vestige of state establishment of religion was swept away in Massachusetts in 1833.) At about the same time that the Federal Constitution was being prepared, many of the churches were reshaping their organizational patterns, especially the Methodists, the Episcopalians, the Presbyterians, and the Roman Catholics.

As a result both of the generally unfriendly attitude of Enlightenment philosophy to revealed religion and the disruptions of church life caused by the Revolution, the vitality of the churches was at a low ebb at the dawn of the 19th century. But this was just at the time of the great movement of population westward. Church leaders felt the need for strong measures; many of them believed that the techniques of revivalism as illustrated by the Great Awakening could save the situation. So they launched what has been known as the "Second Great Awakening." In the East, the Awakening operated largely within the regular patterns of church life. It was effective in reviving the churches, and in gathering support for missionary outreach in the West and overseas. In the West, the revivals tended to be more intensely emotional, and the "camp meeting" was developed. In the 1820's, under the leadership of Charles G. Finney (1792–1875) and others, the "new measures" (protracted meetings, unseasonable hours, harsh language, the anxious bench) were adopted. New-measure-revivalism combined some of the features of eastern and western revivalism, and was widely employed.

Closely related to the spread of revivalism in Protestantism was the rise of many national voluntary societies for the promotion of missions, the publication of Bibles and religious tracts, and the improvement of life through moral and social reform movements. A pioneer agency was the American Board of Commissioners for Foreign Missions (1810), which was basically Congregationalist but which also drew support from Presbyterians and Reformed. Besides many denominational missionary societies there were also organized such nondenominational agencies as the American Education Society (1815), the American Sunday School Union (1817–24), the American Tract Society (1825), and the American Temperance Society (1826). The American Home Missionary Society (1826) was created to carry out the provisions of the Plan of Union (1801) which provided for the virtual merger of Congregational and Presbyterian work on the frontier. In the 1830's these voluntary societies, profiting from the vitalities released by revivalism, grew in size and effectiveness. The movement was correlated into a "benevolent empire" under an "interlocking directorate" of Protestant leaders, many of them Presbyterian or Congregationalist. The benevolence movement did much to promote mission and revival activity, and to conduct crusades for good causes and against moral and social evils.

Though revivalism was the most conspicuous phenomenon in American religion in the first half of the 19th century, it had its opponents. Under the impact of the Enlightenment, Unitarian thought had developed, especially in Congregationalism. Led by William Ellery Channing (1780–1842), the Unitarians formed a new denomination in the early 19th century, pulling many of the Congregational churches with them. They were critical of revivalism; radical Theodore Parker (1810–60) was especially vehement. But revivalism was attacked from the theological right also. In the German Reformed Church, under the leadership of John W. Nevin (1803–86) and Philip Schaff (1819–93), there arose a thoughtful though not very successful protest against the "system of the new measures" on behalf of the "system of the catechism." Of greater influence was the work of Congregational pastor and theologian Horace Bushnell (1802–76). His *Christian Nurture* (1847) challenged the revivalist idea that an emotional conversion experience was essential for entrance into the Christian life. Bushnell's other writings, especially *God in Christ* (1849) and *Nature and the Supernatural* (1857) shifted the attention of Protestant thought from an emphasis on exact dogma to be demonstrated to the mind, to a stress on religious feeling to be conveyed to the heart. Resistance to the revivalist emphasis and its outreach through the volun-

tary societies also contributed directly to a thirty-year schism (1837–38 to 1869–70) in Presbyterianism. The "Old School" was distrustful of men like Finney and was not willing to entrust missionary tasks to societies not under church control; the "New School" accepted revivalism and was strong in support of the voluntary societies.

Revivalism appealed to the religious emotions, and created a spiritual atmosphere conducive to the rise of new religious movements. The Christian Churches, or Disciples of Christ, became a major body in 1832 through the fusion of several revivalistically inclined bodies led by Alexander Campbell (1788–1866) and Barton W. Stone (1772–1844). Disciples hoped to unite all Christians in a restoration of primitive patterns. In western New York, the "burned-over district" where revival fires had swept back and forth, a number of new groups arose. Among them were the Latter Day Saints, or Mormons (1830), and the various Adventist bodies following the failure of the prophecy of William Miller (1782–1849) that the Lord would return in 1844. Religious community movements, especially the Shakers, profited from the excitement stirred by the revivals.

In the first half of the 19th century, denominations which utilized fully the patterns of revivalism mushroomed in size. Methodists excelled in this type of evangelism, and were especially vigorous on the frontier, where the circuit-riders planted many churches as civilization moved westward. By 1850, Methodists claimed over 1,250,000 adherents and had become the largest Protestant group. Baptists were second in size by that date; the "farmer-preacher" helped spread Baptist views in the West, while in the older settlements revivalistic measures were effectively used.

There was another major source of church growth, however—immigration. The influx of immigrants greatly strengthened the Roman Catholic Church, so that by 1850 it was the largest single denomination, with an estimated membership of over 1,700,000. On a smaller scale, Lutherans were also gaining numerically from the influx. The new elements predominantly stood for a "confessional" Lutheran position against a trend to "Americanism." The patterns of Jewish development were also greatly affected by 19th century immigration; the earlier Sephardic (Spanish and Portuguese) type of Judaism was overwhelmed as Ashkenazic (German) immigrants poured into the land.

The sectional tension over slavery which led to the Civil War also caused disruption in the churches. One of the causes espoused by the benevolent empire was abolition. The American Anti-Slavery Society was founded in 1833. Under the leadership of Theodore Dwight Weld (1803–95), the sentiment of many Northern evangelicals was won for antislavery. In the South, however, earlier gradualist antislavery feeling was replaced in the third and fourth decades of the century by a growing proslavery feeling, with the approval of many churchmen. The consequence was the division of several of the denominations, especially Methodists and Baptists in 1844–45. After the war came the rapid growth of the Negro denominations, with Baptist groups winning the majority of Negro Christians, and Methodist bodies a sizable minority.

In the years following the Civil War, the churches were confronted both with the impact of scientific, evolutionary and historical thinking on inherited modes of thought and with the transformation of patterns of daily living by technological developments, especially in the fields of transportation and communication. A number of influential pastors and teachers argued for an interpretation of Christian faith which took account of developments in the scientific and scholarly worlds, in particular the theory of evolution and the historical study of the Bible. Leaders in the rise of liberal theology were such men as Biblical scholar Charles A. Briggs (1841–1913), preacher Phillips Brooks (1835–93) and theologian William Newton Clarke (1841–1912). The latter's *Outline of Christian Theology* (1898) was one of the clearest systematic expressions of liberal theology, and enjoyed a wide circulation, especially in the North.

As the impact of technology and urbanization transformed the nation's social structures in the post-Civil War period, the conservative social theories held by many Protestants seemed to most liberals to be quite irrelevant to the new realities. Approaches to social questions in terms of individualism, charity and moral reform seemed inadequate to a group of leaders who had become aware of the growing tension between capital and labor and of the existence of social injustices in American life. The "father" of the "social gospel" was liberal Congregational pastor Washington Gladden (1836–1918), who argued in many books for a deeper awareness of social issues. The most distinguished leader of the social gospel was Walter Rauschenbusch (1861–1918), Baptist pastor and professor. His books, *Christianity and the Social Crisis* (1907), *Christianizing the Social Order* (1912), and *A Theology for the Social Gospel* (1917) were widely read, and for a generation the social gospel was an important ferment in Protestant life. Its force was felt especially in the Congregational, the Episcopal, and the (northern) Methodist, Baptist, and Presbyterian churches.

In the latter decades of the 19th century the floods of immigration increased; in the first fifteen years of the 20th century the annual influx passed the million mark six times. The flow came increasingly from southern Europe, greatly augmenting Roman Catholic numbers. The growth of that church was so rapid that in 1920 a membership of over 17,000,000 was estimated. The consciousness of a common Americanism during the crisis of World War I helped to overcome tensions among Catholics of differing national backgrounds, while the organization of the National Catholic War Council, later renamed the National Catholic Welfare Conference, did much to consolidate the growing unity of American Catholics. Led by Cardinal James Gibbons (1834–1921), and following the principles presented in the encyclical *Rerum Novarum* (1891) of Pope Leo XIII, American Catholics were seriously concerned with social questions in the 20th century.

The wave of immigration also brought many Jews into the country, especially a large number from Russia and Poland. Three main streams of interpretation of the Jewish heritage (Reform, Conservative and Orthodox) were defined and given formal organization. Many Christians of Eastern Orthodox background, especially Russians and Greeks, came into the country in sizable numbers in the late 19th and early 20th centuries.

In the 1920's, the Protestant world was torn by the bitter fundamentalist-modernist controversy. While the liberal theology had been gaining considerable support, especially in the North and East, many other Protestants, especially in rural America, had remained staunchly conservative. The revival tradition, as perpetuated by Dwight L. Moody (1837–99) and those who copied his methods, was conservatively oriented and resisted the critical approach to the Scriptures. As liberalism advanced in the 20th century toward "modernism," fundamentalism arose in reaction. Many revivalists, especially William A. Sunday (1863–1935) backed the fundamentalist movement, and as some of the country's leading seminaries adopted liberal positions, a number of very conservative Bible schools were founded. The leader of the fundamentalist crusade was William Jennings Bryan (1860–1925), but his death following the famous Scopes trial in Tennessee (1925) weakened the drive to capture control of the major denominations. Fundamentalism survived as a minority movement in the denominations; many of its supporters took refuge in splinter churches.

The period since the Civil War had also seen the rise and growth of many small indigenous movements, often called "sects" or "cults." Some of these have been oriented to fundamentalism, while others have focused around the quest for perfection, or have emphasized the theme of the imminent return of the Lord. Some of the newer religious movements, such as the New Thought and religious science groups, have been deeply concerned with the scientific and philosophical thought of the time.

The movement for Christian co-operation and unity among Protestants and Orthodox matured in the 20th century. In 1908 the Federal Council of Churches of Christ was founded to develop co-operative relationships among the denominations. It was influential in spreading social gospel thought, and in co-ordinating church effort in World Wars I and II. In 1950 it combined with a number of other interdenominational agencies (including those for home missions, foreign missions, and Christian education) to form the National Council of the Churches of Christ in the U. S. A., sponsored by more than thirty denominations. The unitive movement has also been expressed in church unions. Some of these have been within denominational families, as in the formation of the United Lutheran Church in America (1918), the American Lutheran Church (1930), and the Methodist Church (1939). Others have been across denominational lines, as in the formation of the United Church of Christ (1957, bringing together the Congregational Christian and the Evangelical and Reformed churches.)

In the years following World War II, a new interest in religion was evident on the American scene. This was illustrated by the highest estimated percentage of church membership with respect to the total population yet recorded (63% for 1958), by a new interest in religious revivalism and religious literature, and by a renaissance in Biblical and theological scholarship.

RELIGIOUS LIBERTY is perhaps the greatest contribution America has made both in the realm of politics and of religion. At the time of the establishment of the American colonies there was no country in Europe without a state church, and everywhere, with the possible exception of Holland, unity of religion was considered essential to the unity of the state. There is a mistaken notion, widely held, that the Reformation more or less automatically brought about religious liberty, but nothing is farther from the truth. The Reformation resulted in the establishment of numerous national churches, as in England, Scotland, Holland and the Scandinavian countries, which were as intolerant of Roman Catholicism and the small dissenting sects as Roman Catholicism was intolerant of them.

Besides the national churches which arose out of the religious and political upheaval of the Reformation, there also developed numerous small sects, generally poor and despised, most of them taking as their pattern the primitive church of the first three centuries. These small minority bodies generally stood for the separation of church and state, and complete religious liberty. It is an important fact to bear in mind that religious liberty and the separation of church and state have been principally advocated by the small minority sects and never by the great state churches. The English Baptists, a small despised sect, took over the principles of the Anabaptists of the continent and held to religious liberty as their first and greatest principle. The Quakers also became the advocates of freedom of conscience. Another source of the principle of religious liberty is found in the 16th- and 17th-century political philosophers such as Sir Thomas More who pictured in his ideal state one where there was complete religious liberty, and John Locke who wrote an important series of essays on religious toleration.

The American colonies became the first place in the world where complete religious liberty was actually tried in a political state. Roger Williams, the founder of Rhode Island, had become thoroughly imbued with this idea and when he established Rhode Island the principle was there put into operation. Another factor which made the American colonies a fruitful place for the growth of this principle was the fact that a majority of the colonies were begun as proprietary grants, where the governments as well as the land were controlled by the same individual or groups of individuals. This meant that, in order to attract settlers to buy and settle the land, persecuted religious groups from almost every country in western Europe were invited to come to these colonies. Thus William Penn, Lord Baltimore and the proprietors of the Carolinas and Georgia welcomed the persecuted sectaries. Still another factor creating an environment in America favorable to religious liberty was the fact that, by the end of the colonial period, a great majority of the population throughout the colonies was unchurched, and unchurched people generally are opposed to granting special privileges to any one religious body. It is an interesting and significant fact that the political leaders who led in the movement to separate church and state, with the establishment of independence, as James Madison and Thomas Jefferson, were non-church members. Of all the colonial religious bodies the Baptists were the most tenacious in their advocacy of religious liberty and as a whole made the largest contribution toward its achievement.

In the colonies south of Pennsylvania the Anglican church was established by law, but only in Maryland and Virginia was it a factor of significance. In Massachusetts, Connecticut and New Hampshire the Congregational church was the privileged body, but by the end of the colonial period the factors noted above had considerably relaxed its control. The great colonial awakenings had strengthened the dissenting bodies especially in the Middle and Southern colonies and the coming of the Revolution gave them an opportunity to bargain for greater privileges. Although there were no direct religious issues involved in the War for Independence, yet the disturbed political and social situation which it created, together with the necessity for the formation of new governments, gave opportunity for the new principle, religious liberty, to be incorporated in the new constitutions as they were adopted. Thus, the new state and Federal constitutions simply took over, in this respect, what already was, to a large degree, in practical operation.

"REMEMBER THE ALAMO." The bitterness of the Texans over the massacres at the Alamo and at Goliad found expression in this battle cry, the words of which had been used by Gen. Houston in a stirring address to his men two days before the battle of San Jacinto, April 21, 1836.

"REMEMBER THE *MAINE*" was a popular slogan current just before and during the war with Spain (1898). Popular opinion, led by such "yellow" journals as the New York *Journal* and *World*, held Spain responsible for the destruction of the battleship *Maine* in Havana harbor (Feb. 15, 1898). The *Journal* boasted that its readers had known "immediately after the destruction of the *Maine* that she was blown up by a Spanish mine." The *World*, by Feb. 20, declared it had "proved" destruction by a mine, and when the report of a naval court of inquiry sustained this position, announced: *"It is in itself a cause of war* if not atoned for. . . . If Spain will not punish her miscreants, we must punish Spain." This sentiment was echoed in the service journals, the *Army and Navy Register* and *Army and Navy Journal,* and in Congress, where one Senator declared, "The battle cry on sea and land will be 'Remember the *Maine!'* " The resentment embodied in the phrase contributed immeasurably to the war spirit.

REMUDA, a Spanish word taken over by the ranching industry: any unit, varying greatly in number, of "saddle" (cow) horses, whether being ridden, scattered over the range, or herded by the horse wrangler (*remudero*). All range and trail work must be done on horseback; hence the *remuda's* importance.

REORGANIZED CHURCH OF JESUS CHRIST OF LATTER DAY SAINTS claims to be the continuation of and successor to the Church of Jesus Christ of Latter Day Saints, organized by Joseph Smith, Jr., on April 6, 1830, at Fayette, New York. The church in 1831 established headquarters at Kirtland, Ohio, where it built the Kirtland Temple, which still belongs to this church. After migrating to Jackson County, Mo., in 1831, the members suffered persecutions, attributable largely to their rapid growth, their antislavery sentiments and the resulting political fears of other settlers. They were forced to move to the neighboring counties of Clay, Ray, Caldwell and Daviess (1833), but were not allowed to remain, and in 1838 were expelled from Missouri by order of Gov. Lilburn W. Boggs on threat of extermination. They then (1839) settled at Nauvoo, Illinois.

Joseph Smith, Jr., their prophet-president, and his brother were killed by a mob at Carthage, Ill., June 27, 1844, while under a pledge of protection by Gov. Thomas Ford. Confusion followed. Many factions were formed. A small proportion followed Brigham Young to Utah; another group followed Sidney Rigdon to Pennsylvania; a third followed James

J. Strang to Wisconsin and Michigan. A number, desiring to maintain the original faith, finally formed a new group in 1852, still under the name The Church of Jesus Christ of Latter Day Saints. To this group came Joseph Smith, III, the oldest son, and Emma Smith, the widow of Joseph Smith, Jr., and were accepted on their original baptism. All of the children, the sister and only surviving brother of Joseph Smith, Jr., and later his descendants, affiliated with this group. In October, 1869, for legal reasons the word "Reorganized" was added to the name. Independence, Mo., was named as the central place for the establishment of Zion, "the pure in heart." There followed a suit in the U. S. Circuit Court, decided in 1894, for possession of the Temple Lot there. In this case, in which the three principal factions of the Church of the Latter Day Saints were involved, the court decided that the "Reorganized Church" was the true successor, with doctrines and practices identical with those of the original church. The pleadings put in issue the question of polygamy and Judge John F. Philips held it was no part of the teaching or practice of the original church, thereby exonerating Joseph Smith, Jr., of responsibility for the teaching. These doctrines and practices of the original church included social ideals, monogamous marriage, a re-establishment of the New Testament Church with the Holy Scriptures as the fundamental basis of teaching. They also accept the *Book of Mormon* as a record of early inhabitants of America and the *Doctrine and Covenants,* a collection of revelations of today. They differ from other Christian churches in the emphasis upon the right to revelation as a body and individually and the spiritual gifts as set forth in I Corinthians 12. They reject the name Mormon because of the association of the name in the popular mind with doctrines and practices which they have always repudiated.

REPUBLICAN PARTY (JEFFERSONIAN) was the first opposition party under the new National Government, its elements appearing in the first two Congresses when the vigorous leadership of Hamilton and his Federalist associates aroused the fear and hostility of various members who disliked the funding system, the revenue acts, the first United States Bank and the general tendency to create a powerful national authority by liberal construction of the Constitution. The frank reliance of the Federalists on "the wise and good and rich," their liking for forms and ceremonies which smacked of the aristocratic, and particularly their horror of the French Revolution and all its works, tended to make the opposition the party of the common man and gave it its title of "Republican."

Thomas Jefferson supplied the necessary leadership and philosophy. Organization spread, at least in rudimentary form, throughout the country, the "Democratic Clubs" playing an important part. Its leaders realized the importance of propaganda and a number of important newspapers were acquired or founded at strategic points. Jefferson won the Presidency in 1800, carried out a series of mild reforms and innovations, and was re-elected by a huge majority four years later, the Federalists henceforth declining to the position of a factious and intransigent minority largely centered in New England (see Essex Junto). With the election of Madison, however, there ensued a period of twenty years when the Republican party, nominally in power, was in reality a collection of sectional and personal factions rather than a genuine cohesive party. Under its auspices, however, there was a gradual broadening of the suffrage, an increasing democratizing of local life, a perceptible emphasis on humanitarian reform, and after the War of 1812 the development of a nationalist spirit in striking contrast to the divisions of the Federalist era. New issues, however, were appearing. The tariff, the Second United States Bank and internal improvements caused a cleavage comparable to that of 1790–1800 and, with the election of Andrew Jackson in 1828, a new and more logical alignment of "National" and "Democratic" Republicans was well established, to evolve, a few years later, into the Whig and Democratic parties respectively.

REPUBLICAN PARTY. The Kansas-Nebraska Act of 1854, which repealed the Missouri Compromise and opened the western territories to slavery, caused a popular revulsion throughout the North and West. Feeling became so strong that a series of local movements appeared simultaneously in many places. These movements rapidly coalesced, and to show their Jeffersonian ancestry they adopted the name "Republican," which name had been discarded by Jackson's followers in favor of "Democratic." Jefferson's influence was the reputed cause of the passage of the Northwest Ordinance of 1787 which had forever banished slavery from the western territory north of the Ohio River. This principle of the nonextension of slavery, made vital by the Free Soil party of 1848, now became the main platform of the new Republican party. It drew probably one third of its strength from the Democrats by way of the Free Soil party. The other two thirds came from the Whigs.

The name Republican was first adopted at a local political meeting held in Ripon, Wis., on Feb. 28, 1854, and also was formally adopted by a state convention which met at Jackson, Mich., on July 6 of the same year. The various local movements rapidly perfected their organizations and accepted the name Republican. Many conventions were held on July 13, the anniversary of the passage of the Northwest Ordinance of 1787 by the Continental Congress. Among these were state conventions in Indiana, Ohio, Vermont and Wisconsin. The Republican party was not founded in the common acceptance of the term

but just grew. It was the expression of a widespread sentiment. Thomas Jefferson, in a real sense, may be reputed the founder of both the Democratic and Republican parties.

John C. Frémont was the first Republican candidate for President, in 1856, and although defeated, succeeded in carrying eleven states. The nomination of Abraham Lincoln in 1860 upon a platform which combined free soil principles with that of a protective tariff united the agricultural and industrial interests of the North and West and, aided by a split in the Democratic party, resulted in electoral triumph. It also resulted in the adoption of the Hamiltonian principles of National Government and commercial advancement, including "sound money" and a protective tariff, which became the underlying basis of Republican policy for the next seventy years.

Before the Civil War there had been a vigorous two-party system in the South, and this condition persisted, to a surprising degree, into the period of Reconstruction. Many Southern Whigs, sympathizing with the position of the Republican party (which had, after all, merely absorbed Whiggery) on economic questions, showed a disposition to co-operate with the Republicans in defending the civil rights of the recently freed slaves, including even their right to vote. Since these "scalawags" in fact generally represented the Southern planter class, their willingness to enter into what was to all intents and purposes a political alliance with the Negroes merely reflected the persistence of old habits of co-operation, the legacy of the plantation. It was the poorer whites, traditionally Democratic and opposed to the Whiggish planters, who bitterly fought the enfranchisement of the Negro, just as they had once fought to make his slavery as binding and degrading as possible.

These antebellum political relations did not break down in some places until the 1890's, although as early as the 1870's the ex-Whigs had begun to find their connection with the Republicans unsatisfactory. But it was not until Southern conservatives themselves raised the specter of Negro domination in order to head off Populism, which in the South contemplated an economic and political alliance of poor whites and poor Negroes, that the cause of white supremacy finally triumphed in the South. It was only then that the South was finally lost to Republicanism.

Meanwhile the Northern Republicans retreated from their championship of the Negro, and the party fell increasingly under the domination of corporate interests. The zenith of business influence was reached in 1896 when Mark Hanna collected from the frightened "money power" a campaign chest estimated as high as $16,000,000. Under Theodore Roosevelt the party moved briefly in the direction of what Roosevelt called "conservative radicalism," or "progressive conservatism," but his desertion of the party in 1912 left it in the hands of the conservative element, where, on the whole, it has remained to the present time.

Hoover, it is true, was a progressive of sorts, but his kind of progressivism seemed inadequate to the disastrous depression which engulfed his administration, and in any case his more adventurous policies were opposed by his own party. The depression and the Second World War constituted a double disaster for the Republicans, the former because they were blamed for it, the latter because it gave President Franklin D. Roosevelt the opportunity to run for a third and then a fourth term. Not until 1952, when a new generation had come to maturity for whom the issues of the '30's and '40's had little meaning, did the Republican party return to power with the aid of the tremendous popularity of Dwight D. Eisenhower. Congress under Eisenhower, however, went Democratic in three out of four elections.

REPUDIATION OF STATE DEBTS was the subject of agitated discussion in this country and abroad in the 1840's and the 1870's. In the 1830's various American states incurred heavy debts in the construction of canals and railroads, and in the creation of banks. By 1839 the public indebtedness of American states amounted to $170,000,000. Frequently, in authorizing these loans, the faith of the state was pledged for the payment of the interest and the redemption of the principal. In many cases the laws specified that the bonds should not be sold below par. In negotiating these loans authorized agents of the states violated the state statutes and American bankers aided and abetted them. In London, Baring Brothers and Co. and other English banking houses introduced them to their clients; in Amsterdam, Hope and Co. Foreign investors bought with avidity these securities because of the guaranty of the states, the high rate of interest they carried, the high standing of the national credit, and the confidence of foreign bankers in the United States Bank. The aggressive salesmanship of American agents abroad somewhat accounts for the lack of caution and prudence upon the part of the European bankers. By 1839 it was estimated that British subjects held the equivalent of about $110,000,000 to $165,000,000 in American securities. When the American financial structure collapsed in the panic of 1837, European bankers tactlessly suggested that the Federal Government assume the state debts. Whatever merits the scheme might have possessed was lost by the hostility created by its supposedly foreign origin and the scramble for votes in the presidential election of 1840.

Between 1841 and 1842 eight states and one territory defaulted on their interest payments. Mississippi repudiated $5,000,000 of Union Bank bonds in 1842 on the ground that the law providing for their issuance was unconstitutional and that the bonds had been sold on credit to the United States Bank in violation of the state statute. Ten years later the people of Mississippi defeated a tax levy for the purpose of paying the interest on $2,000,000 of Planters'

Bank bonds; and in 1875 an amendment to the state constitution was ratified by the people prohibiting the state from redeeming or paying the Union Bank bonds and the Planters' Bank bonds. In 1842 Florida disavowed her responsibility for $3,900,000 of bank bonds on the ground that the territorial legislature was not empowered to issue them. In 1842 Michigan repudiated a portion of a $5,000,000 loan on the ground that the state had not received payment for the bonds obtained by the United States Bank.

There were many reasons for the growth of repudiation sentiment at this time. The sneers and jeers of the foreign press at American integrity fanned the flames of national prejudices; while the universal indebtedness gave an impetus to the movement in favor of repudiation. Repudiation resulted from a series or combination of forces—speculative mania, ignorance of sound banking, a ruinous depression, blatantly demagogic leadership, and the stupidity of the bondholders in refusing to consider propositions that might have resulted in partial payments of their holdings. While it is true that the meagre resources of the American people at that time made it impossible for them to meet their obligations when they fell due, an inability to pay was no justification for refusal to pay.

The second attack of the disease of state repudiation came with the funding of the state debts incurred during the Reconstruction era. These bonds were issued by governments that were not representative of the Southern states. Foreign investors were warned not to purchase them. The forced repudiation of the Confederate war debts by the Fourteenth Amendment strengthened the Southerner's opposition to the payment of the "bayonet bonds," especially since a large proportion of these securities were held by the "conquerors of the north" who had foisted and maintained the hated Reconstruction governments in the South. The ravages of the Civil War, the misrule of the Reconstruction period, and the hard times following the panic of 1873 increased the heavy burdens of the Southern people; but in no case were the debts scaled or repudiated until it was apparently impossible to discharge them. In 1876 Alabama repudiated $4,705,000 of railroad bonds. In 1884 Arkansas, after a long dispute, repudiated $500,000 of bonds held by James Holford of London along with other obligations incurred during the carpetbag regime. In 1876 the supreme court of Florida declared unconstitutional and void $4,000,000 of railroad bonds. In 1876 Georgia repudiated railroad bonds whose minimum face value amounted to $9,-352,000; and the following year the legislature approved a constitutional amendment confirming the repudiation statutes. The total amount of Louisiana's repudiations between 1875 and 1884 was approximately $22,000,000. In 1879 North Carolina scaled its debt and repudiated over $12,000,000 of bonds. In

1873 South Carolina repudiated $5,965,000 of "conversion bonds."

Foreign creditors had been prevented by the Eleventh Amendment to the Federal Constitution from seeking redress. In December, 1933, the Principality of Monaco which had come into possession of some of the repudiated Mississippi bonds asked leave to bring suit in the U. S. Supreme Court against the State of Mississippi; but on May 21, 1934, the Court unanimously held that the Principality could not sue the State of Mississippi.

RESACA DE LA PALMA, BATTLE OF (May 9, 1846). The day following Gen. Taylor's minor triumph at Palo Alto, Texas, the Mexican army under Mariano Arista fell back five miles to the Resaca de Guerrero, where natural defenses offset the effectiveness of superior American cannon and necessitated reliance on infantry and cavalry. In these branches Arista had a numerical advantage, and when Taylor attacked in mid-afternoon the Mexicans at first held firm. After a fierce hand-to-hand combat in the underbrush and chaparral, however, the Mexican left gave way before the insistent hammering of Taylor's troops. Arista's flank was turned, and his army crumbled under the American assault. A precipitant flight ensued, Taylor's men pursuing the Mexicans to the bank of the Rio Grande, which the latter crossed with difficulty and without order. Mexican losses were 547 killed, wounded, or missing. The American losses were 33 killed, 89 wounded. Taylor wrote his report at the Resaca de la Palma, which gave the battle its name.

RESERVED POWERS OF STATES. The Constitution of the United States created a government of enumerated powers. The framers intended that all powers not conferred upon the National Government by the Constitution nor denied by that document to the states should be retained by the states. In the ratifying conventions questions were raised as to why such an important matter had been left to inference. The first Congress reflected this feeling of uneasiness in proposing a series of amendments. Ten of these were ratified by the states. The Tenth Amendment contained the following language:

"The powers not delegated to the United States by the Constitution, nor prohibited by it to the states, are reserved to the states respectively, or to the people."

This amendment securely established the United States as a Federal state composed of a central government and a number of constituent state governments each possessing powers independent of the other.

One who is desirous of ascertaining the powers of the states at any given moment must do so by a negative process. He must first conceive of all of the potential powers of government as a reservoir from which the people have abstracted certain powers to be given to the National Government. These are found principally in Article I of Section 8 of the Constitution where, in seventeen clauses, the powers of Congress are set forth. Except in a few instances no state may exercise any of these. To the powers expressly conferred upon the National Government by the Constitution, the U. S. Supreme Court has, by a consistent policy of broad construction, added many implied powers. It has also pointed out that the National Government possesses certain inherent powers by virtue of its sovereign character. No state may invade these fields. These are the powers delegated to the United States which are referred to in the Tenth Amendment.

The powers prohibited to the states by the Constitution are found principally in Article I, Section 10, and in the Fourteenth, Fifteenth and Nineteenth Amendments. By Article I, Section 10, the states are forbidden absolutely to enter into treaties, alliances or confederations; to grant letters of marque; to coin money; to emit bills of credit; to make anything but gold or silver coin tender in payment of debts; to pass bills of attainder, ex post facto laws or laws impairing the obligation of contracts; or to grant titles of nobility. They are also prohibited, except with the consent of Congress, from laying duties on imports or exports (with certain exceptions), from laying duties of tonnage, keeping troops or ships of war in time of peace, entering into agreements or compacts, or engaging in war. The Fourteenth Amendment forbids the making or enforcing of any state law which shall abridge the privileges and immunities of citizens of the United States; the deprivation of any person of life, liberty or property without due process of law; or the denial of equal protection of the laws. The Fifteenth and Nineteenth Amendments restrain the power of the states to define the qualifications of electors by forbidding discrimination on the grounds of race, color, previous condition of servitude or sex. All of these things states may not do except upon the conditions specified in the Constitution. But all remaining powers of government are theirs.

The Supreme Court of the United States is the final arbiter in case of conflict between a state and the National Government over the right to exercise a governmental power. On occasion, as in the Child Labor Cases, the Court has declared acts of Congress invalid because they invaded the reserved powers of the states. On many other occasions state statutes have been declared void as invasions of the power of the National Government. Only by such a process may our Federal Union be preserved.

RESERVED POWERS OF THE PEOPLE. The Tenth Amendment reserves all powers not granted to the United States by the Constitution, nor prohibited by it to the states, to the states respectively or the people. It seems clear that the people referred to were the people of the several states, not the people of the United States. Thus viewed, the phrase "to the people" is a pronouncement of a political theory of popular sovereignty—a recognition of the right of the people to create and alter their state governments at will.

If the people of a state merely established a government, placing no limitations upon its powers, the legislative branch would possess all of the authority implied by the Tenth Amendment. But state constitutions commonly go much further than this. Bills of rights to protect the citizen of the state from his state government are found in every state constitution. In many states the people have reserved to themselves the power to propose new laws through the initiative or to require the submission to popular vote of laws passed by the legislature through the referendum. As state constitutions grow longer, more and more subjects are removed from legislative competence and are made subject to alteration only by popular vote. Such reservations of power as these give content to the final phrase of the Tenth Amendment.

In another sense it may be said that the effect of the Amendment was to guarantee to the citizens of the states the continuation of the legal rights and duties which had been built up by the courts in the common law. Or from still another point of view it is an embodiment in legal phraseology of the right of revolution asserted in the Declaration of Independence. Thus it may be interpreted as an effort on the part of the first Congress to suggest that each citizen might possess a sphere of privacy which should be inviolate from interference by his government. During the period of individualism in America this privacy was a reality in many areas of life. But in recent years control, by both state and Federal governments, has become increasingly pervasive.

REUNION was a French colony established in 1854 near Dallas, Texas, by French Socialists who were followers of François Fourier under the immediate leadership of Prosper Victor Considerant, who explained that Reunion would serve as a center from which would radiate numerous lines leading to other colonies to be established by people who had imbibed the doctrines of Fourier. Some attempts were made in Houston, Texas, and one, by the purchase of 50,000 acres, at Uvalde, Texas, but, like Reunion, they were never successful. Some writers estimate that the population of Reunion reached 500, but a safe estimate would be approximately 300. The colony continued, with varying degrees of success and failure, until 1867 when it was disbanded and its assets were distributed.

REVERE'S RIDE. Paul Revere, a Boston silversmith and a trusted messenger of the Massachusetts Committee of Safety, foreseeing an attempt of the British troops in Boston against the military stores collected in Concord, had arranged to signal a warning to the Whigs in Charlestown. In the late evening of April 18, 1775, he was told by Dr. Joseph Warren, chairman of the Committee of Safety, that the British were about to cross the river to begin their march to Concord. Revere signalled the fact by two lanterns (Longfellow's "two if by sea") hung by a friend from the tower of the North Church, probably the present Christ Church in Boston. Then, using a secreted boat, he managed to cross the river in spite of British patrols, and borrowing a horse in Charlestown, started for Concord. Blocked by British officers from the Cambridge road, he rode via Medford, alarming the country as he went. About midnight he arrived in Lexington, and at the house of the Rev. Jonas Clarke roused John Hancock and Samuel Adams, who were thus enabled to seek safety. Joined by William Dawes (sent by Dr. Warren via Roxbury) and by young Dr. Samuel Prescott of Concord, Revere then set forward with his news, only to be intercepted, a few miles farther on, by a patrol of British officers. Prescott leaped a fence and escaped, carrying the alarm to Lincoln and Concord. Dawes fled back toward Lexington; but Revere was taken. Assuring his captors that the country was roused against them, he so alarmed them that they set him free. He returned to Lexington, helped to save Hancock's papers, and saw the first shot fired on the green. Revere did not reach "the bridge in Concord town," but his feat was of quite as great importance as Longfellow supposed.

REVIVALS have occurred in America at frequent intervals from the early 18th century to the present. The Great Awakening, which marks the beginning of this type of religious activity, had three distinct phases: the New England, the Middle Colony and the Southern or Virginian. The New England revival began under the preaching of Jonathan Edwards in Northampton, Mass., in December, 1734, and continued in successive waves for nearly ten years. The entire Connecticut Valley was affected and from 25,000 to 50,000 members were added to the New England churches. The Middle Colony revival centered at New Brunswick, N. J., as the result of the preaching of a group of young men who had been trained in William Tennent's "Log College" at Neshaminy, Pa. It was largely a Presbyterian revival and resulted in greatly expanding the influence of that communion. The Southern or Virginian revival had also three distinct phases: a Presbyterian phase (1750–60) under the leadership of Samuel Davies; a Baptist phase (1760–70) under the leadership of two New England farmer-preachers; and a Methodist phase (1772–80), which marks the real beginning of Methodism in America. The connecting link between all these phases of the colonial Awakenings was George Whitefield, who made seven evangelistic tours of America, between 1738 and 1770, and ranged up and down the colonies from Maine to Georgia, working with all the evangelical churches.

The latter years of the 18th century were a period of religious deadness, to be followed by the Second Awakening (1797–1805) which swept the nation. This movement was particularly spectacular in the West. Here, in great outdoor meetings, many people under great emotional strain were affected by strange physical exercises called the "jerks" and the "falling exercise." While adding tens of thousands to the frontier churches it also left some unfortunate results. The eastern phase of this revival began in the colleges and spread throughout that section. President Timothy Dwight of Yale College was the most conspicuous leader. From this time forward revivalism became the accepted method of work adopted by Congregationalists, Presbyterians, Baptists, Methodists and later the Disciples, and its influence can be traced in the more conservative Lutheran and German Reformed bodies.

The outstanding pre-Civil War revivalist was Charles G. Finney who had many imitators as well as critics. Lyman Beecher and his more famous son, Henry Ward Beecher, were revivalistic preachers as were all the more prominent preachers of the time. The Yale Divinity School, under the inspiration of Nathaniel W. Taylor, turned out a stream of revivalistic preachers for several student generations, and the denominational colleges throughout the land were centers of revivalistic influence and effort.

An unusual revival began in 1857, as a result of a Wall Street panic, in a prayer meeting on Fulton Street in New York City, and soon the nation "was on its knees." It was in this quiet laymen's movement that Dwight L. Moody began his religious activities which in the years following the Civil War made him the outstanding revivalist of his time. The period of Moody's activity as a revivalist covered the years from the close of the Civil War to his death in 1899. He, associated with his great song leader Ira D. Sankey, conducted meetings in every large city in the country, and held two great evangelistic campaigns in Great Britain (1873–75; 1881–84). Though a man without education and with no ecclesiastical organization back of him, Moody was probably the greatest single influence for religion in 19th-century America.

The last six decades in the history of revivalism may be fittingly termed the period of the professional evangelist. It was the period in which B. Fay Mills, Sam Jones, R. A. Torrey, J. Wilbur Chapman and "Billy" Sunday, to name only a few among the better-known revivalists, were occupying the center of the evangelistic stage. This type of revivalism was characterized by high-powered organizations, great tabernacles and the collection of large sums of money. Rev. William A. Sunday, the most conspicuous of these revivalists, was a converted baseball player who began his career as a professional evangelist in the 1890's. His greatest meetings were held from 1910 to 1920, but he continued active until his death in 1935.

Since 1920 this type of revivalism has been on the decline, though revivalistic methods are still extensively used, especially among the numerous pentecostal and holiness bodies.

REVOLUTION, AMERICAN. It is the prevailing notion that the American Revolution was the direct result of a series of acts of the British government restricting, in important particulars, the freedom of the American colonies and designed at the same time to strengthen the hand of the home government in colonial control. The idea is essentially correct, but requires explanations and qualifications. Those acts of the British government commonly cited as causes of the Revolution did indeed, by their cumulative effect, provoke the colonies into revolt, yet these acts were rather the agencies that loosened political, economic and social forces long accumulating and long pent up. The genesis of the Revolution is therefore to be sought primarily in the conditions that had developed in the colonies through a long period of years. What, in brief, had taken place was that the colonies, far separated from the mother country, thrown largely upon their own initiative, long accustomed to directing their own affairs, each according to its situation and its lights, had become imbued not only with a spirit of self-reliance, but with its necessary complement, a spirit of self-determination. Parental respect and affection abode with them still; parental guidance and protection, when needed, they continued to welcome; but let parental concern take on the character of excessive parental domination, and resentment would inevitably ensue; and resentment might easily grow into revolt. It was just such a development that brought on the Revolution. England and her American colonies had grown apart. Economic interests had diverged; political and social ideas had taken different trends. In consequence the bonds that bound the colonies to the mother country had become attenuated, and no great strain was required to break them. The attempt of Great Britain to assert a greater degree of control over the colonies furnished that strain. As these conditions manifested themselves, however, only in the presence of definite provocations, so the provocations find their full interpretation only in their relation to these undercurrents of colonial life.

When we consider the years preceding the Revolution, we seem to perceive this growth of a colonial consciousness of self-sufficiency reaching something like a climax with the close, in 1763, of the long rivalry between England and France, a rivalry that had had always its American phases, involving the colonies in dangers and in consequent measures of defense. This last war (*see* French and Indian War) in particular had been fought to determine whether French or English should be master of the American continent. Victorious England was now in possession not only of Canada on the north, whence had come threats of French aggression, but also of the vast region to the westward, which the French had sought to colonize, but upon which the English colonies had long cast covetous eyes. There followed a sense of relief from danger, of freedom to pursue their own ways, and a turning of the eyes toward the west with an ever greater yearning. Without being quite aware of it, the colonies straightway set out upon a march that, in a dozen years, was to bring them to the verge of separation from the maternal leading-strings.

Even before the events of 1763 had given their new and powerful impulse to the thought that British-America should be master in its own house, voices had been heard that carried the self-same note. There was, for instance, that notable speech of James Otis of Boston, in 1761, against writs of assistance, of which John Adams later declared that "then and there the child Independence was born." Adams was in error, as have been many who have come after him, in assuming that the child Independence, in the sense meant by him, really had a birthday. The child just grew. This is not to maintain that it could not have failed to grow. It was the diet. Much the same may be said of the utterance of Patrick Henry in the famous Parson's Cause, some two years later. The voices of Otis and Henry were in essential unison in that each in his way had proclaimed the doctrines of government—not new doctrines in the world by any means—that the colonies would presently grasp as their main weapons of defense.

It is not to be overlooked that there was also a British side to the picture. Great Britain had become an empire, an empire stretching across all the seas and embracing many peoples of many modes of thought and practice. That empire must needs be defended and strengthened, and, what was of the utmost importance, its unity must somehow be preserved. It was primarily upon the ways and means of promoting these purposes that Great Britain and her colonies clashed. This problem of imperial organization, which was of such vital consequence to Great Britain, was for the moment of little concern to the colonies; yet, when at long last they had gained their independence and upon them, in turn, devolved the task of laying the foundations of a nation, it was upon the proper solution of just such a problem that in great measure depended the nation's future. Indeed, from first to last, it was the failure of mutual understanding and sympathy that brought upon the two great branches of the British empire their mutual woes.

The trouble began when, in 1764, the British ministry decided, quite reasonably, that it was necessary to maintain a small military force in the colonies for their defense, and, also quite reasonably, that the colonies ought to bear at least a part of the expense. The colonies, on their part, objected to anything like a standing army; they objected also to contributing toward its upkeep; but most of all they objected to the methods adopted for raising the necessary revenue. One of the means was by a more rigid enforce-

ment of the Navigation Acts, hitherto more breached than observed by the colonists. This was annoying enough, but when the Sugar Act, forbidding the colonies to trade with the French and Dutch West Indies, followed, colonial exasperation boiled over. But worse was yet to come. So far only the commercial colonies were affected. The withers of the Southern colonies had not been wrung. It was the Stamp Act, passed early in 1765, proposing to collect internal taxes in all the colonies, that stirred a storm of protest throughout their length and breadth, a protest that did not limit itself to words, but employed also measures of forcible resistance. At this distance of time the act would not seem to have been particularly obnoxious in character, for a similar law was then in force in Great Britain, and one of the colonies, Massachusetts, had of its own accord adopted a like measure. But the colonies did not like it, and the keenest colonial minds set to work to evolve good reasons for their dislike of it. The good reason evolved was that it was taxation without representation, and that, they asserted, was contrary to the spirit of the English constitution. Their own colonial assemblies, in which they were represented, might lay taxes, yes; but the British Parliament, in which they were not represented, no. But, ran the British argument, that principle of the constitution means no taxation without representation in the House of Commons, and the colonies, as all other British peoples, were represented in the House of Commons. No, replied the colonies, we do not vote for representatives in the House of Commons, therefore we are not represented in that lawmaking body. And the more they argued over what constituted representation, the more they disagreed, with the result that the knot could be untied only by the Alexandrian method. In addition to fixing in the colonial mind the idea of fundamental colonial rights and the basis of them, the agitation against the Stamp Act had the result of stimulating efforts to bring the colonies together into some sort of unified organization. One such effort took the form of promoting Associations, or boycotts of English goods. Another resulted in the Stamp Act Congress, designed to unite the colonies more effectually in their resistance to the British policies. The final outcome of the agitation was to convince the British authorities that discretion was the handmaiden of wisdom, and the act was repealed. For a little while everybody seemed happy; but not for long.

The author of the Stamp Act and its associated measures, George Grenville, was followed in the ministry by Charles Townshend, who, in his turn, took a look at the colonial problem, and, having observed that the colonies had indicated a willingness to accept external taxation designed for the regulation of trade, decided that the solution would be to give them external taxes. The Townshend Acts (1767) not only provided for raising a revenue by means of certain import duties, they also set up measures of control that touched the colonies in exceedingly sensitive spots. If, in that matter of external taxation, the American expounders of the English constitution seemed for a moment to have been hoist with their own petard, it was only for a moment. Without more than a momentary hesitation, they shifted their platform from "no taxation without representation" to "no legislation without representation." In fact, one of the most notable of the protests against the Stamp Act, the resolutions fathered by Patrick Henry in the Virginia House of Burgesses, had scarcely fallen short of proclaiming that very doctrine. The clamor that had arisen against the Stamp Act was scarcely more than a rehearsal beside that which now arose against the Townshend Acts. External in hue and color these new measures might be, but any measure, contended the colonists, that created an expense was in essence a tax. Away with it! Accordingly all the means of protest and resistance employed against the Stamp Act, violent as well as peaceful, were brought into play, including that formidable weapon, nonimportation. The result was that once again the British government retreated and repealed the acts; that is, all except the tax on tea. Enter that stubborn monarch, George the Third, who wished to maintain the parliamentary right in question, as he also sought, in season and out of season, to uphold the royal authority. As in the case of the Stamp Act, resistance to the Townshend Acts had led to proceedings in the colonies that were to have consequential importance, notably, for one thing, the Massachusetts Circular Letter (1768), fathered by Samuel Adams, designed to bring the colonies into closer co-operation in resisting British policies and containing moreover the declaration that there was no aim at independence; and, for another, the Virginia resolves of the following year, which included a forceful statement of the constitutional principles upon which the rights claimed by the colonies were based. In each case the proceeding resulted, on the one hand, in the dissolution of the assembly concerned, and, on the other, in enthusiastic responses from the other colonies.

The repeal of the Townshend Acts once again brought a lull in the colonies, and the lull might have developed into real peace and quiet, if the temperature of colonial heads had entirely subsided, and if some British heads had not forgotten their lessons. It was just one more instance of British ineptness that sullied the fair prospect; a decision, and for a reason that had little or nothing to do with the colonial problem, to make use of the Tea Act. The importation of cargoes of tea led to the famous Boston Tea Party, and to several other tea parties as well, quite as significant if not so famous; and the Boston Tea Party naturally stirred the British authorities to take punitive action against that nest of sedition called Boston. There followed a group of repressive measures, termed by the colonists the Intolerable Acts, most noteworthy among them being that for closing the

port of Boston. The Quebec Act, passed about the same time, was in no sense punitive in its intent, but it was interpreted by the colonies as designed to cut them off from the rich western territory, and their wrath was increased accordingly.

If Great Britain had been swift to punish, the colonies were just as swift to take measures for the defense of their precious rights. It was now that committees of correspondence sprang into luxuriant growth, with the result that the colonies speedily became well informed of one another's feelings and doings. Likewise it soon became evident that the other colonies would come to the support of the afflicted Massachusetts; for, so they reasoned, the fate of one colony would in all probability ultimately be the fate of all. Out of this network of committees speedily arose the suggestion that a general congress of the colonies be assembled to concert and agree upon measures for the redress of their grievances and the maintenance of their rights. The outcome was the assembling in Philadelphia in September, 1774, of what has come to be known as the First Continental Congress.

Thenceforward the Continental Congress became the focus of the whole Revolutionary movement; for by this time it was becoming tolerably clear that something like a revolution was under way. Eagerly as most of the colonies had espoused the cause of Massachusetts as their own, when, in their congress, they sought to concert and agree, they found themselves wide apart with regard to ways and means, and not at all in agreement as to the ends. Some would yield not a jot nor a tittle to British contentions, others were disposed to compose the differences, while still others chose, at nearly all hazards, to avoid breaking with the established government. What the Congress actually did was to adopt a declaration of rights and grievances, an Association or boycott of British goods, and to propose the assembling of a second Congress in the following May, in the event that their grievances had not meanwhile been redressed. The interval was anything but a time of idling, for the local committees were busily occupied in enforcing the Association.

As May, 1775, approached, no sign of redress had become evident; on the contrary, the conflict had become intensified, for an actual clash of arms had taken place at Lexington and Concord (April 19); and, within little more than a month after the assembling of the Congress, had come the bloody battle of Bunker Hill. The instructions to most of the delegates, drawn before the events of April, had spoken of the restoration of harmony as a chief objective of the Congress; but unexpectedly the Congress found itself with a war on its hands. To all appearances redress of grievances would be obtained only by force of arms, and a very different sort of harmony would have to be sought for. Congress had no mandate to conduct a war; it had no mandate even to constitute itself into a government; but it was the only body in existence that to any degree embodied the wills of the several colonies, and there was no time to wait for advice or instructions. Accordingly, Congress rose to the occasion and with no ado assumed the powers of government. It proceeded to advise, to plan, and even to instruct; it organized an army, appointed the chief officers, and then, to meet the costs, it issued its own promises to pay. Without so much as a yea or a nay, Congress had appropriated to itself most of the attributes of sovereignty, and ere long it would become as jealous of its dignity and authority, such as it was, as the old Parliament itself.

The question might well have been asked at the outset—and Congress did in time ask itself that question—whether it was the part of wisdom to enter upon a test of strength with such a power as Great Britain with no more unity than was manifest in a heterogeneous body of representatives, of uncertain powers and uncertain tenure, with no directive authority anywhere except as might be uttered in a majority vote of the colonies represented. Such an arrangement could but give rise to deep dissatisfactions and put a premium upon hesitancy and inefficiency. And what greatly added to the inefficiency of Congress as an agency for directing such a contest was the deep-seated fear of an efficient government that permeated the colonies. At the very bottom of the controversy was an antagonism to increased efficiency on the part of the home government, and it was a like antagonism in the main that was responsible for the persistent refusal of the states to equip their congress with adequate powers for carrying on the war and for other necessary business of an efficient government. Indeed, Congress itself exhibited the same watchful jealousy toward the army of its own creation, fearing lest the creature might turn and rend its creator, as it likewise did in long refusing to delegate important executive functions.

The first few months of the contest, whether it be measured for its military accomplishments or for the progress of other phases of the Revolutionary movement, were in great part a period of marking time. Not that the wheel of revolution stood still; for there were efforts to thrust it forward, as there were also efforts to turn it backward. Both contestants were maneuvering for advantage. On the colonial side there was as yet indecision whether to provoke a battle or listen to voices of conciliation. They had, in a manner, joined hands, but a complete unison of minds was lacking. Strangely enough, there was a hesitancy, in some quarters almost a repugnance, toward any effective bond of union. This was made particularly evident when, in July, Congress declined to give serious heed to a form of confederation which Franklin had proposed. There was, however, probably another reason. It was just then that the moderates were prevailing with their plea to offer the king one more humble petition, an "Olive Branch."

The spell of hesitating and waiting came to an end when it was learned that not only had the king refused to accept their olive branch, but had proclaimed the colonies in a state of rebellion and had declared that he would use the might of his realm to bring them to obedience. And, worse yet, it appeared that he was preparing to go outside his realm for a part of his might by hiring some Hessians to fight his battles. The colonies had from the beginning, even if at times with tongue in cheek, professed loyalty to the king, firing their arrows of criticism the while at a vicious and stupid Parliament and a wicked ministry; but from this time on they disliked King George the Third immensely. The Congress even had a long debate one day in March, 1776, whether they might not be better advised to charge the king, instead of the ministry, with being "the author of their miseries," a sentiment that Thomas Paine's pamphlet, *Common Sense*, published in early January, was doing much to cultivate. The proposition was not then accepted, but soon, very soon, Congress would be ready to charge King George with all manner of high crimes and misdemeanors.

For by this time colonial thought was moving rapidly toward acceptance of independence. The idea of independence, but a half-suppressed whisper in the summer and early autumn of 1775, had, by the spring of 1776, attained to cyclonic volume and force. In a few short weeks the demand for independence would sweep down upon a faltering Congress and swiftly demolish every other plea and every other argument in its mighty onrush. Not a little of the tempest's force is to be ascribed to that same pamphlet *Common Sense*, whose scathing denunciation and ridicule of the royal person had so effectively turned the wrath of the colonies upon their sovereign lord and master, King George. Even more effectually Paine persuaded Americans to set independence as their one true goal, the goal of peace, happiness and greatness for which they yearned. On the 15th of May the Virginia Convention instructed the delegates of that colony to offer in Congress a resolution for independence; the motion was made on June 7, and on July 2 every colony except New York cast its vote for the resolution. On the fourth of July, the formal Declaration of Independence was adopted; and a few days later the New York delegates also gave their assent. For weal or for woe the die was cast.

These were culminations on the central stage; in the meantime, however, another phase of the Revolution was in process in what were now the independent states. The royal governments in the several colonies had, in fact, long since almost entirely broken down, and Provincial Congresses or Conventions had taken their places. In mid-July, 1775, Congress had advised the colonies to organize committees of safety to serve as governments when the congresses or conventions were not in session; and a little later it was suggested to three of them (New Hampshire, South Carolina and Virginia) that they might do well to establish their own governments. Now, when independence began to loom over the horizon like a threatening storm cloud, all the colonies were counseled to complete their own governmental organizations (May 10, 15). It is to that process, begun at once and actively continued through much of the Revolutionary period, that we must look for many of the significant results of the Revolution; for, although the creation of an efficient government of the United States in their collective capacity would be a consummation of supreme importance, it was in the individual states that new social and political ideas were to bear their most important fruit.

As for the great Common Cause, that was now independence; nothing less and, until that should be won, nothing more. Ceased now all clamor about rights and grievances; ceased also much of the declamation about the nature and principles of government—much, though not all, for they would have to set up some sort of government for their United States, even if only for the duration of the war. The colonies knew and their Congress knew that to win independence they would have to fight, and that to fight effectively they would need to be bound to one another with stronger bonds than the fragile ties that then held them together. So well had this fact been recognized that the formation of a confederation had been one of the elements embodied in the resolution for independence. Not less strong was the conviction that they would need outside aid; therefore the same resolution called for a plan of foreign treaties. Both projects were immediately set on foot, but it was long before either attained to its chief aim. Commissioners sent to France were able to obtain some aid secretly, but for an alliance with that power they had to await a favorable turn of events. Meanwhile, Congress strove mightily through many months and with much anguish of spirit to formulate an instrument of union, but it was not until Nov. 15, 1777, that it was able to reach an agreement upon the content of that instrument—the Articles of Confederation. It was still necessary to obtain the ratifications of all thirteen states, and most of the states found it unsatisfactory. In fact, it was not until March 1, 1781, that the last of the thirteen states, Maryland, was prevailed upon to give her assent.

It was while the states were hesitating over the Articles of Confederation that the commissioners in France were enabled at last to effect treaties of alliance and commerce with that power (Feb. 6, 1778); for it was not until the victory over Gen. Burgoyne in the preceding October that the French government had become willing to risk espousing the American cause (see Franco-American Alliance of 1778). Learning of this alliance, the British government decided to be beforehand with France, if possible, by offering the one-time British colonies terms of conciliation such as had never been offered before. Accordingly

there was something of a race between Great Britain's offer of conciliation and the French treaty, which should reach Congress first. Had the British commissioners, bearing the proposals of conciliation, arrived first, the subsequent story of the American Revolution might have been different. But the French treaty won the race. To Congress, then (May 2, 1778) sitting at York, Pa., and in the dark shadow of what appeared to be almost certain defeat, the alliance with France was a boon from Heaven. Many another dark shadow would fall upon that assembly of delegates before it would be able to emerge from the struggle victorious, but for the moment it was basking in the bright noonday sun. With the aid of France they were bound to win. Their exultant mood was abundantly manifest when, closely following the French treaty, came the British commissioners on conciliation bound. Short of complete independence, they offered practically everything that the Americans had ever asked for; but they had come too late, and they were accordingly bidden, in terms none too polite, to depart.

The alliance with France brought the much needed aid of money, men and ships, an aid so essential that without it the cause would doubtless have been lost; but the alliance also brought to Congress its full quota of troubles and responsibilities, not the least of which, as the contest dragged wearily on, were some pointed queries propounded in 1779 by the French minister, Gérard. To what lengths, queried Gérard, were the United States prepared to go in the prosecution of the war? When it came to a peace settlement—and most certainly the time would come when the United States, France and Great Britain would gather around the peace-table—what would the ultimata of the United States then be? These were most vexatious questions, and Congress spent many weary months debating them. Foremost of them was of course that respecting boundaries. That was of vital concern to all the states. Then there was the question of the free navigation of the Mississippi River, of especial interest to the Southern states. But, rather strange to tell, the question that stirred the bitterest of all the long and bitter wrangles was whether the United States should refuse to make peace unless the New Englanders were allowed to retain their old fishing privileges on the northeastern coast. Here was fuel in abundance for the fires of sectionalism, and the fires were kindled. Later, when the war, as it turned out, was actually drawing to a close, the new French minister, La Luzerne, prodded Congress with another exceedingly vexatious question: Would Congress instruct its peace negotiators to take no important steps without full consultation with the minister of his Most Christian Majesty? And Congress, sorely distressed and heavily pressed, deemed it the part of wisdom to answer yes. When peace-making time was at hand, however, the American negotiators arrogated to themselves a modicum of the fund of wisdom and broke the congressional injunction. To this day historians of that eventful episode dispute over the question whether Congress or its commissioners had the larger share of that fund.

From the virtual termination of the war (*see* Yorktown Campaign), in the closing months of 1781, two years elapsed before the final consummation of the peace (*see* Paris, Treaty of, Sept. 3, 1783); and, strange almost beyond the power of comprehension, many Americans appeared to have all but lost interest in that consummation which would place the United States of America among the nations of the world. The states seemed to be saying, "Great Britain has at last withdrawn from us her heavy, noxious hand; we are individually free and independent states; why worry more?" It was only with the greatest difficulty that a sufficient representation could be gathered in Congress to ratify the treaty of peace (Jan. 14, 1784); but it was done. The independence of the United States of America was at long last a recorded fact. A question of even greater import, nevertheless, remained as yet unanswered. Now that the American states had their independence, what would they do with it? It was a hard lesson they had set for them; yet in time they would master it. (For military phases of the Revolution *see* article, *The Revolutionary War*; also various articles on separate battles and campaigns.)

Financing of the Revolution was, because of colonial hatred of any form of taxation, one of the most difficult tasks that faced the Continental Congress. Following hostilities at Bunker Hill, an issue of $2,000,-000 in bills of credit was voted, based on the credit of the states. Unsatisfactory as this method proved, Congress continued until Nov. 29, 1779, to emit paper money to the amount of $241,552,380, to be redeemed by the states. Depreciation set in shortly, and by March, 1780, in spite of legal-tender laws and an attempt to fix prices, the value of continental currency in silver had fallen to forty to one. Debtors pursued their creditors and "paid them without mercy," according to a contemporary sufferer; prices rose to unheard of heights; while excessive speculation and counterfeiting demoralized the whole financial structure of the struggling colonies. "Not worth a Continental" became a phrase of derision and stark reality.

A system of direct requisitions on the states for corn, beef, pork and other supplies, was resorted to in 1780, but proved equally discouraging, for it lacked an efficient plan of assessment and record. Other means used to obtain funds included domestic and foreign loans; quartermaster, commissary and purchasing agent certificates; lotteries; and prize money received from the sale of captured enemy vessels. Domestic loans were offered for sale from time to time at high rates of interest, and although $63,-289,000 was subscribed, its real value was but a small percentage of that amount. Certificates of purchasing agents were used extensively in payment of supplies for the army, and Hamilton estimated in 1790 that they were outstanding to the amount of $16,708,000. Foreign loans secured from France, Spain and Holland through the influence of Franklin and John Adams proved invaluable. French loans from 1777 to 1783 amounted to $6,352,500; Spanish loans, to $174,017; and Dutch loans, to $1,304,000—making a total of $7,830,517. These, and an outright gift from France made largely through the agency of Beaumarchais in the first years of the war, did much to strengthen colonial morale and finance.

On Feb. 20, 1781, Robert Morris was appointed by Congress to the new office of Superintendent of Finance. He brought some order out of the existing chaos, but was hampered by local jealousies, continued state refusal to levy taxes, and by inadequate financial provisions of the Articles of Confederation. It remained for the new Constitution and the financial genius of Hamilton to establish the United States on a firm national and international credit basis. The cost of the Revolution in gold has been estimated at:

Paper money	$41,000,000
Certificates of indebtedness	16,708,000
Loan-office certificates	11,585,000
Foreign loans	7,830,000
Taxes (requisitions on states)	5,795,000
Gifts from abroad	1,996,000
Miscellaneous receipts	856,000
State debts	18,272,000
	$104,042,000

Revolutionary Committees. The American Revolution was fomented by committees, organized by committees, and, in great measure, conducted by committees. At the first sign of trouble with the mother country committees sprang up here, there and everywhere, to give voice to the general protest; and, by the time the break came with Great Britain, the whole country, from the colonial capital to the remotest community, was afire with committees. If anywhere they were not already in existence by the summer of 1775, they were speedily promoted. For the conflagration known as the American Revolution was not only fanned from below, to no small degree the flame was projected downward by a vigorous draft created at the top.

First in the procession of these laborers in the Revolutionary cause were the committees of correspondence, so called because they were chiefly engaged in gathering information and propagandizing their doctrines by means of the quill. There followed another group, generally known as the committees of safety (quite as often called councils of safety), whose function it was to keep the revolutionary spirit alive and assist in its formulation. In some instances these colonial committees, of whatever name, were instrumental in establishing provincial congresses, which constituted the revolutionary governments of the colonies for the time being, as they were also the chief agencies, either directly or through the provincial congresses, in calling together that convention of colonial committees, called the First Continental Congress, which met in September, 1774.

The First Continental Congress, in its turn, gave a new impetus to committees, for in that boycott of British goods which it proposed, called the Association, it recommended that committees be chosen in every county, city and town, "whose business it shall be attentively to observe the conduct of all persons touching this association"; that is, to enforce the Association. Such committees (usually called committees of observation and inspection, committees of inquiry and the like) were set up accordingly; and they not only observed, inspected and inquired, they took action, usually as courts both of first and last resort. When the Second Continental Congress met in May, 1775, upon the call of the First, it soon became the head and center of the Revolution, and, with its aid and comfort, there presently began a new era both in provincial congresses and in committees. As a first essential step, in the collapse of the old colonial governments, the timid and hesitant Congress advised the colonies to appoint committees of safety to serve as *de facto* governments, "in the recess of their assemblies and conventions." Only when Congress had grown bolder did it urge the completion of the revolutionary process.

The committees that were created in this period varied widely, from colony to colony, in constitution and powers, but in general the central committee was appointed by the Provincial Congress, with designated powers to be exercised between sittings of the Provincial Congress or Convention, and with some degree of authority over the local committees. This authority did not, however, always subsist. The local committees were much disposed to act independently. In fact, it was the local committees that became, in great measure, the effective agencies of the Revolution. It was they chiefly that dealt with Tories, as in many other matters they promoted the cause of the Revolution in ways that to them seemed good. They have had their later models in the frontier vigilante committees, but, unlike the vigilantes, they chose to implement their authority by such means as tar and feathers, rather than with the noose. In short, reform, not execution, was their main objective. Execution was a very serious business; reform might have its accompaniment of downright fun.

Not all of the Revolutionary committees can be classed under the categories mentioned. Some colonies, for instance, had councils of war or boards of war, which might or might not act independently of the committee of safety. There were also, occasionally, various other committees designed to aid in the prosecution of the war, as, for instance, committees of supplies. Finally, there were organizations quite out-

side any official enclosure, such as the Sons of Liberty, that played no insignificant part in the Revolution.

There were some survivals after the organization of state governments, but for the most part committees, of the sort described, thereafter vanished from the picture. At the same time, however, the shifting of the Revolutionary center of gravity to the Continental Congress gave rise to the development of another type of committee that had an important part in the conduct of the Revolution and likewise in the development of our system of government. Like every other legislative body, Congress had perforce to do much of its work through committees of its own members; and such were the importance and the permanence of the tasks devolving upon some of these committees that they came to be called "standing committees." Because of the fluctuating membership of Congress it frequently came about that the personnel of these committees became depleted, and their business fell into neglect accordingly. The first serious effort by Congress to remedy this state of affairs was in the creation of mixed boards, composed partly of members and partly of outsiders, the latter to constitute a sort of permanent staff. The next step was to erect these boards into executive departments, composed entirely of nonmembers, or with single executive heads. This last step was not taken, however, until 1781, when the war was approaching an end. Several of these executive departments, still functioning when the Constitution was adopted, passed over to the new government intact, and became departments in the so-called Cabinet. What was first a Committee of Secret Correspondence, then a Committee for Foreign Affairs, later a Department of Foreign Affairs, became the Department of State. What was the Board of War developed into the Department of War. The business of the treasury, beginning with a committee and developing into a board, passed for a time into the hands of a single executive, the superintendent of finance, then back into the board form, thence into the Treasury Department under the new government. The Navy Department similarly had its origin in the Marine or Naval Committee, which became for a time a Department of Marine. The most important of the standing committees of the Continental Congress that did not become one of the early Cabinet departments was the Committee of Commerce, or Commercial Committee, of which the earliest progenitor was the Secret Committee (not to be confused with the Committee of Secret Correspondence).

Revolutionary War Profiteering. One of the most difficult problems which confronted the Continental Congress was the procuring of supplies of all kinds for the army. Many individuals purchased large stores of provisions and then when the currency rapidly depreciated demanded exorbitant prices. Naturally such persons were considered profiteers. The agents sent to confiscate the Loyalists' property in many cases pocketed a large share of the funds.

Congress on March 3, 1776, directed Silas Deane to go to France and purchase artillery, munitions, clothing and arms for 25,000 men. Deane was one of five merchants who were authorized to procure colonial goods, ship them abroad, sell them, and with the proceeds to buy supplies. In France, Deane was closely associated with Beaumarchais who had established the firm of *Hortalez et Cie* to aid the Americans. Loans and large gifts of money and supplies were received from the French government. Deane, in the meantime, had made connections with the commercial firm of Willing and Morris in Philadelphia. Faction, intrigue and jealousy, largely engineered by Arthur Lee, caused Congress to recall Deane early in 1778. Charges of "unlimited robbery and treason" were made on the basis that the supplies were all gifts of the French government, and that Deane and Beaumarchais were "planning merely to line their own pockets." These charges were never proven, but were responsible for ruining the career of an able patriot whose only fault was in not being meticulous in separating his private commercial interests from his public business. Factions in Congress, economic interests and sectionalism were largely accountable for a great injustice.

Charges of profiteering and of growing rich by "thievish speculation" were likewise brought against Robert Morris on several occasions. Morris had great business acumen and lost no opportunity, while in private or in public life, to make his profit in a deal. He bought great quantities of supplies, taking very great risks, and no doubt made large profits. In 1779 Morris was formally charged with speculation in flour, of "engrossing" it. Growing richer and richer, Morris became the object of envy and jealousy of many, especially the poor who resented his wealth. In 1779 Paine, through the press, made a bitter attack on Morris for conducting private commercial enterprises while holding public office. Henry Laurens, likewise, made charges of fraud against the firm of Willing and Morris. A congressional investigation reported no foundation for such charges and commended Morris for his "fidelity and integrity." The truth was that Morris' services were invaluable and he gave the leaders of the war financial assistance and moral support without which the army would have perished.

When the states established fixed prices for materials, some enterprising merchants purchased supplies in one state and transported them on fast sailing ships to states where prices were higher. These men were charged with profiteering. Again the risks were great and there were few who were successful. Most of the censure, if any censure is justifiable for these conditions, can be explained by the ineptitude of the Congress.

REVOLUTIONARY WAR, THE. The fighting began near Boston, Mass., which had been especially active in resistance to English colonial policies, and hence troops were sent there. On April 19, 1775, a British attempt to seize military stores brought on the double battle of Lexington and Concord. New England militia assembled about Boston, and on June 16, 1775, they began to fortify a spur of Bunker Hill, overlooking Boston. The British broke up this attempt on June 17, but the blockade continued. The independence of the colonies was declared July 4, 1776, and the insurgent forces were reorganized under command of George Washington.

Meanwhile, attempts were made to invade Canada. These failed, but one of the preliminary moves was the capture of Ticonderoga, May 10, 1775, which gave the colonists an excellent train of artillery. These guns were moved to Boston as soon as freezing weather made transportation possible; their employment rendered Boston untenable, and the British garrison was withdrawn to Halifax on March 17, 1776.

England now assumed the offensive. The point of attack was New York, and the general idea was to gain control of the Hudson River and cut the colonies in two. Gen. Howe returned from Halifax, and his brother, Admiral Lord Howe, brought a powerful fleet. Washington had foreseen this move, and transferred his army to New York, occupying Manhattan and Brooklyn.

The British attack came first upon the Brooklyn force, which was driven out in the battle of Long Island, Aug. 27, 1776. Howe then pressed Washington northward out of Manhattan, and began to extend toward Philadelphia. Washington established a strong post in the Highlands of the Hudson, and with his field force retired through Jersey behind the Delaware. The British operations lacked vigor, for the Howe brothers, under orders from England, continually endeavored to open peace negotiations. Washington's defensive plan was to keep inshore from Howe, moving as he moved; to this end he established his "line of communications," a chain of supply depots just above the heads of navigation on the main rivers. He made brilliant counterstrokes at Trenton (Dec. 26, 1776) and Princeton (Jan. 3, 1777), forcing Howe back to New Brunswick; then established himself for the winter at Morristown, on Howe's inshore flank.

For 1777 the British plan called for opening the Hudson from both ends—Howe from New York and Burgoyne from Montreal. A column under Col. St. Leger was to co-operate with Burgoyne, moving down the Mohawk Valley. But Howe, not in sympathy with this plan, took advantage of a certain vagueness in his orders from home to turn his main force toward the "rebel capital" at Philadelphia, leaving at New York a force too small for effective operations up the Hudson. St. Leger's column was defeated at Oriskany and Fort Stanwix (Aug. 6). Burgoyne himself suffered a serious reverse on Aug. 16, when a strong detachment was beaten at Bennington, Vt. His main body pushed south to the region of Saratoga, and on Sept. 19 attacked the Americans at Freeman's Farm. A counterattack by Gen. Arnold almost succeeded, but Gen. Gates, in chief command, refused to support Arnold, and Burgoyne held his ground. He renewed the attack on Oct. 7, and this time was badly beaten and forced to surrender (Oct. 17, 1777).

Howe, meanwhile, had moved his main force south by sea, landed at the head of Chesapeake Bay on Aug. 25, and marched for Philadelphia. Washington tried to check him at the Brandywine River on Sept. 11, but was outflanked and almost trapped. Howe entered Philadelphia on Sept. 26. Washington attacked at Germantown on Oct. 4, but failed, and took up position for the winter at Valley Forge, 25 miles up the Schuylkill. In spite of the great hardships suffered here, advantage was taken of the opportunity for reorganization and training, under the supervision of Gen. von Steuben; and news of the French alliance helped to keep up spirit.

In May, 1778, Howe was relieved by Gen. Clinton, who promptly gave up Philadelphia and marched for New York. Washington struck his flank at Monmouth Court House on June 28, but Clinton made good his withdrawal. Washington established himself at White Plains. Operations in the north after this were unimportant.

In the autumn of 1778 Clinton sent an expedition south, which occupied Savannah and Augusta. In 1779 a French fleet under Admiral d'Estaing arrived to co-operate with the Americans under Gen. Lincoln. Siege was laid to Savannah, but d'Estaing was compelled by approach of the stormy season to return to the West Indies. Lincoln fell back to Charleston, and was besieged by Clinton, who brought reinforcements from New York; Lincoln surrendered on May 12, 1780. Clinton then returned to New York, leaving Cornwallis in command.

Congress sent Gen. Gates to command in the south. On Aug. 16 he was utterly defeated at Camden; Gen. Greene succeeded him. Cornwallis advanced northward, but was weakened by the loss of two strong detachments—Maj. Ferguson's at King's Mountain, Oct. 7, 1780, and Col. Tarleton's at the Cowpens, Jan. 17, 1781. Greene conducted a masterly retreat to Virginia; and Cornwallis, finding his force too small and his line of communications too long for further pursuit, fell back to Wilmington, N. C. Then, leaving a small detachment in the Carolinas, he took his main body to Virginia to join British troops already there. Greene soon drove the Carolina detachment into Charleston, where it remained for the rest of the war.

In Virginia, Cornwallis effected his junction with the other British forces, and found himself opposed only by a small force under Lafayette. After some successful operations, he fortified himself at Yorktown to await Clinton's decision as to the next move.

The French alliance now made itself felt. A French land and naval force under Gen. Rochambeau had established itself at Newport in the summer of 1780, and in the spring of 1781 Admiral DeGrasse brought another French squadron into American waters. By very skilful maneuvering the entire French force, land and naval, with the bulk of Washington's army on the Hudson, was concentrated before Yorktown, and a siege was opened on Oct. 6. Cornwallis surrendered on Oct. 19. Military operations after this time were insignificant, although the Definitive Treaty of Peace was not concluded for almost two years.

The Navy in the Revolution. The Continental Navy had its origin Oct. 13, 1775, when Congress appointed a Naval Committee of three to purchase two vessels. On Oct. 30 Congress ordered two more vessels purchased, and added four members to the committee. This Naval Committee laid the foundations of the navy. In November, 1775, it purchased the four vessels authorized: the *Alfred, Columbus, Andrew Doria* and *Cabot;* on Nov. 5 it appointed Esek Hopkins commander in chief; on Nov. 10 two battalions of marines were provided for; on Nov. 23 it formulated regulations for the navy based on current British practice; and on Dec. 22 submitted to Congress a list of eighteen officers already appointed. On Nov. 25 Congress provided for admiralty courts and the sale of captured vessels, and on Dec. 13 it authorized the construction of thirteen frigates. The next day it appointed a Marine Committee which superseded the Naval Committee. The Marine Committee was superseded in 1779 by a Board of Admiralty, but in 1781 this board was abolished and Robert Morris was made Agent of Marine in charge of naval affairs, a position held by him until the close of the war.

During the Revolution the naval vessels were employed principally in seizing British supply ships and merchantmen, the transport of munitions from France and the carriage of diplomatic agents and despatches to and from Europe. In May, 1777, Capt. Lambert Wickes with three small vessels made a spectacular raid in the Irish Channel, and in August–September, 1779, Commodore John Paul Jones made his celebrated cruise round Great Britain, ending in the capture of the *Serapis* (*see Bonhomme Richard* and *Serapis,* Engagement between the). The greatest service that the navy performed, however, was on Lake Champlain, at Valcour Island, when Benedict Arnold in October, 1776, fought a delaying action which effectually prevented a British invasion in 1776, contributing to American success at Saratoga in 1777. During the war the navy employed 260 naval officers, 124 marine officers and 73 vessels of all descriptions. Due to capture, sale and shipwreck, but one of these vessels, the frigate *Alliance,* remained in 1785.

Revolutionary Army. A few days before the battle of Bunker Hill (June 17, 1775), the Continental Congress took over the force blockading Boston and called it the Continental army. Washington was appointed Commander in Chief, June 14, and hastened to Cambridge, taking command July 3.

The first problem before him was to train officers and men in the rudiments of military discipline. The army was composed of "rough and ready" farmers and mechanics whose conduct was decidedly colored by the personal independence of the frontier. Often the men elected their own officers, and in the early days there was practically no line drawn between officers and enlisted men. Washington said "they regarded an officer no more than a broomstick." Discipline and efficiency in the army were largely the work of von Steuben who began his drill-work in March, 1778.

The army consisted of two distinct elements: the Continentals organized by Congress, and the militia of the states. The militia were enlisted for three, six, or nine months, although the men were always ready to serve for a few weeks unless their "services were required far from their homes." Brave and able, these men were not efficient and were unfit for long periods of inactive camp life or garrison duty.

The Continentals were enrolled for one year or longer and were more thoroughly trained. Washington pleaded for long-term enlistments, for he knew that a standing army could not be properly trained in a year. Congress offered bounties to those serving in the regular forces, but some states offered higher bounties. Before long the bounties were so high that $200 was an average bonus. In paper money, a soldier insisted on $1000 and "in Virginia even twelve thousand dollars could not always buy a soldier." The states passed draft laws to recruit the militia, even imposing fines and imprisonments, penalties Congress could not impose. In Maryland, one of Washington's recruiting officers was arrested for enlisting two men for the artillery.

No accurate figures are available as to the number of men who served. The rolls indicate that altogether there were 231,771 in the Continental army, and 164,087 in the militia. The forces Washington commanded varied from 8000 during the struggle about New York, to as low as 4000 after the winter at Valley Forge, to as high as 26,000 in November, 1779. Other generals seldom had more than 6000.

Desertion was common and difficult to combat. Washington once wrote: "We shall have to detach one half the army to bring back the other." Officers were known to have urged their men to desert in order to find an excuse to follow them. There were plowing, corn to hoe, hay and grain to harvest, sick families, or they were "neglected, starving and freezing." Cold weather brought on the "terrible disorder of Homesickness." Hunger, nakedness and pay in depreciated currency took a heavy toll.

The army used all sorts of guns—many were homemade. The firelock musket and the smoothbore gun were most common. The sharpshooters from the frontier used the rifle which was of greater range than any the British had. The musket was loaded from the muzzle and fired by the flintlock. In the main most of the arms came from abroad.

Powder and lead were scarce, and since the firearms were not uniform, soldiers melted lead and cast it in their own bullet-molds. The cartridge used was a paper envelope which held the charge of ball and powder, and after emptied of its contents was used as a wad, and pushed into the barrel with a ramrod.

There was a decided lack of artillery. Cannon were captured from the royal arsenals and the British army. Some crude ones were homemade but were unpopular with the army. France and Holland were the chief sources of supply.

The need of transport was also serious. Naturally the colonials used the water routes for moving supplies any great distance. Vehicles were scarce while roads were few and bad. There were not enough oxen or horses and sometimes the privates were used as beasts of burden. Farmers were loath to sell supplies for depreciated money—often worthless paper. Engineers were too few to build enough roads, bridges and forts, while the deficiency in maps was somewhat compensated by the officers' intimate knowledge of the country.

Inadequate transport was serious in the case of food and clothing, and often the army was starving in a land of plenty. Soldiers went without meat for an entire week, and in winter the horses and oxen died for want of forage and care. There is a grim humor to the phrase, "no pay, no clothes, no provisions, no rum," chanted by the men at Valley Forge. There was never a satisfactory supply of vegetables and milk. Sickness was rampant while the army was in camp, hospital stores were almost unknown, even the sick died on the frozen ground for lack of blankets or straw. At Valley Forge, Washington reported 3000 men unfit for duty because of their nakedness.

Not only was the soldier ill-armed, but he was worse clothed, often shoeless. One found every variety of dress. Farmers in their usual clothes, and frontiersmen in buckskin with the loose hunting shirts, were the nearest to any uniformity in dress. In Greene's southern campaign many men were naked save for breech cloths. In the north the soldiers often lacked boots in the winter, and could be traced in the snow by bloody footprints. Toward the end of the war, the army was described as "illy clad, badly fed, and worse paid." Too often the military chest was "totally exhausted" and the paymaster with not a dollar in hand. Credit was usually strained and sometimes the troops were "in a state not far from mutiny," which might have been serious but for Washington's firmness and astuteness. Some of the officers, driven by scanty pay to "low and dirty arts," were dishonest, encouraged misbehavior in their men, led plundering raids and refused to restore stolen goods. The causes for these conditions were: the lack of any military traditions, failure to insist upon long-term enlistments, the ineptitude of Congress and sectional jealousy. It is unsurpassed evidence of Washington's ability and genius that he kept the army from disintegration and destruction.

Foreign Volunteers in the Revolutionary Army. The ideal of human liberty actuating the colonies in 1776 found response in the hearts of many Europeans, especially in France. A small proportion of those who wrote Franklin offering their services actually reached America. The first Secret Aid ships of Beaumarchais, the *Mercure* and the *Amphitrite,* landed about thirty volunteers in March and April, 1777, at Portsmouth. A few stragglers and four Royal Engineers, the latter sent for by Congress, reached Philadelphia in June, from the West Indies, while Lafayette and his eleven officers, making their way over intolerable roads from Charleston, arrived in July. More than half of these men were rejected by Congress and had their expenses paid back to France.

Among the most notable of those commissioned were: Armand, Marquis de la Rouërie; Pierre-Charles l'Enfant, later designer of the insignia of the Cincinnati and of the National Capital; Tronson du Coudray, drowned in September in the Schuylkill; Kosciuszko, a Pole, who arrived in 1776, and built the fortifications at West Point; Louis Lebègue Duportail, who fortified Valley Forge; Gouvion and Villefranche, who were Duportail's assistants; and Pulaski, a Polish count, who was killed at Savannah.

Only two of Lafayette's officers were retained by Congress: DeKalb, killed at Camden, and the latter's aide Dubuisson, wounded and made prisoner there.

The last Secret Aid volunteers to arrive came on the *Flamand* in December, 1777, sent by Beaumarchais: among them were von Steuben, and his interpreter, Duponceau, the latter of whom remained in America and became a noted lawyer in Philadelphia.

RHODE ISLAND was founded between 1636 and 1647. In June of the former year, Roger Williams settled at Providence. The second town, Portsmouth, was established in April, 1638, by former residents of Massachusetts, who had left that colony because of the Antinomian controversy. Newport was founded in May, 1639, as an offshoot of Portsmouth; and Warwick came into existence 1643-47 through the efforts of a religious mystic and staunch individualist, Samuel Gorton. At first largely independent of each other, the four original settlements entered into a united colonial government in May, 1647, under the parliamentary charter of 1644, secured by Roger Williams.

Previous to 1636, the coast of Rhode Island was visited by several white explorers. Miguel Cortereal, the Portuguese navigator, was probably in the region in 1511, and in 1524 Giovanni da Verrazzano visited Narragansett Bay. His comment that an island in the vicinity, probably the present Block Island, reminded him of the Isle of Rhodes in the Mediterranean, led in a roundabout fashion to the present name of the state. The Dutch navigator, Adriaen Block, explored the coast in 1614, leaving his name attached to Block Island, some ten miles off the mainland. William Blackstone, an Anglican clergyman and a recluse, settled in 1635 in what is now Cumberland, R. I., but which was then considered a part of Massachusetts.

Founded on the principle of religious freedom, of which Roger Williams was the most pertinacious advocate, Rhode Island became a refuge for sects that encountered discrimination elsewhere in British America. After 1657 the colony acquired a large Quaker element, and a small though influential Jewish group. No single religious sect, however, dominated colonial affairs in the 18th century; the Baptists, Quakers and Episcopalians were all strong, with the Congregationalists in a minor position. Rhode Island secured its second charter in 1663, from Charles II. This document gave official sanction "to hold forth a livelie experiment" in the separation of church and state, which Rhode Island consistently observed, save for the deprivation of suffrage to Roman Catholics, 1664-1783, which worked little hardship as there were then few of that persuasion in the state.

From the mid-17th century to the Revolution, the colony engaged in nine wars. Rhode Islanders carried on privateering against the Dutch, 1652-54, and were prepared to engage in similar activity during England's later wars with Holland, 1664-67 and 1672-74, although little warfare materialized on this side of the Atlantic. King Philip's War wreaked considerable damage on the colony. Roger Williams was unsuccessful in keeping the Narragansetts out of the conflict. The winter encampment of that tribe was destroyed Dec. 19, 1675, after which scattered bands of Indians descended on Warwick and Providence. King Philip was trapped in Bristol by Capt. Benjamin Church, and killed Aug. 12, 1676. For a short time, 1685-89, Rhode Island was a part of the Dominion of New England.

During the four wars fought between 1689 and 1763, Rhode Islanders took part as privateersmen and soldiers on campaign in many parts of New England and New York. Privateering received such a stimulus from the early French wars that it tended to continue as freebooting, but this activity was suppressed before long. Twenty-six pirates were hanged near Newport in July, 1723.

Farming was the chief occupation in the colonial period, although shipbuilding and commerce became important in the 18th century. There was an extensive triangular trade—rum to Africa for Negroes, slaves from thence to the West Indies and molasses from the latter to Rhode Island for the manufacture of more rum. Iron works were first established in 1671 at Pawtucket, by Joseph Jencks, Jr. In South County were large landed estates, run with Negro labor, which were similar to Southern plantations. Rhode Island College, now Brown University, was chartered in 1764, but the state did not have a public school system until after 1800. John Smibert, Robert Feke and Gilbert Stuart were the best known early artists; fine examples of colonial architecture still survive in Providence, Newport, Bristol, Wickford and elsewhere.

Resistance to British colonial regulations, which foreshadowed the Revolution, began in June, 1765, with an attack on the *Maidstone* in Newport harbor. In 1769 the British revenue sloop *Liberty* was scuttled, and in June, 1772, the *Gaspee* was burned off Warwick. Rhode Island raised 1500 troops immediately following the battle of Lexington, and on May 4, 1776, declared her independence from Great Britain. The only important engagement fought in the state was the battle of Rhode Island, in Portsmouth, Aug. 29, 1778; it was an inconclusive struggle, but one which prevented the British from advancing farther into the state from their base at Newport, which they held from December, 1776, to October, 1779. Rhode Island contributed many leaders to distant fields of operation, particularly Esek Hopkins, Commander in Chief of the Continental Navy, 1775–77, and Gen. Nathanael Greene, hero of the 1781 campaign in the far South.

The Revolution cost the state about $1,000,000, and led to a disastrous monetary inflation which was not checked until 1786. Rhode Island was not represented at the Convention of 1787, and it did not ratify the new Constitution until May 29, 1790, by the close vote of 34–32. Rhode Island, the last of the original colonies to enter, considered it to her interest to remain outside the Union, in the hope that she could herself use the customs revenue from her import trade.

RICE CULTURE AND TRADE. After an unsuccessful attempt in 1647 to grow rice in Virginia, it was discovered that the warm, moist lowlands of South Carolina were especially favorable to the propagation of the grain. It is asserted that initial impetus was given to its cultivation by the gift of seed rice brought from Madagascar to Charleston by a storm-driven ship in about 1694. Whether this story is true or not, intensive cultivation of the grain came soon after that date, and its growing and export offered the best opportunity for industrial profit which 18th-century America afforded. After a temporary setback caused by the American Revolution, the industry was revived, and by the time of the Civil War it was the basis of a wealthy aristocracy of a few hundred planters living within the narrow range of the tidal flow near or in Georgetown, Charleston and Beaufort in South Carolina and in the adjoining areas of North Carolina and Georgia.

During the colonial period inundations necessary for the most effective cultivation of the grain were achieved by the impounding of rain and brooks above inland swamps. But the scarcity of water of this origin led after 1783 to the adoption of the system of tidal-flowing. Lands lying within range of the fresh-water tides were equipped with banks, ditches and sluices used for the flooding and draining of these areas thrice each year. They were cultivated by gangs of Negro slaves. At the same time that the tide-flowing system was adopted, drills and harrows were substituted for hand labor, and water-driven threshing mills replaced sticks and wind-fans. About 1820 steam was adopted as the motive power of these mills and they were moved from the plantations to the towns. Before the Civil War the plantations were large semi-capitalistic enterprises, but that event gave the industry a staggering blow from which there was partial recovery for two decades and then gradual annihilation. The free black labor failed to function efficiently in the unhealthful swamps; the improved machinery bogged in the soft soil; crop after crop was ruined by freshets and coastal storm; and the competition of the Southwestern plants brought ruinous prices. By the beginning of the 20th century the Carolina rice fields had returned to their original marshes.

Rice culture began in Louisiana as early as 1718, but for a long time it was unimportant and confined to the lower delta of the Mississippi. After the Civil War landowners of that state eagerly turned to it as an escape from recent impoverishment. Their lands were suitable for the new agricultural machinery, and the grain gave immediate and uniform returns. By 1877 they were able to claim that their product equaled Carolina's best, that their plantation life was healthier, and that they were producing 30% of the nation's total rice. After 1884 prairie regions in Louisiana, Arkansas and Texas were found to be suited for rice; the lands were level; the rivers and bayous were suitable for irrigation; and there were no cataclysmic storms or destroying floods. At present the great bulk of the national crop is produced in those areas.

RICHMOND, CAMPAIGN AGAINST (1864–65). Strictly speaking the campaigns against Richmond began under McDowell in July, 1861, and continued throughout the war, but the final campaign is usually assigned this terminology. It began early in May, 1864, when Grant crossed the Rapidan River and entered the Wilderness in command of an army of 122,000 men. His military objectives were to destroy Lee's army and capture Richmond. With a much smaller force Lee contested Grant's purpose for eleven months. A terrific but fruitless two-day struggle in the battle of the Wilderness was followed by a flanking march to Spotsylvania Courthouse, where another bloody and indecisive conflict took place. Another move to his left by Grant brought the two armies together on the North Anna River; but Grant declined battle and, by a flanking march, reached Cold Harbor, where, in sight of Richmond, his troops were devastated in direct attack on Confederate intrenchments. Stalled north of the James River, Grant, by another flanking move late in June, crossed the river and sought to force the Confederates out of Richmond by cutting its railway connections with the lower Confederacy. Failures before Petersburg in June and in the battle of the Crater, July 30, reduced operations to a long-drawn-out siege of Petersburg. By the following spring the strength of the Confederacy was sapped, and the forces defending Petersburg and Richmond were no longer adequate. It was necessary for Lee's army to evacuate Petersburg and abandon further defense of Richmond. In attempted withdrawal to southwestern Virginia, Lee's troops were surrounded at Appomattox and compelled to surrender.

This final campaign against Richmond was a feature of a more extensive strategy involving both Butler's expedition up the James River and Sherman's marches in Georgia and the Carolinas.

RICHMOND, THE BURNING AND EVACUATION OF, was the dramatic and tragic end of the Confederate capital, in the first days of April, 1865. On Sunday the second, the Union forces captured the outer works around Petersburg. On notice from Lee, Davis and his officials left Richmond. Mobs temporarily took control, looting shops and warehouses. By military order of the Confederates, bridges and warehouses, along with shipping, were fired. Once started, the fire, driven by high wind, spread to the business district. On their arrival, Union troops were used to extinguish the fire and restore law and order. The burning and evacuation of Richmond signalized the overthrow of the Confederacy.

RIFLE. The rifle has played a brilliant part in American history and it is probable that greater technical contributions to its development have been made in the United States and in the colonies from which this nation was formed than anywhere else. Originally invented in Vienna about 1500, the rifle, a firearm depending for accuracy and velocity on spiral grooves in the barrel which impart to the projectile a rotary motion about an axis parallel with the line of flight, was brought to America by Swiss and German immigrants early in the 18th century. In Lancaster, Pa., then a frontier settlement, the rifle was developed primarily as a hunting arm. As the hunters traveled long distances in search of game, light balls or bullets and a piece accurate enough to avoid waste were essential. Continuous and eager competition among the gunsmiths—the Lemans, Terrees, Strugels, Allbrights, Lefevres, Henrys and Rossers—evolved, before the time of the Revolution, a long-barreled, small-bored piece with a muzzle velocity of some 1500 feet per second and said to be as accurate as modern rifles up to 100 yards.

By 1775 these rifles were in the hands of frontiers-

men from the Carolinas to Vermont; they were unknown, however, on the coast and the early battles such as Lexington and Bunker Hill were fought with smooth-bore muskets, ineffective except at close range. Washington, being familiar with the frontier, made great efforts to assemble riflemen from Virginia and Pennsylvania and by midsummer 1775, he had gathered 1400 of them at Cambridge where they amazed the inhabitants by hitting targets seven inches in diameter at two hundred and fifty paces. Stories of this performance, carried by spies to the British army, spread terror among the regulars and this fear of the American riflemen, which grew as the war progressed, is said to have been an important factor in the winning of the Revolution.

The great difficulty with these rifles was in their loading, done from the muzzle with a greased patch and hickory ramrod. Though the Ferguson breech loader was invented in 1776 in England, it seems to have had little use during the war. In 1831 a breech-loading carbine was patented by John Hall. From 1835 breech-loading revolver-pistols and revolver-rifles were invented by Samuel Colt and were used effectively against the Seminole Indians in Florida (1838–42) and later by Texas Rangers and by the army in the Mexican War. By the time of the Civil War nineteen different breech-loading "systems" including the Sharps (1848), the Maynard (from 1851), the Burnside (1856), the Starr (1858) and others were in use. The army was slow in its adoption of the breech-loading rifle and it was used, in the Civil War, largely by mounted troops. The Springfield breechloader came in 1865. In the same year the magazine arrived with the Winchester rifle. In the Spanish-American War the army was equipped with the Krag-Jorgensen magazine rifle and with the old single-shot Springfield (1884). In 1904 the new clip-loading short Springfield was officially adopted.

There was nothing new in the development of the military rifle until after World War I. It was then evident that the next improvement must be an increase in the rate of fire. The light machine gun used in the war was still not light enough to replace the rifle for the infantryman. In the early 1920's, therefore, U. S. Ordnance determined to design a semi-automatic rifle which should require no manual operation for reloading and cocking. The gas-operated mechanism needed to achieve this presented such problems in relation to the weight of the arm that it was not until 1928, when John Garand began his experiments at the Springfield Arsenal, that there was much prospect of success. By 1936, however, he had perfected the M1 or Garand semiautomatic rifle which weighed 9½ pounds and was officially adopted for the army. Later, he developed the M2 carbine which, as it weighed but 5 pounds, could be conveniently used by paratroopers. A second model of this carbine was adapted to both semi- and fully automatic fire, *i.e.*, it could either operate like the M1 or fire uninterruptedly as long as the trigger was held.

RINGS, POLITICAL. A political ring is a comparatively small group of persons, usually headed by a political boss, organized to control a city, county or state, and primarily interested in deriving therefrom large personal monetary profit. Political rings have been found here and there throughout the country periodically as far back as colonial days, but they occupy a particularly colorful position in American history of the second half of the 19th century.

William Marcy Tweed did more to bring political rings into the limelight than any other person. The famous political ring which bears his name, and which for boldness has probably never been surpassed, was organized in 1869 and composed of Tweed, Mayor Hall, Comptroller "Slippery Dick" Connolly and "Brains" Peter B. Sweeny.

Although less notorious than the Tweed Ring, the Philadelphia Gas Ring actually exerted greater political influence, but indulged in less peculation. Whereas the Tweed Ring came to grief within three years of its founding, the Gas Ring wielded great political power from 1865 until 1887.

Less well known than either the Tweed or Gas Rings were the Butler Ring, the Ames Ring and the Ruef Ring. "Colonel" Edward Butler built a political ring in St. Louis in the 1890's with himself as master mind and a select group of members of the two houses of the city council as members. This ring disposed of valuable franchises to the highest bribers. About 1900 "The Genial Doctor," A. A. Ames, constructed a ring around the Minneapolis Police Department which preyed upon thieves, gamblers and other crooks. The "Curly Boss" Abraham Ruef used members of the San Francisco board of supervisors as associates, and "sold" numerous official favors to public utilities during the first decade of the 20th century.

RIO DE JANEIRO CONFERENCE (Aug. 15–Sept. 2, 1947). This meeting of 19 American republics (Nicaragua and Ecuador did not take part) was in line with the long-standing United States practice, as exemplified in Pan-Americanism, of encouraging cooperation among the 21 republics. Wishing to give permanent form to principles of hemispheric solidarity embodied in the Act of Chapultepec (March 3, 1945), the participating countries signed the Inter-American Treaty of Reciprocal Assistance (Sept. 2, 1947), also known as the Pact of Rio. The treaty had great significance because it was the first regional collective security agreement as authorized by Article 51 of the United Nations Charter. Under the treaty it became the duty of each member of the Pact to assist in meeting an armed attack by a country against an American country, pending action by the United Nations; or if an American country were threatened by a situation not involving an armed attack by another country (for example, a revolution), the members would immediately meet to decide on what measures should be taken. The importance attached to the conference by the United States was indicated by President Truman's journey to Brazil to address the final session.

RIO GRANDE first became a significant term in American history as a direct result of the Louisiana Purchase. Many American expansionists felt they had bought southward and westward to that great river. Acceptance of the Sabine boundary, with the purchase of Florida, 1819 (*see* Adams-Onís Treaty), was most unpopular on the southern frontier. The filibustering expedition of Dr. James Long was in direct protest against the Florida treaty.

Mexican independence and liberal land grants by Mexico to American *empresarios*, such as Moses and Stephen F. Austin, temporarily assuaged the westerners. When friction again developed, it broke into the flames of Texan revolt, secession from Mexico and independence. The Texas Republic always maintained and never surrendered the principle that the Rio Grande, from its westernmost head springs to the Gulf, constituted its southern and western boundaries. The United States inherited these claims with the annexation of Texas. Mexico's unwillingness to accept the Rio Grande as a boundary was an immediate cause of the Mexican War.

The Treaty of Guadalupe Hidalgo, 1848, utilized the river as an international boundary from its mouth to El Paso. Since that date no serious boundary question has arisen along the Rio Grande. Most naturally it has been the scene of some lawlessness, jurisdictional disputes, and diplomatic incidents, particularly during irresponsible, revolutionary eras in Mexico. On the whole, the river has been a rather satisfactory boundary, and even less productive of untoward episodes than the survey boundary westward from El Paso.

RIO GRANDE, SIBLEY'S OPERATIONS ON (1861–62). In June, 1861, Maj. H. H. Sibley resigned his commission with the United States Army, and received permission from the Confederacy to raise a force to drive the Federals from New Mexico. A regiment, mostly Texans, was raised at San Antonio and marched to Fort Bliss, near El Paso, which had recently fallen into the hands of the South. From here he moved up the Rio Grande toward Fort Craig, where Col. Canby, in command of the department of New Mexico, made his headquarters. A severe fight occurred Feb. 21, 1862, known as the battle of Valverde, in which Canby was driven across the river into the fort. Sibley continued on up the river and took Albuquerque without a fight, but all the stores had been destroyed by the Federals upon their evacuation. Desperate for provisions for man and horse, Sibley continued on toward Santa Fe. He was met,

March 28, by Col. Slough, from Fort Union, and at Glorieta, in a terrific hand-to-hand battle, Sibley was stopped and began his retreat back down the Rio Grande. Finding himself caught between the armies of Col. Canby on the south and Col. Slough on the north, he made a 100-mile circuit around Fort Craig through the pathless mountains. Forced to abandon his wagons he was soon without food, water and supplies and much suffering occurred. On July 6, 1862, the unfortunate army crossed back into Texas. They had lost over 500 men, killed, dead from disease, or prisoners, and the Federals still held New Mexico.

RIVER NAVIGATION. The primitive means of navigating American rivers was by bull boats (coracles), bark canoes and pirogues; and the whites added to these bateaux, keelboats and barges. Where the nature of the river permitted, sailing craft were utilized, as on the Hudson, Delaware and Potomac Rivers; and it was often possible for ships to ascend far upstream. On such streams as the Connecticut and most of the western rivers, the bateau and keelboat were preferred because rowing or poling were more feasible than sailing.

Boatbuilding was among the earliest activities of the colonists, especially in New England and New Amsterdam, and on Delaware Bay. Flatboats, known also as arks and Kentucky boats, were built at the headwaters of eastern and western rivers for the transportation of produce, coal, cattle, immigrants, etc., and continued in use until after the Civil War. Their number is incalculable, and so is the amount of freight they carried and the number of immigrants they transported, but they were certainly a vital factor in the development and peopling of the West, particularly by way of the Ohio and Tennessee Rivers.

Regular packet boats were rare in the keelboat age on the western rivers, and their services were not long continued, but in the East they existed on the Hudson and Delaware. The Spanish maintained a fleet of "galleys" on the Mississippi for military purposes, and the United States built a number of gunboats during the Revolution and the following years. Gunboats and keelboats were used by the army against the Indians on the western rivers as late as the War of 1812, and thereafter steamboats took their place. A steam gunboat was an important factor in the victory at Bad Axe in 1832. From about 1792 to about 1817 there were built on the western rivers approximately sixty ships which were floated downstream and put into ocean service. The practice, however, did not prove economical and was discontinued. A second spurt of ocean vessel building came in the 1840's and many wooden and iron ships were built at Pittsburgh, Marietta and other points for use in world commerce.

Fulton's *Clermont* was launched on the Hudson in 1807, and a battle royal was soon initiated between river and coastwise steamboats and sailing packets, with the former, of course, destined to eventual victory. Fulton's *Orleans*, or *New Orleans*, was put into operation between Natchez and New Orleans in 1811 and was of some assistance to Jackson's army in 1814 and 1815 (*see* New Orleans, Battle of). Fulton's boats were built with deep hulls which were unsuited to the shallow western rivers and it was not until Henry Shreve's *Washington* was launched in 1816, with its boilers on the deck, that a craft was found suitable for western river navigation. The title "packet" as applied to the western passenger steamboat was a misnomer, as they rarely operated on schedule, but the eastern river steamboats were more reliable. The use of high-pressure boilers resulted in so many explosions that in 1852 Congress set up a system of licensing and inspection. The average life of a western steamboat was about four years.

By 1850 the railroads had begun to sap the trade from the steamboats and from the canals both in East and West. The tremendous volume of transport needed during the Civil War gave the steamboats a new lease on life and this continued for a couple of decades due to the fact that the railroads crossed rather than paralleled the rivers. Barges (the modern form of flatboat) came into general use for carrying coal, oil and other heavy goods and were towed by steamboats. During this second great age of the steamboat, lines of packets were formed and schedules became more honored by observance. "Low water boats" were even developed to cater to mail and passenger needs during the summer. By the 1880's, however, the competition of the railroads parallel to the rivers was rapidly displacing steamboats in the West and had won a victory in the East. It was partially in a desperate sectional effort to block the railroads that the Federal Government was pushed into western river improvements after 1879. A magnificent system of dams and other water controls today make the rivers of the Mississippi basin important highways for heavy freight, such as steel and coal, carried chiefly in barges, and affords a check to railway rates as well.

RIVER TOWNS OF CONNECTICUT were Windsor, Hartford and Wethersfield, together with Springfield until it was discovered that the latter lay within the boundaries of Massachusetts. The settlement of these towns represented a group migration, begun in the summer of 1635 and continued through 1636, from Massachusetts Bay Colony. Thus, practically the whole of the Bay town of Dorchester removed to Windsor; Newtown (Cambridge) removed to Hartford; Watertown removed to Wethersfield. For a short time the original Massachusetts town names were applied to the new settlements on the Connecticut River.

Various reasons were given for the removals, but probably the motivating reason lay in that urge which during the next two and a half centuries drew Americans ever westward. With this migration from the Bay to the Connecticut River, the Westward Movement began.

And, interestingly enough, these Massachusetts pioneers found themselves in a situation which came to be a commonplace of western settlement: they were squatters, though they knew not the word, on land to which no clear title was available. The legal title lay with the Council for New England which, however, at a series of meetings held in London from February to April, 1635, had voted to surrender its patent to the king and had divided its domain between its eight active members. To the Earl of Carlisle had gone the parcel on which the three River Towns of Windsor, Hartford and Wethersfield were established. There is no evidence that the settlers of these towns asked, or received, any authorization from the Council or from Carlisle.

Simultaneously with the migration of the settlers from Massachusetts and the legal activities of the Council in London, a group of Puritan "lords and gentlemen" in England put forth a claim to the Connecticut country through a deed or patent allegedly derived from the Earl of Warwick, and in the summer of 1635 sent over young John Winthrop as governor, and with orders to build a fort at Saybrook. The settlers of the River Towns made no objection to the fort, but promptly ejected a party which attempted to take up land where Windsor was to be founded. Nor were the agents of the Plymouth trading post, which had been established in the same neighborhood some two years earlier, treated with more consideration. The Massachusetts people had come to take the land, they had the manpower to do it, and neither legal title nor claims of title nor incidental prior occupation was to stand in their way.

Possession of the land was promptly followed by the establishment of a federated form of government under a General Court, the first meeting of which, on April 26, 1636, was presided over by Roger Ludlow, former deputy governor of Massachusetts Bay and the leader of the migration.

With the growth of the original settlements, the founding of new towns and the adoption of the Fundamental Orders, the River Towns evolved into the commonwealth of Connecticut.

RIVERMEN OF THE OHIO. The first rivermen of the Ohio were Indians of the canoe age of navigation. Long before the coming of white men the Indians had standardized their craft. Then as now the fabrication of river craft was an art, and ports of entry and departure were determined by land routes of travel. As the Indian craft were well suited to the needs of white explorers and traders, they were taken over by them. When white immigrants began to push into the Ohio Valley, larger and more substantial craft than canoes were needed for the transportation of the ever-increasing numbers of people, their household and kitchen furnishings and their livestock. This led to the flatboat and the keelboat and their numerous modifications. The operators of these craft were known as rivermen, of whom Mike Fink and others were notorious.

In time the half-horse and half-alligator Fink type of men of flatboat and keelboat days gave place to the rousters, gamblers and bullies of the passenger packet days of Ohio River navigation. While the rousters, notably the Negroes, were making a place for themselves in verse and song, gamblers in the cloistered retreats of the passenger packets lay in wait for "gullible folk" whom they gamed out of their cash and in some instances of their clothing and their Negro slaves. Meanwhile by fighting like bulldogs, chewing and biting, bullies kept alive the traditions of the keelboatmen; others, for instance Enoch Enochs, became notorious for petty pilfering; and the bargemen developed a class of rivermen all their own.

The best human products of the heyday of the passenger packet on the Ohio, which extended from about 1840 to about 1855, were its gentlemen captains. In dress and bearing they rivaled the ocean captains of that day, and many of them were very popular. As described by one Gurley in the Cleveland *Plain Dealer:* "The cusses put on as much airs as the New York ocean captains." Following the Civil War the passenger packet captains recovered a measure of their former elegance, but the present rivermen of the Ohio are the captains, pilots, engineers and rousters who man tuglike boats which, like ships that pass in the night, make few or no stops. They are products of the machine age.

RIVINGTON'S GAZETTE (1773–83) was one of the more important colonial newspapers, with a circulation that extended into several colonies. James Rivington named his paper *Rivington's New York Gazetteer, or the Connecticut, New Jersey, Hudson's River, and Quebec Weekly Advertiser* but this title was soon shortened. It was a strongly partisan sheet, favoring the Tories during the Revolution. A group of armed Patriots destroyed Rivington's press in November, 1775, and forced suspension of the paper until October, 1777, when it was revived under the patronage of the king's government. The *Gazette* was useful to the English in publishing proclamations, revealing the misrepresentations of Patriot newspapers, and in perpetrating misrepresentations to aid the Loyalists. Rivington remained in New York City at the end of the war, trying to continue publication, but the last issue printed was Dec. 31, 1783. Thereafter he continued business only as a bookseller.

ROAD WORKING DAYS. Until the development of modern highways in the motor vehicle era, the "working out of road taxes" was a common system in rural America. A regular scale of payment was allowed for men, horses and equipment, and work was in charge of township or road district supervisors. "Road working days" were usually fixed at a time when farm work was not pressing and were occasions for neighborhood gossip and jollification rather than hard work. Construction was almost always unsatisfactory, and abolition of the system was one of the first recommendations of the "good roads" movement. Increasing technical demands and the rigid requirements of state and Federal aid have served to eliminate the system in most localities, and taxes are paid in cash.

ROADS. In 1639 the Massachusetts Bay Colony court ordered that roads be laid out so as to provide "ease and safety for travelers; and for this end every town shall choose two or three men, who shall join with two or three of the next town, and these shall have power to lay out the highways in each town where they may be most convenient. . . ." The New England township system likewise specified the construction of roads. With the establishment of government in other colonies—particularly in New York and Pennsylvania—one finds similar official steps taken for the construction of roads and bridges. Even in the Virginia Statutes at Large for the period 1619–60 one reads that highways shall be "layd out" and that "surveyors of highwaies and maintenance for bridges be yearly kept and appointed in each countie court respectively." Colonial laws pertaining to roads should not be taken too seriously. As the result of official action, precious little was done toward actual improvement in the means of overland transportation, with the exception of occasional tree and stump clearings.

In 1685 private coaches appeared on Boston's cobbled streets for the first time. But the increase in vehicles was slow, and not until the middle of the next century were they widely used. The inauguration of stagecoach passenger and mail service, and the introduction (particularly in Pennsylvania) of the Conestoga wagon freight business during the 18th century, provided the necessary inducement for road improvements. So extensive were these improvements that at the time of the Revolutionary War there existed dirt and corduroy roads throughout the more thickly settled areas of the northern and central colonies with thoroughfares even extending into the normally aquatic-minded Maryland, Virginia, the Carolinas and Georgia.

Land companies were not without their effect upon early road building, for certainly it was under the auspices of the Ohio and Transylvania companies that the first trails were blazed into the Old Northwest and Kentucky respectively. It was in March, 1775, under the direction of the Transylvania Company, that Daniel Boone and his party left the Watauga, where the Treaty of Sycamore Shoals had just been completed, to cut a wagon trail into Kentucky. From just north of Long Island of Holston the route moved west through Cumberland Gap, north for fifty miles along "Warriors' Path" and then again west through dense forests to the Kentucky River where Boone founded the town of Boonesborough. This route was

fittingly called "Wilderness Road"; and in view of the thousands of settlers who jolted their way over it en route to old "Kaintuck," it is scarcely without a peer among the historic highways of the land.

The rapid development of civilization in trans-Appalachia at the opening of the national period was accompanied by an acute transportation problem. Heavy goods were floated on the rivers, but Spanish possession of the mouth of the Mississippi created a potentially dangerous national situation. It was partly to overcome this hazard and partly to establish faster means of communication between the East and the West that the new United States Government took steps toward the construction of roads under Federal auspices. In the act of 1802 granting statehood to Ohio provision was made for an East-West road—a road which, when extended, was destined to become the famous National, or Cumberland, Road.

Toward this end science lent a hand. It had been discovered by John Loudon MacAdam, a Scotchman, that if crushed rock of less than one inch diameter were spread on either a dirt or stone foundation ten inches deep, the roadbeds would become not only harder but stronger with use. During 1792–94 the Philadelphia and Lancaster Turn Pike Co. had demonstrated this superior roadmaking method by constructing a 66-mile toll turnpike road between the above-named cities, albeit at a cost of $465,000. It "is a masterpiece of its kind," wrote Francis Baily, a traveler; "it is paved with stone the whole way, and overlaid with gravel, so that it is never obstructed during the most severe season."

The immense flow of freighters, stagecoaches and ordinary vehicles over the Lancaster Turnpike was sufficient revelation to the Federal authorities not only of the practicability of this new method of road building but of the volume of traffic that would accompany the construction of well-built roads through populous areas. Now, with a crying demand from the West for better transportation facilities, the Government was ready to act. Congress, as stated, first took action leading to construction of the Cumberland Road in 1802—a road from Cumberland, Md., to Wheeling, Va. (now W. Va.). Then in 1806 the decision was reached to expand it into a national road to extend from the Atlantic Ocean to the Mississippi River (St. Louis), and it was toward this end that actual construction began two years later. Constitutional questions were raised; and due to political obstructionism it was not until about 1819 that the road reached Wheeling. Thereafter the National Road continued to be a political football, and while new surveys and constructions were occasionally made, it never got beyond Vandalia, Ill., which point it reached in 1852. As far as Terre Haute, Ind., the road was superbly built—in keeping with MacAdam's principles—but from that point west it remained a dirt road. Although tolls were collected, its success from a social and economic point was unquestioned. "As many as twenty four-horse coaches have been counted in line at one time on the road," wrote one of the early historians of the National Road, "and large broad-wheeled wagons, . . . laden with merchandise and drawn by six Conestoga horses were visible all the day at every point, . . . besides innumerable caravans of horses, mules, cattle, hogs and sheep." The financial burden which this enterprise entailed and the protracted fight over the constitutionality of internal improvements contributed to a reduction of Federal road aid by Jackson's time, and ultimately the National Road was completely abandoned by Congress and was ceded to the states through which it passed. This likewise appears to have been the fate of other Federal or pseudo-Federal roads, which during the early decades of the 19th century had been built for military or social purposes. The coming of the railroads to America by 1828 was likewise a factor explaining why, at this time, the U. S. Government left the matter of road building to state, county and private agencies, which, if their accomplishments in both road and canal construction during the decades of the 1830's and 1840's are an index, were only too happy to assume this responsibility. Not until the advent of the automobile, early in the 20th century, did the Federal Government again become a prominent road builder.

It has often been stated that as frontier society moved steadily westward it repeated certain phases of its evolutionary social processes. This idea is particularly applicable to the subject of roads. During the time of the construction of the Cumberland Road the Far West was still a land of Indian trails. Before long, fur traders and missionaries were headed for the Oregon country and in so doing they marked out what by 1841 became widely known as the Oregon Trail—a route extending from St. Joseph, Mo., to the Willamette Valley, Ore., a route which in a rough way followed the south bank of the Platte River, and after passing through South Pass moved along the Green and Snake Rivers and then over Immigrants Pass to the banks of the Columbia. By following or floating down this massive river gorge the immigrants could reach their destination. In 1843 nearly 1000 pioneers moved westward over the Oregon Trail and for many succeeding years the number remained large. Less permanent, but nevertheless of historical significance, were such routes as the Santa Fe and Mormon trails.

With the discovery of gold in California in 1848 migration westward took on greater magnitude. Many who lived on the Atlantic seaboard preferred either a five-month sea voyage or the fever-ridden Isthmus route to overland travel. But most of the argonauts from the Middle West used the Oregon Trail to a point slightly west of Fort Hall (Idaho) and from there they turned southward and continued on over the thirsty Carson Sink, across the high Sierras south of Lake Tahoe and on to Hangtown, Calif. Within a

decade following the gold discovery California's population rose from a mere 15,000 to almost 380,000, half of which are believed to have passed over the seemingly endless stretches of the Oregon-California Trail. In view of this sudden rush of people into California, nearly half of which hastened off to almost inaccessible mountain retreats, the transportation difficulties seemed insurmountable. It was not long, however, before some trails were converted into passable roadways, and as early as the autumn of 1849 teamsters, using horses, mules, or oxen, were able to haul supplies to some of the more accessible mining towns. And while local and private agencies did much toward the construction of roads, bridges and ferries, we have the words of the Britisher Frank Marryat that "no one knows what a wagon will undergo until he has mastered California trails and gulches."

Hardly had the settlers and miners come to the Pacific coast before they commenced to clamor for a transcontinental railroad. Surveys for such were made, but to discerning persons it was then clearly evident that years would elapse before such a costly enterprise could be consummated. And so the "claim of the people of the West," to use the words of Congressman R. H. Stanton in 1850, "to have an immediate, safe, and practical overland route, to serve until a railroad is built, I think fair, reasonable, righteous, and a constitutional claim." It took much congressional debating before action came, but in 1857 the Overland California Mail Bill became a law. And while this measure did not prescribe Federal aid in road construction, it did empower the Postmaster General to provide a liberal subsidy to a firm which he might select "for the conveyance of the entire letter mail from . . . the Mississippi River . . . to San Francisco . . ." The route selected and provided ran from St. Louis to Little Rock, and then through El Paso and Yuma to its western terminus. It became popularly known as the Butterfield, or Southern Overland route, and between 1858–61 a semiweekly passenger and mail service was maintained over this road. In 1860 this stage road was extended northward from San Francisco to Portland, Oregon—making a total length of 3600 miles. The outbreak of the Civil War necessitated switching the Butterfield route into northern territory, and thereafter it followed in a general way the old Oregon-California Trail. Not until May 10, 1869, when the first transcontinental railroad was completed, did this important stage road lose its economic significance and popularity.

The great expansion and the excellence of the American railway system partly account for the protracted lull in good road building during the last part of the 19th century. But significantly enough the Federal Government was once again to become interested in roads. In 1893 Congress appropriated $10,-000 for an inquiry into good road management. With the advent and use of the automobile after 1900 this renewed interest increased in view of the inadequacy of state and county roads for motor travel. Just what the condition of American roads was as late as 1908 may be indicated by the fact that there was then not a single mile of concrete highway, and only 650 miles of macadam, in the entire United States. For directions to go from Albuquerque to Los Angeles in 1908 the secretary of an automobile club was typically enough told to: "Follow this mountain range eighty miles south to a stick in the fork of a road, with a paper tied at the top. Take the rut that leads off to the right."

In 1912 a plan was proposed for the construction of a direct transcontinental road to be called the Lincoln Highway. And while this enterprise was not completed until 1930, it marked the beginning of widespread Federal and state aid for highway construction, much of which was to be hard surfaced.

Starting with the Highway Act of 1916, the federal government matched state expenditures for arterial roads. By the late 1920s the total annual investment in roads was larger than in steel, railroads, or any other branch of industry or transportation. Furthermore, appropriations grew in good times and bad. By 1958 the combined local state and federal expenditures on roads came to over 10 billion dollars annually. In 1958 Congress passed a bill authorizing payment for 90 per cent of the cost of a new limited access highway system. The total cost was estimated in 1960 at about 40 billion over the next decade. This sum, as appropriated by Congress from year to year, would be in addition to the subsidies to match state expenditure for the older type of highway.

ROBINSON-PATMAN ACT (1936) was primarily intended to protect the independent merchant against the preferential wholesale prices which chain stores were able to command because of their great purchasing volume. It prohibited discrimination in price or terms of sale between purchases of commodities of like grade or quality, prohibited questionable brokerage or advertising allowances, and attempted to prevent the setting of unreasonably low prices for the purpose of destroying competition.

ROCKET INVENTIONS. Robert H. Goddard of Clark University built and launched the first non-munitions rocket (munitions rockets were used in the Revolutionary War) in America in 1926—a liquid-propellant device which burned for 2.5 seconds and achieved a velocity of only 60 miles per hour. In 1932, Goddard succeeded in launching a liquid-propellant rocket to an altitude of 2000 feet and with a velocity of 500 miles per hour. Working with funds supplied by Harry F. Guggenheim and the Government, Goddard made several improvements on his basic liquid-propellant power plant and facilities in Roswell, N. Mex., and later in Annapolis, Md. There are many basic patents in the Goddard name, and

although a solitary worker, he must be recognized as the engineer-father of modern rocketry.

Fortunately for America, in the middle 1930's one of the world's greatest physicists, Prof. Theodore von Karman, of the California Institute of Technology, had the courage to espouse the cause of rocketry. Von Karman combined theoretical physics with engineering genius, and he is truly the author of thousands of ideas which were translated into patents by his students and fellow workers. The resulting amazing complex of inventions and innovations includes patents in the areas of liquid and solid propellants and power plants; pumps, pressure vessels, many forms of turbines, ignition systems, airframes, controls; indeed, to shorten a long narration, from many forms of aerodynamic devices down through the long corridor of science, to the motors involving basic knowledge of the kinetics of chemical reaction to corpuscular radiation, his most recent field being magneto-fluiddynamics. His students and fellow workers include such important present-day rocketry inventors as Frank J. Malina, John S. Parsons, Martin Summerfield, E. S. Forman, A. M. O. Smith, H. S. Tsien, and the hundreds of scientists who worked under his direction at Cal-Tech and Aerojet. No commentary would be complete without crediting Prof. Fritz Zwicky (Cal-Tech and Aerojet) with his morphological matrix—evolved in 1943—which pointed the way to all fields of invention in the entire ambit of rocketry.

During the 1930's many of the United States contributions to rocketry and astronautics were made within the framework of the American Rocket Society [A. R. S.], organized in 1930 as the American Interplanetary Society. Under the direction of G. E. Pendray and H. F. Pierce, and with the aid of A. Africano and others, the Society's first rocket motor took shape, based on the German *Repulsor* designs. It operated on gasoline and liquid oxygen, was pressure-fed, and produced 60-pound thrust. It underwent a successful static test schedule in 1932. Under the leadership of Bernard Smith, Rocket No. 2 was constructed. On launching day in May of 1933, it fired for only two seconds, reaching 250 feet. An explosion in the oxygen tank caused the malfunction, but in spite of this, the experimenters were jubilant because a liquid rocket had at last left the ground.

Spurred by this success, new rockets were designed and built. Smith and Pendray prepared Rocket No. 3; John Shesta, No. 4. The Shesta motor had four nozzles, a feature designed to strengthen its construction, and it was water-jacket-cooled. This rocket reached a calculated velocity of 700 miles per hour.

The American Rocket Society also developed a "heat sponge" motor, wherein blocks of aluminum absorbed large amounts of heat. By 1935, a test stand was constructed, permitting motors to be thoroughly checked out before actual flight-firing. This facility led to further basic knowledge of rocket engine operation, which enabled the Society's members (J. Wyld and P. Van Dresser had been added to the original member list) to devise better and more reliable motors. The U. S. Government exhibited little official interest in rocketry. The Navy exhibited some interest in pilotless aircraft and remote-controlled bombs in the late 1930's, and the Army's Col. George Holloman realized the significance of guided missiles, but neither effort really recognized the ultimate possibilities of rocket propulsion. In 1932, L. A. Skinner, of the Army Ordnance Department, began tests on his own initiative, with limited funds and facilities, at Aberdeen, Md. He was primarily interested in the possibility of accelerating a shell by means of a solid or liquid-propellant rocket motor.

It was also during this period that Robert Goddard developed a self-contained gyroscopic stabilization system for his test rockets, with jetavator vanes for missile control. He also launched the world's first supersonic rocket.

In August, 1941, the first solid-propellant JATO, whose propellant was developed by J. W. Parsons, was successfully flight-tested on a small liaison type airplane. In April, 1942, liquid-propellant JATO, utilizing nitric acid and aniline, developed by Martin Summerfield, was successfully tested in an exhaustive series of flights on an A-20 attack bomber. These flights were the first jet-assisted take-offs carried out in the United States.

During World War II, only two rocket developmental centers existed, namely, Aerojet Engineering Corporation in Azusa, California, of which Andrew G. Haley was wartime president, and Reaction Motors Corporation of Rockaway, N. J., of which Lovell Lawrence was wartime president. From this small industrial beginning and from the great basic contributions of Goddard and Von Karman and those already mentioned, has arisen in a few years the greatest era of invention and scientific achievement ever known. One indication of the greatness of the scientific complex is that literally thousands of inventions and innovations in all fields of science are involved.

ROCKY MOUNTAIN FUR COMPANY (1822–34) was a simple partnership of traders. An announcement published in St. Louis, upon behalf of William H. Ashley, on March 20, 1822, asked for the enlistment of "one hundred young men to ascend the Missouri River to its source, there to be employed for one, two, or three years." The business agreement behind this announcement marked the beginning of the company. The company later passed under control of other partners, of whom Jedediah S. Smith, David Jackson and William L. Sublette were the best known.

This company, in its brief history, opened up the wealthiest fur sections of the West. It was the first company to depend primarily upon directly trapping beaver rather than securing the skins by trading with the Indians. Knowledge of the geography of the West was greatly increased by the explorations incidental to the activities of its members. The regions of the Platte, Green, Yellowstone and Snake Rivers were explored by them. The region around the Great Salt Lake was trapped, and Smith made his way from there into California, and then along the coast into Oregon, being the first white man known to have covered most of this great distance. Guides for later fur trade and settlement enterprises received their training with this company.

ROCKY MOUNTAINS. Spanish pioneers were the first white men to see the Rocky Mountains, first in Mexico and then (Coronado, 1540) in the United States. The geologic upheaval that produced the Rocky Mountains had brought the conditions for ore-making. And the presence of the precious metals induced the earliest exploration and first settlements, by Spaniards in the southern portion of the Rockies.

From the East, via the Great Lakes, came the French. As early as 1743, Verendrye saw the "Shining Mountains" in the Wyoming region. Frenchmen and then Englishmen, hunting furs, followed Canadian streams to the western mountains. Then came pelt-hungry Americans up the Missouri and its tributaries. These trappers and traders, first gathering beaver skins and later buffalo robes, became the Mountain Men who were the real trail-blazers of the central Rocky Mountain West. Their pack trains, and later their wagons, broke the practicable trails into and over the mountains.

The Louisiana Purchase of 1803 was without definite boundaries, but the original French claim to the drainage area of the Mississippi indicated the crest of the Rockies as the western boundary. Lewis and Clark in the Northwest, and Z. M. Pike in the Southwest, led the first official expeditions for the United States into the Rocky Mountains. Their reports were more favorable than that of Maj. Long (1820), who came to the base of the mountains and labeled the adjoining high plains, "The Great American Desert." To the west-moving flood of homeseekers these plains, the Rocky Mountains and intervening plateaus were uninviting for settlement and they traveled another thousand miles to the Pacific coast, over trails determined by mountain topography. In southern Wyoming, where the Rockies flatten to a high plain, South Pass became the gateway to Oregon. The Mormon trek (1847) and the rush of the Forty-niners to California took the same crossing of the continental divide. Gold discoveries during the 1850's and 1860's brought permanent settlement in the Rockies, and the formation of the mountain states.

RODEOS, or roundups, may be considered (1) as factors of the range industry, and (2) as public spectacles.

The first ranching (Spanish) in America was on

the open range, and open-range conditions existed through a long period of expansion of the industry by English-speaking rangemen, until the advent of barbed wire. Cattle and horses on the open range always drift, fences not altogether confining them. As a result, the working of stock on any unfenced range concerned neighboring—and even far distant—stockmen as much as the immediate controller of that range. While Texas and California were still Mexican territory, laws were added to custom to regulate the gatherings of stock. Riders from far and near participated in these rodeos. A *juez de campo*—judge of the plains —presided with full authority. Beeves and cows were selected for slaughter, their only value on the Pacific slope until in the late 1840's being the worth of hide and tallow; colts, calves and unbranded animals were branded; young horses were caught for breaking; *manadas* (bands of mares, each kept in charge by a stallion) were "shaped up"; animals belonging on distant ranges were cut out, etc.

During the 1870's and 1880's, while the Great Plains and adjacent territory developed into the cattle empire, roundups that dwarfed the original rodeos became systematized. Their times, limits and manner of procedure were during their heyday regulated by cattle associations of Texas, Colorado, Wyoming and other states. As many as two or three hundred riders—though lesser roundups were far more common—representing scores of brands, fed by dozens of chuck wagons and having in their *remudas* from six to ten horses for each rider, would concentrate against some natural boundary, mountain or stream. The general roundup boss would then direct various units as to each day's work. Daily a big piece of country was "combed" and out of the cattle brought together calves would be branded, beeves held for shipping and strays to be returned to their proper ranges cut out. The "cuts" were kept under herd and were daily driven to each new roundup ground, and thus were constantly augmented. The "work" might end more than 100 miles from where it started.

Rodeos and roundups alike brought together, socially, men leading isolated lives; they were festivals of a kind. Horse racing and betting were inevitable. Fancy riding and expert roping were displayed by horsemen of a class that has always been proud of its "profession" and its expertness. Poker and other games went on upon blankets spread out in the firelight. Cowboys exchanged songs. Occasionally there was an "augering match"—a contest in storytelling. Long before the range was all fenced in the Southwest, riding and roping contests became popular features of fairs and barbecues.

Buffalo Bill's Wild West Show proved the popular interest in a dramatization of the horseback West. About the opening of the century, Booger Red and other "stove-up" cowpunchers were enterprising bronc-riding exhibitions and charging admission. In 1908 the Millers of Oklahoma put their 101 Ranch exhibition on the road. In 1897 Cheyenne began its annual exhibition, famous now all over the continent as Frontier Days. The Calgary Stampede and the Pendleton Roundup, both started later, are equally famous. These, with the Southwestern Exhibition and Fat Stock Show at Fort Worth, the Last Roundup at Dodge City, rodeos at Miles City, Prescott, Las Vegas, and at many other places, now draw millions of spectators annually. The rodeo is a feature in New York's Madison Square Garden and Chicago's Coliseum; it has been to London. Professionals follow the big rodeos; but all over the range country there are held, each summer and fall, rodeos in which only local talent—ranch people—participate. The rodeo— with its steer and bronc riding, wild-cow milking, bull-dogging, calf roping and other features, has become as much an American institution as bullfighting is Spanish or the Olympic games were Greek.

ROGERS' RANGERS. This most colorful corps in the British-American army during the French and Indian War was commanded by Maj. Robert Rogers with such capable soldiers as John Stark, Israel Putnam and James Dalyell as lieutenants. The unit of 600 frontiersmen, serving as the eyes of Abercromby's and Amherst's armies, in scores of raids scouted enemy forces and positions and captured prisoners.

The Rangers took part in daring and bloody engagements. On Jan. 21, 1757, they cleverly escaped extermination by a greatly superior French force between Crown Point and Ticonderoga. The Battle on Snowshoes, fought to the south of Ticonderoga on March 13, 1758, did not end so well, for Rogers lost 130 of his 180 men and barely escaped himself, according to tradition by making the Indians believe he had descended the steep promontory on Lake George now known as Rogers' Rock. In 1759 the Rangers boldly wiped out the village of the St. Francis Indians, and during the next year Rogers journeyed as far west as Detroit to receive the surrender of the French posts.

The great strength of the Rangers came from adopting the best features of Indian warfare. Each Ranger was an extremely mobile and highly self-sufficient military unit. He was clad in buckskin and carried a smooth-bore firelock, sixty rounds of powder and ball, a heavy hatchet and a small supply of dried meat and biscuit. Extremely vigilant, the Rangers marched through the forest silently in single file with a cloud of skirmishers to the front and sides. In battle they fought from behind the heavy covert of shrubs and bushes. If outnumbered, they retired with slow, enchafing fire and, under cover of night, melted away in a hundred directions to the appointed rendezvous many miles away. Their dashing courage, incredible hardihood and humorous pranks made them famous alike in England and the colonies.

ROOT-TAKAHIRA AGREEMENT (Nov. 30, 1908), made by Secretary of State Elihu Root and the Japanese Ambassador Takahira, declared the wish of the two governments to develop their commerce in the Pacific; their policy to maintain the status quo and defend the open door and the independence and integrity of China; their resolve, reciprocally, to respect the territorial possessions of each other in the Pacific; and a willingness to communicate with each other if these principles were threatened. (An earlier proposal for such an arrangement by Ambassador Aoki, in October, 1907, had been repudiated by the Japanese government but the suggestion was renewed when the Katsura Ministry came into power in Japan.) The proposal was welcomed by the United States as helpful in quieting the widely held belief that war between the two countries was impending, a belief stimulated by the disputes over Japanese immigration and the anti-Japanese measures in California. The agreement was enthusiastically received in European capitals but did not please the Chinese who feared that it would strengthen Japan's position in China.

ROSENBERG CASE. On April 5, 1951, Julius Rosenberg and his wife, Ethel, natives of New York City, were sentenced to death for furnishing vital information on the atomic bomb to Soviet agents in 1944 and 1945. Rosenberg had been an electrical engineer. Evidence against the pair was supplied by Mrs. Rosenberg's brother, David Greenglass, who was himself sentenced to fifteen years. Also involved was Morton Sobel, sentenced to thirty years. The Rosenbergs were executed at Sing Sing on June 19, 1953.

ROUGH RIDERS. This most widely publicized single regiment in American military history was recruited for the Spanish-American War from the cattle ranges, mining camps and from the law enforcing bodies of the Southwest, its personnel offering brilliant copy for the flamboyant, uncensored and unrestrained war correspondents of the era. Its commanding officers were the final touch. Leonard Wood, of the Army Medical Corps, left his post as White House physician to accept the colonelcy; Theodore Roosevelt became lieutenant colonel. Neither was trained for line command, but they had the fire of crusaders and colorful personalities.

The First U. S. Cavalry Volunteers, the official designation, had a brief training period at San Antonio, spring of 1898; thence it entrained for Tampa. There its horses were abandoned; and in the chaos of embarkation, but little more than half the regiment left Florida. The fragment that did reach Cuba lived up to its advance publicity. From Las Guásimas, after which Wood was promoted to a brigade, to San Juan Hill their attacks were often unconventional but usually successful.

ROYAL COLONIES. With the exceptions of Connecticut and Rhode Island, all of the original thirteen colonies began as chartered or proprietary provinces —and those two exceptions shortly came to be chartered colonies. Governmental problems caused most proprietors to surrender their charters to the Crown. Massachusetts Bay Colony lost its charter in 1684. The new form of government was known as a royal province, and began first in Virginia in 1624. At the time of the Revolution only Connecticut, Maryland, Pennsylvania and Rhode Island retained the earlier forms of government. Thus the royal province became the standard type of colonial government in America.

In the royal province no legal limitations stood between the king and the people. The king was represented by a royal governor, appointed and removable at will, whose authority rested upon a commission and a set of instructions. The first conferred authority, the latter directed how the authority was to be exercised. Together these documents constituted a written constitution, subject to change by the Crown. The governor was assisted by a council of twelve, appointed by the Crown.

Each colony had an elected assembly representing the people, which had complete control over lawmaking, taxation, and the handling of public revenues. Most royal governors were dependent upon the assembly for financial support. This opened the way for extensive popular control of government in America by the assemblies, and by 1764 the royal provinces were quite fully self-governing commonwealths. Georgia was the only original colony supported directly by parliamentary appropriations. In 1767 the royal governors and other civil officers were made independent of the assemblies, and were paid directly from the American revenue.

Judges were appointed by the Crown, usually for good behavior. After 1760 they could be removed by the Crown the same as governors, and under the act of 1767 were no longer paid by the assemblies. All laws had to be sent to England and were subject to the royal veto. All unsold public land belonged to the Crown and could be granted by the governor. The colonial government articulated with England, by way of the Board of Trade, in ordinary civil matters; with the Secretary of State for the Southern Department in major political affairs; with the Treasury Department in matters of customs duties; and with the Admiralty office in matters of admiralty.

ROYAL DISALLOWANCE. In addition to possessing authority to review cases on appeal from colonial courts, the Privy Council had the power to approve or disallow colonial legislation. By 1730 this applied to all the colonies except Connecticut and Rhode Island. Laws contrary to English common or statute law, to a colonial charter or to governor's instructions, laws manifestly inequitable or badly drafted, were principal targets of the disallowance procedure. While only a very small percentage of colonial laws were disallowed, the practice helped to tighten the mercantilist vise upon the colonies, as frequent objects of royal disapproval were laws affecting English trade and shipping interests, establishing debt moratoria and inflation, and fostering colonial manufactures.

RUBBER, SYNTHETIC. Plantation, or natural, rubber has been produced for centuries, but the perfection of the vulcanizing process greatly widened its areas of use. Major production of natural rubber is in southeast Asia where soil and climatic conditions are favorable to the growth of rubber trees which are tapped for latex, the basis for rubber. Other important areas are in South America, particularly in the Amazon valley region. The great growth of the industry resulted from the demands of the automobile industry and increasing use in other ways.

When World War II began, with Japan largely in control of the major rubber-producing areas, western Europe, particularly Germany, and the United States speeded up the development and manufacture of synthetic rubber which, while a substitute for natural rubber, is in no way identical in its chemical and physical properties. Synthetic rubber is made from a variety of chemical products in combination, one of the most important and widely used being a hydrocarbon called butadiene. Buna S, polymer of butadiene, and styrene are used for automobile tires. Other combinations or synthetics are used for manufacturing special-purpose products.

When the United States entered the war in December, 1941, natural rubber usage was nearly 100%; the 1945 United States consumption was about 15% natural rubber and 85% synthetic rubber. During the four-year period 1941–1945, synthetic rubber had largely replaced natural rubber, not only for tires but also for a wide variety of rubber products. Production had increased from 25,000 short tons in 1942 to nearly one million tons in 1945. By 1960, though natural rubber usage in the United States had increased to over one-half million tons, synthetic rubber consumption was over one million tons. In fact, in 1960, the United States produced 85% of the world's total production of synthetic rubber.

RULE OF REASON is a principle of judicial interpretation which might with propriety be applied to any piece of legislation, the purpose and intent of which were open to serious question. Actually, the application of the phrase has been largely restricted to the interpretation of the Sherman Antitrust Act of 1890. This measure, either by accident or by design, was so poorly drawn that even with the passage of approximately half a century, no one has ever known precisely what it meant. If it meant what it appeared to mean, it would not only be unenforceable, but socially and economically unsound, and probably unconstitutional as well. In the effort to evade the latter issue, the Supreme Court in Standard Oil Co. v. U. S. (221 U. S. 1, 1911) and U. S. v. American Tobacco Co. (221 U. S. 106, 1911) enunciated the rule of reason. Henceforth, as a result of this process of judicial amendment, the prohibition of "all combinations in restraint of trade" set forth in the act, should mean "all *unreasonable* combinations in restraint of trade." The Court developed and elaborated upon the concept in U. S. v. St. Louis Terminal Railway Association (224 U. S. 383, 1912).

RULE OF THE WAR OF 1756. In 1756 the French, because of England's maritime supremacy, opened their colonial trade to the neutral Dutch. This resulted in a notification by Great Britain to the Netherlands that Great Britain in the future would not allow neutrals to engage in time of war in a trade from which they were excluded in time of peace. The British prize courts enforced this dictum, since known as the Rule of the War of 1756.

During the wars of the French Revolution and Napoleon, the neutral American carrying trade endeavored to circumvent and circumnavigate the Rule of the War of 1756 by taking French colonial goods to American ports and re-exporting them as American goods. In the case of the *Polly,* decided by British prize courts in 1802 (a war case actually decided in an interval of peace), it was held that this circuitous voyage, broken at a neutral port, did not constitute a violation of the Rule of the War of 1756. In making this decision the court did not consider the question whether the payment of drawbacks of import tariff charges when the imported goods were re-exported nullified the Americanization and made the exports subject to capture under the Rule of the War of 1756. In the case of the *Essex,* decided in 1805, after the renewal of the war, the British prize courts decided that payment of drawbacks on colonial goods re-exported by way of neutral countries nullified the neutralization of those goods and subjected them to capture and condemnation under the Rule of the War of 1756. This ruling was the cause of much diplomatic dispute between Great Britain and the United States.

RUM TRADE, COLONIAL. Begun in the New England colonies in the 17th century, it was vital to the existence of a people unable to produce staple crops. The climate of Massachusetts and Rhode Island being unsuitable to such large staples as tobacco, which maintained the Southern colonies, agriculture was confined, there, to the subsistence farms. The lumber and fishing industries of New England were unable to find markets in England large enough to pay for the manufactured goods imported from the mother country. They were forced, therefore, to seek a market in the West Indies. Here lumber and fish were paid for by molasses, the main product of the island. The manufacture of rum, from this molasses, thus became one of the earliest of the New England industries. The rapidity with which this industry grew is evident from the fact that, in 1731, 1,250,000 gallons of rum were manufactured in Boston from molasses brought in from the French West Indies.

It was presently understood by the Yankee traders that the most pressing need of the island planters was for slaves. The more adventurous of the New England sea-captains were familiar with the African Gold Coast before the end of the 17th century. The celebrated "triangle," therefore: molasses to New England, rum to Africa, slaves to the West Indies, was a logical invention and maintained the prosperity of the Northern colonies through the 18th century.

These colonies, however, soon came into conflict with England through the rum trade. Yankee traders found it more profitable to deal with the French, Dutch or Spanish islands than with the English. First, Catholic populations formed a fish market; second, the sugar supply of the English islands was inadequate; third, the sugar of the English colonies was more expensive. In France, legislation designed to protect native brandy forbade importation of rum from the colonies so that most of the molasses supply of the French islands was available to the Yankees. The English Parliament attempted, in 1733, to limit this trade by imposing high duties on non-British molasses imported into New England. This legislation was the celebrated Sugar Act. It was consistently evaded; smuggling became an accepted practice and achieved an enormous scale. It has been estimated that, of 15,000 hogsheads of molasses imported into Massachusetts in 1763, the duty (9d per gallon) was paid on only 1000.

In this year the conflict came to a crisis largely because of the war between England and France. England attempted to enforce the Sugar Act by the navy, by the appointment of customs commissioners and by the Writs of Assistance, which are recognized as a cause of the Revolution. By this time, however, smuggling was regarded by New Englanders as a patriotic exercise.

The rum trade was an important factor in the development of colonial shipping; it was partly responsible for the design of fast ships and for the skill of Yankee skippers.

RUMSEY'S STEAMBOAT. On Dec. 3, 1787, James Rumsey exhibited at Shepherdstown, Va., now West Virginia, in the presence of a crowd of spectators, a boat which was propelled by water forced out through the stern by a pump operated by a steam engine. Gen. Horatio Gates, Maj. Henry Bedinger and other prominent men who were present gave Rumsey certificates stating that they had had the pleasure of seeing his boat "get on her way, with near half her burthen on board and move against the current at the rate of three miles per hour by the force of steam, without

any external application whatever." On Dec. 11 at another trial a speed of four miles an hour against the current was attained. Being without funds to carry on further experiments, Rumsey went to Philadelphia where, shortly after his arrival, the Rumseian Society was formed. In May, 1788, that organization provided funds for him to go to England to carry on his steamboat experiments. There, after suffering untold disappointments and hardships, he died Dec. 20, 1792, a few days before he was to make a public trial of his boat. The following February his boat made a successful trip on the Thames at the rate of four knots an hour. In 1785 Rumsey invented a water-tube boiler of the type employed today in the United States and the British navies and in various steam plants where high pressure is a requisite.

RUNIC INSCRIPTIONS. The discovery in 1824 of a runic record in Greenland, and the publication in 1837 of Rafn's mistaken attempt to read the marks on Dighton Rock as a Norse inscription, led to an enthusiastic search for Norse relics in America. More than a score of rocks, from Maine to Virginia and from the Atlantic to the Pacific, have been credited with bearing runic inscriptions of the Vinland period. Some were proveably fraudulent. Some were misinterpreted natural marks and stains, or unintended scorings by ploughs. Many were haphazard scribblings by colonial Indians. Only two of them are actually in genuine runic characters. One, at Kensington in Minnesota, is still in dispute, warmly defended by some as a true Scandinavian record of 1362 and confidently asserted by others to be a modern fraud. The other, on No Man's Land in Massachusetts, bears the name "Leif Eriksson" and the date MI. There are strong reasons for believing that it was carved sometime within the present century, either as a practical joke on the owner of the island or as an innocently conceived private tribute to Leif.

RURAL FREE DELIVERY (1896) was established to provide an extension of the postal service to a considerable part of the population living beyond urban limits. Although the "village delivery" system of mail to small communities, introduced in 1890, had been discontinued in slightly more than two years, it led to lively agitation for an enlargement of the system into thinly populated areas. In 1891 Mortimer Whitehead of New Jersey brought the subject to the attention of the National Grange, and within a few months he presented before a committee of Congress his proposal for free rural delivery of mails. Early in 1893 James O'Donnell of Michigan introduced into the House of Representatives a bill for rural mail service, but it was never brought out of committee. Through the influence of the state granges, the movement was kept alive. Two appropriations, one of $10,000 in 1893 and the other of $20,000 the following year, for this purpose were not immediately used, but were added to the $10,000 made available in 1896 for experimental service, which in less than a year was opened on routes in West Virginia. The first complete county service was inaugurated in 1899 in Carroll County, Md.

While the benefits of the free delivery of mail in the rural area are not limited to those engaged in agricultural work, its establishment may be credited to the farmer. It has diminished the isolation of rural areas. With the daily delivery of newspapers the farmer has become informed concerning markets, and has been able to receive other instructive advantages already enjoyed by the urban citizen. Undoubtedly the rural free delivery system was one of the many factors in bringing about the parcel post service seventeen years later. It helped to prepare the way for making possible the contact of the large mail-order houses with their country patrons.

RUSSELL, MAJORS AND WADDELL. William H. Russell of Missouri and Alexander Majors, a Kentuckian, formed a partnership in 1855 and procured a contract for carrying government supplies from Fort Leavenworth to the plains and mountain army posts, for which work they used about 350 wagons. The sending of an army force to Utah in 1857 brought them a greatly increased business; they took in another partner, Waddell, and in 1858 they carried 16,000,000 pounds of government freight. To achieve this, they increased their equipment to 4000 men, 3500 wagons, 1000 mules and 40,000 oxen. When the Pikes Peak gold rush began, Russell, against his partners' wishes, formed a partnership, in 1859, with John S. Jones as the Leavenworth and Pikes Peak Express. The new company was soon in financial difficulties, and Russell, Majors and Waddell took it over. They also absorbed Hockaday and Liggett's stage line from St. Joseph to Salt Lake City, reorganized as the Central Overland California and Pikes Peak Express. In 1860–61 they operated the Pony Express. Their losses in these ventures were so heavy that they were forced out of business. In March, 1862, Ben Holladay took over the Salt Lake stage line on foreclosure, and soon afterward, the famous partnership was dissolved.

RUSSIAN FLEETS, VISIT OF (1863). In September, 1863, six Russian warships under Rear Admiral Lisovskii arrived at New York, and, in October, six more warships under Rear Admiral Popov anchored off San Francisco. The North warmly welcomed both fleets, believing that they came as possible allies. Popov, indeed, when a threatened attack on San Francisco by the Confederate raiders *Alabama* and *Sumter* was reported, ordered his ships to "clear for action." On April 25, 1864, both fleets were ordered home. The Russians did not come as Northern allies, but, fearing war with Great Britain and probable blockade, both fleets had been ordered to neutral ports, from which, if war were declared, they might make raids on British merchant shipping.

RUSSIAN TERRITORIAL CLAIMS. The creation of the Russian-American Company, in 1799, was the first occasion for Russia to define its claims to North American lands. The charter, granted by Paul I, established a monopoly of Russian-American trade and, of necessity, gave some indication of the territorial limits within which the trade could be carried on. These extended from 55° N. Lat. to Bering Strait, and included the "Aleutian, Kurile, and other islands situated in the northeastern ocean."

That was only the beginning, for the company was empowered to make new discoveries to the south as well as to the north of 55°. This privilege the company soon began to exercise, as well as an additional privilege of attempting trade with neighboring or attainable peoples, like the Japanese. It was soon learned that the great market for furs was at Canton, China, so the statesmen of the company, notably Count Rezanof, planned a great trade route which should embrace the Asiatic Islands, Japan, etc., and tie all in with the Alaska fur trade with Canton.

The problem of securing supplies for the Alaskan establishments, however, caused the Russians to look toward the Spanish settlements far to the south. Rezanof himself made a voyage to Spanish California in order to procure food for the Alaskans; and he was interested in making a farming settlement in the valley of the Columbia, but failed to enter the river. Finally, it was decided to plant a colony on the California coast above the Spanish settlements. Fort Ross, begun in 1809, at Bodega Bay, was intended as a supply station for meat and grain. No agreement was ever made with the Spaniards in regard to the California lands thus occupied; and finally, in 1841, the Fort Ross settlement was abandoned as no longer useful.

In 1821 on renewing the charter of the Russian-American Company the Russian government declared its authority would extend as far down the coast as 51° N. Lat.

The ukase setting forth that claim alarmed Great Britain and the United States, both of whose governments were by that time (1821) claiming territory on the northwest coast. In consequence, both these governments protested successfully and each succeeded in limiting Russia's exclusive claim to the southern line of 54° 40′ N. Lat. The British-Russian treaty of 1825 also delimited the Russian claims from the coast inland, thus establishing the basis for the boundary of Alaska as granted by Russia to the United States in 1867.

RUSTLER WAR was a conflict centering in Johnson County, Wyo., between ranchmen and a large group of alleged cattle thieves or "rustlers," and their friends. Finding it impossible to stop cattle stealing or to secure convictions in the local courts, owing to the fact that jurors and county officials were either intimidated by the "rustlers" or sympathized with them, the cattlemen resolved to take matters into their own hands. In April, 1892, they brought in a group of hired "gunmen" from Texas, and organized an expedition of about forty-five men to hunt down and kill some seventy men who they claimed were known to be cattle thieves. The expedition first visited the K. C. Ranch, where two men, alleged to be thieves, were killed. The cattlemen soon met resistance, however, and took refuge in the buildings of the T A Ranch, where they were besieged for three days by a force of some two hundred men. Upon the request of the governor of Wyoming, the President sent United States troops, commanded by Col. James Van Horn from Fort McKinney, to the scene of disorder. To these the beleaguered men, whose situation had grown desperate, gladly surrendered. They were delivered over to the civil courts for trial, but were all eventually acquitted.

RYSWICK, PEACE OF (1697), ended King William's War. By its provisions all conquests made during the war were to be mutually restored; but the ownership of the lands lying around Hudson Bay was to be decided by an Anglo-French joint commission. Such a commission met in 1699, but failed to reach a decision.

SACCO-VANZETTI CASE. On April 15, 1920, the paymaster and guard of the Slater and Morrill shoe factory at South Braintree, Mass., were shot dead and robbed of $15,776. Nicola Sacco, an Italian-born edger at a Milford, Mass., shoe factory, and Bartolomeo Vanzetti, an Italian-born fish peddler, were arrested on May 5 and charged with the crime. Their joint trial began May 31, 1921, at Dedham before Judge Webster Thayer. On July 14, 1921, both were found guilty of murder in the first degree. After the trial, motions for a re-hearing were made to Judge Thayer; they were denied and the supreme court of Massachusetts declined to intervene. But the demand for an impartial review of the case continued, and on June 1, 1927, Gov. Alvan T. Fuller appointed President A. Lawrence Lowell of Harvard, President Samuel W. Stratton of Massachusetts Institute of Technology and former probate judge Robert Grant to an advisory committee, the purpose of which was to report on the fairness of the trial and on the justification for the conviction. Meanwhile Governor Fuller made his own investigation, and on Aug. 3 announced that he and the committee agreed that the trial was fair and the defendants guilty. After midnight, Aug. 22, 1927, the two men were electrocuted.

The case was highly controversial. Both defendants had been draft dodgers; both were philosophical anarchists. The criticism was made that their radicalism had been improperly emphasized during the trial.

The claim was also made by Herbert B. Ehrmann, one of their attorneys, that the crime was actually committed by the Morelli gang. Ehrmann made much of the confession of a certain Celestino F. Madeiros to "being in the shoe company crime." It was true that no money was traced to the defendants. And it was not proved that they were in possession of the car in which the killers fled.

Felix Frankfurter, then on the faculty of the Harvard Law School, was the most eloquent champion of Sacco and Vanzetti. Justice Oliver Wendell Holmes of the U. S. Supreme Court denied the petition for stay and extension of time in which to apply for a writ of *certiorari*.

SACHEM is a term of Algonkin origin appearing in colonial writing about 1625. In New England the sachem was the chief, or leader, of two or more allied tribes. Later the term was used as synonymous with chief. Sagamore, from the Abenaki name for chief, had a similar meaning, but came to be used for chiefs of inferior rank to sachems. In government and territorial distinctions, sachemship signified the territory and jurisdiction of a chief. The Tammany Society adopted the title sachem for its head men, as Grand Sachem, Sachem, etc.

SACKETTS HARBOR OPERATION. In the War of 1812 the importance of naval control on Lake Ontario made the Sacketts Harbor naval base, near its foot, a hive of shipbuilding activity. Here seamen, shipwrights, and stores were assembled for Commodore Isaac Chauncey's flotilla, and in 1814 some six hundred workers were building two immense three-deckers of over one hundred guns. The base underwent two British attacks, the first, July 19, 1812, being limited to an ineffective two-hour naval bombardment. The second, May 27–29, 1813, was a combined operation by Commodore Yeo's squadron and over one thousand British regulars and Indians under Gov. Gen. Sir George Prevost. Although the base was well fortified and manned by equal forces, the New York militia fled at the first landing of British troops. As the British approached the blockhouse and barracks, however, they were held up by sharp fire from regulars and artillery. Gen. Jacob Brown, in chief command, rallied the militia, and at this reinforcement the British retreated to their boats. Losses were about equal, numbering for the British 48 killed and 208 wounded. Stores valued at $500,000 were burned to prevent capture, but two ships on the stocks escaped with slight damage.

SACKVILLE-WEST INCIDENT. In September, 1888, Lord Sackville-West, the British minister at Washington, received a letter, signed Charles F. Murchison, saying that the writer was a naturalized Englishman who desired advice as to how he should vote in the coming election. Without suspecting that the letter was only a decoy and that he was being made the victim of a hoax, the minister replied that he thought Cleveland more friendly to England than Harrison. The Republicans promptly published the correspondence, expecting that the incident would turn the Irish vote away from Cleveland. Sackville-West's explanations only made matters worse. When Lord Salisbury refused to call him home, he was dismissed.

SADDLES, AMERICAN. Saddles for men have been of three principal types: (a) "English"—a flat tree with low pommel and cantle, introduced into America during the early colonial period and still the popular style throughout the Eastern states; (b) "army"—first fully developed during the Civil War and, in this initial form (the McClellan), an English tree modified by heightening pommel and cantle, dishing the seat and lengthening the stirrup leathers; (c) "stock," interchangeably termed also "cowboy," "cow," "Mexican," "Western" or "range."

The progenitor of the stock saddle was brought to Mexico by Cortez in 1519. Of the same pattern as that which the Moors carried into Spain during their 8th-century invasion, it was a deeply dished tree with wall-like pommel and cantle. The rider sat in it, rather than on it. Upon the pommel of the Cortez saddle Mexican *vaqueros* presently attached a vertical protuberance (the "horn") to which the lariat could be fastened. This Mexican saddle was adopted by western Americans when in 1823 they began ranching. It became, and is today, the standard saddle of the West. By permitting lariat throwing from horseback, riding of bucking broncos and traveling great distances, it hastened the spread of civilization throughout the plains.

Women at the outset of the colonial period used a pillion (a pad fastened behind the saddle occupied by a rider) on which they sat facing sideways. Soon the pillion was supplanted by the "side saddle"—in its ultimate form, a copy of the man's English tree altered by omitting the right-hand stirrup and adding hooked-shaped pommels which imprisoned the horizontally bent right knee and prevented the left foot from losing its stirrup. When, in approximately 1900, eastern women commenced visiting western ranches where they had to ride astride—few broncos would tolerate a side saddle—the side saddle began everywhere to disappear.

Pack saddles for conveyance of goods were of two sorts, the wooden "crossbuck" and the leathern *aparejo*. These originated in Spain and came without change of form by way of Mexico into the United States.

SAG HARBOR, Long Island, was one of the leading colonial whaling ports. During the Revolution it was, for a time, used by the British as a depot for military stores. In the spring of 1777 the Americans, angered

by the destruction of Danbury by Tryon, planned a raid on Sag Harbor, and on May 23 Lt. Col. Meigs with 234 men in thirteen whale boats crossed the Sound, made a surprise attack, destroyed the military supplies at Sag Harbor and took ninety prisoners.

By the middle of the 19th century the increasing use of petroleum began seriously to affect the whaling industry. The fleet of Sag Harbor dwindled, and it is said that the last whaling ship, the *Myra*, sailed out of the harbor in 1871.

SAGADAHOC is the alternative ancient Indian name for the Kennebec region and river, especially that stretch of the stream from Merrymeeting Bay south to the Atlantic. The first recorded English settlement in New England was made at the mouth of the Sagadahoc, by Popham, in 1607. The region was remarkably rich in fish and furs, and many of the first settlers were fishermen or traders with the Indians. Settlements were established along this waterway at Georgetown, Merrymeeting Bay, Bath and Arrowsic, near the middle of the 17th century. The river was the scene of bitter fighting in the century of Indian warfare.

SAGINAW TREATY. On Sept. 24, 1819, Lewis Cass negotiated a treaty with the Chippewa Indians at Saginaw (Michigan Territory) in which a large land cession, located chiefly in Michigan Territory, was obtained from the tribe. There were sixteen reservations to the tribe within the lands ceded and several other smaller reserves for specified individuals. For the cession the United States agreed to pay annually forever $1000 in silver and to convert all previously promised annuities into payments in silver. The United States promised to furnish the natives with a blacksmith, cattle, farm tools, and persons to aid them in agriculture, in return for the privilege of building roads through their country.

The sequel throws much light on the history of Indian land cessions. On June 16, 1820, at Sault St. Marie, Michigan Territory, the Chippewa tribe ceded to the United States sixteen square miles of land on St. Marys River. On July 6, 1820, at L'Arbre Croche and at Michilimackinac, the Chippewa and Ottawa tribes ceded the St. Martin Islands in Lake Huron. At Chicago, Aug. 29, 1821, the Chippewas surrendered more of their lands to the Federal Government. Again on Aug. 19, 1825, at the Treaty of Prairie du Chien the Chippewas, together with several other tribes, ceded lands to the United States. Another treaty was secured from the Chippewas at Butte des Morts on Aug. 11, 1827, in which additional lands were secured by the National Government.

ST. AUGUSTINE, FLA., was founded by Pedro Menéndez in September, 1565, to establish Spanish authority in the mainland, protect shipping in the Bahama Channel and demolish the French settlement at Fort Caroline. Menéndez hoped to make St. Augustine the center of an ambitious expansion, a dream never realized, but it remained the garrisoned settlement, generally poor and needy, from which radiated mission enterprise to the south, west and north. As the colonial rivalry of England and Spain developed, it was attacked by British corsairs and by expeditions from the southern colonies. It was defended by San Marco (now Fort Marion), begun in 1672 and completed in 1756.

When Florida became British, St. Augustine was the government seat of East Florida and although most of the inhabitants left, the town shared the plantation prosperity of the region. Restoration to Spain turned it into a sleepy, unprogressive, little garrison town, for Spain's interests lay elsewhere; but it was still the administrative seat of East Florida and, as such, the object of attack by the "Patriots" in 1812. It was also one of three Spanish forts when the United States purchased the Floridas.

ST. CLAIR'S DEFEAT (Nov. 4, 1791). Gen. Harmar's failure to subdue the northwestern Indians compelled the American Government to send a second army against them. President Washington obtained from two small regular regiments) were "wretched men, and appointed Gov. Arthur St. Clair to command it.

Plans were made to have the army in readiness at Fort Washington (Cincinnati) by July 10, when it was to march to Fort Wayne and conquer the hostile Indian confederacy. From beginning to end, however, everything went wrong. October had arrived before as many as 2000 men could be assembled. Considered as an army, their quality was deplorable. The supplies provided were poor; the commissary department was both corrupt and incompetent; the commander was sick and incapable; the soldiers themselves (apart from two small regular regiments) were "wretched stuff," consisting of raw militia and six-months' levies "purchased from prisons, wheelbarrows and brothels at two dollars a month."

Thus composed, the army stumbled northward through the Ohio wilderness; about sunrise of Nov. 4, it was furiously assailed in its camp at present-day Fort Recovery, and after two hours the survivors fled madly back to Fort Jefferson, 22 miles away. Two thirds of the army—900 men—had been killed or wounded. Efforts to make St. Clair a scapegoat for the sins of others proved unavailing; responsibility for the disaster rested squarely upon the Government and the American public in general, which entered upon a difficult war without troubling to undertake the preparations essential for success.

ST. FRANCIS, ROGERS' EXPEDITION AGAINST. In September, 1759, because of the activities of the St. Francis Indians against Gen. Amherst's army while it lay at Crown Point, Maj. Robert Rogers, commander of Rogers' Rangers, proposed to Amherst that he be allowed to attack and destroy St. Francis (on the St. Francis River, three miles above its confluence with the St. Lawrence). Amherst agreed, and Rogers left Crown Point on Sept. 13, 1759, with 17 whaleboats and a force of 220 Rangers, among them several Stockbridge Indians and Mohawks. Two days later forty members of the expedition returned to Crown Point, ostensibly because of sickness. The remainder rowed on, arriving in Missisquoi Bay, at the northern end of Lake Champlain, on Sept. 23. The detachment hid its boats and set off through the forest for St. Francis. On Sept. 25 the boats were discovered and burned by French and Indians, leaving Rogers without a base. He sent a messenger to Gen. Amherst asking that supplies be deposited at the juncture of the Lower Ammonoosuc and Connecticut Rivers; then went on. For nine days Rogers and his men marched through a spruce bog, sleeping at night in the branches of felled trees. On Oct. 5 the detachment, reduced to 142 men, sighted St. Francis; and at dawn on Oct. 6 Rogers attacked, burning the town, killing 200 Indians, releasing 5 whites who had been held captive, and keeping 5 Indian children as prisoners. An hour after the attack he commenced his homeward trip with no provisions but dried corn. His second-in-command, Capt. Amos Ogden, had been shot through the body, but contrived to keep up. On Oct. 14, near Lake Memphremagog, the detachment ran short of food. Rogers divided his force into "small companies," so that they might live off the country, and ordered them to rendezvous at the mouth of the Ammonoosuc. On Oct. 16 one of the companies was ambushed by French and Indians, and destroyed. Several days later Rogers arrived at the mouth of the Lower Ammonoosuc to find that Amherst had sent provisions as requested, but that they had been taken away a few hours before his arrival. He built a raft and on Oct. 27 set off down the Connecticut to get supplies for his starving men. With him went Capt. Ogden, another Ranger, and one of the Indian boys captured at St. Francis. On Oct. 28 the raft was wrecked at White River Falls. Too weak to swing a hatchet, Rogers obtained logs for another raft by burning down trees, saved it from destruction at Wattoquitchey Falls with his last reserve of strength, and on Oct. 31 arrived at the fort at Number 4 (Charlestown, N. H.). He returned at once to the mouth of the Ammonoosuc with food for the survivors of the expedition. Lt. Samuel Stephens, the Ranger officer who had gone with provisions to the mouth of the Ammonoosuc but failed to wait, was court-martialed and found guilty of neglect of duty. Of the 142 men who attacked St. Francis, 93 returned to Crown Point.

STE. GENEVIEVE LEAD-MINING DISTRICT. One of the earliest references to lead in Missouri was made by Father Gravier in an account of his trip in 1700. Later in the same year, an expedition headed by LeSueur was sent up the Mississippi from its mouth for the special purpose of investigating minerals in the valley. The report was inadequate, but it mentioned that the savages in the Merrimac River (Mo.) area had lead mines.

Le Moine d'Iberville was interested in the report to the extent that he asked the French government, in 1701, for the exclusive right of lead mining and fur trading in the Missouri area, but died before the petition was granted. The French authorities gave a similar but enlarged grant to Anthony Crozat in 1712. Crozat's governor, de la Motte Cadillac, investigated the lead producing area, but little was done in the way of developing lead production until Crozat's successor to the grant of the monopoly, John Law, of the Company of the Indies, commissioned Philip Renault in 1723 as director general of mining operations. A rapid development followed, and lead was carried to Kaskaskia to be shipped down the Mississippi. By 1735 the activities of the lead miners and fur traders had become so general on the west side of the river that Ste. Genevieve was established and became the shipping point for the lead-mining district of the hills a few miles to its west.

The French, like the Indians, continued to use the primitive shallow-pit method of mining until Moses Austin moved to the district in 1798 and developed shaft mining and other tendencies toward modern methods. With the building of a railroad connecting the "Lead Belt" with St. Louis, Ste. Genevieve lost its lead-shipping industry. Flat River became the most important of a number of mining towns in St. François County which continues to be one of the greatest lead-producing areas in the world.

ST. JOSEPH, FORT. St. Joseph, near modern Niles, Mich. (close by the St. Joseph-Kankakee Rivers portage), was one of the earliest centers of French activity in the Great Lakes area. Here LaSalle (1679) and uncounted other travelers passed; here Father Allouez labored and died (1689); here for sixty years (*ca.* 1700–1760) French soldiers kept guard; here a British garrison was destroyed (1763), a Spanish army raided (1781), an American army sojourned (en route to establish Fort Dearborn in 1803).

ST. JOSEPH, MO., originally known as "Blacksnake Hills," was founded by Joseph Robidoux as a trading post in 1826. The town was platted in 1843 and incorporated in 1845. Population jumped from 964 in 1846 to 2257 in 1853. St. Joseph's economic growth, particularly in grain and livestock, was stimulated by outfitting Oregon and California immigrants and furnishing supplies to military posts. In 1859 the Hannibal and St. Joseph Railroad was completed; in 1860 the Pony Express linked St. Joseph with California. During the Civil War decade population increased from 8932 to 19,565: thereafter the construction of stockyards, the completion of the Missouri

River bridge and the extension of the railroad accelerated St. Joseph as a grain and cattle mart.

ST. LAWRENCE RIVER was explored by Jacques Cartier in 1535 as far as the island of Montreal, Cartier having discovered the Gulf of St. Lawrence in his voyage of the previous year. The name was first given by the explorer to a bay on the gulf, and later extended to the gulf and river. In 1541 Cartier carried his exploration to the second rapid above Montreal. It is not certain who first ascended the river from there to Lake Ontario, but it is known that the missionary Simon LeMoyne traveled to the villages of the Onondagas south of Lake Ontario in 1653 and returned the following year by way of the upper St. Lawrence. The St. Lawrence River, with its tributary, the Ottawa, and with the Great Lakes which geographically are part of the same river system, formed the main water thoroughfares from the sea to the interior of the continent. From Quebec or Montreal set forth explorers, missionaries and fur traders, bound for the west or the southwest; Champlain up the Richelieu to Lake Champlain, and by the Ottawa to Lake Huron; LaSalle, Marquette and Jolliet to the Mississippi; Radisson, Duluth and Allouez to Lake Superior and the country south of it; LaVérendrye to the plains of Manitoba, the Missouri and the Yellowstone. Fur-trading brigades of the North West Company left Montreal bound for Mackinac, Grand Portage, Lake Winnipeg, the Saskatchewan and the Columbia. Trading goods came from overseas up the St. Lawrence to Montreal, and thence in canoes to the west; and furs came down to Montreal and over to the London market. The colonial wars, the Revolutionary War and the War of 1812 each found the use or mastery of the St. Lawrence waterways a factor to be striven for.

ST. LAWRENCE SEAWAY. With a minimum depth of 27 feet and a length of 2350 miles, the Seaway extends from Lake Superior to the Atlantic. As part of a combined navigation-power project, it was improved through the co-operative efforts of the United States and Canada and was officially opened by Queen Elizabeth and President Eisenhower on June 26, 1959.

The improvements of the 1950's, it should be emphasized, were only the latest of many which have been made by the North American peoples since the discovery of the St. Lawrence by Jacques Cartier in 1535. From the early 1700's the Canadians carried out a construction program, which by 1903 afforded 14-foot navigation from the Atlantic to Lake Erie. Beginning in 1823, the United States improved the connecting channels of the Great Lakes, by 1914 making available 21-foot navigation for upbound and 25-foot navigation for downbound traffic from Lake Erie to Lake Superior. Between 1913 and 1932 Canada built the Welland Canal, with a 25-foot depth to bypass Niagara Falls.

However, with the rapid expansion of trade, and the corresponding increase in the size of ships, even the deepest of the improved channels soon were outmoded. Rail rates were high and the railroads proved incapable of handling wheat and manufactured goods pouring out of the Great Lakes region. On both sides of the boundary farmers and exporters—supported by private and public agencies interested in cheap electricity—insistently demanded the co-operative improvement of the waterway.

Mainly because of the opposition of sectional interests and economic groups, a treaty, signed July 19, 1932, was rejected by the U. S. Senate in 1934. An agreement signed in March, 1941, was never able to obtain the required majority approval of the two houses of Congress. As one means of ending the impasse, in 1952 President Harry S. Truman and Prime Minister Louis St. Laurent agreed that New York and Ontario should develop the power of the International Rapids section, while Canada alone should build the waterway. But the following year Congress decided that the United States should have a voice in the Seaway's construction and control. Very reluctantly, Canada abandoned her own construction plans and admitted the United States into a new partnership arrangement. Construction was started in the summer of 1954 and completed five years later. The dream of half a century had finally become a reality.

ST. LOUIS, BRITISH ATTACK ON (May 26, 1780), was part of the British strategy of the Revolutionary War, and the successful defense of this village is generally accounted a victory for the United Colonies. It shared with King's Mountain the sum total of victories over the British in 1780. Instructions had been received by the British Gen. Haldimand on June 16, 1779, to reduce the Spanish and Illinois posts. In consequence he organized a force of Indian bands including Menominee, Sauk, Fox, Winnebago and Sioux, under Emmanuel Hesse, together with some Canadians, traders, and their servants. Sent by various routes, these combined into a body of about 1200 for a surprise attack upon St. Louis. It was generally supposed that Cahokia, about five miles farther south, was the first British objective, but the garrison at St. Louis had some warning the previous day that they would be first attacked. In consequence the British, who had planned a surprise attack, were themselves astonished. The village was successfully defended by 50 soldiers and 280 townsmen, including a small reinforcement from Ste. Genevieve, with a loss of 104 men. The attackers were so badly demoralized and delayed that the whole expedition collapsed and the British menace from the West was entirely removed.

ST. LOUIS, MO., was founded Feb. 15, 1764, by Pierre Laclede Ligueste, a Frenchman commonly known as Laclede. He was at the time commander of an armed force and commercial enterprise organized in New Orleans to take over for a period of eight years the exclusive privilege to "trade with the savages of the Missouri and all nations residing west of the Mississippi River." When placed at the head of his "considerable armament," Laclede moved his outfit, containing a large quantity of merchandise and supplies, to Ste. Genevieve and thence across the river to Fort Chartres, where he found temporary housing. After searching the west bank of the Mississippi above this point to the mouth of the Missouri for a suitable place to build his establishment. Laclede found, in December, 1763, the best location at the present site of St. Louis: perched on a limestone bluff forty feet high and two miles long, backed up by terraces of higher ground around which the river flowed in the shape of a bow. Here he blazed with his own hands a number of trees to mark the place, and returned to Fort Chartres. There he announced that he had chosen a spot which, on account of its many natural advantages, would become one of the finest cities in America. The following February Laclede sent a party of thirty, including "two dependable men," with Auguste Chouteau to clear off the trees and begin necessary buildings on the chosen ground. In April, 1764, Laclede followed, selected the spot for his own dwelling and laid out the exact plan of the village, which he named St. Louis in honor of the patron saint of Louis XV, reigning King of France. St. Louis early became the center of the fur trade and the starting point of most expeditions and trails into the western country. Here they outfitted and gathered supplies for their journeys and from here *voyageurs*, trappers, traders and soldiers plied their labored way along the streams into the wilderness.

In 1762 in the secret treaty of Fontainebleau, France ceded to Spain all of the territory of Louisiana west of the Mississippi River and also New Orleans, but it was several years before local authorities knew of the transaction, and the first Spanish governor was driven away. Even after 1770 when Spanish Lt.-Gov. Pedro Piernas came into command at St. Louis, the village continued to be predominantly French. It was not incorporated until 1808. Soon after the purchase of Louisiana from France by the United States, the town was overrun by a large number of speculative New Englanders, who launched a very considerable boom. In course of time a new town grew up beside the old one. Here began almost perceptibly a line of cleavage between the new industrial speculative type and the old conservatives, which ultimately divided the city into two groups of different social and political caste. Racial changes in the course of time greatly altered the character of the population. Many Virginians, Kentuckians and North Carolinians moved into Missouri in the Spanish days and also after the purchase. These settled largely in rural districts but a goodly number settled in St. Louis and participated in the early fur trade, Santa Fe and Oregon expeditions as well as local merchandising. These people mixed well with the French, were accustomed to African slavery and found no antagonism in the native trend. In the early days the slaves numbered about one third of the total population.

With the advent of the steamboat St. Louis rose very rapidly in both population and wealth. From 1811 to 1882 the assessed valuation of real estate in St. Louis was multiplied about fifteen hundredfold. With a great river at her feet, and near to the outlets of many other rivers there came to her wharf river craft of every shape and kind from the many boatable tributaries of the Mississippi. Iron, lead and zinc from nearby mines; bituminous coal from across the river; farm and garden products from rich valleys nearby; hemp, cotton and sugar from the South; all contributed to make St. Louis the great river capital of the West and the second largest railroad center of the United States.

In the late 1820's a German by the name of Duden wrote many letters and stimulated considerable immigration from his native land. This influx was followed by another and larger German immigration in 1848–49. Most of these German immigrants were industrialists and became strongly allied with the New Englanders. They opposed slave labor as a kind of aristocratic paternalism, a menace to free labor and a phase of social life to which they had never been accustomed. When the sectional war excited by the crusaders against slavery was seen to be approaching, large numbers of privately drilled, unofficial German military bodies early joined in a movement to suppress the militia and block the legislative and executive departments of the state. Thus identified with the Union cause and constituting a large portion of the victorious element in the Civil War, the German population of St. Louis increased rapidly in numbers and political power.

In 1960 the population was 750,026.

ST. MARYS FALLS SHIP CANAL,

opened in 1855, is an artificial waterway on the St. Marys River connecting Lake Superior with Lake Huron. In 1797 the North West Company of Montreal constructed a small canal and lock on the north shore of the rapids of St. Marys River, where the water of Lake Superior descends some twenty-one feet to the level of Lake Huron. An American canal was projected by Michigan in 1837. It became imperative after the commencement of copper and iron mining in the next decade. Congressional aid was sought, and in 1852 a land grant of 750,000 acres was provided for this purpose. The state contracted with an eastern corporation to construct the works, and the canal was ready for use in June, 1855. Tolls were charged, but they were inadequate for the maintenance and necessary improvement of the waterway. In 1869 the legislature invited Federal operation. This was effected in 1881, when the state ceded the canal to the United States, which abolished tolls and assumed maintenance and control. The War Department is in charge and through the U. S. Engineer Corps has enlarged the canal and locks, the largest of which are 1350 feet long. The tonnage on this route considerably exceeds the combined tonnage passing through the Panama and Suez canals.

ST. MIHIEL, OPERATIONS AT

(Sept. 12–16, 1918). The front between the Moselle River and the Argonne forest having been selected as the field for American operations, after the successful Aisne-Marne offensive, in which many American divisions participated, the American First Army was organized, Aug. 10, and immediately began gathering its troops between the Moselle and Verdun. Marshal Foch and Gen. Pershing planned that this army should direct its first blow against the German salient at St. Mihiel. Nine American divisions, numbering 550,000 men, and four French divisions under Pershing's command, numbering 70,000, were assembled. Seven American divisions were placed on the south face of the salient, two American and two French divisions on the west face, and two French divisions around its tip. The Germans held this front with nine divisions of the Gallwitz Army Group, under Fuchs (about 60,000 men).

On the morning of Sept. 12, after a violent artillery bombardment, the First Army advanced into the salient and by midnight the southern attack had penetrated to an average depth of five miles. Just after daylight, Sept. 13, the 1st Division, from the south, and the 26th Division, from the west, met at Vigneulles-les-Hattonchatel, trapping 16,000 Germans in the point of the salient. Altogether 443 guns were captured. By Sept. 16 the salient was entirely obliterated. American losses had aggregated 7000.

SALEM, MASS.,

was founded by John Endecott and the colonists sent out by the Massachusetts Bay Company in the ship *Abigail*. They reached Salem Sept. 6, 1628, with a copy of the charter, which superseded the rights of the Dorchester Company under the Sheffield Patent in the area now Massachusetts. A few settlers of the defunct Dorchester Company had moved up from Cape Ann and built some huts on the peninsula of Salem as early as 1626. In 1629 came the ministers Skelton and Higginson, and there was founded on Aug. 6 the first Puritan Congregational Church modeled to a large extent on the Separatist Church at Plymouth. Roger Williams was minister of the church in 1633–35, and was forced out by the magistrates of Boston over the protests of the Salem people for political reasons. The famous Hugh Peter was the next minister, and was instrumental in starting the fisheries, on the products of which a foreign trade with Spain, Portugal and the West Indies was built up, which largely accounted for the prosperity of Salem for the next 150 years.

John Winthrop and his fleet landed at Salem on

June 12, 1630, and then proceeded to Boston Bay, around which they settled later in the summer.

In 1692 a wave of the witchcraft delusion, which had spread all over Europe, reached Salem, and an hysterical outburst of accusations occurred, chiefly at Salem Village (now Danvers). The accused were tried in Salem, and eighteen persons were hanged. All the convictions and executions occurred between June and September, 1692. The jury and most of the judges not long afterward made public confession of their error.

The town aided vigorously in all the colonial wars, and Benjamin Pickman was a dominant factor in promoting the crusade against Louisburg in 1745. The capital of Massachusetts was twice transferred to Salem; under Gov. Burnet in 1728, and under Gov. Gage in 1774. The first provincial congress was organized there in October, 1774, and the first armed resistance to the British troops occurred at the North Bridge on Feb. 26, 1775. A Salem ship, the *Quero*, carried the first news of the Battle of Lexington to England, and another, the *Astrea*, brought the first news of the treaty of peace to America. About one tenth of the privateers of the Revolution, some two hundred or more, were sent out of Salem Bay.

After the Revolution for forty years Salem ships sought out trade in every corner of the world, and actually began the foreign trade with more different ports than all other American ports combined.

SALK VACCINE. Research by and under the direction of Dr. Jonas E. Salk of the University of Pittsburgh, begun in 1949, resulted in the development of a vaccine or immunizing agent against the virus which causes poliomyelitis (infantile paralysis, so-called). Widely tested in 1954, the vaccine has been successfully administered to great numbers of people; the results obtained would indicate that active immunization against polio is now possible.

SALT was important in the domestic economy of the colonists, who, in the absence of refrigeration and canning processes, employed it not only to preserve fish and meat for home use, but for commercial manufacture when an active trade developed with the West Indies. Salt making was one of the earliest industries attempted in Virginia, New York and New England, and was carried on with varying vigor and success under the impetus of monopolies or bounties throughout the colonial period. The fishermen cured their fish chiefly, however, with salt imported from the Barbadoes, West Indies and Southern Europe, taken usually in ballast.

The interruption of foreign trade by the Revolution occasioned distressing scarcity of salt, and produced numerous small establishments along the shore from Cape Cod to Georgia. The states, urged by the Continental Congress, encouraged the industry by offering bounties and by some ventures at state salt works.

As the western country opened up after the Revolution, salt was carried over the mountains at great expense by pack horses. Saline springs and salt "licks" in many parts of the Mississippi Valley awaited capital for development. The Onondaga salines in New York were worked only after 1787, though they had been known through Jesuit priests since 1652, and remained the chief source for the West until 1810 when the strong salt of the Kanawha Valley in western Virginia offered strong competition. The famous wells in southwestern Virginia remained undeveloped until about 1782.

The discovery of salt wells in Michigan on the eve of the Civil War was opportune, for the Mississippi Valley had been depending chiefly on the Kanawha salt and on foreign importations at New Orleans. So active was Michigan competition with New York salt that the price in the North averaged 87½ cents a bushel, while in the South it soared to $35 and more.

In the 20th century the United States became the world's greatest producer of salt. The great "domes" of rock salt of Louisiana, the beds in Texas, as well as the salt lagoons along the coast, and the sheets of rock salt found in New York and Michigan, have been exploited. Discovery of a salt field in Kansas, while boring for natural gas, was fortunate for the packing industry in the vicinity. The solar system of evaporation has proved practicable on the shores of the Great Salt Lake and on San Francisco Bay. Manufacturing processes have been greatly improved and the production increased by the demand for salt in chemical manufactures and ore reduction plants. Since 1892 the country has produced more than it has consumed.

SALT LAKE CITY, UTAH. Laid out in 10-acre squares with streets 132 feet wide, following the plan of the "City of Zion" prepared in 1833 by Joseph Smith, Salt Lake City was founded by Brigham Young and the Mormons in 1847. The city is the headquarters of the Church of Jesus Christ of Latter-Day Saints, or Mormons, and is noted for its many fine structures, including the Mormon Temple and Tabernacle. The Temple is of Utah gray granite from the Wasatch Mountains and was forty years in course of construction (1853–93). In 1960 the population was 189,454.

SALZBURGERS IN GEORGIA. In 1734 a group of 78 Salzburgers, who had been driven out of their European home by the Bishop of Salzburg, landed in the new colony of Georgia. They were settled by James Oglethorpe up the Savannah River at a place which they called Ebenezer. Being dissatisfied with their original location, they were moved to a more convenient spot on the river itself, bringing the name Ebenezer with them. By 1741, 1200 Salzburgers were living in Georgia, mostly in Ebenezer and the surrounding territory, but a few had settled on St. Simons Island. Lutheran in religion and German in language, they were largely ruled over by their ministers.

SAN ANTONIO, TEXAS, was founded in 1718 by the establishment of a mission and *presidio,* or military camp. Some of the soldiers were married, and their families formed the nucleus of a village, or civil settlement. Several years later a chain of missions was established in the valley below San Antonio, and in 1731 the village was reinforced by a small colony from the Canary Islands. The settlement thus became the civil and military capital of Texas during the Spanish-Mexican regime.

The prominence of San Antonio in state and regional life and literature is derived chiefly from its historic past. During the Texas revolution, it was first captured from its strong Mexican garrison by siege (December, 1835) and later recaptured by Santa Anna in the tragic assault on the Alamo (March, 1836), only to be regained by the Texans as a result of their victory at San Jacinto (April, 1836), which practically established the independence of the Republic of Texas. As the largest settlement on the southern and western frontier, San Antonio was exposed to raids from Mexicans and Indians. During 1842 it was twice occupied by Mexican raiders and was the scene of desperate fighting in which a considerable proportion of the Comanche leaders were massacred after having assembled for a council to discuss terms of peace. Soon after the annexation of Texas by the United States, San Antonio became the chief military post in a line of forts that the Federal Government established to guard the southern and western frontier.

Prior to the development of ranching on the west Texas plains, in the early 1880's, San Antonio was the headquarters of the Texas cattle industry. The population in 1960 was 687,718.

SAN DIEGO, CALIF., named after Didacus de Alcalá, a Franciscan saint, was founded in 1769 by Gaspár de Portolá, governor of Lower California. A military post until 1835, it occupied the site known today as Old Town, while Mission San Diego lay five miles up so-called Mission Valley. Being a seaport and close to the Mexican border, San Diego loomed large in the disturbances following Mexico's emancipation from Spain and in the later conflict between Mexico and the United States. Though a civil government was established in 1835, the town had in 1840 only 150 inhabitants. It was practically extinct when eight years later California became a state. The present metropolis, three miles below Old Town, was founded in 1867 by A. E. Horton, a merchant prospector of San Francisco. At San Diego in 1846 the United States flag was officially raised for the first time on California soil. The population in 1960 was 573,224.

SAN FRANCISCO, CALIF. The peninsula site of the present city of San Francisco was first occupied in 1776. Called Yerba Buena until 1847, the isolated Spanish-Mexican outpost was for sixty years distinguished only by a derelict *presidio* and mission. In 1835 it became a station for New England whalers and hide traders. From that date San Francisco was in all but fact an American community. Yankee economic superiority over the rival Hudson's Bay Company was speedily achieved and the U. S. Government became aware of the strategic value of the great landlocked harbor into which drain the river systems of the Sierra Nevada. After a decade of unsuccessful bargaining with Mexico over the purchase of the Bay region, U. S. Marines were landed on July 9, 1846, and American rule was established without opposition.

The discovery of gold in 1848 transformed San Francisco suddenly from a quiet port into one of the world's richest and most famous cities. In the score of years between the gold rush and the completion of the transcontinental railroad in 1869, perhaps 400,000 people came to San Francisco. These extraordinarily diverse and talented immigrants created out of their own resources, and in isolation, the most splendid society yet raised on any frontier. Not the least of their achievements was securing the state for the Union cause in 1861. Offsetting this was a legacy of lawlessness and violence inherited from the gold era. The city government's failure to deal effectively with crime led in 1851 and 1856 to the organization of citizens' vigilance committees and the execution or exile of the most conspicuous criminals. But politics continued corrupt until 1906, when a sweeping graft investigation brought about the victory of a reform party.

The coming of the railroad coincided with the passing of the pioneer phase of frontier exploitation, and with it San Francisco began a difficult period of economic and social adjustment. By 1876 the city recovered sufficiently from the silver panic to extend itself to almost its present limits. At the turn of the century the growth of industry and agriculture, together with the development of the Alaskan and Pacific trade, gave San Francisco a position among the nation's ten leading cities. Then, in three days of April, 1906, the city was destroyed by earthquake and fire. Four square miles were burned and $500,-000,000 worth of property destroyed; 500 people were buried in the debris and another 250,000 fled homeless to the parks and beaches. The city was rebuilt in haste on its old foundations rather than to the magnificent plans prepared by Daniel Burnham. In the era between the fire and World War II San Francisco held international expositions marking the opening of the Panama Canal and the completion of bridges linking the city with Oakland and Marin County; experienced a series of bitter waterfront strikes which ended in the decline of the once great port; and was the scene of the historic conference which drafted the charter of the United Nations. San Francisco has remained secure in its position as the financial capital of the West. Its population in 1960 was 742,855.

SAN ILDEFONSO, TREATY OF. By this treaty, exe-cuted in preliminary form on Oct. 1, 1800, and made effective on Oct. 15, 1802, Louisiana was re-ceded by Spain to France in return for an Italian kingdom of Etruria.

Sovereign over Louisiana only since the French and Indian War, Spain had developed neither economic profit nor colonial attachment, but in surrendering the province, the king of Spain ignored vital issues of strategy and national prestige. He negotiated without the knowledge of his minister, Manuel Godoy, who, on learning the facts, was shocked by the levity with which an empire had been alienated. Godoy's chagrin equaled the elation of Lucien Bonaparte, Napoleon's brother, who assumed much credit for the French success. While Spain was losing a vast but unprofit-able domain beyond the Mississippi, Napoleon be-lieved himself restorer of the colonial empire lost so ignominiously by his Bourbon predecessors.

Rumors of the pending transfer rekindled Thomas Jefferson's interest in the Mississippi Valley and moti-vated the dispatch of James Monroe to France in 1803 and the resultant purchase of Louisiana.

SAN JACINTO, BATTLE OF (April 21, 1836). On March 11, 1836, five days after the Alamo debacle, Gen. Sam Houston took command of 374 men at Gonzales and two days later began his retreat from Santa Anna's advance. Extermination of forces under Fannin and King left Houston's band the sole body under arms in the republic. Difficulties were increased by the flight of the government and of the civil population toward the United States border and the Gulf ports. For 37 days Houston retreated, adding to the force he held together by the exercise of personal authority, while Santa Anna divided his army in pur-suit. With 800 men, on April 20, Houston intercepted Santa Anna, with 910, at a ferry over the San Jacinto. Brushing aside a Mexican reconnaissance in force, Houston waited for 540 men under Cos to join Santa Anna the following morning, in order, he later said, not "to take two bites of a cherry." Then, cutting down a bridge protecting his own as well as the Mexicans' avenue of retreat, Houston formed up under a screen of trees and attacked. Santa Anna's surprise was complete. A thinly held barricade protecting his camp being quickly overrun, organized resistance was at an end in twenty minutes. The rest was slaughter. Texan figures on enemy casualties—630 killed, 208 wounded, 730 prisoners—are inexact, the total rep-resenting 200 more men than Santa Anna had on the field. Texan losses were 16 killed, 24 wounded in-cluding Gen. Houston. Santa Anna, a prisoner, signed armistice terms under which the other divisions of his army immediately evacuated Texas.

SAN JUAN HILL AND EL CANEY. After the with-drawal of Spanish outposts from Las Guasimas, the key points defending Santiago, Cuba, against Shafter's advance, June, 1898, were along the line San Juan Hill, northeasterly to El Caney. The former was di-rectly in the path of the American advance; the latter protected the city from envelopment by the American right wing.

On July 1 the Americans attacked along the entire line. Lawton's division, on the right, carried El Caney. The attack against San Juan Hill was not so well timed. Kent's division and the dismounted cavalry, including the Rough Riders, advancing as much from desperation as by design, captured San Juan. This placed the American army in control of high ground overlooking the city, and in position to isolate the city. Admiral Cervera, alarmed by possibilities of American artillery on hills overlooking the bay in which his fleet was anchored, sought safety, July 4, in a dash to sea—and destruction. Santiago surrendered July 17.

SAND CREEK MASSACRE is the most controversial subject in Colorado history. Following repeated Indian raids and depredations in 1864, giving the Indians control of all lines of travel between Denver and the Missouri River, thus cutting off supplies, and with the Government unable to render effective defense be-cause of the Civil War, local military authorities de-cided that punitive measures were necessary. Col. J. M. Chivington, commanding the District of Colorado, on Nov. 29, 1864, with about 900 soldiers made a surprise attack at Sand Creek near Fort Lyon on a camp of Cheyennes and some Arapahoes, containing about 200 warriors and about 500 women and chil-dren. Estimates of Indians killed range from 150 to 500 with a loss of 10 soldiers. Controversy still rages over whether these Indians were peaceful or hostile; whether they considered themselves under protection; justification for killing women and children; responsi-bility for the attack and other points.

SANITARY COMMISSION, UNITED STATES, was created by the U. S. Government in June, 1861, under the presidency of Rev. H. W. Bellows, a noted Uni-tarian divine, who had been active in organizing war-relief work. Its purpose was to assist in the care of sick and wounded soldiers and of their dependent families. It was supported mainly by private contri-butions. Most of the local Aid Societies, active since the very first days of the war, immediately affiliated as branches of the national organization.

The Commission developed an elaborate organiza-tion and at times employed as many as five hundred agents. Its work covered almost every conceivable form of aid, such as field and hospital medical in-spection, field ambulance and hospital service, and hospital cars and steamers. It also maintained feeding stations and soldiers' lodges, and supplied assistance to dependent families. Funds were raised by churches, private contributions, and especially by Sanitary Fairs. Camp life was much improved by its work.

SANITATION, the preservation of health, has grown from the taking of simple precautions against epidemics during early American history to the complex regulations of the present. In colonial and later times, health officers were stationed at the Atlantic ports to inspect incoming ships. Subject to yellow fever particularly, coastal towns adopted elaborate precautions to prevent the introduction of disease. The dearth of scientific information, however, led to many regulations which seem ridiculous in the light of subsequent knowledge. As late as 1797 a Pennsylvania law regulating the "importation of Germans" provided that the ship at sea weekly burn charcoal or tobacco between decks and wash down the ship with vinegar. On the other hand, we get both a respect for the medical profession and a picture of the American city from a letter written by the College of Physicians of Philadelphia to the governor of the state, suggesting measures to be taken to mitigate the yellow-fever menace. It was proposed that the city be cleaned up, that sewers be closed and that filth be quickly removed.

Satisfactory precautions could not usually be taken against disease until the nature of disease itself was known. These precautions followed Pasteur's discoveries. The simplest measures would be obtaining a constant water supply, sewage disposal and refuse collection. It was only with regard to the first that American cities made any noticeable progress before 1880. Boston had a water-pipe system as early as 1652. The emphasis in the water-supply systems, however, was on quantity instead of quality. Although sand filters were introduced in Poughkeepsie in 1885, as late as 1908 few other cities had followed its example. As more sewer systems contaminated the rivers, New York and other large cities began to pipe their water from uninfected sources.

American cities were frequently swept by epidemics. With the exception of vaccination for smallpox, introduced into this country in 1799, the precautions taken in all cases were too late, consisting of efforts to confine diseases within communities by means of quarantine laws and within the communities themselves by means of pesthouses. It was an epidemic of unusual severity in Memphis in 1879 which focused national attention on sewage disposal. Over 5000 people died of yellow fever. Congress acted; a National Board of Health was set up which investigated conditions in the city. The nation was shocked at the conditions exposed. Shortly after (1887) the Massachusetts Board of Health undertook a systematic study of methods of sewage disposal. Septic tanks proved a failure. Around 1915 Milwaukee and Cleveland developed the aerated sludge system by which sewage was nitrified and purified by means of aerating in series of tanks. Too expensive for cities with population under 25,000 people, its cost was subsequently reduced by making the purified sewage available as fertilizer.

Garbage removal was a third basis of better sanitation. At first garbage was dumped in waste lands, where it provided a breeding place for flies and rats. The first garbage furnace was built by Lt. H. J. Reilly of the U. S. Army in 1885 on Governors Island, New York Harbor. Slowly municipal incinerators have been making progress against dumping grounds. Cleveland reclaimed some of the cost by selling the residue as a low-grade fertilizer. One other improvement was the use of covered cans for garbage collection.

Control of epidemics, pure water supply, sewage disposal and garbage removal constitute only a beginning in public sanitation. Demand for drugs of a decent standard led in the 1840's to appointment of drug inspectors at the ports and to the subsequent Pure Food and Drugs Acts of 1906 and 1938. Publicity attending the information on the large number of deaths caused by adulterated meats in the Spanish-American War together with Upton Sinclair's *The Jungle* led to the Meat Inspection Act of 1906. Since the turn of the century two factors have enlarged the scope of sanitary regulations: more accurate information on the origin and spread of diseases, and increased communal activities. With regard to the first, sanitary regulations are designed to rid the country of disease carriers. With regard to the second, great industries have developed which have taken the place of small-scale or home activity in the past. Milk distribution, bread making and meat packing are only a few. Amusements have been commercialized with the result that swimming pools, tourist camps and theaters, for example, must be controlled for cleanliness and ventilation. The relation between noise and the health of city dwellers is also receiving increased attention.

SANTA FE. Abandoning their first settlement in New Mexico, on the Rio Chama, the Spaniards selected for their capital a more suitable site twenty-five miles to the southeast. Here in 1609 Gov. Peralta founded the present city of Santa Fe. In 1630 the town numbered about 1050 inhabitants, of whom 250 were Spaniards. It suffered severely during the Pueblo Revolt in 1680 and was always exposed to Navaho and Comanche raids. After the reconquest (1693) and during the first half of the 18th century, Santa Fe with its 1500 inhabitants was the objective of Mexican traders from Chihuahua and of French traders from the Mississippi Valley, whose activities after 1763 were continued by the Americans over the famous Santa Fe Trail. During the first decades of the 19th century and the later troubles between the United States and Mexico it was often the scene of political disturbances. Gen. Kearny occupied the city in 1846 and suppressed the revolt that broke out the next year. Santa Fe remained the capital when, in 1850, Congress organized New Mexico into a territory and in 1912 made it a sovereign state.

SANTA FE TRAIL, famed in history and fiction, was an important commerce route for the 59 years between 1821 and 1880. Since the greater extent of its 780 miles lay across the plains and avoided the rivers, wagons could easily traverse it. As the trail was extended south from Santa Fe for an additional thousand miles through El Paso, Chihuahua and Durango, wagon masters continued to find natural roads the entire distance.

Prior to the opening of the trail, Santa Fe was supplied with goods brought by mule back at great expense from the Mexican seaport of Vera Cruz, over a roundabout path, the last 500 miles of which were infested with Apaches, whose very name signifies robber. Thus, while Santa Fe was rich in silver, wool and mules, she lacked the simplest manufactured articles. News of this condition came to the Mallet Brothers of Canada, who crossed the plains to Santa Fe in 1739. In succeeding years more Frenchmen passed at intervals from the Missouri or from Arkansas Post to the Rio Grande. Zebulon M. Pike, American Army lieutenant, arriving in 1807, met two Americans, Baptiste LaLande and James Purcell, who had preceded him to Santa Fe in 1804 and 1805 respectively.

American attempts at Santa Fe trade met with summary action by Spanish authorities, who arrested twelve St. Louisans in 1812 and imprisoned them for nine years, and arrested A. P. Chouteau's St. Louis fur brigade in 1815 for merely trapping on the Upper Arkansas. Chouteau's property, valued at $30,000, was confiscated, but he was released after 48 days. Information that Mexico had overthrown Spanish rule and that traders were welcome in Santa Fe came to three Indian traders on the plains late in 1821. First of the three to arrive was William Becknell, of Arrow Rock, Mo., who reached Santa Fe Nov. 16 and sold his Indian trade goods at from ten to twenty times higher than St. Louis prices. Thomas James of St. Louis and Hugh Glenn, Osage Indian trader, arrived later and also were welcomed. There was no well-defined Santa Fe Trail prior to Becknell's journey. The Mallets, LaLande and Purcell followed the Platte River part way to the mountains. Chouteau and Glenn traversed the Osage trail from southwest Missouri to the Arkansas. James crossed the present Oklahoma and Arkansas from the Mississippi.

Becknell, father of the trail, started from the steamboat landing of Franklin, Mo., followed the prairie divide between the tributaries of the Kansas and the Arkansas to the Great Bend of the Arkansas, then followed the Arkansas almost to the mountains before turning south to New Mexico. His route became the Santa Fe Trail of history. All early travelers transported their goods by pack horse. In 1822 Becknell, on his second journey, carried part of his merchandise in wagons. After that wagons were generally employed. The Missouri River terminus was first Franklin, then Independence and finally Westport (now Kansas City). At the western end the trail turned south to Santa Fe from the Arkansas by three different ways. The Taos Trail diverged from the Arkansas at the Huerfano River. A middle course branched from the Arkansas west of the mouth of Purgatory River to cross Raton Pass. The shortest and in later times the most-traveled route was the Cimarron Cutoff, leaving the Arkansas near the present Cimarron, Kans. (this crossing varied), and proceeding southwest across the Cimarron Valley.

Merchants traveled in caravans, the wagons moving in parallel columns so that they might be quickly formed into a circular corral, with livestock inside, to repel Indian attacks. Indians seldom risked battle with well-organized caravans. Such phrases as "the trail was red with blood" or "bleached bones marked the trail" are pure romance. Up to 1843 Gregg reported the Indians killed but eleven men on the trail. Losses were greatest from 1864 to 1869, the bloodiest year being 1868 when seventeen stagecoach passengers were captured and burned at Cimarron Crossing. In that year Gen. Custer's *Wild Life on the Plains* lists 45 deaths on or near the trail.

Santa Fe trade brought to the United States much-needed silver, gave America the Missouri mule and led to the conquest of New Mexico in the Mexican War. Here are comparative figures as to westward-bound traffic on the trail at three different periods: Gregg reported that 350 persons transported $450,000 worth of goods at St. Louis prices in 1843, the largest year up to that time. Lt. Col. Gilpin's register shows 3000 wagons, 12,000 persons and 50,000 animals in twelve months of 1848–49, a large part of the number being bound for California. The register at Council Grove, Kans., in 1860 showed 3514 persons with 2567 wagons, 61 carriages and stagecoaches, 5819 mules, 478 horses and 22,738 oxen. Federal mail service by stagecoach was instituted in 1849. Completion of the last section of the railroad from Topeka to Santa Fe in 1880 ended the importance of the wagon road.

SANTANTA'S WARS ranged from Texas to Kansas in the period following the Civil War. An accomplished warrior and an adept at the art of deception, the Kiowa chief caused trouble for Custer, Sheridan and Sherman in numerous raids. Cattlemen and settlers also felt his heavy hand. He was at the Battle of Adobe Walls (1874). After imprisonment in Texas, he was paroled, raided again in Texas, was reimprisoned, and finally killed himself rather than serve a life sentence. At the Medicine Lodge Treaty in 1867 Santanta stated the case of the irreconcilables in the following words:

"I love the land and the buffalo and will not part with it. I want the children raised as I was. I don't want to settle. I love to roam over the prairies. A long time ago this land belonged to our fathers; but when I go up the river I see camps of soldiers on its banks. These soldiers cut down my timber; they kill my buffalo; and when I see that it feels as if my heart would burst with sorrow."

SANTIAGO, BLOCKADE AND BATTLE OF. Ten days after Cervera's four armored cruisers arrived in Santiago de Cuba on May 19, 1898, they were blockaded by Sampson and Schley with the battleships *Massachusetts, Iowa, Indiana, Oregon* and *Texas,* and by the armored cruisers *New York* and *Brooklyn.* At nine o'clock on the morning of July 3 Cervera dashed out to avoid being caught in a trap by the army encircling the city. As the flagship, *Infanta Maria Teresa,* headed westward, followed by the *Vizcaya, Colon* and *Oquendo,* the blockaders quickly closed in and concentrated on the *Teresa,* which within fifteen minutes was set on fire and three quarters of an hour later driven ashore, as was also the *Oquendo.* By eleven o'clock the *Vizcaya* was crippled and beached, and at one o'clock the *Colon,* a new and fast ship, already under fire from the 13-inch guns of the *Oregon,* lowered her colors and turned shorewards. Meanwhile the *Gloucester* had forced the Spanish destroyer *Pluton* ashore, where she soon blew up. Another Spanish destroyer, the *Furor,* was sent to the bottom by a heavy shell from the *New York.*

The greater Spanish loss, 600 killed, as compared with one American killed and one seriously wounded, was due primarily to the American rapid-fire guns, which swept the decks, ignited the woodwork and drove the gunners from their stations. The victory removed all chance of Spanish naval resistance in the New World, and greatly increased the respect which Europe held for the American Navy.

Schley, second in command, had been on the *Brooklyn* in the very forefront of the engagement, so close indeed that when the *Teresa* turned toward the *Brooklyn* as if to ram, Schley circled back and narrowly avoided a collision with the other ships. As Sampson was not within firing distance during most of the fight, having gone in the *New York* for a conference with Gen. Shafter, a controversy arose as to who should receive the chief credit for the victory.

SARAH CONSTANT, flagship of the three vessels conveying the founders of the first successful English settlement in the New World, sailed down the Thames for Virginia Dec. 20, 1606 (O.S.). She (100 tons) and her consorts, the *Goodspeed* (40 tons) and the *Discovery* (20 tons), were under the command of Christopher Newport. Delayed off the coast by contrary winds until February, Newport followed the southern route via the West Indies. Arriving at the entrance of the Chesapeake Bay, a landing was made April 26, 1607 (O.S.), at the cape which was named Henry. After sailing well up the Powhatan, or James, River in order to have better protection against attacks by Spaniards, the colonists established themselves upon "an extended plaine and spot of earth, which thrust out into the depth and middest of the channel." Here the *Sarah Constant* and her sister ships were "moored to the trees in six fathoms of water," and the site was named James-Forte or Jamestowne.

SARATOGA, SURRENDER AT (Oct. 17, 1777). After his defeat at the second battle of Freeman's Farm on Oct. 7, Gen. John Burgoyne with his 4500 men slowly retreated northward. He neglected to crush a detachment of 1300 Continental militia commanded by Gen. John Fellows, which had been posted to block his retreat, but instead took up a strong position near Old Saratoga (now Schuylerville, N. Y.). The British troops were dead tired, and their supplies were running low. The American forces under Gen. Horatio Gates now consisted of about 5000 regulars and more than 12,000 militia. Gates almost made a fatal mistake by ordering an attack against the British position on Oct. 11 under the misconception that it was defended only by a rear guard, but he finally changed his mind, perhaps at the suggestion of Col. James Wilkinson.

Burgoyne could not decide what to do, though a prompt and complete retreat was the only logical course left open to him. While he hesitated, Gates surrounded his position. Burgoyne finally asked for terms on Oct. 13. Gates at first demanded an unconditional surrender but on Oct. 15 weakly accepted Burgoyne's "convention," which provided that the British troops should be returned to England on condition that they would take no further part in the war. Burgoyne, having heard that Sir Henry Clinton had captured the Continental forts near West Point (Highlands, 1777–81) and was sending an expedition against Albany, now tried to delay the surrender. The negotiations came to resemble a comic opera, but on the afternoon of Oct. 16 Burgoyne accepted the inevitable, and the formal laying down of arms took place on the next day. Burgoyne, with a graceful bow, said, "The fortune of war, General Gates, has made me your prisoner," and Gates courteously replied, "I shall always be ready to testify that it has not been through any fault of your Excellency." This event marked the turning point of the American Revolution, since France now decided to enter the war as an ally of the thirteen United States.

SAULT STE. MARIE, FRENCH MISSION AND TRADING POST AT. The sault or rapids of St. Marys River, which discharges the waters of Lake Superior into Lake Huron, were a favorite rendezvous in colonial days for Indians and traders. The limitless supply of excellent whitefish to be found in the rapids was a lure to the Indians, who, moreover, if they came from the North, had to pass through this locality on their trading trips to the lower St. Lawrence. The designation, Sault Ste. Marie (St. Marys Falls or Rapids), originated with the Jesuit missionaries. The first white man to reach the Sault appears to have been Etienne Brulé, *ca.* 1622, followed in 1634 by Jean Nicolet, and in 1641 by the Jesuits, St. Isaac Jogues and Father Charles Raymbaut, who gave the place its first distinct mention in the records. In 1668 Father Jacques Marquette opened on the south (American) side of the rapids, at their foot, a mission post around which grew up the earliest settlement of whites in Michigan. He is generally taken to be the founder, as he was the first chronicler, of Sault Ste. Marie.

The Jesuit mission was in 1670 a square enclosure of cedar posts twelve feet high with chapel and residence within. The Indian population of the Sault numbered some 2000 souls, among them the Chippewa or Saulters, so called from their customary habitat at the rapids. As a trading center and crossroads the place began early to decline, owing, among other causes, to the enterprise of the Hudson's Bay Company, which directed much trade to the North, and to Cadillac's policy of concentrating the Indians at Detroit. Later came a revival, the North West Company, and afterward the American Fur Company, maintaining important posts at the Sault. The mission also declined toward the end of the 17th century, the last resident pastor, Father Albanel, dying in 1696, after which date there was no resident clergyman of any denomination at Sault Ste. Marie until 1831.

SAVANNAH was the first settlement in the colony of Georgia. Having made friends with the Yamacraw Indians who occupied the site, James Oglethorpe on Feb. 12, 1733, landed his colonists and immediately laid out a town with numerous squares breaking the monotony of the streets—a plan adhered to in the subsequent growth of the city. The principal thoroughfare was named Bull for William Bull, a South Carolinian, who aided the settlers in the early days. Each colonist was given five acres for a building lot, a garden and land to cultivate on the outskirts of the city. Though other settlements were made, Savannah continued for the next century to be the principal town in the colony and state. It became the seat of the local governmental division (called first Christ Church Parish and after 1777 Chatham County) and it remained the capital city until 1786. The first commercial house carrying on foreign trade was Harris & Habersham, founded in 1744, and the first printing press was set up here by James Johnston in 1763, which began the same year to publish the *Georgia Gazette,* the first newspaper in the colony. The Anglicans, Presbyterians and Jews early established congregations and erected houses for worship, the first-named being served during 1736 and 1737 by John Wesley.

Savannah was the center of opposition to British authority as the Revolution drew near. During the exciting years of 1765–66, Liberty Boys spiked royal cannon and rolled them down the river banks, burned in effigy the royal governor, drove out the stamp agent, and forced the removal of the stamps. A Council of Safety was appointed in 1775, and here the various provincial congresses met preparatory to driving out of the colony in 1776 the royal governor Sir James Wright. In December, 1778, the British seized the city and held it until 1782, making it again the capital of the royal government and in the mean-

time beating off in October, 1779, a furious attack by the French and Americans.

In 1786 Savannah ceased to be the capital, losing the prize to Augusta. Its growth in population and trade though steady was never spectacular. In 1810 it had a population of about 5000; twenty years later it had about 7700; in 1850 there were 14,000; and at the end of the Civil War it was 24,000. Its exports in 1773 were valued at about $380,000; in 1788 the first bale of cotton was shipped out; in 1800 its exports, coastwise and foreign, amounted to over $2,000,-000, which had increased in 1860 to $18,000,000.

The city has been visited by two disastrous fires, 1796 and 1820, the latter being the greatest conflagration to strike any American city up to that time. In ante-bellum times the city was visited by two yellow-fever epidemics, 1820 and 1854.

Early in the Civil War the city's outer defenses (Fort Pulaski) fell, and in December, 1864, Gen. Sherman captured the city. After the war its growth was marked, though its prosperity has been somewhat marred by the decline in its naval stores and cotton exports. In 1960 the population was 149,245.

SAVANNAH (steamship) was the first ship to cross the Atlantic Ocean, propelled or aided by steam. Built in New York as a sailing ship with auxiliary steam power, it was bought by a shipping company in Savannah, Ga., whence it sailed for Liverpool on May 22, 1819, arriving 29 days later.

SAVINGS AND LOAN ASSOCIATIONS began with the Oxford Provident Building Association founded in 1831 in a suburb of Philadelphia. Early associations were simply co-operative clubs, usually created by working-class people of limited resources to build themselves homes. Gradually they became more formal, opened offices and sought members who did not plan to build. The number grew rapidly after the Civil War, reaching 5800 by 1893. They were usually called building and loan associations, but they were also known as "co-operative banks" in New England and "homestead associations" in Louisiana. Since the 1930's they have favored the name of "saving and loan association." Lenders and borrowers both are voting members of these mutual organizations. Persons placing savings with them are, strictly speaking, not depositors but shareholders and receive dividends, not interest.

Bank failures and withdrawals of bank savings in the depressed early 1930's limited mortgage loans, held back home building, and thus blocked an important route to economic recovery. The Hoover administration by act of July 22, 1932, set up the Federal Home Loan System with eleven regional Banks and a Home Loan Bank Board in Washington to facilitate again the flow of mortgage funds. Anyone familiar with the American dual banking system of state and nationally chartered banks and the Federal

Reserve System will recognize much the same pattern in the savings and loan world. The Home Owners Loan Act of June 13, 1933, provided for the first time for nationally chartered Federal Savings and Loan Associations. These had to belong to the Federal Home Loan Bank System but state associations might also become members. Member associations' purchases of stock and their deposits in Federal Home Loan Banks provide those institutions with much of their capital. The Home Loan Board also directs the Federal Savings and Loan Insurance Corporation, created by law of June 27, 1934, to insure savings accounts. State member associations are not obliged to belong to it although most large ones do.

Between 1933 and 1959 total associations declined from 10,956 to 6230. Of the latter, 1841 were Federal and 3976 were insured. About 94% of all savings accounts were insured up to $10,000. Savings and loan associations were among the fastest growing of savings institutions in this period. Their savings accounts grew from a modest $4,800,000,000 to a large $54,500,000,000, putting them in much the same class as commercial banks' time deposits, life insurance companies' paid-up policies and U. S. Savings Bond issues. Associations normally invest about 80% of their funds in mortgages and they had about $50,000,000,000 so invested in 1959. During the 1950's savings and loan associations supplied between 29% and 38% a year of all monies loaned to finance nonfarm homes. Savings made available through these associations are in considerable part responsible for the fact that nonfarm home ownership grew from 41% in 1940 to 61% in 1960.

SAYBROOK PLATFORM was a revision of the ecclesiastical polity of the colony of Connecticut, drawn up by a synod meeting at the call of the legislature in Saybrook, Sept. 9, 1708. Its chief feature was an accentuation of the principle of "consociation" or rule by councils, away from the independency of early Congregationalism. The Platform was the outcome of a wide feeling in conservative circles that the Cambridge Platform, which gave to synods a right merely to "advise" individual churches, did not furnish adequate authority for keeping all churches in line. At Saybrook the churches were organized into county associations, ruled by a council of ministers and lay delegates, which was given extensive disciplinary powers over erring congregations, and supervision over the choice of new pastors; county associations then sent delegates to an annual assembly which regulated the whole colony. A similar movement in Massachusetts, resulting in the ministerial Proposals of 1705, failed because of a lack of legislative support and the attacks of John Wise; in Connecticut, governmental support of the Platform effectively transformed the polity of the 18th century into a centrally administered unit, making the church practically a form of Presbyterianism.

SCALPING AND SCALP BOUNTIES. Among many tribes of American Indians the scalp proper, a circular patch of skin and hair at the crown of the head, was allowed to grow long and abundant as a conspicuous ornament. The remainder of the hair was shaved or cut short. Before contact with the white man, the only Indian tribes to scalp their foes were the Iroquois, Muskhogean Choctaws, Chickasaws and Creeks. The process was extremely painful but not always fatal. A circular incision was made about the scalp lock, and it was alternately pulled and cut from the head. If taken as a trophy, nearly the whole scalp might be peeled off, stretched on a hoop, cleaned and dried, painted on the underside and fastened to a short pole.

The white frontiersmen quickly adopted the Indian custom, and British, French, Colonial and United States governments all came to offer rewards for the taking of enemy scalps. It was customary to justify the bounties by pointing to "the Cruel & Barbarous Practice of Scalping our Inhabitants" followed by the enemy Indians and to the "absolute necessity in Retaliation to Pursue the same Methods." Scalps of grown men usually brought about twenty-five to fifty dollars (though the colony of Massachusetts once offered as much as £100), and those of women and children half that amount. Occasionally a humane provision of the bounty laws offered double the scalp bounty for prisoners, but, of course, scalps could usually be transported more easily than prisoners. Urged on by the bounties, which were still offered during the Indian wars of the 19th century, and by thousands of "scalping knives" given or sold by traders and government agents, the gruesome practice of scalping spread among the Indians of the central and western United States.

SCHENK v. UNITED STATES (249 U. S. 47, 1919). The Espionage Act of 1917 penalized any attempt to cause disloyalty in the Army or Navy or to obstruct recruiting. Schenk, secretary of the Socialist party, circulated leaflets encouraging resistance to the draft. He was convicted and the act was sustained in an opinion in which Justice Holmes made his famous statement that "the words used" in every case must tend "to create a near and present danger" of substantive evils which Congress has a right to prevent.

SCHOOL LANDS. When Congress created new states out of the public domain it reserved to itself the management and disposal of the public land within their boundaries. However, it granted land to the states for various purposes, chief of which was to aid the development of elementary schools. Beginning with 1803, Congress granted one section in each township for school purposes to the new states as they were admitted into the Union; in 1850 the grant was increased to two sections in each township and in 1896 it was again increased to four sections in each township. Twelve states received one section, thirteen states received two sections and four states received four sections in each township.

The pressure of public opinion prevented these lands being held for high prices and induced the legislatures to take early action for this disposal. Ohio, the first public-land state, tried a number of experiments in managing its school lands, among them being short-term leases, perpetual leases for 12 cents per acre, 99-year leases at 6% of appraised valuation, one-year leases and sale at a minimum price of $5 per acre. Some states, like Ohio, held the lands and proceeds from them as trustees for the townships while others, like Indiana, turned them over to the townships. Local management generally led to favoritism, careless administration and reckless use of the funds derived from the sale. State management frequently played into the hands of large speculator groups as in Wisconsin where individuals acquired as much as 57,000 acres of school lands. Wisconsin and Nebraska loaned their school-land funds to individuals, taking mortgages on the lands of these persons as security and when payments were delayed were forced to foreclose. The more common procedure was to require that the school funds should be invested in state bonds paying 6% interest. Despite the haste in selling, the mismanagement of the funds and the actual diversion of receipts by some of the states the lands did aid materially in making possible elementary schools in communities where the tax base was insufficient to permit the establishment of schools or where school taxes were opposed.

Management of school lands in the newer states of the Far West has been more successful than it was in Ohio, Illinois or Wisconsin, partly because Congress attempted to prescribe more fully the conditions under which the lands should be sold and partly because the states have been more prudent in their administration of them. Such states as Minnesota, North Dakota and Washington, to cite only a few, have accumulated large funds from their school lands, the income from which comprises a substantial part of the state contribution to the public schools.

SCHOONER. In its pure form, this vessel originated at Gloucester, Mass., in 1713–14. It is fore-and-aft rigged, originally small (50- to 100-ton), with two masts, designed for coastwise trade, but developed in the 1880's and 1890's to vessels of two or three thousand tons, having 4, 5 and even 6 masts, engaged also in foreign trade. Only one 7-master was attempted (1901–2), the *Thomas Lawson*, 368 feet long, of 5200 tons.

The schooner has always stood as the favorite and distinctive rig of American waters.

SCIOTO COMPANY. In July, 1787, through the agency of Manasseh Cutler, the Ohio Company's representative, a group of New York speculators, headed by William Duer, Secretary of the Treasury

Board, secured from Congress an option to a great tract of land lying north and west of the Ohio Company purchase and extending to the Scioto River on the west. As later surveyed, it contained 4,901,480 acres. Payment was to be made in six installments at 66⅔ cents an acre, the first payment due six months after the boundary had been surveyed. A number of New York and Massachusetts speculators divided the thirty shares among themselves with Duer, Royal Flint and Andrew Craigie acting as trustees, and Richard Platt as treasurer. Joel Barlow was sent to France as their agent and organized, with William Playfair, an unscrupulous Englishman, the Compagnie du Scioto to sell the Scioto lands. Although sales were active at first, little cash came in and the French company presently collapsed. The financial panic of 1792 swept away the fortunes of the leading American partners, and the Scioto Company defaulted on its contract with the Government. Gallipolis was the only settlement resulting from its efforts.

SCOPES TRIAL. A Tennessee statute of March 21, 1925, forbade any educational institution supported by public funds "to teach the theory that denies the story of the divine creation of man as taught in the Bible." In a test case, John T. Scopes, a teacher of biology in the public schools of Dayton, Tenn., was tried in the following July for violation of the act, the trial attracting world-wide attention. Clarence Darrow and other distinguished counsel volunteered their services for the defendant, and William J. Bryan represented the state. The latter's appearance on the witness stand as an expert on the Bible constituted the climax of what the state supreme court afterward characterized as "this bizarre case." Scopes was convicted, but while the state supreme court upheld the constitutionality of the statute, sentence was set aside inasmuch as the trial court imposed a fine in excess of its authorized maximum. Further appeal was thereby prevented, but the trial not only added to the gaiety of nations, but undoubtedly led to the withdrawal of similar legislative projects in other states.

SCOTCH-IRISH in the American colonies and the United States emanated from the Scottish Protestants who were transplanted to Ulster, Ireland, chiefly during the 17th century, and from their descendants. By the close of the 17th century adverse economic conditions and political and religious disabilities arose to cause them to leave Ireland. Their farms were owned by absent English landlords who demanded high rentals; parliamentary regulation, 1665–80, seriously impaired their cattle-raising industry; the Woolens Act of 1699, which forbade the exportation of wool from Ireland, rendered sheep raising unprofitable; an act of Parliament in 1704, excluding Presbyterians from holding civil and military offices, denied them a voice in government; and the government taxed them to support the Anglican Church in which they did not worship. Consequently, thousands of these people from Ulster, with their Scotch heritage, with their experience in colonization, and with their Presbyterian faith, came to the American colonies.

SEA OTTER TRADE. Europeans and Americans first came to the North Pacific coast of America for sea otter skins. While beaver trapping was drawing furmen from the Atlantic seaboard into the interior of North America, the sea otter trade caused mariners to push into the North Pacific, where they established bases whence they ran the coast from the Aleutian Islands to Lower California. In China sea otter furs were exchanged at good profit for prized oriental goods.

Russia and Spain were the pioneer nations to engage in this trade. After the Bering expeditions of the early 18th century, *promishleniki* (fur traders) pushed eastward until in 1784 the first permanent Russian settlement in America was established on Kadiak Island. In the same year Spain organized a sea otter trade between California and China. The great fur rush to the Northwest coast was caused by published accounts of Capt. Cook's last Pacific voyage, 1776–80. English and American vessels led the drive, but within a decade the former had practically withdrawn. At the opening of the 19th century American and Russian traders entered the California sea otter fields where in the face of strong opposition they poached throughout the Spanish period. After 1821 the liberal commercial policy of independent Mexico stimulated the California otter trade, and many Americans became Mexican citizens in order to participate in the business.

The number of skins obtained in the sea otter trade can only be estimated. From 1804 to 1807 it was reported that 59,346 furs were taken by American vessels, while the period 1808 to 1812 yielded 47,962. The greatest number of skins known to have been taken from the California coast in any one year was 10,638 in 1811. By 1818 the number decreased to 4500.

The sea otter trade came to an end when ruthless hunting, intensified by the introduction of firearms, exterminated the animals. In general, the fur areas were exhausted in the order in which they were opened, and at approximately the following dates—Kamtchatka and the westernmost Aleutian Islands, 1790; Kadiak, 1805; Sitka to Nootka Sound, 1820; and California, 1840.

SEAL, GREAT, OF THE UNITED STATES. The day the Continental Congress declared the United States an independent nation it appointed a committee to devise a great seal with which to authenticate its formal, official documents. The necessity was obvious; but after more than six weeks the committee could suggest only a weird jumble of impossible heraldic detail and biblical legend. It took Congress six years more to obtain a satisfactory design. The obverse of the seal finally adopted was the design of Secretary Charles Thomson. William Barton's idea was selected for the reverse. Both obverse and reverse are pictured on the United States one-dollar note (series of 1935). The Great Seal is kept by the Secretary of State and is affixed only on the signed order of the President. A circle of special white paper, with serrated edge, is attached to the document, and the seal impressed through both by a metal die. From 1856 to 1869 a special wax impression (about 6 inches in diameter), enclosed in a gold or silver box, was attached to treaties by silken cords. Although recut three times (1841, 1883 and 1902) to improve its artistic appearance the Great Seal has always been precisely as decreed by the Continental Congress, June 20, 1782.

SECESSION, RIGHT OF. The Southern states of the American Union were advancing no new theory when they appealed to and exercised the right of secession in 1860. Publicists and statesmen had championed the right from the beginning of American independence. The right of a people to establish, alter and abolish their government, and to institute a new one if their safety and happiness demanded it was a fundamental principle of the American Revolution (*see* Declaration of Independence). This idea was the basis of the threat of both Vermont and Kentucky to separate from the Confederation and set up independent governments, or to ally with some foreign power, during the 1780's.

More specifically the right of secession was based upon the doctrine of state sovereignty and the compact theory of the Union. James Madison stated this theory very clearly when he wrote: "Our governmental system is established by *compact*, not between the Government of the United States and the State *Governments* but between the STATES AS SOVEREIGN COMMUNITIES, *stipulating* EACH with THE OTHER. . . ."

The first serious threat of secession came in 1798 when the Democratic Republicans (*see* Republican Party, Jeffersonian), smarting under Federalist legislation, talked of separation. John Taylor of Caroline openly advocated secession but the more moderate views of Jefferson prevailed, and Virginia and Kentucky adopted their Resolutions condemning the legislation as unconstitutional, null and void, and proclaiming the right of the states to interpose or nullify such acts. Jefferson's purpose was to appeal to the people in the election of 1800, rather than to apply either nullification or secession.

After Jefferson's victory in 1801 the New England Federalists sought a remedy against Democratic domination. Sen. Timothy Pickering said that "the principles of our Revolution point to the remedy—a separation." The purchase of Louisiana further antagonized the Federalists and the Essex Junto planned a new confederacy composed of New England and New York, "exempt from the corrupt . . . influence and oppression of the aristocratic democrats of the South." Alexander Hamilton blocked their efforts but Josiah Quincy still maintained in 1811 that the admission of Louisiana would dissolve the Union. The disgruntled Federalists of New England resorted to treasonable action in opposing "Mr. Madison's war," and in 1814 met in the Hartford Convention behind closed doors and in utmost secrecy. There is little doubt that their object was the dissolution of the Union and the formation of a New England Confederacy if their program of constitutional reform failed. Fortunately the news of the peace treaty prevented action.

The next rumblings of discontent were heard in the Southern states. Threats of separation were made over both the Missouri question (see Missouri Compromise) and the Indian controversy (see Cherokee Nation v. Georgia), and the tariff issue brought these threats to the very threshold of action. South Carolina nullified the tariff acts of 1828 and 1832 and signified her intention of seceding if the Federal Government attempted to coerce her (see Nullification).

Slavery in the territories caused both North and South to threaten to secede. John Quincy Adams thought the free states would secede if Texas were annexed, and the Southern leaders threatened separation if slavery were excluded from the Mexican cession. This controversy culminated in the assembling of the Nashville Convention of 1850 and of state conventions in several Southern states. These conventions reluctantly accepted the Compromise of 1850 and secession was halted. The abolitionists called a convention of all the free states to meet at Cleveland in 1857 to consider separation, but the depression prevented the meeting.

The threat of secession had been the last resort of the minority to protect its interests under the Constitution, and had been constantly present from the Revolution to the Civil War.

SECESSION OF SOUTHERN STATES. Upon Lincoln's election the governor of South Carolina recommended and the legislature called a state convention (that being the method by which the Constitution of 1787 was ratified) which met amidst great excitement and on Dec. 20, 1860, by a unanimous vote, passed an ordinance dissolving "the union now subsisting between South Carolina and other States." The convention issued a "Declaration of Immediate Causes," expressing the state rights view of the Union, and appointed commissioners to other Southern states and to Washington. To many who favored further efforts to secure constitutional rights (through an all-Southern convention, appeals to the North, or compromise through Congress) this action seemed precipitate. But South Carolina had assurances that other states would follow, and many thought that better terms might be

made out of the Union than in it. Overriding minorities, six other states by conventions passed ordinances of secession: Mississippi, Jan. 9 (84 to 15); Florida, Jan. 10 (62 to 7); Alabama, Jan. 11 (61 to 39); Georgia, Jan. 19 (164 to 133); Louisiana, Jan. 26 (113 to 17); and Texas (over the opposition of Gov. Houston), Feb. 1 (166 to 8), thus completing the secession of the lower South. Nearly all who voted against secession did so because they doubted its expediency, not the right.

Buchanan, believing secession unconstitutional but considering himself without authority to coerce, and anxious not to give the upper South cause for secession, was determined not to risk war by an overt act in protecting Federal property (forts, arsenals, post offices, etc.) and sustaining the operation of Federal laws. The South Carolina commissioners, sent to negotiate with Buchanan for the peaceful division of property, debts, etc., demanded that Maj. Anderson, then occupying Fort Sumter in Charleston harbor, evacuate that post as inconsistent with the sovereignty of South Carolina. This he refused. Meanwhile Congress, despite an address from some Southern members saying that "All hope of relief in the Union, through the agency of committees, Congressional legislation, or constitutional amendments, is extinguished," was sifting compromise proposals. Of these the Crittenden Compromise, involving the extension of the Missouri Compromise line, was the more hopeful, but it failed to get the support of the Republican leaders, as did Crittenden's suggestion for a national referendum. More certain was the failure (because opposed by the extremists on either side) of the Washington Peace Conference (Border Slave State Convention) which, two months later, presented proposals similar to Crittenden's.

With compromise failing and with Buchanan taking a firmer attitude as he became less hopeful of peace and union (he sent the *Star of the West* to reinforce Sumter) representatives from the seceded states met at Montgomery (Feb. 4, 1861) to organize a new nation. Lincoln's inaugural promise "to hold, occupy, and possess the property and places belonging to the government," coupled with his assertion that "physically speaking, we cannot separate," seemed none the less threatening by his assurance that "the government will not assail you." Peaceful secession seemed remote after Lincoln's fateful decision to relieve Fort Sumter, the firing on the fort and Lincoln's call for volunteers. This practical state of war compelled the states of the upper South to make a reluctant choice between the Confederacy and the Union.

One month after Lincoln's inauguration the Virginia convention voted against secession (88 to 45), preferring a conference of the border states and further discussions with Lincoln. But two days after the call for volunteers the convention (April 17) adopted the ordinance of secession (88 to 55) which was ratified by popular vote on May 23, although the convention had entered into a military league with the Confederacy on April 24. In Arkansas opinion was very evenly divided (a popular referendum had been set for Aug. 5), but the governor rejected Lincoln's call for militia and on May 6 the convention passed the secession ordinance (65 to 5). Tennessee, like Virginia, had large nonslaveholding sections where many people for geographic, economic or social reasons did not feel that their interests would be served by the Confederacy. The legislature on Jan. 19 provided for a popular vote for delegates to a convention and for the convention itself which was rejected (69,675 to 57,798). After the firing on Fort Sumter and the threat of coercion, the legislature ratified a league with the Confederacy (May 7) and authorized the governor to raise a force of 55,000 men. On June 8 the people voted for secession (104,913 to 47,238). The opposition to secession in western Virginia led to the formation of a separate state (West Virginia); a like movement in eastern Tennessee proved abortive. The unanimous vote for secession by the convention of North Carolina, the last state to secede (May 20), was clearly the result of Lincoln's proclamation. The border slave states of Kentucky, Maryland, Delaware and Missouri did not secede and Kentucky's attempted neutrality failed.

SECTIONALISM. The older American historians were inclined to regard the sectional struggles that culminated in the Civil War and Reconstruction as essentially a contest between freedom and democracy on the one hand and slavery and oligarchy on the other. But a later and more dispassionate generation of scholars, whose historical philosophy has been given classic expression in the later writings of Frederick Jackson Turner, look upon sectionalism as the permanent product of climate, soil, geography, race and natural resources. The basic factors of sectionalism being thus regarded as permanent, sectional conflict within the United States is frankly recognized as not having begun with the slavery issue nor as having come to an end with emancipation. Indeed sectionalism has been accepted as a continuing reality in American life.

While the United States is divided into several natural regions, politically these areas have usually aligned themselves into three or four sections. Before 1860, in a general sense, these groupings were the East, the South and the West. The social and economic interests of the dominant groups of the East centered in commerce, industry and finance, while the dominant groups as well as the masses of the South and West were engaged in agriculture. The East desired a protective tariff, a national bank, internal improvement at national expense, and it opposed territorial expansion and free lands for settlers —until it became clear that the settlers might become political allies. The South asked little of the National Government in domestic affairs, but was imperialistic

in foreign affairs. It favored territorial expansion and free land until it became apparent that such lands would be settled by immigrants unfriendly to the South. It opposed a protective tariff—except in 1816 while still under the shadow of the War of 1812; it objected to a national bank and internal improvements at national expense. In fact the South opposed the entire program of the East. The West was agreed with the South on all save two items: it wanted internal improvements at national expense and it was not averse to a protective tariff. An alliance between the South and West was, therefore, a natural consequence of the near identity of interests of the two sections. When it is recalled that the majority of the inhabitants of the Old Northwest were of Southern origin or descent as late as 1850 it will be even more obvious that a political alliance between South and West was the normal thing until the end of the first half of the 19th century.

The combination of South and West was not made —or if made was not strong enough to gain control of the National Government—until the election of 1800. During the preceding twelve years the East through the medium of the Federalist party had controlled the Federal Government and had put much of its program into operation to the supposed detriment of the rest of the country. After the Jeffersonian party came into power in 1801, the combination of South and West, with three exceptions, elected the President and usually held a majority in Congress until 1860. It is a mistake, however, to say that the South controlled the National Government during this time. Perhaps it is not incorrect to say that the South determined selection of the President, and that it usually had more influence with the President than did the Western or the Eastern Democrats. But the South did not control Congress—nor the judiciary until after John Marshall's death. Despite the ability of the South to designate the presidential nominee and despite the fact that Congress more often than not had a majority of Democrats, the South had no control over Congress on issues of a sectional nature. Turner has made a microscopical study of sectionalism from 1820 to 1850 and he has found that political lines broke down in the face of sectional issues, so that Eastern and Western Whigs and Democrats often voted side by side against Southern Whigs and Democrats.

Reconstruction, following upon Civil War, was an attempt to form an alliance between the East and South by means of the Negro vote and the disfranchisement of the white leaders. This alliance was successful only long enough to place Grant and Hayes in the White House. Its aftermath was the Solid (white) South and the virtual disfranchisement of the Negro race. Perhaps an unexpected result of Reconstruction was the creation of a Republican West which remained the steadfast ally of the East for many years.

One of the issues that transcended sectional and

party alignments was slavery. While the South before the Missouri Compromise agreed in the abstract with the other sections that slavery was an evil, after that event and under the attack of the radical abolitionists, it reversed its position and defended slavery on principle. Since the extension of slavery into the territories involved the balance of power between the East and the South, if not between the slave and free states, it was inevitable that the slavery issue should be injected into politics. The moral and religious fervor which the radical abolitionists added to the political controversy over slavery made it inevitable that slavery should become a sectional rather than a party issue, and it was the mutual hostility aroused in the West and the South over the right of extension of slavery into the territories that finally destroyed the political alliance of those two sections and contributed powerfully to the creation of the East-West combination that brought the Republican party into power, and precipitated the secession of the South. However, it is not meant to state positively that slavery was the cause of secession and the Civil War. It was, without much doubt, the most potent single cause; but the conflicting economic and social interests that had characterized the sections, and had created sectionalism before the slavery issue became important, were even greater in 1860 than ever before, and furnished the underlying causes for the South's attempted withdrawal from the Union.

While the East has been the dominant power since Reconstruction—usually symbolized by Wall Street—the other sections of the country have not failed to fight for what they considered their own interests. The Greenback Movement, the Granger laws, the Populist party, the Interstate Commerce Commissions, Free Silver, the Federal Reserve Banking System, the Agricultural Adjustment Administration programs and the antitrust laws were moves of the hinterland sections against the dominant East.

SELDEN PATENT was the first and most bitterly contested of all the automobile patents. The original application for a patent on a vehicle propelled by an internal combustion engine was filed in 1879 by George B. Selden, a lawyer of Rochester, N. Y., but was kept pending while Selden attempted to interest capital in his ideas, and the patent (No. 549,160) was not issued until 1895. First purchased by the Pope Manufacturing Co., several shifts in control finally brought the rights into the possession of the Electric Vehicle Co. In 1900 this concern began a vigorous enforcement of its patent rights by filing suit against the Winton Motor Carriage Co. The case dragged along for three years, only to be abandoned when Winton and nine other companies organized themselves into the Association of Licensed Automobile Manufacturers and agreed to pay royalties.

Henry Ford, however, refused to take part in the agreement and in 1903 an infringement suit was filed against him. Outstanding legal talent was engaged for both sides of the controversy, and the amazing case was spun out for eight years, amassing 36 large volumes of testimony. A principal argument made by the defense was that the Selden patent contemplated use of the Brayton two-cycle motor, and not the Otto four-cycle engine then being used in practically all cars. This argument was strengthened by a contemptuous entry in Selden's diary characterizing the Otto motor as "another of those damned Dutch engines." The lower court upheld the claim of infringement but the court of appeals, which ruled in Ford's favor, stated that although the patent was valid, it was not being infringed by manufacture of vehicles using the Otto type motor.

SELECTMEN. From the earliest times the New England town meeting has chosen these executive officers. Their performances are interwoven with the literature and history of the region. The usual number has been three, although five to nine in some larger communities, and annual election has been the prevailing rule. The selectmen constitute an executive committee for the town and handle its administrative affairs. In the earlier period they were vested with police and educational functions now usually transferred to other authorities. Their general functions are determined by state law, and while varying in different states, usually involve the preparation of the warrant for annual or special meetings, supervision of local highways, valuation and assessment of property, election control, issuance of licenses, poor relief, etc. Special duties not otherwise provided for may be authorized by the town meeting. The office has served as a training school for local political leadership and administration.

SENECA FALLS CONVENTION, the first modern woman's rights convention, called through the initiative of Lucretia Mott and Elizabeth Cady Stanton, was held in the Wesleyan Chapel at Seneca Falls, N. Y., July 19 and 20, 1848. At the gathering a Declaration of Sentiments, listing the many discriminations existing against women, was read, and a series of eleven resolutions, one of them calling for woman suffrage, were adopted. This convention launched the organized modern woman's rights movement.

SEPARATISTS, OR INDEPENDENTS, were radical Puritans who refused to wait for a Puritan reformation within the Church of England, but set up churches outside the established order. Robert Browne gathered the first Separatist church at Norfolk in 1581; later Separatists were dubbed "Brownists," but the groups did not constitute an organized movement. As with the Scrooby congregation in 1602, a Separatist church resulted whenever a number of earnest Puritans concluded that the true Biblical polity had to be achieved "without tarying for anie." In the main, Separatists proposed a Congregational or "Independent" form of church polity, wherein each church was to be autonomous, founded upon a formal covenant, electing its own officers and restricting the membership to visible saints. Separation was held a major offense by the regular Puritans as well as by Anglicans and royal authorities; yet the Puritans who settled Massachusetts Bay already believed that Congregationalism rather than Presbyterianism was the polity of the New Testament, and when founding churches at Salem and Boston, 1629 and 1630, sought advice from the Separatists at Plymouth. In England during the 1640's the minority wing of the Puritan party maintained Congregationalism against the majority in the Westminster Assembly and the Parliament, and were known as "Independents," but the multitude of sects which arose out of the disorders of the time also took unto themselves the title of Independents, so that the term came to be a vague designation for opponents of Presbyterianism. Orthodox New England Puritans, although practising a Congregational discipline, always denied that they were either Separatists or Independents.

SEVEN DAYS' BATTLES (June 25–July 1, 1862) were the succession of battles in which Lee's (C.) army forced that under McClellan (U.) to abandon its threatening position east of Richmond and retreat to the James River.

McClellan had pushed his right wing, 30,000 strong, under Porter, northward across the Chickahominy, hoping that McDowell's corps would join it from Fredericksburg. Aware that Porter was separated from McClellan's main force of 75,000, Lee ordered Jackson, with 18,500 men from the Shenandoah Valley, to fall upon Porter's right and rear. Simultaneously Lee with 40,000 of his 68,000 troops, crossing the Chickahominy north of Richmond, would assail Porter in front.

Lee attacked at Mechanicsville (June 26) but, Jackson not arriving, was repulsed. Porter withdrew to Gaines' Mill, where next day the Confederate Army, including Jackson's command, drove him across the Chickahominy. The Federal base on the Pamunkey River was now exposed, but McClellan transferred it by water to Harrison's Landing on the James, and marched his army thither. June 29 his covering troops repulsed Confederate attacks at Savage's Station. Discovering that his adversary was retiring on the James, Lee hurried columns to Frayser's Farm. Here his desperate assaults on June 30 failed to interrupt McClellan's retreat, while at White Oak Swamp Jackson was equally unsuccessful in crushing his rear guard. McClellan, continuing his retirement, occupied Malvern Hill, where (July 1) Lee's final attack suffered decisive repulse. McClellan now fortified his army at Harrison's Landing, having lost 16,000 men in total casualties, while Lee had lost 20,000.

SEWING MACHINE. American sewing machines developed with explosive suddenness about 1850 from inventions perfecting ideas previously current in America and Europe. These were recorded in patents by Elias Howe, John Bachelder, Allen B. Wilson, I. M. Singer, W. O. Grover, James Gibbs and others between 1846 and 1860. A flood of improvement patents followed. In the early 1850's three companies were manufacturing machines for the general market. In 1856 the "Albany Agreement" pooling the principal patents was concluded by leading makers. Under this, 130,000 machines were sold within three years. The industry's rapid expansion and quick success in creating a popular market were possible because automatic machinery and standardized parts were already familiar in America. Sewing machine factories soon ranked among the country's largest manufacturing establishments. By 1870 the annual output had reached 500,000 machines.

SHACKAMAXON, TREATY OF, traditionally known as the "Great Treaty." Much doubt still remains about the details. There is no doubt, however, that William Penn met the Indians in 1682 at Shackamaxon (now Kensington), the chief village of the Delawares, and entered into negotiations with them for friendly relations and good feeling. On June 23, 1683, several agreements were signed with the Indian chiefs granting to Penn and his heirs land in southeastern Pennsylvania. All of these were duly witnessed by both whites and Indians. The leading representative of the Indians was Tammanen (Tammany). No valid reason exists for rejecting the traditional story of Penn's meeting the Indians seated under a large elm. This event has been made familiar by Benjamin West's painting and Voltaire's allusion as "the only treaty never sworn to and never broken." Penn described the seating arrangements of a meeting with the Indians in a letter to the Free Society of Traders written on Aug. 16, 1683.

SHAKERS, AMERICAN SECT OF, officially known as the United Society of Believers in Christ's Second Appearing, was founded by (Mother) Ann Lee of Manchester, England, who came to this country in 1774. Its origin was in the Quaker church, but its tenets were those of a distinctive social-religious culture. The Shakers believed in a dual deity and messiahship; in confession, celibacy, sex equality, separation from the world, consecrated labor and common property. Between 1787–94 eleven communities were established in New York and New England, and in the first quarter of the 19th century, seven more in Ohio, Kentucky and Indiana. These societies were divided into "families" and grouped into bishoprics, a central ministry at New Lebanon, N. Y., directing affairs through subordinate ministers, elders, eldresses and trustees. As fine agriculturists and mechanics, particularly as makers of furniture, as moral purists or perfectionists and as successful communists, the Shakers exerted considerable influence in 19th-century America.

SHARECROPPER is the general term used, particularly in the South, to describe the type of tenant farmer, white or black, owning neither tools nor working stock, who receives a share of the crop—usually half—in return for the labor of himself and his family. While varying in detail, the landlord generally provides the land, a cabin, fuel, tools, working stock, and feed for stock, the seed and half the fertilizer. Since few croppers can maintain themselves until the crops are gathered they must have credit. A landlord may keep a "commissary" from which a few staple articles of food and clothing are issued in limited amounts; or credit to a fixed sum is secured from a merchant, who is protected, more or less, by a lien on the tenant's share of the growing, or even the unplanted crops. When the crop—cotton or tobacco—is gathered, all these advances, and half the cost of ginning and fertilizer, are deducted from the tenant's share. With unfavorable weather conditions or a low price for the product all concerned are likely to lose.

SHARE-THE-WEALTH MOVEMENTS IN THE UNITED STATES. At the lowest ebb of the great depression, in the winter of 1932–33, two impressions were stamped on the popular mind by the publicity concerning "Technocracy." They were, first, a prophecy of impending doom and, second, a promise of potential utopia. "The nation stands at the threshold of what is simultaneously opportunity and disaster," announced the foremost "Technocrat." These two ideas together with the acute distress of the unemployed, the insecurity of the middle class and the deepening plight of the aged, formed the common basis of appeal for the great mass organizations that sprang into existence in the South and West between 1933 and 1936. Among those declaring their purpose to be the redistribution of wealth were the Townsend Plan, Father Coughlin's National Union for Social Justice, Sen. Long's Share-Our-Wealth Clubs, William Lemke's Union party and Upton Sinclair's EPIC.

Differing widely in their proposals, these organizations joined in disclaiming any desire to destroy the capitalist order, and all, except the EPIC, depended fundamentally upon a core of inflationist doctrine. Following American middle-class traditions of utopianism, mingled with religious zeal, they adopted such new techniques as national radio "hook-ups," skilled publicity methods of pressure politics, huge mass meetings, or "conventions," swayed by frenzied emotionalism, and blind trust in spectacular individual leaders rather than in the slow education of a party. Moving in and out of alliance with the New Deal and with one another, according to the whims or mutual jealousies of their leaders, they ran the gamut of reform tactics: the whirlwind drive for power of an individual leader, the attempt to capture an old party, the trial of the third party method, disciplined backing of congressional candidates of either old party who pledged support of "the plan," and finally sporadic drives to perfect schemes within single states. Revealed in all these movements was the anxious disillusionment, the distress, the experimental frame of mind of the lower middle class and the complete unreality of party divisions in the United States.

SHARPS RIFLE. One of the earliest successful breech-loaders, it was invented by Christian Sharps about 1850. It first attracted wide attention during the Kansas Border War (1855–56) when some 900 of them, often called "Beecher's Bibles," were used by the Free State party. About half of these were supplied by officers of the New England Emigrant Aid Company. These rifles gave the Free State side a moral, if not a military, superiority throughout the conflict. They probably saved Lawrence from attack during the Wakarusa War, and were undoubtedly a factor in provoking the Proslavery men to acts of violence. Later they were used by Montgomery in the border war and by John Brown at Harpers Ferry. The Sharps rifle was considered for adoption by the U. S. Army in 1856, and though not finally adopted, some 80,000 were used by the North during the Civil War. It had a high reputation for range and accuracy.

SHAYS' REBELLION (August, 1786 to February, 1787), in western and central Massachusetts, was the outstanding manifestation of the discontent widespread throughout New England during the economic depression following the Revolution. Many small property holders in Massachusetts were losing their possessions through seizures for overdue debts and delinquent taxes; many faced imprisonment for debt. Town meetings and county conventions petitioned for lightening of taxes (disproportionately burdensome to the poorer classes and western sections), sought suspension, abolition or reform of certain courts, as well as revision of the state constitution, and especially urged the issue of paper money, but were stubbornly opposed on most points by the legislature. Lacking, in many cases, property qualifications for voting and thus unable to look for relief through the ballot, the malcontents, beginning at Northampton, Aug. 29, resorted to massed efforts to intimidate and close the courts to prevent action against debtors. Fearful they might be indicted for treason or sedition by the supreme court at Springfield, in September, they appeared there in armed force. Daniel Shays, Revolutionary veteran and local officeholder of Pelham, emerged as leader, demanding that the court refrain from indictments and otherwise restrict its business. A clash with neighborhood militia under Maj. Gen. Shepard was avoided when both bands agreed to disperse. The court adjourned.

In January the insurgents returned to Springfield for supplies from the Confederation arsenal there, a move foreseen by state and Federal authorities. Federal preparations for arsenal defense were masked by announcement that requisitioning of forces was necessitated by menacing Indians on the frontier. Adequate government funds were not forthcoming for either Federal or state troops, but Gen. Lincoln secured for the latter some $20,000 from private individuals. Shepard's forces repulsed the Shaysites' attack on the arsenal (Jan. 25); Lincoln's men dispersed a near-by insurgent force under Luke Day. Marching to Petersham through a blinding snowstorm Lincoln surprised and captured most of the remaining insurgents early in February, and the rebellion soon collapsed. Shays escaped to Vermont; eventually, with about a dozen others condemned to death, he was pardoned. Bowdoin, governor during the insurrection, was defeated at the next election; reforms in line with the Shaysites' demands were soon made, and amnesty granted with few exceptions. Alarmed by "this unprovoked insurrection" of "wicked and ambitious men" some conservatives despaired of republican institutions. Far greater numbers viewed the rebellion as proof of need for a stronger general Government, capable of suppressing such uprisings, or, better still, preventing them by improving economic conditions throughout the United States. Thus, indirectly, the rebellion strengthened the movement culminating in the adoption of the Federal Constitution.

SHEEP, domesticated, were introduced into the Americas by European colonists—into Mexico by the Spanish, into Virginia (1609) and Massachusetts (1629) by the English, into New York (1625) by the Dutch and into New Jersey (1634) by the Swedes. These animals were unimproved.

In colonial times sheep were raised as a part of self-sufficient agriculture to supply wool for home-spun clothing and not for commercial purposes. Because of wolves, improper care and English competition, the number of sheep remained relatively few and the quality and quantity of the wool poor. The industry improved somewhat during the Revolution, but slumped after peace and the resumption of British trade.

The first decades of the 19th century witnessed a marked change. Two events of importance occurred: the introduction of Merino sheep, and the exclusion of English competitors from the American market by the various nonintercourse acts and the War of 1812. The first Merinos were imported in 1801–2 from France and from Spain. With the passage of the Embargo Act (1807), native mills increased, wool prices skyrocketed and the demand for fine-wool sheep was insatiable. A Merino craze followed. Merino wool sold for $2 a pound and the early importers sold sheep for $1000 a head. In the midst of this craze the Napoleonic armies broke the Spanish restrictions on the exportation of Merinos, and between 1808–11 approximately 24,000 Merinos were imported into the United States. Sheep raising entered its commercial phase.

After 1815 British woolen importations again depressed the industry. The growth of the factory system and the tariff of 1828 revived it. Woolen manufactures doubled in a decade, the price of wool went up and eastern flocks increased tremendously. In the 1830's 60% of American sheep were in New England and the Middle Atlantic states. After 1840, because of westward migration, improved transportation facilities, easy access to cheap western land and an increase in the prices of foodstuffs, the center of sheep raising shifted westward. By 1850 it was in the Ohio Valley.

The Civil War produced a second Merino craze. After the war, sheep raising continued to travel West to the Rocky Mountains and Pacific coast states. In 1935, 60% of all the sheep in the United States were in the western states. Meanwhile the animals were improved. Through importations of European breeds and selective breeding, the average weight per fleece increased from 2 pounds in 1840 to 7.9 pounds in 1935. Its quality also improved.

Progressively as the Far West shifted to wool production, the East under the stimulus of growing urban markets turned to mutton production. English mutton breeds were introduced—the Leicesters, Southdowns, Shropshires and similar breeds. After 1890 even the Far West placed more emphasis on dual-purpose sheep and mutton production; lamb feeding developed in this area.

SHEEP WARS, WESTERN. Spanish colonists introduced the sheep industry to the West when they occupied New Mexico, Arizona, Texas and California. But not until long after the intrusion of the Anglo-Americans were there causes for range wars. After the Homestead Act of 1862 the free prairie range rapidly diminished and three decades later range wars had begun. The average cowboy looked with scorn upon the drab routine of the lowly shepherd (*pastor*). But this did not lead to conflict; the causes for trouble were more tangible. The sharp hoofs of feeding sheep destroyed the turf and a range was often made barren after months of occupancy. Moreover, cattle would not drink from watering places of sheep. Thus the sheepmen had a natural advantage in range controversies. And when the *pastores* were driven from a favorite range by their enemies because of superior numbers, they could usually find a redress of grievances in near-by courts.

By 1875 clashes between these natural rivals occurred along the New Mexico-Texas boundary. New Mexicans drove their flocks upon the Canadian range of Col. Charles Goodnight. But Goodnight's cowhands drove more than four hundred sheep into the Canadian River and drowned them. Later a New Mexican court found judgment in favor of the sheepmen. In 1876 Goodnight and the sheepmen agreed on a division of a Staked Plains range. The shepherds were allowed the range of the Canadian Valley and

Goodnight was to graze undisturbed the Palo Duro canyon.

Other range controversies ended in bloodshed. In Colorado, Nevada, Idaho, Wyoming and Montana thousands of sheep were killed in the bitter wars, and shepherds and cowboys were slain. During the 1880's and 1890's sheepmen controlled the Arizona range from Ashfork to Seligman, and threatened to drive the cowmen from other choice ranges. This led to the Graham-Tewksbury feud in which twenty-six cattlemen and six sheepmen lost their lives. During this period also Wyoming cowmen attacked the shepherds who had invaded their ranges and drove more than 10,000 sheep into the mountains to be eaten by coyotes and mountain lions. Another clash near North Rock Springs was won by the cowmen who then destroyed 12,000 sheep by driving them over a cliff. But rivalries subsided with the occupation of the country by landowners and the fencing of the range.

SHELBY'S MEXICAN EXPEDITION (1865). After the downfall of the Confederacy in 1865, Gen. Joseph O. Shelby, one of the ablest Southern cavalry commanders, rather than surrender, called on his men to follow him into Mexico and there enlist in the army of the Emperor Maximilian, then precariously maintaining his throne.

With 1000 men, including many Confederate notables, such as Generals E. Kirby-Smith, John B. Magruder, T. C. Hindman, C. M. Wilcox, and Governors Murrah of Texas, Morehead of Kentucky and Allen of Louisiana, Shelby crossed the Rio Grande to Piedras Negras from Eagle Pass, Texas, burying the Confederate flag in the river on July 4, 1865. At Piedras Negras, four cannon were exchanged for gold to buy supplies, and Shelby's expedition began fighting its way across northern Mexico toward Monterrey, being impeded by guerrillas supporting Benito Juarez, the Mexican Republican leader who was fighting Maximilian.

At Monterrey, the expedition broke up into several sections, parts going to Canada, British Honduras, Sonora, and even joining the French army in Mexico. Shelby, with the remnant of his men, marched to Mexico City. The vacillating Emperor Maximilian, however, refused the offer of Shelby's sword, fearing the displeasure of the United States, and the Confederates attempted to establish a colony on land given them by the Empress Carlotta. The overthrow of Maximilian and his execution, June 19, 1867, however, made the colony untenable, and most of the Confederate exiles returned to the United States or went elsewhere.

SHENANDOAH. This was the last armed cruiser to carry the Confederate flag and, next to the *Alabama*, was the most destructive to United States shipping. Purchased in England September, 1864, the *Sea King* sailed to Madeira, where Capt. James Waddell equipped her as an armed cruiser and named her the *Shenandoah*. The cruiser was a fast, well-armed vessel of 790 tons register, powered with steam and sail. From Madeira, she began a cruise to the Pacific by way of the Cape of Good Hope and Australia, which resulted in the capture of nearly forty prizes valued at about $1,400,000. On August 2, 1865, Capt. Waddell learned from a British ship that the war had ended. He then sailed for Liverpool by way of Cape Horn, reaching the English port in November, 1865. The British government transferred the cruiser to the United States, by whom it was sold to the Sultan of Zanzibar. Later it was lost at sea.

SHENANDOAH VALLEY is that part of the great valley between the Allegheny and the Blue Ridge Mountains extending from the Potomac River at Harpers Ferry south to the watershed of the James River a few miles southwest of Lexington. There are three parts of the Shenandoah Valley: the lower, extending from the Potomac forty miles south, settled chiefly by English immigrants from tidewater Virginia; the middle, from near Strasburg to the vicinity of Harrisonburg, settled almost wholly by Germans; and the upper, from Harrisonburg to the waters of the James, originally more wooded than the middle and lower valley. This last was the part chosen by the Scotch-Irish immigrants, most of whom came down from Pennsylvania.

There were travelers into the Valley at least fifty years before Gov. Spotswood's expedition of the Knights of the Golden Horseshoe in 1716 and the larger movement of Germans led by Joist Hite in 1732 and of Scotch-Irish led by John Lewis in the same year. Bona fide settlers were known near Shepherdstown in 1717; Adam Miller had settled in the present Page County by 1726; and there were settlers near Luray in 1727.

The lower valley became the seat of slavery and tobacco, and adhered to the Church of England, while the middle valley, Lutheran in religion, marked by large barns and rolling meadows, was settled by quiet home-loving "Valley Dutch" people. The upper valley, Presbyterian in its life, Scotch-Irish in its politics, was known for its fierce democracy, its exploring hunger for land, and its Indian wars. The lower valley was linked closely with tidewater Virginia geographically and socially; George Washington served in the House of Burgesses as delegate from Frederick County before he represented Fairfax. The middle valley was largely self-contained. The upper valley, including the famous Augusta County, extended to "the Great South Sea, including California" and held its county court at times near Fort Duquesne, the present Pittsburgh.

SHERIDAN'S RIDE. During the Shenandoah Campaign of 1864, Gen. Early (C.) attacked Sheridan's army (U.) at dawn on Oct. 19, along Cedar Creek near Strasburg. Two Federal corps, awakened from sleep, were quickly thrown into panic. Other troops, however, rallied and resisted the Confederate advance, though they were slowly forced back. Gen. Sheridan, returning from a visit to Washington, had stopped at Winchester on the night of the 18th. Awakened next morning by the distant sound of artillery firing, he left for the front, and soon began to meet the routed commands, who told him that all was lost. He reached the battlefield about 10:30 A.M. and his presence quickly restored confidence. By mid-afternoon the Confederates were in retreat, losing heavily in artillery and supplies. A poem written several months later by T. Buchanan Read, with its refrain, "And Sheridan twenty miles away" (in reality, the distance was less than fifteen), fixed his ride in the public mind as one of the heroic events of history.

SHERMAN ACT OF 1890 was the upshot of political higgling. At the time this bill was laid before Congress, a certain group was anxious to enact the McKinley Tariff Bill, and the advocates of silver currency were urging the enactment of a bill providing for the free coinage of silver. While the silver advocates had a majority in the Senate, powerful enough to force the House into line, they were advisedly fearful that President Harrison would veto a free coinage bill even if it were attached as a rider to a tariff bill which he otherwise favored. As a practical solution to this dilemma the "Silver" senators determined to adopt not a free coinage measure but the nearest possible approach to it, namely, the Sherman Act of 1890, which became a law July 14, 1890. The act provided for the issuance of legal tender notes sufficient in amount to pay for 4,500,000 ounces of silver bullion each month at the prevailing market price. Then enough silver dollars were to be coined from the bullion purchased to redeem all the outstanding Treasury notes issued in this manner. The notes were made full legal tender except where otherwise expressly stipulated in the contract, and were made redeemable on demand either in gold or silver coin at the discretion of the Secretary of the Treasury, although the act went on to declare it to be "the established policy of the United States to maintain the two metals on a parity with each other upon the present legal ratio or such ratio as may be established by law."

With the passage of the Sherman Act of 1890 there were three kinds of currency, substantial in amount, which the Federal Government had to keep at par with gold, namely, greenbacks, silver certificates and Treasury notes. The direct effect of the Sherman Act was twofold: First, it increased the circulation of redeemable paper currency in the form of Treasury notes by $156,000,000, and second, it accentuated the drain on the Government's gold reserves by requiring the Treasury notes to be redeemed in gold

as long as the Treasury had gold in its possession. The financial crackup in Argentine and the resultant liquidation in Great Britain, involving the failure of Baring Brothers, eventually forced an exportation of gold from the United States to Great Britain, and this exodus, coupled with an extraordinary stringency in the money market induced by unusually heavy demand for funds evoked by the industrial activity in the West and South, created a situation bordering on panic in the latter part of 1890.

Some respite from this taut financial situation was gained by the extraordinary grain crop of 1891 in the United States and the European crop shortage, as a consequence of which the exports of gold were transformed into imports, which in turn made bank reserves ample and the money market easy. However, this respite was short-lived. The arbitrary issues of Treasury notes again began to undermine public confidence. The Treasury's already precarious position ensuing from a policy of increased governmental expenditures, the marked growth of our indebtedness to foreign nations, the reduction in custom receipts brought about by the McKinley Tariff Law, was aggravated by the additional drain upon the Treasury's resources which the redemption of the Treasury notes entailed. The cumulative effect of the foregoing factors culminated in the panic of 1893 which was characterized by a fear of the abandonment of the gold standard due to the depletion of the Government's gold reserve. The panic was checked in the autumn in 1893 by the repeal of the Sherman Act.

SHERMAN ANTITRUST LAW has been one of the great landmarks in the relation of American Government to business. Hostility to monopoly has been traditional among English-speaking people. Some centuries ago laws in England existed against forestalling, monopolizing and regrating. The tradition has taken firm root here. Combination activity which finally induced the passage of the Sherman law began on a considerable scale in the decade from 1870 to 1880. The first Standard Oil trust was formed in 1879, and revised in 1882. This stimulated combination in like form among other growing businesses. The so-called trust movement has developed through a number of stages—pools, simple business trusts, holding companies, combinations in the form of amalgamations and mergers, and finally combinations of nonrelated businesses. Active legislation against the "trusts" started in several states about 1885. These acts culminated in the Federal law of 1890, now known as the Sherman Antitrust law. Only one specific kind of combination was named in the act—"trusts"—but a blanket phrase covered all others, whether present or future. Thus the first line of the law reads, "Every contract, combination in the form of trust or otherwise, or conspiracy, in restraint of trade or commerce among the several States, or with foreign nations, is hereby declared to be illegal." The act contains eight sections and is a model of brevity and clarity, wherein are stated methods of procedure and penalties for violation. But some years passed before the Government obtained notable success with the law. Resort of business to the holding company device under the General Corporation Act of New Jersey (1899), which made possible organization of a pure finance company under a general statute, temporarily provided a means of escape. One of the first major successes was the dissolution of the American Tobacco Co. and of the Standard Oil Co. (1911). The "unscrambling" of combinations presented many difficulties. The device employed with the two companies just named was to dissolve the old organizations into a number of competing units. The properties of the old companies were transferred to the new. The stock was distributed ratably among the stockholders. Complete consolidation put many companies on firmer ground, since it could be maintained that the various divisions of the organization did not compete and consequently were not contrary to the law. Subsequently, the methods of attack were relaxed under the application of the rule of reason, and in some cases by consent decrees.

SHERMAN'S MARCH TO THE SEA. With a vivid and daring imagination and against Grant's judgment, Gen. W. T. Sherman conceived the plan of marching across Georgia from Atlanta to Savannah. His purpose was to destroy the food supplies of a region on which Lee largely depended and to break the will of the people to continue the war. On Nov. 15, 1864, he burned Atlanta, preparatory to setting out on his march the next day. With four army corps and 5000 cavalrymen, in all numbering 62,000 men, he pointed his course toward Milledgeville, Sandersville, Louisville, Millen and Savannah. Gen. O. O. Howard commanded his right wing; Gen. H. W. Slocum, his left, which Sherman, himself, accompanied; and H. J. Kilpatrick led the cavalry force. The army was spread out sufficiently to cover a course sixty miles wide through the state.

Cutting all communications, Sherman lived off the country through which he marched. His regularly organized raiding parties ranged widely, returning at the end of each day heavily laden with food, livestock, vehicles of various kinds and a great deal of nondescript property secured through pillage. Within a week the left wing reached Milledgeville but not in time to capture the fleeing state officials. In keeping with the general picnic spirit of the march, the soldiers held here a mock session of the legislature in which they repealed the secession ordinance. On Dec. 10 the army drove in the pickets before Savannah, and after a ten-day siege forced the Confederates to flee across the Savannah River into South Carolina. Sherman sent his famous message to President Lincoln giving him the city for a Christmas present. As Gen. Hood at the outset of the march retreated into Tennessee, Sherman had no opposition except the in-effectual raiding of Gen. Joe Wheeler. Sherman estimated that he had inflicted damages amounting to $100,000,000—$80,000,000 being "simple waste and destruction."

SHILOH, BATTLE OF (April 6–7, 1862). Grant's capture of Forts Henry and Donelson opened the Cumberland and Tennessee Rivers to Union water traffic and pierced the center of the Confederate far-flung defensive line so that Columbus, Ky., had to be evacuated. Buell could occupy Nashville, Tenn., with the Army of the Ohio, and Halleck on March 1 could order C. F. Smith with 30,000 troops of the Army of the Tennessee by water up that river to concentrate at Pittsburg Landing 25 miles north of the Confederates under Albert Sidney Johnston at Corinth, Miss. Grant arrived and assumed command on March 16. Buell's 25,000 were to join by marching overland from Nashville preparatory to a vigorous combined thrust southward as the next logical step in the campaign for the conquest of the Mississippi Valley.

On April 3 Johnston moved out of Corinth, 50,000 strong, to strike Grant's force before the junction could be effected. On April 6, after a slow massed march, undetected by Grant, Johnston made a sudden surprise attack early in the morning against the unfortified and incompletely covered Union position. Vigorous Confederate attacks drove in Grant's outlying units, shattered the hastily formed lines in all day fighting, costly for both sides, and pushed the Union troops against the river.

Grant personally was absent when the massed assault struck. He hurried to the scene, approved arrangements McPherson had made in his stead, coordinated the defense, concentrated rear units, and—Buell arriving by night—counterattacked next morning. The Confederates were disrupted and confused by their own violent attacks and the death of their commander, Johnston. Grant's stroke, with the fresh troops of Buell and Lew Wallace, aided by portions of Sherman's and McClernand's commands, swept them from the field toward Corinth.

SHIPBUILDING in America has been a "feast or famine" industry, with frequent sharp ups and downs, particularly in recent years. So long as it was a matter of wooden sailing vessels, American shipbuilders, with ample oak and pine growing almost down to the water's edge, could build almost one third more cheaply than the British, who had to import much of their ship timber from the Baltic or elsewhere. After steam and iron or steel began to supplant sail and wood in the mid-19th century, a similar advantage in cost passed to the British and other Europeans with their superior technological development and supplies. During the earlier sail-wood period, the construction of warships and merchantmen was very similar; by the end of the 19th century they were beginning to differ radically.

The New England colonists took to shipbuilding very early; the sloop *Virginia* was built by the short-lived Popham colony on the Kennebec as early as 1607. By 1700, Boston ranked after London and Bristol among all the British ports in its shipping. Under the Navigation Acts, vessels built in the colonies enjoyed all the privileges of English registry; because of their cheapness, large numbers were sold to British shipowners. By the eve of the Revolution, about one third of all the tonnage in British registry was American-built, some of it being owned in Britain and the rest in the colonies.

During the age of wood and sail, building methods remained fairly uniform. As in house construction, there were no specialized naval architects at the outset; the builder generally did his own designing, often carving out a "half-model" from which the lines could be taken. The hull consisted of the frame or "skeleton" and the planking or "skin." The former, generally of white oak or tough Southern live oak in the better vessels, included the keel or "backbone" and the numerous frames or "ribs." Outside of that was fitted the planking, also usually of oak, generally two to four inches thick. Lateral beams, supported by right-angle "knees" ran from side to side, and on those was laid the planking of the decks, sometimes of pine. The masts and spars were generally of pine, sometimes of fir. Usually sailcloth, cordage and ironware were the only materials not available locally. Vessels usually fell into four major categories according to rig and size. Largest were the full-rigged ships, with three masts, all square-rigged; then came the brigs, with two masts, also square-rigged; then the schooners, an American innovation, with two or more masts fore-and-aft rigged, and finally, the sloop, with a single mast. There gradually developed several variations, such as barks, brigantines, topsail schooners, and the like.

A very distinctive American achievement was the clipper, in which capacity was sacrificed for speed. The term was first applied to fast little Baltimore schooners early in the century, but its principal association was with the big full-rigged ships built in mid-century for the China and California trades. Most celebrated was the *Flying Cloud* which twice made the New York-San Francisco run in 89 days. She was almost the same size as the other most famous American sailing vessel, the frigate *Constitution*, designed by Joshua Humphreys and others in 1794.

The *Flying Cloud* and several of the other fastest clippers were designed and built by Donald McKay at East Boston. Numerous other crack clippers, plus some of the best packets and steamers, were built on New York's East River by William H. Webb, Smith & Dimon, Westervelt, and others. The North River, south of Boston, produced much good shipping in the early national period, but the bulk of the rank and file of the merchant sail during the 19th century came from yards in Maine, particularly from Bath on the Ken-

nebec; in 1860, the Bath district produced more tonnage than the whole southern coast from North Carolina to Texas.

Gradual introduction of steam and iron eventually changed that pattern. Engines and boilers for the early steamers had been built in separate "iron works" around New York and other ports. Construction in iron received a stimulus from the Civil War building of monitors. By 1870, the center of building in steam and iron shifted to the Delaware River, where John Roach was combining the various processes under one head. Most of the hulls of wooden warships were built in navy yards, but the coming of the steel "New Navy" in the 1880's shifted that to the Roach, Cramp and other Delaware yards. By the end of the century, the "big three" of private yards were the Newport News Shipbuilding and Dry Dock Co. on Hampton Roads, the New York Shipbuilding Co. at Camden, N. J., and the Fore River yard, later Bethlehem Quincy, at Quincy, Mass. The Navy had to send its young constructors to Britain for their naval architecture until M. I. T. was able to take over that function.

World Wars I and II each produced a tremendous emergency program of cargo ships, initially to offset submarine losses. With the regular yards busy with the more intricate naval construction in each case, new yards sprang into being to handle the fairly standardized merchant types. In World War I, the largest yard was Hog Island near Philadelphia, whose fifty shipways built a hundred-odd good steel freighters. Altogether that first emergency program, continuing to 1921, produced some 700 large steel freighters, 575 smaller ones, and a number of less satisfactory wooden and concrete ships. The Navy built more than 200 "four-stacker" destroyers during those same years. Between the wars, naval and commercial shipbuilding fell off so sharply that even the strongest yards had difficulty in keeping going. The "construction-differential" subsidies of the Merchant Marine Act of 1936 were designed primarily to enable them to compete with the cheaper foreign building costs.

World War II saw tremendous construction programs, in which the Navy under Vice Adm. Edward L. Cochrane spent some $19,000,000,000 building everything from landing craft up to superdreadnoughts and carriers, while the Maritime Commission under Vice Adm. Emory S. Land spent some $13,000,000,000 in constructing 5777 ships, including 2708 of the standardized 10-knot Liberty ships; 414 of the faster 16½-knot Victory ships, also of around 10,000 dead-weight tons; 541 of the "C-2's," "C-3's" and other "tailor-made" ships of the long-range program; and 702 tankers, along with some military and minor types. In most cases, these wartime vessels were welded in place of the previous riveting. Another post-war slump had struck the shipyards by 1956, when only two freighters and six tankers were built. The postwar construction, however, did produce some distinctive new types. The liner *United States,* built in 1952, established a record as the fastest afloat. The new atomic power was first installed in the *Nautilus,* followed by several other nuclear submarines, and then in the huge carrier *Enterprise* and the merchant ship *Savannah.*

SHIPS-OF-THE-LINE, or line-of-battle ships, were the 18th- and early 19th-century counterparts of modern first-class battleships, ships fit to engage the most formidable enemy ships in battle line. As planned for the U. S. Navy, they were about 190 feet long, of about 2600 tons displacement, mounted at least 74 guns on three decks, though the largest, the *Pennsylvania,* mounted 120 guns. Our first ship of this type, the *America,* was launched at Portsmouth, N. H., Nov. 5, 1782, and was given to our French allies. Congress authorized six "Seventy-fours" in 1799, but none were built, and again in 1813 authorized four more. These were named the *Franklin, Independence, Washington* and *New Orleans.* The latter, built at Sackets Harbor on Lake Ontario, was never launched. The *Franklin* was converted into a steamer in 1854, the *Washington* was broken up in 1843 and the *Independence* served as a naval receiving ship until her sale in 1913.

In 1816 Congress authorized nine more ships-of-the-line. They were the *Columbus, Ohio, Pennsylvania, Vermont, Virginia, Delaware, Alabama, New York* and *North Carolina.* The *Virginia* and *New York* were never completed. The *Pennsylvania, Columbus* and *Delaware* were burned at the Norfolk Navy Yard, April 20, 1861. The *Vermont, North Carolina* and *Ohio* were long used as receiving ships at navy yards; and the *Alabama,* renamed the *New Hampshire* in 1864, and the *Granite State* in 1904, was used as a training ship by the New York Naval Militia until 1921. None of these ships was ever engaged in battle. The introduction of steam, explosive shells and armor plate rendered them obsolete before they could be used in actual warfare.

"SHOT HEARD ROUND THE WORLD." This phrase from Emerson's poem, written for the dedication of the monument at Concord Bridge in 1836, and carved on the base of Daniel Chester French's Minute-Man statue erected there in 1875, has been accepted by the American public as expressing the patriotism which, risking everything in an immediate crisis, began the war which led to American independence.

> By the rude bridge that arched the flood,
> Their flag to April's breeze unfurled,
> Here once the embattled farmers stood
> And fired the shot heard round the world.

SIBERIAN EXPEDITION. In the summer of 1918 the United States, with the other Allied powers approving, joined Japan in military action to aid friend-ly Russians and Czechoslovak soldiers in eastern Siberia against dangers from the Russian Soviet government. In August the 27th and 31st United States Infantry regiments, with auxiliary troops, left Manila, P. I., and landed at Vladivostok. This American Expeditionary Force in Siberia, eventually reinforced from the United States to a strength of about 9000, was commanded by Maj. Gen. William S. Graves, though the Japanese commander in chief, Gen. Kikuzo Otani, was in supreme command of the allied Japanese, American and Chinese forces.

The Americans garrisoned Vladivostok and served in detachments as railway guards on certain sections of the Trans-Siberian and Chinese-Eastern railways. These sections totaled 316 miles and included one, from Verhnudinsk to Mysovaya, near Lake Baikal, which was 1700 miles west of Vladivostok. While performing their duties 36 American soldiers were killed in conflicts with armed partisans. The American forces were withdrawn from Siberia early in 1920, the last troops leaving Vladivostok for Manila, April 1, 1920.

"SIC SEMPER TYRANNIS" (thus ever to tyrants), Latin motto of Virginia from 1776, recommended by George Mason, its probable originator, is popularly associated with Lincoln's assassination, April 14, 1865, in Ford's Theater, Washington, by the deranged John Wilkes Booth, who shouted *"Sic semper tyrannis! The South is avenged!"* as he fired.

SILVER CERTIFICATES were first authorized (by the act of Feb. 28, 1878) to be issued in denominations of not less than ten dollars. The act of Aug. 4, 1886, authorized one-, two- and five-dollar denominations, and the act of March 14, 1900, limited denominations of over ten dollars to 10% of the total. Silver certificates were made full legal tender by the Joint Resolution of June 5, 1933. The Gold Reserve Act of 1934 authorized the President to issue silver certificates against deposited silver bullion as well as coined silver dollars.

SILVER DEMOCRATS was a term used at various times after 1878 to distinguish those members of the Democratic party who were active advocates of free coinage of silver at the 16 to 1 ratio. More general use followed the inauguration of President Cleveland in 1893 and the special session of Congress called by him to repeal the Sherman Act of 1890. This proposal split the party wide open, with silver Democrats in opposition to the Administration, which in turn used every means at its command to force Democrats in Congress to support the Administration's plan. From that time until the national convention of July, 1896, the silver Democrats were a large faction of the party at odds with the official leadership. That convention was a test of strength between the Administration and the silver Democrats, and had the latter lost, undoubtedly many of them would have joined the other free-coinage factions in support of a fusion candidate. Its complete victory in the convention made the silver Democrats the regulars beyond question and the term tended to fall into disuse. This result was encouraged also by the disappearance of the issue from politics. Nevertheless the platform of 1900 was a silver-Democratic document, and only in 1904 was free coinage repudiated by the party's candidate, A. B. Parker.

SILVER LEGISLATION may be deemed to refer to the totality of American legislation which in any way involved silver coinage. Or it may be considered to refer only to monetary statutes passed in the interests of silver as a metal and silver miners as a class. Both types of legislation have loomed large in American history. The details of the specific statutes of both types will be found under their appropriate titles. Silver legislation is here considered from the general standpoint of its place in American history.

It was the intention of the founders of the nation to establish a genuine bimetallism. From the dollar to the tiny "half-disme" silver coins had free coinage and were unlimited legal tender. It has been generally accepted by historians that this policy was based upon the theory, actually offered by Hamilton in his *Mint Report,* that under bimetallism there is a more plentiful supply of money. An equally cogent reason was the fact that the principle of subsidiary silver coinage was unknown to science or to history, and bimetallism was a necessity if small silver was to be coined.

The bimetallic system was a failure. Revision of the legal ratio in 1834 and 1837 created an adequate gold coinage but drove out the limited silver coinage in circulation. From 1834 on, American silver coins as standard money ceased to play a part in the life of the nation. The establishment of subsidiary silver coinage in 1853 confirmed this situation legally. By an accident, fraught with dire consequences for the country, the silver dollar was overlooked in 1853. It was left a standard coin, at a ratio of 16 to 1, although the market ratio continued to make its coinage impossible. In a revision of the statutes in 1873 the unknown piece was dropped.

In 1873 the world market ratio of silver to gold fell below 16 to 1, for the first time in history. This decline coincided with the opening of rich silver mines in the West, with the post-Civil War deflation, and with a deep depression which sorely afflicted the country. The consequence was a political movement, promoted by the silver interests and embraced by the agrarian and inflationary elements, for the restoration of bimetallism. The pressure has never ceased, though it has been relaxed in prosperous periods. Eventually there developed in the Senate and less definitely in the House a nonpartisan "silver bloc," made possible by the meager population and mine-owner control of the silver states of the West.

In the 1870's and the 1890's, as well as in 1933, the unceasing labors of this pressure group, reinforced by the popular clamor for inflation, almost achieved bimetallism. Just failing in this endeavor, they have at intervals extracted from Congress legislation which gave a cash subsidy of some sort to the producers of silver. Among the measures were the creation of the trade dollar in 1873, with a "joker" in the statute making it legal tender; the coinage of a wholly superfluous 20-cent silver piece in 1875; the passage of a premature resumption of silver coinage act in 1875; the Bland-Allison Act of 1878 (passed over Hayes' veto); the Sherman Act of 1890 (approved by Harrison and repealed on the insistence of Cleveland); the Pittman Act of 1918 (approved by Wilson); the Silver Purchase Act of 1934 (approved by F. D. Roosevelt); and the presidential proclamations from 1933 to 1938 which gave subsidies to domestic silver miners. Reference should be made also to illegal or unauthorized Treasury action in connection with silver coinage, which had the effect of aiding the silver interests. Such action was taken by Treasury secretaries from 1853 to 1862, by Richardson in 1873, by Bristow in 1875 and by Sherman in 1876. The Silver Purchase Act of 1934 had for its objectives a government subsidy to silver, the establishment of a hybrid monetary standard of mixed gold and silver, and the issue of silver certificates to swell the currency. During the depression beginning in 1929 the price of silver fell to unprecedented levels. A flood of proposals for subsidies to silver were urged upon Congress. The futile 1933 World Economic Conference at London enacted, under pressure of United States members, an agreement for stabilizing silver, under cover of which, by presidential proclamation, the United States paid from 64.64 cents to 77 cents per ounce for domestic silver whose value was 45 cents. Unable to achieve bimetallism at 16 to 1 (the market ratio was 70 to 1), even with the provisions of the Thomas Amendment, the silver interests finally forced the passage of the Silver Purchase Act. It provided for the nationalization of domestic stocks of silver and the purchase of silver by the Treasury until the price should reach $1.2929 per ounce or the amount held should equal one third of the value of the Government gold holdings. The immediate effect was a speculative rise of silver to 81 cents an ounce, which destroyed the currency systems of China and Mexico.

In 1939 the President's powers to debase the gold standard and buy silver were renewed, and Congress was allowed to set the price for domestic silver. It was pegged at the beginning at 71 cents, 36 cents above the market price.

In World War II a shortage of silver developed and the price rose rapidly. Under the leadership of Senator McCarran, measures were blocked which would have provided silver for defense production, for industrial use in nonwar industries, and for our allies. Finally, in 1943, the Green Act provided that our industries might buy silver at the high price originally paid for it, and large amounts of silver were lent to our allies, all of which was returned for burial in our vaults. The purchase of foreign silver was stopped in 1941, but as late as 1960 the Silver Purchase Act of 1934 was unrepealed, and domestic silver was still acquired at a price fixed by Congress.

SILVER PROSPECTING AND MINING. Silver sometimes occurs in ore as native silver in lodes or veins which run to great depths underground. The outcroppings of such ores identify the lode to the prospector. This silver can be recovered by crushing the ore in a stamp mill, passing it over copper plates coated with mercury, and separating the amalgam by driving off the mercury with heat.

Most silver ores, however, are more complex. Silver is usually chemically combined with gold, lead, copper, or other metals, and the identification of these ores is much more difficult than those containing native silver. The complex ores also require more intricate metallurgical processes for separation. Concentrating mills and smelters, necessary for treating complex silver ores, were not available in the United States until after 1868, when the first successful smelter was erected at Blackhawk, Colo., by Nathaniel P. Hill. For these reasons, although silver mining in the United States began at an early period, the total amount of silver produced was extremely limited and of rather inconsequential significance prior to 1870. The Spanish had worked small mines during their occupation of New Mexico, California, and Texas. Small amounts of silver also were recovered by mining in New Hampshire after 1828 and in Virginia and Tennessee after 1832–34.

Large-scale silver mining had its beginning in Nevada after 1859 when Peter O'Reiley and Patrick McLaughlin, prospecting the area eastward from the California gold fields, staked the Ophir, or Comstock lode. They were looking for gold, but their happy discovery developed into a bonanza mine that yielded more silver than gold. The Comstock ores were so rich that within two decades more than $300,000,000 worth of silver and gold had been extracted.

The Comstock experience of gold-seekers finding silver became a pattern repeated in various parts of the West in the years that followed. At Georgetown, Colo., an original gold placer camp developed as the center of a silver producing district after the opening of the Belmont lode in 1864. Also in Colorado, the gold camp of Oro City was almost a ghost town when ores of carbonate of lead, with rich silver content, were discovered in 1877 and the greatest of Colorado silver cities, Leadville, was born. Again, gold prospectors accidentally discovered the Bunker Hill and Sullivan mines in the Cœur d'Alene district of Idaho.

The prosperity of the silver mining industry in the United States during the 19th century was intimately related to the currency policy of the Federal Government, particularly after the demonitization of silver in 1873. Many of the largest producing silver mines in the country, including those at Leadville, Aspen, and Silver Cliff in Colorado, those of the Silver Reef district in Utah, the Idaho mines, and the mines in the Butte district in Montana, were opened after 1873. During the quarter century that followed, while the nation debated the questions of silver purchases and coinage, the huge quantities of silver produced by these mines depressed the price, already reduced by the demonitization. With the repeal of the Sherman Silver Purchase Act in 1893, the domestic silver market fell to levels so low that many mines suspended operations.

The industry recovered sufficiently to make the years from 1911–15 the peak years in volume of production. Then the advent of World War I, the continuing low prices for silver and the high production costs severely limited activity in mining. After 1920 the leading silver producing regions of the United States were the Cœur d'Alene district of Idaho, the Summitt Valley (Butte) district of Montana, and the West Mountain (Bingham) district of Utah.

The Bureau of the Mint has estimated that from 1493 to 1957 the total world production of silver was 20,716,063,100 fine ounces, of which the United States produced approximately one fifth.

SILVERSMITHING was popular in the colonies as early as 1650, as it offered a secure way of preserving capital. Its quality, evident in the earliest pieces, was due to the adoption of the European apprenticeship system with its attendant seven years' indenture. The centers of the craft in the 17th century were Boston and New York. The output consisted of beakers, tankards, caudle cups and porringers for secular use, as well as beakers, cups and baptismal basins for ecclesiastical usage. In Boston these were based upon the current English styles and are marked by their vigorous simplicity. The early artisans there were English-trained Robert Sanderson and his partner John Hull. The early 18th century, with the introduction of luxuries, ushers in the golden age of American silversmithing with the richly ornamented standing salts, chocolate pots, sugar boxes and imposing loving cups by the American-trained Jeremiah Dummer (1645–1718), John Coney (1656–1722) and Edward Winslow (1669–1753). By the second quarter of the century the studied simplicity of the English Queen Anne style is reflected in the work of Jacob Hurd (1702–58). The popularity of tea drinking added to variety of form. The exuberant rococo and its succeeding reserved classic styles of the last half of the 18th century are best seen in the work of Paul Revere (1735–1818).

The origin of the New York style is a combination of Dutch and French as reflected in the names of the early artisans: Cornelius Vanderburg (1653–99), Jacob Boelen (1654–1729) and his son Henricus (1697–1755), Jacobus Vanderspiegel (1668–1708), Bartholomew LeRoux (*ca.* 1688–1713) and his sons John and Charles (1689–1745), as well as Simeon Soumain (1685–1750). Surfaces were more richly ornamented and a high standard set. After 1750 styles were anglicized. In the early 18th century Newport and Philadelphia became important centers, Samuel Vernon (1683–1737) in Newport, and the Richardson and Syng silversmithing dynasties in Philadelphia, where silversmithing reached its peak *ca.* 1790. In the early 19th century Baltimore had its group of craftsmen, among them Samuel Kirk (1793–1872). In Boston George C. Gebelein is carrying on the early traditions. The most comprehensive public collections are those of the Museum of Fine Arts, Boston; The Metropolitan Museum of Art; Museum of the City of New York; Philadelphia Museum of Art; Baltimore Museum of Art; and the Mabel Brady Garvan Collection, Gallery of Fine Arts, Yale University.

SINGLE TAX. This plan of Henry George was set forth in his famous work *Progress and Poverty* published in 1879. In place of all other taxes George advocated a single tax which would appropriate for government use all of the economic rent of land. His proposal was intended as much more than a mere fiscal device. It was set forth as an engine of social reform.

On the ground that land was a gift of nature, not a product of man's effort, George condemned private property in land which he considered the cause of economic and social ills. Land values, he held, were due to social or community causes. The State, therefore, and not the individual, should be the beneficiary of these values and any increases therein. "What I, therefore propose," he wrote, "as the simple yet sovereign remedy, which will raise wages, increase the earnings of capital, extirpate pauperism, abolish poverty, give remunerative employment to whoever wishes it, afford free scope to human powers, lessen crime, elevate morals, and taste, and intelligence, purify government, and carry civilization to yet nobler heights, is—to appropriate rent by taxation."

SKYSCRAPERS. The skyscraper may be defined as a multistory elevator business building, usually of skeleton frame construction. Its foundations were laid on American soil in the last quarter of the 19th century, but since that time its form has been borrowed by many countries throughout the world.

Its beginnings can be traced back to such structures as the Equitable Life Building (Gilman, Kendall and Post, 1868–70), the Western Union Building (George B. Post, 1873–75), and the Tribune Building (Richard M. Hunt, 1873–75), all in New York, in which the potentialities of the elevator as it relates to the rental of high office space was first exploited.

Skeleton frame construction which made buildings of more than ten stories economically feasible was perfected in Chicago by William LeBaron Jenney in the Home Life Insurance Building (1883–85) and by Holabird & Roche in the Tacoma Building (1888–89). In the Wainwright Building (St. Louis, 1890–91) Adler and Sullivan clad the metal frame with a functional design that expressed not only its structural system but also its use as a tall office building, producing one of the finest examples of early skyscraper architecture.

In the East, architects were moving in a different direction. The Ames Building by Shepley, Rutan & Coolidge (Boston, 1889) represented the Romanesque mode as revived by H. H. Richardson. The New York Life Insurance Building by McKim, Mead & White (Kansas City, 1890) employed Italian Renaissance garb. Bruce Price, in the American Surety Building (New York, 1894–95) conceived of the skyscraper as a classic column divided into base, shaft and capital. The tower concept had many followers, as exemplified by the Singer Tower (Ernest Flagg, 1906–8), the Woolworth Building Tower (Cass Gilbert, 1913), the Chrysler Tower (William Van Alen, 1929) and the tallest of all, the Empire State Building (Shreve, Lamb & Harmon, 1930).

Rockefeller Center (Reinhard & Hofmeister; Hood, Godley & Fouilhoux; Corbett, Harrison & MacMurray, 1928–40) marked the beginning of the present trend to open large-scale planning. The tendency toward modest development and landscaped environment has been continued in such works as Lever House (Skidmore, Owings & Merrill, 1952) and the Seagram Building by Miës van der Rohe and Philip Johnson (New York, 1958).

SLAUGHTER HOUSE CASES (16 Wallace 36, 1873), are considered as the Supreme Court's first interpretation of the due process clause of the Fourteenth Amendment and the most important decision of that Court since the Dred Scott case. In 1869 the carpetbag legislature of Louisiana, probably under corrupt influences, granted a monopoly of the slaughtering business within the city limits of New Orleans in favor of a single corporation, thereby depriving some thousand persons of their occupation. This monopoly was challenged in the courts mainly as a violation of the Fourteenth Amendment particularly with reference to the "privileges and immunities" clause, the denial by the state of the equal protection of the laws, and a deprivation of property under the due process clause. Justice Miller, delivering the majority opinion of the Court, declared that the "one pervading purpose" of the Amendment was the protection of the Negro freedman and not that of transferring the control over the entire domain of civil rights from the states to the Federal Government. This decision was in flagrant violation of the intent of the Radical

Republican framers of the Amendment, who had desired to bring about Federal protection of corporations and other businesses from discriminating state legislation, as well as to achieve social guarantees for the Negro. The Slaughter House Cases are significant as a temporary reversal in the strong trend of Federal centralization evident since the Civil War.

SLAVE CODES, emanating from specific enactments to meet current problems, took the form of general police laws based upon cumulative experience, supplemented periodically by additional legislation as new issues arose. The Barbadian assembly passed a series of acts beginning in 1644 which were brought together in a general law of 1688. After experimenting with specific statutes, South Carolina in 1712 adopted much of the Barbadian law, but added further regulations in 1740 following a servile revolt. Georgia adopted the South Carolina system in 1770, Florida drew upon the Georgia code in the 1820's, and other states utilized the same sequential sources. Several 17th-century Virginia acts culminated in a general police law of 1680, subsequently drawn upon by neighboring colonies and western slaveholding states. In Louisiana the liberal Code Noir of 1724 served throughout the French and Spanish eras, but was subjected to material changes in the American period. Northern colonial legislatures enacted laws regulating slave status, and all, whether North or South, passed acts affecting Indian slavery.

Negro slave codes, designed to protect property rights and white society, varied in character but certain provisions were common to many. These restrained freedom of assembly, trade, transit and the bearing of arms; provided for the return of absconders and penalties for theft and homicide; forbade any one to instruct them in reading and writing, or to sell them liquor without the owners' consent; specified compensation for slaves executed for capital crimes; and permitted testimony in court only in cases involving other slaves. Occasionally an act guaranteed adequate clothing and rations, limited working hours, or prevented separate sale of mothers and small children. Codes were severest in the West Indies, harsher on the rice coast than in the tobacco area; everywhere enforcement was lax. Except in Delaware and the North, a Negro was presumed to be a slave.

SLAVE INSURRECTIONS. It is difficult to estimate the extent of slave unrest leading to attempted insurrections in the United States, because of the obvious policy of silence regarding such events, the difficulty of distinguishing between personal crimes and organized revolt, and the quick spread of baseless rumors. A unique record of slave convictions in Virginia, 1780–1864, shows out of a total of 1418, 91 for insurrection and conspiracy and 346 for murder. Fifty-three cases of slave ship mutinies, 1699–1808, have been listed. In 17th-century Virginia two or three plots involving white servants and slaves were discovered. In the early 18th century there were a good many scares in Virginia and South Carolina—the outbreak at Stono, S. C., 1740, probably being the most formidable. The New York outbreaks of 1712 and 1741 were both "more notable for the frenzy of the public than for the formidableness of the menace."

The insurrections in San Domingo growing out of the French Revolution led to a new series of plots in Virginia, South Carolina and Louisiana. Gabriel's uprising near Richmond in 1800 was marked by a real plan and followed by numerous plots and rumors from Virginia to Louisiana (with one in York, Pa., in 1803), lasting to about 1816. The plot of Denmark Vesey (Charleston, 1822) is probably the most noteworthy. Nat Turner's insurrection in 1831 led to another wave of plots and rumors. In Louisiana especially a succession of plots, 1835–40, was followed by a succession of reports finally proved baseless. In 1856, connected in Southern minds with the rise of the Republican party, there was believed to be a widespread conspiracy covering the whole South. Harpers Ferry was followed in 1860 by reports of arson and poison plots from Texas to Virginia. In 1861 the question became important in the North and throughout the war the possibility of a slave insurrection figured prominently in Northern policies and politics.

The plots were marked naturally by poor planning, participation of some whites and free Negroes, betrayal by some slave. Each episode brought a new crop of repressive legislation often relaxed and evaded when fears subsided. Negro historians tend to stress the amount of slave unrest and U. Phillips admits that the actual revolts and plots "were sufficiently serious to produce a very palpable disquiet from time-to-time and the rumors were frequent enough to maintain a fairly constant undertone of uneasiness."

SLAVE SHIPS, which brought slaves from Africa to America, sailed under the flags of all nations—but Dutch, Spanish and English were most active in the trade. As the New England colonies developed, their vessels entered the trade also.

The ships were usually sloops or schooners of fifty to one hundred tons burden with a deck three feet below the regular deck on which the slaves were crowded, unable to stand erect.

They carried a crew of eight to fifteen men in addition to the captain. The crew received wages and the captain received a commission and frequently the right to transport and sell for his own profit.

On the voyage to Africa the ship was loaded with hogsheads of rum and trinkets for trading. On its return all available space below deck was filled with slaves. The horrors of "the middle passage," as the trip to America was called, beggar description. Slaves were kept shackled. They suffered from the tropic heat, overcrowding and seasickness. Epidemics of scurvy and smallpox decimated them. Often food and water ran short and the death rate was high.

However, the slave ship was a profitable investment and owners of such vessels made fortunes out of the trade.

SLAVE TRADE, AMERICAN. The beginning of traffic in Negro slaves is lost in antiquity but the modern trade dates from 1444, when a Portuguese trader imported ten Negro slaves from Africa. Two years later a trading company was organized and the trade soon became systematized. Columbus brought the first Negro to America in 1492 and the trade in Negro slaves to America was recognized ten years later. Charles V granted Lorenzo de Gomenot the exclusive right to supply the West Indian Islands with 4000 Negro slaves in 1518. This was done at the suggestion of Las Casas and others to lighten the burden of the red men. John Hawkins, the first Englishman to engage in the African slave trade, brought a cargo of Negroes from Sierra Leone and sold them in Hispaniola in 1562.

The first Negro slaves introduced into the English continental colonies were landed at Jamestown by a Dutch vessel in 1619. They seem to have been sold as indentured servants for life. The importation of slaves for a number of years thereafter was occasional and incidental. At first there was little demand for slaves and in 1650 they numbered only about 300. As tobacco culture became more profitable the demand for slaves increased, and in 1661 slavery was given legal recognition. Between that date and the chartering of the Royal African Company in 1672 several shiploads of slaves were imported into Virginia. Slavery was introduced into Massachusetts from the West Indies in 1636 and given legal status in 1641. Importation of slaves increased rapidly during the latter half of the 17th century and slavery was given legal recognition in all the English colonies in America.

Much of the slave trade during the early part of the 17th century was a secondary one from the West Indies, and was largely carried on by the Dutch. The Royal African Company was given a monopoly of the English slave trade in 1672 and entered largely into the traffic. Between 1680 and 1688 this company sent out some 249 ships which landed 46,396 slaves in America. The importance of this company declined after 1688 when it lost its privileged position. The Asiento of 1713 between Spain and England gave the latter a monopoly of the Spanish slave trade for thirty years. Under this agreement England was to supply the Spanish colonies with 144,000 slaves at the rate of 4800 per year. The first colonial ship to engage in the trade was built at Marblehead in 1636. The trade became very profitable to the shipping colonies and Massachusetts, Rhode Island, Connecticut and New Hampshire had many ships in the triangular trade. Rhode Island alone had 150 vessels engaged in this

traffic in 1770. The largest number of English vessels engaged in the trade in any one year was 192 in 1771. Reports indicate that the horrors of the middle passage were more unbearable in New England than in English ships.

Rapid growth of slave population during the 18th century led the colonial assemblies to place restrictions on the trade. Opposition to the increase of slavery in the planting or Southern colonies was based upon fear of slave insurrection, while the argument that slave labor was unprofitable was largely used in the farming or middle colonies. The moral argument against slavery arose early in the New England shipping colonies but it could not withstand the profits of the trade and soon died out. Most colonial laws restricting the trade were disallowed by the king in council because of the advantages of the trade to England. The trustees of Georgia at first forbade slavery, but the settlers clamored for Negro laborers and slave trade and slavery were legalized in that colony in 1750.

The total number of slaves imported into the thirteen English colonies can never be known, but the Negro population in 1776 has been estimated at 502,-132. Negro slaves were distributed as follows: 15,000 in New England; 32,000 in the middle colonies; and the remainder in the South: 16,000 in Georgia, 75,-000 in North Carolina, 110,000 in South Carolina and 165,000 in Virginia.

Upon the outbreak of the American Revolution the colonies were able to restrict the slave trade. Virginia forbade importation of slaves from England in 1768 and was shortly followed by the other colonies. In 1774 the Continental Association also forbade importation from England. Reasons for this action may be summarized as follows: slavery was economically unprofitable in the northern colonies; the Southern colonies feared slave insurrections; the American market was overstocked; traders feared their ships would be captured by the English; human bondage was incompatible with the natural rights philosophy of the period; and, it was believed that nonimportation would force England to redress colonial grievances. Jefferson condemned the slave trade in the original draft of the Declaration of Independence but the New England traders joined the planters of Georgia and South Carolina to strike out the clause. The Articles of Confederation made no mention of the slave trade but the Constitution prohibited Congress from interdicting the trade before 1808. All the states, however, ended the importation of foreign slaves before 1803. South Carolina removed her restrictions in 1804 and some 40,000 slaves were imported into that state during the next four years. In 1808 Congress exercised the power bestowed on it by the Constitution and forever put an end to legal importation of slaves.

Both the New England traders and Southern planters opposed the action of Congress and smuggling soon became a profitable enterprise. It is estimated that up to 1816 more than 15,000 slaves were annually smuggled in. Barataria and Amelia Island were important centers for this illicit trade. Drake, a famous smuggler, had a depot in the Gulf of Mexico where he at one time had a supply of 1600 Negroes awaiting a purchaser. More than 10,000 slaves were smuggled into New Orleans in one year alone. Congress at first made little attempt to enforce the law, but after 1820, when the slave trade was made piracy, an agency was set up to enforce it. It is worthy of note, however, that no person was executed under this act until the outbreak of the Civil War. The price of slaves mounted in the 1850's and Southern planters began to agitate the reopening of the foreign slave trade. As a result of the agitation smuggling rapidly increased in the years just preceding the war. The *Wanderer,* last slave ship to land a cargo of African Negroes in the United States, was owned by Georgia planters. Stephen A. Douglas estimated that 15,000 slaves were imported in 1858, and 85 vessels are reported to have sailed from New York in 1859–60 to engage in the trade. The Confederate Constitution forbade the foreign slave trade in spite of the interest of the planters to reopen it.

A local domestic trade developed soon after slavery was introduced into America. All purchasers could not buy direct from the shipper and a local market was established. When a planter abandoned his business for any reason or a slaveholder died without heirs the slaves had to be disposed of. Some slaveholders had no need for the natural increase of their slaves and the surplus had to be sold. Planters had no hesitancy in advertising the sale of slaves at public auction before the county courthouse or at their residence. The early trade was chiefly confined to American-born slaves but not entirely restricted to such, for planters often desired to sell refractory Africans. The trade was small in the beginning but reached sizable proportions in the last quarter of the 18th century. Partly casual and partly systematic it became a well-organized business by 1800. The close of the African slave trade in 1808 was a potent factor in the increase of the domestic trade between the Upper and the Lower South. As the new lands of the Southwest were opened to settlers the demand for slaves on the part of the cotton and sugar planters increased by leaps and bounds. The only source of supply was the domestic trade. Slavery was becoming less profitable on the worn-out lands of the old tobacco belt and the profits to be derived from the trade were sufficiently large to induce many men to engage in it. As a rule, however, there was a stigma attached to the business.

In the towns of the Upper South, there were many local dealers and brokers who bought surplus Negroes to sell either direct to planters who came to the local market, or to the long-distance trader who shipped slaves to the markets of the Southwest. Local dealers were often employed as regular agents of the shipping firms. With the rise in prices some planters of the Upper South deliberately encouraged a rapid birth rate among the breeding Negroes.

The long-distance trade was systematically organized. Trading companies had assembling headquarters in the Upper South and distributing markets in the Southwest. In addition to purchasing from the local dealer the shippers had field agents who combed the countryside for slaves. They advertised widely in local papers offering to pay cash prices for likely or prime Negroes. Some traders used the local jail, taverns, or warehouses for assembling their slaves, others owned their pens and stockades.

Franklin and Armfield, one of the best-known firms, owned an assembling plant in Alexandria, and sold in the markets at Natchez and New Orleans. The Alexandria plant was equipped with brick office and residence, two whitewashed stockades or courts for men and women, eating quarters, a hospital and sleeping barracks. All were clean and sanitary. Armfield was in charge of the plant. Isaac Franklin, who became a wealthy and respected planter as well as slave dealer, disposed of the purchases in the Southwest markets.

Slaves were transported to market by boat around the Florida peninsula and through the Gulf, or down the Mississippi after being driven overland from Alexandria. Some were transported in hired ships, others in ships owned by the trader. Some slaves were driven in coffles all the way to New Orleans. Some of these might be sold at local markets or to individual planters along the route. Slaves were well fed and cared for in transit so that they might be in good or prime condition when they reached the market. Slaves generally dreaded being sold down the river not only because it meant breaking family ties but also because the institution was less patriarchal in the Southwest.

The public auctions, whether local or general, exhibited all the worst features of the trade. Auctioneers, usually coarse, cruel fellows, had little or no sympathy with the finer feelings of the slave. Human beings were placed on the block to be examined by the prospective purchaser as if they were mere livestock. The markets and auctions were found in all the chief towns of the Old South but centered in Alexandria, Richmond, Charleston, Savannah, Mobile, New Orleans, Natchez, Memphis, Louisville and Lexington. There were, of course, markets in some inland towns.

All the Southern states made some effort to regulate and restrict the domestic trade. Laws were passed prohibiting the export of slaves from the state, but Delaware alone really enforced the law. Other laws forbade the importation of slaves for sale and prohibited the sale of young children away from their mothers. Most such laws were ineffective. Congress forbade the trade in the District of Columbia as a part of the Compromise of 1850.

The volume and value of the domestic slave trade cannot be fixed with any degree of accuracy since no statistics of the trade were kept. Virginia, Maryland,

Kentucky, Missouri and the Carolinas were almost exclusively exporting states; Texas, Florida and Arkansas were exclusively importing states; and Georgia, Alabama, Mississippi, Louisiana and Tennessee were both importing and exporting states. The latter group chiefly imported up to 1850 but exported considerable numbers to the newer states in the decade of the 1850's. During the period from 1830 to 1860 Virginia exported about 220,000 slaves. Mississippi imported about 102,000 in the fourth decade and exported about 1000; the figures for the fifth decade are 58,000 and 3000; and for the sixth decade of the century 56,000 and 8000. For the decade of the 1850's the estimate for all the states is an annual turnover of about 80,000 valued at $59,000,000.

SLAVERY. Chattel slavery had practically disappeared from Europe before the discovery of America; serfdom was declining and had already been destroyed in England, but the expansion of European states in the 16th century, and of England during the following century, resulted in the revival of the institution of slavery in their colonial possessions and of serfdom in a modified form. In the North American colonies of England the unsatisfactory attempts to enslave the Indians were followed by the use of white indentured servants, men and women who contracted to serve and to subject themselves to their masters for a period of years, thus supplying a small population with what was considered a necessary type of labor for a new, undeveloped country. "Redemptioners," convicts and political prisoners constituted the source of this labor, and each colony received its share. As late as 1818 a cargo of "redemptioners" was landed in Philadelphia. The opportunities offered by a new country encouraged indentured servants to jump their contracts, while a general disinclination and physical inability to perform the kind of labor demanded in the Southern colonies resulted in the exploitation of another source.

The development of the plantation system in Virginia, and its spread to other Southern colonies during the 17th century led to the introduction and adaptation of Negro slave labor for the agricultural industry, and a corresponding experimentation in the provinces to the north. It was not, however, until the first quarter of the 18th century that a rapid development is noted, and the lively trade direct to Africa transformed Newport and Bristol (R. I.) to flourishing centers of the traffic.

By 1776 some 500,000 slaves, out of a total population of 2,500,000, were distributed along the Atlantic seaboard, their treatment and occupation differing according to section. In the New England colonies they were generally employed in trades and domestic duties; in the Middle Atlantic region far more were used in agriculture; and in the South, where they were present in the largest numbers and agriculture was the chief occupation, the institution became basic to the social and economic system. This new element

in colonial society led first to the modification of the laws regulating indentured servants to meet the needs of the community, and then to positive legislation defining the legal, political and social status of Negroes in a white society. When the American Revolution broke out Virginia led the group with 200,000 slaves, South Carolina, 100,000, Maryland and North Carolina, 70,000 each, New York, 25,000, Georgia, 10,000, New Jersey and Pennsylvania, 6000 each, Connecticut and Massachusetts, 5000 each, Rhode Island, 4000, New Hampshire, 700, with no data for Delaware. (These figures, which are necessarily estimates, are based on J. F. Jameson, *The American Revolution Considered as a Social Movement.* For a different estimate *see* article on the Slave Trade, in which the figures are based on J. D. B. DeBow, *Industrial Resources of the South and West.*)

New England farmers grew no produce which found a ready and widespread market to encourage the enlargement of their agricultural units and the industries found slave labor too expensive and too difficult to train for the skilled trades, and, according to John Adams, the white laborers disliked competition with the Negro slaves. Moral and economic considerations promoted antislavery sentiment in the Middle Atlantic provinces. Colonial leaders were aware of the inconsistency of the doctrines of natural rights and the enslavement of a half million Negroes and scarcely needed to be reminded by Lord Mansfield that slavery was "so odious that nothing could be suffered to support it but positive law." Humanitarians who attacked the institution were found in every section, John Usselinx, James Edward Oglethorpe, Roger Williams, John Eliot, Anthony Benezet, John Woolman, Henry Laurens and Thomas Jefferson, for example, were voices crying against it from 1624 to 1776. Indeed, the official attitude of the English government had been far less liberal than that of many of the colonies. Massachusetts, Connecticut, Rhode Island, Pennsylvania and Virginia attempted to abolish the slave trade only to find that such action interfered with the Royal African Company and was nullified by royal disallowance. The First Continental Congress (1774) approved a nonimportation agreement prohibiting the slave trade, and by 1786 all of the states, except Georgia (in 1798), abolished the foreign trade. Antislavery societies were organized on the eve of the Revolution, the first by Philadelphia Quakers, to curb slavery and to promote manumission. Many of these organizations were found in the South.

Emancipating the slaves in the Northern colonies was comparatively easy, since they were few in proportion to the whites, and were not deemed essential to the economic system. Where there were considerable numbers, emancipation was gradual. By legislative action Rhode Island freed her slaves in 1774; Vermont, by her constitution (1777); court decisions in Massachusetts (1781) and New Hampshire (1783) put an end to slavery there; Pennsylvania (1780),

Connecticut (1784), New York (1799) and New Jersey (1804) adopted gradual emancipation laws, the latter two requiring until 1827 and 1846 respectively to effect complete abolition. The Southern states debated the problem, but the large number, the force of custom, the race question and the economic value of the system to agriculture prevented emancipation. More liberal manumission laws were passed, however, with the result that Virginia freed more slaves by private action than there were in Massachusetts, Rhode Island and New Hampshire combined. From 1790 to 1860 there was an actual decline in the number of slaves in Delaware and Maryland, and two thirds of all the free Negroes in the South in 1860 were in these two states and Virginia. Jefferson's proposal to exclude slavery from the Old Northwest Territory found its way into the Ordinance of 1787. The framers of the Federal Constitution of 1787 regarded the question of emancipation as a state matter, and their concern with a general framework of government excluded such a consideration as much as the relations between an employer and his clerk. Nevertheless, the congressional powers over commerce, the three-fifths clause, the mutual obligations of states as members of the Union, and congressional powers in the territories were potential sources of controversy.

The invention of the cotton gin by Eli Whitney (1793) and the introduction of sea-island cotton (1784) relieved the depressed South Atlantic states, revived slavery, and showed the value of the Negro to the industry. It was cotton more than any other staple that gave new strength to a moribund institution. The Negro seemed perfectly adapted to its growth, and women and children could be utilized in numerous ways. Established, embryonic and aspiring planters moved into the southern piedmont, swung south and westward, and each decade thereafter saw a growth in the number of slaves, the bales of cotton, and a corresponding diminution in the southern liberality of 1776.

Climatic and geographical factors divided the South into four zones of staple production—(1) Tobacco: Maryland, Virginia, Kentucky and North Carolina; (2) Cotton: South Carolina, Georgia and the Gulf states; (3) Sugar cane: Georgia and Louisiana; (4) Rice: South Carolina and Georgia. Slavery sought its climatic and geographical level, being found even in the southern portions of the free states along the Ohio River. Slavery was unevenly distributed, its irregularity following that of the plantation belts, and nearly one half of all slaves in 1860 were found in the cotton states. Of the total white population of that area, namely over 8,000,000, only 383,000 owned slaves, less than one third of that number owned over 10 slaves each, while only 2292 owned 100 or more each. Less than one half the whole area of the South was in the cotton zone, and less than one half its people were engaged in its production.

The Southern farm and plantation had an almost equal division of slaves, and on both they were classified as field hands and house servants. The latter took pride in their privileged position and were the envy of their less fortunate brethren. The industrial and social life of the field hands was strictly regulated: they lived in quarters, received regular rations of food and clothes, labored in gangs, usually, under the supervision of an overseer or the owner, and were not allowed to leave the premises without a pass. Overseers were given detailed instructions as to the administration of the plantation, the industrial direction of the slaves, and even their punishment. The degree of regimentation depended upon the size of the plantation or farm, the staple grown and the locality. While house servants by no means enjoyed full freedom, their lot was far better than that of the field hands, and they were not subject to such strict control.

Family life was encouraged among the slaves, and the majority of the adults were apt to be married. Cast-off furniture and ornaments found their way to the quarters, articles of slave manufacture, gardens and perhaps a few chickens gave an air of domesticity to the little cabins. Medical attention was given by the master's physician, and on the large plantations a hospital might be found. Generally, the slaves were well-fed, even if the food was coarse, reasonable rest periods were observed, and while the hours of labor were long, there was no systematic exploitation of the workers. Slaves represented capital, and no owner would risk its loss any more than the owner of a valuable horse or a registered bull. Moreover, most of the slaveowners were fully aware that their property were human beings and treated them accordingly, such treatment being commensurate with the character, temper and intelligence of the master. Religious instruction was given at regular intervals on the large plantations, and frequently the slaves attended their master's church. Truancy, sullenness, the refusal to obey orders, etc., brought punishment, usually whipping, the degree being in proportion to the nature of the offense.

Slaves were employed to some extent in industry, but experimentation with slave labor in cotton mills and railroad construction proved unsatisfactory. Some worked as stevedores, carpenters, masons, plasterers and mechanics, furnishing a mobile labor supply, and were hired out frequently to individuals desiring such workers, the profits accruing to the owner.

The nature of the institution, antislavery sentiment, latent and active, in the North, and political expediency injected the issue into national politics and made the course of our territorial expansion difficult. The first important controversy came over the application of Missouri for admission as a state in 1818. Some politicians from the Middle Atlantic states, tired of the rule of the Virginia dynasty, saw an opportunity to break its hold on the Republican party (Jeffersonian) through the slavery question, by presenting it in such a way as to force the South to set the bounds to its expansion, and consequently lose political power in the National Government, or reject it, and thus alienate the northern wing of the party. James Tallmadge, of New York, introduced an amendment in the House (1819) excluding slavery from Missouri, and so heated were the arguments in Congress that such leaders as John Adams and Thomas Jefferson were thoroughly alarmed. The settlement of the question would be a precedent for other states carved from the major part of the Louisiana Purchase of 1803. The compromise of 1820, admitting Missouri with slavery but excluding it from the territory north of 36° 30′, removed the question from public arenas for some time (see Missouri Compromise).

Geographical proximity, the activities of land speculators, and the expansion of the southern frontier resulted in the settlement of the Mexican state of Texas by Americans, and its successful revolution in 1836 raised the question of annexation to the Union. Slavery existed in Texas, and if admitted to the Union the political advantage would be to the South. The panic of 1837 postponed the matter, but subsequent debates and sharp political division kept it in the foreground. In general the majority of the Democrats favored annexation, the majority of the Whigs opposed. By the end of 1844 it seemed impossible to secure the necessary two thirds of the Senate to annex Texas by a treaty, so a joint resolution of Congress was adopted in 1845, the offer rushed to Texas just before the Tyler administration retired, and Dec. 29, it was admitted as a state. The annexation of Texas led directly to the War with Mexico (1846–48), and again political expediency was fateful in its results. David Wilmot (Pa.) introduced the famous proviso to an appropriation bill (1846) calling for the exclusion of slavery from any territory acquired from Mexico. It passed the House of Representatives, was defeated in the Senate, and the passions thus aroused, aggravated by Abolitionist demands for the emancipation of slaves and the abolition of the slave trade in the District of Columbia, with the counter demand of Southerners for an equal share in the territories and a better fugitive slave law, led to an organized secession movement in the South. Conservatives and moderates in Congress adopted the Compromise of 1850 which admitted California as a free state (its constitution forbade slavery), organized Utah and New Mexico as territories with no reference to slavery, abolished the slave trade in the District of Columbia, and provided a more stringent fugitive slave law. The Southern Convention meeting at Nashville (Tenn.) in 1850 accepted the Compromise as a permanent solution of the question, but warned that any future interference with slavery in the states or the domestic slave trade, or the refusal by Congress to admit a state because of slavery would be met with resistance even to the point of secession.

As things stood in 1850, every square inch of territory had been divided between slavery and freedom;

the Missouri Compromise took care of the Louisiana Purchase and the northern part of Texas; that of 1850, California and New Mexico; Oregon did not feature in the dispute. The great majority, North and South, took this as the final settlement, and the elections of 1852 and 1856 seemed to prove that the country was weary of the controversy.

The contest was raised again by the Kansas-Nebraska Act of 1854. Stephen A. Douglas (Ill.), chairman of the Senate committee on the territories, was highly desirous of organizing a territorial government for the region so as to facilitate the construction of a transcontinental railroad to the Pacific. Jefferson Davis (Miss.) and others planned a similar project from New Orleans and following the southern route to the Pacific, the line passing through a territory already organized. Others favored a line running north of Kansas. The result was the reporting of a bill organizing both regions. Sen. Archibald M. Dixon (Ky.) proposed an amendment repealing the Missouri Compromise, and all efforts to have him withdraw the motion failed. The bill passed. This put the slavery issue, politically, where it was in 1819. The doctrine of popular, or "squatter" sovereignty, advocated by Douglas and Lewis Cass (Mich.), left Kansas to be controlled by the first groups arriving, and the struggle that ensued over the framing of the constitution and the control of the government was a prelude to the Civil War. The Republican party was organized on this issue.

The decision of the U. S. Supreme Court on March 6, 1857, in Dred Scott v. Sanford was an effort to suppress the dispute and take the question out of politics. The right of Congress to prohibit slavery in a territory was denied, and the Missouri Compromise was pronounced unconstitutional and void. This seemed to be an approval of Calhoun's doctrine that slavery followed the flag into the territories.

The controversy was settled, after an appeal to arms, by a victorious North standing unquestioned over a prostrate South. The Thirteenth Amendment to the Constitution, legally abolishing slavery, passed Congress in 1864, and Secretary of State William H. Seward announced Dec. 18, 1865, that the requisite number of states had ratified, including eight states of the former Confederacy.

SLAVERY, ATTITUDE OF THE CHURCHES TO.
All the larger colonial churches accepted slavery without question. The Society for the Propagation of the Gospel instructed its missionaries to give attention to the religious instruction of slaves, but did not condemn slavery as such. Prominent New England ministers owned slaves and respectable New England citizens were interested in the slave trade. Several of the smaller German sects (e.g., Mennonites, Dunkers) opposed slavery and the Quakers had taken steps to eliminate slaveholding members by 1787.

The first antislavery movement came from two main

sources: the increased humanitarian impulse coming out of the 18th century revivals; the revolutionary philosophy embodied in the Declaration of Independence, which states that "all men are created equal." Responding to these influences the American churches during the last quarter of the 18th and the first quarter of the 19th centuries became increasingly antislavery. It was during this period that the Northern states rid themselves of slavery. New England Congregationalism became actively antislavery under the leadership of Samuel Hopkins; the Methodists passed antislavery legislation at their organizing conference in 1784; the Presbyterians took strong antislavery positions in 1787 and 1818; and various Baptist associations took similar action.

The churches began to recede from this strong antislavery position after 1830, due to the influences arising out of the agricultural revolution taking place in the South and the rise of the rabid abolition movement in the North. Slaveholding church members and even slaveholding ministers became an accepted fact in the South, while in the North condemnation of slaveholding church members came to be increasingly virulent.

The general church officials, having in charge national church bodies, attempted to keep down controversy within the church, fearing for its unity, and until 1840 they generally occupied a moderate position and condemned abolitionism. William Lloyd Garrison at first found considerable support for his radical movement among church people, but his violent methods soon alienated them and after 1840 his movement found little church support. As a result, Garrison developed an anticlerical and antichurch obsession, and he and his disciples were responsible for the legend that the American churches were the chief bulwarks of American slavery.

After about 1836 a new antislavery movement began among church people led by Theodore Dwight Weld and a group of Oberlin graduates, which swept throughout central and western New York, Ohio, western Pennsylvania and Michigan. This Oberlin movement was particularly strong among New School Presbyterians, slavery having been one of the causes leading to the Old School-New School division in 1837. The Weld influence was largely responsible for sending the first antislavery members to Congress, and for a time Weld acted as an extremely effective lobbyist. Growing differences over the slavery issue divided Methodists and Baptists in 1844–45 into Northern and Southern bodies, the Northern section of the churches becoming increasingly antislavery, the Southern bodies increasingly proslavery. Roman Catholics and Episcopalians generally avoided all agitation of the question and thus avoided a slavery schism.

SMITH ACT (June 28, 1940). This act reflected American anxiety over Germany's rapid conquest of Western Europe in World War II and over Com-

munist-inspired strikes intended to injure American defense production. The act provides for the registration and fingerprinting of aliens living in the United States, and declares it unlawful to advocate or teach the forceful overthrow of any government in the United States, or to belong to any group advocating or teaching such action. The act has been strongly criticized on the ground that it interferes with freedom of speech, guaranteed by the First Amendment. In a famous case (Dennis v. United States) concerning the conviction of eleven Communists under the act, the Supreme Court in 1951 upheld its constitutionality.

SMUGGLING, COLONIAL. The extent of smuggling and its effect upon the imperial relationship offer one of the most perplexing problems of colonial history. That smuggling existed there can be no doubt. Parliament was surprisingly negligent in providing for the enforcement of the Navigation Acts. It provided regulations in 1660 and 1663 governing exportations and importations. But not until 1673 did it create officials to enforce them, and not until 1696 did it give them the powers granted customs officers in England. The colonial charters complicated problems of enforcement already made complex by natural geographic conditions. The lengthy coastline, numerous sheltered coves, afforded tempting opportunities for clandestine activities. Accounts of tobacco packed in flour barrels and foreign wine masquerading as New England rum, of the connivance of officials, forgery of certificates, and tarring and feathering of informers, all show that violations occurred.

A quantitative analysis of colonial trade, however, throws a clearer light on the extent of smuggling. Although obviously no statistical records of surreptitious activities exist, official records showing the great volume of tobacco and other enumerated products moving in legal channels and the quantities of European manufactures coming to the colonies from England as the laws prescribed demonstrate that the bulk of the trade with Europe was legitimate. Any other assumption would greatly exaggerate colonial productive and consumptive capacities. Violations of the Molasses Act, however, were a different matter. The amount of rum produced in the Northern colonies demonstrates that a flourishing illicit trade existed with the foreign West Indies. It is more difficult to estimate the extent of smuggling during the revolutionary period, but the probabilities seem to be that it was held in check by increased enforcement activities.

Many elements were required to precipitate the American Revolution, and smuggling did more than add spice to the formula. The very fact that the European clauses of the laws were reasonably well enforced, left the colonists with an unfavorable balance of trade in the Old World. The monopolistic advantages enjoyed by the English factors kept Southern planters in a state of continual indebtedness which served to intensify any irritation aroused by other causes. After the Molasses Act, illicit trade with the foreign West Indies was an economic necessity. Its treasonable aspect during the French and Indian War aroused British resentment, and subsequent attempts to restrain it awakened such active opposition in the colonies as to warrant John Adams' remark that "molasses was an essential ingredient in American independence."

Equally important, the other commercial reforms which Britain initiated at the same time attempted too much. The new duties in America and the decreased drawbacks on goods which the colonists were obliged to acquire in England either tended to increase smuggling or added economic grievances to political irritation. The rearrangement of the duties on tea, which offered a legal supply at lower prices, aroused smugglers whose profits were threatened, while the demand for bonds even when shipping non-enumerated articles, the burdensome restrictions on the coasting trade, and worst of all arbitrary adherence to the letter of the law injured even the "fair trader." At first the merchants expressed their resentment in the form of nonimportation agreements, but such attempts at peaceful coercion soon led to acts of "riot and rebellion."

SNELLING, FORT, was established in 1819 by Col. Henry Leavenworth as part of a general plan of frontier defense. Its site, at the junction of the Mississippi and Minnesota Rivers, was originally selected in 1805 by Lt. Zebulon M. Pike. It was at first called Fort St. Anthony, but in 1825 its name was changed to Fort Snelling in honor of Col. Josiah Snelling, who became commandant in 1820 and erected permanent buildings and fortifications. The fort was the headquarters for the Indian agency, of which Maj. Lawrence Taliaferro had charge for twenty years; and it served to protect the headquarters of the American Fur Company, located across the Minnesota River at Mendota, and the pioneer settlers of Minnesota. It was never the scene of a hostile demonstration. It was abandoned in 1858 and reoccupied in 1861.

SOCIAL GOSPEL is an emphasis in American Protestant Christianity which has developed since the Civil War. The rise of labor organizations and the resulting labor disturbances of the 1880's brought the accusation from labor that the church was more sympathetic with capital than labor. This stirred liberal church leaders to a study of the implications of the teachings of Jesus on social and economic questions. Among the early leaders in this movement were Washington Gladden, Walter Rauschenbusch and Shailer Mathews. Their teachings and writings were soon exercising widespread influence, and a lively social consciousness was created in all the major denominations which has led to their adoption of definite social programs.

SOCIAL SECURITY. Social security systems were developed in the populous, industrialized nations of Europe considerably in advance of similar measures in the United States. With the depression of 1929, however, this country's need for a plan, national in scope, became clearly imperative. States, localities, and private charities proved unable to cope with prolonged mass economic distress. Mounting unemployment prompted emergency Federal programs for public works and relief. More significantly for the future, it spurred a search for ordered ways of providing safeguards against the various social and economic hazards common to all that can lead to destitution and dependency in a modern economy where most people must rely on continuing money income for everyday necessities.

In 1934 President F. D. Roosevelt appointed a Committee on Economic Security whose recommendations were transmitted with a special message to Congress. After study of this report and extensive hearings, Congress passed the Social Security Act, which became law on Aug. 14, 1935.

Title II of the Act established the basic program of social security, the Federal old-age retirement system financed through taxes on employers and employees in commerce and industry. In 1939 the law was amended to provide benefits for certain dependents and survivors of workers protected by the system. Benefits for totally disabled workers age 50 and over were included in the law in 1956, and benefits for their dependents were added in 1958. About 14,000,000 persons received benefits in early 1960, at an annual rate of some $10,000,000,000.

The coverage of the system was broadened in 1950 to include regularly employed farm workers and domestics and the nonfarm self-employed. In 1954, 1956 and 1958 further extensions brought in farm operators, most self-employed professionals, and members of the armed forces. Thus, virtually all gainful employment was covered, except that of some government workers who had separate retirement protection and self-employed doctors of medicine.

Benefit amounts, maximum earnings taxable and creditable for benefits, and earnings permitted without suspension of benefits were adjusted a number of times beginning in 1950 in recognition of the rising level of the economy. Under the tax schedule established in 1958 the contribution rate in 1960 was 3% each for employer and employee and 4½% for self-employed.

Other titles of the Social Security Act, designed to supplement social insurance, provided for Federal grants to the states to help finance public assistance for the needy aged, dependent children in broken homes, blind, and, beginning in 1950, permanently and totally disabled persons. Under these state-administered programs, intended for needy persons not eligible for benefits under Title II or whose benefits were too small for basic necessities, almost 6,000,000 persons in early 1960 received cash assistance or medical care.

The law also established Federal grants for maternal and child health services, services for crippled children, and child welfare services, and provided also for a system of unemployment insurance.

The Federal agency originally responsible for administering the provisions of the act was the Social Security Board. After various reorganizations, responsibility was placed with the Social Security Administration in the Department of Health, Education and Welfare for all programs except unemployment insurance, which is now administered by the Bureau of Employment Security in the Department of Labor.

SOCIAL SETTLEMENTS.

The settlement-house movement was the most important American reaction to the basic social problem represented by the labor unrest of the 1870's, the revolutionary socialism of the 1880's, the isolation of "colonies" of immigrants in congested tenements, unemployment, and the progressive lowering of the standard of living, factors furnishing rich soil for unscrupulous politicians. In 1886 Stanton Coit and Charles B. Stover, following the example of Toynbee Hall, London, established the Neighborhood Guild (later University Settlement) in New York, "to cultivate friendly relations between the educated and the uneducated and thus uplift the latter."

Others followed: College Settlement, New York, 1889 (Vida D. Scudder and Jean G. Fine); Hull House, Chicago, 1889 (Jane Addams); East Side House, New York, 1891; Northwestern University Settlement, 1891 (Harriet Vittum); South End House, Boston, 1892 (Robert A. Woods); Henry Street Settlement, New York, 1893 (Lillian Wald). Economic distress brought rapid increase after 1893, especially: Hudson Guild, New York, 1895 (John L. Elliott); University of Chicago Settlement, 1894 (Mary McDowell); Chicago Commons, 1894 (Graham Taylor); Hiram House, Cleveland, 1896 (George A. Bellamy); Greenwich House, New York, 1902 (Mary Kingsbury Simkhovitch). Although new houses continued to be established until World War I, few were established thereafter. A national federation, organized 1911, had 160 members in 1930. Of 300 nonmember houses, most were church-supported. About twenty houses were supported by Catholics (1922) and twenty-eight by Jews. The Y. M. C. A., Y. W. C. A. and other national agencies carried on similar work.

The greatest single service of the settlements has been in Americanization. In addition, they have sponsored group study of music, art, literature and handicrafts; provided clinics, visiting nurses, classes in cooking and child care, playgrounds, summer camps, employment bureaus; revived national festivals, and helped inspire the Little Theater Movement.

SOCIAL WORK.

Although the late 18th century produced a few pioneers like Dr. Benjamin Rush and Thomas Eddy, modern social service in the United States had its beginning in organizations like the Society for Prevention of Pauperism (New York, 1818) and the Association for Improving the Condition of the Poor of the 1840's. Early workers were philanthropic merchants and professional men, or members of their families. The Charity Organization Movement of the late 1870's, although chiefly dominated by volunteer workers, brought the first conscious development of social service as a profession.

Multiplication of social-service institutions after 1880 brought specialization of work. Relief of poverty became social case work, or family work, producing the "case worker." Social settlements aroused interest in housing, community betterment and slum clearance, producing such specializations as group workers and settlement workers, and led to work in community organization. Educational and preventive social work introduced teachers, recreational and playground directors, visiting nurses, social medical workers and legal-aid officers. Psychiatrists and housing experts were called into service. Social case work was the most important and characteristic, and best represented the principles of scientific sociology, biology and psychology. It marked clearly the departure from the spirit of early 19th-century reform with its exclusive interest in saving individuals. The new purpose was to analyze and change the environment deemed responsible for the individual's or family's plight.

SOCIALIST MOVEMENT.

Socialism may be defined as a system of philosophy which requires that the instruments of production, distribution and exchange shall be owned, controlled and operated by society co-operatively for the advantage of all rather than privately and competitively for the benefit of a few. It necessarily involves the abolition of private wealth, except perhaps in consumption goods.

During the early 19th century, there were many experiments in the United States based upon the theories of such utopian reformers as the Welshman, Robert Owen, and the Frenchmen, Etienne Cabet and Charles Fourier. Among Americans interested in these new movements were Albert Brisbane, Horace Greeley, William Cullen Bryant, Charles A. Dana and Nathaniel Hawthorne. Brook Farm, Cabet's Icarian colony and Owen's New Harmony were typical of many utopian communities.

Modern socialism, however, is identified with Karl Marx and Friedrich Engels. Their fundamental theories were incorporated first in the *Communist Manifesto* (1848). Marx and Engels concerned themselves with an analysis of industrial conditions, economic tendencies and social forces which, they believed, would destroy capitalism and lead to socialism. Their doctrines included the economic interpretation of history, which attributes to economic forces the predominant role in determining historical development; the class struggle, which posits an irreconcilable conflict between the possessing and the propertyless classes; the theory of value and surplus value, which holds that labor creates all value and produces a surplus that is expropriated by the capitalist; and the law of capitalist development, according to which capitalism is digging its own grave through the concentration of capital, recurring economic crises, increasing unemployment, disappearance of the middle class, and increasing misery of the masses. The inevitable overthrow of the capitalistic system through social revolution is predicted.

The American socialist movement, from the organization of the Socialist Labor party in 1874, has embraced these doctrines. The Social Democracy of America was formed in 1897. Unwilling to accept its utopian aims, Eugene V. Debs and Victor Berger organized the Social Democratic party of America. In 1901 the Socialist party came into existence, and ever since has championed opportunistic socialism. Debs retained leadership until his death in 1926, and was succeeded by Norman Thomas.

From the beginning, the movement has suffered from internal dissension, relentless opposition by adherents of capitalism, the relatively high status of American wage-earners, and the conservatism of trade unionism. Reflecting the Russian Revolution (1917), it split into three distinct groups. The opportunists remained in control of the Socialist party; the extreme left wing formed the Communist party; and the center-left wing organized the Communist-Labor party. Because of violent differences and internal strife, the collectivist movement has become hopelessly divided.

SOD HOUSE. This type appeared (1830–1910) when settlement began on the prairies away from the streams where timber was obtainable. The Plains Indians had long made their permanent winter homes from dirt, and the white man adapted the Indian habitation to his needs. In the early days in the area beyond the Missouri River, in many counties, 90% of the people at one time or another lived in sod houses.

In building a sod house, the settler plowed half an acre of ground. The thick strips of turf were cut into three-foot bricks with a spade. These bricks were then hauled to the building location and laid up like a brick wall. The first layer was laid side by side around the base except where the door was to be. The cracks were then filled with dirt and two more layers were placed on these. The joints were broken as in bricklaying. Every third course was laid crossways to bind the sods together. A doorframe and two window frames were set in the wall and sods built around them at the proper time. Sometimes hickory withes were driven down into the walls for reinforcement.

The gables were built of sod or frame according to the means of the builder. Poorer settlers built a roof in the crudest manner. A forked pole set in each end of the cabin furnished support for the ridge pole. The rafters were made of poles and the sheeting consisted of brush covered with a layer of prairie hay. Over this a layer of sod was placed. Those who could afford it sometimes used lumber sheeting covered with a light layer of sod. The cracks were filled with fine clay. In a short time growths of sunflowers and grass appeared on the roof. Sometimes the inside was plastered with ashes and clay. Often the outside was hewn smooth. The dirt floor was sprinkled in dry weather to keep down the dust. In wet weather the water-soaked roof dripped constantly, making puddles on the floor. The whole structure was built for less than five dollars. These little cabins often housed a dozen people. The three-foot walls were warm in winter and cool in summer but the houses were ill-ventilated and dark. As soon as possible the family moved into a frame structure, leaving the old house to the stock.

SOMERS, MUTINY ON THE (1842). The U. S. brig *Somers* was en route from the African coast to New York when, on Nov. 26, 1842, the purser's steward reported to Commander A. S. Mackenzie, that Acting-Midshipman Spencer had attempted to induce him to aid in seizing the ship, murder the officers and turn pirate. Two seamen were also named as Spencer's accomplices. The three men were held prisoner and a court of inquiry was convened which adjudged them guilty. Commander Mackenzie caused them to be hanged on Dec. 1. Subsequently Mackenzie was tried by court-martial for his act, but was acquitted.

SOMME OFFENSIVE (Aug. 8–Nov. 11, 1918). Three American divisions, the 33rd (Bell), 27th (O'Ryan) and 30th (Lewis), participated in the Somme offensive under the British 4th Army (Rawlinson). Elements of the 33rd Division aided in capturing Hamel, July 4, Chipilly Ridge and Gressaire Wood, Aug. 9, and Etinehem Spur, Aug. 13.

The 27th and 30th Divisions constituted the American 2nd Corps (Read). After serving in the Ypres-Lys operation in August, Read's corps entered the line east of Peronne. In the 4th Army attack, Sept. 29, the corps assaulted and broke through the Hindenburg Line at the Bellicourt Canal Tunnel. Alternating in attack with the Australian Corps (Monash), the Americans between Oct. 9 and Oct. 21 captured Brancourt-le-Grand, Premont and Vaux-Andigny, crossed the Selle River, Oct. 17, conquered Ribeauville, Mazinghien and Rejet-de-Beaulieu, and nearly reached the Sambre River. When relieved Oct. 21, the two divisions had advanced 11½ miles against resistance and lost 3414 killed and 14,526 wounded.

SONS OF LIBERTY (Revolutionary) was organized in the American colonies at the time of the Stamp

Act controversy. Societies sprang up simultaneously in scattered communities, an indication that while leadership was an important factor in agitating American independence, there existed among the people a considerable discontent which had been aggravated by parliamentary interference. New York and Boston had two of the most energetic and spirited chapters. The Sons of Liberty constituted the extralegal enforcement arm of the movement for colonial self-government. Members circulated patriotic petitions, tarred and feathered violators of patriotic decrees, and intimidated British officials and their families. They stimulated a consciousness of colonial grievances by propaganda. They conducted funerals of patriots killed in street brawls. They promoted picnics, dinners and rallies, drank toasts to the honor of historic leaders of liberty, sang songs, denounced British tyranny and hanged unpopular officials in effigy. Upon discovery of governmental impotency they issued semiofficial decrees of authority, and impudently summoned royal officials to Liberty Trees to explain their conduct to the people. Nothwithstanding faults, the organization was a vigorous recrudescence in man's age-long struggle to improve his economic and political conditions.

"SOONERS" were those persons who illegally entered certain lands in the Indian Territory prior to the date that had been set for the opening of the lands to settlement. The term was first used in connection with the settlement of the "Oklahoma Lands," which occurred at noon, April 22, 1889. A proclamation issued thirty days earlier by President Benjamin Harrison had set this date and hour for these lands to be settled and had forbidden any person to enter them earlier. Those who did so came to be called "Sooners." The term was also used at later openings of Indian Territory lands to settlement.

SOUTH CAROLINA was first visited by Spaniards in 1521, and temporarily settled by them under Ayllon in 1526. In 1562 the French Protestant, Jean Ribaut, attempted to establish a colony on Parris Island, but was thwarted by Spaniards. England claimed the region also, but the charter granted to Sir Robert Heath in 1629 was allowed to lapse, and in 1663 Charles II granted Carolina (including the present North Carolina) to eight of his favorites. By a second charter (1665) the grant was extended to include the territory from 29° on the south to 36° 30′ on the north and stretching from "sea to sea." Under the government of the proprietors, chief of whom was called the Palatinate, legislation was to be "by and with the advice, assent and approbation of the freemen," and religious freedom was permitted but not required. In 1669 a plan of government was prepared by John Locke in the elaborate and unworkable Fundamental Constitutions. The first permanent settlement (Albemarle Point, April, 1670) was later (1680) moved across the Ashley River to the present site of Charleston.

Almost from the first the colony prospered, partly because of the excellent harbor and the advertising ingenuity of the proprietors, and partly because of the influx of English Dissenters and French Huguenots. During the proprietary rule (1663–1719) there were wars with Spain (1686, 1702–4) and France and Spain (1706), as well as with the troublesome pirates (1718) and the native Indians in the bloody Yamasee War (1715). Internally there was friction between the absentee proprietors and the people who feared the effects of the Fundamental Constitutions and who were loath to pay the quitrents. In 1693 the commons house won the right to initiate legislation equally with the governor and council. A religious controversy, resulting in the establishment of the Church of England (1706–78), together with the failure of the proprietors to approve needed legislation and to protect the colonies, served to further weaken the hold of the proprietors, and in 1719 the commons house usurped control of the colony. The Privy Council took this opportunity to appoint a royal governor, and in 1729 Parliament provided for the purchase of the proprietors' land titles. In 1730 a preliminary boundary was fixed between the two Carolinas which had been separately governed except for one period (1691–1712).

The period of royal control (1719–1776), with the increased export of skins, rice and indigo, and with the flourishing Indian trade, was an era of prosperity. Also important were the growing influence of the commons house and the decline of the authority of the governor and council, who found the commons peculiarly stubborn in the contests for control of the purse and for "constitutional rights."

Unhappy experiences with the men and methods of royal control and a desire for local self-government brought resistance to the Stamp Act and delegates were sent to the Stamp Act Congress (1765). Subsequent British legislation fanned the flame, and in July, 1774, a provincial congress elected delegates to the Continental Congress and practically assumed the government of the colony. On Sept. 15, 1775, the royal governor fled, and on March 26, 1776, a constitution was signed.

The British hope of taking Charleston and uniting with the Tories of the upcountry was dashed at the battle of Fort Moultrie (June 28, 1776), and it was not until 1780 that the city fell. The sporadic attacks of the partisan leaders, Sumter, Marion and Pickens, served to keep alive the patriot cause, and the victories of King's Mountain (Oct. 7, 1780) and Cowpens (Jan. 17, 1781) put some restraint upon the British, although Charleston was not evacuated until December, 1782. South Carolina ratified the U. S. Constitution on May 23, 1788.

Prior to the Civil War, the state was the first to adopt (unanimously) an ordinance of secession (Dec.

20, 1860), and the war began with the firing on Fort Sumter in Charleston Harbor (April 12, 1861).

The defeat of war was crowned by the march of Sherman through the state and the burning of Columbia (Feb. 17, 1865). The social upheaval and economic ruin were made more distressing by the refusal of Congress to accept the re-established civil government (December, 1865). Under congressional Reconstruction the grant of Negro suffrage and the disfranchisement of many whites meant the establishment (under the constitution of 1868) of a government of "carpetbaggers," "scalawags" and Negroes. Then followed eight years of fraud and corruption until the white Democrats "redeemed" the state (1876).

SOUTH DAKOTA, consisting of the southern half of Dakota Territory, was admitted as a state on Nov. 2, 1889. The state is divided by the Missouri River into two sections of about equal size. East of the river is rolling prairie, which has developed as agricultural land: general farming, wheat growing and grazing. West of the Missouri River the land is rougher, culminating in the Badlands and the Black Hills.

When the state was admitted all of the area west of the Missouri River, except the lands between the Forks of the Cheyenne River (which included the Black Hills), consisted of the Great Sioux Reservation, created by the Treaty of Laramie in 1868. On the east side of the Missouri were the Yankton, Wahpeton and Sisseton reservations. In all 25,000 Indians, mostly of Sioux stock, lived on these reservations under the jurisdiction of the Federal Government.

In 1890, 3,840,000 acres of the Great Sioux Reservation were opened to white settlement, and the Indians limited to reservations within the former territory, as follows: Pine Ridge Reservation, Rosebud Reservation, Lower Brule Reservation, Cheyenne River Reservation and Standing Rock Reservation.

In the same year (1890) came the Messiah War, caused by religious frenzy and culminating in the battle of Wounded Knee.

In 1892 the Sisseton Indian Reservation, consisting of 384,000 acres, was opened to white settlement pursuant to an agreement ratified by act of Congress. Twelve years later (1904) 416,000 acres of the Rosebud Reservation, along the south line of the state west of the Missouri, were opened to settlement by previous registration, priority determined by lot. One hundred and six thousand persons entered these lands. The succeeding years saw a rush of homesteaders to the trans-Missouri territory, and, side by side with this rush of settlement, went extensions of the railroads across the state—into the Black Hills in 1908 and through the northern part of the state the following year. In 1909 the Cheyenne River and Standing Rock reservations were opened to settlement west of and adjoining the Missouri River.

SOUTH IMPROVEMENT COMPANY was utilized by John D. Rockefeller and associates (*see* Standard Oil Company) in their first attempt (1871–72) to secure a monopoly of the petroleum industry by means of exclusive rebates from the railroads of the oil region. Resistance from producers, public indignation and annulment of its charter defeated the scheme.

SOUTH PASS. This is the most celebrated of the passes in the Rocky Mountains, because over it passed the great emigrant trail to Oregon and California. It is located in Wyoming at the southern end of the Wind River Mountains. The approach to the pass is so easy and gradual that, to use the words of John C. Frémont, "the traveller, without being reminded of any change by toilsome ascents, suddenly finds himself on the waters which flow to the Pacific Ocean." There are claims that John Colter discovered the South Pass in 1807 or 1808, and that Robert Stuart and the returning Astorians crossed it in 1812, but both claims are disputed. It is certain that the effective discovery was made in 1824 by Thomas Fitzpatrick, a fur trader. Capt. Bonneville first took wagons over the pass in 1832, and a few years later it became the mountain gateway through which passed the Oregon Trail.

SOUTHEAST ASIA TREATY ORGANIZATION (S.E.A.T.O.) was set up by a treaty signed Sept. 8, 1954, at Manila, P.I., by the United States, Britain, France, Australia, New Zealand, the Philippine Islands, Pakistan and Thailand. The treaty covered the "general area of Southeast Asia" and the western Pacific and provided that in case of aggression its members are to "consult immediately in order to agree to measures which should be taken for common defense." Hong Kong and Formosa were excluded from the treaty, but a protocol to the treaty extended coverage to Cambodia and Laos and the free territory under the jurisdiction of the state of Vietnam. India, Burma, Ceylon and Indonesia declined to join.

For the United States, the importance of the treaty was that it could be used to meet either internal or external aggression. An "understanding," added by the United States, stated that provisions of the treaty "apply only to communist aggression," but "in the event of other aggression or armed attack," the United States will consult the other signatories to the treaty as to what action should be taken. The United Kingdom was released of sole responsibility to maintain peace in the area. France signed the treaty as the only guarantee to the political independence and territorial integrity of Cambodia, Laos and South Vietnam.

S.E.A.T.O. came into effect as a result of a pact signed at its headquarters in Bangkok in February, 1955. Some complications in Southeast Asia resulted from the proclamation of Malayan independence in mid-1957, but Malaya did not join S.E.A.T.O. Although the organization was loosely held together, no member withdrew from it. It was generally thought that hostility to S.E.A.T.O., particularly on the part of the Southeast Asian nonsignatory nations, was less evident than it had originally been, though opposition by Soviet Russia and communist China was still strong.

In 1959 and 1960 aggressive activities of communist-led forces in northern Laos gave cause for alarm. Although not a member of S.E.A.T.O., Laos was one of the countries designated by the protocol to the treaty to which action against aggression should apply. Communist action in Laos as well as in neighboring Cambodia and South Vietnam was, therefore, of obvious concern to S.E.A.T.O., primarily a regional defense system against communism. In August, 1960, fighting began in northern Laos that was only ended some ten months later after the communist-inspired Laotian rebels had occupied much of eastern Laos and driven a wedge between Laos and Cambodia. In early May, 1961, a truce was agreed on. At a subsequent meeting, the S.E.A.T.O. nations and Canada, communist China, Poland, India, Burma, Cambodia, North Vietnam and Soviet Russia would work out a formula for the independence and neutrality of Laos. For the first time, the real contenders over Laos and the entire defense policy in Southeast Asia came face to face in Geneva, Switzerland, the place of the meeting.

SOUTHERN COMMERCIAL CONVENTIONS. The most notable gatherings to which this name applies were the sessions of the so-called Southern Commercial Convention, which met successively at Baltimore, Memphis, Charleston, New Orleans, Richmond, Savannah, Knoxville, Montgomery and Vicksburg between December, 1852, and May, 1859.

The original object of the Southern Commercial Convention was to devise remedies for Southern "decline." The South was not keeping pace with the North in population, manufacturing, railroad building, shipping and other lines of economic development. This was galling to the pride of loyal Southerners. It was taken as proof that the section was not prospering as it should. Thoughtful Southerners felt that the industrial and commercial dependence of their section resulted in Southern earnings being drained away to build up the North. The superior population and wealth of the free states were giving them an advantage in the bitter struggle over slavery. The convention canvassed a wide variety of proposed remedies, such as, building a railroad to the Pacific by a southern route, promotion of trade with Latin America, direct importation of European goods and encouragement of Southern manufactures by bounties or by discriminatory taxation of Northern-made articles.

Although in effect mass meetings, the earlier sessions of the convention were representative of all parts of the South and all shades of opinion. As time went

by and the convention failed to produce tangible results moderate men ceased to attend, and the sessions came to be dominated by the secessionists of the lower South, who contended that the Union was an obstacle to Southern economic development. Finally a question was injected which threatened seriously to divide the disunionists themselves, namely the desirability of reopening the foreign slave trade. Secessionist leaders then exerted themselves to bring the convention to an end. The net result of the gatherings was to promote Southern sectionalism.

Similar to the Southern Commercial Convention, and forerunners of it, were the "direct-trade" conventions held in Augusta and Charleston, 1837–39, and in Richmond and Norfolk, 1838, and the Southwestern Convention in Memphis, 1845.

SPANISH-AMERICAN WAR. This war was an outgrowth of the Cuban insurrection against Spanish rule, which began in February, 1895, and was waged with ruthlessness for three years by both Spanish and insurgents. American investments in Cuba (estimated at $50,000,000) suffered, and the destruction of the sugar and tobacco crops by the insurgents reduced the trade between Cuba and the United States to the vanishing point. Many commercial firms along the Atlantic and Gulf coasts of the United States desired intervention to stop the war, but business interests in general were opposed to interference by the United States. Humanitarian or sentimental sympathy with the Cuban people in their struggle for independence, and popular indignation at the cruelty of the Spanish methods of warfare, were inflamed by a one-sided picture of the Cuban war presented in the sensational press. A large section of the religious press, also, preached the sacred duty of intervention to put an end to Spanish misrule.

President Cleveland (1893–97) resisted all pressure for intervention, and so at first did his successor, President McKinley (1897–1901). In Spain the Liberal Sagasta ministry, assuming control in 1897, abandoned the more objectionable military methods in Cuba and offered a limited autonomy to the Cubans. A peaceful settlement seemed in prospect, but the destruction of the United States battleship *Maine* in Havana harbor (Feb. 15, 1898) led to a new outburst of anti-Spanish feeling in the United States. Though advised by the United States minister in Madrid that the Spanish government was making all the concessions which public opinion would permit, McKinley sent to Congress (April 11, 1898) a message asking authority to end the civil war in Cuba. Congress promptly (April 19) passed resolutions recognizing the independence of Cuba, demanding that Spain withdraw from the island, and authorizing the President to use the armed forces of the United States to effect those ends. A fourth resolution disclaimed all purpose of annexing Cuba. Spain at once severed diplomatic relations, and on April 25

Congress declared the existence of a state of war, retroactive to and including April 21.

A blockade of Cuban ports was instituted April 22, but the first dramatic event of the war occurred in the Far East. On the morning of May 1, Commodore George Dewey, commanding the U. S. Asiatic Squadron, entered Manila Bay in the Philippine Islands and completely destroyed the antiquated Spanish fleet which defended it. Dewey's squadron remained in Manila Bay and before the end of July was reinforced by an army of some 10,000 men under Gen. Wesley Merritt. The city of Manila was occupied Aug. 13.

Meanwhile, Spain's Atlantic fleet, under Admiral Cervera, had entered the harbor of Santiago, Cuba, on May 19, and was there blockaded by an American fleet under Rear Admiral W. T. Sampson. The capture or destruction of this Spanish fleet now became the immediate military objective of the United States. An army of 18,000 regulars and volunteers, assembled at Tampa, Fla., was transported to the Cuban coast east of Santiago before the end of June. Commanded by Gen. W. R. Shafter, it stormed the heights overlooking Santiago in the battles of El Caney and San Juan Hill, July 1. The Spanish position in Santiago now became untenable. Cervera was ordered by Capt. Gen. Blanco to lead his fleet out of the harbor. His sortie on July 3 resulted in the total destruction of his squadron by the blockading fleet.

The destruction of Cervera's fleet practically ended the war. The city of Santiago was surrendered July 16. On July 25 an army under Gen. Nelson A. Miles landed in Puerto Rico and occupied that island almost unopposed. The Spanish government now initiated peace negotiations through the French ambassador in Washington, and on Aug. 12 hostilities were terminated by a protocol under which Spain relinquished Cuba, ceded to the United States Puerto Rico and one of the Ladrone Islands (later fixed as Guam), and agreed to the occupation of Manila by the United States until the disposition of the Philippine Islands should be determined by the definitive treaty of peace. This was to be negotiated by commissioners meeting in Paris. The treaty, signed in Paris Dec. 10, 1898, and approved by the Senate Feb. 6, 1899, supplemented the above terms by providing for the cession of the Philippines to the United States, the payment of $20,000,000 by the United States to Spain and the retention by Spain of liability for the Cuban debt.

The war had cost the United States about $250,-000,000 in money and over 5000 lives. Of the dead, however, fewer than 400 had been killed in battle or died of wounds. The balance represented the toll of disease. At this cost the United States had acquired a colonial empire of 120,000 square miles and some 8,500,000 people and had risen suddenly to a position of prominence in world affairs, particularly in the Caribbean and the Far East.

SPANISH CONSPIRACY. This series of more or less closely related intrigues, between Spain and certain western Americans, began in 1786 and continued for a score of years thereafter. The main purpose of Spain was to defend Louisiana and Florida by promoting the secession of the West from the United States through bribery, the manipulation of commerce on the Mississippi River (over which Spain retained some control until 1803), and the exploitation of sectional antagonism between East and West. Before the United States obtained the free navigation of the Mississippi by the Pinckney Treaty of 1795, some of the American conspirators were probably sincere in their profession of secessionist aims; but after 1795 their sole purpose and at all times their main purpose seems to have been to advance their own personal interests by obtaining from Spain money, commercial privileges, support for colonization schemes, and other advantages. The first intrigue, a short-lived one begun in 1786 by Diego de Gardoqui and James White, was related to the Muscle Shoals speculation. The central figure in these intrigues, however, was James Wilkinson and their focal point was in Kentucky. In 1786 great indignation was aroused in the West by the decision of Congress not to press the United States' claim to the free navigation of the Mississippi; and in 1787 Wilkinson, who had won a prominent place in Kentucky politics, went to New Orleans to try his hand at direct negotiation with the Spanish officials of Louisiana. The upshot was that he won some commercial privileges for the Western people and more for himself, took an oath of allegiance to the Spanish crown and became the principal agent of Spain in its secessionist intrigue, with a pension of $2000 a year (later raised to $4000), which was paid to him at intervals for many years after he became an officer in the United States Army (1791). Benjamin Sebastian, Harry Innes and a few other influential Kentuckians joined in the intrigue; but they often worked at cross-purposes with Wilkinson, Spain and each other. The existence of the conspiracy was widely suspected almost from the beginning, some partial revelations of it were made in the 1790's, and many of the details were exposed in 1806 by the *Western World* (a Kentucky newspaper) and in 1809 by Daniel Clark's *Proofs of the Corruption of . . . Wilkinson;* but full legal proof was lacking. Wilkinson retained his commission in the army and continued to enjoy the apparent confidence of Presidents Jefferson and Madison as he had that of Presidents Washington and Adams. The exposure did, however, put an end to the conspiracy which had long since become a farce. The secessionist plan was never put into action. What few advantages the conspiracy yielded were reaped by the Americans, and Spain footed the bill.

SPANISH MILITARY SUPPLIES FROM NEW ORLEANS (1776–79). When armed hostilities began between England and her North American colonies in 1775, commercial intercourse with the mother country was suspended, and British fleets blockaded Atlantic ports to prevent importation of munitions and other supplies from foreign countries. In this emergency the colonists turned to Spanish New Orleans as a source of needed supplies, since Spain was a traditional enemy of England and was eagerly watching developments, in the hope of recovering territory and prestige lost to the British in the French and Indian War. Spain resented British West Florida trade with Louisiana, and wished to end this menace. Spain was also jealous of British expansion and increasing influence over the Indians west of the Alleghenies, which endangered Spanish control of Louisiana.

The Spanish government was exceedingly cautious to avoid war with England; and Unzaga, Spanish governor of Louisiana, reflected this caution in his dealings with American agents sent to New Orleans in 1776. However, through the influence of Oliver Pollock, these agents were permitted to purchase guns, gunpowder, blankets and medicines, especially quinine, from Spanish sources in that port. These supplies were rowed up the Mississippi in boats carrying the Spanish flag, to prevent their seizure by British authorities at West Florida posts above New Orleans.

Bernardo de Galvez, who succeeded Unzaga as governor of Louisiana in 1777, was bolder than his predecessor in assisting American agents in New Orleans, since he was unperturbed by the prospect of war with England in consequence of such unneutral acts. Through Galvez's assistance the traffic in supplies up the Mississippi from New Orleans went on apace, and from this source the Americans procured the sorely needed supplies which enabled George Rogers Clark to defeat the British in the Old Northwest in 1778 and 1779.

The chief obstacle to this trade was the lack of colonial funds to purchase supplies available in New Orleans, the treasuries of the central and state governments being chronically empty. Pollock extended his credit to the limit to finance this trade and became bankrupt through tardiness of the revolutionary governments concerned in repaying the advances made by him in their behalf. When France joined the United States in the war in 1778, her fleets landed supplies at Atlantic ports, thus reducing the dependence upon the New Orleans trade; and after Spain entered the war against England in 1779, secrecy was no longer necessary in this up-the-river trade.

SPANISH TRAIL, an important overland route between Santa Fe, N. Mex., and Los Angeles, Calif., dates from 1775–76, during the Spanish occupation. Two Franciscan monks first traversed most of it, Father Garcés traveling its westerly section in 1775–76, and Father Escalante its eastern portion in 1776. Jedediah Smith came up the western half of the trail but the first American to cover its full length was William Wolfskill, a Kentuckian, who led a company of trappers over it in 1830–31. From that period annual caravans passed over it in trade, the trail being sufficiently far north to avoid most Apache incursions while finding water across the desert. It later was an important immigrant route, and the Mountain Meadows Massacre took place on it in 1857.

The Spanish Trail led from Santa Fe up the Chama River through Durango, and followed the Dolores. It crossed the Grand and Green Rivers, passed through the mountains up the Sevier Valley, followed the line of the Santa Clara and Virgin Rivers southwest, and cut across the desert to the Mojave River, thence over the mountains to Los Angeles.

SPECIE PAYMENTS, SUSPENSION AND RESUMPTION OF. Until 1934 the general rule was that fiduciary money should be redeemed on request in standard money (called specie when monetary standard is metallic) by the issuing authority. Thus, when the country was on a gold-coin standard, all its moneys were ultimately redeemable in gold coin. There were several exceptions to the rule, of which the following are noteworthy. (1) The Government as well as the national banks assumed responsibility for the national bank notes. (2) Banks might redeem in legal tender, which included some paper money after 1862. (3) Early in the 19th century state banks often refused to redeem their notes in specie knowing that the only penalty would be having the notes pass at a discount. (4) Silver certificates, first issued in 1878 and legally redeemable only in silver dollars, in practice have been redeemed in gold to keep them at a parity.

Specie payments have been wholly or sectionally suspended in the United States during eight emergency periods, 1814–17, 1819–22, 1837–38, 1839–43, 1857–58, 1861–78, 1917–19, 1933–34. All banks except those of New England suspended specie payments after the capture of Washington, Aug. 24, 1814. The banks' recent unregulated credit expansion as well as the war was responsible. Resumption took place Feb. 20, 1817. During the depression years, 1819–22, most banks in the South and West refused to pay specie.

The years following 1830, notable for westward expansion and internal improvements, culminated in a period of land speculation. The Treasury's "specie circular" of July 11, 1836, permitting agents to accept only specie for public lands, embarrassed many banks. On May 10, 1837, New York City banks led in a widespread suspension of specie payments. Resumption on Aug. 13, 1838, was premature. Pennsylvania banks suspended again Oct. 9, 1839, followed by those of other states. Resumption occurred gradually, by regions, throughout 1842.

The decade of the 1850's witnessed railroad expansion and industrial development on a large scale. Overspeculation, European depression, and finally the bankruptcy of the Ohio Life Insurance and Trust Co. in August of 1857 caused all but one New York City bank (the Chemical) to suspend payments on Oct. 13. Nearly all banks elsewhere followed. Resumption took place slowly between November and February.

The suspension of specie payments during the Civil War began in New York City, Dec. 30, 1861. It was caused by the unfavorable course of the war, the *Trent* affair, and Secretary Chase's increasing use of demand Treasury notes and his failure to recommend an adequate tax program to Congress. It was not owing to issues of United States notes, "greenbacks," which began Feb. 25, 1862, but the suspension was prolonged because of them. By 1865 there were about $735,000,000 in various kinds of money in circulation, $431,000,000 being greenbacks. The gold value of $100 in currency averaged $49.50 that year. Several methods of resumption were suggested. Under the Funding Act of April 12, 1866, greenbacks in circulation were gradually reduced to $356,000,000 on Feb. 4, 1868, when further retirement was stopped. The amount was temporarily raised to $382,000,000 by 1872. In 1874 Grant vetoed the Inflation Bill, intended to raise the greenback circulation permanently to $400,000,000. On Jan. 14, 1875, a Republican lame-duck Congress passed Sen. George Edmunds' Resumption Act, providing that greenbacks be reduced to $300,000,000 and resumption begin Jan. 1, 1879. Delay in accumulating a gold reserve, the free silver threat and Congress' halting the greenback reduction at $346,681,000 on May 31, 1878, made resumption on time seem unlikely for a while. Thanks to Secretary Sherman's efforts the premium on gold disappeared Dec. 17, 1878, and resumption took place Jan. 2, 1879. In summary, resumption was accomplished partly by retiring greenbacks. Of at least equal importance, however, was the fact that during this period the country's business needs grew up to the larger currency supply.

Attention in passing is called to the panics of 1893 and 1907 when specie payments were entirely suspended at clearinghouses and partially so in banks in New York City for several weeks. The years 1893–95 are memorable because the Treasury barely managed to obtain enough gold to redeem the Treasury notes presented.

Our entry into World War I caused President Wilson to issue orders on Sept. 7 and Oct. 12, 1917, placing an embargo on gold exports. Although this did not result in a formal suspension of specie payments by the Federal Reserve Banks, the unnecessary use of gold coin was officially discouraged. It is usually regarded as a *de facto* suspension of the gold standard. All restrictions were removed June 9, 1919.

The last suspension resulted from the depression following the panic of 1929. In 1930–32 there were 5102 bank failures, a new record; England abandoned the gold standard in September, 1931, and gold flowed out of the United States on net balance every month of 1932 from January to July. These large gold exports and the publicity of the Reconstruction Finance Corporation's loans to banks frightened the public. The first "banking holiday" was declared in Nevada, Oct. 31, 1932. Public confidence declined further that winter. On Feb. 14 Gov. W. A. Comstock of Michigan declared a bank holiday. Other states followed, New York on Saturday, March 4. On March 6 President F. D. Roosevelt announced a four-day nationwide banking moratorium. Congress met on the 9th and hastily passed the Emergency Banking Act. The President imposed a temporary embargo on gold exports and ordered every one to turn gold in to the Government for other money. By March 29, 12,800 out of about 18,000 banks had been licensed to open on an unrestricted basis, but specie payments were not resumed. On April 20 a second presidential embargo on gold exports signaled the indefinite abandonment of the gold-coin standard.

The Gold Reserve Act and presidential order of Jan. 30–31, 1934, established a new dollar of 13.71 grains of fine gold, and made it possible, with the approval of the Treasury, to obtain gold bullion for making international payments. It has been impossible since then to get any money redeemed in gold coin or bars for domestic use.

SPENCER RIFLE, a self-loading, repeating weapon, was patented by Christopher M. Spencer in 1860, and shortly thereafter adopted by the United States Army. It was the first effective and widely used magazine repeater; 106,667 pieces in rifle and carbine form were bought by the Government from Jan. 1, 1861 to June 30, 1866, for $2,861,024.38. Many officers of the Civil War declared it to have been the best arm of its time. The magazine capacity was 9 rounds, rimfire cartridges of .56 caliber. Sixteen shots per minute could be fired. Eight Spencer patents were obtained during the years 1860–73. The weapon had a weakness in its tendency to explode shells carried in the magazine.

SPIES, IN EARLY AMERICAN HISTORY. Little documentary evidence exists concerning their work, as the nature of their activities made the keeping of written records an additional and unnecessary hazard. The young American spy, Nathan Hale, who was hanged by the British in New York, Sept. 22, 1776, was, doubtless, the most noted spy of the Revolution. Another spy, the Quakeress Lydia Darrah, is credited with once saving Washington's army, and another spy, Charles Morgan, penetrated Lord Cornwallis' lines at Yorktown in 1781 and secured valuable military secrets for Lafayette. On the British side the most notable spy was Maj. John André, captured in civilian clothes with despatches from Gen. Benedict Arnold and hanged Oct. 2, 1780. Spying for the British government on the Continent were the Americans, Dr. Edward Bancroft, Benjamin Franklin's supposed friend; Paul Wentworth, who directed an intricate espionage system on the Continent; the Rev. John Vardill, once assistant minister of Trinity Church, New York; and Capt. Joseph Hynson, a Maryland seaman, who stole despatches destined for the Continental Congress.

During the Civil War large numbers of men and women, North and South, performed heroic service as spies, a few of whose names stand out: Allan Pinkerton, who organized the United States Secret Service; his agent, Timothy Webster, captured and hanged in Richmond; Emma Edmonds, Army nurse, who penetrated the Confederate lines eleven times; Lafayette C. Baker, who entered Richmond as an itinerant photographer; Harry Young, Gen. Philip H. Sheridan's chief spy; and Elizabeth L. Van Lew, Gen. U. S. Grant's most valued spy in Richmond. On the Confederate side, Belle Boyd, Walter Bowie, Mrs. Rose O'Neal Greenhow and many others supplied Lee's army with invaluable military information.

SPOILS SYSTEM. "To the victor belong the spoils," is the slogan of the spoilsmen, coined in 1832 by Sen. William L. Marcy of New York. The spoils system makes loyalty and service to a party the chief qualification for appointment to a public office. Under the system officeholders are ruthlessly removed to make room for those who have been faithful to the victorious party. These removals are justified on the ground that rotation in office is a proper principle to apply under a democratic system. The theory is that one person is as well qualified as another to perform the duties of an office. In its worst form the spoils system is characterized by the assessment of officeholders to raise money for the party's expenses. The system makes possible the building up of a party machine ready to do the bidding of the leaders. It makes impossible a career in public service and so discourages the best qualified citizens from seeking governmental offices.

When the Government of the United States began functioning under the Constitution, it could hardly be said that the spoils system was a new phenomenon. Ancient as well as modern history abounds with examples of it. But it is under a two party system such as has prevailed in this country that the spoilsmen operate most effectively.

President Washington, at the beginning of his first administration, made loyalty to the Constitution the chief qualification for appointment to office. Later, after the rise of the party system, he made appointments on the basis of faithfulness to the Federalist party. Certainly, his successor, President John Adams, made appointments on a purely partisan basis as was illustrated by his 1801 "midnight appointments." President Jefferson went even farther. While pro-

fessing to make fitness for office the test for appointments, he was careful to select men of his own party. Nor did he hesitate to remove Federalists to make room for loyal Democratic-Republicans.

Since the three Presidents who followed Jefferson were of the same party they had little occasion to disturb the officeholders, so few removals were made. Meanwhile the spoils system was firmly established in some of the states, notably in New York and Pennsylvania. When President Jackson assumed office in 1829 the situation was favorable for a wholesale introduction of the system into national politics. Jackson's followers confidently expected him to sweep the offices clean and to appoint to the vacancies men who had helped him achieve his triumph at the polls. In his inaugural address he encouraged this expectation by alluding to "reform" as inscribed "on the list of Executive duties, in characters too legible to be overlooked."

Historians have been prone to accept, without examining the record, the charge that Jackson introduced the spoils system into national politics. He did make partisan removals; he placed his own followers in offices, including some unfit for their positions; and he took advantage of the Four Year Act of 1820 to replace incumbents when their four-year terms expired. Jackson believed in the theory of rotation in office and he used officeholders in developing an effective party machine. The charge that officeholders were assessed for party purpose during his administration has, however, never been proved but merely asserted. In the final analysis, Jackson was not a wholehearted spoilsman. During the period when he was alleged to have made a clean sweep of the officeholders, he and his subordinates actually replaced 919 or one eleventh of the whole number. Not over one fifth of those whom he found in office were replaced during his eight years in the Presidency. The worst that should be said of President Jackson is that his administration merely marked another step toward the establishment of the spoils system. He hardly deserved any more blame than President Jefferson for its introduction. Each removed about the same proportion of officeholders and each filled vacancies on a partisan basis.

When the Whigs came into power in 1841 they proceeded to make the clean sweep that Jackson has been falsely accused of making. Thereafter, with each change of administration, officeholders were removed wholesale and were replaced by faithful supporters of the successful candidate.

The spoils system continued to operate without hindrance until after the Civil War. Though feeble attempts were made to secure reform, no substantial success was achieved until 1883 when Congress passed the Federal Civil Service Act.

SPOTSYLVANIA COURTHOUSE, BATTLE OF (May 8–21, 1864). Warren's (U.) 5th Corps, leading

Grant's southward march from the Wilderness, was stopped northwest of Spotsylvania Courthouse by Kershaw's (C.) division, leading Anderson's corps. Sedgwick's (U.) 6th Corps joined Warren's left and late in the afternoon these corps assaulted Anderson, but were repulsed. During May 9, Ewell's (C.) and Hill's (C.) corps extended Anderson's line northeast to McCool's house and thence south to Spotsylvania Courthouse, entrenching a front four miles long. Hancock's (U.) 2nd Corps joined the 5th and 6th, while Burnside's (U.) 9th Corps, marching from Fredericksburg, approached Hill at Spotsylvania. At McCool's, Ewell's corps occupied a salient separating Burnside from the three corps of the Federal right. May 10, the latter three corps, assaulting Anderson and Ewell, suffered another repulse. On the 12th Hancock attacked and captured Ewell's salient but was driven back to the outside of the entrenchments. Hancock being reinforced by Wright and Burnside, the opposing masses fought all day hand-to-hand at this, the "Bloody Angle." About midnight Ewell retired to an inner line. Thereafter for some days Grant gradually withdrew his right and pushed his left southward and on May 20 marched toward Hanover Courthouse. At the North Anna River, however, Lee again blocked him. Grant's losses at Spotsylvania were 17,000; Lee's, 8000.

"SQUARE DEAL" was a picturesque phrase used with political significance by Theodore Roosevelt while he was President, to symbolize his personal attitude toward current topics of the period. He first used the phrase in Kansas while on a tour of the Western states as he explained the principles later to be embodied in the platform of the Progressive party. The "square deal" included Roosevelt's ideals of citizenship, the dignity of labor, nobility of parenthood and the essence of Christian character. Later it was applied to industry. The phrase was extremely popular in 1906.

STAGECOACH TRAVEL. The first successful stagecoach lines in the United States were established in the Northern colonies in the two decades before the Revolution, most of them running to near-by places from the three largest cities, Boston, New York and Philadelphia. The only lines connecting large cities were those between Boston and Providence, between New York and Philadelphia, and between Philadelphia and Baltimore. In each instance a short land journey was substituted for a long water passage. No stagecoaches ran south of Annapolis in colonial times.

These lines were halted by the Revolution, but most of them were again in motion before the treaty of peace was signed. They were aided financially and clothed with greater public interest when, in 1785, Congress first provided for the carrying of the mail by stagecoach over roads where it had grown too heavy for horse and rider. Slowly the mail stage

network widened, the Post Office encouraging and frequently, through its mail contracts, giving financial assistance to proprietors who established lines through new territory. Such assistance resulted in 1803 in the first line connecting the Central Atlantic states with the Carolinas and Georgia. The Ohio Valley was first penetrated by a line established to Pittsburgh in 1804. Rapid development of stagecoach facilities west of the Alleghenies did not take place until the Jacksonian era when Post Office subsidies became heavy. The mileage of mail stage lines tripled between 1828 and 1838, the latter date representing approximately the peak of staging activity east of the Mississippi River.

As lines were thrust westward with the advancing frontier, service on the older roads in the East grew more rapid and more frequent, and additional local routes were established until there were few villages that did not have a stagecoach arriving and departing several times a week. On the busier roads stagecoach companies ran both "limited" mail coaches, taking but a few passengers through rapidly at higher fares, and "accommodation" coaches which traveled more slowly, stopped more frequently along the way, and allowed the full resting time at night. Landlords of taverns where the stages stopped were usually partners in the line, a community of interest along the road being thus established. Stages of rival lines stopped at rival taverns. Eventually, large stagecoach companies controlled the paying lines in certain areas, and these companies in turn formed working agreements with each other. The Post Office because of its interest in efficiency and smooth connecting arrangements generally tolerated these large combinations of interest.

After railroads invaded the heaviest routes of travel the stage lines became extensions of advancing railheads or feeders from fertile tributary areas. The amount of staging, all told, did not necessarily decline at once, for the railroads encouraged travel and shipping and often furnished the stages with more business than they had previously known. Ultimately, however, when the railroads had completed their trunk lines and built branches into the more profitable tributary regions, the stagecoach was forced back to a marginal fringe which it did not pay the railroads to develop. In mountainous regions in both East and West it lingered, serving isolated valleys and villages, until the coming of the motor bus.

STAKED PLAINS (*Llano Estacado*) is the name applied to the high level part of northwest Texas and eastern New Mexico which lies above the Cap Rock escarpment. Coronado led the first expedition of white men across it and later other Spaniards visited it. It was so named, perhaps, because one such expedition drove stakes at intervals by which to retrace their route. The fierce Comanche Indians occupied it until about 1880, and the whites did not consider it worth wresting from them. Within the decade 1880–90 the buffaloes were extinguished, the Comanches were expelled, the Fort Worth and Denver Railroad was built across the region, and the huge XIT Ranch was being formed by the Capitol Syndicate out of the three million acres which were granted to it by the State of Texas. The region soon became a cattle country and later, in part, a dry farming section.

STALWARTS was a term applied to certain conservative Republican leaders led by Sen. Roscoe Conklin of New York. They opposed the Southern policy and the civil-service reform program of Hayes' administration and dubbed his adherents "Halfbreeds." Though the Stalwarts were unsuccessful in securing Grant's nomination for a third presidential term in 1880, one of their henchmen, Chester A. Arthur, was awarded the vice-presidential nomination. After Conklin's retirement from politics in the 1880's the designation soon passed out of use.

STAMP ACT (1765). By 1763 British and colonial arms had driven French power from Canada. The extension of colonial empire raised new and serious problems. The conquest of Canada brought under British rule disaffected French and hostile Indians. In 1763 the Indians, under the leadership of Pontiac, fearing British rule and colonial encroachment on their land, fell upon the frontier settlements in a devastating attack. Clearly it was necessary to station garrisons on the long border to guard the colonists against Indian attack and the Indians against predatory whites. It was equally clear that the control of frontier affairs could no longer be left to the separate colonies with their conflicting interests. Frontier problems became more than ever a matter of common concern to be met and solved by the British government as the central authority.

The garrisoning of the border meant a heavy expense, and at once the financial question became a decisive factor. The estimates fixed £320,000 as the cost of supporting an American army of ten thousand men for defense in the mainland colonies and the West Indies. Where should this financial burden fall? The French war had doubled the British national debt, bringing it to the sum of £130,000,000 with a yearly interest charge of £4,500,000. In addition to the support of a colonial military force, increased estimates were necessary to maintain British naval supremacy. So heavy was the strain upon the British taxpayer that the ministry decided to call upon the colonies to share the expense of the American army. This decision once made, another decisive question arose. Should the colonial share be levied by the several colonial representative bodies or by the British Parliament? In the past, Parliament had not taxed the colonies for revenue purposes. In time of imperial wars, royal requisitions were sent to the colonies to raise and pay troops to co-operate with the British forces. But the realities of the late war plainly showed

that the requisition system was inefficient and unfair. A general lack of vigorous co-operation impaired military operation. The military burden was not equitably distributed, a few colonies responded loyally, some half-heartedly, others far short of their abilities. This conduct led during the war to proposals to tax the colonies by act of Parliament. The Indian uprising under Pontiac further revealed that the colonies could not be depended upon for adequate frontier defense nor would they share the burden equitably.

These facts decided the British ministry to resort to the levy of a parliamentary tax upon the colonies. The first step was the passage of the Sugar Act of 1764. The old severe duties on colonial trade with the foreign West Indies were reduced in the hope that it would yield some revenue, probably £45,000. This was held to be less than the colonial share, and Sir George Grenville, Chancellor of the Exchequer, proposed a stamp tax upon the colonies. He deferred the plan a year to give the colonies an opportunity to suggest means more to their liking. They protested strongly against a stamp tax and suggested nothing more than taxation by the colonial assemblies as of old. Grenville conferred with the colonial agents in London, among them Benjamin Franklin of Pennsylvania and Jared Ingersoll of Connecticut. The agents pleaded for the old method of raising revenue in the colonies. To this Grenville countered by asking if the colonies could agree on the quotas each should raise and whether it was certain every colony would raise its quotas. In the light of past experience, the agents had no answer to these questions. And so Parliament proceeded to the passage of the famous Stamp Act of 1765 with a heavy majority. The use of stamps was required on all legal and commercial papers, pamphlets, newspapers, almanacs, cards and dice. The law provided for a Stamp Office in London, an inspector for each of the colonial districts, and a stamp distributor for each colony. The estimated yield from stamps ranged from £60,000 to £100,000, collected in both mainland colonies and the West Indies. The combined revenues of the Sugar and Stamp Acts, £105,000 to £145,000, would meet less than half the cost of the American garrison forces.

Few in England realized the significance of the stamp tax. Parliament, in harmony with the rule not to receive petitions against revenue bills, did not heed the colonial protests. The ministers and Parliament felt that the law was a fair solution of a pressing problem. Even the colonial agents failed to understand the colonial temper. Franklin nominated a stamp distributor for Pennsylvania and Ingersoll accepted the post for Connecticut. News of the Stamp Act blew up a colonial storm. Parliamentary taxation for revenue was an innovation which threatened the very foundation of colonial self-government and outraged the precious right of Englishmen to be taxed only by their consent. Colonial opposition nullified the Stamp Act.

STAMP ACT CONGRESS (1765). The Stamp Act and other recent British statutes menaced self-rule in all the colonies and thus furnished a principle of union. The House of Representatives of Massachusetts, appreciating the value of united effort, issued in June a call to all the colonies to send delegates to New York. Nine colonies responded and a total of 27 delegates met in the City Hall in October. They framed resolutions of colonial "rights and grievances" and petitioned king and Parliament to repeal the objectionable legislation. They held that taxing the colonies without their consent violated one of the most precious rights of Englishmen. Since distance precluded colonial representation in the British Parliament, they could be taxed only by their local assemblies in which they were represented. The Congress is significant in that parliamentary threats to colonial self-control fostered the movement which slowly brought to maturity the spirit and agencies of national unity.

STANDARD OIL COMPANY, an Ohio corporation, was incorporated in January, 1870, with a capital of $1,000,000, the original stockholders being John D. Rockefeller (2667 shares); William Rockefeller (1333 shares); Henry M. Flagler (1333 shares); Samuel Andrews (1333 shares); Stephen V. Harkness (1334 shares); O. B. Jennings (1000 shares); and the firm of Rockefeller, Andrews & Flagler (1000 shares). It took the place of the previous firm of Rockefeller, Andrews & Flagler, whose refineries were much the largest in Cleveland and probably the largest in the world. Important extensions were immediately made. Thanks partly to these, partly to superior efficiency, and partly to the threat of the South Improvement Co., the Standard early in 1872 swallowed practically all rival refineries in the Cleveland area. The roster of stockholders on Jan. 1, 1872, was slightly increased, and the capital raised to $2,500,000. Coincidentally with the conquest of Cleveland, the Standard began reaching out to other cities. In 1872 it bought the oil-transporting and refining firm of J. A. Bostwick & Co. in New York; the Long Island Oil Co.; and a controlling share of the Devoe Manufacturing Co. on Long Island. In 1873 it bought pipelines, the largest refinery in the oil regions, and a half-interest in a Louisville refinery. The acquisition of the principal refineries of Pittsburgh and Philadelphia was carried out in 1874–76, while in 1877 the Standard in a terrific war defeated the Pennsylvania Railroad and the Empire Transportation Co., taking possession of the pipelines and refineries of the latter. Another war with the Tidewater Pipeline resulted in a working agreement which drastically limited the latter's operations. By 1879 the Standard, with its subsidiary and associated companies, controlled from 90% to 95% of the refining capacity of the United States, immense pipeline and storage-tank systems, and powerful marketing organizations at home and abroad. Under

Rockefeller's leadership it was the first company in the world to organize the whole of a huge, complex and extremely rich industry. In 1875 the stock of the Standard was increased for the last time to a total of $3,500,000, the million dollars of new stock being taken by Charles Pratt & Co., Warden, Frew & Co., and S. V. Harkness. In 1879 there were 37 stockholders, of whom John D. Rockefeller, with 8984 shares, held nearly three times as much as any other man.

While the Standard Oil of Ohio remained legally a small company with no manufacturing operations outside its state, practically it was the nucleus of an almost nation-wide industrial organization, the richest and most powerful in the country. Its articles of incorporation had not authorized it to hold stock in other companies or to be a partner in any firm. It had met this difficulty by acquiring stocks not in the name of the Standard of Ohio, but in that of some one prominent stockholder as trustee. Henry M. Flagler, William Rockefeller, J. A. Bostwick and various others served from 1873 to 1879 as trustees. Then in 1879 the situation was given more systematic treatment. All the stocks acquired by the Standard and held by various trustees, and all the properties outside Ohio in which the Standard had an interest, were transferred to three minor employees (George H. Vilas, Myron R. Keith, George F. Chester) as trustees. They held the stocks and properties for the exclusive use and benefit of the Standard's stockholders, and distributed dividends in specified proportions. But while this arrangement was satisfactory from a legal point of view, it did not provide sufficient administrative centralization. On Jan. 2, 1882, therefore, a new arrangement, the Standard Oil Trust Agreement, set up the first trust in the sense of a monopoly in American history. All stock and properties, including that of the Standard Oil proper as well as of interests outside Ohio, were transferred to a board of nine trustees, consisting of the principal owners and managers, with John D. Rockefeller as head. For each share of stock of the Standard of Ohio, twenty trust certificates of a par value of $100 each were to be issued. The total of the trust certificates was therefore $70,000,000, considerably less than the actual value of the properties. The Standard's huge network of refineries, pipes, tanks and marketing systems was thus given a secret but for the time being satisfactory legal organization, while administration was centralized in nine able men with Rockefeller at their head.

This situation lasted until 1892, the Standard constantly growing in wealth and power. Then as the result of a decree by the Ohio courts the Standard Oil Trust dissolved, and the separate establishments and plants were reorganized into twenty constituent companies. But by informal arrangement, unity of action was maintained among these twenty corporations until they could be gathered into a holding company

(Standard Oil of New Jersey). Then in 1911 a decree of the Federal Supreme Court forced a more complete dissolution. Rockefeller remained nominal head of the Standard until 1911, but after 1895 he had surrendered more and more of the actual authority to his associates, with John D. Archbold as their chief.

STANDING ORDER. For nearly two centuries New England was dominated by a close association of the clergy, the magistrates and the well-to-do, which consciously controlled political, economic, social and intellectual life. This control rested on popular acceptance, a limited suffrage and the special legal position of the Congregational church, and was so firmly established as to win the name of the Standing Order. Its members were aristocratic and intensely conservative, and failed to hold out against the growing democracy of the early 19th century.

STANSBURY EXPLORATION, made by Capt. Howard Stansbury of the U. S. Army in 1852, had for its object a survey of the valley of Great Salt Lake, an inspection of the Mormon colony, and an examination of a new route through the mountains. These were all accomplished in the face of difficulties, and Stansbury's illustrated report and accompanying atlases make it one of the most interesting and valuable explorations ever made under government auspices.

STANWIX, FORT. In 1758 the old fort at the Oneida carrying place, which had been destroyed by Gen. Webb after the French captured Oswego in 1756, was rebuilt and named Stanwix after its builder, Gen. John Stanwix. Its strategic location between the upper Mohawk and Wood Creek made it an important point of defense during the colonial period and a center of Indian trade and treaties. After the conclusion of peace with the French in 1763 it was allowed to fall into disrepair, and at the beginning of the Revolution was found to be untenable. It was rebuilt and for a time called Fort Schuyler in honor of Gen. Philip Schuyler. It was here that in 1777 St. Leger was held back on his way to Albany. With the conclusion of peace the usefulness of the old fort was over. Immigrants from New England swarmed into the region. A village, the present city of Rome, was founded on the site of the fort.

STANWIX, FORT, FIRST TREATY OF (1768). At the time of the Proclamation of 1763 it was evidently intended that another Indian boundary line farther west than the Proclamation Line would be established by means of treaties with the Indian tribes. This plan was forgotten until late in 1767 when Lord Shelburne received letters from America warning him of dangers of Indian warfare unless something were done. The Lords of Trade and the Privy Council discussed the matter and Shelburne was authorized to instruct the two Indian superintendents in America to negotiate with the Indians with a view to establishing a boundary line.

Upon receipt of these instructions Sir William Johnson summoned the Iroquois Indians and their allies to meet him at Fort Stanwix in September, 1768. Twenty boatloads of presents were alluringly displayed before the covetous eyes of the Indians, who were told that all these attractive goods would be theirs if they would make a grant of land to the king. The prospect, together with well-placed private gifts, won the desired result late in October. The Iroquois agreed to cede their claims to lands east and south of a line which was indicated in detail in the treaty. This line ran from the vicinity of Fort Stanwix on the upper Mohawk southward to the Delaware, then in a general southwestwardly direction across and along both branches of the Susquehanna to the Allegheny River, and down that stream and the Ohio to the mouth of the Tennessee. The extension of the line to the Tennessee River was an afterthought, and was apparently included because of the intrigues of certain traders, although the Iroquois themselves requested permission to cede land south of the Ohio in order to prove their claims to the region as against the Cherokees.

The Indian boundary line was continued southward by treaties made by John Stuart, the most important being those made at Hard Labor in 1768 and Lochaber in 1770, by which the Cherokees ceded their claims to lands in the present State of West Virginia. These two treaties have a close connection with the Treaty of Fort Stanwix, for between them they opened to settlement large areas of land in southwestern Pennsylvania and in the region back of Virginia. Whether the British authorities intended the making of these treaties to authorize settlement west of the Proclamation Line is not clear, but American settlers indicated their own interpretation by moving in large numbers into the country between the two lines.

STANWIX, FORT, SECOND TREATY OF (1784). The powerful Iroquois Indians had been greatly weakened by the vigorous campaigns of Sullivan and Brodhead during the Revolutionary War and their leaders recognized the futility of further resistance to the white advance. Consequently at Fort Stanwix in October, 1784, they ceded a small tract of land in western New York, and all that part of Pennsylvania north and west of the Indian boundary line established by the first Treaty of Fort Stanwix in 1768 (constituting about one fourth of the area of the state). They also relinquished their claim to land west of the Ohio River—a claim, however, which was disputed by other tribes.

STAPLES, COLONIAL. The continental British-American colonies had three important staple crops— tobacco, rice, indigo. Tobacco was a major crop in

Virginia, Maryland and parts of North Carolina. Tobacco was an enumerated product and found its chief market in England and Scotland where it was graded, processed and shipped to the various markets of the world. Rice was mainly grown on the lowlands of South Carolina and Georgia. It found its chief market in England, the West Indies and in Southern Europe. As England could not use the entire crop it was permitted to be marketed in Europe south of Cape Finisterre. Indigo was produced only in South Carolina and some of the West Indies. It had to have rich soil and special treatment. It was encouraged by British bounties and was marketed almost entirely in England. In the British West Indies, especially in Barbados, sugar was another important staple crop. This product, like the others, was enumerated and was shipped largely to England where it was refined and marketed throughout the British Empire and Europe. Molasses was an important by-product of this industry and was used directly by the rum distilling industry in England and America.

The staple industries had several things in common. Each tended to become a plantation type of crop where the labor was almost exclusively done by slaves. Such single-crop types of farming tended to develop irregular production, absentee landlords and dependence upon foreign financing and foreign markets. All, except indigo, were bulky and required extensive shipping to carry them to England.

STAR ROUTE FRAUDS. Star Routes were roads, principally in the West, where mail was carried under contracts by wagons or horses and not by railroad or steamboat. Extensive frauds in the Post Office Department caused great financial losses to the Government. Departmental officials, contractors, sub-contractors and an ex-Senator were in conspiracy. This "gang" demanded more congressional appropriations for starting new and useless routes; fraudulent and padded petitions supported their demands for money to expedite old routes; worthless bonds and securities were imposed on the Department; and contractors exacted fines and profits from sub-contractors. One $90,000 contract was let on the affidavit of one contractor. Another route with $761 income annually was expedited in speed and number of trips at a cost of $50,000, although for 39 days no papers or letters were carried over that road. Analysis of the specifications of John M. Peck, one contractor, showed requirements that each horse had to travel twenty hours daily and the rider forty hours daily! Congressional investigations, special agents, Pinkerton detectives and attorneys brought about more than 25 indictments. Trials in 1882 and 1883 proved frauds on 93 routes. But no convictions resulted and the Government was defrauded of about $4,000,000.

"STAR-SPANGLED BANNER" was inspired by the British attack on Fort McHenry, Sept. 13, 1814.

On the night of the attack, Francis Scott Key, a young Baltimore lawyer, together with a group of friends had gone to the British admiral to seek the release of a prominent physician who had been captured by the British. Because of plans for the attack, Key and his companions were detained on ship in the harbor and spent the night watching the British bombard the fort. Key felt sure that the attack had been successful, but when dawn disclosed the flag still flying Key's emotions were so stirred that he wrote the words of "The Star-Spangled Banner" on the back of an envelope, adapting them to a then popular drinking song, "To Anacreon in Heaven." The original version was printed as a handbill the next day; a week later it appeared in a Baltimore newspaper. Later Key made a complete draft which is now in a private collection in Baltimore. The song soon became in fact the national anthem, but it was not until 1931 that Congress officially recognized it as such. Despite its prominence there are few people who know more than the first stanza of the "Star-Spangled Banner" and even fewer who can sing the difficult melody. Numerous attempts have been made to simplify the music, but none have been generally accepted.

"STARVING TIME" is the term used to refer to the food shortage at Jamestown in the spring of 1609. There was a similar shortage of food at Plymouth in the spring of 1622. The Jamestown starving time was relieved by the arrival of a ship from England, that at Plymouth by the arrival of a fishing vessel via Virginia.

STATE, DEPARTMENT OF. During the Revolutionary War foreign affairs were handled by committees of Congress, until a Department of Foreign Affairs was set up in 1781. The first Secretaries for Foreign Affairs were Robert R. Livingston, who served from Oct. 20, 1781, until June 4, 1783, and John Jay, who took office in December, 1784, and continued to act, without further appointment, until Thomas Jefferson took office as Secretary of State in March, 1790.

The first Congress under the Constitution provided for a Department of Foreign Affairs in July, 1789, but changed the name to Department of State in September, 1789, when it decided to entrust to the Department the conduct of domestic affairs that did not fall within the jurisdiction of the other two executive departments, War and Treasury. The Secretary of State administered "home affairs," as well as foreign affairs, until the establishment of the Interior Department in 1849.

When Jefferson took office, his staff consisted of five clerks. There were two American diplomatic representatives abroad, and only four foreign governments were represented in the United States. Several of the Republic's great statesmen—John Marshall (1800–1), James Monroe (1811–17), John Quincy Adams

(1817–25), Henry Clay (1825–29), Martin Van Buren (1829–31), Daniel Webster (1841–43 and 1850–52), and James Buchanan (1845–49)—followed Jefferson as Secretaries of State, but the Department continued to be a small organization. In 1820 it had a staff of only fifteen persons, and until 1853, when provision was made for an Assistant Secretary of State, the Chief Clerk was the ranking officer under the Secretary. For lack of personnel, communications from diplomatic representatives abroad often went unanswered, and documents in foreign languages could not be translated. At times, original papers were sent to the Senate because no copies were available. The Department was strengthened and became more efficient after the Civil War and especially during the period (1869–77) when Hamilton Fish was Secretary of State.

Two officers, whose combined service covered 72 years, gave continuity to the Department's work during the latter part of the 19th century. William Hunter was Chief Clerk, except for a brief period, from 1852 until 1866, and Second Assistant Secretary of State from 1866, when the office was created, until his death in 1886. His successor as Second Assistant Secretary was Alvey A. Adee, who had been Third Assistant Secretary since 1882 and who died in office as Assistant Secretary in 1924. Adee for decades decided all but the most important questions of policy, and his advice on important matters was sought, and followed, by successive Presidents and Secretaries of State.

In 1901 the Department had three Assistant Secretaries and 63 clerks. There was no technical staff except the Solicitor and the Assistant Solicitor, who advised on legal matters, and there was no one whose duty it was to be specially informed about the problems of any region or country. Few if any of those working in the Department had had service abroad. Correspondence with foreign diplomats in Washington and with American diplomatic missions abroad was handled by a Diplomatic Bureau where clerks were assigned to groups of countries arranged alphabetically. The Foreign Service was still more inadequate, for most diplomats and consuls were appointed solely for political reasons.

Changes were clearly needed if the United States was to discharge creditably the obligations that it was assuming as a world power, but reforms came rather slowly. In 1909 Congress made provision for eight "drafting officers" to assist the higher officials in dealing with questions of policy, and in the same year the first geographical divisions were established in the Department, under officers who had some knowledge of the regions with which they were dealing. The consular service was reorganized after 1906 and the diplomatic service was made somewhat more efficient. In 1915 Congress authorized the assignment of diplomatic and consular officers for service in the Department, for periods of not more than four years at one

time, and thus made it possible to provide a more experienced staff for the geographical divisions. Economists were added to the staff, for the first time, in 1919. Though the volume of work increased rapidly during and after World War I, increases in personnel made it possible to deal with it in a fairly adequate way during the interwar period. The Foreign Service was greatly improved after the passage of the Rogers Act in 1924.

World War II and the postwar years brought new problems. The United States had responsibilities of leadership which compelled it to take an interest in the affairs of many countries with whose problems it had hitherto had little concern. New military and economic commitments and the greatly increased importance of cultural relations and propaganda called for a great expansion of staffs abroad and in Washington, and the involvement of many other departments of the Federal Government in these matters created new problems of liaison and co-ordination. The State Department was also called on to absorb the activities and part of the personnel of several wartime agencies, like the Office of Strategic Services, the Office of War Information, and the Office of Inter-American Affairs. The result was a considerable measure of administrative confusion which led to several more or less successful efforts at reorganization.

The most important change was effected as a result of the work of a committee appointed by the Secretary of State in 1954 under the chairmanship of Dr. Henry M. Wriston, president of Brown University. The committee recommended the prompt integration of a large part of the Department's staff into the Foreign Service, to create a unified group that would serve both at home and abroad. Before 1954, foreign service officers formed the larger part of the staff of many divisions in the Department; but there had also been many civil service employees, and some offices, like those dealing with economic and legal problems, were manned almost entirely by persons permanently located in Washington. Integration had been recommended by other groups that had studied the Department's organizational problems, and had been accepted in principle as a policy, but little had been done to achieve it. Between 1954 and 1956 the program recommended by the Wriston Committee was substantially carried out.

Some difficulties were encountered. Since there were few foreign service officers qualified by training for some branches of technical work, a number of positions had to be withdrawn from the dual service category and redesignated as civil service positions. Several hundred officers in the Department and a smaller group in the Foreign Service declined to enter the new combined service. In general, however, amalgamation was achieved. A vigorous program was inaugurated to obtain a larger number of qualified candidates for the lower ranks of the new service, and the program of in-service training under the Foreign Service Institute was expanded.

The way in which diplomatic relations are carried on has changed greatly since the State Department was first set up. When communication was by sailing ship, or even by steamer, diplomatic representatives had to act on general instructions and to use their discretion in dealing with new situations when there was no time to consult the home office. The submarine cable, and later the telephone, changed this situation, but did not diminish the diplomat's responsibility as the only official who was in close touch with the government to which he was accredited. In modern times, partly because the airplane has made travel easier and far more rapid, the use of special envoys to deal with important problems has increased, and personal conferences between ministers of foreign affairs and even between heads of states have become much more common. There has been an equally notable increase in the number of international conferences attended by representatives of several states, frequently to deal with matters that would not formerly have been considered subjects for diplomatic negotiation.

The State Department's increased responsibilities in the postwar period made it necessary for the Secretary of State to have a far larger staff and especially a larger number of assistants of high rank. On June 1, 1959, there were two Undersecretaries of State and two deputy undersecretaries. Each of the five geographical bureaus was headed by an assistant secretary, and there were also assistant secretaries for international organization affairs, economic affairs, administration, public affairs, congressional relations, and policy planning. Other important officials were the Counselor, the Legal Adviser, the Director of Intelligence and Research, and several "Special Assistants." The International Co-operation Administration, under its Director, was an autonomous agency within the Department.

STATE BIRDS AND FLOWERS. Alabama: *Yellowhammer, Goldenrod.* Alaska: *Willow Ptarmigan, Forget-me-not.* Arizona: *Cactus Wren, Giant Cactus* or *Saguaro.* Arkansas: *Mockingbird, Apple Blossom.* California: *Valley Quail, Golden Poppy.* Colorado: *Lark Bunting, Columbine.* Connecticut: *American Robin, Mountain Laurel.* Delaware: *Blue Hen Chicken, Peach Blossom.* Florida: *Mockingbird, Orange Blossom.* Georgia: *Brown Thrasher, Cherokee Rose.* Hawaii: _____, *Hibiscus.* Idaho: *Mountain Bluebird, Lewis Mock Orange.* Illinois: *Cardinal, Butterfly Violet.* Indiana: *Cardinal, Peony.* Iowa: *Eastern Goldfinch, Carolina* (*Wild*) *Rose.* Kansas: *Western Meadow Lark, Sunflower.* Kentucky: *Cardinal, Goldenrod.* Louisiana: *Brown Pelican, Magnolia Grandiflora.* Maine: *Chickadee, Pine Cone.* Maryland: *Oriole, Black-eyed Susan.* Massachusetts: *Chickadee, Trailing Arbutus.* Michigan: *Robin, Apple Blossom.* Minne-

sota: *American Goldfinch, Showy Lady-slipper.* Mississippi: *Mockingbird, Magnolia.* Missouri: *Bluebird, Hawthorn.* Montana: *Western Meadow Lark, Bitterroot.* Nebraska: *Western Meadow Lark, Goldenrod.* Nevada: *Mountain Bluebird, Sagebrush.* New Hampshire: *Purple Finch, Purple Lilac.* New Jersey: *Eastern Goldfinch, Purple Violet.* New Mexico: *Road Runner, Yucca.* New York: *Eastern Bluebird, Rose.* North Carolina: *Cardinal, Dogwood.* North Dakota: *Western Meadow Lark, Prairie Rose.* Ohio: *Cardinal, Scarlet Carnation.* Oklahoma: *Scissor-tailed Flycatcher, Mistletoe.* Oregon: *Western Meadow Lark, Oregon Grape.* Pennsylvania: *Ruffed Grouse, Mountain Laurel.* Rhode Island: *Rhode Island Red, Violet.* South Carolina: *Carolina Wren, Carolina* (*Yellow*) *Jessamine.* South Dakota: *Ringnecked Pheasant, Pasqueflower.* Tennessee: *Mockingbird, Iris.* Texas: *Mockingbird, Bluebonnet.* Utah: *Sea Gull, Sego Lily.* Vermont: *Hermit Thrush, Red Clover.* Virginia: *Cardinal, American Dogwood.* Washington: *Willow Goldfinch, Rhododendron.* West Virginia: *Cardinal, Rosebay Rhododendron.* Wisconsin: *Robin, Butterfly Violet.* Wyoming: *Meadow Lark, Wyoming Painted Cup.*

STATE FAIRS. The first state fair of continued existence was held in Syracuse, N. Y., in 1841. By 1860 eighteen states had established fairs. Permanent sites near urban centers were the rule by 1900. State fairs have aided in improving livestock, popularizing new inventions and providing a gala day on which rural and urban people intermingle.

STATE-MAKING PROCESS. The original thirteen states had their origin as colonies of Great Britain and, following their successful war for independence, they formed the original United States of America. The Constitution of the United States went into effect in 1789 following its ratification by conventions in eleven of the states. North Carolina and Rhode Island were included soon after. The State of Vermont may possibly be considered as belonging to the same class of original states since its people formed a constitution and declared themselves independent in 1777, and the state was admitted into the Union in 1791 by act of Congress. Kentucky, originally a part of the State of Virginia, was formed into a county of that state in 1776. The people of this district asked Virginia to consent to the creation of a new state. The consent was given in 1789 and Kentucky was admitted as a state in 1792. Also, North Carolina originally included the territory comprising the State of Tennessee. This latter was transferred to the Union and was admitted as a state in 1796. All creations of states and admissions to the Union were, of course, authorized by act of Congress.

By virtue of the Definitive Treaty of Peace of 1783, with Great Britain, the territory of the United States was extended to the Mississippi River. Further annexations of lands during the succeeding years, such as the purchase of Louisiana and Florida and the cessions from Mexico added to this wide extent of national possessions. The State of Texas was originally an independent nation from 1836–45, having successfully won its independence from Mexico. It was annexed to the Union by joint resolution of Congress in 1845. With the exception of Texas and the State of Maine which was separated from Massachusetts in 1820 the remainder of the states were carved out of the public lands owned by the United States as the result of the various cessions and annexations.

Immediately following the American Revolution the Continental Congress took the first steps in organizing the then western lands with a view to preparing the inhabitants for local self-government and organization into territories not only for this purpose but also with the objective of their final admission as states into the Union. The famous "Northwest Ordinance" or "Ordinance for the Government of the Territory of the United States Northwest of the River Ohio," was passed on July 13, 1787. It contained three very important provisions: first, there was a grant to the inhabitants of the territory of those fundamental political and personal rights which are presumed to be the basis of American liberty; second, there was a statement of a plan for the immediate government of a territory; and third, there was a statement of the policy of the Federal Government with regard to the final status of such a territory. This ordinance was the basis upon which all public lands and even foreign possessions of the United States have been organized in various degrees for their administration during the succeeding one hundred years.

For the immediate government of an organized territory all powers were vested in a governor, a secretary and a court of three judges, all of whom were to be appointed by the Continental Congress. At first there was to be no legislature but the above officials had the authority to adopt and promulgate the laws of the already existing states as they considered them best suited to the needs of the territory. While these laws were to be reported to Congress they were supposed to go into effect unless disallowed by that body. This concentration of executive and legislative power in the same hands was a violation of fundamental American ideas of free government, but was justified on the grounds of temporary expediency. A more complete government was to be substituted as soon as there were five thousand free male inhabitants in any one of the territories, then or in the future to be created. There was to be a legislative body consisting of a house of representatives on a certain arbitrary numerical basis of apportionment and an upper house or council of five members to be chosen by Congress upon nomination of the lower house of the legislature. The governor and legislature under a delegation of power by act of Congress were to pass all laws needed for local government, but there was no provision for

a veto by the governor. A further provision required that the two houses of the legislature in joint session should elect a delegate to Congress who should have a seat in that body with a right to participate in debate but no vote. This plan as contained in the Ordinance of 1787 forms the basis upon which has been built up since that time in the various stages of development the system of government for the future states of the United States. The first United States Congress under the new Constitution passed an act on May 26, 1790, which provided that a like plan of government should be created for the Southwest Territory which lay south of the Ohio River. Ohio, the first state to be founded under the Northwest Ordinance, was admitted to the Union in 1803.

As soon as an organized territory had maintained self-government under these conditions and had grown in population to a position sufficient to justify, in the varying public opinion of the times, its admission as a state, the United States Congress has passed a specific enabling act under which the people of the territory have chosen delegates to a territorial constitutional convention. The general procedure has been for this convention to draw up a constitution for the prospective state which usually was modeled upon the constitutions of the original or other early states already in the Union. Upon adjournment of the convention this constitution was submitted to the people of the territory for their ratification and generally has been accepted by them. The prospective state has then applied to Congress for admission to full status in the Union. Congress has usually passed the necessary enabling act and upon a like acceptance by the people and government of the territory a new state has been formally admitted into the Union. When finally admitted, each new state acquires complete equality with all the other states and a like possession of all reserved powers not specifically delegated to the National Government according to the provisions of the United States Constitution.

In the course of time new problems of social and political importance have arisen and these have on various occasions caused Congress to impose certain restrictions upon the states in the form of mandatory requirements of provisions in their constitutions before an enabling act for their admission is passed. This procedure in reality began in the original provision in the Ordinance of 1787 which forever prohibited slavery within territories soon to be organized. Also, when the Southern states were "readmitted" to the Union in the years following the Civil War, Congress required the inclusion in their respective constitutions of certain provisions, among which the abolition and future prohibition of slavery were the most important.

In illustration of the above may be given the procedure in the admission of Utah to the Union. Congress refused to pass the enabling act until Utah included in its constitution a provision prohibiting polygamy within the prospective state, which then was admitted in 1896. Also in 1910 the territories of New Mexico and Arizona were given congressional permission to frame constitutions and apply for admission to the Union. This procedure was completed by the territories within the next year but, due to the inclusion in the proposed Arizona constitution of a provision for the popular recall of judges, admission of the territories was refused. For political reasons, the case of New Mexico was included with that of Arizona. In the year 1912 the Arizona constitution had been amended to exclude the clause to which there was objection and both states were admitted to the Union. Alaska, the forty-ninth state, and Hawaii, the fiftieth, were admitted in 1959.

STATE SOVEREIGNTY as a doctrine appeared shortly after 1776. "Among the first sentiments expressed in the first Congress," said James Wilson in the Convention of 1787, "one was that Virginia is no more, that Pennsylvania is no more, etc. We are now one nation of brethren. We must bury all local interests and distinctions. This language continued for some time. No sooner were the State governments formed than their jealousy and ambition began to display themselves. Each endeavored to cut a slice from the common loaf, to add to his morsel, till at length the confederation became frittered down to the impotent condition in which it now stands." So intolerable had the evils of particularism become by 1787 that Henry Knox wrote: "The State systems are the accursed things which will prevent our becoming a nation. The democracy might be managed, nay, it would be a remedy itself after being sufficiently fermented; but the vile State governments are sources of pollution, which will contaminate the American name for ages—machines that must produce ill, but cannot produce good."

There was sound reason for the display of state loyalty in 1787. State governments were known and trusted; they had carried the people through the war with Great Britain while the impotent Congress of the Confederation had been unable to achieve the objects for which it was created. It followed that not only did men distrust a national government, but they also failed to understand that two jurisdictions largely co-ordinate could work toward a similar end. They imagined that co-ordination meant antithesis, and feared lest the surrender of a portion of the power wielded by the states would end in the destruction of personal liberty. It could therefore be argued that the National Government must rest in part on the states.

The part the states should play in the American political system was the subject of prolonged debate in the Convention of 1787. Hamilton, who wanted the states reduced to "corporations for local purposes," was poles asunder from members who argued for the complete sovereignty of the states. As he listened to the debate, Dr. William Samuel Johnson of Connecti-

cut remarked that "the controversy must be endless whilst gentlemen differ in the grounds of their arguments; those on one side considering the states as districts of people composing one political society; those on the other considering them as so many political societies." Finally, a compromise was reached whereby the states were secured against encroachment by the National Government through their equal representation in the Senate (*see* Connecticut Compromise).

The problem of sovereignty remained unsolved when the government under the Constitution was inaugurated in 1789. The prevalent opinion was that somehow sovereignty had been divided between the states and the Union. This view was staunchly maintained by James Madison and was enunciated by the Supreme Court in Chisholm v. Georgia (1793). Up to the time when the theory of Calhoun became influential, the characteristic American doctrine was that in the United States the sovereignty had been divided into several portions without the destruction of its life principle.

Calhoun, in insisting that sovereignty in the United States is indivisible, returned to the issues debated in the Federal Convention. He declared that to the people of the several states sovereignty devolved upon the separation from Great Britain, and it was through the exercise of this sovereignty that the state constitutions as well as the Constitution of the United States were created. In other words, the Constitution of the United States was ordained and established by the people of the several states, acting as so many sovereign political communities, and not by the people of the United States, acting as one people, though within the states.

The accepted statement of the states' rights doctrine was set forth by Calhoun in his *Disquisition on Government* and his *Discourse on the Constitution and Government of the United States*. The influence of Calhoun is without question; his political theories became the dogma of the states' rights party and found expression in the constitution of the Confederate States.

The nationalist theory of the Union was defended by Daniel Webster, who insisted that the Constitution is an agreement among individuals to form a national government. "It is established," he said, "by the people of the United States. It does not say by the people of the several States. It is as all the people of the United States that they established the Constitution." Between the party of Calhoun and that of Webster the division of opinion was identical with that observed by Dr. Johnson in the Federal Convention. State sovereignty was made to rest upon the idea that the people of the United States constitute a number of political societies among whom a treaty or agreement was made to form a national government. The Constitution was not, as the nationalists maintained, a fundamental law ordained and established by the whole people of the United States. The controversy remained for the clash of arms to settle, but the victory of Grant at Appomattox settled the question in favor of the defenders of nationalism.

STATES' RIGHTS. As a political or constitutional principle states' rights is an outgrowth of colonial particularism. The spirit of particularism or states' rights manifested itself during the Revolution and the Confederation, and presented a major problem to the Constitution makers of 1787. The classic and constitutional basis of states' rights, as maintained under the Constitution, may be found in the Tenth Amendment adopted in 1791: "The powers not delegated to the United States by the Constitution, nor prohibited by it to the States, are reserved to the States respectively, or to the people" (*see* Reserved Powers of States).

STATUE OF LIBERTY, properly "Liberty Enlightening the World," on Bedloe's Island, New York Harbor, was conceived by Frederic Auguste Bartholdi, Alsatian sculptor, who built it in Paris during the 1870's and early 1880's. A gift to the United States from the people of France, costing approximately a million francs, raised by subscription, the colossal copper figure was shipped in sections in 1885, and unveiled Oct. 28, 1886. Cleveland accepted it in a belated commemoration of a century of American independence. The statue with its upraised torch, standing 152 feet above the pedestal and 300 feet above sea level, forthwith became the symbol of welcome to immigrating thousands.

STEAM POWER. The first successful steam engine in the American colonies was put into operation in 1755 at the Schuyler Copper Mines, near Newark, N. J., for pumping water from the mines. The engine, a Newcomen model, was built by the Hornblowers, an English firm of engine builders. It was in operation until the eve of the American Revolution when work at the mines was abandoned except for surface digging. In 1792 the engine again operated, but only for a short period. Before 1775 several English engines were imported into New England and a few built in the colonies. They were not successful.

During the last part of the 18th century when Watt and others in England were pushing their inventions from an experimental to a practical stage, Henry, Colles, Fitch, Rumsey, Evans, Donaldson, Latrobe, Kinsey, Voight, Thornton, Hall and others were experimenting with steam power in this country. Many were interested in applying steam to navigation. As early as 1787 John Fitch demonstrated a steamboat on the Delaware River before members of the Constitutional Convention, but not until Robert Fulton's *Clermont* appeared on the Hudson River in 1807 was the success of the steamboat assured. Oliver Evans and others led attempts to apply steam power

also to land conveyances, but success was delayed until the introduction of steam railroads.

The development of steam power for driving machinery was retarded in the United States largely by the abundance and cheapness of water power. In 1800 there were only six engines in successful operation. They were designed on the Boulton and Watt plan, but most of the parts were made here. The high-pressure engine perfected by Oliver Evans opened the way for utilizing steam for driving machinery. By 1812 at least ten engines of this type provided power for sawmills, gristmills, sugar mills and textile mills. In the following decades New England slowly adopted the steam engine, but still relied to a large extent upon water power. In the rest of the country, especially in the Pittsburgh region and in the growing West, the introduction of the stationary steam engine made more rapid progress. In the period following the Civil War steam power was in general use, industrially.

Among the inventors who improved the steam engine in the United States, the name of George H. Corliss ranks high. The most important of his many inventions was his "drop cut-off" mechanism. A great Corliss engine provided power for all the machinery at the Philadelphia Centennial Exposition in 1876. Another American inventor, Charles G. Curtis, combined the ideas of Gustaf de Laval, a Swedish engineer, and Charles A. Parsons, an English engineer, in producing an improved steam turbine.

STEAMBOATS. The idea of steam-powered boats intrigued men before the days of James Rumsey, John Fitch and Robert Fulton. Practical steamboat experiments began with the double-acting engine in 1782; both Rumsey and Fitch operated their boats before Washington's inauguration. Successful commercial navigation, however, is usually dated from the voyage of Fulton's *Clermont* in 1807. Thereafter steamships were launched for deep-sea passage; steamboats for the swift streams of the tidewater and Mississippi Valley whose tortuous curves and shallow sand-bar studded waters required high-powered, light draft boats. The first steamboat on western waters, the *New Orleans,* was built from Fulton-Livingston patents in 1811. She was a 300-ton, two-masted side-wheeler with boiler, engine and vertical stationary cylinder placed in her open hold. The bow was reserved for freight—the cabins were aft of the machinery. In 1813 Daniel French launched the 25-ton *Comet,* a stern-wheeler featuring vibrating cylinders. The *New Orleans* and *Comet* served as models until 1816, when Henry Shreve built the *Washington,* the first real steamboat on western waters. Shreve contributed three ideas to his 403-ton craft: he placed the machinery and cabin on the main deck, used horizontal cylinders with vibrations to the pitmans, and employed a double high-pressure engine. Subsequent marine architecture simply improved on these features.

A generation passed before the floating palaces of the Mark Twain era evolved. Steamboats increased in tonnage, boasted ornate cabins and private staterooms, bars and barber shops, bands and orchestras, steam whistles and calliopes. Steam was used to work the capstan, handle the spars, or swing the stage. An auxiliary engine, or doctor, pumped water into the boiler. Coal gradually replaced wood, the electric searchlight was substituted for the wood-torch. Spacious decks with promenades were built high above the main deck—the "Texas" (for the crew) and the pilot house being placed high above all. In 1843 the second *J. M. White* was launched at Pittsburgh. She was 250 feet long, 31 feet beam, 8½ feet hold, had seven boilers, 30-inch cylinders and a 10-foot stroke. In 1878 the third *J. M. White* was built at Louisville at a cost of over $200,000. She was 325 feet long, 50 feet beam and 11½ feet hold. She had ten boilers 34 feet long and her cylinders were 43 inches in diameter with an 11-foot stroke. The main cabin was 260 feet long. She could carry 8500 bales of cotton. The record load of 9226 bales of cotton was carried by the *Henry Frank* in 1881. It would have taken a season of hard work for the *New Orleans* to carry this amount.

Steamboat Racing reached its zenith in 1870 when the *Robert E. Lee* raced from New Orleans to St. Louis in three days, eighteen hours, fourteen minutes, defeating the *Natchez* by over three hours. All America was agog, telegraphic reports were flashed to Europe, and more than a million dollars in bets is said to have changed hands. Although editorials denounced the practice as dangerous, fast boats were popular with travelers and shippers. Moreover, few explosions occurred while boats were racing, for engineers were more alert. Many races were against time, captains endeavoring to break records between ports. By 1840, when steamboats were attaining a high standard in marine architecture, the average speed was about six miles per hour upstream, and ten to twelve miles per hour downstream. Fast boats could average better than ten miles per hour upstream. Thus, in 1844 the *J. M. White* ran from New Orleans to St. Louis in 3 days and 23 hours, a record that stood for years. In 1815 the *Enterprise* churned from New Orleans to Louisville in 25 days; by 1853 the *Eclipse* had reduced this time to 4 days, 9 hours, 30 minutes. The *Cataract* raced from St. Louis to LaSalle, Ill., in 1854, in 23 hours, 45 minutes. The *James H. Lucas* ran from St. Louis to St. Joseph on the Missouri in 1856 in 2 days, 12 hours, 52 minutes; and the *Hawkeye State* sped from St. Louis to St. Paul in 1868 in 2 days and 20 hours. On a short run from St. Louis to Alton in 1853 the *Altoona* made 25 miles in 1 hour and 35 minutes.

Steamboating on Western Waters was inaugurated by the *New Orleans* in 1811. Scarcely a dozen steamboats were built by 1817, but in the next two years over sixty were launched for traffic on the Mississippi, the Missouri and the Ohio. By 1834 there were 230 steamboats, aggregating 39,000 tons, on western waters. Of the 684 steam craft constructed by the close of 1835, the Pittsburgh district contributed 304, the Cincinnati district 221 and the Louisville area 103. So phenomenal was the growth that steam tonnage on western waters soon exceeded steam tonnage in the British merchant marine. The cost of running the 1190 steamboats on western waters in 1846 was estimated at $41,154,194. At that time fully 10,126,160 tons of freight valued at $432,621,240 were transported annually. This was nearly double the United States foreign commerce. Pittsburgh, Cincinnati and Louisville were great Ohio ports, while New Orleans dominated the Lower Mississippi. In 1854 New Orleans and St. Louis ranked second and third respectively in enrolled steam tonnage in the United States. Six years later St. Louis recorded 1524 steamboat arrivals from the Upper Mississippi, 767 from the Lower Mississippi, 544 from the Illinois, 277 from the Ohio, 269 from the Missouri, 35 from the Cumberland, 31 from the Tennessee and 7 from the Arkansas.

The first steamboat navigated the Missouri in 1819, the Tennessee in 1821, the Upper Mississippi in 1823 and the Illinois in 1828. Before the Civil War, over forty tributaries of the Mississippi system had been navigated by steamboat. Captain-ownership was followed by the formation of powerful corporations such as the Cincinnati and Louisville Mail Line, the Anchor Line on the Lower Mississippi, the Northern Line on the Upper Mississippi and the Union Packet Line on the Missouri. The attempts of "tramp" boats or new lines to enter a profitable trade led to cut-throat competition and ruinous rates. River towns collected staggering wharfage fees but failed to provide adequate terminal facilities. Expensive litigation, unbusinesslike methods, uncertain rates and the limited season of navigation were additional handicaps. The Civil War ruined steamboating on the Lower Mississippi and contributed to the decline on the Ohio River, already locked in a death struggle with the railroads. Corporations were re-established on the Lower Mississippi after the Civil War, and St. Louis advertised lines to the Arkansas, the Red, the Ouachita, the Tennessee and other streams. But the halcyon days were soon gone: not even the race of the *Natchez* and the *Robert E. Lee* in 1870 could revive them. The Mississippi was paralleled by rails and trussed with bridges that were frequently hazardous to navigation. The iron horse reached St. Joseph on the Missouri in 1859, Council Bluffs in 1867, Bismarck in 1872. Most river improvements came after steamboating had virtually died. The gradually increasing tonnage on the Ohio and Mississippi since World War I reflects the persistence of steamboating on western waters.

STEEL TRAP. In *Book 14, Orders and Wills of York County, 1709–1716* (Williamsburg, Va.), Capt. Daniel

Taylor's inventory of personal property includes "steele traps." This is probably the earliest record of the steel trap in America. By the middle of the 18th century it was in use wherever Europeans traded for furs with the Indian. The records of the British trade are especially revealing in this respect, and there are a few dated traps of this period in American collections. The *Sir William Johnson Papers* contain a requisition of 1764 for 5000 beaver traps valued at ten shillings each. British and French traps were carried far into the interior, and by 1797 were in use on the Lower Red River. In October, 1804, the Lewis and Clark party found steel traps in use by the Mandan Indians, who explained that they had been obtained from the French.

The British traders of Canada and the Pacific Northwest imported from England or manufactured locally a trap of distinctive design, which found use in India as well as in America. The Hudson's Bay Company factors recognized the American-made trap as superior to this British product and obtained it as occasions permitted. By 1853 the Newhouse trap made by the Oneida Community was recognized throughout America as standard for design and quality, although it had competitors. One of the best collections of traps in the United States is possessed by the Bucks County Historical Society, Doylestown, Pa.

STEVENS' INDIAN TREATIES (1854–59). Gov. Isaac I. Stevens of Washington Territory was also superintendent of Indian affairs for his territory. Late in 1854 and continuing into 1855 he negotiated a number of important treaties with the Indian tribes north of the Columbia River and west of the Cascade Mountains. Joel Palmer, the superintendent of Indian affairs for Oregon, co-operated with Stevens in the joint negotiation of some of the most important of these treaties and the general policy for the treaties followed the one worked out by Palmer in Oregon. This plan was to concentrate the Indians on a few reservations and pay for their lands with useful goods and instruct them in farming. The Medicine Creek Treaty, signed Dec. 26, 1854, by 62 chiefs and headmen representing the Puget Sound tribes, accepted the reservation policy. In 1855 three added treaties with the Canoe Indians of the Sound region were signed.

The great council for the interior was opened in the Walla Walla Valley in May, 1855, and the treaty was proclaimed June 12, 1855. It accepted the reservation policy for the powerful tribes of the interior. The outbreak of a series of Indian wars, and friction between the Indian agents and Federal military officers delayed the ratification of these Walla Walla treaties by the Federal Government until March 8, 1859.

STEVENS' RAILROAD SURVEY. Isaac I. Stevens of Massachusetts in 1853 was appointed as governor of the newly created Washington Territory and given two important added duties, that of Superintendent of Indian Affairs for the Pacific Northwest and director of the survey to find a route for a Northern railway to the Pacific. Stevens was a trained army engineer and excellently qualified for his job. Capt. George B. McClellan, assigned to assist in the active direction of the survey, was directed to explore the Cascade Mountains for a practicable pass. Stevens' personal command, while on the overland trip to the coast, explored the passes in the Rocky and Bitter Root mountains. The Marias Pass, later used by the Great Northern, was missed by Stevens' exploring parties although they were searching especially for it because Indians had told them of its existence.

The location of a suitable pass into the Puget Sound region (across the Cascades) proved the most difficult problem of the survey. McClellan was instructed to explore the Naches Pass but failed because he was too easily convinced it was impassable. A. W. Tinkham received orders at Walla Walla to attempt passage of the Snoqualmie Pass, and with the aid of two Indians guides made the trip through it and discovered grades practicable for a railway. Between Oct. 7, 1853, and Feb. 1, 1854, Tinkham covered some 1164 miles of new country. McClellan long stubbornly contested the practicability of the route discovered by Tinkham but it was accepted by Stevens.

STILLWATER CONVENTION (1848). When Wisconsin was admitted to the Union in 1848, a large part of what is now eastern Minnesota was excluded from the new state. A demand for a territorial government by the people of this unorganized area led to a public meeting on Aug. 4, 1848, and a "convention" on Aug. 26, both held at Stillwater. Sixty-one delegates, including most of the prominent men in the Minnesota country, signed memorials to Congress and to the President recommending the "early organization of the Territory of Minnesota." To further that purpose, the convention named Henry H. Sibley a delegate to "visit Washington and represent the interests of the proposed territory." In October, acting upon the assumption that the Territory of Wisconsin was still in existence, the people of the excluded area elected Sibley as delegate to Congress, and in January, 1849, to his great surprise, he was seated.

STOCKYARDS, GROWTH OF. Travelers along the Cumberland Road and other highways leading into the West of the 1820's and 1830's were accustomed to the familiar sight of droves of cattle fattened on the frontier farms of the Middle West on their way to the markets of the Eastern seaboard cities. The extension of the railroads into the West in the two succeeding decades changed all this, so that by the outbreak of the Civil War, livestock had become one of the chief freight items of the western roads. This change in the marketing of livestock resulted in new business methods. At the various western termini, accommodations for holding livestock, commission firms to handle the consignments for the shipper, and packing plants to process a portion of the shipments appeared as component parts of a great business community.

The early stockyards in these terminal cities were either private yards or yards owned and operated by the railroads. As the traffic increased, need for a consolidated yard became clear to all. On Christmas Day, 1865, the Union Stockyards in Chicago were opened. Under a charter granted by the Illinois legislature, a company, known as the Union Stockyard and Transit Co., was formed with a capital of $1,000,000. The railroads running into Chicago took most of the stock and on the board of directors were to be found officials of most of the roads. As the trade in Western cattle grew, yards were opened in other cities: Kansas City in 1871, St. Louis in 1872, Cincinnati in 1874, Omaha in 1884 and St. Paul and Denver in 1886.

The rise of Chicago to a position of supremacy in this business was due to its favorable location, the convergence of nine important railroad lines there, the advantage of an early start given it by the concentration of supplies for the Northern armies during the Civil War, and the enterprise of its citizens in furnishing those factors indispensable for the efficient marketing of livestock: commission houses, stockyards and packing plants. With the concentration of the packing business in Chicago—Nelson Morris in 1859, Armour in 1867 and Swift in 1875—and the mounting flood of cattle pouring in from the Western ranges, Chicago became the greatest livestock center in the world.

In and around the "Yards" in the various cities, there grew up distinctive communities. The great packing companies built their plants near by and around them sprawled the "Packingtowns" made famous in Upton Sinclair's *Jungle*. In the "Yards" were to be found a lusty crowd of commission men, cattle and horse buyers, railroad men, reporters of stock news, cattlemen and their cowboys from the Western ranges and stock detectives representing Western livestock associations. They formed a vigorous, distinctive and colorful group in the business community of the West.

STONY POINT, CAPTURE OF (July 16, 1779). This rocky peninsula on the west bank of the Hudson was connected with Verplanck's Point on the east shore by King's Ferry, a link between two main traveled roads leading from New England to Pennsylvania. On May 31 the British occupied the two points and began to fortify them strongly. Washington himself carefully reconnoitered Stony Point. Deciding that a surprise of the position was practicable, he chose "Mad Anthony" Wayne and the American Light Infantry, a picked corps of 1300 men, for the attack. "I'll storm Hell if you'll plan it," Wayne is reported to have told him. The attack took place at midnight. While a small detachment in the center fired noisily to divert the attention of the defenders, two silent columns, their empty muskets surmounted by bayonets, swarmed over the fortifications to kill and wound 123 men and to take 575 prisoners. Though Washington abandoned the works on July 18, the expedition had done much for the morale of his army.

STOURBRIDGE LION was the first steam locomotive to run on a track in America. The Delaware and Hudson Canal Co. built a railroad line between its mines at Carbondale, Pa., and its canal terminus at Honesdale, and had four locomotives built in England, of which one, the *Stourbridge Lion*, was tested at Honesdale on Aug. 8, 1829. It weighed seven tons, whereas the company had specified only three. The company's engineer bravely drove it over trestles which trembled under its weight, but that first trip was its last; it was discarded as being too heavy for any bridge. What became of the other three engines is unknown.

STRATFORD HALL, Westmoreland County, Virginia, was the birthplace on Jan. 19, 1807, of Robert E. Lee. One of the great architectural monuments of the colonial period, it was erected *ca.* 1725 by Thomas Lee, resident manager for the Fairfaxes on the Northern Neck, and president of the Governor's Council. It has been opened to the public by the Robert E. Lee Foundation.

STREET RAILWAYS. The first street railway in America was laid on the Bowery and Fourth Avenue, from Prince Street to Murray Hill, New York City, in 1832–33. A portion of it was put into operation in June, 1833. The horse-drawn cars had bodies like stagecoaches, and two passengers might ride on the dickey, or driver's seat. This road met much opposition because its rails were slotted so deeply that they damaged the wheels of other vehicles. It was a financial failure, and not until 1836 was another car line attempted, this one in Boston. Thereafter, little was done in street railways until about 1850; between that date and 1855, six new lines were built in various cities. In 1855 the Boston line tried a rail with a slot only seven-eighths inch deep, and in the following year, the modern type of streetcar rail was designed for a Philadelphia line, which greatly accelerated the development of the business. Between 1855 and 1860 thirty new lines were built; between 1860 and 1880 eighty more came into being. By 1890 there were 769 such railways in the principal cities of the country.

As cities grew larger and distances greater, horses became too slow for the longer lines. Beginning in the 1870's, steam cars were tried in some cities, but they were highly objectionable. The continuous cable, running in a slot under the surface, the cars attaching themselves to it by a clutch or grip, next became the most popular form of rapid transit. The first such line was completed in San Francisco in 1873, and was found well adapted to the steep hills of that city. During the next fifteen years most of the larger cities had one or more cable lines, but such systems were very costly—about $100,000 per mile. Electric cars, introduced between 1880 and 1890, rapidly superseded all other systems. In 1912 there were 41,065 miles of electric railways in the United States, but the rapid development of the automobile and then the motor bus was already beginning to threaten their existence. By 1920 street railways in most places were losing money heavily. Fares—which had always been five cents for almost any length of ride—were being raised practically everywhere save in New York City, but this only increased competition. After 1930 the railway lines began to disappear more and more rapidly and were replaced by motor buses.

STUART'S RIDE (June 12–15, 1862). As Lee (C.) prepared to resist McClellan's (U.) attempt to capture Richmond, it was necessary to know the exact position of the Federal right. On June 13 Stuart's (C.) cavalry accomplished this. Then, Stuart decided to ride around McClellan's army, because he thought such a movement would be unexpected. On June 14 Stuart was in McClellan's rear; on June 15 the cavalry rode into Richmond, having traveled over one hundred miles. As a result of Stuart's ride McClellan changed his supply base to the James River; Lee was supplied with the information he required. The moral value of the ride was tremendous; from a military viewpoint its value was questionable.

SUBLETTE'S CUT-OFF (1841–69) was a dry branch of the Oregon Trail between South Pass and Bear River, Wyoming, 53 miles shorter than the better watered Fort Bridger detour. Part of the cutoff was used in 1832 for pack mules by William Sublette, hair-trigger fur man and congressional aspirant. Capt. Bonneville's wagon train followed the route in 1832. Others took the same general course. Father DeSmet crossing South Pass (1841) ahead of the Oregon migration found two trails, one bearing south, the other west across the desert. One became the Oregon Trail. The other—Sublette's—was also called Meek's, Greenwood's or Hedspeth's cut-off. Both were traveled extensively until 1869.

SUBMARINES. The first practical submarine was built in 1775 by David Bushnell of Saybrook, Conn. Named *Turtle,* this one-man boat was the first to use piston pumps to fill and empty ballast tanks. Hand-operated by Ezra Lee of Lyme, Conn., *Turtle* was also the first submarine to be used in actual warfare, although its attempted attacks on the British fleet in New York harbor failed (1776). Another American, Robert Fulton, completed his *Nautilus* (1801), the first of many submarines to bear that name. Fulton

introduced all-metal construction, stern horizontal diving planes, the propeller (which he called "the fly") and dual means of propulsion—hand power submerged and sail for the surface. Repeated demonstrations attended with considerable success failed to interest the governments of France, England and the United States. For nearly half a century, with the exception of the work of Wilhelm Bauer, no important developments in submarine design appeared.

In the Civil War, the Confederate States, eager to break the Union blockade, began the construction of the spar torpedo-carrying semisubmersibles called "Davids." One such "David" rammed and damaged the formidable *New Ironsides* (1863). The first submarine to sink an enemy ship was the hand-powered *Hunley.* Designed by Barriens, built by Hunley and McClintock at Mobile, Ala., this cigar-shaped boat made of boiler plate and manned by a crew of nine took the lives of 35 volunteers in five successive trials. Known as the "Peripatetic Coffin," *Hunley* was ordered to operate as a surface vessel. On the night of Feb. 17, 1864, she drove her spar torpedo into *Housatonic* anchored at the entrance to Charleston harbor. *Hunley* went down with her victim. The Union's one attempt to construct a submarine proved abortive. Her chief effort went into semisubmersibles such as *Stromboli* and *Spuyten Duyvil.*

At this time the evolution of the submarine shifted to Europe. France (Burgois, Brun, Goubet), England (Campbell and Ash, Waddington, Garrett), Sweden (Nordenfelt using Garrett's design), Russia (Drzewicki) and Spain (Peral) all contributed practical experience to submarine construction. But it was the American, Irish-born inventor John P. Holland who became known as the "father of the modern submarine." Holland built six submarines and as many designs and models (1875–97). In 1893 he won the U. S. Government's competition for the design of a practical submarine. This boat was launched at Baltimore (1897), but its cumbersome propulsion system of steam and electricity led the inventor to build independently a smaller craft, the 53-foot *Holland.* Launched May 17, 1897, at Elizabethport, N. J., *Holland* was accepted by the United States on April 11, 1900, and commissioned the following October. This boat became the first submarine of the U. S. Navy, prototype for the seven A-class boats which followed, and the basic design with which Great Britain and Japan inaugurated their modern submarine fleets. Holland boats were plunging types. They set the propulsion pattern of internal combustion engine (diesel engines were introduced after 1911 in E-class) and battery-operated dynamo for submerged power. Special tanks were arranged for the compensation of lost weight (torpedoes expended, fuel consumed, etc.), enabling these boats to maintain a fixed center of gravity. In 1898 the Holland Torpedo Boat Co. merged with Electric Boat, now a division of General Dynamics Corp. Simon Lake of Bridgeport, Conn., pursued the submarine's potential for underwater salvage and exploration. *Argonaut* (1897, rebuilt in 1898) had wheels for travel on the ocean floor and airtight chambers for the egress and ingress of divers. Lake applied bow diving planes, substituted neutral buoyancy for the "tender" state of a positive reserve buoyancy, thus permitting his ships to submerge on an even keel. Lake's company built seven submarines for Russia (1901–6), twenty-seven for the United States, the first completed in 1911.

Though Germany entered the competition late (U-1, 1904), she demonstrated beyond all doubt the effectiveness of the submarine as an instrument of war (1914–18). American L-class boats were stationed abroad in World War I, but they saw little action.

In World War II, boats of the P-class and later the fleet submarines of *Flasher* type sank 1314 naval and merchant ships in the Pacific theater (1941–45). By the close of the war, radar forced submarines to increased operation submerged and the snorkel enabled diesels to "breathe" and recharge batteries without completely surfacing.

Postwar development was rapid. The first nuclear-powered submarine *Nautilus* was launched at Groton, Conn. (1954). Of 3000 ton displacement, 320 feet long, *Nautilus* cruised 60,000 miles on her initial fuel, traversed the Arctic Ocean under the pack ice, crossing the North Pole Aug. 3, 1958. This last feat has been duplicated by the American nuclear submarines *Skate* (twice) and *Sargo* (1960).

Armament, from the first Whitehead torpedo (1868) and early dynamite guns (as in Holland's *Fenian Ram,* 1881) to the present, has kept pace with the evolution in size and design. The *Tunny*-class guided missile submarines; *Pompon*-class radar picket boats, and nine authorized fleet ballistic missile submarines of which *George Washington* is the first to join the fleet, have been of revolutionary importance for the U. S. Navy. *Triton,* powered by twin nuclear reactors, displacing 5000 tons and 447 feet in length, was the world's largest submarine in 1960. With the return to the porpoise-shaped hull of the original *Holland* in *Albacore,* combined with nuclear power in *Skipjack* (launched at Groton in 1958), the true submarine, fictionalized by Jules Verne and anticipated by John Holland, has arrived.

SUBSTITUTES, CIVIL WAR. No conscription in the North during the Civil War was absolute. Always there was the opportunity for the drafted man to hire a substitute, if he could afford it. This was first allowed in the militia draft of 1862 on the theory that, so long as each name drawn from the wheel produced a man, it made no difference whether the drafted person or one hired to take his place appeared for muster. The Conscription Act of March 3, 1863, definitely legalized this method of draft evasion, and each later amendment perpetuated it. Until the act of Feb. 24, 1864, the conscript could take his choice

between hiring a substitute or paying the Government $300 as commutation of service. Thereafter, substitution alone was permitted, except for conscientious objectors. Furthermore, exemption by furnishing a substitute extended only till the next succeeding draft, when the principal again became liable. At once the prices of substitutes rose far above the $300 to which the commutation clause had held them. For this reason legal draft evasion became the prerogative of only the unusually well to do. In the last two years of the war 118,010 substitutes were enlisted, as contrasted with 52,067 conscripts.

The Confederacy also allowed a limited substitution system from early days of the war. The first Conscription Act permitted substitutes from men not legally liable to service to the extent of one man a month in each company. Frauds in the supplying of such substitutes approximated those in the North, as did also the cost of such service (in comparative values). The second Conscription Act (Sept. 17, 1862) made men previously furnishing substitutes again liable to service, thus causing much dissension and legal action. The whole system was abolished by the end of the year 1863. The number of substitutes has never been accurately compiled.

SUFFOLK RESOLVES (Sept. 9, 1774). Of the many meetings held in Massachusetts in 1774 to protest the Coercion Acts, the best known was that of delegates from Boston and other towns in Suffolk County, held at Dedham on Sept. 6 and adjourned to Milton on Sept. 9. There Dr. Joseph Warren presented the resolves, which vigorously denounced the actions of England; refused obedience to the recent acts, or to officials created under them; urged weekly militia musters, nonpayment of taxes and nonintercourse with Great Britain; and suggested the need of a provincial congress to meet at Concord in October. The resolves were passed unanimously and taken by Paul Revere to the Continental Congress at Philadelphia, which by endorsing them moved another step toward independence.

SUGAR ACTS, COLONIAL. The British Empire was dependent upon its West India islands for sugar. The rich sugar planters, residing in England, became politically powerful, and in 1733 secured the enactment of the Molasses Act. Under this law foreign molasses, imported into any British colony, was subject to an import duty of sixpence per gallon. The object was not taxation, but to give the British sugar planters a monopoly of the American molasses market. The law was opposed by the New England merchants, especially Massachusetts and Rhode Island, on the ground that the resultant increased price of rum would injure both the fishing industry and the trade to Africa. The protests were ineffective and the dire results failed to develop. Opposition to the law died down, especially as there was little systematic effort to enforce it.

The sugar planters discovered the Molasses Act was of little value to them and what they most needed was a larger market in Europe, which they got through a rebate of the import duties on sugar exported to the continent. In time the British rum distilleries absorbed the British molasses while there was no market for that from the growing French sugar industry. This situation made French molasses cheap and there developed a well-organized colonial evasion of the import duty.

In 1764 Grenville had enacted a new Sugar Act by which he undertook to end the smuggling trade in foreign molasses and at the same time secure a revenue. The duty on foreign molasses was lowered from six to threepence a gallon, the duties on foreign refined sugar were raised, and an increased export bounty on British refined sugar bound for the colonies was granted. The net result was to give the British sugar planters an effective monopoly of the American sugar market; smuggling of foreign sugar became unprofitable, and the old illicit trade in foreign molasses was disturbed. Americans had been importing large quantities of foreign molasses on which they paid, by collusion, total sums that averaged somewhere between half a penny and a penny a gallon. Most of this money went into the pockets of the customs officials instead of the treasury. Under the act of 1764, the threepence was more than the traffic would bear, if the law was enforced. There were violent protests at first; two years later the duty was lowered to one penny a gallon, applied alike to foreign and British imports, and the protests on the molasses duty came to an end. At this lower rate it was an important revenue producer and yielded annually from 1767 to 1775 an average of £12,194 per year.

Other phases of the Sugar Act of 1764 were far more irritating than was the lowered duty on molasses. One was a new duty on wine imported from Madeira, which prior to this time had come in duty free and was the main source of profit for the fish and food ships returning from the Mediterranean. This part of the Sugar Act led to few direct protests, but did produce some spectacular attempts at evasion, such as the Capt. Malcolm wine running episode in Boston. The provisions that produced the most irritation were new bonding regulations compelling ship masters to give bond, even when loaded with nonenumerated goods. The worst feature was a provision that bond had to be given before any article enumerated or nonenumerated was put on board. Under American conditions it was impossible for a shipmaster to give a new bond at a custom house before he took on board every new consignment of freight. The universal practice was to load first, then clear and give bond. Under the Sugar Act any ship caught with any article on board before bond covering that article had been given was subject to seizure and confiscation. The Customs Commissioners made this provision a source of private profit to themselves. The most

notorious seizures for technical violations of the bonding provision included John Hancock's sloop *Liberty* and the *Ann* belonging to Henry Laurens of South Carolina.

SUGAR INDUSTRY, EARLY. Until the Louisiana Purchase the only sugar made in the United States was from maple sap for household use and frontier trading. Cane sugar from the West Indies was refined by colonial "sugar bakers" who remelted raw sugar and poured it into moulds topped with wet clay whence water percolated through the mass, washing out impurities and leaving the traditional sugar loaf of our forefathers. About 1810 New Orleans already refined sugar locally and shipped raw sugar for refining to St. Louis, Louisville and Cincinnati. By 1830 New Orleans had the "largest refinery in the world" with an annual capacity of 6000 tons. With the introduction of steam melting, boneblack clarifying and centrifugal drying about this time plants became larger, so that by 1856 one New York refinery reported an investment of nearly $1,000,000.

Sugar mill improvements before 1850 included steam power to crush cane and vacuum pans and triple effects—an epoch-making Louisiana invention of the 1840's—to evaporate juice. These made mills more expensive and centralized manufacturing, like refining, in larger establishments. In the 1880's unsatisfactory attempts were made to extract juice from cane by the diffusion process, which is universally employed in making beet sugar.

SULLIVAN-CLINTON CAMPAIGN (1779) was planned by Washington in an effort to curb the attacks of the Indians and Tories on the frontiers of New York and Pennsylvania. Originally planned in 1778 as a westward movement along the Mohawk, the main drive was shifted in 1779 to the Susquehanna. The command, first offered to Gen. Gates and curtly refused, was given Gen. John Sullivan. To hold the eastern tribes of the Iroquois in check, Gen. James Clinton, who was in charge of the New York wing of the army, sent Col. Van Schaick in April to make a surprise attack on the Onondagas.

The major force of the campaign was mobilized in Easton, Pa. On June 18 Sullivan with about 2500 men under Generals Maxwell, Hand and Poor moved toward Wyoming, Pa. Here, disappointed at not finding the supplies he expected, he delayed for over five weeks while, with difficulty, supplies were collected. On Aug. 11 the army reached Tioga, and the following day the greater part of the troops were pushed forward to attack the Indian town of Chemung. The Indians fled, and being pursued by Gen. Hand ambushed a part of his men, killing six. Sullivan fell back to Tioga, where Fort Sullivan was built as a base for supplies. Here, on Aug. 22, he was joined by Gen. Clinton, with 1500 men, who had proceeded southwestward from Canajoharie on the Mohawk, destroying the Indian villages on the upper Susquehanna. On Aug. 26 Sullivan moved his whole force toward the territory of the Cayugas and Senecas. At Newtown, near the present city of Elmira, the Indians and Tories made their only stand. The fatalities on both sides were not large. The Indians and Tories were driven from the field. From Newtown the army pushed forward, skirting the eastern shore of Lake Seneca, to old Genesee Castle. Forty Indian villages were burned and 160,000 bushels of corn destroyed. Failing to make a junction with Col. Brodhead, who had left Fort Pitt on Aug. 11, Sullivan felt the season was too far advanced to attempt the capture of Niagara as had been planned and returned to Easton.

SUMMIT CONFERENCES.

As generally used, the term refers to the belief entertained by some people after World War II that a necessary step toward closing the rift between the communist and free-world countries is for the heads of government of at least three and probably four of the leading powers (certainly the United States and the Soviet Union, and probably Great Britain and France, too) to meet together, face to face, in one or more conferences, perhaps without fixed agenda, to reach a broad measure of agreement. Since Stalin's death (March 5, 1953) Russia has occasionally suggested convening a summit conference; and on May 11, 1953, Prime Minister Churchill called for one. The United States departed from its usual postwar insistence on lower-level conferences with fixed agenda when President Eisenhower met with the new British Prime Minister Eden, Premier Faure of France, and Premier Bulganin of Russia at Geneva (July 18–23, 1955). They discussed German unification, European security, disarmament (Eisenhower urged his "open sky" proposals), and closer East-West contacts. No agreement was reached except to instruct their four foreign ministers to meet at Geneva in October, 1955, in order to consider again the same four points.

Further summit conferences have frequently been proposed; and agreement was reached Dec. 30, 1959, for the heads of government of the United States, the Soviet Union, Great Britain and France to meet at Paris May 16, 1960. Nothing came of this attempted meeting.

SUMNER-BROOKS AFFAIR

(May 22, 1856). Sen. Charles Sumner, in the course of his famous speech, "The Crime Against Kansas," ridiculed Sen. Andrew P. Butler of South Carolina for his devotion to "the harlot, Slavery." Three days after these remarks, during Butler's absence from Washington, his nephew, Preston S. Brooks, a member of Congress from South Carolina, sought out the Massachusetts Senator at his desk and, rebuking him for his insult, struck him over the head repeatedly with a cane. When the attack ended Sumner sank to the floor with injuries that incapacitated him for some years. This demon-

stration, and the investigation ordered by the House, heightened the tension of the sectional controversy. Brooks, who was saved from expulsion by the two-thirds rule, was praised in the South and rewarded with re-election.

SUMPTUARY LAWS AND TAXES, COLONIAL.

The term "sumptuary laws" is usually meant to refer to legal attempts to regulate food, clothing, morals, amusements, church attendance and Sabbath observance. In this respect there were sumptuary laws in all of the colonies. Some of these were general statutes enacted by the colony, others were local regulations, others were applications of what was understood to be the common law applicable to local situations and still others were the fixed customs of the people of the different colonies. Custom and practice are as much a part of the total laws of a community as are the formal statutes, although their enforcement is different. The most discussed collection of such laws is the famous "Blue Laws of Connecticut." These were originally compiled by Reverend Samuel Peters in 1781. For many years people accepted or denounced this account of the Connecticut colonial code. In 1898 Walter F. Prince published in the *Report of the American Historical Association for 1898* a detailed analysis of the Peters laws based upon careful research. He found that one half did exist in New Haven, more than four fifths existed in one or more of the New England colonies, others were inventions, exaggerations, misunderstandings, or the result of copying from other writers on New England history.

The laws against wearing gold decorations, lace, hatbands, ruffs, silks and similar materials when one's station in life did not warrant such expensive clothing were confined mostly to the 17th century and were not peculiar to New England. In 1621 directions were sent to Virginia limiting the right to wear such apparel to members of the Council. Enforcement was usually by fine, although in Massachusetts the wearer might have his assessed valuation raised to £300 in addition to a fine. Connecticut had no definite laws regulating dress, while in Massachusetts the regulations were very detailed. Laws against Sabbath breaking were common to all of the colonies, and, in most of them, church attendance was prescribed by law. Enforcement was probably stricter in New England than elsewhere. In all but the Middle Colonies everybody was taxed to support the local church and its minister. In New England doctrinal uniformity was prescribed by law. Quakers were punished and driven from Massachusetts and three were hanged for persistent return. Baptists were also beaten and imprisoned. Alleged witches were proscribed and several hanged, all in the latter half of the 17th century. Yet with all this reputation for harshness, there were far fewer death penalties provided by law in New England than in the English statutes of the same time.

Laws against sex immorality were similar in all the

colonies, although in the South they were directed particularly against amalgamation with the Negroes. Seating at church in accordance with one's rank in the community was common, and students' names in the catalogue of Yale were arranged in a similar way as late as 1767 and at Harvard till 1772.

SUNDAY SCHOOLS are generally considered to have had their origin in the movement begun by Robert Raikes, editor of the *Gloucester* (England) *Journal*, in 1780. His attention was called to the deplorable condition prevailing among the children of the Gloucester poor, many of whom, being employed in a pin factory during the week, were turned loose on Sunday, their only holiday, to engage in rough and vicious sport. Thinking that their conduct was largely due to ignorance he conceived the plan of gathering them into schools on Sundays, where they were taught to read and were also given instruction in the catechism. The movement spread rapidly and schools were established in other towns and cities—where John Wesley, in his wide travels, came upon them, gave them his encouragement, and soon introduced them as a feature of his societies.

The situation which gave rise to Sunday Schools in America was quite unlike that which brought them into existence in England. Here the Sunday School was formed solely to give religious instruction, and from the beginning they were closely associated with the church. Some of the New England churches, such as that at Plymouth, early gave instruction to children on Sundays during the intermission between the morning and afternoon services. But this was not a uniform practice. Francis Asbury, with Wesley's encouragement, organized what was probably the first Sunday School in America, in Hanover County, Va., in 1786. Four years later (1790) the American Methodists officially adopted the Sunday School, stating that the establishment of Sunday Schools in or near the places of worship was to be encouraged—the first official recognition of Sunday Schools in the United States by an ecclesiastical body.

In 1790 Bishop William White of the Protestant Episcopal Church formed a Sunday School in Philadelphia; and the same year he with Dr. Benjamin Rush and others of Philadelphia organized the First-Day or Sunday School Society, an interdenominational body and the first of its kind. Sunday Schools now began to appear in numerous places: Pawtucket, R. I., in 1797; New York in 1801–4; Pittsburgh in 1809. Though endorsed and adopted by individual churches the early Sunday School movement in the United States was more largely an interdenominational movement, and Sunday School Unions or Societies were numerously formed in many of the larger towns and cities during the first two decades of the 19th century. In 1824 the American Sunday School Union was organized which incorporated many of the previously formed Sunday School Societies as its auxiliaries. The

same year the Union began the publication of its *Sunday School Magazine* which marks the beginning of a vast Sunday School literature. In 1830 the Sunday School Union reported 5901 Sunday Schools, 52,663 teachers and 349,202 scholars throughout the United States.

The formation of state and denominational Sunday School Societies now followed in rapid succession; the Massachusetts Sunday School Union, made up of Congregationalists and Baptists in 1825; the Sunday School Union of the Protestant Episcopal Church in 1826; that of the Methodist Episcopal Church in 1827. All of these bodies were active in the publication of Sunday School papers and other literature.

The first national convention of Sunday School workers was held in New York in 1832. A great advance was made in Sunday School work in 1866 when Dr. John H. Vincent projected a uniform system of teaching. This bore fruit in the establishment of the *Berean Series* of lessons, 1870, and in the *International Series* in 1873. The Chautauqua Assembly, begun in 1874 under the leadership of Dr. Vincent to bring together Sunday School teachers and workers for systematic training, was soon duplicated in many sections of the country. In 1893 there were in the United States and Canada 11,669,956 Sunday School members. In 1908 a system of graded lessons was adopted. In 1903 the Religious Education Association was formed to raise the teaching standards of Sunday Schools. It has introduced a more definitely Church point of view and has led to an increased efficiency.

SUPERIOR, LAKE, the largest body of fresh water in the world, was discovered probably by Étienne Brûlé about 1620. It is thought that Brûlé reached the lake by way of the St. Marys River from Lake Huron. The Jesuit missionaries Isaac Jogues and Charles Rambault established a mission at the outlet of the lake in 1641; René Ménard spent the winter of 1660–61 with the Ottawa Indians on the south shore, and in the summer of 1661 lost his life in an attempt to cross over to the Hurons on Green Bay; Pierre Esprit Radisson and Médard Chouart discovered the western end and part of the north shore the same year; Claude Jean Allouez reached the lake in the autumn of 1665, and named it Lac Tracy, after the then Viceroy of New France; he founded a mission on Chequamegon Bay, and explored part of the south shore. Daniel Greysolon Duluth was in the country around the western end between 1678 and 1682. His brother, Charles de Greysolon, Sieur de LaTourette, built trading posts on the north shore between 1678 and 1686. Zacharie Robutel de LaNoüe built a post at the mouth of the Kaministikwia River in 1717, and made his way inland as far as Rainy Lake. Pierre Gaultier de Varennes, Sieur de La Vérendrye wintered at Fort Kaministikwia in 1731–32, and in the spring explored the Grand Portage route to Rainy Lake and the Lake of the Woods. In the days of the fur trade three canoe routes were used from Lake Superior to the West, by way of Grand Portage, the Kaministi-kwia River, and the St. Louis River at Fond du Lac; and important posts were maintained at Sault Ste. Marie and Grand Portage, the latter being removed in 1801, by the North West Company, to Fort William, at the mouth of the Kaministikwia. The search for copper mines led to the building of the first sailing ship on Lake Superior in 1737; that was the beginning of an immense commerce, and the gradual spread of population particularly along the south shore.

SUPREME COURT. The highest court in the judicial system of the United States, the Supreme Court is one of the three branches of government established by the Constitution. Article III of the Constitution states that "the judicial power of the United States, shall be vested in one supreme Court, and in such inferior Courts as the Congress may from time to time ordain and establish," provides that judges shall hold office during good behavior and defines the jurisdiction of the Supreme Court. The question of the nature and organization of the judiciary was left to the discretion of Congress. The foundation of the judicial system of the United States was laid by the Judiciary Act of Sept. 24, 1789. That act provided for a Supreme Court consisting of a chief justice and five associate justices, divided the United States into thirteen districts in each of which a district court consisting of one judge was established, and created three circuit courts composed of the district judges included in that circuit, together with two Supreme Court justices. The Judiciary Act spelled out in detail the procedure, powers, and respective jurisdictions of the Federal courts. The most important provision of the act was Section 25 which made the Constitution "the supreme law of the land," authorizing the Supreme Court to pass upon the validity of state legislation, and to review the decisions of state courts whenever constitutional questions were answered in favor of the states.

John Jay was appointed chief justice and the Supreme Court held its first session on Feb. 2, 1790, in New York City. The first decade of the history of the Court, however important its work was in establishing abiding precedents, was noncontroversial. With the elevation of John Marshall to the chief justiceship in 1801 the Court was thrust into the storm center of politics where it intermittently has been ever since. Of the fourteen chief justices who up to 1960 have presided over the Supreme Court, Marshall is indisputably "the great Chief Justice," for he, more than any other, left his imprint upon the future development of constitutional law. In a series of notable decisions, beginning with Marbury v. Madison and extending through the years of his chief justiceship, Marshall firmly established the role of the Supreme Court as the authoritative expounder of the Constitution.

The most important and distinctive power of the Supreme Court is judicial review—the right to veto any law, congressional, state or local, which in the justices' opinion contravenes the provisions of the Constitution. The most publicized aspect of judicial review has been the review of congressional acts. The number of such acts invalidated, however, has been comparatively few and (the 1934–36 decisions of the Court nullifying the measures of the New Deal excepted) seldom of sufficient importance appreciably to affect the course of our history. Far more important has been judicial review of state acts. Emphasis on judicial review, both "national" and "federal," has tended to obscure another important power of the Supreme Court: its right to interpret the laws passed by Congress.

The number of justices on the Supreme Court has changed a number of times over the years. In 1789 the Court consisted of six justices; in 1801, the number was reduced to five, but the following year was restored to six; in 1837 the number of justices was increased to nine where it remained until 1863 when an additional justice was added. During the turbulent years of Reconstruction the number was twice changed—it was lowered to seven in 1866 (it actually never got below eight) and restored to nine in 1869. For ninety-odd years there has been no change, by far the longest period in our history without one.

Several acts have revised other aspects of the Federal court system established by the Judiciary Act of 1789. In 1869 circuit court judges were provided for to help relieve the overburdened Court of some of its work, but the justices were still required to attend one term of circuit court every two years. In 1891, a Circuit Court of Appeals consisting of three judges was established and the justices of the Supreme Court finally were relieved of circuit court duty. More important than these changes in the organization of the Court were the jurisdictional changes made by the Judiciary Act of 1925. By that Act the right to appeal to the Supreme Court as a matter of course was taken away and the Court was made the judge, in most cases, of whether an appeal to it would be received. "The Judiciary Act of 1925," Justice Felix Frankfurter has said, "was aimed to extend the Court's control over its business by curtailing its appellate jurisdiction drastically. Relief was given by Congress to enable this Court to discharge its indispensable functions."

Judged by the standards of its decisions on governmental powers and individual liberty, the history of the Supreme Court may be divided into five periods. The first was from the inauguration of the Government until the death of Chief Justice John Marshall (1789–1835). During this period the Court's emphasis was on the supremacy of the National Government and the protection of its powers against the inroads either of the states or other branches of the Federal Government. The second period was from the appointment of Roger B. Taney as Chief Justice to the Civil War. Whereas national supremacy was the keystone of John Marshall's constitutional jurisprudence, the Taney Court emphasized the Tenth Amendment which states that "The powers not delegated to the United States by the Constitution, nor prohibited by it to the States, are reserved to the States respectively, or to the people." The Court under Taney thus regarded itself as the arbiter between two equal "sovereign" powers. The third period, stretching from the Civil War until about 1890, was a period of transition. The Court gradually recovered from the loss of prestige brought on by its own caution and cowardice during the Civil War and Reconstruction. In a series of cases during the 1870's and 1880's the Court refused to secure for Negroes the rights presumably guaranteed them by the Fourteenth and Fifteenth Amendments and, at first cautiously, assumed the guardianship of property against infringements by state or national legislation. The fourth period, from about 1890 to 1937, was one during which the Court substituted judicial supremacy for judicial review. By striking down state and Federal legislation the Court became, in the words of Justice Louis Brandeis, "a super-legislature" and exercised power to which, as Justice Oliver Wendell Holmes remarked, there was "hardly any limit but the sky." The fifth period extends from 1937 until the present. Inaugurated in 1937 by President Franklin D. Roosevelt's proposed "Courtpacking" plan, this period has seen numerous reversals of earlier precedents. The Court has ceased to be the special guardian of property rights and has insisted that the best safeguard against government encroachments on such rights is not judicial restraint but reliance on the will of the people as expressed through their popularly elected representatives. On the other hand, legislative and administrative infringements of civil rights—except for occasional deviations like those occurring during the chief justiceship of Fred Vinson—have been subjected to more exacting scrutiny. Under the pressure of depression, war, and cold war, the Court also has emphasized, as did the Court of John Marshall, the supremacy of national power.

Throughout our history the idea has popularly prevailed that the Supreme Court should be kept above criticism and out of politics. For at least three quarters of a century, furthermore, most Americans have regarded the Court with a respect and reverence denied any other department of government. This deference doubtless has been due to the knowledge that a system of government based, as is ours, on a written constitution cannot function effectively without judicial arbitration of constitutional issues. The Court, however, has always exercised political as well as legal power, a fact attested not only by decisions like that in the Dred Scott case—perhaps the most conspicuous example of judicial lawmaking before the outlawing of segregation in 1954—but by decisions

on issues ranging from strikes in wartime and loyalty programs, to conflicting state and Federal claims to tidelands oil.

Because of such decisions and because it is less responsive to the public will than the other two branches of our government, the Supreme Court frequently has been the object of attack. The attack seldom has been that the Court is an undemocratic institution; the charge has rather been that the justices usurp powers that rightfully belong to the executive or legislative branches. Following the lead of Thomas Jefferson who reproached his fellow-Virginian, Chief Justice John Marshall, for usurping powers not granted by the Constitution, the political branches of the Government often have attempted to curb the Court's power. The easiest and favorite method has been the exercise of the presidential and congressional power to increase or diminish the number of justices. During the administrations of Jackson, Lincoln, Grant, and the two Roosevelts, Congress thus either altered or threatened to alter the Court's size. The only other checks on the power of the Court are: (1) The right of the Senate to reject a newly appointed justice; (2) the right of Congress to impeach a justice (tried only once in our history and then unsuccessfully); and (3) the right of the public to reverse a decision by amending the Constitution (exercised only three times in our history).

Whatever the usurpations of power in the past, however persistent the criticism of the Supreme Court as an undemocratic institution, the Court has played a constructive role in safeguarding the American Federal system. This aspect of the Court's task has best been described by Justice Oliver Wendell Holmes: "I do not think the United States would come to an end if we lost our power to declare an Act of Congress void," he wrote. "I do think the Union would be imperiled if we could not make that declaration as to the laws of the several States. For one in my place sees how often a local policy prevails with those who are not trained to national views and how often action is taken that embodies what the Commerce Clause was meant to end." The Court, in brief, has been and remains the guardian and arbiter of our Federal system.

SURVEYORS, EARLY. One of the first white men to appear in a frontier district was the pioneer surveyor. In the New England colonies he preceded the settlers, ran the township lines and laid out the lots into which the rectangular township was divided. The New England surveyor followed an orderly system in which tier after tier of townships were surveyed as additional land was required for settlement, but the surveyor was never far from places of abode. In the Southern colonies surveying was done privately for speculators who were locating lands in advance of settlement or for squatters who had preceded the surveyor. There the rectangular system was not adopted and the surveyors' lines had to conform to the squatters' improvements no matter how irregular they were.

Early surveyors operating mostly in uninhabited areas encountered many hardships and risks in the performance of their work. During the winter the heavy snow made walking difficult, food and forage were scarce and it was more difficult to cover up one's tracks to prevent pursuit by unfriendly Indians. In the summer the mosquitoes were intolerable, the heat intense, the underbrush almost impenetrable, numerous streams had to be forded and fever and ague were likely to lay the surveyor low. The danger from the lurking Indian or wild animals was always present and intimidated all but the most intrepid.

Save for the steel tape and the solar compass, surveyors in 1750 had available every basic instrument of modern surveying, including the compass, the bubble level, the telescopic sight, and the chain. But, as a rule, frontier surveyors were supplied with these instruments only in their crudest and most elementary form. The Mason and Dixon Line was run with wooden rods and the Military Tract of New York was surveyed by the magnetic compass without due regard for the three-degree declination from the true meridian. The United States surveys were let out on contract, the compensation depending upon the nature of the land. The contract system encouraged "running" of the lines, errors in measurements and calculations, poorly marked corners and outright fraud. When land activity was great and when surveys were being rapidly pushed, many individuals who possessed only the bare rudiments of surveying were able to secure government contracts and it was but natural that errors should be made by them.

Early surveyors like Christopher Gist, James Harrod, Isaac Shelby and Daniel Boone combined exploring and search for fertile land with actual surveying. As they appeared in the Indian country before it was ceded by the red men their coming produced conflicts such as Pontiac's Conspiracy and Dunmore's War. To many frontiersmen whose principal occupation was exploring and buying and selling land, knowledge of surveying was essential. Among the outstanding Americans who had early experience in surveying were Washington, Jefferson and Lincoln. The first official surveyor and "geographer" of the United States was Thomas Hutchins of New Jersey who, between 1785 and 1789, had charge of the survey of the Seven Ranges in eastern Ohio. On his staff was Rufus Putnam who later surveyed the tract of the Ohio Company of Associates.

The notebooks of the early surveyors are an invaluable source for a description of the geography, flora and soil of the public land states as they were before settlement entered them.

SUSQUEHANNAH COMPANY was a merging of a number of smaller groups of Connecticut farmers who organized at Windham, Conn., in 1753, for the purpose of settling on lands in Wyoming Valley in Pennsylvania, basing their claim on the Connecticut Charter of 1662. Leading citizens of Connecticut were shareholders in this company, such as Ezra Stiles, Phineas Lyman, Eliphalet Dyer and Jedediah Elderkin, and it was supported by Governors Wolcott and Trumbull, though Thomas Fitch and his followers opposed the company's claims. The company leaders engaged John Lydius to effect a purchase of lands from the Six Nations, and this was done at the Albany Congress in 1754, though there is reason to believe Lydius used devious means to secure the deed and the Pennsylvania authorities bought a part of the same land from some of the same Indians at the same congress. The Susquehannah Company merged with the First and Second Delaware Companies, started a settlement at Wyoming in 1763 (which was wiped out by Indians), sent Eliphalet Dyer to London in 1764 to obtain a charter for a separate colony, and, after the Treaty of Fort Stanwix (1768), began in 1769 to settle the lands with the establishment of the town of Wilkes-Barre. But the first Yankee-Pennamite War interrupted this settlement until 1772 when permanent settlement of the region by Connecticut settlers began. The company laid out townships five miles square throughout the 41st parallel of latitude from a line ten miles east of and parallel to the Susquehanna River to a line 120 west of the river. The jurisdiction of this territory was awarded to Pennsylvania in 1782 and at once the second Yankee-Pennamite War broke out, resulting in the dispossession of most of the Connecticut settlers. But under the stimulus of John Franklin's leadership a horde of "half-right" men invaded the upper Susquehanna from Connecticut and in 1786 made an abortive attempt to erect a separate state in this region, with Athens, Pa., as its capital. The next year Pennsylvania, urged on by land operators of Philadelphia who were tired of the conflict, passed the Confirming Act recognizing titles under the Susquehannah Company in seventeen townships which had been settled prior to 1782. This act was repealed in 1790, but the region remained thereafter in comparative quiet until an act of 1803 enabled the holders of Connecticut titles in the seventeen townships to exchange them for Pennsylvania titles. By then John Franklin had ended his twenty-year fight to make a success of the Susquehannah Company's claim and had retired to Athens. The company in its half-century of existence succeeded in populating the northeastern section of Pennsylvania with Connecticut stock and in giving to the heterogeneous population of Pennsylvania a new element which has not been without its influence in the history of the Commonwealth.

SUTRO TUNNEL. Adolph Sutro, operator of an ore stamp mill at Virginia City, Nev., conceived the idea of a tunnel into the side of Mount Davidson to intercept all the mines on the Comstock silver lode, drain them of water and gases and make ore removal easier. His franchise specified that work must begin in 1866 and be completed in eight years, but the time was later extended because of his difficulty in raising money. He was fought by mine owners and financial interests, and only his indomitable will carried the project through. Ground was broken in 1869. Unable to obtain funds in America, Sutro finally found backers in England. The tunnel broke through into the Savage Mine July 8, 1878, but by that time the best days of the Comstock lode were over. The tunnel property was sold in 1889 to satisfy the English investors' bond mortgage. It was reorganized, but continued a losing venture.

SUTTER'S FORT, on the site of what is now Sacramento, Calif., is one of the most familiar names in American history because it was near this stronghold, and on land belonging to the Swiss Capt. John August Sutter, that gold was discovered on Jan. 24, 1848. The fort was erected in 1841 with walls five feet thick and twelve feet high and room for a garrison of a hundred men. Guns and other equipment were moved from the Russian Fort Ross. Here Sutter lived in baronial style, possessing at one time 4000 oxen, 1200 cows, 1500 horses and mules and 12,000 sheep. His fort was a stopping place for army officers and early California pioneers. Following the discovery of gold in California an eruption of squatters dispossessed Sutter and most of the movable parts of the fort were carried away.

SYCAMORE SHOALS, TREATY OF (1775), was perhaps the most important treaty ever made with a southern Indian tribe. A group of North Carolinians, headed by Judge Richard Henderson, conceived a plan to acquire a vast western domain from the Cherokee Indians. In 1769 Daniel Boone was employed to make a reconnoissance of the Kentucky country. On Aug. 27, 1774, a company was organized, the name first assumed being the Louisa Land Company (changed in January, 1775, to the Transylvania Company); and Henderson soon visited the Overhill Cherokees, who deputed their great Chief Attakullakulla to go home with Henderson and continue negotiations. March 14, 1775, was agreed upon as the time and Sycamore Shoals of the Watauga as the place for holding the treaty. On March 17 a treaty was signed which conveyed to the members of the Transylvania Company the vast domain lying between the Kentucky River and the south watershed of the Cumberland River—large portions of the Kentucky and Tennessee countries. The recited consideration was £2000. A smaller tract was conveyed by a separate instrument called the "Path Deed," because this tract connected the larger territory with the white settlements.

TAMMANY HALL is the headquarters of the New York County Democratic Committee and of the Society of Tammany, or Columbian Order. This oath-bound society was formed, shortly after the signing of the Definitive Treaty of Peace in 1783, to uphold the new experiment in democracy, but was not organized until May 12, 1789. Its name was borrowed from the Sons of St. Tammany, whose patron was Tammanend, or Tammany, a Delaware chief. Its members were allies of the Sons of Liberty in the prelude to the American Revolution. The society has a ritual patterned on Indian customs, and is governed by thirteen sachems; it has no political test for membership. By 1800 most of its Federalist members withdrew. On April 9, 1805, it was incorporated as a charitable organization. Now it boasted a fixed meeting place, or wigwam: the long room of Martling's tavern, where Republicans, later called Democrats, foregathered. These partisans were known as Martling men until the close of the War of 1812, when they were dubbed Tammanies.

The enfranchisement of propertyless whites (1822), which Tammany had championed, was the source of its gradual growth of power. During the early political struggles for control, the sachems denied the use of Tammany Hall to ambitious factions, and decided disputed nominations. When this usurpation was first challenged (1852), and the sachems were reminded that the society was independent of the party, and incorporated solely for charitable ends, they replied that the society's fame as a political organization was "too extended to need mention."

Until the advent of William M. Tweed as leader (1860), Tammany Hall differed from other urban political organizations only in degree. He made it a smoothly running juggernaut, which has served as a model for most city machines. He controlled the mob by catering to its religious and racial groups, and by gifts to the poor; he managed rival political groups by bribing their leaders. "This population is too hopelessly split into races and factions to govern it under universal suffrage, except by the bribery of patronage, or corruption," said Tweed. He established another tradition by making himself supreme, and glorified in his title of "Boss." Subordination to his will was a prerequisite to appointment or election to office. He raised Tammany to state power when he elected his candidate for governor (1868). Then emerged the Tweed Ring, and the disclosure of its systematized stealings temporarily halted Tammany's pace. This was the first of several major public scandals in which outstanding Tammany leaders have been involved.

Tammany wielded still greater power when Brooklyn, Long Island City and scores of villages, with old New York, were merged into the present metropolis (1898). In 1910 Tammany again elected a governor, and thenceforward ruled the state, both party and government, save for six years, until 1932. In 1928 its *de facto* leader, Alfred E. Smith, was nominated

913

for President. Four years later, Franklin D. Roosevelt, in reprisal for Tammany's refusal to make his nomination for President (1932) unanimous, attempted to control the organization, and failing, reduced it to the status of a county organization.

TAOS, N. MEX., an old Indian-Spanish-American town, is located some seventy miles up the Rio Grande from Santa Fe. Within three miles of one another stand an old and large Indian pueblo and a town, begun by Spaniards before 1680, whose life and architecture even now show a strong Indian influence. The pueblo, with its curious pyramidlike dwellings of three and four stories, was discovered in 1540 by some of Coronado's men. Oñate's expedition arrived there in 1598 and gave it its present name, though other names were used until an American postmaster in 1884 fixed the name Taos permanently.

The Taos Indians played an important part in the early history of New Mexico. With Taos as headquarters, the Indian leader, Popé, planned and carried out in 1680–82 a general revolt against Spanish rule which succeeded in killing or expelling all Spaniards from the province. When twelve years later DeVargas reconquered Santa Fe and the southern part of the province, he encountered a continued and stubborn revolt among the Taos Indians until he defeated them in 1696. Again, in 1847, it was mainly some Indians of Taos with a few Mexicans who scalped and killed Charles Bent, first American governor of New Mexico, while at his home in Taos, and attempted to raise a general revolt against American authority. With the execution of a few leaders, the revolt subsided. The dress and habits of the Taos Indians make them colorful subjects for American artists.

Spaniards came to Taos as missionaries early in the 17th century and later established both a village and a permanent mission. The only newspaper in New Mexico before the American period was issued by a printing press at Taos in 1834. The white population, previously much less than the Indian, was gradually increased after the arrival of American traders, such as LaLande in 1804, William Becknell and associates in the Santa Fe trade in 1822, Ewing Young and James O. Pattie about 1824 and Kit Carson in 1826. Indians and Spaniards had traded in Taos before this. During most of the 18th century, and perhaps later, annual fairs were held at which goods of various kinds were bartered, since no money was available. Chihuahua traders who sent wagons to Taos seem to have reaped enormous profits. Americans after 1822 made Taos the center of a very active fur trade. Most notable of all these Americans was Kit Carson who at seventeen years of age arrived, in 1826, to make his future home in Taos and to get a reputation as the greatest of American scouts.

TAOS TRAIL was already called the "Old" Taos Trail when Jacob Fowler traversed it in 1822. It first served as a road for Spaniards going north to the Rockies and for Plains Indians attending the Taos fair. Later the American fur trappers of the Rockies followed the trail south to enjoy the friendliness and hospitality of Taos. It also served as the westernmost branch of the Santa Fe Trail and was used as such until 1880. The route of the Taos Trail varied considerably. Roughly it ran north from Taos, crossed the Sangre de Cristo Range at La Veta Pass and followed the Huerfano River to the Arkansas.

TARIFF is a duty levied on goods coming into the ports of the nation from foreign sources (called a *specific* duty if levied at so much per article or unit of weight or measure; *ad valorem* if at so much per dollar value). As a practice and as a philosophy of the National Government, it was born with the Constitution. The stipulation was clearly made that exports should not be subject to duties. Tariffs may be in their simplest purpose either revenue-raising or protective; that is, a low tax may be levied that discourages importations only a little but brings in money to the treasury for helping maintain the government, or on the other hand, a high tax may in whole or in part block the flow of incoming goods and thus theoretically encourage domestic production. A policy of absolutely unhampered economic intercourse is described as free trade. This practice of levying no duties either on imports or on exports is based on the premise that each politico-geographic unit should produce what it can produce best and most cheaply. Thus without the maintenance of high-cost production and its consequent high prices, consumers, whether they be buyers of finished goods or purchasers of raw materials for processing, would enjoy both quality and cheapness.

"Tariff for Revenue Only." The Democratic party, under whatever name it has been designated since the beginning of the nation, has traditionally though not exclusively sponsored low tariff rates. As a consequence it was long referred to as a "free trade" party. The term, in fact, was habitually applied both in Europe and in the United States to all parties and individuals advocating low duties. Sensing the inaccuracy of the term "free trade," the Democrats came eventually in the late 19th century to designate their policy as "tariff for revenue only." Even that was a selective term, for it meant, whether specifically put into words or not, revenue exacted from those most able to pay or from those who bought extravagantly. Salt, sugar, coal, flour and other essentials of human beings regardless of their incomes were exempted whenever possible. Leather for harness, coarse cloth, cheap dishes, lumber and similar products used by the poor in their quest of livelihood were taxed lightly on the theory that even if there was no competition for the maintenance of the government until 1860 domestic manufacturers might use the rates as an

excuse for maintaining high prices. Luxuries, however, might bear heavier levies than protectionists would demand. Whether the rates were high or low, revenue has been an important aspect of the tariff. With the exception of two years, 1814–15, during the war with England, and a short period in the middle 1830's, when the land boom was at its height, money was derived overwhelmingly from the customs dues. From 1868 until the end of the first decade of the 20th century the tariff, thoroughly protectionist, was, except for a half dozen years in the 1890's, still the greatest single contributor of revenue.

The two basic premises of the argument of the advocates of low tariff rates were: that in the short run unrestricted trade prevented exactions of the many by the few, and in the long run promoted a rising standard of living among all the people. In the years after the Civil War many noted intellectuals joined the farmers, workmen and others in a vigorous attack on the high rates. Before the Wilson administration, however, only a few abortive reductions were achieved.

Tariff for Protection. The theory of a protective tariff has origins deep in American history. Colonial experience shaped some of the protectionist thought; and in the early years of the government, especially after the War of 1812, it became obvious that the development of basic domestic industries was necessary if the people wanted to escape the economic-financial subservience of colonial days. Although the first tariff laws were in part dictated by a deep concern with encouraging domestic industries, protection as such did not begin until after 1816, suffered a decline in the 1840's and 1850's, and rose to dominance with the burgeoning industry of the second half of the 19th century.

The two primary arguments of the protectionists were: first, that high duties defended infant industries against competition and permitted them to grow into producers for the nation; and, second, that the high duties benefited the workman by giving him more days of work at higher rates of pay. Prosperity and protection as allies were set forth in bold strokes by Alexander Hamilton and brilliantly portrayed by Henry Clay, but it was in the twenty years preceding 1900 that the full dinner pail, the smoking factory chimney, and the happy laborer were forged into a seemingly indestructible industrial montage. There were other arguments. Political, economic, and often patriotic groups declared vehemently for protection of home industries against specific low-cost foreign competition (as, at times, in the case of sugar) even though the cost to consumers was frequently much higher than the gain to the producers. Others demanded tariffs to equalize in general the disadvantages of the United States in competition with the low-cost, low-wage products of the world. And always there was the argument, emphasized again since World War II, that preservation and promotion of strategic industries and arts is essential to national survival.

But whatever the theories advanced, high tariffs were achieved largely through promises of prosperity by eminent political leaders, backed by aggressive and generous manufacturers. Effective, too, was the fact that legislators, whatever their importance, were forced to support bills providing protection of products of other regions in order to obtain privileges demanded by the economic interests of their own constituents. The bitterest criticisms of protection were that industrialists, selling in a closed market, exacted unwarranted profits from consumers, that high tariffs mothered trusts and monopolies, that "infant industries" never grew to maturity, and that the duties were a tax as clearly (as Grover Cleveland put it) as though the tax gatherer called at stated intervals and collected the tolls.

TARIFF COMMISSIONS

The Revenue Commissions. Section 19 of the Internal Revenue Act of March 3, 1865, authorized the Secretary of the Treasury to appoint a commission of three persons to "inquire and report" on how much money should be raised by taxation to meet the needs of the government, the sources from which it should be drawn, and the "best and most efficient mode of raising the same." The Commission was neither impartial nor nonpolitical. David A. Wells, scientist, teacher, and author and recent but ardent convert to protection, was chairman. Stephen Colwell, former lawyer, iron maker, and active member of the American Iron and Steel Association, was also an Easterner and a protectionist. Western agrarian, Democratic, and other minority interests were represented by Samuel S. Hays, comptroller of the City of Chicago. Wells and Colwell were anxiously watched and carefully instructed by Henry C. Carey, Philadelphia's high priest of high tariff.

Colwell became within a short time merely an adviser to the industrialists as to how to organize and present their demands. Wells, on the other hand, began to question protection, especially after the new tariff bill, based in part on his recommendations, was put before the House on June 25, 1866. Pressures for upward changes became so powerful that a Representative cried out "there is no end to it." In July leaders of the hopelessly entangled Congress substituted for the Commission a new office of Special Commissioner of the Revenue. Wells, appointed to the position, began the basic preparation for another bill, which he soon found was doomed to failure. Even the Commissioner himself was drawn into the welter of confusion that was created by the interplay of selfish interests and was finally beaten into the ranks of the tariff reformers. The office came to an end on June 30, 1870.

Tariff Commission of 1882. In December, 1881, President Chester A. Arthur, confronted with domestic and foreign economic disturbances and plagued with a treasury surplus of $100,000,000, recommended a Tariff Commission. The Democrats bitterly opposed the measure not only on the premise that the Commission would be protective but also on the assumption that the Congressmen were more familiar with the needs of the people than the members of a commission could be. Not a single member of the Commission as appointed was an advocate of tariff reform. John L. Hayes, Secretary of the Wool Manufacturers' Association, was named chairman. But in spite of the bias, the report of the Commission as submitted to Congress cited facts to show that some of the high rates were actually injurious to the interests supposed to be benefited. Reductions in the general tariff were recommended, though sometimes, as the chairman of the Commission wrote, as "a concession to public sentiment, a bending of the top and branches to the wind of public opinion to save the trunk of the protective system." No basic changes were made, and the Democrats, when they returned to power in the House in December, 1883, let the Commission die.

Tariff Board. Sensing the difficulties that might arise in applying reciprocity provisions (limited reciprocity plans had been included in both the McKinley and the Dingley tariffs), the Republicans in the Payne-Aldrich tariff of 1909 authorized the President to employ such persons as might be required in the discharge of his duties. Taft, using the loosely worded authority that was his, created in September a Tariff Board with Henry C. Emery, professor of political economy at Yale, as chairman. The Board, in cooperation with the State Department, made studies of discriminatory practices on the part of foreign states and, in addition, investigated American industries in relation to cost of production, duties demanded, and duties already exacted for their benefit. But its life was short. The protectionists, already under heavy challenge, feared it was a new threat to their supremacy. The Democrats, suspecting anything Republican as protectionist, refused in 1912 to make appropriations for its continuance.

Tariff Commission of 1916. President Woodrow Wilson in 1916 appointed what is often referred to as the first nonpartisan Tariff Commission. There was, he said, a world economic revolution and the changes accompanying it were so rapid that Congressmen, already overwhelmed by the magnitude of their duties, had neither time nor means for the inquiry necessary to keep them informed. Headed by Prof. Frank W. Taussig until 1919, the Commission in one form or another still survives, though at various times accused of partisanship and occasionally of incompetence.

The work of the Commission was first used in the preparation of the incongruous Fordney-McCumber tariff of 1922. That legislation, in fact, not only continued the Commission but increased its powers as well. The President was authorized—on recommendation of the Tariff Commission—to raise or lower duties by not more than 50% of the *ad valorem* rate on articles that threatened to capture American markets because of our higher cost of production. Though it was obvious that Europe could pay its huge debt to the United States only through the shipments of goods, the Tariff Commission under the Hawley-Smoot tariff continued its cost investigations.

International political and economic complexities since the 1930's have shown the United States, a major force in the free world, the necessity for building tariffs on the soundest knowledge available. Moreover, since tariff making had actually become a world affair shaped in part by such international organizations as the General Agreement on Tariffs and Trade, a deliberative body like Congress could no longer respond quickly enough to meet the rapidly changing economic and political challenges that were occurring. The first major step in adjusting the tariff to the disturbed world of the present was the Trade Agreements Act of 1934. By that legislation the President became and has remained the active power in executing tariff agreements and applying tariff details. Realistic technical and statistical data became imperative in the new program. Congress could shape general policy only if it possessed accurate information, and the President could use his delegated authority wisely only if he was fully aware of world developments, real or impending. The Tariff Commission, in its beginnings an ineffective adviser to the Congressmen, became in fact if not in theory the essential unit in tariff making and tariff application. Its influence grew rapidly in the Truman and Eisenhower administrations. Recent legislation has made acceptance of its recommendations in escape clause cases obligatory if supported by a two-thirds vote of both houses of Congress. The proposed creation of the European Common Market requires new studies of tariff incidence and rates where U. S. foreign trade is concerned.

TARIFF POWERS OF THE PRESIDENT

Always a potentially significant force in the direction of the tariff in spite of the jealously guarded rights of the legislators, the President in the 20th century has become a powerful factor both in shaping and in applying the tariff. The authority necessary to carry out the reciprocity provisions of the tariffs of 1890 and 1897 were carefully circumscribed, but in 1909 the President was given rather broad powers in the Payne-Aldrich bill. These powers were further enlarged in 1922, when, in the Fordney-McCumber Tariff Act he was delegated the right, after hearings and a favorable report by the Tariff Commission, to raise or lower established duties by 50% without further reference to Congress. Challenged by a New York importer, this action was upheld in J. W. Hampton, Jr., & Company v. United States (276 U. S. 394, 1928). The cost equalization formula that, until the early 1930's, underlay the flexible provisions tended to increase the tariff.

The presidential authority in tariff matters during the administrations of Franklin D. Roosevelt changed less in form than in purpose and method of achievement. By the Trade Agreements Act of 1934 the President could still shift duties by 50%, but these changes were achieved through reciprocal trade agreements. The tendency in theory and in fact has been in general to lower tariffs, and to lessen discrimination in international commerce. During the Roosevelt, Truman, and Eisenhower administrations the act was extended (and sometimes amended) eleven times.

HISTORY OF THE TARIFF

The forces that have made tariff a subject of concern to the American people have varied from time to time both as to nature and as to intensity; the purposes for levying duties have been always complex and sometimes uncertain. Generally speaking, the history of the tariff in the nation can be divided into two great periods: from 1789 to 1860, and from 1860 to well into the second quarter of the 20th century. A third period may well be in the making, beginning roughly in the depression years of the 1930's and taking form in World War II; for then the old system of international commerce broke down in many ways, and multilateral trade all but came to an end as nations with needs but no money bartered their physical or political assets for world position or for the goods of survival.

The Tariff of 1789. Controversy over tariff for revenue only and tariff for protection began with the beginning Congress. The bill of 1789, presented by James Madison as a simple means of raising money, emerged as a partially protective measure. Several states, particularly Massachusetts and Pennsylvania, were able to impose *ad valorem* duties ranging from 5% to 15% in defense of leading articles of manufacture in the new nation. Some agricultural products were included also, and specific duties with the obvious intent of promoting home output were levied on certain articles of common use such as nails and glass.

As early as 1790 Alexander Hamilton had begun to collect information on the condition of and the attitude toward industry in the various states. On Dec. 5, 1791, he submitted his brilliant "Report on Manufactures," but his pleas for further protection were ignored. Congress did make many changes by increasing duties on special items and by enlarging the free list of raw materials, but the general level remained much the same.

The Tariff of 1816. In less than a fortnight after war was declared in 1812, Congress doubled all import duties and levied additional restrictions on all goods brought in in foreign bottoms. An embargo a year later almost destroyed the already crippled commerce. Rehabilitation began immediately after the war. All restrictions (both on tonnage and on goods) based on nationality of vessels were repealed—providing, of course, that all foreign discriminations were abolished also. American commerce, less restrained than it had ever been, began to flourish. But the per capita debt of the nation had more than doubled, prices were declining, and England, eager to regain her sales abroad, began dumping her surplus goods onto the markets of the United States for whatever they would bring.

The tariff problem was confused. John C. Calhoun, though warned of the penalties that must fall on agriculture, sponsored high duties in the hope of stimulating cotton manufacturing and cotton sales. Other nationalists, especially in the South and West, hostile toward England and resentful of the nation's dependence on Europe for munitions and military supplies of various kinds, joined the clamor for high rates. But it was the owners of the iron mills and textile plants that had grown up with such astounding rapidity during the war who cried out the loudest. "Infant industries" that had saved the nation, deserved, they said, rates high enough to make their continued operation possible even though they were obviously inefficient. To further complicate the traditional alignment on the tariff question, Daniel Webster spoke out against protection for New England, where the commercial and shipping aristocracy, though weakening, still dominated.

The bill that was finally passed in April, 1816, marks the beginning of tariff for protection. Cotton and woolen goods and pig iron and hammered and rolled bars were especially favored. Estimates of the general average rate of protection have varied from 30% to 45%. The argument for higher rates continued. Henry Clay wished to protect the "home market" for the benefit of agrarians and industrialists alike and the profits derived would be used for internal improvements. His "American system" envisioned increasing wages for the industrial workers and rising prices for the farmers. The situation, however, was changing. The South was becoming a bitter enemy of a tariff system that seemed to benefit only manufacturers. Deluded by false hopes of quick prosperity that would spread transportation across the Appalachians and bring pounding factories to their section, growers of foodstuffs and also of hemp, flax and wool in western Pennsylvania, Ohio, Indiana, Illinois, Kentucky and Missouri joined the Middle Atlantic states in an incongruous protectionist alliance and in 1824 passed a new tariff that not only raised the rates of 1816 substantially but also placed duties on such untaxed products as lead, glass, hemp, silk, linens and cutlery.

"The Tariff of Abominations." The woolen manufacturers especially were dissatisfied with the protection afforded by the tariff of 1824, and the mild recession of 1825 spread discontent. In 1827 the deciding vote of Vice-President Calhoun alone defeated a bill that would have raised the *ad valorem* duty on the most used woolen cloth to about 70%. That same year delegates from more than half the states in a meeting at Harrisburg, Pa., spoke out dramatically for general tariff increases. Angry protests arose against what was regarded as unneeded and unwarranted levies, particularly in the South. The tariff issue, in fact, had become not only sectional but partisan as well. Andrew Jackson, smarting from the injustices of the assumed "corrupt bargain" of 1824, was determined to win enough followers to send him to the Executive Mansion. His supporters are charged with constructing a tariff in such a way that its anticipated defeat would isolate New England but bring enough support in New York, Pennsylvania and the West—when joined with the vote of the South—to elect the General. Jackson was not personally involved in the plan and neither were at least some of the men who pushed the measure through Congress in 1828, but there was some substance to the remark of John Randolph that the bill was concerned only with the manufacture of a President.

Cottons, woolens, iron, hemp, flax, wool, molasses, sailcloth, and whatever else could be protected was protected in the new bill. The tax on raw wool, molasses and sailcloth, along with many others, irked the New Englanders, but enough of them voted for the measure to pass it. Nobody was pleased; the phrase "tariff of abominations" was bandied about everywhere and in the South became a rallying point for nullificationists.

The Compromise Tariff of 1833. The protests of 1828, coupled with the budding Treasury surplus, soon forced the protectionists to desert in part the "infant industry" doctrine in favor of the pauper-labor argument. Clay, hoping to quell rising criticism, pushed through Congress in 1832 a bill that removed most of the objectionable features of the "abominations" tariff and lowered general duties slightly below those of 1824. But in November South Carolina declared the act (as well as its predecessor) null and void. Jackson—with much meaningless bluster—took a firm stand. He swore he would collect the revenue and he asked Congress for a force act authorizing the use of military power in dealing with the situation.

Clay and Calhoun worked out a compromise plan to give seeming victory to all involved. By skillful congressional manipulation they both revised the tariff and passed the force bill on the same day— March 1, 1833. To please the South they enlarged the free list and stipulated that all rates above 20% should be lowered to that level by June 30, 1842. To placate the protectionists they provided for gradual reduction of one tenth every two years until 1840 (the remaining six tenths was to be removed in the last six months). The compromise tariff was replaced shortly after it expired by a hurriedly prepared measure that reversed temporarily the downward trend of duties. But, financial and business conditions having improved, the trend turned downward again in the Walker Act of 1846 and further reductions were made in 1857.

The Morrill Tariffs. The first of the Morrill tariffs, enacted March 2, 1861, was precipitated by the panic of 1857, which drastically affected Federal revenue. Succeeding acts in 1862, 1864, and 1865 raised the rates to hitherto undreamed of heights. Revenue was not completely forgotten, but the need to assuage American manufacturers upon whose products heavy internal revenue taxes had been levied was far more important. The end of the war and a growing Treasury surplus soon brought repeal of most of the internal revenue levies except for those on such items as liquors and tobacco. The Morrill tariffs, however, remained basically undisturbed until 1890, when they were raised. Though some modest efforts at tariff reductions began soon after the war, the moderate proposals of 1866, 1867, 1872, 1875, 1883, and other years brought no real changes.

The Democrats won the speakership in 1875 (and held it with the exception of one term until 1889), but it was not until December, 1883, that the southern and border states tariff-revisionist wing of the party—with the help of midwestern farmers— stripped the chair from Samuel J. Randall of Pennsylvania, staunch friend of industry, and elected John G. Carlisle of Kentucky. Early in 1884 William R. Morrison introduced a bill to reduce the tariffs by a horizontal 20%, with no rates lower than those of the Morrill bill of 1861. But Randall and his forty protectionist followers representing Ohio wool growers, Louisiana sugar producers, and a handful of other small interests in the House defeated the measure. The election of Grover Cleveland in 1884 brought no immediate help. A depression had strengthened the protectionists, silver had disturbed the political situation, and, though *Puck* issued a cartoon making the point that "The Old Hose Won't Work" any more (bloody shirt issue in putting out the tariff reform fire), the party—to the profit of the industrialists— still lay faintly in the shadow of the political charges of treason. Moreover, Carlisle was too theoretically democratic to be ruthless, Cleveland was too adamant to be politic, and the Democrats were too divided to use effectively their power.

President Cleveland, after the Morrison bills had failed again in 1885 and 1886, decided to make the tariff alone the subject of his message to Congress in December, 1887. In July the next year a very real reform tariff prepared by Roger Q. Mills was passed in the House with only four Democratic votes in opposition. Randall had lost his power, and the decision on protection was left to the Republican Senate.

McKinley Tariff of 1890. The Republicans chose to regard the election of Benjamin Harrison to the Presidency as a mandate for higher tariffs. William McKinley's bill, pushed by sheer ruthlessness through the House by Speaker Thomas B. Reed, was reshaped in the Senate. That body, in fact, was for the next 19 years the major force in tariff making. Taxes on tobacco and alcohol were reduced, but the tariff duties were raised appreciably and with protection as the primary purpose. Bounties were given sugar growers and for the first time a reciprocity provision was included.

The Wilson-Gorman Tariff of 1894. Since they had won the House in the fall elections of 1890 and the Presidency and the Senate two years later, success seemed within reach of the tariff-reform Democrats, but the golden hopes of reductions soon faded. The Harrison administration had stripped the Treasury of its surplus, a paralyzing panic fell on the country in April, and Cleveland split his party into bitter factions by his determined repeal of the Sherman Silver Act in a special session of Congress in the late summer of 1893. The bill which William L. Wilson introduced in the House early in 1894 fell in the Senate into the hands of Arthur P. Gorman of Maryland, a protectionist Democrat, and was completely reshaped; 634 amendments were added by the interests. The House majority made a dramatic stand, but the Senate had its way, and Cleveland, having declared that "party perfidy and party dishonor" had been involved in its making, let the Wilson-Gorman bill become a law without his signature.

The Dingley and the Payne-Aldrich Tariffs. After victory in the campaign of 1896 the Republicans turned not to gold but to the tariff, and, in spite of swelling opposition to protection even within their own party, maintained for more than a decade the highest duties in American history up to that time. It took just thirteen days to push through the House the bill which Nelson W. Dingley introduced in March, 1897. After 872 amendments and two months of argument in the Senate the bill finally emerged from Congress with the highest duties ever passed. But with growing opposition from the intellectuals and increasing protests from the people and their liberal representatives, tariff was becoming politically dangerous. Theodore Roosevelt chose to avoid the issue altogether. By 1908, however, pressure for reduction had become so great that even the Republican party seemed in its platform to promise downward revision.

The moderate House bill which Sereno E. Payne submitted early in 1909 was quickly passed. Nelson W. Aldrich reshaped it in the Senate; a total of 847 amendments were made, almost wholly in the interest of higher duties. In spite of some concessions to the President and brilliant opposition by the Republican insurgents, the tariff remained protectionist, and Taft ineptly praised the measure as the best ever passed.

The Underwood Tariff of 1913. In tariff philosophy Woodrow Wilson represented not only the majority of his party but also the thought of the intellectuals, who had long been questioning the prevailing protectionist practice of the nation. Comprehending in part at least the currents of change that were sweeping the nation into the world, he turned his knowledge of theoretical and practical politics to the task of reshaping domestic policy in many fields. Soon after Oscar W. Underwood of Alabama revealed his tariff proposals to the special Congress in 1913 the long-familiar lobbyists, a significant force in tariff making, flocked into Washington. The President struck out in a biting condemnation and the "third house" departed. Approved by the Senate with few changes, the measure became effective in October, providing the first real and consistent reductions since the tariffs of 1846 and 1857. The free list was greatly enlarged, 958 rates were reduced, 307 were left unchanged, and fewer than a hundred were increased. An income tax, legalized by Constitutional amendment, was also enacted. Rates averaged roughly 26%; some had not been lower since the first tariff.

Unfortunately the low duties never had a chance to prove themselves in a warring world. The conflict with Germany and her satellites, when the nation joined the Allies, brought not only increasing prices but also new producing plants, hurriedly and expensively built. The inevitable cry against foreign competition would come up when war's end brought reconversion to peacetime needs with its accompanying costly production and its shrinking days of work, declining wages, and lessening demand for agricultural and other extractive products. New industries —the "war babies"—would fight, too, for benefits.

The Fordney-McCumber and the Hawley-Smoot Tariffs. Pulling the nation out of its economic difficulties by increasing protection in the dozen critical years after World War I was attempting the impossible. An emergency tariff of 1921 sought to soothe the discontented farmers and check some beginning imports from Europe. But it was the bill introduced in the House by Joseph W. Fordney the next year and taken up in the Senate by Porter J. McCumber that sought to withdraw the nation from the economic world as others were attempting to isolate it from the political world. Equalization in a rabid form in part determined the details and blind nationalistic ambitions gave it spirit. The farmers were again promised impossible prosperity by levying duties on a product with smothering surpluses at home. The rates in general were the highest in American history, and a flexible provision by which the President could revise rates up or down by 50% insured maintenance of the equal-cost-of-production principle. Conditions did not improve materially, and seemingly the only answer politics had to offer was more protection. The rates of the Hawley-Smoot bill of June, 1930, set a new record in restrictive legislation and brought much-deserved criticism. More than a thousand members of the American Economic Association petitioned President Hoover to veto the bill. Other economic and financial organizations as well as individuals joined the rising protest that spread over the world. European nations not only spoke out boldly but also passed retaliatory laws. The depression grew worse, war-debt payments from Europe ceased, and, from a combination of circumstances, world economy ground to a standstill.

Tariffs by Reciprocity Agreements. Cordell Hull of Tennessee was among the few men in Congress during the depression who insisted that national prosperity depended on freeing the commerce of the world rather than restricting it. He became Secretary of State in the administration of Franklin D. Roosevelt and in 1934, by authority of the Reciprocal Trade Agreements Act of that year, inaugurated a series of executive agreements with foreign nations by which he in part freed trade not only for the United States, but, by applying the "most-favored-nation" clause, for other nations as well.

After the appalling destruction of World War II there was no possible return to isolation in the United States. Old nations and new were plagued with dollar shortages and their people in many cases had not the means with which to rehabilitate themselves. The task of vitalizing commerce and reestablishing buying power was further complicated by the rise of aggressive communism. For the first time in the history of the nation tariff ceased to be merely a domestic problem. Foreign considerations became a part of tariff making, and the Secretary of State displaced the Secretary of the Treasury as the dominant executive officer in shaping the legislation.

The liberalization in trade that Secretary Hull had launched culminated after World War II in the establishment in January, 1948, of the General Agreement on Tariffs and Trade (GATT), an international organization devoted in large part to the reduction of trade barriers and trade discriminations in international commerce. Multilateral treaties were again made possible by the creation of GATT. The

United States as a member is still directed by the Trade Agreements Act of 1934, extended for the eleventh time in 1958. Congress remains the general directive power, the President is the outward agent of the government, while the Tariff Commission advises both the legislative and the executive departments. Though significant changes have been made, particularly in 1958, the basic factor still remains, as at the beginning, the ability of the President to raise or lower rates within limits without reference to Congress. Safeguards are provided through "peril point" judgments and injustices are righted through "escape clause" decisions. The first is the rate of duty determined through study by the Tariff Commission *before* negotiations are entered into and below which, the Commission believes, the President cannot drop the tariff without injury to the particular industry in question; if he disregards the judgment he must explain his reasons to Congress. The second provides for relief from injuries *after* agreements have been made. The President, the Congress, the Tariff Commission itself, or any interested party can invoke the clause on the assumption that the existing tariff rates are resulting in impositions on an industry or industries. The Commission after investigation makes its recommendations to the President, which he may or may not accept. By amendment in 1958, however, the President, if he rejects the recommendations, may be reversed by a two-thirds vote of Congress.

The reciprocity policy of the United States, while it sometimes runs counter to other actions of the government in world rehabilitation, has removed many of the restrictions and discriminations that have bound commerce. There are many means employed by economic and political groups, however, in circumventing the making of reciprocity agreements—surviving laws from the depression years, the Defense Production Act, the Buy American Act, riders to military appropriations bills, quotas, and many others—but tariff rates in the nation and over the world have been greatly reduced. What effects the removal of the fear of communist domination would have on the international structure is not clear.

TAXATION is the imposition of compulsory contributions on the subjects of a government for meeting all or part of the expenditures of that government, local, state, or national. The taxes imposed during the course of American history have changed as the United States has undergone transition from a colonial, agricultural-mercantile economy to a predominantly industrial, urban world power. The American tax system has reflected modifications in the ownership and control of property and business enterprise and has responded to the rise of a government bureaucracy, capable of improving economic records, tax-appraisal-valuations, and collection techniques. The clash of different economic and social groups over the desirable goals of government expenditures and the proper means of raising revenue accounts for much of the specific tax legislation proposed and enacted over the years. Some influence on tax policy has come from national statesmen, reformers, and fiscal experts who placed the national welfare, as they saw it, above narrow partisan politics. The advancement of social welfare through wise governmental fiscal policy in peace and war justifies the dictum of the late Justice Holmes: "Taxes are the price we pay for civilization."

Colonial Period

Throughout the 17th and the first few decades of the 18th century government expenditures of the thirteen colonies were relatively simple and limited. Both colonial taxations and the custom duties imposed by the British trade and navigation laws in this period were light. The taxing systems of the colonies varied according to the economic and political conditions in three main sections of the country. The New England colonies favored a poll tax; a tax on the gross produce of the land, which was finally developed into a general property tax; and a faculty tax (an arbitrary tax upon the assumed income or earnings of laborers, artisans, and tradesmen). The Southern colonies, dominated by large landowners, preferred import and export duties, supplemented at times by the poll tax. The Middle colonies evolved a mixed system of import duties, excises on beverages, and property taxes. All the colonies resorted at one time or another to import and export duties for revenue purposes. The colonies, notably New England, used an indirect form of taxation or forced loan from their people whenever they issued paper money that depreciated greatly in value. Although Parliament prohibited the further issue of legal-tender bills of credit in 1751 in New England and in 1764 in all the other colonies, as late as 1774 some $12,000,000 in such paper money was estimated to be in current use. In all the proprietary colonies, except New Netherland, quitrents (very light annual feudal payments on all grants of land) were imposed, but widespread resistance by the colonists brought very little revenue except in Maryland, Virginia and Pennsylvania.

The local colonial governments maintained themselves by fees, fines, and compulsory contributions of services; by voluntary monetary contributions early in colonial history; and by taxes on real and personal property throughout the rest of the colonial period. The poll (capitation or head) tax was a tax levied upon all persons, generally adult males, in a community, free or slave, without any regard for the size of the income or property of the person upon whom the tax was based. Although the poll tax was usually low, it bore most heavily, except in the case of the slave-owners, upon the low-income groups, especially in wartime. The poll tax was utilized in all the colonies, particularly in the South during the 17th century. The local governments of Virginia, North Carolina, and Maryland relied very greatly upon poll taxes to meet their needs. Payment was frequently made in produce, e.g., tobacco.

The property tax developed in the 17th century in New England and then spread to the Middle colonies. It never took root in the Southern colonies, which used it for a few years during the fiscal crises of war. Property in New England was originally supplementary as a tax base to the poll and to the "faculty" or income-earning capacity of the tradesmen, craftsmen and professional groups. Property taxes were frequently imposed only upon selected types of real and personal property, especially land, houses, livestock, ships and mills. Often these types of property were taxed according to rather arbitrary schedules of statutory values, and with different rates applicable to different types of property. Both the colonial and local governments in New England and the Middle colonies used these property taxes as important sources of revenue, but the Southern ruling groups resisted the use of such taxes until the American Revolution.

Until the end of the French and Indian War, England never attempted to collect much revenue from the colonies, and that little chiefly for the regulation of trade according to the Navigation Acts. In 1765 Parliament passed the historic Stamp Act which, contrary to precedent, was an internal tax imposed from without. The resentment against this tax, and the 1764 Sugar Tax, was intensified by the economic depression following the 1763 Peace Treaty with France, and led the colonists to oppose all forms of taxation by England on the new principle of "no taxation without representation." Although the Stamp Act was repealed the next year, Parliament in 1767 revived its tax policy and imposed import duties upon certain commodities through the Townshend Acts. A strong colonial nonimportation movement caused Parliament in 1770 to repeal all these duties, except that on tea. The reconciliation with the colonists lasted two years; it ended with the Boston Tea Party, Parliament's Coercive Acts, and the battles of Lexington and Concord.

Revolution and Confederation Period

The organization and support of the Revolutionary militia were sustained at first by the various colonies, which obtained the requisite funds out of the established revenue sources and the issuance of paper money. In 1775 the Continental Congress authorized a continental army and navy, a committee for foreign affairs, the supervision of the frontier Indians, and the administration of the post office. Revenue was needed for these activities. Although heavy war taxes might have been desirable, the colonies had not granted to the Continental Congress the power to levy taxes. The Congress assumed the power to contract debts, but it could only apportion the sums that it needed among the colonies and ask them to remit. These requisitions upon the colonies could not be imposed by force by any central authority and were little honored. The total receipts from the colonies, measured in gold, has been estimated at $5,800,000. In 1780 Congress demanded tax payments through specific supplies of food and fodder, but this new system resulted in great waste and inefficiency and proved to be of small value. The consequence was that Congress depended for its revenue mainly upon the issuance of paper money and upon domestic and foreign loans. The colonial or state governments, unlike the Continental Congress, had the power to levy taxes. The New England states, New Jersey and Maryland used this power during the Revolution to cover their expenses, to retire their own early currency issues and to raise part of their contributions to the Continental Government. New York, Pennsylvania and the Southern states made no attempt to levy direct taxes, but raised some revenue from indirect taxes, and relied generally upon their own paper money and loans to meet their needs.

In 1781 the Articles of Confederation went into effect after the Continental Congress had been carrying on for some years as a revolutionary, extralegal but *de facto* national co-ordinating and directing, if not centralized, government. The Articles did not confer upon the Congress the right to levy taxes, but it empowered Congress to contract debts and to apportion the sums needed to cover its expenses among the states in proportion to the value of the land, buildings and improvements thereon within each state. The taxes for paying that proportion were to be *laid and levied by the authority and direction of the legislatures of the several States,* within the time agreed upon by the United States, in Congress assembled." Some states attempted to meet the requisitions of Congress, but the majority of the states proved indifferent. In order to obtain funds for current expenditures or payment of interest on the national debt, Congress proposed, first in 1781 and then in 1783, that it be granted power to levy specific customs duties upon certain classes of imports. These proposals were blocked by Rhode Island in the first instance, by New York in the second. Efforts in 1781–82 to secure approval for a Confederation land tax, a poll tax and a liquor excise were equally fruitless.

1789–1865

The Confederation Government never managed to obtain enough revenue from its requisitions to cover its expenditures between 1781 and September, 1789, and had to depend upon foreign and domestic loans to meet most of its current expenses. Although the achievements of the Confederation are greater than many of its past critics have allowed, there is no doubt that the framers of the new Constitution of 1787 strengthened the National Government by em-

powering Congress "to lay and collect taxes, duties, imposts and excises to pay the debts and provide for the common defense and general welfare of the United States." But certain limitations were imposed: all duties, imposts and excises were to be (geographically) uniform throughout the United States; direct taxes were to be laid in proportion to the population; no duties were to be imposed by Congress upon articles exported from any state. On the other hand, no export or import duties were to be imposed by any state without the consent of Congress. Direct taxes were generally understood at that time to be taxes on land and poll taxes; this interpretation was sanctioned by U. S. Supreme Court decisions from 1796 until 1881. The general welfare clause was capable of a narrow and a broad construction in relation to the spending and taxing powers of Congress, but after a century and a half of debate the Hamiltonian interpretation has come to prevail against Madison's more restricted one, and Congress has been deemed the authority fit to decide the proper objects of government spending and the appropriate tax measures needed therefor. Congress was not originally circumscribed in its taxing power by constitutional tax exemptions for the instrumentalities of state government, the salaries of state and Federal judges, and the holders of state and municipal offices. These limitations on Congress came from acts of judicial legislation by the Supreme Court after the Civil War.

The first use by Congress of its tax powers was in the passage of the tariff act of July 4, 1789; from that date until the Civil War the Federal Government derived its main revenue from its receipts from customs duties upon goods imported into the United States. The American people were by their past political experience hostile to internal taxation. But when the early customs duties failed to produce sufficient revenue, Congress established an internal revenue system that has grown from a few excise taxes on distilled spirits, carriages and other commodities or transactions to personal and corporate income taxes, estate and gift taxes, railroad compensation taxes, social security taxes and unjust enrichment taxes. In addition to these tax receipts, the National Government over the 170 years since has received income from such other sources as the sale of public lands, surplus postal receipts, the proceeds of Government-owned securities, Panama Canal tolls, proceeds from the sale of surplus property, and seigniorage. From 1791 to 1802 Congress experimented with excise taxes on distilled spirits (1791); and on carriages, the sale of certain liquors, snuff-manufacture, sugar-refining and auction sales (1794); with stamp duties on legal transactions, including a duty on receipts for legacies and probates of will—the first step in the development of the Federal inheritance tax (1797). The first direct tax was imposed in 1798 upon all dwelling houses, lands, and slaves between twelve and fifty. Congress set the specific sum to be collected and then apportioned it among the states according to the size of each state's population.

The unpopularity of these taxes led to the Whiskey Rebellion in 1794, and was a major factor in the 1802 abolition of the whole Federalist system of excise duties and direct taxes, with the exception of the salt tax (eliminated in 1807). For revenue Jefferson relied upon the customs receipts, land sales and the postal services. The War of 1812 forced Congress to adopt new internal taxes; direct taxes upon houses, lands, and slaves were levied in 1813, 1815 and 1816 for some $12,000,000 and apportioned among the states on the basis of the 1810 census. Congress also enacted duties on liquor licenses, auction sales, carriages, refined sugar, distilled spirits and certain other articles. But these duties and the direct taxes were repealed late in 1817 in response to popular pressure. If the war had not ended in 1815, Congress might have adopted the inheritance tax and income tax recommended early that year by Alexander J. Dallas, Madison's Secretary of the Treasury. From 1817 to the outbreak of the Civil War the National Government made no use of excise, stamp, income, inheritance, or direct property taxes. Government expenses were met principally from customs duties, supplemented by the income from the sale of public lands. When the revenues for brief periods were inadequate, the Treasury secured temporary loans and thus avoided new internal taxes even during the war with Mexico. Between 1817 and 1857 it was necessary fourteen times to issue Treasury notes or to raise loans, but the revenues in the following years restored the balance in favor of the Government.

The panic of 1857, the consequent drop in national income, and the failure to tap new tax resources resulted in a series of Treasury deficits that were increased by the secession of Southern states and the outbreak of the Civil War. S. P. Chase, Secretary of the Treasury, feared to impose heavy taxation and wished to rely mainly upon the sale of government bonds, tariff increases, and the proceeds from public-land sales. But the public and Congress proved to be wiser than he and backed the introduction of a massive internal tax program. Congress passed a series of internal revenue bills between 1861 and 1865 that revived the direct tax, introduced the first national income tax and genuine national inheritance tax, restored such old excise taxes as those on spirituous and malt liquors, tobacco and carriages, and developed an immense number of new excise taxes on manufactured goods, especially luxuries, the gross receipts of transportation and insurance companies, the circulation, deposits, and capital of banks, stamps on legal documents and instruments of evidence, and licenses for carrying on certain trades, professions, and businesses. The Civil War income tax laws granted exemptions to those with income first under $800, then under $600. The principle of progressive income

taxation was embodied in both the 1862 and 1864 internal revenue acts, as was the important administrative device of "tapping revenue at the source." No exemption was given to income derived from state instrumentalities until the U. S. Supreme Court ruled in Collector v. Day, 11 Wall. 113 (1870) that Congress could not tax the instrumentalities of state government, including the salary of a state judge. (This doctrine was later extended in Pollock v. Farmers' Loan & Trust Co. (1895) to exempt the holders of state and municipal bonds from paying national income taxes on income from such securities.) Although the Confederate States of America failed to establish an independent Southern nation, their tax system deserves some brief mention. Jefferson Davis' successive Secretaries of the Treasury, Memminger and Trenholm, had an impossible task. But they persuaded their Congress to pass a direct tax; an income tax; a property tax on naval stores, agricultural products, and all kinds of money and currency on hand and on deposit; a tax upon profits from any business; and a license tax. These taxes, enacted between 1861 and 1865, were insufficient, and the Confederacy resorted to issuing bonds and paper money, only to end in fiscal chaos and military defeat.

1866–1913

Once the Civil War was over, national governmental expenditures declined, and taxes were reduced. Internal revenue taxes were gradually repealed between 1866 and 1883, after which the only commodities taxed were liquor and tobacco. The political pressure activities of diverse manufacturing and banking groups led first to the reduction of the income tax in 1867 and 1870 and then to its expiration in 1872 in spite of the opposition of the merchant and farm groups who feared that abolition of the income tax would strengthen governmental reliance on the protective tariff for revenue. The taxes on legacies and successions were repealed in 1870 for the same reasons as the income tax. Yet agrarian and labor discontent from 1873 on resulted in repeated proposals for the restoration of the income tax by Southern and Western Congressmen, the Greenback, Anti-Monopoly, and Populist parties, and the Knights of Labor. In 1894 Congress passed a 2% tax on all personal and corporate income over $4000; gifts and inheritances were included in income. The Supreme Court had held in 1796 that the only direct taxes in a clear constitutional sense were poll taxes and taxes on land (Hylton v. United States, 3 Dallas 171). The Civil War income tax laws had been upheld by the Supreme Court in 1881 (Springer v. United States, 102 U. S. 586) on the ground that an income tax was not a direct tax. But powerful financial interests feared the impact of the 1894 income tax law upon the accumulation of great fortunes and brought three suits before the Supreme Court that resulted in the Court handing down two decisions in 1895 which reversed a century of legal precedent (Pollock v. Farmers' Loan and Trust Co., 157 U. S. 429, 158 U. S. 601). The first decision (April 8, 1895) declared that the tax on rents or income from property was a direct tax, had to be apportioned among the states according to population, and unless so apportioned, was unconstitutional. The tax on income from municipal bonds was nullified as an infringement by the National Government on the borrowing power of the state and its instrumentalities. On May 20, 1895, the full Court, by a five to four decision, ruled that a tax on income from personal property was a direct tax. Although the whole Court agreed that a tax on the income from professions, trades or employments was valid, the majority of five held the entire income tax invalid. This judicial veto of Congress led to intense political pressure by small business, farm, and labor groups through the Populist, Democratic, Socialist Labor, and Socialist parties for the adoption of the Sixteenth Amendment to the Constitution. With its ratification in 1913, the taxation of personal income by the National Government became a valid, permanent, and major source of revenue.

The Spanish-American War forced the sound-money, conservative war finance group in Congress to nearly double the tobacco and beer taxes, to adopt special stamp and occupation taxes, and to accede to a tax on legacies and distributive shares of personal property, graduated both according to degree of relationship and amount of the estate, with general exemption for estates under $10,000 and for all property passing to the surviving husband or wife. The rate rose to 15% on bequests from estates of over $1,000,000 to more distant relatives, strangers in blood, and "bodies politic or corporate." The emphasis of the tax was on the transmission of the property; this made the tax in a technical sense a modified estate duty rather than an inheritance tax.

The passage of this radical statute was partly due to the resurgence of the inheritance tax movement in the late 1880's and '90's. Although there had been several state inheritance taxes of one kind or another before 1885, New York passed a collateral inheritance tax law in 1885 which became a model for many states adopting such taxes in the next few years. In 1892 New York, by imposing an inheritance tax upon direct heirs, gave an impetus to other states. The Supreme Court had upheld the constitutionality of the Federal Civil-War inheritance tax in 1874 in Scholey v. Rew, 23 Wall. 331, and of state inheritance taxes in 1896 and 1898 in United States v. Perkins, 163 U. S. 625, and Magoun v. Illinois Trust and Savings Bank, 170 U. S. 283. To get around the restrictions of the 1895 Pollock decision, the Court held in Knowlton v. Moore, 178 U. S. 41 (1900), that the 1898 Federal inheritance tax was valid as an indirect excise tax not subject to the Constitution's apportionment requirement and not violating its uniformity requirement. Shortly thereafter Congress first lowered many, and then repealed all, of the war revenue taxes.

The continuing resentments of small businessmen, farmers, and workers against big business erupted into a Progressive movement that had as a major objective the passage of a Federal income tax law notwithstanding the 1895 decisions. To prevent this, conservative Republicans put through Congress in 1909 the first Federal corporation tax since the Civil War, a mild 1% tax on the net income above $5000 of every corporation organized for profit. This was an extension of the general taxation of corporations by states, which Pennsylvania had initiated in 1840 with a tax on dividends and had developed by 1868 into a tax on corporate net income. Opponents of this new form of Federal taxation appealed to the Supreme Court to follow the Pollock precedent, but the Court decided that the 1909 tax was not a direct tax but an excise that could be based upon the entire corporate income including income from nontaxable property such as municipal bonds and other property not directly or actively used in the corporate business. In 1913 the Sixteenth Amendment was finally adopted with its explicit grant of power to Congress to levy income taxes without apportionment among the states. This sanctioned the 1913 Federal income tax law with a progressive rate scale that had as its maximum a 7% tax on personal net income over $500,000, as well as a 1% tax on corporate net income. The Supreme Court affirmed the constitutionality of the 1913 income tax in Brushaber v. Union Pacific Railroad Co., 240 U. S. 1 (1916).

1914–1940

The outbreak of World War I led to increased American defense and (after 1917) war expenditures and a series of new tax laws designed to meet about one third of the total war costs, with the remainder to be met by large-scale public borrowings. Congress passed four major revenue acts between October, 1914, and February, 1919, which increased the rates of the recently adopted corporation and personal income taxes to unprecedented heights and added a special tax upon munitions manufacturers, an estate tax, an excess-profits tax, a war-profits tax, transportation taxes, and a wide variety of new excise taxes on goods and services, mainly luxuries and amusements. The duties on fermented liquors, wines and tobacco were raised. The principle of progression was applied to the corporation, estate, personal income, excess-profits, and war-profits taxes so as to increase the burden upon high incomes and large fortunes. The income tax exemption was lowered to $1000 for single persons and $2000 for married persons. The tax on personal incomes rose to 77% on income over $1,000,000. The excess-profits tax was based on the profits in excess of the normal prewar profits during 1911–13, measured as a percentage of the invested capital for the taxable year, and was designed to minimize high war profits that represented "wind-falls" to those engaged in wartime business enterprise. A tax was imposed on undistributed corporation profits that were retained as surplus above the requirements of the business for income-tax avoidance purposes, but this provision proved ineffectual and was repealed in 1918. All these taxes, especially the income and excess-profits taxes, brought in a higher percentage of the Federal Government's war revenue than the taxes in the Civil War or any other previous American war. The Treasury resorted to four great bond issues during 1917–18; the four Liberty Loans brought in a total of $17,000,000,000. This bond total was increased to $21,500,000,000 by the 1919 Victory Loan. Most of these loans carried tax-exemption privileges that made them attractive to investors and offered opportunities for tax-avoidance. Two factors that reduced the war revenue from taxes were the sharp drop in imports and customs duties that followed the outbreak of war in Europe, and the loss in revenue caused by state and Federal prohibition laws passed between 1914 and 1918.

After World War I, Congress gradually repealed the special war taxes, especially the excess-profits tax, and made sharp reductions in corporate and personal income, as well as estate, tax rates. A Federal gift tax was introduced in 1924 to counteract widespread avoidance of Federal estate taxes, but this provision was abolished in 1926, only to be restored in 1932 as a permanent part of the Federal tax structure. In 1924 Congress tried to promote uniformity in state inheritance taxation by providing credit up to 25% of the Federal estate tax for the amount of any estate, inheritance, legacy, or succession taxes paid to any state or territory on any property included in the gross estate. This credit was increased to 80% in 1926 and has remained at that level ever since. But this tax credit did not produce much uniformity in the form of state taxes or in state tax rates. Most states absorbed the Federal credit by supplementing their inheritance taxes with estate taxes.

The 1929 depression forced Congress and Hoover into late antidepression fiscal spending and into raising the corporate and personal income tax rates, doubling the estate tax rates, re-enacting the gift tax, and imposing numerous manufacturers' excise taxes, sales taxes on gasoline, luxury and sporting articles, and special taxes on bank checks, bond transfers, and telephone, telegraph and radio messages in a futile effort to balance the Federal budget. With the inauguration of Franklin D. Roosevelt and his New Deal policies for relief, recovery, and reform, massive government spending to finance unemployment relief and public works destroyed the balanced Federal budget. Taxation was passed "to prevent an unjust concentration of wealth and economic power," and to induce business to adopt certain recovery policies. In 1933 Congress enacted a corporation excess-profits tax, a capital stock tax, and an increase in the gasoline

tax. Under the Agricultural Adjustment Act farmers were paid for curtailing their acreage of certain commodities through taxes imposed on the first processor of the commodities in question. This tax was given up after the Supreme Court's annulment of the A. A. A. in 1936. In 1934–35 the surtax rates on personal income and the rates of the estate and gift taxes were increased and a tax was imposed upon the undistributed net income of personal holding companies. In 1935 the corporate income tax and the excess-profits tax were made higher, on a progressive scale. That same year the Social Security Act established old-age insurance for qualified workers through payroll taxes upon both employers and employees, and unemployment insurance through a payroll tax upon employers, with a 90% credit for an unemployment tax paid to any state. In 1936 a graduated undistributed corporate income or profits tax was levied in order to induce corporations to distribute their earnings to their stockholders. This highly controversial measure was modified in 1938 and repealed in 1939. Partly as compensation for this repeal, the corporate income tax was increased in 1938 and 1939. The Public Salary Act of 1939 extended the Federal income tax to the salaries of Federal judges and of state employees and officials; in return, the Federal Government permitted nondiscriminatory state taxation of the salaries of Federal employees and officers. The Court supported this reciprocity-action in Graves v. O'Keefe, 306 U. S. 466 (1939).

1940–1960

The invasion of Poland by Nazi Germany in September, 1939, and the Japanese attack on Pearl Harbor in December, 1941, put the economy of the United States first on a semi-, then on a full-fledged, war basis in military expenditures and revenue measures. The Federal Government spent almost $300,-000,000,000 on war expenditures between 1940 and 1945, over 80% of total Federal expenditures. The national debt rose from $36,000,000,000 at the end of 1940 to $270,000,000,000 at the end of the fiscal year 1946. Of the $380,000,000,000 received as revenue during the period June, 1940–December, 1945, about 40% came from taxes. This was a higher percentage than that of World War I or the Civil War. This record was achieved by the passage of six important revenue bills between June, 1940, and May, 1944. These acts raised progressively the rates on personal income to a maximum of 94% on income over $200,000 while lowering the exemption to $500 per person, whether married, single, or dependent, so that the number of income-tax payers rose from 4,000,000 in 1939 to 42,700,000 in 1945. The lowering of the exemption was a means of restraining inflation and was accompanied by the enactment of heavy excises on commodities, the consumption of which would have affected the war effort adversely. To prevent war profiteering, drastic increases in corporate and excess-profits taxes were enacted along with price controls and war-contract renegotiation. The excess-profits tax, reintroduced in 1940, rose to a gross rate of 95% and a net rate of 85.5%, inasmuch as a postwar credit of 10% of the amount due was given. Excess profits, as finally determined, were those in excess of (a) 95% of the average earnings of the base period, 1936–39, or (b) the amount of a specified percentage of the invested capital. The combined normal and surtax corporation tax rate was raised from 19% in 1940 to 40% by 1942. But these high personal and corporate tax rates were tempered by various provisions. Individuals were given the benefit of personal deductions for unusually large medical expenses, a generous optional standard deduction, and the rule that no person was required to pay more than 90% of his income in taxes. Similarly, the aggregate of the corporation and excess-profits tax could not exceed 80% of the income. Business losses, suffered by either individuals or corporations, could be carried back or forward for two years to reduce taxable income. An important innovation was the transfer of the personal income tax from a deferred to a current basis of payment. Congress forgave about three fourths of the taxes due in 1942 to ease the shift. Substantial revenue was obtained from the excise taxes on distilled spirits, wines, fermented malt liquors, tobacco, transportation of persons and property, telephone and telegraph messages, theater admissions, and manufactures. The rates of the estate and gift taxes were greatly increased in 1941, mainly by making the maximum rate of each apply to that portion of net estates and net gifts exceeding $10,000,000 in place of the former figure of $50,000,000.

Congress had lagged behind the Treasury on the percentage of war expenditures that might be paid out of taxes. The consequence was that the United States financed World War II primarily through borrowing. The Treasury offered three different types of savings bonds, as well as the usual long-term bonds; short-term obligations to corporations and high-income investors; certificates of indebtedness; Treasury bills running for 71–91 days; and tax savings notes, acceptable at par and accrued interest. Starting in December, 1942, a series of seven war bond drives, followed by a final Victory drive at the close of 1945, succeeded in selling between $13,000,000,000 and $26,000,000,000 at each drive, a total of $156,900,-000,000. Although individuals bought about 25% of the total defense-war offerings of the U. S. Government, the commercial banks and the Federal Reserve Banks took 38%. The consequence was a doubling of the money supply between 1941 and 1945, which did not affect the price level proportionately until the removal of price controls after the war.

Shortly before Japan surrendered in September, 1945, Congress began easing the tax capital-reconversion burdens of American business through the

1945 Tax Adjustment Act. That November, Congress passed a Reconversion Tax Act that repealed the capital-stock tax and the excess-profits tax, the latter effective at the end of 1945. Corporate and personal income tax rates were moderately reduced, and tax exemptions were given to members of the armed forces below the rank of a commissioned officer on service pay received during the war. With presidential support, Congress postponed reduction of many of the wartime excise taxes which were due to expire. Most of these "temporary" taxes have continued to the present. In 1948 Congress overrode President Truman's veto and made large reductions in the personal income, estate and gift taxes. Husbands and wives were allowed to split their incomes on joint income tax forms and thereby reduce their tax. The new estate- and gift-tax law permitted a husband or wife in a common-law state to transfer one half of his or her property to a spouse without taxation, provided that the receiver of the property obtained complete control of it and included it in his or her estate at death for taxation purposes. This marital deduction provision eliminated the long-standing advantage that residents of community-property states had over the residents of the common-law states. The trend to lower taxes was halted by the outbreak of the Korean War in June, 1950, and America's defense of South Korea. Congress in three revenue bills, enacted during 1950–51, raised personal and corporation income taxes to World War II levels, in some instances even higher; reimposed an excess profits tax; and increased excise taxes above the World War II rates. In 1954, one year after the Korean War ended, Congress repealed the excess-profits tax and put through a comprehensive downward revision of the income tax, partly to stimulate business enterprise, partly to remove inequalities in the treatment of taxpayers. Between 1950 and 1958 the Social Security taxes and the accompanying benefits were raised on five different occasions. A few changes in the excise taxes were made, the biggest of which were the increases on motorists to aid in financing the highways. In 1958 the so-called temporary World War II tax on freight transportation was abolished, and numerous other changes were made, some of which, including measures designed to aid small business, resulted in important alterations in tax structure and considerable loss in revenue. Congress in 1959 reduced the tax on the transportation of persons, repealed the 10% tax on "general"—i.e., local exchange—telephone service, and imposed a tax on the taxable investment income, operating gains, and capital gains of life insurance companies.

State and Municipal Taxation

State taxation in the United States during the 19th century rested mainly upon the general property tax although some states tapped other sources of income such as special bank taxes, insurance company taxes, general corporation taxes and inheritance taxes. None of these levies, however, produced more than a slight fraction of the total state revenue. Toward the end of the 19th century the states began to depend to a larger extent upon taxes other than the general property tax, which as late as 1902 furnished 52% of the states' revenue. Corporation and personal income taxes became increasingly important after 1911; after 1920, gasoline taxes became another leading state revenue source. By 1940 property taxes supplied only one sixteenth of state tax revenue. By 1959 the ratio was one thirtieth. Since the 1930's the chief state taxes, in addition to the corporation and individual income taxes, have been the general sales tax, the gasoline tax, and the payroll tax for unemployment insurance. Specific state taxes on the retail sale of tobacco products and alcoholic beverages have also been productive of revenue, although they and the state inheritance and estate taxes have brought in considerably less revenue than the "big" four state taxes. The most common form of sales tax is a tax paid by the consumer on purchases at retail, whether obtained from retailers, wholesalers or manufacturers, of all commodities, except those specifically excluded, and, in some states, of certain services, usually public utilities and amusements. A few states include in their sales tax structure fractional rate business occupation levies on sales by manufacturers or wholesalers, or both. A very few states use the retail sales tax supplemented by business taxes on the gross receipts of businesses at all stages of production and distribution, including the retail. One state, Indiana, has no true sales tax, but imposes a gross income tax on receipts of all businesses, including retailers, as well as on personal income. The payroll taxes of the states are due to the establishment of a 90% credit to each state for the tax that each employer otherwise would have been required to pay in full to the Federal Government under the Social Security Act of 1935.

During the 19th century, counties, municipalities, and other local governing authorities relied on the general property tax as their principal source of revenue, but after 1850 the cost of local government increased with the accelerated growth of cities. The consequent shift from low to high rates in the general property tax led to severe criticism of the prevailing undervaluation of real property and inadequate assessment of personal property, especially of stocks, bonds, notes, and mortgages. Improvements in tax administration, the establishment of local boards of review and equalization and of state tax commissions were accompanied by a marked development in the practice of dividing certain state-collected taxes between the state and local governments and by the trend in the 20th century for the state governments to rely less upon the taxation of property. Several states ceased to tax property and left that source to cities, counties and other local units of government. Most cities and some counties have also derived some revenue from local licenses, permits and various fees. To an increasing extent since World War II local governments have been imposing payroll, income, sales, gasoline, auto, and miscellaneous taxes as supplements to their property taxes. Nevertheless, nonproperty taxes in 1957 for all cities averaged $17 per capita while property taxes came to $44 per capita. This postwar period also was marked by widespread attempts to improve the local property tax.

Trends in Tax Policy

Certain major trends in the American tax system deserve careful consideration. Total American tax collections, local, state, and Federal, increased 150% from 1890 to 1913, over 400% from 1913 to 1920, dropped slightly in the early 1930's, doubled from 1933 to 1940, and increased ninefold from 1940 to 1959, except for a dip in the mid-1940's. The critical international situation has made it necessary for the U. S. Government to maintain and increase military and foreign aid outlays. These, combined with heavy postwar Federal debt interest, veterans' aid costs, domestic welfare expenditures and farm aid, prevent any significant reduction in Federal taxes. At the same time state and local governments, with the great war and postwar demands for schooling, housing and other services, have had, and will have, need to raise the revenue they receive through taxes. These unprecedented revenue demands have come while the economy has expanded with a fivefold gain in national income since 1940. Tax yields have risen at the same time that most taxpayers have been able to increase their consumer purchases. Before 1940 Federal tax collections constituted about one third of the total for all governmental units—local, state, and Federal. The Federal tax proportion rose in World War II to 80%, by 1959 seemed stabilized at a 70% level, and appears destined to exceed the state or local percentage throughout the foreseeable future. Of all the taxes in the American tax system the personal income tax is the most important, responsible for 34% of the total revenue in 1958. Its main importance is as a Federal source. Next in importance are business taxes, principally corporation taxes, with a yield of 20% of the total, if one does not count property and payroll taxes. Sales, commodity, and service excise taxes, especially those on tobacco and liquor, form about 12% of the 1958 total. If gasoline and motor vehicle licenses are included in the consumption taxes, this group accounts for almost 20% of the nation's tax revenue. Fourth in rank is the property tax, until the early 1940's the most important; it still dominates local finance and supplied 44% of the combined state and local tax revenue in 1958.

"TAXATION WITHOUT REPRESENTATION" became an issue in the American colonies when Charles Townshend (1767) sought to impose taxes on such commodities as glass and tea, and provided means for the enforcement of the taxes. That James Otis, in arguing against Writs of Assistance in 1761, first used the expression "Taxation without Representation is Tyranny!" may be doubted. The phrase in various forms was in common use during the period preceding the outbreak of the Revolution. The colonists agreed with Camden and with Chatham that in the matter of internal taxation they were free from parliamentary control. External taxes for the regulation of colonial trade could be levied by Parliament but only with the consent of the colonies. Colonial statesmen admitted the authority of Parliament over the colonies but sought to establish the principle that there were some things Parliament could not do. The real grievance of the colonists lay in the defective system of parliamentary representation which permitted the manipulation of the "rotten boroughs" so that there was always a standing majority in support of the ministers.

At first the representation was held to be one of land but was later shifted to the assertion that in Parliament all British subjects find a virtual representation. "We virtually and implicitly allow the institutions of any government of which we enjoy the benefit and solicit the protection," declared Samuel Johnson. He denied that in the case of the colonies the disfranchised were unrepresented. "They are represented," he said, "by the same virtual representation as the greater part of England." But the theory of virtual representation was attacked in England and was wholly rejected in the colonies. To the colonists it was identified with political corruption and appeared irreconcilable with the dogma that government derives its just powers from the consent of the governed. Colonial debaters could not believe that a man was represented who stood under a personal incapacity to become an elector. "If every inhabitant of America had the requisite freehold," said Daniel Dulany, "not one could vote, but upon the supposition of his ceasing to become an inhabitant of America, and becoming a resident of Great Britain." The colonial argument therefore insisted that representation was achieved only through an assembly of men actually elected by the persons they were intended to represent. That is not to say the colonists desired a representation in Parliament. What the colonists desired was the confirmation and continuance of the authority of their local assemblies to legislate, especially in matters of taxation. From external taxation they claimed to be wholly free.

TEA, DUTY ON. Tea coming to America was subject to British import and excise or inland duties. The import duties were practically fixed at 11⅔%, and the inland duties varied from four shillings in 1723 to one shilling plus 25% *ad valorem* in 1745. In 1748 a rebate of the inland duty was given on tea exported to the colonies or to Ireland, and in 1767 the Tea Act provided a rebate of the import duty as well as

the inland duties, so that tea left England duty free. In the same year the Revenue Act levied an American duty of threepence per pound collected at the American ports. This American duty became the center of a political agitation that finally resulted in actual resistance. The changes made in 1767 lowered costs of tea in America and resulted at first in increased exports, in spite of an organized agitation against the use of tea and an attempted boycott against its importation. Apparently Americans would have their tea and, between 1767 and 1774, more than 2,000,000 pounds were imported and paid the regular American duty.

In 1772 a change was made in the law by which the East India Company was permitted to export tea directly to America and set up wholesale markets on this side. Four centers, Boston, New York, Philadelphia and Charleston, were determined upon. Agents were appointed and quantities shipped in accordance with estimates of probable sales. Immediately there was precipitated an agitation in America not unlike that over the sale of stamps. There had been no change in the tax since 1767, but the tea ships with their loads of taxed freight became a symbol of taxation tyranny. The discussion was not confined to the local ports, but involved the whole country. The tea must be prevented from landing. Efforts were made by the East India Company to arrange for the payment of the American duties in England, ship the tea in bond, and enter it at the local customs house without visible payment of the tax. Both a newspaper and a pamphlet war developed. Tories claimed the tea was coming in without paying any tax. Whigs exposed the subterfuge. It was in this warfare that Alexander Hamilton won his first reputation as a political writer. Every tea ship was turned back, had its tea destroyed, or its cargo was landed under agreement it would not be sold. After 1774 the Association enforced an effectual boycott on most English imports. Some tea, however, filtered through, was entered at the customhouses and paid the regular duty. During the life of this duty, 1767–75, taxes on tea totaling £31,768 were collected.

TEA PARTIES. The term "tea party" is applicable to several pre-Revolutionary episodes concerning this particular symbol of British taxation. Of these the first (Dec. 16, 1773) was held at Boston. Previously, citizens of New York had persuaded consignees to refuse to receive any tea; and the first cargo at that port (April, 1774) was turned back. A consignment discovered on board another vessel was, after the Boston precedent, thrown into the river. At Portsmouth, N. H., and Philadelphia tea ships were turned away.

At Annapolis, Md., public resentment against importation included the importer, when unmasked citizens in broad daylight forced the owner of the offending vessel to put it to the torch. This incident has been called the "Peggy Stewart Tea Party" after the name of the ship that was burned. Edenton, on the coast of North Carolina, held what was known as the "Ladies' Tea Party," so called because the women of the neighborhood met and openly proclaimed their allegiance to the principles of colonial self-government through endorsing the action of the Continental Congress and passing resolutions against the use of tea until the impost thereon should be repealed. South Carolina held a "tea party" during the Revolution, when a considerable quantity of the proscribed leaf that had been seized at Charleston was sold and the funds used to promote the cause of independence.

TEAPOT DOME OIL SCANDAL. Teapot Dome, Wyoming, was the second of the Naval Oil Reserves leased as a unit. The lease was executed, April 7, 1922, by Secretary of the Interior Albert B. Fall with H. F. Sinclair, president of the Mammoth Oil Co., the lessee, without competitive bidding. Its provisions were generally similar to those of the Elk Hills lease, and as in that case the special Federal prosecutors brought a civil suit to cancel the lease, and a suit for criminal conspiracy, against Fall and Sinclair. The Federal District Court of Wyoming held the lease valid, but was reversed by the Circuit Court, and the reversal was upheld by the Supreme Court, Oct. 10, 1927. Sinclair was tried on the conspiracy charge before a jury in the District of Columbia and acquitted April 21, 1928; the indictment against Fall was dismissed in June, 1932, he having been meanwhile convicted on a bribery charge in connection with the Elk Hills lease.

TECHNOCRACY MOVEMENT. As in all periods of acute industrial depression, the slump which began late in 1929 stimulated profound misgivings and wide questioning of the salutariness of the current capitalistic organization of industry. The same conditions excited widespread speculation upon alternative modes of organizing the economy, and panaceas were in order. One of these was the technocracy movement which had its birth in the depths of the depression of 1931–32.

The central idea it embodied was somewhat older. In 1923 Thorstein Veblen in a book entitled *The Engineers and the Price System* had elaborated upon the growing discrepancy between the potential productivity of modern mechanized industry and the actual productivity made available under the current method of its control, *i.e.*, business guided by the profit motive. It was Veblen's thesis that only by placing the control of production in the hands of technicians guided by technical considerations could the full efficiency of industrial equipment be realized.

Starting with these ideas, a study group was organized in the early 1930's which focused its inquiry upon a survey of the development of automatic processes and a determination of the actual capacity of industry to turn out goods. Ignoring the value prob-

lem, and concentrating upon a calculation of productivity in "weight and tale" terms, it is not surprising that these technicians uncovered much evidence of undercapacity output. They professed even to foresee the elimination, shortly, of all need for manual labor. While no definite program for "taking over" control was propounded, it was clearly suggested that the use of money in the distribution of goods would have to be abandoned and the market displaced. The mystery in which this rather esoteric group enveloped its "findings" was in no small part responsible for the feverish excitement awakened among a perplexed public by its "revelations," and with the dissipation of this mystery the movement quickly subsided.

TEHERAN CONFERENCE (Nov. 28–Dec. 1, 1943). Held between the two Cairo Conferences, this was the first one attended by President Roosevelt, Prime Minister Churchill, and Marshal Stalin. It was convened because of the evident need, as the time approached for opening a second front in Europe, to co-ordinate Western military plans with those of Russia. Moreover, Roosevelt and Churchill considered it essential to placate Stalin, whose displeasure over postponement of a second front was embarrassingly obvious, by meeting with him face to face. The three leaders took important military decisions regarding a second front, and discussed the boundaries of Poland and the future of Germany. Roosevelt afterwards reported to Congress that he "got along fine" with Stalin at Teheran.

TELEGRAPH. After a century of experimenting, mostly in Europe (though some attempts were made in America and messages actually sent), Samuel F. B. Morse, a painter, at the cost of twelve years of hard work and miserable poverty, produced the first practicable telegraph instrument. With the aid of a $30,000 appropriation by Congress, a line of wire was strung from Washington to Baltimore. While it was under construction, frequent messages were sent from Washington to the end of the line and back, and on May 1, 1844, when it had reached Annapolis Junction, news of the Whig nomination in Baltimore of Henry Clay for the Presidency was telegraphed to Washington, arriving an hour before a train brought the news. On May 24 the line was formally opened to Baltimore, with Morse himself in Washington ticking off the message, "What hath God wrought!"—often erroneously referred to as the first message by wire—and Alfred Vail, his assistant, who had played no small part in developing the instrument, receiving it.

For nearly three years the Government owned this 44-mile line, while Congress was pondering whether to take over the patent and make the telegraph a government agency, as is the post office. For eleven months after the opening, messages might be sent free, but almost no one sent any. Meanwhile, private companies were being organized under Morse patent privileges to build lines throughout the East, always with the proviso that the Government might eventually assume control. However, on April 16, 1847, Congress decided that the telegraph was not destined to be a lucrative business, and so turned the Washington-Baltimore line over to the Magnetic Telegraph Co., organized by two of Morse's partners. But at that very time, enthusiasm for the new device was developing everywhere, notwithstanding the fact that it was so imperfect that there was constant and even furious complaint. Little was known of insulation until the glass insulator was discovered about 1850, and during rainy weather the current was often so feeble that messages could not come through. A line consisted of only a single wire, which might become so crowded that messages were delayed for days. Construction was flimsy, wires frequently attached to trees instead of poles, and broken almost daily. The New York-Boston line was once broken or grounded in 170 places within 30 miles.

Litigation also tormented the business for years. New instruments were being patented: Royal E. House's automatic printing telegraph in 1846; Alexander Bain's chemical telegraph (which made marks on a sort of litmus paper) in 1848; David E. Hughes' printing telegraph in 1855; and all these brought on lawsuits. Henry O'Reilly, a dynamic promoter, built 8000 miles of line in the Middle West and South, but he was accused of violating his contract with the Morse patentees at the very start, and litigation followed, which was fought with much bitterness. In 1848 O'Reilly's line across Kentucky was destroyed by order of a Federal court. With the rise of the Western Union in the latter 1850's, an era of consolidation began. During the Civil War, the telegraph, as operated by the Federal Government with experts taken over from the great commercial companies, was used by armies in the field for the first time in history. Remarkable feats were performed in setting up lines as the armies moved, sometimes during battle, and in sending messages under fire. The Confederate Army's telegraph was much less mobile than that of the North. The invention of the stock ticker in 1866 was another milestone in telegraph history. After 1900 printing telegraphs began slowly to displace the Morse clicking key, and the coming of the teletype still further depleted its numbers, though a few are still in use.

TELEPHONE. Between 1872 and 1875, Alexander Graham Bell of Boston, a teacher of diction and of the deaf, and Elisha Gray, an electrical inventor of Highland Park, Ill., were both working along similar lines toward the development of a telephone, though both had started with the idea of producing a harmonic telegraph. On Feb. 14, 1876, Gray and an attorney acting for Bell entered the Patent Office in Washington at different hours and filed applications, Bell's being for a patent, while the more cau-

tious Gray merely filed a caveat—a notice that he had his invention well under way. Later a dispute arose over this coincidence. The Patent Office maintained that Bell's paper was the first to be filed by two or three hours and therefore had a sole right—while Gray and his supporters charged that he had been first and that his caveat had been falsely placed after Bell's application. Bell's patent was granted on March 7. Three days later he succeeded in transmitting speech over his telephone. Improvements followed rapidly, not only by Bell, but by other inventors. Thomas A. Edison invented a carbon transmitter in 1878 which was better than Bell's; and about the same time Emile Berliner, an obscure clerk in a Washington dry goods store, produced another transmitter, which was better still.

After 1881 Bell did not take an active part in the telephone business, though he was called upon frequently to testify in law suits to defend his original patent and a second issued in 1877. Several suits reached the U. S. Supreme Court. In every one of them, the Court upheld Bell's rights.

No other invention before the automobile so quickly became a popular convenience and then a necessity. Doctors, newspaper offices and businesses were among the first to recognize the telephone's value. The first telephone was placed in the White House in 1878 when Rutherford B. Hayes was President. Seventy-five years later, the country's 50,000,-000th telephone was installed on the desk of President Dwight D. Eisenhower.

The first commercially successful long-distance line —running 45 miles between Boston and Providence, R. I.—opened for business in 1881. New York and Chicago were linked by telephone in 1892. The first transcontinental telephone line, New York-to-San Francisco, opened in 1915. Transatlantic telephone service, by radiotelephone, was inaugurated in 1927 between New York and London. The first transoceanic telephone cable, across the North Atlantic, was opened for service in 1956. A year later, a similar cable system was completed between California and Hawaii.

Through the years, the quality of telephone transmission has been improved. In 1920, speaking over the telephone was equivalent to two people talking to each other while they were some fifty feet apart. Forty years later, transmission had been improved to a point equivalent to their talking to each other face-to-face—that is, only six feet apart.

After World War II, telephone services were expanded rapidly. By 1959 there were more than 67,000,000 telephones in the United States, three times as many as in 1940. The difference between local and long-distance service was beginning to disappear. Dialing of long-distance calls by customers was introduced on a trial basis in one city in 1951. Within less than ten years, this service was available in more than 1400 American communities. In the

Bell Telephone Laboratories, entirely new all-electronic telephone switching systems were under development by 1959.

Many kinds of communications were being carried over telephone lines, including voice, pictures, data and television. Telephone inventions also played a part in outer-space research. Bell solar batteries and transistors, the tiny electronic devices designed to do almost anything vacuum tubes can do, provided the communications power in the United States' first Vanguard satellite, launched in 1958.

TELEVISION dates from 1923, when Vladimir Zworykin, a naturalized citizen of the United States, applied for his first patent on the iconoscope an all-electric television tube. Before that, a whole list of inventors had worked on a mechanical scanning system which finally proved to be impractical, both from the standpoint of light and synchronized sound. David Sarnoff, who had hired Zworykin to work for R. C. A., never lost faith in the electronic process developed by Zworykin and invested, over the years, $9,000,000 of R. C. A. earnings in this process. The proof of his faith came in 1935 when N. B. C. successfully demonstrated the practical use of the Zworykin tube with experimental signals sent from the tower of the Empire State Building in New York City and received in the R. C. A. Building twenty blocks away. In 1939, television was demonstrated at the New York World's Fair by R. C. A. and in 1941, the Federal Communications Commission, on the advice of an all-industry engineering committee, authorized standards for television transmission for full commercial operation on 18 UHF channels (later reduced to 12) at 525 scanning lines to the inch to cover the entire United States. World War II interrupted the development of television but four stations, two in New York and one each in Schenectady and Philadelphia, continued to operate until peace was declared in 1945.

In 1960 there were approximately 600 stations in the United States of which 55 were educational noncommercial operations, authorized under the Sixth Report and Order of the Federal Communications Commission in 1952. There were four networks, three commercial and one noncommercial. The commercial networks were tied together by microwave and coaxial cable relays; the noncommercial network was operated by air transfer of video tape recordings.

The first television programs were received either on tinted screens or in black and white, but multicolor television was introduced in 1950. Two rival systems were introduced, one using the old rotating disc, the other the iconoscope tube with a myriad of additional tubes to control color. Inasmuch as the rotating disc introduced an incompatible system in which color and black and white could not be received on the same set, the Federal Communications Commission, again with the help and advice of an all-industry committee, finally set up standards for color involving the iconoscope tube, which are in use today. Two of the leading networks by 1958 had developed programs of different types. The C. B. S. network proceeded along traditional lines: big sponsors, big programs, regular scheduling. N. B. C. on the other hand emphasized (1) the magazine concept which involved multiple sponsorship of programs, such as the early morning program TODAY and the late evening program TONIGHT, (2) spectaculars—huge, expensive programs presented intermittently on an irregular schedule and (3) documentaries—costly programs of a public-service nature on current subjects in the news. The Dumont network disappeared in 1955 and the A. B. C. network assumed the third-place position. Meanwhile, the educational tape network grew and assumed fourth position in audience measurement.

The total audience for television is now measured in many millions. There were approximately 60,000,000 homes provided with television receivers in 1960. There were also over 60,000 schools receiving television programs regularly in the classrooms.

TEMPERANCE MOVEMENT. Although the temperance movement originated in the sporadic attempts to curb the use of intoxicants during the 17th century, the first temperance society in English America was formed in 1808 at Moreau, Saratoga County, N. Y., by Dr. Billy J. Clark, a physician who had been much impressed by Benjamin Rush's *An Inquiry into the Effects of Spirituous Liquors on the Human Mind and Body* (first published in 1784), for it confirmed his own ideas based upon long observation of intemperance among the people to whom he ministered. The 44 members of the unique society signed a pledge to "use no rum, gin, whisky, wine or any distilled spirits . . . except by advice of a physician, or in case of actual disease." This was no ironclad pledge, but it became the model for other groups opposed to intemperance. More important than the work of Dr. Clark was the influence of Lyman Beecher, pastor at East Hampton, L. I., who was inspired by Dr. Rush's essay to preach a series of sermons in 1810 against the current drinking customs. Entering upon a pastorate at Litchfield, Conn., the following year, Beecher persuaded the political and ecclesiastical leaders of the "standing order," fearful of the tendency of the ungodly to join the Jeffersonian ranks, that it was essential to organize in order to save the state from "rum-selling, tippling folk, infidels and ruff-scruff." From this agitation came the Connecticut Society for the Reformation of Morals (May 19, 1813), which was dedicated to the suppression of drunkenness, gambling and general lawlessness. Meanwhile, the Massachusetts clergy, supported by Federalist politicians, had organized their campaign against intemperance (February, 1813) under the leadership of

Jedidiah Morse and Jeremiah Evarts. Auxiliary societies were soon formed in New England and New York, but for a decade no phenomenal victories were won.

Not until 1825 were the forces of evangelical Protestantism really mobilized for the temperance crusade. In that year Lyman Beecher again stirred his parishioners with powerful sermons which were printed and widely distributed. The response to his appeal quickly took form; on Feb. 13, 1826, sixteen clergy and laymen in Boston signed the constitution of the American Society for the Promotion of Temperance. Their action revealed a new spirit. The temperance reformers were now under divine compulsion to send out missionaries to preach the gospel of total abstinence from the use of ardent spirits. Using an effective system of state, county and local auxiliaries, the Boston society soon claimed to be national. Voluntary contributions enabled it to support agents who visited every part of the country striving to affiliate all temperance groups with the national society. By 1834 there were auxiliaries in every state with which approximately 5000 locals and 1,000,000 pledge signers were affiliated. Two years later there were eleven weekly and monthly journals devoted solely to temperance, while many religious periodicals carried news of the reform. Despite limited financial resources, the reformers printed and distributed millions of tracts. In song and story, in pageant and play, in essay and sermon, the temperance plea was presented to the nation.

In 1836, at the annual convention of the American Temperance Union (sponsored by the American Temperance Society), dissension appeared within the ranks. The delegates wrangled over three proposals: (1) to denounce the antislavery reformers and placate the Southern temperance societies; (2) to sponsor legislation against the liquor traffic; (3) to adopt a pledge of "total abstinence from all that can intoxicate." The convention avoided a decision on the first two proposals, but by a narrow majority adopted the total abstinence pledge. As a result there was a noticeable decline in the membership of the societies affiliated with the A.T.U., for many insisted that abstinence and temperance were not synonymous, and vigorously opposed placing wines and malt beverages under the ban. But the ground thus lost was more than regained during the decade of the 1840's, as the Washingtonian revival brought a remarkable increase in pledge signers. Labeling themselves as reformed drunkards, the Washingtonians in the spring of 1841 began to stage sensational "experience meetings" which aroused the interest of thousands who had not been reached by the literary propaganda of the older societies. The emotionalism of such meetings was contagious, and the most successful temperance lecturer of the day, John B. Gough, soon utilized it in winning converts. While Washingtonianism was at its height, Father Theobald Mathew, whose campaign against intemperance among his Irish fellow countrymen had

won world-wide acclaim, undertook a speaking tour through the United States. Between July, 1849, and November, 1851, according to the *New York Herald,* he traveled 37,000 miles and administered the pledge to almost 500,000 Catholics.

Beneath the surface the temperance movement had been slowly converted into a campaign for prohibition. A few leaders had long been eager to direct the force of law against the liquor traffic; they had denounced the licensing of retail dealers in intoxicants; they had supported such legislation as the "fifteen gallon law" of Massachusetts (1838) which forbade the sale of spirituous liquors in less quantity than fifteen gallons "and that delivered and carried away all at one time." The demand for state-wide prohibition was most ably expressed in Maine, where Neal Dow, a successful merchant of Portland, had committed the temperance groups to the policy of legal coercion. In 1846 the legislature passed an act which prohibited the retail sale of intoxicants. Not satisfied, Dow's followers secured a truly prohibitory statute in 1851. Thereafter, the temperance forces, wearied from the long effort to combat intemperance by persuasion, turned to the "strong arm of the law." Their objective was statewide, then national, prohibition.

TENNESSEE, STATE OF. In 1541 Hernando De Soto discovered the Mississippi River, presumedly within the bounds of present-day Tennessee at the site of Memphis, and it is also believed probable that he had already crossed the southeastern corner of the state on his journey from Florida. This visit was not followed by Spanish occupation; therefore, it was the English and the French who, more than a century later, became rival claimants for the possession of the region. In 1673 two Virginia traders, James Needham and Gabriel Arthur, visited the Indians who resided in the southeastern part of Tennessee; and in the same year the two French voyagers, Marquette and Jolliet, touched the western edge of the present state when they landed on the eastern bank of the Mississippi River. Nine years later LaSalle built Fort Prudhomme at the mouth of the Big Hatchie during his voyage down the Mississippi.

Soon thereafter the English and French traders engaged in bitter rivalry for the trade and friendship of the Indian tribes which occupied or claimed portions of the Tennessee country. For a time the Shawnee lived in the Cumberland Valley, but early in the 18th century they were driven northward across the Ohio River by the Cherokee and Chickasaw. The Chickasaw towns were situated south of the Tennessee line in northwestern Mississippi but they claimed possession of the whole of West Tennessee and part of Middle Tennessee. The Cherokee occupied the southeastern part of the state and claimed the remainder of East Tennessee and all of Middle Tennessee. In 1739 the French built Fort Assumption at the site of Memphis within the Chickasaw domain as a part of an unsuccessful effort to destroy that tribe. In an attempt to retain the friendship of the "Over Hill" Cherokee the English in 1756–57 built two forts on the banks of the Little Tennessee River. The more important of these, Fort Loudoun, constructed and garrisoned by an expedition from South Carolina, was for a time the most western English fort in America.

Lured on by the tales of hunters and agents of land companies who had been traversing the western country, the first permanent settlers came into Tennessee from the "back country" of Virginia and the Carolinas about 1769. Under the leadership of William Bean, James Robertson and others, they settled along the Watauga, Nolichucky and Holston Rivers in the northeastern corner of the state. Finding themselves outside the bounds of organized government and on Indian land, they set up in 1772 a "homespun" government called the Watauga Association. They succeeded in negotiating a lease of their lands from the Cherokee, which they converted into a purchase in 1775 when Richard Henderson and the Transylvania Company bought an extensive tract of land in Middle Tennessee and Kentucky from the same tribe.

Soon after the outbreak of the Revolution the Wataugans organized the district of Washington, the first local division of government to be named after the commander in chief of the Revolutionary army. In 1777 the district was annexed to North Carolina, which gave the name Washington County to the whole of its territorial claim west of the mountains. During the war the Wataugans not only defended their homes successfully from Indian attacks, but also participated in campaigns east of the mountains, notably at King's Mountain. They also sent forth the expeditions which founded Nashville in Middle Tennessee in 1779–80.

When North Carolina ceded her western lands to the United States in 1784, the settlers in the East Tennessee region organized the State of Franklin, and although the cession act was quickly repealed, they attempted unsuccessfully to maintain themselves as a separate state. Both the Franklinites and the Cumberland settlers participated in an intrigue with the Spanish in 1788, which was brought to an end by North Carolina's second cession of her western claim in 1789. The region ceded was organized in 1790 as the "Territory South of the River Ohio" with William Blount as governor, and admitted to the Union as a state on June 1, 1796.

Following the election of Lincoln in 1860 and the secession of seven Southern states, the people of Tennessee refused to call a convention to consider secession. With the beginning of hostilities, however, public sentiment rapidly changed, and in June, 1861, the people voted by an overwhelming majority in favor of separation from the Union. Tennessee was the last of the eleven states to leave the Union, and she did so by the unique procedure of declaring her independence rather than adopting an ordinance of secession.

From 1862 to 1865 Tennessee was under the military governorship of Andrew Johnson. Under the control of the Reconstruction governor, William G. Brownlow, elected March 4, 1865, Tennessee was the only ex-Confederate state to ratify the Fourteenth Amendment prior to the forcible establishment of the Negro-carpetbag regimes in the South. In consequence of this action, in July, 1866, Tennessee was immediately reinstated to its position in the Union, and thus escaped the harsh congressional program of military reconstruction applied to the other states of the Confederacy.

TENNESSEE RIVER, formed by the confluence near Knoxville of the Holston, which rises in southwest Virginia, and the French Broad, which has its source in western North Carolina, follows a serpentine course into northern Alabama and thence northward to the Ohio River at Paducah, Ky. The length of the main stream is 652 miles, and the total drainage area is 40,569 square miles. Called for a time the Cherokee River, it was used extensively by Indians on their war and hunting expeditions, especially by the Cherokee, some of whose towns were located along the branches of the river in southeast Tennessee. The Tennessee Valley played an important part in the Anglo-French rivalry for the control of the Old Southwest which culminated in the French and Indian War; and the river was an important route of migration of settlers into the Southwest following that struggle. The use of the river for navigation purposes was handicapped by the presence of serious obstructions, especially the Muscle and Colbert Shoals at the "Great Bend" in northern Alabama. The Muscle Shoals region became the scene of numerous land speculative undertakings, beginning as early as 1783. The problem of removing or obviating the obstructions to navigation has been a perennial one, and has received spasmodic attention from the Federal Government as well as from the states of Tennessee and Alabama, including a grant of public lands to Alabama in 1828 for the construction of a canal, and several subsequent surveys and appropriations. In the 20th century the emphasis shifted from navigation to power production and flood control, and the construction during World War I of the Wilson Dam and nitrate plants at the Muscle Shoals initiated a nationwide controversy over the question of public or private ownership and operation of power facilities. Since 1933 the Tennessee Valley Authority has been engaged in an extensive program involving navigation and flood control, fertilizer experimentation, the production and sale of electric power and the social and economic transformation of the Tennessee Valley.

TENNESSEE VALLEY AUTHORITY. During World War I, the Wilson Dam and power plant were built on the Tennessee River to produce nitrates for munitions. For fifteen years thereafter a contest between proponents and opponents of public power held that installation largely inactive.

In May, 1933, upon recommendation of President Franklin D. Roosevelt, the Tennessee Valley Authority was created by act of Congress. The Authority is governed by a board of three directors, appointed by the President. The original board consisted of Harcourt A. Morgan, David E. Lilienthal and Arthur E. Morgan, Chairman. In the President's words, it was to be "a corporation clothed with the power of government, but possessed with the flexibility and initiative of a private enterprise." Its aim was the unified development of the Tennessee River system by a single program for all useful purposes, especially national defense, flood control, navigation, power development, fertilizer development, improvement of agriculture and forestry. In operation other values developed, including elimination of malaria, development of recreation facilities and improvement of fisheries.

The Tennessee, the largest branch of the Ohio, drains 40,000 square miles, mostly in Tennessee, but partly in Kentucky, Virginia, North Carolina, Georgia, Alabama and Mississippi. The French Broad and Holston Rivers unite above Knoxville to form the Tennessee, which flows southwest and west through Tennessee, north Alabama, and northeast Mississippi, and then north across Tennessee and Kentucky to the Ohio. It has a total fall of 515 feet in its length of 580 miles.

Annual precipitation in the area, averaging 51 inches, is one of the heaviest in the United States, varying in different years from 38 to 63 inches. The total annual runoff has varied from 11 to 33 inches. The extreme low flow of the river has been 4500 cubic feet per second, and the maximum about 500,000 cubic feet per second. Control by reservoirs has greatly lessened these extremes.

The T. V. A. was created during the great depression, when increase of employment was a major issue. Beginning in June, 1933, with no organization whatsoever, in four months two great dams were under construction, which were finished in less than three years, turning waste man-hours into enduring structures which will continue to produce wealth through the centuries.

Greatly improved standards of human relations in the construction industry were given application by adoption of the labor relations policy recently developed and applied on the Miami flood control project in Ohio. Also following that Ohio precedent and using a core engineering staff trained there, the T. V. A. carried out its major works without letting contracts, but with its own engineering and construction staff. This enabled construction to begin quickly during the depression, and created an able staff which has built twenty dams and some of the largest steam power plants in the world. The peak of T. V. A. employment, in 1942, was about 30,000 persons.

The thirty dams which the T. V. A. has built or owns or controls have a storage capacity of about 12,000,000 acre feet. The Tennessee River is now a chain of lakes. Water regulation is centered in the Chief Engineer's office. With a widespread system of recording and forecasting, the total water supply is manipulated in the interest of flood control, navigation, power development, malaria control, recreation and fisheries. The values from this complex operation are far greater than could be realized by any possible unco-ordinated undertakings.

Navigation. With nine-foot navigation for the 627 miles from the Ohio River to above Knoxville, and with locks being brought to the present standard of 600 feet long and 110 feet wide, the river traffic in 1959 was 65 times as great as in 1933, or 2,130,000,000 ton miles. During that year 75,000 vessels passed through the locks. Estimated annual savings in transportation costs are $25,000,000, which, after paying costs of operation, leaves a profit of about 10% on the $190,000,000 charged to navigation.

Flood Control. Flood control and navigation have first claim on T. V. A. reservoir capacity. With no great general floods during summer, it is possible in some degree to use the same storage capacity, partly for flood control and partly for power. According to T. V. A. estimates, the system has prevented $35,000,000 flood damage at Chattanooga, and can lower flood stages two to four feet at the mouth of the Ohio. A similar increase of Mississippi River flood protection by raising levees probably would cost much more than the $183,000,000 charged to T. V. A. flood control.

Electric Power. With the energetic initiative of David E. Lilienthal, one of the original directors, there was developed a program for marketing the large amounts of power generated at T. V. A. dams. Because of the great power demands of the atomic energy program, steam plants have been added, two of them the largest in the United States, until in 1960 T. V. A. was the largest power producer and the largest purchaser of coal in the United States, with three times as much steam as waterpower capacity. It was the sole source of power over 80,000 square miles, about twice the area of Ohio, with a population of about 5,000,000 people. It sold power at wholesale to 99 municipalities, to 51 rural electrical co-operatives, and to 30 large industries, while more than half of its total sales were to the U. S. Government, largely for the atomic energy program.

T. V. A. prescribes conditions and maximum rates at which municipalities shall sell its power. According to official reports, during 1959 the average annual residential use in the T. V. A. area was 7863 kilowatt hours, at a cost of 1.03¢ per kwh, whereas the average residential use by the United States as a whole was 3450 kwh, at a cost of 2.52¢ per kwh.

This difference results in part from the inherent economy in the construction of an integrated river control system for all purposes, which makes construction less expensive than where a single purpose must bear the entire expense. Also, the unified operation of thirty dams and reservoirs in a single system makes possible an economy and effectiveness in the use of water quite beyond that of a single plant.

Lower cost and resulting larger use have been somewhat favored by the fact that, whereas private utilities would be required to pay about 52% of net earnings (about 9% of the operating cost) for income tax, the T. V. A. and its distributing municipalities pay no income tax. According to the T. V. A. Annual Report for 1959, nearby private utilities pay state and local taxes amounting to 8.6% of the total operating cost, while the T. V. A. and its distributing municipalities pay 6.8%, a difference of 1.8% of the operating cost. While private utilities pay 2.5% or more interest on their investment, T. V. A. estimates interest at 2%, a difference of perhaps 2.5% of the operating cost.

The T. V. A. electric service has been of a high order, and has markedly advanced the economy of the region. Active promotion by T. V. A. and associated public agencies, together with lower unit costs, has greatly expanded the use of electric power. In 1959 about 1,200,000 homes were served with T. V. A. power, of which about 250,000 are heated entirely by electricity, which increases the use in the home by nearly five times.

In 1959 the total investment in T. V. A. power was about $1,700,000,000. Large additional installations were under way. According to T. V. A. reports, its power business pays all costs and makes a profit of about 4% on the net investment for power, which is used to increase plant or to repay the cost. The 1959 Congress authorized the Authority to sell bonds, not more than $750,000,000 to be outstanding at any one time, to finance further growth.

Fertilizer. The T. V. A. statute provided for the production and sale of cheap nitrogen fertilizer. Dr. H. A. Morgan, one of the directors, believed the great need of Southern soils was phosphates, and that exclusive use of nitrates robbed the soil of essential plant nutrients. He therefore promoted phosphate fertilizers and their experimental distribution. This accelerated use of phosphates substantially advanced Southern agriculture, turning it from cotton and corn to grass and livestock, reducing soil erosion.

Forestry. Half of the T. V. A. area is forest. Beginning with the first years of the T. V. A., with cooperation of national and state forestry services, studies were made of forest conditions and possibilities, and steps were taken to increase forest productivity. This coincided with a general movement to the same effect over the country, and with technological developments for using hardwoods for papermaking. T. V. A. area forests are steadily increasing in productiveness.

Malaria Control. Before the T. V. A., endemic malaria was a chief handicap of lowland areas. In some locations more than a quarter of the population was infected. Since malaria is carried by mosquitoes which breed in standing water, the process of turning the Tennessee into a series of lakes threatened to make the region uninhabitable. An early action of the T. V. A. Board was to appoint Dr. Eugene L. Bishop to deal with this problem. He did a masterly job, and the disease was eliminated from the region. It is stated that during ten years no cases have been reported except a few brought in from outside.

Recreation. With malaria eliminated, T. V. A. lakes are a major recreation area. Seventy-five state and local parks along their shores have public facilities, and there are thousands of summer cottages. In 1959 there were 45,000 recreational craft on the lakes. Fishing in T. V. A. lakes has steadily improved. Tests indicate that less than a fifth of the fish are ever caught. (The commercial fish catch amounted to about 4,700,000 pounds in 1959.)

The over-all result of the Tennessee Valley Authority has been a release of productive capacity, and a complex of values not achieved by any other river development program in the nation.

TENNIS was introduced into this country from England about 1874 and rapidly became a popular game in the fashionable circles of American life. At first a gentle as well as a genteel pastime, played by both men and women, it evolved only slowly into the more active modern game with its hard, overhead service, back court drives and smashes at the net. The formation of the United States Lawn Tennis Association (1881), institution of its annual tournaments at Newport (1881), and the beginning of the Davis Cup matches (1900) marked the important stages of its early growth. By the end of the 19th century a group of outstanding players had emerged from the ranks— R. D. Sears, Robert D. Wrenn, Dwight F. Davis, William A. Larned—and tennis began to be played more and more widely throughout the country. With the new century America began to produce players who could carry off international honors, the most outstanding being William T. Tilden II, and what had originally been the polite pastime of society became one of the country's most popular amateur, participant sports.

TENURE-OF-OFFICE ACT, passed by Congress March 2, 1867, over Johnson's veto, was designed to restrict greatly the appointing and removing power of President Johnson. The Senate's consent was required for removals in all cases where this consent was necessary for appointment. At first the design seems not to have been that of protecting any particular cabinet member—these officers being expressly excepted—but rather Republican appointees in general. But after considerable debate there was substituted for the cabinet exception a proviso that cabinet members should hold office during, and for one month after, the term of the President who made the appointment, subject to removal only with the Senate's consent. Violation of the act was made a high misdemeanor. When Johnson attempted to remove Secretary of War Stanton, the Radical Republican Congress proceeded with its long-laid plans for the impeachment and trial of the President. It was shown, however, that, as Stanton was not a Johnson appointee, the act could not apply to him. Passed during, and as part of, the struggle between Johnson and Congress over Reconstruction, the act was virtually repealed early in Grant's first administration and entirely repealed in March, 1887.

TEPEE, TEEPEE, OR TIPI. The Dakota Indian word *tipi,* meaning "where I live," was adopted by frontiersmen to designate a conical skin-covered shelter supported by a framework of poles. An alternate term is lodge. The tipi differs from a pointed tent by possessing an opening at the top through which the poles extend two feet or more. The poles range from 12 to 18 feet in total length and vary from 12 to 15 in number. Generally, the name tepee is applied to any such conical pole structure, covered with skins, mats, bark or cloth. The geographical distribution of the tipi is from Texas to Canada (formerly skin-covered, now using cloth), from Nova Scotia into Siberia (covered with birchbark and occasionally with mats).

TERRITORIAL GOVERNMENTS are similar to state governments in form but differ essentially in that they are completely subject to Congress. The first territorial government, established for the Northwest Territory by the Ordinance of July 13, 1787, has furnished the prototype for those subsequently organized. As modified in 1789, the Ordinance provided for a governor, secretary and three judges, all appointed by the President with the consent of the Senate. The governor, appointed for three years, was also head of the militia and superintendent of Indian affairs. The secretary, appointed for four years, recorded the territorial laws and served as governor in the latter's absence. The judges, who served during good behavior, had common-law jurisdiction only.

Under the first or temporary stage of government, the governor was authorized to establish townships and counties, appoint their officials, and, in conjunction with the judges, adopt laws for the territory. Laws thus adopted were subject to revision by Congress, and also by the territorial legislature after the organization of the permanent government. This consisted of a house of representatives, elected for two years by the resident freeholders, a council, appointed by the President for five years, and a delegate to Congress, elected by the house and council together. The delegate had the privilege of debate but no vote. The governor had authority to convene, prorogue and dissolve the legislature, and he had an absolute veto over its enactments.

Slavery was prohibited by the ordinance, but this prohibition was not extended to the Southern territories. Otherwise the governments established for the Southwest, Mississippi and Indiana territories, organized in 1790, 1798 and 1800 respectively, differed but little from that described above. Thereafter, however, changes in the original form were made by Congress with increasing frequency, either by the organic acts, by acts applied to specific territories, or by general laws extended to all the territories. In the main, these modifications tended to (1) increase the powers of the legislature, (2) widen the electoral base and increase the powers of the electorate, and (3) extend the jurisdiction of the courts. Innovations adopted for one territory were not always extended to the others, but with the organization of Minnesota Territory in 1849 the evolution of the territorial government was essentially complete. The government of that territory, as established by its organic act and by previously enacted statutes applicable to all territories, illustrates the changes introduced in the preceding half century.

The Minnesota governor, secretary and judges were appointed for four years. The members of the council and the congressional delegate were elected by the territorial electorate for two-year terms. The governor's appointive power was subject to the consent of the council, and his veto was subject to overrule by two-thirds vote of the legislature. The legislature was empowered to apportion its representation, fix the qualifications for suffrage and organize the judicial districts. Acts of the governor and the legislature were subject to the approval of Congress. Most of the township and county officers were elective, and the freehold qualifications demanded of the early territorial voter and officeholder were replaced by residence requirements. The judicial power was vested in supreme, district, probate and justice-of-the-peace courts, with the judges of the supreme and district courts possessing equity and chancery as well as common-law jurisdiction.

The above description is, in general, applicable to the territories organized after 1849. In the later territories the governmental organization becomes more elaborate and more specialized, and the powers and duties of the territorial officers and agencies are described in greater detail in their organic acts.

TERRITORIES OF THE UNITED STATES are parts of the national domain which have been separately organized by Congress. Their governments are similar to those of the states in form but not in authority; they are dependent on Congress for their status and power, and their chief officers are appointed by the President and the Senate. All the states except the original thirteen and Vermont, Kentucky, Maine, Texas, California and West Virginia have passed through the territorial stage. Most of the territories were formed by the breaking up of the major or parent territorial areas. The successive delimitations through which the territories passed prior to their admission as states are too involved to permit of even approximate description in every case, but the following illustrations are typical.

The territory northwest of the River Ohio, as organized by the ordinance of July 13, 1787, was bounded by the New York and Pennsylvania state lines, the Ohio and Mississippi Rivers, a line drawn north from the headwaters of the Mississippi to Canada, and the international boundary. In 1800 that part west of a line drawn north from the mouth of the Kentucky River, on the Ohio, to Fort Recovery, thence north to Canada, was organized as Indiana Territory. From the remaining territory, the State of Ohio, with approximately its present boundaries, was admitted March 1, 1803. Indiana thus comprised all the original Northwest Territory except Ohio until reduced by the creation of Michigan and Illinois territories, and Michigan was in turn reduced by the formation of Wisconsin Territory. The dates of the acts organizing these territories, and the dates of their admission as states, are: Indiana, May 7, 1800– Dec. 11, 1816; Michigan, Jan. 11, 1805–Jan. 26, 1837; Illinois, Feb. 3, 1809–Dec. 3, 1818; Wisconsin, April 20, 1836–May 29, 1848. Part of Minnesota (March 3, 1849–May 11, 1858) was also originally in the Northwest Territory.

The territory south of the River Ohio was organized May 26, 1790, from the region west of the present states of North Carolina and Georgia to the Mississippi, north of parallel 31. The northern part was admitted as the State of Tennessee, June 1, 1796. The lower third of the remainder was organized as Mississippi Territory, April 7, 1798, but was later enlarged to comprise what is now included in Mississippi and Alabama. Mississippi was admitted as a state, with its present boundaries, Dec. 10, 1817, and at the same time the remaining eastern half was organized as Alabama Territory. Alabama became a state Dec. 14, 1819.

Louisiana, purchased from France in 1803, extended from the Mississippi to the western boundary of the Mississippi drainage basin. Orleans Territory, comprising approximately what is now Louisiana, was organized March 26, 1804, while the rest of the Purchase was established as Louisiana Territory, March 3, 1805. Orleans became the State of Louisiana, April 30, 1812, and in the same year Louisiana Territory was renamed Missouri. The latter became a state Aug. 10, 1821, but the remaining undivided part of the Purchase retained the name Missouri Territory until 1854. In addition to those mentioned, all or part of the following territories were created from this region: Arkansas, March 2, 1819–June 15, 1836; Iowa, June 12, 1838–Dec. 28, 1846; Kansas, May 30, 1854–Jan. 29, 1861; Nebraska, May 30, 1854–Feb. 9, 1867; Colorado, Feb. 28, 1861–Aug. 1, 1876; Dakota, March 2, 1861–Nov. 2, 1889; Montana, May 26, 1864–Nov. 8, 1889; Wyoming, July 25, 1868–July 10, 1890. During this period Florida became a state (March 30, 1822–March 3, 1845), and the great areas of the Northwest and Southwest were organized.

The Oregon country was held jointly by the United States and Great Britain until 1846, when the northern boundary was fixed at parallel 49. The country south of this line to parallel 42, and west to the Rocky Mountains, was organized as Oregon Territory (Aug. 14, 1848–Feb. 14, 1859), and the remainder as Washington Territory (March 2, 1853–Nov. 11, 1889). Idaho (March 3, 1863–July 3, 1890) was formed from parts of Washington, Dakota and Nebraska. The region acquired from Mexico in 1848 was divided into the territories of Utah (Sept. 9, 1850–Jan. 4, 1896), Nevada (March 2, 1861–Oct. 31, 1864), and parts of New Mexico (Sept. 9, 1850– Jan. 6, 1912), Arizona (Feb. 24, 1863–Feb. 14, 1912), Wyoming and Colorado. California was admitted directly as a state, Sept. 9, 1850.

Alaska, purchased from Russia, March 30, 1867, was made a territory Aug. 24, 1912. It became a state on June 30, 1958. The Republic of Hawaii, annexed July 7, 1898, and given territorial status June 14, 1900, became a state in March, 1959. None of the other possessions of the United States have been designated by Congress as territories, although Puerto Rico has been given many of the privileges of territorial status.

TEXAN–SANTA FE EXPEDITIONS. After Spain's establishment of Santa Fe and San Antonio as centers respectively of New Mexico and Texas, joining the two areas was an enduring frontier objective, but there interposed between them as barriers the uncharted southern end of the Great Plains and the Plains Indians. Small parties led by Pedro Vial and José Mares traveled across the intervening country, 1786–89; in 1808 Capt. Francisco Amangual led 200 men from San Antonio to Santa Fe. Spanish efforts, however, never effected a satisfactory communication.

The Texan-Santa Fe Expedition of 1841 was occasioned by Texas' claim of New Mexican territory and President Mirabeau B. Lamar's desire to divert to Texas the regular Santa Fe trade. Gen. Hugh McLeod commanded a force totaling 321 men, which was harassed by Kiowas and broken up by the adversities and limitations presented by the Great Plains environment, eventually to be captured in sections by New Mexican troops under Gov. Manuel Armijo.

The Texans were subjected to many indignities en route to Mexico City, where they became the subject of a heated diplomatic controversy between the United States and Mexico. Most of the prisoners were released in April, 1842. Although generally considered a failure, the expedition stimulated a renewal of interest in Texas within both the United States and Mexico.

TEXAS. *Early History.* The history of Spanish Texas divides itself into three periods: (1) discovery and exploration, 1519–1684; (2) Spanish and French colonization of and rivalry for, 1685–1762; and (3) reorganization, and Spanish-United States competition for, 1762–1821.

The period of discovery and exploration was initiated by Alonso de Pineda, who, in 1519, explored for Spain the entire coast of the Mexican Gulf from Florida to Mexico. A period of active exploration followed the first glimpses of the Texas coast by Pineda. The southern and western sections of the state were traversed by such well-known explorers as Cabeza de Vaca (1528–36); Coronado (1541); Espejo (1583); Castaño de Sosa (1590); Oñate (1601); Martín and Castillo (1650); Guadalajara (1654); and Domínguez and López (1684). In East Texas the famous DeSoto expedition explored probably as far west as the Brazos River in 1542.

The period in which Spain's interest in Texas was undisputed and merely incidental ended about 1684. The next year Spain's title to Texas was formally disputed for the first time by a rival aggressor, France. The ill-fated French expedition under LaSalle to the Lavaca Bay region brought about the explorations of Alonso de León (1688–90) from the present Eagle Pass region, northeastward, by way of Lavaca Bay, to the region east of the Trinity, and also to the temporary Spanish occupation of East Texas between 1690 and 1693. Renewed aggressions of the French in Louisiana after 1712 stimulated the Spaniards to establish by 1721 six missions and two *presidios* between the Trinity and Red Rivers; three missions and one *presidio*, save for a two-year period (1719–21), remained there continuously until after 1762. From 1722 until 1773 the capital of Spanish Texas was at Los Adaes, fifteen miles west of the French post of Natchitoches on the Red River. To serve chiefly as a stopping place from Coahuila to East Texas, San Antonio was founded in 1718, and within less than two decades it had become the principal Spanish settlement in the province. To effect better control over outlying Indian tribes and to consolidate their opposition against Indian allies of the French, temporary Spanish missions and *presidios* were established among the Tonkawas of central Texas (1746–55) and among the Apaches on the San Saba River, beginning in 1757. In southeast Texas, chiefly in order to check aggressions of French traders along the Gulf coast, a mission and a *presidio* were maintained for a few years near the mouth of the Trinity River, beginning in 1756. Present Texas south of the Nueces River was never a part of Spanish Texas.

By the Treaty of Fontainebleau with France in 1762 Spain acquired western Louisiana. As a result, Spain was relieved of problems of frontier defense in the Texas-Louisiana sector. Accordingly, in 1773 the remaining three missions and one *presidio* and several hundred colonists between the Trinity and Red Rivers were withdrawn, and the capital of Spanish Texas was removed to San Antonio. This abandonment proved to be temporary, for by 1790 most of the evicted settlers had returned to their former homes, and Nacogdoches had been established as the chief Spanish center in East Texas.

Western Louisiana, with indefinite boundaries, was receded by Spain to France in 1800 and three years later it was sold, with the same indefinite boundaries, to the United States. A diplomatic dispute between the United States and Spain at once arose concerning, in part, the western limits of the Louisiana purchase. President Jefferson, as early as 1804, claimed that Louisiana, as purchased by the United States, extended to the Rio Grande; and Spain, on the basis of the occupation and administration of Texas as a separate province since 1721, denied that Louisiana had ever extended farther west than Natchitoches. Threatened hostilities were averted between the two nations in 1806 by the extra-regular Neutral Ground Agreement. By this agreement—reached by United States and Spanish military commanders—Americans and Spaniards were to refrain from exercising jurisdiction in the territory between the Sabine River and the Arroyo Hondo, a small stream a few miles west of Natchitoches. Thirteen years later—on the basis of incontrovertible evidence submitted by Spain in the form of a masterful argumentative proof of Spain's title to Texas that had been drafted some years earlier by Father José Antonio Pichardo—the western boundary of Louisiana was formally agreed upon by Spain and the United States. This treaty, which was ratified in 1821, had the effect of fixing the eastern and northern boundaries of the Spanish province of Texas along the Sabine from its mouth to the 32nd parallel, thence north to the Red River, along that river to the 100th meridian, thence north to the Arkansas River and along it to its source, thence north to the 42nd parallel, N. Lat., and west on that parallel to a point due north of the source of the Rio Grande.

Texas Revolution resulted from complex social, political and economic incompatibilities between the Mexican government and the Anglo-American colonists introduced under Mexican federal and state colonization laws. From 1832 to 1835 there was a more or less active rivalry in Texas between a small group of impatient malcontents and the great mass of the settlers who were content to wait awhile in the hope that time would quiet Mexican disorders and bring them ever-increasing measures of local autonomy. The confidence of the pacifists was shaken by Santa Anna's violent revision of the federal constitution to fit the forms of his dictatorship, and was wholly undone by his evident determination to garrison Texas strongly with federal troops.

Though there had been armed conflicts during 1832, the first clash of the final revolution occurred at Gonzales on Oct. 2, 1835. A few days later the Texans captured Goliad with valuable supplies; and in December the strong Mexican force at San Antonio surrendered. In the meantime, Santa Anna was preparing for an overwhelming invasion. Toward the end of February, 1836, the main column, commanded by Santa Anna in person, began to concentrate around San Antonio, where a Texan force held the Alamo. While a strong force commanded by Gen. José Urrea marched along the coast, Santa Anna took the Alamo by assault on March 6, and put to death all defenders. William B. Travis, James Bowie and David Crockett perished here with 180 followers. Urrea "mopped up" several detachments in the coastal area, and on March 19 captured a force of roughly 400 men near Goliad, commanded by J. W. Fannin. A week later these men, except a few who escaped or were spared by individual intervention, were executed by order of Santa Anna.

Fannin's men and most of those who died in the Alamo were recent volunteers from the United States. During March and April, however, a considerable force of old settlers joined Gen. Sam Houston, as he retreated across Texas from Gonzales to the Brazos River. Leaving Houston encamped on the Brazos, Santa Anna rashly crossed the river, with a small division, lower down and marched rapidly to capture the Texan provisional government at Harrisburg. The government escaped to Galveston Island. Santa Anna pursued to the bay shore and on his return found Houston blocking his way at San Jacinto. There the decisive battle was fought on April 21, 1836. Santa Anna was captured, ordered his main army to evacuate Texas, and promised to use his influence to obtain recognition of Texan independence.

The "Consultation" of the provisional government had declared on Nov. 7, 1835, that the Texans were in arms to protect the republican constitution of Mexico. The incidents of the war and failure of Mexican liberals to co-operate with Texas caused a new convention to declare the independence of Texas on March 2, 1836. *De facto* independence was established by Houston's fortunate victory at San Jacinto.

Republic of Texas (1836–46) was created during the Texas Revolution by the convention of March, 1836, which declared independence from Mexico, drafted a constitution, and set up a provisional government. With the battle of San Jacinto, independence became an established fact, and in October, 1836, the provisional government was superseded by

the duly elected constitutional authorities, with Sam Houston as president. Houston's administration devoted its attention largely to problems of insuring economic and political stability, of establishing peaceful relations with Indian tribes, and of obtaining recognition from the United States, with hopes for immediate annexation.

Mirabeau B. Lamar succeeded Houston in 1838 and launched a positive foreign policy with a view to laying a basis for permanent independence. Discussion of annexation was stopped; diplomatic relations were established with France and England; attempts were made to negotiate with Mexico; a program of commercial expansion was undertaken; and efforts were made to strengthen the army and navy. In domestic affairs, aggressive warfare was waged against the Indians; plans were made for developing the natural resources of the country; a new land policy was formulated; the basis was laid for a system of public education; and futile attempts were made to establish a sound financial organization.

Returning to the presidency in 1841, Houston found expenses running far ahead of receipts, treasury notes depreciated to about fifteen cents on the dollar, and the public debt increased to about $8,000,000. He inaugurated a drastic program of retrenchment, in spite of renewed threats from Mexico, and in spite of sectional conflict between East and West Texas over such questions as frontier defense and the location of the capital. In foreign affairs, his interest was centered primarily in reopening the question of annexation. By using England and France as intermediaries between Texas and Mexico he probably contributed toward hastening favorable action in the United States. As a result, Anson Jones, who succeeded him in 1844, was able to present to the Texans a choice between annexation on the terms of the Joint Resolution and continued independence acknowledged by Mexico. With the acceptance of the annexation offer in the summer of 1845 and the installation of state officials in February, 1846, the transition of Texas from a frontier Mexican province to a state of the American Union was completed.

Annexation. By the Adams-Onís Treaty of 1819–21 the United States ceded a legally plausible but historically feeble claim to the territory of Texas as a part of the Louisiana Purchase. John Quincy Adams, while President, endeavored to obtain from Mexico, which had succeeded Spain in the sovereignty of Texas, a readjustment of the boundary in such a way as to give the United States all of the present State of Texas. Jackson, without success, continued these efforts throughout his two administrations. The Texas Revolution gave the problem a new turn.

In September, 1836, the Texans voted almost unanimously in favor of annexation to the United States. Congress expressed its readiness to recognize the independence of Texas, and one of Jackson's last official acts was to name a *chargé d'affaires* to Texas, but annexation was another matter. Possibilities of international complications and the violent opposition of the free states to the further extension of slave territory were obstacles not easily overcome. Van Buren definitely declined to consider a Texan proffer of annexation in August, 1837, and the subject dropped from public discussion until 1842. Then it was quickened by fear of English designs to control Texas.

The movement which led finally to annexation was inaugurated by President Tyler in the autumn of 1843. In April, 1844, he submitted to the Senate a treaty that proposed to annex Texas as a territory. This, for reasons hard to determine, the Senate rejected in June. In the meantime, the Democratic National Convention had nominated James K. Polk and pledged the party to the immediate "re-annexation" of Texas. The Democrats won the election in November, and Congress, with little opposition, passed a joint resolution authorizing the President: (1) to offer Texas annexation as a state; or (2) to conclude with Texas a new annexation treaty. Tyler acted upon the first alternative (March 1, 1845); Polk concurred and carried the negotiations with Texas to a successful conclusion. The Texan constitution was accepted by Congress, and Texas was admitted to the Union on Dec. 29, 1845. Recognition of the rising commercial importance of Texas and apprehension growing out of England's friendly intervention in behalf of Texas with Mexico were influential in weakening Northern antagonism to southward expansion.

State of Texas (1845 f.). The immense size of the state caused the insertion of a provision in the annexation resolution permitting the state to divide itself into as many as five states. From time to time, either because of hostility between sections or because of political ambition to create more offices, an issue has been made of the subdivision question. No reduction of the state has occurred, however, except that in the Compromise of 1850 Texas was to sell to the United States its lands north of latitude 36° 30′ and that part of the present New Mexico lying east of the Rio Grande. With the money received Texas paid its public debts, thus satisfying the chief purpose for which it had been permitted by the annexation resolution to retain its public lands. Even after this reduction, however, Texas had more than 100,-000,000 acres of public domain. A little of this was sold, some was given to soldiers, a great deal was granted to early railroads, to educational institutions, for the erection of public buildings, and the remainder was set aside as a permanent endowment for public schools. Both the University of Texas and the public school system are now benefiting from the discovery of oil on their lands.

Since the leading men of property in the state supported slavery and states' rights, Texas became involved in the secession movement of 1860. In spite of Gov. Sam Houston's efforts to prevent it, Texas seceded and on March 2, 1861, formally joined the Confederacy. Houston was forced from office and Lt. Gov. Edward Clark succeeded him. Texas furnished to the Confederacy a number of soldiers estimated at from 50,000 to 65,000, most notable of whom were "Terry's Texas Rangers." Valuable supplies were sent from the state, and through it from Mexico, to the Confederate armies in the southeast. Texas suffered little from military engagements on its own soil. Galveston, Brownsville and Matagorda were taken by Federals, but Galveston was recaptured by a Confederate force in a somewhat spectacular engagement. More famous was the repulse of a Federal Army of 5000 men and the capture of 350 prisoners by Lt. Dick Dowling and his 47 men at Sabine Pass.

Reconstruction began favorably for Texas. Under President Johnson's "ten per cent" plan, A. J. Hamilton, a citizen of Texas formerly honored with high offices, was appointed temporary governor, a new constitution was adopted in 1866, and in the following election a government of Texans headed by Gov. J. W. Throckmorton was chosen. Texas was returning to prosperity and normal order. But the congressional Reconstruction Act of 1867 brought an end to the "loyal" white man's government and replaced it with one of the "carpetbag" variety. E. M. Pease was appointed to succeed Gov. Throckmorton, the radical constitution of 1869 was substituted for the constitution of 1866, and in 1870 the Republican party elected the state officers headed by Gov. E. J. Davis. As usual in other Southern state governments of that time, there were despotism, extravagance, mounting state debt and increased taxation. In 1872 the Democrats won a majority in the legislature, and in 1874 they forced the unwilling Davis from office and inaugurated a Texan governor, Richard Coke. With cotton, cattle and lumber aided by an expansion of railroads, Texas began to recover from the blight of reconstruction. A new constitution was enacted in 1876.

TEXAS RANGERS. As early as 1826 Texas colonists had from "20 to 30 Rangers in service" against Indians. For years the Texas Rangers were loosely and impermanently organized minutemen. About 1840, while Texas was a republic, a definite corps with *esprit* developed under Jack Hays and other captains. It ranged out mostly from San Antonio against marauding Indians and Mexicans and made the six-shooter the weapon of the horseback West. During the Mexican War the Rangers achieved fame. In the 1870's they reached their zenith of usefulness in bringing law and order along the Rio Grande border, holding back the wild Indians across a frontier stretching from Brownsville to the northern edge of the Staked Plains, and clearing horse thieves, feudists and bad men of all kinds—types that followed the Civil War and flourished during Reconstruction disorders—out of the country.

The Rangers have never been uniformed, the only standardized features of their dress being six-shooter and saddle gun. For range men—expert trailers, tireless riders—a slicker and saddle blanket afforded bedding and a "Spanish dinner" (which means taking up the belt a hole) nourishment for more riding. They have never drilled, notched a gun, or learned to salute officers. Their mobility is extraordinary. Their quiet reserve has become a proverb. They have always been picked men.

THAMES, BATTLE OF THE (Oct. 5, 1813). The surrender of Detroit and Michigan Territory in August, 1812, gave the British control of practically all the region tributary to the Upper Lakes. Thereafter the American objective was to recover, the British to retain, Detroit and the Northwest; the two outstanding leaders were Gen. Procter (Br.) at Detroit and Amherstburg, and Gen. William Henry Harrison (Amer.). Harrison established Fort Meigs (above Toledo) as an advanced base, which Procter, carrying the war to the Americans, twice attacked (April-May and July, 1813). Meanwhile Perry built at Erie the fleet which on Sept. 10 won the Battle of Lake Erie. Loss of naval control rendered Procter's position untenable, and a grim race ensued, Procter seeking to retire to Lake Ontario, while Harrison, convoyed by Perry's fleet, hotly pursued, in the hope of destroying him.

The route of the armies along Lake St. Clair and the Thames River is closely paralleled by the modern highway from Windsor to Hamilton. The race ended when Procter was brought to bay a few miles east of Thamesville. Harrison's strength was overwhelming and there could be but one issue to the battle. The weary Forty-first Regiment held the British left, while Tecumseh's Indians occupied the right. Col. Richard Mentor Johnson's mounted regiment charged the hostile line and quickly rode over the British left, which, caught between the cavalry behind and Harrison's infantry in front, promptly surrendered. The Indians fought until Tecumseh fell, when they melted into the forest. After ravaging the near-by Moravian Indian settlement, Harrison returned to Detroit, and his Kentucky levies to their homes. Lake Erie and the Thames restored the American dominance in the Northwest which Hull had lost in August, 1812. The glory won at the Thames proved a potent factor in the subsequent elevation of Harrison to the Presidency and of Johnson to the Vice-Presidency of the United States.

THANKSGIVING DAY. After the first harvest of the Massachusetts colonists, Gov. Bradford appointed a day of thanksgiving and prayer. Another in 1623 celebrated a fall of rain after a drought. After 1630 an annual thanksgiving came to be observed after harvest, and other New England colonies took up the practice in desultory fashion. During the Revolutionary War the Continental Congress recommended days of thanksgiving, and decreed a special one in 1784 for the return of peace. President Washington proclaimed one in 1789, at the setting up of the new government, and another in 1795 for general benefits. President Madison in 1815 again asked the nation to give thanks for peace. By 1830 New York had adopted the day as an annual custom, and other Northern states followed its lead. In the South the custom did not appear until 1855, when it was adopted by Virginia, and thereafter by the other Southern states. President Lincoln in 1864 began the practice of a national proclamation, fixing the fourth Thursday (later it came to be regularly the last Thursday) in November, though he had no power to order a holiday in the various states. In 1939 President Franklin D. Roosevelt upset the precedent of several decades' standing by proclaiming Nov. 23. Many governors refused to accept this date, and in their states Nov. 30 was the accepted festival, though a few actually authorized the celebration of both dates.

THEATER. Throughout the early colonies, social disinterest and religious prejudice combined to delay theater building and to oppose any form of dramatic activity. Such was the unyielding Puritan ban on play acting in northern settlements, the scarcity of experienced theater workers, the lack of cultural interest in drama and its literature, and still more restrictive, the widespread official insistence that play acting and attendance interfered dangerously with colonizing labor. Even in Virginia, legal action was taken in 1665 against a group of youths who had written and acted a play.

There was a strong desire, however, among seamen aboard British merchantmen and gunboats moored for long periods in coastal harbors, for theater entertainment such as they enjoyed in England on shore-leave. It is believed that their eagerness was the chief reason for the establishment in 1736 of the earliest enduring playhouse, the Dock Street, in Charleston, S. C. It opened with a production of Otway's *Orphan* by a British troupe of professional actors who had performed the previous year in crudely inadequate quarters.

Soon afterwards other playhouses were established under similar conditions: the East Baltimore Street Theater in Baltimore and a still earlier one—the first actual theater structure in any colony—built in Williamsburg, Va., in 1716, but which for lack of patronage was soon afterwards converted into the Town Hall.

During the Revolution, while British ships were blockading the coastal harbors, acting was in great

941

demand—even in Puritan Boston. In 1775–76, a play, *The Blockade of Boston,* by General Burgoyne, was staged there in the imposing new Federal Street Theater, which in 1749 had replaced the city's ill-suited New Exhibition Room, till then the city's only playhouse. But Burgoyne's play was ironically interrupted by the attack that ended the British occupation of city and harbor. As a result of a riot of ticket buyers the year following, Massachusetts prohibited further play acting, a ruling strictly enforced until 1792.

Theater development of a more normal kind gradually spread elsewhere. In 1690 Harvard students wrote and staged a play; and in 1702 students of William and Mary College in Williamsburg performed a "Pastoral Colloquy." The professionals Charles and Mary Stagg, for whose acting the Williamsburg Theater of 1716 was built, imported, as was often done in later years, a supporting cast of actors and painted scenery from London. Also in that same Virginia town, a famous British family of actors, the Hallams, who were the first to bring to America a supporting cast of their own, began a tour throughout the colonies in 1752 with a production of *The Merchant of Venice,* staged in a new theater of their own built to replace the original theater that was then the Town Hall.

The first city to become a theater capital was Philadelphia, where plays were first presented in a sail loft over a warehouse. In 1749 the Chestnut Street Theater carefully reproduced the design and elegance of the Royal Theater of Bath, England. Also famous was the Southwark Theater with a talented acting company of its own.

Like other colonial theaters the Southwark was frequently host to leading stars from England, as when, in 1749, the management welcomed the Murray-Kean company following its brilliant engagement at Charleston's Dock Street Theater. The Southwark was also reputed for its staging of new American plays. It was a high honor for a young playwright to have his work acted there.

At the Southwark, the first full-length play of literary quality written by an American, *The Prince of Parthia,* by Thomas Godfrey, was produced in 1767, two years after the dramatist's death. The fact of its being the first such play produced in an American theater was due to coincidence, for another all-American play of a satirical nature, *The Disappointment,* by Col. Thomas Forrest, was already in production at the Southwark, but was withdrawn because it was found to be a caricature of certain Philadelphians.

At Philadelphia's Chestnut Street Theater the famous London tragedian, Thomas Abthorpe Cooper, appeared in *Macbeth* in 1796. Still more sensational was the appearance there of G. Frederick Cooke, whose Othello was unrivaled. More and more British stars had begun touring American theaters because

payment made them in America was already considerably higher than in established British playhouses.

In New York, unlike Philadelphia, dramatic enterprise encountered many hindrances. In 1699 Richard Hunter petitioned Lt. Gov. Nanfan for the right to stage plays, but with no apparent results. The following year professional acting is known to have begun in a remodeled room of a commercial building. In 1703–4 a newly arrived British actor, producer, and critic, Anthony Aston, together with a fellow actor, also a "fencing master" at London's Lincoln Inn, produced in New York a musical, *The Fool's Opera; or, The Taste of the Age.* Whether or not the said "fencing master's" influence was responsible, New York's governor in 1709 forbade all "play acting and prize-fighting." Not until 1732, it is believed, was normal theatrical production established in New York with the staging of Farquhar's *Recruiting Officer* by a visiting London company. On March 5, 1750, Thomas Kean and Walter Murray opened a season of acting in *Richard III,* staged in the old Nassau Street house and followed by more British repertory, including the *Beaux' Stratagem* and *Love for Love.*

Two years later the touring Hallams from Virginia took over this playhouse; it was so run down that they had a new one built, which they opened with Richard Steele's widely influential comedy of manners, *The Conscious Lovers,* a play of new "sentimentalism." In it their son Lewis made his debut as Archer, having to act in old and shabby scenery brought to America fifteen years before by his parents—play settings that could not be replaced, because scene painters were not yet to be found in America.

Most lastingly important of New York productions of the 18th century was the first American play on American social life of its time: Royall Tyler's *The Contrast,* first staged at the John Street Theater in 1787. Its performance was attended by George Washington, a drama enthusiast, who headed the subscription list to insure the play's publication.

At about this time there emerged William Dunlap (1766–1839), playwright, manager, scenic artist, and stage historian. His assistants in management were Lewis Hallam and Joy John Hodgkinson, the latter recently come from England. Dunlap's *History of the American Theater* pictured a group of play lovers who met after each new production to discuss its merits and determine what should be written as criticism in the press—an important custom unfortunately abandoned by later generations of newspaper critics.

Dunlap was also involved in the opening near City Hall of the new Park Theater (1798) that superseded the old John Street Theater, by then too small and shabby for the rapidly expanding theater life of New York. During the Park's first season,

Dunlap's most popular play, *André*, was presented there with his British actor friends, Cooper and Hodgkinson, in the leading roles.

The Park Theater continued under the management of Cooper and Steven Price from 1808 to 1815 as the city's most fashionable playhouse. When in the latter year Cooper withdrew, Price not only continued as its manager but, like Augustin Daly and Gilbert Miller of the 19th century, he also took over the management of a London theater, the Drury Lane.

During the early 19th century, audiences were attracted more by the actor's than by the playwright's art, and touring of acting companies extended from coast to coast. The earliest of these journeys to stir great interest started in 1815 by wagon from Albany to the headwaters of the Allegheny River, then continued by boat down that tributary and the Ohio. After a performance in Pittsburgh, the actors were carted overland to Frankfort and Lexington, Ky., thence to Cincinnati, where they performed in that city's fifteen-year-old playhouse. Again by water, the company reached Natchez and New Orleans for a performance in that city's new French Theater.

Additional playhouses were soon to be opened: at Mobile (1824); St. Louis (1819); and Chicago, first in a two-story hotel (1837). A decade later a completely equipped theater was erected in Chicago. Finally a theater troupe reached San Francisco in January, 1850. By the end of that year four new theaters had been erected there.

With the rapid spread of railways and increase in ocean transport, theater touring became more prevalent. By the end of the century, centers like New York, Boston, Philadelphia, and Chicago were visited almost annually by foreign companies with carloads of scenery. Sir Henry Irving and Ellen Terry came with Shakespearean and Tennysonian repertory, Sir Johnston Forbes-Robertson with his colloquial delivery of Hamlet's lines that forecast the end of the forced declamation of earlier Shakespearean stars; from Paris, Sarah Bernhardt, Réjane, the Coquelins; and from Italy, greatest of them all, Eleanora Duse.

Great acting, rather than great playwriting had been the chief attraction of theater-goers during the 19th century. Still familiar are the names of John Howard Payne (1791–1852), Edwin Forrest (1806–72), Edwin Booth (1833–93), Charlotte Cushman (1816–72), Joseph Jefferson (1829–1905), E. L. Davenport (1816–77), his daughter Fanny (1850–95), and Minnie Maddern Fiske (1865–1932).

During the present century American playwrights have come more conspicuously to the fore in Europe as well as in the United States. Among the more important have been: Eugene O'Neill, Paul Green, Tennessee Williams, William Saroyan, Maxwell Anderson, and Arthur Miller. Their interest and talents have been inspired, at least indirectly, by two widespread American theater developments: courses in playwriting in colleges and universities and the rapidly multiplying "little theaters," in which some young writers like Saroyan have made their first contacts with the high standards of "naturalistic" or poetically symbolic and "expressionistic" dramaturgy and stagecraft of this century.

From such unprofessional theater experience was created in 1919 New York's most influential theater organization, The Theater Guild, which in its own playhouse or in others has brought before the public plays superbly staged, representing some of the most advanced theater creations of this century, both European and American.

THEOCRACY IN NEW ENGLAND is the term usually applied to the political regime set up by the founders of Massachusetts Bay and New Haven colonies. It is a correct description to the extent that the leaders deliberately intended to create a "Bible Commonwealth," a society where the fundamental law would be the revealed Word of God, and God regarded as the supreme legislator. Thus John Winthrop announced the program before the settlement, "For the worke wee haue in hand, it is by a mutuall consent . . . to seeke out a place of Cohabitation and Consorteshipp vnder a due forme of Government both ciuill and ecclesiasticall," the "due forme" being that enacted in the Bible. John Cotton later argued that the New England colonies, having a clear field before them, were duty-bound to erect a "Theocracy . . . as the best forme of government in the commonwealth, as well as in the Church." Consequently the political theory assumed that the colonies were based upon the Bible and that all specific laws must be required to show Biblical warrant.

In a still more fundamental sense, the governments of the two colonies were true theocracies in that all society was held to be ordained by God as a check upon the impulses of depraved human nature, and therefore that all politics should ideally be directed to the ends prescribed by God. Hence, John Winthrop explained in 1645, after men have entered a body politic they thereafter have freedom not to do what is good in their own eyes, but only that "which is good, just and honest," only that, in other words, which God demands. The purpose of the state was universally agreed among the first settlers to be the enforcement, by all possible external means, of the observance of God's laws on the part of every member of the society.

On the other hand, the term "theocracy" is a misnomer if it is taken, as it often is, to mean that the ministers directly ruled the colonies. It was well recognized that the Bible defined a distinct sphere for the civil government, and the secular authorities in both colonies were jealous of any clerical invasion of their province. The ministers did indeed possess great influence; in doubtful cases or at times of crisis their opinion was asked, though it was not always followed exactly as they desired.

THIRD PARTIES. The vast majority of American voters have supported one or the other of two great political parties throughout most of the period since the adoption of the Constitution. Since 1825, however, there have been many voters, in the aggregate, who have been temporarily dissatisfied with the principles, policies or leadership of the two major parties, and accordingly have started independent, or "third party," movements. The earliest of our third parties was the Anti-Masonic party, which arose suddenly in 1826, and disappeared within a decade. Then came the Liberty party about 1840, and the Free Soil party in 1848, soon to be followed by the Native American or Know-Nothing party of 1852–56. In 1854–56 the present Republican party was first organized as a third party. The campaign of 1872 saw the birth of the short-lived Labor Reform party, the forerunner of the Independent or Greenback party of 1876–84, and of the Prohibition party, the longest-lived of all our third parties if we except the Republican party. Of much greater importance than any of these was the People's or Populist party, which polled two million votes in the presidential election of 1892, only to disintegrate after its partial coalition with the Democrats in 1896. The National Progressive party, organized in 1912, likewise disappeared when Theodore Roosevelt returned to the Republican party in 1916. The Socialist party, organized about 1897, survived many internal schisms to become an apparently permanent feature of the political landscape. The LaFollette Progressives of 1924 were hardly an organization, since they entered no local candidates. The same applies to the Wallace Progressives and to the States' Rights Democrats, or "Dixiecrats," of 1948. The latter, however, carried four Southern states for J. Strom Thurmond of South Carolina.

Of considerably less significance have been the Constitutional Union party of 1860; the Liberal Republicans of 1872; the Anti-Monopoly, Union Labor, and United Labor parties, 1884–88; the Socialist Labor party, 1892–1944; the Union (Lemke) party of 1936; and the Communist party from 1928 until it was outlawed. Other short-lived parties have appeared from time to time in state and local politics.

Although minor parties polled enough votes in pivotal states to affect the result of presidential elections in 1844, 1848, 1884 and 1912, no third party has risen to a commanding position in national politics since the Republican victory of 1860. In fact, there have been only three presidential elections since that year in which third parties together have polled more than 10% of the popular vote: the Populists in 1892; the National Progressives in 1912;

and the LaFollette Progressives in 1924. In 1948 the combined third parties polled only 5.75% of the total vote. At most presidential elections since 1860, not one vote in twenty has been cast for the candidates of all minor parties together; they have elected very few members of Congress; and, except in 1892, 1912, 1924 and 1948, have failed to carry any of the states.

THIRD-TERM DOCTRINE. The Convention of 1787 did not place in the Constitution any provision with regard to the eligibility of the President for re-election. Washington declined a third term, although in his Farewell Address he based this refusal on personal reasons only. Thomas Jefferson likewise refused a third term in 1808. His successors, James Madison and James Monroe, served for two terms each. Thus there grew up a custom of only two terms by a sort of tacit consent. When Andrew Jackson was completing his second term, in 1836, there was a strong movement for a third term, but he positively refused. He himself favored a constitutional amendment which would limit the President to a single term.

In December, 1875, when President Grant showed signs of wishing a third term, the House of Representatives resolved by a vote of 234 to 18 that a third term was "unwise, unpatriotic, and fraught with peril to our free institutions." Again in 1928, after President Coolidge's equivocal notice that "he did not choose to run," the Senate by a vote of 56 to 26 condemned a third term in nearly the same words. On the other hand Theodore Roosevelt attracted considerable popular support when he ran for the Presidency in 1912, although his success would have given him, in effect, three almost complete (although not successive) terms in office.

The long tradition opposing a third term notwithstanding, Franklin D. Roosevelt was comfortably elected for the third time in 1940, and for the fourth time in 1944. In 1940 the third term was a major issue—perhaps the leading issue—of the campaign, and the result showed that a majority of Americans, in this as in other matters, were willing to sacrifice custom to what they regarded as the exigencies of the moment. There is no question that the war in Europe created an atmosphere favorable to Roosevelt's candidacy, since it enabled his supporters to argue that in times of international crisis continuity of foreign policy was imperative.

In the full flood of reaction against the New Deal, Congress in 1947 passed the so-called Bricker Amendment, limiting the President to two terms in office. In 1951, having been ratified by three fourths of the states, this provision became the Twenty-second Amendment to the Constitution. The amendment was framed so as to exclude President Truman from its provisions.

The chief objections raised by opponents of the amendment are not only that it may at any time deprive the country, rather arbitrarily, of the services of an outstanding man, but that by making mandatory the retirement of a President after his second term, it prematurely weakens his power as a party leader.

THRESHING MACHINE. The credit for developing a complete thresher, one combining in a single unit machinery for accomplishing all three processes, goes to Andrew Meikle of Scotland, who, in 1788, patented a thresher, in 1789 added a separator, and in 1800, a fanning mill.

Such a machine as this could not be operated by hand. Sometimes water power could be used, but this sacrificed essential mobility. Until the application of the steam engine in farming operations, the only solution was the use of horse power. At first stationary and later portable treadmills and capstan-like sweeps were manufactured.

Because such machines were too expensive for the ordinary farmer, two developments are to be noted. The cheap hand-driven fanning mill became a part of the standard equipment of most farmers. Then, in the early 1820's, Jacob Pope put on the market a cheap hand-operated thresher; in the next decade scores of such machines were patented and sold.

In the 1840's we have the real advance in thresher making. Wheeler and Melick developed a small, cheap thresher-separator, and in 1844 Jerome I. Case began to turn out a similar machine in Racine, Wis. The first American machine to combine the three operations, threshing, separating and cleaning, was built by John and Hiram Pitts of Winthrop, Maine. In 1840 John had established a factory at Albany, N. Y., which was later moved to Buffalo. Hiram Pitts in 1847 began manufacturing threshers in Alton, Ill., moving to Chicago in 1851. Like the plow and the harvester, the manufacture of the thresher tended to follow the extension of the wheat-growing area into the Northwest. By the 1860's most of the threshers had a cleaning attachment, and by the 1880's the old hand-driven fanning mill was a museum piece.

The thresher was too expensive for the average farmer to own. The owner of such a machine with its portable "power" moved from farm to farm during the threshing season. Sometimes such an entrepreneur supplied the threshing crew, but more often the "hands" were the farmers in the neighborhood formed into a simple co-operative group.

Up to the late 1870's the horse continued to be the source of power. Then, in the Far West, where wheat growing was carried on, on a large scale, the steam tractor came into general use. Here too the thresher was attached to the harvester, making a single unit, the "combine." It was not until the coming of the cheap portable gas engine, however, that the old "horse power" finally disappeared from most American farms.

TICONDEROGA, CAPTURE OF (1775). The suggestion for reducing this British post has at various times been credited to Will Gilliland, John Brown of Pittsfield, Ethan Allen and Benedict Arnold. The immediate object of the attack was not only to take the dilapidated fort, but also to obtain cannon for the siege of Boston. The Hartford Committee of Correspondence raised more than fifty men and £300 and urged the Green Mountain Boys to take part in the expedition. It was decided that Ethan Allen should command, and the rendezvous was set for Hand's Cove on the eastern shore of Lake Champlain. Meanwhile, Col. Benedict Arnold had been commissioned by the Massachusetts Committee of Safety to raise 400 men, and with a single servant he arrived at Hand's Cove in time to claim the command. When the Green Mountain Boys refused to participate in the expedition without their own officers, it was agreed that Allen and Arnold should enter the fort side by side at the head of the column. Early in the morning of May 10, Allen, Arnold and 83 men crossed the lake in two boats. After a harangue by Allen, the expedition passed through the ruined walls and without bloodshed quickly subdued the sleepy garrison, consisting of Capt. Delaplace, Lt. Feltham, and 43 men.

The ensuing plan of Congress to abandon Crown Point and Ticonderoga aroused so much opposition in New England and New York that it was finally dropped. Not until the winter of 1775–76 were the Ticonderoga cannon removed to Cambridge. Col. Henry Knox, a young artillery officer of twenty-four, laid the plans for transporting the ordnance. Knox arrived at Ticonderoga on Dec. 5, 1775, and arranged to move 14 mortars and coehorns, 2 howitzers and 43 cannon, weighing a total of 119,900 pounds. The guns were taken in groups by water to Fort George at the southern end of Lake George. On sleds drawn by oxen and horses, they progressed past Fort Edward, Saratoga, Albany and Kinderhook to Claverack. Their route then turned east through the mountains to Springfield, Worcester and Cambridge. Citizens along the way were impressed by the great guns, and one mortar known as the "old sow" was fired off several times for the people to hear its deep roar. By Jan. 24, 1776, the first section of the artillery train was in Cambridge, and Washington was enabled to force the British from Boston.

TIDELANDS are the off-shore limits of the ocean, navigable streams and bays. Controversy with respect to navigable streams and bays is usually concerned with the exact boundary location, whether at mean high tide, at low tide, etc.

Where the extension of boundary limits into the ocean from the shore line is involved the case becomes important, especially where valuable so-called mineral rights, usually oil and gas, are concerned. The first producing off-shore oil well was completed in 1938 in shallow water one mile off the Louisiana coast; the second was not brought in until 1947, at a point eleven miles out to sea off Terrebonne Parish, La. A major controversy, extending over a period of years, was thus generated. It was finally decided, May 31, 1960, when the U. S. Supreme Court handed down a ruling fixing the off-shore boundary limits of the five states bordering on the Gulf of Mexico, namely, Florida, Alabama, Mississippi, Louisiana and Texas. The court ruled that Mississippi, Alabama and Louisiana owned the rights to the off-shore submerged lands for a distance of 3½ miles from their coast-line boundaries; Texas and Florida rights were ruled as extending three leagues, or approximately 10½ miles, from their coast-line boundaries. The more extended ruling as to Texas and Florida was based on boundary provisions of the state constitutions. In the case of Texas, the claim to special boundary limits was recognized by Congress in the Treaty of Guadalupe-Hidalgo of 1848 which ended the war with Mexico. The ruling as to Florida was based on congressional approval when the state was received back into the Union, June 25, 1868, after the Civil War.

The controversy grew out of the "ill-drawn" Submerged Lands Act of 1953, designed to overturn decisions of the Supreme Court in 1947 and 1950, which held that the Federal Government had "paramount rights" in all off-shore lands. At stake were valuable reserves of crude oil and gas lying under the water and extending to the outer edge of the continental shelf. To Florida, Alabama and Mississippi, the ruling is presently meaningless because, so far as developed, no such resources exist. In relation to Louisiana and Texas, a large potential of revenue is involved, particularly to Louisiana. It is estimated that some 15 billion barrels of oil are available in the Gulf off-shore, nearly 50% of proved reserves for the whole of the United States, and that 10 billion barrels are in the Louisiana off-shore area. Nearly 1600 producing off-shore wells are in the disputed Louisiana zone lying between the 3½ mile- and 10½-mile limit. Royalties derived from these Louisiana wells, as well as from the few in the similar Texas area, were kept in escrow. Unless the Supreme Court ruling is overturned by an act of Congress these will go to the Federal Government, as will any future royalties.

The coastal boundary as defined by the so-called Chapman Line was accepted by those concerned as the shore line from which the limits are to be measured. Clarification of the shore line may take years. The then Secretary of the Interior Oscar Chapman, who drew the line in 1956, did so without reference to "geographical realities."

TIDEWATER is a term commonly used in American history to designate that part of the Atlantic coastal plain lying east of the points in rivers reached by oceanic tides. This region, first occupied by settlers from the Old World, became slowly the habitat of comparative wealth. Merchants and shippers in the towns, and planters growing tobacco, rice, indigo and cotton, dominated the tidewater population. Since in New England the tidewater coastal area is so narrow the terminology is more applicable elsewhere, particularly in the Middle Atlantic and South Atlantic regions of the English colonies and the later states of the Federal Union. First on the ground and earlier established economically, socially and politically, the inhabitants of the tidewater regions secured control of the government. Almost inevitably they used the machinery of government for their own benefit, and in accordance with their traditions and ideals, and resisted any effort to weaken their control. But the later population, composed largely of small farmers, which moved beyond into the Piedmont region, found this tidewater domination of government both unfair and injurious. A serious and long-continued sectional conflict resulted.

TILLMANISM, a South Carolina aspect of the agrarian movement, was inaugurated by Benjamin R. Tillman in 1885 by a series of letters to the Charleston *News and Courier* vividly expressing the grievances of the white rural population against the dominant forces of the post-Reconstruction period in that strongly Southern commonwealth. This farmer-agitator accused the merchants of extortionate charges for advances to farmers; the oligarchy under Wade Hampton of greed and of failure to be progressive; the state college of improper expenditure of Federal appropriations for agricultural education; and the Negro of trying to recover his Reconstruction privileges. He set the country against the town; the upcountry against Charleston; the farmer against the lawyer and the businessman; and the common man against the aristocrat. His formula for success was effective appeal to the prejudices of the majority against the minority. Yet he possessed constructive notions, notably the demand for an agricultural college. In 1890, after arousing unparalleled enthusiasm for his person and measures by a canvass of the state, Tillman won complete control of the state government. Notable results followed. Officeholders were supplanted by Tillman partisans; Negro suffrage was destroyed and the white masses, through a wider application of primary elections, gained greater political power; colleges were founded for the vocational education of white boys and girls; corporations were forced to pay a greater share of taxation; and the Dispensary, a state liquor monopoly, was established. Tillman's elevation to the U. S. Senate in 1895 was followed by an abatement of the partisan and reformist zeal of his movement and by a gradual revival of the forces he had fought. But Tillmanism was not without permanent results. Within definite limitations it gave a progressive tone to events in an otherwise reactionary commonwealth, and it gave a new life to white democracy. It also lowered the quality of the public service, made reactionary attitudes toward the Negro a permanent policy, and made the Blease movement possible.

TIME. In our early history, a community's time was dictated by a town clock in a church steeple or public building, which was set as nearly as possible by the sun. In later years it might follow the time of the railroad running through the town. But among the railroads of the country there were no less than 75 systems of time! The resulting confusion became so great that the American Meteorological Society appointed a committee in 1879 to study the subject —with the result that Congress in 1882 authorized the President to call an international conference to select a common prime meridian for reckoning longitude and regulating time throughout the world. Delegates from 26 countries met in Washington on Oct. 1, 1884, but could not agree on a prime meridian, though most of them favored that of Greenwich, England. But just before this conference met, the United States and Canada had agreed upon a series of time zones in multiples of 15° corresponding to one hour of sun time difference. For the United States, these were Eastern, centered roughly on 75° west of Greenwich, Central (90° west), Mountain (105°) and Pacific (120°). For several years, many communities still clung to sun time, and often the two systems were found functioning in the same area; but gradually standard time prevailed. (*See also* Daylight Saving.)

TINTYPE, a distinctively American style of photograph, made by the wet process on black japanned metal, was patented by Hamilton L. Smith of Gambier, Ohio, in 1856. Originally introduced as the *melainotype* and the *ferrotype*, it is now universally called by the popular term tintype. Small tintype medals of the presidential candidates widely distributed in the campaign of 1860 first brought national recognition, but the tremendous popularity of the tintype occurred during the Civil War. Small tintypes in oval cutout mounts, known as "gems," have been made in prodigious numbers by itinerant photographers. They are still produced by modern materials.

TIPPECANOE, BATTLE OF (Nov. 7, 1811). The opposition of Tecumseh to the steady advance of the white race in the Northwest produced a situation which could be resolved only by a test of military might. The crisis came in the summer of 1811, when the Indian leader, after renewing his demands upon Gov. Harrison at Vincennes, departed to rally the tribes of the Southwest to the confederacy he was organizing. Urged on by the frantic frontier settlers, Harrison determined to anticipate Tecumseh's blow by striking first, and the Tippecanoe campaign followed.

The Indian capital was on Tippecanoe Creek, 150 miles north of Vincennes, and Harrison began his northward advance on Sept. 26, with an army of 1000 soldiers, equal in quality, probably, to the best America could produce. Most of October was consumed in constructing Fort Harrison at Terre Haute, to serve as an advance base. On Oct. 29 the march was resumed, and a week later the army was within striking distance of Prophetstown. For several miles it advanced in line of battle, with numerous warriors hovering on its front and flanks; then, with the town in sight, and immediate victory within his grasp, Harrison unaccountably yielded to belated appeals for a conference, and, turning aside, encamped on an elevated site a mile distant from the village. The camp site was like an inverted flatiron and the best the vicinity afforded. Although mutual promises were exchanged that no hostilities would be indulged before the morrow, the soldiers slept on their arms at their appointed stations, in readiness for instant action. Meanwhile the warriors, a mile away, were stirred to frenzy by the Prophet's appeals, and shortly before dawn (Nov. 7), without leaders and largely without a plan, they drove in Harrison's pickets and furiously stormed the still-sleeping camp. The soldiers sprang to action, and the battle raged, either hand-to-hand or at close range, until daylight came, when a series of charges drove the warriors from the immediate field. Following the action, Harrison visited and razed the Indian town, and then began the weary retreat to distant Fort Harrison.

Although Tippecanoe was popularly regarded as a great victory, Harrison's triumph was dearly bought and far from decisive. Under circumstances highly advantageous to himself he had struck an indecisive blow; with almost one fourth of his followers dead or wounded he retreated to Vincennes, where the army was disbanded or scattered, and the frontier became as defenseless as before the campaign. Since Tecumseh's plans were not yet matured, it suited his policy to make light of the Tippecanoe affair, yet it was obvious that the war must be continued to a conclusion, and equally obvious that if war between America and Great Britain should eventuate, the northwestern Indians would make common cause with the British. This came to pass the following summer, when the War of 1812 was declared.

"TIPPECANOE AND TYLER TOO!" was the campaign slogan of the Whigs in 1840, when William Henry Harrison, the hero of the battle of Tippecanoe, and John Tyler were their candidates for the Presidency and Vice-Presidency respectively. The party cry typified the emotional appeal of the Whig canvass. Deliberately avoiding issues, its supporters wore coonskin caps, built campaign log cabins in almost every town of consequence and freely dispensed hard cider to the voters, who were persuaded that Harrison had saved the country from untold Indian atrocities.

Few American political slogans have been such un-adulterated demagoguery.

TITHINGMEN were town officers of colonial New England, charged with the responsibility of getting out church attendance and maintaining decorous conduct on the Sabbath day. The symbol of office according to tradition was a wand tipped with feathers or a fox tail with which to awaken the drowsy during protracted sermons, while mischievous youngsters were rapped with the hard end.

TOBACCO, the most important export staple of the colonial period, has always held a major place in American economy.

Encouraged by the success of John Rolfe, who in 1612 began experimenting to develop a tobacco suitable for commerce, his fellow-Virginians adopted the leaf as their chief product and by 1627 annually produced about 500,000 pounds. From Virginia the culture of tobacco soon spread to Maryland and to North Carolina. Such was the energy applied to the crop that on the eve of the Revolution the yearly exports averaged about 100,000,000 pounds. Most of the tobacco eventually reached the continent, though as an "enumerated article" under the mercantile system it had to be sent first to Great Britain. For the successful marketing of tobacco there evolved in Virginia, and later in Maryland and in North Carolina, inspection systems to guarantee the quality of the exported staple. The problem of controlled quantity was less easily solved, and excessive crops periodically drove the price to profitless levels. Many planters, overestimating the income to be derived from their produce, became hopelessly indebted to British merchants.

During the American Revolution the tobacco industry suffered an inevitable setback. There was temporary recovery about 1790, but international trade difficulties, a new demand for wheat and the rivalry of cotton postponed a permanent revival until about 1820, when the production of tobacco regained its old levels.

Soon after the War of 1812 tobacco culture expanded into the Mississippi Valley; especially noteworthy were the crops of Kentucky, Tennessee, Ohio and Missouri. By the early 1840's the planters in those states were raising more tobacco than their brethren east of the Alleghenies, and, with a product grown on virgin soil, were displacing in foreign markets the leaf of the older section. The planters of the Atlantic seaboard were forced to improve their technique of production and sale. Fortunately for them they found a home market in the factories of the Virginia and North Carolina piedmont, which by 1860 were manufacturing over 61% of the nation's finished product, other than cigars. In this period before the Civil War the making of cigars evolved into important enterprises centering in New York and Philadelphia.

The staple produced distinctive patterns of slavery on the plantation, where the necessity for intense supervision led to comparatively small slaveholdings, and in the factories, where the initiative of the slave was stirred by relative freedom and a system of bonuses.

Types of tobacco other than the colonial dark fire-cured have been extensively cultivated since the middle of the 19th century. White burley, useful in manufacturing because of its peculiarly absorptive properties, originated in Ohio during the 1860's and from there spread to Kentucky and other states. In the cultivation of cigar leaf, localized in the Connecticut Valley, in Pennsylvania, in Ohio and Wisconsin, a notable innovation after 1875 was the adoption of Havana seedleaf. About 1900 a shade-grown cigar wrapper was introduced in the Connecticut Valley and in Florida. Although bright or flue-cured manufacturing was developed in the ante-bellum period, its culture was restricted to a small area until after the Civil War, when it spread over large parts of piedmont Virginia and North Carolina. The cultivation of bright tobacco extended into the eastern sections of North Carolina and South Carolina about 1890; later into Georgia. Originally used as a wrapper for chewing tobacco, bright tobacco has proved especially adapted for cigarette manufacture. The production of all types of tobacco increased from 434,000,000 pounds in 1859 to 1,800,257,000 pounds in 1959–60.

The annual product of the factories was by 1860 valued at less than $31,000,000; by 1919, at over $1,000,000,000. This expansion of manufacturing was characterized by the concentration of production into fewer and larger units, the application of machinery to processes formerly carried on by hand, and the energetic pursuit of both domestic and foreign markets.

Around the production of machine-made cigarettes James B. Duke in 1890 organized the American Tobacco Co., which by 1910 had obtained virtual control of all branches of the tobacco manufacturing industry, save cigars. In 1911 the Supreme Court declared the American Tobacco Co. a monopoly contrary to the provisions of the Sherman Antitrust Act. Its properties were divided among sixteen companies, among them being a less powerful American Tobacco Co.

TOBACCO AS MONEY. Due to the scarcity of metallic money, Virginia, Maryland and North Carolina used tobacco as currency throughout most of the colonial period. In 1619 the Virginia legislature "rated" tobacco at "three shillings the best and the second sort at 18d. in the pound," and a statute of 1642 made tobacco a legal tender. Maryland began to use tobacco for money soon after the founding of that colony, and nearly all business transactions were in terms of tobacco, and all governmental levies, except customs duties, were payable in this commodity. Alsop, writing in 1660, said: "Tobacco is the current Coyn of Maryland and will sooner purchase Commodities from the Merchant, then [sic] money." Oldmixon, writing about fifty years later, said: "Tobacco is their Meat, Drink, Clothing and Money." In 1715 the North Carolina legislature fixed the price of tobacco at 10 shillings per hundredweight. This colony used tobacco as money until the outbreak of the Revolution, though in lesser degree than either Virginia or Maryland.

Overproduction of tobacco led to sharp fluctuations in its market price, in spite of the laws. There was also a tendency to pay debts in inferior tobacco, in spite of numerous inspection laws designed to remedy this evil. It was also found to be impracticable to transfer large quantities of tobacco from hand to hand. Accordingly, Virginia, in 1727, adopted the system of using "tobacco notes," which were certificates issued by the official inspectors of government warehouses. These notes formed a more convenient medium of exchange than the tobacco which they represented and they constituted the most important source of money in Virginia at that time. Apparently Maryland made little use of tobacco notes, though that colony did establish government warehouses in 1747.

Tobacco did not possess many of the qualities of a good money and was never entirely satisfactory as a medium of exchange. It was not easily portable; it had divisibility but lacked homogeneity; and it lacked stability of value due to the uncertainty and variability of production. Nevertheless its use as money proved to be a great boon to colonial Virginia and Maryland.

"TOM THUMB" LOCOMOTIVE was built by Peter Cooper for use on the new Baltimore & Ohio Railroad which, at the beginning, used horses as motive power. In its test, Aug. 28, 1830, the engine, on a double track line out of Baltimore, raced against a car drawn by a horse and would have beaten it had not a pulley belt slipped off.

TOMAHAWK seems to have been derived from an Algonkin word, to cut. In 1607–9, Capt. John Smith wrote that an English hatchet was a tomahawk, as did Strachey in 1610. In New York, Van der Donck (1650) says the Indians use small axes or tomahawks, instead of warclubs. The early tomahawks made by the English and French had wide chopping blades and at the top a kind of hook. Later, French traders introduced one with a pointed blade, obviously a weapon. By 1700 metal tomahawks were the preferred hand weapons of the Alkonkin and Iroquois-speaking Indians.

The history of the pipe tomahawk, one with a hole through the handle and a pipe bowl where the head of the hatchet should be, is obscure, but early

in 1700 it displaced other forms. Among the prized types are handsome, engraved blades of bronze. The handles are of wood and usually Indian-made.

TOMBSTONE, a famous silver-mining town of the Southwest, is located in the valley of the San Pedro River of Arizona, some 25 miles north of the Mexican boundary. The common tradition is that Ed Schieffelen, a prospector who discovered a large silver deposit there in 1878, gave the location its name because he had been told by scoffers at nearby Fort Huachuca that he would find nothing more than his tombstone in that region. Production of silver on a large scale began in 1880. During the next twenty years the district yielded about $40,000,000 worth of silver and $3,000,000 in gold. Tombstone attained notoriety because of its extravagant social life, its numerous gunmen such as Sheriff Wyatt Earp and his brothers and foes, and the violent feuds among the miners, gamblers and outlaws who made up a considerable part of what was, at one time, said to be a population of 15,000. In the 1890's the mines began to be flooded with underground water, and, despite expensive efforts to drain them, were nearly all abandoned by 1911. From that time Tombstone declined steadily in population and importance, as the mining interests of Arizona were shifted from silver to copper.

"TOO PROUD TO FIGHT." At Philadelphia on May 10, 1915, three days after the sinking of the *Lusitania*, President Wilson, speaking to some newly-naturalized citizens, said *inter alia*, "The example of America must be a special example. The people of America must be the example not merely of peace because it will not fight but of peace because peace is the healing and elevating influence of the world and strife is not. There is such a thing as a man being too proud to fight. There is such a thing as a nation being too proud to fight. There is such a thing as a nation being so right that it does not need to convince others by force that it is right." The phrase "too proud to fight" was caught up by critics, especially in England, but it revealed the President's mind and probably helps to explain why he did not make the sinking of the *Lusitania* a cause for war.

TOPEKA MOVEMENT AND THE TOPEKA CONSTITUTION. The movement for statehood, launched by Free State Kansans in opposition to the proslavery territorial government, was inaugurated in late summer, 1855, and was directed by an executive committee headed by James H. Lane. A "People's" assembly at Topeka, Sept. 19, called an election for members of a constitutional convention on Oct. 9. Fifty-one delegates were chosen but only thirty-seven signed the constitution. The convention was held Oct. 23 to Nov. 12, 1855. Thirteen of the delegates were natives of Southern states, ten of New

York and Pennsylvania, eight of the Old Northwest, four of New England and two of foreign countries. On the basis of former politics, there were twenty-one Democrats, nine Whigs, four Republicans, two Independents and one Free Soiler. Lane, an erstwhile popular sovereignty Democrat who posed as an Administration spokesman, was chosen president.

The constitution was not unlike other organic acts in its provisions for the forms and functions of government. A resolution endorsing popular sovereignty, adopted by a majority of two, temporarily revived former political affiliations; the following day it was reconsidered and postponed indefinitely. Sections in the bill of rights prohibited slavery and declared invalid Negro indentures executed in other states. The service of free Negroes in the militia was prohibited, but the fundamental question of admitting them to Kansas was referred to the voters along with the constitution and a general banking law. On Dec. 15 the instrument was ratified, 1731 to 46; the banking law was approved; and a provision to exclude free Negroes was adopted by a majority of nearly three to one. A month later state officials, including Charles Robinson as governor, were chosen. Lane was dispatched to Washington to present Congress with a memorial petitioning admission. On March 4, 1856, the legislature assembled at Topeka and elected United States senators. The House of Representatives passed a bill July 3, 1856, to admit Kansas under the Topeka constitution; five days later the Senate substituted its own measure authorizing a constitutional convention. Practically, the movement terminated with senatorial rejection, although subsequent sessions of the legislature convened, the last on March 4, 1858.

TORDESILLAS, TREATY OF (1494). The discovery of America by Christopher Columbus raised a question of claims of Spain and Portugal, respectively, to the newly discovered regions. Pope Alexander VI, a Spaniard, settled the dispute by a series of papal bulls in 1493, which awarded to Spain exclusive dominion and sovereignty over all lands not already belonging to any other Christian prince, discovered and to be discovered "west and south" of a line to be drawn from the North Pole to the South Pole, 100 leagues west of the Azores and Cape Verde Islands. All lands to the east and south of the demarcation line were to go to Portugal. The kings of Portugal and Spain subsequently agreed by the Treaty of Tordesillas to shift the demarcation line to a point 370 leagues west of the Cape Verde Islands. This treaty received papal approval in 1506. Though the treaty line never was surveyed, in effect it cut off a big eastern triangle of South America. Northern Brazil very roughly derives its claims to sovereignty from the Portuguese share of this ancient treaty.

TORNADOES AND CYCLONES. Lexicographers make no clear distinctions between hurricanes, torna-

does and cyclones; but common practice in America has made the hurricane a marine or West Indian gale, the tornado or cyclone a land storm, usually a gigantic whirlwind. This type of storm has been most prevalent in the mid-Western prairie states and in parts of the South. Destructive winds have often occurred in the East, but the whirling or cyclone type has been very rare east of the Alleghenies. Benjamin Silliman, the scientist, observed one, however, near New Brunswick, N. J., in 1835. The life of a cyclone may be only a few minutes or an hour or so. That which assailed Little Rock, Ark., on Oct. 2, 1894, lasted only three minutes, but in that time did a million dollars' damage, killed four persons and injured many. A cyclone is therefore known usually by the name of one town where it does its worst execution—as, the Grinnell, Iowa, cyclone of 1882, which destroyed nearly all of the town, including the buildings of Iowa College, and killed more than 100 people. Kansas was perhaps the most frequent sufferer from these storms in the 19th century, and it became common practice for farmers and villagers to construct cyclone cellars apart from the dwelling, stoutly roofed and covered with earth, in which the family took refuge when menacing clouds were seen. All the prairie states, including Wisconsin, Illinois and Indiana, have been attacked by these fatal and destructive storms. Early in the 20th century Alabama and Mississippi suffered so much from them that cyclone cellars were built in many neighborhoods. Only rarely have cyclones attacked large cities. St. Paul was considerably damaged by one in 1904. Another killed 170 persons, injured more than 250 and did great damage in Omaha on March 23, 1913. On the evening of March 27, 1890, a tornado passed through Louisville, causing the deaths of more than 100 and destroying many large buildings, including the Union Railway Station. Far more destructive was the cyclone which tore through the south-central portion of St. Louis on the afternoon of May 27, 1896, killing 400 persons, injuring 1200 and inflicting enormous property damage. It crossed the Mississippi River, wrecking a number of steamboats and a part of the city of East St. Louis. On March 18, 1925, a cyclone crossed southern Illinois from Missouri to Indiana, leaving 830 dead and 3800 injured in its wake. Two such storms developed in Georgia in 1936 within four days' time: on April 2 Cordele and on April 6 Gainesville were stricken, with great property losses. At Gainesville 185 were killed and more than 1700 injured. The tornado that struck St. Louis on February 10, 1959, killed 21 and caused $10,000,000 in damage.

TOTEM POLES are tall tree trunks erected in front of their houses by the coast tribes of Indians between Sitka and Puget Sound. Upon the front of these columns, conventionalized representations of animals, birds, fish and human beings are carved in relief, their character emphasized by painting. These carvings symbolize the family histories of the persons dwelling in the house, their mythical ancestors in particular. A similar series of carvings may be found upon the interior massive posts supporting the roof of the house. Wooden columns similar to totem poles were raised over graves as monuments, or memorials. Most of the aboriginal totem poles have disappeared, but in Indian cemeteries carved marble monuments take the place of the former memorial columns. Totem poles were in use when these Indians were first discovered, but the introduction of metal tools gave this art a new impetus, reaching its maximum about 1850.

TOWN GOVERNMENT, the most important local jurisdiction within the New England colonies and states, had its precedents in local authorities in rural England dealing with churches, poor relief, highways, schools and other neighborhood concerns. The founders of New England, actuated by their community of interests, settled compactly in villages surrounded by farms, meadows, pastures and woodland. They looked to the General Courts (the colonial legislatures) for recognition or incorporation of these villages and their environs as towns, privileged to enjoy local autonomy and to be represented in the legislature, usually securing these town privileges only after a probationary period as "plantations." Sometimes a second church "gathered" within a community became the nucleus of a new town; often discontent with local conditions led to a group exodus or petition for a separate incorporation. Most of the adult male inhabitants assembled in town meetings to discuss and decide public business, levy taxes, and elect local officials, the most important of whom were the selectmen who administered affairs along lines determined in town meeting. Constables (peace officers) were elected, and provisions made for public education and local courts. "Town lands" at first were bought from the Indians or bestowed by the General Court upon "town proprietors"; later the legislatures sold colony lands for township sites to secure public revenue. Distributed according to decision in town meeting, in equal division (sometimes by lot) or according to "ratable estates" or otherwise, early landholdings were sufficiently similar in value to encourage economic and political democracy within the towns. But in the 18th century speculation in "town rights" and town sites by proprietors, often nonresidents, introduced serious evils of absentee ownership. These proprietors, intent on financial gain, discriminated against settlers with no legal proprietary rights, excluding them from common lands, ignoring them in making new divisions, and seeking drastically to restrict their part in town meetings. Other inequalities, too, appeared. Nevertheless, the town governments retained much of their vitality and on the eve of the Revolution were notably effective in formulating and directing public opinion through committees of correspondence and by instructions to their representatives in the colonial legislatures.

Early in the 19th century President Jefferson felt "the foundation of Government" shaken under his feet "by the New England townships" which relentlessly opposed his Embargo policy. Impressed by the effectiveness of New England town government, Jefferson advocated a similar form of "elementary republics" to make every man feel "that he is a participant in the government of affairs." But later in this century the industrialization and urbanization of much of New England, and the influx of European immigrants, difficult to assimilate, greatly impaired the community of interests characteristic of the earlier towns. Throughout New England, however, town government survived, although losing some of its functions to larger local jurisdictions and somewhat modernized, as by the introduction of limited town meetings, advisory committees and town managers. Its continued importance is largely due to the fact that, in contrast to the practice in other sections where townships exist, the town government in New England functions as the chief local government for many villages and small urban communities as well as serving the surrounding rural districts. Sometimes claiming powers by long-established right, independent of current statutory provision, sometimes, on the contrary, dubbed "mere agencies of the state," the New England town may be justly termed "a quasi corporation . . . high in the scale of corporate life," which performs numerous services as a political subdivision of the state and at the same time manages corporate property of its own and regulates many matters of local concern.

TOWN MEETINGS, in their most highly developed form, are assemblies of the voters of the New England towns. With modifications they are reflected in the town and township meetings in the northern tier of central states where westward-moving New Englanders carried their institutions with them. Faintly foreshadowed by vestry meetings in rural England, such assemblies are chiefly a product of conditions of settlement in the New England colonies. General participation in local government by the men who shared in the establishment of local settlements seems to have been taken for granted. A system soon developed in which the men dwelling in a town were generally accepted as town freemen regardless of requirements for the colony franchise, and even if they were not among the proprietors to whom the town lands were confirmed by the General Court. These men assembled in annual town meetings for the election of selectmen, constables and other officers, and, upon due call, attended special town meetings. By majority vote at these assemblies town lands were distributed, local taxes levied, and action taken on other matters of local concern, such as town schools, roads, bridges, trainbands and the local church. Differences of opinion in these meetings were often acute and hotly argued, especially in the 18th century when profiteering proprietors sought to dominate the towns regardless of the nonproprietary interests. The controversial and critical faculties thus exercised were turned against British management of colonial affairs so conspicuously that the Parliamentary Act of 1774 revising the government of Massachusetts decreed that no town meetings should be held without the royal governor's written permit except for election of town officers and representatives to the General Court. Nothing daunted, town meetings continued to voice protests against England and, after Independence, against such state and national policies as displeased any of them.

Despite 19th- and 20th-century factors which have tended to handicap town government, town meetings have continued to furnish to hundreds of communities open forums on local affairs. The town government's authority is greatest and town meetings best attended in New England, where they usually serve as the chief local government agency in villages and small cities as well as in rural portions of the townships. Although only qualified voters are summoned by the warrant which calls the meeting and specifies its business, inhabitants in general are admitted and sometimes participate in debate. A date in the spring is most usual for the annual meeting. Called to order by the town clerk, the typical town meeting proceeds to the election of a moderator (often honored by a long series of re-elections), then proceeds to the business stated in the "warning," or call for the meeting. Although some transactions may have been prearranged by informal caucus or special advisory or finance committees, the open discussion is often spirited and effective. Town business is so extensive as sometimes to require adjourned sessions of the annual meeting as well as occasional special meetings. Although fixed within certain limits by state law, it includes a wide variety of subjects, such as maintenance of schools, roads, bridges, waterworks, libraries, cemeteries, parks, poor relief, band concerts, public health, old-home week and the eradication of insect pests.

Some of the larger New England towns have provided "limited town meetings," restricted chiefly to elected members representing subdivisions of the town. In many sections, outside of New England, townships exist only as minor local units, without provision for town meetings. In New York, New Jersey and in more than half of the north central states town meetings are called but generally attract little interest, often being, in effect, only gatherings of township officials.

TOWNSEND PLAN, or the Old-Age Revolving Pension, announced on Jan. 1, 1934, by its originator, Dr. Francis E. Townsend, speedily enrolled millions of supporters in one of the most astonishing social movements of the period. As embodied in a bill endorsed by Townsend the Plan provided that every person sixty years of age and over, who is a citizen of the United States and has been for at least five years, shall on application receive from the U. S. Treasury an an-

nuity "not exceeding $200 per month," provided he "shall not engage in any gainful pursuit," and shall spend within the United States all of each month's annuity during the month it is received or five days thereafter. The $20,000,000,000 a year held by proponents of the Plan to be necessary in financing was to be raised not by a tax on income or wealth, but by a "duty of 2 per centum upon the gross dollar value of each transaction done within the United States." In effect this would amount to a general sales tax of such proportions, say its critics, that wholesale inflation would result. The authors of the Plan regarded it as no mere old-age pension but as a solution for virtually all economic ills.

Combining the American traditions of pressure politics, reform by monetary manipulation, and evangelical utopianism, the Townsend Plan was only one of several such movements produced by the social distress and insecurity following the panic of 1929.

TOWNSHEND ACTS take their name from Charles Townshend, Chancellor of the Exchequer and head of the British government at the time they were enacted. There were four acts and all were passed between June 15 and July 2, 1767.

The first, passed on June 15, suspended the New York assembly from further legislative activities until it complied with the provisions of the Quartering Act of 1765 which required colonies to supply barracks, or other shelter; straw for bedding; cooking utensils; firewood for cooking and heating purposes; and the antiscorbutic ration of rum, cider or vinegar. Pontiac's Conspiracy had just occurred and had demonstrated the danger of leaving the army units scattered in small garrisons throughout the West where they could be attacked and destroyed in detail. Gen. Gage, commander in chief in America, decided to skeletonize the western garrisons and concentrate all available troops in central reserves to be dispatched to any place where they were needed. New York was selected as the best place for the reserves, and troops were ordered there, which imposed an unforeseen financial burden upon that province. Apparently the amount of expenditures would vary, not with the plans of the assembly, but with the whims of the commanding general. The New York assembly made its usual appropriation for a limited number of troops, but refused to appropriate for additional quarters in New York, especially as there was still ample room in the barracks at Albany. The Suspending Act forbade the assembly to carry on any other business until it had met fully the demands of Gen. Gage. As assemblies were summoned, prorogued, and dissolved by order of the governor, representing the Crown, this assumption of authority on the part of Parliament created serious concern in America. It was a weapon that might be used to invade other American rights, and enforce other laws that the colonists considered unjust and unconstitutional.

The second and third acts were passed on June 29, 1767. One provided for an American revenue, and the other set up a special board in Boston to collect the revenue.

The Revenue Act levied import duties payable at American ports on white and red lead, painters' colors, various kinds of paper, glass of all kinds, and threepence a pound on tea. All of these articles were legally importable only from Great Britain. It was the second time in the history of the Empire that commercial regulations affecting the colonies had been adopted for revenue purposes. All other laws, except the Sugar Act of 1764, had been for the purpose of protecting some industry within the Empire. For this reason men like Pitt, Burke, Trecothic and others assailed this law as anticommercial. Instead of encouraging British industry, it discouraged English manufacture, and by taxation encouraged a competing industry in the colonies or discouraged the use of the articles singled out for taxation.

The revenue arising from these new colonial taxes was to go first to the cost of collection, then to support an independent civil establishment in America—that is, judges, governors and other Crown employees were paid from this fund instead of being dependent, as they always had been for their salaries, upon annual appropriations of the local assemblies. This use of the money struck at the very foundation of American political liberty. During the past half century the colonies had achieved almost complete local self-government through financial control of the royal officers. To put judges and governors beyond all local control, and at the same time make them dependent upon the Ministry for the tenure of their offices and their pay was to set up what many Americans considered despotic control.

Resistance to a program of political enslavement took the form of agitation, nonimportation agreements, open evasion of the duties in some cases, promotion of American spinning, weaving, glass and paper industries, and open hostility to the enforcing officers.

The new taxes were to be collected by a Board of Customs Commissioners (the third act) stationed at Boston, which was given complete control over all customs in America. They were empowered to revise and reorganize the entire American customs; discontinue old or establish new ports of entry; appoint customs officers, searchers, spies; hire coast-guard vessels, provide them with search warrants, and in general do whatever seemed to them necessary to enforce the revenue laws.

Costs of this new and very costly establishment were to be paid out of the revenue and out of seizures. As the revenue law itself was unpopular and considered by the colonists unconstitutional, the enforcement officers met with resistance in some cases as in the seizure of the *Liberty* and the burning of the *Gaspee*. The real or fancied opposition led the customs commissioners to ask for troops, and large forces were hurried to Boston in September, 1768, where they were quartered in the city contrary to the Quartering Act. For more than nine months Boston was practically under military rule. There was friction between the people and the soldiers. The people of Massachusetts appealed to other colonies through protests and through *The Journal of the Times,* an ostensible day-to-day account of actual conditions in Boston. This was widely published in American and British papers. Most of the troops were withdrawn in 1769, but two regiments were left. One of these, the Twenty-ninth, was involved in the Boston Massacre, March 5, 1770, after which all troops were withdrawn. With the repeal of all duties, except those on tea in 1770, the controversy gradually quieted down, until aroused anew by the tea controversy and the Boston Tea Party in 1773.

The fourth act repealed the inland duties on tea in England and permitted it to be exported to the colonies free of all British taxes.

It has been said that Townshend sought to raise a revenue in America by enforcing the Navigation Acts. Such statements are without foundation. The only navigation act that could yield a revenue was 25 Charles II which levied export duties on enumerated products shipped from one British colony to another. This was purely regulative and only designed to prevent enumerated products being shipped to Europe in competition with the direct trade from England. The collections under this law after 1767 were not increased; for the fifteen years, 1749–63, the collections had averaged £1395 annually; and for the six years ending with 1774 under the Townshend Acts, they averaged only £778 per year—an actual decrease of more than £600 per annum under the Townshend Acts. The increased revenues came from the Sugar Act and from the Townshend Revenue Act.

TOWNSHIP SYSTEM. As provided for in the Ordinance of 1785, this was an adaptation of a system of local governmental units involving a system of land survey, ownership and settlement. The term had been used rather vaguely in England. It was at one time a subdivision of a parish, with certain officers for the subdivision. The words town and township have been, and still are, much confused. In parts of New England a town is a subdivision of a county, likewise in Wisconsin. In other parts of New England the county subdivision is called a township, as is the case over a large part of the country.

Our townships are, with a few exceptions, six miles square, divided into 36 square miles, called sections. The sections are numbered, beginning in the northeast corner from east to west, forth and back. In the "Seven Ranges," surveyed under the Ordinance of 1785, the numbering of the sections begins in the southeast corner and runs from south to north for all tiers. Ohio has two tracts of townships five miles square.

The township came to be a basic unit in the land system of the country, but of just as much importance, it has become a basic unit of government. Each township, or each "town" (which may be more or less than the congressional township of 36 sections of land) is a unit of local government. Varying much from place to place, these local governments have important functions to perform respecting schools and roads, as well as in the more general matters of keeping the peace, and providing poor relief. These local units of government elect tax assessors, and in many states collect the taxes. In New England the town government is more significant than the county. Over most of the country the town functions and responsibility are distinctly subordinate to those of the county.

TRADE, DOMESTIC. One difficulty which confronted early new communities in the United States was to find something to ship beyond its confines which other communities wanted. Until after 1860 hundreds of settlements scattered over the country were faced with this problem. Thus, in the early years, much of the trade which we call domestic was within towns, villages and growing cities. Trade is based on differences in products and services. Differences of some description must exist for commerce to move. But another factor of great importance is required. This is transportation. In the commercial development of this country the most significant additions to our trade facilities have been the improvement of waterways, the building of railways, and since 1900 the enormous extension of surfaced roads. Widened markets made possible higher prices for the products of forest, fields and mines, while at the same time they made lower prices for goods brought into the communities in return for products shipped out. Improved transportation brought about growing specialization in goods in which the communities had advantages; at all times the favored conditions of domestic trading, unhampered by duties, or other forms of taxes, gave this country an unusual opportunity for the development of its domestic trade. In short, a great free market was open to manufacturers and merchants everywhere.

A few examples will illustrate the importance of adequate means of transport. The Great Lakes region has become one of the most important markets of the country. Prior to the opening of the Erie Canal in 1825 this was one of our most inaccessible regions. Before that date, wheat from western New York was shipped down the Susquehanna River to Baltimore as the cheapest route. According to a report to the legislature of New York in 1817 the cost of shipment from Buffalo to New York City was $100 a ton, which was three times the usual market value of wheat, six times that of corn, twelve times that of oats. With the opening of the canal the rates to New York ranged from $5.00 to $13.00, and by 1852 from $3.00 to $7.00, depending on the season of the year and the conditions

of the traffic. At any time from the first settlement of the interior to about 1825 the charge for transporting a ton of merchandise from Philadelphia to Pittsburgh was from $100 to $150. Before 1817 it cost as much to bring a similar weight upriver from New Orleans. Flatboats, which were the usual means of conveyance before the advent of the steamboat, were unable to return upstream. Hence, northbound trade was carried in keelboats, operated by manpower. These devices had only a small capacity for freight, and the voyage was intermittent.

The steamboat, introduced on the Ohio-Mississippi system in 1811, brought relief from these difficulties. A writer of the times estimated the importance of the new facility in the following terms: "It has contributed more than any other single cause, perhaps more than all other causes combined, to advance the prosperity of the West." This statement was borne out by the facts.

The history of domestic commerce has been characterized by the successive opening of new markets. The earliest trading areas were along the north Atlantic seaboard. Cereals and flour were of some importance in inter-regional trade, with the Middle Colonies being the chief sources of production. In addition to a small export, and to a demand to meet the sailor's trade, limited quantities were sold in New England, and to some extent in the Southern areas. While the fish and lumber and timber products of New England, the tobacco of Virginia, and the rice and indigo of Carolina were destined mainly for foreign export they provided the means for purchase of a considerable variety of foreign goods which subsequently became articles of domestic trade. Meanwhile, even in the early years of settlement, some seaboard communities enjoyed trade with the natives which, from their point of view, was important, because it supplied furs and skins, unique products for export. In the course of time this trade became an important branch of domestic enterprise, and it continued to grow in significance until about 1860. At one time St. Louis was the fur-trading center of a region which ultimately comprised practically all the country west of the Mississippi River to the Pacific. In 1763 Albany and Philadelphia were still fitting out places for trade with the Indians of the interior. Meanwhile, the leading Atlantic cities were becoming the source of supply of hardware and dry goods distributed over the entire interior.

A second important market to receive development was along the Ohio River south of Pittsburgh. This city, along with Cincinnati and Louisville, became manufacturing centers. The output included various articles of iron and steel, machinery, engines for steamboats and for flour and lumber mills, boots, shoes, clothing, packing house and related products. The markets were mainly in the river towns as far south as New Orleans.

A third market area to come into prominence was

along the Great Lakes. The introduction of steam navigation on these waters in 1819 and the opening of the Erie Canal were the major contributing factors. Canal transport provided an easy access to the interior not only for human beings but for their belongings. Great migrations moved into the areas which are now tributary to the lake cities. Farming, trading and manufacturing were developed to supply not only local needs, but demands in distant areas. Chicago, Cleveland, Toledo, Buffalo became the leading industrial and commercial cities—gathering points for commodities in the regions roundabout, and points of distribution for goods brought in from a wide area.

The marketing area west of the Mississippi was originally in the hands of merchants of St. Louis. Eventually, with the building of western railroads, Chicago became a competitor for this commerce, particularly in all the area west and north of the great bend of the Missouri River. Trade lines branched mainly in three directions; one to the southwest to the old Spanish town of Santa Fe, and eventually into old Mexico; to the mid-mountain area in the direction of Denver, which city became the marketing center for the new mining camps in Colorado; and to the Far West over the Oregon Trail.

The southern market, particularly east of the Mississippi, had received attention from merchants and manufacturers of the Ohio River cities as early as 1820. This trade was extended to cover not only the whole area east of the Mississippi but, after 1840, to the regions of Texas. With the development of manufacturing in the South, notably after 1880, with the growth of the lumbering industry, and after 1900 of petroleum production and refining, the whole South became a marketing region of great significance.

The development of trade with the Pacific received its earliest stimulus from the gold rushes, 1848 to 1860, and subsequently to the opening of the first transcontinental railroad in 1869. After 1914 the opening of the Panama Canal was a further trade advantage. These developments caused an opening of the great nonferrous metal resources of the Rocky Mountains, the timber resources of the Northwest, and agriculture along the Pacific, notably citrus fruit in California and certain cereals in the north Pacific.

Although rather complete records have been kept of foreign commerce even from colonial days, little definite information could be obtained about domestic trade until the census of 1930. In this prior period we are able to obtain information here and there which indicates the magnitude and direction of growth. Commercial journals of the time contain scattered information which is sometimes helpful. We are informed from such sources that the trade of New Orleans with the interior, which had been about $8,700,000 in 1815, became $185,200,000 in 1860, and that about 1852 the total commerce of the Mississippi and its tributaries was about $339,500,000, and that the estimated value of the commerce of the Mississippi Valley was

$653,900,000. Since this was growth from almost nothing in 1790 it is a truly remarkable record of commercial expansion.

From such sources, also, we are informed that the trade west of the Mississippi expanded to considerable proportions, beginning shortly before 1860. In that year the total investment in the trade of the Plains, including wagons, teams, merchandise and wages of men, was estimated at $5,500,000. The merchandise shipped from Missouri River points was said to have been $10,000,000, of which the New Mexican trade took about $3,000,000, the Pikes Peak gold area about $6,000,000, the Utah trade about $500,000, and the remainder was trade with the Indians. Kansas City enjoyed the largest share of this commerce but found competitors in Leavenworth, Atchison, Nebraska City, St. Joseph and Omaha.

The rapid expansion of railroad building brought the whole country into one great market. The operated railway mileage was about 4000 in 1842; it became 30,600 in 1860 and 254,800 in 1934. This development was aided, notably with the lines west of the Mississippi, by Federal land grants and in some cases by guarantee of certain types of railroad bonds. Mainly since 1900 the development of interurban electric transport, and the building of surfaced roads, have added enormously to the facilities for moving passengers and freight.

As highways improved, motor trucks increased both in number and in size and railroads lost relatively to this more facile vehicle that transformed the long established station-to-station into door-to-door. Between 1930 and 1958 the number of railroad cars of revenue-freight loaded fell from 45,000,000 to 30,000,000; the actual tonnage carried, however, increased slightly. Coal and coke led in total shipments. In intercity freight traffic between 1940 and 1957, the railroad carriage fell from 63% to 47%, but motor carriage increased from 9% to 19%. The percentage of the new pipe lines grew from 9% to 17%. Powerful towboats, pushing huge barges of oil, crushed stone, building materials, and similar products on inland rivers have increased in recent years. The airplane in special fields has achieved some significance in freight transportation.

Retail trade in 1958 amounted to $200,370,000,000; $133,474,000,000 of that was spent in 189 standard metropolitan areas, with New York, Los Angeles, and Chicago in order leading all the rest. Nineteen years before, retail sales had amounted to only $42,000,000,000. In 1939 the five leading groups in trade were: the food group ($10,164,000,000), the general merchandise group ($5,665,000,000), the automotive group ($5,548,000,000), eating and drinking places ($3,520,000,000) and the apparel groups ($3,258,000,000). In 1958 the rank was: the food group ($49,224,000,000), the automobile dealers ($31,905,000,000), the general merchandise group ($21,971,000,000), eating and drinking places

($15,295,000,000), and the lumber-building group ($14,326,000,000). The Middle Atlantic States (New York, New Jersey and Pennsylvania) and the Middle Western States (Indiana, Illinois, Michigan and Wisconsin) have maintained by far the greater sectional sales—almost equal, if California, Oregon and Washington are omitted, to that of all the other states and the District of Columbia combined. The outstanding feature of the swelling trade was the increase on the Pacific coast, though the South Atlantic States made unusual increases also.

TRADE, FOREIGN. The United States throughout its history has been relatively self-sufficient, yet foreign trade has since colonial beginnings been a dominant factor in the growth of the nation. The colonies were founded basically for the purpose of commerce: the shipment of products, particularly raw materials, to the mother country and the sale of finished goods from the shops of England in the colonies. Even had colonial plans not been centered around the welfare of Englishmen at home, the results could scarcely have been different. The Atlantic coast is particularly suited to commerce on the high seas. Deep harbors in the North and bays, indentations, and rivers and smaller streams from New York southward provided excellent ports for loading and unloading the ships of the day. Moreover, the settlements, clustered around the places where the ships came in or scattered along the rivers and creeks, were almost completely isolated from each other. As late as 1794 it took a week under the most favorable conditions to make the trip by coach from Boston to New York. Though the seas were infested by privateers and pirates (and the distinction was sometimes a thin one), and the ships were small and the journey long, the hazards of overland trading were still greater and the returns were more uncertain.

Colonial Period. Foreign trade was primarily in outgoing raw materials and incoming manufactured goods. It was simple economic necessity that turned the colonists to agriculture: each had to eat. When surpluses of food became possible economic specialization appeared. Dictated by climatic and soil conditions as well as by a host of other factors, production in each section determined the course of its commerce. The trade of the colonies south of Pennsylvania was chiefly with England. Ships from British ports called at the wharves of plantations along the rivers of Maryland and Virginia for tobacco and the next year returned with goods ordered from the shops of London and other cities. Furs, skins, naval stores, and small quantities of tobacco made up the early cargoes that went out from the Carolinas, but after 1700 rice quickly gained the lead as the most important export. Before the middle of the century indigo had become a profitable crop not only because it offered employment for the slaves when they were not busy in the rice fields but also because the demand for the dye in England had induced Parliament to vote a bounty. On the eve of the Revolution indigo made up by value about 35% of the exports of South Carolina.

The commerce of New England and the Middle Colonies ran counter to economic plans of empire. Grain, flour, meat, and fish from the sea made up the major products of Pennsylvania and New Jersey and the colonies to the northward. Yet shipment of these materials to England would endanger long-established interests of Englishmen at home, and, after 1660, violate parliamentary legislation. Though small amounts of naval stores, iron, ships' timber, furs, whale oil and whalebone, oak and pine plank, and staves, barrels, and hoops went off to London, other markets had to be sought in order to obtain means of paying for the large amounts of goods bought in England. The search for sales brought what is often referred to as the "triangular trade." Southern Europe, Africa, and the West Indies bought three fourths of the exports of New England and more than half of those of New York and Pennsylvania. On the eve of the Revolution the Middle Colonies were shipping annually to southern Europe over 500,000 bushels of wheat and more than 18,000 tons of bread. Fish, meat, grain, ship timbers, lumber, and materials for barrels, kegs, and casks also went out in large quantities from Pennsylvania, New York and New England. Rum was exchanged in Africa for slaves and the slaves in turn sold in the West Indies for specie or for more molasses for New England rum distilleries. These islands, in fact, provided an inexhaustible market for fish, meat, foodstuffs and live animals, as well as pearlash, potash, cut-out houses, lumber, and finished parts for making containers for sugar, rum and molasses. Corn, wheat, flour, bread and vegetables found here their greatest outlet.

Unfortunately the sellers of raw materials—the colonists—were almost always in debt to the manufacturers of finished goods—the British. Carrying charges by English shipowners ate up the favorable balance of the Southerners and the debts of the planters became virtually hereditary. Northern commercial men, selling more than they bought everywhere except in England, gained enough specie to settle their accounts in London with reasonable promptness. The persistent drainage of money to the mother country, however, was a significant factor in the discontent that grew up in America.

1776–1814

Though the Revolution did not destroy American trade even with the British, the former colonies obviously lost their preferred position in the world of commerce and also the protection of the powerful empire fleet. The British Navigation Act of 1783 (emphasized by further acts in 1786 and 1787) closed the ports of the West Indies to the ships of the new nation and protected others by heavy tonnage duties. Only Sweden and Prussia agreed to reciprocity treaties. Yet the "critical period" was far less discouraging than is sometimes pictured. Varying tariffs in the ports and hostile action and counter-action among the states did keep commerce in perpetual uncertainty and prevented retaliation against European discriminations, but trade went on either in traditional channels or in new markets. In May, 1785, the *Empress of China*, "fresh" from Canton, returned to New York, and in August the *Pallas*, manned by lascars, put into Baltimore with its cargo of tea, china, silks, satins, gauzes, velvets, umbrellas, paper hangings and similar items from the Orient. Soon other ships were unloading at Eastern ports. Means were found, too, for evading the restrictions in the West Indies, and enough luxuries were brought in from England to disturb the already uncertain economic situation.

Shipping interests in the new Congress under the Constitution secured legislation favoring American-owned ships. The tonnage registered for foreign trade increased in the years 1789–1810 from 123,893 to 981,000, and imports and exports in American bottoms jumped roughly from 20% to 90%. Great ships from the larger ports sailed the high seas, but even the smallest towns sent out cargoes of lumber, horses, hay, grain and other wanted products to the West Indies. The China trade increased with Capt. Robert Gray's journey in 1792. But there were difficulties. The British and the French were hostile in the West Indies, treaty privileges were sparingly and grudgingly given everywhere, and France for several years engaged in what amounted to an undeclared war on the United States. The Barbary pirates preyed on the ships of the young nation, and England began impressment.

The Napoleonic Wars turned production forces to military goods, drove merchant ships from the seas, and pushed prices upward rapidly. Though many ships were seized, American merchant captains and the nation as well prospered until Jefferson, seeking to maintain peace, induced Congress in 1807 to pass an Embargo Act. Exports dropped from $108,343,000 to $22,431,000 within a year; imports fell from $138,500,000 to $56,990,000. Repeal of the Embargo brought some revival, but other restrictions and the war against England drove exports to $6,927,000 in 1814 and imports to $12,965,000. Domestic economy and foreign trade had been dealt a severe blow; both recovered quickly, however, when at the end of the war all restrictions on tonnage and on goods based on nationality of ship were repealed on a reciprocity basis.

1815–1860

Foreign trade in the years between 1815 and 1860, though fluctuating often, moved generally upward. Agricultural products made up the major part of the exports. Cotton led all the rest—production mounted from 60,000 bales in 1821 to 3,800,000 in 1860, 80% of which was sold abroad. Great Britain and France were the two greatest purchasers, but Germany, Austria, Belgium, Holland and Russia bought appreciable quantities. The West Indies and South America took large amounts of grain and flour and English demands increased steadily after the repeal of the corn laws in the middle 1840's. Tobacco, rice, meat and meat products, as well as lumber, naval stores, barrels and kegs, staves and hoops moved out in large quantities. Cottons, woolens, silks, iron, cutlery, china, and a miscellany of other items made up the bulk of the incoming cargoes. But the glory of the clipper ship was being obscured by the iron-hulled steamers that came from the British shipyards; the day of the whalers was ending even before oil began to flow out of the first well at Titusville in Pennsylvania in 1859; and not only were agricultural goods declining relatively in exports and markets shifting but special foods, beverages, liquors, fibers and condiments from the far corners of the earth were pressing hard for first place in inbound merchandise.

1860–1940

The years since the Civil War have been primarily industrial years, and, until World War II, domestic production and domestic trade were the basic concerns of the nation. Railroads knit marketing centers together and economic specialization reached maturity. Agriculture, spreading into the West, increased each year its outpouring of foodstuffs, and industry, entrenched behind a high protective tariff, grew with astounding rapidity. The American merchant marine declined rapidly as investors turned their dollars into railroads and other industrial ventures at home. The percentage of foreign trade carried in American bottoms decreased from 66.5% in 1860 to 7.1% in 1900. That did not mean, however, any lessening in total ocean commerce. The value of exports and imports combined rose from $686,192,000 in 1860 to $4,257,-000,000 in 1914. Cotton, wheat, flour and other farm products continued to move out in ever-larger amounts, but it was obvious that agriculture was losing out to manufactured goods. Finished articles in outgoing cargoes rose percentagewise from a yearly average of about 15% in 1871–75 to something more than 31% in 1914. Incoming manufactured items, averaging roughly 40% of imports in 1870, had dropped to about 24% in 1914. The changing nature of exports and imports clearly revealed the fact that Europe was becoming each year relatively less important in American foreign trade. Shipments to and from Asia, Oceania, Africa, Canada and Latin America were growing rapidly. Cotton, wheat, petroleum, tobacco, metals, and a great variety of manufactured goods flowed out to the new trading centers from ports on the Atlantic, the Gulf, and the Pacific. The return flow was made up of tropical foods and materials, coffee, sugar, wool, rubber, silk, paper and paper stock, and a growing amount of raw materials. Two world wars and a depression completed the revolution.

World War I restored temporarily the supremacy of Europe as a consumer of American agricultural products. But strange goods also made up large portions of the cargoes—chemicals, explosives, firearms, special woods for airplane propellers, barbed wire, and a host of other needs of fighting forces. The value of exports and imports more than doubled during the war (about $4,000,000,000 to $9,000,000,000), rose to somewhat less than $14,000,000,000 in 1920, and dropped back to $9,000,000,000 in 1929. But neither the trade of the war years nor that of the decade of the '20's was normal. The huge purchases of the Allies were based on government credits in the United States, and the slow growth for the next decade was financed largely by American loans. The economic structure fell apart in 1929. Prices declined sharply everywhere, world credit and world finances broke down, foreign exchange transactions were curtailed or taken over completely by government in many places, and the principal powers sought to maintain themselves by hiding behind high tariffs, trade licenses, and fixed quotas. The United States had for a decade been shutting herself from the world. The climax was reached in the Hawley-Smoot Tariff of 1930, which brought retaliatory restrictions from other nations. Foreign trade of the nation dropped to $2,933,000,000 in 1932. The slow climb upward to $6,646,000,000 in 1940 was largely due to the patient insistence of Cordell Hull that reciprocity agreements rather than trade restrictions were essentials in commercial revival. By authority of the Reciprocal Trade Agreements Act of 1934 he made a series of executive agreements with foreign nations by which he encouraged American trade, and, by applying the "most-favored-nation" clause, spread the gains widely over the world.

1941–1960

In the years 1941–45 more than $50,000,000,000 in goods went out of American ports and $17,536,000,-000 came in. But roughly $32,887,000,000 of the exports were lend-lease war materials to fighting allies for which no payment was expected. With the end of the war total foreign trade slumped temporarily and then jumped upward astoundingly: $13,805,000,000 in 1945; $32,370,000,000 in 1959. But the figures are deceptive. Multilateral trade all but came to an end with the war. The United States, fearful of communism and convinced that people must be fed beyond the mere point of subsistence if traditional nations were to be maintained and new governments were to be established on the principle of freedom of choice, set up the Marshall Plan, challenged the communists in Korea, and assumed the task of maintaining international trade. The Economic Cooperation Administration (E. C. A.), working with the Committee of European Economic Co-operation (C. E. E. C.) and a host of other organizations, sought to create a workable assistance plan. The Reciprocal Trade Agreements Act of 1934, designed to release world trade from hampering restrictions, was in 1958 extended for the eleventh time. A General Agreement for Tariffs and Trade (GATT) was created also for the purpose of developing multilateral economic exchange by international agreements in international conferences. Europe set up a "Common Market" in an attempt to remove its paralyzing nationalistic barriers.

But however drastic the changes in detail, basic trends long observable still prevailed. Manufactured goods gained over crude materials in exports and declined in imports. New markets continued to grow in importance as scientists, planning their devices in relation to strange new needs and not according to the resources nationally available, scanned the earth for the exact product or products needed. Canada and Latin America outstripped Europe as the principal trading area of the nation—Canada buys more than one fifth of all our exports and sells us more than one fifth of our imports. Asia, Oceania, and Africa have become significant, too. The so-called underdeveloped countries in the 20th century provide basic essentials in ordinary economic life (such as rubber and coffee) or critical materials in what is often referred to as world survival (the Belgian Congo, for instance, supplies 60% of the world's uranium and 90% of its radium). Between July 1, 1945, and June 30, 1956, the United States advanced $57,000,000,000 to 75 nations in underdeveloped areas.

But the role of the nation is not merely that of financial abettor. It produces and consumes more than one third of the goods and services of the globe, though it possesses less than 7% of either the land area or the population. The chief exports at the beginning of the 1960's were industrial machinery, iron and steel, chemicals, automobiles and parts, cotton, wheat and flour, coal and coke, electrical machinery, petroleum and products, and textile manufactures; the leading imports were petroleum and products, coffee, machinery and vehicles, paper and paper manufactures, textiles, cane sugar, meats and fish, copper, crude rubber, and ore. (*See also* Merchant Marine.)

TRADE, TRIANGULAR. Unlike the tobacco and sugar colonies, the mainland English colonies north of Maryland did not, from their beginnings, have great staple products readily exportable directly to England in exchange for European goods. Yet, in order to maintain their accustomed European standards of living and to support an expanding economy, their relatively heavy populations demanded large imports of European manufactured wares—hardware, kitchen utensils, furniture, guns, building materials, farm tools, textiles, etc. Thus, from earliest times their imports from England exceeded their direct exports to England; moreover, after 1660, many of their exportable surpluses—fish, cereals and meats—were forbidden in England. As they were unable or forbidden by law to manufacture their needs in the colonies, they were forced to balance their trade by engaging in complex trading enterprises, to dispose of diversified surpluses in non-English markets in order to provide purchasing power in England. One such means to redress the unfavorable English trade balance was the Triangular Trade, sometimes called the "three-cornered," or "roundabout," trade.

The Triangular Trade did not conform to a constant mercantile pattern. In its simplest form, near the mid-18th century, its three "corners" were, in sequence: a port in the Northern colonies (most commonly Boston or Newport, R. I.), the Gold Coast of Africa, a port in the West Indies (often Kingston, Jamaica), and thence home. For example, the brigantine *Sanderson* of Newport sailed (March, 1752) with a crew of nine and a cargo of 8220 gallons of rum, some short iron bars ("African iron," used as currency among African natives), flour, pots, tar, sugar, shackles, shirts, provisions and water. Reaching Africa, the cargo was exchanged for 56 slaves, 40 ounces of gold dust and about 900 pounds of pepper. Proceeding to Barbados (June 17, 1753), the captain sold the slaves at £33 to £56 per head and disposed of the gold dust and pepper—with net proceeds of £1324. Of this, £911:17s. was spent for 55 hogsheads of molasses and 3 hogsheads, 27 barrels of sugar; the remainder due the captain was paid in bills of exchange drawn upon Liverpool. The *Sanderson* then returned to Newport.

Cargoes, routes and ports varied. Though the main cargo on the first leg was generally rum and "African iron," it sometimes consisted of cloth or trinkets; the chief cargo on the second leg of the voyage—famous as the horrible "middle passage"—was slaves, but occasionally it consisted of gold dust, condiments, ivory, or wines purchased en route at the Wine Islands, Spain, or France; and on the homeward voyage, besides molasses and sugar, salt, wines, condiments, cotton, dyewoods, rice, tobacco, silver, bills of exchange and slaves occasionally made up the cargo—any wares, in fact, that could be used at home or sold in England. Another variant of the trade ran as follows: a New England, New York, or Philadelphia vessel carried fish, tobacco, or lumber to Lisbon, Cadiz, Gibraltar, or other Mediterranean ports, exchanged the cargo for European goods, traded in the West Indies for molasses, sugar, silver, or bills of exchange, and returned home.

Roots of the Triangular Trade extended into early Massachusetts commerce, though the trade itself did not flourish until after 1700. In the 1640's New England sales of fish and lumber in Spain and concurrent commerce with the West Indies must have suggested the "roundabout" trade; and in the 1650's New England vessels engaged directly in the African slave trade. But the monopoly of the Royal African Company (1672–97) closed to colonial vessels legal slave trade to the West Indies. Meanwhile, New England trade with the sugar colonies reached enormous proportions, and the uses of rum in the Indian trade and in the fisheries came to be widely recognized. Twenty-five years after Parliament threw open the slave trade (1697), rum—increasingly of New England origin—displaced French brandy in the African slave trade. Rum distilleries arose everywhere in New England after about 1700; Newport alone had 22 in 1730, Massachusetts had 63 in 1750. To a lesser extent they also developed in New York and Philadelphia. By 1770 three fourths of the imports from the West Indies to Northern colonies consisted of rum, molasses and sugar. After 1715 much of these derived illegally from the French sugar islands, giving rise to English demands for the widely ignored Molasses Act of 1733 and the revolution-provoking Sugar Act of 1764. The importation of rum's baser cane equivalents and the growth of distilleries in the colonies were in direct proportion to the growth of the Triangular Trade.

Centered in New England, principally at Newport and Boston, the Triangular Trade extended to New York and Philadelphia, engaged hundreds of vessels before the Revolution, mostly small ships of 100 tons or less. Prominent merchants, notably Peter Faneuil of Boston, took the lead in the business, sold countless slaves in the West Indies, whence most were distributed to Spanish colonies, some to New England, New York, Philadelphia and the Southern mainland. Profits arising from the trade not only materially assisted to balance the colonies' trade with England (adverse to the extent of £1,232,000 in 1770), but also accumulated great private capital surpluses in the colonies, capital of great value in developing subsequent American business enterprise.

TRADE-MARKS. The first Federal act permitting trade-mark registration was passed in 1870. Registrations averaged less than 1000 per year for the first ten years, and never reached 2000 in any one year until 1902. The act of 1905 made registration of a trade-mark *prima facie* evidence of ownership.

TRADING POSTS, FRONTIER. From the establishment of Jamestown (1607) until the end of Indian treaty-making (1871), traders and trading posts have been important factors in border relations. By 1774 Albany and Oswego (N. Y.) were important trade centers for the Iroquois and other northwestern tribes. At both places Indians would exchange their furs for guns, ammunition, hatchets, scalping knives, kettles and blankets. And during the period of colonial rivalries Spain and France, also, had their strategic trading posts. Mobile (1710), Natchitoches (by St. Denis, 1713), Natchez (by Bienville, 1716), and St. Louis, Mo. (by LaClede and Chouteau, 1764) were only a few maintained in the Mississippi Valley and from New Orleans to Pensacola.

After American independence, President Washington proposed, and Congress inaugurated (1796), the setting up of government factories and trading posts, and every border fort became a trade center. But bitter opposition of individual traders led to the abandonment of the policy in 1822. Moreover, American influence with frontier tribes up to 1814 was hampered by British trader influence. Not until 1795 would England agree to surrender occupied posts within the northern boundary of the United States. And English traders at Detroit continued to sell war supplies to tribes of the Ohio and Mississippi valleys until after 1814.

Shortly after American occupation of the Louisiana Territory (1804), trading posts were established throughout the trans-Mississippi West. St. Louis was the center for supplying traders and posts within the Pacific northwest and central west, and New Orleans the southwest. Missouri traders had built Fort Lisa by 1813 and Fort Benton (at the mouth of the Big Horn, not to be confused with Fort Benton on the Upper Missouri) by 1821, and John Jacob Astor had set up a post at Astoria on the Columbia River in 1811. Astor's organization encountered severe competition from the Hudson's Bay Company which had several posts in the same region. Sutter's post on the American River (1841) in California was the best-known trading station in California; and farther east, Fort Bridger and Fort Laramie became well known by the early 1840's.

In the greater Southwest, posts were equally important as factors in advancing the frontier. At the three forks of the Arkansas, in present Oklahoma, A. P. Chouteau and other traders had established their posts by 1815; and Chouteau built another near present Purcell (1835). The best-known trading post in the Southwest during the 1830's was Bent's Fort on the Arkansas, begun by Charles and William Bent, Ceran St. Vrain, and Benito Vasquez (1828–29). In Texas, posts were established during the days of the republic near modern Waco (Torrey's), and higher up on the Brazos. From these and others, here and there, went vast quantities of trade goods for furs and buffalo hides taken by the Indians.

TRAIL DRIVERS were cowboys in the act of moving cattle from a home range to a distant market or another range. The typical herd consisted of around 2500 head of cattle; though the average herd was smaller, herds of 3000 head were not uncommon; one of 5000 was exceptional. To move, water and graze more than 5000 cattle in one herd was virtually impossible.

The typical outfit consisted of a boss, who might or might not be the owner; from ten to fifteen hands, each of whom had a string of from five to ten horses; a horse wrangler (or *remudero*), who drove and herded the cow horses; and a cook, who drove the chuck wagon—or, in the earlier stages of trail driving, carried his kitchen and chuck on pack animals. The wagon carried the bed rolls; tents were considered excess luxury. The men drove and grazed the cattle most of the day, herding them by relays at night. Ten or twelve miles was considered a good day's drive, as the cattle must thrive on the route.

TRAIL OF TEARS was the journey of the eastern Cherokees to Oklahoma in 1838. By the treaty of New Echota, signed by a minority of the tribe in 1835, the Cherokees were to surrender their lands in Georgia and remove west of the Mississippi to the Indian country. The majority bitterly opposed removal and refused to go until forced to do so by troops under Gen. Winfield Scott. Soldiers drove the Indians into concentration camps, from which they were later released and detachments formed for the journey. In October and November, 1838, over 15,000 started westward, mostly on foot, since wagons were provided only for small children and the old and infirm. Winter came on and cold, rain and poor food brought sickness. Heartbroken at being compelled to leave their old homes, many fell an easy prey to disease. Exact figures cannot be found, but it is probable that nearly 10% of those who started died on this tragic journey.

TRAIN ROBBERIES were more frequent in America than anywhere else in the world in the latter half of the 19th century. This was in part due to vast stretches of sparsely inhabited country which permitted the robbers to escape undetected, but was in part due to carelessness and lack of adequate protection. The first train robbery on record was that of an Adams Express car on the New York, New Haven and Hartford Railroad which was rifled of $700,000 between New York and New Haven in 1866. In the same year occurred the first train holdup by the Reno gang in southern Indiana. They took the express messenger's keys from him at gun point, and robbed the safe of $13,000. Some members of the gang were arrested, but never tried, and a year later another gang repeated the exploit in the same neighborhood. For an arrest of one of the Renos in 1867, the remainder of the gang staged a number of bold-faced bank and train robberies in southern Indiana and Illinois in 1868. They were traced by the Pinkerton Detective agency, just then coming into prominence, arrested and jailed, but the entire family of brothers, except John, were executed by vigilantes before their cases came to trial. The Farringtons operated in 1870 in Kentucky and Tennessee; and Jack Davis of Nevada started operations at Truckee by robbing an express car of $41,000. He had learned his trade robbing stagecoaches in California a few years earlier.

The year 1870 marked the climax of train robberies, East and West. An express car was robbed at Albany in that year and the messenger shot. In those days care was not taken to lock the express and baggage end doors and the cars were frequently used for loafing and smoking. The picturesque and daring James gang began to operate in 1873 near Council Bluffs, Iowa. No other train robbers are so well known, and legends and songs cluster about their deeds. For nine years they terrorized the Middle West, and it was only after Jesse was shot by a confederate and Frank retired to run a Wild West show, that trainmen could breathe freely. Sam Bass in Texas, the Dalton Boys in Oklahoma and Sontag and Evans in California are other robbers with well-known records. After 1900 the number of holdups declined conspicuously.

TRAINING DAY IN NEW ENGLAND was the day for drilling the "trainbands." New England inherited the medieval custom of a militia periodically drilled; by 1600 the organization in England, outside of London, had fallen into decay and the shire militia in 1640 was little better than a mob, but frontier conditions in New England made efficient administration necessary. The local militia was organized only for drill or for emergency defense; the actual fighting, as in King Philip's War, was done by special companies of "troopers," recruited from the various bands and officered by men appointed by the General Court. The militia on the contrary was largely self-governing, electing its own officers, who had merely to be approved by the court.

On training day all able-bodied men, with the exception of a few professions such as ministers, magistrates, town herdsmen and millers, met to elect officers, drill, and converse. The clerk of the band called the roll and the companies themselves inflicted fines upon absentees. In 1649 the General Court defined the purposes of the day as drilling and fortification; in the 17th century the days were often devoted to constructing palisades, watch houses, and even churches. The day was always opened and closed with prayer and there was often a sermon. In contrast to such occasions in England, the New England days were at first models of propriety, so that John Winthrop could boast that when 1200 men trained on Boston Common no man was drunk, no oath was sworn, and nobody was hurt.

At first captains were required to train the companies every week; in 1636 eight days in every year were ordered; in 1660 the number was reduced to six; in 1679 to four. The town bought arms and supplies and sold them to individuals; the equipment was varied and often not efficient. There were no uniforms. Because the militia organization was an integral part of the community life, the training day became a gathering of the whole town; transactions of every sort were then performed and by the end of the century the day had become a sort of bazaar. By this time the clergy were complaining that it was an occasion for intoxication and quarrels.

TRANSCENDENTALISM, a philosophical term developed by Kant embodying those aspects of man's nature transcending, or independent of, experience, became the inspiration of a liberal social and cultural renaissance in New England during 1830–45 and received its chief American expression in Emerson's individualistic doctrine of self-reliance. In 1836 Emerson and a radical wing of Unitarians formed the Transcendental Club as a discussion group, Margaret Fuller's *Dial* later becoming its leading organ. Experiments in "plain living and high thinking" like Brook Farm and Fruitlands attracted the exponents of a new self-culture; and social utopians, from vegetarian enthusiasts to abolitionists, found a congenial atmosphere within the movement.

TRAPPERS' RENDEZVOUS. An advertisement appearing in the *Missouri Republican* of St. Louis, Mo., in the spring of 1822 read as follows: "To enterprising young men. The subscriber wishes to engage one hundred young men to ascend the Missouri River to its source, there to be employed for one, two, or three years. . . . [Signed] William H. Ashley." Out of this recruiting grew an organization of mountain men destined to institute a unique method of trapping and trade in the beaver country.

Following established practice, Ashley's men (Rocky Mountain Fur Company) held to the valley of the Missouri and depended upon Indians and white trappers to come to their forts to trade. Pushed by the competition of the Missouri Fur Company, Ashley relinquished the Missouri Valley and carried his operations to the west side of the Rocky Mountains. Here he dropped the practice of conducting trade from fixed points, and relied upon itinerant parties equipped to trap rather than trade, so obtaining his beaver directly from the streams. Such giants of the fur trade era as Andrew Henry, Jedediah S. Smith, the four Sublette brothers, James Bridger, Thomas Fitzpatrick, Henry Fraeb, Robert Campbell, David Jackson and Étienne Provost, are identified with the expeditions launched by Ashley. The parties penetrated the untapped regions of the Green, the Snake and the Salt Lake basin. The new method of doing business necessitated annual gatherings of the itinerant parties, at which time pack outfits from St. Louis delivered equipment, supplies, trade goods—and liquor—and picked up the product of the trappers' work. Naturally, to these meetings came hordes of Indians to participate in the trade and hilarity. These notable fairs in the wilderness became known as annual *rendezvous*. The first one, a mild affair on the Sweetwater (Wyo.) in 1824 was held for the convenience of scattered parties of Ashley's men under Fitzpatrick, who had trapped the Wind River country in 1823–24. In the summer of 1825, Ashley, himself, assembled his parties, joined by a Hudson's Bay Company group, on Henry's Fork of the Green River. The next year, Ashley met with his company at a site near the present Ogden, Utah. Here, with great profit he disposed of his interests in the Rocky Mountain Fur Company to some of his associates, who continued with the rendezvous method. Succeeding assemblages, in some of which rival companies participated, were held at Bear Lake, Utah, 1827; Ogden, Utah, 1828; Popo Agie, Wyo., 1829, 1830 and 1838; Big Hole near the Salmon River, 1831; Pierre's Hole, Idaho, 1832; Green River at Horse Creek, 1833, 1835, 1836, 1839 and 1840; Green River on Ham's Fork, 1834; and Wind River, Wyo., 1837.

TRAPPING continues to be a part-time occupation for many rural Americans. Until the middle of the 19th century trapping was a prime factor in the process of westward movement, for professional trappers and traders not only developed a source of wealth for a growing nation but, more important, they explored the rivers, blazed trails through unmapped forests, brought hostile Indians under control, made known the agricultural values of the wilderness, and extended American holdings to the very Pacific itself. The American trapper, as a type, may well be identified as that picturesque mountain man of the Rocky Mountain region who during the first half of the 19th century worked out of the fur trade center, St. Louis, in a struggle against nature and British antagonists in winning the West for the United States. This American trapper did not, however, arrive ready-made to succeed Lewis and Clark in further penetration of our western country. He evolved through many stages from the Pilgrim trapper of 1620, from the Dutch trader of the Connecticut and the Hudson, from the Frenchman of Green Bay, from the British North West Company agent, from the Hudson's Bay Company *voyageur*, and from the backwoodsman of Kentucky and Tennessee. From some of these, he inherited a psychological character that made him indomitable; from all, he borrowed his technique and his material equipment. The upper Missouri trapper of 1830 was a composite picture of the many types that had dared the wilderness through two hundred years of westward progress. With him he took a method that had its beginnings in the Indian trade on the St. Lawrence and the Potomac, and a paraphernalia that sprang from roots deep in the countries of Europe. Many of his items of equipment and objects of trade had changed not a whit in two centuries of use in America.

In following his profession, the trapper of the upper Missouri traveled with a company of companions employed by one of the established trading firms of St. Louis or worked out of that city as free and independent trappers. Zenas Leonard, writing of his arrival with the Gant and Blackwell party in beaver country at the junction of the Laramie and Platte Rivers, Aug. 27, 1831, gives the following description of procedure: "Captain Gant gave orders to make preparations for trapping. The company was divided into parties of from 15 to 20 men, with their respective captains placed over them, and directed by Captain Gant in what direction to go. Captain Washburn ascended the Tiber Fork; Captain Stephens, the Laramie; Captain Gant, the Sweetwater—all of which empty into the River Platte near the same place. Each of these companies were directed to ascend these rivers until they found beaver sufficiently plenty for trapping, or until the snow and cold weather compelled them to stop, at which event they were to return to the mouth of the Laramie River to pass the winter together."

TRAVERSE DES SIOUX, TREATY OF (July 23, 1851). By this treaty, signed at Traverse des Sioux on the Minnesota River, the Upper Sioux ceded to the United States all their lands in Iowa and Minnesota east of a line following the western bank of the Red River through Lake Traverse, thence southwesterly to the Big Sioux River and along the western bank of that river to the Iowa line. The chief consideration to the Indians was an annual interest payment of $68,000 for fifty years, of which $40,000 was to be cash. According to the "Traders' Paper," signed by the chiefs directly after the treaty, $210,000 was designated to liquidate their debts to the traders. The reservation assigned them extended along the upper Minnesota River, ten miles wide on either side. Later, on Aug. 5, the Lower Sioux ceded the same lands in a treaty at Mendota differing essentially from that at Traverse des Sioux only in the amounts of money. Their reservation continued along the Minnesota from the upper reserve nearly to New Ulm. These treaties, ratified at Washington June 23, 1852, with amendments later accepted by the Indians, were proclaimed by President Fillmore, Feb. 24, 1853. Dissatisfaction of the Indians with these treaties and their nonfulfillment culminated in the Sioux War of 1862.

TRAVOIS. A characteristic method of transportation employed chiefly by plains Indians, consisted of poles, lashed on the back of a horse in such manner that the ends dragged behind. Usually in moving camp these were teepee poles, the teepee cover, food, luggage and even persons, riding on the dragging ends. Sometimes especially constructed travois, consisting of two springy poles and a litter, were employed for transportation of children or aged persons. Dogs were often employed to drag small travois.

TREASON: "IF THIS BE TREASON, MAKE THE MOST OF IT." There are several versions as to the exact wording of this part of Patrick Henry's Stamp Act speech. Wirt's version reads: "Caesar had his Brutus, Charles the First his Cromwell, and George the Third—['Treason' cried the Speaker . . .] may profit by their example. If *this* be treason, make the most of it." Since, however, several witnesses, writing independently, included a reference to Tarquin, the most accurate rendition would seem to be the W. W. Henry version: "Tarquin and Caesar had each his Brutus; Charles the First, his Cromwell; and George the Third"—interrupted here by cries of "Treason!" Henry concluded: "may profit by their example. If *this* be treason, make the most of it."

TREASURY, DEPARTMENT OF THE, was established by Congress by the act of Sept. 2, 1789. The law provided also for the appointment by the President of a Secretary of the Treasury who was to be the head of the Treasury Department. The Secretary was directed to digest and prepare plans for the management and improvement of the revenue and the support of the public credit. He was also authorized to superintend the collection of revenue, to report budget estimates, etc. The act placed the Secretary in intimate connection with Congress by providing that calls for financial information be made direct to the Treasury without going through the President.

In addition to providing for a Secretary of the Treasury, the law authorized the appointment of a treasurer, comptroller, auditor, register and an assistant secretary, all save the last-named being purely accounting officers with special functions of checking accounts and payments to be sure no unauthorized expenditures were made by the Treasury.

Although the number of officers has been increased from time to time as the business of the Treasury increased, there has been no radical change of functions from those specified in the act of 1789. Since that act, however, a number of bureaus of the Treasury Department have been created. The customs service, established by the act of July 31, 1789, automatically came under the control of the Treasury Department after the passage of the act of Sept. 2. The office of Director of the Mint was assigned to the State Department by Washington in 1792, but was transferred to the Treasury Department in 1795 at the request of Hamilton. The mint was not legally made a bureau of the Treasury, however, until the act of Feb. 12, 1873.

Collectors of Internal Revenue were first authorized by the act of July 16, 1798, but the existing office of Commissioner of Internal Revenue was not established until July 1, 1862. The National Bank Act of Feb. 25, 1863 (re-enacted June 3, 1864) established the office of Comptroller of the Currency as a Treasury bureau, and the act of March 3, 1877, established the Bureau of Engraving and Printing. The Bureau of the Budget was created by an act of June 10, 1921.

Alexander Hamilton was appointed by Washington as the first Secretary of the Treasury on Sept. 11, 1789.

TREATIES WITH FOREIGN NATIONS. Under the Constitution, the President is empowered to make treaties, with the advice and consent of the Senate, provided that two thirds of the Senators present concur. He usually negotiates treaties through representatives who are given special "full powers" to sign them. The agreements do not take effect until the formal exchange of ratifications after Senate action. *Note.* In using this general study of treaty making, the reader will find it important to refer to the expanded articles on major treaties which are included in this book under their specific names.

The United States' first treaties were made before the Constitution was adopted. The alliance with France in 1778 helped to make independence possible, and the Treaty of 1783 with Great Britain ended the Revolutionary War. Other treaties were made with the Netherlands (1782), Sweden (1783), Prussia (1785), and Morocco (1786).

In the first forty years after the establishment of the Federal Government, only a relatively few treaties were signed, but most of them were of major importance. Among these were the Jay Treaty of 1794, which averted a dangerous crisis in relations with Great Britain, the Treaty of Ghent of 1814, which ended the War of 1812, and the commercial convention with Great Britain of 1815. Pinckney's treaty with Spain, in 1795, was considered a notable success for American diplomacy. The Louisiana Purchase Treaty of 1803 with France, and the treaty of 1819 by which Spain ceded the Floridas and the Oregon territory to the United States added great areas to the national domain.

In the subsequent period, and more especially during the past 75 years, the United States made treaties with a great number of foreign governments, dealing with a vast range of subject matter. Many of these dealt with commerce and navigation, the rights of consuls, pecuniary claims, and the extradition of criminals. Treaties with Turkey (1830), with Muscat and with Siam (in 1833), with China (1844 and 1858), and with Japan (1854) testified to an increasing interest in countries outside of Europe. American citizens obtained extraterritorial rights in several oriental countries, including the Turkish Empire, China and Japan. Boundary disputes with Great Britain were adjusted by the Webster-Ashburton Treaty of 1842 and the Oregon Treaty of 1846; and the Treaty of Guadalupe Hidalgo (1848) and the Gadsden Treaty (1854) fixed the boundary with Mexico. Alaska was purchased from Russia by treaty in 1867. Another notable agreement was the Treaty of Washington with Great Britain in 1871, which provided for the arbitration of the Alabama claims and settled several other troublesome questions. A number of agreements with Great Britain dealt with fisheries questions.

American interest in the Caribbean and in the construction of a transisthmian canal led to the negotiation of several treaties, beginning with the agreement of 1846 with Colombia and the Clayton-Bulwer Treaty of 1850 with Great Britain. The Treaty of Paris with Spain in 1898 freed Cuba and gave the United States Puerto Rico, the Philippines and Guam. Two agreements with Cuba, the Permanent Treaty of 1903, which incorporated the Platt Amendment, and the Reciprocity Treaty of 1902, defined relations with the newly established government in that country. The Platt Amendment was abolished by another treaty in 1934. In 1901 the Hay-Pauncefote Treaty with Great Britain freed the United States from the restrictions which the Clayton-Bulwer Treaty had imposed on its freedom of action in building the transisthmian canal, and in 1903 a treaty with Panama provided for its construction. Important modifications of American rights in the Canal Zone were accepted in later treaties signed with Panama in 1936 and 1955. Colombia received $25,000,000 from the United States in compensation for the loss of Panama under a treaty signed in 1914 but not ratified until 1921. Other important agreements, motivated in part at least by considerations related to the security of the Canal, were the customs receivership treaty of 1907 with the Dominican Republic, the treaty of 1915 with Haiti, and the treaty by which the United States acquired the Virgin Islands from Denmark, signed in 1916.

One of the principal subjects dealt with by treaty has been the protection and promotion of international trade. The general treaties of commerce and navigation have been revised or replaced from time to time as conditions have changed. Most of the trade treaties made after 1923, unlike those of an earlier date, included an unconditional most-favored-nation clause. Reciprocity agreements, providing for mutual concessions with respect to customs duties, were concluded with many countries during the 19th and the first part of the 20th century. Since the enactment of the Trade Agreements Act of 1934, tariff concessions have usually been dealt with by agreements that do not require ratification by the Senate.

Another prime objective of United States treaty-making has been the promotion of international peace. This was the purpose of the multilateral conventions signed at the Hague conferences of 1899 and 1907. After 1908 bilateral arbitration conventions were entered into with many countries, and in 1913–14 treaties for the advancement of peace sponsored by Secretary of State William J. Bryan were signed with more than twenty governments. The Briand-Kellogg pact for the renunciation of war, signed in 1928, was ratified by nearly all civilized states. The problem of maintaining peace was approached from a different angle in the Treaty for the Limitation of Naval Armaments drawn up at the Washington Con-

ference of 1921–22 and the London Naval Treaty of 1936.

The advancement of peace within the Americas has been the purpose of a long series of inter-American treaties, beginning with a convention for the compulsory arbitration of pecuniary claims signed at the first Pan-American conference in 1889. Subsequent conferences drew up increasingly comprehensive measures for the peaceful settlement of disputes, culminating in the American Treaty of Pacific Settlement, signed at the ninth Pan-American conference at Bogotá in 1948. The same conference adopted the Charter of the Organization of American States, the basic agreement of the inter-American community of nations. Other inter-American agreements have dealt with economic and cultural cooperation and many other matters including hemisphere defense. One of the most important treaties to which the United States is a party is the Inter-American Treaty of Reciprocal Assistance, signed at Rio de Janeiro in 1947.

Matters of interest to large groups of nations have often been dealt with by multilateral conventions. Among the earlier ones were the Red Cross Convention of 1864, to which the United States adhered in 1882, the Industrial Property Convention of 1883, the Submarine Cables Convention of 1884, and the General Act for Suppression of the Slave Trade, 1890. The subjects dealt with in more recent multilateral agreements are too numerous to enumerate; weights and measures, bills of lading, health problems, the liquor traffic in Africa, radio communication, aviation, safety at sea, and the protection of the whale fishery may be mentioned as examples.

The signature of the Charter of the United Nations Organization, on June 26, 1945, was a landmark in modern history. Other important recent agreements have been the North Atlantic (NATO) Treaty of 1947, and the peace treaties with Italy, Hungary, Rumania, Bulgaria, and Finland in 1947; with Japan in 1951; with the German Federal Republic in 1952; and with Austria in 1955.

A controversy over the treaty-making power arose when a "genocide" convention and a convention on human rights, drafted under the auspices of the United Nations in 1949 and 1951 respectively, aroused apprehension lest treaties be used to accomplish purposes that the Federal Government could not accomplish by legislation. Under Article VI of the Constitution, treaties, like Federal statutes, are the supreme law of the land. To avert the possibility that a treaty might infringe on the constitutional rights of individuals or of the states, Senator John W. Bricker of Ohio introduced a constitutional amendment which would have provided that treaties and other international agreements should become effective as internal law in the United States only through legislation valid in the absence of international agreement. The "Bricker Amendment," in various forms, was introduced in several sessions of Congress, and it seemed to have much support in the Senate, but it was opposed by President Truman and later by President Eisenhower as an unwise restriction of the President's treaty-making power.

It should be observed that a great number of international agreements are not treaties, which require approval by the Senate, but Executive Agreements. These are equally effective and valid as international acts. Many of them are made under statutory authority or in compliance with a joint resolution of Congress. Of this type are the postal conventions, the first of which date from the 18th century, and the more recent reciprocal trade agreements, as well as a great many arrangements covering other sorts of governmental activity. Other executive agreements are made by the President on his own authority, in cases where he does not consider a formal treaty necessary or advisable. Sometimes these have dealt with matters of major importance, and there has been a question whether they should not have been submitted to the Senate for approval. In 1905, for example, when the Senate failed to act on a treaty for the establishment of a customs receivership in the Dominican Republic, President Theodore Roosevelt made temporary arrangements for the receivership under a *modus vivendi*. The requirement for approval by a two-thirds majority of the Senate of course makes it more difficult to conclude a treaty, and there have been cases where a majority of Congress resorted to action by joint resolution to accomplish what a treaty could not accomplish because a two-thirds majority of the Senate could not be mustered for its approval. Perhaps the most notable examples were the annexation of Texas in 1845 and of Hawaii in 1898.

TREDEGAR IRON WORKS. Rolling mills rose at Richmond almost as soon as at Pittsburgh. The Tredegar rolling mill, privately built in 1836, was first operated by the Tredegar Iron Co., Jan. 2, 1838. Joseph Reid Anderson, a West Point graduate, the company's third commercial agent, saved it from failing in 1841. In 1843 he leased, and in 1848 bought the works. By 1860 he had enlarged them, and successfully manufactured for a national market nearly every type of iron, including 1200 cannon for the U. S. Government. Produced largely by skilled slave labor, Tredegar iron, because of its great tensile strength, ranked as one of the three leading charcoal irons of America. Without the Tredegar the Confederacy would have collapsed, since, until 1863, it constituted the government's only source for cannon other than by capture. It served as a laboratory for Confederate military and naval experiment, and a reservoir of munitions; it equipped the army with nearly 1100 cannon; it made mandatory the defense of Richmond, and thus the removal of the capital from Montgomery for psychological reasons. Rein-

corporated, after the war, as the Tredegar Company, with Anderson as president, it led in rebuilding the new South.

TRENT AFFAIR. The disputed doctrine of the freedom of the seas was involved in this incident. In the autumn of 1861 the Confederate government selected as diplomats James Murray Mason of Virginia for London and John Slidell of Louisiana for Paris. The commissioners successfully ran the blockade to Havana, Cuba, where they took passage, Nov. 7, 1861, on the *Trent*, a British ship. The next day, without instructions, Capt. Charles Wilkes of the U. S. S. *San Jacinto* stopped the *Trent*, searched the vessel, arrested the two Confederate commissioners and their secretaries, and removed them to the *San Jacinto*. The *Trent* was permitted to continue its voyage, but the commissioners were taken as prisoners to Fort Warren, in Boston Harbor. Capt. Wilkes had made the mistake of searching the ship and seizing the agents on board a neutral vessel at sea instead of bringing the ship into port for adjudication. The *Trent* might have been seized, however, for performing an unneutral service. The ship's "cargo," though, could not be legally condemned except by bringing the vessel before a prize court and receiving a judicial decree to that effect.

When the news of the *Trent* affair reached the American public, there was naturally great rejoicing in the North because Union victories on the battlefield thus far had been few. In England, however, news of the incident was followed by a wave of indignation. In fact, a demand for war spread through the British Isles. Lord Russell drafted a demand for an apology and for the immediate release of Mason and Slidell. If this demand were not met, Lord Lyons, the British minister at Washington, was to come home. Fortunately, the Prince Consort, who was on his deathbed, softened the British note, and Lyons presented the position of his government as tactfully as possible. The British government rushed 8000 troops to the defense of Canada and forbade temporarily the exportation of arms and ammunition.

A majority of Lincoln's cabinet had rejoiced with the public, and failed to question Wilkes' act. The House of Representatives even voted Wilkes a gold medal. Lincoln, fortunately, was cautious, and Secretary Seward soon realized that a mistake had been made. Nothing was done, however, prior to the arrival of the British note, except to instruct Charles Francis Adams, American minister to England, to inform Lord Palmerston that Wilkes had acted without instructions.

Upon realizing that the alternative to the surrender of the commissioners must be war with England, Seward, in a communication, Dec. 26, "cheerfully liberated" them because Wilkes had erred in not bringing the ship into port for adjudication, and because he had violated American established policy of freedom of the seas. The dispatch was written to soothe the American public and also to satisfy the British. Although successful in this endeavor, Seward lost for the United States an opportunity to secure British acquiescence in the principle of freedom of the seas.

TRENTON, BATTLE OF (Dec. 26, 1776). Following Washington's evacuation of New Jersey, Howe (Br.) had established two unsupported cantonments of 1500 Hessians each, at Bordentown and Trenton. Col. Rall, the commandant at Trenton, scorning the American soldier, refused to fortify the village. To Washington, facing the dissolution of his army and sure the enemy only awaited the freezing of the Delaware to seize Philadelphia, the exposed position of these posts offered an opportunity. He accordingly planned a simultaneous surprise movement against both, with the main blow falling at Trenton.

On Christmas night, with 2500 troops, he crossed the Delaware at McKonkey's Ferry, eight miles above Trenton. Delayed by floating ice and a storm of sleet and snow, it was eight o'clock and broad day when his two columns, under his own and Sullivan's command, reached the village. The Hessians, who, as Washington had foreseen, had spent Christmas night in celebrating, were completely surprised. "They made no regular stand" (Washington); their firing was ineffective as their powder was dampened by the storm; and Rall, who had ignored warnings of the attack, seemed not to know what to do. The Americans, among whom were many expert riflemen, fired from houses, cellars, from behind trees and fences, while their artillery raked the two main streets of the town. In the battle, lasting scarcely forty minutes, the Hessians lost 22 killed (including Rall), 84 wounded and 1000 taken prisoner, while the patriots had only two officers and two privates wounded. Two supporting divisions failed to cross the river until the following day; meanwhile the Hessians at Bordentown safely withdrew.

Coming so swiftly after a succession of bitter defeats, this victory infused new life into the patriot cause, restored confidence in Washington both at home and abroad, strengthened the resolution of Congress and, coupled with Princeton, practically freed New Jersey of British control.

TRIANGLE FIRE (1911). The Triangle Waist Co., occupying the three top floors of a ten-story loft building in New York City, suffered a disastrous fire on March 25, 1911, in which 147 lives, mostly those of women and girl workers, were lost. The proprietors of the business were indicted and tried, but acquitted. Public opinion had been aroused, however, and the disaster led to sweeping reforms in building and factory laws, especially as to precautions against fire.

TRUMAN DOCTRINE. On March 12, 1947, President Truman asked Congress for $400,000,000 for the defense of Greece and Turkey from the pressure of Soviet communism. On May 15, Congress, although the country was officially at peace, voted the money, thus sanctioning a radical departure from the traditional policy of "nonentanglement" in European affairs. That this departure was to be more than temporary, Truman indicated when he declared it to be a general principle of American policy "to help free peoples to maintain . . . their national integrity against aggressive movements that seek to impose upon them totalitarian [*i.e.*, communist] regimes."

TRUSTS. Authorities on trusts agree that the term has been so broadly used that a precise definition is impossible. Eliot Jones limits it to an industrial monopoly, and that is the general practice, although banking combines have been known as "money" trusts, public utilities have been called "power" trusts, and railroad companies and labor organizations have been prosecuted under the Federal antitrust laws. The attempt or the ability to control a large portion of the market is what makes a concern a trust.

In the late 19th century improving technology created problems of overcapacity or overproduction in a growing number of industries, especially those using expensive equipment. There were four basic solutions to such overproduction. One was to find new markets for the greater output and this led to great advances in marketing; a second was to demand higher tariffs to keep out foreign competition; a third was to cut costs; and the last to form a monopoly to limit output and put up prices. The adage, "If you can't beat them, join them" was often the solution adopted. The monopoly solution in turn had serious faults. These were exploitation of the consumer, unfair competition to kill off would-be competitors, unnecessary unemployment, and too great concentration of economic and political power in the hands of powerful directors of big industry.

The monopolistic tendency on a national scale of American industry first took the form of pooling agreements limiting production, fixing prices, centralizing selling, and setting quotas, but since these were unenforceable under the common law, they were often broken. The first trust was the Standard Oil whose form of organization, secret in 1879 but amended and publicized in 1882, originated the name. The stockholders in numerous refining, pipeline and other companies assigned their stock to a board of nine trustees at a stipulated price and received trust certificates. The trustees had legal and voting rights in the stocks; and the stockholders received the profits. This ingenious system was shortly copied by other industries; the American Cotton Oil Trust was set up in 1884, the National Linseed Oil Trust in 1885, and the Distillers and Cattle Feeders Trust, known as the "whiskey trust," in 1887.

Public agitation over the size and power of these giant organizations led to the testing of their legality in state courts, which decided that entering into such agreements was beyond a corporation's powers. Congress passed the Sherman Antitrust Law July 2, 1890, section 1 of which states that "Every contract, combination . . . or conspiracy in restraint of trade or commerce among the several states . . . is . . . illegal." Between 1891 and 1897 there were only fifty combinations of over a million dollars formed. The depression covering much of this period was, of course, also a discouraging factor.

The antitrust legislation was not effective for long. The Supreme Court seemed to draw the teeth of the Sherman Act in 1895 in the Knight case (U. S. v. E. C. Knight Co.) by ruling that the control of 98% of the sugar refining in the country was not illegal because it took the form of manufacturing in one state and not commerce between states. Said the Court, "Commerce succeeds to manufacture, and is not a part of it." In addition a satisfactory substitute for the trustee device was found when New Jersey in 1889 and 1893, then Delaware, Maine and other states, authorized corporations receiving charters from them to hold stock in other corporations, a right previously not enjoyed. The holding company thus made possible differed from the trustee system in that ownership was substituted for trusteeship.

Between 1898 and 1903 trusts were formed in rapid succession. The census of 1900 showed 185 industrial combinations, 73 of them capitalized at $10,000,000 or more, turning out 14% of the industrial products of the nation; 1901 witnessed the founding of the billion-dollar United States Steel Corp.; and by 1904, 318 trusts controlled two fifths of the manufacturing capital of the country. The "rich man's panic" of 1903 brought the movement to a close.

Meanwhile the Government had won a few minor cases with the Sherman law, Theodore Roosevelt had become President, and a fever of reform had begun to sweep the nation. The "trust busting" movement began with the Supreme Court decision of March 14, 1904, against the Northern Securities Co., a holding company formed to unite two great competing railroad systems in the Northwest. Suits were brought against 44 trusts and combinations in Roosevelt's administration and against ninety more under President Taft.

The trusts became better behaved. Ruthless extermination of rivals that had characterized the oil and cash-register trusts gave way to a more tolerant system of letting the independents live if they would adhere to the trust's price policy and so keep business stable and profits at a maximum. These milder tactics bore fruit in 1911 when the Supreme Court announced in its *obiter dicta* in the Standard Oil and American Tobacco cases that these trusts were being dissolved because they were acting in "unreasonable" restraint of trade. The implication of this renowned "rule of reason" was that "good" trusts would not be broken up in the future. The following year the Court went a step farther in the Terminal Railroad Association

case (224 U. S. 383) and contended that even a trust which had acted in restraint of trade should be tolerated, if it could be used for legitimate purposes.

In 1912 Woodrow Wilson popularized his "New Freedom" whose keynote was the restoration of free competition in trade and industry, and in 1914 his administration secured the Clayton and Federal Trade Commission acts. The Clayton Act condemned such business practices as local price discrimination, tying contracts, interlocking directorates, and even the acquisition by one corporation of the stock of another in the same business, if the consequences were monopolistic. The Federal Trade Commission Act forbade "unfair methods of competition in commerce," a broad term which it was left to the commission to enforce and the courts to continue to interpret. But the "New Freedom," handicapped by greater judicial tolerance of trusts and by the outbreak of the World War, died young.

There are several explanations for the public's less hostile attitude toward trusts after World War I. The war taught businessmen in all lines the advantages of concerted action; it showed the public that a rising price level was probably caused more by monetary factors than by monopoly exploitation; and it bred a cynical attitude toward reform. The Webb-Pomerene Act of 1918 and the Merchant Marine Act of 1920 permitted American concerns to combine to some extent in their foreign business. When the Supreme Court did not dissolve the U. S. Steel Corp. in 1920 (251 U. S. 417), despite its control of over half the steel output, and such evidence as a price of $28 a ton for steel rails maintained for ten years, a new trust movement got under way. The merger was now the chief method of combination because the Clayton Act virtually forbade large-scale commercial combination by stock purchase. However, public utility empires were built with the holding-company device. It has been estimated that there were over 500 combinations in the Coolidge administration alone. During the prosperous 1920's businesses in the same line were permitted to an increasing degree to compare recent statistical information, basing point systems grew in popularity, and finally, in the Appalachian Coal Case (288 U. S. 344) in 1933 a joint sales agency, including producers of 75% of the output, was judged not contrary to the antitrust laws.

The great amount of price-cutting that took place during the depression after 1929 led to criticism of the predatory character of competition and to considerable talk of the need for a more planned economy. The F. D. Roosevelt administration under the National Industrial Recovery Act of 1933 permitted trade associations and other industrial groups to control prices and determine production, and encouraged them to draw up codes of fair competition, promising that any action taken in compliance with an approved code would not subject them to prosecution under the antitrust laws. The Federal Trade Commission was to enforce these codes. Within the first month over 400 of the eventual total of 677 were filed, and many were too hastily approved. Code groups were allowed to do many things the antitrust laws forbade, and this was especially true of the soft coal, petroleum, lumber and cleaning and dyeing businesses. The suspension of over forty years of antitrust legal precedents left the courts bewildered. However, the Supreme Court's adverse decision in the Schechter case in May, 1935, brought this experiment in industrial self-government to an end.

Two subsequent laws slightly altered antitrust legislation. The Robinson-Patman Act (1936) attempted to define more clearly the types of wholesale price discrimination that were prohibited. The Miller-Tydings Act (1937) gave force in interstate commerce to the resale price maintenance laws most states have, and represented a lessening of competition.

The recession of 1937 saw a revival of trust prosecutions, notably against the Aluminum Co. of America and the cement industry. On June 16, 1938, Congress authorized the appointment of the Temporary National Economic Committee (the T. N. E. C.), with Sen. Joseph O'Mahoney as chairman, to investigate the growing concentration of economic power and recommend appropriate legislation. That committee's lengthy hearings starting Dec. 16, 1938, and its final report indicated the need again to curb the trusts. Thurman Arnold of the Antitrust Division of the Justice Department had many big companies haled into court. Then World War II broke out and, just as in World War I, the Government suspended prosecution of the trusts and encouraged co-operation among industries in the interest of efficiency. The Office of Price Administration even found this concentration of economic power useful in effecting price controls.

In 1946 the Antitrust Division reported, "The monopoly problem in American industry today is more serious and widespread than at any time since the passage of the Sherman Act." The Division began investigations of 122 companies. Chief of their targets were the Aluminum Co. of America (the Government sold its war-built plants to competitors of Alcoa), du Pont with its large General Motor holdings (Antitrust won this case in 1957), the Atlantic and Pacific Tea Co. controlling 5% of the grocery business, and the Pullman Co. But Antitrust's greatest victory was the Supreme Court's order in 1948 to the Cement Institute to abandon the basing point system which was a subtler version of Pittsburgh Plus. This obliged some 25 other industries, among them steel, to give up theirs, too. By the 1950's Antitrust had a large staff and ample funds and was able to investigate and prosecute many trusts simultaneously. In its eyes great size had become tantamount to monopoly. But the 1950 monopolies bore little resemblance to those of the 1900's. They were more subtly organized and better behaved in general.

The trust or monopoly situation had changed in a number of ways in half a century. Since the 1930's there had been increasing talk of the evils of oligopoly (a few big producers, for example, General Motors, Ford and Chrysler, recently controlled 97% of American passenger car production). Also many critics argued that the Nation's most powerful monopolies were no longer industries but some large unions. Yet these by legislation (1914, 1932) and political attitudes were virtually exempt from antitrust prosecution. Finally, the Federal Government itself, from the 1930's on, when faced with overproduction or overcapacity problems, organized or encouraged its own monopoly as the solution to the problem, somewhat as John D. Rockefeller had once done. The Agricultural Adjustment Administration of 1933 was essentially a Government-sponsored farmers' trust to limit production and raise the level of farm prices. Admittedly the Government, not private citizens, directed this, but this monopoly, like others, exploited the consumers.

America and England have used seven methods to deal with trusts. They are: regulating the industry, which Congress did to the railroads by the act of 1887; setting up a government yardstick as the Tennessee Valley Authority allegedly does; doing nothing and hoping that competition will somehow reappear; doing nothing except imposing heavy taxes on monopoly profits; keeping tariffs low to make foreign competition effective (England did this up to 1931); nationalizing offending industries (as England has also done); and ordering the trusts to break up, as the Supreme Court did to Standard Oil of New Jersey in 1911. American antitrust legislation has used dissolution as its chief solution and form of punishment but that has not been especially successful. The 34 pieces of Standard Oil of New Jersey remained for a time after 1911 a trust operating under an interlocking directorate.

TRYON'S LINE. William Tryon, as royal governor of North Carolina, in pursuance of agreements made with the Cherokee on Oct. 20, 1765, and June 13, 1767, caused to be run a line between North Carolina and the Cherokee hunting grounds. Under instructions from London, this line was run in the summer of 1767 as a part of the line referred to in the Proclamation of 1763. Tryon named three commissioners who ran the line from Reedy River, where the North Carolina-South Carolina line terminated, to the top of Tryon Mountain of the Blue Ridge; thence by a straight course to Chiswell's Mine (the present Austinville, Va.) on New River. Tryon then issued a proclamation forbidding any purchase of land from the Indians and the issuance of grants beyond and within a strip one mile east of the line.

TURNER'S REBELLION of Aug. 21, 1831, at Southampton, Va., seventy miles from Richmond, raised Southern fears of a general servile war to their highest point. As a "leader" or lay Negro preacher, Nat Turner exercised a strong influence over his race. He believed himself a supernatural instrument to lead his people out of bondage. On the fatal August night, he led a band of sixty or seventy slaves to the large plantations, killing fifty-five whites before the community could act. This outbreak, following repeated disclosures of slave plots in Virginia and elsewhere, exercised a profound influence upon the attitude of the South toward slavery. After a consideration of the arguments of emancipationists during the legislative session of 1831–32, Virginia rejected them in favor of strengthening the police measures against the slave. Other Southern states, fearing a repercussion of Nat Turner's insurrection, attributed in some quarters to abolitionist propaganda, passed more stringent slave laws and Negro education became more than ever an object of suspicion.

TURNPIKES, EARLY. These were roads on which tolls were collected from users to meet the costs of construction and maintenance. The idea of thus financing highways was imported, toward the end of the 18th century, from England, where the turnpikes were publicly owned and administered by trustees. In America, however, they were generally built with private capital and operated by corporations for profit under state regulation, although outside New England public funds were sometimes so invested.

The greatest activity in company organization and road construction occurred between 1795 and 1810. The growth of commerce, which called for road betterment, and an easing of capital combined to encourage this activity. One hundred seventy active turnpike companies were chartered in New England between 1792 and 1810. They invested over $5,000,000 in building or improving nearly 3000 miles of road. By 1807 New York had 88 different operating companies, representing a capital investment of over $5,500,000 and operating over 3000 miles of road; Pennsylvania had 88 companies operating 1807 miles by 1821.

Costs of construction varied in New England between $200 and $13,000 per mile. Companies which built entirely new roads, especially those in metropolitan areas, invested heavily in land. Other companies simply took over old public roads without purchase. Those roads built in tidewater areas often required an artificial roadbed, while others required only cleaning and grading. The number of bridges required affected costs of construction significantly, as did the type of road surface desired. Turnpikes in New England were rarely surfaced, since the sand content of its soil is generally high. In New York, Pennsylvania and some of the Southern states, however, an artificial gravel surface was common.

Turnpike corporations were responsible for a decided improvement in road conditions generally. Cities and villages were brought closer together. The ex-

tensive business done by stage lines and the rapid increase in the number of privately owned traveling vehicles between 1800 and 1830 attest to the encouragement of travel by turnpikes. In freight carriage they were important as feeders to water transportation facilities, but ineffective as competitors with water routes.

In spite of this stimulus to land travel and transportation, especially the former, as business enterprises the turnpikes were miserable failures. By 1825 turnpike stocks were generally worthless, since maintenance charges were only slightly, if any, less than toll receipts. During the turnpike era, 1800–40, probably not over a dozen turnpike roads paid their proprietors even reasonably well. An overwhelming majority lost the whole amount of original investment. The trouble lay in overbuilding. Naturally well-situated roads should have been built less expensively and less well-situated roads should not have been turnpiked at all. The inherent inefficiency of horse-drawn vehicles for long-distance travel or hauling could not be overcome by the expensive multiplication or improvement of highways.

TUSKEGEE INSTITUTE was established by the Alabama legislature in the post-Reconstruction period. Its first session began with thirty students, July 4, 1881, under Booker T. Washington. His plan of education included the correlation of academic courses with industrial training. His successors, Robert Russa Moton and Frederick Douglass Patterson, with a Negro faculty and friends North and South, co-operated in making Tuskegee one of the Negro's great achievements.

TWEED RING, THE, robbed the New York City treasury of a minimum of $30,000,000 in the thirty months ended July 31, 1871. Another audit estimated that the Tweed Ring proper, which began in 1869, and its immediate forerunner, looted the city of between $45,000,000 and $50,000,000 in the three years and six months beginning Jan. 1, 1868. An aldermanic investigation (1877) raised this figure to $60,000,000. Matthew J. O'Rourke, a journalist who, while county bookkeeper, bared the frauds, reckoned $200,000,000 as the total stealings of the Ring and the lesser Tweed rings from Jan. 1, 1865, to July 31, 1871. This included fraudulent bond issues, the sale of franchises, tax reductions and other official favors, of an approximate worth of $125,000,000.

When the Ring came into being on Jan. 1, 1869, it seemingly had nothing to fear. Tweed's man, John T. Hoffman, had that day been inaugurated governor of the state; and in the metropolis, Tweed was sovereign. He controlled the police, the district attorney, the courts and most of the newspapers. A Democrat, he silenced the Republican party by putting scores of its leaders on the payroll—his own or the taxpayers'. He took over the city's lone reform organization in like manner.

The Ring members were Mayor A. Oakey Hall, surnamed "The Elegant One"; City Comptroller Richard B. Connolly, alias "Slippery Dick"; City Chamberlain Peter Barr Sweeny, otherwise "Bismarck," or "Brains"; William M. Tweed, president of the Board of Supervisors and leader of Tammany Hall.

The Ring's methods called for unscrupulous contractors, merchants and others who dealt with the municipality. The original plan called for mulcting the city out of one dollar for every two paid out. The Ring's share was gradually increased until, drunk with avarice, members drew checks to imaginary individuals, firms, hospitals and other charitable institutions.

The Ring's recklessness and the magnitude of its thefts shoved the city to the verge of bankruptcy. This, coupled with a struggle between Tweed and Samuel J. Tilden for party control, led to the Ring's undoing.

Promises to publish a complete list of the Ring's beneficiaries and to sue them all were broken because too many influential ones were involved. Three of the Ring judges, George G. Barnard, John H. McCunn and Albert Cardozo, were impeached. The first two were removed. Cardozo resigned. Tweed, reputedly worth $12,000,000 at the peak of his power, was made the scapegoat. He made a partial confession. His offer to tell all if permitted to die outside prison walls was spurned. He died in Ludlow Street jail (1877).

TWIN CITIES. St. Paul and Minneapolis are situated at the head of navigation on the Mississippi River. Pierre Parrant staked a claim on the site of St. Paul in 1838, and in the summer of 1840 a group of Catholic French-Canadians settled in what is now the heart of that city. Father Lucian Galtier built a log chapel there in October, 1841, which he dedicated to St. Paul, and from it the city received its name. The settlement thus established was designated the capital when Minnesota was organized as a territory in 1849, and was incorporated as a city in 1854.

Minneapolis, about ten miles north and west of St. Paul, was originally two communities—St. Anthony on the east bank of the Mississippi, and Minneapolis on the west. St. Anthony was settled in the 1840's and Minneapolis grew up after 1849. The two were united in 1872 and by 1880 had a population of 46,887. The older community of St. Paul had already fallen behind with 41,473 inhabitants. In 1960 Minneapolis had a population of 482,872, and St. Paul, 313,411. Protestant New Englanders and Scandinavians predominated in the population of Minneapolis, while in the settlement of St. Paul there were many French, Irish and German Catholics.

From early times, St. Paul developed as a commercial metropolis and Minneapolis as an industrial center. Steamboats connected St. Paul with points downstream, and trade developed with the Red River settlements. The city became an important market for furs, livestock and farm products, and a wholesale distributing point in the 1850's and 1860's, decades when industrial plants, particularly lumber and flour mills, were growing up about the Falls of St. Anthony in Minneapolis. In addition to developing as the marketing, manufacturing and wholesale distributing point of the Northwest, the Twin Cities have become the financial, cultural and educational center of a wide region.

TYPEWRITER. Beginning with a patent for a "writing machine" issued in 1714 to Henry Mill, an engineer of London, numerous variations of the typewriting principle appeared in France, England and the United States in contrivances frequently using embossed letters intended primarily for the blind. Thus, in 1829 William A. Burt of Detroit patented a boxlike device with type arranged on a segment of a circle. Other inventions before 1867, however ingenious, usually proved to be too slow in operation or to involve costs that were prohibitive.

The invention of the first practical typewriter has been attributed to the work of Christopher L. Sholes, editor and politician of Milwaukee, and his associates, S. W. Soule and Carlos Glidden. Influenced by the "Pterotype," an English invention, they patented in 1867 a machine that was both accurate and rapid, although crude, which they called "the type-writer." In 1873 Sholes and Glidden concluded a historic contract for the manufacture of typewriters with E. Remington and Sons, famous gunmakers of Ilion, N. Y. The first users of this machine were court reporters; then came lawyers, editors, authors and clergymen. Once the union of the typewriter and stenography was consummated the success of the invention was assured. By 1923 the typewriter served 84 language groups in every portion of the globe. The pioneer Model 1 Remington, printing solely in capital letters, was replaced in 1878 by Model 2 which added the shift key and had two letters mounted on each type bar.

Although Sholes had turned over his royalty rights to a partner, he felt gratified to witness the social revolution wrought by his machine in the status of women. The typewriter aided materially in giving that sex economic emancipation and opportunity for greater participation in public life.

"UNCLE SAM" is a nickname of the United States Government. Arising in the War of 1812, and coming into notice in the autumn of 1813, the term was first applied somewhat derisively to customhouse officers and then to soldiers by those opposed to the war, but was avoided by the "war hawks"; and, as contemporary newspapers show, was doubtless a jocular expansion of the letters U. S. on uniforms and government property.

UNCLE TOM'S CABIN; OR, LIFE AMONG THE LOWLY, by Harriet Beecher Stowe, was published serially in the Washington *National Era* (June 5, 1851–April 1, 1852) and appeared in book form March 20, 1852. Mrs. Stowe came into intimate contact with the bitter criticism of the Fugitive Slave Law in New England and determined to write an account of slavery as she had known it in Cincinnati. She intended to condemn the system, not the slaveholder, and expected a favorable hearing in the South. Based on fact, the book was not, however, an accurate picture of the system, although it did show both the strength and weakness of Southern society. The book had a popular reception never before accorded a novel. Three hundred thousand copies were sold the first year and more than one million by 1860. Dramatized and produced on the stage, it reached millions who never read the book. Northern people were incensed and aroused against the inhuman system. Many Southerners read the book; some wrote ineffectual replies; others forbade its circulation. Measured by its emotional appeal and lasting influence the book ranks high as reform propaganda. Most potent of all accounts of slavery, it lighted a new torch in the North and was a contributing cause of the Civil War.

UNDERGROUND RAILROAD. This was an informal, secret system of aiding fugitive slaves to attain freedom in the free states and Canada. It was operated, generally at night, by Quaker, Negro, Covenanter, Wesleyan Methodist, and other antislavery people, who, using all sorts of hiding places, and sometimes disguising their passengers, passed the fugitives from station to station. Slaves first heard of Canada from veterans of the War of 1812. They sang of that "promised land" and learned from friendly whites of the north star as their guide. A master losing trace of his chattel at Ripley, Ohio, is said to have been the first to apply the name of "underground road" to the method of escape. The system developed until it extended through fourteen Northern states from Maine to Kansas and Nebraska, inclusive. Networks of routes ran northward through eastern and western Pennsylvania, all of Ohio and Indiana, and eastward through southern Michigan. Another network extended eastward through southern Iowa and northeast through Illinois. Numerous routes ran through eastern Massachusetts and New Hampshire and through western Massachusetts and Vermont. Hundreds of fugitives came to New England as stowaways from Southern ports, and some were shipped to New Brunswick, Nova Scotia and England. From the coast towns of Lakes Ontario, Erie and Superior thousands entered Ontario. The Underground's business increased until 1861, and was probably used by 75,000 slaves.

UNEMPLOYMENT has traditionally been viewed in America as a problem in personal adjustment. In colonial times an abundance of land provided a ready employment opportunity for every man willing to pioneer. Under such conditions unemployment was identified with unemployability. Following English precedents the colonial authorities distinguished between "impotent beggars" and "sturdy beggars." The former, consisting of the ill, the physically and mentally defective, together with the aged and children, were cared for by outdoor relief or in almshouses, while the latter were dealt with as vagrants, indentured, flogged, put in the stocks and sometimes branded or mutilated. During periods of depressed business, the self-sustaining colonial economy enabled the population for the most part to continue to produce and distribute the basic means of subsistence. Indian wars and the vicissitudes of the seasons were more important factors in the well-being of the masses than general economic trends.

The modern view of unemployment as a problem in industrial organization presents a sharp contrast to this earlier conception. Many authorities now refuse to include idleness due to personal characteristics of the worker within the definition of unemployment at all, and limit the term to lack of economically remunerative work on the part of persons of working age who are able and willing to work but can find no opportunity to do so on account of maladjustments within a given industry, or within the general economic organization of society. The former are problems for social case work; the latter are the concern of industrial reorganization.

Little is known of the extent of unemployment in this sense until recent years. As long as the daily routine of toil in shop, store and field changed but little from generation to generation, the gradual emergence of the phenomenon was not noted. But after the Civil War the rapid development of industry brought with it extreme division of labor, marked changes in occupations and a system of production dominated by price, profit and the market, and the working population became dependent for jobs and income upon the steady flow of goods for exchange, and hence upon the maintenance of the purchasing power of consumers. Even agriculture became dependent on the exchange system, and farmers began increasingly to suffer from crises which left them unaffected as producers, but bankrupted them as merchants.

Mass unemployment now appeared, and in 1890 the United States Census for the first time took cognizance of the fact. From these and other data it is estimated that for the past half century unemployment has varied from 5% in good years to upward of 20% in bad. At the depth of a depression in 1933, it affected from twelve to fifteen millions, approximately one third of the working population.

Economists recognize that an irreducible minimum of normal unemployment, affecting 1% or 2% of the working population, is unavoidable in a free market, where workers are at liberty to leave their jobs and seek other employment in whatever locality it is to be found. Normal unemployment was much greater in the United States than in western Europe before the advent of war; since this type of unemployment rises in areas where economic expansion is declining, it has substantially increased in many countries during the postwar periods.

Seasonal unemployment is characteristic of certain trades in which the weather conditions production, as in agriculture, lumbering, fishing and the construction industry, or in which climatic changes or annually recurring conventions and customs influence consumer demand, as in coal mining and the garment and luxury trades.

Technological unemployment is the displacement of workers either by improved machinery or by more efficient methods of business organization and management. Although it has been generally acknowledged to affect the total volume of employment favorably in the long run, its dislocation of workers within certain industries has often been severe.

Cyclical unemployment, or the increase of joblessness due to recurrent business crises, is, however, the most serious aspect of mass unemployment.

UNICAMERAL LEGISLATURES. Colonial assemblies, with only two or three exceptions, originated as unicameral bodies. Charters and patents vested the management of affairs in a governor and a small council or board of directors and granted, vaguely or expressly, for the purpose of consultation and advice, a voice to the freemen through their chosen deputies. These two groups, governor and council on the one hand and the locally elected deputies on the other, developed sharp differences of opinion over matters of taxation, internal policy of government and status of civil rights, a prolonged conflict in which the deputies, as the representatives of the freemen, ultimately gained a coequal voice in lawmaking. At the beginning of the 18th century only two colonies, Delaware and Pennsylvania, had one-house legislative bodies. When state governments were formulated during the Revolutionary period, all except two, Georgia and Pennsylvania, adopted bicameral legislatures. When Vermont became a state in 1777, its constitution provided for a unicameral lawmaking body. Georgia's one-house legislature was in operation only twelve years and gave way to a bicameral body under the second constitution, adopted in 1789. The unicameral legislature of Georgia was one house in name only since a board of censors acted practically as a second house. In Pennsylvania also a board of censors so thwarted the rights and prerogatives of the legislature that the latter assumed the responsibility of calling a constitutional convention. The new constitution provided for a bicameral legislature. Vermont retained its unicameral legislature until 1836 when the force of example of the other states and of the national Congress influenced the vote of the people. The unicam-

eral idea did not assume importance again until the second decade of the 20th century when it was considered in several states. In 1934 Nebraska adopted a one-house legislature.

UNION, FORT (N. Dak.), was built on the northerly side of the Missouri River, just above the mouth of the Yellowstone, by Kenneth McKenzie in 1829 for the American Fur Company. It was in longitude 104° 02′ 07″, which location is within the boundaries of the present State of North Dakota. This was the most important and pretentious fort of the company, palisaded with poplar logs and stone bastions. The *chevaux-de-frise* was quite 20 feet high and had towered blockhouses 24 feet square, with embrasures for cannon, rising from the southwest and northeast corner to a height of 30 feet. Around the second stories were balconies for observation purposes and along the inside of the enclosure was a raised walk for shooting firearms over the top in case of attack. The enclosure was about 60 feet north of the river bank, the fort proper having a front of 220 feet and depth of 240 feet. In the fort were some eight or ten log houses, stores, kitchen, council rooms and a powder magazine of fifty thousand pounds capacity. There were accommodations for more than 150 horses. The fort was built for trading with the Assiniboine Indians and as a central depot to the scattered outposts, from which unification it derived its name. Fort Union was not completed for several years, although functioning meanwhile. This accounts for varying descriptions by different visitors to the place from time to time. On Feb. 3, 1832, a fire broke out in the west quadrangle 24 x 120 feet in size, where clerks, interpreters, mechanics, *engagés* and their families were quartered. These buildings with large stores of building materials, furs, etc., were destroyed. McKenzie said that the whole fort would have been destroyed if the wind had blown otherwise than from the east. In 1834 the fort was finally completed and continued in existence until 1867, when it was bought by the United States, wrecked, and the materials used to complete Fort Buford about two miles down the Missouri. Many celebrated persons were entertained at Fort Union while it reigned in splendor as the king of trading forts. Fort Union was never Fort Floyd, as some writers have supposed. These forts were coexistent in 1830 as shown by a letter of McKenzie, dated Fort Union, May 5, 1830.

UNITARIANS. From the English Presbyterian Unitarians the name, originating in Poland and Transylvania about 1600 A.D. among the Socinian disciples of Erasmus, was transferred to a group of about 125 of the old Puritan churches of New England. Their members, under the leadership of the great Boston preacher, William Ellery Channing, came in 1819 to an open break with the Calvinist tenets of the Trinity, predestination, total depravity, Biblical inerrancy.

They believed that Christ taught none of these doctrines but saved souls by the simple truths of the universal Fatherhood of God, salvation through integrity and charity of life, and the eventual brotherhood of Man in the kingdom of God on earth, of which Christ was the appointed Messiah. To such beliefs Harvard College had been won in 1805, although the erstwhile Anglican King's Chapel in Boston had become virtually Unitarian in 1785; Rev. Joseph Priestley, the discoverer of oxygen, a leader of British Unitarianism, had founded a Unitarian society in Philadelphia in 1796. The American Unitarian Association was formed in 1825.

In 1838 Ralph Waldo Emerson, a disciple of Channing and a former Unitarian minister of Boston, in his Harvard Divinity School Address, enlarged Channing's liberal Christianity into a Transcendentalist version of the ethical theism of Plato, the Stoics and Kant, co-ordinated with the nascent evolutionist science of the day and the newly explored mysticism of the ancient East. This new religious philosophy, as construed and applied by the Boston preacher Theodore Parker and other disciples of Emerson, included the other great ethnic faiths with Christianity in a universal religion of Humanity and through its intellectual hospitality operated to open Unitarian fellowship to evolutionists, monists, pragmatists and humanists.

In 1900 the American Unitarian Association undertook the organization of the International Association of Liberal Christian and Religious Freedom, a world-wide fellowship of over fifty liberal religious bodies, committed to universal ethical theism, with a constituency of about 20,000,000 members, and headquarters at Utrecht, Holland.

In 1960 there were about 110,000 Unitarians in the United States and Canada.

UNITED COLONIES OF NEW ENGLAND. This was a confederation consisting of the four colonies of Massachusetts, Plymouth, Connecticut and New Haven, from which Rhode Island and Maine were excluded because of their political and religious uncongeniality. Suggested as early as 1637, it gradually evolved after the outbreak of the Puritan Revolution from a complexity of motives, chief of which was defense. The infant colonies realized that they would be particularly exposed to danger of attack from other countries while England's attention was taken by troubles at home, while the menace of the Indians was increasingly apparent after the Pequot War. Perhaps also they may have feared being drawn into the vortex of civil war in England. In addition to defense, they had in mind the well-being of their state religion and the spread of the gospel according to its doctrines; and there were many intercolonial problems such as control of runaway servants and prisoners for which the need of united action was felt.

According to the articles of agreement adopted, the confederation government consisted of a board of eight commissioners, two from each member colony, and a vote of six was necessary to make action legal. If six could not agree, the business in question was then to be referred to the General Courts of the four constituent colonies. The commissioners were to meet annually and oftener if necessary. Although a permanent center was projected for the future, for the time being the confederation was to be itinerant, meeting twice out of every five times at Boston. The commissioners had power to make ordinances concerning general matters of a civil nature and to act as a sort of court of arbitration in the settlement of conflicts between members or with foreign countries or colonies. In case of war, offensive or defensive, the burden of expense and of soldiers was to be borne in proportion to the size of the male population between the ages of sixteen and sixty. Provision was made for emergency action in case of sudden invasion, but even though help of member colonies had been thus invoked, the confederation was not to bear the expense if upon examination the colony or colonies concerned were at fault in the action provoking the war.

Equal representation and proportional support contained an element of unfairness to Massachusetts, but there was no other way to prevent her exercising a preponderance of influence in the affairs of New England. As it was, she sometimes defied the confederation when she disapproved of its decisions, and there was no way of coercing her to obedience.

In spite of its inherent weaknesses, the confederation performed a very real service for New England during its first twenty years. Although it lost prestige and influence after Connecticut's absorption of New Haven in 1662, it continued to exist until the new order of things following the annulment of the Massachusetts charter in 1684.

UNITED EMPIRE LOYALISTS was the name applied to those inhabitants of the thirteen colonies who remained loyal to the British Crown at the time of the Revolution, and particularly to those who migrated to what is now Canada. In 1783 and 1784 the United States lost between fifty and sixty thousand refugees, who became the backbone of pioneer settlement in Canada. They went mainly from New York, Massachusetts and Connecticut to Nova Scotia, New Brunswick and Prince Edward Island, in 1783, and to Upper and Lower Canada, now Ontario and Quebec, in 1784.

UNITED NATIONS CONFERENCE, SAN FRANCISCO (April 25–June 26, 1945). Attended by 50 countries (46 of them signatories of the United Nations Declaration), this conference was held as German surrender in World War II drew near, for the purposes of putting into final form the proposals for an international peace organization drafted at the Dumbarton Oaks Conference. In naming the American delegation, President Roosevelt, who died shortly before the conference met, had evidently had in mind avoiding President Wilson's mistake of failing to include members of Congress in the delegation that participated in drafting the League of Nations Covenant after World War I. Roosevelt named two members of the Senate and two of the House. The rift between East and West, indications of which had already appeared, made itself felt during the conference. Three main points of contention developed, with respect to each of which the United States and Russia took opposing stands: over the disposition of dependent peoples; over regional collective security arrangements; and over voting in the Security Council. After some acrimony these controversies were resolved (in a manner more favorable, on the whole, to the United States than to Russia), and the United Nations Charter was unanimously approved June 26, 1945.

UNITED NATIONS DECLARATION. Soon after Japan's attack on Pearl Harbor (Dec. 7, 1941), Prime Minister Churchill hastened to Washington and with President Roosevelt announced a "Declaration by United Nations," open to all nations, the signatories to which constituted a military alliance against "Hitlerism." The Declaration was signed Jan. 1, 1942, by the United States (making its first military alliance since the French alliance of 1778), the United Kingdom, and 24 other "United Nations": the Soviet Union, China, Australia, Belgium, Canada, Costa Rica, Cuba, Czechoslovakia, the Dominican Republic, El Salvador, Greece, Guatemala, Haiti, Honduras, India, Luxembourg, the Netherlands, New Zealand, Nicaragua, Norway, Panama, Poland, South Africa and Yugoslavia. Subsequent signers were Bolivia, Brazil, Chile, Colombia, Ecuador, Egypt, Ethiopia, France, Iceland, Iran, Iraq, Liberia, Mexico, Paraguay, Peru, the Philippines, Saudi Arabia, Turkey, Uruguay and Venezuela. Below(*), the text of the Declaration.

UNITED STATES OF AMERICA (origin of the name). Our national name was first used officially in the Declaration of Independence, where, however, it merely took the place of "United Colonies," etc., hitherto employed, although in varying forms. The "United Colonies of New England" was the name of the so-called New England Confederation, and it was therefore quite natural that "United Colonies" should be used to designate the new union. The earliest official use of the designation in the Revolutionary period appears to have been in a communication of the Massachusetts convention, May 16, 1775, embodied in the *Journals of the Continental Congress* under June 2. The term was used by Congress itself in a resolution of June 7, 1775, again in a resolution of June 10, then definitely in Washington's commission, June 17, and in his instructions, June 20. Thereupon, both officially and unofficially, "The United Colonies," in variant forms, came into general use. Among the earlier forms used were, "all the English colonies on this continent" (the fast-day proclamation of June 12), "all the colonies from Nova Scotia to Georgia" (pledge of support to Gen. Washington, June 17), and "associated colonies" (committee report, June 19). In official documents thereafter the name was usually "The United Colonies of America," or "of North America" (more often the latter), and frequently with "twelve" or "thirteen," as the case might be, prefixed, sometimes also preceded by the word "English." For instance, the imprint of the Rules for the troops, June 30, 1775, names the governing authority as "the Twelve united English Colonies of North-America."

As the idea of independence grew and the term "colony" came to connote a status of dependence, writers came more and more to employ the term "states" to designate the American political entities. The term was accordingly used in the Virginia Resolutions of May 15, 1776, whence came the resolution proposed in Congress June 7, "That these United Colonies are, and of right ought to be, free and independent States." It was therefore a matter of course that, in the Declaration of Independence, the name "United Colonies," etc., should give place to "The United States of America." From the Declaration the name was taken over into the Articles of Confederation (1777) and thence into the Constitution (1787).

Curiously enough, for a brief period the name of this nation was "The United States of North America."

* The Governments signatory hereto,

Having subscribed to a common program of purposes and principles embodied in the Joint Declaration of the President of the United States of America and the Prime Minister of the United Kingdom of Great Britain and Northern Ireland dated August 14, 1941, known as the Atlantic Charter,

Being convinced that complete victory over their enemies is essential to defend life, liberty, independence and religious freedom, and to preserve human rights and justice in their own lands as well as in other lands, and that they are now engaged in a common struggle against savage and brutal forces seeking to subjugate the world, *Declare:*

(1) Each Government pledges itself to employ its full resources, military or economic, against those members of the Tripartite Pact and its adherents with which such government is at war.

(2) Each Government pledges itself to co-operate with the Governments signatory hereto and not to make a separate armistice or peace with the enemies.

The foregoing declaration may be adhered to by other nations which are, or which may be, rendering material assistance and contributions in the struggle for victory over Hitlerism.

The prevailing inclination to use "North America" had found official expression in the Declaration on Taking Arms (June 6, 1775), and again (probably through Franklin's preference for that form, as witness his proposed articles of confederation, July 21, 1775) in the treaty with France (Feb. 6, 1778), in which the name is set down as "the thirteen United States of North America." Thereupon (May 19, 1778) Congress adopted "the Stile of the Treaties of Paris" (letters of President Laurens May 19, 20, 23); but, on July 11 following, that action was rescinded, and the word "North" dropped from the name.

U. S. v. E. C. KNIGHT CO. (156 U. S. 1, 1895) was the first Supreme Court case involving the Sherman Antitrust Act, which forbade combinations restraining interstate commerce. The American Sugar Refining Co. purchased four independent concerns, giving it control of 98% of the country's output. The Court held that the acquisition of refineries and the business of sugar manufacturing within a state bore no direct relation to interstate commerce, and hence were not in violation of the act. The decision stimulated the formation of trusts.

"UNITED WE STAND, DIVIDED WE FALL," favorite toast, in varying forms, of political orators from Franklin to Lincoln, gained currency from John Dickinson's "Liberty Song," published July 18, 1768, in the Boston *Gazette,* containing the lines:

Then join hand in hand, brave Americans all—
By uniting we stand, by dividing we fall!

Renewed popularity came three quarters of a century later with the appearance of G. P. Morris' "The Flag of our Union," which quoted the sentiment as given above, from the motto of Kentucky, adopted in 1792.

UNIVERSALISTS. Opposition to the preaching of eternal torment and the predestination of the elect had been growing in England and New England during the 17th and 18th centuries, but it was not effectively preached in this country until the arrival of the Rev. John Murray from London in 1770. Murray's preaching in Gloucester, Mass., and vicinity was paralleled in Philadelphia by the Rev. Elhanan Winchester and in New Hampshire by the Rev. Caleb Rich. In 1790 these three movements united in a general convention in Philadelphia. After 1805 the Rev. Hosea Ballou of Massachusetts, who opposed both eternal damnation and the doctrine of the Trinity, became denomination leader for the next fifty years.

Universalism spread into New York State and the Middle West, although the majority of its churches have always been in New England. About 69,000 persons belonged to the Universalist Church of America in 1958. In 1961 they joined with the Unitarians.

URSULINES were a prominent order of French nuns. On Sept. 13, 1726, the order signed a contract with the Company of the Indies, which then controlled Louisiana, to send a group of their members to New Orleans to take charge of the hospital and to establish a school for girls. With Marie Tranchepain de St. Augustin as Mother Superior, the group arrived in 1727. In 1770 they were relieved of their duties in connection with the hospital, but the convent and school for girls which they established, the first of its kind in the Mississippi Valley, is still in existence in New Orleans.

USEFUL MANUFACTURES, SOCIETY FOR ESTABLISHING, was founded by Alexander Hamilton to show America the way to independence of European manufactures by establishing an emporium of great factories producing a variety of products for common use. A perpetual charter granted by the New Jersey legislature (Nov. 22, 1791), authorized the Society to engage freely in manufacturing and selling, to acquire real estate, improve rivers, dig canals, collect tolls on improvements, and to incorporate a municipality at the site chosen, to be called Paterson, in honor of Gov. William Paterson. Seven hundred acres were purchased (May, 1792) at the Great Falls of the Passaic River where a small cotton factory was built. Since 1796, when manufacturing was abandoned due to financial reverses, the Society's chief business has been to lease sites, furnish water and electric power and capital to establish useful manufactures by others. Repeated efforts to break the Society's charter and to terminate its tax immunity have failed.

UTAH, the 45th state of the Union, was named for the Ute, or Eutaw, Indians. The eastern portion is traversed by mountain ranges running north and south, excepting the Uintah Mountains, running east and west, the only range so situated in the United States. The western half of Utah is in the Great Basin, or bed of Lake Bonneville, the remnant of which is Great Salt Lake. The first white men known to have entered Utah were soldiers in the army of Coronado, who in 1540 came searching for the mythical Seven Cities of Cíbola. In 1776 two Spanish friars, Escalante and Dominguez, from Santa Fe entered Utah seeking a direct route to California but were unsuccessful and returned. Next came the trappers of the early 19th century. The first permanent settlers were the Mormons, religious outcasts driven from Illinois after the slaying of their leaders Joseph and Hyrum Smith. Brigham Young, who succeeded Joseph Smith as president of the Mormon Church, led his people to the Salt Lake Valley, the first company arriving July 24, 1847. The Mormons planted colonies in all parts of the desert, and to them more than to any others is due the redemption of the arid West. Their industry made the desert blossom and the Great Basin habitable. Upon the arrival of the Mormons, a provisional government was set up and in 1849 Congress was petitioned to accept that government as the State of Deseret. This petition was denied, but in 1850 Congress created the Territory of Utah. Brigham Young, who was acting as governor in the provisional government, was appointed governor and served two terms. Near the close of his second term friction arose between Utah and the Federal Government based upon false reports made by Utah Federal officers. They said the territorial records had been burned and the people were in rebellion. Without an investigation President Buchanan sent an army to suppress the supposed rebellion and to install Alfred Cumming of Georgia as governor to succeed Brigham Young. This army under Albert Sidney Johnston entered Salt Lake City in 1858, but moved forty miles south and established Camp Floyd where they remained for a considerable time. The true condition eventually became known in Washington and the troops were withdrawn. Gov. Cumming was received and loyally supported by the Mormon people. From that time forth, while Utah remained a territory, Federal appointees, who were men from other states, with few exceptions were unfriendly to the Mormons. Many attempts were made to obtain statehood, but due to the internal strife, and the question of polygamy as practiced by the Mormons before 1890, these failed until Jan. 4, 1896.

UTRECHT, TREATY OF (1713), concluded Queen Anne's War. The terms of peace pertinent to American history were included in treaties between France and Great Britain (April 11, 1713), and between Spain and Great Britain (July 13, 1713). France restored to Great Britain Hudson Strait and Bay within boundaries to be defined by commissioners; and the English Hudson's Bay Company was to be indemnified for losses incurred through French action in times of peace. France conceded to Great Britain the island of St. Christopher, Acadia, Newfoundland and its adjacent islands; but retained Cape Breton and the islands of the St. Lawrence. French fishermen retained the right of drying fish, caught off Newfoundland, on shores between Cape Bonavista and Point Riche. Frenchmen in newly acquired British territory might exercise the Roman Catholic religion so far as British laws allowed. France acknowledged British sovereignty over the Five Nations of Iroquois; and both parties agreed not to interfere with Indians under their respective influence. For her part Spain pledged that no portion of Spanish America would ever be transferred to any foreign power. Spain granted to Great Britain, for thirty years, the *Asiento,* together with a depôt on the Rio de la Plata and the right of sending an annual ship to trade with Spanish America.

VACCINATION, INTRODUCTION OF. The copy of Edward Jenner's *Inquiry into the Causes and Effects of the Variolae Vaccinae* (1798), which John Coakley Lettsom of London forwarded to Benjamin Waterhouse of Boston, was the earliest to reach this country. Waterhouse, the first professor of theory and

practice at Harvard, read with interest the thin quarto, bound in boards, selling for 7s. 6d., and reviewed it in a newspaper (*The Columbian Sentinel,* March 12, 1799) under the title, "Something Curious in the Medical Line." After repeated efforts, Waterhouse succeeded in obtaining vaccine virus from Jenner's stock, with which he vaccinated his offspring (July 8, 1800), starting with Daniel Oliver Waterhouse (the first vaccinated American). Waterhouse then exposed his children in William Aspinwall's private Smallpox Hospital at Brookline, where smallpox matter was inserted by punctures into one of these children, and an infected thread passed through his skin. The dreaded smallpox did not develop, and Aspinwall, who had made a fortune through the old inoculation, acknowledged the superiority of the new inoculation. Waterhouse's experiment on his family removed the *variolous papule* as the most appalling menace on the American continent.

VALLANDIGHAM INCIDENT (May, 1863). Clement L. Vallandigham, Dayton, Ohio, Copperhead leader and ex-Congressman, was arrested on May 5 for violating Gen. Burnside's "General Order No. 38" in a speech at Mount Vernon, Ohio, on May 1 in which he appealed from Order No. 38 to Order No. 1, the Constitution. Tried by military commission at Cincinnati, he was sentenced to jail for the duration of the war; Lincoln commuted the sentence to banishment beyond the Federal lines, which was done on May 25. Passing through the Confederacy to Canada, Vallandigham, now Democratic candidate for governor of Ohio, conducted an unsuccessful campaign against John Brough.

In February, 1864, Vallandigham appealed through counsel to the U. S. Supreme Court for revision of the sentence of the military commission. His petition was denied for lack of jurisdiction. Vallandigham, returning to the United States in June, 1864, to take part in the political campaign, was not further molested by the Federal authorities.

VALLEY FORGE, the encampment ground for the Continental army from Dec. 19, 1777, until June 19, 1778, is situated on the west bank of the Schuylkill River, in Montgomery and Chester counties, Pa., 22 miles northwest of Philadelphia.

After the Americans had been defeated at Brandywine, Paoli and Germantown, and after the British had occupied Philadelphia (then the National Capital) Washington led 11,000 regular troops to Valley Forge from Whitemarsh to take up winter quarters. The site was chosen for strategic reasons. Its high ground commanded the roads from Philadelphia to the ironworks, gunneries and powder mills of Warwick and Coventry in northern Chester County. Valley Forge also lay close to the great road, now called the Lancaster Pike, which tapped the interior of

Pennsylvania, and the site dominated the route from the South that led through Coryell's Ferry to West Point and New England. Valley Forge was in easy reach of the fertile farm lands of the pro-Revolutionary Pennsylvania Germans, and it was only eight miles distant from a famous health resort at Yellow Springs which could readily be adapted for hospital use. Du Portail, French fortification engineer with the army, believed that the sloping hills, flanked by the Schuylkill and supported on the rear by the high, winding, wooded gorge of Valley Creek, could be made impregnable against attack. As a further safeguard, picket parties were detached to watch the movement of the British.

Washington's plans were well drawn and his staff was efficient in carrying out their duties, but negligence and mismanagement on the part of others, particularly in the commissary department and in the transport service, almost destroyed the Continental army during the encampment. An unexpectedly early winter, with heavy snows and abnormally freezing weather in Christmas week, prevented the receipt of regular supplies. A January thaw brought mud so deep upon the roads that hundreds of army wagons had to be abandoned. Even when transport was available, however, the neglect of the army by the Continental Congress and the failure of the commissary officers to forward food, clothing and supplies by the most available routes, increased the sufferings of the men. On several occasions, Washington expressed his fears that only extraordinary efforts could prevent the army from disbanding. Camp fever, probably of the type now called typhus, and smallpox were epidemic during the army's stay at Valley Forge. Medical supplies were lacking. Hundreds of men died and were buried in unmarked graves.

During the encampment period, however, much constructive good was accomplished, particularly in the restoration of morale and in the insistence upon proper discipline. Baron Steuben introduced efficient drilling. The Franco-American Alliance, known in camp about May Day, brought new supplies of money and especially of adequate arms and clothing. Ten days after the army left Valley Forge, it met the British army withdrawing from Philadelphia, and fought with it on equal terms at Monmouth.

VANCOUVER, FORT (located on the north bank of the Columbia about 100 miles from its mouth, at the present site of Vancouver, Wash.), was the western headquarters of the Hudson's Bay Company from 1825 to 1845. Under the direction of George Simpson, American governor of the company, the site was selected in 1824. The buildings were dedicated in March, 1825, and replaced Fort George as the chief western post with Dr. John McLoughlin as chief factor.

The first location was almost a mile from the river; but in 1829 the fort was rebuilt on the banks of the river. With the declining importance of fur trade in the Columbia region, combined with fear of unfriendly relations with incoming American settlers, the principal western headquarters were transferred to Victoria on Vancouver Island in 1845.

Old Fort Vancouver and its lands were later purchased by the United States Government and the site used for a military post.

VANCOUVER'S EXPLORATION (1791–95). To carry out the terms of the Nootka Sound Convention Capt. George Vancouver was sent to meet the Spanish commissioner at Vancouver Island. His expedition consisted of the sloop-of-war *Discovery* and the armed tender *Chatham*, with the equipment and personnel for scientific research. He sailed from England in January, 1791, with instructions to survey the American shore line from 30° to 60° North Latitude. He was especially instructed to see if there might be interlocking river systems opening communication into the interior of the continent.

Vancouver reached the American coast off California on April 17, 1792. He skirted the northern California and southern Oregon coast rather far out, naming Cape Orford and noting only a few major landmarks. He observed the mouth of the Columbia River but mistook its true nature. Giving the coast to the north a more minute survey, he noted the Strait of Juan de Fuca and sailed into the great waterways opening into it. Puget Sound was explored in detail. Principal geographical features were named, many of the names becoming established in permanent usage.

During his subsequent months of exploration Vancouver and his officers gave detailed examination and made charts of the coast from California to 60° N., including the lower hundred miles of the Columbia River which had been recently discovered by Capt. Robert Gray. The charts were accurate enough to be readily compared with the ones in use at the present time. He ended his four years of exploration in 1795.

"VANDALIA COLONY" was the term applied to a project for a settlement on the Ohio River, sponsored in the early 1770's by the Grand Ohio Company, often referred to as the Walpole Company. While the colony never materialized, the movement behind it was typical of the great land speculation schemes which were so numerous in England and America in the 18th century. This particular project had a long and extremely complex history and counted among its backers many persons of prominence on both sides of the ocean. It became deeply involved in politics in both England and America.

The plan contemplated the establishment of a new colony with a separate government of the royal type, with ownership of most of the land vested in the proprietors of the Grand Ohio Company. Though many of the proprietors were Englishmen holding high official positions, the project encountered strong opposition from influential British quarters and from rival speculative interests in Virginia. In 1773 the grant appeared about to materialize but there were further delays, and the outbreak of hostilities in America in 1775 ended all hope of success. In 1781 Wharton and certain other Americans who were interested tried to persuade Congress to recognize the abortive Vandalia grant, but the opposition was too strong and the enterprise finally lapsed.

VENEZUELA BOUNDARY CONTROVERSY. When Great Britain annexed the territory of British Guiana in 1814, there was no definite boundary along the western side. In 1840 a British agent, Robert Schomburgk, surveyed a line to the westward of the British settlements and the government, after a few years, adopted this as its definite claim.

In 1885–86 the British authorities suddenly extended their claims to include some 30,000 square miles to the westward of the Schomburgk line, in a region where gold was reported. The Venezuelan government protested hotly and, securing no satisfaction, broke off relations. Finally in June, 1895, Secretary Richard Olney injected a new note by demanding a settlement, under the authority conferred upon the United States by the Monroe Doctrine, which he interpreted as equivalent to a virtual protectorate over the western hemisphere. When the Marquis of Salisbury refused to accept this interpretation of the Doctrine and reiterated the refusal to accept unrestricted arbitration, President Cleveland, in great indignation at the "grab" of 1886, asked Congress for authority to determine and maintain the legal boundary, under the Monroe Doctrine. Salisbury not only did not resent the American demand but, expressly waiving the Monroe Doctrine, offered to discuss the problem with Secretary Olney as the representative of Venezuela, being pushed to this by the overwhelming pressure of British public and parliamentary opinion. In the negotiations which followed, the British still refused any form of unrestricted arbitration and no progress was made until Olney suggested that settlements in existence for sixty years be guaranteed. After reducing sixty years to fifty, Salisbury accepted this solution and a treaty was signed in 1897. Olney's provision enabled the arbitrators in 1899 to award to Venezuela the land "grabbed" in 1885–86, the rest of the boundary following approximately the Schomburgk line. Usually described as a British triumph, the award did, in fact, accomplish the main purpose that Cleveland and Olney desired, the blocking of the 1886 seizure.

VERA CRUZ (1914). When Victoriano Huerta seized the Mexican presidency in 1913, the United States refused to recognize him. Early in 1914, when Tampico was under martial law, some United States marines were arrested there, but quickly released and apologies made. President Wilson, however, insisted that a salute of 21 guns to the American flag also be fired. When this was not forthcoming, he ordered a fleet to Vera Cruz. Troops were landed on April 21, and, aided by bombardment, the city was taken with an American loss of 17 killed and 63 wounded. Continued American political pressure forced Huerta out in July, and he fled to Jamaica.

VERA CRUZ, SIEGE AND CAPTURE OF (1847). With 10,000 troops and a siege train, Gen. Winfield Scott, during the Mexican War, landed on the beach near Vera Cruz, March 9, 1847. Without serious opposition intrenchments were dug, the city was completely invested, and, on the 13th, summoned. Gen. Juan Morales, with 1200 soldiers in San Juan de Ulúa castle and 3800 in the town, refused to capitulate. Scott opened the bombardment on the 22nd. Naval guns, borrowed and manned from the fleet, planted 800 yards from the walls, opened breaches and partially destroyed the city. Ulúa was undamaged, but pressure from the terrified populace induced Morales to yield. He relinquished command to Gen. Landero, who, on the 29th, raised the white flag. American losses were 19 killed, 63 wounded; Mexican, 80 military casualties and 100 civilians killed. Landero and his troops were paroled; the city was cleaned and garrisoned by Scott. Thereafter, throughout the war, it served as the port base of the invading army.

VERENDRYE EXPLORATIONS. In 1728 Verendrye (Pierre Gaultier de Varennes) was stationed by the French government of Canada at a small outpost on Lake Nipigon. Here he heard from the Indians of a river flowing west into a salt sea. He knew nothing of the Rocky Mountains and he conceived the idea of an overland commerce between Lake Superior and the Pacific Ocean to bring the goods of the Far East to France by way of Montreal. The cost of this route could, he was sure, be defrayed from the profits of his fur trade.

Obtaining from the governor general of Canada a trade monopoly in this vast territory, he established a line of posts westward from Lake Superior to Lake-of-the-Woods and Lake Winnipeg, and up the Red and Assiniboine Rivers. On the latter stream he built Fort La Reine, now Portage La Prairie, at the point where the old Indian trail from the Great Plains led across the river northward to York Factory on Hudson's Bay. In 1738, in search for the westward-flowing river, he led a party south from this point to Star Mound in Canada. This was the First Mountain mentioned in his journal and was the site of an abandoned Hidatsa village on the old trail. He next records passing Turtle Mountain on the north side and from this point his guides led him far out of his course to an ancient Hidatsa site on Antler Creek.

From this point he went directly south to a fortified Hidatsa village he called Fort La Butte, recently identified as near Minot, N. Dak. While here he sent his son to a second Hidatsa village, a day's journey distant, located on the Missouri at Old Crossing at the present site of Sanish, and he reported that he had found there a westward-flowing river.

In 1742 Verendrye sent his two sons from Fort La Reine across the Missouri River at Old Crossing. From the account in their journal, the party traveled west and southwest until they came within sight of the Big Horn Mountains, west of the Black Hills. Here, on the banks of the North Platte River (erroneously called by their guides the Missouri), they buried a lead plate inscribed with the date and the names of three of the party. How this lead plate came to be found in 1913 on the west bank of the Missouri River at Fort Pierre, S. Dak., may be explained from the lively curiosity of the Indians where the plate was originally buried and from the naïveté of the Verendrye sons, who appeared to believe they had successfully concealed the plate under a pile of stones on a bluff overlooking the river.

From their own account the party returned by the same route over which they had already traveled. It is worthy of note that after crossing the Missouri again they spoke of Fort La Butte as being a day's journey from Old Crossing.

VERMONT was discovered in 1609 by Samuel de Champlain. Decades of predatory warfare and organized battle followed, making settlement uncertain and transient. In 1666 the French built Fort. St. Anne on Isle La Motte. In 1724 the English built Fort Dummer near Brattleboro. Both were military outposts and marked a definite approach of the two nations that was to result inevitably in a major clash for control of the strategic Champlain Valley. In 1731 the French, advancing farther south, erected Fort St. Frédéric.

Lake Champlain now became the key to rival campaign strategy. On the English side Winthrop's campaign (1690) and Nicholson's first and second campaigns (1709, 1711) all ended in failure. The French gained an advantage by throwing up Fort Carillon (1756), later Ticonderoga, at the southern end of the lake, which, with its advanced position, backed up by Fort St. Frédéric (1731), served as an operative base for raids and as a constant threat to the northern colonies in any concerted campaign. French attacks on Vermont during this period included Bridgman's Fort, Fort Massachusetts, Number Four across the Connecticut, and Hobbs Fight. Blocking further French progress, the English had Fort William Henry (1755) at the southern end of Lake George, where it faced off against Carillon, being backed up by Fort Edward (1755) as Carillon was backed by Fort St. Frédéric. In the valleys of Lake George and Champlain armies of thousands of men were now on the move. Then came Amherst (1759), driving the lilies of France down Champlain into their Canadian strongholds.

In 1749 Benning Wentworth, governor of New Hampshire, had made the first official grant of land in the territory now known as Vermont, but it was not until the capture of Fort Frédéric, or Crown Point, by Gen. Amherst ten years later and the subsequent destruction of the St. Francis Indians in lower Canada that settlement on an extensive scale began. The territory was now called the New Hampshire Grants, and the classic controversy arose between New Hampshire and New York as to which had jurisdiction over it. The claim of New York, based on a grant made by Charles II to the Duke of York in 1664, was sustained by the Crown, and New York immediately began chartering townships within the Grants. Some of these conflicted with charters already granted by Gov. Wentworth, and when an effort was made to enforce the New York claim the settlers stood on what they considered their rights, appealing to the New York courts for protection. The courts decided in favor of the New York claimants. Deprived of legal defense, the settlers sent Samuel Robinson to England to present their grievance. The Crown issued an injunction restraining New York from making grants, pending his Majesty's pleasure, but New York, putting its own interpretation on the injunction, continued its former practice, and the settlers, resorting to physical measures, organized the Green Mountain Boys and other protective bodies to safeguard their interests.

The controversy was interrupted by the outbreak of the Revolution, which again brought war upon the settlements. On March 10, 1775, Ethan Allen and his Green Mountain Boys took Ticonderoga. The Battle of Hubbardton was fought July 7, 1777, under Warner. Vermont arms were prominent at the important Battle of Bennington, Aug. 16, 1777.

It was in 1777 that Vermont, threatened with invasion by Burgoyne on the one hand and dismemberment by three neighboring colonies on the other, declared herself an independent commonwealth and set up the machinery of government which became operative in 1778 with a unicameral legislature and Thomas Chittenden as the first governor. Political differences with the neighboring states and Congress, in which Vermont played a lone and victorious diplomatic hand, continued until 1791, when the conflicting claims of all parties were satisfactorily settled and Vermont was admitted into the Union (March 4, 1791) as the 14th state.

VERSAILLES, TREATY OF. Signed on June 28, 1919, by the United States, the British Empire, France, Italy and Japan, and twenty-three other Allied and Associated Powers, and Germany, it consisted of 15 parts comprising 440 articles. Part I was the Covenant of the League of Nations. Part II de-

979

fined the boundaries of Germany in Europe: she lost Alsace-Lorraine to France, West Prussia and Posen to Poland, and two small areas to Belgium; she surrendered the Saar and Danzig to the League of Nations, and Memel to the Allied Powers; she agreed to plebiscites in North Schleswig, Allenstein and Marienwerder, and Upper Silesia. Part IV deprived Germany of her overseas possessions, which were made mandated territories under the League of Nations, and of various rights and interests in China, Siam, Liberia, Morocco, Egypt, Turkey and Bulgaria. In Part III Germany consented to the abrogation of the neutrality of Belgium and Luxembourg and to the exclusion of the latter from the German Customs Union. She acknowledged and promised to respect the independence of Austria. She accepted the demilitarization of the Rhineland and a zone extending 50 kilometres east of the Rhine. She ceded to France the coal mines of the Saar as compensation for the destruction of French mines during the war.

Part V provided for the disarmament of Germany, "in order to render possible the initiation of a general limitation of the armaments of all nations." Her army was limited to 100,000 men, recruited by long-term enlistment; the general staff was abolished; military and naval air forces were forbidden. The manufacture of munitions was limited, their import forbidden; poisonous gases were also forbidden. Her navy was restricted to a small number of old ships. Inter-Allied commissions were established to supervise the execution of these clauses.

Part VI dealt with prisoners of war and graves. In Part VII William II, the former Emperor, was indicted for "a supreme offense against international morality and the sanctity of treaties," and he was to be tried by the five Principal Powers. Germany also promised to deliver any of her nationals who might be accused by the Allies of having violated the laws and customs of war.

Part VIII dealt with reparation, beginning with the famous Article 231: "The Allied and Associated Governments affirm and Germany accepts the responsibility of Germany and her allies for causing all the loss and damage to which the Allied and Associated Governments and their nationals have been subjected as a consequence of the war imposed on them by the aggression of Germany and her allies" (the purpose of this article was, not to assess a moral judgment, but to establish the legal liability of Germany for reparation, to which she had agreed in the Armistice of Nov. 11, 1918). Germany undertook to make compensation for "all damage done to the civilian population" of the Allies "by land, by sea and from the air," which was defined in a manner large enough to include military pensions and separation allowances; Germany had furthermore to reimburse Belgium, with interest, for all sums borrowed from the Allies. A reparation commission was to determine, by May 1, 1921, the amount which Ger-

many should pay; in the meantime, Germany was to pay in gold, commodities, ships, securities or otherwise $5,000,000,000. Elaborate clauses provided in great detail for the delivery of goods in kind. The Allied Powers reserved the right to take whatever measures they deemed necessary in the event of "voluntary default" by Germany. Part IX was concerned with financial clauses. Part X dealt with tariffs, business contracts and the like; in particular the Allies obtained the right to seize German private property in their territories on account of reparation. Many of these financial and economic clauses were of a temporary character. Part XI had to do with aerial navigation. In Part XII, which dealt with ports, waterways and railways, international control of the Rhine, Oder and Elbe, was established in the interest of land-locked states. The Kiel Canal was opened to all nations. Part XIII established the International Labor Office as an autonomous branch of the League of Nations.

Part XIV provided for guarantees. The Allies were to occupy the Rhineland and its bridgeheads for 15 years, certain zones to be evacuated at the end of 5 and 10 years. Article 430 empowered the Allies to reoccupy the region at any time thereafter if Germany defaulted on reparation payments. Germany was to pay the cost of the armies of occupation. Part XV dealt with miscellaneous items.

By the treaty Germany did not become a member of the League of Nations or the International Labor Office, although in time she might be eligible to both. She lost more than 25,000 square miles of territory and more than 6,000,000 inhabitants in Europe, besides many valuable resources abroad. The Treaty of Versailles was regarded by German opinion as a *Diktat* (a dictated peace) and a violation of the Fourteen Points, on the basis of which Germany had surrendered and the Allies had promised to make peace. In Allied countries, the treaty was considered as just punishment to Germany for the war which she had brought on the world in August, 1914. In the United States, the treaty was received with mixed feelings.

The treaty was promptly ratified by Germany and more slowly by the Allied Powers. It came into force on Jan. 10, 1920, without being ratified by the United States, and it was rejected by the Senate on March 19, 1920. The war between the United States and Germany was formally ended in 1921 by the Treaty of Berlin.

VESEY REBELLION. The mulatto Télémaque Vesey (his first name was corrupted to "Denmark") was the leader of what might have been a spectacular uprising of the slaves of South Carolina. Vesey, who bought his freedom in 1800 after winning $1500 in a Charleston lottery, was evidently inspired by the Negro revolt in Santo Domingo. A carpenter, a member first of the Second Presbyterian Church and then of the African Methodist congregation, he was the ringleader of a group that planned to seize Charleston on June 16, 1822. He was, however, betrayed by a Negro, and he and 35 other Negroes were hanged after a trial. Thirty-four other Negroes involved were sent out of the state, and 61 were acquitted. Four whites were also tried, fined and imprisoned for their part in the conspiracy.

Since Vesey and his henchmen died without making any revelations, the exact extent of their ambition will never be known, and what use the plotters would have made of the daggers, pikes and bayonets they had been accumulating must be left to conjecture.

VICE-PRESIDENCY. This office is one of the few disappointments in the scheme of government outlined in the Constitution. Suspended in a constitutional limbo between executive and legislative and in a political limbo between second-class impotence and world-shaking authority, the Vice-President is an essentially unhappy officer who must rely almost exclusively on the good will and confidence of the President for any power he may exercise. Such power, as in the cases of Alben Barkley and Richard M. Nixon, will always be personal rather than official in nature and persuasive rather than commanding in method.

The Vice-Presidency was established primarily to provide an uncommitted presiding officer for the Senate and a constitutional heir for the President, and it was expected to be filled at least some of the time by the second most popular and distinguished man in the nation. The ratification of the Twelfth Amendment, which made the elections of President and Vice-President two separate affairs, doomed the office to a dull future. Throughout most of its history it has been occupied by a man who was far from being second only to the President as a political figure, even of his own party.

A measure of the relative unimportance of the Vice-Presidency is the fact that there have been fifteen occasions, adding up to a total of more than 36 years, when the nation had no Vice-President and never knew the difference. Seven died in office. One, John C. Calhoun, resigned. Seven succeeded to the Presidency and thereby bore witness to the cogency of the first Vice-President's observation that he (John Adams) was "nothing *in esse*," but "everything *in posse*." The death of Franklin D. Roosevelt and the three illnesses of Dwight D. Eisenhower inspired many sober thoughts about the necessity of placing first-rate men in this second-rate office, and there is a general expectation that more eminent men will be nominated for it by the party conventions in the future.

The office was given a visible boost in prestige, if not in lasting authority, by the combined efforts of Eisenhower and Nixon. It is safe to say that no President in history relied more heavily on his Vice-President nor gave him more useful tasks to perform. The Eisenhower-Nixon relationship, however, was almost unique, matched in its display of mutual admiration and trust only by the affinity of Andrew Jackson and Martin Van Buren. The strained relationship of Jackson and John C. Calhoun or cool relationship of Calvin Coolidge and Charles G. Dawes has been the more normal pattern.

The problem of the Vice-Presidency, which is essentially one of giving the office genuine authority without endangering the unity of the Presidency, remains to be solved.

VICKSBURG, MISS., on the high eastern bank of the Mississippi at the Yazoo's mouth, occupied an old, important site; nearby the French built Fort St. Pierre (1715); there Spaniards built Fort Nogales (1791); Spain's American successors (1798) called it Walnut Hills, its name under England; Fort Nogales became Fort McHenry.

Settlement began with Newitt Vick, Virginia Methodist preacher, about 1812. He set aside (1819) 200 acres for a town site. Settlers thereon incorporated as the town of Vicksburg (1825). Although property was somewhat disturbed by Vick Estate litigation, prosperity followed opening the Mississippi-Yazoo Delta for settlement after removal of Choctaws by the Treaties of Doak's Stand (1820) and Dancing Rabbit Creek (1830). The Delta was fabulously fertile cotton country; Vicksburg stood at the junction of the rivers bounding it; thus Vicksburg began to rival Natchez as Mississippi's center of wealth and political power. Its population in 1860 was 4600 (Natchez, 7100).

Famous in Vicksburg was an "under the hill" section surpassing in disrepute that at Natchez. Outraged citizens in 1835 lynched five gamblers in a batch.

Vicksburg depended on river traffic; the decline of steamboating reduced its importance after the Civil War, though population continued to increase.

VICKSBURG IN THE CIVIL WAR. Until after the fall of New Orleans in April, 1862, Vicksburg was practically undefended and probably could have been easily captured. In May, however, Vicksburg's importance as an obstacle to Union control of the Mississippi River had become evident. At the direction of Gen. Mansfield Lovell (C.) construction of fortifications was rushed. On June 28, 1862, several ships from Farragut's squadron (U.), under cover of heavy bombardment, went upstream past the Vicksburg batteries and anchored. On July 15 the Confederate ram *Arkansas* steamed out of the Yazoo River and down the Mississippi past the Union fleet to safety under the batteries. In the last days of July the Union fleet returned to New Orleans, and Vicksburg was free of any menace until the following year.

In October, 1862, Gen. Earl Van Dorn (C.), who had succeeded Lovell, was replaced by Gen. J. C. Pemberton (C.). Early in December, 1862, Gen. U. S. Grant (U.) began his campaign against Vicksburg, his troops moving from Memphis through northern Mississippi. The advance, under Sherman (U.), was decisively beaten at Chickasaw Bluffs. Four subsequent unsuccessful attempts to reach Vicksburg culminated in the burning of the Union supply depot at Holly Springs, Miss. The Union troops had floundered about in the water and morass of the numerous bayous without coming near to their objective. In a final desperate effort, Grant decided to abandon his base at Memphis, move down the west bank of the Mississippi, live off the country, cross below Vicksburg and try to get at the city by coming to it from the east through the back door. By skilful leadership and earnest determination on the part of the troops, the plan was successful.

The Confederate commander, governed by events, waited on the man of action. Unexpectedly Grant's army was across the Mississippi, but only a small force opposed it. Within three weeks Vicksburg was in a state of siege. Though nearly cut off from supplies and reinforcements and with Union ships in control of the river, Pemberton might still have escaped and joined forces with Gen. J. E. Johnston, near Jackson, before Grant surrounded Vicksburg. Divided counsel, long-distance control and personal antagonisms prevented.

The Confederate soldiers fought bravely against odds of superior strength and vacillating leadership. Aided by bombardment from the river fleet under Porter, Grant assaulted the Vicksburg lines three times on May 22. Each attack was repulsed with heavy loss. In spite of numerical superiority it now became evident to Grant that Vicksburg could only be taken by siege operations. Dwindling food and ammunition, mounting casualties, sickness and the hopelessness of reinforcement or relief finally induced Pemberton to open surrender negotiations. On July 4, 1863, he capitulated, officers and men being paroled as prisoners of war. Port Hudson, 300 miles down the river, surrendered July 9. The Mississippi flowed "unvexed" to the sea. Vicksburg thenceforth became a Union base of operations.

VIEUX CARRÉ ("Old Square") is the name commonly applied to the old French and Spanish section of New Orleans. It is bounded by the Mississippi River in front, Rampart Street in the rear, Canal Street above, and Esplanade Avenue below.

VIGILANTES. Western vigilance committees operated in border communities before law courts were organized and peace officers were elected. In 1844 an English traveler in Texas noted that settlers had a "primitive system of administering justice." Since state and county service could not be had, substantial citizens sought by mass action to drive desperadoes from their midst. The best example of the employment of such corrective measures was the work of the San Francisco Vigilance Committee (1851). The inrush of thousands of people following gold discovery in January, 1848, brought many outlaws. Soon outlaw rule made unsafe the life and property of all residents, and a band of thugs actually crossed the bay and raided Berkeley in open day. But soon the vigilantes began the weeding out of outlaw leaders by summary executions, and others scattered to other parts of the West.

Desperadoes who fled from the California vigilantes found only temporary tenure in Arizona and Nevada. California had been successful with its committees; other Rocky Mountain communities took up the movement. In some instances action was little more than that of a mob; in others it was deliberate and well planned. Missourians in June, 1854, set up near Leavenworth, Kans., the Squatters' Claim Association which included a committee of thirteen pledged to protect the rights of slaveholders; others were organized in Linn County, Council City and elsewhere. An early publicist, A. D. Richardson, found a vigilance committee in Denver, and other Colorado towns caring adequately for their outlaw problem. In Montana (1864) a large outlaw gang, headed by Sheriff Henry Plummer, terrorized the citizens in the mining communities until the vigilantes broke it up. During the month of January, 1864, twenty-one desperadoes were hanged. John X. Beidler from Pennsylvania is said to have presided at many of these trials.

Much effective vigilance committee work was done in Texas, New Mexico and Kansas after the Civil War. That of the committee at Fort Griffin, Texas, is best known. The Dallas *Herald* (April 23, 1876) comments that here a "vigilance committee is now astonishing the authorities . . . by the off-hand way it does business." And the Denison *News* (March 23, 1874) speaks of a "neck or two stretched" when thugs had congregated there after the Missouri, Kansas and Texas Railroad had reached the Red River. The Topeka *Commonwealth* (July 14, 1875) indicated that Kansas was keeping stride with Texas by announcing that a vigilance committee had been organized at Dodge City to rid the Arkansas Valley of "a bold gang of horse thieves." Like California, all the Western states and territories broke up organized bands of cutthroats by vigilance committee operations.

VILLA RAID AT COLUMBUS (March 9, 1916). Mexican depredations against American persons and property on both sides of the border culminated on the night of March 8–9, 1916, with Villa's raid on Columbus, N. Mex. Units of the 13th U. S. Cavalry, totaling 12 officers and 341 enlisted men, stationed at Columbus, were quickly aroused and drove the

Mexicans, variously estimated as from 500 to 1000 men, back across the border. American losses were: seven soldiers killed, five wounded, eight civilians killed, two wounded; Mexicans: approximately 190 killed or wounded. This raid marked the zenith of Villa's career and was directly responsible for Pershing's punitive expedition into Mexico.

VILLASUR EXPEDITION (1720). In the summer of 1720 Don Pedro de Villasur left Santa Fe with 42 soldiers and 60 Indian allies for a reconnaissance of the French thrust from the east into Spanish territory, which had been going on for several years. On Aug. 13 the party was attacked and routed by a band of Pawnee Indians, allies of the French, the scene of the battle being on the south side of the North Platte River, in the vicinity of the present town of North Platte, Nebr. The killed, 44 in number, included Villasur, the Franciscan chaplain, Father Juan Minguez and the interpreter, Juan de l'Archevêque, erstwhile companion of LaSalle.

VINCENNES. The French government, in order to protect its claim to territory in the New World reaching from Quebec to New Orleans, early in the 17th century began the erection of a chain of fortified posts. One was built at Detroit (1701). An Indian village on the east bank of the Wabash River, 150 miles above its mouth, was selected as a suitable site for another such fort, and around this post a permanent settlement grew up. The date of the settlement is uncertain, but fur traders probably made this important Indian village their headquarters as early as 1700. It was visited by missionaries about the same time.

François Morgane Sieur de Vincennes with a considerable body of French troops was stationed there in 1736. The promotion of actual settlement by the French government followed the surrender by the Company of the Indies of their charter (1732) granting them exclusive control of the fur trade in the Illinois and Indiana country. From the Indians the Vincennes settlers received a large tract of land on both sides of the Wabash River. Five thousand acres of this grant were laid off as common fields and enclosed with pickets. Adjoining the village were the narrow, ribbonlike strips of land, from one half to a mile long and varying in width from ten to forty rods, common to French settlements.

Influenced by the victory of George Rogers Clark (1779), immigrants from Kentucky and Virginia with land warrants for service in the Revolution began coming to Vincennes. Before his return to Kaskaskia, Clark set up a form of government at Vincennes by appointing Capt. Leonard Helm as civil and military commandant.

In 1790 Knox County, the first organized government in Indiana, was formed with Vincennes as the county seat. Its jurisdiction embraced an area larger than the present State of Indiana. Ten years later (1800) Indiana Territory, which included practically all of the Northwest Territory, excluding Ohio, was created by an act of Congress. On Jan. 10, 1801, William Henry Harrison arrived at Vincennes, which had been made the capital—then a town, including the area in and around it, of some 2500 inhabitants. Gov. Harrison's duties as Superintendent of Indian Affairs occupied the greater part of his time and from 1802 to 1809, six of the eight treaties by which the Indians were driven from their domain in Indiana were conducted at Vincennes.

By an act of the Territorial Assembly, March 11, 1813, after a bitter contest, the capital was located at Corydon because of its more central situation within Indiana Territory. Vincennes continued to be an important trade center.

VINCENNES, TREATY OF (1803). Next to his victory at Tippecanoe, William Henry Harrison is best known for his many successful Indian treaty negotiations. Appointed governor of the newly created Indiana Territory in 1800, Harrison was instructed by the Federal Government to gain title to Indian lands in the area, in order to remove the source of constant friction between traders, settlers and Indians. After a preliminary conference in the fall of 1802, in which he had difficulty reconciling the jealousies of the chieftains, Harrison succeeded in getting a formal treaty signed at Fort Wayne, June 7, 1803. This provided for the cession by nine tribes (Shawnees, Potawatomis, Miamis, Weas, Eel Rivers, Delawares, Piankashaws, Kaskaskias and Kickapoos) of the land about Vincennes, extending along the Wabash River from the mouth of the White River about 25 miles north and from 12 miles west of that river to 72 miles eastward. By a supplementary treaty signed at Vincennes (Aug. 7, 1803) several tracts were ceded for way-stations from Clarksville to Kaskaskia via Vincennes.

VINLAND. It is impossible with certainty to determine the location of the Vinland said to have been explored in the 11th century by the Norwegian Leif Ericsson. Besides the northern limit of wild vines the *Tale of the Greenlanders* gives this clue: "The days and nights there were of more nearly equal length than in Greenland or Iceland. On the shortest day of winter the sun was up between 'eyktarstad' and 'dagmálastad.' " By astronomers this has been calculated as indicating the most northerly latitude of 49°, but it could be farther south. The *Tale* also says that there was no lack of salmon there; accordingly it could not lie beyond the southern limit of this fish, which is Long Island Sound. Hence Vinland is probably to be sought somewhere on the coast of New England.

VIRGIN ISLANDS, THE, are Saint Thomas, Saint Croix and Saint John, with about 50 adjacent islets and rocks, formerly known as the Danish West Indies. They are located about 40 miles east and south of Puerto Rico, and have a total area of 138 square miles with a population in 1960 of 31,904. Since 1927 the inhabitants have been citizens of the United States, and under the Organic Act of 1936 all who can read and write can vote, if of age. A governor is appointed by the President. Two municipal divisions have been formed, each with a colonial council. These form the legislative bodies and meet yearly. The islands are under the general jurisdiction of the Secretary of the Interior. Saint Thomas has an excellent harbor. Its splendid location, 1440 miles from New York, 1020 miles from Colon and 500 miles from LaGuaira, Venezuela, makes it a port of great value to American commerce, especially since the construction of the Panama Canal. The chief exports from the islands are sugar and rum.

Long owned by Denmark, the value of these islands to the United States as a naval station was, during the Civil War, recognized by President Lincoln and Wm. H. Seward who started negotiations for their purchase. Denmark, in need of cash because of defeat in the war with Prussia and Austria, was willing to sell. A treaty was agreed upon, and a plebiscite was held in the islands, which showed that the inhabitants were overwhelmingly in favor of the transfer, but political conditions connected with Reconstruction, led the Senate to refuse ratification (1870). This put the United States in a peculiar situation because of the Monroe Doctrine. If Denmark should want to dispose of the islands, the United States would either have to allow another nation to purchase them, or change her mind on purchasing them herself. Attempts to secure the islands were made in 1893 and 1902 but they failed, the last time by the act of the Danish *Landsthing*. The consideration at that time was $5,000,000. Many Danish people felt that the islands were a financial burden to their country and favored sale to the United States. The outbreak of World War I created a new situation. It was believed that Germany, if victorious, would insist on obtaining the islands in order to secure a foothold in the Caribbean. It was undoubtedly to forestall such a possibility, as well as to secure the Saint Thomas harbor for the United States, that negotiations for the purchase were taken up for the fourth time. Robert Lansing, Secretary of State, and Constantin Brun, Danish Ambassador to the United States, concluded a treaty, Aug. 4, 1916, which was duly ratified by the Senate and the Danish *Rigsdag*. A plebiscite was held in the islands which showed that the inhabitants still favored the transfer. Ratifications were exchanged Jan. 17, 1917, and the formal transfer took place March 31, 1917. The purchase price was $25,000,000.

VIRGINIA. *Colony.* After Raleigh's attempts at Roanoke Island, a permanent settlement was estab-

lished in 1607, following the issuance of a charter to the Virginia Company of London in 1606. The first colonists of about 100 men and boys were sent out in the *Sarah Constant,* the *Goodspeed* and the *Discovery,* all being under the command of Christopher Newport. On May 24 (N. S.) the settlers disembarked on a site which they named James Fort, or Jamestown.

Besides Newport, a number of these pioneers were men who had acquired reputations for distinguished service in England, in transatlantic exploration, or in foreign countries. Outstanding leaders were Capt. Bartholomew Gosnold, Edward Maria Wingfield, Capt. George Percy, Gabriel Archer, Capt. John Martin, Capt. John Smith, Capt. John Ratcliffe; and the Rev. Robert Hunt, who ministered to the spiritual welfare of the settlers. The entire group, from the highborn Percy to the lowliest laborer, represented a cross section of contemporary English life.

The settlement began happily as all went to work, "every man to somewhat." Sentinels were placed down the river to warn of threatened attacks by the Spaniards, while fortifications and palisades were erected for protection against the Indians, who very shortly made a fierce night assault.

Several causes soon brought the colony to desperate straits. Neighboring swamps bred mosquitoes with consequent malaria, so that disease alone is believed to have carried off from one half to two thirds of all new settlers during several summer seasons, unless by chance the newcomers sought high ground on which to build. Again, the colonists were required to hold supplies and produce in common, so that the poorer sort lived at the the expense of the industrious in a "comunitie" plan, that was later attempted at Plymouth with similar ill results, until four years later success was forecast when Sir Thomas Dale (1611–16) allowed private ownership of property. Shortly thereafter, John Rolfe discovered a method of curing tobacco which made "the weed" a profitable commodity for export.

In 1622 the Indians executed a widespread surprise attack in which several hundred settlers were slain. This "Great Massacre" cut short an extensive plan to convert and civilize the savages, for whom schools and a college were under construction, with George Thorpe, scholar and philanthropist, in charge.

In 1609 and again in 1612 the Virginia Company in London had secured charters which transferred matters of colonial government from the Crown to the company. These patents led in 1618 to what has been called a constitution for self-government; so that in the summer of 1619 the first legislature in the New World met at Jamestown under Gov. Sir George Yeardley. In the same year the first Negroes were brought to Jamestown in a noncommissioned English-manned Dutch frigate. Since records of release from service have been found, it seems clear that these Negroes were indentured for a term of years, much as many white immigrants whose services were "sold" in payment for their transatlantic passage. In 1624 James I procured the dissolution of the London Company, whereupon Virginia became a royal colony.

Under the lead of Gov. Sir William Berkeley, Virginia was strongly royalist and, despite the triumph of Oliver Cromwell, declared for the exiled Prince, afterwards Charles II. The Civil War that had thus ended in England seemed about to break out in Virginia. Cromwell's commissioners, however, offered liberal terms of agreement and Berkeley retired. Virginia was subsequently awarded the complimentary title of the "Old Dominion," with the status of a "fifth kingdom." Restored to power after the fall of Cromwell's Commonwealth, Berkeley became tyrannical, and dissatisfaction broke out in open rebellion (1676) under the leadership of Nathaniel Bacon. At the height of the uprising, with Berkeley driven across the Bay, Bacon died of fever, and the rebellion collapsed.

Despite the oft-quoted expression of thanksgiving by the despotic Berkeley that there were no free schools in Virginia, a few had been established by private endowment. Throughout the colonial period after the Berkeley regime a great number of tutorial schools were maintained. These were small, for Virginia remained almost wholly agricultural, with few towns, even in the tidewater section. A college for the colony, first projected in 1620, was finally realized in the establishment of William and Mary in 1693.

From the beginning many of the colonists were given to writing, as may be seen from the first return voyage of Admiral Newport in 1607, which bore a "report" on Virginia; a "Relatyon"; Tindall's "Journal" and map; and narrative letters addressed to the Prince of Wales, the Earl of Salisbury and other notables. A few years later, the first English literature in America was written by George Sandys in a translation of Ovid's *Metamorphoses,* published in London in 1626.

The establishment of the capital at Williamsburg (1699) was followed by the "Golden Age" of Virginia colonial history, in which Gov. Spotswood played a prominent role. He it was who turned general attention to the "Great Valley" beyond the Blue Ridge; and in 1749 Thomas Lee recorded the accustomed English claims in the statement that the western boundary of Virginia was "the Great South Sea, including California." When the clash came with the French for the control of the transmontane region, the Shenandoah Valley had become peopled not only by eastern Virginians, but by Scotch-Irish, Irish and Germans. The tidewater planters had always in mind western expansion. This ambition led in 1748 to the formation of the Ohio Company. Subsequently, the concern of the Virginians over the prospective shutting off of this western development was shared by Gov. Dunmore (1771–75); and clashes with the Indians led to a war under Dunmore's administration in which George Washington and his lordship saw eye to eye in opposition to British policy.

During this period of the French and Indian War, Virginia was developing a number of political philosophers who were largely instrumental in setting forth the colonial attitude toward the policies of the mother country and the subsequent shaping of the principles that were to guide the creation of independent states and the Federal Republic. The first or foremost of this group of political pamphleteers was Richard Bland, who, as early as 1764, announced the doctrine that England and her various colonies were co-ordinate entities under the Crown.

In resisting the Stamp Act and other revenue measures enacted by Parliament, the Virginia leaders made it clear that their opposition was not based on "taxation without representation" in the British Parliament, which representation they did not want, but on the principle of "taxation without the consent" of the colonial assemblies. Again, while Virginia immediately and wholeheartedly took up the cause of Massachusetts in the matter of the Intolerable Acts that brought on the clash of arms, the Old Dominion was directly concerned with the Quebec Act, which aimed to cut off the western territory she long regarded as her own. Chance only prevented in Virginia a clash of arms simultaneously with that at Lexington and Concord. Lord Dunmore took refuge on the *Fowey,* whence he issued a proclamation of emancipation with a view to arousing the Negroes, some of whom were enlisted. The royal navy controlled the sea, but after the bombardment of Norfolk and neighboring towns, the British did not descend upon Virginia in force until the closing year of the war. Virginia was then an independent state and had strengthened its claim to the Northwest by authorizing the expedition of George Rogers Clark, who, supplied by Virginia men and money, defeated the British and took possession in the name of the Commonwealth.

State of Virginia. Turning from colonial status, she called upon her ablest leaders to prepare the constitution of the independent commonwealth; and George Mason drafted that portion of the instrument known as the Declaration of Rights, which was to become a model for other states and ultimately of the United States. The constitution that formally created the state was adopted June 29, 1776, several days before the Continental Congress approved the Declaration of Independence. Ravaged by both armies, Virginia was first to cede her Western lands to Congress; she suffered by having no delegate to plead her interest at the Paris peace table, where commercial not agrarian rights were defended. Though Washington presided over the Federal Convention of 1787, and though Virginians contributed the basic plan of the strong central government on which was grounded the Constitution, Virginia in part tried to defeat the Constitution which, when finally ratified on June 25, 1788, enabled the courts to order planters to settle with British merchants.

Virginia seceded from the Union on April 17, 1861. The western part of the state which refused to secede later became West Virginia. Virginia returned to the Union in 1870.

VIRGINIA, ARMY OF NORTHERN. On June 1, 1862, after the wounding of Gen. J. E. Johnston, President Davis personally placed Robert E. Lee in command of the Confederate Army and officially designated it the Army of Northern Virginia. Henceforth, until the surrender at Appomattox, nearly three years later, this most famous and best known of Confederate armies was commanded by Lee. During this period he established his reputation as one of the most skilful of American generals. Likewise, the Army of Northern Virginia became one of the most effective fighting weapons ever constituted. Jackson's foot cavalry, Longstreet's and A. P. Hill's fighters, "Jeb" Stuart's horse, and Pelham's, Pegram's and other batteries were among its famous personnel. The army—its members varying in age from fifteen years to sixty-five, many of them often marching and fighting barefooted and hatless in slacks and shirt— was the embodiment of faith and determination. It included many world-famous soldiers among its leaders. Always it fought against numerical odds. It won battles with skill and lost only to try again in the hope of better luck. As an army, its personnel was truly representative of the Southern Confederacy. Leaders and men in the ranks alike came from Virginia, from the Border and Gulf states, from the Eastern seaboard and from the Deep South. At Gettysburg nearly one half of the regimental organizations and of the corps and division commanders were from the lower South, the remainder being from Virginia and North Carolina.

Originally organized in divisional form, after the Second Bull Run it was divided into two corps under Longstreet and Jackson. Following Jackson's death after Chancellorsville it was reorganized into three corps under Longstreet, Ewell and A. P. Hill. This division was preserved for the remainder of the war. Its effective battle strength was at a maximum in the Seven Days' Battles when it exceeded 90,000. From this time it declined, after each battle, until at Appomattox, decimated by deaths, desertions, absentees and from other causes, only 8000 men were in line.

VIRGINIA, THE UNIVERSITY OF, was founded and designed by Thomas Jefferson. Developed from an academy charter of 1803, its buildings were started in 1817 and eight schools were opened in 1825. Its foundation was one of the landmarks in the development of higher public education in America. Jefferson spoke of himself as its "father," and in writing the inscription for his tombstone, mentioned his connection with its foundation as one of the three achievements of his life by which he wished to be remembered.

VIRGINIA AND KENTUCKY RESOLUTIONS were resolutions passed by the legislature of Virginia, Dec. 24, 1798, and of Kentucky, Nov. 16, 1798 and Nov. 22, 1799. The first two are those usually referred to and are the more important, though the word "nullification" first appears in the third. The Kentucky Resolutions were written by Thomas Jefferson, though the authorship long remained unknown, and the Virginia one by James Madison. The immediate occasion was to protest against the passage of the Alien and Sedition Acts by the Federalist administration, but the problems considered were much wider in scope, having to do with the nature of the Federal Union. Both sets of Resolutions took the sound position that the Federal Government was one of limited and delegated powers only. But there was the further question, who should judge whether the central government was overstepping its rightful powers or not.

Jefferson stated that the National Government could not be the final judge of its own powers, and that the states—perhaps even one state—should be. Madison's words were less emphatic, but all three resolutions, unless we are very careful to interpret political terms and philosophy in their contemporary significance, can easily be made to appear as advocating the doctrines of state sovereignty, nullification and secession as those doctrines were later developed. We have to consider, however, the prevailing theory of divided sovereignty; and in 1828 when Calhoun was preaching his versions of state sovereignty and nullification, Madison pointed out that the Union was a Constitutional one, not a mere League, and that his Virginia Resolution of 1798 could not be considered as affording a basis for Calhoun's interpretation. In the earlier year, the Government was facing unsolved problems. If it appeared illogical that a central government of merely delegated powers should be the judge of whether it had overstepped them, the other horn of the dilemma, that of making the states judges, offered equal practical difficulties.

The resolutions, as passed in 1798 and 1799, were forwarded for comment to the legislatures of the other states, which proved cool to the suggestions made, and in a number of cases replied that states could not decide on the constitutionality of Federal laws because that power belonged to the judiciary. There, in the course of our development, it was finally to be lodged, but the resolutions may have helped by bringing the problem to a head and causing John Marshall to develop his theory of the functions of the Supreme Court. Later, the resolutions were used to buttress the doctrines of states' rights as promulgated particularly in the South, and their political influence was great. By many, the resolutions came to be considered as almost a part of the Constitution, and to have a legal authority which in fact they never possessed.

VIRGINIA CAPES, BATTLE OF (Sept. 5, 1781), was an indispensable factor in the Yorktown Campaign. In close harmony with Washington and Rochambeau, the French Admiral de Grasse had brought from Haiti to the Chesapeake all the troops and ships available. Anchored in Lynnhaven Bay, his fleet of 24 ships of the line was soon confronted by a British fleet of nineteen ships commanded by Admiral Graves. Standing out to sea, de Grasse prepared to give battle. The British delayed to bear down until center might oppose enemy center, and van enemy van; their rear (Hood's division of seven ships) never got into the fighting. The British suffered greater losses, but at the end of the day the issue was still undecided. For four days the two fleets sailed along parallel courses without renewing the battle. Meanwhile de Barras, with a fleet and siege guns from Newport, had slipped into the Chesapeake to augment the French forces. Relief and reinforcements being barred from the British, Cornwallis the following month was forced to surrender.

VIRGINIA CITY, the largest and most famous of Nevada's early mining towns, came into existence in 1859. It had every characteristic of a frontier mining community: huts, shacks and tents of every description; a cosmopolitan population, with few women; and numbers of lawless characters. By 1861 it was a town of importance with a population of more than 3000. Soon it had hotels, churches, banks, an opera house and an Odd Fellows hall. It declined in the 1880's when the ores of the great Comstock mining region failed.

VIRGINIA COMPANY OF LONDON (1606–24). The individual effort at the close of the medieval period that revealed itself in other phases of economic development was especially prominent when, in 1606, the Society of Adventurers to trade in Virginia was organized by letters patent of that year "to Sir Thomas Gates, Sir George Somers and others, for two several Colonies and Plantations, to be made in Virginia, and other parts and Territories of America. [Dated] April 10, 1606." Articles IV and V of the document specify two colonies, called "the first Colony" and "the second Colony." The "first Colony" included "any place upon the said coast of Virginia or America" between latitudes 34° and 40°. The second colony allowed Thomas Hanham and others "of the town of Plimouth in the county of Devon or elsewhere" to begin a plantation between latitudes 38° and 40°, but neither one was to "plant" itself within 100 miles of the other. Article VII provided that each colony should have a council to "govern

and order all matters and causes, which shall arise" within the colony. To investors were left the privileges of raising funds, furnishing supplies and sending out expeditions. However, affairs were to be conducted by the king through a council in England called "our Council of Virginia," created by himself, and responsible to himself, resembling private companies for trade based on ancient charters. It was a modification of this form of management to which the government of the London Company reverted after its dissolution in 1624, and again at the end of the century when royal colonies were substituted for proprietary and corporate forms throughout America.

From 1606 to 1609 the body of undertakers had little influence even in commercial interests. Business management was left to joint-stock companies and the magazine was controlled by a treasurer and two clerks elected by the president and council in the colony. But the government of the colonies and of the territory of Virginia was reserved to the Crown through the Council of Thirteen for Virginia, which was to be appointed by the king and to reside in England. It nominated to the king persons to whom lands were to be granted and appointed the first council in Virginia.

In 1609 a "Second Charter" was granted to the company, erecting it into a corporation and body politic "for . . . enlargement . . . of the said Company and first Colony of Virginia. . . ." It was to be "called and incorporated by the name of, The Treasurer and Company of Adventurers and Planters of the City of London for the first Colony in Virginia." The "limits of the colony" were expressed in terms of distance from "Cape or Point Comfort," 200 miles to northward and 200 miles to southward and from "sea to sea, west and northwest." The undertakers, with Sir Thomas Smith as treasurer, became distinctly proprietary, retaining the commercial responsibilities but assuming governmental functions in place of the king. The investors desired more authority. They feared that desire to placate Spain, or religious consideration, might lead the Crown to abandon the scheme. Certain it is that "petitioners" wished to secure more direct authority and larger investments. The council of the company in London chosen by the adventurers therefore acted as a standing committee for them and exercised controlling authority in place of the king.

The charter of 1612 erected a commercial company and made it overlord of a proprietary province. Matters of importance were decided in the quarter courts. A system for joint management of land and trade to extend over a period of seven years promised dividends to the adventurers and support to the planters.

After 1619 Virginia was still a proprietary province with a commercial company as overlord and the company was still the immediate source of government in the colony. It adopted "Orders and Constitutions" to secure legality of action and they were read at one quarter court each year. The forms and usages followed in other commercial companies, in other corporate bodies and in Parliament greatly influenced the decisions of the company. Through reward or by purchase an individual might own land and not purchase stock, but he might secure the latter within three years by "planting" or peopling his land. Ownership of land and possession of freedom of the company were not always coexistent. Each involved the possibility of the other. The company, domiciled at London, was thus a body of adventurers that had gained the freedom of the company by payment of money, by rendering of service or by settlement of land in Virginia. It was presided over by a treasurer chosen by itself at will and conducted all of its business through its regularly elected officers or committees or by special committees. According to the "Orders and Constitutions," it kept a complete record of its actions in the courts and compelled its committees to do the same.

Between 1619 and 1622 factions developed in the company due to the administration of Samuel Argall, deputy governor of the colony, under whom both the lands and trade of the company were recklessly exploited for his own benefit and that of his friends. The incident resulted in an administration under the Earl of Southampton, Lord Cavendish, Sir Edwin Sandys and John and Nicholas Ferrar. No radical change in policy took place. Gradually certain developments occurred. Emigration by laborers, artisans and apprentices was encouraged to attain production of grain and to install industry. As stated by Osgood, "introduction of free tenancy and the development of private plantations in addition to the company's land was all the time . . . preparing the way for its transition from the plantation to the provincial type."

Doubtless in 1622 the catastrophe of the Indian massacre added to complications in the colony and in England. Also, political difficulties arose. The Sandys-Southampton party supported parliamentary opposition in England and the king and Sandys were bitterly hostile.

On April 17, 1623, a committee headed by Lord Cavendish was summoned before the Privy Council to defend the company against the "grievances of Planters and Adventurers." As a result, the first blow was struck at the liberty of the company when the Privy Council announced that a commission had been appointed to inquire into the state of the Virginia and Somers Island plantation. On Nov. 4, 1623, the writ of *quo warranto* was issued out of the Court of the King's Bench. Judgment was rendered on May 24, 1624, and the Virginia Company was thereby dissolved. The patent roll, dated July 15, 1624, records appointment of "the commission and certain others" to supplant the Virginia Company and establish the first royal province in America. The commission was composed of the lords of the council and

"certain others," and the council register seems to indicate that it was usually the council sitting as a commission. Papers, letters and instructions, and commissions to the councilors and to governors of the colony passed the Privy Seal and were engrossed on the patent roll, and the letters or papers from the colony were addressed to the council.

Although advice of the company was sought by the king on questions affecting the government of the colony, Sir Edwin Sandys was unsuccessful in his attempt to secure new letters patent. The *Discourse of the Old Company* was issued later in reply. A new charter for the company was never granted and its function as a trading organization ceased.

The mass of materials that form the records between 1619 and 1624 is much greater than in the earlier decade. The minutes comprise two volumes of the "court book" and fill 741 large manuscript pages. Between November, 1623, and June, 1624, Nicholas Ferrar was busily engaged in having these documents transcribed. These transcripts were secured by Thomas Jefferson and are now in the Library of Congress.

VIRGINIA DECLARATION OF RIGHTS was formulated by George Mason and adopted by the Virginia Convention, June 12, 1776, preceding by seventeen days the adoption of the constitution that made Virginia an independent state. It furnished a model for similar declarations in other state constitutions (*see* Bills of Rights, State), as also for the first ten amendments to the Federal Constitution, or the Bill of Rights.

VIRGINIUS **AFFAIR.** News reached the United States Nov. 5, 1873, of the capture in British waters by a Spanish gunboat of the *Virginius*, a ship of American registry engaged in carrying arms to Cuban rebels. Two days later information followed that four of the captives had been executed, one of them an American. On Nov. 12, confirmation arrived that Capt. Fry of the *Virginius* and 36 men had been executed as "pirates" by Gen. Juan Burriel, the governor of Santiago.

The case against Spain was thus extremely serious. The *Virginius* was of American registry and her pursuit and seizure on the high seas, with the ensuing massacre, not only violated international law but excited public resentment in the United States. Weakening these claims, however, was the fact that registration papers had been fraudulently obtained, the vessel's actual owners being Cubans. Both governments understood the weakness in their respective cases. But in the first wave of indignation Secretary of State Hamilton Fish drafted a virtual ultimatum, which lost nothing in its presentation by Gen. Sickles, American minister at Madrid, whose maladroit maneuvers appear to have been motivated by a personal desire for war.

Transferring the negotiation to Washington, Secretary Fish and Admiral Polo, the Spanish minister, achieved a compromise. The attack upon the *Virginius,* whatever her defects of registry, was an injury. The *Virginius,* then, and her survivors, must be restored to the United States, from Spanish waters, and with the American flag at mast. On the vexing question of punctilio concerning a salute to the flag, opportunity was granted for further research into conflicting claims.

The *Virginius* was surrendered on Dec. 16, 1873, but foundered before reaching port. As Fish wrote shortly afterward, there was no *"unnecessary* war undertaken for a dishonest vessel."

VOLSTEAD ACT. The Eighteenth Amendment needing a law to enforce it, the National Prohibition Act, introduced by Andrew J. Volstead of Minnesota, was passed through Congress in October, 1919. It was vetoed by President Wilson (Oct. 27), repassed by the House the same day and by the Senate the following day. It construed intoxicating liquor as that containing as much as ½% of alcohol by volume. It fixed penalties for liquor sales, provided for injunctions against and the padlocking of hotels, restaurants, etc., found to be selling liquor, contained a search and seizure clause, and oddly enough, continued the taxation of a product which had been outlawed. It permitted the retention of private stocks of liquor bought before the act went into effect, and likewise the manufacture of beer by brewers, on condition that they reduce the alcoholic content to ½% before sale. The Eighteenth Amendment was repealed by the ratification of the Twenty-first Amendment in 1933.

VOTING. In American history the election of public officials by popular vote dates back almost to the beginning of the colonial period. Originally the process of voting, particularly in the royal colonies, was an adaptation of the contemporary English practices, always *viva voce*—acclamation, "ereccion" of hands, or individual announcement. The most common procedure was to require each voter to face the election officials and openly state his choices, which, while the favored candidates bowed and murmured their appreciation, were entered upon the books. Concomitant applause, mingled with jeers, enlivened the occasion.

The first signal departure from English precedent came in New England. As early as 1634, Massachusetts set up the innovation of using a paper ballot. Other states gradually followed her example, though in some localities a preference was shown for beans or kernels of corn, black for one candidate and white for the other. By 1800 almost all the states had adopted the paper ballot, at least for some purposes. Oral voting, however, long persisted in parts of the South, Kentucky (1890) being the last state to give up the practice.

The paper ballots were unofficial, each person furnishing his own. Shortly after the beginning of the 19th century, therefore, political parties began to capitalize on the situation by supplying their own tickets for the convenience of the voter. To make identification possible, each party printed tickets of a separate color—"vest-pocket" ballots they were termed, from the puzzled voter standing in the presence of the clerk, fumbling in his vest pockets for the missive he intended to have recorded. That voting was politically controlled is evident from the expression, "straight-arm voting," which described the common spectacle of lines of persons being marched to the polls holding their colored ballots above their heads to show that they were observing orders or fulfilling promises.

By the time of the Civil War, election processes everywhere in the United States were falling into disrepute. Violence, intimidation and bribery were prevalent, especially in the cities; and although statutes were enacted, it was difficult to suppress the train of evils so long as each person could discern how the others were voting.

The importation of the Australian ballot, late in the 19th century, provided the necessary element of secrecy. Now the citizen came to the polls, gave his name, and received the official ballot, which he marked in the shelter of a booth. Where the precinct adopted the voting machine, the citizen was protected by curtains. Everywhere today the statutes make it illegal to campaign close to the polls, to divulge how one has voted, to bet on the election results, to offer bribes or threats, or to create election disturbances. The purpose of this legislation is to preserve the secrecy and freedom of the franchise.

VOYAGEURS, or *engagés,* in American and Canadian history, were a class of men employed by fur traders—especially by the North West, the American, and the Hudson's Bay companies—to paddle their canoes and perform other menial tasks connected with the securing of furs and the maintenance of posts in the interior. They begin to be mentioned as such by French writers about the middle of the 17th century when it became necessary to travel (*voyager*) long distances into the interior in order to get furs. From that time until the third quarter of the 19th century these men formed a rather distinct class that was recognized as such by their contemporaries. Most of the canoemen were born in parishes along the lower St. Lawrence, but in time their descendants in the fur country were also recognized as *voyageurs,* in so far as they followed their ancestors' calling. Perhaps 5000 was an average number for the *voyageurs* to be found in Canada and the United States in any one year of the late 18th and early 19th centuries.

They were generally divided into two classes: (1) according to experience, the pork-eaters and the winterers; and (2) according to skill, the guides, middlemen and *bouts*. The pork-eaters (*mangeurs de lard*) were the novices; the winterers had spent at least one winter in the interior. The guides were the men capable of directing the course of a brigade of canoes. The middlemen (*milieux*) sat in the middle of the canoe and merely propelled it in unison without attempting to guide its course, which was governed by the *bouts* (the two men who stood in the prow and stern respectively), *i.e.*, by the *avant* in the prow, and the steersman (*gouvernail*) in the stern. In the interior the *voyageurs* at the posts helped construct them, cut shingles and made canoes, fished and hunted, went out among the natives, and generally were more or less versatile. They even served their countries during the American Revolution and the War of 1812 as soldiers, certain companies, especially in the Canadian armies, being composed and named by them.

WABASH AND ERIE CANAL. This great waterway, the object of such fond hope in early Indiana, planned to follow the Maumee and Wabash Rivers from Lake Erie to the Ohio River, was agreed upon by the states of Ohio and Indiana in 1829. State lands were sold in Indiana to raise money; $200,000 was borrowed; and in 1832 that state began excavation. Ohio was to build eastward from the Indiana line, but delayed action for several years. Progress in Indiana was slow. By 1841 the canal was in operation only from Fort Wayne to Logansport, and the panics of 1837–39, plus mismanagement, graft and unexpectedly high costs, had well-nigh ruined the state's finances. In 1843 Ohio completed the eastern section of the canal, and some real prosperity now came to the Maumee and upper Wabash valleys. In 1844 the fastest canal packet service in the country was operating between Toledo, Fort Wayne and LaFayette. The canal was opened to Terre Haute in 1849; but flood damage and the competition of railroads being built parallel to its course foreshadowed its end. In 1856 it reached Evansville, 452 miles from Toledo, making it the longest canal in the United States—but it was already dying. The portion below Terre Haute was closed in 1860, and the last short stretch near LaFayette was abandoned in 1875.

WADE-DAVIS BILL, passed by Congress July 2, 1864, provided that the government of a seceded state could be reorganized only after a majority of the white male citizens had taken the oath of allegiance, and a constitution acceptable to the President and Congress was adopted. Henry W. Davis and Benjamin F. Wade, sponsors of the bill, and other Radical Republicans believed that Reconstruction was the prerogative of Congress rather than of the President. Lincoln's pocket veto of this bill, which was the response of Congress to Lincoln's plan of Reconstruction, angered the Radicals and presaged the contest over Reconstruction between Johnson and Congress.

WAGON BOX FIGHT (Aug. 2, 1867). Sioux under Red Cloud attacked a wood-cutting detail under Capt. James Powell near Fort Phil Kearny, Wyo. Thirty-two white men retreated to a corral built of wagon boxes from which they repulsed all attacks of the Sioux. Lt. J. C. Jenness and six men were killed. Powell estimated the Indian loss at 180 killed and wounded.

WAGON TRAINS. For purposes of protection and efficiency, California, Oregon, Santa Fe and other traders and emigrants of the trans-Mississippi West before 1880 customarily gathered their wagons into more or less organized caravans or trains. There is some doubt as to who first used wagons of the "prairie schooner" or canvas-covered type over the transmontane trails to the Far West, but apparently William L. Sublette, one of the partners in the reorganized Rocky Mountain Fur Company, conducted a ten-wagon mule-drawn train over the Oregon Trail from St. Louis as far as the company's Wind River rendezvous between April 10 and July 16, 1830, arriving back at St. Louis on October 10. To Capt. Benjamin L. E. Bonneville's fur-trading expedition is usually ascribed the dictinction of first taking wagons through South Pass, when in July of 1832 his twenty-wagon train, drawn by oxen and mules, reached the Green River by that route. It was not until 1843 that the celebrated "cow column" Oregon emigrant party of about 1000 persons under Peter H. Burnett, Jesse Applegate and Dr. Marcus Whitman brought most of its 120 wagons over the trail to arrive near the Columbia River on October 10, the first wagon train to reach Oregon. Separating from the main emigration of 1843 at Fort Hall, Joseph B. Chiles left Joseph R. Walker to guide a portion of his party with three wagons and reach California after abandoning their wagons just east of the Sierra Nevada at Owen's Lake. The so-called Stevens-Murphy-Townsend party of some fifty persons in October–December of the following year, with five of its original eleven ox-drawn vehicles, is claimed to have been the first group to bring wagons all the way from Missouri and through the Sierras by the California Trail, Donner Lake and Truckee Pass, guided by Caleb Greenwood. William Becknell, a Missouri merchant, took the first wagon train, of three wagons, to Santa Fe in May–July, 1822; and the first wagon trail from Santa Fe on to southern California seems to have been marked during the Mexican War by Lt. Col. Philip St. G. Cooke with his Mormon Battalion (Oct. 19, 1846–Jan. 29, 1847), by way of Guadalupe Pass and the Gila River and Colorado Desert to San Diego. The eastern section of the Old Spanish Trail, from the Wasatch Mountains through Utah, Colorado and New Mexico to Santa Fe, seems to have been seldom if ever traversed by wagons, although Mexican pack trains had used it at least as early as 1830. The western section of this trail, however, through southwestern Utah and across Nevada and California to the vicinity of Los Angeles, was used frequently during the gold rush days by wagon trains of emigrants turning southward from Salt Lake City. A number of well-marked wagon routes ran across Texas from its coast towns and from Louisiana, Arkansas and the Indian Territory to El Paso or other points on the Rio Grande, whence connections could easily be made with the Gila Trail.

The number of wagons making the overland journey annually from 1843 to 1848 is difficult to determine with accuracy. But some idea of the increased emigration by wagon train, after the news of the California gold discovery was confirmed in the East, may be gathered from the report, dated June 23, 1849, that already that year 5516 wagons had passed Fort Kearny on the Platte River, bound for California or the Columbia Valley. In 1865, when the "prairie schooners" were beginning to carry rather more freight than passengers, from thirty to fifty canvas-topped wagons, each capable of transporting from 4000 to 7000 pounds, and drawn usually by five or six yoke of oxen, urged on by "bull-whackers," were said to make up an ordinary train, and trains five miles in length were occasionally reported.

The organization and daily routine of a wagon train depended upon the danger expected from Indians, the nature of the country to be traversed and the number and character of the parties composing the train. Some trains, such as those of the Mormon migrations, had a semi-military formation, others were very loosely bound together. It was customary to elect a "captain" as central authority, and several "lieutenants" were put in charge of assigned sections of the train, their duties being chiefly to execute the commands of the captain, to keep order in their sections and to place them properly in designated positions when the train paused for its encampments. One function of the captain was usually to select each night's camping site in accordance with the advice of a guide or the reports of horsemen sent out in advance during the day. At night the wagons were commonly drawn up in a circle or square, end to end, so as to form a corral for at least the more valuable horses, mules and cattle, as well as a fortress for the passengers. Frequent causes for these precautions were Indian thefts, buffalo herds, storms and other alarms which might stampede the domestic draft animals. Horse- or mule-drawn wagons could make as a rule from ten to fifteen miles a day, the more dependable ox-drawn trains seldom more than ten, under average conditions of travel.

WAKARUSA WAR (December, 1855) was an episode in the rivalry between Free State and proslavery forces in Kansas. The murder of an antislavery settler and threatened retaliation loosed pent-up tension, and 1200 proslavery Missourians and Kansans assembled at Franklin on the Wakarusa River for an attack upon Lawrence. Charles Robinson and James H. Lane prepared to defend the town against attack. To prevent bloodshed, Gov. Wilson Shannon hastened to the scene, signed a "treaty" with Lane and Robinson, conferred with proslavery leaders, and secured their reluctant acquiescence. Both parties disbanded their forces without a resort to arms.

WALK-IN-THE-WATER was the first steamboat to navigate the Upper Great Lakes. Built by Noah Brown, it was launched May 28, 1818, at the Black Rock shipyard at the mouth of Scajaquada Creek (now Buffalo, N. Y.). On August 23, she left port on her maiden voyage, commanded by Job Fish, and continued in service until wrecked off Buffalo, Nov. 1, 1821.

WALKING PURCHASE. In Indian land sales the extent of the purchase was sometimes determined by the distance a man could walk within a specified time. In 1686 the Delaware Indians deeded to William Penn a tract in the fork of the Delaware and Lehigh Rivers, in depth "as far as a man can go in a day and a half"—forty miles as walked by Penn. When, in 1737, the Delawares agreed to a new release of this tract, Thomas Penn employed experts, one of whom, starting near Wrightstown meeting-house in the head line of the deed of 1682, and walking in a northwesterly direction over a prepared route, reached the Poconos, a distance of 66½ miles, within the allotted time. The land thus obtained, about 1200 square miles, and extending northeastward to the Delaware, included portions of the present Bucks and Carbon counties, nine tenths of Northhampton and about a fourth of Monroe and Pike counties. When the Delawares complained of the manner and extent of the walk Penn called in the Iroquois who expelled them from the purchase. Charging fraud and unjust dispossession they then allied themselves with the French and made war upon the province. Penn later relinquished to the Six Nations the northern half of the purchase (1758) while the colony settled with the Delawares for £400 (1762).

WALLA WALLA SETTLEMENTS began with the establishment of the Indian trading post, Fort Nez Percé, in 1818 by Donald MacKenzie and Alexander Ross for the North West Company on the east bank of the Columbia at its junction with the Walla Walla River. This post was often called Fort Walla Walla. A farm was maintained in connection with it. Waiilatpu, the Whitman mission, twenty miles up

991

the river from the post, built in October, 1836, was the next white settlement. Agriculture was carried on there. It served (quoting Mrs. Whitman) "as a resting place for weary travelers." This settlement was destroyed when the Indians killed Dr. and Mrs. Whitman and some twelve other men, women and children, temporary immigrant and missionary residents, Nov. 29, 1847. Later, a new settlement sprang up near by, known as Whitman or French Town, made up of Catholic French-Canadians and half-breeds.

A few white families had settled in the Walla Walla Valley by 1855 at the time of the Indian uprising in eastern Washington. These were ordered out by the United States Indian agent. He also forced Fort Nez Percé to be abandoned at the same time. A new Fort Walla Walla, a United States military post, was erected in November, 1856, about 28 miles up the river of that name.

Walla Walla County was created by the Washington territorial legislature in 1854. By 1859, with the close of the Yakima Indian Wars, 2000 white settlers were located in this valley. In 1862 the city of Walla Walla was incorporated and Wallula at the mouth of Walla Walla River was laid out as a town. A railroad connecting these two points was completed in the early 1870's. These towns were very prosperous during the period of the rush to the gold mines in eastern Oregon and western Idaho, 1860 and afterward.

WAMPUM is an Indian word meaning a string of shell beads. When the whites settled along the northern Atlantic seaboard certain shell beads were highly prized by the Iroquois and their neighbors. The former exacted tribute in wampum of the tribes they conquered. It had, in addition, a ceremonial value. From the beginning the Dutch and English accepted wampum from the Indians as money. In 1640 Massachusetts made it legal tender. According to Roger Williams six white and three black beads were equivalent to a penny; 360 white and 180 black beads were considered a fathom, valued at 5 shillings. The term "string of wampum" at one time signified strung wampum, about one foot in length, and was rated at twelve and one half cents. In Virginia the use of wampum began early, but glass beads were imported as a cheap substitute and in 1621 a glass furnace was built to manufacture them at home. Adulteration eventually set in among the Dutch and in New England, causing wide fluctuations in the value of wampum. Machines were built to turn out wampum beads in quantity. Two such factories are known to have existed, one in Hackensack, N. J., the other in Babylon, L. I. In 1650 the Council of New Netherland attempted to fix the value of wampum, but counterfeiting continued on such a scale that the use of wampum as currency declined, vanishing at the end of the 17th century. However, the Indians continued to value it for gifts, peace pledges and ceremonial purposes well into the 19th century.

After the middle of the 17th century beaver skins began to rival wampum in the Indian trade and soon became legal tender. For a time beaver skins and wampum were equated, as one beaver to two fathoms of white and one fathom of black wampum, but later we find a different quotation, two strings of wampum for one beaver. In the Canadian trade the value of a beaver was rated in goods directly, and not in terms of wampum, as may be noted in the reports of the Hudson's Bay Company.

WAMPUM BELT. This was an Indian symbol of a message of good will, peace or war, often between individuals but sometimes between tribes or confederacies. The use of such belts was highly characteristic of the Iroquois-speaking tribes, especially the Six Nations, but to a less degree among all the tribes of northeastern United States. None of the belts in collections is believed to be of great age for most of the beads in them are of Dutch and English manufacture. All the belts known are made of cylindrical or tubular shell beads, the wampum of colonial times, strung or woven in bands two to four inches wide and of varying length. When a treaty was made belts were exchanged as symbols or pledges. The tradition is that the Iroquois declared war by sending a belt painted red, but that this was more than figurative language is uncertain. On the other hand a belt was sometimes carried by a messenger to call out warriors from the allied or subject tribes of the Six Nations. The colors of wampum beads varied with the natural color of the shells used, the prevailing colors being white, black (dark blue) and shades of purple. Simple designs were formed by arranging beads of these colors. In most cases these designs were geometric but in a few existing belts there are crude figures of houses and of men holding hands. The so-called reading of the belts seems to have been little more than a verbal narrative of the occasion and the reasons for presenting the belts in question, the differences in design and size serving to identify them.

WAR CRIMES TRIALS. In November, 1945–October, 1946, at Nuremberg, the surviving leaders of the Nazi regime in Germany were tried before an International Tribunal (the United States, Great Britain, Russia and France) as "war criminals," charged with violations of international law, with having waged aggressive warfare, and in general with "crimes against humanity." Of 22 high officials brought to trial, 19 were found guilty. Twelve, including Goering, Ribbentrop and Seyss-Inquart, were sentenced to death, and of these eight were eventually hanged. In addition a number of lesser officials were tried, most of whom were convicted.

Comparable trials of Japanese leaders were held at Tokyo, June, 1946–April, 1948, with similar results.

The trial of war criminals rested on the assumption that aggressive warfare was a crime, and on the still broader assumption that the principles of jurisprudence as developed in England and the United States applied to international relations as well. Yet many people objected that these principles were themselves disregarded in the trials. Thus it was charged that to try men for committing acts which were only later designated as crimes was to pass judgment *ex post facto*. The only answer to this was that the crimes of the Nazi leaders—the full magnitude of which became apparent only as the trials unfolded—were so horrible as to deserve, if not to demand, such punishment.

"WAR HAWKS" was the term applied to those members of the Twelfth Congress (1811–13) whose advocacy of war with Great Britain brought on the War of 1812. Their leaders, among whom were Clay and Johnson of Kentucky, Porter of western New York, Grundy of Tennessee and Calhoun of South Carolina, came chiefly from the West and South, the regions least affected by British interference with "free trade and sailors' rights." Their enthusiasm for war may be attributed partly to their youthful exuberance—they were nearly all young men; but as spokesmen for their sections they envisioned concrete advantages as the fruit of war. Men of the Northwest commonly held the British responsible for their troubles with the Indians (exemplified in the activities of Tecumseh and the bloody encounter at Tippecanoe, Nov. 7, 1811) and expected to end these difficulties by driving the British from Canada. Southerners planned to conquer Florida from Spain, Great Britain's ally. Thus the "war hawks" represented the expansionist aims of the frontier.

WAR OF 1812, THE, was provoked by Great Britain's maritime policy in her war with Napoleon and by her overfriendly relations with the Indian tribes of the American Northwest; its advent was facilitated by the desire of the West and South to secure possession of Canada and Florida.

Neither England nor France, in their life-and-death struggle (1793–1801, 1803–15), paid much heed to the rights of neutrals. While Napoleon, through a series of decrees, issued at Berlin, Milan and elsewhere, sought to exclude neutral ships from all trade with Great Britain, British Orders in Council forbade neutral ships to trade with France or with French dependencies except after touching at English ports. Thus American ships conforming to the demands of one belligerent were subject to confiscation by the other. Meanwhile, Great Britain insisted upon the right of her naval officers to "impress" from American ships on the high seas deserters from the royal navy or other British subjects liable to naval service, and bona fide American citizens were frequently the victims of this practice.

The dispute over British practices became acute in 1806 and reached a climax in 1807, when the British frigate *Leopard* fired upon the U.S.S. *Chesapeake* and removed four sailors, three of them American citizens. Finding it impossible to adjust the disputes with the belligerents by negotiation, and unwilling to resort to war, Jefferson experimented with a policy of "peaceful coercion." At his request Congress passed the Embargo Act of 1807, forbidding the departure from American ports of both American and foreign vessels, except those American ships engaged in the coastwise trade. When the Embargo proved more injurious to the United States than to its intended victims, France and England, it was repealed (March, 1809), and in its place a Nonintercourse Act merely forbade trade with the offending powers. This in turn gave way to a new measure (May, 1810), which reopened trade with all the world, but promised that if either England or France would revoke its obnoxious measures, nonintercourse would be revived against the other.

Napoleon, through a pretended revocation of the Berlin and Milan Decrees, inveigled President Madison into reinstituting nonintercourse against Great Britain (November, 1810), and when the British government, nevertheless, refused, until too late (June, 1812, when the Orders in Council were in fact repealed), to modify its policy toward the United States, Madison called Congress a month ahead of time and on Nov. 5, 1811, recommended that that body prepare the country for hostilities.

The Twelfth Congress, which received Madison's bellicose message, proved to be dominated by the "War Hawks." This group of young men, chiefly from the West and South, resented the injuries inflicted on the country by Great Britain and wished to avenge them. In their eyes, British crimes were not confined to the high seas. While western agriculture, like that of other sections, suffered from the British blockade of France, the West had peculiar grievances which were not felt along the seaboard. On the northwestern frontier, in Ohio and in the territories of Indiana, Illinois and Michigan, the Indians, led by the enterprising Shawnee chief, Tecumseh, were showing a new disposition to unite in opposition to further encroachments upon their lands. It was no secret that British agents in Canada were sympathetic toward Tecumseh and his policy. It was known that the Indians received British arms and ammunition, and it was believed (somewhat unjustly) that the British were actively inciting the Indians to hostilities against American settlers. Even as Congress met, a western army under Gen. William Henry Harrison, governor of Indiana Territory, suffered severe losses in an attack by the Indians near the village of Tippecanoe. Almost with one voice, the Northwest held England responsible for this bloodshed and demanded the expulsion of the British from Canada as the only remedy for Indian troubles.

The northwestern demand for Canada was balanced by a southwestern and southern demand for the conquest of East and West Florida. These Spanish provinces were coveted because of their strategic position, their navigable rivers draining American territory, and the harborage which they gave to hostile Indians and runaway slaves. The United States had long claimed a portion of West Florida as part of the Louisiana Purchase, and had begun absorbing it piecemeal. The fact that Spain was an ally of Great Britain offered a plausible excuse for seizing the remainder of both provinces in the event of war.

These frontier grievances and ambitions occupied a prominent place in the war debates in Congress. It is impossible to disregard them in estimating the causes of the war. On the whole, it seems safe to say that it required a combination of the maritime and the frontier grievances to bring about war with Great Britain; that neither set alone would have been sufficient. Certain it is that it was the hope of the "War Hawks," as one of them phrased it, "not only to add the Floridas to the South, but the Canadas to the North of this empire."

Unfortunately, the Congress which on June 18, 1812, approved war by an ominously close vote (19 to 13 in the Senate, 79 to 49 in the House) had spent seven months in debating without making adequate military, naval or financial preparation for war. The consequence of congressional trifling, of insufficient and ill-trained troops, of military incompetence in high command and of defective strategy was a series of military disasters which, had not England's hands been tied in Europe, might have spelled national calamity. The first year of war witnessed the surrender of Gen. William Hull at Detroit, the failure of Generals Van Rensselaer and Smyth on the Niagara River and of Dearborn at the foot of Lake Champlain. The year 1813 saw the recovery of Detroit and the defeat of the British at the Thames by Gen. Harrison, but closed with the complete failure of Gen. James Wilkinson's campaign against Montreal, and with the capture of Fort Niagara and the burning of Buffalo by the British. By the summer of 1814, the competent hands of Generals Jacob Brown and Winfield Scott had imbued the northern army with excellent discipline and a fighting spirit, but British veterans were now present in such force that the Americans could hope for nothing more than to hold their own. The hard fighting at Chippewa, Lundy's Lane and Fort Erie demonstrated the prowess of the United States Army but failed to conquer any territory. Meanwhile, a British army landed on the shores of Chesapeake Bay, burned Washington, but failed to take Baltimore. Another, advancing from Montreal, reached Plattsburg, on Lake Champlain, but retreated hastily when the accompanying fleet was destroyed. At New Orleans on Jan. 8, 1815 (two weeks after the signing of the peace treaty), Andrew Jackson inflicted upon a British army under Gen.

Pakenham the most crushing military defeat of the war.

Meanwhile, the United States Navy had given a good account of itself. The victories on Lake Erie (September, 1813) and Lake Champlain (September, 1814) gave the United States control of those important waterways. The numerous single-ship actions on the high seas proved the mettle of the navy, but failed to diminish the overwhelming superiority of the British fleet, which gradually tightened its blockade upon the American coast.

As an indirect result of an offer of mediation by the Czar of Russia, American and British peace commissioners met at Ghent in the summer of 1814. The Americans (Gallatin, J. Q. Adams, Clay, Bayard and Jonathan Russell) were in no position to ask for territory and soon found it necessary to drop even their demands for concessions in regard to neutral rights and impressments. The British commissioners, in their turn, abandoned their demands for boundary readjustments and for a permanent Indian barrier state in the Northwest and at length accepted the American ultimatum of peace on the basis of the *status quo ante bellum* as to territory. The British right to navigate the Mississippi and the American right to engage in inshore fishing on the coasts of British North America, both provided in the Definitive Treaty of Peace of 1783, were allowed to lapse. The fact was that both nations were war-weary, and the British government was advised by the Duke of Wellington that it could not hope for better terms without an expenditure of energy which it was unprepared to make.

The Treaty of Ghent, signed Dec. 24, 1814, though it gained not one of the ends for which the United States had gone to war, was joyously received in this country and unanimously ratified by the Senate. It nipped in the bud a rising sectional opposition to government policy which had appeared rather ominously in the Hartford Convention.

Although, measured by military achievement or by the terms of the treaty of peace, the war was a failure, it is not wholly correct so to regard it. Through it the West and South, although indirectly, achieved their principal objectives. Canada was not conquered, but the war shattered British prestige among the Indians, ended British interference in their affairs, and left them powerless to check the American advance. In the South, though efforts to seize Florida were blocked by northern opposition, Jackson's campaign against the Creek Indians (1813–14) opened for settlement an enormous area in Georgia and Alabama and started the train of events which ended with Spain's surrender of Florida by the Adams-Onís Treaty of 1819. The cessation of impressments and of interference with neutral trade, though due almost entirely to the termination of the war in Europe, doubtless contributed to the feeling that the war, though ill-fought, had not been wholly devoid of profit.

Blockade of U. S. Seaboard. Although Congress declared that a state of war existed with Great Britain on June 18, 1812, the British government delayed giving orders for a blockade of the United States until November, when it instructed Admiral Warren to blockade rigorously Chesapeake and Delaware bays. The blockaded areas were gradually extended to include New York, Charleston, Port Royal, Savannah and the mouth of the Mississippi in the spring of 1813; Long Island Sound in November, 1813; and the entire eastern seaboard (including New England, previously exempt because of pro-British sentiment in that section), in May, 1814.

To enforce the blockade, the British Admiralty maintained off the American coast at least ten ships-of-the-line (necessitated by the superiority of the American 44-gun frigates over the British "thirty-eights") and a large number of frigates and sloops-of-war. So effective was their work that only rarely was a swift American vessel able to steal through, and maritime trade practically ceased. This was true of coastwise no less than of foreign trade; even the sounds and inland channels of the southern coast were penetrated by the ubiquitous blockading ships.

The effect was disastrous upon both private business and government revenues. Only from Georgia, by way of Spanish Florida, and from New England up to the summer of 1814, could American produce be exported. Exports from Virginia fell from $4,800,000 in 1811 to $17,581 in 1814. New York and Philadelphia suffered almost as heavily. The destruction of exports, ruinous to the farmer, forced the suspension of specie payments by all banks south of New England by the early fall of 1814. Imports, likewise, practically ceased, save through the favored New England ports, and import duties fell proportionately. Revenue from this source, over $13,000,000 in 1811, declined to less than $6,000,000 in 1814, and from the ports south of New England fell close to the zero mark. Economic ruin and governmental bankruptcy were averted only by the timely termination of the war.

(*See also* the following battles and campaigns: Bladensburg; Borgne, Lake; Canada, American Invasion of, 1812–14; *Chesapeake* Captured by *Shannon; Chippewa, Battle of; Constitution* and *Guerrière* Engagement; Erie, Lake; Lake Champlain in the War of 1812; Lundy's Lane; Mims, Fort, Massacre at; New Orleans, Battle of; Niagara Campaigns; Plattsburg; Queenston Heights; Sacketts Harbor; Thames.)

WARRIORS PATH, GREAT, was the war road between the northern and southern Indians, that is, between the Shawnee and Wyandot of the Ohio country and the Catawba and Cherokee of western North Carolina. The road ran from opposite the mouth of Scioto River along the eastern portion of what is now Kentucky, past the Upper Blue Licks and the Red River branch of the Kentucky to the Cumberland Gap; thence it passed down Powell's Valley, crossed the Clinch River and the north fork of the Holston. There it divided, the eastern end going on to the Catawba towns, the western across Nolachucky and the French Broad Rivers to the heart of the Overhill Cherokee Indian towns.

The Great Warriors Path was mentioned in 1750 by Dr. Thomas Walker in his western explorations. It was plainly marked in Powell's Valley when Boone and Finley came out in 1769. Except at the Cumberland Gap it was avoided by explorers, because of danger from passing Indians.

It was shown on the map of Lewis Evans in 1755; on that of Thomas Hutchins in 1778. On Filson's map of Kentucky, 1784, there are two branches, one direct from the Scioto mouth, the other passing westward crossing the Ohio at Cabin Creek and proceeding to the Mingo towns on a branch of the Scioto.

WARS: COSTS OF MAJOR UNITED STATES WARS. Any estimate of war costs must be based on arbitrary assumptions as to what kinds of expenses are properly chargeable to war. Granting that wartime military expenditures by the government are a basic element of war costs, should not one deduct from these the normal peacetime operating costs of the military establishment which would have been incurred anyway? It is arguable, too, that both the prewar build-up of military expenditures in anticipation of hostilities and the postwar taper-off of such expenditures should be included. Should one deduct from military appropriation figures the costs of feeding, clothing, and housing military personnel, considering, on the one hand, that these would have had to be provided for anyway, but, on the other, that they would have been productively occupied? What about property damage, and the lost economic value of people killed or disabled in war, not to mention the costs of wartime economic disruption, or the "negative" cost—*i.e.,* economic gain—of a wartime boom? Part of the cost of war is transferred to future generations in the form of interest charges on war debts, and these charges usually continue long after the debts themselves have lost their identity in the total debt of the nation. In a similar category are the costs of veterans' pensions and bonuses, medical and hospital care, and the like. Finally, the fluctuating value of the dollar must be kept in mind in comparing the costs of various wars, even though it may not be practicable to translate all the long-term costs of a particular war in terms of a fictitious constant dollar.

The estimates given in the table are limited to expenditures by the Government; they do not include any general economic, human, or enemy (except Confederate) costs. With a few exceptions the periods of actual hostilities have been extended, for

	NET MILITARY COSTS	DEBT INTEREST	VETERANS' BENEFITS	TOTAL
		(IN MILLIONS OF DOLLARS)		
Revolution	101	84	70	255
War of 1812	90	50	49	189
Mexican War	71	35	64	170
Civil War				
Union	3,183	2,593	8,541	14,317
Confederacy	1,520	?	?	1,520
Spanish War	283	83	4,117	4,483
World War I	24,269	20,468	20,294	65,031
World War II	315,227	62,278	46,800	425,305
Korean War				
Korean operations	18,000	338	2,825	21,163
Net Defense (a)	34,065	1,483	2,825	38,373
Net Defense (b)	79,097	1,483	2,825	83,405

purposes of computation, to include the entire fiscal year in which hostilities began (for World War II, the preceding year as well) and one or two fiscal years following the end of hostilities, in order to make allowance for the prewar and postwar overlap factor mentioned above. Military costs are "net"; that is, they have been reduced by the estimated normal peacetime costs of the military establishment for an equivalent period. For costs of veterans' benefits, the computations of the Veterans Administration have been used; they extend through Fiscal Year 1956. U. S. Treasury computations for the cost of interest on particular debts have been used when available; in other cases they have been estimated.

For the Revolutionary War, estimates include the specie value of Treasury expenditures and certificates of indebtedness for the years 1775 through 1783, foreign loans, and state war debts assumed by the Federal Government. The estimate of war costs of the Southern Confederacy is based solely on military appropriations by the Confederate Congress; since no effort has been made to estimate other categories of loss to the Confederacy, no valid figure for total Civil War costs can be arrived at. Allied war debts owed to the United States from World War I have not been included in the costs of that war. Costs for World Wars I and II have been reduced by the value of surplus assets of the armed services; they also include expenditures by certain nonmilitary agencies. World War II costs include lend-lease transfers valued at $50,200,000,000, reduced by the amounts subsequently repaid by some of the recipient countries. Allowance has also been made for recoveries of excess profits under the World War II renegotiation process.

The Korean War presents a special problem, in that it is virtually impossible to separate the costs growing out of operations in Korea from those of the mobilization and expansion of military strength during the same period resulting from the expecta-

tion of new communist aggressions in Europe and elsewhere. Moreover, estimates of "normal" peacetime military costs for the post-World War II period are complicated by the fact that defense expenditures following the Korean War continued at a high level. Any estimate of Korean War costs based merely on the increase over low prewar expenditures for defense must be justified by the assumption that the whole rearmament effort of 1951–53 grew out of the communist aggression in Korea. Nevertheless the table includes such an estimate, in order to follow the pattern of estimates for earlier wars. Three sets of figures are shown for the Korean War: one based on the Defense Department's estimate (in 1955) of military expenditures "in the Korean area alone," and two estimates of "net" costs representing, respectively, the increase over average peacetime levels (a) during both the pre-Korea and post-Korea years, and (b) during the pre-Korea period only.

WARS: LOSS OF LIFE IN MAJOR UNITED STATES WARS. Few historical statistics are as unreliable as those showing forces engaged and loss of life in war, particularly those for earlier wars and for the Confederacy in the Civil War. In most United States wars the system of volunteering permitted varied terms of enlistment, shorter than the duration of the war, with the result that many soldiers re-enlisted several times; these multiple enlistments are seldom reflected in the statistics. The figures are further complicated by the traditional practice of allowing conscripts to purchase substitutes, by the falsification of identities attendant on giving bounties for volunteering, and by the sheer confusion and error incident to most wartime recordkeeping. Casualty records are, of course, subject to the additional uncertainties of battle, particularly with respect to the causes of death.

The table shown states official U. S. Department of Defense figures (1957) of total numbers of personnel

	TOTAL WHO SERVED	BATTLE DEATHS	OTHER DEATHS	TOTAL DEATHS
Revolution (1775–83)	(250,000)	4,435	?	(4,435)
War of 1812 (1812–15)	286,730	2,260	?	(2,260)
Mexican War (1846–48)	78,718	1,733	?	(1,733)
Civil War (1861–65)				
Union	2,213,363	140,414	224,097	364,511
Confederacy	(900,000)	(74,524)	(90,457)	(164,981)
Spanish War (1898)	306,760	385	2,061	2,446
World War I (1917–18)	4,734,991	53,402	63,114	116,516
World War II (1941–45)	14,903,213	291,557	113,842	405,399
Korean War (1950–53)	5,720,000	33,629	20,617	54,246

who served in the wars indicated, and of loss of life among military personnel (Coast Guard data are not included). Figures in parentheses are estimates not officially endorsed by the Department of Defense. The "number serving" figure for World War II is for the period Dec. 1, 1941, through Aug. 31, 1945, although the deaths figures cover the period through Dec. 31, 1946, when the emergency was officially terminated.

WARSHIPS. Until almost the end of the 19th century, the U. S. Navy consisted almost entirely of wooden cruisers, except for the monitor interlude during the Civil War. Except for a few occasional ships of the line which never served together as a major fleet, it did not go in for capital ships until 1890, when Capt. Alfred Thayer Mahan first stressed the importance of such maximum force in contesting for control of the seas. Eventually, the Navy not only achieved great strength in battleships but also branched out into destroyers, submarines, cruisers, and, eventually, aircraft carriers which finally replaced the battleship as the major unit of sea power.

During the American Revolution most of the vessels acquired under national or state authority were frigates or lesser cruisers of moderate size; one of them at least, the *Hancock*, was of very superior design and construction but, like most of the rest of the Continental Navy, was not adequately handled. By 1785 the last vessel of that first Navy was gone, and for several years the Americans had no navy at all.

One of the most effective steps in American naval construction came in 1794 when the United States decided to build six ships for a new navy. Just how much credit is due to Joshua Humphreys of Philadelphia is not certain, but he did have a part in the decision to build three of the ships as superfrigates, strong enough to defeat the conventional 36-gun and 38-gun frigates of other navies, and fast enough to escape from anything stronger. This resulted in the 44-gun *Constitution* built at Boston, the

United States at Philadelphia, and *President* at New York. The victories of 1812 were due in part to their superior strength. The early Navy also contained some frigates of more conventional size, some sloops of war, and some gun brigs and schooners. When Commodore Preble asked for a few little gunboats for the Barbary wars, Jefferson persuaded Congress to build more than 200 of the quite worthless little craft.

In the field of steam, the U.S. Navy achieved several "firsts" even though it did not follow them up as vigorously as the British or French. During the War of 1812, Robert Fulton conceived the idea of a steam floating battery to attack the blockaders off New York. The resultant *Demologos*, or *Fulton the First*, the first steam warship, was launched in 1814 but was not completed until the spring of 1815 when the war was over and Fulton dead. In 1823, the *Sea Gull*, a little river steamer taken by the Navy for service against the West Indian pirates, was the first steam warship in action. Thirdly, the United States Navy also had the first warship with a screw propeller instead of the vulnerable paddle wheel; this was the *Princeton*, completed in 1844 through the initiative of Capt. Robert Stockton, just ahead of the British *Rattler*. The nation might also have had the first seagoing ironclad, had it given continued support to the project of the inventive Stevens family of Hoboken, whose ironclad "battery," undertaken in 1843, was rusting, partly completed, when the Civil War began.

That conflict led to further innovations, though the United States had lagged behind Britain and France in the meantime. They had not only gone quite thoroughly into steam but had produced the ironclad *Gloire* in 1859 and *Warrior* in 1860. With the coming of war, the Confederacy converted the sunken steam frigate *Merrimack* into an ironclad. The North, advertising for suggestions, built a substantial seagoing armored vessel, the new *Ironsides*, but she was overshadowed by the *Monitor*, "cheese-box on a raft," designed by John Ericsson, the Swedish engineer who was also a prime inventor of the screw propeller; her contribution to the development of naval architecture was the revolving turret. Her encounter with the *Merrimack* at Hampton Roads in 1862 gave undue prominence to a type of limited utility; Congressmen liked these ships because they could defend home ports, and the Navy built altogether too many.

After the Civil War, the U. S. Navy lagged behind while other navies were making steady progress with steam and iron. For this Adm. David D. Porter was partly responsible; he laid up the cruiser *Wampanoag*, the fastest vessel afloat, and tried to keep the Navy's scattered cruisers under sail as far as possible.

In 1881, Secretary of the Navy Hunt began the movement for the "New Navy" of steel ships. It resulted in the "White Squadron" of the *Atlanta, Boston,* and *Chicago,* and the despatch boat *Dolphin.* More cruisers quickly followed, and in 1890, Secretary Tracy sponsored the move for battleships proper, with heavy armor, resulting in the *Indiana, Massachusetts,* and *Oregon* for a start. By 1898, in the war with Spain, the Navy won spectacular and easy victories at Manila Bay and Santiago. Then, thanks in part to the stimulus of President Theodore Roosevelt, battleship construction on a large scale resulted. Late in 1907, partly to meet a Japanese threat, he sent the "Great White Fleet" of 16 battleships around the world. They were already obsolescent, for Britain's *Dreadnought* in 1906, with "all big guns" instead of only four, forced other nations to start afresh. By the time the "Great White Fleet" returned, the *Delaware,* first of the American dreadnoughts had been launched.

Despite the heavy emphasis on battleships, other types were also taking form. In 1900, the Navy purchased and commissioned the *Holland,* usually regarded as the first regular submarine. It was also following the British in adopting the swift little "torpedo boat destroyer" which would soon become the submarine's principal adversary; the first of the Navy's 950-odd destroyers was the 420-ton *Bainbridge* in 1901.

The next important type to develop was the aircraft carrier, with which the British experimented during World War I. The first American carrier was the converted collier *Jupiter,* renamed the *Langley* in 1920. Next came the huge *Lexington* and *Saratoga* of 33,000 tons, converted from battle cruisers after the Washington Naval Conference of 1921–22, which sharply restricted capital ship construction, and led to a long "holiday" in battleship building. By World War II, the carrier was supplanting the battleship, and instead of the old "line ahead" of the dreadnoughts, the "fast carrier task force" of cruisers, destroyers and even new battleships escorting the carriers at 33 knots or better became the principal naval offensive formation.

Finally, the decade 1950–60 saw the most drastic transformation of any period in naval construction and tactics. The two new features were atomic power, which would give vessels an almost unlimited cruising radius without having to return to base, and guided missiles which gradually replaced the old naval guns which, even at their 16-inch best, could reach only some twenty miles. Atomic power, developed through the primary initiative of Adm. Hyman Rickover, first appeared in the *Nautilus,* completed at Groton, Conn., in 1955, followed by several others, some of which had the new fast "teardrop" design. At the same time, constant experimentation was producing new guided missiles, not only for use against attacking planes but also against land targets. The two movements combined dramatically and effectively in the "Polaris" ballistic missile with a range of 1500 miles or more which can be fired from a submerged atomic submarine. With a considerable number of those, plus a new atomic-powered carrier, the Navy feels that it has developed a powerful "deterrent" for the national defense against aggressors.

WASHINGTON, D. C. Congress located the permanent seat of government of the United States on the Potomac River and accepted the cession of ten miles square from Maryland and Virginia to form the District of Columbia. Over this territory the Constitution gave to Congress exclusive authority in order to prevent such indignities as the Continental Congress had suffered in the nine cities in which it successively assembled. Boundaries and the planning were left to President Washington, as was also the selection of three commissioners to survey and mark the district and to provide buildings for Congress, the President and the public offices. The City of Washington in the Territory of Columbia was the name chosen by the Commissioners in consultation with Jefferson and Madison.

President Washington (1791) sent Andrew Ellicott (experienced in running state and international boundaries) to survey an area ten miles square, to include Georgetown in Maryland and Alexandria in Virginia, prospective centers of western commerce. He accepted the proffered services of Maj. Pierre-Charles L'Enfant to design the city plan. L'Enfant, trained as an architect and engineer, came to America in 1777 as a French lieutenant. He suffered the privations of Valley Forge, was wounded, captured and exchanged at Savannah, and was commissioned major in the Continental Army. He established a reputation as an arbiter of taste, designed the insignia of the Order of the Cincinnati, and remodeled Federal Hall in New York (where Washington was inaugurated), reputed the finest building in the country.

During 1791 Ellicott and L'Enfant worked as companions. Ellicott was 37 and L'Enfant the same age. Riding over the ground, Washington and L'Enfant selected commanding sites for the Capitol and the President's House; the two men consulted at Mount

Vernon as the plans progressed. Putting aside Jefferson's sketch for a town one third the size of L'Enfant's, with a gridiron street plan, Washington readily responded to L'Enfant's enthusiasm for a city area as extensive as that of the Paris of their day, with public buildings connected by broad avenues arranged to create fine vistas, open spaces for landscape effects, and with canals and fountains to provide embellishments such as L'Enfant had been familiar with in the gardens LeNôtre had made at Versailles and Fontainebleau for Louis XIV. The plans for the extension of Paris were still only on paper (the Tuileries gardens a stone quarry and the Place de l'Etoile an apple orchard) when L'Enfant drew his plan for that park connection between "the Federal House" and "the Presidential Palace" which (prolonged to the Potomac in the plan of 1901) forms the central composition of Washington.

L'Enfant regarded (with some reason) the plan as his personal property; the President sent his drawing (now in the Library of Congress) to Congress for information, and when L'Enfant refused to encourage speculation by yielding it to the Commissioners, Ellicott prepared for publication the L'Enfant plan with minor changes approved by Washington. With characteristic extravagance and disregard for private rights, L'Enfant proceeded to open streets beyond the financial ability of the Commissioners, whose funds came from the sale of the moiety of city lots divided with the proprietors. After a year of strenuous labors, L'Enfant's service was ended with the President's reluctant assent. Refusing what he regarded as inadequate payment and declining a professorship (in 1812) at West Point, L'Enfant, importunate and embittered, lived in poverty with compassionate friends until his death in 1825.

In the meantime the city had been laid waste by the British in the War of 1812. In the evening of Aug. 24, 1814, the Capitol, the White House and the Treasury Building were burned by a detachment of troops headed by Maj. Gen. Robert Ross and Rear Adm. Sir George Cockburn; by the following noon the buildings housing the Departments of State and War were in ruins, and so were two ropewalks, a tavern, and the office of the *National Intelligencer*.

In later years the inherent excellence of L'Enfant's plan could not be overlooked, despite many serious mutilations in time of peace. Notably the Mall (the park between the Capitol and the President's House) was dismembered; railway tracks bisected it; axial relations, dear to both Washington and L'Enfant, were destroyed in the casual location of the Washington Monument. Like all other American cities during the 19th century the National Capital had a haphazard growth. Then came the Chicago World's Fair of 1893 to reveal the value of orderliness, convenience and beauty in planning cities.

In 1901 Sen. James McMillan secured Senate sanction for plans to develop the park system of the District of Columbia and for the location of future public buildings and monuments. For the task he selected the designers of the Chicago Fair, D. H. Burnham, C. F. McKim, Augustus Saint-Gaudens and F. L. Olmsted, Jr., recommended by the American Institute of Architects. After a visit to European capitals and a study of the sources of L'Enfant's inspiration (particularly in LeNôtre's gardens), the Senate Park Commission presented plans restoring the authority of L'Enfant's plan, curing mutilations of it and extending it to comprise the entire District of Columbia. The McMillan plan (officially so called) is the L'Enfant plan brought up to date; it has guided the development of Washington since 1902. Tardily, fittingly, on March 28, 1909, the remains of L'Enfant, recovered from a casual grave on the Diggs farm, were borne in honor to the Capitol and thence to Arlington National Cemetery.

The rapid growth and diversification of government functions, beginning with the Spanish-American War (1898), caused an imperative demand for departmental buildings; also for the removal of the Supreme Court from the Capitol to a home of its own. On the initiative of President Coolidge, Congress in 1926 began a public-building program more extensive than ever before undertaken by any nation, and still in progress. Washington (now coextensive with the District of Columbia) has grown by 1960 to a city of over 763,956 within the seven miles square to which it was reduced by the retrocession of Virginia's portion in 1846. Naturally the political center of the country, government service (supplemented by the Smithsonian and Carnegie institutions) has gathered a great body of scientists; the Library of Congress compares with leading libraries of the world both in size and richness; the Corcoran, the Freer, and the Phillips Memorial galleries, as well as the National Gallery of Art, represent the world of art from the United States to the Far East, and from antiquity to the 20th century: all contributions to cultural life, wherein our capital has previously lagged. Park extensions now under way will cause the Potomac to flow through a continuous park for thirty miles from Great Falls to Mount Vernon. Washington never will be finished; it will continue to progress with the Republic.

WASHINGTON, STATE OF, was, until 1844, inhabited largely by some 25,000 Indians: Chinooks, Flathead, Nez Percé, Cayuse and others. Probably the first white man to sight the Washington shore was the Spaniard Juan Perez, who in 1774 discovered the Nootka Sound and Mt. Olympus. In 1775 the Spaniard Bruno Heceta landed on Washington soil at 47½°, barely missing the discovery of the Columbia River.

English and Americans followed. In 1778 Capt. Cook sojourned at Nootka, recorded native words, which later became the Chinook jargon, and opened the Northwest fur trade. Spain's and England's controversy over Nootka, in 1790, ended in favor of the latter. In 1792 George Vancouver mapped Puget Sound, named Hood Canal, Mt. Rainier and Puget Sound. On May 11, 1792, Robert Gray sailed over the bar into the river which he named Columbia in honor of his ship, thus giving America her first claim to the Oregon country. This claim was strengthened when Lewis and Clark crossed the continent and reached the Pacific, November, 1805.

The British and Americans raced for the possession of "Oregon." David Thompson explored and mapped the Columbia Valley in 1810. In 1811 John Jacob Astor of the American Fur Company founded Astoria, which was taken over by the British in 1812, but restored in 1818. Spain and Russia surrendered their claims to this region in 1819 and 1824, respectively. Between 1824 and 1846 Dr. John McLoughlin of the Hudson's Bay Company ruled the Northwest firmly and wisely from Fort Vancouver, controlling the Indians and helping American settlers. In 1818 England and the United States agreed to hold the territory for ten years, and in 1827, joint occupancy was extended indefinitely. Meanwhile, newly arrived American settlers organized a provisional government in Oregon in 1843, and the slogan of the Democratic party "Fifty-four forty or fight" added to the other factors influenced England in 1846 to accept the 49th parallel as her southern boundary.

Until 1853 "Washington" was part of the Oregon Territory. Encountering the difficulty of traversing the distance to the capital at Salem, the settlers north of the Columbia petitioned Congress to organize the Territory of Columbia. Supported by the Oregon legislature, Congress created Washington Territory, March 2, 1853.

From 1853 to 1889 Washington as a territory developed many typically American institutions. Mining booms in the eastern section and in British Columbia in 1855–84 brought prosperity, population and Indian troubles. In 1854–55 Gov. Isaac Stevens entered into treaties with the Indians, but encroachments upon Indian lands led to rebellions. Later, in 1885–86, labor agitators instigated mobs who expelled Chinese from many communities. Riots in Tacoma and Seattle were quelled by Federal troops when martial law was declared.

When Oregon became a state in 1859 Washington acquired the eastern territory, including Idaho, parts of Montana and Wyoming. In 1863, when the Idaho Territory was created, Washington was given her present eastern boundary. From 1863 to 1889 the Washington legislature resisted schemes for detaching parts of the eastern section to be annexed to Oregon, or to form an Inland Empire Territory. From 1867 to 1889 Washington conducted a campaign for statehood. After defeating propositions to call constitutional conventions in 1869, 1871 and 1873, the people approved in 1876. A constitution was drafted in 1878, but despite numerous bills and memorials, it was not until Feb. 22, 1889, that Congress passed the enabling act and admitted Washington into the Union, Nov. 11, 1889.

WASHINGTON, TREATY OF, concluded between the United States and Great Britain May 8, 1871, settled amicably the Alabama Claims and other differences between the two nations. Much of the groundwork for it had been discreetly laid by Secretary of State Hamilton Fish in 1869–70. During 1870 British reluctance to negotiate was removed by the Franco-Prussian War and the ensuing denunciation of the Black Sea agreement by Russia, which threatened European complications; by pressure from financial interests; and by the appointment of the conciliatory Lord Granville as Foreign Secretary. The reluctance of some American elements to negotiate was modified by difficulties with Spain; pressure from American bankers; and general realization that the hope of peaceable annexation of Canada was vain. When John Rose, recently a Canadian statesman and now a London financier, came to Washington in January, 1871, Fish and he readily made arrangements with the British minister, Sir Edward Thornton, for submission of the various disputes to a Joint High Commission. This had been Fish's desire since taking office. The British Commissioners (Earl de Grey and Ripon of the Gladstone Cabinet, Sir Stafford Northcote, Prof. Montague Bernard of Oxford, Sir John MacDonald, Prime Minister of Canada, and Thornton) were soon at work in Washington with the American Commissioners (Fish, Rockwood Hoar, Robert C. Schenck, Justice Nelson of the Supreme Court and Sen. George H. Williams). The principal questions at issue were the Alabama Claims, the rights of American fishermen in Canadian waters, and the water-boundary between British Columbia and the State of Washington. The fisheries question was settled by agreement that a mixed commission should sit at Halifax and determine the relative value of certain reciprocal privileges granted each other by the two nations. The northwestern or San Juan boundary dispute was submitted to the German Emperor. Most important of all, the first eleven of the forty-three articles of the treaty provided that the Alabama Claims should be adjudicated at Geneva by five arbitrators, appointed respectively by the Presidents of the United States and Switzerland, and the rulers of Great Britain, Italy and Brazil.

The treaty was distinguished by two unprecedented features. One was the British confession of wrongdoing incorporated in the preamble, where the imperial commissioners expressed regret for the escape of the *Alabama* and other cruisers. The other was agreement upon three rules of international law for the guidance of the Geneva Tribunal in interpreting certain terms used in the treaty. The chief of these rules asserted that "due diligence" to maintain absolute neutrality "ought to be exercised by neutral governments" in exact proportion to the risks to which belligerents were exposed by breaches. The other two made explicit the impropriety of letting a vessel be constructed, equipped and armed under such circumstances as attended the building of the *Alabama;* and dealt with the use of neutral territory by belligerent vessels. The compact was defective in only one particular. It failed to touch on the so-called "indirect claims" of the United States for prolongation of the war by the cruisers, an evasion of a delicate question which almost wrecked the Geneva Arbitration. But the treaty remains a great landmark in the history of peaceful relations between Britain and America. Credit for it belongs chiefly to Fish, but in some degree also to Rose, Thornton and Lord Granville.

WASHINGTON CONFERENCE ON THE LIMITATION OF ARMAMENTS (1921–22) was called on Anglo-American initiative in November, 1921, for the purpose of adjusting the international problems of the Pacific Ocean and Eastern Asia in accordance with a schedule of limitation of naval armaments. The following nations participated: the United States, Great Britain and the Dominions, Japan, France, Italy, the Netherlands, Portugal, Belgium and China. Germany, ejected from the Far East by the results of World War I, and Russia, paralyzed by revolution, were not invited. The conference arrived at a peaceful adjustment of existing problems—notably in the Far East—by a network of treaties, principally multilateral, accompanied by a Sino-Japanese treaty (for the evacuation of Shantung) and an American-Japanese treaty (for regulation of Yap Island). A perpetual Nine-Power Treaty bound all the powers to the principle of the Open Door and the integrity of China and pledged the signatories not to take advantage of disturbed conditions in China to seek special concessions or favors for themselves. A ten-year (later extended to fifteen years) naval treaty brought naval tonnage in capital ships of the five naval powers down to a ratio of 5 (United States)—5 (Great Britain)—3 (Japan)—1.7 (France)—1.7 (Italy), with limitation of island fortifications to the existing *status quo* in certain regions of the Pacific. A Four-Power (United States, Great Britain, France, Japan) consultation treaty in effect replaced the Anglo-Japanese Alliance; the Lansing-Ishii Agreement of 1917 was abrogated as a result of the Nine-Power Treaty.

The result of the treaties was to leave Japan as a preponderant naval and military power in the Far East in return for her pledges not to take advantage of conditions in China for further special privileges for herself. This was the fallacy of the settlement, to expect a power like Japan to hold to this pledge in the face of a national revival of China. In 1931 Japan, taking advantage of the economic prostration and political divisions of the Occident, brushed all treaty restrictions aside, began her conquest of China,

and bolted the protesting but impotent League of Nations. The naval limitations treaty expired Dec. 31, 1936.

The Washington conference saved the peace for ten years in the Orient, and in the Occident for fifteen. It can be interpreted to have relieved the United States from the sole sponsorship of the doctrine of the Open Door and the integrity of China, an embarrassing legacy of American diplomacy stemming from the acquisition of the Philippines.

WASHINGTON MONUMENT. This marble shaft, 555 feet high, on the Mall in Washington, D. C., was designed by Robert Mills to commemorate George Washington. Begun in 1848, the monument was completed in 1884.

WASHINGTON'S FAREWELL ADDRESS (Sept. 19, 1796) had for its main purpose the elimination of himself from the third presidential election. He had hoped to evade his second election and had roughed out a declination at that time; but political pressure and the critical state of our foreign relations forced a change of purpose. Reasons for the inclusion of other matters than a simple declination of candidacy are to be found in Washington's habit of mind and honest love of his country. The first part of the address gives his reasons for retiring; the second, and most important part, presents his reflections on the necessity of a strong union of the states and the principles upon which permanent domestic contentment could be maintained and foreign respect compelled; the third, and briefest part, justified his neutrality toward France and England, and merged that justification into the more important principles of the address, which flowered from his deeply rooted, personal experiences in managing a revolutionary army for eight years of disheartening war, and directing an untried form of republican government for eight years of difficult peace. The unselfish honesty of his hope that the address would be of some occasional good in moderating the fury of party spirit, of warning against foreign intrigue, and guarding against the impostures of pretended patriotism does not entirely conceal the deep wound inflicted on his sensibilities by the malignant and unscrupulous political enemies of his administration; but the address is, nevertheless, one of the world's remarkable documents. It still remains a wholesome political guide to the people of the nation to whom it was addressed. It was never publicly read by Washington, and was first published in the Philadelphia *Daily American Advertiser*. The senseless controversy over authorship credit is now recognized as a mixture of egoistic pedantry and ignorant partisanship.

WASP, a sloop-of-war commanded by Master-Commandant Jacob Jones, on Oct. 18, 1812, about 500 miles east of the Chesapeake Capes, captured the

British brig *Frolic*, Capt. Thomas Whinyates, escorting a convoy of six vessels. During a furious action of 43 minutes at close quarters, the Americans had five killed and five wounded and the British suffered ninety casualties. Both vessels were severely injured in spars and rigging, and the British ship-of-the-line *Poictiers*, appearing soon after the action, captured the *Wasp*, which was unable to flee, and took her to Bermuda.

Wasp, The Second (sloop-of-war), commanded by Master-Commandant Johnston Blakely, sailed from Portsmouth, N. H., on May 1, 1814. Capturing eight prizes on the voyage to her station off the English Channel, early on the morning of June 28 she fell in with the British brig *Reindeer*, Capt. William Manners. After two hours of skilful maneuvering for position, the *Wasp* secured the advantage and raked the *Reindeer*, repelled an attempt to board, and then boarded the enemy, who surrendered after an action of only 19 minutes. The British lost 25 killed, including Capt. Manners, and 42 wounded; the American loss was 5 killed and 21 wounded. In men and armament the *Wasp* had the advantage by about three to two.

After making six more prizes during a second cruise, on the evening of September 1, Blakely destroyed the British brig *Avon*, Capt. James Arbuthnot, after an engagement of 45 minutes. The *Avon* lost 9 killed and 33 wounded; the *Wasp*, 2 killed and 1 wounded. Sailing with dispatches for Savannah, the *Wasp* captured the *Atlanta* off the Madeiras and was last seen about 900 miles farther south. The fate of the little man-of-war is one of the mysteries of the sea.

WATAUGA SETTLEMENT AND ASSOCIATION. Into the Treaty of Fort Stanwix, 1768, bordermen in Virginia and North Carolina willingly read permission to venture their fortunes in the farther West notwithstanding the claim of the Cherokees to the region. Following the collapse of the first phase of the Regulation in North Carolina a few of the Regulators moved to the Holston and Watauga; but William Bean of Pittsylvania County, Va., became in 1769 the first permanent settler in Tennessee, on the Watauga. Soon there gathered around him relatives and friends from that Virginia county. Another nucleus of settlers was farther up the Watauga under James Robertson; and gradually the gap between the two was filled by immigrants. For protection against horse thieves and outlaws, they formed, in 1772, a government under written articles known as the Watauga Association. The Brown Settlement, begun in 1771 on the Nolachucky, later (1775) adhered to this government, which existed until Washington District was established. In 1772 the people of Watauga took a ten-year lease of all lands on that stream from the Cherokees. A court of five men, with legislative powers, was their governmental body.

The laws of Virginia were taken as guide "so near as the situation of affairs would admit." Wataugans joined their brethren of the Holston Settlement in the campaign of 1774 against the Indians on the Ohio and fought in the battle of Point Pleasant.

These two settlements in the Tennessee country were the seed-plot of the civilization of the Old Southwest. The founders, or their descendants, aided in establishing the Transylvania government in Kentucky. James Robertson led fellow settlers to the Cumberland where was established the nucleus of Middle Tennessee. They furnished the first governors of Tennessee, Kentucky, Missouri and Arkansas, and the first senators in Congress of Tennessee, Missouri, Indiana and Arkansas. At the breaking out of the Revolutionary War, these settlements were the "advance guard of civilization," in the western wilderness and during the war they swarmed into the farther West to have and to hold against Great Britain and the Indian allies of that power.

WATERWAYS, INLAND. Inland water transportation was very important to the early settlers as the rivers furnished the best means of transportation. There were no important inland settlements away from the rivers, as nothing but a self-sufficing economy could exist. As a result, the rich resources located away from their banks were not utilized.

Prior to the Revolution, intercolonial commerce was very small. The British government had discouraged this trade as it desired each colony to trade directly with the mother country. Except in densely populated areas, roads were few and poor. As a result, the short streams flowing into the Atlantic were of vital importance. The first settlers to migrate westward, about 1720, settled in the Appalachian Mountain valleys in Pennsylvania where the Susquehanna River cut through the mountain ranges.

It was not until the end of the Revolution that the settlement of the West began and not until the Constitution was accepted and a strong National Government created, that it reached large proportions. By 1800 the frontier had expanded so rapidly that its population stretched along both banks of the Ohio and parts of the Mississippi, Tennessee and Cumberland Rivers. This advance of the frontier was contrary to Washington's advice, as he wanted it to proceed in an orderly manner. However, it proceeded along the lines of most attraction and least resistance.

From a national standpoint, the early history of our inland transportation was concerned largely with plans to break through the Appalachian Mountain ranges. Sectionalism was rampant and commercial intercourse between the East and West had to be established. However, the mountain wall proved to be a formidable barrier for several decades. During this period, the frontiersmen found the route down the Ohio and Mississippi to New Orleans their best avenue of transportation for their surplus production.

These river systems accounted for the westward spread of the population, but they served to isolate still further the two sections of the country.

But this route was not without its handicaps. River travel was dangerous, difficult and hazardous. Until the invention of the steamboat in 1807, it was mostly a one-way route, as man power only could bring boats up against the current. Spain controlled the mouth of the Mississippi River and for several years it refused the Americans official permission to use New Orleans as a place of deposit, largely because of the frontier disputes in Florida. In 1795, however, the Federal Government obtained a treaty which allowed the use of this port (Pinckney's Treaty), but this permission was withdrawn again in 1802 when Spain secretly ceded the Louisiana territory to France (Treaty of San Ildefonso). As this treaty did not designate another place of deposit as required, the United States realized that its westward expansion was seriously threatened. Jefferson suggested an alliance with Great Britain to fight France whenever war should break out between the two countries. However, Napoleon's ill-fated expedition to crush a revolt in Santo Domingo caused him to drop his project of a western empire and in 1803 he sold the entire territory to the United States, thus creating a free outlet for western commerce.

The War of 1812 emphasized the weakness of river transportation and the lack of good roads for troop transportation. This factor combined with a greater desire to settle in the West created a strong demand for improved inland water transportation. Many rivers and lakes throughout the United States were canalized and a few artificial waterways were constructed. The longest were built by New York, Pennsylvania and Maryland, and of these the Erie Canal exerted the strongest influence in reducing transportation costs, facilitating commercial intercourse between the East and West, and relieving somewhat the ever-present problem of sectionalism. By 1840 the active period of canal construction was concluded as the supremacy of the railroad was recognized. By this time over $100,000,000 had been spent to create about 3300 miles of improved waterways and practically all of it was lost as the railroad net spread over the country.

It was not until the advent of the 20th century that interest in these waterways was revived. Its revival then was due to the desire to conserve natural resources, control floods, create a more adequate national transportation system, set up a competitor to railroads and secure a cheaper form of transportation. While local governments and private capital financed most of the early projects, the Federal Government is now chiefly responsible for their construction.

Between 1824 and 1906 the Federal Government spent about $500,000,000 on navigation improvements. This was mostly for improvement of harbors on the coasts and on the Great Lakes. During the entire period from 1824 through 1957, the Federal expenditures for navigation improvements, including new construction and maintenance and operation, have totaled about $4,000,000,000 of which about $2,000,000,000 has been for the inland and intracoastal waterways.

Traffic on the nation's inland waterways has been increased. Waterborne commerce of the United States in 1922, excluding commerce on the Great Lakes, totaled 282,000,000 short tons, compared with 396,-000,000 in 1936. By 1957, the total had risen to 914,-000,000 tons.

WAXHAWS, BATTLE OF (May 29, 1780). At the time of the capture of Charleston by the British, May 12, 1780, Col. Buford, with 380 Virginia troops, was marching to its assistance; but hearing of its fall, he retreated rapidly northward. Lord Cornwallis sent Tarleton with nearly 300 cavalry in pursuit of him. Tarleton overtook the Americans at the Waxhaws, near the North Carolina line. He first sent an officer ahead to demand capitulation. This Buford refused. But when his wearied men on foot were attacked by cavalry, most of them threw down their arms in offer of surrender. Little quarter was given them, however; 113 were slain outright, 150 were so badly maimed that they could not be moved, and only 53 prisoners were carried off by the British. Col. Buford and some of his mounted men escaped. The British loss was only twenty. "Tarleton's quarter" thereupon became a common expression for butchery.

WAYNE, FORT, built by Gen. Wayne at the junction of the St. Joseph and St. Marys, commanding the strategic Maumee-Wabash portage, was named by Col. John F. Hamtramck, its commandant, at its dedication, Oct. 22, 1794. The place had been an important Indian trading center and French and English forts (to 1763) had once occupied the site. The American fort, moved to a new location in 1800, was the scene of important Indian treaties (1803, 1809) negotiated by Gov. William Henry Harrison of Indiana Territory, and was a center for distributing annuities and supplies. In August, 1812, Indians under British influence besieged the garrison of seventy or eighty men but Harrison relieved the fort Sept. 12. The loss of Forts Dearborn and Detroit made the retention of Fort Wayne important to American defense of the Northwest. It was abandoned as a military post, April 19, 1819.

WAYNE, FORT, TREATY OF (Sept. 30, 1809), was one of the most important treaties made by the United States with the Indians. Concluded by William Henry Harrison, then governor of Indiana Territory, with the Delaware, the Potawatomie, the Miami and the Eel River tribes, the treaty ceded to the United States three tracts of land containing over 2,500,000 acres on the upper Wabash River. Ancillary treaties confirming the Fort Wayne purchase were made with the Wea and the Kickapoo tribes on Oct. 26 and Dec. 9 (1809), respectively.

The Fort Wayne Treaty aroused bitter opposition among the Indians. Tecumseh (who, with his brother, the Prophet, had since 1807 been organizing a confederation of the Indians of the Old Northwest) denounced it violently. He denied the validity of the purchase, asserting that the Indian chiefs had no right to alienate land because all the Indian tribes owned the land in common. He openly declared his intention of uniting the Indians in order to check the encroachments of the white men. He so stirred up the Indians that during 1810 and 1811 the frontier was kept in a state of alarm and tension. This strengthened Gov. Harrison's suspicions as to the designs of Tecumseh and the Prophet, and led to his attack against the Prophet's encampment on Tippecanoe Creek, November, 1811. The Treaty of Fort Wayne was thus a factor in precipitating hostilities against the Indians of the Northwest, and contributed to their decision to join the British against the United States in the War of 1812.

WAYNE CAMPAIGN (1792–95). Since the northwestern Indians were determined to retain, and the white settlers to possess, the region northwest of the Ohio River, the Indian warfare of 1790–95 may be said to have been inevitable. The failure of two successive armies (led by Harmar and St. Clair) to conquer the savages induced President Washington, early in 1792, to assign the task to Gen. Anthony Wayne, who had made a brilliant record in the Revolution.

Wayne moved deliberately to organize an army competent to his task, and almost two years were consumed before he brought it to the scene of combat. Not until the spring of 1793 did he advance to Fort Washington (modern Cincinnati), where months of further drill and seasoning ensued. In the autumn he advanced to Greenville, 81 miles north of Cincinnati, and from here sent a detachment to build Fort Recovery, on the scene of St. Clair's defeat.

Another winter of drill and preparation followed. The savages now took the initiative, and on June 30, 1794, 2000 warriors began a two-day assault on Fort Recovery. Defeated, the northern or "Lake" warriors returned to their homes, abandoning their southern allies to their fate. This failure and desertion marked the turning point in the five-year war. Following it, Wayne resumed his own advance northward. At the junction of the Glaize and the Maumee, where his hope of striking a decisive blow was defeated by the withdrawal of the Indians, he built Fort Defiance. From here, on Aug. 15, he resumed his pursuit of the savages, who had retreated east-

ward down the Maumee. At Fallen Timbers, where a tornado had uprooted the trees, they made their stand, and here on Aug. 20 were decisively defeated.

The fleeing warriors were pursued to the walls of British Fort Miami, where Wayne engaged in a spirited exchange of notes with the commandant. Several score of Detroit militia had fought in the Indian ranks, and the general conduct of the British fell barely short of open alliance with them. After thoroughly razing the property of both Indians and British traders, Wayne marched up the Maumee to the Wabash Portage, the objective of Harmar and St. Clair, and there built Fort Wayne. From here he returned to Greenville, where he awaited the fallen foemen to dictate terms of peace. The treaty of Greenville, signed Aug. 3, 1795, gave southern and eastern Ohio to the United States, recognized the Indian title to the remainder of the Northwest, subject to the condition that they could sell it only to the United States, and gave to the latter sites for forts at numerous strategic points, together with the free passage of the rivers and portages connecting them.

Wayne's achievement was of epochal importance in the history of America. He terminated a generation of warfare in the Ohio Valley, during which thousands of settlers had been slain or carried into a captivity frequently worse than death. The peace dictated at Greenville endured until the conditions which had evoked it passed away, being broken only by the belated movement of Tecumseh for Indian independence.

"WE ARE COMING, FATHER ABRA'AM, THREE HUNDRED THOUSAND MORE" was the refrain of one of the most popular Civil War songs. The poem, written by the Quaker abolitionist, James Sloan Gibbons, was first printed anonymously, July 16, 1862, in the New York *Evening Post* after President Lincoln's call (July 2) for 300,000 more volunteers following McClellan's defeat at Richmond. Several composers set the words to music, including Stephen C. Foster, but the most popular setting was by Luther Orlando Emerson (1820–1915).

"WE HAVE MET THE ENEMY AND THEY ARE OURS." On defeating, spectacularly and decisively, the British fleet under Robert H. Barclay in the Battle of Lake Erie, Sept. 10, 1813, Oliver Hazard Perry, commander of the American fleet, dispatched one of the most famous messages in military history to Maj. Gen. William Henry Harrison, commander of the western army at nearby Seneca town. Written in pencil on a soiled envelope for delivery by a midshipman, it read: "Dear Gen'l: We have met the enemy, and they are ours, two ships, two brigs, one schooner and one sloop. Yours with great respect and esteem. O. H. Perry."

WEATHER BUREAU. Weather observations in the United States were first taken by Josiah Meigs, Commissioner General of the General Land Office, who in 1817 started a system of tridaily observations in the land offices. In 1819 similar observations were instituted by the Surgeon General of the Army at military posts. In 1841 the Patent Office and in 1847 the Smithsonian Institution began to record observations. It was not until 1849, however, that Joseph Henry of the Smithsonian Institution inaugurated the first published weather forecasts, based on simultaneous telegraphic observations. Twenty years later Cleveland Abbe, director of the Mitchell Astronomical Observatory, paved the way for regular forecasts by collecting observations from thirty stations by telegraph and preparing a chart of weather forecasts.

The weather service was first established as part of the U. S. Army Signal Service, later the Signal Corps, by Joint Resolution of Congress, Feb. 9, 1870 (16 Stat. L., 369), for the benefit of navigation along the seacoast and on the Great Lakes. The value of its services, however, was soon realized by commercial, agricultural and industrial interests. The service was expanded in an effort to meet these wide demands, but the need for a new organization with more real scientific apparatus was apparent and by act of Congress Oct. 1, 1890 (26 Stat. L., 653) the Weather Service of the Signal Corps was transferred to the Department of Agriculture, effective July 1, 1891, and was named the Weather Bureau. Under authority of the President's Reorganization Plan IV, effective June 30, 1940, the Bureau became a part of the Commerce Department. This transfer was caused by an increasing demand for meteorological information by the nation's expanding commercial enterprise.

An extensive program of meteorological observation is carried on by the Weather Bureau. Complete synoptic observations are made at six-hour intervals and abbreviated observations at intermediate three-hour intervals at about 300 Bureau stations located in the continental United States, its territories and possessions; in the Atlantic and Pacific oceans and the Gulf of Mexico; and in the Arctic and Antarctic regions. This network is supplemented by observations from United States military land stations and vessels; from other Federal agencies; from merchant vessels of all nationalities; and from foreign countries under international agreements. These observations cover the readings of the barometer, dry and wet bulb, the thermometer, the anemometer, the wind vane, and the rain and snow gauge. Upper air observations are obtained from over 90 stations twice daily and from 22 stations four times daily. The meteorological information is charted on base maps and analyzed to enable the preparation of forecasts of the weather over the United States at least every six hours during the day and night.

Weather Bureau stations supplemented by observations from over 600 airports operate 24 hours a day. They collect reports and disseminate forecasts. They offer pilot "briefing" service and provide an up-to-the-minute picture of weather conditions existing at the point of departure, along the flight route, and at the destination. In addition, the stations collect and issue forecasts in areas threatened by hurricanes, severe local storms, frosts, floods, and forest fires.

Over 12,000 voluntary and co-operative observers in areas not served by regular Bureau stations participate daily in the making of necessary observations and reports and in the disseminating of forecasts and warnings.

Research programs of the Weather Bureau include extensive studies of hurricanes, tornadoes, severe local storms, the stability of cloud elements, the physical processes involved in precipitation, and the role of solar and terrestrial radiation.

For the information of meteorologists, climatologists, and the general public the Weather Bureau publishes various maps and bulletins including the *Daily Weather Map,* the *Monthly Weather Review, Climatological Data,* and the *Weekly Weather and Crop Bulletin.*

WEBSTER-ASHBURTON TREATY (1842). This treaty, and accompanying exchanges of notes, made great headway in the settlement of a number of vexing Anglo-American issues of the middle of the century. Of these, boundary disputes were the most prominent. The dispute over the northeastern boundary (Maine and New Brunswick) had brought nationals of the two countries to the verge of armed hostility (Aroostook War); this was settled by what then appeared to be a wise compromise of territorial claims which provided the present boundary line. Actually it was a concession which knowledge of Franklin's "Red-Line Map," discovered in 1932, would have made unnecessary. The boundary was also rectified at the head of the Connecticut River, at the north end of Lake Champlain, in the Detroit River, and at the head of Lake Superior. There was a useful extradition article, and another providing for the free navigation of the St. John River. Exchanges of notes covering the slave trade assured the United States against "officious interference with American vessels," and the protection of "regularly-documented ships" by the flag they flew.

WEBSTER-HAYNE DEBATE (January, 1830). This was one of the most significant constitutional debates ever held in Congress; in it the two opposing philosophies of American government—nationalism and states' rights—were clearly enunciated and forcefully championed. It started over public lands; ranged over tariff, slavery, local patriotism, and sectionalism; and finally narrowed down to a discussion of the Constitution and the nature of the American Union. Samuel A. Foot of Connecticut introduced a resolution in the Senate (Dec. 29, 1829) looking toward the restriction of the sale of public lands. Thomas Hart Benton of Missouri attacked the resolution (Jan. 18, 1830) as a manifestation of Eastern hostility to the West and called upon the South to protect the West. Robert Y. Hayne of South Carolina, seeking to strengthen the alliance between the South and West and thus defeat the protectionist forces, responded (Jan. 19), denouncing the "selfish and unprincipled" attitude of the East and expressing the fear that consolidation tendencies in the Federal Government threatened the independence of the sovereign states. Daniel Webster of Massachusetts defended the East (Jan. 20) and cleverly led Hayne to expound and champion the states' rights philosophy and nullification spirit of Calhoun's *Exposition*. Webster was thus enabled to meet Hayne on his own chosen field, and Foot's resolution was soon forgotten. Hayne added little to Calhoun's theory but fell into an error in stating that the Federal Government was a party to the compact between the states. Webster's reply was one of the greatest speeches ever delivered in Congress. Largely ignoring Hayne's economic arguments, he centered his fire upon his theory of the Constitution. He showed the fallacy of 24 separate states interpreting the Constitution; maintained that the Constitution was the work of the people; and that "liberty and Union" were "one and inseparable." Hayne was correct in his historical arguments but Webster's was the new, growing spirit of nationalism.

WELLS, FARGO & COMPANY. The founders of the American Express Co., Henry Wells, William G. Fargo and associates, organized this new company in 1852 to function as a western ally of the American. The two companies were to divide the continent approximately at the Mississippi and Missouri Rivers. Wells, Fargo & Co. at once installed ocean service between New York and San Francisco via Panama, erected a fine office building in San Francisco and began to operate, not only in the gold region of California, but over the entire Pacific coast. In less than ten years it had either bought out or eliminated nearly all competitors and become the most powerful company in the Far West. It was the chief dependence for letter-carrying of citizens in remote mining camps where the mails had not yet penetrated; and, even after the mails came, was often preferred as being more dependable. It spread rapidly through the entire Rocky Mountain region. It carried more gold, silver and bullion by many millions than any other agency. It took over the famous Pony Express after the failure of the original projectors. It extended its operations to western Canada, Alaska, Mexico, the West Indies, Central America, Hawaii, and for a short time even carried letters to China and Japan. Later, it pushed its service eastward to the Atlantic coast. Along with all the other expresses, it was merged with the American Railway Express Co. in 1918, but as a separate corporation continued to function on 14,000 miles of railway in Mexico and in Cuba.

WEST COAST HOTEL COMPANY v. PARRISH (300 U. S. 379, 1937) was a decision by the U. S. Supreme court involving the constitutional validity of a Washington statute creating a commission with power to fix minimum wages for women in the state. The court thought that the close division by which the case of Adkins v. Children's Hospital (holding a similar act unconstitutional) had been decided, and changed economic conditions since that case, called for a fresh consideration of the validity of minimum-wage legislation. The question was: Does minimum-wage legislation constitute an undue infringement of the freedom of contract guaranteed by the "due-process" clause of the Fourteenth Amendment of the Constitution? Chief Justice Hughes, speaking for the Court (Justices Brandeis, Stone, Roberts and Cardozo concurring), contended that the fact that both parties were of full age and competent to contract, did not mean that the state could not interfere, where it appeared that the parties were not equal in bargaining power, or where public health required that the weaker party be protected against himself.

The Court pointed out that the health of women is peculiarly related to the vigor of the race, that women are easily overreached, and that denial to them of a living wage is not only detrimental to their health and well-being, but casts a burden on the community to support them. The enactment of a minimum-wage law for women, therefore, said the Court, was not a taking of "liberty" without "due process of law," and the Adkins case, being wrongly decided, should be overruled. Justices Sutherland, Van Devanter, McReynolds and Butler, reiterating the arguments of the Adkins case, dissented.

WEST FLORIDA CONTROVERSY. The area between the Iberville and Perdido Rivers on the Gulf of Mexico coast was included in Spain's claims by discovery from 1492 on, but from 1695 to 1763 France occupied it as part of Louisiana. Great Britain held it, with an enlarged Florida boundary, from 1763 (*see* Paris, The Treaty of) until the Definitive Treaty of Peace of 1783 provided for its return to Spain. After 1803 the United States claimed it as part of the Louisiana Purchase, coveting it for commercial control of rivers rising in the Southwest Territory. Spain refuted the claim due to the separation of the area from Louisiana in 1763, but could not defend it. Congress by the Mobile Act of 1804 authorized the President to assume control, but nothing definite was done then. Frontiersmen from the United States, who had settled the Baton Rouge district, rebelled against Spain in 1810, whereupon this country seized that portion of the province which was included in the new state of Louisiana in 1812. The remainder was added to Mississippi Territory in 1813. United States troops made the occupation permanently effective in 1814. Spain relinquished all claim in the Adams-Onís Treaty of 1819, but the negotiators of that agreement intentionally failed to state who had owned West Florida before.

WEST JERSEY. In 1674 Edward Byllynge, a Quaker, possibly acting for his Society, purchased Lord Berkeley's interest in New Jersey. John Fenwick, another Quaker, agreed to manage the property for a share in it. Dissatisfied with his share, Fenwick asked William Penn to arbitrate and accepted a one-tenth interest. Becoming involved in debt, Byllynge assigned his rights in trust to Penn and two other Quakers. Inequity of the division, and Penn's desire to have a free hand to test his ideas of government, led to the execution of the "quintipartite deed" of 1676. By this deed a line running from Little Egg Harbor northwesterly to a point on the Delaware River at the 41st parallel of latitude divided the province, Carteret receiving the eastern portion, henceforth called East Jersey, and the Quaker associates the remainder, West Jersey. In 1675 Fenwick founded a colony in his "tenth," at Salem. Two years later, 1677, Burlington was founded and became the chief port and capital of the province. West Jersey was governed by the most liberal charter drawn up to this time, the "Concessions and Agreement." About 1691 the province passed into the hands of the West Jersey Society which governed it until the surrender to the Crown in 1702.

WEST POINT, N. Y. The swift collapse of the Hudson River defenses in October, 1777, when in a fortnight Gen. Sir Henry Clinton brought under British control the entire area from Manhattan Island north to Kingston, impressed on the Continentals the need of a proper defense. Moved to action by the urgent pleas of Gen. Washington, the Provincial Congress of New York initiated a new survey of the Highlands, with the result that West Point was chosen as the site of the citadel for a strong system of defenses. The location was ideal. A plateau, of about forty acres, lying more than 100 feet above the river level, formed a peninsula which dominated the water of a double right-angled bend of the river, as well as the river approaches, north and south, within cannon range. Moreover, the crests of two ridges west of the plateau could be fortified to meet a land attack.

The original plans were largely those of a French engineer officer, Lt. Col. de la Radière. In their execution, a brigade under Gen. Samuel H. Parsons began breaking ground Jan. 20, 1778. Weather conditions could not have been worse (it was the Valley Forge winter). In spite of extreme suffering among the men, the construction of gun emplacements at the river's edge and of a stone fortress at the nose of the peninsula, Fort Arnold (later, Clinton) was pressed vigorously. In March, 1778, Tadeusz Kosciuszko, ap-

pointed by Washington engineer in charge, took over the construction work which continued to the end of the war.

Washington, who referred to West Point as the "key to America," made his headquarters there for the four months following July 28, 1779. He was impelled to take charge by the urgencies of Baron Von Steuben who, writing of British plans of campaign, declared: "Whatever means they employ, I am positive their operations are directed exclusively to getting charge of this post and of the river as far as Albany. . . . On their success depends the fate of America." It proved to be the year of greatest activity, with some 2600 men, aside from the garrison troops, engaged in the work. In April of the previous year a great sixty-ton chain had been stretched across the stream to Constitution Island, closing it to navigation. Protective water batteries on both sides, including the remodeled fortifications of Constitution Fort, effectively barred the channel. On the first ridge west of the plateau, Forts Webb, Wyllys and Putnam protected the land approaches. These in turn were covered by four redoubts on a ridge lying west and south. The strongest of these, and the fort into which Benedict Arnold was to have admitted the British, was Fort Putnam. Its possession by the British would have destroyed American resistance in the Highlands, with consequences already described. The seizure of West Point was always present in the British plans of campaign after 1777. Except for Arnold's treason and Gen. Clinton's nibbles at the Highlands when he twice seized Stony Point, it was never threatened.

A Corps of Invalids (Veterans) created by act of Congress, June 20, 1777, was transferred four years later to West Point, with the intention of using them as a *cadre* for the instruction of candidates for commissions. The germ of the idea which ultimately produced the United States Military Academy existed in that plan. However, in June, 1784, Congress declared that "Standing armies in time of peace are . . . dangerous to the liberties of a free people," and accordingly reduced the army to 80 men, of which 55 were detailed to guard stores at West Point.

When domestic violence and foreign embroilments later forced Congress to increase the army, West Point became the garrison station of a corps of artillerists and engineers. Finally, in 1802, Congress took the step which legally established the United States Military Academy at West Point. That step ensured the fact that it was to be the oldest United States military post over which the country's flag has continuously flown.

WEST VIRGINIA, the 35th state in the Union, was originally a part of Virginia and shares her early traditions. The first white settlement of record in present West Virginia was made by Morgan Morgan in 1731 near Bunker Hill, Berkeley County, but recently discovered church records indicate the possibility of earlier settlements. First settlers were Scotch-Irish and Germans (Pennsylvania Dutch) with sprinklings of English, Welsh and Dutch. Most of the English settlers came from eastern Virginia, Maryland and New Jersey. The others came mostly from Pennsylvania in search of cheap lands. Among all of them there were many dissenters in church and state who, together with their descendants, favored religious liberty and American independence.

With the termination of the Indian wars in the Upper Ohio Valley following the American Revolution and the purchase of Louisiana, the inhabitants of present West Virginia tended to particularism in things political, but with the awakened interest of trans-Allegheny in industry, internal improvement and banking following the War of 1812, inhabitants of northwest Virginia developed a decided trend to nationalism. This tendency was quite pronounced about 1830, when eastern and western Virginia were said to be at the parting of the ways. These sectional differences were reconciled somewhat by the influence of the Abolition agitation, by the reforms of 1830 and 1851 in the state government, and by concessions which eastern Virginia made meanwhile in such things as internal improvements, appointive and elective officers, and free public schools, but the safeguards considered necessary by the east for the protection of slave property caused an irreparable breach between the two sections.

As a consequence of this difference the adoption of the Virginia Secession Ordinance was seized upon by northwest Virginia as sufficient cause to assert nationalism in the form of loyalty to the Union. The Virginia state government was, therefore, restored on a loyal basis with its capital at Wheeling, and when the Civil War which followed did not end quickly as expected, the Virginia Restored Government gave its consent to the formation of West Virginia which became a separate state on June 20, 1863, in accord with an act of Congress signed by the President on Dec. 31, 1862.

WESTERN EXPLORATION. The activities of the French and English explorers, hunters and traders had made the portion of the United States east of the Mississippi River well known by 1783, when that area, north of Florida, was included within the boundaries of the new nation. On the other hand, the region west of the Mississippi was comparatively unknown to Americans when the Louisiana Purchase was made in 1803.

Fifty years later this entire area was so well known that substantially accurate maps could be published. This accomplishment was the result of the explorations, observations and writings of a large number of individuals and groups. While the official explorations directed and financed by the Federal Government receive principal attention in the following summary, it must be remembered that important contribu-

tions to geographical knowledge were made by fur traders, scientists, adventurers and surveyors of possible routes for railroads to the Pacific.

The expedition of Lewis and Clark to the Pacific coast brought to fulfilment a dream of western exploration long cherished by Thomas Jefferson. Starting from St. Louis in May, 1804, the party proceeded up the Missouri River and wintered among the Mandan Indians. The following year they explored the Missouri to the headwaters of the Jefferson Fork, crossed the Bitter Root Mountains, descended the Columbia River, and reached the Pacific early in November. The return journey was accomplished between March and September, 1806.

Contemporaneously with Lewis and Clark several other exploring expeditions were sent into the region west of the Mississippi River. During the winter of 1804–5 William Dunbar and Dr. George Hunter explored the lower Red River and the Ouachita. In 1806 Thomas Freeman ascended the Red River about 600 miles. After returning in 1806 from an exploration of the Upper Mississippi, Zebulon M. Pike received instructions from Gen. James Wilkinson to explore the country drained by the Arkansas and Red Rivers. Setting out in the summer of 1806 Pike led his party westward into the present Colorado, crossed the Sangre de Cristo Range, and found himself on the Conejos, a small tributary of the Rio Grande. Here he and his men were captured by a company of Spanish soldiers, held prisoners for a time, and finally conducted to the Louisiana frontier and released. Pike's report stimulated American interest in the Spanish town of Santa Fe, and laid the groundwork for the myth of the Great American Desert.

Twelve years now elapsed before there was another governmental expedition into the Far West. In the interval, John Shaw, John Bradbury, Henry M. Brackenridge, Henry R. Schoolcraft and Thomas Nuttall made private ventures west of the Mississippi, most of which resulted in published reports or journals of considerable value.

In 1819 Stephen H. Long was directed by the War Department to lead a small party to the Rocky Mountains for the purpose of discovering the sources of the Platte and Red Rivers, exploring the upper Arkansas, and gathering scientific data regarding the country. Long reached and explored portions of Colorado and went as far south as the Canadian River. A section of his party descended the upper Arkansas River. The report of Long's expedition reinforced Pike's statements concerning the unsuitability of much of the country traversed for habitation by white men.

Thus far all the official explorations of the Far West, with the exception of the Lewis and Clark expedition, had been confined to the country east of the Rocky Mountains. Fur traders, however, became familiar with the vast region between the Rockies and the Pacific coast. For instance, there is reason to give Jedediah Smith and Thomas Fitzpatrick credit for discovering the South Pass in 1824; while between 1826 and 1829 the former made two trips into California, traversed almost the entire length of California, and crossed the present State of Oregon. Capt. B. L. E. Bonneville and Joseph Walker also made important expeditions in the Great Basin and the Northwest.

With the growth of interest in the Oregon country early in the 1840's, the Government decided that more detailed information should be secured regarding the country beyond the Rockies. John C. Frémont was selected to lead expeditions with this object in view. In 1842 he went as far as the region around the South Pass. His most famous expedition (1843–44) took him into Colorado, northward to the South Pass, southwestward to the Great Salt Lake, and then over the route of the Oregon Trail to The Dalles on the Columbia River. At this point he turned south and traveled across central Oregon, into Nevada, across the high Sierras into California, south nearly as far as Los Angeles, then eastward by the old Spanish Trail. He visited Utah Lake, re-entered the Colorado region, descended the Arkansas some distance, and then struck off across the prairies to St. Louis. On his last official expedition in 1845 Frémont journeyed to California by a more central route. His published reports were widely read and contributed greatly to the spread of knowledge regarding the Far West.

WESTERN LANDS. When the thirteen colonies declared their independence of Great Britain seven of them had overlapping and conflicting claims to western lands which were based on royal grants and charters. These claims, which extended to the Mississippi River, had been cut off by the Proclamation of 1763 and the Quebec Act of 1774, but with independence the states revived them and Virginia undertook a campaign to recover her territory. Virginia had the largest claim, which included present Kentucky and West Virginia and the territory north of the Ohio and east of the Mississippi. Cutting across this northwest territory of Virginia were the claims of Massachusetts, Connecticut and New York. South of Virginia were the claims of North and South Carolina and Georgia which included the land between their present boundaries and the Mississippi.

The ownership of such vast areas by a few states aroused jealousy and ill-feeling among the small states which had no western lands. It was feared that the western lands would give the states owning them too great power in the Confederacy, and Maryland refused to ratify the Articles of Confederation until the landowning states should surrender their claims to the new government. The Continental Congress urged the states to cede their land claims to the central government and promised that the territory so ceded would be erected into new states having full equality with the old. Thus assured, New York and Virginia ceded their claims, the latter, however, with qualifications

which were not acceptable. New York's claims rested on Indian treaties of doubtful legality but the cession by this state was of importance in starting the movement. By 1781 Maryland had become sufficiently convinced that other states would follow this example and her delegates therefore ratified the Articles of Confederation.

In 1783 Virginia again offered to cede its lands north of the Ohio on condition of being allowed to reserve for itself the Military District between the Scioto and Little Miami Rivers in the present State of Ohio to satisfy military grants made during the Revolution. This offer was accepted. Virginia also retained its land south of the Ohio which was organized as the State of Kentucky and permitted to enter the Union in 1792. In 1785 Massachusetts ceded its claim to a belt of land extending across present Michigan and Wisconsin, and in the following year Connecticut ceded its western lands. Connecticut reserved to itself a tract of 3,800,000 acres in northeastern Ohio—called the Western Reserve—a part of which was set aside for the relief of Connecticut sufferers whose property had been destroyed by the British during the Revolution (Firelands) and the remainder was sold to the Connecticut Land Company. South Carolina ceded its narrow strip of land in 1787 and North Carolina transferred its western lands in 1790. After long delay Georgia was induced to make a satisfactory cession in 1802 but not until it had sold vast tracts in the Yazoo Valley to land speculating companies. These sales had been revoked by a later legislature, but the Yazoo Land Companies claimed they were valid despite the notorious fraud involved in them, and demanded from the state or Federal Government restitution of the lands or compensation for the losses sustained. The Yazoo land question embroiled the political waters for a generation before relief was granted by Congress.

These cessions of western lands gave to the Confederation a vast public domain in which it owned the land and over which it had governmental jurisdiction. Within present Kentucky and Tennessee, however, the soil had already been granted to Revolutionary War veterans, settlers and land companies by Virginia and North Carolina and the Confederation received no land but only political jurisdiction. Some 221,987,000 acres of the public domain resulted from the land cessions. In 1785 a Land Ordinance was adopted by the Confederation to provide a method of disposing of the vast territory and in 1787, in response to demands of the Ohio and Scioto Land Companies, which were negotiating for the purchase of large tracts of land north of the Ohio, the Northwest Ordinance (*see* Ordinances of 1784, 1785 and 1787) was adopted to provide a form of government for what came to be known as the "Old Northwest" (*see* Northwest Territory). The land and government systems were not extended to the territory of the Southwest until later.

WESTERN RESERVE, a part of northeastern Ohio lying along the south shore of Lake Erie and once belonging to Connecticut, may be roughly described as a somewhat irregular quadrilateral with Conneaut, Youngstown, Willard and Port Clinton at the corners. The charter which the Connecticut River Towns obtained from Charles II in 1662 fixed the colony's boundaries North and South by parallels extending westward to the South Sea. With royal disdain for the inconveniences of geography King Charles granted parts of the same region to the Duke of York and to William Penn, while King James had already given Virginia a basis for a claim to all the territory included in Connecticut's boundaries beyond Pennsylvania. The thirteen states faced for the future serious territorial disputes. Confederation during the Revolution was delayed by the small states without western lands, particularly Maryland, loath to enter a union with great inequalities in public lands. Congress pointed the way out by proposing that the states cede their western lands, all or part, to the Confederation, promising to use such for the benefit of the whole and the admission of the territories formed therefrom as new states on equal terms with the original thirteen. The states accepted the plan and the Confederation was launched. In 1786 Connecticut ceded its lands west of Pennsylvania, except a portion, the Western Reserve, attempting by the reservation to secure for itself some compensating advantage for its relatively small size, and proceeded at once to plan for an advantageous disposal of its western estate. In 1792 500,000 acres from the western end were assigned to the inhabitants of the Connecticut towns along the Sound as compensation for losses inflicted by raids of the British Army during the Revolution. "The Sufferers' Lands" or "The Firelands," as the region was called, drew in after years a steady stream of immigrants from Connecticut. In 1795 the remaining portion of the Western Reserve, supposed at the time to amount to more than 3,000,000 acres, was sold to the Connecticut Land Company, a body composed of 35 Connecticut landowners who sought to enlarge their estates by a western speculation. Each shareholder gave a mortgage on his Connecticut real estate, due in five years, interest to begin after the second year. Moses Cleaveland, one of the purchasers, general agent of the company, went west in 1796 to supervise a survey and other preparations for sale and settlement. History has not been concerned with the struggle of the speculators to dispose of their lands or their losses or gains in the end. Conditions were long unfavorable for extensive sale of the heavily forested area along the south shore of Lake Erie. The absence of any form of local government was also for many years a barrier to settlement. In 1800 Connecticut and the United States arranged by a joint agreement that the Western Reserve should be attached as a county to the newly formed Ohio Territory. Gov. St. Clair gave it the name Trumbull County and proceeded to organize local government. In later years as conditions in the new West became favorable, particularly after the completion of the Erie Canal (1825), the population grew and Trumbull County was divided and redivided into many counties. The term Western Reserve ceased to have any territorial meaning, and lingered merely as a memory of the old settlers or as a local name for various enterprises, mercantile, banking and the like. Only in such instances as the Western Reserve Historical Society and the Western Reserve University has the phrase survived to puzzle a larger public. But Connecticut's Western Reserve by the process of development became an extension of New England into the West. Names of families and towns, architecture and social customs carried evidence of this transfer of population, and marked Western Reserve apart from other parts of the country until industrialization and a new immigration blurred origins and made the name wholly meaningless to all but the historically minded few.

WESTERN UNION TELEGRAPH COMPANY was the outgrowth of a company organized in 1851 by Hiram Sibley and Samuel L. Selden of Rochester, N. Y., to use the House printing telegraph instrument. Sibley saw opportunities for great expansion in the Middle West, and reorganized the company as the Western Union in 1856. It absorbed smaller companies rapidly, and by 1860 its lines reached from the Atlantic to the Mississippi River, and from the Great Lakes to the Ohio River. Its progress during the next few years was well-nigh fantastic. Its capitalization rose from $385,700 in 1858 to $41,000,000 in 1867. Now top-heavy with stock issues, it was also threatened by rival companies, among them the Atlantic & Pacific, of which Jay Gould obtained control in 1874. In 1881 Gould sold this and another company to the Western Union on terms which raised the latter's capital stock to $80,000,000 and gave him control of it. Its position as the chief telegraph power on the continent was never thereafter seriously menaced.

WESTPORT, MO. In 1831 Rev. Isaac McCoy, a Baptist missionary, purchased land in western Missouri about four miles south of Chouteau's warehouse on the Missouri River. John C. McCoy, his son, erected a store on the land to trade with near-by Indians and settlers, and in 1833 laid out the town of Westport at that place. Other trading houses were soon established there. Westport's Indian trade, at first only local, eventually extended to the Great Plains and Rocky Mountains. During the late 1840's and early 1850's, together with Kansas City, it superseded Independence as an outfitting and starting point for Santa Fe traders, trappers, emigrants and explorers. Its period of greatest prosperity was between 1854 and 1860. During the Civil War its trade decreased. After that conflict, with the advent of railroads and growth of Kansas City, the town declined in importance. It was annexed to Kansas City in 1899.

WESTWARD MOVEMENT. The movement of people which resulted in the settlement of America constitutes one of the most fascinating and significant topics in the history of the United States. In character, volume and rate of progress the westward movement in America is not fully paralleled elsewhere in world history. Invading armies have swept over many lands. There have been numerous colonial projects, fostered by governments and rulers. Nowhere else has an area of equal size been settled in so short a time almost entirely as a result of the initiative of individuals and small groups.

Treated fully, the history of the westward movement might well include the establishment of the English colonies in America. It is true also that there is still a considerable movement of people westward even in the 20th century. In general usage, however, the westward movement is considered to have begun with the first expansion from Atlantic tidewater settlements into the interior. In most respects the movement lost its typical characteristics around the closing years of the 19th century, when there could no longer be said to be a frontier line.

Thus limited, the story may well begin in 1635, when a group of Massachusetts Bay colonists, led by Roger Ludlow, moved westward into the Connecticut Valley. Windsor, Hartford, Wethersfield and Springfield soon appeared, and thereafter settlers pushed up the Connecticut as far as Deerfield and Northfield. King Philip's War (1675–76) temporarily checked expansion, and during the series of struggles between the French and the English the New England frontier settlements suffered from frequent Indian raids. It speaks volumes for the hardihood, courage and persistent land hunger of the New England pioneers that by 1754 the frontier had been extended well into Vermont, New Hampshire and Maine.

The settlement of interior New York was long delayed, because of geographical obstacles, hostility of the Iroquois Indians, exposure to French attack, but especially because of the unenlightened land policy of the colony. The only notable activity before the French and Indian War was that of German immigrants, fleeing from the desolation of the war-ridden Palatinate. Beginning in 1710 they settled on both banks of the Hudson near Saugerties. A few years later some of these Germans made homes for themselves along the Schoharie River; and still later others went far up the Mohawk and established the settlement known as the German Flats.

Pennsylvania presented a striking contrast. The religious toleration, liberal land policy, and widespread advertising of that colony attracted a host of immigrants who rapidly moved into the interior. By 1750 the frontier settlements extended along the foot of the mountains from Easton southwestward to the Maryland line. This westward expansion was largely the work of Germans and Scotch-Irish, with a mingling of Swiss Mennonites, who began pouring into Pennsyl-

vania by the thousands in the early decades of the 18th century.

South of Pennsylvania, frontier expansion was the achievement of two streams of settlers: one which pushed westward from the tidewater regions, and the other which flowed southward from Pennsylvania. Virginia was well occupied as far west as the "fall line" by 1700. During the first quarter of the 18th century the settlement of the country between the fall line and the Blue Ridge was in full swing, as small farmers were crowded out of the tidewater section by large plantation owners. The Shenandoah Valley received some settlers from eastern Virginia, but its settlement was accomplished mainly by Germans and Scotch-Irish moving southward from Pennsylvania between 1730 and 1750. The occupation of the piedmont and mountain regions in the Carolinas came a little later and in about the same manner, with Scotch-Irish, Germans, and others from the North pioneering the way in the upland back country.

Thus, by 1750 settlements extended far into the interior of New England, there were agricultural outposts up the Mohawk in New York, and from Pennsylvania southward settlers were living close up against the Appalachian barrier and there were scattered cabins on westward-flowing streams. Here the advance was halted by the French and Indian War, and the frontier line even receded temporarily.

No sooner, however, had Fort Duquesne and the other Western posts of France been captured in 1758 and 1759 than the westward march was resumed and the frontier crossed the mountains in complete disregard of the royal Proclamation of 1763. By Braddock's Road settlers from Maryland and Virginia moved inland as far as the Forks of the Ohio, where they were joined by others coming across Pennsylvania by Forbes' Road. In Virginia, the Carolinas and Georgia, cabins appeared farther and farther up the streams flowing into the Atlantic and even in Powell's Valley and on such westward-flowing rivers as the Cheat, the Holston, the Clinch and the French Broad. About 1769 pioneers from Virginia began to settle along the Watauga River, in what is now southeastern Tennessee, and after 1771 they were joined by discouraged "Regulators" from North Carolina. Before the beginning of the Revolutionary War numerous settlements were made in West Florida. By this time also settlements had been established in central Kentucky around Boonesborough.

This was the situation at the close of the Revolutionary War, when the new American nation came into existence. The small stream of settlers that had begun to trickle over the mountain passes now swelled to an ever-increasing torrent that spread with amazing rapidity over the great interior valley, and within scarcely more than a half-century deposited outposts of settlement on the Pacific coast. The decennial reports of the Federal census, beginning in 1790, are valuable sources for the study of this great westward movement of land-hungry settlers. The dates of the creation of territories and the admission of states are other indications of the volume and direction of the movement. A series of shaded maps, in the *Report of the Eleventh Census,* 1890, showing population density and the spread of settlements by decades, tells the story even more graphically. But to gain an intimate, firsthand view of the process by which our country was settled one must go to the letters, diaries, journals of travel, newspapers and other writings of those who saw the movement when it was in progress.

These latter sources tell of roads crowded year after year, during the months from early spring to late fall, with settlers moving westward, singly, by families, or in groups. The typical migrating unit was the family, moving to a new home in the West with their belongings in a single covered wagon and with perhaps a cow or two. There is frequent mention, however, of well-equipped cavalcades of well-to-do farmers or plantation owners. On the other hand, a two-wheeled cart, pulled by a horse or an ox, was the only vehicle of many; while others made the journey on horseback or on foot.

Thousands of settlers placed their possessions, often including livestock, on flatboats on the upper Ohio and floated down that great highway to their destination in the West, or on down the Mississippi. Similarly the canal boats on the Erie Canal, after its completion in 1825, were often crowded with emigrants on their way to western New York or to Michigan and northern Ohio, Indiana and Illinois. Steamboats later played a large role in transporting settlers upstream to lands along the Mississippi and the Missouri.

The close of the Revolutionary War was followed by a great outpouring of people, principally from Virginia and North Carolina, into central Kentucky and Tennessee. Across the Ohio River there also appeared the vanguard of the stream of emigrants who soon transformed that region into a land of homes and farms and towns. The principal effects of the westward movement down to 1810 were seen in Ohio, Kentucky and Tennessee. The next decade witnessed the so-called "Great Migration" following the War of 1812, when the entire frontier moved westward. So many settlers poured into the Old Southwest that Mississippi and Alabama were admitted into the Union before the close of the decade. The movement into the Old Northwest resulted in the creation of the States of Indiana and Illinois. Across the Mississippi the influx of settlers set the stage for the great struggle over the admission of Missouri. By 1830 not only had all the Western states received large accessions of population, but the tide of settlers was moving into the territories of Michigan and Arkansas, and there were probably 20,000 Americans in Texas, which still belonged to Mexico.

During the decade of the 1830's the movement to Michigan and Arkansas, especially to the former,

reached such large proportions that two new states were admitted. Illinois nearly trebled in population and two new territories (Wisconsin and Iowa) were created. The "fabulous forties" were notable years in the history of the westward movement. Not only was the frontier expansion into Wisconsin and Iowa so vigorous that there were two additions to the roster of states, but thriving American settlements appeared on the Pacific coast. Early in this decade there began the movement of pioneers over the long Oregon Trail to the Pacific Northwest. In 1846 and 1847 the Mormons made their famous hegira from Nauvoo to their new home in Utah. Then just at the close of the decade came the mad rush of thousands of people of every description to the newly discovered gold fields in California.

During the decade of the 1850's migration to Oregon, California and Texas continued unabated. New converts swelled the population of the Mormon colony in Utah, and the Territory of New Mexico attracted thousands of settlers. The struggle for Kansas brought streams of zealous emigrants from the North and the South into that turbulent territory, which had a population of more than 100,000 in 1860. But in many respects the most significant phase of the westward movement of this decade is to be found in the fact that the population of the eight states of the upper Mississippi Valley increased by more than 3,350,000, or more than 167%. This growth, due partly to natural increases but mainly to the westward migration of Americans and hosts of foreign immigrants, definitely established the numerical and economic superiority of the North and had profound political effects.

The Civil War naturally checked the westward movement. And yet, even during those troubled years, there was a surprisingly large migration to the Far West, for this was the period of constantly recurring gold and silver discoveries in Colorado, Nevada, Oregon, Idaho and Montana. For instance, an observer writing in 1863 stated that the road at Omaha was "covered most of the time with the wagons of those bound for Colorado, California and Oregon; one train of nine hundred wagons was noted, another of twelve hundred. On the Kansas route this year a traveler from Colorado, sixteen days on the road, met on an average five hundred wagons a day going to Colorado and California." After the close of the war the movement to the Far West was greatly augmented, and was notable in the South as well as in the North, and particularly in the Border States where large numbers of Southern sympathizers left their homes for the West.

It was during the decades of the 1870's and the 1880's that the Great Plains—the last American frontier—received the greatest number of westward-moving settlers. This was the region long known as the Great American Desert. Then it became the scene of an extensive range-cattle industry. But steadily and inexorably the settlers moved westward and the great cattle range disappeared. By 1890 Kansas and Nebraska were populous states and the newly admitted states of North and South Dakota had substantial populations. Just at the close of the decade of the 1880's the dramatic rush to Oklahoma recalled scenes which had been witnessed many times when Indian lands were opened to settlement.

With the closing decade of the 19th century the story of the westward movement in America may well close. The farmers' frontier had advanced into some part of almost every section and region, and the pioneer phase of the occupation of the land within continental boundaries of the United States, excluding Alaska, was finished.

WHALEBACKS were first constructed in the 1880's at Duluth, Minn., by a Capt. McDougall. These ships were both passenger and freight vessels, although only one of the former—the *Christopher Columbus*—was built. This passenger ship was 360 feet long and was first used in 1892. It was scrapped in 1934. Whaleback freighters were smaller, measuring from 250 to 325 feet in length; they were also different in that the machinery was placed aft, whereas in the *Christopher Columbus* it was placed amidships. The freighters of this class were so designed that the greatest possible clear open-hold space was provided for carrying bulk cargoes. Whereas old freighters had numerous beams to strengthen the sides of the ships, the arch of the side of the whaleback made such beams unnecessary. Underwater, the bodies of most whalebacks were shaped at the ends like ordinary freighters, but others were like a cigar, with the round point forward. Whalebacks are being replaced by still more modern ships. These latter vessels have retained the arch used in whalebacks, thus leaving the space in the hull entirely open for bulk freight.

WHALING in the 18th and 19th centuries was a staple industry that provided oil for lamps and spermaceti for the candles of a nation. It had likewise a marked influence upon the territorial expansion of the United States and the management of diplomatic relations. Largely because of the activities of American whalemen an envoy was sent to South America before the War of 1812, Capt. David Porter doubled the Horn in the first American navy vessel to sail the Pacific, Lt. Charles Wilkes explored the coast of California and the South Seas, Commodore Perry opened Japan to occidental trade, and Hawaii and Alaska became American territories.

Whaling was early pursued by the settlers of southeastern Massachusetts and Long Island. Nantucket became the great whaling port of the world. Important fishery grounds were Davis' Strait, the Gulf of St. Lawrence and the Strait of Belle Isle. Between 1770 and 1775 the industry grew to an extent theretofore unparalleled. At the outbreak of the Revolution colonial ships had ventured south of the equator. The

war seriously crippled American whaling. Hundreds of Nantucket seamen emigrated from New England to sail under the French or English flags. A Nantucket captain in a British ship had the distinction of first exploiting the rich Australian grounds. The first whaleship to round Cape Horn was English fitted (cleared London, 1797), manned by a crew of Nantucket sailors. The mate, an American, killed the first sperm whale known to have been taken in Pacific waters.

The Pacific fishery grew rapidly and, after the War of 1812, was a virtual American monopoly for nearly one hundred years. By 1846 America had more than 700 ships at sea. New Bedford became the greatest whaling port the world has ever known, sending ships to the Pacific by way of Cape Horn or the Cape of Good Hope. Yankee captains discovered many tiny islands, at first considered worthless, but which discoveries have since perfected the right of American sovereignty to lands necessary for the development of transpacific airplane routes.

The Arctic Ocean grounds were discovered (1846) when an American ship in a dense fog drifted northward through Bering Strait. Adjacency to the new grounds and the advent of steam whalers (1879–80) promoted San Francisco to first rank as a whaling port, although many ships that outfitted there were owned and registered at New Bedford. The long four- or five-year voyages of the 1840's and 1850's from Atlantic ports were now reduced to less than one year out of San Francisco. In 1889 the *Nicoline* made the experiment of wintering in the North. After two years it returned to San Francisco without the capture of a single whale. The *Grampus* and *Mary D. Hume* wintered at Herschel Island at about the same time, with rich success. The latter ships were owned by a firm of Western capitalists who ventured the construction in San Francisco of large works for the treatment of oil. Prior to this experiment oil and bone had been shipped East, first around the Horn from San Francisco or Hawaii, or across the Isthmus of Panama. With the advent of the transcontinental railroad, oil and, especially, bone were commonly shipped by rail to Eastern centers of industry. In the early days of Pacific whaling captains frequently sold their oil in Australia.

American whaling came to a virtual end during the first decade of the 20th century. The discovery of petroleum, the development of electricity and the scarcity of whales were attributes which contributed to its decline. Considering physical risks and pecuniary hazards, the whaling industry was never extremely, nor consistently, profitable.

WHEAT, in the United States, was first planted in Virginia in 1618. Subsequently both spring and winter wheats were introduced into the colonies. New England attempted raising wheat, but was forced to give up its culture. In the South, only Virginia and Maryland used it as a cash crop. But the Middle Colonies became famous for their wheat, especially after "the blast" of 1664 drove the grain first into western Massachusetts and Connecticut, thence into the Genesee country of New York, the limestone region of Pennsylvania and the Shenandoah Valley of the South.

Production reached 84,000,000 bushels by 1839, with Ohio, Pennsylvania, New York and Virginia producing 60% of the nation's wheat. After the second westward movement (1859), the North Central Region became the national granary, harvesting 173,104,000 bushels of wheat.

Until 1879 the old Middle West was still the great producing area because wheat was the great cash crop, withstood transportation better and had a world market. But the Great Plains, supreme in 1889, never again relinquished first place in national production. The final transition westward occurred after 1890 when the Columbia Valley produced wheat for the Orient.

Meanwhile America kept the old Common White Wheat and introduced four new classes: (1) Soft Red Winter (1840); (2) Hard Red Spring (1860); (3) Hard Red Winter (1873); and (4) Durum (1892). Of these, Hard Red Spring and Hard Red Winter are best for bread flour; while Soft Red Winter, Common White and Durum mill the pastry and macaroni flours. Of these it is variously estimated that the United States produces 250 to 275 varieties.

All in all, wheat has been very important in the growth of our nation. It stimulated interstate and international migration into the West. Its changing varieties alone made possible the economic revaluation of the Great Plains. Its new methods made the American family the world's greatest producing unit. It hastened the shift from self-sufficiency to commercial agriculture. It revived large-scale farming. It revolutionized the whole milling process. It caused the rise of storage systems. It created new divisions of labor. It brought about organizations of farmers. It inspired basic economic changes in tractive power from oxen to horses to steam and gas engines. It prompted the organization of the Wheat Pit. It brought in its train the building of turnpikes, canals and railroads. It made America the granary and the bread basket of Europe.

Turkey Red Wheat and the Mennonites. Little Mennonite children, selecting seed in their fathers' bins in the Crimea in 1874, gave Turkey Red wheat to the Southwest Plains. Our story begins when the German states were instituting compulsory military service. The Mennonites, most of whom lived in Germany, were and are pacifists. Part of them fled to America to become the Amish. Others accepted an invitation in 1783 of Catherine the Great of Russia to settle in Crimea, which she had taken from Turkey. She promised exemption from the army for one hundred years. Her hope was that the industry of

the Mennonites would be an example to her shiftless Tatar subjects.

Ninety years later the Mennonites, realizing that their century of exemption would soon end, began a migration to the United States and Canada. Three scouts sent out in 1873 returned to induce 500 families to move to central Kansas. The first band of 24 families migrated to Kansas in 1874 and the others soon followed. While in Crimea the Mennonites had found the Turks growing a dark, hard wheat of desirable strength for bread baking. They improved it by seed selection and named it Turkey Red. Each family bound for Kansas took a small quantity of the Turkey wheat as seed. Since they could carry very little with them, they hand-picked it, a grain at a time, to insure that none but the finest was taken to the new land.

This tedious task was assigned to little children, for the elders had the heavier work to do. Anna Barkman, who as an eight-year-old child selected a peck of seed for her father, recollected in her old age that it required a week to pick a peck. She examined each individual grain for hardness and the dark red color, an appalling task when we know that about 250,000 grains are needed for a peck.

Turkey Red did so well in Kansas where no other wheat had been successful that the neighbors bought seed from the Mennonites. It has spread over the Southwest Plains states and to the Argentine. Kanred, Blackhull and some lesser varieties are derived direct from Turkey, and Tenmarq is a cross of Kanred and Marquis. Because of the high-protein content of Turkey and its offspring, they are blended with low-protein wheat to bring up baking strength.

WHIG PARTY. This was an opposition party that took form in the early 1830's to challenge the achievements of a triumphant Jacksonian democracy. Charging executive tyranny against "King Andrew," the representatives of the vested property interest of the North and the South recurred to an 18th-century formula that promised to be effective in rallying his opponents. Originally used (in 1832) by the anti-tariff leaders of South Carolina in close association with the "principles of 1798"—the Virginia and Kentucky Resolutions—the term, "Whig," soon came to be applied to all elements which found themselves opposed to the Jackson or Democratic party. Jackson's proclamation against nullification resulted in Henry Clay's co-operation with the nullifiers and their sympathizers in enacting the "Compromise Tariff" of 1833, which was dictated by the antitariff forces. Jackson's war on the Bank of the United States brought new recruits to the opposition, both from the South and from the North. His promotion of Martin Van Buren for the presidential succession alienated another group, the supporters of the aspirations of Judge Hugh L. White of Tennessee. Even before this most of the former National Republicans and the remnants of the Anti-Masonic party had joined the opposition. Van Buren's subtreasury policy brought an accretion of Democratic "conservatives" and the "Log Cabin" campaign of 1840 for William H. Harrison added important strength in the back country, which had previously seen little attraction in Whiggery.

The Whig success of 1840 imposed upon it the obligation of a temporarily dominant majority charged with the responsibilities of power. Clay promptly laid down a nationalistic program to which the majority of the party rallied, despite President Tyler's insistence in continuing what were to him the true Whig traditions of the 1830's. Read out of the party, the President watched in dismay the acceptance of the Clay formula by the vast body of Whigs. The issue of the annexation of Texas and of the extension of slavery into the territories in time proved a menace to solidarity of the party. The election of 1844 showed the loss of expansionist forces that had in 1840 yielded to the lure of "Hard Cider." The conservative property interests of leading Whigs, however, made them opponents of the Mexican War and of expansion; the "no territory" resolutions which they supported were largely sponsored by their Southern leaders. While some of the Northern element were antislavery men (Conscience Whigs), others were sufficiently proslavery to earn the label, "Cotton Whigs." In the crisis of 1850–51 the Southern element was prominent among the Union forces that fought secession (see Compromise of 1850). By 1852 the logic of sectional allegiance was so strong that the party began to disintegrate and suffered a defeat which marked the beginning of the end.

WHIP, PARTY, is a party officer in Congress, whose duties are particularly to see that members of his party are present for important roll calls and that they vote right. This kind of officer has been used in the English Parliament at least since 1836, but was first formally introduced into our House of Representatives in 1899, when Rep. James E. Watson of Indiana was designated as whip by the House Republican caucus, and into the Senate in 1913, when Sen. James Hamilton Lewis of Illinois was similarly designated by the Senate Democrats. Since that time whips have been regularly chosen by each party in each house, and their work has become of increasing importance, so much so that the Democrats in the House recently provided for fifteen assistant whips chosen by geographical districts, and required at least four to be on the floor of the House at all times.

WHISKEY INSURRECTION. The American back country in the 1790's was intensely democratic in its views and resented the way in which Alexander Hamilton's fiscal policies concentrated power in the hands of the upper classes. Other grievances accentuated Western resentment, notably the failure to open the Mississippi to navigation, the dilatory conduct of the Indian war, the speculative prices of land, arduous and ill-paid militia duty, scarcity of specie and the creation of a salaried official class. The excise law of 1791 which taxed whiskey, the chief transportable and barterable Western product, furnished a convenient peg on which to hang these grievances, and for three years the opposition to this measure increased.

The fact that noncomplying distillers from western Pennsylvania had to go to York or Philadelphia for trial (a procedure that would cost the value of the average Western farm) formed so legitimate a grievance that in May and June, 1794, Congress passed a measure making such offenses cognizable in state courts. While the bill was in Congress the U. S. District Court of Pennsylvania issued a series of processes returnable to Philadelphia. The fact that these processes were not served until July, six weeks after the easing measure was passed, angered the citizens of the southwestern counties. A Federal marshal was attacked in Allegheny County while serving a process and on July 17 several hundred men, led by members of a local "Democratic society," attacked and burned the home of Gen. John Neville, the regional inspector of the excise.

The attackers would probably have stopped with this action but certain leaders robbed the mail and found in the stolen letters expressions that they used in stirring up the people to attack Pittsburgh. A muster of the southwestern militia was called at Braddock's Field for Aug. 1. The citizens of Pittsburgh were so alarmed that they exiled the odious townsmen and thus averted the wrath of the recalcitrants. The militia march on Pittsburgh on Aug. 2 was carried through without violence.

On Aug. 14–15 delegates from the Monongahela country met at Parkinson's Ferry, but were prevented from drastic measures by the parliamentary tactics of the moderates. A committee appointed by Washington met with a Western committee and arranged that the sentiment of the people of the western counties concerning submission be taken on Sept. 11. The vote was unsatisfactory and Washington set in motion the militia army which had meanwhile been gathering in the East. The western counties were occupied during November and more than a score of prisoners sent to Philadelphia. All of them were acquitted, pardoned, or dismissed for lack of evidence.

The result of the insurrection was simply to strengthen the political power of Hamilton and the Federalists, and circumstantial evidence seems to indicate that Hamilton promoted the original misunderstanding and sent the army West solely for that purpose. It is likely also that the defeat of the democrats encouraged investors to accelerate the economic development of the region which they had already begun.

WHISKEY RING. Subsequent to becoming Secretary of the Treasury in Grant's cabinet in June, 1874, Benjamin H. Bristow procured the indictment and conviction of three government officials and a journalist in St. Louis, Mo., and of a government official in Washington. The charges involved conspiracy between Internal Revenue officials and whiskey distillers, located chiefly in St. Louis, and accomplices in Washington to divide certain illegal abatements of taxes on whiskey. The facts revealed would have been of little historical importance had not allegations been made that the illegal abatements of taxes were to raise funds for the Republican party, especially to procure a second and third term for Grant and that the improprieties involved not only Grant's private secretary, but in a measure the President himself. All of this made the matter a political scandal of the first water. While the private secretary was acquitted and the nation as a whole gave slight credence to the charges reflecting upon Grant himself, the revelations undoubtedly had an effect upon public sentiment in the ensuing presidential campaign.

WHITE HOUSE, THE, was familiarly so called from early times, because the Aquia Creek sandstone of which it was built was painted white. Originally named the President's House, in President Lincoln's day it was officially The Executive Mansion and so continued until President Theodore Roosevelt adopted the commonly used appellation. President Washington and Maj. L'Enfant selected for the Capitol and the White House two commanding sites in the city of their planning (*see* Washington). The fact that the locations were a mile and a half apart was welcomed by the courtly L'Enfant as conducing to ceremonial intercourse, and by the practical President as mitigating the importunities of legislators, a waste of time he suffered in New York and Philadelphia. As the result of a competition in which nineteen designs were submitted (including an anonymous one by Jefferson) the commissioners selected that of James Hoban, architecturally trained in Dublin. Washington approved the choice as combining elegance with simplicity and dignity; and it appealed to Jefferson by its adherence to classical precedents. In fact Hoban designed a gentleman's house of his period.

In October, 1800, Mrs. John Adams found an unfinished and unfurnished White House in which to spend an uncomfortable winter. President Jefferson, coming five months later, gave to the furnishings a French touch that has persisted.

After Washington was burned by the British in 1814 Hoban superintended the repairs. The east and west terraces, and the south and north porticoes were added by B. H. Latrobe prior to 1824.

During the century, the combination of President's office and residence in one building resulted in mutilations to the house and unspeakable discomforts to its occupants. In 1902 Congress charged President Theodore Roosevelt with drastic renovations. He selected McKim, Mead and White as architects. Between May and November, 1902, the interior was entirely rebuilt and refurnished, reverently restoring and preserving the architecture of the historic White House while giving to the interior all the facilities of elegant and comfortable living and entertaining.

WHITE PLAINS, BATTLE OF (Oct. 28, 1776). After the Battle of Harlem Heights both the American and British armies were inactive for about three weeks. The next military movement came from Howe. With the main part of his army he moved up the East River in order to get in the rear of the Americans and at the same time cut off communication with Connecticut and the other New England states. So slowly did he advance, however, that he did not reach New Rochelle until Oct. 21. His delay gave Washington time to move north and take up a strong position across the roads leading up the Hudson and to New England. Strongly entrenched on the high ground northwest and northeast of the village of White Plains he waited for Howe's next move. On Oct. 28 Howe was ready to attack. The action was short, sharp and creditable to the Americans. Avoiding a direct attack on Washington's front, Howe sent a detachment to gain Chatterton Hill, a rocky eminence west of the Bronx River, and near the village. The British were forestalled, however, by Gen. McDougall, who gained the hill first and held it until British reinforcements forced a retreat to the village. During the night Washington drew back his line and strengthened it. Howe waited for reinforcements before continuing the attack. On the night of the 31st, however, Washington withdrew into the "Hills" five miles to the northwest.

WICKIUP. This term, from an Algonkin Indian word, a variant of wigwam, came into use in the early years of the 19th century to designate a rude brush shelter, usually temporary. In recent years the tendency has been to restrict its use to the conical brush-covered homes of the Great Basin Indians in Utah and Nevada. The type structure is a tripod of forked poles covered with brush.

WIGWAM is an Abenaki Indian word meaning "dwelling," but similar forms of the word are found in most Algonkin languages. Wickiup is a variant of the same term. The English settlers adopted the word from the first, thus giving it a definite place in English speech. The wigwam in New England was a dome-shaped structure or a similar elongated form, covered with bark—birch-bark whenever available. In some cases the winter covering was of mats or thatch. However, the English extended the name wigwam to all Iroquois and Algonkin dwellings, thus covering the area from the Atlantic to the Mississippi, and north of Carolina and Tennessee into Canada. Later, the term wigwam was applied to tepees. In modern literature the tendency is to use wigwam for oval and elongated bark houses and tepee for conical structures of the tepee type.

WILD WEST SHOW is an original American entertainment featuring exhibitions typical of the life of cowboy, Indian and soldier. The first was the "Wild West, Rocky Mountain and Prairie Exhibition" of William F. Cody ("Buffalo Bill") and Dr. W. F. Carver, opening at Omaha, Nebr., May 17, 1883, with Maj. Frank North, Gordon W. Lillie ("Pawnee Bill") and Capt. A. H. Bogardus in the cast. It was reorganized in 1884 by Cody, Bogardus and Nate Salsbury. Annie Oakley, "Little Sure Shot," joined in 1885 and Sitting Bull was with the show that season. "Buffalo Bill's" Wild West toured Europe in 1887, 1889–92 and 1902–7. At the Chicago World's Fair in 1893 a "Congress of Rough Riders of the World" was featured. Carver, Lillie and Buck Taylor were also in the field. "Buffalo Bill" merged with "Pawnee Bill" in 1908 and with the Sells-Floto circus in 1913; his last appearance was with the Miller Brothers "101 Ranch Wild West Show" in 1916. Financial troubles were attributed to motion-picture competition. Zach T. Miller failed to repeat Cody's 1893 triumph with the 101 Ranch at the Chicago World's Fair of 1933 and Col. Tim McCoy's attempt to revive the Wild West Show in the grand manner in 1938 was a quick failure. The rodeo is a closely related form of entertainment.

WILDERNESS, BATTLES OF THE (May 5–7, 1864). On May 4 Grant's (U.) army was across the Rapidan River, preparing to attack Lee's (C.) army. The move had been anticipated. Instead of attacking the Union troops in the act of crossing, as might have been expected, Lee preferred to engage Grant in The Wilderness where the Union two-to-one superiority in numbers and artillery would be somewhat neutralized. Grant directed his main movement at Lee's right, hoping to get clear of The Wilderness before effective resistance could be offered. Lee, however, moved rapidly to check this attempt. Road divergence separated his two wings; Longstreet (C.), expected to support either wing, was late in arriving. On May 5 Grant attacked. Ewell (C.) on the left and A. P. Hill (C.) both held firm. Night ended the fighting.

The next day Grant resumed his attack. Hill's troops were driven in confusion. Lee personally rode among the fleeing men to rally and lead them back into battle. As the cry, "Lee to the rear" rose on every side, Longstreet's tardy command arrived and struck with suddenness and fury, driving Grant's men back. Ewell, on Lee's left, repulsed all attacks.

In the midst of success, Longstreet was wounded by his own men, as Jackson had been at Chancellorsville. Soon afterward fighting ceased for the day.

It is doubtful if Longstreet's wounding had any important effect on the outcome of the day's fighting. The troops on both sides were much disorganized, the hour was late and little more could have been accomplished. During the 7th the two armies faced each other from behind their hasty breastworks. The two days had seen bitter fighting in a region difficult either to receive or deliver battle. Thousands of acres of tangled forest, interlaced undergrowth and scrub trees were on every hand with here and there only narrow roads, some of them mere paths. Cavalry was useless and artillery hardly less so. Vision was limited to short distances and once the fighting began, control passed to local commanders. The brush caught fire and many wounded were burned to death. Dense smoke filled the air. The Wilderness became a tract of doom and over all was the shadow of death.

Perceiving the uselessness of again assaulting Lee's lines, Grant decided to move by the flank toward Richmond, thus forcing Lee to come and meet him. The goal was Spotsylvania Courthouse. As Grant's advance troops reached this objective Lee's men were in position to meet the threat. The first act of a campaign, bitterly fought and replete with brilliant strategical and tactical movements, was completed.

WILDERNESS ROAD ran from eastern Virginia (where it linked up with the Maryland and Pennsylvania roads from the north and the Carolina and East Tennessee roads from the south) through the mountain pass, known as Cave or Cumberland Gap, to the interior of Kentucky and thence to the Ohio and beyond. A rudimentary road already existed when, in March, 1775, Daniel Boone and a party of about thirty woodsmen undertook to clear and mark out a trail from the Indian treaty-ground at Fort Watauga, in what is now East Tennessee, by way of Cumberland Gap and through the rugged mountains and rolling canelands of Kentucky, to the mouth of Otter Creek, on the Kentucky River, a site chosen for a fortified town and forthwith named Boonesborough. Later the road forked at the Hazel Patch, in Laurel County, one branch leading by the Crab Orchard and Danville to the Falls of the Ohio at Louisville. This primitive road, made up in large part of a succession of irregular woodland paths trodden down and worn bare by wandering herds of buffalo and roving Indian hunters or war parties, was blazed by Boone at the instance of the Transylvania Company. Its total length was close to 300 miles, and fully two thirds of the distance had to be opened and marked to guide an endless train of plodding pioneers who followed in the wake of Boone and his fellow road builders. At first little more than a footpath or pack-horse trail, spasmodic but insufficient measures were taken by the Virginia government to enlarge and improve the crowded thoroughfare, but a score of years elapsed before it was passable by wagons. After Kentucky became a separate state, renewed efforts to grade, widen and reinforce the road were put forth. Sections of the road were leased to contractors who, in consideration of materials and labor furnished to maintain the road, were authorized to erect gates or turnpikes across it and collect tolls from travelers. In legislation on the subject, the road was generally called "The Wilderness Turnpike Road." Blockhouses were erected and manned at intervals along the way to protect travelers against marauding Indians and other outlaws. For more than half a century after Boone blazed the way in 1775, the Wilderness Road was a principal avenue for the movement of immigrants and others to and from the early West. The Ohio River afforded the only alternative route; and over these converging highways to the great inland empire of the new nation, thousands upon thousands of Americans of the pioneer period passed and repassed in a never-ending procession. The Wilderness Road is still an important interstate arterial roadway and constitutes a part of U. S. Route 25, otherwise known as the "Dixie Highway."

WILLIAM AND MARY, COLLEGE OF. The third attempt to establish a college in Virginia was successful when King William and Queen Mary granted to Rev. James Blair a charter and endowment Feb. 8, 1693. The Wren building, erected 1695, used for classes and dormitories, was rebuilt after a fire in 1705. An Indian school was supported by part of the income from a fund bequeathed for philanthropic purposes by the distinguished physicist, Hon. Robert Boyle. The grammar, philosophy and divinity schools, modeled on English predecessors, were fully established by 1729. Many of the alumni were leaders in the American Revolution, including Thomas Jefferson, James Monroe, Richard Bland, Peyton Randolph, Edmund Randolph and Benjamin Harrison. The buildings were damaged by Revolutionary troops and the endowment was seriously impaired as a result of the war. In 1776 the Phi Beta Kappa Society was organized by a group of students. In 1779 the grammar, Indian and divinity schools were replaced by schools of modern languages, medicine and law. In 1859 the Wren building was burned a second time and rebuilt; it was burned a third time in 1862. The College was closed from 1861 until 1865, when instruction was resumed and continued until 1881. In 1888 a small grant from the state enabled the College to reopen. In 1906 the property of the College was deeded to the State of Virginia. It became coeducational in 1918. The Wren building, President's house, and Brafferton Hall were restored in 1929 by John D. Rockefeller, Jr.

WILLIAM HENRY, FORT, MASSACRE AT (Aug. 10, 1757). The Marquis de Montcalm, the French commander, with an army numbering more than 8000 including 2000 Indians, laid siege to the British fort at the head of Lake George early in August. Lt. Col. Monro with fewer than 2500 men bravely defended the post, while Col. Webb, at Fort Edward, cravenly refused to lead his 4000 troops to the rescue. Monro was finally forced to surrender on the 9th, though Montcalm allowed him fair terms and agreed to give the garrison safe conduct to Fort Edward. However, the French Indians treacherously killed the wounded British, plundered the fort and camp, and at last began a general massacre. Montcalm and his chief officers were able to restrain the Indians only with the greatest difficulty and at the risk of their own lives. "Kill me, but spare the English who are under my protection," exclaimed Montcalm. Though some accounts put the number massacred as high as 1500 persons, the best evidence shows that only about fifty were killed, though six or seven hundred were carried off, stripped and otherwise mistreated. The massacre served for long as an "atrocity story" and has often been called a blot on Montcalm's record.

WILLIAMSBURG, VA., had its origins in a central section of Middle Plantation, a palisaded outpost established between the James and York Rivers in 1633 against the Indians. The town received its present name in 1699 in honor of William III, the then reigning British monarch, at which time it became the second capital of the colony of Virginia. The College of William and Mary had been established at this point six years prior to that time. From 1699 to 1779 Williamsburg remained the economic, educational, religious and social, as well as the governmental center of the colony. Being the urban center for a large and dispersed civilization, this city of one or two thousand inhabitants became a metropolis of five or six thousand persons during court seasons and other "public times."

Williamsburg was the scene of much political activity in the period immediately preceding the American Revolution and toward the end of that struggle was occupied in turn by British and American forces. Owing to the exigencies of the war and to the desire for a more central capital on the part of an expanding population, the seat of government was removed to Richmond in 1779. Until its restoration, except for intervals during the Civil War and World War I, Williamsburg remained a quiet county seat and college town. During the Battle of Williamsburg in 1862, Federal troops occupied the town and remained there until 1865.

The restoration of Colonial Williamsburg was begun in 1928, financed by John D. Rockefeller, Jr.

WILMOT PROVISO. Soon after the Mexican War began, President Polk requested $2,000,000 from

Congress with which to negotiate peace, it being understood that territory would be acquired from Mexico. On Aug. 8, 1846, a bill to appropriate the sum was moved in the House. David Wilmot, a Democrat from Pennsylvania, hitherto identified with the administration, proposed the following amendment to the bill: "Provided, That, as an express and fundamental condition to the acquisition of any territory from the Republic of Mexico by the United States, by virtue of any treaty which may be negotiated between them, and to the use by the Executive of the moneys herein appropriated, neither slavery nor involuntary servitude shall ever exist in any part of said territory. . . ." This amendment became famous as the Wilmot Proviso. It precipitated a bitter debate over the question of slavery in the territories.

An effort was made in the House to amend the Wilmot Proviso by limiting its application to the region north of the Missouri Compromise line, but this was defeated. The appropriation bill carrying the Wilmot Proviso was then passed by the House by a vote of 87 to 64. The bill as amended was then sent to the Senate; but the Senate adjourned for the session before a vote was taken.

In the next Congress, a bill to appropriate $3,000,-000 for peace negotiations was introduced in the House, and Wilmot again moved his Proviso. The bill as amended was carried in the House, Feb. 1, 1847, by a vote of 115 to 106. The Senate refused to consider the amended bill, but passed one of its own appropriating the desired sum. After bitter debate the House concurred in the Senate bill, and the $3,000,000 became available to President Polk, without Wilmot's conditions.

In the meantime debates over the Proviso had aroused the country, North and South. State legislatures and other public bodies approved and condemned the principle incorporated in the Proviso. Sectional animosity was heightened. The principle of the Proviso, contained in other legislation, continued to provoke sectional debate. The modern Republican party was later founded on this principle, and Abraham Lincoln was elected on a platform pledged to carry it out.

Modern historical scholarship recognizes that more is involved in the Wilmot Proviso than meets the eye. Polk was unpopular with Northern Democrats in 1846 because of his recent settlement of the Oregon question, the Walker tariff of 1846, and his recent veto of a rivers and harbors bill. Votes for the Wilmot Proviso were calculated to embarrass the President. The motive of David Wilmot, an administration Democrat, has been puzzling. The usual theory is that he merely served as an accommodating mouthpiece for an antiadministration Democrat, Jacob Brinkerhoff. Some historians now maintain that Wilmot, not Brinkerhoff, was the real author of the plan, and that his motive was not unconnected with a de-

sire to regain the support of his Pennsylvania constituency, alienated by his recent tariff vote.

WILSON'S CREEK, BATTLE OF, was fought Aug. 10, 1861, between Federal troops under Gen. Nathaniel Lyon and an army of the Missouri State Guard under Gen. Sterling Price, co-operating with a force of Confederates from Arkansas under Gen. McCulloch. Lyon had 5400 men and Price and McCulloch had nearly 11,000. Lyon attacked the combined force at Wilson's Creek, Mo., ten miles southwest of Springfield, at 5 o'clock in the morning. He sent Gen. Franz Sigel to make a flank attack but McCulloch defeated him and both armies turned on Lyon. At the critical moment Lyon was killed. The Federal army retreated toward Rolla. The total casualties, about equally divided between the two armies, were 2544 or nearly 16% of all those engaged. This was the first success of the Confederates in Missouri.

WINCHESTER, BATTLE OF (May 25, 1862). The disaster to Kenly's forces at Front Royal, Va., placed the command of Gen. N. P. Banks at Strasburg, consisting of some 10,000 Federal troops and 16 guns, in grave peril from Confederate forces operating in the Valley of Virginia under Generals "Stonewall" Jackson and R. S. Ewell. Reluctant to retire, Banks delayed starting for Winchester until he was all but outflanked. With Jackson striking at his flank and rear and Ewell striving to intercept him, he finally reached Winchester late in the afternoon of the 24th and took position south, west and east of the town. There at dawn on the 25th, Banks was attacked by Ewell, soon reinforced by Jackson, their combined troops and guns double his own. Against these odds Banks retreated five or ten miles beyond Winchester, where the Confederates, unable to break his columns, allowed him to proceed unmolested to the Potomac River. Rejoined there by his wagon trains, he crossed the river at Williamsport next day.

WINCHESTER, BATTLE OF (Sept. 19, 1864). On Aug. 7, 1864, Gen. P. H. Sheridan (U.) was placed in command of all troops in the Shenandoah Valley, was given both authority and means and was directed to halt the offensive operations directed by Gen. J. A. Early (C.), and to drive the Confederates from the Valley. With reinforcements from Grant's (U.) army, Sheridan forced Early up the Valley and when the latter was also reinforced, Sheridan withdrew northward. Early, following in pursuit, divided his force about the same time that his reinforcements were recalled by Lee. Sheridan with superior force attacked the Confederates and forced them back. Reinforced by concentrating detachments, Early halted, attacked and drove the Federals back. He then took position behind Opequon Creek to the westward and in front of Winchester. Sheridan, again reinforced, counterattacked, on Sept. 19, 1864, using his cavalry effectively. After severe fighting, which lasted throughout the day, the Confederate left was turned and Early's troops were forced back in some confusion. After dark, the Confederate Army retired southward through Winchester, finally halting at Fisher's Hill.

WISCONSIN was discovered by the French in 1634 when Champlain sent Jean Nicolet to explore for a route to the Western ocean and to the Orient. In 1671 all this region was formally annexed to the Kingdom of France by a ceremony at Sault Ste. Marie. In 1673 its chief waterway, the Fox-Wisconsin, was opened by Jolliet and Marquette who discovered the Mississippi. The Indian name for its principal river gave its name to the state.

The French regime lasted for over a century. Missions were maintained at the forts and a central Jesuit mission at DePere. Settlements were begun at Green Bay, LaPointe and Prairie du Chien. During the Fox wars of the early 18th century French expeditions invaded Wisconsin in 1716 and in 1728. During the French and Indian War, Indians from Wisconsin, led by Charles de Langlade, helped defeat Braddock, 1755, and served under Montcalm, 1759.

The cession of all interior North America to Great Britain and the withdrawal of the French garrisons from LaPointe and Green Bay put an end to the control of what is now Wisconsin by the French government. Nevertheless, the French language persisted, and French methods of conducting the fur trade endured during all the British regime. The British built Fort Edward Augustus at Green Bay in 1761, but the garrison was withdrawn during Pontiac's conspiracy (1763), and never reinstated. The period of British supremacy was the time of the greatest development of the fur trade. Great companies were organized such as the North West Fur Company, and Wisconsin Indians were encouraged to hunt and bring furs to the trading posts. The region of the upper Mississippi, the south shore of Lake Superior, and the interior lakes had many fur-trading posts. During the American Revolution the fur trade was disorganized; emissaries of the British, Americans and even of the trans-Mississippi Spanish visited the Indian villages. Milwaukee village was strong for the American cause.

At the close of the Revolution Wisconsin became nominally a part of the Northwest Territory. In reality, as the British refused to surrender the Northwest posts, the fur trade regime continued under British control. While a part of the Northwest Territory, Wisconsin became part of Indiana Territory in 1800; of Illinois Territory in 1809; of Michigan Territory in 1818.

When the War of 1812 broke out, the Indians and few settlers of Wisconsin all sided with the British. In 1814 an expedition from St. Louis mounted the Mississippi and built an American post—Fort Shelby—at Prairie du Chien, which raised the first American flag in Wisconsin. A month later a British force from Mackinac captured this fort, the only military clash on Wisconsin soil between Great Britain and the United States. The next year, after the treaty of peace, the British evacuated Prairie du Chien and the American regime began in Wisconsin with the building in 1816 of Fort Howard at Green Bay and Fort Crawford at Prairie du Chien.

The military occupation of Wisconsin continued until the organization of the territory in 1836. In 1825 a great treaty was held at Prairie du Chien to induce the Indians to keep the peace. In 1827, however, the Winnebago War occurred, occasioned largely by the trespass of lead miners on the lands of this tribe. When it was suppressed by the surrender of Red Bird, Winnebago chief, mining rapidly increased, and there was a rush to the southwest that built the settlements of Platteville, Potosi, Mineral Point, Dodgeville, Shullsburg and others.

Fort Winnebago was built in 1828 at the Portage to control the Indians and to safeguard the Fox-Wisconsin waterway. During the Black Hawk War of 1832, the miners of southwest Wisconsin "forted" at numerous small forts, and Dodge raised a troop of rangers that aided in defeating Black Hawk at the Battle of Wisconsin Heights.

After this last Indian war immigration increased rapidly. The Indian claims south of the Fox-Wisconsin were extinguished, American settlers came in at the Lake Michigan ports, land offices were opened and southern Wisconsin had by 1836 over 12,000 population. That year Wisconsin Territory was organized from what had been a part of Michigan, Dodge was appointed governor, and Madison was chosen the capital.

The twelve years of territorial life saw enormous gains in population, chiefly from the New England states and New York. The census for 1840 was 30,000. Foreigners, mostly Germans, began coming by 1838 and continued with accelerated rate. Norwegians, Belgians, Swiss, as well as English-speaking foreigners came in also during the territorial period. In 1848 Wisconsin, after rejecting one constitution and accepting a second, entered the Union.

WITCHCRAFT. Belief in witchcraft was universal and sincere, and came to America with the colonists. Margaret Jones was executed for witchcraft in Boston in 1648. Soon after Mary Parsons of Springfield was indicted for witchcraft, but actually executed for murdering her child. Mrs. Anne Hibbins was hanged in Boston, June 19, 1656. Other accusations, some of them with fatal results, occurred in scattered points in New England and the other colonies. Even William Penn presided over the trial of two Swedish women for witchcraft, but the acquittal of Bridget Bishop in 1680 in Salem, and the execution of a woman named Glover in Boston in 1688, largely on the evidence of a Goodwin child thirteen years old, whose case was studied by Cotton Mather, most closely paralleled the Salem hysteria. The latter probably made Mather the champion of the witchcraft persecution.

In the spring of 1692 in Salem Village, now Danvers, a group of young women and girls, who had been amusing themselves during the long winter listening to the lurid tales of Tituba, an old Negro slave of the minister, Rev. Samuel Parris, showed signs of hysteria. These "afflicted children" presently began to accuse persons of bewitching them. They fell down in fits supposed to be caused by the alleged witches, who were also accused of pinching them and sticking pins into them. The local physician could not see that the children had any malady, so Parris called in other ministers to confer on the strange manifestations. A powerful and inflammatory sermon was preached at the village by a visiting clergyman against the machinations of the devil. The civil magistrates entered the case. A special court to try the cases was appointed by the governor, and between May and September, 1692, several hundred persons were arrested, nineteen were hanged and many imprisoned. The cases were tried in Salem in an atmosphere of terror and tense excitement. No one knew who would be accused next and condemned on charges by the "afflicted children." Resistance to the delusion, at first terrorized into silence, grew rapidly, however, and by October the people came to their senses. Many strong characters exhibited high courage in resisting the excitement at the risk of their lives. Early in the next year all those arrested had been released with or without trial and the episode was over.

No witch was ever burned in Salem. Giles Corey, who was pressed to death, was so treated under an old English law for refusing to plead to the indictment, not for witchcraft. Nowhere except in Massachusetts did the participants in such a delusion have the courage to confess their errors publicly. The General Court passed a resolution to that effect Dec. 17, 1696. Judge Sewall handed to his minister a confession to be read in his meeting house while he stood in his pew, and the twelve jurymen signed a statement admitting their error and asking forgiveness.

While a few later cases of witchcraft persecution occurred in Virginia in 1706, in North Carolina in 1712, and perhaps in Rhode Island in 1728, this fiery outbreak at Salem Village practically ended witchcraft in America.

"WITH MALICE TOWARD NONE; WITH CHARITY FOR ALL" are the opening phrases of the last sentence of Abraham Lincoln's second inaugural address, March 4, 1865. By many Americans these words, with the sentiments of tolerance and sym-

pathy which follow them, are accepted as the perfect expression of Lincoln's nobility of character.

WOLVES were originally found throughout the continent of North America, from central Mexico to the Arctic. Several local varieties may be distinguished, differing more or less in color and size, but these variations do not in general represent any real differences in species. The two main species most commonly referred to are the gray or timber wolf (*canis occidentalis*) and the prairie wolf or coyote (*canis latrans*). The timber wolf is somewhat larger than the coyote and is distinguished by its howl, which is quite different from the high-pitched dirge of the coyote. The coyote is found principally in the Great Plains and Rocky Mountain area, while the gray wolf is more widely distributed.

Wolves have always been present in considerable numbers along the American frontier and the accounts of early western travelers contain innumerable allusions to them and their deep-throated nocturnal howling. These travelers are likely to be inaccurate in their descriptions and in the names which they apply to different varieties. Still, there is a remarkable unanimity in their accounts of the habits of the wolf and the great nuisance involved in its presence. From the very beginning of settlement the wolf was a problem. It preyed upon livestock and in winter would hover in the vicinity of farms and ranches, seeking its victims. While wolves often hunted in packs during the winter, there are few authenticated instances where they attacked man. The settlers from the start waged a war of extermination against wolves and as early as the 1630's bounties seem to have been offered for wolf scalps in Virginia and Massachusetts. The aid of Indians was sometimes enlisted in the war upon them. With the rise of sheep and cattle ranches in the trans-Mississippi West, the wolves constituted a serious economic problem. Most of the Western states and territories resorted to the bounty system while professional "wolfers" were sometimes engaged to hunt the animals. Traps and poisons were imported in an effort to eradicate the pest. Bounties are still paid in some localities but expert opinion differs as to the effectiveness of this method of exterminating wolves. Lack of conformity of bounty laws has led to abuses of the system while the "counterfeiting" of wolf scalps has even been resorted to. The gradual extension of settlement has been more effective than any laws. Wolf skins have always constituted an item in the North American fur trade, although they do not have a relatively high value. From the accounts of early observers it appears that the Indians were fond of wearing wolf heads and skins in ceremonial dances, and the wolf played its part in their folklore. Wolves have practically disappeared from the region east of the Mississippi and south of the Great Lakes, although even in recent years wolf drives have not been unknown in certain localities in the Middle West. Notwithstanding its destructiveness to game and livestock, the wolf seems to have served at least one useful purpose as a carrion-eater and scavenger.

WOMAN'S CHRISTIAN TEMPERANCE UNION

had its origin in the Woman's Temperance Crusade of 1873–74. Inspired by a temperance address delivered by Dr. Dio Lewis, noted health advocate at Hillsboro, Ohio, in December, 1873, the women of the town began a praying crusade against the saloon. Hymns were sung and prayers offered within and without the saloons. The liquor traffic was swept from some 200 towns in a score of states in less than two months. Realizing the possible temporary effects of the crusade because the saloon enjoyed the protection of the law, and sensing the need of a permanent organization to complete the victory, the leading church women of Chautauqua, N. Y., called a national convention of temperance women. Delegates from 17 states attended these meetings at Cleveland, O., Nov. 18–20, 1874, at which the Woman's Christian Temperance Union was founded.

The new organization grew rapidly and became a real force in public affairs. By the turn of the century every state required scientific temperance instruction in its public schools. The prohibition victories of the next two decades may be traced to voters educated as children concerning the evil effects of alcohol. The Anti-Saloon League, formed in 1893, was mainly a result of the work of the W. C. T. U. Based on high ideals of good morals and clean living, the Union worked to convince the American people that drinking was morally wrong. It mercilessly fought the saloon as the destroyer of the home and the ally of corrupt politics and crime.

To the energetic leadership and guidance of Frances E. Willard the Woman's Christian Temperance Union owes the scope of its program. With twenty distinct departments of work headed by experts, working principally through schools, churches, press, politics, contests and petitions, it is organized in every state, territory, and dependency of the United States.

Largely through the efforts of Miss Willard, the World Woman's Christian Temperance Union was founded in 1883. It is now organized in seventy countries of the world.

WOMAN'S RIGHTS MOVEMENT.

In 17th- and 18th-century America, the subordinate position of women arose from the common-law heritage of the British colonies, and the teachings of the Protestant churches. When a woman married she lost all separate legal identity. Women voted only in sporadic instances; the last possibility of exercising the franchise was barred to them in 1807 in New Jersey.

A conscious movement for improving the position of women arose from the same social causes that produced a democratic industrialized society in the United States. Immediate factors were: the growing need for women workers, initially in the New England textile mills; the rational and humanist thought of the French Revolution; the growth of other reform movements, especially that for abolition of Negro chattel slavery; and the loosening of social restrictions along the constantly westward-moving frontier, where women played a crucial role as pioneer homemakers and producers.

Women won the right to speak in public (originally permitted only by the Quakers) in the abolition struggles, led by Sarah and Angelina Grimké in 1838. Among those who followed them on the platform were Quakers like Lucretia Mott and Susan B. Anthony, or graduates of the earliest institutions to offer women improved education: Elizabeth Cady Stanton attended Emma Willard's academy in Troy, N. Y., and Lucy Stone went to Oberlin, the first co-educational college.

The first woman's rights convention, held on the initiative of Mrs. Stanton at Seneca Falls, N. Y., July 18 and 19, 1848, produced a far-reaching Declaration of Principles demanding wider educational and professional opportunities, abolition of legal inequities, and the franchise. The earliest remedial legislation, in the form of Married Women's Property Acts, was passed state by state as the result of energetic efforts by small groups of women and their male supporters; the vote did not become a real issue until after the Civil War.

Educated by ten years of woman's rights conventions, widespread lecturing, and the writings of Sarah Grimké (*The Equality of the Sexes,* 1838) and Margaret Fuller (*Woman in the 19th Century,* 1844), women organized to support the Northern cause during the Civil War, in the National Woman's Loyal League. The experience prepared them to organize in their own behalf, when the Republican Party not only excluded them from the provisions of the Fourteenth and Fifteenth Constitutional Amendments, but raised the issue of whether women were actually citizens by including the word "male" in the Fourteenth Amendment.

A militant group led by Mrs. Stanton and Miss Anthony organized the National Woman Suffrage Association in 1869; the American Woman Suffrage Association, founded by Lucy Stone and her husband Henry Blackwell in the same year, was more conservative. The two groups did not merge until 1890.

Women first won the vote in Wyoming Territory in 1869, led by Esther Morris. A few weeks later the Mormon Territory of Utah gave women the franchise, which they lost in 1887 by an act of Congress aimed at penalizing Mormon plural marriage practices. Both Wyoming (1890) and Utah (1896) came into the Union with woman suffrage. Women were given the vote in Colorado (1893) and Idaho (1896) by referendum vote. No further gains were made until the successful suffrage referenda in Washington (1910) and California (1911).

Such victories were the exceptions in half a century of disheartening defeats in state suffrage campaigns, unsuccessful annual congressional hearings on the Anthony Woman Suffrage Amendment (first introduced in 1870), and steadily mounting opposition to suffrage, which came largely from two sources: business concerns which feared women as a "reform" factor in politics, particularly the brewing and liquor interests; and the Southern delegation in Congress, which believed that granting woman suffrage would open the door to voting rights for the Negro.

In the first decade of the 20th century, suffrage received fresh impetus from the militant movement in Great Britain. Harriot Stanton Blatch (daughter of Elizabeth Cady Stanton) and Mrs. Carrie Chapman Catt began organizing at the political precinct level. In 1914 Alice Paul, who had spent a year working with Emmeline Pankhurst in England, founded the Congressional Union (later the Woman's Party), aimed at reviving interest in the suffrage amendment. A year later Mrs. Catt, replacing Dr. Anna Howard Shaw as head of the National Suffrage Association, galvanized it into fresh activity. Although women had the vote by then in eleven states west of the Mississippi, and the presidential ballot in Illinois (1913), the breakthrough did not come in the East until New York State, which had defeated a suffrage referendum in 1915, passed it in 1917. No real suffrage movement ever developed in the "deep South."

During the period when the country was in World War I, the large numbers of women in industry and war work helped to foster the public opinion needed to compel congressional action, and to strengthen President Wilson's support of the suffrage amendment. Suffragists continued to press for the vote: the Woman's Party picketed the White House and won wide publicity because many of its members were arrested and went on hunger strikes. The National Association's strategy, conceived by Mrs. Catt, combined pressure on Congress with state referendum campaigns, despite difficult wartime conditions.

The suffrage amendment passed the House of Representatives of the 65th Congress on Jan. 10, 1918, and was defeated in the Senate on Oct. 1. It was passed again by the House in the 66th Congress on May 20, 1919, and by the Senate on June 4 by exactly the needed two-thirds majority. Ratification required 14 months' additional campaigning; the 36th state was won only after a bitter battle in the lower house of the Tennessee legislature, which ratified by a majority of 1 on Aug. 18, 1920. (Kentucky and Texas were the only other Southern states to ratify.) The Nineteenth Amendment was proclaimed on Aug. 26th.

Women had won equality in principle on other fronts long before they won the vote. The higher education of women developed during the second half of the 19th century, following the pioneering efforts of Emma Willard, the founding of Mount Holyoke Seminary by Mary Lyon (1838), the opening of Vassar (1865) as the first institution which aimed at a collegiate level, followed by Smith and Wellesley (1875), the Society for the Collegiate Instruction of Women (1882) which became Radcliffe College (1893), Mills College (1885), and Bryn Mawr (1885). The Morrill Land Grant Act (1862) aided the growth of state institutions in the West and Middle West, which admitted women in increasing numbers.

Entry into some professions preceded the opening of colleges to women. The first woman to receive a medical degree was Elizabeth Blackwell, who graduated from Geneva College Medical School (1849). The first woman minister to be ordained was Antoinette Brown (1852). The first woman to be admitted to a state bar to practice law was Arabella Mansfield in Iowa in 1869.

Many women found a wider scope for their lives in clubs, beginning with Sorosis, which was founded by Jennie C. Croly in New York (1869), and the New England Woman's Club in Boston (1869). These organizations grew rapidly in number, and the General Federation of Women's Clubs was founded in 1890. Frances Willard, dynamic president of the Woman's Christian Temperance Union (1879–98), built up a powerful organization by linking together work for temperance and woman suffrage with a broad program of social activities.

Women workers first organized effectively for higher pay and better working conditions in the Lowell, Mass., textile mills, under the leadership of Sarah Bagley (1845–46). The first national labor unions to admit women to membership were the Cigar-makers (1867) and the Typographers (1869). Women in many trades attempted to organize independently, without lasting success, and developed such leaders as Augusta Lewis, who first organized women typographers in New York (1869), Kate Mullaney, who led striking collar and laundry workers in Troy, N. Y. (1868–69), and Leonora M. Barry, women's organizer in the Knights of Labor (1886–90). In 1892 the American Federation of Labor appointed Mary E. Kenney as an organizer for a few months. The lasting organization of women workers finally took place following the great strikes of 1910 and 1911 in the New York and Chicago shirtwaist and garment trades, and was materially aided by the work of the National Woman's Trade Union League, founded in 1903; women won improved conditions in the retail field through the support of the National Consumers League, founded in 1898. State legislation protecting hours and working conditions for women workers was first approved by the U. S. Supreme Court in Muller v. Oregon (1908).

The nature of American Negro women's efforts for equal rights was largely determined by their condition during 150 years of chattel slavery, and their special problems in the ante-bellum South, where they lacked opportunity for education and adequate legal safeguards for their personal dignity.

Negro women were active before the Civil War in the abolition movement, particularly the escaped slave Harriet Tubman, Sojourner Truth (who was freed by New York State law in 1827), and the poet and lecturer Frances E. W. Harper. Frederick Douglass, leading Negro abolitionist, bore witness to the fact that the anti-lynching protest movement of the 1890's was sparked by the journalist and lecturer Ida Wells-Barnett, who was also instrumental in founding a number of women's clubs to improve the position of colored women. Others who took part in this work, which led to the founding of the National Association of Colored Women (1896), were Hallie Q. Brown, Fannie Barrier Williams, Margaret M. (Mrs. Booker T.) Washington, Josephine St. Pierre Ruffin and Mary Church Terrell.

Since the passage of the Nineteenth Amendment in 1920, state by state legislation has abolished most legal discrimination against women; inequities remain in a few states with respect to jury service, guardianship of children, marriage and divorce. Unequal pay remains a source of economic inequality; only 18 states have equal pay laws, with varying degrees of coverage, whose enforcement leaves much to be desired. A proposed constitutional Equal Rights amendment would bar discrimination in any form; the measure has aroused opposition on the grounds that it would threaten safeguards won for women in industry by state laws, without giving them comparable effective protection. Women have made their way slowly in politics, beginning with the election of Jeannette Rankin of Montana to the House of Representatives (1916); Hattie W. Caraway of Arkansas was the first woman elected to the U. S. Senate (1932). Nellie W. Ross served as governor of Wyoming; Miriam A. Ferguson, as governor of Texas. The first woman appointed to the cabinet was Frances Perkins as Secretary of Labor (1932).

WOMEN IN THE MILITARY SERVICES. American women figured in the Revolutionary, Civil, and Spanish-American wars. They ran canteens and nursed the sick, and Molly Pitcher and Deborah Sampson actually took part in the fighting during the Revolution.

The admission of women as official members of the military services is, however, a phenomenon of the 20th century. Naturally enough, women were welcomed first as nurses. The Army Nurse Corps came into being in 1901, the Navy Nurse Corps in 1908. During World War I the Army which was authorized to enlist *men* employed several thousand civilian women. The Navy and Marine Corps interpreted their enabling act to enlist *persons* as authorizing the enlistment of some 11,000 yeomanettes and 305 marinettes.

Early in World War II the Congress realized that the man-power shortage made it urgent to draw on woman-power for military duty. The Women's Army Auxiliary Corps (WAAC) was authorized on May 14, 1942. On July 31, 1942, a bill was signed admitting women to the Naval Reserve. The Navy WAVES (Women Accepted for Volunteer Emergency Service) were pleased when, in 1943, the WAAC was authorized to drop its "auxiliary" title and became the WAC, a component part of the Army. This helped the public to believe that the 250,000 wartime volunteer women were not mere "auxiliaries," but were full-fledged members of the Army, Navy, Coast Guard and Marine Reserves. In World War II and since, the Marine Corps has avoided any official nickname for its women. The Coast Guard SPARS take their name from the initial letters of the motto, "Semper Paratus; Always Ready."

In 1947 the two nurses corps again led the way and together with a new organization, the Army Women's Medical Specialist Corps, became the first to be given permanent commissioned status. In 1948 the Women's Armed Services Integration Act clarified the status of women in all the services and today provides for both regular and reserve status. Shortly after the passage of the Integration Act, the Air Force which had formerly been a part of the Army, became a separate service and admitted women, designated as WAF, and established the Air Force Nurse Corps and Medical Specialist Corps.

The peacetime complement of women is small, providing a nucleus of experienced military personnel in case of future need for expansion. The military services continue to be essentially male organizations. Women are not permitted in combat or in combat planes or vessels and may not be assigned to "tasks beyond their strength." They are all volunteers and with few exceptions hold ranks no higher than lieutenant colonel or commander, with one woman in each component holding the rank of colonel or captain while she serves as the ranking woman officer in her component, the title differing from service to service. Career opportunities, retirement rights, pay and allowances are available for women as they are for men. Women in uniform perform a variety of functions, skilled and unskilled, and demonstrate that American women are capable of adapting themselves to the discipline of military life. Meanwhile, the military organizations have shown themselves capable of adapting their procedures so that women lose none of their womanliness as they assume military responsibility.

WORCESTER v. GEORGIA (6 Pet. 515). In this case the U. S. Supreme Court handed down a decision in 1832 in the controversy between Georgia and the Cherokee Indians, in which John Marshall held that the Cherokees were a nation under the protection of the United States and free from the jurisdiction of Georgia. The case arose over the arrest of Samuel A. Worcester and ten other missionaries for having violated a Georgia law forbidding white men to reside in the Cherokee country without first taking an oath of allegiance to the state and securing a permit. Sentenced to four years in the penitentiary, nine accepted a pardon, but Worcester and Elizur Butler appealed their case, which resulted in Marshall's decision. Georgia spurned an appearance in court and refused to obey the decision. President Jackson, who liked neither Marshall nor the Indians, allowed the decision to go unenforced.

WORLD WAR I (1914–1918). The assassination at Sarajevo on June 28, 1914, of the Austrian archduke Francis Ferdinand led in a few weeks to a conflict involving the Allies (England, France, Russia, Belgium, Serbia, Montenegro, and Japan) and the Central Powers (Germany, Austria-Hungary, and the Ottoman Empire). Americans felt the effects immediately: travelers abroad were repatriated with difficulty; stock markets crashed and exchanges closed; markets abroad were disrupted and business depression made the winter of 1914–15 one of hardship. Soon, however, war orders from the Allies, who controlled the seas, started a boom which lasted until after the Armistice.

Issuing a proclamation (Aug. 4, 1914) warning citizens to observe wartime regulations and abstain from participation in hostilities, Wilson later called for neutrality of spirit as well as act, but opinion rapidly took sides, stimulated by propaganda from all belligerents. Sentiment afforded the Allies better opportunity except in parts of the West. Sentiment worked with economic interest of those profiting by increased trade or having bought bonds floated by J. P. Morgan, who became purchasing agent for all the Allies.

Immediately diplomatic issues arose from neutral trade and from a blockade attempting to isolate Germany and her associates. American precedent from Civil War times made a basis for extension of continuous voyage doctrine through ultimate destination to ultimate consumption, thus affecting European neutrals as well as belligerents. The contestants were asked whether the Declaration of London (1909) would be observed, but while Germany, standing to gain, agreed if the others would, the Allies refused to be bound and gradually limited the free list until it was negligible. Complaints about seizures and diversions mounted, while interference with mails and establishment of a blacklist irritated, until in 1916 many feared a breach with England. But Wilson, believing a German victory would be calamitous, though authorizing vigorous protests, did not push the issue to a breaking point. In Congress an attempt to embargo munitions, favorable to the Central Powers, was blocked by Wilson who asserted a change of rules during the war would be unneutral.

Attention was diverted from neutral trade by Germany's submarine warfare (starting February, 1915) and, when the *Lusitania* was sunk (May 7) with loss of 124 Americans, Wilson so strongly demanded apology, reparation and promise to desist that Bryan resigned as Secretary of State and Lansing succeeded him. Bryan had contended Americans should be warned from belligerent merchantmen and that defensively armed vessels should be denied American ports, maintaining this was a practice, antagonistic to Germany, which would lead the United States into war. After the *Arabic* was sunk (August, 1915) Germany modified its policy and the issue was quiescent until revived by the *Sussex* case (March 24, 1916) when another series of notes brought a promise not to sink without warning.

Meantime submarine warfare raised the question of American preparation for possible war. Many agreed with Secretary of War Garrison in demanding increase of armed forces, but opposition was voiced by those who held the United States was not menaced and arming would incite to belligerency. In late 1915 Wilson swung to limited preparedness but not far enough for Garrison who resigned to be replaced by Baker. Preparedness had a prominent part in the presidential campaign of 1916 as did Wilson's policy toward the World War and toward Mexico. The narrow Democratic victory was attributed by many to belief Wilson had kept the United States out of war, as indeed he tried, for he sought opportunity to help to peace through mediation, utilizing Col. House who, however, never quite understood or sympathized with the President. In December, 1916, with contestants apparently deadlocked, Germany hinted at American mediation although making clear her ambitions in Central and Eastern Europe. Risking the charge of pro-Germanism, Wilson asked the belligerents to state their aims, which the Allies did somewhat more explicitly than Germany. This offered Wilson opportunity to state (Jan. 22, 1917) the position of America if drawn in: he proposed a negotiated peace guaranteed by world organization. Meantime German navalists had persuaded the Kaiser that France and England could be crushed by unrestricted submarine warfare before America could be effective, and announced through Ambassador Bernstorff, who opposed the step, intention to start the policy Feb. 1. Bernstorff was dismissed and Gerard recalled from Germany. Then was published (Feb. 24) the Zimmermann Note inviting alliance with Mexico, whence Pershing's expedition had just been withdrawn, and co-operation with Japan, holding out to them a prospect of securing American territory. Two days later Wilson asked power to arm American merchantmen, and, Congress failing to act, proceeded under an old law. Armed forces were increased. After reports of sinking American vessels Wilson called together the new Congress (April 2, 1917) to read his War Message and four days later signed the resolution declaring its existence. Strongly in support of the action was sentiment among Americans who had been keyed up by the war in general and especially by atrocity stories, submarine operations and real or suspected subversive acts by German agents in the United States.

Allied missions visited the United States to plan co-ordination of effort, secure credits and facilitate flow of war materials. Congress immediately started a legislative basis for participation. A Selective Service Act (May 10, 1917), inaugurating compulsory service, caused enrollment of 10,000,000 men of whom some 4,000,000 were drafted; the regular army was strengthened, the National Guard brought under stricter Federal control and a great navy program started. A token force under Pershing was sent to France (June 10) although it was not till a year later that significant numbers were abroad to help stop the German advance. Russia's defection through revolution, Italy's retreat, Rumania's collapse, and yielding of the Western Front made the situation so desperate that in December, 1917, Pershing, seconded by House who relayed the Allies' pleas, stated that without effective aid a German victory was imminent. Stimulated thus and by American impatience for action, men were rushed over until by July, 1918, a million had reached France; by the Armistice 2,000,000 were there and as many more preparing to follow. At first Americans were brigaded with French and British, but Pershing, backed by Wilson, insisted on a separate American army.

German determination to break the Western Front brought in 1918 four drives which were not stopped until after enormous gains, and Paris was threatened. After June increasing American aid helped stem the rout; it figured at Cantigny, Château-Thierry, Belleau Wood and elsewhere; it participated in a counter-drive (St. Mihiel, Argonne), and, with a second army, was ready to drive toward Metz in the spring, but the Armistice (Nov. 11) made this unnecessary. Some aid in Italy and participation in the North Russian expedition and in Siberia were among American activities. The Navy aided principally in convoys and patrolling sea lanes.

To keep the army in the field and support the Allies necessitated organization on the home front. A Council of National Defense (August, 1916) set up committees from which emerged the War Industries Board which, especially after the Overman Act (May 20, 1918), centralized control of production, apportioned materials with preference for war industries, advised on prices and, through its divisions, practically dominated key industries. Herbert Hoover as Food Administrator, especially after the Lever Act (August, 1917), by persuasion and without recourse to rationing, enormously stimulated food production. Fuel was under Harry A. Garfield. The transportation system by autumn, 1917, threatened to break down and McAdoo (Treasury) was put in charge of all railways and later of express companies. Telegraphs were co-ordinated under the Postmaster General. The U. S. Shipping Board, organized in 1916 to stimulate the merchant marine, created the Emergency Fleet Corporation which, after a period of dissension, by building, purchase, lease and by confiscation of German interned bottoms, built up a fleet of ten million tons by the end of the war, although the "cost-plus" system had encouraged waste and extravagance. The War Trade Board (October, 1917) co-operated with the Shipping Board to control commerce through licensing, while the Alien Property Custodian took over and turned to American use German properties and patents. Labor, being scarce, necessitated co-ordination provided by a National War Labor Board working under policies framed by a War Labor Policies Board.

Opinion was guided by the Committee on Public Information, while opposition to the war and its conduct, never very serious, was restricted by the Espionage (June 15, 1917) and Sedition (May 6, 1918) Acts which went farther than ever before in curtailing expression of opinion. State and local Committees of Public Safety, while often doing effective work, sometimes exceeded legitimate objects and left a memory of unjust repression in many communities. No formal censorship existed but its ends were achieved by pressure, while prosecution of objectors, sometimes sustained by the Supreme Court, brought a good many convictions for political crimes.

Some two thirds of war expenses, including loans to Allies, were met by bond issues widely oversubscribed; taxation was heavy and vexatious, but even at the time some, usually in silence, regretted that more emphasis had not been placed on taxation and less on borrowing. While there was in general less waste and corruption than in the Civil War there could not fail to be some; perhaps the greatest scandal rose from the failure of an ambitious airplane program where hundreds of millions were spent and almost no planes sent abroad.

In the winter of 1917–18 there was popular and congressional criticism of America's delay in getting an effective force into France, with Secretary Baker the principal target. In Congress there was agitation for an investigation, probably looking to a war cabinet, which Wilson interpreted as indicating lack of confidence. He demanded and obtained defeat of the proposition and then Congress bestowed upon him (Overman Act, May 30, 1918) almost unlimited power to reorganize, co-ordinate and centralize governmental functions. Thereafter there was little vocal objection to the conduct of the war, although when, before the congressional elections (November, 1918), Wilson appealed for return of a Democratic majority, he lost support and incurred opposition for what was interpreted as a reflection upon the loyalty of Republicans.

Throughout the war, as before America's entrance,

Wilson looked for openings leading to peace, but, as time went on, he envisaged a peace based upon complete defeat of the Central Empires. He emphasized drawing a distinction between the German people and their government which, he maintained, was based upon Prussian militarism. From time to time he defined his country's position and objectives and, on Jan. 8, 1918, enunciated his Fourteen Points as a basis upon which lasting peace, maintained by a League of Nations, might be established. A month later he discussed before Congress the replies of the Allies and the Central Powers, again laying blame upon German militarism. In August the Pope's offer of mediation was declined both by Allies and the United States. In September, with German armies in retreat and Austria-Hungary on the verge of collapse, the latter put out feelers for a conference, but Wilson said there could be no bargaining for peace. A suggestion from Germany brought questions whether the old military clique was still in power and whether Belgium and France would be evacuated. What seemed a favorable response was rejected by the President who seemed to be affected by the sweep of opinion in the United States that Germany must be completely defeated and humiliated; hence it was not until a new German government, after the Kaiser fled to The Netherlands, sued for an Armistice that firing stopped on Nov. 11, 1918.

(*See also* American Expeditionary Forces; Armistice of Nov. 11, 1918; Army of Occupation; *and* the following battles and campaigns: Aisne Defensive; Aisne-Marne Operation; Belleau Wood; Cantigny; Champagne-Marne Operation; Château-Thierry Bridge; Meuse-Argonne Offensive; Oise-Aisne Operation; St. Mihiel; Somme Offensive; Ypres-Lys Operation.)

The Navy in World War I. The United States Navy's notable contribution to Allied victory lay in services against submarines and in transporting troops and their supplies across the Atlantic Ocean. Allied defeat was imminent in the spring of 1917 because more than 850,000 tons of essential shipping was being sunk per month by German submarines. Reinforcements of American destroyers, yachts and gunboats made possible a system of convoys that cut shipping losses nearly two thirds by November, and thereafter held them at safe levels. Our overseas escorting vessels were based principally at Queenstown, Brest and Gibraltar, all forces in Europe being commanded by Vice-Admiral W. S. Sims with headquarters in London. Approximately 18,600 ships were escorted. Another major antisubmarine effort was a huge mine barrage across the North Sea from the Orkney Islands to Norway. Of a total of 70,263 mines, 56,611 were planted by ten large American mine-layers in thirteen expeditions. This project

under Admiral Joseph Strauss was not quite complete at the Armistice but had sunk possibly eight submarines besides damaging others, and its moral effect was great.

A method of hunting submarines by underwater sound detection devices was developed for use on destroyers and "sub-chasers," a special type of craft of only eighty-five tons displacement. Of the latter 120 crossed the Atlantic and served in northern waters or the Mediterranean, manned principally by Naval Reserves. A group of eleven under Commander Nelson screened British and Italian heavy ships during their bombardment of Durazzo on Oct. 2, 1918. Sound detection devices were installed on American submarines and seven of them sent to Europe under Capt. Hart. In four attacks on enemy submarines one was destroyed.

Naval aviation was also employed on an extensive scale in patrolling for and attacking submarines, in assisting convoys and in bombing submarine bases. At the Armistice overseas aviation personnel had expanded to 16,000 and equipment to 500 planes, 3 dirigibles and 50 kite balloons. Twenty-two thousand war-flights had been made from 27 operating bases covering 1,000,000 miles.

The British Grand Fleet, reinforced by a squadron of American battleships under Admiral Hugh Rodman, gave general protection to antisubmarine and convoy operations against possible attack by the German main fleet. Toward the war's end the Germans sent six submarines successively to the American coast as a diversion. They laid mines and attacked single ships and were combatted by "sub-chasers," destroyers and airplanes while our convoys sailed uninterruptedly.

The foregoing antisubmarine measures saved enough merchant shipping, which, together with new construction, made possible the transatlantic transport of nearly 2,000,000 American troops and their supplies—in addition to meeting Allied demands. Despite great obstacles the Transport Force under Admiral Albert Gleaves grew to nearly 50 troopships, and 450 supply ships were also organized under the Navy. By midsummer of 1918, 300,000 troops were being transported per month. The margin of American troops prevented imminent defeat in early 1918 and brought unexpected victory by November. American naval vessels transported 911,000 troops and escorted many more moving in foreign ships. The *Leviathan* alone carried 96,804 soldiers to France. The principal debarkation port at Brest was under Admiral H. B. Wilson who also directed special destroyer escorts for troop convoys. A few transports were torpedoed while homeward bound and nearly empty and the troop losses at sea were inconsiderable. About 30,000 Marines reinforced the Army in combat operations in France and a Naval Railway Battery of five 14-in. long-range guns also saw action ashore.

Economic Mobilization. The vast armies placed in the field by the various belligerents from 1914–18 made new methods for supply and maintenance necessary. When the vision of a short war faded at the Marne in 1914, preparations had to be made for a war of attrition. This called for the mobilization of economic resources as well as man power. Germany was the first country to realize the importance of an economic mobilization for war. Early in the war Dr. Walter Rathenau foresaw the pressure of the Allied blockade and urged the creation of a section in the War Ministry to control the supply of raw materials (*Kriegsrohstoffabteilung*). By November, 1916, the *Kriegsamt* had virtual control of the entire economic resources of Germany. In England and France the progress toward this goal was slower and took the form of a munitions ministry.

In the United States some progress was made toward the mobilization of industry prior to 1917, but, with the system of free enterprise firmly entrenched, little could be done in the direction of economic mobilization until the war emergency called for extreme measures. The Committee of National Defense established in 1916 was charged with providing economic and industrial preparations for defense. Steps were taken in 1917 for this committee to act with the various industries through one man, but the Committee of National Defense lacked authority to compel adherence to its decisions. When Congress declared war in April, 1917, it pledged the entire resources of the United States to its prosecution, but no effective attempt was made to mobilize all the economic resources of the nation until March 4, 1918, when the War Industries Board was given wide powers by executive order of the President.

Once fortified with power, the various committees of the War Industries Board carried out an economic mobilization unprecedented in American history. The ancient rights of free enterprise were annulled and all resources and manufacturing facilities came under the orders of this agency. The immense work of this board was divided between many subcommittees. A requirements division attempted to reconcile the needs of the military services with the available material and facilities. When additional manufacturing facilities were required, this agency planned their construction with a view to labor, transportation and other considerations. This tended to reduce the dangerous congestion of manufacturing establishments in the New England area, which had caused a virtual breakdown of transportation in the winter of 1917–18. A conservation committee reduced waste in materials and nonessential services. Prices were fixed by one committee and the distribution of each important commodity was entrusted to a committee made up of members of the Board and members of the trade.

The result of these changes was "a systematic scheduling of production in practically all industrial plants in the United States in accord and synchronization with the war program." Within a few months America achieved a mobilization of resources and industry. The mobilized industry of America was described by Bernard Baruch as a "weapon of offense or defense more potent than anything the world has ever seen, more terrible, I think, than the mind of any man has ever imagined." So carefully was the distribution of all commodities supervised that it was impossible to purchase a ton of steel in the United States after March, 1918, without the approval of the War Industries Board. The wartime experience of the United States in the realm of economic mobilization was later incorporated in the Revised Industrial Mobilization Plan of 1933.

Financing. After entering World War I, the United States Government decided to finance its participation by borrowing approximately two thirds of the required amount and by raising the remaining third through taxation. Three methods of borrowing were employed. Through the use of certificates of indebtedness, the Treasury borrowed for short periods from the Federal Reserve banks, retiring the certificates as income was received. A more permanent form of borrowing was through the sales of Liberty Bonds. To reach those of small means, war-savings certificates were issued. These held twenty war-savings stamps, each of which had a maturity value of $5.00. Thrift stamps were also sold for 25 cents. Sixteen of these could be exchanged for a war-savings stamp.

To provide the needed taxes, Congress enacted special revenue laws on Oct. 3, 1917, and Feb. 24, 1919. These acts greatly increased the income-tax rates, imposed war excess profits taxes, and provided for many other special taxes. From April 6, 1917, to June 30, 1919, a total of $9,384,278,708 was received from taxes. This amount, together with $21,-432,918,450 received from five bond issues and $1,116,076,438 realized from the sale of war saving certificates and thrift stamps, made up the war revenues of the United States.

Propaganda and Undercover Activities. The outbreak of World War I in August, 1914, was followed by an intense competition between the Allies and the Central Powers for the support of American public opinion. Allied propaganda was facilitated by pre-existing linguistic, cultural and financial ties with the United States, by Allied control over European news services and cables, and by the mistakes and difficulties of the Central Powers. In September, 1914, the British established a propaganda bureau at Wellington House, 8 Buckingham Gate, London, under the direction of Charles F. G. Masterman. Sir Gilbert Parker, in charge of one of its divisions, undertook to mold public opinion in the United States. This division made weekly reports to the British cabinet on the state of American public opinion, kept in close touch with American newspaper correspondents and assisted them in arranging interviews with prominent Englishmen, supplied 360 American newspapers with a weekly news service, and inspired the preparation of vast quantities of books, pamphlets, articles and motion pictures for distribution in the United States. In 1917 Wellington House as a propaganda center was supplanted by a Department of Information under the direction of John Buchan, assisted by an Advisory Committee headed by Lord Northcliffe. In June, 1917, Lord Northcliffe brought a special mission to the United States which resulted in the establishment of the British Bureau of Information in New York City. A further reorganization of British propaganda took place in February, 1918, with the creation of a Ministry of Propaganda under Lord Beaverbrook.

The principal agents of German propaganda in the United States were diplomatic and consular officials, notably Ambassador J. H. von Bernstorff and Capt. Franz von Papen; representatives of German banks and shipping companies; German-American associations and societies such as the National German-American Alliance under the presidency of Dr. J. C. Hexamer; as well as numerous sympathizers in the academic and journalistic fields. An important center of German propaganda in the United States was the office of Dr. Bernhard Dernburg in New York City, under whose direction a press bureau was established and a weekly periodical, *The Fatherland*, devoted to the idea of fair play for Germany and Austria-Hungary. The propaganda activities of the Central Powers were less skillfully executed than those of the Allies and ultimately culminated in exposures that led to the imprisonment or expulsion from the United States of some of their agents.

On April 14, 1917, subsequent to the entry of the United States into the war, the President by executive order established a Committee on Public Information composed of the Secretaries of State, War and Navy with George Creel as chairman. This famous Creel Committee, under the vigorous leadership of its chairman, soon became a mammoth propaganda agency enlisting the services of more than 150,000 persons. From the time of its creation until its disestablishment on June 30, 1919, it operated at a cost of $4,912,553. As it finally took shape the Committee comprised two main sections, domestic and foreign. The domestic section, with fifteen divisions, supervised the dissemination of governmental news; issued an official daily newspaper; assembled the artists of America for the production of posters; mobilized the advertising forces of the country; planned various types of war exhibits; organized and directed societies and leagues of foreign language groups; created a nation-wide network of speakers' bureaus; distributed motion pictures; gathered together leading novelists, essayists and publicists;

arranged special kinds of propaganda activities designed to appeal to the women of the country; and interpreted war aims to the public through pamphlets and books prepared by outstanding scholars. One of the most extraordinary activities of the domestic section was the creation of an organization of Four-Minute Men which commanded the volunteer services of 75,000 speakers operating in 5200 communities.

The foreign section, with three divisions, operated a world-wide news service, a foreign mail press service, and distributed propaganda films throughout the world. It had offices in practically every neutral and Allied country.

The work of the Creel Committee, and for that matter the effectiveness of Allied propaganda generally, was greatly enhanced by the speeches and writings of President Wilson, such as his address to Congress on April 2, 1917; the Flag Day address of June 14, 1917; the message to Congress on Dec. 4, 1917; the Fourteen Points speech on Jan. 8, 1918; and the speeches on Feb. 11, April 6, and July 4, 1918. They proved to be unparalleled weapons for propaganda purposes. It was only necessary for the Creel Committee to translate and publicize Wilsonian principles and statements into popular terms.

World War I propaganda greatly affected the subsequent history of propaganda. It gave the word a more invidious connotation. It stimulated the rise of state propaganda machines and influenced the propaganda techniques of unofficial economic, political and social groups. The growing interest in the study and analysis of public opinion and propaganda is traceable in large part to propaganda activities during World War I.

Peace Conference (1919). In May, 1917, preliminary steps preceded a request by President Wilson to Col. House (September, 1917) which produced the Inquiry, an organization of nongovernmental experts under Sidney E. Mezes which explored ethnic, historical, economic and other phases of issues opened by the war. Neither Inquiry nor State Department, not always working together harmoniously, planned procedure, as had the British, or had a program, hence Americans were hampered during the negotiations. Furnished with results of the investigation and accompanied by the experts, the American delegation (Wilson, House, Lansing, Bliss and White) reached France Dec. 13, 1918. Delays, partly due to British, French and Italian desire to counteract Wilson's personal popularity and to disparage his Fourteen Points, prevented the Conference's formal meeting till Jan. 18, 1919, although already the Supreme War Council (Wilson, Lansing and Allied premiers) had roughly outlined procedure. The Council of Five (Supreme War Council and Japan) was instituted (Jan. 19) with the understanding that other Allied belligerents should be consulted on issues affecting them and neutrals might be called in. The Council of Ten (executive heads plus foreign ministers) was an inner cabinet which made final decisions until March when the Council of Four (Wilson, Clemenceau, Lloyd George and Orlando) functioned alone.

Closest to Wilson's heart was a proposed League of Nations, approved in principle by the second plenary Conference (Jan. 25), and he was made chairman of the Commission to formulate its constitution. The next day Clemenceau, president of the Conference, appointed committees to work on such things as reparations, responsibility, waterways, labor legislation and other questions before the Conference. Each committee with its experts worked almost exclusively on its own problem so that nowhere, except belatedly in the Council of Four, were the cumulative effects of the treaty realized.

The League Commission completed its draft of the Covenant which Wilson presented to the Conference Feb. 14, the day he left Paris for the United States. In his absence Allied delegates, especially the French, regretted their tentative approval, and in the United States Wilson found a disposition to question the project. This, on his return, brought reopening of the subject and modifications including a safeguard of the Monroe Doctrine. Before leaving Paris, Wilson had been asked by the Yugoslavs to mediate the Adriatic question, but the Italians refused his services. In March, after his return, the Italians threatened to leave the Conference unless they got Fiume, and on April 28, after Wilson's conference with them and his appeal to the Italian people, they returned to Rome where they were upheld by their Parliament and people. It was at this time that Wilson himself threatened to leave Paris on account of the intransigeant attitude of French and Italians.

On May 7, the Italians having returned, a treaty was ready to present to German delegates who (May 29) protested terms which stripped them of much territory including colonies, disarmed them, obligated them to indefinite reparations and provided sanctions until compliance. Earlier there was an intention of the Allies, following customary procedure, to draft demands and then work out a treaty with German delegates. Fear that their own ranks might split, impatience of their peoples spurred by a press kept in the dark, and a desire not to rework the treaty made it a unilateral affair. German protests, emphasizing the Fourteen Points, were generally unavailing and the Treaty of Versailles was signed June 28. Americans and their associates knew it was imperfect and harsh, but Wilson, having seen his Fourteen Points emasculated or ignored, counted on the League to rectify injustices.

American Relief in Europe extended from 1914 through 1923, but several agencies continued special projects after 1923. During the war, relief was mainly in Allied countries by organizations for aid to the wounded, refugees, children, war widows, etc., and this work continued during reconstruction. But, except for the Commission for Relief in Belgium, the period of mass relief was after the Armistice when government finance, cash sales, and benevolence poured millions of tons of supplies into Central and Eastern Europe where 200,000,000 people were in need. This pacific American intervention contributed greatly to the rehabilitation of Europe and particularly to the establishment of the new states formed by the peace treaties. "Benevolence," through the American Relief Administration alone, amounted to $134,000,000 after the Armistice, and total supplies to over $1,000,000,000. About $6,000,000,000 worth of American food and other supplies were sent to Europe, 1914–23. United States Government subsidies and loans for supplies were $624,000,000 during the Armistice, and $81,000,000 in reconstruction and the Russian famine.

The American Relief Administration was created early in 1919 to administer a congressional appropriation of $100,000,000 for European relief, to be partially repaid by the countries aided. Herbert Hoover, U. S. Food Administrator, went to Europe in November, 1918, to study the need and initiate relief, and was soon appointed Director-General of Relief for the Allies under the Supreme Economic Council. He formed and directed the A. R. A., to carry out the American share of the program. The needs were so appalling that financing by all governments was necessary, but 80% of the supplies came from the United States and were distributed by the A. R. A., Allied commissions, foreign governments and private agencies. The A. R. A. used the machinery for purchase and transport created by the Food Administration but formed local committees for distribution, with final control in American hands, and encouraged both governments and citizens to donate services. In all, over 4,000,000 metric tons were sent to 21 countries. The original United States appropriation excluded enemy countries, but their condition was such that special finance was immediately found (Joint Allied Finance, United States loans to Allies, cash payments by enemy States, etc.) and after the Allied blockade was relaxed, from February through July, 1919, $282,000,000 worth of supplies went to Germany and $98,000,000 to Austria. The A. R. A. instituted child-feeding; transported or allocated food for private agencies; and transmitted $6,000,000 in cash from individuals or groups in the United States to persons in Europe. At liquidation of the Armistice program on June 30, 1919, the A. R. A. had delivered 1,728,000 metric tons of supplies at an operating cost of 53/100 of one per cent of sales value, and returned $84,000,000 of the congressional appropriation to the U. S. Treasury in foreign government obligations.

Thereafter, the A. R. A. operated as a private agency, though it administered three other congressional appropriations: one (1920) for sale of flour on credit, and two (1921–22) for famine and medical relief in Russia. It co-operated closely with other agencies and, 1920–21, with eight others (European Relief Council) raised $29,000,000 in the United States for children's relief. It fed some 8,000,000 children, entered refugee work, the control of epidemics, relief to special groups, and delivered $22,-000,000 worth of food purchased in America for persons or groups in Europe. In 1921 it made an agreement with the Soviet government for famine relief, under which most of the American agencies worked, and at the peak of this relief, 1921–23, fed some 10,000,000 Russians, delivered large shipments of seed grain, food packages and bulk sales, and operated a medical unit which inoculated 8,000,000 persons in epidemics and delivered $3,000,000 worth of Red Cross supplies to 14,000 Russian hospitals and institutions.

The American Red Cross spent overseas 56 cents on each dollar collected, 1914–19, and some $200,-000,000 altogether in Europe, 1914–23. Its greatest work was naturally medical relief, health service and control of postwar epidemics, but it also engaged in child-care and refugee work, allocated funds or supplies (clothing or medical) to other agencies, and had units in 24 countries in 1919. It worked in Russia and Siberia, 1917–18, and in the famine of 1921–23 it contributed the $3,000,000 worth of medical and hospital supplies mentioned above.

The American Friends Service Committee (Quakers) was organized on our entry into the war, but American Quakers had previously worked with British Quakers in war relief. They sent small units wherever the need was greatest and were among the first to reach enemy territories. The American Friends' greatest achievement was child-feeding in Germany, 1919–22, where they distributed $9,000,-000 worth of relief, about $6,000,000 allocated by the A. R. A. or European Relief Council. The Friends raised over $1,000,000 from German-Americans, and when they withdrew, 1922, helped to provide another $4,000,000 for child-feeding by Germans through 1924. They were also active in Poland, Austria, Serbia, Yugoslavia and Russia.

The Jewish Joint Distribution Committee was formed, November, 1919, to distribute relief funds for American Jewish societies, and at the end of 1926 had spent $69,000,000 abroad. They distributed through other organizations until 1920, and worked closely with the A. R. A. through 1923, sending a vast number of food packages and bulk sales to Poland, Austria and Russia. In 1920 the Jewish Distribution Committee began its own medical work and reconstruction, and in 1921, refugee and child-care, repatriation, and cultural work in twelve European countries besides Palestine, continuing much of this after 1923.

Near East Relief derived from a committee organized, 1919, by Henry Morgenthau, United States Ambassador to Turkey, for Armenian-Syrian relief, and distributed most of the American relief in Near East countries. The A. R. A., Red Cross and others made large allotments to Near East Relief, which, 1919–23, distributed some $28,000,000 in supplies—$16,000,000 from government credits and the rest from benevolence. It did refugee and resettlement work, child-care and child-placing, especially of orphans, and continued after 1923, raising funds by its own American campaigns.

Other organizations, notably Young Men's Christian Association and Young Women's Christian Association, gave large amounts of relief to all European countries, often for special groups, such as students or the intelligentsia. The Federal Council of Churches, Knights of Columbus, and National Catholic Welfare Council were members of the European Relief Council, and three foundations—Rockefeller Foundation, Laura Spelman Rockefeller Memorial, and Commonwealth Fund—made large gifts to the A. R. A. and other agencies for children's relief or special purposes.

WORLD WAR II. By 1939, the international situation had become so delicate that isolationism was no longer a creed, except to a small segment who were pacifists or "America First" advocates. Militarist-dominated Japan was by then clearly embarked on the conquest and domination of eastern Asia. Hitler in Central Europe was recognized as a danger to us, as well as to his neighbors and to humanity at large. The invasion of Poland was the handwriting on the wall.

Background to Pearl Harbor

After her defeat and disarmament in World War I, Germany eventually fell into the hands of extreme nationalists. The National Socialists rearmed the nation, re-entered the Rhineland, forced a union with Austria, seized Czechoslovakia with false promises, made a nonaggression pact with Russia to protect her eastern frontier, and then overran Poland in 1939, bringing France and Great Britain into war against her in consequence of their pledge to maintain Polish independence. In May, 1940, a power thrust swept German troops forward through France, drove British forces across the Channel, and compelled France to surrender. An attack on England, aimed to deny use of Britain as a "springboard" for reconquest of the Continent, failed in the air and did not materialize on land. Open breach of the nonaggression treaty was followed by a German invasion of Russia in June, 1941.

Meanwhile, Japan had been fortifying Pacific islands in secret violation of 1921 treaties, encroaching on China in Manchuria and Tientsin in 1931 and in Shanghai in 1932, starting open war at Peking in

1937, and thereafter, as Germany's ally, planning further conquests.

The United States opposed this Japanese expansion diplomatically by every means short of war, and military staff planning began as early as 1938 to think of a two-ocean war as bound to come, and to calculate that the issues in the Orient would have to be largely decided in Europe. It would be our safest course in the long run, it was felt, to maintain the integrity of the Western Hemisphere by preventing the defeat of the British Commonwealth. Ever since the Russo-Japanese War of 1905, our army had been convinced that we could not hold Manila. We had agreed in 1921 not to fortify further there or on Guam. It was felt that our eventual western defense line must run from Alaska through Hawaii to Panama.

Rearmament started at home, developing and producing new weapons and new planes, and speeding up motorization of our land forces. A Uranium Committee was created in 1939, a National Defense Research Committee in 1940, and the Office of Scientific Research and Development in 1941 to develop radar and antisubmarine devices. Formation of a Council of National Defense to co-ordinate industry, finance, transportation and labor in the event of open war, showed a high level realization of the seriousness of impending events. Prior to our formal entry into war, we assisted France and Britain by shipping tanks and weapons, and furnishing much material to help equip the British Home Guard. We turned over naval destroyers to Britain to hold down the submarine menace. We ourselves patrolled large areas of the Atlantic against the German U-boats, and our ships were involved in prewar shooting incidents with them. We took over rights and responsibilities at defense bases on British possessions bordering the Atlantic.

In 1940 our course was mapped by rapidly passing events. The April and May invasions of Norway, Denmark, Holland, Belgium, Luxembourg and France triggered our actions. In his Chicago speech of 1937, President Roosevelt had promised to quarantine aggressors. In his Charlottesville speech on June 10, 1940, he went further. He not only indicted Germany's new partner Italy, but also issued a public promise of help to "the opponents of force." In June also, he assured himself of bipartisan political support by appointing the Republicans Knox and Stimson to head the Navy and War Departments. Military expansion began in earnest.

The Selective Service and Training Act of Sept. 16, 1940, instituted peacetime conscription for the first time in our history, registering 16,000,000 men in a month. Also—following Woodrow Wilson's technique of 1916—it brought the National Guard into active Federal service to harden and weed and ready it for combat. In July, 1940, an Export Embargo Act was passed, which was to be used as a war measure,

followed by the Lend Lease Act of March, 1941, to help our prospective allies and others in need of aid. Our military leaders strongly preferred to avoid a war with Japan, believing that we were not ready for it. In November, 1940, Admiral Stark and General Marshall jointly declared that our major course of action for the time being would therefore be: (a) to rearm, (b) to avoid provoking attack, and (c) to restrict Pacific actions so as to permit major offensive action in the Atlantic theater, should war actually come. In January, 1941, in view of possible future developments, there were Anglo-American staff conferences in Washington. In August, 1941, President Roosevelt and Prime Minister Churchill met at Argentia, Newfoundland, and formulated war aims, and with their staffs delved into over-all strategy and war planning. For the first time in our history we were for all practical purposes militarily allied before war came. At this meeting was established the Atlantic Charter and what we know as the Four Freedoms declaration. In September, 1941, with the signs clear as to the future, the draft act was extended beyond its previous limit of one year, even though by the slim margin of a single vote in Congress, and the full training, reorganization, and augmentation of our forces began.

Organization, Preparation, and Strategy

On Dec. 7, 1941, a sneak attack by Japanese carrier-based planes surprised and severely crippled our fleet at Pearl Harbor, dooming our forces in the Philippines. Japan was now free to expand into Southeast Asia and the East Indies toward Australia. The very next day Congress declared war on Japan and on Dec. 11 met declarations from Italy and Germany—allied to Japan by treaties—by similar declarations put through in a single day of legislative action in committees and on the floor of both houses of Congress. There was no choice. We had been attacked by one power and had had war declared on us by two other powers.

Before the month of December was out, Winston Churchill was again in Washington, bringing with him military and naval experts for what has been called the Arcadia conference, and within weeks there was created in Washington the Combined Chiefs of Staff, an international military, naval, and air body which was used throughout the war to (a) settle strategy, (b) establish unified interallied command in the separate theaters of war, and (c) issue strategic instructions to theater commanders. Allied to it were a Munitions Assignment Board to allocate materials to the different theaters, and also a Combined Raw Materials Board and a Combined Shipping Assignment Board, neither of which however played an extremely important role.

Almost instantly upon the declaration of war, under the first War Powers Act there began reorganization and expansion of the Army and the Navy, including the National Guard already in Federal service. Increasing numbers of reservists were called to active duty, not as units but as individuals, to fill gaps in existing units, to officer the training centers, and to officer new units being formed. Additional divisions were created and put into training, bearing the numbers of World War I divisions in most cases, but with scarcely any relation to them in locality or to previously existing reserve divisions in personnel. Field artillery regiments were broken up, and greater flexibility was achieved with separate battalions. Cavalry units were transformed into armored forces. Antiaircraft units were improved and greatly increased in number, later to be armed with the new proximity fuse for their projectiles. New types of troops were formed: mountain units, armored divisions, airborne divisions. The old square infantry divisions were altered to the new triangular division pattern for greater mobility and increased fire power. New activities were created for psychological warfare, and for civil affairs and military government in territories to be liberated or captured. The Air Force also underwent a great expansion, in personnel, in units, and in planes. Some units were assigned to coastal defense on the Atlantic and Pacific Coasts, the latter then actually vulnerable to invasion. Others were sent to overseas stations. Notable was the creation and shipment to England of high level, precision daylight bombing units, which worked with the British to rain tons of bombs on enemy centers. Later they assisted the invasions and major attacks. Increasingly by their bombing they disrupted German factories and rail lines and, weakening the entire economy of Germany, were extremely important in forcing Hitler to his fall. Lighter units of fighter bombers were trained to work closely with our front line ground forces on critical occasions. The armed forces of the United States, in general, expanded their strength and put to use a host of details in tactics and in equipment which had been merely experimental in the long stretch of economy years preceding. From new planes to new rifles, from motorization to emergency rations, from field radio telephones to long-reaching radar, progress was widespread.

The War Department was completely reorganized in March, 1942. Combat branch chiefs were abolished and new broader agencies took over—the Air Forces, the Ground Forces, and the Services of Supply. A new and important Operations Division was created for strategic planning. The Air Forces were separated from the Army for all practical purposes, and were represented co-equally with the Army and Navy in staff meetings.

To previous American concepts of war, not only had there been added new concepts of operation and new and improved mechanized materiel; there had also been added a reasoned and complete concept of an all-out popular effort, a greater national unity and a greater systematization of production, and especially more intense emphasis on technology. The efforts of World War I were far surpassed. Our effort would truly be, as Churchill predicted after the Dunkirk defeat, "the new world with all its power and might" stepping forth to "the rescue and liberation of the old." Quickly there came from Congress the First War Powers Act of Dec. 18, 1941, and the Second War Powers Act of March 27, 1942. There came Emergency Price Control, with its Office of Price Administration, and the Office of Economic Stabilization, the War Production Board, the War Labor Board, and the Office of War Information. In many fields volunteer civilian assistants administered to the people the local details of contact and control. Critical items of food, coffee, sugar, meat, butter and canned goods were rationed for civilians, and heating fuels and gasoline, too. Rent control was established. Two thirds of the planes of civilian air lines were taken over by the Air Force. Travel was subject to priorities for war purposes. There was also voluntary censorship of newspapers, under only general guidance from Washington.

There was special development and production of escort vessels for the Navy, of landing craft, small and large, for beach invasions, of planes for the Air Force on a program so huge that the public gasped when the figures were announced, of high octane gasoline, and of synthetic rubber. It was recognized and accepted that, as Secretary Stimson said, "in wartime the demands of the Army enter into every aspect of national life." Local draft boards had been given great leeway in drawing up their own standards of exemption and deferment from service and at first had favored agriculture over industry; but soon controls were established according to national needs. By 1945 we had engaged more than 16,000,000 men under arms, and still improved our economy. Production was needed to save the war, and indeed production would very nearly win the war, with its pipelines of supply flowing to the fronts a great mass of material which our enemies could not match. At one time, it has been calculated, it took half the total resources of the nation in materials and labor to support our forces and to help our allies. It was a war of "power and might," as Churchill had predicted.

Vitally important was the successful development of new air and sea methods of protecting the delivery of troops and munitions across the distant Pacific and especially across the submarine-infested Atlantic to beleaguered Britain. German submarines were active against all transocean shipping, and also along the eastern coast of the United States against oil shipments from the Caribbean and the Gulf of Mexico to our Atlantic coastal ports. The challenge was severe, but it was met by inventiveness as well as by determination and organization, by air and sea action against enemy underwater craft, and by the construction of two great pipelines to bring oil from Texan fields to the eastern seaboard by an overland route.

The grand strategy, from the beginning, was to defeat Germany while containing Japan, a strategy maintained and followed by the Combined Chiefs of Staff, closely co-ordinated with the thinking of President Roosevelt and Prime Minister Churchill— except on one occasion when in the early summer of 1942 Admiral King and General Marshall met the news that there would be no attempt to create a beachhead in Europe that year by suggesting a shift of our power to the Pacific, and President Roosevelt promptly overruled them.

Campaign in the Pacific: 1941 – Spring, 1945

Almost immediately after the strike at Pearl Harbor, the Japanese invaded the Philippines and overran our garrisons on Guam and Wake in late December. They soon captured Manila, then conquered our forces on the Bataan peninsula by April 8, 1942, and our last stronghold on Corregidor on May 6. Japan then feinted into the North Pacific, easily seizing Attu and Kiska in the Aleutian Islands in June, 1942. She continued to attract our attention and some troops toward Alaska until her forces were withdrawn in March, 1943.

Gen. Douglas MacArthur had been pulled out of the Philippines before the fall of Corregidor and sent to Australia to assume responsibility for protecting that continent against Japanese invasion, increasingly imminent since Singapore and Java had been taken. Limited numbers of troops were sent to him, because in this area there was to be only a containing effort and these troops had to come to him and be supplied over a long sea route protected only by the occupation of some intervening islands in the Pacific. With great skill, Gen. MacArthur used American and Australian forces to check Japanese inroads in New Guinea at Port Moresby, and land and sea forces to push the Japanese back from spot to spot to take Buna and Sananda, although not until January, 1943. To block a hostile thrust against his communications through New Zealand back home, Marine and Infantry divisions were thrown into the Solomon Islands, where Guadalcanal was ours by February, 1943, after bitter touch-and-go land, sea, and air fighting. The push north continued to Bougainville in November, 1943, and Green Islands in February, 1944, leaving many hostile stations in the Solomons cut off from supply and destined to futility. Unwilling to perform merely containing operations, Gen. MacArthur then used air and sea power to leapfrog his ground units along the northern coast of New Guinea and west to Morotai by September, 1944, employing to the full the new capabilities of modern planes, and using amphibious assaults to capture Japanese airfields. In his forward movements he got excellent aid from the Australian airmen to cover

his open left flank, to neutralize bypassed Japanese forces, and to assist in supporting landings on Tarakan and Borneo.

Previously and almost concurrently, the Navy with Marine and Army troops was attacking selected Japanese bases in the Pacific, moving steadily westward and successfully hitting the Marshall Islands at Eniwetok and Kwajalein, the Gilberts at Makin and Tarawa, and—turning north—the Marianas at Guam and Saipan in June and July, 1944, largely bypassing Truk and the Carolines and leaving them and many other individual spots to be mopped up at leisure. To assist the Army's move on the Philippines, the Navy and Marines also struck westward at the Palau Islands in September, 1944, and had them in hand within a month. Our control of the approaches to the Philippines was now assured. In the Coral Sea and also in the open spaces near Midway, in May and June, 1942, respectively, the U. S. Navy had severely crippled the Japanese fleet. Air and submarine strikes closer in had had a serious weakening effect. It was the result of these efforts, equally with the Army advance in the New Guinea area, that enabled Gen. MacArthur's forces, supported by Adm. Halsey and the Third Fleet, in October, 1944, to return to the Philippines on the island of Leyte. Their initial success was endangered by a final, major Japanese naval effort there near Leyte, which was countered by a naval thrust of our own which wiped much of the Japanese fleet from the waves. Army progress through the Philippines was thereafter steady. Manila and Corregidor were again ours in February, 1945. Mindanao was cleared in March.

Our land and sea forces were now in position to drive north directly toward Japan itself. Marines had landed on Iwo Jima on Feb. 19 and invaded Okinawa on April 1, both within good flying distance of the main enemy islands. The Japanese navy and air force were so depleted that in July, 1945, our fleet was steaming off the coast of Japan and bombarding almost with impunity. Between July 10 and Aug. 15, 1945, forces under Admiral Halsey destroyed or damaged 2084 enemy planes, sank or damaged 148 Japanese combat ships, and sank or damaged 1598 merchant vessels, in addition to administering heavy blows at industrial targets and war industries.

Until the island hopping brought swift successes in 1944, it had been expected that we would need the China mainland as a base for an attack on Japan. Japanese southward moves had dug into Burma and imperiled India. Gen. Stilwell had been sent out there (a) to command American forces in China, (b) to serve Chiang Kai-Shek as chief of staff, and (c) anomalously, to serve under the British commander of the Burma-India theater of operations. Efforts to reinforce the Chinese against the Japanese on the Asia mainland had not been fully successful. Cargo planes had tried to fly sufficient supplies over "the Hump" from India and Burma. An attempt was made to build a road from Lashio in Burma over the mountains to Kunming and Chungking, but Japanese thrusts forced Gen. Stilwell out of China and Burma in disastrous retreat. Nevertheless, the sea and land successes of Gen. MacArthur and the Navy admirals Nimitz, Halsey and Mitscher had brought us to positions where in the spring of 1945 it was possible to think of an actual invasion of Japan without using China as a base at all. This situation had been achieved as a result of some factors that made for greater and swifter successes than had been planned for this "containing" operation in the Pacific. These factors were: (a) the new naval technique of employing the fleet as a set of floating air bases, as well as for holding the sea lanes open, (b) the augmentation and improvement of our submarine service to a point where it was fatal to Japanese shipping, sinking more than 200 enemy combat vessels and more than 1100 merchant ships and thus seriously disrupting the desperately needed supply of Japanese troops on the many islands, and (c) Gen. MacArthur's "leap-frogging" tactics, letting many advanced Japanese bases simply "die on the vine." Not to be overlooked was MacArthur's own energy and persuasive skill. He got more troops than had been originally calculated to be furnished him, and he and the Navy got by 1944 as many beach landing craft as were assigned to all Europe, so that the British had complained that the operations in the Pacific were too expansively progressive for the broad strategic plan that had been established. Not to be overlooked, either, was the monumental performance of the Air Force, bombing ahead of the Army from spot to spot, smashing enemy airplanes and airfields, and crippling Japanese supply lines.

These results had been accomplished while our major national effort had been diverted toward Europe, and with limited materials. They had demonstrated great skill in the co-ordination of air power with land and sea power, and the weight of even a restricted part of our production. The Japanese had foolishly challenged the man power and the industrial power, the skill and fighting spirit of the United States, and had been driven along the road to defeat by only that portion of our resources which we could spare for the Pacific area. And this had happened in spite of the initial, serious and dangerous crippling of our naval concentration at Pearl Harbor. We were simply too strong to be beaten, even though we were at the same time fighting another war across the Atlantic.

Campaigns in Africa and Italy: 1942 – Spring, 1945

In Europe, our first participation was to furnish materials to Britain, and air bombardment units, and a small but steadily growing number of ground troops. Also, planes and tanks were flown and shipped to and around Africa to bolster the defense of Egypt, threatened by German successes in the Western Desert. Special facilities were set up in the Persian Gulf to furnish tanks and trucks through Iran to Russia, our other ally. The Office of Strategic Services collected data from inside enemy lines, and sent parachute personnel to drop behind those lines and work with local resistance groups.

Pressures, notably from Russian leaders, early began building for an invasion of the European mainland on a "second front." There not being sufficient buildup in England for a major attack across the Channel in 1942, even for a small preliminary beachhead, our troops were moved, some from Britain with the British and some directly from America, to invade northwest Africa from Casablanca to Oran and Algiers on Nov. 8, 1942. The aim was to save that area for the French, and to seize Tunisia and block from the rear the German forces now retreating before a British drive from Cairo. After the long coastal strip had been seized and the temporarily resisting French brought to our side, the Anglo-American forces pushed east. The Germans were reinforced and concentrated. Sharp and costly fighting by air, army, and armor attacks and counterattacks, notably in February, 1943, at the Kasserine Pass, ended, however, with the Allied conquest of Tunisia and a great German surrender at Tunis and Bizerte and Cape Bon on May 12, 1943. The operation was conducted with Gen. Dwight D. Eisenhower in command, using a mixed Anglo-American staff. Shortly before this, at Casablanca in late January, a high level interallied conference declared for an "unconditional surrender" by the German nation. It would be a war to the finish, not a negotiated, temporary peace.

The next step was an Anglo-American invasion of Sicily, beginning in July, 1943, using large-scale parachute drops and perfected beach-landing skills, as a step toward knocking Italy out of the war. On Sept. 3, Italy proper was invaded, the British crossing the Messina strait and the Americans landing at Salerno near Naples. Five days later Italy surrendered, but the Germans occupied Rome and took control of the Italian government. After a long check midway up the boot of Italy on a line through Cassino, a dangerous landing was made at Anzio, Jan. 22, 1944. Fierce German counter-attacks there were stopped short of success, and a following breakthrough carried our forces past Rome, which fell June 4, 1944, and the next month to the line of Florence and the Arno River, the British on the east and the Americans on the west. Thereafter, although some Anglo-American advances were made and a final offensive in April, 1945, carried our troops to the Po Valley, Italy ceased to be the scene of major strategic efforts, and the theater was drained to support the Normandy invasion by a landing in southern France.

Campaigns in France and Germany: 1944 – Spring, 1945

For the principal invasion of France, an inter-allied planning staff had been created in March, 1943, in London. In May, the first tentative attack date was set, to be early in May of the following year. That same summer, some of our troops from the Mediterranean theater began to be withdrawn and shipped to England. The build-up of units and supplies proceeded steadily for nearly a year, and was helped greatly by improved successes against German submarines aimed at our sea-going convoys. There was a one-month delay in the target date for the invasion of France, to secure more landing craft and more troops to make a broader beach base for the initial thrust. Finally, after a day's further delay owing to bad weather conditions, on June 6, 1944, the greatest amphibious invasion in history was launched across the English Channel, 12,000 fighters parachuting from planes and over 5300 ships and landing craft carrying the rest. Mine sweepers preceded. Naval ships assisted with gunfire from battleships, cruisers and destroyers. Aerial bombers flew over to attack enemy fortifications. It was a huge, carefully and intricately co-ordinated land, sea and air action, with a precisely scheduled flow of reinforcements and supplies. To hit from Dover to Calais would have been shorter, but inland thence the terrain was cut by many water lines. Brittany was too far by water and by air. To land in Normandy would provide better flank protection by the Seine and Orne rivers, and ample maneuver space, and would be just within practicable air fighter support. So it was on the Normandy coast, from the Cherbourg peninsula to the mouth of the Orne that the landings were made at selected beaches, the Second British Army and the First Canadian Army on the east and the American First Army on the west, all ground forces under the command of the British Gen. Montgomery, and our Gen. Eisenhower as Supreme Allied Commander. The flanks of the landing force were assisted and protected by costly but successful parachute and glider drops by British and American units.

The battle on the Normandy beaches on June 6 was vicious, particularly on "Omaha" in front of Calvados where a reinforcing German division had just arrived, and only raw courage and determination brought success. Yet, the invaders moved inland in spite of losses and confusions. The build-up of reinforcements had been carefully planned and scheduled, as was the forwarding of supplies. Over the beaches the shallow-draft landing craft passed along a steady stream of men and materials, seriously interrupted only once, when a four-day storm starting June 19 prevented beach debarkations and destroyed a large but temporary pier on the American beach, so that at one time our First Army was down to one day's supply of ammunition. By that time, we had about 314,514 American troops ashore, and about the same number of British. All were reorganizing and pressing inland. The weather cleared; we had a good foothold, as did the British on our left; by June 26 Cherbourg had fallen; and we had a seaport and were ready to spin about and go south.

The Germans had been reinforcing their positions, although badly hampered by aerial bombardments of road and rail lines and convoys in motion. There followed a month of almost pedestrian fighting through thick hedgerow country to establish a forward line through the road center at St. Lô. Then, late in July, with the British holding and drawing to their front by Caen a large proportion of the German forces, particularly much of their armor, the American infantry and tanks, aided by a massive air bombardment, pierced the enemy line near St. Lô and swung rapidly to the southwest toward Coutances, making many captures of outflanked German troops.

At this juncture, Gen. Montgomery relinquished command of all ground troops and took over only the British 21st Army Group while Gen. Omar Bradley moved from command of the American First Army to that of the 12th Army Group, including both First and Third Armies.

The Germans reacted to this penetration by finally drawing their reserve Fifteenth Army out of the Calais area, where it had been held by a deception ruse and the threat of a second beach landing there. They struck directly west across our front to try to cut off our leading troops who had already begun entering Brittany. This German effort was blocked by Gen. Bradley's forces; the British pushed slowly but inexorably southwards; the American First and Third Armies mostly abandoned the drive in Brittany and Brest and raced eastwards toward Paris. At the same time they circled northeast around Falaise to pocket against the advancing British a large force of Germans who were killed and captured in vast numbers. German resistance in northern France now crumbled. On Aug. 25, Paris fell to American and French divisions with scarcely a battle.

The Germans retreated rapidly and skillfully for the distant frontier and their defense lines, except where they at points resisted the British in order to try and hold the seaports along the northern coast. There were some substantial captures, notably at a large pocket near Mons, but the German withdrawal was generally successful. In spite of our enormous support build-up on the Normandy beaches, in spite of emergency supply by airplane, and in spite of immobilizing some units to use their trucks to carry food and ammunition and gasoline to the most forward units, forward supply was seriously lacking to our forces. Some troops actually at times had to subsist on captured German rations. It was not possible to hit the distant German frontier line soon or hard enough.

While these events were taking place, a landing had been made in southern France on Aug. 15, 1944, by a Franco-American force under American command, which swept from the Riviera coast up the Rhone valley, made contact with the previously exposed right flank of our racing Third Army, and then turned east and northeast to extend the front of our forces which had come east across northern France from Normandy. By early September, Brest fell into our hands, and a German army in southwest France had surrendered, completely cut off. Also by early September our general eastward advance was checked by well-fortified Germans at about the frontier line, largely because we had run ahead too fast for our supplies. But France was almost completely liberated from German occupation.

For more than two months, with the British moving up on our left, and some French on our right, American armies moved up through very difficult country against hard German resistance and at the cost of heavy casualties, all the while rebuilding forward supply and preparing to push into the Palatinate and on to the Rhineland plain toward Coblenz and Cologne. The over-all strategic idea was to make the final major Allied effort over the Rhine north of Cologne and through the relatively open country north of the Ruhr. But we were still miles from the Rhine. As infantry and tanks slugged forward aided by exceptional air support, Aachen fell in October and the line of the Roer River and the Eifel mountains was reached. Applying pressure on our left, we thinned our center. There the Germans struck hard on Dec. 16 in the wooded and hilly Ardennes, in their final bid with a newly trained and reorganized force. During five days of fierce fighting, the Americans held strongly on the shoulders of the penetration, which was aimed northwest at Liège and Antwerp; our First Army was regrouped to check the main drive to the northwest, we threw in some divisions which had been out of line—either to exploit a possible success or to meet just such a threat as this—swung our Third Army to block from the south near Bastogne, and received reserves from the British. Split from our Third Army, the First was temporarily placed under Montgomery's command. Then, at the peak of the German penetration, not far from the Meuse River, leading German units, out of gasoline, were captured. Our air bombardments, both close and deep, had seriously weakened German transportation, both rail and road. They could not get their motor fuel up nor capture ours. On our side, our losses had been serious; but by Jan. 1, every lost tank and artillery piece had been replaced from our "pipeline" of supply. Germany could not match the weight of American industrial support. In bitter January winter weather, the Germans stubbornly resisted, but our troops dogged and chewed them up and slowly forced them out of the bulge they had made. This had been their final major effort. They had used up their last major resources and had failed to defeat us.

By a phenomenon of large-scale production and mass transportation, our air forces in Europe had been built to high strength so that they could take severe losses and still beat the enemy down. From bases in Britain and from bases successively in North Africa and Italy our bombers had struck at the heart of the German economy. By large-scale air raids, like those on Ploesti, Roumania, a decisive proportion of German oil refinery production was knocked out. German planes and tanks faced being starved for fuel. German fighter planes, beaten back by the British in 1940, were later cut down by our own heavily armed bombers and their long-range fighter escorts. Except for a short, sharp, and costly new campaign in the final month of 1944, German planes had ceased to be a serious major threat, and at the same time our fighter-bombers were taking the air under conditions over the Ardennes when they should not have flown at all, and aiding the ground troops. German flying bombs (V-1) and rocket bombs (V-2) had continued to blast Britain until their installations were overrun, but they had no effect on ground operations or on air superiority as a whole.

In February, 1945, our armies struck out into the Palatinate and swept the German forces across the Rhine. The enemy destroyed bridges as they crossed— all but one. On March 9, an advanced armored unit of our First Army approached the great railway bridge at Remagen, a little downstream from Coblenz, found it intact, dashed over it, tore the fuses from demolition charges, and drove local Germans back. Plans had not existed for a crossing here, but the opportunity was promptly exploited. Troops were hustled over the bridge for several days before it collapsed from damage, but by then pontoon bridges were in. Our east bank holdings were slowly expanded against sharp German resistance attracted there, thus making easier the planned crossing later north of Cologne by the British and by our own Ninth Army, and letting troops of the Third Army upriver cross with comparative ease, at one place without a defensive shot being fired against them.

Avoiding the heavily wooded Ruhr region in the center, the previously planned northern crossing of the Rhine was effected with navy, air, and parachute help on March 23, 1945; all arms drove directly eastwards into Germany while the First and Third Armies drove eastwards below the Ruhr, the first of these soon swinging north at the end of March through Giessen and Marburg to make contact at Paderborn and Lippstadt with the northern force. More than 300,000 Germans were thus enclosed in the Ruhr pocket.

Germany's military strength had now practically collapsed. The British on our left raced toward Hamburg and the Baltic. Our First Army pressed through to Leipzig, and met the Russians on April 25, 1945, at Torgau on the Elbe River, which had been established at the Yalta Conference as part of the post-hostilities boundary with the Russians. Our Third Army dashed toward Bavaria to prevent possible German retreat to a last stand in the south. Our southernmost flank swung southwards toward Austria at Linz, and toward Italy at the Brenner Pass, our Seventh Army troops on May 4 meeting the Fifth Army there coming up out of Italy where German resistance had likewise collapsed. Germany asked for peace, and signed it at Allied headquarters at Rheims on May 7, 1945.

Surrender of Japan

Progress in the Pacific by this time had been substantial. Our ships and planes were dominating sea and air close to Japan. Troops were soon to be redeployed from the European theater. Protracted clean-up operations against now isolated Japanese island garrisons were coming to a close. Our planes were bombing Tokyo almost with impunity. A single raid on that city on March 9, 1945, had devastated 16 square miles, killed 80,000 persons, and left 1,500,000 people homeless. But the Japanese were still unwilling to surrender. Approved by President Roosevelt, our scientists under military direction had devised a devastating airplane bomb, based upon atomic fission. A demand was made upon Japan on July 26 for surrender, threatening with repeated warnings the destruction of eleven Japanese cities in turn. The Japanese rulers scorned the threats. Then, President Truman gave his consent for the use of the atom bomb and, on Aug. 6, Hiroshima was hit. There were more warnings, and still no surrender. On Aug. 9, Nagasaki was bombed and two square miles wiped out. Five days later, on Aug. 14, the Japanese agreed to surrender. The official instrument of surrender was signed on Sept. 2, 1945, on board the battleship *Missouri* in Tokyo Bay.

(*See also* Air Force, U. S.; Army, U. S.; Defense, National; Draft; Merchant Marine; Navy, U. S.)

WORLD'S COLUMBIAN EXPOSITION. This, the most successful and influential of all world's fairs in the United States, was held in Chicago from May 1 to Oct. 30, 1893, a year after the 400th anniversary of America it was intended to celebrate. Nearly 28,000,000 visitors filed through the turnstiles of the so-called "White City" on the South Side.

Except for the Fisheries Building by H. I. Cobb and the Transportation Building by Louis Sullivan, the architecture of the fair spelled out the triumph of the classic revival promoted by McKim, Mead & White and R. M. Hunt of New York and their Chicago admirer D. H. Burnham. Burnham's partner, John Root, who might have insisted on a more original program, died before the Fair was launched.

"Do you realize that this is the greatest meeting of artists since the 15th century?" called out the sculptor Augustus Saint-Gaudens in the midst of a conference in which McKim and the others had had their say. R. M. Hunt was more businesslike. "Hell!" he said. "We haven't come out here on a missionary expedition. Let's get down to work."

Louis Sullivan, who had no respect for the classic revival, argued that the damage wrought by the fair would last for half a century. "It has," he said, "penetrated deep into the constitution of the American mind, effecting there lesions significant of dementia." Sullivan may have exaggerated. His own practice dwindled thereafter, but it is doubtful that the Fair was to blame. And Frank Lloyd Wright, Purcell & Elmslie, W. B. Griffin and others built so many buildings in the quarter century following that the Chicago School, of which Sullivan was the leader, was not eclipsed until the coming of World War I. Moreover, scholars have pointed out that the City Beautiful type of planning, represented by Burnham's plans for Chicago, Cleveland and other cities, not to forget the revival of L'Enfant's plan for Washington, owes much to the splendid lagoons of the fair grounds.

The fair focused the attention of the entire world on Chicago, and on the public spirit that endowed the Art Institute of Chicago, founded in 1879; Hull House, opened by Jane Addams in 1889; and the Chicago Symphony Orchestra, launched in 1891.

WOUNDED KNEE, BATTLE OF (Dec. 29, 1890), last important clash of Indians with United States troops, climaxed the Ghost Dance trouble. Big Foot's band of Sioux, which fled into the Badlands after the killing of Sitting Bull, Dec. 15, 1890, was captured by the 7th Cavalry at Wounded Knee Creek, S. Dak., December 28. Col. J. W. Forsyth, the following day, ordered the Indians disarmed. When a few resisted, general firing began in which more than 200 Indian men, women and children were slaughtered, including Big Foot. The white losses were 29 dead and 33 wounded. Many wounded Indians, left on the field, froze to death in a blizzard the next night.

WRITS OF ASSISTANCE were general search warrants issued to the customs officers by the superior courts of the various colonies. They were first issued in Massachusetts in 1751. Neither the issue nor the use of such writs seems to have excited controversy prior to 1761. In that year new writs were applied for as the old ones were expiring. These were opposed as unconstitutional by some merchants through their attorney, James Otis. There was some delay but the writs were issued (1762) after instructions had been received from England supporting their legality. That closed the controversy in Massachusetts.

The Townshend Revenue Act (1767) authorized writs of assistance, but did not specify any form. A form was prepared by the customs officers similar to the one that had been granted in Massachusetts. Every customs officer in America was sent a copy of the desired writ and directed to request the Attorney General of his colony to secure such writs from the superior court. This action made writs of assistance an issue in the superior court of every province in

America. The form of the writ was novel to the judges and seemed to encroach upon important rights of citizens. The term "writ of assistance" as used in the law was a common legal expression used to designate a search warrant. It was difficult, however, to convince the judges that such words meant general search warrants. There was delay in most of the courts and the issue dragged through 1768 to 1772, resulting in a direct refusal by the courts of Connecticut, Rhode Island, New York, New Jersey, Pennsylvania, Maryland, Virginia and North Carolina, although the judges offered to issue "writs of assistance," in particular cases, "as directed by law." In some cases the refusals stated the forms presented to the judges were novel and unconstitutional. Finally in 1772 the customs officers reported that they had secured writs in East Florida, West Florida, South Carolina, Bahama, Bermuda, New Hampshire, Nova Scotia and Quebec. It is obvious that the controversy over writs of assistance was not a Massachusetts affair only, and it was not the speech of Otis that made their issue a cause of the Revolution, especially as his speech did not become generally known until long after the Revolution was over. It was the raising of the issue in every superior court in America, dragged through five years, that made writs a common grievance as stated in the Declaration of Independence.

WYOMING. Mystery cloaks the first entry of the white man into the area now included in Wyoming. The Verendrye brothers, French-Canadian fur traders, may have penetrated to the central part of the Wyoming country in the winter of 1742–43, but it seems probable that they did not go farther west than the Black Hills of South Dakota. Early in the 19th century came trappers and traders: John Colter who passed through the Yellowstone Park region in 1807; Andrew Henry, the Western partner of Manuel Lisa, who entered western Wyoming in 1809; Jacques Laramie, an employee of the North West Company; Jim Bridger, one of the partners in Ashley's Rocky Mountain Fur Company, who explored much of Wyoming; and many others.

Capt. Bonneville, on leave of absence from the army, led a fur-trading expedition of 110 men into the Wyoming region in 1832, taking the first wagons over the Continental Divide, on the way to Pierre's Hole. Lt. John Frémont explored the country for the Government, 1842–43. On the heels of the trappers and explorers came missionaries: Whitman, Spalding, DeSmet and White.

The Oregon Trail became the great highway across Wyoming in the 1840's: for Whitman, who led a thousand settlers with 200 wagons over the Trail to Oregon in 1843; for Brigham Young who led a party of Mormons over the Trail in 1847; for those who participated in the gold rush to California in 1849 and after. The opening of the Overland and Bozeman

Trails provided new courses for population flow. The telegraph reached Wyoming in 1861; the Union Pacific, in 1867.

The first permanent settlers in Wyoming were a party of Mormons who came to Fort Bridger in 1853. Gold discovery at South Pass in 1867 led to the foundation of mining towns and to the establishment of Carter County with the approval of the Dakota legislature in December, 1867.

Wyoming contains lands obtained from the Louisiana Purchase, Texas Annexation, the Oregon Treaty and the Mexican Cession of 1848. Parts of the Wyoming country were included in the Unorganized Country, 1834–54; Oregon Territory, 1848–53; Utah Territory, 1850–68; Washington Territory, 1853–63; Nebraska Territory, 1854–63; Dakota Territory, 1861–63, 1864–68; and Idaho Territory, 1863–68. Wyoming Territory, with the same boundaries that the state was to have, was created July 25, 1868, from portions of Dakota, Idaho and Utah territories. Territorial government was organized in 1869. Woman suffrage was granted in the Territory, Dec. 10, 1869; in 1870 a woman served as justice of the peace and women served on juries.

The numerous Indian tribes of the region caused much trouble for the whites who first traversed, explored and settled Wyoming. Government commissioners met the several tribes in council at Fort Laramie in 1851, outlined tribal boundaries, and promised annuities. Increased traffic along the trails, particularly along the Bozeman Trail, opened in 1863, and the arrival of stage lines, pony express, telegraph and railroad provoked Indian attacks which led to military retaliation. In the late 1860's and 1870's all of the tribes except the Shoshone and Arapaho were removed from the Territory. The Shoshones and Arapahoes were placed on the Wind River Reservation in west central Wyoming where they still remain.

Between 1870 and 1890 the population of Wyoming Territory increased tenfold. Statehood was achieved July 10, 1890, Wyoming entering as the 44th state of the Union.

WYOMING MASSACRE (July 3–6, 1778), the "surpassing horror of the Revolution," included the Battle of Wyoming, July 3, and subsequent atrocities.

Unlike Indian raids, this battle between Butler's Rangers, with Tories and Iroquois, and the Connecticut settlers in the Wyoming Valley, Pennsylvania, under Col. Zebulon Butler, had a definite line of attack and defense.

The able-bodied men of the settlement were with Washington's army, but Zebulon Butler, home on furlough, gathered the families in Forty Fort, upon the British approach, June 30. On July 3, overruled by rash counsel, Butler led the small garrison, about three hundred, against a force four times their number. The thin line held, then, overwhelmed by the

Indians, broke into confusion. The wounded were ruthlessly killed, or slain later by the half-breed Queen Esther.

Barely sixty escaped to surrender on July 4. Butler lost control of the Indians, who disregarding the capitulation terms destroyed the settlers' possessions.

A pivotal battle of the Revolution, stimulating the patriots to activity and union, the Wyoming massacre decided Washington to send the Sullivan Expedition (1779) to destroy the Iroquois, while it created English opposition to the policy of employing Indians.

XYZ AFFAIR was the most dramatic incident in the bitter dispute between the French Directory and the United States. Incensed at our negotiation of Jay's Treaty with Great Britain, France issued decrees against American shipping and refused to receive Charles Cotesworth Pinckney, the newly appointed American minister. President John Adams held to a pacific course and sent a mission to Paris composed of Pinckney, then in Holland, John Marshall and Elbridge Gerry, the first two Southern Federalists, the last a Massachusetts Republican.

The American ministers arrived just after their supporters in the French legislature had been destroyed by the *coup d'etat* of Sept. 4, 1797. The Directory's armies were victorious in Italy and the Rhineland, and Talleyrand, the new foreign minister, thought he could take advantage of the bitter feud between Federalists and Republicans (Jeffersonian) in the United States and embarrass the Federalist administration without running any risk of war. Reports from the United States showed the Republicans were gaining ground, and even Jefferson had suggested to the French consul general that France would profit by temporizing.

Talleyrand received the envoys unofficially on Oct. 8, 1797, and stated that they would have an audience with the Directory as soon as a report could be prepared on American affairs. Weeks of official silence ensued. Meanwhile, three unofficial agents of the foreign minister, Hottinguer, Bellamy and Hauteval, called on the Americans suggesting a gratuity of $250,000 for Talleyrand, a loan to France, and an indemnity for Adams' criticism of France in his speech to Congress on May 15, 1797. The ministers were willing to consider a payment to Talleyrand after a treaty had been signed, and they even proposed that one of them return to confer with Adams regarding a loan, provided the Directory would cease its attacks on American shipping and negotiate with the two ministers who remained. Not even these concessions could secure the reception of the ministers by the Directory.

On Jan. 17, 1798, Pinckney, Marshall and Gerry presented a dignified statement of the American position, defending Jay's Treaty, offering France the same privileges Britain enjoyed under that document

and demanding compensation for the losses of American shipping. Talleyrand deferred his reply until March 18 when he made an insulting proposal to treat with Gerry alone, characterizing him as the only one of the ministers friendly to France. Although Gerry refused to negotiate with Talleyrand, he remained in Paris after the departure of his colleagues, in the honest but erroneous belief that his presence there prevented war.

The publication of its ministers' despatches by the American Government created such a stir in this country that the affair acquired a unique place in the popular mind. The incident was given a mysterious quality by the substitution of the letters X, Y, and Z for the names of Talleyrand's agents. The Federalists made political capital of the situation, and Congress abrogated the treaties of 1778 (*see* Franco-American Alliance), suspended commercial relations with France, authorized the seizure of *armed* French vessels and strengthened the nation's naval and military forces. Talleyrand, thoroughly alarmed, sought valiantly to prevent a declaration of war. The wise policy he and President Adams then pursued led to the Convention of Sept. 30, 1800, which ended the misunderstanding.

YADKIN RIVER SETTLEMENTS. The Yadkin River Valley of North Carolina was not settled until after 1740, though Henry McCulloh, Arthur Dobbs, and several other prominent men received an extensive grant of land in that region in 1737. In 1746 a few families removed from the Cape Fear region of southeastern North Carolina "to the west of the Yadkin where they joined others who had already broken into that wilderness." About 1750 there were a few German settlers along the Yadkin, and in 1753, Moravians from Bethlehem, Pa., planted the Wachovia Colony and founded three towns, Betharaba, Bethania and Salem. From that date to the outbreak of the American Revolution, thousands of Scotch-Irish and Germans moved from Pennsylvania to the Yadkin River Valley of North Carolina, coming down the "wagon road," the terminal points of which were Lancaster, Pa., and Salisbury, N. C. The latter town was begun about 1755.

YAKIMA INDIAN WARS (1855–58). The Yakima Indians, in alliance with the Klickitats, started this war which finally involved the principal tribes of the Pacific Northwest. Before the Indians were forced to submission the conflict had ranged over what is now eastern Washington and northern Idaho, reaching the coast at Puget Sound, and being stopped in its threatened invasion of western Oregon at the Cascades of the Columbia. Throughout, the leading spirit and organizer of the Indians was the remarkable chieftain, Kamiakin, of the Yakimas.

In August, 1855, parties of prospectors passing through the Yakima country were attacked by the

Indians. When the Indian agent, A. J. Bolon, went alone to confer with Kamiakin, he was killed. A small detachment of regulars under Maj. Granville O. Haller left The Dalles to arrest the murderers, but was forced to retreat before superior numbers of hostiles. All regulars from the western posts were put into the field and companies of volunteers were called from Oregon and Washington. The Federal military officers were generally critical of the volunteers, and Maj. Gen. John E. Wool, in command of the department of the Pacific, became involved in a bitter quarrel with the territorial authorities of both Oregon and Washington, needlessly prolonging the struggle.

Regulars under Maj. Gabriel J. Rains and volunteers under J. W. Nesmith jointly invaded the Yakima country during November and December, 1855. Although there was no decisive engagement they swept the hostiles from the country.

During the time of the action in the Yakima section, Lt. Col. James K. Kelly conducted a campaign in the Walla Walla Valley where he became involved in a winter campaign, ending, for the regulars, after a four-day battle in early December, which drove the Indians across the Snake River; but the poorly equipped and provisioned volunteers endured a severe winter in the Indian country.

The war had many outcroppings in widely separated regions. The regular army was aroused from its indifferent handling of the Indian war by a defeat suffered under Lt. Col. Edward J. Steptoe in the Spokane country (May, 1858). The military authorities then accepted the territorial view of the seriousness of the situation and pushed the war rigorously. Col. George Wright, in charge of the campaign in the Spokane country, finally broke the power of the Indians and forced them to submission in the fall of 1858.

YALE UNIVERSITY was founded in October, 1701, as the "Collegiate School within his Majesties Colony of Connecticot." In that year, so runs tradition, ten Congregational ministers met at the Rev. Samuel Russel's parsonage in Branford, each with a gift of books. Classes were first taught at Killingworth, now Clinton, in the house of the first Rector, the Rev. Abraham Pierson. Upon Pierson's death in 1707 the College moved to Saybrook, and in 1716 to New Haven whose citizens had outstripped other communities in subscribing sums toward a building. Two years later help came from Elihu Yale, a retired East India merchant, New England born, then living in London. He sent nine bales of East India goods, which brought at sale for the College, £562 12s., and the institution, in gratitude, took his name. The philosopher, George Berkeley, afterward Bishop of Cloyne, gave the College his farm in Rhode Island and a collection of valuable books in 1731–33.

The first brick building, Connecticut Hall (still standing), was built in 1752; the first professorship, a chair in divinity, was established in 1755; others in mathematics, physics and astronomy were added in 1771.

The University in 1959 comprised twelve schools: Yale College (founded 1701); the School of Engineering (1932); the Freshman Year (1919) which is common to the two preceding; the Graduate School (1847); School of Medicine (1813), Divinity School (1822); School of Law (1824); School of Art and Architecture (1866); School of Music (1894); School of Forestry (1900); School of Nursing (1923); School of Drama (1955).

Yale had the first gallery of fine arts among American colleges (1832), and conferred the first degree of Doctor of Philosophy in America in 1861.

The *Yale Literary Magazine* is the oldest literary periodical in this country; the *Yale Daily News* the oldest college daily paper.

There were in 1959 more than 60,000 living Yale alumni who resided in every state in the Union and in more than 55 foreign countries. Twenty-four graduates of Yale were members of the Continental Congress, four signed the Declaration of Independence, and four were members of the convention which framed the U. S. Constitution.

Women were permitted to enroll for the first time in the Yale Graduate School in 1892 for the Ph.D. degree. In 1959 there were 500 women students in the graduate and professional schools, but no women in the undergraduate college.

The total Yale enrollment in 1959 was about 7500 students, of whom 4000 are in the undergraduate schools. Upperclassmen in these schools live in groups of about 200 in any one of ten undergraduate colleges: Berkeley, Branford, Calhoun, Davenport, Timothy Dwight, Jonathan Edwards, Pierson, Saybrook, Silliman and Trumbull. The undergraduate college plan was made possible by the gift of Edward S. Harkness, '97.

Plans were underway in 1959 to construct two additional residential colleges with the support of a $15,000,000 gift from Paul Mellon, '29.

The Faculty then numbered about 1700. The University Library contained over 4,000,000 volumes, including one of the most valuable collections of rare manuscripts in the world.

YALTA CONFERENCE (Feb. 4–11, 1945) of President Roosevelt, Prime Minister Churchill, and Marshal Stalin came at a turning point of World War II when the imminent collapse of Germany made it necessary to make plans for administering Europe. In addition, Roosevelt envisaged another personal meeting with Stalin (following that of the Teheran Conference) as a final means of winning the latter's confidence in American goodwill, and thereby ensuring a peaceful, free postwar world.

After amicable discussions Roosevelt, Churchill,

and Stalin announced publicly (Feb. 11) agreement on: (1) the occupation of Germany by the United States, Great Britain, Russia, and France in four separate zones; (2) a conference of the signatories of the United Nations Declaration to open at San Francisco April 25, 1945, for the purpose of establishing a world peace organization; (3) a (then secret) big-power voting formula in the new organization; (4) an eastern boundary of Poland following mainly the Curzon line (which handed over to Russia about one third of prewar Poland) with compensation for Poland in the north and west by unspecified German territory, and a new, freely elected, democratic Polish government; (5) freely elected democratic governments for other liberated European nations. A supplementary secret agreement (Feb. 11) provided for Russian entry into the war with Japan in two or three months after Germany surrendered, and in return British and American acceptance of: (1) the *status quo* of Outer Mongolia; (2) restoration to Russia of her position in Manchuria before the Russo-Japanese War (1904–5), with safeguarding of Russian interests in Dairen, Port Arthur, and the Manchurian railways; (3) the cession to Russia of the Kurile Islands and the southern half of Sakhalin.

The conference has been harshly criticized, on the grounds particularly of the American and British "betrayal" of Poland and their "unnecessary" (since Japan collapsed before much Russian power was brought to bear against her) concessions to Russia at the expense of China.

YAMASEE WAR (1715–16) was waged in southeastern South Carolina. Possibly instigated by Spaniards, the Indians certainly were incensed at land encroachments and at numerous evils incident to their extensive peltry traffic with Carolinians. At dawn, April 15, 1715, about ninety traders and their families were slain. Subsequently, Yamasee bands raided plantations, burning and murdering. Most of the Indian nations between Saint Augustine and Cape Fear, and some in the interior, allied themselves with the Yamasee, but usually did not go beyond the murdering of traders in their towns. Aided by supplies from New England and a few troops from North Carolina and Virginia, South Carolina gradually gained the upper hand; in the autumn the Yamasee were driven far southward into Florida. For its persuasive effect, a force of 300 Carolinians was sent among the powerful Cherokee, wavering between peace and war. That nation chose peace (January, 1716), while the Lower Creek, openly hostile, migrated westward to obtain protection of the French at Mobile. Thus the far-reaching conspiracy against Carolina collapsed. Although costly in men, money and trade, the war facilitated the subsequent establishment of Georgia and ushered in a long period of generally peaceful relations between South Carolina and its Indian neighbors.

"YANKEE DOODLE" is our most popular national air or march, easy to remember, adaptable to fife and drum, and with an appeal to the sense of humor. The origin of the tune, like that of the words, is uncertain. It probably was derived from an old air, possibly Dutch, and in its English form said to have been called "Nancy Dawson," "Lucy Locket," or "Kitty Fisher." It is supposed to have been introduced to the colonies by an English fife-major of the Grenadier Guards about 1750, played in a Philadelphia ballad opera in 1767 and by English bands in America as early as 1768. It seems to have first appeared in print in Aird's *Scotch, English, Irish and Foreign Airs* about 1782 and to have been first published in America in 1794. The words originated probably after 1764 and with many variations were probably embodied in their present form:

> Yankee Doodle came to town,
> Riding on a pony,
> Stuck a feather in his cap
> And called him [or "it"] Macaroni.

about 1775, probably from the pen of a Tory or Briton. The early versions of the song with many and various verses, running into scores, were obviously composed at various times by various individuals. The origin of these was probably a satirical ballad, *The Yankee's Return from Camp*, printed between 1810 and 1813. These verses are obviously the product of Americans.

YANKEE-PENNAMITE WARS occurred in 1769–72, 1775 and 1784 when settlers under Connecticut titles and those under Pennsylvania disputed their private claims by force while the Pennsylvania-Connecticut Boundary Dispute was pursuing its official and legal course. In 1769 the Pennsylvanians dispossessed Maj. Durkee from the blockhouse and fort at Wilkes-Barre. The next spring the Connecticut settlers, led by Lazarus Stewart and his Paxton Boys, recaptured the fort. In 1771 Stewart, or one of his party, killed an attacking Pennamite and the leader of the Paxton Boys fled to Connecticut where he was shielded by the Susquehannah Company and even, it appears, by Gov. Trumbull. By the summer of 1772 the Connecticut people had gained permanent possession of the region and peaceful settlement began. There was a threat of renewal of the war in December, 1775, when Sheriff Plunkett of Northumberland County led a "posse" (in reality a militia troop of 500 men) against the Wyoming settlements, but he was repulsed in a brief engagement at the lower end of the valley. In 1784 the second so-called Pennamite-Yankee War broke out when local authorities of Pennsylvania, acting in close co-operation with Pennsylvania claimants, dispossessed those holding Connecticut titles. These "wars" were conducted by disciplined companies acting under military leaders, forts were built and besieged, articles of capitulation were drawn up and signed, and in general the formal rules of 18th-century warfare were observed. Some bloodshed, some misery and a great deal of lasting bitterness resulted. But in general the "wars" were carried on by private persons unsupported by governmental authority.

YAZOO FRAUD. In 1795 the legislature of Georgia passed a law granting the greater part of the territory now making up Alabama and Mississippi to four land companies for the sum of $500,000. These companies, bearing the names Georgia, Georgia-Mississippi, Upper Mississippi and Tennessee, received varying amounts, the first-named receiving the most. They were composed of people in all walks of life and from various parts of the country, including even a sprinkling of the legislators who passed the law. In this fact and also in the light of proof that all who voted for the law, with one exception, were bribed in one way or another to support the measure, grew up the charge of fraud. With the wrath of the Georgians fanned by William H. Crawford and James Jackson, who resigned from the U. S. Senate to return to Georgia and fight the fraud, a new legislature was elected in 1796 which rescinded the act. To show further indignation, the legislature in a solemn formal meeting burned the Yazoo act and all papers relating to it; and the state constitutional convention of 1798 inserted a clause ratifying the rescinding act and declaring the land in question inalienable.

The fraud received its name from the Yazoo River which ran through a part of the territory sold, and it had as an important element in its background the dispute of ownership of these western lands. Georgia claimed them as coming within her colonial limits; the United States claimed them as part of the spoils of the Revolution; Spain claimed, until 1795, all south of 32° 28′; and various tribes of Indians claimed and occupied them. Surrounded with these uncertainties, Georgia had sold most of this land in 1789 to three companies, who, failing to comply with all the terms of the law, lost their rights. Finally in 1802 Georgia sold all her claims west of the Chattahoochee River to the United States for $1,250,000.

The Yazoo claimants denied Georgia's right to rescind the sale and sought a remedy from Congress. For years this body debated the subject, and after the U. S. Supreme Court had decided in the Fletcher v. Peck case that the rescinding law was unconstitutional, Congress paid the claimants, in 1814, $4,282,-151.12½.

YELLOW FEVER. In that indispensable sourcebook, John Winthrop's *History of New England,* we find the first reference to yellow fever (1647), referring to yellow fever from the West Indies (Barbadoes Distemper). The effort of the Court on this occasion to exclude the crew and the cargo from

Massachusetts was this country's initial enforcement of quarantine. The British ships that sailed from Boston to capture Martinique returned without the island, but with an epidemic of yellow fever (1694). Despite its endemic focus on the African coast, yellow fever emerged as a peculiarly American disease (the "American plague"). If syphilis is the Indian's revenge on his white captors, malaria and yellow fever are the Negro's retaliation, as these two diseases spread through America with the African slave trade. With the single exception of smallpox, the most dreaded verdict on the lips of a colonial physician was yellow fever, and long after immunity was secured from smallpox, there was no protectio against yellow fever. The summer or autumn tha brought the Yellow Jack to America heard the death-carts through the streets, and the never-forgotten cries of the grave-diggers, "Bring out your dead! Bring out your dead!"

The outstanding epidemic of yellow fever, which doomed the supremacy of Philadelphia among American cities, was described by an eyewitness, the bookseller and publisher, Mathew Carey (1793): "People uniformly and hastily shifted their course at the sight of a hearse coming towards them. Many never walked on the foot-path, but went into the middle of the street, to avoid being infected in passing houses wherein people had died. Acquaintances and friends avoided each other in the streets, and only signified their regard by a cold nod. The old custom of shaking hands fell into such general disuse that many shrank back with affright at even the offer of the hand. A person with crape or any appearance of mourning was shunned like a leper. And many valued themselves highly on the skill and address with which they got to windward of every person whom they met." The tragedy of this behavior lies in its utter uselessness, since yellow fever can never pass from man to man.

Benjamin Rush, the medical oracle to whom all turned for succour, was relentless in his insistence on bloodletting, calomel and jalop. Rush's reign of blood, and his mercurial thunderbolts did not stop the epidemic. Rush, after noting a meteor, a dead cat, and that mosquitoes were numerous ("the usual attendants of a sickly autumn"), decided the yellow fever was caused by spoiled coffee on a wharf. Many years were destined to pass before the *Ædes ægypti* was proved guilty.

The prevention of yellow fever depends upon the elimination of the yellow-fever mosquito. Walter Reed, an army doctor from Virginia, tracking pestilence in Cuba with his devoted associates, demonstrated that the female mosquito carries the unknown parasite of yellow fever. The work of Walter Reed, James Carroll, the martyred Lazear, and the immune Aristide Agramonte sent William Crawford Gorgas, of Alabama, on his quest of the mosquito. Handicapped for years at Panama by uncomprehending officials ("Do you know, Gorgas, that every mosquito you kill costs the United States Government ten dollars?"), he hunted the wriggling larvae on that narrow strip of jungle, transforming the death-trap of the tropics into a health resort. The United States was able to break the barrier between the Atlantic and the Pacific by building the Panama Canal because this modern Theseus slew two mosquitoes—the devouring Minotaurs of malaria and of yellow fever.

"YELLOW JOURNALISM." James Gordon Bennett was the first American publisher to introduce the sensational manner in presenting news, but it was not until the 1880's that the term "Yellow Journalism" was applied to this type of news presentation. In this decade the development of pulp paper and the increase in advertising made possible a general reduction in newspaper prices and a consequent extension of the field for subscribers.

Advertising paid a large share of the publishing costs and since space rates were based on distribution, there was constant pressure for increase in the number of subscribers. Joseph Pulitzer, of the New York *World*, used high-pressure methods to accomplish this end. One of his innovations was a Sunday edition, carrying special articles and comic strips. One of these strips featured a "Yellow Kid" and it was from this character that the name "Yellow Journalism" was derived. This type of journalism gained a new recruit in William Randolph Hearst, publisher of the San Francisco *Examiner*, who in 1895 acquired the New York *Morning Journal* and began a subscription war with the *World*. This struggle resulted in an intensification of the methods of "Yellow Journalism."

The Cuban question was made to order for the sensational methods of the two publishers. Typical of the journalistic activities of the period were the propaganda methods used in reporting the concentration camps, the DeLome letters and the sinking of the *Maine*.

At the turn of the century the scare head, the scandal section, the sob sister and the elaborate Sunday features had become permanent features of the sensational press.

Some newspapers never adopted the extreme methods of the Yellow Journal press, but a considerable number of the metropolitan papers used some if not all of the innovations that appeared in the newspapers of the 1880's.

YELLOWSTONE RIVER EXPEDITIONS (1819–25) were planned by John C. Calhoun, Secretary of War, to overawe British fur traders and the Indians of the upper Missouri. As a means of impressing the Indians five steamboats were commissioned to ascend the Missouri, where no steamboat had ever been, and carry the expedition of 1100 men commanded by Gen. Henry Atkinson. Unfortunately the steamboats were unsuited for Missouri navigation. Two turned back at the start and only one reached Council Bluffs, half way to the Yellowstone, after voyaging the entire summer of 1819. The expedition failed for lack of funds, except that Maj. Stephen H. Long led an overland party to the Rockies.

Continued Indian attacks on fur traders resulted in a second expedition in 1825 with 476 men under Atkinson, accompanied by Benjamin O'Fallon, Indian agent. Among subordinate officers were Henry Leavenworth, Stephen W. Kearny and Bennett C. Riley, western soldiers, whose names are perpetuated in Forts Leavenworth, Riley and Kearny. Atkinson's party voyaged in eight keelboats, arrived at the Yellowstone in August and returned the same season. The Indians were so impressed by the show of force that O'Fallon and Atkinson were able to conclude treaties with fifteen tribes.

YORKTOWN CAMPAIGN (1781). Lord Cornwallis, retreating to Wilmington, N. C., after the Battle of Guilford Court House, decided to move into Virginia and add the forces of Arnold and Phillips to his own. He left Wilmington April 25, 1781, and on May 20 reached Petersburg, Va., where he met the Arnold and Phillips troops, giving him about 5000 men. Lafayette, who had been sent by Washington to watch Arnold, was then at Richmond with 3000 men, two thirds of them green troops. Cornwallis tried to persuade Sir Henry Clinton to abandon New York and concentrate on Virginia, but the latter refused. Cornwallis then moved against Lafayette, who retreated north of the Rapidan, where new accretions increased his force to more than 4000. He now blocked a raid by Tarleton and became so threatening that Cornwallis thought it wise to place himself nearer the coast. He retired to Richmond, and on June 20 moved farther down the Peninsula to Williamsburg. Lafayette, now reinforced by Steuben with 1000 more men, was close upon his heels, and had a brush with him on July 6, losing 145 men. In the first week in August, Cornwallis settled himself in Yorktown, and added the Portsmouth, Va., garrison to his force, giving him an army of 7000. Lafayette paused at Malvern Hill. On Aug. 31 Admiral DeGrasse arrived in Chesapeake Bay with a powerful squadron and disembarked 3000 troops under St. Simon, who were added to those of Lafayette. The latter, on Sept. 7, drew his line, now numbering 8000, across the Peninsula at Williamsburg, thus blocking Cornwallis' possible escape. Meanwhile, DeGrasse had beaten off the English fleet on Sept. 5.

Cornwallis, with his seasoned veterans, might still have broken through Lafayette's militia and ill-equipped regulars, and returned to the Carolinas; but he was relying on the British fleet and he was unaware that Washington, kept constantly informed by Lafayette, had conceived the daring plan of shifting his and Rochambeau's forces from New York to Virginia, some 400 miles, to overwhelm Cornwallis. Keeping Clinton at New York, still fearful of an attack upon him, Washington left the Hudson River on Aug. 19, five days after hearing that De-Grasse was heading for the Chesapeake, marched through Philadelphia to the head of the bay and began embarking his troops on Sept. 6. Washington himself reached Lafayette's headquarters on the 14th and assumed command, and his army arrived in detachments between the 18th and the 26th. A few days later, the full force, 16,000 strong, was drawn in a semicircle around Yorktown and began its bombardment with seventy cannon. On Oct. 6 the first parallel of works was opened by Gen. Lincoln. On the 11th the second parallel, only 300 yards from the British works, was opened by Baron Steuben. On the 14th two British redoubts were stormed by American and French troops under Alexander Hamilton and Baron DeViomenil. A British sortie on the 15th failed, and on the 17th Cornwallis asked for terms, the surrender of his 7247 men being completed on the 19th. Although not so regarded at the time by either side, this was really the deathblow to the British cause in America. There was no more fighting of consequence thereafter.

"YOUNG AMERICA" was a popular and widespread figure of speech culturally generic to the period 1840–50 and designating anything that exhibited the youthful spirit of energy and enterprise characteristic of the times; historically, a concept related to ideas of capitalistic progress and romantic individualism. Also an aggressively nationalistic term, it combined Young Europe's democratic universalism, imported by scholars and refugees, with the manifest destiny espoused by elements in the Democratic party after 1844, notably George Nicholas Sanders. A more elevated nationalistic interpretation was best stated by Emerson (1844). Intermingling with these sources was political Young Americanism, beginning with Edwin DeLeon (1844), influenced by younger party leaders and by George Henry Evans (1845 ff.), and culminating in the amorphous Young America Democratic faction (1851–56). The latter, headed by Sanders and the *Democratic Review* (1852), sought to revitalize its party by uniting all sections on a platform of free trade, foreign markets, a subsidized merchant marine, annexation southward and the encouragement of republican movements abroad. Fundamentally an attempt to construct issues apart from sectional controversy, this premature experiment had no lasting effects. After finding scattered literary and political expression, Young Americanism gradually disappeared, having made chiefly a contribution to native democratic idealism.

YOUNG MEN'S CHRISTIAN ASSOCIATIONS. The first such organizations in America were formed in Montreal and Boston in 1851, following the plan of a society organized in England in 1844. Forty more units were organized within the next three years, and an international convention was held at Buffalo in 1854. Thereafter, annual conventions took place until the Civil War disrupted the movement considerably, the surviving organizations working mostly among the soldiers in the field. After the war, a period of rapid growth ensued, and buildings which steadily developed into residential hotels as well as religious, cultural, and recreational centers were erected in all of the larger cities. During World War I, the Y. M. C. A. operated in every place where Americans trained or served, and handled nine tenths of the welfare work among the American forces in Europe. Just before the armistice in 1918, it had 1397 stations in France, and operated 2029 stations during the following winter when the troops were awaiting orders to return to America. During the five years following the war, it gave educational assistance to more than 100,000 ex-servicemen studying in schools and colleges. In World War II, the Y. M. C. A. was one of the six organizations that founded the United Service Organizations (U. S. O.) to provide recreation programs for American troops. Religious and other services to prisoners of war were provided under the auspices of the World Alliance of Y. M. C. A.'s in World Wars I and II. During 1958, memberships were held by 3,342,931 different persons in 1823 Y. M. C. A.'s in the United States. Among youth of high school age, 15,466 Hi-Y Clubs for boys and Tri-Hi-Y Clubs for girls were active.

YOUNG PLAN. This is the popular name of a plan recommended by a committee of experts, in its report of June 7, 1929, for the final settlement of the German reparation problem. This plan was largely adopted by the governments concerned. Its popular name was derived from the fact that Owen D. Young, one of the American experts, was elected chairman of the committee.

The Young Plan set forth a schedule of annuity payments by Germany which, it was felt, would be within the capacity of that country to pay, and established the machinery for transferring such payments in the form of the Bank for International Settlements. This institution not only had the function of transferring reparation payments from Germany to the Allied powers, but was given important banking powers in dealing with central banks.

YOUNG WOMEN'S CHRISTIAN ASSOCIATION of the U. S. A. (the Y. W. C. A.) is a voluntary membership organization with a Christian purpose. Founded in 1855 in London, England, the Y. W. C. A. started in New York City in 1858 as the Ladies' Christian Association "to labor for the temporal, moral and religious welfare of self-supporting young women." In 1866 the Young Women's Christian Association of Boston was established, with employment and boarding directory bureaus as adjuncts, and two years later it set up a boardinghouse of its own. Associations were formed in other cities, and in 1871 an International Conference of Women's Christian Associations was held at Hartford, Conn. The first college unit was formed at the Normal University, Normal, Ill., in 1873. In 1886 a National Association of Y. W. C. A.'s was formed, and reorganization took place in 1891–94 and in 1906.

In 1959 there was Y. W. C. A. work in seventy countries and territories of the world, and the Y. W. C. A. of the U. S. A. in 1958 helped 29 other national Y. W. C. A.'s either through advisory secretaries, program grants or trainees brought to the United States for observation and study—or through a combination of all three methods.

In 1959 in the United States there were approximately 2,000,000 members and/or participants in Y. W. C. A. programs in 441 Community Associations and in more than 200 registered Y. W. C. A.'s and on more than 500 college campuses. The Y. W. C. A. of the U. S. A. meets in Convention once every three years and accepts policies which set goals and direction for the national organization.

The Y. W. C. A. works consciously to include in its membership women and girls from different economic, racial, occupational, religious, cultural and age groups. As a local, national and world movement, the Y. W. C. A. develops programs and services which take into account the needs and concerns of its members in the changing community. Its program of health, education, recreation, housing and counseling anticipates the need of women as they change with the times. To fit the pattern of living today, the Y. W. C. A.'s program includes men and boys and reaches out to the families of the girls and women it serves.

YPRES-LYS OPERATION (Aug. 19–Nov. 11, 1918). In July the pressing need of the British for troops caused the American 27th (O'Ryan) and 30th (Lewis) divisions, breaking their training period, to be placed in line near Ypres with the 2nd British Army (Plumer). Later Plumer attacked and the American divisions from August 31 to September 2 advanced some 2000 yards, capturing Lankhof Farm and Voormezeele and occupying Vierstraat Ridge and parts of Mount Kemmel and Wytschaete Ridge.

In October, the 37th (Farnsworth) and 91st (Johnston) divisions were withdrawn from the American 1st Army and sent to reinforce the French 6th Army (de Boissoudy), advancing toward Brussels, in Belgium. From Oct. 30 to Nov. 4 the 37th Division, attacking east, cleared Cruyshautem Ridge and crossed the Scheldt River at Eyne and Heurne. On its right the 91st Division flanked and captured

Spitaals-Bosschen and took Audenarde. Returning to line Nov. 9, the 91st crossed the Scheldt and both divisions progressed some distance east of it by Nov. 11. Each division suffered about 1600 casualties in the Belgian operations.

YUKON. Rising as the Lewes, in the mountains east of Skagway (lat. 59°) within a score of miles of the Pacific, the river takes the name Yukon at the confluence of the Lewes and the Pelly at Selkirk. Joined by numerous tributaries on its northward course, it enters Alaska 90 miles north of Dawson about latitude 65°. At the Arctic Circle, where it is joined by the Porcupine, it bends and flows southwestward discharging through numerous channels over an immense delta into Bering Sea. The Yukon is the largest river in Alaska, fifth largest in North America, draining an area of 330,000 square miles. About 1600 of its 2300 miles are navigable for large steamboats.

In 1842 the Russian Zagoshkin explored part of the river. In 1850 Robert Campbell of the Hudson's Bay Company descended the river from Fort Selkirk to Fort Yukon, proving the identity of the Yukon and the Kwikpak. In 1866 Robert Kennecott surveyed a route for the Western Union Telegraph Co. for a line by way of Alaska and Siberia to Europe. The plan was abandoned with the death of Kennecott. In 1873 gold seekers began to arrive. The Klondike gold rush in 1896, and after, influenced conditions in the Yukon region. In 1898 the U. S. Geodetic Survey mapped the delta of the Yukon.

YUMA, FORT. From the late 18th century the Yuma Indians operated a crude ferry service at the confluence of the Colorado and Gila Rivers for traders and travelers between California, Sonora and Santa Fe. After the Treaty of Guadalupe Hidalgo, United States boundary surveyors and their military escort camped on the California side at this Indian ferry, and in 1849 John Glanton and other Americans are said to have seized the ferry from the Indians and operated it for emigrants. The hostile conduct of the Yumas toward the ferrymen and westbound emigrants, particularly the massacre of about fifteen Americans at Glanton's ferry on April 23, 1850, led to the establishment of a permanent military camp at this point on Nov. 27, 1850. Maj. S. P. Heintzelman, in charge of United States troops brought from San Diego, named the new post Camp Independence, but in March, 1851, the name became Camp Yuma. Abandoned in December, 1851, it was reoccupied on Feb. 22, 1852, as Fort Yuma. Across the river in what is now Arizona, a town site laid out after the completion of the Gadsden Purchase in 1854 was variously known as Colorado City, Arizona City and the present Yuma. Fort Yuma flourished as a station on early stagecoach lines beginning in 1857. The lands included in the military reservation of Fort Yuma lay at first partly in California, partly in Arizona; this was changed on June 22, 1874, the land on the Arizona side being given to the Department of the Interior. The fort, on the California side, was turned over to the same department on June 9, 1884, for use as an Indian school, located at the center of what is now the Yuma Indian Reservation. Meanwhile, in 1877, the Southern Pacific Railroad had built across the reservation into the town and across the river, supplanting gradually the old stage route eastward. The importance of Fort Yuma was thereafter for many years determined more by the flow of railway traffic than by any other factor, especially after steamboat navigation on the Colorado River declined.

ZANE'S TRACE AND GRANTS. In 1796 Congress authorized the President to contract with Ebenezer Zane, whose home was on the south branch of the Potomac River in Maryland, to build a "trace" through Ohio. This was first a bridle path from the Ohio River at Wheeling by way of the sites of Zanesville, Lancaster and Chillicothe to Limestone (Maysville), Ky. The path east of Zanesville later was developed into the National Road, and the trace became one of the most important pioneer highways in the state. For locating and building the trace, Congress gave Zane the privilege of locating military warrants upon three sections of land amounting to 1920 acres. The first of these was at the crossing of the Muskingum River, the second at the Hockhocking River and the third at the Scioto River crossing. At the Scioto, Zane was obliged to locate his warrant on the east side of the river opposite Chillicothe, as the western shore lay within the Virginia military grant.

ZENGER TRIAL (Aug. 4, 1735). From his arrival in 1732 William Cosby, colonial governor of New York, provoked controversy. His prosecution of the interim governor, Rip Van Dam, and his removal of Chief Justice Lewis Morris, stirred up an opposition party. This group established John Peter Zenger as printer of the *New York Weekly Journal* (Nov. 5, 1733), the first newspaper in America to be the organ of a political faction. Strictures published in this paper led the governor to have Zenger arrested and put in jail. His cause became that of the people, and when the governor arbitrarily debarred his New York counsel, Andrew Hamilton of Philadelphia, the most distinguished advocate in the colonies, consented to serve.

The printer was charged with seditious libel. Hamilton admitted the publication, but denied that it was a libel unless false, and sought to prove the truth of the statements. The court held that the fact of publication was sufficient to convict, and excluded the truth from evidence. Hamilton made an eloquent appeal to the jury to judge both the law and the fact, and the verdict was "not guilty." Zenger was

released, and the Common Council voted Hamilton the "Freedom of the Corporation." It was a notable victory for the freedom of the press, and set a precedent against judicial tyranny in libel suits.

ZIMMERMANN NOTE (January, 1917) was a telegram from Alfred Zimmermann, German secretary for foreign affairs, to the German minister to Mexico. Declaring that unrestricted submarine warfare would begin on Feb. 1, and fearing the United States would not remain neutral, Zimmermann directed that an alliance be formed with Mexico and that Japan be detached from the Entente. Mexico was to attack the United States on its southwestern border and recover Texas, New Mexico and Arizona. This telegram was intercepted by the British and delivered to the United States Government. Its publication strengthened President Wilson's position and caused popular indignation against Germany to mount even higher.

ZONING, a police power granted by the state through enabling legislation, is a modern practice governing land use. It had its origin in the industrialization and the resultant expansion of American cities. The first zoning law was enacted in New York City in 1916 as a reaction to some of the disagreeable manifestations of its nuisance industries such as slaughtering houses, tallow and chemical factories, etc. The first zoning case to come before the U. S. Supreme Court was decided in 1926. It upheld the validity of zoning regulations in some 400 communities.

Zoning is designed primarily to prevent adverse mixtures of land use, to set standards for use and growth and to guide community expansion. Good zoning may control the density and character of population growth, control land use, keep down taxes, particularly school taxes, and give a distinct character to the zoned areas. Zoning ordinances vary widely because each zoned area has different needs, conditions and trends in land utilization.

Zoning, however, is "only as good as its administration and maintenance." Lax enforcement, too frequent and unrealistic granting of variances and erratic, selfish and unintelligent amendment of zoning ordinances can prevent constructive use and ordered growth, destroy the value and benefits of zoning and render it worse than useless.

ZOUAVES, distinguished by a drill and uniform derived from the Zouaoua tribe in French service in Algeria (*ca.* 1830), were popularized in the United States by Elmer E. Ellsworth and others after the Crimean War. In the Civil War Ellsworth's 1st New York Fire Zouaves (11th New York Infantry) attracted much attention, but was mustered out a year after the death of its colonel. There were some ten other Zouave regiments, but the Zouave idea was soon abandoned under field conditions.

INDEX

INDEX

In the following Index, all entries of principal articles are distinguished by their setting in **bold-face** type and the first numeral following the entry (also in bold-face) is the page designation for the principal entry. Other mention of the same topic is noted thereafter in roman type. Italic type is used in citation of the names of ships and also of the titles of newspapers, periodicals and books.

Hannastown Resolution, 419
Hannibal and St. Joseph Railroad, 790, 848
Hard Labor, Treaty of, 419; and Indian land cessions, 454; and new Indian boundary line, 769; and First Treaty of Fort Stanwix, 895
Hard Money, 420
Hard Shell Baptists, 88
Hardee, W. J., and battle of Missionary Ridge, 616
Harding, Warren G., and campaign of 1920, 144; and the filibuster, 356; and the League of Nations, 547; and naval oil reserves, 644; and normalcy, 685; and the Presidency, 759; and the radio, 786
Harkness, Edward S., and Harvard University, 423; and Yale University, 765, 1041
Harkness, Stephen V., original stockholder of Standard Oil Company, 894
Harlem, Battle of, 420
Harmar, Fort, Treaties of, 420
Harmar's Expedition, 420; and the Wayne campaign, 340, 1004; and Northwest Indians, 847
Harmony Society, 420, 219
Harney, W. S., and battle of Ash Hollow, 66; appointed to Indian commission, 467
Harper, Robert Goodloe, and "Millions for defense, etc.," 614
Harpers Ferry, Capture of, 420; and battle of Antietam, 40; and Lee's Lost Order, 571
Harpers Ferry Raid, 421; Sharps rifles used in, 865; and slave insurrections, 875
Harriman, Edward H., and the Northern Securities case, 689; and the Union Pacific Railroad, 798
Harris, Harwell H., architect, 48
Harris, Joel Chandler, author of Uncle Remus books, 559
Harris, W. T., and philosophical thought and writings, 316
Harrison, Benjamin (1726?–1791), signer of the Declaration of Independence, 284; alumnus of William and Mary College, 1018
Harrison, Benjamin (1833–1901), elected to Presidency, 141; defeated for Presidency, 142; and Neagle case, 651; and the Presidency, 759
Harrison, Carter H., and Haymarket Riot, 426
Harrison, Fort, advance base in battle of Tippecanoe, 947
Harrison, Peter, architect, 44, 677
Harrison, Wallace K., architect, 47
Harrison, William Henry, and Cabinet, 128; and the Presidency, 138; and Perry's message after battle of Lake Erie, 332; and the Law Act of 1800, 421; and Indian treaties, 456; appointed governor of Indiana Territory, 477; and Fort Meigs, 601; elected President, 759; wins battle of the Thames, 941; and battle of Tippecanoe, 947; and "Tippecanoe and Tyler Too!" 947; arrives at Vincennes, 983; and Treaty of Vincennes, 983; suffers severe losses at Tippecanoe, 993; and battle of the Thames, 994; negotiates treaties at Fort Wayne, 1003; and the Whig party, 1015

Harrison Land Act, 421; and public land sales, 537
Harrison's Landing, and the Peninsular campaign, 719
Harrisse, Henry, historian, 559
Harrod, James, locates and begins building Harrodstown, 422; as early surveyor, 912
Harrodsburg, 422; first permanent settlement in Kentucky, 104
Hart, Charles, and Quantrill, 783
Hart, John, signer of the Declaration of Independence, 284
Harte, Bret, and fiction, 559
Hartford, **422;** in battle of Mobile Bay, 621
Hartford, Treaty of (1650), 669
Hartford, Treaty of (1786), and the State of New York, 676
Hartford Convention, 422; effect on campaign of 1816, 136; and the Essex Junto, 333; and the Federalist party, 354, 641; and nullification, 691; and secession, 861; and the War of 1812, 994
Hartford Wits, 422
Harvard University, 422; founded, 134; and colonial period, 312; and the printing press, 765; and the Unitarians, 973
Harvester, first patented by McCormick, 341
Harvey, George, antagonistic to the League of Nations, 546
Harvey, W. H. ("Coin"), author of *Coin's Financial School,* 205
Hassler, Ferdinand R., and the Coast and Geodetic Survey, 199
Hastings' Cutoff, 423
Hat Act of 1732, and British colonial policy, 211; and colonial manufacture, 581
Hatch Act of 1887, and agricultural experiment stations, 11
Hatchet, Burying the, 423
Hatfield-McCoy Feud, 423
Haughwout Building, first practical passenger elevator installed in, 46
Hauptmann, Bruno, and Lindbergh kidapping case, 556
Havana, Pan-American conference at, 706
Haverford College, and the Quakers, 782
Hawaii, 424; and "manifest destiny," 367; as an insular possession, 480; annexed by the United States, 580; admitted as the 50th state, 900; as an incorporated territory, 937
Hawkins, James, John, and William, explorers, 33
Hawkins' Zouaves, 1047
Hawk's Peak Episode, and the Bear Flag Revolt, 92
Hawley, Gideon, and education, 314
Hawley-Smoot Tariff, 425, 149, 916
Hawthorne, Nathaniel, and Brook Farm, 117; and the Concord Group, 221; and books, 558; and the Socialist movement, 883
Hay, John, and the Boxer Rebellion, 111; and Lincoln, 325; and the Olney-Pauncefote treaty, 696; and Panama, 707; and the Perdicaris affair, 725; and Lincoln's plan of reconstruction, 805